THE EARLY SERIAL PUBLICATIONS OF THE HAWAIIAN VOLCANO OBSERVATORY

VOLUME 1. Special Report of the Hawaiian Volcano Observatory (1st through 4th); Special Bulletin of the Hawaiian Volcano Observatory; Bibliographic References to Volcanoes and Volcanic Activity on the Island of Hawaii

VOLUME 2. Weekly Report, Weekly Bulletin, and Monthly Bulletin of the Hawaiian Volcano Observatory (1913-1920)

VOLUME 3. Monthly Bulletin of the Hawaiian Volcano Observatory (1921-1929)

Edited by **Darcy Bevens, Taeko Jane Takahashi,** and **Thomas L. Wright**

Published by the Hawaii Natural History Association, Hawaii National Park, Hawaii, 1988

ISBN 0-940295-03-2
ISBN 0-940295-05-9

The paper used in this publication meets the minimum requirements of the American National Standard for Permanence of Paper for Printed Library Materials Z39.48-1984

The logo on the cover and title page of this volume first appeared in Number 436 of the Volcano Letter, June 1936. We use it here to indicate that these are companion volumes to the reprinted edition of the complete Volcano Letter, published by the Smithsonian Institution, January 1987, on the occasion of the 75th anniversary of the founding of the Hawaiian Volcano Observatory.

PREFACE

With these volumes we complete the reprinting of the early serial publications of the Hawaiian Volcano Observatory (HVO), begun with the reprinting of *The Volcano Letter* by the Smithsonian Institution (Fiske and others, 1987). The contents of these volumes are as follows:

Volume 1. *Special Report of the Hawaiian Volcano Observatory* (first through fourth); *Special Bulletin of the Hawaiian Volcano Observatory*; a bibliography of all technical and many non-technical references to volcanoes on the island of Hawaii, exclusive of HVO serial publications, complete through 1955.

Volume 2. *Weekly Report, Weekly Bulletin,* and *Monthly Bulletin of the Hawaiian Volcano Observatory*, 1913-1920, inclusive.

Volume 3. *Monthly Bulletin of the Hawaiian Volcano Observatory*, 1921-1929, inclusive.

Each volume is separately paginated and indexed, using the index of the reprinted *Volcano Letter* as a rough guide. Our emphasis in indexing has been on capturing passages where active volcanic processes are particularly well-documented or interpreted and where quantitative measurements have been made. The indexing is necessarily subjective, and no two indexers would agree on all of the citations, either as to importance or as to the subject heading assigned. Nonetheless we have aimed to pull out of an otherwise continuous narrative information useful to a researcher interested in original observations and interpretations of active Hawaiian volcanism. Syntheses of some of these observations are made in articles published outside the HVO serial publications (see remarks on the bibliography below). Routine descriptions of seismic and volcanic activity are not indexed, as they are found chronologically in each weekly and monthly bulletin. The second through fourth special reports have been indexed less specifically, as these each contain a table of contents to guide the interested reader.

It has been especially satisfying to be able to index a comprehensive list of references to papers published before the founding of the Hawaiian Volcano Observatory, as well as those published in outside journals in the decades covered by the HVO serial publications (1912-1955). Our bibliography updates the superb annotated bibliography published by Gordon Macdonald in 1947 (reference number 530 of the bibliography in volume 1). We have included in our list only those references in Macdonald (1947) pertaining to Hawaiian volcanic activity published in outside journals. Thus, we have excluded the following: (1) articles in *The*

Volcano Letter and in the HVO publications reprinted in the present volumes; (2) articles on hydrology, and most references to the geography and geomorphology of Hawaii that do not appear to contain information on volcanic processes; (3) a few articles on Hawaiian volcanic activity where Macdonald's annotations indicate either that the observations are undated or are entirely quoted from earlier sources cited elsewhere in the bibliography; (4) articles about tsunami generated by distant earthquakes; and (5) articles on botany, with the exception of those that deal specifically with revegetation of lava flows.

We have found a few additional early references and have added references published between 1947 and 1955, using a variety of sources, including an unpublished bibliography prepared by Chester Wentworth in 1959. We have indexed the new references and have also incorporated Macdonald's index (Macdonald, 1947, p. 177-191).

ACKNOWLEDGEMENTS

The inspiration for this project came from the reprinting of *The Volcano Letter by* Dick Fiske, Tom Simkin, and Elizabeth Nielsen (1987)*. The success of that project made it obvious that the reprinting of the early serial reports of the Hawaiian Volcano Observatory should, and could, be completed. We are indebted to the Hawaii Natural History Association for its generous funding of this project, and we gratefully acknowledge the support of the following individuals without whom the project could not have been completed:

The late Gordon Macdonald, whose scholarly annotated and indexed bibliography of publications through 1946 was a critical resource which made possible the preparation and indexing of references extending back to the earliest voyages of discovery.

Patrick McNally of the Hamilton Library, University of Hawaii at Manoa, Junko Nowaki and Coreen Ishimaru of the University of Hawaii at Hilo, and U.S. Geological Survey librarians Barbara Chappell, Harry Allan, and Carmen O'Neill at Reston and Jacqueline Freeberg and Ellen White at Menlo Park, who, together with other members of their library staff, researched and provided copies of original reference material not available at HVO.

---

* Fiske, R.S., Simkin, T., and Nielson, E.A., eds., 1987, The Volcano Letter, 1925-1955 [compiled and reprinted; originally published by the Hawaiian Volcano Observatory]: Washington, D.C., Smithsonian Institution Press [unpag.].

Tom English and Wil Tanigawa, for computer and word-processing support throughout the project.

Elizabeth Nielsen, for providing her *Volcano Letter* index on a computer file.

John P. Lockwood, for providing additional references to the early eruptive activity of Mauna Loa.

Helen Bevens of the Hawaii Volcanoes National Park library for assistance with references from their rare book collection and for providing copies of some of the HVO bulletins.

Nelson Ho, for assistance with pagination of the reprinted volumes.

Edwards Brothers, Incorporated, for their high quality reprinting of these bulletins on acid-free paper.

Darcy Bevens, Taeko Jane Takahashi, and Thomas L. Wright

INTRODUCTION

The first through fourth *Special Report of the Hawaiian Volcano Observatory* cover a wide range of topics. The first report summarizes the activity of Kilauea in the years before and just after the establishment of the Hawaiian Volcano Observatory (HVO), describes the founding of HVO, and summarizes the earliest attempts to measure the temperature of the long-lived lava lake at Halemaumau. The second report evaluates tidal influences on the activity at Kilauea and contains a valuable chronology of Kilauea activity from 1865 to 1924. The third and fourth reports stray from the immediate observation of Kilauea, but contain some interpretations of Kilauea's two historic explosive eruptions, those of 1790 and 1924. The third report is a comprehensive treatise on ash deposits of Hawaii and forms the definitive reference for all subsequent work on that topic. The fourth report emphasises the activity of Mount Pelee, with a brief section comparing its eruption with that of Kilauea in 1924.

These four reports are supplemented by a remarkable address delivered by T.A. Jaggar to the Hawaii Volcano Research Association (H.V.R.A.) in December, 1913, and published as a *Special Bulletin of the Hawaiian Volcano Observatory*. In his address to the H.V.R.A., Jaggar discussed the history of volcanology and of the infant HVO and laid out a vision for the future science of volcano observation in the following words: "Keep and publish careful records, invite the whole world to cooperate, and interest the business man." Jaggar's Hawaiian Volcano Observatory took the lead in all three of these principles, and the first two are mainstays of the present HVO, with its extensive observational databases now stored on high-speed computers and with its many collaborative projects with scientists from universities and government agencies, both domestic and foreign. The last aim ultimately failed, though not because of any lack of effort on Jaggar's part. We are today faced with an unfortunate gap between the practical results of science done at HVO and the imperfect understanding and use of these results by those responsible for land-use planning or by investors in such ventures as geothermal energy or residential construction on the slopes of Hawaii's active volcanoes.

The *Bulletin* series, taking up where the first *Special Report* ended in 1912, contains a continuous record of observations made at HVO from 1913 to 1929. In later years, the *Weekly Report, Weekly Bulletin,* and *Monthly Bulletin* overlap with, and were eventually supplanted by, *The Volcano Letter*, which began publication after the great collapse of Halemaumau in 1924. The emphasis in the *Bulletin* differs from that of *The Volcano Letter* in that the material is almost solely restricted to the descriptions of Kilauea and Mauna Loa eruptions, the monitoring of the continuous activity in Kilauea caldera, and the record of the seismograph located at Kilauea summit. The *Bulletin* series contains the *only* descriptions of Kilauea eruptions in the years 1918-1923, except for the reprinting of selected information in the Hawaiian Annual for those years, and are a primary reference for the Mauna Loa eruptions of 1914, 1916, and 1919, as well as for the 1924 eruption of Kilauea.

The *Bulletin* gives an interesting picture of the importance attached to various monitoring activities, most of which are still carried on at HVO. The greatest emphasis was placed on narrating the continuous activity in Kilauea caldera. There are particularly good descriptions of the rise and fall of the lava lake, circulation within the lake, and the formation and destruction of islands or crags of solidified crust within the lake. Much attention was paid to temperature measurement and gas collection. The former was only partly successful, but included among the latter are some of the best gas samples ever collected at an active volcano. Attention was also paid to the recording of earthquakes and measurement of ground tilting. These observations are colored by Jaggar's interest in tidal influences on volcanic cycles and with the idea that all of the active volcanoes were interconnected at depth. Thus, interpretations of seismic activity and ground tilt measured at Kilauea, as well as interpretation of the rise and fall of Halemaumau lava lake, are closely tied to activity at Mauna Loa.

Today we would interpret the shallow plumbing systems of each volcano as being separate, and we have demonstrated that at present there is no relation between earthquake activity and ground deformation at one volcano with eruptive activity at the other. Yet the earlier observations made at Kilauea during Mauna Loa eruptions are sufficiently compelling to raise the question of whether Kilauea *does* respond to activity at Mauna Loa when Kilauea's system is open to the surface.

The things that were not monitored are equally fascinating. There is not a single lithologic description of erupted lava, even during the 1921 eruption, when the olivine content was notably higher than in eruptions before and since. There was evidently no systematic sample collection for either chemical or petrographic analysis, nor were maps prepared to show distribution of erupted lava. What little data we have on the chemistry of Kilauea in this period came from scientists associated with universities, the Carnegie Institution, or the mainland U.S. Geological Survey, who either collected samples themselves, or had them sent by Jaggar. Likewise, the chemistry of early Mauna Loa eruptions was determined from samples collected long after the eruption was over. Observations on the volcanoes were, with a few exceptions, not plotted or synthesized on a regular basis. We have indexed the summaries that *do* exist, and the *Bulletin* contains sufficient information to construct yearly plots of Halemaumau lake level. Tilt and seismic data collected before 1929 were treated more thoroughly in issues of *The Volcano Letter* published in the 1950's.

At this writing Kilauea has been erupting on its east rift zone since January 1983 (continuously since July 1986). A lava shield is being constructed near Kalalua cone, surmounted by a lava lake that exhibits much of the behavior seen on a larger scale in Halemaumau in the early part of this century. The material reprinted in these volumes provides a valuable perspective for observations being made today. In reading the early literature, we find that many of the present-day observations were also made, some in great detail, during earlier periods of Mauna Loa or Kilauea activity. For example, the eight-month-long construction of the small shield Mauna Iki in 1920 parallels the growth of both the Mauna Ulu shield (1969-1974) and the present (1986-) shield. Yet there are also many differences in comparing Kilauea's recent activity with that of the early twentieth century, and it seems evident that, following the 1924 enlargement of Halemaumau, the relationship between summit and rift activity at Kilauea has changed in a rather fundamental way. We can ask whether this change is part of a repeating cycle, and how each type of activity relates to larger cycles marked by caldera collapse. These and other questions can only be answered through study of the entire historic volcanic record, and it is to this end that the material contained in the early serial reports of the Hawaiian Volcano Observatory is being reprinted.

Thomas L. Wright

BULLETIN OF THE TECHNOLOGY STATION, KILAUEA, HAWAII,
JUNE 28, 1913

Kilauea Rumbles an dRoars, but Lava Does Not Rise; Activity Now Expected to Begin July 3.

Hawaiian Volcano Observatory. The observatory is largely supported by the Hawaiian Volcanic Association, made up of leading citizens of the Territory. Photos by T. A. Jaggar, Jr.

DISTANT QUAKE AND 16 LOCAL SHOCKS RECORDED.

TECHNOLOGY STATION, Kilauea, June 28, 1913.—The time of the summer solstice, which reached its culmination June 22, has shown its usual terrestrial effects in the recently reported earthquakes in Martinique and Bulgaria, with loss of life in the last place, and in volcanic eruptions of Asama in Japan and of one or more volcanoes in the upper Alaskan Peninsula. Also, as shown in Mr. Wood's report below, a strong distant earthquake was recorded on our seismographs the evening of June 25, and sixteen local shocks have been noted in the last two weeks. As yet the crater of Kilauea has not responded to the tidal strain.

Halemaumau Dormant.

Halemaumau remains dormant. The glow reported last week died away. On June 22 the fumes appeared thin and there was some faint blowing noise with an interval of forty seconds like Old Faithful playing in cavities beneath the floor over 600 feet down. There were occasional avalanches: a heavy one was reported in the early morning of June 20. On June 24 the fumes had become heavier, there was no noise, and weak talus slides were heard. This morning, June 26, there was no sliding heard, the blowing noise was faintly audible, and the fumes were still dense.

Mauna Loa has been clearly visible today morning, noon and night without the faintest trace of vapor jets. Mr. Wood has calculated that a second culmination in the tidal stresses of the solstice period is reached July 3. It remains to be seen whether any response to this stress will be evidenced by rising lava in either Kilauea or Mauna Loa.

For the Whitney Laboratory of Siesmology Mr. W. O. Wood makes the following report:

Seven Shocks Recorded.

During the past week seven earthquakes have been registered, six small local shocks and one feeble teleseism.

June 19, from 2:17:02 a.m. to 2:18 a.m. H. S. T. Intensity, high II Cancani scale; about 0.4 the minimum perceptible unit. Origin distant about 15

June 19, from 3:38:32 a.m. to 3:40:15 a.m. H. S. T. Intensity, III-IV Cancani scale: not felt, but about the value of the minimum perceptible unit. Origin distant about 20 miles.

June 19, from 4:27:25 a.m. to 4:29 a.m. H. S. T. Intensity, III-IV Cancani scale; not felt, but about the value of the minimum perceptible unit. Origin distant about 15 miles.

June 21, from 10:38:27 a.m. to 10:40:47 a. m. H. S. T. Intensity, III-IV Cancani scale; just below the minimum perceptible unit. Origin distant about 14 miles.

June 22, teleseismic chief-phase waves from 3:31:5 a.m. to 3:27:5 a.m. H. S. T. Earlier phases were not registered. Distance of origin unknown. This shock manifested only moderate power at its source.

June 22, from 5:46:46 p.m. to 5:48:5 p. m. H. S. T. Intensity, medium I Cancani scale; about one-tenth the minimum perceptible unit. Origin distant a little over 40 miles.

June 25, from 8:20:19 a.m. to 8:20:36 a.m., H. S. T. Intensity, III-IV Cancani scale; not felt, but about the value of the minimum perceptible unit. Origin distant not over 6 miles.

Also, in the early evening hours of June 25, motion of a powerful, world-shaking telesecism was recorded for several hours, motion of large amplitude being recorded for over an hour. This record has not yet been measured with care. Approximately, the origin was distant a little over 3000 miles.

T. A. JAGGAR, Jr., Director.

Cancani Scale.

Those in charge of the Observatory at the Volcano have prepared a table explaining the Cancani dynamical scale by which seismic intensity is measured. The scale is based on millimeters per second. The intensity of acceleration from one given point to another in the scale enables the observers to state definitely the system of the shock, as follows:

		From	To
I.	Instrumental	0.0	2.5
II.	Very slight	2.5	5.0
III.	Slight	5.0	10.0
IV.	Sensible, mediocre...	10.0	25.0
V.	Rather strong	25.0	50.0
VI.	Strong	25.0	50.0
VII.	Very strong	100.0	250.0
VIII.	Ruinous	250.0	500.0

Inner cone and pit at Halemaumau, as seen from the concrete pier on the observatory porch. Daily photographs are taken of this scene to show changes in fumes, clouds and atmospheric conditions.

WEEKLY REPORT OF HAWAIIAN VOLCANO OBSERVATORY

From the Pacific Commercial Advertiser, July 7, 1913.

TECHNOLOGY STATION, Kilauea, July 3.—The reported activity of Vesuvius, June 29, adds another to the list of eruptions following the solstice. At Kilauea, June 27, between 11:30 a. m. and 2:30 p. m., the blowing noises had ceased to be audible, and subsidence of the lava was indicated by heavy avalanches and small slides from the N.E. side of the bottom of the pit. The fumes appeared heavier and were irrespirable on the east and south edges of the pit. June 29 the avalanching had diminished and a faint blowing was heard again.

June 30, at 11 a. m., a prolonged hissing occurred at intervals of about 50 seconds, each hissing lasting from 20 to 30 seconds. It appeared to come from about the middle of the bottom area, and was heard best on the north or windward edge. Rare light sliding of rocks was heard and one avalanche at 11:40 a. m. Below the north station the wall far down could be seen flaring inward, the talus has slipped far below where it was in March last, and there is a sulphurous patch high under the west station. The N. bench 60 feet down is all gone except a clinging remnant 3 to 4 feet wide under the N sta-

INSTRUMENT SHELTER,
Built on the north edge of Halemaumau.

TECHNOLOGY STATION,
The building on the lava near the edge of the fire pit.

tion. The Postal Rift at 2 p. m., June 30, 1913, had a temperature of 316 Cent., a fall of only 7 C. since April 1.

July 1, between 10:30 a. m. and noon, two long slides and a number of small slides were heard and some hissing could be heard from time to time lasting from 10 to 15 seconds.

The first reports of work done at this station by Mr. Perret in 1911 have been published in the American Journal of Science monthly February to June, 1913.

Some Activity.

Up to the time of writing no response of the magma column to the culumination of stress on this date, mentioned in the last report, has been noted other than this—that the sounds of eruption, chiefly hoarse breathing noises, which had become inaudible on June 27, have again increased in energy. In view of the general low stage of eruption at present, more than this could scarcely be looked for with confidence. Large talus-avalanches, usually considered to indicate sinking magma, have been heard several times in the past week.

Seismic Records.

The routine report of the Whitney Laboratory of Seismology follows:

Up to June 30 six shocks have been recorded, the first being the strong teleseism mentioned last week, the others weak local shocks.

The world-shaking earthquake on the 25th of June was registered from a sharp beginning at 6:33:51 p. m. H. S. T. to a vague ending at 8:45—p. m. H. S. T. Its origin was about 3000 miles distant from this station. Among earthquakes of great power it was only a moderate shock.

June 28, from 5:58:27 p. m. to 6:02 p. m. H. S. T. Intensity, III-IV Cancani scale; not felt, but about the value of the minimum perceptible unit. Origin distant about 30 miles.

June 29, from 11:32:03 a. m. to 11:32:15 a. m. H. S. T. Intensity, low III Cancani scale; about 0.6 the minimum perceptible unit. Distance of origin indeterminate.

June 29, from 11:32:20 a. m. to 11:32:27 a. m. H. S. T. Intensity, III-IV Cancani scale; not felt, but about the value of the minimum perceptible unit. Distance of origin indeterminate.

June 29, from 11:34:10 a. m. to 11:34:31 a. m. H. S. T. Intensity, medium III Cancani scale; about 0.7 to 0.8 the minimum perceptible unit. Distance of origin indeterminate.

June 30, from 11:12:27 a. m. to 11:13:5 a. m. H. S. T. Intensity, low I Cancani scale; about 0.1 the minimum perceptible unit. Origin distant about 25 miles.

Also in July two local shocks have been registered.

July 1, from 9:27:00 a. m. to 9:29:54 a. m. H. S. T. Intensity, medium III Cancani scale; about 0.8 the minimum perceptible unit. The registration of this shock was witnessed and it definitely was not perceptible to the senses. Origin distant about 30 miles.

July 1, from 2:21:06 p. m. to 2:21:36 p. m. H. S. T. Intensity, medium I Cancani scale; about 0.2 the minimum perceptible unit. Distance of origin indeterminate. Very respectfully,

T. A. JAGGAR, JR., Director.

Weekly Report of Hawaiian Volcano Observatory

From the Pacific Commercial Advertiser, July 14, 1913.

TECHNOLOGY STATION, Kilauea, July 10.—Earthquakes have been reported in Italy with some damage to buildings; this brings the number of districts in the world where seismic and volcanic disturbances of an unusual sort have been reported up to six, without counting those places which have not attracted newspaper notice. All of these happenings have come at a time when the earth was under nutation strain by reason of the sun's northing. The observers at the Hawaiian Volcano Observatory expected some change of activity at Kilauea at this season, because of the record of the volcano since the return of the lava in the autumn of 1907, the record showing rise winter and summer and subsidence spring and autumn, as follows:

Winter 1907-1908, rising lava.
Spring 1908, moderate.
Summer 1908, increase.
Autumn 1908, collapse.
Winter 1908-1909, high.
Spring 1909, lower.
Summer 1909, higher.
Autumn 1909, subsidence.
Autumn and winter 1909, high.
Spring 1910, low.
April and June 1910, high.
Summer and autumn 1910, lower.
Winter 1910-1911, moderate.
Spring 1911, no measure.
Summer 1911, high.
Autumn 1911, low.
Winter 1911-1912, highest.
Spring, 1912, lower.
Summer 1912, high.
Autumn 1912, low.
Winter 1912-1913, higher.
Spring 1913, very low.

It will be seen that this has been fairly systematic, the exceptions being the two cases capitalized. The beginning of this period of activity followed within nine months the cessation of activity on Mauna Loa.

Kilauea during the past week shows no change. July 4, 1913, two avalanches were heard about four o'clock in the afternoon, and an occasional very deep booming from the lava in the depths. On the afternoon of July 7 one avalanche at the W. was heard at three o'clock, and rare faint blowing sounds. On July 9 the blowing was more distinct. At some time during June, 1913, a large portion of the S.E. high rim of Halemaumau has fallen, removing a formerly protruding crag.

Seven Earthquakes Recorded.

For the Whitney Laboratory of Seismology the following report is submitted by H. O. Wood:

Seven earthquakes have been registered here during the interval covered; two of these were very feeble teleseismic movements, the others weak local shocks.

July 4, from 8:22:40 a.m. to 8:23:32 a.m. H. S. T. Intensity, III-IV Cancani scale; not felt but about the value of the minimum perceptible unit. Origin distant about 21 miles.

July 6, from 2:59:23 p.m. to 2:59:58 p.m. H. S. T. Intensity, III-IV Cancani scale; not felt but about the value of the minimum perceptible unit. Origin distant about 16 miles.

July 7, from 7.15:26 a.m. to 8.33 a.m. H. S. T. Intensity, locally very slight, probably of only moderate energy at its origin, for a strong shock. Origin distant not less than 2200 miles nor more than 3900 miles phases ill-defined so that more precise determination is impossible.

July 8, from 1:55:38 p.m. to 2:35 p.m. H. S. T. This shock had only moderate energy, for a strong shock, at its origin; very feebly registered here.

Distance of origin cannot be determined.

July 9, from 2:24:00 a.m. to 2:25:03 a.m. H. S. T. Intensity, medium III Cancani scale; about 0.75 the minimum perceptible unit. Origin distant about 26 miles.

July 9, from 5:08:59 a.m. to 5.10:35 a.m. H. S. T. Intensity, I-II Cancani scale; about 0.25 the minimum perceptible unit. Origin distant about 22 miles.

July 9, from 6.35:44 a.m. to 6:37:11 a.m. H. S. T. Intensity, I-II Cancani scale; about 0.25 the minimum perceptible unit. Origin distant about 25 miles.

T. A. JAGGAR, Jr.,
Director.

VIEWS SHOWING ACTIVITY IN PIT OF KILAUEA.

(Photographs by Prof. T. A. Jaggar, Jr.)

First Stage: S. Bench of 1912; looking down from S. Station 11 a. m., Jan. 14, 1913. White line shows what fell away in second stage.

Second Stage: S. Bench of 1912; looking down from S. Station 11 a. m., March 29, 1913, after greater part of bench had fallen away.

S. part Halemaumau pit Dec. 3, 1912. From S. W. Station. Portion marked by white line has fallen during June, 1913.

Looking eastward and down from Old Rest-house 6:10 p. m., March 23, 1913. Entire bench beyond white line fell during week following.

WEEKLY BULLETIN OF HAWAIIAN VOLCANO OBSERVATORY

From the Pacific Commercial Advertiser, Honolulu, July 21, 1913.

TECHNOLOGY STATION, July 17. —The only noteworthy change in the behavior of Halemaumau during the past week has happened during the last twenty-four hours, when the blowing noises became louder. Since the last report the crater has remained smoky, the fumes acrid and unbreathable, the noise a faint rhythmic blowing, and rock slides few.

It may be of interest to state here briefly the present condition of the Hawaiian Volcano Research Association. This society is a voluntary one, made up of subscribers to scientific work which is being executed by the Massachusetts Institute of Technology.

Source of Support.

There are twenty-six subscribers in Hawaii and Massachusetts, both firms and individuals. A group of firms and persons in Hilo built the main observatory building in the spring of 1912. Publications to date have been weekly reports since the summer of 1911, a memoir by Daly in the Proceedings of American Academy of Arts and Sciences in 1911, articles by the director in the Technology Review 1911 and the Honolulu Chamber of Commerce Annual 1912, articles by H. O. Wood in the Bulletin of the Seismological Society of America, and articles by Perret in the American Journal of Science. The Massachusetts Institute will publish the quarterly reports.

From now on this weekly bulletin as it appears in The Advertiser will be reprinted as a leaflet and sent to regular annual subscribers to the work of the association. L. A. Thurston is chairman of the active committee of the subscribers and C. H. Cooke is treasurer. New subscribers who are interested in our volcanoes will be welcomed in the association. The association aims: (1) To record volcanic activity and earthquakes in Hawaii; (2) to attract scientific men hither for special studies; (3) to promote by every legitimate means the establishment of volcano observatories all over the world.

Fourteen Earthquakes.

The following report from the Whitney Laboratory of Seismology is submitted by H. O. Wood:

During the interval covered by this report fourteen earthquakes have been registered at the observatory; all were of local origin and four wrote records of considerable amplitude.

July 9, from 4:55:10 p. m. to 4:56:54 p. m. H. S T. Intensity, medium I Cancani scale; about 0.15 the value of the minimum perceptible unit. Origin distant about 12 miles.

July 10, from 3:07:03 p. m. to 3:07:12 p. m. H. S. T. Intensity, I-II Cancani scale; about 0.25 the minimum perceptible unit. Origin distant about seven miles.

July 10 from 4:54:51 p. m. to 4:56:03 p. m. H. S. T. Intensity, low I Cancani scale; about 0.07 the minimum perceptible unit. Origin distant about 30 miles.

July 11, from 4:06:34 p. m. to 4:07:39 p. m. H. S. T. Intensity, high I Cancani scale; about 0.2 the minimum perceptible unit. Origin distant about 13 miles.

July 11, from 10:19:24 p. m. to 10:20:45 p. m. H. S. T. Intensity, medium I Cancani scale; about 0.1 the minimum perceptible unit. Origin distant about 13 miles.

July 12, from 1:31:30 a. m. to 1:33:03 a. m. H. S. T. Intensity, medium I

CLIFF-WALL UNDER THE OBSERVATORY.

COTTAGE AND INSTRUMENT SHELTER OF HAWAIIAN VOLCANO OBSERVATORY.

Cancani scale; about 0.1 the minimum perceptible unit. Origin distance is indeterminate.

July 12, from 2:29:42 a. m. to 2:30:31 a. m. H. S. T. Intensity, low I Cancani scale; about 0.06 the minimum perceptible unit. Origin distance is indeterminate.

July 12, from 3:39:32 a. m. to 4:02:17 a. m. H. S. T. Intensity, III-IV Cancani scale; not felt here, but about the value of the minimum perceptible unit. Felt at Kapapala. Origin distant about 30 miles.

July 12, from 4:37:03 a. m. to 4:38:48 a. m. H. S. T. Intensity, low I Cancani scale; about 0.06 the minimum perceptible unit. Origin distant about 10 miles.

July 13, from 8:06:57 a. m. to 8:08:49 a. m. H. S. T. Intensity, II Cancani scale; about 0.4 the minimum perceptible unit. Origin distant about 30 miles.

July 13, from 11:50:03 a. m. to 11:50:55 a. m. H. S. T. Intensity, low I Cancani scale; about 0.1 the minimum perceptible unit. Origin distance is indeterminate.

July 18, from 5:14:43 p. m. to 5:15:28 p. m. H. S. T. Intensity, low I Cancani scale; about 0.06 the minimum perceptible unit. Origin distance is indeterminate.

July 14, from 9:59:56 p. m. to 10:00:45 p. m. H. S. T. Intensity, medium I Cancani scale; about 0.1 the minimum perceptible unit. Origin distance indeterminate.

July 15, from 1:28:50 p. m. to 1:30:39 p. m. H. S. T. Intensity, III-IV Cancani scale; about the value of the minimum perceptible unit, though not felt here. For one value of the amplitude the acceleration rises far about the value of the minimum perceptible unit, but this probably was caused by a superposition of thrusts in succession, for such a value, if real, would have been felt generally. Origin distant about 14 miles.

Very respectfully,

T. A. JAGGAR JR., Director.

*** ——— ***

Cancani Scale of Seismic Intensity.

Expressed by accelerations measured in millimeters per second.

I.	Instrumental . . .	0.0	2.5
II.	Very slight	2.5	5.0
III.	Slight	10.0	25.0
IV.	Sensible, mediocre	10.0	50.0
V.	Rather strong	25.0	50.0
VI.	Strong	25.0	50.0
VII.	Very strong	100.0	250.0
VIII.	Ruinous	250.0	500.0
IX	Disastrous	500.0	1000.0
X.	Very disastrous	1000.0	2500.0
XI.	Catastrophic . . .	2500.0	5000.0
XII.	Great catastrophe	5000.0	10000.0

Grade IV. is ordinarily the minimum perceived by the senses; and in grade XII. the acceleration, or rate of change of motion (jerk) reaches that of terrestrial gravitation.

The Whitney Laboratory of Seismology is equipped with two Bosch-Onori 100ky tromometers registering N-S and E-W motion, a heavy Onori tromometer registering E-W motion and an Onori "ordinary Seismograph" designed for registering strong earthquakes in all three components of motion. These are seated on concrete piers in a closed basement room having practically constant temperature, beneath the chief Observatory building near the hotel. For the present time is referred to a rated chronometer, loaned by the College of Hawaii. At the substation by the edge of the active pit an Onori two-component tromometer with light steady masses is mounted on a concrete pier placed directly on the fresh lava surface.

WEEKLY BULLETIN OF HAWAIIAN VOLCANO OBSERVATORY

From the Pacific Commercial Advertiser, Honolulu, July 28, 1913.

TECHNOLOGY STATION, July 24. —The week at Kilauea began without marked change, the pit smoky and the glow of the lava or burning gases invisible beneath a mantle of crust and rock tumble, as in the weeks past. An important change took place July 23, and the visible fire returned. About June 19, 1913, glow and flames in cavities were last seen during a short-lived rise, which came to an end within a few days. The active lava pool of the past winter subsided and crusted over early in April, and since that time has been hissing and rumbling at a depth of over 600 feet below the 3700-foot contour, the level of the north rim of Halemaumau.

The slight increase of blowing noise reported last week for Thursday, July 17, did not develop any great intensity. July 18 blowing could be heard by listening intently near the Old Rest-house on the north rim, the puffs lasting from 8 to 13 seconds. About 11:30 a.m. and 11.45 a.m., two rock-slides were heard, lasting each about four minutes. July 20 the noises were a little stronger but there was very little sliding. July 22 the blowing noise was very faint, and could not be heard at all from the east side of the pit. Throughout the period from July 17 to July 22 the fumes rose in dense clouds of hard outline.

Signs of a Rise.

On the morning of July 23 the fume cloud as seen from the Observatory appeared less dense, smaller and of softer outline. The wind-eddy opened from time to time the southeast half of the pit, so that the walls, the low-lying talus at their foot and the inner ring of fuming holes could be clearly seen. At 11 a.m. from the S. and SE. stations strong hissing noises from the bottom area could be heard every 60 to 70 seconds and lasting from 5 to 10 seconds. The fumes as seen from the edge appeared much thinner and their odor was much less acrid and more breathable, than of late. These changes have all been observed in the past to be the characteristic of rising lava.

At 4:30 p.m. July 23 the hissing was still louder accompanied by an occasional deep rumbling note like subterranean lava in a cavern. The blowing had become almost continuous with a rhythmic puff-puff like a freight engine on a steep grade interrupted every now and then by a long hiss. The short puffs were at intervals of about two-fifths of a second. The recurrent deep grumble was timed and found to have no regularity, the intervals being 20, 30, 35, 90 seconds, etc. Occasional light rock slides were heard, principally NE, W and N.

The Postal Card Rift at 6 p.m. had a temperature of 313 degrees C., a fall of 3 degrees sine June 30, 1913.

After dark at 8 p.m., July 23, a glowing and probably flaming chimney was seen in the northeast part of the bottom area of the pit during temporary clearings of the fume-cloud. It appeared to be in the location whence the blowing noises proceeded and about where the Old Faithful fountain was last seen. It was seen from the E, SE, S and SW stations.

For the Whitney Laboratory of Seismology Mr. H. O. Wood reports the somewhat unusual condition that there have been no earthquakes registered during the past week. Very respectfully, T. A. JAGGAR, Jr., Director.

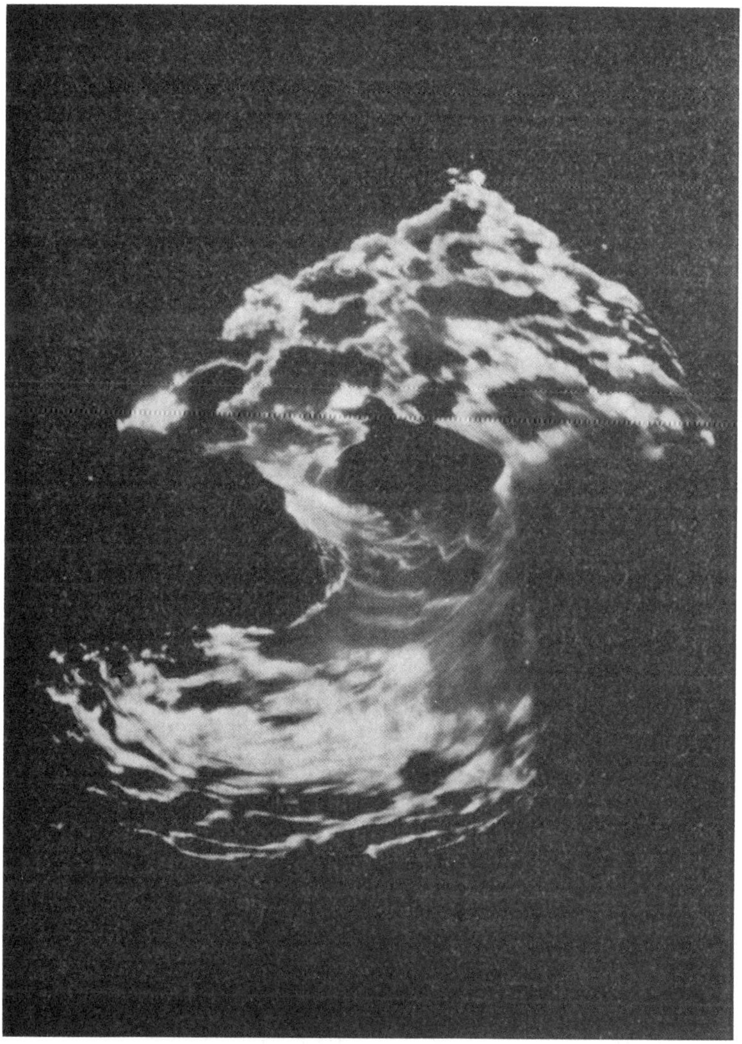

THE LAVA POOL WHEN LAST SEEN.

Feb. 24, 1913 at 8 p. m., from the East. Two great torrents of melt were pouring around an island from West to East.

Cancani Scale of Seismic Intensity.

Expressed by accelerations measured in millimeters per second.

I.	Instrumental . . .	0.0	2.5
II.	Very slight	2.5	5.0
III.	Slight	10.0	25.0
IV.	Sensible, mediocre	10.0	50.0
V.	Rather strong	25.0	50.0
VI.	Strong	25.0	50.0
VII.	Very strong	100.0	250.0
VIII.	Ruinous	250.0	500.0
IX	Disastrous	500.0	1000.0
X.	Very disastrous	1000.0	2500.0
XI.	Catastrophic . . .	2500.0	5000.0
XII.	Great catastrophe	5000.0	10000.0

Grade IV. is ordinarily the minimum perceived by the senses; and in grade XII. the acceleration, or rate of change of motion (jerk) reaches that of terrestrial gravitation.

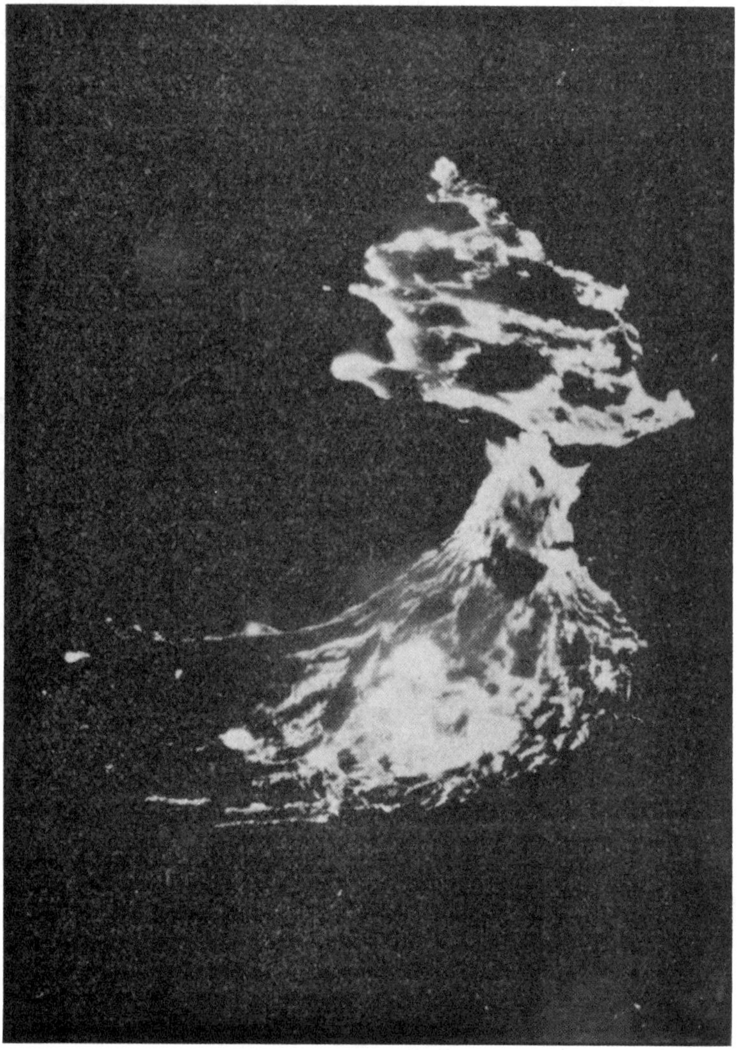

The Lava Pool at 9 a. m., Feb. 26, 1913, from the East. The island has become a peninsula, on the left.

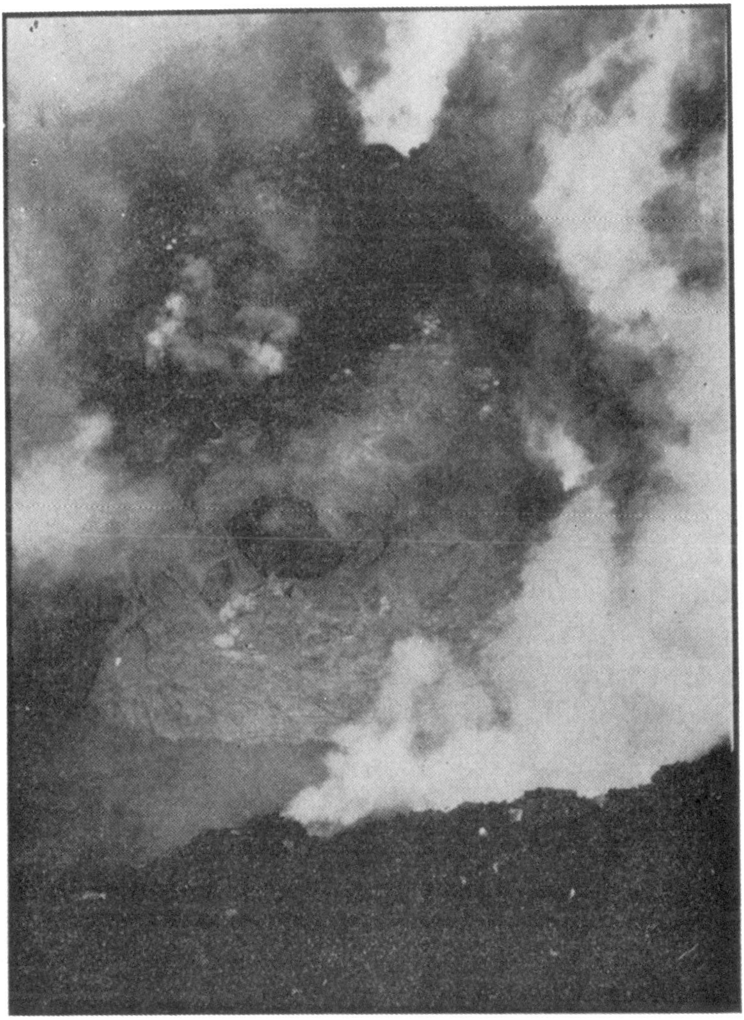

The Lava Pool after temporary rise at 9 a. m., March 10, 1913, from the East. After this it sank away and became gradually obscured by fumes.

The Whitney Laboratory of Seismology is equipped with two Bosch-Omori 100ky tromometers registering N-S and E-W motion, a heavy Omori tromometer registering E-W motion and an Omori "ordinary Seismograph" designed for registering strong earthquakes in all three components of motion. These are seated on concrete piers in a closed basement room having practically constant temperature, beneath the chief Observatory building near the hotel. For the present time is referred to a rated chronometer, loaned by the College of Hawaii. At the substation by the edge of the active pit an Omori two-component tromometer with light steady masses is mounted on a concrete pier placed directly on the fresh lava surface.

WEEKLY BULLETIN OF HAWAIIAN VOLCANO OBSERVATORY

From the Pacific Commercial Advertiser, Honolulu, August 4, 1913.

TECHNOLOGY STATION, Kilauea, July 31.—The glowing chimney in Halemaumau seen last week was short-lived. On the morning of Thursday, July 24, from ten o'clock to noon noises of hissing, rumbling and pulsating exhausts were audible as on the previous day. Heavier and more continuous avalanches of rock took place, sometimes continuing for five minutes or longer, especially on the west side of the pit. In the morning the fumes appeared as before, relatively thin, but in the afternoon they appeared denser, with hard edges to the rising billows. These signs were all indicative of subsiding lava beneath. In the evening continued avalanches were reported and no glow was seen.

Heavy Avalanches Witnessed.

On July 25, from ten o'clock to noon, the fumes rose straight up with little wind, overriding the edges first east, then west. Further confirmation of subsidence after the rise of two days before was presented by the acridity of the fumes to any one breathing them, the sulphuric acid being very strong, whereas on July 23 the smoke had been respirable. About eleven a.m. by a rare chance of the eddying fumes the whole bottom tract of Halemaumau was seen clearly. It was an immense flat funnel of slide-rock with the inner talus continually sliding. There was no hole in the middle, but the fumes rose from orifices in the rock tumble about the periphery of the slide-rock area.

One fumarole high on the west wall is cemented with plastered lava, moulded in talus which has now slipped away to a lower position. The bare, steep rock walls extend down from two to four hundred feet almost sheer, and in places with some overhang. By good fortune the writer saw one very heavy avalanche of talus when the entire funnel ring slid inward with a tremendous roar which could be heard at a considerable distance away from the pit, and clouds of brown dust were thrown up in the center. The effect was as though the lava floor under the talus were withdrawing its support by subsidence. The slide lasted a full minute.

On this date a grumbling noise like pounding lava deep down was heard the sound becoming almost continuou after eleven a.m. At ten-thirty in the morning from the East an occasional faint blowing was heard. After eleven o'clock the fumes closed in and the pit was obscured.

Uwekahuna Moving.

At nine-fifteen in the morning July 25 a landslide was seen from the observatory on the west wall of Kilauea south of Uwekahuna Bluff. At the foot of this cliff on the lava floor there are two talus cones, and the slide augmented the southern and lighter colored one. The source of the slide at the top of the cliff was seen to be one of the Uwekahuna cracks, suggesting that those cracks are perhaps "working," that is, the great rock spalls on the side of the subsiding lava of the pit may be tending to slip down a little. There is a series of such spalls under Uwekahuna Bluff making terraced steps in the wall of Kilauea Crater. Light brown dust rose from the slide, and similar dust clouds marking slides at the same place arose repeatedly during the day and the following four days. At eleven forty-five a.m. July 27, there was a strong slide there.

Saturday, July 26, at 8:30 a.m. sliding rocks in Halemaumau could be heard occasionally, the fumes were strong, and partial views of the bottom area from the southeast and south stations showed nothing new. From the north a very faint and rare breathing noise was heard, but the dominant noise was sliding stones. The Postal Rift at ten-thirty a.m. had a temperature of 313 degrees C., temperature of the air 20 degrees C.

On July 29, at three-twenty p.m., the temperature of the Postal Rift remained the same, 313 degrees C. On this date there was a slight rumble from the pit, having tendency to the Old Faithful period (40 seconds). The now Uwekahuna slide was examined and photographed; it was found that a chasm at the top of the cliff is extending itself northward in the direction of the many parallel cracks.

Six Shocks Recorded.

For the Whitney Laboratory of Seismology the following report is submitted by H. O. Wood:

Since the last report six local earthquakes have been registered here, none of which was strong enough to attract the notice of any person. In all cases the amplitude of movement was small, but in two cases it was unusually rapid, denoting a relatively high acceleration.

July 25, from 11:29:57 p. m. to 11:31:22 p. m. H. S. T. Intensity, very low I Cancani scale; less than 0.1 the minimum perceptible unit. Origin distant about 47 miles.

July 27, from 9:16:40 a. m. to 9:18:25 a. m. H. S. T. Intensity, medium I Cancani scale; less than 0.2 the minimum perceptible unit. Origin distant about 50 miles.

July 28, from 10:03:08 p. m. to 10:03:44 p. m. H. S. T. Intensity, doubtful—acceleration measures twice the minimum perceptible unit, but the amplitude was very small and the shock was not felt—the motion was exceedingly rapid. Origin distant about 12.5 miles.

July 29, from 12:44:08 (midnight) to 12:44:51 a. m. H. S. T. Intensity, doubtful—higher acceleration than that of the minimum perceptible unit, but not felt—motion very rapid. Origin distant about 13 miles.

July 29, from 6:07:48 a. m. to 6:09:15 a. m. H. S. T. Intensity, medium III Cancani scale; about 0.5 the minimum perceptible unit. Origin distant about 12.5 miles.

July 29, from 6:37:20 a. m. to 6:38:35 H. S. T. Intensity, medium III Cancani scale; about 0.8 the minimum perceptible unit. Origin distant about 18.6 miles.

Besides these feeble earthquakes there has been a noteworthy registration of the motion due to volcanic vibration. At this station this motion is seldom or never absent completely from the seismogram. There are, however, sporadic waxings in amplitude which give rise to conspicuous groups of waves which may run for a few seconds up to several minutes, rarely longer. Fundamentally these do not differ from weak local earthquakes, except perhaps in point of causation; but on the seismogram they differ from typical earthquake records because they increase in amplitude gradually from minimum to maximum and then decrease gradually again. Thus they do not present the well-marked phases commonly distinguishable even with very feeble near-by shocks.

Since July 18 there have been registered between 125 and 150 distinct groups of these vibrations. This is at least twice as many groups as for any corresponding interval, probably three times as many. Also the energy of these groups has been far greater than usual. In one instance the acceleration measures nearly twice the minimum perceptible unit, but as in the cases of the shocks discussed above this is due to exceedingly rapid motion, not to moderately large amplitude, and consequently such motion was not actually perceptible. No interpretation of the meaning of this marked augmentation in volcanic vibration can be hazarded.

Very respectfully,

T. A. JAGGAR JR., Director.

VIEWS TAKEN AT KILAUEA.

Upper—Blister lava· An extraordinary flow which solidified in a hollow sheli in the northeast part of the Kilauea lava field.—Lower—Sulphur crystals in cavities at the Sulphur banks, Volcano House.

Cancani Scale of Seismic Intensity.

Expressed by accelerations measured in millimeters per second.

I.	Instrumental . ..	0.0	2.5
II.	Very slight	2.5	5.0
III.	Slight	10.0	25.0
IV.	Sensible, mediocre	10.0	50.0
V.	Rather strong	25.0	50.0
VI.	Strong	25.0	50.0
VII.	Very strong	100.0	250.0
VIII.	Ruinous	250.0	500.0
IX	Disastrous	500.0	1000.0
X.	Very disastrous	1000.0	2500.0
XI.	Catastrophic . ..	2500.0	5000.0
XII.	Great catastrophe	5000.0	10000.0

Grade IV. is ordinarily the minimum perceived by the senses; and in grade XII. the acceleration, or rate of change of motion (jerk) reaches that of terrestrial gravitation.

The Whitney Laboratory of Seismology is equipped with two Bosch-Omori 100ky tromometers registering N-S and E-W motion, a heavy Omori tromometer registering E-W motion and an Omori "ordinary Seismograph" designed for registering strong earthquakes in all three components of motion. These are seated on concrete piers in a closed basement room having practically constant temperature, beneath the chief Observatory building near the hotel. For the present time is referred to a rated chronometer, loaned by the College of Hawaii. At the substation by the edge of the active pit an Omori two-component tromometer with light steady masses is mounted on a concrete pier placed directly on the fresh lava surface.

WEEKLY BULLETIN OF HAWAIIAN VOLCANO OBSERVATORY

From the Pacific Commercial Advertiser, Honolulu, August 11, 1913.

TECHNOLOGY STATION, KILAUEA, August 7.—No important changes have taken place at Halemaumau. On Thursday, July 31, there was some blowing noise in the pit and a few rock slides. On August 1 there was a rumbling noise from the depths resembling thunder, more or less continuous. On both days the fumes were dense.

On the evening of August 1, at about six o'clock, there was a rock fall at the new slide from the wall of Kilauea Crater south of Uwekahuna Bluff. Sharp tilting of the ground northward was recorded by the seismographs during the night. In the early morning of August 2 two more rock slides were reported at this place.

August 3 at the pit no noise at all was audible in the afternoon, and there was very little talus sliding. On Monday, August 4, there was blowing and rumbling. August 5, from one to three p. m., the blowing noise was almost continuous as heard from the north rest-house. The fumes appeared thinner from a distance, but were not easily respirable on the edge. A thunderous reverberation accompanied the puffing. The latter had no rhythmic quality, but seemed to wax and wane with the thundering of lava in caverns. The puffing was in general of the "freight engine" kind.

August 5, at four p. m., the temperature of the Postal Rift was 313 degrees C.

August 6. at three p. m., the noise had diminished. There was thudding and rumbling and a rare breathing noise. It could be heard only on the windward edge, and occasionally augmented. There were no avalanches and the fumes were irrespirable and dense. There was no good seeing. The rumbling was nearly continuous, but not loud. At five p. m. the fumarole high on the western wall was seen to be smoking strongly, with sulphur stain. At four-thirty p. m. the intervals between the beginnings of the rumbling sounds were timed and found to vary from twenty to fifty seconds, and the duration of each rumble varied from five to fifteen seconds.

The fuming vents on the high northeastern slope of Mauna Loa were plainly visible from the Observatory at sundown on the evenings of August 5 and 6.

Large Lava Tube Explored.

A notable happening of the week was an exploration on the morning of August 2, by a party headed by L. A. Thurston, of a large lava tube or cavern leading northeast from the bottom of Kaluaiki Crater, the northern of the twin craters. This cave opens from the wall twenty-five feet above the ground and extends 1914 feet about N. 55° E. It is some twelve feet in diameter at the entrance, of nearly circular section, with a flat floor like a masonry water conduit.

Chambers within the tube are thirty feet wide and eighteen feet high. The floor is encumbered in two or three places with tumble from the roof, one of these opening a shallow shaft to daylight, but otherwise for a third of a mile a man may walk erect through the tunnel. Stalagmites in groups of spires dot the floor in places, one to two feet high and four to six inches across at the base, and corresponding stalactites are suspended from the roof. These accretions are of the water-made variety. The tunnel ends abruptly in a wide chamber with roof sloping down to the floor.

No Local Shocks Recorded.

For the Whitney Laboratory of Seismology, H. O. Wood submits the following report:

During the past week no local earthquakes have been recorded and there has been nothing noteworthy about the registration of the local volcanic vibration. Sharp earth-tilt has been recorded, but not more notably than on former occasions.

During the week three teleseismic records have been written. In all three cases the energy transmitted to this station was slight, so that the earlier phases were not well delineated; consequently no accurate measure of origin distance is possible in any of the cases. It is sure that these shocks were not of unusual power in the vicinity of their origins, though of course they were strong shocks. They were registered as follows:

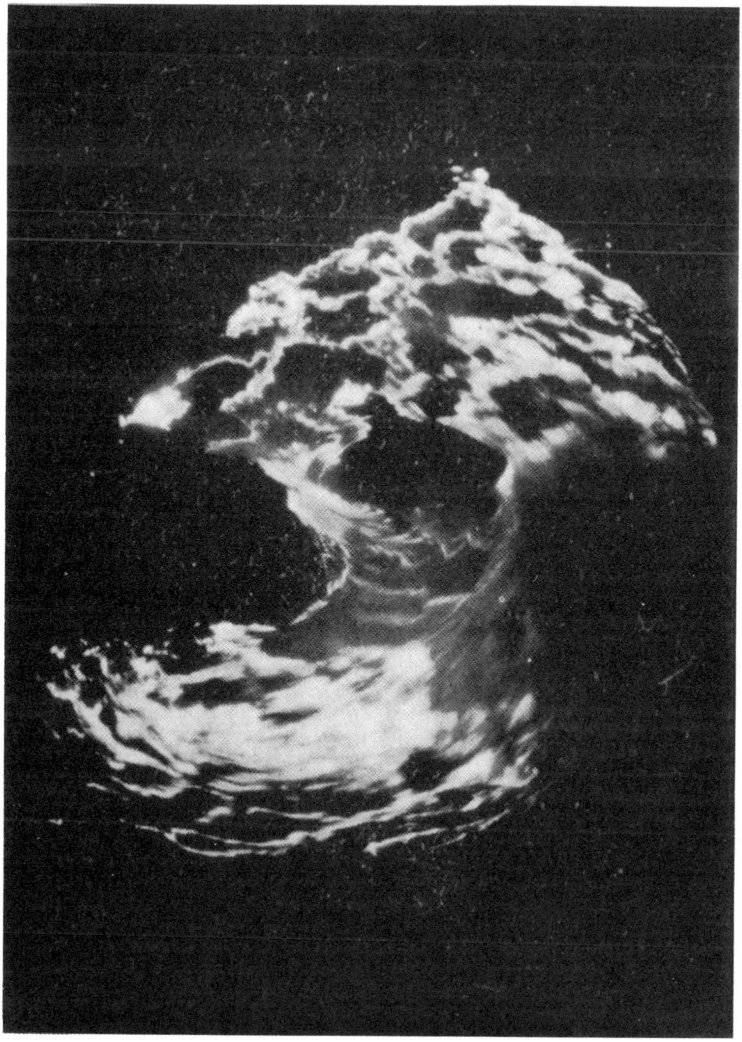

THE LAVA POOL WHEN LAST SEEN.
Feb. 24, 1913 at 8 p. m., from the East. Two great torrents of melt were pouring around an island from west to east.

July 31, from 5:32:37 a. m. to 5:45 approx. a. m. H. S. T. Only the chief-phase action was registered.

August 1, from 7:01:37 a. m. to an indefinite ending about ten minutes later. Also only the chief phase was registered.

August 5, from 3:31:32 p. m. to an indefinite ending about ten minutes later. Part of the early motion was vaguely inscribed in the case of this shock. Very respectfully,

T. A. JAGGAR JR., Director.

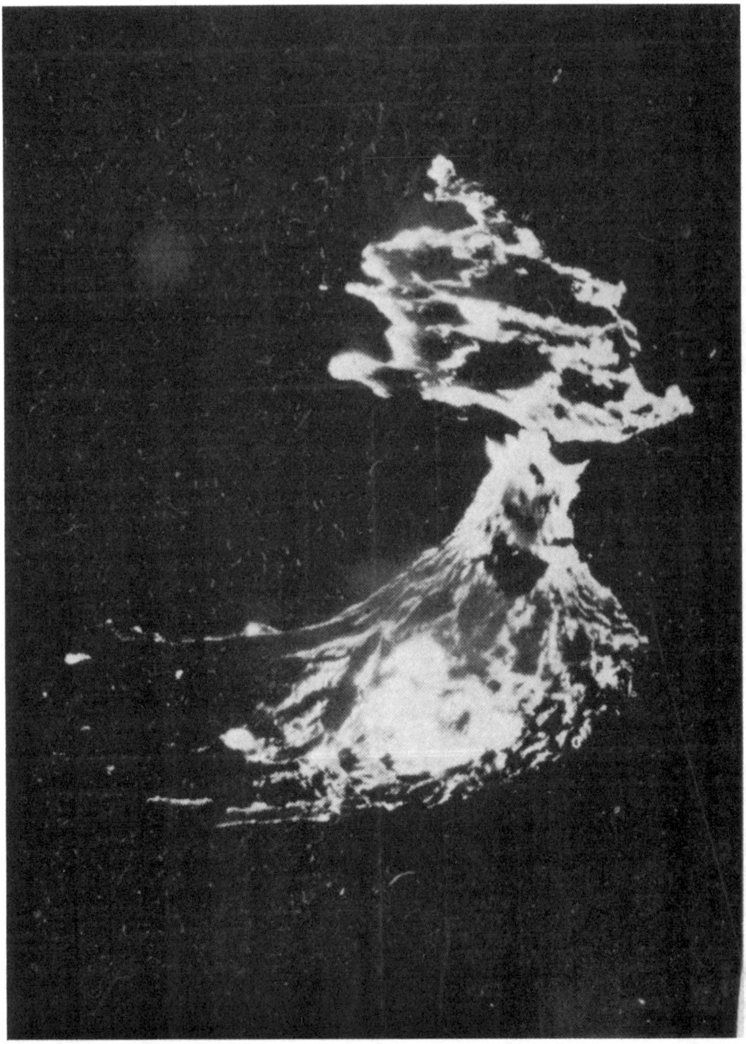

The Lava Pool at 9 p. m., Feb. 26, 1913, from the east. The island has become a peninsula, on the left.

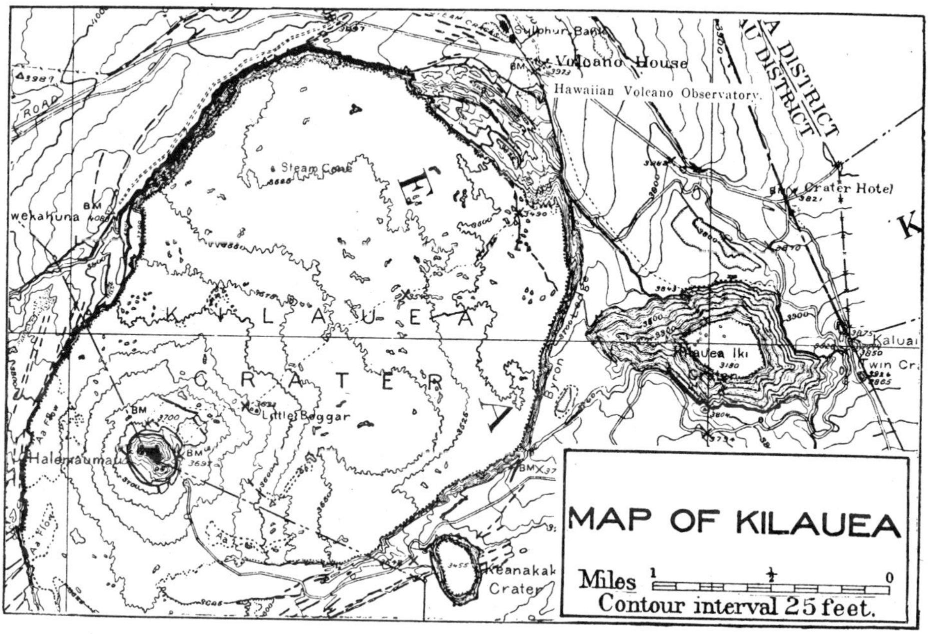

HAWAIIAN VOLCANO RESEARCH ASSOCIATION.

This society is a voluntary one, made up of subscribers to scientific work which is being executed by the Massachusetts Institute of Technology.

There are twenty-six subscribers in Hawaii and Massachusetts, firms and individuals. A group of firms and persons in Hilo built the main observatory building in the spring of 1912. Publications to date have been weekly reports since the summer of 1911, a memoir by Daly in the Proceedings of American Academy of Arts and Sciences in 1911, articles by the director in the Technology Review 1911 and the Honolulu Chamber of Commerce Annual 1912, articles by H. O. Wood in the Bulletin of the Seismological Society of America, and articles by Perret in the American Journal of Science. The Massachusetts Institute will publish the quarterly reports.

This weekly bulletin as it appears in The Advertiser will be reprinted as a leaflet and sent to regular annual subscribers to the work of the association. L. A. Thurston is chairman of the active committee of the subscribers and C. H. Cooke is treasurer. New subscribers who are interested in our volcanoes will be welcomed in the association. The association aims: (1) To record volcanic activity and earthquakes in Hawaii; (2) to attract scientific men hither for special studies; (3) to promote the establishment of volcano observatories all over the world.

WHITNEY LABORATORY OF SEISMOLOGY.

The Whitney Laboratory of Seismology is equipped with two Bosch-Omori 100kg tromometers registering N-S and E-W motion, a heavy Omori tromometer registering E-W motion and an Omori "ordinary Seismograph" designed for registering strong earthquakes in all three components of motion. These are seated on concrete piers in a closed basement room having practically constant temperature, beneath the chief Observatory building near the hotel. For the present, time is referred to a rated chronometer, loaned by the College of Hawaii. At the substation by the edge of the active pit an Omori two-component tromometer with light steady masses is mounted on a concrete pier placed directly on the fresh lava surface.

CANCANI SCALE OF SEISMIC INTENSITY

Expressed by accelerations measured in millimeters per second written "per second per second."

I.	Instrumental	0.0	2.5
II.	Very slight	2.5	5.0
III.	Slight	5.0	10.0
IV.	Sensible, mediocre....	10.0	25.0
V.	Rather strong	25.0	50.0
VI.	Strong	50.0	100.0
VII.	Very strong	100.0	250.0
VIII.	Ruinous	250.0	500.0
IX.	Disastrous	500.0	1000.0
X.	Very disastrous	1000.0	2500.0
XI.	Catastrophic	2500.0	5000.0
XII.	Great catastrophe....	5000.0	10000.0

Grade IV. is ordinarily the minimum perceived by the senses; and in grade XII. the acceleration, or rate of change of motion (jerk) reaches that of terrestrial gravitation.

Weekly Bulletin of Hawaiian Volcano Observatory

From the Pacific Commercial Advertiser, Honolulu, August 18, 1913.

TECHNOLOGY STATION, August 14.—The inner lava pit of Kilauea, Halemaumau, continues in a state of repose, the only mark of activity of the lava beneath being clouds of whitish fume which either fill the pit, diffused by the strong tradewind, or eddy over the edge at one or more places so as to leave one side open to view. The most common point of view under the northeast trade is from the south or southeast, and here one looks down into an enormous caldron, with vertical walls extending down two to four hundred feet, beyond which sliderock continues down funnelwise to where the fumes are seen rising through the tumble of talus. Beyond all is concealed by the fume-fog.

During the last three months the only marks of activity which have fluctuated have been noises of blowing and rumbling, greater or less suffocating quality to the fumes when breathed, and very rare glimpses of flame seen two or three times at night. The sliding of talus blocks, either heard or seen, increases when the bottom is sinking.

Unusually Quiet Conditions.

The past week has been unusually quiet, corresponding with a marked cessation of local earthquakes for three weeks past. On August 10, at eleven forty-five a.m. there was no noise except a weak working of the W talus. At ten a.m., August 11, there was not even any sliding heard. On August 12 at four p.m. one or two blocks of rock were heard slipping, but otherwise all was quiet. The fumes seemed a little more breathable. Today, August 14, at eleven a.m., four fumaroles around the bottom area could be seen S. SE and E, the southeastern one emitting white fume very vigorously.

The talus was sliding a little W. the fumes were very irrespirable, and there was no blowing or rumbling.

For the Whitney Laboratory of Seismology the following report is submitted by H. O. Wood:

Local seismic action continues to be of slight energy. During the interval covered by this report no local earthquakes have been registered and no noteworthy tilting or volcanic-vibration groups have been recorded. During the past three days microscopic waves have been strong, but not of unusual energy.

Peruvian Earthquake Recorded.

The strong earthquake of August 6, reported from Caraveli in West-central Peru, was registered here. It wrote a peculiar record. The first phase, beginning sharply at 12:06:17 (noon) H. S. T., was unusually vigorous and of unusually large amplitude, but it died away quickly and became lost to view completely, among moderate microscopic waves, except in the north-south component. No indication of the registration of the second phase can be discerned on any of the seismograms. The chief phase began vaguely, but surely, at about 12:23:20 p.m. H. S. T.; except in the north-south component in which its beginning was very vague. This interpretation of the record is justified by the periods of waves measured, as well as by the fact that the time interval between the beginning of the first and chief phases, thus interpreted, denotes a distance for the origin of somewhat over 4000 miles—a close approximation to the actual value. In appearance, however, the record more closely resembles a record of the chief phase of two weak distant shocks with a short time interval intervening, so strong relatively is the motion of the first phase. A reasonable interpretation of this record would point to a very short, sharp shock of moderate destructive energy at the source, so that the energy of the chief phase, and especially of the second phase, would be relatively slight. Motion of this shock was not registered later than 1:35 p.m. Very respectfully; T. A. JAGGAR, Jr.
Director.

One of the rewards of exploration in the vast lava-crusted caldron of Kilauea.

Looking out through the entrance of Keanakakina (Thurston's Cavern).

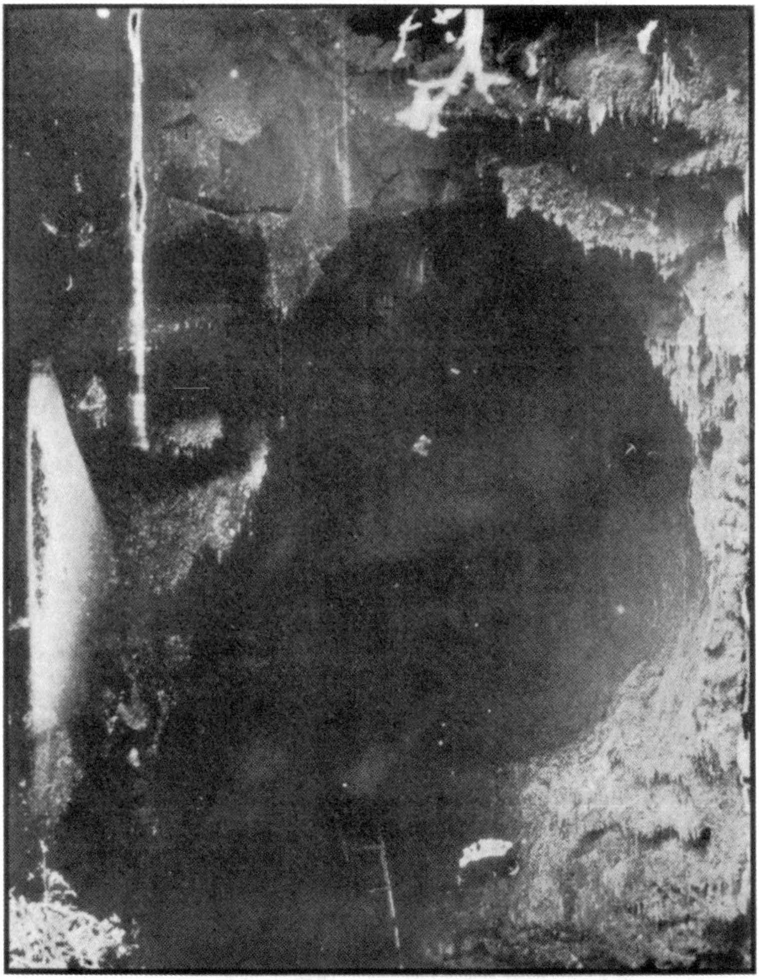

Looking into entrance of Keanakakina

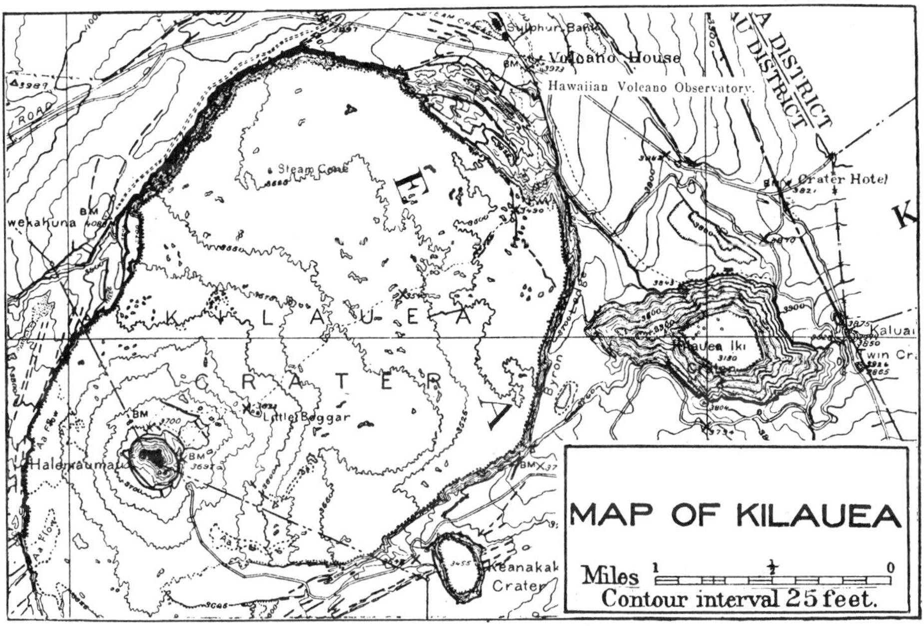

MAP OF KILAUEA

HAWAIIAN VOLCANO RESEARCH ASSOCIATION.

This society is a voluntary one, made up of subscribers to scientific work which is being executed by the Massachusetts Institute of Technology.

There are twenty-six subscribers in Hawaii and Massachusetts, firms and individuals. A group of firms and persons in Hilo built the main observatory building in the spring of 1912. Publications to date have been weekly reports since the summer of 1911, a memoir by Daly in the Proceedings of American Academy of Arts and Sciences in 1911, articles by the director in the Technology Review 1911 and the Honolulu Chamber of Commerce Annual 1912, articles by H. O. Wood in the Bulletin of the Seismological Society of America, and articles by Perret in the American Journal of Science. The Massachusetts Institute will publish the quarterly reports.

This weekly bulletin as it appears in the Advertiser will be reprinted as a leaflet and sent to regular annual subscribers to the work of the association. L. A. Thurston is chairman of the active committee of the subscribers and C. H. Cooke is treasurer. New subscribers who are interested in our volcanoes will be welcomed in the association. The association aims: (1) To record volcanic activity and earthquakes in Hawaii; (2) to attract scientific men hither for special studies; (3) to promote the establishment of volcano observatories all over the world.

WHITNEY LABORATORY OF SEISMOLOGY.

The Whitney Laboratory of Seismology is equipped with two Bosch-Omori 100kg tromometers registering N-S and E-W motion, a heavy Omori tromometer registering E-W motion and an Omori "ordinary Seismograph" designed for registering strong earthquakes in all three components of motion. These are seated on concrete piers in a closed basement room having practically constant temperature, beneath the chief Observatory building near the hotel. For the present, time is referred to a rated chronometer, loaned by the College of Hawaii. At the substation by the edge of the active pit an Omori two-component tromometer with light steady masses is mounted on a concrete pier placed directly on the fresh lava surface. Hawaiian standard time (H. S. T.) is 10 hrs. 30 m. slower than Greenwich time.

CANCANI SCALE OF SEISMIC INTENSITY

Expressed by accelerations measured in millimeters per second.

I.	Instrumental	0.0	2.5
II.	Very slight	2.5	5.0
III.	Slight	5.0	10.0
IV.	Sensible, mediocre	10.0	25.0
V.	Rather strong	25.0	50.0
VI.	Strong	50.0	100.0
VII.	Very strong	100.0	250.0
VIII.	Ruinous	250.0	500.0
IX.	Disastrous	500.0	1000.0
X.	Very disastrous	1000.0	2500.0
XI.	Catastrophic	2500.0	5000.0
XII.	Great catastrophe	5000.0	10000.0

Grade IV. is ordinarily the minimum perceived by the senses; and in grade XII. the acceleration, or rate of change of motion (jerk) reaches that of terrestrial gravitation.

WEEKLY BULLETIN HAWAIIAN VOLCANO OBSERVATORY.

Technology Station, August 21, 1913.

At Kilauea the past week has been uneventful. There has been no marked change in the activity of Halemaumau, there have been no earthquakes, and nothing unusual or noteworthy has been observed in the registration of microseismic motion, or of volcanic vibrations.

In the early forenoon of Friday, August 15, a strong south to southwest wind set in which blew, with diminishing energy, until late Sunday evening, August 17. During the first day of its duration, this wind brought heavy rain, the precipitation amounting to more than two inches in twenty-four hours. Associated with this storm there was immediate, sharp southward tilting of the rock surface at the Observatory, of unusually large amount, with less marked but still considerable westward tilting. This response is considered to be due to sudden and unusual loading with rainfall of the adjacent south and southwest region.

At Halemaumau at 2 p.m. on Saturday, August 16, the wind was south, sweeping dense fumes over the 1894 shelf at the northwest. Fumes were rising at the southeast, south, southwest and west. Here they were sharp and irrespirable. At the west one rumble and some slipping of talus was heard. One long continuous blast was heard, due either to a general talus slide or to a puff.

Partial views from the old rest house showed that there were not many fumaroles working on the north side. At this point the fumes were perhaps a little more respirable.

At about 10 a.m. on Sunday, August 17, there was a light south wind and drizzling rain at the edge of the pit, and at the old rest house there was heard from time to time a sharp crackling -- or single snaping sounds -- at first thought to be due to single rocks falling. However, with a favorable wind change the fumes cleared from the whole pit of Halemaumau affording a splendid view of the entire bottom. There were six marked fumarole places, one at the west being most active, and largest. From this place came the snapping noise -- now thought to be due to rocks cracking under great heat, like the cracking of a lamp chimney. Two talus slides were heard, one at the northwest and one at the west.

Under the west station and just above the talus there are two rock caverns revealed by the breaking away of the lower walls, which are new. The southernmost of these is a cave in the wall, opening downwards at about forty-five degrees. The other is a craterlet with a vertical tube about ten feet in diameter, extending downwards. These are in the same general region with Perret's cavern and the one under the west station, but much lower down.

In the bottom of the pit two of the fumaroles yield fumes much more fluish than the others. The bottom area appears even flatter than when last seen previously, and no lower. It is the sliding away of the lowermost talus which has revealed the west caves.

On the north wall at its bottom the vertical cliff gives place to an insloping rock face of much flatter angle. At the joint between the two is an active fumarole at a fissure in the wall. This is where active fuming undermined the north shelf earlier in the year, but now the source of the fumes is seen to be from the wall itself, all the talus having slipped lower. Amongst the talus material still farther down on the side there are one or two ledges which suggest an inner rock wall. Occasional rumbling noises and rare breathing sounds were heard. With the resumption of the trade wind, nothing could be seen or heard on Monday or Tuesday, August 18 and 19.

WEEKLY BULLETIN OF HAWAIIAN VOLCANO OBSERVATORY

From the Pacific Commercial Advertiser, Honolulu, September 1, 1913.

TECHNOLOGY STATION, August 28.—Conditions at Kilauea remain without change. uring the past week northeast trade winds have blown steadily, so maintaining almost continually a swirl of fumes in the Halemaumau pit. No view into the depths has been afforded to the writer and, so far as can be learned, only one party of visitors has been more fortunate. This party reported that the caves leading into the west wall were visible but that no view of the very bottom was obtained. No sounds of eruption have been heard by any.

One sharp local earthquake has been recorded but it was not felt by any one in the vicinity of the cald-ra. As has been the case several times recently its rate of vibration was very rapid and in consequence of this its acceleration value was considerably above that fixed as the minimum perceptible unit, but on the other hand its maximal amplitudes were small so that the motion did not become perceptible to the senses. For, in reality, the perceptibility of seismic motion depends upon both acceleration and amplitude, though the former is the more important factor. This shock was registered as follows

August 21, from 9:04:48 a. m. to 9:07 a. m. H. S. T. Intensity, III-IV Cancani scale; in the neighborhood of the value of the minimum perceptible unit. Origin distant about 14.3 miles.

There has been nothing noteworthy in the registration of other earth motions during the past week Very respectfully,

H. O. WOOD, Associate.

Evidence of Former Activity at Kilauea

A meandering, distributing lava flow (top) from near the old margin of the former "New Lake," and (lower) doming, with fracture of ropy-festooned lava surface, from the eastern margin of the main crater.

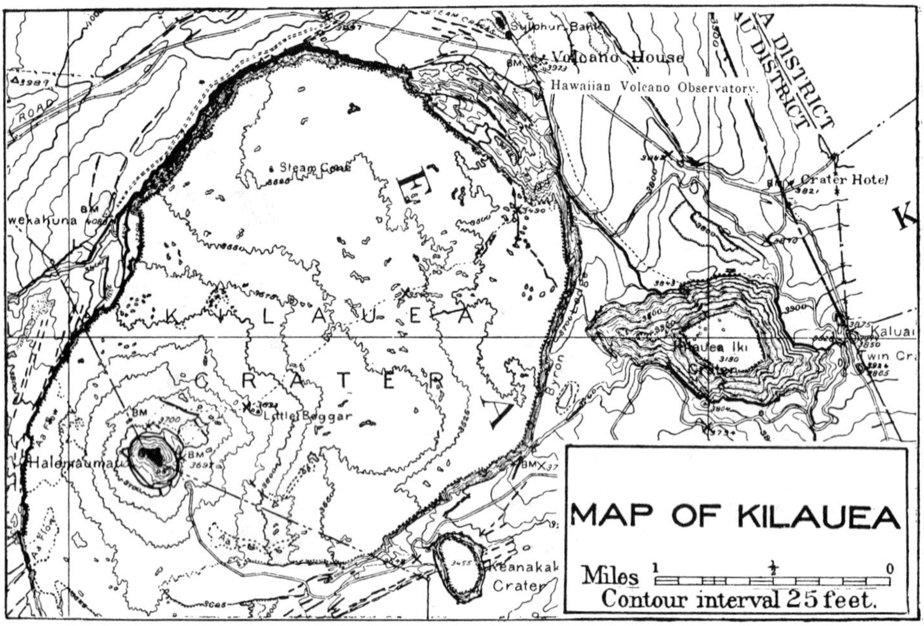

HAWAIIAN VOLCANO RESEARCH ASSOCIATION.

This society is a voluntary one, made up of subscribers to scientific work which is being executed by the Massachusetts Institute of Technology.

There are twenty-six subscribers in Hawaii and Massachusetts, firms and individuals. A group of firms and persons in Hilo built the main observatory building in the spring of 1912. Publications to date have been weekly reports since the summer of 1911, a memoir by Daly in the Proceedings of American Academy of Arts and Sciences in 1911, articles by the director in the Technology Review 1911 and the Honolulu Chamber of Commerce Annual 1912, articles by H. O. Wood in the Bulletin of the Seismological Society of America, and articles by Perret in the American Journal of Science. The Massachusetts Institute will publish the quarterly reports. This weekly bulletin as it appears in the Advertiser will be reprinted as a leaflet and sent to regular annual subscribers to the work of the association. L. A. Thurston is chairman of the active committee of the subscribers and C. H. Cooke is treasurer. New subscribers who are interested in our volcanoes will be welcomed in the association. The association aims: (1) To record volcanic activity and earthquakes in Hawaii; (2) to attract scientific men hither for special studies; (3) to promote the establishment of volcano observatories all over the world.

WHITNEY LABORATORY OF SEISMOLOGY.

The Whitney Laboratory of Seismology is equipped with two Bosch-Omori 100kg tromometers registering N-S and E-W motion, a heavy Omori tromometer registering E-W motion and an Omori "ordinary Seismograph" designed for registering strong earthquakes in all three components of motion. These are seated on concrete piers in a closed basement room having practically constant temperature, beneath the chief Observatory building near the hotel. For the present, time is referred to a rated chronometer, loaned by the College of Hawaii. At the substation by the edge of the active pit an Omori two-component tromometer with light steady masses is mounted on a concrete pier placed directly on the fresh lava surface. Hawaiian standard time (H. S. T.) is 10 hrs. 30 m. slower than Greenwich time.

CANCANI SCALE OF SEISMIC INTENSITY

Expressed by accelerations measured in millimeters per second per second.

I.	Instrumental	0.0	2.5
II.	Very slight	2.5	5.0
III.	Slight	5.0	10.0
IV.	Sensible, mediocre	10.0	25.0
V.	Rather strong	25.0	50.0
VI.	Strong	50.0	100.0
VII.	Very strong	100.0	250.0
VIII.	Ruinous	250.0	500.0
IX.	Disastrous	500.0	1000.0
X.	Very disastrous	1000.0	2500.0
XI.	Catastrophic	2500.0	5000.0
XII.	Great catastrophe	5000.0	10000.0

Grade IV. is ordinarily the minimum perceived by the senses; and in grade XII. the acceleration, or rate of change of motion (jerk) reaches that of terrestrial gravitation.

WEEKLY BULLETIN OF HAWAIIAN VOLCANO OBSERVATORY

From the Pacific Commercial Advertiser, Honolulu, September 8, 1913.

TECHNOLOGY STATION, September 4.—The week has produced a slight increase of activity in Halemaumau, marked by the return of blowing noise from the bottom. From August 28 to August 31, 1913, conditions remained quiet. On September 1 marked blowing noise was heard from the southeast, the wind being southerly. On September 2, at eleven-thirty in the morning, the wind was from the south and a fair view was obtained of the north half of the interior of the caldron of Halemaumau. No pronounced change in the condition of the interior of the pit was observed, except that the western fumaroles appeared more extensive. A strong periodic blowing noise, with the Old Faithful period of about forty-five seconds, was audible from the northern brink. There was very little talus sliding.

A heavy thunderstorm gathered over the Mauna Loa slopes during the morning of September 2, and broke as a torrential rain over Kilauea in the early afternoon, nearly two inches of rain falling, with heavy thunder claps and much lightning.

Today, September 4, at ten in the morning, the blowing noises continue at Halemaumau and the northeast trade wind has brought cooler weather.

J. W. Green, magnetic observer of the United States Coast and Geodetic Survey, has arrived at the Observatory, detailed by the chief of the survey to make special magnetic observations for some weeks at Kilauea. These observations are made at the request of the Hawaiian Volcano Research Association, and have in view both the occupancy of certain magnetic stations to determine local changes in magnetism throughout periods of years, and also to experiment on fluctuations in magnetic declination in relation to the observed changes of activity in Halemaumau.

H. O. Wood reports as follows for the Whitney Laboratory of Seismology:

A single very small earthquake of local origin was recorded between eleven and twelve a. m. on September 2. The exact times of phases and the dimensions of this shock will be given in a later report.

The heavy rain September 2 to September 3 produced notable northward tilt deviation. There has not been any further noteworthy seismic registration. Very respectfully,

T. A. JAGGAR JR., Director.

SCENES AT KILAUEA.

Taking temperature of the Postal Rift (upper), and view of recent landslide on west wall of Kilauea crater.

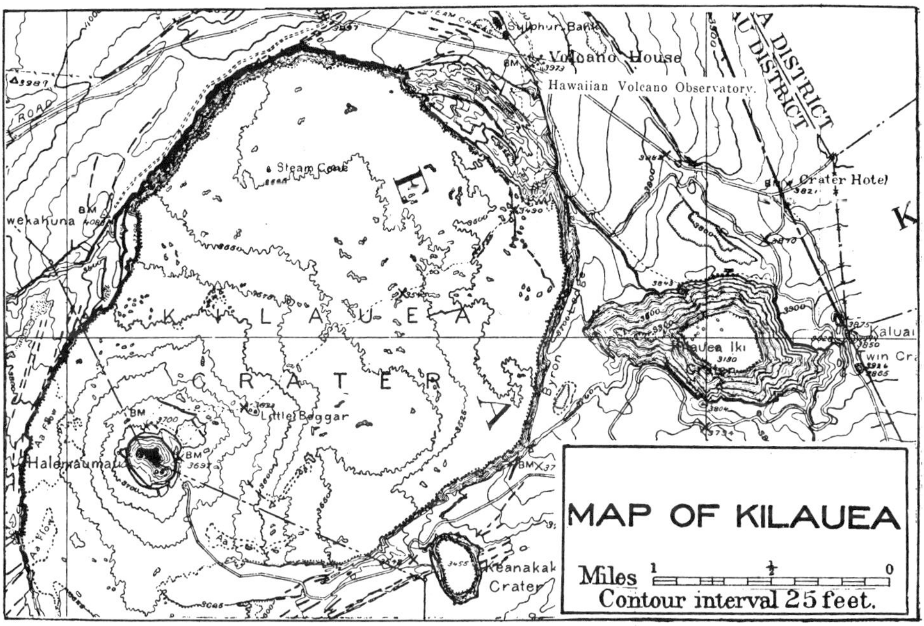

HAWAIIAN VOLCANO RESEARCH ASSOCIATION.

This society is a voluntary one, made up of subscribers to scientific work which is being executed by the Massachusetts Institute of Technology.

There are twenty-six subscribers in Hawaii and Massachusetts, firms and individuals. A group of firms and persons in Hilo built the main observatory building in the spring of 1912. Publications to date have been weekly reports since the summer of 1911, a memoir by Daly in the Proceedings of American Academy of Arts and Sciences in 1911, articles by the director in the Technology Review 1911 and the Honolulu Chamber of Commerce Annual 1912, articles by H. O. Wood in the Bulletin of the Seismological Society of America, and articles by Perret in the American Journal of Science. The Massachusetts Institute will publish the quarterly reports.

This weekly bulletin as it appears in the Advertiser will be reprinted as a leaflet and sent to regular annual subscribers to the work of the association. L. A. Thurston is chairman of the active committee of the subscribers and C. H. Cooke is treasurer. New subscribers who are interested in our volcanoes will be welcomed in the association. The association aims: (1) To record volcanic activity and earthquakes in Hawaii; (2) to attract scientific men hither for special studies; (3) to promote the establishment of volcano observatories all over the world.

WHITNEY LABORATORY OF SEISMOLOGY.

The Whitney Laboratory of Seismology is equipped with two Bosch-Omori 100kg tromometers registering N-S and E-W motion, a heavy Omori tromometer registering E-W motion and an Omori "ordinary Seismograph" designed for registering strong earthquakes in all three components of motion. These are seated on concrete piers in a closed basement room having practically constant temperature, beneath the chief Observatory building near the hotel. For the present, time is referred to a rated chronometer, loaned by the College of Hawaii. At the substation by the edge of the active pit an Omori two-component tromometer with light steady masses is mounted on a concrete pier placed directly on the fresh lava surface. Hawaiian standard time (H. S. T.) is 10 hrs. 30 m. slower than Greenwich time.

CANCANI SCALE OF SEISMIC INTENSITY

Expressed by accelerations measured in millimeters per second per second.

I.	Instrumental	0.0	2.5
II.	Very slight	2.5	5.0
III.	Slight	5.0	10.0
IV.	Sensible, mediocre	10.0	25.0
V.	Rather strong	25.0	50.0
VI.	Strong	50.0	100.0
VII.	Very strong	100.0	250.0
VIII.	Ruinous	250.0	500.0
IX.	Disastrous	500.0	1000.0
X.	Very disastrous	1000.0	2500.0
XI.	Catastrophic	2500.0	5000.0
XII.	Great catastrophe	5000.0	10000.0

Grade IV. is ordinarily the minimum perceived by the senses; and in grade XII. the acceleration, or rate of change of motion (jerk) reaches that of terrestrial gravitation.

WEEKLY BULLETIN OF HAWAIIAN VOLCANO OBSERVATORY

From the Pacific Commercial Advertiser, Honolulu, September 16, 1913.

TECHNOLOGY STATION, September 11.—The week at Kilauea has been marked by first a diminution and then an increase of the blowing noises in Halemaumau, and by an earthquake about 11:38 a.m., September 8, perceptible at the Volcano House and sharply felt at Hilo.

On Friday, September 5, 1913, the blowing noise was inaudible from the east station in the morning but was heard faintly in the afternoon. One rock slide was heard in the morning. On September 7 there was some blowing. At 9 a. m., September 8, the blowing was moderate and rhythmtic with the usual 40-second interval. It was heard from the north. A few stones were heard moving on the W. slides. There was some thudding noise and faint rumble. The fumes were acrid but moderate in volume, and under the NE. trade obscured all view east or north.

On September 10 strong blasts were reported, one lasting 20 seconds.

Seismology Report.

From the Whitney Observatory of Seismology the following report is submitted by H. O. Wood:

Since the last systematic report the following six earthquakes have been registered here:

August 30, from 7:45:40 p. m. to 7:48:50 p. m. H. S. T. Intensity, medium I Cancani scale; about 0.1 the minimum perceptible unit. Origin distant about 25 miles.

August 30, from 8:12:36 p. m. to 8:13:32 p. m. H. S. T. Intensity, medium I cancani scale; less than 0.1 the minimum perceptible unit. Origin distant about 12.5 miles.

September 2, from 11:37:49 a. m. to 11:39:21 a. m. H. S. T. Intensity, medium I Cancani scale; more than 0.1 the minimum perceptible unit. Origin distant about 27.5 miles.

September 3, from 10:39:02 a. m. to 11:16:3 a. m. H. S. T. An ill-registered teleseismic disturbance, probably of relatively small energy at its origin. The phases are indeterminate, hence its origin-distance is unknown.

September 8, at 11:37:56 a.m. H. S. T. A local shock felt at the margin of Kilauea; felt sharply in Hilo. Intensity estimated at IV F-R scale, at VI Cancani scale. All pens of the more sensitive tromometers swept off recording cylinders instantly. Origin-distance approximated at 14 miles. Data uncertain on account of the mutilation of the record.

September 8, from 4:38:45 p. m. to 4:39:49 p. m. H. S. T. Intensity, medium I Cancani scale; about 0.1 the minimum perceptible unit. Origin distant about 16 miles.

Very respectfully,
T. A. JAGGAR, Jr.,
Director.

Upper photo shows north edge of Halemaumau, taken from northeast station; lower shows ash beds under lava of Uwekahuna Bluff on the west wall of Kilauea: both taken on July 29, 1913.

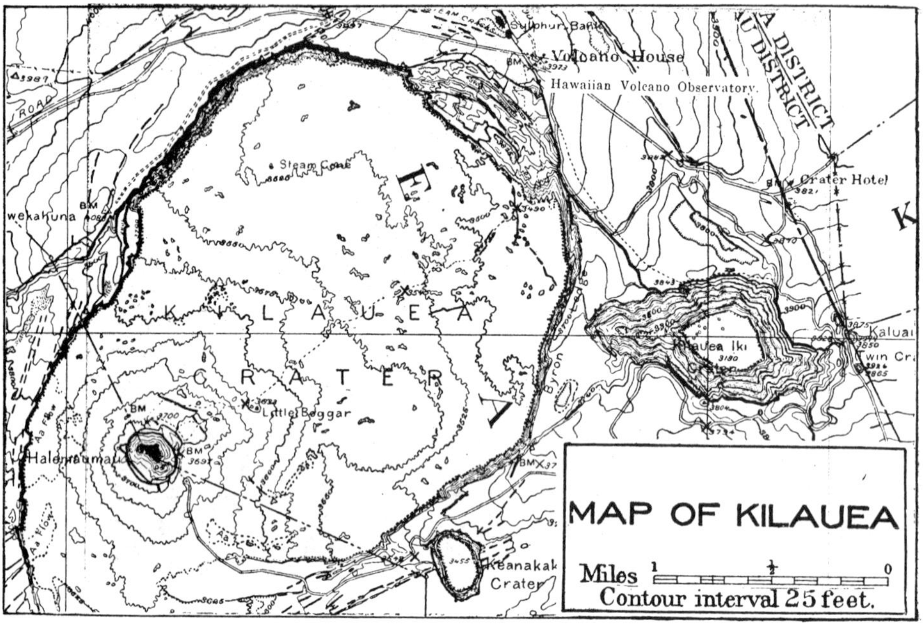

HAWAIIAN VOLCANO RESEARCH ASSOCIATION.

This society is a voluntary one, made up of subscribers to scientific work which is being executed by the Massachusetts Institute of Technology.

There are twenty-six subscribers in Hawaii and Massachusetts, firms and individuals. A group of firms and persons in Hilo built the main observatory building in the spring of 1912. Publications to date have been weekly reports since the summer of 1911, a memoir by Daly in the Proceedings of American Academy of Arts and Sciences in 1911, articles by the director in the Technology Review 1911 and the Honolulu Chamber of Commerce Annual 1912, articles by H. O. Wood in the Bulletin of the Seismological Society of America, and articles by Perret in the American Journal of Science. The Massachusetts Institute will publish the quarterly reports.

This weekly bulletin as it appears in the Advertiser will be reprinted as a leaflet and sent to regular annual subscribers to the work of the association. L. A. Thurston is chairman of the active committee of the subscribers and C. H. Cooke is treasurer. New subscribers who are interested in our volcanoes will be welcomed in the association. The association aims: (1) To record volcanic activity and earthquakes in Hawaii; (2) to attract scientific men hither for special studies; (3) to promote the establishment of volcano observatories all over the world.

WHITNEY LABORATORY OF SEISMOLOGY.

The Whitney Laboratory of Seismology is equipped with two Bosch-Omori 100kg tromometers registering N-S and E-W motion, a heavy Omori tromometer registering E-W motion and an Omori "ordinary Seismograph" designed for registering strong earthquakes in all three components of motion. These are seated on concrete piers in a closed basement room having practically constant temperature, beneath the chief Observatory building near the hotel. For the present, time is referred to a rated chronometer, loaned by the College of Hawaii. At the substation by the edge of the active pit an Omori two-component tromometer with light steady masses is mounted on a concrete pier placed directly on the fresh lava surface. Hawaiian standard time (H. S. T.) is 10 hrs. 30 m. slower than Greenwich time.

CANCANI SCALE OF SEISMIC INTENSITY

Expressed by accelerations measured in millimeters per second per second.

I.	Instrumental	0.0	2.5
II.	Very slight	2.5	5.0
III.	Slight	5.0	10.0
IV.	Sensible, mediocre	10.0	25.0
V.	Rather strong	25.0	50.0
VI.	Strong	50.0	100.0
VII.	Very strong	100.0	250.0
VIII.	Ruinous	250.0	500.0
IX.	Disastrous	500.0	1000.0
X.	Very disastrous	1000.0	2500.0
XI.	Catastrophic	2500.0	5000.0
XII.	Great catastrophe	5000.0	10000.0

Grade IV. is ordinarily the minimum perceived by the senses; and in grade XII. the acceleration, or rate of change of motion (jerk) reaches that of terrestrial gravitation.

WEEKLY BULLETIN OF HAWAIIAN VOLCANO OBSERVATORY

From the Pacific Commercial Advertiser, Honolulu, September 24, 1913.

TECHNOLOGY STATION, Kilauea, September 18, 1913.—The increase of activity noted last week continues at Halemaumau. On Friday, September 12, there was a lull with no noise whatever of blowing. There were dense fumes and some avalanching, indicating a temporary subsidence of the lava beneath. September 13 there was continuous hissing. On September 15 this continued and was louder, and there was some puffing heard. September 16 long and loud hissing was heard even at the east station, where the noise is generally drowned by the wind. September 17 the hissing was moderate and periodic, but today (the eighteenth) the blowing has become harsh and very loud, so that it can be heard at some distance back from the edge of the pit. The blasts were noted at intervals of twenty-five seconds, with occasional exceptionally loud puffs.

For the Whitney Laboratory of Seismology, H. O. Wood reports that during the past week one extremely feeble local earthquake has been registered, which will be detailed in a later report. Nothing noteworthy has been observed in connection with the registration of other seismic motion.

J. W. Green of the United States Coast and Geodetic Survey has already obtained very striking results in magnetic measurement at stations near the edge of Halemaumau, his observations showing very unusual fluctuations in dip and declination within short distances. Very respectfully,

T. A. JAGGAR JR., Director.

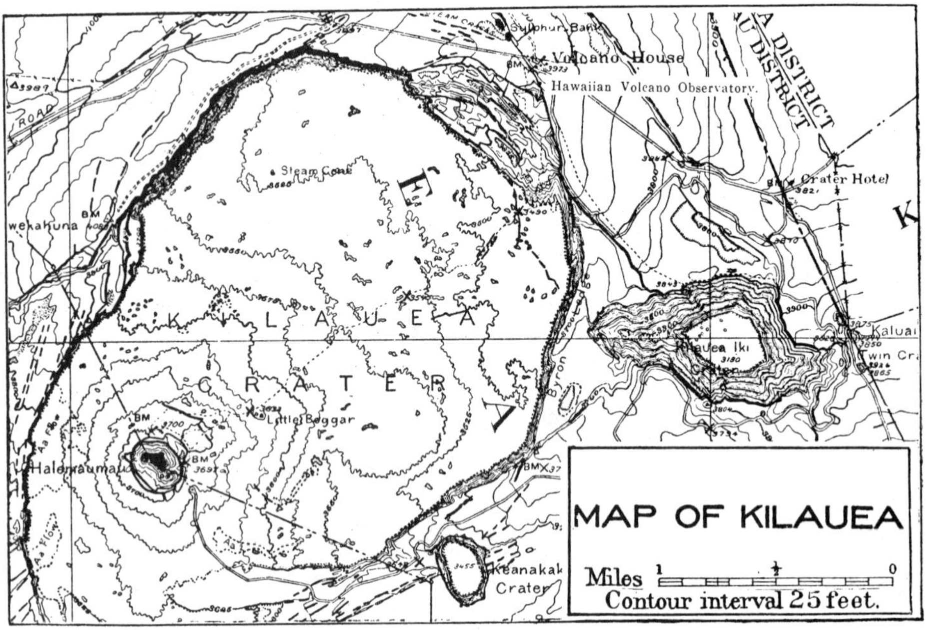

HAWAIIAN VOLCANO RESEARCH ASSOCIATION.

This society is a voluntary one, made up of subscribers to scientific work which is being executed by the Massachusetts Institute of Technology.

There are twenty-six subscribers in Hawaii and Massachusetts, firms and individuals. A group of firms and persons in Hilo built the main observatory building in the spring of 1912. Publications to date have been weekly reports since the summer of 1911, a memoir by Daly in the Proceedings of American Academy of Arts and Sciences in 1911, articles by the director in the Technology Review 1911 and the Honolulu Chamber of Commerce Annual 1912, articles by H. O. Wood in the Bulletin of the Seismological Society of America, and articles by Perret in the American Journal of Science. The Massachusetts Institute will publish the quarterly reports.

This weekly bulletin as it appears in the Advertiser will be reprinted as a leaflet and sent to regular annual subscribers to the work of the association. L. A. Thurston is chairman of the active committee of the subscribers and C. H. Cooke is treasurer. New subscribers who are interested in our volcanoes will be welcomed in the association. The association aims: (1) To record volcanic activity and earthquakes in Hawaii; (2) to attract scientific men hither for special studies; (3) to promote the establishment of volcano observatories all over the world.

WHITNEY LABORATORY OF SEISMOLOGY.

The Whitney Laboratory of Seismology is equipped with two Bosch-Omori 100kg tromometers registering N-S and E-W motion, a heavy Omori tromometer registering E-W motion and an Omori "ordinary Seismograph" designed for registering strong earthquakes in all three components of motion. These are seated on concrete piers in a closed basement room having practically constant temperature, beneath the chief Observatory building near the hotel. For the present, time is referred to a rated chronometer, loaned by the College of Hawaii. At the substation by the edge of the active pit an Omori two-component tromometer with light steady masses is mounted on a concrete pier placed directly on the fresh lava surface. Hawaiian standard time (H. S. T.) is 10 hrs. 30 m. slower than Greenwich time.

CANCANI SCALE OF SEISMIC INTENSITY

Expressed by accelerations measured in millimeters per second per second.

I.	Instrumental	0.0	2.5
II.	Very slight	2.5	5.0
III.	Slight	5.0	10.0
IV.	Sensible, mediocre....	10.0	25.0
V.	Rather strong	25.0	50.0
VI.	Strong	50.0	100.0
VII.	Very strong	100.0	250.0
VIII.	Ruinous	250.0	500.0
IX.	Disastrous	500.0	1000.0
X.	Very disastrous	1000.0	2500.0
XI.	Catastrophic	2500.0	5000.0
XII.	Great catastrophe....	5000.0	10000.0

Grade IV. is ordinarily the minimum perceived by the senses; and in grade XII. the acceleration, or rate of change of motion (jerk) reaches that of terrestrial gravitation.

WEEKLY BULLETIN OF HAWAIIAN VOLCANO OBSERVATORY

From the Pacific Commercial Advertiser, Honolulu, September 28, 1913.

TECHNOLOGY STATION, September 25,—The activity of the inner crater Halemaumau continued to increase to the time of the equinox (September 22) and beyond, with stronger blasting of hot gas through the bottom talus, until at length a glowing lava conelet has appeared about the locality of strong blowing, and the blasting noise has become continuous and loud. The last time a glow was seen was on July 23, 1913, when in the evening, after greatly increased puffing for several days, a glowing spot could be seen faintly through the fumes for a short time, but its nature could not be determined. It was probably a glowing cone, as at present. Accompanying the present increase of activity is a distinct rise of temperature of the Postal Rift fumes, a few hundred feet north of the Halemaumau edge.

On Friday, September 19, increasingly loud blasts were heard from the bottom, lasting each for twenty seconds, followed by lighter puffing for from twenty to twenty-five seconds, when a new blast would begin. September 20, in the evening, the noise was louder, resembling somewhat the roar of a breaking surf. September 21 the blowing noise continued.

September 22, Monday, a record was kept from 10 a. m. until 4 p. m., omitting the hour 12 to 1, to show the average duration of the long puffs and the quieter intervals for a five-minute period at the beginning of every ten minutes. Once an hour throughout this time the temperature of the Postal Rift was read, for six hours. During the same day Mr. J. W. Green made minute to minute observations of magnetic declination at a station northeast of and near Halemaumau. The long puffs averaged about thirty seconds, followed by ten or fifteen seconds usually of diminished hissing, but sometimes the strong hiss would be continuous for from forty to fifty seconds, and then would be augmented in violence by the beginning of a new puff. The Postal Rift remained at a constant temperature, namely, 323 degrees Cent., and the magnetic declination exhibited no unusual phenomena.

The high temperature of the Postal Rift is noticeable, 323 degrees being the same temperature recorded March 25, 1913, when the lava pool was on its final decline before the crusted period of the past summer. The fall in temperature of the Postal Rift appears to have coincided with the subsidence of the lava, and if causally so the present rise in temperature may imply a rise in the lava commensurate with the stand of the end of March last. The following list shows temperatures of Postal Rift:

March 25, 1913, 323 degrees Cent.
March 28, 1913, 318 degrees Cent.
March 29, 1913, 317 degrees Cent.
Lava lake reported ''stagnant, low and approaching a stationary condition.''
June 30, 1913, 316 degrees Cent.
July 23, 1913, 313 degrees Cent.
July 26, 1913, 313 degrees Cent.
July 29, 1913, 313 degrees Cent.
August 5, 1913, 313 degrees Cent.
September 22, 1913, 323 degrees Cent.

At 1:45 p. m. of this date (September 22) an eddy from the light and variable east wind opened the west and northwest sides of the pit to view, showing the bottom with its active fumaroles west and north, the cavern and craterlet at the foot of the west wall, and glimpses were had of the tumble of rocks on the bottom in the center, where now and then a whitish jet seemed to correspond with the noise of blowing. A very hot-looking beehive cone had developed around the north fumarole. A visit to the S. station on the edge of Halemaumau revealed the fact that the western part of the south high bench has lately fallen away. Rock slides were heard occasionally.

Tuesday, September 23, hissing of the same character was in progress, but less loud. At 4:30 p. m. September 24, however, a fine view of the bottom from the north instrument house was obtained, and a glowing conelet was seen in the midst of the funnel of talus. This cone lay to the south of the north fumarole, about the middle of the bottom, not far from the Old Faithful position. Whether the glow in the fissures of the cone was lava or burning gas it was not possible to determine in the short time of vision before the fumes again closed in. The border fumaroles were purling very actively, but the vapors were white and quickly dissipated, and the fumes breathed at the edge were less strong than usual. The hissing was continuous and very loud, and the glowing cone appeared to be the source of the hissing, but no vapor could be seen rising from it. There was some appearance of lava splash around the cone.

Today, September 25, at 4 p. m. continuous hissing could be heard from the old resthouse, but much less loud. There was some faint crackling, rumbling and rock sliding. Little could be seen. The hissing stopped for an instant at one time, only to be immediately resumed. Apparently the volcano is marking time, and the lava falling very slightly since yesterday. In general this period represents the highest activity since early in April.

Seismology Report.

For the Whitney Laboratory of Seismology, the following report is submitted by H. O. Wood:

Since the last systematic report the following earthquakes, all of local origin, have been registered:

Sept. 13; from 10:06:01 a. m. to 10:07:08 a. m. H. S. T. Intensity, low I Cancani scale; about 0.06 the minimum perceptible unit Origin distant about 12.4 miles

Sept. 14, from 7:59:00 a. m. to 8:00:28 a. m. H. S. T. Intensity, low I Cancani scale; about 0.9 the minimum perceptible unit. Origin distant about 12.4 miles.

Sept. 20, from 8:14:29 a. m. to 8:16:49 a. m. H. S. T. Intensity, III-IV Cancani scale; not sensibly felt, but measures above the minimum perceptible unit. Origin-distant 12.4 miles.

Sept. 20, from 8:20:22 a. m. to 8:20:40 a. m. H. S. T. An exceedingly feeble shock, leaving the phases, magnitudes and origin distance practically indeterminable.

Sept. 20, from 8:22:25 a. m. to 8:24:22 a. m. H. S. T. Intensity, medium I Cancani scale; about 0.15 the minimum perceptible unit. Origin distant about 31 miles.

Sept. 24, from 1:10:49 a. m. to 1:12:07 a. m. H. S. T. Intensity, low I Cancani scale; about 0.08 the minimum perceptible unit. Origin distant about 12.5 miles.

Besides these shocks a considerable number of groups of volcanic vibrations have been recorded in the past fortnight, and particularly during the past week. These have, for the most part, been of small amplitude and, except for the unusual quiet of the preceding weeks, they would not be regarded as worthy of note in this routine report. Rapid tilting has been registered during the past week, but it has not been of unusual character.

Very respectfully,

T. A. JAGGAR JR.,
Director.

Northeast Rim, Halemaumau, Photographed in July.

Northwest Rim, Halemaumau, Photographed in July.

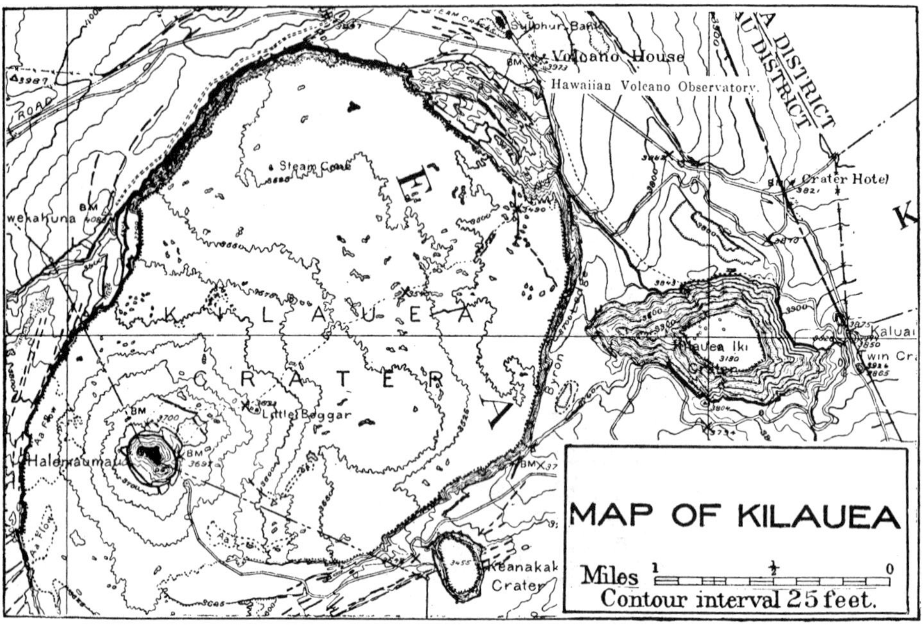

HAWAIIAN VOLCANO RESEARCH ASSOCIATION.

This society is a voluntary one, made up of subscribers to scientific work which is being executed by the Massachusetts Institute of Technology.

There are twenty-six subscribers in Hawaii and Massachusetts, firms and individuals. A group of firms and persons in Hilo built the main observatory building in the spring of 1912. Publications to date have been weekly reports since the summer of 1911, a memoir by Daly in the Proceedings of American Academy of Arts and Sciences in 1911, articles by the director in the Technology Review 1911 and the Honolulu Chamber of Commerce Annual 1912, articles by H. O. Wood in the Bulletin of the Seismological Society of America, and articles by Perret in the American Journal of Science. The Massachusetts Institute will publish the quarterly reports.

This weekly bulletin as it appears in the Advertiser will be reprinted as a leaflet and sent to regular annual subscribers to the work of the association. L. A. Thurston is chairman of the active committee of the subscribers and C. H. Cooke is treasurer. New subscribers who are interested in our volcanoes will be welcomed in the association. The association aims: (1) To record volcanic activity and earthquakes in Hawaii; (2) to attract scientific men hither for special studies; (3) to promote the establishment of volcano observatories all over the world.

WHITNEY LABORATORY OF SEISMOLOGY.

The Whitney Laboratory of Seismology is equipped with two Bosch-Omori 100kg tromometers registering N-S and E-W motion, a heavy Omori tromometer registering E-W motion and an Omori "ordinary Seismograph" designed for registering strong earthquakes in all three components of motion. These are seated on concrete piers in a closed basement room having practically constant temperature, beneath the chief Observatory building near the hotel. For the present, time is referred to a rated chronometer, loaned by the College of Hawaii. At the substation by the edge of the active pit an Omori two-component tromometer with light steady masses is mounted on a concrete pier placed directly on the fresh lava surface. Hawaiian standard time (H. S. T.) is 10 hrs. 30 m. slower than Greenwich time.

CANCANI SCALE OF SEISMIC INTENSITY

Expressed by accelerations measured in millimeters per second per second.

I.	Instrumental	0.0	2.5
II.	Very slight	2.5	5.0
III.	Slight	5.0	10.0
IV.	Sensible, mediocre....	10.0	25.0
V.	Rather strong	25.0	50.0
VI.	Strong	50.0	100.0
VII.	Very strong	100.0	250.0
VIII.	Ruinous	250.0	500.0
IX.	Disastrous	500.0	1000.0
X.	Very disastrous	1000.0	2500.0
XI.	Catastrophic	2500.0	5000.0
XII.	Great catastrophe....	5000.0	10000.0

Grade IV. is ordinarily the minimum perceived by the senses; and in grade XII. the acceleration, or rate of change of motion (jerk) reaches that of terrestrial gravitation.

WEEKLY BULLETIN OF HAWAIIAN VOLCANO OBSERVATORY

From the Pacific Commercial Advertiser, Honolulu, October 5, 1913.

TECHNOLOGY STATION, October 2 —The increased activity noted last week has continued at the inner pit of Kilauea, a spouting, puffing and rumbling lava cone is growing in its bottom, and new Pele's hair is being distributed over the lava to leeward.

At 5 p. m. Friday, September 26, a light continuous hissing could be heard, but nothing could be seen through the fume cloud. At 4:30 p. m., September 27, only the louder hisses could be heard from the east station, and from the old resthouse on the north the hissing was fainter than the previous day and fluctuating. No rock slides were heard. The intervals between the louder puffs were about 70 seconds long. At 5:10 p. m. the temperature of the Postal Rift was 320 degrees Cent. a fall of 3 degrees since September 22.

At 4 p. m., September 29, the noise had changed to a distinct puffing at intervals of from one to two seconds, louder at the end of every minute. For about forty seconds the puffing would be loud and then die away during the last twenty seconds. There was no longer any continuous hiss and at times the puffing was fairly loud. This puffing noise continued, growing more strident and irregular the next two days and finally, at 8 p. m. October 1, flaring at night on the fume cloud over Halemaumau was detected from the Volcano House. At the pit the wind was W.N.W., and from the S.E. station strong glow could be seen. The fumes occasionally overran the edge but they were tolerable to breathe.

Nothing could be seen from the northern stations. The glow would flare up accompanied by loud snorts from the lava cone below, the snorting being clogged and accompanied by a thudding sound, and the loudness was very irregular with intervals of complete silence for a few seconds. Sometimes the blowing was very loud with a noise like a rocket.

Lava Splashing.

During slight clearing from the S.E. at 11 p. m., October 1, a glowing crack apparently eight or ten feet long, was seen, presumably the apex of the lava cone, in the same position as the cone seen September 24. This fissure was the source of the muffled blasts which came with a roar every thirty to forty seconds. With the blasts the crack sputtered sparks and lava splash. It slowly changed to the shape of an oven open northward and ejecting lava sidewise in that direction. Flames were observed playing about the opening. The depth to the lava cone was estimated to be between 500 and 600 feet, and it will be measured when there is sufficient seeing to permit. Only glimpses have been obtained as yet.

KATMAI VOLCANO, ALASKAN PENINSULA, IN AUGUST, 1913.

Pele's Hair Blown Out.

Today, October 2, the wind has been from the SW., and the humidity high, making the fume cloud dense and obstructive to seeing. Strong puffing continued at 3 p. m., when the crater was visited by the writer, the puffs lasting from five to fifteen seconds, followed by intervals of nearly complete quiet averaging about thirty seconds. There were a few light rock slides. The fumes were respirable. Fresh Pele's hair was found scattered to leeward in small tufts, partly coarse hairs of spun glass, but largely a fine whitish down. The roar of the gas blasts at the lava cone in the pit could be plainly heard at the fumarole zone of the Postal Rift to leeward. At 4 p. m. the temperature of the Postal Rift was 320 degrees Cent. At 4:30 the same sputtering noise as last night, like gas explosions clogged with liquid lava, was heard from the lava cone.

Off to Mokuaweoweo.

September 29, an expedition from the observatory departed for Mokuaweoweo the summit crater of Mauna Loa, by the Ainapo route, over the trail recently buillt by Mr. Julian Monsarrat, The party consisted of Mr. H. O. Wood, of the observatory staff, seismologist and geologist, and Mr. J. W Green, magnetician of the Coast Survey. They plan to stay four days at the summit and carry on magnetic and geological investigations. They were accompanied by men from Kapapala Ranch and by Alex. Lancaster.

The complete report of the Whitney Laboratory of Seismology for the week will be made after Mr. Wood's return. Seismically nothing of importance happened until September 30 to October 1, when a remarkable tilt towards the north immediately preceded the increased activity of the crater October 1; this was followed by a number of small local earthquakes, including one felt at the Volcano House about 7:30 a. m. October 2. Very respectfully,

T. A. JAGGAR, JR.,
Director.

* * * * * * * * * * * * * * * *

These remarkable pictures were taken by M. Hohner, during the past summer, and sent to Professor Jaggar, at the Kilauea observatory, by A. H. Bradford, a graduate of Technology. Katmai, the volcano pictured on the preceding page, was in violent eruption in the summer of 1912, and strewed ashes over much of Alaska. The crater was quite inaccessible for many months, and these are among the first pictures taken near it. The picture on this page is that of a great rock, hurled a mile and a half by Katmai.

* * * * * * * * * * * * * * * *

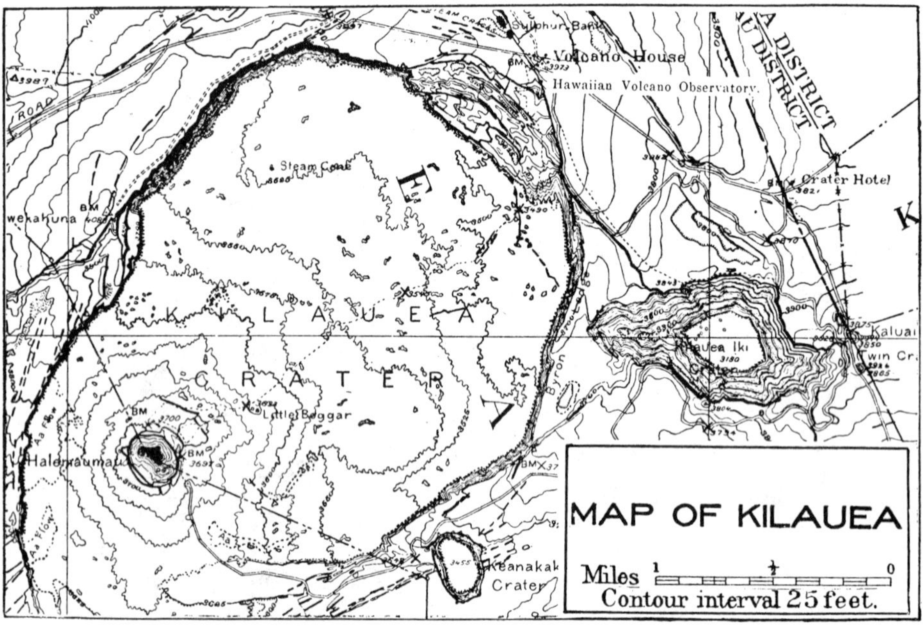

HAWAIIAN VOLCANO RESEARCH ASSOCIATION.

This society is a voluntary one, made up of subscribers to scientific work which is being executed by the Massachusetts Institute of Technology.

There are twenty-six subscribers in Hawaii and Massachusetts, firms and individuals. A group of firms and persons in Hilo built the main observatory building in the spring of 1912. Publications to date have been weekly reports since the summer of 1911, a memoir by Daly in the Proceedings of American Academy of Arts and Sciences in 1911, articles by the director in the Technology Review 1911 and the Honolulu Chamber of Commerce Annual 1912, articles by H. O. Wood in the Bulletin of the Seismological Society of America, and articles by Perret in the American Journal of Science. The Massachusetts Institute will publish the quarterly reports.

This weekly bulletin as it appears in the Advertiser will be reprinted as a leaflet and sent to regular annual subscribers to the work of the association. L. A. Thurston is chairman of the active committee of the subscribers and C. H. Cooke is treasurer. New subscribers who are interested in our volcanoes will be welcomed in the association. The association aims: (1) To record volcanic activity and earthquakes in Hawaii; (2) to attract scientific men hither for special studies; (3) to promote the establishment of volcano observatories all over the world.

WHITNEY LABORATORY OF SEISMOLOGY.

The Whitney Laboratory of Seismology is equipped with two Bosch-Omori 100kg tromometers registering N-S and E-W motion, a heavy Omori tromometer registering E-W motion and an Omori "ordinary Seismograph" designed for registering strong earthquakes in all three components of motion. These are seated on concrete piers in a closed basement room having practically constant temperature, beneath the chief Observatory building near the hotel. For the present, time is referred to a rated chronometer, loaned by the College of Hawaii. At the substation by the edge of the active pit an Omori two-component tromometer with light steady masses is mounted on a concrete pier placed directly on the fresh lava surface. Hawaiian standard time (H. S. T.) is 10 hrs. 30 m. slower than Greenwich time.

CANCANI SCALE OF SEISMIC INTENSITY

Expressed by accelerations measured in millimeters per second per second.

I.	Instrumental	0.0	2.5
II.	Very slight	2.5	5.0
III.	Slight	5.0	10.0
IV.	Sensible, mediocre	10.0	25.0
V.	Rather strong	25.0	50.0
VI.	Strong	50.0	100.0
VII.	Very strong	100.0	250.0
VIII.	Ruinous	250.0	500.0
IX.	Disastrous	500.0	1000.0
X.	Very disastrous	1000.0	2500.0
XI.	Catastrophic	2500.0	5000.0
XII.	Great catastrophe	5000.0	10000.0

Grade IV. is ordinarily the minimum perceived by the senses; and in grade XII. the acceleration, or rate of change of motion (jerk) reaches that of terrestrial gravitation.

WEEKLY BULLETIN OF HAWAIIAN VOLCANO OBSERVATORY

From the Pacific Commercial Advertiser, Honolulu, October 13, 1913.

TECHNOLOGY Station, October 9.—The Mauna Loa expedition returned in good health after a successful four days at the summit. The party, consisting of Mr. Wood, Mr. Green and Alex. Lancaster left the Volcano House by automobile September 29, at eight a. m., reached the bull-pen of Kapa pala (near the Halfway House) at eight thirty a. m., left there on horseback with two Hawaiian kamaainas and a pack train of four animals at nine twenty a. m., and arrived at the watertank above Ainapo at twelve forty five p. m, where camp was made. This point is about the lower terminus of the new trail.

At Crater Four Days.

The next morning camp was broken at six fifteen a. m., and the crater reached at ten ten a. m., where the four-day camp was made some distance south of the old Wilkes campground on the east side of Mokuaweoweo. The packers here left the party and returned below with the animals. Perfect weather and nearly cloudless skies characterized the whole week. At night at the summit the mercury registered below freezing. The expedition slept in cone tents of oiled silk, pegged down with bowlders, cooking was done with alcohol stove, and water was found in abundance in the ice-lined cracks near the edge of the crater.

During the next three days from October 1 to October 3, Mr. Wood explored the region and Mr. Green set up magnetic stations and made readings for dip and intensity, and secured one determination of approximate declination, though he had only dip-circle with compass attachment. No unusual activity of the volcano was observed, the fuming cracks on the floor being about as they were in 1912. Mr. Wood made the entire circuit of Mokuaweoweo on foot, and descended to the floor and explored it. Both observers obtained photographs. A remarkable feature noted by Mr. Wood is the row of large cones extending northeastward from the north end of the crater. These are continuous with the line of many craters down the northeast slope of Mauna Loa, which have been the source of nineteenth century flows, and this slope ought to be provided with an alpine hut as a substation of the Hawaiian Volcano Observatory, for there is in that vicinity a vast field for exploration and observation.

The packers returned to the summit with the animals at eight-thirty a. m. Saturday, October 4, the return start down the mountain was made at nine fifteen a. m., Ainapo was reached at two forty five p. m., and the rendezvous on the highroad at four twenty p. m., where the motor car was in waiting.

Simple Route Now Open.

A plain trail has been built from the water tank to the crater, although much of the way is a-a lava.

The Observatory is very grateful to Messrs. Julian Monsarrat and C. E. Wright of the Volcano Stables Company, for courtesies in the accomplish ment of this trip, and the public should now be able to make closer acquaintance with Mauna Loa through this simple route to the summit. The Observa tory party suffered from no mountain sickness, and had no serious difficulties of any kind, but they learned that military folding cots would be desirable, as the ground is very rough for a bed, and good sleep is essential to good work at that altitude. With good sleep and good warm food, very few people would be at all seriously troubled by the altitude of Mokuaweoweo, after a day's acclimatization.

Quiet Week at Halemaumau.

After the revival recorded last week at Halemaumau another week of quiet follows. Some faint glow was seen on the evenings of October 3 and 4. Saturday, October 4, the blowing noise at the bottom of the crater was continuous.

On the morning of October 5 at ten o'clock the SE amphitheater cleared from time to time, and showed the usual fumaroles through the talus at the bottom, a continuous slope of slide-rock leading down into the funnel SE, S and SW, and the whole west half of the high S bench was seen to be gone, only the east remnant of that bench clinging to the wall sixty feet below the S station.

The blowing noises from the lava cone could be heard from the Old Rest-house and from the SE. These noises had changed in quality. They were now short sudden coughs like the noise from the exhaust-pipe of a gasoline en-

gine. There was occasional longer hissing, and much of the coughing noise sounded like explosions coming through pasty lava. The bottom could not be seen.

Glow Not Visible.

Tuesday, October 7, occasional strong hissing puffs could be heard in the morning from the eastern stations, but by five p. m. the noise had diminished remarkably, so that even from the Old Resthouse on the north, where under a projecting ledge the best hearing is obtained with northeast winds, the only sounds were very faint and distant rhythmic puffs like a far-away freight engine, sometimes dying away altogether, and at times interrupted by short coughs. At five p. m. a good view was obtained from the southeast nearly to the middle of the bottom area, but no glow was seen nor could the detail of the lava cone region be made out. The fumes on this day were more acrid. At about four p. m. the writer heard a distinct deep rumble while in the cavern known as Pele's "drawing room," just back of the Technology station.

In a preliminary report for the week for the Whitney Laboratory of seismology, H. O. Wood reports earthquakes as follows:

A short sharp felt shock October 3, 1913, a little before 6 p. m.

Very feeble shock Monday October 6 a few minutes after 9 a. m.

Very feeble shock Tuesday, October 7, shortly before 3 a. m.

Very slight shock Tuesday, October 7, shortly before 3 p. m.

Very respectfully,
T. A. JAGGAR JR.,
Director.

Mokuaweoweo, October 1, 1913, from photographs taken by H. O. Wood, during exploration of crater at summit of Mauna Loa. Preceding view is taken from the southeast side of south pit, looking north by northwest; fresh, thin lava cascade from south platform into south pit. This view looking south-southeast from southern promontory on west wall; south lunate platform, fresh flow on the right, and gap beyond leading into south pit.

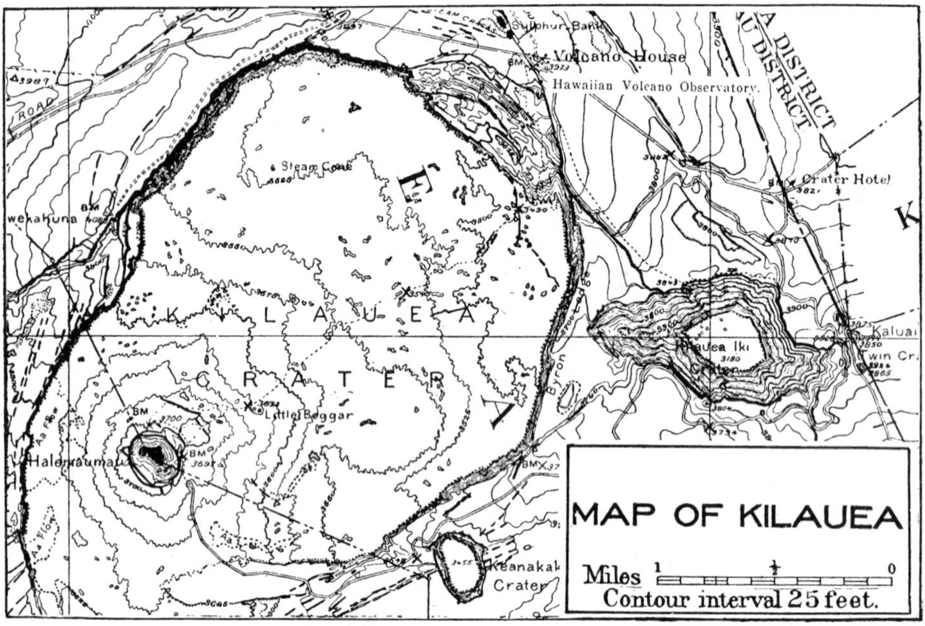

HAWAIIAN VOLCANO RESEARCH ASSOCIATION.

This society is a voluntary one, made up of subscribers to scientific work which is being executed by the Massachusetts Institute of Technology.

There are twenty-six subscribers in Hawaii and Massachusetts, firms and individuals. A group of firms and persons in Hilo built the main observatory building in the spring of 1912. Publications to date have been weekly reports since the summer of 1911, a memoir by Daly in the Proceedings of American Academy of Arts and Sciences in 1911, articles by the director in the Technology Review 1911 and the Honolulu Chamber of Commerce Annual 1912, articles by H. O. Wood in the Bulletin of the Seismological Society of America, and articles by Perret in the American Journal of Science. The Massachusetts Institute will publish the quarterly reports.

This weekly bulletin as it appears in the Advertiser will be reprinted as a leaflet and sent to regular annual subscribers to the work of the association. L. A. Thurston is chairman of the active committee of the subscribers and C. H. Cooke is treasurer. New subscribers who are interested in our volcanoes will be welcomed in the association. The association aims: (1) To record volcanic activity and earthquakes in Hawaii; (2) to attract scientific men hither for special studies; (3) to promote the establishment of volcano observatories all over the world.

WHITNEY LABORATORY OF SEISMOLOGY.

The Whitney Laboratory of Seismology is equipped with two Bosch-Omori 100kg tromometers registering N-S and E-W motion, a heavy Omori tromometer registering E-W motion and an Omori "ordinary Seismograph" designed for registering strong earthquakes in all three components of motion. These are seated on concrete piers in a closed basement room having practically constant temperature, beneath the chief Observatory building near the hotel. For the present, time is referred to a rated chronometer, loaned by the College of Hawaii. At the substation by the edge of the active pit an Omori two-component tromometer with light steady masses is mounted on a concrete pier placed directly on the fresh lava surface. Hawaiian standard time (H. S. T.) is 10 hrs. 30 m. slower than Greenwich time.

CANCANI SCALE OF SEISMIC INTENSITY

Expressed by accelerations measured in millimeters per second per second.

I.	Instrumental	0.0	2.5
II.	Very slight	2.5	5.0
III.	Slight	5.0	10.0
IV.	Sensible, mediocre. . . .	10.0	25.0
V.	Rather strong	25.0	50.0
VI.	Strong	50.0	100.0
VII.	Very strong	100.0	250.0
VIII.	Ruinous	250.0	500.0
IX.	Disastrous	500.0	1000.0
X.	Very disastrous	1000.0	2500.0
XI.	Catastrophic	2500.0	5000.0
XII.	Great catastrophe. . . .	5000.0	10000.0

Grade IV. is ordinarily the minimum perceived by the senses; and in grade XII. the acceleration, or rate of change of motion (jerk) reaches that of terrestrial gravitation.

WEEKLY BULLETIN OF HAWAIIAN VOLCANO OBSERVATORY

From the Pacific Commercial Advertiser, Honolulu, October 20, 1913.

TECHNOLOGY STATION, October 16.—The volcano continues in minor eruptive phase. Frequent irregular explosive noises have been heard throughout the past week, varying from puffing sounds to sharp explosions accompanied by rumbling like deep distant thunder, waxing and waning but, on the whole, increasing in volume and energy. Intervals between noises have varied from twenty seconds to over a minute, and these have been distributed without order.

Sliding of talus on a small scale has been heard during the week, but it is thought to denote readjustments among the blocks rather than pronounced movement of the magma column.

Great volumes of fumes continue to be given off. To measure these is next to impossible but the writer considers their volume now much greater than some weeks ago — and increasing. Views into the pit, particularly to its very bottom, are consequently rare and fortuitous. The gases appear to be rushing from the bottom fumaroles on the north and west as though under considerable pressure. This was especially noted Wednesday, October 15.

Lava Visible at Bottom.

Late in the afternoon on Friday, October 10, J. W. Green obtained a good view of the bottom of the pit when, for about twenty minutes, the bottom region was kept free of fumes. A small area of incandescent lava was visible and at irregular intervals when especially hard blowing took place a jet of molten spray was shot out of this orifice to a height of a few feet, at a slight angle from the vertical.

The ordinary activity described above continued, with fluctuations, until just before noon, Wednesday, October 15, when it was noticed that the explosive noises were becoming distinctly sharper. At about 2:30 p. m., an unusually loud and energetic explosive sound was heard, after which these sounds were accompanied by a swashing noise like that of a much disturbed heavy fluid. After hard blasts the patter of falling lumps, presumably from lava jets, was heard. Mr. Green mentions also a sound resembling that of rock snapping from heat. After nightfall at long intervals brilliant flarings were seen from the Volcano House, despite a bright moonlight illumination of the fume cloud.

Earthquakes Recorded.

Since the last systematic report from the Whitney Laboratory the following shocks have been recorded:

September 25, from 1:58:09 a.m. to 1:58:52 a.m. H. S. T. Intensity, I Cancani scale; about 0.15 the minimum perceptible unit. Origin distant about 12 miles.

October 2, from 7:29:02 a.m. to 7:31:02 a.m. H. S. T. Intensity, II-III Cancani scale; felt but measures only about 0.8 the minimum perceptible unit. Origin distant about twenty-eight miles.

October 3, from 5:58:14 p.m. to 6:00:12 p.m. H. S. T. Intensity, V-VI Cancani scale; about 5 to 8 times the minimum perceptible unit. Distinctly felt. Origin-distance in doubt.

October 6, from 9:20:31 a.m. to 9:21:23 a.m. H. S. T. Intensity, low I Cancani scale; less than 0.1 the minimum perceptible unit. Origin distant a little over six miles.

October 7, from 2:54:31 a.m. to 2:54::56 a.m. H.S.T. Intensity, high I Cancani scale; over 0.2 the minimum perceptible unit. Origin distant about 10.5 miles.

October 7, from 2:41:00 p.m. to 2:42 p.m. H. S. T. Intensity, II-III Cancani scale; not felt, from 0.4 to 1.0 the minimum perceptible unit. Origin distant about six miles.

October 10, from 3:32 p.m. to 3:47 p.m. H. S. T. Feeble registered waves of a very distant earthquake, chief phase only. Hence not a shock of very great power. Origin distance indeterminate.

October 10, from 6:05 p.m. to 6:27 p.m. H. S. T. Waves of a very distant earthquake, registration beginning with the chief phase. This was not a shock of very great power. Its origin distance is indeterminate.

October 13, from 9:47:34 p.m. to 11:08 p.m. H. S. T. A distant earthquake of only ordinarily great power, originating at a distance of about 2300 miles from this Observatory. Very respectfully,

H. O. WOOD, Associate.

From the north part of the west rim, looking southward. This shows a block of the original summit area, partly engulfed and tremendously fissured.

From the central part of the east rim, looking southward. Shows the southeast "Lunate platform," an old pahoehoe surface, weathered and fissured, probably part of the original surface.

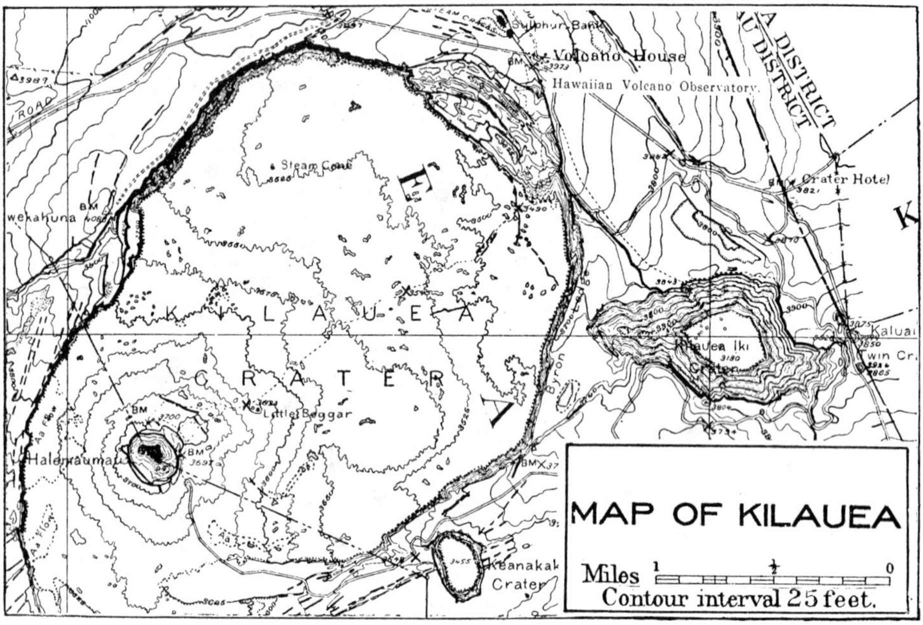

HAWAIIAN VOLCANO RESEARCH ASSOCIATION.

This society is a voluntary one, made up of subscribers to scientific work which is being executed by the Massachusetts Institute of Technology.

There are twenty-six subscribers in Hawaii and Massachusetts, firms and individuals. A group of firms and persons in Hilo built the main observatory building in the spring of 1912. Publications to date have been weekly reports since the summer of 1911, a memoir by Daly in the Proceedings of American Academy of Arts and Sciences in 1911, articles by the director in the Technology Review 1911 and the Honolulu Chamber of Commerce Annual 1912, articles by H. O. Wood in the Bulletin of the Seismological Society of America, and articles by Perret in the American Journal of Science. The Massachusetts Institute will publish the quarterly reports.

This weekly bulletin as it appears in the Advertiser will be reprinted as a leaflet and sent to regular annual subscribers to the work of the association. L. A. Thurston is chairman of the active committee of the subscribers and C. H. Cooke is treasurer. New subscribers who are interested in our volcanoes will be welcomed in the association. The association aims: (1) To record volcanic activity and earthquakes in Hawaii; (2) to attract scientific men hither for special studies; (3) to promote the establishment of volcano observatories all over the world.

WHITNEY LABORATORY OF SEISMOLOGY.

The Whitney Laboratory of Seismology is equipped with two Bosch-Omori 100kg tromometers registering N-S and E-W motion, a heavy Omori tromometer registering E-W motion and an Omori "ordinary Seismograph" designed for registering strong earthquakes in all three components of motion. These are seated on concrete piers in a closed basement room having practically constant temperature, beneath the chief Observatory building near the hotel. For the present, time is referred to a rated chronometer, loaned by the College of Hawaii. At the substation by the edge of the active pit an Omori two-component tromometer with light steady masses is mounted on a concrete pier placed directly on the fresh lava surface. Hawaiian standard time (H. S. T.) is 10 hrs. 30 m. slower than Greenwich time.

CANCANI SCALE OF SEISMIC INTENSITY

Expressed by accelerations measured in millimeters per second per second.

I.	Instrumental	0.0	2.5
II.	Very slight	2.5	5.0
III.	Slight	5.0	10.0
IV.	Sensible, mediocre....	10.0	25.0
V.	Rather strong	25.0	50.0
VI.	Strong	50.0	100.0
VII.	Very strong	100.0	250.0
VIII.	Ruinous	250.0	500.0
IX.	Disastrous	500.0	1000.0
X.	Very disastrous	1000.0	2500.0
XI.	Catastrophic	2500.0	5000.0
XII.	Great catastrophe....	5000.0	10000.0

Grade IV. is ordinarily the minimum perceived by the senses; and in grade XII. the acceleration, or rate of change of motion (jerk) reaches that of terrestrial gravitation.

WEEKLY BULLETIN OF HAWAIIAN VOLCANO OBSERVATORY

From the Pacific Commercial Advertiser, Honolulu, October 27, 1913.

TECHNOLOGY STATION, October 23.—The activity of Kilauea in October, 1913, has been similar to that of October, 1912, in that the month started with a revival, followed by sluggish phases and occasional withdrawals of the lava, as though a contest were in progress between a rising lava column and a subsiding tumble of debris which tends to choke and chill the hot fluid beneath. The past week has been an illustration of this, in that the fumes have been dense, the glow repressed, and the noises less, everything pointing to a suppression of the rising column by the great quantity of talus fragments which must needs be taken into solution by the magma before its seemingly limited supply of hot gases can sufficiently assert their power to make a vigorous lava lake.

Lakes of Lava Active.

Throughout the week there have been sounds as of the swashing of a heavy liquid. This noise had a tendency to increase and decrease every few seconds, accompanied at short intervals by spattering sounds, such as are made by the falling of lumps of molten lava.

At longer and quite irregular intervals, a minute, more or less, sharp blowing noises have been heard, followed usually by much of the spatter sound.

Glow on the Clouds.

In the evenings of October 18, 19, and 20, Saturday, Sunday and Monday, particularly the 19th, there was visible from the Observatory (and the Volcano House) a dim but steady glow on the fume cloud with brilliant flaring at considerable irregular intervals.

On the morning of October 20, D. Lycurgus reported a view of the bottom which disclosed a well-marked cone with an orifice at the apex some ten feet in diameter, out of which lava jets spurted at fairly long intervals.

Today, October 23, at 4 p. m., the weather was rainy and foggy and little could be seen. A puff, not at all loud, could be heard from the east and north stations about once a minute, sometimes repeated two or three times at intervals of ten seconds, with some sound of splash. The fumes were strong and disagreeable to breathe.

Magnetic Work Continues.

J. W. Green continues his magnetic work and is now engaged in establishing magnetic stations on the rim of the greater crater of Kilauea. He has found that owing to its content of magnetic minerals the Kilauea basalt is itself variously magnetic in small specimens, a fact which promises to greatly complicate the use of the magnetic needle in this region.

There has been almost nothing to report this week for the Whitney Laboratory of Seismology. What few feeble movements have been recorded will be embodied in a later report by Mr. H. O. Wood. Very respectfully,

T. A. JAGGAR, JR.,
Director.

AT THE EDGE OF MOKUAWEOWEO.
Photograph of the Camp Ground of the Scientific Party which ascended Mauna Loa. Taken October 4.

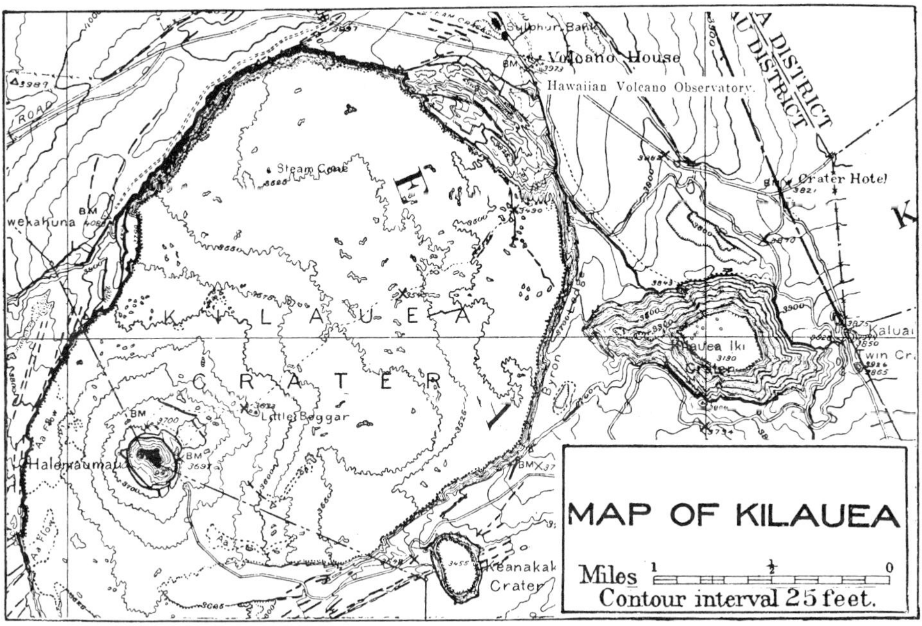

HAWAIIAN VOLCANO RESEARCH ASSOCIATION.

This society is a voluntary one, made up of subscribers to scientific work which is being executed by the Massachusetts Institute of Technology.

There are twenty-six subscribers in Hawaii and Massachusetts, firms and individuals. A group of firms and persons in Hilo built the main observatory building in the spring of 1912. Publications to date have been weekly reports since the summer of 1911, a memoir by Daly in the Proceedings of American Academy of Arts and Sciences in 1911, articles by the director in the Technology Review 1911 and the Honolulu Chamber of Commerce Annual 1912, articles by H. O. Wood in the Bulletin of the Seismological Society of America, and articles by Perret in the American Journal of Science. The Massachusetts Institute will publish the quarterly reports.

This weekly bulletin as it appears in the Advertiser will be reprinted as a leaflet and sent to regular annual subscribers to the work of the association. L. A. Thurston is chairman of the active committee of the subscribers and C. H. Cooke is treasurer. New subscribers who are interested in our volcanoes will be welcomed in the association. The association aims: (1) To record volcanic activity and earthquakes in Hawaii; (2) to attract scientific men hither for special studies; (3) to promote the establishment of volcano observatories all over the world.

WHITNEY LABORATORY OF SEISMOLOGY.

The Whitney Laboratory of Seismology is equipped with two Bosch-Omori 100kg tromometers registering N-S and E-W motion, a heavy Omori tromometer registering E-W motion and an Omori "ordinary Seismograph" designed for registering strong earthquakes in all three components of motion. These are seated on concrete piers in a closed basement room having practically constant temperature, beneath the chief Observatory building near the hotel. For the present, time is referred to a rated chronometer, loaned by the College of Hawaii. At the substation by the edge of the active pit an Omori two-component tromometer with light steady masses is mounted on a concrete pier placed directly on the fresh lava surface. Hawaiian standard time (H. S. T.) is 10 hrs. 30 m. slower than Greenwich time.

CANCANI SCALE OF SEISMIC INTENSITY

Expressed by accelerations measured in millimeters per second per second.

I.	Instrumental	0.0	2.5
II.	Very slight	2.5	5.0
III.	Slight	5.0	10.0
IV.	Sensible, mediocre....	10.0	25.0
V.	Rather strong	25.0	50.0
VI.	Strong	50.0	100.0
VII.	Very strong	100.0	250.0
VIII.	Ruinous	250.0	500.0
IX.	Disastrous	500.0	1000.0
X.	Very disastrous	1000.0	2500.0
XI.	Catastrophic	2500.0	5000.0
XII.	Great catastrophe....	5000.0	10000.0

Grade IV. is ordinarily the minimum perceived by the senses; and in grade XII. the acceleration, or rate of change of motion (jerk) reaches that of terrestrial gravitation.

WEEKLY BULLETIN OF HAWAIIAN VOLCANO OBSERVATORY

From the Pacific Commercial Advertiser, Honolulu, November 2 and 3, 1913.

TECHNOLOGY STATION, October 30, 1913.

A Notable Week.

"The week at Kilauea has been a notable one, characterized by a rising lava column in Halemaumau with finally overflow of the cone in the bottom, and by an earthquake strong enough to dismantle the more sensitive seismographs of the station — the strongest experienced here since the station was established in January, 1912.

"Mr. J. W. Green today finishes his magnetic work, and the Volcano Research Association has reason to be grateful to him and to the U. S. Coast and Geodetic Survey for this excellent addition to our knowledge of the physical peculiarities of Kilauea. It is to be hoped that this preliminary magnetic reconnaissance of a region which shows extraordinary magnetic variations, will lead eventually to a complete magnetic survey of this island.

"At Halemaumau from the SW station at 8:45 a. m. October 24, moderately loud puffs could be heard every fifty seconds. The weather was calm. There were occasional intermediate puffs, and sometimes a rocket-like noise, but no sound of splashing. At 9:05 a. m., a faint rhythmic 'freight engine' puffing was heard. At 9:25 and 9:35 a. m. respectively, small rock slides were heard W and S. At night from 10 to 12 p. m., steady glow on the fume-cloud could be seen from the Volcano House with occasional flaring, showing that the lava cone was spouting.

The Earthquake.

"After midnight, during the first hour of October 25, the fume products of the pit settled northeastward over the Volcano House, making breathing very disagreeable. The night was very still. About 1 a. m. the earthquake occurred, the stronger portion lasting five or six seconds and shaking the buildings vigorously so that some objects fell, pictures swayed and were left awry, everyone was awakened, and numerous rock slides were started in Kilauea and Kilauea-iki, which could be heard roaring and rumbling through the mist of fumes. These slides left numerous brown fresh scars especially on the north walls of the two craters. Two of the tromometers of the seismograph cellar were broken, and a crack was made in the concrete wall, on the north side. A record of the earthquake was written by the Omori ordinary seismograph. The first rock falls were heard in the direction of Kilauea-iki, suggesting that the movement was from the eastward. Mr. Green reported hearing the rumble of the earthquake receding toward the southwest before the noise of the rock falls began.

A Quick Inspection.

"An inspection of Halemaumau from two to four a. m. revealed an illumined fume cloud, with light NE wind, and fog hanging over the region of the Twin Craters. In four places rocks had fallen from the banks into the Crater Road. Looking down into the pit from the Old Resthouse on the north side, a cavity on the bottom was seen to be spouting lava at intervals of forty to fifty seconds, with chiefly a splashing noise, and occasionally large sputterings would fall on the rock floor with thuds. The opening was in the top of a cone or dome, roughly rectangular, continuously open, and showing a seething pool within. Cracks extended from the four corners, as though the aperture had been made at the intersection of two main fissures. Its estimated length was from ten to twelve feet, width five to six feet, with walls three or four feet thick. The spurting was oblique northward. The pool appeared about in the Old Faithful position, as compared with last spring. The flaring on the fume-cloud was made by the spurts, but the fumes were continuously illumined.

"The earthquake had wrought no

conspicuous change in the eastern or northern rim of Halemaumau. There was little rock-sliding. At the volcano station a stadia rod had fallen into the middle of the room from the southern frame timbers, and a bottle had fallen over on the table. The rocks of the east wall of the Old Resthouse had tumbled southward at the entrance. At about 2:30 a. m. the talus was still sliding in Kilauea Iki.

Crater Walls Shaken.

''At 10 a. m. an inspection of the craters by daylight showed:

''In Kilauea Iki, at least four falls from the north wall and two from the east; the eastern falls are from the southern sides of two pronounced scars high up on the precipitous cliff, which are themselves the product of some earthquake of the nineteenth century, perhaps 1868.

''In Kilauea, fresh fallen material at the northern end of Uwokehuna cliff, and a number of breaks along the cliffs under the Volcano House. Near the northern end of Byron's ledge one fresh brown scar is seen.

New Earth Cracks.

''Four small crevices had opened in the hard brown earth of the path up the hill back of the Volcano House, near the water tanks and in the line of the large steam crack. The maximum gaping was one-half inch. All the crevices are side by side in a distance of fifteen feet, and they extend in the line of the cliff and the steam cracks, implying some slight movement on the large steam crack. No other fresh cracks were found, although they were looked for along the stable paths and from the Sulphur Banks southward.

''October 26, 1913, at 3:40 p. m., the fumes cleared away and the detail of the bottom of Halemaumau was clearly seen by daylight. The cone of black fresh masalt was spurting lava at about fifty-second intervals. The cavity in the top had changed its form and become roundish, perhaps five feet in diameter, and the liquid splashed out often in heavy masses. Approximately the cone was twenty feet wide and fifteen feet high. From it extended black flows some hundred feet to the northwest, and among them was another black cavity, which appeared to have been recently active. The active cone was ejecting its liquid in an easterly direction.

''The fumaroles toward the west were very active, very hot and crackling, sulphur stained and emitting rapidly bluish fumes. These fumaroles west and north are at least one hundred feet above the active cone, and emerge from the top of the talus slopes that surround the active area. On the north side of the ring of talus is a bright salmon-colored bank of red rock, with blue fumes rising from rock cracks back (N.) of it. The axis of the active area in the bottom, cone and flows, lies about in the line between the SE. and NW. stations on the rim.

''During the next three days activity of the same sort continued, and moderate glow was seen on the fume-cloud at night.

Lava Splashing.

''Today, October 30, at 10:30 a. m., with moderate NE. wind, the lava cone could be heard spouting vigorously every fifteen to forty seconds, and the splash of the falling lava spray could be heard some distance back from the edge; at 10:45 a new noise was heard, which was at first mistaken for continuous rock-sliding low down, and a rumble as of lava in a cavern. At 11:10 a. m. a view of the cone was obtained, and the sliding and rumbling were explained: a splendid lava flow was pouring westward from the top of the cone, in three streams, bubbling out continuously like an artesian well, with floods added to it by the spasmodic vomitings of the fountain in the cone. The lava-filled area was much larger than it had been when last seen, L-shaped, with its new extension to the west. The flows poured on with distributary branchings.

''At 11:20 a. m. the temperature of the air was 23 degrees Cent., and of the Postal Rift 310 degrees.

''At 11:30 a. m., from the hot fumaroles on the SW. side, came a noise of snapping of hot rocks, like musketry, superimposed on the continuous noise of the streaming lava.

''All of this indicates that the lava column at the moment is rising rapidly, but there is still a vast amount of talus for it to dissolve, and while lava may rise into the hot and crackling SW. fumaroles and pour thence in cataracts, more periods of stagnation are to be expected before the bottom of the pit is clear for the formation of a large pool. At present the lava torrent is a magnificent spectacle, but it may become choked and invisible within twenty-four hours.

From the Pacific Commercial Advertiser, Monday, November 3, 1913

Much importance is attached to the shocks of October 25, 1913, by Professor Jaggar and his associates at the observatory. They are anxious to secure data on the distribution of earthquake intensity. This will be valuable in determining a distribution for simple observation instruments which the scientists will place at different points on Hawaii and the other Islands. There is little doubt but the shock was felt all over the Island of Hawaii and possibly on others of the Islands.

Want People to Aid.

Professor Jaggar has called upon the newspapers to aid in securing this data. What is wanted is a report from every person on the Islands as to whether or not they experienced the earthquake on the morning of October 25. To aid in making the work more thorough, reports are asked from persons who did not feel the shock as well as those who did. A full list of questions has been prepared. Residents of the Islands are asked to fill these out and send them to Professor T. A. Jaggar at the Volcano House, Kilauea, Hawaii. Following are the questions:

List of Questions.

Earthquake of October 25, 1913; Information Blank.

What is your name, occupation, and P. O. address?

Did you feel the earthquake October 25, 1913, about 1 a. m.?

How many shocks did you feel?

At what locality were you? Describe place as exactly as possible.

Were you indoors or outdoors, and if indoors, on what floor of house?

Were you walking, riding, standing, sitting or lying down?

At what time did the shock or shocks occur, as nearly as you know?

How long, in your judgment, did the shock or shocks last?

At your locality.

(1) Was the earthquake felt by few or many persons?

(2) Did doors and windows rattle, or buildings creak?

(3) Did hanging objects, like pictures swing?

(4) Did plaster crack?

(5) Was furniture moved about?

(6) Did bottles, vases, etc., fall?

(7) Did church bells ring?

(8) Were people generally awakened?

(9) Were pendulum clocks stopped?

(10) If so, in what direction did the pendulum swing? (answer north-south, east-west, etc.)

(11) Were many people frightened?

(12) Were many people made dizzy or sick?

(13) Did trees, doors, etc., swing slowly, or did they quiver?

(14) Was water in tanks observed to swing slowly, or splash quickly?

(15) Did chimneys fall?

(16) Did brick masonry crack?

(17) Did window glass break?

(18) If so, what directions did most of the broken windows face?

(19) Did concrete masonry crack?

(20) Were any buildings destroyed?

(21) Was there any damage to wooden buildings?

(22) Were there any landslips, cracks in the earth or new springs formed?

(23) What noise did you hear, if any, before, during or after the earthquake?

(24) Was there general evidence that objects shook or fell in one direction, or one line of direction, as north-south, east-west, etc.?

(25) Were animals or fowls restless, noisy or unusually quiet before the earthquake?

(26) Were there any other noteworthy happenings?

(27) Persons of scientific training who receive this are invited to write here a complete brief description of phenomena observed.

Since the last systematic report from the Whitney Laboratory of Seismology, Mr. H. O. Wood reports that earthquakes have been registered as follows:

Oct. 15, from 5:37:19 a.m. to 5:38:06 a.m. H. S. T.

Intensity, medium II Cancani scale; about 0.3 the minimum perceptible unit. Origin distance about 16 miles.

Oct. 18, from 3:12:11 p.m. to 3:13:7 p.m. H. S. T. Intensity, medium I Cancani scale; about 4.15 the minimum perceptible unit. Origin distance unknown.

Oct. 19, from 5:31:38 a.m. to 5:32:23 a.m. H. S. T. Intensity, medium I Cancani scale; about 0.15 the minimum perceptible unit. Origin distant about 18.7 miles.

"October 25, beginning at 12:57:37 (mdt.) a.m. a shock sufficiently energetic to disable all the delicate, continuously recording seismometers, and to stop the pendulum time-marking clock, at 12:57:39 a.m., whose pendulum swung in a north-south direction, very closely in the true meridian. There was no further continuous registration for some hours.

"While this was a strong shock instrumentally, from the geological point of view it was only a strong weak-shock here at Kilauea—the phenomena in this vicinity corresponding unusually well with those which define Grade VI of the Rossi-Forel scale, or Grade V-VI of the Mercalli scale.

"The silk-fibre suspensions of both the Bosch-Omori tromometers were snapped off, and the Cardan lamella of the N-S component was broken. The delicate Omori tromometer had its sub-pendulum dislodged and slightly bent by its fall, and some pivots in the universal joints of the magnifying lever system were sprung from their sockets and injured.

"The Omori ordinary seismograph recorded motion for two or three minutes. One or two seconds elapsed before the motion it recorded became large enough to be limited by the safety stops of the instrument, indicating very vaguely an origin from ten to twenty kilometers distant. The origin probably lay in the Hilo direction. The strong part of the motion began one or two seconds after the first movement and lasted from four to six seconds.

"Here at Kilauea the perceptible duration of the shock was from sixteen to eighteen seconds, according to an approximate second-count by Mr. J. W. Green and an estimate by Mr. H. O. Wood. These were independent determinations.

"In this vicinity all persons were wakened, but no one was alarmed. A few unstable objects, a mirror, two or three bottles, etc., were tipped over.

"Small but noisy falls of loosened rock blocks occurred along the northwest pali of the main crater, on the Byron's ledge section of the crater wall, and also from the high, steep pali on the northeast in Kilauea-iki.

"Minute cracks were opened in earth in a filled-in place along the course of an old steam crack.

"A single crack was opened from top to bottom of the concrete wall on the north of the seismograph cellar. In view of the loose-block character of the rock foundation here at the very edge of the pali, this is not surprising or significant of high energy, but formally such an effect cannot be correlated with other phenomena here since ordinarily it would denote very strong motion.

The motion was preceded and accompanied by an earth sound, a roaring noise heard before the roar of the rock falls, which appeared to move progressively southwestward.

"Vague information indicates that the shock was little, if any, stronger at Hilo than here, but at intermediate places it seems to have been stronger—tending to confirm the probability of the intermediate location of the origin.

"Between 12 o'clock noon and 12 o'clock midnight on October 25 five very feeble shocks were recorded. One of these was of the usual magnitude of local small shocks, the others were exceedingly feeble. These were recorded only by the Bosch-Omori east-west component and, owing to settling movements following readjustments necessitated by the strong shock, the traces of the seismograph are confused by overscoring so that the times and dimensions of these shocks cannot be measured precisely."

Oct. 26, from 10:31:39 a.m. to 10:32:00 a. m. H. S. T. Intensity, high I Cancani scale; about 0.22 the minimum perceptible unit. Origin distance about 13 miles.

Between about 2 p.m. of Oct. 26 and 6 a.m. of October 27 there were registered several, from 6 to 10, very feeble shocks whose times and dimensions cannot be measured precisely.

Oct. 27, from 9:44:26 a.m. to 9:45:21 a.m. H. S. T. Intensity, low II Cancani scale; about 0.3 the minimum perceptible unit. Origin distant about 13 miles.

Oct. 28, from 5:05:57 a.m. to 5:06:29 a.m. H. S. T. Intensity, low II Cancani scale; about 0.35 the minimum perceptible unit. Origin distant about 14.3 miles.

Oct. 28, from 8:45:10 a.m. to 8:47:08 a.m. H. S. T. Intensity, high III Cancani scale; a little less than the minimum perceptible unit; not felt perceptibly. Origin distant 13 miles.

Oct. 28, from 1:00:18 p.m. to 1:01:22 p.m. H. S. T. Intensity, low I Cancani scale; about 0.08 the minimum perceptible unit. Origin distance unknown.

Oct. 29, from 5:49:29 a.m. to 5:49:48 a.m. H. S. T. Intensity, high I Cancani scale; about 0.2 the minimum perceptible unit. Origin distant about 13.7 miles.

Very respectfully,

T. A. JAGGAR, JR.,
Director.

WEEKLY BULLETIN HAWAIIAN VOLCANO OBSERVATORY.

Technology Station, November 6, 1913.

A crusted lava pool has continued to sputter idly in the bottom of Halemaumau during the past week. The week has been uneventful Seismically and accordingly no report of the Whitney Laboratory of Seismology is here included.

At 9:10 p.m. Oct. 30, 1913, the flows which had been seen earlier in the day had so filled up the the bottom area as to nearly drown the cone, and the effect was as of a pool of crusted lava, cherry red, elongate east and west, with considerable sputter over the buried cone. Every now and then the crust would crack open with a sharp report and a wide band of liquid lava would well up the crack. The rim of the pool showed bright glow lines. Glows was also seen in the SE and SW fumaroles. When the crust was rent asunder and the liquid welled up, a bright flare was made on the fume cloud above, which was seen from a distance. The noisy crackling which was made by the splitting of the crust in all directions probably is identical with the noise heard in the morning, supposed to be the snapping of hot rocks in the SW fumarole.

Nov. 1 at 11:30 a.m. a light NE wind was blowing, the SE station was fumy, but there was occasional seeing from the north stations. A sluggish belching noise came from the E end of the pool, as of vicious lava confined. At very irregular periods came rocket blasts, and there was some rumbling as of thudding lava under a crust. At noon from the Old Resthouse intervals between the blasts were respectively 42, 100, 35, 25, and 10 seconds. A glimpse showed the pool black and crusted, the puffing coming from the E end, where the cone had been. The fumaroles were mostly emitting thin fumes sluggishly, except the low SW one which was very active. A faint very light crackling noise could be heard. At night the fumes obscured the view, though there was glow on the cloud.

Nov, 2 in the evening a bright flare was seen once or twice from the Observatory, otherwise the fume cloud appeared nearly dark.

Monday and Tuesday, Nov. 3 and 4, there was a mild puffing and no seeing, the noise being louder at 9:30 a.m. Nov, 4 than on the previous afternoon. At 6: p.m. on Nov. 4, a glimpse was had of two spouting cracks at the east and west ends of the pool, and occasionally there were extra loud rocket blasts, but very little sound of splashing or falling lava. The glow on the cloud after dark was slight.

In the evening of November 5 the fume cloud in the moonlight appeared almost without glow from beneath. Today Nov. 6 at 10:45 a.m. the wind was light from the NE, and the fumes appeared thin. From the old Resthouse the noise was found to have changed in character during the last two days; there was the spatter of heavy falls of lava on a rocky floor, the continuous sliding noise of a running lava-flow, a grumble from the W and a blowing noise mixed with splash from east. The suggestion was that there is an open pot toward the position of the former eastern cone from which a flow is pouring.

New slides about Kilauea, generated by the earthquake of Oct. 25, 1913, have been discovered near the base of Waldron's ledge, where a single large block has fallen out near the trail, and from the low cliff west of the foot of the trail leading from the Volcano House to the crater. This last place is a broad fresh notch, marking the scar of a landslip of considerable magnitude, as shown by the talus heaps beneath.

WEEKLY BULLETIN OF HAWAIIAN VOLCANO OBSERVATORY

From the Pacific Commercial Advertiser, Honolulu, November 17, 1913

TECHNOLOGY, STATION, November 13.—The volcano has remained quiet throughout the heavy rainstorm of the week. The rain began on Saturday, November 8, and since that time to today, November 13, eleven inches of rain have fallen at the observatory, with nearly four and one-half inches in one day, between Tuesday and Wednesday, November 11 and 12.

November 7, in the evening, visitors were able to see the floor of Halemaumau, where at two points lava was spurting. November 8, at 11:30 a. m., the floor could be seen from the old resthouse, and the festoons of the new lava flows appeared light brownish, as though powdered with the dust of avalanches. Strong blowing could be heard from two fissures which were splashing lava at the east end of the floor.

The crackling noise of a lava flow could be heard but its source was not evident through the fumes. The crusted pool appeared to have increased in size. Around the edges were some glowing cracks. The humidity of the air on this day was extraordinarily low and the fumes appeared thin. The blowing noises were incessant, with some variations in loudness.

November 9 and 10 there was no seeing, but at midnight of the 10th, a view of the pit by moonlight from the observatory revealed no glow or flaring on the fume-cloud. November 11 all was enveloped in rain and mist.

Veiled in Steamy Fumes.

November 12 at 3 p. m., a partial view through steamy fumes from the northwest showed all conditions to be similar to November 8, one glowing crack at the east end of the floor was faintly seen, and stones were heard sliding from the west and north walls. The noises of blowing had decreased and once in three or four minutes a louder blast came from the region of Old Faithful.

Today, November 13, at noon, the noises were the same with some rock-sliding, but nothing could be seen. Excessive volumes of fumes continue to be given off from fumaroles all around the talus ring within the pit, and the talus is slowly sliding inward and retarding the progress of the rising lava column. It is still impossible to get any observations of depth with instruments, owing to the incessant veil of fumes.

In the earthquake report which follows, and in these reports since August 27, 1913, time has been referred as heretofore, to a rated chronometer, but it has been possible to check the rate with solar observations. These were first kindly furnished by Mr. J. W. Green, in connection with his magnetic work, and later the solar observing has been done by Mr. Wood, with aid of a transit with solar attachment loaned to the observatory by the College of Hawaii.

The following report is submitted by H. O. Wood for the Whitney Laboratory of Seismology:

Earthquake Report.

Since the last systematic report the following earthquakes have been registered here.

October 29, from 2:08:24 p.m. to 2:09:03 p.m., H.S.T. Intensity, medium III Cancani scale; more than 0.5 the minimum perceptible unit. Origin distant about fourteen miles.

November 1, in late afternoon or early evening; overscoring makes it impossible to determine the precise time limits. Intensity, high I Cancani scale; about 0.2 the minimum perceptible unit. Origin distant between twelve and fourteen miles.

November 3, in the late evening (or possibly in the early morning of the fourth). Precise time limits are indeterminate owing to overscoring. Intensity, low II Cancani scale; about 0.25 the minimum perceptible unit. Origin distant about 12.5 miles.

November 6, from 2:54:30 p.m. to 2:55:19 p.m., H.S.T. Intensity, medium I Cancani scale; about 0.1 the minimum perceptible unit. Origin distant about thirteen miles.

November 7, from 10:07:41 a.m. to 10:08:38 a.m. H. S. T. Intensity, low I Cancani scale, about 0.5 the minimum perceptible unit. Origin distant about forty-eight miles.

November 7, from 12:35:41 p.m. (noon) to 12:37:18 p.m. H.S.T. Intensity III-IV Cancani scale; about the minimum perceptible unit. Felt in Hilo, but not felt in the vicinity of the crater. Origin distant about 13.3 miles.

November 7, from 7:01:50 p.m. to 7:02:05 p.m. H.S.T. Intensity, medium II Cancani scale; about 0.3 the minimum perceptible unit. Origin distant about ten miles.

November 8, from 4:27:45 a.m. to 4:28:01 a.m. H. S. T. Intensity, high II Cancani scale; about 0.4 the minimum perceptible unit. Origin distant about twelve miles.

November 9, from 10:27:38 p.m. to 10:28:39 p.m. H.S.T. Intensity, low I Cancani scale; about 0.05 the minimum perceptible unit. Origin distant about 20.3 miles.

November 10, from 11:04 to 11:30 approximately H.S.T. Waves of the chief phase of a very distant teleseism, probably of only ordinarily strong energy at the origin.

November 10, from 1:13:33 p.m. to 1:13:58 p.m. H.S.T. Intensity III, approximately, Cancani scale; less than the minimum perceptible unit. Origin distant about twenty-six miles.

November 12, from 9:23:08 a.m. to 9:23:33 a.m. H.S.T. Intensity, II Cancani scale; about 0.35 the minimum perceptible unit. Origin distant indeterminate. Very respectfully,

T. A. JAGGAR, Jr.,
Director.

WEEKLY BULLETIN OF HAWAIIAN VOLCANO OBSERVATORY

From the Pacific Commercial Advertiser, Honolulu, November 23, 1913.

TECHNOLOGY STATION, November 20.—A quiet period in the present state of activity at Kilauea accompanied continued heavy rain from the time of the preceding report, November 13, to the afternoon and evening of Tuesday, November 18. Heavy winds from the northeast brought much fog and mist with frequent heavy showers many of which were of prolonged duration, thus setting up conditions of swirling fumes and steam under which it is practically impossible to see the lower portion of the Halemaumau pit, even in brief glimpses.

During this stormy interval no views were obtained. However, throughout this time the fume cloud was not perceptibly illuminated, not even by flaring. It was conspicuously dark on Monday evening, November 17.

On Tuesday afternoon, November 18, one instantaneous glimpse of a small area at the bottom of the pit showed spots of glowing lava. The blowing noise of escaping gas was moderately loud and practically continuous, though the usual irregular variations in the volume of sound, supposed to follow the irregular action of Old Faithful, were heard. Also at intervals was heard the spatter sound made by the falling of lumps of molten lava after vigorous fountain action.

Throughout the evening and night of November 18-19 the fume cloud was continuously illuminated by the molten lava rising and flowing in the bottom of the pit, with frequent brilliant flarings at the usual irregular intervals of Old Faithful. However, the wind and rain made seeing impossible from all sides of the pit.

Activity Increases.

This activity continued on November 19, when, in the afternoon, a view of the bottom disclosed two fountain places where at intervals the molten lava welled over the banks onto the surrounding floor. Steady glow, with occasional flaring, was seen throughout the evening and night.

A view early on Thursday morning, November 20, showed a pool at the bottom of the pit in which the molten magma was surging vigorously. Later in the forenoon the lake crust was breaking up, particularly along the edges, and the bottom of the pit was filling at a comparatively rapid rate. The noise of escaping gas was much louder than on Tuesday.

Rainy weather has obscured the sun at noon for a considerable time past, preventing observations for time to check the rates of the chronometer and clock. On this account the systematic report from the Whitney Laboratory will be given at a later time. However, only one earthquake, instrumentally only a moderately small shock, has been registered since the last report. It occurred early in the afternoon of November 18.

Very respectfully,

H. O. WOOD, Associate.

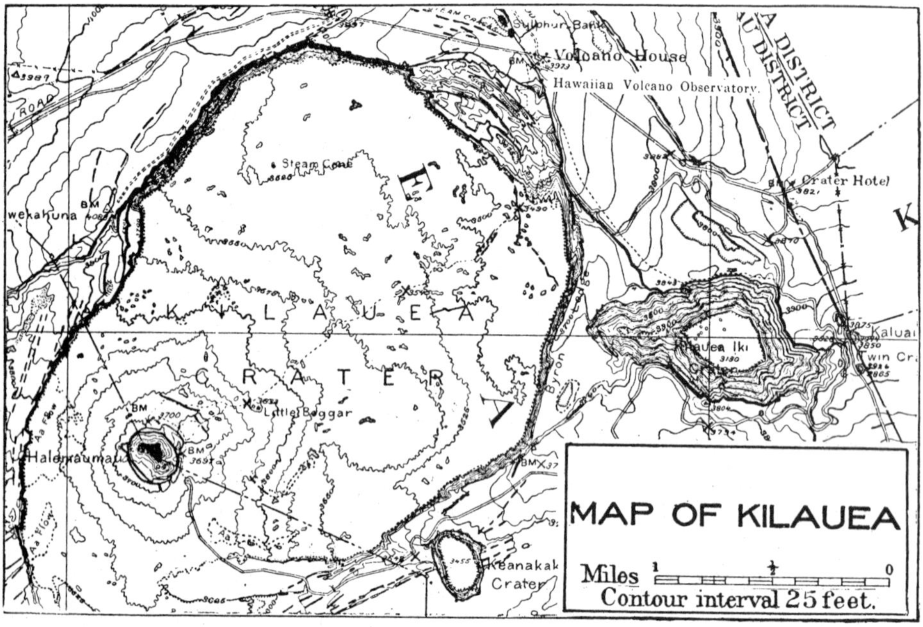

HAWAIIAN VOLCANO RESEARCH ASSOCIATION.

This society is a voluntary one, made up of subscribers to scientific work which is being executed by the Massachusetts Institute of Technology.

In 1913 there were 26 subscribers in Hawaii and Massachusetts, firms and individuals. A group of firms and persons in Hilo built the main observatory building in the spring of 1912. Publications to date have been weekly reports since the summer of 1911, a memoir by Daly in the Proceedings of American Academy of Arts and Sciences in 1911, articles by the director in the Technology Review 1911 and the Honolulu Chamber of Commerce Annual 1912, articles by H. O. Wood in the Bulletin of the Seismological Society of America, and articles by Perret in the American Journal of Science. The Massachusetts Institute of Technology will publish semi-annual reports.

This weekly bulletin as it appears in the Advertiser will be reprinted as a leaflet and sent to regular annual subscribers to the work of the association. C. H. Cooke is president of the Board of Directors of the association and R. W. Shingle is treasurer. New subscribers who are interested in our volcanoes will be welcomed in the association. The association aims: (1) To record volcanic activity and earthquakes in Hawaii; (2) to attract scientific men hither for special studies; (3) to promote the establishment of volcano observatories all over the world.

WHITNEY LABORATORY OF SEISMOLOGY.

The Whitney Laboratory of Seismology is equipped with two Bosch-Omori 100kg tromometers registering N-S and E-W motion, a heavy Omori tromometer registering E-W motion and an Omori "ordinary Seismograph" designed for registering strong earthquakes in all three components of motion. These are seated on concrete piers in a closed basement room having practically constant temperature, beneath the chief Observatory building near the hotel. For the present, time is referred to a rated chronometer, loaned by the College of Hawaii. At the substation by the edge of the active pit an Omori two-component tromometer with light steady masses is mounted on a concrete pier placed directly on the fresh lava surface. Hawaiian standard time (H. S. T.) is 10 hrs. 30 m. slower than Greenwich time.

CANCANI SCALE OF SEISMIC INTENSITY

Expressed by accelerations measured in millimeters per second per second.

I.	Instrumental	0.0	2.5
II.	Very slight	2.5	5.0
III.	Slight	5.0	10.0
IV.	Sensible, mediocre	10.0	25.0
V.	Rather strong	25.0	50.0
VI.	Strong	50.0	100.0
VII.	Very strong	100.0	250.0
VIII.	Ruinous	250.0	500.0
IX.	Disastrous	500.0	1000.0
X.	Very disastrous	1000.0	2500.0
XI.	Catastrophic	2500.0	5000.0
XII.	Great catastrophe	5000.0	10000.0

Grade IV. is ordinarily the minimum perceived by the senses; and in grade XII. the acceleration, or rate of change of motion (jerk) reaches that of terrestrial gravitation.

WEEKLY BULLETIN HAWAIIAN VOLCANO OBSERVATORY

Technology Station, November 27, 1913

At the time of writing the last report a marked increase of activity was just beginning in Halemaumau. This increase continued throughout Thursday afternoon and evening, November 20. In the evening of this day quiet air made it possible to observe the surface action from the station at the Old Rest House for comparatively long intervals. Elsewhere swirling fumes interfered. The steady action in the Old Faithful pool resembled that of a boiling spring--the magma rising steadily and flowing rapidly away under the crust in several varying directions, occasionally overflowing onto the neighboring crust for a few minutes. During this time the lava was rising steadily, lifting and at times cracking the thin black crust which covered most of the lava lake. Now and then a miniature flow would well out through one of these cracks. In a general way this system of cracks was permanently maintained and the glowing lava could be seen through them all along their course.

Even on Thursday, Nov. 20, conditions were not favorable for the routine work which is carried on when the fumes will permit. Consequently the depth to the lake surface and its dimensions were not measured; but the bottom area has definitely risen above recent previous marks by a considerable amount; and the lake area was of moderate size, probably not less than 100 feet in the E-W direction by 60 feet in the N-S direction.

At frequent intervals fountain action disturbed the steady flowing in the Old Faithful pool, sending spasmodic momentary flows and down the small, low, south and east slopes of the spatter cone which enclosed the figuration. Throughout the evening and night of November 20 the fume cloud was brilliantly lighted and brilliant flares were seen frequently.

This was the crisis of this eruptive stage. On Friday, Nov. 21, no view could be obtained on account of the wind. In the evening and night the illumination of the fumes was steady, but low, and flaring was less conspicuous.

Since then strong winds have made seeing altogether out of the question. But diminished illumination of the fume cloud--sometimes almost to the vanishing point--has indicated clearly a cessation of the marked rising and overflowing.

Hissing and swashing sounds, with the sounds of falling spatter, have been heard whenever the pit has been visited, but they have not been so loud as previously.

Nothing of interest in the registration of seismic motion has occurred during this week.

[This page has been retyped from an original typewritten insert.]

WEEKLY BULLETIN OF HAWAIIAN VOLCANO OBSERVATORY

From the Pacific Commercial Advertiser, Honolulu, December 7, 1913

TECHNOLOGY STATION, December 4.—The quiet stage in the activity in Halemaumau has continued without observed change, since the last writing. At the bottom of the pit there is a level area of black lava—the thickly frozen surface of the magna lake—probably somewhat larger in dimensions than the values given last week. However, it has not enlarged in the meantime, merely better views have been obtained of it, enabling better judged estimates to be made. It is judged to be in the neighborhood of 200 feet long, east and west, and about 150 feet wide, north and south. It is wider near the east end than near the west, an irregular polygon with curving sides. Several jagged peaks of low altitude rise around the place of Old Faithful, the remnants of its collapsed cone.

At the Old Faithful place, and at a point on the south shore of the lake area near its west end, are groups of small glowing orifices, two or three in each instance, out of which gas is discharged noisily. No fountain action, or flowing, has been observed. The fume cloud is dark at night. The fumes continue to issue in abundance from fumaroles all about the lake border.

Despite the quiescent state at present the evidence of activity is much greater than two months ago.

The weather has continued cloudy at and around noon, completely preventing observations for time. Since we are now undertaking to give the times with precision in the systematic reports from the Whitney Laboratory, such a report for the present period must be delayed still a little longer. However, several light, local earthquakes have occurred since the last writing.

Also in the afternoon and evening of December 3, the registration of volcanic vibrations was very pronounced, and individual groups of these waves were of comparatively long duration, from five to ten minutes. Very respectfully,

H. O. WOOD, Associate.

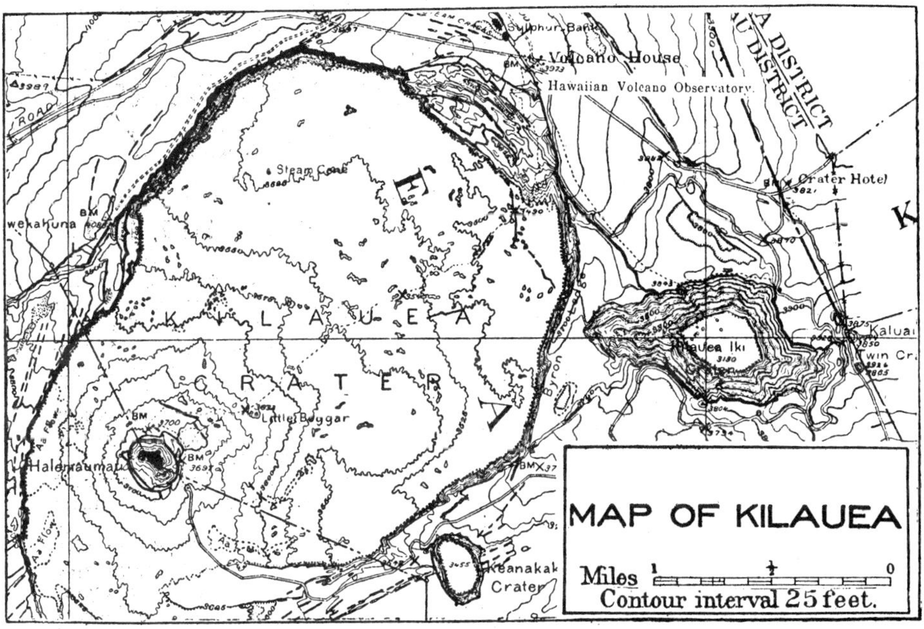

HAWAIIAN VOLCANO RESEARCH ASSOCIATION.

This society is a voluntary one, made up of subscribers to scientific work which is being executed by the Massachusetts Institute of Technology.

In 1913 there were 26 subscribers in Hawaii and Massachusetts, firms and individuals. A group of firms and persons in Hilo built the main observatory building in the spring of 1912. Publications to date have been weekly reports since the summer of 1911, a memoir by Daly in the Proceedings of American Academy of Arts and Sciences in 1911, articles by the director in the Technology Review 1911 and the Honolulu Chamber of Commerce Annual 1912, articles by H. O. Wood in the Bulletin of the Seismological Society of America, and articles by Perret in the American Journal of Science. The Massachusetts Institute of Technology will publish semi-annual reports.

This weekly bulletin as it appears in the Advertiser will be reprinted as a leaflet and sent to regular annual subscribers to the work of the association. C. H. Cooke is president of the Board of Directors of the association and R. W. Shingle is treasurer. New subscribers who are interested in our volcanoes will be welcomed in the association. The association aims: (1) To record volcanic activity and earthquakes in Hawaii; (2) to attract scientific men hither for special studies; (3) to promote the establishment of volcano observatories all over the world.

WHITNEY LABORATORY OF SEISMOLOGY.

The Whitney Laboratory of Seismology is equipped with two Bosch-Omori 100kg tromometers registering N-S and E-W motion, a heavy Omori tromometer registering E-W motion and an Omori "ordinary Seismograph" designed for registering strong earthquakes in all three components of motion. These are seated on concrete piers in a closed basement room having practically constant temperature, beneath the chief Observatory building near the hotel. For the present, time is referred to a rated chronometer, loaned by the College of Hawaii. At the substation by the edge of the active pit an Omori two-component tromometer with light steady masses is mounted on a concrete pier placed directly on the fresh lava surface. Hawaiian standard time (H. S. T.) is 10 hrs. 30 m. slower than Greenwich time.

CANCANI SCALE OF SEISMIC INTENSITY

Expressed by accelerations measured in millimeters per second per second.

I.	Instrumental	0.0	2.5
II.	Very slight	2.5	5.0
III.	Slight	5.0	10.0
IV.	Sensible, mediocre	10.0	25.0
V.	Rather strong	25.0	50.0
VI.	Strong	50.0	100.0
VII.	Very strong	100.0	250.0
VIII.	Ruinous	250.0	500.0
IX.	Disastrous	500.0	1000.0
X.	Very disastrous	1000.0	2500.0
XI.	Catastrophic	2500.0	5000.0
XII.	Great catastrophe	5000.0	10000.0

Grade IV. is ordinarily the minimum perceived by the senses; and in grade XII. the acceleration, or rate of change of motion (jerk) reaches that of terrestrial gravitation.

WEEKLY BULLETIN HAWAIIAN VOLCANO OBSERVATORY

Technology Station, December 11, 1913

Kilauea still remains in a semi-dormant stage. In general the conditions described in the previous report persist. Good views, for brief intervals, were obtained on both Thursday and Friday, Dec. 4 and 5, but nothing noteworthy was then observed.

On Saturday afternoon, Dec. 6, during several intervals of from ten seconds to two or three minutes duration, large parts of the bottom area were visible from the north and northwest parts of the rim of Halemaumau. Glowing spots were seen at the Old Faithful place and on the south margin of the lake area near its western extremity. At this time there was no visible boiling, flowing, or spouting of molten lava. The fumaroles in the talus at the southwest were unusually productive, yielding copious quantities of both snow-white and thin, blue fumes. At this time a fumarole was discovered almost directly under the N station, less than 200 feet below the rim, the fumes issuing directly out of the precipitous rock wall, nearly 300 feet above the next highest fuming place. This fumarole had been noticed, but not reported, about a week earlier than this by the old guide, Alex Lancaster. As yet only a small amount of vapor, blue in color, is coming from this place. In the evening and night intermittent illumination of the fume cloud could be observed though there was bright moonlight. One or two of the flarings were very brilliant.

At sundown on Saturday, Dec. 6, the steam jets on the northeast slope of Mauna Loa were visible for more than half an hour -- being conspicuous for the first time in many weeks. The amount of vapor visibly issuing from them was as great as, probably greater than, has been observed hitherto.

Good views into the pit were obtained on Sunday, Dec. 7, but no new manifestations were observed. Save for one or two isolated flarings, which could barely be seen, there was no illumination of the fume at night.

On Dec. 6, no view of the bottom could be obtained but there was no sound of falling spatter from the molten lumps after fountain discharges. The noise of the eruption appeared slightly increased.

[This page has been retyped from an original typewritten insert.]

On Dec. 9, there was no seeing, owing to a strong and gusty northeast wind.

On Dec. 10, a swerving southwest breeze made it impossible to see into the pit, but noises of swashing and of the falling of lumps of molten lava were heard, chiefly in the vicinity of the Old Faithful place.

On the morning of Dec. 11 brief but clear glimpses of portions of the bottom disclosed nothing new, except that the Old Faithful place was surrounded by fresh spatter lumps; and that a blowing cone under thc south station near the edge of the lake area was also surrounded by fresh spatter fragments. Gas was rushing noisily from this orifice, from that at the southwest and from Old Faithful.

It is still necessary to withhold any systematic report from the Whitney Laboratory on account of uncertainty in regard to time correction factors. There was extreme tilting during the run of 8-9 December, and a feeble local shock was registered in the early afternoon of the 9th.

[This page has been retyped from an original typewritten insert.]

WEEKLY BULLETIN OF HAWAIIAN VOLCANO OBSERVATORY

From the Pacific Commercial Advertiser, Honolulu, December 22, 1913.

Weather conditions during the past week have been such that it has been diffcult to observe conditions at Halemaumau. However Madame Pele has not given much evidence of renewed activity according to reports from the observatory. The only marked feature has been in slides in the talus of the roaring and blowing sounds showing that active forces are continuing at work. Under date of December 18, Observer H. O. Wood, writing from the technology station at Kilauea makes the following report:

"Conditions at Halemaumau remain practically without change. The weather during the past week has not been favorable for observing; owing to steady winds only quick glimpses of the bottom region have been obtained.

"On Friday, December 12, a brief glimpse was obtained in the afternoon. Glowing spots were observable in the places heretofore noted. At irregular intervals slides were occurring in the talus. One of these was seen to run down into a deep, smoking hole about 100 feet above the bottom of the pit at a point a little to the south of the west end of the pit. No illumination of the smoke cloud was observed during the evening or night.

"On Saturday, December 13, nothing was noted except the continued visibility of the glowing blow-holes and snorting sounds of eruption. No illumination was observed at night.

"On Sunday, December 14, the deep, smoking hole seen on Friday was choked with talus. The bottom could not be seen. The usual sounds of eruption were heard. At intervals slight sliding took place in the talus. At night a faint illumination of the fume cloud could be seen, before moonrise, with occasional flaring.

"On Monday, December 15, nothing was observed except a continued, faint illumination before moon-rise.

"On Tuesday, December 16, at about 10:30 a. m. a considerable slide took place under the west station lasting for some sixty seconds. Numerous smaller slides were noted during the day. The sounds of blowing, rumbling, and snorting continued undiminished. By day the bottom could not be seen. At night the glowing spots were visible and the fume cloud was faintly illumined.

"Wednesday, December 17, a moderately high wind prevailed and no visit was made to the pit. The faint illumination at night continued.

"Below is submitted a systematic report from the Whitney Laboratory of Seismology covering to date the interval not hitherto reported upon.

"November 18, from 1:30:53 p. m. to 1:33:02 p. m. H. S. T. Intensity, about III Cancani scale; something less than the minimum perceptible unit. Origin distant about 20 miles.

"November 23, from 12:58 p. m. to 12:59:37 p. m. H. S. T. Intensity, low I Cancani scale; about 0.05 the minimum perceptible unit. Origin distance indeterminate.

"November 27, from 1:27:39 p. m. to 1:29:59 p. m. H. S. T. Intensity, III Cancani scale; about 0.8 the minimum perceptible unit. Origin distant about 46 miles.

"November 29, from 6:50:35 a. m. to 6:51:07 a. m. H. S. T. Intensity, low I Cancani scale; less than 0.1 the minimum perceptible unit. Origin distant about 12.4 miles.

"November 29, from 8:11:35 a. m. to 8:12:29 a. m. H. S. T. Intensity, about III Cancani scale; probably less than the minimum perceptible unit. Origin distant about 13 miles.

"November 29, from 6:21:25 p. m. to 6:22:55 p. m. H. S. T. Intensity, I-II Cancani scale; more than 0.2 the minimum perceptible unit. Origin distant about 12.4 miles.

"December 1, from 11:16:29 a. m. to 11:16:50 a. m. H. S. T. Intensity, II Cancani scale; about 0.5 the minimum perceptible unit. Origin distant about 13 miles.

"December 3, from 12:51:22 p. m. to 12:53:21 p. m. H. S. T. Intensity, about III Cancani scale; probably less than the minimum perceptible unit. Origin distant 13 miles.

"December 9, from 10:51:02 p. m. to 10:51:59 p. m. H. S. T. Intensity, III Cancani scale; about 0.5 the minimum perceptible unit. Origin distant 13 miles.

"December 14, from 5:33:04 a. m. to 5:36:05 a. m. H. S. T. Intensity, III Cancani scale; about 0.6 the minimum perceptible unit. Origin distant 68 miles.

"December 15, from 3:33:37 a. m. to 3:35:15 a. m. H. S. T. Intensity, I Cancani scale; a little over 0.1 the minimum perceptible unit. Origin distant about 20 miles.

H. O. WOOD, Associate.

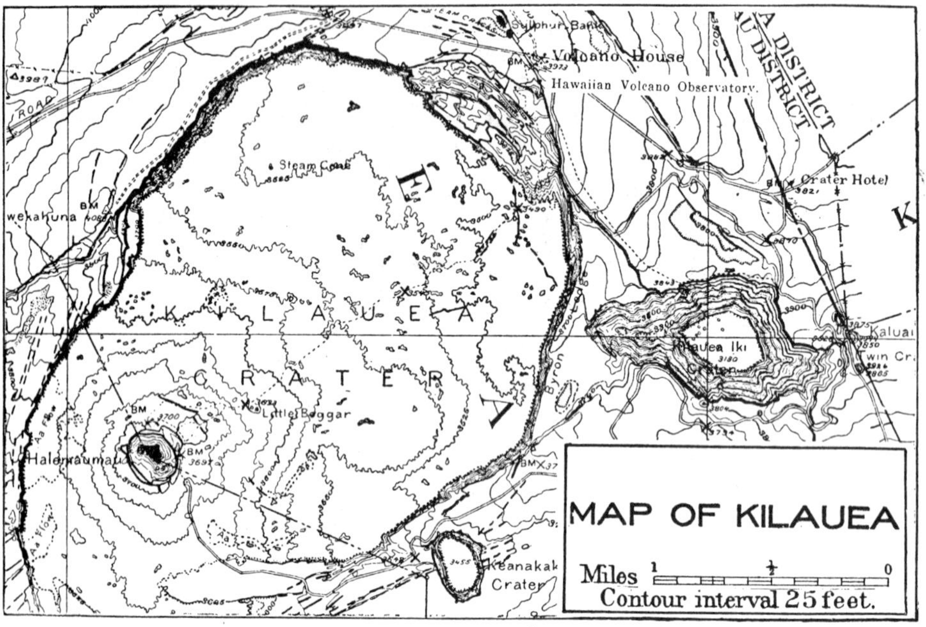

HAWAIIAN VOLCANO RESEARCH ASSOCIATION.

This society is a voluntary one, made up of subscribers to scientific work which is being executed by the Massachusetts Institute of Technology.

In 1913 there were 26 subscribers in Hawaii and Massachusetts, firms and individuals. A group of firms and persons in Hilo built the main observatory building in the spring of 1912. Publications to date have been weekly reports since the summer of 1911, a memoir by Daly in the Proceedings of American Academy of Arts and Sciences in 1911, articles by the director in the Technology Review 1911 and the Honolulu Chamber of Commerce Annual 1912, articles by H. O. Wood in the Bulletin of the Seismological Society of America, and articles by Perret in the American Journal of Science. The Massachusetts Institute of Technology will publish semiannual reports.

This weekly bulletin as it appears in the Advertiser will be reprinted as a leaflet and sent to regular annual subscribers to the work of the association. C. H. Cooke is president of the Board of Directors of the association and R. W. Shingle is treasurer. New subscribers who are interested in our volcanoes will be welcomed in the association. The association aims: (1) To record volcanic activity and earthquakes in Hawaii; (2) to attract scientific men hither for special studies; (3) to promote the establishment of volcano observatories all over the world.

WHITNEY LABORATORY OF SEISMOLOGY.

The Whitney Laboratory of Seismology is equipped with two Bosch-Omori 100kg tromometers registering N-S and E-W motion, a heavy Omori tromometer registering E-W motion and an Omori "ordinary Seismograph" designed for registering strong earthquakes in all three components of motion. These are seated on concrete piers in a closed basement room having practically constant temperature, beneath the chief Observatory building near the hotel. For the present, time is referred to a rated chronometer, loaned by the College of Hawaii. At the substation by the edge of the active pit an Omori two-component tromometer with light steady masses is mounted on a concrete pier placed directly on the fresh lava surface. Hawaiian standard time (H. S. T.) is 10 hrs. 30 m. slower than Greenwich time.

CANCANI SCALE OF SEISMIC INTENSITY

Expressed by accelerations measured in millimeters per second per second.

I.	Instrumental	0.0	2.5
II.	Very slight	2.5	5.0
III.	Slight	5.0	10.0
IV.	Sensible, mediocre	10.0	25.0
V.	Rather strong	25.0	50.0
VI.	Strong	50.0	100.0
VII.	Very strong	100.0	250.0
VIII.	Ruinous	250.0	500.0
IX.	Disastrous	500.0	1000.0
X.	Very disastrous	1000.0	2500.0
XI.	Catastrophic	2500.0	5000.0
XII.	Great catastrophe	5000.0	10000.0

Grade IV. is ordinarily the minimum perceived by the senses; and in grade XII. the acceleration, or rate of change of motion (jerk) reaches that of terrestrial gravitation.

WEEKLY BULLETIN
OF
Hawaiian Volcano Observatory

Vol. II. HONOLULU, HAWAII, JANUARY 7, 1914 No. 1.

From the Pacific Commercial Advertiser, Honolulu, December 28, 1913.

TECHNOLOGY STATION, December 25.—The Christmas season of the winter solstice brings no revival of activity in Kilauea as yet. The gradual rise of the lava of Halemaumau in October and November reached a stationary level at some time early in this month and the movement since, if there has been any, has been a sinking rather than a rising. Until this week the fumes have been too dense for measurement; an approximate measure of depth last Monday, December 22, shows that the present level of the bottom crust is about where it was last April.

Saturday, December 20, with fair weather and northeast wind, the fumes appeared relatively light and the pit quiet. There was no seeing, but from the north edge faint puffs could be heard with the usual irregular intervals of from half a minute to a minute. Some rock sliding from the north side of the pit could be heard. Time of the observations, 10:30 a. m.

On December 21, at 5 p. m., conditions were much the same, but the fumes were very dense. No slides were heard, and in this respect the present week has been quieter than last week. At about 3 p. m., however, a pronounced rock slide was reported by one party. At night three glow spots in the floor could be distinguished. A faint, steady glow could be seen from the Observatory, which brightened toward midnight.

Heavy Rock Slides.

December 22, at 10:30 a. m., good views of the bottom and the ring of fumaroles were obtained from the south and southeast stations. Occasional sliding noises and puffs were heard, and heavy rock slides occurred about 11:10 a. m. The sliding could not be seen through the fumes, but it sounded as though it were mostly from the west. Approximate measurements with alidade and plane-table were made from the south and southeast stations, determining the depth of the pit to a fuming hole at the south border of the floor to be 568 feet, and the depth to a fumarole on the south margin of the talus ring, almost under the south station, 394 feet. This would make the height of the rocky cliff, under the eastern A-frame near the automobile terminus, about 400 feet. The wind was very light and from the east, causing the fumes to rise in a column on the north and northwest walls, sometimes overriding the north edge and burying the stations there in smoke clouds.

WEEKLY BULLETIN
of
Hawaiian Volcano Observatory

Published at Honolulu, Hawaii, by the **Hawaiian Volcano Research Association**

Editor..............Howard M. Ballou
Professor of Physics, College of Hawaii

Application pending for entry as second-class matter at the post-office, Honolulu, Hawaii.

December 23 and 24 the glow seen from the Observatory was very faint at night. At 3 p. m. December 24, the west wall was seen and faint puffing was heard, but no slides.

Today, December 25, at 11:30 a. m., the wind was light from the southwest, and from the southwest station puffs could be heard, recorded at intervals as follows: 65, 90, 27, 30, 17, 60, etc., seconds. One rock slide was heard at 11:40 a. m. From the northwest station the floor and western fumaroles could be seen. Large fuming patches in the talus were seen west and north of the bottom area, a high one in the rock wall north, and dimly the lava floor of the bottom could be made out, apparently overridden by talus. The two holes in the west wall now appear about halfway up.

There have been no unusual seismic happenings this week.

T. A. JAGGAR JR.,
Director.

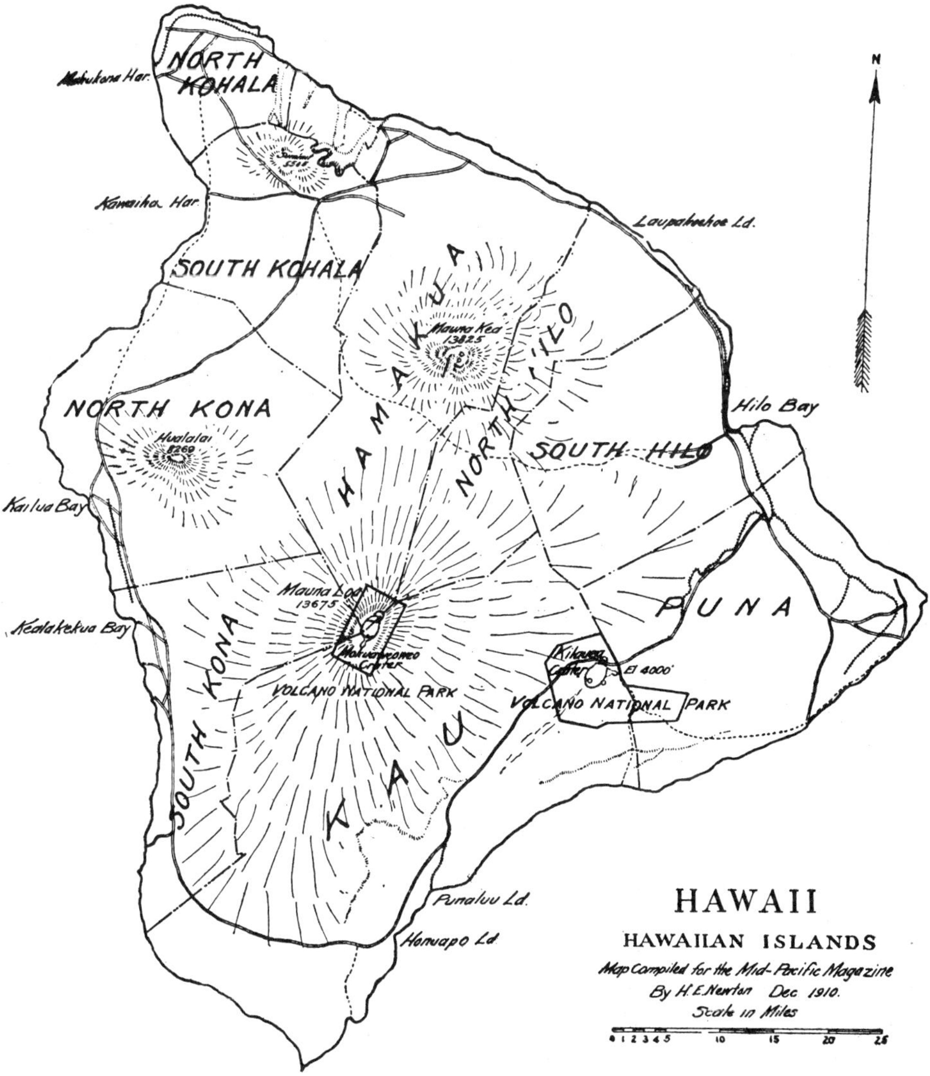

HAWAII

HAWAIIAN ISLANDS

Map Compiled for the Mid-Pacific Magazine
By H. E. Newton Dec 1910.
Scale in Miles

0 1 2 3 4 5 10 15 20 25

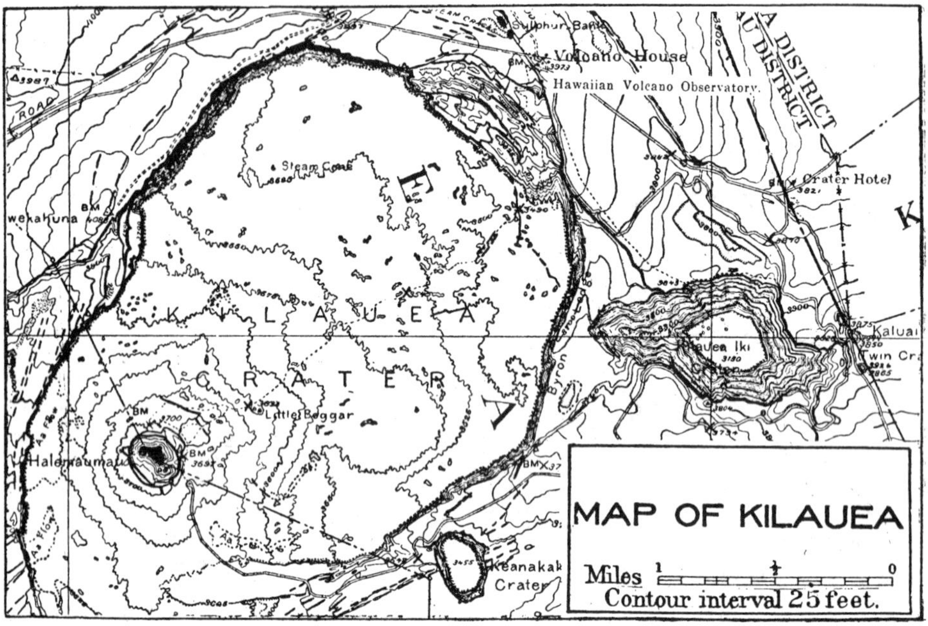

HAWAIIAN VOLCANO RESEARCH ASSOCIATION.

This society is a voluntary one, made up of subscribers to scientific work which is being executed by the Massachusetts Institute of Technology.

In 1913 there were 26 subscribers in Hawaii and Massachusetts, firms and individuals. A group of firms and persons in Hilo built the main observatory building in the spring of 1912. Publications to date have been weekly reports since the summer of 1911, a memoir by Daly in the Proceedings of American Academy of Arts and Sciences in 1911, articles by the director in the Technology Review 1911 and the Honolulu Chamber of Commerce Annual 1912, articles by H. O. Wood in the Bulletin of the Seismological Society of America, and articles by Perret in the American Journal of Science. The Massachusetts Institute of Technology will publish semi-annual reports.

This weekly bulletin as it appears in the Advertiser will be reprinted as a leaflet and sent to regular annual subscribers to the work of the association. C. H. Cooke is president of the Board of Directors of the association and R. W. Shingle is treasurer. New subscribers who are interested in our volcanoes will be welcomed in the association. The association aims: (1) To record volcanic activity and earthquakes in Hawaii; (2) to attract scientific men hither for special studies; (3) to promote the establishment of volcano observatories all over the world.

WHITNEY LABORATORY OF SEISMOLOGY.

The Whitney Laboratory of Seismology is equipped with two Bosch-Omori 100kg tromometers registering N-S and E-W motion, a heavy Omori tromometer registering E-W motion and an Omori "ordinary Seismograph" designed for registering strong earthquakes in all three components of motion. These are seated on concrete piers in a closed basement room having practically constant temperature, beneath the chief Observatory building near the hotel. For the present, time is referred to a rated chronometer, loaned by the College of Hawaii. At the substation by the edge of the active pit an Omori two-component tromometer with light steady masses is mounted on a concrete pier placed directly on the fresh lava surface. Hawaiian standard time (H. S. T.) is 10 hrs. 30 m. slower than Greenwich time.

CANCANI SCALE OF SEISMIC INTENSITY

Expressed by accelerations measured in millimeters per second per second.

I.	Instrumental	0.0	2.5
II.	Very slight	2.5	5.0
III.	Slight	5.0	10.0
IV.	Sensible, mediocre....	10.0	25.0
V.	Rather strong	25.0	50.0
VI.	Strong	50.0	100.0
VII.	Very strong	100.0	250.0
VIII.	Ruinous	250.0	500.0
IX.	Disastrous	500.0	1000.0
X.	Very disastrous	1000.0	2500.0
XI.	Catastrophic	2500.0	5000.0
XII.	Great catastrophe....	5000.0	10000.0

Grade IV. is ordinarily the minimum perceived by the senses; and in grade XII. the acceleration, or rate of change of motion (jerk) reaches that of terrestrial gravitation.

WEEKLY BULLETIN OF Hawaiian Volcano Observatory

Vol. II. HONOLULU, HAWAII, JANUARY 14, 1914. No. 2.

From the Pacific Commercial Advertiser, Honolulu, January 5, 1914.

TECHNOLOGY STATION, January 1, 1914.—The last week of the year 1913 has shown no marked change in the Halemaumau lava pit. It is a huge funnel between 500 and 600 feet deep, with a thickly crusted lava pool in its bottom, flat slide-rock slopes around the pool, one and possibly two spatter cones showing glowing lava on the floor, and at least two glowing fumaroles in the talus, one at the floor level S.W. and another much higher in the N.W. slide-rock slope.

Vast quantities of white smoke rise from a ring of very hot and active fumaroles about the top of the talus from 100 to 150 feet above the floor level. Bluish smoke comes from the large central spatter cone in the floor, supposed to represent the site of Old Faithful fountain. Two fuming holes in the solid rock of the wall of the pit high above the talus occur N. and N.E. Two dark cavernous openings without fumes are in the W. wall halfway down to the talus.

There is no present activity in Mauna Loa. Earthquakes are not more prevalent than usual. It is worthy of note that Mr. J. L. Fleming reports that on December 11, 1913, at 1 p. m., the steamer Mauna Loa on the W. side of the Island of Hawaii off Hualalai, opposite McGuire's, encountered small dead rock-fish on the water scattered along about two miles of her course. For the past week the wind has been almost continuously from the S.W., blowing the fumes from the crater over the Observatory and the Volcano House, so as to make breathing difficult, wilting many plants and notably killing the slugs and cut-worms. Today the wind has changed to the east.

A Glimpse of Activity.

Friday, December 26, at 10 a. m., the wind was light southerly and one good view of the bottom of Halemaumau was obtained from the old north rest-house. Glowing lava was seen in the westermost of two built-up cones on the floor. Blue fumes were rising from the lava. Very active peripheral fumaroles were seen, the southern one on the edge of the floor, the N. and W. ones higher. The talus has slipped down until it is very flat. The noises are louder than on the previous day, and once spatter fall was heard on the rocks, and some splashing noise coupled with the blowing. One rock-slide was heard.

At 11:30 a. m. on December 27 atmospheric conditions were similar. There was no seeing from the east and southeast stations, but the puffing could be heard from the latter. From the N.W. station several views of the bottom of the pit were obtained, sufficient for photographic records, but not for good pictures. The fumes were not particularly disagreeable to breathe on the leeward side of the crater.

At the N.W. station the puffing was quite loud and irregular. The loud puffs came at intervals of from one to three minutes. In the intervals there were sometimes prolonged and faint soft blowing sounds. The loud puffs sometimes came in groups. No spatter fall was heard. A small fumarole in the rock high on the wall of the 1894 bench N.E. was noticed for the first

WEEKLY BULLETIN
of
Hawaiian Volcano Observatory

Published at Honolulu, Hawaii, by the
Hawaiian Volcano Research Association

Editor..............Howard M. Ballou
Professor of Physics, College of Hawaii

Application pending for entry as second-class matter at the post-office, Honolulu, Hawaii.

time. Slight slides were heard N.E. and W. At 11 a. m. the temperature of the air was 17 degrees C., (62.6° F.) and of the Postal Rift 315 degrees, with the wind S.E.

December 28, conditions were similar. December 29, at 5:30 p. m., the weather was still and foggy. The fume column was rising almost vertically, hugging the walls of the pit, and obscuring all view of the bottom and of the glowing vents after dark. Rock sliding was heard W., E., and S. and in fact small rocks were moving on the talus most of the time. At least five strong slides took place in the course of an hour. The noise of puffing was rare and weak. The great increase of sliding on this day suggested renewal of subsidence.

December 30, at 8 p. m., three marked glowing spots in the pit could be seen, one of them the high W.N.W. fumarole at the top of the talus. The other two are the S.W. fumarole at the margin of the floor and one of the spatter cones. These holes make considerable glow on the fume cloud when it rises and this can be seen from the Observatory at night. The puffing noises were as usual, and there was little sliding.

New Year Phenomena.

Today January 1, 1914, at 10:45 a. m., measured intervals between the puffs were 40, 20, 50 and 30 seconds. The wind was N.E. and from the N.W. a good view of the bottom was obtained. There was little sliding and the puffing was as usual. Fumaroles N. and N.W. in the talus were cloudy and giving off thin fumes. The westermost cone in the floor gave blue fumes, N.E., W.N.W., W., and S.W. were very active fumaroles giving small hard outlined jets with cauliflower outlines of white vapor rising in tails through the stones, and here sulphurous incrustations appeared on the stones. The floor was of brown pahoehoe. The high W.N.W. fumarole was particularly active and appeared to be undermining the slope above it so that rocks would slide down into it from time to time. This is one of those which glow at night.

A few small earthquakes have been recorded during the week, one of them perceptible at the Volcano House. They will be formally reported on later by Mr. H. O. Wood, in charge of the Whitney laboratory of seismology.

T. A. JAGGAR, JR.,
Director.

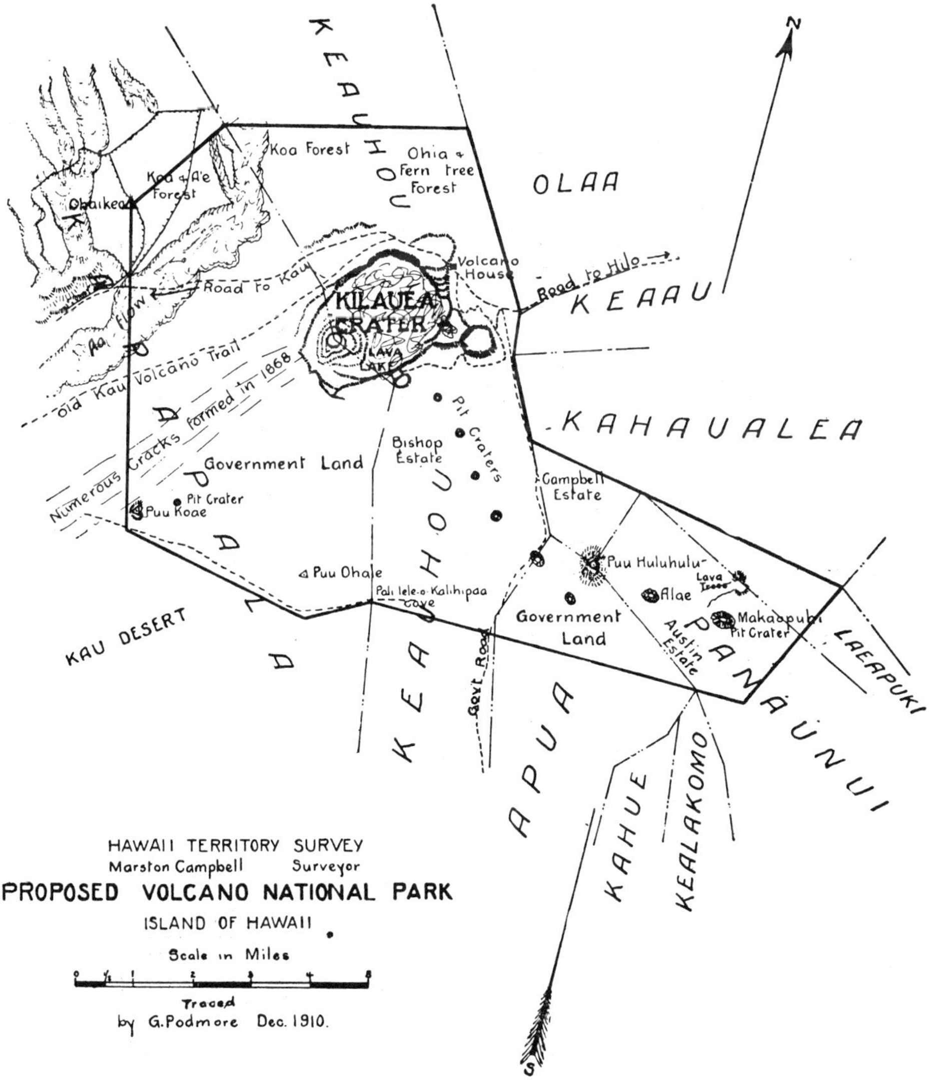
KEAUHOU
OLAA
KEAAU
KAHAUALEA
KAPAPALA
KEAUHOU
APUA
PANAUNUI
LAEAPUKI
KAHUE
KEALAKOMO
KAU DESERT
Koa Forest
Ohia & Fern tree Forest
Koa & A'e Forest
Ohaikea
Volcano House
Road to Hilo
Road to Kau
Aa Flow
KILAUEA CRATER
LAVA LAKE
old Kau Volcano Trail
Numerous Cracks formed in 1868
Government Land
Bishop Estate
Pit Craters
Pit Crater
Puu Koae
Campbell Estate
Puu Huluhulu
Lava Trees
Alae
Makaopuhi Pit Crater
Government Land
Austin Estate
Puu Ohale
Pali lele-o-Kalihipaa Cave
Govt Road
N
S
HAWAII TERRITORY SURVEY
Marston Campbell Surveyor
PROPOSED VOLCANO NATIONAL PARK
ISLAND OF HAWAII
Scale in Miles
0 ½ 1 2 3 4 5
Traced by G.Podmore Dec. 1910.

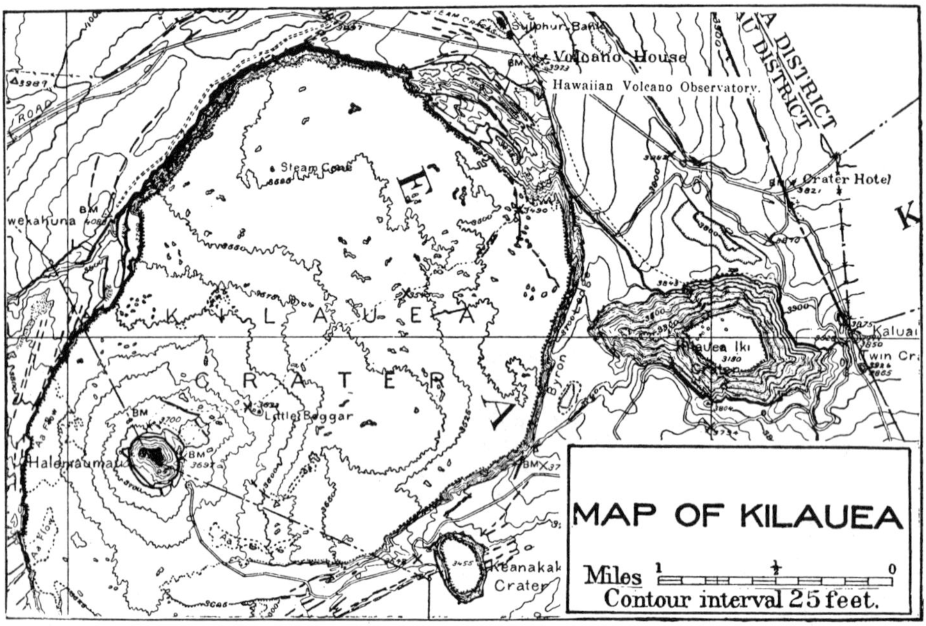

HAWAIIAN VOLCANO RESEARCH ASSOCIATION.

This society is a voluntary one, made up of subscribers to scientific work which is being executed by the Massachusetts Institute of Technology.

In 1913 there were 26 subscribers in Hawaii and Massachusetts, firms and individuals. A group of firms and persons in Hilo built the main observatory building in the spring of 1912. Publications to date have been weekly reports since the summer of 1911, a memoir by Daly in the Proceedings of American Academy of Arts and Sciences in 1911, articles by the director in the Technology Review 1911 and the Honolulu Chamber of Commerce Annual 1912, articles by H. O. Wood in the Bulletin of the Seismological Society of America, and articles by Perret in the American Journal of Science. The Massachusetts Institute of Technology will publish semi-annual reports.

This weekly bulletin as it appears in the Advertiser will be reprinted as a leaflet and sent to regular annual subscribers to the work of the association. C. H. Cooke is president of the Board of Directors of the association and R. W. Shingle is treasurer. New subscribers who are interested in our volcanoes will be welcomed in the association. The association aims: (1) To record volcanic activity and earthquakes in Hawaii; (2) to attract scientific men hither for special studies; (3) to promote the establishment of volcano observatories all over the world.

WHITNEY LABORATORY OF SEISMOLOGY.

The Whitney Laboratory of Seismology is equipped with two Bosch-Omori 100kg tromometers registering N-S and E-W motion, a heavy Omori tromometer registering E-W motion and an Omori "ordinary Seismograph" designed for registering strong earthquakes in all three components of motion. These are seated on concrete piers in a closed basement room having practically constant temperature, beneath the chief Observatory building near the hotel. For the present, time is referred to a rated chronometer, loaned by the College of Hawaii. At the substation by the edge of the active pit an Omori two-component tromometer with light steady masses is mounted on a concrete pier placed directly on the fresh lava surface. Hawaiian standard time (H. S. T.) is 10 hrs. 30 m. slower than Greenwich time.

CANCANI SCALE OF SEISMIC INTENSITY

Expressed by accelerations measured in millimeters per second per second.

I.	Instrumental	0.0	2.5
II.	Very slight	2.5	5.0
III.	Slight	5.0	10.0
IV.	Sensible, mediocre....	10.0	25.0
V.	Rather strong	25.0	50.0
VI.	Strong	50.0	100.0
VII.	Very strong	100.0	250.0
VIII.	Ruinous	250.0	500.0
IX.	Disastrous	500.0	1000.0
X.	Very disastrous	1000.0	2500.0
XI.	Catastrophic	2500.0	5000.0
XII.	Great catastrophe....	5000.0	10000.0

Grade IV. is ordinarily the minimum perceived by the senses; and in grade XII. the acceleration, or rate of change of motion (jerk) reaches that of terrestrial gravitation.

WEEKLY BULLETIN
OF
Hawaiian Volcano Observatory

Vol. II. HONOLULU, HAWAII, JANUARY 21, 1914. No. 3.

From the Pacific Commercial Advertiser, Honolulu, January 11, 1914.

TECHNOLOGY STATION, January 8.—The new year has brought no change in the condition of Halemaumau. The crater remains smoky, the fumes strong and difficult to breathe; the noises of blowing and splashing have diminished, and there is hardly any glow on the smoke-cloud at night visible from the Observatory. The bottom is generally invisible, except for partial openings through eddies in the smoke-cloud west and southeast.

Saturday, January 3, at 3:30 p.m., the wind S. E. and the weather misty, Halemaumau was enveloped in fumes and mist and nothing could be seen. One rock-slide was heard and faint puffs from the floor vent.

January 5, at 4 p.m., the wind was strong from the NE with drizzle. Faint blowing noises could be heard at intervals of from one to three minutes. No sliding was heard and there was no seeing.

January 7, at 4 p.m., faint puffs could be heard at rare intervals, and a partial view of the west wall was obtained from the old resthouse. Once or twice a distinct splashing noise was heard, and there was a little sliding toward the west. The fumes were strong and not easily respirable.

The following report from the Whitney Laboratory of Seismology is submitted by H. O. Wood:

Since the last systematic report earthquakes have been registered as follows:

1913—December 19, from 12:21:12 p.m. to 12:22:23 p.m. H. S. T. Intensity, II Cancani scale; about 40 per cent to 50 per cent of the minimum perceptible unit. Origin distant about 13 miles.

December 20, from 4:03:50 a.m. to 4:04:52 a.m. H. S. T. Intensity, I Cancani scale; about 13 per cent of the minimum perceptible unit. Origin distance indeterminate.

December 20, from 11:28:51 p.m. to 11:29:45 p.m. H. S. T. Intensity, I Cancani scale; about 20 per cent of the minimum perceptible unit. Origin distant about 13.7 miles.

December 22, from 2:55:42 p.m. to 2:56:08 p.m. H. S. T. Intensity, II-III Cancani scale; about 50 per cent of the minimum perceptible unit. Origin distant about 12.5 miles.

December 26, from 2:26:03 a.m. to 2:28:29 a.m. H. S. T. Intensity, I Cancani scale; about 13 per cent of the minimum perceptible unit. Origin distant about 18.6 miles.

December 26, from 6:47:48 a.m. to 6:49:06 a.m. H. S. T. Intensity, I Cancani scale; about 15 per cent of the minimum perceptible unit. Origin distance indeterminate.

December 26, from 11:16:19 a.m. to 11:17:02 a.m. H. S. T. Intensity, III Cancani scale, less than the minimum perceptible unit. Origin distant about 13 miles.

December 26, from 12:16:33 p.m. to 12:19:10 p.m. H. S. T. Intensity, IV Cancani scale; about the value of the minimum perceptible unit. Felt at the Volcano House by one person lying down. Origin distance about 14.3 miles.

December 26, from 12:39:13 p.m. to 12:41:26 p.m. H. S. T. Intensity, I Cancani scale; about 7.5 per cent of the minimum perceptible unit. Origin distance indeterminate.

December 28, from 2:24:59 a.m. to 2:26:06 a.m. H. S. T. Intensity, III

WEEKLY BULLETIN
of
Hawaiian Volcano Observatory

Published at Honolulu, Hawaii, by the
Hawaiian Volcano Research Association

Editor..............Howard M. Ballou
Professor of Physics, College of Hawaii

Application pending for entry as second-class matter at the post-office, Honolulu, Hawaii.

Cancani scale; about 60 per cent of the minimum perceptible unit. Origin distant about 13 miles.

December 28, from 5:02:25 a.m. to 5:03:49 a.m. H. S. T. Intensity, I Cancani scale; about 20 per cent of the minimum perceptible unit. Origin distant about 17 miles.

December 31, from 9:04:50 p.m. to 9:05:38 p.m. H. S. T. Intensity, II Cancani scale; about 30 per cent of the the minimum perceptible unit. Origin distant about 17 miles.

December 31, from 10:58:52 p.m. to 10:59:46 p.m. H. S. T. Intensity, I Cancani scale; about 12 per cent of the minimum perceptible unit. Origin distant about 13 miles.

1914—January 2, from 12:30:41 p.m. to 12:31:25 p.m. H. S. T. Intensity, I Cancani scale; about 20 per cent of the minimum perceptible unit. Origin distant about 13.6 miles.

T. A. JAGGAR, Jr., Director.

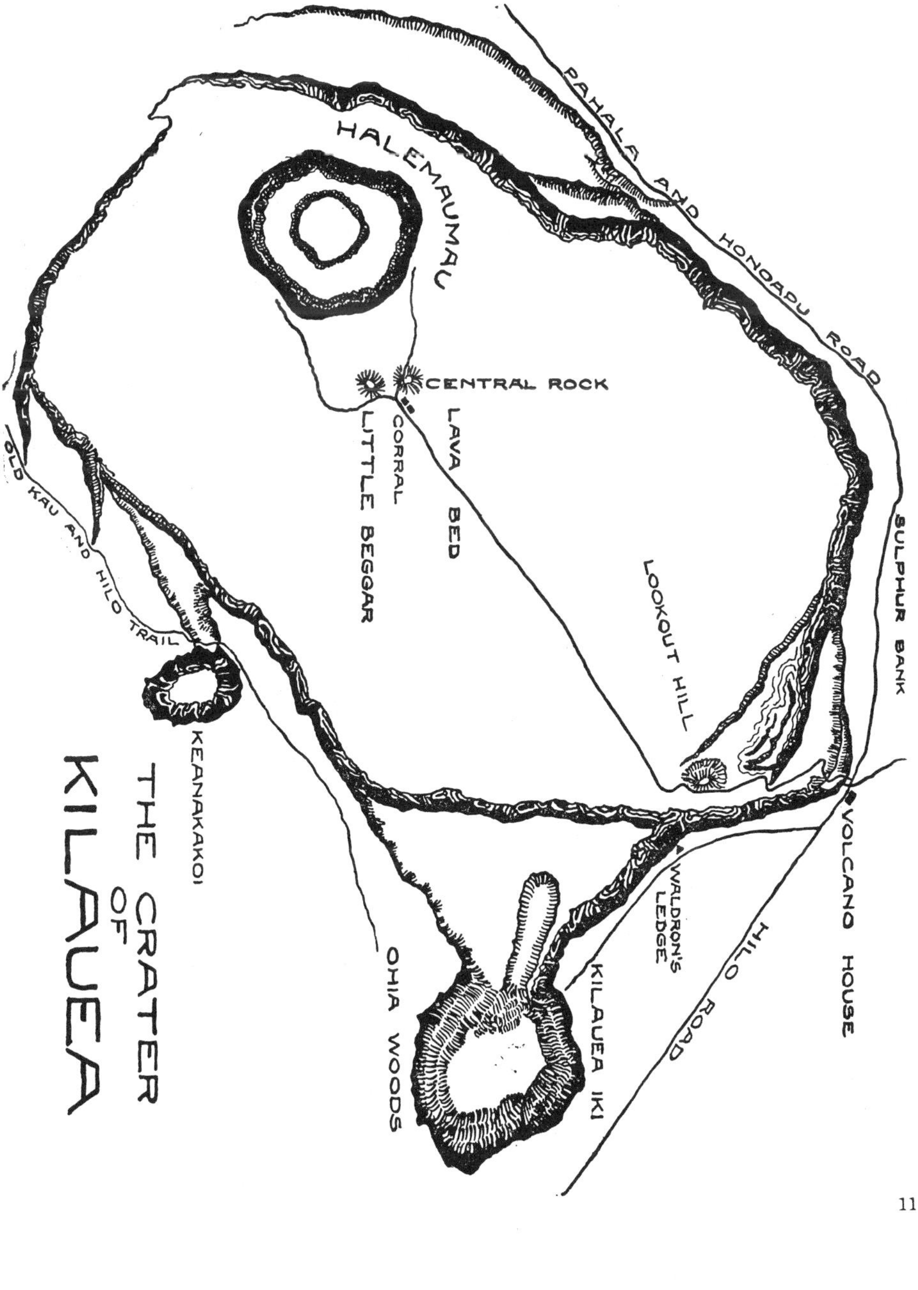

THE CRATER OF KILAUEA

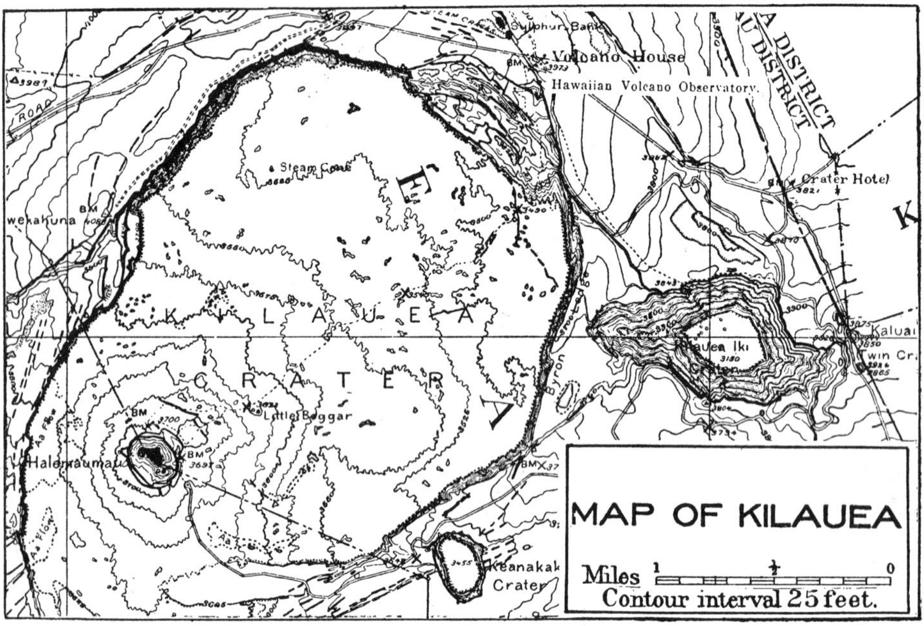

HAWAIIAN VOLCANO RESEARCH ASSOCIATION.

This society is a voluntary one, made up of subscribers to scientific work which is being executed by the Massachusetts Institute of Technology.

In 1913 there were 26 subscribers in Hawaii and Massachusetts, firms and individuals. A group of firms and persons in Hilo built the main observatory building in the spring of 1912. Publications to date have been weekly reports since the summer of 1911, a memoir by Daly in the Proceedings of American Academy of Arts and Sciences in 1911, articles by the director in the Technology Review 1911 and the Honolulu Chamber of Commerce Annual 1912, articles by H. O. Wood in the Bulletin of the Seismological Society of America, and articles by Perret in the American Journal of Science. The Massachusetts Institute of Technology will publish semiannual reports.

This weekly bulletin as it appears in the Advertiser will be reprinted as a leaflet and sent to regular annual subscribers to the work of the association. C. H. Cooke is president of the Board of Directors of the association and R. W. Shingle is treasurer. New subscribers who are interested in our volcanoes will be welcomed in the association. The association aims: (1) To record volcanic activity and earthquakes in Hawaii; (2) to attract scientific men hither for special studies; (3) to promote the establishment of volcano observatories all over the world.

WHITNEY LABORATORY OF SEISMOLOGY.

The Whitney Laboratory of Seismology is equipped with two Bosch-Omori 100 kg tromometers registering N-S and E-W motion, a heavy Omori tromometer registering E-W motion and an Omori "ordinary Seismograph" designed for registering strong earthquakes in all three components of motion. These are seated on concrete piers in a closed basement room having practically constant temperature, beneath the chief Observatory building near the hotel. Time is referred to a rated chronometer, checked at intervals by solar observations with a transit. Both instruments are loaned by the College of Hawaii. At the substation by the edge of the active pit an Omori two-component tromometer with light steady masses is mounted on a concrete pier placed directly on the fresh lava surface. Hawaiian standard time (H. S. T.) is 10 hrs. 30 m. slower than Greenwich time.

CANCANI SCALE OF SEISMIC INTENSITY

Expressed by accelerations measured in millimeters per second per second.

I.	Instrumental	0.0	2.5
II.	Very slight	2.5	5.0
III.	Slight	5.0	10.0
IV.	Sensible, mediocre....	10.0	25.0
V.	Rather strong	25.0	50.0
VI.	Strong	50.0	100.0
VII.	Very strong	100.0	250.0
VIII.	Ruinous	250.0	500.0
IX.	Disastrous	500.0	1000.0
X.	Very disastrous	1000.0	2500.0
XI.	Catastrophic	2500.0	5000.0
XII.	Great catastrophe....	5000.0	10000.0

Grade IV. is ordinarily the minimum perceived by the senses; and in grade XII. the acceleration, or rate of change of motion (jerk) reaches that of terrestrial gravitation.

WEEKLY BULLETIN
OF
Hawaiian Volcano Observatory

Vol. II. HONOLULU, HAWAII, JANUARY 28, 1914. No. 4.

From the Pacific Commercial Advertiser, Honolulu, January 18, 1914.

TECHNOLOGY STATION, January 15.—The week has been very stormy, windy and cold at the volcano, the wind northeasterly, and there has been much rain and drizzle. The Halemaumau pit has entered into a period of almost complete repose, so far as can be judged by the observers hearing nothing and seeing little at the edge. Even the talus has ceased active sliding, so that there is no sign of considerable rising or falling of the lava column.

The rock floor has not been visible this week, owing to the great volume of rain fog added to the volcanic fumes. There have, however, been times of clearing out of the southeast part of the pit, showing that part of the great circle of fumaroles actively spouting through the stones great jets of white vapor, about four hundred feet below the verge of the chasm, this vapor swirling into cumuli above, which incessantly roll away to leeward.

It should be borne in mind by those visiting the volcano that this vomiting of fumes in large volume is not wholly to be regarded as a disappointing mark of inactivity. It marks a new and interesting phase in the activity of Kilauea, which in times of real inactivity within the last twenty years has shown the bottom clear, with practically no fumes. Experienced observers of the volcano who have seen it for fifty years assert that this dense smoke is unprecedented.

The fumaroles whence the smoke rises appear to be places of multiple orifices through pores among broken stone, and in places the gases have recently been burning with blue flames, the hottest and most active fumaroles yielding quick jets of bluish white vapor, while the less active vents give up slower purling whitish clouds. There has been no glow on the cloud seen from the observatory this week. There is every reason, however, to suppose that the liquid lava is not far below the floor, the hot fumaroles marking its location, for had the lava column subsided the bottom would have collapsed and produced noisy avalanches.

January 8 and 9, 1914, were rainy, with some slipping of stones in the crater, and no seeing. January 11, from 3 to 3:30 p.m., the southern part of the pit was open to view, and there were many small avalanches inside the talus ring. The fumaroles at the 400-foot level were photographed. Much blue smoke could be seen near the south end of the bottom area, but the floor could not be distinguished. Rare puffs of gas at intervals of from four to five minutes could be heard both from the southeast station and from the old north rest-house.

January 13, after a rainstorm with high northeast wind in the morning, the afternoon cleared partially, and at 4 p.m. imperfect views of the fumaroles were obtained from the southeast station. From the old rest-house no blowing or rock sliding was heard.

This morning, January 15, at 10 a.m., the wind was northeast and the weather cloudy to rainy. The fumes smelled acrid and there was no seeing nor hearing from any station. The temperature of the air at 10:30 a. m. was 13 degrees Centigrade (55.4 deg. Fehr.), and of the Postal Rift 314 degrees Cent. (597.2 deg. Fahr.).

WEEKLY BULLETIN
of
Hawaiian Volcano Observatory

Published at Honolulu, Hawaii, by the **Hawaiian Volcano Research Association**

Editor..............Howard M. Ballou
Professor of Physics, College of Hawaii

Application pending for entry as second-class matter at the post-office, Honolulu, Hawaii.

H. O. Wood reports for the Whitney Laboratory of Seismology that the week has been very quiet seismically.

The eruption of Sakura is undoubtedly a great one. This volcano, in Osumi Province, the southernmost in Japan, must not be confused with Ontake, a volcano over 10,000 feet high in Central Nippon. Sakura lies near the north end of the long chain of active volcanoes of the Luchu Islands, and rises 3506 feet high, making an island in Kagoshima bay, on which is the village of Take. Kagoshima is recorded by Murray as having a population of 59,000 and appears on the map to be about six miles from the central crater of Sakura. This relationship makes Sakura one of the dangerous volcanoes of the world.

Last Eruption in 1779.

The last great eruption of Sakura is said to have taken place in 1779, and to have been commemorated at the island by a monthly festival. This should interest us in Hawaii, where the last great explosive eruption of Kilauea took place in 1790; and it will be remembered that prior to the terrific earthquake of 1908 at Messina no such disaster had been known there since 1783.

Sakura has two craters, northwest and southeast respectively, the southeast one, on the side remote from Kagoshima, being by reason of its hot solfataras the one most probably in action in the present eruption. There is a line of important active volcanoes extending north from Sakura into Kyushu.

T. A. JAGGAR, JR.,
Director.

The Hawaiian Volcano Research Association at a meeting held Jan. 19 passed resolutions asking its director, Dr. Thomas A. Jaggar, Jr., to proceed at once to Kogoshima and the scenes of the other volcano disasters in Japan and render every aid in his power to the Imperial Earthquake Investigation Committee in its investigations.

Following is a copy of the resolutions adopted,

Whereas, The recent eruption of the volcano of Sakura in the Empire of Japan, involving great loss of life and property, is of such a character as should be scientifically investigated and definite data concerning the same secured and reliable records made thereof, with a view, ultimately, to devising ways and means of minimizing the dangers incident to volcanic activity;

And Whereas, A large percentage of the residents of this Territory are subjects of the Empire of Japan, and it is appropriate, both from a scientific standpoint and as showing the friendly interest which the people of Hawaii feel toward their nearest neighbors on the west, that this association should offer to assist the Imperial Earthquake Investigation Committee of Japan in the work above set forth;

Now Therefore Be It Resolved: That the Hawaiian Volcano Research Association hereby requests its Director, Dr. Thomas A. Jaggar, Jr., to proceed as soon as practicable to the scene of said eruption, there to offer his services in connection with the work aforesaid, and cooperate with and assist the said committee and such others as may be engaged in such work, making such investigation and securing such maps, photographs and other data and information concerning the said eruption and any matters incidental thereto as he may think proper.

PROF. THOMAS A. JAGGAR, JR.

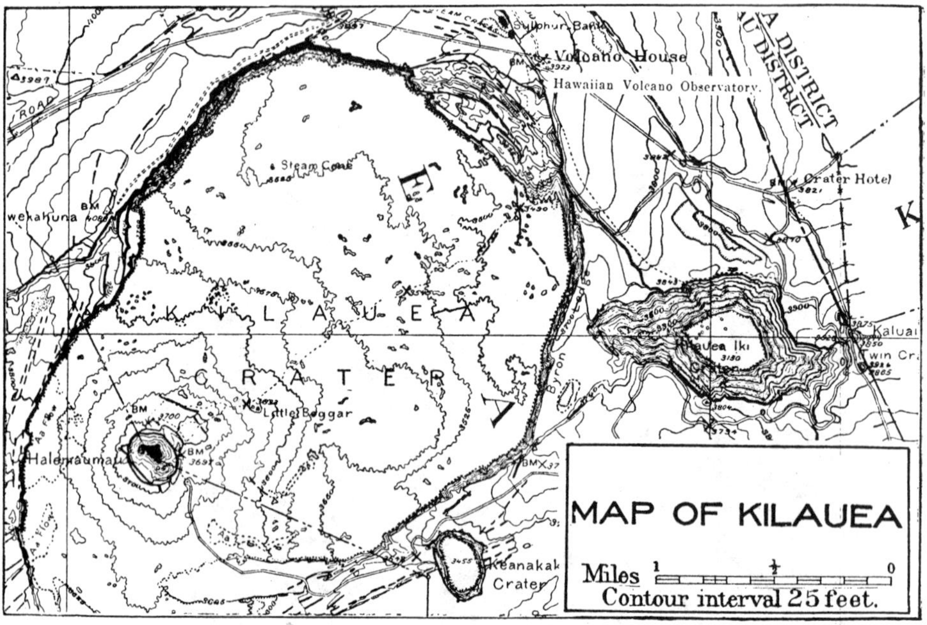

HAWAIIAN VOLCANO RESEARCH ASSOCIATION.

This society is a voluntary one, made up of subscribers to scientific work which is being executed by the Massachusetts Institute of Technology.

In 1913 there were 26 subscribers in Hawaii and Massachusetts, firms and individuals. A group of firms and persons in Hilo built the main observatory building in the spring of 1912. Publications to date have been weekly reports since the summer of 1911, a memoir by Daly in the Proceedings of American Academy of Arts and Sciences in 1911, articles by the director in the Technology Review 1911 and the Honolulu Chamber of Commerce Annual 1912, articles by H. O. Wood in the Bulletin of the Seismological Society of America, and articles by Perret in the American Journal of Science. The Massachusetts Institute of Technology will publish semi-annual reports.

This weekly bulletin as it appears in the Advertiser will be reprinted as a leaflet and sent to regular annual subscribers to the work of the association. C. H. Cooke is president of the Board of Directors of the association and R. W. Shingle is treasurer. New subscribers who are interested in our volcanoes will be welcomed in the association. The association aims: (1) To record volcanic activity and earthquakes in Hawaii; (2) to attract scientific men hither for special studies; (3) to promote the establishment of volcano observatories all over the world.

WHITNEY LABORATORY OF SEISMOLOGY.

The Whitney Laboratory of Seismology is equipped with two Bosch-Omori 100 kg tromometers registering N-S and E-W motion, a heavy Omori tromometer registering E-W motion and an Omori "ordinary Seismograph" designed for registering strong earthquakes in all three components of motion. These are seated on concrete piers in a closed basement room having practically constant temperature, beneath the chief Observatory building near the hotel. Time is referred to a rated chronometer, checked at intervals by solar observations with a transit. Both instruments are loaned by the College of Hawaii. At the substation by the edge of the active pit an Omori two-component tromometer with light steady masses is mounted on a concrete pier placed directly on the fresh lava surface. Hawaiian standard time (H. S. T.) is 10 hrs. 30 m. slower than Greenwich time.

CANCANI SCALE OF SEISMIC INTENSITY

Expressed by accelerations measured in millimeters per second per second.

I.	Instrumental	0.0	2.5
II.	Very slight	2.5	5.0
III.	Slight	5.0	10.0
IV.	Sensible, mediocre....	10.0	25.0
V.	Rather strong	25.0	50.0
VI.	Strong	50.0	100.0
VII.	Very strong	100.0	250.0
VIII.	Ruinous	250.0	500.0
IX.	Disastrous	500.0	1000.0
X.	Very disastrous	1000.0	2500.0
XI.	Catastrophic	2500.0	5000.0
XII.	Great catastrophe....	5000.0	10000.0

Grade IV. is ordinarily the minimum perceived by the senses; and in grade XII. the acceleration, or rate of change of motion (jerk) reaches that of terrestrial gravitation.

WEEKLY BULLETIN
OF
Hawaiian Volcano Observatory

Vol. II. HONOLULU, HAWAII, FEBRUARY 4, 1914. No. 5.

From the Pacific Commercial Advertiser, Honolulu, January 26, 1914.

TECHNOLOGY STATION, Kilauea, January 22.—Cloudy weather and strong winds, at first from the N.E., later from the S.W., have prevailed during most of the week past, causing very unfavorable conditions for observations of all kinds. There has been no change in the behavior of the volcano.

On Friday evening, January 16, a brief glimpse of the central glow-hole was obtained. No avalanches were heard and the noises of eruption were very subdued.

On Sunday, January 18, nothing could be seen on account of swirling fumes. No sounds of eruption of any sort whatever could be heard. No avalanching or sliding of talus was heard.

On Monday, January 19, the same conditions prevailed.

On Wednesday, January 21, though nothing could be seen, a short, sharp, but faint puffing sound was heard at considerable intervals, from twenty to thirty minutes, and during much of the time a low, grave, rumbling sound, suggestive of reverberations in a cave, could be heard. One heavy avalanche of short duration was noted, occurring under the northwest cliffs.

Fumes continue to pour out without abatement.

No sun observations for the correction of time have been possible since the last report from the Whitney Laboratory of Seismology; hence no systematic report can be included here. However, the week has been very quiet seismically—only two very trifling earthquakes have been registered, and no noteworthy earth-action of other sort.

H. O. WOOD, Associate.

Minutes of the Meetings of the Board of Directors.

The first meeting of the Board of Directors of the newly reorganized Hawaiian Volcano Research Association, was held at the University Club, Friday, Dec. 12th, 1913 at 12 m. Present: Messrs. Lorrin A. Thurston, Albert F. Judd, A. Lewis, Jr., W. R. Castle, directors, Richard Cooke, representing C. H. Cooke, J. L. McLean, representing J. A. Kennedy, Thos. A. Jaggar, Jr., and Howard M. Ballou.

The following officers of the Association were unanimously elected.

President, Clarence H. Cooke; 1st Vice-President, Lorrin A. Thurston; 2nd Vice-President, Albert F. Judd; Treasurer, Robert W. Shingle; Secretary, Howard M. Ballou.

Voted: that the President be ex-officio member of all committees.

Voted: that the following members be appointed on the Finance Committee: Robert W. Shingle, Geo. F. Davies, Geo. R. Carter, A. Lewis, Jr.

Voted: that the following members be appointed on the Membership Committee: E. L. Withington, Albert F. Judd, J. L. McLean and Ed Towse.

Adjourned.

HOWARD M. BALLOU,
Secretary.

WEEKLY BULLETIN
of
Hawaiian Volcano Observatory

Published at Honolulu, Hawaii, by the **Hawaiian Volcano Research Association**

Editor.............Howard M. Ballou
Professor of Physics, College of Hawaii

Application pending for entry as second-class matter at the post-office, Honolulu, Hawaii.

At a meeting of the Board called by direction of Vice-President L. A. Thurston for Tuesday, Jan. 6, 1914, there were present only L. A. Thurston, director, and H. M. Ballou, secretary.

Adjourned: No quorum.

The second meeting of the Board, called by direction of Pres. C. H. Cooke, was held at the University Club, Monday, Jan. 19, 1914, at 12 m.

Present: Messrs. Cooke, Judd, Lewis, Shingle and Thurston, directors, H. M. Ballou, secretary, and Dr. T. A. Jaggar, Jr.

Minutes of the first meeting were read and approved.

Dr. Jaggar addressed the Board on the subject of the recent eruption of Sakura volcano.

Mr. Thurston offered the following resolution, which was unanimously carried:

Whereas, The recent eruption of the volcano of Sakura in the Empire of Japan, involving great loss of life and property, is of such a character as should be scientifically investigated and definite data concerning the same secured and reliable records made thereof, with a view, ultimately, to devising ways and means of minimizing the dangers incident to volcanic activity;

And Whereas, A large percentage of the residents of this Territory are subjects of the Empire of Japan, and it is appropriate, both from a scientific standpoint and as showing the friendly interest which the people of Hawaii feel toward their nearest neighbors on the west, that this association should offer to assist the Imperial Earthquake Investigation Committee of Japan in the work above set forth;

Now Therefore Be It Resolved: That the Hawaiian Volcano Research Association hereby requests its Director, Dr. Thomas A. Jaggar, Jr., to proceed as soon as practicable to the scene of said eruption, there to offer his services in connection with the work aforesaid, and cooperate with and assist the said committee and such others as may be engaged in such work, making such investigation and securing such maps, photographs and other data and information concerning the said eruption and any matters incidental thereto as he may think proper.

Dr. Jaggar read a cablegram from President Maclaurin of the Massachusetts Institute of Technology approving of his expedition.

Voted: that Dr. T. A. Jaggar, Jr., be elected Director of the Hawaiian Volcano Observatory.

Voted: that there be an editorial and publication committee consisting of Messrs. Thurston, Jaggar and Ballou.

Voted: that the Secretary be directed to continue the publication of the weekly reports of the Hawaiian Volcano Observatory in a weekly bulletin reprinted from the Advertiser, for free distribution among members of the Association and scientific libraries.

Voted: that the bulletin be distributed only to patrons and members of the Association and to such libraries and scientific societies as may be designated by the publication committee.

Adjourned.

HOWARD M. BALLOU,
Secretary.

LAVA LAKE AT KILAUEA AT THE BEGINNING OF SUBSIDENCE.

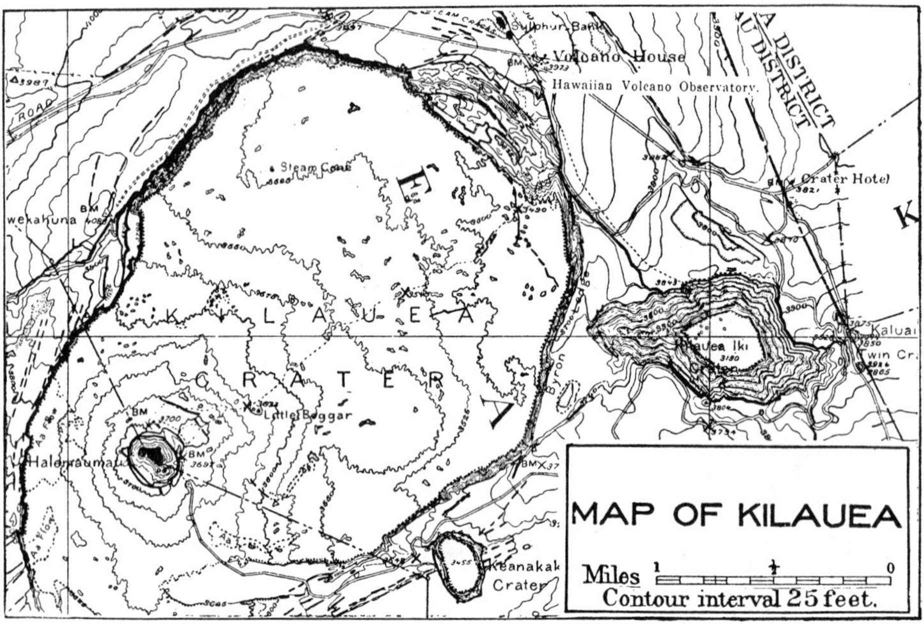

HAWAIIAN VOLCANO RESEARCH ASSOCIATION.

This society is a voluntary one, made up of subscribers to scientific work which is being executed by the Massachusetts Institute of Technology.

In 1913 there were 26 subscribers in Hawaii and Massachusetts, firms and individuals. A group of firms and persons in Hilo built the main observatory building in the spring of 1912. Publications to date have been weekly reports since the summer of 1911, a memoir by Daly in the Proceedings of American Academy of Arts and Sciences in 1911, articles by the director in the Technology Review 1911 and the Honolulu Chamber of Commerce Annual 1912, articles by H. O. Wood in the Bulletin of the Seismological Society of America, and articles by Perret in the American Journal of Science. The Massachusetts Institute of Technology will publish semiannual reports.

This weekly bulletin as it appears in the Advertiser will be reprinted as a leaflet and sent to regular annual subscribers to the work of the association. C. H. Cooke is president of the Board of Directors of the association and R. W. Shingle is treasurer. New subscribers who are interested in our volcanoes will be welcomed in the association. The association aims: (1) To record volcanic activity and earthquakes in Hawaii; (2) to attract scientific men hither for special studies; (3) to promote the establishment of volcano observatories all over the world.

WHITNEY LABORATORY OF SEISMOLOGY.

The Whitney Laboratory of Seismology is equipped with two Bosch-Omori 100 kg tromometers registering N-S and E-W motion, a heavy Omori tromometer registering E-W motion and an Omori "ordinary Seismograph" designed for registering strong earthquakes in all three components of motion. These are seated on concrete piers in a closed basement room having practically constant temperature, beneath the chief Observatory building near the hotel. Time is referred to a rated chronometer, checked at intervals by solar observations with a transit. Both instruments are loaned by the College of Hawaii. At the substation by the edge of the active pit an Omori two-component tromometer with light steady masses is mounted on a concrete pier placed directly on the fresh lava surface. Hawaiian standard time (H. S. T.) is 10 hrs. 30 m. slower than Greenwich time.

CANCANI SCALE OF SEISMIC INTENSITY

Expressed by accelerations measured in millimeters per second per second.

I.	Instrumental	0.0	2.5
II.	Very slight	2.5	5.0
III.	Slight	5.0	10.0
IV.	Sensible, mediocre....	10.0	25.0
V.	Rather strong	25.0	50.0
VI.	Strong	50.0	100.0
VII.	Very strong	100.0	250.0
VIII.	Ruinous	250.0	500.0
IX.	Disastrous	500.0	1000.0
X.	Very disastrous	1000.0	2500.0
XI.	Catastrophic	2500.0	5000.0
XII.	Great catastrophe....	5000.0	10000.0

Grade IV. is ordinarily the minimum perceived by the senses; and in grade XII. the acceleration, or rate of change of motion (jerk) reaches that of terrestrial gravitation.

WEEKLY BULLETIN
OF
Hawaiian Volcano Observatory

Vol. II. HONOLULU, HAWAII, FEBRUARY 11, 1914. No. 6.

From the Pacific Commercial Advertiser, Honolulu, February 5, 1914.

TECHNOLOGY STATION, Kilauea, January 29.—During the past week there has been no change in the activity of Kilauea.

Long watches were kept on January 22, 23, 24 and 28; a shorter stay at the crater was made on January 25; and a brief visit was made on January 26. On January 27 weather conditions, fog and wind, were so unfavorable that no visit was made. On January 28 a good view of the bottom of the pit was obtained. No other view has been obtained during this week.

The noises of eruption have undergone no change: faint, barely audible puffing can be heard at long, irregular intervals; a deep-toned rumbling sound, weak in volume, can be heard at frequent intervals. Either of these sounds is inaudible in a high, rushing wind.

One heavy, prolonged avalanche has been noted during the week on January 23, at about 10:30 a. m., lasting for about ten minutes. This took place at the south side of the pit.

Just before noon, on January 28 a lull and an eddy in the wind cleared the pit of fumes and permitted a good view of the bottom for about ten minutes. Fumes were issuing copiously from a low cone about ''Old Faithful,'' but glowing lava could be seen in the orifice at the top of the cone. Also at the low cone near the west end on the southern margin of the ''frozen'' surface, fumes were pouring out furiously, but glowing lava was seen. The peripheral fumaroles in the talus showed unabated activity, also the high fumarole in the wall under the north station. The floor remains unchanged in appearance—so, as yet, there is no evidence of conspicuous subsidence. Occasional slight movements of readjustment among the talus blocks are heard.

Owing to adverse weather conditions at apparent noon, no systematic report from the Whitney Laboratory of Seismology can yet be given. One earthquake not felt, but moderately strong instrumentally, was registered during the week.

H. O. WOOD, Associate.

WEEKLY BULLETIN
of
Hawaiian Volcano Observatory

Published at Honolulu, Hawaii, by the
Hawaiian Volcano Research Association

Editor..............Howard M. Ballou
Professor of Physics, College of Hawaii

Application pending for entry as second-class matter at the post-office, Honolulu, Hawaii.

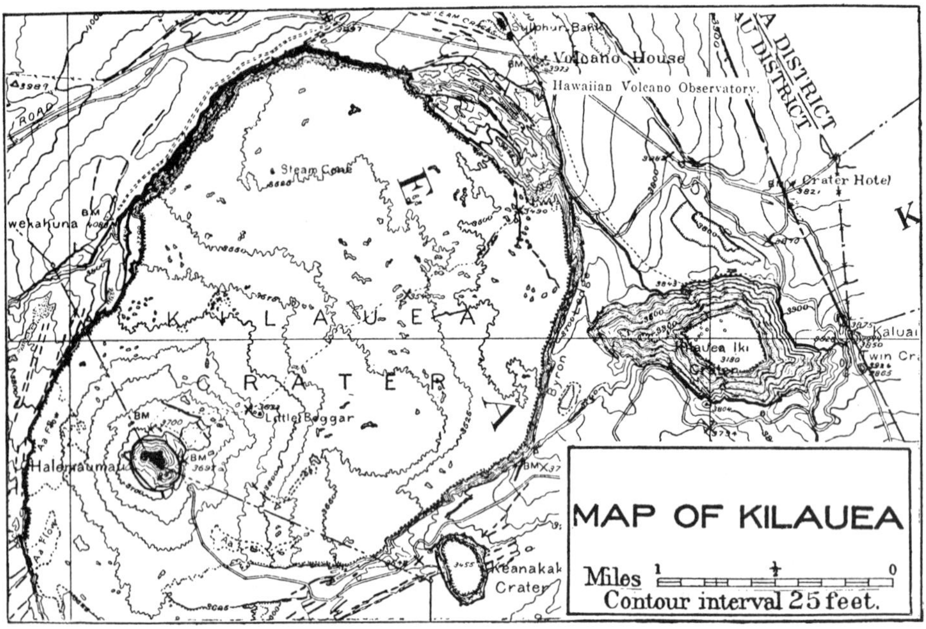

HAWAIIAN VOLCANO RESEARCH ASSOCIATION.

This society is a voluntary one, made up of subscribers to scientific work which is being executed by the Massachusetts Institute of Technology.

In 1913 there were 26 subscribers in Hawaii and Massachusetts, firms and individuals. A group of firms and persons in Hilo built the main observatory building in the spring of 1912. Publications to date have been weekly reports since the summer of 1911, a memoir by Daly in the Proceedings of American Academy of Arts and Sciences in 1911, articles by the director in the Technology Review 1911 and the Honolulu Chamber of Commerce Annual 1912, articles by H. O. Wood in the Bulletin of the Seismological Society of America, and articles by Perret in the American Journal of Science. The Massachusetts Institute of Technology will publish semi-annual reports.

This weekly bulletin as it appears in the Advertiser will be reprinted as a leaflet and sent to regular annual subscribers to the work of the association. C. H. Cooke is president of the Board of Directors of the association and R. W. Shingle is treasurer. New subscribers who are interested in our volcanoes will be welcomed in the association. The association aims: (1) To record volcanic activity and earthquakes in Hawaii; (2) to attract scientific men hither for special studies; (3) to promote the establishment of volcano observatories all over the world.

WHITNEY LABORATORY OF SEISMOLOGY.

The Whitney Laboratory of Seismology is equipped with two Bosch-Omori 100 kg tromometers registering N-S and E-W motion, a heavy Omori tromometer registering E-W motion and an Omori "ordinary Seismograph" designed for registering strong earthquakes in all three components of motion. These are seated on concrete piers in a closed basement room having practically constant temperature, beneath the chief Observatory building near the hotel. Time is referred to a rated chronometer, checked at intervals by solar observations with a transit. Both instruments are loaned by the College of Hawaii. At the substation by the edge of the active pit an Omori two-component tromometer with light steady masses is mounted on a concrete pier placed directly on the fresh lava surface. Hawaiian standard time (H. S. T.) is 10 hrs. 30 m. slower than Greenwich time.

CANCANI SCALE OF SEISMIC INTENSITY

Expressed by accelerations measured in millimeters per second per second.

I.	Instrumental	0.0	2.5
II.	Very slight	2.5	5.0
III.	Slight	5.0	10.0
IV.	Sensible, mediocre....	10.0	25.0
V.	Rather strong	25.0	50.0
VI.	Strong	50.0	100.0
VII.	Very strong	100.0	250.0
VIII.	Ruinous	250.0	500.0
IX.	Disastrous	500.0	1000.0
X.	Very disastrous	1000.0	2500.0
XI.	Catastrophic	2500.0	5000.0
XII.	Great catastrophe....	5000.0	10000.0

Grade IV. is ordinarily the minimum perceived by the senses; and in grade XII. the acceleration, or rate of change of motion (jerk) reaches that of terrestrial gravitation.

WEEKLY BULLETIN
OF
Hawaiian Volcano Observatory

Vol. II. HONOLULU, HAWAII, FEBRUARY 18, 1914. No. 7.

From the Pacific Commercial Advertiser, Honolulu, February 9, 1914.

TECHNOLOGY STATION, Kilauea, February 5.—Still there is little or no change to report in the action at Kilauea. During the past week the winds have been light, allowing the pit to clear of fumes, so that several good views have been obtained. There has, however, been no opportunity suitable for photography.

On January 30, there were frequent views into the interior of Halemaumau, but no view of the very bottom. At a little before eleven o'clock in the forenoon, and a few minutes after twelve noon, heavy and prolonged avalanches occurred, the first at the south near the west end, the second at the north; these lasted ten and eight minutes respectively. Throughout the intervening interval, and the remainder of the day, there were frequent slight slidings—probably only readjustments among the disturbed talus. Neither puffing nor rumbling noises could be heard.

On January 31, nothing was observed except small slides at considerable intervals. These also were probably only movements of readjustment.

On February 1, excellent views of the floor of Halemaumau were had at frequent intervals for nearly two hours in the early afternoon. The black floor remained level and unbroken, though much material had fallen upon it at the SW and NW margins. The orifices where glowing lava has been seen during preceding weeks were clearly visible; blue fumes were issuing vigorously, but no glowing lava could be seen. A gash appears to be developing in the wall at the west as the avalanching clears away the loose material of the wall. No slides were noted, except a few trifling readjustment movements. If any subsidence has been going on since the formation of the black floor in November, the floor has gone down as a whole without collapse or fracture. No depth measurement was undertaken because the views, while excellent, could be obtained only from the neighborhood of the old resthouse.

On February 2, quiet air again permitted good views. The conditions observed were similar in all respects to those of the first. No noises of eruption could be heard.

On February 3, on account of fog and wind from the southwest, no watch was maintained.

On February 4, again a good view was obtained; conditions were the same as on the first and second, except that small slides were more frequent, the rumbling sound of eruption was again audible, and glowing lava could be seen in small amount within the "Old Faithful" orifice.

Since the last systematic report from the Whitney Laboratory of Seismology earthquakes have been registered as follows:

January 7, from 9:00:17 p.m. to 9:01:05 p.m. H. S. T. Intensity, medium III Cancani scale; at least 70 per cent of the minimum perceptible unit. Origin distant about 12 miles.

January 10, from 8:52:29 p.m. to 8:53:09 p.m., H. S. T. Intensity, high I Cancani scale; 16 per cent to 21 per cent of the minimum perceptible unit. Origin distant about 27 miles.

January 15, from 5:26:52 a.m. to

WEEKLY BULLETIN
of
Hawaiian Volcano Observatory

Published at Honolulu, Hawaii, by the **Hawaiian Volcano Research Association**

Editor..............Howard M. Ballou
Professor of Physics, College of Hawaii

Application pending for entry as second-class matter at the post-office, Honolulu, Hawaii.

5:27:35 a.m., H. S. T. Intensity, medium III Cancani scale; about 85 per cent of the minimum perceptible unit. Origin distant about 20 miles.

January 18, from 4:19:09 a.m. to 4:21:12 a.m. H. S. T. Intensity, medium I Cancani scale; about 16 per cent of the minimum perceptible unit. Origin distant about 13 miles.

January 21, from 7:13:09 p.m. to 7:14:09 p.m., H. S. T. Intensity, III-IV Cancani scale; less than the minimum perceptible unit, although it measures higher; very rapid motion. Origin distant about 14 miles.

January 22, from 5:16:40 a.m. to 5:17:31 a.m. H. S. T. Intensity, I Cancani scale; about 7.5 per cent of the minimum perceptible unit. Origin distant about 27 miles.

January 25, from 4:24:54 p.m. to 4:28:14 p.m. H. S. T. Intensity, here only III Cancani scale; about 60 per cent of the minimum perceptible unit. Felt at Hilo, (but not felt at this point), so that the origin probably lay in the Hilo direction. Origin distant about 20 miles.

January 29, from 10:29:58 a.m. to 10:31:29 a.m., H. S. T. Intensity III-IV Cancani scale; this shock measures, in acceleration value, from 120 per cent to 180 per cent of the minimum perceptible unit, but it very definitely was not felt at the Observatory. The writer was sitting quietly at a writing table when the "Ordinary seismograph" began recording, and definitely did not feel any motion. Origin distant about 7 miles. The shock was felt distinctly in Hilo.

February 1, from 4:48:50 p.m. to 4:49:26 p.m. H. S. T. Intensity, medium II Cancani scale; about 35 per cent of the minimum perceptible unit. Origin distant about 10 miles.

February 3, from 5:01:21 a.m. to 5:03:03 a.m. H. S. T. Intensity, II Cancani scale; about 48 per cent of the minimum perceptible unit. Origin distant about 26 miles.

H. O. WOOD, Associate.

Looking Eastward from the Northernmost Point of Margin of Halemaumau, Kilauea Volcano.

The points of interest shown in this view are:

(1) The spur, projecting southward in the middle foreground—thought to designate the northern entrance of the master, NE-SW, rift through Kilauea.

(2) The broken irregularly subsided region in the distant middle ground—illustrating, at an unfinished stage, the mode of formation of the main sink-crater of Kilauea, by fracture and subsidence of segments of the summit dome.

(3) The greatly fissured and exceedingly rough character, in miniature, of the floor of the crater at the north end.

(4) The distant, high ground N-E of Kilauea-iki, thought to be a former summit point of Kilauea.

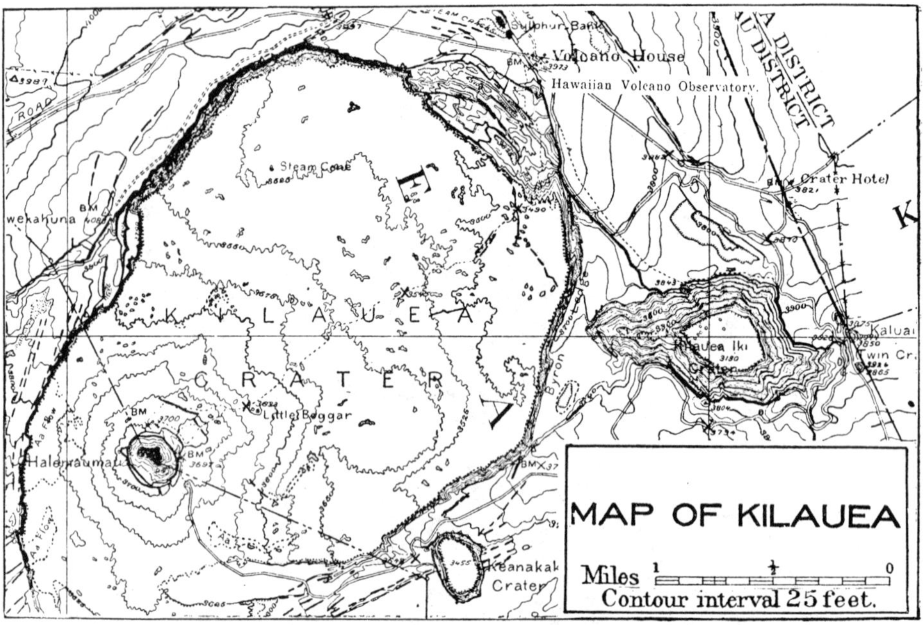

MAP OF KILAUEA

HAWAIIAN VOLCANO RESEARCH ASSOCIATION.

This society is a voluntary one, made up of subscribers to scientific work which is being executed by the Massachusetts Institute of Technology.

In 1913 there were 26 subscribers in Hawaii and Massachusetts, firms and individuals. A group of firms and persons in Hilo built the main observatory building in the spring of 1912. Publications to date have been weekly reports since the summer of 1911, a memoir by Daly in the Proceedings of American Academy of Arts and Sciences in 1911, articles by the director in the Technology Review 1911 and the Honolulu Chamber of Commerce Annual 1912, articles by H. O. Wood in the Bulletin of the Seismological Society of America, and articles by Perret in the American Journal of Science. The Massachusetts Institute of Technology will publish semiannual reports.

This weekly bulletin as it appears in the Advertiser will be reprinted as a leaflet and sent to regular annual subscribers to the work of the association. C. H. Cooke is president of the Board of Directors of the association and R. W. Shingle is treasurer. New subscribers who are interested in our volcanoes will be welcomed in the association. The association aims: (1) To record volcanic activity and earthquakes in Hawaii; (2) to attract scientific men hither for special studies; (3) to promote the establishment of volcano observatories all over the world.

WHITNEY LABORATORY OF SEISMOLOGY.

The Whitney Laboratory of Seismology is equipped with two Bosch-Omori 100 kg tromometers registering N-S and E-W motion, a heavy Omori tromometer registering E-W motion and an Omori "ordinary Seismograph" designed for registering strong earthquakes in all three components of motion. These are seated on concrete piers in a closed basement room having practically constant temperature, beneath the chief Observatory building near the hotel. Time is referred to a rated chronometer, checked at intervals by solar observations with a transit. Both instruments are loaned by the College of Hawaii. At the substation by the edge of the active pit an Omori two-component tromometer with light steady masses is mounted on a concrete pier placed directly on the fresh lava surface. Hawaiian standard time (H. S. T.) is 10 hrs. 30 m. slower than Greenwich time.

CANCANI SCALE OF SEISMIC INTENSITY

Expressed by accelerations measured in millimeters per second per second.

I.	Instrumental	0.0	2.5
II.	Very slight	2.5	5.0
III.	Slight	5.0	10.0
IV.	Sensible, mediocre....	10.0	25.0
V.	Rather strong	25.0	50.0
VI.	Strong	50.0	100.0
VII.	Very strong . ,.....	100.0	250.0
VIII.	Ruinous	250.0	500.0
IX.	Disastrous	500.0	1000.0
X.	Very disastrous	1000.0	2500.0
XI.	Catastrophic	2500.0	5000.0
XII.	Great catastrophe....	5000.0	10000.0

Grade IV. is ordinarily the minimum perceived by the senses; and in grade XII. the acceleration, or rate of change of motion (jerk) reaches that of terrestrial gravitation.

WEEKLY BULLETIN
OF
Hawaiian Volcano Observatory

Vol. II. HONOLULU, HAWAII, FEBRUARY 25, 1914. No. 8.

From the Pacific Commercial Advertiser, Honolulu, February 17, 1914.

TECHNOLOGY STATION, Kilauea, February 12.—The energy of eruption has increased definitely since the last writing. Just at the close of the previous week, on February 4, glowing lava had reappeared within the "Old Faithful" orifice.

On February 5, quiet air made good seeing possible from the north and northwest rim of the pit. Glowing lava was seen plainly both by day and by night in the "Old Faithful" orifice and, as well, in the orifice at the apex of a miniature cone near the southeast end of the lake area. No slides of any notable magnitude occurred and no noises of eruption were heard.

On February 6, again there was a good view from the northwest part of the rim of Halemaumau. Conditions were nearly the same as on the previous day, glowing lava being visible in both orifices. In the afternoon small avalanches were heard occasionally. Only one of these was notable, this lasting a little over two minutes. The low, rumbling noise of eruption could be heard again plainly.

On February 7, seeing was again possible and again the two glowing orifices were conspicuous. Up to late afternoon there were no noises of eruption except the low, rumbling sounds; but about nightfall explosive hissing sounds began to be heard at irregular intervals of two to three minutes.

In the afternoon of February 8, these sounds had increased in frequency and energy, occurring at intervals of five to sixty seconds, the usual intervals being those so common to "Old Faithful," 15-20 to 35-45 seconds. Frequently this harsh blowing sound was almost continuous for minutes together. The noise was sharp and harsh at the same time, and rather loud—as loud as in the early part of October, 1913, though not nearly loud enough to be heard at a distance of from 100 to 200 yards from the rim of the pit, as was the case in the latter part of September. The rumbling noise was continuously punctuated by a muffled coughing sound. In the afternoon the two glowing orifices were seen. In the evening these two and three others were noted. It was reported by a visitor present in the early evening that jets of lava were thrown up from the orifice at the edge of the lake area just under the north station near the old rest-house. No glowing lava was seen in that orifice during the day. No avalanches were heard on this date.

On February 9, the harsh blowing and rumbling sounds were heard plainly, but a fresh breeze prevented seeing.

On February 10, a strong wind prevailed, with stormy and threatening weather. No prolonged watch was maintained. However, the blowing and rumbling continued, possibly a trifle increased.

On February 11, again there was a strong wind, preventing any good view into the pit. The loud, explosive, hissing sounds were occuring at intervals of from five to seven seconds. Some blasts were of considerable duration, the noisy outrush of gas continuing for about ten seconds.

Throughout the week there has been bright moonlight in the evenings. No glow has been discerned on the fume cloud. The fumes continue to pour out

WEEKLY BULLETIN
of
Hawaiian Volcano Observatory

Published at Honolulu, Hawaii, by the **Hawaiian Volcano Research Association**

Editor..............Howard M. Ballou
Professor of Physics, College of Hawaii

Application pending for entry as second-class matter at the post-office, Honolulu, Hawaii.

in undiminished volumes from fumaroles in the talus all about the margin of the lake area.

No observations for the correction of time have been secured during the week. Hence no systematic seismological report can be included here, but nothing notable in the way of seismic motion has been registered, though two or three extremely small local shocks have been recorded.

H. O. WOOD, Associate.

Northwest Station, rim of Halemaumau, taken July 16, 1913, showing A-frame used in temperature tests.

View of the Volcano, looking southwest from the most northerly point on the margin of the main crater, directly along the course of the cleft, or master rift, through Kilauea, showing the high northwestern wall with its cliffs and talus slopes; the summit point, Uwekahuna; and the partly down-faulted portions of the old summit surface in the middle distance.

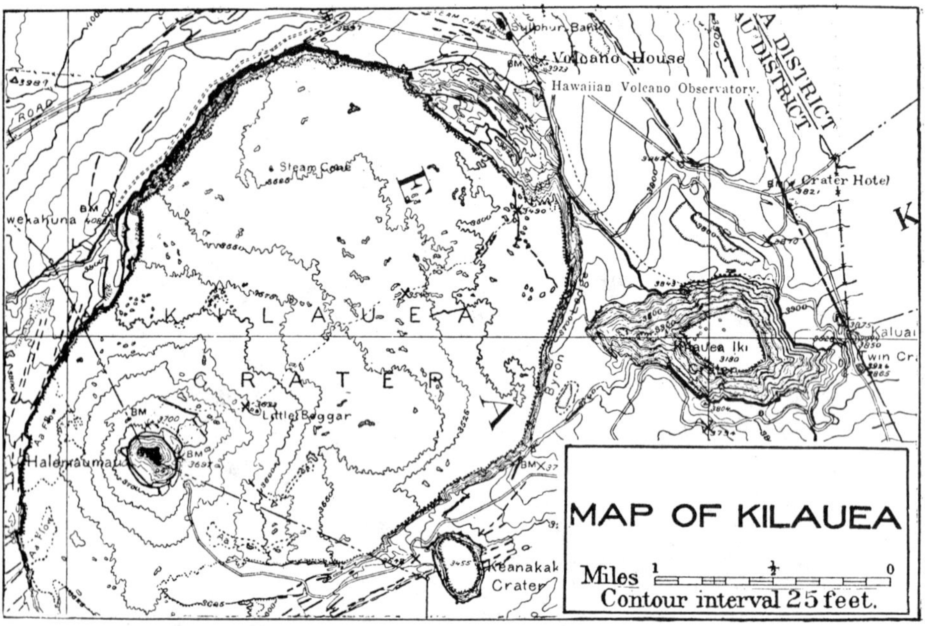

HAWAIIAN VOLCANO RESEARCH ASSOCIATION.

This society is a voluntary one, made up of subscribers to scientific work which is being executed by the Massachusetts Institute of Technology.

In 1913 there were 26 subscribers in Hawaii and Massachusetts, firms and individuals. A group of firms and persons in Hilo built the main observatory building in the spring of 1912. Publications to date have been weekly reports since the summer of 1911, a memoir by Daly in the Proceedings of American Academy of Arts and Sciences in 1911, articles by the director in the Technology Review 1911 and the Honolulu Chamber of Commerce Annual 1912, articles by H. O. Wood in the Bulletin of the Seismological Society of America, and articles by Perret in the American Journal of Science. The Massachusetts Institute of Technology will publish semi-annual reports.

This weekly bulletin as it appears in the Advertiser will be reprinted as a leaflet and sent to regular annual subscribers to the work of the association. C. H. Cooke is president of the Board of Directors of the association and R. W. Shingle is treasurer. New subscribers who are interested in our volcanoes will be welcomed in the association. The association aims: (1) To record volcanic activity and earthquakes in Hawaii; (2) to attract scientific men hither for special studies; (3) to promote the establishment of volcano observatories all over the world.

WHITNEY LABORATORY OF SEISMOLOGY.

The Whitney Laboratory of Seismology is equipped with two Bosch-Omori 100 kg tromometers registering N-S and E-W motion, a heavy Omori tromometer registering E-W motion and an Omori "ordinary Seismograph" designed for registering strong earthquakes in all three components of motion. These are seated on concrete piers in a closed basement room having practically constant temperature, beneath the chief Observatory building near the hotel. Time is referred to a rated chronometer, checked at intervals by solar observations with a transit. Both instruments are loaned by the College of Hawaii. At the substation by the edge of the active pit an Omori two-component tromometer with light steady masses is mounted on a concrete pier placed directly on the fresh lava surface. Hawaiian standard time (H. S. T.) is 10 hrs. 30 m. slower than Greenwich time.

CANCANI SCALE OF SEISMIC INTENSITY

Expressed by accelerations measured in millimeters per second per second.

I.	Instrumental	0.0	2.5
II.	Very slight	2.5	5.0
III.	Slight	5.0	10.0
IV.	Sensible, mediocre....	10.0	25.0
V.	Rather strong	25.0	50.0
VI.	Strong	50.0	100.0
VII.	Very strong	100.0	250.0
VIII.	Ruinous	250.0	500.0
IX.	Disastrous	500.0	1000.0
X.	Very disastrous	1000.0	2500.0
XI.	Catastrophic	2500.0	5000.0
XII.	Great catastrophe....	5000.0	10000.0

Grade IV. is ordinarily the minimum perceived by the senses; and in grade XII. the acceleration, or rate of change of motion (jerk) reaches that of terrestrial gravitation.

WEEKLY BULLETIN
OF
Hawaiian Volcano Observatory

Vol. II. HONOLULU, HAWAII, MARCH 4, 1914. No. 9.

From the Pacific Commercial Advertiser, Honolulu, February 26, 1914.

TECHNOLOGY STATION, Kilauea, February 19.—There has been a further increase in eruptive energy at Kilauea since last week, though no marked change has been noted during the last four days. No molten pool has appeared nor have any fountains, jets or sprays been observed either by the writer or any other accustomed observer.

On February 12 no view was obtained on account of swirling fumes. Noises of snorting and prolonged sharp blasts, in quality like the sound of steam escaping from a safety valve, were audible for intervals of one to ten seconds, often at considerable distance from the margin of Halemaumau. Sounds of rumbling, with interrupted coughing noises, were almost continuous and appeared to come from the cleft region at the west end of the lake area. These sounds were louder than on previous days. No slides were heard.

Explosive Noises Become Louder.

On February 13 the fumes again prevented seeing. The sounds described above were heard but they were even louder than before—the loudest blasts at intervals of two or three minutes being plainly audible at the old corral on the trail, nearly a third of a mile northeast up the wind, from the edge of the pit. Thudding sounds like the patter of falling lumps of molten or viscous lava-spray were heard. However, these probably were muffled explosive coughings, because subsequent views have not revealed any sign of lava jetting during the present spasm of increased activity. For a short time in the late evening on this date the fume cloud was definitely, though dimly, illuminated—seen plainly from the Volcano House. It is inferred that the top of one of the blowing cones collapsed, but soon congealed again.

On February 14 there was no view. Loud blasts were audible at the old corral down the trail, and the rumbling noise was very loud. The noises of snorting and hissing seemed to emanate from several separate orifices at the bottom of the pit. Also the sound like that of falling lava spray was heard.

On February 15 a very brief daylight view revealed glowing lava in the orifice at the top of the "Old Faithful" cone. No other glimpse of "fire" was seen. The rumbling, snorting and hissing sounds were very loud.

On February 16 the gas blasts were still very loud and plainly audible at the old corral. Both rumbling and hissing sounds seemed to come from several different vents.

Glowing Lava Is Seen.

On February 17 a good view of the bottom area was secured for a very brief time. Glowing lava was seen in the "Old Faithful" orifice. The cone at the southeast margin and that at the north margin of the lake area were smoking furiously, emitting bright blue fumes, but, by daylight, no molten lava was discernible in their vents. Great quantities of bright blue fumes were rushing out of the cleft at the west, whence a loud and continuous rumbling noise emanated. As before, all the noises of eruption were very loud, the hard blasts still being audible as fa away as the old corral. The sound of rumbling could be heard distinctly to

WEEKLY BULLETIN
of
Hawaiian Volcano Observatory

Published at Honolulu, Hawaii, by the **Hawaiian Volcano Research Association**

Editor..............Howard M. Ballou
Professor of Physics, College of Hawaii

Application pending for entry as second-class matter at the post-office, Honolulu, Hawaii.

the north of the hot fissure situated some forty to fifty yards from the margin of the crater. On this date the blasts and hissing sounds all seemed to come from the "Old Faithful" orifice.

On February 18, on account of a strong southwest wind, with frequ showers, no visit was made to the pit; for these weather conditions preclude satisfactory observing.

Still no systematic seismological report can be rendered. One weak and three extremely feeble earthquakes have been registered. No noteworthy seismic motion of other sort has been recorded.

H. O. WOOD, Associate.

Sulphur Banks about 500 feet from the Volcano House, Hawaii.

Snow on the Summit of Mauna Kea, Hawaii.

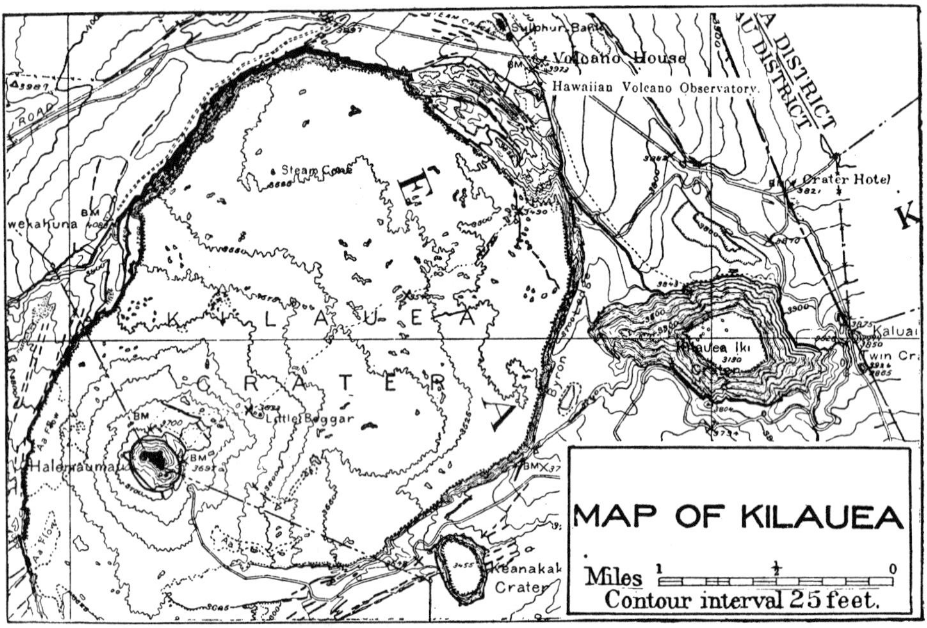

HAWAIIAN VOLCANO RESEARCH ASSOCIATION.

This society is a voluntary one, made up of subscribers to scientific work which is being executed by the Massachusetts Institute of Technology.

In 1913 there were 26 subscribers in Hawaii and Massachusetts, firms and individuals. A group of firms and persons in Hilo built the main observatory building in the spring of 1912. Publications to date have been weekly reports since the summer of 1911, a memoir by Daly in the Proceedings of American Academy of Arts and Sciences in 1911, articles by the director in the Technology Review 1911 and the Honolulu Chamber of Commerce Annual 1912, articles by H. O. Wood in the Bulletin of the Seismological Society of America, and articles by Perret in the American Journal of Science. The Massachusetts Institute of Technology will publish semi-annual reports.

This weekly bulletin as it appears in the Advertiser will be reprinted as a leaflet and sent to regular annual subscribers to the work of the association. C. H. Cooke is president of the Board of Directors of the association and R. W. Shingle is treasurer. New subscribers who are interested in our volcanoes will be welcomed in the association. The association aims: (1) To record volcanic activity and earthquakes in Hawaii; (2) to attract scientific men hither for special studies; (3) to promote the establishment of volcano observatories all over the world.

WHITNEY LABORATORY OF SEISMOLOGY.

The Whitney Laboratory of Seismology is equipped with two Bosch-Omori 100 kg tromometers registering N-S and E-W motion, a heavy Omori tromometer registering E-W motion and an Omori "ordinary Seismograph" designed for registering strong earthquakes in all three components of motion. These are seated on concrete piers in a closed basement room having practically constant temperature, beneath the chief Observatory building near the hotel. Time is referred to a rated chronometer, checked at intervals by solar observations with a transit. Both instruments are loaned by the College of Hawaii. At the substation by the edge of the active pit an Omori two-component tromometer with light steady masses is mounted on a concrete pier placed directly on the fresh lava surface. Hawaiian standard time (H. S. T.) is 10 hrs. 30 m. slower than Greenwich time.

CANCANI SCALE OF SEISMIC INTENSITY

Expressed by accelerations measured in millimeters per second per second.

I.	Instrumental	0.0	2.5
II.	Very slight	2.5	5.0
III.	Slight	5.0	10.0
IV.	Sensible, mediocre....	10.0	25.0
V.	Rather strong	25.0	50.0
VI.	Strong	50.0	100.0
VII.	Very strong	100.0	250.0
VIII.	Ruinous	250.0	500.0
IX.	Disastrous	500.0	1000.0
X.	Very disastrous	1000.0	2500.0
XI.	Catastrophic	2500.0	5000.0
XII.	Great catastrophe....	5000.0	10000.0

Grade IV. is ordinarily the minimum perceived by the senses; and in grade XII. the acceleration, or rate of change of motion, (jerk) reaches that of terrestrial gravitation.

WEEKLY BULLETIN
OF
Hawaiian Volcano Observatory

Vol. II. HONOLULU, HAWAII, MARCH 11, 1914. No. 10.

From the Pacific Commercial Advertiser, Honolulu, March 2, 1914.

TECHNOLOGY STATION, Kilauea, February 26.—The energy of eruption has definitely increased during the past week. At night the fume cloud, as seen from the Volcano House, has been definitely illuminated, and the amount of illumination and the strength of the flaring has definitely increased. It is still, however, a very feeble illumination.

The latest date covered by the preceding report was February 17. No visit was made to the pit on February 18 owing to weather conditions unfavorable for observing.

On February 19, the pit was reached early in the forenoon, when it was remarked that a conspicuous diminution had come about in the harsh hissing and blowing sounds produced by spasmodic outrush of gases. The rumbling sound, however, had undergone no diminution—if anything it had increased in energy. During the forenoon many small talus slides were heard, and early in the afternoon one avalanche lasting for twenty-two seconds was noted. During the day no view of the bottom area was obtained on account of swirling fumes, but in the evening glowing lava was seen in the "Old Faithful" orifice.

On February 20, no view was obtained. The rumbling and hissing sounds were heard much as on the ninteenth. At considerable intervals small talus slides were heard.

On February 21, the blowing sound was again somewhat louder than on the two previous days. Brief but clear views of the bottom disclosed glowing lava, seen in daylight, in the orifice of the "Old Faithful" cone, and at the apex of a blowing cone under the southeast station. The opening in "Old Faithful" was larger than heretofore during the present revival of activity. Nevertheless it was still a small opening, estimated at a little over three feet in diameter. Trivial talus slides were heard at irregular intervals. The greater part of the rumbling sound still seems to emanate from the cleft region nearly under the west station.

Jets of Molten Lava Seen.

On February 22 numerous clear views were obtained by many visitors. Both by day and night glowing lava was seen in the orifices of the blowing cones. In the evening four glowing orifices were seen — the two already mentioned, one nearly under the north station and one relatively high under the south station. Small jets of molten lava were seen by some visitors. The noises of eruption were as on the previous day. For the first time, during this revival, faint flaring in the illumination of the fume cloud could be definitely distinguished from the Volcano House.

On February 23, small lava jets, throwing molten spray, or "sparks" from "Old Faithful" were seen plainly in bright forenoon light. The glowing orifice at the top of the southeast cone was also seen plainly. The noises of eruption were continuing without change. Small movements of sliding in the talus, from twenty-five to forty-five seconds in duration, were heard from time to time. Many large and small boulders are seen resting on the frozen lake area, and its margins are nearly hidden by fallen talus. The southeast blowing cone appears as a small island in the talus. It was thought that glow-

WEEKLY BULLETIN
of
Hawaiian Volcano Observatory

Published at Honolulu, Hawaii, by the **Hawaiian Volcano Research Association**

Editor..............Howard M. Ballou
Professor of Physics, College of Hawaii

Application pending for entry as second-class matter at the post-office, Honolulu, Hawaii.

ing lava was visible by light of day in the high south orifice, about one hundred feet above the lake surface, but this was uncertain.

On February 24 no visit was made to Halemaumau.

On February 25, both by day and by night molten spray was seen spurting from both the "Old Faithful" orifice and from that in the top of the southeast cone. Fresh lava could be seen all about the "Old Faithful" vent. In the late evening a large orifice was observed under the south station, about one hundred feet above the floor of the pit, out of which shone a bright light, but no incandescent lava was seen in this vent. No sliding was noted. The noises of eruption were the same as usual recently. The fumes continue to pour out copiously through vents in the talus at points all around the periphery of the lake area.

Since the last systematic report from the Whitney Laboratory of Seismology, earthquakes have been registered as described in the list below. Of these all but one were very feeble shocks, except instrumentally, and most of them were feeble even from this point of view. Even the one exception noted was not perceived by the senses in this neighborhood; but it was a smart shock, nevertheless, and its acceleration measures well above the perceptible minimum, but the motion was excessively rapid.

February 4, from 10:54:42 p. m. to 10:55:57 p. m.—H. S. T. Intensity, high III Cancani scale; 80% of the minimum perceptible unit. Origin distant about 9.3 miles.

February 7, from 1:18:41 p. m. to 1:19:26 p. m.—H. S. T. Intensity, high II Cancani scale; 45% of the minimum perceptible unit. Origin distant about 13 miles.

February 9, from 10:40:45 a. m. to 10:41:33 a. m.—H. S. T. Intensity, low III Cancani scale; 65% of the minimum perceptible unit. Origin distant about 13 miles.

February 12, from 6:21:13 a. m. to 6:23:03 a. m.—H. S. T. Intensity, medium III Cancani scale; 70% of the minimum perceptible unit. Origin distant about 20 miles.

February 12, from 12:33:21 p. m. to 12:33:53 p. m.—H. S. T. Intensity, medium I Cancani scale; 13% of the minimum perceptible unit. Origin distance indeterminate.

February 12, from 11:26:00 p. m. to 11:26:59 p. m.—H. S. T. Intensity, medium II Cancani scale; 35% of the minimum perceptible unit. Origin distant about 11.2 miles.

February 13, from 10:23:20 p. m. to 10:24:04 p. m.—H. S. T. Intensity, low III Cancani scale; 65% of the minimum perceptible unit. Origin distant about 11.8 miles.

February 14, from 3:13:18 p. m. to 3:14:00 p. m.—H. S. T. Intensity, high II Cancani scale; 45% of the minimum perceptible unit. Origin distant about 10.5 miles.

February 14, from 7:49:04 p. m. to 7:50:53 p. m.—H. S. T. Intensity, (?) III-IV (?) Cancani scale; measures more than twice the minimum perceptible unit, but vibratory movement is excessively rapid. Origin distant about 11.2 miles.

February 20, from 1:47:34 a. m. to 1:48:29 a. m.—H. S. T. Intensity, low II Cancani scale; 30% of the minimum perceptible unit. Origin distance indeterminate.

February 20, from 1:53:27 a. m. to 1:54:15 a. m.—H. S. T. Intensity, medium III Cancani scale; 75% of the minimum perceptible unit. Origin distant about 6.8 miles.

February 21, from 2:04:59 a. m. to 2:05:47 a. m.—H. S. T. Intensity, high II to low III Cancani scale; 40-70% of the minimum perceptible unit. Origin distant about 11.2 miles.

February 23, from 10:15:25 a. m. to 10:18:05 a. m.—H. S. T. Intensity, high III Cancani scale; 80% of the minimum

February 23, from 2:35:29 p. m. to 2:36:39 p. m.—H. S. T. Intensity, low III Cancani scale; 60% of the minimum perceptible unit. Origin distant about 13 miles.

February 23.—In the early evening (about 6:38 p. m. H. S. T.) the seismographic time-marking clock stopped, without discovered cause. Subsequent to this time there occurred one very slight local shock, even very small instrumentally, the times of which cannot be made out even approximately, and the dimensions cannot be ascertained with precision.

H. O. WOOD,
Associate.

View of Driblet Cone northwest of Halemaumau, taken July 16, 1913.

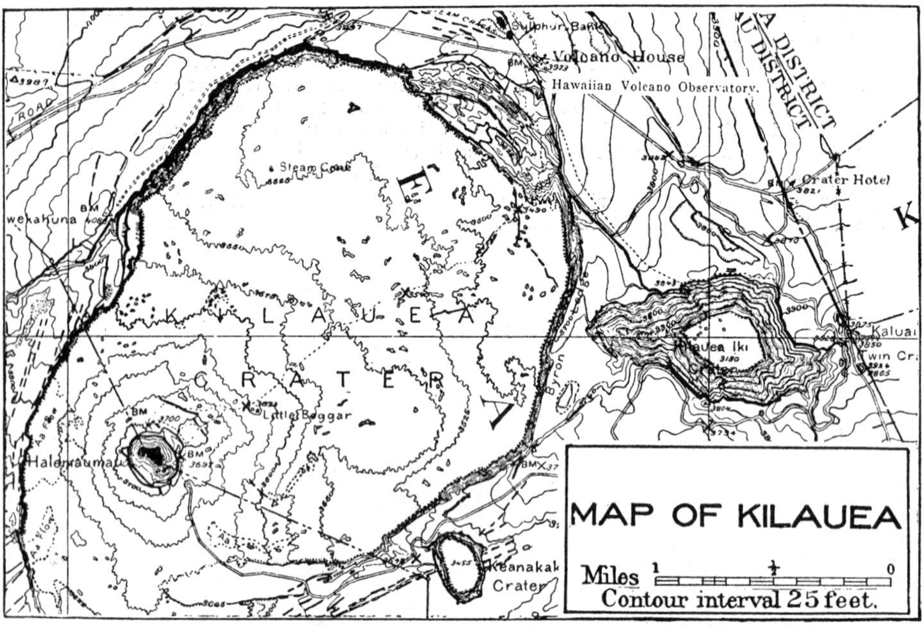

HAWAIIAN VOLCANO RESEARCH ASSOCIATION.

This society is a voluntary one, made up of subscribers to scientific work which is being executed by the Massachusetts Institute of Technology.

In 1913 there were 26 subscribers in Hawaii and Massachusetts, firms and individuals. A group of firms and persons in Hilo built the main observatory building in the spring of 1912. Publications to date have been weekly reports since the summer of 1911, a memoir by Daly in the Proceedings of American Academy of Arts and Sciences in 1911, articles by the director in the Technology Review 1911 and the Honolulu Chamber of Commerce Annual 1912, articles by H. O. Wood in the Bulletin of the Seismological Society of America, and articles by Perret in the American Journal of Science. The Massachusetts Institute of Technology will publish semi-annual reports.

This weekly bulletin as it appears in the Advertiser will be reprinted as a leaflet and sent to regular annual subscribers to the work of the association. C. H. Cooke is president of the Board of Directors of the association and R. W. Shingle is treasurer. New subscribers who are interested in our volcanoes will be welcomed in the association. The association aims: (1) To record volcanic activity and earthquakes in Hawaii; (2) to attract scientific men hither for special studies; (3) to promote the establishment of volcano observatories all over the world.

WHITNEY LABORATORY OF SEISMOLOGY.

The Whitney Laboratory of Seismology is equipped with two Bosch-Omori 100 kg tromometers registering N-S and E-W motion, a heavy Omori tromometer registering E-W motion and an Omori "ordinary Seismograph" designed for registering strong earthquakes in all three components of motion. These are seated on concrete piers in a closed basement room having practically constant temperature, beneath the chief Observatory building near the hotel. Time is referred to a rated chronometer, checked at intervals by solar observations with a transit. Both instruments are loaned by the College of Hawaii. At the substation by the edge of the active pit an Omori two-component tromometer with light steady masses is mounted on a concrete pier placed directly on the fresh lava surface. Hawaiian standard time (H. S. T.) is 10 hrs. 30 m. slower than Greenwich time.

CANCANI SCALE OF SEISMIC INTENSITY

Expressed by accelerations measured in millimeters per second per second.

I.	Instrumental	0.0	2.5
II.	Very slight	2.5	5.0
III.	Slight	5.0	10.0
IV.	Sensible, mediocre	10.0	25.0
V.	Rather strong	25.0	50.0
VI.	Strong	50.0	100.0
VII.	Very strong	100.0	250.0
VIII.	Ruinous	250.0	500.0
IX.	Disastrous	500.0	1000.0
X.	Very disastrous	1000.0	2500.0
XI.	Catastrophic	2500.0	5000.0
XII.	Great catastrophe	5000.0	10000.0

Grade IV. is ordinarily the minimum perceived by the senses; and in grade XII. the acceleration, or rate of change of motion (jerk) reaches that of terrestrial gravitation.

WEEKLY BULLETIN
OF
Hawaiian Volcano Observatory

Vol. II. HONOLULU, HAWAII, MARCH 18, 1914. No. 11.

From the Pacific Commercial Advertiser, Honolulu, March 8, 1914.

TECHNOLOGY STATION, Kilauea, March 5.—Activity in Halemaumau continues to increase, though slowly and irregularly. As yet there is no molten pool, but, when the swirling fumes permit, glowing lava can be seen especially at night, in the ''Old Faithful'' place, in the apex of the cone at the southeast, in an orifice about one hundred feet above the floor at the south, in an orifice at the west, and in one at the north. An occasional jet of molten lumps is seen, and the sound of falling spatter has been heard at rather long, but irregular, intervals.

The fume cloud is faintly illuminated at night, punctuated by feeble but well-defined spasmodic flarings. The harsh blowing noise has again become very loud—at times almost explosively sharp. The deep-toned rumbling is loud and continuous. Sounds like those of surging and swashing of the heavy molten fluid can be heard plainly.

On February 26 a good view was obtained of the ''Old Faithful'' cone and the southeast cone. Several small cones were seen—one at the south-southeast, in the talus, between twenty and fifty feet above the floor. Talus slides were frequent and prolonged. The rumbling sound continued unabated, and the blowing sound, though not so loud as earlier, was the same as on the foregoing days.

On February 27 no view was obtained. The noises were as usual. There were frequent talus slides, some lasting fully half a minute.

Glowing Lava Cone.

On February 28 a good view of ''Old Faithful'' was obtained. Glowing lava could be seen within the cone. No molten spray could be seen, even when the blasts were hard. The blowing sound was about the same as on the previous day. The rumbling was as usual. The southeast cone was seen, and glowing lava was visible in it at the apex; but no gas blasts were issuing from it—only from ''Old Faithful.'' Blue fumes were issuing copiously from a large orifice on the floor between the south and southeast stations; also from the western crevasse.

On March 1 only a fleeting view was obtained. Three glow-holes, possibly each three to four feet in diameter, were seen at the apex of the ''Old Faithful'' cone. Thin and scanty blue fumes were seen to be rising constantly out of the talus at the south, less than one hundred feet below the summit rim. The rumbling was loud and continuous and had a pulsating quality. The blowing noise had greatly increased in energy and the blasts were occasionally prolonged, at irregular intervals, lasting from thirty to one hundred and fifty seconds. Blue and white fumes were issuing copiously from the southeast group of fumaroles in the talus.

Gas Blasts Frequent.

On March 2 a good view was obtained. Three large orifices exhibiting molten lava were seen plainly at the apex of the ''Old Faithful'' cone. Gas blasts were issuing from these every two or three seconds, and the noise was very loud. The rumbling was as usual. Every few seconds a flash of light was seen within the large crevasse at the west-northwest, and there were three blowing orifices close by.

WEEKLY BULLETIN
of
Hawaiian Volcano Observatory

Published at Honolulu, Hawaii, by the **Hawaiian Volcano Research Association**

Editor..............Howard M. Ballou
Professor of Physics, College of Hawaii

Application pending for entry as second-class matter at the post-office, Honolulu, Hawaii.

An Excellent View.

On March 3, in the early part of the day no view was obtained. However, visitors reported that just before nightfall there was an excellent and prolonged view. Glowing lava was visible in several orifices in the talus, as well as, probably, in the "Old Faithful" place. Small jets of molten spray were seen. On this day the blowing noises were much louder than on Sunday, the 1st, and the rumbling was as usual.

On March 4 no view of the bottom was obtained. Again blue fumes were seen rising from the talus less than one hundred feet below the southern rim, from the spot from 150-200 feet below the rim under the north station, and in very great volume from the crevasse at the west. The sounds of blowing were much louder than on the first, and the quiet intervals were shorter, but no prolonged blasts were heard. Rumbling was heard as usual. One trivial talus slide occurred.

At night, in bright moonlight, distinct flaring was seen at the irregular short intervals so characteristic of the fountain action of "Old Faithful," but while the moon was shining no continuous illumination from the molten lava could be made out. After moonset, both on the third and on the fourth of March, a faint but steady illumination of the fume cloud was seen.

Slight Earthquakes.

During the week five slight local earthquakes have been registered. One, on March 1, was felt distinctly a few miles in the direction of Hilo, and was fairly heavy at Kapapala, but in the immediate vicinity of the Volcano House it was just barely perceptible under day conditions—about II Rossi-Forel. No systematic report upon these earthquakes can be rendered this week.

H. O. WOOD, Associate.

The Trail down into the Crater of Kilauea, Hawaii.

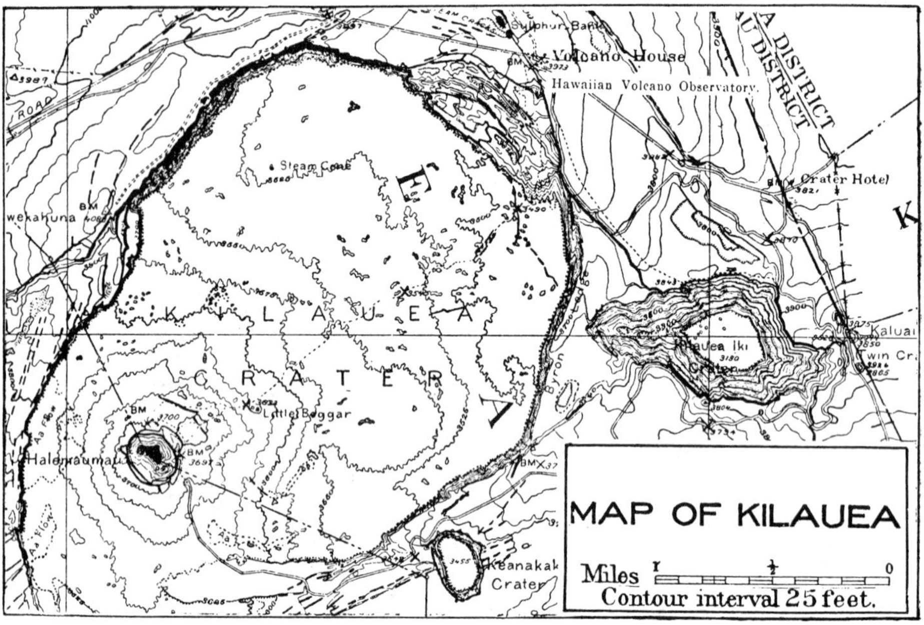

HAWAIIAN VOLCANO RESEARCH ASSOCIATION.

This society is a voluntary one, made up of subscribers to scientific work which is being executed by the Massachusetts Institute of Technology.

In 1913 there were 26 subscribers in Hawaii and Massachusetts, firms and individuals. A group of firms and persons in Hilo built the main observatory building in the spring of 1912. Publications to date have been weekly reports since the summer of 1911, a memoir by Daly in the Proceedings of American Academy of Arts and Sciences in 1911, articles by the director in the Technology Review 1911 and the Honolulu Chamber of Commerce Annual 1912, articles by H. O. Wood in the Bulletin of the Seismological Society of America, and articles by Perret in the American Journal of Science. The Massachusetts Institute of Technology will publish semi-annual reports.

This weekly bulletin as it appears in the Advertiser will be reprinted as a leaflet and sent to regular annual subscribers to the work of the association. C. H. Cooke is president of the Board of Directors of the association and R. W. Shingle is treasurer. New subscribers who are interested in our volcanoes will be welcomed in the association. The association aims: (1) To record volcanic activity and earthquakes in Hawaii; (2) to attract scientific men hither for special studies; (3) to promote the establishment of volcano observatories all over the world.

WHITNEY LABORATORY OF SEISMOLOGY.

The Whitney Laboratory of Seismology is equipped with two Bosch-Omori 100 kg tromometers registering N-S and E-W motion, a heavy Omori tromometer registering E-W motion and an Omori "ordinary Seismograph" designed for registering strong earthquakes in all three components of motion. These are seated on concrete piers in a closed basement room having practically constant temperature, beneath the chief Observatory building near the hotel. Time is referred to a rated chronometer, checked at intervals by solar observations with a transit. Both instruments are loaned by the College of Hawaii. At the substation by the edge of the active pit an Omori two-component tromometer with light steady masses is mounted on a concrete pier placed directly on the fresh lava surface. Hawaiian standard time (H. S. T.) is 10 hrs. 30 m. slower than Greenwich time.

CANCANI SCALE OF SEISMIC INTENSITY

Expressed by accelerations measured in millimeters per second per second.

I.	Instrumental	0.0	2.5
II.	Very slight	2.5	5.0
III.	Slight	5.0	10.0
IV.	Sensible, mediocre....	10.0	25.0
V.	Rather strong	25.0	50.0
VI.	Strong	50.0	100.0
VII.	Very strong	100.0	250.0
VIII.	Ruinous	250.0	500.0
IX.	Disastrous	500.0	1000.0
X.	Very disastrous	1000.0	2500.0
XI.	Catastrophic	2500.0	5000.0
XII.	Great catastrophe....	5000.0	10000.0

Grade IV. is ordinarily the minimum perceived by the senses; and in grade XII. the acceleration, or rate of change of motion (jerk) reaches that of terrestrial gravitation.

WEEKLY BULLETIN
OF
Hawaiian Volcano Observatory

Vol. II. HONOLULU, HAWAII, MARCH 25, 1914. No. 12.

From the Pacific Commercial Advertiser, Honolulu, March 15, 1914.

TECHNOLOGY STATION, March 12. —During the past week, conditions at Halemaumau have undergone little change, but there has been no diminution in activity; probably a slight increase.

On Thursday, March 5, no visit to the active pit was made from the Observatory, but visiting tourists reported the blowing noise to be loud, the rumbling continuously audible, and views of glowing lava after nightfall visible in the usual orifices.

On March 6 a very prolonged watch was kept. Many brief views were obtained. Throughout the day and evening molten lava was ejected in flying lumps from the "Old Faithful" orifice, at an interval of about forty-five seconds. Some of these jets of molten spray shot up from forty to fifty feet. Brightly-glowing lava was seen in late afternoon and evening in the large gash, or crevasse, on the floor leading into the cliff under the northwest station. Glowing spots were seen on the floor at the southeast, and in the talus near the floor at the southwest. The blowing noise was louder and harsher than on previous days. The rumbling was much as usual. At night the fume cloud was illuminated brilliantly by flaring for instants, though there was bright moonlight.

Because of wind, and of the prolonged watch on the previous day, no visit was made to the pit on March 7.

On March 8 the blowing noise, though frequently prolonged and quite loud, had lost much of its harsh, shrill quality. This probably resulted from the enlargement of the orifices from which gas is escaping. The rumbling was as usual. "Old Faithful" was seen plainly—three small orifices at the apex of the cone, within which glowing lava was visible. No lava jets were seen, nor no sound of falling spatter was heard. Glowing lava was seen at the southeast on the floor, at the southwest a little above the floor in the talus, and in the gash leading into the wall at the northwest. This latter was by far the largest and hottest orifice. Here the rock was snapping sharply from the increasing heat. At times flame appeared to be playing above it. Here blue fumes were exhaled in great abundance. Blue fumes were again noticed escaping from several orifices high up in the south talus, and from the high north fumarole. Brief slides were heard.

On March 9 the rumbling noise was not so loud, but the blowing was fully as loud, possibly louder than on the 8th. Lumps of molten lava were sprayed up from "Old Faithful," falling as spatter about the cone. Many small slides were heard, and several lasting from forty-five seconds to a minute were noted. The moving material in most of the small slides, and at least one of the longer ones, ran down into the gash orifice under the northwest station.

On March 10 wind prevented any view. There were many small slides, and one of about one minute's duration, which occurred at the southeast. The sounds of blowing and rumbling were as usual.

On March 11, in early evening, a brief view from the southeast station showed "Old Faithful" and the southeast cone, both with glowing orifices, and both ejecting showers of molten

WEEKLY BULLETIN
of
Hawaiian Volcano Observatory

Published at Honolulu, Hawaii, by the **Hawaiian Volcano Research Association**

Editor..............Howard M. Ballou
Professor of Physics, College of Hawaii

Application pending for entry as second-class matter at the post-office, Honolulu, Hawaii.

spray at intervals. The blowing noise was very loud, particularly the blasts from "Old Faithful." The rumbling was as usual. No slides were heard. Smoke prevented any view of the west-northwest orifice.

No systematic seismological report can be rendered this week. However, five slight earthquakes have been registered, one early in the morning of March 8 being strong enough to be barely perceptible to the senses.

H. O. WOOD,
Associate.

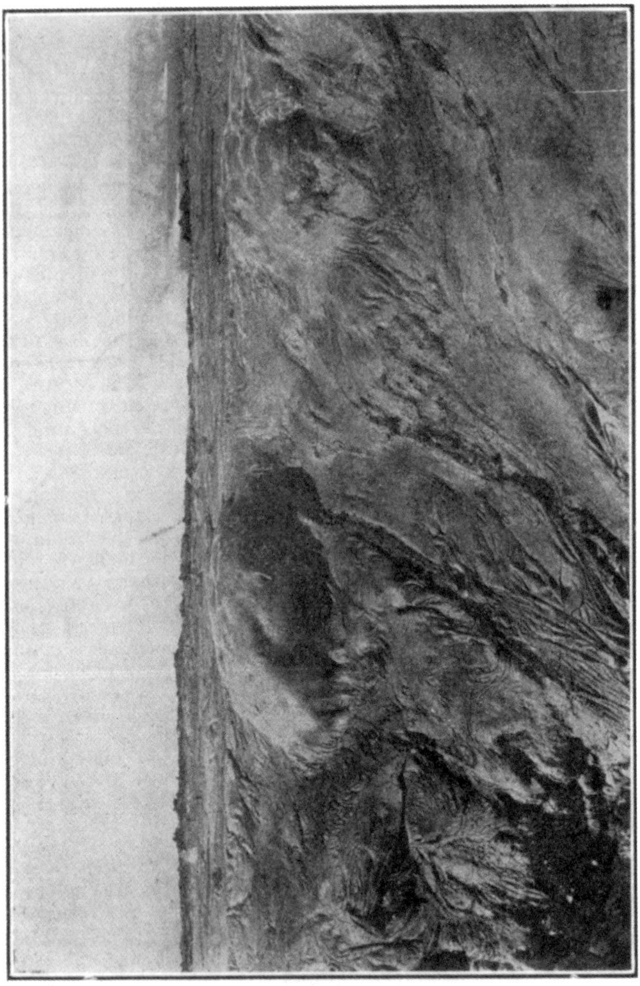

Smooth Lava (Pahoehoe).

“Table” or “Stack” of lava in depression north of Halemaumau, showing former position of lava surface here before subsidence occurred.

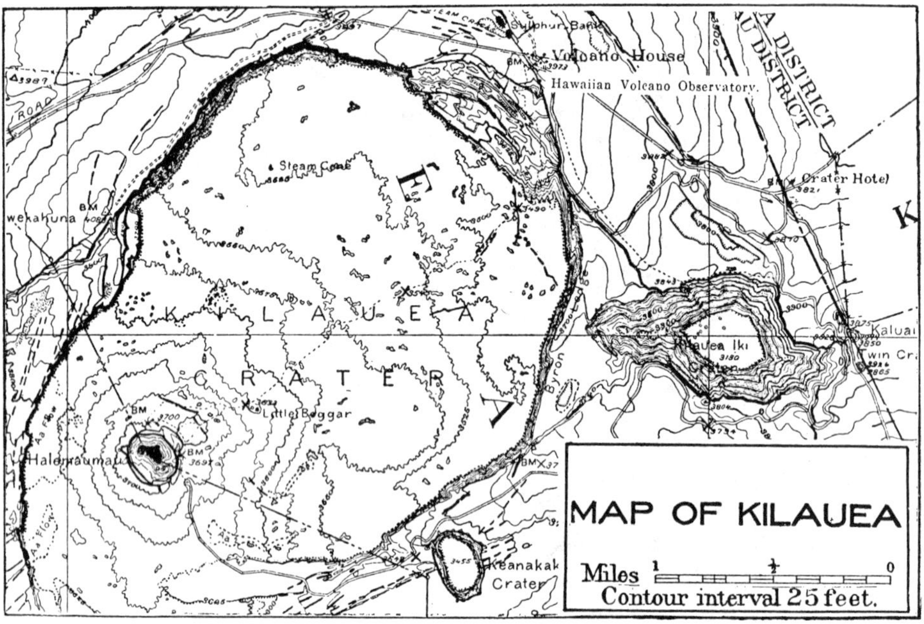

HAWAIIAN VOLCANO RESEARCH ASSOCIATION.

This society is a voluntary one, made up of subscribers to scientific work which is being executed by the Massachusetts Institute of Technology.

In 1913 there were 26 subscribers in Hawaii and Massachusetts, firms and individuals. A group of firms and persons in Hilo built the main observatory building in the spring of 1912. Publications to date have been weekly reports since the summer of 1911, a memoir by Daly in the Proceedings of American Academy of Arts and Sciences in 1911, articles by the director in the Technology Review 1911 and the Honolulu Chamber of Commerce Annual 1912, articles by H. O. Wood in the Bulletin of the Seismological Society of America, and articles by Perret in the American Journal of Science. The Massachusetts Institute of Technology will publish semi-annual reports.

This weekly bulletin as it appears in the Advertiser will be reprinted as a leaflet and sent to regular annual subscribers to the work of the association. C. H. Cooke is president of the Board of Directors of the association and R. W. Shingle is treasurer. New subscribers who are interested in our volcanoes will be welcomed in the association. The association aims: (1) To record volcanic activity and earthquakes in Hawaii; (2) to attract scientific men hither for special studies; (3) to promote the establishment of volcano observatories all over the world.

WHITNEY LABORATORY OF SEISMOLOGY.

The Whitney Laboratory of Seismology is equipped with two Bosch-Omori 100 kg tromometers registering N-S and E-W motion, a heavy Omori tromometer registering E-W motion and an Omori "ordinary Seismograph" designed for registering strong earthquakes in all three components of motion. These are seated on concrete piers in a closed basement room having practically constant temperature, beneath the chief Observatory building near the hotel. Time is referred to a rated chronometer, checked at intervals by solar observations with a transit. Both instruments are loaned by the College of Hawaii. At the sub-station by the edge of the active pit an Omori two-component tromometer with light steady masses is mounted on a concrete pier placed directly on the fresh lava surface. Hawaiian standard time (H. S. T.) is 10 hrs. 30 m. slower than Greenwich time.

CANCANI SCALE OF SEISMIC INTENSITY

Expressed by accelerations measured in millimeters per second per second.

I.	Instrumental	0.0	2.5
II.	Very slight	2.5	5.0
III.	Slight	5.0	10.0
IV.	Sensible, mediocre....	10.0	25.0
V.	Rather strong	25.0	50.0
VI.	Strong	50.0	100.0
VII.	Very strong	100.0	250.0
VIII.	Ruinous	250.0	500.0
IX.	Disastrous	500.0	1000.0
X.	Very disastrous	1000.0	2500.0
XI.	Catastrophic	2500.0	5000.0
XII.	Great catastrophe....	5000.0	10000.0

Grade IV. is ordinarily the minimum perceived by the senses; and in grade XII. the acceleration, or rate of change of motion (jerk) reaches that of terrestrial gravitation.

WEEKLY BULLETIN
OF
Hawaiian Volcano Observatory

Vol. II. HONOLULU, HAWAII, APRIL 1, 1914. No. 13.

From the Pacific Commercial Advertiser, Honolulu, March 22, 1914.

TECHNOLOGY STATION, March 19.—As a spectacle Kilauea is again in action—at night affording to the patient watcher, unless a strong wind blows, fitful views of jets of molten lava flung upwards to heights sometimes exceeding one hundred feet, these jets springing up every few seconds from three or four different orifices. The pit is theatrically illuminated by the glow from several small caves and orifices in its depths. As yet, however, there is no molten pool.

On March 12, at frequent intervals, lava was violently ejected, but in small quantity, from the ''Old Faithful'' orifice and from that in the southeast cone. Noise of blowing and rumbling was as usual. A large orifice was noted, for the first time, under the northeast station at the very edge of the lake area. Here the gas was issuing in spasmodic blasts, but no lava jets were noticed. The glow on the fumes here was very bright. No slides were heard. At times a blue flame was seen playing over ''Old Faithful.''

On March 13 jets of molten lava were seen issuing from ''Old Faithful'' and from the southeast cone, and glowing lava could be seen in the orifice of the northeast cave. The blowing sound was very loud indeed. The jets from ''Old Faithful'' were thrown up from forty to fifty feet. Blue flames were playing above its cone. No slides were heard.

On March 14 conditions had undergone no change, except that nearly all the marks of activity had slightly increased. No incandescence, however, could be seen at the northeast orifice, but simply bright illumination of the fumes there. A new, small orifice was observed under the northwest station at the edge of the lake area, in which glowing lava was seen.

On March 15 wind prevented seeing in afternoon and early evening. It was noted that the blowing sound, remaining fairly loud, had become continuous, but that it was punctuated at intervals of from one-half to two seconds by explosive snorting and coughing sounds. Further, at intervals of twenty to one hundred seconds there occurred still other louder and heavier gas blasts. Rumbling was heard as usual. There were frequent snapping sounds, loud and sharp, as of rock cracking from heat. There was heard, doubtfully, the sound of falling spatter.

In the late evening, as reported by visitors, jets of molten lava were flung up from forty to fifty feet from ''Old Faithful,'' and a flow cascaded to the floor from the low gash-orifice at the W. N. W. Though there was a southwest wind, blowing the fume cloud toward the Observatory, from here bright and prolonged flares were seen at times.

On March 16 a very strong southwest wind prevailed, preventing all views. This wind set up and maintained a state of vibration of the foundation piers of the seismographs exceeding in amplitude the vibrations commonly produced by violent activity in the pit. At Halemaumau a few trivial slides were heard; also, as usual, sounds of rumbling and of continuous blowing punctuated by snorting and coughing sounds. There were subdued, but heavy, sounds as of considerable bodies of lava in motion. The sound of falling spatter was

WEEKLY BULLETIN
of
Hawaiian Volcano Observatory

Published at Honolulu, Hawaii, by the **Hawaiian Volcano Research Association**

Editor..............Howard M. Ballou
Professor of Physics, College of Hawaii

Application pending for entry as second-class matter at the post-office, Honolulu, Hawaii.

plainly heard, and the flaring, seen at the pitside, was very bright.

On March 17 conditions had undergone no change. The large W. N. W. orifice had partly closed, but the rumbling there was very loud. No glowing lava could be seen in it until evening, when very small incandescent holes could be seen. Jets of molten lava, sometimes in considerable amount, were flung from "Old Faithful" at every eruptive spasm. The blowing noise was continuous, but the coughing and snorting was less pronounced. Trivial slides were heard, and much material was seen to have fallen to the floor since the early part of the week here under report. The southeast cone was nearly covered with talus. After nightfall many small glowing orifices were seen in the talus, and cliff wall, near the edge of the lake area—up to one hundred feet above the floor of the pit. Despite the swirling fumes views, satisfactory from the spectacular point of view, were frequent throughout the evening.

On March 18 general conditions remained the same. Lava jets from "Old Faithful" sometimes exceeded one hundred feet (estimated) in height. At these times tons of molten lava were flung into the air from this orifice. Incandescent lava was seen plainly in the W. N. W. gash. Numerous small, glowing places were seen again in the cliff walls and in the talus high above the bottom of the pit. The southeast cone was seen to be almost buried under talus. Jets of lava were springing obliquely out from the northeast cave. No blue flames were seen. A few trivial slides were heard. The sharp sound of rock snapping from heat was heard plainly.

Seismically the week has passed uneventfully. No systematic report can yet be rendered.

H. O. WOOD, Associate.

From the Pacific Commercial Advertiser, Honolulu, March 24, 1914

KAGOSHIMA, Japan, February 20. —I have to report that I left Honolulu per S. S. Korea, January 22; arrived Yokohama February 2; spent February 3 in Tokio with Professors Omori and Koto; sailed the same day; arrived Nagasaki February 6 and remained there until Monday, February 9.

On that day, accompanied by Mr. Mihara, an employe of Holme, Ringer & Company of Nagasaki as interpreter, I left by rail for Kagoshima, arriving the same night and stopping at the Satsuma Hotel. Every possible courtesy was shown me in Tokio and Nagasaki.

Arrived at my destination, I was met by Professor Sasamoto, a geologist and teacher of this city, and by Mr. Atsumi, an associate of Professor Omori and a member of the staff of the Imperial Meteorological Observatory at Kagoshima. February 10 I called on the acting governor of the prefecture, Governor Tanaguchi being absent in Tokio on official duty connected with the eruption. The acting governor, Mr. Hattori, immediately sent a guide about the city with me and placed at my disposal the training ship Nishiki Maru, and extended other courtesies. Mr. Wm. L. Schwartz, an American teacher and man of letters here, has worked for me most assiduously in accumulating photographs and records, as well as offering me the hospitality of his home. One and all have been most kind, and I cannot say enough in praise of the hospitality, scientific interest and intelligent efficiency of the government and people of Kagoshima.

As to the eruption of Sakurajima, it proves to be an epoch-marking event in Japan, and this expedition was amply justified. I am glad to hear that Mr. Perret is coming, and I hope that some gas chemist will come when the more violent explosions now in progress have subsided.

The unusual feature of the eruption for Japan is the outflow of two floods of a-a lava of the composition of hypersthene andesite. It is not unusual for this volcano, for the same thing appears by the old records to have happened at Sakurajima in 1779 and 1476, but there are few volcanoes like it in Japan. At the time Professor Omori left, January 28, he estimated ten square kilometers had poured out, and the depth of the east flow in places is not less than 500 feet, as it fills a channel fifty-five fathoms deep and is piled two hundred feet high above sea-level.

Sakurajima is a wonderfully impressive peak, as it towers before the city of Kagoshima. It has a serrate summit, somewhat like the Dents du Midi as seen from the Lake of Geneva. It made a round island two miles from the city and right in front of it, in a bay which is elongate right and left as one faces the waterfront.

Back of Sakurajima a point of land jutted out from the province of Osumi within a quarter of a mile of the island. A population of 20,000 fishermen and farmers occupied sixteen villages along the shore of the island.

My first glimpse of the volcano was from the train at night, approaching the city, and I saw a great column of smoke rising from the east base of the mountain, with a fitful flare of dull red lava below. It appears that the mountain was rent asunder along an east-west vertical fracture. The summit craters played no part in the eruption, and six or eight new craters were formed east and west at elevations from 500 to 1500 feet above sea-level, ejecting first stones, gas and dust, and within a day, lava.

The eruption was essentially Vesuvian in quality. Premonitory were eruptions of Kirishima, the next volcano thirty miles north, in June, November and December last, and an unusual earthquake last July. The past year has been excessively dry here. Doctor Friedlaender published a warning in 1910 to the effect that an eruption might be expected, heralded by strong earthquakes.

The phases of the eruption were:

Three hundred and seventy earthquake shocks during some 27 hours, January 11 to the morning of January 12. On January 12 at 8:30 a. m. curbed hot springs at Arimura, on the south shore of Sakurajima, rose suddenly about three feet.

Simultaneously with this gush of springs, white threads of vapor rose above the southern summit crater. At 2 p. m. the previous day similar white vapor had been seen.

At 10 a. m., January 12, an explosion with black "cauliflower" smoke took place on the side of the volcano towards Kagoshima, the west side, the earliest photographs indicating some obliquity of the jet westward.

About ten minutes later, according to the masters of vessels to the south, who could see both sides of the mountain, a similar column of black smoke rose at the eastern base of the volcano.

At first the rumbling noise was not very strong, but it increased during the day to tremendous detonations, and for three days those who stayed in the city were almost deafened by the detonations, coupled with the noisy jar of the screen-doors of the Japanese houses (shoji) incessantly vibrating by atmospheric concussion. The earthquakes continued. The explosion column of smoke and ash from the west side rose over 20,000 feet and bent eastward, while at first the eastern column appeared smaller and whiter under the overarching column from the west vents.

At 5:30 p. m., January 12, strong earthquake shocks were felt at Arimura on the southeast shore of the island and this time was said by the officers of the Nishiki Maru to be the culmination of the western explosions. There were tremendous revivals that night at midnight and on the next evening (13th) a marvelous fiery display, but this time was probably the maximum explosive gas pressure before the lava rose to the craters. And the southeast earthquakes of 5:30 p. m. probably marked the wider opening and rise of lava in the eastern vents.

At 6:30 p. m., January 12, a strong and somewhat prolonged earthquake shook Kagoshima, wrecked stone walls and killed about twenty persons. Others were wounded. The earth wave was east to west, from the direction of the volcano, north to south walls falling and east to west ones resisting.

A bright flare over the volcano was seen simultaneously with the earthquake. This I attribute to the fact that the lava wedge with its hot gases split its final passage to the craters at 6:30, cracking suddenly the foundation of the volcano along a W-NW vertical plane connecting the east and west craters and so producing the earthquake as a result of the sudden fracture. From the alignment of the east craters it is clear that such a rift exists, and this line accords with that of the two principal west craters. There are at least four main east crater vents and three western ones.

At midnight, January 12, there was a second special culmination of explosive activity with occasional flarings, visible incandescent blocks describing trajectories upward and outward and vanishing in their downward course to the earth. In daylight they left trails of smoke. The east craters were not carefully observed, as there were no scientific observers on that side. Lightning was seen in the cauliflower jets, first stellar, then linear flashes. They were not seen to pass from cloud to earth, or to the bay. Lightning was seen January 12, 13 and 14, that of the 13th being more elongate. There was rain and local thunderstorms the evening of the 13th.

The midnight crisis of January 12 may be attributed to the culmination of free flow of gas liberated by the lava which had risen to the craters at 6:30 that evening.

On January 13 there were few earthquakes and of no great strength. The crisis had passed.

The explosive activity continued, however, with great force, and the event of this date was the beginning of lava flow down the slopes of the mountain east and west, eventually burying the deserted villages at Yokoyama, Waki, Arimura and Seto. The flow on the west side became visible soon after 3 p. m.

An earthquake sufficiently strong to be startling was recorded at the observatory at 4:09 p. m. At 7 p. m. the lava was flowing rapidly with colossal cauliflower explosions at the west craters and the greatest noise and fire of the eruption took place from 8 to 8:30 p. m. of this date January 13th.

Ship's officers on the Kagoshima waterfront at this time saw houses burning at Hakamagoshi, the promontory straight across the channel from Kagoshima. When I visited this place later, I found evidence of a horizontal blast outward and downward from the craters, and this is probably what ignited these houses, for the lava flow was not near them. Trees were uprooted and shredded and scarred with horizontally flying stones, and they were thrown over in lines directly away from the volcano. This blast of the Pelee type, therefore, probably took place about 8 p. m., January 13, when the explosion debris in the air was weighing down on the upjets and the atmosphere over the volcano had become surcharged with solid matter. This was the only locality where I saw evidence of such a blast, and moreover this blast was headed directly for Kagoshima only two miles across the strait.

Had the lava not flowed, and the explosions gone on increasing in violence on the west side, Kagoshima might well have suffered the fate of St. Pierre in Martinique. As it was, however, this small blast of the evening of the 13th was the only manifestation of this sort and the great display of 8:30 that night was the final performance so far as the western craters were concerned. It was probably occasioned by ebullition of gas released from the lava column when rapid overflow started great quantities of fluid from the depths.

January 14, the noises had changed. Up to the evening of January 13 continual quick detonations like artillery were the rule. After the lava flowed and the great display of 8:30 p. m. was over, the noise settled down to rumbles and growls, with detonations and felt earthquakes increasingly rare. When I reached Kagoshima, February 9, the occasional noises from Sakurajima, best heard when the wind was easterly, were precisely like the rumbling of heavy balls in a bowling alley, and the duration of the rumble about that which precedes a ten-strike. Occasionally this was varied by one or more loud "booms," like cannon, and all the screens and shutters of the house would rattle with the concussion.

On January 14, the western lava flow was well back from the shore, and the cauliflower explosions of the west craters appeared still dominant over those from the east craters.

January 15 the western lava reached sea-level and started the building of what has become a large promontory of new land. Explosion on the west had now greatly diminished, while the explosion on the east maintained great violence, with lava flow as well.

About January 20 the small island Karasushima on the west was reached by the advancing promontory of lava and buried under it. At this time explosion practically ceased from the west craters, but it continued on the east, and is still in vigorous activity at this time (February 20, 1914), and the lava flows are still in motion on both sides of the volcano. From time to time minor explosions in the new lava fields took place after January 20 on the west, but most of these were due to local accumulation of gas and some of them to spring water which accumulated under the hot lava, made contact with it, and so produced superficial steam explosion. There are craterlets, doubtless due to this mechanism, in the fields of hot ash and stones on the western foot slopes.

February 1 was the historic date when Sakurajima ceased to be an island and became a peninsula. The eastern lava-flow had been coursing onward from January 13 presumably, balancing on the east side, the outflow on the west, and eventually piling up to much greater heights. The lava at sea level on the east is a chaotic mass of a-a 150 to 170 feet high, whereas it is only about 50 feet high on the west.

On February 1 the east lava front closed the channel and made contact with the Osumi peninsula. February 13 a survey was made showing contact with the shore for two hundred feet and lava sixty feet high. February 19 I visited the place and found 330 feet of shore in contact with the lava and the latter piled up 150 feet high. For several hundred feet in both directions the lava was nearly on the shore, separated from it by a channel fifty feet wide of hot sea-water at a temperature of 138 degrees Fahrenheit. Earlier measurements of the temperature of water at the west lava-front were reported by the Navigation School to be 153 degrees Fahrenheit.

From February 1 to the present time the history of the eruption has been slow decadence. Earthquakes have diminished in number and intensity since January 15. During my stay (February 9 to February 20) the explosions of the east craters have shown diminished violence and the lowest of three prominent craters on that side has practically gone out of explosive action, though lava continues to pour from it.

The lava east and west flows slowly in tubes under heavy a-a crusts. The east lava is plastered deep with banks of sand, pumice and ash. Pumice floats in scums and patches all over Kagoshima bay, the larger stones being four inches in diameter. Ash fell all over the country, on January 14 even as far as Tokio, and ranges in depth from a fraction of an inch to seven feet. There was no sympathetic eruption of the Volcanoes Kaimon, Kirishima or Aso as at first reported. There were no geysers in the bay.

Mr. Katsuno, the efficient director of the meteorological observatory, remained at his post throughout the eruption, kept excellent record of everything, and is still at his post, and furnished me with much valuable information. The stories of his suicide were malignant gossip wholly without foundation or justice.

The loss of life was about twenty-four persons, missing about eighteen, wounded unknown. Most of the deaths were from earthquake. The death zone would have involved at least 20,000 persons if they had stayed in their homes. They migrated without panic and were cared for in neighboring towns. Then in a week, when reassured, they came back, at least to Kagoshima. Probably on Tuesday, January 13, there were not 1000 persons, of a population of 70,000 in Kagoshima. In all about 90,000 people migrated. When we compare Messina with a death roll of 130,000, and St. Pierre, 26,000, the record here of forewarning and efficient self-protection is without parallel. The government immediately took control. Doctor Omori, of the Imperial Earthquake Investigation Committee, came to Kagoshima, examined conditions, and issued a statement, on the basis of which the people returned, and that statement has proved to be correct. Plans are now being perfected to rehabilitate the Sakurajima people in a safer land in the Province of Hyuga.

The eruption is now a magnificent spectacle and should be visited by everyone coming to Japan. It is a scene not to be duplicated once in a century. There is no reason for nervousness nor apprehension of further outbreaks, at least in the Kagoshima district, for years to come, as the safety valve is open, lava has flowed freely, and the gases are pouring forth from an open vent. There may be earthquake shocks occasionally and some further lava and gas activity, but the essential features of a periodic volcanic eruption here are finished.

T. A. JAGGAR, Jr., Director.

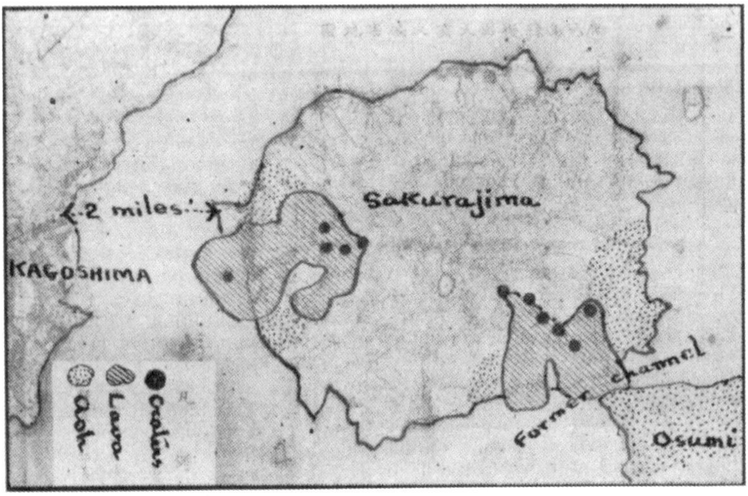

VESTIGES OF THE MOLTEN GLOBE. PART II. THE EARTH'S SURFACE FEATURES AND VOLCANIC PHENOMENA.

By Wm. Lowthian Green,
Honolulu, 1887, pp. 337, 8 vo.

A few copies of this important work, (new, though slightly shop-worn) are still obtainable. Price $3.00, post free, Howard M. Ballou, Secretary Hawaiian Volcano Association, Box 353, Honolulu, Hawaii.

Dr. Jaggar writes of this book as follows:

No more remarkable book on the fundamenta of geology was written in the nineteenth century than Green's ''Vestiges,'' except possibly Darwin's ''Coral Reefs.'' Mr. Green was a scholarly man of business, inspired by the unique volcanic environment of a home in mid-ocean islands, and his acute power of observation during many visits to Kilauea and Mauna Loa led to generalizations which have won acceptance from men of science the world over. Michel Levy and De l'Apparent in France, Emerson and Daly in America, and many others have followed Green in his ideas of a tetrahedral earth and a fluid substratum, while his studies of volcanoes must ever remain among the classics in the library of the volcanologist. The first volume dealt with the tetrahedral earth and is very rare. The second volume is of more interest to the general reader and summarizes the first, extending the work to special studies of volcanoes and of Hawaii in particular.

This book is all too little known and ought to be reprinted and in the possession of all the libraries of the world. It deals with the figure of the earth, special strains in tropic zones, distribution and origin of the oceans, the meaning of volcanism and Hawaiian volcanism in particular, the chemistry of volcanoes and the peculiarities of fracture systems in the crust of the earth.

Later, in a lecture, Dr. Jaggar thus mentions the work:—

Green, the man of business, in his leisure moments student of volcanic life and of the inspiring heights and depths of the globe, conceived to scale, with its film of waters and its blanket of gas, wrote a remarkable book in two volumes, ''Vestiges of the Molten Globe.'' His second volume deals especially with Hawaiian volcanoes, which he visited many times, and of it Professor Daly of Harvard writes: ''It is certainly a pity that the second part of Green's work is not more generally known. The book is almost as remarkable a contribution to the philosophy of vulcanism as Part I, 'On the Tetrahedral Theory of the Earth,' is important in cosmogonic philosophy.'' Green's work foreshadowed theoretic conceptions which modern thought has fixed more firmly, and his interest, as a business man, in the affairs of pure science was forerunner of the wider interest of many business men (and intelligent women) of Hawaii who now make up the Hawaiian Volcano Research Association.''

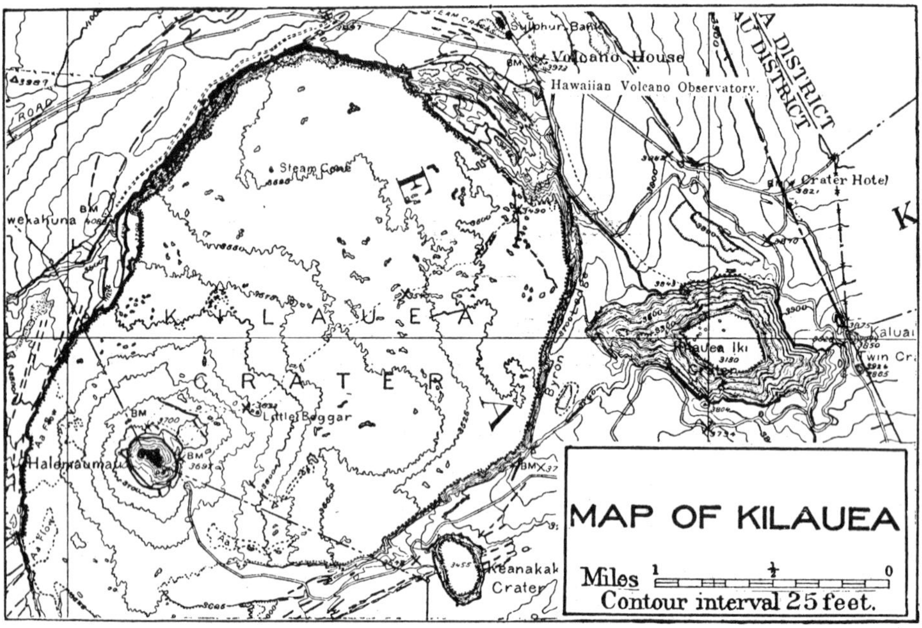

HAWAIIAN VOLCANO RESEARCH ASSOCIATION.

This society is a voluntary one, made up of subscribers to scientific work which is being executed by the Massachusetts Institute of Technology.

In 1913 there were 26 subscribers in Hawaii and Massachusetts, firms and individuals. A group of firms and persons in Hilo built the main observatory building in the spring of 1912. Publications to date have been weekly reports since the summer of 1911, a memoir by Daly in the Proceedings of American Academy of Arts and Sciences in 1911, articles by the director in the Technology Review 1911 and the Honolulu Chamber of Commerce Annual 1912, articles by H. O. Wood in the Bulletin of the Seismological Society of America, and articles by Perret in the American Journal of Science. The Massachusetts Institute of Technology will publish semi-annual reports.

This weekly bulletin as it appears in the Advertiser will be reprinted as a leaflet and sent to regular annual subscribers to the work of the association. C. H. Cooke is president of the Board of Directors of the association and R. W. Shingle is treasurer. New subscribers who are interested in our volcanoes will be welcomed in the association. The association aims: (1) To record volcanic activity and earthquakes in Hawaii; (2) to attract scientific men hither for special studies; (3) to promote the establishment of volcano observatories all over the world.

WHITNEY LABORATORY OF SEISMOLOGY.

The Whitney Laboratory of Seismology is equipped with two Bosch-Omori 100 kg tromometers registering N-S and E-W motion, a heavy Omori tromometer registering E-W motion and an Omori "ordinary Seismograph" designed for registering strong earthquakes in all three components of motion. These are seated on concrete piers in a closed basement room having practically constant temperature, beneath the chief Observatory building near the hotel. Time is referred to a rated chronometer, checked at intervals by solar observations with a transit. Both instruments are loaned by the College of Hawaii. At the substation by the edge of the active pit an Omori two-component tromometer with light steady masses is mounted on a concrete pier placed directly on the fresh lava surface. Hawaiian standard time (H. S. T.) is 10 hrs. 30 m. slower than Greenwich time.

CANCANI SCALE OF SEISMIC INTENSITY

Expressed by accelerations measured in millimeters per second per second.

I.	Instrumental	0.0	2.5
II.	Very slight	2.5	5.0
III.	Slight	5.0	10.0
IV.	Sensible, mediocre....	10.0	25.0
V.	Rather strong	25.0	50.0
VI.	Strong	50.0	100.0
VII.	Very strong	100.0	250.0
VIII.	Ruinous	250.0	500.0
IX.	Disastrous	500.0	1000.0
X.	Very disastrous	1000.0	2500.0
XI.	Catastrophic	2500.0	5000.0
XII.	Great catastrophe....	5000.0	10000.0

Grade IV. is ordinarily the minimum perceived by the senses; and in grade XII. the acceleration, or rate of change of motion (jerk) reaches that of terrestrial gravitation.

WEEKLY BULLETIN
OF
Hawaiian Volcano Observatory

Vol. II. HONOLULU, HAWAII, APRIL 8, 1914. No. 14.

From the Pacific Commercial Advertiser, Honolulu, March 29, 1914.

TECHNOLOGY STATION, KILAUEA, March 26—Kilauea grows more spectacular, though no molten lava lake has yet formed. Up to the evening of March 22 the eruptive energy continued definitely to increase. Since that time the condition tnen reached has been maintained at practically a stationary point, but with minor increases and decreases in energy. The sound of rumbling continues unabated, but the blowing sound produced by the outrush of gases has markedly declined in harshness and volume, owing, probably, to the opening of new orifices. Correlatively, though jets of lava spring up at frequent irregular intervals, the molten lumps are not flung so high nor with such seeming violence, and seemingly the volume is not so great as at the time of the last report. No outflows of molten lava have been witnessed, but flaring, seen from the Observatory, has suggested flowing, and freshly cooled lava is seen on the floor of the pit.

On March 19 jets were seen to rise from "Old Faithful" to heights of fifty to one hundred feet or more, and incandescent streaks were seen all over the floor. The cone under the west station was blowing loudly. The glow was very marked at the northeast cave, and from the west-northwest orifice. Rumbling was as usual, and a few trivial slides were heard.

On March 20 a high southwest wind with heavy rain prevented observation.

On March 21 jets of lava from fifty to one hundred feet in height were flung from "Old Faithful." Small jets were springing from the cone under the west station. Blowing was loud at the northeast orifice, and a brilliant glow was seen there. Incandescent lava was seen in the west-northwest orifice. During the evening the activity increased. The "Old Faithful" orifice became a long, narrow rent, at least twenty feet long by two to three feet wide, with a secondary opening about four by six feet. The jets of this evening were very violent. A blue flame played continuously at a minor orifice in the "Old Faithful" cone. Incandescent lava was seen at many points on the floor.

On March 22 no observations were made. Visitors reported conditions much as described above. It was said that seething, molten lava was seen in the west-northwest place.

On March 23 conditions were much as before, except that the jets were less energetic. Lesser jets were seen from "Old Faithful" and from the west cone, and incandescent lava was seen in the west-northwest orifice. Many cracks were seen in the frozen lake surface, through which incandescent lava shone. A new orifice had appeared under the east station, and many small orifices were seen on the floor.

On March 24 jets were seen from "Old Faithful," also, for the first time, from the west-northwest orifice. At the west cone the blowing and rumbling noises were decreased. Fresh lava was seen on the floor. "Old Faithful" was seen to have built a steep cone, with a broken-in top. The scene in early evening was unusually spectacular; also, in the night, the illumination of the fume cloud was striking and brilliant.

WEEKLY BULLETIN
of
Hawaiian Volcano Observatory

Published at Honolulu, Hawaii, by the **Hawaiian Volcano Research Association**

Editor..............Howard M. Ballou
Professor of Physics, College of Hawaii

Application pending for entry as second-class matter at the post-office, Honolulu, Hawaii.

On March 25 jets from "Old Faithful" were few and small, but the orifices in the cone were of good size and were glowing brightly. Bright glow was seen at the west-northwest cave and in that at the northeast. Numerous small orifices were seen on the floor. Rumbling was as usual, but the sound of blowing was a trifle louder than on the previous day. Many trivial slides were heard. Blue fumes were issuing copiously from all the usual orifices, but no blue flames were seen.

Even yet no systematic earthquake report can be rendered. One earthquake strong enough to rattle gently the windows in the Observatory occurred early in the forenoon of March 25.

H. O. WOOD, Associate.

Rough Lava (aa) near the summit of Mauna Kea.

Cascade of pahoehoe, from region of Halemaumau, over walls of an area of subsidence, situated one-quarter of a mile north of present pit. Tube and bubble surface structure.

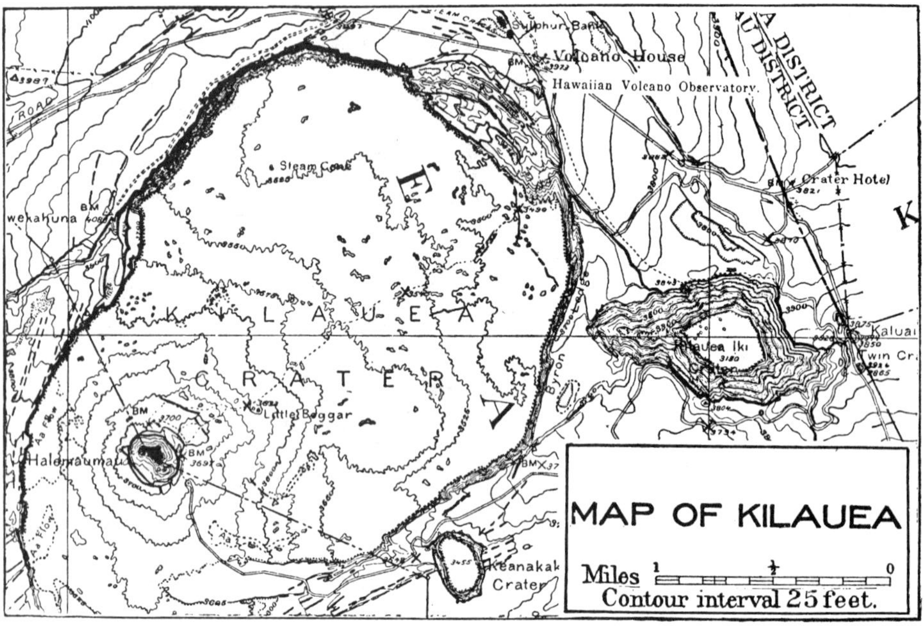

HAWAIIAN VOLCANO RESEARCH ASSOCIATION.

This society is a voluntary one, made up of subscribers to scientific work which is being executed by the Massachusetts Institute of Technology.

In 1913 there were 26 subscribers in Hawaii and Massachusetts, firms and individuals. A group of firms and persons in Hilo built the main observatory building in the spring of 1912. Publications to date have been weekly reports since the summer of 1911, a memoir by Daly in the Proceedings of American Academy of Arts and Sciences in 1911, articles by the director in the Technology Review 1911 and the Honolulu Chamber of Commerce Annual 1912, articles by H. O. Wood in the Bulletin of the Seismological Society of America, and articles by Perret in the American Journal of Science. The Massachusetts Institute of Technology will publish semi-annual reports.

This weekly bulletin as it appears in the Advertiser will be reprinted as a leaflet and sent to regular annual subscribers to the work of the association. C. H. Cooke is president of the Board of Directors of the association and R. W. Shingle is treasurer. New subscribers who are interested in our volcanoes will be welcomed in the association. The association aims: (1) To record volcanic activity and earthquakes in Hawaii; (2) to attract scientific men hither for special studies; (3) to promote the establishment of volcano observatories all over the world.

WHITNEY LABORATORY OF SEISMOLOGY.

The Whitney Laboratory of Seismology is equipped with two Bosch-Omori 100 kg tromometers registering N-S and E-W motion, a heavy Omori tromometer registering E-W motion and an Omori "ordinary Seismograph" designed for registering strong earthquakes in all three components of motion. These are seated on concrete piers in a closed basement room having practically constant temperature, beneath the chief Observatory building near the hotel. Time is referred to a rated chronometer, checked at intervals by solar observations with a transit. Both instruments are loaned by the College of Hawaii. At the substation by the edge of the active pit an Omori two-component tromometer with light steady masses is mounted on a concrete pier placed directly on the fresh lava surface. Hawaiian standard time (H. S. T.) is 10 hrs. 30 m. slower than Greenwich time.

CANCANI SCALE OF SEISMIC INTENSITY

Expressed by accelerations measured in millimeters per second per second.

I.	Instrumental	0.0	2.5
II.	Very slight	2.5	5.0
III.	Slight	5.0	10.0
IV.	Sensible, mediocre....	10.0	25.0
V.	Rather strong	25.0	50.0
VI.	Strong	50.0	100.0
VII.	Very strong	100.0	250.0
VIII.	Ruinous	250.0	500.0
IX.	Disastrous	500.0	1000.0
X.	Very disastrous	1000.0	2500.0
XI.	Catastrophic	2500.0	5000.0
XII.	Great catastrophe....	5000.0	10000.0

Grade IV. is ordinarily the minimum perceived by the senses; and in grade XII. the acceleration, or rate of change of motion (jerk) reaches that of terrestrial gravitation.

WEEKLY BULLETIN
OF
Hawaiian Volcano Observatory

Vol. II. HONOLULU, HAWAII, APRIL 15, 1914. No. 15.

From the Pacific Commercial Advertiser, Honolulu, April 5, 1914.

TECHNOLOGY STATION, Kilauea, April 2.—A lull has followed the energetic activity in the Volcano which prevailed and was increasing up to about one week ago. The week just past has been exceptionally unfavorable for eye and ear observation at Halemaumau. High winds from the southwest, with fumes, fog and rain, have prevailed much of the time. Consequently views have been fewer, and watches less prolonged, than just previously.

However, the violent up-jetting of molten lava from orifices in the floor has greatly declined; has indeed ceased almost altogether, and the blowing sound has diminished in like manner.

Despite this, all the orifices previously mentioned remain open, and through them the brightly glowing lava shines. If anything, the bottom area appears hotter. It seems merely as though the spasmodic uprush of gases had diminished. On account of the cessation of jetting the scene is less spectacular and the illumination of fumes at night less brilliant on the average.

On March 26 the weather conditions were bad for observing. In early evening brief glimpses of the usual orifices were afforded at rare intervals. No slides were heard and no flames were seen. The sound of blowing had diminished, but the rumbling was as usual. No lava jets were seen.

On March 27 violent winds from the southwest made it futile to undertake observation.

On March 28 conditions for observation were very unfavorable. No views were obtained. Small slides were heard, one under the south station lasting at least 45 seconds. The rumbling was as usual. The blowing, while diminished, was about the same as on the 26th.

On March 29 no watch was maintained, owing to bad weather, until early evening. Visitors obtained brief glimpses of the usual glowing orifices. No jets or flames were seen and no slides were heard. The noises of eruption were much the same.

On March 30 a good view of the bottom was obtained in early evening. The usual orifices were glowing brightly, but no jets were seen. The sound of blowing was very subdued. The rumbling was as usual. A few trivial slides were heard.

On March 31 no observations were undertaken, owing to unfavorable conditions for seeing.

On April first once again all the usual orifices were seen, with glowing lava showing brightly, in early evening. The brilliant appearance of the northeast, the "Old Faithful," and the west northwest orifices was particularly noted. No jets or flames were seen. The blowing was not loud. Rumbling was as usual. A few trivial slides were heard.

Owing to continued dull weather at noon no observations for the correction of time have been possible for nearly a month. In consequence of this the systematic seismic reports have necessarily been withheld. The week has been quiet seismically except that in the late afternoon, evening and early morning of March 29-30 several disturbances were recorded. One of these

WEEKLY BULLETIN
of
Hawaiian Volcano Observatory

Published at Honolulu, Hawaii, by the **Hawaiian Volcano Research Association**

Editor..............Howard M. Ballou
Professor of Physics, College of Hawaii

Application pending for entry as second-class matter at the post-office, Honolulu, Hawaii.

was the chief phase, with rudiments of earlier motion, of a distant earthquake which, while strong, was not a great shock at its origin.

Another shock was of near origin, as distinguished from local, its distance not yet determined, which was of only moderate energy—not felt in the neighborhood of the Observatory, but felt by Mr. L. A. Thurston lying in camp at a considerable altitude on the southeast slope of Mauna Loa. This was in early evening.

The other shocks, three in number, were very slight, and were strictly local earthquakes.

H. O. WOOD, Associate.

Lava Tree Moulds, Island of Hawaii.

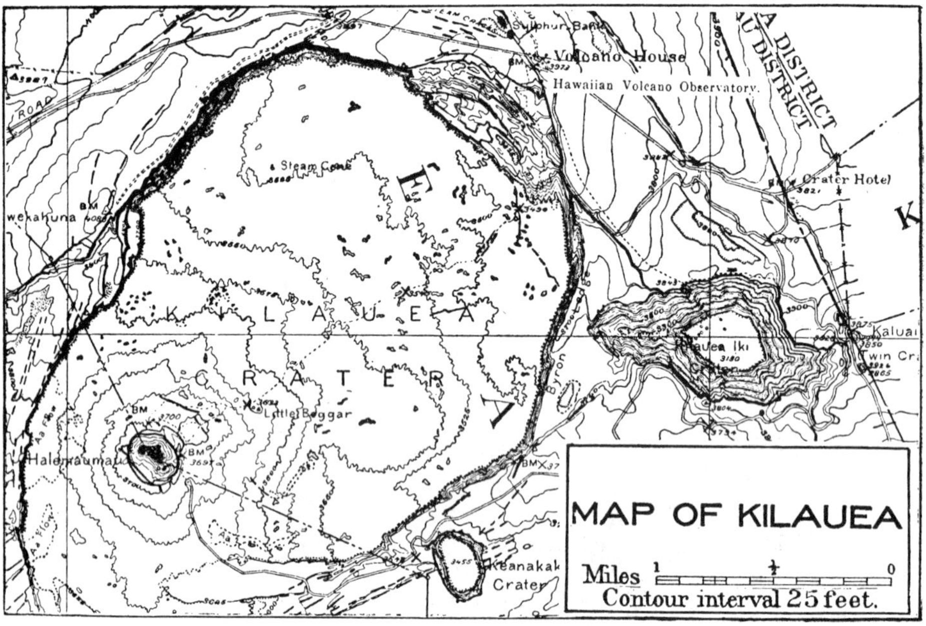

HAWAIIAN VOLCANO RESEARCH ASSOCIATION.

This society is a voluntary one, made up of subscribers to scientific work which is being executed by the Massachusetts Institute of Technology.

In 1913 there were 26 subscribers in Hawaii and Massachusetts, firms and individuals. A group of firms and persons in Hilo built the main observatory building in the spring of 1912. Publications to date have been weekly reports since the summer of 1911, a memoir by Daly in the Proceedings of American Academy of Arts and Sciences in 1911, articles by the director in the Technology Review 1911 and the Honolulu Chamber of Commerce Annual 1912, articles by H. O. Wood in the Bulletin of the Seismological Society of America, and articles by Perret in the American Journal of Science. The Massachusetts Institute of Technology will publish semi-annual reports.

This weekly bulletin as it appears in the Advertiser will be reprinted as a leaflet and sent to regular annual subscribers to the work of the association. C. H. Cooke is president of the Board of Directors of the association and R. W. Shingle is treasurer. New subscribers who are interested in our volcanoes will be welcomed in the association. The association aims: (1) To record volcanic activity and earthquakes in Hawaii; (2) to attract scientific men hither for special studies; (3) to promote the establishment of volcano observatories all over the world.

WHITNEY LABORATORY OF SEISMOLOGY.

The Whitney Laboratory of Seismology is equipped with two Bosch-Omori 100 kg tromometers registering N-S and E-W motion, a heavy Omori tromometer registering E-W motion and an Omori "ordinary Seismograph" designed for registering strong earthquakes in all three components of motion. These are seated on concrete piers in a closed basement room having practically constant temperature, beneath the chief Observatory building near the hotel. Time is referred to a rated chronometer, checked at intervals by solar observations with a transit. Both instruments are loaned by the College of Hawaii. At the substation by the edge of the active pit an Omori two-component tromometer with light steady masses is mounted on a concrete pier placed directly on the fresh lava surface. Hawaiian standard time (H. S. T.) is 10 hrs. 30 m. slower than Greenwich time.

CANCANI SCALE OF SEISMIC INTENSITY

Expressed by accelerations measured in millimeters per second per second.

I.	Instrumental	0.0	2.5
II.	Very slight	2.5	5.0
III.	Slight	5.0	10.0
IV.	Sensible, mediocre....	10.0	25.0
V.	Rather strong	25.0	50.0
VI.	Strong	50.0	100.0
VII.	Very strong	100.0	250.0
VIII.	Ruinous	250.0	500.0
IX.	Disastrous	500.0	1000.0
X.	Very disastrous	1000.0	2500.0
XI.	Catastrophic	2500.0	5000.0
XII.	Great catastrophe....	5000.0	10000.0

Grade IV. is ordinarily the minimum perceived by the senses; and in grade XII. the acceleration, or rate of change of motion (jerk) reaches that of terrestrial gravitation.

WEEKLY BULLETIN
OF
Hawaiian Volcano Observatory

Vol. II. HONOLULU, HAWAII, APRIL 22, 1914. No. 16.

From the Pacific Commercial Advertiser, Honolulu, April 12, 1914.

TECHNOLOGY STATION, KILAUEA, April 9.—Following the slight decrease noted last week, a slight increase in activity of Kilauea has been evident since that time. The orifices have slightly enlarged and jetting lava has been seen. The noises of blowing and rumbling have again increased slightly, as there have been short intervals during which these sounds were very loud. As a spectacle, however, the volcano is not so fine as it was just before the end of March. Nevertheless, though the behavior is not easy to interpret, the writer inclines to the opinion that the surface activity is still greater than at that time. The rising fumes seem much thinner during three or four days past, as noted by all accustomed to see the crater, though the phenomenon is impossible of measurement. This is considered to indicate rising temperature at the top of the magma column, a condition usually due to elevation of the column. There are more and larger orifices, and in at least two of these seething lava has been seen plainly.

Sulphur Fumes Heavy.

Also, at the east-northeast, along a system of deep cracks about 100 yards back from the rim of Halemaumau and peripheral to it, blue fumes of sulphur of a very acrid kind are issuing copiously. This phenomenon began to attract attention about the first of the year, but very recently the action has increased noticeably both in the amount of the fumes and in the degree of their acridity. No sort of quantitative measurement has been possible with our equipment, but the discomfort caused by these fumes has greatly increased within a fortnight. It is possible, of course, that this aspect of the matter is accidental.

No observations were made on April 2. Visitors reported conditions much as usual. Views of the glowing orifices were obtained, and the blowing and rumbling was as usual.

On April 3 an excellent view of the floor region disclosed new lava a little to the west of "Old Faithful," in a position suggesting that it had welled up through a fissure in the floor. The orifice at the top of the "Old Faithful" cone appeared much enlarged. At considerable intervals jets were flung out from "Old Faithful." The lava thus ejected was in large amount, but it was not thrown very high. Small jets were springing from the west cone. Glowing lava was seen in the west-northwest orifice. In all, six orifices were seen, four on the floor and two, at the west-northwest and at the north-east, at a slight elevation above it. No flames were seen. Small slides were numerous. The sound of blowing was very subdued, and even the rumbling noise was less than ordinary.

Flaring Seen From Observatory.

On April 3 boiling and seething lava was seen in the west-northwest and in the northeast orifices. For all that the blowing and rumbling was less. Jets were seen springing from "Old Faithful" and from the west cone, but small in amount and height. In addition to the six orifices seen yesterday a small

WEEKLY BULLETIN
of
Hawaiian Volcano Observatory

Published at Honolulu, Hawaii, by the **Hawaiian Volcano Research Association**

Editor..............Howard M. Ballou
Professor of Physics, College of Hawaii

Entered as second-class matter January 20, 1914, at the post-office at Honolulu, Hawaii, under the Act of August 24, 1912.

glow hole was discovered under the southwest station, about 100 feet above the floor. No flames were seen. One or two trivial slides were heard.

On April 5 no routine observations were made. The usual conditions were reported by visitors.

On April 6 conditions were as above described, except that both the blowing and the rumbling sounds were much less than common. Jets from "Old Faithful" were rare and very small. A large blue flame was seen issuing from this orifice, fluttering like a banner. Smoke concealed both the northeast and the west-northwest orifices. About midnight very bright flaring was seen from the observatory.

On April 7 in early afternoon there occurred a spasm of violent blowing; short, sharp gas blasts in quick succession, with greatly increased rumbling. This more violent phase wore away toward evening, but the sounds still remained louder than on previous days. Smoke concealed the west-northwest and northeast orifices. Small jets were thrown from "Old Faithful." No flames could be seen. Several small slides occurred.

On April 8 conditions remained without significant change. Blowing and rumbling had decreased slightly in loudness. No lava jets were seen, though incandescent lava could be seen plainly in the usual orifices. No flames were seen. Small slides occurred frequently.

Seismically the week has passed uneventfully.

H. O. WOOD, Associate.

Part of the Crater of Haleakala, Maui.

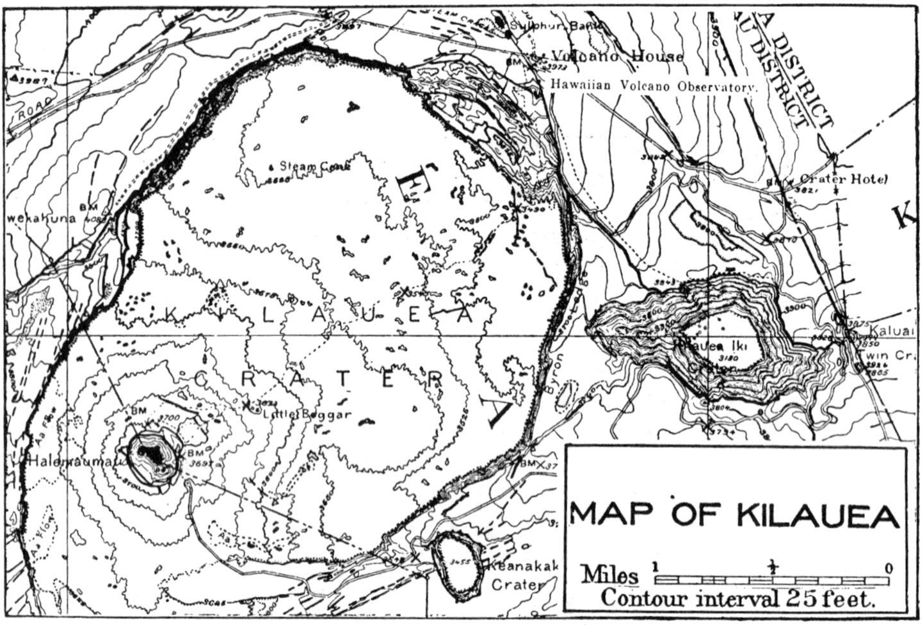

HAWAIIAN VOLCANO RESEARCH ASSOCIATION.

This society is a voluntary one, made up of subscribers to scientific work which is being executed by the Massachusetts Institute of Technology.

In 1913 there were 26 subscribers in Hawaii and Massachusetts, firms and individuals. A group of firms and persons in Hilo built the main observatory building in the spring of 1912. Publications to date have been weekly reports since the summer of 1911, a memoir by Daly in the Proceedings of American Academy of Arts and Sciences in 1911, articles by the director in the Technology Review 1911 and the Honolulu Chamber of Commerce Annual 1912, articles by H. O. Wood in the Bulletin of the Seismological Society of America, and articles by Perret in the American Journal of Science. The Massachusetts Institute of Technology will publish semi-annual reports.

This weekly bulletin as it appears in the Advertiser will be reprinted as a leaflet and sent to regular annual subscribers to the work of the association. C. H. Cooke is president of the Board of Directors of the association and R. W. Shingle is treasurer. New subscribers who are interested in our volcanoes will be welcomed in the association. The association aims: (1) To record volcanic activity and earthquakes in Hawaii; (2) to attract scientific men hither for special studies; (3) to promote the establishment of volcano observatories all over the world.

WHITNEY LABORATORY OF SEISMOLOGY.

The Whitney Laboratory of Seismology is equipped with two Bosch-Omori 100 kg tromometers registering N-S and E-W motion, a heavy Omori tromometer registering E-W motion and an Omori "ordinary Seismograph" designed for registering strong earthquakes in all three components of motion. These are seated on concrete piers in a closed basement room having practically constant temperature, beneath the chief Observatory building near the hotel. Time is referred to a rated chronometer, checked at intervals by solar observations with a transit. Both instruments are loaned by the College of Hawaii. At the substation by the edge of the active pit an Omori two-component tromometer with light steady masses is mounted on a concrete pier placed directly on the fresh lava surface. Hawaiian standard time (H. S. T.) is 10 hrs. 30 m. slower than Greenwich time.

CANCANI SCALE OF SEISMIC INTENSITY

Expressed by accelerations measured in millimeters per second per second.

I.	Instrumental	0.0	2.5
II.	Very slight	2.5	5.0
III.	Slight	5.0	10.0
IV.	Sensible, mediocre....	10.0	25.0
V.	Rather strong	25.0	50.0
VI.	Strong	50.0	100.0
VII.	Very strong	100.0	250.0
VIII.	Ruinous	250.0	500.0
IX.	Disastrous	500.0	1000.0
X.	Very disastrous	1000.0	2500.0
XI.	Catastrophic	2500.0	5000.0
XII.	Great catastrophe....	5000.0	10000.0

Grade IV. is ordinarily the minimum perceived by the senses; and in grade XII. the acceleration, or rate of change of motion (jerk) reaches that of terrestrial gravitation.

WEEKLY BULLETIN
OF
Hawaiian Volcano Observatory

Vol. II. HONOLULU, HAWAII, APRIL 29, 1914. No. 17.

From the Pacific Commercial Advertiser, Honolulu, April 23, 1914.

TECHNOLOGY STATION, Kilauea, April 16.—Since the last writing there has been a steady increase in activity at Kilauea, manifested by an increase in the size and the apparent hotness of the glowing orifices, by increased loudness in blowing and rumbling, and by jet action.

On April 9 a strong wind prevented seeing. Puffing, blowing and rumbling were as usual, and trivial slides were heard.

On April 10 no visit was made to the pit on account of an exceptionally strong S. W. wind, accompanied by fog and light rain.

On April 11 seething lava was seen in the W.N.W. orifice, above which wavered a blue flame. At intervals the puffing sounds, chiefly from "Old Faithful," were quite loud. Lumps of molten lava were flung from "Old Faithful" and from the cone under the southeast station. Blue flames were issuing from a subsidiary orifice in the "Old Faithful" cone. In all, nine glowing orifices were visible. Many trivial slides took place, some lasting for 30 seconds. The rumbling sound was loud.

On April 12 the orifices showed distinct enlargement. Molten lava was surging about, making a distinct rushing sound in addition to the louder blowing, puffing and rumbling noises. Seething lava was seen in "Old Faithful" and especially in the W.N.W. orifice, now almost large enough to be called a pool, where in early evening a miniature flow was poured out. The illumination of the walls and the rising fumes was highly spectacular. At long intervals blue flames flashed above 'Old Faithful." No jets were seen and no slides worth mention were noted.

On April 13 a good view of the W.N.W. center of activity was obtained where several orifices are now clustered; the larger, almost a pool, exhibited seething lava and blue flames. The sounds of blowing and rumbling were louder, but good views of "Old Faithful" and of the southeast cone did not disclose any jet action. Trivial rock falls occurred.

On April 14 jet action had begun again at the "Old Faithful" orifice but nowhere else. Blowing and rumbling was still louder than on the previous day. No flames were seen. No slides were heard. Swirling fumes prevented clear views so that the larger orifices were not seen.

On April 15 excellent views showed seething lava in the W.N.W. orifice into which loose talus was seen to be sliding—some of the slides lasting 40 seconds. Many trivial slides took place. Rumbling and blowing was very loud in the early evening, but jet action was not observed until later, when "sparks" were flung up from the southeast cone. In mid-evening the "Old Faithful" cone collapsed, making a large orifice where splashing lava was visible, thus greatly augmenting the illumination of the walls and fumes.

WEEKLY BULLETIN
of
Hawaiian Volcano Observatory

Published at Honolulu, Hawaii, by the **Hawaiian Volcano Research Association**

Editor..............Howard M. Ballou
Professor of Physics, College of Hawaii

Entered as second-class matter January 20, 1914, at the post-office at Honolulu, Hawaii, under the Act of August 24, 1912.

Observations for the correction of time now permit the following systematic report from the Whitney Laboratory of Seismology, a report delayed for some weeks by adverse weather. Earthquake shocks have been registered as follows:

February 27, from 11:55:14 a. m. to 11:56:04 a. m. H. S. T. Intensity, II Cancani scale; 35 to 50 per cent of the minimum perceptible unit. Origin distant about 13 miles.

February 28, from 8:32:59 a. m. to 8:34:04 a. m. H. S. T. Intensity, III Cancani scale; above 78 per cent of the minimum perceptible unit. Origin distant about 12 miles.

February 28, from 10:04:07 a. m. to 10:05:44 a. m. H. S. T. Intensity III Cancani scale; 90 to 120 per cent of the minimum perceptible unit. Origin distant about 12 miles.

March 1, beginning about 9:22:03 a. m. H. S. T. a shock strong enough to throw the recording pens from the cylinders. The shock was not felt, but it caused the windows to rattle. Owing to its strength the records are defective and further information cannot be derived from them.

March 3, from 7:37:43 a. m. to 7:39:47 a. m. H. S. T. Intensity, II Cancani scale; 30 to 50 per cent of the minimum perceptible unit. Origin distant about 24 miles.

March 4, from 2:15:28 p. m. to 2:18:08 p. m. H. S. T. Intensity, III-IV Cancani scale; greater than the minimum perceptible unit, but not sensible at the Observatory. Origin distant about 5.6 miles.

March 5, from 1:43:28 a. m. to 1:43:59 a. m. H. S. T. Intensity, III-IV Cancani scale; greater than the minimum perceptible unit, but not noticed at the Observatory. Origin distant about 5 miles.

March 8, from 2:07:55 a. m. to 2:09:33 a. m. H. S. T. Intensity, about VI Cancani scale; several times the minimum perceptible unit; wakened one sleeping person. Origin distant about 6.8 miles.

March 8, from 2:33:18 p. m. to 2:33:58 p. m. H. S. T. Intensity, II Cancani scale; about 45 per cent of the minimum perceptible unit. Origin distance is indeterminate.

March 10, from 5:15:40 p. m. to 5:17:31 p. m. H. S. T. Intensity, II-III Cancani scale; less than 60 per cent of the minimum perceptible unit. Origin distant less than 4 miles.

March 21, from 1:21:57 a. m. to 1:24:17 a. m. H. S. T. Intensity, I Cancani scale; about 20 per cent of the minimum perceptible unit. Origin distance indeterminate.

March 25, beginning about 9:38:05 a. m., a shock strong enough barely to be felt at the Observatory; on account of its strength the records are defective and yield no further information. Intensity, probably VII Cancani scale; from 10 to 12 times the minimum perceptible unit.

March 25, from 11:25:07 a. m. to 11:26:56 a. m. H. S. T. Intensity, low I Cancani scale; about 8 per cent of the minimum perceptible unit. Origin distant about 37 miles.

March 25, from 7:49:41 p. m. to 7:50:18 p. m. H. S. T. Intensity, III Cancani scale; about 60 per cent of the minimum perceptible unit. Origin distant about 32 miles.

March 25, from 8:46:00 p. m. to 8:47:47 p. m. H. S. T. Intensity, low I Cancani scale; about 6 per cent of the minimum perceptible unit. Origin distant about 31 miles.

March 26, from 5:44:01 a. m. to 5:44:44 a. m. H. S. T. Intensity, high II Cancani scale; about 45 per cent of the minimum perceptible unit. Origin distant about 33.5 miles.

March 26, from 5:01:55 p. m. to 5:02:32 p. m. H. S. T. Intensity, low III Cancani scale; about 60 per cent of the minimum perceptible unit. Origin distant about 13.7 miles.

March 26, from 5:06:30 p. m. to 5:06:34 p. m. H. S. T. Intensity, medium II Cancani scale; about 40 per cent of the minimum perceptible unit. Origin distance indeterminate.

March 26, from 5:06:49 p. m. to 5:07:42 p. m. H. S. T. Intensity, low IV Cancani scale; a little above the minimum porceptible unit, but not noticed at the Observatory. Origin distant about 13 miles.

March 27, from 5:47 a. m. to 5:57 a. m. there was registered a portion of the chief phase of a distant earthquake. Nothing could be made out concerning either the distance or the energy of this earthquake.

March 29, from 2:27 p. m. until later than 3:00 p. m. waves of the chief phase of a distant earthquake were registered. The origin distance of this shock could not be determined; but it could be seen that it was only a moderate strong shock.

March 29, from 3:47:41 p. m. to 3:49:34 p. m. H. S. T. Intensity, low I Cancani scale; about 14 per cent of the minimum perceptible unit. Origin distant about 14 miles.

March 29, from 8:04:12 p. m. to 8:12:53 p. m. H. S. T. Intensity, at Observatory, IV Cancani scale; about 1.5 times the minimum perceptible unit, though unnoticed here, probably owing to occupation and inattention. Origin distant about 180 miles. Felt on the southeast flank of Mauna Loa, and more strongly on Maui and Oahu.

March 29, from 11:08:27 p. m. to 11:09:13 p. m. H. S. T. Intensity, low I Cancani scale; about 9.5 per cent of the minimum perceptible unit. Origin distance indeterminate.

March 30, from 10:19:54 a. m. to 10:20:34 a. m. H. S. T. Intensity, low I Cancani scale; about 8 per cent of the minimum perceptible unit. Origin distant about 8 miles.

April 3, from 10:30:17 p. m. to 10:31:32 p. m. H. S. T. Intensity, III-IV Cancani scale; about the minimum perceptible unit, but not noticed at the Observatory. Origin distant about 12 miles.

April 4, from 8:14:15 a. m. to 8:15:50 a. m. H. S. T. Intensity, high I Cancani scale; about 19 per cent of the minimum perceptible unit. Origin distant about 12 miles.

April 4, from 7:06:21 p. m. to 7:07:37 p. m. H .S. T. Intensity, III-IV Cancani scale; about the minimum perceptible unit, but not felt at the Observatory. Origin distant about 14 miles.

April 6, from 3:20:35 p. m. to 3:21:22 p. m. H. S. T. Intensity, II Cancani scale; about 35 per cent of the minimum perceptible unit. Origin distant about 13 miles.

April 9, from 3:13:56 p. m. to 3:14:30 p. m. H. S. T. Intensity, high III Cancani scale; 80 to 90 per cent of the minimum perceptible unit. Origin distant about 12 miles.

April 12, from 11:27:36 p. m. to 11:28:24 p. m. H. S. T. Intensity, low III Cancani scale; about 60 per cent of the minimum perceptible unit. Origin distant a little over 11 miles.

April 13, from 00:48:23 a. m. to 00:49:01 a. m. H. S. T. Intensity, medium III Cancani scale; about 70 per cent of the minimum perceptible unit. Origin distant about 14.3 miles.

April 13, from 4:15:37 a. m. to 4:17:08 a. m. H. S. T. Intensity, IV Cancani scale; a little above the minimum perceptible unit, but not noticed at the Observatory. Origin distant about 29 miles.

April 13, from 1:01:58 p. m. to 1:03:03 p. m. H. S. T. Intensity, high II Cancani scale; about 40 per cent of the minimum perceptible unit. Origin distant about 10.6 miles.

April 13, from 9:58:37 p. m. to 9:31:31 p. m. H. S. T. Intensity, IV Cancani scale; a little over the minimum perceptible unit; barely, and at the time doubtfully, felt here. Origin distant about 30 miles.

April 15, from 1:57:28 a. m. to 1:50:52 a. m. H. S. T. Intensity, IV Cancani scale; a little above the minimum perceptible unit, but not noticed at the Observatory. Origin distant about 13.7 miles.

H. O. WOOD, Associate.

From the Pacific Commercial Advertiser, Honolulu, April 19, 1914.

HONOLULU, April 15, 1914.—In continuation of the report published in The Advertiser March 24, 1914, I have to conclude my narrative of the journey authorized by the Hawaiian Volcano Research Association with some account of visits made to the volcanoes Kirishimayama, Asosan and Bandaisan and of cooperation started with Dr. Omori in the construction of certain earthquake instruments for general use by amateurs in Hawaii.

February 9 to February 24 I remained in Kagoshima and vicinity. I then went to Miya on the high slopes of Kirishima volcano, the eastern peak of which contains an active and somewhat dangerous vent which has destroyed life and property in the past. A Frenchman was wounded and his guide killed by flying stones here only a few years ago, so that it is sometimes difficult to get anyone to accompany the traveler to the summit. Fortunately just at present Kirishima is quiet, and I secured a guide and made the ascent to the crater on the afternoon of February 25. A great explosion took place November 8 last, which left a magnificent bread-crust bomb twelve feet in diameter on the edge. I looked down into a quietly steaming cauldron, with an inner circular black cavity, while outside of the high cone on the west was an extraordinary scour-gulch produced by volcanic avalanches accompanying recent eruptions. Gigantic boulders were buried and half-buried in the ground, or split in fragments about the depressions made by their fall.

The next day we crossed Kirishima past the middle and western peaks of the volcanic mass, which is as a whole a dome more than fifteen miles long crowned by cinder cones somewhat like Mauna Kea, and rising to a summit 1700 meters above sea-level. The whole mountain shows ash sections everywhere, indicating that explosive eruption has been dominant in its later upbuilding.

The eruption of November, 1913, was followed by others December 9, and January 8, and then came the Sakurajima outburst January 12, which seems to have relieved the subterranean region of Kirishima so that the latter became quiet. The eruptive activity appears to be migrating southward, for in February the volcano island Iwojima still farther south in the Luchu chain broke out, and then about March 20 another volcano on the island Suwanose in the same line and more to the southward began exploding. The sequence was remarkable and the suggestion strong that some volcano still farther in the direction of Formosa might be heard from in April. All this activity in the Luchus must be relieving the magma of the under-earth at Kagoshima, and is favorable for an early cessation of the explosions and lava-flow at Sakurajima.

Asosan was reached and the active craters studied February 28. This volcano is intensely active as a cauldron of boiling mud and steam, and has been explosively active many times since the eleventh century, with culminations of lava activity in the fourteenth century, and of ash and lava in the seventeenth, eighteenth and nineteenth centuries.

The last considerable eruptions were from 1906 to 1908. Asosan has the reputation of being an ash volcano and of having the largest crater in Japan, and so of being "Japan's greatest volcano."

On close acquaintance several things about Asosan surprised me. Lava makes up the greater part of the dome, and is in evidence abundantly on the very summit and about the active vents, appearing as recent flows in the vicinity of the four active pits. Two of these pits contain warm lakes, and two are boiling violently, with hundreds of tails of white vapor rising with a roar from the bottom, three to four hundred feet down, amid pools of fountaining black mud. It is a mixed volcano, with both ash and lava in its structure, and very much lava.

As to its being "Japan's greatest

volcano,'' I think that conclusion is questionable. Its highest peak is only 1500 meters high. There is an outer ring of cliffs of elliptical plan with greatest diameter fourteen miles. This is called the ''great crater.'' It is a collapsed dome of heavy lava flows, such as Kilauea would become if merged with Kilauea Iki and Keanakakoi, and general collapse took place back of the Volcano House, so as to make the crater say ten by fourteen miles in dimensions. Then in Asosan four rugged inner volcanic mountains have been built up, and the active crater is a row of pits within one of these. The outer wall is in some sense a ''crater'' doubtless, just as the Nuuanu Pali is, but we can hardly gauge the size of volcanoes by the size of the hole made when they cave in or collapse.

The same mistake has been made by those who claim that the Plinian ''crater'' of Vesuvius in the year 79 A.D., when Pompeii was destroyed, can be reconstructed by prolonging Monte Somma circularly. Indeed in that case there is no evidence that the 79 crater was not within the present active cone. The resemblance of Asosan to Kilauea or Mauna Loa, partially buried under mixed accumulations, is striking, and leads one to wonder whether all volcanoes, could we dissect them, would not be found to possess a Kilauea for pediment.

I returned to Nagasaki March 2 and met there Mr. Frank A. Perret on his way to Kagoshima. He was at Kagoshima through March, and was slightly injured by exploding lava. He expects to come to Hawaii about May 1 and to visit again our volcanoes.

My next objective was Bandaisan, in northern Honshu, which I reached March 22, after visits to all the larger cities to collect copies of newspapers and of newspaper photographs dealing with the early days of the Sakurajima eruption. Bandaisan is on a line of active volcanoes in the central region of Japan, north of Tokyo, and is famous as the scene of a terrific explosion in July, 1888, when the whole north side of the mountain was blown out, and rocks and earth filled up deep basins and valleys, flowed miles, and dammed drainage to produce numerous large lakes. Several hundred persons were killed and villages engulfed or swept away. The eruption was said to be from the end mountain of a group, to have exhibited no lava, and to be purely a steam explosion. These statements all seem to me questionable after seeing and exploring Bandai and its crater.

It is an isolated distinct volcano, surrounded by valleys and lowlands. There are scattered fragments of porous black lava, like complete units of an a-a surface, to be found here and there in the debris of the avalanche. The gases now rushing from the solfataras in the crater are full of sulphur, and at 205° Fahr., somewhat above the boiling point for that altitude (1100 meters), and hence it seems probable that they were much hotter and contained much besides water when the great eruption occurred. There is ample evidence in the topography that similar eruptions have occurred at Bandaisan before, and I believe the ''avalanche-explosion'' habit of this volcano to be merely a stage of decadence of volcanic activity more advanced than Sakurajima, but occasioned by the same under-mechanism of a rising lava surcharged with gas.

My adventures in the Bandaisan crater were somewhat Arctic, as there were eight-foot snowdrifts partially crusted and occasional rock avalanches occasioned by the war of snow and ice with hot vapors. Also there was dense fog, and my guides lost their way, so that we had to steer out of the snowy wilderness with the aid of the compass needle. Also there was much rain and some snowfall, but in the course of a four-day trip we saw enough and secured enough photographs to reward us for the journey. I had with me for interpreter Suito, a Japanese photographer, who rendered efficient service.

From March 26 to April 4 I gave much time to conferences with Professor Omori, chief of the imperial earthquake investigation committee of Japan. It has long seemed desirable to have a seismograph available for voluntary observers in Hawaii, which they would buy as they might a barograph, and which would record with ink the time and relative intensity of ordinary earthquakes. Such an instrument we drew up a design for, with the aid of Mr. Mitsubori, chief engineer of the Educational Appliance Company of Tokyo.

A sample instrument is to be made and tested by Doctor Omori, and if satisfactory some of the instruments will be sent to our observatory and distributed in Kona, Kau, Hilo and Kohala. It is to be a horizontal pendulum, portable, with a twenty-four-hour drum wound with white paper rolled from a spool. The magnifying lever will write with ink on the paper, and minute and hour marks will be pricked in the paper parallel to the pendulum record. The magnification will be from fifty to seventy-five times the earth movement to be recorded. It is expected that the cost of the instrument will be under fifty dollars. If successful this instrument should fill a need long felt in places like California, where it is of the utmost interest to know what small earth movements take place locally and to know with some accuracy the time, number and intensity of such movements, apart from hearsay or the sensitiveness of individuals.

I sailed from Yokohama on the Manchuria April 6, arriving at Honolulu April 15, 1914.

T. A. JAGGAR, JR.,
Director.

Kagoshima and Sakurajima, January 14, the volcano in active eruption.

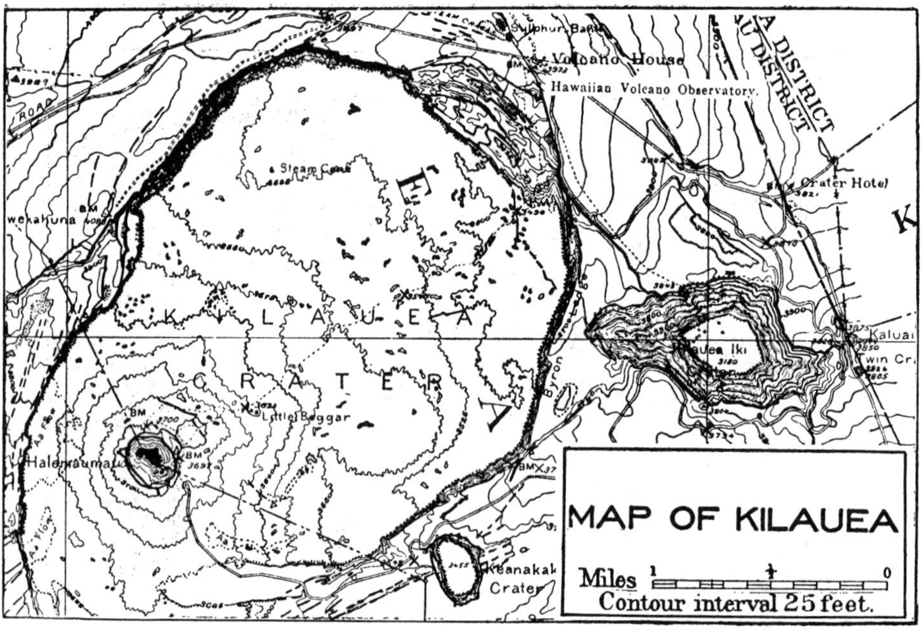

HAWAIIAN VOLCANO RESEARCH ASSOCIATION.

This society is a voluntary one, made up of subscribers to scientific work which is being executed by the Massachusetts Institute of Technology.

In 1913 there were 26 subscribers in Hawaii and Massachusetts, firms and individuals. A group of firms and persons in Hilo built the main observatory building in the spring of 1912. Publications to date have been weekly reports since the summer of 1911, a memoir by Daly in the Proceedings of American Academy of Arts and Sciences in 1911, articles by the director in the Technology Review 1911 and the Honolulu Chamber of Commerce Annual 1912, articles by H. O. Wood in the Bulletin of the Seismological Society of America, and articles by Perret in the American Journal of Science. The Massachusetts Institute of Technology will publish semiannual reports.

This weekly bulletin as it appears in the Advertiser will be reprinted as a leaflet and sent to regular annual subscribers to the work of the association. C. H. Cooke is president of the Board of Directors of the association and R. W. Shingle is treasurer. New subscribers who are interested in our volcanoes will be welcomed in the association. The association aims: (1) To record volcanic activity and earthquakes in Hawaii; (2) to attract scientific men hither for special studies; (3) to promote the establishment of volcano observatories all over the world.

WHITNEY LABORATORY OF SEISMOLOGY.

The Whitney Laboratory of Seismology is equipped with two Bosch-Omori 100 kg tromometers registering N-S and E-W motion, a heavy Omori tromometer registering E-W motion and an Omori "ordinary Seismograph" designed for registering strong earthquakes in all three components of motion. These are seated on concrete piers in a closed basement room having practically constant temperature, beneath the chief Observatory building near the hotel. Time is referred to a rated chronometer, checked at intervals by solar observations with a transit. Both instruments are loaned by the College of Hawaii. At the substation by the edge of the active pit an Omori two-component tromometer with light steady masses is mounted on a concrete pier placed directly on the fresh lava surface. Hawaiian standard time (H. S. T.) is 10 hrs. 30 m. slower than Greenwich time.

CANCANI SCALE OF SEISMIC INTENSITY

Expressed by accelerations measured in millimeters per second per second.

I.	Instrumental	0.0	2.5
II.	Very slight	2.5	5.0
III.	Slight	5.0	10.0
IV.	Sensible, mediocre....	10.0	25.0
V.	Rather strong	25.0	50.0
VI.	Strong	50.0	100.0
VII.	Very strong	100.0	250.0
VIII.	Ruinous	250.0	500.0
IX.	Disastrous	500.0	1000.0
X.	Very disastrous	1000.0	2500.0
XI.	Catastrophic	2500.0	5000.0
XII.	Great catastrophe....	5000.0	10000.0

Grade IV. is ordinarily the minimum perceived by the senses; and in grade XII. the acceleration, or rate of change of motion (jerk) reaches that of terrestrial gravitation.

WEEKLY BULLETIN
OF
Hawaiian Volcano Observatory

Vol. II. HONOLULU, HAWAII, MAY 6, 1914. No. 18.

From the Pacific Commercial Advertiser, Honolulu, April 27, 1914.

TECHNOLOGY STATION, KILAUEA, April 23. — During much of the past week conditions for observing at Kilauea have been unfavorable. However, another halt in the increase of energy of eruption has occurred. For four or five days past the noises of eruption, and all the visible manifestations, have been undergoing sporadic increase and decrease either side of the condition reached on Saturday, April 18, as an average or stage of reference. There is no reason to think that any quasi-permanent diminution in eruptivity has occurred. The condition appears merely to be one of the customary lulls.

On April 16 continual small jets of lava were seen to spout from ''Old Faithful'' and blue flames played above it; and boiling magma was seen plainly in the west-northwest orifice, out of which small jets were seen to spring at considerable intervals. Incandescent lava was seen in the openings of all the cones hitherto described, being particularly brilliant in the northeast orifice. Also a new, brightly glowing orifice was seen about fifty feet above the bottom of the pit at the west-southwest.

The noise of rumbling was very loud. Blowing and rushing sounds were produced frequently and were of much volume, but were somewhat lacking in harshness and intensity. An unusually large number of medium-sized talus slides occurred, many of which lasted for nearly a minute. Most of these plunged down into the large west-northwest orifice, causing the magma there to surge and splash. During the previous twenty-four hours a great deal of readjustment in the talus materials had taken place, in consequence of which the southeast cone was nearly buried. All things considered the activity on this date was greater than at any other time thus far during the present revival of eruption.

On April 17, so far as could be ascertained, the conditions of eruption were almost as on the previous day, but the rising fumes were kept aswirl by a fresh wind, so that no really good view was obtained. Sounds of blowing and rumbling were little if any diminished, and the fumes were brilliantly illuminated in the neighborhood of the larger orifices, particularly at the west-northwest. A brief view of ''Old Faithful'' showed the action there to be as on the day before. Only a few talus slides were heard.

On April 18 there was little if any further diminution in the intensity of the phenomena. Flaring, for instance, seen from the Observatory, was very brilliant, but no jets were visible at the pitside. Swirling fumes prevented any but brief glimpses, during which the conditions seen were much as on previous days. However, throughout the hours devoted to observation talus slides were occurring almost continuously, and many of them were of prolonged duration. Nevertheless it is considered that no fresh rock was dislodged, but merely an extensive readjustment of the loose material brought about.

On April 19, in the forenoon, swirling fumes prevented views, but noises

WEEKLY BULLETIN
of
Hawaiian Volcano Observatory

Published at Honolulu, Hawaii, by the **Hawaiian Volcano Research Association**

Editor..............Howard M. Ballou
Professor of Physics, College of Hawaii

Entered as second-class matter January 20, 1914, at the post-office at Honolulu, Hawaii, under the Act of August 24, 1912.

of rock-fall and the blowing and rumbling sounds of eruption were plainly heard, as also was the case in early afternoon. But as the afternoon wore on all sounds decreased and the interval separating eruptive spasms increased until in early evening no noises could be heard and nothing could be seen—not even a faint illumination of the fumes, which were eddying violently, not even in the neighborhood of the orifices. It was feared that a collapse had occurred.

On April 20, however, brief and poor views in early evening through the fumes revealed incandescent lava in the chief orifices, "Old Faithful," the west-northwest and the northeast orifices. The usual rumbling-sounds were audible, little if any subdued, but the blowing sound was faint and low. Probably the conspicuous readjustments in the talus during the day or two previous had the effect of choking the vent and of depressing the temperature of the top of the magma column. The fume cloud, seen from the Observatory, was definitely illuminated at night, with feeble flaring.

On April 21 conditions for observing were so unfavorable that no visit was made to the pit. At night the fume cloud was seen to be faintly but definitely illuminated, with feeble flaring.

On April 22 nothing could be seen on account of high winds and eddying fumes. The rumbling was as usual and the blowing noise was again very loud. At night blinding rain shut out the view of the pit from the Observatory.

No noteworthy seismic action has been recorded since the last report, merely two or three exceptionally small shocks. On these no systematic report can be made this week.

H. O. WOOD, Associate.

Minutes of the Meetings of the Board of Directors.

The third meeting of the Board, called by direction of Pres. C. H. Cooke, was held at the University Club, Tuesday, April 28, 1914, at 12 m.

Present: Messrs. Cooke, Castle, Lewis, and E. M. Campbell, representing R. W. Shingle, directors; H. M. Ballou, secretary; Dr. T. A. Jaggar, Jr., and T. Clive Davies.

Dr. T. A. Jaggar, Jr., presented the following report concerning his expedition to Japan, which was accepted and ordered to be printed.

To the Directors, Hawaiian Volcano Research Association.

Gentlemen:—Concerning my trip to Japan I have already reported in the Bulletins published in the Advertiser. I have in preparation a longer article with eighty illustrations to be sent on approval to the National Geographic Society. Last week I addressed four audiences in Honolulu on different phases of the Japan work.

I brought back a full note-book, and purchases in Japan for the observatory to the amount of $362.80. These include two light transits for crater surveys, between 400 and 500 photographs, a dozen charts, a number of new books, a nearly complete set of Transactions of the Seismological Society of Japan 1880-1894, about 800 feet of moving picture film of the Sakurajima eruption, 109 colored lantern slides from my own and other photographs, and files of Japanese and English journals dealing with Sakurajima. I also collected specimens on Sakurajima and three other volcanoes, and took photographs. I obtained a small model of Fujiyama and specimens from Vries Island. Dr. Omori gave me for the Observatory a list of all the publications of the Earthquake Investigation Committee of Japan, and on my checking the list, will make our set complete of both English and Japanese publications.

I trust that my visit to Japan will stimulate the Japanese to the establishment of more volcano observatories. A temporary observatory has been started on Sakurajima, and for some years an observatory has been in operation on Asama, but only during the summer months.

Dr. Omori is cooperating with me in having some new instruments made in Tokyo, for the use of voluntary observers in recording local earthquakes.

Mr. F. A. Perret is expected in Honolulu April 29th,* by the Mongolia from Japan, where he too has been studying Sakurajima, and I hope he will be with us here for some weeks. He plans to visit our volcano. He has with him, I think, lantern slides of his recent studies of Stromboli and Etna, and I hope he will give a lecture, the proceeds of which should be devoted to the benefit of his work.

The treasurer will show you the present condition of the finances of the Association. The Japan trip will not burden the Association at all. Ten subscribers subscribed for this expedition $770, all paid. My travelling expenses cost $802.60, and I made purchases in addition to the amount of $362.80. No portion of the travelling expenses will be charged to the Association, and it would appear at present as though the Association could well afford these purchases, to judge from the estimated income and expenditures for the year.

There appears to me to be urgent need for action on the part of the membership and finance committees in recruiting new patrons and members. I ask permission myself to devote some months to steady writing of reports for publication, for this is all-important, and we are backward in this work.

It will be of interest to the Directors to know that the first part of a new and great work ''Der Vulkanismus,'' by Professor Wolff, has just appeared in Germany; that Dr. Friedlaender has established his Volcanologic Institute in Naples with his own money, put up a great stone laboratory, and begun the publication of a Journal of Volcanology.

With regard to the Japanese Earthquake Investigation Committee, I made careful inquiry of Dr. Omori in Tokyo, as to ways and means, and learned that he possesses extraordinary advantages due to low cost of labor: he has the direction of an appropriation of about $9000 from the Earthquake Committee; but his plant is part of the University and he holds a professorship there. He can get extra appropriations of about $1500 when he takes a trip for the inspection of a disaster, as to San Francisco in 1906. He has to do no systematic recording, as that is all done by the weather bureau stations, 135 of them in Japan, and some 1500 voluntary observers. He has at his own station 19 instruments. His staff includes one assistant professor, 5 scientific assistants at about $20 per month, 4 skilled workmen at about $12 per month, and he can publish a large memoir with 60 plates in color and collotype for $450! His assistants include a draughtsman, an instrument man, a computer, a photographer, a woodworker, a machinist and a bookkeeper. He also has expert associates, university professors, who give their services to the Earthquake Committee free.

Splendid collotype work is done in Japan and I believe that, even with the duty added, illustrations could be made there better and cheaper than anywhere else, for publications here.

Very respectfully,

T. A. JAGGAR, JR.,
Director.

The Treasurer's report from January 1 to April 28 was read, accepted, and ordered placed on file.

On motion of Mr. Lewis it was voted that all patrons and officers of the Association be enrolled among the members, and that a firm contributing as a patron shall have the right to designate one of its members to be so enrolled.

On motion of the Secretary the following contributors, having been unanimously approved by the Membership Committee, were elected members of the Association.

* Prof. Perret did not arrive as expected.

Members of Hawaiian Volcano Research Association.

Mrs. B. M. Allen,
Mr. Carl B. Andrews,
Mr. R. W. Andrews,
Mr. Chas. H. Atherton,
Mr. F. C. Atherton,
Prof. Howard M. Ballou,
Dr. W. D. Baldwin,
Mr. Chester E. Blacow,
Mr. A. W. T. Bottomley,
Mr. Cecil Brown,
Prof. W. A. Bryan,
Mr. G. F. Bush,
Mr. J. W. Caldwell,
Mr. A. N. Campbell,
Mr. J. C. Cannon,
Mr. Geo. R. Carter,
Mr. Bruce Cartwright, Jr.,
Mr. Alfred L. Castle,
Mr. Geo. P. Castle,
Mrs. Geo. P. Castle,
Mr. J. B. Castle,
Mr. W. R. Castle,
Mr. Robt. Catton,
Mrs. H. C. Coleman,
Mr. A. F. Cooke,
Mr. Clarence M. Cooke,
Prof. R. A. Daly,
Mr. T. Clive Davies,
Hon. Sanford B. Dole.
Mr. Jas. D. Dole,
Dr. N. B. Emerson,
Mr. W. L. Emory,
Mr. Wm. C. Furer,
Prof. A. F. Griffiths,
Mr. J. F. Hackfeld,
Mr. J. F. C. Hagens,
Prof. C. H. Hitchcock,
Mr. Henry Holmes,
Dr. T. A. Jaggar, Jr.,
Mr. P. C. Jones,
Hon. Albert F. Judd,
Mr. F. A. Klamp,
Mr. C. H. Kluegel,
Mr. A. Lewis, Jr.,
Mr. Wm. A. Love,
Dr. A. Marques,
Mrs. E. M. O. Marques,
Mr. Benj. L. Marx,
Mr. Jas. L. McLean,
Dr. Iga Mori,
Mr. Wm. C. Parke,
Dr. J. S. B. Pratt,
Mrs. E. K. Pratt,
Mr. J. L. P. Robinson,
Mr. Mark P. Robinson,
Mr. Georg Rodiek,
Dr. W. G. Rogers,
Mr. F. A. Schaefer,
Mr. R. W. Shingle,
Mr. W. O. Smith,
Mrs. Edw. I. Spalding,
Mr. Walter T. Spalding,
Mr. F. M. Swanzy,
Hon. Wade Warren Thayer,
Mr. L. A. Thurston,
Mrs. Harriet P. Thurston,
Mr. Ed Towse,
Mr. James Wakefield,
Mr. J. W. Waldron,
Mr. Walter E. Wall,
Mrs. Edward E. Waters,
Mr. Norman Watkins,
Rev. Wm. D. Westervelt,
Mrs. W. D. Westervelt,
Master Andrew C. Westervelt,
Mr. Jas. A. Wilder,
Mr. J. N. S. Williams,
Mr. H. O. Wood,
Mr. H. P. Wood,
Mr. D. L. Withington,
Prof. John M. Young,

HOWARD M. BALLOU,
Secretary.

Scientists and societies favoring us with copies of their publications in exchamge are requested to mail them to our observatory, Volcano House, Hawaii, and not to Honolulu.

WEEKLY BULLETIN
OF
Hawaiian Volcano Observatory

Vol. II. HONOLULU, HAWAII, MAY 13, 1914. No. 19.

From the Pacific Commercial Advertiser, Honolulu, May 4, 1914.

TECHNOLOGY STATION, Kilauea, April 30. — Again there has been a slight increase in activity in Halemaumau. Readjustments among the talus blocks produce frequent trivial rock-slides, occasioned probably by the melting and subsequent fluid movement of the lower layers. Nevertheless, the state of heat at the bottom of the pit near the top of the magma column seems to be increasing steadily, though the balance of the surface conditions which make for spectacular display vary in a partly regular, partly irregular way.

It may be appropriate to call attention again to the tolerably close agreement between this observed change in activity and theoretical variations in earth-strain produced by the action of sun and moon components of attraction. It is a tentative opinion, or hypothesis, that this variation in apparent activity noted from week to week is controlled partly, or largely, by this variation in earth-strain.

On April 23 conditions at the pit were as usual; brief glimpses of the incandescent orifices were obtained, but no flames or jets were seen. A few trivial slides occurred. There was nothing specially noteworthy about the blowing or rumbling sounds.

On April 24, owing to weather conditions unfavorable for observing, no visit was made to the pit.

On April 25 nothing could be seen on account of swirling fumes. The blowing and rumbling had become loud.

On April 26 no watch was maintained at the pit, but visitors reported the usual conditions.

On April 27 intermittent lava jets were seen playing out of "Old Faithful" and from the southeast blowing cone to heights closely approximating but not exceeding seventy-five feet. Blue flames wavered above the "Old Faithful" orifices. Rumbling and blowing was loud, the latter at considerable intervals being very loud indeed. No slides were heard and almost no symptoms of readjustment among the fallen blocks. Fumes obscured the west northwest and the northeast orifices but in the neighborhood of these the illumination of the fumes was brilliant.

On April 28 no lava jets were seen during the brief glimpses obtained of the "Old Faithful" and the southeast cones, but sounds of blowing and rumbling were very loud, the former of staccato quality. No prolonged slides were heard but the movement of individual rocks was noted frequently.

On April 29 an excellent series of views was obtained. Seething lava was again visible in the west northwest orifice. Small lava jets, twenty to twenty-five feet in height, were springing from the "Old Faithful" orifice, and blue flames were playing there. Nowhere else were jets noted. Blue flames were playing at the southeast cone also. Prolonged trivial slides were occurring frequently.

No systematic seismological report can be rendered at this time. The week passed without noteworthy seismic behavior until shortly before three in the afternoon of April 29, when a weak local earthquake, barely perceptible to the senses here at the Observatory, occurred.

H. O. WOOD,
Associate.

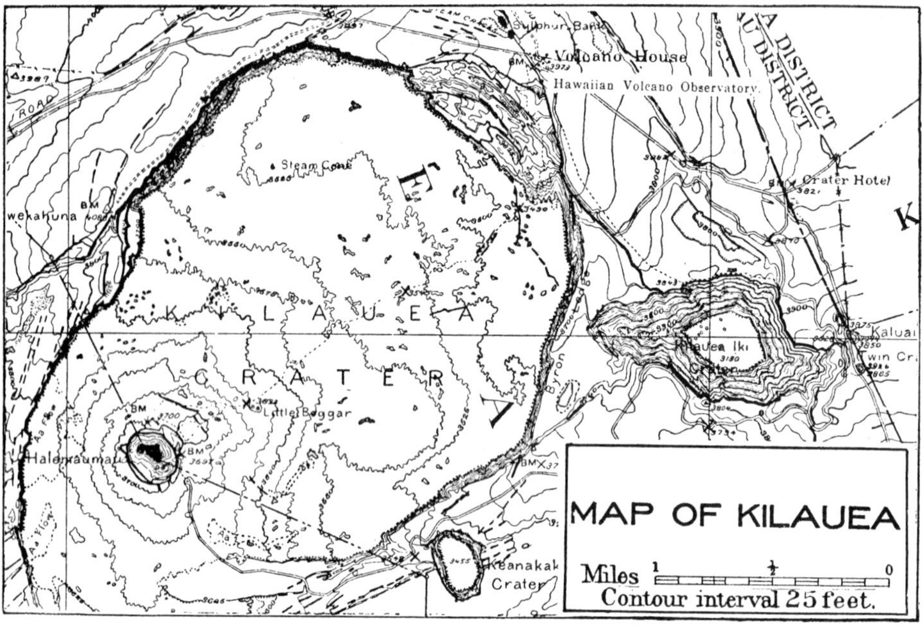

HAWAIIAN VOLCANO RESEARCH ASSOCIATION.

This society is a voluntary one, made up of subscribers to scientific work which is being executed by the Massachusetts Institute of Technology.

In 1913 there were 26 subscribers in Hawaii and Massachusetts, firms and individuals. A group of firms and persons in Hilo built the main observatory building in the spring of 1912. Publications to date have been weekly reports since the summer of 1911, a memoir by Daly in the Proceedings of American Academy of Arts and Sciences in 1911, articles by the director in the Technology Review 1911 and the Honolulu Chamber of Commerce Annual 1912, articles by H. O. Wood in the Bulletin of the Seismological Society of America, and articles by Perret in the American Journal of Science. The Massachusetts Institute of Technology will publish semiannual reports.

This weekly bulletin as it appears in the Advertiser will be reprinted as a leaflet and sent to regular annual subscribers to the work of the association. C. H. Cooke is president of the Board of Directors of the association and R. W. Shingle is treasurer. New subscribers who are interested in our volcanoes will be welcomed in the association. The association aims: (1) To record volcanic activity and earthquakes in Hawaii; (2) to attract scientific men hither for special studies; (3) to promote the establishment of volcano observatories all over the world.

WHITNEY LABORATORY OF SEISMOLOGY.

The Whitney Laboratory of Seismology is equipped with two Bosch-Omori 100 kg tromometers registering N-S and E-W motion, a heavy Omori tromometer registering E-W motion and an Omori "ordinary Seismograph" designed for registering strong earthquakes in all three components of motion. These are seated on concrete piers in a closed basement room having practically constant temperature, beneath the chief Observatory building near the hotel. Time is referred to a rated chronometer, checked at intervals by solar observations with a transit. Both instruments are loaned by the College of Hawaii. At the substation by the edge of the active pit an Omori two-component tromometer with light steady masses is mounted on a concrete pier placed directly on the fresh lava surface. Hawaiian standard time (H. S. T.) is 10 hrs. 30 m. slower than Greenwich time.

CANCANI SCALE OF SEISMIC INTENSITY

Expressed by accelerations measured in millimeters per second per second.

I.	Instrumental	0.0	2.5
II.	Very slight	2.5	5.0
III.	Slight	5.0	10.0
IV.	Sensible, mediocre....	10.0	25.0
V.	Rather strong	25.0	50.0
VI.	Strong	50.0	100.0
VII.	Very strong	100.0	250.0
VIII.	Ruinous	250.0	500.0
IX.	Disastrous	500.0	1000.0
X.	Very disastrous	1000.0	2500.0
XI.	Catastrophic	2500.0	5000.0
XII.	Great catastrophe....	5000.0	10000.0

Grade IV. is ordinarily the minimum perceived by the senses; and in grade XII. the acceleration, or rate of change of motion (jerk) reaches that of terrestrial gravitation.

WEEKLY BULLETIN
OF
Hawaiian Volcano Observatory

Vol. II. HONOLULU, HAWAII, MAY 20, 1914. No. 20.

From the Pacific Commercial Advertiser, Honolulu, May 10, 1914.

TECHNOLOGY STATION, Kilauea, May 7.—The week at Halemaumau has shown a marked increase of activity, culminating in a fiery display May 4 and 5, with lava flows from the cone-lets on the floor, but at a very great depth within the pit. All signs indicate a progressive slow rise of the lava from week to week, the fumarole action being very strong high up the walls, and the great mass of talus material being now in large measure consumed, so that bare rock walls extend nearly to the floor. For more than a year the low-lying lava column has been melting up this vast body of tumbled rock, its benches and overflows of 1912, the conflict between the heat supply and the inslipping slides proceeding by pulsations of about a fortnight's duration each, marked by alternations of quiet and activity.

Thursday, April 30, there was no seeing on account of smoke, but the rumbling was loud and the blowing noise very loud, with occasional exceptional blasts.

May 1 at 5:20 p. m., the pit was clearly visible from the north. The Old Faithful cone was blowing and rumbling and emitting blue flames from its cracks. A strong avalanche lasted 45 seconds. At 8 p. m. from the southeast station strong glow could be seen in the west-northwest cavity under the wall and at some other spots, but there were no lava drops or spatters ejected. Slides continued.

May 2, at 5:40 p. m., the Old Faithful cone was seen to be spattering and the west-northwest hole was glowing, as seen from the north. Blowing and rumbling noises continued. At 6:10 p. m., from the same point of view a clearing out of the fumes revealed the fact that new lava flows had poured all over the floor, surrounding the Old Faithful cone, the source apparently being a conelet under the southeast station. Glowing streaks could be seen where the flows had cracked. Slides were still plentiful. The west cone on the floor was occasionally rumbling and blowing out glowing spatter. At 6:30 p. m., all the pots and craterlets were seen to be flaring, Old Faithful was vomiting spatter from its main lateral cavity, and blue flames from a crack on its crest.

May 3, from 6 to 8 p. m., conditions were similar, the various pots bubbling and flaming, with noises of puffing and splashing, the seeing being best from the southeast station. The fumaroles were very rapid in their puffing, one being seen not more than 100 feet below the south station. In the same zone of vapor as the postal rift, back from the edge of Halemaumau, but more to the eastward, east of the Volcano House trail, a fumarole has developed acid fumes which are like those of the floor, intensely disagreeable and probably injurious.

May 4, 3 to 4 p. m., the bottom area was plainly visible from the northwest for from twenty to thirty minutes. Old Faithful exhibited a small triangular orifice and the southeast cone was glowing. These were both spatter-heaps at the floor level, the floor being made up of flows. On the south side of the floor two small glowing spots were seen. In the large west-northwest orifice there

WEEKLY BULLETIN
of
Hawaiian Volcano Observatory

Published at Honolulu, Hawaii, by the **Hawaiian Volcano Research Association**

Editor..............Howard M. Ballou
Professor of Physics, College of Hawaii

Entered as second-class matter January 20, 1914, at the post-office at Honolulu, Hawaii, under the Act of August 24, 1912.

was marked activity concealed by fumes. Two small glow spots appeared under the northwest station. The high fumarole in the north wall was very active. The northeast cave was glowing. No lava jets were seen. Rumbling was strong, and the blowing noise comparatively weak.

From 9 to 11 in the evening of May 4, and again at 4 a. m., the most intense glow which has been seen over the pit from the Observatory for many months was observed, due to extensive lava flows on the floor, as was proved next day. These were seen still in eruption on the afternoon and evening of May 5. As on May 2, the source of the principal flows was the southeast cone, now become an oven opening to the north and vomiting out an immense flow which covered the whole east end of the floor. There were other spattering flows from Old Faithful, nearer the middle of the floor, this also being an oven open to the north. There was little sliding, and the noise was mostly splashing and puffing. Seeing was from the south and southeast, the whole southeast end of the pit being continuously clear, and in general the fumes less obstructive than of late, though the ring of fumaroles around the low talus adjacent to the floor was intensely active, emitting hundreds of tails of white vapor. Dimly the western holes could be seen in action, and there were western lava flows, but their detail could not be made out. High over the floor in the northeast wall a large craterlet was fuming and flaming. Under it near the floor level were several glowing holes and a black cone illumined by the incandescence of the lava flows. Now and again the flows would crust over, blacken and then rend asunder, the glowing orange-colored melt welling up in streaks and ribbons. Altogether it was a glorious display, and lasted for hours. There were at least three main flows and seven glowing craterlets.

May 5, 8 to 10 p. m., the depth was measured with the new Japanese simplex transits and very accordant results were obtained from three readings, making the elevation of the south and southeast stations above the Old Faithful and southeast cones 585 feet approximately.

May 6 the evening glow indicated diminished activity, confirmed May 7, 11 a. m., when the floor was concealed, the noises that of puffing, with one slow avalanche heard.

T. A. JAGGAR JR.,
Director.

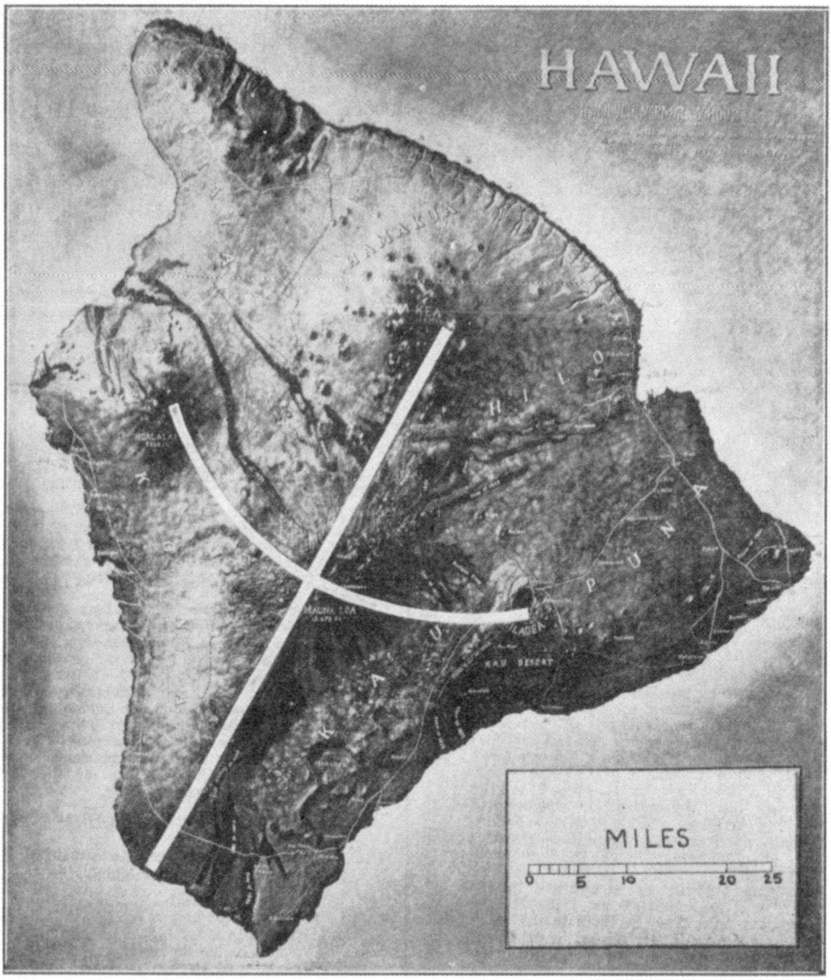

Relief map of the Island of Hawaii, the cross showing the symmetrical cruciform location of the volcanoes.

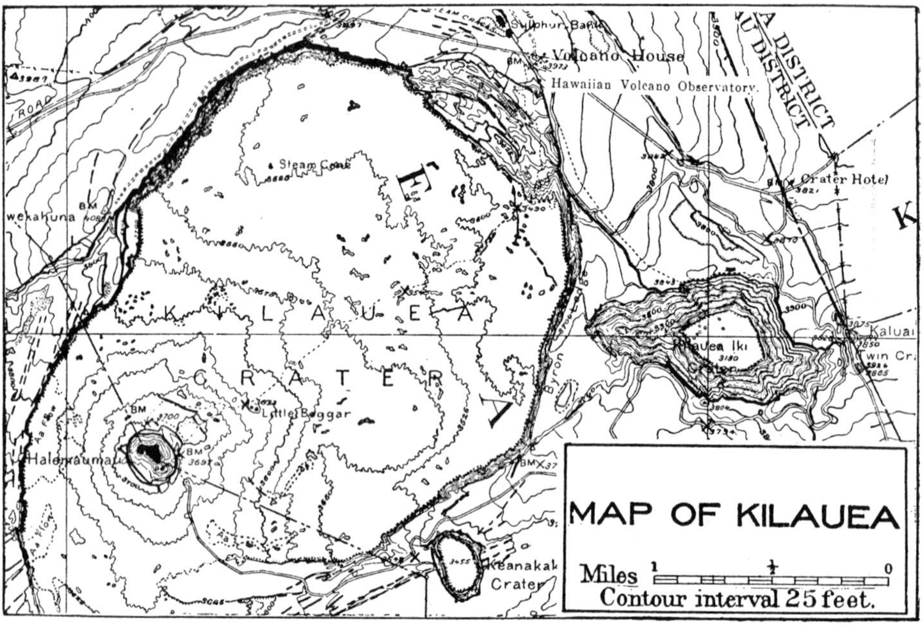

HAWAIIAN VOLCANO RESEARCH ASSOCIATION.

This society is a voluntary one, made up of subscribers to scientific work which is being executed by the Massachusetts Institute of Technology.

In 1913 there were 26 subscribers in Hawaii and Massachusetts, firms and individuals. A group of firms and persons in Hilo built the main observatory building in the spring of 1912. Publications to date have been weekly reports since the summer of 1911, a memoir by Daly in the Proceedings of American Academy of Arts and Sciences in 1911, articles by the director in the Technology Review 1911 and the Honolulu Chamber of Commerce Annual 1912, articles by H. O. Wood in the Bulletin of the Seismological Society of America, and articles by Perret in the American Journal of Science. The Massachusetts Institute of Technology will publish semiannual reports.

This weekly bulletin as it appears in the Advertiser will be reprinted as a leaflet and sent to regular annual subscribers to the work of the association. C. H. Cooke is president of the Board of Directors of the association and R. W. Shingle is treasurer. New subscribers who are interested in our volcanoes will be welcomed in the association. The association aims: (1) To record volcanic activity and earthquakes in Hawaii; (2) to attract scientific men hither for special studies; (3) to promote the establishment of volcano observatories all over the world.

WHITNEY LABORATORY OF SEISMOLOGY.

The Whitney Laboratory of Seismology is equipped with two Bosch-Omori 100 kg tromometers registering N-S and E-W motion, a heavy Omori tromometer registering E-W motion and an Omori "ordinary Seismograph" designed for registering strong earthquakes in all three components of motion. These are seated on concrete piers in a closed basement room having practically constant temperature, beneath the chief Observatory building near the hotel. Time is referred to a rated chronometer, checked at intervals by solar observations with a transit. Both instruments are loaned by the College of Hawaii. At the substation by the edge of the active pit an Omori two-component tromometer with light steady masses is mounted on a concrete pier placed directly on the fresh lava surface. Hawaiian standard time (H. S. T.) is 10 hrs. 30 m. slower than Greenwich time.

CANCANI SCALE OF SEISMIC INTENSITY

Expressed by accelerations measured in millimeters per second per second.

I.	Instrumental	0.0	2.5
II.	Very slight	2.5	5.0
III.	Slight	5.0	10.0
IV.	Sensible, mediocre....	10.0	25.0
V.	Rather strong	25.0	50.0
VI.	Strong	50.0	100.0
VII.	Very strong	100.0	250.0
VIII.	Ruinous	250.0	500.0
IX.	Disastrous	500.0	1000.0
X.	Very disastrous	1000.0	2500.0
XI.	Catastrophic	2500.0	5000.0
XII.	Great catastrophe....	5000.0	10000.0

Grade IV. is ordinarily the minimum perceived by the senses; and in grade XII. the acceleration, or rate of change of motion (jerk) reaches that of terrestrial gravitation.

WEEKLY BULLETIN
OF

Hawaiian Volcano Observatory

Vol. II. HONOLULU, HAWAII, MAY 27, 1914. No. 21.

From the Pacific Commercial Advertiser, Honolulu, May 18, 1914.

TECHNOLOGY STATION, Kilauea, May 14.—The week at the fire-pit has been one of steady continuance of activity, with probably some rising.

May 7, at 11 a. m. a partial view of the interior of the pit was obtained. Under the south station for a depth of at least 300 feet is a bare insloping rock wall ending below in a V of talus rising on each side.

Much of the enormous quantity of slide-rock which filled the south end of the pit last year is gone, engulfed in the magma column below. There still remains a remnant of the high south bench sixty feet below the rim. On this date the wind was diffusing the fumes in the pit, Old Faithful was hissing continuously, there was no sound of very great activity, and a slow avalanche was heard tumbling toward the west.

There was some glow during the night of May 8-9, and at 1 p. m. May 9, Old Faithful was seen from the northwest station to be a small pool about 25 feet in diameter, with flows running over the edge on the floor toward the northwest and toward the southeast. The west cone on the floor was ejecting incandescent lava jets.

Blowing, rumbling, and breaking noises were very loud. At 1:15 streaming currents could be seen in the Old Faithful pool. The cavern in the wall westnorthwest was throwing out lava jets from time to time and the floor below it was covered with fresh lava. In the evening from 8 to 10 p. m., the seeing was best from the south station. The whole bottom was visible; two cones with glowing filagree in the westnorthwest wall, the western floor-cone, Old Faithful an open pot with hanging stalactites, showing streaming within, and sometimes splashing out. The southeast cone of the two days before was now submerged under fresh lava-flow from Old Faithful.

The noise of strongest loud blowing seemed to come from the southwest margin of the floor, where were puffing fumaroles. The floor was divided into halves, the western evidently higher than the eastern, and a cascade of lava poured down a slope from west to east across the dividing line. This cataract was a narrow ribbon, and at its lower end was pouring into Old Faithful. The noise of the lava stream was a peculiar and characteristic crackling rumble. Other noises were sharp hisses and splashes, and a little rock-sliding. The whole east floor showed the glowing cracks of a fresh lava flow.

At 5 p. m. Sunday, May 10, there was no clear seeing and the noises were the same. At 3:20 p. m., May 11, the Old Faithful pot, with streaming lava within, was visible from the east station, and the noises were blowing and loud rumbling. From the southeast station at 4:20 p. m. the Old Faithful pot was seen to be overflowing, and there was glow in a southeast crack in the floor.

May 12 at 3 p. m., the seeing was poor; the noise was a continuous hiss, with rumbling and occasional loud puffs. The Old Faithful glowhole could be dimly seen splashing. Fumaroles around the bottom were very ac-

WEEKLY BULLETIN
of
Hawaiian Volcano Observatory

Published at Honolulu, Hawaii, by the **Hawaiian Volcano Research Association**

Editor..............Howard M. Ballou
Professor of Physics, College of Hawaii

Entered as second-class matter January 20, 1914, at the post-office at Honolulu, Hawaii, under the Act of August 24, 1912.

tive southeast and south, and one high one was noticed about 100 feet above the floor in the wall east. The rumble was loud enough to be heard at the Technology Station about 100 feet back from the edge of the pit. At 5 p. m. from the southeast station the east end of the floor could be seen; Old Faithful was an oven with hanging stalactites open to the east, there was another small beehive cone on the floor southeast, and a small glow spot could be seen in the west pool. A very high fumarole in the wall was discovered at the top of the talus just to the south of the west station.

May 13 at 4 and 6 p. m. seeing was bad, the triangular orifice of Old Faithful could be made out from the southeast station, and the noise was the usual loud rumbling and blowing. The blowing of late has had no very definite period, but has been continuous, with sporadic louder puffs. I have never yet been able to identify visible jets of vapor with the sounds perceived, nor by any other means satisfactorily to localize the sounds.

H. O. Wood reports that continued cloudy weather at noon has prevented observations for the correction of time, so that no systematic report from the Whitney Laboratory of Seismology can yet be given. The week has been quiet seismically except for a shock at about 9:05 p. m. May 12. This was sufficiently energetic to start the ordinary seismograph, and barely to be perceived in the vicinity of the Observatory. Vague reports indicate that it was stronger to the senses on the southern slopes of Mauna Loa, a circumstance considered probable, since its origin would appear by the trace on the seismogram to be 30 to 40 miles from the Observatory.

The director, on the evening of May 14, is to repeat in Hilo the lecture on the eruption of Sakurajima, with illustrations, previously delivered in Honolulu.

T. A. JAGGAR, JR.,
Director.

Hitchcock's painting, (1910), of ''The Lake of Fire,'' Halemaumau, Hawaii,

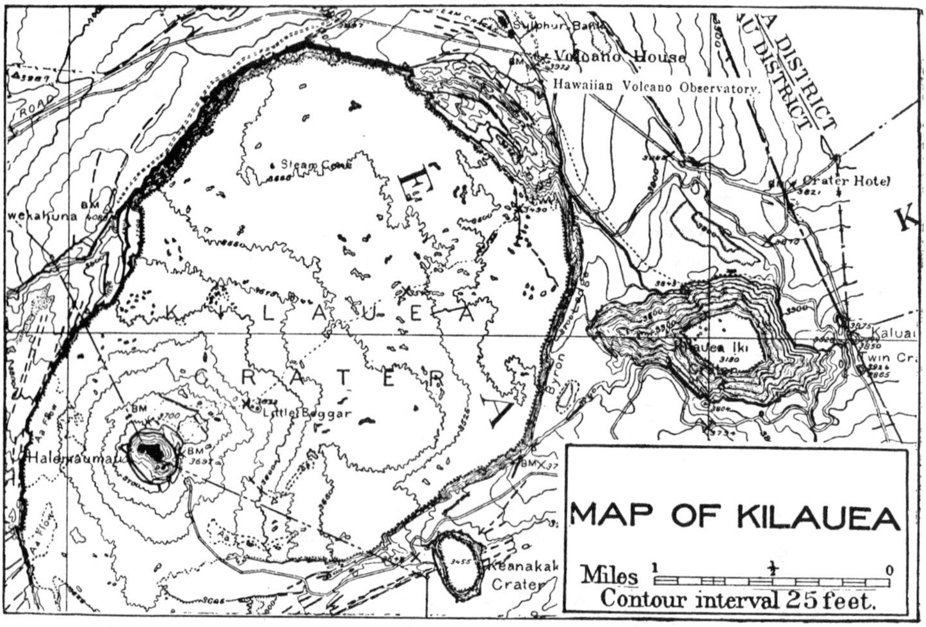

HAWAIIAN VOLCANO RESEARCH ASSOCIATION.

This society is a voluntary one, made up of subscribers to scientific work which is being executed by the Massachusetts Institute of Technology.

In 1913 there were 26 subscribers in Hawaii and Massachusetts, firms and individuals. A group of firms and persons in Hilo built the main observatory building in the spring of 1912. Publications to date have been weekly reports since the summer of 1911, a memoir by Daly in the Proceedings of American Academy of Arts and Sciences in 1911, articles by the director in the Technology Review 1911 and the Honolulu Chamber of Commerce Annual 1912, articles by H. O. Wood in the Bulletin of the Seismological Society of America, and articles by Perret in the American Journal of Science. The Massachusetts Institute of Technology will publish semi-annual reports.

This weekly bulletin as it appears in the Advertiser will be reprinted as a leaflet and sent to regular annual subscribers to the work of the association. C. H. Cooke is president of the Board of Directors of the association and R. W. Shingle is treasurer. New subscribers who are interested in our volcanoes will be welcomed in the association. The association aims: (1) To record volcanic activity and earthquakes in Hawaii; (2) to attract scientific men hither for special studies; (3) to promote the establishment of volcano observatories all over the world.

WHITNEY LABORATORY OF SEISMOLOGY.

The Whitney Laboratory of Seismology is equipped with two Bosch-Omori 100 kg tromometers registering N-S and E-W motion, a heavy Omori tromometer registering E-W motion and an Omori "ordinary Seismograph" designed for registering strong earthquakes in all three components of motion. These are seated on concrete piers in a closed basement room having practically constant temperature, beneath the chief Observatory building near the hotel. Time is referred to a rated chronometer, checked at intervals by solar observations with a transit. Both instruments are loaned by the College of Hawaii. At the substation by the edge of the active pit an Omori two-component tromometer with light steady masses is mounted on a concrete pier placed directly on the fresh lava surface. Hawaiian standard time (H. S. T.) is 10 hrs. 30 m. slower than Greenwich time.

CANCANI SCALE OF SEISMIC INTENSITY

Expressed by accelerations measured in millimeters per second per second.

I.	Instrumental	0.0	2.5
II.	Very slight	2.5	5.0
III.	Slight	5.0	10.0
IV.	Sensible, mediocre	10.0	25.0
V.	Rather strong	25.0	50.0
VI.	Strong	50.0	100.0
VII.	Very strong	100.0	250.0
VIII.	Ruinous	250.0	500.0
IX.	Disastrous	500.0	1000.0
X.	Very disastrous	1000.0	2500.0
XI.	Catastrophic	2500.0	5000.0
XII.	Great catastrophe	5000.0	10000.0

Grade IV. is ordinarily the minimum perceived by the senses; and in grade XII. the acceleration, or rate of change of motion (jerk) reaches that of terrestrial gravitation.

WEEKLY BULLETIN
OF
Hawaiian Volcano Observatory

Vol. II. HONOLULU, HAWAII, JUNE 3, 1914. No. 22.

From the Pacific Commercial Advertiser, Honolulu, May 25, 1914.

TECHNOLOGY STATION, Kilauea, Hawaii, May 21, 1914:—

The rise at Halemaumau continues, though the bottom of the pit is over six hundred feet below the rim in places, according to recent measurement. The deepest parts are at the west end of the floor. Flows over the floor from various vents have made a brilliant flaring glow at night, seen from the Observatory, while in the daytime seeing has been variable, the fume-cloud sometimes being obstructive. In general it has been a week of brilliant nocturnal displays for visitors. It should be noted that the temperature of the Postal Rift was unusually low last week; on May 12, at 4:30 p..m., the temperature of the air was 20 degrees C., (68 degrees F.); of the hot gases in the rift 308 degrees C. (586 degrees F.); usually in the past two years the Postal crack has given a temperature measurement of from 315 to 323 degrees C. (599 to 613 degrees F.)

At 3:52 p.m., May 14, a long slide was heard from the southwest part of the pit, lasting about 45 seconds, and small slides thereafter. At 6:25 p.m. the Old Faithful oven was spouting lava; three holes in a line appeared beyond as seen from the southeast station, one of them emitting blue flames. The southeast cone on the floor occasionally blew out spray. A bright glow-hole appeared under the northeast station, another under the east station, and the blowing and rumbling noises continued as of late. At 6:50 p.m. a flow appeared on the floor pouring from the west toward Old Faithful.

May 15 at 4:30 p.m., seeing from the southeast and south stations was sufficiently clear for a partial survey of the bottom with a transit. The floor was very active from at least eighteen points. A flow from the southeast cone showed glowing cracks and rim, and covered the eastern floor. The principal active holes visible were the west cone, Old Faithful, a pot just west of Old Faithful, the southeast cone, the northeast chimney, a glowing spot on the east side of the floor, and the two high west chimneys. By "chimneys" I refer to craterlets in the wall at some height above the floor, and exhibiting glow. The noises were sharp hisses, bubbling and rumbling and some rock-slipping southwest. I was able for the first time to identify the hisses with jets from the southeast cone, which visibly coincided with the noise, and this place was clearly at the source of the lava flow spreading over the east floor under its own crust.

The flow in solidifying tended to choke its orifice, hence the hisses of hot gas which kept the orifice open, and kept pumping a narrow stream of incandescent lava under the crust to swell and spread the accumulation on the floor. The west cone and Old Faithful were both splashing pots occasionally ejecting spray.

The measurements revealed a rise of the eastern floor of from seven to eight feet in the past fortnight, the mean depth below the south-southeast rim being 575 feet to the southeast cone, 574 feet to Old Faithful, 583 feet to the pot just west of Old Faithful, and 605 feet to the southwest cone.

WEEKLY BULLETIN
of
Hawaiian Volcano Observatory

Published at Honolulu, Hawaii, by the **Hawaiian Volcano Research Association**

Editor..............Howard M. Ballou
Professor of Physics, College of Hawaii

Entered as second-class matter January 20, 1914, at the post-office at Honolulu, Hawaii, under the Act of August 24, 1912.

The long downward slope here revealed from Old Faithful, as a built-up cone toward the west end of the floor, indicates how much the activity of the eastern floor during the past few weeks has been constructive by overflow, in contrast to the west end. The distance from Old Faithful to the southeast cone was 110 feet, and to the southwest cone 243 feet. The whole flat cone of overflow, which we have been calling "floor," is at least 550 feet long from east to west and perhaps 200 feet wide.

May 16 at 11 a.m., conditions were the same, seeing poor. May 18 at 6 p.m. activity was strong, Old Faithful was blowing out jets of lava, the front of a flow was in motion at the east end, the southeast cone was puffing spray, and the noises were loud. At 6:10 a flow was pouring from the north toward Old Faithful.

May 19 at 1:30 p.m., there was continuous hissing and puffing with no definite period that could be timed. There was some rumbling and what little could be seen of the floor from the southwest and south stations showed a black surface with gaping, glowing pots at Old Faithful and vicinity. There were no flows seen in motion. Two high fumaroles at the top of the talus occur east and west of the southwest station. Further down in the pit there is a flat remnant of the 200-foot bench of 1912, its top cracked in many directions, fuming, and discolored with sulphur. East of the bench under the south station, at the foot of the vertical wall that bounds the pit there is an extraordinary downsloping gully, almost a crevasse, probably produced by the sagging outward toward the pit of a block of bench or wall material.

May 20 at 6 p.m. from the southeast station a flow was again seen to be pouring from the west into Old Faithful. This would imply that the summit region of the floor is slowly migrating westward. A cone under the east station was blowing jets of lava 40 to 50 feet into the air. The southeast cone was emitting blue flames. Bright glow showed in the northeast chimney, and the floor showed the crackled glowing pattern of the recent lava flow. Two orifices appeared in the Old Faithful position.

Owing to bad weather preventing solar observation for the correction of time, the report of the Whitney Laboratory of Seismology will be deferred. The week has been quiet seismically.

T. A. JAGGAR, Jr., Director.

Harold Bauer, the distinguished musician, who has been visiting Madame Pele and viewing the entrancing spectacle that the Fire Goddess is now presenting at Kilauea, has become a patron of the Hawaiian Volcano Research Association and has subscribed liberally towards the fund by means of which the scientific work at the Volcano is now being carried on. Mr. Bauer, who spent the evening of Friday, May 15, with his wife on the edge of Halemaumau, entranced with the gorgeous display of spouting lavas, fire fountains and brilliant flows, is enthusiastic over the Volcano itself and as much so over the work being done in the study of the Volcano and its phenomena by Professor Jaggar and his associates, writing as follows:

"The value of this experience is something I can never over-estimate, for it has been truly a revelation. Such work undertaken in the cause of humanity cannot fail to inspire the sympathetic and enthusiastic interest of every observer. I cannot believe that the lack of financial support will prove of long duration, for I am convinced that the time is ripe for every human being to understand the far-reaching importance of scientific research into the underworld, more immediate and vital in its relation to our lives than many other branches of study upon which time and wealth have been lavished in abundance. In enclosing herewith a modest contribution towards the funds of your Association, I earnestly trust that the necessary movement in public feeling may shortly be manifested and your endowment rapidly attain such proportions as to enable you to prosecute your labors to the fullest and most permanent advantage.''

A very large audience attended the lecture in Hilo May 14 by the director on ''The Japanese Volcanic Disaster,'' and the proceeds netted $123.00 to the Hawaiian Volcano Research Association.

Rough Lava.

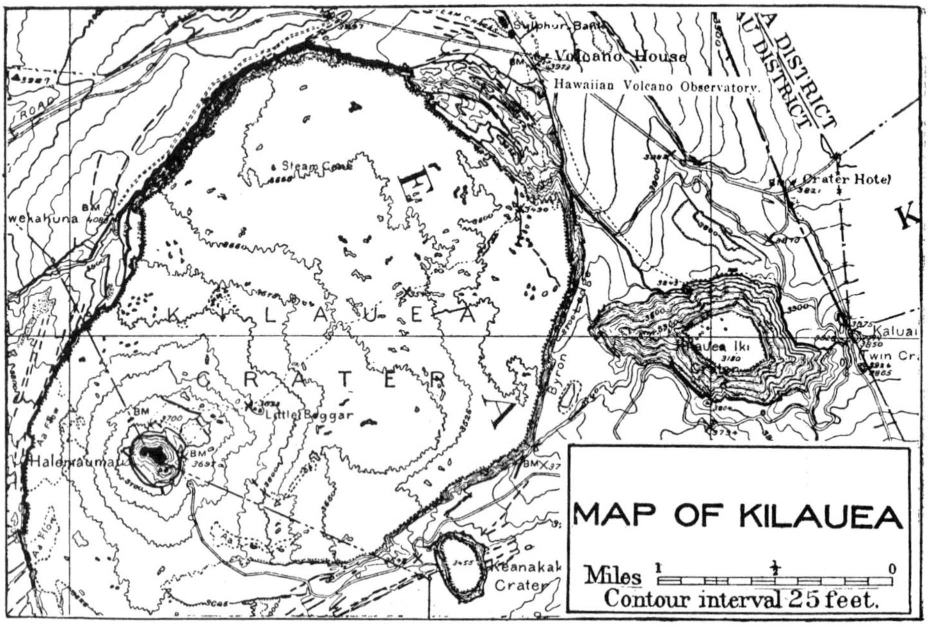

HAWAIIAN VOLCANO RESEARCH ASSOCIATION.

This society is a voluntary one, made up of subscribers to scientific work which is being executed by the Massachusetts Institute of Technology.

In 1913 there were 26 subscribers in Hawaii and Massachusetts, firms and individuals. A group of firms and persons in Hilo built the main observatory building in the spring of 1912. Publications to date have been weekly reports since the summer of 1911, a memoir by Daly in the Proceedings of American Academy of Arts and Sciences in 1911, articles by the director in the Technology Review 1911 and the Honolulu Chamber of Commerce Annual 1912, articles by H. O. Wood in the Bulletin of the Seismological Society of America, and articles by Perret in the American Journal of Science. The Massachusetts Institute of Technology will publish semiannual reports.

This weekly bulletin as it appears in the Advertiser will be reprinted as a leaflet and sent to regular annual subscribers to the work of the association. C. H. Cooke is president of the Board of Directors of the association and R. W. Shingle is treasurer. New subscribers who are interested in our volcanoes will be welcomed in the association. The association aims: (1) To record volcanic activity and earthquakes in Hawaii; (2) to attract scientific men hither for special studies; (3) to promote the establishment of volcano observatories all over the world.

WHITNEY LABORATORY OF SEISMOLOGY.

The Whitney Laboratory of Seismology is equipped with two Bosch-Omori 100 kg tromometers registering N-S and E-W motion, a heavy Omori tromometer registering E-W motion and an Omori "ordinary Seismograph" designed for registering strong earthquakes in all three components of motion. These are seated on concrete piers in a closed basement room having practically constant temperature, beneath the chief Observatory building near the hotel. Time is referred to a rated chronometer, checked at intervals by solar observations with a transit. Both instruments are loaned by the College of Hawaii. At the substation by the edge of the active pit an Omori two-component tromometer with light steady masses is mounted on a concrete pier placed directly on the fresh lava surface. Hawaiian standard time (H. S. T.) is 10 hrs. 30 m. slower than Greenwich time.

CANCANI SCALE OF SEISMIC INTENSITY

Expressed by accelerations measured in millimeters per second per second.

I.	Instrumental	0.0	2.5
II.	Very slight	2.5	5.0
III.	Slight	5.0	10.0
IV.	Sensible, mediocre....	10.0	25.0
V.	Rather strong	25.0	50.0
VI.	Strong	50.0	100.0
VII.	Very strong	100.0	250.0
VIII.	Ruinous	250.0	500.0
IX.	Disastrous	500.0	1000.0
X.	Very disastrous	1000.0	2500.0
XI.	Catastrophic	2500.0	5000.0
XII.	Great catastrophe....	5000.0	10000.0

Grade IV. is ordinarily the minimum perceived by the senses; and in grade XII. the acceleration, or rate of change of motion (jerk) reaches that of terrestrial gravitation.

WEEKLY BULLETIN
OF
Hawaiian Volcano Observatory

Vol. II. HONOLULU, HAWAII, JUNE 10, 1914. No. 23.

From the Pacific Commercial Advertiser, Honolulu, June 1, 1914.

TECHNOLOGY STATION, Kilauea, May 28. 1914.—The week at Halemaumau has been one of continuous activity of the same order as that recently reported, with lava jets and spatter from time to time from the pots in the floor, and flaming chimneys around the border of the floor area. There was a slight subsidence, to judge by depth of lava in the pots, from May 21 to 23, and thereafter some rising, but this appearance needs checking by measurement, as the pulsatory overflow and spatter on the floor may by building up simulate lava-sinking, just as the engulfment of slide-rock and floor crust when it all slides down may simulate lava-rising. There is evidence in the south talus of such a downslip in the latter part of the period, probably on the night of May 24-25, and this was immediately followed by renewed overflow of lava jets from the Old Faithful oven.

May 21, 1914 at 8:30 p. m., seen from southeast and south stations, a narrow vent just west of Old Faithful emitted a rapid-flowing ribbon of glowing lava down a steep slope as seen from the south into Old Faithful. The lava within the Old Faithful pot appeared to be streaming rapidly eastward, and to be from eight to twelve feet below the solidified crust. There were many dull red cracks all over the eastern half of the floor, apparently persistent. The southeast cone was quietly glowing, but there was greater activity in two northeast places at and just above the foot of the wall. At the north was one conspicuous orifice and two or three were dimly seen in the fumes to the west. There were rare low jets from Old Faithful, tinkling sounds of cracking crust, occasional local rock falls, and bright illumination of the fume-cloud and walls.

May 22 at 11:20 a. m. the high northwest chimney was seen from the north rest-house to be surmounted by a cone about ten feet high, with a large orifice at the top, an opening in its side, and boiling lava within which occasionally surged up to high levels without overflowing or jetting. Five other chimney vents in a line beyond this one showed glow. Rumbling noises were more marked than hissing, and there were many slides. At noon from the same point Old Faithful could be seen, a roundish hole in the floor about 20 feet wide, its edge some five feet above the surging lava within, which occasionally spattered out. Fire showed also in the northeast chimney. At 4:20 p. m., the various vents were more active, and at 8 p. m. from the southeast station the cracks in the floor east were glowing, the east cone ejecting moderately high jets, and the lava pots and chimneys generally active, but there were no moving flows seen.

May 23 at 6 p. m., dim views from the south station showed the usual glow-holes and a bright flame in the northeast chimney. The west end of the floor area exhibited a bright flare, but what occasioned it was obscure. The noises were a continuous puffing and splashing. The southeast fuma-

WEEKLY BULLETIN
of
Hawaiian Volcano Observatory

Published at Honolulu, Hawaii, by the **Hawaiian Volcano Research Association**

Editor.............Howard M. Ballou
Professor of Physics, College of Hawaii

Entered as second-class matter January 20, 1914, at the post-office at Honolulu, Hawaii, under the Act of August 24, 1912.

roles in the talus exhibited a smoking rift trending northeast, gaping open and lined with whitish sulphur, as though the lower portion of the talus had started to slide away from the upper portion. Two days later this was all changed and the whole slide had gone lower, implying that the hot lava under these most active vents is rapidly consuming the slide-rock. From the northwest station at 6:30 p. m. there was no seeing, but the bright flare over the west end of the bottom area was accompanied by a splashing and booming which sounded like the fountains of a pool. Conditions on the evening of May 24 were fumy; the usual glow-holes were seen.

May 25 at 3:30 p. m. from the north rest-house the noises were steady hissing and a thudding rumble like the boiling of a viscous fluid. At 4:20 p. m. from the southeast the floor was seen to be black without moving flows, with conelets east and southeast, a triangular orifice at Old Faithful, a similar smaller one in the northeast vent, and the great V of insloping wall under the south station had extended down much lower than on the 23rd, in consequence of bodily subsidence of the fumarole talus beneath. The sulphurous crevasse was gone, only some whitish bowlders revealed where it had been. The southeast wall has by the recession of the talus become remarkably high and steep, and about 100 feet down a great red protuberant portion actually overhangs.

May 26 at 6:30 p. m., the Old Faithful hole appeared about 3 x 5 feet in diameter, with surging lava within, and the other glow-holes appeared scattered about the floor. At 7 p. m. Old Faithful was splashing lava out on to the floor, the northeast chimney was flaming, and the east cone was jetting spray. Rumbling and blowing noises continued.

May 27 was a rainy day, and a weak glow was seen over the pit in the evening, at which time also a southwest wind began, carrying the fumes over the Observatory and the Volcano House. This has today, May 28, developed into a southerly storm. There has been much rain for months past at the Volcano House.

Changes in the cracks back of the rest-house at Halemaumau have accompanied the low level floor (about 600 feet plus) of the past year and the rising lava of the past few months. Evidently the cracks concentric to the pit bound immense spalls of rock, crescent-shaped in plan, like the 1894 bench, which tend to sag out into the pit and subside. The outer ring of fumaroles, of which the Postal Rift is the type, is a continuous echelon of such cracks extending down to the hot lava probably, and recently movements on this ring east and southeast have opened the way to the passage of very acid fumes which are intensely irritating. One place straight back of the east rest-house shows bluish fume. Probably lava is rising beneath this ring just as in the case of the inner ring of talus fumaroles. Moreover cracks parallel to the edge of the pit from ten to thirty feet from the edge between the north rest-house and the northwest station have gaped a few inches, and in one case at least, the outer block has subsided, these cracks being from three to thirty inches wide. The rock on the pit side of a twelve-inch crack forty feet in front of the Technology Station has settled four inches in sixteen months. The rock filling of a thirty-inch crack in the trail back from the northwest station has settled three inches in the same period, indicating that the crack has gaped. No motion can be detected at the north station, the trail from the north to northeast stations, nor about the east station.

The seismological report will be deferred until clear weather at noon permits a time observation. One distant earthquake was recorded May 25-26.

T. A. JAGGAR, JR.,
Director.

On the Summit of Mauna Loa.

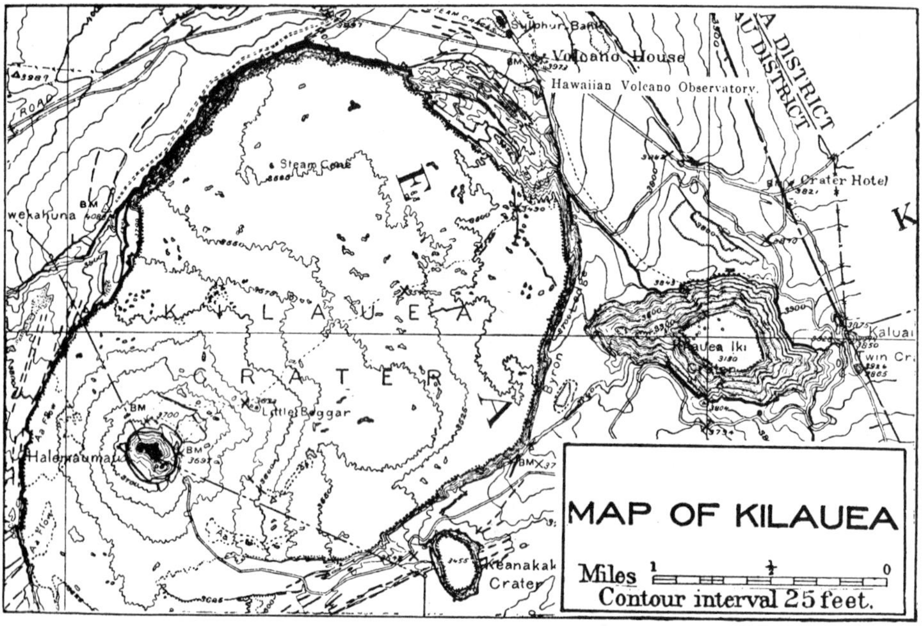

HAWAIIAN VOLCANO RESEARCH ASSOCIATION.

This society is a voluntary one, made up of subscribers to scientific work which is being executed by the Massachusetts Institute of Technology.

In 1913 there were 26 subscribers in Hawaii and Massachusetts, firms and individuals. A group of firms and persons in Hilo built the main observatory building in the spring of 1912. Publications to date have been weekly reports since the summer of 1911, a memoir by Daly in the Proceedings of American Academy of Arts and Sciences in 1911, articles by the director in the Technology Review 1911 and the Honolulu Chamber of Commerce Annual 1912, articles by H. O. Wood in the Bulletin of the Seismological Society of America, and articles by Perret in the American Journal of Science. The Massachusetts Institute of Technology will publish semi-annual reports.

This weekly bulletin as it appears in the Advertiser will be reprinted as a leaflet and sent to regular annual subscribers to the work of the association. C. H. Cooke is president of the Board of Directors of the association and R. W. Shingle is treasurer. New subscribers who are interested in our volcanoes will be welcomed in the association. The association aims: (1) To record volcanic activity and earthquakes in Hawaii; (2) to attract scientific men hither for special studies; (3) to promote the establishment of volcano observatories all over the world.

WHITNEY LABORATORY OF SEISMOLOGY.

The Whitney Laboratory of Seismology is equipped with two Bosch-Omori 100 kg tromometers registering N-S and E-W motion, a heavy Omori tromometer registering E-W motion and an Omori "ordinary Seismograph" designed for registering strong earthquakes in all three components of motion. These are seated on concrete piers in a closed basement room having practically constant temperature, beneath the chief Observatory building near the hotel. Time is referred to a rated chronometer, checked at intervals by solar observations with a transit. Both instruments are loaned by the College of Hawaii. At the substation by the edge of the active pit an Omori two-component tromometer with light steady masses is mounted on a concrete pier placed directly on the fresh lava surface. Hawaiian standard time (H. S. T.) is 10 hrs. 30 m. slower than Greenwich time.

CANCANI SCALE OF SEISMIC INTENSITY

Expressed by accelerations measured in millimeters per second per second.

I.	Instrumental	0.0	2.5
II.	Very slight	2.5	5.0
III.	Slight	5.0	10.0
IV.	Sensible, mediocre....	10.0	25.0
V.	Rather strong	25.0	50.0
VI.	Strong	50.0	100.0
VII.	Very strong	100.0	250.0
VIII.	Ruinous	250.0	500.0
IX.	Disastrous	500.0	1000.0
X.	Very disastrous	1000.0	2500.0
XI.	Catastrophic	2500.0	5000.0
XII.	Great catastrophe....	5000.0	10000.0

Grade IV. is ordinarily the minimum perceived by the senses; and in grade XII. the acceleration, or rate of change of motion (jerk) reaches that of terrestrial gravitation.

WEEKLY BULLETIN
OF
Hawaiian Volcano Observatory

Vol. II. HONOLULU, HAWAII, JUNE 17, 1914. No 24.

TECHNOLOGY STATION, Kilauea, June 4, 1914.—The week at Kilauea has passed uneventfully. No unusual phenomena have been observed nor any fluctuation in activity of noteworthy sort. Owing to rain and wind the volcano has been less under observation than ordinarily.

No visit was made to the pit on Thursday, May 28.

On Friday, May 29, fitful glimpses were obtained showing the usual orifices on the floor as well as those at the northwest and east, higher than the floor. All were brightly incandescent, exhaling fumes copiously but with comparatively little noise of eruption. Frequent trivial slides were heard, indicative, in the judgment of the writer, of slow rising disturbing the lower stratum of talus blocks and thus producing sliding readjustments. Snapping sounds, as of rock cracking from heat, were heard very frequently, indicative of increasing heat at the top of the magma column. Neither lava jets nor flames were seen.

On Saturday, May 30, conditions indicated a slight rise. Jets were springing from the west-northwest, the northeast, and the east cones and the noises of eruption had much increased. In the course of the evening the top of the northwest cone was blown off and a flow poured out, gradually covering the floor of the pit. No flames were seen. Short slides were frequent.

On May 31, no flowing lava was seen. Lava jets were visible and the noises of eruption were relatively loud. No flames were seen and slides were comparatively rare.

On June 1, no visit was made to the pit.

On June 2, conditions indicated a slight decrease. Jets, or sprays, of molten lava were thrown from "Old Faithful" and all the usual orifices were glowing brightly, particularly a long fissure in the wall under the east station. But no flows occurred, no slides were heard, and no flames were seen. Noises of eruption were not quite so loud.

On June 3, again a slight increase appeared to be indicated. Jets were springing to greater heights and the sounds had increased in volume. Swirling magma was visible in "Old Faithful," which exhibited a somewhat enlarged orifice. No slides were heard and no flames were seen.

H. O. WOOD, Associate.

WEEKLY BULLETIN
of
Hawaiian Volcano Observatory

Published at Honolulu, Hawaii, by the **Hawaiian Volcano Research Association**

Editor..............Howard M. Ballou
Professor of Physics, College of Hawaii

Entered as second-class matter January 20, 1914, at the post-office at Honolulu, Hawaii, under the Act of August 24, 1912.

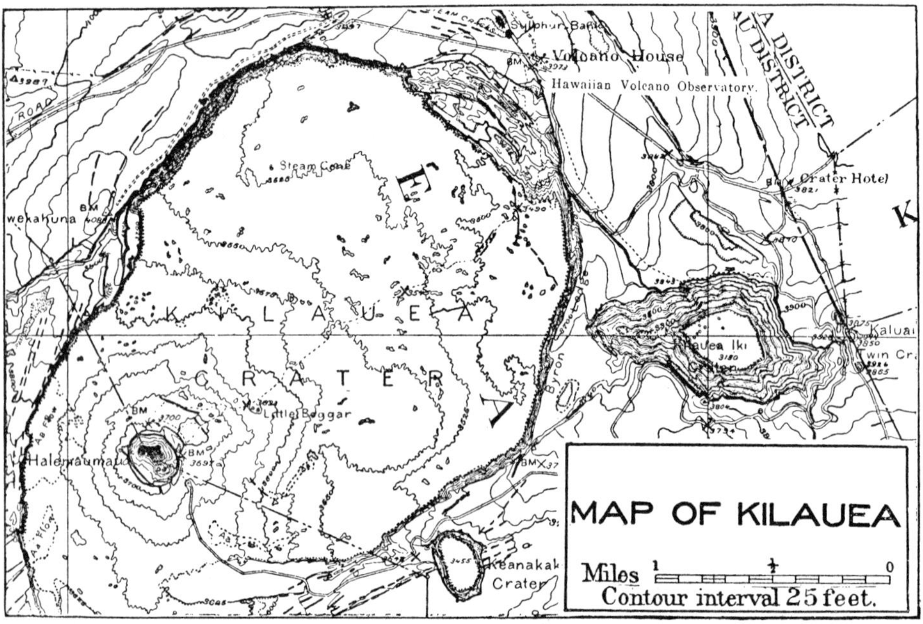

HAWAIIAN VOLCANO RESEARCH ASSOCIATION.

This society is a voluntary one, made up of subscribers to scientific work which is being executed by the Massachusetts Institute of Technology.

In 1913 there were 26 subscribers in Hawaii and Massachusetts, firms and individuals. A group of firms and persons in Hilo built the main observatory building in the spring of 1912. Publications to date have been weekly reports since the summer of 1911, a memoir by Daly in the Proceedings of American Academy of Arts and Sciences in 1911, articles by the director in the Technology Review 1911 and the Honolulu Chamber of Commerce Annual 1912, articles by H. O. Wood in the Bulletin of the Seismological Society of America, and articles by Perret in the American Journal of Science. The Massachusetts Institute of Technology will publish semiannual reports.

This weekly bulletin as it appears in the Advertiser will be reprinted as a leaflet and sent to regular annual subscribers to the work of the association. C. H. Cooke is president of the Board of Directors of the association and R. W. Shingle is treasurer. New subscribers who are interested in our volcanoes will be welcomed in the association. The association aims: (1) To record volcanic activity and earthquakes in Hawaii; (2) to attract scientific men hither for special studies; (3) to promote the establishment of volcano observatories all over the world.

WHITNEY LABORATORY OF SEISMOLOGY.

The Whitney Laboratory of Seismology is equipped with two Bosch-Omori 100 kg tromometers registering N-S and E-W motion, a heavy Omori tromometer registering E-W motion and an Omori "ordinary Seismograph" designed for registering strong earthquakes in all three components of motion. These are seated on concrete piers in a closed basement room having practically constant temperature, beneath the chief Observatory building near the hotel. Time is referred to a rated chronometer, checked at intervals by solar observations with a transit. Both instruments are loaned by the College of Hawaii. At the substation by the edge of the active pit an Omori two-component tromometer with light steady masses is mounted on a concrete pier placed directly on the fresh lava surface. Hawaiian standard time (H. S. T.) is 10 hrs. 30 m. slower than Greenwich time.

CANCANI SCALE OF SEISMIC INTENSITY

Expressed by accelerations measured in millimeters per second per second.

I.	Instrumental	0.0	2.5
II.	Very slight	2.5	5.0
III.	Slight	5.0	10.0
IV.	Sensible, mediocre	10.0	25.0
V.	Rather strong	25.0	50.0
VI.	Strong	50.0	100.0
VII.	Very strong	100.0	250.0
VIII.	Ruinous	250.0	500.0
IX.	Disastrous	500.0	1000.0
X.	Very disastrous	1000.0	2500.0
XI.	Catastrophic	2500.0	5000.0
XII.	Great catastrophe	5000.0	10000.0

Grade IV. is ordinarily the minimum perceived by the senses; and in grade XII. the acceleration, or rate of change of motion (jerk) reaches that of terrestrial gravitation.

WEEKLY BULLETIN OF Hawaiian Volcano Observatory

Vol. II. HONOLULU, HAWAII, JUNE 24, 1914. No 25.

TECHNOLOGY STATION, Kilauea, June 11.—The week at the observatory on Kilauea has been notable for a very welcome visit from Frank A. Perret, K. I. C., the distinguished volcanologist of the Springfield Volcanic Research Association who started our work here in Hawaii in 1911, and who has since published in the American Journal of Science a remarkable series of articles on the results of his Kilauea studies. He is on his way back to Naples from Sakurajima in Japan, where he made an investigation for the Volcanologic Institute founded in Naples by Immanuel Friedlaender. It was an inspiring experience to have a few days in the field at Kilauea with Mr. Perret, collecting gases and specimens and making photographs.

The lava during the week has continued rising vigorously, though the floor is still much obscured by fumes, and it has not yet developed an open liquid pool. There are signs, however, that such a pool is forming by collapse of the crust in the west part of the floor. The mechanism of spouting cones has been replaced by quiet welling up of flows which spread over the floor, emitted either from cracks or from conelets. There are two well marked open pots with splashing lava within at the extreme border of the floor north and east northeast. Blazing chimneys with glowing lava within are increasing in size along great tangential cracks at the east and west ends of Halemaumau, high above the bottom, as though slices of the wall-rock were there splitting away with lava rising behind them.

June 4 at 3 p. m. from the old north resthouse the noises in the pit were of bubbling, hissing and thudding. Walking around the pit by the northwest, west and southwest stations, a fifteen inch open crack was found between the two latter, parallel to the edge of Halemaumau and fifty feet back of it, with warm sulphurous gas rising from it and the walls coated with a yellow deposit that is waxy in appearance and tastes like alum. It appears to be a mixture of alum and sulphur. This same deposit was found in the eastern fissures which have recently been newly emitting acrid fumes. On test by Mr. Perret, the cracks in question gave no reaction for hydrogen sulphide or hydrochloric acid. From the south station at 6 p. m. partial views of the floor showed a flow pouring toward its east northeast margin, where it ended by cascading downward—apparently into a pot which has since been seen there. This flow was approximately eighteen feet wide and sixty feet long, and the visible glowing part poured from under a crust or skin having a zigzag edge. Several gash-like glowing chimneys appeared in the east wall.

On June 5 an expedition was made with Mr. Perret to the Cone Crater and pits in the Kau desert. June 6 he took me to a spatter cone near the Kau road on the edge of Kilauea crater in its northwest corner, where it is possible to collect glass droplets of many different shapes, as they were ejected from this cone and fell unbroken into the soft soil.

June 7 at 10 a. m. from the south station Halemaumau was puffing loudly and the noises indicated great activity. A pot in the east northeast

WEEKLY BULLETIN
of
Hawaiian Volcano Observatory

Published at Honolulu, Hawaii, by the **Hawaiian Volcano Research Association**

Editor..............Howard M. Ballou
Professor of Physics, College of Hawaii

Entered as second-class matter January 20, 1914, at the post-office at Honolulu, Hawaii, under the Act of August 24, 1912.

border of the floor was belching and splashing with liquid lava. There was a continuous roaring hiss west. The south and southwest fumaroles under the cliff appeared more active than of late. On the sloping remnant of the 200-feet bench southwest a fumarole increasing in activity has developed in a network of cracks on the surface of the bench with yellow deposits. A similar yellow stained fumarole is in the talus just east of this bench. The southeast talus fumaroles were very active, one of them appearing to puff softly. The southeast cone on the floor was ejecting a flow from an oven on its southeast side. The northeast pot was boiling very actively and Old Faithful was a cone spouting lava from a triangular opening in its southeast side. The west and west northwest holes could not be seen, but were heard hissing like a freight engine, four puffs at a time.

The northeast gashes in the wall were glowing and the whole floor was a glistening black pahoehoe surface of fresh basalt. Everything indicated active rising. At 4 p. m. the pit was much quieter, the noise a mild plashing and blowing. The main blowing noises came from northeast and west. At 4:30 p. m. a flow was seen pouring over the surface from Old Faithful westward, the cone of the latter being submerged, but there was some jetting at the source of the flow. Cones were seen southeast, east and northeast. Occasional sharp hisses came from the west. Mr. Perret made collections of the mixed gases from the pit and the gas from the Sulphur Banks near the Volcano House.

June 8 at 6:30 p. m. from the southeast station a long lava flow was seen pouring out of the southeast cone on the floor and flowing northeast. It appeared to be 20 feet wide. From the south station at 7 p. m., many small flows were seen welling up in different parts of the floor, Old Faithful was occasionally spouting, and the noises were as usual.

June 9 at 5:30 p. m. the transit was set up at the south station, but fumes prevented sufficient continuous seeing to secure a measure of depth. Occasional glimpses revealed the east end of the floor where a very large black spatter cone has been built up, with glistening rounded surfaces and a hole on top. The east northeast pot had grown very large, it was at the edge of the floor against the wall and lava was splashing within. The southeast cone could be seen, but not Old Faithful. There were many glowing cracks and points of flame on the floor, indicating the outlines of recent flows and the noises of blowing and splashing were loud.

June 10 at 6:30 p. m. from the northwest the bottom could be seen. A strong flow which appeared to be thirty feet wide was pouring eastward over the floor. The whole floor appeared to be made up of recent glowing flows. At 7 p. m. small flows were welling up in different places, and from the south station a small cone under the east station was seen to be jetting lava. The noises were loud. At 9 p. m., occasional seeing from the south station showed the whole floor covered with crackling, glowing and flaming crusted flows. Hot lava welled up from cracks here and there. The open pot against the east northeast wall was smaller than the day before. Another was seen at the northern edge of the floor. Beside the large cone in the eastern part of the floor and a little to the north of it was a smaller one with multiple openings emitting blue spears of flame. Old Faithful could not be identified. The long vertical north-south gash was glowing and flaming high above the floor in the east wall. Another one is high above the floor at the west end. In the west part of the floor was a foundering crust area with zigzag edge and flows welling up cracks, appearing like a lake or a pocled part of a large flow. The floor appeared larger than ever before during this year: active rising is evident. The illumination of the fume-cloud was moderate.

T. A. JAGGAR, JR.,
Director.

Halemaumau from Northeast rim, Autumn 1909.

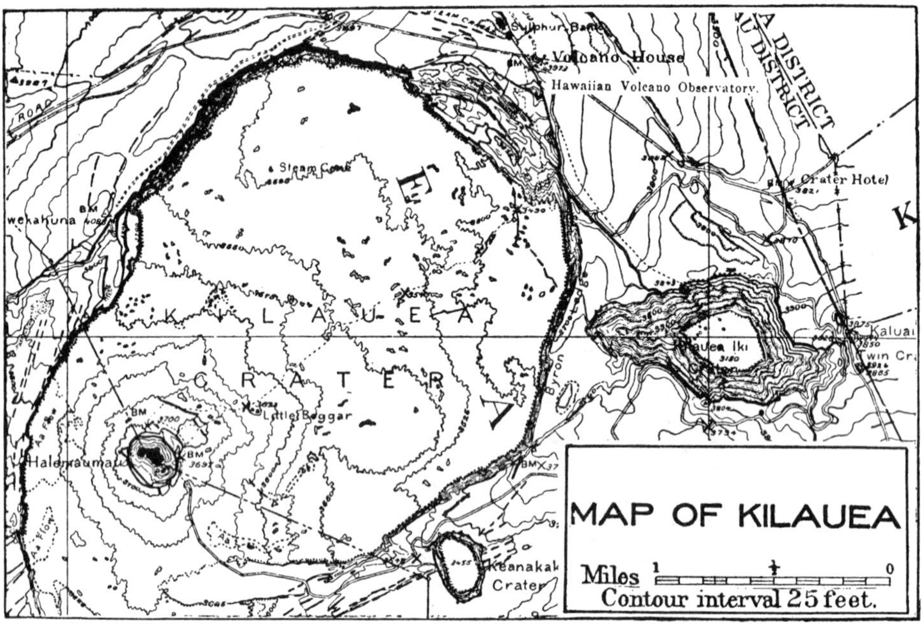

HAWAIIAN VOLCANO RESEARCH ASSOCIATION.

This society is a voluntary one, made up of subscribers to scientific work which is being executed by the Massachusetts Institute of Technology.

In 1913 there were 26 subscribers in Hawaii and Massachusetts, firms and individuals. A group of firms and persons in Hilo built the main observatory building in the spring of 1912. Publications to date have been weekly reports since the summer of 1911, a memoir by Daly in the Proceedings of American Academy of Arts and Sciences in 1911, articles by the director in the Technology Review 1911 and the Honolulu Chamber of Commerce Annual 1912, articles by H. O. Wood in the Bulletin of the Seismological Society of America, and articles by Perret in the American Journal of Science. The Massachusetts Institute of Technology will publish semiannual reports.

This weekly bulletin as it appears in the Advertiser will be reprinted as a leaflet and sent to regular annual subscribers to the work of the association. C. H. Cooke is president of the Board of Directors of the association and R. W. Shingle is treasurer. New subscribers who are interested in our volcanoes will be welcomed in the association. The association aims: (1) To record volcanic activity and earthquakes in Hawaii; (2) to attract scientific men hither for special studies; (3) to promote the establishment of volcano observatories all over the world.

WHITNEY LABORATORY OF SEISMOLOGY.

The Whitney Laboratory of Seismology is equipped with two Bosch-Omori 100 kg tromometers registering N-S and E-W motion, a heavy Omori tromometer registering E-W motion and an Omori "ordinary Seismograph" designed for registering strong earthquakes in all three components of motion. These are seated on concrete piers in a closed basement room having practically constant temperature, beneath the chief Observatory building near the hotel. Time is referred to a rated chronometer, checked at intervals by solar observations with a transit. Both instruments are loaned by the College of Hawaii. At the substation by the edge of the active pit an Omori two-component tromometer with light steady masses is mounted on a concrete pier placed directly on the fresh lava surface. Hawaiian standard time (H. S. T.) is 10 hrs. 30 m. slower than Greenwich time.

CANCANI SCALE OF SEISMIC INTENSITY

Expressed by accelerations measured in millimeters per second per second.

I.	Instrumental	0.0	2.5
II.	Very slight	2.5	5.0
III.	Slight	5.0	10.0
IV.	Sensible, mediocre....	10.0	25.0
V.	Rather strong	25.0	50.0
VI.	Strong	50.0	100.0
VII.	Very strong	100.0	250.0
VIII.	Ruinous	250.0	500.0
IX.	Disastrous	500.0	1000.0
X.	Very disastrous	1000.0	2500.0
XI.	Catastrophic	2500.0	5000.0
XII.	Great catastrophe....	5000.0	10000.0

Grade IV. is ordinarily the minimum perceived by the senses; and in grade XII. the acceleration, or rate of change of motion (jerk) reaches that of terrestrial gravitation.

WEEKLY BULLETIN
OF
Hawaiian Volcano Observatory

Vol. II. HONOLULU, HAWAII, JULY 1, 1914. No. 26.

TECHNOLOGY STATION, KILAUEA, June 18.—The lava column of Kilauea, during the week June 11-18, has overflowed the floor and risen rapidly, and a measurement secured June 15 shows depth to the floor below the south rim of 530 feet, indicating since the last measurement a rise of the eastern floor of forty-five feet in thirty-one days, or an average rise of 1.45 feet per day.

This marked rise on the approach of the summer solstice is quite in accord with the rule of the last seven years. Another phenomenon of the week which is in agreement with records of the last decade is the boiling up of the melt in the west and flow towards the east, and it now seems probable by all signs that if the present rise continues the first open pool will appear in the west end of Halemaumau. The thick fumes are still very obstructive to good seeing, but on Sunday night, June 14, the whole floor was revealed, covered with spactacular flows.

Thursday, June 11, 1914, at 7 p. m., from the south station, a small cone at the east end was seen to be blowing spray of incandescent lava out on the floor, and the floor was streaked with fire. From the old north resthouse, at 7:15 p. m., a cone on the floor west-northwest was seen to be ejecting jets, and so was a central fountain, presumably Old Faithful. The rumbling and blowing noises were loud, but no slides were heard and no flows seen.

At 5:45 o'clock on the evening of June 12 an attempt at surveying from the south station was defeated by the thick fumes. A glowing crack could be seen on the southeast part of the floor, and stalactites hung in front of glowing caverns on the north and northeast edges, while in the eastern part a small pool on the surface of the floor, with zigzag edges, was discernable from time to time, apparently a flow. A slide of talus west was heard about 5:40 p. m. The principal noise was moderate puffing and a continuous hiss at the west end. On the evening of June 13 the seeing was poor.

At sundown and long thereafter on June 13 three vapor jets were seen in the usual place on the high northeast flank of Mauna Loa, estimated by Mr. H. O. Wood to be at least 600 feet high. There were some others of smaller size. These jets are seen frequently at this time of the year when the air is still on the heights and the sinking sun in its summer northing gets behind the highest cones of the northeast rift, this being the place where the jets are seen. Mr. Perret tells me he frequently saw them in 1911.

Sunday evening, June 14, from 5 p. m. on, the pit exhibited a wonderful spectacle as darkness revealed its glowing depths. At first very loud roaring blasts were heard in rushing spasms, the sound coming first from one place, then from another, as heard from the southeast station, where the seeing was at first cut off by the curtain of vapor from the southeast fumaroles. From the south station there was occasional lifting of the curtain.

Everything indicated rapid rising; the loudest blasts were heard from the west. A flow covered with festoons of skin was seen pouring from the Old Faithful region to the south talus. As the flow crusted over, new toes would push out from under its skirts. A bubbling small fountain was seen at

WEEKLY BULLETIN
of
Hawaiian Volcano Observatory

Published at Honolulu, Hawaii, by the **Hawaiian Volcano Research Association**

Editor..............Howard M. Ballou
Professor of Physics, College of Hawaii

Entered as second-class matter January 20, 1914, at the post-office at Honolulu, Hawaii, under the Act of August 24, 1912.

about the Old Faithful position, with a flow flaring out westward from it. Dimly a big cone could be seen on the western end of the floor. The large cone on the eastern floor described June 9 and 10 had disappeared. At many points small holes on the surface were seen, apparently each at the source of flows, with confined gases rushing out in puffs and spitting lava. The wall pots east, northeast and north, were small but very active. The high gashes in the eastern wall were flaming and glowing within as usual. There was a fountaining pot in the middle of the western floor.

The noises in general were unusually loud at 5 p. m., and diminished markedly at 7 p. m.

As darkness approached, the west end was seen to be a large body of liquid lava with ragged flow-lines. The two high chimneys at the west were glowing. A narrow cascade developed at the east end from a half-cone built up against the wall, and the orifice discharged a flow which flared out below with festoons, the spatter from the craterlet appearing like dross from an anvil.

Finally, when darkness was complete, the whole floor was revealed, and a great fountain was seen welling up at the extreme northwest end of the floor area, sending a mighty flood of molten basalt like a river eastward over the whole bottom, forking into two leaf-like lobes north and south, and doubtless eventually making a new layer over the entire floor. The west central pot maintained its fountaining right through the surface of the new flow. The flow showed the usual zigzag lines bounding semi-crusted areas, these lines being mostly drawn out in the direction of flow.

June 15, at 2:20 p. m., the noises in general had diminished. The gases were hissing continuously at the east end. Strong puffing and spouting sounds came from the west. At 5:15 p. m. a change of wind made some seeing possible from the south station, and vertical and azimuth angles were obtained with transit from the south and southwest stations on a boiling pot in the floor against the northeast wall. These gave a depth of 528 feet below the south station and 531 feet below the southwest station, which is slightly higher. No incandescent flows were seen.

Since this time it has been rainy and the seeing has been unsatisfactory. At 6 p. m. Tuesday, June 16, from the south station a glimpse of the floor showed no flows, but a little jetting from the middle of the floor and the northeast border. The noises were as usual.

There has been glow of moderate brightness on the fume cloud during the week as seen from the Observatory. June 17, at 11:30 a. m., there was no seeing southeast or northwest. The wind at times seems to blow in convectionally from both sides of the pit, and no eddy whatever forms to make an opening. On this date the puffing was toward the west; a steady hiss could be heard in the central region and toward the east, and the fumes which rose around the Old Resthouse were very acrid. At 5:30 p. m., from the southeast station, a central pot was seen to be blowing lava out on to the floor, and some orifice under the east station was puffing very loudly. The noises of this date compared in intensity with those of June 14.

The week has been quiet seismically.

T. A. JAGGAR, JR.,
Director.

WEEKLY BULLETINS
OF THE
Hawaiian Volcano Observatory

Vol. II. HONOLULU, HAWAII, AUGUST 1, 1914. No. 27.

TECHNOLOGY STATION, June 25. —The time of the solstice of June 22 has been, as usual, marked by volcanic and seismic happenings. There have been volcanic eruptions in California and in the Philippines, the lava of Kilauea displays rising activity, and for June 19 and 20 the seismographs recorded two local and one distant earthquakes.

Halemaumau crater continues to exhibit rising lava with occasional brilliant displays, the whole floor, about 520 feet down, being occasionally visible at night, dotted with spouting and flaming cones. There has been fair seeing recently from the Old Resthouse, with thinner fumes. The rising proceeds in pulsations of two orders, the one of a few hours and the other of about a half-weekly period; that is, there is a marked diurnal fluctuation, and there are brilliant displays of overflow of the bottom about twice a week. This suggests accumulation and periodic expulsion of hot gas from the lava column.

Thursday, June 18, from 5 to 8 p. m., there was at first little seeing from the south station, but with a slight change of wind from northeast to north as the evening advanced, the eddy carried the fumes up the west wall and revealed the bottom. The eastern floor, from 6:30 to 7:30 p. m., showed many spitting holes and small wall-pots northeast and north. There appeared to be a cavern at the border of the floor east under the high flaming gashes. The southeast conelet had developed a high inclined spatterhorn. Old Faithful was spurting incandescent "tears" fifty feet high at forty-second intervals. A spot just west of Old Faithful showed pasty lava bubbling sluggishly.

At nightfall a magnificent spectacle was presented near the southwest border of the floor, where a large flat dome burst into eruption like an artesian well of fire, with a lava fountain on top which poured radial flows down all sides, the largest flowing eastward, where it widened and forked into lobes. At the west there was a spouting cavern under the wall which ejected splash down a half-cone onto the floor. At the northwest and west flaming cones could be seen. Fierce hissing noises came from a northeast cone on the floor and from Old Faithful. Everything pointed to intense rising activity, and the southeast talus fumaroles appeared to be ever creeping higher, widening radially, and consuming the slide.

From 4 to 10 p. m., June 19, conditions remained as on the previous day and the evening display was very brilliant. The noises were loud, the eastern cone and Old Faithful ejected lava spray, a flow was pouring past the south side of Old Faithful eastward, the floor was streaked with incandescent cracks and dotted with flaming holes, and the flaring glow on the fume-cloud was bright as seen from the Volcano House.

A lull in this activity occurred during the next two days. June 20, from 5 to 6 p. m., from the south station, the floor appeared black, without active flows, there was slight puffing, and fire could be seen in the northeast pot, the east cone, the high east gashes and at Old Faithful. June 21, at 5 p. m., from the Old North Resthouse continuous blowing could be heard east and west, and in the middle Old Faithful uttered a great blast once in from forty to sixty seconds. After some of these puffs the

WEEKLY BULLETINS
of the
Hawaiian Volcano Observatory

Published Monthly at Honolulu, Hawaii, by the Hawaiian Volcano Research Association

Editor..............Howard M. Ballou
Professor of Physics, College of Hawaii

Application pending for entry as second-class matter at the postoffice, Honolulu, Hawaii.

spatter could be heard falling on the floor.

Occasionally there was a secondary puff from Old Faithful after from 10 to 12 seconds. As a whole the pit was noisy and sometimes a deep thud or rumble could be heard. Two rock slides were heard from the northeast wall. Fumes from the southeast fumaroles were very acrid east, southeast and south of the pit. All the conditions point to temporary subsidence. Between 6 and 7 p. m. there was some seeing from the northwest station.

For the first time in many months I obtained a good view of the west corner of the floor. This was seen to extend westward into a sharp point in plan, with three cones along the west-northwest border flaming and spurting sluggishly, the noises having diminished markedly within two hours. These west cones on the floor are what were taken for high chimneys in the wall as seen through the fumes from the south station recently. The round black crater-like hole high in a projection of the west wall was seen to be wholly without activity, unchanged since last year.

Monday, June 22 at 3 p. m., from the southeast station a flow was seen pouring from the middle of the floor toward the southeast. Noises were very loud from the west. At 5 p. m. Old Faithful was spouting and the flow had stopped.

June 23 at 8:30 p. m., the noises were loud and the seeing was altogether from the west and northwest. The noises had decreased by 10:30 p. m. From the northwest station the whole floor was revealed, shaped like a boot, with the toe at the west, the instep bending around the great southern talus slopes, and the back, heel and sole at the foot of immense cliffs, east, north and northwest. Sluggish pots were bubbling along the northeast wall. The western cones were all spurting, and glowing cracks made a network in the floor. It was impossible to tell whether the floor was level, though it appeared so, and banners of flame waved over many vents.

On June 24 from 8 to 9 p. m., the appearance was much the same but less active; two spatter cones were building on the floor under the northwest wall, jetting spray which partly hardened before it fell to distances of ten or twenty feet. Around the actual orifices liquid lava splashed out. A large cone with an open orifice was spouting west-northwest and another smaller oven at the point of the west cove. Flames were numerous, the blowing was mild, and but one small slide was heard on the west. The greater activity of these western spouting cones over the eastern suggests what has been the rule for years past in the case of the open pools, that the rising under the crust is at the west and the streaming and down-sucking towards the east. In the crusted condition, then, these most active cones correspond to the "baby fountains" of the liquid pools.

This week has produced the brightest glow on the fume cloud at night which has been seen this year.

There was a small local earthquake about 11:14 a. m., June 19, a distant earthquake was recorded about 7:53 p. m., local time, June 19, which wrote its record for about one hour, and a moderate local shock which was felt in Hilo and disturbed the Ordinary Seismograph took place about 1:40 p. m. June 20, 1914. Another local shock took place this morning, June 25, strong enough to start the Ordinary Seismograph.

T. A. JAGGAR, JR.,
Director.

TECHNOLOGY STATION, July 2.—The end of June 1914, presents Kilauea in a state of pronounced rising activity, the maximum following the solstice being not yet reached. The highest measured level of the year was recorded as 517 feet below the south southeast rim, the lava in a lateral conelet on the south talus reaching 39 feet higher; this record being of date June 28.

Friday, June 26, from the southeast station at 4 p. m. the floor could be seen without incandescence, while the sounds of puffing and hissing were mostly from the west. At 7:30 p. m. from the south station there was evidence, in the glowing outline and fire streaking, of a recent flow within three hours covering the whole floor and apparently having origin at the west end. Border cones west northwest and northwest were spurting lava out on the floor. The noises were loud.

June 27 at 6:30 p. m. from the southeast station a cone on the floor at its east end was seen to be blowing out jets of lava. The noises were loud. As darkness approached, at 7 p. m., from the south station the floor was seen to be streaked with glowing lines, two northwest cones were spitting, and some rock sliding was heard.

June 28 from the south and southeast stations at about 7 p. m. measurements were made with transit. A recently developed cone on the lower slope of the south talus proved to be 478 feet below a mean point of the south southeast rim, while an open pot in the middle of the eastern part of the floor at about the Old Faithful position measured 517 feet down. This would make the talus conelet 39 feet above the middle of the floor, and probably still higher above the border, supposing the floor to be flatly conical. This conelet had poured lava down the slope below it to the floor level in a cascade now frozen, showing one of those remarkable mechanisms whereby the basalt foam may be pumped by its contained expanding gas 40 to 50 feet above the average level of the presumed liquid lake under the crust at the top of the main lava column.

The bottom of the crater at this time was mildly hissing, fresh small flows could be seen at various places on the floor, fanning out and glowing on the northeast portion. There were two open pots in the middle, an openwork glow cone at the east end, wall pots along the eastern border, and the strongly glowing edge of a new flow southeast.

June 29 at 5:30 p. m. the floor could be seen clearly from the northwest station, and eleven cones, some of them quite high, could be counted on the floor. Only a few were jetting lava. The hissing noises were moderate, and a few rock slides were heard towards the west. These continued at 7 p. m., and darkness revealed the usual network of glowing cracks on the floor.

July 1 indicated that the temporary lull of two days before was being replaced by renewed activity. Loud rhythmic puffs and strong hissing could be heard all the afternoon and rock falls were heard at 6:15 and at 7 p. m. From the south station the many glowing cones were seen, and open pots at the west end, at Old Faithful, east of Old Faithful and at the east end. The glowing cone on the south talus had increased in size. About 7:15 Old Faithful caved in and became a large pot, almost a pool, about 40 feet long in a north to south direction and 25 feet wide. A liquid pool within surged violently, making a bright glow which flared on the cloud above.

The eastern pot appeared also as an opening with liquid lava splashing within, and with huge stalactites hanging within its lip. The eastern high chimneys appeared to have diminished in size and brightness. A fresh flow was glowing on the southeast floor, and the southeast talus fumaroles were emitting very voluminous smoke.

The earthquake record of the Whitney Laboratory of Seismology for the week has shown nothing unusual, and the summit of Mauna Loa appears sparklingly clear and free from vapor in the evening light on this date, July 2, 1914.

T. A. JAGGAR JR.,
Director.

TECHNOLOGY STATION, July 9.—The lava of Halemaumau continues to rise slowly and the flat floor of black lava to increase in size. It is now about one thousand feet long, with partly vertical walls five hundred feet high, east, north and west, and sloping remnants of talus and benches on the south. A gigantic gas-cone built of spatter, fully thirty feet high, has been raised within two weeks on the south talus, its base being about twenty feet above the floor, and it is surrounded by frozen cascades of lava that extend down to the floor.

The crust that forms the floor, while it has been built of flows from many vents, now appears like the flat, frozen surface of a large lake, the more so in that a pool about eighty feet long and twenty feet wide appeared around the fountain Old Faithful July 6, with very active bubble fountains in the intervals of the larger explosions, this time being coincident with great seismic activity, as reported by Mr. Wood hereafter; at present the activity and size of the Old Faithful pool has somewhat diminished.

Both volcanic and seismic activity thereby coincided remarkably with expectable luni-solar strain. This season's results, added to those of the past three years, promise important conclusions to the effect that Kilauea is in some sense a barometer of earth tides.

July 2, at 7 p. m., the activity was moderate with hissing noises, a cone over Old Faithful, an open pot east, numerous flames, and the cone in the south talus spurting gas and spatter and increasing in height. On the evening of July 3 the puffings were louder, Old Faithful had developed a splashing pot by collapse, ten or eleven cones could be counted, besides the high one on the south talus, and the great chimneys east were flaming. A fountain could be seen in the Old Faithful pot, and lava stalactites hung on its rim. July 4 conditions were the same, the noise of plashing fountains being added to the hissing and puffing sounds.

From six to seven o'clock on the evening of July 5, the Old Faithful pot had enlarged to the northwest and the fountaining was more violent. July 6, from 5 to 7 p. m., from the south station (all the foregoing observations were from this station) the high south cone was spitting lava from the southwest side of its summit, and Old Faithful had broken away into a long pool in the floor trending northwest to southeast, about eighty by twenty feet in dimensions and with walls eight or ten feet above the liquid flood within, pointed at the ends in plan. The glowing lava of the pool was boiling with many baby fountains, and occasionally the great fountain would dome up and splash the walls. The noise at the east end was a continuous hiss, but the south cone emitted loud puffs of gas every three to four seconds. The southern high fumarole, at about the 200-foot level below the rim, was emitting very dense fumes. The east flaming chimneys were very active, with much blue smoke.

July 7 at 5:30 p.m. the temperature of the Postal rift was 308 deg. C. (586 deg. F.) and of the air 22 deg. C. (72 deg. F.). The noises from the north were general bubbling, rumbling and hissing. From the south station at 6 to 8 p.m., conditions were as before with possibly greater activity, the Old Faithful interval twenty-five to thirty seconds, and the walls of the pool about twelve feet high hanging with stalactites. The south cone appeared to be about thirty feet high. July 8 the appearances were the same, with glowing cracks over the floor probably indicative of new overflow, and hence rising.

The following report from the Whitney Laboratory of Seismology is submitted by H. O. Wood:

During the week ending July 8 sixteen local earthquakes were registered. All but two of these occurred within a period of forty-eight hours on July 5, 6 and 7, eleven of them between 2:44 p.m. July 5 and 1:41 a.m. July 6. It is interesting to note that this group of shocks occurred at the maximum of the hypothetical fortnightly variation in earth strain due to the action of lunar declination compounded with that of solar declination. Also, on the basis of this hypothesis, which we are testing at Kilauea, the maximum in question is one of the six high maximums of the year. The shocks of the week occurred at the following approximate times:

July 1, 6:39 p.m.; July 2, 5:32 p.m.; July 5, 2:44 p.m. 3:18 p.m., 3:54 p.m., 4:38 p.m., 6:45 p.m., 7:20 p.m., 7:32 p.m., 8:06 p.m., 9:39 p.m.; July 6, 1:41 a.m.; July 7, 11:07 a.m., 12:47 p.m. (noon), 1:25 p.m.

Of these, four, all of the July 5-6 group, were instrumentally strong or moderately strong. All the others were instrumentally feeble shocks. The shock at 7:20 p.m. on July 5 was distinctly felt by people staying in cottages about two miles toward Hilo from the Observatory, but no one in the close neighborhood of the Observatory noted it with certainty. Besides this the shocks at 3:18 p.m. and 4:38 p.m. on July 5 were instrumentally strong enough to belong to the perceptible class, though they passed unnoticed. This was true also of the shock which occurred at 1:41 a.m. on July 6.

T. A. JAGGAR, JR.
Director.

TECHNOLOGY STATION, July 16. —The week July 9 to 15, inclusive, at the lava pool of Kilauea volcano shows no diminution in the tendency to rise by overflow and the building of driblet cones. The main lava pool around Old Faithful fountain grows no larger, but other pots have from time to time increased in size so as to merit the name of pools, and the floor area has distinctly increased in size and encroached on the talus. The fumes have probably diminished somewhat in volume during the week and there have been several occasions of good seeing in the daytime from both the southeast and northwest rims of the pit. From the old north resthouse it has been possible to see the whole floor and even to obtain photographs of part of it, although its approximate depth is still five hundred feet.

At night there have been fine spectacles of lava-flow welling over from the pots and cones onto the floor, and in one instance pouring down into a pot where the liquid was engulfed amid bubbling fountains.

On July 9, Thursday, at 11:30 a. m., there was partial seeing from the south station under the veil of fumes. The noises were light puffing from the west and hissing from the east. At 12:30 p. m., from the north resthouse, the wind veered for an hour to the east and opened the floor to good seeing. A small fuming talus appeared under the north wall; otherwise the walls of rock east, north and northwest descended directly to the lava floor. A glowing vertical crack in the wall, parallel to the border of the floor, was flaming a few feet above it on the northwest side of the bottom. Three cones had been built on the floor near the west end, the middle one, the largest, piled like a haystack against the wall. The west corner was now nearly a right angle in plan; when last seen it was acutely pointed. Old Faithful was an elongate pot with black stalactites hanging in its lip, with sluggishly boiling lava within like thick, black mush. All was coated with a mobile black skin, and the activity was mild, without high domings. The south cone was emitting sharp puffs, and Old Faithful was rumbling. A little talus-sliding was heard west-southwest and south, all the conditions indicating temporary stagnation.

Twelve fuming places were counted in the periphery and on the floor. There were two cones on the middle part of the floor in a line west from Old Faithful. The gas cone on the south talus could be plainly seen across the floor, and it appeared certainly thirty feet high, its base well up the talus slope, with black flows from it down to the floor.

Old Faithful sluggishly exploded every thirty-five to forty seconds, with an occasionally subordinate interval of twelve to fifteen seconds. Sometimes it would splash incandescent lava over the whole rim of its pot. The length of the pot was about one-twentieth of the floor, or say fifty feet. The inactive round craterlet high up the northwest wall remained unaltered. The larger west-northwest cone on the border of the floor showed openwork glow. The floor exhibited glossy, thin surface flows of pahoehoe of different luster from those beneath, and the whole floor appeared very flat.

On the evening of July 10, 7 to 8

o'clock, from the south to east stations, Old Faithful was seen boiling and spurting to some height and the south cone was noisily ejecting spatter. July 11 at 3 p.m., and at other times that day the smoke from the pit seemed unusually brown. There were hissing noises east and west in the pit. At four p.m. Old Faithful could be seen, and a northeast cone on the floor, while the northernmost of the three west cones had three openings and a small frozen flow around them. In the evening a thin flow was seen covering the west half of the floor, with two or more sources in the west cones.

Sunday, July 12, seeing was poor, while the hissing noise was loud especially from the west, but no rock sliding was heard. July 13, from 5 to 6 p.m., there was faint seeing from the south station. The south and southeast fumaroles in the talus were belching dense vapor, the south cone was hissing strongly in blasts every three to five seconds and occasional puffs could be heard from the west end. The large east chimney was glowing, as well as a line of three or more cavities back of a thin slab of the vertical eastern wall. A cone could be seen east-northeast and an open pot against the northeast wall, the east end of Old Faithful was pointed, and a cone occupied the middle of the southeast floor.

The evening of July 14 was spectacular. From 8 to 9 p.m. the floor was completely visible from the Old Rest-house (north). Along the northeast wall from northwest to southeast poured a sheaf of lava over the floor, fountaining continuously at its source and cascading down into a large pot about thirty feet in diameter at its termination. The pot terminus boiled with baby fountains. This stream was perhaps 100 feet long, and shaped like a spindle. From it a large lobate flow spread over the southeast floor. Another small flow, with much spatter at its source, bubbled out of a northeast wall orifice at the edge of the floor. Old Faithful was a round 30-foot pot fountaining violently in the middle region, most of it was a cone with a gash-like opening up which lava surged and spouted spray to a height of forty feet or more, and the western cones and wall chimney flamed with a blowpipe brightness. A small openwork cone in the southwest part of the floor bubbled feebly.

Old Faithful was at first overbrimming, but later sank a foot or two into its pot. This performance of intense activity, with rising, lasted a half-hour with something like ten-minute pulsations of alternate rising and ebbing; then the ebbing became dominant, activity diminished at all the vents and the west cones became less luminous at their flame vents. The northeast flow totally ceased, its source became a dim cone, and its terminus became an open pot like Old Faithful in size and shape, containing many baby fountains continuously active. There were two glowing holes under the north talus; in all 23 glow holes of all sizes were visible on the floor and walls. At 10 p.m. a flow started from the west corner, spreading around the two southwest cones on the floor. The most intense heat on this evening, to judge by the glow, was the yellow incandescence about the flaming west cones and wall chimney.

July 15 at 4 p.m. from the east station a strong avalanche was heard and the Old Faithful and northeast pots were seen to be low and sluggish. In the evening Old Faithful and a hole west of it showed bubble fountains about ten feet down, the noises were steady hissing, and three light slides were heard.

Mr. H. O. Wood reports for the Whitney Laboratory of Seismology that the week has been quiet seismically.

T. A. JAGGAR, JR.,
Director.

TECHNOLOGY STATION, Kilauea, July 23.—During the week ending with July 22 the action of Kilauea has been more than commonly instructive, though perhaps a little less brilliant and spectacular than just previously.

On July 16, for over an hour, from noon to one o'clock, there was good seeing from the northeast, north and northwest stations. From the north station the cone on the floor in the west corner, some twenty feet high, was seen clearly. From this cone came the flow seen at 10 p.m. on July 14. Against the west-northwest wall there was a cone with a long east to west slot-like opening out of which lava was slopping. North of this there was a north to south chimney in the wall. ''Old Faithful'' was an open pool with active glowing lava at a depth of about ten feet below the adjacent surface. It was rimmed with stalactites. In it were bubble-fountains playing continuously and moving from east to west, and with occasional large fountaining movements. The east end of the ''Old Faithful'' pool was crusted over and surmounted by a low cone in which there showed a small opening. From the south cone came a loud, steady, hissing sound. The base of this cone was still high above the floor on the talus. At the northeast there were five open pots and cones. One avalanche was heard in the talus in the eastern part of the pit.

On July 17 there was good seeing a little after noon from near the Old Rest-house. Conditions were practically the same as on July 16. Most of the noise of eruption came from the south cone, a steady, sharp hissing.

In the afternoon on July 18 the seeing was not very good. From the south station conditions were seen to be much the same as on July 16 and 17. A triangular pot was noticed on the floor at the northeast. The ''Old Faithful'' pool was smaller, but it still showed active fountain action. The sounds of eruption were as usual.

In the early morning of July 19 the fume cloud was brilliantly illuminated with a steady light, punctuated with very bright flaring. From 10 a.m. till after noon there was partial seeing from the north station. ''Old Faithful'' was an active, fountaining pool the size of which enlarged considerably during the interval of watching. There was sound of steady hissing, probably coming from the south cone.

On July 20 in the early morning hours there was a very prolonged and very brilliant illumination of the fumes, with bright flaring, indicating, probably, a large flow of considerable duration. From about 4 p.m. until 9:30 p.m. there was good seeing from the vicinity of the Old Rest House. Before nightfall there were a number of prolonged intervals, some of several minutes duration, during which the pit was almost free of fumes. The floor area was covered with coarsely festooned, fresh, bronze-tinted lava the surface of which presented a ''checked'' appearance somewhat like the ''check'' patterns in cross-sections of dry wood, or the bark of some trees. A very fresh flow, probably that of the morning, from the two cones at the north edge of the floor covered from two-thirds to three-quarters its area, extending to the edge all along the northern and eastern borders of the floor. This had almost obliterated, temporarily, the ''Old Faithful'' orifice, which now consisted of a narrow crack with an aureole of very small cracks marking its periphery, all evidences of a cone having disappeared. The central crack perceptibly enlarged during the watch, but the pool did not re-open. There were two active ''bee-hive'' cones in a line northwest from ''Old Faithful,'' from both of which at considerable intervals small red-hot lava fragments were ejected. Similar ejections took place from the northwest and west-northwest cones, in the neighborhood of which were small fresh flows with complexly draped surface forms. There were several gash orifices in the floor along its east-northeast margin and at the north and northwest. Besides these, the high east-northeast chimney and an orifice a little lower down at the south were seen very distinctly.

From this latter orifice a fresh lava cascade fell down the talus slope to and out onto the floor. Though well developed when first seen this cascade was still in action, and continued to work throughout the stay at the pit. Its action was very instructive. No description of such behavior has come to the writer's notice, though it must have been observed many times in former days at this volcano. The cascade was seen clearly by daylight and the surface color of its lava, where cooled, was strongly suggestive of a straw-yellow transparent color laid over a metallic bronze. Its surface structure, or miniature physiography, appeared as a system of tubes, probably from six to eighteen inches in external diameter, some leading in a fairly straight line down the slope, but many very completely contorted and so arranged as to suggest a badly tangled knot of fire-hose or hawsers, all leading down fan-fashion to the floor and then out upon it, appearing there as a group of "toes" or "pushes." An incessant crackling sound, with a subdued tinkling note, proceeded from this cascade, due to the rending of cooled crusts as the action described below went on.

First from one and then from another of these tubes tiny, sluggish flows were seen oozing out. These soon cooled over, thus extending and complicating the tube system. Some of these outbreaks occurred at or near the ends of the tubes on the floor, others broke out higher up the slope forming new tubular segments branching from a small parent tube. The supply of lava welling up at the source was scanty, and it appeared to be very viscous, oozing slowly down the tubes. This action, while much less spectacular than a "waterfall of lava," and in no sense like such a down-pouring, was extremely instructive, illustrating clearly the mechanism and manner of formation of the tubular cascades, so many of which may be seen in various parts of the main crater.

An intermittent flame was flaring at the orifice at the head of the cascade, while a yellowish-white flame burned for some seconds at a small orifice in the surface of the fresh northern flow early in the evening. The usual blue flames were flaring from all or nearly all the well defined orifices.

Rhythmic gas discharge sounds were heard coming from the south cone and a continuous surging sound punctuated with booming noises from all parts of the floor. Relative to earlier stages of the present revival of activity these sounds were not loud. A few very trival rock-falls occurred.

In the afternoon and evening of July 21 there were excellent views of the floor from the Old Rest House. All the cones and orifices seen on the previous day were seen clearly. The "Old Faithful" place had again become a small pool with incessant boiling and occasional doming-fountain action when large splashes of molten lava were thrown out upon the floor. Similar action was seen in the cone under the west northwest station. Altogether there were fifteen orifices in the floor area in which boiling lava was plainly visible. Besides this there were many cracks in the floor, through which brightly glowing lava could be seen. More than at any time of late the appearance of the floor suggested a great lava lake beneath, with a comparatively heavy "ice" of lava-crust breached by numerous cracks and "breathing holes."

No flows occurred and no avalanches were heard, though steady hissing was heard from the south cone, interrupted by loud puffing sounds.

In the late afternoon and early evening of July 22 there was good, but interrupted, seeing of the eastern part of the pit-bottom from the south and southeast stations. "Old Faithful" was a pool of nearly rectangular form with rounded corners, about twenty-five by thirty-five feet in dimension, in which at a depth of from six to ten feet below the adjacent surface there was incessant boiling with appearances of streaming from west to east. Occasionally at irregular intervals of more than one minute, there was the characteristic doming-fountain action, but no out-splashing was observed. Heavy stalactites rimmed the pool. Small, short radial cracks were seen leading from the high active east-northeast chimney. The gash orifices in the floor at the east and northeast were as usual, and the usual hissing and puffing emanated from the south cone. Brief glimpses of parts of the western part of the pit disclosed the conditions seen on July 20 and 21 without significant change.

Just before 8 p. m. a slight change in the wind drove the fumes up over the southeast margin of the pit, necessitating a somewhat prolonged exposure to them, which fixed attention on the fact that the fumes from the pit itself are now much sharper, though thinner, than earlier in the year.

Following is a report from the Whitney Laboratory of Seismology: During the fortnight ending with July 22 sixteen earthquakes were registered all of which, except one, were imperceptible to the senses of persons in the vicinity of the Observatory, and all except three were shocks of very, very small magnitude.

Two of the number were simply the chief-phase portions of feeble distant earthquakes; one, on July 16, vaguely beginning at 8:51:04 p. m. H. S. T. and ending even more vaguely about fifteen minutes later; the other, on July 21, beginning quite clearly at 12:15:09 p. m. H. S. T. and ending vaguely at about 12:36:09 p. m. H. S. T.

All the rest were local shocks occurring at the following times:

July 8, from 11:47:39 a. m. to 11:48.5 a. m. H. S. T.; 7:21:45 p. m. to 7:23:28 p. m. July 9, 9:36:43 a. m. to 9:38:25 a. m.; 1:31:57 p. m. to 1:33:11 p. m.; 1:38:04 p. m. to 1:39:46 p. m.; 2:18:19 p. m. to 2:19:02 p. m.; 5:24:51 p. m. to 5:25:29 p. m. July 14, 9:19:23 p. to 9:20:51 p. m. July 16, 6:17:07 a. m. to 6:17:50 a. m. July 17, 12:11:20 a. m. to 12:13:28 a. m.; 8:39:55 p. m. to 8:41:23 p. m. July 19, 8:50:47 a. m. to 8:51:22 a. m. July 20, 4:03:20 a. m. to 4:06:33 a. m. July 22, 9:09:24 a. m. to 9:10:08 a. m. H. S. T.

The shock at about 9:37 a. m. on July 9 had a maximum acceleration in the east to west component just below the least perceptible value, but less than a third this strength in the north to south component. The shock was not felt.

The shock on July 19 was not felt by anyone; it measures just higher than the theoretica' least perceptible value in the east to west component, but only half this value in the north to south component.

The shock on July 20 was distinctly felt by two persons lying awake and one or two more were wakened at the time of its occurrence but did not realize the cause. These were probably sleeping very lightly. It probably reached an intensity of only II-III R.-F.

H. O. WOOD, Associate.

A systematic report from the Whitney Laboratory of Seismology covering the period beginning April 21, 1914, and ending July 22, 1914, is submitted here. Systematic reports upon the shocks of earthquake registered during this interval were delayed for a long time by repeated failure to secure measures for the correction of time, and subsequently owing to a short absence from the Observatory of the writer.

April 21, from 7:24:13 a. m. to 7:25:08 a. m. H. S. T. Intensity, medium III Cancani scale; 30% to 70% of the minimum perceptible unit. Origin distant about 12.4 miles.

April 29, from 2:50:10 p. m. to 3:15 approx. H. S. T. Intensity, II R.-F., VI-VII Cancani scale; a felt shock: from 5 to 25 times the minimum perceptible unit. Origin distant about 20 miles.

April 29, from 2:59:36 p. m. to 2:59:54 p. m. H. S. T. Intensity, V-VI Cancani scale; about 4 times the minimum perceptible unit: the second maximum in the felt shock.

April 29, from 6:37:25 p. m. to 6:38:15 p. m. H. S. T. Intensity, low I Cancani scale; 5% to 6% of the minimum perceptible unit. Origin distance indeterminate.

April 30, from 3:18:42 a. m. to 3:19:46 a. m. H. S. T. Intensity, low III Cancani scale; about 65% of the minimum perceptible unit. Origin distance indeterminate.

April 30, from 11:28:30 a. m. to 11:30:00 a. m. H. S. T. Intensity, low III Cancani scale; about 70% of the minimum perceptible unit. Origin distant about 18.6 miles.

May 12, from 11:12:30 a. m. to 11:13:00 a. m. H. S. T. Intensity, III-IV Cancani scale; about the minimum perceptible unit, but not felt. Origin distance indeterminate.

May 12, from 9:10:14 p. m. to 9:12:34 p. m. H. S. T. Intensity, I R.-F., III Cancani scale; but less than 90% of the minimum perceptible unit. Origin distant about 15.5 miles.

May 12, from 9:59:36 p. m. to 10:00:13 p. m. H. S. T. Intensity, high II Cancani scale; about 45% of the minimum perceptible unit. Origin distant about 12.4 miles.

May 13, from 3:41:54 p. m. to 3:42:31 p. m. H. S. T. Intensity, medium IV Cancani scale; about 2.5 times the minimum perceptible unit, but yet not felt. Origin distant about 10 miles.

May 15, a feebly registered teleseism, distance indeterminate, E. at 9:50 approx. a. m. H. S. T. F. wholly indefinite.

May 22, from 4:38:26 a. m. to 4:39:25 a. m. H. S. T. Intensity, medium II Cancani scale; about 35% of the minimum perceptible unit. Origin distant about 13 miles.

May 23, from 7:52:24 p. m. to 7:54:01 p. m. H. S. T. Intensity, II Cancani scale; about 30% of the minimum perceptible unit. Origin distant about 25 miles.

May 24, from 5:27:35 a. m. to 5:28:59 a. m. H. S. T. Intensity, II-III Cancani scale; about 50% of the minimum perceptible unit. Origin distant about 13 miles.

May 26, from 2:01:49 a. m. to 2:02:24 a. m. H. S. T. Intensity, high II Cancani scale; about 40% of the minimum perceptible unit. Origin distant about 13 miles.

May 26, from 4:05:17 a. m. to 5:16 approx. a. m. H. S. T. A teleseism. Intensity, locally negligible, at origin uncertain, but not a very great shock. Distance of origin about 6,000 miles.

May 27, from 3:30:18 p. m. to 3:31:58 p. m. H. S. T. Intensity, medium I Cancani scale; about 14% of the minimum perceptible unit. Origin distant about 30 miles.

May 28, from 9:17:27 a. m. to 9:18:57 a. m. H. S. T. Intensity, high I Cancani scale; about 24% of the minimum perceptible unit. Origin distant about 9.3 miles.

May 29, from 8:23:26 p. m. to 8:24:22 p. m. H. S. T. Intensity, medium III Cancani scale; about 80% of the minimum perceptible unit. Origin distant about 10 miles.

June 1, a felt shock, III R.-F., began 6:29:28 a. m. H. S. T., then pens off. Intensity, beyond instrumental range.

June 1, from 12:16:03 p. m. to 12:16:51 p. m. H. S. T. Intensity, II-III Cancani scale; 50% to 60% of the minimum perceptible unit. Origin distant about 6.9 miles.

June 2, from 5:15:02 a. m. to 5:15:40 a. m. H. S. T. Intensity, low I Cancani scale; about 6.5% of the minimum perceptible unit. Origin distance indeterminate.

June 2, from 5:25:37 p. m. to 5:26:28 p. m. H. S. T. Intensity, medium III Cancani scale; about 65% of the minimum perceptible unit. Origin distant about 7.5 miles.

June 2, from 6:24:45 p. m. to 6:25:22 p. m. H. S. T. Intensity, medium III Cancani scale; about 65% of the minimum perceptible unit.

June 5, from 4:54:14 p. m. to 4:55:35 p. m. H. S. T. Intensity, medium II Cancani scale; about 32% of the minimum perceptible unit. Origin distant about 15 miles in a northeasterly direction.

June 11, from 10:06:49 p. m. to 10:08:37 p. m. H. S. T. Intensity, medium I Cancani scale; about 11% of the minimum perceptible unit. Origin distant about 27 miles.

June 15, from 1:54:50 p. m. to 1:55:10 p. m. H. S. T. Intensity, medium to high I Cancani scale; 20% of the minimum perceptible unit. Origin distance indeterminate.

June 17, from 8:43:03 a. m. to 8:44 approx. a. m. H. S. T. Intensity, low I Cancani scale; 5% to 6% of the minimum perceptible unit. Origin distant about 12 miles.

June 19, from 11:20:20 a. m. to 11:21:29 a. m. H. S. T. Intensity, III-IV Cancani scale; 60% to 100% of the minimum perceptible unit, but not felt. Origin distant about 19.4 miles.

June 19, a feebly registered teleseism from 8:59:26 p. m. to 9:32 approx. according to H. S. T. Origin distant about 3,700 miles. Phases measured.

June 20, from 12:47:30 a. m. to 12:48:18 a. m. H. S. T. Intensity, II-III Cancani scale; about 50% of the minimum perceptible unit. Origin distant about 11.7 miles.

June 20, from 1:46:00 p. m. to 1:48:38 p. m. H. S. T. Intensity, IV Cancani scale; nearly 2 times the minimum perceptible unit, but not felt. Origin distant about 10 miles.

June 22, from 5:22.8 p. m. to 5:40.7 p. m. H. S. T. A teleseism, no phases. Origin distance indeterminate.

June 25, from 9:29:08 a. m. to 9:32:25 a. m. H. S. T. Intensity, III-IV Cancani scale; 90% to 120% of the minimum perceptible unit, but not felt. Origin distant about 20 miles.

June 25, from 6:28.9 p. m. to 8:06.9 p. m. H. S. T., a weakly registered teleseism, with defined phases. Origin distant about 3,500 miles.

July 1, from 2:28:01 a. m. to 2:28:55 a. m. H. S. T. Intensity, low I Cancani scale; about 5% of the minimum perceptible unit. Origin distant about 20 miles.

July 1, from 5:37:09 p. m. to 5:38:30 p. m. H. S. T. Intensity, II-III Cancani scale; about 50% of the minimum perceptible unit. Origin distance indeterminate.

July 2, from 5:30:13 p. m. to 5:31:13 p. m. H. S. T. Intensity, II-III Cancani scale; about 50% of the minimum perceptible unit. Origin distance indeterminate.

July 5, from 2:42:15 p. m. to 2:44:11 p. m. H. S. T. Intensity, medium I Cancani scale; 11% to 19% of the minimum perceptible unit. Origin distant 12.4 miles.

July 5, from 3:16:01 p. m. to 3:21.6 approx. p. m. H. S. T. Intensity, V Cancani scale; about 3 times the minimum perceptible unit, probably perceptible but unnoticed. Origin distant about 12.4 miles.

July 5, from 3:51:43 p. m. to 3:53:05 p. m. H. S. T. Intensity, III-IV Cancani scale; about the minimum perceptible unit, but not noticed. Origin distant about 12.2 miles.

July 5, from 4:36:00 p. m. to 4:37:27 p. m. H. S. T. Intensity, low II Cancani scale; about 27% of the minimum perceptible unit. Origin distant about 13 miles.

July 5, from 6:42:25 p. m. to 6:44:04 p. m. H. S. T. Intensity, low I Cancani scale; about 11% of the minimum perceptible unit. Origin distance indeterminate.

July 5, from 7:18:14 p. m. to 7:20:58 p. m. H. S. T. A felt shock. Intensity, VI Cancani scale; from 3 to 6 times the minimum perceptible unit. Origin distant about 13 miles.

July 5, from 7:25:42 p. m. to 7:27:38 p. m. H. S. T. Intensity, low III Cancani scale; about 54% of the minimum perceptible unit. Origin distant about 11.3 miles.

July 5, from 7:30:02 p. m. to 7:31:50 p. m. H. S. T. Intensity, very low I Cancani scale; 8% to 9% of the minimum perceptible unit. Origin distance indeterminate.

July 5, from 8:03:49 p. m. to 8:04:16 p. m. H. S. T. Intensity, low I Cancani scale; about 13% of the minimum perceptible unit. Origin distance indeterminate.

July 5, from 9:37:06 p. m. to 9:39:17 p. m. H. S. T. Intensity, low I Cancani scale; 5% to 8% of the minimum perceptible unit. Origin distant about 20 miles.

July 6, from 1:39:03 a. m. to 1:40:37 a. m. H. S. T. Intensity, III Cancani scale; 75% to 95% of the minimum perceptible unit. Origin distant 13.7 miles.

July 6, from 11:05:19 a. m. to 11:07:01 a. m. H. S. T. Intensity, low I Cancani scale; about 7% of the minimum perceptible unit. Origin distant 13 miles.

July 6, from 12:45:34 p. m. to 12:47:18 p. m. H. S. T. Intensity, high I Cancani scale; about 22% of the minimum perceptible unit. Origin distant 20 miles.

July 6, from 1:23:15 p. m. to 1:24:56 p. m. H. S. T. Intensity, low I Cancani scale; 6% to 7% of the minimum perceptible unit. Origin distant about 13 miles.

July 8, from 11:47:29 a. m. to 11:48.5 approx. a. m. H. S. T. Intensity, low I Cancani scale; 5% to 6% of the minimum perceptible unit. Origin distance indeterminate.

July 8, from 7:21:45 p. m. to 7:23:28 p. m. H. S. T. Intensity, low I Cancani scale; about 8% of the minimum perceptible unit. Origin distant 13 miles.

July 9, from 9:36:43 a. m. to 9:38:25 a. m. H. S. T. Intensity, III Cancani scale; about 80% of the minimum perceptible unit. Origin distant about 6.9 miles.

July 9, from 1:31:57 p. m. to 1:33:11 p. m. H. S. T. Intensity, low I Cancani scale; about 7.5% of the minimum perceptible unit. Origin distant about 6.9 miles.

July 9, from 1:38:04 p. m. to 1:39:46 p. m. H. S. T. Intensity, low I Cancani scale; about 19% of the minimum perceptible unit. Origin distant about 13 miles.

July 9, from 2:18:19 p. m. to 2:19:02 p. m. H. S. T. Intensity, low II Cancani scale; about 30% of the minimum perceptible unit. Origin distance indeterminate.

July 9, from 5:24:51 p. m. to 5:25:29 p. m. H. S. T. Intensity, low II Cancani scale; about 30% of the minimum perceptible unit. Origin distant about 10 miles.

July 14, from 9:19:23 p. m. to 9:20:51 p. m. H. S. T. Intensity, medium I Cancani scale; about 16% of the minimum perceptible unit.

July 16, from 6:17:07 a. m. to 6:17:50 a. m. H. S. T. Intensity, low I Cancani scale; about 9% of the minimum perceptible unit.

July 16, a feebly registered teleseism no phases, e. 8:51:04 p. m. H. S. T. and F. 9:06:04 p. m. H. S. T.

July 17, from 12:11:20 a. m. to 12:13:28 a. m. H. S. T. Intensity, I Cancani scale; about 11% of the minimum perceptible unit. Origin distant about 19.3 miles.

July 17, from 8:39:55 p. m. to 8:41:23 p. m. H. S. T. Intensity, low I Cancani scale; 3% to 6% of the minimum perceptible unit. Origin distance indeterminate.

July 19, from 8:50:47 a. m. to 8:51:22 a. m. H. S. T. Intensity, III-IV Cancani scale; 50% to 110% of the minimum perceptible unit, but not felt. Origin distant about 11.8 miles.

July 20, from 4:03:20 a. m. to 4:06:33 a. m. H. S. T. A felt shock. Intensity II R.-F., IV-V Cancani scale; about 2.5 times the minimum perceptible unit. Origin distant about 20 miles.

July 21, from 12:15.9 p. m. to 12:36.9 p. m. H. S. T. The chief phase only of a feebly registered teleseism.

July 22, from 9:09:24 a. m. to 9:10:08 a. m. H. S. T. Intensity, high II Cancani scale; about 40% of the minimum perceptible unit. Origin distance indeterminate.

H. O. WOOD,
Associate.

Interior of Technology Station at Halemaumau, Showing Crater Seismograph.

WEEKLY BULLETINS
OF THE
Hawaiian Volcano Observatory

Vol. II. HONOLULU, HAWAII, SEPTEMBER, 1914. No. 28.

TECHNOLOGY STATION, KILAUEA, July 30.—Until the very end of the week under report there had been very little change in the eruptive behavior at Kilauea. But in the last two days, ending with July 29, avalanches in the talus were noted with increasing frequency of occurrence and large increase in the volume of rock fragments set in motion. Fitful glimpses of the east end of the pit-bottom in the late afternoon of July 29 showed that the fresh pahoehoe in this area was traversed by ugly peripheral and radial cracks, and that large amounts of coarse talus blocks had run down upon and out onto the floor in this part of the pit.

As most of the observed avalanching has been in the west part of the pit, similar phenomena have probably taken place there. Such action is considered to mean sinking of the magma column. Such sinking is expectable in this part of the year. However, on this afternoon "Old Faithful" was a large, open pool in which surging magma was seen, in size comparable with the magnitude observed on the previous day, mentioned below. The east-northeast chimney, high on the wall, also emitted its usual bright glow and seemed as active as ever. All the rest of the pit was hidden in the fumes. Large avalanches occurred at the west and at intervals of several minutes. A few tinkling rock-falls occurred under the east wall. The eruptive noises were much as usual, except that no rhythmic blasts were proceeding from the south cone.

During the past week work at Halemaumau has been hindered and interrupted by the heaviest fall of rain since the establishment of the observatory—a total precipitation of 20.94 inches for the week, with a maximum daily fall of 12.75 inches from 9:30 a. m. July 26 to 9:30 a. m. July 27.

In the evening of July 23 a small, fresh flow, about sixty feet long by thirty feet wide, was observed running from an orifice in the south cone out onto the floor. A smaller flow poured out onto the floor at the northeast, and a still smaller flow was seen in the center of the floor area. The entire floor area showed streaks of fire, and small jets sprang occasionally from many small cones, most of which were near the edge of the floor area. Both rumbling sounds and noises of blowing were very loud, especially the blasts from the south cone. Here a blue flame was flaming steadily. No slides were occurring. Late in the evening a considerable flow took place, illuminating the fume cloud more brilliantly for about twenty minutes than at any time during more than a year previously. This flow was crusted over and had apparently ceased moving before it came under observation. Incandescent streaks over its entire surface marked its area completely.

In the afternoon and evening of July 24 conditions, so far as observable, were as on the previous day, except that flowing was less in evidence. Yet small flows were seen.

In the afternoon of July 26, in the midst of the heavy downpour, a clear view of the entire pit-bottom was obtained. All the boiling pots and cones recently described were seen, most of them somewhat enlarged, except for "Old Faithful"; in all but one or two, at the northwest, boiling lava was seen, again strongly suggesting a great molten body thickly crusted over at the bottom of the pit. At this time "Old Faithful" was no larger than several other openings in this crust. A few

WEEKLY BULLETINS
of the
Hawaiian Volcano Observatory

Published Monthly at Honolulu, Hawaii, by the Hawaiian Volcano Research Association

Editor..............Howard M. Ballou
Professor of Physics, College of Hawaii

Entered as second-class matter January 20, 1914, at the post-office at Honolulu, Hawaii, under the Act of August 24, 1912.

trivial rock-falls occurred. Sounds of eruption were much as usual, except that a distinct sizzling sound, doubtless due to the excessive downpour of rain, was added to the rest. So heavy was the rain at this hour that water in considerable volume was cascading down the terraces below Uwekahuna to the crater floor, a veritable waterfall. Steam was rising from the Perret cone in unusual abundance, and nearer Halemaumau the response to this unusual rainfall was very positive and interesting. Where the trail from the Volcano House divides, near the northeast margin of Halemaumau, is a well-known region of peripheral crevasses from which steam and fumes of sulphur constantly arise. On this day the behavior of these cracks, from the trail or a little northwest of it on to the region of the Devil's Kitchen and thereabouts, was much as usual. Little or no additional steam was issuing. Around the Devil's Kitchen, however, there was marked increase, and from the trail along the belt of cracks toward the motor depot the increase in steam emanation was very marked, the steam issuing so violently as to produce a roaring sound of considerable volume at a spot only a few paces eastward from the trail. At the west-northwest of Halemaumau, also, there was a region showing marked increase in steam output. In general there seemed to be increase in steam emanation along radial tracts leading north-northeast and east-northeast from the center of the pit. These observations were made during an interval when rain was falling at a rate surely in excess of five-tenths inch per hour, with momentary showers far heavier.

On July 27, in early evening the "Old Faithful" orifice was again considerably enlarged, and in it boiling magma was seen plainly. At considerable intervals molten lava was flung out onto the floor. The usual cone orifices were glowing brightly. No flows occurred. There were a few small talus slides, chiefly at the south and southwest. Rumbling and blowing sounds were quite loud, particularly at the south cone. It was still raining plentifully, though not as on the previous day, and the steam phenomena were much as described above. In addition it was noted that much steam was coming from a great number of cracks in the hanging 1912 shelf or platform under the south station.

On July 28 "Old Faithful" was still more enlarged, again measuring about thirty feet in the east to west direction by about twenty feet in the north to south direction. No change in its behavior was observed. A circular orifice about fifteen feet in diameter was seen under the east station, and in this molten magma was surging to and fro. The many small cones were glowing brightly. Rumbling and blowing noises were loud, but the pronounced blasts from the south cone were no longer heard, but only a feeble wheezing. No flowing was observed. Very many short, small slides took place at the south, southwest and west. One was noted under the northeast wall.

The phenomena observed in the afternoon of July 29 have been detailed in the opening paragraph of this report.

In the Whitney Laboratory of Seismology but two very small shocks of earthquake have been registered during the week ending July 29.

July 22, from 8:36:20 p. m. to 8:37:36 p. m., H. S. T. Intensity, II-III Cancani scale, thirty per cent to fifty-five per cent of the minimum perceptible unit. Origin, distant about thirteen miles.

July 23, from 3:41:59 a. m. to 3:43:33 a. m., H. S. T. Intensity, medium I Cancani scale, ten per cent to fourteen per cent of the minimum perceptible unit. Origin, distant about six and nine-tenths miles.

H. O. WOOD, Associate.

TECHNOLOGY STATION, August 6.—For the first week in August the active lava column of Kilauea shows pronounced subsidence, with small avalanches of talus, open pots where there were recently cones of overflow, the molten matter very deep within the pots, and while Old Faithful still fountains up and flares fitfully upon the dense fume-cloud above, the general appearance of the floor indicates a sinking. The week has been so rainy and the fumes so dense that it has not been possible to obtain a measurement of depth, but I estimate the lava surface to be about 550 feet down. The red glow on the fume-cloud at night is still visible from the Volcano House.

July 30 and 31 were rainy. On the evening of the 31st the only seeing was from the southeast station where Old Faithful and the other eastern pots and chimneys exhibited no marked change. Two avalanches were heard and the glow on the cloud was moderate.

On the morning of August 1 there was no seeing on account of the dense fumes, and the noises were very faint. The smoke from the east and southeast fumaroles rose above the edge of the pit in rapid puffs, and even in the evening at 8 p.m. with a northerly wind there was no seeing from either side of the pit. There was some flaring, indicating the usual fountains in the pot of Old Faithful, and splashing noises could be heard from the east station. One slight rock slide was heard. The fumes were very dense and acrid.

At 9 p.m. the party of Dr. Wm. T. Brigham, who has honored us with a visit this week, saw the Old Faithful pot boiling, with stalactites hanging around the rim, and also the eastern pots and chimneys, and heard small talus slides.

August 2, the wind was strong from the northeast and the pit was filled with fumes. August 3, at 11 a.m., there was a little seeing from the southeast and south stations, though there was still a high wind blowing from the northeast which drove the fumes down into the pit. The southeast end of the floor was piled with new fallen talus. A part of the eastern high chimney on the wall appeared caved away, making an overhanging cavernous recess at the base of the wall. The V-shaped area of the rock wall southeast was extended much lower than when last seen and the talus on either side of it was continuously sliding. Faint puffing could be heard from the floor, but the noises are incomparably fainter than in early July. The south conelet on the talus could not be distinguished. The general effect is pronounced subsidence.

August 4, at 9 p.m., the weather was calm and the fumes were rising straight upward with indraught east and west, making seeing difficult. One glimpse from the old north resthouse showed a very low floor, with four pots along the northeast wall, apparently funnel-shaped and deep, one or two of them showing surging lava far down. Old Faithful was quite large, perhaps 70 feet long as a pot, the lava within fairly active, skinning over and then rending the skins, and fountaining. This made brilliant flares on the cloud. There were two open pots northwest, where recently there have been cones, and two near the foot of the north slope. The plashing noise was fairly pronounced.

Mr. H. O. Wood reports for the Whitney Laboratory of Seismology that the week has been very quiet seismically. Mauna Loa exhibits no unusual phenomena, the vapor jets on the high north-east slope were seen one evening against the sunset.

T. A. JAGGAR, JR., Director.

TECHNOLOGY STATION, August 13.—After a nine-days' subsidence ending about August 4, the lava of Halemaumau has risen for eight days so as to restore a condition of activity and overflow from cones on the floor quite similar to the conditions of June and July, except that the period of sinking caused much new slide-rock to tumble from the walls and bury the borders of the floor. Again the dominant place of overflow at the beginning of the new rise is at the west end.

The rising and falling movements of 1914 to date have been between levels 700 feet and 500 feet below the rim. Below 600 feet, measurements are generally impossible because of the dense fumes, and at the end of 1913 the pit was a funnel over 600 feet deep with dim glowing cones on a small lava floor. The floor remained stationary with a subsiding tendency from December 28, 1913, to February 3, 1914.

From February 4 to March 15 a definite rise was inaugurated with increasing puffing from the vents, lava spatter thrown high from the conelets on the floor, increased glow on the fume cloud and finally lava flows on the bottom. This period lasted forty days.

A period of subsidence followed from about March 16 to May 2 (forty-eight days), inaugurated and characterized by many rock slides, and what was described as "a lull" or "a halt" in the energetic activity which had started, with marked diminution in jets of lava and blowing noises. Cones collapsed and pots increased in size, characteristics of subsidence.

From May 3 to June 22 (51 days) we find "a marked increase in activity with lava flows," and a definite rise by overflow measured with transit.

May 5, 1914, 585 feet below rim.
May 15, 1914, 574 feet below rim.
June 15, 1914, 530 feet below rim.

The net movement of the lava column since that time has been upward, for we find,

June 28, 517 feet below rim.
August 12, 501 feet below rim.

After the solstice for thirty-four days to July 26, the rising progressed more slowly with pronounced stationary intervals, with the average per day for a month, following June 28, of only one-half foot, as against a rise per day of one and three-quarters feet the preceding month (before June 15). From June 15 to June 28 the average rise was about one foot per day. In general the July activity showed fewer overflows on the floor than the May-June activity, enlarged pots, and very large spouting gas-cones.

From July 27 to August 4 there was a sharp subsidence, with a tendency for the floor to collapse funnelwise and crack around the border, while the latter became strewn with fallen debris. From about August 5 to the present a reverse movement of rising appears to have lifted the floor bodily, and overflow has started again from the western corner of the floor.

Summed up and divided roughly by months, the record of Halemaumau for the year to August shows a stagnant period in January following the winter solstice, a revival in February, a lull in March and April around the time of the equinox, a revival in May to a maximum of activity about the summer solstice June 22, and a high level maintained through the greater party of July.

From 6 to 7 p. m., August 6, 1914, a puffing noise could be heard occasionally from some northeastern vent, a plashing noise from the bubble fountains in Old Faithful pot, and a heavy splash at intervals from the periodic large fountain of Old Faithful. From the southeast and south stations the floor could be seen at dusk. Old Faithful appeared a nearly circular pot with steep walls plastered on the west side with big stalactites hanging down into the surging lava within. The pot was about sixty feet in diameter, bubble fountains played actively on the lava, there was streaming from west to east, and the large fountain broke at the usual intervals. Three deep pots in a line parallel to and near the northeast walls showed glare on their inner walls, but the lava within was too deep to show. This suggests that if the lava under the floor is at a common level, the Old Faithful pot in the center, which shows the lava, is at the lowest part of a funnel-like subsidence of the floor.

There was a pot under the east northeast wall, and the high east chimney was glowing brightly. Between the southeast fumaroles and the wall behind them a flat gray place has been left bare by the sliding talus, which appears like solid rock, almost horizontal; the south rock wall appears to bell inward toward the middle of the pit. The high south conelet, which formerly rose from the talus, appears to have been destroyed. A western pot, probably the west central one in the floor, was seen dimly.

August 7 from 6 to 7:30 p. m., conditions were about the same. Heavy stalactites bordered Old Faithful all around, and the surface streaming in Old Faithful was still to the east. The southern of the three northeast pots showed some lava in its bottom, there was very bright flaring and loud splashing from Old Faithful, and in general the lava was a little higher than on the previous day. There were no avalanches and the eastern chimney was very bright.

August 8 there was no marked change reported. On August 7 the lava in Old Faithful pot was from 12 to 15 feet down beneath the rim of the pot, but on August 9 at 8:30 p. m. it was only 2 to 3 feet down and splashing over the rim. The streaming had reversed its direction and was now from east to west. Evidently a marked rise had taken place. The pot had diminished its diameter to about 50 feet, a common result of rising and rampart building, with a straight edge on the southwest, circular otherwise. Explosions of the main fountain were recorded at intervals of 30, 45, 55, 40 and 35 seconds. In the interval there were bubble fountains, but thick black skins often formed before the main explosions, the latter being very heavy, with a noise like surf breaking on a rocky shore. There was hissing toward the west, and from the southeast station two glow holes could be seen beyond Old Faithful, at the west end. Two others appeared southwest from Old Faithful, two under the north wall, four along the northeast wall, one with a beehive conelet near it under the east northeast wall, while the high east chimney was flaming brightly, with the highest luminosity shown anywhere in the pit.

The fumes appeared less than of late. Lava did not show in any pot but Old Faithful, but spatter jets could be seen in two pots northeast. The largest northeast pot appeared almost dark with a few sparks jetted up far down it now and then. The great dome explosions of Old Faithful filled the whole pot; in the intervals spears of blue flame could be seen from under the skin around the borders. Blue flames also appeared at other pots north, northeast and southwest.

The Observatory was honored this week by a visit from Professor E. C. Franklin, a distinguished chemist of Stanford University. Professor Franklin has had experience on the Selby Commission for investigation of damage resulting from smelter fumes, and after going to leeward of Halemaumau and breathing the direct fume cloud as it emerges from the crater, he expressed the opinion that roughly the content of sulphurous acid gas cannot be more than from twenty five to seventy-five parts in a million, for it is quite respirable, and one hundred parts in a million is the utmost limit of human endurance, according to the tests of that commission.

Monday, August 10, there was very heavy rain. On both August 10 and 11 there was strong glare from the pots on the fume cloud. August 12 from two to three o'clock the wind blew from the eastward and opened to view the floor from the northwest and north stations so as to make possible a brief survey for depth. Readings were obtained on the west end and the pot in the center next west of Old Faithful, which determined the floor to be essentially level, and at a depth below the north rim of 501 feet. A large cone at the west northwest border was determined to be about eight feet high.

New talus overlapped the floor west, west northwest, southwest and northeast. A great new sheet of glistening brown lava flows covered the western half of the floor, in marked contrast to the gray and dusty older surface, and the source was three border vents in the extreme west corner. Old Faithful was an oval pot with longer axis northeast to southwest, and with a distinct rampart built around it. Fire holes appeared in the northeast talus. Two spurting pots southwest of Old Faithful had maintained themselves through the new lava flows. Two cones and a slot chimney appeared along the northwest border of the floor, with the great haystack dome beyond to the west, all these features being persistent from a month ago. A southeast cone on the floor could be dimly seen, and a strong fumarole was smoking through the southwest talus. The noises were pounding, spatter, fall, splash and puff. Two heavy rock slides were heard from the east, and one southwest.

T. A. JAGGAR, JR., Director.

TECHNOLOGY STATION, August 20.—The new rise at Halemaumau, reported last week, continued to August 13 inclusive; then there was slight subsidence to August 16, which then ceased, and the lava column remained almost stationary, with slight rise, to the 19th. The week has been rainy, and in consequence apparently of the extraordinarily heavy rain of the last week in July, a large steaming patch has developed on the Kilauea floor between the Volcano House and Halemaumau. This is in the region of the group of largest lava domes, and the steaming area covers over three hundred acres. The development of this steam in sequence upon the heaviest rainfall we have recorded here gives additional weight to the view that the outlying steam vents of Kilauea are from heated rain cisterns.

After midnight following August 13, a very bright glow on the fume cloud over Halemaumau was visible from the Observatory, suggesting new flows on the floor. Such flows could not afterwards be identified, but the seeing of the week has not been good.

From 9 to 10 p. m. Friday, August 14, the floor could be seen from the old north rest-house. Twenty glowing spots were counted. Seven cones on the floor at the west end were brightest and emitting flames. The lava of Old Faithful was low, in a long, narrow pot, pounding among heavy stalactites. In a large glowing pot with double orifices, west of Old Faithful, there was steady high glow without motion, except some sparks thrown up at rare intervals. This appears to be either incandescence in the inner walls or mere reflection of lava beneath, more probably the latter, though the very high glow, even in the daylight, is suggestive of incandescence. Spurting was taking place also at the west "haystack" cone and at Old Faithful. The bubble fountaining in the intervals of the larger explosions goes on in Old Faithful, but the streaming is no longer noticeable. Liquid lava could be seen in one of the northeast pots.

It should be noted that the orifices along the west and northwest walls are spatter cones, those on the floor and at the north are pots with more or less rampart built around them, and those along the northeast wall are distinct pits. This has been the general arrangement for months past, and the highest glow and the greater number of flows have come from the west end.

August 15, from 3 to 4 p. m., the floor could be seen from the northern station. It showed no marked change, the lava in Old Faithful was very low and lava could be seen streaming within a northeast pot. The noises were splashing at Old Faithful and hissing to the west. No new flows could be identified on the floor. A long avalanche was heard from the northeast, and there was much new talus on the northwest floor.

On this day I crossed the area of new steam near the large lava domes in the northeast central part of Kilauea. Very hot steam was coming out quietly from numerous holes in the vicinity of collapsed caverns, and it seems probable that this is a cavernous region of lava tubes where rain water accumulates below, is heated, and its vapor accumulates and condenses in the tubes so that it emerges as an excess of visible vapor even on dry days.

In the evening of August 15 avalanching extended around to the high north wall and several tons of rock from the high edge of Halemaumau in front of and to the left of the Old Rest house fell in, leaving there a distinct notch. The sliding of debris on the inner slopes responds with extraordinary sensitiveness to a slight sinking of the lava.

August 16 at 5:45 p.m. the lava appeared a little higher in the Old Faithful pot, which had become oval in shape, and the stalactites were smaller. The double orifice of the hole west of Old Faithful had changed to a single L-shaped orifice, with steady glow within. The large cone at the west end was hissing and spattering and had an open oven on its north aspect hung with stalactites. The larger northeast pot had changed its shape. The main fountain of Old Faithful made heavy surging noises. There was a fumarole under the north wall of the pit which may by its undermining have induced the fall by the Old Resthouse. One stone was heard sliding toward the east on this evening, but no avalanches. Eighteen glowing places were counted on the floor and the high chimney at the east end was seen to be still flaming. The cumuli of vapor from the eastern inner fumaroles were on this day rising very rapidly.

August 17 the glow at night was steady and moderate.

August 18 from 8 to 9 p. m. a dim view of the bottom was obtained. There were no avalanches, Old Faithful was flaring, there was slight spatter from the western "haystack," which had changed the shape of its summit to a double orifice on opposite sides of an arch separating them.

August 19 at 10:30 a. m. there was no seeing, the splashing was loud from Old Faithful and the hissing from the west cone was somewhat louder than the night before. In the evening the glow was bright, with flaring at the usual Old Faithful intervals.

T. A. JAGGAR, JR., Director.

TECHNOLOGY STATION, August 27.—Again the week has been very rainy at the volcano, making the seeing bad, but there has been little change in the condition of the top of the lava column; however the aggregate movement of the week has been in the direction of rising, shown by new flows on the floor and entire absence of such symptoms of subsidence as avalanching or noises of talus sliding.

At 7 p. m., Friday, August 2, the floor could be dimly seen from the southeast station. The site of the former southeast cone on the floor was occupied by a small glow-hole shaped like a figure eight. The Old Faithful pot was about sixty feet long, pointed in plan west, and rounded east, the lava bubbling up to the edge and splashing over during the dome explosions very actively, with surface streaming eastward in the intervals. In the northeastern pots and chimney there was glow.

August 23 at 9 p. m. there was a fine view of the pit from the south station. Old Faithful had eaten away its north wall to become somewhat more circular. The activity was very great and in the course of an hour the surface streaming changed directions, first southward, then westward and then to the more usual direction eastward. This change in direction of surface streaming is frequently coincident with rapid rising, and probably later on this night there were overflows from the west end. The southeast locality had changed to an oval pot fully thirty feet long, full of lava, with a brightly glowing cave in its north border, where the incandescent liquid boiled and splashed. The lava in Old Faithful appeared to be at a little higher level than in this southeast pot. Several cones were dimly seen at the west end and there a constant blowing noise could be heard. In an openwork glowing cone to the northeast a prolonged hissing roar revived every six to eight minutes, lasting for a minute or so with gradual weakening; there was clearly some sort of a gas chamber with accumulation beneath.

August 25 at 11 a.m. from the south station, the lava of Old Faithful was seen to have subsided about twelve feet. The wall of the pot was hung with heavy stalactites, and the lava could be seen extending into cavernous spaces underneath them. New fresh brown lava flows were identified, surrounding Old Faithful and extending to and submerging the southeast pot. Whether they came from Old Faithful or the west end could not be determined owing to the fumes. The southeast pot had been filled and converted into a blow-cone with a small glowing orifice.

A remnant of the south spatter-cone, which formerly stood on the talus, was seen to be still standing, now on the edge of the lava floor, the flows having built up to its level. It showed no activity. The new flows extend much farther east than those described on August 12.

There was much talus on the eastern and southern parts of the floor. The remnant of the 200-foot bench southwest has diminished in size and increased its inward slope; it has fumes still rising from sulphur-stained cracks at its upper border. Very bright blue semi-transparent fumes were rising rapidly from the high east flame-chimney in marked contrast to the dense and more sluggish white fumes from the southeast fumaroles, which are blown aside when their volutes mingle with the gases rising from the chimney. There are very thick, white, active fumes rising from the talus south southwest. A strong splashing noise was coming from Old Faithful, but there was no marked blowing anywhere. Blowing noises indicating increased gas pressure always accompany rising in the present crusted condition of the pool.

At 11 a.m., August 26, from the southeast station there was dim seeing of Old Faithful and the southeast hole. No change was evident. The noise was splashing, without blowing. There has been no rock sliding heard during this week.

The Whitney Laboratory of Seismology has been undergoing repair. There have been no felt earthquakes, and there is no sign of activity on Mauna Loa, as seen from the Observatory.

T. A. JAGGAR, JR., Director.

TECHNOLOGY STATION, September 3.—During several days of the week preceding September 2 the surface activity in Halemaumau has been decidedly more spectacular than usual. Small sprays of molten lava have fountained from the cones, and numerous small flows have welled out from them onto the floor of the pit. Also in brilliant moonlight the fume cloud has been illuminated with a more persistent and lively glow than at any time since the revival of activity a little less than a year ago. But this manifestation of increased activity has begun already to decline.

It is interesting to note that this spasm of rising and increased surface action has corresponded almost precisely with a fortnightly maximum of solilunar earth strain, computed on the basis of a hypothesis which we are evolving and testing, which fell near the moon's first quarter. Such a correspondence is more than usually favorable to the hypothesis because, when the maximum falls near the moon's quarter its effectiveness is hypothetically less than when it falls near conjunction or opposition. Hence a definite increase and decrease in action when the variation in strain is hypothetically less effective indicates the probable reality of action according to this hypothesis in preference to others hitherto proposed.

It was reported that the molten lava was standing at a higher level in the "Old Faithful" pot in the evening of August 27 than on previous days.

On August 28 lava was spurting from most of the holes in the floor that could be seen from the east and southeast margins of the pit. During its explosions the lava in "Old Faithful" rose and overflowed the margins of the orifice. At 7:45 p.m. a flow from the cone at the west end began. Up to this time a strong blowing noise was heard here which now was replaced by the gentle rushing sound of the flow.

The illumination produced was strong enough to penetrate the fumes rising as a curtain along the wall under the Old Rest House. The flow divided at the cone into two branches, the larger and longer making along the south margin of the floor, the smaller along the north margin. The south branch flowed some 400 feet in about half-an-hour.

The flows on this evening were considered by Director Jaggar to be the most spectacular witnessed by him this year. Later in the evening, from 9 to 10 p.m., the whole floor of the pit was seen clearly from the east and southeast stations.

A triangular hole west of "Old Faithful" was partially overwhelmed by the lava flood, but it was maintained as an open orifice of diminished size by the action of gas blowing up through it.

The "Old Faithful" pot grew smaller by the building about it of a flat cone by the cooling of the outwelling gushes or splashes, many of which amounted to small flows on all sides.

The glow in the east chimney appeared less than usual. The holes at the northeast showed brightly and were blowing. The streaming action in "Old Faithful," from north to south previous to 7 p. m., changed at about that time to from west to east. At 10 p. m. the flow along the south margin was moving in pulsations like meal from a sack, not nearly so rapidly as earlier, when it ran as a heavy liquid, like mercury.

At about 11 a. m. on August 29 the lava in the "Old Faithful" pot was ten to twelve feet below the surrounding margins. The flow had covered nearly all the floor, except a relatively small strip at the southeast. It had surrounded "Old Faithful." At 11:30 a rock slide occurred in the northeast part of the pit. Blowing sounds were heard from the holes at the northeast, and pounding and splashing sounds from "Old Faithful."

At noon the lava had risen to the brim in "Old Faithful" and the southeast cone. The orifice of this cone had grown larger. Strong blowing was now heard at the west end. The east chimney was seen plainly, and a blue flame was playing out of it. No glow was seen in it in daylight. Two vertical gashes were seen in the northeast wall. These appeared to be undermining the wall here. They were immediately over blowing cones on the floor. In the early afternoon jets of lava were springing from the west cone and splashes were welling out of "Old Faithful."

In the early and middle evening of August 30 lava flowing from cones and orifices at the west end of the pit covered all the floor, according to reports by visitors accustomed to the action in Halemaumau.

In the forenoon of August 31 a good view of the floor showed a carpet of new lava everywhere. Lava was splasbing out of "Old Faithful." At long intervals loud puffing and rumbling sounds could be heard. The east cone also was very active, and from another cone, at the west-southwest, sprays of lava were jetting out. Very small rock slides were frequent, and occasionally a short, heavy slide took place.

On September 1, in the late afternoon and early evening, the "Old Faithful" pot was still large, and from it splashes and sprays of molten lava were thrown out upon the floor. It was a surging pool of quadrangular outline, possibly forty feet across. All the holes in the floor were glowing brightly. Many long, glowing cracks were seen. No flows were occurring, however, and no evidence could be seen of flowing on the previous day. Evident decline in surface action had begun. Blowing and rumbling sounds were quite loud, and a few small slides occurred from time to time.

On September 2 the "Old Faithful" orifice had become nearly clogged. Sound of blowing had become very faint. However, rumbling and surging sounds remained quite loud. No slides were heard. All the usual holes in the floor were glowing brightly. A strong wind prevented more than momentary glimpses into the bottom of the pit.

H. O. WOOD, Associate.

TECHNOLOGY STATION, Sept. 10.—The activity in Halemaumau during the week ending with September 9 has undergone little change. First was noted a slight gradual decrease in vigor of action, soon followed by an apparently stationary stage with minor temporary increases and decreases. With the date of the equinox only two weeks off it may be well again to draw attention to the fact that since the early part of July—up to which time there was pronounced rising and increase of surface action, which then halted—there has been little or no sinking of the magma surface, and the decrease in surface activity, while sufficient to be noticeable, has as a whole been slight. This is construed to indicate a gradual increase in the action of Kilauea independent of the semi-annual variation and it encourages an expectation of pronounced rise and increase of surface action during the fall season. This is in no sense put forward as a prediction. It is simply a statement made to enable readers of these reports to comprehend our interpretation of the observed conditions in terms of our tentative hypothesis.

In the late afternoon and early evening of September 3 views obtained showed the ''Old Faithful'' opening to be about fifty feet long, east and west, by twenty feet wide, and of quadrangular shape. In it molten magma was boiling vigorously over a surface sufficiently high for small amounts of the molten material to surge over the brim occasionally. A small cone under the east station was throwing out molten lava spray at irregular intervals. Blowing noises and sounds of surging and swashing were quite loud. Small glowing holes and cracks were seen in all parts of the floor. No avalanches were heard.

On September 4 general conditions had not changed, but the fountain action in ''Old Faithful'' was a trifle more vigorous; also, at the east cone, and at a cone on the floor between the east and northeast stations molten spray was being ejected more forcibly. The noises, too, were louder. Early in the evening lava was swashing over the brim of a pot under the northwest station.

On September 5 it was observed that the ''Old Faithful'' orifice was much smaller. In other respects no change was noted. Twelve cones with glowing orifices were seen on the floor. Out of several of these molten spray was spurted at intervals. Blue flames were seen playing from them. The noises, if anything, were louder than on the previous day.

On the sixth of September the noises had become very conspicuous—not so loud as when the entire bottom was choked with talus, but still very loud. More than at most times they took on something of a terrifying quality. The blowing sounds were very sharp and short and came from several different cones in so rapid succession as to seem almost continuous. The other noises were merely louder than usual. The small open pot under the east station was surging furiously, and almost continuously flinging very small amounts of lava over its brim. ''Old Faithful'' showed as a very small, comparatively quiet opening. Several small cones along the north margin from the northeast to the northwest were almost every instant throwing out small, spray-like jets with obvious force.

In the middle evening of September 7, after hard rain, a bright, steady illumination of the fumes, indicating a flow on the floor, led to an impromptu visit. When the rim was reached the flow had ceased. It was very small, covering only a portion of the floor in the vicinity of the eastern margin, where many brightly glowing cracks marked its limit. The noises were very loud and could be heard very distinctly for about two hundred yards back to the northeast from the margin of Halemaumau. There was only a light breeze blowing. In all other respects the action was as on the previous day.

On the eighth of September there was a slight decline in action in that molten lava was being thrown out from ''Old Faithful'' only, and then only at considerable intervals. Also the blowing and rumbling noises were less loud.

The cracking sound of rock breaking from heat was heard.

On the ninth of September small quantities of molten spray were being ejected feebly from "Old Faithful," and the magma was seen to be surging furiously in the pot under the east station where masses were frequently swashed out over the brim. This pot is now the largest orifice in the floor. The noises were still very loud.

H. O. WOOD, Associate.

TECHNOLOGY STATION, September 17.—At Kilauea the week ending with September 16 has been marked by a conspicuous minor increase in activity, followed by a short lull, which has given place to a further minor increase. These variations tally with expectable behavior on the basis of luni-solar stress control, the first subsidiary maximum of activity corresponding well with a declination stress maximum, the second with a stress maximum, probably of less effectiveness, due to the practically coincident occurrence of perigee and conjunction. In addition, as hitherto mentioned, there appears to be a slow, steady increase apart from these short-term fluctuations.

In the afternoon and evening of September 10 symptoms of increased activity were observed. At the orifice of the cone under the northeast station the magma was boiling vigorously and frequently splashing over the brim. The blowing sound from "Old Faithful" was very loud, its pot was boiling actively, and now and then blue flames could be seen flaring from it.

During the afternoon the sound of cracking of the lava crusts could be heard occasionally, and in the early evening about half the floor was marked by glowing cracks, indicating that a small flow had taken place. Molten lava was jetting from several cones. From a small one under the east station, about a hundred feet out from the edge of the floor, the jets were leaping forty to fifty feet into the air. In mid-evening "Old Faithful" was seen to be larger, with an irregular opening about sixty feet east and west by thirty feet north and south. Rumbling became very loud.

On September 11 lava was boiling and splashing out upon the floor from "Old Faithful" and the northeast cone almost continuously, and this was happening also at all of a group of eight small orifices close together under the east station. Marked activity was apparent at all the open spots on the floor. Blowing and rumbling sounds were conspicuously loud. Also the high cone under the south station, which has been quiet for a few weeks past, was blowing feebly at intervals and glow holes were seen at its top. Although no flow occurred during this period of observation the action appeared more vigorous than on the tenth.

On September 12, late in the afternoon, a small flow was seen running over the floor from the north and north-northwest margin toward the middle of the pit. Later it was seen that a larger flow, proceeding from the cones under the west to northwest stations, had run all the way to the margin under the southeast station. This flow, as indicated by glowing streaks, had a width of nearly or quite half that of the floor itself. At the southeast margin it bent around and sent a tongue along the edge to a point under the east station. All the cones on the floor showed boiling lava, which was slopping out almost continuously onto the floor. Every place in the pit was in unusually vigorous action. The noises were sharp and very loud.

On September 13 there had come a lull in the activity. The "Old Faithful" opening was of much less size, but still a pot with lava boiling vigorously in it some feet below the adjacent surface. No other boiling pot was seen, but all the usual orifices showed glowing lava. Under the east station, smoking steadily, were two "beehive" cones, whose domes were traversed by cracks arranged in something like a mud-crack pattern. A similar cone stood about midway between "Old Faithful" and the southeast margin. A single lazy jet of lava was seen to spring from one of the subsidiary orifices in the floor. The noises were subdued. Fresh lava in great folds was seen to cover the southeast and east parts of the floor.

On September 14 lava was splashing out onto the floor from "Old Faithful" and small jets were springing from the small beehive cones under the east station. The noises from "Old Faithful" were quite vigorous. Elsewhere only boiling pots were seen. In early evening a heavy avalanche, the rock tumbling continuously for upwards of three minutes, took place under the west station, and a little later a short slide, only some four seconds long, but very heavy, started from the very brim between the east and southeast stations.

On September 15 activity was again slightly increased. Much molten lava was splashing out of the "Old Faithful" orifice, and the whole floor was marked by glowing streaks. In late afternoon considerable avalanches, starting from the very brim between the east and southeast stations, broke through the crust and thus caused a small flow of short duration. A little later a larger flow, of slow motion, was seen running toward the middle of the pit from the northwest station. Lava was seen boiling vigorously in all the open holes.

On September 16 a considerable flow was seen moving on the floor of the pit at the east end, from the cone under the east station toward the southeast. This flow, when first seen, was estimated to be some twenty feet wide and seventy long. The cone it started from was boiling over steadily. Small jets were springing up in many places. All the sounds were loud. Blue flames were playing above nearly all the boiling pots. No avalanches were observed, but occasionally a few boulders would drop from various parts of the walls.

H. O. WOOD, Associate.

TECHNOLOGY STATION, Kilauea, September 24.—During the week ending with September 23 the activity in Halemaumau has undergone only slight changes. There have been no conspicuous increases or decreases, merely slight variations, in both directions, from day to day.

On September 17 all the usual glowing orifices were seen, and out of several molten lava was splashing at intervals. No flows were seen and no talus slides were heard. Occasional jets were spurting up but without any great force. All the noises were loud. Blue flames were flaring conspicuously from several boiling pots.

On September 18, while no lava was seen flowing there were other indications of a slight increase. The noises of eruption were much louder, and molten jets were being flung out with much force, sometimes to estimated heights of fifty feet. There was no open pool on the floor, but several of the orifices were much enlarged. At these places boiling lava could be seen vigorously splashing over the brim.

On September 19, the activity, as regards most of the manifestations, was only ordinary, but a small flow occurred at the west end.

On September 21 the noises were conspicuously loud, but no flowing or spouting lava was seen. Unusually large blue flame-banners were flaring from the larger orifices. These orifices were at the tops of well marked cones in every case. There was no pool on the floor.

On September 22 a fine view of the floor region by daylight showed that several small, short flows, proceeding from the cones under the northwest to west rim, had taken place in previous days without being observed. Molten spray was issuing from these cones at intervals. Magma was splashing out of the top of the "Old Faithful" cone, now about twenty feet high and with a large top. Small amounts of lava were being flung from the cones under the east and southeast stations, but only at intervals. Eighteen cones from ten to twenty feet high were counted. The noises of eruption were very loud. Blue flames flared from many of the orifices.

On September 23 lava was splashing so vigorously out of the northwest cone that at one time a small flow made away from it. All the cones at the west and south, as well as "Old Faithful," were blowing vigorously. The noises continued to be very loud. Flames were seen as usual. A few small talus slides were heard.

H. O. WOOD, Associate.

WEEKLY BULLETINS
OF THE
Hawaiian Volcano Observatory

Vol. II. HONOLULU, HAWAII, OCTOBER, 1914. No. 29.

Honolulu, Hawaii, September 21, 1914.

Volcano research at Kilauea, which has been in progress since 1909, has produced important discoveries published in the United States, Italy, Switzerland, Germany, France and England. Specialists who have worked here during the last six years are Daly and Curtis from Harvard, Jaggar from the Massachusetts Institute of Technology, Brun of the Sorbonne and of Geneva, the late Tempest Anderson of York, Day and Shepherd of the Carnegie Institution, Birdseye and Green of Government bureaus in Washington, Wood of the California Earthquake Committee, Perret of Springfield, Friedländer of Naples, and Arnold Heim of Zurich. The results give positive experimental data on measurement, circulation, rise, fall, flow, temperature and consolidation of lava, on gas action and composition, water vapor, magnetism and earth motions. This knowledge is revivifying the science of volcanology, and new text-books, societies, experiment stations and expeditions, especially in Germany, Italy and Japan, attest the growth of a definite propaganda. The Kilauea observatory this year materially extended its influence by sending an expedition to Japan.

The Hawaiian Volcano Research Association maintains a station hospitable to workers of all nationalities. The published results bear on the origin of our soils and waters, on minimizing disaster from lava or earthquake, and on fundamental subjects of pure science. The publicity from this laboratory, financed within the Territory, is much wider than could be obtained from one supported by some mainland institution.

The Research Association is supported by the voluntary subscriptions of patrons. Over and above the membership fee of $5.00, the subscriptions range from one dollar to two thousand dollars. New lists were subscribed in October, 1911, and July, 1912, and owing to recent decline in support it becomes necessary for the Directors of the Association to appeal earnestly to firms, business men, planters and the general public in the Territory of Hawaii to make new subscriptions for the years 1915 and 1916.

(Signed) CLARENCE H. COOKE,
L. A. THURSTON,
ALBERT F. JUDD,
A. LEWIS, JR.,
WILLIAM R. CASTLE,
JAMES A. KENNEDY,
Board of Directors Hawaiian Volcano Research Association.

Executive Chamber,
Honolulu, Hawaii, Sept. 26, 1914.

I approve of this work, and of legislation providing for trails, refuge houses, maps and scientific studies in the regions of active lava flows on Mauna Loa, with a view to preventing disaster, as well as the advancement of science.

(Signed) LUCIUS E. PINKHAM,
Governor of Hawaii.

Honolulu, September 28, 1914.

The Advertising and Subscription Committee of the Chamber of Commerce of Honolulu, approves of the work herein outlined and approves, also, of the campaign for additional funds.

By order of the Committee.

(Signed) RAYMOND C. BROWN,
Secretary.

MINUTES OF THE MEETINGS OF THE BOARD OF DIRECTORS.

As directed by the President, the fourth meeting of the Board of Directors of the Hawaiian Volcano Research Association was held at the University Club, Friday, September 18, at 12:15 p. m. Present: W. R. Castle, C. H. Cooke, A. F. Judd, L. A. Thurston, directors; H. M. Ballou, secretary, and T. A. Jaggar, Jr., director of the Observatory.

The membership committee presented the following list of patrons and members who were duly elected to membership in the Association: Harold Bauer, George Carroll Curtis, Mrs. Harold G. Dillingham, Dr. I. Friedlaender, Hilo Board of Trade, Hilo Electric Light Co., Miss Harriet C. Hitchcock, Mrs. Mary T. C. Hitchcock, Hilo Railroad Co., Inter-Island Steam Navigation Co., Juan I. de Jongh, Kilauea Volcano House Co., H. A. Morss, L. Tenney Peck, Robert W. Sayles, Alfred M. Tozzer, A. S. Wilcox, and G. N. Wilcox.

The following report from the Treasurer was received and accepted:

STATEMENT OF CASH RECEIPTS AND DISBURSEMENTS FROM JANUARY 1, TO SEPTEMBER 15, 1914.

RECEIPTS.

Check from C. M. Cooke, retiring Treasurer	$ 217.45
From Donations	4900.00
From Patrons	441.00
From Membership Fees	390.00
From Lectures by Dr. Jaggar	189.50
	$6137.95

DISBURSEMENTS.

Salaries	$3000.00
Services	1642.85
Purchases	445.35
Printing	361.69
Repairs	125.20
Freight	66.35
Travel	26.50
	$5667.94
Balance on hand	$ 470.01

E. & O. E.: E. M. Campbell, for R. W. Shingle, Treasurer.

The following report from the publication committee was read, accepted, and ordered printed. The publication committee was authorized to prepare the pamphlet suggested therein:

To the Directors, Hawaiian Volcano Research Association.

Gentlemen:—Your editorial and publication committee have to report that there have been published in 1914, to date, by this Association, twenty-six weekly bulletins and two monthly bulletins. The monthly form has been adopted since July. In association with the Massachusetts Institute of Technology a first Boston report has been issued, covering the years 1909 to 1911 inclusive at Kilauea, this publication being printed at the expense of the Institute. Other such reports are in preparation for the years 1912, 1913 and 1914. The publications are sent to about 250 addresses.

A scientific paper has been published in the Bulletin of the Seismological Society of America by H. O. Wood, dealing with the limits of sensibility of measured earthquakes, and a paper on "Education and the Philosophy of Change" by the Director as the commencement address at the College of Hawaii.

In finished manuscript there are three articles awaiting publication—one by Professor Jaggar on "The Eruption of Sakurajima," with 114 illustrations, and two by Mr. H. O. Wood, dealing respectively with the 1868 earthquake in Hawaii, and with the response of Kilauea to earth strain.

There are now on hand the following publications, some of which are available for distribution, which have appeared from time to time since 1911:

Weekly Bulletins, Vol. I, of the last half of 1913.

Weekly Bulletins, Vol. II, 1914.

1st Report of the Hawaiian Volcano Observatory. Boston:1914.

The Hawaiian Volcano Observatory, by T. A. Jaggar. Boston:1912.

The Hawaiian Volcano Observatory, by H. O. Wood. Bull. Seis. Soc. Amer., 1912.

Scientific Work on Hawaiian Volcanoes, by T. A. Jaggar, Jr. Honolulu: 1913.

The Cross of Hawaii, by T. A. Jaggar, Jr. Chamber of Commerce Annual, Honolulu:Jan., 1913.

Constitution of the Hawaiian Volcano Research Association.

Investigations at Kilauea in the Summer of 1911, by F. A. Perret. American Journal of Science, 1913.

There is no comprehensible statement of the aims and organization of the Hawaiian Volcano Research Association in print. Your committee would recommend the preparation of such a book to be freely distributed to tourists, scientific men, and at the San Francisco Exposition. A placard should also be printed inviting prospective patrons and members to join the Association, and exhibited at such places as the hotels and the Promotion Committee rooms.

A member of your committee has interviewed Mr. H. P. Wood concerning an exhibit of volcano photographs at San Francisco, and Mr. Wood offers for our use a large koa revolving stand with hanging frames. He also suggests that the directors submit a proposition to the Fair Commission for Hawaii concerning the cost of an exhibit, with a view to getting from the Hawaiian Fund an appropriation for the volcano exhibit.

There can be no question but that such an exhibit will be a benefit to the Association, and there is ample material obtainable to make a fine photographic display, showing the activity of Kilauea and Mauna Loa for the last thirty years.

Very respectfully,
H. M. Ballou,
L. A. Thurston,
T. A. Jaggar, Jr.,
Publication Committee.

Dr. Jaggar read the following report as to the financial outlook, which was accepted, and ordered printed:

To the Directors, Hawaiian Volcano Research Association.

Gentlemen:—The principal subjects to come before this meeting are the finances of the Association and the reports of membership and publication committees. In the absence of the treasurer, I have asked Mr. Campbell to submit a statement of receipts and disbursements to September 15 for 1914, which is before you. The pledges of 1914 amount to $7381, which would permit an expenditure of $615 per month. The average cost of the work per month, January-June, was $635.67, not including the Japan expedition, and with practically no purchases during my absence in Japan for three months. The pledges of 1915 amount to $6631 if all are paid, permitting only $552 average expense per month.

To show the gradual retrenchment, and consequent decline in our equipment, and increase in our burden of work since 1912; the average expense per month was:

First half of 1912	$1219.35
Second half of 1912	923.28
First half of 1913	746.71
Second half of 1913	851.49
First half of 1914	635.67
Prospective in 1915	552.58

By dint of continual watchfulness we have avoided deficits. A small deficit of $216 against the Japan expedition will be met by funds coming in in the autumn, and I anticipate no deficit at the end of this year. But the reduction of income has steadily been met by reduction of field work, which is expensive, and this, of course, means reduced efficiency in the end. We are not properly prepared for

WEEKLY BULLETINS
of the
Hawaiian Volcano Observatory

Published Monthly at Honolulu, Hawaii, by the Hawaiian Volcano Research Association

Editor.............Howard M. Ballou
Professor of Physics, College of Hawaii

Entered as second-class matter January 20, 1914, at the post-office at Honolulu, Hawaii, under the Act of August 24, 1912.

an eruption of Mauna Loa, and we are undermanned for proper study of Kilauea. Fortunately, the activity of Kilauea has been moderate of late, and we have marked time and devoted ourselves to writing reports; labor relatively inexpensive.

The reduction of income is due to death, withdrawal and retrenchment of patrons. About $4000 per annum has been withdrawn, in the last two years. We cannot do the work without money. Of the original Hawaiian subscribers of 1911, there are only seven left, making $3600 of the guaranteed $5000. By my personal solicitation the additional funds have been obtained, with the aid of the approval of the Chamber of Commerce, so that actually the Hawaiian subscription fund has never fallen below $5000, but it will do so next year, unless it is vigorously recruited. The Hawaiian Volcano Observatory cannot be operated on $552 per month, therefore a new subscription blank must be issued, endorsed by whatever leading commercial and social bodies we can interest, and new patrons must be obtained.

I submit a letter in form to be signed by the President and Treasurer of the Association, as a basis for a statement to be drawn up by the finance committee and made the heading of a new subscription list. It is suggested that the approval of the Governor, the Regents of the College of Hawaii, and the Chamber of Commerce be sought and their comment subscribed on this heading.

We undertook last year to increase the income of the Association to $12,000 per annum and failed on account of sugar depression. This year should be more favorable, and now is the time also to make clear to the community that the work must be made permanent or it will fail of its object. I have just returned from lecturing on Kauai, and expect to lecture there again in December, and also in Honolulu, on "Recent Discoveries at Kilauea Volcano."

Very respectfully,
T. A. JAGGAR, JR.,
Director of Observatory.

Adjourned to Monday, September 21, at 12:15 p. m.

HOWARD M. BALLOU,
Secretary.

The fifth meeting of the Board of Directors of the Hawaiian Volcano Research Association was held at the University Club, Monday, September 21, at 12:15 p. m. Present: W. R. Castle, C. H. Cooke, A. F. Judd, L. A. Thurston, Directors; H. M. Ballou, Secretary, and Dr. T. A. Jaggar, Jr., Director of Observatory.

Voted: That a circular be sent out, signed by the Directors, soliciting support for the Association.

Voted: That the Pacific-Panama Fair Commission be asked to appropriate $250 for a photographic exhibition of the Volcano.

Voted: That a stated meeting of the Board of Directors be held Friday, December 4, 1914.

Voted: That the President appoint a committee to nominate members of the Board of Directors for the ensuing year, this committee to report December 4.

Adjourned.

HOWARD M. BALLOU,
Secretary.

WEEKLY BULLETIN
OF THE
Hawaiian Volcano Observatory

Vol. II. HONOLULU, HAWAII, NOVEMBER, 1914. No. 30.

TECHNOLOGY STATION, October 1.—During the week ending with September 30, the activity in Halemaumau has stood still, nearly—there has been no symptom of increase and no well-marked symptom of decrease, though an interval of halt always seems to carry the suggestion of decreasing vigor of action. At this season such a stand is expectable.

September 25 there were no flows, but lava is jetting from "Old Faithful." All the active cones were blowing loudly, and from several blue flame-banners were steadily flaring. Rumbling noises were very loud. No slides occurred.

September 26 there was no boiling lava visible in any of the breathing holes or cones, though the incandescent walls were plainly visible. No lava jets were seen, save one very feeble outburst from one of the minor cones under the northeast rim. The blowing sound had decreased to a soft hissing, and the rumbling had become very deep-toned and far-away. These sounds were incessant. All the open holes were at the tops of cones from fifteen to thirty feet high, from which thin blue fumes rose. Cave-like openings in the wall under the northeast were seen fully 100 feet above the floor. These were dark. The high east-northeast chimney was glowing brightly. In general the fumes were thin.

September 28 sounds of blowing and rumbling were very low, and the molten lava was deep within the cones; but it was plainly visible. Only at the west-north-west was molten lava splashing out, with a loud boiling sound. Fifteen breathing holes, with flame-banners, were counted.

September 29 the sounds of eruption were hardly audible and the molten lava had sunk too low within the cones to be seen. No jets were seen. No slides occurred.

September 30 the noises of eruption had grown comparatively loud again and from the cones along the margin of the floor from east to north-east blue flames were flaring, and molten lava spray was occasionally thrown out. "Old Faithful," and the cones to the south, were relatively quiet. Those from the west to the west-north-west were concealed by the fumes.

The Whitney Laboratory of Seismology, which had suspended registrations about the middle of August, owing to the necessity of renovation and repairs, has now been put in order after a prolonged intermission due to unforeseen delays. Routine registration was resumed Monday, September 28, and there was an interval of trial registration, beginning early on the twenty-seventh of September.

During the past week a seismic spasm has occurred, beginning on the morning of the twenty-seventh. Before the seismographs were started writing two earthquakes occurred, both strong enough to operate the starting mechanism of the ordinary seismograph. These occurred at ten-ten and ten-twelve in the morning approximately. A little later the seismographs were set writing and, with one or two intermissions of an hour or more, for work of readjustment, they continued to write until Monday forenoon. Seven additional earthquakes were registered during the afternoon and night of September 27-28. Monday forenoon was devoted to readjusting the instruments and the writing of test seismograms. Continuous registration was resumed just before noon. During the remainder of the run, up to early forenoon of September 29, four shocks were registered. It was reported to the writer that at Kapapala twenty-nine shocks were felt from the morning of the twenty-seventh to the evening of the twenty-eighth. None of these shocks

WEEKLY BULLETIN
of the
Hawaiian Volcano Observatory

Published Monthly at Honolulu, Hawaii, by the Hawaiian Volcano Research Association

Editor.............Howard M. Ballou
Professor of Physics, College of Hawaii

Entered as second-class matter January 20, 1914, at the post-office at Honolulu, Hawaii, under the Act of August 24, 1912.

was felt at the observatory, but, despite the interruptions in registration, about one-half as many were registered here.

Without question the forty-eight hours from ten a.m., September 27, to ten a.m., September 29, was a period more active seismically than any interval of like duration since the establishment of this station. Details of time and magnitude for these shocks will be given later in systematic form.

Despite the continuation of rainy weather several clear views of Mauna Loa have been obtained, covering all times of day. No sign has been seen of any response to this seismic spasm on the part of the big mountain.

H. O. WOOD, Associate.

TECHNOLOGY STATION, Kilauea, October 8.—During the week ending with October 7, following the stationary stage described in the previous report, there has been a marked and apparently ''permanent'' increase in the action in Halemaumau. About the ''Old Faithful'' orifice as a center an open pool of magma has formed, which has enlarged rapidly—without symptoms of down-sinking or of marked rise—until at the date of writing it has become a lake of the kind so well known in Kilauea, a semi- molten surface, upon which thin black crusts form continually, only to be torn up and engulfed every minute or so by the uprush and fountain-doming of large magma lumps, or so-called bubbles. Also there are many small fountains in it, and a conspicuous action of surging against and up onto the banks of the spatter ramparts which confine the pool. No clear streaming in definite directions has been observed as yet.

Needless to say the opening of this ''permanent'' lake has made the scene much more spectacular and brilliant. In bright moonlight the fumes are illuminated by an unquenchable ruddy glow, more fiery than in any previous displays since March, 1913. A continued, fluctuating increase is expectable.

On October 1 conditions were very much as described previously. Early in the afternoon small amounts of magma were being flung as spray out of the ''Old Faithful'' cone. Blue flames were flaring conspicuously in broad daylight from the cones under the east and northeast stations and from an orifice close by about twenty-five feet above the floor. Later on, in the evening, molten spray was being flung from nearly all the cones on the floor. The action had definitely increased over that of the previous day.

On October 2 there was little change in behavior, but more orifices were seen than at any previous time in recent weeks. Twenty-two brilliantly glowing cones were counted. Blue flames were flaring from nearly all and many were spouting molten spray vigorously—particularly the cones under the northwest station.

On October 3 the ''Old Faithful'' cone structure had collapsed, resulting in the formation of a pool about fifty feet long by forty feet wide, of triangular shape, with its sharpest apex to the west. In this the magma was boiling violently and splashing over the margin in considerable amount. Molten spray was being flung from the east cones. In all respects increase of action was noted.

On October 4 the ''Old Faithful'' pool had enlarged, despite the active building of spatter ramparts, until its dimensions were at least one hundred by seventy feet. It was still triangular, with the sharp apex to the west. At intervals of no great length portions of the spatter banks collapsed into the pool, thus continually enlarging it. Furious boiling and surging followed such collapses. The more or less regular fountain action of ''Old Faithful'' was going on as formerly. All the orifices, together with some newly formed ones, were glowing brightly, but no molten spray was seen. A high orifice showing a bright, but deep, red glow was seen in the talus under the southwest station.

On October 5 the dimensions of the pool were estimated to be two hundred by one hundred feet. It had become egg-shaped, with irregular boundaries. The action in it was very vigorous, but the spatter walls had grown so high that only occasionally were small amounts of the melted rock flung out beyond these onto the floor. The surf-like rushing roar had become very loud. In other parts of the pit the action was as usual.

On October 6 the roaring sound was still louder, and despite the spatter walls a considerable amount of the molten lava was being flung out onto the floor. The lake area was still larger than on the previous day, but the increase in size was not so great as during the first two or three days after its formation. At the smaller orifices all was as usual, except that no lava jets were seen.

On October 7 a very high wind accompanied by rain made seeing impracticable. In the early morning hours of October 8 the glow on the fumes indicated that the activity was undiminished.

The seismic spasm of last week was quickly over. Nothing unusual has occurred during the past week. Several small shocks have been registered. All these shocks will be reported upon in systematic form as soon as the necessary time and instrumental corrections can be worked out.

H. O. WOOD, Associate.

TECHNOLOGY STATION, October 15.—The month of October has inaugurated the return of Pele's active and spectacular lava pool. The mechanism of the return of the lake recalls its disappearance in March of 1913, the conditions being strikingly similar, except that it is rising now and was sinking then. The new pool as at that time is about 470 feet down, its shape is elongate northwest to southeast, with surface streaming also in this direction, Old Faithful boils in the east central region, and smoking wall fumaroles encircle the lake. The volume of smoke is still large, but may be confidently expected to diminish greatly if the lake rises another hundred feet. A gradual rise from now on until December, after the equinox and approaching the solstice, is quite in order if the habit of previous years is preserved.

During the past few days the weather at the Volcano has been sunny and dry, and Mauna Loa has been under inspection for many hours at a time with perfectly clear seeing. There is not a trace of smoke or vapor visible over any part of the mountain. No earthquakes have been felt in a camp of cattlemen on the northeast slope.

The week has greatly increased the size of Halemaumau lake by temporary subsidence and collapse of the lake walls.

October 8, 1914, at four-forty-five p. m. Old Faithful was fountaining violently and splashing over the banks of a pool estimated 300 feet long northwest by southeast, by 150 feet wide, south-west by north-east. At six p.m.

The Summit Lake on Mauna Kea, (From a Painting by D. Howard Hitchcock).

in the gathering darkness fifteen fiery cones could be counted on the floor of overflow surrounding the molten lake, especially along the base of the steep north-east and north-west walls at the border of the floor. These showed glow within numerous orifices, from which generally banners of blue flame shot up, and there was some blowing noise. In the transition stages of this week, from a small to a large pool, and consequently an increasingly large open surface of boiling lava, this blowing of the outlying cones has ceased, just as the subsidence of the lava at the end of last week caused it to cease spattering out of the blowing cones.

October 9 from five to six-thirty p.m. conditions were much the same with the pool lengthening towards the north-west. A large cone at the north-west border of the floor was ejecting lava spray. Two open pots lay in a line northwest of the pool near it, and two others away from the border of the floor lay east and south of the lake. The eastern one showed lava boiling within. The Old Faithful fountains occasionally splashed over the rim.

On October 10 from four to six p.m. the pool seen from the southeast station had extended itself to include the two north-west pots. It now appeared 400 feet long. At six-ten p.m. a noisy traveling fountain was seen to start near the middle of the lake and migrate to the east bank.

At four p.m. on October 11 the lake as seen from the south-east was shaped like a balloon with narrow neck toward the west end, from which a steady surface streaming proceeded to the open oval of the south-east end. The surface of the lava was covered with skins occasionally rending along zigzag lines. Old Faithful burst sluggishly toward the east end, there were some small fountains in the narrow west neck, and a place of fountaining bombardment on the north bank. At three-thirty p.m. a portion of this north bank, which was quite high, fell in with a crash, followed by a great surging and boiling around the engulfed fragments. This is turn was followed for a time by a chilling and stagnation of the lava in that region. The pool appeared to be 500 feet long and subsiding, with considerable enlargement going on by the process of caving of the walls. There were glow holes in the eastern floor and a large black hole in the floor just south of the pool. The east wall was smoking very actively from cracks high up in the face of the precipice.

Measurements made with transit between 4 and 5 p. m. October 12 showed a glowing cone on the northeast floor to be 471 feet below the southeast rim of Halemaumau, and the northeast edge of the active lava to be 498 feet down, or twenty-seven feet below the floor level. A very clear view obtained for a few minutes showed a vertical wall over 25 feet high around the pool, with stalactites on the north side hanging into the flood beneath, and at a point further west in the north wall a cascade of molten lava was rushing out from under the wall into the pool.

The streaming was from the west and south away under the northeast wall. Streaming lava could be seen at the bottom of the black southern hole in the floor which was fully twenty feet in diameter. The glowing eastern chimney in the outer wall appeared not more than twenty feet above the floor level, showing how the floor has risen by overflow in the last two months.

October 13, at four forty-five p. m., the pool was at least 600 feet long with extensions which included the two black pits in the floor to the east and south. This completely changed its shape to an irregular T, with Old Faithful at the meeting point of arms extending northwest, southeast and south. The streaming proceeded from the narrow west neck southeastward, under the northeast bank opposite Old Faithful, and into the southeast and south coves. There were few fountains, slow streaming skins and a splashing noise only. At six p. m., intervals of Old Faithful counted were thirty-five, fifty-five and fifteen seconds. I saw the southwest wall of the west arm of the lake cave in and the west wall of the new south cove. There was in each case a violent attack on the place of engulfment, for from one to three minutes with streaming toward the place of inbreak. This was followed by stagnation and crusting. There was a very bright pit in the floor about 10 feet in diameter near the east border in the line of the new east extension of the pool. This extension occupies the site of what was a black pot the preceding day. The whole lake appears like a great river of lava pouring from west to east.

On October 14, from ten to twelve a. m., a change in wind permitted the floor to be seen from the northwest station. The active pit-lake within the black ledge which we have hitherto called the floor was now seen to be bordered by a broad floor remnant southwest and north. A group of five glowing cones, the largest at least 15 feet high, occupied the northwest end of the floor. Several of these had annular tops with wide cavities within. Along the east wall on the floor was a row of big black holes of ragged caved-in aspect, each with a ring of white gypsum stain around it. The walls of the lake were high and continually falling in and the eastern cove was longer than yesterday. The west and northwest wall of Halemaumau showed evidences of recent falls, in that a small high cavern and a vertical hole in a projection of the wall have both disappeared.

T. A. JAGGAR, JR.,
Director.

TECHNOLOGY STATION, October 22.—Slow subsidence accompanying the development of a large pool by the caving in of its banks has continued this week, as last week, with a total sinking of the liquid lava surface of about twenty feet in nine days. Such subsidence has commonly followed the opening of new pools, owing perhaps to the chilling effect of the engulfed material from the collapse of the cones. The floor as a whole has subsided somewhat, this being indicated by border cracks and cracks near the edge of the inner pit. The general condition at present is a large oval floor fully 1000 feet long in northwest-southeast direction, a little less than 500 feet down. Four glowing and fuming "haystack" cones are along the northwest border. Four or five roundish black pits, luminous within and ten to twenty feet across, are along the southeast border.

In the middle and with extensions east and south, is the great fiery lava lake in a pit of its own, twenty feet deep and over six hundred feet long. It is nearer the southeast border of the floor than the northwest. In plan it is pointed toward the west, has a round cove extending south, and a ragged cove eastward, continually lengthening as brown avalanches tumble into the flood. This extension is now almost undermining the vertical east wall of Halemaumau. Very active fumaroles are working in that wall high up, the lower ones glowing, so that now and then falls of rock take place. The southeast patch of fumaroles has greatly diminished its activity, but the bench remnant southwest is smoking more than ever, with the development of two crater-like chimneys in the slope above the floor at different elevations. The lava lake is streaming from west to east, with changes about the east end, where sometimes a torrent pours westward and joins the main current about the Old Faithful fountain, where with tumultuous upheavings and splashings the streaming melt rushes under the north bank. At other times the united current flows under the southeast bank, or else the south cove is stagnant and there is a majestic march of the whole surface of the pool west to east, black skins tearing zigzag over blood-red slag in daytime, a flood of liquified gold lace at night.

The total volume of fumes from Halemaumau slowly diminishes with the growth of the hot lake. The heat of the lake can now be felt on the edge, and in the early morning forms a high raincloud to leeward over the desert.

Thursday, October 15, at ten-thirty a. m., the east and southeast coves appeared enlarged. There was a line of fountains up the middle of the pool with streaming west to east into the east cove. Spatter benches of black lava could be seen around the lake shore, suggesting temporary rise relative to the banks. The liquid surface was mantled with patches of black lava skin. The seeing was from the southeast.

October 16 at noon subsidence was going on. The streaming was into both the east and south coves, and the lava was pouring with violent ebullition into a cavern between the two coves. There was much falling in of broken rock from the banks into the lake. At four p. m. the cavern had become submerged under a temporary rise, or what would produce the same effect, a relative sinking of the whole floor.

October 17 at four p. m. the inner wall around the pool was reported to be only about fifteen feet high. There was some rumbling and occasional very strong fountaining at the west end. The streaming was from west and east, meeting and pouring southeast under the point between the two coves. It was reported lower in the evening, so that the record for this day appears to have been rising in the morning and sinking in the evening.

From eight to nine p. m. October 18 a marvelous golden torrent, almost a cascade, was pouring from the northeast under and into the end of the east cove, meeting the west-flowing stream opposite the point between the two coves in a line of fountains, the united current pouring under the point of rock. The surface stream from the west also poured into the south cove, bombarding its inner end. On the rapid flowing surface of the east torrent scintillating points of light appeared, brighter than the golden flood, probably bubbles of gas which burst and oxidized in small flashes of flame. After about forty minutes a dark skin formed over the pool and the torrent disappeared as though the lake had risen. At nine-fifteen it reappeared again, but this time it bent northward and joined the current from the west in flowing under the northeast bank, and the flow into the south cove was replaced by quiet scum.

A pot under the east wall of Halemaumau was glowing very intensely within, and a high banner of bluish flame played above it. From the lurid glow within these eastern pots the lava inside would appear to be at about the level of the main pool, fifteen or twenty feet down. A small fall of rock took place from the high fuming east wall of the greater Halemaumau crater.

October 19 the pit was obscured by fumes in the afternoon; in the evening the glow was strong as usual.

October 20, six to seven p. m., the surface activity was sluggish and all signs pointed to a sinking. Crusts formed over the west end, which broke away and floated eastward from time to time. There were bubble fountains along the north bank and the east-setting current streamed under the north side of the east cove. The south cove was stagnant. A ragged edge of skin lay over the liquid at the point of origin of the flowing, west. Four glowing cones were seen on the border of the floor west and north. The surface of the lake showed alternations of apparent active flow and stagnation. A night photograph of the lake was obtained for the first time in nineteen months.

October 21 at three p. m. seeing was clear from the north and northwest stations. Transit measurements made the depth to the lava surface between the east and south coves 518 feet. That the floor as a whole has subsided as well as the liquid lava appears from the fact that the inner wall appeared relatively low, and from cracks around the periphery of the floor and near the edge of the inner pit. Heavy caving was seen to take place at the end of the east cove, sending up clouds of brown dust. There was continuous fountaining near Old Faithful and east of it, where the streaming from the west and east met and poured under the northeast wall. Spatter rims showed on the bank for six or eight feet above the lake, indicating temporary apparent rise. The south cove was rather stagnant, but at four p. m. two big fountains, one near Old Faithful and one in this cove, began to boil furiously and continuously with much noise, this phenomenon lasting some minutes. The two new chimneys in the southwest talus are elongate slots parallel to the edge of the floor, fuming vertical holes, about twenty and fifty feet long, respectively, below and above, the lower about twenty feet above the floor, the other 100 feet.

For the Whitney Laboratory of Seismology, H. O. Wood reports that during the week ending October 21 two very slight local earthquakes have been registered, as follows:

October 18, from 3:08:39 p. m. to 3:10:39 p. m., H. S. T.; intensity medium I Cancani scale, seventeen to eighteen per cent of the minimum perceptible unit. Origin distant about twenty miles.

October 21, from 2:50:29 a. m. to 2:51:14 a. m., H. S. T., intensity medium I Cancani scale, about sixteen per cent of the minimum perceptible unit. Origin distant about sixteen and two-tenths miles.

T. A. JAGGAR, JR., Director.

TECHNOLOGY STATION, October 29.—The past week has been one of renewed rising and greatly increased activity within the inner pit of Halemaumau, with some overflow of the western part of the floor. A survey of the lake October 23, 1914, gives the following dimensions: Length of lava pool, 375 feet; width of pool, 150 feet at Old Faithful; length of floor, east-west, 660 feet; width of floor, 550 feet, approximately; wall of inner pit at noon on this date, ten feet high at west end, level with lava at east end.

The floor slopes down from west to east, being about 460 feet below the north station at the west end, 470 feet in the middle and 480 feet down at the east end. The three cones at the border of the floor west, are respectively, from south to north, nineteen feet, twelve feet and seven feet high. The east and south coves of the lake extend for from eighty to ninety feet from their entrances.

The change from sinking to rising within the inner pit happened about October 22. October 23 the lake rose until it was brimming at noon, and two small flows poured out of the west-northwest cone. Throughout the morning the activity was tremendous, the surface currents rushing in various directions and pounding on the banks with formation of spatter ramparts. The noises of puffing, splashing, pounding and rumbling made the pit seem like a manufacturing city in full activity as one looks down the smoke from a hilltop. At ten a. m. there was a wall about ten feet high at the west end of the lake. At noon there was only a low rampart west, and the liquid was up to the edge on the east. Heavy bombardment was going on on the north side of the lake. In the west-northwest cone the lava was throwing up spray within an opening ten feet across.

This became roofed over in the form of a dome in the course of the day, leaving a filagree pattern of openings. There is a very marked gradation in the height and form of the border cones going from west to east around the north wall. The highest are at the west, they are half broken down in the middle region, and at the east they are wholly broken in, to form ragged-edged pots. High in the northeast wall there is a black chimney without fumes.

The streaming was mostly from under a blanket which formed about the junction of the two coves with the main pool, the currents pouring into the two coves and westward in the main pool, against the northwest bank and under the bank at the extreme west end—an exact reversal of the prevalent streaming. This appeared characteristic of rising stages, for at two-thirty p. m., during a temporary subsiding stage the east flow was resumed and the blanketed area was engulfed, while the current poured under the north shore near Old Faithful. Rising was resumed at four p. m., again with westward flow.

The fumes of this period are extremely acrid and hard to breathe. At noon the pool was rising so fast it could be seen to well up its edges. Very much Pele's hair was seen; in one case a tangle floated by in the hot fumes which was fully fourteen inches long by five wide.

At one-thirty p. m. there was a temporary sinking with bombardment against the southwest bank. At one-forty-five a flow on the floor began from both sides of the largest western cone; at two-thirty this flow had stopped, after traveling about fifty feet on the lake side. On the wall side the flow was only ten or fifteen feet long.

The Old Faithful fountainings were not very large during this activity, and the interval was long, about sixty seconds. About one p. m. a pot in the floor near the northeast wall was seen to be full of liquid lava almost to brimming, and lava was also welling up northeast between the wall and the edge of the floor. At three-thirty p. m., during the sinking phase, the lava in the northeast pot had sunk about five feet.

From eight to ten p. m. blue flames were very conspicuous, playing over the bank above the splash of the grottoes and out of the glowing cones. There was a rise, with tremendous noisy bombardment, from nine to ten p. m. The heat of the lake was plainly felt on the rim. Some stones were heard falling. The streaming was west to east, with rush into the south and east coves. The east wall chimney still glows and a glowing spot is visible at the extreme southwest border of the floor.

This kind of activity continued during the ensuing days. On the evening of October 24 the lake was spattering over its ramparts and changing its streaming, rising and falling within a small range.

October 25, at three p. m., the lake appeared about ten feet under its rampart on the west, five feet on the east. It was active and streaming from west to east. There is one large active fumarole still in the southeast talus. The high southwest fumaroles remain as they were in the summer. Some spatter construction has taken place around the east pots. In the evening seeing was fair from the north, and about ten p. m. a collapse of the bank of the pool caused much noise, violent fountaining and bright glare. The illumination of the fumes at night is at present very brilliant.

October 26, between four and five p. m., the high activity continued, though there was no evidence of new overflows. There were cavings of the bank from both the north and south sides. In the evening the seeing was poor. From the southeast the pool could be discerned streaming from west to east, bombarding the north shore and east end, with occasional traveling fountains that migrated along with the streaming as though a confined gas pocket were pushed along beneath the surface layers of viscous lava. Several flaming grottoes were the scenes of splashing and puffing under the bank in the south cove. A skin lay over the pool at the west end, where the lava was from fifteen to twenty feet below its bank.

October 27 the pit appeared smoky, and no change was reported in its action.

October 28, at ten-thirty a. m., the pool was high and active, but very fumy. At noon the surface streaming was into the south and east coves; the lava appeared to be six feet below the bank in the south cove, where it was bombarding. The noise was a steady bubbling with an occasional puffing in the south grottoes. At eight-thirty p. m. the pool was down about eight feet lower, and at nine p. m. the northeast bank collapsed, causing great ebullition and disturbance for forty mintues.

H. O. Wood reports for the Whitney Laboratory of Seismology that early in the week ending with October 28 two trivial local earthquakes were registered. Since their occurrence there has been no disturbance. Microseismic waves have been unusually strong during the greater part of the week.

T. A. JAGGAR, JR., Director.

TECHNOLOGY STATION, November 5.—The lava pool about the 480-foot level in Halemaumau has held its own during the past week, with a subsidence the first of the week and later some rising, the activity continuing about the same, the fumaroles smoky, and the shape of the lake undergoing no essential change. There has been no overflowing onto the floor observed. The weather has been fair, Mauna Loa is clearly seen free from smoke, and seismic activity is slight.

October 29, at six-thirty p. m., from the south station the whole pit was seen in spectacular grandeur. The pool was lowered within its banks about twenty feet. There was slow streaming from east and west toward Old Faithful and thence from a dividing point a little east of Old Faithful the current poured in two directions, under the north bank and into the south cove. The noises were of rumbling and splashing, mostly from grottoes of inrush under the northeast wall and in the south cove. Stalactites were seen in the overhang at the east end. Slow skins formed over the lake's surface and were rent apart, and traveling fountains appeared from time to time in the Old Faithful region. On the floor or black ledge there were flaming cones west and six flaming pots east. Two of the latter were under the east wall, the larger exhibiting for its full width, possibly ten feet, a blue flame which flared up steadily fully eight feet. The talus fumaroles were active, southeast and southwest. From time to time some tinkle of falling stones could be heard.

October 30, at one p. m., the level of the lava appeared still lower, about twenty-five feet within the inner pit along the west wall of the same, and the streaming was eastward into the east and south coves. The northwest cones were puffing, but not visibly spurting. Glow was seen in a northeast and an east pot. At three p. m. the lake was in noisy ebullition all over its surface.

At one-thirty p. m. October 31 the lake had risen about ten feet and the activity was greater than on the previous day. The streaming was still to the south and east coves. At three p. m. the activity was high, the lava splashing up onto the banks. At four p. m. the northwest cone on the floor was ejecting spurts of lava and the cones farther west were puffing.

November 2, at noon, from the old north rest-house a fall of rock from the bank into the lava was seen, followed by great activity. The west banks appeared about fifteen feet high, and the northwest blowing cone occasionally threw out a spurt of liquid. The glowing pot northeast, which a week ago was full of lava, has become a dark, cavernous hole. At three p. m. the level was lower, with twenty feet of bank west and fifteen feet east. There has evidently been caving around the shores of the east cove and along the promontory between the east and south coves, as shown by notches in the high bank and the recession of the promontory so that it is no longer a pointed cape. At this time there was continuous boiling and some traveling fountains in the Old Faithful locality, the fountains traveling into the south cove. In addition there were the periodic explosions of Old Faithful. There was noisy boiling under the bank east and south, and quiet outflow from under black skins at the west. Along the edges of the lake, southwest and northwest, small bubble fountains appeared from time to time. Northeast of the pool in the floor were fuming cracks more or less parallel to the edge of the bank. A cone at the north edge of the floor was glowing and flaming, in addition to the northwest cone, and a new glow-cone was forming in the talus west-northwest. No fresh flows could be detected on the floor. Three northeast pots were dark. A heavy spatter border had formed at the lake's edge between the east and south coves, as though from a long stationary stand of the lava. The fumes hugged the east wall of Halemaumau and appeared to rise very rapidly and to be very brown. At three p. m. from the northwest the streaming was from the west end to Old Faithful and thence northeast, east and south.

November 3, at eleven a. m., from the southeast station the bank of the south cove was only about five feet high, showing continued rising. A change of current again accompanied the rise, the streaming from the east cove being westward, from the west end being eastward, and from the union of these currents southward into the cove. The east cove was completely blanketed over except for some small fountains at its inner end. There was a river-like flow with much fountaining from the west end into the south cove. At the end of the south cove there was bombardment. The noise was moderate, without rumbling. At five p. m. the streaming was similar, with two additional places of bombardment against the northeast bank of the pool. The lake was so high that it spattered over onto the flat east and south, while at the northwest end it splashed up against a higher wall. It was very active in spells, but not noisy. At one time the south cove became stagnant, the flow being directed against the northeast wall.

November 4 was windy and smoky and there was no seeing, but the usual noise, not very loud. In the evening the glow over the pit was moderate.

H. O. Wood reports that during the

two weeks ending with November 4 six local earthquakes, all of trivial magnitude, have been registered at the Whitney Laboratory of Seismology, as detailed below. During the past week there has been no noteworthy seismic motion of other sorts.

October 21, from 6:49:58 p. m. to 6:50:52 p. m., H. S. T. Intensity high I Cancani scale; about 24% of the minimum perceptible unit. Origin distant about twenty-one miles.

October 23, from 8:29:31 p. m. to 8:30:56 p. m., H. S. T. Intensity medium I Cancani scale; about 14% of the minimum perceptible unit. Origin distant about fifteen miles.

November 3, from 9:03:37 p. m. to 9:03:55 p. m., H. S. T. Intensity medium III Cancani scale; about 70% of the minimum perceptible unit. Origin near, distance indeterminate.

November 3, from 9:03:54 p. m. to 9:05:08 p. m., H. S. T. Intensity high I Cancani scale; about 21% of the minimum perceptible unit. Origin near, distance indeterminate.

November 3, from 9:08:22 p. m. to 9:08:37 p. m., H. S. T. Intensity low I Cancani scale; about 9.5% of the minimum perceptible unit. Origin near, distance indeterminate.

November 4, from 3:03:37 a. m. to 3:05:09 a. m., H. S. T. Intensity medium I Cancani scale; about 17% of the minimum perceptible unit. Origin distant about fifteen miles.

T. A. JAGGAR, JR., Director.

TECHNOLOGY STATION, November 12.—The lava pool of Halemaumau continues gradual rising, with overflow from the border cones and hence some building up of the floor. The activity during the week has been strong, with vigorous fountains from Old Faithful, traveling fountains and streaming from west to east, along with splashing and bombarding in the grottoes. Outrushes of gas and flame with hissing and puffing take place over the rim grottoes of the lake and the border cones of the floor. New glowing cones and chimneys have formed in the last three weeks in the southwest and northwest talus, and the new flows on the floor are slowly encroaching on the talus and widening the floor area.

Thursday, November 5, at 5:30 p. m., the pool from the east was dimly seen streaming like a curve in a river from the west end to the south cove, the east cove being stationary with some bombardment in the grotto at its end. The lava stood at a high level about five feet below the floor.

At 6:30 p. m. the lake, seen from the north rest-house, was rising. Signs of this were seen in the dark flexible blanket which had formed over the whole surface of the pool west of Old Faithful, the quiet liquid here streaming east and south from under a ragged edge of skin. In the eastern part traveling fountains and shore bombardments were lively, with shifting positions of activity, first in the south cove, then the east cove, then the northeast bank and lastly the north bank. The fluid welled up until on a level with the floor, brimming but not overflowing, between the south and east coves.

At 7:30 the maximum height was reached and then subsidence went on for an hour to a depth of about six feet below the floor east, with increased boiling and more rapid streaming. The motion tore up the western surface blanket and the whole pool resumed its more usual aspect. With the loss of support, a great accumulation of built up rampart, almost the whole length of the bank between the east and south coves, caved in with commotion. Such a rampart in the south cove formed a shell over the grotto there, with a small hole in the bank perhaps two feet wide spouting lava spray. This evening the blowing of spray under gas pressure from the grottoes and the sputter phase of Old Faithful were very pronounced. In the south cove the spurts shot up over thirty feet.

The northeast pot's glowed dimly and the western cones were all very active, five of them glowing. The two larger ones northwest and westnorthwest showed lava pools bubbling and slowly streaming within. The westnorthwest one had a large window with a stalactitic screen across its north side, which had grown from the driblets of the fountains at work inside.

Blue flames played above all these cones. The noises this evening were quiet plashing during the rising stage, and plashing with rumbling during the sinking. The south grotto was more open during the subsidence.

November 6 in the afternoon a climax of rising for the week was reached, which took effect in overflows around the periphery of the floor rather than from the pool. The maximum overflow was from the west end. From 4 to 5 p. m. the lake was brimming and a large flow was pouring eastward from the extreme west end along the southwest floor. A glistening black zone of festoons widening downstream extended down the middle of the flow from the source, while the lower part of the flow was a wide series of overlapping puddles of bronzy sheen. There were glow lines at the sides of the zone of festoons and about the front, where toes put out from time to time, making the aggregate movement of the front as viewed from the south station, about 100 feet in thirty minutes.

The source of this particular flow was an opening in a cone at the extreme west corner of the floor, but at least three other northwest cones were overflowing. The greater flow was fully 450 feet long. At 8:30 p. m. the lake was very active, with rumbling, blowing and splashing, and a rapid rush into the south cove and sometimes into the east cove. A blue flame was flickering from a pot at the base of the eastern cliff. At this time a large area in the great southwest flow foundered in a circle, increasing its diameter by concentric inbreaking. The yellow fluid welled up within an area about 100 feet in diameter, and as new cracks formed back from the edge of this well, the fresh liquid melt would rise in the cracks along a feather shaped line or band, spreading from a glowing midrib right and left. Quickly the circle cooled leaving a texture different from the festooned flow around it. Some glowing toes pushed out from the circular pudding, which appeared to be slightly higher than the flow in the midst of which it had arisen. The streaming in the main lake was from the west end into the south cove, the east cove and the west end being both covered with skin.

November 7 in the morning the flows on the floor had ceased to move, the seeing was poor, the pool was high, and the noise a splashing. At 2:15 p. m. from the southeast the lake appeared to be about ten feet below the floor and stalactites were hanging in the south grotto. At 4:30 it was rising again, the west end was skinned over, and the east cove was seen be decidedly smaller by reason of the building inward of its banks by spatter during the recent rise. The shore fountains were splashing over on the floor northeast and east and there were many bubble fountains.

At 3 p. m., November 8, the pool appeared a little lower. The point between the east and south coves has receded until the shore is almost a straight line.

The streaming was from the west into the south cove. The lake was very active with blowing noises strong and continued. There were baby fountains around the Old Faithful region. The glowing chimney in the southwest talus was puffing. At 4 p. m. the lake was covered with quiet blankets of partly solidified lava and was rising, with stagnant surface in the east cove and streaming from the west end into the south cove.

November 9 at 3 p. m. measurement with transit showed the lake in the south cove to be 469 feet below the north rim of Halemaumau. Clear seeing from the north and northwest stations showed that the rising and overflowing had taken place from one at least of the northeast pots as well as from the west cones during the recent rising spell, and all of these east pots had been converted by spurting into cones.

Six cones could be counted along the northeast wall at the edge of the floor, and fifty feet above the floor the northeast high chimney, a flaming crevice in the rock, was still glowing. There are still higher strongly fuming crevices in this wall. The new east flow was from the middle of the row of cones north ward along the wall. Large cracks have developed along the floor northeast near and parallel to the row of cones, between them and the lake. The northwest cones were puffing, and new flows were seen to have poured out from under three of them, both toward the lake and along the wall northward. The great northwest cone was domed over with a glowing filagree. The lake appeared about five feet down with a spatter rim all around, streaming from the west into the east and south coves.

November 10 at 2:30 p. m. conditions

were the same, the lava being lower in the early afternoon and rising at 4:30, about five feet below its banks. Seven cones were counted northwest and seven northeast. The streaming was as usual from the west into the east and south coves. The noise at 2:30 was plashing and rumbling with bubble fountains; at 4:30 the lake was very quiet with skins east and west. Greater noise and ebullition accompanies temporary subsidence, though an increase in the aggregate noisiness is a characteristic of rapid rising. The reason for this is that during rapid rising the elevation of the lava column proceeds in pulsations, the upward movements being short, swift and quiet, with intervening longer movements of noisy retirement of the lava and escape of gas.

A small earthquake shock was felt at the volcano house before midnight November 10. At 4 p. m., November 11, the lake appeared about ten feet below the floor, enlarged by caving shores. The streaming was as usual and there were hissing noises from the south cove and the west cones. The large northwest cone was again open with spurting lava within.

T. A. JAGGAR, JR., Director

TECHNOLOGY STATION, November 19.—The week November 12-18, inclusive, at the lava pit of Kilauea has been an eventful and very spectacular one with great and irregular enlargement of the lake of liquid lava and some overflows. There have been many small local earthquakes recorded on the seismographs. Mauna Loa remains clear and free from smoke. There have been at least two thunder storms during the week, one on Mauna Loa November 12, and one in the Hilo district November 18.

November 12 it was becoming evident that the lake lay in a depression of the floor surrounding it, and not at the apex of a flat cone as is more usual. This accounts for the lack of overflow away from the edges of the lake; the lake brims over but against an insloping shore, so that the only effect is a slight enlargement temporarily of the lake area, followed by a subsidence. At two p. m. the pool was very active and about twelve feet below its rim. The eastern cove had widened greatly by collapse of its north bank, whither the current streamed under the bank rapidly in the direction of the northeast cones. At three p. m. the lake was only five feet down below its bank at the west end, where there were fuming holes eight or ten feet back from the edge of the bank. At this time there was tremendous bombardment of the shore between the east and south coves. Large lumpy accretions of lava spatter had accumulated on the banks of the east cove. At three-thirty p. m. the lava was brimming along the western shores, showing that there has been general subsidence of the western floor or an equivalent rise east during the last fortnight, for in its recent brimmings the west end has always shown a cliff while the east nearly overflowed.

The northwest and west-northwest cones had openings above and the west-northwest one was spurting lava jets. The northwest cone was very large, high and symmetrical. A large cone east-northeast had collapsed and was now a pot full of lava, while between it and the lake at the east cove dense fumes were rising from cracks; this fuming in less degree extending all along the northeast cracks and cones. Yellow sulphurous deposit appeared around a pot at the edge of the floor east. The large cracks across the northern part of the floor were fuming. The noises on this day were splashing, blowing and rumbling. The streaming was from west to east.

November 13 at four p. m. conditions at the pool were much the same. The streaming was from the west end into the south and east coves. Subsidence was in progress, the lake about five feet below its banks, and tremendous ebullition with traveling fountains migrated from the Old Faithful region towards the east cove. The east lava pot was an oven-shaped half-cone puffing and spurting, and the west-northwest cone was also in commotion. The south side of the east cove was overhung with stalactites. The grotto at the end of the south cove was roofed over with two spouting apertures above. The promontory between the south and east coves as seen from the north appeared to be a five-foot crust over a continuous pool. At four-twenty p. m. rising recommenced. The high east chimney was glowing, and the cracks in the northern floor appeared to be growing in number and width. About seven-fifty p. m. a light earthquake was felt at the observatory.

From the southeast station at four p. m. November 14, the pool appeared to be bordered by a six-foot cliff and very active, with streaming from west to south and heavy spatter banks. The noise was variously blowing and plashing, and the current poured under the point between the east and south coves. The "spouting horn" over the south cove has built up into a cone and the eastern oven now appeared to be a closed cone. A block of the bank on the north side of the east cove appeared cracked away and just ready to topple into the flood. At four-fifteen p. m. the lake was rising.

On the afternoon of November 16 a great change had taken place in the lake. There is some ground for supposing that this happened in the small hours of the early morning of November 15, when the seismograph at the pit station recorded excessive tremors for an hour. The entire line of northeast cones and three or more of the northwest cones were engulfed in lava which rose from below, converting the northeast line into an elongate arm of the lake trending from the east cove northerly, and the northwest line into a separate pond of sluggish lava. The streaming in the main pool was from the west end around the new point formed between the main pool and the east arm and northward into this arm. The streaming in the northwest pond was eastward. A small outlying pot of lava boiled a few feet north of the northern end of the east arm.

At eleven to twelve a. m. November 17 and thereafter in the afternoon the enlarged lake was clearly seen and photographed from the northwest station. The east arm, extending northward along the border of the floor, occupies what before was a crusted extension of the lake along the peripheral cracks of the floor lava. It was fissures in this crust which had been smoking so violently, and here had been the line of pots, then cones of spatter, and finally all had caved in and made an arm of the lake. In like manner a pond had been made by the collapse of cones underlaid by lava northwest. In view of these developments revealing positive sub-crustal channels filled with liquid lava locally, which announced themselves long in advance by flame and smoke and lava jets, it seems doubtful whether the main floor where these phenomena are absent is a crusted pool. The first impression of a scientific observer is that the liquid lava extends outward everywhere under the floor, the latter being a crust over a much larger pool than appears liquid. The writer has doubted this for some time, observing that this floor was constructed by repeated flows from various vents, which merely masked talus below by a smooth filling which has the appearance of a crusted lake. The actual lake from the start has grown by the coalescence of collapsed vents, these maintaining rather constant positions, the start being from the Old Faithful vent, as usual. New vents are formed over cracks, which break across the floor from time to time, and here may be expected new developments of the lake, beginning as coves.

Accompanying the developments of November 15 to 16 three flows along the floor border, one from the sulphurous east border pot southward, one from the end of the new east arm northward, and one from the north side of the new northwest pond northward. These are all short flows not more than 100 feet long. From time to time they are added to, and the flow from the east arm was seen in motion on this day November 17. The streaming was to the east in the northwest pond as well as in the main lake, in the latter bending into the three coves to pour into grottoes at their ends. The east cove has enlarged in the directions of its south bank, that is, in the direction opposite to the east arm, which extends northeastward, and this east cove will hereafter be called the southeast cove. A small pond of lava and great cracks extended northward from the end of the east arm. The sag around the edge of the floor which had received the small flows appeared to be due to a gradual sinking inward towards the center of the floor area. The great cracks in the northern part of the floor gaped more than ever. The pool was rising and falling every few minutes, with excessive fountaining and rumbling on the fall and quiet plashing on the rise. The west cones, of which three persisted, were puffing and spurting, and occasionally a long whistling puff would come from one of them. Spatter ramparts were built along the east side of the east arm and in the south cove.

The east arm was about 150 feet long and the northwest pond about 100 feet long. The little northeast pond was about twelve feet long. Estimating the length of the main pool at 400 feet, the entire length around the bend with the east arm added would be over 500 feet. There is no evidence of any marked change in the height of lake, which by last measurement was 469 feet below the rim of Halemaumau.

At two-thirty p. m. it was evident that the entrance to the east arm was widening and that the southeast cove was enlarging itself by bombardment. The blast from the west cone was growing louder. From nine to ten p. m. the lake was a splendid sight. It had sunk about twelve feet below its rim, and stalactites hung over the western grotto of inflow and the south, southeast and east grottoes of outflow. The southeast grotto was undermining the actual foot of the east cliff of Halemaumau, and with the subsidence falling stones, loosened from the precipice above, fell into the lake. At one time the northwest pond, which was crusted over, suddenly broke up with a seething noise and the crusts foundered rapidly, gliding northward under the bank and being replaced with bright yellow liquid. This in turn cooled rapidly and the pond skinned over and resumed a slow eastward streaming. Flames were playing from all the cones and grottoes. A lava curtain had formed in front of the grotto on the east side of the east arm, where the lava was rushing under the bank. The current in the afternoon had been swiftest in the channel leading from the main lake into the southeast cove. This evening it was swiftest in the east arm. There was much rumbling. Heat from the lake could be plainly felt on the face at the northern stations.

The east high chimney was ejecting a high flame. An oven had formed over the east end of the northwest pond. There was a glowing cone at the north border of the floor, and also over the south cove. Bubble fountains sometimes formed in the rapid part of the surface of the lake, but these little fountains have not been so active this year as in 1912-13. There was dense fume rising, red in the transmitted light of the pool, from the north end of the east arm and from the east end of the northwest pond.

T. A. JAGGAR, JR., Director.

The following report from the Whitney Laboratory of Seismology is submitted:

Local shocks were registered as follows:

July 29, from 10:45:39 p. m. to 10:46:15 p. m. H. S. T.

Intensity, medium I Cancani scale; about 10% of the minimum perceptible unit. Origin distant about 26 miles.

August 6, from 1:24:42 a. m. to 1:26:00 a. m. H. S. T.

Intensity, medium I Cancani scale; about 17% of the minimum perceptible unit. Origin distant about 26 miles.

August 6, from 7:15:03 a. m. to 7:15:51 a. m. H. S. T.

Intensity, medium I Cancani scale; about 12% of the minimum perceptible unit. Origin distant about 19.3 miles.

August 6. from 8:19:24 a. m. to 8:20:12 a. m. H. S. T.

Intensity, III-IV Cancani scale; about the minimum perceptible acceleration but not perceptible to the senses. Started the ordinary seismograph, but definitely not felt in the Observatory work-room. Origin distant about 12.4 miles.

August 8, a shock of moderate energy from an origin at moderate distance. The beginnings of the earlier phases are not very surely delineated, as is often the case with shocks of moderate energy, so the determination of origin-distance is less sure than usual. The best approximation possible fixes the origin at a distance of about 140 miles from the Observatory. The distance is not less than this amount. The vague beginning of the first phase occurred at 8:57:49 a. m., and action was perceptibly registered until a few minutes after 10 a. m. by the Hawaiian

Standard Time. The second phase began, probably, at 8:58:14 a. m., the chief phase at 8:58:40 a. m. quite definitely, and the greatest amplitude at 9:00:12 a. m. The direction of the origin cannot be estimated from the seismogram. No report has come to notice of the shock having been felt.

August 10, from 2:30:00 a. m. to 2:30:32 a. m. H. S. T.

Intensity, low III Cancani scale; about 60-75% of the minimum perceptible unit. Origin distance indeterminate, but very small; probably less than one mile.

August 10, from 4:00:43 p. m. to 4:01:59 p. m. H. S. T.

Intensity, high II Cancani scale; 30-40% of the minimum perceptible unit. Origin distant about 13 miles.

August 12, from 7:20:41 a. m. to 7:21:29 a. m. H. S. T.

Intensity, medium I Cancani scale; about 16% of the minimum perceptible unit. Origin distant about 19.3 miles.

Registration suspended until September 28, 1914.

H. O. WOOD,
Associate.

The following systematic report from the Whitney Laboratory of Seismology is submitted, registration having been resumed after an interval of about six weeks:

Sept. 27, at about 10:06 a. m., a shock strong enough to exceed the range of the sensitive seismometers; not registered, but observed.

Sept. 27, at about 10:08 a. m., an instrumentally strong shock; not registered, but observed.

Neither of these shocks were felt at the Observatory but were felt at neighboring places.

Sept. 27, from 1:11:27 p. m. to 1:14:29 p. m. H. S. T.

Intensity, IV Cancani scale; 145% of the minimum perceptible unit, but not felt here. Origin distant about 21 miles.

Sept. 27, from 1:58:53 p. m. to 2:00:03 p. m. H. S. T.

Intensity, I-II Cancani scale; about 27% of the minimum perceptible unit. Origin distant about 21 miles.

Sept. 27, a shock in mid-afternoon; the record is so overscored that the time and dimensions cannot be worked out.

Sept. 27, from 9:54:23 p. m. to 9:56:11 p. m. H. S. T.

Intensity, high I Cancani scale; about 25% of the minimum perceptible unit. Origin distant 20-21 miles.

Sept. 28, from 1:38:40 a. m. to 1:40:08 a. m. H. S. T.

Intensity, I-II Cancani scale; about 27% of the minimum perceptible unit. Origin distant 21-22 miles.

Sept. 28, from 1:50:17 a. m. to 1:51:21 a. m. H. S. T.

Intensity, medium I Cancani scale; about 12% of the minimum perceptible unit. Origin distant 20 miles.

Sept. 28, from 6:40:48 a. m. to 6:41:44 a. m. H. S. T.

Intensity, low I Cancani scale; about 8% of the minimum perceptible unit. Origin distant 16 miles.

Sept. 28, from 6:45:30 p. m. to 6:47:42 p. m. H. S. T.

Intensity, low II Cancani scale; about 38% of the minimum perceptible unit. Origin distant 20 miles.

Sept. 28, from 8:40:52 p. m. to 8:42:44 p. m. H. S. T.

Intensity, low I Cancani scale; about 8% of the minimum perceptible unit. Origin distance indeterminate.

Sept. 28, from 10:41:31 p. m. to 10:42:01 p. m. H. S. T.

Intensity, II-III Cancani scale; about half the minimum perceptible unit. Origin distant 19.3 miles.

Sept. 28, from 11:17:49 p. m. to 11:18:37 p. m. H. S. T.

Intensity, medium II Cancani scale; about 35% of the minimum perceptible unit. Origin distant 14.3 miles.

Sept. 29, from 12:45:15 p. m. to 12:46:59 p. m. H. S. T.

Intensity, high III Cancani scale; about 95% of the minimum perceptible unit. Origin distant 18.5 miles.

Sept. 29, from 5:05:31 p. m. to 5:07:16 p. m. H. S. T.

Intensity, medium I Cancani scale; about 12% of the minimum perceptible unit. Origin distant 18.6 miles.

Oct. 2, from 12:56:54 p. m. to 12:58:42 p. m. H. S. T.

Intensity, I-II Cancani scale; about 28% of the minimum perceptible unit. Origin distant 14.3 miles.

Oct. 2, from 6:50:31 p. m. to 6:50:57 p. m. H. S. T.

Intensity, medium I Cancani scale; about 16% of the minimum perceptible unit. Origin distance indeterminate.

Oct. 3, from 12:46:57 a. m. to 12:49:13 a. m. H. S. T.

Intensity, high II Cancani scale; about 40% of the minimum perceptible unit. Origin distant about 15 miles.

Oct. 3, from 7:15:.. a. m. to 7:22:.. a. m. H. S. T. The very feebly registered chief phase of a teleseism of no great original energy.

Oct. 4, from 5:20:06 a. m. to 5:21:06 a. m. H. S. T.

Intensity, medium I Cancani scale; about 11% of the minimum perceptible unit. Origin distant about 20 miles.

Oct. 6, from 3:33:21 p. m. to 3:34:04 p. m. H. S. T.

Intensity, II-III Cancani scale; less than 31% of the minimum perceptible unit. Origin distant about 16.8 miles.

Oct. 7, from 2:21:26 a. m. to 2:22:25 a. m. H. S. T.

Intensity, low I Cancani scale; 5 to 6% of the minimum perceptible unit. Origin distance indeterminate.

Oct. 10, from 1:28:40 a. m. to 1:29:48 a. m. H. S. T.

Intensity, low I Cancani scale; about 8% of the minimum perceptible unit. Origin distant 18 miles.

Oct. 10, from 3:24:17 a. m. to 3:26:04 a. m. H. S. T.

Intensity, medium I Cancani scale; 16 to 18% of the minimum perceptible unit. Origin distant 16.75 miles.

Oct. 12, from 3:03:51 a. m. to 3:04:46 a. m. H. S. T.

Intensity, high II Cancani scale; about 45% of the minimum perceptible unit. Origin distant 9.3 miles.

Oct. 13, from 11:56:43 p. m. to 11:58:15 p. m. H. S. T.

Intensity, medium I Cancani scale; about 15% of the minimum perceptible unit. Origin distant 17.4 miles.

H. O. WOOD,
Associate.

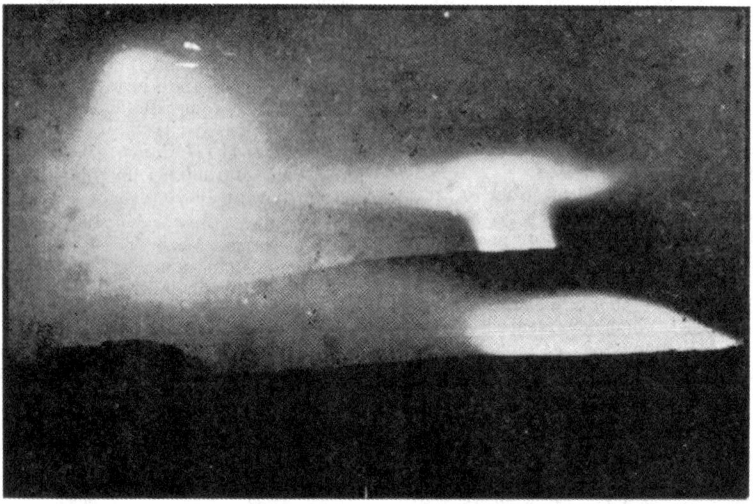

The new outbreak of Mauna Loa. View from motor road near Keanakekoi, Friday, Nov. 27, 1914, 12 midnight to 12:25 a. m. In the middle right is the Halemaumau cloud, illuminated. Above it, towards the left is the illuminated cloud above Mokuaweoweo. In the upper left hand part is the streak of the moon, traveling downwards for twenty-five minutes. Note the dim profiles of the mountains, due to moonlight illumination.

WEEKLY BULLETIN
OF THE
Hawaiian Volcano Observatory

Vol. II. HONOLULU, HAWAII, DECEMBER, 1914. No. 31.

WATER AND VOLCANIC ACTIVITY.

By A. L. Day and E. S. Shepherd. A Review by Frank T. Dillingham.

(Read Before the Hawaiian Chemists' Association.)

The authors, Day and Shepherd, begin their paper on "Water and Volcanic Activity" by quoting from two distinguished observers of volcanic activity, namely Wm. L. Green, an Englishman, for many years in the service of the government of these Islands, and Albert Brun, a Swiss chemist.

Green's conclusion from his study of the activity of Kilauea was as follows: "What we mainly wish to contend for and to impress upon geologists—for reconsideration, at least—is, that it may be a mistake to assert, as is so often done in the most positive manner, that water and steam are inseparably connected with volcanic activity. On the contrary it would appear that elastic vapors have nothing to do with the liquidity of the Hawaiian basic lavas, and that as a matter of fact they do not seem to come up with them from below, whilst the basic minerals themselves give no indications in the main eruptions of having been in contact with water, highly susceptible as they are to such an influence." This conclusion, which was supported by many facts of observation, has received much consideration from geologists in general.

Brun's conclusions are entirely similar. He says: "It is therefore absolutely certain that the active volcano does not give off water. The proof is complete. The large white cloud is composed of solid and anhydrous particles. The water theory must therefore disappear from science."

With the exception of these two instances students of volcanoes have generally concluded that water is usually, if not always, the chief agent of volcanic activity.

The authors, Day and Shepherd, next proceed to discuss in some detail what they call the novel conclusion of Green and Brun; the conclusion, namely, that water has no part in the volcanic activity of Kilauea. They produce evidence to show that while the observations of the facts noted by both Green and Brun may be exactly as described, yet their conclusion, that water is not exhaled by the volcano, may well be erroneous.

Some of their arguments are as follows: "When the lava is high enough to completely flood the floor of the basin, these cracks (in the inclosing banks) are closed, and all the gases emitted emerge directly from the surface of the lava into the atmosphere and have the temperature appropriate to the surface of the liquid (1000° to 1200°). At this temperature the gases (sulphur and hydrogen, for example) burn promptly on contact with the oxygen of the air and remain nearly or quite invisible." (This is the condition of no cloud described by Green).

"When the lava level in the lake has fallen ten or twenty feet (which is an almost daily occurrence and often takes place within an hour), only part of the gases set free come from the free surface of the lava, and considerable quantities now appear through the shattered floor surrounding the basin. The gases bubbling out from the lava basin re-

WEEKLY BULLETIN
of the
Hawaiian Volcano Observatory

Published Monthly at Honolulu, Hawaii, by the Hawaiian Volcano Research Association

Editor..............Howard M. Ballou
Professor of Physics, College of Hawaii

Entered as second-class matter January 20, 1914, at the post-office at Honolulu, Hawaii, under the Act of August 24, 1912.

main as transparent as before, and for the same reasons; but the gases appearing from the cracks in the floor and from the surrounding talus are now cooled to such an extent in passing through the cracks that they no longer burn on reaching the oxygen of the air. Free sulphur is then set free in considerable quantities, unburned; this we were able to collect without trouble, both at the point of emergence and on the crater rim. It is this finely divided free sulphur which is mainly responsible for the beautiful white cloud above the crater, and not crystalline chlorides as supposed by Brun. In fact only a minute quantity of chlorine or its salts (less than 0.02%) could be found in the emanations from the Kilauea basin during the period of our visit.''

''Our observation of the appearance and behavior of this cloud is therefore in full accord with the observations of both Green and Brun, so far as recorded; but there is nothing in the facts thus established to show whether the sulphur is accompanied by water vapor or not.''

The remainder of Brun's observations of the apparent absence of water vapor may find appropriate explanation in the fact that they were made in an **unsaturated** atmosphere at a distance of more than 250 feet from the point of emergence of the gases, and the further fact that the cloud not only carries sulphur, but two of its oxidation products, SO2 and SO3, both of which in these circumstances are effective drying agents. It may very well happen that water is given off in considerable amount by the volcano and yet remains invisible; for, in addition to the portion disappearing as vapor in the unsaturated atmosphere, a considerable additional quantity will condense about the finely divided sulphur particles serving as nuclei of condensation. . .

The authors decided that it was a matter of great importance to collect gases from Kilauea before they had come into contact with air at all. In this connection they state: ''Hot gases of more or less complex composition discharged from an active volcanic vent into the air undergo immediate and violent chemical and temperature changes, the consequences of which, with our present limited knowledge of gas relations at these temperatures, can be only partly inferred. It is, therefore, a matter of the first importance to collect the gases directly from the liquid lava or the explosive vents before contact with the air has given opportunity for these alterations to occur.''

To make such a collection it was necessary to go down upon the floor of the pit directly adjacent to the liquid lava. In the interval between May 1st, 1912, and January 1st, 1913, there occurred but two favorable opportunities for such a purpose.

About the last of May, 1912, it was noted that a column of liquid lava had worked its way up through the floor close beside the large active basin and had there formed an active lava fountain several feet in diameter. This fountain quickly built for itself an inclosing wall which soon formed a completely inclosing dome. The gases escaping from narrow slits in the dome could be seen burning at night with a pale blue flame which showed that there was an excess of pressure within the dome and that the gases released from the liquid lava first came in contact with the air on passing out from these openings.

Regarding these domes, the authors state: ''The domes from which these gases were collected were built up by the lava itself on the floor of the crater and were both chemically and physically ideal gas collectors, being lined with fresh splashes of liquid lava of the same temperature and chemical composition as that from which the gas had just emerged. They formed at the level of the lava lake and, as could be plainly seen after the collapse of the domes, were directly connected with the lake by channels of liquid lava just below the surface crust.''

The descent into the crater was made in safety and the gases were collected in a continuous series of ten glass tubes of about one-half liter capacity each. To one end of this series of tubes a glass pipe line was attached which led directly into one of the cracks of the dome. That portion of the pipe line which led into the dome consisted of an iron tube, partly lined with glass, so that, except for twelve inches of iron pipe within the dome, the gases came into contact with no substance other than cold glass and a few short rubber connectors. The other end of the system of tubes was connected with a piston pump which insured a rapid passage of the gases through the entire system. The gases entered the pipe line at a temperature of about 1000° C. Pumping was kept up for fifteen minutes in order to completely displace the air originally contained in the pipe line and connecting tubes, after which the pipe line was sealed off with pinch-clamps.

It was noted that water began to condense in this pipeline with the first stroke of the pump. At the end of fifteen minutes about 300 c.c. had accumulated in the collecting tubes. This water was clouded with free sulphur, partly from the original gases and partly from the action of the iron tube on the SO2 of the gases.

Knowing Brun's conclusion, the authors state that in making this first collection of gases they had provided apparatus for collecting fixed gases only. They were not prepared for the reception of any gases which might condense during passage through the collecting tubes.

What they actually obtained at this time was a quantity of fixed gases and water. The water was in considerable excess owing to the fact that it was not pumped through the tubes with the fixed gases, but condensed and remained principally in the first three or four tubes. Hence there is no way to estimate from the results of this collection the proportion of water to the total quantity of volatile matter discharged from the lava. Shepherd and Day regard this as a fortunate mischance inasmuch as they were thus able to collect a sufficient quantity of water to establish its existence without doubt among the volatile substances exhaled by the volcano.

Steps were at once taken to prepare vacuum tubes for the collection of a further supply of the volcanic gases. These tubes were of one-half liter capacity each, and were provided with a long stem, on the further end of which a thin glass bulb was blown. The plan was to attach these tubes to a long pole and thrust the end having the thin bulb into the dome where the heat might be expected to explode the thin glass at once, allowing the tube to fill with the gases and as quickly be sealed again by melting down the broken end. But by the time these tubes were prepared the top of the dome had fallen in and there was no more opportunity at that time to collect gases under conditions which would avoid contamination from the air.

A second opportunity for the collection of gases occurred in December of the same year. A second dome formed on the edge of the lava lake. This time the gases were collected in the vacuum tubes exactly as was planned. Six tubes were filled with gases under these conditions.

On descending into the crater for this second collection of gases, it was found that in addition to a long crack across the top of the dome from which the gases were escaping, there was a second opening near the base which was not noticed before the descent. This opening gave access to air at the base of the dome and thus behaved like an air-blast in a furnace. The gases were therefore partly burned within the dome, and the tubes which were filled at the upper opening were consequently found to contain mainly burned gases.

Hence, although the identity and something of the relation of the gases can be established from a study of the material collected in May, the determination of the exact proportion of water to the other gases present must wait for another favorable opportunity.

The authors, however, have carried on and are still carrying on a laboratory study of the relations between the gases already found; and in their paper offer a preliminary discussion of the results thus far attained. This discussion offers evidence that the composition of the gases varies within considerable limits, so that the exact proportions of the gases given off at any given moment may prove to be of less importance than was at first believed.

Their analyses of **liquid lava** dipped from the middle of the lake and of **solid lava** taken from the floor of the crater near the pit are substantially identical, and agree well with other recent analyses of Hawaiian lavas. The most noteworthy feature of the new analyses is the presence of a small amount of Molybdenum (Mo. O3, trace to 0.01%) which appears to have escaped detection previously.

The following analyses were made of the **fixed gases** collected in the series of glass tubes, May, 1912. The tubes were numbered from 1 to 20 in the order in which the gases entered from the volcano. All the tubes contained condensed water; number one contained nearly 100 cubic centimeters.

Table 2.

The Gases from Halemaumau (Kilauea), May, 1912.

Percentage by volume.

	Tube 1.	Tube 2.	Tube 8.	Tube 10.	Tube 17.
CO_2	23.8	58.0	62.3	59.2	73.9
CO	5.6	3.9	3.5	4.6	4.0
H_2	7.2	6.7	7.5	7.0	10.2
N_2	63.3	29.8	13.8	29.2	11.8
SO_2	none	1.5	12.8	none	none
Rare gases	none	none	none	none	none
Hydrocarbons	none	none	none	none	none

During the fifteen minutes pumping in the first collection of gases, the short length of iron pipe which extended into the dome was partly destroyed by the joint action of the sulphur and SO2. Owing to the high temperature and the splashing of the molten lava, neither glass nor porcelain would have withstood the ordeal, and a silica tube was not at hand.

The authors, however, present abundant proof to show that the effect of this small section of iron pipe on the relations between the gases collected in the tubes is not as great as might at first appear.

Among other things they say: "It might be assumed, further, that the free hydrogen present would be partly oxidized to water in reducing the ferrous oxide formed from the SO2 and iron (this is one of the reactions when these components are brought together at this temperature in the laboratory), but if this reaction has had a share in the disposition of our exposed bit of iron, we must admit its presence in overwhelming magnitude over the entire inner surface of the dome, which is everywhere lined with liquid lava containing nearly 10% of ferrous oxide. The assumption of this reaction would, therefore, have the immediate effect of establishing the presence of water in quantity among the volcano gases and at the same time relegate the influence of the iron tube to a position of entire insignificance." . . .

To this reaction assumed to be going on between hydrogen and ferrous oxide may be added another and much more important one in which the iron has no part. The free hydrogen liberated by the volcano reacts with sulphur dioxide at 1000° to form water and free sulphur. . . . It will also be remembered that carbon dioxide and hydrogen undergo a similar reaction at this temperature, as in the manufacture of water gas. . . .

$$H_2 + CO_2 \rightleftharpoons CO + H_2O.$$

It follows as a result of this that the chemical analyses of volcano gases offered by Brun in support of his contention that the emanations from Kilauea and other volcanoes are anhydrous, show on their faces the clear proof that his conclusion is erroneous. Neither CO2 nor SO2 can be associated with free hydrogen at temperatures of approximately 1000° without the formation of water.

The relative quantity of the gases discharged by the volcano is not well established by these samples because of the unexpected presence and condensation of water in the collecting tubes. After the collection of gases had been made, the tubes each contained a quantity of the condensed water in which the fixed gases are individually soluble in different degrees both during and after cooling. There is also some reaction between the gases and water. Nearly a year elapsed between the date of collecting the gases and their analysis in Washington, and this gave opportunity for such readjustments to proceed practically to completion. For example the SO2 has gone over in part or altogether to SO3, and entered into solution, as a result only two out of the five tubes analyzed now show SO_2 as such.

For this reason some importance may be accredited to a preliminary and very hasty analysis of the contents of tube number three, made only four days after the collection. This examination was made in the chemical laboratory of the College of Hawaii. Owing to the limited facilities, at that time, it was not possible to make a complete analysis; but on shaking the tube with water the total volume of the gas was reduced by 51.6%, which may fairly be assumed to represent the SO_2 in this particular tube, in excess of that quantity of SO_2 which had already gone into solution in the condensed volcano water of that tube. The carbon dioxide of this tube amounted to 39.8%, but was probably contaminated with some SO_2. The carbon monoxide amounted to 5.5%. The hydrogen and nitrogen could not be determined, but there was not enough hydrogen in the residual gas to form an explosive mixture when mixed with an equal volume of air. The water in this tube gave only a very slight turbidity with acid silver nitrate.

The water which was collected in the first tubes of the series may fairly be assumed to contain practically all of the halogens. The analyzes of this water is given in the following table, No. 3.

Table 3.

Analyses of Material contained in the Water collected in the Tubes.

	Amounts in Grams. Tube 1	Tube 2
Na_2O	0.0214 gms.	0.031 gms.
K_2O	0.0102 "	0.011 "
CaO	0.0120 "	0.14 "
Fe_2O_3) Al_2O_3)	0.080 "	0.010 "

(The major portion of these may have come from the glass or from Pele's hair.)

Cl	0.220 "	0.206 "
F	0.565 "	0.492 "
NH_3	0.0018 "	none "
TiO_2	0.005(?) "	none "
Total S as SO_3	0.480 "	0.508 "

In speaking of this table the authors say: "It is not improbable that most of the alkalies, lime, and alumina have resulted from the action of the acid liquid on the glass tubing, but it is of the greatest importance to establish the fact that the entire quantity of gas pumped through the "wash bottle" (i.e condensed water) yielded no more than 0.4 grams of chlorine. If this be calculated in the form of gas, it will correspond at most to 0.02%, assuming that approximately 1000 liters of gas were drawn into the tubes. Fluorine seems to be present in about twice this quantity, but in no sense can these halogens be regarded as forming more than a very minor part of the crater exhalation.

After all the active gases had been removed from the various tubes during the analyses, there was found to be an inactive residue which consisted mainly of nitrogen. This volume of residual gas was brought into contact with oxygen in a spark tube and subjected to an alternating current spark discharge of considerable intensity for several hours. The final residue of gas thus obtained was subjected to a thorough spectroscopic examination by Prof. R. W. Wood of Johns Hopkins. No trace of any rare gases could be found. The residual gas was therefore composed entirely of nitrogen. It is thus shown that the gases collected from Halemaumau in May contain nitrogen, but no argon. This, the authors state, furnishes a most desirable confirmation of their belief that the volcano gases were successfully collected before they had come into contact with atmospheric air at all. It also offers support to the view that the volcanic nitrogen is not of atmospheric origin.

The gases which were collected in vacuum tubes in December, 1912, afford less information than was obtained from those of the May collection. This was due entirely to the fact, already stated, that the second dome proved on closer examination to be an imperfect one, in that it allowed the entrance of air and a partial combustion of the gases within the dome. On opening these tubes they were found to contain mixtures of volcano gases and air, as was expected. Concerning these gases the authors say: "The analyses at best add but little to the knowledge already obtained."

Several collections and analyses of gases from a number of the hot cracks which occur outside the rim of the Halemaumau pit were made for purposes of comparison with the gases exhaled from the liquid lava.

Concerning these the authors state: "With regard to the chemical products along this circular track about the crater basin of Halemaumau, we can sum up by saying that water, although no doubt partly of meteoric origin, was always present at the time of our visit, and the gases were prevailingly high in carbon dioxide, sulphur dioxide, and sulphur trioxide. Only at the automobile road terminus was chlorine found to be present in an amount sufficient to show appreciably in a field test. Cracks farther removed from the Halemaumau pit show in some cases small amounts of SO2, but more frequently exhale merely steam. Thus in caves where stalactites are forming at a temperature of about 40°, the gas present was, in all the cases examined, merely air and steam and contained no more CO2 than is normally contained in the air. The formation of the stalactites in this cave is accompanied by the formation of gelatinous silica in the presence of some kind of green algae. As might be expected, neither carbon monoxide nor hydrogen was detected in the gases taken from these cracks."

To sum up the evidence presented; it has been shown that the gases given off from the hot lava are N2, H2O, CO2, CO, SO2, free H, and free S, with comparatively small quantities of Cl, F, and possibly NH3,. (No argon or other rare gases and no hydrocarbons). It follows then, that this particular group of gases cannot be associated together in equilibrium at a temperature of 1000°, and that chemical action is still going on between them.

For example, free sulphur could not remain long in stable association with CO2, nor could free hydrogen exist in stable relations with CO2 and SO2 at 1000°. Furthermore as the pressure continues to lessen during the upward progress of the gases, the quantity of gas released from solution, and consequently free to enter into new relations, must constantly and rapidly increase, up to the moment of discharge into the air.

Two consequences follow from this action. First, the rapid expansion of the gases with the release of pressure is a cooling phenomenon, which, if the expansion takes place suddenly from a high pressure into the air, may be extremely rapid. Second, the interaction between the gases thus set free in constantly increasing quantity is accompanied by evolution of heat, which naturally raises the temperature of the surrounding lava as long as the reacting gases remain in contact with it. The heat generated by these reactions, in the region near the surface where the amount of gas is large, may easily be much more than enough to counteract the cooling effect of the expansion within the rising lava column, which may thus become hotter and not cooler as it approaches the surface. We have here, therefore, an enormous store of volcanic energy which reaches its maximum temperature at the surface itself.

In accordance with the positive conclusion that these particular gases can not exist together in stable equilibrium at the temperature at which they are found, the statement of their analyses (already given) shows that their composition varies from one tube to another. The successive tubes of gases collected at the same time show that the individual gases are not present in the same proportions, but rather in proportions which change with every bubble which bursts from the liquid lava.

If it now be granted that water is present as an active constituent of the liquid lava, it is necessary to inquire whether this water is magmatic or meteoric in its origin. No positive answer can be given to this question as yet. Three views are possible; first, water may have entered by infiltration of sea water from the surrounding ocean; second, by deep seated infiltration of water originally meteoric; third, the water may be considered to be entirely magmatic in character and an original constituent of the lava.

Owing to the conditions surrounding the volcano it is somewhat arbitrary to attempt to assign the water found in the lava to one or other of these three possible sources. None the less, the authors point out some definite indications towards one specific source; as follows: "First and most important, in our opinion, is the fact that the nitrogen found in the emanation is free from argon. It is plain that if atmospheric water is to reach a hot lava column at a temperature of 1000°, or higher, it must do so as a gas, and therefore on the same terms as other atmospheric gases. Argon is invariably contained in the air in measurable quantity and forms no chemical compounds. Whence it follows that if the gases of the atmosphere had reached the liquid lava in any manner whatsoever, the argon would be released with the others; but no trace of argon was found.

"The second difficulty is to conceive a mechanism whereby atmospheric or surface water of whatever origin can make its way into a lava column or basin at a temperature of 1000° or more. . . . This temperature passed (374°, critical temperature of water), water must make its way precisely like any other gas by diffusion through pores or by overcoming whatever chemical or mechanical conditions it may encounter. The prospect is not an encouraging one. The hydrostatic pressure at great depths of the sea would appear to be the only sufficiently powerful agent to drive water against a high adverse temperature gradient, but to invoke this would be to invite nice distinctions of where magmatic water begins and meteoric water ends. The presence or absence of chlorine is not a conclusive factor one way or the other, because the physical processes of infiltration through porous rock and of distillation are alike of such a kind as gradually to leave the dissolved salts behind.

"To us, therefore, such evidence as there is appears to indicate that the water released from the liquid lava when it reaches the surface is entitled to be considered an original component of the lava with as much right as the sulphur or the carbon."

TECHNOLOGY STATION, Kilauea November 27.—The past week culminated in an outbreak of lava and fume columns in Mokuaweoweo at about three forty-five Wednesday afternoon, November 25, 1914, the beginning of the belated eruption of Mauna Loa which has been expected for three years past at this observatory, and especially of late, owing to increased numbers of local earthquakes recorded by the seismographs and felt in Hamakua, Hilo, Kau and Kona.

The first column of white vapor was seen shortly before four p. m. at Pahala, rising rapidly from the north side of the summit of Mauna Loa, then four other columns rose in rapid succession beside it and next south of it, and when night came these quiet slender vapor stems were brilliantly illumined by bright yellow light from the lava below. The spectacle was splendid from Halemaumau and from the Kau road a short distance from the observatory.

At the Observatory there was a thin rain cloud. The fume jets merged above into a broad cloud mushroom of tabular form, themselves making collectively a wide stem to the mushroom, apparently from four main fountaining centers within the whole length of Mokuaweoweo. The vapor columns were rising rapidly, but with no trace of explosion cauliflowers or of black dust. In the distance they appeared almost still, as though the dome of Mauna Loa were crowned with a delicate luminous halo coronet.

The glow over Kilauea was much more conspicuously red, making the Mauna Loa illumination appear white by contrast. In the light of the western moon, seen from the gravel banks near Halemaumau, the spectacle of the two craters one above the other, with the hard profile of the great mountain between, and the billowy fumes moving silently southward from Kilauea, was surpassingly beautiful. Kilauea continued its activity with some rising, but as yet with no effect sympathetic with the sudden awakening of Mauna Loa.

The week at Kilauea, as might be expected after the rising activity of last week, has shown subsidence and same caving and enlarging of the great double lake which was created by the collapse of the eastern cones. As the report of the Whitney Laboratory shows, the seismic activity of the last three weeks in Hawaii has been the strongest yet recorded at this station; there has been an unusually large number of local earthquakes.

November 19, at 10:45 a. m., the lake seen from the northwest station was about ten feet below its rim (which is about 460 feet below the edge of Halemaumau), and was streaming actively from the west to the south, east and northeast coves. Traveling fountains were moving from the region of Old Faithful toward the eastern arm. The current swept around the point very rapidly into the east arm, with hard boiling in the entrance to the east arm. Some of the traveling fountains migrated into the east cove.

At eleven a. m. the lake had risen five feet. The northwest pond was very quiet, covered with a skin of lava, which moved lazily occasionally. The cone in the west corner of the floor puffed at intervals. At two p. m. the lake had sunk again to ten feet below the bank, showing that the rise observed happened about noon. Activity was very great in the south cove and at the end of the east arm. The general changes of this day, noted about five p. m. from the north rest-house, were a lengthening of the east arm northwestward, and of the west end of the northwest pond by the collapse of the next western cone. Also the western part of the main lake appeared wider.

November 20, the seismograph record showed a large number of local earthquakes for the preceding twenty-four hours. Mauna Loa was clear on the afternoon and night of this day, and showed absolutely no vapor or glow.

At eight p. m. from the south and southeast stations there was clear seeing. The lake appeared fully fifteen feet below its banks.

The streaming was, as usual, from the west to the east and south. The torrent poured under the east cliff at the end of the east cove, and under the northeast cliff near the end of the east arm of the lake. These two points of inpouring are nearly under the two ends of the 1894 bench, and if much undermining went on there this bench might well subside farther. The high eastern chimney flame was very bright. The northwest pond appeared low within its walls and to be elongating itself eastward. The east arm was elongating westward in the direction of effecting a junction with the northwest pond. The portion of it which lay under the northeast cliff appeared as straight as an artificial ditch.

A group of small fountains played incessantly at the Old Faithful locality, and Old Faithful burst at intervals, sometimes in multiple domes. The most rapid streaming was in the east arm at the point of outrush under the northeast bank. No falling stones were heard, but the general nature of the activity suggested a subsiding phase, rapid streaming and fountaining, and no sluggish skins. About half way up the northeast cliff there is a very active fumarole, back of a slab which protrudes high above the east chimney.

November 21, the pool again presented the phenomenon of a noon rise. At 11:15 a. m. from the south station it appeared about twenty feet below its banks, actively fountaining and rumbling, some of the fountains traveling around the bend into the east arm. At two p. m. the activity was much less, as befits a rising phase, with some fountaining in the middle, east and northeast. By 2:15 the lake had risen to within five feet of the floor level. This was seen from the north, whence the north end of the east arm was seen to be prolonged into a trench bordered by great cracks. The northwest pond was boiling and streaming eastward under a cone at its east end slowly. The west-northwest cones were blowing noisily. At three p. m. the lava level had settled down again to ten feet below the rim with strong activity.

November 22 from 2:30 to 4 p. m., as seen from the north, the pool appeared to be down only from ten to fifteen feet below its bank and rising, with quiet skins on its surface and slow streaming and fountaining. A striking change accompanying this rise was the reversal of direction of streaming in the east arm, now from north to south from under the zigzag edge of a skin within the cove. Otherwise the streaming was from the west as usual, into the south cove, and through a rather constricted channel into the southeast cove. There was a large cone over the east end of the northwest pond, and the overflow along the edge of the floor eastward from that pond appeared to be augmented. The lake as a whole appeared to be growing larger.

At one p. m. Monday, November 23, from the southeast station the lake appeared twenty-five feet below the floor level and very active with a strong renewal of bubble fountaining or baby fountains over much of the surface. The streaming was toward the east and northeast, the current running around the bend into the east arm. The south cove was quiet. At three p. m. conditions were the same, with much rumbling and plashing.

On the afternoon of November 24 there was no clear seeing on account of high wind and rain. Glimpses indicated a low lake and much fume.

T. A. JAGGER JR.

The report of earthquake shocks recorded at Whitney Laboratory of Seismology at Kilauea from November 4 to November 24 tells plainly the story of the subterannean struggle that was going on in the immediate vicinity of Mokuaweoweo. There is scarcely a day in that time but the director in charge, did not discover the tracings of from one to four temblors on the delicate instruments which are installed at the observatory to detect earthquakes and locate as near as possible their source.

In the three weeks ending November 24 the observatory secured records of fifty-six earthquake shocks, all of them with one exception ranging from five to thirty miles of Kilauea. On November 20 there were ten distinct shocks recorded there.

The one quake which did not originate close to Kilauea was recorded on the morning of November 24 and had a duration of about five minutes. It was what the scientists class as a "weak shock of the strong class," possessing only moderate energy for a shock of the strong class at the origin. It was figured that the shock originated at a distance of about eighteen hundred miles from the observatory.

In the seismic report, Professor Jaggar says:

"Besides these, eight or more shocks occurred early in the afternoon of November 25, beginning shortly after noon with a continuous shaking, having several maxima, extending over several minutes—or, perhaps better, several shocks in rapid succession. These were followed at longer intervals by the others. Later in the afternoon, at about four o'clock, it was noticed that white smoke columns were rising from the summit of Mauna Loa. This was reported from several sources, but, owing to driving mists, nothing was noticed at the observatory until about six-fifteen p. m. when the glow was plainly seen through the curtains of mist. These shocks of the afternoon of November 25 have not yet been measured. No shocks were registered after the mid-afternoon.

"While as yet experience and the body of knowledge is not developed far enough to have justified a prediction, based on the increase in earthquake frequency and energy, that a state of eruption was culminating—nevertheless, there is little doubt that the earthquakes here reported constitute a seismic prelude to the volcanic outbreak. Any discussion of the geophysical meaning of this is too long to be included here. However, this prelude was anticipated by the writer, despite the strongly substantiated statements that oubreaks in Mokuaweoweo are frequently unheralded by shocks of earthquake. Bearing on this point it is noteworthy that, so far as has been learned, the shocks of the afternoon of November 25 attracted no attention on the eastern slope of Mauna Loa, except instrumentally."

TECHNOLOGY STATION, December 3.—The week that has passed since the outbreak in Mokuaweoweo, ending December 2, has proved unfavorable, on the whole, for observation of Mauna Loa, either from the observatory or from nearer vantage points. Many brief views have been afforded but, both by night and day, rains, clouds, and driving mists have sadly interfered with seeing. Also the party led up the mountain by Director Jaggar came to grief, being stopped and driven back by a very severe wind and snow storm when near the summit, but before the crater was reached—forced, in fact, to abandon the camp equipment temporarily. So far as is known, only one party has reached the summit as yet.

They reported fire fountains to be playing there, as is customary in such outbreaks. At second hand, their report stated that they witnessed twelve fountains, of which one was spurting to heights of from three hundred to four hundred feet, that there was no molten lake, or flow, merely fountains with pools about them.

Neither of the members of this party has been interviewed directly by the writer, and consequently no attempt can be made here to introduce their testimony responsibly. Also, the report of the attempted ascent by Director Jaggar must await his return. At a distance of a mile, or upwards, from the crater a deep-toned murmuring sound was heard, which was considered to emanate from the activity there.

It can be stated as a virtual certainty that no flows on the mountain slopes have yet occurred.

At Halemaumau nothing has been observed that could be thought to indicate any response in activity to the outbreak in Mokuaweoweo. The usual oscillations in height, and minor changes in activity, of the molten surface have gone on, but the configuration of the magma lake and pool and the disposition and behavior of the blowing cones remain as before, no marked changes having taken place.

Since the cluster of earthquakes which immediately preceded the outbreak only two (with possibly a third) small shocks have been registered.

On November 26, a clear view of the summit profile of Mauna Loa at about nine a. m. showed a cluster of fume columns, merging into a fluted curtain of thin bluish-white fumes rising quietly to a position subtending an angle above the summit about two-thirds as great as that subtended by the summit above the level of Kilauea, hence attaining an altitude of 6000 to 7000 feet above the summit, where a scanty cumulus crown of condensed vapor hung.

Presumably this was condensed water vapor. All about it was a very thin, much diffused bluish haze of uncondensed fumes. By day the effect was disappointingly slight. Drifting clouds during forenoon and afternoon made seeing uncertain. Toward sundown, however, clear seeing was again afforded. Seen in sunset lighting, partly by reflected, partly by transmitted light, the thin fume curtain—now chiefly a north and a south column—displayed a succession of color tints of distinctly fluorescent character, as follows; (a) just before sunset, with the sun on the mountain profile well south of the summit, the fumes showed a dirty saffron tint, seen largely by reflected light; (b) at about ten minutes after sunset this had gradually turned to a brown, in which a distinctly greenish cast was seen; it was still a muddy color, though seen largely by transmitted light; (c) about twenty minutes after sunset the tone had become a deep, translucent brown, still of somewhat muddy consistency.

Seeing in the evening was much interrupted by mist. Meteorological conditions at the summit were unquestionably less favorable for a spectacular display than on the evening of outbreak. Nevertheless it appeared certain that the active area had decreased, though there was no suggestion that the intensity of action was diminishing. There were two well-marked columns of rising fumes, the southern larger and better illuminated. Usually these were separated by a blank space of clear sky, but at times illuminated drifting fumes intervened.

On November 27, by day only brief glimpses of the top of the fume column were obtained. At night the scene was essentially unchanged, though somewhat more spectacular than on the previous evening.

On November 28, forenoon views were like those of the preceding days. Heavy rain set in about noon and there was no further seeing.

On November 29, no view was obtained till late afternoon and evening. The summit was seen to be covered with snow down to about 12,000 feet. There was no significant change in the action from that seen on Friday evening, November 27.

On November 30, at about ten a. m. the north fume column was seen to be very much lessened. At night in bright, hazy moonlight the display was brilliant and quite as spectacular as at any time except the first evening and night. Nevertheless the output of fumes was less than on the preceding evenings. The south column of fumes was much the larger, and better illuminated. The dark space intervening between it and the north column was occasionally filled with drifting fumes well lighted.

On December 1, an overcast day with very high clouds, the fumes showed faint brown tints against the cloud background in early forenoon. A stratum of very thin, cerulean blue fumes, with a faint but distinctly defined limiting plane at the bottom, rested upon the mountain, above about 10,000 feet. In the afternoon only the south fume column was any longer visible. This rose, straight and slender, from 9000 to 10,000 feet above the summit, and there a ragged cumulus crown hung stationary in a streaked, wavy network of blue haze. In the evening the slender fume column was faintly illuminated and soon obscured by drifting clouds. While this would apparently indicate decreasing activity, such an opinion must be scanned cautiously —for the spectacle depends very greatly upon meteorological conditions at the summit.

On December 2, no view was obtained until evening. Then, at first the single south fume column appeared dimly lighted, almost invisible in the bright light of the full moon, but soon fumes appeared to be rising more copiously and more rapidly and the column became very brilliantly lighted, as much so as at any time except on the night of outbreak.

There can be no question that, so far, the most brilliant spectacle was afforded on the evening and night of the outbreak. Nevertheless it is conjectured that there has been no significant change in the intensity of the action in Mokuaweoweo, but it is practically sure that the area of action has decreased, and it is highly probable that there are fewer playing fountains. But there still is a magnificent scene to be observed at close hand in the great caldera.

Observations at Halemaumau

On November 25, the molten surface was approximately 25 feet below the floor of the pit. The relatively vigorous surface action so common of late was going on—both traveling fountains, or better, migrating boiling places, were moving, and torn crusts were streaming, toward the northeast wall and the east cove. There was much activity in the south and east coves and around the site of ''Old Faithful.'' The noise was like that of heavy surf. During a couple of hours the surface rose four or five feet.

On November 26, in the late forenoon the molten surface was about ten feet below the floor and exhibited rapid streaming of torn crusts around the bend, where the two arms of the lake join, toward the wall under the northeast. Boiling action was vigorous in many parts of the lake. The northwest pool was very active and the west cone was blowing very loudly.

On November 27, the conditions of surface activity were practically unchanged. The fumes rising near the east margin were exceptionally sharp. Wherever vigorous fountain action was going on, particularly under the cliff margin in the small arm of the lake near its southeast end, there was much splashing of molten spray with spinning of Pele's hair. Streaming in both arms was toward this place of fountaining. Subordinate strong fountain action was going on under the central part of the north margin of the main arm and there was subordinate streaming toward this place. The northwest pool was relatively sluggish. The molten surface was from ten to fifteen feet below the floor.

On November 28 a very heavy rain prevented observation.

On November 29, the molten surface had sunk to twenty-five or thirty feet below the floor. The encircling spatter margin, seen clearly for the first time recently, was built up surprisingly little. The configuration of the lake remained unchanged. The surface action was somewhat less vigorous than on the twenty-seventh. Slow streaming with slow tearing of the crusts was going on as then. Later this streaming became more rapid. At one time a spasmodic breakup of the entire crusted lake occurred, almost explosive in character, accompanied by a foot or two of sudden sinking and a dull, explosive splashing sound. A few minutes of exceptionally vigorous surface action ensued. Fountain action with great spattering was most vigorous under the cliff margin of the smaller arm of the lake near its southeast end. At long, irregular intervals a harsh blast was blown by the westernmost of the high south cones. Blue flames were playing from the cones. The sound like that of heavy surf was continuous.

On November 30 no change worthy of description was observed.

On December 1 the streaming was frequently changing in direction, and was taking place in several directions simultaneously in different parts of both arms of the lake. Fountains were flinging spatter vigorously, particularly at the east margin of the east cove. The molten surface had risen slightly, being from fifteen to twenty-five feet below the floor.

On December 2 it was observed that two flows had occurred on the floor. One had burst out from under the cliff wall at the west end of the pit, beyond the west cones, and flowed along the west and north margins of the pit along the cliff wall as far as the talus heap below the north station. When seen it had crusted over, but was still issuing sluggishly from the source. The fresh lava shone through numerous cracks in the surface of the flow. This flow had gone partly into the open pool at the northwest. This was now more sluggish than usual. On the cliff side the pool seemed to be nearly level with the floor, but the walls toward the center were from six to ten feet high. The north boiling pot had enlarged almost to a small pool. The second small flow, originating near the cliff margin somewhere near the east cove (the origin being continuously hidden by fumes), had also worked along the northeast margin of the pit as far as the talus heap under the north station. This talus heap was all that had prevented the meeting of the two flows. The molten surface of the lake was somewhat higher than on December 1, but no numerical estimate was made because there was always a veil of thin fumes. The general activity had slightly increased, and much spatter was being flung from the fountains, particularly that under the cliff wall in the east cove.

The sound of rock cracking from heat was heard at intervals, presumably from the fresh flows. Blue flames were flaring, even from one cone almost submerged by the western flow. There was the noise of heavy surf. On one occasion the fountain action under the northeast wall was so violent that a pronounced vibration of the rock was perceptible at the Old Rest House.

During the week there has been no opportunity for the making of an observation for the correction of time. In consequence of this and of unusual pressure of routine, no report from the Whitney Laboratory of Seismology can be included in this report.

H. O. WOOD, Associate.

TECHNOLOGY STATION, December 10.—During the past week the visible glow and fume column on Mauna Loa has ceased to appear, and Kilauea has increased its area of liquid lava and shows rise by survey on December 9. Kilauea is very active and a splendid spectacle, as was expected for this season of approach to the solstice. The depth of the lava surface is 446 feet below the rim.

From the observatory on December 3 in the evening Mauna Loa cleared under high clouds, showing a single smoke column more voluminous than on previous days and more spectacularly illuminated. December 4 and 5 there was rain, but a faint diffused illumination of the cloud cap was seen at night. December 6, at half-past nine p. m., Mauna Loa cleared off, showing a single slender column of fume with orange light of about the same color as Halemaumau, rising rapidly in puffs discernible even at this great distance (twenty-two miles) to a height of about 6000 feet, and there spreading into a diffuse mushroom or balloon of thin vapor, illumined ruddy. The topmost detectable glow reached to at least 10,000 feet above the summit. The next morning, Monday, December 7, at eight a. m., Mauna Loa was revealed with a wide snow cap, and from its middle rose a very slender column of white vapor, diffused above into a bluish haze. On the next morning, December 8, the mountain was brilliantly clear and showed not the faintest trace of a fume column, and there was no night glow seen, though the mountain was clear at 4 a. m., December 10.

Halemaumau on December 4, from four forty-five to five forty-five p. m., was a remarkable spectacle from the northwest and west stations. There were the main lake, the east arm along the northeast wall, coves south and southeast, the outlying pond along the wall northwest, moving glowing flows from this region along the north wall at its base, glowing and hissing cones on the west floor and in the southwest talus, and at the wall end of the southeast cone a splashing pot had opened within the rock gash in the wall, which had been for so long the high east chimney. The lava in the pot appeared to be at the lake level. At first there was a crust separating the east arm from the main lake. About five twenty o'clock this broke up and great activity ensued with westward streaming, and the surface of the northwest pond was seen to be broken up also into vigorous surface action. The small flow in progress along the northeast margin of the pit exhibited glowing cracks. Shore bombardment with spatter was going on on the north side of the main lake, in the south cove and on the east side of the east arm. The inner portion of the northeast arm was crusted over more than of late, but otherwise the surface action was more intense. There were the usual surf noises, a steady, harsh blowing from the west cones, and one of the latter was an open pot with surging magma. There appeared to be further collapse of the floor north, away from the pit margin, leaving a gulf between the floor block and the wall strata, on the northeast and north sides. A broad blue flame banner was playing from the entrance to the east chimney pot.

December 5, three to four p. m., the lake was about five feet below the floor, streaming westward around the bend from the east arm into the main lake. Jets of spray shot high in the south cove. The northwest pond was streaming eastward, with a five-foot wall overhanging it on the side toward the lake. The west cones and a cone fifty feet up the southwest talus were blowing out spurts of liquid lava. The southwest cone made a loud blast with every spurt. The northwest pond was also spattering its bank.

December 6, at three-thirty p. m., lava had been rising through the west cones to such extent that a long new steel-colored flow flowed the whole southwest border of the floor from west to east, reaching to a point under the south station, where it surrounded the old south cone on the border of the floor. It was more than 500 feet long. The floor has receded from the east wall and in the crack or gully so formed the lake has undermined the wall and poured small festooned flows ten feet below the floor level. A torrent was pouring from the east arm into the main pool, and the streaming was westward and to places of bombardment north and south. The southeast cone was crusted over, but the east chimney pot at its end was spattering. The east arm was partially blanketed, and its walls appeared higher than those of the lake, which on this day were about ten feet high. There was a glowing cone on the floor at the west end of the lake, and smoke from cracks in the floor north and south, and within the new flow there were glowing cracks and the west cones were flaming. The northwest pond was streaming eastward. The lake was plashing and a sharp puffing noise came occasionally from the high southwest cone.

On the afternoon of December 7 the most significant change was further collapse of a marginal area of the floor north, making a trench between the east arm and the northwest pond, the floor block between this trench and the middle of the pit being upraised and tilted toward the lake. New glowing lava occupied part of this trench. The north pot was almost choked and the northwest pond sluggish and active by turns. The southwest cone was spurting a little regularly. There was heavy and steady fountain action near the east bend, near Old Faithful, in the middle of the lake, and in the south cone. The lake was about ten feet below its margin.

December 8, at 5 p. m., the lake had sunk so that the cliff around it was fully thirty feet high. This had nearly cut off the east arm from the main pool, revealing a promontory protruding from the upturned central floor block into the east arm. A narrow cascade poured from the east arm into the lake. There were crusts on the pool which broke up from time to time. A lava curtain with a slot in it had formed before a grotto at the northwest end of the main lake. Old Faithful was spattering violently. The streaming changed direction so as to run in three directions from a middle point east of old Faithful. The noise was of plashing with puffs from the southwest cone.

December 9 I made a survey of the lake about three p. m. and obtained some unusual views of the floor from the southwest and west stations, owing to a southerly wind. The north side of the main lake was 446 feet below the southwest station; the high pinnacle of upturned floor north of it 388 feet down; the floor level at the west cones 434 feet; the east end of the northwest pond 441 feet; and the floor level above the west end of the lake 440 feet.

The most striking feature of these measurements, which also was obvious to the eye from these points of view, is the upturned rock pinnacle, now fifty-eight feet high above the lake, constructed of the northern half of the floor, which has been bodily upheaved on the pit margin side, leaving a trench between it and the wall, and a pronounced slope towards the lake. This mass appears to be becoming a large island, and will do so if the lake rises fifteen feet higher.

There were new small flows trickling east from the west cones and from overflow of the northwest pond westward. The streaming in the lake was westward and the pool was only six feet below its rim. Rapid rising had taken place since the previous day. Smoke was rising from cracks in the tilted block of floor. The border talus is consumed and buried east, north and west; the southeast talus fumarole has dwindled, and dense white fume clouds are rising from talus fumaroles south and southwest. The 1912 sloping bench still persists 250 feet above the lake southwest, and a remnant of the sixty-foot bench clings to the wall under the south station. At the west and east end of the floor the walls of Halemaumau have steepened as the result of undermining by the lava, and the fresh raw rock shows some white bodies, more or less rectangular in section, which appear to be a different rock from the old lava flows, and possibly intrusive.

The length of the lake by measurement east-west is 435 feet, and of the floor 750 feet.

T. A. JAGGER JR., Director.

THE OUTBREAK OF MAUNA LOA.

The scientific staff of the Hawaiian Volcano Observatory has been awaiting an eruption of Mauna Loa since 1911. On October 21 of that year the writer recorded this expectation and the statistical data on which it was based, as follows:*

"It is fair to expect that Mauna Loa will renew activity with a lava pool at the Mokuaweoweo center, and without flows at first, before February 1, 1915. After lakings and fountains, with intervals of retirement of the lava, one outflow is expectable in the course of the five years following the outbreak (average duration since 1868).

"As the last flow in 1907 was to the south, the next by the law of alternation, which has held since 1868, should be on the north side of the mountain. These north flows have not commonly been accompanied by strong earthquakes. As the flows on each side, north and south, have been progressively higher since 1868, and there is no sign of collapse like that which led to the 1868 crisis, the new flow on the north side may be expected at a higher level than the Dewey crater of 1899. Thus the flow may be looked for somewhere near the high crater of 1843 northeast, or near the vent of 1859 on the northwest slope."

In accordance with such precedent the great lava fountain appeared in the summit crater on Thanksgiving Eve, November 25, 1914, about three-forty-

*Report of the Hawaiian Volcano Observatory, January-March, 1912, Mass. Inst. Tech., Boston. Also Chamber of Commerce Annual, Honolulu, 1912.

five p. m., Hawaiian Standard Time. This date brings to a close an interval of repose which in length is within two months of equaling the maximum recorded interval of the last half century, namely, the eight years from 1888 to 1895 inclusive. At that time, as at present, the long repose period followed one of the southern outflows. The summit outbreak of April, 1896, inaugurated an active epoch which culminated in the northern outflow of July 4, 1899.

The four seismographs of the Whitney Laboratory of Seismology of the Massachusetts Institute of Technology, in charge of H. O. Wood, in the basement of the observatory, have abundantly recorded a seismic prelude to this eruption, fifty-six earthquakes, all but one local, being registered in the twenty-one days preceding the outbreak.

Moreover, throughout the year there have been strong recurrent seismic spasms, sometimes accompanied by strongly felt shocks, especially in the region of the Mauna Loa longitudinal axis. The seismic activity of the above mentioned twenty-one days was greater than any similar period of the last three years.

On November 25, in the early afternoon there were eight or more shocks, beginning shortly after noon with a continuous shaking, having several maxima, extending over several minutes. No shocks were registered after the midafternoon. These shocks attracted no attention except instrumentally, showing that the statements that the outbreaks of Mauna Loa are frequently unheralded by shocks of earthquake are loose assertions and refer only to earthquakes of perceptible magnitude. The action of the instruments about noon on November 25 was so peculiar that Mr. Wood called my attention to it and mentioned the probability that an outbreak of Mauna Loa was the cause.

Kilauea cannot be said to have shown the slightest instantaneous sympathy with the Mauna Loa revival. Throughout 1914 Kilauea has gradually increased in the activity of a rising lava column, following upon marked dormancy in 1913. As a whole the lava column of Kilauea rose gradually from 1906 to 1910, its revival taking place just before the culminating outflow of Mauna Loa in 1907.

In the winters of 1910 and 1912 the Kilauea lava column rose to within sixty feet of the rim of the Halemaumau cone, but did not overflow. Since 1912 the lava has gradually receded, and even now, while brilliant, is very low, 460 feet below the rim.

There were thus three years of rise, two years of high level and three years of subsidence in Kilauea, with minor semi-annual and monthly fluctuations. And this term of eight years checks closely with the repose period of Mauna Loa. If the lava of Kilauea disappears in 1915, and during the term of the active epoch of Mauna Loa remains dormant, we may well suspect a sympathy of alternation between the two volcanoes.

During the week of November 15, 1914, Mr. Conant of Kona, with Charles Ka as guide, went to the summit crater of Mauna Loa, Mokuaweoweo, and found conditions as usual, the 1907 cone on the floor of the crater just as it has been in the last eight years, with a few sulphurous cracks vaporing on the floor near the cone. Therefore in the week before the outbreak there was no significant visible change.

At the observatory notes have been kept for months past on the appearance of Mauna Loa, not a trace of vapor being seen above Mokuaweoweo. From time to time since 1912 high, thin, vapor columns have been recorded, rising several hundred feet above three old conelets on the northeast rift line of the mountain, the highest of many such cones which appear in profile from the observatory, and about in the position where the next flow might be expected. This locality exhibited five vapor jets on the evening of December 1, 1914, but it has not been especially active this year.

On the afternoon of November 25, 1914, Wednesday, shortly before four o'clock, the observatory was enveloped in a drizzling mist, but at Pahala, on the southern flank of Mauna Loa, the summit was clearly seen, and a column of white vapor suddenly rose from the north side of the summit; then four other columns rose in rapid succession beside it and next south of it, occupying apparently an arc of the mountain top about equal to the diameter of the main Mokuaweoweo basin. There was no noise and no earthquake.

When darkness came the fume columns were brilliantly lighted from below, and then there was some good seeing from the observatory on Kilauea. The slender vapor stems over Mauna Loa reflected bright yellow light from what must have been immense fountains of lava below, and they made collectively a wide trunk for a spreading mushroom of vapor above.

The night was moonlit, and a photograph was made by the writer from the gravel flats east of Kilauea near Keanakakoi crater, looking westward across Halemaumau at Mauna Loa. This was made with Zeiss Tessar F 6.3, Wratten panchromatic plate, exposed twenty-five minutes, beginning at midnight. It shows the Kilauea fume cloud below on the right, blown toward the left with the trade wind. Right over it is the great "pino" or pine tree of smoke rising above Mauna Loa, and the profile of both domes is shown in the volcanic glare.

The Mauna Loa column, twenty-two miles away, rises in still air from its high base (13,675 feet, 4168 meters), and spreads above into a diffuse table of fume. In the sky on the left is a glare made by the track of the moon.

Kilauea was very active and made a bright reddish glow on its fume cloud, but the Mauna Loa column appeared almost silvery in its whiteness by contrast. The writer would judge the color to have been the yellow resembling a coal-gas flame.

The Mauna Loa column was made up of from four to six thin, wavy strands, apparently separate fume jets above separate fountains, appearing almost stationary at the great distance of observation. One strand, to the right (north), maintained its distance from the others, so as to leave a dark belt of sky beyond between it and them, which shows even in the photograph.

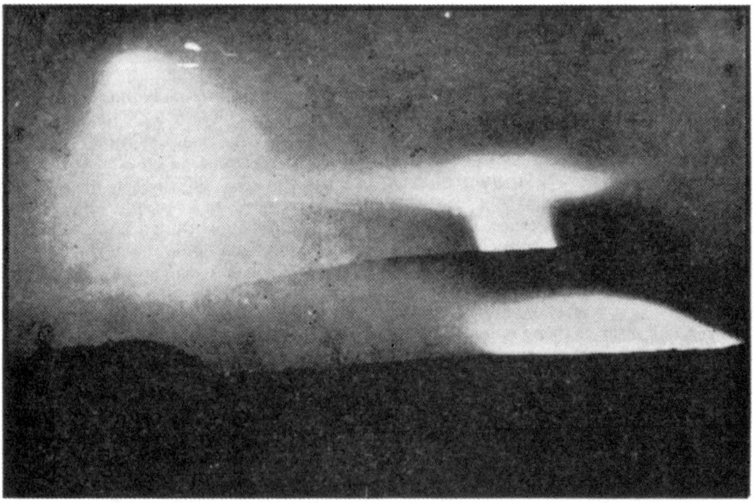

This first night was unquestionably the most brilliant, and up to the present (December 10) represented the maximum fountain activity. On the night of November 27 the summit was clearly seen from Puu Lehua, on the northwest slope, by the writer, when the brightest column rose from the south side of the band and there was a secondary smoky strand on the north side with a dark zone in between, and the color was orange.

Fortunately, in view of the stormy weather which followed, an ascent was

The Crater Lake on Mauna Kea, (12,000 feet), Hawaii.

made by two good observers, Messrs. Leslie Forrest and L. C. Palmer, from Pahala on the evening of November 27, and they spent the night on the edge of Mokuaweoweo southeast near the Wilkes station. I am indebted to these gentlemen for the following description and the accompanying plan. They reached the rim in the early evening, watched the fountains off and on all night, and returned down the mountain next morning. The activity was confined to the main central basin of Mokuaweoweo, where an elongate area of new lava overspread the middle part of the floor in a northeast-southwest direction and seemed to overlap the northern lunate platform of the Alexander map. Mr. Palmer did not see the remnant of that platform at all. This new lava was an elongate fountaining pool at the south, and apparently overflows on the floor at the west and north.

There were eight main fountains, mostly playing continuously, the southernmost a tremendous sheet fountain, estimated 150 feet wide, apparently playing above a north-south crack which determined its elongate character. As seen from the east it varied in width (length) like a flickering flame on a ragged, flat lamp wick, but played continuously to heights estimated between 300 and 400 feet. The height was estimated by comparison with the west wall behind it.

The other fountains were lower, forty to fifty feet high, the southern ones having in part the character of shore jets working in grottoes. Several mounds had been built up by spatter, and some of the fountains were concealed behind these mounds, or possibly within them.

At F2 (see diagram) was a spasmodic fountain which erupted at varying intervals, sometimes ten minutes, sometimes an hour or more, resembling a fiery flower pot, and shooting up to heights estimated at 200 feet.

The new lava flows glowed from time to time, especially between two and four a. m. November 28, when there was general recrudescence. There was white vapor on the south lunate platform and all around the northern end of the lava field. In the greater fountains the lava jets reached the curved upper limits of their trajectories still red and blackened in their downward course.

The following is the text of Mr. Palmer's description of the sketch-map:

"If the southern platform is 550 feet down (Alexander), the lake of lava must have been about 600 feet below the top of the mountain. Circles are fountains (F). 'M' are mounds with fountains back of them or else cones with fire coming through them. (Mr. Palmer identified no definite flames.) I could not tell at night, and by morning there did not seem to be any lava coming over them at all.

"F1 is a large fountain, varying in width, as it sometimes included a small fountain to the south; about 150 feet was the average width, but that is only a guess. The great fountain played continuously about half the height of the west wall of the crater, sometimes higher, particularly between two and four a. m., when it must have reached a height two-thirds or three-quarters that of the west cliff.

"F2 is a fountain which sent up a single column of lava at irregular intervals, not as high as F1. "S" is steam or vapor. Most of the night there was black crust over most of the lava area, but towards morning, between two and four, it disappeared, particularly in the northern part, where the surface was all red for a while, but by daylight it looked black again. Between the lake and the east wall (x), the lava was the same level as the lake, but black, except that a little fire showed through at x."

The next night, November 28, the writer's party reached the summit area, but were driven back by a severe sleet storm. In camp, at a distance of about three miles from Mokuaweoweo west, distinct rumbling could be heard from the crater at intervals, resembling the rumbling heard at Kilauea during activity, a few feet back from the edge of Halemaumau. Messrs. Palmer and Forrest on the previous night described the noises of the fountains as heard at about one mile distant from the east rim as rumbling and splashing, but not very loud or different from the sounds usually heard at Kilauea.

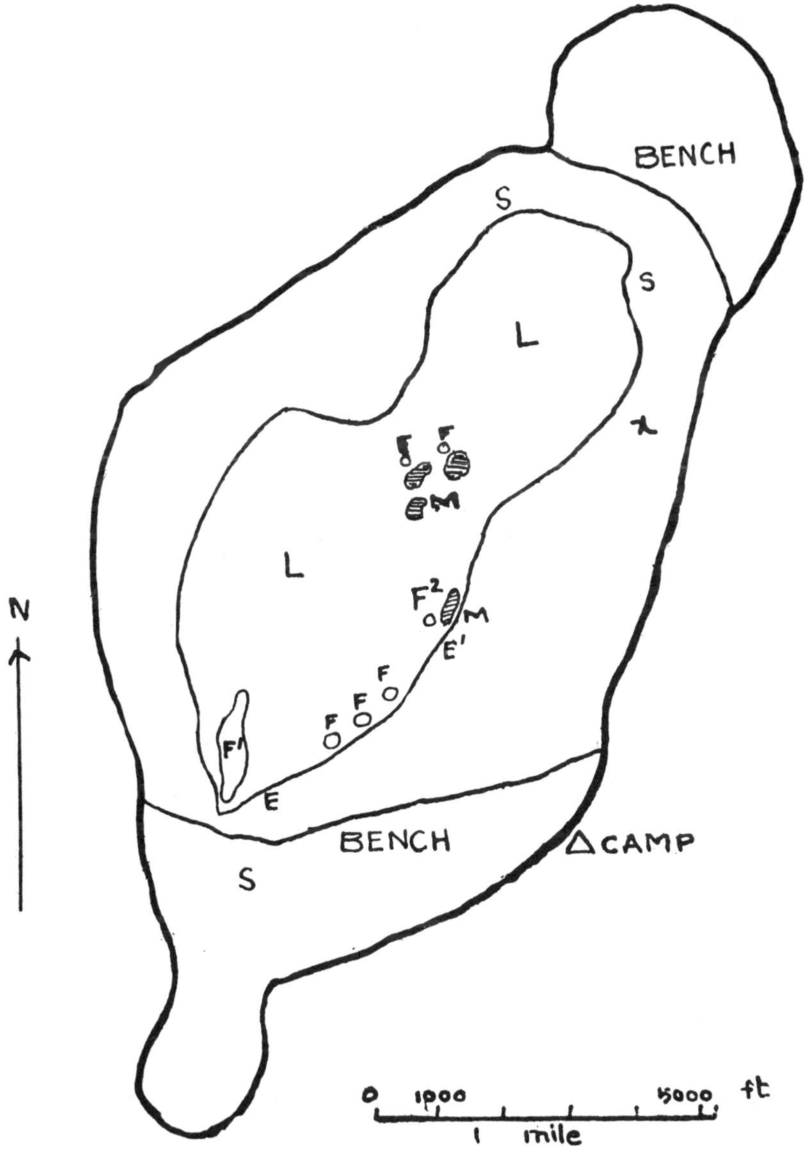

X—Glowed a little.
L—New lava, mostly flows.
EE'—Edge of distinct pool.
F'—Large fountain.
F—Fountains.
S—Steam (white vapor).
M—Mounds.
F2—Irregular fountain.

Outline of Mokuaweoweo, November 27-28, 1914. Sketched by L. C. Palmer from the J. M. Alexander map of 1885.

Stormy weather followed and covered the summit area and the floor of the crater with ice and snow. A second party, consisting of Charles Ka, Hawaiian guide, and an assistant, was sent up by the writer December 3, 1914, to recover abandoned camp equipment. They reported four fountains in the southern part of the crater, the northernmost the largest, the whole four corresponding in position with the large fountain F1 of November 27. Such dwindling corresponds with the appearance from below. Ka saw the mounds, and identified the cone of 1907 as still in place in the western part of the crater. He described the entire eastern half of the crater and the eastern plateau as plastered with heavy ice. He saw very little smoke.

December 6, from the observatory at Kilauea at 10 p. m., the summit of Mauna Loa was clear, with only a single slender vapor column rising and spreading at a height of perhaps 7000 feet above the summit into a thin illuminated balloon of flame. The color of the light was orange.

On the morning of December 7, Mauna Loa was capped with snow, and a thin faint column of fume could be seen widening above into very tenuous blue films in the upper atmosphere. The smoke has the same quality as that from Kilauea, brown in transmitted light and blue in reflected light. It is undoubtedly sulphurous. but as yet its odor has not been perceived by any one.

On the morning of December 8 the weather was brilliantly clear and not the faintest trace of a fume column over Mokuaweoweo could be detected with powerful glasses. There was a snow cap on the mountain and heavy masses of snow on the summit cones of Mauna Kea. December 9 also revealed the summit of Mauna Loa in the morning free from fumes. In the nights of December 7 and 8 Mauna Loa was concealed by clouds.

This morning, December 10, in the darkness of 4 a. m., Mauna Loa was clear, without any trace of glow on the summit.

There has been much talk about a lava flow. As shown in the first paragraph of this article, the lava flow of this period of activity of Mauna Loa may break out at any time in the next five years and it is likely to emerge on the Hilo side. Because the summit fountains cease activity, as they may do soon, it is no sign that the eruption is ended. The eruption will not be finished until a flow floods the mountain slope and so relieves the accumulated gas and lava pressure within. The conditions of the beginning of this eruptive epoch closely resemble those of 1896, which culminated in the Dewey Crater flow of 1899.

Whether the flow will menace Hilo or Kona no one can say, but we Americans must not be behind the Japanese, as at Sakurajima, in our orderly preparations for engineering such a crisis. Governor Pinkham wrote as follows on the appeal for more funds of the Hawaiian Volcano Research Association, September 26, 1914: "I approve of this work, and of legislation providing for trails, refuge houses, maps and scientific studies in the regions of active lava flows of Mauna Loa, with a view to preventing disaster, as well as the advancement of science."

The work of the observatory has no more than barely kept alive during the last two years owing to shortage in funds. It is no great burden for every interested person in the Islands to join the association at five dollars a year, and with a thousand members instead of one hundred, the scientific work would be much more effective. Furthermore, we want the patronage, and that means a subscription of from $100 to $500, of every interested corporation and plantation. By "interested" is meant not only those having business houses, ranches and mills in the danger zone, and that includes all of Hilo, Puna, Kau and Kona, but all who are public-spirited enough to take an interest in the efforts of a few, supported by an engineering school in Boston, to be prepared, in the interest of science and public safety.

We need about $3000 extra right now to open a way and construct stone refuge houses along the northeast rift line of Mauna Loa, for it is almost certain that the coming flow will burst out along that line. I have been trying to get this for years, knowing the difficulties that would confront us when the eruption came.

In the recent summit fountaining, all the marvelous exhibit was confined to the first twenty-four hours; no one saw it. For two clear, brilliant nights it was impossible to get either horses or men who would make the ascent. On the third night the activity had probably dwindled, according to my photographic record from a distance and the report of Forrest and Palmer, to at least one-third of its first intensity. And when I finally got there by a long, circuitous route, I was baffled and defeated by bad weather.

If Hawaii wishes to maintain its record for scientific efficiency, in which it has been successful in the sugar industry (but pitiably unsuccessful in some other lines, such as road maintenance, infant hygiene and dairying), it has an opportunity now to do an epoch-making feat in science and engineering; to call back a topographic party of the United States Geological Survey, and complete rapidly a reconnaisance map of the north slope of Mauna Loa; to appoint a commission of engineers to co-operate with the observatory in preparation for the lava flow, making an exhaustive study and report upon probable paths of flow, orifices of exit, past experience and critical divides where deflection might be accomplished artificially in case valuable property were menaced; and to appropriate money for trails and refuge houses so that these studies may be made from proper camps where supplies may be stored and both animals and men protected from inclement weather.

Whether property is eventually endangered or not, the record of complete preparation will redound to the credit of the Territory or of whoever accomplishes the work as one of the romances of science, like the story of the British engineers in India in preparation for the bursting of the Gohna dam in 1896.

The time is now.

The place is here.

The opportunity will not come again for ten years. And scientific men, however willing, cannot do the work without assistance and money.

The following report is submitted from the Whitney Laboratory of Seismology:

Nov. 4, from 10:35:46 p. m. to 10:36:12 p. m. H. S. T. Intensity, low II Cancani scale; about 35% of the minimum perceptible unit. Origin distant about 16.8 miles.

Nov. 5, from 9:00:29 p. m. to 9:02:27 p. m. H. S. T. Intensity, low II Cancani scale; about 38% of the minimum perceptible unit. Origin distant about 13.7 miles.

Nov. 5, from 9:04:52 p. m. to 9:06:54 p. m. H. S. T. Intensity, I-II Cancani scale; about 26% of the minimum perceptible unit. Origin distant about 15.5 miles.

Nov. 6, from 3:06:33 p. m. to 3:07:55 p. m. H. S. T. Intensity, low I Cancani scale; about 8% of the minimum perceptible unit. Origin distant about 13.7 miles.

Nov. 6, from 7:24:00 p. m. to 7:24:19 p. m. H. S. T. Intensity, IV Cancani scale, but not felt; about of perceptible magnitude. Origin distant about 11.8 miles.

Nov. 7, from 6:42:59 a. m. to 6:44:26 a. m. H. S. T. Intensity, high I Cancani scale; about 22:5% of the minimum perceptible unit. Origin distant about 32.4 miles.

Nov. 7, from 10:29:52 a. m. to 10:31:00 a. m. H. S. T. Intensity, medium I Cancani scale; about 16% of the minimum perceptible unit. Origin distant about 29.2 miles.

Nov. 7, from 11:36:25 a. m. to 11:37:41 a. m. H. S. T. Intensity, low II Cancani scale; about 30% of the minimum perceptible unit. Origin distant about 20 miles.

Nov. 7, from 8:33:25 p. m. to 8:35:06 p. m. H. S. T. Intensity, high III Cancani scale; about 80% of the minimum perceptible unit. Origin distant about 13 miles.

Nov. 8, from 3:01:27 a. m. to 3:01:48 a. m. H. S. T. Intensity, low I Cancani scale; about 7% of the minimum perceptible unit. Origin distance indeterminate.

Nov. 8, from 5:29:20 a. m. to 5:29:50 a. m. H. S. T. Intensity, medium I Cancani scale; about 12% of the minimum perceptible unit. Origin distant about 13 miles.

Nov. 8, from 7:10:24 a. m. to 7:11:10 a. m. H. S. T. Intensity, low I Cancani scale; about 6.5% of the minimum perceptible unit. Origin distant about 29.2 miles.

Nov. 10, from 10:41:02 a. m. to 10:-42:21 a. m. H. S. T. Intensity, low I Cancani scale; about 9.5% of the minimum perceptible unit. Origin distant about 14.3 miles.

Nov. 10, from 6:42:33 p. m. to 6:43:— p. m. H. S. T. Intensity, low I Cancani scale; about 10% of the minimum perceptible unit. Origin distant about 19.3 miles.

Nov. 10, from 6:43:13 p. m. to 6:44:46 p. m. H. S. T. Intensity, low II Cancani scale; about 30% of the minimum perceptible unit. Origin distant about 20 miles.

Nov. 10, from 11:38:43 p. m. to 11:-40:33 p. m. H. S. T. Intensity, low III Cancani scale; about 60% of the minimum perceptible unit. Origin close at hand, but distance indeterminate. A felt shock.

Nov. 11, from 8:25:00 a. m. to 8:25:39 a. m. H. S. T. Intensity, medium II Cancani scale; about 37% of the minimum perceptible unit. Origin distant about 13 miles.

Nov. 13, from 1:34:42 p. m. to 1:36:10 p. m. H. S. T. Intensity, high I Cancani scale; about 24% of the minimum perceptible unit. Origin distant 10.6 miles.

Nov. 13, from 7:57:36 p. m. to 7:59:46 p. m. H. S. T. Intensity, low IV Cancani scale, but not reported as felt. From 120% to 160% of the minimum perceptible unit. Origin distant about 15.5 miles.

Nov. 13, from 11:20:33 p. m. to 11:-21:35 p. m. H. S. T. Intensity, III-IV Cancani scale; about the minimum perceptible unit, but not reported as felt. Origin distance indeterminate.

Nov. 15, from 12:50:39 p. m. (noon) to 12:53:29 p. m. H. S. T. Intensity, low IV Cancani scale; felt gently. About 220% of the minimum perceptible unit. Origin distant about 11.7 miles.

Nov. 16, from 1:23:01 p. m. to 1:24:39 p. m. H. S. T. Intensity, low III Cancani scale; about 55% of the minimum perceptible unit. Origin distant about 20 miles.

Nov. 17, from 3:12:29 a. m. to 3:13:15 a. m. H. S. T. Intensity, low IV Cancani scale; about 110% of the minimum perceptible unit, but not reported as felt. Origin distance indeterminate.

Nov. 17, from 7:29:00 a. m. to 7:29:15 a. m. H. S. T. Intensity, low II Cancani scale; about 35% of the minimum perceptible unit. Origin distant about 13 miles.

Nov. 17, from 5:44:44 p. m. to 5:46:15 p. m. H. S. T. Intensity, high II Cancani scale; about 42% of the minimum perceptible unit. Origin distant about 14.3 miles.

Nov. 17, from 8:30:15 p. m. to 8:30:46 p. m. H. S. T. Intensity, medium I Cancani scale; about 12% of the minimum perceptible unit. Origin distance indeterminate.

Nov. 18, from 9:40:25 a. m. to 9:41:17 a. m. H. S. T. Intensity, medium I Cancani scale; about 16% of the minimum perceptible unit. Origin distant about 15.5 miles..

Nov. 18, from 11:15:36 a. m. to 11:-17:07 a. m. H. S. T. Intensity, low II Cancani scale; about 30% of the minimum perceptible unit. Origin distant about 20.3 miles.

Nov. 18, from 1:43:08 p. m. to 1:44:10 p. m. H. S. T. Intensity, I-II Cancani scale; about 25% of the minimum perceptible unit. Origin distant about 13 miles.

Nov. 18, from 4:37:30 p. m. to 4:38:55 p. m. H. S. T. Intensity, medium I Cancani scale; about 19% of the minimum perceptible unit. Origin distant about 16.2 miles.

Nov. 19, from 2:31:45 a. m. to 2:32:34 a. m. H. S. T. Intensity, medium I Cancani scale; about 19% of the minimum perceptible unit. Origin distant about 10.5 miles.

Nov. 19, from 2:44:03 a. m. to 2:44:52 a. m. H. S. T. Intensity, high II Cancani scale; about 40% of the minimum perceptible unit. Origin distant about 10.6 miles.

Nov. 19, from 4:46:17 p. m. to 4:46:45 p. m. H. S. T.. Intensity, medium IV Cancani scale, but neither felt nor perceptible owing to the smallness of the amplitude. Acceleration measures 280% of the value of the ordinary minimum perceptible unit. Origin distant 5.3 miles.

Nov. 19, from 7:17:27 p. m. to 7:19:01 p. m. H. S. T. Intensity, medium I Cancani scale; about 17.5% of the minimum perceptible unit. Origin distant 13 miles.

Nov. 19, from 8:06:36 p. m. to 8:08:03 p. m. H. S. T. Intensity, low III Cancani scale; about 70% of the minimum perceptible unit. Origin distant about 10 miles.

Nov. 19, from 8:09:08 p. m. to 8:09:52 p. m. H. S. T. Intensity, low III Cancani scale; about 70% of the minimum perceptible unit. Origin distance indeterminate. .

Nov. 20, from 3:09:41 a. m. to 3:10:40 a. m. H. S. T. Intensity, low I Cancani scale; about 6.5% of the minimum perceptible unit. Origin distance indeterminate.

Nov. 20, from 3:13:14 a. m. to 3:14:13 a. m. H. S. T. Intensity, low I Cancani scale; about 5% of the minimum perceptible unit. Origin distance indeterminte.

Nov. 20, from 3:44:17 a. m. to 3:45:23 a. m. H. S. T. Intensity, low I Cancani scale; about 4% of the minimum perceptible unit. Origin distance indeterminate.

Nov. 20, from 3:54:44 a. m. to 3:55:57 a. m. H. S. T. Intensity, medium I Cancani scale; about 18% of the minimum perceptible unit. Origin distant about 20 miles.

Nov. 20, from 6:11:02 a. m. to 6:12:36 a. m. H. S. T. Intensity, I-II Cancani scale; about 27% of the minimum perceptible unit. Origin distant about 4.5 miles.

Nov. 20, from 6:15:13 a. m. to 6:16:15 a. m. H. S. T. Intensity, low I Cancani scale; about 6.5% of the minimum perceptible unit. Origin distance indeterminate.

Nov. 20, from 10:27:13 a. m. to 10:-27:55 a. m. H. S. T. Intensity, low I Cancani scale; about 6.5% of the minimum perceptible unit. Origin distant about 18.3 miles.

Nov. 20, from 11:46:08 a. m. to 11:-46:31 a. m. H. S. T. Intensity, I-II Cancani scale; about 30% of the minimum perceptible unit. Origin distance indeterminate.

Nov. 20, from 1:48:41 p. m. to 1:49:16 p. m.. H. S. T. Intensity, high II Cancani scale; about 45% of the minimum perceptible unit. Origin distant about 18.6 miles.

Nov. 20, from 5:39:01 p. m. to 5:39:42 p. m. H. S. T. Intensity, II-III Cancani scale; about half the minimum perceptible unit. Origin distant about 12.4 miles.

Nov. 21, from 4:00:17 p. m. to 4:01:37 p. m. H. S. T. Intensity, III-IV Cancani scale, but not felt; about the minimum perceptible unit. Origin distant about 14.3 miles.

Nov. 21, from 6:03:25 p. m. to 6:05:27 p. m. H. S. T. Intensity, high III Cancani scale; about 90% of the minimum perceptible unit. Origin distant about 13 miles.

Nov. 22, from 3:56:40 a. m. to 3:57:30 a. m. H. S. T. Intensity, low I Cancani scale; about 7% of the minimum perceptible unit. Origin distance indeterminate.

Nov. 22, from 11:55:56 p. m. to 11:-56:10 p. m. H. S. T. Intensity, high II Cancani scale; about 45% of the minimum perceptible unit. Origin distance indeterminate.

Nov. 23, from 6:23:29 a. m. to 6:24:58 a. m. H. S. T. Intensity, high I Cancani scale; about 20% of the minimum perceptible unit. Origin distant about 32 miles.

Nov. 23, from 10:11:07 p. m. to 10:-11:20 p. m. H. S. T. Intensity, I-II Cancani scale; about 25% of the minimum perceptible unit. Origin distance indeterminate.

Nov. 23, from 11:30:05 p. m. to 11:-30:50 p. m. H. S. T. Intensity, low I Cancani scale; about 6.5% of the minimum perceptible unit. Origin distance indeterminate.

Nov. 24, from 1:32:51 a. m. to 2:23: plus a. m. H. S. T. A teleseism of moderate energy, probably, at its origin a weak shock of the strong class. The technical phase-times follow—eP 1:32:51 a. m., eS 1:37:31 a. m., iLM 1:40:47 a. m., M 1:47:37 a. m., C 1:43: plus, F 2:23: plus. All these are given here in Hawaiian Standard Time. To reduce to Greenwich Time add 10 hours and 30 minutes. Owing to strong microseismic waves it was difficult and uncertain work fixing upon the times of beginning of the fore-phases. Consequently the distance of the origin is in some doubt. The best approximation makes it a little over 1800 miles. The record of the chief phase was sharply written, but with a small amplitude, indicating only moderate energy, for a shock of the strong class, at the origin.

Nov. 24, from 9:53:47 a. m. to 9:55:05 a. m. H. S. T. Intensity, high III Cancani scale; about 83% of the minimum perceptible unit. Origin distant about 10 miles.

Nov. 24, from 9:57:38 a. m. to 9:58:02 a. m. H. S. T. Intensity, low I Cancani scale; about 6.5% of the minimum perceptible unit. Origin distance indeterminate.

H. O. WOOD, **Associate.**

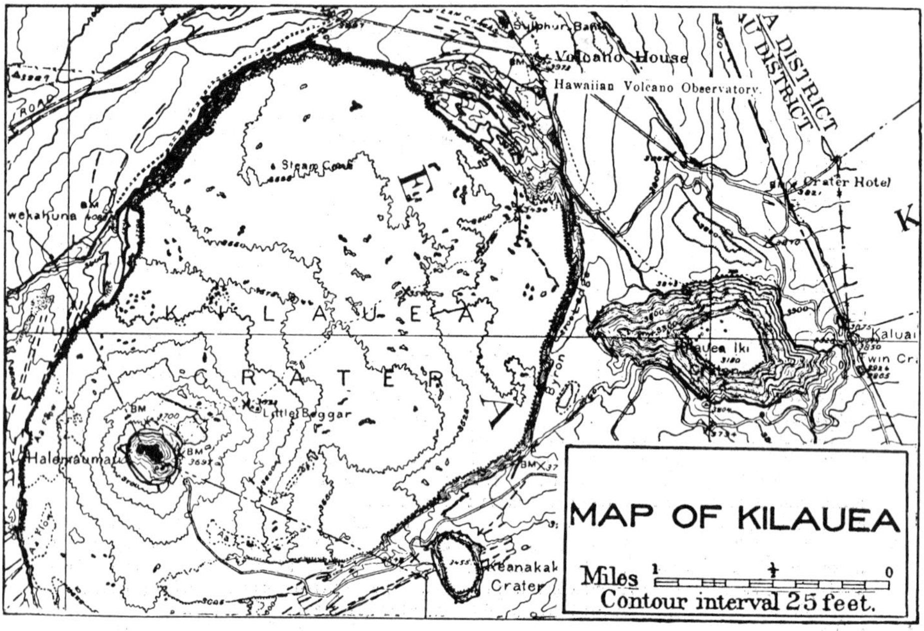

HAWAIIAN VOLCANO RESEARCH ASSOCIATION.

This society is a voluntary one, made up of subscribers to scientific work which is being executed by the Massachusetts Institute of Technology.

In 1913 there were 26 subscribers in Hawaii and Massachusetts, firms and individuals. A group of firms and persons in Hilo built the main observatory building in the spring of 1912. Publications to date have been weekly reports since the summer of 1911, a memoir by Daly in the Proceedings of American Academy of Arts and Sciences in 1911, articles by the director in the Technology Review 1911 and the Honolulu Chamber of Commerce Annual 1912, articles by H. O. Wood in the Bulletin of the Seismological Society of America, and articles by Perret in the American Journal of Science. The Massachusetts Institute of Technology will publish semiannual reports.

This weekly bulletin as it appears in the Advertiser will be reprinted as a leaflet and sent to regular annual subscribers to the work of the association. C. H. Cooke is president of the Board of Directors of the association and R. W. Shingle is treasurer. New subscribers who are interested in our volcanoes will be welcomed in the association. The association aims: (1) To record volcanic activity and earthquakes in Hawaii; (2) to attract scientific men hither for special studies; (3) to promote the establishment of volcano observatories all over the world.

WHITNEY LABORATORY OF SEISMOLOGY.

The Whitney Laboratory of Seismology is equipped with two Bosch-Omori 100 kg tromometers registering N-S and E-W motion, a heavy Omori tromometer registering E-W motion and an Omori "ordinary Seismograph" designed for registering strong earthquakes in all three components of motion. These are seated on concrete piers in a closed basement room having practically constant temperature, beneath the chief Observatory building near the hotel. Time is referred to a rated chronometer, checked at intervals by solar observations with a transit. Both instruments are loaned by the College of Hawaii. At the substation by the edge of the active pit an Omori two-component tromometer with light steady masses is mounted on a concrete pier placed directly on the fresh lava surface. Hawaiian standard time (H. S. T.) is 10 hrs. 30 m. slower than Greenwich time.

CANCANI SCALE OF SEISMIC INTENSITY

Expressed by accelerations measured in millimeters per second per second.

I.	Instrumental	0.0	2.5
II.	Very slight	2.5	5.0
III.	Slight	5.0	10.0
IV.	Sensible, mediocre....	10.0	25.0
V.	Rather strong	25.0	50.0
VI.	Strong	50.0	100.0
VII.	Very strong	100.0	250.0
VIII.	Ruinous	250.0	500.0
IX.	Disastrous	500.0	1000.0
X.	Very disastrous	1000.0	2500.0
XI.	Catastrophic	2500.0	5000.0
XII.	Great catastrophe....	5000.0	10000.0

Grade IV. is ordinarily the minimum perceived by the senses; and in grade XII. the acceleration, or rate of change of motion (jerk) reaches that of terrestrial gravitation.

WEEKLY BULLETIN
OF THE
Hawaiian Volcano Observatory

Vol. II. HONOLULU, HAWAII, DECEMBER 31, 1914. No. 32.

TECHNOLOGY STATION, December 17.—The week at Kilauea has been marked by the high activity, with overflow of the floor area at the bottom of Halemaumau, expected at this season. We have also succeeded this week in reaching Mokuaweoweo and taking photographs and notes of the fountaining activity which continues there.

There have now been five parties which reached the summit area, and only one of these, the first, Messrs. Forrest and Palmer, on November 27, succeeded in spending the night there. Owing to high winds and snow the December parties have had to content themselves with daylight views. The parties named were Forrest and Palmer, November 27; Jaggar, November 28; Charles Ka, December 3; Baker and Bowdish, December 11; Volcano Observatory expedition, December 15.

Three of the expeditions attempted to camp at the summit and failed, owing to weather conditions. The expense, in the case of the observatory's trips, has been enormously out of proportion to the small results achieved, owing wholly to the lack of any shelter in the summit area. The lessons learned in this respect, however, have been of great value. The Mauna Loa summit region cannot be a place of good scientific observation and survey until a shelter hut and stable have been erected there.

The expedition of this week left Volcano House Monday, December 14, at 9 a. m., by motor car for the upper cattle pen of Kapapala ranch, below the Halfway House. At 10:30 the pack train was loaded and it reached the water tank and camp ground in the forest reservation, at an elevation of about 8000 feet, at 4 p. m. and camp was made for the night. There were eight men, with riding animals and five pack animals. The party was H. O. Wood, D. Lycurgus, Mr. Withers, Mr. Hannon, Alex Lancaster, Joe de Mello and H. Kaukine, besides the writer.

December 15 start was made for the summit with the packs at 7:30 a. m., and before noon, in the snow-covered summit region, a gale of wind from the southwest sprang up. This was bitterly cold and the animals could barely make progress against it. The weather was cloudy but without snowfall or rain.

The snow of the summit plateau was deep and crusted over, so that it generally supported horses without their plunging through the crust, but one or two of the animals went through. There was perhaps the equivalent of a foot of snow on the level, drifted into the hollows, and revealing points of rocks.

As there was no diminution of wind on the summit plateau, which was reached at 12:30 p. m., I sent the pack animals back to the lower camp and all but the two packers proceeded to the crater. It was quite impracticable to make camp in such a gale, and in deep snow, with every prospect of a possible storm.

There are no ridges to offer protection, only a waste of pahoehoe and a-a blanketed with snow and occasional concealed crevasses. This plateau extends about four miles from the edge of the crater on the east side, but the west or Kona side is the actual summit of Mauna Loa and slopes off rapidly westward .

We reached the east margin of Mokuaweoweo at one-fifteen p. m. above the east end of the south lunate platform as mapped by Alexander in 1885. We looked across the south half of the main crater circle, which in general is much like the greater crater of Kilauea, and saw a large red fountain playing continuously in the southwest part of the crater. The fountain rose from the

WEEKLY BULLETIN
of the
Hawaiian Volcano Observatory

Published Monthly at Honolulu, Hawaii, by the Hawaiian Volcano Research Association

Editor..............Howard M. Ballou
Professor of Physics, College of Hawaii

Entered as second-class matter January 20, 1914, at the post-office at Honolulu, Hawaii, under the Act of August 24, 1912.

northwest corner of an oval pool of crusted pumiceous lava. and back of the fountain was a huge half-cone of its own building. All of this was a mile away, as though one looked from the Volcano House at Kilauea at a fountain playing near the foot of Uwekahuna bluff, the great west cliff of Kilauea crater.

The fountain played steadily to a height of about a hundred feet, and its horizontal diameter was about the same. Above this it sent up jets fifty feet higher, which parted into many fragments, cooling through shades of cherry red to claret color and black, and these black ejecta, instead of falling heavily, floated away and fell slowly like burnt paper, showing that the lava was of a very light, pumice-like quality.

The falling spatter from the fountain was to the west and north, and here on the edge of the pool was a black mound, probably crescent-shaped in plan, and steep or overhanging on the side of the fountain like the oven ramparts that build over grottoes around the borders of the Kilauea lake.

This spatter heap was at least seventy-five feet high and made part of the background of the great fountain. Lower ramparts engirdled the oval lake, which stood relatively high above a region of black pools and flows south of it and from it. The west side of the lake exhibited other lower fountains, one of them building a small mound, and mostly in the line of the big fountain and along the shore of the pool. Other fountains broke through the crust of the pool from place to place and time to time, seemingly indicating that the black crust was foamy or light and easily punctured. The fountains were indescribably different from the relatively heavy domes like old Faithful in Halemaumau.

They appeared to me much redder in daylight and more like flames than a heavy liquid. The suggestion was rather as of an exceedingly light and gas-charged liquid, which cooled and changed color even more quickly than the fluid of Kilauea, and which boiled to much greater heights because of its aeriform consistency.

In the high wind which was blowing very little smoke showed. Above the fountains, however, a blue fume developed in volutes and rose. Between the large fountain and the fume above it appeared a semi-transparent space with strong uprushing heat-movement lines, which gave me the impression of being a bluish flame which in darkness would have shown as such. The only smoking area was in the vicinity of the heated pool and the flows below it to the south.

The rest of the crater appeared much as in 1912 and 1913, except that new detail of small mounds appeared along a fissure line northward from the large fountain and beyond the great mound or cone of 1907. Mr. Palmer's map, reprinted from my report of last week, will serve to illustrate the line of this fissure, and no doubt there are new flows from this fissure over the middle region of the crater. The larger central mounds, however, shown on his map are not new, but are the old cones of 1907, somewhat modified by the new eruption. The detail of these changes, and perhaps some dimensions, I hope to work out from the photograph studied in comparison with earlier ones.

No changes were seen in the walls of Mokuaweoweo nor in the north or south pits, though we could not see into the latter. The southern lunate bench and parts of the crater floor were covered with snow, but not the central, southern and north central parts of the main crater, implying, perhaps, that all of that region is warm. Remnants of the north lunate bench still persist and show no change since last year. The north gateway to the crater formed a frame for a striking view of Mauna Kea, with its snow-covered upper cones.

The party left the summit at two p. m. and reached the lower camp at five. One of the animals was quite exhausted and was unable to hold out through the return trip next day. On December 16 we left the camp at eight-forty-five a. m. and reached the high-road soon after noon.

Halemaumau.

At three-thirty p. m., December 9, 1914, a curious meteorological phenomenon was seen over the northwest part of Kilauea crater. It was drizzling and the wind was southerly, and great volumes of visible steam were rising from the cracks of the floor, partly ionzed by the smoke from Halemaumau. The low rain cloud effected a junction with this steam in the shape of a long vertical filament of cloud with a central hollow or pipe which showed lighter than the main whirl, the whole thing looking like a waterspout. At the crater floor it threw the steam into a whirl. The spout migrated slowly northwestward, and once or twice broke in two, and then rejoined. Finally it broke away and was sucked up into the cloud above.

December 10, at noon, the lake in Halemaumau was about 5 feet below the rim. Streaming was from the east arm westward and into the southeast and south coves. The southwest cone, high above the floor, was spouting and blowing out lava spurts. The northwest pond was streaming eastward and the activity was strong.

December 11. at three-fifteen p. m. the temperature of the air was 16 degrees C., (61 degrees F.) and of the Postal Rift 307 degrees C., (585 degrees F.)

Halemaumau was about the same but with very intense fountaining occasioned by opposed currents meeting. The places of meeting were first the narrow entrance to the east arm, then near Old Faithful; then there was tremendous continued bombardment of the southwest bank, then the west bank of the south cove. The pool was about five feet below the banks. The streaming changed, first radial from the middle, then westward. When the bombardment became transferred to the north shore, great spatter blocks of the rampart fell into the flood. Later there was some sinking.

December 12 and 13 new flows poured along the walls along the border of the floor south and north from the west cones. The general tilt to the old floor had now made the edge of the lake much higher at the east end than the west. The west end was only about three feet above the lake and the east end five feet. There was heavy fountaining, various streaming, and conflicting currents. The northwest pond appeared to have migrated out from the wall, with broad flows back of it. For the first time this year overflow took place from the edge of the lake, two such flows pouring southward from the main pool.

December 16, at six-thirty p. m. conditions were much the same, with very high activity, new flows, glowing cracks, and the southwest cone gone along with the lower talus of that wall. There was now a rock chimney southwest. The four west cones were flaming and blowing, flames were rising from the west grotto of the main pool, and from the east vents. The heat of the lake could be strongly felt on the edge of Halemaumau. Very bright boiling pots lay alongside of the northwest pond. The lake was about ten feet below its banks and the streaming was various and tumultuous.

A correction concerning the outbreak of Mauna Loa, November 25, is to the effect that herders of Kapapala ranch saw the smoke between noon and one p. m., just when the seismographs registered prolonged motion. There was evening glow on Mauna Loa, December 10 and 13, and thereafter and occasional fumes seen by day.

T. A. JAGGAR, JR., Director.

TECHNOLOGY STATION, Kilauea, December 24, 1914.—The summit glow and fume column on Mauna Loa during the past week have been visible in clear weather over Mokuaweoweo without marked change.

The level of the lake in Halemaumau has been as follows:

Dec. 17, below NW. station......409 ft.
Dec. 19, below SE. station.......414 ft.
Dec. 23, below E. station........405 ft.

The level of the floor around the lake has been:

Dec. 17, below E. station, about..407 ft.
Dec. 19, below E. station, about..411 ft.
Dec. 23, below E. station, about..390 ft.

Full discussion of the overflows and floor movements of the past week will have to be deferred, as they have been remarkable. Just at the solstice, as expected, a rise occurred which continued for five days, December 18 to 22 inclusive. Instead of progressing by overflow from the lake, the overflow was from the west cones and northwest pond, with great flows along the walls which encircled and poured into the lake.

The lake itself remained relatively stationary, but a block of floor lava involving the accumulations of the early part of this year tilted and rotated about a horizontal east-west axis, so as to lift a crag on the north and sink beneath new flows on the south side of the lake.

The basin of the lake itself, hollowed into this older block, has shifted slightly. The new flows built up the floor about twenty-one feet in actual elevation, but probably more in thickness of filling on the south. The top of the tilted crag, by measurement December 23, was only 347 feet below the east station, or fifty-eight feet above the lake.

December 17 no marked change in general configuration was seen, the lake was two feet below the banks, the streaming was westward, and the new filling of south flows sloped towards the lake markedly. The suggestion is strong that the heavy southern talus is subsiding and pushing the floor block with it. From cracks in the floor and crag much smoke arose.

On December 18 at three p. m. tremendous flows poured from the northwest pond, north and south, reaching the east arm and the main lake southwest, with inflooding torrents, the lake preserving its outline and the northeast crag and west cones rising as islands in the hot flood.

The heat was very strong on the rim and the noise was a high, steady roar and hiss. The rapid current at the source was estimated to flow from half a mile to one mile per hour. The flowing diminished at four-thirty, revived at five p. m., ceased before eight p. m., revived about ten-forty p. m., was still in action at one a. m., and the next morning at ten-thirty a. m. had quieted. At this time (December 19) the streaming in the lake was to the west, north and south from the east arm, the old south cone in the talus was buried under new flows, the crag appeared as high as ever; the southwest cone was now reforming on the floor and wide flow lava appeared between the east arm and the northeast wall.

December 20, at five-fifteen p. m. and at ten p. m., flooding from the west was again in progress with all the features of December 18, one of the sources of the great southern flow being the larger west cone on the floor as well as the northwest pond. The flow was cascading into the lake southwest and puddling in an immense circle on the floor south. There were many flames and the lake was tumultuous.

December 21. at three p. m.. flooding was still in progress in the same fashion. On the southern floor two holes were receiving from the flow steady cascades near the site of the southwest cone. and another south of the south cone. These cascades poured thus into voids for an hour and were still pouring when the writer departed. The lake in its temporary rises would meet the fall pouring into it sometimes at a brimming level, so that the surface currents and the inflowing torrent met in conflict at a common plane.

December 22 flowing continued in diminished volume during the day, the lake subsided from two to six feet below its banks, and increased fumes, snapping sounds, puffing, and in the afternoon a few rock slides from the crag and from the northeast wall gave evidence of the beginning of general sinking.

December 23 the lake and northwest pond were fifteen feet down, there was a little rock sliding and harsh blasts at thirty-second intervals southwest.

T. A. JAGGAR, JR., Director.

First Photographs of 1914 Activity In Mokuaweoweo Sent To Honolulu, Taken December 15

THE PANORAMA of the active crater of Mokuaweoweo, shown in the upper reproduction, is the first photograph of the recent activity to be taken. The various plates from which this panorama is made up, were exposed by Professor Jaggar for The Advertiser on December 15, and show the south lunate platform on the left; next, the fire fountains as they appeared that day; next, to the right, the cone of 1903-7 in the middle and the new mound, formed in the present activity. On the right is Maunakea and the north bay of the crater. The group photograph reproduced is that of the Observatory party at the summit, with the exception of Professor Jaggar, who took the picture. The photograph gives a splendid idea of the bleak surroundings of the crater and the severe cold with which the scientists had to contend.

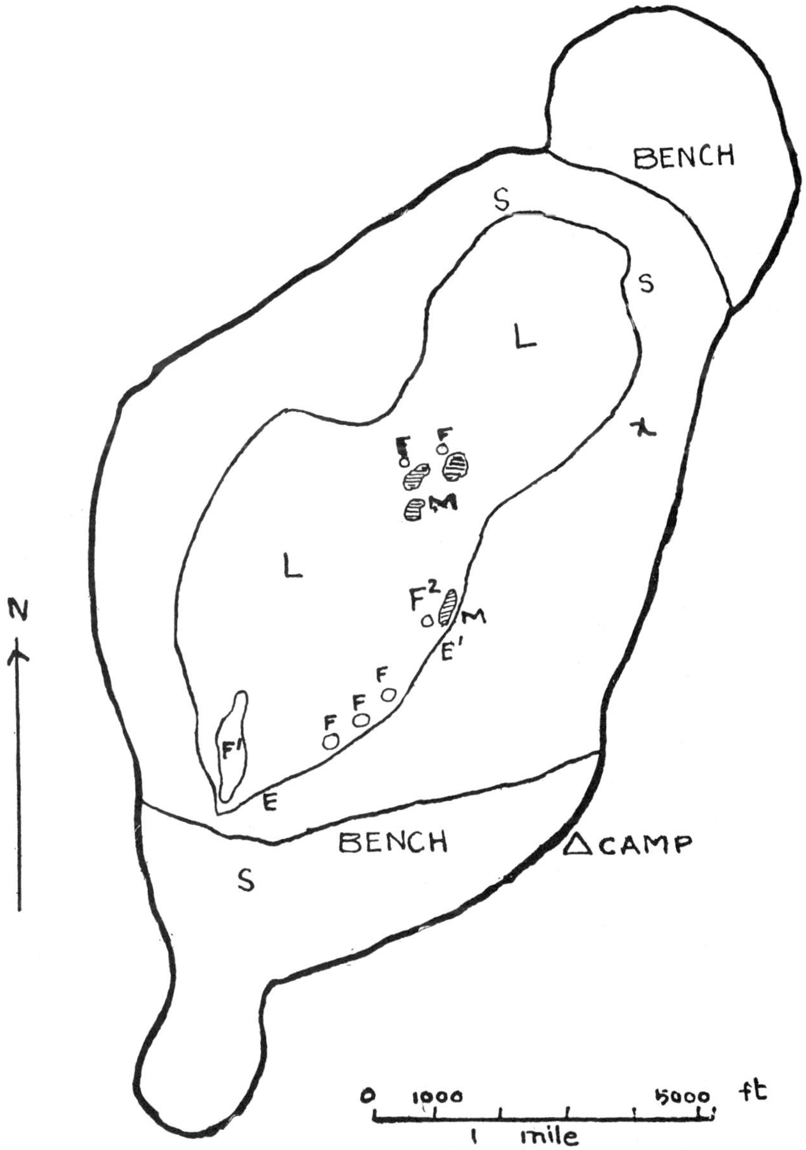

X—Glowed a little.
L—New lava, mostly flows.
EE'—Edge of distinct pool.
F'—Large fountain.
F—Fountains.
S—Steam (white vapor).
M—Mounds.
F2—Irregular fountain.

Outline of Mokuaweoweo, November 27-28, 1914. Sketched by L. C. Palmer from the J. M. Alexander map of 1885.

TECHNOLOGY STATION, December 31.—The fume column on Mauna Loa has been very clearly visible this week owing to exceptionally transparent air. It makes a visible gauge of wind direction on the summit, often quite different from the wind below.

December 26, the slender single fume column was glowing in the evening. December 27, from 7 to 9 a. m., with light northeast wind at Volcano House, the fume column on Mauna Loa rose high, bent eastward and thinned out over Puna to a bluish iridescent fume cirrus, quite unlike any rain cloud in color and luster. It showed a slight transverse ripple-marking in the middle part of its course. There was possibly a slight increase in volume of fumes, which has continued through the week, but owing to varying conditions of wind and of clear atmosphere, with frequently no seeing at all, it is impossible to judge slight changes accurately.

An increase of fumes is to be looked for, by analogy with the habit of Kilauea, if the fountains in Mokuaweoweo are still diminishing. The glow at night continued through the week. December 28, in the morning, small volutes of fume were rising; December 29, a straight column in still air; December 30, the same, bending in a counter current eastward in the upper atmosphere, while the wind was northeast below.

At 1 p. m. the high column was bending southward, the puffs showing brownish below and blue above. This morning, December 31, with northeast wind continuing below, the fume puffs of Mokuaweoweo are blowing away westward, implying that the wind below and above is now one and the same, and that the trade-wind stratum has in the last few days thickened to above 14,000 feet.

Halemaumau suffered a temporary subsidence December 22 to 24 inclusive, but since that time has risen vigorously so that the lake of basalt is twenty-five feet higher than on December 23, the present level (measurement of December 28) being 380 feet below the rim.

General conditions remain the same, with overflowing both from the lake and from the western pots and pond. The island-like crag continues to rise with the elevation of the floor, being on December 28 about 333 feet below the southeast rim, 47 feet above the lake.

December 24, in the evening, there were no flows. December 25 was stormy. December 26, at 10 a. m., fresh hot flows were on the floor, violent fountaining across the lake near Old Faithful was occasioned by meeting currents, and the lake was almost brimming. Streaming was westward from the east arm, from under an arch of crust formed over the strait at the entrance to the arm. The northwest pond was active, and there were splashing pots in the floor southwest and off the end of the southeast cove. In the afternoon and evening flows from the west renewed their cascading into the southwest pot.

December 27, 8 to 10 p. m., the floor was covered with fresh glowing flows and from the north rest house an oven was seen in the southwest part of the floor, opening from the north side of an eruptive cone. Into this oven a lava stream from one of the western flows was pouring, and every minute or so a belch from within hurled out a great splash of lava, repelling the inflow. There was a pot of lava within at nearly the same level as the flow. With every belch tremendous spurts shot upward from the hole in the top of the cone, ejecting incandescent blobs at least fifty feet upward and sidewise. The west cones were submerged under splashing pools and a small flow poured southward from one of them. From time to time the skins on the northwest pond and the east arm broke up, and both the lake and the northwest pond were brimming full. There was hissing from an eastern cone.

December 28, 3 p. m., flows were pouring north and south from a west cone on the floor. On the southwest floor was an open grotto or cavern opening southeastward and into it cascades of glowing lava from a flow were dripping. Against the wall, southwest, a pot was boiling, and here the remnant of the 200-foot bench of 1912 was being undermined. The lake was brimming; at the southeast cove it was welling over in splashes and building a spatter cone; there was crust over the strait leading to the east arm; the streaming was from the east arm, southeast, south and west, meeting with tumult as eastward current about Old Faithful, while west of there the westward streaming was resumed.

The crag was still high, and a few blocks of freshly fallen talus appeared on the south floor.

From two boiling pots at the site of the west cones flows poured south and east, the latter following the edge of the floor to the east arm; the east arm brimmed over and made small flows toward the northeast wall. At 3:15 p. m. a heavy festooning flow overwelled the whole length of the east arm, filled up the space between it and the wall, and there poured into an open old lava tube or cavern in the northeast wall of Halemaumau, which has been a landmark for some months past. The torrent rushing into the cavern made a loud, crackling noise like the burning of a wood fire, probably due to the sudden contact of the hot fluid and the cold rock in the cave; it continued to pour in for an hour and probably longer when concealed under its crust. This intrusion in old caverns is probably the process which makes the whitish intrusive bodies seen in the Kilauea and Halemaumau cliffs. At 4 p. m. the lake overflowed from the south side of the southeast cove, making a broad flood over the southeast part of the floor. At 4:30 the eastward flow from the west cone, which started with a bifurcation uniting under the north wall, was cascading into the northwest pond on its north side, as well as flowing along the wall beyond to the east arm. The east arm appeared obliterated under flows, with the one spitting hole. An oval area of collapse formed eastward from the cascade grotto southwest, and a crack south of it was spurting. There was a small blowing cone near the east wall. The dominant streaming in the lake was westward as usual.

December 29, at 8 a. m., from the observatory, with low humidity, the fumes over Halemaumau appeared thinner than ever before during this year. The southwest wall of Kilauea crater could be seen through them plainly. At 11 a. m., from the southeast station it was evident that active rising had continued with much overflow. Two great sheets of overflow from the lake east and west of the south cove covered the whole southeastern floor, and new flows from the west covered the southwest floor. The southwest cone under the wall had increased in height and a fountain was playing continuously on its summit, with rills of lava flowing down its flanks. One of these was cascading continuously for two hours and longer into a hole at the site of the cascade grotto of the previous day.

December 30, at 5:30 p. m., streaming in the lake was westward as usual, there were new fresh flows glowing, three pots were boiling on the western floor, the northwest pond was stagnant, an active flow was pouring along the southwest wall, the east cone was hissing and fresh flows were glowing along the north wall. A large spatter lump protruded into the northeast side of the east arm. The southeast cove and the east arm crusted over and broke up from time to time. The lake was about three feet below its banks and was rumbling in the grottoes. A crack spurted occasionally on the southwest floor.

T. A. JAGGAR, JR., Director.

The following systematic report is submitted from the Whitney Laboratory of Seismology:

Nov. 25, from 12:17:49 p. m. to 12:19:30 p. m. H. S. T. Intensity, low I Cancani scale; about 9.6% of the minimum perceptible unit. Origin distance estimated at from 20 to 25 miles.

Nov. 25, from 12:23:43 p. m. to an indefinite moment, H. S. T. Recording pen swept from cylinder. Intensity, IV plus, Cancani scale; more than the minimum perceptible unit, but for all this *definitely not felt.* Origin distant 21-22 miles.

Nov. 25, from 12:25:50 (?) p. m. to 12:27:14 p. m., H. S. T. Intensity, low II Cancani scale; about 30% of the minimum perceptible unit. Origin estimated from 20 to 25 miles distant.

Nov. 25, from 12:27:50 p. m. to 12:29:26 p. m., H. S. T. Intensity, high I Cancani scale; about 21% of the minimum perceptible unit. Origin estimated from 20 to 25 miles distant.

Nov. 25, from 12:30:02 p. m. to 12:30:50 p. m., H. S. T. Intensity, medium I Cancani scale; about 16.5% of the minimum perceptible unit. Origin estimated from 20 to 25 miles distant.

Nov. 25, from 12:53:26 to 12:54:47 p. m., H. S. T. Intensity, low II Cancani scale; about 32% of the minimum perceptible unit. Origin estimated from 20 to 25 miles distant.

Nov. 25, from 12:57:24 p. m. to 12: 59:09 p. m., H. S. T. Intensity, low I Cancani scale; about 6.5% of the minimum perceptible unit. Origin estimated from 20 to 25 miles distant.

Nov. 25, from 1:17:18 p. m. to 1:18:36 p. m., H. S. T. Intensity, low I Cancani scale; about 6.5% of the minimum perceptible unit. Origin estimated from 20 to 25 miles distant.

Nov. 25, from 1:26:57 p. m. to 1:28:44 p. m., H. S. T. Intensity, medium I Cancani scale; about 18% of the minimum perceptible unit. Origin distant 24 miles.

Nov. 25, from 12:53:26 p. m. to 12: 54:47 p. m., H. S. T. Intensity, low II Cancani scale; about 32% of the minimum perceptible unit. Origin estimated from 20 to 25 miles distant.

Nov. 25, from 1:49:01 p. m. to 1:50:07 p. m., H. S. T. Intensity, low I Cancani scale; about 5% of the minimum perceptible unit. Origin estimated from 20 to 25 miles distant.

Nov. 25, from 2:13:10 p. m. to 2:17:48 p. m., H. S. T. Intensity, about IV Cancani scale, but definitely not felt. Origin distant about 23 miles. This shock was the last of the group which ushered in the outbreak of eruption.

Nov. 26, from 11:16:08 p. m. to 11: 17:29 p. m., H. S. T. Intensity, low I Cancani scale; about 11% of the minimum perceptible unit. Origin distant about 23 miles.

Nov. 27, from 6:48:05 p. m. to 6:49:05 p. m., H. S. T. Intensity, low II Cancani scale; about 32% of the minimum perceptible unit. Origin distant about 25 miles.

Dec. 9, from 10:55:01 a. m. to 10: 55:55 a. m., H. S. T. Intensity, low I Cancani scale; about 11% of the minimum perceptible unit. Origin distant 32 miles.

Dec. 10, from 8:21:36 a. m. to 8:22:20 a. m., H. S. T. Intensity, low I Cancani scale; about 11% of the minimum perceptible unit. Origin distant about 20 miles.

Dec. 13, from 7:40:13 p. m. to 7:41:33 p. m., H. S. T. Intensity, about IV Cancani scale; about the minimum perceptible unit. Shock not felt. Origin distant about 20 miles.

Dec. 17, from 7:05:51 p. m. to 7:06:53 p. m., H. S. T. Intensity, IV plus Cancani scale; more than the minimum perceptible unit, but not perceived here. Origin distant 12.4 miles, approximately.

Dec. 18, from 7:52:40 a. m. to 7:54:13 a. m., H. S. T. Intensity, low I Cancani scale; about 7% of the minimum perceptible unit. Origin distance indeterminate.

Dec. 19, from 4:42:38 p. m. to 4:44:12 p. m., H. S. T. Intensity, low II Cancani scale; about 27% of the minimum perceptible unit. Origin distant about 20 miles.

Dec. 19, from 9:05:58 p. m. to 9:06:58 p. m., H. S. T. Intensity, low I Cancani scale; about 8% of the minimum perceptible unit. Origin distance indeterminate.

Dec. 22, from 8:37:45 p. m. to 8:38:04 p. m., H. S. T. Intensity, high III Cancani scale; about 90% of the minimum perceptible unit. Origin distant about 10.5 miles.

Dec. 22, from 11:03:01 p m. to 11: 03:58 p. m., H. S. T. Intensity, medium I Cancani scale; about 17.5% of the minimum perceptible unit. Origin distant about 29 miles.

Dec. 23, from 3:47:32 p. m. to 3:48:43 p. m., H. S. T. Intensity, medium I Cancani scale; about 13.5% of the minimum perceptible unit. Origin distant about 18 miles.

Dec. 27, from 8:47:47 a. m. to 8:49:12 a. m., H. S. T. Intensity, high I Cancani scale; about 22% of the minimum perceptible unit. Origin distant about 29 miles.

Dec. 28, from 00:49:07 a. m. to 00: 50:12 a. m., H. S. T. Intensity, medium I Cancani scale; about 11% of the minimum perceptible unit. Origin distant about 29 miles.

Dec. 28, from 5:09:13 a. m. to 5:09:43 a. m., H. S. T. Intensity, III Cancani scale; about 70% of the minimum perceptible unit. Origin distance indeterminate.

No additional shocks during the remainder of December, 1914.

HARRY O. WOOD,
Associate.

(End of Volume II.)

WEEKLY BULLETIN
OF THE
Hawaiian Volcano Observatory

Vol. III. HONOLULU, HAWAII, JANUARY, 1915. No. 1

TECHNOLOGY STATION, January 7.—The first week of the new year 1915 finds the Hawaiian volcanoes Mauna Loa and Kilauea both in a state of activity, the former with one or more fountains of brilliant lava foam continuously playing in the southwestern part of the summit crater Mokuaweoweo, the latter with a lively lake and three smaller lava ponds 368 feet below the rim of the crater pit Halemaumau. Kilauea has been in almost continuous action since the autumn of 1906, Mauna Loa has been fountaining at the summit only since November 25, 1914, forty-three days to date.

The fume and glow over Mokuaweoweo have continued constant. December 31, the fume was blowing to the northwest. January 1, the fume blew westward, making the column a low dome as seen from the Observatory, with glow at night.

January 2, there was northeast drizzle with tremendous squalls of wind at the Observatory; the Mauna Loa fume appeared to be blowing southeast. In the afternoon there was a crown of rain-cloud above the snow-line on Mauna Loa, with the blue fume funnel rising vertically from its midst and bending east above. The sunset was brown-yellow, with the fume-streak crossing it. The night was clear, showing not only the illumined fume-column but a marked radiant glow spreading upward in the atmosphere above the summit fountains.

January 3, very small puffs of fume showed, apparently blowing west and this continued January 4, the nights showing the radiant glow and occasionally the low illumined fume. January 5 was similar, but the fume dome rose higher and at night there was a high luminous zone and rare glimpses of the fume top. There was fresh snow on the mountain. January 6, the fume was blowing northwestward.

The smoke from Halemaumau has been remarkably thin and transparent, this accompanying active rising lava in accordance with its habit. Extraordinarily low humidity occurred at the same time, and the invisibility of the water-vapor in the column added to the effect.

December 31 the Halemaumau fume appeared only a thin veil, and in the evening at sundown, with no unusual humidity conditions, for all the steam jets of the crater floor showed voluminously, the veil as seen from the Observatory was so thin that the sunset clouds and the south wall of Kilauea crater were clearly visible through it.

January 2, the fumes appeared extraordinarily thin at 8 a. m. The relative humidity during the morning was high, but at 4 p. m. it had gone down to 49 per cent, an unheard-of dryness for this climate, so that woodwork actually crackled noisily. January 3, the thin fumes continued; January 4, they appeared denser, and since that time, while thinner than usual, they have not been remarkable. The thinness of fume accorded with rapidity of rising and overflowing lava in Halemaumau.

Since January 4, the intense rising activity has diminished and by measurement the lava column has been at a standstill since January 2.

At noon January 2, 1915, the lake of lava was 368 feet below the east station, and the northeast crag which rises between the east arm and the main lake was 345 feet down, or 23 feet above the lake. January 6 at 3 p. m. the depth was the same, 368 feet below the southeast rim. In both cases the point measured was the contact of lava and shore at the cape or promontory north, where the streaming surface flow

WEEKLY BULLETIN
of the
Hawaiian Volcano Observatory

Published Monthly at Honolulu, Hawaii, by the Hawaiian Volcano Research Association

Editor..............Howard M. Ballou
Professor of Physics, College of Hawaii

Entered as second-class matter January 20, 1914, at the post-office at Honolulu, Hawaii, under the Act of August 24, 1912.

pours around the bend from the east arm into the main lake.

December 31, 1914, after 8 p. m., the fiery spectacle within the Halemaumau pit was the most remarkable of the year which the writer has seen. It was obvious from the Observatory that extraordinary activity was in progress, the fumes being very thin and the glow intense and roseate, with flaring.

At 8 p. m. from the southeast station two lava cascades were seen to be plunging into the west end of the lake. The pool was about ten feet below its banks. The cascades were from a broad ribbon flow pouring straight from the northwest pond to the lake.

The slope over which the falls poured was steep. There was a curtain of skin between the two cascades, probably with lava pouring beneath. On the floor southwest, an orifice in the top of a cone was spurting jets at least 100 feet into the air. Everywhere on the floor new flows were glowing.

The east arm was crusted over at first but broke up at 9 p. m. From the south station at 9 p. m. the western cascades were seen to crust over and the skin on the northwest pond broke up. At 8:45 a large flow southward from the west end was seen to revive. The southeast cove this evening was divided into two, with a protruding spatter lump between.

The northern division of this cove was a remarkable caldron containing seething and fountaining lava. The caldron was open to the lake, but the streaming and skinned over basalt of the lake flowed by the entrance and surged against the entrance to the caldron at the lake level, while the caldron maintained a level two or three feet lower, with incessant fountainings which seemed to burst out from under the lake skins. The latter migrated slowly into the caldron and were sucked down. The southern division of the southeast cove maintained a brimming high level of the usual sort.

Flames were numerous from the southeast cove, south cove, southwest cone, east cone and elsewhere. At 9:15 p. m. the cascades revived. The streaming was from the east arm into the southeast cove, the south cove and along the whole length of the lake westward. At the west end of the floor an arch-like cone with openings north and south was the vent of flows in both directions from ovens in its flank.

At 9:45 p. m. a second flow, in addition to the cascade flow, was pouring from the northwest pond eastward towards the east arm. Seen from the north resthouse at 10:15 p. m. the cone at the west was vomiting a flood of lava like an artesian well, which bulged into a spindle shape in plan, and fell into the northwest pond. By 11 p. m. this flow was blanketed over with dark skin except at the vent. Great flows were pouring from the east arm to the northeast wall.

A platform or black ledge of overflow along the north shore of the lake had formed, separating the lake from direct contact with the long slope of the uplifted crag, and indicating that the rise of the lake had been more rapid than that of the crag. This has been proved by measurement; on December 9 and December 23 the crag was 58 feet above the lake on each measurement, the lake mean time having risen 41 feet. The crag block was thus rising with the lake.

December 28, the lake had risen 25 feet more, but the crag was now only 47 feet above the lake, which had thus gained on it 11 feet. On January 2, the lake had risen 12 feet more and the crag was only 23 feet above the lake, so that the lake had gained on it 24 feet, the crag having bodily subsided 12 feet.

At 11 p. m. December 31, the lake was only 2 feet below its banks. The southwest cone had ceased its spurting, but its banner of blue flame still flared and occasionally it would blow a prolonged blast of gas. Throughout the evening there was much puffing from grottoes and flaming pots. January 2 at 11 a. m., the crag area was much smaller, surrounded by new flows. There was a gale blowing and much new talus, perhaps started by wind, lay on the floor east and southeast. The lake was about one foot below the bank and was streaming westward, and a pot was boiling at the source of the western flows.

January 3, there were new flows on the southeast floor and ponds west and northwest. There was a large flat puddle of new hot lava southwest, pushing out at its border. Broad skins were streaming straight in ribbons from east to west over the surface of the lake. Two rock slides took place at 11:30 a. m. and 12:30 p. m. from the west wall. The southeast cove had lost its medial partition. The noises were of hissing, plashing and pounding. There was more encroachment on the crag area. The northwest pond was enlarged.

January 5 at 11 a. m., from the south station there were new flows on the floor from the south and southeast coves, and a definite pond had formed southwest. There were now three ponds in a semicircle around the west end of the lake, all about the same size and shape, 100 feet long and oval, northwest, west and southwest. A pot was splashing in the floor near the end of the south cove, and another very brilliant one with a shell cover open in the middle, near the east wall of the pit, and boiling hard within with high incandescence. The cliff over the lake appeared four feet high north and two feet high south. The crag appeared a little higher relatively to the lake. The three ponds were full of lava boiling sluggishly a foot or two down.

The southeast cove was deep and pointed. From time to time large fountains against the south wall of the southwest pond burst up explosively.

A cone lay adjacent to the pond and southwest of it. Floor cracks westward from the west end of the lake were fuming.

From 9 to 10 p. m., the southwest pond was found to have filled up and overflowed and the west pond was doing the same. The streaming in the lake was from east to west, about two and a half miles per hour. The lake appeared about 4 feet below its banks. The southeast cove was stagnant, the east arm crusted, Old Faithful was explosive, jetting sometimes forty feet high, the streaming varied its point of attack, sometimes against the north bank, sometimes against the west end.

Lines of traveling fountains formed from Old Faithful to the west end owing to the conflict of these two currents. There was a flaming pot in the south talus, under the large fumarole there. The surface of the northwest pond was streaming from west to east. Flames appeared above the southeast cove and the east pot. Sometimes the flame, pale blue, rising from the east pot was wholly without visible fume and fluttered like burning alcohol; at other times it fumed strongly, possibly owing to nucleation from the fumarole smoke blown down over it. The flow from the southwest pond moved eastward.

January 6 at 3 p. m., the southwest pond had become an oval pit in the floor twenty feet deep with a sunken black crust for a floor and walls of basalt layers. A cascade of molten lava was tumbling across the west corner of its bottom and from its southwest side within a fountain exploded from a hole at intervals. The lake appeared ten feet below its walls with very active bubble and traveling fountains and swift westward streaming. The east arm was active and mostly free from skin. The west pond was crusted over, the northwest pond active, the east pot active, and a branch of the lake streaming was into the south cove. Old Faithful was making large fountainings and there was some appearance of increase in size of both the lake and the east arm. At 4:20 p. m. the cascade in the southwest pond began to pool and flow over the bottom crust.

T. A. Jaggar, Jr., Director.

TECHNOLOGY STATION, January 14.—The week has fulfilled every expectation based on the hypothesis that Hawaiian volcanoes respond to the solstice and subside thereafter, for the lava of Halemaumau has been rapidly sinking and on January 11 the fume column and glow of the Mokuaweoweo fountain ceased.

The time of the solstice, or maximum declination of the sun south, was from December 20 to 24 inclusive, the turning point being reached December 22; calling the eruptive period of Mokuaweoweo forty-eight days, from November 25 to January 11 inclusive, the middle day of the period, twenty-four days after the outbreak, was December 18-19. January 4, 1915, appears to have been the date of highest tide in Halemaumau, when the last overflows of the lake took place at an elevation 363 feet below the southeast rim of the pit; on January 13 the lake had fallen about thirty-five feet below this, or 398 feet below the rim.

Kilauea was intensely active and in general rising all through December, and in accordance with the measurements of preceding years it was fully expected at the Observatory that it would sink in January. The movements of the lava column, though as a whole lower, have been remarkably parallel to those of 1911-12, when also there was a maximum on January 4.

For those who intend to visit the volcano, the time to come is now. Positive predictions are not possible, but there is great likelihood of increase of fumes and poor seeing in February or March, with a very low level of the lava on the equinox. At present the lake is magnificent and spectacular.

There was glow over Mokuaweoweo January 6, 1915, and a tuft of fume like white cotton appeared on the morning of January 7, apparently blowing away to the west. For the previous fortnight there had been no marked changes, except that a diffuse glow had appeared at night distinct from the light reflected from the obvious fume cloud, and frequently in the air around the fume column. This was attributed to atmospheric conditions. At and around two p. m. January 6, streamers of white cloud rose in tufts from the high or cone region on the northeast slope of Mauna Loa, quickly disappearing and having no resemblance in color to the fume. On January 7 between one and two p. m. the same thing happened again, mostly above the snow line, along the northeast cone line, and at one time over Mokuaweoweo itself, the color of the white tufts being quite distinct from the blue fume against which it showed. At three-thirty p. m. these white jets were still at work near the two upper cones where similar jets have been seen from time to time during the past three years. January 9 there was a strong column of fume rising high and bending southward, and in the evening bright glow with some visible fume, blowing to the southwest.

On January 10 at the Observatory the weather was brilliant with strong northeast wind. The fume was seen in Kona, but day and night there was no trace of fume or glow seen from the observatory at Kilauea. No fume or glow has been seen since, nor is any reported from other points. Today, January 14 at eight a. m. the weather was calm with the Kilauea fume rising high and spreading into a mushroom. There is no evidence of a high wind current which might blow the fume on Mauna Loa away. With clear seeing and powerful field glasses not the slightest trace of fume can be detected over Mokuaweoweo.

Halemaumau on January 7 and 8, 1915, showed slight subsidence of the lava column and a cracking of the floor. January 9 at three-thirty p. m. from the southeast station the wall around the inner pit made by the subsiding lake appeared about fifteen feet high. Cracks in the floor had developed parallel to the south side of the southeast cove, the northeast side of the east arm, and along the base of the northeast wall of Halemaumau. An immense crack had opened ten feet back from the whole southwest shore of the lake, extending westward toward the west pond into smoking fissure fumaroles in the floor. Other large cracks extended from the west margin of the southwest pond westward. All of this means that the floor is breaking up over a strongly subsiding lava column.

The lake also showed the characters of subsidence. The coves and east arm were free from skin, a few bubble fountains were playing in the west part, streaming was slow from east to west, and the lava within the east pot, really a fissure extension of the southeast cove, was seething and streaming southeastward.

The southwest pond was a pit with a crusted bottom, apparently a crust of collapse, with very slight splashes of lava into the southwest part of its bottom. The northwest pond was active and a dim glow could be seen in the region of the west pond, which during a glimpse exhibited a wall on its west side and frozen overflows east. In the evening about nine o'clock the surface of this pond broke up and the lava welled out a little eastward.

The chimney in talus south glowed and displayed a blue flame at night, as did also the east pot. The southwest cone was smoking. The crag appeared very high above the east arm of the lake and a few new-fallen stones could be seen on the east and southeast floor.

January 10 from eleven to twelve a. m. everything appeared the same except that a new short straight flow had poured from the overflow side of the west pond to the southwest pond. The fumes appeared thin. January 11 was rainy, and though the glow was bright at night the fumes appeared denser.

January 12 marks of subsidence were numerous, the pool larger by tumbles from the banks, the banks higher, the end of the east arm extended northward, slides falling in the high talus west of the south station, blowing noises in the southwest pond, the cracked block on the southwest border of the lake lower, and the activity of fountaining higher and the streaming more rapid.

By survey the lake was 495 feet long, and the east arm 250 feet long from its entrance. The depth to the lake at the bend was 391 feet below the southeast station, and to the floor south of the southeast cove 363 feet, making the height of inner wall over lake 28 feet.

Many stalactites hung over the splashing and pounding lava at the west end of the lake. The fume sources had greatly increased in number and the seeing was poor. The glow-hole in the south talus was fuming more, a new line of cracks and smoke extended from the southeast cove to the east pot, a smoking crack extended westward from the southwest cone, and there was increase of smoke from the cracks around the lake and extending westward therefrom, and from the crag. There was very rapid streaming under the west end of the lake. The lava seen through the circular opening in the east pot was streaming rapidly southeastward. The southwest pond had become a black pit. The noises were of fountaining, blowing and rumbling.

January 13 from six to seven p. m. the lake was well displayed from the southeast and appeared still lower, thirty-five or forty feet below the floor. It now occupies a pit or well in the floor. Travelling fountains were moving from the Old Faithful regions westward. Heavy curtains and mobile stalactites of newly splashed up lava hung along the bombarded overhang at the west end. An active surface stream poured from the inner end of the east arm to the lake, then westward with branches into the southeast and south coves. The east pot had collapsed to an irregular opening, and was larger, with the lava of the southeast cove streaming beneath it southeastward. Under the northeast crag and beyond the head of the east arm, a flaming pot revealed lava streaming westward. The west and northwest ponds had become deep pits like the lake. The west pond was smoking with dim glow, and from the Old Resthouse the northwest pond was seen to be active, the glowing lava surface in its bottom pouring through an orifice westward, and otherwise streaming out radially from a patch of skin on its surface. Lava was spattering occasionally into the bottom of the southwest pond on two sides. The crack at the southwest cone showed a flame. The noises were of plashing and rumbling.

There have been a few local earthquakes renewing seismic activiy of late. One of these was felt in Hilo on the evening of January 13.

T. A. Jaggar, Jr., Director.

TECHNOLOGY STATION, January 21.—The Halemaumau pit continues to be a splendid spectacle at night, but slow subsidence continues. No activity has been observed on Mauna Loa during the past week.

January 15 at two-thirty p. m., conditions were about as reported for January 13. The lava of the lake was within an inner pit about forty feet deep, streaming was from the east arm to the west and southeast. The material between the long cracks southwest of the lake and the lake was gradually sinking to become a slope of talus. Fallen rocks were seen on the floor.

January 16 at three p. m., from the southeast station the lake appeared a little higher, but at the moment subsidence was apparently in progress for at three-twenty p. m. a rock slide took place in the high talus southwest.

January 17 conditions were similar, with streaming westward in the main lake, and southeastward in the east pot, which, though joined beneath the floor with the southeast cove, was separated by a bridge of cracked crust from the lake.

January 18 at two p. m., the continued subsidence had produced the expected result and the bridge between the east pot and the southeast cove had collapsed, thereby greatly widening and lengthening the southeast cove. The streaming was now eastward in both the main lake and the east arm, rushing to a rapid downflow in the southeast cove. There was torrential in-pouring at the north end of the east arm. The lake appeared over forty feet below its pit rim, with continuous bubble fountaining at the Old Faithful locality, as well as the usual large fountains at the Old Faithful interval of from forty seconds to one minute. From three to three-twenty p. m. a pronounced rise in the lava took place of about five feet, with rapid flow from the west and down-sucking along the east bank. Intense incandescence in the southeast cove was accompanied by a greenish-blue flame five feet high. Folded skins piled up against the eastern banks and thick yellow fumes arose from the cracks in the floor above. At three-thirty-five p. m. a compensatory sinking of five feet had taken place, with a cessation of fountaining and an infolding downsucked skin line along the middle of the pool.

At three-forty p. m. Mr. A. Hannon, to whom the writer is indebted for notes of this period, threw stones into the lava of the east cove, and the places where the stones struck the skin remained glowing spots which streamed along with the surface current. From the north station at four-thirty p. m. the northwest pond was seen to be very active with westward flow, forty feet down within the pit, and hard boiling at its west end.

The distinctive features of activity January 19 were cavings-in of the inner pit walls, with the lake slowly sinking, and intense fountaining. The streaming was from the north end of the east arm, estimated ten miles per hour. It seemed to flow under the cracked eastern floor remnant and pour out again into the southeast cove. Another current bent westward and was joined by a stream from the south side of the lake. At three-fifteen p. m. a heavy tumble of ledge matter fell into the southeast cove, and at three-twenty-five there was a noisy slide on the west side of the lake. An old rim fissure between the south and southeast stations on the high rim of Halemaumau was found hot enough to scorch paper black. At four-twenty-five p. m. some of the edge of the northwest pond fell in. The streaming in the west pond was westward.

Wednesday afternoon, January 20, the fumes were thick and troublesome. An orifice was seen about three feet above the lava level at the west end of the lake from which lava cascaded into the lake every few minutes. Several large fountains were breaking. Bubble fountains were active in the east arm, whence the streaming was from east to west through the pool, with a branch southeastward into the southeast cove. About four-thirty p. m. the streaming reversed in the main lake and there was tremendous surging against the east banks so that vibration could be felt on the southeast rim. The lake at the same time rose three feet. At four-forty-five the old current was resumed and the bombardment had ceased. At eight p. m. the lake appeared to be about sixty feet below the inner cliff.

TECHNOLOGY STATION, January 28.—Conditions at the active lava pit of Kilauea are about stationary with the liquid pool about 440 feet below the rim and the black ledge (former floor) about 370 feet. Cracking of the ledges and fuming has continued with tumbles of rock into the lake and some sliding in the higher talus slopes. The pit is a fine night spectacle and in the daytime is smoky, with seeing at intervals. No further activity has been observed on Mauna Loa. Seismically the week has been quiet.

Thursday, January 21, five to six p. m., the walls of the inner pit around the lake appeared about 60 feet high. A marked reversal of streaming had taken place in the southeast cove, where the surface current was now streaming out, joining the current out from the east arm to pour westward the length of the lake.

A glowing torrent was pouring from under a cavernous overhang at the north end of the east arm. There were glowing spots on the inner walls well above the lake at the west end of the lake and at the end of the east arm. Spatter levels of new black lava appeared above the north shore of the lake, indicating that the stand of the lava had been the same for some time, with only minor fluctuations. The noise was of plashing, activity was normal, and there were no slides in the high talus. A bit of the edge of the inner cliff fell in at the west end of the lake.

The southwest chimney in the talus was flaming. Glow appeared in a southwestern crack in the floor. The northwest pond was active. The surface of the crag between the main lake and the east arm appeared flatter than of late, as though that block were sinking back to a more level position. Large bowlders on the southern floor have been there since January 18.

Measurements January 23 about three p. m. made the length of lake 513 feet, width opposite south cove 160 feet, length of east arm 420 feet, depth from rim to southwest chimney in talus 330 feet, height of chimney above floor 45 feet, depth to south floor 375 feet, to lake 440 feet, height of north cliff of inner pit above liquid lava 74 feet.

Conditions January 23 indicated subsidence, the phenomena being similar to those of February, 1913. The lake was streaming east to west with a fan pattern of skins, and a whirlpool formed from time to time in the south cove 100 feet in diameter with rotation counter-clockwise. Very heavy discharges took place from time to time from Old Faithful and a golden torrent poured from the east arm. Spatter bank accumulations collapsed off the north wall.

The noise of fountaining was loud and occasionally the western fountains of the main lake spurted high. The west pond had become a deep tumbled pit with glow. The northwest pond was active, making now and then a noisy spurt. At the northern stations the smoke from the crag was acrid and very disagreeable, while at the west station the white vapor from the higher wall fumaroles in the south and southwest talus was quite breatheable. One clinking rock fall was heard. The lava in the northwest pond was low, with high pit inner walls just as in the main lake. Smoking cracks extended west from the crag, and also along the southeast border of the floor.

January 24 at six p. m., conditions were in general similar but with an appearance of temporary rising, crusts had formed over the east arm and southeast cove, streaming was into the latter and westward in the main lake from under the skin of the east arm. Flaming glow cracks had formed along the southeast edge of the floor, apparently with lava in them. There were some glowing spots on the southwest floor.

From the southeast station, four p. m. January 25, the east part of the main lake and most of the east arm were crusted over. By five-thirty p. m., the east arm had become active. The principal noise was of plashing. From the old north rest house the eastern end of the southeast cove appeared to be a pond separated from the mouth of the cove and at a higher level. The streaming in the east arm was now reversed to the north, that is, into the cove. The small active pond deep in the bottom of the northwest pit was streaming westward. There was glow in the remains of the southwest pit and at two other points in this neighborhood, as well as along the southeast margin of the floor. The southeast cove had widened very greatly southward, and there was a lower ledge within its northern part where the lava was bombarding. At six p. m. there came a change in the surface circulation of the lava in the east arm. It had been stagnant and covered with black skin near the entrance. This skin tore away and the streaming of the lake poured into the east arm, into the southeast cove, and towards the west end, arising from the south banks of the main lake. The depression of the east arm now extended far to the north almost under the old resthouse, the crag becoming more and more a peninsula. A slight blowing noise could be heard from the northwest pond.

January 26, from three to four p. m., from the north and northeast glimpses through the fume revealed two deep channels at the entrance to the southeast cove, the whole cove being a collapsed amphitheater, containing apparently a bridge separating an inner active pot from the entrance, streaming in the lake was westward. There were noises of plashing and rumbling, an occasional explosive eruption from Old Faithful, and noises which sounded like rock falls from the crag. The west pit smoked and glowed, there were flames and glow cracks southeast. The northwest pond was skinned over and streaming westward, and a spooned depression could be detected in the floor extending eastward from the pit where the southwest pond had been. A landslip fell into the northwest pond at 4 p. m. The southeast cove was now bounded wholly on the east by the old whitish wall of Halemaumau, from which the new lava of the past year had completely fallen away. There were smoking cracks located as follows: in floor southwest of lake, east of northwest pond, west of northwest pond, around the west pond, now a tumbled pit, in the southwest pond region, at southeast edge of floor, from the crag, in the pit west end of east arm, on south side of southeast cove. The places named gave off blue fume, but in the high tumble of 1912 benches southwest and south are two large fumaroles which yield white vapor, much of which is probably steam, for these are much more easily breathed than the bottom fumes. All this fuming greatly hampers observation and photography.

January 27 from nine to ten a. m., seeing was fair from the south and conditions were about the same. One small tinkling slide was seen in the talus under the south station. The cracks which bound the crag on the north now are smoking in a line which nearly reaches through to the northwest end of the lake, as though the crag block were going to become an island by toppling out to the southeast. The lake and east arm appeared skinned over as though rising were going on and there were no cavernous overhangs around the lake such as would imply sinking.

T. A. JAGGAR, JR., Director.

WEEKLY BULLETIN
OF THE
Hawaiian Volcano Observatory

Vol. III. HONOLULU, HAWAII, FEBRUARY, 1915. No. 2

TECHNOLOGY STATION, February 4.—At the end of January there was some slight rising of the lava column of Kilauea, but in general the past week has been characterized by the phenomena of continued subsidence such as whirlpools and inbreaks, with increased brilliant streaming and whirling activity during the last three days. The level of the lake surface has not significantly changed except for rapid daily fluctuation about a mean point. Seismically the week has been normal, and Mauna Loa remains without fume or glow.

January 28 from 5:30 to 6 p. m., from the northwest, the lake was streaming rapidly from out of the east arm westward, with fan-shaped pattern of skins. The southeast cove showed an inner pond with bubble fountains. The northwest pond was bubbling with some violent fountaining against its east wall. Inside its entrance the lava of the east arm was pounding and splashing high on its east bank, and a hole in the spatter ledge above was blowing, spurting lava and flaming. At west end of lake were bubble fountains, and Old Faithful, in addition to its normal action, occasionally gave vent to heavy explosions. The east arm was mostly crusted except for a small area of splashing lava near its head. The fumes from the pit as a whole seemed a little thinner.

January 29 at 4 p. m. the walls over the lake appeared about 70 feet high. The streaming was the same, the plashing noises subdued, but at 5 p. m. the activity became noisy. At 4:35 p. m. an avalanche fell from the west wall of Halemaumau to the floor. The northwest pond was quiet with northward flow. Three or more glowing cracks appeared in the floor southeast and southwest. At 4:40 p. m. the north side of the crag collapsed and thereafter the fuming from the summit of the crag ceased, but fumes strong with sulphuric acid rose from the depression under the crag to the north. At 4:50 p. m. a small fountain was breaking every 30 seconds in the northwest pond. The southeast cove appeared to be a source of the large quantities of Pele's hair newly fallen in Kilauea; in addition to its bubble fountains it was spurting from its south wall across to the north. The blow hole east of east arm had gone out of action, but not the surging on the bank. Dense fumes were rising from the northeast and southeast edges of the floor.

January 30 at 11 a. m. measurement with transit gave the following depths below southeast rim:

Fumarole northeast edge of floor, 365 feet; northwest rim of main lake, 436 feet; summit of crag, 376 feet; cliff edge north above lake, 396 feet.

These figures make the cliff north of the lake 40 feet high above the liquid lava, while the edge of the old floor northeast of the east arm was 71 feet above the lava level. The summit of crag was lower and about 60 feet above the lava and 20 feet higher than the north cliff-edge.

There were stalacites about the lake, the streaming was westward and other conditions remained unchanged. The plotted measurements showed that the north edge of the lake had been migrating northward, probably by caving in.

January 31 at noon there was seeing from the south station. At eleven-fifteen a. m. a prolonged grating noise was heard from the west end of the pit which sounded like a slide. The lake appeared about the same, walls fifty feet high, streaming from the east arm westward and into the southeast cove. The skins were arranged fanwise from the entrance to the east arm westward.

WEEKLY BULLETIN
of the
Hawaiian Volcano Observatory

Published Monthly at Honolulu, Hawaii, by the Hawaiian Volcano Research Association

Editor..............Howard M. Ballou
Professor of Physics, College of Hawaii

Entered as second-class matter January 20, 1914, at the post-office at Honolulu, Hawaii, under the Act of August 24, 1912.

A dim view could be had of the pit at the head of the east arm and it seemed to be extending itself westward. The whole southwest part of the old floor had subsided, leaving a border bench, and fuming cracks were elongating themselves southward from the southeast cove. A spatter rim about the lake shore five or six feet higher than the present lake level gave evidence of the range of recent fluctuation. The noise was of plashing, and there was no evidence on the south floor or elsewhere of considerable recent landslides. At twelve-five p. m. the east end of the southeast cove caved in with a crash, sending up a great column of red dust in cauliflower volutes, which as seen from the Volcano House were reported to resemble a crateral explosion. There was slight tremor on the east edge of the pit. The writer photographed the puff from the south station. The southeast cove was lengthened by the collapse about thirty feet along the southeast wall of Halemaumau. The masses of dust-laden fume were salmon-red and shot up for a few seconds with great rapidity several hundred feet above the edge of Halemaumau, and then mingled with the general cloud of fume, coloring it. Within three or four minutes only quick blue fume was rising from the depression left by the landslip. This caving was along the line of fuming cracks flaming and glowing southward from the southeast cove, where there is undoubtedly a subterranean extension of the lake. For a few seconds the phenomenon was altogether like the well-known cauliflower clouds of Stromboli and Vesuvius.

February 1, 1915, there was no change. February 2, intense activity of streaming and boiling was inaugurated. At eight-thirty p. m. a wide, rapid torrent was rushing from the east arm into the main lake at a rate of perhaps ten miles an hour, toward the south cove, and then with a clockwise rotation around Old Faithful in a powerful vortex. A standing rapid was maintained opposite the southeast cove. The heat was very strong, the noise was of plashing, bubble fountains broke incessantly through the torrent, and where the latter fanned out to slower speed there seemed to be actual convexity to the surface of the stream, the riven skins parting and slipping down slopes right and left.

This kind of activity continued on February 3 at eleven a. m. A loud blowhole had formed in the northwest pond, so that droplets of lava of some size fell at the northwest station. Lava poured out of the southeast cove westward under a bridge of crust. The fumes appeared thinner. At twelve-twenty-five p. m. a small landslip took place from the west ledge of northwest pond, and yellow dust arose.

T. A. JAGGAR, JR., Director.

TECHNOLOGY STATION, February 10.—The week at Kilauea has shown the lava column to be at a standstill, though there was every evidence of subsidence in the whirlpool mechanism which developed in Halemaumau, and in the marked collapse of the former floor, now a black ledge around tumbled crags which border the lake. The seeing at night is still good in fine weather, and occasionally very fine spectacles are staged within the pit, but it is desirable for those coming to see the volcano to stay long enough to see it at its best; rainy and foggy weather makes very poor seeing.

Mauna Loa continues quiet and earthquakes are few. The weather has been various, with high northeast gales and drizzle, moderating to a normal trade wind and fine weather.

The intense whirlpool activity which had been inaugurated February 2, was still in full swing on February 4 at five

p. m. From the east station the observer looked down upon a most extraordinary spectacle of vortical downsucking about Old Faithful, the skins upon the streaming lava arranging themselves in a spiral like a snail shell, with Old Faithful in the midst of the coil. The rotation was from left to right, or like the hands of a clock. The spiral was fed by a rapid golden torrent from the east end of the lake, which poured out of the east arm and the southeast cove from undercrusts. Great blocks of skin and crust shot down this rapid, westward, and were broken up by innumerable bubble fountains which burst through the stream. There was a back eddy in the south cove and another at the west end. Standing rapids were noticeable in the swiftest part of the current, which may have reached a rate of fifteen miles per hour or faster. Excellent photographs were secured of this whirlpool. At six p. m. a small rock fall was heard in the southeast cove. Among the noises from the torrent and the fountains there was some strong rumbling heard. Everything pointed to subsidence.

February 5, at two-thirty p. m., there was no seeing into the pit on account of the terrific northeast gale that was blowing; sand and gravel was literally streaming up the leeward edge of Halemaumau, blown by the wind, and on the windward edge it was not safe to approach the rim except stretched at full length on the lava. The noises of the lake were normal, but nothing could be seen.

From six to seven p. m. on February 6 there was much smoke and some faint seeing from the south, southeast and east stations. The lake was stagnant and all the torrent action had ceased. Slow engulfment of surface skins was going on in Old Faithful. Heavy masses of rock fell into the lake somewhere towards the northwest. There was no marked streaming. From the south station a prominent crag could be discerned between the southeast and south coves, and a tumbled slope was dimly visible back of the south cove, backed in turn on the south by a bench remnant of the floor. Glowing spots could be seen in this slope and along the cracks, smoking, on the southeast margin of the floor.

February 7, at five p. m., streaming in the lake was from west to east, large skin patches formed and broke on the surface, the west end was crusted over and the general quiet appearance, interrupted only by the bursts of Old Faithful, suggested rising. The northwest inner pit showed glow. The southeast tumbled area of the old floor was seen to consist of a large block of the floor, down-sunken about thirty feet, and cracked radially away from the south cove so that the great crevasses looked more like valleys than fissures. Measurements, made with difficulty on account of high wind and much smoke, showed the crag at the down-sunken level between south and southeast coves to be about 400 feet below the southeast rim of Halemaumau, and the lake forty feet lower. The east and southeast arms were crusted over and smoking, and the south chimney was flaming brilliantly.

Monday evening, February 8, at seven p. m., conditions were essentially the same. Some groups of traveling fountains moved eastward. Some glow was seen at the southwest border on the floor, where the southwest cove formerly was, and there was smoke from the site of the southwest pit. A filagree crust had formed over part of the south chimney. A flare appeared, like a flame, on the bench between the southeast cove and the east arm. At the entrance to the east arm the lava appeared stagnant. Streaming in the main lake was eastward from the zigzag edge of skins over the west end.

T. A. JAGGAR, JR., Director.

TECHNOLOGY STATION, February 18.—The week at the Halemauman lava pit has shown few marked changes. There have been strong northeast gales, and owing to fumes the seeing in daytime has been difficult. The lava column is probably sinking slowly and carrying the tumble of concentric benches with it. The fumes are becoming more unbearable to breathe, and bubble fountains along with four or five large standing fountains attest shrinkage of lava surface and concentrated escape of gas—phenomena distinctive of subsidence. The writer is indebted to Mr. Arthur Hannon for crater observations on several days.

On February 11 about 11 a. m., as seen from south station, the lake appeared relatively high within its walls. The lava surface was roaring with many fountains and the heat felt on the rim of Halemaumau was strong. The south chimney in talus was flaming hotly and the fume rising was gray-blue, even in the heavy fumarole above, whereas the southeast fumaroles were white and the southwest ones moderately so. The lake appeared rising, with overlapping skins on its shore and streaming from west to east. It appeared to have a new rampart around it, an inner bench. This makes the sixth concentric bench around the present pool, counting from the south margin, the uppermost the rim of Halemaumau, then the 50-foot bench and the 200-foot bench of 1912, next the floor edge and inner tumble of 1914, last the new rampart of 1915.

Between the southern crags over hanging the lake and the bench remnant of floor south there was now a deep crevasse or valley full of debris. The black ledge at the 360-foot level extends around the west end of the pit, with tumble ground below it. The crag north of lake was still in place and of the same general shape as when last seen. The west pit, formerly the west pond, was now continuous with the northwest pit as a depression or huge trench, backed with bare spots of the raw ancient red rocks of the Halemaumau wall. This trench appeared to be continuous under the north wall of Halemaumau through to the east arm. The latter appeared wider and the northeast wall bench narrower, and the east arm was seen to be choked with tumbled rocks.

There were bubble fountains all over the lake and they were pounding against the north wall. The streaming was from under a zigzag edge of skin at the west. Five or six large fountains were bursting at once. The north wall above the lava appeared about 60 feet high. There were two blowing grottoes at the west end of lake.

Saturday, February 13, at 3 p. m., the lake appeared stagnant as to streaming, with three very large and several small fountains, and its level was ten feet below the new rampart. A small slide fell from the south chimney to the floor. February 14 there was no change. February 15 at 3 p. m. the streaming was toward the west; at 3:30 it was eastward, rapid, with traveling fountains and many bubble fountains.

February 16 at 11:30 a. m. the fumes were thick and white, and around the northern stations they were painful to eyes, nose and throat. The lake was making a steady boiling noise and appeared about ten feet below the inner rampart. The best seeing was from the south and east. At 11:50 a. m. it was clear that several fountains were playing continuously, each nearly as large as Old Faithful. The streaming was slight, radial outward from the center. At 12:10 p. m. the streaming was slow, westward, with steady playing of fountains.

The south glowing chimney developed very hot blue fumes over heat waves of an invisible flame which flared twenty feet high. From the crag above the fumes rising were dense white.

A pond of red lava had formed in the region of the southwest pond with rapid streaming, too fast to crust over. At 12:35 p. m. a blowing noise could be heard near the northwest wall of the lake, where there were grottoes with much surging. A block of the main red wall of Halemaumau about 50 feet by 20 feet, which has been watched of late, suspended on an eastern projection of the wall, was seen to have slid down into the southeast cove. At 1:15 p. m. the southwest pond was seen to be much lower, and a spine of old ledge 30 feet high was standing upright on the south shore of this pond. Much fume had developed around the pond. Its north shore was a 30-foot cliff of old ledge, otherwise its shores were talus slopes. Conditions on February 17 appeared the same.

T. A. JAGGAR, JR., Director.

TECHNOLOGY STATION, February 25, 1915.—In the last fortnight the lava lake of Halemaumau has subsided twenty feet, but not that much within its inner pit. The walls and slopes of debris around that inner pit have been going down with it, so that the streaming and splashing of the surface basalt fluid has built a considerable marginal platform at the apparent lava-level, the subsidence of the debris at times probably exceeding that of the lava column and so producing the border effects of a temporary rise. That sinking was in progress was evidenced by the intense continuous fountaining activity, collapses in the fumaroles, development of new smoke-holes, and rapid fluctuations of level and streaming. The pit still remains an interesting spectacle night and day, the surface of the active lake standing 460 feet below the rim.

The observatory is fortunate in having as scientific visitors for some months to come Dr. Sidney Powers, Sheldon Travelling Fellow of Harvard University and a graduate of Williams College and of the Massachusetts Institute of Technology, and Mr. J. F. Haworth of Pittsburg with a staff of kite experts, to make bird's-eye photographs of the Hawaiian volcanic landscape. Dr. Powers will study geological and physiographic problems in the Islands, and Mr. Haworth will investigate certain meteorological and astronomical problems, the latter of great interest in comparison of the Hawaiian Volcanoes to those on the moon.

At 8 p. m., February 18, 1915, the lake seen from the southeast station was spectacular and very active, with large and small fountains playing continuously, and surface streaming from the west end eastward to the bend under the high north crag, where the current curved northward against the bank of crusts formed over what was formerly the long east arm, now a trench full of tumbled rocks. The lake was now an irregular oval pit opening into smoky trenches at its east end, the tumbled remnants of its east and southeast coves. North of the lake rose a precipice about fifty feet high topped by a sloping crag, which stood like an island in the midst of the north part of Halemaumau, bounded on the east, north, and west by a great trench formed by subsidence out of the former northwest pond now joined to the former east arm. The south shores of the lake were now irregular cliffs and slopes made of the tumble of the wide southern floor of last December. This tumble consists of toppling crags on the lake side, backed on the wall side by a rift valley surmounted by a remnant black bench that still clings to the old talus slope above, this bench being all that is left of the floor. It extends from a point under the southeast station to a point under the west station. The crevassed valley is continuous in a horse-shoe by way of the old southwest and west pits, into the north trench. Smoke in great volumes rises from all the pits and cracks and there are high talus fumaroles south and southwest. In general then, the lake is an oval against the actual cliff wall of Halemaumau on the east, surrounded south, west, and north by a horse-shoe ridge of insunken floor ledge, and this ridge in turn leaves a gaping valley of crevasses around the periphery of the filling of Halemaumau. Outside of all this rise the walls of the main pit, steep north, east, and west, but with talus on the south, remnant from 1912.

At 3 p. m., February 19, seen from the southeast station, the lake appeared about five feet below its rim bench, with large and small perpetual fountains. The streaming had changed and was now pouring westward. Lava spray was shooting up with blowing noises about the site of the former southwest pond. Glow appeared with blue flames in the southeast cracks on the 1914 bench remnant of the recent floor.

In the morning of February 21 the blowing vent was still active southwest. Pele's hair was rising. A new fumarole was smoking in the south valley of debris and the higher south chimney appeared to have less fumes and less heat. Where the southwest pot of lava was last week there was now only fume. At 11:35 a. m. a sudden burst of blue fume rose from the high south chimney in the talus, and shot up above the rim of Halemaumau, possibly due to a collapse within the conduit of the chimney. It shot to this height in a mushroom cloud in the face of a strong gale of wind. At 11:40 the gas jet from the fumarole became stationary with a height of twenty feet. By 12:15 p. m. this chimney had become almost inactive and with very little glow. Four fountains were boiling continuously in the lake, all of about the size of Old Faithful; the latter was breaking at twenty second intervals. A noon rise was evident, the lake having been about twenty feet below the inner ledge at 10 a. m.; at 12:30 it had risen three feet and the gas blowing southwest had diminished. The southeast cracks were yellow and yellow and white fumes rose from the southeast extension of the inner pit.

February 22 at 3 p. m. the pool was in violent ebullition with large and traveling fountains and many bubble fountains, blowing, splashing, and rumbling noises, and the streaming was irregular but dominantly into the south cove of the lake where strong bombardment was flinging the lava over the bank. Traveling fountains were moving southward with great commotion and the borders of the lake were very smoky.

Towards noon on Tuesday, February 23, the lava was level with the inner bench, but at 3:15 p. m. it was five feet down. Activity was still strong at the south cove with lava flung over the ledge, and continuous ebullition of large and small fountains was still in progress over the northern part of the pool.

February 24, measurements 10 to 11 a. m. showed the lake to be 460 feet below the southwest station. Curtains of stalactites at 10 a. m. hung before fountaining grottoes southeast and east, but at noon these stalactites were submerged under a temporary rise. Blue fumes rose from the south chimney and the region of the southwest pit. Spurting lava could be seen in the tumbled region of the west pond. Streaming at 10 a. m. was from west to east, but at the time of the noon rise the streaming was divergent from a central region of the lake, with traveling fountains moving from east to west in the Old Faithful part. The lava pots at the west end occasionally hissed violently, and the blue fume southwest puffed upward under strong pressure from time to time. There was much continuous fountaining and the general noise of the lake was of plashing. The whole north inner crag was clearly seen on this day, and it had changed its shape very little, its peak being to the north, the slope of its surface southward, bending into steep cliffs over the lake and over the east trench. From 8:30 to 10:30 p. m. the lava pool in the western trench was seen to be covered with a crust seamed with glowing cracks. Eleven vents blew out steady blue flames, and three vents were spattering lava. At 9 p. m. a hard rain chilled the surface skins of the main lake; the crust so formed cracked and a blue flame shot up from the crack over 100 feet long and at least fifty feet high, flaring thus for at least a second.

The record of a distant earthquake was made on the seismographs February 24-25. A systematic earthquake report will be made later by Mr. H. O. Wood. No further activity has been observed on Mauna Loa.

T. A. JAGGAR, JR., Director.

TECHNOLOGY STATION, March 4. —The conditions of activity in the lava lake of Halemaumau have remained during the past week essentially the same as the week before. A pronounced temporary rise took place February 25 and February 26, and with these sudden fluctuations. which are very characteristic of a time of general subsidence, there were four new driblet cones built in the west trench on the site of the former pots and cones that were the sources of so many outflows in November and December, 1914.

On February 25 the lake, seen from the south station at seven p. m., had rapidly risen within three hours well above the lower bench, for it was reported at five p. m. to be well below the bench, though splashing up over it. The lake was fountaining and spurting at the west, but there were large quiet skins over all the eastern part. Spraying fountains, with spurts fifty to eighty feet high, broke through the skin south, southeast and east. The lake widened greatly by encroachment on the southern talus. There was in the region of Old Faithful a glowing pool with surface streaming from southeast to northwest. There was also streaming out from under the skin against the southeast and east banks, the large medial skin area being the place of departure of currents east and west. Between the south cove and the east end there was an area of cherry red overflows on the lower bench, with glowing and sparkling bubbles or flame vents on its surface. A glow at the rim of the inner crust could be discerned within the southeast arm. The blanketed and active areas changed their shapes. Noises of blowing and rumbling could be heard. Heavy fumes rose from the south fumarole and from the southeast arm and its extension into cracks. The south chimney was flaming. Shore bombardment was in progress at the northwest end of the lake. Within the west trench a few active fountains were playing through a crust.

February 27, at four p. m., the lake was about twenty feet below the lower ledge and the streaming was towards the west end and into the south cove. At four-fifteen there appeared to be centripetal streaming to a place of downsucking opposite the south cove. The intervals between Old Faithful explosions timed on this day were very irregular, the shorter intervals being from ten to twenty seconds and the longer ones from forty to sixty seconds.

February 28, at two p. m., seen from the east, the lake was only about two feet below the second ledge, with great activity of many continuous fountains on the west. Again it had drowned the lower ledge completely by a sudden rise. A small cone was puffing loudly in the southwest crevasses. At two-thirty p. m. the lava had subsided at least five feet and was streaming toward the southeast cove with much boiling and rumbling. From the southwest station, at three p. m., the surface streaming was seen to have changed its direction to westward, with traveling fountains. In the trench under the northwest station, about fifty feet below the 1914 floor level, two large cones were puffing loudly, with glowing holes on top, from which lava spray was occasionally ejected.

March 1, from ten to twelve a. m., the lake had fallen again to about ten feet below the lower ledge. Fresh flows from the rapid rise of the previous day lay spread over the second bench, the overflow having taken place from the southwest side of the pool. The streaming was westward, with increasing skins over the east end marking a noon rise. With the rise the fountaining activity diminished. At two-thirty p. m. the westward current bombarded the shore in two division, northwest and southwest. From the west station, at three-thirty p. m., four cones, from fifteen to twenty feet high, were seen to be glowing and spurting with liquid lava within the west trench. Two growing cones could be seen in the southwest tumble. By four-fifteen p. m. the activity of the lake had increased, migrating fountains were moving westward, where stalactitic aprons had formed over cavernous grottoes.

The next morning, March 2, 1915, at ten a. m., conditions were similar, with westward flow, stalactite aprons west, increased bubble fountain activity, and general level about ten feet lower. A portion of the crust south-southeast formed a new floor at a still lower level. In the east and southeast coves there was eastward streaming, and in the southeast cove this developed a rapid clockwise vortex, with an inrush at the rate of at least six miles an hour, calling the normal westward streaming two miles an hour. At two-thirty p. m. there was noisy fountaining, and the seeing was from the west and southwest. Streaming was east and west from a skin area in the east central part of the pool, and the rim around the pool appeared only about fifteen feet high, suggesting that there had been again a noon rise. There were blowing noises and traveling fountains. The north crag appeared as usual. The causeway between the west trench and the main lake was seen to be narrowing by collapse on each side, so as to now only be about 150 feet wide, and the west wall of the west trench had scaled off so as to leave the bare old red rock of the Halemaumau cliff. A sulphur-stained cone was built up in the south trench. and four glowing cones of considerable height appeared in the western pit.

March 3, at four-fifteen p. m., with light southeast wind, there was good seeing from the north and northwest stations. Streaming was east and west from a medial zone of skins. A torrent was pouring into a southeast pot, the pot maintaining a level a few feet lower than the lake, so as to produce the effect of a cascade into a void. The lava in the pot sometimes whirled. At four-thirty all rose to a common level and skinned over. The lake at first appeared twenty feet below the lower bench, but at four-thirty it temporarily rose a few feet. A new flow of last week's rise was seen covering the floor of the east arm. Cracked crags lay between the east arm and the west trench, the two trenches being connected only by crevasses, not by a continuous gulch. A very marked wide crevasse was seen back of the southwest tumble of the 1914 floor. A high sulphur cone has developed south. One glowing cone appeared in the middle of the east arm and several in the western trench.

T. A. JAGGAR, JR., Director.

WEEKLY BULLETIN
OF THE
Hawaiian Volcano Observatory

Vol. III. HONOLULU, HAWAII, MARCH, 1915. No. 3

TECHNOLOGY STATION, March 11.—A general slight increase in the amount and intensity of surface action in Halemaumau has gone on during the past week ending with March 10. This has, of course, been punctuated with the usual subsidiary variations in energy. This increase has occurred in spite of the fact that the molten surface stands about twenty-five feet lower than during the previous week. No marked oscillations in the depth-altitude of the molten surface have been observed, though the usual irregularly timed risings and fallings of from two to five feet, more or less, have been noted during all prolonged watches. The general depth of the surface below the rim of the pit has stood at approximately 460 feet.

To a much greater extent than usual the action has been characterized by the freezing over of large parts of the lava surface, sometimes almost the whole area of the lake, which then have remained quiet for several minutes only to give way to sudden breakups of the crusted region with turbulent flowing in several directions simultaneously, interrupted by boiling-fountain action, often accompanied by vigorous spatter-fountain action especially from under the lake margins. Also linear arrangements of small boiling-fountains traversing the lake in the east-west direction have several times been observed. There has been no consistent directioning of surface flow for any considerable time. Nearly all parts of the lake margin and several central loci, that of "Old Faithful" being most conspicuous, have been in turn regions of approach and regions of departure of flow. Thus, more than commonly, the suggestion of shifting, surficial eddy-currents has been emphasized.

For sundry details of information and observation the writer is indebted to Mr. Arthur Hannon and to Dr. Sidney Powers.

In the late afternoon of March 4 there was steady streaming action from the northeast part of the lake toward the west. Small boiling fountains were located not far from the origin of the streaming.

In the forenoon of March 5 the depth of the molten surface measured 466 feet below the south station, while the depth of the south fumarole, on the 1914 shelf, measured 440 feet. The eastern half of the lake remained largely crusted over during an interval of nearly two hours, except for a very small spot at the extreme east, where there was westward streaming. In the western half of the lake there was steady streaming with rapid motion toward and under the southwest margin. In mid-forenoon a southerly streaming was observed, and later a slight easterly streaming at the east end. There were at first many small fountains in the central part of the lake but later skins formed frequently and the surface was relatively quiet.

In the evening the eastern part of the lake exhibited streaming, and boiling fountains were at work in the west part.

In the early afternoon of March 6 good views were obtained from the south and southeast stations. The molten surface was about fifteen feet below the third lava floor. Large boiling fountains to the number of four to six were active simultaneously, during much of the time, and small boiling fountains were conspicuous. The streaming was directed toward the west and northwest in under the lake margins. At about three p. m. blue flames could be seen playing from the

WEEKLY BULLETIN
of the
Hawaiian Volcano Observatory

Published Monthly at Honolulu, Hawaii, by the Hawaiian Volcano Research Association

Editor.............Howard M. Ballou
Professor of Physics, College of Hawaii

Entered as second-class matter January 20, 1914, at the post-office at Honolulu, Hawaii, under the Act of August 24, 1912.

high south-southwest cone, fifty feet above the second lava floor, and an intermittent blowing noise proceeded from the recently developed south cone on the second floor. At this hour the direction of streaming had shifted, setting to the northeast. A little later it was seen that the pool under he northwest station which has been choked and crusted over for some weeks past, had re-appeared as an oval area twenty-five feet wide by about forty feet long in which vigorous boiling-fountain action was going on. Glow spots also were seen near the tops of the driblet cones near the pool. Later on the streaming became exceedingly variable in direction.

In the forenoon of March 8 measurements of the depth of the molten surface showed it to be, in general, 460 feet below the rim, at an estimated depth of twenty-five to thirty feet below the third floor. At intervals of only a few minutes spatter-fountain action and the action of molten surf was observed at practically all parts of the lake margin in turn. The northwest pool, forty by fifty feet in diameter, exhibited active streaming in from the north and out at the southeast.

During the evening of March 9 there was good seeing almost continuously from the north part of the rim. The northwest pool, estimated three times larger than on March 7, when first seen was boiling lazily, then crusted over but showing a pulsing, wavy motion of the skin, followed by break-up and collapse of the crust with brilliant spatter-fountain action—molten droplets being flung not less than seventy feet into the air. This cycle was frequently repeated, requiring roughly from fifteen to twenty minutes for its accomplishment. Southeast of this pool there opened a small triangular orifice out of which spatter fragments were flung vigorously. The lava seen in this orifice, only a few feet from the pool, stood at a lower lever than in the pool itself. In the pool there was streaming in from the north and out to the southeast toward the lower level of the small orifice.

Throughout the evening a very bright glow and a brilliant blue flame were seen at the orifice of the high south-southwest cone whence, nevertheless, copious white and bluish white fumes emanated.

At different times at various points of the lake margin heavy spatter-fountain and surf action were going on, accompanied by the very loud and deep surf-pounding noise so characteristic of this sort of action. At times this action was so energetic that a trembling motion was communicated to the rook at the rim. Deep down in a peripheral crevice which has converted the southwest part of the floor into a fissured crag, a brightly illuminated fumarole was seen but no molten lava. A small group of small glow holes were seen near the foot of the pit wall under the north station in the deep crevice north of the high crag that divides the main lake from the frozen over northeast arm. Except for one short interval when the entire lake was crusted over, large boiling fountains were active in a central region of the lake west of the ''Old Faithful'' bursting place. Recurrent small-scale action of sinking and rising was observable at irregular intervals. At times the floating, tearing crusts were so thin as to exhibit a fiery sheen owing to great numbers of fire-points showing through. On this evening the fumes were much less copious and less acrid than for some weeks past. At the extreme east end were seen two small glow holes, one several days old, the other, larger, opened since March 7.

In the late afternoon and early evening of March 10 the activity was similar in character to that of the previous evening, but of less intensity. Some of the time the east part of the lake was frozen over. The surf sound was replaced by an incessant splashing noise. During one of the brief sinking phases at about six p. m. a splendidly developed stalactite apron was seen from the south station, hanging from the northwest wall, with some of the lava icicles as much as ten feet long, Streaming, so far as any general tendency could be noted, was from the center of the lake to the west and south.

During the week five or more exceedingly small local earthquakes, all from near origins, have been registered in the Whitney Laboratory. During the whole time there has been a strong tilt to the west and a moderately strong tilt to the south. At times both have been excessive. There has been nothing noteworthy about the registration of microseismic motion or of volcanic vibrations .

H. O. WOOD, Associate.

TECHNOLOGY STATION, March 18. —During the past week, ending March 17, there has been a small, well-marked subsidence of from fifteen to twenty feet of the surface of the molten lake and pools in Halemaumau, attended by apparent diminution in surface activity, although as a consequence of the sinking, streaming has at times been more vigorous than usual. Some moderately heavy avalanches, involving broken material of the collapsing 1914-15 benches, have been seen and heard. No significant falls from the old walls have occurred. Such subsiding of the magma is expectable at this time, with equinox only a few days off.

During the forenoon of March 11 observations were made from the west and northwest stations. The surface action was normal or sub-normal. Splashing was seen as follows: At about ten a. m., along the east-northeast rim of the lake; at ten-fifteen, in a cave south of the northwest pool; at about ten-thirty, vigorous splashing at the west end of the lake; and after eleven, at the southeast margin of the lake.

Streaming was noted as follows: Until ten-thirty a. m., steadily toward the southwest lake margin, then toward the west end; at ten-forty-five, to and down along a short line of east-west baby fountains in the western lobe of the lake. At times the lake would appear quiet for a brief interval, only to resume its normal surface activity.

The spatter cones recently active were quiet. Heavy surf sounds came from under the east margin of the lake. The usual loud, splashing noises were heard. Measurement fixed the depth of a splashing cave south of the northwest pool at about 465 feet. In mid-evening a small avalanche fell from some location at the north. There was vigorous splashing at the west margin, and the surface of the northwest pool showed great activity.

In the late afternoon of March 12 streaming toward the southeast cove, and also toward the northwest cove, was steadily maintained. A few large boiling-fountains were in action in the central region of the lake, and numerous smaller ones were seen in the lines of streaming. The molten surface appeared to be about ten feet below the third platform. The pool under the northwest station, roughly quadrangular in outline, seemed to have diameters of about sixty feet. Small boiling-fountain action characterized its surface. Molten spray was ejected from two blow-holes near the wall between the northwest and the west.

During the forenoon of March 13 the characteristic action was that of small boiling-fountains, arranged in lines and clusters in various regions of the lake at different times, with streaming towards these places and towards, in turn, several parts of the lake margin. Marginal splashing was at times sufficiently vigorous to hurl spray high in air. There was observable a tendency for the lake to crust over at the east. Similar action also prevailed during the greater part of the afternoon. Blue flame banners flared from the spatter cones, and occasionally large boiling-fountains were in vigorous action. Very loud and heavy surf sounds preponderated. The depth of the molten surface below the third platform was estimated at from ten to twenty feet at different times during the day.

In late evening on the fourteenth of March it was seen that the northwest pool had enlarged considerably and some talus avalanches had taken place in its vicinity. The general activity was as usual in character and somewhat greater in intensity.

On the fifteenth the usual action of streaming and of small boiling-fountains, in variable directions and positions, was noted, but with less intensity than usual. Intermittent marginal splashing, sometimes vigorous, was observed, but there appeared to be no predominant direction of streaming. Heavy falls of broken 1914-15 bench material occurred in late forenoon and afternoon, partially choking the enlarged northwest pool, while a small pool, twenty feet from the main lake, had appeared at the southeast.

Measurements gave for diameters of the main lake in the east to west direction 500 feet, and in the north to south direction 150 feet. Owing to adverse conditions, depth measures of the molten surface varied considerably; the average was about 480 feet.

In the afternoon of the sixteenth of March the seeing was poor. Glimpses showed that marginal splashing was going on at variable points. Streaming southeast, south and southwest was fairly steady, so far as could be ascertained. From the southeast pool spray was flung into the air to a height, say, of thirty feet.

On March 17 in the afternoon, again seeing was poor. However, it was observed that the northwest pool was crusted over, as in fact was the case on the preceding day. This pool has engulfed some talus material on the north side, and to the west and northwest it has enlarged so that it is now tangent to the cliff wall there. Its north to south diameter has enlarged to 230 feet. So far as it was visible or audible, the activity was as usual.

By measurement, the dimensions of the main lake were 490 to 510 feet in the east to west direction by 150 to 180 in the north to south direction. Measures of the depth of the molten surface indicated it at from 475 to 482 feet below the rim.

During the week seven or more small, local earthquakes have been registered. Of these only one was of moderate instrumental intensity—unfelt here, but capable of overturning a very top-heavy vase filled with long-stemmed flowers. There has been nothing notable about microseismic registration or that of volcanic vibrations.

The tilt to the south and west, so marked during the week previous, has continued conspicuous during the week now ending, but its amount has been less than earlier.

H. O. WOOD, Associate.

TECHNOLOGY STATION, March 25, 1915.—During the week ending with March 24 the molten surface of the lava in Halemaumau has receded still further from the rim-level of the pit. This withdrawal of the magma has led to further conspicuous collapsing of the 1914 and 1915 floors, benches, or platforms adjoining the molten lake. These are traversed by new systems of fissures and their surfaces are warped and broken anew in complicated ways—all contributing to down-letting toward the center except for minor reversals of slope due to the rotating of the blocks, much as in the case of large landslides. Small avalanches, of course, have accompanied this downsinking. Such withdrawal of magma at this time is, it is necessary often to point out, an expectable circumstance. The surface activity, however, on this occasion has shown little or no diminution of energy. During most of the intervals of observation there was normal streaming with energetic boiling- and splashing-fountains.

During the afternoon of March 18 there was temporary rising. A small flow overbrimmed the northwest pool, flowing into a near-by cone orifice. This flow attained a width of 20 feet, and continued in action about a half-hour. Near-by molten spray was blown to a considerable height from a cone to the right (seen from the north station) of the pool, near the cliff wall. On this afternoon the estimated dimensions of this northwest pool were 100 feet in the north-south direction and 60-

70 feet in the east-west direction. Active boiling fountains along the margin characterized the action of the east pool, whose diameters were estimated at 60x70 feet. The surface of the main lake was comparatively quiet, ten feet below the third floor, with comparatively quiet streaming toward the northwest cove.

In the afternoon of March 19 the magma had subsided 10 feet or more in both the northwest pool and the main lake. Both were characterized by vigorous boiling and splashing-fountains, as was also the smaller pool at the east. The cone beside the northwest pool was still ejecting molten spray to a considerable height. In the main lake there was steady streaming toward the northwest cove and a more vigorous and rapid streaming toward the east pool.

A description of the conditions and activity on the afternoon of March 20, so far as these could be seen in unfavorable weather, would be simply a repetition of the description for the foregoing day.

On Sunday, March 21, the conditions were observed both in forenoon and in evening. In the main lake the lava was slightly lower but the amount of this sinking, not measured, was trifling. The splashing-fountain action, particularly in the evening, was unusually vigorous, molten spray being flung to far greater heights than usual, resulting in the spinning of much new Pele's Hair. The cone near the northwest pond was still ejecting molten spray. There was steady and strong eastward streaming. The noises of eruption were conspicuously loud.

By the afternoon of March 22 great changes, on the small scale of course, had taken place in the pit. There had been abrupt sinking, with in-caving of the lower benches and platforms as summarized above. Maps and profiles, based on surveys, would be required to indicate these changes clearly and briefly. The surface was relatively quiet though the usual doming-fountains broke through, and there was quiet streaming to the north and the east. The depth-altitude had become 500 feet, the molten surface standing more than 50 feet below the 1915 platform. The lake diameters were: East to west, 560 feet; north to south, 170 feet. The northwest pond, however, measured only 483 feet down, with diameters: North to south, 260 feet; east to west, 30 feet.

In the afternoon of March 24 further measurement showed the depth to be still 500 feet to the surface of the main lake, while the surface of the northwest pond had sunk to 495 feet. In the northwest pool there was rapid streaming, at the rate of 10 miles per hour, along the narrow southern part, with cascading around a small projection from the east, into the northern lobe and on under the north bank. The main lake was characterized by boiling fountain action in the central region with very energetic streaming into the pool and thence into the cave at the east end. The doming-fountains reached unusual heights, bursting at heights of from 20 to 40 feet. Small avalanches took place at the south of the main lake.

During the past week only one earthquake has been registered, a shock of moderate instrumental amplitude, in the early forenoon of March 24. The strong west and south tilt has been maintained with slight variations in amount.

H. O. WOOD,
Associate.

TECHNOLOGY STATION, April 1, 1915.—"The week ending Mar. 31, 1915, at Kilauea Volcano has been marked by continued strong activity in the lava pool about 500 feet below the rim, and one strongly felt earthquake on Sunday morning, March 28. The signs of subsidence in Halemaumau continue, avalanches and swirling and rushing torrents of melt.

"March 25, from three to four a. m., the main lake, seen from the north, was very active with eastward streaming and traveling fountains. The liquid appeared about fifteen feet below the lower bench. At the east end a channel, perhaps forty feet wide and sixty feet long, had formed at the entrance to the southeast cove, and into this the lava was rushing in a torrent at a rate of about fifteen miles an hour, the channel terminating in an overarching spatter-grotto against the east wall of the pit. A few fountains broke through the current. The northwest pool was actively fountaining, streaming from the cavern at its west end against the northwest wall, and the lava level in this pool was about ten feet below the inner bench. At two-thirty p. m. an avalanche fell from the east wall into the channel torrent.

"At three p. m. March 26 streaming in the main lake was east and west from a medial zone, and fountaining was especially active about the south cove. At four p. m., from the north rest house, it was discovered that an active pool was boiling on the site of the inner end of the former northeast arm, separated by a bridge of crust four or five feet thick from the lake, and under this bridge a stream was running into the lake and out of the pool. Many bubble fountains played on the surface of this northeast pool.

"March 27, at three p. m., the lake, seen from the north, appeared the same, with streaming east and northwest. The northwest pool at the west end was partially buried under debris from a recent avalanche, and similar effects were seen near its east end on the wall side, where the tumble had left a scar in the cliff above.

"March 28, at noon, the lake could be seen from the west and northwest, with eastward streaming in the lake and northward streaming in the northwest pool. The tumble of benches around the lake shows great confusion; the northeast crag block has subsided so that its summit is well below the December floor remnants of 1914, and the region of the former southwest pond is occupied by a deep L-shaped crevasse, smoking fiercely amid toppled crags. The upper surface of the northeast crag, last remnant of the September floor, is much narrower than a month ago by scaling off of the cliffs on both sides. At seven p. m., from the northeast station, a good view was obtained of the northeast pool, separated by a bridge of crust from the lake. Streaming was now from the lake under this bridge into the northeast pool, and the inrush into the pool was torrential, bending into a whirl that rotated counter-clockwise. Occasional small avalanches were heard at the west.

"March 29, at three p. m., from the east the lake appeared twenty feet below the inner bench, and the northeast pool was crusted over and buried under avalanche material. The northwest pool was active, the cavern at its west end had reopened and from it a rapid current of lava was streaming into the pool. At three-ten p. m., twenty feet of the south bank of the lake fell in.

"March 30, at three p. m., there had been some rising, the lava surface being about ten feet below the lower bench. There was noisy fountaining activity in the direction of the south cove. Streaming was from a middle point in three directions, northwest, south and east. The northwest pond was active but its west end was covered with slides. The northeast pool was crusted but glowing in spots. In the southwest part of the pit much blue fume arose from a hole in the second bench.

"On March 31, avalanches were numerous and were recorded as follows: Two-thirty p. m., small avalanche southwest; two-forty p. m., loud avalanche southwest; two-fifty-five p. m., small avalanche east; three-eight p. m., small avalanche south; four-twenty-five p. m., small avalanche east. Two other small slides took place before five p. m.

"Streaming on this day, March 31, was eastward, the current forking into the east cove and under the northeast bridge, the latter pouring around the bend very rapidly. The northwest pool showed many bubble fountains traveling northward and the lava surface was only three feet below the inner bench. There was rapid inrush into the east cove of the main lake.

"By survey, March 31, the lake was 490 feet long east to west, about 250 feet wide and 507 feet below the northwest rim. The west pond was 175 feet long by about seventy feet wide, the greater length being north to south. The bottom of the pit at the lava level was about 800 feet long in an east-southeast direction by 425 feet wide, including the northwest pond in the length and the northeast pond in the width. The summit of the northeast crag was 391 feet below the northwest rim. These measurements show pronounced diminution in the size of the lake and of the northwest pond since March 22.

"The following report from the Whitney Laboratory of Seismology is submitted by H. O. Wood:

" 'During the week ending with March 31 eight local earthquakes were registered here, all but one of which were, as usual, of very small amplitude, even as instrumentally recorded. The other shock, which occurred just before eight-thirty a. m. on Sunday, March 28, was a perceptible shock of more than usually complex characteristics, and, though light, only about IV-V of the Rossi-Forel scale, nevertheless it was the second in point of intensity registered here since the establishment of this observatory. During a continuous shaking from five to seven seconds in duration, six definitely separated maxima were detected by the writer. Of these the third, though shorter than the second or fourth, was much the strongest—suggesting, momentarily, an earthquake of great energy. Throughout, the motion was slower than is generally characteristic of felt shocks here. Toward the southwest the shock was lighter than toward the northeast. Also fewer maxima were perceived near Hilo. All the information received thus far suggests an origin in the Hilo direction, possibly even beyond Hilo. The shock was instantaneously too strong for our registering seismometers, sweeping the writing points off at once, to the south and east. No further seismometric data are determinable. At the observatory the shock was not strong enough to stop clocks, but at Waiohinu one clock is reported to have stopped. It is worthy of note that the shock was stronger at Waiohinu than at nearer points in the southwest direction, though the motion there was slow rather than sharp. All things taken together, there is a vague indication that the origin was located on the northeast segment of the Mauna Loa rift.

" 'The seismograph pens were replaced within a few minutes after the shock, and from the start motion of considerable amplitude and relatively slow period was registered for over an hour. This suggests the practically contemporaneous arrival of the waves of a distant shock of small energy. If this was the case, the early phases were lost and no determination of origin-distance can be made. If this motion was due to the local shock, it is unusual and requires study.

" 'A shock of intensity IV-V of the Rossi-Forel scale was felt at Kealakokua just before midnight on the twenty-seventh of March, but this shock was not felt on the east side of the island and it was not registered seismometrically here.

" 'Moderate microseismic motion with sporadic, moderately strong volcanic-vibration spasms have been registered through the week.

" 'With irregular fluctuations in amount, the pronounced tilting to the south and west has continued and gradually grown larger until it has necessitated a readjustment of the seismometers to a new position of equilibrium.' "

T. A. JAGGAR, JR., Director.

TECHNOLOGY STATION, April 8, 1915.—"The subsidence of the lava columa recorded last week by measurement and indicated by avalanches ceased about April 3, and a slight rise has taken place since that time, so that avalanches have ceased falling; the fumes are somewhat thinner, there have been occasions of very clear seeing, and measurement demonstrates a rise of the pool to less than 500 feet below the rim. With this rise flaming chimneys have developed at the east end and a large spatter dome on the bank of the northwest pond.

"At three p. m. April 1 the lava lake appeared to be about fifteen feet below the inner bench, boiling actively with traveling fountains migrating eastward with the effect of streaming under the crusts of the east arm and the southeast cove. Both of these embayments were by now trenches filled with fallen debris. At three-thirty p. m. the streaming was dominantly into the south cove and there was ebullition under the banks south, west, northwest, north, and east, the last with a torrential inrush. At four-ten p. m. an avalanche from under the 1894 bench east lasted about three seconds. At eight-thirty p. m. the northwest pond was seen to be active, there was streaming radially inward from all directions to a north-south line of traveling fountains which was moving southward from the region to the south of Old Faithful. East of Old Faithful there was a belt of quiet skin over the melt across the lake north-south, and this appeared to be a place of rising, for the surface streaming poured east and west from it. From it eastward there was a rapid rush into the east cove, and there behind a bridge of crust on the site of the former southeast cove a glowing pot was visible from the southeast station where down-sucking was in progress.

"The gases rising from the south chimney were under unusually high pressure, the flaring flame and blue fume rushing upward vigorously. Above this chimney, which was a hole in the talus, rocks rolled down from time to time following the hollow between the two remnants of the high 1912 bench south.

"The lake as a whole had become an irregular oval, with rounded coves west and south and a V-shaped one east. It was coated with quiet skins, parting along the usual zigzag lines. The noises were chiefly those of the traveling fountains, plashings, enhanced sometimes by increased bombardment of the south bank with spurts of spray more than fifty feet high. The wall above the lake under the north crag appeared fully 100 feet high. Dense fumes were rising in the pit east, southwest and north. Recently the outlying fume vents of the ring of the Postal rift, to the northeast of Halemaumau, have become very acrid and unpleasant to breathe.

"At two-thirty p. m., April 2, seen from the east, there were no significant changes observed and no rock falls were heard. On the evening of April 3 there was very clear seeing, the glow was brilliant, the northwest pond was still active, and one rock fall was observed into the lake from its north wall. During April 4 and 5 the change from sinking to rising appears to have taken place and avalanching came to an end. On Tuesday noon, April 6, the pit was smoky, but there was dim seeing from the south station. There lake was boiling noisily about Old Faithful. Streaming was very sluggish, mostly eastward. The lava level appeared twenty feet below the inner ledge. During one hour no rock falls were heard. The east wall of Halemaumau was freshly scarred by recent falls into the southeast cove. The group of pulpit rocks or pinnacles formed of the fallen bench southeast was in place.

"A newly tumbled block appeared, fallen from the lower western half of the 1912 bench south. There were five or six recently fallen large whitish boulders on the 1914 bench under the south chimney. At the latter the fumes were still gushing under pressure. The southeast corner of the 1914 floor was no longer full of fuming cracks, all of that part has tumbled in, but fumes rise there from below the bench. This 1914 bench, the floor level of last December, still clings to the wall from the southeast around by the west end to the edge of the northwest pit. Beyond that point it is all collapsed into the north trench.

"At nine-fifteen p. m., April 6, seen from the southeast, the general appearance of the activity and size and shape of the lake were strikingly like the evening of April 1. Traveling fountains moved into the south cove, a torrent poured into the east cove, streaming was to the south and east, and dark skins on the surface of the lava were tearing apart and being engulfed in the Old Faithful downsuck and in the east cove. At the east end several boiling pots were belching out immense flaring flames. The south chimney was red and puffing. Glow could be seen within the southwest fumarole in the bench tumble. The main streaming was west to east. The lake appeared very low, twenty-five feet at least below the inner ledge. One of the east pots was spitting. The outline of the glowing lake was ragged, an effect increased by an irregular crust attached to the west end.

"At noon, April 7, the lake had risen fully fifteen feet. Measurements made the lake shore 492 feet, the summit of the crag 385 feet, and the white stones on the southern 1914 bench 376 feet below the southwest rim station. The lake was ten feet below the inner bench. Streaming was eastward with acceleration into the south and east coves, the northwest pond was streaming eastward also and a large spatter dome glistened on its southeast bank and glowed on the side of the pond. The craggy cavities over the east cove flamed high above the lake level. The streaming changed once so as to pour westward as well as eastward from Old Faithful.

"H. O. Wood reports that during the week ending April 7 two small earthquakes have been registered at the Whitney laboratory of seismology. Both were local shocks of very small instrumental amplitude. Microseismic motion has been continuously moderate to moderately strong, but the accompanying weather conditions have not been unusual in any way. Volcanic vibrations have been as usual. The tilt to the west and south has fluctuated during the week, but without noticeable increase or decrease as a whole."

T. A. JAGGAR, JR., Director.

TECHNOLOGY STATION, April 15. —The week ending April 14, at Kilauea has shown only slignt changes in the lava lake. The level of the lava surface has been essentially stationary except for diurnal fluctuation. The latter has been marked and of considerable range, spatter levels being visible on the shore wall of the inner pit fully twenty feet above the lake at times, and quick changes of streaming and fountaining mark sudden reversals from rising to falling and vice versa.

On the evening of April 8 from eight to eleven p. m. the lake appeared relatively high and active; there was clear seeing from the south, streaming was east and west from a belt of skin west of Old Faithful, the eastward currents poured into the south and east coves and traveling fountains moved southeastward between these two coves. There were glowing pots in the east arm and on the southwest bench and in the southeast cove, a high spatter dome with flaming holes east and the south chimney in the talus flamed and puffed. The northwest pit was active. One fall of rocks was heard on the east.

April 9 at two p. m. the lake appeared ten feet below the lower bench with much fountaining and southward streaming. At four p. m. the lake had risen five feet, and streaming was into the east as well as the south coves. At four fifteen p. m. infolding black skins were being engulfed along a medial line.

April 10 at two-thirty p. m. from the southeast station the lake appeared ten feet lower or about fifteen feet below the lower bench. Streaming was eastward with traveling bubbles and fountains and a rush into the east cove. At three p. m. the northwest pond was observed from the west station; the surface was active with eastward streaming and bombardment against the northwest wall of the pond. From the west the main lake could be seen pouring under a lava bridge and cascading into a hole at the east end. The spatter cone above appeared ten feet high. Occasional rock falls could be heard from the north wall.

Monday, April 12 at eleven a. m. the activity was strong but subsidence on this day was in progress, for avalanches were numerous. The northwest pond was active with eastward flow. As the seeing was from the north the east arm came into view, revealing there a pool 100 feet long with no visible streaming and active fountains in its midst. The main lake showed strong eastward flow increasing to a rush at the east end at the rate of from fifteen to twenty miles an hour, where two torrents divided about a peninsula in the east cove and poured into voids against the east wall of Halemaumau and under the crust of the southeast cove. The fumes of the south chimney had lost their pressure, they were yellowish rather than blue, and in daylight no glow could be seen there. The north crag was scaling off from time to time as pieces of rock were heard to fall, fumes were strong and thick, and Pele's hair was floating up from the pit.

At two-fifteen the lake appeared ten feet below the lower bench. The northwest pond was very quiet with only two small active spots. At four p. m. the crust broke up and the pond became active with boiling.

Avalanches were noted as follows: two twenty-two p. m., short lived avalanche southwest; two thirty-four p. m., another in the same place; two fifty-four p. m., prolonged avalanche south, many large bowlders rolled down, estimated to last one minute; three thirty-eight p. m., avalanche from between the south and southwest stations, material of the high 1912 bench.

April 13 at noon the lake appeared fifteen feet below the lower bench. The surface was sluggish, but moved slowly east and south, faster at the east end, and there was overhang with stalactites at the east end. The noises were rumbling and plashing. There are now three benches below that of the 1914 floor—first, the broken ground, now a distinct bench; second the bench of the southeast pinnacles; and third the lower bench of recent accumulation. No avalanches were heard. The southwest pot in the broken ground was ejecting puffs of white fume, but the fume from the south chimney rose quietly. The crag appeared narrower than ever before in a north-south direction. The northwest pond, seen from the west station was surging hard and streaming against its northwest wall with blowing and rumbling noises.

The big spatter dome observed last week on a bench in the northwest pit was gone, and the pit appeared larger and deeper. At three p. m. the bombardment into the stalactitic grotto at the east end developed into a remarkable spectacle as seen from the northern stations. The southeast cove became very active, ejecting spurts of lava; then it appeared that the lava of the lake was there rushing over a submerged ledge like a great waterfall, and pouring with the noise of a cataract into a cavernous space beyond, where it whirled about and disappeared into an abyss. A number of small rock falls were heard in the afternoon.

Measurement from the east and southeast stations to the lava level in the south cove at three-thirty p. m. April 14, made the level of the lake below the east rim of Halemaumau just 500 feet, or about eight feet lower than seven days previous. The lake appeared rising, with the lower bench gone, either submerged or fallen away. The streaming was completely reversed, flowing from east to west, with quiet skins over the east end. Boiling was in progress in a southeast pot. The south chimney was again an open black hole fuming and flaming. The crag appeared to have fallen off much along a thin edge on its southeast aspect, so that this edge has migrated back to the northwestward. At six p. m. the streaming was eastward again, with pouring resumed into the voids. At eight p. m. the east end had again filled and become quiet and the westward streaming was resumed.

H. O. Wood reports that during the week ending with April 14, five weak local earthquakes have been registered at the Whitney Laboratory of Seismology, two of which were strong enough to set the "ordinary seismograph" in motion. One of them was barely perceptible to persons lying awake at the Volcano House. Microseismic registration has manifested no unusual characteristics. Volcanic vibrations have been steadily a little stronger than for some weeks past but without reaching any very notable intensity. Tilt to the south and west has continued but without increase.

T. A. JAGGAR, JR., Director.

TECHNOLOGY STATION, April 22. —The past week at the lava pit of Halemaumau has shown pronounced sinking of the lava surface, one heavy avalanche and many small ones, and crusting and terrace-building of the lava lake so as greatly to diminish its width and somewhat its length. Smoke has increased so that seeing is at times difficult in daytime, though the lake is still a wonderful spectacle at night. In the progress of the subsidence of the last three months, the transition stage from an increasing area of lake to a diminishing one appears to be well past, the increase at first being due to caving in of the banks, the present diminution to choking from excessive caving along with sinking, cooling, and congealing.

At eight p. m. Thursday, April 15, the lake was streaming eastward with a cataract pouring from it into a pot at the east end, making a marvelous spectacle. The whole width of the lake poured over a submerged ledge in a gigantic cascade at least fifty feet high, with a smaller trickle tumbling at one side, and this Niagara of fire rushed into a vast hole at the east end where the lava surged and bubbled at the lower level with terrific fury. This outrush produced no appreciable effect visibly on the level of the lake, which must have been continuously replenished by upwelling at the west. And the process had been going on at intervals since December, when the same phenomenon was observed in the same place but on a smaller scale.

There was hissing on the southwest shore of the lake. Avalanches fell south and north. The northwest pond was dull, and a small pot of lava could be seen in the east arm trench. The seeing was from the north and west.

April 16 in the afternoon the lake, seen from the east and north, was still streaming east and bombarding the east end actively, but the cavernous cascade was no longer in action. Traveling fountains migrated toward the south cove, the northwest pond was sluggish, and at three-ten p. m. there was a small avalanche southwest.

About ten a. m. April 17, a heavy collapse of debris took place and the whole western remnant of the fifty-foot bench south, a relic of 1912, fell over the south chimney and smothered it. A cloud of brown dust rose, seen from the observatory, and a coating of dust showed on the fresh black ledges. Thin fume continued to rise from the talus blocks covering the chimney. There was some general readjustment of the material in the pit and a rapid temporary rise of the lake about noon. The lower bench disappeared, and the bench separating the northwest pool from the lake had warped down with widened fissures. The lava in the northwest pond became visible from the south station. The rising from eleven a. m. until one-twenty p. m. was accompanied by a quiet lake with crumpled skins streaming slowly eastward, while miniature flows welled over the crusts. For several hours there was no fountaining, not even from Old Faithful. The northwest pond was actively flowing and swirling, and at its northwest border was a cave curtained with stalactites, some of them ten to fifteen feet long. Owing to the disappearance of the lower bench the main lake appeared unusually wide.

The next day, April 18, at two p. m. the lake appeared level with a lower bench with traveling fountains streaming notheastward. At two-forty the lake overflowed the bench. Old Faithful was as usual. At two-fifty an avalanche fell into the lake with much commotion from the north crag.

April 19 at eleven a. m. the northwest pond was boiling on its west side but crusted otherwise, and the main lake was very quiet and crusted over on its southwest and east sides. Streaming was east and south. The north crag was broken in two where avalanches had fallen from it east and west. Old Faithful broke seldom and then very small. White fumes were rising on the site of the former south chimney. At eleven-forty-five a. m. a slight rise took place but the general level appeared about 510 feet below the rim. Some rock falls were heard. The seeing was from the southeast. The southeast rim of the pit is dangerous near certain cracks which have been widening, just to the south of the southeast station. A portion of the rim is likely to fall soon.

At noon, April 20, there was some seeing from the west and northwest stations. The lake appeared thirty feet below the lower bench. It was very smoky and sluggish, crusted southwest, boiling mildly south of the middle. There were a few rock tumbles heard. The northwest pond appeared small and sluggish. The former crust of the southeast and east arms appeared to be very high above the lake, with lava terraces at lower levels. Avalanches were noted at one-fifty northwest, at two-twelve p. m. northeast, at three p. m. southwest, and another into the northwest pond, and there were many small rock slides during the afternoon. At two p. m. the lake was active with fountains traveling eastward, and the northwest pond showed increased activity with northeastward streaming and fountaining. At three p. m. the lake was seen to have formed a new lower terrace, especially south, and to be growing small and narrow.

Wednesday, April 21, conditions were essentially the same. A large spatter grotto had formed on the northeast shore of the lake, streaming was eastward, a narrows nearly divided the lake in two formed by a promontory from the southwest. Behind a partition a pit could be seen in the east arm. Three glowing places appeared on the north bank of the lake high above it. There was a noon rise of the lake level with quiet skins over the lava. Occasional rocks fell and one short slide was heard. If Old Faithful was present it was under the south promontory, which had somewhat the aspect of a cone with grottoes under it. This cone was part of a lower shelf ten feet above the lake, and another bench appeared about thirty feet higher.

Measurements about noon, April 25, made the lake level 525 feet below the southwest station, and the top of the crag 387 feet down, and the 1914 bench south 381 feet down. The length of the lake was 460 feet, thirty feet less than on March 31; its width at the narrows was only about sixty feet and at the widest part not more than 150 feet, or 100 feet narrower than on March 31.

H. O. Wood reports that during the week ending with April 21, four small local earthquakes have been registered in the Whitney laboratory of seismology. None were unusual. Micro-seismic registration has gone on as usual. At times, but without discernable significance, volcanic vibrations have been stronger than usual. The pronounced tilt to the south and west maintained during recent weeks has continued. It has, however, undergone greater variation than hitherto, and has reached both less and greater extremes during the past week than in any previous interval. As the week comes to an end it stands at a value nearly as great as the maximum recently measured. The tilt to the south is more pronounced, relative to previous stands, than the tilt to the west.

T. A. JAGGAR, JR., Director.

WEEKLY BULLETIN
OF THE
Hawaiian Volcano Observatory

Vol. III. HONOLULU, HAWAII, APRIL, 1915. No. 4

KILAUEA AND MAUNA LOA IN 1914.

ADDRESS delivered at annual meeting of Hawaiian Volcano Research Association, in Honolulu, March 10, 1915, by T. A. Jaggar, Jr., Director of Hawaiian Volcano Observatory.

Present Activity of Mauna Loa.

THE title of this heading will probably excite some curiosity in the minds of those readers who imagine that Mauna Loa has ceased activity after an outbreak in November and December, 1914. It is true that the superficial evidence of lava fountains in the summit crater, smoke, and glow at night, have for the time being come to an end; but if we examine the past record of the volcano and analyze the meaning of a complete eruption, we shall see that the 1914 outbreak was merely the beginning. For the complete eruption of any volcano is first a violent discharge of lava foaming under pressure of contained gases, and second, the outflow of the liquid somewhat relieved of its gas content. The end of an eruption then is a lava flow, and there has been no flow as yet from the outbreak of Mauna Loa in 1914. Moreover, Mauna Loa in the past has always obeyed this law.

The last two eruptions, marked by the northern flow from the Dewey Crater in 1899 and the southern flow in Kahuku in 1907, in each case really began with the outbreak in the crater of Mokuaweoweo three years before, in 1896 and 1903. These first outbreaks lasted only fifteen and sixty days respectively, and were followed by years of seeming repose, but it is probable that those years would have exhibited to a careful observer living on the mountain (had there been any such) very hot gases rising through cracks and possibly occasional small trickling lava flows in the summit crater, showing that the lava was accumulating and changing from a foamy to a liquid condition.

Comparing the present condition, therefore, with the records of the last thirty years we may truly consider the volcano Mauna Loa at present, in 1915, to be in an active condition, with a white hot column of lava in cracks underground at an unknown depth below the fountain vents of Mokuaweoweo. Probably vast quantities of the gases of carbon, hydrogen and sulphur are rising through the summit vents or elsewhere, this ebullition producing a gradual change whereby the liquid within the mountain grows heavier and less foamy, preparatory to its eventual escape as a lava flow in about three years, if the analogy with the last two eruptions holds good. It will be seen that the basis for prediction is nothing mysterious or occult, but merely a common sense reasoning from the events of the past, all too imperfectly recorded in this Hawaiian land. If we only had the diary of such a devoted observer as is above referred to, one who had dwelt in camps for many years within the desert

WEEKLY BULLETIN
of the
Hawaiian Volcano Observatory

Published Monthly at Honolulu, Hawaii, by the Hawaiian Volcano Research Association

Editor.............Howard M. Ballou
Professor of Physics, College of Hawaii

Entered as second-class matter January 20, 1914, at the post-office at Honolulu, Hawaii, under the Act of August 24, 1912.

wastes of Mauna Loa, and had occasionally thrust a thermometer into the hot cracks or taken photographs of the vapor puffs and located these puffing places upon his map, we would have a much more complete story to tell of the habits of the monster on whose back we make our dwellings.

Function of an Observatory

This harking back to the past, including even the recent events of the nineteenth century, indicates something of the meaning of a scientific observatory, as contrasted with an experiment station. An experiment station in the work of any science may be established for a short period in a favorable place. An observatory, on the other hand, such as is maintained by the astronomer or meteorologist, is permanently located for the purpose of keeping up a routine of accurate observation, and recording as truthfully as possible the facts observed. Often many of the facts so recorded have no meaning whatever at the time of observation. They may acquire great significance, however, when after many years the same seemingly insignificant event is found recurring in association with other happenings of known significance. The most interesting discoveries of science often come from men who have compiled the patient labors of others and have put together in tables, curves and diagrams thousands of measurements on rainfall, temperature, or movements of the stars. By such compiling science learns to recognize regular repetition and definite orderly spacing and the rate of movement of things, where before all was seemingly haphazard.

In the popular mind, an active volcano is supposed to be the most disorderly and haphazard thing imaginable. But when, at the suggestion of business men in Honolulu, influenced by the Massachusetts Institute of Technology, the town of Hilo in 1912 subscribed the money to build an Hawaiian volcano observatory at Kilauea, there was evidenced a scientific spirit in the community far in advance of the popular conception. It became the function of the new observatory to study the two active volcanoes (Mauna Loa and Kilauea) from year to year as closely as possible with a view to finding out, apart from all prejudice, whether the gases and lavas come out from the earth's interior in some orderly pulsation or otherwise. The gradual growth of the science of volcanology from an hysterical history of disaster has been well begun in Italy, Japan and elsewhere since the terrible catastrophe of St. Pierre in Martinique in 1902, and the foundation of the Hawaiian Observatory was a sound step in advance. It is my purpose to show here certain orderly results of three years' watching and to urge the necessity of extending our facilities so that the summit crater of Mauna Loa will be more accessible.

Community Gives Support

In spite of hard times and hard prospects, the scientific work on the volcano has received encouragement from the community. The Hawaiian Volcano Research Association has been organized, and anyone who is interested may join and receive the weekly bulletins of the association, which tell of the progress of the activities at Kilauea. We have members in Europe, United States, Central and South America and Japan The Massachusetts Institute of Technology is a large subscriber and contracts to carry on the scientific work of the association. Co-workers have made important experimental studies here who have come from Italy, Switzerland, France, England and United States. We have taken part in investigating the great disaster of Sakurajima, in Japan, by sending an expedition thither. The leading business firms of these islands have subscribed to the scientific work being done here and the officers and directors of the society have been leaders in the educational and commercial life of Honolulu. While Hilo took an important part in the initiation of the work it is to be regretted that the Reseach Association has not more Hilo members, and it is hoped that a substantial addition to the membership list will soon be made through the increased interest of persons living on the Island of Hawaii. For surely the inhabitants of this island have every reason to take an interest in the fires beneath their feet.

Routine of the Observatory

For three years the observatory at Kilauea volcano, under the scientific direction of the Massachusetts Institute of Technology, has recorded the rise and fall of the lava in the pit of Halemaumau, has mapped the outline of the lava pool, has noted the nature of the activity and the temperature of some of the gas vents, while the seismograph pendulums in the basement of the observatory have written from second to second a story of the local earthquakes and the tiltings and tremblings of the ground, and the meteorological instruments have made similar records of the rainfall, humidity, temperature, and pressure of the air.

Tides in the Rock

It has long been known that the crust of our rocky globe rises and falls with a tide similar to that of the ocean. Like the latter, this slow creaking wave that passes through the rocks to a depth of many miles is occasioned by the pull of the sun and moon acting upon the revolving earth. The earth bulges somewhat in a zone around the equator, and every month the moon moves north and south of the equator, while the sun does so only every year. Each half year the sun reaches its farthest south or its farthest north, while the moon does so each half month. These great celestial swings make a squeeze upon the bulging crust of the equatorial belt over and above the normal tides which depend upon the daily rotation of the earth and the conjunction and opposition of sun and moon, popularly known as the times of new and full moon. There are other factors, such as the times when the sun and moon are respectively nearest to the earth, which modify the daily, semi-monthly, and semi-annual squeezes which are crunching the rock crust on which we live, and a diagram showing all the complications of tidal theory and its effect at any point on the globe no one living is at present competent to construct. But from direct experiment, Professor Chamberlin, geologist, and Professor Michelson, physicist, of the University of Chicago, have recently proved a tidal movement in the solid earth, up and down, of about a foot, twice each day, and varying in amount through the lunar month and the solar year; and more than twice as great in a north and south direction as east and west. It is easy to understand how important such a movement is here in the equatorial belt of the globe where relatively small cracks going down forty or fifty miles are filled with liquid lava between walls of rock subjected to this rise and fall as well as to sidewise pressure—that is, to the passage of earth waves.

With knowledge of this ebb and flow in the rocky shell of the globe, we would expect careful measurements of the rise and fall of the lava column of Kilauea to show some kind of daily tides, some monthly change and a maximum every half year. Beyond this, in terms measured in years and centuries, there should be greater crisis of some sort. but in how far they should be tidal and how far dependent on the construction of the volcano is at present unknown. By construction of the volcano I mean the building up of inner cones by lava overflow so as to confine the otherwise steadily rising lava column, as is the present case with Halemaumau, and complications of hot gas and congealing lava underground which may determine the relationships of Mauna Loa and Kilauea.

Daily Lava Tides

There is definitely a daily movement marked by a maximum and minimum of lava level in Halemaumau every few hours, and there seems to be a tendency to marked rising about noon and midnight, the times of most barometic pressure. There is also a pulsating movement which I once recorded for twenty-two hours (in January, 1913) making a measurement once an hour of the height of the lava surface. The lava as a whole was rising, but the record showed a succession of quick jumps followed by slow sinking for three or four hours, each jump happening within the course of an hour and rising to a point slightly above that of the last previous jump. This jumping movement was probably occasioned by gas accumulation and release, while the net rise in the course of a day may have been tidal. It is to be hoped that some day we shall have the means during a time of high activity of Kilauea to keep a staff of assistants at work with a transit on the edge of the pit every fifteen minutes throughout a lunar month, and thus construct a diagram showing the details of tidal movement. This would necessarily be more expensive work than is now possible.

Lava Charts 1912-14

Diagrams (see cut) have been prepared to show for the years 1912, 1913 and 1914 the rise and fall of the surface of the liquid lava measured from the edge of the pit Halemaumau, which is at an elevation of 3700 feet above sea level. The average height of the lava for each five days has been shown as a black vertical line drawn with reference to a scale of depths below the rim of the pit indicated on the side of each diagram so that the tops of the black lines fluctuate in height in accordance with the measurements. From left to right across the diagram are monthly divisions, each month of thirty days being represented by six of the vertical lines or columns, and the fluctuation in height to the top of the columns thus expresses for each month graphically the fluctuation of the lava.

These diagrams beginning with January, 1912, reveal on the whole a gradual sinking of the lava throughout that year and until May, 1913, when the pit became so smoky and the lava sank so low, that for just one year no accurate measurement was possible. The year in question was from May, 1913, to April, 1914, when the lava was in general over six hundred feet below the rim of Halemaumau. From May, 1914, to the end of that year, the lava gradually rose , but not so high as previously. From January 5, 1915, to the end of March, 1915, it has gradually been sinking until it is more than five hundred feet below the rim of the pit.

Bi-Monthly Lava Tides

Examining the details of these diagrams from month to month, it is easy to see that every month there is a distinct bend in the movement of the lava. The lunar month contains twenty-eight days and therefore does not check perfectly with the calendar month. Allowing for this, we find that there are thirteen crises in the year 1912 about a month apart, as follows: December-January high, January-February low, February high, March low, April-May high, June low, July high, August low, September high, September-October low, October high, November low, December high. The incomplete diagrams of 1913 and 1914 show similar features and it becomes clear from a study of these diagrams that there is a complete rise and fall of the lava column, a flow and ebb, every two lunar months. In general, rising takes place faster than falling, though this is not invariable.

High and Low Level Changes

We next come to a marked characteristic of the movement of the Kilauea lava column: namely, the semi-annual high level. That this is connected with the change in declination of the sun north and south of the equator seems probable because both the changes in the sun's angle and the rise and fall of the lava are gradual, and the quarterly culminations correspond. The 1912-1913 diagrams show high level (1911) November-January, low level February-April, high level May-July, low level August-October, high level November-January, low level February-April. The high levels are times of solstice, the low levels times of equinox. This movement became so definite that it has been used during the past year for prediction, and the December rise of 1914 was expected, the prediction published, as was the expectation that there would be a fall in January, 1915, and thereafter, and these things have come true.

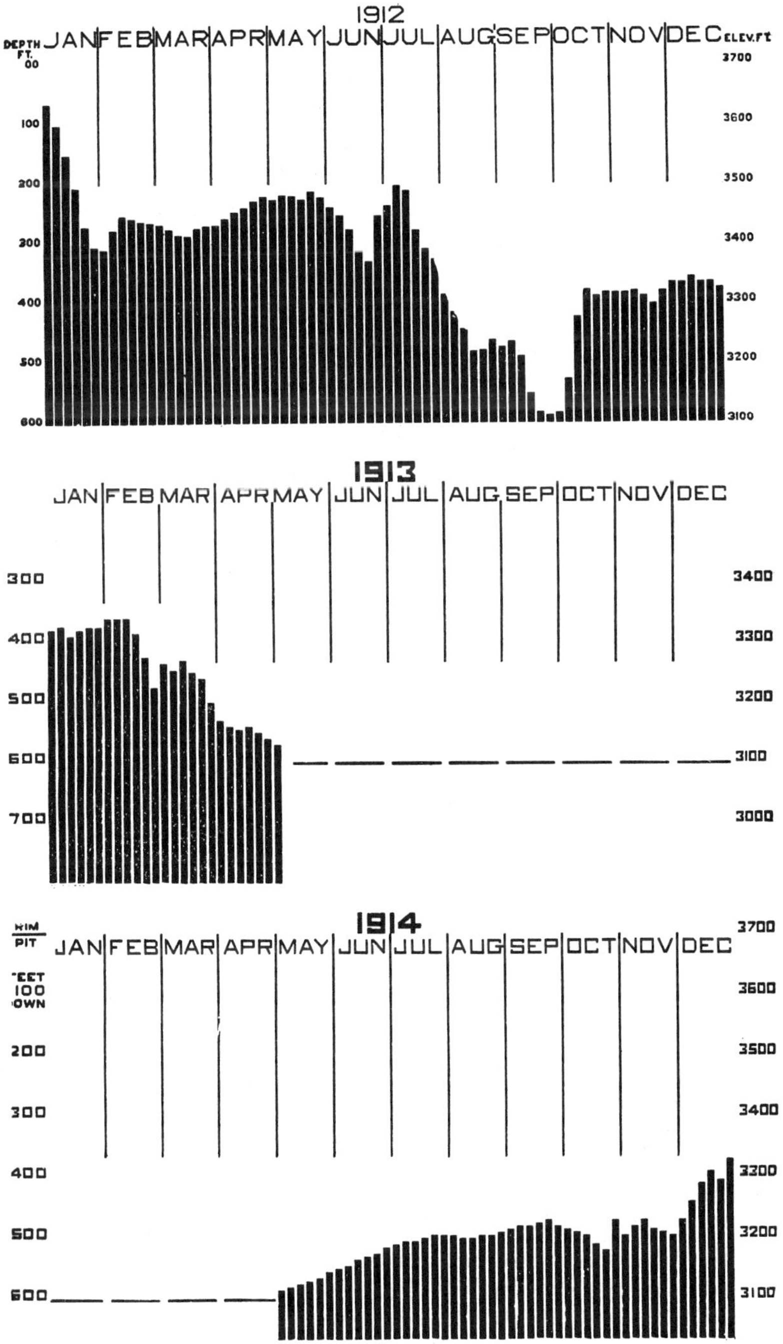

Diagrams showing the rise and fall of Kilauea lava column below rim of Halemaumau, and above sea-level from 1912 to 1914 inclusive.
(Broken line marks a time where pit was too smoky for measurement.)

Meaning of Lava Tides

There are thus short and long period movements of some regularity within a single year and these are gradually being verified by the accumulation of records for several years. The rising and falling of the Kilauea lava column is a sensitive index of the addition or subtraction of hot gases to a much larger mass of liquid deep in the earth and is also a sensitive measure of any compressing together or opening apart of the walls of the larger lava chamber underground to which the pool in Halemaumau is merely a small window. Geologists think that the lava comes from a substratum potentially melted at least fifty miles down and probably the passage leading down to this large mass of lava is nothing more than a crack or fissure. Kilauea has been built as a cone by the overflow of lava above this crack, and this overflow has built up a central hole and radiating flows so that the lengthwise trend of the fissure beneath is entirely masked by the mechanism of a central pit above. Squeezing together the walls of a fissure containing liquid which opens into a small tube above will cause the liquid to rise and fall in the tube, and something of this sort takes place when a tidal squeeze warps out of shape the whole body of the earth, be it ever so slightly. As only three years of measurement have yielded such important results we may expect that a half century of work at the Hawaiian Observatory will create a new science. The work must go on, it must unceasingly increase in accuracy of method and completeness of record, and it must be extended to other volcanoes around the Pacific Ocean for comparative results.

Long Term Eruptions

Even with the casual notes of travelers and scientific men made since the time of Vancouver's voyage in 1794, it is possible to glimpse something of the meaning of the relationship between Kilauea and Mauna Loa and of the long term happenings at Kilauea which are marked by tremendous cataclysms. There have been two such catastrophes at Kilauea in historic times, the explosive eruption of 1790 and the tremendous earthquake of 1868. In both cases there was collapse of the bottom of Kilauea crater, and afterwards a new period of building up the bottom by means of lava overflows. We know nothing of what sympathy Mauna Loa may have shown with the 1790 explosion, but we know positively that Mauna Loa shared in every way in the earthquake and lava flows of 1868.

For Mauna Loa the 1868 crisis inaugurated lava flows at the south end of the mountain and since that time the eruptions of Mauna Loa have happened about once in ten years, with flows alternating north and south. The 1868 flow was south, that of 1880 north; the 1887 flow was south, that of 1899 north; the 1907 flow was south, and accordingly the flow to be expected from the present eruption about ten years later, say 1917 or 1918, should come from the north.

The outbreaks of Mauna Loa every ten years or so, beginning with gas-lava fountains at the summit and ending with lava flow from the flank of the mountain, seem to mean that some great force tends to steadily push gas and lava upward, while a restraining structure, the great slag heap of the mountain nearly 14,000 feet high confines the lava within the oven so built up and compels it to erupt in spasms and at intervals instead of continuously. There is some reason to think that all volcanoes have passed through stages from free flowing continuous lava emission to greatly confined gas lava explosion.

Kilauea volcano is not so high as Mauna Loa, and after its evisceration in 1790, the lava, with many blowing cones and poolings within the crater, began to overflow and construct there a floor which was slowly built up into an inner cone, this cone-building by overflow being continuous throughout the nineteenth century until 1894, except for temporary interruptions by lateral outflow to the sea in 1823, 1840, and 1868, and possibly 1887. From 1894 to the present time Kilauea has failed to overflow the inner Halemaumau cone, and this period of twenty-one years, more than a fifth of a century, must be an important episode in the approach toward another great crisis like those of 1790 and 1868. Both Mauna Loa and Kilauea have shown diminution of volume of lava poured out from 1790 to the present time.

Sympathy Between the Volcanoes

It has frequently been asserted that there is no sympathy between the activities of Mauna Loa and Kilauea. This statement seems to me a loose one, unsubstantiated by facts. If there were a deep seated connection somewhere between the surface of the earth and the substratum fifty miles down whereby both the Mauna Loa and Kilauea lava-gas columns come together, and the mechanism of the rising and falling columns is dependent on a squeezing earth crust and on hot gas which maintains a heat circulation in a liquid subject to rapid congealing, then we are not to look for any hydrostatic balance between the two columns. We have clearly to do with an uprising stream of liquid on each side of the system, that is in Mauna Loa and in Kilauea respectively, which is restrained by its own tendency to solidify above when chilled, and is maintained by the release of hot gas and lava under pressure from below. If one of the two vents suddenly split open wider and so released to the air lava and gas under pressure, the other vent might be expected to be robbed of heat and of expending gas and consequently to congeal and its lava to subside. It might well be that for a time in the case of the sudden opening of one of the vents, the other vent would show a sympathetic kick or rise in the lava, followed by subsidence as suggested above. The evidence of sympathy, therefore, in the behavior of the two vents would be complex and would depend on the sizes and heights of the orifices, the source and mechanism of the heat supply, the depth and size of the connection between them and the volume and pressure of the foaming body of lava available for the particular eruption in question. This last factor is doubtless dependent on the time interval which has elapsed since the last eruption, in the case of a volcano like Mauna Loa, if we suppose the succession of eruptions to be the spasms of a steadily accumulating fluid which tends to escape.

The records of the nineteenth century are too incomplete, especially as concerns the stagnant times at Kilauea, to give us any clear evidence as to whether Kilauea lava went down when Mauna Loa lava came up, and vice versa, as might be expected from the above analysis. The record of the last thirty years, however, suggests such a relation. After the Mauna Loa outflow of 1887 there was revival and vigorous activity of Kilauea culminating in 1894. During this time Mauna Loa was quiet except for a small summit outbreak in 1892. Kilauea lava subsided and disappeared after 1894 and Mauna Loa revived in 1896 and poured out lava from the Dewey Crater in 1899. Kilaeuea showed a little life but at a very low level in 1900 to 1902, and Mauna Loa remained quiet. Mauna Loa became active in 1903, with outflow in Kahuku in 1907. Kilauea revived after the Mauna Loa flow of 1907, rose to its highest level three years later, in 1910, remained high for the three years from 1910 to 1912, and sank slowly, as shown by our diagrams, from 1912 to 1914. During all this time Mauna Loa remained quiet. In 1914 Mauna Loa revived, and at present (1915) Kilauea is subsiding, to what end remains to be seen.

This sequence of events suggests a more or less periodic eruption of Mauna Loa about once in ten years and Kilauea activity during the repose periods of Mauna Loa. These ten-year periods are probably controlled by influences of lava accumulation and release rather than by any tidal strains. It may well be, however, that in the critical time of approach to the end of a repose period that an exceptional tidal stress in the crust of the earth will act as trigger to release an eruption. Other crises at still longer intervals in the history of these volcanoes are very likely always accompanied by sympathetic displays in both volcanoes as in 1868 when the sympathy was unquestioned and in 1790, concerning which the accounts are very meagre; we know nothing whatever of Mauna Loa or of the earthquakes and lava flows of that time.

Exceptional Tide Dates

Where there is accumulated stress underground from gas or lava pressure, it has been above suggested that the critical times of tidal squeeze, summer and winter, may act as trigger to release the gas or liquid and start an eruption. There are some dates when the earth squeeze is unusually strong, and these dates do not recur every year, as they are dependent on coincidence of several variable relations of the sun, moon and earth. Thus either sun or moon may be at their nearest points to the earth, both may be farthest north or farthest south of the equator in their periodic swings, and they may be pulling together on opposite sides or on the same side of the earth. It is rare for all of these extreme positions to occur on the same day, but there was such an occurrence January 4. 1912, the time of the very highest rise of the Kilauea lava column shown in our diagrams. Also on the same day the tide gauges in Hawaii showed the highest ocean tide ever recorded on them. The reason was that the moon was farthest north and the sun was farthest south, both were nearest to the earth and the moon was full; that is, it was pulling on the opposite side from the sun. Events of the year, of the half year and the month conspired on one day to make a rare event of the combination which only happens at long intervals. It can be easily understood that such a day of unusual stress on our globe would press the button to start explosion or earthquake if volcano or straining earth crust were ready to be touched off.

Sequence of Typical Eruption

Science is still very ignorant about volcanoes and about the physical chemistry of hot lava filled with gas. Laboratory and field studies are working together, however, in demonstrating that the course of typical volcanic eruptions is everywhere the same in kind, differing only in degree; some volcanoes showing dominantly explosion and gas, while others are comparatively quiet with liquid lava as their chief product. Without discussing here the complex reasons for what happens, which would take us far afield, it is generally agreed that a typical eruption proceeds as follows:

Earthquakes

(1) Unusual earthquake strain near the volcano for days, weeks, or months with an abnormally large number of small earthquakes and some strong ones.

Gas Explosion

(2) A foamy lava rushes upward with a cracking open of the mountain through the central crater, the foaming being due to the gases contained in the fluid, very hot and very greatly compressed. According to the intensity of this gas pressure the eruption may be a tremendous explosion which blows the lava foam to dust, or it may be a violent foam fountain with oxidation of the combustible gases making flames. The first case is that of Sakurajima or Vesuvius, the second that of Mauna Loa. The rise of the lava foam in any volcano follows upon a longer or shorter term of rest, and in general the longer the term the more explosive the outbreak. Like volcanoes are apt to have like terms of repose, and the length of these quiet intervals appears be one of the distinctive characters of a given volcano, though some volcanoes are much more regular than others. Given an average repose period drawing to a close for a particular volcano, and numerous earthquakes marking the underground stress, we can look for an eruption as most likely to come near the solstice or on some date when the celestial tide strain is strongest.

Gas Release

(3) The adjustment of gas to liquid underground, a complex relation little understood at present, next takes place through the escape of large quantities of gas in the form of bubbles rising through the liquid, and if the upper part of the lava column is in any sense a froth, then this froth or foam may be conceived to sink or settle down as its bubbles burst. The gas itself, imagined to be contained in solution in the lava far down, passes from the dissolved to the bubble stage somewhere in the depths and there-above expands and rises with dissociation and some chemical reactions which have various

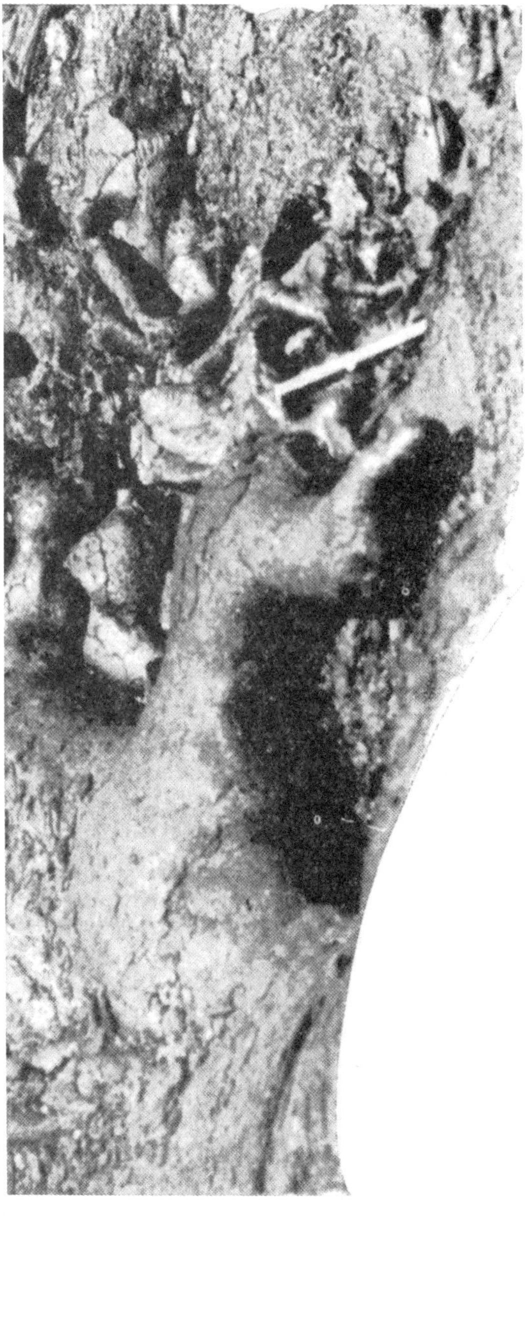

LAVA TOES, FLOOR OF KILAUEA CRATER.

cooling and heating tendencies, the net result of which is volcanic eruption. Until these processes are imitated in the laboratory science will know little about them, but the actual observation of volcanoes demonstrates without question that gas rushes forth for days or weeks after the first outbreak. This outrush may gradually decline, or it may be periodically renewed as though pulsating under alternate confinement and release. The term of gas escape before the liquid lava flows may be short or long, measured in hours or in years. There is no hard and fast line between explosive lava and liquid lava, and in a sense the lava flows from the instant that a volcano begins exploding, the transitions between explosion clouds, foam fountains, frothy flow, lava flow and the rise of stiff lava plugs is represented in all gradations in different volcanoes and sometimes two or more of these processes are simultaneously at work in different parts of the same volcano.

Liquid Release

(4) The liquid lava rises and escapes from the volcano in some form of lava flow, and this stage is generally sharply marked as a term of days or months when the mobile melted rock is either welling up in the summit crater and higher, like a stiffening dome of very viscous slag, or the mountain rifts open along some ancient fissure and the liquid lava, perhaps spurting at first to the summit crater for a temporary display, finally makes a new crater lower down and pours a flood of melt for days or months down the flanks of the volcano in accordance with the habits of such volcanoes as Etna and Mauna Loa. The first type mentioned, with the stiff dome rising above the crater, is now known to be common in the West Indies, Aleutian Islands, Japan and elsewhere, but was unknown to geologists before the eruption of Mount Pelee in 1902. This escape of lava is the culminating achievement of volcanic eruption, that for which the eruptive process is devised in the economy of nature and hence brings the eruption to a close by relieving the strain due to accumulation. The gases have been allowed to expand, the froth and gas charged liquid to escape and to cool.

Solidification

(5) The cooling and congealing extends to a certain small depth below the crater and a term of repose ensues. Whatever the ultimate cause of the upward pushing force, be it gas pressure or the compressive stress of a shrinking globe, we know that the force is there. The lava has to escape once in so often and the machinery of eruption adds so much new rock to the surface of the earth.

Accumulation

(6) A new term of accumulation in the deep region begins. There may be a few small earthquakes occasioned by the settling of the rocks over the void left by the lava flow, but in general the years immediately following a complete eruption constitute a time of unusual quiet with little activity, either seismic or volcanic. By complete eruption is meant the escape of the final lava flow for a given eruptive period, for some volcanoes have recurrent flows for several years before an eruption is finished.

Mauna Loa in 1914

Summarizing the six stages of a typical volcanic eruption they may be briefly expressed as (1)earthquake stress, (2)gas foam explosion, (3) gas release, (4)liquid release, (5) solidification, and (6) new accumulation. Mauna Loa in 1914 illustrated the end of a period of accumulation (6), and a year of earthquake stress (1) initiating gas-lava foaming (2) in Mokuaweoweo, the summit crater, November 25, 1914, and gas release (3) took place through the summit orifices throughout December and January and probably continues at the present time (spring 1915) with subsidence for the time being of the lava froth.

That the approach to the solstice (December 22) and the earth's nearest approach to the sun (perihelion) about the same season induced effective stresses touching off the accumulated strain is probable. For in November there were sixty local earthquakes, at the end of the month the summit fountains broke out and this activity endured until twenty days after the solstice, when the glow and fumes died away.

There remain yet to come in the present eruption of Mauna Loa stages 4, 5 and 6; namely, the escape of liquid lava, its solidification and the beginning of a new repose period. By this analysis it should be plain that Mauna Loa is now active and must be so regarded until the lava flow comes.

Preparation for the Eruption

It will now be profitable to review what the Hawaiian Observatory has done in preparing for and observing this eruption of Mauna Loa. The studies of men of science who have come to Hawaii from a distance—Dana, Friedlaender, Daly, Brun, Perret, Day, and Shepherd, and the work of Brigham and Hitchcock, resident here, have thrown new light on sequences, intervals, and the meaning of volcanic gases, and these things are the basis of the deductions outlined in this lecture. Four of these workers have co-operated with the observatory. The staff of the observatory has made continuous records of the processes of Kilauea and has visited the summit crater of Mauna Loa at least once a year.

Prediction

From these records I have worked out a tentative philosophy of the two volcanoes, as herein outlined, with a view to the practical service rendered the community in securing some basis of prediction, however inadequate and faulty our first attempts may be. Mr. H. O. Wood has been studying carefully the present day local earthquakes and the records of the terrific Hawaiian earthquake of 1868, and with me has been watching attentively the seismic and volcanic activities in their relation to the tidal and other stresses set up in the globe by the sun and moon. Mr. Wood has made a special study of the theoretical effects of the declination of the sun and moon north and south of the equator. From all these studies of records of the past, records of the present and of the processes of physics and astronomy, it became possible to foresee that Mauna Loa would have a summit outbreak between 1911 and 1915, that it was most likely to come near June or December, and this much has been verified in 1914. By similar reasoning there remain as yet unverified expectations (1) a very low level of the lava of Kilauea; (2) a lava flow from Mauna Loa, probably within four years and most probably in not less than three years; (3) the occurrence of a short lived summit outbreak before the flow; (4) the time of this outbreak probably near June or December, this combination making January or July of 1918 likely times for the eruption to culminate; and lastly, (5) the lava flow should break out from a vent on the north side of the mountain, probably somewhere above the Dewey Crater of 1899. All this sounds like unwarrantably precise prediction, but the basis for it has been explained above. To such extent as such prediction proves useful and leads to proper preparation and precaution, it is justifiable.

Exploration of Mauna Loa Expensive

In expectation of a coming eruption it was desirable for the observatory to have a station on Mauna Loa occupied frequently for purposes of recording temperatures of fumaroles, local earthquakes, weather conditions or any other phenomena that might bear on the approaching outbreak. But it early became evident that this ideal could not be realized with the funds at the disposal of the Research Association. Mauna Loa is a vast desert waste without water and rising to an immense height. Every expedition to the summit exhausts the energies of the men and animals employed and the animals are frequently crippled and have their legs cut by the rough block lava. Consequently the ranchers will not rent good animals at any price, and as there is no shelter on the summit, little water, no feed, violent winds and low temperatures, the men who can with difficulty be induced to go and act as guides or packers, object to remaining over night. The wages paid them and the hire of animals are high. All of this means that it costs several hundred dollars in order to take an unsatisfactory trip to the summit, see the crater and returu before any real scientific work can be done and even before the party is acclimated to the unusual altitude. In the winter time there is deep snow on the summit plateau, and snow flurries or violent thunder storms with heavy gales of wind may occur at any season and make havoc in a camp of tents. There is no soil, so ordinary tent pegs cannot be used, and there is no flat ground on which to sleep. There is no fuel of any sort there and no hillocks or valleys to offer shelter. The crater Mokuaweoweo is surrounded by vertical precipices from three hundred to eight hundred feet high and the floor is accessible only by arduous climbing. The area of exploration for proper study of hot vents whence lava flows may issue, and of the seven or eight summit vents (pits and cones) including the great crater, is fully twenty miles long by three wide, not including the separate area of flows in Kau to the south thirty miles away. It will be seen from this that Mauna Loa presents a problem of extensive exploration under difficult conditions and is not like Kilauea in possessing a single lava pit conveniently accessible.

Annual Visits to Mauna Loa

The most that the observatory has been able to do, therefore, in dealing with Mauna Loa during its repose was to send an expedition to the summit once each year and to record the observations of other travelers whenever such were available. Observatory expeditions visited Mokuaweoweo in August, 1912, and October, 1913, and no unusual phenomena were noted, the only activity being very slight vaporing from cracks both in the bottom of Mokuaweoweo and in outlying fissures. These steaming fissures extend both northeast and south from the crater, the directions in which large rifts trend down the mountain along lines of historic lava vents.

Premonitory Earthquakes of 1914

In 1914 the Whitney Laboratory of Seismology in the basement of the observatory, equipped with seismographs, registered groups of earthquakes from time to time in seismic spasms, and reports came from Kau and from the ranchers on Mauna Kea of sudden strong earthquakes in the line of the axis of Mauna Loa's greatest length. In November, 1914, the registration of about sixty earthquakes in three weeks, the greatest number ever recorded in like time since the instruments were set up, greatly stimulated our attitude of expectancy. On November 25, 1914, about 12:45 p. m., the instruments showed prolonged earthquake movements of an unusual character, and at the same time cattle herders on Kapapala Ranch saw thick fume clouds puff up suddenly above the summit crater of Mauna Loa. After that the earthquake activity diminished.

Outbreak

The eruption became visible from the observatory as darkness approached, November 25, and photographs were made of Mauna Loa from the vicinity that night and on succeeding days and nights. These photographs show the column of glowing fumes, the glow diminishing rapidly after the first night.

Expeditions

November 26 I started for the summit by way of Kona, being unable to get men or horses for the Kapapala trail in Kau. I reached the summit area in a blinding sleet storm November 28 and was unable to do any work on account of the storm. Fortunately two young men from Kau, Messrs. Forrest and Palmer, pushed their way to the summit on the previous night (November 27) and furnished the observatory with a sketch map and notes. They saw ten or twelve fountains of lava along a north-south rift in the bottom of the crater, one of these in the southern part being between three hundred and four hundred feet high. December 2 Charles Ka was sent to the summit by the writer and saw only four fountains. Similar conditions were noted a few days later by Messrs. Baker and Bowdish, and on December 15 an expedition from the observatory reached the summit on the Kau side and saw only one large fountain about one hundred and fifty feet high and a few small ones. These were photographed, but conditions were too stormy to permit an extended stay on the summit.

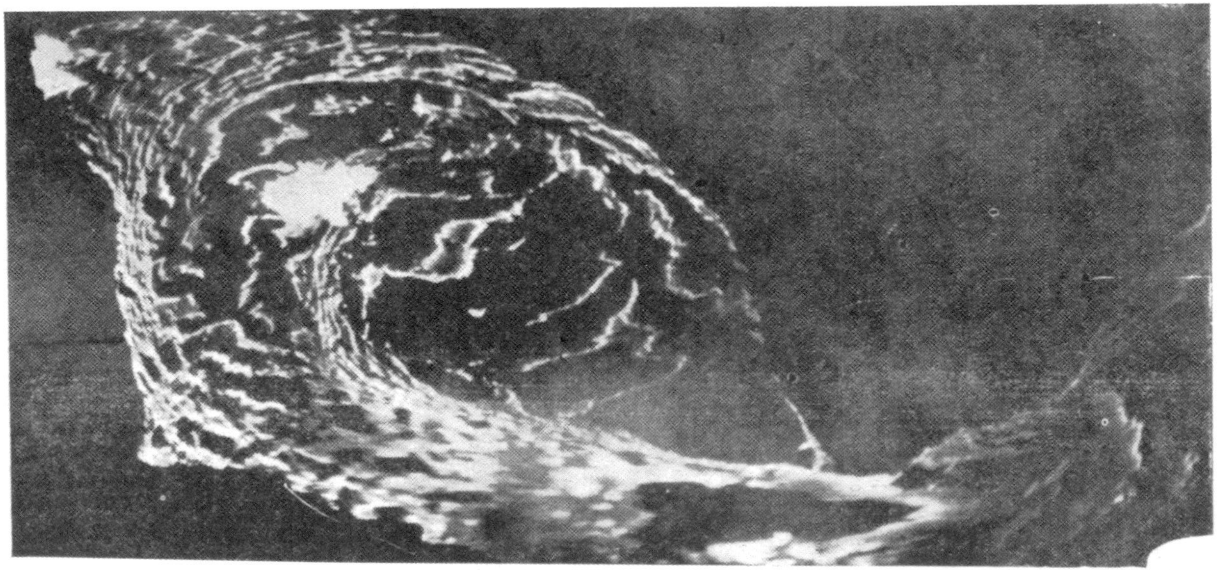

WHIRLPOOL IN SINKING LAVA LAKE OF HALEMAUMAU AT NIGHT, JANUARY, 1915, FROM THE SOUTH-EAST, LOOKING DOWN, SHOWING TORRENT RUSHING IN FROM THE EAST.

End of First Phase

Throughout December a watch was kept at the observatory on the fume column over Mauna Loa. It was occasionally photographed and it persisted until January 10, 1915, showing a line of bluish fume by day and a dull glow over the mountain at night. After that date it disappeared, the fountains probably subsiding and the lava solidifying.

The Study of the Coming Lava Flow

The observatory has a difficult and expensive task before it if it is to make adequate record of the spectacular closing stages of this eruptive period of Mauna Loa. We have learned a useful lesson of the futility of attempting a scientific siege of the crater fortress in winter time without houses built in advance to shelter men and animals. Such houses ought to be built of stone both at the summit and on the north flank of the mountain near the probable site of the expected flow. The escape of the liquid lava after the months of temporary repose which we are now living through will begin with more fountains at the summit. With a slight earthquake prelude to warn us, and a shelter camp, we ought to be able to have photographers ready to make pictures of the fountains at their highest. A probable time for this outbreak is about December, 1917, when the summit will be cold and snowy, but it may come sooner. It is certain that nothing can be done of scientific value at such a season without a summit hut and a shelter for horses.

The next stage will be a lava flow from a lower vent, probably several miles to the northeast of the summit crater. A secondary camp should be prepared in this neighborhood so that photographs and measurements may be made of the fountains which generally shoot to an enormous height when the flow breaks forth, and thereafter of the flow itself in following its course or courses down the slope.

The Money Needed

These camps and the survey of trails to them will cost at least three thousand dollars, and to maintain them and explore the field in their vicinity will cost three thousand dollars more. The work of survey and construction should be provided for at once without delay, but there is no possibility of the observatory doing this with its present means. It has no means to do anything beyond the recording of the activity of Kilauea and is barely able to do this owing to steadily decreasing income from subscriptions since 1912.

Governor Pinkham has gone on record as favoring legislative aid for this work, for the protection of the community and for the advance of science. Whether the money be furnished by the government, business corporations, an educational institution, wealthy individuals, Honolulu, Hilo, or the County of Hawaii, or by all of these in concert makes no difference in the result, but it makes a very great difference if no one will furnish it. I suppose there is no question in anybody's mind but that the work ought to be done in accordance with the appeal of the directors of the Hawaiian Volcano Research Association, approved by the governor and by the Honolulu Chamber of Commerce. It should not be a heavy burden to raise two thousand dollars per annum for three years—1915, 1916 and 1917—and to turn this over to the Hawaiian Volcano Research Association with instructions to devote the money to systematic preparation for a survey of the expected lava flow from Mauna Loa.

The most that can be expected from the writer as director of the observatory is a statement of why this should be done, what should be done and its probable cost. This he has attempted in this article. Mauna Loa has mobilized its forces and declared war. The problem of furnishing the sinews of war cannot be left to the scientific staff.

T. A. JAGGAR, Jr., Director.

WEEKLY BULLETINS.

TECHNOLOGY STATION, April 29, 1915.—In general the sinking of the lava of Kilauea has continued during the week ending April 28, 1915. The weather has been rainy and the pit smoky with little satisfactory seeing. Avalanching has been less than the previous week and there have been temporary risings of the lava surface and at times every appearance of stationary condition. So far as can be seen changes have been few. Large cracks fifteen or twenty yards back from the rim of Halemaumau southted a little warm sulphur vapor and deposited sulphurous alum, have gaped wider open in the last three weeks, with some downslipping of the blocks bounding the crevasses on the pit side.

April 22 at 11 a. m. measurement made the northeast cavern at the lava level 530 feet beneath the level of the southeast station on the rim of the pit. This is the lowest recorded level of the year to date.

The lake was almost divided in two by the peninsula built out into it from the southwest. The surfaces of the two halves were sluggish with eastward streaming. The lake was much crusted and the active part diminished in area by crusting, a wide bench being built out over the south cove, and crusts over the east and west ends. Old Faithful fountain was not to be seen. Bombardment of the banks was at the northeast cave and the northwest end. A rock fall was heard at 10:30 a. m., and numerous others occurred during the morning, mostly from the slopes north and south of the remnants of the north crag, which appeared high but small. The trenches left by the former southeast cove and east arm contained much rock debris but no lava pots. Fume clouds were dense and numerous.

From the position of points by survey the lake basin appears to have migrated westward during the slump of the last month; the west end of the lake is seventy-five feet west of where it was on April 1, 1915, largely, no doubt, by the caving away of the partition bench between the main lake and the northwest pond. The summit of the crag has also migrated west twenty-seven feet since April 1, this also probably by maximum caving on the east side.

Measurement April 23 at 3:30 p. m. made the northeast corner of the lake 522 feet below the southeast station. This rise of eight feet checked with the appearance of the pool, for the strait between the two halves had widened, the southwest peninsula was smaller, and there was dark skin over the western half of such as forms over a rising pool, and streaming east and south in the eastern half. Shore bombardment was in the south cove and the northeast cavern. Heavy falls of rock took place from the southwest bank of the lake and from the north crag. At 3:50 p. m. the skin was over the middle region, with streaming from it both east and west. A very small fountain sluggishly breaking in the strait at the edge of the skin may have represented Old Faithful. Stalactites hung in the northeast cavern. The northwest pond was active with westward streaming. A break has been forced in the surface of the bench between the two pools. Markers placed in cracks between the west and southwest stations have fallen in, showing marked gaping and displacement on the fissures. The offset shows subsidence of the rock on the pit side of the cracks. Mr. Hannon made these observations.

At 10:20 a. m. Saturday, April 24, from the south station the lake was seen to be streaming east and south, with two subordinate currents against places of bombardment northwest and southwest. From the southwest and west stations the northwest pond was found to be very active with streaming and bombardment against its west bank. Old Faithful was not seen. The lake level appeared to be about 540 feet down. Rocks were falling from the north crag. At 11:30 a. m. a small avalanche fell from the wall west of the northwest pond. At noon the lake was very quiet, probably during the usual noon rise.

Mr. Hannon recorded the following movement on the southwest sulphur crack, a fissure two to three feet across bounding a segment of the high southwest edge of Halemaumau. In the last three days this crack, by located markers, had opened over two feet and the segment towards the crater had gone down thirteen inches. New markers were placed in position. These movements are of great interest in conjunction with the pronounced tilting to the south and west going on at the observatory on the border of the greater crater, the suggestion being of a general slump of the floor of Ki'auea.

The next days were rainy, and on April 26 from 10 to 11 a. m. a little could be seen from the southwest station under very smoky and rainy conditions, showing the northwest pond streaming from west to east with a stalactite grotto on its north wall, and the west end of the main lake with eastward streaming. There was little noise, mostly the splash of the northwest pond. No avalanches were heard, there was no appearance of greater depth, and no measurement was possible.

Mr. H. O. Wood reports for the Whitney Laboratory of Seismology that during the week ending with April 28, 1915, only three earthquakes have been registered, and these exceptionally small local ones. Micro-seismic motion has been less vigorous than usual. Volcanic vibration has been somewhat more vigorous than in other recent intervals. Action of tilting has fluctuated only slightly during the week but its general amount has increased to the south and west.

T. A. JAGGAR, JR., Director.

TECHNOLOGY STATION, May 6.—The record of the past week is particularly interesting at Kilauea because it reveals a distinct rise in the lava of Halemaumau. At this season, the first week in May, and at this time when Mauna Loa is potentially active, the probabilities of the continuance of this rise in Kilauea to a higher level at the June solistice are nicely balanced.

If the sympathy by alternation with Mauna Loa is to be shown immediately, this rise should be slight, followed by strong sinking. If the lava of Halamaumau, however, is to sink away during 1915, as gradually as it rose in 1914, then it may be expected to show response to the solstice by some rising.

If, on the other hand, there is to be no immediate sympathetic sinking of Kilauea lava, there may come, during the present Mauna Loa lull, a strong Kilauea rise, with fluctuations for many months to come, culminating in high levels and even overflow, followed by collapse.

This is what happened after the short December outbreak of Mokuaweoweo in 1892; in a year and a half the Halemaumau lava rose over 400 feet, it built up or lifted the rim of the pit half that amount, and it formed a large lake, over a thousand feet long most of the time, recurrently overflowing. Then, on July 11, 1894, it sank two hundred feet in ten hours and thereafter subsided and disappeared.

The time of the sudden drop on that occasion was exactly midway between two premonitory eruptions of Mauna Loa forty months apart—the second one, in April, 1896, lasting fifteen days, whereas the 1892 outbreak had continued only three days. The final lava flow did not come until 1899, in July, thirty-eight months later, and endured less than a month.

The week ending April 21, 1915, showed strong sinking with avalanches. The week ending April 29 showed rather stationary condition, the lowest measured level of the year (April 22) being 530 feet below the rim. April 23 it was eight feet higher, or 522 feet down.

April 29, three-thirty p. m., the northwest pond was seen to be loudly boiling and spurting from many fountains. The main lake was slightly below its spatter bench, active with traveling fountains and eastward streaming. A small pot of fluid lava occasionally boiled up in the lower bench south of the lake, about ten by five feet in dimensions. The glow of Hala-

MAUNA LOA ERUPTION FROM THE NORTHWEST, NOVEMBER 27, 1914, THIRD NIGHT OF THE ERUPTION, CAMP GROUND AT PAU LEHUA.—ERUPTION HAD GREATLY DWINDLED.

maumau at night during these days was dull and smoky.

April 30, five p. m., south station, the northwest pond was seen to be streaming eastward with numerous fountains, and the main lake showed divided streaming from a middle area of skin, one current running northwestward and the other east and south; occasional active bombardment and spurting in the south cove.

At eleven a. m., May 1, from the south station, the lake was streaming very slowly eastward, with thick skins that folded up into ridges perhaps five feet in height as they passed the narrow medial part of the lake. The northwest pond was surging in a cave to the west. Old Faithful fountain still failed to appear. There was some blowing noise northwest.

The scar of a large slide appeared in the southwest part of the pit, notching both the 200-foot ledge of July, 1912, and the 1914 ledge, leaving a big chasm about seventy-five feet wide below. A few rocks were seen rolling down the south slide of talus. The 1914 ledge had caved in slightly at its east end. Further movement of a few inches was indicated by the markers in the southwest fissure. At three p. m. both pools were rumbling and boiling noisily.

May 2, eight to nine p. m. there were alternations of strong hissing and standing fountains (in five or six border pools kept open through a general crust) and quieter times with larger streaming pools in the crust and an appearance of rising. This blowing-pot activity was a totally new feature.

The noise was very loud of the rush of gas through the standing fountains, which were bright, continuous, spurting high, and building border benches with their splashing.

The northwest pond was quite visible from the southeast station, showing that the partition bench between it and the main lake had subsided somewhat and that the pond had risen. The partition, however, was still intact with its cracked, flat top. The pond was pounding and puffing on its west wall. The lakes do not appear low, probably something over 500 feet.

In the southwest tumble, two glowing and flaming filagree cones of lava-sputter appeared high above the lake level. There were others in the talus north of the lake and west of the north crag. The latter appeared small and peaked. The lake at times opened pools between the central crust and the shore at its east and west ends, with streaming in each, respectively eastward and westward. Old Faithful was not in action. The south talus fumed but did not glow or emit flames.

May 3rd.—In the morning conditions were the same—isolated blowing pools in the crust. Seeing was poor, fumes were dense and in the evening there was rain.

May 4, at three p. m., with southwest wind and drizzle, there were partial openings through the fume east and north. The lake was covered with skins, showed a few border fountains, eastward streaming, no marked blowing, and there was no change in level which was obvious. The noise was of splashing. Mr. Hannon's markers in the southwest rift have again fallen in within the past days, indicating a gaping of more than an inch.

Measurements on May 5, 1915, after three-fifteen p. m. gave the depth from the south station to the main lake as 511 feet; to the northwest pond, 508 feet; to the 1914 ledge south, 390 feet; length of lake, east-west, 470 feet; length west side of pond to east end 675 feet.

These measurements show a rise of about nineteen feet since April 22 and a slight increase in the length of the lake (ten feet) since April 21. The width at the narrows has greatly increased. There has been general subsidence of rock material, as the 1914 bench is ten feet lower than on April 21, and twenty-seven feet lower than when it was formed in January.

Appearances on May 5 indicated general rising. A fresh spatter ledge fifteen feet high encompassed the lake. The reversed westward streaming, so frequently observed during rising, was in progress at three-fifteen p. m., and at four-fifteen p. m. the streaming was divergent northwestward and southward.

Black polygonal skins covered the lake, broken by vigorous, rumbling shore bombardment, north, northwest,

PERRET'S COVE, STEAMING DRIBLET CONE ON NORTH FLOOR OF KILAUEA CRATER.

west, south, and east. Stalactitic caves and curtains suggested a temporary subsidence after the noon rise. The northwest pond was large, but active only in the caverns. A point protruded into the middle of the main lake from the southern bench, covered with fresh splashes of lava. Glowing places could be seen on the north bank where the high spatter bench was pierced by flaming pots.

The north crag appeared high and pointed and the southeast crags, with their radial fissuring, were still in position. There is yellow sulphur stain at the east end of the 1914 bench. At long intervals there is some breaking of the middle skin of the lake, which suggests a return of Old Faithful. Very strong bubble-fountaining is a new feature, and goes hand in hand with all the other evidences of a rise. At night the glow was bright and the pit largely free from fume.

On the morning of this day, Messrs. Haworth and Porter succeeded in lowering a moving picture camera to one of the lower ledges in a tripod cage, and operating it from above with a long wire belt to roll off the film, the lower wheel being connected to the camera by flexible shafting.

Mr. H. O. Wood reports that during the week ending with May 5 a distant earthquake, of world-shaking magnitude but probably of only moderately great energy in this class, was registered in the evening of April 30, from six-thirty-eight-fifty-five p. m. to about nine-ten p. m., by the seismographs in the Whitney Laboratory of Seismology. All the usual phases of the motion, and reflected phases of the waves of the second kind, were well registered. The distance of the origin is determined satisfactorily at about 3300 miles from this station. The waves of the third phase were larger in the north-south seismogram than in the east-west record. This suggests that the origin lies to the west or east—west in this instance.

Besides this, five local shocks have been registered. One of these, though very feeble, was of instrumentally moderate amplitude, the others were very small in all respects. Motion of volcanic vibration and micro-seismic motion have been registered as usual. The tilt to the west and south, so conspicuous of late, is still maintained, with usual fluctuations. Possibly it is a trifle greater than hitherto.

T. A. JAGGAR, JR., Director.

TECHNOLOGY STATION, May 13—

The past week has brought a lull in the rising activity inaugurated the week before and there has probably been some pronounced sinking in the last few days, but the measurements are as yet inadequate to prove it. Today veritical angles were read from the southeast station and by comparison with angles read in April on equivalent points those of today are higher; thus the lake, at the south point which protrudes into it, was 530 feet down on April 22, and the higher angle of today would make it 550 feet down, if the distance were about the same. It was impossible, owing to smoke, to secure intersection from a second station and so determine the distance. The rising continued during the first few days of the week with very pronounced development of outlying pots, especially to the east. Otherwise the changes in the condition of Halemaumau have been slight.

Between three and four p. m. May 6, 1915, the main lava lake was vigorously boiling under the bank south, west, northwest, and east, with continuous fountains which spattered and rumbled, and the surface streaming was eastward and into the south cove. The lake was level with the lower bench and the western half was crusted over. At three p. m. the bombardment at the south cove broke away a part of the bank; nine fountains were spurting at once, the jets at the west end rising at least forty feet. At three-thirty p. m. the lake crusted over leaving only five boiling spots. At four p. m. it was evident from the overflow of the lower bench that rising was in progress. The northwest pond was actively fountaining and streaming eastward and a pot was boiling and spurting lava in the northeast trench.

Friday, May 7, appears to have been about the culmination of this rising spell. At three p. m. the northwest pond appeared about twenty feet higher than on the previous day and unusually long, fountaining with great activity; the main lake was fountaining with energy around the border, streaming eastward, puffing and overflowing into the northeast pot. The noise was unusually loud and a rise of fully twenty feet appeared to have taken place in the course of two hours.

May 8, at three p. m., the lake was five feet below the third or lower bench (third, counting the 1914 bench as number one), streaming eastward without fountains and the northwest pond was very still. At three-twenty there was one fountaining spot at the east end of the lake and at four p.m. there was some rising and eastward streaming. The point protruding into the middle of the lake from the south appeared to have grown, reducing the width of the lake, and the lower bench appeared covered with new lava all around the lake.

May 9 at eight p. m. the lake was slowly streaming eastward with bombardment against the south bank, some inrush into a northeast grotto, and stalactities hanging along the northwest bank. Traveling fountains formed and moved southeast. Old Faithful has resumed its fountaining, at rather irregular intervals. There was some activity in the northwest pond. Evidence of the recent rise appeared in the presence of two flaming chimneys in the east trench, two filagree spatter heaps flaming in the east cove, and some glow to the southwest. The level of the lava showed no conspicuous change.

From May 10 to 12 there was no marked change. May 13 accurate measurement was prevented by the fumes, but the lake appeared as low as at any time this year, which would make it 530 feet below the rim at least. The fumes were sharp. The lake was narrower in the middle, the lower bench broad and apparently about fifteen feet above the lake. The northwest pond was small and crusted with cavernous overhang on the west side. The southwest glow-cone had collapsed and was replaced by a smoking circular pot. The southeast crag had partly collapsed to a talus slope on its southeast side. Two boiling pots were bubbling in the east arm trench. Old Faithful had resumed its outbreaks at intervals of from twenty to ninety seconds and there were bubble fountains in the northeast part of the lake. The recently formed bench was built high against the north crag, and the latter appeared low and crumbly. The lengthwise cracks in the bench between the two pools were wider, implying that that bench is crumbling. A high level glowing crack could be seen above the northwest pond.

H. O. Wood reports that during the week ending with May 12 five earthquakes have been registered at the Whitney Laboratory of Seismology, one of these was the chief phase only of a feeble teleseism. None of the other characteristics of this shock are determinate. The four remaining shocks were weak local earthquakes of the usual kind.

Microseismic registration has been as usual without noteworthy crises. Volcanic vibration has been registered more strongly than in recent weeks, and the stronger motion has been of much more continuous character. The tilt to the south and west prevailing so strongly of late has been subject to the usual fluctuations, but its amount has definitely decreased during the latter part of the week.

Last week at the observatory has been notable on account of the visit of the congressional party on May 9. At the request of Mr. Thurston, the director addressed them on that afternoon at the Volcano House on the subject of the scientific study of volcanoes. On May 11 an exhibit of more than 125 photographs mounted on a post in hinged frames was opened to inspection in the Hilo library. This is the exhibit of the observatory to be sent to the Panama exposition in San Francisco, and shows the changes in the activities of the volcanoes for thirty years past, their characteristic landscape forms and formations, and some maps, diagrams, and photographs illustrating the work of the Hawaiian Volcano Research Association. The exhibit will be displayed in the Library of Hawaii, in Honolulu, beginning May 18 for a few days.

T. A. JAGGAR, JR., Director.

TECHNOLOGY STATION, Kilauea, May 20.—There has been but little change in Halemaumau during the past week. The usual irregular fluctuations in the height of stand have been observed, but the general depth level appears to have undergone no noticeable change. No depth measures have been secured during the week.

The action of streaming with the tearing, crumpling and engulfment of thin crusts or skins, broken through by bubbling fountains of all sizes, has continued as usual. Traveling fountains have been noted more frequently and persistently than commonly.

On Friday morning, May 14, the following observations were noted: The scene from the south and southeast was like that of the previous day. Bubble fountains were seen traveling to the east and south. The magma stood from eight to ten feet below the surrounding platform. In the northwest pond the action was sluggish. This pool was crusted over, showing glow only along the edges. "Old Faithful" was regularly in action, bursting at intervals of from 20 to 40 seconds.

East from it extended a line of bubble-fountains and traveling fountains, all situated in the eastern part of the lake. In the west part only streaming skins were seen—with a heavy spatter bombardment at the west side of the point. The tip of the point had broken off since the previous day. The lake appeared wider and higher, with symptoms of rising. Glowing spots were seen in the east arm, at a point west of the talus west of the crag, and at the south end of the north-west pond. About the latter deposits of sulphur were seen. The south fumarole in the talus exhibited only very slight activity. At the top of the south talus there were steaming places around which "wet dirt" areas were seen and a patch of green, wet sulphur was seen at the fumarole at the east end of the 1914 bench. At the southwest a big cavity was seen in the 1914 bench and in the 200-foot bench.

On Sunday, May 16, in early afternoon there were many large fountains in the lake, some traveling toward the east concurrently with the tendency to streaming. "Old Faithful" was in action as usual. The noise of eruption was unusually loud. There was unusual surface action in the smaller pool. The magma stood about ten feet below the surrounding third platform. Blue fumes were rising copiously from the south fumarole directly beneath the 1912 shelf at the south station.

On Monday afternoon, May 17, the action in the northwest pool was very sluggish, barely exhibiting glow. The chief lake was in vigorous action with large bubble fountains, some traveling, with the streaming tending toward the east. The noise of eruption was loud. The magma had fallen to about twenty-five feet below the third platform, but had again begun to rise.

On Tuesday afternoon, May 18, the magma was seen to be a little more than fifteen feet below the adjacent platform, but a relatively rapid rising tendency was observed in progress throughout the interval of watching. The action was as described for the previous days—with the tendency to streaming and fountain-travel toward the southeast.

On Wednesday afternoon, May 19, the lake was seen from the south station to be in vigorous action at a depth of about fifteen feet below the third platform. The direction of streaming, and of fountain travel, had changed to the southeast. Besides the bursting of large bubble-fountains, there were many baby fountains playing all over the surface of the pool.

An in-fall of a large bit of the spatter bench at the southwest was followed, as is often the case, by a marked action of boiling over the whole surface of the lake. Owing to swirling fumes no view of the northwest pool was obtained.

Only four very small local earthquakes have been recorded during the past week in the Whitney Laboratory of Seismology.

The tilt to the south and west, though still continuing very much in excess of the value in late winter, has decreased further in the course of its fluctuations during the week past.

There is nothing which requires mention concerning the registration of volcanic vibrations or of microscopic action.

H. O. WOOD,
Associate.

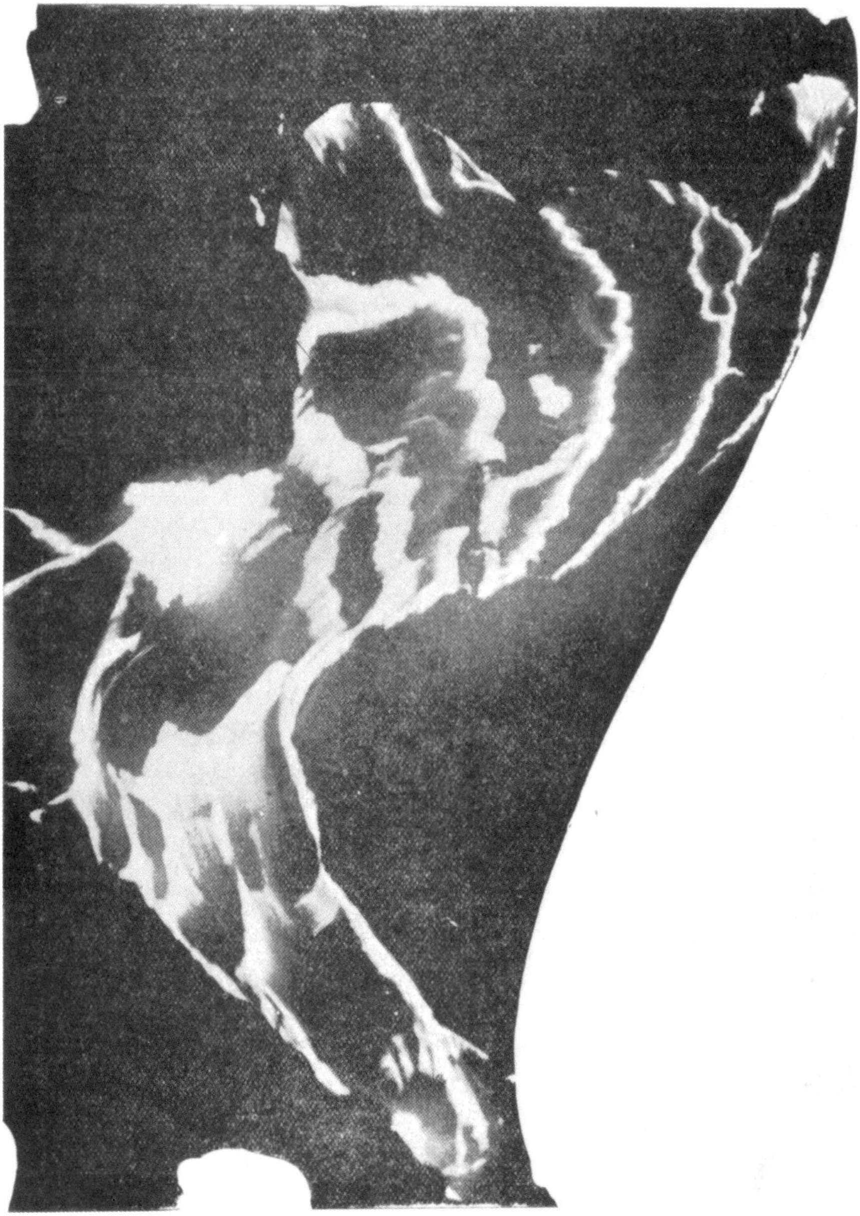

LAVA LAKE OF HALEMAUMAU AT NIGHT, DECEMBER, 1914, FROM THE SOUTHEAST, LOOKING DOWN.

TECHNOLOGY STATION, May 27. —For the week ended May 26, 1915, the lava pit of Kilauea Volcano has shown few significant changes. The level of the lakes remains something more than five hundred feet and evidence from caving of the banks and avalanches seems to indicate slow subsidence. The south cove has increased in size through collapse of the lower bench. Old Faithful fountain has become re-established in its customary place.

May 20, at three-thirty p. m., it was evident that about a half of the lower bench in its eastern part had fallen in. The lake appeared about twelve feet below the bench,, streaming northeastward with many fountains, large and small. By reason of the collapse, the lake appeared wider. At the east end a tunnel from the lava level appeared to have penetrated beneath the old bench or floor, and a small cone was glowing above. At the southwest the pit in the second bench had increased in size and was emitting thick blue fumes. In the course of an hour the lake rose to within three feet of the level of the lower bench.

Lake Shaped Like "U"

Friday, May 21, at three p. m., seen from the southeast station, the lake was active and about ten feet below the bench. Streaming was to the southeast, with traveling fountains and the Old Faithful fountain boiled up from time to time in the middle region west of the south point. Thick fumes rose to the southeast. The lake was now shaped like a wide "U," with a peninsula protruding from the southwest side to give it the "U" shape, and the south cove was now so widened as to present two angular corners. The north crag had become a knife-edge ridge. The small northwest pool was still in action with fountains around the border and in the middle.

May 22, at four p. m., conditions were the same, with the lake about five feet below the bench and great activity in the northwest pond.

May 24, at three p. m., seen from the north, the northwest pond appeared high and active with westward streaming and bubble fountains. At three-thirty p. m. the main lake appeared ten feet below the bench, active principally along the shore with few central fountains. The streaming was eastward. A small specially active pool in the crust formed in the northeast part of the lake. At three-forty-five p. m. an avalanche took place from the region of the north crag. There was evidence in the border fissure southwest of Halemaumau of further sinking of the outer block and gaping of the crack.

Large Grotto Develops

May 25, at six-thirty p. m., as seen from the south station, the lake was active, streaming from west to east but crusted over its west end. A large grotto with hanging stalactites could be seen on the west side of the northwest pond; bombardment was going on in the main la keeast and south. Old Faithful was in action, glowing cones could be seen in the east and southeast trenches high above the lake, and the southwest pit showed glow within. Heavy masses of white smoke rose from below the second bench southwest; the lower bench at the peninsula appeared tipped back to the southward and raised in a peak at the point over the lake, the point thus developing into a crag which would become an island if the lake should rise. The second bench south and southeast still retains its craggy character and deep clefts.

Four Local Earthquakes

H. O. Wood reports that during the week ending with May 26 four local earthquakes have been registered at the Whitney Laboratory of Seismology. Three of these were very small—of the usual imperceptible sort. The fourth was a weak, felt shock, perceived by several at the Volcano House as a s'ow swaving movement.

The tilting has fluctuated more than usual during the past week but there is no significant change in it as a whole.

The small micro-seismic waves and those designated as volcanic vibrations have been somewhat stronger than usual, but not to a marked degree.

T. A. JAGGAR, JR., Director.

WEEKLY BULLETIN
OF THE
Hawaiian Volcano Observatory

Vol. III. HONOLULU, HAWAII, MAY, 1915. No. 5

A CONSIDERATION OF RECENT EARTHQUAKES LOCAL TO HAWAII, AND OF THE SEISMOLOGICAL PROBLEM THEY INDICATE.

By Harry O. Wood.

Slight earthquakes, the great majority of which can be detected only by seismographic means, occur very frequently on the Island of Hawaii; while moderate perceptible shocks occur occasionally, stronger shocks more rarely, and at long, uncertain intervals come shocks of great power. This, therefore, is a province of moderately high seismicity.

Hawaii is the largest and the youngest, in certain respects at any rate, of the islands of the Hawaiian Group. It stands the southeasternmost of these. On it is the great, recurrently active volcano, Mauna Loa,—and Kilauea as well, universally known on account of its remarkably continuous activity. By some the latter is regarded as a subordinate vent on the flank of Mauna Loa, but others, probably the majority, consider it a separate and generally independent volcano. Besides these, here are situated the volcanic mountains, Hualalai, active in 1801; Mauna Kea, of very recent aspect geologically but extinct in the sense that there is no record or tradition of activity; and Kohala, a deeply eroded volcanic mass, extinct presumably in the strictest sense.

As earthquakes always attend the more violent phases of volcanic activity, it is natural that action in these volcanoes should be regarded generally as the cause of shocks here on Hawaii, as in the case of volcanic neighborhoods elsewhere. All the more does such opinion prevail since there is no thorough understanding of the mechanism of volcanic action *in extenso,* and the more widely current speculations in regard to it are favorable to such a view.

Early in August, 1912, shortly after the Hawaiian Volcano Observatory began operations, a registering seismometer was set at work here in the Whitney Laboratory of Seismology. In the spring of 1913 this equipment was improved by the addition of two seismometers of later type. Repairs, alterations and improvements have necessitated three or four brief interruptions of registration. Otherwise registration has been conducted continuously to the time of writing (May 14, 1915). The apparatus at this Observatory comprises the only registering seismographs on Hawaii. There is a Milne Seismograph, a very sensitive type, maintained in operation at the magnetic Station of the U. S. C. & G. S. at Ewa, on the Island of Oahu.

During less than two years and a half, taking account of the times of interruption, some 604 local earthquakes have been registered here. By careful and close measurement of the time-duration of the fore-phases, and the employment of Zeissig's table for Δ, it has been possible to determine, subject to the minute errors involved in the method, the origin-distances from the seismometer station for 441 of these shocks. In the case of the remaining 163 shocks, whose origin-distances could not be so determined, the indefiniteness in almost every instance has been due to too feeble or too imperfect registration of the early motion; but there is no suggestion in any of their characteristics that these shocks differ from those more satisfactorily registered in being, as a class, either of nearer or of farther

WEEKLY BULLETIN
of the
Hawaiian Volcano Observatory

Published Monthly at Honolulu, Hawaii, by the Hawaiian Volcano Research Association

Editor..............Howard M. Ballou
Professor of Physics, College of Hawaii

Entered as second-class matter January 20, 1914, at the post-office at Honolulu, Hawaii, under the Act of August 24, 1912.

origin than the average. The following discussion, however, is based necessarily on the 441 shocks whose origin-distances could be determined.

Upon tabulating and classifying the distances of these it develops that numerous shocks have originated near to each and every unit distance between 5 kilometers and 50, with sixteen other shocks scattered along at irregular distances up to 500 kilometers. Summarizing, the shocks have been spaced out as shown in Table 1, following.

If only the stronger shocks are counted, disregarding all whose intensity did not rise above grade I of the Cancani scale, we obtain numbers and percentages which also appear in Table I. The whole number of such shocks is 227.

TABLE I.

Δ Km	441 Shocks No.	441 Shocks Per Cent	227 Stronger Shocks No.	227 Stronger Shocks Per Cent
0—10	15	3.3+	9	3.9+
10—15	25	5.5+	20	8.7+
15—20	51	11.3+	39	17.0—
20—25	150	33.1+	88	38.3±
25—30	34	7.5+	10	4.4—
30—35	82	18.3+	41	17.9
35—40	27	6.0—	10	4.4—
40—45	26	5.8—	8	3.4±
45—50	25	5.6±	1	0. ±
50 and over	16	3.6±	4	1.7
	451	100.0±	230	100.1±
Deduct, counted, twice	10	Basis of 451 shocks	3	Basis of 230 shocks
Totals	441		227	
15—25	201	44.7	127	55.3
30—40	109	34.2	51	22.2

In considering this distance distribution it is important to take note that the seismometer station is situated on the verge of the main crater of Kilauea, only about 3.5 kilometers northeast from Halemaumau, the inner pit-crater in which the continuous action for which Kilauea is famous has its theatre. Also bring to mind the fact that volcanic earthquakes are almost, if not quite, universally *considered* to spring from very shallow origins, usually from one to five kilometers in depth, and seldom if ever in excess of ten kilometers. Also note that the crater of Mokuaweoweo, on the summit of Mauna Loa, is distant almost exactly 35 kilometers from the seismometer cellar, and at a height in excess of 2900 meters above it. Moreover the rift extending northeast from it approaches the station more closely still, passing at no greater distance than 20 kilometers, possibly less yet.

Therefore, from this work of distance measurement and its statistical examination two noteworthy facts stand out:

1. Few shocks, or none at all, have originated in or very near to the recognized volcanic axis of Kilauea, Halemaumau;

2. There has been a very marked tendency for shock origins to cluster at distances between 20 and 25 kilometers from the station, and again, to a less extent, at distances between 30 and 35 kilometers.

Working seismologists will at once discern that these distances correspond to phase difference time-intervals of 2 to 2.5 seconds and of 3 to 3.5 seconds respectively, where the distances are determined by the Zeissig Δ—table. Wherefore they may suspect the clustering here indicated to be due to systematic error dependent upon the personal equation in measuring these intervals. So far as possible this has been guarded against by measuring the intervals in hundredths of inches and computing the second fractions with the slide-rule. Moreover, to an even greater extent, shock origins have tended to cluster at distances between 16 and 25 kilometers for the larger group, and between 30 and 40 kilometers for the second group—but in taking these distance intervals the probability of systematic error is greatly reduced. There is no doubt that the clustering is real and approximately of the values determined.

The first of these generalizations indicates clearly that the great majority of these shocks are not associated with explosive outbursts or sudden expansions in the magma conduit—a conclusion a priori deducible from the quiet character of the action in Halemaumau. Further, owing to the small values of origin-distance for these shocks, they cannot probably be associated with any such action deep in the magma chamber (if such action can occur), unless its superior envelope is at small depth. *Our want of knowledge in regard to this raises one of the chief volcanological problems* here. However, shocks of perceptible magnitude attract notice much more frequently low on the flanks of Kilauea than high on its dome—whence, in view of all this, we consider that these shocks are probably not of the same genetic nature as those, typifying volcanic earthquakes, which accompany violent volcanic eruptions. For these latter usually originate directly beneath the craters and often rend the caldera walls asunder.

This suggestion, based primarily upon this consideration of seismometric data, raises abruptly the question—are these shocks of volcanic causation in the ordinary meaning of the terms? We revert to this below.

The second generalization raises the query—is this tendency to clustering within certain distance-ranges accidental, or does it point to a specialized arrangement of the places of origin; and in the latter, more likely event, is there a haphazard arrangement within the discrete, peripheral zones, or within suitably distanced group-localities, or are the orgins distributed along one or more linear courses, such as zones of faulting, which traverse the distance zones in such a manner as to induce the observed clustering?

Unfortunately it has rarely been possible here to determine seismometrically the direction of an origin from the station, and in only a few instances have other clues to the direction been definite; so, of course, definite answers cannot be given directly to the alternative terms of the above query.

But in passing it may be pointed out that accidental clustering to the extent found is logically unlikely, as is also the relatively artificial alternative of clustering by haphazard placement in discrete peripheral zones. Grouping in restricted localities would be a reasonable arrangement, but the a priori more conspicuously likely localities, the calderas and their purlieus, are not within the distance ranges characterized by the most conspicuous clustering. This is especially true of Kilauea. There is thus a certain presumption in favor of the linear, or fault-zone, distribution which is greatly strengthened by geological considerations—whatever mechanism of causation is appealed to—as we shall see.

As mentioned above, with the overwhelming majority of the shocks thus far measured no estimate, even, could be made as to origin-direction, aside from a priori reasoning. On the human side this has been due to the sensory imperceptibility of most of the shocks, and where felt shocks are in question, to a sparse and practically linear distribution of the neighboring population. On the side of seismometry the failure is due to (a) feeble initial seismic agitation, (b) the employment of mechanical registration on sooted paper in a chamber ranging in temperature from 75 to 85 degrees F. in which the air remains near to saturation, with the inevitable undesirable amount of friction at the writing point, and (c) to a rate of motion of the registering cylinder not rapid enough to yield a record sufficiently "open" to differentiate distinctly the early vibrations when these are very rapid and very small—all these conditions combining to render doubtful the directions of initial excursions, or those of any surely identifiable phase. Also there is available no vertical motion seismometer so that the determination of azimuth would be ambiguous in any event.

Obviously, with the origin-distances well enough determinted for a large number of shocks, but with the origin-directions unknown, not even indicated, except in a very few instances, it is not possible to locate the places of origin in any absolute or precise way. Nevertheless it will be interesting and, in large measure, profitable to examine their distance-distribution in the light of our knowledge of the dynamical-structural geology of the island, especially in view of the fact that certain strong earthquakes which have occurred here exhibit many of the characteristics of tectonic shocks—as the writer has recently pointed out.*

Such a correlation requires a brief outline of the significant geological features of Hawaii.

GEOLOGICAL FEATURES OF HAWAII.

Hawaii is an island of markedly triangular shape with apices at the north, east and south.

Its slightly arcuate boundary from the E. point to the S. point is quite surely controlled by a fault-system; one of the escarpments, standing inland from the present strand from two to five kilometers, runs parallel to this leg of the triangle for more than half its length. To the writer there seems little doubt that in 1868 extensive vertical readjustments took place along submarine segments of this zone. Therefore there is a strong presumption that small shocks originate here at intervals. However, none of the lot under consideration are surely identified with it. No exact indication of the direction or of the width of this zone can be placed on the map, merely a generalized line to suggest its position and course. (See Map, Plate I.) It seems probable that the perpendicular distance of this line from the Observatory should be in the neighborhood of 30 kilometers, but that branching parts of the zone must pass considerably nearer.

A similar off-shore fault-zone is strongly suspected along the coast from the E. point to the N. point, owing to the general straight line course of the coast, and to the physiographic peculiarities of the Kohala block, a deeply eroded mountain mass which meets the sea on the northeast in a very high, nearly vertical cliff, recessed a little from the adjoining segments of the shore, and remarkably rectilinear throughout its length of nearly 20 kilometers. Of course, in this case also, the width and exact course of the zone as a whole—if indeed it actually exists—can be indicated by a general line only. Its perpendicular distance from the station at Kilauea is at least 45 kilometers and, in consequence, it is sure that not many of the shocks considered here have emanated from it, if, indeed, any of them have done so.

Of still less importance to the present study, but of equal geological importance with these, is the north-south off-shore fault zone along the west coast of Hawaii. This is a line suspected from the physiography and to a considerable extent confirmed by the eruptions of 1801 and 1877, the later submarine, as well as by the occurrence of certain earthquakes. The perpendicular distance of this zone from Kilauea must be more than 70 kilometers, so that few or none of the shocks here considered can be associated with it.

Of the greatest importance to this study is the great crust-fracture, or fault, whose course is in part unequivocally indicated by the innumerable open fissures leading to the southwest, and curving to the south, from the caldera of Kilauea. This appears to be a broad fault zone limited on the west by a low, broken, east-facing escarpment, whose segments are arranged *en echelon*, masked in places by overflow of lava from Mauna Loa. In the neighborhood of Kilauea the zone is confused with numerous subordinate fissures radial to, and peripheral about, the caldera. Northeast from the crater the country is a dense, practically unexplored jungle; but for a considerable distance the feature may be followed with the eye as a broad, gentle depression; and a similar feature in its projected course, south of Hilo village, appears to indicate its continuance to the sea. Whatever may be thought as to the causation of the shocks the fact that the large number here considered exhibit a definite tendency to cluster within certain distance-ranges leads the writer to the judgment that many of these, possibly a majority of them, have origin-

* On the Earthquakes of 1868 in Hawaii, by H. O. Wood, Bull. Seis. Soc. Am., IV, 4, Dec., 1914.

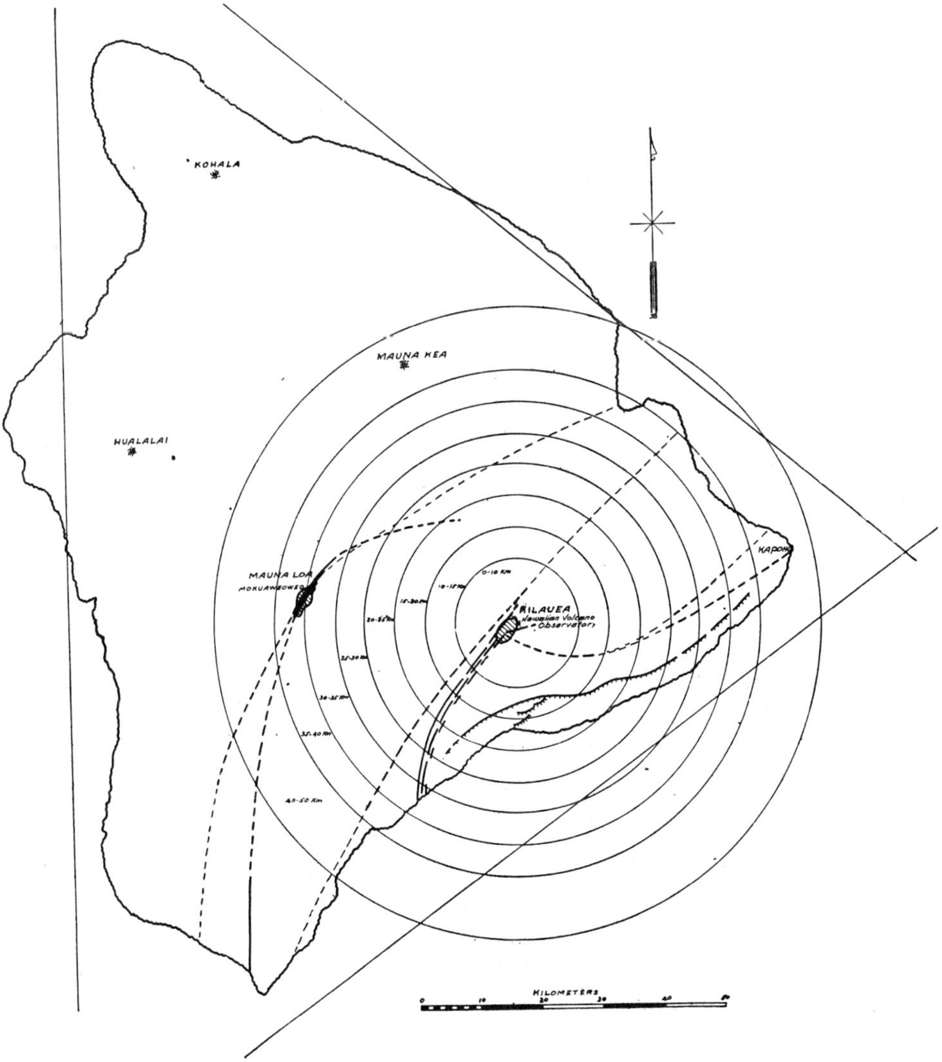
KOHALA
MAUNA KEA
HUALALAI
MAUNA LOA
MOKUAWEOWEO
KILAUEA
Hawaiian Volcano Observatory
KAPOHO
0-10 Km
10-15 Km
15-20 Km
25-30 Km
35-40 Km
40-50 Km
KILOMETERS
0
10
20
30
40

PLATE I.

ated along this conspicuous zone of weakness in the dome of the volcano. The fact that few of them have originated near to the caldera will be discussed a little later.

A feature, probably of subordinate importance but nevertheless not negligible, is the belt of fissures leading from Halemaumau to the E.N.E. through the subordinate crater, Kilauea-iki. There is no evidence, nor is there suggestion in the landscape, that this radial fissure system extends far. Nevertheless in less than a century it has been rejuvenated three times—in 1832, in 1868 and in 1877. On each occasion molten lava was ejected from the freshly opened fissures. There were no great, nor significantly strong earthquakes attendant upon the 1832 or the 1877 events; and the chief origin of the 1868 shock was certainly not along this line. Hence the writer is disposed to think of this as a subordinate feature only. No part of its known or suspected course extends beyond 10 kilometers from the Observatory and therefore it has no prominent role in this study.

Eastward from Kilauea along a line which exhibits a considerable curve convex to the south are subordinate craters which near the summit are chiefly pits but near the sea crateriform cones. Deep fissures and sunken areas help to mark the course of this line. From it the flow of 1840 burst out, while the molten fluid was ejected from several places along its course higher up the mountain than the chief source. There is strong indication that certain earthquakes have originated upon it but there is no strict proof of this. It certainly is worthy of consideration as a shock cluster line.

Last, and surely as important geologically as is the main fault zone through Kilauea, though possibly of slightly less importance in the present correlation, is the great crust-fracture through Mokuaweoweo and, almost certainly, through the whole dome of Mauna Loa. This broad belt of deep fissures is known to traverse Mokuaweoweo and to lead from its ends down the slopes to the northeast, and to the south-southwest, for long distances. Also from the coast line a little to the west of the south point of the island a great, deep system of fissures extends along the base of a west-facing escarpment up towards the summit. On this, some sixteen kilometers from the shore, is the source of the 1868 flow. But the fissure system continues beyond this up the mountain for an unexplored distance. There is little doubt that it is continuous with the summit system. It is probably a broad zone, for the sources of the 1887 and 1907 flows, also from fissures, lie a little to the west of the probable continuation of the obvious, open cracks of 1868.

The belt of fissures, and along it the sources of outbreak of numerous historical flows, continues certainly for many kilometers to the northeast from Mokuaweoweo, and in all probability on to the coast and beyond, though its lower course is concealed and modified by recent flows and thick jungle growth.

In passing it may be said that there is strict proof, in the sidelong offsets which resulted in 1868, that the chief fissure systems of both Kilauea and Mauna Loa are geological faults, as well as eruption fissures.

In either case we have good reason for thinking of these as earthquake cluster lines.

Having determined the number and the percentage number of shocks for succeeding distance-ranges of 5 kilometers, it should be instructive to determine and correlate with them the segment lengths and their percentages of these fault lines, as cut off by the limiting surves of each 5-kilometer zone. At best this can be done only doubtfully for we do not know the breadth limits nor the exact courses of these faults—and this is especially true for the case of the submarine zone along the southeast coast of the island.

However, before undertaking any critical comparison between shock-numbers or shock-percentages and fault-segment-lengths or length-percentages for the different zones, it must be pointed out and *emphasized* that (1) very few shocks have been registered from a distance greater than 50 kilometers, and (2) that fewer and fewer of the feebler shocks would be determinably registered at the station as more and more remote origin zones are dealt with. These things are true because at greater distances greater initial energy would be required to produce given effects at the station; and, *for such instruments as are employed here for registering shocks of the category now under consideration a distance of about 50 kilometers appears to be the limit of effective registration.* This is indicated by the statistics of the present study, for there certainly is no reason, a priori, to suppose that shocks do not originate frequently at near-distances greater than 50 kilometers. Also such a conclusion was reached by the writer, long before these facts were known to him, from studies of the occurrence of shocks in Central California up to the summer of 1912, based on the performance there of instruments of the same type as are here employed. This judgment is further strengthened by the following incident:

Just before midnight of the night of March 27-28, 1915, a shock was felt on the west side of Hawaii strong enough to waken all sleepers and to disturb domestic animals. A careful observation indicated that the earth motion was directed along a line a trifle north of east to south of west. This determination was independent of structural indications. The perceptible shaking lasted six seconds, or more. The distance from the place of observation to the station at Kilauea was, in direct line, only about 68 to 70 kilometers. How much farther or nearer the origin of the shock lay can not be known, for this shock was not registered at Kilauea. And there is much reason for thinking that this is not an unique incident.

It is pertinent also to direct attention to the geometrical fact that when lines are segmented by zones determined by equally spaced concentric curves at or near to tangency with an inner limiting arc, the segment-length will be proportionately greater in the case of a zone of large radius than in the case of a zone of small radius. This obviously may affect the correlation of the following table, Table II, with that of the occurrence of shocks.

TABLE II.

Distance Ranges	Kilauea—Main Rift	Kilauea—Kapoho Rift	Kilauea-Kilauea-Iki Rift	South-Coast Fault Zone	Mauna Loa Main Rift N-E Segment	Mauna Loa Main Rift S-W Segment	Total Segment Lengths	Segment Length Percentages	Excluding S Coast Fault Zone	
									Total Segment Lengths	Segment Length Percentages
Km	Km	Km	Km	Km	Km	Km	Km	%	Km	%
0—10	20	11	5±	.....	.....	....	36±	9.5+	36±	12.—
10—15	11±	6—	....	.....	.....	....	17±	4.5+	17±	6.—
15—20	11±	6.5±	....	.....	3.5±	.....	21±	5.6+	21±	7.—
20—25	11±	6.5±	....	..	19.5±	.....	37±	9.8±	37±	13.—
25—30	11±	6.5±	....	17±	19.5±	.....	54±	14.4±	37±	13.—
30—35	11±	6.5±	....	23±	18.5±	.....	59±	15.7—	36±	12.+
35—40	11±	6.5±	....	15.5±	7±	13.5±	53.5±	14.3+	38±	13.+
40—50	21+	11+	....	26.5±	12±	18.5±	99±	26.4±	625±	22.—
Totals	107±	55.5±	5±	82±	80±	32±	375.5±	100.2±	284.5±	100.±

The diagram, Plate II, exhibits clearly and graphically whatever discernible relationships exist between shock-occurrence percentages and fault segment-length percentages.

Owing to the doubtfulness of the procedure no emphasis can be placed upon conclusions suggested by such a correlation as this. However, taking account of the foregoing qualifications, to the writer the correlation strengthens statistically the view suggested by geological considerations—that the tendency of these shocks to cluster at certain distances is very likely due to the location of their origins upon some or all of the faults here considered. Examination of the Map, Plate I, will show how and at what distance the various faults enter and traverse the distance-range zones. Attention is particularly invited to their situation within the 15-25 kilometer and the 30-40 kilometer distance zones—especially in regard to the two chief rifts.

Most of the shocks studied here which were perceived by the senses were felt all along the way between the villages of Hilo and Waiohinu—a N.E.—S.W. line of approximately 100 kilometers length. Some of these also have been felt in Kailua, about 95 kilometers from Hilo and from 75 to 80 kilometers from Waiohinu. As none of these shocks were really strong, only one being popularly considered so, at any of the places of report, moderately deep origins are indicated—and this suggests, in view of the prevailing ideas and definitions, that they are shocks of non-volcanic character.

Speaking of felt shocks, in several instances when the direction of origin could be estimated with fair assurance the origin has been indicated as lying to the N.E. or S.W. from Kilauea. In several other instances an origin to the N. or N.W. has been indicated. In the case of shocks generated within the 50-kilometer distance no other directions have been indicated with any emphasis. But of course it is true that there has been no reliable indication at all in most instances.

This is an appropriate point for mere reference to the registration of volcanic vibrations briefly described and defined in an earlier paper.* The seismometers here register continuously, strictly without cessation, (and also without the abrupt changes in period and amplitude which characterize phase beginnings in the spasmodic records of earthquakes), vibrations of very short period of the order of 0.5 second, and of very variable amplitude which is always very small indeed, of the order of 1 to 5 microns, possibly 10 microns at the greatest maxima. It is a general truth that these vibrations are more pronounced when there is unusual surface motion in Halemaumau; and, now, in several instances, exceptional groups or ''storms'' of these waves have been directly correlated with great surface turbulence in Halemaumau, produced by the in-slumping of large segments of the thickly crusted pit floor. There is little doubt, if any, that these continuous vibrations originate in the action in the magma—that these are the *truly volcanic earthquake* disturbances here at Kilauea in its latter-day phases of action. Even when these vibrations attain an intensity, or acceleration, as great as that of the small local shocks, seismographically they still differ in all essential points from the waves of spasmodic shocks. For despite their small dimensions they wax and wane gradually and exhibit distinctly a sinusoidal character. Sharp changes are almost never seen.

Thus the writer has been led gradually by various independent circumstances to think of the local earthquakes registered here as generated by rock-slip, occurring at crises in elastic crust-strain, at various loci distributed along the known faults,—in most instances somewhat remote from the caldera margins.

So it now should be pointed out that the calderas, particularly that of Kilauea, are encompassed by many, deep, peripheral fissures distributed outwards over a wide zone so that they almost completely isolate these great pits from the more continuously solid, basalt dome-structures lower down the mountains. Also many comparatively short radial cracks are seen. These facts, together with the plausible idea that this completely broken mosaic may repose upon, and in a sense may be locally lubricated by, a viscous, molten fluid, make it easy to understand that excessive elastic strain in the crust ought not to accumulate in the close vicinity of the calderas. It seems to the writer

* The Hawaiian Volcano Observatory, by H. O. Wood, Bull. Eeis. Soc. Am., Vol. III, 1, March, 1913, pp. 17-18.

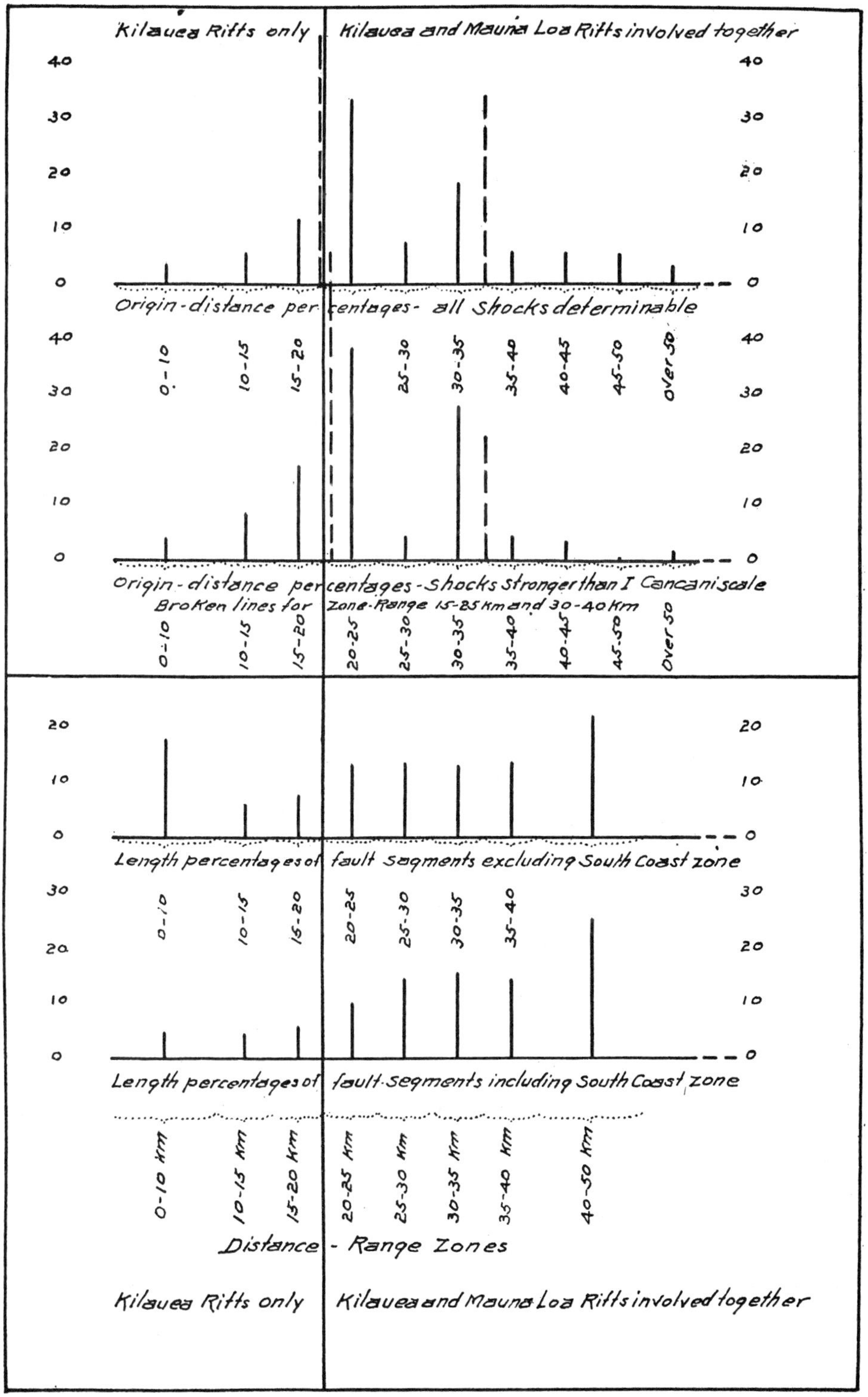
Kilauea Rifts only
Kilauea and Mauna Loa Rifts involved together
Origin-distance percentages - all Shocks determinable
0-10
10-15
15-20
25-30
30-35
35-40
40-45
45-50
Over 50
Origin-distance percentages - Shocks stronger than I Cancani scale
Broken lines for Zone-Range 15-25 Km and 30-40 Km
20-25
Length percentages of fault segments excluding South Coast zone
Length percentages of fault-segments including South Coast zone
0-10 Km
10-15 Km
15-20 Km
20-25 Km
25-30 Km
30-35 Km
35-40 Km
40-50 Km
Distance - Range Zones
Kilauea Rifts only
Kilauea and Mauna Loa Rifts involved together

PLATE II.

that only comparatively trivial block movements are to be expected near them (excluding from consideration the possibility of further major breakdown of the mountain summits). Also, at such close quarters, any rapid expansions in the magma short of genuine explosion should be easily accommodated in the crater and the loose mosaic without the production of sharp shocks. The relative, if not complete, absence of earthquake origins near Kilauea is in accord with such a view.

Also, in passing, it is desirable to indicate that such a broken mosaic would possess in marked degree the property of damping out and dissipating vibrational energy. This accords with the facts (a) that local shocks manifest less violence near the crater than lower down the slopes, and (b) that comparatively few teleseismic shocks are registered here.

Therefore, without attempting here to re-define, or to examine critically the variant readings of the terms, volcanic and tectonic, as applied to earthquakes—it appears to the writer that most of the shocks dealt with in this study are of the tectonic sort, as the term is most generally understood.

Such a view and its implications with reference to the mechanism of volcanic eruption from lava cones like these on Hawaii, or fissure-systems, raises abruptly seismological problems of profound importance both in a general sense, to the development of earth-science, and in a special sense, to human welfare, in regions subjected to such kinds of volcanic ejection. This province thus affords a testing ground of great scientific and economic or humanitarian interest.

For, here in Hawaii, precise seismometric investigations would surely go far toward elucidating problems of this nature.

In order that such investigation may be effective and, in the end, economical there will be required the establishment of numerous seismometric laboratories —so located that all parts of the land area of the islands, particularly of Hawaii and Maui, shall be within fifty kilometers of two, preferably of three, stations, as far as possible.

In locating such a system of stations especial care should be taken in the districts known to be traversed by fissure, or fault-zones to make the best available placement. Having in mind the present development and distribution of population the system presented in the accompanying table, Table III, is suggested. But there is no need for rigid adherence to this as against some other suitable disposition of stations.

TABLE III.

Suitable locations, desirably spaced, for a system of seismemetric laboratories for the Hawaiian Group:

Waiohinu Kealakekua Kilauea Hilo Waimea Kohala	Island of Hawaii.
Kipahulu [Ulupalakua] Lahaina	Island of Maui.
Palawai	Island of Lanai.
Kaunakakai	Island of Molokai.
Koko Head [Ewa] Waialua Kahuku	Island of Oahu.
Lihue Hanalei Waimea	Island of Kauai.
....	Island of Niihau.

16 [19] stations in all.

For the most effective service all these laboratories should be of uniform design, construction and equipment, in all respects up to the hour and especially arranged for and adapted to this region, and its peculiar, local problems. The time service should be excellent and common to all the stations, best controlled by wireless time-signals.

Primarily there should be at each station a suitable, dry, underground chamber in which a practically constant temperature can practicably be maintained, and in which provision can be made for the installation and maintenance of apparatus as follows:

(A) Continuously registering seismometers for each of the three usually recorded components of motion.

For this province these should be constructed to write an unusually open record and, at the same time, have a high degree of sensitiveness adapted for shocks like the feeblest which occur here; also considerable range of energy must be registered, between the limits of the weakest and the stronger of the ordinary local shocks. Hence two or more sets of seismometers may be required to meet the situation completely. Other peculiarities in construction should be contemplated, looking to the greater efficiency of the apparatus.

(B) There will be greatly needed continuously registering devices for the measurement of earth-tilt, installed in strictly constant temperature chambers, and:

(C) Meteorological apparatus, both direct-reading and registering, especially adapted for the seismic problems will be very useful. For wind direction and velocity, and the barometric and thermometric gradients have effect on the intensity of loading of small localized districts, and have been thought to exhibit relationships with the occurrence of certain earthquakes.

(D) Also provision should be made for the installation, testing and employment of additional or experimental apparatus as experience may indicate.

Of course provision for the accurate keeping of time is essential.

———

Following the establishment and satisfactory operation under common direction of such a system of seismometric laboratories, two categories of very important results can be expected confidently to issue from the thorough analysis and measurement of the seismograms, with critical co-ordination of all the data thus obtainend.

I. This should afford at first a very closely approximate, later on a very accurate location of the region of origin for a great majority of the earthquakes, often with approximate knowledge of the limits of depth, and, at least sometimes, serviceable ideas as to the size and shape of the focal region.

Consideration of such knowledge of the placement and dimensions of the origins taken in connection with the frequency of recurrence of shocks will prove enlightening as to their character and mechanisms of causation—and, practically, of the stage and intensity of accumulating crust strains with the localization and delimitation of zones of failure. Knowledge of these conditions is a necessary precedent to any efforts in the direction of prediction of place, and eventually of time, for the occurrence of future shocks whether great or small. The practical and scientific importance of this needs no emphasis.

This work of measurement and co-ordination will also yield knowledge in regard to

(a) The total energy;

(b) The distribution of intensity and circumstances of radiation;

(c) The speeds of transmission of the various seismic waves, and

(d) The dimensions and characteristics of these waves for the shocks registered, *especially in the local province, a wide region of very unusual homogeneity of rock material which in several respects approximates to the average for the surface regions of the globe.*

It would be difficult to exaggerate the importance such results would have—

(a) Both in their local practical bearing (for the catastrophic shocks of 1868 must not be lost sight of) and

(b) In their more general scientific bearing, both along new lines and also along lines already investigated but in need of more refined delineation.

But such results can not be obtained by working with inferior or inadequate equipment, nor with good equipment at too few localities.

II. Clear exposition of the expectable results of the second category requires a brief introduction.

The physical study of seismic motion, with the consequent discussion of the data of seismometry in relation to the general theory of wave-motion in an elastic solid has led already, in a decade and a half, to rapid advancement of knowledge and to the establishment of important generalizations in seismology.

Seismograms, particularly of earthquakes originating at great distance, exhibit a natural division into phases, or groups of waves, differentiated by the later and later arrivals of vibrations of different character, and of the reflected and refracted portions of these. Analysis of the phenomena has already taught much concerning the state and properties of the matter, and the distribution and variation of its density and elastic quality, in the deep regions of the globe.

Beneath a portion of the Island of Hawaii unquestionably, possibly beneath the Hawaiian Group as a whole, is a body of molten matter—exhibited as visibly tangent to the surface in the crater of Kilauea (and at times in that of Mauna Loa, also), during a large percentage of the time in recent years.

As yet the shape, extent and vertical dimensions of this body are quite unknown.

However, at its envelope, particularly the superior surfaces of this boundary, there must be a change from a relatively rigid to a relatively fluid condition which may take place quite suddenly, but which more likely is accomplished by a gradual transition. There are certain reasons for thinking this boundary, or zone of transition, at small depth; others for judging it to be much deeper.

The speed, direction and reflection of the first-phase, or longitudinal, seismic waves should be definitely affected upon arriving at the boundary of this body, and in transit through it. If it is in a genuinely fluid condition the second-phase, or transversal, seismic waves cannot be transmitted through it; but must either be subjected to reflection with characteristic changes, or be absorbed within the transition zone, either wholly or in part. Therefore it is reasonable to expect that very sensitive registering seismometers adapted to the region, with suitably adjusted rates of registration and factors of magnification, may write seismograms exhibiting characteristic phase divisions peculiarly controlled by the local subjacent conditions.

In view of the dimensions and delimitations, heights and profiles of the volcanic mountains of these islands, particularly of the surely active Loa and Kilauea (see the profile drawing, Plate III), it is reasonable to anticipate that a seismometric survey, in the course of time, may result in a fairly accurate determination of the size, shape and physical condition of the actually or potentially molten reservoir below; providing that its upper bounding surface does not lie too deep. In any case, in addition to all the results of the first category, the correlation of earthquake occurrences with the amounts, periods and directions of earth-tilt—all taken in connection with the behavior in the craters—should ultimately prove very illuminating with regard to the grand mechanism of volcanism here. This is the most intimate of the contacts of the seismic problem with that properly pertaining to the action of the volcanoes.

Surely nothing need be said of the need for, or value of, experimental studies in this connection, or the pursuit of additional special inquiries such as gravity surveys, magnetic surveys, etc.

In conclusion it may be well to say definitely, however, that this study is an effort to present the seismological and geo-dynamical problem offered in the Hawaiian Group—as distinct from the volcanological and geo-chemical problem. For these sciences, though in close contact here at many points, have, nevertheless, special goals of their own.

Hawaiian Volcano Observatory,
14 May, 1915.

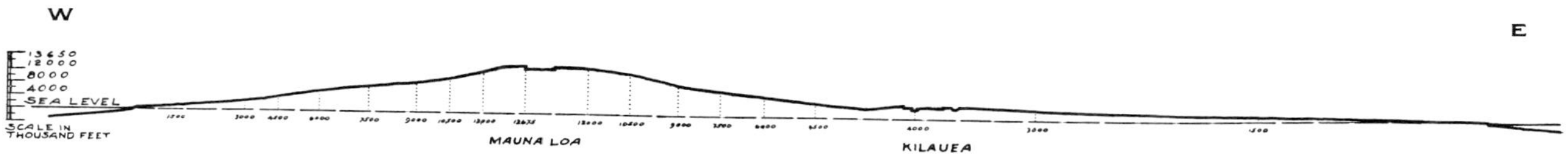
W
E
13650
12000
8000
4000
SEA LEVEL
SCALE IN THOUSAND FEET
MAUNA LOA
KILAUEA

PLATE III

WEEKLY BULLETIN

OF THE

Hawaiian Volcano Observatory

Vol. III. HONOLULU, HAWAII, JUNE, 1915. No. 6

TECHNOLOGY STATION, June 3. —The action in Halemaumau during the week ended with June 2 has corresponded with marked exactness with that expectable on the basis of the incomplete and imperfect hypothesis of tidal control which we have been working out at this Observatory. Through considerable daily fluctuations in height of stand, the magma surface has definitely risen, with accompanying changes in the minute configuration of the molten lake and of the complex talus mosaic about it. Unfortunately no depth measure has been secured, but a positive rise, greater in amount than the daily range, has surely occurred—thus building to a higher level the "third" platform which immediately surrounds the molten pools. Vigorous fountain action and miniature marginal overflows have made the scene more brilliant than usual and the action correspondingly more energetic. All this has corresponded in time with a theoretical fortnightly strain crisis of greater magnitude than common, with the usual factor of lag.

In the afternoon of May 26 the magma surface was about twenty-five feet below the surface of the third platform, which was itself lower then than later in the week. The melt was streaming toward the east, carrying along numerous baby fountains, singly and in groups. Large bubble-fountain action was vigorous in the center of the pool and at changeable spots along the sides. Some of the fountains were projected to considerable heights, particularly from the pool under the northeast station. The noise of eruption was quite loud.

In the afternoon of May 27 the magma was still about twenty-five feet below the third platform. Streaming to the eastward still prevailed, together with the action of bubble-fountains and baby fountains. Avalanches were noted, particularly under the north station. These were small and in the light of subsequent observation probably they were merely movements of readjustment in the loose talus. Infalls from the margin took place, producing the usual surface turbulence for a few minutes following the infall.

In the afternoon of May 28 the magma stood only ten feet below the surface of the third platform at the beginning of the observation; it rose comparatively rapidly until it reached the level of the third platform and overflowed on to it—thus building the platform surface to a higher level. Eastward streaming prevailed and the vigorous action of large and small fountains continued. In the small pool under the northwest station fountains were spurting to heights of thirty to forty feet. The noise of eruption was very loud.

In the afternoon of May 29 conditions were much the same. In the course of the afternoon the lava rose from a depth of three feet or so below the third platform to level with it and with overflowing. In the main lake large traveling fountains moved with the stream to the southeast and east. In the northwest pool fountains were spurting to considerable heights. Contemporaneous with the rising several small avalanches occurred under the east station.

On May 31 fountains were spurting to heights of thirty to forty feet under the Northeast station. In all other respects conditions were as on pre-

WEEKLY BULLETIN
of the
Hawaiian Volcano Observatory

Published Monthly at Honolulu, Hawaii, by the Hawaiian Volcano Research Association

Editor..............Howard M. Ballou
Professor of Physics, College of Hawaii

Entered as second-class matter January 20, 1914, at the post-office at Honolulu, Hawaii, under the Act of August 24, 1912.

vious days. The magma was seen to rise from a depth of about two feet below the third platform to level with it and overflowing.

On June 1, in the afternoon the action continued as described above. However, there was no observed fluctuation in the depth of the magma surface, which appeared to stand a foot or so below the third platform (which, of course, had now been built up an unknown amount higher than its position earlier in the week). Big traveling fountains following with the streaming eastward were still conspicuous.

In the afternoon of June 2, the magma stood level with the third floor on which evidence of fresh flowing was clear. The action was just as on the previous days. The noise of eruption was unusually loud, for an open lake. During this morning no avalanches were heard.

Six very small local earthquakes have been registered at the Whitney Laboratory during the past week.

There has been considerable fluctuation in the amount of tilting, but the net result appears to be a considerable decrease in the amount of the pitch to the south and west which has been referred to in all recent reports. The tilt to the south and west is still large, however.

The registration of microseisms has gone on as usual.

The volcanic vibration movements were stronger than normal early in the week, but later subsided to normal values.

H. O. WOOD, Associate.

TECHNOLOGY STATION, June 10. —The rising of the lava in Halemaumau continues with the approach to the solstice. The division between the two lakes is low and both have built wide floors of overflow. The north crag has crumbled low and the floor about the main lake has so built up that the overflows will soon break through the notch west of the north crag and overflow the northeast trench. There are flaming cones east and southwest. "Old Faithful" fountain has again gone out of action.

At three p. m. June 3 the lake appeared three feet below the floor of overflow, splashing against the south point and throwing the molten lava over it. The shore was thus built high. Streaming was from west and east and in under the overhang of the south point where there was much boiling up of gas. The northwest pond was stagnant, with glowing shoreward cracks, and loud gas puffing.

At three p. m. June 5 the northwest pond was active around the border with a few large fountains in the middle, the lava being level with its floor of overflow. The main lake was streaming west to east with many fountains and shore activity southeast, southwest and northwest. It was overflowing the bench with splashes of melt. Fresh flows covered nearly half the bench apparently encircling the lake from overflow at the west. No avalanches were observed.

June 7 at four p. m. the lake was about five feet below the bench. Two central fountains were in action and there was border activity. The small pond (northwest) was actively streaming northward bombarding a cavern in the bank north, and there were numerous fountains with rumblings and puffings. A blowing cone about five feet high, glowing and flaming, could be seen against the base of the east wall of Halemaumau.

June 8 at three p. m. the streaming was reversed to the westward. The lava appeared five feet below the bench. There was strong noisy fountaining in both the large and small pools, some of those in the small pool spurting to heights of thirty feet.

On June 9 at four p. m. streaming

was from west to east with little fountaining except at the eastern border. Polygonal skins moved across the surface. Spatter knobs make a rampart all around the lake, especially high and protuberant northeast and east. "Old Faithful" fountain nowhere appeared, nor any large central fountains. The lake appeared about 460 feet below the rim. The rifted crags southeast were still in place. The fumes were thin. There was no fume at all at the site of the former south chimney, but some increase of fuming under the west end of the fifty-foot bench south. The platform of overflow around the lake was widest southwest, and the bench dividing the northwest pond and its platform from the main lake has become a mere low isthmus. The southwest pot in the second bench shows a glow-cone within.

The streaming in the northwest pond was toward the northeast with bombardment against the north bank. The north crag appeared only about forty feet high. The 1914 bench appeared more broken and collapsed both east and west. There were fumaroles east, southeast, southwest and north.

H. O. Wood reports for the Whitney Laboratory of Seismology that during the week ending with June 9 no earthquakes have been registered. Motion of volcanic vibration has been stronger than usual, especially at sporadic intervals. Microseismic motion has continued as usual. There has been no significant change in the amount of tilting and its fluctuation in amount has been less than usual.

The director has spent twelve days from May 29 to June 9 in making a circuit of the island of Hawaii with Mr. Sidney Powers, studying the geology.

T. A. JAGGAR, JR., Director.

TECHNOLOGY STATION, June 17. —Until June 14, inclusive, rising of the lake and overflow of the lower bench continued in Halemaumau. This was accompanied by remarkable thinning of the fumes over the crater as seen from a distance. On June 15 the density of the fumes was markedly greater and thereafter the lake appeared sunken by at least thirty feet below the lower bench, the bench being broken so that the eastern half made an escarpment overhanging the western. Measurements on June 16, however, did not confirm the appearance of subsidence, but made the level of the lake 482 feet below the south station, exactly the same figure as on June 14. Measurements in duplicate from different stations on both days checked satisfactorily, so that it is hard to explain the discrepancy between measurements and appearance except by assuming that the floor benches had risen bodily—a possibility which has been suspected on other occasions. Further measurements will throw light on the problem.

On June 10 about two p. m. the lake had risen level with the lower bench and was active with central and peripheral fountains and eastward streaming. June 11 at two p. m. the lake was five feet below the bench, but the glowing cracks in a fresh flow on the bench could be seen, its source being at the west end. At three p. m. the northwest pond was stagnant but brimming level with the bench around it. The noises were of fountaining and some puffing.

Between three and three-thirty p. m. June 12 the lava rose from three feet below the bench to a level flush with it and splashing over, with the usual fountaining and eastward streaming. The northwest pond was also splashing high.

Measurements on June 14 at three p. m. gave the following levels below the southeast rim of the pit:

Lake, 480 feet down.

Overflow bench, 465 feet down.

Southeast crag, second bench, 401 feet down.

1914 bench south, 392 feet down.

These measurements indicate that the 1914 bench has slightly subsided since May 5 and the southeast crag has considerably risen since May 13. Evidently the inner benches have shared somewhat in the recent movement of rising of the lava. The summit of the southeast crag, the crevassed inner portion of the 1914 floor which subsided to make a second bench in January, is now only nine feet below the rim portion of the 1914 floor which is preserved on the south side of the pit. The rim portion has slid down with the upper talus, while the inner bench has tilted back and lifted up with the rising lava. This lifting power of the rising lava recalls the hill which was raised on the rim of Halemaumau in 1894.

On this date, June 14, there was steady hot fountaining making bubbles under the skins, sporadic bursts and traveling line of ebullition. The streaming was from west to east, the noise that of splashing and heat from the lake could be felt on the rim strongly. The northwest pond was active and the fumes were thin.

Large flows of recent date could be seen on both sides of and around the north crag filling the northeast trench with new lava as predicted last week. The north crag appeared only about twenty feet high and there was a second pinnacle beyond it to the northeast. The bench between the two lakes appeared not more than ten feet high. Blue fumes rose from under the fifty-foot bench beneath the south station.

On June 15 the fumes were much denser. June 16 at noon the lake appeared at first glance fallen about thirty feet within an inner pit bounded by the lower bench. The western half of the lower bench including the south point had fallen along a diagonal rift line so that it was only a few feet above the lake, and the eastern half of the same bench overhung it as an escarpment. West, north, east and southeast the bench overhung the lake as a high cliff. The partition between the lakes appeared high, as did also the north crag. No avalanches were heard and the lake appeared active and rising.

The lake appeared larger by incaving of banks. The streaming was toward a central fountaining area and there were many baby fountains. The noise was of splashing without rumbling, and thick skins formed over the southeast part of the lake as though rising were in progress. Measurement made the lake 484 feet below the southeast rim in no way confirming the appearance of a thirty-foot subsidence.

H. O. Wood reports that during the week ending with June 16 six ordinary small earthquakes of nearby origin were registered in the Whitney Laboratory of Seismology. None were of perceptible magnitude at the observatory. The usual waxing and waning of microseismic waves and of those designated as volcanic vibrations has gone on without any marked characteristics. The action of tilting has changed in such a way as to decrease considerbaly the tilt to the southward without any accompanying marked change in the east-west tilting. There is still a considerable residual of tilting to the southwest over the status at an earlier time in the year. There has been fluctuation in amount through the week as usual.

T. A. JAGGAR, JR., Director.

TECHNOLOGY STATION, June 24. —The movement of the lava lake of Halemaumau showed slight subsidence from June 15 to June 21, and slight rising thereafter. The time of the solstice as usual has been marked by seismic and volcanic events in various parts of the world such as the renewed activity of Lassen's Peak in California, earthquake disaster in Lower California about the Imperial Valley and across the Mexican border, and the outbreak of a new submarine volcano in the Bonin Isles of Japan.

On June 17 at noon there was no marked change in the lava lake of Kilauea. The surface currents were streaming rapidly from the west end to a middle zone of perpetual fountains across the lake. East of these fountains the lake was covered with sluggish skins drifting eastward. The cliff over the molten flood appeared about twenty-five feet high on the north, the east and the southeast. It was only about ten feet high from the south point westward.

The southeast crags, the southeast part of the lower bench, and the block bounding the lake on the north and west appear in the recent movement of June 15 to have tilted upward as independent blocks, their surfaces sloping southward, while the lake only slightly subsided, or else unperceived subsided greatly in a few hours and as quickly recovered. The northwest pond on June 17 appeared large and active. An occasional large fountain in the lowest central part of the lake broke about every thirty seconds; this may be the return of "Old Faithful."

June 18 at 2:30 p. m. the bench cliff over the lake appeared about twenty feet high, and small fountains were abundant and the streaming was eastward; the northwest pond was also active.

June 19 at 3 p. m. conditions were the same in the main lake and the "Old Faithful" fountain appeared to be at work. The northwest pond was quiet with only a few glow streaks visible bordering its crust.

On the morning of June 21 the fumes from Halemaumau appeared thick and measurements from the southeast rim determined the depth to the lava surface to be 490 feet.

The lake was 480 feet long by 175 feet wide at the narrowest part. There were stalactities hanging under spatter rims attached as a series of lumps to the border cliff. The wall at the east end of the lake appeared about thirty feet high. The two north crags and the western partition between the pools appeared high. In the northeast trench were two pots revealing streaming lava within, apparently at the lake level and connected through to the lake in a cavernous space. A cone glowed on the bench at the east end. The northwest pond was sluggishly boiling.

The streaming of the main lake was from west to east against the north bank. There was violent turbulence at 2 p. m. succeeded by quiet at 3 p. m. There was border splashing northeast, northwest and in the south cove. Noisy perpetual fountaining was in progress in the west central region. The pit was very smoky and seeing was bad.

At 9 p. m. a flame could be seen in the southwest pot in the second bench. The streaming had become reversed so that the skins moved from east to west. The northwest pond could be seen from the north stations dimly, and was an oval pool with streaming northwestward. "Old Faithful" appeared to be in action.

At 8 p. m. June 22 the lake appeared to be rising, for there was a crust over its west end, the streaming was from west to east, the three high eastern holes and the southwest pot were all glowing, there was a medial line of fountains in the lake, and the partition from the northwest pond appeared about forty feet high. The noise was purely of splashing and the smoke appeared thin.

From a distance the smoke appeared thinner on June 24 and measurement at noon made the depth of the lava below the south rim of the pit 484 feet. There was no change in the appearance of the lake. The border cliff appeared about 25 feet high. New tumbles of rock could be seen on the bench west of the north crags. The northwest pond was pounding in a cave at its northeast end. Portions of the spatter rampart on the northwest side of the main lake fell in under bombardment. Large knobs of spatter had formed at the east end of the lake. The streaming was eastward and the main places of shore bombardment were north and east, changing occasionally to the northwest bank. "Old Faithful" appeared to be in action.

H. O. Wood reports that during the week ending with June 23 five small local earthquakes were registered in the Whitney Laboratory of Seismology. None were of perceptible magnitude at the Observatory. The condition of tilt to the south and west has undergone the usual fluctuation but there seems to be no mean change. It remains strong compared to spring and winter value. Microseisms have fluctuated in intensity more than usual but have not been strong. The registration of volcanic vibration has been as usual."

T. A. JAGGAR, JR., Director.

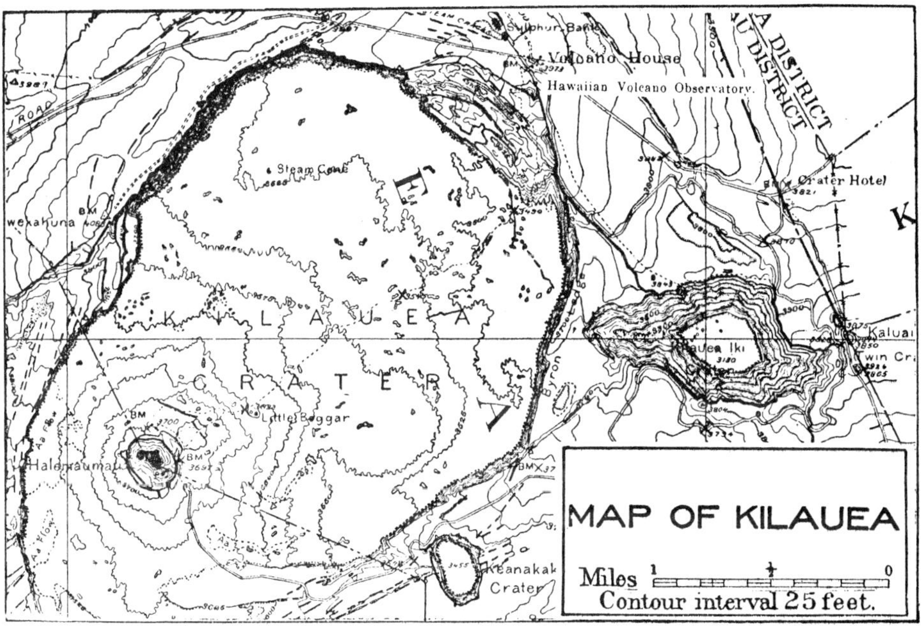

HAWAIIAN VOLCANO RESEARCH ASSOCIATION.

This society is a voluntary one, made up of subscribers to scientific work which is being executed by the Massachusetts Institute of Technology.

In 1915 there are about 100 subscribers in Hawaii and elsewhere, firms and individuals. A group of firms and persons in Hilo built the main observatory building in the spring of 1912. Publications to date have been weekly reports since the summer of 1911, now reprinted in Honolulu in monthly form. The Massachusetts Institute of Technology will publish annual reports, of which the introductory number was printed in 1912.

The weekly bulletin as it appears in the Advertiser is reprinted as a leaflet and sent to regular annual subscribers to the work of the Association. L. A. Thurston is president of the Board of Directors of the Assocíation, and R. W. Shingle is treasurer. New subscribers who are interested in volcanoes will be welcomed in the Association. The Association aims: (1) To record volcanic activity and earthquakes in Hawaii; (2) to attract scientific men hither for special studies; (3) to promote the establishment of volcano observatories all over the world. The annual dues of regular members are $5; patrons of the Assocaition subscribe larger amounts.

WHITNEY LABORATORY OF SEISMOLOGY.

The Whitney Laboratory of Seismology is equipped with two Bosch-Omori 100 kg tromometers registering N-S and E-W motion, a heavy Omori tromometer registering E-W motion, and an Omori "ordinary Seismograph" designed for registering strong earthquakes in all three components of motion. These are seated on concrete piers in a closed basement room having practically constant temperature, beneath the chief Observatory building near the hotel. Time is referred to a rated chronometer, checked at intervals by solar observations with a transit. Both instruments are loaned by the College of Hawaii. At the substation by the edge of the active pit an Omori two-component tromometer with light steady masses is mounted on a concrete pier placed directly on the fresh lava surface. Hawaiian standard time (H. S. T.) is 10 hrs. 30 min. slower than Greenwich time.

CANCANI SCALE OF SEISMIC INTENSITY.

Expressed by accelerations measured in millimeters per second per second.

I.	Instrumental	0.0	2.5
II.	Very slight	2.5	5.0
III.	Slight	5.0	10.0
IV.	Sensible, mediocre	10.0	25.0
V.	Rather strong	25.0	50.0
VI.	Strong	50.0	100.0
VII.	Very strong	100.0	250.0
VIII.	Ruinous	250.0	500.0
IX.	Disastrous	500.0	1000.0
X.	Very disastrous	1000.0	2500.0
XI.	Catastrophic	2500.0	5000.0
XII.	Great catastrophe	5000.0	10000.0

Grade IV. is ordinarily the minimum perceived by the senses; and in grade XII. the acceleration, or rate of change of motion (jerk) reaches that of terrestrial gravitation.

In the standard form of report the maximum intensity or acceleration, designated by the symbol a, or max. a, is given in the conventional unit, **the milligal**. The milligal is a measure of acceleration, such that 1 milligal = 1/100 mm. per sec. per sec. = 10 μ per sec. per sec. The Cancani scale, here defined in terms of millimeters per sec. per sec., can therefore be expressed in **milligals** by multiplying each of the numbers by 100.

WEEKLY BULLETIN
OF THE
Hawaiian Volcano Observatory

Vol. III. HONOLULU, HAWAII, JULY, 1915. No. 7

TECHNOLOGY STATION, July 1—The rising lava of last week in Halemaumau reached its culmination June 25 and thereafter fell off slightly but the fluctuations of the month of June were all slight. The record of the last two months at Kilauea shows a net rise of sixty-five feet between April 22 and June 10, 1915, with low levels in April and May and culminations of rising twice in June, the minima of height being about 530 feet below the rim of Halemaumau and the maxima being about 465 feet below it. The movements have been small and gradual as compared with former years, excepting 1914 when the slow rising of the year had this same quality. As compared with last December (1914) the maximum of the present summer solstice time is 100 feet lower.

On June 25 at three p. m., both large and small pools were level with their bench shores. The small pool was fountaining around its border noisily and the bench showed that it had overflowed. The main lake had many large fountains. Two small blowing cones were at work on the bench at the east end. At four o'clock the lake was overflowing the bench while large fountains played in its midst. Probably the lake level was about 470 feet below the rim on this day.

At two-thirty p. m. June 26, seen from the east station the lake was ten feet below the bench. The streaming was easterly, pouring against the bank northeast and east. Noisy fountaining continued in the middle with much bubble fountaining in the west central area. The small northwest pond appeared to be about five feet below its bench, fountaining in only one place against the northwest bank.

On June 27 at three p. m. from the north the lake appeared to be only five feet below the bank with only one central fountaining area and bombardment against the southeast bank. The northwest pond was level with its shore and active only on its northwest side. At four p. m. the main lake had risen until nearly level with the bench and many big fountains were playing along the medial line of the pool, the fountains themselves migrating eastward with the surface streaming. The splashing noise was very loud and there was bombardment east,, north and west.

By measurement June 28 at three p. m. the two pools were 484 feet below the south rim. The fumes at a distance appeared thin and blue. The streaming was from the south cove northward and eastward, and from a patch of skin in the western part of the lake westward and eastward. The lake appeared from twenty-five to thirty feet below its bank, there was heavy bombardment of the shore north, east and west with much rumbling. There aws perpetual fountaining in the middle of the lake.

There appeared to be a strong insuck of the fluid under the north and northeast banks with violent fountaining and an accelerating current as the bank was approached, with many bubble fountains. This mechanism suggested rapid subsidence. In the northwest pond the streaming was to the northeast and at four p. m. a collapse of the bench into this pond produced violent ebullition of bubble fountains. Fresh lava spatter and overflow showed on the benches at the west end of the lake and around the small pool, and there were spatter rim lines built against the cliff over the lake north and east. The open pot with glowing lava within still showed in the east bench.

WEEKLY BULLETIN
of the
Hawaiian Volcano Observatory

Published Monthly at Honolulu, Hawaii, by the Hawaiian Volcano Research Association

Editor..............**Howard M. Ballou**
Professor of Physics, College of Hawaii

Entered as second-class matter January 20, 1914, at the post-office at Honolulu, Hawaii, under the Act of August 24, 1912.

From the southeast station at three p. m. June 29 the lake appeared thirty feet below the bench, streaming was against the northeast and east banks, there were few large fountains and much bubbling. The fountain "Old Faithful" appeared to be distinguishable bursting at intervals in the same place.

On July 1 at eleven a. m. the fumes were thick again and seeing from the southeast station was difficult. The most conspicuous change was a collapse from the east inner wall of Halemaumau low down into the southeast trench making a niche in the wall under the east station; still lower a crevasse appeared between the wall and east bench, and involving apparently another spall from the wall, as though the lava lake extension under the bench were tending to eat away the east wall and undermine it. For a year past this wall has been threatened by the direct bombardment of the lava lake. The lake was very active with intense hot fountaining and hardly any streaming. There were large steady fountains in four or five places and some bubble fountaining. The only noise was of plashing. At the south point the cliff over the lava, which was part of the bench recently overflowed, appeared about fifteen feet high.

H. O. Wood reports that during the week ending with June 30, 1915, some seven local earthquakes were registered in the Whitney Laboratory. During this week the volcanic vibrations have been stronger than usual, both on the average and with reference to particular groups of waves. Microscismic motion has fluctuated as usual. The tilt has varied more considerably than usual. There has not been much net change in regard to the E-W component, though during the week larger tilts to the west have been noted than during recent weeks. This has decreased again. Also considerable tilt to the south was noted at one time but the tendency of the week was readjustment toward the north. In spite of variation in recent weeks the general status is a tilt to the southwest greater than that in the past winter.

T. A. JAGGAR, JR., Director.

TECHNOLOGY STATION, July 8.—Another addition to the volcanic happenings of the solstice period of the summer of 1915 was the outbreak of Yakeyama in Japan, June 6. This volcano in Shinshu Province, near the borders of Hida, among the Japanese Alps, is in one of the wildest mountain countries of central Japan, midway between the Asama group of active volcanoes and the scene of the terrible Mino-Owari earthquake of 1891. The eruption of Yakeyama after three days is said to have covered ten square miles of country with rocks, ash and mud up to four feet in depth, destroyed the forest, and dammed the Azusagawa River with a barrier sixty feet high, making a lake a mile and a half long. The waters of the river cut a spillway over the dam, which they rushed down in a cataract a quarter of a mile long. This river is one of the headwater affluents of the Shinanogawa, the largest river in Honshu, the Japanese mainland.

Kilauea has remained stationary during the first week in July, but has again developed a spectacular turbulent whirlpool and down rushing cascade of lava at the east end of the fire pit. The lava lake is tremendously active at a depth of 480 feet below the rim. Fine summer weather has begun and visitors to Halemaumau are repaid by seeing a wonderful spectacle which shows no signs yet of abating.

July 2 at ten a. m. the lake appeared no more than ten feet below the low southwest bank. The northwest pond was making blowing and bubbling sounds as though the shores were caving in. The lava had worked into the east bench region, creating a new cove out of the pot which has been there. The streaming was eastward with a stagnant area at the east end, over a hot plashing pool, which appeared rising. The bench blocks around the lake were now tipped and cracked in great confusion especially east, southwest and northeast. The former north crag was now a low pinnacle south of a much higher crag formed by a floor block parting from the northwest wall.

Over the east end of the lake there was increased caving, with a glow hole in its midst. The glow hole to the southwest had become a splashing lava pot at least sixty-five feet above the lake level. Fume had diminished in this vicinity and also generally, but the relative humidity of the air was low and this would make the water content of the fumes invisble anyway. There is no question but that there is a marked water vapor effect in the general fume cloud from Halemaumau, and the high inner fumaroles of the pit south show wet places in the soil around them. There is much more visible steam mixed with the sulphur fume on cold and wet days than at other times.

The southeast bench over the lake had caved in since the previous day. There was new tumble of rocks around the northern crags. There were blowing border grottoes and much bubbling on the west shore of the northwest pond. The smoke in the south talus, where the chimney was buried up, had totally ceased. The vapor under the high south bench must be wholly water vapor, for it was today quite invisible. New spatter rims were observed around the lake, showing fluctuation in level since the previous day.

During the next three days there were no marked changes. July 5 in the morning the lake appeared about fifteen feet below the lower bench.

Measurement on July 6 at nine a. m. gave depth to the lava surface below the southeast rim of the pit as 480 feet. There was now a definite small cove with a narrow entrance at the east end of the lake. Across the entrance there was a crust, but the lava was splashing inside. The west end of the lake was skinned over, streaming was eastward and against the north bank, and there was a rapid surface stream pouring out of the corner of the south cove next east of the south point. The overhang in the east wall of Halemaumau at the southeast trench made a deeper niche as though there had been more caving there. Old Faithful was in action and the northwest pond was active and appeared unchanged. In the afternoon the lava was cascading from the lake down into a void or caldron at the east cove, the fall taking place at the narrow entrance to the cove, just as has happened repeatedly at that end of the lake since December of 1914.

Floes of crust or skin pitched over the edge of the cataract and broke up in the churning tumultuous fiery melt below, probably thirty feet down. From eight to eleven p. m. the direction of flow had changed, probably with a change from sinking to rising, the east caldron had filled up and there was streaming into the lake westward from the east cove with very hot activity, and much fountaining. At eleven-fifteen p. m. after vigorous inflow for hours, the current reversed again and the lava began to sink, and there was outflow into the east cove with some downrush. At the same time the wind veered to the east and the pit became fumy, just about the hour of the night barometric maximum. At the same moment there was a small rock slide to the southeast. The rush into the east cove would last a few minutes, then lessen and stagnate; this again would continue for a few minutes and then there would begin a swifter downrush into the cove. These repetitions went on until the cove was again a caldron, receiving a cascade from the lake.

The southwest chimney was flaming. There was very intense fountaining against the north bank. The western cavern of the northwest pond was rumbling. There was streaming away from the shore on both sides of the south point.

On July 7, from five to seven p. m., the whole lake was streaming eastward and pouring in a torrential cataract twenty feet down into the fiery flood of the east caldron with a roar, and the lava within churned and whirled about in high incandescence. Old Faithful was bursting at intervals and perpetual fountains were at work, mostly in the middle near Old Faithful. There was a flaming cone on the east bench. The northwest pond was as usual showing a splashing cavern at the west shore. Skins on the lake migrated east, broke up and rushed down the cascade. Steam was rising on these two days again from under the west end of the sixty-foot bench south. Stalactites appeared on the northwest side of the lake and along the shore of the northwest pond. The seeing on these days was from the south station.

On the morning of July 8 at nine a. m. humidity was very low and the pit very clear as seen from the south station. The lake appeared thirty feet below the bench on the south point, with many spatter rims. The east cove was no longer a caldron, there was slow streaming from the lake into it and some splashing in its inner extremity. The streaming in the lake was eastward with boiling west, middle and east. There was hard bombardment with rumbling in the grottoes of the west pond. Smoke rose from the southeast crag, the second bench above the lake south, the southwest pot and the base of the south high walls. The southeast trench appeared to be a very deep cleft, and there were deep rifts in the flows of the northeast trench filling, very recently formed by overflow. The fume column at noon as seen from the observatory appeared very small and thin as seen in the dry air and light wind from the northeast.

Mauna Loa has been under inspection with clear air many times in the last five months, and no trace of fume or glow has been seen over Mokuaweoweo.

H. O. Wood reports that during the week ending with July 7, six small local earthquakes were registered in the Whitney Laboratory of Seismology. None were of perceptible magnitude. Microseismic waves have varied in amplitude from quite strong values to very slight, with much fluctuation. Throughout the greater part of the week volcanic vibrations were stronger than usual. The tilt has fluctuated as usual. Referred to recent positions, the east-west tilt changed between moderate and strong inclinations to the west and the north-south tilt changed from strong to very slight inclination to the north.

T. A. JAGGAR, JR., Director.

TECHNOLOGY STATION, July 15. —During the week ending with July 14 the molten lava surface in Halemaumau has fallen slightly, and the depth has fluctuated considerably within a range of thirty to forty feet. Toward the end of the interval the surface has shown a marked tendency to congeal, thus reducing the area of the fluid part. Moderately thick crusts have formed over the west part of the main lake, and along its north margin, and over the northeast bay. The general activity, though reduced in amount, remains the same in character. Slow streaming in changing directions, with vigorous fountain action in several places simultaneously, and with accelerated streaming has been the rule.

On July 9 the magma surface was level with the third bench. In the afternoon the surface action was rather quiet but in the evening it became very vigorous. There was streaming and counter-streaming from the center of the lake to the west and to the east, and vice versa. There was intermittent vigorous spatter fountain action at various spots eventually covering nearly all parts of the larger lake. A large spatter bank broke in along the west end causing the usual commotion. There were gentle cascade streams of short duration running into the northeast bay and into the southeast cove.

On July 10 the magma surface was still level with the third bench. The action at the surface was as on the ninth, with no characteristic differences.

On July 11 the surface had fallen very slightly without other change— except that symptoms of further sinking were observable. Along the west bank of the large lake a considerable infall of the isthmus which divides the two lakes was observed in the evening. Trifling rock-falls from the walls were noted, and small movements of readjustment in the loose talus.

By the afternoon of the twelfth of July, the lava surface had subsided below the third bench possibly as much as fifty feet. The surface action was very vigorous, and strong and persistent streaming from west to east and into the northeast bay was observed.

On July 14 the surface had risen slightly, being from twenty-five to thirty feet below the third bench. Thick crusts covered the southwest, west and north margins, and the surface of the northeast bay. Surface action was moderate and there was streaming and counter-streaming in various directions.

Thin but certain and definite fumes have been seen rising, or standing, above Mokuaweoweo, usually visible only just at sunset. The writer saw these at sunset on the tenth, eleventh and thirteenth of July. Fog and clouds obscured the summit on the twelfth and fourteenth. It is possible that jets of fume were seen, by an inexperienced observer, on the afternoon of the tenth. Another person, also an inexperienced observer, reported a faint glow of very short duration seen at about eleven-thirty p. m. on the tenth. Shortly after noon on the fourteenth several persons saw fumes above the summit. The fume displays at sunset have been seen by all who have had attention drawn to them. Therefore there can be no doubt as to the reality of their appearance, or reappearance. Whether this means a revival of summit action or merely exceptional seeing conditions, making visible again fume emanations which have been given off continuously since the autumn outbreak, is not clear, for, under good seeing conditions, no glow has been visible, except in the instance cited.

The steam jets on the northeast slope of Loa have been seen as usual, without change in amount or character.

There has been nothing unusual about the occurrence of earthquakes during this week. Only four small local shocks have been registered in the Whitney Laboratory of Seismology.

Microseismic motion and that of the volcanic-vibration sort has been somewhat stronger than normal.

Except for the usual fluctuations tilting has undergone no notable change.

H. O. WOOD, Associate.

TECHNOLOGY STATION, July 22.—A very pronounced rise of the lava took place between the twelfth and the sixteenth of July amounting to from forty to fifty feet, and since that time there has been slight subsidence. In general the June-July level of the lava has been constant with a small daily or weekly range about a mean depth of the lava surface below the rim of the pit of 475 feet. The faint fume over the summit of Mauna Loa seen last week has not this week been conspicuous.

On July 15 there was no marked change in the lake of liquid lava in Halemaumau. From two to three p. m. on July 16 the liquid rose about ten feet to the point where it was nearly level with the lower bench at the west end. The surface streaming was eastward with traveling and bubble fountains.

The southwest blowing cone in the tumble of the benches was ejecting spray to a height of twenty-five or thirty feet. Old Faithful fountain was playing in its usual position. The maximum shore bombardment was northeast where the splash was thrown up twenty-five or thirty feet. The small northwest pond was quiet, and its streaming was northward; there were boiling grottoes on its border west and north. This pond had diminished in size. There was a blowing cone on the southwest bank of the main lake. July 17 and 18 there were no marked changes.

At noon July 19 from the south the lake appeared large and streaming westward. The lava was about fifteen feet below the lower bench. A small point had developed in the shore northeast. During the previous week the piles of spatter on the eastern and southwestern high blowing cones had grown considerably. In the afternoon one avalanche was reported at the east end.

July 20 there was clear seeing from the south about nine a. m. The new overflows of the last few days were conspicuous on the lower bench northeast and southwest. The streaming was eastward and into the cove at the east end. The noise was of plashing and Old Faithful was sometimes violent. During an hour the lava rose rapidly from fifteen feet below the ledge to five feet below it. Measurement made the west pond 472 feet below the south station and the shore level of the main lake northeast 467 feet. This would imply a mean rise since July 6 of only ten feet. The lake is now very irregular surrounded by a vast tumble of crags. The general shape is an elongate S in an east-west direction, with five irregular benches over the lake on the south, an uptilted crag separating the two lakes on the west, and two benches and two crags on the north, the lower of the latter being the last remnant of the floor of October, 1914, which went through a complicated history of upheaval and depression for nine months. Beyond the western crag is the small pond and above it a remnant of the 1914 floor clinging as a bench to the wall.

July 21 at nine a. m. from the south station the lake appeared little changed. There was a small lower bench to be seen at the south entrance to the east cove. The lake appeared fifteen to twenty feet below the bench. There were stalactites around the borders and there was rumbling noise in addition to the plash of the fountains. There was little streaming and such drift of the surface skins as there was mostly toward permanent fountains in the middle of the lake. The liquid splashed in grottoes northeast, north and northwest, and on the west and north sides of the west pond. Thick white smoke rose from cracks in the south point bench and from the shelf next above as though these places were undermining. The wall over the lake was higher north and northeast than at the south point. The east cove was quiet. The fume cloud from the pit as a whole was moderate and the fountaining intense and hot. The dominant crag in the bottom area is now the bench between the two lakes, its surface sloping southward and its north end reared high like the prow of a sinking ship. The space southeast of the southeast crags, between them and the wall of the pit is full of tumbled blocks and gravel.

H. O. Wood reports that during the week ending with July 21, only two small local earthquakes have been registered in the Whitney Laboratory of Seismology. Microseismic motion has been registered as usual. Volcanic vibrations have continued to occur in groups, and steadily, with greater amplitudes than normal. In the first part of this week tilt to the north grew so pronounced that an instrumental readjustment was necessitated. Since then, except for fluctuation, there has been no change. East-west tilt has undergone no change except the usual fluctuations.

The exhibit of the Observatory has been set up in the Hawaii Building at the Panama-Pacific exposition in San Francisco. The Board of Directors of the Hawaiian Volcano Research Association met on July 17 and adopted a report having in view a proposal that the United States government take over the scientific work now being carried on by the Hawaiian Volcano Observatory, with a view to making permanent the observing and recording and to safeguard for all time the important records, charts and photographs which are now incessantly in danger of destruction by fire.

T. A. JAGGAR, JR., Director.

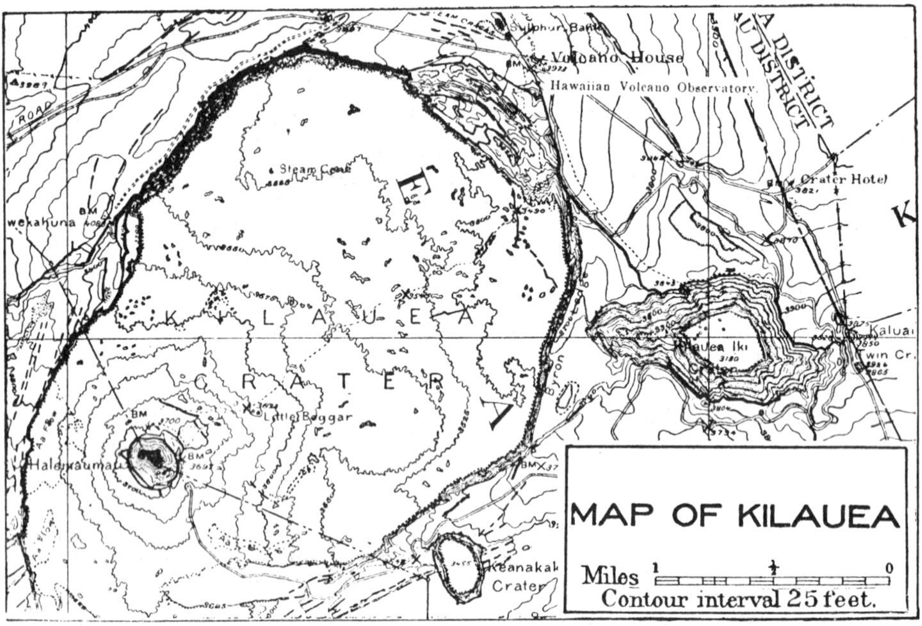

HAWAIIAN VOLCANO RESEARCH ASSOCIATION.

This society is a voluntary one, made up of subscribers to scientific work which is being executed by the Massachusetts Institute of Technology.

In 1915 there are about 100 subscribers in Hawaii and elsewhere, firms and individuals. A group of firms and persons in Hilo built the main observatory building in the spring of 1912. Publications to date have been weekly reports since the summer of 1911, now reprinted in Honolulu in monthly form. The Massachusetts Institute of Technology will publish annual reports, of which the introductory number was printed in 1912.

The weekly bulletin as it appears in the Advertiser is reprinted as a leaflet and sent to regular annual subscribers to the work of the Association. L. A. Thurston is president of the Board of Directors of the Association, and R. W. Shingle is treasurer. New subscribers who are interested in volcanoes will be welcomed in the Association. The Association aims: (1) To record volcanic activity and earthquakes in Hawaii; (2) to attract scientific men hither for special studies; (3) to promote the establishment of volcano observatories all over the world. The annual dues of regular members are $5; patrons of the Assocaition subscribe larger amounts.

WHITNEY LABORATORY OF SEISMOLOGY.

The Whitney Laboratory of Seismology is equipped with two Bosch-Omori 100 kg tromometers registering N-S and E-W motion, a heavy Omori tromometer registering E-W motion, and an Omori "ordinary Seismograph" designed for registering strong earthquakes in all three components of motion. These are seated on concrete piers in a closed basement room having practically constant temperature, beneath the chief Observatory building near the hotel. Time is referred to a rated chronometer, checked at intervals by solar observations with a transit. Both instruments are loaned by the College of Hawaii. At the substation by the edge of the active pit an Omori two-component tromometer with light steady masses is mounted on a concrete pier placed directly on the fresh lava surface. Hawaiian standard time (H. S. T.) is 10 hrs. 30 min. slower than Greenwich time.

CANCANI SCALE OF SEISMIC INTENSITY.

Expressed by accelerations measured in millimeters per second per second.

I.	Instrumental	0.0	2.5
II.	Very slight	2.5	5.0
III.	Slight	5.0	10.0
IV.	Sensible, mediocre	10.0	25.0
V.	Rather strong	25.0	50.0
VI.	Strong	50.0	100.0
VII.	Very strong	100.0	250.0
VIII.	Ruinous	250.0	500.0
IX.	Disastrous	500.0	1000.0
X.	Very disastrous	1000.0	2500.0
XI.	Catastrophic	2500.0	5000.0
XII.	Great catastrophe	5000.0	10000.0

Grade IV. is ordinarily the minimum perceived by the senses; and in grade XII. the acceleration, or rate of change of motion (jerk) reaches that of terrestrial gravitation.

In the standard form of report the maximum intensity or acceleration, designated by the symbol a, or max. a, is given in the conventional unit, **the milligal.** The milligal is a measure of acceleration, such that 1 milligal = 1/100 mm. per sec. per sec. = 10 μ per sec. per sec. The Cancani scale, here defined in terms of millimeters per sec. per sec., can therefore be expressed in **milligals** by multiplying each of the numbers by 100.

WEEKLY BULLETIN
OF THE
Hawaiian Volcano Observatory

Vol. III. HONOLULU, HAWAII, AUGUST, 1915. No. 8

TECHNOLOGY STATION, July 29.—The week at the Hawaiian volcanoes has been an interesting one in that Kilauea had a spectacular rise of lava in the pit of about forty feet, and a party headed by Alfred L. Castle climbed Mauna Loa on foot by the Kapapala trail and saw fumes rising from the southern part of the Crater Mokuaweoweo, but no lava activity. The Kilauea rise reached its maximum July 27 and since then the lava has remained high about 432 feet below the eastern edge of Halemaumau.

At Halemaumau, seen from the southeast July 22, 1915 at one p. m., the pit showed no important changes. There was an abrupt cliff around the lava lake about ten feet high. The South point of the lower bench and also the West end of the same bench southwest of the lake had slipped down along cracks parallel to the lake shore as to make two new lower benches.

On the lake there were thick skins East and West with fountaining in the middle: the noise was of plashing and the streaming was eastward. The eastern spatter cone on the bench had built an annular margin shaped like a doughnut, with an orifice five or six feet in diameter. At the moment bombardment was against the South point. The East cone was in a gravelly pit as was also the southwest pot.

July 23 from two to four p. m. the lake rose about five feet and overflowed the northeast bank. Streaming was eastward with little fountaining. At three p. m. traveling fountains were migrating eastward and the southwest hole was puffing. After overflowing at four p. m. the liquid sank a foot or more with noisy fountaining.

On Saturday, July 24, at three p. m. the view from the southeast showed that a definite rise had begun; the wide southwest bench was nearly half covered with new flows and the lake was puffing and fountaining around the borders, building up spatter ramparts on all sides, a very distinctive characteristic of determined rising. The small West pond was very active with both middle and border fountains. Two blowing cones were forming on the lower bench near the new flows and occasionally spurting incandescent lava.

July 25, overflows were reported and July 26 at four p. m. these flows completely covered the west end of the lower bench and a solidified slender cascade appeared which had trickled across the south end of the partition crag from the west pond to the main lake. The smaller pond was at a considerably higher level than the larger lake. The fumes were thin and the lake appeared hotter and higher than for many months, with increased gas pressure indicated by blowing sounds. The streaming was slow and various in direction. There was much quiet skin over the lake. Sharp puffs came from the southwest cone and hissing from the east end region. Both the East and southwest blowing cones had overflowed and enlarged. The new blowing cone was in action back of the new flows on the lower bench southwest. The flow across the partition had poured on to the west end of the lower bench from the south end of the west pond. Bombardment was against the north bank and around the borders of the lake there was the most fountaining.

A block of the point at the north entrance to the east cove had dropped down and there was a smoking chasm behind it, as seen from the south station. The general drift of the surface skins was eastward. There were high glowing and flaming chimneys over the

WEEKLY BULLETIN
of the
Hawaiian Volcano Observatory

Published Monthly at Honolulu, Hawaii, by the Hawaiian Volcano Research Association

Editor.............Howard M. Ballou
Professor of Physics, College of Hawaii

Entered as second-class matter January 20, 1914, at the post-office at Honolulu, Hawaii, under the Act of August 24, 1912.

east cove. Blowing noises could be located around the shores of the lake at fountaining places, while the middle skins formed quiet polyhedra separated by zigzag lines of parting. In the west pond the lava was pounding against the west wall.

At five p. m. the lake overflowed its banks and a flood of lava came pouring down into the lake at its west end from the south end of the west pond. At nine p. m. these fresh flows were glowing. At ten p. m. new flows poured across from the west pond, widening the belt of new material which now connected the two pools, and it was evident that the lake and the pond were rapidly approaching a common level.

A survey at three p. m., July 27, made the lake 434 feet below the southeast station and the southwest pot only five feet higher. There was tremendous rising activity. The east cone was replaced by a small oval pool. The southwest pot was belching great splashes of glowing lava from an oval mouth, and these joined the lava flow from the west which was majestically advancing to cascade into the lake.

The source of this flow was a succession of pulsating overflows from the south end of the west pond, and these flooded the southwest bench region and cascaded into the lake with a drop of two or three feet along a length of shoreline of about sixty feet. The lake was covered with skins which streamed eastward and the fountaining was mostly around the borders. The noises were puff, belch, thud and plash. The two north crags, the partition crag northwest, and the southeast crags were all still in place. In general the events of this period, especially the torrent from the west pouring into the lake, are a repetition of what took place December 31 and thereafter, 1914.

The rising must have culminated during the night July 27-28 for on the morning of July 28 the fumes appeared thinner than at any time since last December. Inspection at ten-thirty a. m. showed large new flows in the northeast trench, and new flows over the bench north of the lake had drowned completely the last remnant of the old north crag of 1914. Seen from the southeast a new small flow had trickled from the region of the southwest pot eastward along the sag back of the southeast crags. The lake was about four feet below its banks and measurement made the depth 432 feet below the southeast station, so that the maximum elevation of the night must have been about 428 feet below the southeast rim of Halemaumau.

The flows at eleven a. m., July 28, were all crusted over except for a small trickle welling up a crack in the new flows of the northeast trench. There was a wide sweep of flows from the west pond to the lake, in general flat as though the two lakes were once more on nearly the same level. Two southern coves of the main lake were tending to merge by collapse of the point between. Streaming was sluggish northward, with splashing against the north bank, in the south cove and elsewhere from time to time. The southwest pot, now a cone, puffed occasionally, and the noises in general were mild plashing and puffing. The eastern pond was crusted over. The lake in a few days had greatly changed its shape; it was now elongate with double coves southwest and south, and single coves east and northwest, and a straight shore northeast. On the north were two beetling crags with a deep crevasse between them and the north wall of the pit. Wide black flows filled the eastern end of this trench even into the space formerly called the southeast trench, between the southeast crags and the eastern wall of the pit. The formation of these tilted crags at times of subsidence has now been watched and photographed several times; they represent old floor benches which gradually topple, leaving sloping scarps. When flows pour around them they stand up as crags; when they topple into the lake they form islands.

H. O. Wood reports that during the week ended July 28 five, or possibly six small local earthquakes have been registered at the Whitney Laboratory of Seismology. The character of one group of feeble waves is in doubt. During the week the amplitude of the microseismic waves has increased from slight values to considerable values. Amplitudes of the volcanic vibration waves have undergone a general decrease during the week. Except for the usual fluctuations there has been no change in the condition of tilt.

T. A. JAGGAR, JR., Director.

TECHNOLOGY STATION, August 5. —The week ending August 4 at Kilauea Volcano has shown slight subsidence of the top of the lava column and has brought to a close the marked rise with overflow which was so spectacular the previous week. In general the lava has been stationary this week about ten to twelve feet below the high-level bench of recent overflow, but between August 2 and 3 there was a small new overflow on the southwest bench, about 435 feet below the east station.

At midnight of July 28 no flows were in action on the floor. July 29 at ten o'clock a. m. the bank over the lake was about 3 feet high on the north and 1 foot on the south; it looks as though the south were tilting down under the weight of the flows as happened last autumn, while the north bottom area lifts. The high northeast and northwest crags show evidence of this tilting action.

The streaming was north and east. Fountaining was strong against the north shore and a portion of the bank collapsed. There was much bubble fountaining and some traveling fountains. The west pond was streaming northward, and a sluggish stream poured northward from under crust at the north end of the little east pond. The southwest cone was coated with white sublimates and occasionally hissed. Glow spots were seen above the east cove. The solidified flows in the northeast arm appeared to have come from the direction of the east pond. A trench fissure without any filling of flows lay between a high clinging northern bench remnant and the northern crags. The southeast crag bench appears to have subsided bodily, and now the southwest cone and flow appeared to be on the lake shore level, as the measurements show them to be. The culmination of rising had passed.

July 30 at three p. m. the lake was five feet below the bank, streaming was east and north, fountaining was violent north, the southwest cone was puffing, and the west pond was quiet with the liquid 2 feet down.

Saturday, July 31 at three p. m. conditions were similar but the lake appeared 10 feet down and the west pond about 8 feet. There were many bubble fountains carried along with the streaming towards the east cove. The west pond was active and streaming northward. There was rapid streaming in the main lake from the west end and against the north bank.

August 2 at 5 p. m. both lakes had cliffs about 12 feet high above the lava. In the main lake the north cliff was higher than the south. There was slow eastward streaming, and perpetual bubbling and blowing fountains were migrating to the northeast from the Old Faithful locality. Old Faithful was very violent, sometimes bursting in multiple domes; its intervals were irregular, as follows: 25, 50, 65, 30, 15, 20, 25, 15, 15, 15, 20, 40, 15, 25 seconds. There was some acceleration of the rate of streaming inside of the east cove; over the inner end of the east cove was a glowing cavity. and beyond was a pot in the northeast trench, indicating that a considerable crusted extension of the east cove extended in that direction, liable to collapse and increase the size of the lake when subsidence takes place.

There were now glowing cones in the northeast trench, on the east bench, to the southwest, and on the cracked benches covered with new flows south of the lake. The great southwest cone, seen best from the southwest station, had a triangular hole in its crest six feet in diameter showing hanging stalactites within, and splashing lava surged up within it from time to time and slopped out at intervals. The east pond had glow at each end, the middle part was all black folded crusts. On the floor north of the lake there was a hump in the new flows where the remnant of the old crag underlay them. The noises were of blowing, fountaining and rumbling, the latter noise characteristic of subsidence. Shore grottoes with stalactites appeared northwest, north and in the east cove. The west pond was streaming north covered with quiet skins.

From five to six p. m. there was rising going on and diminished rumble. The upper ten feet of cliff over the lake exhibit spatter horizons showing that for the last few days there has been oscillation of the lava level but no overflow.

Fresh overflows can always be told by their blackness and lustre, qualities lost within three days under the attack of fumes. There was fresh yellow stain of solfataric deposit in the trench back of the southeast crags. Blue fumes rose from the southwest cone and the fumes in general were a little heavier than last week. The heaviest smoke was from the southeast trench.

At ten a. m. August 3 there was one small new overflow on the southwest floor showing that there had been a temporary rise, probably in the night. The southwest cone was enlarged and the orifice was closed except for a crack. Both lakes appeared 10 or 12 feet down. There was much cracking along a line of flaming cones at the edge of the second shelf of the south bench. The south bench was markedly lower than the north wall over the lake, so that the observed overflow may have been due to increased tilting of the bottom rather than to any marked rise of the lake.

August 4 at six p. m. the lake appeared 15 feet below the bank north and was crusted across the west end and sluggish. The streaming was various in general toward the perpetual fountains near the north bank. At the west end a pool opened in the crust and then streaming was westward in that pool and eastward in the eastern lake. The west pond was moderately active against its west bank and streaming northward. The southwest cone had collapsed again and was flaming and fuming from an orifice in its summit.

H. O. Wood reports that during the week ending with August 4 six earthquakes were registered in the Whitney Laboratory of Seismology. Of these five were of the usual, slight, local sort. The sixth was a shock of distant origin and of moderate world-shaking power, or possibly greater. The approximate focal distance is 3500 miles from this station.

There have been only the usual fluctuations is energy in the case of microseisms and volcanic vibrations.

In general the tilting has not changed. And its variations have been of smaller amount than usual.

T. A. JAGGAR, JR., Director.

Technology Station, August 12.—Subsidence of lava in Halemaumau pit has continued during week ending August 11, 1915, and with it the lower bench of overflow has also subsided, especially southwest of the lake. The west pond has gone down step by step along with the main lake. There have been spectacular avalanches of rock into the lake from the western crag which separates the two pools. The total subsidence of the lava column amounted to 30 feet in the week from August 2, to August 9. Faint fumes have been seen occasionally at sundown and in the afternoon over Mokuaweoweo during clear weather.

August 5, at nine a. m., the air was dry but the fumes from Halemaumau appeared thick. At two p. m., from the south east station, the lava appeared to be about fifteen feet below the lower bench with eastward streaming and fountains northeast; Old Faithful burst occasionally. The west pond was quiet.

August 6, at three p. m., from the southeast station, there was much bubble fountaining in the main lake, no marked change in the relative levels of the lava and the south bench and the eastward streaming surface current poured into a tunnel in the east cove with much commotion. From the west station the small pool west was seen to be quiet with northward streaming.

August 7, at three p. m., from the southeast station, the lake appeared lower, perhaps 20 feet below the bench, and very active in the middle with traveling fountains moving eastward.

August 8, at eleven a. m., from the south station, evidence of subsidence of the south bench began to appear. This bench had parted along the east-west crack which has lately been marked by a row of spatter cones and the strip between the crack and the lake had sunk down with eastward slope so that its eastern end was submerged beneath the lava making an effect like a bench of the east side of the south point.

Back of this strip the remainder of the bench stood as a cliff twelve feet high above the subsided portion. The northeast bench had also subsided along a series of cracks parallel with the shore so as to change the bank from a cliff to a slope. The whole north platform under the north crag was cracked, the east cove appeared wider and the point at its north entrance appeared ready to break away to form a peninsula or an island. New lava films lapped over the northeast and south sunken shore-lines showing that there had been intense bombardment at these places. There were stagnant slow skins over the east end of the lake, the streaming was north from the southwest bank, eastward in the east part of the lake and into the east cove and toward the down-sunken bench westward in the region of the south cove. At the east and west ends of the lake the cliff appeared 15 feet high and even higher over the shores of the west pond. There was a black hole in the bench above the south end of the west pond. Glow appeared in the insunken top of the southwest cove and at the north end of the small east pond.

There were fountains against the west shore of the west pond and in the main lake north and west with bubble fountains at the south point. The fumes from the east end were dense and also in the northeast trench.

Measurements at eleven a. m. on August 9 made the depth of the lake surface below the southwest rim of Halemaumau 465 feet with subsidence in progress. The west end of the lower bench southwest of the main lake, formed only a fortnight ago by flows, had collapsed in a semi-circle leaving a marked cliff bounding the bench on the side of the partition which separates the two lakes . This bench was much cracked in lines parallel with southwest margin of the lake. The south point was about 5 feet above the lake level, while east and west cliffs 20 to 25 feet high rose above the lake. The streaming was north and east and all signs pointed to subsidence.

The night view August 10 at 9 p. m., from the southeast showed flames around the border of the lake, from the southwest cone, the east pond and a place in the northeast trench. At first the streaming in the lake was eastward and slow. Then great tumbles of rock crashed down from the west crag, a large portion of which caved away into the lake, and there appeared to be other falls of rock into the west pond. After the avalanche for a few minutes the surface streaming of the main lake was diverted westward against the bank where the rocks had fallen in. At the northern entrance of the east cove the point of rock had broken away and subsided and was converted into a peninsula joined by only a narrow neck to the bench on the north.

August 11 at ten a. m. seen from the southeast station, the lake appeared to have risen somewhat as it was flooding the south bench. This may, however, have been an effect of subsidence of the bench. There was crust over the lake and fountaining pools around the border. An avalanche was heard to fall from the north crag, fresh white talus slopes appeared along the north and west crags and the whole west end of the lake was much enlarged by collapse of the banks including a considerable portion of the south bench.

The noises were of puffing and splashing. The lava sank 3 feet between ten and eleven a. m., leaving the south point emerged by that amount while elsewhere cliffs over the lake ranged from 20 feet at the east end to 60 feet at the west crag. The large southwest cone displayed an open crater glowing within. A 20-foot cliff surmounted the semi-circular curve of the southwest bench. The west pond was splashing. By eleven a. m. the crusts in the main lake had broken up and increased activity accompanied the subsidence, while thin skins formed which drifted eastward.

During the week ending with August 11 five small local earthquakes were registered in the Whitney Laboratory of Seismology, all occurring in the early part of the week.

Microseismic motion has varied irregularly between moderate and moderately strong values. Similarly volcanic vibrations have varied from moderate to moderately strong sustained motion.

During the week there has been a slight general increase in the inclination of the tilting to the north which has been subject to the usual diurnal, and longer, fluctuations. The condition of east-west tilt has in general remained unchanged but has been subject to the usual short term changes.

T. A. JAGGAR, JR., Director.

TECHNOLOGY STATION, August 19.—After a slight rise of the lava in Halemaumau pit ending about Friday, August 13, pronounced subsidence again took place, resulting during the past week in great increase of fume, collapse of the partition separating the main lake from the west pond, and a resumption of the cascading and whirlpool action in the east cove which has been a characteristic of subsidence for nine months past. In consequence of these changes, the present lake merged with the west pond, is longer than at any time since early in the year 1912.

August 12 the temporary rise following subsidence of the preceding days, continued. August 13 at two-thirty p. m. seen from the southeast station, it was evident that pulsations of rising and sinking were in progress, the sinking phases resulting in more crumbling of the western crag so that the saddle between the two lakes had become a jagged edge.

Another evidence of recurrence of subsidence was the rush of surface lava into the east cove which recurred every ten to fifteen minutes with quiet times between. The walls over the lake appeared thirty feet high east and west, the south and north banks about six feet high. The west end of the lake was crusted over, with boiling pools at the margin of the crust and streaming was eastward with bombardment of the north bank and the east cove. The southwest cone sputtered lava slightly, although it was now high above the lake level. The glowing cones appeared at the site of the east pond. Blue fumes arose from the south banks and the southwest pit, white fumes from the southeast crags and the south end of the west pond. The latter was fountaining. The west end of the lake appeared wider and the west crag showed change of shape and was lower than before.

August 14 at three p. m. from the southeast station, a great change was seen to have taken place. The saddle between the two lakes had fallen in and was replaced by a strait uniting the lakes into one. The west crag north of this strait had fallen to pieces and a large block of the north bank was tilted toward the lake and bounded at its east end by a new fingering cove into which the lava rushed. This cove had been a deep grotto before. The east cove and the west pond (the latter now part of the main lake) were relatively quiet. Bombardment and over-spatter were in progress on the northeast bank, and a continuous fountain played in the middle of the east end of the lake.

A fairly complete survey on this day with clear seeing from the east and south made the combined lake 690 feet long with an average width of about 150 feet; the greatest length was in an east-western direction.

The west pond was about 225 feet long north-south, the mean depression of the surface of the lake below the southeast rim of the pit was 458 feet, seven feet higher than on August 9. The southwest cone at its summit was forty-two feet above the lake level and the north crag fifty-three feet above the lake. Streaming in general was from the southwest cove, north, west and east with rapid streaming around the peninsula which separated the eastern cove from the main lake and some southward rush against the bank in the south cove.

August 15 at eleven a. m. the pit was very smoky with occasional seeing from the southeast station. The lake appeared about ten feet lower than on the previous day and the strait leading to the west pond was now a cove of the lake, the crust over the strait making a slight bench. Spatter ramparts appeared all around the lake and stalactites were hanging in the grottoes.

In the east cove the rampart was at least ten feet high, streaming was east and north from the southwest cove, there was bombardment against the north shore and the north finger cove was narrow and stagnant, curved to the west at its inner end; the noises were of plashing and rumbling and a long hiss was heard occasionally from the region of the southwest cone. There was no sign of any more avalanches but every sign of general subsidence with more crusting and higher spatter banks.

August 16 at eleven a. m. measurement made the level of the lava below the southeast rim 459 feet, only one foot lower than on August 14, and of the summit of the southwest cone 419 feet or three feet lower than on August 14. The most striking feature was the rush of lava into the past cove, which now amounted to a cataract.

There was also streaming into the cove from under the crust of the northeast trench and from under the crust over the isthmus which connected the island block with the north bank immediately to the west of the cove. This last torrent was the most rapid and the three torrents meeting in the cove made there a tremendous whirlpool. There were no other conspicuous changes.

August 17 at four-thirty p. m. the lake appeared still lower and the pit was still more smoky. The measurement made the depth to the lava surface from the southeast station 474 feet, or sixteen feet lower than on the 14th. A dim view from the northwest station showed activity along the border of the west pond. The east side of the south point appeared to be caving back into a cavernous grotto under bombardment. The southwest cove and the cove opposite the west strait showed increased definition with deep banks, the north finger had become a mere narrow cleft, streaming was eastward and against the north bank from the southwest cove and also into the west cove; stalactites appeared at the south point and the north bank, quiet skins covered most of the lake and the noise was of plashing.

From time to time intense fountaining took place near the east end of the lake. At four-forty-five the inrush at the east cove began again, showing that the down-sinking at that point was intermittent. No glow could be seen in the southernmost of the two cones on the east bench, the northern one was a large round glowing lava pot. The southwest pit appeared deeper by collapse.

On August 18 from six to eight p. m. the smoke in the pit was so dense and so blown by the wind that there was no good seeing from any side. Dim views of the lake after dark showed no marked change, there was moderate activity in the east cove but no rush of streaming there. The bank at the south point appeared fifteen feet high at least. Occasional blowing was heard from the southwest.

There was no continuous connection of moving lava seen through the strait from the west pond to the main lake. From the northwest rim of the pit the west pond could be seen covered with quiet skins streaming northward. Otherwise the streaming and fountaining was the same as during the last few days.

Four local earthquakes have been registered in the Whitney Laboratory of Seismology during the week ending August 18. One of these, about five-twenty a. m.. August 15, was felt at the Volcano House and vicinity. Microseismic and volcanic vibrations have been moderate during the week and the tilt to the north and west has fluctuated as usual.

On Tuesday morning August 17 at seven a. m. an expedition from the observatory to the summit of Mauna Loa was despatched in charge of H. O. Wood. It is the purpose of this expedition to collect photographs and specimens from the scene of the activity of December 1914 and to explore the rift extending northeast from the crater Mokuaweoweo.

The first party consisted of Mr. Wood and Alex Lancaster with packers and guide supplied by the Volcano Stables Company and Kapapala Ranch. Mr. Wood and Lancaster proceeded to the summit to camp there for a fortnight, while the packers returned to the lower camp with the animals. J. F. Haworth plans to join the party at the summit August 22. Leaving the road at the Kapapala cattle pen at nine a. m., the expedition reached Ainapo at nine-fifty, the forest reservation at one-twenty-five p. m. and the lower camp ground, elevation 7800 feet, at two p. m. A beacon fire built at the camp ground at seven p. m. was plainly seen at the Observatory.

At five-fiffteen a. m. August 18 Mr. Wood left the camp ground on foot and arrived at Mokuaweoweo in five hours twenty-five minutes, ten-forty a. m. The pack train left camp at six-thirty a. m. and arrived at the summit at ten-twenty-five a. m. There was no smoke to be seen in the crater and practically no steam, at the time of arrival.

T. A. JAGGAR, JR., Director.

TECHNOLOGY STATION, August 26.—The week ended August 25 at the lava pit Halemaumau has been characterized by pronounced rising of the lava column at least seventy-five feet so that the lake at the end of the week was about 400 feet below the rim of the pit. Wide new platforms of overflow have been built and lava has poured and trickled out of lateral cones east, south, southwest and west. The last remnant of the west crag has been buried under flows and a majestic torrent has continuously poured from the west pond into the main lake. The peninsula at the northern entrance of the east cove has been converted into an island. Altogether the lava lake is at present as spectacular and free from fume as at any time during the past year and it is larger than at any time for years past, extending from wall to wall of the pit from northwest to east.

On the morning of August 19, a marked change from the thick fumes of the preceding subsidence period was noted from the Observatory, the fumes appearing thin and diffuse so that the remoter walls of the crater could be seen through them. At six p. m. from the south station it became clear that this change was occasioned by a sudden rise of about twenty-five feet. A broad torrent was pouring from the west pond to the lake, there were blowing cones on the sites of the east peninsula and the north finger and a continuous hiss could be heard from the vicinity of the southwest cone. There was evidently very high gas pressure accompanying the rise and occasional violent hisses were heard from the blowing cones. The eastern cone occasionally spurted lava spray to heights estimated as between sixty and 100 feet. There were fresh overflows at the end of the east cove and over the north and southwest platforms between six and six-fifteen p. m. after a temporary sinking spell during the preceding quarter of an hour.

At six-twenty p. m. the west torrent was broader and slower and the south end of the west pond was covered with a ragged skin. The entire north bench became flooded with lava which merged with the overflow from the north side of the east cove. At six-twenty-five p. m. subsidence began again and the speed of flow eastward in the east cove and west channel increased, the line of border fountains formed along the north bank, tremendous spurts shot up from the eastern blow-hole and lava splashed up in the north cone. There was some spurting in a blow-hole in the northeast trench. Fountaining took place at the north and south ends of the west pond, a continuous fountain played in a small cove west of the south point and Old Faithful broke occasionally as a small dome near the north bank.

From nine to eleven p. m. this mechanism of alternations of rising and falling at intervals of about twenty minutes continued. At nine p. m. the lava was relatively lower and a rapid narrow torrent poured eastward from the west pond, apparently down a slope to the main lake and the lava of the lake streamed westward to meet the torrent in an overlapping surface layer.

The east blowing cone was spurting moderately and a blue flame flared above its orifice. About ten p. m. rising was in progress with overflows on the benches. At ten-thirty p. m. a tremendous rise took place and cataracts rushed into the northeast trench from the north bench and east cove, and others tumbled into voids northwestward from the north bench, filling the hollows among the crags there. The eastward stream across the surface of the lake backed up, stagnated and reversed until the streaming was westward in the west channel, and then the west pond overflowed its northern bank and poured a torrent into the north trench. The main lake became a great flood of overflows in all directions with zigzag glow lines and quiet skins. The rise during the hour must have been twenty feet at least, and reached an elevation fully forty feet above the level of the preceding day.

At ten-fifty p. m. there was a sudden change to sinking. The lake resumed its west to east river-like quality and its normal outline again asserted itself, while the overflows on the benches cooled and blackened. The greatest spurting and gas pressure was during the rising periods, when also the surface currents slowed down and the fountaining became less. Rapid currents and intense fountaining accompanied the subsidence. At eleven p. m. subsidence was in progress.

On August 20 the fumes were a little denser, there was some slight subsidence and the activity showed much fluctuation, and change in direction of streaming.

On the morning of August 21 the fumes again had greatly decreased and rapid rising was in progress. At noon the lake was brimming, a rapid torrent poured from the west pond, there were over-spatter cones on the bank north, south, and at the north end of the west pond. The east blowing cone had become a round convex lens with a small hole in its summit which was hissing very violently from time to time, showing a spear of flame, like a blow-pipe, which increased with each hiss. The southwest cone was hissing continuously. The north crag was surrounded by new floor and two smoking remnants of the west crag protruded through the floor. The east cove was quiet, brimming full and surrounded by flat floor. There were broad new flows north, southwest, and along the whole length of the northeast trench from the east cove to the north end of the pond. Old Faithful was small and insignificant. The heat from the lake was great. During the two hours from eleven a. m. to one p. m. there were fresh overflows northeast, north, southwest, and at the end of the east cove. In the north trench at the base of the northeast cliff could be seen a glowhole where a slight cavern had been undermined in the old wall. Measurements made the lake 427 feet below the southeast rim, the summit of the southwest cone 409 feet and the north crag about 403 feet.

August 22 at five p. m., the lake was still brimming and rising with eastward streaming as before. There had evidently been spells of pronounced sinking and collapse of the banks, for the eastern cone had disappeared and the north bank was eaten back for a stretch 100 feet long by bombardment. The southwest pit was now a pond mostly crusted over, with a fountain at its west end. The torrent from the west pond backed up and became stagnant during a rising spell from five to five-fifteen p. m., after which temporary subsidence caused it to resume its eastward flow. New high level flows could be seen west of the southwest cove of the main lake from a pot south of the west pond, the lake appeared to be about on the level of the base of the southwest cone, which would make it about fifty feet higher than on August 17, or say 424 feet below the rim of Halemaumau. The southwest pond appeared to be at the same level. Puffing at intervals could be heard from the southwest cone. There were oversplash ramparts south, north, southwest, east, at the end of the east cove, at the north end of the west pond and at the west end of the southwest pond. Great blocks of skin floated down the torrent from the west pond like ice-floes in a river, and the pattern of skins on the lake fanned out from this torrent eastward. The main bombardment was against the north bank.

During the next two days, August 23 and 24, there was slight subsidence, and the increased activity which accompanied the sinking, along with the emergence of an island at the east end and the rush of two streams of lava around it, added greatly to the spectacular quality of the scene.

From nine to ten p. m. August 23 the pit was fumy but the lake could be seen through the fumes from the southeast and northwest stations. The pattern of skins and fountains was most various and tumultuous, streams poured eastward on both sides of the island at the entrance of the east cove and against the east face of the island there was tumultuous inrush where the two streams joined. A new pot with surging lava and flame appeared in the southeast ledge, and lava surged up in the southwest cone which was built high by spatter. A continuous fountain played on the west side of the southwest cove which was otherwise crusted over. A high knob appeared at the west side of a new embayment in the north bank. Two pots were glowing and sputtering on the east bench, the west torrent backed up and reversed its current every little while and now and again a vortex would form with counter-clockwise rotation, near the lower end of the torrent against the north bank. From a glowing pot south of the west pond a ribbon of lava poured into the pond and there was a small overflow in motion at the north end of the west pond.

At seven p. m. August 24 no conspicuous changes were seen from the southeast station, small flows were flowing around the southwest cone from the southwest pit and the flow from the west pot northward into the west pond continued. The glowing pots east and southeast were no longer in evidence. The south point appeared to be twenty feet high, glowing outlines indicated fresh flows in the north trench and from the west pot to the southwest cove.

On August 25 the fumes appeared a little thicker during the day, but pronounced overflowing took place as was revealed on the following day.

No earthquakes were recorded in the Whitney Laboratory of Seismology during week ending August 25, and the microseismic and tilting motions fluctuated but slightly. Volcanic vibrations were unusually strong at intervals during the week.

J. F. Haworth joined the Observatory party on the summit of Mauna Loa August 22 to remain with them there for a week.

T. A. JAGGAR, JR., Director.

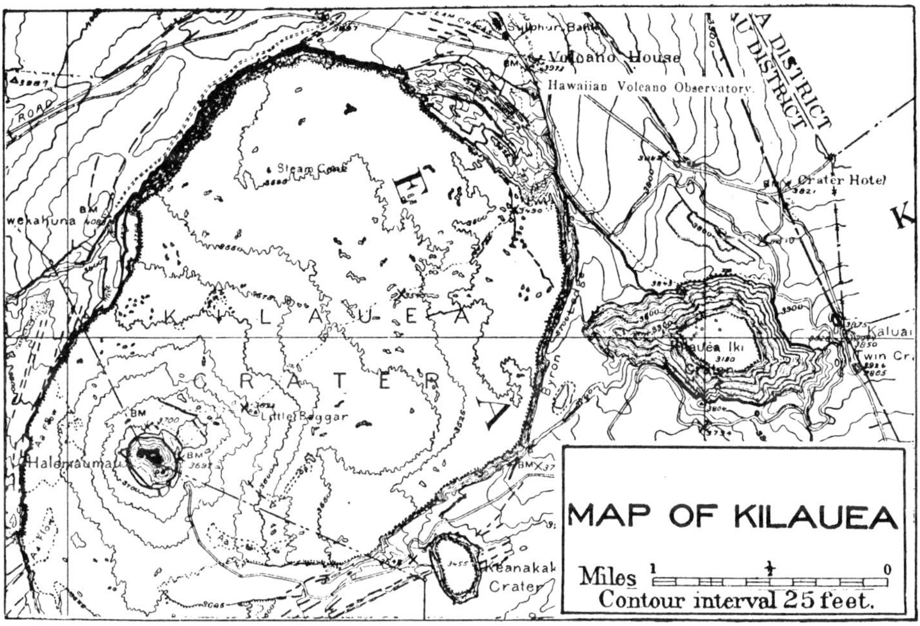

HAWAIIAN VOLCANO RESEARCH ASSOCIATION.

This society is a voluntary one, made up of subscribers to scientific work which is being executed by the Massachusetts Institute of Technology.

In 1915 there are about 100 subscribers in Hawaii and elsewhere, firms and individuals. A group of firms and persons in Hilo built the main observatory building in the spring of 1912. Publications to date have been weekly reports since the summer of 1911, now reprinted in Honolulu in monthly form. The Massachusetts Institute of Technology will publish annual reports, of which the introductory number was printed in 1912.

The weekly bulletin as it appears in the Advertiser is reprinted as a leaflet and sent to regular annual subscribers to the work of the Association. L. A. Thurston is president of the Board of Directors of the Association, and R. W. Shingle is treasurer. New subscribers who are interested in volcanoes will be welcomed in the Association. The Association aims: (1) To record volcanic activity and earthquakes in Hawaii; (2) to attract scientific men hither for special studies; (3) to promote the establishment of volcano observatories all over the world. The annual dues of regular members are $5; patrons of the Assocaition subscribe larger amounts.

WHITNEY LABORATORY OF SEISMOLOGY.

The Whitney Laboratory of Seismology is equipped with two Bosch-Omori 100 kg tromometers registering N-S and E-W motion, a heavy Omori tromometer registering E-W motion, and an Omori "ordinary Seismograph" designed for registering strong earthquakes in all three components of motion. These are seated on concrete piers in a closed basement room having practically constant temperature, beneath the chief Observatory building near the hotel. Time is referred to a rated chronometer, checked at intervals by solar observations with a transit. Both instruments are loaned by the College of Hawaii. At the substation by the edge of the active pit an Omori two-component tromometer with light steady masses is mounted on a concrete pier placed directly on the fresh lava surface. Hawaiian standard time (H. S. T.) is 10 hrs. 30 min. slower than Greenwich time.

CANCANI SCALE OF SEISMIC INTENSITY.

Expressed by accelerations measured in millimeters per second per second.

I.	Instrumental	0.0	2.5
II.	Very slight	2.5	5.0
III.	Slight	5.0	10.0
IV.	Sensible, mediocre	10.0	25.0
V.	Rather strong	25.0	50.0
VI.	Strong	50.0	100.0
VII.	Very strong	100.0	250.0
VIII.	Ruinous	250.0	500.0
IX.	Disastrous	500.0	1000.0
X.	Very disastrous	1000.0	2500.0
XI.	Catastrophic	2500.0	5000.0
XII.	Great catastrophe	5000.0	10000.0

Grade IV. is ordinarily the minimum perceived by the senses; and in grade XII. the acceleration, or rate of change of motion (jerk) reaches that of terrestrial gravitation.

In the standard form of report the maximum intensity or acceleration, designated by the symbol a, or max. a, is given in the conventional unit, **the milligal.** The milligal is a measure of acceleration, such that 1 milligal = 1/100 mm. per sec. per sec. = 10 μ per sec. per sec. The Cancani scale, here defined in terms of millimeters per sec. per sec., can therefore be expressed in **milligals** by multiplying each of the numbers by 100.

WEEKLY BULLETIN
OF THE
Hawaiian Volcano Observatory

Vol. III. HONOLULU, HAWAII, SEPTEMBER, 1915. No. 9

TECHNOLOGY STATION, September 2.—The pronounced rise of the lava in Halemaumau inaugurated on August 19 has continued during the past week at a fairly uniform rate. The lake has enlarged, the benches have been flooded repeatedly both by flows from the lateral cones and by overflow from the lake. The crags have consequently become increasingly submerged under solidified flows so that only small remnants of them protrude above the general level. The lake has risen to within a few feet of the bench remnants of the floor of December 1914, and has overflowed the down-sunken remnants of that bench on the southeast. The fumes over the pit have been extraordinarily thin, and blue flames from the cones and the border grottoes have been very conspicuous.

On August 26, 1915, at nine o'clock in the morning extensive fresh overflows of the preceding thirty-six hours were seen in the southeast valley and over the east, north and west benches. A floor of overflow had formed between the southeast crags and the lake. Overflows had poured from the southwest pond, now a bay in the general floor, to the lake. The south point was built high by spatter and a spatter-bench appeared around the lake, in places six feet high. The south half of the west pond was covered with skin and the lake was streaming eastward with much fountaining and puffing. The stream from the west pond eastward divided about a small island shoal, apparently a submerged block fallen from a notch to the southwest. The southwest cone was about fifteen feet high with a glowing hole in the summit surrounded by a ring of spatter. A new south cone had formed on the back slope of the southeast crags with radial trickels of lava about it.

Only a small talus now divided the east bench from the new flows in the southeast valley. The west cone sent a sheaf-like flow northward into the west pond which passed under a bridge of crust; another sluggish flow moved down a straight slope from this cone eastward into the lake. Bombardment was taking place in a grotto in a large half-cone at the north end of the west pond. Fresh flows were glowing on the east bench. The last remnants of the west crags were covered with new flows. A conelet was building in the southwest embayment. At the base of the old wall southeast a yellow stained niche, or cavity, appeared, about twenty feet high, probably the orifice of the southeast chimney which was so persistent throughout 1914. On the evening of this date, the lake overflowed the island at the east end.

On August 27, the fumes were extremely thin and it became evident that a pronounced rise was in progress. So clear was the seeing in daylight that for the first time in many months, photographs and measurements were made from the western stations.

A complete survey of the floor made the depth to the lake below the northwest station 416 feet, length of lake 700 feet, width 220 feet, length of floor 780 feet in a southeast-northwest direction and width 730 feet east-west. The west pot was 20 feet above the lake level and the east bench 9 feet above it. The 1914 bench south was 392 feet below the rim.

There was a slight subsidence nine to eleven o'clock a. m., and rising from eleven o'clock a. m. to twelve-thirty o'clock p. m. The heat from the lava felt on the rim of the pit was strong. The west cone appeared to be the principal source of the rising lava and the highest orifice on the floor.

WEEKLY BULLETIN
of the
Hawaiian Volcano Observatory

Published Monthly at Honolulu, Hawaii, by the Hawaiian Volcano Research Association

Editor.............Howard M. Ballou
Professor of Physics, College of Hawaii

Entered as second-class matter January 20, 1914, at the post-office at Honolulu, Hawaii, under the Act of August 24, 1912.

Flows poured from it north and east, the torrent poured eastward from the west pond and general streaming was to the east. A steady small cascade poured into the southwest cove of the lake from under a crust. Fresh floods of overflow floored the southeast valley but the east bench was covered with flows separated from the lake by a spatter rampart and evidently from border cracks rather than from overflow; at twelve-thirty o'clock p. m. the crusts on this bench broke up and incandescent lava overflowed through the cracks. The lake maintained a rampart about three feet high. Glowing fresh lava extended from the north end of the west pond eastward in the depression between the north crag and the wall of the pit. Large spatter cones were maintained at the northeast corner of the lake, above three grottoes at the north end of the west pond and on the north side of the lake. The lake had greatly widened south of the island at the east end. The noises were of splashing, pounding and occasional hissing. At one o'clock p. m. subsidence was in progress.

During the following days the mechanism of rising showed the same general features with a lessening of the hissing gas pressure and much quiet flooding of the benches. The lake was almost continuously brimming level with its banks, so that in daytime an inexperienced observer might have difficulty in determining the boundaries between the lake proper and the floor of overflow.

On August 28 at ten o'clock a. m., from the southeast, the principal changes were the junction of the flows of the southeast valley and the east bench between the southeast crags and the wall; a very large spatter cone on the north bank which was the scene of the maximum bombardment; the island was smaller; the west pond and the west cone appeared now to be on the same level; and the western outlier of the southeast crag was now buried under flows. The main smoking places were the crags and the west margin of the southwest embayment.

On August 29 the crags were still more submerged, the floor southeast overlapped the bench remnant of 1914 and there were now five cones from east to west around the south margin of the floor which were sources of border flows. General overflow from the lake had taken place at the west but not at the east, north or south, where the border filling of the floor was fed from border vents. The southeast crags were now three pinnacles rising through the floor, and the west end of the north crag was all submerged. The island has been flooded and was square and flat-topped. A northern lower bench remnant of 1914 was now submerged under new flows. At six-thirty o'clock p. m. the southwest cone had collapsed on the lake side and a torrent was continuously foutaining from under it like an artesian well and pouring into the lake. Flows advanced by flooding and cracking on the south and north benches and the island had disappeared beneath the rising lake.

On August 30 at nine-thirty o'clock a. m., the lake was still brimming but the stream between it and the southwest cone was reversed in direction and now cascading into the pit under the cone. Flows were moving on the benches, the north spatter cones of the lake and the west pond had disappeared and the lake was overflowing northeast.

The rising and flooding continued throughout August 31. At eight o'clock p. m., the southwest cone was seen to be again built up into a dome, vomiting lava spasmodically northward and westward from its summit. A ribbon of lava poured northward from under crusts east of it. The crags were still more submerged. Large violent blue flames under pressure and from two to four feet high shot up from grottoes in the east bank, and from an orifice back of the east rampart and an immense banner of flames played above the fountaining grotto at the north end of the west pond. Flames were everywhere conspicuous, burning under strong gas pressure.

On September 1 from nine to ten o'clock a. m., the lake was rising but thereafter subsidence took place, so that at noon the lava was about five feet below the rampart. The lake appeared greatly enlarged east and southwest. The southern bench of 1914 was completely submerged, hot flows were crackling, the crags north and southeast were small and only fifteen to twenty feet high. The southwest embayment was now occupied by an elongate cove of the lake into which two cascades of lava poured from opposite sides of the southwest cone.

Measurements on the morning of September 1 showed the lake to be 380 feet below the south station, a rise of 36 feet since August 27 indicating that the rate of rising per day has been 7 feet. The lake was now 720 by 250 feet in dimensions the floor was 900 feet long by 700 feet wide.

During the week ending with September 1 six local earthquakes were registered in the Whitney Laboratory of Seismology. Three of these occurred in one day. One of them was distinctly felt here and two were felt in Hilo. They were, however, very weak shocks.

In the later days of the week microseismic motion has waxed from slight to strong. With some ordinary fluctuations the amplitude of volcanic vibration has been considerable throughout the week. This motion has been maintained strong steadily, and ''storms'' of these waves have occurred also.

Tilting has undergone little change in the east-west direction except fluctuation. In the north-south direction, however, tilt to the north has increased in a very marked manner necessitating readjustment of the pendulum to accommodate it. This has been especially the fact in the latter part of the week. Fluctuation has been marked in this component also.

The Mauna Loa expedition headed by H. O. Wood returned August 29 after ten days of exploration of the floor of the crater, its rim and the northeast rift. Many photographs were obtained. The vents of December 1914, appear to have closed almost completely, the fumes observed by the party being even less than usual and there was no evidence of any extraordinary heat from crevices in the crater floor or elsewhere.

T. A. JAGGAR, JR., Director.

TECHNOLOGY STATION, September 9.—The lava in Halemaumau continued to rise during the past week, but more slowly than before, the rate of upbuilding of floor from September 1 to September 8 being not more than a foot and a quarter a day.

During the first part of the week the lake subsided below its banks, but the cones around the border of the floor continued to eject flows. During the latter half of the week there has been some return of high gas pressure and overflowing of the lake margin. The fumes continue to be very thin and the whole floor of the pit is clearly visible from the rim day and night.

On September 2 at eleven-thirty o'clock the east cove appeared larger, extending nearly to the east wall, a new glistening black flow covered three-fourths of the southeast valley, other new overflows appeared about the south end of the west pond and large spatter cones appeared at the south border of the lake and on the north bank.

Bombardment was in progress under a very large and broad north cone. The southwest cone was belching out a flood of lava northward, and beside it a cascade poured into the southwest cove from under the crust of the southeast floor. The east end of the lake was brimming, the west end about two feet below the banks, streaming was north in the west pond and east in the lake.

Bubble fountains appeared in the rapid current that was rushing under the north spatter cone. What was formerly the point at the east entrance of the southwest cove was now a large island with a splashing grotto under its south side and the lava streaming eastward between it and the south shore of the lake. The island appeared to have been recently flooded with layers of new lava. This island was entirely different in location and origin from the submerged island in the east cove which disappeared on August 29.

Throughout this rising period, Old Faithful had not been definitely marked or regular in its eruptions.

On September 4 at eleven o'clock the lake was subsiding slightly, but by noon it had started to rise. Streaming was westward from skins over the east cove, eastward from the west end, and there was inrush against the north bank, east of the island, and into a void under the southwest cone. The south cone exhibited an open splashing pot whence a crusted flow westward cascaded into the cracks near the southwest cone. The southwest cone was rent asunder along an irregular fracture.

A singular and cruel tragedy was seen in the pit at this time. Flexible black skins bounded by zigzag fiery lines were moving eastward across the lake as usual. A pair of white "bos'n" birds were encircling about the interior of Halemaumau, as they frequently do, attracted by night by the glow and daytime by the warmth and motion of the lava.

One of the birds allowed his curiosity to carry him too far; he lighted on the moving skins over the liquid, was instantly overcome by the gases and heat and in a few seconds flashed into flame and was slowly engulfed as a glowing ember. The incident exhibited Halemaumau in a new capacity, namely, a natural death trap.

On September 5 in the afternoon the lake was brimming full. At six-thirty o'clock it had sunk about ten feet, five or six fountains were spattering strongly, a cascade tumbled from the lake into a pot under the broken southwest cone, stalactites hung from the north grotto and in general the lake appeared wider. The south cone on the floor was ejecting flows east and west and the floor showed glowing lines and flames. The only noise was of plashing, all the hissing of the previous week having ceased.

On September 6 at six-thirty o'clock the lake was about five feet below its banks and the southeast floor was still covered with glowing flows from the south cone. A flow westward from this cone poured into the fracture chasm of the southwest cone. The latter, however, was no longer receiving an inrush from the lake, but was sending out a golden stream over the crusts of the southwest cove.

Streaming in the lake was east and west from the ends and against the north and southwest banks. Glowing skins covered the east pond, which is a definitely marked oval pit in the bench. The island off the southwest cove was small but still in place and five or six standing fountains played in the middle region of the lake.

On September 7 at eight o'clock a marked change had taken place by increase of gas pressure; there were hissing fountains traveling from west to east which spurted spray and flame, the border grottoes were spurting high and about every thirty seconds the southwest cone shot a burst of spray fifty feet into the air.

This cone had re-formed as a low circular spatter heap. The lake was only about one foot below the bench and exhibited a motley pattern of east flowing skins. The central island was enlarged and the streaming skins divided around it. The southwest cove and the south end of the west pond were crusted over. Bubble fountains developed from time to time in the east cove.

There were new glowing flows all over the south platform originating at the south cone. The north end of the west pond was overflowing over the north platform. Between 8 and 9 o'clock a lava flow broke through the crusts of the south bench and poured northward first, cascading into a cavity in the bench and then pushing on to the lake border cascaded into the lake. This action became continuous.

On the morning of September 8 at ten-thirty o'clock conditions were about the same with the lake one foot below the bench and rising. After eleven-thirty o'clock it began to sink. The island had developed a plump shape, pointed at the ends, with the westward end raised higher than the eastward. It was forty-five feet long and about ten feet high. It was quite rigid and the current streamed eastward on both sides of it.

The bombardment of the north shore had entirely ceased. Old Faithful fountain was distinguishable between the island and the north bank, with an average interval between eruptions of about forty seconds. A continued festooned lava flow from the south cone poured straight northward across the bench and cascaded into the lake.

The promontory southeast of the west pond appeared to have become almost an island through the development of a deep cove extending from the main lake westward to the south end of the west pond. The latter was extended somewhat southward.

Fresh overflows appeared all around the lake north, west and south, but not east and northeast. The main smoking places were the southeast corner, the southeast crag and the north crag. The high gas pressure of the previous night had ceased and the southwest cone was dormant, but some hissing could be heard from the east. The east pond rose and fell with the lake.

Measurement on September 8 made the lake level 369 feet below the south rise of Halemaumau. The bench was about four feet higher, and the remnant of the December bench of 1914 appeared at the west end to be about eight feet higher still.

Another ascent of Mauna Loa by the Kapapala trail was made on September 7 by Messrs. Balsh, Thompson and Howes to the crater Mokuaweoweo. Conditions there showed complete dormancy as in August.

During the week ending with September 8 six small local earthquakes were registered in the Whitney Laboratory of Seismology. Besides these, in the morning hours of September 6 there was registered the chief phase only of a moderate teleseism and in the afternoon hours of the same day, Hawaiian time, a somewhat stronger teleseism was registered without defect of phase. This latter almost surely was the earthquake which has been reported as destructive in Guatemala.

During the week both the microseismic waves and those of the volcanic vibration series have gradually decreased in amplitude, though with fluctuations. There has been much fluctuation in tilt in the north-south component, little in the east-west component and no maintained changes in either.

T. A. JAGGAR, JR., Director.

Technology Station, September 16.—Very slowly the magma has continued to rise during the week ending with September 15. On September 10, the molten surface stood 366 feet below the rim. In spite of its actual slow upbuilding, during most of the time in the past week the magma has stood slightly below the surrounding platform which now has built to a higher level than the platform of December, 1914, except for a very narrow marginal tract under the southwest wall. Even this has been reduced in area by overflow in the week past. The fumes appear thinner than hitherto since July, 1912. Nevertheless the surface action is only ordinary—quiet streaming with simply the usual doming fountains. There are brief spasms of greater activity.

In this report the writer is indebted to the director for observations on September 9, and to Dr. Sidney Powers for measurements, and notes on September 10, 11 and 12.

In the forenoon on September 9 the lava was rising and there were new overflows at the west. A cone with splashing lava had built completely over the north end of the west pond. The promontory at the south entrance of the west pond was now an island. The southwest cove was masked by new overflows. The southwest cone was quiet. The south cone was a heaving pot with trickling overflows. The orifice just back of the south bank where the flow had been cascading in had now become a source of radial overflow, though a stream was still pouring into it from the south cone. The southeast crag appeared smaller, the north crag unchanged. The east pond was masked by overflows.

There was streaming to the east on both sides of the western island which is large, and has a grotto and spatter ridge on its east side and piled up skins on its west side. The island in the center had changed shape. There were flows over the south end of the west bench of December last.

In the early forenoon of September 10 the lake stood two feet lower than on the previous day. A long arm had opened reaching along the north from the west end of the lake, separated from the lake by a crag about 18 feet in height. This crag presented the appearance of positive uplift, with tilting and subsidence of the eastern end. It was cracked across at its junction with the floor. There was streaming toward the east with splashing caves at the east end.

The east pond was covered by fresh flows and was not visible. The eastern cove of the southwest arm was frozen over.

The south bench had apparently subsided slightly as the lake in rising, at eleven-thirty a. m., spilled over onto it. Also it had been flooded on the previous night from the southeast arm. The south cone was quiet. Near the edge of the lake north of it a new pot had opened. The southwest pot was quiet. Both islands had undergone minute changes of shape. On September 11 further changes in the shapes of the islands were noted, and the west island had almost disappeared beneath the molten surface. Magma was splashing upon it. The magma was rising, brimming on the south and confined by a low, spatter wall on the north.

The new crag was relatively lower owing to the rise of magma. The crack at its junction with the bench had widened. At the lake edge there was a spatter grotto on the south side of the crack. In the new north arm lava was pouring in from the west and running over onto the floor. Thin smoke was issuing from under the 1912 talus, from under the 1912 ledge at the south station, from the north crag, from the crack in the west crag, from the rift between the north and west crags, and from the floor west of the southwest arm and south of the south cove.

A violent torrent poured out of the south cone on the south. A flow was observed issuing from the region of the east pond and moving southward. There were also flows over the south part of the floor from the southwest arm. There were prolonged, steady, hissing noises due to outrush of gas from the south cone, and loud, spasmodic blasts from the southwest cone. A short-lived pot made its appearance south of the south cone. The southeast crag had been submerged by flows from the region of the east pond. In the afternoon the lake had fallen away some two feet and a new pot had opened just west of the southwest arm. The south part of the floor had been flooded successively from the main lake, from the southwest arm, and from the south and east pots.

On September 12 the lake stood some six feet lower than the platform, somewhat below the stand of the previous day. Thus the islands appeared in their usual places without significant change of form, but standing higher above the molten surface. This sinking served to crack and tilt further toward the lake the already tilted, tumbled crag of 1912 near the southwest arm. This arm now showed its true outline within the platform. The tumbled crag was enveloped by spatter walls. During the previous night the south part of the floor was again flooded from the east pond, and probably also from the south cove. All the pots were merely glowing quietly. A new fumarole was seen in the hanging talus just under the west station. The spatter cone at the crack margin of the new crag was smoking more vigorously. The issuing gases were hissing quietly.

On September 13 in the afternoon the lava was streaming vigorously east and northeast in the main lake, this flowing being accompanied with many large traveling fountains. In the north arm there was vigorous streaming into a boiling place near its east end. The lava stood at a depth of about one foot below the platform. A prolonged flow ran out of the southeast cone over the south part of the floor. The east pond opened and overflowed onto the surrounding platform. During the afternoon the lava sank away slightly.

On September 14 the lava stood from three to five feet below the level of the southern platform. In the main lake there was quiet streaming to the eastward and to the northeastward near the east end. Doming fountains breaking around and under the island near the center were the most vigorous manifestations seen. This island was reduced in area and obviously much undermined. There was quiet streaming into the main lake out of the southwest arm in the north arm there was quiet streaming toward the east where near the end there was an area of vigorous boiling. The smoke, while exceedingly thin, was issuing from a dozen or more places on the floor and at its margin, with one high fumarole under the south station. The fumes were very sharp and hot. The cones and pots were all in quiet action, and only the deep-toned surf noise attracted attention. The east pond, thinly skinned over, was heaving lazily.

On September 15 the lava stood about five feet below the 1914 floor. Large fountains travelling eastward, with the stream were seen. There had been a further flow over the southwest floor, and the glow could still be seen, in daylight, through cracks in the crust of this. Loud blowing sounds could be heard at intervals from the cones.

During the week ending with September 15 six small local earthquakes were registered in the Whitney Laboratory of Seismology. The registration of microseisms and of volcanic vibrations has presented nothing out of the ordinary. There has been a slight increase in the energy of the volcanic vibrations toward the end of the week. Save for the usual fluctuations the condition of tilt has undergone little change, merely a very slight shift southward in the north-south component.

H. O. WOOD, Associate.

TECHNOLOGY STATION, September 23.—The week preceding the equinox of September, 1915, has been marked by numerous earthquakes of small magnitude, and by a pronounced sinking of the lava in Halemaumau more than forty feet. The pit has again become smoky with poor seeing in the daytime. Torrential downpouring of lava into a void at the east end has begun again, this movement having been the precursor of marked subsidence frequently during the past year.

September 17, at 3 p. m., the lake was very large, over 700 feet long east-west, with north and south arms extending eastward from the west end following peripheral cracks around the floor, so as to give the whole lake somewhat the shape of the letter E. The streaming was eastward in all three arms, and an island occupied the middle of the west end. The liquid was about three feet below the floor. At 9 p. m. flames were conspicuous in nine places, and even the central fountains showed blue flames against the dark quiet skins that covered the surface of the pool. The bank now appeared about ten feet high above the liquid.

The next afternoon, September 18, the lake appeared five feet lower. A great block of the spatter rampart tumbled into the flood from the north bank. The middle island had reappeared as the lava subsided around it, but it appeared to stand as a spatter mushroom on a rather narrow stem. There were two glowing pools in the east pond, the south arm was quiet, Old Faithful was in operation, and at 6:15 p. m. the current began to rush into the end of the north arm as though subsidence were in progress there in excess of that of the main lake.

On September 19, at 8 p. m., the middle island had disappeared, probably by collapse, as the lake appeared no higher. Flames of bluish color were again very conspicuous.

Travelling fountains moved eastward, the streaming was from a narrow crust at the west end, stagnant heavy blankets covered the east end, and the noises were of rumble, blow, plash and spatter. Occasionally almost all the central fountaining ceased. The southwest cone had now become a violent flaming and spurting grotto. Inrush at the north arm, with strong spurting and flaming at the grotto at its end, took place from time to time, and was always accompanied by strong gas spurting from the north grotto of the main lake. These were probably times of accelerated subsidence. There was a flaming pot in the bench west of the southwest cove. The south arm was quiet with steady blue flames at its east end. There were glowing cracks on the northeast bench.

On September 21, at 3 p. m., it was evident that rapid subsidence was going on. The banks were twenty-five feet high. The west island was again a peninsula joined to the bench southwest of it. The lava of the east pond had withdrawn faster than the lake, and a tremendous cataract was pouring from the lake into it under an arch at the east end.

This was revealed through the opening of the pond above, which had become a pit, and through this as through a window from the southeast station one looked down into a churning pot of bright yellow lava, probably forty feet below the lake level, receiving a great cascade from the lake almost vertically, while another small stream poured into the cauldron from the south side.

The most astonishing feature of this Niagara of fire was its noiselessness; only a slight rushing sound could be heard, even when the observer was almost directly over it. The crusted south arm showed a trickle of festooned lava moving west. There was slow inrush under the bank at the southwest cone.

From the east pit blue fume puffed up from the cauldron and condensed to gray smoke above. A small remnant of the north crag was fuming, another of the southeast crag, and the north bench fumed, but elsewhere as yet no cracking of the benches showed. A fresh scar indicated recent falls from the north bank.

Measurement September 22, at 10 a. m., made the lake 384 feet below the southeast rim and the bench 341 feet down, or forty-three feet above the lake. This means that 341 feet was the maximum position of the recent rise about September 12. The average rate of subsidence therefore for ten days has been 4.3 feet per day.

On September 22 the smoke was very troublesome. Conditions were about as on the previous day. At 9 p. m. however the southwest cove was crusted over and occasional violent splashes were ejected from irregular fissures about the region of the southwest cone. From the north the surface lava could be seen to cascade into a circular grotto lined with stalactites opposite the east pit and the glow from that fiery cauldron was a greenish flare. The steepness of the cascade had somewhat diminished.

H. O. Wood reports as follows for the Whitney Laboratory of Seismology: "The week ending with September 22 has exhibited marked seismic activity. In the morning hours of September 16, (H. S. T.) there was registered the chief phases only of a weak teleseism. In the following six days sixteen well marked local earthquakes were registered. None of these were felt close by the observatory, but several, one in particular, were felt at Hilo, Kapapala and on the Hamakua coast.

"Most of these, while distinctively of local origin, were from more distant sources than the average of local shocks. Besides these there were thirteen, more or less, seismic disturbances grading in character and energy from well marked earthquake wave-groups to those usually considered as volcanic-vibration wave groups. All these were of very small amplitude; and there is no genetic distinction between an earthquake record and a volcanic-vibration record. The former is a group of earth waves with a distinct indication of fore-phases. Though Mauna Loa shows no sign from the observatory, the possibility that these disturbances point to renewed action there cannot be overlooked.

"During the week microseismic motion has declined in amplitude from moderate to slight values. The motion of volcanic vibration has fluctuated, in amplitude, but has tended to increase in the latter part of the week. Except for diurnal changes there has been no change in tilting."

Arrangements are being perfected for the building of trails and rest houses up the northeast flank of Mauna Loa.

T. A. JAGGAR, JR., Director.

KILAUEA TECHNOLOGY STATION, September 30—The week ending September 29, 1915, at Kilauea volcano has been a very eventful one with rapid sinking of the lava column in Halemaumau at the average rate of sixteen feet per day during the six days September 22 to September 28. A sudden acceleration in the subsidence took place September 25-26, causing a chaotic tumble of benches in the pit and obliterating the north and south arms and the east pond. During the same twenty-four hours there was a most extraordinary swarm of local earthquakes. The lake subsided about 100 feet with some recovery on September 29.

On September 23 conditions remained as last described after a week of seismic activity coupled with subsidence. The lake was down thirty or more feet making an inner pit of irregular outline within the sagging bench of recent formation. This bench was slightly cracked and had caved away on the actual shores of the lake but not elsewhere. A great cascade was pouring through a tunnel at the east end from the lake under the bench into the boiling caldron of the east pit. This, in fact, appeared to be the main drainage vent of the subsiding lake and continued to be so until September 25. Until that day rock sliding in the pit was rare and cracking in the benches inconspicuous.

At two p. m. September 24 the wall over the lake as seen from the southeast station appeared about forty-five feet high, some seven fountains were in action, the east torrent was flowing and the southwest cove was quiet and crusted. Smoke had greatly increased.

At two-thirty p. m. September 25 the wind was blowing hard so as to make the seeing very dim from the southeast station. There was much fountaining and eastward streaming but the torrent into the east caldron had stopped. The caldron, however, was seething with small bubble fountains. Broken rocks could be seen on the bench at the east indicating that rocks had fallen from the high walls. The inner wall over the lake appeared about 50 feet high.

At five-thirty p. m. September 26 it was evident that a great crisis of collapse had followed the cessation of flow of the cascade. The middle of the north bench as seen from the south had fallen away completely so as to reveal beneath the white ancient wall rocks of Halemaumau, and east of there the bench wall above the lake appeared at least eighty feet high. The east bench had so collapsed that the arch leading from the lake to the east pond was entirely gone and the pond istelf was a mass of black debris and smoke. New glowing cracks back of the south bench showed that bench to be sinking between the east pond and the south arm.

The latter was choked with debris, but a glowing crack was spitting lava at the site of the southwest cone and a glowing crack could be seen at the east end of the south arm. The west end was obscured by smoke but a remnant of the west island could be seen and a torrent rushed eastward in the north arm and generated a whirlpool. The middle and eastern islands of some weeks ago had reappeared, revealed as the flood subsided, and they now stood as high pinnacles in the lake The eastern island was attached by crust to the south shore and the middle one to the north shore. Both appeared at least 25 feet high and showed the ring markings of sucessive levels of the sinking lava.

About five-forty-five p. m. a great fall of debris into the lake took place from the east part of the north bench. On the highest southern talus rocks were sliding just below the southwest station. Old Faithful was fountaining in the middle of the lake and there were many shore crusts in different places with river-like streams pouring between them, suggesting that everything was jumbled and out of adjustment with different parts of the lake subsiding at different rates. In general the streaming was east in the main lake and the eastern coves, and west from a skin which made a band across the lake, just west of Old Faithful. A specially large and rapid torrent amounting to a cascade poured from the middle pool eastward on the south side of the middle island. Great volumes of smoke rose from the wreck of the east pond and from the north and west benches.

At five p. m. September 27 the lake was much lower. The north wall appeared still higher, the south bench had slumped greatly, glow could no longer be seen in the bench cracks south nor in the south arm, and there was more crust on the lake with scattered pots showing activity through it. South of the middle island a golden cascade tumbled eastward, met below by a westward flowing stream which overlapped the cascade in the pool at its base. It was evident that the east end, as usual, was subsiding faster than the middle and west parts of the lake. A few rock falls were heard from the northeast bank of the lake and from the western talus.

The rapid subsidence appears to have continued through Tuesday, September 28. About two-thirty p. m. two northern avalanches were heard, lasting each about three seconds. At two-fifty p. m. an avalanche fell from under the northwest station. About thirteen other small avalanches were heard in the course of two hours, many of them from the crumbling bench on the northeast side of the lake. A portion of that bench now stood as a peak west of a great cone of slide rock north of the middle island. The islands still stood as high pinnacles and the streaming and fountaining continued as before.

At ten a. m. September 29 it was evident that the lake was slightly higher, and was building spatter rims and benches. The islands appeared much lower, avalanches were fewer and the smoke, while thick, cleared away sufficiently to reveal glimpses of the west end. The south bench had continued to slump so that the last remnant of the pit of the east pond was obliterated. The region of promontory between the Old Faithful pool and the north arm must have been previously connected by a channel under the bench, for it had completely collapsed leaving the western end of the promontory as a high island in a greatly widened lake basin. The western bench had collapsed but details of the west end could not be seen.

There was rapid inrush into a small northern cove west of the north pinnacle. The noises were of plashing and blowing. One small fall of rock into the lake was heard. Old Faithful was not working, but there was a heavy spatter lump built on the shore near its site.

Measurements at ten a. m. September 29 made the lava at the northeast shore of the lake 472 feet below the southeast rim of tho pit. The depth on the previous day, September 28 therefore, was at least 480 feet below the rim.

At five-forty p. m. September 23 Mauna Loa was seen very clearly after sundown and three marked jets of vapor appeared in the usual places along the northeast profile of the mountain. It was calm in the summit region although a cold northeast wind was blowing below. The usual faint fume over Mokuaweoweo could be detected. There was nothing unusual in these appearances except possibly unusually clear seeing.

Active preparations for building a northeast trail on Mauna Loa continue. On September 28 a party consisting of Messrs. Thurston, Burdick, Jaggar and Dent, accompanied by Lieutenant Philoon of the Twenty-fifth United States Infantry, climbed the mountain from Keauhou ranch to about the 7000-foot level above the water hole Keawewai. With permission of the departmental commander a company of officers and men of the Twenty-fifth Infantry have volunteered to do the work of trail and house building, and it is proposed that the committee having charge of the project secure the necessary transportation to this end.

The following report from the Whitney Laboratory of Seismology is submitted by H. O. Wood.

The week ending with September 29 has been marked by extraordinary local, seismic activity—though none of the earthquakes registered have been felt at the observatory or at the Volcano House. However, within three miles in the direction of Hilo several have been felt, particularly on September 26, some quite sharply.

The disturbances registered have been well defined earthquakes of from moderate to small instrumental amplitude, well defined earthquakes of very minute instrumental amplitude, and groups of earth waves in large number—some of which probably are not different from the usual spasmodic waxings in the registration of volcanic vibrations, but others of these groups exhibit abrupt beginnings, though without the development of seismic phases, and thus are to be discriminated from the ordinary groups of volcanic vibration waves.

Disturbances were registered during the twenty-four-hour periods, ending in the forenoon of the dates specified, as follows:

September 23, three well-marked shocks and about nine other disturbances; September 24, one well-marked shock and about five others; September 25, two well-marked shocks and one other; September 26, the day of the crisis, forty-four well-marked shocks, thirty-seven definite shocks of lesser amplitude and eighty-three other wave-groups, some of which almost surely were minor earthquakes; September 27, ten well-marked shocks and twelve others, more or less; September 28, ten well-marked shocks and three others; and September 29, one well-marked shock and eight other disturbances. The total for the week, therefore, is 108 definite earthquakes about half of which were of very small amplitude, and none of large amplitude, and 121 other definite wave-groups, many of which probably were minute earthquakes and many, doubtless, only groups of volcanic vibrations.

Accompanying this seismic spasm there has been a rapid subsidence in Halemaumau. However, few, or none, of these shocks originated in the neighborhood of the crator of Kilauea, or within it, and some have emanated from local sources so distant, up to about sixty miles, as to make it imprudent to infer a Kilauean origin for them.

It is better not to attempt any determinate explanation of this seismic crisis until more definite and complete information is at hand.

Except as above mentioned there has been nothing remarkable about the registration of microseismic motion, or that of volcanic vibration.

During the early part of the week a sharp tilt to the south and east took place during a day or two, but the movement was only temporary. There appears to have been no net change.

T. A. JAGGAR, JR., Director.

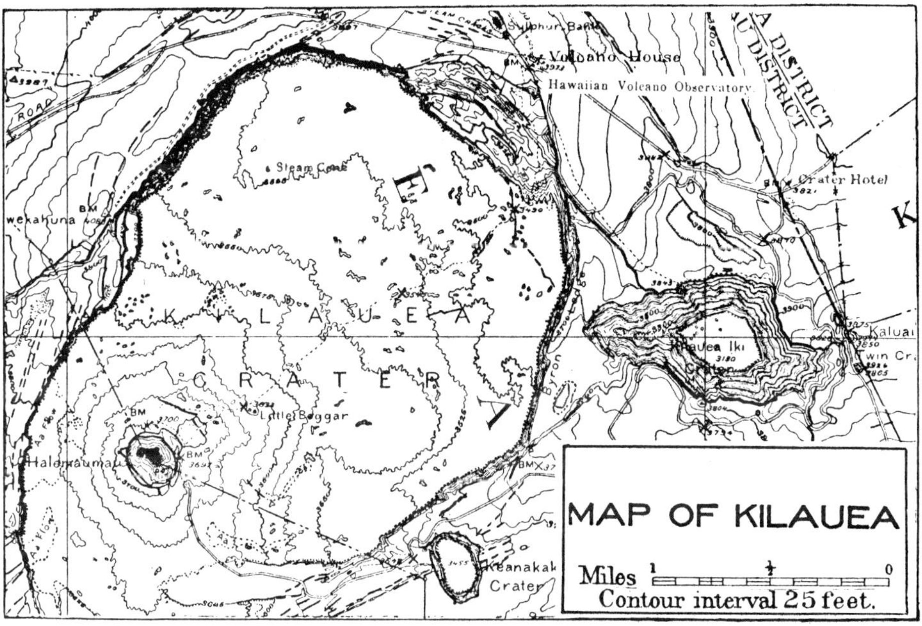

HAWAIIAN VOLCANO RESEARCH ASSOCIATION.

This society is a voluntary one, made up of subscribers to scientific work which is being executed by the Massachusetts Institute of Technology.

In 1915 there are about 100 subscribers in Hawaii and elsewhere, firms and individuals. A group of firms and persons in Hilo built the main observatory building in the spring of 1912. Publications to date have been weekly reports since the summer of 1911, now reprinted in Honolulu in monthly form. The Massachusetts Institute of Technology will publish annual reports, of which the introductory number was printed in 1912.

The weekly bulletin as it appears in the Advertiser is reprinted as a leaflet and sent to regular annual subscribers to the work of the Association. L. A. Thurston is president of the Board of Directors of the Association, and R. W. Shingle is treasurer. New subscribers who are interested in volcanoes will be welcomed in the Association. The Association aims: (1) To record volcanic activity and earthquakes in Hawaii; (2) to attract scientific men hither for special studies; (3) to promote the establishment of volcano observatories all over the world. The annual dues of regular members are $5; patrons of the Assocaition subscribe larger amounts.

WHITNEY LABORATORY OF SEISMOLOGY.

The Whitney Laboratory of Seismology is equipped with two Bosch-Omori 100 kg tromometers registering N-S and E-W motion, a heavy Omori tromometer registering E-W motion, and an Omori "ordinary Seismograph" designed for registering strong earthquakes in all three components of motion. These are seated on concrete piers in a closed basement room having practically constant temperature, beneath the chief Observatory building near the hotel. Time is referred to a rated chronometer, checked at intervals by solar observations with a transit. Both instruments are loaned by the College of Hawaii. Hawaiian standard time (H. S. T.) is 10 hrs. 30 min. slower than Greenwich time.

CANCANI SCALE OF SEISMIC INTENSITY.

Expressed by accelerations measured in millimeters per second per second.

I.	Instrumental	0.0	2.5
II.	Very slight	2.5	5.0
III.	Slight	5.0	10.0
IV.	Sensible, mediocre	10.0	25.0
V.	Rather strong	25.0	50.0
VI.	Strong	50.0	100.0
VII.	Very strong	100.0	250.0
VIII.	Ruinous	250.0	500.0
IX.	Disastrous	500.0	1000.0
X.	Very disastrous	1000.0	2500.0
XI.	Catastrophic	2500.0	5000.0
XII.	Great catastrophe	5000.0	10000.0

Grade IV. is ordinarily the minimum perceived by the senses; and in grade XII. the acceleration, or rate of change of motion (jerk) reaches that of terrestrial gravitation.

In the standard form of report the maximum intensity or acceleration, designated by the symbol a, or max. a, is given in the conventional unit, **the milligal.** The milligal is a measure of acceleration, such that 1 milligal = 1/100 mm. per sec. per sec. = 10 μ per sec. per sec. The Cancani scale, here defined in terms of millimeters per sec. per sec., can therefore be expressed in **milligals** by multiplying each of the numbers by 100.

WEEKLY BULLETIN
OF THE

Hawaiian Volcano Observatory

Vol. III. HONOLULU, HAWAII, OCTOBER, 1915. No. 10

TECHNOLOGY STATION, October 7.—The week at Kilauea has been marked by gradual subsidence of the lava quite in accordance with what is expectable at this season following the autumnal equinox. There has been little marked change in the Halemaumau pit.

On September 30 at two in the afternoon the sunken bench of 1915 appeared about fifty feet above the lake, which was boiling in many places and streaming eastward from the middle island. The eastern island appeared much lower than the middle one. About three o'clock rapid rising was in progress and no avalanches were heard in the afternoon, but in the evening heavy rock falls from the north bench were reported. Blue fume rose rapidly from the margin of the broken bench on the southeast. A blow hole southwest about twenty feet above the lake occasionally emitted a loud hiss. The northeast bench had largely fallen away.

On October 2 at two o'clock in the afternoon a definite new bench around the lake was observed and the strait had narrowed between the middle island and the south shore. This island was now at the tip of a peninsula extending from the north bank, and what was left of the east island was merely a blow hole on a peninsula extending from the south bank. The lake was about five feet below the new bench. Continuous puffing could be heard southwest and northwest and rocks were occasionally heard sliding. The west end of the lake appeared to surround a large island.

On October 3 in the afternoon the lake appeared level with the lower bench, and in the evening a sharp hiss was heard from time to time on the southwest.

On October 4 at eleven o'clock in the morning the noise was of plashing and there was much dense white, yellow and blue smoke, especially at the east end. The lake appeared three feet below its banks, there was slow inrush southwest with bubble fountains, streaming was east and west from a skin southwest of the middle island, and east from the west pond region. A new island lay northwest of the middle island in the vicinity of the Old Faithful position. A whistling hiss now and then could be heard, but not located. A very hot solfatara with blue fumes and white sublimates had formed at the site of the former east pond. A broken pinnacle stood at the end of the former south promontory. The south arm was now merely a tumble of red debris. The south end of the west bench had all fallen away. Hot fumaroles occupied the inner end of the south arm and the bench east of it. The south talus was sliding in two places. Heavy fumes rose from the west end and yellow smoke from the north bench.

On October 5 at eleven o'clock in the morning the lake appeared to be ten feet below the lower bench. The Old Faithful island was the only one of the four so-called islands in the lake which still had liquid lava all around it. The lake was very irregular in shape with a middle pool, a west pond and an east pond. A riverlike stream poured from the west pond into the middle pool, and again under a crust from the middle pool to the east pond. The old mechanism of more rapid sinking at the east end still persisted. A high crag made of the broken north bench towered above the middle of the lake on the north. For several days the Old Faithful foun-

WEEKLY BULLETIN
of the
Hawaiian Volcano Observatory

Published Monthly at Honolulu, Hawaii, by the Hawaiian Volcano Research Association

Editor..............**Howard M. Ballou**
Professor of Physics, College of Hawaii

Entered as second-class matter January 20, 1914, at the post-office at Honolulu, Hawaii, under the Act of August 24, 1912.

tain had ceased to be recognizable. The west island, like the middle island, was now connected to the north shore by a strip of bench.

At six o'clock in the evening on October 6 conditions were much the same, but the lake was more crusted and sluggish. The west end was crusted over as well as the eastern half of the middle pool. Blue flames could be seen in several places. Streams east and west in the middle pool bent northwestward to rush under the bank, sliding was still going on in the south talus and the pit was very smoky.

Mr. Burdick, a territorial engineer, made a second expedition up Mauna Loa on October 4, through the Keauhou Ranch lands, accompanied by K. Pea as guide. He reached Puu Ulaula by a very direct route and marked a way for a trail which crosses very little of the rougher lava. He also made a reconnaissance for a short distance up the slope above Puu Ulaula. A favorable place for the proposed house was found on flat, gravelly ground, in the shelter of Puu Ulaula, on its south side.

The following report from the Whitney Laboratory of Seismology is submitted by H. O. Wood:

The pronounced seismic spasm which occurred last week passed off rapidly. So far as the present status of seismology allows of an interpretation, this would indicate only a minor crisis in rock strain; but such a conclusion must be only tentative.

During the week now ending, October 6, there have been registered five ordinary small local earthquakes, none felt, and five very small wave groups of the ambiguous sort intermediate between well defined shocks and waxing groups of volcanic vibration.

In addition the recent strong earthquake in California was registered. The record written here would indicate this to be a weak shock of the strong, or world-shaking class; that is, a shock locally destructive but not approaching great earthquakes in total energy. However, on account of the unsuitable, shattered foundation rock here at Kilauea this conclusion must be stated guardedly.

During the week, especially the latter part of it, microseismic motion has displayed moderately large amplitude.

Nearly every day has seen the registration of numerous prolonged groups of volcanic vibrations of unusually large amplitude. The week has shown a gradual movement of tilting to the east over and above the usual daily fluctuations, and a moderately strong tilting to the south in the early part of the week which was reversed and neutralized in the latter part so that no net change is observed.

T. A. JAGGAR, JR., Director.

TECHNOLOGY STATION, October 14—The week ending October 13, 1915, at Halemaumau has shown no great changes in the height or condition of the active lava pool. The pit has remained smoky with poor seeing in the day time and the views at night have been various, but sometimes spectacular. In general there was subsidence until October 9, a slight rise to October 12, and thereafter a stagnant and sinking lava column.

On October 7 at three p. m. the lake from the southeast station was seen to be level with the lower bench, fountaining vigorously and streaming eastward. For three seconds rocks were heard sliding at the west end of the pit and the talus there continued to move for some time. Blue fumes were dense at the southeast benches.

On October 8 at about two-thirty p. m. the lake was lower, the banks being about five feet high. Streaming was rapid in the east channel, there were bubble fountains at the east end and fumes were thick.

At two-thirty p. m. October 9 the lake was ten feet below the lower bench and other conditions appeared as of late, but the smoke made seeing very difficult. On October 10 the seeing was still bad and the fumes very dense. The glow on the smoke cloud as seen from the Observatory was dim on these evenings.

On October 12 from 5 to 6 p. m. there was some improvement in the seeing, the fumes being thinner because of a positive rise. From the south station the whole lake could be seen, with a strong flow westward from the middle pool to the west pond. This west flow in the western channel is very unusual, and generally marks a relatively sudden rise, reversing the usual convection currents. There was violent bombardment along the whole length of the west bank of the west pond.

In the eastern part of the lake the streaming was eastward from a crust south of the middle island. The three islands, were still in place but attached by crusts as peninsulas to the shores. Old Faithful fountain was not definitely in action but there was perpetual fountaining at its location. A new southwestern glow cone had formed above a crack on the high bench above the locality of the former southwest cone. There were some caverns with stalactites at the border of the lake. Once rocks were heard falling into the lake. There was a deep northern arm of the lake, an extension of the Old Faithful pool. Blue fumes were conspicuous southwest and west, and for a short time there was vigorous spatter on the west side of the middle island. There were flaming glow holes southwest, south and northeast and a small incandescent pond on the bench to the south of the eastern island. Dense fumes rose from the benches east, southwest, west and north.

On Wednesday, October 13, at two p. m. the open part of the pit was transferred to the southwest and west owing to a southeast wind. The lava was much more sluggish, the lake appeared to be about eight feet below the lower bench with spatter rims above it. Streaming in the west channel had resumed its normal eastward course and the west pond was covered with skin. The north cove had become an isolated pond separated from the lake by a strip of crust. The clear seeing revealed the north crag much lower than a week ago and overhanging the immediate bank of the Old Faithful pool. The high southwest glow cone appeared in daylight to be a yellow fumarole. A high remnant of the 1915 bench was seen clinging to the north wall. There was the usual eastward streaming at the east end of the lake, while streaming from east and west met in the Old Faithful pool to bend northward.

Old Faithful was in action making a splashing noise with bubble fountains at work during the intervals between the large domings.

During the week a 5000 gallon tank has been built in the Observatory grounds to supply the camp of the soldiers who are coming to build the Mauna Loa trail, and two other smaller tanks have been shipped up the mountain to a camp ground near the timber line.

The following report from the Whitney laboratory of seismology is submitted by H. O. Wood.

During the week ending with October 13 nine weak local shocks were registered; also five wave-groups of very small amplitude which may prove to be true shocks.

Throughout the week the amplitude of microseismic motion has ranged from moderate to moderately large values. This holds true also of the motion of volcanic vibration. Short "storms" of these latter waves have been frequent.

Tilting has shown larger and more rapid fluctuations than usual, but without definite net change.

T. A. JAGGAR, JR., Director.

TECHNOLOGY STATION, October 21.—The lava lake of Halemaumau continues very active and of irregular outline with its surface about 475 feet below the rim of the pit. Measurements made on October 15 made the depth to the lake surface 450 feet. There appears to have been at that time a rising movement which continued to about October 12. Thereafter there was sinking to October 17 and from that time to the present there has been a slight rise. The fluctuation of the last three weeks, however, appears to have been within a range of forty feet.

On October 15 at 2:30 p. m. rocks were avalanching at the west end for about three seconds. The bench over the lake was five feet high, there were many fountains, large and small, and a small active pool had formed in the southeast lower bench about ten feet in diameter. A second avalanche of short duration was heard toward the northwest at 3 p. m. Evidently at this time the lava was sinking.

At 3 p. m., Monday, October 18, the lake was only one foot below the lower bench, fountaining was vigorous and streaming was eastward. The southeast pot in the bench was spurting vigorously, throwing lava spray from twenty-five to thirty feet high. All avalanching had ceased. There were signs of recent caving in the high wall of Halemaumau under the east station. At 8 p. m. rising was evidently in progress, for the southeast pond overflowed the bench and the flow from it cascaded northward into the lake. Other bench ponds were seen northeast and northwest. The west end of the lake was streaming eastward, the middle pool streamed northward and the east arm streamed eastward, with occasional accelerations, due doubtless to temporary subsidence. A rhythmic fountain like Old Faithful was playing in the narrower part of the east arm, Old Faithful itself was very active in the middle pool, and violent bombardment was going on against the north bank of the middle pool under the northern crag. The lake in the region of the southeast cascade appeared to be about ten feet below the bench.

On October 19, at 10:30 a. m., measurement made the lake 475 feet below the southeast station. The north crag appeared to have subsided. Old Faithful was playing. The crag at the entrance of the south niche appeared lower. Streaming was eastward, and in the middle pool northward. There was bubble fountaining and puffing in the east arm and in general the noises were of plashing and blowing. Two glow holes appeared in the southwest tumble of benches at different levels with much yellow sulphur stain about the upper one. The lower bench appeared not more than three feet above the lake and at the south there were fresh overflows on the surface of the bench. On October 20 conditions were similar but the pit was very smoky.

On October 15, thanks to the cooperation of the Matson Navigation Company, a first detachment of thirty men under Lieutenant Philoon arrived on the Matsonia from Honolulu and proceeded to establish camp near the Volcano House, on the bench near the trail leading to the crater. A pipe line supplying the camp ground with water from the observatory tanks had been prepared. On October 17 the remainder of Company E of the Twenty-fifth Infantry (colored), commanded by Captain Bates, arrived on the steamer Mauna Kea and went into camp. On October 19-20 the officers, guided by Mr. Burdick and accompanied by L. A. Thurston and H. O. Wood, went up Mauna Loa over the route of the proposed trail, and Captain Bates and Mr. Burdick remained over night on the mountain, exploring as far as Puu Ulaula. At the half-way camp ground on the mountain two 2000-gallon tanks have been erected to supply the trail builders with water and a third tank has been placed at Keauhou ranch for their use. Work on the trail has actively commenced.

The following report from the Whitney Laboratory of Seismology is submitted by H. O. Wood:

During the week ending October 20 only six ordinary small local earthquakes have been registered. One of these, on the evening of October 16, was felt in Hilo but not at the Volcano House.

Microseismic motion has been ordinary during the week.

T. A. JAGGAR, JR., Director.

TECHNOLOGY STATION, October 28.—The week at Kilauea has been marked by a slight rise of the lava and enlargement of the main pool by the formation of a deep bay to the northwest.

On October 20 at ten a. m. conditions suggested slow rising, as the island crags appeared lower owing to overflow of the benches about them and there was much spattering on banks and a blowing noise. There was rapid streaming and fountaining in the east pool. The southwest glow hole was spitting and occasionally emitted a sharp hiss. Old Faithful fountain was very noisy. A crag hung out from the 1915 bench at its east end. The pot in the northeast bench was churning and splashing.

On October 22 at 3 p. m. the lake was five feet below the lower bench, fountaining actively and the occasional loud hiss from the southwest vent was very pronounced. The middle pool was bombarding its north bank. Between the middle pool and the east pool there was now a bridge of heavy crust. From under this bridge a narrow torrent streamed eastward in the east pool. Streaming continues eastward from the west pond into the middle pool.

On October 23 at three p. m. the bank around the lake was only two feet high and the pools were noisy and smoky. There was much rumbling. At three-ten p. m. a heavy avalanche took place owing to the collapse of the 1915 bench northeast. The slide lasted nearly five minutes and the pit filled with dust and smoke. At eight p. m. from the southeast station the lake appeared to consist of two symmetrical torrents sweeping between three rather regularly spaced ponds.

From the west pool a stream rushed into the middle pool bombarding the north bank of the latter; and from the middle pool a stream rushed into the east pool bombarding its north bank. In both cases the stream rushed around an island crag, these crags being attached to the north wall by isthmuses of bench material, in which were several boiling pots indicating their bridge-like character. A large grotto with stalactites occupied the northwest shore of the middle pool. In the midst of this pool Old Faithful was bursting. A seething pot was spitting lava spume near the north bank of the east pool and the high southwest pot was spitting and flaming. The lake appeared higher, but the rapid streaming and heavy bombardment suggested temporary subsidence. The south side of the west pond was covered with crust.

At eight p. m. on October 24 the seeing was very dim from the southeast station. The site of the northeast pot had become a cavern in the bank of the lake and there was a small glow spot in the bench beyond. There was heavy bombardment on the north side of the middle pool and the streaming in both pools was active.

At six p. m. Monday, October 25, there appeared to be subsidence. The northeast grotto was higher and a deep lava pot was splashing at the foot of the cliff beyond it to the north. There were caverns with hanging stalactites on the northwest side of the middle pool and a square glowing pot in the bench north of the western island. The southwest pot was spouting spray fifty to sixty feet in the air. The streaming was eastward and there were no pronounced changes in general form or condition of the lake.

Measurements from the southeast and south stations at nine-thirty a. m. October 26 made the depression of the lake surface 452 feet. This indicates a rise of twenty-three feet since October 19. The shore bench appeared about five feet high. In the bench were pots northeast and southeast. There was much blowing in the eastern grottoes. The north crag appeared very low and the middle and eastern islands had become mere lumps surrounded by bench overflows. A very marked change had taken place in the middle pool on its northwest side, where all of the bench material surrounding the pots and grottoes of the previous day had collapsed, making a deep bay in that direction. Streaming was eastward in the east pool and in the channel leading from the west pond, and the surface current in the middle pool curved northward into the new bay.

On October 27 at nine-thirty a. m. it

was evident that a slow rise of the lava was building up the lower bench. The northeast pot could not be identified owing to burial under its own overflows. The east island was gone, and in its place was only a flat peninsula. The middle island was now a very small lump. There were new flows on the bench southeast, northeast and south. The southeast pot in the bench was still visible. The noises were quieter than on the previous day, there were fresh spatter rims around the shores of the lake, which at the moment was about two feet below the bench.

The fumes on the southeast rim of Halemaumau emitted from some crack northeast of there have of late been disagreeable and acrid with sulphuric acid.

During the week ending with October 27 there have been four local earthquakes registered in the Whitney Laboratory of Seismology. One of these in the early morning of October 21 probably was felt in this vicinity.

Movement of tilting has been slight and the microseismic and volcanic vibrations have been moderately strong.

T. A. JAGGAR, JR., Director.

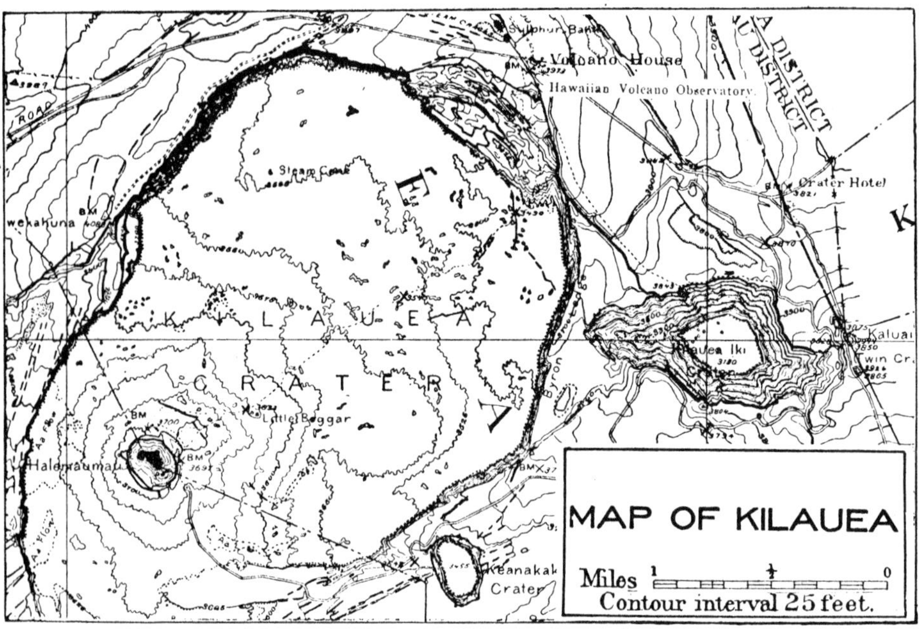

HAWAIIAN VOLCANO RESEARCH ASSOCIATION.

This society is a voluntary one, made up of subscribers to scientific work which is being executed by the Massachusetts Institute of Technology.

In 1915 there are about 100 subscribers in Hawaii and elsewhere, firms and individuals. A group of firms and persons in Hilo built the main observatory building in the spring of 1912. Publications to date have been weekly reports since the summer of 1911, now reprinted in Honolulu in monthly form. The Massachusetts Institute of Technology will publish annual reports, of which the introductory number was printed in 1912.

The weekly bulletin as it appears in the Advertiser is reprinted as a leaflet and sent to regular annual subscribers to the work of the Association. L. A. Thurston is president of the Board of Directors of the Association, and R. W. Shingle is treasurer. New subscribers who are interested in volcanoes will be welcomed in the Association. The Association aims: (1) To record volcanic activity and earthquakes in Hawaii; (2) to attract scientific men hither for special studies; (3) to promote the establishment of volcano observatories all over the world. The annual dues of regular members are $5; patrons of the Assocaition subscribe larger amounts.

WHITNEY LABORATORY OF SEISMOLOGY.

The Whitney Laboratory of Seismology is equipped with two Bosch-Omori 100 kg tromometers registering N-S and E-W motion, a heavy Omori tromometer registering E-W motion, and an Omori "ordinary Seismograph" designed for registering strong earthquakes in all three components of motion. These are seated on concrete piers in a closed basement room having practically constant temperature, beneath the chief Observatory building near the hotel. Time is referred to a rated chronometer, checked at intervals by solar observations with a transit. Both instruments are loaned by the College of Hawaii. Hawaiian standard time (H. S. T.) is 10 hrs. 30 min. slower than Greenwich time.

CANCANI SCALE OF SEISMIC INTENSITY.

Expressed by accelerations measured in millimeters per second per second.

I.	Instrumental	0.0	2.5
II.	Very slight	2.5	5.0
III.	Slight	5.0	10.0
IV.	Sensible, mediocre	10.0	25.0
V.	Rather strong	25.0	50.0
VI.	Strong	50.0	100.0
VII.	Very strong	100.0	250.0
VIII.	Ruinous	250.0	500.0
IX.	Disastrous	500.0	1000.0
X.	Very disastrous	1000.0	2500.0
XI.	Catastrophic	2500.0	5000.0
XII.	Great catastrophe	5000.0	10000.0

Grade IV. is ordinarily the minimum perceived by the senses; and in grade XII. the acceleration, or rate of change of motion (jerk) reaches that of terrestrial gravitation.

In the standard form of report the maximum intensity or acceleration, designated by the symbol α, or max. α, is given in the conventional unit, **the milligal.** The milligal is a measure of acceleration, such that 1 milligal = 1/100 mm. per sec. per sec. = 10 μ per sec. per sec. The Cancani scale, here defined in terms of millimeters per sec. per sec., can therefore be expressed in **milligals** by multiplying each of the numbers by 100.

WEEKLY BULLETIN

OF THE

Hawaiian Volcano Observatory

Vol. III. HONOLULU, HAWAII, NOVEMBER, 1915. No. 11

TECHNOLOGY STATION, November 4.—The week ending November 3 at Halemaumau has been marked by relatively small fluctuations of level of the lava column, with subsidence probably dominant, but the weather has been too windy and rainy for making depth measurement. The most striking development of the week has been the formation of a tremendous cascade of lava from the middle pool into the northeast pot recurrently subsiding at intervals usually of from ten to twenty minutes, and so permitting the lake fluid to pour like a cataract into it.

This process was first seen on October 28 at eight p.m. from the southeast station. The whole lake was visible and its outline in plan had now become somewhat symmetrical to the right and left of a northeast axis extending through Old Faithful. The southwest shore was a long curve terminated southeast and northwest by the east and west pools respectively. These pools were each separated from the middle pool by an island promontory jutting out from the northeast shore line. Between these promontories in turn the middle pool was bifurcated northeastward into the northwest bay and the northeast caldron.

This last feature, the northeast caldron, was new and had been created by the collapse of the bridge which had separated the northeast pot from the lake. A torrent cascade was pouring from the place where Old Faithful occasionally fountained into a swirling caldron with a drop of from ten to fifteen feet. This caldron was the northeast pot greatly enlarged. As a consequence of this development, and the recent enlargement of the northwest bay, the middle and west islands have once more become almost completely surrounded by moving liquid. The streaming was in general eastward with divergent currents into the northwest bay and the northeast caldron and into a cavern hung with stalactites on the north side of the east pool. This place appeared to be separated by only a narrow bridge from the northeast caldron. The recurrence of cascading from the lake into an outlying vent, and the enlargement of the lake by collapse suggests that sinking is in progress.

On October 29 and 30 the pit appeared smoky and there was much rain. On October 31 at three p.m. a fresh northeast wind blew the fumes down into the pit and made seeing difficult. There was great activity, the east pool was wider, the southeast pot in the bench was splashing with the liquid lava and now and then a strong hiss could be heard from the southwest cone. It was evident that the lake had been overflowing the southeast bench. The cascade from the middle pool into the northeast caldron was still at work, changing to a slower stream from time to time when the pot seemed to fill up. Thus at three p.m. there was a slow stream with splashes of bombardment at the end of the caldron completely overflowing the narrow isthmus which separated this pot (now an arm of the middle pool) from the east pool. At three-fifteen p.m., however, the lava in the pot had so subsided that the stream had become a cataract.

At six-thirty p.m. on November 1 there was still a high wind and very dim seeing from the east. The cascade still poured at intervals into the northeast caldron. From time to time there was prolonged blowing at the southwest cone, the southeast pot was full of lava and there was great turbulance at the west end in the region of the Old Faithful. There was no bridge across the strait south of the middle

WEEKLY BULLETIN
of the
Hawaiian Volcano Observatory

Published Monthly at Honolulu, Hawaii, by the Hawaiian Volcano Research Association

Editor..............Howard M. Ballou
Professor of Physics, College of Hawaii

Entered as second-class matter January 20, 1914, at the post-office at Honolulu, Hawaii, under the Act of August 24, 1912.

island, the east arm being continuous with the middle pool with eastward streaming.

On November 2 at six p.m., the wind had somewhat abated and apparently the lake was rising. There was much better seeing, heavy puffing was heard at the southwest and the streaming was westward in the west channel, an unusual reversal which has been a sign of rising in the past. At six p.m. the northeast caldron was crusted over and dark. Suddenly the lake overflowed this crust and rapid whirlpool action started in the caldron. By 6:10 this had ceased and the caldron area skinned over. At 5:15 the lava column of the caldron subsided faster than the lake and the cascade from the lake into the caldron began. The east pool also subsided somewhat so as to increase the speed of the current into it. In the south bank of the northeast caldron there was a flaming and spurting hole. In a few minutes this caldron again filled up, quieted, and grew dark. This process continued rhythmically, cascading commencing about every ten minutes, and the rapid rushing lasting about two minutes. The west flowing current in the west channel stagnated about six-fifteen p.m.. and at six-twenty the flow there was slowly eastward.

Old Faithful had been in action at six p.m., but at six-thirty it was replaced by perpetual and migrating fountains. At the same time the whole south of the northeast caldron had ceased to spurt lava spray but was emitting blue flames vigorously. An open pot could be seen northwest of the western island. The north crag was now a mere spatter bank. The noises were of plashing and blowing, there was hiss from a small glow-hole in the south bench tumble, stalactites hung above boiling lava in the southeast pot, and a small second orifice in the bench had formed beside this pot and to the south of it. The west pond was streaming eastward, and during the time of the westward current in the west channel the two streams conflicted at the narrows with violent bombardment on the banks.

On November 3 there was a heavy rain storm from the northeast and more than five inches of rain fell at the Observatory.

In the Whitney Laboratory of Seismology there have been registered in the week ending November 3 four very small local earthquakes, three of them October 31 and November 1. On October 31 about nine p.m., occurred the prolonged registration of a distant earthquake. Microseismic motion has been moderate during the week, volcanic vibrations were strong early in the week and less toward its close, while tilting was strong to the north and east about October 31, moderating thereafter.

Captain Bates of Company E, Twenty-fifth Infantry, has succeeded in marking a trail through to the red cone on the northeast slope of Mauna Loa and is building a way through the worst parts of it so as to make it passable for pack animals. He is now at work reconnoitering a way from the red cone to Mokuaweoweo.

T. A. JAGGAR, JR., Director.

TECHNOLOGY STATION, November 11.—The past week at Halemaumau showed continued subsidence of the lava until November 8, but since that time owing to a heavy storm that has precipitated more than twenty inches of rain at the Obesrvatory there has been no opportunity for observation of the crater. The principal development of the week has been the revival of the three islands, east, middle and west, by collapse of the bridges which have connected them with the outer benches.

On November 4 at eight p. m. there was fair seeing from the southeast station, though a drizzle was falling at the time. The lake appeared about fifteen feet below the lower bench and the middle pool was sending a rapid current into the northeast embayment but there was no cascading there. The caldron appeared so low that the view of the lava within it was partially obstructed by the ledge in front of it. The lake had subsided an equal amount thus accounting for the cessation of cascading.

In the east arm streaming was against the north bank. There was a large dark skin over the north middle part of the middle pool resting against the point which divided the two northern bays. Heavy bombardment was going on against the south end of the west island promontory. Two or three pots were splashing in the bench to the northwest of the western island as though a liquid connection from the northwest bay to the west pond were nearly established. There were now two pots in the southeast bench. The southwest cone which now showed a glowing filigree pattern, occasionally gave vent to a strong puff. The west pond was largely skinned over. Streaming was eastward in the west channel, northward in the northwest arm, northeastward in the northeast arm and eastward in the east channel, the surface of the lake in general moving away from the long curve of the southwest shore.

The next evening, November 5, at six p. m., there was evidence in the south talus that sliding of the tumble of fragments had been going on carrying the talus cones to a lower level and leaving scored sulphur-streaked rock visible beneath. The west side of the middle island had been bombarded and eaten into along a series of scallops, the largest re-entrant making a nearly circular spouting horn in which the liquid lava was splashing and spurting at a level somewhat above that of the lake. Old Faithful was not in motion.

On the evening of November 6 conditions were similar but the middle island was now isolated from the north bank by a narrow stream which swept through from the northeast caldron to the east arm.

On the evening of November 7 there was probably some elevation of the surface of the lake and the channel northeast of the middle island had again crusted over.

On November 8 at two p. m. there was unusually clear seeing of the whole lake from the south and southwest stations and it became possible to make a fairly complete survey of the lake for the first time in many weeks. The plain seeing was not, however, occasioned by a rise of the lava with diminution of fumes, for all signs pointed to marked subsidence. Rocks were sliding on the talus east, south and southwest and the shore of the lake was in many places a cliff from fifteen to twenty feet high. Especially striking was the renewed isolation of the east and west islands. The east island stood in the widened east pool as a flat topped pinnacle with vertical walls about ten feet high, and the lava streamed eastward both north and south of it. The west island was a long craggy mass with nearly vertical walls and a flattish top highest at the west end. From the west pond streaming was eastward through channels north and south of this island and in the eddy of these currents at the east end of the island there was vigorous bombardment. The west island was about twenty feet high.

The middle island was connected by a slight bridge of crust to the shore on the northeast. The northwest bay had extended itself northward and was bounded by a definite point at its east end. Streaming was everywhere eastward and the noises were of plashing and occasional rock sliding. A clear view was obtained on this day of the western remnant of the bench of August 1915. This appeared very high above the lake and under it, as on the south, there was a second bench made up of subsided portions of the August floor, while at a still lower level there was a third bench built of recent overflows.

Measurement on November 8 made the greatest length of the pool 600 feet, its maximum width 250 feet and its depth below the southern rim 467 feet.

On November 9 and 10 there was a severe storm at first from the northeast and later with wind veering to the southeast.

On November 5 during an intermission in the rainy weather Captain Bates and Messrs. Philoon and Burdick made a rapid ascent from Puu Ulaula to Mokuaweoweo and back. They reached the north rim of the crater by way of the northeast line of cones and found practicable route for the trail to the summit, passing many interesting features including hot steam cracks, at the sources of the great flows which have poured down the mountain during the nineteenth century.

The following report from the Whitney Laboratory of Seismology is submitted by H. O. Wood:

During the week ending with November 10 only three, possibly two, very small earthquakes have been registered. The amplitude of microseismic motion and that of volcanic vibration has fluctuated very slightly, remaining at normal value during by far the greater part of the time. The motion of tilting has been very slight in amplitude, and of normal character.

T. A. JAGGAR, JR., Director.

TECHNOLOGY STATION, November 18.—The behavior of Kilauea during the week ending with Nov. 17 has presented little out of ordinary. The level of the lava has fluctuated, reaching in the afternoon of the 16th a higher point than at any time the rapid subsidence late in September. This rise was accordant with a theoretical, fortnightly maximum of earth-strain, with the usual factor of lag. Afterward the surface subsided slightly.

On Thursday, Nov. 11, after 20.5 inches of rain in 48 hours (the total for the ten days ending with this report has been 28.85 inches), a great fume cloud was developed which rose in immense cauliflower forms over the crater. The ring of encircling fumaroles was particularly dense. There was a great increase in the exhalation of white water-vapor fumes on the S.W. wall at the top of the S. talus, all over the 360-foot bench of August, 1915, and, in general, in the border fumaroles, S.E., E., and N.

In the evening the lake was very active, with high gas pressure. There was occasional good seeing from the S.E. Strong blowing from the higher and lower vents at the S.W. was noted. Those higher were flaming continually, and rocket action was also taking place from them. The lower vents were spurting continually. There was a row of glow holes from the S.W. chimney to the lake. Sliding in the S. talus was noted from time to time. The middle island was joined to the shore by a N.E. bridge, but the E. and W. islands remained isolated. "Old Faithful" was not in action, but there was a fountain playing rhythmically in the E. pool. Streaming was eastward throughout the lake. A remnant of the E. part of the W. island now made a separate island about 40 feet away to the east. The W. island was much smaller than on Nov. 8. The S.E. pot had enlarged to a small pool.

On Nov. 13 fountain action was pronounced and many fountains were traveling with the eastward streaming. The lava surface stood about five feet below the adjacent, third floor. Loud, shrill blowing noises emanated from a blowhole S.W. of the lake. A cone, from 15 to 20 feet high had been built on the floor east of the lake.

On Nov. 15 the lava surface had risen level with the third floor. Streaming eastwardly was still characteristic, with many traveling fountains of small size. Loud blasts continued to come from the S.W. The blow-hole there had grown into a small cone.

On Nov. 16 the lava had risen so as to overflow the second, subsided floor, surrounding it, reaching a level higher than any since the collapse in late September. The cone at the east was submerged; the islands were awash; and the peninsula destroyed or buried so that the lake had become one single body. The lava lacked only three feet of overflowing onto the first, subsided floor. The S.W. blow-hole had become a spatter cone from which came, spasmodically, thick sprays of magma, and very loud blowing noises. Many fountains were seen traveling eastward with the streaming into a well defined whirlpool at the S.E. Thick blue fumes were rising from the talus at the S. about 100 feet above the first, subsided floor of 1915.

On November 17 action was as usual except that westward streaming, and a lava cataract, were seen in the forenoon in the W. part of the lake. Elsewhere the streaming was westward as usual. The lava had subsided to a stand about three feet below the second floor. A new and very active spouting blowhole had developed on the floor at the south.

Only three, or possibly four, very small local earthquakes have been registered in the Whitney Laboratory of Seismology during the week ending with November 17.

Microseismic motion has been slightly greater than ordinary—motion of volcanic vibrations rather less.

Marked fluctuations in tilting have occurred, with sharp departures, to the E. and S., followed by return to normal.

H. O. WOOD,
Associate.

TECHNOLOGY STATION, November 25.—During the week ending with November 24 the surface of molten lava in Halemaumau has risen slowly, but comparatively steadily with little oscillating, until all the low-lying floors, benches and crags have been submerged, except the large, high crag at the north. The state of action has been ordinary and usual.

On November 18 overflowing was seen all along the southeast, south and west, and lava jets were springing from the pot at the end of the southeast cove. Streaming from the west to the northeast, east and southeast was steady. No unusual phases of the action were seen.

On November 19 overflowing was still in progress at the southeast and west. Some fresh slumping of talus and wall-rock, under the east station, had developed a gash out of which dense fumes were rising. There was general streaming to the east and northeast from the north and south—but at times this was interrupted, and complicated, by the movement of cakes of crust in divergent directions over the surface of the main pool. Though constantly breaking up the lake was overcrusted more than usual.

On November 20 overflowing in recent hours had been considerable. Thin crumpling skins which almost completely covered the lake were moving along and around the peninsula into the northeast cove where they were engulfed in a boiling area. The directions of this streaming were as usual. The general action was very sluggish.

On November 22 there was rapid streaming from the northwest to the east, but otherwise the action was quiet. The surface had subsided about three feet. Nevertheless, magma jets were playing from the cone at the southwest.

On November 23 the lava had again risen level with the floor and there was much fountain action in most parts of the pool, but the usual streaming from the west to the northeast, east and southeast prevailed, carrying along the minor fountains.

On November 24 the lava had again overflowed the margins, but afterward it had subsided some five feet. A thin scum covered the lake and only two spots showed persistent action. Streaming continued as usual, and magma jets issued with loud noises from the cone at the southwest. Fumes were issuing in considerable volume at the southeast.

Only one small local earthquake and one well-marked teleseism of moderate amplitude (but whose early phases are only vaguely delineated) have been registered during the past week at the Whitney Laboratory of Seismology.

Microseismic waves have been registered constantly with larger amplitudes than usual.

The amplitudes of the motion of volcanic vibration has been small throughout the week.

Fluctuations in tilting in both directions, and in both components, have been larger than usual, but no net change has been suspected.

H. O. WOOD, Associate.

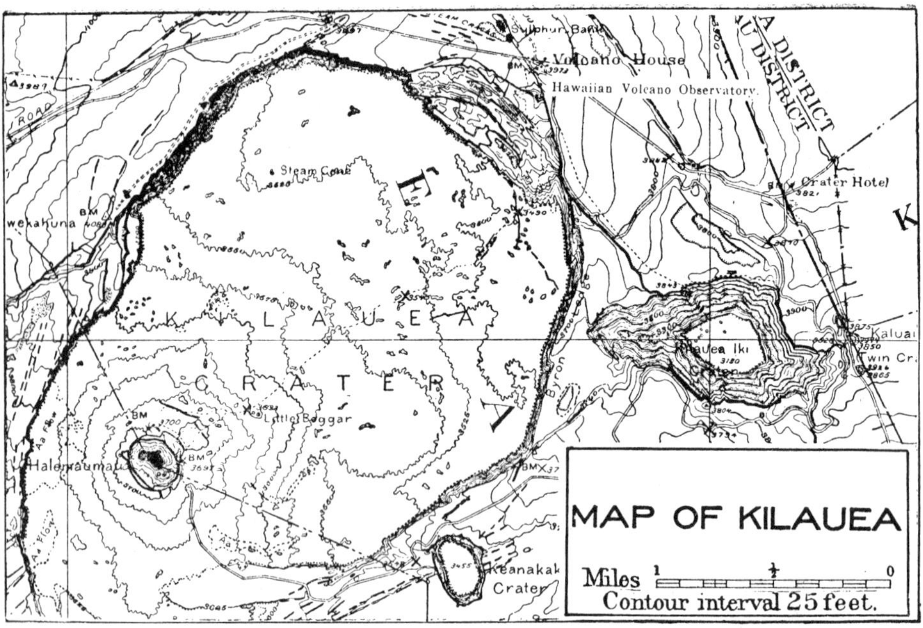

HAWAIIAN VOLCANO RESEARCH ASSOCIATION.

This society is a voluntary one, made up of subscribers to scientific work which is being executed by the Massachusetts Institute of Technology.

In 1915 there are about 100 subscribers in Hawaii and elsewhere, firms and individuals. A group of firms and persons in Hilo built the main observatory building in the spring of 1912. Publications to date have been weekly reports since the summer of 1911, now reprinted in Honolulu in monthly form. The Massachusetts Institute of Technology will publish annual reports, of which the introductory number was printed in 1912.

The weekly bulletin as it appears in the Advertiser is reprinted as a leaflet and sent to regular annual subscribers to the work of the Association. L. A. Thurston is president of the Board of Directors of the Association, and R. W. Shingle is treasurer. New subscribers who are interested in volcanoes will be welcomed in the Association. The Association aims: (1) To record volcanic activity and earthquakes in Hawaii; (2) to attract scientific men hither for special studies; (3) to promote the establishment of volcano observatories all over the world. The annual dues of regular members are $5; patrons of the Assocaition subscribe larger amounts.

WHITNEY LABORATORY OF SEISMOLOGY.

The Whitney Laboratory of Seismology is equipped with two Bosch-Omori 100 kg tromometers registering N-S and E-W motion, a heavy Omori tromometer registering E-W motion, and an Omori ''ordinary Seismograph'' designed for registering strong earthquakes in all three components of motion. These are seated on concrete piers in a closed basement room having practically constant temperature, beneath the chief Observatory building near the hotel. Time is referred to a rated chronometer, checked at intervals by solar observations with a transit. Both instruments are loaned by the College of Hawaii. Hawaiian standard time (H. S. T.) is 10 hrs. 30 min. slower than Greenwich time.

CANCANI SCALE OF SEISMIC INTENSITY.

Expressed by accelerations measured in millimeters per second per second.

I.	Instrumental	0.0	2.5
II.	Very slight	2.5	5.0
III.	Slight	5.0	10.0
IV.	Sensible, mediocre	10.0	25.0
V.	Rather strong	25.0	50.0
VI.	Strong	50.0	100.0
VII.	Very strong	100.0	250.0
VIII.	Ruinous	250.0	500.0
IX.	Disastrous	500.0	1000.0
X.	Very disastrous	1000.0	2500.0
XI.	Catastrophic	2500.0	5000.0
XII.	Great catastrophe	5000.0	10000.0

Grade IV. is ordinarily the minimum perceived by the senses; and in grade XII. the acceleration, or rate of change of motion (jerk) reaches that of terrestrial gravitation.

In the standard form of report the maximum intensity or acceleration, designated by the symbol a, or max. a, is given in the conventional unit, **the milligal.** The milligal is a measure of acceleration, such that 1 milligal = 1/100 mm. per sec. per sec. = 10 μ per sec. per sec. The Cancani scale, here defined in terms of millimeters per sec. per sec., can therefore be expressed in **milligals** by multiplying each of the numbers by 100.

WEEKLY BULLETIN
OF THE
Hawaiian Volcano Observatory

Vol. III. HONOLULU, HAWAII, DECEMBER, 1915. No. 12

TECHNOLOGY STATION, December 2.—During the week ending with December 1 the action in Halemaumau has been sluggish. Slow eastward streaming has prevailed continuously. The slow rising of magma went on during the previous week ended with it, and a subsidence ensued, followed by oscillation of stand about a depth-level some thirty feet or more, lower.

During the past fortnight the fume cloud has afforded an index of the height of the magma stand. During the rising of the first week the visible fumes diminished gradually almost to the vanishing point, but with the falling they increased again in a marked way. Since the establishment of the observatory there has hardly been so immediate a response to the changing conditions in the pit by the fume emanation.

On November 25 the magma had fallen about ten feet below the newly constructed floor and its surface was covered by a thin black scum. Only three boiling places were observed—one in the east cove, one in the northeast cove and the third at the center of the north margin.

On November 26 the magma had fallen five or ten feet further and the surface action was still more sluggish; only two boiling places in evidence. Thick blue fumes were issuing from the tops of the cones.

On November 27 the lava had fallen still lower by fifteen or twenty feet, a total depth below the new floor of thirty-five to forty feet. A portion of the peninsula jutting out from the north had collapsed, leaving its tip as an island. Also a part of the east bank had fallen in. Very thick blue fumes were coming from this collapse.

On November 29 the magma stood at about the same level, with very sluggish surface activity. Blue fumes issued copiously from under the east station and many other places. There had been further collapse. A considerable mass had fallen from the northeast side and a small place on the east had fallen in. The floor region between the east and northeast had warped down perceptibly.

On November 30 the lava had risen some fifteen or twenty feet. The surface action had increased notably; and thus the continuous streaming to the east was rendered more conspicuous. In the afternoon the lava was rising at a visible rate.

On December 1 the lava had subsided again some five feet or more. The surface action was sluggish again. The island had been reduced in area by undercutting and appeared near collapse. Under its margin were two areas of continuous action.

During the week ending with December 1 three small, local earthquakes, and possibly two more, have been registered in the Whitney Laboratory of Seismology.

Throughout the week microseismic motion has been of larger amplitude than normal. At the beginning of the week the amplitude of the motion of volcanic vibration was small, but it has increased gradually until of greater value than usual.

There has been nothing unusual or noteworthy concerning tilting action.

H. O. WOOD, Associate.

WEEKLY BULLETIN
of the
Hawaiian Volcano Observatory

Published Monthly at Honolulu, Hawaii, by the Hawaiian Volcano Research Association

Entered as second-class matter January 20, 1914, at the post-office at Honolulu, Hawaii, under the Act of August 24, 1912.

TECHNOLOGY STATION, December 9.—During the week ending with December 8 the magma surface has risen slowly in Halemaumau, with considerable oscillation of level; and the vigor of surface action has undergone a definite and easily recognizable increase. However, the height of stand of a fortnight since has not been reached again, as yet.

On December 2 the action of boiling fountains and of baby spurting fountains was more marked than just previously, but the fumes were thick enough, nevertheless, to prevent clear seeing. The magma had not risen appreciably—though it stood a little higher than the lowest recent stage, on November 27-29.

On December 3 the action was sluggish, but the surface had risen to a depth hardly greater than twenty feet below the floor, possibly no more than fifteen feet. Streaming to the eastward prevailed, except that this was diverted to some extent in under the east region of the island.

On December 4 it was discerned that the fumes appeared thinner from the observatory and this was confirmed by what was seen at the pit. In character the action was unchanged, but its vigor had again increased and the depth of the molten surface was now no more than fifteen feet below the surrounding platform. Rising could be seen in progress and molten lava could be seen in the bottom of a sink between the southeast and the east.

On December 5 the surface had risen still higher and there was oversplashing at certain places along the wall which were subjected to fountain bombardment. Rising was in progress, indicated by a steady rapid streaming into the lake from a spring in a depressed place on the floor at the south—and by the out-jetting of ponderous masses of the molten lava from blowholes at the southwest and south.

Bombardment by fountain action was conspicuous under the east end of the island, and at various other places, temporarily, along the lake margin especially at the north and east. The lake was crusted less than usual in recent days. Doming fountains were seen as well as steady boiling action and spiteful spray-flinging fountains which were spinning Pele's hair.

On December 6 the surface was less than five feet below the surrounding floor. The action of up-welling and streaming continued as on December 5. then.

On December 8 the lava was still a little below the floor but higher than on previous days. The fumes were much thinner. The surface action was somewhat less energetic.

During the week eight local earthquakes, more or less, have been registered in the Whitney Laboratory of Seismology. Two of these were of considerable seismographic amplitude. One was felt by one person lying down at the Volcano House. The other was not noticed though of undoubtedly greater intensity. Two other shocks were definite and distinct though well below the perceptible value. And there were four, more or less, rather sharp disturbances of the kind not easy to distinguish from groups of waves of volcanic vibrations.

During the week there has been nothing noteworthy about the registration of other sorts of seismic motion.

H. O. WOOD, Associate.

TECHNOLOGY STATION, December 16.—During the week ending with December 15, the surface of molten lava in Halemaumau rose slowly for a day or two, then fluctuated in height for three or four days, perhaps with a slightly rising tendency—and then for a day or two fluctuated with a definite sinking tendency. The surface action has been more vigorous than in the provious weeks, but no unusual effects have been witnessed.

On December 9 the lava was rising but it stood a trifle below the surrounding floor. The usual eastward streaming was rapid, especially near the east end, and vigorous boiling fountains were at work there, along the north bank nearby, and under the east end of the island.

On December 10, when first seen, the lava stood somewhat lower than on the ninth, but it rose until level with the lower parts of the floor. The usual streaming and boiling action was going on. Spatter action was adding to the height of the cones, particularly that at the southwest, which had been built up about twenty feet. From the southwest there was seen, under the east station, a long crack in the wall about 100 feet above the floor of the pit, which exhibited incandescence and emitted copious fumes. In early evening a considerable portion of the east end of the island broke away and slumped into the lake.

On December 11 the surface had subsided a few feet and the cones about the margin were smoking. The surface action was less vigorous, the lake being covered largely by black skins. These were moving rather rapidly from the west, around the small remnant of the island, to the east, where there was considerable boiling fountain action.

On December 12 the surface had risen slightly and spatter action was vigorous against the walls at the east end, and against a segment of the southwest wall. In general the surface action was vigorous, the surface hot, and both fountains boiling; fountains and spraying fountains were conspicuous at all times. An occasional doming fountain broke in the middle part of the lake. The island had been largely rebuilt by spatter action, and had taken on the shape of a loaf of bread. Streaming was as usual, and with it went an occasional travelling boiling-fountain—one of these was observed to move steadily and slowly, with vigorously continued action, from the east end of the island to the east end of the lake. Heavy spatter and viciously flung spray were ejected from the cones and pots on the floor south of the lake.

On December 13 it was seen that overflow onto the floor had taken place, with subsequent subsidence of a few feet. Action was as usual.

On December 14 the lava surface was only a foot or so lower than the floor when first seen, but action of sinking was in progress. Apparently still more overflowing onto the floor had taken place. Magma was jetting out from the southwest cone.

On December 15 further subsidence had taken place; the surface being ten feet or more below the floor. Action was as usual, but more energetic than average. The cones were smoking, and a new fuming place had developed on the floor at the north-northwest. The fumes had definitely increased in volume.

During the week six small, definite, local earthquakes have been registered in the Whitney Laboratory of Seismology; and besides these some seven very small disturbances of earthquake character, but without definitely indicated phase-beginnings.

Volcanic vibration has slightly increased in amplitude in the latter part of the week.

Nothing of note has occurred in the registration of microseismic motion, or that of tilting.

H. O. WOOD, Associate.

TECHNOLOGY STATION, 23 December, 1915 — During the week ending with December 22 there was little net change in action in Halemaumau. The lava level oscillated considerably, with a slight sinking tendency throughout most of the week, but with an apparent rising tendency at the end.

On December 16 action was, as usual of late, with conspicuous boiling places under the island and in the east cove—with prevailing eastward streaming. The magma surface was a few feet below the surrounding floor, which exhibited new fuming cracks in considerable number along its northeast part. A little cone had formed on the top of the island, and fumes were issuing from this. A considerable rock-fall from the wall at the ESE. had taken place.

On December 17 the level of the magma surface was a very little lower. There was vigorous action around about the east cove, but fully three-quarters of the area of the lake was covered with black scum. Fumes were swirling in the pit and were thick enough to prevent good seeing.

On December 18 there had been a further slight subsidence accompanied by the infall of a considerable fragment of the lake embankment at the northeast and east. In the afternoon there was a further infall of a large selvage on the southwest. As a result the lake was widened a little. A well-like hole, with lava boiling at the bottom, had formed by collapse, under the east station against the wall. Action in the lake was as usual.

On December 20 the surface stood a trifle higher, with a somewhat more active condition prevailing. A further slight collapse of the embankment under the east station had taken place, and also a more considerable infall along the northeast bank. Several small, deep holes had formed by collapse in the floor south of the lake.

On December 21 the surface had fallen again perceptibly. The island had nearly disappeared. A few large fountains, and many small ones, were boiling in the coves at the east and northeast. The southwest cone had collapsed, producing a small round hole in the floor. At the east collapses had resulted in bringing the edge of the lake quite to the wall of the Halemaumau pit.

On December 22 the lava surface was still low, but a definite action of rising was in progress, with increase in the number of breaking fountains of small size, and the resumption of fountain action on the larger scale.

During the week ending with December 22 only three very small local earthquakes have been registered in the Whitney Laboratory of Seismology—with a few groups of small waves of doubtful character. Microseismic waves have shown larger amplitudes than average; and this has been true also of those of volcanic vibration. There has been little fluctuation of the movement of tilting, and no net change has been noted.

Very respectfully,

(Signed) H. O. WOOD,
Associate.

TECHNOLOGY STATION, December 30.—Little change has been noted in Halemaumau during the week ending with December 29. However, observation was effectively interrupted by the severe kona storm which prevailed from the twenth-fourth to the twenty-seventh of December, inclusive. Gusty wind of gale strength with driving rain of variable amount, totalling 16.23 inches in four days, made the usual routine at the pit impracticable. Views were obtainable only during lulls in the storm,—by any fortunate enough to be present at such times. No reports indicate any overflowing onto the pit floor during the week; but all views have found the lava surface at various depths between ten and twenty feet below the floor,—thus oscillating practically at a stand slightly lower than a fortnight since.

On December 23 the surface stood from fifteen to twenty feet below the floor, distributed by many big boiling fountains, and the usual eastward streaming. Seeing was less satisfactory than usual, owing to changeable winds. In the afternoon considerable in-falls of the solidified crust were seen to occur along the banks at the north.

On December 24 no view was obtainable from any part of the rim. The kona wind had begun to blow, with gusts of gale strength, but rain had not yet set in.

In the evening of December 26 the magma stood at about the same level as on the twenty-third. The usual action was seen, and nothing more.

On the twenty-seventh the action was as usual. No estimate of depth was feasible through the fumes.

On December 28 the surface was seen to stand a trifle higher, about 10 feet below the pit floor. Streaming continued as usual, and there was much boiling-fountain action in the middle of the pool. An avalanche of considerable magnitude took place at the southwest, and frequent small rock-falls were noted.

On the twenty-ninth the stand of the magma surface seemed about the same. No unusual action was noted in the pool, while the usual boiling and streaming prevailed, with many baby fountains travelling with the stream.

During the week three, small, local earthquakes, and two or more indeterminate groups of earth-waves, were registered in the Whitney Laboratory of Seismology.

Accompanying the storm there was great increase in the amplitude of microseismic waves; and the motion of volcanic vibration, and possibly that of small shocks also, was completely masked by vibrations produced by the rocking of the Observatory and its foundations under the blasts of the wind. During the greater part of the time from the morning of the twenty-fourth to the afternoon of the twenty-sixth, with some later spasms, such motion predominated.

Also water invaded the seismograph cellar, driven through all crevices in the Observatory by the force of the wind.

Rapid tilting accompanied the storm,—to the west in considerable amount and to the south in excessive amount, necessitating readjustment of the suspensions of the seismometers. Since the storm passed there has been only partial recovery from this, especially in the north-south component. Such action occurred about a year ago in connection with a similar storm,—and then also there was only partial recovery.

For the greater part of the week the work of the station was badly interfered with by the storm.

H. O. WOOD, Associate.

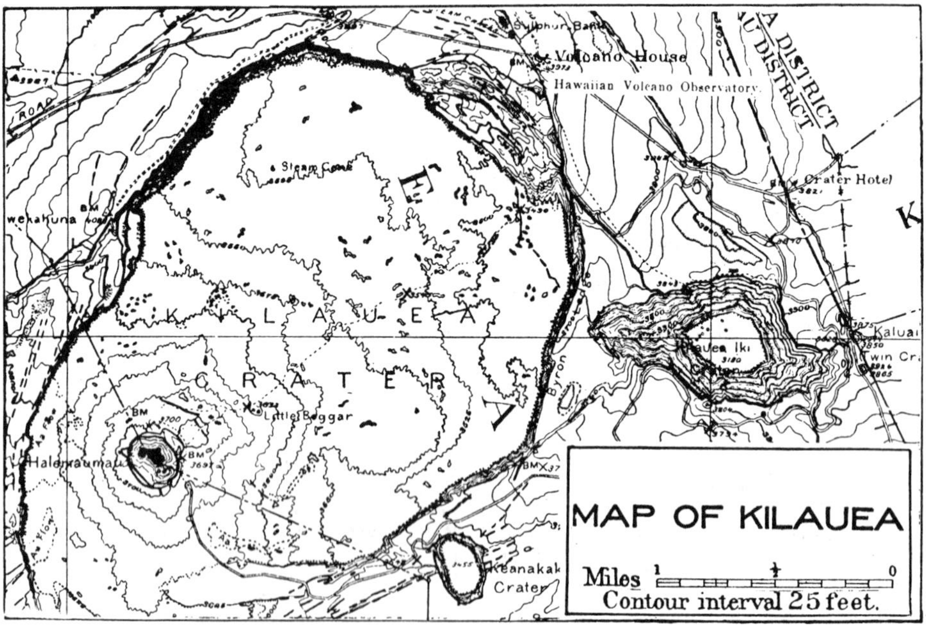

HAWAIIAN VOLCANO RESEARCH ASSOCIATION.

This society is a voluntary one, made up of subscribers to scientific work which is being executed by the Massachusetts Institute of Technology.

In 1915 there are about 100 subscribers in Hawaii and elsewhere, firms and individuals. A group of firms and persons in Hilo built the main observatory building in the spring of 1912. Publications to date have been weekly reports since the summer of 1911, now reprinted in Honolulu in monthly form. The Massachusetts Institute of Technology will publish annual reports, of which the introductory number was printed in 1912.

The weekly bulletin as it appears in the Advertiser is reprinted as a leaflet and sent to regular annual subscribers to the work of the Association. L. A. Thurston is president of the Board of Directors of the Association, and R. W. Shingle is treasurer. New subscribers who are interested in volcanoes will be welcomed in the Association. The Association aims: (1) To record volcanic activity and earthquakes in Hawaii; (2) to attract scientific men hither for special studies; (3) to promote the establishment of volcano observatories all over the world. The annual dues of regular members are $5; patrons of the Assocaition subscribe larger amounts.

WHITNEY LABORATORY OF SEISMOLOGY.

The Whitney Laboratory of Seismology is equipped with two Bosch-Omori 100 kg tromometers registering N-S and E-W motion, a heavy Omori tromometer registering E-W motion, and an Omori "ordinary Seismograph" designed for registering strong earthquakes in all three components of motion. These are seated on concrete piers in a closed basement room having practically constant temperature, beneath the chief Observatory building near the hotel. Time is referred to a rated chronometer, checked at intervals by solar observations with a transit. Both instruments are loaned by the College of Hawaii. Hawaiian standard time (H. S. T.) is 10 hrs. 30 min. slower than Greenwich time.

CANCANI SCALE OF SEISMIC INTENSITY.

Expressed by accelerations measured in millimeters per second per second.

I.	Instrumental	0.0	2.5
II.	Very slight	2.5	5.0
III.	Slight	5.0	10.0
IV.	Sensible, mediocre	10.0	25.0
V.	Rather strong	25.0	50.0
VI.	Strong	50.0	100.0
VII.	Very strong	100.0	250.0
VIII.	Ruinous	250.0	500.0
IX.	Disastrous	500.0	1000.0
X.	Very disastrous	1000.0	2500.0
XI.	Catastrophic	2500.0	5000.0
XII.	Great catastrophe	5000.0	10000.0

Grade IV. is ordinarily the minimum perceived by the senses; and in grade XII. the acceleration, or rate of change of motion (jerk) reaches that of terrestrial gravitation.

In the standard form of report the maximum intensity or acceleration, designated by the symbol a, or max. a, is given in the conventional unit, **the milligal.** The milligal is a measure of acceleration, such that 1 milligal = 1/100 mm. per sec. per sec. = 10 μ per sec. per sec. The Cancani scale, here defined in terms of millimeters per sec. per sec., can therefore be expressed in **milligals** by multiplying each of the numbers by 100.

WEEKLY BULLETIN
OF THE
Hawaiian Volcano Observatory

Vol. IV. HONOLULU, HAWAII, JANUARY, 1916. No. 1

TECHNOLOGY STATION, January 6.—During the week ending with January 8, little change has been seen in Halemaumau, though a definite rising tendency manifested itself throughout this interval, and a greater degree of surface action was observed. For nearly two months there has been little or no change in the character of this action—only changes in its intensity. No overflowing onto the floor has been observed since early in December, since when the surface has risen and fallen periodically through a range of thirty to forty feet—often standing only a foot or two below the surrounding platform.

On December 30 a tendency to rising was observed with the usual streaming and boiling. Jets of lava were flung regularly from the apex of the southwest cone—once to a height estimated at seventy-five feet.

On December 31 the surface seemed to be at a standstill at a few feet below the floor. The jet action continued, with a loud, deep, muffled, explosive sound; like that of a distant blast

On January 1 a rising tendency was again obvious, with lessened evidence of surface action. Small jets were flung from the southwest cone, and, in subdued volume, the explosive sound was heard.

On January 4 seeing was much obscured by fumes kept swirling by a strong north wind, but the magma surface was a little higher and much more active, with constant eastward streaming and boiling, always at the east end and often in other places as well, with occasional spatter bombardment along the walls. Gradually, without any permanent retirement of the lava, the lake has widened through the falling in of segments of the floor-platforms along its margins—so that it is now of larger area than for months past. Jet action from the southwest cone continued, but the muffled explosions were much subdued.

On January 5 the lava surface was standing a few feet below the floor. It had been suspected on January 4 that slight overflowing onto the floor was in progress, but it was now seen that this had not taken place. Nevertheless, the surface appeared still higher than on January 1.

During the week three teleseisms and seven definite local earthquakes, with doubtful wave-groups to the number of ten or more, have been registered in the Whitney Laboratory of Seismology.

One of the teleseisms was sharply registered and many maxima of considerable amplitude appeared in sequence in the record of the chief phase waves; the others were less well registered, and wrote movements of smaller amplitude and less energy. Both of the feebler shocks preceded the greater one, and all three were shocks of world-shaking power. These doubtless—in the case of the greatest, it is sure, had origin in San Salvador, whence news comes of a catastrophic shock on New Year's Day.

Central America lies in the junction of two well marked zones, each of which nearly encircles the earth, along great circles of the globe, in which are located the origins of a great majority of earthquakes on record. In recent years this region, with Southern Mexico, appears to be the most frequently and most profoundly shaken part of the earth, not excepting Italy or Japan. This occurrence in quick succession shortly after solstice of three world-shaking shocks, one, and possibly all, originating there, is of great interest in

WEEKLY BULLETIN
of the
Hawaiian Volcano Observatory

Published Monthly at Honolulu, Hawaii, by the Hawaiian Volcano Research Association

Entered as second-class matter January 20, 1914, at the post-office at Honolulu, Hawaii, under the Act of August 24, 1912.

connection with our developing study of seasonal variations in ear-strain.

There has been nothing of note regarding microseismic registration this week; nor that of volcanic vibration, except for a slight increase in energy in the latter part of the interval.

Tilting has undergone no net change, and there has been no further recovery from the permanent, or semi-permanent, change which accompanied the onset of the recent kona storm.

H. O. WOOD, Associate.

TECHNOLOGY STATION, January 13—During the week ending with January 12, though no hard storm has prevailed at Kilauea, still on several days southwest winds have been fairly steady during the day, accompanied by lighter to heavier showers, making conditions for observing at Halemaumau difficult to impossible. Nevertheless, it is certain that there has been little or no change in general conditions in Halemaumau, or in activity, for there have been numerous intervals, usually short, of good seeing. There has been no tendency to general subsidence during the week, but though the lava reached the highest point in about a month, it would be misleading to say that a rising tendency has prevailed. Rather, the magma has stood at a point a little below the floor, with oscillation about such a mean level. During one of the temporary rises, the date of which is unknown, a small thin overflow took place onto the floor at the southwest.

So unsatisfactory have been the conditions for seeing, or rather for observing, that for this week no attempt is made to give a day to day description of the action. On every occasion when the lake has been seen clearly, either by the writer or by others who are familiar with it, the surface has stood below the platform by small amounts, from three to five, or ten, feet: and the activity has been of the sort described so often recently; steady flowing, with tearing and crumpling of thin surface skins, from west to east and northeast where, in an area of vigorous boiling, skins and crusts continually are engulfed. There have been occasional doming fountains breaking in all parts of the lake, but chiefly east of its center. Now and then an outbreak of spatter fountains has taken place, with the area of action slowly migrating, usually with the stream, but sometimes against it especially when acting along the banks. The breaking of baby fountains has varied in the usual sporadic way. The southwest spatter-cone has been at work steadily, and has grown to considerable height.

The lake continues to widen gradually, though change of this sort in the past week has been small. The island near the west end is ever changing in outline and area, through spatter-building and collapse. It now has taken on a crescentic outline, with apex to the west and horns pointing eastward down the course of surface flow.

For two weeks past the fumes seem to have been decreasing in volume, but they are issuing now from numerous vents all around the margin of the floor platform, while a month ago they were coming more copiously but chiefly from a few vents along the north margin. Hence, though thinner now, they prevent really clear seeing by day more effectively than then. They are rarely dense enough, however, to obscure the spectacular seeing at night. But they make observation of details somewhat troublesome.

The recent heavy rainfall has brought about a resumption of copious steaming from many fissures in parts of the main crater ordinarily free of vapor; especially between the northeast bank and Halemaumau. Similar action followed the heavy rains of July, August and September, 1914. In many places this vapor issues with a hissing noise.

During the past week three local earthquakes were registered in the Whitney Laboratory of Seismology. Two of these were felt in Hilo, in early evening on the tenth. Neither was noticed in the vicinity of the Observatory, though they measure well above the perceptible minimum.

The amplitude of microseismic motion and of volcanic vibrations both continue greater than normal.

Fluctuations in tilting during the week have been of less range than usual.

H. O. WOOD, Associate.

TECHNOLOGY STATION, January 20.—The past week at Kilauea has been eventful. It began, on January 13, with a slight, but nevertheless markedly noticeable increase in surface action in Halemaumau: and it has ended with a kona storm of severity unequalled in recent years, the wind culminating in strength in the forenoon of Tuesday, January 18, when it stripped the roof from the main part of the observatory, admitting rain to the work rooms and the seismograph cellar with much resultant damage and interruption of work.

Strong wind from the southwest began early Sunday morning, January 16, and it reached normal gale strength early in the forenoon; it maintained this force until the early morning hours of the seventeenth when for a few hours, shortly after rain began to fall, the wind declined slightly. In the early afternoon of the seventeenth it regained steady, normal, gale strength with gusts which reached high values within the gale range. By noon of the seventeenth rain was falling in torrents, driving nearly horizontally. The storm gained steadily in strength, excepting a brief interval of moderate violence only, at about midnight of the seventeenth-eightenth, reaching its greatest violence at about 10:30 a. m. on the eighteenth when the gusts of wind were little short of hurricane violence. At this time the observatory roof was torn off, without warning, within the space of one to two seconds. The roof-frame and corrugated iron were distributed over a distance of two to three hundred yards to the north-eastward.

Though there was no warning of this, in the way of previous cracking or straining sounds in the roof-structure proper, nevertheless the walls of the building had been warping in and out in an alarming way and the whole structure had been trembling violently from the beginning of the storm. The wind continued with little or no abatement until late evening of the eighteenth; and it remained strong until late afternoon of the nineteenth. Practically no rain fell on the sixteenth. The rain was measured at ten a. m. on the seventeenth at one p. m. on the eighteenth, and at five p. m. on the nineteenth, with the following results, —0.49 inch, 7.15 inches, and 0.52 inch, a total of 8.26 for the storm. Fortunately the greater part fell before the unroofing of the building. Up to the time of writing no visits to Halemaumau have been made since the evening of the sixteenth. To have approached the edge of the pit without secure anchorage would have been foolhardy, if other weather conditions had been favorable, so strong and so gusty was the wind.

In the early afternoon of January 13 the surface of the lava stood a trifle, say two feet, below the floor platform around it, but it had only just ceased overflowing onto this floor at the southwest where a thin flow of pahoehoe still exhibited glow-cracks in its surface, visible by afternoon light. As usual, recently, boiling action was pronounced at the east and northeast with steady streaming towards this area. The cone under the southwest station, now grown quite large, was blowing very loudly, and ejecting lumps of magma at intervals. In the evening of this day there as an interval of practically no wind, with a light drift of air from the southwest. During this time the periodic explosive blasts from the southwest cone could be heard at the Volcano House very plainly. These sounds were quite loud and were absolutely unmistakable in character,—quite as loud and as well characterized as when the hearer is only fifty to a hundred yards from the pit-edge under ordinary conditions of hearing. This occurrence is unique since work was begun at this Observatory.

On January 14 the surface had fallen slightly and the explosive sounds made by the southwest cone had greatly diminished. Rapid streaming to the east cove was observed, with the usual activity noted there, and many large boiling fountains in many parts of the pool.

On January 15 the surface had subsided a little further, standing about ten feet below the floor platform. The surface action had diminished and about three-quarters of the surface was chilled and covered with black skins. In the forenoon a roaring sound was heard which could not be localized nor correlated with observed action. In the afternoon only rumbling and boiling sounds were audible, without any blowing noises or explosive blasts. The northwest island was smaller and was now shaped like a figure seven.

On January 16 the lava still stood several feet below the floor, but there were certain symptoms of vigorous rising outside the margins of the lake. A very liquid flow poured out from the southwest cone onto the floor adjacent to it, and lava welled out at two other orifices at the south and west. A small cascade of lava, running very rapidly, poured from a vent in the bank at the west-southwest and ran briskly into the main lake. Noises of eruption were louder than usual. The kona wind had already attained gale force and proved very disagreeable to visitors on this date. To the time of writing (early evening of January 19), no subsequent visit has been made so far as the writer is aware.

During the early part of the week now ending, with January 19, one very distant teleseism was registered in the Whitney Laboratory of Seismology. No other shocks were registered before the storm put a stop to further registration. Previous to the storm microseismic waves began to exhibit larger and larger amplitudes, but no extraordinary values were written prior to its arrival. There was nothing noteworthy about the registration of volcanic vibrations. A very pronounced tilt to the west was noticed which increased in magnitude up to the time of the culmination of the storm.

The seismograms which registered the interval from the morning of the seventeenth to the morning of the eighteenth were destroyed while still on the record cylinders by the entry of water shortly after the destruction of the roof. They were seen before this, however, and were remarkable for the extraordinary amplitude of vibrations generated by the wind—almost without cessation—much in excess of ordinary, small, local earthquake movements: and also for microseismic waves of very unusual amplitude. These wind vibrations, it must be understood, were tremblings of the buried concrete basement, not air-motions, due partly to vibrations set up in the concrete by the trembling of the frame structure which rested upon it. It is suspected, however, that in part these were due to the violent blasts of the wind against the neighboring cliff wall. Strong vibrations of this sort were registered also from the 16th to the 17th.

H. O. WOOD, Associate.

TECHNOLOGY STATION, January 27.—Although the scene in Halemaumau has been under observation much more than usual during the week ending with January 26, owing to the complete interruption of other work caused by the unroofing of the observatory, nevertheless there is little to say of its action. A day to day account again would be a wearisome repetition of details. The lake remains practically unchanged, extending from wall to wall in the east-west direction with a north-south width of about 200 to 220 feet.

Near the west end is the small island which undergoes slight changes in shape through spatter accretion and in-slumping. In general it is crescent shaped with its convexity to the west. Day after day the steady streaming of the magma from west to east continues, and there almost always is a boiling area at the east end, sometimes elsewhere temporarily especially on the north near the west end.

A periodic doming fountain which behaves exactly as "Old Faithful" has again begun to work, but this breaks very close to the east end of the lake instead of near the center. Fumes appear to have increased slightly in volume and now sometimes they interfere considerably with seeing by day, and to a less extent at night. The height of stand has not been seen to vary much during the week—from level with the platform, perhaps overflowing on the 20th of January, to a depth of three to five feet below the platform at the lowest stage of the week.

The southwest cone is growing in height through the outflinging of spatter lumps. This section was particularly noticeable during the evening of the twenty-fourth. On this date also there was little or no wind in the afternoon—what breezes there were blew from all quarters at intervals—and loud, spasmodic blowing sounds, due to gas escaping from this cone, were heard plainly, and as loudly as sometimes close by the pit, at points all along the west margin of the main crater, and also along the trail as near to the Observatory as the bridge which crosses the wide fissure in the lava floor.

There is no report from the Whitney Laboratory of Seismology for this week. Some little time will elapse before seismic registration can be resumed.

H. O. WOOD, Associate.

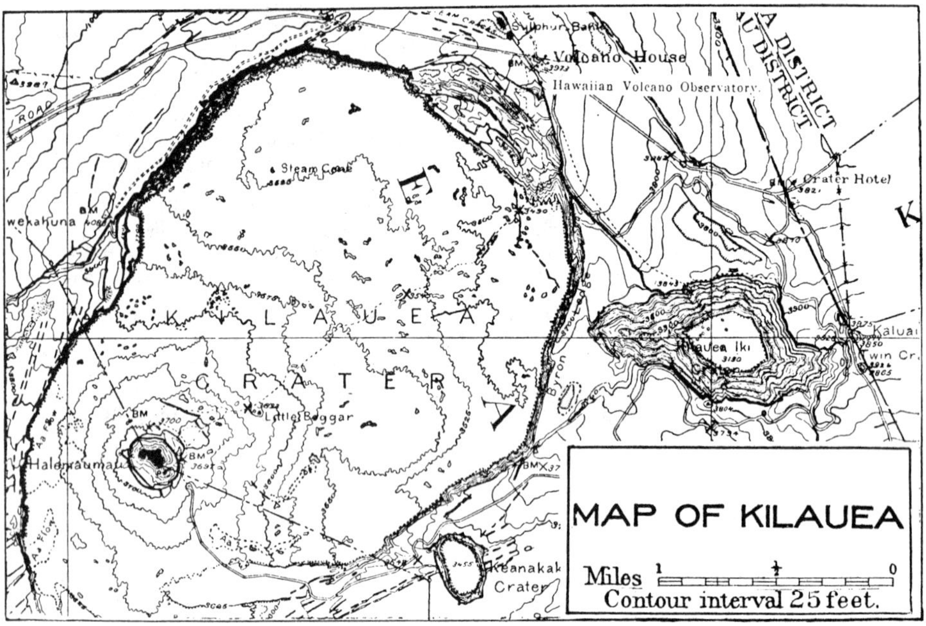

HAWAIIAN VOLCANO RESEARCH ASSOCIATION.

This society is a voluntary one, made up of subscribers to scientific work which is being executed by the Massachusetts Institute of Technology.

In 1915 there are about 100 subscribers in Hawaii and elsewhere, firms and individuals. A group of firms and persons in Hilo built the main observatory building in the spring of 1912. Publications to date have been weekly reports since the summer of 1911 now reprinted in Honolulu in monthly form. The Massachusetts Institute of Technology will publish annual reports, of which the introductory number was printed in 1912.

The weekly bulletin as it appears in the Advertiser is reprinted as a leaflet and sent to regular annual subscribers to the work of the Association. L. A. Thurston is president of the Board of Directors of the Association, and R. W. Shingle is treasurer. New subscribers who are interested in volcanoes will be welcomed in the Association. The Association aims: (1) To record volcanic activity and earthquakes in Hawaii; (2) to attract scientific men hither for special studies; (3) to promote the establishment of volcano observatories all over the world. The annual dues of regular members are $5; patrons of the Assocaition subscribe larger amounts.

WHITNEY LABORATORY OF SEISMOLOGY.

The Whitney Laboratory of Seismology is equipped with two Bosch-Omori 100 kg tromometers registering N-S and E-W motion, a heavy Omori tromometer registering E-W motion, and an Omori "ordinary Seismograph" designed for registering strong earthquakes in all three components of motion. These are seated on concrete piers in a closed basement room having practically constant temperature, beneath the chief Observatory building near the hotel. Time is referred to a rated chronometer, checked at intervals by solar observations with a transit. Both instruments are loaned by the College of Hawaii. Hawaiian standard time (H. S. T.) is 10 hrs. 30 min. slower than Greenwich time.

CANCANI SCALE OF SEISMIC INTENSITY.

Expressed by accelerations measured in millimeters per second per second.

I.	Instrumental	0.0	2.5
II.	Very slight	2.5	5.0
III.	Slight	5.0	10.0
IV.	Sensible, mediocre	10.0	25.0
V.	Rather strong	25.0	50.0
VI.	Strong	50.0	100.0
VII.	Very strong	100.0	250.0
VIII.	Ruinous	250.0	500.0
IX.	Disastrous	500.0	1000.0
X.	Very disastrous	1000.0	2500.0
XI.	Catastrophic	2500.0	5000.0
XII.	Great catastrophe	5000.0	10000.0

Grade IV. is ordinarily the minimum perceived by the senses; and in grade XII. the acceleration, or rate of change of motion (jerk) reaches that of terrestrial gravitation.

In the standard form of report the maximum intensity or acceleration, designated by the symbol a, or max. a, is given in the conventional unit, **the milligal.** The milligal is a measure of acceleration, such that 1 milligal = 1/100 mm. per sec. per sec. = 10 μ per sec. per sec. The Cancani scale, here defined in terms of millimeters per sec. per sec., can therefore be expressed in **milligals** by multiplying each of the numbers by 100.

WEEKLY BULLETIN
OF THE
Hawaiian Volcano Observatory

Vol. IV. HONOLULU, HAWAII, FEBRUARY, 1916. No. 2

TECHNOLOGY STATION, February 3.—Though its range has been small, there has been much more oscillation in the height of stand of the molten surface in Halemaumau during the week ended with February 2 than in any previous week for more than a month. There has been corresponding variety in the surface activity, so that the scene has grown more spectacular.

On January 27 the surface was nearly level with the floor platform, and the configuration of the lake and island was as usual. Small masses of molten lava were ejected from the southwest cone with harsh explosive noises. But the eastward streaming which had so long prevailed was interrupted. A rapid current was swinging around from the west to the north at a point near the middle of the lake, and towards this place there was radial streaming from the eastern and southern parts of the lake.

On January 28 a subsidence of the molten surface of from fifteen to twenty feet had taken place, apparently rapidly, since the southeast part of the floor platform neighboring the lake was cracked and warped down lower than the adjacent southwest part, which previously had stood at a lower level. A small, nearly circular area of the floor platform, northeast of the southwest spatter-cone and tangent to it, had collapsed completely, forming a small magma pool in which slender fountains were playing up from thirty to forty feet. Partial collapse of the southwest cone had occurred and its action had practically ceased. A small rock-fall had taken place at the extreme west; and at the east more considerable avalanches had choked the east end of the lake, so that it no longer reached to the wall at this point. Streaming from west to east prevailed as usual.

On January 30 general conditions had undergone no further change, except that at the east end streaming was so steady and rapid, in under the jumble of fallen rock, as to resemble a steep cascade.

On January 31 the surface had risen slightly, possibly to five feet below the platform. The cascade at the east continued. The island had become a peninsula, joined to the northwest bank by a narrow arm. Streaming was irregular.

On February 2, when first seen, the lake stood from twenty to twenty-five feet below the flatform, and was very stagnant, with a slow eastward streaming. The southwest lava pool appeared completely clogged. Within a short time the lake was seen to be rising steadily; and a torrential flow set in to the westward, coursing along north of the island. This flowing was far more rapid and turbulent than commonly is the case, and the magma surged and tossed so violently as to suggest the action of rushing water, rather than the more sluggish mechanisms seen in the flow of heavy liquids.

The writer has never seen a more vigorous and rapid flow in action in Halemaumau. This went on throughout the period of observation—the lake plainly rising all the while, so that the surface stood no more than fifteen feet below the platform about an hour after this action began. The southwest lava pool was rejuvenated; spatter action in the southwest and south cones was resumed; and fountain action in the lake grew more pronounced. The rapid current mentioned altered the mechanism of surface streaming, making it irregular and changeable in direction, with the production of unusual and striking fire patterns, and the conspicuous wrinkling and tearing of surface skins.

H. O. WOOD, Associate.

WEEKLY BULLETIN
of the
Hawaiian Volcano Observatory

Published Monthly at Honolulu, Hawaii, by the Hawaiian Volcano Research Association

Entered as second-class matter January 20, 1914, at the post-office at Honolulu, Hawaii, under the Act of August 24, 1912.

TECHNOLOGY STATION, February 10.—During the week ended with February 9 there was slight rising of the molten surface in Halemaumau, with greater short-term fluctuations in its height, and more diversified surface action than has been usual of late. The lake has not been seen to overflow its margins, and there is no reason to think that it has done so; but the floor platform, particularly at the south, has been covered over with new lava. However, the new stratum probably is a thin one.

In the afternoon of February 3 the molten surface appeared about twenty feet below the platform at the south, with the usual vigorous boiling at the east end toward which the streaming tended as usual. On this date about three-quarters of the lake, at the west end, was covered with black skins. Lava spray was flung high out of the cone at the southwest, occasionally with a very loud blowing noise. Few big fountains were seen, but many baby fountains characterized the action of boiling at the east end.

On February 4 in the afternoon in general these conditions still persisted, modified, however, by the circumstance that a rapid streaming was going on around the point of the peninsula and then northwestward into a cove, making a very loud noise. Elsewhere the eastward streaming continued sedately. At intervals the lake surface was disturbed by the breaking of large doming fountains in various parts of the pool. A large avalanche had fallen from the side of the main wall between the west and northwest stations. Blue fumes hovered in quantity all over the floor on this date.

On February 5 the surface of the lake had risen slightly and many large fountains were boiling in various parts of it. Near the east end the general eastward stream divided vaguely—, one current setting to the east cove, where the usual boiling prevailed, and another to a southeast cove also marked by a boiling area. The southwest cone was spurting lava spray very high with loud blowing sounds. From the little pool nearby came an overflow onto the south floor which ran half-way around the cone and reached to the wall of talus. As the afternoon wore on the surface action in the lake increased until nearly all the surface was disturbed and at frequent intervals numbers of large fountains broke practically at the same instant.

On February 7 the surface stood apparently ten feet below the platform. Into the lake poured a stream of lava which welled up in the small pool near the southwest cone. This action made a very loud noise. The surface action in the lake was usual in character, but of increased vigor.

On February 8 the lava level seemed the same, but the streaming was distributed—a current setting to the southwest, another to the northwest, and a third to the east cove: many large fountains were boiling in various parts of the lake. Nearly all the floor at the southwest had been covered with new lava from the southwest pool, now only a group of little holes. As a result the apparent height of the southwest cone seemed much diminished. However, at the east the old floor was still visible, so this fresh lava did not form a very thick layer. Three small cones had formed on the northeast side of the lake. The surface was rising during the interval of observation.

On February 9 an easterly wind kept the fumes swirling in the pit. Many fairly good glimpses were afforded, but no sustained good seeing. The lake surface appeared to stand from ten to fifteen feet below the south platform—now slightly upbuilt during the past three days—with steady streaming to the east where the usual boiling area was in action.

Ordinary surface activity prevailed. The southwest cone was still in evidence and mildly active, but the pool nearby had completely disappeared, and nearly all the south floor was formed of new lava. The tinkling sound made by rock cracking from heat—frequently due to slow overflowing which rends its crust already cooled—was the most prominent sound; but no flowing could be made out. The surface appeared to be subsiding slightly during the interval of observation.

It will interest many to know that the new trail to the summit of Mauna Loa, by way of Puu Ulaula (apparently destined to be known as Red Hill), where the rest-house was built recently, is finding favor. The latest party to traverse it, F. B. Dodge and J. W. Driscoll, left the Volcano House at nine-forty five a. m., on January 25, with saddle horses and a pack-horse; walking all the way they reached Camp Bates at about one p. m., where they remained for about an hour before resuming the climb; they reached the new house at Red Hill at about five-fifteen p. m., finding the trail good for horses all the way to this station. The house is well situated and attractive and proved very comfortable, though as yet it is scantily provided with furniture.

The next day, January 29, at about six-thirty a. m., they set out for the summit on foot.

This part of the way is not yet a built trail and so would be risky for horses, especially with a thin cover of snow such as is usual at this season. Mr. Dodge reached the edge of the summit crater at about eleven forty-five a. m., after a long walk over soft snow in a dazzling sun. After a brief stay he started down, reaching the house about five o'clock in the afternoon. The rift-cones and steaming cones seen along the way commanded attention, and the many unusual features of interest which characterize this trail were commented upon. Exposure to the spotless snow under the cloudless tropical sky led to disagreeable burning of the face and eyes, which made the second night at Red Hill uncomfortable.

On the thirtieth, the party started down from Red Hill at about eleven a. m., and reached the Volcano House at four-thirty p. m.—a trip of five hours and thirty minutes of continuous going.

The trip to Mokuaweoweo is now an easy one for qualified trampers and mountaineers, and offers besides many features of great interest along the way.

H. O. WOOD, Associate.

TECHNOLOGY STATION, February 17.—In Halemaumau the week ending with February 16 has been characterized by minor oscillation in height of stand, accompanied by slight changes in the energy of surface action; with a definite rising tendency toward the end of the interval.

On February 10 the surface stood about ten feet below the floor platform at the northeast. The pool near the northeast side of the southwest cone had re-opened and become a pot of surging lava, nearly level full. The southwest cone gave out loud blowing sounds. Streaming and boiling action were as usual—with moderate energy of flow and fountaining.

On February 11 the surface had fallen some six to eight feet, and the surface action had grown more turbulent. In the northeast area both large and small fountains were breaking incessantly. Though standing lower, the surface was in process of rising. A very rapid magma current was setting around the peninsula toward the northeast cove—distributed from the general current to the east and northeast. There was loud blowing from the southwest cone, and occasionally molten spray was ejected to a considerable height. The small pool near the cone had increased in activity and in it appeared a confused rushing of surface currents. A new small cone had formed on the northeast side of the pool, in a direct line with the southwest cone and the pool, and molten spray was jetting from this to heights of twenty to twenty-five feet.

On February 12 the surface stood about five feet below the floor and the action was comparatively quiet, boiling being conspicuous only in the east area, where action has been practically uninterrupted for several months. The eastward streaming prevailed, but the current was slow and thin black lava skins made up the surface, which was rising.

On February 14 the lava had fallen slightly, standing some ten feet below the floor. Except for vigorous fountain action in the east and northeast areas the surface was very quiet. A second small pool had opened near the southwest cone, in line with the cones and the earlier pool.

On February 15 the lava had risen further. The barriers between the pools and the main lake had dropped in, making a long, narrow southwest trench or cove, extending to the base of the southwest cone. In this a very rapid current of magma was setting from the lake toward the cone. In the lake area streaming was as usual, with numerous baby fountains breaking and shifting with the stream. Steady boiling was manifested in the south cove and the east area. Elsewhere the lake surface was quiet.

Occasionally large masses of lava would be thrown out from a large orifice on the south side of the southwest cone.

Throughout afternoon and evening the surface was rising slowly, but no overflowing onto the floor was seen.

On February 16 the action and the conditions of the surface were substantially, as on the preceding days; but, though symptoms of rising were general, no overflowing onto the floor was observed.

Repairs to the observatory, necessitated by the action of the Kona gale of mid-January, have now been completed, and the structure has been strengthened and improved. Considerable progress has been made in cleaning and repairing the seismographic mechanisms and accessory apparatus; but some little time must elapse still before routine registration can be resumed.

H. O. WOOD, Associate.

TECHNOLOGY STATION, February 24.—The week ending with February 23 has seen slight changes in Halemaumau—minor oscillations, with a definite rising tendency in the earlier part of the week and a disposition to stand, or fall slightly, at the end.

On February 15 the lava stood a few feet below the margin of the floor platform, but this appeared tilted away from the lake, especially at the southwest, as though up-forced by rising magma. A large part of the southwest floor had been overrun by a thin, slow-flowing lava sheet whose surface was one of miniature flow-tubes ending in lava-toes. Flowing and toeing out was still in progress. This overwelling was not from the main lake, but from the southwest pool; and the position of the new lava emphasized the tilted state of the floor. Action of streaming and boiling was as usual, and more than half the surface was covered almost completely with thin black skins.

On February 19 overflowing was still going on slowly, and except for streaming the action showed little change. There was somewhat greater fountain activity at the east end of the lake. The surface streaming was divided into three parts, one coursing to the southwest, one swerving into the southeast cove and the remaining one continuing straight on to the east.

On February 21 the surface was some five feet below the floor margin, and there was no fountain action except at the east end. Yet a flow burst out near the wall under the southeast station and ran toward the lake, spreading rather widely from its course. The northwest peninsula had again become an island, small in area.

On February 22 the lava stood about five feet below the floor, but it was rising slowly. There was much sporadic fountain activity in all parts of the pool. Under the northwest station a new pool of small area had opened, and lava was jetting up from it to considerable heights from time to time.

On February 23 there was much surface activity with both large fountains and small traveling along with the eastward streaming. The surface stood five feet, more or less, below the floor. There had been a further collapse of the debris at the east, forming a deep hole out of which thick clouds of fumes were rising.

An earthquake has been reported to the writer, strong enough to throw down a rude stone house situated on the trail leading from Kilauea to Mauna Kea at a point not far from the course of the Mauna Loa rift-belt. This occurred in late evening of February 15. There is no report that this shock was felt except by ranchmen who happened to be in camp along the trail. This is of interest as a shock almost surely emanating from the northeast segment of the Loa rift-system. The anticipation of eruption on this flank adds to its interest.

A slight earthquake was felt at the Volcano House in the early morning hours at about four o'clock on February 23.

There were, of course, no seismographic records of these or other shocks.

H. O. WOOD, Associate.

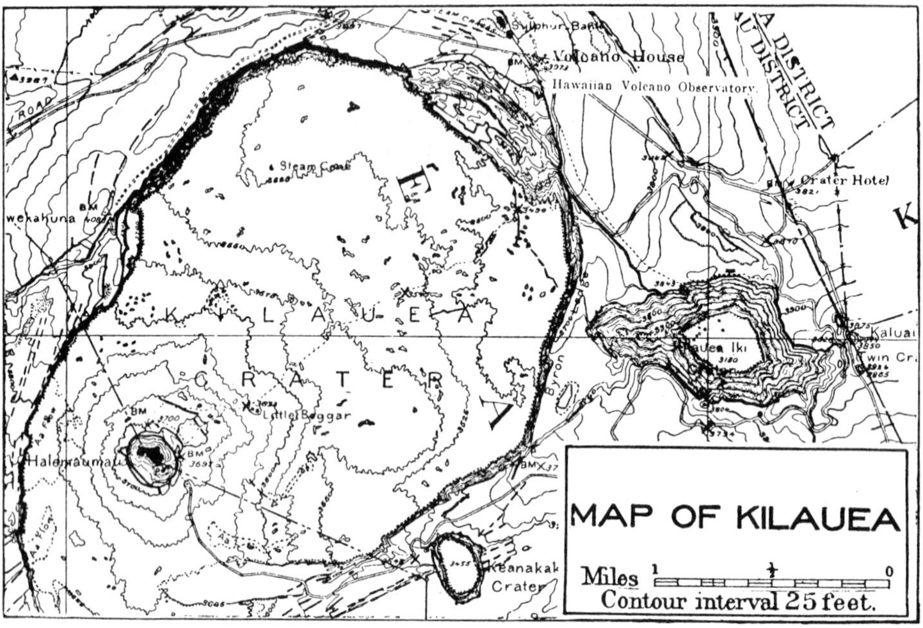

HAWAIIAN VOLCANO RESEARCH ASSOCIATION.

This society is a voluntary one, made up of subscribers to scientific work which is being executed by the Massachusetts Institute of Technology.

In 1915 there are about 100 subscribers in Hawaii and elsewhere, firms and individuals. A group of firms and persons in Hilo built the main observatory building in the spring of 1912. Publications to date have been weekly reports since the summer of 1911 now reprinted in Honolulu in monthly form. The Massachusetts Institute of Technology will publish annual reports, of which the introductory number was printed in 1912.

The weekly bulletin as it appears in the Advertiser is reprinted as a leaflet and sent to regular annual subscribers to the work of the Association. L. A. Thurston is president of the Board of Directors of the Association, and R. W. Shingle is treasurer. New subscribers who are interested in volcanoes will be welcomed in the Association. The Association aims: (1) To record volcanic activity and earthquakes in Hawaii: (2) to attract scientific men hither for special studies; (3) to promote the establishment of volcano observatories all over the world. The annual dues of regular members are $5; patrons of the Assocaition subscribe larger amounts.

WHITNEY LABORATORY OF SEISMOLOGY.

The Whitney Laboratory of Seismology is equipped with two Bosch-Omori 100 kg tromometers registering N-S and E-W motion, a heavy Omori tromometer registering E-W motion, and an Omori "ordinary Seismograph" designed for registering strong earthquakes in all three components of motion. These are seated on concrete piers in a closed basement room having practically constant temperature, beneath the chief Observatory building near the hotel. Time is referred to a rated chronometer, checked at intervals by solar observations with a transit. Both instruments are loaned by the College of Hawaii. Hawaiian standard time (H. S. T.) is 10 hrs. 30 min. slower than Greenwich time.

CANCANI SCALE OF SEISMIC INTENSITY.

Expressed by accelerations measured in millimeters per second per second.

I.	Instrumental	0.0	2.5
II.	Very slight	2.5	5.0
III.	Slight	5.0	10.0
IV.	Sensible, mediocre	10.0	25.0
V.	Rather strong	25.0	50.0
VI.	Strong	50.0	100.0
VII.	Very strong	100.0	250.0
VIII.	Ruinous	250.0	500.0
IX.	Disastrous	500.0	1000.0
X.	Very disastrous	1000.0	2500.0
XI.	Catastrophic	2500.0	5000.0
XII.	Great catastrophe	5000.0	10000.0

Grade IV. is ordinarily the minimum perceived by the senses; and in grade XII. the acceleration, or rate of change of motion (jerk) reaches that of terrestrial gravitation.

In the standard form of report the maximum intensity or acceleration, designated by the symbol α, or max. α, is given in the conventional unit, **the milligal.** The milligal is a measure of acceleration, such that 1 milligal = 1/100 mm. per sec. per sec. = 10 μ per sec. per sec. The Cancani scale, here defined in terms of millimeters per sec. per sec., can therefore be expressed in **milligals** by multiplying each of the numbers by 100.

WEEKLY BULLETIN
OF THE
Hawaiian Volcano Observatory

Vol. IV. HONOLULU, HAWAII, MARCH, 1916. No. 3

TECHNOLOGY STATION, March 2. —During the week ending March 1 the lava lake of Halemaumau has remained relatively stationary at a depth of 470 feet below the southern rim of the pit. The lake extends from wall to wall of the pit in its lengthwise direction east and west, and is bordered on its north bank by a craggy platform only a few yards wide, while its south bank follows the edge of a broad floor covered with new flows. Apparently the same mechanism of overflow of the southern floor has been going on during the past winter as in the preceding year. This both weighs down the southern floor and widens it while the north bank of the lake keeps its height above the liquid. In general the lake has been from ten to fifteen feet below its bank during the past week.

On February 24, at two o'clock in the afternoon, the lake was fifteen feet below the rim, very active on the northeast, and streaming into coves northeast and east. The black skins were conspicuous and moving very slowly, only a few fountains broke the surface at the east end and cones on the southern floor were not puffing. There were no avalanches. At three o'clock from the north station a small pool next to the northeast wall could be seen boiling and spurting. It appeared to be twenty feet long by ten wide.

On February 25, at two o'clock, from the southeast station the lake appeared fifteen feet below the floor with ebullition on the northeast side, many bubble fountains and eastward streaming. Most of the lake was quiet. Old Faithful fountain appeared to have resumed activity in the east central part of the lake. At half-past two o'clock the slide-rock between the west and southwest stations was sliding, indicating that subsidence was in progress.

On February 26, at half-past two o'clock, from the southeast station the lava appeared to be rising slowly, the border cliff appeared to be about ten feet high and the only active fountaining was at the east end. The southwest cone on the floor was making loud puffing noises. There were some falls of rock from the east end of the 50-foot bench under the south station.

On February 28, at two o'clock, the streaming was eastward from under a skin which covered the west end of the lake. There were really two islands adjacent to the northwest corner of the lake, though in appearance the island nearest the shore seemed to be a peninsula. But its connection with the shore was only a crust. A smaller islet protruded into the middle of the western part of the lake with a current pouring by it eastward on both its north and south sides. High glowing cracks were seen along the western border of the lake and of the floor area, and it is evident that from these cracks recent flows have poured eastward. One hundred and twenty feet higher at the west end a clinging remnant of the 1915 high level bench still persisted.

From the southeast station at three-twenty-five o'clock a rock slide took place from the wall talus west-southwest. The fountaining activity was moderate in the eastern part of the lake and the streaming steady, eastward and northward. Some hissing could be heard apparently from the southern smoke cone on the floor. Several more slides took place to the southwest. The east end of the southern fifty-foot bench has crumbled away so that the bench is smaller. Old Faithful fountain was erupting at intervals of from forty to sixty seconds with perpetual fountaining in the middle of the lake east of it. During the afternoon

WEEKLY BULLETIN
of the
Hawaiian Volcano Observatory

Published Monthly at Honolulu, Hawaii, by the Hawaiian Volcano Research Association

Entered as second-class matter January 20, 1914, at the post-office at Honolulu, Hawaii, under the Act of August 24, 1912.

it was evident that the lava had been rising and falling in pulsations of a half hour or less, with increased hissing noise during the rises and with rumbling and rock-sliding during the sinkings. The net movement of the lake surface from two o'clock to four o'clock appeared to be a rise of about ten feet. In the southern talus there is a fumarole jetting white smoke vigorously from a point perhaps forty feet above the floor, where the slide-rock is much stained with the sulphur. The lake has a narrow arm extending straight into the bench from it southwestward to the southwest cone. The floor areas north, southwest and west are greenish and old, but the south and southeast floor is covered with fresh flows. There are freshly fallen stones on the floor at the east end and a talus slope at the actual lake edge east. The glowing northeast pot was still in action on this date.

On February 29, at three o'clock, a survey from the southeast and south stations made the lava of the lake 472 feet below the rim, the base of the southwest cone at the floor level 467 feet down, and the 1915 bench at the west end 342 feet below the edge of Halemaumau. As the cliff over the lake west of the southwest arm was at least fifteen feet high it was apparent that the floor sloped back to the base of the cone.

Conditions in the lake were little changed. Small slides took place south and southwest. The noises were of puffing and fountaining. The streaming was eastward in the lake and inward into the southwest arm, and the liquid was pounding and fountaining in the northern, northeastern and eastern grottoes. A smoking crack at the edge of the floor southeast appeared to be an extension of the eastern grotto. In the same way the northeast grotto led under the bank toward the northeast wall pot, while the southwest cone lay at the end of the southwest arm, the latter being evidently the development of a former tunnel in that direction. The southern cone in the middle of the floor also may have a tunnel connection with the lake, for opposite to it on the edge of the lake there is a large glow-hole.

Blue fumes were rising from the east end, southwest cone and south cone. A fan pattern of skins radiated out on the lake from the west end. The fumes from the south talus were much whiter and without noise. Hissing could be heard at the west end.

The entire floor of Kilauea crater shows much more visible steam than is usual, owing to the excessive rainfall of the past winter. There is also much steam in the fumes from the pit, but generally at present the lake can be clearly seen day and night and the area of molten surface is large. The slide-rock around the borders of the lake has been increasingly dissolved by the lava and the walls are growing steeper, especially to the south and southwest, so that we have had during the past winter the unusual condition of a floor nearly 1000 feet long at a depth over 450 feet below the rim of the pit.

The director returned from Washington February 20. The projects of turning the observatory over to the United States Weather Bureau and of creating an Hawaiian National Park are both before congress. The annual meeting of the Hawaiian Volcano Research Association has been called for April 7 at three o'clock in the chamber of commerce rooms, Honolulu, and some account will be given of these projects and of the plans for the future of the Research Association.

T. A. JAGGAR, JR., Director.

TECHNOLOGY STATION, March 9. —The week ending March 8, 1916, at Kilauea volcano has been characterized by rising activity of the lava lake and a heavy rain and wind storm from the south-west. The pronounced tumbling of debris on the talus slopes, observed during the previous week came to an end with the return of the lava to the lip of the inner pit, and at the same time new flows from the west spread over the whole southern floor.

On Wednesday March 1, at two p. m., seen from the north, the lake was twenty feet below its rim with active fountaining northeast and east. Streaming was eastward in the main lake and a current was running rapidly into the southwest arm. Old Faithful fountain occasionally erupted. It was evident that the old rampart along the southwest shore of the lake was being tilted southwestward under the weight of the flows accumulated between it and the wall of the pit. There was actual uplift of the lake margin and subsidence of the wall margin thus converting the bench into a ridge or crag. The sinking of the under floor along the base of the southwest wall was the cause of the frequent movement which there took place in the slide-rock. At three p. m. the west arm of the lake was boiling and sputtering to such a height that the droplets of lava fell upon the bench above.

On March 2 at one p. m., the lake was seen from the south station to have risen so that the banks were five feet high at the west end and ten feet high at the east. The south-west crag was still more tilted with fresh flows from the west arm between it and the wall. The north and southeast coves were greatly enlarged, the northeast grotto submerged, Old Faithful explosions could not be distinguished as definite in location or regularity, and the southern glow hole at the edge of the lake had become a cone topped with a filagree of lava spatter. Rock sliding was still in progress on the south-west. The middle portion of the 340-foot bench at the west end had fallen away. The glowing cracks at the west end which were sources for the lava flows on the south bench, now appeared to be at the lake level, and practically to have become part of the west arm of the lake. The western island had been flooded over with new lava. Streaming in the lake was slight and indefinite in direction.

On March 3 at six p. m., the lake was visible from both the northern and southern stations and its surface was very quiet, covered with skins, with little streaming action, some fountaining at the east end and but little noise of activity. The crag on the southwest appeared high and strong avalanches were tumbling east, southwest and southeast.

A heavy Kona storm from the southwest interrupted all observations at the lava pit for the next two days. Ten inches of rain fell at the Observatory.

At six p. m. on March 6 the first view obtained after the storm was from the southeast station and it was evident that the lake had been rising, the banks at the east end being only about four feet high, and much of this constructed by the spatter. A new glowing flow extended along the southwest and south edges of the floor. There was glow in the south and southwest floor cones and a flaming window in the cone at the south edge of the lake. The surface of the lake was streaming majestically eastward into the southeast cove and on the northeast shore a knob of spatter protruded into the lake. Skins were forming and breaking in the southwest arm. The west end of the lake was shaped in plan like the head of a goose, the bill making a long arm extending southwestward against the west wall of the pit. Shore bombardment was in progress southeast, east, north-east and north-west. There was occasional fountaining in the middle region of the east end of the lake and strong bubble fountaining with rapid inrush was exhibited at the northeast and southwest ends of a wide southeastern cove. There was inrush also on the northeast. The pattern of the skins on the surface of the lake was generally in crescents with the points eastward. The flows on the floor made crackling noises, one rock fall was heard to the south, and hissing occasionally took place from the end of the south-west arm. The prevailing noise however, was the splash of fountains. The fumes along the south-east wall were dense and white but those of the south fumarole were thin.

On March 7 at six p. m. it was evident that the lake was definitely rising. Thick new flows from the west covered the south floor, and the south cone was spouting liquid lava. One small slide was heard at the east end. The lake was crusted at the west. The streaming from the west end diverged against the banks on all sides and was rapid into the south-west arm. There were ten localities of bombardment and overspatter around the shores of the lake, with pockets built in the bank at each place where the liquid boiled and sputtered to construct a semicircular niche. The lake at this time was very spectacular and free from obstructing fumes.

At noon on March 8 measurement from the south and south-east stations made the lake 460 feet below the rim, indicating a rise of twelve feet in eight days.

The rising activity continued with the same general mechanism as on the previous day. In addition to the southwest crag there is a second crag of old floor tilted southward under the southeast wall of the pit opposite the southeast cove of the lake. The degree of tilt in this eastern crag appears to be the same as that of the southwest crag, indicating that the two are the ends of a cake of floor material occupying the southern half of the pit which has been weighted down bodily by the heavy flows that have submerged it.

There were seven splashing niches on the north, large coves had now developed northeast and southeast, and five symmetrical scallops bordered the southeast cove giving it an appearance like a scalloped shell. The greater part of the southern floor was covered with a wide plain of new flows. The south cone had built higher and was spitting weakly. The south fumarole in the talus was about forty feet above the floor, emitting thick blue fumes. A tumbled bench and fumarole occupied the site of the recent north-east lava pot. The south-west cone was buried under the new flows and the lava of the southwest arm was boiling sluggishly.

At nine p. m. conditions were about the same with fresh glowing liquid lava pushing out from the flows on the floor, and rapid oscillations in the level of the lake.

T. A. JAGGAR, JR., Director.

TECHNOLOGY STATION, March 16.—The lava lake of Halemaumau continued to rise gradually until March 13 and since that time it has slightly subsided. The fumes from the pit have been remarkably thin and during good weather the entire interior of the cauldron has been visible. The weather, however, most of the week has been drizzly with northeast winds.

On March 9 at two-thirty p. m. the lake was crusted at the west, streaming eastward with bombardment on the banks north-west, north, north-east and south-east. The point which separated the northeast and south-east coves had disappeared and it is probable that its collapse into the lake was seen on the evening of March 8, when a remarkable crag with a flat top was seen to lift itself through the liquid and remain for half an hour as an island before it broke up and subsided. The niches in the bank north, north-east, east and south-east had become spatter cones, large ones being conspicuous north-east and south-east several feet back from the rim of the pool.

The lake was brimming full, level with its margin. A small remnant of the western island could still be seen among the quiet skins of the middle of the west end. There was glow on the wall margin of the floor north-east and new flows had poured thence to the lake. The south cone and the border cone on the south margin of the lake were both partially submerged by new flows. The south-west arm was stagnant with a hissing cone at the inner end, fumes from the south fumarole were thin and the seeing was everywhere distinct. A little smoke arose from the scarps of the south-west and the south-east crags. A shallow cavern about twenty feet high has developed in the wall south-east where the south-east crag had broken away. Flows glowing through the fissures covered the south floor.

On March 10 at six p. m. the lake was overflowing on all sides especially north-east, east, south and west. The two crags were still more submerged under flows, the shore cones and the south cone had disappeared. A trickling flow poured from the east end of the lake into the hollow between the south-east crag and the wall, forking as it ran. Another flow trickled into this hole from the floor flows on the south side of the crag. Eleven border fountains were in action and one in the south-west arm. Gas issued with a roaring noise from border fountains in the south-east cove. The west end was crusted and streaming was from west to east. The south-east crag had greatly diminished in size. The south floor was covered with swelling flows, the west arm had widened at its south end. Occasional slips took place in the south talus.

On March 12 at seven p. m. conditions were much the same. The south cone had rebuilt and was smoking. A blue flame played on the north rim of the lake and the level of the lava was slightly below the rim.

On March 14 at eleven-thirty a. m. from the south station there was very clear seeing and it was evident that the floods of lava on the south floor had latterly been pouring over the edge of the lake southward, westward and eastward, the pronounced overflow from the west end having ceased. Long trains of festoons in the skin of the flows radiated west and south from the south-west arm and eastward from the shore of the lake a little farther to the east. Both crags appeared greatly submerged, the eastern one now rising only about eight feet above the bench and the south-west one fifteen feet at its highest part. Its western end had almost disappeared. The west island was gone. The hole east of the south-east crag was filled up with new lava. The south fumarole appeared about ten feet above the floor which had widened all around the pit. The west end of the lake no longer showed a long arm extending southward. The lake was about three feet below the spatter rim with eastward streaming, bombardment north and east, stalactites on the north, hissing to the west, and bubble fountains in the east end. The noise was chiefly a plashing. The south-west and south cones had reasserted their presence through the flows on the floor. The northern and eastern talus slopes were greatly diminished by burial under new flows.

On March 14 at three-thirty p. m. and again at five-forty-five p. m. pronounced thin blue fume appeared over Mokuaweoweo on Mauna Loa. With change in the sun's angle about sunset, the fume disappeared completely in the course of ten minutes showing that its visibility was largely due to favorable conditions of illumination.

For the Whitney Laboratory of Seismology, H. O. Wood reports that about twelve-thirty a. m., March 10, an earthquake ocurred strong enough to start the clock of the ordinary seismometer. More than a minute elapsed before the electric contact starting pendulum quieted sufficiently to allow of re-setting. No records were written as the seismographs are still out of commission. Some time before the early forenoon of the eleventh, this power clock was again started but the time is unknown. Neither shock was felt at the observatory.

Much progress has been made in rehabilitating the seismographic equipment but further repairs are found necessary to delicate parts of the writing fechanism so that a further delay, not foreseen, will intervene before the resumption of registration.

T. A. JAGGAR, JR., Director.

TECHNOLOGY STATION, March 23.—The last two weeks at the volcano have been characterized by cold and windy weather with high cirrus clouds and north-east gales followed by warmer weather with rain from the north-east. The lava lake continued to subside during the first three days of the week ending March 22, and thereafter rising activity was resumed with overflows of the bench which is at present about 425 feet below the rim.

On March 16 at nine-thirty a. m. the fumes were forced down into the pit by the north-east gale making seeing difficult. From the south station the lake appeared about eight feet below its rim with eastward streaming and five fountaining areas toward the east; stalactities were conspicuous in grottoes north-west, north-east and in the south-west arm; a new niche appeared at the base of the cliff wall south-east where a block of the wall was sliding down and there were fresh talus slides south-east and south-west. The floor was much cracked. The east crag appeared unchanged.

On March 17 at nine-thirty a. m. dim views through the fumes were obtained from the north rest house and the south-east station. The lake appeared fifteen feet below the floor west and ten feet down on the east. An arch of crust between the south-west crag and the wall overhung a cavernous extension formerly the west arm of the lake. The south floor showed sluggish lava welling up cracks. These was a row of fountains up the middle of the lake, the south-west talus was sliding, the south-west crag appeared about thirty-five feet high at its eastern end and grottoes with stalactites were conspicuous as before.

At nine-thirty a. m. Saturday, March 18, the high north-east wind appeared to be thrown into a whirl by the rising heat column from the pit so that the fume, which was very thin in appearance, was whirled over the edge suffocatingly south-east, south and south-west and there was no clear seeing. The lake appeared higher, overflows from the west again appeared on the southwest floor and trickle-flows rising from cracks had increased in size on the south floor. The south-west crag appeared lower, the east crag unchanged. The lake was streaming eastward, its surface was about three feet below the rim and at the east end it spattered over the bank slightly. The fountaining had diminished and the stalactites had disappeared. There was bombardment on the shore east and north. Smoke rose from the south-west cone on the floor. The cavern at the base of the south-east wall appeared to have deepened, and a wet fumarole appeared in the wall about 100 feet above it. Rocks were sliding a little east and south-west but the wind might have occasioned this.

On March 20 at four p. m. the lake was rising strongly and overflowing north, south-east, south and west. It was flush with its northern rim. Spatter lumps had formed on the bank east, south-east and south. Streaming was eastward and a rapid current poured into the southwest arm. Old Faithful fountain appeared to be playing at intervals of about sixty seconds. The west end was covered with skin. The only noises were the plash and roar of the fountains. There was heavy surging in the grottoes under the crag in the southwest arm.

The south-west crag was evidently tilting back rapidly toward the south-west wall under the weight of new flows on its south-west slope. A recent spatter rim on the lake shore at the east base of the crag had been uplifted bodily and tilted and the west end of the crag was now rising and lifting the flow material on its back. The east crag on the other hand jutted through new flows to a height of only about three feet. The south-east wall cavern was filled higher with new flows. Fresh lava toes were moving on the south floor which was now built up to the base of the south talus fumarole. The latter was smoking very slightly. Fumes rose from the two crags, from a jutting ledge at the base of the north-east wall, from the high wet fumarole south-east and from the edge of the floor beneath. Rocks were falling from the wall under the east end of the 1894 bench about 200 feet down.

On March 21 at six p. m. rising continued. The floor was so much built up that the east crag was submerged and the floor was extended in area on all sides. Lava trickle welled up through cracks in the flows and occasionally a large area would break up so that the crusts foundered in the melt beneath. When this took place small bubble fountains were abundant in the flow lava. The south-west crag was still more tilted back and a new shore bench at its base was raised about three feet. A considerable width of floor had now formed east of the lake and a narrow bench separated the lake from the western wall of the pit in marked contrast to conditions of a month ago when the lake extended from wall to wall. There was very clear seeing and the thin fumes made only a faint bluish veil above the pit as viewed from a distance, but high in the air to leeward water vapor drawn in from the sides condensed in cumulus clouds. On March 22 the rising continued.

Nothing unusual has been observed in seismic conditions as recorded by one seismograph which was started March 20.

T. A. JAGGAR, JR., Director.

TECHNOLOGY STATION, March 30.—The lava lake of Halemaumau during the week ending March 29, 1916, has displayed intense rising activity interrupted by only a slight tendency to fall a few feet between March 26 and 27. The southwest crag has continued to tilt backward and has become essentially an island in the midst of lava floods. These floods over the floor both from the lake and from smaller vents have been maintained in such volume that it is hard to distinguish the outline of the lake proper and the heat on the faces of observers at the rim of the pit is intense. The flooded area is the largest since December of 1911, owing to the steepness of the cliff walls and the absence of slide-rock slopes. The fumes have almost totally disappeared so that every detail of the interior of the pit is visible from all sides night and day.

On March 30 it appeared from the south station that rising had continued and there were almost no visible fumes, the gases rising in a thin blue haze. The lake was streaming eastward and bombarding its north, northeast and east shores. A cascade from southwestern flows poured into the end of the southwest arm and a continuous fountain played midway between the southwest crag and the southwest wall. The crag was more tilted up and its west end appeared as high as the east end. The ends were smoking slightly as was the projection at the northeast margin of the floor. The floor was everywhere covered with glistening, curtained flows, a large area south swelling and breaking up occasionally by the cracking and foundering process, revealing floods of melt beneath, bubbling with gas. At noon the east end of the lake was overflowing and the southwest cascade had increased to a torrent.

A survey on March 23 at eleven a. m. showed the lake was 407 feet below the south rim, 670 feet long, the west summit of the crag forty-six feet high above the lake, the east summit twenty-seven feet, and the floor area measured 950 feet south-east north-west by 770 feet north-east south-west.

At midnight on March 23 and again at ten a. m., March 24, the floor had built higher, the southwest arm was covered wtih an arch of crusted flows under which the cascade poured from the southwestern fountaining pool, and around the lake were spatter lumps and new overflows. The floor area south of the crag was now larger than the entire lake and northern rim of floor bordering the lake. There was some rumbling noise as well as the usual plash and hiss characteristic of rising. The heat on the rim was strong.

At eleven a. m. on March 25 the lake was brimming to its margins and streaming eastward, and building border spatter. The streaming was from under thin skins which covered the west end and the entrance to the southwest arm.

A half cone of spatter had built on the northeast shore. An islet appeared in the lake near its northwest shore. The crag had so tilted that four distinct shore benches, raised one above the other, were visible at its eastern base. The southwest pool was fountaining and cascading under a crust into the southwest arm. This cascade had migrated westward, suggesting that the arm was extending itself, and the oval southwest pool showed a distinct rampart as though the lava had some depth. There were three pooled areas on the floor southeast, south and southwest, and at eleven a. m., the southeastern one broke up and extended its engulfing of the crust westward until it tapped the southern area. A torrent then poured for many minutes from this southern pool forming festoons on its surface and indicating that the general grade of the floor was downward from west to east.

On March 26 at eleven-thirty a. m., rising had continued, the southwest arm appeared to extend to the southwest fountain, streaming was eastward in both the lake and the arm, the crag appeared to be more submerged and the island was overflooded with new lava. Some twenty fountains were in action on the north and east, in the lake and along the shores, and among them a large periodic fountain appeared to represent Old Faithful. In the evening the lake tended to subside at intervals with inrush toward a pot in the middle of the southwest arm where the sinking went on faster than in the lake.

On March 27 at ten-thirty a. m. this process was clearly evident and the lake was about four feet below its banks. The inrush into the pot amounted to a two-sided cascading at the south corner of the crag, the site of the former inner end of the southwest arm.

Into this cavernous void, roofed with stalactites, the lava of the lake cascaded from the east and that of the southwest pool from the west. The southwest pool was distinctly oval in form with a perpetual fountain at its west end. There were now two islands in the lake near the north bank opposite the crag. On the north-northwest bank a large half dome of spatter had formed. There was an occasional cracking noise like a pistol shot, there was heavy rumbling from the grottoes and occasionally a prolonged, unexplained hiss came from the floor area. White fumes rose from the two ends of the crag. One small slide took place southwest. The flows on the floor were of silky appearance and bronzy tarnish, somewhat cracked, but no liquid welled up the cracks. The larger islet stood about four feet above the lake, which was streaming eastward.

On March 28 at noon the rising had been resumed, the lake was brimming and the heat from the bottom of the pit was intense. There was almost no fume visible. A little white vapor arose from the crag and bluish gas from the fountains. A wide river of lava poured from the south-west pool to the lake, there was a fountain in the midst of the south floor, streaming was eastward, Old Faithful was active, the islands were submerged and there was splash on the banks east, southeast, north and north-west. The bronzy lava of the previous day was submerged under new flows except for a rim of it along the south base of the crag which had been raised up with the continual tilting of that mass.

Three distinct ages of tilted lava could now be distinguished on the back of the crag, and four bench lines on the lake side. Crackling noises were heard and blowing to the south-west. There was maximum rising activity from eleven-thirty a. m. to twelve noon and a slight subsidence thereafter. At six p. m. on this date there was slight sinking with stagnant lava at the entrance of the south-west arm and streaming into the south-west pot.

On March 29 at nine-thirty a. m. tremendous rising was in progress, the lake was overflowing on all sides and a blowing cone was spurting violently at the edge of the south-west pot. Six shore benches could now be counted at the east base of the crag. The lake was stagnant in its middle and western parts and streaming very slowly in the east. The inner wall of the pit west of the south station was scaling off so that small stones tumbled occasionally. The rising was so rapid between nine-fifteen and ten a. m. that the line of bronzy floor edge of March 27 at the south base of the crag became submerged.

A survey at nine-thirty a. m. on March 29 showed that the lake was

381 feet below the south-east rim of the pit; the west end of the crag forty feet and the east end thirty-two feet above the lake; while the floor measured 1030 feet from north-west to south-east, and 857 East-northeast to south-south-west. The crag from summit to summit measured 315 feet in length. Its west summit in the six days since March 23 had moved fifteen feet southward while the east summit had moved 100 feet south-west in the process of tilting. Meanwhile its height above the lake had remained almost constant.

The following report from the Whitney Laboratory of Seismology is submitted by H. O. Wood:

Though not in final adjustment as yet, one of the seismographs, the Omori Major Tromometer, has been registering since the morning of March 20. During the interval ending with the morning of March 29 only one very feeble local shock has been recorded, together with two, or three, disturbances of local character. Microseismic motion has been small in amplitude. Volcanic vibration has been moderately strong. Nothing can be stated in regard to tilting owing to the uncertain adjustment of the pendulum.

T. A. JAGGAR, JR., Director.

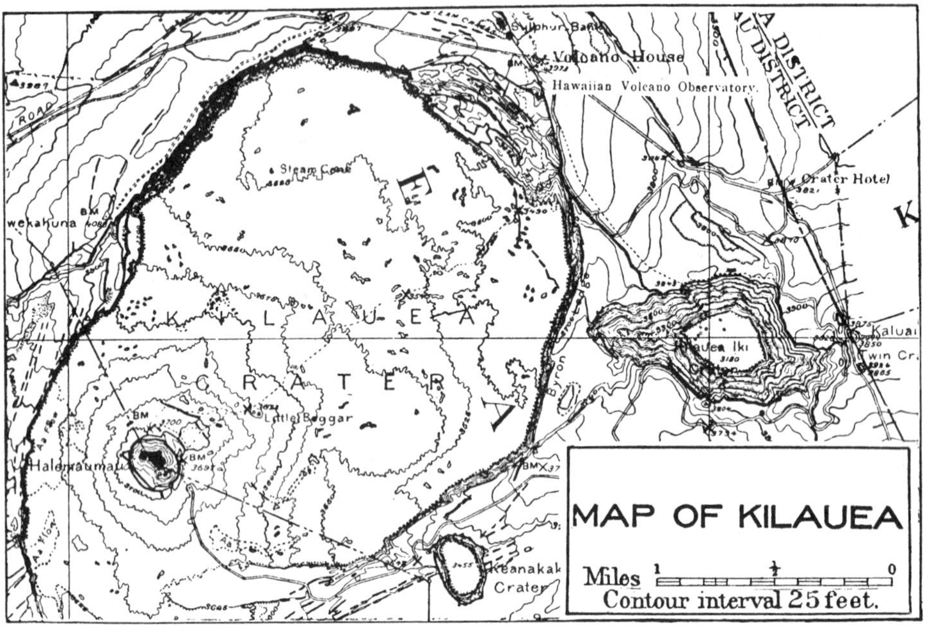

HAWAIIAN VOLCANO RESEARCH ASSOCIATION.

This society is a voluntary one, made up of subscribers to scientific work which is being executed by the Massachusetts Institute of Technology.

In 1915 there are about 100 subscribers in Hawaii and elsewhere, firms and individuals. A group of firms and persons in Hilo built the main observatory building in the spring of 1912. Publications to date have been weekly reports since the summer of 1911, now reprinted in Honolulu in monthly form. The Massachusetts Institute of Technology will publish annual reports, of which the introductory number was printed in 1912.

The weekly bulletin as it appears in the Advertiser is reprinted as a leaflet and sent to regular annual subscribers to the work of the Association. L. A. Thurston is president of the Board of Directors of the Association, and R. W. Shingle is treasurer. New subscribers who are interested in volcanoes will be welcomed in the Association. The Association aims: (1) To record volcanic activity and earthquakes in Hawaii; (2) to attract scientific men hither for special studies; (3) to promote the establishment of volcano observatories all over the world. The annual dues of regular members are $5; patrons of the Assocaition subscribe larger amounts.

WHITNEY LABORATORY OF SEISMOLOGY.

The Whitney Laboratory of Seismology is equipped with two Bosch-Omori 100 kg tromometers registering N-S and E-W motion, a heavy Omori tromometer registering E-W motion, and an Omori "ordinary Seismograph" designed for registering strong earthquakes in all three components of motion. These are seated on concrete piers in a closed basement room having practically constant temperature, beneath the chief Observatory building near the hotel. Time is referred to a rated chronometer, checked at intervals by solar observations with a transit. Both instruments are loaned by the College of Hawaii. Hawaiian standard time (H. S. T.) is 10 hrs. 30 min. slower than Greenwich time.

CANCANI SCALE OF SEISMIC INTENSITY.

Expressed by accelerations measured in millimeters per second per second.

I.	Instrumental	0.0	2.5
II.	Very slight	2.5	5.0
III.	Slight	5.0	10.0
IV.	Sensible, mediocre	10.0	25.0
V.	Rather strong	25.0	50.0
VI.	Strong	50.0	100.0
VII.	Very strong	100.0	250.0
VIII.	Ruinous	250.0	500.0
IX.	Disastrous	500.0	1000.0
X.	Very disastrous	1000.0	2500.0
XI.	Catastrophic	2500.0	5000.0
XII.	Great catastrophe	5000.0	10000.0

Grade IV. is ordinarily the minimum perceived by the senses; and in grade XII. the acceleration, or rate of change of motion (jerk) reaches that of terrestrial gravitation.

In the standard form of report the maximum intensity or acceleration, designated by the symbol a, or max. a, is given in the conventional unit, **the milligal.** The milligal is a measure of acceleration, such that 1 milligal = 1/100 mm. per sec. per sec. = 10 μ per sec. per sec. The Cancani scale, here defined in terms of millimeters per sec. per sec., can therefore be expressed in **milligals by multiplying each of the numbers by 100.**

WEEKLY BULLETIN
OF THE
Hawaiian Volcano Observatory

Vol. IV. HONOLULU, HAWAII, APRIL, 1916. No. 4

ANNUAL ADDRESS OF THE DIRECTOR, APRIL 7, 1916.

APPENDIX.

1. Summary Report 1915, work of Hawaiian Volcano Observatory.
2. Approximate Routine of the Staff of Hawaiian Volcano Observatory.
3. Report of Committee of Hawaiian Volcano Research Association appointed to consider method of making the Hawaiian Volcano Observatory a government institution.
4. Report of the Secretary of Agriculture on government work in volcanology.
5. Bill to establish Hawaii National Park.
6. Report of T. A. Jaggar to Secretary of Interior on Hawaii National Park Bill.
7. Report of Committee on Public Lands, recommending passage of Hawaii National Park bill. (Including report of Secretary of Interior.)
8. Publications of Hawaiian Volcano Observatory.
9. Publications of T. A. Jaggar, 1911-1916.
10. Publications of H. O. Wood, 1911-1916.
11. Publications of F. A. Perret, R. A. Daly and others, 1911-1916.

THE PROPOSED HAWAIIAN VOLCANO MUSEUM.

By T. A. Jaggar.

Introduction

Each year of investigation of the scientific secrets of Kilauea and Mauna Loa since 1911 has shown definite progress toward a goal. The vision of this goal or end to be achieved was in the hearts and minds of the scientific writers who studied Kilauea in the last century. The Hawaiian Volcano Research Association gave the vision substance. There remains the task of giving to that substance permanency.

What was the goal? It was clearly not the attainment of a discovery which should in any sense be final. Dr. Brigham many years ago—in 1869—expressed his idea of the pressing need for continuous seismological study in Hawaii. The thing needed was an organization which should live on indefinitely to make careful record of the truth concerning the activities of the volcanoes, however much the individuals composing the institution might perish or fall by the wayside. The goal, then, was an institution rather than an achievement.

In 1911 first studies were made at the crater by Mr. Perret and Dr. Shepherd; in 1912 a little frame building was put up near the Volcano House by the people of Hilo, and about twenty-five subscribers constituted the original Research Association; in 1913 the Research Association adopted a constitution and enlarged its membership to eighty or ninety persons; in 1914 a volcanologic expedition was sent to Japan

WEEKLY BULLETIN
of the
Hawaiian Volcano Observatory

Published Monthly at Honolulu, Hawaii, by the Hawaiian Volcano Research Association

Entered as second-class matter January 20, 1914, at the post-office at Honolulu, Hawaii, under the Act of August 24, 1912.

and an outbreak of Mauna Loa was studied; and in 1915 the Association succeeded in getting a new trail and rest house on Mauna Loa, made an exhibit in the San Francisco exposition, and opened definite negotiations in Washington for expanded volcanologic work around the Pacific, for possible taking over of the Kilauea observatory by the government and for the establishment of an Hawaiian National Park. (See Appendix 1 and 2.)

Negotiations with the United States Government

On July 17, 1915, your Board of Directors adopted the report of a committee appointed to consider method of making the Hawaiian Volcano Observatory a government institution. (See Appendix 3.) The committee consists of L. A. Thurston, W. D. Westervelt and T. A. Jaggar. They outlined the history of the Hawaiian Observatory and its future requirements, the objects of a United States bureau of volcano observatories, the reasons for making such observatories permanent and establishing them in Central America, California, Alaska, the Philippines and the Ladrone Islands, and they proposed that Professor Jaggar should go as delegate to Washington and introduce a suitable measure in Congress which would convey the observatory to the government and insure its operation in perpetuity as an observing station. This report was later approved by the Honolulu Chamber of Commerce and Professor Jaggar was asked by that body and by the Superintendent of Public Works to represent the national park project in Washington and present it to the Committee on Public Lands of the House of Representatives.

He arrived in Washington in December and secured the approval of the Secretary of Agriculture to a project for taking over the Hawaiian Observatory by the United States Weather Bureau, under a division of volcanology of that bureau. The matter was introduced to the Committee on Agriculture of the House on January 10, 1916, by Secretary Houston in a letter to the Hon. A. F. Lever, chairman of the committee, and the secretary expressed his approval as follows: "From informal information and advices obtained from other branches of the Government interested in these important studies I am convinced that the Government should undertake this work and that the Weather Bureau, because of its extensive field organization of trained and experienced observers, is in the best position to conduct the studies with the least possible expense and the most effective results."

The Secretary of Agriculture introduced a supplemental estimate to the Agricultural Appropriation Bill of $18,000 for the first year. (See Appendix 4.) Two hearings were given the project, one on January 10 and one on January 18 and the plan received a strong backing from the Chief of the Weather Bureau and the Secretary of Agriculture. The Massachusetts Institute of Technology approved the decision of the directors of the Research Association that the Observatory and its appurtenances should be turned over to the government in the event of the creation of a Division of Volcanology by Congress.

The bill to establish a national park in the Territory of Hawaii was introduced January 20, 1916, given a favorable hearing by the Committee on Public Lands February 3, 1916, and reported favorably with an amendment February 7. The bill provides that 75,295 acres be set aside including the craters of Mauna Loa, Kilauea and Haleakala, four-ninths of the area being public land, the three tracts constituting the Hawaii National Park. (See Appendix 5, 6 and 7.)

No appropriation is carried by the bill, and it is provided that no appropriation shall be made until proper conveyances in the matter of the private lands shall be made to the United States such as the Secretary of the Interior shall find necessary. Otherwise existing claims and privately owned lands are unaffected by the bill. The Secretary of the Interior and his associates heartily endorsed this bill and Secretary Lane wrote a favorable report, which was embodied in the report of the committee to Congress recommending that the bill pass.

These two matters, namely, the proposal for volcano study by the United States Weather Bureau and the bill to establish the Hawaii National Park, are now before Congress, but I understand that the former, at least so far as the appropriation under the Agricultural Bill is concerned, has not been reported by the committee. Whatever may be its fate this year, we have reason to hope that it will be introduced in the regular estimates of the Department of Agriculture next year. The Weather Bureau is already empowered to carry on seismological work, and we have made a definite move in the direction of coöperation with the Seismological Division of that bureau, with the approval of the Chief of the bureau and the Secretary of Agriculture.

Original Aims of Association

In June of 1912 an agreement was entered into by the board of directors of the Association with the Massachusetts Institute of Technology whereby the latter institution was to supervise a seismological station at the crater for five years from July 1, 1912, and to furnish the income of the Whitney Research Fund (about $1000), provided that the subscribers in Hawaii would produce at least $5000 per annum toward expenses for the five years ending July 1, 1917. Both contracting parties to this agreement have done their shares since that time so that we have had $7000 to $8000 per annum to work with. With this we have observed the craters, published a little monthly bulletin, sent notices to the newspapers, maintained a weather record for the government, accommodated occasional scientific specialists, provided for four frame buildings on Kilauea, and, through the Mauna Loa trail Committee, two additional ones on Mauna Loa; issued occasional seismologic reports in the international form and published special articles from time to time as result of the reasearch in volcanology and seismology of the director and his associates. (See Appendix 8, 9, 10 and 11.)

The original aims of the Research Association under its constitution are to maintain an observatory at Kilauea, to promote the science of volcanology, to invite scientific men to come here for study, and to publish reports and make collections. All of these aims have in a measure been subserved in the history of growth above outlined. We have now to ask ourselves, however, what is to be the future of the Association, what is its task at just the present juncture while these government measures are pending, and which of its four original aims will become the center of its future activities.

For it must not for a moment be supposed that the Hawaiian Volcano Research Association, after inaugurating such a program as is embodied in its constitution can afford to retire on the strength of work begun, and leave future progress to others. If the Association should adopt such an attitude at this time all that has been done would be wasted effort. The government projects are in their infancy and may require years before they will reach accomplishment. And the Massachusetts Institute of Technology intends to continue its interest in the work begun in Hawaii, so far as the seismological funds at its disposal are concerned.

Need of Popularizing

The vision of the early explorers has materialized in modest measure, but to me as the director of the scientific activities of the Association and of the Observatory there has been, and is, one thing greatly lacking in our organization. We have no effective mechanism within the Association for promoting and actuating internal enthusiasm. We need a place of resort for our own members. I believe that there is no lack of enthusiasm, and both patrons and members have been faithful in supplying money to the extent of their promises. There is needed, however, a center of activity for the study, illumination and illustration of these volcanoes, which shall be so attractive to both members and their friends, that real growth in enthusiasm and in membership will result. We need something more than a center of routine record and research by specialists. We want a place where the members will be tempted to do some work on their own account. This should be preferably at the volcano, where everyone who has been fascinated by Pele may, under the fresh spell of that fascination, read books, look at pictures, study maps, models and specimens freely, and perhaps hear occasional lectures. In short, the publicity end of the work of the Hawaiian Volcano Research Association has been neglected.

There are two possible media for giving wider publicity to the interesting features of the scientific work of the Association. One is increased publication with abundant illustrations, and the other is the establishment of a museum and reading room in conjunction with the Observatory at the volcano. Increased publication would reach more people at a distance, and will be done as we have the means, but so far as illustration is concerned, there are long periods at Halemaumau when photographic illustrations would show very little change in conditions, and when the smoke is so obstructive as to make all photographs poor.

The need for a museum and reading room at the volcano, on the other hand, is very real and constantly demanded. The demand, moreover, is increasing with the coming of larger numbers of tourists and with the growth of better facilities for transportation and housing of visitors. The question ''Where can I read about the volcano?'' or ''Are visitors allowed at the Observatory?'' is incessantly asked at the hotels, and the keen interest which visitors feel after they have been gazing at the wonderful scene displayed in the fiery pit is in itself advertisement for Hawaii, which ought to be cultivated and stimulated by every possible means.

Moreover, there is needed a new slogan for our promoters in addition to ''See Hawaii first.'' It is ''Don't come to the volcano unless you can stay a week.'' There is too much to see for a mere day's visit; a visit of one rainy day gives the place a bad reputation; the seasick folk work themselves injustice by a short stay; the **changes** in the crater are its most impressive features; and your one-day visitor sees nothing of the wonders of the crater floor, the desert, the great lava flows and caverns, and the botanical marvels of the Mauna Loa forests. I have made a study for four years of the people who stay a day and the people who stay a month. Only the latter group see and understand the real wonder and mystery of our volcano.

There should be provided a convenient, well-lighted room next the present observatory with a broad veranda commanding an unobstructed view of the volcanoes, with the great Curtis model of Kilauea crater in its midst, and abundant accessible books, photographs, diagrams, charts and specimens exhibiting volcano lore within easy reach; placards inviting subscription and membership in the Association; these things would take advantage of the public interest and would offer to regular members occupation for rainy days and opportunity to increase their information and their enthusiasm.

The purpose of the Observatory is to accumulate records and publish synthetic studies of the meaning of these records when compared with the story of other volcanoes. This work has in a sense been hampered during its early years by the urgent necessity of popularizing in order to win money enough to pay the salaries of the scientific staff. The popular interest in the shape of visitors to the working laboratory is a nuisance. As it is only through popular interest, however, that the money is forthcoming to do any useful investigating, perhaps it is as well for us to make a careful study of the attitude of travellers as a phenomenon of itself worthy of record and stimulation. The interest is there, the possibilities of growth are manifold and the expense which would be necessary to promote such growth need not be large.

Proposed Research Association Building at Kilauea

The preceding introductory remarks will serve to indicate the principal aim of this address, which is to create at the crater of Kilauea a substantial Volcano Association building. It has been by a series of public addresses, in each case making an appeal, that scientific work has at length come to be systematically carried on at Kilauea. The first talk was by your present director in February, 1909, and a subscription list resulted. The second was by Mr. F. A. Perret in November, 1911, at the University Club, Honolulu, when a committee was appointed to found an observatory. The third was by the director in December, 1913, when the Association adopted a membership fee and a constitution. The fourth was by the director in March, 1915, urging the vital necessity of a trail and rest houses on Mauna Loa, and by the end of the year trail and rest houses were provided for, with contributions from the Territory, the County and the public. The present address is therefore the fifth of a series and this is the fifth year of our effort to develop permanent study of volcanology in Hawaii. As each appeal in the past has been so generously responded to, I may be pardoned for confident belief that the present appeal will be given earnest consideration and will lead in some measure to fulfillment.

We have passed the stage where our Association need appear before the community as soliciting charitable aid. The $42,000, more or less, which has been contributed since 1911 for instruments, buildings and operating expenses is an investment in promotion of volcano knowledge. Our Observatory is an accomplished fact with four years of record behind it and the records have gone into the libraries of the world where they are treated with respect and appreciation. Our Association has gone before Congress and received earnest attention in a project for government volcanological work here and elsewhere. Scientific experts have come to us and made maps, models, photographs and analyses and published reports of their investigations, and others are planning to come. All this is good, but as an association we are at fault in that we are not making public the final results of our work here at home, where as an association we are almost unknown.

We have few regular meetings. Our membership contains few Honolulu firms, almost no plantation folk, hardly anyone in Hilo or outside Honolulu, and is recruited rarely from the tourists who visit us. We are not even mentioned in Thrum's Hawaiian Annual nor are we placarded in the hotels or Promotion Committee rooms. If we have a membership committee no results of its activity have appeared in increased membership or increased patronage. The scientific staff has lived and worked in shacks, two of which have been blown to pieces by winter storms, and the main so-called observatory is so cheap a structure that it has been flooded repeatedly and it was completely deroofed by a hurricane on January 18 of this year so as to force suspension of seismological work for two months. Surely in this time of prosperity and abundant wealth in Hawaii, when scientific institutions are suffering profoundly in Europe, these conditions can be remedied.

What is now demanded at the crater of Kilauea, on the land which is leased gratuitously to this Association, is a good Research Association building designed to give wider publicity to the work which the Association is fostering, to provide collections and reading matter in a comfortable place, and to secure safety, accessibility and permanency to the scientific archives.

It has been suggested that possibly the Bishop Museum might consider establishing a geological branch of its exhibition rooms at the volcano and this, no doubt, would be as good a way as any other to accomplish the end sought for. What I have to present to you, however, as the Hawaiian Volcano Research Association, is not a suggestion of ways and means, but rather a definite plan of what is needed. I leave the ways and means to you and the community.

The Association must have a house for members, for visitors, and for safe storage of valuable property. It is not proposed to rebuild the Observatory, which is a fire-trap, but will do well enough for the present routine work. There is needed an additional building which will serve (1) as a place for visitors apart from the Observatory, (2) a place for occasional lectures where folding chairs may be arranged and a stereopticon screen erected, and (3) a place for the library and librarian of the Observatory, this officer to attend to the wants of visitors, to enroll new members and to keep systematically and securely the records of the Observatory and the collection of books, periodicals, reprints, maps, photographs, lantern slides, publications, seismograms, thermograms, barograms, negatives, correspondence, exchanges, specimens, models and drawings, and to sell such products of the Association as are saleable. In short, the proposed building and its attendant represents a vital need of our work for more safety and more publicity, demanded alike by the scientific staff, the members of this Association and the general public.

Safety

The above list of kinds of accumulated scientific material, now housed in a light pitchpine building, liable to be demolished in a storm, as was proved this winter (we had five Kona gales of great severity), and lighted with the most unsafe forms of illumination, such as kerosene and acetylene, gives only a hint of the growing burden of responsibility which rests on the Director and his associate in storing what the outside scientific world recognizes as valuable collections of data. We now have thousands of photographic negatives, seismograms, maps, drawings, etc., which came very near being utterly ruined this winter when the roof blew off. A kerosene stove in one part of the building has several times flared up in the absence of the attendant and filled the house with soot, producing imminent danger of fire. Visitors come to the Observatory building at all hours, and there is no permanent attendant in charge of the building, so that theft is quite possible and complaints of inability to inspect the scientific records are frequent. Hawaii is an earthquake land, and a severe earthquake at night while lamps are burning might easily overturn them and destroy everything. I would not be doing my duty to this Association, in view of the respect extended to this Association by scientific establishments elsewhere, if I failed to present most urgently the facts of the dangers to which our archives are exposed.

Publicity

The remedy for this situation lies clearly in constructing a new building which shall be strong and fireproof, and shall also, if possible, contain within itself those elements of popularity which will promote the growth of the Association to the end that the outlay shall be in some measure justified. We do not any of us, the lay members of this Association, visit or study the volcanoes enough. Every member who can stand the altitude ought to climb Mauna Loa by the new trail during the next five years. Every member ought to come to the volcano during the summer and spend a month, not merely at play, but in the study of volcanology. To permit and promote this, something more than dull little weekly bulletins is needed. The members who saw the collections of photographs that we exhibited in the Hawaiian building of the Panama Pacific Exposition, saw only a fiftieth part of what exists in collections of that kind, which ought to be drawn together and properly framed and labelled.

In December I visited the studio of Mr. George Carroll Curtis in Boston and inspected the new circular naturalistic relief of Kilauea crater which he is sculpturing. The model is thirteen feet in diameter and shows every detail of relief, structure and color in natural proportions and with the utmost fidelity. This embodies Mr. Curtis' field work of 1913 and Mr. Haworth's kite photograph data of 1915. The first copy of this model is for the Harvard University Museum. It will be losing a valuable opportunity if we are unable to order a second copy of this model for permanent exhibition in the Territory of Hawaii, and the proper place for such installation and exhibit is the proposed reading room and museum of this Association at the volcano.

The librarian or curator of the building proposed will be quite as essential a new institution within our society as the house itself. He will be a paid official of the Association whose duties will be manifold, but his main charge will be as keeper of the archives. He will be the volcano representative of the secretary of the Association. It will be his function to systematize the volcano and earthquake records, to make card catalogues, to keep track of periodicals and subscriptions thereto, to keep the exhibits labelled and well arranged and to provide for proper cleaning of the exhibition room. In library work he will assist the Director of the Observatory with correspondence incidental to collecting old photographs of the volcano and similar records, and he will always have some such task wherewith to busy his odd moments. He will be attentive to travelers and use his influence to advertise the society, win new members and distribute judiciously the publications, lantern slides and photographs which result from the scientific activities of the Observatory. In large measure this officer will be the acting secretary of the society and will relieve the Secretary of clerical duties.

In saying that we are not making public here in Hawaii the work of the Association, I do not refer to the routine work of the Observatory as reviewed by newspapers. I refer rather to the kind of publicity that advertises the Association as such, that popularly illustrates the methods and adventures of the scientific staff, that invites subscription to the work of the Association, that furnishes information to eager curiosity seekers, that sells the photographs, lantern slides and publications of the Observatory and which through the pride and interest of a growing membership, places on the community the responsibility for popularizing increased study of volcanoes, rather than leaving it all to the scientific observers.

There are many visitors who stay a week or longer at the volcano, there should be many more, and there is little occupation for rainy days. These visitors sit in the writing room of the Volcano House and pore over the recent hotel record books, which contain a very little science, and a very large quantity of silly doggerel and vulgarity. By way of contrast, imagine yourself, an intelligent member of this Association, privileged to cross the road and enter the new Research Association building. It would be a long room with an open stone fireplace on one side, some comfortable chairs and one or two window tables with writing materials. All about would be portraits of volcano workers, Coan, Green, Brigham, Dana, Dutton, Wilkes, Sereno Bishop and Hitchcock. In the art metal library stacks at one end of the room you could read the English publications of the Earthquake Investigation Committee of Japan, or an account of the volcanoes of South America, or the government report of the Charleston earthquake, the description of the Krakatoa explosion of 1883, or of the Martinique disaster of 1902. On a table the librarian would have spread out for you recent numbers of the Volcanological Journal, the Bulletin of the Seismological Society of America, the American Journal of Science, the Monthly Weather Review, etc., and in these magazines you could look up all the latest news about Lassen's Peak and its eruptions in California. You could find at a moment's notice the report of Day and Shepherd on their experiments here in 1912. In the center of the room would be the great model of Kilauea, on which you could trace out your walk of yesterday and the one that you plan for fair weather on the morrow. Four other smaller models in the corners of the room would exhibit the shape of the bottom of the Pacific, with the great Hawaiian ridge in its midst; Sakurajima volcano, in south Japan, as modelled by the Japanese government; a Dutch model of Bromo volcano in Java, and a beautiful Italian model of Etna, in Sicily. In the windows would be large colored transparencies showing Haleakala, Mokuaweoweo, some of the craters on Mauna Kea and Hualalai, the craters on the moon, and the fire fountains of Kilauea. On well-lighted racks on one side of the room would be displayed labelled photographs in series showing all the changes in the Hawaiian craters from 1825 to the present time, and the detailed surveys made by our volcano observatory during the last five years. Some of the racks would contain a complete series of Mr. Perret's wonderful photographs of Vesuvius, Stromboli, Etna, Teneriffe, Sakurajima and Kilauea, and yet other series would show Lassen's Peak, Mont Pelé, Soufrière in St. Vincent, Bogoslof in the Aleutian Islands, and the volcanoes of Japan and Java. In specimen cases, under glass and well labelled, would appear collections of lava stalactites, Pele's hair, basaltic pumice, and all the manifold odd forms of Hawaiian lava which are not seen in the field by the casual tourist. In storage cases would be petrographic and geological specimens for the use of experts. A photographic laboratory adjacent to the museum would be available for amateur photographers.

This alluring picture contains nothing which is not easily obtainable and at moderate expense. Much of the material above described is already in the stores of the Observatory. We need only the room, the models, the furniture and the librarian, and the means for their upkeep.

Cost of Building Proposed

As in all cases where an estimate is demanded, the outlay and running expense of such an establishment as is here outlined might be any sum from $5000 to $50,000, according to the scale on which the plan is developed. In view of the elements of safety and permanency, however, and the increasing value of the collections, it is wholly out of the question to make use of a cheap frame building. The building should be of concrete or stone with a tile or asbestos roof and not less than 20x40 feet in ground plan. Possibly $6000 would build such a house of reinforced concrete if, as is probable, the county would furnish broken stone and perhaps assist in furnishing labor. The furniture and the models would require an allotment of at least $5000 additional, making $11,000 for first outlay. The running expense per annum, including salary of librarian, heating, lighting and upkeep of building would be as least $2000.

For $11,000 outlay, then, and $2000 per annum upkeep as minimum suggested sums, the proposed studio of the Hawaiian Volcano Research Association at Volcano House could be created. For double these amounts we would have a building to be proud of. It matters not whether this building be named museum, rest house, studio, reading room or library, whether it be named and endowed for the family of the donor or as a memorial to someone deceased, nor is it even essential that it be wholly in the name of this Research Association, provided a room in the building be set apart for the Association, where its library and archives may be kept. The more distinctly educational the proposed building can be made, the better it will serve the community, provided, however, that the general public be not excluded and that the aim of all exhibits be to simplify rather than to make technical. No question of interference by any institution is involved, unless possibly the Bishop Museum might take the matter up, and the Massachusetts Institute of Technology is interested only as a current subscriber to this Association.

In the subject of the present appeal all residents of the Territory and all travelers hither should be interested. A comfortable and attractive library, reading room and exhibition room at the volcano, wherein one may spend long hours delving into volcano secrets, cannot but appeal to any thinking man, woman or child who has ever visited the fiery pit. Moreover, from the commercial standpoint a dozen bodies may be named—the railroads, three steamship companies, the promotion committees, the chambers of commerce and the hotel syndicates—who will see in this volcano museum an added motive to produce travel, to prolong and repeat the visits of travelers, and to advertise Hawaii generally. If the Maui Chamber of Commerce is interested in the promotion of Haleakala, then it, too, would rejoice to see the Kilauea museum started, for Haleakala is famous in the annals of science. Kauai is likely to be the first of our islands to be geologically surveyed by the Government because it is the oldest island and the best mapped. The Director of the United States Geological Survey recently assured me that he was greatly interested to see geological surveys of the Hawaiian Islands started, and it is hoped that co-operation with the Territory may soon permit this. Therefore the Kauai people should favor the Kilauea volcano library, which will teach visitors the value of geological surveys. And Oahu needs no teaching in these matters, for it is the center of all our progress.

I might say more to this society about forcing the growth of our membership, procuring new patrons and subscribing more money for the scientific work. But all of these things will necessarily result, if the building here asked for is generously subscribed and promptly made a reality. In the appendix to this address as printed there appears the full report of your committee appointed last July to consider method of making our observatory a government institution. In this report appears the following comment on the future of the Hawaiian Volcano Research Association: "The Association can then devote its energies to building up a museum of volcanology which will be a center for scientific visitors, will accumulate a great library of volcanology, and will continue to publish the reports of those special workers of the Association who may continue to take aggressive interest in scientific problems connected with the volcanoes of Hawaii."

Appendix No. 1.

SUMMARY REPORT 1915 WORK OF HAWAIIAN VOLCANO OBSERVATORY.

There have been subscribed approximately eighty-five hundred dollars ($8500.00) per annum or forty-two thousand five hundred dollars ($42,-500.00) total in five years. Three-fourths of this was contributed in Honolulu.

Six frame buildings have been provided for, three at Volcano House, one at Halemaumau crater, and two on Mauna Loa, twenty and thirty miles away, with a thirty-mile trail connecting the summit with the Observatory.

Five sets of reports have been issued, viz:—

Perret Volcanologic series work of 1911;

Observatory Volcanologic series weekly 1912 to 1915;

Weather Bureau series monthly 1913 to 1915;

International Seismologic series formally begun 1914;

Reports Massachusetts Institute of Technology begun January, 1912.

Of the last two, which are summary reports, only the first few issues have as yet appeared; the second and third Technology reports are ready.

The first two series have been published, and the weekly bulletin continues without cessation in two newspapers in Hawaii, and is reprinted monthly and sent to subscribers and libraries all over the world.

The Weather Bureau in Honolulu is now publishing monthly the Volcano Observatory weather data.

Special articles have been published elsewhere, (Appendix 9, 10, 11,) and a long article on the Japanese eruption by the Director has been accepted by the National Geographic Magazine.

The expedition to Japan occupied three months, January to April, 1914 and was privately subscribed.

The Hawaiian Volcano Research Association was formally organized in December, 1913, and numbers about 100 persons.

All the work at the Observatory has been done by the Director and his associate without any staff of clerks, draftsmen or machinists.

Appendix No. 2.

APPROXIMATE ROUTINE OF THE STAFF OF THE HAWAIIAN VOLCANO OBSERVATORY.

Daily Routine

Drive 7 miles to inner crater 8 a. m.; survey and photograph inner crater 8:30 to 10 a. m.; return 10 to 10:30 a. m.

9 a. m. to 12:30 p. m.—Record wet and dry bulb thermometers, maximum

and minimum thermometers, rain gauge, wind and clouds; in seismograph cellar change record-sheets and record time comparisons on four seismographs; check time clocks with chronometer; take daily photograph of crater from Observatory porch.

1.30 to 4:30 p. m.—Develop photographs, compute surveys, draw maps, enter readings, measure seismograms, carry on research, receive visitors.

7 to 9 p. m.—If weather is favorable drive to Halemaumau and make night photographs.

Weekly Routine

Wind eight-day clock, barograph and thermograph, and change record sheets; make and compute solar observation for time.

On Thursdays compose and typewrite five copies weekly report, usually of five pages, and mail to four addresses.

Sundays and Thursdays send off correspondence on semi-weekly steamers. Weekly weather report on Thursdays. The Director usually drives to Hilo (31 miles) once a week for purchase of supplies and dictation of letters and reports, and direction of shop-work.

Fortnightly Routine

Steamers of the Matson Line from San Francisco arrive with from 50 to 100 tourists, many of whom visit the Observatory, some bringing letters of introduction. Often scientific visitors are among them. Steamers of other lines arrive occasionally (Great Northern and Northern Pacific), bringing 300 tourists or more.

Monthly Routine

Weekly bulletins reprinted in standard form, Seismological bulletin compiled, U. S. Weather Bureau monthly report sent off in duplicate, bills listed and approved and sent to Treasurer for payment.

Quarterly Routine

The Director proceeds to Honolulu (250 miles) for the meeting of the Directors of the Hawaiian Volcano Research Association, and for conference with the Treasurer and to give what aid he can in recruiting funds. Sometimes salaries have been delayed owing to delayed collections.

Semi-annual Routine

Expedition organized to visit summit crater of Mauna Loa, 30 miles by pack train, 13,800 feet above sea-level.

Annual Routine

Annual meeting of Hawaii Volcano Research Association, election of officers, address by Director of Observatory.

In addition to these routine duties there are repairs, construction, special reports and auxiliary schemes such as the San Francisco exhibit or the bills before Congress; in 1913 the Director made a report for the United States Navy on the geology of the foundation of the collapsed Pearl Harbor drydock; he has lectured on four of the islands; and scientific men have been entertained as visitors for protracted periods.

Appendix No. 3.

HAWAIIAN VOLCANO RESEARCH ASSOCIATION.

Report of Committee Appointed to Consider Method of Making the Hawaiian Volcano Observatory a Government Institution.

[Adopted and recommendations approved to go into effect July 17, 1915, by the board of directors, Hawaiian Volcano Research Association. By them transmitted for indorsement and publication to the Honolulu Chamber of Commerce with recommendation to that body that the Hawaiian National Park bill be pressed at the same time. This recommendation duly adopted by Honolulu Chamber of Commerce.]

PART I.

PROPOSED UNITED STATES BUREAU OF VOLCANO OBSERVATORIES.

History of Hawaiian Volcano Observatory.—The Hawaiian Volcano Observatory was first planned in 1909 by subscribers in Honolulu at the suggestion of Prof. T. A. Jaggar, of the Massachusetts Institute of Technology. In 1911 the Massachusetts Institute of Technology sent an expedition to Kilauto volcano headed by Mr. F. A. Perret, and scientific studies at the crater were inaugurated. In 1912 an observatory building was presented by the town of Hilo, and systematic records of volcano and earthquake activity have been maintained since that time under the direction of Dr. Jaggar. Funds were furnished by the Massachusetts Institute of Technology and subscribers in Hawaii. In December, 1913, the committee in charge of the Hawaiian funds organized the Hawaiian Volcano Research Association and adopted a constitution as a voluntary association (a) to promote investigation of volcanoes, b) to maintain an Hawaiian observatory, (c) to invite scientific visitors to Hawaii and (d) to publish reports and make collections. The present function of the Hawaiian Volcano Observatory is to serve as a laboratory at Kilauea volcano for preservation of records and assistance of scientific visitors, under the Hawaiian Volcano Research Association, to which society the Massachusetts Institute of Technology is subscriber and contractor for the volcanologic recording. This recording is being done by Mr. Jaggar, assisted by Mr. H. O. Wood, as seismologist. Mr. Jaggar retains his professorship in the Massachusetts Institute of Technology on leave of absence for purposes of research for five years from July 1, 1912. His salary during this term is paid by the Hawaiian Volcano Research Association.

At the present time, in 1915, records have been made of the activities of Mauna Loa and Kilauea volcanoes in Hawaii for three and a half years, and during this time also record of weather and earthquakes has been maintained. Special studies of the resident staff have concerned lava mechanism, tidal phenomena evidenced by the rise and fall of the lava, relationship between the two adjacent volcanoes, and the relationships of the local earthquakes to the volcanic activities. Specialists from the United States Geological Survey, United States Coast and Geodetic Survey, and the Carnegie Institution of Washington have made topographic maps, magnetic surveys, and analyses of volcanic gas as scientific visitors. Other persons on scientific missions from many lands have been here from time to time.

Future Requirements of the Hawaiian Volcano Observatory

The net result of the first four years of work at these most active volcanoes in the world is a demonstration that the product is of far-reaching value, provided two essentials are preserved; namely, permanency of record and hospitable encouragement of the work of scientific visitors.

Permanency of record means the construction of fireproof buildings and disasterproof vaults for the archives of the observatory, and either endowment or Government support which will maintain for all time a system of noting, measuring and recording the changes of activity in the lavas and gases of the volcanoes, and the quality and quantity of the quakings and tiltings of the ground.

Hospitable encouragement of scientific visitors means much more than appears at first sight. This function of the observatory is not a mere amiable side issue, but a first essential. The reason for this is that no resident staff can ever be large enough to inaugurate all the experimental work that the new science of volcanology demands for its healthy growth. Hawaiian volcanoes attract the attention of geologists, astronomers, meteorologists, chemists, and physicists as a field laboratory which they are anxious to experiment upon. Their results add to the store of material essential for the improvement, from time to time, of the recording done by the resident staff. By the simple device of hospitable encouragement, meaning provision of some laboratory facilities and occasional correspondence urging the visits of certain specialists, we may succeed in securing scientific data at the hands of the most skilled experts which will make for the prime object of our Association; namely, the promotion and improvement of volcano investigation. This principle has been adopted in other research establishments, such as the zoölogical experiment stations and the astrophysical observatories, with marked success.

Object of a United States Bureau of Volcano Observatories

Whatever private endowment might do for the immediate purposes of the

Hawaiian station, there is no question but that scientific intervention in volcanology by the United States Government, having in view permanent observatories at widely distributed active volcanic vents around the Pacific, and within the American domain, would be much more far-reaching. At first mention, such work would seem too specialized and technical to deserve a bureau by itself, and the question might be asked, "Why is not this within the province of the Government Geological Survey?"

In answer to this question, two points covering volcano study must be strongly insisted upon and emphasized even at the risk of repetition. The first is that volcano recording is no more geology than it is economics or meteorology. It is in a measure all of these, but it no more concerns fossils, coal, and iron, and the history of the earth, than it does the origin of the gases and dusts of the atmosphere or the vital needs of mankind when a time of frightful earthquake or lava disaster is approaching. The geologist maps the distribution of ancient deposits on the land and interprets the past history of the rocks. The volcano observatory maps the changes from day to day at a volcanic vent with a view to interpreting the probable changes of the future for the benefit of science and of mankind. The geologist is vitally interested in the products of volcano recording, for only by this means can he learn to understand the lavas and ore deposits of the ancient volcanic lands. But the training and equipment of geological surveyors is all for the study of ancient history and not to maintain observatories of present-day happenings. The second point is that volcano recording has an eventual humane and commercial bearing quite remote from economic geology. The terrible disasters of the twentieth century due to earthquake and volcanic eruption are fresh in the public mind and need no recounting here. Volcanoes are critical centers of such disaster and in the science of the globe are physically related to earthquakes. The records of volcano observing stations, when such have been established a few score years, will as vitally improve conditions of life and engineering construction in earthquake lands as the Government weather service has improved agriculture, and, coupled with magnetism and astronomy, has removed the terrors of navigation. These two points, then, distinguish volcano observing from geology: It involves perpetual recording at permanent stations like astronomy or meteorology, and it concerns the present and the future of the dwelling places of men.

The specific objects of a Government volcano service in the United States would be more closely related to the work of the United States Coast and Geodetic Survey and that of the Weather Bureau than to that of any other Government offices. In order to keep record of distributed centers of emission of gases and lava from the earth, and to compare these records with each other and with earthquake reports as collected by the Weather Bureau, the United States should maintain volcano observatories in Hawaii, the Philippines, Aleutian Islands, Alaska mainland, California, and Nicaragua. It would be advisable also, by coöperation or otherwise, to maintain an observatory in Mexico and if possible, from Guam as a center, in the Ladrone Islands. It is obvious to anyone who has given close attention on the one hand to volcano science and on the other to the present organization of scientific bureaus in Washington that there is no one Government bureau at present especially adapted to take under its wing a division of volcano observatories. Volcanology is peculiar in that its stations would, many of them, be on islands in the ocean and so would require visitation with the aid of ships, such as those of the Coast Survey, Coast Guard, Navy, or Army transport service. So far as connection with seismology is concerned, both the Coast Survey and Weather Bureau now maintain earthquake recording stations. The Weather Bureau, with its meteorological observers and instruments scattered from Porto Rico to the Philippines, and now empowered by Congress to study earthquakes, is in many respects better suited for affiliation with a division of volcano observatories than any other Government agency. The connection, moreover, between volcanoes and the study of the atmosphere is very close, for Prof. Abbott has recently drawn attention to the effect of volcanic dust on climate, and recent studies of volcanoes have accentuated the importance of gas; all active volcanoes are continually, in some degree, adding to and changing the composition of the air.

Contrast Between Volcanology and Seismology

As the layman is very apt to confuse the study of volcanoes with the study of earthquakes, a word should be said defining the distinct purpose of the volcano observatories proposed. A few years ago the Geological Society of America issued an appeal urging upon Governments the establishment of volcano *and* earthquake observatories.

Partly as a result of this, Congress has approved earthquake study by the Weather Bureau. A seismological observatory maintains delicate pendulums which write automatically, year in and year out, with pens actuated by the pulsations of the ground, a story of earthquakes far and near. Earthquake science is a branch of earth physics. The records are compiled and published by an international committee having headquarters at Strassburg, Germany. There are already many public and private earthquake recording stations. A strong earthquake sends out waves through the globe which write their records wherever these delicate pendulums are set up. The study of these records of world-shaking earthquakes gives information to a physicist about the physical condition of the inside of the globe. Again, many districts have small local earthquakes not strong enough to permeate the world, so to speak, and these also are recorded on local seismographs and are chiefly of interest in connection with local engineering and geology, or local volcanoes, or as the aftermath of some great earthquake. Earthquakes, destructive or otherwise, may occur anywhere, and there have been disastrous ones in eastern Canada, the Mississippi Valley, in South Carolina, California, Alaska, Hawaii, the Philippines, and some other places within the territory of the United States. All of this interests the science of seismology.

In contrast to this science, the study of volcanoes, or volcanology, is concerned with the quality and quantity of active vents in the crust of the earth which occasionally or continuously emit gas, lava dust, and liquid lava. Such a place is an active volcano and there are about 425 of them known in the world. They are largely in or near the great oceans, but some, like Lassen's Peak in California, are, exceptionally, quite a distance inland. Small earthquakes invariably occur in the vicinity of active volcanoes and sometimes great ones; it is perhaps this fact which leads so many people to associate volcanoes with the idea of earthquakes. As a matter of fact, however, many of the greatest earthquakes have been nowhere near living volcanoes as, for example, the Charleston earthquake of 1886 or the San Francisco earthquake of 1906. The only volcano observatories in the world are those on Vesuvius and Etna in Italy, Kilauea in Hawaii, Asama in Japan, and Taal in the Philippines. And these are not all of them continuously occupied by a resident staff. The oldest of them is the Royal Vesuvian Observatory which was founded about 50 years ago. There has never been any concerted plan of uniform recording among these observatories and their publications have not been consecutive or uniform. It is the object of the Hawaiian Volcano Observatory and the Hawaiian Volcano Research Association to reform volcano observing in this respect, if possible, and to spread a propaganda of uniform and orderly observing, with publications standardized and issued at stated intervals. It should be obvious after this explanation, that the task of a volcano observatory which accumulates not only seismograms, but also maps and measurements of changing craters, hot cracks, temperatures, dust explosions, and the relation of all these to the lunar tides and the weather, is quite distinct from an earthquake laboratory, which may be placed anywhere on the globe and takes account only of the quivering of pendulums. If only we had a record of the rise and fall, from day to day, of the volcanic activities for the last four years at Colima, Mexico; Lassen's Peak, Cal.; Akutan near Unalaska, and Farallon de Pajardos near Guam, to compare with what we have observed of the habits of Kilauea in Hawaii during the same period, we could probably state definitely some great tidal laws concerning the squeezings of the crust of our earth ball by the sun and moon and the effects of these squeezings on volcanoes. We have proved at Kilauea alone that some things about volcanic eruption are definitely predictable. In almost every volcanic chain there are certain key volcanoes, like Stromboli or Kilauea, which are continuously active in some sense, so that there is always some change to observe.

Reasons for Permanent Volcano Observatories

Enough has been said to indicate the purposes of scientific observation of volcanoes. Persons not trained in geology are apt to think of volcanoes as places quiescent most of the time and dangerously explosive at long intervals. This is true of some volcanoes, but even at these places in the repose periods there are hot sulphurous gases and waters oozing out of cracks called solfataras, and these would show changing composition and temperature and, in addition, underground noises and measurable tiltings and tremblings of the ground would vary from day to day and be worthy of measurement and record, the interest growing as some of these things increased in vehemence during the months preceding an eruption. But, as stated above, it is not necessary to select a wholly sleeping volcano for the location of an observatory, as there may generally be found in every volcanic region such as the Philippines, the Japanese mainland, the Ladrone Islands, or the Territory of Hawaii, one or more vents perpetually active and perpetually changing. Near these places the observatories should be located, each observatory keeping within its sphere of influence a watchful eye upon the quieter neighboring volcanoes with the aid of voluntary observers and such means of communication and transportation as are available.

It is just because of the intermittent and long interval quality of great volcanic eruptions, and because of the time element in its bearing on prediction and change, that permanency and stability of method are needed in volcano study. Just as the physician uses the microscope to subdivide tissues into their ultimate units, so the student of the great changes in the universe must devise an apparatus for subdividing the events which happen in time into their smaller component parts. An observatory, whether it be recording the motions of the stars, the changes of the weather or the fluctuations of the ground, is a time microscope, and it is the duty of science, in view of the short-lived limitations of the individual observer, to create institutions which will live through the centuries and observe the process as a whole with the aid of the minute records which a succession of observers accumulates. Great generalizations, like Darwin's statement of evolution, have only come about as the result of the patient labors of many investigators who classified and catalogued species.

In volcanology, as, for instance, with the workers at the Hawaiian Observatory, it has been found continually necessary to hark back to the meager accounts of many casual observers who wrote notes on the volcanoes during the last century. It is most baffling and frequently disheartening when one is working on the question of the periods of recurrence of eruption in a volcano like Mauna Loa to find whole decades of the past history utterly unrecorded and to be able to get no information whatever earlier than 125 years ago, a time when Kilauea exploded and produced a tremendous catastrophe. There is no information extant on the condition of the crater during the 20 years after Capt. Cook discovered the Hawaiian Islands. Such a tremendous crisis will occur again after an interval of 150 or 200 or 300 years, and such long intervals are by no means uncommon with either volcanoes or earthquakes. Therefore it is that permanent institutions are needed, just as in astronomy, which shall faithfully preserve measurements and charts to serve the future generations and make continuously for the advancement of science.

Palmieri, founder and first director of the Royal Vesuvian Observatory, deserves all honor and credit for being the first to point out clearly the necessity for regular secular recording of the activity of volcanoes. And the Italian Government has the honor of being the first to put this idea into effect. Even today there are geologists who consider consecutive routine study of the earth's interior through volcanic vents as unnecessary and hopeless, and whose sole interest in volcanoes is to send expeditions thither when unusual eruptions occur. These expeditions commonly arrive on the scene after the eruption is all over, and precise or instrumental record of what led up to and accompanied the crisis is generally wanting. A so-called eruption of a volcano is merely a paroxysmal phase of the escape of gas from inside the earth, which is going on there all the time. Surely, then, it is the duty of science to attach its measuring instruments to the gas vent, a marvelous place, the orifice of a shaft leading down scores of miles into the hot globe, and learn its secrets. The volcano observatory has this great advantage over the earthquake observatory, viz, its location is defined in the economy of the globe as one of the relatively few deep holes which have been there from time immemorial and which unquestionably yield evidence of change when a great change is approaching. Even from what little we know about the science today, there is no doubt whatever but that great volcanic eruptions are predictable; the location is assured and premonitory symptoms occur. In earthquake science there is no such assurance with respect to either place or time. Moreover, if seismology is to arrive at possibilities of prediction, perhaps the most hopeful line of investigation to follow in starting on the quest will be to begin with the study of volcanoes and find out definitely how they are related to the strong earthquakes which sometimes happen in their vicinity. The Messina earthquake was an illustration in point, possibly predictable if science had really understood all the workings of Mount Etna.

Number of Volcanoes in United States Territory

The United States probably possesses more than a quarter of the active volcanoes on the globe. The catalogue of the late G. Mercalli made the total number of volcanoes in the world about 417, and of these on American soil there are about 60 in Alaska and the Aleutian Islands, and probably as many more in the Philippines, Hawaii, and western United States. We have, then, over 100 active volcanoes and our affiliation with Nicaragua and possession of the canal route through that republic, as well as our interest in Central America because of the Panama Canal, would justify a scientific bureau of the United States Government in extending its operations to the Nicaraguan volcanoes.

Number and Location of Proposed American Observatories

For a beginning the observatories should be placed so as to secure as much as possible the same sort of advantage as is possessed by the Hawaiian Volcano Observatory, namely, (1) continuous measurable volcanic activity, (2) facilities of transportation and communication for subordinate stations and general observations at other volcanoes, and (3) proximity to a center of civilization. The third requirement obviously can not always be satisfied, as some of the most interesting and important volcanic vents are remote from civilization. In case of such remoteness, the station ought to be equipped with a large power boat or other means of transportation so as to keep reasonably in touch with a base of supplies.

In the western United States there are two places of great importance for experiment and measurement in volcanology, namely, Lassen's Peak in California and the geyser district of Yellowstone Park. These are both scenes of very ancient expiring volcanic activity, the Yellowstone the most so.

An observatory in Nicaragua, even close to the capital, Managua, would cover the activities of several volcanoes typical of the volcanism of Central America and of greater intensity than that of Lassen's Peak. The isthmian vicinity is of great interest also because of the relationship of severe earthquakes to decadent volcanoes, as in the cases of the Quetzaltenango earthquake of 1902 and the Costa Rican earthquake of 1910—the latter right in the line of the Nicaraguan volcanoes, where experts earlier employed by the Nicaraguan Canal Commission believed earthquake conditions relatively harmless. The great Cartago earthquake of 1910 conclusively demonstrated the wisdom of the choice of the Panama route.

In Alaska there should be one observatory near Unalaska village, covering the activities of Akutan and Bogoslof Volcanoes, and provided with a strong power boat. Akutan is well known to navigators but is unknown to science, and, like Stromboli, is continuously active; it should prove a most valuable index volcano for the Aleutian chain. Another observatory should be placed on the Alaskan peninsula near whatever volcano is there most steadily active and convenient to a base. It will require a reconnaissance to choose the most favorable site. This Alaskan volcano line is of intense interest to science, for it is a place of transitions from volcanoes under the sea to volcanoes elevated above the sea on the backbone of a continent, and the whole process of volcanic eruption in conjunction with upheaval and earthquakes is probably as rapid on the Alaskan peninsula as anywhere in the world.

In the Philippines there is a small observatory which has been erected by the insular government near Taal Volcano as a precautionary measure since the terrible disaster of 1911, when some 2000 people lost their lives in the rush of dust and gas from a sudden explosion of the crater. Taal has the advantage of being relatively near Manila, but whether it is the most suitable place for a permanent observatory in the Philippines is not known to your committee. There are many other active volcanoes in the archipelago.

In the Ladrone chain of islands, which extends southward from the Bonin Isles of Japan, there are active volcanoes, some of them perennially emitting clouds of gas and dust, and this chain is particularly interesting as representing the greatest circle of active volcanoes in the world, known as the Sunda Arc. This arc begins on the west with the Andaman Islands and extends in a circle through Java and Sumatra, the Moluccas and the Ladrone Islands to the Bonin Islands and Japan. The Philippines lie in the center of this circle. The Ladrones would thus offer a type of volcanism representative of one of the great primitive features of the globe and of a large oceanic area outside of the territory of the United States. The volcanic activity there should be closely akin to that of the Aleutian Islands, but at present there is almost no information about it. The establishment of an observatory in this chain might be expensive owing to the remoteness of the station, but it could not fail to be of interest. The active volcano Farralon de Pajardos is well known to navigators and is generally passed by the Army transports going to and from Manila. It is said to be always "smoking," and from the photographs which have been taken of it, it has every appearance of being similar to Akutan and a good subject for study if there is any other island less formidable as a dwelling place, which may be used as a base.

Lastly, coming to the island of Hawaii, we have there to do with the two most active volcanoes on earth, Kilauea and Mauna Loa, and being in the middle of the North Pacific close to Honolulu, which is on steamer routes in all directions, the place possesses a strategic value from the scientific standpoint which is unsurpassed. If the United States Government is to take up the work which the Hawaiian Volcano Observatory has started, and extend it to the other Pacific lands which that government owns or controls, it could find no better place for a headquarters of a bureau of volcano observatories than Honolulu. The Hawaiian Volcano Observatory would then become the main central volcano experiment station, and there is much about the Hawaiian volcanoes which justifies their selection for this purpose. The central administration of an American volcano observatory service at Honolulu would have the advantage of being in touch by steamer and cable or wireless with Panama, Tehuantepec, California, Seattle, Vancouver, Japan, Guam, the Philippines, Samoa, Fiji and New Zealand. There is certainly no American community so sympathetic with the aims which such a Federal bureau would have as the business men of Honolulu, who have given evidence of this sympathy by their liberal subscription to the funds of the Hawaiian Volcano Research Association.

Present Status of Volcano Study in the Pacific

The following is a brief review of what has been done in the last few years in Government study of Pacific and Cordilleran volcanoes:

Japan in 1891 after the serious earthquake of that year appointed and financed a committee of seismologists and engineers to study what could be done to prevent disaster from earthquakes. This committee has existed ever since and has published many memoirs in English as well as in Japanese. Part of their work has dealt with the study of the active volcanoes of Japan and they have given increasing attention to the study of volcanoes in the last few years. Small seismological observatories have been placed on or near several active cones, and Dr. Omori, chief of the committee, has recently given close attention to Asama volcano and published several memoirs as a result of his studies there. An especially noteworthy feature of the Japanese administration of such scientific work is the economical coöperation which exists between the several government bureaus concerned and between all of these and the Imperial University of Tokyo. Dr. Omori is professor in the university, his laboratory is there, and he has at his service all the stations of the Central Meteorological Observatory, which corresponds to our Weather Bureau. The efficiency of the Earthquake Investigation Committee of Japan in volcanology was well shown when Sakurajima erupted in 1914. Hardly any lives were lost, and at least 90,000 people were temporarily deported and returned to their homes in safety under competent scientific advice.

The Bureau of Science in the Philippines maintains an observatory of meteorology and seismology in Manila administered by the Jesuit fathers, and these men have done most valuable work in compiling what is known of the Philippine volcanoes and observing Taal volcano.

The United States Geological Survey has mapped the geology of Yellowstone Park, encouraged physical studies of the geyser activities there, and very lately, in conjunction with the Forestry Service, has caused a watch to be kept on the activity of Lassen's Peak in California. The Geological Survey has also published some catalogues of earthquakes and geological papers dealing with the Hawaiian volcanoes.

The United States Weather Bureau has for many years operated a seismograph in Washington, and lately the bureau has been empowered to extend its seismological work.

The United States Coast and Geodetic Survey has for many years maintained certain observatories for the study of earth magnetism, and some of these places have been equipped with seismographs. There is such an observatory near Honolulu, and in 1913 the Coast Survey made special magnetic observations at the craters of Kilauea and Mauna Loa. Formerly also this bureau made determinations of terrestrial gravity in the Hawaiian Islands.

The United States Revenue-Cutter Service (Coast Guard) at the request of the National Geographic Society has done some work in visiting and reporting upon active volcanoes in the Aleutian Islands.

The following Government agencies have from time to time, by loan of instruments or otherwise, assisted the Hawaiian Volcano Observatory: United States Geological Survey, Hawaiian Territorial government, United States Weather Bureau, College of Hawaii,

United States Army, and the United States Coast and Geodetic Survey.

Future of the Hawaiian Volcano Research Association

It should not be understood that the Hawaiian Volcano Research Association will go out of existence in case the observatory be taken over by the Federal Government. The maintenance of an observatory is only one of the four objects of the Association. The other three are to promote volcano investigation all over the world, to invite scientific visitors to study the volcanoes of Hawaii, and to produce publications and make collections in volcanology. If the Association succeeds in inducing the Government to maintain the observatory and to build others in other places; it will have abundantly succeeded in its first two objects. The Association can then devote its energies to building up a museum of volcanology which will be a center for scientific visitors, will accumulate a great library of volcanology, and will continue to publish the reports of those special workers of the Association who may continue to take aggressive interest in scientific problems connected with the volcanoes of Hawaii.

PART II.

PROPOSED METHOD OF BRINGING VOLCANO OBSERVATORY BILL BEFORE CONGRESS.

Delegation to Washington.—The foregoing part of this report makes it clear that no other Government has greater reason to take scientific interest for humane, practical, and theoretical ends in observing systematically the volcanoes of the Pacific than the United States. Scientific societies and academies in Europe, America and the Orient have earnestly recommended that Governments take up this work. The recent visit to Hawaii of a large delegation of Senators and Congressmen in 1915 makes this a favorable time to present the matter to the American Government in the form of a bill creating a bureau of volcano observatories. Many of the Senators and Representatives expressed themselves as favorable to the project of having the Federal Government take over the Hawaiian Volcano Observatory and perhaps extend the work to other volcanoes in the Federal domain. The director of the Hawaiian Volcano Observatory was urged by some of these gentlemen to bring the matter before Congress, and it is with this in view that this report is presented. It will require advice which can only be obtained in Washington to determine what department or existing bureau of the Government can best further the interests of volcano research, and therefore the actual drafting of a bill should be done in Washington. Your committee would recommend that the Hawaiian Volcano Research Association send Prof. Jaggar as its delegate to Washington in November, 1915, provided conditions at the national capital at that time are peaceful, and empower him to have a suitable bill drafted in accordance with advice which he may secure there.

Consultation.—The delegate of the Association should be instructed to consult with the chiefs of scientific bureaus, notably those which have been in any way concerned with the work already done on volcanoes around the Pacific. He should also consult with interested Congressmen, seeking advice as to the method to be pursued with Congress in drafting a bill and presenting it most advantageously to secure the establishment of volcano observatories in some department, so that whatever work is already under way may be organized and coördinated and thus develop into a government system for complete study of volcanic phenomena especially as bearing on safety of life and preservation of property.

Conveyance of Hawaiian Volcano Observatory to the Government.—Your committee would recommend that the Hawaiian Volcano Research Association go on record as favoring, subject to the approval of the Massachusetts Institute of Technology, the conveyance of the Hawaiian Volcano Observatory and its appurtenances to the United States Government in the event of the creation of a Bureau of Volcano Observatories, or in the event of its being taken over by some existing bureau.

Your committee believes, however, that the Research Association, in conveying the observatory and its records to the Government in such event, should further go on record as strongly favoring the continuation of present policy in the conduct of the observatory in the two vital principles enunciated in the first part of this report, namely, (1) that recording of volcanic activity by the resident staff be systematically published and permanently maintained and (2) that the policy of inviting skilled scientific visitors to make use of the facilities of the observatory is a sound policy and results in the greatest possible economy of scientific production and most favorable development of volcanology.

L. A. THURSTON,
W. D. WESTERVELT,
T. A. JAGGAR,
Committee.

Appendix No. 4.

REPORT OF THE SECRETARY OF AGRICULTURE ON GOVERNMENT WORK IN VOLCANOLOGY.

Department of Agriculture,
Washington, D. C., Jan. 10, 1916.

Hon. A. F. Lever, Chairman,
Committee on Agriculture,
House of Representatives.

Dear Mr. Lever: Referring to the question of the Government performing certain work in volcanology, especially in the Hawaiian Islands, Alaska, California, the West Indies, and in the vicinity of the Canal Zone, it is desired to have included in the appropriation for the Weather Bureau an amount of money sufficient to establish this work during the fiscal year ending June 30, 1917.

This subject has been fully discussed with Dr. T. A. Jaggar, of the Massachusetts Institute of Technology, who is director of the Hawaiian Volcano Observatory. From informal information and advices obtained from other branches of the Government interested in these important studies, I am convinced that the Government should undertake this work and that the Weather Bureau, because of its extensive field organization of trained and experienced observers, is in the best position to conduct the studies with the least possible expense and the most effective results.

At first sight it may appear that the study of volcanology is not in any way connected with meteorology or agriculture. This, however, is a mistake. Some of the most fertile fields in the world are in the vicinity of great volcanoes, as in Hawaii and, notably, around Mount Vesuvius. Moreover, from time to time volcanoes burst forth and eject tremendous quantities of finely divided dust particles, which are thrown to very great heights in the upper atmosphere. The heavier particles of dust ejected fall quickly to the earth. The volcanic activity may also be accompanied by the flow of lava and by other things that not only affect the lives of people in the vicinity but make great changes in the surface cover of the surrounding region. Recent studies have shown that the most finely divided dust particles thrown into the upper atmosphere remain suspended there for many months, and even years, before finally settling to the earth. Throughout this period the presence of this dust in the upper atmosphere materially modifies the transmission of solar radiation to the earth's surface and causes effects that appreciably change the climatic conditions for the time being. Only within recent years has the importance of the study of these phenomena of nature come to be properly and fully recognized. The prosecution of this study will add to the fund of the knowledge of the operations and processes of nature and be beneficial to mankind in general.

It is estimated that when fully organized the work will involve an expenditure of approximately $25,000 per annum, but as time will be required to effectively organize the work it is estimated that if a sum of about $18,000 for these investigations is added to the appropriation for the Weather Bureau, the work can be put on a satisfactory operating basis in the beginning. The exact amount and the manner in which it should be apportioned can not be submitted at this moment, owing to the absence from Washington of Dr. Jaggar, who, however, expects to return on Wednesday of this week, at which time full details for providing for this work will be prepared and submitted without delay.

Very truly yours,

D. F. HOUSTON,
Secretary.

Appendix No. 5.

NATIONAL PARK BILL.

64th Congress, 1st Session.

UNION CALENDAR NO. 47.
H. R. 9525.

[Report No. 131.]

In the House of Representatives.
January 20, 1916.

Mr. Kalanianaole introduced the following bill; which was referred to the Committee on the Public Lands and ordered to be printed.

February 7, 1916.

Reported with an amendment, committed to the Committee of the Whole House on the state of the Union, and ordered to be printed.
[Insert the part printed in italic.]

A BILL

To establish a national park in the Territory of Hawaii.

Be it enacted by the Senate and House of Representatives of the United States of America in Congress assembled, That the tracts of land on the island of Hawaii and on the island of Maui, in the Territory of Hawaii, hereinafter described, shall be perpetually dedicated and set apart as a public park or pleasure ground for the benefit and enjoyment of the people of the United States, to be known as Hawaii National Park. Said tracts of land are described as follows:

First. All that tract of land comprising portions of the lands of Kapapala and Keauhou, in the district of Kau, and Kahaualea, Panaunui, and Apua, in the district of Puna, on the island of Hawaii, containing approximately thirty-five thousand eight hundred and sixty-five acres, bounded as follows: Beginning at a point on the west edge of the Keamoku Aa Flow (lava flow of eighteen hundred and twenty-three), from which point the true azimuth and distance to Government survey trigonometrical station Ohaikea is one hundred and sixty-six degrees twenty minutes, six thousand three hundred and fifty feet, and running by true azimuths: (First) Along the west edge of the Keamoku lava flow in a northeasterly and northwesterly direction, the direct azimuth and distance being one hundred and ninety-eight degrees ten minutes, fourteen thousand seven hundred feet; (second) two hundred and fifty-six degrees, eleven thousand four hundred feet, more or less, across the land of Kapapala and Keauhou to a marked point on the Humuula trail; (third) three hundred and twenty-eight degrees fifteen minutes, eight thousand seven hundred and twenty-five feet, across the land of Keauhou to the top of the fault north of the Kau road; (fourth) along the fault in a northeasterly direction, the direction azimuth and distance being two hundred and fifty-one degrees and thirty minutes, four thousand three hundred and thirty feet; (fifth) two hundred and forty-five degrees, six thousand feet, to a point near the southwest boundary of the land of Olaa; (sixth) three hundred and thirty-seven degrees ten minutes, eight thousand six hundred and fifty feet, more or less, to the junction of the Hilo and Keauhou roads; (seventh) three hundred and thirty-three degrees and twenty minutes, three thousand three hundred feet, more or less, to the southwest corner of the land of Keaau; (eighth) three hundred and thirty-two degrees and ten minutes, seven thousand feet, along the land of Kahaualea; (ninth) two hundred and eighty-one degrees, thirty thousand three hundred and seventy-five feet, more or less, across the land of Kahaualea, passing through the north corner of the land of Panaunui, to the north corner of the land of Laeapuki; (tenth) thirty-one degrees thirty mniutes, thirteen thousand two hundred feet, more or less, along the land of Laeapuki and across the land of Panaunui; (eleventh) eighty-nine degrees and ten minutes, thirty-two thousand nine hundred feet, more or less, across the land of Panaunui, Apua, and Keauhou to "Palilele-o-Kalihipaa," the boundary point of the Keauhou-Kapapala boundary; (twelfth) fifty-one degrees and thirty minutes, five thousand and five hundred feet, across the land of Kapapala; (thirteenth) one hundred and two degrees and fifty minutes, nineteen thousand one hundred and fifty feet, across the land of Kapapala to a small cone about one thousand five hundred feet southwest of Puu Koae trigonometrical station; (fourteenth) one hundred and sixty-six degrees twenty minutes, twenty-one thousand feet, across the land of Kapapala to the point of beginning.

Second. All that tract of land comprising portions of the lands of Kapapala and Kahuku, in the district of Kau, island of Hawaii; Keauhou second, in the district of North Kona; and Kaohe, in the district of Hamakua, containing seventeen thousand nine hundred and twenty acres, bounded as follows: Beginning at Pohaku Hanalei of Humuula, a small cone on the brow of Mauna Loa, and at the common boundary points of the lands of Humuula, Kapapala, and Kaohe, from which the true azimuth and distance to Government survey trigonometrical station Omaokoili is one hundred and ninety-five degrees twelve minutes eighteen seconds, seventy-eight thousand two hundred and eighty-six feet, and running by true azimuths: First, two hundred and ninety-eight degrees, five thousand two hundred and forty feet; second, twenty-eight degrees, thirty-six thousand nine hundred and sixty feet; third, one hundred and eighteen degrees, twenty-one thousand one hundred and twenty feet; fourth, two hundred and eight degrees, thirty-six thousand nine hundred and sixty feet; fifth, two hundred and ninety-eight degrees, fifteen thousand eight hundred and eighty feet, to the point of beginning.

Third. A strip of land of sufficient width for a road to connect the two tracts of land on the island of Hawaii above described, the width and location of which strip shall be determined by the Secretary of the Interior.

Fourth. All that tract of land comprising portions of the lands of Honuaula and Kula, in the district of Makawao, and Kipahulu, Kaupo, and Kahikinui, in the district of Hana, on the island of Maui, containing approximately twenty-one thousand one hundred and fifty acres, bounded as follows: Beginning at a point called Kolekole, on the summit near the most western point of the rim of the crater of Haleakala, and running by approximate azimuths and distances: First, hundred and ninety-three degrees forty-five minutes nineteen thousand three hundred and fifty feet along the west slope of the crater of Haleakala to a point called Puu-o-Ili; second, two hundred and sixty-eight degrees twenty-three thousand feet up the western slope and across Koolau Gap to the point where the southwest boundary of Koolau Forest Reserve crosses the east rim of Koolau Gap; third, three hundred and six degrees thirty minutes seventeen thousand one hundred and fifty feet along the southwest boundary of Koolau Forest Reserve to a point called Palalia, on the east rim of the crater of Haleakala; fourth, along the east rim of the crater of Haleakala, the direct azimuth and distance being three hundred and fifty-four degrees fifteen minutes eighteen thousand three hundred feet to a point on the east rim of Kaupo Gap, shown on Hawaiian Government survey maps at an elevation of four thousand two hundred and eight feet; fifth, eighty-eight degrees forty-five minutes three thousand three hundred feet across Kaupo Gap to a point called Kaumikaohu, on the boundary line between the lands of Kipahulu and Kahikinui; sixth, one hundred and two degrees and thirty minutes forty thousand seven hundred and fifty feet along the south slope of the crater of Haleakala to the point of beginning.

Sec. 2. That nothing herein contained shall affect any valid existing claim, location, or entry under the land laws of the United States, whether for homestead, mineral, right of way, or any other purpose whatsoever, or shall affect the rights of any such claimant, locator, or entryman to the full use and enjoyment of his land. Whenever consistent with the primary purposes of the park the Act of February fifteenth, nineteen hundred and one, applicable to the location of rights of way in certain national parks and the national forests for irrigation and other purposes, shall be and remain applicable to the lands included within the park. The Secretary of the Interior may, in his discretion and upon such conditions as he may deem wise, grant easements or rights of way for steam, electric, or similar transportation upon or across the park.

Sec. 3. That no lands located within the park boundaries now held in private or municipal ownership shall be affected by or subject to the provisions of this Act.

Sec. 4. That the said park shall be under the executive control of the Secretary of the Interior whose duty it shall be, as soon as practicable, to make and publish such rules and regulations as he may deem necessary or proper for the care and management of the same. Such regulations shall provide fór the preservation from injury of all timber, birds, mineral deposits, and natural curiosities or wonders within said park, and their retention in their natural condition as nearly as possible. The Secretary may in his discretion grant leases for terms not exceeding twenty years, at such annual rental as he may determine, of parcels of land in said park of not more than twenty acres in all to any one person, corporation, or company for the erection and maintenance of buildings for the accommodation of visitors; but no such lease shall include any of the objects of curiosity or interest in said park or exclude the public from free and convenient approach thereto or convey, either expressly or by implication, any exclusive privilege within the park except upon the premises held thereunder and for the time granted therein; and every such lease shall require the lessee to observe and obey each and every provision in any Act of Congress and every rule, order, or regulation of the Secretary of the Interior concerning the use, care, management, or government of the park, or any object or propeťy therein, under penalty of forfeiture of such lease. The Secretary may in his discretion grant to persons or corporations now holding leases of land in the park, upon the surrender thereof, new stipulations contained in their present leases, with such modifications, restrictions, and reservations as he may prescribe. All of the proceeds of said leases and other revenues that may be derived from any source connected with the park shall be expended under the direction of the Secretary, in the management and protection of the same and the construction of roads and paths therein. The Secretary may also, in his discretion, permit the erection and maintenance of buildings in said park for scientific purposes: *Provided, That no appropriation for the maintenance, supervision, and improvement of said park in excess of $10,000 annually shall be made unless the same shall have first been expressly authorized by law*: *And provided further, That no appropriation shall be made for the improvement or maintenance of said park until proper conveyances shall be made to the United States of such perpetual easements and rights of way over private lands within the exterior boundaries of said park as the Secretary of the Interior shall find necessary to make said park reasonably accessible in all its parts, and said Secretary shall when such easements and rights of way have been conveyed to the United States report the same to Congress.*

T. A. JAGGAR'S REPORT ON

Appendix No. 6.

HAWAII NATIONAL PARK.

Bill H. R. 9525.

January 20, 1916.

Report by T. A. Jaggar, Director of the Hawaiian Volcano Observatory, Professor of Geology, Mass. Inst. Technology.

The Bill

The writer has been instrumental in preparing and modifying this bill as the authorized Agent in Washington of the Honolulu Chamber of Commerce, and of the Superintendent of Public Works Charles R. Forbes, acting under the instructions of the Governor of Hawaii. Mr. Forbes has recently left Washington to return to the Territory, but the present draft of the bill was fully discussed with him before he left.

History of the Bill

In its original form a bill to establish a National Park in the Territory of Hawaii was introduced in the House in

1911 by the Delegate from Hawaii under authority from Governor Walter F. Frear. This bill defined two tracts of land, including respectively the craters of the active volcanoes Mauna Loa and Kilauea, and a reservation for a roadway between them. The bill called for an appropriation of $50,000 to be used in part for the purchase of private lands within the areas defined, and the negotiations which were privately carried on by persons interested in the proposed Park showed unanimity of sentiment in favor of the Park, but developed protracted delays with the trust estates which owned the land as to definite metes and bounds. Most of the land would unquestionably be ceded at a nominal price as it consists of a waste of barren lava. About one-half of the original tracts was public land. In 1912 the proposed Park was surveyod by topographers of the U. S. Geological Survey and still later the outline was modified by the territorial surveyor. The bill was reintroduced in the House in December, 1915, and the present substituted bill January 20, 1916.

Contents of Bill

The present bill is designed to establish a National Park in Hawaii consisting of the two original tracts as modified by later surveys, and an additional tract consisting of the great crater of Haleakala Volcano, on the Island of Maui. The total acreage is about 75,295 acres, divided as follows:

Mauna Loa Tract—17,920 acres, about one-half public land.

Kilauea Tract—35,865 acres, about four-ninths public land.

Roadway Tract—360 acres, about one-half public land.

Haleakala Tract—21,150 acres, about one-third public land.

Four-ninths of the total area is public land, but the balance is mainly desert or worthless cattle land belonging largely to benevolent trust estates interested in the public welfare. Probably nine-tenths of the private land will be ceded to the territory at such time as the territory will take the matter in hand under a definite authorization such as the passage of this bill will create, to secure for a National Park all the land obtainable within definite metes and bounds. Therefore, this bill is drawn solely for the purpose of creating a Park, it calls for no appropraition from the National Treasury and the Park so created will consist at the outset only of the public lands within the boundaries defined.

Section 2 provides that no existing claim, location or entry within the Park shall be affected and that the usual provision for rights of way, etc., may be made by the Secretary of the Interior. Section 3 provides that no lands privately owned shall be affected by or subject to the provisions of this act. Section 4 provides that the Secretary of the Interior shall have executive control over the Park and may use the proceeds of leases and other revenues in protection and management of the same.

National Character of Hawaiian Craters

There is the same justification for creating a National Park about the three great volcanoes of Hawaii that there was for setting aside the wonders of the Yellowstone Geyser District, the big trees of California and the great Canyon of the Yosemite. The Hawaiian volcanoes are truly a national asset, wholly unique of their kind, the most famous in the world of science, and the most continuously, variously and harmlessly active volcanoes on earth. Kilauea crater has been nearly continuously active with a lake or lakes of molten lava for a century. Mauna Loa is the largest active volcano and mountain mass in the world, with eruptions about once a decade, and has poured out more lava during the last century than any other volcano on the globe. Haleakala is a mountain mass ten thousand feet high with a tremendous crater rift in its summit eight miles in diameter and three thousand feet deep with many high lava cones built up inside the crater. It is probably the largest of all known craters among volcanoes that are technically known as active. Haleakala erupted less than two hundred years ago. The crater at sunrise is the grandest volcanic spectacle on earth.

Comparison with Other National Parks

The following summary by the Hon. L. A. Thurston of Honolulu, is a just comparison of the natural wonders of

Hawaii with those of other National Parks:

"The Yellowstone has its beautiful lake and river and its geysers of hot water.

"The volcano of Kilauea has its lake of molten lava, its islands of rock, its natural sulphur factories; while the volcano of Mauna Loa forces columns of liquid lava hundreds of feet into the air, and every few years pours forth billions of tons of lava in a few days. Both of these volcanoes are within the proposed park.

"The Yosemite has its grand precipices and granite peaks.

"The Hawaiian reservation contains a mountain, Mouna Loa, 13,675 feet high, three active volcanoes, pit craters with perpendicular walls rising sheer, in one instance, for 1500 feet, and innumerable other craters, cones, pits, wells, sinks, caverns, lava tubes, and other volcanic structures with every possible diversity in form, color and detail, making such a fascinating study of the world in the making as is found nowhere else in the world.

"The Yellowstone, Yosemite and Sequoia Parks contain big trees, beautiful groves, and landscape such as artists love.

"The proposed Hawaiian Park contains groves of sandalwood now nearly extinct elsewhere in the Pacific; magnifiicent Hawaiian mahogany trees, with trunks over twenty feet in circumference; forests of tree ferns up to forty feet in height with single leaves twenty feet long; tropical jungles with scores of varieties of the most exquisite and delicate ferns and mosses, many of them found nowhere else in the world; numerous song birds of brilliant hues, many of them found nowhere else but in Hawaii, and nearly extinct except in this particular locality. There are rolling, grassy meadows, dotted with tropical trees, shrubs and ferns giving a park-like effect. Many of the trees are botanical treasures known only in this locality and of great rarity, and great destruction is being wrought among them by pigs and cattle. There is now no public reservation accessible to the people, where these features are preserved and where the right exists to camp or picnic, or even carry on scientific observation. The heart of the tree ferns makes excellent pig food, and hundreds of them are cut every year in the area proposed to be reserved. If this is not stopped the tree ferns will be exterminated. With the disappearance of the trees and ferns, the birds disappear also."

The marvelously spectacular quality of the lakes of lava at Kilauea is indescribable, but those who visit them unhesitatingly pronounce the scene the most wonderful sight on earth. President Charles W. Eliot, of Harvard University, visited the crater in 1912 after a trip around the world and pronounced it the most wonderful scene he had ever watched. It is a lake of fire a thousand feet long, splashing on its banks with a noise like the waves of the sea, while great fountains boil through it fifty feet high, sending quantities of glowing spray over the shore with hissing of gases, rumbling and blue flames playing through crevices. It is ever changing and the record of these changes is being kept from day to day photographically and otherwise, by the Hawaiian Volcano Observatory. There have been occasional crises during the last century when the active crater was upheaved into a hill, and thereafter collapsed into a deep pit with marvelously spectacular avalanches, fiery grottos and clouds of brown dust. Through many years the crater was overflowing. Frequently islands form in the molten lake, owing to the infall of large pieces of the shore. Cascades, whirlpools and rapids of glowing melt are common. There are vapor cracks so hot that a stick may be charred in them in a few minutes. A line of thirteen pit craters extends southeast from the active vent for about ten miles, showing every variety of form and color, width and depth, some of them being only a few feet across and 250 feet deep. These are all within the proposed reservation. There are walks and horseback rides in all directions through splendid forests or barren deserts, with weird lava forms built into pinnacles or festoons, and rifted into mighty chasms.

"Mauna Loa is capped with perpetual snow, and ice may be found in cracks as a source of water supply even in summer. In the winter time there is every variety of climate to be found from sea level to the summit of Mauna Loa, from the warmth of the tropics to arctic blizzards on the mountain top.

"There are petrified trees in a national monument reservation in Arizona; in the proposed Hawaiian Park there are trees of lava formed by an intensely liquid flow of lava rushing through a forest, congealing around the trunks, and then flowing off, leaving standing a perfect mould of the tree trunks.

"There are deposits at Kilauea of yellow and green pumice, as light and airy as sea foam, side by side with rocks weighing tons, all having rained down from overhead after an explosive eruption about 1790. There are fields of 'Pele's Hair' lava blown out like spun glass by the wind as the fiery spray is dashed into the air on the surface of the molten lake of lava."

Development as a Tourist Resort at Present.

Kilauea crater is the main feature at present visited by travelers from all over the world. The climb to the summit craters of Mauna Loa and Haleakala is more arduous, requiring horseback and camping, and is taken by only the more adventurous spirits. Kilauea is thirty miles from the port of Hilo, which in turn is about two hundred miles from the capital, Honolulu. There are two good hotels at Kilauea, reached by automobile roads from Hilo and from the south end of the Island of Hawaii, and an automobile road extends from the hotels seven miles to the inner lake of lava, which may thus be visited without any walking whatever. About one thousand tourists visit the crater every year, and three or four times that number of local visitors. The crater is not a steep mountain top, but a broad forested plateau beneath which is a lava sink three miles in diameter surrounded by cliffs three hundred feet high, and the cool climate attracts many local visitors through the summer months to the hotels and cottages. The volcano is the main local summer resort of the residents of the Hawaiian Islands.

There are many trails to the desert, the pit craters, the lava caverns, and the forest glades. Through the cooperation of the territorial government, the U. S. Army, and private subscription there has recently been built a trail thirty miles long up Mauna Loa to the summit and provision has been made for two rest houses on the way. There are two other trails up Mauna Loa from opposite sides of the mountain. In the case of Haleakala crater there is a roadway and trail and a concrete rest house on the summit which has been provided through subscription and the enterprise of the Maui Board of Trade. The Island of Maui is on the steamship route from Honolulu to Hilo and about half way.

Steamships ply between Honolulu and Hilo on an average of about three times a week with occasional large vessels from the coast in addition to the regular inter-island service. The steamship service is excellent and the journey from Honolulu to the Island of Maui is about six hours and from Honolulu to Hilo is about fifteen hours.

There is a disastrous lack of proper guardianship of the roads, trails and natural curiosities at present. There is no regular policing of the edge of the lava pit, visited during active times by hundreds of irresponsible people from week to week. There have been automobile accidents and occasional parties have been lost in the desert, and in one instance at least a too adventurous climber fell into the crater and was rescued with great difficulty. In the summer of 1913 scientific explorers discovered a wonderful lava cavern full of rare stalactites and delicate spires of lava and this cave at once became a popular resort. As a result all the delicate specimens were immediately broken away and carried off and the natural beauty of the place was ruined, and all sorts of nuisances committed. The same thing is true with regard to the insect, bird and plant life of the crater region, there being no adequate protection of these things by law. The establishment of a National Park with suitable guardians would remedy this situation.

Scientific Research at the Craters

During the nineteenth century many scientific men visited Kilauea, and Professor J. D. Dana of Yale University wrote an important book based on Hawaiian volcanoes entitled, 'Characteristics of Volcanoes.' Many records were written in large blank books preserved for the purpose by the Kilauea Volcano House.

In 1911 systematic keeping of records and establishment of seismographs in Observatory buildings was started through the Massachusetts Institute of Technology, by the writer, and this has been kept up since that time and is now likely to pass into the control of the United States Weather Bureau. There is no place on the globe so favorable for systematic study of volcanology and the relations of local earthquakes to volcanoes as in Hawaii, and for this reason alone, if for no other, it would be appropriate to set aside a National Park in this wonderland of volcanic activity, where the earth's primitive processes are at work making new land and adding new gases to the atmosphere.

Appendix No. 7.

COMMITTEE REPORT ON NATIONAL PARK.

Report of Committee on the Public Lands, recommending passage of Hawaii National Park Bill, including report of Secretary of the Interior.

HOUSE OF REPRESENTATIVES.

64th Congress, 1st Session.

Report No. 131.

NATIONAL PARK OF HAWAII.

February 7, 1916.—Committed to the Committee of the Whole House on the state of the Union and ordered to be printed.

Mr. Ferris, from the Committee on Public Lands, submitted the following report:

[To accompany H. R. 9525]

The Committee on the Public Lands, to whom was referred the bill (H. R. 9525) to create a national park in the Territory of Hawaii, having had the same under consideration, report it back to the House with the recommendation that it do pass with amendment as follows:

Page 8, at the end of the section, add the following provisos:

Provided, That no appropriation for the maintenance, supervision or improvement of said park in excess of $10,000 annually shall be made unless the same shall have first been expressly authorized by law: *And provided further,* That no appropriation shall be made for the improvement or maintenance of said park until proper conveyance shall be made to the United States of such perpetual easements and rights of way over private lands within the exterior boundaries of said park as the Secretary of the Interior shall find necessary to make said park reasonably accessible in all its parts, and said Secretary shall when such easements and rights of way have been conveyed to the United States, report the same to Congress.

The bill proposes to establish the Hawaii National Park, including the three crater areas and natural wonders of the three great volcanoes of Hawaii, respectively, Mauna Loa volcano, Kilauea volcano, and Haleakala volcano.

By the provisions of this bill 75,295 acres are set aside, four-ninths of which is public land, and the balance, chiefly waste land, belongs to educational and eleemosynary trusts said to be willing to cede the land in large measure.

No appropriation is carried by the bill, and it is provided that no appropriation shall be made until proper conveyances in the matter of the private lands shall be made to the United States such as the Secretary of the Interior shall find necessary. Otherwise existing claims and privately owned lands are unaffected by the bill.

Strong reasons for creating a national park in this district are that the craters in question are among the most remarkable of natural wonders. Kilauea is the most continuously active volcano, Mauna Loa the largest volcano, and Haleakala, the largest and most spectacular crater in the world. There is urgent need for the protection of curiosities now being damaged. Scientific studies in inaccessible parts of the area, of importance for the public safety, will be furthered by Federal control and park improvement. Scientifically and popularly, the volcanoes are a national rather than a local asset, and the opinions of travelers appear to be unanimous that this area is of national importance for park preservation.

The Secretary of the Interior favors the bill and his report is printed herewith:

February 2, 1916.

My Dear Mr. Ferris:

Your letter of January 22 has been received, inclosing H. R. bill 9525, with request for report thereon. This bill proposes the establishment of a national park in the Territory of Hawaii, such park to include two of the great craters on the Island of Hawaii and one on the Island of Maui. I am in favor of the preservation of these great natural wonders, and would be glad to see them made a part of our national park system.

Cordially yours,

FRANKLIN K. LANE,
Secretary.

Hon. SCOTT FERRIS,
Chairman Committee on the Public Lands, House of Representatives.

Appendix No. 8.

PUBLICATIONS OF HAWAIIAN VOLCANO OBSERVATORY.

1. Six Illustrated **Weekly Reports**, by F. A. Perret, August 17 to September 22, 1911. Pacific Commercial Advertiser, Honolulu. (Republished without illustrations in Thrum's Hawaiian Annual for 1911, and in First Report of Hawaiian Volcano Observatory, Boston, Jan.-Mar., 1912.)
2. **Weekly Reports** of Observatory, T. A. Jaggar in charge from Jan. 25, 1912, to June 21, 1913, Pac. Com. Adv., Honolulu.
3. **Weekly Reports** of Hawaiian Volcano Observatory, T. A. Jaggar in charge, from June 28, 1913, to July 14, 1913, Pac. Com. Adv., Honolulu, and republished as leaflets by Hawaiian Volcano Research Association.
4. **Weekly Bulletin** of Hawn. Vol. Obser., T. A. Jaggar in charge, July 21, 1913, to June 18, 1914, Pac. Com. Adv., Honolulu; republished, weekly form by Hawn. Vol. Res. Assn., editor H. M. Ballou. The numbered series begins with Vol. II, No. 1, Jan. 7, 1914, ending with No. 32, Dec. 31, 1914. (The following numbers are unpublished: Aug. 21, Nov. 6, Nov. 27 and Dec. 11, 1913.)
5. **Special Bulletin**, Hawn. Vol. Obser., Dec. 11, 1913; Scientific Work on Hawaiian Volcanoes by T. A. Jaggar, Hawn. Vol. Res. Assn., Honolulu.
6. **Weekly Bulletins** of Hawn. Vol. Obser., T. A. Jaggar in charge, Aug., 1914, to Aug., 1915, Pac. Com. Adv., Honolulu; republished monthly form by Hawn. Vol. Res. Assn., editor H. M. Ballou. (Vol. III, No. 1, Jan., 1915.)
7. **Seismometric Bulletin** of Hawn. Vol. Obser., Vol. I, Nos. 1 to 4, bi-monthly, 1915. Systematic reports of the Whitney Laboratory of Seismology; international notation; by H. O. Wood. Hawn. Vol. Res. Assn., Honolulu.
8. **First Report Hawn. Vol. Obser.**, T. A. Jaggar, Director; Boston, Mass., Jan.-Mar., 1912. Published by the Society of Arts, Massachusetts Institute of Technology. 75 pp, 32 figs.
9. **Constitution of the Hawaiian Volcano Research Association.** 4 pp. Honolulu, December, 1913.

Appendix No. 9.

PUBLICATIONS OF T. A. JAGGAR, 1911 TO 1916.

1. **The Technology Station in Hawaii.** The Technology Review, Vol. XIII, No. 8, Boston, pp. 508 to 515, Nov., 1911; 4 figs.

2. **The Cross of Hawaii.** Annual of Honolulu Chamber of Commerce, 1912. 12 pp., 1 fig.
3. **Report of the Hawaiian Volcano Observatory,** Jan.-Mar., 1912. Massachusetts Institute of Technology, Boston. 75 pp, 32 figs.
4. **Scientific Work on Hawaiian Volcanoes,** Special Bulletin Hawaiian Volcano Association, 1913; 15 pp.
5. **Education and the Philosophy of Change.** Commencement address College of Hawaii, June, 1914; published by the Star-Bulletin Co., Honolulu. 6 pp.
6. **Kilauea and Mauna Loa in 1914.** Address annual meeting Hawn. Vol. Res. Assn., Mar. 19, 1915, Bulletin Hawn. Vol. Obser., pp. 20 to 42, Vol. III, No. 4, 13 figs. (Also Science Conspectus, pp. 85 to 103, Boston, Vol. V, No. 4, 1915, under the title Notes from a Volcano Laboratory. Republished in Scientific American Supplement.)
7. **The Outbreak of Mauna Loa, Hawaii, 1914.** American Journal of Science, Vol. XXXIX, Feb., 1915, pp. 167 to 172. 2 figs.
8. **The Problem of Volcanism.** (Review.) The Nation, Vol. 101, No. 2613, July 29, 1915, pp. 155 to 157.
9. **Problems of American Geology.** (Review.) The Nation, Vol. 101, No. 2618, Sept. 2, 1915, pp. 296 to 298.
10. **Activity of Mauna Loa, Hawaii, Dec.-Jan., 1914-15.** Amer. Jour. of Science, Vol. XL, Dec., 1815, pp. 621 to 638, 13 figs.
11. **The Hawaii National Park.** Report to the Secretary of the Interior on H. R. 9525, Hearing before the Committee on Public Lands, Feb. 3, 1916, Washington, Government Printing Office.
12. **On Making the Hawaiian Volcano Observatory a Government Institution.** (Including Committee Report Hawn. Vol. Res. Assn.) Hearings before Committee on Agriculture, House of Representatives, Jan. 18, 1916. Washington, Government Printing Office.
13. **Eruption of Sakurajima and Notes on Other Japanese Volcanoes.** Bul. Hawn. Vol. Obsvy., Vol. II, No. 13, pp. 48 to 52, 1 fig., April 1, 1914, and Vol. II, No. 17, pp. 70 to 73, 1 fig. April 29, 1914.

Appendix No. 10.

PUBLICATIONS OF H. O. WOOD, 1911 TO 1916.

1. **The Observation of Earthquakes.** Bulletin Seismological Society of America. June, 1911, pp. 48 to 82.
2. **On the Region of Origin of the Central Californian Earthquakes of July, August and September, 1911.** Bul. Seis. Soc. Amer., Vol. II, No. 1, March, 1912, pp. 31 to 39, 1 fig.
3. **Seismographic Bookkeeping.** Bul. Seis. Soc. Amer., Vol. II, No. 2, June, 1912.
4. **The Registration of Earthquakes at the Berkeley Station, from Oct. 30, 1910, to Mar. 31, 1911.** Univ. of Cal. Publications, Bul. of the Seismographic Stations, No. 1, pp. 1-10, 1912.
5. **The Registration of Earthquakes at the Berkeley Station, from April 1 to Sept. 30, 1911, and the Lick Observatory Station from May 23 to Sept. 30, 1911.** Ibid. No. 2, 1912.
6. **The Registration of Earthquakes at the Berkeley Station and at the Lick Observatory Station from Oct. 1, 1911, to Mar. 31, 1912.** Ibid. No. 3. 1912.
7. **Volcanic Eruptions in the Philippines, etc.** By Rev. M. S. Maso, S. J. (review). Bul. Seis. Soc. Amer., Vol. II, No. 3, pp. 213-215, 1912.
8. **Ueber Eine Dynamische Skala Zur Schätzung Von Makroseismischen Bewegungen.** By Fürst B. Galitzin (review). Bul. Seis. Soc. Amer., Vol. III, No. 2, pp. 90-93, 2 figs. 1913.
9. **The Hawaiian Volcano Observatory.** Bul. Seis. Soc. Amer., Vol. III, No. 1, March, 1913, pp. 14 to 19.

10. **Concerning the Perceptibility of Weak Earthquakes and Their Dynamical Measurement.** Bul. Seis. Soc. Amer., Vol. IV, No. 1, March, 1914, pp. 29 to 38, 3 figs.
11. **On the Earthquakes of 1868 in Hawaii.** Bul. Seis. Soc. Amer., Vol. IV, No. 4, Dec., 1914, pp. 169 to 203, 2 figs.
12. **The Seismic Prelude to the 1914 Eruption of Mauna Loa.** Bul. Seis. Soc. Amer., Vol. V, No. 1, March, 1915, pp. 39 to 50.
13. **A Consideration of Recent Earthquakes Local to Hawaii, and of the Seismological Problem They Indicate.** Bulletin Hawaiian Volcano Observatory, Vol. III, No. 5, May, 1915, pp. 53 to 65, 3 figs.
14. **On a Possible Causal Mechanism For Heave-Fault Slipping in the California Coast Range Region.** Bul. Seis. Soc. Amer., Vol. V, No. 4, Dec., 1915, 3 figs.

Appendix No. 11.

PUBLICATIONS OF R. A. DALY, F. A. PERRET AND OTHERS. 1911-1916.

By R. A. Daly:

1. **The Nature of Volcanic Action.** Proc. Amer. Acad. Arts and Sciences, Vol. XLVII, 1911.
2. **Magmatic Differentiation in Hawaii.** Jour. Geol., Vol. XIX, No. 4, 1911, pp. 289 to 316, 1 fig.
3. **Igneous Rocks and Their Origin.** McGraw-Hill Book Co., 1914, 563 pp., 205 figs.

By F. A. Perret:

4. **The Lava Fountains of Kilauea.** Amer. Jour. of Science, Vol. XXXV, pp. 139 to 148, 1913, 7 figs.
5. **The Floating Islands of Halemaumau.** Amer. Jour. of Science, Vol. XXXV, pp. 273 to 282, 1913, 6 figs.
6. **The Circulatory System in the Halemaumau Lake During the Summer of 1911.** Amer. Jour. of Science, Vol. XXXV, No. 208, April, 1913, pp. 338 to 349, 6 figs.
7. **Subsidence Phenomena at Kilauea in the Summer of 1911.** Amer. Jour. of Science, Vol. XXXV, No. 209, May, 1913, pp. 469 to 276, 6 figs.
8. **Some Kilauean Ejectamenta.** Amer. Jour. of Science, Vol. XXXV, 1913, pp. 611 to 618, 7 figs.
9. **Some Kilauean Formations.** Amer. Jour. of Science, Vol. XXXVI, No. 212, Aug., 1913, pp. 151 to 159, 7 figs.
10. **Volcanic Research at Kilauea in Summer of 1911.** By F. A. Perret with a report by Dr. Albert Brun on the material taken directly from "Old Faithful." Amer. Jour. of Science, Vol. XXXVI, No. 215, Nov., 1913, pp. 475 to 488, 5 figs.

By E. S. Shepherd:

11. **Temperature of the Fluid Lava of Halemaumau, July, 1911.** First Report Hawn. Vol. Obsvy., Boston, 1912, pp. 47 to 51.

By J. F. Rock:

12. **Mauna Loa on February 17, 1912.** First Report Hawn. Vol. Obsvy., 1912, Boston, p. 73.

By F. T. Dillingham.

13. **Water and Volcanic Activity.** (Review of Day and Shepherd.) Bul. Hawn. Vol. Obsvy., Vol. II, No. 31, Dec. 1914, pp. 149 to 155. (See Bul. Geol. Soc. Amer., Vol. XXIV, No. 4, 1913, pp. 573-606, 12 figs.)

By A. L. Day and E. S. Shepherd:

14. **L'eau et les gaz magmatiques.** Comptes Rendus 157, 1913, pp. 958-961.
15. **Water and Volcanic Activity.** Bul. Geol. Soc. Amer., Vol. 24, pp. 573-606, pls. 17-27, Dec., 1913.

By G. C. Curtis:

16. **Work Going on at Kilauea Volcano.** Science N. S., Vol. XXXVIII, No. 975, Sept. 12, 1913, pp. 355-358.

By J. W. Green:

17. **Magnetic Observations at Kilauea and Mauna Loa.** U. S. Coast and Geodetic Survey, Special Publ. No. 20, 1914, pp. 12-27-29.

By Whitman Cross:

18. **Lavas of Hawaii and Their Relations.** U. S. Geol. Survey; Prof. Paper, 88, 98 pp., 4 pls., 1915.

By Sidney Powers:

19. **The Recent Activity of Kilauea and Mauna Loa, Hawaii.** Science N. S. XLII, No. 1074, 1915, pp. 147-154, 2 figs.

By C. H. Birdseye and A. O. Burkland:

20. **Topographic Map of Proposed Kilauea Volcano National Park.** U. S. Geol. Survey, Advance Sheet, 1912. (Surveyed in coöperation with the Territory of Hawaii.)

By Arnold Heim:

21. **Lavafelder des Kilauea, Hawaii.** Geol. Charakterbilder. Heft. 16. Borntraeger, Berlin, 1913, 12 pp., 4 figs., 8 pls.

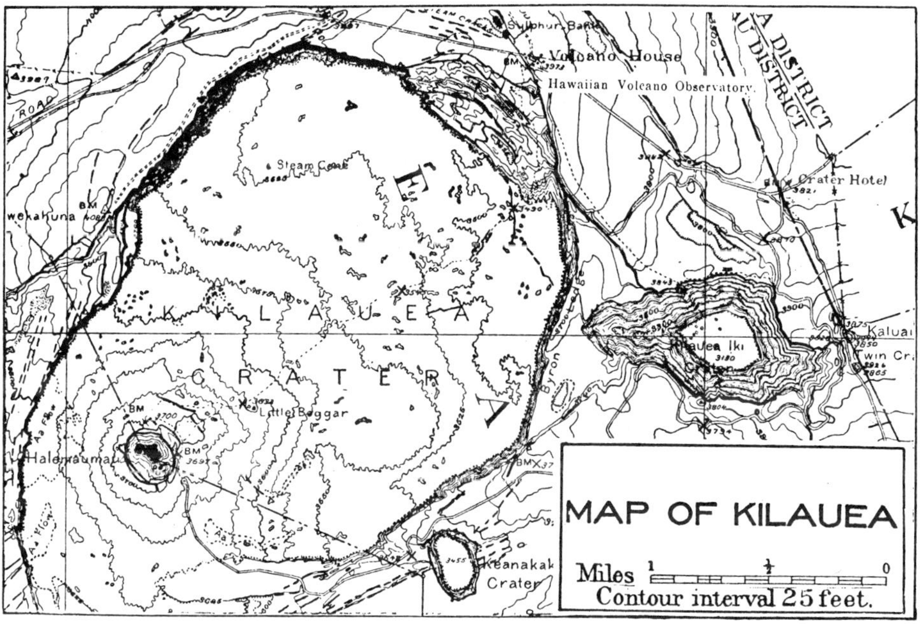

HAWAIIAN VOLCANO RESEARCH ASSOCIATION.

This society is a voluntary one, made up of subscribers to scientific work which is being executed by the Massachusetts Institute of Technology.

In 1915 there are about 100 subscribers in Hawaii and elsewhere, firms and individuals. A group of firms and persons in Hilo built the main observatory building in the spring of 1912. Publications to date have been weekly reports since the summer of 1911, now reprinted in Honolulu in monthly form. The Massachusetts Institute of Technology will publish annual reports, of which the introductory number was printed in 1912.

The weekly bulletin as it appears in the Advertiser is reprinted as a leaflet and sent to regular annual subscribers to the work of the Association. L. A. Thurston is president of the Board of Directors of the Association, and R. W. Shingle is treasurer. New subscribers who are interested in volcanoes will be welcomed in the Association. The Association aims: (1) To record volcanic activity and earthquakes in Hawaii; (2) to attract scientific men hither for special studies; (3) to promote the establishment of volcano observatories all over the world. The annual dues of regular members are $5; patrons of the Assocaition subscribe larger amounts.

WHITNEY LABORATORY OF SEISMOLOGY.

The Whitney Laboratory of Seismology is equipped with two Bosch-Omori 100 kg tromometers registering N-S and E-W motion, a heavy Omori tromometer registering E-W motion, and an Omori "ordinary Seismograph" designed for registering strong earthquakes in all three components of motion. These are seated on concrete piers in a closed basement room having practically constant temperature, beneath the chief Observatory building near the hotel. Time is referred to a rated chronometer, checked at intervals by solar observations with a transit. Both instruments are loaned by the College of Hawaii. Hawaiian standard time (H. S. T.) is 10 hrs. 30 min. slower than Greenwich time.

CANCANI SCALE OF SEISMIC INTENSITY.

Expressed by accelerations measured in millimeters per second per second.

I.	Instrumental	0.0	2.5
II.	Very slight	2.5	5.0
III.	Slight	5.0	10.0
IV.	Sensible, mediocre	10.0	25.0
V.	Rather strong	25.0	50.0
VI.	Strong	50.0	100.0
VII.	Very strong	100.0	250.0
VIII.	Ruinous	250.0	500.0
IX.	Disastrous	500.0	1000.0
X.	Very disastrous	1000.0	2500.0
XI.	Catastrophic	2500.0	5000.0
XII.	Great catastrophe	5000.0	10000.0

Grade IV. is ordinarily the minimum perceived by the senses; and in grade XII. the acceleration, or rate of change of motion (jerk) reaches that of terrestrial gravitation.

In the standard form of report the maximum intensity or acceleration, designated by the symbol a, or max. a, is given in the conventional unit, **the milligal.** The milligal is a measure of acceleration, such that 1 milligal = 1/100 mm. per sec. per sec. = 10 μ per sec. per sec. The Cancani scale, here defined in terms of millimeters per sec. per sec., can therefore be expressed in **milligals** by multiplying each of the numbers by 100.

WEEKLY BULLETIN
OF THE
Hawaiian Volcano Observatory

Vol. IV. HONOLULU, HAWAII, APRIL-MAY, 1916. No. 5

TECHNOLOGY STATION, April 6—During the week ending April 5 the magma surface has risen slowly and steadily in Halemaumau, visibly overflowing from the lake and outlying magma springs on the south and southwest at almost all times. No tendency to subsidence of the main lake has been observed except on April 1. Frequently its outlines have been indistinct on account of the flowing about its margins. In general the surface activity has been relatively sluggish, though the moving flows have made the scene brilliant, especially at night. At times, for short intervals, fountain action has been vigorous also.

On March 31 at 10.30 a. m. fresh flows were in motion on the floor at the south. Smoke was rising from the east end of the crag and from the northeast jut. The east bench of the crag was about three feet above the floor. There was a torrent pouring out of the southwest arm and cascading down into a boiling pot at its mouth, opposite the peninsula of raised benches joined to the crag. The lake likewise was rushing into this boiling pot.

The southwest pool was seen to break up with the accompaniment of great quantities of bubble fountains. The tilting of the crag has progressed with larger sudden movements at first and smaller ones later, as evidenced by seven spatter rims with wide intervals between the higher ones and narrow below. There were spatter cones on the shore at the south and east, and three coves in the lake at the east, northeast and north. A wide margin of tarnished flows of two days earlier separated the new lava of the southwest pool from the base of the crag.

A deep bay was seen in the crag on the north, and a narrow low isthmus separated the two summits. Some travelling fountains were seen near the east end of the lake whose surface appeared as subsided about eight inches. Noise of splashing predominated. In the afternoon a raincloud was noticed forming above Halemaumau with a very rapid boiling up of cauliflowers over the swift convection current from the lava surface. The convectional updraft evidently reached a high level. A system of cracks was seen cutting across the crag near its east end.

On April 1 at 10 a. m. the lake surface appeared two feet lower than the floor. The southwest pool had well defined boundaries. It was oval in shape and stood slightly lower than the floor. Inrush at the east base of the crag was seen, and spatter action about the lake borders. No other changes were observed except some border debris on the floor.

On April 2 at 10 a. m. the lake was again level with the floor. It was seen that during the subsidence of the previous day the crag broke in two along a vertical plane which joined the southwest inner pot and the big bay on the north side of the crag. The east part had swung back to the eastward, bringing its flat service back into a horizontal position. A stream of magma seventy-five feet wide was pouring from the southwest pool to the west part of the lake between the two separated parts of the crag. The former southwest arm had been obliterated by the rotation of the east part of the crag. This had brought the highest of the tilted shore benches back to a level position about three feet above the lake surface. All the lower ones were submerged.

New flows were seen on the floor on all sides. Those at the southeast appeared older. Three large spatter niches were seen along the north shore of

WEEKLY BULLETIN
of the
Hawaiian Volcano Observatory

Published Monthly at Honolulu, Hawaii, by the Hawaiian Volcano Research Association

Entered as second-class matter January 20, 1914, at the post-office at Honolulu, Hawaii, under the Act of August 24, 1912.

the lake. The northeast jut had been submerged under flows. There were cones along the southeast shore and south side of the east part of the crag. The fountain previously so conspicuous in the southwest pool had now ceased to act.

On April 3 the lake was everywhere brimming and its margin could be distinguished only by the crumpling of the streaming skins. About noon one heavy landslide fell. There was steady streaming eastward in the main lake and eastward and northward in the southwest arm. A few boiling fountains were in action near the east end, and there were several conspicuous spatter niches at the shore margin. Thin flows spreading by crust-foundering, slowly spread from several sporadic centers at the southwest, south, southeast and east over the whole south and east floors. Fuming places were almost absent, but considerable quantities of cobalt blue fumes were emitted in puffs when the larger fountains broke, and lesser volumes of these rose from the steady fountaining places. A strong wind distributed these so that at almost all times a blue haze, quite transparent to vision, but intensely actinic, curtained the whole scene. The surface of the lava was estimated to be about ten feet below the bench remnants of the high stands in 1914 and 1915.

On April 4 the surface action, in afternoon, had increased. In various parts of the lake many fountains were boiling. The magma was still rising. It was established that the bench remnants were only about three feet above the floor. The streaming in lake and arm continued as on the third, and lava was seen flooding the south and southeast part of the floor. The walls of the spatter niches at the east had increased in height and size.

On April 5 the walls of the spatter niches had collapsed and disappeared, and lava from the lake was rapidly overflowing the east and northeast part of the floor. The streaming in the lake and arm continued without change. The floor at the south and southeast was still being flooded visibly. The surface was still below the bench remnants of 1914-15. There was some fountain action in the east part of the main lake, and the sporadic breaking of Old Faithful was observed.

During the week one earthquake has been registered which was felt sharply in Hilo, and perhaps barely felt at the Observatory, near midnight. Besides this two or three doubtful wave-groups have been registered.

Other motion has been registered as usual, with no conspicuous features.

H. O. WOOD, Associate.

TECHNOLOGY STATION, April 13. —After the rising and overflowing recorded for the previous week the lava column of Halemaumau reached a level where it has remained stationary with daily fluctuations of from two to three feet. This level is approximately 350 feet below the south rim of the pit and the present floor is almost even with the bench remnants of September, 1915, the uptilted crags being fifteen or twenty feet higher. As result of the stationary and slightly subsided condition of the lake, it has greatly enlarged by collapse of the northern banks, and the southwestern pool shows sharp definition as a large arm of the lake.

On the afternoon of Friday, April 7, the streaming was from west to east, there were four or five fountaining areas toward the east and pronounced enlargement of the lake along its north bank had taken place during the previous two days. The banks were from one to two feet high so that the lake was definitely outlined. A cresent shaped half-dome of spatter had formed along two-thirds of the eastern shore beginning at the south with a height equal to one-fifth of its length. Lava was still welling up over the south floor, probably from the southern cone vent and was spreading theron by the cracking and foundering process. One avalanche took place from under the south station. Fumes rose from the eastern crag, the lake margin and from the rim of the floor north, and blue fumes puffed up from the bursting fountains.

On Monday, April 10, from four to seven p.m., the scene in Halemaumau was very different from that of a fortnight previous. The lake was about four feet below its banks and with the south pool and the river of melt pouring from that pool northward, exhibited one of the largest areas of liquid bounded by definite shores which have been seen here since 1912. The south pool and lake both streamed eastward from under skins at the west ends. An elongated cape made out into the lake from the northeast corner of the west crag, and another point of spatter separated the northeast and southeast coves. The south cone locality in the floor was a circular pot fifty feet in diameter which after six-thirty p.m., slowly filled with a lava pudding through which gas sputtered lazily. During the night several short flows poured out radially on the floor from this pot. The floor otherwise was surfaced with bronzy flows wrinkled like stiff drapery. The action in the lake was a mild streaming with swifter flow against the east end, into the bank east of the east crag, and in the river between the crags. There was a little fresh tumble of rock debris at the edge of the floor south and the blue fume from the pit was slightly stronger and denser than the previous week.

On April 11 at four p.m. the lake was slightly higher, about two feet below the bank, otherwise conditions were unchanged. Six radial flows around a driblet cone replaced the south pot of the day before. The pit was very free from fume, only a little blue smoke and spatter at the east end.

On April 12 at 4 p.m. the lake was again about four feet down and the south cone had overflowed further so that the flows reached to the base of the east crag There was a large spatter ridge built up at the east end, otherwise conditions were the same. It was evident that the lake was essentially stationary with rising pulsations that caused slight overflow of the south cone.

For the Whitney Laboratory of Seismology, H. O. Wood reports that four earthquakes have been registered in the latter part of the week ending April 12.

There have thus been five earthquakes in the last ten days, apparently coincident with the cessation of rapid rising in Halemaumau, and it is noteworthy that that rising has just reached the level of last year and stopped.

The Director returned from Honolulu April 9 after the annual meeting of the Hawaiian Volcano Research Association held April 7 in Honolulu. At that meeting a committee was provided for which should take up the question of founding a permanant Volcano museum at Kilauea as repository for the records of the observatory, and as a home for the Association where anyone may study maps, models, photographs and books dealing with volcanoes.

T. A. JAGGAR, JR., Director.

TECHNOLOGY STATION, April 20. —During the week ending April 19, 1916, the lava lake of Halemaumau has risen slowly, the time of slight subsidence of the previous week coming to an end on April 15. The last remnants of the bench of 1915 have now been completely submerged under new flows and the level of the lake surface is approximately 340 feet below the rim of the pit.

On Friday, April 14, at five p.m. the lake was one foot below its banks with very slow eastward streaming. Traveling fountains played between infolding skins toward the south-east, the skins sinking with rapid downsuck along the line of fountains. Where the skins came against the bank they would tear and pale blue flames arose from the rents. Flames could also be seen above the border fountains.

From time to time there were periods of increased fountaining and inrush to the southeast during increased subsidence. There were large cracks in the floor in general parallel to the shoreline on the southeast and others all around the northeast and north banks. A flow was in motion on the floor from the south cone and there were other flows which had formed during the preceding forty-eight hours. There was a new festooned flow from the west end to the shore of the southwest pool and this pool had overflowed its eastern bank. One avalanche was heard from the southwest wall. The blue veil of fume rising from the pit was slightly thicker than of late.

An examination of the Postal Rift north of Halemaumau showed greatly increased visible fume and changes in the arrangement of the cracks in the highly altered and whitened surface lava. It is evident that this solfaratic area is continually slumping under the corrosive action of the acid gas. The increase in visible vapor is probably due to the excessive rainfall of the last few months.

On April 15 at eleven a.m. the fume veil had again become almost invisible, the lake was brimming full and from the southeast station it was evident that overflow had taken place east of the middle crag, along the east and north shores, and southward from the southwest pool. The region of the south cone was evidently higher and surmounted the new flows. There were more fresh flows at the west end and the surface lava rushed toward the bank on the southwest, otherwise conditions remained the same.

At eleven-thirty a.m. on April 16 the rising continued, there were more overflows on all sides and the south cone remained a roundish area rising above new flows which had met on the floor from overflow of both pools. It was evident from the tilted shorelines, ten feet high at the southeast end of the west crag and about eight feet high on the west face of the east crag on opposite sides of the river of melt which poured northward, that both the crags were in process of tilting away from each other, the western crag northwestward and the eastern crag eastward. This for the western crag was at right angles to its former direction of tilting which had been southwestward.

The cracks in the floor were now submerged. The 1915 benches were about five feet above the floor level. The west ends of both pools were crusted over. There were fifteen or twenty fountaining areas playing in and around the lake.

On April 17 from five to six p.m. the lake rose and overflowed the entire bench area clear to the walls on all sides during the hour and the last remnants of the greenish bench of 1915 were submerged west and north. This meant that the lake level was 342 feet below the south rim of the pit. There was very great heat on the edge and Pele's hair was being made by the sputtering fountains in great quantities so that the air to leeward was full of it in single strands and tangles. The width of the new flows between the west wall and the crag had greatly increased. The south cone was now completely submerged and the point extending northward from the west crag was overflowed. The middle crag showed cracking through its center from south to north. The west end of the west crag appeared more submerged than its east and this corresponded with the evidence cited for its tendency to tilt westward. The streaming was slow eastward as usual.

On April 18 at noon the lake rose about one foot from a level two feet below its banks and overflowed the south corner of the southwest pool where was a spatter cone of horseshoe shape open on the side of the pool. There were other spatter cones on the southwest, and south and northeast of the middle crag. There was a rim of spatter along the southeastern and northern shores of the lake.

The surface currents were most rapid in the river between the crags. At the east end skins were folding inward and being sucked down. There were wide crusts at the west ends of the two pools which occasionally broke up by the cracking and foundering process. There were pronounced new tilt benches at the foot of each crag on the river side. On the floor were cracked crusts which sagged from the border inward on all sides and there were occasional crackling noises. A little smoke rose from the crags.

On April 19 at nine-thirty a. m. the lake was brimming, the surface was very quiet and the middle of the northern main pool was stagnant. In the river between the crags there was a reversed current flowing southward to meet the north flowing current from the southwest pool along a line of fountains. The meeting point slowly migrated from north to south and then maintained its position along a line joining the southern corners of the two crags. Here the surface skins of the two currents met and foundered while at each end of the line the currents were deflected against the banks with much fountaining. There was the usual streaming toward the bank southeast with down-folding skins and fountains.

From time to time a general hissing noise was heard which appeared to come from the surface of the floor. The west crag in the course of its westward tilt appeared to be shifting its position somewhat, the west end appearing farther north than formerly. It is these shiftings and tiltings in such heavy crags which have led some observers to call them "floating islands." They show not the slighest sign of flotation, and are massive deep blocks of floor material resting below against the funnel walls of the pit but frequently undermined by the lava channels which form around them so that they slip and tip until they are finally submerged or consumed. They are no more buoyed up by the lava than the floor is and a sudden subsidence of the lake to a depth of 50 or 100 feet would reveal a narrowing pit in the floor with insloping walls and leave both floor and crags as an upstanding bench.

It is worthy of note that there is remarkably little fountaining in this lake of large area in contrast to the many fountains of the smaller lake of the summer of 1912.

The following report from the Whitney Laboratory of Seismology is submitted by H. O. Wood:

During the week ending with April 19 three, or four, very weak local earthquakes have been registered; and one world-shaking teleseism of great energy. Registration of the latter began between 6 and 7 p. m. H. S. T. on April 17 and continued for two hours or so. Its origin was distant from this station between 2200 and 2300 miles. From our records no clue as to direction can ordinarily be gained. Microseismic motion has been as usual or weaker. Volcanic vibration has been strong and "stormy". Tilting has occurred toward the west slightly with considerable diurnal variation.

T. A. JAGGAR, JR., Director.

TECHNOLOGY STATION, April 27. —During the week ended April 26, the lava lake of Halemaumau has continued to overflow its banks and as result of the continued tilting of the eastern crag, a great block of the south-east floor has subsided so as to unite the south-western and northern pools, thus producing one great elliptical lake in which the eastern crag now stands as a true island. The western crag is still a peninsula extending from the west floor.

At two p.m. on April 20 the lake was about one foot below the floor, the eastward streaming was very slow and the two crags rose high above the river of lava which streamed northward between them. At two-thirty p. m., the lake rose and overflowed the floor to the wall of the pit on the east and south.

On April 21 the great change took place whereby the crag in the middle of the lake became converted into an island and the southern and southeastern floor subsided as described above

At ten a. m. April 22, there was a large elliptical lake and it was evident from the raised spatter rims on the south corner of the west crag, and on the west side of the island that the tilt of these two crags away from each other had been going on more strongly than ever. Seven spatter benches, one above the other could be counted on opposite sides of the river between the crags, The upper surfaces also now showed the tilt, the island sloping eastward and the western peninsula westward. It was undoubtedly the downward movement of the eastern part of the east crag, compensating this upward movement at the river, which carried the new floor in the region of the south cone down with it and so developed the new southeast channel between the island the remaining floor. This region was already undermined and full of cavities which had acted as conduits for the lava flows which had poured out of the south cone. The site of that cone was now definitely beneath the surface of the lake.

If the pronounced tilting westward goes on in the west crag, it too will become an island with a channel between it and the west wall. Already there had developed large glowing cracks around the west border of the crag and these perhaps marked the beginning of such a channel.

The lake was about 330 feet below the rim of the pit. The west sliderock above the former 1915 bench remnant was nearly submerged, and the floor southeast was level with the wet fumarole in the wall.

The streaming in the new lake was eastward on both sides of the island, the two currents meeting in a line between the island and the southeast shore. Here the skins were sucked down with occasional development of travelling fountains. The streaming was slow making a pattern of long wrinkled skins. Scalloped spatter banks had formed southeast and northeast and the latter caved in with much commotion at ten-thirty a.m.

This is the first lake which has developed the tendency to circular form since January 1912.

From five to six o'clock in the evening the lake rose at least four feet and overflowed the whole floor. The west talus was submerged, a wide flood of new lava filled the space between the west wall and the base of the upturned part of the crag and only one southeastern spatter cone protruded through the new lava. The eastern base of the island was completely submerged, only the tilted part remaining visible. Fountains spurted thirty to fifty feet in the air on the north and northeast and there was inrush on the north side of the island. After six-thirty o'clock in the evening the lake subsided sufficiently to exhibit its elliptical outline.

In the evening of April 23 from nine to ten o'clock the lake appeared about two feet below its banks, the crag and island stood high above it, there was a long peninsula north from the west side of the island and high spatter lumps had formed on the shore of the lake northeast and south. The southern one was a niche of horseshoe shape. The channel between crag and island was stagnant, while north and south there was quiet, slow streaming eastward. Against the southeast bank the lava would rush under occasionally with overspash on the bank. There were some stalactites. Glowing flows covered the floor everywhere. Fountains were few and flames could be seen around the border of the lake. The noises were of plashing and rumbling.

On April 24 at two o'clock in the afternoon conditions were similar with flows on the floor and two principal fountaining areas northeast. At three o'clock there was increase in activity with twelve fountains in action and overflow of the shelf on the east side of the island.

At eleven o'clock on the morning of April 25 the lake was perhaps 325 feet below the rim, but in general at this time the rate of rising had decreased, so as to allow heavy spatter benches to build. Some of these became overweighted and fell into the lake from time to time. The channel between crag and island was stagnant. A rounded point of shore was extending itself into the south side of the lake.

On April 26 at three o'clock in the afternoon with south wind the lake was inspected from the southeast and north stations. It was brimming full and semi-circular spatter cones on the bank were overflowing northeast, east and south. Crusts covered the northwest and southwest ends from which the streaming proceeded. From the north station it was evident that the north and west floors were wider than the east floor and while the south floor was still wider the lake was more nearly central to the pit than it has been at any time since January, 1912. The island, moreover, was almost central to the lake. On this date there was no sign of much recent overflow.

The following report from the Whitney Laboratory of Seismology is submitted by H. O. Wood:

''During the week ending with April 26 no local earthquakes have been registered. Three or four doubtful wave-groups are found. One fairly well-marked teleseism of small apparent amplitude occurred. Besides this there was recorded with very small amplitude the chief phase of a feeble teleseism; and possibly of a second—the latter so feeble that it is uncertain. Microseismic motion has been of small amplitude, increasing slightly toward the end of the week. Volcanic vibration has been stronger than usual, with short and long 'storm' intervals. Tilting has been as usual.''

T. A. JAGGAR, JR., Director.

TECHNOLOGY STATION, May 4.—The week ending on May 3 on Kilauea Volcano has been stormy, with southerly wind and thunder and lightning the first part of the week and northeasterly rains the latter part. The lightning storms of the week on Hawaii have been the heaviest in many years.

The lava pit of Halemaumau has sown a slight net rise in the lava pool with considerable oscillation of level. The lake and floor are the largest since January 4, 1912. Fumes have slightly increased in volume. On April 27 and 28 no visits were made to the pit on account of the stormy weather.

At two p. m. Saturday, April 29, the lake of lava, seen from the south station, was brimming and overflowing, the channel between the crags was much wider, and the floor had been overflowed so as to raise its margin several feet as shown by landmarks in the bordering wall.

While a crust could be seen between the west floor and the west crag, nevertheless that crag was now practically an island, the crust having a margin rampart on the west. This crag was now tilting again to the south-west instead of west, and its north point was uplifted twenty feet. The eastern island appeared also to have tilted back to the southwest, submerging the raised spatter bench which had been visible on the channel side. This island looks as though it had moved to the northeast. On the floor on four sides there were trickling leaf-like flows of overspatter. The wall fumarole southeast had disappeared. The lake appeared to be two or three feet below its banks. It had overflowed in the late afternoon, for there were glowing flows all over the floor. There were spatter grottoes and flames around the margin.

Measurements on April 30 at eleven-thirty a. m. made the lake 321 feet below the south rim of the pit, the west crust measuring thirteen feet higher than the lava in the southeast grottoes. The summit of the east island was forty-one feet above the lake and the west island fifty-five feet. The lake east-west was 775 feet long by 665 feet wide north-south. The floor northwest-southeast measured 1110 feet long and southwest-northeast about 1000 feet wide. The west island was 400 feet long and the east island 250 feet long. The channel between the islands was 150 feet wide.

The lake on April 30 was about 4 feet below its banks. The western crag was definitely an island. The floor had again been overflowed. Streaming was eastward north and south of the island, and northward in the channel between them. The platform around the east island was horizontal, while that of the west island was tilting strongly to the south-west. Slight coves were developing in the lake on the west, south-west south and south-east, but the north shore retained an elliptic curve. There was spatter on the banks south-west, south-east and north-east, and also on the north-east side of the eastern island with occassional inrush against the island. Slight falls of rock from the wall of the pit took place on the west, east and south-east. The floor sagged away from the walls leaving a raised lip around. Stalactites were visible in the grottoes. Blue fumes rose north-east of the east island, from the south-east bank, and from the fountains.

On May 1 at eleven a. m. the lake was overflowing on all sides. From eleven to twelve o'clock it subsided slightly. A steady crackling noise at the east end appeared to be due to a flow pouring into a marginal crack in the floor under its crust.

Cracking and foundering of the crust was going on at the west end. There was downsucking in the lake east of the island. The west island was still tipping southwestward. The streaming in the channel between the islands was now southward.

On May 2 at three p. m. the lake was only one foot below its banks but it had been much lower evidently, for large cracks had opened in the south floor both parallel and at right angles to the lake margin and there was avalanche debris all around the south margin of the floor from east to west. There was increased blue smoke, especially from the new cracks, where also white sublimates were deposited. The western island was still more tilted back to the south-west, five bench levels, each ten or more feet high, apbearing along its northern and eastern crags.

The eastern island was bordered by a horizontal platform not tilted at all. The crackling noise continued. Two small flows on the floor of recent origin appeared south-west and north. On the south-west violent border spatter was splashing high over the bank and dripping down into the cracks there.

There was a crust over the west end, thin blistered skins covered the lava emerging and streaming east from under this crust, the skins thickened towards the east, and north-east of the east island was a line of downsucking with fountains. Here "Old Faithful" was again in action at intervals from thirty to forty-five seconds. A large steady fountain played in the channel between the islands, which was now streaming northward again. Cracking and foundering occasionally broke up the west crust. Grottoes with stalactites could be seen north, north-east, east, south-east and south-west.

The following report from the Whitney Laboratory of Seismology is submitted by H O. Wood:

"During the week ending with May 3, three small local earthquakes have been registered. One of these was felt in Hilo, though not in the neighborhood of the observatory. There is no knowledge that the others were perceived. Microseismic motion has exhibited moderate to strong amplitudes during the week, particularly in the early part. In storms the amplitude of volcanic vibrations has been large instrumentally. During the latter part of the week there has been a slight progressive tilting to the east and north with moderate to strong diurnal variations."

T. A. JAGGAR, JR., Director.

TECHNOLOGY STATION, May 11.—During the week ending May 10, 1916, the lava lake of Halemaumau has continued to rise very slowly with overflows of the floor bench around the lake, but with only minor changes in the two islands. The platform of the east island has been slightly overflooded with new lava on its west side owing to its westward tilt.

On May 4, 1916, at six p. m. the lake was about three feet below its banks and the floor bench around it had been completely renewed by overflow during the preceding two days and glowing cracks could be seen in these flows after nightfall. A white spot in the north wall which had been a few feet above the floor was now covered. The pattern of the surface on the south floor was partly that made by cracking and foundering and this process was in progress breaking up the crusts of the west end of the lake.

There was no avalanche material on the floor and the fumes had decreased. An examination from the northwest station showed that one corner of the western island at its west end was still connected by an arch of crust with the border platform of the lake. There was seen to be a deep cove in the north-west end of the west island. The eastern island was in process of tilting to the south-west, two lifted shore benches showing along its north-east margin and the surface of its platform exhibiting distinct slope south-westward.

Explosion clouds from Mauna Loa, south-west flank, about
Photographed by Mr. H. O. Wood fro

,000-foot level, May 19, 1916, from 7:45 a. m. to 9:05 a. m.
the Hawaiian Volcano Observatory.

The explosion cloud from the Observatory at 8:30 a. m., showing double column and cloud rising over 20,000 feet above the vent.—Photo H. O. Wood.

On May 5 at eleven a. m. there was little change except that the south shore platform of the lake showed new lava formed by cracking and foundering. It was not clear whether the source of this lava was from border cracks in the floor bench or from crusted overflow. The flows on the bench were very hot and glowing, there were niches in the bank of the lake especially south-east, east and north-east; the bank was about one foot high at the west end and three feet high at the east end. At five p. m. there was no marked change.

On May 7 at one p. m. the lake was nearly brimming with spatter slopping over on the north-east and south-east. The surface was generally quiet and the whole west half of the lake was blanketted over. There was occasional fountaining north-east of the east island and the streaming was various with general eastward trend. There were fresh flows on the south-west floor apparently from the lake and no fresh rock falls.

At three p. m. on May 8 the lake was overflowing south-east, south, south-west, west and north-west. There were no fresh flows north-east and east. New tumbles of rock from the walls lay on the floor platform east, south and north-west. The lake was so high that the east island was narrowed by overflow on its west side, and the lowest of the five benches of the west island was submerged. There was spatter north-east and south-east and fountaining at the Old Faithful locality, east of the east island, and in the channel between the two islands.

The streaming was eastward north and south of the islands and northward in the channel. The west end was crusted. The eastward streaming surface skins moved with the current and the noise was of plashing. The correspondence of overflow and rockfalls on the western floor bench as against the absence of these things north-east suggests a slight weighing down of the western floor to loosen the rocks above.

On May 9 at noon the floor platform had been built still higher and there were active overflows all around the lake especially south, west and north. The eastward streaming surface skins from north-west and south-west met in a line of vigorous fountaining trend- east island. The spatter rampart at the ing eastward from the east point of the east end of the lake was seen to cave in and the lake broke through and overflowed the eastern platform to the wall. On the south-east a spatter wall was building along the bank. The rock-falls at the south margin of the floor were not yet covered by new flows. The islands were unchanged. At the edge of the pit the fumes were strong but wholly transparent.

On this day a warm cavern in the northeastern part of Kilauea crater which has been frequently entered in the past was found to be wholly impenetrable owing to the heat of the steam emerging from it. The cavern north of Halemaumau known as "Pele's Reception Room" is also very warm in contrast to its condition two years ago, this access of steam to the chambers in the lava crust of the crater being due to the excessive rainfall of the past winter. In the cool of the early mornings at the present time vast volumes of visible steam rise from the whole surface of the floor of the greater crater, and with the right atmospheric conditions are sucked in to the hot gas column above the lake and may condense as a high spectacular cumulus rising at least 3000 feet above the edge of Halemaumau. On warm, dry days, on other hand, the gas column from the lava rises and is blown away to leeward without any condensation of visible steam whatever, although the steaming postal rift one hundred yards from the crater rim always emits clouds of visible water vapor, whatever the relative humidity of the air.

The fume from the boiling lake is transparent, blue in reflected light and very faintly brown when seen against the sky. This color is at present so slight that at three p. m. May 5, on approaching Halemaumau from the desert to the south, two miles away, no trace whatever of the rising fume could be seen by the writer to guide him toward Halemaumau. On a similar trip a fortnight earlier the faint brown fume served as a guiding landmark.

On May 10 at eleven-thirty a. m. from the southeast station the lake appeared relatively stationary, the floor platform showing that slow rising had continued. Fresh flows occupied a zone between the edge of the lake and the wall, and the heat at the border of the pit was oppressive. The light southerly wind made clouds of Pele's hair rise in the eddy up the southeast and southwest walls. A horseshoe niche had been built on the northeast bank of the lake. Streaming was eastward and there were meeting currents in the channel between the islands and east of the east island. There was some rumbling noise as well as plashing. The lake was about one foot below the bank, the lower benches of the islands showing distinctly. The last remnants of the southwest talus slopes still rise above the floor of the pit about 20 feet.

The following report of the Whitney Laboratory of Seismology is submitted by H. O. Wood:

"During the week ending with May 10 two small local earthquakes have been recorded,—and two or more wave groups of doubtful character. The earlier shock occurred late in the afternoon on May 4 and was felt perceptibly in the open at the margin of Halemaumau but not at the observatory or at the Volcano House. Origin at the southwest is indicated therefore. Motion of volcanic vibration has continued strong, sporadically, and microseismic motion has been as usual. The slow tilt noted earlier to the north and east has halted and tilting to the southwest, in compensation, has set in.

The observatory has this week been honored by a visit from Dr. Herbert E. Gregory, Silliman professor of geology in the Yale University and successor in that institution to the late honored James D. Dana, an ardent student of Hawaiian volcanoes. Professor and Mrs. Gregory have been traveling in Australia and remained at the volcano from May 4 to May 8.

T. A. JAGGAR, JR., Director.

TECHNOLOGY STATION, May 18. —The week ending May 17, 1916, at the inner lava pit of Kilauea volcano has produced extraordinary changes in the two islands in the lake, along with continued rising and moderate overflowing of the floor bench around the lake. The lake is now less than 300 feet below the rim. A heavy mat of Pele's hair has been built all over the north wall of the pit and covers the north floor bench at the border of the lake, resembling brown moss. The heat is very strong on the edge.

Especially remarkable through all these weeks is the absence of visible fume. Seen from the Volcano House the well known steam of the postal rift and the road terminus localities rises in dense white clouds, but the vastly greater volumes of gas pushing upward through the boiling lava is hardly discernible except as a faint bluish puff at the moment of fountaining. There is no smoke from the floor bench or walls. That the gas is there is amply evident when the observer is caught in the invisible cloud, the strong sulphurous acid being almost unbearable. That water vapor must be in very small quantity in this gas is shown by the total absence of any condensation to leeward, even when the ring of outlying steam jets is condensing heavily.

A pronounced rise between Thursday, May 11, and Saturday, May 13, dislocated the great block or blocks beneath the lake, the peaks of which make the islands, so that they moved eastward and the larger western one also moved northward against the bank. This movement was undoubtedly a rotation and sliding of the blocks on the saucer-like sides of the cup containing the lake, the movement being in the general direction of that deepest hole under the Old Faithful fountain, which is always revealed when the lake goes down and out.

It will be remembered that on May 10 at 11:30 a. m. the lake was down very slightly with rumbling, and the southwest talus stood twenty feet above the floor. The larger island was against the west bank, the smaller island out near the center of the lake and the streaming on both the north and south sides of the little island was eastward.

On May 11 at 2 p. m. both islands had moved eastward gradually, the large western one the more, so that the channel between the islands was narrowed, and a considerable channel had opened between the large island and the west bank. There were splashing grottoes west, north and northeast and the streaming was all toward the northeast bank, and from a point on the west bank. There was a surface stream through the new channel northeastward, another around the south side of the islands in a curve southeast, east and north, and a branch northward through the channel between the islands.

In this last channel there was much fountaining, and Old Faithful could be identified northeast of the small island. There was new overflow on the southeast floor. The lake was about one foot below the banks. The large island appeared thirty feet high on its east side sloping to the lake level on the west. The small island appeared five feet high. This day's position seemed to indicate that the island block had straightened up to occupy the middle of the funnel.

On May 12 at 2:30 p. m. conditions were similar but the larger island had moved northward. Fountaining had diminished. At 3 p. m. there was a rise with increased activity.

At 8 p. m. on May 13 from the east and southeast stations glowing cracks could be seen all over the south bench showing that strong overflow and rising had taken place. The large island had migrated bodily northward as though by rotation in a horizontal plane so that its western horn impinged against the north bank and the U-shaped cove on that side of the island was nearly closed. The channel between the islands was narrowed. The small island was nearly submerged, but still exhibited slight southwesterly tilt to its surface. There was no marked change in the tilt of the large island. The west end of the lake was now its widest part and the streaming arose on the northwest and flowed around the islands to the northeast and through the channel northward.

On May 14 at 10 a. m. the lake was brimming and there were fresh flows north, west and south and three small festooned flows on the east bench. The large island showed four uptilted benches on its northeast side. The small island was a triangle only a few feet high. The lake was flush with the shore on the west and about one foot down on the east. There were fountains west and northeast of the small island and a triangular patch of tranquil skin lay north of it with north flowing currents on both sides. Looking down on the large island from the northwest station, it lay directly below, it was shaped like a huge inverted V with its west leg against the bank and a slight opening between the bank and its east leg.

The southwest floor had built up at least fifteen feet, and only the extreme tips of the southwest talus cones remained visible. There were spatter grottoes north, east and south.

On May 15 at 11 a. m. the lake had lowered to a point about two feet below the banks, revealing the fifth bench of the large island and a larger platform around the small island. There was now a channel about two feet wide between each horn of the large island and the bank.

On May 16 at 11 a. m. the only marked change was the presence of fresh small overflows on the bench all around the lake. A very small fall of rocks took place from the southwest wall to the floor. A raised bench on the southwest side of the large island suggested that it was now tilting to the northeast. Streaming was especially rapid in the channel between the islands. The lake was covered with glistening, thin, rapid-moving black skins. It was elliptical in outline except for a cape at the south.

On May 17 at noon the observed tilt of the previous day in the large island had taken effect in bringing the northeast horn of the island against the bank and opening the channel of the northwest horn so that the lava was streaming into this channel from the west. Along with this movement both islands appeared to have migrated farther northeast with a slight tilt to the southwest. In the northern cove-cavern of the large island cracking and foundering were in progress. The small island was now heart-shaped with the point on the southwest and a cove on the northeast. Five distinct benches could be counted on the east side of the large island. Both the channel between the islands and that east of the small island were narrower. The south point of the large island was now east of the center of the lake. The greater lake was now west of the islands, where before it was northeast of them.

The streaming was out into the lake from under the west bank where a slight cove had formed. There was pronounced blistering and minute bubble fountaining in this hot area of outward streaming, in marked contrast to the thicker festooned skins without blisters at the east end of the lake. Travelling fountains moved in a line northeastward toward the point of the small island and northward from its northwest point. Old Faithful was vaguely identifiable at the south end of this last line. There were fresh overflows on the floor bench, east, south, west and northwest, the last two following the bench around respectively southward and northward. A small tumble of freshly fallen rocks lay on the south edge of the floor.

The following report from the Whitney Laboratory of Seismology is submitted by Mr. H. O. Wood:—

During the week ending with May 17 four very small definite local earthquakes have been registered,—and two to four wave groups of doubtful character.

The amplitude of microseismic motion has continued moderate; that of volcanic vibration relatively large, especially in storms. A strong progressive northerly tilt has gone on during the week—with a very slight tilt to the east.

T. A. JAGGAR, JR., Director.

TECHNOLOGY STATION, May 25. —During the week ended with May 24 the magma surface in Halemaumau has continued to rise with oscillations in height of stand quite as in recent weeks. Minor changes in activity and in configuration have occurred and the islands have shifted in position in complicated ways. These details will be described by the Director in a later report. Space is needed here for an account of the outbreak of Mauna Loa.

OUTBREAK AT MOUNA LOA.

The beginnings of this eruption were noticed first in the early morning of May 19.

Information at second hand states that a smart earthquake was felt at sea off the south shore of Hawaii at about two a. m. in the morning of May 19 and that then or slightly after a glow was seen high up on the south slope of the mountain.

During the morning and afternoon hours of May 19 a swarm of local earthquakes was registered. All were very feeble movements, even when judged from the seismographic point of view. The earliest was recorded at a little before three in the morning. A lull followed, beginning in late forenoon. Later on frequent occurrence was resumed.

On the evening of May 18 and the night, morning and forenoon of May 19 the weather was brilliantly clear. Nearly the whole profile of Mauna Loa was outlined sharply against the sky. From late evening on there was brilliant moonlight. Until midnight, and at six-fifteen a. m., no signs of eruption were seen from the vicinity of the observatory.

At about seven a. m. a group of cloud-forms appeared high on the flank of Loa at the south. In this vicinity these were first seen by Joseph Moniz. Though these were peculiar in appearance and development they were thought to be clouds for some time, and more than a half-hour elapsed before they were called to the attention of the writer, at about seven thirty-five a. m. By this time it was sure that these were fume clouds rising rapidly above a place of outbreak.

The writer immediately began making a series of photographic records of this section,—twelve views in all. The first was made at seven forty-five a. m and the last at noon.

When first seen by the writer there were two chief standing columns in which fumes were rushing rapidly straight up to merge in a double cumulus crown. The column higher up the slope was larger and taller and it was separated from the other by a space clear of fumes of about its own width, say 1000 feet. The higher column rose probably 10,000 to 12,000 feet above the mountain profile and the lower from 8000 to 10,000 feet. The place of outbreak was at an altitude judged to be about 8000 feet. It surely was less than 10,000 feet. As it was hidden behind the mountain profile accurate estimate was impossible. Very quickly other subordinate columns appeared and very soon all had merged into a single pillar of uprushing fumes much larger in diameter than the whole when first seen. At 7.45 there was still a double crown indicating the position of the two dominant fume columns. Also a smoke ring was seen enclosing the upper part of the column below the crown.

The form of this eruption cloud underwent rapid changes as continued emanation of fumes added to its bulk and the convection currents and the winds at different altitudes continually reshaped it. By eight a. m. the crown had reached a height of 20,000 feet or more, and the diameter of the column had increased to a mile and a half or over.

Shortly after eight o'clock the uprush of fumes began to diminish, and by eight-thirty the two dominant columns were again distinctly separated. The cloud had developed a beautiful mushroom shape with two stalks. By nine a. m. or a little later the flumes were greatly diminished and the cloud form was much frayed. By ten o'clock it required keen observation to detect further emanation of fumes, and by noon nothing could be seen but a frayed stratum of high cloud overspreading the sky above the mountain. This showed rippling; and it persisted until after sunset.

A small amount of lava was ejected at the time of this outbreak. This was seen by men high on the slopes back of Naalehu and Kahuku. But this action was quickly over.

At sunset on the nineteenth very thin wisps of fume were seen rising at or near this place of outbreak. No fumes were seen on the twentieth, but again at time of sunset on the twenty-first they were seen in the same place; and they then appeared a trifle more pronounced.

After a lull of less than twenty-four hours small local earthquakes began to be registered again with greater frequency and greater amplitude than before. Intervals of quiet were short. This action continued and led to expectation of the outbreak of flow.

Flow broke out, lower down the slope than the place of first outbreak, in the late evening of May 21. It was seen earliest, at eleven-fifteen p. m., by the writer,—so far as present information extends. It was at once brought to the attention of the Director, and others at the Volcano House, and from there the news was spread.

Probably the outbreak was noticed almost as soon as it occurred. The night was clear except for a low bank of clouds at the north-east. At ten p. m. there was no suggestion of illumination anywhere along the southern segment of the mountain profile. At about eleven-fifteen p. m. the writer went to the observatory to see that seismographs were in good working order before retiring. The moon had just risen but it was hidden behind the bank of clouds at the northeast. A very faint diffuse moonlight was spread over the sky. Upon mounting the observatory porch a faint light was seen radiating from a point behind the mountain profile much lower down the slope than the place of first outbreak. The effect was similar to that sometimes produced here just as a planet or a bright star drops below the profile. However, after inspection of the seismographs,—perhaps three minutes later,—this radiating light had become more definite although the illumination of the sky by the moon had grown brighter. Almost immediately it took on a pinkish hue. Then the news was spread at once.

Judging by the rapidity of its development in the first ten minutes after it was discovered the outbreak did not take place earlier than eleven p. m. H. S. T., and probably not earlier than eleven-ten p. m.

In the first ten or fifteen minutes after its discovery the light at the fountain head grew rapidly and a small diffuse cloud of fumes appeared. This increased also and the glow grew brighter and more ruddy. Shortly the fumes at the top began to drift to the northwest up the mountain slope behind the profile. At the same time we detected a progressive extension of a faint ruddy illumination down the slope behind the profile. Flow had begun.

Between eleven-forty-five p. m. and six-forty-five of the next morning the Director and the writer motored from the observatory to a point beyond the western branch of the flow of 1907 and back again, making many stops to observe and photograph between Waiohinu and the turning point. Emanation of fumes at the fountain head increased steadily and the brilliancy of the illumination also, until daylight intervened. From the upland flats near Kahuku and westward a long line of faint red illumination was seen extending to the right from the fountain head. At first it was thought to be light from the surface of a pool, but as it elongated rapidly it was soon thought to be a line of illumination above a flowing stream. This afterwards was confirmed. Its course was estimated to be about south south-east.

Upon returning to the observatory the true azimuth of the apparent center of the fume column was determined at South 66 degrees West. This projected upon the map indicated a source on the south-southwest flank of the mountain near the line of the upper branch of the flow of 1907 at an altitude of about 7000 feet,—a little above Puu o Keokeo. This has since been confirmed (though it seems likely that a multiple source will be found).

Early in the evening of May 23, as a member of a party of six, the writer again reached the upland flats west of Waiohinu, and after the clouds lifted a great change was seen. A flow had progressed rapidly down the Southwest slope toward Honomalino in Kona, and a great band of fire-light reaching not less than three quarters of a mile above the mountain profile to the layer of clouds overhead and not less than seven and a half miles from the fountain head to the front, illuminated the scene. The road was congested with motors and wild rumors were current. After going to within four or five miles of Honomalino we were warned to turn back on account of the supposed rapid approach of the flow to the road and uncertainty as to its exact course. Accordingly after a long uncertain wait, we returned to Kahuku flats and spent the night in watching from there. After midnight the glow above the flow toward Honomalino rapidly decreased and before morning it had practically vanished.

Between twelve and half-past one o'clock a. m. a rapid spread of illumination to the right of the fountain head was interpreted as a flow toward Kahuku. It was soon over. This has been confirmed.

By eleven o'clock a. m. of May 23, the writer reached the front of the Kona flow, about three miles by trail from the road at Honomalino. It was already moving very slowly. At the front it was a flow of a-a and the details of its behavior must be left for a later report. It appeared to have a width of one-fourth to one-third of a mile. In the late afternoon of this day its forward motion had stopped altogether. On the twenty-fourth loud explosive sounds led to the report that it had been rejuvenated but these were due to the action of the hot lava on vegetation. This flow has stopped at a considerable distance from the road. Its further motion is problematical.

On the night of May 23, and again on May 24, the illumination seen from the observatory was very brilliant. There was no suggestion of diminution in action at the source. The location and elongation of the fume cloud, however, pointed to a flow toward Kahuku. This has been verified by a visit by the Director at two p. m. on May 24, and by visits by others at seven p. m. on the twenty-fourth and at two a. m. on the twenty-fifth. On the twenty-fourth its front was eight miles from the road and a day later it had advanced a mile or more along a course trending between the flows of 1868 and 1887.

According to a report from a visit to the source by parties from the Kona side the source of this later flow is below Puu o Keokeo * while that of the Kona flow was above it. This report made mention of the usual spectacular phenomena seen at a fountain head.

At last reports this Kahuku flow was still moving at a slow rate which

* Erroneous.

if maintained, would bring it to the road after several days.

A party consisting of Messrs. J. W. Waldron and T. Hardy reached a point about 6500 feet above sea in Kahuku and spent the night of May 22-23 there. They were able to confirm the inferences regarding the two earlier minor flows to the south-southeast and south and they saw fire-fountains of unknown height at the source. They also saw the upper reaches of the Kona flow. They communicated many details regarding their observations which must await place in later reports. Thus far the event has been complicated and conditions not favorable for sustained work. More coherent and detailed accounts of it will be given later.

Hundreds of weak local earthquakes have been registered in the interval since the beginning and these continue. Only three or four have been felt in the vicinity of the observatory; but many more were felt in the south part of the Island.

H. O. WOOD, Associate.

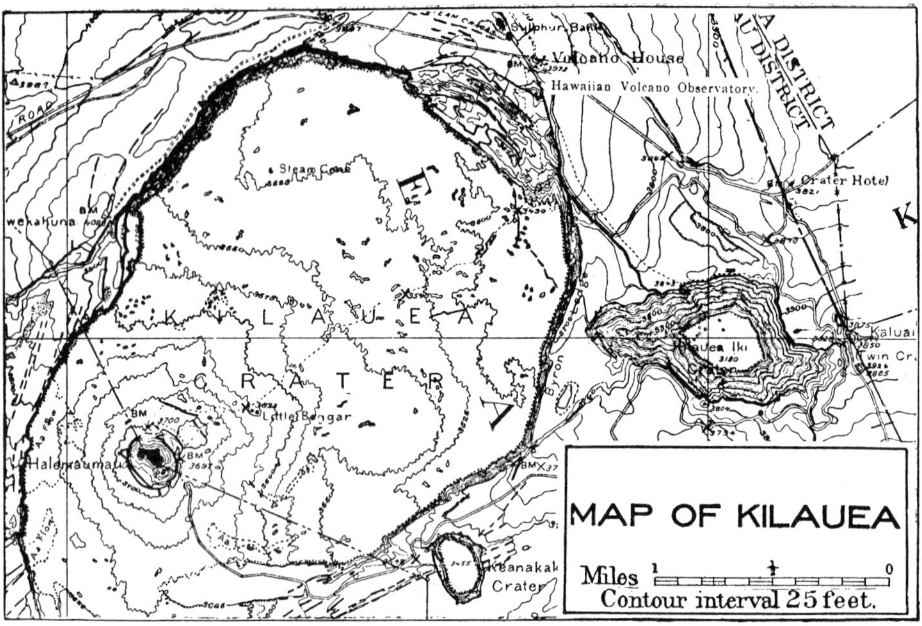

HAWAIIAN VOLCANO RESEARCH ASSOCIATION.

This society is a voluntary one, made up of subscribers to scientific work which is being executed by the Massachusetts Institute of Technology.

In 1915 there are about 100 subscribers in Hawaii and elsewhere, firms and individuals. A group of firms and persons in Hilo built the main observatory building in the spring of 1912. Publications to date have been weekly reports since the summer of 1911, now reprinted in Honolulu in monthly form. The Massachusetts Institute of Technology will publish annual reports, of which the introductory number was printed in 1912.

The weekly bulletin as it appears in the Advertiser is reprinted as a leaflet and sent to regular annual subscribers to the work of the Association. L. A. Thurston is president of the Board of Directors of the Association, and R. W. Shingle is treasurer. New subscribers who are interested in volcanoes will be welcomed in the Association. The Association aims: (1) To record volcanic activity and earthquakes in Hawaii; (2) to attract scientific men hither for special studies; (3) to promote the establishment of volcano observatories all over the world. The annual dues of regular members are $5; patrons of the Assocaition subscribe larger amounts.

WHITNEY LABORATORY OF SEISMOLOGY.

The Whitney Laboratory of Seismology is equipped with two Bosch-Omori 100 kg tromometers registering N-S and E-W motion, a heavy Omori tromometer registering E-W motion, and an Omori "ordinary Seismograph" designed for registering strong earthquakes in all three components of motion. These are seated on concrete piers in a closed basement room having practically constant temperature, beneath the chief Observatory building near the hotel. Time is referred to a rated chronometer, checked at intervals by solar observations with a transit. Both instruments are loaned by the College of Hawaii. Hawaiian standard time (H. S. T.) is 10 hrs. 30 min. slower than Greenwich time.

CANCANI SCALE OF SEISMIC INTENSITY.

Expressed by accelerations measured in millimeters per second per second.

I.	Instrumental	0.0	2.5
II.	Very slight	2.5	5.0
III.	Slight	5.0	10.0
IV.	Sensible, mediocre	10.0	25.0
V.	Rather strong	25.0	50.0
VI.	Strong	50.0	100.0
VII.	Very strong	100.0	250.0
VIII.	Ruinous	250.0	500.0
IX.	Disastrous	500.0	1000.0
X.	Very disastrous	1000.0	2500.0
XI.	Catastrophic	2500.0	5000.0
XII.	Great catastrophe	5000.0	10000.0

Grade IV. is ordinarily the minimum perceived by the senses; and in grade XII. the acceleration, or rate of change of motion (jerk) reaches that of terrestrial gravitation.

In the standard form of report the maximum intensity or acceleration, designated by the symbol a, or max. a, is given in the conventional unit, **the milligal.** The milligal is a measure of acceleration, such that 1 milligal = 1/100 mm. per sec. per sec. = 10 μ per sec. per sec. The Cancani scale, here **defined** in terms of millimeters per sec. per sec., can therefore be expressed in **milligals by multiplying each of the numbers by 100.**

WEEKLY BULLETIN
OF THE
Hawaiian Volcano Observatory

Vol. IV. HONOLULU, HAWAII, JUNE, 1916. No. 6

TECHNOLOGY STATION, June 1, 1916.—The fortnight ending May 31, 1916, has been marked by the outbreak of Mauna Loa and by a culmination of the long continued rise of the lava in Kilauea, followed by subsidence. The lava in Kahuku flowed vigorously from the evening of May 21 to May 27 and thereafter appears to have diminished in activity. The seismographic registration of earthquakes has also diminished almost to the normal.

Mauna Loa Outbreak

By T. A. JAGGAR, JR., Director.

"The lava flows of May 21, and thereafter on Mauna Loa add two more expected episodes to the sequence of the recent eruptive period of that volcano. This sequence was fully described in the Director's annual address before the Hawaiian Volcano Research Association in Honolulu, March 10, 1915. (This Bulletin, April, 1915.) It was there pointed out that there should be yet to come (1) a low level in Kilauea, (2) a short lived summit outbreak of Mauna Loa near June or December within four years from the beginning of 1915, and (3) a lava flow from Mauna Loa. By analogy with the lava flows of 1899 and 1907 and some others during the previous thirty years, the flow was not expected quite so soon as the present date, and it was not expected on the south side of the mountain.

The occurrence of two Kahuku flows within ten years is contrary to the habit of the volcano since 1868. It was expected, however, that the next flow on the south side would come from a vent higher than that of 1907, and this has happened. It was further expected from the experience of the past that the next south flow, like former ones, would be accompanied by many earthquakes in Kau; and this also has happened in the present instance.

The attempt at forecast, therefore, made by the writer as far back as 1911 and published in 1912, has been verified in the Mokuaweoweo outbreak of November 25, 1914, in the interval of eighteen months of quiet following it, in the high gaseous explosion of Mauna Loa May 19, 1916, and in the relatively quiet outburst of flowing lava at a lower point forty hours later, this point being somewhat higher than the place of last eruption on that side of the mountain; and in the occurrence of all these happenings at dates near the solstice.

The expectable low level in Halemaumau occurred in 1913-14, and anticipated by a year the visible emission of lava from Mauna Loa, so that only in a general way and through a long term may the two volcanoes in this case be said to alternate eruptions. The alternation will be fairly satisfactory, however, if Kilauea exhibits strong rising and perhaps overflow during the next three years. For conclusion of the theoretical complete sequence in Mauna Loa, there remains to come the period of solidification of the present lava flows and a repose period of six or seven years to follow.

A summary of events in this eruptive episode on Mauna Loa is as follows:

(1) Explosion of gas and foamy lava 7:15 a. m., May 19, 1916, on the great southwest rift of Mauna Loa about the 10,000-foot line, reaching by 8 a. m. a height of 20,000 feet above the vent and spreading from north to south along the rift for a distance between one and two miles. This ejection ceased about 10 a. m. Many small earthquakes accompanied this eruption.

WEEKLY BULLETIN
of the
Hawaiian Volcano Observatory

Published Monthly at Honolulu, Hawaii, by the Hawaiian Volcano Research Association

L. W. de Vis-Norton........Secretary

Entered as second-class matter January 20, 1914, at the post-office at Honolulu, Hawaii, under the Act of August 24, 1912.

(2) On May 20 and 21 earthquakes were very numerous in Kau and were occasionally of moderate strength. They were felt principally in Hilea, and were stronger and more numerous at a homestead five miles northwest of Hilea in the direction of Puu o Keokeo. Hundreds of local earthquakes were recorded by the seismographs of the Observatory.

(3) At 11:15 p. m. May 21, a faint glow over Kahuku was seen from the Observatory and developed intensity during the night. On making the half circuit during the night of Puu o Keokeo by the government road, a column of fume illumined red from below was seen by the writer at apparently about the same distance inland everywhere from Waiohinu to Kapua. It was evident that Puu o Keokeo was approximately at the center of the disturbance at an elevation of 6900 feet. All along the road a brilliant radiance could be seen extending southeast and east from the fume column, indicating that an extensive pool or flow of lava was spreading eastward from the vent. All was dark to the westward. W. Vredenburg, manager of the Kahuku Ranch, rode at 2 a. m. May 22 to the edge of the upland between the 1868 and 1887 flows above the koa forest, and saw two aa flows in rapid motion headed respectively southeast and south south-east.

These were about ten miles from the road. At 5 a. m. May 22 from Kahuku Ranch gate, the main fume column was seen to extend itself in a series of puffs developing to the right; that is, up the rift northeastward. It is possible that this represented a splitting open of the fissure in that direction to develop the vent which gave rise to the Kona flow. However, it is, asserted that the first vent of all, on May 21, opened some miles above Puu o Keokeo.

(4) During the day May 22, the accumulated lavas of the upland were discharging southwestward from a vent about two miles above Puu o Keokeo. As no glow was seen west of the vent before 6 a. m., this southwest flow across Honomalino Ranch must have progressed at least six miles in twelve hours, for at 6 p. m. it was within three miles of the road at Honomalino.

The settlement here lies in a valley and the flow was headed directly for the houses. The timber could be seen burning from the road and the flowing lava, advancing down a ten degree slope, from the housetops. Detonations from exploding gas, and the crash of falling trees, could be heard. The homes were temporarily evacuated but fortunately the flow stopped at this point, its front resting on a hillside forested with lehua, kukui and guava. This flow was rugged aa eight to twelve feet in thickness and an eighth of a mile wide along its lower course.

At 8 o'clock on this night, Monday May 22, the fiery radiance above the fountain head and the flows probably reached its greatest brilliancy. Unlike the night before, the glow was now all to the west of the column of fountain fumes which shot up in purling volutes on the right spreading to the west in a high cloudy haze, which was lighted from below a bright red from the glowing river of melt in Honomalino. On the left a great purplish swirl of smoke from the burning forest rose and curled over to the east. There was darkness over the Kahuku flow, showing that for the time the lavas on that side were sluggish and congealing.

(5) During the night May 22-23 there was revival in Kahuku. Messrs. Waldron and Hardy found the front of the first flow nearly motionless at altitude 5500 feet by aneroid. At 1 a. m. May 23, an arm of this flow more southerly in trend developed near the

source and for two hours advanced brilliantly. Then it became sluggish, cooled down and stopped. About daylight the western glow and the fountaining at the source had both diminished.

(6) On May 22 motion within the Honomalino flow diminished rapidly. In the morning flowing lava could be seen and trees were still being overturned. At 3 p. m. high ohia trees were still standing in the midst of the flow, their trunks blazing, a few blocks were tumbling at the front but no pasty lava was to be seen. The side of the flow resembled a heap of burning anthracite coal, with flames playing through incandescent blocks, and the only odors were a strong smell of burnt charcoal and occasional coal-gas.

At 7 p. m. the glow seen from the south indicated distinctly a revival of the south-east flow toward Kahuku. All was dark west of the fume column. There was a tapering line of reflected light on the clouds trending SSE, and in the same direction along the ground below could be seen a low straight-topped film of smoke, highest near the source and lowest at the lava front. Over this smoke could be seen the radiant glow from the lava.

(7) May 24. On this date the writer inspected the Kahuku flow eight miles from the road and in the region between the 1868 and the 1887 flows. At about seven miles there is a broad rolling paddock with sparse koa. Above this is a steeper slope of koa forest, down which the ancient aa flow, Pele o Iki, had cut a swath. Above this forest is an extensive bushy upland consisting of old pahoehoe and aa which stretch out as far as the eye can reach toward distant cones and on the west to the rugged ridges of the 1887 flow.

On reaching the upper edge of the koa slope, it was found that the fronts of the new flow had moved down more than a mile since the previous morning and were now close to the forest. On riding up the west side of the flow, which was in process of overriding Pele o Iki, we came to the moving lava advancing in billows and cascades of red hot viscous liquid and overflowing the already cooled aa surface of the previous day. The moving liquid lay in streams from 100 to 300 feet in width and one of these only a hundred yards from us was coursing down the main lobe of the previous day, driving in front of it a fan-shaped pool of dark red color with a sugary surface which advanced at the rate of perhaps a half a mile per hour. The cascades above carried huge rafts and boulders of aa ten to thirty feet in diameter, and these blocks moved along majestically in a procession, about as fast as a man might walk. The advancing flood became deflected to the west and tumbled over the bank of congealed lava into the vegetation at our feet not fifty yards away. The liquid would develop a cindery surface and then congeal into what appeared to be a glowing mass of coals.

The only odor was of the carbon gases and these were strong and oppressive, particularly as we were directly to leeward and a fresh breeze was blowing from the northeast. The heat was intense, and occasionally fierce small whirlwinds developed at the edge of the hot flood and moved along the border with a whistling noise, carrying up clouds of grit and smoke. Out in the molten river gigantic bubbles would occasionally burst with a thud but there were no fountains as in Halemaumau. Cascade beyond cascade could be seen up stream vanishing into the hot vibrant fume of the distance and I was much impressed by the piling-up effect of this motion, the advance being always by overflow. This is in marked contrast to the usual mechanism of pahoehoe flow where the new floods push out from beneath in tongues which break through the skin, or else a crust breaks up and founders in the rising melt. No crusts whatever were seen forming on this aa. There were moving blocks and there was the red hot flood. When it cooled, it appeared to cool as a unit and the new floods overflowed it. There were one or two patches of roundish shape in the chilled part of the flow which resembled pahoehoe. These were probably blocks transported from far above where near the vent the flow actually was pahoehoe.

The front of the overriding flow was advancing in the direction S.15° E. The under-flow was in two lobes, one leaf-shaped and headed in this direction, and one more to the east pushing forward very slowly at a rate estimated at sixty feet per hour.

Between 2 p. m. and 7 p. m., according to Messrs. Bonesteel and Moses, the fan-like advance pool which we had seen, overran the leaf-shaped lobe and coursed down the koa slope carrying the forest before it, following the western margin of Pele o Iki. This became the main Kahuku front and flowed a mile farther stopping in the forest about seven miles from the road. The flood would surround the trees, burn them and uproot them, and in some cases the koas were seen to be carried along upright like blazing torches before they toppled over and were engulfed. At the front the flow was only a few hundred feet wide.

An interesting mechanism which occurred whenever the flow poured over old cavernous pahoehoe was furnished by gas explosions in caves. This was probably coal gas mixed with air. Detonations were frequently heard, and the writer saw the dust from one of these explosions a few feet away, puff up through cracks above a cavern. The old rock was very hot, and it was evident that some of the hot gases and perhaps the new lava had penetrated a subterranean tube. L. A. Thurston in the same region on the following day found several of these places where the whole roof of the cavern had blown off and large blocks of rock were strewn about several feet from the orifice.

The noise of the lava itself in motion was not great. It was a splashing sound, and where the pasty lava dripped the quickly cooled droplets fell with a tinkle. The bubbles bursting made thudding noises, but there was no sustained explosive fountaining such as the writer had imagined. In general the advancing floods were unexpectedly noiseless. The horses advanced fearlessly to within two hundred feet of where the liquid lava to windward was actually cascading on to the grass and bushes, and showed as complete indifference as they would to a camp fire. In the forest, of course, there were the noises of falling timber and crackling flames.

The various estimates of rate of motion of lava flows which different observers reported of these flows, were based usually on observed progress of the runways compared to a man's pace. But the runways are no measure of the movement of the lobe as a whole, nor is the movement of a lobe a measure of the advance of the whole arm of lava which may be slowly pushing down a grade. The flows progress apparently by impulses of overflooding into hollows, the central vent above feeding a great pooled area. Somewhere the margin of this area finds outlets. From what the writer saw he would judge five miles an hour to be a fast rate for the rush of the runways, and a half-mile an hour for average general progress of a flow as a whole during its most rapid advance on a steep slope. This progress appears to be not gradual, but in spasms, with intervals of many hours of stagnation.

At midnight May 24, the profile north from the Kahuku gate showed a column of dark smoke thought to be burning forest, bright flames at two points shooting up on its right, and strong radiance both east and west of the smoke column. The smoke and flames were at the front of the Kahuku flow, and so nearer the observer, while the radiance was from the floods of molten stuff in the distance.

R. McWayne about this time reported for the head of the Honomalino flow a cone about the 7000 foot level ejecting with a roar high lava fountains and blocks of rock. There were two main vents in action, both above Puu o Keokeo and in a line with it, the higher feeding several tongues in motion toward Kona, the lower supplying the Kahuku flows.

(8) Vredenburg left the Kahuku flow at 2 a. m. May 25. The main lobe had then advanced three quarters of a mile in twelve hours, and the eastern lobe had pushed forward along the east margin of Pele o Iki. The main front was stagnant and three hundred feet in width, widening above. The main direction was about S. 15° East.

During this day the main flow advanced a quarter of a mile farther, there was some activity and burning forest on the front of the east lobe, and to the westward glowing lava could be seen in motion overriding the flows already cooled.

At 11 p. m. May 25, the mountain profile showed a red general glow behind a screen of cloud, with rapid rising white cumulus over the fountain head.

(9) May 26. A second visit to the Honomalino flow on this day showed that it had cooled off remarkably. Only a few glowing and flaming cavities a few inches across could be found. The surface aa was cold. One could walk out over the middle of the flow. Nearly all the imprisoned timber had fallen. There was little smoke, but a hot refraction haze over the profile of aa showed that all was glowing inside, and this was evident when one looked into the deep cavities. Rare small explosions were heard. Many leaves on the fallen trees in the flow were still partially green. There was no channel discernible in the middle of this arm. The slope of the ground was carefully measured and found to be ten degrees.

L. A. Thurston's party visited the Kahuku flows. Motion was seen in a stream carrying a procession of large blocks within a branch flow extending south southwest from the upper part of the main flow. Rapid flow was seen in overriding layers of the main arm upstream. Vredenburg made his way on foot around the foot of the west branch, which he found nearly stagnant at the front and climbed Puu o Keokeo, a cone about 200 feet high. From there looking up the line of cones northeastward he saw a line of fuming vents, two nearer ones vomiting lava. The first was a throbbing pit in a cinder-cone seventy-five yards away sending a stream twelve feet wide towards Kahuku. The second, much farther away, was a cone with a red stream flowing down its Kona flank. The thunderous noise and a whiff of overpowering sulphurous gas drove him back along the line of white stained cracks which extends from Puu o Keokeo to the source of the 1887 flow. The flows of 1916 at the source are in part at least a rough pahoehoe.

(10) May 27, 1916. Messrs. Farrell, Bryan, Forbes and Barnes visited the source region from Papa. Mr. Farrell describes a line of fuming cracks as far as the eye could see up Mauna Loa north-northeast. A few miles north was a cone that appeared to be the first source of this lava eruption. From this a fresh flow had poured southward to a second nearer cone which was spouting lava in jets every few seconds. This flowed down in a northern branch of the Kona flow toward Papa, and was a very rough glistening sponge-like pahoehoe. Sulphur smell was noticed and the noise was a heavy roar attributed to the thudding fall of the fountain material. Lava could be seen in motion toward Kahuku from the vent to the south. Some Pele's hair was seen. There was no trembling of the ground observed.

The mountain profile from the south at 9 p. m. on May 27 showed marked dwindling of size of fume column and of glow. The fountain fume rose in small, rapid, bright jets and a band of slight radiance extended a short distance east from it; then came a wide zone of darkness and finally a slight whitish glare, probably a forest blaze at the extreme east limit of the lava. From the Volcano Observatory at Kilauea only a faint radiance was seen.

(11) At 8 a. m. May 28, Vredenburg was at the vents and saw sluggish pahoehoe emerging from the Kahuku vent, and occasional spasmodic spouting from the northern cone. He could see no lava flowing towards Kona. No movement was seen in the Kahuku flows.

(12) May 30 and 31, H. O. Wood and D. Lycurgus made the circuit of the Kahuku flows on the south, east and north. The fountaining at the sources was ceasing, and motion in the flows had stopped.

No glow has been seen over Kahuku from the Observatory since May 27 and no further reports of activity have come in. Registration of earthquakes has dwindled, but one very sharp shock was felt in Kau and recorded on the seismograms about 8:15 p. m. May 30.

Activity of Kilauea

During the fortnight May 18 to May 31, 1916, the rising lava column in the pit Halemaumau reached its highest point on May 25 at an elevation of 265 feet below the rim, then turned and subsided slowly until it was twenty-five feet below the floor of overflow, and an inner pit was formed. The two islands tended to subside with the lake, the small island more than the large one. If there has been sympathetic movement between Kilauea and the Mauna Loa eruption, it has been in the accentuated rise of the former from May 19 to May 24, the period of outbreak and maximum activity on the larger volcano, and in the unusual and definite subsidence of Kilauea lava from May 25 to May 31, corresponding with the gradual cessation of the Kahuku activity. By analogy with former years at the time of the June solstice, the present subsidence of Kilauea should be short lived, and there should be a revival of overflow of the bench toward the end of June. As usual with sinking lava in Halemaumau, the smoke in the pit has increased.

At 2 p. m. on May 18 the bank around the lake was about one foot high, the larger island lay with its eastern horn against the north bank, the smaller island lay midway between it and the east bank, and the surface streaming took its rise at the west end of the lake and flowed east and north. There was fountaining along the shore southwest, south, southeast and northeast. The central region was quiet except for an occasional fountain south of the larger island and heavy perpetual fountaining in Old Faithful region north of the small island. At 3 p. m. the lake had risen and was brimming on its western bank.

On May 19 at 12:30 p. m. the shore was four feet high on the east and one foot high on the west. The smaller island appeared larger and tilted eastward, rising four feet above the lake on the east side and seven feet on the west. The larger island had crushed the north bank of the lake, maintaining a channel ten feet wide between its western horn and the northwest bench. A new small islet about eight feet long and five feet wide appeared beside Old Faithful and east of it.

It appeared to be a submerged reef extension of the north point of the small island with a channel about one hundred feet wide between it and that point. Both the eastern channels appeared narrower as though the islands had migrated farther in that direction. Streaming continued eastward and northward, and there was inflow to the bank on both sides of the contact of the large island with the shore. At the northern border of the west cove from which the streaming proceeded, a rampart of broken crusts lay on the bench at the lake's edge. There were large areas on the bench southwest of recent cracking and foundering. Under the bank there were grottoes on the west and stalactities southeast and northeast.

As this was the day of the high explosion on Mauna Loa, a second visit was made to the pit at 8 p. m. From the south station the lake was seen to be overflowing the west bank in several places, and a golden torrent was pouring north between the islands, and fountains were spattering over the south bank ejecting a spray of droplets eighty feet high. There was not much central fountaining. The fumes were unpleasant. One small rock slide was seen in motion at the base of the southwest wall.

At noon on May 20 there was tremendous overflowing of the bench all around the lava lake. The small island was nearly submerged, only a little fuming knob above the liquid surface marking its location. On the large island the lake had risen to the second bench. One spatter knob of the southeast bank protruded above the flood, otherwise the shore of the lake was wholly submerged. The lake had risen at least ten feet in twenty-four hours. West and south, fountains were overflooding the border region. Occasional reports were heard. The heat on the rim was intense. The noises were of plashing and of puffing. The flood on the bench consisted of cracking and foundering lava and of melt welling up through heavy skins out to the edge of the floor. Streaming was slow from west to east and north-east, and the large island appeared to stand out away from the north bank but the position of the bank could be judged only by occasional fountains.

On May 21, the day of the Mauna Loa outflow, the rising continued, the lake at 2 p. m. being only a few inches below the bench. In twenty-five hours the two islands had completely shifted their positions, the large island moving across the lake to the south-west, its western horn resting against the western bank. The small island had tilted over to the south-east so that only its northern edge emerged from the lake, and its triangular shape had changed to an elongate oval with axis east-west. The large island showed a broad platform surrounding it at the level of the second bench. Its tilt appeared nearly unchanged and the new platform appeared horizontal. Apparently its motion had been pivotal to the west around a vertical axis in the neighborhood of its south point.

Along with this shift in the islands, the surface streaming of the lake was completely reversed. The channel between the islands was wider and the current now poured southward on both sides of the small island. This current started from crusts northwest of the large island. At the southwest corner of the large island an east-flowing current met the other and wrinkled the skins, and similarly a short east-flowing eddy blocked the westward flow on the south-east bank, making turbulent fountaining and overspatter.

There were fresh overflows everywhere on the floor which appeared wider south and south-east. There were stalactities in grottoes under the large island. The space between the large island and the south-west bank was narrow and the main lake now lay wholly to the north-east of the two islands. During a rising spell, the bay in the north end of the large island overflowed and the lava rose well up the back slope of the second bench on the island. During pronounced rising as on these two days, the islands do not float up with the flood but remain rigid while the liquid rises on their shores. On the other hand, when pronounced sinking occurs, the island blocks may slip down along the funnel walls of the deep basin which contains the lake, and this has recently happened. If the lake recovers and rises again, the heavy island blocks cannot float up but they may rise for a time by tilting.

On May 23 at 6 p. m. conditions were about the same with heavy stagnant skins over the lake. The lake was brimming, with overflows north and south, and by 6:15 p. m. this overflowing was going on all around. Much Pele's hair was floating straight up in the heated current of still air. Fountain activity increased until there were about twenty border fountains jetting spray at least seventy-five feet upward and the noise increased with blowing sounds. The skin in the northern embayment of the large island broke up twice within a quarter of an hour and then solidified. Smoke was rising from the small island. Overflowing diminished at 7 p. m.

On May 24 at 6 p. m. the lake seen from the south-east station was brimming and there were fresh glowing flows on the bench. The larger island was separated from the west bank by a channel. The small island had resumed triangular shape and moved toward the east bank. There were border fountains north, north-east, east and south-west, the latter building two half-cones. Old Faithful was active but irregular. Streaming was from a stagnant area north-west of the large island, eastward, south-westward and southward. Opposed streams rushed into the narrow channel east of the small island making perpetual fountains at the meeting point.

At 6:30 p. m. on this date rapid subsidence began, grottoes with stalactites formed under the south-east point of the large island, the east side of small island and along the northern bank. The southern point of the small island collapsed with much commotion and the perpetual fountaining migrated to this locality. Fountaining activity increased with rows of fountains between the islands, and a wild bombardment throwing out spatter far out over the lake and over the eastern island developed in the northern and eastern grottoes. Blue flames occasionally burst through heavy blankets of skin in the middle of the lake. Rumbling and blowing noise greatly increased. This was probably the beginning of the pulsations of subsidence which took effect in the next few days.

On May 25 at 6:30 p. m., the islands

were still as before close respectively to the west and east banks, streaming was southward, there was noisy fountaining and increased smoke from the floor and banks. The blue fume from the pit as a whole was more visible than of late. The large island still stood as a very high crag but the small island was low and flat. There were some falls of material observed from the shores of the islands. Flame was playing between the small island and the bank, and at that point there was inrush from the lake on both sides of the island.

The lake now was in process of sinking. In the afternoon of May 26 the wall of the inner pit was from eight to ten feet high. On the morning of May 27 the lake was fifteen feet below the bench but at 5 p. m. it had risen five feet and was rising. The next evening, May 28, the lake was relatively high and the large island was in process of moving from the west end toward the north shore. No one has seen actual movement in these islands, as the shiftings are very slow.

On May 29, at 11 a. m. streaming was reversed to its old course eastward and northward, and the large island had moved over its old course to a point near the north bank but there was still a channel north of it. The east island was against the east bank and its flat top was ten feet below the bench. It had sunk. The bench was fifteen feet above the lake, and was coated brown with Pele's hair. Around the border of the inner pit and near the edge over the lake cracks were forming. Fallen stones around the edge of the floor and increase in smoke gave further evidence of subsidence. Smoke was rising from the north, southeast and southwest banks and from the small island. The latter showed tilt northward. The south point of the large island lay near the middle of the lake, its north side being close to the N.N.W. bank and it appeared fully thirty feet high.

At 4 p. m. on May 30 the pit was quiet and smoky and the lake a little lower, about eighteen feet below the bench. There was rapid inrush to the east bank both north and south of the small island, which was nearly covered with newly folded skins. A grotto under the bank east of it was building a spatter heap on the flat top of the island. There appeared to be a north-south crack developing through the center of the large island and its lower spatter bench indicated some tilt to the north. There were five benches in the profile of the south end of the large island. Its western horn lay under the northwest station and almost against the bank.

At 5:30 p. m. on May 31 the lake appeared about three feet lower or twenty-one feet below the bench, and its action was quiet with skins being engulfed near Old Faithful and elsewhere. Fumes rose in intolerable gusts at the southeast station, coming from the north and east sides of the lake and from the small island, and obscuring the view. Pele's hair was abundant and it was increasing in drifts on the lower bench. This bench showed large cracks from twenty to forty feet from the edge of the lake, and at the west end a large cracked block of the bench appeared ready to fall. One small rock fall was heard. The large island stood twenty feet from the north bank. The small island exhibited a three foot wall over the lake and on its eastern surface there was a knob and broken fragments which appeared to be blocks fallen from the bank. Streaming was east and north with border fountains southeast and northeast.''

THE GREAT COLLAPSE AT HALEMAUMAU.

By T. A. JAGGAR, JR.

TECHNOLOGY STATION, June 8, 1916.—The week ending June 7, 1916, has been one of the most sensational in the history of Kilauea, in that on June 5 the lava sank nearly 400 feet in twenty-four hours.

On June 1, 1916, the pit was smoky. On June 2 at ten-thirty a. m. the small east island seen from the north showed a rim two feet above the lake and the large island near the north bank a lower bench five feet high. The wall of the inner pit appeared twenty-five feet high and the lake rising, with a quiet surface and the smoke, mostly east and south, thinner. Fresh lava or spatter from a recent rise or wave was plastered high on the north and west sides of the large island. It is probable that this was occasioned by the fall of the cracked block of bench seen at the west end two days previously, for that block was now gone, leaving a cove from which the surface streaming proceeded. The streaming was eastward on both sides of the large island, and against the bank southeast, northeast and between the small island and the cliff.

At 7:30 p. m. on June 1 a meteorite fell to the southwest with extraordinary brilliancy and a trail of sparks, making a bright flare as it reached the horizon.

On June 3 at six-thirty p. m. the lake seemed a little higher and spatter rims appeared above it about two feet higher still. The surface was extraordinary quiet. Streaming was slow to the east and north. Spatter grottoes formed occasionally northeast, east and southwest. Old Faithful was playing weakly. There was a channel fifteen to twenty feet wide, north of the large island, and the small island showed skins piled up against its edges. A permanent crust formed across the bay in the north end of the large island had greatly diminished the indentation.

On Sunday, June 4, at eleven a. m. the lake appeared the same or a little higher, and the fumes were less. A crack appeared wider in the south bench, tending to break off the south point. No fresh avalanche material appeared on the bench. The large island showed on the north four main benches and five on the south side. The lowest was about a foot high and made a wide platform on both sides of the north bay. Bubble fountains were playing in the Old Faithful locality and the noise was a gentle plashing.

Measurements on June 4 at eleven-thirty a. m. made the floor level under the west-southwest cliff 265 feet below the east station, and the lakeshore south 302 feet down, or thirty-seven feet below the highest point reached on May 25 (265 feet). The top of the large island was forty feet above the lake and the east side of this island was 382 feet long.

On the evening of June 4 the lake was reported to show increased fountaining and rapid streaming, and one or two avalanches were heard. The seismographs at the observatory indicated local earthquakes.

On June 5 at eight-thirty a. m. from the south-east the lake appeared at least sixty feet below the bench, the islands were subsiding with it, and the south point had fallen making a tumble of debris which rose above the lake level. In two hours the lake fell forty feet and falls from the south inner cliffs become frequent and spectacular, as the bench matter, made of recent overflows, was red hot within, and broke or crumbled like masses of hard cheese. Sometimes this material flowed in a sugary fashion. The great blocks formed an incandescent talus slope below, which spread into a crumbling south promontory. The large island lay farther west than before, and a torrent pouring eastward around its south point received repeatedly great infalls of gigantic fragments from this promontory.

It early became evident that one of the great volcanic spectacles of all time was in progress and the southwest station was selected as a viewpoint. Here notes and photographs were made until twelve-thirty p. m. immediately over the great benches as they fell. Then the north-west station was occupied throughout the fall of the northern benches. Then a survey was made with transit from the north and northwest stations. For the remainder of the day and in the evening the south station was occupied, while terrific avalanches of the old wall materials sent down and up creamy, salmon colored, terra cotta, white, brown and black cauliflowers of dust making the most gorgeous display of volcanic clouds the writer has ever seen.

While the edge trembled slightly, and there were occasional perceptible earthquakes, a remarkable feature of the whole cataclysm was the rigidity of the upper walls. The south bench remnant of 1912 under the A-frame at the south station was carried away at two-fifty p. m. in a succession of appalling avalanches, but at no time did the writer see a single block drop from the high rim. There was undoubtedly some slight scaling off the rim due to concussion and jarring, and a few cracks opened slightly back from the edge, but otherwise the plan of the pit at the surface remained unchanged.

The maximum subsidence was probably from eleven a. m. to three p. m., and thereafter it continued more slowly for the next twenty-four hours; measurements of the lake surface were as follows:

Previous day, June 4,
Depression of lake measured....302 ft
June 5, 8:30 a. m. estimated....340 ft
June 5, 10.30 a. m. esitmated...380 ft
June 5, 3 p. m. measured ......540 ft
Next day,
June 6, noon, measured ....673 ft

At eleven-fifty-four an enormous block south-west fell directly into the lake converting the south-west torrent for the moment into a violently boiling pool and reversing the streaming to inrush towards it. Within one minute the eastward streaming was resumed. The violent boiling and the freshly exposed incandescence in the talus greatly increased the perceptible heat on the rim of the pit.

At twelve noon the old red rock wall east and south was now stripped bare of 1916 benches leaving a small remnant southeast. Bright red dust clouds began to rise in contrast to the chocolate brown puffs which always shot up when the new benches fell. By this time avalanching was incessant with detonations, roars and crashes waxing and waning, to which was added the deep rumble of the boiling lake when the talus plunged into it. An avalanche would start below almost silently in a great salmon colored cauliflower showing frequently that the old wall was stripped bare far below the clinging remnants of the black and incandescent lava above. Then the undermining would extend upward, great crevasses in the bench would yawn and open, and with an increasing roar, the mighty slab would topple outward and then crumble into the glowing slope below. Clouds of grit fell in showers on the edge of the pit, and later the whole country to leeward was coated with red dust.

A small pool at this time south of the small island sank faster than the lake and a cascade developed from the lake into it.

At twelve fifty five p. m., the whole north bench fell at once and the most colossal brown cauliflower of the day shot up from Halemaumau and was seen many miles away. A bench from seventy-five to one hundred feet wide and 265 feet below the rim extending around the north side of the pit from northeast to west, fell inward as a unit leaving hardly any remnants clinging to the walls. This mass fell 250 feet and for the moment completely swamped the lake, a body of molten lava not less than 600 feet long.

The lake splashed all over the island remnants and at least 150 feet up the south talus, plastering it with pitchy black glass, and then the wave swung back and rose on the north shore fifty or sixty feet. The lake surface blackened and blistered, then at a new level it resumed sluggish streaming.

A few minutes later there developed at the west end of the lake a glowing lava cascade pouring like a spring from a vertical crack in the wall back of the talus and pushing its way over the slide-rock down forty feet into the west pool where it built lobes and festoons on the crust.

A wonderful feature of the entire subsidence up to this time was the absence of smoke. There was white steam far down the southern wall where the ground water seeped inward and the walls were seen to be wet.

Heavy gusts of wind carried up wads of Pele's hair dislodged from the drifts of that material matted against the walls. Whirlwinds on the south and southeast edge of Halemaumau became so severe that twice the writer had to lie down to prevent his being hurled into the pit.

At two-fifty p. m. a succession of tremendous avalanches south and west carried away the 1912 bench completely.

At three-fifty p. m. from the south station Halemaumau was now a terrible black void overhung by brown avalanche clouds, the successive rockfalls sending up hard-edged billows in marvelous colors made by brick-red dust, white steam, blue-gray smoke and ever changing shadows. All of this, coupled with an occasional roaring collapse that started the lake into violent boiling and made a great flare of fire below, while the slopes glowed cherry red, produced such a volcanic spectacle as few have been privileged to see. To the noise of thunder and musketry were now added an occasional explosive bellow and thud from the southeast vent which was building a spatter cone.

In the evening the avalanching had somewhat diminished but the talus slopes were in motion with blocks tumbling into the lake which had extended itself in a southeasterly direction. The island remnants were still visible.

On June 6 in the morning. Halemaumau was a smoke-filled void with nearly continuous clatter of falling stones and occasional avalanches. A survey at noon showed the lake to be an oval pool in talus 673 feet down, 500 feet long and 250 feet wide. The shifting slides had moved the lake bodily 125 feet to the southeast in the last twenty hours and the two islands had disappeared under the debris.

How this happened was illustrated at twelve-fifteen p. m. when a southwestern avalanche developed with a tremendous roar into a general slide into the lake which boiled hotly into a thousand fountains and clouds of brown smoke shot upward. Snorting, spouting cones on the margin gave vent to loud blasts. The clatter of falling material had diminished by 1 p. m.

On June 7 a large brown avalanche cloud rose from the pit at 11 a. m. At 4 p. m. there was little to be seen except smoke, some avalanche clatter was heard and from the west the lake could be seen with a few fountains and crusts cracking and foundering. The walls were steeper and all the country to leeward of the pit was plastered with red dust.

The following report from the Whitney Laboratory of Seismology is submitted by Mr. H. O. Wood:

The earthquake spasm that accompanied the outbreak of Mauna Loa drew to a close with the decline of activity. The interpretation of this relationship must be left for thorough discussion elsewhere.

A brief interval of comparative seismic quiet ensued, extending over the last four or five days of the previous week and the first four days of the week ending with June 7, 1916, now under discussion. A second seismic spasm then began, in the early part of the twenty-four-hour interval ending in the forenoon of June 5. Many shocks were registered. A very large number of shocks followed in the succeeding twenty-four hours ending June 6; and a considerable number in the interval ending June 7.

These were all local shocks of feeble character,—though many of them were felt at the observatory, and at the margin of Halemaumau. This series attracted no attention at Hilo or at Pahala. None of the shocks were stronger than III of the Rossi-Forel scale, and most of them were feebler than this. Instrumentally many of them exhibited large amplitude. At times for upwards of an hour there was continuous registration of earthquake motion without cessation, though with waxing and waning in amplitude.

These shocks proceeded from origins nearer to the observatory than those comprised in the earlier spasm; but they appear to have originated at distances in excess of ten miles. The seismograms have not been measured systematically as yet, but the duration of preliminary motion is seen by inspection to be about two seconds.

These were associated with a rapid drainage of Kilauea, similar to that witnessed in September, 1915, but on a larger scale and of more spectacular nature. The interpretation of the association must be left for thorough discussion later.

Waves of the chief phase only of a feeble teleseism were registered in the latter part of the twenty-four-hour interval ending on June 6. Nothing further can be said of it prior to systematic measurement.

Microseismic motion during the week has been of normal character. Volcanic vibration appears to have maintained a somewhat larger amplitude than usual throughout the week. Tilting has not been excessive but the changes have been noticeable. With the null-points adjusted as at present, the swing was to the east and north in the early part of the week followed by a return, and then a departure to the west and south in the latter part of the week.

TECHNOLOGY STATION, June 15, 1916.—The great collapse in Halemaumau was quickly over and recovery appears to have begun. The tumbled masses of rock blocks have been engulfed, for the most part; and an encrusted magma lake of considerable area is visible at the bottom of the pit. Rising is in progress.

No noteworthy falls have taken place from the old rim, though old cracks about the margin have been rejuvenated and extended and new ones have formed.

The illumination at night, almost quenched for a day or two, has grown stronger and steadier.

In the afternoon on June 8 there was a hard wind and a considerable volume of fumes, so that no clear seeing was obtained. No general avalanches occurred, but at intervals large rock blocks fell, with bounding, to the bottom of the pit. There were four places in which boiling lava could be seen. These were along a straight line in a sort of trench.

In early and mid-afternoon on June 9 several considerable avalanches occurred on the north, east and south sides of the pit; and large rock blocks fell at intervals. There was fair seeing from the northwest station. Fumes had decreased markedly. The molten lava at the bottom of the pit had engulfed the greater portion of the intumbled blocks, and a flat lake surface about 200 feet wide by 400 to 500 feet long was visible. Boiling fountains at times were very active, and from south quarters there was streaming to the northwestward toward the middle of the lake area.

In late afternoon and evening on June 10 there was very little fuming. But fumes from the postal-card crack were swirling down into the pit. A few rock falls and one large avalanche were noted. The latter fell at about nine-fifty p. m. from the 1894 bench at the north, building a new talus shore for the lake thus changing its shape into a plump crescent. After this fell there were a few moments of pronounced action followed by an interval of greatly reduced activity.

On the floor there was cracking and foundering and a few sluggish fountains. At the south-southeast the lava was boiling up in the talus against the wall and making a higher outlying pool from which three small flows were cascading down over the talus toward the lake, distributing over the slope and building a lobate delta at the lake edge.

It was seen that about 300 feet of the 1894 bench, in the middle portion between the northeast station and the bench under the east station, had slumped off, the fall involving a depth, back from the edge, of ten to twenty feet.

On June 11 the fumes were still thinner, and in the morning there were few slides and a quiet condition of the lake. The cascade at the south-southeast was a black slope. Snorting sounds emanated from that part of the pit. In the evening the avalanches were small. There were two fountain areas on the floors, and flows were trickling slowly down the slope to the lake from the high south-southeast pool in which action was comparatively sluggish. Later there was cracking and foundering on the floor with rising and the building of toes into the talus. This was accompanied by increased outflow from

June 5, 1916. 9 a. m. Beginning of the great subsidence. Lake and islands from S.W. station. Depression of lake 300 feet, depression of bench around it 253 feet. Dimensions 780x675 feet.

June 5, 1916. About 11:20 a. m. Main lake from S.W. station. End of small island broken off, shoals revealed on north side of lake, large island showing emerging. New bench on the left.

June 5, 1916. About noon. East bench has collapsed completely and lake is choked with débris. Bench cracking away on the right preparatory to further falls.

June 24, 1916. 11:30 a. m. N. end of Lava Lake from S.W. station after recovery. Lake 900 feet long, and depression below rim of pit 592 feet.

the south-southeast pool which then built a leaf-like delta westward over the crust on the lake. There was exhaust puffing in the south-southeast pool. The lake appeared slightly higher and larger.

On June 12 in early afternoon, the floor area was a level black surface in which two small boiling fountains were seen. A single considerable flow was cascading from the high south southeast pool to the floor. Several small avalanches fell from under the west and southwest edges. In mid-afternoon the floor area began to crack and founder with outflow of fresh lava and rising; and the action increased in the south-southeast pool until three, and later four, small streams were cascading from it over the encrusted talus to the lake surface.

On June 13 in the forenoon there were four streams cascading from the south-southeast pool, but in the afternoon this action had declined and only one was seen at work, and that was partly crusted over. At the southwest and west small avalanches fell. The floor showed only two boiling pots active continuously, but at intervals there was cracking and foundering with definite rising. Two blow-holes against the wall in the south-southeast pool area were making loud blowing noises.

On June 14 the cascading from the south-southeast pool had increased considerably. The two boiling fountains on the floor were both ejecting molten lumps to considerable heights. The floor area had risen very considerably so that it was estimated to be only twenty-five to thirty feet below the surface of the south-southeast pool. A few very small avalanches were heard.

In the Whitney Laboratory of Seismology the seismic spasm that preceded and accompanied by drainage of Kilauea, continued with diminishing energy into the early part of the present week, ending with June 11, during the first four days of which a considerable number of small, local earthquakes were registered. In the three succeeding days it has declined to normal.

One felt shock, shortly before seven a. m. on June 12, deserves notice. This was a triple shock, three distinct, perceptible maxima in a total duration of about five seconds. This shock, too strong for instrumental registration, was a slow, gentle rocking motion of somewhat larger amplitude than usual. It was strong enough to stop the seconds-pendulum clock in the Whitney Laboratory, thus indicating an intensity of VI of the R.-F. scale (but probably low in the range of that grade). Though nothing like so strong as the shock in October of 1913, it was next to that the strongest shock experienced here since the foundation of the observatory. In Hilo it was stronger than at the observatory.

Microseismic motion has exhibited its usual characteristics. Volcanic vibration, while stronger than normal, has not shown unusual energy. Tilting has been as usual.

H. O. WOOD.

RECONNAISSANCE OF THE KAHUKU FLOW OF 1916.

By H. O. WOOD.

The writer, with one companion (Mr. D. Lycurgus) and a native guide, spent two days—May 30 and 31, 1916—in an arduous and rapid reconnaissance of the Kahuku branch of the 1916 flow down the south flank of Mauna Loa. This branch, which began flowing just before midnight on May 21, showed no forward movement later than the 27th or the 28th. It was still very hot, however, on May 31.

Narrative

The writer and companion left the Hawaiian Volcano Observatory in the early evening of May 29, and motored to the village of Waiohinu where the night was spent. Early next morning we motored on to the gate of the Kahuku ranch just west of the ranch buildings. Here we were joined by the guide and the party set out on horseback at 8 a. m., going up the mountain between the flows of 1868 and 1887. At 10:30 a. m. we reached the southernmost "toe" of the front of the Kahuku branch. Here we turned off to the right to pass around this flow and up on the east and north of it. We followed an upland trail toward Kapapala until we came into a kipuka (a long narrow belt of forest land extending up the mountain between two barren streams of aa), called Kipuka Akala.

At the lower end of this we left our horses. We reached this shortly before noon, and at noon we set out on foot up the mountain, in a northwest course, towards the general source of the 1916 flow, north of a cluster of conspicuous cinder cones which culminate in Puu o Keokeo, a point 6870 feet above sea. As we were destined to spend the night near the source we were necessarily laden with food, water, photographic equipment and so forth, and blankets or extra clothing, a moderate load for each man. For about an hour we made our way upward alongside the kipuka, going chiefly over old aa. At about 1 p. m. we came out into a barren complex network of aa flows, of varying direction and age, over which we climbed and walked until a little after 5 p. m. We then reached an old cinder cone situated between two and three miles from Puu o Keokeo in a direction a trifle east of north. This cone was between an eighth and a quarter of a mile east from the eastern margin of the rift-line source of the 1916 flow, described below. We were still a considerable distance below the upper limit of this source, which had been our goal, but it became impracticable to go on further. In the lee of this old cinder cone we passed the night, practically all of which the writer devoted to observation of the action and conditions along the visible length of the rift-source.

At 4:50 a. m. on the 31st we began the descent. At 9:40 a. m. the horses were reached, and at 10:15 a. m. we started on our way to Puu o Keokeo, going around the southern end of the Kahuku branch of the flow and upon the western side of it. By noon we reached a flat clearing where we dropped our camp equipment and immediately proceeded upward on horseback to a point very near to Puu o Keokeo, on a low ridge of ancient pahoehoe which extends a short distance eastward from the conspicuous cluster of cinder cones. In clear weather this slight eminence would afford an expansive view to the northward, and much wider views still could be obtained from the summits of the cones nearby. Through driving fog and clouds, and in brief clear spells between small local showers, we obtained partial views. This point of outlook was reached at 2:20 p. m. It was practically impossible to keep horses here overnight, and this, with the unfavorable conditions of seeing and the further impracticability of remaining in rainy weather without camp equipment, made it practically necessary to descend soon. So the return was begun at 2:35 p. m. and the camping place was reached at 3:50 p. m. So far as conditions had permitted, the work we had undertaken was done. From 10 a. m. on, rain had fallen in brief showers, some of which were heavy, and bad weather still threatened. Consequently it was decided to return to Waiohinu instead of camping with meagre equipment. Continuing on, we reached the ranch gate at 6:40 p. m. and Waiohinu at 8:30 p. m. The night was passed here and the observatory was reached by motor just before noon on June 1.

We passed completely around the Kahuku branch of the flow, except for its breadth near its source. In this way, especially on the foot journey (and also from the lava ridge near Puu o Keokeo), a good general survey was obtained of conditions along the flow and at its source; and in limited localities, particularly those encountered on foot along the eastern side of the Kahuku branch, many matters of detail were observed. A sufficient knowledge of the work which must be done on this eastern branch was obtained.

Circumstances of footing, distance and weather, prevented survey of the upper limits of the source of action and of conditions on the side toward Kona, and the making of photographic records. This last especially was much regretted. For in good weather excellent illustrative views could be obtained.

Geographical Notes

The closely grouped cluster of old cinder cones, of which Puu o Keokeo (6870 feet above sea) is the highest, forms a low but conspicuous landmark on the S. S. W. flank of Mauna Loa. Extending eastward from this for a mile or less is a low ridge of ancient pahoehoe from ten to thirty, possibly even to fifty feet in height. A long, narrow belt of country, characterized by many cinder cones (double semi-cones built on either side of rift cracks) in parallel linear arrangements, leads from this conspicuous group first in a direction a little west of north, then northwardly and finally in directions gradually swinging to the east of north on and up to the western side of the summit plateau of Mauna Loa. North of this lava ridge and east of this belt of cinder cones (and very probably west of it also, though this was not seen), is a flat area. For several miles to the northward toward the summit the surface of this stands at a lower altitude than the summit of Puu o Keokeo, and its eastward extension from the belt of cones, though variable, has a width of from two to three miles. This is a very conspicuous flat area on a very flat dome surface. South of the chief cones the usual gentle slope of the mountain is resumed. At the southeast and east the broad irregular flat passes imperceptibly into the irregular broken slope of the dome. Several miles to the north of Puu o Keokeo the flat passes rather quickly though the region of transition is indefinite, into the somewhat steeper slopes which rise to the summit plateau. Viewed from the lava ridge south of this flat, Mauna Loa appears a distinct mountain, until the genetic significance of the long belt of cones is grasped.

This belt of cones marks an unmistakeable rift-zone which joins at the summit with that leading down the northeast flank of the mountain—a great crust fracture, slightly curved and convex to the northwest, through the whole dome of Mauna Loa. This stretches northwardly across the flat and bounds on the west that part of it seen on this expedition.

Sources of Eruption.

The sources of the eruption of 1916 were in this rift-zone. Both the sources of the earliest outbreak high on the dome and the sources of flow lie in it. Both appear to be linear segments in the rift zone.

A long fissure line marked by constant emanation of steam (or fumes) was seen leading from the western side of the summit plateau of Mauna Loa down the S. S. W. side of the upper slopes of the dome nearly to the region where this grades into the great flat—a distance of several miles. For the most part the steam was clinging to the surface along the line of fissure; but at one point (and possibly another) it was rising definitely in small volume. Unquestionably this marks a rejuvenation in 1916 of the action of rifting through Mauna Loa, and in this upper segment were the orifices, large and small, from which came the outrush of fumes in the morning of May 19. The place (or places) where steam appeared to be rising definitely,was well up the slope beyond its transition into the flat. This leads the writer to consider that the orifices of the earliest outbreak may have been situated at a higher altitude than appearances from the Observatory indicated,—perhaps as high as 9,500 or 10,000 feet above sea. The line of fissure marked by steam emanation is possibly interrupted and perhaps offset en echelon. This could not be determined surely when seen from so considerable a distance.

This fissure leads down into line with the system of double semi-cones which stretch across the flat along the rift zone northwardly from Puu o Keokeo.

This line of new steam emanation was seen definitely, but through atmosphere haze, mist and showers, at all times when the upper slopes were in the field of vision.

Only a portion of the source of flow was seen definitely. A line of rifting, in the direction of, and within the limits of the broad rift zone, marked by fresh outflow at the side, and by new, small cinder cones some of which were still building, was seen to extend for a distance of more than three miles in a direction a trifle west of north from Puu o Keokeo across the flat toward the summit. The upper limit was not reached. It may be four miles or more above Puu o Keokeo. Only the eastern side of the newly developed rift source was seen. Possibly more than one rift crack opened. There may very well be parallel lines on the west.

The writer was told that on the west

of Puu o Keokeo the rift source extends down the mountain for a mile or so further. This he did not see personally.

From this rift crack came the molten lava which streamed away toward lands in Kona, and towards Kahuku, dividing above the group of old cones. The Kahuku branch was the only one seen in this expedition.

Our bivouac for the night of May 30-31 was in the lee of an old, triple-peaked semi-cone, in the re-entrant where it straddled an ancient cinder-choked fissure. The cone was elongated in the north-south course of this fissure. It had been the source of an ancient eruption of pahoehoe. This station was between two and three miles from Puu o Keokeo in a direction a trifle east of north. Just west of us, from one-eighth to one-quarter of a mile away, was one of the larger cinder cones of 1916, from 75 to 100 feet in height. The eastern line of the new rift source passed through this reaching northward from the old cone Puu Olohia near Puu o Keokeo. Both north and south of this new cone were numerous other cones. I am told that the ranchmen recognize seven new cones; but this neglects numerous small and inconspicuous mounds which are no less true cones than the larger ones. Only a very narrow tongue of aa (1907?) separated us from the eastern line of vent of the present activity.

Though greatly diminished, there was still vigorous action at many points along this line.

When we first reached this station, the most active vent (Hale Pohaha) was at the northern base of Puu Olohia, between two and three miles due south of us. Though this was down the wind (which, however, was gentle) explosive coughing sounds could be heard at frequent irregular intervals, and occasionally red hot masses were thrown up into our field of vision. This action continued throughout the evening and the early part of the night. During this interval the glow above this vent was considerable, though less than that ordinarily seen above Kilauea as viewed from the observatory at about the same distance, yet it was comparable with it. However at about 8:45 p. m., May 30, a short, sharp earthquake occurred, plainly felt by all three of us sitting or reclining on the cinders in the re-entrant of the cone. This shock was felt sharply at Waiohinu and at Kapapala. At Hilea it was felt as the strongest shock of the entire series connected with this eruption. Within less than a minute after the shock there occurred a spasm of greatly increased action at this vent, with the jetting of lumps of lava and a great increase in the flow. This quickly declined to normal. Afterward the action at this vent declined, at first slowly, but toward 1 a. m., May 31, more rapidly; by 3 a. m. the situation of this vent could barely be made out. When seen again in mid-afternoon on May 31, from near Puu Olohia, only a low smoking cone appeared.

In the late afternoon of May 30, a glowing cone was seen, with an oven-like orifice, at a distance of two hundred to three hundred yards to the northeast of this most active vent. In the night the glow above this was negligible.

Between the new cone directly west of our bivouac and the place of greatest activity just described, fumes were rising steadily from numerous larger and smaller vents and cones. After darkness fell, three of these fuming places exhibited glow. From our viewpoint the glow came and went intermittently, but this appearance seemed due to drifting fog and fumes alternately concealing and disclosing the illumined fume columns.

The larger new cone just west of our bivouac, showed steady vigorous glow on the fumes at both its north and south vents. These were separated by a dark interval of, say, 200 feet. No incandescent matter was thrown from this cone into our field of vision.

To the northeast, at a distance judged to be about a mile, hence probably all of three miles from Puu o Keokeo in a direction a trifle west of north, was a cone which in one respect exhibited the greatest activity of any of the vents, though it was not conspicuous for glow. Indeed, it was remarkable for the apparently trifling amount of fumes which spread from it. By daylight this was not seen clearly, owing to drifting fog and fumes, but at night it became plainly visible. It was still building. There were numerous gashes and glow-spots on its sides which remained without substantial change throughout the hours of the night. These were interpreted as true gashes and orifices in the shell of the cone, through which shone the incandescent core. Almost incessantly, red hot masses were thrown out of this cone into the air. Most of these barely cleared the summit to tumble and roll down the sides of the cone. The relative motion of these between and among the practically permanent orifices created the illusion of a steady fountain play of fiery particles rising and falling like droplets at the top of a jet of water. It required prolonged observation to correct this impression. At intervals of twenty seconds to three to five minutes larger masses would be projected into the air high above the apex of the cone. These usually would describe free parabolic curves to fall, apparently, beyond the base of the cone. In most such instances no rolling was seen. The writer was observing from too great a distance to venture more than a guess at the height of projection. Taking the height of the cone at 100 feet, and its distance at about one mile, the best estimate that could be made in the dark of the height of projection was fully 250 feet above the base of the cone, or 150 feet clear of its apex. Some of the ejected masses appeared large. On the basis of the other estimates the largest appeared to have diameters of at least six feet, possibly as much as ten feet or more. Though the cone was estimated to be a mile away across the wind, a steady, gentle drift of air, loud, staccato, explosive booms could be heard from the cone occasionally.

This was the most spectacular center of activity remaining of those which came within our field of vision.

On the southwest side of it there was an intermittent illumination of the thin fume, of a sort which suggested outflow of lava coursing away in the southwest direction, but this was an inference merely, without further support.

This cone appeared to lie west of the course of the rift-source, or more properly, west of the eastern side of this.

Further north, but in line with the eastern side of the rift-source, was a glowing orifice, like an oven, probably a gash in a quiet cone.

A little beyond, a lava ridge made the local northern horizon, and by daylight only rising fumes were seen behind this from this station. These showed no illumination at night.

At night, nine places were distinguished where rising fumes were illuminated. Seven of these were arranged in line northward from the chief vent at the foot of Puu Olohia. The other two, one an oven orifice, the other the spouting cone, lay one to the east and the other to the west, of this line and near to it.

Small quantities of new pumice, usually in elongated stringers, were seen in close proximity to the rift-source. Much pumice of much older origin was seen in the interstices between the blocks of the older aa surfaces. There was more and more of this as the rift was approached more and more closely. Thus there is suggestion that the lavas of earlier eruptions from nearby sources were more highly charged with gas.

The length of the eastern side of the rift-source of outflow, as seen from this bivouac, was not less than three miles nor more than four, but its upper limit was not in sight. It had been planned to go to the source and explore it, but the going, all over aa, proved too exhausting.

In the upper reaches of the rift-source, the lateral outflow on the eastern side was little. Whether there was much flowing down the course of the rift was not seen. However, near the station occupied, the grade was all but imperceptible, so much flowing seemed unlikely. On the western side nothing could be seen. South of our station the Kahuku branch departed in an irregular, sprawling, many-tongued flow to the southeast and south.

All the material seen in the Kahuku branch of the flow was aa except that small areas of pahochoe have formed as the last products of outflow at the vent just north of Puu Olohia.

The Kahuku branch of the 1916 flow runs in south and southeast directions from points along the rift source beginning just north of the cluster of old cones at Puu o Keokeo and extending up the line for nearly two miles. For example, on our foot journey from 3 p. m. on May 30, we kept seeing little fuming areas south of our route. These indicated the course of the new flow and its tongues. Toward the end we approached quite closely to these as we neared the rift source at a point more than two miles north of Puu o Keokeo. Possibly lava was contributed to it from still higher up the rift source; but if this is so the fact must be determined by detailed survey. On this western side the flow departs from the source just north of the old cones where it starts eastwardly to pass around the end of the ridge of ancient pahoehoe that juts out to eastward from the cluster, before it swerves southwardly down the mountain. At an early stage of the action, as quoted in the Weekly Bulletin, it was reported that the source of this branch was lower down the mountain than Puu o Keokeo; but this definitely was an error.

The western edge of this branch was encountered by our party only at several isolated points. At these it was aa, piled irregularly from twenty to forty feet high or deep, still hot and fuming on May 31. Smells of subliming sulphur, sulphur acids, charcoal and the smell of cinders were very noticeable. Also there were smoke smells from burning vegetation. Probably tongues or toes project from the main stream on its western side, as others report who viewed it before it ceased flowing, but we found no opportunity to follow the margin closely and did not note any conspicuous projections. However, in passing from its southermost point to the eastward and northward around the branch, we encountered many thin narrow tongues, from five to eight or ten feet in depth and from fifty to 200 yards in width, radiating to the southeast and east. These departed from the main stream at higher and higher points. Wherever junctions were seen the departures of these minor branches appeared capricious—i. e., no evidences of local damming or pooling were seen. Though much thinner and less massive than the main stream, these were still fuming, and in varying degrees the air above them was in a state of shimmer from heat. The emanation of the fumes, however, furnished a more reliable indication of their course than the heat-disturbed air above them.

The cartographic delineation of the complex out-branching of this Kahuku part of the flow can be accomplished only by actual topographic survey.

A general conception of a long narrow flow to the southeast and south, of a somewhat sinuous course and with offshoots to the east and southeast, is all that can be developed as a result of this reconnaissance.

Exceedingly little pahoehoe was encountered or seen on this flat or on the adjacent upper slopes at the southeast. The few small patches found were ancient. The old mountain surface here is an ancient rusty red aa with very scanty, low-grown ohelo and other shrubs growing in pockets of soil between the blocks. This surface is nearly covered by a thickly meshed irregular network of aa flows of recent times —though the dates of these are unknown, mostly. The latest of them are the relatively thin narrow tongues of the flow of 1907, and now of 1916 These are relatively small in area and in volume, but they are conspicuous on account of their fresh appearance. It is worthy of note that we have not previously heard of these Kahuku tongues of the flow of 1907, leading for short distances eastward and southeastward from their rift-line source north of Puu o Keokeo. But they have been known to the ranchmen; and one tongue was seen by the writer bridging an old straight fissure which seemed surely to be the fissure opened in 1868. This fissure is discussed below. There seems little doubt that important minor flows ran out in 1907 upon this upland flat which passed unmentioned and perhaps unnoticed.

In close neighborhood of the well-marked rift zone several fissures were encountered which ran parallel with it up and down the mountain. These were best marked where they passed across tracts of the old surface. They were neither so numerous nor so well developed as might have been expected, yet they were deep, sustained fissures.

The very complicated weaving of these very thin aa flows has given the surface of the flat a very rough and tumbled character in miniature and the varying color of the different flows, against the ruddy red surface of ancient aa, gives the appearance of coarsely woven fabric when viewed at a distance.

Fissure of 1868 (?)

On the return foot journey the last part of the traverse, before entering the kipuka, Akala, at its upper end, was made over the ancient aa surface which hereabouts for a considerable area was less overlain with new flows. A short distance, possibly a mile but probably less, above the upper end of the kipuka, we encountered a long straight fissure. This was a simple fissure from three to six feet wide and indefinitely deep. It was choked with fallen blocks. There were few side-cracks and these were small and apparently discontinuous. This fissure could be seen stretching up the mountain toward the eastern margin of the summit plateau for a long distance. It was finally lost to sight amid the irregularities of the surface. Down the mountain a few rods from where we crossed it, it was bridged by a tongue of recent aa, cold, and therefore not of 1916 date.

There were indications, in the postures and conditions of the fractured surfaces and coigns of the riven blocks that choked it, that this fissure was of no great age. It was found near to the projected course which the 1868 fissure should have, and its course down the mountain would take it to the head of the 1868 flow. Between it and the source of the latest flow no other great fissure was encountered. The fissure of 1868 could not pass eastward or southeastward of this one without exhibiting marked and unlikely curvature. Hence there seems much probability that this was the fissure of 1868. If so it is remarkable for its simplicity, considering the earth-paroxysms which attended its opening, and for its great depth for so narrow and simple a fracture. Also it is remarkably rectilinear.

Conditions Near Puu o Keokeo.

As mentioned already, from the cluster of cones at Puu o Keokeo there leads eastwardly a low ridge of ancient pahoehoe, which for a mile or so, rises somewhat above the general elevation of the flat to the north. South from this the normal downward slope of the mountain is resumed. The surface of this and much of the ancient lava to the south and southeast above timber line, or more strictly above the well-wooded region, exhibits tube forms of all sizes from very large to small. In this ancient surface are numerous irregular cracks and fissures, irregular collapsed areas and collapsed tube-courses, caves, lava bridges, and so forth. These conditions become more conspicuous the closer the cone cluster is approached, and the size of the features increases likewise. The ridge stands from ten to thirty, and possibly as much as fifty feet above the surface of the flat to the north.

The suggestion, which appears to have originated with S. E. Bishop, that Puu o Keokeo is a subordinate but distinct vent needs thorough investigation. The fact that it is a comparatively inconspicuous feature in the course of a marked rift zone through the whole mass of Mauna Loa is adverse to such an opinion, but this cannot be considered wholly conclusive.

From this ridge, in good weather, and even better from the summits of the adjacent cones, good seeing can be had and instructive views can be made. It is also a good center from which to make explorations.

TECHNOLOGY STATION, June 22, 1916.—At the very beginning of the week ending with June 21 a marked rising tendency was exhibited by the molten surface in Halemaumau. This was checked by a sudden, small subsidence. Later a tendency to stand was noticed, followed by rising with oscillations in height which has continued to the time of writing. Though the rising since the great collapse has been moderately rapid, the lake surface still stands at great depth. However, there is a lake of large size filling completely the bottom of the steep-walled pit, except for small protuberant bodies of talus at the north, west and southwest. The surface action has been relatively quiet.

On June 15 the whole floor area was repeatedly broken up by the process of crust foundering with surface outflow. Only one persistent fountain was seen; this was on the N. E. margin of the lake: it threw splashes of molten lava to considerable heights. The surface of the lake had risen nearly level with the surface of the pool at the southeast, from which there was rapid streaming toward the center of the lake. Many small avalanches occurred and at times large blocks fell free and clear into the lake making large splashes as they struck its surface. It was noted that a well-marked crack along the upper rim of the pit on the W. S. W. appeared to have opened out, accompanied by a subsidence of the inner block, indicating decreased stability of a considerable mass of the wall along this part of the pit.

On June 16 a subsidence of about ten feet was noticed. Under the north station a new cascade. about twenty feet wide, was seen. This had broken out higher up than the lake surface and it was pouring very rapidly into the lake. Also there was a small flow on the northeast side. Between the west and the south-west another cascade was seen welling out at a height of about 150 feet above the floor and plunging down into the lake. One persistent fountain was seen. which displayed the irregular. periodic characteristics of Old Faithful. This was in the north-east part of the lake near the margin.

On June 17 the lake appeared at about the same height as on the previous day. The southeast cascade was running rapidly, but the other cascades had ceased action. A glow spot emitting blue fumes was seen at the head of the west-southwest cascade. Crust foundering and surface outflow was seen. Small avalanches fell from several parts of the walls.

On June 19 the surface had risen perceptibly. The cascade had stopped running. The fountain at the northeast margin continued to break after the manner of Old Faithful, with intervals of from fifteen to twenty seconds. A small avalanche fell from the south wall. There was much evidence of rising, and repeated crust foundering with surface outflow was conspicuous.

On June 20 rising had continued, and the persistence of the northeast fountain and its resemblance to Old Faithful were marked. A considerable avalanche fell from the east wall. Many of the larger boulders went into the lake and were engulfed immediately. Intermittent activity of the southeast cascade was noted.

On June 21 rising was in progress and surface action was increased somewhat. Besides the Old Faithful fountain, there was seen a large central fountain which traveled slowly toward the northeast: and two boiling pots near the northeast margin. All these ejected molten lumps to a considerable height. The level of the lava was nearly as high as that noted on June 15. A small avalanche fell from the west wall.

During the early part of the interval under report four small local earthquakes have been registered in the Whitney Laboratory of Seismology. None were of perceptible magnitude. Therefore it may be stated that the seismic activity has again fallen to normal value.

Other sorts of seismic motion have been registered as usual, without noteworthy characteristics.

H. O. WOOD.

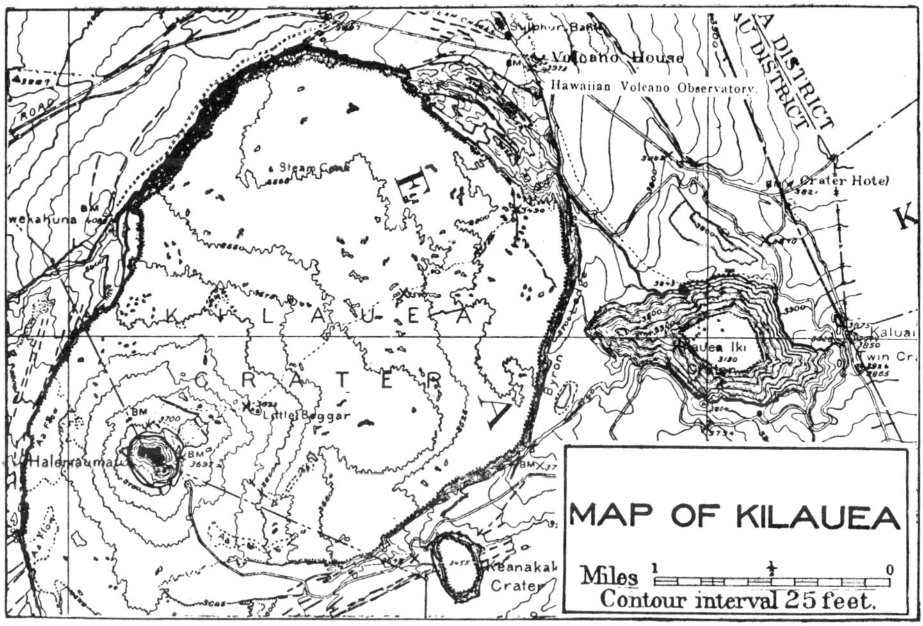

HAWAIIAN VOLCANO RESEARCH ASSOCIATION.

This society is a voluntary one, made up of subscribers to scientific work which is being executed by the Massachusetts Institute of Technology.

In 1915 there are about 100 subscribers in Hawaii and elsewhere, firms and individuals. A group of firms and persons in Hilo built the main observatory building in the spring of 1912. Publications to date have been weekly reports since the summer of 1911, now reprinted in Honolulu in monthly form. The Massachusetts Institute of Technology will publish annual reports, of which the introductory number was printed in 1912.

The weekly bulletin as it appears in the Advertiser is reprinted as a leaflet and sent to regular annual subscribers to the work of the Association. L. A. Thurston is president of the Board of Directors of the Association, and R. W. Shingle is treasurer. New subscribers who are interested in volcanoes will be welcomed in the Association. The Association aims: (1) To record volcanic activity and earthquakes in Hawaii; (2) to attract scientific men hither for special studies; (3) to promote the establishment of volcano observatories all over the world. The annual dues of regular members are $5; patrons of the Assocaition subscribe larger amounts.

WHITNEY LABORATORY OF SEISMOLOGY.

The Whitney Laboratory of Seismology is equipped with two Bosch-Omori 100 kg tromometers registering N-S and E-W motion, a heavy Omori tromometer registering E-W motion, and an Omori "ordinary Seismograph" designed for registering strong earthquakes in all three components of motion. These are seated on concrete piers in a closed basement room having practically constant temperature, beneath the chief Observatory building near the hotel. Time is referred to a rated chronometer, checked at intervals by solar observations with a transit. Both instruments are loaned by the College of Hawaii. Hawaiian standard time (H. S. T.) is 10 hrs. 30 min. slower than Greenwich time.

CANCANI SCALE OF SEISMIC INTENSITY.

Expressed by accelerations measured in millimeters per second per second.

I.	Instrumental	0.0	2.5
II.	Very slight	2.5	5.0
III.	Slight	5.0	10.0
IV.	Sensible, mediocre	10.0	25.0
V.	Rather strong	25.0	50.0
VI.	Strong	50.0	100.0
VII.	Very strong	100.0	250.0
VIII.	Ruinous	250.0	500.0
IX.	Disastrous	500.0	1000.0
X.	Very disastrous	1000.0	2500.0
XI.	Catastrophic	2500.0	5000.0
XII.	Great catastrophe	5000.0	10000.0

Grade IV. is ordinarily the minimum perceived by the senses; and in grade XII. the acceleration, or rate of change of motion (jerk) reaches that of terrestrial gravitation.

In the standard form of report the maximum intensity or acceleration, designated by the symbol a, or max. a, is given in the conventional unit, **the milligal.** The milligal is a measure of acceleration, such that 1 milligal = 1/100 mm. per sec. per sec. = 10 μ per sec. per sec. The Cancani scale, here defined in terms of millimeters per sec. per sec., can therefore be expressed in **milligals** by multiplying **each of the numbers by 100.**

WEEKLY BULLETIN
OF THE
Hawaiian Volcano Observatory

Vol. IV. HONOLULU, HAWAII, JULY, 1916. No. 7

By T. A. JAGGAR, JR.

TECHNOLOGY STATION, July 1.—During the week ending June 28, the molten lake in Halemaumau has continued to rise, chiefly by overflow of the southern half of the bench. The lake is of very great size and the bench narrow. The fumes have been thin so that there has been no difficulty in securing photographs and measurements. The depression of the lake surface below the rim is now less than 570 feet.

Measurements on June 23 from the east and southeast made the depression of the lake 592 feet, its length in an eastsoutheast-westnorthwest direction 893 feet, and its width at right angles to this 512 feet. The lake is larger than it was before the great collapse of June 5.

There were four fountains in the lake and five spatter grottoes on the bank. The surface of the lake was covered with quiet skin and the streaming was various. Old Faithful lay close to the north-northeast shore. Some glowing pots were sputtering lazily at the base of the north wall where the lava cascade of June 16 had solidified. Perpetual fountaining was in progress southwest of the center of the lake. The southeast cascade of the previous week had now become completely submerged so that the pool, formerly the source of the cascade, was now a cove of the lake ending squarely against the wall. A few rock slides were heard on the northeast where the largest talus slope rests against the wall under the 1894 bench. One slide was heard on the west.

On June 24 at ten-thirty in the morning, the lake by measurement had risen fifteen feet, its depth below the rim being now 577 feet. Its spatter rampart was built to a height of about two feet at the southeast and five feet to the northwest, and the northwestern bench appeared much higher than the bench at the opposite end of the lake. The streaming was more rapid and definitely from north to south, with fountains migrating southward from the central region and intermittent fountaining at Old Faithful. The interval between Old Faithful explosions was forty seconds. The heat felt on the rim was strong. There was bubble fountaining and rapid streaming against the northwest bank. The skins were blistered and thin. A grotto lined with stalactites appeared east of the southeast cove.

By watching closely, pulsations lasting several minutes could be detected of alternate quiet rising and more boisterous sinking spells. At six in the evening the lake was seen to break through the rampart and overflow the bench on the south. There was on this day very little rock sliding. The smell of the fumes was strong on the southwest rim. The principal white fumes rose from the north cascade locality, and a little blue smoke puffed up from the fountains. The bench around the lake was of fairly uniform width with a marked secondary terrace on the north and northeast. The eastern wall, 200 feet above the lake, showed white solfataric stain, cavities, and a wet steaming area. Freshly fallen talus blocks lay on the bench west and northwest. The principal talus slopes were northeast, northwest and southwest; on the west were only small scattered heaps.

On June 25 at four-thirty in the evening it was evident that the south bank had been overflowed. The lake

WEEKLY BULLETIN
of the
Hawaiian Volcano Observatory

Published Monthly at Honolulu, Hawaii, by the Hawaiian Volcano Research Association

L. W. de Vis-Norton........Secretary

Entered as second-class matter January 20, 1914, at the post-office at Honolulu, Hawaii, under the Act of August 24, 1912.

was brimming, streaming was from north to south, and large surface skins were being sucked down with commotion in the southern region. Old Faithful broke regularly, throwing up first a tree-shaped body of liquid which fell as a disk with a slapping sound, this being followed by the usual droning explosion. The streaming was from a large quiet northern skin. Occasionally there was bombardment at the southeast cove where outward streaming from the cove met the main current.

The north and east benches were mossy with Pele's hair, while the platform south and southwest was covered with fresh lava. A recently exposed cavern could be seen half way down the western wall. The spurting and flaming pot under the north wall continued active. Occasional abortive fountains in the lake would throw back a leaf of skin without exploding, leaving visible for an instant a patch of cherry red melt which would skin over at once.

On June 26 at five-thirty p. m. there was little change except that for the time slight subsidence was in progress. The talus was sliding on the northwest and west, twelve fountain areas could be counted and the smoke had slightly increased. There was occasional strong inrush at the southeast cove. The bank appeared ten feet high on the north, three feet high on the south, the rampart material at the south bank was shattered and at the north cascade locality distinct cracks were visible emitting smoke. There was much fresh Pele's hair to the leeward of the pit.

On June 27 at two-thirty p. m. the streaming was reversed, now flowing from south to north, and the lake was overflowing vigorously. The surface was covered with thin blistered skins in long carpets. The bench was overflooded east, southeast, south, and southwest to the wall. There were fountains near the shore northwest, northeast (Old Faithful), and southwest, and a niche had been built over the southeastern grotto.

The southeast cove was obliterated by overflow and the flows were spreading northward along the bench. On the north, however, the bank still appeared from two to three feet high. The fumes were thinner. At the base of the west wall was seen a large slab parted from the wall by a fifteen-foot chasm, the base of the slab on the lake side being buried in talus.

Except for two earthquakes felt at the observatory about one a. m. and eight a. m. on June 24, the week at the volcano has been quiet seismically; and the microseisms, volanic vibrations and tiltings have been normal.

The observatory during the past fortnight has been honored by visits from Professor Phelps of Yale, Professor Leuschner of the University of California, and Dr. A. L. Day of the geophysical laboratory of the Carnegie Institution of Washington. On June 27 Dr. Day left for the new lava flows of Mauna Loa accompanied by H. O. Wood and Alex Lancaster.

By T. A. JAGGAR, JR.

TECHNOLOGY STATION, Hawaii, July 8.—During the week ending July 5, the lava lake has continued to rise and with it the north bordering bench has risen and the south bench subsided. On the northwest and west the rising has proceeded by overflow from cracks more than one hundred feet above the lake. On the south the rising has been by overflow of the lake.

On June 29 at 8 p. m. there was a marked wall over the northeast side of the lake where Old Faithful broke at intervals over the bank. There was a tendency in the Old Faithful locality for the lava to heave rythmically at a point, with a rising and falling surge without ebullition. The streaming was from northwest and southeast, both ends being covered with skin while a bright zone remained open across the middle of the lake.

Fountains were numerous. The crusts tended to thicken and then they would crack along fissures which extended themselves gradually, making an unusual pattern. Above the skins south of Old Faithful about 9 p. m. there suddenly flashed out a yellow flame which bounced along the surface with a flickering effect, divided into smaller flames and went out. This the writer had never seen before.

On July 1 at 6 p. m. the northwest bank was at least fifteen feet high and showed three spatter benches; the southeast bank was only five feet high in a single bench. It was evident that the basin containing the lake was subsiding on the southeast and this movement had an undermining effect, for there was a large, fresh fall of debris east of the southeast cove and a small tumble on the west bench.

Here on the west appeared a new trickling lava cascade from a crack at the base of the wall at least seventy-five feet above the lake and south of the former cascade on that side. This probably started flowing on June 30. There were fresh festooned flows on the south bench and a new conspicuous boulder on the bench west. The activity was strong. Twelve fountains could be counted at once and Old Faithful was both puffing and splashing over the bank at intervals of from twenty to thirty seconds. Streaming was in currents from northwest to southeast, meeting in the middle region.

On July 2 at 4 p. m. Old Faithful had become a covered cone with two orifices on a new lower bench level, spouting lava and blowing every four or five minutes and quite irregularly. North-northwest there were now five spatter levels revealed above the lake. The south bench, on the other hand, showed every evidence of continued subsidence, there was a new tumble of wall rocks on the south edge of the southeast cove and fresh lava had invaded this tumble. The streaming was changeable, first toward the center and then away from it.

On the south, wrinkled and piled-up skins appeared, whereas on the north and northwest a beach-like bench was emerging. At 4:50 p. m. the lake rose rapidly and overflowed the benches, for a few moments all fountaining ceased, and three festooning overflows poured on to the bench from the south edge of the lake, where there was a place of pereptual fountaining. These merged into a single wide flow. Old Faithful cone became half surrounded by the rising lava and the explosions increased in violence and were accompanied by an adjacent shore fountain. At 5 p. m. there was a bubbling inrush against the north bank.

Measurements at 2 p. m. on July 4 made the depression of the lake 533 feet below the south rim of the pit and showed that the north bench was 28 feet high. This measurement indicated a rise of about three feet per day during the last fortnight, and a rise of the north bench in relation to the lake surface of about two feet per day in the same period. This singular movement resembles the tilting of the crags which has been measured before, only in this case it is the whole shore bench of the lake in a ring which is tilting about a horizontal axis northeast and southwest.

The new terrace north was about four feet high while the south bench stood about two feet above the lake. Streaming was from the southwest shore, meeting south-trending currents in a row of fountains which travelled southeastward. Wide blistered carpets of skin were formed and there was violent fountaining at the north and south ends of the lake. Old Faithful was reduced to a small smoking hole in the northeast lower bench and an occasional weak fountain under the bench. A wide cascade had developed at the new western locality, trickling steadily under its crust and dripping under the bank into the lake. The south bench was overspattered and overflowed with new lava which had obliterated the new southern rock tumble. Heat was strong on the rim and the fumes were thin.

The chasm at the base of the west-northwest wall was now brimming full of black lava and trickling over, glowing in spots. A similar chasm was developing back of the large northeast talus heap, and this tendency indicated a gaping at the base of the north semicircle of wall in accordance with an actual uplift of the bench ring.

At 9 p. m. streaming was in all directions, two cascades were trickling west-northwest and west, Old Faithful at long intervals spurted and snorted violently, and continuously emitted a blue flame through one of a group of glow holes in the bank. At 9:15 the writer saw again the white flame bubbles leap through a skin in the center of the lake and drift in a wind current like sea-foam over the skin until reduced to small flames and then extinguished. The phenomenon can best be described as a flaming froth. Its color was yellowish white like a coal flame. At one place a heavy blanket of skin was seen to rend apart and emit a sheaf of blue flame.

On July 5 at 11:30 a. m. large new solidified cascades were seen west and northwest and new delta benches at the edge of the lake below them. The large boulder on the northwest bench was surrounded by the cascade lava.

The lake was streaming variously, with thin hot blistered skins showing drawn surfaces and there was vigorous bubble fountaining along that bank southeast and west. There were fresh festooned overflows on the south bench which was widening to make a re-entrant point into the south end of the west talus. The fresh tumble southeast, however, was not yet invaded by overflow.

It was now quite evident that actual uplift of the north bench was taking place. The several terraces sloped down to lake level along the east and west sides of the basin. This tilt was indicated by the presence of two benches on the east, three benches northeast, four benches north-northeast, and five benches on the north under the old cascade. The latter had cracked away from the wall and showed a chasm behind it which extended into a marked valley behind the taluses on each side of it. Probably the lake had made for itself a bowl lining of solidified lava on the cup of slide rock from the recent collapses which lie beneath it. The overflowing of the south bank is overweighting that end of the bowl so that it goes down on the south and rises on the north.

The week has been very quiet seismically and there has been no unusual microseismic or volcanic vibration. Tilt of the ground has been strong to the westward.

On June 30 the Director, accompanied by A. J. W. Mackenzie made an expedition to Camp Bates and the Red Hill by the new trail. The new rest house at Red Hill on the northeast slope of Mauna Loa was found to be in good condition and an ample water supply had accumulated. An estimate was made of the furniture and equipment needed to complete the house as a habitation. Some of the large cones at the sources of lava flows were explored and photographed and the lower portion of the upper trail was examined, the markers being found in good condition. The party returned July 1.

Dr. Day, Mr. Wood and Alex Lancaster returned from their trip to the sources of the recent flows on July 4 and reported complete cessation of all activity. They were able to walk over the new lava and penetrate the craters without difficulty and a fine collection of photographs was obtained.

BY T. A. JAGGAR, JR.

TECHNOLOGY STATION, July 14—During the week ending July 12, the lava lake of Halemaumau has continued to rise slowly while the bordering bench on the north side of the lake has risen faster than the lake. The south bench has been overflooded as before and there have been some rock falls from the wall on the southeast and east.

On July 6 at two p. m. the lake appeared about five feet below the south bench and the streaming was toward the northwest. At two twenty-five and again at two-thirty, avalanches fell from the walls under the south station leaving a considerable hollow. Probably these falls were occasioned by the tendency of the south bench to subside, compensating the upward movement on the north.

At two p. m., July 7, there was new material poured out in the west cascade and the north smoke appeared thicker. At two-thirty p. m. an avalanche fell from the southeast wall.

At two-thirty p. m., July 8, the activity was the same and very large blocks of rock from the wall had fallen upon the southeast bench. At five-thirty p. m., ten areas could be counted fountaining steadily, on the southeast the lake was brimming, and the streaming was variable but mostly away from a skin which lay against the bank at the Old Faithful locality northeast. A line of fountains extended through the middle of the lake north and south. There were cracks in the bank above Old Faithful.

On July 9, at eleven a. m., the streaming was radial away from Old Faithful, the latter being a small semicircular grotto in the bank without fountaining. The lake appeared one foot down on the southeast and there was fountaining southeast and west. There was fresh glistening overspatter at the south margin, and the skins were thin and blistered.

Measurements on July 11, at nine-thirty a. m., made the lake level 520 feet below the south rim, indicating a rise of thirteen feet since July 4, or a rate of about two feet per day. The north bench at the smoke hole was thirty-seven feet above the lake, nine feet higher above the lake than on July 4, but actually twenty-two feet higher than on July 4 with reference to fixed bench marks. In other words the north bench had risen twenty-two feet in seven days while the lake was rising thirteen feet.

After the great collapse of June 5 the lower inner walls of Halemaumau scaled off extensively so as to greatly enlarge the lower part of the pit and straighten the walls. Measurement showed that the upper limit of this caving in on the northwest was 184 feet below the rim, and on the west 249 feet.

On this date, July 11, there were rock falls from the east walls. In the morning a steady cascade was pouring from the lake into a boiling pot at the Old Faithful locality. At 12, noon, the outflow stopped and the place became a quiet fountain. Before this change the streaming was radial from a central skin. Afterwards the streaming was northward and against the bank northeast, northwest and southeast.

There were fresh festooned overflows on the bench south and there had been fresh overflow at the southeast cove on the new avalanche material. The fumes were thin, the lake very hot and covered with thin blistered skins and a spatter rampart was built on the south. There was much cracking in the raised bench northwest, north and northeast. At nine p. m. the lake appeared slightly lowered with a vigorous line of fountains west of the center. Old Faithful was a quiet grotto with hanging stalactites. There was glow and flame at the head of the west cascade. Rocks were still falling from the east wall.

H. O. Wood reports that during the week ending July 12 four small local earthquakes have been registered in the Whitney Laboratory of Seismology. One of these in the late evening of July 11, was felt feebly locally. The others were too small to be perceptible.

Microseisms have been of weak to moderate amplitude throughout the week. Volcanic vibrations have ranged from weak to strong and back to moderate values in amplitude. Strong tilt to west has prevailed throughout the week but no corresponding north-south tilt has been registered.

By T. A. JAGGAR, Jr.

TECHNOLOGY STATION, July 21—The week ending July 19, 1916, has shown continued rising of the Kilauea lava column, the rise increasing in vigor on July 15 and thereafter. A marked event of the week was the fall of a large part of the east end of the 1894 bench.

On July 13 at noon, a black lava stack was seen rising thirty feet above its base in the chasm west of the north smoke crack and close to the wall. This was a spatter cone of remarkably straight sides like a stove pipe, and from its summit lava was spurting which fell back into the chasm. About five p. m. the east end of the 1894 bench fell with a crash and a red dust cloud arose. Where the platform of overflow of 1910 had been, just under the east rest house, there was left a gulch with sliding stones in its bottom. This was the platform frequently visited in the past by those who clambered down the trail to the 1894 bench.

The avalanche fell directly into the lake and added a southern extension to the large northeastern talus. The lake was so violently displaced that it flooded the whole south and west bench with a film of lava and rose fully forty feet up the southwest wall leaving a black mark. A return wave plastered the northeast bench.

On July 14 at four-thirty p. m. the lake was still rising and brimming at the southeast end. It was building a new bench against the base of the new east talus, there piling up folded skins in a heap. There was a spatter rampart along the south bench. A glow crack appeared at the head of the west cascade. There was very violent fountaining mostly along a north-south line west of the center of the lake. Old Faithful was no longer identifiable. The north bench was still rising as shown by a new lower terrace extending from the large northern smoke crack to the eastern corner of the lake making six terraces on the east side of the smoke crack. West of the smoke crack the rising appeared less in evidence, the eastern block tending to become a rising crag bounded by large fissures.

Stones were still sliding in the avalanche gulch in the east end of the 1894 bench, and the large crack between the southeast station and the east station was found to have widened from twelve to eighteen inches in places. At present, and as long as the slopes below continue to work, the east station opposite the east rest house is unsafe. Visitors should be very cautious at the present time, for the walls of the pit are in a dangerous condition and the upper edge should be avoided in these places where below rocks are seen falling. There have been heavy falls during the past week on both sides of the east station, which is the terminus of the main trail hitherto visited by everybody.

On July 15 at ten-thirty a. m. the lake appeared little changed, the streaming was from north to south, smoke rose from the north cracks and the west cascade, there were many fountains, no new overflows appeared on the south bench and the bench under the new east talus appeared about one foot high. Stones were still sliding from under the east station.

At some time in the afternoon rapid rising began. At nine p. m. the lake was overflowing the southern banks in floods, the streams spreading out in rapid festooned flows and the northwest cascade broke out at the wall and flowed to the lake in two forks. The west cascade chasm was also spouting and a heaving skin in the chasm showed that the cleft was full of molten lava. Fountaining areas developed in various parts of the lake, the streaming being mostly southward. The north stack was ejecting incandescent spray.

On July 17, at three p. m., the bench east, south and southwest was continuously flooded. Streaming in the lake was from north to south, and ten fountains could be counted, mostly in the south central area. The noise was mostly plashing, with some hissing on the northwest. The south bench had greatly increased in width. The rising lava had submerged the two lower terraces, so that on the northwest the number was reduced from four to two, and east of the north smoke crack from six to four. There was no evident increase of tilt. From the west station the north stack was now seen to be a spatter cone greatly reduced in height. A large cavern was seen in the west wall about 300 feet down.

On July 18, at eleven a. m., measurement made the lake surface at the northwest bank 482 feet below the southeast rim of the pit. Streaming in the lake was from north to south, and at eleven-thirty a. m. the lake was rising and exhibited six border fountains and three central ones. Old Faithful had reappeared as a pot in the lower terrace northeast, ejecting heavy splashes at intervals or from thirty to sixty seconds. The streaming was away from a quiet skin at the base of the west cascade. A fountain grotto had been built under a half-cone at the southeast cove and a similar niche could be seen building at the foot of the northwest cascade.

A remarkable phenomenon at the southeast grotto was the inflation of large blisters in surface skins that were being sucked into the grotto. The heavy skins would become bellied upward with gas from the lava below, and this inflation would proceed for a distance of from eighty to one hundred feet northward from the grotto until the point of the bag so formed reached a zigzag glow line, where it burst and at once deflated the whole blister so that it fell in collapsing folds. The effect was quite like that observed when the wind gets under a large sheet of canvas and momentarily balloons it upward. It was clearly evident that excessive gas was rising in the neighborhood of the grotto, and this particular skin must have been unusually gas-tight.

There was a large new tumble of white stones on the southeast bench which had fallen from the solfataric patch in the wall. There was a shore rampart five feet high along the south bench. A small rock fall appeared on the bench south, which was greatly widened and covered with festooned flows. Along the north side of the lake a new bench had emerged, making five terraces east of the north smoke crack. Rocks were sliding east and southeast, under the east station.

On July 19, at eight-thirty a. m., the fume from the pit was very thin, and that which was rising from the north inner bench and in two other similar places at the west cascade appeared to be mostly white steam. The lake was streaming northward and southward from the middle region. Old Faithful was quiet except for occasional puffs of gas. The rim about the lake was one foot high and the fountaining varied, being sometimes noisy in patches and sometimes almost entirely absent. There were new overflows on the bench south and east. The northwest cascade had flooded eastward along the base of the northwest talus. The west chasm had so filled with new lava that the large slab in it had disappeared. The splash mark of the avalanche of July 13 now rose only about three feet above the built-up bench.

The following report from the Whitney Laboratory of Seismology is submitted by H. O. Wood:

''During the week ending with July 19 two very slight local earthquake movements have been registered and two or three doubtful groups of waves. Microseismic motion has varied from moderate to slight values in amplitude. The amplitude of volcanic vibration waves has varied spasmodically through a considerable range. There has been no noteworthy change in tilt.

By T. A. JAGGAR, Jr.

TECHNOLOGY STATION, July 27—During the week ending July 26, 1916, the lava lake of Kilauea has continued to rise with intervals of stagnation, the average rate being four feet per day. Two of the cascade localities, respectively north and west, where within a month lava has poured down into the lake from wall fissures, have now become chasms, owing probably to the cessation of cascade flow under the crust, and the collapse of the crust in each case into the tube beneath.

On July 21 at ten p. m. the bank southeast appeared about three feet high and the bench, which had been overflooded on the south side of the lake within a few hours was covered with crusted flows showing glowing cracks. There were flaming spatter grottoes on the southeast, south and northwest. There was inrush at the north chasm. Twice white flames were seen from ignited gas which burst through surface skins. The skins were heavy and the fountaining was slight. There was a fountaining spot at the Old Faithful locality. The surface streaming was various. A fresh rock tumble lay on the southeast bench. The lowest northeast terrace was submerged.

On July 22 at five p. m. the lake from the south station showed a glow crack in the bench over Old Faithful, a spatter cone on the bank west of the north chasm, a new cracking at right angles to the lake shore in the west cascade, and the lava-filled chasm along the wall at the head of that cascade exhibited settling. A belt of skin lay across the southern end of the lake with streaming southeastward on both sides of it and there was local streaming toward the bank at Old Faithful. The new flows on the south bench had started to spread along the wall back of a great slab of rock which lay somewhat detatched from the wall along the southwest quarter of the pit. This slab appears like a talus but is in reality solid rock separated from the wall by a chasm filled with debris which is continuous with the chasm farther north that gave vent to the cascades.

On July 23 measurement at noon indicated that the west border of the lake was 463 feet below the southeast station making the rise of the lake surface nineteen feet in the previous five days. At eleven a. m. there was rapid overflowing of the south bench, masses of lava pouring across the bench to the wall of the pit showing that the rising had taken a vigorous spurt. This continued for more than two hours. At the other end of the lake in the north chasm, which had grown by collapse to a width of about 75 feet, a double fountain was continuously doming in a cauldron with much noise and a slight insuck toward it of the surface of the lake. On the northeast bank at the Old Faithful locality a crack in the bench showed lava from the lake trickling inward and downward to a pot under the bench where a fountain below splashed occasionally. A large shore fountain was playing on the southeast. Streaming was in general from the west shore. There were fountains in the middle of the lake which was otherwise covered with striated and blistered thin skins. The heat from the lake was strong. There was much fume on the north and west.

There were thus two seemingly opposed processes at work at opposite ends of the lake. On the north the lake was pouring down into holes in the bank. On the south the lake was overflowing the bank. The explanation is that the overflowing on the south was overweighting the lake basins like a saucer on that side, and so raising the terraced rim of the north side. With reference to that north rim therefore the lake was deserting its shores and so giving rise to all the phenomena of subsidence. Fissures in the north bank gaping open below the lake level while the rim was tilting up, caused the lake to flow into the open spaces. Consequently the lake, in reality rising, appeared to be rising on the south and sinking on the north.

On July 24 at one p. m. the south bench showed that the rising had continued. On the previous day this bench had been covered with festooned skins. To-day it was smooth with the crack-and-founder pattern. There was a slight new fall of debris southeast. Fresh small over-spatter flows appeared on the south. At the north chasm there was slow inflow from the lake and rocks were tumbling at its inner end where also there was a grotto lined with stalactites. At one-thirty p. m. a hissing and sputtering pot opened at the head of the west cascade. There were shore grottoes northwest and southeast. The streaming was north, northwest and southeast. Six terraces could be counted east of the north cauldron, the lowest of very recent date. White smoke rose from the north chasm and blue from the west cascade.

From five to seven p. m. the cavern in the west wall about one-hundred feet above the lake was seen to have fresh black lava folds within it, as though invaded by rising lava from within. It is possible that this cavern communicates with the great southwest rift, which on the upper edge of Halemaumau has recently gaped wider open by several feet. At night spears of flame were visible from the puffing west cone and from the glow crack over Old Faithful.

On July 25 at eleven a. m. the bank of the lake was four feet high on the north and two feet on the south. There was a fresh small overflow southeast. There was sluggish inflow to the north chasm, the action of the lake surface was quiet, large crusty skins covered its western half and the streaming was northward and southeastward. At 12:40 p. m. a small slide fell from the lower south cliff to the bench.

The west chasm filling showed cracking and there was no spurting at the west cone. The north-northwest chasm where the stack had been was seen to be full of debris. The north chasm showed red walls and red debris from the upraised bench indicating that under the action of the fumes oxidation of this recent lava had proceeded very rapidly.

On July 26 at nine-thirty a. m. the lake was very hot and fresh overflows covered the bench southwest, south and southeast. The western cascade had now collapsed into a chasm like that on the north, this chasm extending from the lake to the wall. A small festooned overflow from the lake lay upon the cascade lava. Again the phenomenon of overflow south and recession from the shore north was in progress. A flow was pouring on to the east bench, while at the Old Faithful locality there was inrush and cascading from the lake to a cavity under the bank. There was a large glowing cone on the bank over Old Faithful. Large steady fountains played south of the center of the lake and near the north chasm. Streaming was sluggish and indefinite. There was a fresh tumble of rocks on the northwest bench; that on the southeast bench was covered by new lava. The west cone was hissing and five terraces only could be counted east of the north chasm. A sulphurous spot in the southeast wall fifty feet above the lake showed a small cavern revealed by the recent downfalls.

The following report from the Whitney Laboratory of Seismology is submitted by Mr. H. O. Wood:—

During the week ending July 26, five, and possibly six, small local earthquakes have been registered; of these two were of barely perceptible strength, the others instrumental only and very slight also. The amplitude of microseismic motion and of that of volcanic vibration has varied slightly from small to moderate values in a wholly irregular way. There has been no significant change in tilt.

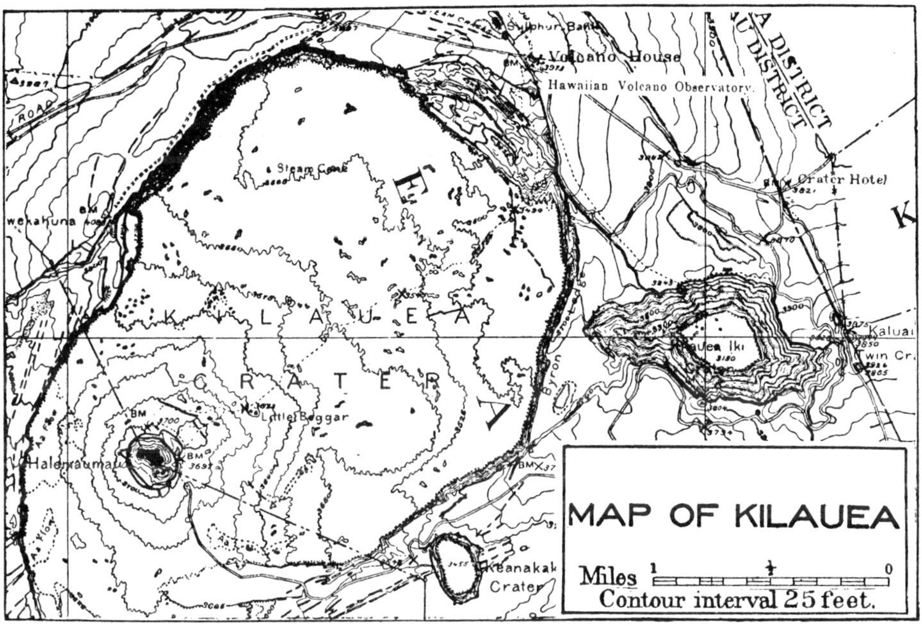

HAWAIIAN VOLCANO RESEARCH ASSOCIATION.

This society is a voluntary one, made up of subscribers to scientific work which is being executed by the Massachusetts Institute of Technology.

In 1915 there are about 100 subscribers in Hawaii and elsewhere, firms and individuals. A group of firms and persons in Hilo built the main observatory building in the spring of 1912. Publications to date have been weekly reports since the summer of 1911, now reprinted in Honolulu in monthly form. The Massachusetts Institute of Technology will publish annual reports, of which the introductory number was printed in 1912.

The weekly bulletin as it appears in the Advertiser is reprinted as a leaflet and sent to regular annual subscribers to the work of the Association. L. A. Thurston is president of the Board of Directors of the Association, and R. W. Shingle is treasurer. New subscribers who are interested in volcanoes will be welcomed in the Association. The Association aims: (1) To record volcanic activity and earthquakes in Hawaii; (2) to attract scientific men hither for special studies; (3) to promote the establishment of volcano observatories all over the world. The annual dues of regular members are $5; patrons of the Assocaition subscribe larger amounts.

WHITNEY LABORATORY OF SEISMOLOGY.

The Whitney Laboratory of Seismology is equipped with two Bosch-Omori 100 kg tromometers registering N-S and E-W motion, a heavy Omori tromometer registering E-W motion, and an Omori ''ordinary Seismograph'' designed for registering strong earthquakes in all three components of motion. These are seated on concrete piers in a closed basement room having practically constant temperature, beneath the chief Observatory building near the hotel. Time is referred to a rated chronometer, checked at intervals by solar observations with a transit. Both instruments are loaned by the College of Hawaii. Hawaiian standard time (H. S. T.) is 10 hrs. 30 min. slower than Greenwich time.

CANCANI SCALE OF SEISMIC INTENSITY.

Expressed by accelerations measured in millimeters per second per second.

I.	Instrumental	0.0	2.5
II.	Very slight	2.5	5.0
III.	Slight	5.0	10.0
IV.	Sensible, mediocre	10.0	25.0
V.	Rather strong	25.0	50.0
VI.	Strong	50.0	100.0
VII.	Very strong	100.0	250.0
VIII.	Ruinous	250.0	500.0
IX.	Disastrous	500.0	1000.0
X.	Very disastrous	1000.0	2500.0
XI.	Catastrophic	2500.0	5000.0
XII.	Great catastrophe	5000.0	10000.0

Grade IV. is ordinarily the minimum perceived by the senses; and in grade XII. the acceleration, or rate of change of motion (jerk) reaches that of terrestrial gravitation.

In the standard form of report the maximum intensity or acceleration, designated by the symbol a, or max. a, is given in the conventional unit, **the milligal.** The milligal is a measure of acceleration, such that 1 milligal = 1/100 mm. per sec. per sec. = 10 μ per sec. per sec. The Cancani scale, here **defined in terms of millimeters per sec. per sec., can therefore be expressed in milligals by multiplying each of the numbers by 100.**

WEEKLY BULLETIN
OF THE

Hawaiian Volcano Observatory

Vol. IV. HONOLULU, HAWAII, AUGUST, 1916. No. 8

TECHNOLOGY STATION, August 1. —It has been found advisable to slightly change the character of the monthly bulletins, and it is hoped that this change will succeed in making them of more real interest to the members of the Volcano Research Association.

It has been objected that some of the reports were too technical for the understanding of the uninitiated, and further, that there was too much "sameness" in the reports month by month. These objections are, perhaps, well sustained, but it should be pointed out that spectacular volcanic happenings are of infrequent occurrence, and that the major part of the work of the scientist in charge, consists in careful and methodical watching, in itself frequently an extremely monotonous task.

The Board of Directors, however, is desirous of adding in every possible way to the interest of the regular reports sent out from the Technology Station at Kilauea, and has therefore arranged that such reports shall be edited by a writer of considerable experience and an enthusiastic supporter of the work and objects of the Association.

In addition to this change, which is first apparent in this present number, it is hoped, if funds permit, to present, each month, a series of illustrations showing the changes taking place at the Volcano during the month under review. It is further proposed to issue, as circumstances allow, supplementary bulletins of an interesting nature upon subjects connected with the routine or other work of the Association, written from a novel standpoint.

Members are advised to keep the illustrations appearing each month, as these will form a constantly enlarging collection of unique and valuable photographs of occurrences never again likely to repeat themselves.

It is hoped, by these and other methods to be announced later, to add to the interest already taken in the work of the Association, and to merit still further generous encouragement of its aims and objects.

L. W. de Vis-Norton, Editor.

The lava lake at Kilauea has continued to rise during the week ending August 2. At two fifteen p. m. on July 27, the lake was visited, position being taken up at the south station, from which point there is generally clear seeing. Fountains were playing in the center and in the channel on the northern side of the lake; the lake was brimming level with the south bank, over which fresh lava had recently flowed, while an overflow onto the west bank was still moving. Old Faithful could be seen in action in a cavern under the northeast bank, an interesting spectacle for visitors. There were small rockfalls on this date, one being seen on the southeast bench and another occurring from the lower section of the southwest wall, at two-forty-five p. m.

The hour was late when the lake was visited on the following date. At eleven p. m. on July 28, rapid lava flow was rushing from the lake into the north channel, which, owing to fresh slides of red rock, had become somewhat wider. A fountain was in action in this channel, and fresh flows were noted in the west chasm. Visitors frequently succeed in getting most interesting time-exposure pictures of these rapid flows at night, but care should be taken to keep the camera perfectly steady.

On July 29 at five p. m. streaming of the flows in various directions was taking place, though the activity as a whole was moderate. The inner end of the north channel appeared to be ex-

WEEKLY BULLETIN
of the
Hawaiian Volcano Observatory

Published Monthly at Honolulu, Hawaii, by the Hawaiian Volcano Research Association

L. W. de Vis-Norton........Secretary

Entered as second-class matter January 20, 1914, at the post-office at Honolulu, Hawaii. under the Act of August 24, 1912.

tending westward. A chasm had appeared under the bank in the locality of Old Faithful, and into this the lake was pouring steadily. The west chasm had become an extension of the T-shaped bench, which had been repeatedly overflowed from the lake, and about the center of this area could be seen a spouting, flaming pot. The south bench had also received overflow on this day.

The lake was visited at six-thirty p. m., on July 30. In the Old Faithful section the lake was still pouring down into a cavern, as on the previous day, but was now flowing between large lumps of spatter which had been built out from the bank during the early hours of the day. Moreover, there was an intensely interesting spectacle in progress at this point, for the cavern, or pot, every half-minute or so would become filled up from within, and then, as the under-pressure increased, there would be a great explosion; the lava would be forced under tremendous pressure, through every hole and crevice, and would spurt in great jets some thirty feet up the bank. The spatter lumps already referred to, were thus subjected to a heavy bombardment, and eventually one of them collapsed, falling into the lake, and causing rapid longshore streaming towards the pot.

At the north arm, there was slow inward streaming, and in the bank to the west of it, several large flaming holes had opened. The center of the lake was occupied by several continually shifting fountains, and the greater part of the surface streaming was towards these fountains, and towards the southeast bank. Over Old Faithful there were more flaming holes, and some also in the west channel. The southern portion of the lake was sluggish at times, and dark, quiet crusts would form over it at intervals.

A visit of inspection at four p. m. on July 31, showed general sluggishness of the lake surface. The west channel was inactive, and a new cone appeared in it. The spatter lumps near Old Faithful had all vanished save one, and the fountain itself was quiet. General streaming towards the southeast was in progress, the skins as a whole were thin, and the north arm was crusted over.

Small new overflows had taken place through the south rampart, and all over the widening south bench appeared a new crack and founder pattern. The southwest slope, composed of fallen debris from above, was fast being buried beneath this bench, but fresh slides of rock appeared on the bench southeast and southwest. At the inner end of the north arm a fresh red talus slide was observed.

The following morning, August 1, the lake was again quiet. Inspection was made at eleven-forty-five a. m., at which time there were but few fountains and almost the whole lake surface was covered with thin, blistered skins. Old Faithful was now covered by a low, wide dome, under which, on the lake-side was an arched cavern, from which every now and then fountains would belch outward. The greatest visible activity on this morning, was somewhat to the north of the center of the lake where there was occasional turbulent fountain play.

The west cone, first noted on the previous day, was now hissing; the southeast bench displayed freshly fallen rock, and slides were heard to fall from the southeast wall. It was quite evident that during the week, the northern and western benches had again risen, for there were now six terraces east of the north channel and the crags on each side of the west channel appeared higher, but on the whole, the lake, during the past six days, has exhibited no very spectacular features, except the display alluded to as occuring on July 30th.

The following report from the Whitney Laboratory of Seismology is submitted by Mr. H. O. Wood:

''During the week ending with August 2, two earthquakes of very small seismographic amplitude, and perhaps a third, have been registered. The amplitude of microseismic motion has been moderate in amount, though somewhat greater than in other recent weeks. The energy of volcanic vibration has fluctuated as usual without specially noteworthy characteristics.

''There has been a slight progressive tilt to the east and north, but its amount has not been strikingly noticeable.''

T. A. JAGGAR, JR.

TECHNOLOGY STATION, August 12.—The great fire-lake is now providing an exceedingly spectacular display, and its increasing size cannot but add daily to its impressiveness. A steady rise of the lake level, at the rate of about 2¾ feet a day, is taking place, although there have been some short periods of falling. The area of the lake was measured on August 1, the dimensions being found to be 820 feet in length with a width of 550 feet, while on that date the surface of the lake was 447 feet below the upper rim of the pit.

Comparatively rapid changes have taken place during the period under review, that of most moment to visitors being the continued avalanches from the eastern rim and the wall below, with a consequent further opening of the large crack on the surface adjacent to the east rest-house. As this rest-house is the usual point of observation for sightseers, it would seem advisable to sound a quiet note of warning, as was done some weeks ago. The trail from the automobile rendezvous leading to the rest-house, is wide and distinct, and there is no necessity for approach to the rim in the neighborhood of the large crack referred to. The rest-house is an excellent point of vantage, but visitors are cautioned not to venture between the ''Danger'' signs and the rim of the pit, as these signs have been placed there in order to prevent risk of possible accident.

Another feature of interest is undoubtedly the increase in fountaining areas, and while these may vary considerably from day to day, visitors at the present time would seem assured of a particularly imposing spectacle.

Commencing on August 1, a daily survey of conditions has been made, and is the subject of this present report. Upon that date levels and dimensions were ascertained, and these have already been alluded to.

At 2 p. m. on August 2 the level of the lake was found to have subsided some five feet, but a few moments prior to ascertaining this fact, there was a small avalanche from the south wall, preceded by similar slides from the wall to the southeast. The channel or north side of lake, referred to in last report, was quiet, but fresh overflows of lava had taken place on the west and also to the southeast.

The following day was remarkable for the great increase in fountaining around the borders of the lake, extending also along the north channel, which was particularly active at 2 p. m. on this day. A surface current poured steadily into the Old Faithful cavity, the bank above this being surmounted by a new cone. Old Faithful fountain was exploding at frequent intervals with considerable violence; thick blue fumes were rising on the north, making seeing a matter of difficulty, but on the southwest bank, stalactites from one to two feet long were seen to have developed under the roof of a large grotto or cave.

August 4 showed that the lake, when visited at 2 p. m., had undergone a further sinking, and changes were taking place in connection with the west channel. The crags forming the entrance to this channel had taken the form of protruding capes and were some 20 feet in height above the lake-surface. Steady streaming was in progress from this west channel, spreading eastward and southward. The southwest bank was about ten feet above the lake, and small avalanches were falling from the walls south and southeast, these having their origin at points some 50 feet above the bench which surrounds the lake in these sections.

Another visit of inspection was made at 9 p. m. on this date, at which time the action of Old Faithful was exceedingly pronounced, the heavy explosions alternating with intervals during which inward streaming of the molten lake-surface took place. The chimney in the third terrace above this point was glowing and emitting flames, while in the north channel steady inward streaming was in progress, and a large glowing hole had made an appearance in the terrace to the west of the channel. There were large glow-cracks behind the lake rampart on the southeast and southwest sides, heavy bombardment was taking place, with loud rumbling noises, on the southeast bank, several large glow-holes made their appearance in the west chasm, while the entrance to the west channel had so widened as to become in reality an arm of the main lake, although the two flanking crags were still conspicuous. There were but few avalanches during the period of night observation, though a slight earthquake about 9:30 p. m. dislodged a small quantity of rock towards the east.

At 3 o'clock on the afternoon of Saturday, August 5, the crags on either side of the north channel had risen considerably, exhibiting no less than seven terraces on the east, and six on the west sides. The western crag was riven with great chasms. A similarly changed appearance characterized the western channel, the flanking crags being terraced in regular stairways. The outflows from this channel had almost completely buried the great debris slope under the northwestern wall of the pit, while to the eastward of this a huge, ragged chasm had opened behind the north crag. The large glow-hole west of the north channel had partly fallen in, converting this portion into a bay towards which surface currents were streaming. A cavern of considerable size had opened above the southeast bench, onto which slight rock-falls had tumbled. Old Faithful was very active, and there were fifteen fountaining areas, some of them very continuous. The great rift on the southwest rim, at some distance back from the edge, was emitting hot blasts of sulphurous air on this day, and at the west station the odor of sulphuretted hydrogen was unpleasantly perceptible. This is very unusual and of rare occurrence in this section.

The general appearance of the lake on 5th August induced a close inspection on the following day, three separate journeys being made from the Observatory to the pit. The first took place at 11 a. m., at which time the lake was rising very markedly, the southeast bench was being overflowed, the south bench was covered with new flows, Old Faithful was exploding in the usual violent manner, and some twelve to fifteen fountaining areas were visible. Heavy smoke was rising from cracks in the summit of the crag east of the north channel, making visibility poor, but as a whole, the activity of the lake was moderate.

In the afternoon the southeast rampart was undergoing a very heavy bombardment, and a glowing cone was visible above the western extension of the lake.

Another visit was made at 10 p. m., when there was strong streaming out from the west channel. The chasm at the head of that channel was now seen to have taken the form of an elongated pond, glowing beneath thin skins. The crags at the entrance of the channel loomed over points of quiet surface skin, but streaming was in action from between these points, traveling eastward and spreading outward in fan shape. Right opposite, on the other side of the lake, there was strong streaming into the Old Faithful grotto, and from this bank, clear across the lake to the west channel, there was a row of traveling fountains migrating eastward. The southeast rampart showed new grottoes hung with stalactites, and the same formations were visible in the west bay of the north channel. That the lake was rising was apparent from the gradual disappearance of the stalactites. There was a considerable amount of flaming, north, northeast and southeast; there were glowing cracks in all the new flows, small rockfalls took place both north and south, and there was much smoke, with consequent obscuration.

Monday, August 7, was without noteworthy incident. Skins were thin on the surface of the lake, there was radial streaming, and the west pond appeared to be higher than the main lake. The crags on either side of the west channel, as well as those flanking the north channel, were showing signs of tilting away from their respective channels; there were cracks visible southwest, south and east in the rampart, and a few had appeared in the bench. There was less smoke than on the previous day, and it was noted that the fallen debris on the south bench had been quite covered by new flows.

The following day the lake had risen, and at 4 p. m. twenty-two fountaining areas could be counted. There was a sound of strong hissing from the west side. Further tilting of the crags flanking both channels was apparent, and on the southwest there was a new, high cave with arched roof lined with stalactites. Heavy bombardment was in progress against the southeast and southern shores of the lake, and the surface streaming was largely southward. The whole shape of the lake showed rapid alterations as the bays on the northwest and southwest developed.

On August 9th streaming was strong from the west and north channels; the wall behind the latter channel appeared to be breaking away, and revealed fresh red slabs underneath. The west pond was thickly crusted, and the only occurrence of note was a further heavy rock-fall from the 1894 bench under the east rest-house.

At 2 p. m., August 10, streaming was north as well as into the Old Faithful grotto, and there was new overflow of crackling lava completely covering the south bench. There was no doubt that the heavy fall of the day before, and further falls under the east rest-house on 10th, had the effect of widening the big cracks on the rim of the pit in that section. This crack now gapes as much as six feet, and should be avoided by visitors.

On August 11th the lake was visited at 2 p. m. There was not much change, but the west lake had again become active and was showing boiling fountains. The north channel appeared to be developing a new pond along the wall, the south bench was covered with fresh flows. Half an hour later the south rampart was brimming over and a flow was pouring across the whole bench.

The Whitney Laboratory of Seismology submits the following report by Mr. Wood:

During the interval beginning with August 3 and ending with August 11, one very small local earthquake, of certain characteristics, has been registered; but a large number of very small wave-groups of the kind difficult to discriminate between definite shocks and "storms" of volcanic vibrations have been recorded, especially in the middle part of the interval. Microseismic amplitudes have ranged from moderate to moderately large values, and then to small values. Volcanic vibration amplitudes have been of moderate to strong values—with the doubtful groups mentioned above. In the early part of the interval there was a small, slow progressive tilt to the westward, followed by a return movement to the eastward, of the same character.

T. A. JAGGAR, JR.

TECHNOLOGY STATION, August 19, 1916.—The week ending August 18, 1916, has been remarkable for the activity of the great fire-lake of the volcano, the changes in shape of the lake, and also for the continuance of the avalanches from the upper rim and benches, in one of which downfalls the northeast observing and signal station was completely destroyed.

The observations of the week commenced as usual on Saturday. On this day, 12th August at 2 p. m., the lake was visited and disclosed fifteen fire fountains in action, their greatest activity being toward the north. It was at this time that the destruction of the northeast station was discovered, it having probably fallen during the preceding night. The Old Faithful cavern was receiving surface streaming, the northeast crags were smoking heavily, but the western and northern arms of the lake were both quiet. The next day, Sunday 13th, was remarkable for a very sudden rise which took place at 5:30 p. m. Heavy flows of lava poured along the south and east benches, meeting at the southeastern point. The accumulations weighted down the bench until the high rampart at the southeast grotto was finally overwhelmed by the flows. Old Faithful was now boiling in an open pot on the northeast shore. The gas pressure was everywhere high, but along the southeastern shore it was intense, and molten spray from the incessant ebullition was shot up eighty feet into the air with loud blowing and rumbling noises. At 6:10 p. m. there was a heavy avalanche close to the former northeast station, thirteen fountain areas were in action and the west and north arms were receiving heavy overflows from the northeast bench. The capes on each side of the west channel were now straight promontories.

The significance of the changes taking place at this time rendered close observation necessary,. and the lake was watched throughout the night. At 2:15 on the morning of August 14, another rapid rise commenced on the western side, and a quarter of an hour later the banks of the lake were everywhere overflowing rapidly. Subsidence began about 3:30 a. m., the lake sinking about three feet below its banks, but the process was reversed at 6 a. m., and there was then a magnificent display of fountaining.

Observations taken at 11:50 a. m. on this date disclosed the fact that the face of the 1894 bench had stripped off, and this process had evidently been the cause of the collapse of the northeast station. The lake at this time was fairly quiet with surface streaming radiating from the west channel. The Old Faithful chimney still existed but there was a large open pot below it. Flows on the east bench had extended behind the northeast talus. A most interesting phenomenon had taken place, for the heavy lava flows to the north had weighed down the margins of the northern bench, causing a pronounced tilting of a section of the northeastern part of the lake basin, and bringing to view an increase of height in the western promontories and also a small island, which had emerged from the liquid surface of the lake.

A few minutes after noon there was another heavy rise, and for an hour the display was brilliant in the extreme. The northwestern corner of the pit received a great overflow, starting with an impressive manifestation of cracking and foundering that extended from the island to the wall clear across the northwest cove. There were two periods of overflow into the north channel, also at the northwest bench, the west pond and the southwest and eastern benches. The northern of the two west promontories exhibited eight strongly titled terraces, the tilt being westward. Measurements were taken on the following day, August 15th at 11 a. m. The floor area of the pit from northwest to southeast measured 1100 feet, while the width from northeast to southwest was 900 feet, the surface level of the lake being 390 feet below the rim, a rise of 33 feet in seven days. The smoking northeast crag was 32 feet above the lake level. There was further rising on this day, the ledge pinnacle and talus at the base of the southwest wall were surrounded with new flows, while the west promontories, the new island and the north-northwest crag all seemed to be higher. At noon there were about a dozen fountains playing, and the benches were overflooding east and southwest. The southwest shore niche had widened but the grotto

Aug. 16, 1916. S. W. pinnacle surrounded by rising lava, from S. E. station

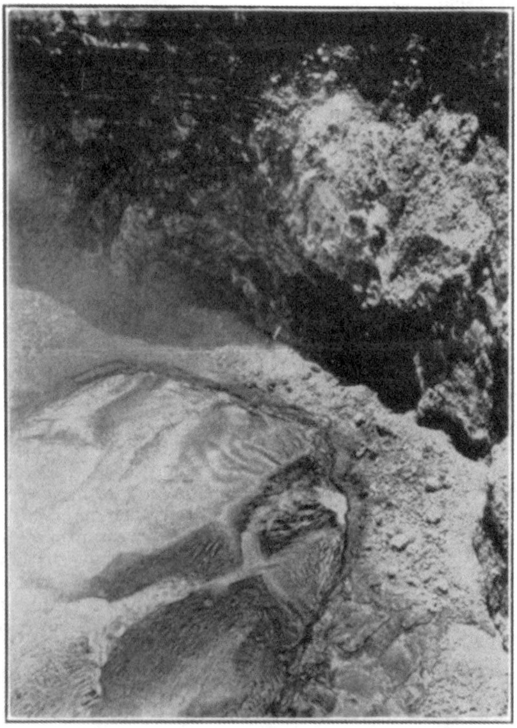

July 31, 1916, from S. W. Avalanche debris on S. bench and south end of lava lake.

Aug. 16, 1916. Notch in 1894 bench, (x) site of former N. E. station, looking from northeast rim across 1894 bench at E. resthouse.

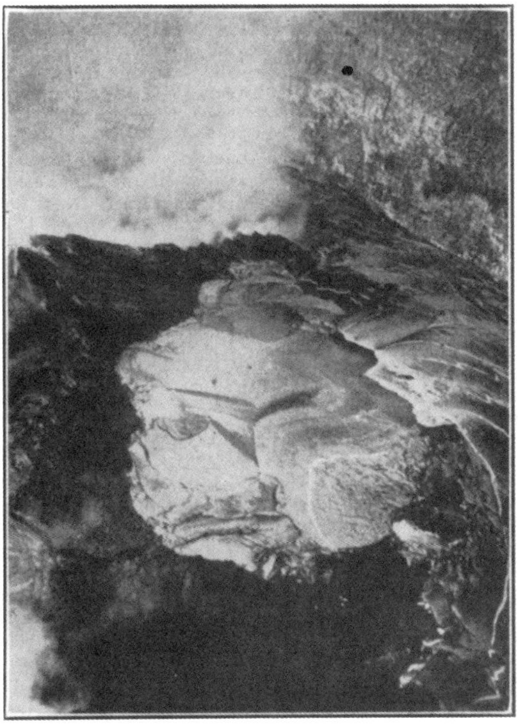

Aug. 23, 1916. New N. W. pond from N. showing overflooding of N. W. bench on the right and new ledges on the left.

on the north had contracted greatly. The north channel, although occassionally overflooded, appeared as a bench raised above the lake level, extending into a wide lower terrace around the old crags, burying the old lower terraces and tending to isolate the crags. At 1 p. m. the lake had fallen to some five feet below its banks and was fairly quiet as regards fountaining, though lines of fountains occasionally formed from the west channel across the entire lake, with larger areas almost in the centre. There were fresh flows in every direction, and cracking and foundering were in progress in the west pond region. August 16th, at 8.30 p. m., there was clear seeing only from the west and south. The new island and the western promontories had risen with amazing rapidity and were now at least fifteen feet above the lake, the island standing out as a pulpit-shaped rock with an isthmus extension towards the south. The lower bench on the west side of the north channel had risen about ten feet. The southern of the two western promontories showed a new crack, and similar cracking was visible on the opposite side of the west channel as well as in the north-northwest bench. A remarkable feature of this sudden uplift is the high red wall of broken rock displayed on the channel side of the uplifted northern promontory. The top and bottom portions of this wall showed the usual spatter markings of black lava, but the intervening portion for at least ten feet in height is vertical and absolutely unmarked, proving that it must have been suddenly raised and have broken away from its extension beneath the channel along a fracture at about the shore line. This means that a western segment of the lake basin has been elevated. Although some might hold that it was caused by a sudden sinking of the lake level, this is easily disproved, because the lake was still overflowing and was still brimming along the southern and eastern shore lines.

Surface streaming was taking place from the west channel, the ramparts along the southern edges of the lake were about two feet high, and the southeast grotto had become a splash dome some ten feet high, with stalactites on the lakeside where fountains were actively playing. Puffing was heard from the north channel and the whole lake was covered with bubble fountains. New benches were seen on the north and south sides of the northwest cove and along the northeast shore.

At 10:20 a. m. there was a temporary subsidence bringing to view the rim of the northwest cove and increasing the apparent height of the ledge between the island and the west promontory. At 7 p. m. there was much fountain activity in the central part of the lake and lava spray was spurting from under the southern ramparts.

On August 17 the lake was inspected at 5 p. m., the shape of the glowing outline being found to have completely changed. The uplifting was still continuing and had brought to view two new islets off the entrance to the northeast cove. There had been rockfalls southeast and southwest. Some fifteen to seventeen fountains were playing, and perpetual fixed fountains played in the west channel and northwest cove. Splashing grottoes were visible on the southeast bank and against the south face of the pulpit island, and there was radiating surface streaming from the west channel. A morning visit on Friday, August 10, showed an upbuilding of the western floor so that new flows were now running into the cavern in this wall. New flows had poured southward along the bench at the base of the northeast wall. The southwestern promontory had almost disappeared, but that on the north side of the west channel stood higher than ever, being twenty feet above the channel and tilted slightly northwestward.

An isthmus connected this point with the pulpit island and, more to the east was a small, low oval island, with a shoal or flat to the southward of it. This flat on the previous day had been an island.

Old Faithful was quiet but emitting heavy smoke; there were fresh flows over the south bench, the crags on the west of the north channel were tilted yet further northwestward, almost shutting off the northwest cove from the main lake. Fresh rockfalls had fallen at the foot of the southwest wall.

A sudden and pronounced rise set in

at 11 a. m., and rapid overflows began pouring radially away from the lake at the west pond and on the southwest, south and southeast portions of the bench. The southwest promontory and shoal were nearly submerged. Then, and finally, a general overflow began all along the east bank. The lake was covered with blistered skins and only eight fountains could be seen, but the general overflowing of the molten lava was exceedingly spectacular, though it was witnessed by only a few chance spectators.

The following report from the Whitney Laboratory of Seismology is submitted by Mr. H. O. Wood:

During the week ending with August 18 two very small local earthquakes have been registered. The amplitudes of microseismic waves have been moderate to small. The amplitude of waves of volcanic vibration has been moderate to large; and this motion has been more noticeable than usual. There has been progressive tilt to the north, but the east-west tilt has undergone little or no change, except for the usual daily fluctuations.

T. A. JAGGAR, JR.

TECHNOLOGY STATION, August 26.—The week ending the twenty-fifth of August has been remarkable for two occurrences which stand out conspicuously among the many minor changes that have taken place in the fire lake of Kilauea. The first of these happenings is comprised in the birth of a series of new crags in the entrance of the great northwest cove. These crags emerged on the twenty-first instant or very early on the twenty-second, and have completely blocked the entrance, converting the cove into an entirely separate lake, which, in sympathy with its great parent, has now also commenced to overflow its banks.

The other occurrence of note may be described as the death of Old Faithful and the birth of a successor Old Faithful has for years been one of the most spectacular features in the fire lake and its surges have commanded the admiration and awe of every visitor.

It will perhaps be remembered that after the great collapse of the lake on June 5, 1916, following the outburst of lava from Mauna Loa, the locality of Old Faithful, was, for a time at least, completely covered by the thousands of tons of debris which fell from the upper walls. It was some considerable time before the well-known feature was again manifest, and even then it was still almost buried. During the period covered by the last report, the cone which had reared itself as a funnel for Old Faithful, had collapsed and its place had been taken by an open pot or hole through which the molten lava spurted at intervals. This glowing hole has now become eliminated to all intents and purposes, and two new fountains have come into being, and have developed all the Old Faithful characteristics. Thus it may be said that Old Faithful has been reborn, and visitors will be greatly interested in the spectacle thus provided.

The steady rising of the lake has continued throughout the week, and many fresh details of note will be found in the report which follows:

Commencing the week's observations at two-twenty p. m. on August 19, the lake was seen to be level with the top of its banks. There were seven areas displaying fountains, while the northwest cove was furiously boiling and rumbling. At three o'clock there was a period of rapid rising and in a few moments the lake overflowed on the south, southeast and west sides, the western flow reaching clear to the wall and flowing to right and left along its base.

The fumes on the following day were so thick that seeing at two fifty-five p. m. was extremely difficult. However, the lake appeared to have fallen some five feet or so, and the activity seemed to have shifted to the north and northwest, though the southwestern shores were undergoing bombardment.

It was on Tuesday, August 22, that the great change in the northwest cove was first noticed. As already stated, the cove had become changed into a complete lake, and a new crag and two inlets had emerged close to the high west promontory. The southwest pinnacle had become still more submerged and the cavern in the west wall was entirely buried under new flows. Surface streaming was outwards from the west channel, with an occasional rapid spurt against the northwest bank. The crag on the west side of the north channel had greatly subsided, but there was a new crag some short distance to the west of it.

It will be remembered that Old Faithful, during the preceding week, was a large open glow-hole: it had now changed into a cone with open top glowing and splashing at intervals. In a cove of the northwest lake a new fountain had started and was playing steadily, while the promontory to the south of the west channel had flattened out and was covered with new skins from overflows. Moving flows in the north channel showed the lava apparently welling up from the wall chasm, and had glowing "toes" pointing southward.

The lake rose strongly at eleven-thirty a. m. on this day, the flows taking place northwest and west, while fountains played in many places and splashed high against the banks almost all round the lake. A further inspection was made the same evening at nine o'clock at which time the steady eastward streaming was forming a magnificent spectacle. A flow was traveling across the north channel from west to east, the fountain in the northwest lake was spurting at intervals, and the whole floor, save only the eastern portion was covered with brightly glowing cracks.

On August 23, fresh flows were pouring from the north-west pond and were traveling north-westward at ten-thirty a. m. All the crags and islets seemed to have risen considerably, although overflowing had taken place in almost every direction. The west promontory was now at least thirty-five feet high, while new cracks were in evidence across the northeast crag terraces and across the upraised edge between the northwest pond and the lake.

It is probable that the heavy overflows at the north-west have overweighted the bench along the wall at this point, and have thus tilted up all the crags referred to. On the rim of the north-west pond there was a large new spatter cone, while in the cove to the eastward of this, were two new fountains playing rythmically. Slow flows were in movement along the base of the north-west wall from wall cracks, and heavy smoke was rising from the north-east crag and from the western promontory. Inspection that night showed a lake subsidence of some six feet; heavy fountains were playing in a large new cavern on the south-east bank, and the two new fountains noted in the morning played at regular intervals. Blue flames were seen from a group of orifices on the north-east bank and there was marked rumbling in the shore grottoes south and south-east. On August 24 at noon, the lake was some three feet below its banks, and comparatively quiet. Streaming was from the west, fountaining was small and the south bank was receiving slight splashing. The pinnacle to the southwest appeared to be still more submerged, and fresh flows had welled up from the wall-cracks south, south-east, east and north-west. There were no marked changes on this day, but it was noticed that the lake was particularly hot.

In the morning of the following day, August 25, the entire south bench was overflooded and there was every evidence of a rapid rise. There were no apparent further uplifts, but a new spurting cone was in action at the inner end of the south-west promontory. There were spatter ramparts southwest, south, south-east, north and at the northern end of the north-west lake. The heat was exceedingly great and was accompanied by heavy smoke from the crags and promontory west and north-north-west. From eleven a. m. until twelve-fifteen p. m., there were spectacular overflows from all sides of the lake, with a small avalanche at noon at the foot of the south-west wall. The original Old Faithful pot on the north-east bench, which has been referred to as having changed into an open glow hole, had almost vanished and the two rythmic fountains in the cove east of the north-west pond appeared to have developed the characteristics of the best-known feature of the lake. It is probable that a new Old Faithful has thus been born and will become a fixed institution.

The Whitney Laboratory submits the following seismological report: "During the week ending August 25, there have been no sure registrations of earthquakes; three or more wave-groups of very small amplitude and abrupt emergence have appeared, however, as well as numerous undoubted 'storms' of volcanic vibration. Amplitudes of microseismic motion have been normal and fairly steady. Volcanic vibration, though not unusual, has been stronger than normal throughout the week. There has been a moderate westward tilting tendency without much change in the north-south levels."

T. A. JAGGAR, JR.

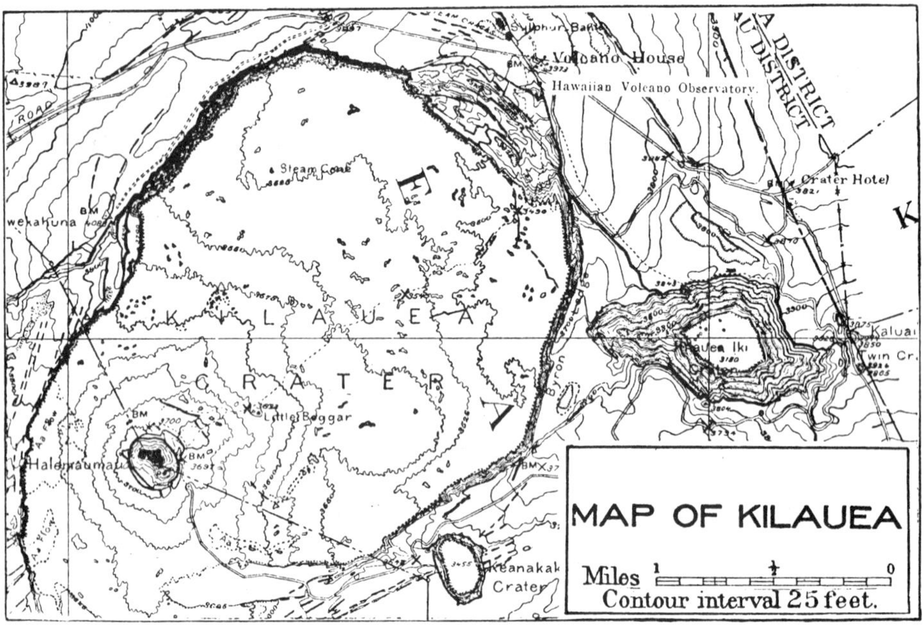

HAWAIIAN VOLCANO RESEARCH ASSOCIATION.

This society is a voluntary one, made up of subscribers to scientific work which is being executed by the Massachusetts Institute of Technology.

In 1915 there are about 100 subscribers in Hawaii and elsewhere, firms and individuals. A group of firms and persons in Hilo built the main observatory building in the spring of 1912. Publications to date have been weekly reports since the summer of 1911, now reprinted in Honolulu in monthly form. The Massachusetts Institute of Technology will publish annual reports, of which the introductory number was printed in 1912.

The weekly bulletin as it appears in the Advertiser is reprinted as a leaflet and sent to regular annual subscribers to the work of the Association. L. A. Thurston is president of the Board of Directors of the Association, and R. W. Shingle is treasurer. New subscribers who are interested in volcanoes will be welcomed in the Association. The Association aims: (1) To record volcanic activity and earthquakes in Hawaii; (2) to attract scientific men hither for special studies; (3) to promote the establishment of volcano observatories all over the world. The annual dues of regular members are $5; patrons of the Assocaition subscribe larger amounts.

WHITNEY LABORATORY OF SEISMOLOGY.

The Whitney Laboratory of Seismology is equipped with two Bosch-Omori 100 kg tromometers registering N-S and E-W motion, a heavy Omori tromometer registering E-W motion, and an Omori "ordinary Seismograph" designed for registering strong earthquakes in all three components of motion. These are seated on concrete piers in a closed basement room having practically constant temperature, beneath the chief Observatory building near the hotel. Time is referred to a rated chronometer, checked at intervals by solar observations with a transit. Both instruments are loaned by the College of Hawaii. Hawaiian standard time (H. S. T.) is 10 hrs. 30 min. slower than Greenwich time.

CANCANI SCALE OF SEISMIC INTENSITY.

Expressed by accelerations measured in millimeters per second per second.

I.	Instrumental	0.0	2.5
II.	Very slight	2.5	5.0
III.	Slight	5.0	10.0
IV.	Sensible, mediocre	10.0	25.0
V.	Rather strong	25.0	50.0
VI.	Strong	50.0	100.0
VII.	Very strong	100.0	250.0
VIII.	Ruinous	250.0	500.0
IX.	Disastrous	500.0	1000.0
X.	Very disastrous	1000.0	2500.0
XI.	Catastrophic	2500.0	5000.0
XII.	Great catastrophe	5000.0	10000.0

Grade IV. is ordinarily the minimum perceived by the senses; and in grade XII. the acceleration, or rate of change of motion (jerk) reaches that of terrestrial gravitation.

In the standard form of report the maximum intensity or acceleration, designated by the symbol α, or max. α, is given in the conventional unit, **the milligal.** The milligal is a measure of acceleration, such that 1 milligal = 1/100 mm. per sec. per sec. = 10 μ per sec. per sec. The Cancani scale, here defined in terms of millimeters per sec. per sec., can therefore be expressed in **milligals** by multiplying each of the numbers by 100.

WEEKLY BULLETIN
OF THE

Hawaiian Volcano Observatory

Vol. VI. HONOLULU, HAWAII, SEPTEMBER, 1916. No. 9

TECHNOLOGY STATION, September 2.—As compared with the occurrences of the last few weeks events at the great fire-lake Halemaumau have been almost devoid of spectacular features, at least in the eye of the trained observer.

Visitors, however, have been treated to fine displays of fountain playing and to several conspicuous overflowings from various sections of the lake.

The level of the lake below the rim has varied but slightly during the week, and while there has been a tendency towards falling there are as yet no indications that the upward movement which has been in progress ever since the spectacular collapse of 5th June, has been arrested. A subsidence might be looked for at the close of the equinoctial period, about the third week in September, but there are no indications of this at moment of writing.

The observations of the week now under review have been much interfered with by greatly increased fuming, which has frequently made seeing quite impossible.

Inspection from the east station at 2:15 p. m., August 26, showed the lake level with its banks, with fresh lava flows covering the benches surrounding it. The northwest bench displayed a moving flow and the pond in this section was steadily overflowing. The new Old Faithful was playing at regular intervals in the north central region, and there was strong fountain activity in every direction.

A further attempt at serious observation was made at 2:45 p. m., but failed, owing to smoke and dense rising fumes.

A few minutes later, however, there was a comparatively clear interval and it was possible to see that a marked rise was in progress, the lake overflowing in every quarter and drowning the small islet towards the north and also covering the southwest promontory. The rising ceased about 3:05 p. m., and the bank surrounding the lake then appeared to be about one foot in height.

On August 29 the lake was visited at 2:15 p. m., and comparatively clear seeing was obtained from the northern station. There was violent disturbance at the southwest, where the new cone was blowing furiously, with the accompaniment of loud rumblings. The lake had subsided some five feet and the northwest pond was quite quiet. Old Faithful broke at regular intervals as usual, but there was considerable fountain action in progress to the south and southeast.

At the same time on the following day, August 30, similar conditions prevailed, although both fountaining and bombardment showed considerable increase. Some bombardment was violent northwest, southwest, south, southeast and also east, with heavy fountaining in the northern part of the lake. There had been one small overflow onto the southwest bench, and a rock-fall was heard from the cliff under the east station.

August 31 showed the lake to have fallen, leaving spatter walls some ten feet in height. The northwest pond had also fallen and was about five feet below its banks, being quiet and heavily crusted over. There had been several avalanches during the preceding night, notably on the southwest, with a large fall under the northwest station. There was much fountaining on this day, the lake boiling furiously in no less than eighteen places; the southwest cone was blowing noisily, streaming, as usual, was spreading out fanwise from the west channel, and Old Faithful was in steady action. On account of the thickness of the smoke

WEEKLY BULLETIN
of the
Hawaiian Volcano Observatory

Published Monthly at Honolulu, Hawaii, by the Hawaiian Volcano Research Association

L. W. de Vis-Norton........Secretary

Entered as second-class matter January 20, 1914, at the post-office at Honolulu, Hawaii, under the Act of August 24, 1912.

seeing was extremely difficult on this day.

The lake on September 1, when inspetion was made at 2:30 p. m., was extremely quict, the only activity being at the northern side. The southern portion of the lake surface was covered with thick skins, and the lake showed maintained depression below its banks. There were no marks of fresh avalanches, and the northwest pond was perfectly quiescent. The blue fumes on this day were unpleasantly thick and seeing was very difficult.

The following report from the Whitney Laboratory of Seismology is submitted by Mr. H. O. Wood:

"During the week ending with September 1, six local earthquakes have been registered. All were of very small amplitude and two were ill characterized, being possibly only waves of volcanic vibration with abrupt beginning. Microseismic motion has been registered as usual. The amplitudes of volcanic vibration waves have been slightly greater than normal and this motion has been more constant at large amplitude than usual. Also 'storms' have recurred frequently. Except for daily fluctuations of ordinary character the movements of tilting have shown no significant change."

TECHNOLOGY STATION, September 9.—During the past week there have been minor changes in the great lava lake of the Volcano Kilauea, the general rising movement having, to a certain extent, ceased, though apparently again about to recommence.

The surface of the lake on September 6, was 332 feet below the south-east rim, some ten feet higher than on August 25.

The director, in this week's report, sounds a note of warning to visitors at the present time. He states quite frankly that the east shelter (that is to say, the roofless shelter at the end of the trail leading from the automobile terminal), is the safest view-point, and that the south station, which is marked by a tall tripod of poles, should be avoided until further notice. The reason for this warning is the presence of suffocating fumes in large quantities along the branch trail parallel with the south and south-east rim.

These fumes are at times so dense that not even the use of a wet noseguard makes it possible for the visitor to breathe. They are accompanied by strong whirlwinds, generated at the border of the hot uprush from the pit. Although there may be no actual danger from the presence of these heavy squalls, they pick up quantities of sand and gravel, mixed with Pele's hair, and therefore are extremely unpleasant to be caught in. Visitors are advised that the presence of fumes may be detected during the daylight hours by their vivid blue color, but care should be taken at night-time when they are not readily perceived.

Observations made at two-thirty p. m. on Saturday, September 2, showed that the high spatter dome above the south-east grotto had collapsed, leaving a cove which extended the lake into the bench close under the south-east cliff. The lava in this cove presently overflowed, pouring along the bench in a westerly direction for a hundred feet or so, in a thirty-foot torrent. The lake then settled down and appeared about five feet below its bordering bench. The north-west pond was entirely quiet, but there was some fountaining in progress toward the north, and considerable debris was noticed on the southwest bench.

At six p. m. on September 4, the lake was seen to have become very irregular in shape, the west channel making a very long arm bordered on both sides by promontories. The north cove showed a high, new islet and there were flaming pots to the north, northeast and west. The north-west pond had a splashing grotto at its northern end, but was otherwise tranquil. Surface streaming radiated from the west channel and the extreme north-west end of the north cove, increasing to a cascading rush under an arch leading to one of the flaming pots. At the site of the original Old Faithful a new vent appeared, gradually building up a beautiful glowing cone, which, however, collapsed at six-fifteen p. m., leaving a large open fiery pot. The lake as a whole was very quiet, only five fountaining areas being present; there were small new overflows south and south-east, new rockfalls in five places south-west and in one place east under the new gulch, while stones were seen falling at the south-west.

The entire bench surrounding the lake appeared to be tilting, becoming depressed at the south-east and rising at the opposite side. This was shown by the level south-east being only about four feet above the lake, while the benches to the west and north had risen to at least ten feet. A very conspicuous flaming pot, shooting banners of flaming gas high over the eastern bank where the lava foamed and surged, occupied part of the south-west promontory and was much commented on by visitors present. On September 5, at nine-thirty p. m., the lake was properly visible for the first time since the previous day. Three pronounced signs of collapse were clearly apparent (1) the south-west promontory had subsided, leaving only a small islet, (2) the Old Faithful pot, referred to on previous day, had broken away and had become a cove of the lake, and (3) a long line of flaming pots connected the head of the west channel with the north-west pond, indicating that the latter would soon connect through with the main lake. The south-eastward streaming now poured through the new channel west of the new islet as well as along its former course to the north of it. The northern crags appeared higher than ever, while the south-east rampart was about five feet high. The north-west pond was quiet but fourteen fountains areas in the main lake were counted in addition to the large periodic north fountain. There was flaming at the head of the west arm and in the western pots.

Intolerably strong, hot fumes swirled over the south-east edge of the pit,, and whirlwinds generated at the border of the hot uprush from the lake made traveling difficult. One of these small tornadoes was seen whirling smoke along the south edge of the lake. This excessive gustiness of the wind on the edge of the pit is a new feature which has been common only during the last few months. That it is connected with the upward current of air from the unusually large lava surface and is wholly local is shown by the fact that these tremendous squalls capable of picking up sand and gravel, occur on the edge of the pit when the wind at the Volcano House is moderate or even light.

The fumes on September 6 were quite unbearable, and only from the north was it possible to study the detail of the north-west pond region. There had been a heavy rockfall from the north-west wall, and the pond was brimming on its north-west side but exhibited a high bank on the south-east. The crags to the east of it showed a new tilt south-westward, and a high escarpment rose forty feet above a channel connecting the north ends of the two lakes. On the north-west side of this crag there was a splash mark of black lava up the talus slope for twenty feet. This had probably been caused by an avalanche from the crag sending a wave of liquid lava back and forth across the lake. The surface of this mass of crags sloped southward to a new subsided channel between the south end of the north-west pond and the former west channel. It is evident that the north-west pond is again merging with the lake, and, incredible as it may seem, the great mass of crags which was FORMERLY THE LAKE BOTTOM, is becoming a huge island. At one p. m., on this day there was a sudden rise of the lake, causing overflow south and south-east, and drowning the south-west islet and the end of the north-west promontory.

On September 7 at six p. m., nine fountains were playing along the border of the lake, streaming was circular from the west towards the south-east and north, and the north-west pond was covered with skins. Flames were seen above the border grottoes which showed high ramparts south-east and south.

The lake as a whole was stationary and rather smoky, but the fumes on this day were the worst the writer has ever experienced at Kilauea. The gas is hot and intensely acrid, and breathing is impossible even with a wet nose-guard. On Friday, September 8, the smoke column appeared more thin than unusal, and observation was possible from the south station. The lake was rising rapidly and two great torrents of overflow swept along the bench from the south-west. Two eastern shore fountains were rumbling heavily and there were loud explosive snortings of gas at the north end of the northern cove. The pit was extremely hot and much Pele's hair was floating upwards from it. Rocks were continually falling from the south-west wall, doubtless due to the subsidence of the bench under the weight of the heavy overflows. At ten-fifty-five a. m., a long line of bombardment against the eastern shore overflooded the bench there, the tilt southward of the northern crags seemed to have increased, the high north end was cracked across and ready to fall, while the low south end of the mass was largely submerged.

During the week there has been one pronounced local earthquake and three or four very small ones recorded by the seismographs. Movement. of tilting and of volcanic and microseismic vibration has shown no unusual characters.

Messrs. H. O. Wood of the Massachusetts Institute, and G. H. Vicars of the Hawaii Publicity Commission, accompanied by Alex Lancaster as guide, left the Observatory on Monday September 4, for an exploring trip up the north-east flank of Mauna Loa They will be absent probably one week.

TECHNOLOGY STATION, September 16—During the week ended September 15, the lava lake of Halemaumau has continued to rise steadily, being interrupted only by a temporary fall of a few feet on September 12—13. The level of the lake at the present time is 326 feet below the southeast rim, its dimensions being 800 feet in length, with a greatest width of 540 feet. The director's report follows:

On Saturday, September 9, at four p. m., the southeast brink of the pit was very fumy, but good seeing was obtained from the northwest. The main lake was about one foot below its borders, with nine fountains in action, some being in grottoes under the bank. A small, glowing cone appeared on the north bench and there were blowing noises from this edge of the lake.

In the Old Faithful locality there was a small cove, the north fountain broke at intervals, the southwest island was again visible, and the usual streaming from the west was in progress. The pond at the northwest was crusted, but occasionally overflowing the bench both eastward and westward. Fresh overflows from the main lake had poured over the north bank, and the channel connecting with the north west pond had widened considerably. The bench all around the lake appeared to be widening, and a deep crack appeared between it and the northwest wall.

Sunday, September 10, the fumes at the south station were bad. The lake had dropped to five feet below the bank, but the northwest pond was slowly overflowing. The promontory, crags and islet northwest were much elevated, no channel was visible between the pond and the west arm, but stalactites were seen at the head of the arm and probably a cavern was in existence below. There were but few fountains in action, the north cove was quiet and streaming was to the southeast.

In the evening of September 11, the northwest pond was discharging a stream eastward to the lake under the high crag.

On September 12, the first inspection was commenced at two p. m. The lake as seen from the east had risen to within a foot of the rim bench, the northwest pond was overflowing into the north cove of the main lake, and there were numerous fountains at work. An avalanche fell from the southwest at two-thirty p. m. followed by a rapid subsidence of the lake, amounting to three or four feet. The northern end of the lake cleared of smoke at four-thirty p. m. and the situation appeared as follows: the lowest shorelines were around the northwest pond: the pond

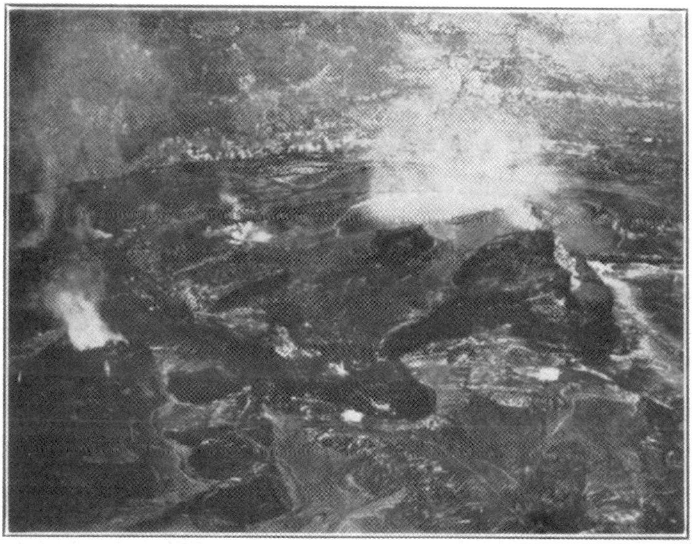

Sept. 14, 1916, looking N. W. from Southeast station. North crag mass and islets, northwest pond in distance, 10:20 a.m. Halemaumau. —Photo Jaggar.

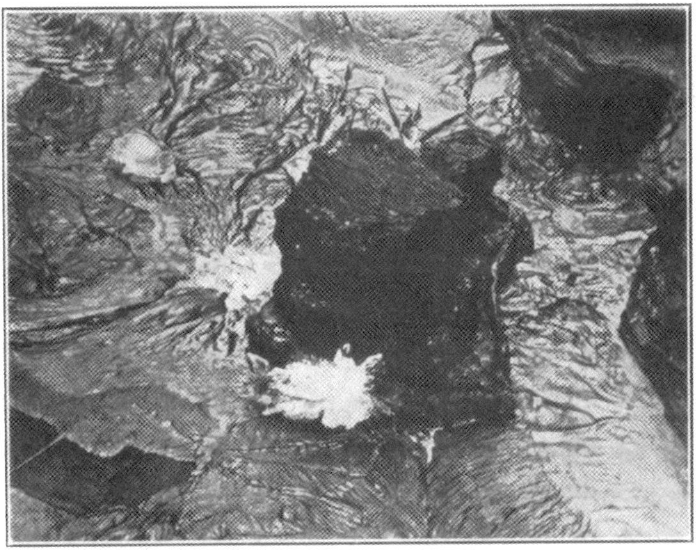

Sept. 13. 1916, 11 a.m., telephoto looking south down from north resthouse. Fountains splashing at base of north islet, Halemaumau. —Photo Jaggar.

Sept. 14, 1916, looking N. from Southeast station. Old north smoke crags overwhelmed by new flows in foreground 10:50 a.m. Halemaumau. —Photo Jaggar.

Sept. 13. 1916, 10:25 a.m. telephoto looking down southwest from north resthouse. Lava rivulet pouring from pond to lake, Halemaumau. —Photo Jaggar.

was considerably higher than the lake and was pouring out a torrent of melt twenty feet wide, which cascaded down into the lake.

The north shore of the main lake was also low, the other banks being from three to five feet high. The northwestern crag was now higher than ever, its summit being a c'iff rising fifty feet above the torren just referred to. A conspicuous broken slab sagged out over the channel, and appeared ready to fall. The islet to the east of the crag had also been bodily elevated, and showed a broad base and twelve spatter levels on its sides, while the channel between it and the crag had become a narrow chasm. At both ends of the northwest pond there were fresh, glowing over-flows. The southwest island had altered in shape and was now elongate in a north-south direction. On either side of it were channels, through which were pouring streams south and east. Only a few fountains were playing in the lake at this hour.

Marked changes had taken place when the lake was observed on the following day, September 13, at nine-thirty a. m. The southwestern avalanche debris had been partially overflowed, and west-southwest the bench showed transverse cracks, these being again visible in the northeast bench across the lake. These benches northeast and southwest had been bodily uplifted about fifteen feet but the northwest and southeast lake margins had, on the contrary, been overflowed. The raised walls were raw broken red rock in the middle, passing into raised spatter benches at the ends. As a result of this uplift the southwest promontory was partly restored, but was still cut off from its island extremity by a narrow channel. From the northwest pond to the west channel there was a distinct curved fracture, and from the north end of the pond a narrow stream poured eastward.

At ten a. m. sudden rise took place in the lake, reversing this flow, and pouring from the lake to the pond. This lasted for some fifteen minutes and then process was reversed once more. At the extreme northern end of the lake, a new islet appeared, splashing grottoes were seen southeast and south and the southeast cove had greatly widened. An avalanche fell from the north crag and in the Old Faithful district there was a grotto into which the streaming sometimes converged.

On the following day, at ten a. m., September 14, measurements were taken, the lake being found to be 326 feet below the southeast rim, indicating a rise of six feet since September 6. The great crag was fifty-two feet above the level of the lake. The dimensions of the lake were: length 800 feet, greatest width 540 feet.

At both the northwest and southeast ends of the lake heavy overflows had poured right and left along the wall, the intervening banks were arched up at least fifteen feet, while the stream was still pouring from the northwest pond eastward to the lake, with a temporary backing up at eleven a. m.

Fumes were thin on this day and mostly from the old northeast crag; talus to the east and northwest was nearly buried under new flows, while the crag mass and islet appeared somewhat higher. Five fountains only were in action in the main lake.

At eight p. m. further glowing flows had taken place all over the bench southwest, south, southeast, west, northwest and north. A small whirlpool was seen in the north cove at the mouth of the torrent, the south bank was being very heavily bombarded, with flames flickering above the ramparts and stalactites hanging below, and nine fountains were playing. Streaming was slow. The southeast cove overflowed at eight-fifteen p. m.

On September 15, at eleven a. m., the southeast cove was overspattering in a short flow that extended to the wall. The lake appeared higher than on the previous day, the north rivulet had stopped flowing and was crusted over, and the benches east and west appeared only ten feet high. At three p. m. there was overflow southeast extending along the bench in both directions. Large cracks in the raised benches east and west appear to be changing these into new crags. The northern crag mass appeared lower, the new northern islet and the north and northwest shores were about two feet high. There was fountaining on the bank to the north, northwest and southeast, with heavy bombardment south.

The following report from the Whitney Laboratory of Seismology is submitted by H. O. Wood:

"During the week ending with September 15 five local earthquakes of very small amplitudes, and energy, have been registered. These were all of seismographic strength only.

"The amplitudes of microseismic motion have varied between moderate and very small values. The amplitudes of volcanic-vibration waves have ranged sporadically between moderately small and moderately large values. There has been no significant change in the state of tilt in the east-west direction but during the past fortnight the strong tilt to the north previously maintained for a considerable interval has been offset by a slight tendency to tilt to the south."

Messrs. H. O. Wood and G. H. Vicars returned from Mauna Loa on September 10. Mr. Wood secured good photographs of the northeastern rift zone.

TECHNOLOGY STATION, September 23—Only minor changes have taken place in the lava lake of Halemaumau during the week ending September 22, 1916. The lake has continued to rise steadily and is now only 312 feet below the east rim of the pit. This indicates a rise of fourteen feet in eight days, a slightly faster rate of rise than during the previous week. No decided changes have occurred in the crag mass or other features occupying the bottom of the pit, and though on one or two days the fumes were exceedingly unpleasant on the southeast rim, during the latter part of the period they were thinner and more bearable. The director of the volcano observatory reports as follows:

"At two p. m., September 16, from the east station, the lava surface appeared only about five feet depressed below its bank northwest and southeast and the northwest pond was more active than the large lake where there was some bombardment southwest at the edge. At two-thirty p. m. the northwest pond had risen until it was nearly overflowing and fourteen fountains could be counted over the whole area of the bottom. The fumes were thick.

"On September 17 at three p. m. the blue fumes rising southeast and south made breathing almost impossible and their source was the grotto fountains at the edge of the lake south, southeast and east. From the east station the bank of the lake was seen to be five feet high north and south and twice that height east and west. There were nine fountaining areas and heavy continuous fountaining was in progress in the cove east of the crag mass, the ebullition there ever migrating to the high north islet where it expended itself in violent bombardment of the shore. The surface liquid appeared excessively viscous as shown by the sticky jets of the fountains which expanded in umbrella-like forms. The west cove and the channel of the north rivulet appeared to be widened. The stream from the northwest pond to the lake was wider and moderately rapid. A small avalanche had fallen onto the west bench. There was no new flow material anywhere and it seems probable that the widening of the coves was revealing subsidence and caving in for there was a new lower spatter level all around the lake and small stalactites in several places. The pit was smoky. Much Pele's hair had accumulated near the south station.

"From seven to nine p. m. on September 18 there was no perceptible difference in the general level of the lakes. At seven-thirty p. m. there was noisy puffing from a cone on the north bank, vigorous fountaining north and south, heavy bombardment on the south bank, a stream pouring from the northwest pond, both lakes very bright and a flow welling up a crack between bench and wall on the southwest and spreading southward. At eight p. m. all this activity dwindled and there may have been some rising in the lake. The smoke was variable. The streaming as usual radiated from the west side of the lake. The south cove had widened considerably in a westward direction.

"On September 19, from four to five p. m., conditions were smoky and rainy, fumes were intolerable southeast and there was dim seeing from the east. The lakes appeared higher, the north cone was puffing noisily and about eight fountains were in action. At about five p. m. the channel rivulet poured from the lake to the pond and at five-thirty p. m. it was pouring from the pond to the lake, surmounted by an arch of crust. The north fountain varied and tended to northwestward migration but it showed none of the rythmic character of Old Faithful.

''On Wednesday, September 20, at ten a. m. the fumes appeared thinner. There were fresh overflows northwest and west. Streaming in the northwest pond was from south to north and out through the channel into the lake. Streaming from the west channel was eastward and southward. There were from six to eight fountains. The crag and islet appeared higher. The lakes were brimming level with their banks southeast and northwest while northeast and southwest the banks were about five feet high. Large cracks were seen in the west side of the crag mass and in the south bench. A smoking scarp curved northward from west of the west channel to the northwest pond presenting a steep wall on the lake side as though the complete lake were tending again to become an ellipse by subsidence of the south end of the crag mass. The southeast cove had overflowed to the wall.

''On September 21 at eight-thirty p. m. there was great activity with violent fountaining north, north-northeast, north side of northwest pond, southwest and south, and strong blasts of gas echoing from the cone on the bench. From four orifices in this cone bright spears of bluish flame played continuously. There were also flames bursting from under skins in the middle of the lake and shooting up as banners of violent fire from border grottoes especially at the northeast end of the northwest pond. From time to time in that pond there were spectacular displays when the dark crust would break up suddenly and migrate eastward to a point of intense bombardment at the northeast end. Sudden northward streaming also took place sometimes in the north end of the larger lake with much spectacular bubble fountaining. By nine p. m. the violent blasts and strong fountaining had ceased and the lake was relatively quiet. A glowing flow next the wall was seen on the northwest bench which may have come from a wall crack. Smoke on this night was distinctly less.

''Measurement on September 22 at four p. m. from the east and north stations determined the level of the lake below the east rim of the pit to be 312 feet, indicating a rise of fourteen feet in eight days or an average of approximately one and three-quarters feet a day.

''The lake was higher and overflowing the north and northwest banks, the channel from the northwest pond was crusted over but under this crust a stream poured from the pond to the lake and then from the lake to the pond. There was violent fountaining followed by quieter conditions. Splashing was going on at the northeast end of the northwest pond. For a time the north and west coves of the main lake were crusted over. There was temporary heavy bombardment southeast. The northern blowing had ceased. The lake was level with its banks northwest and southeast but in the middle region the shore appeared five feet high.''

The following report from the Whitney Laboratory of Seismology is submitted by H. O. Wood:

''During the week ending September 22 one exceedingly feeble earthquake has been registered, along with one or two doubtful wave groups. Microseismic motion has been registered with the usual changes and characteristics. The amplitude of the motion of volcanic vibration has varied irregularly from small to moderate values. There has been no marked change in the east-west tilt but in the north-south direction there was a movement to north of rather sharp character followed by a gradual return. The diurnal wandering of the pens in the east-west direction has been greater than normal.

''An exhibit of photographs was displayed by the observatory at the Hawaii County Fair in Hilo, September 22-24. Three first prizes were awarded this collection, respectively for remarkable subjects, speed photography and best enlargement.''

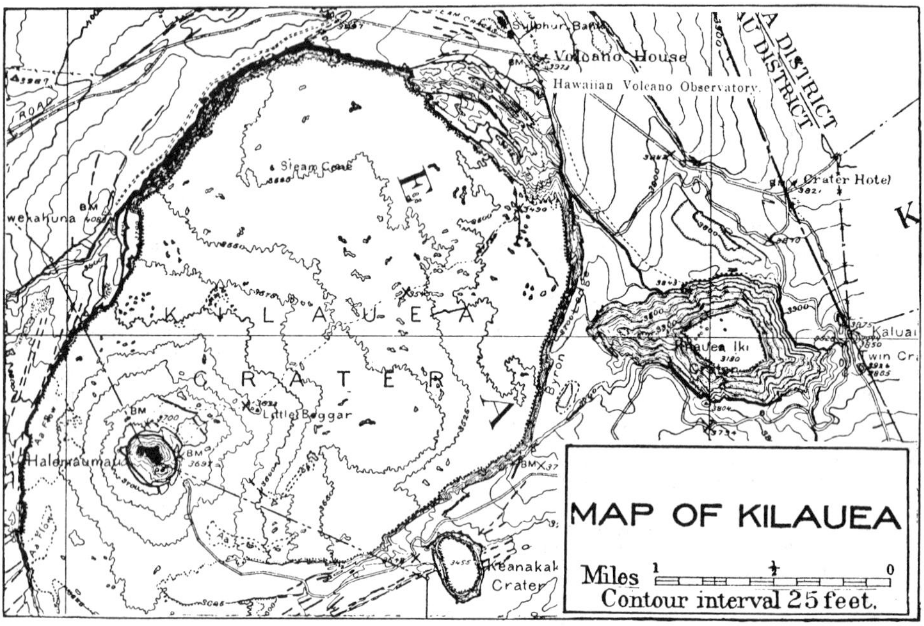

HAWAIIAN VOLCANO RESEARCH ASSOCIATION.

This society is a voluntary one, made up of subscribers to scientific work which is being executed by the Massachusetts Institute of Technology.

In 1915 there are about 100 subscribers in Hawaii and elsewhere, firms and individuals. A group of firms and persons in Hilo built the main observatory building in the spring of 1912. Publications to date have been weekly reports since the summer of 1911, now reprinted in Honolulu in monthly form. The Massachusetts Institute of Technology will publish annual reports, of which the introductory number was printed in 1912.

The weekly bulletin as it appears in the Advertiser is reprinted as a leaflet and sent to regular annual subscribers to the work of the Association. L. A. Thurston is president of the Board of Directors of the Association, and R. W. Shingle is treasurer. New subscribers who are interested in volcanoes will be welcomed in the Association. The Association aims: (1) To record volcanic activity and earthquakes in Hawaii; (2) to attract scientific men hither for special studies; (3) to promote the establishment of volcano observatories all over the world. The annual dues of regular members are $5; patrons of the Assocaition subscribe larger amounts.

WHITNEY LABORATORY OF SEISMOLOGY.

The Whitney Laboratory of Seismology is equipped with two Bosch-Omori 100 kg tromometers registering N-S and E-W motion, a heavy Omori tromometer registering E-W motion, and an Omori "ordinary Seismograph" designed for registering strong earthquakes in all three components of motion. These are seated on concrete piers in a closed basement room having practically constant temperature, beneath the chief Observatory building near the hotel. Time is referred to a rated chronometer, checked at intervals by solar observations with a transit. Both instruments are loaned by the College of Hawaii. Hawaiian standard time (H. S. T.) is 10 hrs. 30 min. slower than Greenwich time.

CANCANI SCALE OF SEISMIC INTENSITY.

Expressed by accelerations measured in millimeters per second per second.

I.	Instrumental	0.0	2.5
II.	Very slight	2.5	5.0
III.	Slight	5.0	10.0
IV.	Sensible, mediocre	10.0	25.0
V.	Rather strong	25.0	50.0
VI.	Strong	50.0	100.0
VII.	Very strong	100.0	250.0
VIII.	Ruinous	250.0	500.0
IX.	Disastrous	500.0	1000.0
X.	Very disastrous	1000.0	2500.0
XI.	Catastrophic	2500.0	5000.0
XII.	Great catastrophe	5000.0	10000.0

Grade IV. is ordinarily the minimum perceived by the senses; and in grade XII. the acceleration, or rate of change of motion (jerk) reaches that of terrestrial gravitation.

In the standard form of report the maximum intensity or acceleration, designated by the symbol a, or max. a, is given in the conventional unit, **the milligal.** The milligal is a measure of acceleration, such that 1 milligal = 1/100 mm. per sec. per sec. = 10 μ per sec. per sec. The Cancani scale, here defined in terms of millimeters per sec. per sec., can therefore be expressed in **milligals by multiplying each of the numbers by 100.**

WEEKLY BULLETIN
OF THE
Hawaiian Volcano Observatory

Vol. IV. HONOLULU, HAWAII, OCTOBER, 1916. No. 10

TECHNOLOGY STATION, September 30—During the week ending September 29, 1916, the usual equinoctial subsidence of the lava lake of Halemaumau has taken place, followed by so rapid a recovery that the net movement of the lava between September 22 and 28, has amounted to a rise of three feet. At the present time the level of the lake is almost stationary at 309 feet, with a new lower bordering bench above which rise crags, pinnacles and tubular elevations in great variety.

On September 23 at eight p. m., when inspection was made, the channel from the northwest pond to the lake was seen to have reopened. Flames were seen in a high stalactite grotto at the lake border south; on the north bank a glowing filagree cone was noisily puffing sparks, while the older cone behind it showed spears of blue flame. The southwest island had lengthened in a north-south direction.

On September 25, at two p. m., a tremendous change was evident. The northeast and southwest benches were at least forty feet high, the southeast end of the lake showed a new island some thirty feet in height, and the large crag mass to the north appeared to be over sixty feet high. The walls of the northwest pond were thirty feet above the liquid lava, which was boiling in one place. The high east and west inner cliffs bordering the lake showed raw, broken reddish walls, the south and east benches were crevassed and tumbled, the lake was cascading into a southeast pot, and there were but few fountains. The fumes were thick and no avalanches were seen.

On September 26, at two-forty-five p. m., pronounced rising had followed the subsidence of the previous day. The east and west banks were twenty feet; southeast about ten feet; at the south end of the crag mass seven feet, and at the north border of the lake, two feet high. The southwest island showed about twenty feet high. Inrush to the southeast cove was in progress, nine fountains were playing and throwing up Pele's hair in large quantities. From the southwest station the southeast island was seen to be only just above the lake level. The northwest pond was brimming full with an overflow on the north bench. At the base of the walls west, northwest, north and northeast new avalanche debris appeared. The Old Faithful location was now a grotto under the bank, and the whole lake was sinking slowly, with the pond and coves tending to crust over. The southeast torrent made a tinkling noise and there was occasional blowing at the north. The bench south was deeply fissured and tumbled, and dense smoke was rising from this point.

On Wednesday, September 27, at noon, the lava was rising and overflowing north and northwest, but half an hour afterwards this was followed by a slight subsidence. The raised benches northeast and southwest appeared about twenty feet high. The southwest island showed a new spatter niche on the east side, and there were new overflows southeast and north. Twenty fountains were counted in action as a line of travelling fountains extending from the promontory of the crag-mass in a southerly direction. A striking feature of the east and west raised benches is that their elevation above the southeast and north floor at the lake level appears to be bodily uplift without tilt, falling off abruptly opposite the west channel and at the northeast crags and less abruptly toward the south.

WEEKLY BULLETIN
of the
Hawaiian Volcano Observatory

Published Monthly at Honolulu, Hawaii, by the Hawaiian Volcano Research Association

L. W. de Vis-Norton........Secretary

Entered as second-class matter January 20, 1914, at the post-office at Honolulu, Hawaii, under the Act of August 24, 1912.

The lake was extremely hot, with thin blistered skins and much Pele's hair. The north end of the crag mass had fallen in, the north islet was now a slender pinnacle, a fresh plaster of black lava coated the lower part of the western inner cliff and the northeast end of the northwest pond was active.

Measurement on the following day, September 28, at noon, made the lake level 309 feet below the south station. The lake was almost stationary and had built a new lower platform, converting the north islet and southwest island into peninsulas and making a wide bench under the rugged cliffs northeast and southwest. There was streaming from north to south in the northwest pond, inrush was in progress at the southeast cove, the lake streaming was various and the heat from the pit and blowing grottoes was strong. New flows had welled up the wall crack south, behind the southwest high bench and it was clear that these elevated benches were isolated bodies which had moved up with shattered and gaping rifts between them and the walls of the pit.

On September 29, at ten-thirty a. m., the lake appeared slightly higher and was level with the new southeastern island and probably overflowing the northwest bench. Strong fountaining was in progress northward and there were very marked crevasses between the northeast and southwest plateau benches and the wall. At noon there was a subsidence of about two feet.

The Whitney Laboratory of Seismology, (H. O. Wood) submits the following report:

During the week ending September 29 one local earthquake of moderate seismographic amplitude and six local shocks of exceedingly small seismographic amplitude have been registered here. There have been a few small wave groups of doubtful character also. Microseismic motion has been registered as usual. The amplitude of waves of volcanic vibration have been larger than usual and the "storms" of these have been more frequent and of longer duration than in previous weeks. There has been a slight progressive increase in tilt to the northward. The observatory on September 29 was honored with a visit from Prof. Dana P. Bartlett of the Massachusetts Institute of Technology.

TECHNOLOGY STATION, Oct. 7, 1916—During the week ending Oct. 6, 1916, the lava lake Halemaumau, has risen steadily, being now only 283 feet below the rim of the pit. The rise has been accompanied by periods of sinking in regular pulsations which occur about every two hours, but which rarely amount to a greater drop than a foot or so at each period.

Inspection at 10 a. m. on Sept. 30, 1916, revealed an aparently stationary lake. A slow flow was moving along the south wall crack in an easterly direction to a point where it found its way outward to the lake in a small stream. The northwest bench was covered with new festooned flows. The pond was heavily crusted over but broke up at noon with loud crackings and foundering of the black crusts. The main lake showed an inner bench from one to two feet in height; the main lake surface was hot and blistery with variable fountains and occasional inflow under the bank on the southeast and northeast. The west arm was crusted over.

Oct. 2, at 3:15 p. m., the lake was much higher, with considerable action in progress. Eight large grottoes showed violent boiling under heavy gas pressure; there were new overflows at the southeast cove, the north edge of the main lake and beside the northwest pond. The crag mass had split at the southeast and the promontory at that end had now become a small islet. The bench along the shore, and the south-island were only about a foot in height; a new small pond had developed at the base of the south wall, with extensions to the east and west and live flows towards the lake. New lava appeared in the wall crack to the east of this and ran to the overflows of the southeast cove. North and west the lake surface was covered with skins from which streaming took place to south and east. The southwest peninsula was again nearly isolated, and bombardment was taking place at four places along the south bank as well as at the northeast end of the northwest pond and elsewhere. The north islet stood as a pinnacle rising from a low flat bench protruding eastward from the crag mass. The raised benches northeast and southwest were heavily crevassed into chasms extending from the pit wall to the lake.

At 11:30 a. m., on the following day, Oct. 3, tremendous overflows were pouring from the northwest pond right and left along the base of the wall, and another flow, five feet in width, rushed from the lake clear over the rampart to the wall, completely filling the depression found there. The wall pond and crack on the south were crusted and glowing; six places in the main lake showed fountains of a shifting character, a great spatter grotto had formed on the southwest and now and again a very violent fountain developed east of the south island. The great overflow lasted for over an hour, finally causing a meeting of the flood over the north bank of the main lake and the bench flow from the northwest pond. This latter flow extended itself eastward to the remnant of the northeast talus of June 1916, where it pushed its way among the stones with fierce crackling noises. The flows met at 12:05 p. m., the great north flood ending on the west midway between the west and southwest stations, and on the east under the north station, while the southeast flow followed the wall crack east and west. One very remarkable feature may be mentioned: at the line where the golden torrent overflowed the border of the northwest pond many small bubble fountains broke through the glowing stream, while none of these could be seen in the torrent which left the lake at the southeast cove. Likewise, skin blisters were most numerous in the north cove. These facts imply that the most gas and hottest lava were rising toward the northwest. The lake fountains generally now rise at various points on the surface and migrate to the banks where they vanish. There are, at the present time, no rhythmic fountains of the Old Faithful type.

We have referred to the rising and sinking pulsations of the lake. Seen on October 4 from the old north rest house, the lake rose from ten-thirty to eleven-thirty a. m., with overflows southeast and northwest. During the next thirty minutes the lake fell and the overflow stream was reversed, the flood pouring back again into the main lake. At twelve-fifteen p. m. rising was once more in progress and the overflows had reached far to the southwest behind the plateau bench. The raised northeast bench was now higher than the old northeast crags; the promontory at the southeast end of the crag mass had again developed by accretion and the southeast overflow was covering the craggy tumble of the old bench. The pond at the foot of the south wall was fountaining; fumes were thin, as a whole; streaming was in progress in the northwest pond, first to the north and then to the south, probably in accordance with the rising and sinking of the lake. Nine fountains were counted in action on this morning.

The same evening at nine p. m. the lake had slightly fallen and the southern shore was being heavily bombarded. Bench flows were glowing, and the overflow northwest of the previous day had extended into the head of the west cove and had there merged with the lake lava. Twelve fountains were seen in action.

On October 5 the two lakes as seen from the north rest house showed rising between ten and eleven a. m., falling during the next hour and then again rising. During the first period heavy overflows took place from the northwest pond and at the southeast cove, while the sinking stage was distinguished by cracking and foundering among the flows from the pond. This cracking and foundering spread toward the pond as though the back draining and lowering of the crust occasioned the cracking. Traveling fountains in the north cove migrated to grottoes on the north bank. The south island was becoming heart-shaped, possibly owing to the constant appearance of fountains at its base, and the crashing of these against the wall; a high grotto was splashing southeast, and there had been a few small rockfalls from the southwest wall. The central and southwest islands were now again promontories, and the old channel from the northwest pond to the lake appeared to have become obliterated. A point of the crag mass had built itself into the pond, making a narrow construction towards the east end.

Survey from south and southeast stations at eleven-thirty a. m. on October 6 made the mean elevation of the southeast rim of the pit above the lake 283 feet, corresponding to a daily rise since September 28 of an average of three and a quarter feet. This indicates conclusively that the stagnation and spasmodic subsidence of September were equinoctial, for the present rising agrees closely with the August tendency. The shore bank around the lake was fourteen feet high, indicating that the depression of the lava October 5 was only 269 feet, six feet lower only than the maximum of the year last May.

Eleven fountains were in action, among them a line of traveling fountains moving northward in the north cove. The lake rose about five feet at noon, but fell again five minutes later. Avalanches were taking place at the base of the north wall, and fresh tumbles were observed north, west and southwest. The fresh overflows on the southeast bench displayed new cracks; streaming was from the west towards the north and southwest; the south wall pond had ceased to fountain and showed a glowing cone; the northwest pond and the south end of the main lake were alternately crusting over and breaking up, and fairly recent overflows have traveled eastward from the north end of the northwest pond.

The Whitney Laboratory of Seismology reports for the week about a dozen local earthquakes, of which only four or five have been of even instrumental significance, the others being merely exaggerated volcanic tremors. Volcanic vibration has been strong at times in spasms lasting several minutes. Microseismic motion has been small. Tilting to the north and east in the early part of the week was followed by recovery to the normal. The weather has been unusually dry, with extended calm spells, the fumes from Halemaumau rising straight into the air, surmounted by a cumulus cloud of atmospheric moisture.

During the week ending October 13, 1916, the lava lake has shown strong fluctuations with heavy overflows produced by rising and marked cessation of such overflow accompanied by subsidence at the end of the week. Consequently the net movement of the lava column has been slight, amounting to a rise of only a little over one foot per day. The border benches of the lava lake have been further elevated northeast and southwest, while the old northeast crags dating from the first of July, 1916, have been completely submerged under bench overflows.

On October 7 and 8 the weather was rainy and there was little change in the condition of the lava pit.

On October 9 at 4 p. m. it was again rainy and from the east and south stations the general shape of the lake and height of the banks appeared as on October 6. At 9 a. m. there had been an overflow at the north cove and the east end of the northwest pond. At noon there had been very intense fountaining. Now at 4 p. m. six fountains were in action, the lower bench bordering the lake was ten feet high, the lower five feet of this representing subsidence since the morning. At the north and southeast ends, however, the shore was only three feet high. The northwest pond exhibited a splashing grotto on its west side. The west arm had widened southward behind the southwest peninsula. The central promontory showed a slight extension southward. The south island stood high and showed slight tilt of its upper surface toward the west. The small pond next to the south wall was crusted over, with a glow cone on its surface close to the wall, while farther east along the wall crack there was a cone showing two open orifices in its summit, through which could be seen the surging lava beneath. Avalanches took place occasionally from the north and southwest walls of the pit.

There were some big infalls of spatter banks bordering the lake on the southwest shore, the west side of the south island, along the east bank, and elsewhere. For a time the south end of the lake remained quiet, covered with skin. Travelling fountains moved north in the northern cove. There were heavy spurts of umbrella shape from some of the northern fountains, which became places of continuous and tumultuous ebullition when once formed, migrating slowly northward to the bank; as their violence increased, the lake surface behind them would stream more rapidly owing to the downsucking of skins into the fountains. The source of streaming appeared to be wholly at the west arm. After a time the quiet south end of the lake broke up and streaming was restored southward. The lake rose and fell a foot or two from time to time in the course of two hours but remained mostly low.

On Oct. 10 at 2 p. m. the lake seen from the east station was much higher than on the previous day and only about one foot below the inner bench. At the shore of the northwest pond it was still higher and overflowing the bench eastward. Fresh festooned flows covered the lower terraces of the old northeast crags on the lake side, and there were other fresh overflows toward the southeast. The glow pots in the filling of the south-southeast wall crack had changed their shape to a small cone with one little fiery orifice. Trickling lava glowed along the wall crack east and northeast. There was a high splashing grotto southwest of the southwest promontory, a border fountain was active at the north cove and a crescent shaped spatter cone appeared at the east end of the northwest pond.

At two-twenty p. m. a rapid, tumultuous rising took place whereby vast floods overwelled the banks of the northwest pond, north cove, southeast cove, west arm and south bench. The overflow southeast poured a stream ten feet wide, which forked east and west, the eastern branch filling a crevasse in the old bench. Then the flood spread out to the wall and expanded east and west. The northern flow drowned the old northeast crags. The northwest and west floods spread all over the bench and moved southward back of the raised southwest bench to a heap of talus under the southwest station. On the south bench the overflow spread only a short distance in the direction of the wall pond.

The flood continued for an hour. At three-ten p. m. a remarkable spectacle was afforded by the northwest pond, which temporarily subsided with great rapidity about four feet. The result was that from its north side the hot flood of lava on the bench poured back into the pond with a roar and a rush, making a gorgeous, noisy cascade. In five minutes an adjustment was reached, the pond filled up again, and from three-twenty to three-twenty-five it was overflowing once more its whole north, northwest and west shore. Meanwhile the main lake subsided a foot and ceased overflowing. This period of flood tide left as a remnant of the old northeast crags only six smoking points of rock, and lava flows enveloped the whole northern and western base of the old northeast debris slope, the tongues penetrating among the stones with a crackling noise. The northeast and southwest raised benches were still left twenty feet high. The lava-filled wall cracks northeast and south did not appear to share in the great rise of the lake. During the rise a fountain at the entrance of the north cove broke occasionally in a huge incandescent dome.

At 3:30 p. m. the northwest pond was still overflowing, the lake was brimming level with the northern bank and in the south-southeast wall crack the cone was hissing. At 4:15 p. m. increased overflow from the northwest pond so augmented the flood on the bench that the northeast crag remnants were completely submerged.

On October 11 the lava lake was much the same with occasional risings without overflow. The bank appeared from two to three feet high.

On Thursday, October 12, at 5 p. m., with wind varying from southwest to calm, the lake from the southeast station appeared extraordinarily quiet and relatively cool and crusted. The surface was about three feet below the banks except at the southeast cove where it was overflowing and level with the glowing fill of a crescent shaped depression occupying the wall crack right and left. There were only three continuous fountaining areas, two on the shore of the north cove and one under a high grotto on the west side of the northwest pond. East-northeast there was fresh avalanche material on the bench. In the south southeast cone a stiff lava was spitting and surging under a flexible skin and through it gas emerged hissing and flaming. The gas pressure under the heavy blankets covering the lake which were nearly stagnant without streaming, most of the time would relieve itself by breaking the crust every fifteen or twenty minutes in three or four places where violent ebullition would develop. At these places violent continuous fountaining threw up heavy umbrella spurts and very high spray, the fountain area in each case migrating to some part of the bank where it expended itself. The migration was various at different times with streaming following in its wake. At other times the only streaming was northward in the north cove. In several places heavily overweighted spatter banks on the lake shore tumbled into the molten lava. This remarkably quiet spell proceeded a sudden movement of sinking.

On Oct. 13 at 9 a. m. the pit was smoky and the lake was extraordinarily depressed below the recent platform around it by about 20 feet in most places, especially northeast and southwest. At the north, however, this bench was only five feet above the lake level and three feet high at the southwest cove. This appeared to indicate that much of the movement which at first sight appeared to be a sinking of 17 feet since the previous day, was really a bodily upheaval of the northeast, and southwest benches. This was further suggested by new gaping cracks across the raised lower bench on the south and southwest. This remarkable movement of rising benches suggests the possibility of local intrusion of the lava beneath.

The lake was covered with hot skins and there was slow streaming south and north from the west arm. A new small promontory extended from the foot of the southwest peninsula. The south island was about 17 feet high. The northwest pond had now become completely divided by the uplift or accretion of the point projecting from the crag mass so that it now formed two ponds which appeared to be about ten feet below the bordering bench. Twelve fountains were in action, including seven in the north cove. There were rock tumbles from the inner cliff into the lake. Smoke rose thickly from clefts on the north, east, northwest, southwest and south-southeast. There was a pile of new white stones, an avalanche talus at the base of the south-southwest wall. Up to 10 a. m. the lake was rising and at that time it was splashing over the southeast bank. Later it subsided again.

Measurements on Oct. 13 between 8:30 and 9:30 a. m. from the east and southwest stations determined the depression of the lake to be 275 feet and of the northwest pond 272 feet below the east station. The bench at the central promontory was 27 feet high and at the grotto west of the northwest pond 17 feet high. These measurements indicate an average rise of the lake for seven days since Oct. 6 of only one and one-seventh feet per day.

During the recent period of calms and light southwest winds (which came to an end Oct. 13), the blowing of the fumes northeastward across the floor of the greater crater produced marked condensation of the steam jets in that region from Halemaumau to Perret's cone, in contrast to the relatively invisible vapor jets elsewhere . The effect extended fully two miles and was sharply perceptible even where the blue-brown crater fume was so thin as

Halemaumau Oct. 24, 1916, from the S. SW. showing the benches and crags elevated bodily around the lava lake.
—Photo Jaggar.

West rim of Halemaumau and the region of the N. W. ponds below, Oct. 24, 1916, from the S. SW.
—Photo Jaggar.

to be almost imperceptible. The relative humidity on these days was from 75 to 81%. The effect was very marked on Oct. 9.

On the rainy days of this calm southerly spell, steam-spouts have been common, rope-like vortex whirls drawing up the steam of the crater floor to join with tails of low-hung cloud pulled downward, the whole structure, like a waterspout, moving slowly across the crater and showing a core more transparent than the condensed vapor around it. These steam-spouts are quite distinctive of this area in such weather.

In the Whitney Laboratory of Seismology for the week ending Oct. 13 five local earthquakes have been registered on the seismographs. One of these was generally felt in southern Hawaii about 11:30 a. m. Oct. 8. Tilt to the northeast has increased during the week and the same is true of the volcanic vibrations. Both the tilt and the volcanic vibrations have shown tendency to occurrence in spasms arising relatively suddenly and continuing for spells of variable duration.

Technology Station,
October 21, 1916.

During the week ending Oct. 20, 1916, the lava column of Kilauea volcano has resumed vigorous rising, and a remarkable incident of the rise has been the mass elevation of the benches and crags surrounding the lakes so that throughout the week there has been almost no overflow of the inner benches. The week has furnished probably the most extraordinary example of this mechanism which has taken place since the Observatory has been here. The impression of an observer who made no surveys would have favored the supposition that the lake was going down, for as a whole the ledges bordering the lava have increased in height above the liquid. Along with this there has been much smoke and some rock tumbles, all supposed symptoms of subsidence. The only sign of pressure from below has been the welling up of viscid lava along the wall crack. Tilting of the ledges which has accompanied uplift has been away from the lake toward the walls. A reasonable explanation of the uplifting force in such a case is that the lava wedged in under and between the ledges below the lake level and solidified as an intrusion.

On October 14 the pit was smoky and conditions appeared unchanged. On October 15 between 3 p. m. and 4 p. m. the fumes at the southeast and east stations were intolerable, north and west they formed an impenetrable veil. Southwest and south there was clear seeing of the lava lakes. The circle of benches had been uplifted so that the rim of the northwest pond appeared 20 feet high and the banks of the lake 6 feet high southeast and north and about 30 feet high elsewhere. The elevated plateaus northeast and southwest appeared at least 50 feet above the lake. The west side of the south island had broken away, the crevasses in the southwest bench were wider, there was fresh rock tumble under the southwest wall, the crag mass appeared higher than ever and there was smoke from all the crags and from the northern bench. The south pond and the wall crack under the east station were piled with new lava, which glowed in the southern locality. The bank of the lake caved in on the northeast. Streaming was from the west and bent northward to a rapid rush in the north cove. Eight or more fountains were in action. Stalactites hung under the banks of the central promontory, the northwest pond and the west cove. The lake appeared hot and active, and made plashing and rumbling noises.

On October 16 from 4 p. m. to 5 p. m. the sketches made by the writer at the south station appear to indicate that on this day the maximum uplift of the crags occurred and that thereafter the lake rose so as to gain on the uplifted shores. The inner benches appeared from 25 to 40 feet high and the south island still higher. A new flat islet had emerged from the lake north of the south island. The lake at 4 p. m. was crusted over toward the south, but this broke up with violent fountaining against the east side of the island. Then the fountaining migrated to the southeast cove. For a time there was streaming from the southeast to the east side of the island, but afterwards this changed until the current was wholly southeastward. There appeared to be a stagnation zone on the surface of the lake between the new islet and the east bank as though continued uplift of the lake bottom would produce a peninsula. The general effect of this day's movement was to make the lakes appear lower. The only sign of fresh overflow was a small festoon of new lava on the southeast bench and a long one westward from the western half of the northwest pond. There were fresh high spatter rims around the lake as though rapid fluctuations were in progress. Between noon and 4 p. m. there was the appearance of at least six feet of sinking of the lakes. The west-northwest pond was crusted over, while the north-northwest one showed glow. On the south-southeast bench were two small glowing cones. Cracks in the south bench were increasing in size and a new crack opening in the high south-west table showed that the rock within was glowing cherry red. A crackling noise came from the lake crust. At times there were from twelve to fifteen fountains. On the east there was a heavy fall of spatter banks, the south island towered high and the rampart at the north cove was higher than the one southeast.

On October 17 at 11:30 a. m. the lake appeared about eight feet higher and rising, and the west-northwest pond was higher and actively fountaining at the tunnel under the thickened crust which led to the north-northwest pond (formerly the east cove of the pond). These tunnels under crusts with hanging stalactites have appeared of late back of the north islet and of the southwest promontory showing that channels remained below which were revealed by uplift. Southeast there was violent fountaining. Around the pond in the south wall crack there was some collapsing and breaking of crusts. East of it were tumbled ledges and there was fresh talus southwest. Small crags had reappeared on the north bench and there was some new talus northeast. A loose pinnacle at the end of the central promontory had fallen into the lake. The small east islet and the south glow cone were still in place but the incandescent cracks southwest had cooled off.

On October 18 at 8:30 a. m. the new east islet was two feet high, but by 10 a. m. it was drowned under rising lava. The lake appeared higher and exhibited less smoke. There was some fresh overflow at the north-northwest pond and southeast cove. The central promontory had broken up into a group of small pinnacles. There was a fresh spatter rim around the lake about five feet high. There was a little fresh talus on the floor northwest and south-west. A new lower bench appeared built by accretion around the south islet and the southwest promontory. There were eight fountains in action and the west-northwest pond was higher and active around its border. Streaming was straight across the lake from the west arm, rapid northward to the west side of the north cove and sluggish southwestward. There was occasional violent fountaining in the southeast and north coves. Gas pressure was higher, the noise was of puffing and plashing, the lake was hotter with thin glistening black skins striated but not conspicuously blistered.

Measurements on Thursday, October 19, at 9:30 a. m., from the south station revealed the following dimensions:

Diameter floor N. W.-S. E.	1125 ft.
Length of lake N.-S.	775 ft.
Width of lake E.-W.	625 ft.
Length of W. N. W. pond	160 ft.
Height of crag above lake	60 ft.
Height lower bench N. E. above lake	14 ft.
Height of upper benches N. E. and S. W.	40 ft.
Depression of lake surface below S. rim of pit	243 ft.

The summit of the crag mass was thus only 181 feet below the rim of the pit. The lake had risen 30 feet since October 13, or at the rate of about five feet per day in six days. It had carried upward with it the entire ring of benches and crags so that generally they retained their relative proportions of height, but as a whole increased their height above the lake.

On this day the fumes appeared thinner and eighteen fountains were in action, especially in the north and southeast coves. Both ponds were higher and the north-northwest one was active. The tabular ledges northeast and southwest showed increased tilt away from the lake, the northeast ledge being highest at the south while the southwest ledge was higher at the north. The lower terrace was only four feet high southeast and north, but elsewhere it was higher. Streaming was faster than usual, skins were thin, spatter ramparts had been built eight to ten feet high southeast and north, a large crevasse had opened back of the southwest promontory and the noises were of plashing and puffing. A small slide was heard southwest. Under the east gulch was a coarse heap of talus twenty feet high.

At 9 a. m. on October 20 the lake appeared eight feet lower, but this may have been further uplift of the bench. The small east islet was again revealed, but by 9:30 a. m. the lake had risen flush with its surface. There was occasional rush, with fountaining, to the east bank. Twelve fountains were in action. The west-northwest pond was high and largely crusted and did not share in the general appearance of subsidence. Its level appeared much higher than the lake. There were stalactite caverns back of the southwest promontory and north islet promontory and the head of the west arm. Streaming was sluggish, there were heavy stagnant skins and there was occasional stormy fountaining. One of the spatter domes on the shore of the north cove had been built into a crescent. A current with bubble fountaining flowed slowly out from the southwest cavern and there was occasional violent inrush with fountaining to the bank just south of it. This appeared to alternate with violent fountaining which would start east of the south island and migrate to the southeast cove. The north cove contained multiple fountains most of the time. There was more white avalanche debris southwest. No fresh overflows appeared.

The seismographs of the Whitney Laboratory have registered a few small local earthquake shocks and one distant earthquake. Tilting to the east has been very strong while that to the north has gradually returned to nearly normal. Microseismic motion has been ordinary and volcanic vibration strong.

TECHNOLOGY STATION, Oct. 28, 1916.—During the week ending Friday, October 27, 1916, the active lava column of Halemaumau has continued to rise with the same extraordinary mechanism of uplift of the benches that prevailed during the preceding week. The rate of rising, however, was somewhat slower, only about two feet per day.

On October 22 at 6 p. m. it was evident that the activity of the preceding forty-eight hours had continued to push up the ledges and islands, including new shoals under the lake, for three small islets had appeared off the end of the southwest promontory. This peninsula was in process of breaking up, invaded from the north by the extension of a cove inward from the west arm. All the crags appeared higher. The east islet stood eight feet above the lake. On north and southeast, however, the shore was still low. Large cracks were developing in the uplifted bench on the south and southwest. The glowing cone on the south-southeast bench was still puffing and flaming, and large blue-green flames played through a crack at the inner edge of the rampart on the north-northeast border of the lake. There were eighteen fountains playing in the lake at one time, and the west-northwest pond showed glow and fountain activity.

On Monday, October 23, at 3 p. m., there were fourteen fountains in action, and in relation to its banks the lake was higher. The east islet now stood only three feet above the liquid, and the end of the southwest promontory had partially subsided. The west arm was much crusted over. The liquid of the fountains appeared viscous to judge by the slaggy umbrella jets that were thrown up. Opposite the southwest cove instreaming and outstreaming currents met with violent ebulition. The new wall pond opposite the end of the west arm was in process of overflow with incandescent toes pushing along the wall crack. The low floors bordering the lake on the north and southeast were covered with a greenish-tan coating of Pele's hair, and there was much of this substance outside of Halemaumau on the south. At the southern stations the heat radiation from the lake was very strong. The noises were not loud, and consisted chiefly of plashing. South of the south island there was a steady fountain playing most of the time where currents from west and east met; here the skins drawn toward the place of boiling would become inflated like balloons before being engulfed in the hot swirl.

At 8:30 a. m. on October 24, the lake was overflowing the southeast floor, the southwest islets were flush with the lake level, the north-northwest pond was overflowing, and there was violent fountaining on the southeast and north, with twelve fountains in action. During the hour, however, to 9:30 a. m., the activity dwindled and the lake sank about four feet, so that at 9:45 a. m. there were only five fountains playing and the islets had emerged, the two outer southwest islets being joined together, while the inner had become joined to the peninsula. There was a little sliding under the southwest wall. The hissing conelet was still in evidence south-southeast, and hissing could be heard from the northwest bench. A heavy spatter rampart had been built all around the north cove, but no overflow could be seen there. The fountains were less viscous than on the previous day, and the lake was covered with glistening black skins, thin and wrinkled but not blistered.

At 6 p. m. the border benches were all higher by about five feet, the southwest islets had united to form a peninsula and fiery grottoes with stalactites had developed on the southeast, southwest, northeast, north, and in the west arm. The wall crack west was ejecting a lava flow. The largest crevasse in the southwest bench showed cherry red glow in its depths and rocks fell occasionally on the southwest talus. The lake was in process of rising, for most of the stalactites were submerged by 6:15 p. m.

On October 25 at 9 a. m. the pit was fumy and the lake again appeared relatively high and flush with the surface of the new extension of the southwestern peninsula. The west-northwest pond was active, five fountains could be counted, the east islet stood about four feet above the lake, streaming as usual was from the west, and there were some stagnant skins in places. The south bench had been rising and cracking still more, and the new southeast overflows showed collapsed crusts. There were smoking cracks on the northeast, north, west, southwest and south.

Measurements on Thursday, October 26, at 10 a. m., made the depression of the lake surface 228 feet below the southeast rim of the pit, indicating a rise of fifteen feet since October 19. The summit of the crag mass was 72 feet above the lake, or only 156 feet below the rim of Halemaumau. This meant that the crag mass had risen 25 feet during the week. The new tip of the southwest promontory formed by the emergence of the three islets had extended the promontory by 100 feet.

On this morning the heat from the lake was more intense than at any time before during the present year. Ten fountains were in action, there were small fresh overflows southeast, and continuous splashing was in progress at a high grotto in the southwest cove where the two currents met from north and west. The northern current here was now pouring through an open chasm which had developed during the night so as to separate the southwest promontory from the shore and permit a torrent to pour through from the head of the west arm. Consequently the southwest promontory was converted into a large island, high at its west end and with its eastern platform about four feet above the lake. The northern end of this island had narrowed the west arm. At 11:30 a. m. there was a marked rise of the liquid with overflow of the southeast floor. The west-northwest pond appeared high. The southwest crags appeared higher than ever and their elevation was greater than that of the northeast crags. There were new rock tumbles on the northeast, southeast and southwest. A small slide was seen in motion under the east gulch. There was a small overflow at the lowest point in the north rampart.

Here the flaming crack continued in action. The south island was very high. The skins on the lake showed many blisters.

On October 27 at 5 p. m. the lake seen from the south station showed little change. There were glowing overflows along the base of the northern wall which had their origin by overflow of the north bench. Glowing lava could also be seen at the base of the west wall, probably oozing up the wall crack. A strong golden stream poured through the new channel between the southwest island and the bench, meeting the current from around the island in a furious fountain which played in the southwest cove. In the same way meeting currents made a fountain south of the south island. A new small islet had risen near the northwest corner of the south island. Six or seven fountains were in action, there were many smoking places, glow and flame continued in the north rampart and on the south-southeast bench. For a time the south end of the lake was stagnant.

During the week ending October 27 the seismographs of the Whitney Laboratory have registered only three very small local earthquake shocks, microseismic and volcanic vibrations have been moderate, and the very strong tilting to the north as well as to the east has been resumed.

Very respectfully,
T. A. JAGGAR JR.,
Director.

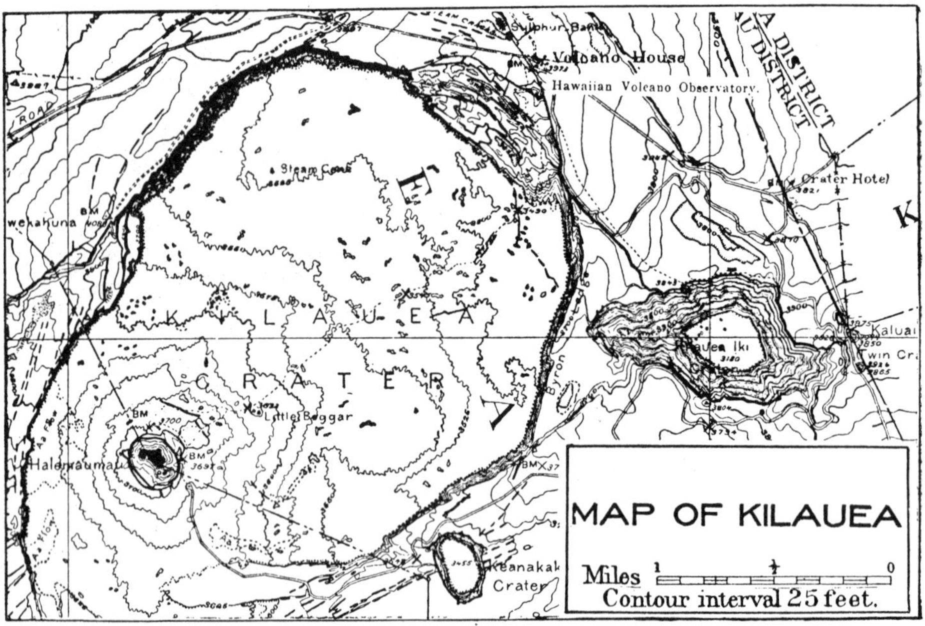

MAP OF KILAUEA

Miles 1 0

Contour interval 25 feet.

HAWAIIAN VOLCANO RESEARCH ASSOCIATION.

This society is a voluntary one, made up of subscribers to scientific work which is being executed by the Massachusetts Institute of Technology.

In 1915 there are about 100 subscribers in Hawaii and elsewhere, firms and individuals. A group of firms and persons in Hilo built the main observatory building in the spring of 1912. Publications to date have been weekly reports since the summer of 1911, now reprinted in Honolulu in monthly form. The Massachusetts Institute of Technology will publish annual reports, of which the introductory number was printed in 1912.

The weekly bulletin as it appears in the Advertiser is reprinted as a leaflet and sent to regular annual subscribers to the work of the Association. L. A. Thurston is president of the Board of Directors of the Association, and R. W. Shingle is treasurer. New subscribers who are interested in volcanoes will be welcomed in the Association. The Association aims: (1) To record volcanic activity and earthquakes in Hawaii; (2) to attract scientific men hither for special studies; (3) to promote the establishment of volcano observatories all over the world. The annual dues of regular members are $5; patrons of the Assocaition subscribe larger amounts.

WHITNEY LABORATORY OF SEISMOLOGY.

The Whitney Laboratory of Seismology is equipped with two Bosch-Omori 100 kg tromometers registering N-S and E-W motion, a heavy Omori tromometer registering E-W motion, and an Omori "ordinary Seismograph" designed for registering strong earthquakes in all three components of motion. These are seated on concrete piers in a closed basement room having practically constant temperature, beneath the chief Observatory building near the hotel. Time is referred to a rated chronometer, checked at intervals by solar observations with a transit. Both instruments are loaned by the College of Hawaii. Hawaiian standard time (H. S. T.) is 10 hrs. 30 min. slower than Greenwich time.

CANCANI SCALE OF SEISMIC INTENSITY.

Expressed by accelerations measured in millimeters per second per second.

I.	Instrumental	0.0	2.5
II.	Very slight	2.5	5.0
III.	Slight	5.0	10.0
IV.	Sensible, mediocre	10.0	25.0
V.	Rather strong	25.0	50.0
VI.	Strong	50.0	100.0
VII.	Very strong	100.0	250.0
VIII.	Ruinous	250.0	500.0
IX.	Disastrous	500.0	1000.0
X.	Very disastrous	1000.0	2500.0
XI.	Catastrophic	2500.0	5000.0
XII.	Great catastrophe	5000.0	10000.0

Grade IV. is ordinarily the minimum perceived by the senses; and in grade XII. the acceleration, or rate of change of motion (jerk) reaches that of terrestrial gravitation.

In the standard form of report the maximum intensity or acceleration, designated by the symbol α, or max. α, is given in the conventional unit, **the milligal.** The milligal is a measure of acceleration, such that 1 milligal = 1/100 mm. per sec. per sec. = 10 μ per sec. per sec. The Cancani scale, here defined in terms of millimeters per sec. per sec., can therefore be expressed in **milligals** by multiplying each of the numbers by 100.

WEEKLY BULLETIN
OF THE
Hawaiian Volcano Observatory

Vol. IV. HONOLULU, HAWAII, NOVEMBER, 1916. No. 11

TECHNOLOGY STATION, Hawaii, November 11—During the week ending November 10 rising of the lava lake in Halemaumau has continued and increased its rate to about three feet per day. The lava has now reached the same level as in the summer of 1912, but the movement of rising is much more gradual than at that time and the fountaining very tranquil in contrast to the hundreds of fountains and violent gas pressure of the years between 1910 and 1912.

On November 4, from eight to nine p. m., the lava lake seen from the south exhibited nine fountains in action, mostly in the north cove, and the surface streaming was in two broad golden bands from the west channel to the north and the southeast. The southwestern and eastern regions were crusted over.

The wall ponds were not glowing, but there was a glowing cone on the south-southwest bench as usual. The level of the lake showed low banks southeast and north, and high walls elsewhere.. The west-northwest pond was high and active. A high stalactite grotto overhung the lake north-northeast. A portion of the inner cliff over the southwest cove had fallen away and there was glow on the bench above.

On the night of November 5 an examination of the pit from all sides revealed brilliant overflowing in progress. From the southeast station at eight-thirty p. m. a brilliant torrent was seen pouring over the southeast bench. The lake was crusted across the middle region, but there were glowing areas north and south. Six fountains were in action. From the south station at nine p. m. the middle skins were seen to break up and the lake subsided slightly, the southeast overflow crusting over.. What appeared to be glowing lava in a crack was seen at the upper edge of the high southwest bench. Looking down from the southwest station, the bench beneath was seen to have crumbled back and the southwest channel had widened. A blow hole was flaming in the northwest end of the southwest islet. The active fountains appeared heavy and viscous.. From the west station at nine-thirty p. m. the west-northwest pond was seen to be bombarding its west bank in a cavern. Still farther west a circular hole in the bench was flaming and occasionally throwing out sparks. The two ponds were mostly crusted over.

The north-northwest pond, however, was overflowing in a ribbon torrent about 100 feet long and eight feet wide which raced down the slope to the wall where it spread right and left in a glowing mass. There were other ribbon flows from this pond and a wide zone of crust showing glow beneath. The basins of the two ponds had been lifted along with the crag mass, the bench around them being cracked and showing increased slope toward the wall. From the northwest station, the north-northwest pond broke up about nine-forty-five p. m. with much cracking and foundering, and the lava of the pond sank sufficiently to cause the ribbon flows to stagnate for a time. Later they revived. One glow spot was seen on the north bench but no overflows. From the east station at ten p. m. the lake appeared quiet, with dark skins and a few fountains. The east islet was about eight feet high.

On Tuesday, November 7, at ten-thirty a. m. the lake level stood about four feet below the southeast bench and the surface was very quiet with from seven to nine fountains, mostly in a line in the north cove. The stalac-

WEEKLY BULLETIN
of the
Hawaiian Volcano Observatory

Published Monthly at Honolulu, Hawaii, by the Hawaiian Volcano Research Association

L. W. de Vis-Norton........Secretary

Entered as second-class matter January 20, 1914, at the post-office at Honolulu, Hawaii, under the Act of August 24, 1912.

tite grotto was still active north-northeast, streaming was sluggish, there were no fresh overflows and the general condition was stagnant. A new extension protruded from the end of the southwest promontory. The pit was smoky.

On November 8, about nine a. m., the lake was high with six fountains in action. Many trickle overflows of recent formation, which had poured through the north rampart, appeared on the north-northeast bench. The north-northwest pond was high and active, and brimming on the west margin. The lake was hot and covered with thin skins and stood level with the lower benches of the southwest promontory. The small islet west of the south island had reappeared covered with broken crusts flush with the lake surface. The noise was of splashing. There was smoke from the eastern, northern and western crags and from the summit of the crag mass. The west-northwest pond was active. There was a continuous band of solidified flow from the wall crack under the northwest station about fifty feet wide, but no fresh flows from the northwest ponds. Both ponds were sunken in their pits about eight feet.

On November 9 at eight p. m. from the north station, the lake was seen to be crusted across the west arm and the southwest cove. The west end of the west-northwest pond was active. There were recent glowing flows on the southeast bench. Against this bench fountains splashed in niches bounded by high knobs, and at one point a hole back of these knobs was spurting lava spray. From seven to nine fountains were in action.

Flames on this night were very abundant, especially above the north-northeast grotto and from under crusts in the southwest cove. Here a line of spears of blue flame shaped like the teeth of a saw burst through a split in the crust and played repeatedly through the crack for several seconds. Then a fountain burst and relieved the gas pressure from under the crusted area. Streaming was slow to the north, southeast and southwest. The new small islet was now an extension of the west side of the south island. The islands appeared high. There was much rumbling on the banks of the lake. At eight-thirty p. m. the lake surface seen from the east station broke up, stalactitic rims appeared around the lake borders and then the surface darkened again. The north-northwest pond was active and a blue flame played from a hole high in its northeast bank. This bank was about eight feet high.

No fresh flows were seen on the north bench and heavy white fume rose from it. The blow hole at the northwest end of the southwest island continued to spurt.

Measurements on November 10 at nine forty-five a. m. determined the mean depression of the lake below the southeast rim of the pit to be 193 feet, indicating a rise of 21 feet in eight days. This is practically the same level reached on July 12, 1912, the maximum of that summer.

At nine-fifteen a. m. on this date the lake was rising. At nine-thirty overflows began in wide floods across the southeast bench immediately filling the hollow to the wall and spreading right and left so that the flood, moving westward, passed beneath the south station and beyond. There were also tremendous overfloods northeast, north and from the north-northwest pond. The west-northwest pond did not overflow. Only two fountains were in action.

The lake was very hot and the middle portion and eastern tip of the southwest island were temporarily drowned, as was also the western extension of the south island. A small overflow took place from the end of the west arm. At 10 a. m. the lake sank back a few inches and seven fountains broke out with bombardment east, southeast and southwest. A new development of surface streaming was the outpouring of a current from the north cove to the southeast and southwest joining with the outward streaming from the west arm. The spatter reached the top of the east islet. All the southeast spatter knobs of the previous evening disappeared under the new overflows and much of the north rampart was covered. The whole northern bench was flooded with new lava clear to the base of the northeast talus, which is now a low heap against the wall, the last remnant of the great debris slopes left by the June subsidence.

The seismographs of the Whitney Laboratory have registered only one small earthquake during the week. Microseismic motion has been rather. strong, volcanic vibration moderate, and the pronounced tilting of the ground to the north and east recovered somewhat toward the end of the week ending Nov. 10, but not nearly to the normal.

TECHNOLOGY STATION, November 18—The week ending November 17, at the lava pit shows continued very rapid rising, averaging for the six days ending November 16 five and one-third feet per day. The lake is now only 160 feet below the rim of the pit and the crags bordering the liquid lava continue to rise. The hissing of the lake recalls the very rapid lifting of the lava column which took place between October and December 1911, and if the present rate of rising continues until the solstice, the lava will be close to the upper rim and the rising crags above it before the new year. The rate of rising for five months past has been over three and a half feet per day.

The changes in the lake are now so numerous and the area of crags, ponds, benches and islands so complicated that it is necessary to abbreviate this weekly report and reserve the details for more complete scientific publication illustrated with maps and diagrams.

On Saturday, November 11, at five-thirty p. m. the lake appeared lower, from seven to nine fountains were in action, five grotttoes were splashing and the cliffs and islands appeared higher than of late. The streaming on the surface of the lake to the southwest was unusually rapid and developed a turbulent fountain where it met a current in the southwest cove that poured out from under the crust which bridged the southwest channel. The only crusted region was the inner part of the west arm and a flame played above a grotto to the south of that arm. Bubble fountains were displayed occasionally toward the south. There was no glow of recent flows on the benches. The fountains were viscous and stringy and the fumes to the southeast were disagreeable.

All these symptoms of subsidence of the lake were verified the next day, November 12, when measurements in the afternoon showed the average depression of the lava to be 195 feet, three feet lower than two days before. An earthquake was felt in the early morning and others were registered by the seismographs. The lake at noon appeared low with overhanging banks which exhibited stalactities, and rocks were sliding under the eastern walls of the pit. From the east station the north-northwest pond was seen to have become an arm of the lake through collapse of a crust on the north side of the crag-mass. Large new crevasses were seen southwest and south. At one p. m. fifteen fountains were in action.

The rising of the crag-mass had gone on during the previous fortnight so that now it was only 119 feet below the rim of the pit where on November 2, it had been 140 feet down. In the interval the lake had risen twenty feet and the crag-mass twenty-one feet, thus maintaining evenly its relative height. The summit of the south island was thirty-seven feet above the lake.

This slight subsidence of November 12 proved only temporary, for at nine-thirty a. m. on November 13 there were fresh overflows on the north and northeast, and rapid lifting of the benches was in progress north and south of the western wall pond. In the evening there were glowing flows all around the base of the north wall and streaming was into the new northwestern arm, and apparently under an arch beyond, to the south end of the northwest pond. Flames were conspicuous and crusts tended to form and break up southwest and west.

At six-thirty p. m. on November 14 the lake was sluggish and crusted. Pele's hair was floating up in large quantities and fresh flows were crackling north and northeast. The streaming into the northwest arm was more sluggish and a flow fed by spatter bombardment from between two huge lumps was trickling down a steep slope back of the north rampart. Flames were again in evidence.

At seven a. m. on November 15 the fume rising from Halemaumau was thin and transparent, and in the calm air rose high in a faintly visible stalk, while above a cumulus of moisture stood over the hot gas column at an elevation of at least 2000 feet.

In the evening this flower-like cloud, illumined rosy by the fire below, lighted the whole country, and the high level of the lava in the pit was evident from the flat angle of the light rays right and left.

Halemaumau at eight-thirty a. m. showed a high lake with rapid surface streaming, hot skins, blue fumes and many fresh overflows. The east island was now a peninsula and the small islet was attached to the south island. The highest portions of the east and west raised benches were now towards the south, and the west wall pond was ruptured at both ends by the drag of the rising crags. The southwest island had risen further and was lengthened toward the east. Inrush had been resumed at the northwest arm and to the inner end of the northwest pond. A lower bench of spatter began to appear around the lake.

Measurements on November 16 at eight-thirty a. m. made the depression of the lake 161 feet. The survey showed that the central promontory had moved horizontally ninety feet southeastward and the summit of the crag mass 125 feet in the same direction. This summit was now only ninety-one feet below the rim of the pit and had therefore lifted in four days twenty-eight feet, while the lake in the same time had risen thirty-five feet. It appeared, therefore, that the rising of the lake was now gaining on the crag mass, whereas for five weeks prior to November 12 the great ledges were rising above the lake by from two to ten feet per week in excess of the lift of the lake surface. With the lake rising eighty-three feet from October 19 to November 16, the crag mass steadily increased in height above the lake surface as follows: October 18, sixty-two feet; October 26, seventy-six feet; November 2, seventy-four feet, and November 12, seventy-seven feet.

On November 16, however, this extraordinary hill in the midst of the pit had lost seven feet of its height above the lake and shifted sideways over 100 feet. This movement must have been a toppling over of the mass on its foundation after the subsidence of November 11-12 so as to slightly arrest the process of its elevation.

November 16, there was again an appearance of susidence. The southwest island was breaking so that large blocks crumbled into the lava making puffs of brown dust and there were similar falls elsewhere. There was a six-foot overhang all around the shore, ten to twelve fountains were in action and occasionally the streaming was rapid. A hissing spot showed lava sputter in the cracked bench south. There were fresh crackling flows on the north and southeast benches. A new islet had appeared in the southern part of the lake. The lake was falling before nine-thirty a. m. but afternoon inspection showed that there had been a rise near noon, with subsidence afterward.

Rising had been resumed on the morning of Friday, November 17, there were few fountains, fresh overflows and spitting driblet cones were building in the western bench crevasses. The crag-mass showed a large north-south crack through its midst and the new islet had disappeared. Nine festooned overflows of recent origin were counted extending from the northwest pools over the north bench, and an overflow from the west arm had poured into the chasm at its head.

The following report from the Whitney Laboratory of Seismology is submitted by Mr. H. O. Wood:—

"During the week ending with November 17, seven, or eight, small local earthquakes were registered. Of these one was a felt shock of ordinary character noticed at the Volcano House and also in Hilo, somewhat more sharply in the latter place. The others were ordinary instrumental shocks. Besides these there were two wave groups of doubtful character. In the latter part of the interval microseismic motion has shown large amplitude increasing from moderately large values earlier in the week. The amplitude of waves of volcanic vibration have been moderately large to large throughout the week, with definite increase over values in previous weeks. The condition of tilt in the east-west direction has shown no marked change: but in the north-south direction there has been a definite increase in tilt to the north."

Technology Station,
Nov. 4, 1916.

During the week ending Nov. 3, 1916, the lava lake at Halemaumau has continued to rise at the average rate of two feet per day and the crags have risen slightly more than the lake, but not so much as during the previous week. The lava column has now reached the same height that it held during the summer of 1912 and the elevated crags and benches are much higher.

On Saturday, Oct. 28, at 12:15 p. m., the lake seen from the south station appeared about five feet lower relative to the benches and islands. The small new oval islet off the west end of the south island stood about five feet above the liquid. The end of the southwest promontory and the surface of the east islet were about ten feet high. The crag mass, the southwest plateau and the south island appeared higher than ever. There was a fresh flow on the southeast platform from the east wall crack. Fresh flows were seen around the base of the old northeast talus apparently spurted up the wall crack there. The northern rampart at the border of the lake was eight feet high but the bench back of it was low. The bench southeast was only two feet high. The channel between the southwest island and the shore was stagnant. The west-northwest pond was glowing but appeared low. Seven fountains were in action and they appeared viscous. The streaming was north and south from the west arm. The east side of the lake was stagnant. The rock wall along the north side of the west channel was being undermined by the construction of the channel produced by the building out of a point from the southwest island and it presented a raw reddish broken surface where the spatter veneer had broken away. The cracks at the base of the west wall of the pit were glowing.

From 9 to 10:30 p. m. the lake was actively rising and overflowing the southeast floor. Fourteen fountains were in action. The west wall crack was overflowing at a higher level than the lake and had been sending a cascade into the head of the west arm. A golden stream was rushing southward through the southwest channel, the west-northwest pond was active but below the rim. General streaming was sluggish and there was shore bombardment north and southeast.

On Oct. 29 at 9 p. m. conditions were much the same. The lake was two feet below the southeast floor and seven fountains were in action throwing up viscous, slaggy umbrella jets. The eight-foot rampart bordering the north cove was almost continuous, showing that the lake surface was keeping pace with the uplift of the floor level there. One fall of spatter veneer was seen to take place from the north bank of the west arm.

The lake seen from the eastern and southern stations between 8 and 9 p. m. on Oct. 30 was at first high and overflowing both the northern and southeastern floors. A glowing flow was visible also at the west wall crack. The whole west arm and the eastern and southern parts of the lake were covered with dark skin. Fourteen fountains were playing in the north and southwest coves and in the two northwest ponds, both of which were in action. About 8:15 p. m. a large fountain broke out at the east base of the south island relieving the pressure of gas accumulated under the dark skin. Tumultuous fountaining was in progress in the southwest cove at the meeting point of the westward streaming from the lake and the southward streaming from the southwest channel. In the northern rampart there was a hole through which spurts of lava and gas were impelled from the shore bombardment with snorting noises. The fountains on this night were noisily rumbling and puffing. The small islet at the west end of the south island was submerged and the lake was brimming level with the extension of the southwest promontory. The fountain liquid was hot and fluent.

At 8:40 p. m. the whole dark crust broke up producing a magnificent display as the golden fluid below welled up the spreading cracks until all the crusts and skins had folded down rapidly beneath the melt and there was left the usual appearance of polyhedral skin patterns and zigzag red lines. The heat evolved during the break-up was intense. It was evident that this breaking up of the crusts accompanied sudden subsidence (or sudden lifting of the benches), for immediately border overhang with stalactites appeared in many places.

On Oct. 31 at 8 p. m. the lake appeared relatively lower, showing a bank three or four feet high southeast and fourteen fountains in action. There were quiet skins in the central and southern region, which broke up about 8:45 p. m. and there was strong fountaining in the southwest and north coves. The west-northwest pond was active but not the north-northwest pond. There was the usual glow crack south-southeast but no glow at the western wall crack. The walls of the southwest promontory, the south island and the central promontory were higher but the small islet west of the south island had not reappeared. A large blue-green flame was jetting from a crack on the west side of the west-northwest pond.

On Nov. 1 at 8 p. m. the lake again appeared a little lower relative to the benches. Twelve fountains were playing, both the northwest ponds were active, both the south and east islands stood high above the lake and there was a grotto in the south bank showing fountaining and stalactites. There were glowing toes piling up in the west wall crack, but no visible overflows anywhere from the lakes. The skins on the lake were dark, there was no very rapid streaming and the fountaining was rather quiet. Fumes rising across the southwest rim of the pit were intolerable.

Measurements at 10 a. m. on Nov. 2 from the east and south stations made the mean depression of the lake 214 feet below the rim and the height of the crag mass above the lake 74 feet. This mass had risen 16 feet in seven days while the lake was rising 14 feet. The depression of the peak of the crag mass below the rim of the pit was thus only 140 feet.

The lake appeared relatively higher. Sixteen fountains were in action, both the northwest ponds were active and there was streaming in a new direction out from the southeast cove northward and westward on both sides of the south island. The east islet was enlarged at its east end and opposite to it on the shore was a short projection making out from the base of the bank. The southwest channel was crusted over. The rampart around the north cove appeared from eight to fourteen feet high. The east islet, the south bench of the south island, and the outer end of the southwest promontory were about eight feet high. The southeast floor was only three feet high. The crags and elevated benches showed no increase of height. Sliding was in progress at the base of the southwest wall. There were heaped up lava driblets at the west wall pond. The crack on the upper bench under the southwest station formerly seen glowing was now smoking and a little wider. There was fresh lava along the wall crack north-northwest and also from under the east station to the southeast cove. It was evident that lava was welling up the crack between the benches and the wall of the pit on all sides. It is also evident latterly that the area of exposed surface of liquid lava is so increasing that some

South Island from S. Station, 7th November, 1916.
—Photo Jaggar.

Crag mass and Southwest Island from South Station, 7th November, 1916.
—Photo Jaggar.

Crag mass from East, 17th November, 1916.
—Photo Jaggar.

Crag mass from Old North Resthouse, 17th November, 1916.
—Photo Jaggar.

West arm from East Station, 17th November, 1916.
—Photo Jaggar.

Northwest pond from Northwest Station, 17th November, 1916.
—Photo Jaggar.

From high Northeast Rim, looking across 1894 Bench at North End of Lake, 17th November, 1916.
—Photo Jaggar.

Crag mass from Southwest, 22nd November, 1916.
—Photo Jaggar.

portions of it now have to crust over. On this day there were quiet crusts east and north and a tendency to the development of motionless skin between the south island and the southwest promontory.

On Nov. 3 at 9 a. m. the lake was a little higher relative to the crags, but the wall ponds all around had been the main sources of rising. Wall floods were continuous from northwest to northeast, up the east wall crack, in the south wall pond where there were fresh glowing crusts and at the west wall pond which was piled high with driblets. The lake within a few hours had been about five feet higher as shown by fresh overflows on the north side of the southwest promontory. At this time it was rising and crusted over with only from five to nine fountains in action. A view from the west station showed that there were recent small overflows from the western rims of both the northwest ponds, these overflows joining along the wall with a rather continuous wall-pond that extended all around the base of the northern walls. Both the northwest ponds were now about ten feet below their rims. One fresh overflow from the lake appeared at the north cove, but none at the southeast cove. There was a high spatter grotto in the north-northeast rampart. Under the south station the crevasses had widened. The fume in the pit interfered with good seeing but was thin as seen at a distance. The west arm was crusted over and also the north-northwest pond, but the latter occasionally broke up with cracking and foundering of the crusts.

In the Whitney Laboratory of Séismology the seismographic instruments have registered only two or three very small local earthquakes during the week ending Nov. 3. The strong tilting of the ground to the east and north recovered somewhat in the early part of the week, especially in the northern component, but after Oct. 30 the northeastward tilt greatly increased, so that by Nov. 3 the writing pens of the east-west pendulums had swung clear off the registration drums. The volcanic vibrations and microseisms have been as usual.

Technology Station,
Nov. 25, 1916.

During the week ending Nov. 24, 1916, the Halemaumau lava column has risen very slightly, the main lake being about 170 feet below the rim and the overflow north, southeast and west tending in the early part of the week to slope down away from the lake toward the walls of the pit. Between these places are the high craggy elevated benches which have continued to rise and to tilt away from the lake. Despite the relatively slight net rise, there have been spectacular overflows and floods of lava from high blowing cones which formed in the border crevasses.

An examination of the pit from Uwekahuna bluff on the evening of Nov. 17 showed that the lake is not yet visible from the high rim of Kilauea crater. A measurement of the temperature of the postal rift 10 to 11 a. m. Nov. 17 at the hottest place gave a reading of 313° C., the temperature of the air being 18° C. This place was about fifty feet west of the hottest crack of 1913-14, and is marked by blue fume emerging with a blowing noise under pressure. The fume is very voluminous and disagreeable to breathe. Other cracks in the neighborhood gave temperatures of 240°, 270° and 298° C. The wind was northeast. This maximum figure of 313° C. is the normal temperature for this crack according to measurements made repeatedly since the Observatory was established. No fluctuation has been observed which accords with the rise or fall of the lava of Halemaumau.

On the afternoon of Nov. 17 a fall of rocks had been heard from the direction of the high 1894 bench northeast and on the morning of Nov. 18 this tumble could be seen on the bench below. The lake on the 18th was active with thin skins and swift inrush to the northwest arm, four or five fountains were playing, spatter grottoes were abundant and a blowing cone on the north border of the northwest arm was seen to collapse to a glowing pot. The crag-mass had risen higher and carried the west bench higher than the northwest floor, showing a sloping down northward in its with it and also lifted the basin of the northwest pond. The driblet cones of the west chasm were broken by crevasses and only hissing slightly.

On November 19 the lake was very hot and spattering over the southeast bank. Very fresh flows from the southeast floor westward were uplifted and cracked by the rise of the southwestern benches. There were a few small fresh rock tumbles on the north bench. Under the south station a driblet cone was building in a crevasse. At 5 p. m. it was evident that there had been overflow southeast and a large driblet cone was seen sputtering in the west chasm. The small southern islet had again appeared.

Measurements on Monday, Nov. 20, 1916, at 10 a. m., showed that the lake was 173 feet below the southeast rim and the summit of the crag-mass 96 feet down. The southern pinnacle of the east bench was 55 feet above the lake, that of the southwest bench still higher, and the south island 38 feet high. The driblet cone in the west chasm was 70 feet above the lake and fully 30 feet above its base. The southwest island had become elongated to the east by an addition of 100 feet since November 12 and the channel between it and the southern islands was now only 60 feet wide.

The spectacular feature of November 20 was the spouting up of lava through the western crevasses, and the northwest ponds. At 10:15 a. m. the big driblet cone to the west began to overflow vigorously from its summit. At 10:45 another cone in the crevasses a few feet farther north began to spout very liquid lava like an artesian well. This poured like a river of blood into the depression of the west chasm and in the course of the day filled the space all along the base of the west wall of the pit and buried the cones completely.

At 11 a. m. the rising lake drowned the south islet. At 11:30 a. m. strong overflowing began from the northwest pond, the northwest arm and the southeast cove. Six festooned torrents poured down the slope from the ponds to the wall and spread right and left.

At 6 p. m. on November 21 the lake was very quiet, partially crusted and exhibited stringy fountains and many flames. The west wall pond was crusted and glowing and there were flaming holes in the southeast bench. Three gottoes were flaming and the overhang of the southeast bench, about five feet above the lake, exhibited a sheet of blue flame made by the rush of gas from under the skins. The flame was fully ten feet wide and fluttered out over the dark skins that covered the surface of the cove so that at times the spurts extended fifteen feet from the bank. The cone under the south station was literally blowing bubbles of melted glass. A small round hole in the top of the cone about three inches in diameter was jetting a steady spear of bright blue flame. About once a minute this hole would clog with incandescent lava from below and immediately the gas pressure from within would blow a bulb of lava which burst noisily and flopped down about the vent like a limp rag. Coarse blobs of glass flew off with the explosion and then a few seconds later there came a long exhaust of gas through the hole followed by the quiet spear of flame for another minute interval. The process was fairly regular with puffs and small spurts during the interval.

On November 22, at 10 a. m., the lake was overflowing strongly on the southeast and the flow poured west along the wall downward in two cascades to the south wall pond. This pond contained a fresh glowing pool of lava fed from the south cone, which was whistling. The lake was covered with hot skins and the south islet was flush with its surface. The crag-mass showed increased tilt to the west, where the T-shaped hollow was now filled well above the lake level with new flows. At 10:25 a. m. sinking set in. Large spatter domes were forming on the lake's edge toward the north.

At 9 a. m., November 23, the lake appeared stationary. From five to seven fountains were splashing in the border grottoes, high spatter rims occasionally became overweighted and collapsed There were flows on the west and north floors from lava which had welled up the wall cracks and the high west lava heap showed a raised growing rim with stalactites at the base of the west wall, indicating that it was liquid under the contact with the wall of the pit. Fresh toes protruded from this west accumulation of fresh lava towards the lake. The south cone was blowing and lava trickled from it to the wall pond. The fume from the pit on these cold clear mornings appears thick in the early morning, but very thin in the bright sunshine of the dry forenoon.

Measurement on November 24, at 10 a. m., made the depression of the lake 168 feet, of the summit of the crag-mass 80 feet, of both east and west benches 103 feet, and of the north floor at the base of the wall 186 feet. Thus there is a slope away from the lake north, and the rim of the north cove is hence a half cone fully 25 feet high. These measurements showed that the lake in four days had risen only five feet while the crag mass had risen sixteen feet. This rise of the crag was produced by the tilt noticed November 22.

On November 24 there were fresh overflows north, southeast and west, the west pond was glowing and there was much fresh rock tumble on the northeast floor. Lava was splashing from a crack on the site of the former west driblet cones. The lake was very quiet and sluggish in its streaming but occasionally, as at 11:30 a. m., the gas from under the skins escaped in a very violent fountain under the south end of the south island with inrush to the place of fountaining and many bubble fountains. The same thing happened in the north cove from time to time.

The following report from the Whitney Laboratory of Seismology is submitted by Mr. H. O. Wood:

During the interval ending with November 24, no local earthquakes have been registered. The chief phase only of a moderately distant teleseism of only moderate energy was registered feebly for a few moments shortly before noon on November 20. The amplitudes of microseismic motion, and of volcanic vibration, have continued larger than normal, but without extreme values. No significant variation in tilt has been observed.

Technology Station,
December 2, 1916.

During the week ending December 1, 1916, Halemaumau has exhibited a lava column slowly rising and still carrying the surrounding crags with it, but the rate of rising for both lava lake and crags has been reduced to a foot and a half a day. There are marked fluctuations of the lake of over ten feet per day frequently, the down-sinkings leaving a high wall all around the lake and the up-risings filling this to the level of the lower terrace. It is probable that these sinkings of the lake relative to the crags correspond to the times when the lava is intruding and solidifying under the crags. There has been more avalanching under the east station so that the gulch slope beneath is now continuous with coarse talus reaching to the east bench. Rock sliding still continues at this place.

On November 29, at 10 a. m., appearances in the pit indicated subsidence. There was seen from the east and south tremendous fountaining against the southwest bank with swarms of bubble fountains. This was where a rapid glowing torrent poured from under an arch of crust across the southwest channel to meet a broad west-flowing surface stream in the southwest cove. The west wall pond had now become a heap of lava from a center west of the crag-mass. There was a slight recent overflow southeast. The lake was hot and covered with thin striated skins, with rapid currents pouring southward and five to seven fountains in action including a line of small travelling fountains from time to time in the north cove. There was high spatter marking against the cliff of the south island. At 10:10 a. m. a strong avalanche fell at the lower end of the east gulch.

From 2 to 3 p. m., on November 27, the lake was brimming against the southeast bank and about fifteen fountains were in action, especially on the north and southeast. From the southwest station a flow was seen pouring from a vent northwest of the crag-mass to the base of the northwest wall of the pit.

On November 28, at 2:30 p. m., the lake seen from the east station was very quiet and sunken below the inner bench about five feet. The lower cliff under the east gulch had been cracking away in huge boulders which were piled so as to make a continuous slope from the gulch to the bench below.

On November 29, at 4 p. m., a circuit of the pit showed that the lake was essentially stationary and building enormous spatter domes southeast and north from which noxious fumes were rising. About ten fountains were in action, a river-like current was pouring westward around the southeast end of the south island and the streaming was outward from the northwest arm. There were fresh wall flows south and north, the two islets had become joined respectively to the southwest and south islands, the southwest channel was closed by crust and the west pond no longer appeared heaped up but was overridden by dribbling flows from the west arm. A spurting cone was hissing on the western end of the southwest island. A very large spatter dome with a splashing grotto open to the lake was a new and spectacular feature of the southeast bench.

Measurements on November 30, at 11 a. m., from the east and south showed the lake to be 160 feet down, the crag-mass 90 feet high above the lake and the south island 45 feet high. These figures indicated a rise of both lake and crag of nine feet in six days.

On this day the lake was about ten feet below the inner bench all around. There was a slight rise at about 11:30 a. m. followed by subsidence. Fresh rock tumble was seen under the south station. There were small fresh overflows southeast. Rocks were falling from the south face of the crag-mass. Ten fountains were in action and ten fuming places could be counted about the floor region. Streaming from the northwest arm was outward into the north cove. There was much overhang around the lake and ten grottoes showed stalactites. The lake was covered with heavy blankets except for a wide stream in the middle which was blistered strongly. The streaming was very slow.

On December 1, at 10:45 a. m., the lake had again risen flush with the lower bench, there were six or seven fountains and broad streaming north and south. The west pond again showed a piled-up appearance, the two southeast shore cones were splashing and fuming and there were blowing noises from the fountains. There was much continuous fountaining in the middle of the north cove where two currents met. The northwest arm and pond were blanketted, the lake at noon was subsiding, there were no new overflows anywhere and the pit was smoky.

The following report from the Whitney Laboratory of Seismology is submitted by Mr. H. O. Wood:

During the week-interval ending with December 1 two local earthquakes of moderately small instrumental amplitude have been registered. Microseismic motion has varied irregularly and at times, particularly in the latter part of the interval, amplitudes have been comparatively large. The amplitude of volcanic vibration has been steadily larger than normal, but storms of these waves have been infrequent. Except for the usual diurnal changes tilting movements have been slight.

T. A. JAGGAR, JR.,

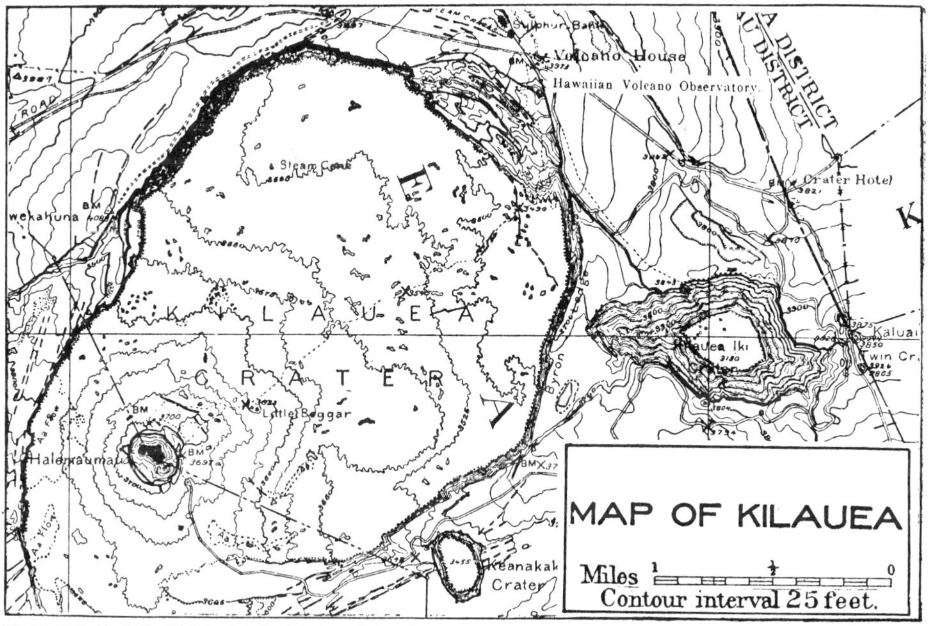

HAWAIIAN VOLCANO RESEARCH ASSOCIATION.

This society is a voluntary one, made up of subscribers to scientific work which is being executed by the Massachusetts Institute of Technology.

In 1915 there are about 100 subscribers in Hawaii and elsewhere, firms and individuals. A group of firms and persons in Hilo built the main observatory building in the spring of 1912. Publications to date have been weekly reports since the summer of 1911, now reprinted in Honolulu in monthly form. The Massachusetts Institute of Technology will publish annual reports, of which the introductory number was printed in 1912.

The weekly bulletin as it appears in the Advertiser is reprinted as a leaflet and sent to regular annual subscribers to the work of the Association. L. A. Thurston is president of the Board of Directors of the Association, and R. W. Shingle is treasurer. New subscribers who are interested in volcanoes will be welcomed in the Association. The Association aims: (1) To record volcanic activity and earthquakes in Hawaii; (2) to attract scientific men hither for special studies; (3) to promote the establishment of volcano observatories all over the world. The annual dues of regular members are $5; patrons of the Assocaition subscribe larger amounts.

WHITNEY LABORATORY OF SEISMOLOGY.

The Whitney Laboratory of Seismology is equipped with two Bosch-Omori 100 kg tromometers registering N-S and E-W motion, a heavy Omori tromometer registering E-W motion, and an Omori "ordinary Seismograph" designed for registering strong earthquakes in all three components of motion. These are seated on concrete piers in a closed basement room having practically constant temperature, beneath the chief Observatory building near the hotel. Time is referred to a rated chronometer, checked at intervals by solar observations with a transit. Both instruments are loaned by the College of Hawaii. Hawaiian standard time (H. S. T.) is 10 hrs. 30 min. slower than Greenwich time.

CANCANI SCALE OF SEISMIC INTENSITY.

Expressed by accelerations measured in millimeters per second per second.

I.	Instrumental	0.0	2.5
II.	Very slight	2.5	5.0
III.	Slight	5.0	10.0
IV.	Sensible, mediocre	10.0	25.0
V.	Rather strong	25.0	50.0
VI.	Strong	50.0	100.0
VII.	Very strong	100.0	250.0
VIII.	Ruinous	250.0	500.0
IX.	Disastrous	500.0	1000.0
X.	Very disastrous	1000.0	2500.0
XI.	Catastrophic	2500.0	5000.0
XII.	Great catastrophe	5000.0	10000.0

Grade IV. is ordinarily the minimum perceived by the senses; and in grade XII. the acceleration, or rate of change of motion (jerk) reaches that of terrestrial gravitation.

In the standard form of report the maximum intensity or acceleration, designated by the symbol a, or max. a, is given in the conventional unit, **the milligal.** The milligal is a measure of acceleration, such that 1 milligal = 1/100 mm. per sec. per sec. = 10 μ per sec. per sec. The Cancani scale, here defined in terms of millimeters per sec. per sec., can therefore be expressed in **milligals** by multiplying **each of the numbers by 100.**

WEEKLY BULLETIN
OF THE

Hawaiian Volcano Observatory

Vol. IV. HONOLULU, HAWAII, DECEMBER, 1916. No. 12

TECHNOLOGY STATION, Dec. 9, 1916.—During the week ending December 8, 1916, strong rising of the lava of Halemaumau has again asserted itself at approximately three feet per day, about double the rate of the previous week. The mechanism of rising has proceeded by alternations of strong overflowing one day, followed by depression the next day of the liquid surface below the surrounding benches five to ten feet, these seeming depressions being probably the times when the lava was intruding under the uptilted benches.

It is doubtful whether there has been so spectacular a lake in the Halemaumau pit at any time during the last twenty-three years as the one which is to be seen there at present. Many of the dramatic events of the early 80's are being re-enacted, such as the piling up of great crags, the building of driblet cones and the formation of circular ramparts. The fumes are very thin and are growing thinner, and it now appears certain that the Christmas season at Kilauea will be of unparalleled interest. Accordingly this is the time for anyone to come who has planned visiting the volcano. It is very probable that there will be subsidence in January, when the pit may become smoky and less interesting. As the activity of the volcano is more or less a matter of course in the newspaper reports, readers are apt not to realize that this is a marvelous time, and one of the rare opportunities of a generation.

On Saturday, December 2, 1916, at 11 a. m., the lake appeared depressed below its inner bench about eight feet and the conditions were very similar to those of November 30. Ten fountains were in action, mostly around the borders. The big cone on the southeast bench was split asunder and stained with white sublimates. No overflows or new rock tumbles were to be seen. The skins blanketting the lake tended to roll over thicker ones pushed by the sluggish surface streaming. The crags and islands stood high, while the lava puffed and splashed in rather stagnant fashion.

Seen from the east at 2 p. m. on December 4 the lake still appeared low and sluggish, but there was fresh overflow still glowing on the north bench. The channel between the south island and the southwest peninsula was nearly closed. At 3 p. m. the lava had risen five feet, illustrating the rapid fluctuation of these days.

At 2:20 p. m. on December 5 the northwest arm was overflooding the north bench and there was great activity in the north cove. The whole northwest floor became flooded with fresh lava, the flow lasting until 2:45 p. m., when the lake sank back about three feet and began fountaining in twelve places.

On December 6 at 2:20 p. m. the inner bench around the lake was about five feet high and some fifteen fountains, great and small, were in action. The driblet dome southeast was throwing up great spurts of lava. At 2:40 p. m. a fragment of the lower east bench fell into the lake, producing violent effervescence. At 3 p. m. strong overflowing started, first in two flows which poured right and left across the southeast bench, and later, about 3:20 p. m., over the north rim of the northwest arm so as to flood the northern floor east and west, the flows extending from the northeast talus to a point under the west station. The southern flows spread until they were under the east station and nearly under the southwest station. At 4 p. m. only six fountains were in action. A cascade thirty feet wide rushed down a twenty-degree slope northward from the northwest arm into the margin of the pooled flow which filled the northern wall valley. This flow was creeping both east

WEEKLY BULLETIN
of the
Hawaiian Volcano Observatory

Published Monthly at Honolulu, Hawaii, by the Hawaiian Volcano Research Association

L. W. de Vis-Norton........Secretary

Entered as second-class matter January 20, 1914, at the post-office at Honolulu, Hawaii, under the Act of August 24, 1912.

and west in a series of minor cascades. The northwest pond was also very high and small flows trickled over its lip. The surface streaming was outward from the northwest arm into the lake. The south channel west of the south island was now completely closed so that the island had become the end of the southwest peninsula. For the first time in weeks there were no islands in the lake. The overflow of this time continued for several hours on the north. The gas pressure was high and there was much puffing and rumbling.

Measurement on Thursday, December 7, determined the depression of the lake below the southeast rim of the pit to be 140 feet, showing a rise of twenty feet in seven days.

On this day overflowing continued in occasional spells. At 9:45 a. m. the northwest arm overflowed for twenty minutes, and at 12:40 p. m. there was overflooding of the benches for a similar period southeast, west and northwest. The fresh flows on the benches were snapping, and at the base of the northeast wall the last trace of the June debris slope was buried. The southeast dome on the bench had an open glowing pot four feet in diameter in its crest, which cooled off to a black hole during the morning. It was evident that the great weight of new flows was tilting up the benches, for small rock slides among the crevasses were seen and heard. A large block fell from the crag mass into the northwest arm.

The west wall pond had become a crater-like depression. There was hissing from the north rampart, which showed flaming cracks in its crest. From seven to eight fountains were in action. A majestic river-like current poured around the south island southward and westward, and the heat immediately above at the southeast station was almost unbearable. It was evident that the channel west of the south island was still open below, for streaming continued there from north to south. Great quantities of Pele's hair were rising. In the evening the southwest cove was crusted and the lake very quiet, with flames playing in five different chimneys. There were fresh flows all over the benches, and from time to time the southwest crust would break up through the migration of a large fountain east to west.

On Friday, December 8, from 10 to 11 a. m., the lake had lowered from five to six feet relative to the lower bench. There was an open arch across the south channel. Five or six fountains were playing. The height of the dome on the southeast bench had increased, and the hole in its summit had dwindled with the building of spatter. There were now three spatter domes at the edge of the lake southeast and three others along the northern rampart. A high cavernous recess had been developed in the cliff that overhung the north side of the west arm. The northwest pond seen from the west station was crusted over and appeared to be at a much higher level than the lake. There was a broad sweep of recent overflows from it to the wall, and similar floods had poured from the northwest arm.

The following report from the Whitney Laboratory of Seismology is submitted by Mr. H. O. Wood:

During the week interval ending with December 8 four local earthquakes have been registered. All were of small seismographic amplitude, though two were sufficiently energetic to rattle windows at the Observatory. Though this effect was sure, no sensation of vibration could be felt. The seismographic amplitude of microseismic motion and of volcanic vibration have been larger than normal, both steadily and in ''storms,'' but less in amount than in the two preceding weeks. The shifting of writing pens through tilt and associated causes has been considerable, with notable fluctuations. At date of writing the net effect is a considerable decrease of the long-accumulated tilt, or shift, to the east, with a very slight diminution of the corresponding effect to the north.

TECHNOLOGY STATION, Dec. 16, 1916.—During the week ending December 15, 1916, the Kilauea lava column has been marking time, the movement of the lava being in the nature of a spreading out around the crags rather than of rising. The crags have also remained essentially stationary.

On December 9 the fumes were thin, as they have been during the entire week. The lake between 10 and 11 a. m. was ten feet below the lower bench, there was deep cavernous overhang in the coves and an arch over the south channel. There were fresh overflows northwest and west. A driblet cone had formed on the north floor, and very large spatter domes were building on the edge of the lake on the southeast and north.

On December 11 at 2 p. m. the inner ledge was again ten feet high, but there had been overflow within a few hours on the northeast bench, the lava there being still incandescent and in motion. At 2:30 p. m. there was a heavy fall from the south side of the crag mass into the west arm which induced prolonged boiling. The lake rose five feet from 2 to 3:30 p. m.

On December 12 at 2 p. m. the lake was only two feet below the lower bench, and fountains were few. There were small fresh overflows. From 4 to 6 p. m. there was occasional overflow southeast, flames were counted in six places around the shores, and sheets of flame burst through cracked skins in the middle of the north cove, when abortive fountains rose. There were six fountaining areas. The spells of rising were quiet, while those of sinking were accompanied by violent central fountaining in the north cove, which would migrate slowly to some point on the bank and then cease. During these sinking spells a glow edge with stalactites appeared around the lake. Sinking predominated over rising. At the west end of the north rampart there was a high grotto hung with four-foot stalactites and surmounted by an eight-foot banner of flame. Another high grotto was in action at the west side of the southeast cove. The eastern dome there had grown very high and was nearly closed over. The driblet cone on the north bench was hissing and a filagree cone glowed on the edge of the north rampart. The wall around the northwest arm appeared five feet high, and the shore bombardment there and at the north and southeast coves was flinging lava over the bank so as to build it up. Flaring chimneys appeared on the north and south sides of the west arm. There was a spurting cone west of the northwest pond. South of the east promontory a large block of the bank of the lake fell in. Confined gas pressure was indicated by puffing noises.

On December 13 at 11:30 a. m. there was the thunderous puffing of confined gas. The lake appeared five feet below the lower bench and five fountains were in action. A high spatter rampart was building at the west end of the southwest cove. Much Pele's hair was floating up from spurts of the southeast cone. About 3:30 p. m. the lake overflowed the southeast cove.

On Thursday, December 14, measurement made the depth of the lake surface below the southwest rim of the pit 138 feet, indicating a rise of only two feet in a week. The northern summit of the south island crag was 50 feet above the lake, and the summit of the crag-mass was 78 feet high. The edge of the floor in contact with the wall of the pit under the south station was only three feet above lake level. On this date the lake was high, the pressure of confined gas was strong, the streaming was swift around the southeast bend, and five fountains were in action. During the morning there were risings and fallings without overflow. There were small flows on the floor of the west chasm, and fresh overflows to the wall from the west side to the northwest pond. This pond had become longer in a north-south direction, and narrower, and a spatter cone southwest of it showed an open glowing hole in its summit, which spurted violently and manufactured great quantities of Pele's hair, which rose in swarms of flossy tangles past the west station. These blowing spasms happened whenever the northwest pond sank and ceased whenever it rose. A large spatter dome had been built on the north side of the northwest cove. There were fresh overflows from the east side of the north cove.

On December 15 from 9 to 10 a. m.

conditions were about the same and streaming was symmetrically balanced from the west arm as a middle axis, flowing in two great semicircles around the long southern peninsula into the southwest cove and around the crag-mass into the northwest arm. Three very high cones were spurting and hissing on the margin of the north cove. There were fresh overflows from the east side of this cove, and a semicircle of festooned flows had poured over the floor for distances from 100 to 200 feet from the northwest arm and the northwest pond. The crusted surfaces of the fresh flows on the northeast floor were making a sputtering tinkle as innumerable small blisters burst through the crust from one to three inches in diameter and ejected the glassy fragments out on to the glassy shell. A very interesting feature of this northeast region of the floor adjacent to these flows was the development of three swollen crustal domes similar to the many with cracked crests seen on the floor of the greater crater. These domes were built by the swelling up from below of the extremity of the last large flow which had swept around the north bench from the northwest. They were unquestionably formed by swelling pressure from below after the crust had become a foot or more thick, the flow beneath in confinement being revived and unable to escape except by doming up the terminal crusted pool. This it did, and the small festooned flows with blistering skins were the products of overflow from the cracks in the domes.

There was puffing and occasional heavy spatter fall at the northern cones. The driblet cone on the north floor had disappeared, probably buried under flows. In the evening there was overflow northeast and southeast.

It will be observed that there have been overflows all through the week, with alternate pulsations of sinking, with practically no net elevation of the lava surface nor of the crags. The south cove has widened and the north floor has extended istelf, the floods in these places encroaching on the uplifted benches. The risings in the lake proper have thus reached a stage where by flooding hollows along the wall they are compensating the recent uptiltings so as to fill in depressions to a common level.

The following report from the Whitney Laboratory of Seismology is submitted by Mr. H. O. Wood:

During the week interval ending with December 15 no earthquakes have been registered. Microseismic motion has displayed larger seismographic amplitudes than normal, especially during the middle of the interval. The seismographic amplitudes of volcanic vibration have remained larger than normal, as has been usual during recent weeks. There has been considerable shifting of the writing levers, but without significant net change. In the early part of the interval there was a sharp return to east and south, restoring the extreme ''tilt'' of earlier intervals, but this was followed by a slow recovery, leaving the median lines only a little further to east and south than their positions as given last week.

TECHNOLOGY STATION, Dec. 23, 1916.—During the week ending December 22, 1916, the lava lake of Kilauea volcano has resumed vigorous rising with but little change in general configuration. The week has been very stormy and rainy, so as to interfere with photographic work. The eastern raised bench inside of Halemaumau pit is now accessible by a steep climb down the east gulch, Mr. W. Spalding and others having descended to the ledge between 2 and 3 p. m. on December 20.

On December 16 at 9:30 a. m. the lake was ten feet below the inner bench, fifteen fountains were in action, and there were fresh short overflows at the east side of the north cove and at the southeast cove. The three southeast spatter domes were now only high parts of the rampart edge. The great north rampart, however, showed five immense half-dome grottoes with stalactites hanging inside, indicating tendency to daily stagnation spells with strong spatter construction on the banks. There was a distinct narrow inner bench all around the lake, with strong overhang below. Streaming was, as usual, outward from the west arm and the northwest arm. The lake was covered with thinly wrinkled black striated skins, showing many glow lines, and there was bubble fountaining at the head of the west arm. There was hissing at the north and southeast ramparts. A little fresh rock fall appeared north-

Dec. 15, 1916. Raised east bench and south part of pit.
—Photo Jaggar.

Dec. 15, 1916. East gulch, 1894 bench and floor.
—Photo Jaggar.

Dec. 15, 1916. Crag mass from northeast rim. —Photo Jaggar.

east and southeast. The fume, very thin as a whole, consisted of white steam from the crags and blue gas from the grottoes.

On December 18 at 2:30 p. m. conditions were about the same, and a spatter bank fell in on the northwest side of the lake. At 2:40 p. m. there was strong activity in the southwest arm. Small tumbles into the lake recurred from time to time. At 3 p. m. the southeast cove overflowed the bench to the wall.

On December 20 from 4:30 to 6 p. m. it was evident that there had been strong overflowing on all sides between 3 and 4 p. m. Strong crackling sounds came from the north floor and puffing noises from the rampart. Nine fountains were in action. At the southeast station the fume from border fountains was intolerable. A small avalanche fell at the east gulch. Glowing filagree accumulations of incandescent lava transmitting burning gases appeared at two places along the north rampart, on the east side of the southeast cove and high up the south cliff of the crag-mass. This last chimney seen from the southwest station showed a flame, leaping from a crack in a projecting corner of the wall 40 feet above the lake, the blue spear of burning gas jetting out horizontally against a dark background of cliff. This would have made an ideal subject for photo-spectroscopic work. The flows on the south floor had become greatly extended to both east and west. A crack was slightly smoking on the high bench under the east gulch. The great spatter domes of the north rampart were hung with stalactitic curtains on the lake side, showing usually an open vertical slit in the middle. The largest one of these was on the west side of the north cove. There was a large cavernous grotto at the west end of the southwest arm. The lava in the northwest arm appeared low, as though the shore had been lifted.

Measurement at 9 a. m. on Thursday, December 21, 1916, determined the depression of the lake to be 117 feet below the southeast rim of the pit, indicating a rise of 21 feet in seven days. The summit of the crag-mass rose 77 feet above the lake, of the east bench 62 feet, and of the south island 50 feet. These crags had thus continued to rise along with the lake, and the highest of them, the crag-mass, was only 41 feet below the rim of the pit.

The condition of activity in the lava lake remained about the same, the liquid being some seven feet below the inner bench. There were eight fountains in action, and fresh small overflows appeared on the north and southeast. Through two tunnels under the peninsula west of the south island the surface streaming was pouring southward.

From 4 to 6 p. m. there was strong puffing gas pressure and heavy overflowing at the northwest pond, northwest arm, the northeast rampart, southeast bench and west arm. The oversplashing on the north rampart was tremendous, so that floods of lava poured down the back slope. The crackling noise was heard from both the southeast and north floors. Parts of the southwest peninsula were overflooded. The cone at the east end of the southeast floor collapsed so as to make temporarily a cove in the rampart. The rising ceased about 5:30 p. m.

At 9 p. m. on December 22 there were again fresh glowing overflows, many flames and all conditions similar to the previous evening. The lake surface suffered very dark crusted spells, and there were several heavy falls from the inner bench into the lake. There was a flaming and puffing cone at the west end of the southwest peninsula and flaming cracks in the southeast bench.

At 9:15 p. m. a very remarkable performance took place in the west wall pond. It will be remembered that this place has been inconspicuous and crusted over for many days. Suddenly it broke up, to a liquid pool violently fountaining, with literally hundreds of bubble fountains which played all over the surface for ten minutes. A cavern and driblet cone were revealed at the north end of the pool. Gradually the bubbling ceased and the pond crusted over. The peculiar intense fountaining at many points recalled the activity of the summer of 1912.

The following report from the Whitney Laboratory of Seismology is submitted by Mr. H. O. Wood:

During the week interval ending with December 22 three small local earthquakes have been registered. Two of these had moderate seismographic amplitudes, but they were not of perceptive energy. The seismographic amplitudes of microseismic motion, and of volcanic vibration, have been as usual in recent weeks—that is, somewhat greater than the general normal value. During the week the pen-shifts ascribed to tilting have indicated a decrease in the pronounced tilt to the north which has prevailed recently, and a slight increase in the tilt to the east, but of small amount compared to the stand of several weeks ago.

TECHNOLOGY STATION, Dec. 30, 1916.—During the week ending December 29, 1916, the great lava lake of Halemaumau has continued to rise and spread out, gaining somewhat on the crags and so widening the bordering platform or floor. The lava fountains in the pit may now be seen from the high rim of Kilauea crater at Uwekahuna bluff, and the crags within the pit with only a little more elevation will be visible from Volcano House.

The lava lake is a very different object from the elliptical pool of last June. Only 100 feet below the rim, it appears like a mighty river of fire amid hills and tilted crags, shaped in general like a "W." Roundish coves north and south are bordered by high ramparts built up by overflow and by continuous fountains, which splashing at one place have constructed huge domes with glowing grottoes inside. Back of these ramparts the overflow surface slopes back to the walls of the pit, so that the lake is really at the top of a low flat inner cone. Higher than these floors on three sides of the lake, but wholly within the pit, are craggy hills benched and fissured, which rise from 40 to 80 feet above the liquid lava.

Other irregularities which add interest to the scene are high flaming and puffing chimneys, outlying ponds of lava and occasional driblet cones which build up over fissures in the floor. Following all the bends, the lake is fully 1800 feet long, with widths of various channels varying from 50 to 200 feet. It would be hard to imagine a more spectacular or varied panorama than is spread before the observer at Halemaumau today, and there are at present daily overflows on the benches. The scene is magnificent from any side of the pit, and there is hardly any obstructing fume.

The writer in the last fifteen years has seen great volcanic eruptions with lava in Japan, Alaska, Italy and the West Indies, and also on Mauna Loa, but for spectacular lava activity he unhesitatingly pronounces the present scene at Kilauea away ahead of them all.

On Monday, December 25, 1916, at 2:30 p. m., the lava in the pit was depressed some fifteen feet below the lower bench, but it was evident from the floods of fresh lava on the north floor that this movement was only temporary. At 2:40 p. m. a large fragment of the lower bench fell from the south island, producing great gas commotion in the lake, and fountaining in general was abundant and noisy.

On December 26 at 2 p. m. the lava had risen to a point only five feet below the inner bench and the lake was quiet and rising. Again there was fresh overflow in evidence on the north bench. At 3 p. m. the lake in the north cove was only one feet below the rampart, and at 3:10 p. m. it was overflowing on the north.

On December 27 at 9:30 a. m. it was evident that strong rising had been in progress since the previous week. The cliffs of the crag mass were now well above the floor of the high west niche of Halemaumau. The domes of the north rampart on the border of the lake were greatly reduced in apparent height by the building up of flows around them.

The lake was brimming level with the lower bench, there were fresh glowing flows on the floor north and southeast, and twelve fountains were in action. Sometimes three immense central fountains were playing at once in the north cove. There was strong continuous hissing from the chimney on the north side of the west arm and from somewhere to the northwest. Streaming was outward from both the west and southwest arms and inward at the northwest arm. Violent bombardment was in progress in the grotto at the east end of the southeast bench, there was a new high rampart on the north side of the southwest peninsula, the southeast channel appeared narrower, and there were fresh overflows at the head of the west arm and into a hollow at the head of the southwest peninsula. The northwest pond appeared depressed, the west wall pond was heaped with fresh glistening pahoehoe, and there was a deep chasm along the wall southwest. Fresh rock tumble lay on the floor in small amounts northeast and west. The fumes were thin. It was evident that the lava floor was filling and spreading out at the expense of the crags south, on the southwest peninsula, northeast and west.

Measurements on December 28, 1916, after 11 a. m., from the north and northwest stations determined the mean depression of the lake to be 107 feet below this higher portion of the rim of the pit or about 100 feet below the southeast rim. The crag mass stood 65 feet above the lake.

At 11 a. m. on this date rising was still in progress and there were fresh overflows northward from the northwest arm and eastward from the east side of the north rampart. During the hour 11:15 to 12:15 p. m. the lake subsided a few feet, with six to ten fountains in action. There was a large glowing cone at the head of the northwest arm. A wide field of fresh lava occupied the area west of the crag mass, with flows at the west pond which had poured from the wall toward the lake. Blisters were snapping all over the surface of the fresh northern flows. The northwest arm was stagnant with inward streaming at its mouth. Streaming was westward in the southwest arm, eastward in the west arm, and northward in the north cove. The driblet cone had reappeared on the floor north of the north rampart. An occasional cracking thud was heard from the region of the crag mass as though it was warping under the weight of the new flows on the floor.

The northwest pond had become completely changed to a pot in the top of a broad cone from which a dozen festooned flows radiated, not only to the west, but also to the east, encroaching on the slopes of the crag mass. At 12:45 p. m. this cone collapsed with a roar, a puff of dust shot into the air, and there was revealed the usual oval pond of glowing, surging melt within, the remains of the cone being an eccentric arched shell over it. The pool of molten lava was from ten to fifteen feet below the shell, boiling turbulently at first and then gradually settling down until there was only a dark red glowing grotto, with some bubble fountains in the pool.

The next morning, December 29, at 9:30 a. m., the lake was high and the northwest pond was overflowing into a big fan-shaped flow northward. The outlines of the pond were obliterated, and it was easy to understand how the boiling fountain dome at the head of the flow might with gradual cooling be left as a pot in the top of a cone. On this occasion, however, at 9:45 a. m., the pond sank suddenly from eight to ten feet, the walls became plastered with the back-flow, and the lava was seen sluggishly pounding within an immense grotto.

The great floods of lava on the northwest floor were seen to be tilting the crag mass in that direction, its lower terraces rising on the lake side.

The southeast cone was again built into a large dome grotto. Six or seven fountains were in action, there was bombardment at the north rampart, and the noises were plashing and rumbling added to the crackle of the new flows. At 10:15 there was a new movement of rising and the northwest pond started overflowing again, the flows augmenting during the next hour.

The following report from the Whitney Laboratory of Seismology is submitted by Mr. H. O. Wood:

During the week interval ending with December 29 one slight local earthquake, of small seismographic amplitude, has been registered. Miscroseismic motion has been registered as usual. The seismographic amplitudes of volcanic vibration waves have, for the most part, been smaller than recently—almost of normal value—except for one prolonged run, of about three hours duration, in mid-forenoon of December 27, when they were continuously greater than usual. This run was not associated with earthquakes nor with any unusual *surface action* in Halemaumau. The lava surface was rising quietly at the time. There has been a slight shifting of the pens in the sense of decreasing tilt to the northward and eastward.

Very respectfully,

T. A. JAGGAR, JR.,
Director.

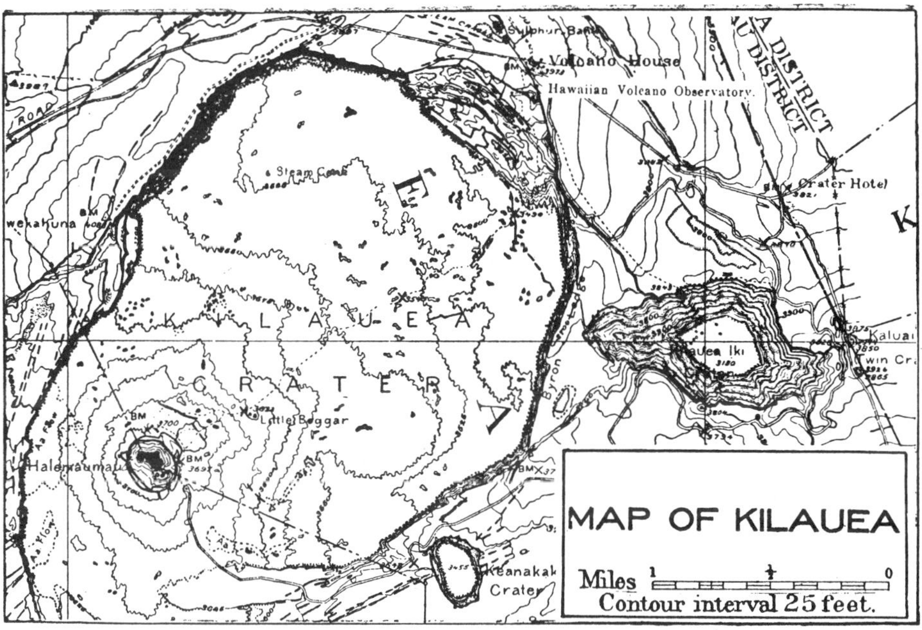

HAWAIIAN VOLCANO RESEARCH ASSOCIATION.

This society is a voluntary one, made up of subscribers to scientific work which is being executed by the Massachusetts Institute of Technology.

In 1915 there are about 100 subscribers in Hawaii and elsewhere, firms and individuals. A group of firms and persons in Hilo built the main observatory building in the spring of 1912. Publications to date have been weekly reports since the summer of 1911, now reprinted in Honolulu in monthly form. The Massachusetts Institute of Technology will publish annual reports, of which the introductory number was printed in 1912.

The weekly bulletin as it appears in the Advertiser is reprinted as a leaflet and sent to regular annual subscribers to the work of the Association. L. A. Thurston is president of the Board of Directors of the Association, and R. W. Shingle is treasurer. New subscribers who are interested in volcanoes will be welcomed in the Association. The Association aims: (1) To record volcanic activity and earthquakes in Hawaii; (2) to attract scientific men hither for special studies; (3) to promote the establishment of volcano observatories all over the world. The annual dues of regular members are $5; patrons of the Assocaition subscribe larger amounts.

WHITNEY LABORATORY OF SEISMOLOGY.

The Whitney Laboratory of Seismology is equipped with two Bosch-Omori 100 kg tromometers registering N-S and E-W motion, a heavy Omori tromometer registering E-W motion, and an Omori "ordinary Seismograph" designed for registering strong earthquakes in all three components of motion. These are seated on concrete piers in a closed basement room having practically constant temperature, beneath the chief Observatory building near the hotel. Time is referred to a rated chronometer, checked at intervals by solar observations with a transit. Both instruments are loaned by the College of Hawaii. Hawaiian standard time (H. S. T.) is 10 hrs. 30 min. slower than Greenwich time.

CANCANI SCALE OF SEISMIC INTENSITY.

Expressed by accelerations measured in millimeters per second per second.

I.	Instrumental	0.0	2.5
II.	Very slight	2.5	5.0
III.	Slight	5.0	10.0
IV.	Sensible, mediocre	10.0	25.0
V.	Rather strong	25.0	50.0
VI.	Strong	50.0	100.0
VII.	Very strong	100.0	250.0
VIII.	Ruinous	250.0	500.0
IX.	Disastrous	500.0	1000.0
X.	Very disastrous	1000.0	2500.0
XI.	Catastrophic	2500.0	5000.0
XII.	Great catastrophe	5000.0	10000.0

Grade IV. is ordinarily the minimum perceived by the senses; and in grade XII. the acceleration, or rate of change of motion (jerk) reaches that of terrestrial gravitation.

In the standard form of report the maximum intensity or acceleration, designated by the symbol a, or max. a, is given in the conventional unit, **the milligal.** The milligal is a measure of acceleration, such that 1 milligal = 1/100 mm. per sec. per sec. = 10 μ per sec. per sec. The Cancani scale, here defined in terms of millimeters per sec. per sec., can therefore be expressed in **milligals** by multiplying each of the numbers by 100.

WEEKLY BULLETIN
OF THE
Hawaiian Volcano Observatory

Vol. V. HONOLULU, HAWAII, JANUARY, 1917. No. 1

TECHNOLOGY STATION, Jan. 6. 1917.—During the week ending Jan. 5, 1917, the lava of Halemaumau subsided twenty feet for the first two days and developed violent cascading downward into a chasm at the extreme southwest. The lake then recovered its level with spasms of return to the cascading process alternating with strong rising and overflow both from the coves and through driblet cones and pots on the floor. The net effect for the week on the lava column January 4 by measurement was a stationary lake 100 feet down with the overflooding expended in spreading out the floor and tending to surround the crags, filling depressions and building ramparts and conelets. The fumes are very thin, but very sharp to leeward. Descents into the pit by the east gulch are now easily made and experimental work with the liquid lava at the edge of the lake is in progress.

On December 30, 1916, at 2 p. m. the lake seen from the northeast station appeared ten feet below its rim and a flow was in motion on the north floor. At 2:20 from the northwest station a dome-shaped cone could be seen on the south border of the northwest pond depression. This pond was crusted but the cone exhibited glowing lava. The pit was smoky.

At noon on December 31, the lake seen from the east appeared twenty feet below its rim with active fountaining at the north and large stalactites in the grottoes. At 12:25 p. m. a large fragment of the crag mass on its northeast side fell into the lake and induced strong fountaining. At 2:30 p. m. and in the evening a cascade had developed from the southwest arm into a cove extending northward from its west end, the lava of the lake pouring downward with great rapidity into a chasm. This cavity had developed by collapse from the blowing and flaming pot which has for weeks past been observed at the west neck leading to the southwest peninsula.

On Monday, January 1, 1917, at 3 p. m. the lake was seen from the northeast to have recovered and at 3:40 it was overflowing on the northeast and southeast. At 4:30 the overflow had extended to the northwest arm and had spread to the base of the wall of the pit.

On January 2 at 3 p. m. the lake was ten feet below its banks and its surface was quiet. At 3:35 subsidence set in, there was rapid streaming westward around the south island with strong fountaining and the cascade again developed from the lake into the southwest chasm making a loud roaring noise. Only a dark pot without glow could be seen at the site of the northwest pond. At 8 p. m. the lake appeared low with the two arches showing west of the south island. Flames were playing from the northwest cone and the high orifice in the wall on the south side of the crag mass. From the east station the driblet cone on the north floor was seen to be ejecting spasmodic spurts and flings of melt from a large hole. The noise which it made was peculiar, a deep gurgling spasm with a bell-like note due to the ringing of the cone cylinder, made of lava glass. Occasionally enormous fountaining areas would develop in the middle of the lake and migrate southeast. Eight or nine fountains were in action, especially in the grottoes of the north rampart, and flames burst from under

WEEKLY BULLETIN
of the
Hawaiian Volcano Observatory

Published Monthly at Honolulu, Hawaii, by the Hawaiian Volcano Research Association

L. W. de Vis-Norton........Secretary

Entered as second-class matter January 20, 1914, at the post-office at Honolulu, Hawaii, under the Act of August 24, 1912.

surface crusts. A glowing cone could be seen near the west wall.

At 11 p. m. the cascading was renewed from the lake into the southwest chasm. From the southwest station this was seen to begin with inrush from the southwest arm to the cove where a cauldron gradually developed by subsidence, thirty feet in diameter and twenty feet deep. The whole end of the southwest arm was sucked down with a roar and there was high incandescence and effervescence of intensely suffocating sulphurous gas. The effect was like a waterfall and inside the cauldron there was tremendous churning and boiling. Simultaneously a sharp crackling noise was heard toward the southeast and the lake was everywhere sinking and showing a stalactitic border.

On January 3 after 11 a. m. the southern region was stagnant and the streaming was northward and from the northwest arm outward. The driblet cone west was high with radial flows, the northwest pit was small and deep, a large sulphur-stained flat cone was crackling southwest of it and from it lumpy short flows had poured westward and a long festooned one south from its east side. There were no fresh flows from the northwest arm.

The north driblet cone was now twenty feet high with an open arch below and a field of hard lumpy pahoehoe around it. Going down by the east gulch the writer, accompanied by Mr. Twigg Smith, explored and photographed this field and the north rampart.

The pahoehoe was making out in incandescent toes covered with a membrane of glassy fibres stiff and flexible. The orange hot melt beneath flowed like very stiff porridge full of bubbles. Dragged out on a stick it stretched much like candy, but in a few seconds became hard as glass. On ascending the rampart which poured forth much yellowish white fume over a grotto, the lake was seen about ten feet below streaming slowly northward and fountaining violently against the rampart a few feet in that direction. The fountains were singularly noiseless heard from this low level, and the skins tearing appeared to consist of thick ropy fibres. The material of the fountains appeared much stiffer than when seen from above, shredding into leathery rods and hard droplets. The gasses eddying up were not oppressive and quite different from the intolerable blue fume which condenses in the air above the fountains and is so unbreathable on the south rim of the pit. The rampart was covered with splashes and droplets of black glossy glistening lava glass. The surface of the lake showed bellying skins with gas beneath, and upfolded and upturned crusts. As a whole, however, it was quite level. The pounding in grottoes produced no shaking and little noise back of the rampart. Noise, heat and fume are all stronger on the high rim of the pit than they are on the floor.

We next walked through the east valley to the southeast floor and up on the southeast rampart. The lake was pounding hard beneath and all along the rampart farther south. There was no great inconvenience from the fume but it was more disagreeable than on the northeast rampart. Great banks of half-decomposed Pele's hair clung to the base of the south wall of the pit, having the appearance of rotten hay seed.

On January 4, 1917, measurement at 10 a. m. made the depression of the lake 101 feet below the southeast rim of the pit and the height of the crag mass sixty-four feet above the lake.

These measurements indicated a stationary condition for the previous week.

There were fresh flows in motion on the north, south and west floors from 7 to 8 a. m. The western floods had nearly joined the southern ones back of the southwest bench. The driblet cone appeared submerged. During the morning the fresh flows, after developing crusts three to five inches thick, collapsed in their middle parts leaving upstanding shells with stalactites around the borders.

At noon the writer, with Alex. Lancaster, Joe Moniz and F. J. Stotts, stood on the northeast rampart after crossing the fresh lava flow and collected an iron pot full of lava by thrusting it beneath the surface of the lake on the end of a long iron pipe. The pot was dipped three times and the specimen resulting will be sent to the Geophysical Laboratory of the Carnegie Institution for analysis of the gases enclosed.

At 12:30 p. m. the inrush cascade at the southwest cove began as before the subsidence. At 1:45 p. m. this stopped during a rising spell. Cascading was resumed at 2:15. This stopped and rising ensued at 2:50 p. m. Thereafter there was a lull in the cascading but at 8:30 p. m. the southwest arm was again tumbling into the void.

On January 5 at 2 p. m. the lake was high with slight fluctuations and new flows southwest, southeast and northeast. Five or six fountains were in action and there was strong blowing at the north rampart. At 4:20 p. m. a powerful true fountain of the ''artesian'' variety started a flow southward from the northwest cone and overflows flooded the benches northwest, east and southeast. At 5:30 p. m. the lake and the northwest pot subsided so that a sharp glow outline appeared around the former about three feet deep with stalactites and the northwest pot became a glowing oven. The flow crusted and violent large fountains started in the lake north, southeast and southwest. There was tremendous hissing emission of gas from under the lake skins along the north and southeast ramparts throwing high spray and puffs of blue fume. There were falls from the spatter benches southwest and elsewhere. During the overflow much of the boundary between lake and floors was obscured by the lava flood. When the west arm settled back there was drip of glowing lava into the lake from the bank under overhanging skins.

The following report from the Whitney Laboratory of Seismology is submitted by Mr. H. O. Wood:

During the week-interval ending with January 5 two local earthquakes, of small and moderately small seismographic amplitude have been registered. These were not of perceptible magnitude. Microseismic motion has been as usual. The seismographic amplitudes of the waves of volcanic vibration have been larger than normal and the conspicuous groups of such waves have been more frequent and of longer duration than usual. In the early part of the week-interval there was a sharp increase in the apparent tilt to the east and north and this has been maintained with little change.

TECHNOLOGY STATION, Jan. 13, 1917.—During the week ending Jan. 12, 1917, the lava lake of Halemaumau has continued to rise at the rate of about two feet per day, with overflows from time to time and lava welling up through cones on the floor, especially at the north and northwest. The crags have also risen, in general keeping pace with the rising of the lake. Experiments have been made during the week by the workers at the Observatory in measuring temperature, collecting gases and photographing the pit from the inner crags.

On Saturday, Jan. 6, the lava had subsided slightly after the strong overflowing of the previous day. On Jan. 7 the writer accompanied by Smith, Lancaster and Moniz adjusted the rope ladders to the west niche of Halemaumau and descended to the northwest floor. Here it was possible to cross the floor to the crag mass and climb to its summit. Photographs were made of the pit walls from the summit and others of the lava lake. Three flaming cones were examined in the vicinity of the northwest pond, the largest of them a glowing orifice three feet in diameter at the southern margin of the pond depression. Flames were playing about the pot and lava could be heard pounding within. The northwest pond itself was a shallow oval depression in broken lava crusts. Two smaller cones about the north margin of the west wall pond were hissing from small holes and lava could be heard splashing inside. There was an extensive fresh flow over the northern and southern benches which had been in motion in the early morning and lava toes were moving red hot in the valley between the southwest crags and the wall. The fumes from the northwest cones were disagreeable to leeward of them, but the air on the upper part of the crag mass was not bad except for occasional whiffs from the large fountains in the north cove. The lake was low and occasional cascading took place into the southwest chasm.

On Jan. 8 a second expedition was made to the northwest cones by Messrs. Wood, Lancaster and Moniz in order to try for gas collection with vacuum tubes. One of the small west cones was broken open in order to enlarge the flaming orifice for insertion of the tubes, but the orifice immediately sealed with lava spatter.

At 10 a. m. the writer inspected the north cone which was putting out lava toes and was now a group of small hummocks a few feet high. From one of these a flame was playing from a narrow vertical slit about eight inches long and there were white sublimates deposited around the glowing orifice which made a whistling noise. The lava in the lake rose and fell through a small range and was in general about ten feet below the rampart. In the evening from 5 to 7 o'clock the lake was still low with numerous fountains and many flames from the grottoes, the wall chimney on the south side of the crag mass and the large northwest cone. The west wall pond was again revealed as a small pool covered with dark blistered skin and showing a quiet glowing grotto at its north end. The north cone was still ejecting sluggish pahoehoe.

On Jan. 9 the lava was high and flows were in motion. On Jan. 10 the lava retained its high levels and there was glow in the northwest cone and in flows around the north cone.

On Jan. 11 at 9 a. m. the lake seen from the east station was brimming level with the rampart, four or five fountains were in action, the recent flows appeared small except for a considerable field of pahoehoe around the north cone.

Assisted by Messrs. Thurston, Smith, H. Johnson and Moniz, the writer made a temperature test with Seeger cones. A battery of six cones of fusible clays, such as are used in the porcelain industry, was enclosed in an iron cylinder, screwed on the end of a galvanized iron pipe and thrust three feet below the surface of the lake. The cones selected ranged in fusibility from 990° C. to 1150° C. The apparatus was immersed in lava for six minutes. Flames from burning gas played around the orifice where the pipe punctured the skin of the lake and these flames were a brilliant greenish yellow color from the zinc of the pipe's galvanized surface. Droplets of metallic zinc and a yellow deposit of zinc oxide were left on the pipe, and this deposit turned white on cooling. The pipe bent sharply at the point where it entered the lava, softened by the heat. On removing and cooling the cylinder, none of the cones showed fusion, indicating that the temperature here, three feet below the surface of the lake, was less than 990° C. Further experiments will be made with cones of lower fusing point.

Overflows began northeast and southeast just as the experiments started, three of them along the northeast rampart, threatening to make the work on the rampart impossible. Fortunately two of these progressed but a short distance and the northernmost only about one hundred feet. The overflowing stopped at 9:30 a. m. and the lake subsided six feet and then recovered three feet. A very large half-dome grotto had been built up southeast and there was occasional heavy fountaining north, and swift streaming westward from the bench at the south island.

Mr. L. A. Thurston experimented by throwing logs of ohia cord wood into the lake. The first, thrown while the lake was overflowing, plunged beneath the skin and remained burning submerged, the flames puffing through the lava and producing some ballooning of the surface, but almost no fountaining. The flames were yellow. The second experiment was after subsidence and during temporary rising. This time the log was hurled down end-on so as to puncture the surface layers of lava over the gas beneath. The result was again flames and puffs of smoke followed by a fountain which spattered thick pasty lava over the bank for several minutes. On neither occasion did the wood show any tendency to float up but burned beneath the surface. Several normal gas flames from the lake were seen which burst from under the crusts and appeared reddish in daylight.

A remarkable fact was noted on this day and previously; namely, that there is practically no odor of sulphurous acid gas to leeward of the moving pahoehoe flows on the north bench. On this day the writer was immediately to leeward of where the golden torrent poured over the rampart with hundreds of small bubble fountains bursting through it. There were oppressive heat waves to leeward but there was none of the acrid and intolerable blue sulphurous fume which reaches the upper rim of the pit from the flaming fountains and grottoes. The suggestion is strong that the oxidation producing the sulphurous acid fume results from union with atmospheric air, and this checks with the observation that not all of the fountains produce flames.

Measurement on Friday, Jan. 12, 1917, at 9:30 a. m., determined the depression of the lake to be 87 feet below the south rim of the pit, indicating a rise of 14 feet in eight days. The south island stood 49 feet above the lake, the east crag 52 feet, the southwest crag 45 feet and the crag mass 65 feet. The length of the lake as a whole was about 800 feet and its width at the west arm 700 feet. The lake was six to ten feet down, first subsiding and thereafter rising with some inrush at the southwest cove with churning in the grotto there. There was southward streaming from under the two arches west of the south island. A sluggish pile of pahoehoe was making incandescent toes over the site of the west pond. There was occasional heavy bombardment in the northeast and southeast rampart grottoes and sometimes very heavy blowing fountains in the north cove. There were two heavy falls of spatter bench material southwest. No marked changes were observed on the northwest floor.

The following report from the Whitney Laboratory of Seismology is submitted by Mr. H. O. Wood:

During the week interval ending with Jan. 12 two local earthquakes have been registered—one with moderate seismographic amplitude and one with small seismographic amplitude—and one wave group of doubtful character. The seismographic amplitude of microseismic motion has varied irregularly between normal and moderate values, rising at the end to strong values. The seismographic amplitude of volcanic vibration has fallen at times to normal values but, though irregular, it has usually been moderately large. There has been an irregular shifting of the pens tending on the whole to indicate a decrease in the tilting to the west and south. This shift has been most marked near the end of the interval.

TECHNOLOGY STATION, Jan. 20, 1917.—"During the week ending January 19, the immense lava lake of Halemaumau has continued to rise and at a still faster rate than during the previous week. The upper portions of the large crag mass are now in full view above the rim of the pit as seen from the Volcano House, and only eight feet below it. The mechanism of rising is remarkably constant with overflow of the north and south ramparts and uplift of the east and west crags. The writer has continued to make experiments in taking direct temperature at the edge of the lake, the results to date indicating that the temperatures just below the surface skins vary between nine hundred degrees centigrade and one thousand degrees centigrade. Away from the grottoes and fountaining areas the lava is stiff and viscous and proves very unwieldy for experimentation owing to its tendency immediately to solidify around any object thrust into it.

"On January 13 and 14 rising was especially conspicuous at the south end of the east crag, indicated by crevasses and uplift of fresh flows at the base of the crag, and compensated by subsidence of the floor under the northeast wall, causing fresh avalanches from the wall.

"On the morning of January 15 the lake was rising and falling from two to six feet. The lava had been piling up from the west and northwest floor vents and the north cone was buried under a smoking tumble of crusts. In the evening the lake overflowed strongly southward and there were avalanche slides at the east.

"With the assistance of Messrs. Thurston, Palmer, Smith and Alex. Lancaster, the writer immersed an iron cylinder three feet below the surface of the lake, on the end of a one-inch pipe, for eleven minutes. This contained six Seeger cones of fusibility ranging from 770 degrees centigrade to 990 degrees centigrade. None of the cones was fused. Possibly the congealed lava on the end of the pipe acted as a non-conductor to prevent heating in the allotted time.

"Next an attempt was made with a Bristol electric pyrometer to determine the rate of cooling of a sample of lava as it solidified. The thermo-element, a couple of wires twisted together which generate an electric current on heating, was fastened in an iron pot which was dipped beneath the surface of the lake and drawn forth filled with lava. Wires leading from the couple to a galvanometer recorded the temperature. The maximum temperature of the lava in the pot registered 420 degrees centigrade, and the rate of loss of temperature for each five minutes was about twenty-two degrees centigrade for the first twenty minutes, then double that amount for the next five-minute interval, and three times that figure for the next five minutes.

"Assisted by Mr. Thurston, the writer next tested the temperature of liquid lava at the edge of the lake with the uncovered thermo-element. The needle swung immediately and steadily to 910 degrees centigrade in a first test and 850 degrees centigrade in the second test. Adding 100 degrees correction to each of these readings for the overheated 'cold junction' which rested against the rampart where the air was very hot, we get 1010 degrees centigrade and 950 degrees centigrade as the measured temperatures for the two cases, the lower temperature in the second case being occasioned by the encrusting of the terminal, which was drawn under the bank by the current. These measurements of temperature check perfectly with the readings made with thermo-element by Shepherd in 1911 and with Fery pyrometer by Daly in 1909.

On January 16 the lake rose and fell in pulsations until four-fifteen in the afternoon, when heavy overflows rushed over the whole south rampart and cascaded down to fill the wall valley, and at the same time strong overflows poured over the north bench from the northwest arm. The overflowing stopped about four forty-five in the afternoon. During the day small avalanches fell from the 1894 bench northeast. there were about eight fountains in the lake, and a large blowing cone had been built up at the extreme end of the northwest arm, which spurted flames and spray with loud puffing noises. It was possible to approach within a few yards of this cone, and just beside it in the northwest arm the writer watched, only a few feet away, a spectacular grotto hung with glowing stalactites, where gas from under the skin blanket made violent outrush with puffing and spraying.

"During the overflow a glowing filigree cone developed at the north cone locality. Occasionally during the day a deep booming sound was heard from the rising east crag, which had been lifted twelve feet within a few days, carrying with it the boulders under the east gulch and the fresh flows near the southeast cove.

"About noon a balloon of skin was raised over the middle of the north cove and extended itself for thirty feet eastward, finally bursting open at its east end and revealing a most beautiful and brilliant cavernous space all glowing and floored with bubbling incandescence. After releasing the flam-

Looking southeast from summit of great crag-mass—showing south crag and connecting peninsula, and lake streaming round crag. —Photo. Jaggar.

Jan. 5, 1917—Crag mass and lava lake from N.E. rampart, standing on edge of lake. —Photo. Jaggar.

ing gas through this archway the bubble slumped. Its outer surface was silvery gray and resembled the back of a hippopotamus.

"The cylinder experiment with Seeger cones of lower fusibility on this day failed owing to an attempt to leave the apparatus in the lava thirty minutes. Heavy skins piled against the pipe where it entered the lake and solidified there. On listening at the upper end of the pipe one could hear distinctly the bubbling noise of the seething lake twenty feet below. On attempting to twist the pipe, it parted at the lava contact where it was heated to redness and immediately the zinc galvanizing of the lining blazed with a strong yellow flame, which played in pulsations for six minutes, leaving a yellow white coating.

"On January 17 at eleven o'clock in the morning the lake was overflowing northeast, and at four that afternoon the north cone gave vent to a flood over the north floor. The lake was then ten feet below its banks. In the evening there was strong outflow from the cones north and northwest.

"On January 18 the lake was low, nine to eleven feet below the inner bench, and a flow was in motion on the north floor with origin somewhere near the site of the north cone, though no cone was visible. There were fresh overflows northeast and southeast and the north rampart had greatly added to the bordering spatter domes, one of these being fully fifteen feet high. Five or more fountains were in action and the surface currents were rapid. The east crag showed further signs of rising.

"Two temperature tests with Seeger cones were made. A new device for holding the cones was used so that they could be inserted one above the other directly in the end of the pipe. The pipe was heated for thirty minutes just above the surface of the lake and then dipped for only one minute. The results showed a cone of fusibility 870° C fused on the edges and one of 970° C very slightly affected, indicating that the temperature was between these limits. The swift currents caught the end of the pipe and strained and bent it so that it was recovered with great difficulty.

"Measurements on Friday, January 19, 1917, at ten-thirty in the morning determined the depression of the lake to be sixty-eight feet below the southeast rim of the pit indicating a rise of nineteen feet in seven days. The crag mass was sixty feet above the lake, the east crag forty-one feet, the south island forty-eight feet, the southwest crag thirty-seven feet and the pinnacle of the south bench thirty-one feet.

"The lake was rising during the morning and overflows took place about 1 p. m. The crag mass showed increasing tilt to the west. There was fresh tumble in the wall valley between the west and southwest stations consisting of very large blocks from the lower part of the cliff. The south bench pinnacle showed elevation and large crevasses had opened near it. There was a very high pile of fresh pahoehoe in the southwest wall valley.

"The following report from the Whitney Laboratory of Seismology is submitted by Mr. H. O. Wood:

" 'During the week interval ending with January 19 three local earthquakes of very small seismographic amplitude, and one doubtful wave group, have been registered. Microseismic motion has been of moderate seismographic amplitude, or less. Volcanic vibration has been of moderate seismographic amplitude, with brief storms of greater energy. Pen shifts in the sense of tilt have indicated an increase in tilt to the south, or more strictly, decrease in tilt to the north, with slight fluctuations in the east-west component without marked net change.' "

TECHNOLOGY STATION, Jan. 27, 1917.—During the week ending Jan. 26, 1917, the lava of Halemaumau has continued to rise and the 1912 level has been passed. The lake is now about 50 feet down. The floor of the west niche is now flooded with fresh lava where the ladders were attached for descent of a 40-foot cliff on Jan. 7. The crags continue to rise and are now in full view from the Observatory. Very heavy and spectacular overflows have taken place during the week from both the north and south marginal ramparts of the lake and the western floor is heaped high with lava that has welled up through vents in the region of the northwest and west ponds. Experiments have been continued in taking temperatures of the grottoes and flames, and in preliminary soundings to determine the depth and consistency of the under liquid of the lava pool.

On Jan. 20, 1917, at 2 p. m. the border bench around the lake was five feet high with lava that has welled up was in the northwest cove. The flow from the vent on the north floor was extending itself by trickling. The wind was southerly and the northeast floor region accordingly fumy. At 2:30 p. m. sudden subsidence of about eighteen inches was accompanied by violent fountaining in the north cove. These fountains tend to migrate to the northeast rampart where they expend themselves.

On Jan. 21 at 2 p. m. the lake was brimming and fountaining violently so as to flood the northeast rampart in streams which forked and spread eastward and northward. At 5 p. m. the lake was very quiet and about five feet down, the flow on the north floor was trickling, a flame played from the south wall of the crag mass, there were glowing spots on the south floor and the fountaining against the north rampart threw up heavy spatter. Later in the evening the northwest cone was seen spurting.

On the morning of Jan. 22 the trickling thick pahoehoe flow was still spreading over the whole northeast floor. Small avalanches were sliding from the east cliff and the 1894 bench. The continued lift of the east crag was carrying with it the rock tumble at the foot of the trail down the east gulch so that it was now easier to descend over the cliff at the east end of the 1894 bench. The northwest cone was now six feet high above a lava heap at the site of the former northwest pond. The lake level was from three to four feet below its margin, eight or more fountains were in action, the ramparts were building high and the wall valleys apparently sinking. There is a sequence every few days of alternative whereby these wall valleys first deepen, and then fill up by overflow.

In order to measure the temperature of the lava actually fountaining and flaming at the lake border in the northeast dome grotto, a one-inch pipe 40 feet long containing six Seeger cones of fusibilities ranging from 590° C. to 1070° C. was thrust into the grotto and allowed to heat for ten minutes in the invisible flame and then for five minutes in the splashing and down-sucking lava. The end of the pipe was sucked down and violently bent and it required the united efforts of five men to withdraw it. Five feet of the end were plastered with lava. All the cones were completely fused but one, and that one, of fusibility of 1070° C., was partially melted showing that the temperature was over 1100° C. Taken along with the results of previous measurements in the non-fountaining lava of the lake, it appears that the liquid in a distance of say 20 feet may change in temperature on entering a boiling grotto through a range of 300° C., or from about 850° C. to 1150° C.

On Jan. 23 with the aid of nine volunteers, an experiment in sounding was tried. Working on the east point and the northeast rampart a length of 200 feet of half-inch pipe was twice thrust over the bank obliquely out into the liquid lava of the lake 20 feet from the shore, and both times the pipe went down to a vertical depth of only about 50 feet when it encountered, not hard bottom, but an increasing resistance which was gradual, and finally caused the pipe to arch upward and fail to penetrate farther. In the first test the submerged lengths of pipe solidified against the bank on the attempt to withdraw it and the lower lengths were lost. In the second test the pipe was recovered, but only through the most strenuous hauling by nine men in line. Twice it stuck owing to accumulations of lava which caught against the bank. The end of the pipe emerged clean and showed no fusion or especial oxidation.

The notable result of this experiment, giving in two different places apparent evidence of increasing viscosity in depths to an impenetrable pudding at about 50 feet down, is the suggestion that the lava lake is cooler and more viscous below than it is at the surface. To confirm this, tests must be made for temperature and viscosity in depth, and such tests are now in preparation.

On this day, Jan. 23, the lake was three to four feet down. There was a glowing flow on the south floor. At the base of the northeast wall recent flows were swollen up into ridges with crusts a foot thick and one of these which had collapsed revealed a cavern three feet high of bright orange glow inside. It looked as though the fresh trickling lava of later date had penetrated beneath these crusts and arched them up, welling out through the cracks, reheating the interior, and then partly escaping. Perhaps it is the slow drip of such secondary intrusion which gives rise to the well-known cavern stalactites and driblet spires.

At 1 p. m. there was overflow at the north and at 5 p. m. very heavy overflows across the south rampart sweeping westward and over the head of the west arm sweeping southward. A spray blast played violently at the southwest cove and there was activity at the northwest cone.

On Jan. 24 at 11 a. m. the lake was down ten feet with few fountains. At 2:45 p. m. the southeast rampart overflowed and the north rampart at 3 p. m.

On Jan. 25 at noon the lava was nearly brimming and rapidly rising and there was fresh lava on the northeast floor. At 2:30 p. m. there was overflow across the north rampart for an hour, the flood pouring east and west.

On Friday, Jan. 26, 1917, the weather was rainy with southwesterly wind, but this wind made conditions favorable for an attempt to walk around the entire circle of the pit on the inner floor following the base of the walls. The descent was made with rope ladder at the west niche, the floor of which was now only seven feet above the fresh lava heapings from the northwest pond. Accordingly the lower ladder was taken up and stored, and this was fortunate, for the next day its position was entirely covered with fresh flows.

A second ascent of the crag mass was made and from its high scarps a good view was obtained of the glowing interior of two high curtained dome grottoes across the north cove to the east. The west slope of the crag mass appeared steeper and more rifted than on Jan. 7 and there were yellow sulphate and alum deposits in the cracks.

Accompanied by Alex Lancaster and Messrs. June and Newton, the writer now made the circuit of the inner floor going first over a high dome of pahoehoe where the west wall pond had been. There were lava flows trickling in the southwest wall valley. We crossed a tumble of boulders which had fallen from the southwest wall and passed the mouths of gigantic crevasses which cut through the southwest crag. On arriving under the A-frame at the south the crusted wall pond there proved to be a distinct depression with a hard floor. After passing the south pinnacle the only disagreeable part of the circuit was encountered, namely crossing the hot flows of the southeast floor through the blue fume of that ever-active rampart. The fume proved bad and it was necessary to move rapidly through a short stretch of it. The lake was about four feet below the rampart. We next passed a deep crevasse south of the east crag and reached the east chasm and the foot of the trail and were now on familiar ground. From there the traverse of the north floor was easy. The northeast cavern was no longer glowing. The remnants of the 1912 ledge under the northwest station were now only six feet above the floor and the cavern in the northwest wall was nearly accessible.

The northwest cone was ten feet across and six feet high with the lava of the roofed-over northwest pond pounding within it at a depth of about twelve feet. There were filagree flaming orifices around the cone about two feet below its summit and the largest of these, ten inches in diameter, made a window on its east side through which could be seen plump glowing stalactites and a gorgeous fiery inner cupola shimmering with orange heat and revealing the splashing lava glass below. Fierce blasts of invisible flame which would have been bluish by night light came from the window and occasionally the gas pressure would increase so that these blasts became rhythmic and noisy like an engine. The extension of the northwest pond north of this cone was arched over with domed lava crusts.

The temperature of the flaming window and the glowing cavity within was measured with a one-inch pipe containing a battery of seven Seeger cones ranging in fusibility from 620° C. to 1130° C. The cupola was blowing hard in pulsations and a whiff of the hot burnt gas from the flame which flew for an instant into the writer's face was a terrific sensation. The pipe was pushed into the window horizontally for three feet and left there nine minutes. First the green-yellow zinc flame appeared until the galvanizing was burnt off. The pipe became incandescent, softened and bent downward.. Then an oxide of iron formed over the surface and glowing drops dripped off the pipe completely liquid. The highest glow played over the pipe just at the entrance to the window where the supply of oxygen from the air was greatest. At this point after nine minutes the pipe was seen to be eaten through and was immediately withdrawn. The whole three feet of iron which had been immersed in the hot gases was a mere black oxidized shell, the end cap was entirely gone but the iron spiral which held the Seeger cones inside the pipe was little affected, showing that the outer reaction was chemical reduction and not fusion. This reaction at such high temperature was probably the union of sulphurous acid with iron to make ferrous oxide and sulphur. The fusible cones indicated a temperature considerably over 1130° C. and probably nearer 1200° C.

The lava lake on this afternoon remained low, from ten to twelve feet below the inner bench, and exhibited six or seven fountains. The north rampart was very high with bulging protuberances and much overhang. There were flaming holes through the rampart which crackled and fumed like a wood fire and showed white deposits.

A young boatswain bird was found alive on one of the west crags and was rescued and given his liberty above.

The following report from the Whitney Laboratory of Seismology is submitted by Mr. H. O. Wood:

During the week-interval ending with Jan. 26 two local shocks of small seismographic amplitude, and one doubtful wave group, have been registered. Microseismic motion, and motion of volcanic vibration, have been registered with variable seismographic amplitudes of values comparable with several previous weeks, but larger than the generally normal values. This holds true more particularly for volcanic vibration. This motion has, for the most part, shown increased amplitudes for nearly three months except for short quiet intervals. In the north-south component there has been a progressive shifting of the pen in the sense of tilt to the south, or of decreasing tilt to the north. In the east-west component the shifting has been variable with no well marked tendency, or net change.

Very respectfully,

T. A. JAGGAR, JR.,
Director.

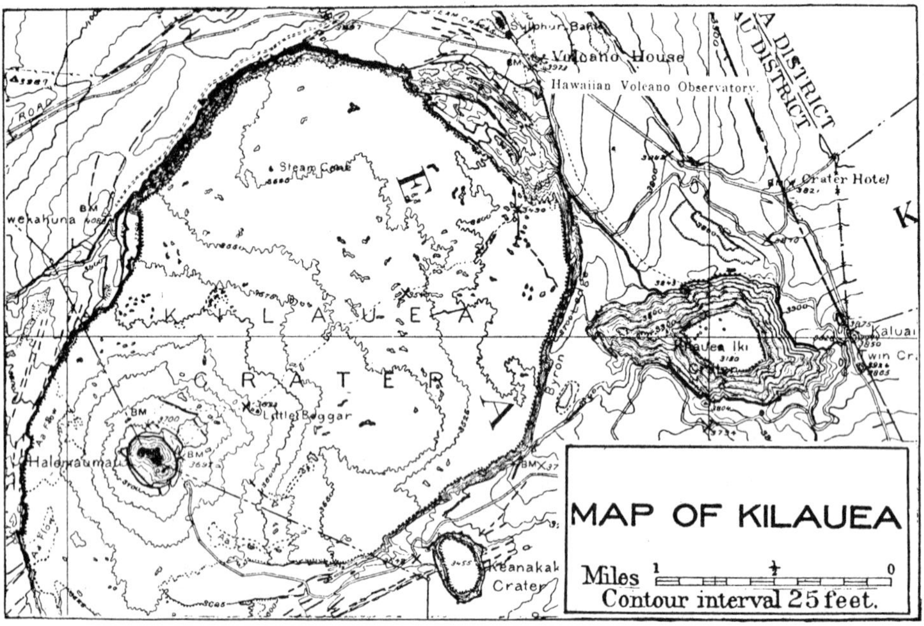

HAWAIIAN VOLCANO RESEARCH ASSOCIATION.

This society is a voluntary one, made up of subscribers to scientific work which is being executed by the Massachusetts Institute of Technology.

In 1915 there are about 100 subscribers in Hawaii and elsewhere, firms and individuals. A group of firms and persons in Hilo built the main observatory building in the spring of 1912. Publications to date have been weekly reports since the summer of 1911, now reprinted in Honolulu in monthly form. The Massachusetts Institute of Technology will publish annual reports, of which the introductory number was printed in 1912.

The weekly bulletin as it appears in the Advertiser is reprinted as a leaflet and sent to regular annual subscribers to the work of the Association. L. A. Thurston is president of the Board of Directors of the Association, and R. W. Shingle is treasurer. New subscribers who are interested in volcanoes will be welcomed in the Association. The Association aims: (1) To record volcanic activity and earthquakes in Hawaii; (2) to attract scientific men hither for special studies; (3) to promote the establishment of volcano observatories all over the world. The annual dues of regular members are $5; patrons of the Assocaition subscribe larger amounts.

WHITNEY LABORATORY OF SEISMOLOGY.

The Whitney Laboratory of Seismology is equipped with two Bosch-Omori 100 kg tromometers registering N-S and E-W motion, a heavy Omori tromometer registering E-W motion, and an Omori "ordinary Seismograph" designed for registering strong earthquakes in all three components of motion. These are seated on concrete piers in a closed basement room having practically constant temperature, beneath the chief Observatory building near the hotel. Time is referred to a rated chronometer, checked at intervals by solar observations with a transit. Both instruments are loaned by the College of Hawaii. Hawaiian standard time (H. S. T.) is 10 hrs. 30 min. slower than Greenwich time.

CANCANI SCALE OF SEISMIC INTENSITY.

Expressed by accelerations measured in millimeters per second per second.

I.	Instrumental	0.0	2.5
II.	Very slight	2.5	5.0
III.	Slight	5.0	10.0
IV.	Sensible, mediocre	10.0	25.0
V.	Rather strong	25.0	50.0
VI.	Strong	50.0	100.0
VII.	Very strong	100.0	250.0
VIII.	Ruinous	250.0	500.0
IX.	Disastrous	500.0	1000.0
X.	Very disastrous	1000.0	2500.0
XI.	Catastrophic	2500.0	5000.0
XII.	Great catastrophe	5000.0	10000.0

Grade IV. is ordinarily the minimum perceived by the senses; and in grade XII. the acceleration, or rate of change of motion (jerk) reaches that of terrestrial gravitation.

In the standard form of report the maximum intensity or acceleration, designated by the symbol a, or max. a, is given in the conventional unit, the **milligal**. The milligal is a measure of acceleration, such that 1 milligal = 1/100 mm. per sec. per sec. = 10 μ per sec. per sec. The Cancani scale, here defined in terms of millimeters per sec. per sec., can therefore be expressed in **milligals** by multiplying each of the numbers by 100.

WEEKLY BULLETIN
OF THE
Hawaiian Volcano Observatory

Vol. V. HONOLULU, HAWAII, FEBRUARY, 1917. No. 2

Technology Station, Feb. 3, 1917.

During the week ending February 2, 1917, the lava of Halemaumau continued to overflow vigorously until February 1, when the flowing was confined to the west floor and there began a subsidence which continued for the next few days. The highest level reached by the lake on February 1 was 45 feet below the rim of the pit. The west pond, however, has piled up fresh lava fully 10 feet above that level.

On January 27 there was overflow across the southeast rampart at 12:35 p. m. and from the northwest pond locality in two powerful springs and from the northwest arm and the south bench. A great heap of lava had accumulated over the west wall pond. The flows continued for over four hours. The southwest peninsula showed tumbling spatter borders when the lava began to subside about 4:30 p. m. A high rampart had been built in front of the southwest crag.

On January 28 overflow began at 1 p. m. from the northwest arm and at 2 p. m. from the southeast cove. A cone had developed at the west end of the southwest peninsula which during the afternoon exhibited a standing fountain similar to the Mokuaweoweo fountains, spraying 40 to 50 feet into the air and manufacturing great quantities of Pele's hair.

On January 29 at 2 p. m. there was much fresh lava on the floors and the lake was very quiet and only about three feet below its banks. On January 30 there was overflow northwest at 1:30 p. m. and an hour later this was extended by a break through the northeast rampart.

On January 31 at 11 a. m. the lake was 10 feet down, fountains were numerous and for four hours there was little change. Ten fountains were in action.

On February 1 at 10:45 a. m. overflow began on the northeast and spread extensively on the bench. At 12:30 p. m. the lake was five feet down. The northwest cone was puffing vigorously and great accumulations of lava west and northwest had built up a rolling surface there which was within three feet of the floor of the large northwest wall cavern.

By this time the three greater crags so protruded above the edge of the pit that they were all in view from the automobile terminus. The crag-mess had been tilting westward. There was a flat ring-shaped cone and crater at the west end of the southwest peninsula. The lake had built immense glowing grotto domes in the northeast rampart and at the west end of the southeast rampart, and under the isthmus adjacent to the south island was a quiet glowing cavern. At 2:30 p. m. the lake was eight feet down and an hour later a striking change in the streaming was observed in the north cove, the surface currents pouring southward for the first time in many weeks. About eight fountains were in action, some of the central ones being very large, spraying to great heights and emitting yellow-brown fume which changed to blue above. Some of these fountain masses were from 60 to 100 feet long. There was a deep grotto exhibiting slow inflow southwest which appeared to communicate with an opening below the southwest cone. At 3:40 p. m. there was sudden sinking of the lake several feet so that the arch west of the south island opened above the subsiding melt.

On Friday, February 2, 1917, at 1 p. m. the lake was ten feet below its rim. The lava heapings northwest were now level with the northwest cavern

WEEKLY BULLETIN
of the
Hawaiian Volcano Observatory

Published Monthly at Honolulu, Hawaii, by the Hawaiian Volcano Research Association

L. W. de Vis-Norton........Secretary

Entered as second-class matter January 20, 1914, at the post-office at Honolulu, Hawaii. under the Act of August 24, 1912.

floor. Flows were trickling in that region. At 7:30 p. m. the lake was nearly brimming but did not overflow. At 9 p. m. the lake had again subsided, there were four great flaming grottoes, and spears of blue flame also rose from the southwest ring cone and the northwest cone. Ten fountains were in action, an especially heavy one occasionally migrating around the south island and expending itself in the southern dome grotto. Here and at a similar grotto southwest the rush of gas threw out lava droplets horizontally which fell upon the crusts of the lake to a distance of from 60 to 100 feet. There were glowing and flaming orifices back of the ramparts northeast and southeast.

The following report from the Whitney Laboratory of Seismology is submitted by Mr. H. O. Wood:

During the week-interval ending with February 2 two earthquakes have been registered. One of these was a local shock of moderate seismographic amplitude but of unfelt magnitude. The other was a great, world-shaking teleseism originating at a distance of a little over 3000 miles from this station. This occurred in late afternoon of January 29. Since no news of it has come to notice it is inferred that the origin was submarine for on land it would have produced certain disaster unless located in the midst of a great wilderness. The seismographic amplitudes of microseismic motion and of volcanic vibration have been variable between moderate and larger values much as in all recent weeks. The pens have continued to shift in a fluctuating way in the sense of increasing tilt to the south and west—or perhaps still, of decreasing tilt to the north and east.

Technology Station, Feb. 10, 1917.

During the week ending February 9, 1917, the Halemaumau lava column has subsided from a maximum height of 45 feet below the rim of the pit to a depth of about double that figure. According to experience this downward movement on the approach of the equinox was to be expected. With the subsidence there has been a sinking of the crags and islands, but not so fast as the going-down of the liquid pool and there have been pronounced falls of rock both from the crags and the old walls of the pit. There has been some overflow on the bench from the western ponds. The present sinking spell is the most pronounced interruption to steady rising which has taken place since June, 1916.

On Saturday, February 3, from 2 to 4 p. m. the lake was 20 feet below its banks and sinking. There were two fresh avalanche falls on the floor south and southwest made of tumble from the high rim of the pit. The places whence these rocks fell were points of emergence of big crevasses. One of these, just beside the south A-frame, had long appeared loose, overhanging and unsteady. There was another fresh tumble at the base of the north wall. The whole southeastern corner of the crag-mass had fallen in including the two pinnacles. Apparently as an effect of the wave or splash of this fall, the long southwestern peninsula was broken through, leaving an open channel where the lava streamed southward from the west arm. The southwest cove had collapsed carrying with it the ring cone so as to extend the end of the southwest arm northward. The west wall pond was again revealed end of the southwest arm northward. as a collapsed pit where the heap of lava had been. This pit was 25 feet across and extended into caverns north and south where the roof would fall in from time to time splashing down into a lava pool twenty feet below. The northwest cone was still in place with an opening on its east side that led to a splashing oven within. There were several glowing caverns on the northwest floor made by collapsed domes. Under the isthmus west of the south island were two high tunnels showing a tumble of broken rock that made a shoal in the lake beneath them. Streaming through these arches had wholly ceased.

The lake showed five fountains, the grottoes were not very active and the largest one northeast was seen to collapse. The skins on the surface appeared heavy and were occasionally broken by violent central fountains and spurts of rapid streaming around the south island. Two balloons of skin were seen inflated by gas on the surface of the north cove. The streaming was southward from the north cove, there were sluggish heavy crusts at the head of the west arm and stalactites in the grotto at the head of the southwest arm. At the site of the southwest grotto there was a shoal at the lake margin. The crevasse at the base of the east crag had widened.

In the evening the south island was seen to sink bodily and the arch west of it collapsed. The south island had been tilting over so as to overhang on its south side and when it sank back it tipped northward and the surface of the peninsula west of it subsided and also tipped to the north.

Measurements on February 3 determined the highest fresh spatter level of the lake surface to be 45 feet below the south rim, the present depression 60 feet and the elevation of the several crags above the lake surface as follows: South island 60 feet, crag-mass 71 feet, east crag 61 feet, southwest crag 40 feet. The south island was thus level with the rim of the pit and the east crag and crag-mass respectively one and eleven feet above it.

After 4 p. m., February 4, the lake was seen to have changed greatly, the margins remaining fifteen to twenty feet high. The south island had sunk bodily twenty-five feet and was separated on the west by a channel from an island remnant of the southwest peninsula. The entire western part of the peninsula was gone except for a small islet near the former southwest cove. Streaming in the southwest channel was now reversed to the east, meeting the other current in the narrows southeast of south island with violent fountaining. A fragment from the west end of the middle island fell into the lake leaving a red hot scar and the entire southeast rampart had fallen away leaving a raw red hot wall. The dome grotto at the west end of the southeast rampart had collapsed.

The east crag appeared higher but the crag-mass lower than on the previous day. The southwest crags were unchanged except for some falls from the rampart. The west wall pond was an open pit eighty feet long. The northwest pond was an irregular open lake 100 feet long with irregular extensions on the side of the crag-mass and the northwest cone was gone. There was a glowing filagree cone under the west station.

The streaming was outward from the west arm and from the northwest arm and ten or more fountains would occasionally break into activity. In the intervening periods thick crusts would form. There were rock falls from the north rampart. Still cavern grottoes were glowing southwest, southeast and northeast.

The west wall pond would rise and fall through a range of fifteen feet. Flames played from orifices in its east wall and the puffing of the flames was in sympathy with a heaving of the dark flexible crust over the pond. This crust would break up with cracking and foundering at the beginning of each subsidence. The sinking spells were rapid and a red hot sugary looking lava wall was revealed of massive scaly aspect like glowing coke, underlying a definite pahoehoe crust shown in section all around this small pit. An intense yellow glow was maintained in the north cavern extension of the pond. Another higher shallow cavern in a flow shell adjacent to the edge of the pit also maintained a high glow.

Flames were very conspicuous southeast, northeast, the north side of the middle island and in the vicinity of the western ponds. There were occasional falls of spatter borders into the lake and one fall was seen from the wall of the southwest crevasse. The liquidity and intensity of glow appeared high in the spatter grottoes and fountains.

On February 5, at 1:30 p. m., the lake remained about twenty feet below its banks but showed rising, and was flush with the lower parts of the southwest island. Fountains were few. At 2:10 and 3:50 p. m. there were falls from the east side of the crag-mass in the lake, starting ebullition. The two western ponds were active and occasionally overflowing.

Seen from the southeast on February 6 the lake appeared ten feet lower or perhaps seventy-five feet below the rim and fountaining had increased. Rocks fell from the northwest side of the crag-mass.

The lake was still thirty feet below its marginal bench at 2 p. m. February 7, 1917, and the surface was very quiet. At 4:30 p. m. it had resumed active fountaining and very rapid streaming southwest and southeast.

At 2 p. m., February 8, the lake appeared forty feet below the bench and very quiet, with one fountain at the south. Slow subsidence was in progress with submergence and thick blue fumes southwest. Collapse northeast had created a new island 200 feet from the shore.

At 1 p. m., February 9, the lake appeared ten feet lower still, with much fountaining. The crag-mass had subsided with increased tilt to the northwest, and with it the west and northwest floor had sunk about twenty feet. Fumes greatly increased.

The following report from the Whitney Laboratory of Seismology is submitted by Mr. H. O. Wood:

During the week-interval ending with February 9 five weak local earthquakes, two of small and three of very small seismographic amplitude, have been registered. The seismographic amplitudes of microseismic motion have varied between normal and moderately large values. The motion of volcanic vibration has been more pronounced than normal both in regard to the magnitude of the seismographic amplitudes and in regard to the frequency of occurrence of well-marked "storms" of these waves. There has been no significant change in the pen shifts ascribed to tilting.

Technology Station, Feb. 17, 1917.

During the week ending February 16, 1917, the lava column of Halemaumau reached a stationary point about 85 feet below the rim of the pit for the first three days, then subsided some twenty-five feet more. This subsidence was followed by rising at the end of the week. There have been more falls of rock from the high rim of Halemaumau east and south. The island crags which were visible above the rim of the pit, through January, from the Volcano House, gradually sank out of sight from that point last week. They are, however, still conspicuous objects within the pit as seen from its rim.

On Saturday, February 10, 1917, at 1:30 p. m., there was no apparent change in the height of the lake. Occasional fountains broke the surface in the northern region but the remainder of the lake was very quiet. There was some caving in from the northeast inner wall starting ebullition below.

On February 12 at 2 p. m. fumes were thick, the lake was sluggish and without fountains and very slow rising was in evidence. At 3 p. m. fountaining started at the southwest and extended to other parts of the lake.

On February 13 at 11:30 a. m. the lake still appeared about 50 feet below the northeast floor with fountaining on that side. At 11:45 a, m| an avalanche tumbled from the east crag into the lake and started many temporary fountains. Thereafter there was central and border fountaining spouting high in the southwest region, and the main streaming was now in that direction through the central part of the lake and originating in the northwest arm.

From 5 to 6 p. m. the general form of the lake as compared with the high level period of a fortnight previous was greatly changed. The high crag-mass and south island had sunk far below the level of the rim of the pit. The south island and peninsula west of it were now attached by isthmuses of crust to the south bench and bordered on the west by a deep cove of the lake. In this cove and out in the center were new islands. In the high floor bench were five pits all around the lake, three of them, west, northwest and north, containing liquid lava. The southwest crags and east crag had subsided less than the central islands and the east crag still protruded somewhat above the edge of Halemaumau. The southeast floor of overflow of January was still high, only about fifty feet below the rim, but the northeast floor had subsided lower. A secondary bench about fifteen feet above the lake marked a transient stand of the lava of the previous week. The south bench pinnacle had lowered and opened a pit beside it filled with tumbled rocks, and a similar pit had developed from the crevasses at the base of the east crag. Streaming was sluggish from the northwest arm to the southwest cove, while south and east the lava was stagnant. At 6 p. m. a fall from the edge of the southeast bench sent up brown avalanche clouds, broke up the crusts on the lake below and sent out a wave that started general cracking and foundering. There were about seven fountains in action. At 5 p. m. the lake had been quiet and rising; at 6 p. m. it was active and sinking.

The crevasses at the east margin of Halemaumau had widened greatly and the concrete monument marking the east station had moved outward ready to fall. On the north floor there was a red hot tumble of glowing crusts. The northwest arm had widened and become a deep gorge. The northwest floor overflows were still heaped irregularly about two feet below Perret's cavern and were piled across the floor of the west niche. These flows sloped down to the northwest pond which lay in a valley, crusted over but glowing.

From the west station an islet was seen in the lake where the southwest ring-cone had been and there was incessant fountaining against its west side. There was also a large grotto cavern splashing under the southwest crags. The west wall pond lay in a pit crusted over and showing glow at its margins. There was great increase of smoke from the north margin of the lake and several places west, southwest and south. The south island crag was low and its summit had crumbled. Between its high western extension and the south bench there were crusted shoals with coves east and west and a small pond in the middle.

Measurements on February 14, 1917, at 11 a. m. made the depression of the lake surface 94 feet below the southeast rim of the pit and in the afternoon the lake had sunk ten feet lower. The dimensions of the lake were 850 feet N.W.-S.E. by 790 feet E.-W. The southern island mass was 450 feet long, the new island in the north central part of the lake 220 feet long, the west pond pit was 160 feet long and the new floor pits north, east and south were from 60 to 80 feet in diameter.

It was evident on visiting the lake on this day that it had risen and subsided again. The new central island had lengthened and become low and flat topped. There were almost no fountains in the lake and much crusting. Fumes had decreased in the pit, there were few rock falls, a vertical sided pit had developed in the north floor where the glow heap had been and the south pinnacle hung out farther and appeared ready to fall.

A most wonderful and beautiful performance throughout this day which afforded a rare spectacle was the cascading of the surface lava of the lake into a great pit at the south where a seemingly insignificant pond in the shoals had been on the previous day. A river-like channel 200 feet long led from the southwest cove bank of the south island mass to this pit which was sixty feet in diameter. A rushing torrent poured through this channel from the lake and at the pit cascaded downward fully forty feet, striking the wall obliquely and being deflected as it fell to join a roaring, surging whirlpool beneath. The noise was like a waterfall. This cascade had formed at some time prior to 11 a. m. and it was pouring continuously until 1 a. m. the following morning. Sometime thereafter it ceased and the pit filled up and crusted over before 8 a. m., February 15. The torrent had singularly little effect as an outlet to the lake, which rose slightly from 11 a. m. to 1:30 p. m., and sank thereafter about ten feet. The cascading action seemed to satisfy the requirements of gas pressure which would ordinarily make fountains, for these were very few and the lake surface was very sluggish. Blue fume condensed above the fiery vortex, festoons of Pele's hair clung to the wall over the cauldron and a spatter knob could be seen forming within. The effect was like a river vanishing into a limestone sink hole. The southeast cove appeared to be a shallow saucer separated by only a narrow partition from the cascade, with the liquid melt idly crusting, cracking and foundering, but showing no connection with the cascade pit.

On February 15 at 11 a. m. the lake was about 110 feet below the southeast rim, the crags appeared lower, the south pinnacle had fallen and the east survey station had fallen. Evidently the net effect of the day of cascading had been subsidence. The cascade pot was crusted over and lava welled out from it slowly westward to meet sluggish inflow at the mouth of the channel. The southwest islet was now two islets; the new central island stood eight feet above the lake. There were fresh and very heavy falls of rock to the floor below from the high edge of Halemaumau between the east and southeast stations where the danger signs have been placed. **The edge at** the present time is distinctly dangerous **and should be avoided.**

There was shore fountaining southeast and only one or two other fountains. At the lower bench southwest, about the site of the former dome grotto, there was a hot spurting pot four feet in diameter probably full of flaming gas. The lake was rising from 11 a. m. to 12 noon but sank lower in the afternoon, and there were more tumbles at the south pinnacle locality.

The next day, however, Friday, February 16, the lake at noon was seen to be rising and nearly level with the surfaces of the new island and the islets. The channel south of the south island was connected through from southeast to southwest with flowing lava. There was a violent shore fountain west with temporary reversed streaming against that bank. Three or four shifting fountains were in action. The northwest and west ponds exhibited occasional fountains at their south ends. The west pit had extended itself northward into a long crevasse which connected in a semi-circle with the northwest arm. This crevasse appeared to be due to a tendency of the crag-mass to change its tilt from westward to eastward, and perhaps likewise from sinking to rising. From 12:30 to 1 p. m. the lake sank about four feet and the two western islets joined in a crescent suggesting the former ring-cone.

Fumes appeared thin this day. The noises during these days have been slight, made by a few puffing fountains and occasional clattering of tumbled lava shells.

The following report from the Whitney Laboratory of Seismology is submitted by Mr. H. O. Wood:

During the week ending with February 16 only one local earthquake of small seismographic amplitude has been registered. Severe Kona winds have produced vibration which have exaggerated, and masked, the motions of volcanic vibration and microseismic motion. However, the seismographic amplitudes of these have been somewhat greater than normal, aside from this.

In the early part of the interval there was a noticeable tendency to pen-shifting in the sense of eastward tilting which was arrested later. Except for the daily fluctuation there was no noticeable change in the north-south component.

Technology Station, Feb. 24, 1917.

During the week ending February 23, 1917, the lava lake has remained stationary but there have been some very extraordinary adjustments among the crags and benches whereby some have risen to compensate rapid subsidence of others. There has also been powerful cascading from the lake into a pot on its northeast shore which has continued for days. The lake is now like a rapid river pouring from northwest to southeast.

On Saturday, February 17, 1917, at 7 a. m., the lake appeared rising and much higher than of late, for the new central island was flush with the lake surface and had evidently been freshly overflowed for it was covered with glow lines. There was fountaining in the northwest pond and in a flaring grotto on the southwest shore. Streaming was outward from an edge of dark

Feb. 22, 1917—Subsided East crag and raised New Island, which came up in a night on Feb. 18. From S.E. station.—Photo. Jaggar.

Feb. 28, 1917—From east station past E. crag to subsided south Island. —Photo. Jaggar.

Feb. 14, 1917—Cascade from lava lake into sinkhole at South Channel, south pinnacle on the left. The surface adjoining the sinkhole was lake bottom in January. From east of S. station.—Photo. Jaggar.

skin that covered the northwest arm and occasionally fountains would form in the north cove and migrate toward the face of the crag-mass, while others would form near the southwest islets and migrate to the southwest grotto. The north pit was glowing. The east crag was the only one of the great summits of January which still surmounted the edge of Halemaumau.

At 11:30 a. m. the next day, February 18, a remarkable transformation had been wrought. This east crag had subsided bodily thirty feet during the night, while opposite it, out in the lake, the low flat central island had risen fully forty feet, so that it was now a high flat-topped mass, its summit an oval table 100 feet long, showing spatter rims of its former level just below the summit for six feet in horizontal bands while for thirty-five feet below was a raw reddish wall sloping outward from the vertical slightly and scored vertically on its south side. Elsewhere this wall was a scaly rough rock which had presumably risen through the crusted margin of the lake as a red hot mass and without giving time for any spatter marks to form. In general appearance it was much like the former south island. The former long northern extension of this central island was now five broken low pinnacle islets extending out to the center of the north cove, the high table rock being eastward between the sunken east crag and the northern peninsula of the south island mass. This latter mass had also risen, the north peninsula of it being heaved up until it was twenty-five feet high with its benches titled westward. The western crag of the mass was rising and cracking, with occasional rock falls, while the east end (former south island- was crumbling and sinking. The great east crag had evidently sunk quietly, for its form was preserved and some iron pipes which we had left on its scarp were undisturbed. The northeast bench had sunk with it and appeared lower than the northwest bench. The east crag was bordered on the south and east by the crevasses along which it had subsided and here were great tumbles of gigantic boulders, partly fallen from the east high cliff.

The shifting of loads whereby the east crag went down and the middle islands came up must have happened after midnight along with a sudden acceleration of the sinking of the east crag and northeast bench due perhaps to the mass suddenly breaking away from its attachment to the east wall of Halemaumau. The balanced action whereby the islands came up as the crag went down lends confirmation to the view that semi-solid matter forms the bottom of the lake and that the liquid lake is very shallow. Probably the recent lengthening of the new island northward was due to the simultaneous subsidence of the northeast bench which pressed out the under substance and squeezed it up under the island.

On this date the lake was rising from 12 to 12:30 p. m. and sinking from 12:30 to 1 p. m. There were fountains in the north, southwest and west coves and in the northwest pond. Crusts bridged the channel between the upraised table island and the east shore. The pit of recent southern cascade was full of lava and overbrimming. The two southwest islets had disappeared. The southwest grotto was in action.

During the next two days, February 19 and 20, the table island became joined to the northeast bench and the pinnacles extending from it became united into a peninsula. The central crags continued to rise and the east crag to sink. The south channel became elevated to a floor above the lake and in it the former cascade pot became transformed into a low rounded sulphurous smoking cone.

On February 21, at 2 p. m., there was rapid streaming of the lake to the southeast cove and violent bombardment at its inner end. The inner bench around the lake was about five feet high, its construction indicating stationary or rising lava. Much of the east and north walls of Halemaumau had been falling to the floor below, indicating subsidence of the inner bench at those places. The inner bench was sagging away from the wall in many places leaving a chasm one to three feet wide. From 10 a. m. to 3 p. m. on this day the lava of the lake surface was pouring continuously as a cascade into a hole under the northeast bench about where "Old Faithful" fountain used to be in June, 1916.

Measurements on Thursday, February 22, 1917, at 2 p. m., determined the depression of the lake below the south rim of the pit to be 106 feet and the inner bench above it at the base of the crag mass, marking recent levels of the lava, to be nine feet higher.

The lower floor was now a distinct feature five to ten feet above the lake in different places. The east crag was still above the level of the southeast bench. On this bench there were fresh falls of rock east, south and southwest. The former south island was now lower than the west end of the south island mass. Streaming was from the northwest arm to the southeast cove ending in a grotto under the inner cliff between the south and southeast stations where there was violent inrush, intense fountaining and a hot fume column rising. The only other fountains were against the bank southwest and in the south end of the west pit. Smoke appeared to be increasing. The southwest cove and the east side of the north cove were both crusted over but from under the crusts broke the southwest fountaining and the northeast cascade, which last continued to pour down steadily under the bank. The north pit was sending up a column of hot fume. The northwest pond was quiet. The northwest bench now appeared level with the northeast bench. All around the pit were fresh falls of rock from the high walls, and crevasses back from the high rim of Halemaumau had gaped open wider on the east, south, southwest, northwest and north.

On February 23, from 4 to 5 p. m., conditions were much the same and the cascade continued to pour from the lake into the northeast pot. This cascade had now been in action for three days without any marked effect on the level of the lake. Strong streaming poured from southwest and northwest, in a river-like current which appeared to slope downward, to the southeast cove, where the same violent boiling and fuming continued under the cliff. The new island and south islands appeared higher, the floor of south channel appeared only about three feet high but the lower bench on the north extension of the south island mass appeared eleven feet high as though that body were lifting. There was a fountain in the northwest arm but the southwest cove was heavily crusted. There was bubbling at the base of the crag mass but no central fountains. The north pit was quiet and the smoke dense, especially northeast and southeast.

The following report from the Whitney Laboratory of Seismology is submitted by Mr. H. O. Wood:

During the week interval ending with February 23, four local earthquakes of very small seismographic amplitude have been registered. The seismographic amplitude of microseismic waves has varied from normal to somewhat larger values. Volcanic vibrations, though more energetic than normal, have developed seismographic amplitudes of less magnitude than in the two or three weeks preceding. The pen shifts in the sense of tilting have shown no pronounced movements apart from the diurnal movement.

Technology Station, March 3, 1917.

During the week ending March 2, 1917, the lava lake of Halemaumau has subsided fourteen feet in eight days and with this subsidence there has been a tendency to collapse in the January bench near the north pit and under the south station. Cascading into sunken pots at the edge of the lake has continued at the northeast and become evident at the southeast. The general form of the lake and crags has not changed and the fumes from the pit have appeared thin, though within it they are locally very dense; and on the southern margins they have been sharp and unbreatheable.

On Saturday, February 24, 1917, the lake appeared higher, its shore bench being three feet above it. At 11:15 a. m. the surface streaming was wholly reversed, flowing from the southeast cove to the north, where the current met the stream from the northwest arm and both united to pour north and northeast. The north inner cliff was notched back and the current poured under it into a wide cavernous space beneath the north pit. The walls adjacent were cracked and smoking densely through the north floor with brownish white fumes which were quite respirable. This smoke would collect in a whirlwind occasionally and shoot up in heavy billows quite unusual for Halemaumau. The torrent at the northeast poured over a ledge V-shaped in plan, with the point of the V toward the lake so as to make a double cascade pouring from two sides like the Horseshoe Falls at Niagara. On one side a ledge protruded through the fall which divided on both sides. From the fall the torrent rushed into a cavern at the base of the cliff about 80 feet wide at the entrance and flame and fume rose above with very brilliant glow at night. The clearly proved ledge under the liquid at the fall showed how shallow was the edge of the lake and revealed a margin of the bottom quite in accord with the recent soundings, which showed a shallow lake only fifty feet deep when the lava was somewhat higher. Great bodies of crust would be carried over the edge into this cascade cavern and broken up.

The January floor benches had been sagging away from the old walls during the February subsidence leaving deep crevasses at the base of the upper cliff from one to three feet wide, especially northwest and southeast, and avalanches from the upper wall followed.

On February 25, at 2 p. m., the lower bench appeared about five feet high and the northeast cascade was tumbling noisily. At 3:30 p. m. the lava had risen level with the bench. At 4 p. m. there was a heavy fall of rock from the north bench starting vigorous fountaining in the lake below.

On February 26, at 2:30 p. m., the lake was ten feet below the bench and the northeast cascade was still in action. The inrush at the southeast had stopped but the river-like streaming in that direction continued. It is noteworthy that during these cascading periods central fountaining almost completely ceases, and that in general the net result of such a period is a lowering of the level of the lava lake.

On February 27, at 1:45 p. m., the lava as seen from the east station appeared level with the lower bench and fountaining was nowhere to be seen. The excessive smoking of the north bench observed on February 24 had ceased, though there was much smoke on the face of the north inner cliff. This appears to have been the culmination of a temporary rise. At 2 p. m. from the northwest station the cascade northeast could be seen racing down into the pot but the entrance orifice had diminished in size. The southwest cove was crusted over. At 3:30 p. m. the lake seen from the west station was sinking; the inner bench being three feet high and few fountains playing. At 6 p. m. streaming was rapid and six border fountains were in action. The northeast cataract was working noisily and other noises were those of blowing and fountaining. The central crags appeared high and the inner bench much higher than in the afternoon. Active spatter grottoes were flaming west-southwest and southeast. Streaming was from the northwest arm to the east, southwest and southeast. The southwest cove was active. There was bright glow at the north pit. The south pot had become a filagree glowing cone. In the remnants of the southwest rampart were two high flaming pots. Some movement of rocks was heard in the eastern talus.

On February 28, at 10 a. m., the inner bench appeared eight feet high and the northeast cascade was still pouring sluggishly. The northwest pond remained a partially crusted area with a circular pit on its west side and the west pit contained an active pond in its depths. The streaming of this pond was northward. There was active fountaining and fuming at the southeast grotto, the southwest cove was stagnant, yellow sublimates stained the rock adjacent to the southwest chimneys and very disagreeable fumes rose from this locality, from a grotto west-southwest, and from the southeast inrush. Occasionally hardened spatter rims fell into the lake and produced immediate boiling. This appears to be the action of air, confined in the vesicles of the hardened lava, on the combustible gases of the liquid melt. At 9 p. m. there was bright glow from the southeast grotto and the cascade pit. Lazy blue flames like burning alcohol played over the southwest chimneys, the larger one being a pot at least six feet in diameter. A spurting blue flame under pressure was seen rising from the bank of the lake in the southeast cove beside a filagree glowing cone adjacent to the southeast grotto. In the northwest arm a small fountain occasionally broke through the crust. There was glow in bench cracks where the floor was deeply crevassed under the south station and at two places northeast. The north pit was glowing and there were brilliant glow, flame and yellowish fume over the northeast cascade pit.

On March 1, 1917, the lake appeared lower and distinctly falling after 11 a. m. There was a heavy tumble of rocks in the region of the south pinnacle under the south station where the January bench promises to fall away completely leaving a gulch. This place is undermined by the former south wall pond, by the inrush grotto southeast and by the south cascade pit (now a cone). The inner bench on this day appeared fifteen feet high and the sinking of the lake revealed cavernous spaces under arches of crust between the central peninsula and the south island mass, under the south channel floor at the inner and the south island mass, under the south channel floor at the inner end of the southeast cove, and under the isthmus connecting the new island with the northeast bench. Four or five fountains were in action including occasional central ones. A new channel appeared between the new island and the pinnacles north of it, with a streaming current from the center of the lake running through it under an arch of crust in the direction of the former cascade, which now appeared to have ceased sucking in the lava of the north cove, unless it were doing it under the crust; no roar, however, was heard. The crag mass showed some subsidence. Halemaumau as seen from a distance was emitting very thin fumes.

Measurements at 10 a. m., Friday, March 2, 1917, made the depression of the lake below the southeast rim of the pit 120 feet in the southeast channel and 114 feet on the extreme west margin of the lake, indicating a downward slope of six feet from the source region at the west to the inrush at the southeast. The shore bench was eleven feet high above the lake, the east crag eighty-one feet, the new island fifty-nine feet and the crag mass eighty-three feet.

The lake appeared about the same but the southeast grotto was now revealed as a definite cascade from the lake into a hole, and also the northeast cascade had reasserted itself a little farther north than before. There were many recent falls of rock on the January bench northwest, north and northeast.

The following report from the Whitney Laboratory of Seismology is submitted by Mr. H. O. Wood:

During the week interval ending with March 2 two local earthquakes of very small seismographic amplitude have been registered, and two other doubtful groups of waves. Besides vibrations due to strong winds in the latter part of this week interval, the seismographic amplitudes both of microseismic motion and of volcanic vibration have rated larger than normal. Aside from the usual diurnal shifts and others resulting from temperature change and strong winds, there have been no pen shifts in the sense of tilt during the week under consideration.

Very respectfully,

T. A. JAGGAR JR.,
Director.

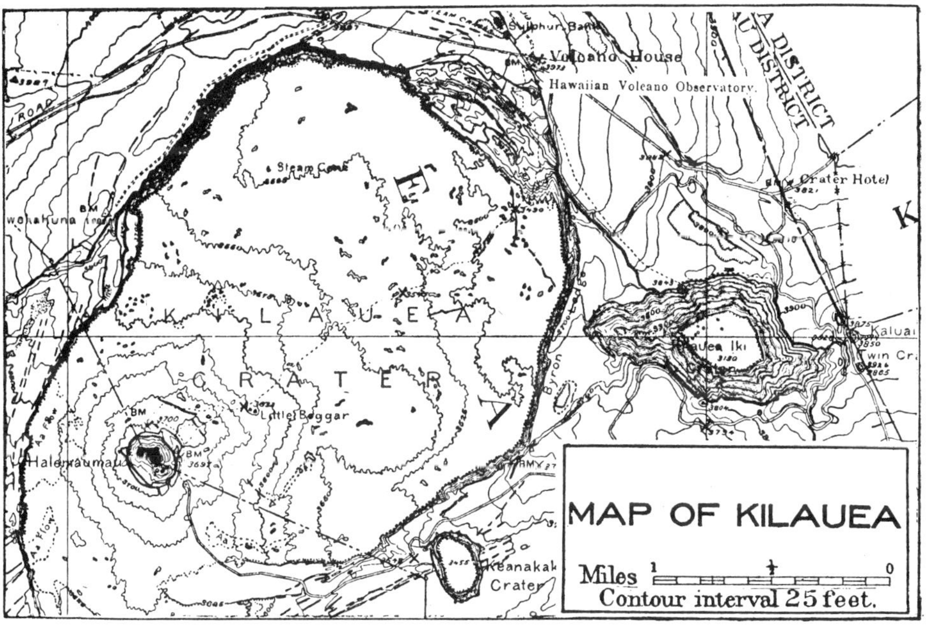

HAWAIIAN VOLCANO RESEARCH ASSOCIATION.

This society is a voluntary one, made up of subscribers to scientific work which is being executed by the Massachusetts Institute of Technology.

In 1917 there are about 150 subscribers in Hawaii and elsewhere, firms and individuals. A group of firms and persons in Hilo built the main observatory building in the spring of 1912. Publications to date have been weekly reports since the summer of 1911, now reprinted in Honolulu in monthly form. The Massachusetts Institute of Technology will publish annual reports, of which the introductory number was printed in 1912.

The weekly bulletin as it appears in the Advertiser is reprinted as a leaflet and sent to regular annual subscribers to the work of the Association. L. A. Thurston is president of the Board of Directors of the Association, and R. W. Shingle is treasurer. New subscribers who are interested in volcanoes will be welcomed in the Association. The Association aims: (1) To record volcanic activity and earthquakes in Hawaii; (2) to attract scientific men hither for special studies; (3) to promote the establishment of volcano observatories all over the world. The annual dues of regular members are $5; patrons of the Association subscribe larger amounts.

WHITNEY LABORATORY OF SEISMOLOGY.

The Whitney Laboratory of Seismology is equipped with two Bosch-Omori 100 kg tromometers registering N-S and E-W motion, a heavy Omori tromometer registering E-W motion, and an Omori "ordinary Seismograph" designed for registering strong earthquakes in all three components of motion. These are seated on concrete piers in a closed basement room having practically constant temperature, beneath the chief Observatory building near the hotel. Time is referred to a rated chronometer, checked at intervals by solar observations with a transit. Both instruments are loaned by the College of Hawaii. Hawaiian standard time (H. S. T.) is 10 hrs. 30 min. slower than Greenwich time.

CANCANI SCALE OF SEISMIC INTENSITY.

Expressed by accelerations measured in millimeters per second per second.

I.	Instrumental	0.0	2.5
II.	Very slight	2.5	5.0
III.	Slight	5.0	10.0
IV.	Sensible, mediocre	10.0	25.0
V.	Rather strong	25.0	50.0
VI.	Strong	50.0	100.0
VII.	Very strong	100.0	250.0
VIII.	Ruinous	250.0	500.0
IX.	Disastrous	500.0	1000.0
X.	Very disastrous	1000.0	2500.0
XI.	Catastrophic	2500.0	5000.0
XII.	Great catastrophe	5000.0	10000.0

Grade IV. is ordinarily the minimum perceived by the senses; and in grade XII. the acceleration, or rate of change of motion (jerk) reaches that of terrestrial gravitation.

In the standard form of report the maximum intensity or acceleration, designated by the symbol α, or max. α, is given in the conventional unit, **the milligal**. The milligal is a measure of acceleration, such that 1 milligal = 1/100 mm. per sec. per sec. = 10 μ per sec. per sec. The Cancani scale, here defined in terms of millimeters per sec. per sec., can therefore be expressed in **milligals** by multiplying each of the numbers by 100.

WEEKLY BULLETIN
OF THE
Hawaiian Volcano Observatory

Vol. V. HONOLULU, HAWAII, MARCH, 1917. No. 3

Technology Station, March 10, 1917.

In contrast to the subsidence of the previous week, the week ending March 9, 1917, exhibits pronounced rising of the lava lake of Halemaumau by about fifteen feet. The rising has been accompanied by cessation of the cascading into border sinkholes and by the building of a marked lower bench all around the lake which is occasionally overflowed. The inner crags are essentially stationary so far during this rising, the liquid lake building up its margin around their bases.

On Saturday, March 3, 1917, at 2:15 p. m., from the east station the lake appeared to be about two feet below its inner bench and very quiet and smoky. Lava from the lake was still cascading into the southeast sinkhole. At 3 p. m. seen from the west, the lake was three feet lower and still quiet and fumy. Seen from the east at 5:30 p. m., the lava had risen level with the inner bench and there was increased activity in the southeast cove, with streaming in that direction. At 6 p. m. a reaction set in with several fountains in the north cove and others in the southeast channel and the cascade from the lake into the border cavern northeast developed to a noisy cataract.

On March 4, at 1:15 p. m., the lake was five feet below the inner bench and showed five fountains and rapid cascading northeast.

On March 5, at 1:30 p. m., there was strong overflow in progress upon the lower bench along the shores of the lake to the south. At 2:15 p. m. the lake had subsided about a foot and there was much fountaining and high spurting in the southeast cave. At 2:45 p. m. from the west station, the northeast cascade could be seen still in action and the length of the ledge over which the lava-fall plunged was fully 100 feet. Surface skins were carried over this fall and downward at an angle beyond into a cavern at the base of the cliff which was thus half tunnel and half pit. It appears to have been in fact an inclined tunnel ending in a pit cauldron.

On March 6 at 11 a. m., the lake was five feet below the inner bench and there was increased fountaining in and around the lake with marked gas puffing. The two cascades had ceased action and all signs pointed to rising conditions. At 4:30 p. m. the lake was brimming at the level of the inner ledge and fountains were numerous.

On Wednesday, March 7, at 1:30 p. m., the lake was again at the inner floor level and actively fountaining. At 2 p. m. a large border grotto at the west cove showed intense fountaining and lava spurting with much plashing and puffing noise. At 5 p. m., seen from the east, the lake showed glowing overflows in the east and southeast coves and marked spatter ramparts in process of building on the west, northeast and southeast. The entrance to the southeast channel had narrowed through construction of the border bench. A slight fall of rock at 5:15 p. m. took place, from the southeast inner cliff into the lake.

On March 8, at 4:30 p. m., the lake was still higher and had been building and widening the inner bench. At the moment its surface was two feet below the bench, and there were six fountains which were noisily blowing and rumbling. Grottoes were now in process of construction at the southeast, northeast, north, west and southwest, all of these being places of previously revealed sinkholes or tunnels below. The main outward streaming into the lake was now entirely from the northwest arm. At the northeast

WEEKLY BULLETIN
of the
Hawaiian Volcano Observatory

Published Monthly at Honolulu, Hawaii, by the Hawaiian Volcano Research Association

L. W. de Vis-Norton........Secretary

Entered as second-class matter January 20, 1914, at the post-office at Honolulu, Hawaii. under the Act of August 24, 1912.

a very large curtained grotto had formed, hung with long stalactites. At the tunnel leading under the inner cliff to the north pit there was continuous fountaining, the lava of the lake being above the top of the arch. Within the north pit there was slow streaming northward to a fountaining grotto within the pit on its north side. Above there was much recent rock-fall on the floor under the old north rest house. The northwest pond no longer showed a pit but in its place was a low smoking cone with stained overflows. The west pit had lengthened by collapsing walls north and south and showed a well three feet across in its bottom containing cherry red incandescent lava which was quiet but occasionally emitted a puff from under its mobile crust. There was an overflow rim around the well. The broken walls of this pit, formed as glistening black glassy overflows only a few months since, were now revealed oxidized through and through to limonite and hematite, yellow and red iron oxides.

Just above the bank of the west cove there had been built a large irregular cone stained sulphur yellow which was crackling, spurting and all glowing through crevices, while a lava fountain pounded in the inner cupola. Just below it at the lake shore was a spatter rampart containing a grotto frequently active. The greatest crackling noise and sharpest blasts from the upper cone happened when this grotto fountain was active. Blue fume rose from both places.

There were other small fountains at various places. The streaming was lively, flames were numerous, the south cone was fuming and the greatest noise came from the north and northeast.

Measurements on Friday, March 9, 1917, made the depression of the lake 102 feet below the southeast margin of the pit. The heights of the crags above the lake were:

East crag, 64 feet.
Crag mass, 63 feet.
Old south island, 23 feet.
New east island, 43 feet.
Central peninsula, 28 feet.
Southwest crag, 72 feet.
Southwest summit of south island mass, 36 feet.

These measurements made the east crag stationary since March 2, the new east island two feet higher than on that date and the crag mass three feet lower.

On the morning of March 9 the lake fluctuated in height between the bench level and about one foot below it. At intervals of about twenty minutes, after quiet accumulation of crust, large fountains would burst in the southeast channel and migrate southward to the bank. The lake would inflate, rise and stagnate during the accumulation, but during the explosion it would sink with rapid acceleration of streaming. During the stagnant spells there would be two or three border fountains active, but during the rapid times there were six or seven fountains. At the southeast cove there was some spattering overflow. Central fountains were more numerous than of late in the three main arms of the lake. The border fountaining over the north tunnel had ceased.

At noon the writer descended to the northeast bench and close inspection of the new island mass revealed the fact that the lower rock which had been pushed up out of the lake was massive and rough and wholly without the horizontal bedding exhibited by the lava flows above. This new island is extraordinarily like the lava plug or dome which was lifted above the summit of Tarumai volcano in north Japan in 1909.

The floor of the northeast bench of January was considerably collapsed and crevassed. Looking down into the north pit, which is about 50 feet in diameter, a very hot churning lava pool was seen 40 feet below the rim, coated with thin black sinks, and heavy fountains pounded against the north and northeast walls. These walls showed spatter layers and stalactites, but very slight grotto overhang. The north grotto here was more of a cavern a few days ago when the lake was lower. The streaming of the pool was northward, changing to a slow rotary movement counter-clockwise.

In the afternoon the lake subsided ten feet and recovered to a level about five feet below the bench.

The following report from the Whitney Laboratory of Seismology is submitted by Mr. H. O. Wood:

During the week-interval ending with March 9 no earthquakes have been registered. The seismographic amplitudes of microseismic motion and of volcanic vibration have decreased from large or moderately large values in the early part of the interval ot values about normal in the latter part of the interval. This is complicated with disturbances of considerable seismographic magnitude due to very strong winds in the early part of the week. These winds also produced pen shifts in the sense of tilting of considerable amount. Aside from these there have been no noteworthy movements of this kind. At the end of the week the pen-positions are normal for the present time.

Technology Station, March 17, 1917.

During the week ending March 16, 1917, the lava of Halemaumau has subsided about 30 feet with spectacular avalanches of debris from both the upper and inner walls. At the end of the week there has been slight recovery with building of a new inner bench. The sudden subsidence of March 11 to 15, following a temporary rise, is in accordance with previous experience at Kilauea at the time of the equinox in March and September.

On Saturday, March 10, 1917, at 2 p. m., the lake surface was about five feet below the inner bench and five border fountains were in action respectively northwest, northeast, southwest, west and southeast. Streaming was vigorous toward the southeast and southwest. There was activity in the north pit and the grotto of the southeast cove was cracking. A flame played above the west cone and heavy white smoke rose from the northeast wall. Subsidence started on this afternoon, at 4 p. m. the lake was two feet lower and a large fragment fell from the crag mass into the lake, starting much fountaining. At 4:15 p. m. a similar avalanche fell from the north inner wall into the lake, followed ten minutes later by a slide from the north outer wall under the old rest house. The north pit was evidently collapsing.

This was confirmed the next day, March 11, when the most subsidence occurred, accompanied by avalanches and small earthquakes. The lava lake sank about 20 feet, violent fountaining was generated by the avalanches and the arch over the channel leading to the north pit collapsed leaving the pit a tumbled chasm in the bench open on the lake side. At 10:45 a. m. the pinnacled point extending westward from the new island collapsed into the lake and about twenty fountains were generated thereby. At 10:35 a. m. a block dropped into the streaming southeast channel from its north side, again starting much fountaining. At 10:45 there was a slide from the north side of the crag mass. At 11:10 another fell from the north inner wall. At 12:05 p. m. part of the northwest wall collapsed and at 12:20 the north side of the north pit fell in. At 1:10 p. m. an immense tumble of rock defaced the whole eastern aspect of the crag mass, followed by a great avalanche from the northwest bench. The resulting fountaining lasted over an hour. At 1:15 p. m. the arch leading from the lake to the north pit collapsed so that that pit became a cove of the lake. After 1:30 p. m. incessant avalanching enlarged the chasm so formed and it was evident that the whole northern inner bench of 1917 was breaking away from a small remnant left clinging to the wall of Halemaumau. A semicircular crevasse bounded the subsiding blocks on the northeast, north and northwest, this crack being concentric with the pit and extending almost continuously from the northeast floor around to the west pond. The northwestern block was toppling outward toward the northwest arm leaving a wide gaping fissure north of it.

On March 12 at 11:30 a. m. the lake appeared 20 feet below the inner bench and its surface was very quiet. At 11:45 there was a heavy tumble of rock from the high rim near the south station and on the evening of this day a still heavier fall west of the south station. About 12:30 p. m. avalanches could be heard in many directions including portions of the 1894 bench. At 2:30 p. m. there was a heavy fall into the lake from the northeast followed by fountaining for an hour. By this time the lava of the former north pit was completely smothered by avalanche debris in the chasm there.

On March 13 at 2:30 p. m., the lake appeared 30 feet below the inner bench and again very quiet and crusted, with avalanches still falling. At 3 p. m. there was a fall from the east side of the crag mass. At 5 p. m. the rush of the current from the main lake to the southeast cove through the channel was very swift with tremendous inrush and fountaining southeast; there was no fountaining elsewhere. At 7:30 p. m. a portion of the southeast bench fell noisily.

On Wednesday, March 14, inspection showed that the fumes had increased; the crag mass and inner islands had strongly subsided with the lava column. The only portions of the bench which remained high were around the margins. The inner bench appeared about 25 feet high, caverns had developed under the floors beside the new east and central islands showing that these connecting isthmuses were really only crusts thickened downward. Streaming was now changed, the current pouring from a crust at the west cove southeastward and northward. The southwest cove was crusted over. Eight fountains were in action and the lake was rising with noises of puffing and plashing. The great rock falls from the crag mass had built a new central promontory extending eastward. There was a cove with occasional inflow on the northeast. To the large cavern opening eastward, adjacent to the central island, there was rapid inflow which terminated in interior fountaining and enormous stalactites like clustered organ pipes had accumulated near the entrance.

The southeast bench was cracked near the margin and parting from the wall of the pit in such a way as to appear as though it were actually rising. The gulch below the south station had widened and the south high rim of the pit had greatly fallen away to a tumble of talus below. The southwest crags had subsided and there were new crevasses back of them. The west pit showed new broken extensions but there was still a pot of live lava in its bottom. The east crag had sunk below the level of the southeast bench and the northeast floor was sinking with it. At 1:30 p. m. there was strong fountaining at the east cove. At 2:45 thirteen fountains were in action and most numerous toward the north.

On March 15 from 4 to 6 p. m., the lake appeared low, eight fountains were in action, there was inrush to the central cavern and explosions within it expelled flames and made strong waves which surged outward. There was fountaining against the south base of the new island and occasional shore fountaining in the southeast cove. In the southwest cove a tunnel from under the south floor, where the February cascade torrent was, showed outward streaming from the pit under the south cone. The streaming in the lake was from sources southwest, west and northwest toward fountains at the northeast base of the crag mass, and at the north, northeast and southeast walls. In general the tops of the crags, islands and benches appeared to be approaching a common level.

A circuit of the pit revealed the following: From the east, the northeast floor was seen to have sunken farther, leaving a shelf under the 1894 bench. From the north, the northern chasm was seen to be a smoky tumble of rock. From the northwest, there was seen a narrow bench remnant below against the wall at the January level, but the broad floor beyond had sagged toward the lake and downward. From the west, the slope of new lava from the west niche to the northwest pond was seen to have cracked and subsided so as to open a crevasse at the old cliff under the west niche. The northwest pond was re-established at its old location as an oval longish pool of quiet glowing lava in a pit and there was blowing and fountaining at its southwest end. Occasionally the surface would crack and founder. Red glowing places were seen among the cracks north, northwest and west, and some of the surface lumps of pahoehoe lava, several months old, were glowing cherry red in places removed from deep cracking, as though reheated through small crevices.

From the southwest, the west pond was seen to contain a rising pool of red hot lava with a flaming blow-hole puffing above its east border. The blowing increased and a small festooned flow emerged from the crusts on the surface of the pool.

Measurement on Friday, March 16, 1917, showed that the lake at the central promontory was depressed 129 feet below the southeast rim, indicating a subsidence of 27 feet in seven days. From 9 to 11 a. m. the lake was rising and falling a few feet, there were four or five fountains in action, including some central fountains. A new narrow bench around most of the lake, especially conspicuous on the north and west, showed that rising was in progress. There were new rampart grottoes at the east cove and against the central promontory of the crag mass. The new island showed tendency to break along two vertical cracks. The central cavern was still flaming and exploding. There were occasional small avalanches and infalling spatter rims, one of the former tumbling from the southwest crags to the shore of the lake. There was much bombardment at the base of the north cliff. Smoke rose densely from the south cone and the north and northwest inner walls.

The following report from the Whitney Laboratory of Seismology is submitted by Mr. H. O. Wood:

During the week ending with March 16 eight local earthquakes have been registered, and two or three doubtful wave-groups. Three of the shocks were of perceptible magnitude. Two were felt in the vicinity of the Volcano House and the Observatory—one quite sharply. The third was strong enough to rattle windows but no vibration was felt. The origins of these were closer at hand than is usual with shocks registered here, yet well beyond the limits of the crater region. Slight but sharply marked subsidence of the lava took place at about the same time, with fracture and partial collapse of considerable parts of the 1917 bench. The seismographic amplitudes of microseismic motion and that of volcanic vibrations have approximated normal values throughout the week. There has been no conspicuous pen shift in the sense of tilt apart from the diurnal fluctuation.

Technology Station, March 24, 1917.

During the week ending March 23, 1917, the lava continued sinking with border cascading southeast, until the evening of March 20 when the depression of the lake below the rim of the pit was at least 135 feet. At that time all signs of subsidence ceased quite suddenly and rising ensued at a rate estimated five feet per day, and continued steadily thereafter. The turning point occurred at the equinox. A remarkable discovery which was made by descending to the eastern lower bench, is that the base of the new island is composed of aa lava. This was the island which rose suddenly out of the bottom of the lake on February 18 and showed a massive lower portion capped by horizontal layers of pahoehoe above. This discovery checks with the belief that the rising lava column of Kilauea, which so rapidly filled the pit after the aa lava flows of Mauna Loa ceased flowing in June of 1916, is identical through subterranean connections in the deep region, with the column that fed Mauna Loa.

On Saturday, March 17, 1917, at 3 p. m., the central cavern was exploding and there were about five fountains in action including a row of spatter grottoes forming a high rampart along the southwest margin of the southeast cove. The streaming was southeastward originating in the southwest cove which was crusted over. It was evident that there had been a heavy fall of rocks into the southeast cove from the high southeast bench, for the whole southern bottom area or lower floor was plastered with a splash of fresh lava as far as the south cone and high up the south side of the old south island. Lesser wave markings of this kind appeared on the banks of the wide southeastern stream channel. The northeast bench showed evidence of further subsidence leaving a secondary ledge below the 1894 wall. The east crag had sunk lower and the east end of the southeast bench showed overhang with a loose slab protruding below. At the northeastern base of the crag-mass a very large slab had broken away and stood out above the lake as a pinnacle. The north chasm had subsided still more. A new tumble of rocks had fallen from the south side of the new island and the debris slope lay at such an angle as to indicate that the stream channel into which it fell was shallow. This fall took place on the previous evening.

On March 18 at 5:15 p. m. the wind was from the south and the pit very smoky. Streaming from northwest and west terminated at the southeast in a torrent which plunged in a tremendous cascade downward, of vivid orange color, at the sinkhole of the southeast cove. On the brink of the final plunge the lava surged up in a high wave with many bubble fountains and travelled with great speed. The noise was a heavy roar. Gusts of suffocating blue fume rose from the abyss. There were five fountains northwest and a furious one in a grotto under the north bench. The lake was temporarily rising with narrowing of the glow rim and drowning of stalactites at the lake margin. March 19 was very rainy.

On March 20 at 2:40 p. m. the cascade was still tumbling at the southeast cove with great rapidity. At 4:15 p. m. from the northeast a heavy avalanche was seen to fall from the southeast bench into the lake and start extensive fountaining with breaking up of the crusts in the channel and the southeast cove. Such are the avalanches which made the wave marks. At 4:40 p. m. another heavy slide fell from the south bench of 1917. Here a long tumbled slope has gullied the bench back under the south station, and extends down to the southern lower floor, which was the bottom of the lake in January, and the scene of the great cascade sinkhole of February 14, now a cone. At 5:30 p. m. from the east station it became evident that pronounced rising had started and at 6 p. m. there was overflow at the east cove and then the southeast cascade pot filled up and brought the cataract to an end.

The next day, March 21, at 11:30 a. m. from the southeast, the lake was seen to be rising vigorously and overflowing the south bottom from the southeast cove, the overflows reaching a maximum about noon. The east and west coves were also overflooded. Streaming was to the southeast and northeast. Spatter niches of crescent shape were building east, southeast, southwest, against the north side of the central promontory, northeast and northwest. The south cone was still in place. The flows on the south floor poured westward on both sides of the spatter crescent there and reached the south cone. The central cavern was submerged but there was fountaining above its entrance. The southern islands appeared tipping eastward. Wave splash now plastered the whole of the old south island. Under the south station great slabs of old wall rock were splitting away, and the southwest crags were settling back to a horizontal position. From the southwest the west pond was seen in its ragged pit to be a single continuous fountain of the artesian or uprising variety, with concentric festoons of pahoehoe crust around, which were being pushed away rather than engulfed. The west cone was submerged by the growth of the west cove and out in the lake were the southwest islet, low and flat, and another smaller one nearer shore. The tunnel leading from the southwest cove to the south cone could be seen with crusts at its entrance. The southwest spatter crescent just west of here become active only at intervals. The northwest pond had risen and was crusted over. Up the slope west of it was a bright hot yellow fuming solfataric area and still nearer the west wall could be seen in daylight the pahoehoe lumps which glowed at night (March 15), now slightly whitened by solfataric action. The northwest arm was flooded and showed some streaming from the lake. After 12 noon floods of lava poured from the lake into the depression of the north chasm past a

Halemaumau from the S.E., 4:30 p.m. March 8, 1917. —Photo. Jaggar.

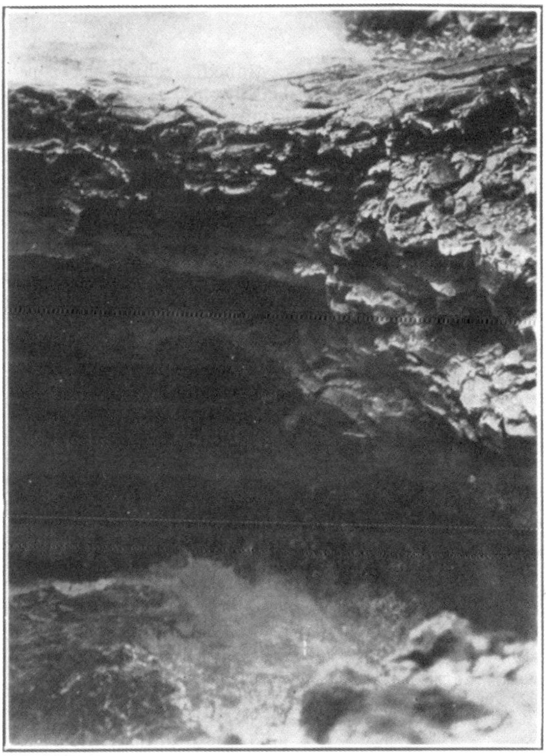

March 9, 1917, 1 p.m. Looking northwest down into fountaining grotto of north pit from its rim, on the January bench. —Photo. Jaggar.

March 9, 1917. Looking south at old South Island, which had surmounted rim of pit in January. —Photo Jaggar.

spatter crescent at its mouth. There were small flows at the lake margin pushing in at the west and northwest coves. The lake was rising, covered with quiet crusts and fountaining was limited to the spatter niches. At 1:30 p. m. the lake was brimming level with the lower bench, with fountaining in the east cove and several fountains in the northern region. In the southeast cove the large grotto niche was at the site of the previous cascade. At 5:30 p. m. there were fifteen fountains, and at 5:45 a fountain started in the east cove.

At 1:30 p. m. on March 22 the lava was level with the bench but about 2:30 p. m. it subsided three feet with much fountaining. The fumes from the pit had greatly diminished. From 5 to 6 p. m. the lake was overflowing so that floods from the east and west joined across the south bottom, those from the west finally dominating the eastern ones as though the tilt eastward of the south island mass determined a slope in that direction. Spatter niches were blowing and spraying southeast, southwest, north, northeast, east and at the central promontory. Glow could be seen over the northwest pond. Streaming was to the southeast and northeast and a very active grotto was throwing high jets under the northeast inner wall. Sinking spells were rare. There were occasional central fountains in the north cove which migrated eastward. Great quantities of Pele's hair were being made.

At 7 p. m. the lava was overflowing from the west cove to the northwest pond. From 10 to 12 p. m. there were spells of rising and sinking, each occupying 20 to 30 minutes, with the rising spells longer than the sinking ones. About 11:30 p. m. a marked subsidence of about two feet developed the form of the true lake and showed the dimmer glow lines of bench flows south and east. In the lake itself all the crusts broke up while twelve or fifteen fountains burst into action. At 10:45 p. m. there was a fall from the southeast January bench into the lake, making a great splash which plastered the old south island and broke up all the crusts of that region. Excessively brilliant fountaining at the east base of the old south island followed the avalanche, while the southeast grotto became quiet. The south cone was now completely submerged. From the northwest pond a stream poured southward, making a glowing festooned current around the end of the crag-mass into the west cove. The southwest cove was crusted and during rising spells dark crusts formed over most of the lake.

At 2 p. m. on Friday, March 23, 1917, from the east the lake was seen to be two feet below the bench and very quiet, with only three fountains in action. At 2:30 p. m. from the south station the west cove was seen to extend all over the northwest pond depression, with one active fountain over the northwest pond vent.

The following report from the Whitney Laboratory of Seismology is submitted by Mr. H. O. Wood:

During the week ending with March 23 one very feeble earthquake probably a near-shock, though the early phases are too indistinctly registered for this to be certain—has been registered. The seismographic amplitude of microseismic motion has been somewhat larger than usual particularly in the early part of the week. The seismographic amplitudes of volcanic vibration have been somewhat larger than normal—especially in prolonged storms in the latter part of the interval. Early in the week-interval, accompanying a strong Kona wind, there was a pronounced shirt of the pens in the sense of tilt to westward; later there was reverse shifting almost completely counteracting this.

Technology Station, March 31, 1917.

During the week ending March 20, 1917, the lava of Halemaumau has oscillated through a range of 20 feet about a depression of approximately 110 feet below the rim of the pit. A pronounced inner bench from the rising activity of the previous week tends to constrict the active lake so that during the present week the inner pit has appeared like a group of three convergent gorges ten to twenty feet deep, the former islands rising as hills within Halemaumau above the inner plateau level. Viewed from this lower flat, the lake has appeared much like the paintings of Tavernier and Furneaux, with extraordinary overhanging bluffs, mushroom islets and marvelous reflected lights and irridescent fumes in the evening.

On Saturday, March 24, after 3:30 p. m., the lake surface was streaming from dark skins on the north and northwest to the west, southwest and southeast. A large half-dome grotto had built at the head of the west cove and the lava flows which had there connected the northwest pond with the lake were now above the lake. The southeast spatter cone had become a high open beehive, flaring and spurting. Heavy falls from the bank took place on opposite sides of the southeast channel. Where the south cone had been there was now only a little smoke through the crust. Looking from the west station the northwest pond region was seen to be covered with crusted flows with a ring-shaped cone spurting on the southwest side. The west pond was also crusted, with a glowing filagree cone and a flaming, hissing orifice east of it. Over the great west dome tremendous splashes of lava were thrown. From the northwest station glow could be seen in the bench northwest and north and the lake on this side was crusted over and no fountaining whatever was going on at the northeast. Apparently the sharp rise had reversed the streaming against the west bank. The north chasm contained a wide area of crusted flows and glow could be seen in cracks of the northeast bench.

A glowing stream poured rapidly along the surface of the lake to the southeast grotto and a small stick of wood thrown in at this point plunged below the thin skin and burned in spasms. The spasmodic lines of flame, bursting through the skin at short intervals as the stick beneath was carried down the current, punctured the surface skin at points progressively farther and farther downstream showing that the undercurrent moved more swiftly than the skin.

On this day, with the aid of men of Company H, 25th U. S. infantry, the writer sounded the channel off the south side of the east island. The half-inch pipe was plunged into the channel and bowed downstream southeastward with the current, but went to the bottom, sticking in stiff material in the lower five or six feet. Forty-six feet of the pipe went below the surface at an angle estimated 40°, making the depth of channel 29 feet. This checks with the supposition that the February subsidence made the lake more shallow for at the end of January the depth was 45 feet.

On March 25 and 26 the lake reacted from its recent rise and subsided. On March 26 there was cascading into the southeast sinkhole. At 4 p. m. on March 27 the lake was depressed 15 feet below its newly constructed inner bench. All around it were vertical and strongly overhanging walls. There was strong overhang beneath the southeast bench and under the old south island, the central cavern was again open and another at the east cove, and the southwest islet was overhanging on all sides like a mushroom. It had evidently increased its surface area as the lake rose. There was general overhang on the west and southwest. Six to eight fountains were in action, streaming was out from the northwest arm, there was a glowing filagree cone on the bench at the east cove and others at the northwest and west ponds. These ponds were crusted but not collapsed. The subsidence appeared to affect chiefly the liquid lake for no avalanches were produced such as occur when the benches subside.

The writer descended the west niche and found his way to the northwest pond and the south end of the crag-mass. Here it was possible to walk out on the lower bench and look into the great west half-dome. It was now raised and inactive, exhibited only a slight niche with stalactites on the lake side, and a vertical wall beneath. The southwest islet mushroom was a most extraordinary object out in the lake, 15 feet high and 50 feet long on the summit but not more than half that length at the lake level. The lake showed quiet, swelling, blistered crusts, fountains were playing in curtained grottoes southwest, the streaming was very slow and the heat was strong.

Returning to the upper bench; I followed around the January floor on the north to the east station. An examination of Perret's cave showed that it was 60 feet deep and ended in a tumble of rocks. Great quantities of yellow-stained alum were forming amid dripping water. Cavern stalactites from the roof were coated with crystals of gypsum and there were driblet cones on the floor which was mossy with Pele's hair.

On the northeast side of the lake there were lower benches of downsunken floor blocks. Fumes had greatly increased over Halemaumau, a dozen places yielding dense white, but breathable, smoke columns. The southeast cone, however, was flaming and producing irrespirable sulphur fume and similar fumes were rising from the glow cones and the southwest grottoes.

On the afternoon of March 28 the lake was lower with inner walls 20 feet high. There was a heavy fall into the southeast channel from the central peninsula. The central cavern was high and deep and a current was rushing into it. The entire bench south of the crag-mass where Alex Lancaster and the writer had stood on the previous day, had fallen into the lake, wrecking the large half-dome and the mushroom islet. The east and southeast cones were less active, there were five or six fountains, streaming was rapid to the southeast and smoke had increased.

At 4:30 p. m. temperature measurements were made with Seger cones at the orifices of the east cone on the lower bench. This cone was about ten feet back from the east cove over the tunnel there. It was about two feet high and ten feet across, consisting of broken stained crusts. The crevices showed a bright cherry red interior by daylight and there was slight blue flame, but no puffing. The glow was distinctly less bright than that of the bright lines on the lake. Seger cones were attached singly by wire to the end of an iron pipe and thrust into the glow about three inches through a crack two inches across. The Seger cone in each test was left heating for five minutes. It would become red hot, of the color of the glow chamber, in about one minute. Four Seger cones were tried as follows:

Seger cone of fusing point 1150° C—no effect.

Seger cone of fusing point 990° C—no effect.

Seger cone of fusing point 920° C—blistered.

Seger cone of fusing point 890° C—end bent down, cone blistered and partially melted within the first two minutes.

Temperature of glow chamber hence over 920° C. This filagree cone was brighter on the day before and almost completely dark on the day following this test.

This careful measurement was of a glowing cavity about the color of the interior of the benches when they break open. As the zigzag lines of the lake crust are brighter, their temperature must be higher than 920° C. As the January measurements made the temperature of the lake three feet below the bright lines much lower than this, we are confronted at once with the query, are not the bright lines heated by oxidizing gases, and is not the thermal gradient of the lava at the actual surface an extraordinarily steep one?

On March 29 at 3 p. m. the lake was rising, with eight to ten fountains and the inner bench fifteen feet high. Streaming was now outward from both the northwest and southwest coves. The central cavern was quiet and appeared to connect through to the southwest cove by a tunnel, for there was fountaining at the other end of the isthmus platform joining the central peninsula with the south island mass. The southwest cove was crusted over and contained two small islets. The west pit showed some subsidence of its crusted pond but its cone and that of the northwest pond were still glowing. There was much bubble fountaining. An interesting feature of the aa surface exhibited in section on the east and west walls of the east island which rose so suddenly February 18, is that this aa shows a curved or humped surface lower on the east and higher on the west, unconformable beneath the bedded pahoehoe layers above. It thus appears at the time of its rising to have swollen up as a mound which sloped towards the sinking east crag; this mound appeared as a shoal in the lake and was plastered by the lake with chilled layers of pahoehoe as a low islet; when the east crag sank suddenly, this hump of aa in the lake bottom rose and produced the table island.

On Friday, March 30, 1917, at 3 p. m., the lake was 12 feet below the inner bench, eight fountains were in action, and very rapid building of border niches was in progress. Quiet crusts covered the lake, there was increased streaming in the late afternoon, small overflows built a new inner bench southeast, east and southwest, and a large spectacular shore cone was built during the afternoon at the east cove. Streaming was outward from the west and northwest and the southwest islets were nearly submerged. Fumes were thinner. A central fountain broke at intervals north of the junction point of the three arms of the lake. There were spatter grottoes northeast, southwest, east and at three points southeast.

At 4:30 p. m. with the aid of volunteer assistants, a temperature measurement was made of the standing bright line near the northeast margin of the stream pouring southeastward along the surface of the lake through the southeast channel. Five Seger cones of fusibilities 830°, 860°, 950°, 970°, and 1010° C were placed in the plugged end of a one-half inch black iron pipe. The pipe was sixty feet long. The end was dabbled in the bright fluid melt of the zigzag line for five minutes, not more than twelve inches of the end of the pipe being allowed at any time to sink beneath the surface of the lake. When the pipe tended to be swept aside and crusted, it was moved back into the bright part, and no fountains broke against it except the small bubblings characteristic of such bright lines.

The experiment was completely successful, for the cones 830° and 860° were fused to powder, 950° was fumed, 970° bent, and 1010° blistered. The temperature was thus approximately 1020° C, as the next cone in series (1030°) would probably have been unaffected. The bright lines are hence at least 100° hotter than the cherry red glow of the bench magma measured March 28 and at least 250° hotter than the lake magma three feet below the surface, as measured in January.

This astonishing surface gradient accouts for some of the discrepancies of the January experiments, when measurement with thermo-couple just at the lake surface gave 1000°+ and measurement with Seger cones plunged three to four feet below the surface and left there for as long as eleven minutes failed to show any trace of fusion on a cone fusible at 770° C. The conclusion is unavoidable that the bright lines are minutely fountaining and flaming and are heated by union of air with escaping combustible gases.

The rapid growth of the east cove shore cone on this afternoon, March 30, was remarkable. At 2 p. m. it was a slight spatter crescent half circling a niche in the shore line where blowing, flaming, spurting, and extensive spinning of Pele's hair was going on with great vigor. So rapidly did it pile up that by 7 p. m. the circle of construction had closed on the lake side making a cone six feet high and ten feet across the base, with an orifice two feet in diameter in the summit where the violent spattering had given place to a flame that rose in puffs one to two feet above the hole and was of a light greenish violet color. Occasional flings of lava surmounted the rim but the violent spurting had stopped. The next morning the cone was destroyed.

The following report from the Whitney Laboratory of Seismology is submitted by Mr. H. O. Wood:

During the week ending with March 30 three local shocks of small seismographic amplitude have been registered. Besides these some twenty-five to thirty earth-jars of a peculiar kind have been noted. These are not earthquakes as ordinarily interpreted—nor groups of conspicuous waves of volcanic vibration as usually manifested. All have been of very brief duration with abrupt beginnings and no division into phases. The periods have been too short for measurement on records as closely written as ours, and their seismographic amplitudes have been very small. No explanation of their meaning is suggested. But they are movements of exceptionally feeble sort and of very local origin.

Registration of microseismic motion and of that of volcanic vibration has been normal and without noteworthy peculiaries. There has been a sharp shift in the sense of tilt to eastward with no corresponding change in the north-south component.

Very respectfully,

T. A. JAGGAR, JR., Director.

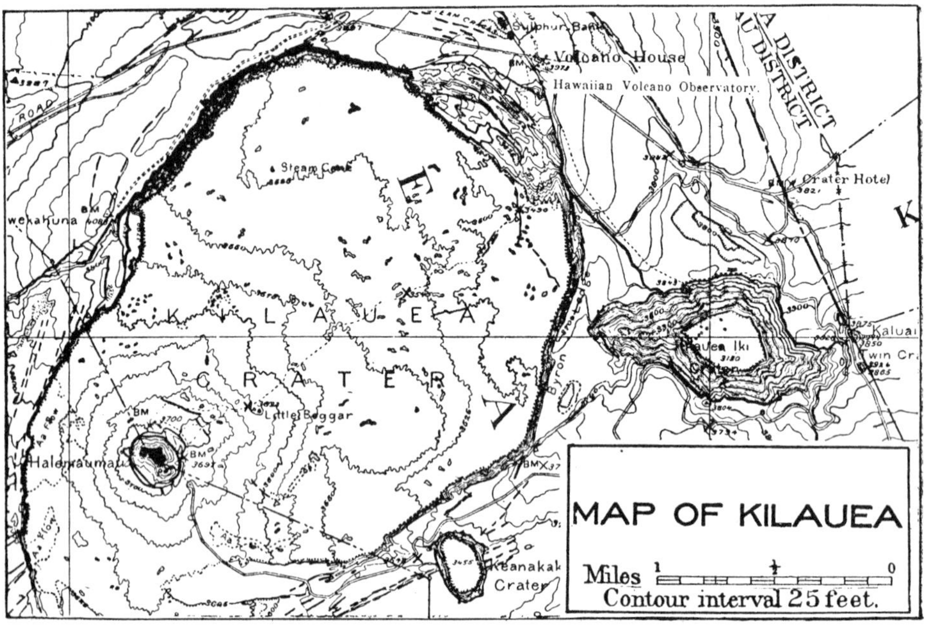

HAWAIIAN VOLCANO RESEARCH ASSOCIATION.

This society is a voluntary one, made up of subscribers to scientific work which is being executed by the Massachusetts Institute of Technology.

In 1917 there are about 150 subscribers in Hawaii and elsewhere, firms and individuals. A group of firms and persons in Hilo built the main observatory building in the spring of 1912. Publications to date have been weekly reports since the summer of 1911, now reprinted in Honolulu in monthly form. The Massachusetts Institute of Technology will publish annual reports, of which the introductory number was printed in 1912.

The weekly bulletin as it appears in the Advertiser is reprinted as a leaflet and sent to regular annual subscribers to the work of the Association. L. A. Thurston is president of the Board of Directors of the Association, and R. W. Shingle is treasurer. New subscribers who are interested in volcanoes will be welcomed in the Association. The Association aims: (1) To record volcanic activity and earthquakes in Hawaii; (2) to attract scientific men hither for special studies; (3) to promote the establishment of volcano observatories all over the world. The annual dues of regular members are $5; patrons of the Association subscribe larger amounts.

WHITNEY LABORATORY OF SEISMOLOGY.

The Whitney Laboratory of Seismology is equipped with two Bosch-Omori 100 kg tromometers registering N-S and E-W motion, a heavy Omori tromometer registering E-W motion, and an Omori "ordinary Seismograph" designed for registering strong earthquakes in all three components of motion. These are seated on concrete piers in a closed basement room having practically constant temperature, beneath the chief Observatory building near the hotel. Time is referred to a rated chronometer, checked at intervals by solar observations with a transit. Both instruments are loaned by the College of Hawaii. Hawaiian standard time (H. S. T.) is 10 hrs. 30 min. slower than Greenwich time.

CANCANI SCALE OF SEISMIC INTENSITY.

Expressed by accelerations measured in millimeters per second per second.

I.	Instrumental	0.0	2.5
II.	Very slight	2.5	5.0
III.	Slight	5.0	10.0
IV.	Sensible, mediocre	10.0	25.0
V.	Rather strong	25.0	50.0
VI.	Strong	50.0	100.0
VII.	Very strong	100.0	250.0
VIII.	Ruinous	250.0	500.0
IX.	Disastrous	500.0	1000.0
X.	Very disastrous	1000.0	2500.0
XI.	Catastrophic	2500.0	5000.0
XII.	Great catastrophe	5000.0	10000.0

Grade IV. is ordinarily the minimum perceived by the senses; and in grade XII. the acceleration, or rate of change of motion (jerk) reaches that of terrestrial gravitation.

In the standard form of report the maximum intensity or acceleration, designated by the symbol a, or max. a, is given in the conventional unit, **the milligal.** The milligal is a measure of acceleration, such that 1 milligal = 1/100 mm. per sec. per sec. = 10 μ per sec. per sec. The Cancani scale, here defined in terms of millimeters per sec. per sec., can therefore be expressed in **milligals** by multiplying **each of the numbers by 100.**

WEEKLY BULLETIN
OF THE
Hawaiian Volcano Observatory

Vol. V. HONOLULU, HAWAII, APRIL, 1917. No. 4

Technology Station, April 7, 1917.

During the week ending April 6, 1917, the lava of Halemaumau has risen slightly with overflows on the south, west and east, but the depression of the lake is still over one hundred feet. The evidence of rising has been erratic as in the autumn of 1916 and the bench crags are again rising. This rising of the crags is now symmetrical about a central point in the pit. This central point is the meeting place of three arms of the lake which lie at angles of 120° to each other. Between these arms are sectors of bench which are sinking around the circumference of the pit and lifting their convergent points near the center. The marginal sinking is started apparently by weight of the overflows and increased by weight of debris from the old benches and from the outer walls. As a result the south island peninsula, the crag-mass and the east island are now all rising, and the east, southwest and northwest floors are sinking. The walls of the inner pit adjacent to the lake, during one of the temporary sinkings, are therefore highest near the center of the pit. As usual the northwest and west ponds are the conduits of uprising liquid lava.

During the week, experiments in measurement of temperature in the depths of the lake have been continued, with the aid of Co. I, 25th Infantry, 4th Co. Coast Artillery, Hilo Boarding School students, and voluntary assistants. The net result of these measurements, made with Seger cones, is that the temperature of the surface of the lake is 1020° C which is 100° C hotter than the lava four feet down; below that point the temperature rises at the rate of 9° C per foot to a depth of 20 feet, the temperature at that depth being approximately 1070° C. Experiments will be continued to determine, if possible, the temperature of the lake bottom and details of the remainder of this remarkable thermal gradient.

On the morning of March 31st, 1917, the lake continued relatively low and sinking during the day, the inner bench walls rising about 15 feet above the liquid lava. At times eight fountains were in action, a large spatter grotto and two islets were seen in the southwest cove; elsewhere a new inner bench about three feet high was being constructed. The cone in the east cove had been destroyed and was covered with slabs from a rise of the previous night. Streaming was mostly slow and there were occasional falls of the spatter bench.

On April 1, at 11 a. m., the lake was slowly rising with few fountains and an inner bench about five feet high. At noon fountaining had increased and the lake had risen to within one foot of overflow. At 4:15 p. m. a collapse northeast developed many fountains and at 6:30 p. m. a similar fall took place on the southwest side of the east island so as to make commotion in the streaming channel there.

On April 2, at 2:30 p. m., the inner walls were five feet high and streaming continued from northwest to southwest and southeast. There was much activity. At 2:50 p. m. portions of the bench on the northeast side of the central peninsula fell into the channel. Fourteen fountains were counted exploding at one time. At 4 p. m. the lake was brimming level with the inner floor on the east.

On April 3 in the morning, the lake was overflowing, and at 2:30 p. m. the inner wall was again five feet high and five fountains were in action, especially at the grottoes east and southeast. At 3 p. m. rapid rising began,

WEEKLY BULLETIN
of the
Hawaiian Volcano Observatory

Published Monthly at Honolulu, Hawaii, by the Hawaiian Volcano Research Association

L. W. de Vis-Norton........Secretary

Entered as second-class matter January 20, 1914, at the post-office at Honolulu, Hawaii. under the Act of August 24, 1912.

at 3:40 p. m. the lake was brimming level with the inner benches, and at 4:20 p. m. it was overflowing at the east cove. At 4:40 p. m. overflows were in progress on all sides, the peninsula crags all appearing surrounded by molten lava and from fifteen to twenty fountains were in action. In the evening the glowing flows lay on the east, south, west and northwest floors but the lake was about three feet down. Eight to ten fountains were in action and the current rushed swiftly from the north bay to the southwest cove. In the southeast channel streaming was more sluggish. Fountains were conspicuous northeast and southeast, in the central region, and on both sides of the southwest cove. A blue flame was flaring above the northwest cone. An overflow had poured from the west corner of the lake into the northwest pond depression.

On April 4 the lake was high but not overflowing. It showed some fresh overspatter at the east cove. There was still much fume. Examination of the western region at 3:30 p. m. showed the west pond to be high, active and level with the floor around it and the northwest cone was spurting and making loud blowing noises.

On April 5 from 10 to 12 a. m. the conditions of activity were much the same and the lake high with five or six fountains in action. At noon and thereafter there was a small trickling overflow in the eastern gulch. In the depression filled with fresh flows on the east side of the east island there was a ridge crossing the flows in a curve from the east cove northward showing that the east island mass was rising while the old northeast bench to the east of it was sinking. There are great smoke holes yellow with sulphur and alum in the northern part of this depression and the edge of the old bench has been crumbling under this faulting movement. The northeast point of the old bench is rising with the island mass.

Looking from the northeast shore of the lake at the central region, a large fountain was seen to burst occasionally in the north central part of the lake. This had some resemblance to the "Old Faithful" of former years. Immense balloons of leathery crust were inflated by gas over the center of the lake, then they would collapse and a great fountain would break through the melt beneath. On the northeast rampart strong grotto fountaining was throwing spatter lumps over the bank and these tended to blow blisters one to three inches across. There was another grotto farther northeast emitting noxious fume.

On Friday, April 6, 1917, the inner little variation. The seismographic amplitude of volcanic vibrations has bench was 10 feet high and sinking increased this to fifteen feet. On this day it became evident that the inner walls were higher (20 feet) near the center of the pit and sloped radially to lower levels with reference to the lake at the ends of the three arms. The summit of the crag-mass was unquestionably rising. Marginal overflow was displacing the bench magma so as to squeeze the pasty substance beneath the crags out towards the region of central lake bottom. There were fountains southwest, northeast, east and southeast. Streaming was from the northwest and was rapid in the southeast channel. There were occasional falls from the raised ramparts.

The following report from the Whitney Laboratory of Seismology is submitted by Mr. H. O. Wood:

During the week-interval ending with April 6, six local earthquakes of small seismographic amplitude have been registered. The motion of microseismic waves has been normal with been steadily larger than normal but without reaching unusual magnitude, and without conspicuous storms. There has been a sharp and considerable shift of the pens in the sense of tilt to westward followed by a sharp return. The net change is inconsiderable. This action was confined to three days in the middle of the interval.

Technology Station, April 14, 1917.

During the week ending April 13, 1917, the lava lake has continued stagnant at a depression somewhat over 100 feet, but with a general tendency toward slight rising. The three sectors of bench magma tipped respectively by the east island, the south peninsula and the crag-mass have continued to rise in the central region of the pit and sink around the margins so that new islets and isthmuses of raised lake bottom tend to subdivide the lake into three pools north, southwest and southeast. The lake has fluctuated in height through a range of 15 feet.

The experimental work of the week has been directed to continued exploration of the thermal gradient of the lava lake using the Bristol electric thermocouple. Tests in the laboratory showed that this instrument could be used without appreciable error by separating the cold junction from the hot junction with a considerable length of copper wire. Accordingly on April 13 the instrument was thus arranged at the lake margin in the east cove, the wires covered with asbestos being led through half-inch iron pipe. The terminal was thrust through a three-inch crust which on that morning tended to cover the whole southeast pool. Trouble was experienced through burnt-out insulation and the temperature measurement made is only tentative but it indicated a temperature of 700° C at a depth of one foot below the thick crust and over 900° C at a depth of three feet. This suggests that the radiation and cooling effect of large crusted areas is effective immediately beneath the crusts for only a few inches, while below there is a gradual rise of temperature. This checks with the measurements of January which showed a low temperature just under the surface crust. On the other hand the surface of the lake, when crusts are tearing and sinking, becomes very hot not only by oxidation of the escaping gases but also through the rapid rising of the liquid melt from several feet down which replaces the less hot surface liquid. This surface liquid immediately under the crusts is heavier than the melt below and during general disturbance of foundering crusts must go down with the crusts.

That the crusts on sinking become centers of solidification of lava was shown in one of these experiments. Five feet of the end of the pipe was covered with a thin shell of solidified lava. This was thrust back into the lake and left for ten minutes in the melt beneath the crust. On withdrawing it the lava accumulation had tripled in thickness showing how rapidly lava partially cooled will act as a nucleus of solidification.

An interesting phenomenon observed with this apparatus was the immediate rise in temperature, by about 60° C, of such a lump of lava on the end of the pipe when it was withdrawn from the lake and exposed to the air. In spite of rapid solidification the temperature rose. The meaning of this appears to be sudden oxidation in air of the gases and also possibly heat of crystallization.

On Saturday, April 7, 1917, the lake appeared lower than on the previous day with inner bench 20 feet high in the southeast channel, central and southeastern caverns both open and showing inward streaming, and southwest islet standing about eight feet above the lake with slight overhang. There was a heavy fresh tumble of rocks from the southern January bench to the floor below. It was becoming evident that these border tumbles, like the overflow of other occasions, act as loads to weight down the bench magma and force the stiff under-fluid toward the center of the pit—in other words, to force up the lake bottom. These fresh-fallen avalanche heaps appear all around the pit along concentric downsunken blocks of bench backed by huge crevasses where these blocks have parted from their former attachment to the old walls of Halemaumau. The northeast bench was subsiding below the 1894 shelf The northeast point, on the other hand, was rising along with the east island. The northwest arm showed a platform of recent overflow above it and the northwest pond was covered with recent overflows from the west cove. The crag-mass, in response to this weighting, showed increased tilt westward.

It has recently been noticed that grapevine stalactites, such as are common in lava tubes, have formed since January in shallow cavernous spaces between lava flows of the northwest broken benches. This indicated that such stalactites are not formed by water drip, but are a peculiar type of feet and formed a secondary conelet under the former cone. The former cone clung to the wall like a bracket, a mere shell of its former structure, but from its under side hung many grapevine stalactites one to two feet long and immediately over the active flaming under-cone. Apparently the great heat from below had produced refusion in the upper cone shell and so developed **in only three days** fully formed stalactites of this type.

The southwest benches had sunk and opened crevasses at the base of the outer Halemaumau wall so as to swallow the heavy talus slopes which had been there. There were new crevasses also at the base of the south wall. The northwest cone was puffing and occasionally lava spurted from adjacent holes in the floor. At 2:30 p. m. the southeast arm sank three feet and there was a heavy fall from the east point of the south island mass.

On April 8 these tumbles into the lake became very numerous and at 2 p. m. it was found that immense falls had taken place from the south side of the east island and the north side of the central peninsula. This last tumble nearly choked the channel leading to the southeast arm showing how shallow the center of the lake was. The promontory making out from the crag-mass had also collapsed and was now represented by two islets five feet high. In the southeast arm the streaming was from the southeast cove, the central cavern and the central channel, the three streams convergent at the east cove. The bench where experiments were made during the previous week, around the south base of the east island, had now entirely fallen away. At 4 p. m. the lake was still sinking, there were more falls from the southeast point and the channel leading to the southeast arm was nearly closed.

On April 9, at 2 p. m., the streaming in the southeast channel was reversed and pouring westward to the central cavern. The elevation of the entrance from the central region to the southeast channel was now complete so that an isthmus connected the east island and the south island mass. The inner benches were 25 feet high in places. At 3 p. m. there was a small avalanche under the east rest house. At 4 p. m. there was slight flow across the isthmus from the north but the main streaming in the southeast pool was eastward from the central cavern. The lake was very quiet. A rhythmic fountain was playing in the north central region and there were shore fountains southwest and southeast. Streaming was outward from a dark skin across the northern part of the lake. A fresh tumble from the bench had left two rocky islets in the southeast cove. Next to the northwest cone a small area of floor over the northwest pond had collapsed leaving a glowing pot.

The spectacular feature of this evening was a revival of the northeast cascade from the lake into an inclined chute under a broad arched cavern at the northeast point. Just south of this point a new pit had opened 20 feet in diameter and this was fuming and flaming vigorously. Looking down into this pit at dusk the lava of the chute could be seen rushing silently eastward like a mill sluice, at a depth of about 20 feet, with glowing gases making a low roar like a furnace and heating the interior of the pit to incandescence. Above the gases condensed to billows of dense white fume which rose rapidly in unusual volume for Kilauea. A few feet to the west of this pit was a sulphur hole also glowing.

On April 10, at 4 p. m., the lake was still low but showed rising tendency, with a new low inner bench which had buried the southeast islets, blocked the entrance to the southeast cove and left a small pool at the inner end of that cove. Four islets lay in a line from the southwest cove to the center of the lake and a rampart grotto was building between the two northern ones. The cone in the west pond had built up and now showed a flaming triangular gash facing westward and revealing clusters of grapevine stalactites inside. The bench on the north side of the northwest arm had collapsed and the high broken northwest bench of January was further split crosswise. The north part of the lake was stagnant, the northeast pit quiet and the northeast cascade locality was fountaining violently without inrush.

On April 11, at 11 a. m., the lake was still low but showed further evidence of rising in fresh bench construction. A hardened flow from the central region lay across the channel isthmus. A high half-dome had been built against the central island. Heavy crusts over the east cove suddenly broke with a gush of gas and loud hissing noise; this was followed by violent spraying, the crust broke up and foundered, an active fountain developed and this migrated to the bank where it expended itself by building a slight crescent rampart. A sudden sinking of the main lake was not shared by the southeast pool, indicating that the isthmus is upraised lake bottom and not an arch of crust.

On Thursday, April 12, 1917, from 2 to 3 p. m., the lake was seen to be definitely higher. Streaming was outward from the central cavern but there was fountaining inside. The northeast sulphur hole was crackling, fuming, glowing and covered with bright yellow sublimates. A strong "sweet" sulphur odor came from this hole quite distinct from the ordinary sulphur dioxide. The northeast pit was entirely inactive and showed black pahoehoe on its bottom where the sluice way had been. The northeast floor of January showed whitish hot areas with cherry red glow in the cracks one to three feet down. No odor whatever was detectable in the hot air rising from these cracks. The north chasm showed a broad solidified festooned overflow from the lake but no activity or fume. At 4 p. m. the lake was rising and level with its inner bench.

On April 13, from 9 to 11 a. m., the lake was relatively high and rising. After 11 a. m. a torrent poured from the north across the isthmus to the lava drip, probably occasioned by reheating due to oxidizing gases. In proof of this, the cone on the northeast corner of the west pond showed on this day a remarkable collection of these stalactites. Three days before the west pond had been level with the floor around it, but now it had sunk four southeast pool and rising from that time on brought the level to within ten feet of the floor level at the east cove. In the morning the southeast pool was heavily crusted from shore to shore. About 10 a. m. this cover broke with violent gas escape and lifting of crusts, followed by a breaking up with intense evolution of heat and bubble fountaining, as well as grotto fountaining. The deflated pool sank two feet. This spell lasted ten minutes and then crusting set in once more, to be finally broken up by the flood from the north. The northeast sulphur hole had developed into an open flaming pot. There was rampart building at the islets and to the northeast and southwest.

The following report from the Whitney Laboratory of Seismology is submitted by Mr. H. O. Wood:

Only three local earthquakes, all of small seismographic amplitude, have been registered during the week-interval ending with April 13. A small number of indefinite wave-groups of lesser magnitude also were recorded. For the most part the seismographic amplitudes of microseismic waves and waves of volcanic vibration have been normal but in the early part of the week-interval moderately large motion occurred. In the first part of the week there was a marked shifting of the pens in the sense of tilt to the east, and then to the west, followed by a steady run without notable net change.

Technology Station, April 21, 1917.

During the week ending April 21, 1917, the Halemaumau lava lake has continued to rise slowly, and this rising now appears to be growing steady, following the stagnation and irregular fluctuation of the equinox period. The inner bench of overflow was 101 feet down on March 30; this bench had been flooded on March 22 and was not again overflowed until April 2. The definite rise which began on April 1 amounted to 14 feet of actual construction in seventeen days, or a rate of one and a fifth feet per day.

On Saturday, April 14, at 2 p. m., the inner bench was seen to have been overflowed east and southeast, the lake now being five feet below it. The southeast cove was now a niche with a hard floor and no liquid pool. The isthmus separating the southeast pool from the main lake was pronounced. There were now three islets instead of four in the main lake, the two middle ones being united apparently into an island at the entrance to the southwest arm of the lake. There was a small islet at the entrance to the north arm, and the older southwest islet was still in place. High spatter half-domes were building on the central island and on the east shore of the southwest arm. A shore pinnacle stood out from the northeast base of the crag-mass. The central cavern was again open and fountaining within, with outward streaming. Smoke was abundant.

Upright laminations in the jointing of the broken southern face of the east island, at the level where aa lava occurs on the opposite side of this upraised mass, may probably be accounted for by supposing them to be the accumulation of foundered crust of Januar. These crusts sink at the lake border and were doing so continuously at that time on the northeast banks, in the region later uplifted to form the east island. The sinking crusts may be laid against the precipitous submerged lake borders in more or less upright layers, and so build out the banks during a rising period. This would account, at such a period, for the invariable contracting of the lake and the widening of the inner benches. Such benches are always built at the shores towards which the streaming and sinking proceed.

On April 16 there was strong rising which obliterated the southeast niche and flooded the south floor from both the east and west sides. An overflow at the east cove poured through a gap in the lower part of the sunken northeast bench of January making a small leaf-shaped flow on that bench under the east shelter. A new inner bench was constructed around the east island. The northeast sulphur hole lost all glow and became a dead cavity. New benches were built at the northwest and west coves.

At 2:30 p. m. on Tuesday, April 17, the three islets and the bench around the southeast pool were eight feet high, streaming was from the central cavern in a curve northward, where a fountaining grotto was revealed under the central isthmus. Streaming in the main lake was from the north and the southwest arm was stagnant. The southeast cone was now ring-shaped with a central pot. The southeast side of the crag-mass appeared much fallen away. Splashing grottoes were building on the northeast, west, southwest and east. A portion of the bank at the east cove collapsed and broke up the heavy crust on the southeast pool. Fumes had greatly diminished. The southeast high bench was gaping away from the wall. The depression of the southeast pool was 105 feet. The noises were of grotto splashing and occasional tinkling falls of rock.

On April 18 from 10 a. m. to 1 p. m. the pools rose from a level four feet below the banks to brimming and then strong overflow. Thereafter until 4 p. m. there was subsidence eight feet. The three central promontories have continued to rise and the border regions of the benches to sink. There were now only two islands in the main lake, in the center and southwest arm respectively, and both of these were flat-topped and larger than before. The northern island appeared to have been submerged. At 11 a. m. the southeast pool was flush with the bench and covered with a crust four inches thick, brown and fibrous, which incessantly crackled, throwing up hundreds of tiny fragments either from cooling strains or bursting gas bubbles. This heavy crust extended for 150 feet across the pool, was arched up slightly by the foaming lava beneath, and was kept broken around the edges as it rose along cracks where a sluggish pudding of lava from beneath would well up with hissing gas pressure. Occasionally at long intervals the crust would break up all over and founder with fountaining and tremendous evolution of heat.

The northeast point of the January bench had now become a pinnacle fifteen feet higher than the bench and

March 30, 1917, 7 p. m. Flaming and spurting border cone, East cove, 20 feet away. Exposure 30 seconds.—Photo. Jaggar.

March 30, 1917, 6 p. m. Flaming and spurting border cone, East cove, 30 feet away. Exposure 90 seconds.—Photo. Jaggar.

April 5, 1917. Aa or block-lava pedestal of East Island. (See Feb. 18 and March 24, this Bulletin).—Photo. Jaggar. Note contrast pahoehoe overflows in foreground, and layers of pahoehoe in cliff.

blocks of rock occasionally fell from it into the small pit on its south side. The overflows on this day poured to the northeast crag wall but not through the gap and they filled the depression at the bottom of the east gulch. Flows poured from the east and from the west a short distance over the south floor. The west pond under the high west wall of Halemaumau was covered with new lava crusts at a high level, as was also the northwest pond. The west cone was built high and had in its summit a small glowing and flaming hole blowing noisily, and the northwest cone was also blowing. There was overflow in the north chasm. In the main lake there was much fountaining in the north central region and against its west, southwest and southeast banks. Everywhere there was strong gas pressure with blowing noises added to the plashing of the fountains. At 6:30 p. m. there was a heavy avalanche into the lake from the southeast side of the crag-mass followed by turbulent fountaining. At 6:30 p. m. the bench along the south side of the east island collapsed en masse and carried away much of the isthmus. Immediately an upwelling of lava started in the southeast pool at the isthmus and during the evening the sluggish crusting which had been characteristic of this pool gave place to strong, hot streaming from under the isthmus, implying apparently that a tunnel had opened connecting the two lakes. There was a tendency to whirlpool pattern in the southeast pool.

Measurements, 2 to 3 p. m. on Thursday, April 19, 1917, showed the depression of the southeast pool to be 87 feet below the southeast rim of Halemaumau. The northeast pinnacle rose above the lake 43 feet, the east island 51 feet and the crag-mass 54 feet. These measurements indicated that the east island had risen 28 feet since March 30, and the crag-mass 17 feet. The dimensions of the southeast pool were 380 by 220 feet; of the main lake 800 by 250 feet; the central and southwest islands in the main lake were each 60 feet long.

The habit of the southeast pool had entirely changed, streaming lava was pouring through a tunnel under the isthmus from the main lake into this pool, which was now very hot and covered with black satiny festoons which moved rapidly to a new grotto at the southeast end of the pool. The skins appeared thin and blistered. The lakes were about four feet below their banks, five or six fountains were in action, there were occasional border tumbles, a rampart encircled the southwest arm and there was glow and flame at the southeast cone. Streaming in the main lake was southward with much bubble fountaining near the central island. The narrow steep-sided crag of the central peninsula was broken and tumbled in the middle and smoking strongly. There was much white smoke from the north inner wall. There were no fresh overflows and the lake appeared sinking in the afternoon, but in the evening it rose rapidly and overflowed the entire southern and eastern floods, pouring again through the northeast gap and greatly widening the leaf-shaped flow on the January bench.

On April 20 at 2 p. m., there was new rock tumble at the edge of the lake under the east end of the high southeast bench. Streaming festoons spread in wide folds from isthmus tunnel toward the southeast station. Two high rampart grottoes had been built at the southwest. There was a noise of incessant grinding crust at the east end of the southeast pool. Only two or three fountains were in action, there was much smoke in the central part of the pit and on the northeast, west southwest and northwest. Streaming in the main lake was from north to south and the banks were about three feet high. The south floor was fast widening owing to the burial of the southern tumble.

The following report from the Whitney Laboratory of Seismology is submitted by Mr. H. O. Wood:

During the week-interval ending with April 20 four local earthquakes of very small seismographic amplitude have been registered—together with a number of wave-groups of indeterminate character and exceedingly small amplitude. Microseismic motion has been normal to weak in energy. Volcanic vibration has varied from normal to moderately strong values—with storms of stronger trembling. There has been little or no net change in pen-shifts in the sense of tilting but in the early part of the interval there were pronounced shifts with strong diurnal movement. In the latter part there has been little shifting of either sort.

———

Technology Station, April 28, 1917.

During the week ending April 27, 1917, the lava lakes of Halemaumau have maintained their level at about 90 feet of depression without marked net rising. There have been fluctuations from day to day within a range of 15 feet.

On April 22 at 2:30 p. m. the inner wall was 15 feet high, the southeast pool was quiet and the main lake active. The central isthmus had subsided on its northeast side so as to show a slope in that direction and a break on the side of the central peninsula. The tunnel connecting the two lakes appeared to be closed. There was streaming from under the southeast bank and slow rising during the afternoon so that at 6 p. m. the lava of the southeast pool was within seven feet of the inner bench.

On April 13 at 2 p. m. both pools were quiet, with banks about ten feet high and fumes thick. At 4:45 p. m. there were numerous fountains in the northern part of the main lake and among these a large rhythmic dome fountain having the aspect of "Old Faithful." The central and southwestern islets stood ten feet above the lake. The west cone showed one glow spot on its southwest side.

On Tuesday, April 24, at 2 p. m. the central cavern open to the east exhibited continuous boiling up of lava and a current poured out of the cavern and across the southeast pool to the north where it expended itself in a line of tumultuous fountaining and downsucking at the south base of the east island. The main lake was quiet and smoky and somewhat higher than the southeast pool, the latter exhibiting inner walls 15 feet high. At 2:30 p. m. a portion of the bank collapsed at the extreme southeast corner producing short-lived fountaining.

The northwest cone was now a tumbled group of pinnacles and the west cone at 4:30 p. m. was heard puffing, indicating rising gas pressure. There was high crusted lava in the west and northwest ponds, a new high bench enclosed the northwest arm and there were recent flows at a high level in the north chasm. On the northeast margin of the lake a high ring-shaped cone had been built with an open flaming orifice on top.

After 5 p. m. the rising in the main lake gradually reached the isthmus level and then the lava flowed across the isthmus to the southeast pool. The arrangement in this pool was peculiar, two open glowing caverns, one above the other, leading into the north side of the isthmus. From the lower of these there appeared to be an outrush eastward of gas and lava on an up grade and this deflected the current from the central cavern so as to produce a succession of waves and noisy longshore fountaining at the base of the east island. The rising and overflowing from the main lake gradually stopped this process by drowning the lower cavern, but the upper cavern then produced a sluggish cascade outward into the southeast pool. When the torrent had poured completely across, the longshore fountaining diminished and the central cavern became drowned. A slow current southeastward replaced the former activity. The southeast cone continued glowing and flaming.

On April 25, 1917, at 3:30 p. m., the banks of the southeast pool were only five feet high and again it was divided from the main lake by the isthmus. The southeast grotto was active and the streaming towards it. There was steady loud hissing from the west cone. Fountains in the main lake played near the middle island, against the northeast wall and in a curtained grotto northwest. The northeast cone was nearly closed above but showed open gashes below leading to large cherry red incandescent chamber. Seen from the northeast bench, the great western crag-mass by tilting westward had entirely changed in profile. The lakes in general appeared crusted and rising.

On this day the south face of the east island was visited and the upright layers noticed there were verified as consisting of wavy crusts of vesicular and deeply oxidized lake lava plastered against the upright aa hillock that forms the foundation of the island. These layers appear to be the sunken crusts of the January activity.

On April 26 at 6 p. m. the lake had subsided, the fumes were thicker and the inner benches 10 to 15 feet high. The southeast pool was crusted, but occasionally a fountain burst in the southeast corner. In the main lake the streaming was from north to south. The great northern rhythmic fountain played at intervals of from 50 to 60 seconds with bubble fountaining between the larger explosions. The central crags were more broken and showed yellow sulphur stain extending to the flat south of them. The central and southwest islets rose about ten feet above the lake with overhanging walls. There was active bombardment at the southwest bank, curtained grottoes to the north, and five or six fountains in all. At 6:30 p. m. the central islet collapsed bodily into the lake producing a wave and a short-lived effervescence. No trace of the islet was left. The west cone was flaming through filagree fused openings. The northwest cone was smoking. The northeast cone was flaming and spurting and the southeast cone flaming. The southeast pool showed streaming out from under the isthmus and occasionally the crust would break up with cracking and foundering.

On Friday, April 27, at 11:30 a. m. the lake appeared still lower and more smoky with inner cliffs 15 to 20 feet high, very slight streaming, a few fountains at the Old Faithful region and in the grottoes, and no trace of the central islet. The southeast floor was smoking strongly. There were now disjointed small crags east, southeast, northwest of east island, west, northwest, and north. The progress of central uplift of the crags has developed two marked bench levels, a newer inner one 10 to 15 feet high corresponding to the level of the isthmus between the two lakes. The higher one, in places 20 feet high, corresponds to the level of the floors south and east. Still higher locally are the January benches northeast and southeast, and the extensions of these north and northwest are now becoming uplifted crags. At still higher levels and at higher angles of tilt are the January crags. The general aspect of the pit as one approaches it from the southeast gives the impression that it is extraordinarily choked with crags and benches, but from the southwest the main lake is seen to be still a large body of liquid lava.

The following report from the Whitney Laboratory of Seismology is submitted by Mr. H. O. Wood:

During the week-interval ending with April 27 nine local earthquakes have been registered, all of very small seismographic amplitude. There have been recorded several very small wave-groups of doubtful character besides. Microseismic motion has been normal. The motion of volcanic vibration was stronger than normal in the middle part of the interval but was normal to subnormal at the beginning and end. During the last four days of the week there has been progressive shifting of the pens in the sense of tilt to westward. Earlier the registration was normal. Of late there has been no noteworthy net change in the north-south component.

Very respectfully,

J. A. JAGGAR, JR.,
Director.

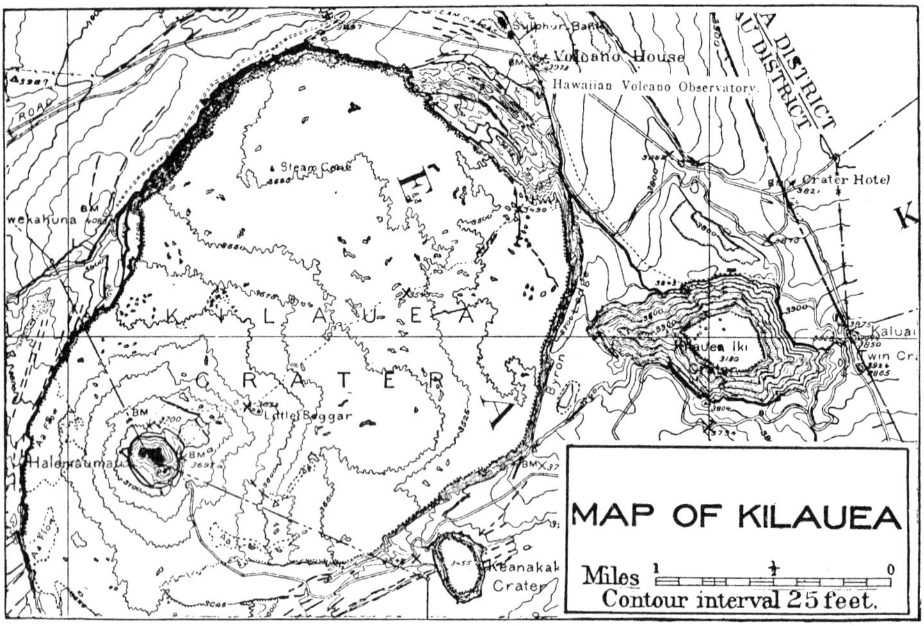

HAWAIIAN VOLCANO RESEARCH ASSOCIATION.

This society is a voluntary one, made up of subscribers to scientific work which is being executed by the Massachusetts Institute of Technology.

In 1917 there are about 150 subscribers in Hawaii and elsewhere, firms and individuals. A group of firms and persons in Hilo built the main observatory building in the spring of 1912. Publications to date have been weekly reports since the summer of 1911, now reprinted in Honolulu in monthly form. The Massachusetts Institute of Technology will publish annual reports, of which the introductory number was printed in 1912.

The weekly bulletin as it appears in the Advertiser is reprinted as a leaflet and sent to regular annual subscribers to the work of the Association. L. A. Thurston is president of the Board of Directors of the Association, and R. W. Shingle is treasurer. New subscribers who are interested in volcanoes will be welcomed in the Association. The Association aims: (1) To record volcanic activity and earthquakes in Hawaii; (2) to attract scientific men hither for special studies; (3) to promote the establishment of volcano observatories all over the world. The annual dues of regular members are $5; patrons of the Association subscribe larger amounts.

WHITNEY LABORATORY OF SEISMOLOGY.

The Whitney Laboratory of Seismology is equipped with two Bosch-Omori 100 kg tromometers registering N-S and E-W motion, a heavy Omori tromometer registering E-W motion, and an Omori "ordinary Seismograph" designed for registering strong earthquakes in all three components of motion. These are seated on concrete piers in a closed basement room having practically constant temperature, beneath the chief Observatory building near the hotel. Time is referred to a rated chronometer, checked at intervals by solar observations with a transit. Both instruments are loaned by the College of Hawaii. Hawaiian standard time (H. S. T.) is 10 hrs. 30 min. slower than Greenwich time.

CANCANI SCALE OF SEISMIC INTENSITY.

Expressed by accelerations measured in millimeters per second per second.

I.	Instrumental	0.0	2.5
II.	Very slight	2.5	5.0
III.	Slight	5.0	10.0
IV.	Sensible, mediocre	10.0	25.0
V.	Rather strong	25.0	50.0
VI.	Strong	50.0	100.0
VII.	Very strong	100.0	250.0
VIII.	Ruinous	250.0	500.0
IX.	Disastrous	500.0	1000.0
X.	Very disastrous	1000.0	2500.0
XI.	Catastrophic	2500.0	5000.0
XII.	Great catastrophe	5000.0	10000.0

Grade IV. is ordinarily the minimum perceived by the senses; and in grade XII. the acceleration, or rate of change of motion (jerk) reaches that of terrestrial gravitation.

In the standard form of report the maximum intensity or acceleration, designated by the symbol a, or max. a, is given in the conventional unit, **the milligal.** The milligal is a measure of acceleration, such that 1 milligal = 1/100 mm. per sec. per sec. = 10 μ per sec. per sec. The Cancani scale, here defined in terms of millimeters per sec. per sec., can therefore be expressed in **milligals by multiplying each of the numbers by 100.**

WEEKLY BULLETIN
OF THE
Hawaiian Volcano Observatory

Vol. V. HONOLULU, HAWAII, MAY, 1917. No. 5

Technology Station, May 5, 1917.

During the week ending May 4, 1917, the lava lake has again risen within its 20-foot range of movement and reached a level slightly higher than on April 19. On April 27, at noon, the depression of the north grotto below the south station was 105 feet. On May 4 the depression of the southeast pool below the east wall of Halemaumau was 83 feet. The fountaining activity varies and Old Faithful, in the north central part of the main lake, appears to be reestablished. In general there is much less tendency to swift streaming than at the beginning of the year and the sluggishness is accompanied by the formation of thick crusts. The construction of driblet cones is again in evidence as part of a general rising tendency.

Experimental work at the lava margin was resumed on Wednesday, May 2, 1917, in spite of the southerly wind and a very fumy pit. The first experiment was to determine the temperature of the bottom of the lake, and simultaneously of the lava at intervals from the bottom upward. For a month past the apparatus has been in preparation. It consists of a steel pipe of 1½-inch internal diameter, 83 feet long, capped with a screw cover at the lower end, and containing a long heavy black annealed steel wire along which were wired nests or cocoons of Seger cones at measured intervals. The cones were enclosed in iron gauze, twenty-nine fragments representing fusibilities from 590° C. to 1290° C. in each cocoon, and twenty of these cocoons were distributed along the wire. There had thus been built a device for exposing twenty thermometers at one time to the heat of the lake at different depths. The cocoons made cigar-shaped swellings in the wire capable of gliding past the joints of the pipe without catching when the wire was withdrawn, the diameter of each cocoon being about one inch. As it takes several minutes for such an apparatus to heat thoroughly and the pipe may be immersed or the wire withdrawn in a few seconds, the error due to immersion and withdrawal of the pyrometer is negligible.

Assisted by Demosthenes Lycurgus, three of his associates and Alex. Lancaster, the writer made the immersion of the pyrometer at the east cove at 2:30 p. m. during a time of crust-breaking, the lava being about four feet below the rampart. The pipe went in at a flat angle owing to its large size and stiffness, but tilted down to 35° in its final position. Seventy-five feet of the pyrometer went into the lake, the lower end finding the resistant bottom lava at a vertical depth estimated at 42 feet. As only a short end of the pipe protruded above the bank, this was held in place by five men holding a taut wire attached to the pipe. The end of the pyrometer wire protruded from the opening of the pipe and was held by the writer. An eight-minute period was allowed for exposure to the heat, three for heating the pipe through and five for fusing the cones, in accordance with previous practice. At the end of the eight minutes the wire was withdrawn without difficulty, no welding or other cementing effect took place in the pipe and the cocoons were all intact with some of the cones fused and others quite unaffected. The pipe was, of course, abandoned.

The results of this measurement indicate a graduated temperature increasing downward as in the measurements of April 5 and 6, at an average rate of 9½° C. for each foot of depth for the whole gradient; for the interval, however, from twelve feet down, where this day's measurement began, to

WEEKLY BULLETIN
of the
Hawaiian Volcano Observatory

Published Monthly at Honolulu, Hawaii, by the Hawaiian Volcano Research Association

L. W. de Vis-Norton........Secretary

Entered as second-class matter January 20, 1914, at the post-office at Honolulu, Hawaii, under the Act of August 24, 1912.

twenty-six feet down the increment was 15° C. per foot, whereas below that point the rate of increase was much slower, 3⅛° C. per foot to the bottom.

On basis of the gradient thus established, the bottom temperature on both April 5 and May 2 was very near 1150° C. and apparently this temperature is characteristic of a zone about ten feet above the bottom. Above that point the lava cools gradually, the rapid cooling effect appearing in the middle zone between twenty-six feet down and sixteen feet down, the range in that region on May 2 being from 1120° C. to 920° C. upward, whereas on April 5, during hot and rapid surface streaming, the range here was from 1130° C. to 1040″ C. There are, unquestionably, differences in the thermal gradient on different days, but the general range is from 920° C. four feet below the crust to 1150″ C. on the bottom. This bottom temperature is close to the temperature of the hotter fountains and is very near the fusing point of the sunken crusts.

It is probable that the combination of high temperature and pastiness encountered at the bottom is occasioned by crust material in process of dissolving through heat generated by reaction of lava gases with the air carried down in the pores of the crusts.

Two other experiments carried out on this day were devised in order to learn the effect of mixing air or oxygen with the lava gases. A quart bottle of oxygen gas was thrown into liquid lava and there immediately resulted quick jets of whitish flame and brown smoke puffing up above the melt. The bottle was slowly carried along beneath the surface and the flame explosions reappeared after about one minute down the current and were repeated several times. Evidently combustible gas in the vesicles of the lava was found and oxidized by the oxygen.

An experiment was made with a tank of compressed air to which a long pipe was attached so that the air could be released beneath the surface of the lake. This produced inconclusive results because the pipe was thrust into the southeast pool when the latter was covered with a very heavy crust. The only positive effects were jets of flame through the orifice around the pipe. Thereafter a gradual lifting of the whole crust took place, followed by cracking, foundering and tremendous fountaining. This happened after the air had been inflating the lava for from four to five minutes, when the tank exhausted itself. The pipe was immersed eight feet at first and later fourteen feet. The break-up came about five minutes after the pipe was withdrawn and there is no proof that it resulted from the experiment, though the central fountaining was unusual for this pool and the activity abnormally strong.

On April 28, at 2:30 p. m., the lake appeared over 20 feet below the inner bench and fifteen fountains were in action. The northeast cone was blowing noisily. There were occasional falls of rock into the lake.

On April 30, at 2:30 p. m., the main lake appeared about ten feet below the inner bench and the only fountaining was in the Old Faithful region. The southeast pool was more active but the fumes obscured the view. The northeast cone was still puffing. At 4:15 p. m. the southeast pool was only six feet below the bench and slowly rising.

On May 1, at 2:30 p. m., both lakes were active and rising, about twelve fountains were in action and there were splashing grottoes east and southeast. The isthmus between the two lakes was two feet high and the inner bench elsewhere five feet high. Streaming in the main lake was outward from the southwest and the northwest. The west side of the central peninsula and the highest northeast pinnacle had fallen. There were great crevasses yawning at the base of the southwest wall of Halemaumau. The southwest island was split along a north-south fissure. The west cone was spouting lava continuously from a hole two feet wide in its west slope so that a lava cascade poured down about three feet to the west pond which was rapidly filling. The pond filled to the level of the hole and overflowed eastward. At 3 p. m. the upward spouting ceased and backflow set in from the pond into the hole with gas explosions at intervals. The northeast cone had collapsed.

On May 2 from 10 a. m. to 1 p. m. the lava rose and overflowed on the north, northwest, southwest and southeast. The southwest point was submerged and flows on the south floor poured from both east and west. The eastern flow was mostly across the site of the former southeast cove to a sinkhole just east of the southeast cone and when the flowing ceased, the cove outline and the sinkhole remained; the latter with lava churning a few feet down. There was border fountaining with strong gas pressure at the east end of the southeast pool, the central and western part being covered with a heavy crust from which streaming proceeded eastward. At noon the two lakes were joined across the isthmus without marked streaming. Once at noon there was very intense blowing off of gas from under the crust at the east cove followed by a break-up and strong fountaining. Streaming in the main lake was southward with the usual fountains.

On May 3, at 6:30 p. m., the banks were three to five feet high, there was sluggish border fountaining, interrupted occasionally by strong gas-pressure fountaining at the Old Faithful locality. Here there would be a noisy tumult of spraying with jets flung up 50 feet and outward in all directions over an area over 80 feet in diameter and this would slowly migrate to the northeast bank. The southeast pool was open and streaming eastward where there was an immense high curtained grotto. There was also a high rampart grotto southeast and flaming cones at the east and west ends of the south floor. The point at the southern end of the southwest cove was reestablished. Streaming was to the northeast and south. The west cone showed bright filagree openings where flaming and blowing took place and there was puffing also from glow spots at the south end of the northwest pond.

Measurements on Friday, May 4, 1917, at 3 p. m., made the depression of the southeast pool 83 feet. There was strong pressure fountaining on the southwest and southeast sides of this pool and in the grottoes of the southwest cove. The lakes were brimming level with the bench, skins appeared thin and blistered and rising was in progress. The southwest island appeared low and high ramparts were building southeast and southwest.

The following report from the Whitney Laboratory of Seismology is submitted by Mr. H. O. Wood:

During the week-interval ending May 4 four local earthquakes of small seismographic amplitude have been registered; and one teleseism of moderate seismographic amplitude only but with well-marked phase beginnings; hence a world-shaking shock of moderately great power is indicated. The registration of microseismic motion has been as usual. The seismographic amplitudes of volcanic vibration were of normal value until the latter part of the interval when they became larger and very small "storms" became frequent. There have been no noteworthy net changes in the direction of the writing levers (tilt) during the week.

Technology Station, May 12, 1917.

During the week ending May 11, 1917, the Halemaumau lava lakes have risen more continuously than of late at an average rate of about two feet per day. Strong overflow into the low places and uplift of the crags have been resumed and the large tabular block of January bench under the northwest station now promises to become a conspicuous elevation, so rapidly is it rising.

On the evening of Friday, May 4, 1917, at 5 o'clock, the southeast pool subsided five feet in the course of ten minutes and remained stationary until 7 p. m. when rising set in. At 7:30 p. m. there were falls of rock from the crag-mass into the lake and from the southeast bank, followed by fountaining activity.

On May 5, at 2:30 p. m., it was apparent that the southeast pool had overflowed at the east cove making a short new flow on the northeast floor. The lake margin was five feet high and there was much fountaining toward the north. A large grotto had formed on the lake margin beneath the crag-mass. Seen from the southwest station at 3 p. m. the main lake exhibited numerous fountains in the northern region. There was much fuming. Recent overflow from the west margin of the lake had flooded the west pond so as nearly to cover the small cone there and pile up crust slabs against it. The cone was puffing loudly.

At 3 p. m. on May 6 the lakes were only three feet below their banks and very quiet. The whole southern floor was covered with fresh flows showing that a strong overflow had taken place southwest during the interval since the last record. At 4 p. m. the main lake was fountaining in several places, ''Old Faithful'' was active and both the west and northwest cones were puffing noisily and rhythmically.

On Monday, May 7, at 3 p. m., the lake was still high and not more than three feet below its banks and there were fountaining grottoes in the east and southeast coves. At 4 p. m. the southwest cove was seen from the south to be building rapidly, by border fountaining, an evenly curved rampart giving circular shape to the pool. The whole lake showed much fountaining and the gas pressure at the west and northwest cones had ceased.

On May 8, at 2 p. m., the banks were five feet high and there was much border fountaining southeast. There was fresh overflow across the south floor from the southeast pool. The west cone was puffing and occasionally throwing out spurts of molten lava, and the puffing from the northwest cone had been resumed.

On May 9, at 2 p. m., the lake was lower with banks ten feet high and a small avalanche fell from the north wall into the lake. The isthmus between the two lakes showed signs of subsidence and a tunnel beneath had been submerged. It stood about five feet above the lake. The fumes on this day were thinner, there was vigorous fountaining towards the north and the western cones were puffing.

Thursday, May 10, was a day of very strong rising and overflowing which reached its maximum between 11 a. m. and noon. At 9:30 a. m. the main lake was overflowing across the isthmus into the southeast pool. At 9:45 a. m. that pool was overflowing at its southeast corner so as to flood the south floor. At 10:30 a. m. there were strong overflows southeast, into the east and north chasms, and into the northwest chasm by overflow of the northwest arm. There were short pooled overflows on the west side of the southwest cove. At 11 a. m. these western overflows were in rapid motion so as to pour southward and eastward back of the rampart of the southwest cove and across the south floor to meet the overflow coming from the southeast pool. At the same time the overflow at the northwest arm had developed a T-shape, pouring through chasms in the broken January benches eastward and southward. There was now a rapid torrent pouring across the isthmus.

From 11 to 11:30 a. m., the overflow from the southeast pool moved rapidly westward in a broad sheet and at 11:30 it met the great flood from the southwest, so that the two flows pooled for the full width of the southern floor area.

This added weight doubtless heaved up the central crags, for the shore-marking under them stood higher above the lake than at the southeast and southwest. Both the central peninsula and the east island crags now show strong southeastward and eastward tilt in their several escarpments.

The southern flood surrounded the southeast cone and buried much of the southern talus. At the south station there was an odor of carbon gases from this great flow but during the strong rising there was little odor of sulphurous acid to leeward of the pit. The north end of the lake was crusted and the streaming was from that region to the southwest, southeast, east, northeast, north, and northwest. There was no overflow at the east cove but the platform under the southeast bench was greatly built up. Spatter niches were building on the north side of the northwest arm and in the rampart at the entrance to the north chasm. "Old Faithful" was in action with occasional very strong fountaining. The southwest island was about five feet high. Both the west and northwest cones were hissing steadily, the latter building a spiracle. The crusts on the west and northwest ponds were covered with broad flat flows which had come from recent overflow of the west shore of the lake. There were puffing shore fountains building ramparts at the several places of overflow, and there was strong longshore fountaining at the west cove.

Subsidence began at 11:45 with strong fountaining around the margins of the lake, especially at the southwest cove and then glowing marginal rims of overhang with stalactites began to appear. In the afternoon the lake subsided five feet and at 8:30 p. m. there was a slide from the northeast side of the east island.

It now began to be evident that the northwest tabular block of the January bench, isolated by chasms on all sides, was becoming a conspicuous rising crag counterpoised by the subsidence of the northeast bench and of the fresh flows in the north chasm.

Measurement on Friday, May 11, 1917, at 10 a. m., determined the depression of the southeast pool to be 80 feet below the rim of Halemaumau and about ten feet lower than the maximum height of the previous day. The following are the heights of the several crags above the lake:

East island, 57 feet.

New eastern summit of crag-mass, 60 feet.

Summit of south island mass, 39 feet.

Southeast January bench, 24 feet.

Southwest island, 19 feet.

The lakes appeared about five feet below most of the shore bench, but only two feet below the isthmus. The marks of the previous day appeared seven feet above the lake under the east islands and only about three feet above it at the extreme southeast. The southwest island was rising rapidly, owing probably to recent copious overflow around the southwest cove which is forcing up the lake-bottom there. The large southeast half-dome grotto was curtained across its entrance with a few glowing orifices left and the blowing within it would depress the skin on the pool outside with each puff. There was occasional central fountaining in the southeast pool. Slides took place from the east side of the northeast peak. There was much blowing noise in the pit, the fumes were thinner and the lake was rising. The northwest arm, which had shown no outline during overflow, was now again outlined and the north end of the main lake was crusted. Long crust slabs of the southeast pool would break and founder, occasioning conspicuous lines of bubble fountaining each time the slabs up-ended and went down.

The following report from the Whitney Laboratory of Seismology is submitted by Mr. H. O. Wood:

During the week ending with May 11, three small local earthquakes of sure characteristics have been registered, and two perhaps of doubtful character. A teleseism of small seismographic amplitude has also been registered—its fore-phase very feebly indicated. A shock of no great original energy, yet of the world-shaking class, is indicated.

The seismographic amplitudes of microseismic motion have varied from small to moderate values. Volcanic vibration has been stronger than usual and "stormy" in occurrence. Pen shifts in the sense of tilt have been marked, to westward and then to eastward, without much net change. The end of the week finds a small net shift to westward which is being reduced by the present eastward tendency.

Technology Station, May 12, 1917.

During the week ending May 18, 1917, the lava column continued to rise about two feet per day, the net building-up of the inner floor for the week amounting to 13 feet. Most of the overflowing was at the beginning of the week followed by a reaction of subsidence, with rapid recovery thereafter. The pronounced rising now in progress is in accord with past experience which shows that rising is usual after the equinox. From February 1 to March 20 there was subsidence.

In the early morning of Saturday, May 12, there were extensive overflows of the inner floor which were fresh and glowing at 10 a. m. At that time the southeast pool had subsided three feet and the main lake somewhat less. After 11 a. m. rising again set in. The earlier fresh flows covered the whole south floor and the northeast floor to a point under the north station. There were fresh flows also in the north chasm and over the sites of the northwest and west ponds going through from the northwest arm to the west cove. The northwest cone was nearly buried. The southeast cone was entirely buried and also the last remnant of the January south island which had been so conspicuous a monolith. Great spatter cones had built on the edge of the lakes north and southeast, each with narrow openings on the lake side. The writer descended to the northeast floor by way of the north end of the 1894 bench and walked through the north chasm to the margin of the lake beside the cone there. This cone was 12 feet high with a fountain pounding against it. The lakes had risen from 11 a. m. to 12:30 p. m., the main lake much faster than the southeast pool so that the heavy crusts at the time of this visit to the shore were flush with the bank. In fact the northwest cove and the southwest shore were overflowing. The west cone was gushing incandescent lava like an artesian well so that the west pond depression overflowed eastward. The main lake overflowed the isthmus so that at noon the two lakes were united. Streaming was south and southeast as usual. The crags had continued to rise and the tabular northwest crag was rising strongly while the north chasm was sinking. This was shown by a cracked down-curving shelf or ridge of fresh flow-lava only two days old along the west side of the north chasm, lifted on the side of the crag and depressed on the side of the chasm, showing a vertical displacement of about six feet from its original position.

The overflowing continued strong, for at 11 a. m., on May 13, the lakes were brimming level with the banks, the fumes were very thin and there were fresh flows everywhere. The northeast floor was now flooded from the main lake on the north as well as from the southeast pool and from the east gulch. The grottoes east, north and southwest were very active and at noon the shores were about three feet above the lakes. There was great activity in the Old Faithful locality with bombardment of the isthmus region. The west cone was hissing and the northwest cone obliterated by flows.

At 5:30 p. m. tremendous overflowing of the benches began and continued for two hours. This flood greatly widened the floors and tended to further constriction of the lakes. On the northeast the flood surmounted the remnants of the January benches and on the northwest the tabular crag was entirely surrounded by new lava. The wall valley southwest received driblet flows from the ends and through the middle crevasse. After 7 p. m. the lakes sank about three feet.

The view from the north and south sides of the pit now showed more than a semicircle floor on the east and south, the only interruption to continuous flooring being the relatively small southeast pool. The greater part of the liquid lava is now wholly west of the middle line of the pit in the main lake, which is elongate in a north-south direction. Even on the west side there are very wide floor spaces, which, however, mask and roof over the northwest and west conduit ponds, represented above only by blowing cones.

On May 14, at 9:30 a. m., the lakes were depressed about five feet delow their banks with about twelve fountains in action. The floods of the previous evening had partially buried the great north dome, but it was being rapidly rebuilt and there was similar strong constructional activity by border fountains southeast, southwest and on the east side of the main lake. The fumes were greatly diminished.

On Tuesday, May 15, 1917, at 2 p. m., the reaction of subsidence had depressed the lakes 15 feet and there was much overhang. Heavy crusts covered the southeast pool, continuously snapping and making a dance of splinters on the surface. These splinters drift in the wind so as to make a ripple pattern on the surface of the lake and when the melt wells up cracks it becomes coated with this grit on the overrolling edges as though with coal dust. The crusts would break up about every 40 minutes. There was a heavy curtain across the southeast grotto which was fountaining inside, and at the lake level under the southeast station three tunnels were revealed by the subsidence, corresponding to three spatter heaps above. These tunnels appeared to lead to a honeycombing in the bench in the direction of the southeast sink-holes of February. There was active fountaining in the main lake with streaming southward.

On this day the writer, assisted by Mr. Horace Johnson, made some experiments at the east cove with air and oxygen. The compressed air tank was connected with forty feet of half-inch pipe, the terminal of which was drilled with small holes. This terminal was immersed in the lake during break-up spells with the air turned on, but except for a little bubbling no definite effects were seen and the tendency to rapid crusting made the conditions unsatisfactory. A glass bottle of oxygen was attached to the pipe and immersed in the lake through a hole broken in the crust, without effect other than the exploding of the bottle. Other bottles were thrown in and either exploded or produced yellow flames through skin. Finally a wooden box full of straw weighted with stones was thrown into the liquid lava and produced a bright flame for some minutes, then explosions as the box sank, then violent fountaining with flames at intervals. Tests by blowing air into a flaming orifice at the northeast margin of the lake produced no effect, showing that combustion was not increased by supplying more oxygen. In general the air tests seem to indicate that the lava, like this vent, is already supplied with air for combustion purposes.

The most interesting result of these experiments was seen on withdrawing the iron pipe, with the perforated end covered with a hot lava shell. On blowing through the upper end, after the pipe had been immersed without air pressure, it was repeatedly shown that a yellow flame burned around the lower orifices, indicating that a combustible gas from the lava had gathered in the pipe. Special experiments will be instituted to discover what this gas is.

On May 16 at 10 a. m., the lake appeared still lower with inner walls about 20 feet high but the crusts were thinner and there was streaming from the central cavern in a curve east and southeast with splashing in the southeast and east grottoes. The pool was very hot and there was overhang all around the borders. The main lake showed several central fountains and many overhanging grottoes, high rampart heaps on the cliff margin north and south and the southwest island stood 20 foot high. All the extensive recent flows showed collapsed surfaces. The east island mass was rising and the northeast floor sinking; the northwest crag was rising and the north chasm sinking; the crag-mass was rising and the northwest pond region sinking; the south island mass was rising and the south floor sinking. The southwest crags, southeast bench, old east crag and northeast peak are being encroached upon and buried by the now flows. The northwest and west cones were both restored to full activity, the former 12 feet high and open on the south side, the latter 20 feet high with an open glowing orifice one foot across showing stalactites within. At 12:30 p. m., the lava had risen four feet. There was a broken cone crater over the southeast grotto.

On May 17, at 10 a. m., the lakes were 10 feet below the floors and rising rapidly. The southeast pool had thin skins and was fountaining on three sides, with streaming mostly eastward. In the main lake the streaming was reversed and poured northward and eastward from the crusted southwest cove with strong bombardment of the northern shores. The southwest point had cracked away and subsided below the southwest bench in a triangular mass 50 feet on a side and was separated from the bench by a crevasse 10 feet wide. Border fountains were puffing and Old Faithful was the only locality of central fountaining.

The northwest cone was hissing continuously and at noon it puffed rhythmically while the west cone threw out pasty lava occasionally from a diminished orifice. There was a high grotto dome on the southwest side of the northwest arm and a cracked pressure ridge extended from it to the northwest pond, smoking strongly as though over a tunnel. Streaming was outward from the northwest arm. Blue smoke rose from the summit of the immense northern grotto dome.

During the morning there was steady rising and at 12 noon the southwest point was mostly submerged, there was much crusting, and strong bombardment southeast. Old Faithful was irregular with explosions averaging about once a minute, through a bubbling spot in a heavy crust. At 12:30 p. m. the lake level was within one foot of overflow at the southeast grotto and at 1 p. m. it was brimming all around both pools. There was not much indication of change of level of the overflow rim of May 13. At 1:15 p. m. there were dribbling overflows at fountaining spots all around and a flow across the isthmus from the main lake. These overflows reached a length of 20 or 30 feet in the east cove and the northwest arm, but subsidence of a few feet followed during the afternoon.

Measurement on May 18, 1917, at 9:15 a. m., made the depression of the southeast pool 70 feet below the southeast rim of Halemaumau, and the level of overflow of the previous day was 57 feet below the rim of the pit.

The lakes were depressed within their inner pits about 15 feet and there were some falls of rock from the inner cliff. The southeast pool was crusted with occasional cracking and foundering, streaming to the southeast and to irregular border fountaining in that direction. The large southeast cone was completely curtained off. A very large dome had been built at the southwest cove, the isthmus was high, the north dome had increased in size with lava puffing and pounding inside it, and occasional cracking was heard from the east and northeast floors. In the middle of the south flood towards the east was a blowing and surging incandescent pot about two feet across, a simple glowing hole through shells of the recent flat flow. The sinking of the lake had completely restored the southwest point, submerged on the previous day. There was bombardment against the south face of the southwest island and open streaming southward from it, the central part of the lake being crusted. The hole in the west cone was still smaller and puffing. The northwest cone was broken and glowing, and fresh driblet flows had poured from it over the site of the northwest pond.

On the lake side of the isthmus there were three grotto tunnels and violent travelling fountains were forming in a semicircle of uncrusted lava and moving from the Old Faithful locality to the northernmost of these. The north end of the main lake was crusted over.

At 1:45 p. m. an unusual northwest wind out of a thunder squall on Mauna Loa blew the pit fumes across the southeast part of Kilauea crater and nucleated there and made visible great quantities of moist warm air rising from the cracks so as to make the whole southeast region appear as though new steam cracks had broken out.

The following report from the Whitney Laboratory of Seismology is submitted by Mr. H. O. Wood:

During the week-interval ending with May 18 three small local earthquakes have been registered, and one feebly-indicated chief phase of a distant teleseism. Throughout the interval the seismographic amplitudes of microseismic motion have been unusually small. Volcanic vibration has been strong and "stormy" throughout the week. Early in the interval there was progressive shift of the pens in the sense of tilt to eastward, restoring balance to the disturbance of the previous week. Afterward there was little change.

Technology Station, May 26, 1917.

During the week ending May 25, 1917, strong rising has continued with flooding of the floors on opposite sides of Halemaumau northwest and southeast, and such rapid rising of the crags that the large crag-mass is now a conspicuous object even from Volcano House. Its summit is now above the southeast rim of Halemaumau. The lake has risen at the rate of 1.3 feet per day and is now only 46 feet below the rim of the pit.

On Saturday, May 19, at 1 p. m., the lake was nearly level with its rim in places, but it subsided about two feet in 20 minutes. There was little fountaining except at the extreme southeast. At 1:30 p. m. the southwest cove overflowed and flooded the whole south

May 28, 1917, 8:30 p. m. Night view of crag mass from northeast.—Photo. Jaggar.

May 29, 1917, at noon. Lava overflows, filling northeast depression.—Photo. Jaggar.

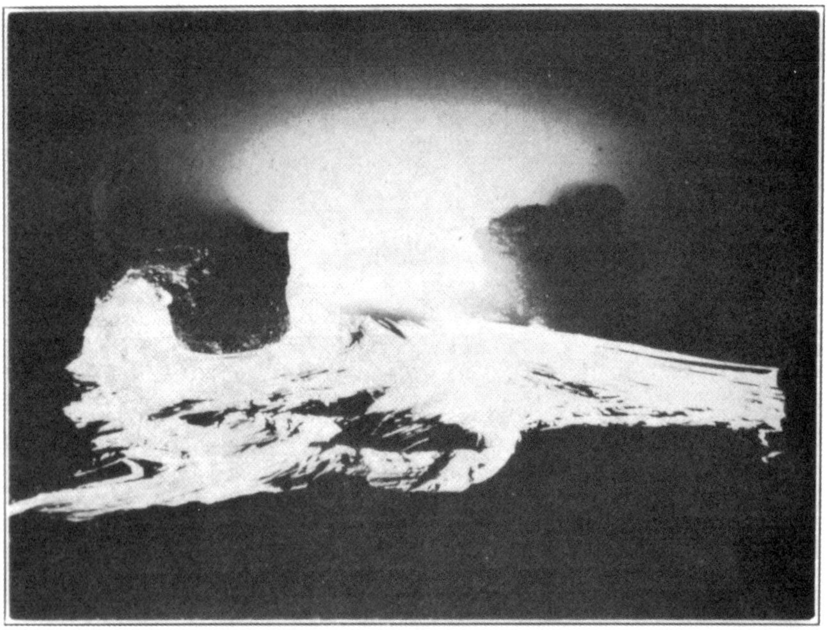

May 28, 1917, 8 p. m. Night view of central cavern and southeast pool during the crag uplift.—Photo. Jaggar.

May 23, 1917. Fountain at East Cove Spinning Pele's Hair; 20 feet distant, exposure 1-100 second; lava spurt about fifteen feet high.—Photo. Jaggar.

floor. At 3:30 p. m. a flow about 200 feet long poured from the northeast bank of the main lake across the northeast floor and an hour later there was overflow at the east cove. The banks of the lake and the southeast island were mostly about two feet high and streaming was rapid from the west. There was much fountaining activity.

On May 20, at 11:30 a. m., there were numerous fresh flows on the northeast floor to be seen from the east station. The lakes were brimming and a broad overflow from the southeast pool extended westward half way across the south floor. This was added to by lava spurting out from the south cone which tended to flow southward. The fumes were thin. At 2:20 p. m. the lakes subsided five feet and there was heavy bombardment southwest. At 2:25 p. m. there were strong falls of rock into the lake from the northeast rampart and from the north dome. At 7:30 p. m. the lakes had again risen and there was overflow into the north chasm.

On Monday, May 21, at 2 p. m., the banks were five feet high with fountaining activity strongest toward the north, and quiet rising in progress in the southeast pool. At 2:30 p. m., there was border fountaining east and northeast.

On May 22, at 10:20 a. m., the inner cliff was ten feet high and there was strong grotto activity southeast and northeast. At 11:30 a. m. there were two rock falls from the bank on the south side of the southeast pool, followed by cracking, foundering and rapid flow towards the east. At 12:10 p. m. there was a heavy avalanche from the rising northwest tabular crag, the debris falling into the northwest arm and producing much fountaining. During the afternoon the lake was stagnant.

The floor levels east and south were now nearly flush with the southeast bench of January. A driblet cone had been built in the middle of the south floor near its east end. The crag-mass was now plainly visible from Volcano House. There was strong fountaining bombardment against the west shore and at the north and northwest. The northeast rampart and the north dome were sulphur-stained. The east island mass was still more upraised on the side of the main lake. The southeast rampart cone was hissing from glowing cracks on its southwest side, the south cone was glowing at its west base, the northwest cone was a glowing tumble of rocks, and the west cone was low with a glowing gash in its middle. A saddle-shaped cone with a lava channel separating its two halves had formed at the northeast rampart, having almost exactly the same location, size, and shape as the January cone at this place. The north half-dome was now 20 feet high, overhanging toward the west and exhibited a continuous flaming fountain within its grotto. There were fresh smooth flows over the sites of the northwest and west ponds with crack-and-founder pattern, mostly from the northwest arm. New floods covered the southwest wall valley. Old Faithful was active and the east side of the main lake appeared to be building points which divided it into coves. Curtained grottoes were numerous. There was much Pele's hair on the south floor.

On May 23, at 8:45 a. m., half of the southeast grotto dome collapsed and this broke up the crusts and started rapid eastward streaming. The southeast pool was about ten feet below the floors. From 10:30 a. m. to 1:30 p. m. the lake rose until it was only two or three feet below the level of overflow. There were numerous fountains and the central crags were obviously rising as the shore spatter levels were higher toward the middle region than elsewhere. There was streaming from the northwest and much quiet crust. The north dome was now curtained and a puffing fountain was active beside it. There was much breathing of gas from under heavy crusts and an occasional uplifting of skins as balloons. It is worthy of note that the large pooled overflows are festooned with a brittle skin when they first flow out but in a short time these skins crack and founder in the pooled lava beneath, releasing great quantities of gas. There results a very thick crust with large blisters on its upper surface six or eight inches in diameter. This crust is much flatter and more stable than the wrinkled shells and the pooled area shows marked slumping through contraction and loss of gas when solidification is complete.

On May 24 at 11:30 a. m. there was a fresh broad festooned overflow from the southeast cove over the south floor. The lake was now 20 feet below the floors and the south side of the isthmus between the two pools had collapsed to an open channel through which was rapid flow from the main lake to the southeast pool amounting at times to a cascade. The southeast, west and northwest cones, and the southwest rampart dome were all glowing. There was a fresh driblet flow in the north chasm and the north dome appeared lower. The west and northwest cones were puffing slightly. The high inner bench and southwest island showed overhang. The main lake was crusted over, but there was shoreward rush and bombardment at the northwest tunnel leading to the northwest pond and at the southwest shore leading to tunnels under the south floor. Smoke had increased. Some very small rock falls were heard and there was much appearance of caving from the inner cliff. At 12:15 p. m. the lake had risen 10 feet and was rising strongly.

On Friday, May 25, 1917, there was strong overflow at 9 a. m., and thereafter until noon the lake subsided about five feet. The lakes were at first joined by a wide channel covering the remnants of the isthmus, and after the subsidence the north side of the isthmus was revealed as a partially sunken large flat islet with channels on both sides of it. The southwest islet was still in place. The overflow floods covered the east and south floors, drowned the south cone and spread all over the northwest and west floors, greatly widening the floor area and encroaching on the talus and the older benches. The south and east talus was now mostly covered. There was tremendous bombardment against the northwest table crag and this table showed an extraordinary uplift of 15 feet since the previous day, carrying with it a bench of fresh flows around its base on the east and north. It showed fresh breaks from north to south in its summit at the east end and at its base at the west end. Instead of tilting this tabular mass is rising bodily owing to inflow beneath it of pasty bench magma impelled by the weight of lava floods much larger than it in area in the lake basin itself and on the floors northwest and northeast.

Measurement on May 25 at 9 a. m. made the southeast pool 46 feet below the rim during the overflow. The floors had now been built up to the January level southeast and northwest and it was very evident that the lake shorelines were tilting toward these directions of maximum overflow. The northeast floor was now the lowest area, but as the northeast shore appeared to be tilting up, no channel was yet available for flooding it. The great overflows east, south and northwest were first covered with broad trains of festooned skin; this would crack and founder and then the whole surface would solidify smoothly, except for hundreds of immense blisters, and subside by several feet. The northwest cone continued to puff.

The following report from the Whitney Laboratory of Seismology is submitted by Mr. H. O. Wood:

During the week interval ending with May 25 one small local earthquake has been registered, and one doubtful wave group.

The seismographic amplitudes of microseismic motion have been of normal value or less. Volcanic vibrations have been strong steadily, with stronger wave groups also. There have been no conspicuous net changes in the direction of the writing levers (tilt)—though the ordinary diurnal changes have taken place.

Technology Station, June 2, 1917.

The week ending Friday, June 1, 1917, has been marked at Halemaumau by gorgeously brilliant spectacles of rising and very rapid uptilting of the inner crags. All of these crags came into full view from the Volcano House recalling the scene pictured in the early eighties, when there were similar crags above the rim of Halemaumau. The overflow level at the southeast bench on May 31 broke all records since 1894, reaching a height only 22 feet below the rim of the pit. The lake itself was only 20 feet down. Fountains and blowing cones during the week have spurted high above the rim of Halemaumau so as occasionally to be visible from the Volcano House. The pit as seen from Uwekahuna bluff was remarkably like a moon crater, showing outer and inner concentric smoking cracks and ridges, irregular peaked inner crags, but differing from the lunar rings in exhibiting an active glowing lava lake. The end of the week shows a sinking of the lava, expectable just before the solstice, by analogy with former years.

At 9 a. m. Saturday, May 26, the lake was nearly brimming and the central crags showed continued rising. Fresh overflows glowed on the southeast and northwest floors. There was much fountaining and the cones were puffing. Streaming was away from the west and northwest coves and through a broad channel to the southeast pool. The lake appeared stationary with much quiet crust. The northwest tabular crag had now again lifted a bank of fresh flows 20 feet high around its base, and rocks falling from its cliffs gave evidence of movement there. The northeast floor and north chasm were clearly subsiding. The west side of the old summit crag of the crag-mass had fallen away. In the evening there began a prolonged period of heavy overflowing destined to continue six days.

In the morning and past noon of May 27 tremendous floods of lava rose at the west and northwest cones and poured over the floors in a great horseshoe encircling the lake on the west, south and east. The northeast floor remained a great depression 25 to 30 feet below the level of overflow, owing to its remoteness from the source conduits, the tendency to build higher at the west maintaining the ancient habit of the pit. During the afternoon the lake subsided 10 feet, glow rims appeared all around the lake and flows and then the latter broke up their crusts by the cracking and foundering process, leaving a smooth surface where before were heavy festoons. Then the gas-vents of the northwest and south cones reasserted themselves where they had been flooded, and the south cone built itself up 3 feet high with splashing and some violent spraying. The southwest crags had been submerged, but they reappeared as low piles of crusts. Southeast and southwest border cones, a fountain above the central cavern locality, and Old Faithful were persistent features.

The northwest wall cavern was now drowned. The west cone maintained itself as a dome with an upwelling fountain beside it. The great half-cone at the edge of the lake southeast grew to be 15 feet high. During the afternoon there was violent bombardment of the north table and the shore of the central peninsula south, but much of the lake was covered with quiet crust. The east and northeast lake margin was rising and thus blocking overflow in that direction.

From 8:30 to 11:30 p. m. the lake was again overflowing, mostly from the west and there was violent spurting above the southeast cone and the southwest rampart, so that the flings of melt could be seen rising high above the edge of Halemaumau.

Rising continued. Apart from the western well-springs, the lava overflowed the lake margin in short driblet flows at the east cove but wholly failed to reach the northeast depression. There were other driblet flows at the north chasm and under the east station. The southeast pool overflowed southward in a wide torrent which curved around to the east, and other overflows poured from the southwest, west and northwest arms of the lake. The south cone at first showed a steady wide blue flame, but this was drowned under the floods. Many flames appeared from under crusts around the lake margin. There was much piling up and scraping of border slabs of crust. In the late evening the southeast cone became quiet, but two fountains over the central cavern built half-ring ramparts.

The high pressure kept up for three hours, but at 11:30 a. m. the lake surface, which had been darkly crusted, cracked up with foundering of crusts and thousands of bubble fountains, then the new flows started cracking and foundering and glow-rims of subsidence appeared all around. The cracking and foundering of the flows began at the northwest and spread from there indicating that the greatest thickness of crusts was first reached in that conduit region.

Measurement at noon Monday, May 28, 1917, made the depression of the southeast bench of overflow 28 feet below the rim of Halemaumau. In contrast to this the bottom of the northeast depression was 59 feet below the rim, and the 1894 bench valley was 65 feet below the rim. The depression of the lake at the moment was 35 feet and above it the heights of the crags were:

Old east crag, 10 feet;
Crag mass, 47 feet;
East island, 45 feet;
Southeast cone, 12 feet.

At 9 a. m. there were short overflows east and west. During the morning the lake subsided 5 feet and then recovered. There was violent bombardment of the east bank, and the streaming was eastward as usual. The crag mass, east island mass and northwest table all appeared higher. One of the flows of the morning had poured from the southeast bench northward to the base of the 1894 ledge. At 1 p. m. the west cone, an open over facing westward, was vomiting out lava which spread over the floor north and south. These flows extended themselves to the south and east as before during the afternoon. The northwest cone had built a high driblet heap.

In the evening a singular cataclysm happened. A brilliant flare and rush of smoke over Halemaumau was seen from the Volcano House at 7:15 p. m. Watchers at the rim of the pit saw a sudden tumble of benches with great clouds of dust and gas brilliantly illumined by multiple fountaining. Apparently the lake subsided about 15 feet in the late afternoon, and a sudden readjustment of the bench magma lifted the central crags and perhaps opened crevasses into which the lake magma flowed so as to lower it temporarily. At 7:45 p. m. there was a profound canyon-like inner pit with the central cavern revealed as a great glowing vault. There was high incandescence and the current was rapid eastward. The southwest island had toppled over to the north.

The south island mass had risen suddenly above the rim of Halemaumau, making a distinct shoulder in fresh glowing flows outpoured only that afternoon. The outer ledge of the east island mass had broken away and risen so as to make a second mushroom beside the earlier east island. The latter had broken away from the eastern escarpment and subsided a little, and adjacent to it on the northwest a lava pond 50 feet in diameter had opened at the site of the sulphur hole. The old east crag and adjacent rampart had risen bodily 10 feet, cracking away from the southeast bench at the site of the former east gulch. The northwest tabular crag was now above the rim of the pit. The crag mass rose so much with westward tilt that its serrate northeast peak had suddenly become its summit, whereas only that morning the middle peak had been the highest. The spatter markings along its base on the lake side were fully 40 feet high.

The northwest cone had become a flaming pile of crusts, and the west cone a glowing hole. There was another similar hole at the west base of the tabular crag northwest. There was noticeable increase of glow in the luminosity of the cracks of the fresh flows, as though oxidation of the gases in the crust cavities had increased, some of the orifices showing whitish yellow heat. Some of the lake fountains also were extraordinarily brilliant. The inner cliffs around the main lake appeared from 40 to 90 feet high. The walls of the southeast pool were horizontally banded with spatter lines for the upper twenty feet, but the lower half appeared massive like aa lava. During the evening the lake rose slowly.

At noon, May 29, the lake by rising had recovered almost its usual aspect and was brimming level with its inner cliff. The sulphur hole pond was fountaining. The northeast depression appeared elevated and the subsidence of the lake edge on that side, next the east island, now made possible an overflow into the depression. This took place, and three overflows poured from the lake north, northeast from the east cove, and east at the east gulch. The east cove flow became dominant and cascaded into the northeast depression in a steady torrent 40 feet wide for two hours. The filling was about 800 feet long and from 10 to 15 feet deep and extended from under the east station to the north chasm. It finally penetrated the middle crevasse of the 1894 ledge with a short driblet flow.

With intermissions the flows continued and at the west cone two high spiracles were built. These spatter heaps were 15 feet high, and at 6 p. m. the southern one was spouting umbrella shaped flings of melt with a gulping noise and a bell-like ring. These spurts could be plainly seen at the Volcano House. There were two cones northwest also, the lower one in process of rapid building. There were strong gas pressure and overflows all around the lake.

On May 30, at 3 p. m., the banks of the lake were 2 feet high, there were few fountains and the hissing was slight at the northwest cone. The west cone was not spurting, but driblet flows were in motion near it on the floor. Otherwise there was no fresh overflow since the previous day. The northeast pond was floored over and a conical spatter heap, now inactive, had been built there. Streaming was from the northwest as usual.

On the morning of May 31, fresh short overflows appeared southeast, east, northeast, north, northwest and west. The depression of the southeast bench at the lake margin was 20 feet and against the wall 22 feet. This was the maximum overflow of this period. The lake subsided from four feet below its bank to twelve feet down during the morning. There was a glowing pond of collapse south of the northwest cones. The west cones were surrounded by domed up flows. The central cavern was visible.

June 1 was rainy, but the crags rose greatly and smoke increased.

The following report from the Whitney Laboratory of Seismology is submitted by Mr. H. O. Wood:

During the week interval ending with June 1, 1917, one small local shock has been registered: and one teleseism, the record of a shock of very considerable energy in the region of the origin.

The seismographic amplitudes of microseismic motion have ranged from small to moderate values.

Volcanic vibration has been strong, both in the steady run, and in sporadic wave-groups or "storms". A well marked storm of considerable duration accompanied the sudden, spasmodic uplift of the crag mass, islands and peninsulas in Halemaumau on the early evening of May 28.

There has been no notable change in pen-shift in the sense of tilt during the week.

Very respectfully,

T. A. JAGGAR, JR., Director.

Editorial Note.

A very complete series of moving pictures of the volcano by day and by night, has recently been made by Mr. Burton Holmes, the noted lecturer. These will be shown in conjunction with Mr. Holmes' lecture tour approximately as follows:

November 15th, commence Philadelphia, Pittsburg, Washington, Baltimore. January 15th, on Sundays and Mondays, New York; Tuesdays, Orange, N. J. Wednesdays, Brooklyn; Thursdays, Wocester; Fridays and Saturdays, Boston.—Editor.

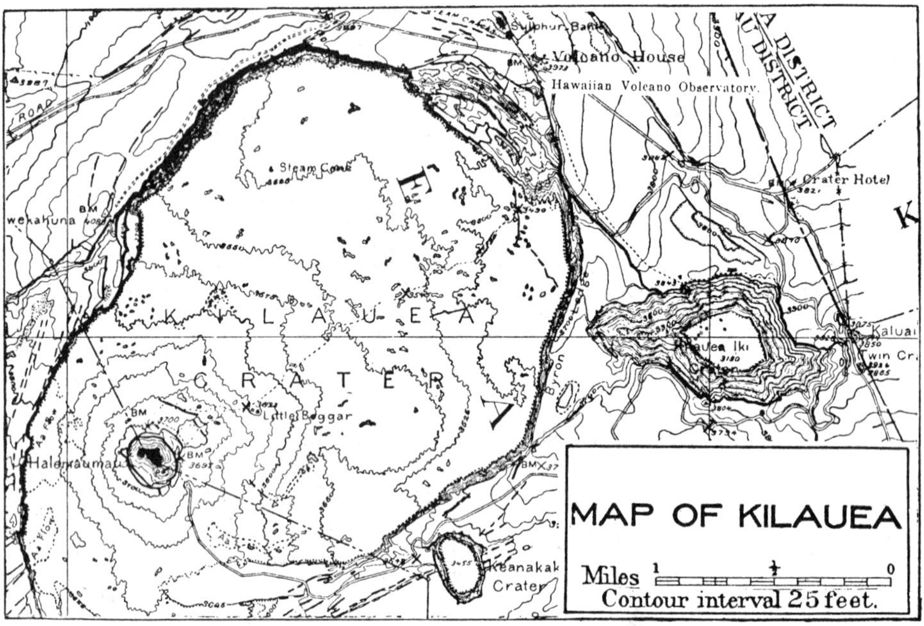

HAWAIIAN VOLCANO RESEARCH ASSOCIATION.

This society is a voluntary one, made up of subscribers to scientific work which is being executed by the Massachusetts Institute of Technology.

In 1917 there are about 150 subscribers in Hawaii and elsewhere, firms and individuals. A group of firms and persons in Hilo built the main observatory building in the spring of 1912. Publications to date have been weekly reports since the summer of 1911, now reprinted in Honolulu in monthly form. The Massachusetts Institute of Technology will publish annual reports, of which the introductory number was printed in 1912.

The weekly bulletin as it appears in the Advertiser is reprinted as a leaflet and sent to regular annual subscribers to the work of the Association. L. A. Thurston is president of the Board of Directors of the Association, and R. W. Shingle is treasurer. New subscribers who are interested in volcanoes will be welcomed in the Association. The Association aims: (1) To record volcanic activity and earthquakes in Hawaii; (2) to attract scientific men hither for special studies; (3) to promote the establishment of volcano observatories all over the world. The annual dues of regular members are $5; patrons of the Association subscribe larger amounts.

WHITNEY LABORATORY OF SEISMOLOGY.

The Whitney Laboratory of Seismology is equipped with two Bosch-Omori 100 kg tromometers registering N-S and E-W motion, a heavy Omori tromometer registering E-W motion, and an Omori "ordinary Seismograph" designed for registering strong earthquakes in all three components of motion. These are seated on concrete piers in a closed basement room having practically constant temperature, beneath the chief Observatory building near the hotel. Time is referred to a rated chronometer, checked at intervals by solar observations with a transit. Both instruments are loaned by the College of Hawaii. Hawaiian standard time (H. S. T.) is 10 hrs. 30 min. slower than Greenwich time.

CANCANI SCALE OF SEISMIC INTENSITY.

Expressed by accelerations measured in millimeters per second per second.

I.	Instrumental	0.0	2.5
II.	Very slight	2.5	5.0
III.	Slight	5.0	10.0
IV.	Sensible, mediocre	10.0	25.0
V.	Rather strong	25.0	50.0
VI.	Strong	50.0	100.0
VII.	Very strong	100.0	250.0
VIII.	Ruinous	250.0	500.0
IX.	Disastrous	500.0	1000.0
X.	Very disastrous	1000.0	2500.0
XI.	Catastrophic	2500.0	5000.0
XII.	Great catastrophe	5000.0	10000.0

Grade IV. is ordinarily the minimum perceived by the senses; and in grade XII. the acceleration, or rate of change of motion (jerk) reaches that of terrestrial gravitation.

In the standard form of report the maximum intensity or acceleration, designated by the symbol a, or max. a, is given in the conventional unit, the milligal. The milligal is a measure of acceleration, such that 1 milligal = 1/100 mm. per sec. per sec. = 10 μ per sec. per sec. The Cancani scale, here defined in terms of millimeters per sec. per sec., can therefore be expressed in milligals by multiplying each of the numbers by 100.

WEEKLY BULLETIN
OF THE
Hawaiian Volcano Observatory

Vol. V. HONOLULU, HAWAII, JUNE, 1917. No. 6

TECHNOLOGY STATION, June 9, 1917.—During the week ending June 8, 1917, the Halemaumau lava column has subsided to a depth of 75 feet below the rim, from a maximum height of only 22 feet depression on May 31. The liquid lake in three days reached its lowest for the subsidence which has so far occurred. Sunday, June 3, showed depression of 78 feet, though only the day before the bench crags had stood at their highest elevation well above the edge of the pit. On June 2, however, the crags subsided gradually and continued to do so during the week, the lake apparently compensating this, perhaps by a rising of its pasty bottom lava, for the level of the liquid surface has fluctuated but little, and has risen slightly at the end of the week. Another high level is to be expected after the solstice about the end of June.

On Saturday, June 2, the lake appeared 20 feet below its inner cliff, or some 40 feet below the southeast Halemaumau rim. At fifteen minutes after noon there were two rock tumbles into the lake northeast, and from the summit of the crag mass, sending up puffs of brown dust. The southwest islet had reappeared. Rocks were falling about the 1894 bench northeast, and from the summit of the crag mass, and all signs pointed to subsidence in progress. In the morning, however, the crags above Halemaumau as seen from the Volcano House had appeared at their highest, and the following by measurement were above the rim of the pit: northeast peak, east island, crag mass, central peninsula, south peak, northwest table. The two east island peaks and the old east crag had risen strongly since May 31, exhibiting south of the east crag a new ridge of elevation in fresh flows.

After noon there was sinking until 3 p. m., the lake showing inner walls 30 feet high. Then the lake appeared to rise somewhat relative to its inner pit. At 3:45 p. m. there were avalanches north and east. At 5:30 p. m. there was a fall of rock from the south side of the southeast pool, inducing much fountaining. The lake appeared rising. At 6:15 p. m. there were heavy falls southeast, and at 6:50 p. m. an avalanche at the east cove. During the afternoon and night the crags sank below the rim, only the cragmass and the northwest table remaining partly visible from Volcano House. The glow at night was moderate and the fumes increased.

Measurement on June 3, 1917, at 9 a. m. made the lake depression southeast 78 feet and that of the east island summit 14 feet. The lake had thus subsided the equivalent of nineteen feet per day for three days. The east island had sunk 30 feet in twenty-four hours. This crag was now 64 feet above the lake.

The inner walls appeared 40 feet high, and the northeast floor had subsided to a much flatter attitude in place of its strong slant northeastward. With it had gone down the east island mass and the northeast peak, and much of the northeast cliff over the main lake had fallen in. Gaping crevasses appeared in the northeast floor, which had subsided 10 feet along with the 1894 bench, carrying down much new debris. Rocks were falling in the valley back of that bench. The southeast shelf remained high, the other floors parting from it along a north-south crack, which became a crevasse under the east station. The southern floor area remained relatively high. The northwest tubular crag had subsided bodily within the elevation ridge around it, and dense smoke rose from cracks at its base on the east, south and west. Rocks were

WEEKLY BULLETIN
of the
Hawaiian Volcano Observatory

Published Monthly at Honolulu, Hawaii, by the Hawaiian Volcano Research Association

L. W. de Vis-Norton........Secretary

Entered as second-class matter January 20, 1914, at the post-office at Honolulu, Hawaii, under the Act of August 24, 1912.

falling from its cliffs. A crevasse extended westward from it, but the western floors were still high. The crag mass had tilted back towards the lake, its three peaks now appearing of equal height. The west and northwest cones were broken heaps and a pressure ridge connected the former with the west cove of the lake. The lake appeared smoky and stagnant, with northern fountaining.

On June 4 at 10:30 a. m. it was evident that sinking continued, though the lake southeast was only 20 feet below the inner bench and exhibited a new spatter level 5 feet above the liquid. The floors were much lower, parting along smoky fissures from the high southeast shelf. The northeast floor had settled back nearly horizontal. There was fountaining southeast and about Old Faithful, and an occasional central fountain migrated eastward through the narrows leading to southeast pool. The northwest table was lower and the crag mass appeared much as in January, the western peak being now again the summit. The south cone was glowing and the fumes appeared thinner. At 2:30 p. m. the lake appeared still higher relative to the subsiding benches, with much fountaining east. That this effect was really subsidence of the benches was shown by abundant falls of rock from the 1894 bench northeast and from the north and northwest walls of Halemaumau.

On June 5 at 3 p. m. the north arm of the lake was found widened owing to the falling away of the northern part of the east island promontory. A grotto northeast near Old Faithful became very active, with high spurting and bubble fountaining.

On June 6 at 4 p. m. the lake was about 60 feet down and the general appearance of Halemaumau was very different from that of the previous week. In general the settling of the floors had followed the scheme of the February subsidence, low northeast and southwest, high northwest and southeast. The recession of the lake in the inner pit and the increased smoke made all but the southeast pool difficult to see, and the first impression of the observer on the brink is of extensive tumbled benches and tabular crags, much smoke, and little lava. The lake really, however, is little changed, and its margins have subsided with it. The south and east island masses have sunk lowest, so that the inner bench about the southeast pool was only 20 feet high except at its southeast end, where the shelf stood twice that height above it. There was much bombardment and building of stalactites under this shelf, and from this cove smoking cracks extended north and south along the break between the lower and higher floors. The southward cracks glowed and led to the glowing heap of the south cone. Crusts were jammed in the western entrance to the southeast pool and from them rapid streaming poured eastward. The southwest cove was crusted over and the southwest islet had become a peninsula attached on the east, while a narrow channel encircled it on the west.

The southwest floor had sunk more than the northwest floor along the crack or tunnel line, which was marked now as a pressure ridge from the west cone to the west cove. The northwest crevasse was widening, with subsidence on the lake side tending to leave a shelf next the wall. The northwest table had sagged downward in the middle along a north-south axis, bending like a plastic substance. Settling had made the northeast floor continuous with the north chasm so that the latter could no longer be distinguished. The cracks in the northeast floor, parallel with the

1894 bench, had widened into crevasses 3 feet across in places; very hot air rose from them, and red glow could be seen in the smaller ones at a depth of four feet.

The new lower inner bench, 4 feet high above the lake, was wide on the southwest and west. The north end of the lake was inactive with southward streaming. Not much motion was in evidence, but a fall from the central peninsula into the southeast channel at 5:15 p. m. showed that subsidence was still in progress. Heavy smoke rose from the northeast inner cliff, from the ends of the northwest table, from the southeast cracks, and from the western pressure ridges.

The lake was 10 feet lower at 3 p. m. on June 7 and the smoke was heavy. There were central fountains and rapid eastward streaming. The west cone was glowing from a gash on its southern side, and the pressure ridge from it extended down the slope to the lake like a long mole-hill.

Measurement on Friday, June 8, 1917, at 10 a. m., made the depression of the lake 73 feet, indicating a rise of 5 feet in 5 days, whereas the summit of the east island had subsided 17 feet in the same period. The summit of the crag mass was the only interior feature now visible from Volcano House. The following were heights above the lake surface:

Marginal bench south of southeast pool	10 ft.
Southeast shelf	46 "
Floor under south station	33 "
Northeast floor	11 "
Summit Crag Mass	64 "
" East Island	42 "
" Northwest Table	63 "
" Central Peninsula south	49 "
" Northeast peak	46 "

Smoke had diminished and the lake was higher in the morning. There was much quiet crusting, and occasional blowoff of gas with fountaining at the central cavern. Streaming was eastward in southeast pool and rapidly southward in the southwest cove. At noon there was subsidence with central and southwestward fountaining. The southeast cove was quiet. The northwest cones puffed slightly.

At 5 p. m. the lake was 5 feet lower and more active. There were fountains southwest, west, at the Old Faithful locality northeast and at the southeast. Streaming was now northward from the southwest cove and from northwest to east and southeast. Flames rose from the south and west cones and in flares from the central cavern. There were occasional falls of spatter margins.

Fresh rock tumbles lay under the upper walls, drawn down by the subsiding floors, on the south, west, northwest, northeast and east. The northwest table was lower, its east end now a sharp pressure ridge, and a valley had developed north of it beneath the wall shelf which extended westward. There was a pressure ridge extending west from the northwest arm. The meaning of these western pressure ridges extending from the sites of conduit wells to the lake, is that tunnels beneath have had their walls pressed together by the wedge effect of the subsidence of the bench magma within a funnel-shaped pit and the tunnel roofs have accordingly arched upward. Such a ridge may thus be an interesting index of a tunnel beneath.

A crevasse in the south and southwest floors was developing parallel to the upper wall, preparatory to making a shelf there as usual if sinking continues, and this merged eastward with cracks under the southeast bench. The west end of the latter was a smoky tumbled slope, where the sinking of the floor had dragged down great masses of rock from the upper cliff.

The Observatory has again the privilege of assisting at chemical investigations of Halemaumau conducted by the Geophysical Laboratory of the Carnegie Institution of Washington. Dr. E. S. Shepherd of that laboratory, who was here in 1911 and 1912, arrived at the volcano on June 8 for a protracted stay, and equipped with improved apparatus for the collection of volcanic gases.

The following report from the Whitney Laboratory of Seismology is submitted by Mr. H. O. Wood:

During the week ending with June 8, 1917, six small local earthquakes have been registered, and the chief phases of two distant teleseisms with small amplitudes and vague indications of phase. Microseismic registration has been as usual. Volcanic vibration has continued to be registered, with seismographic amplitudes somewhat greater than normal, both in the steady run and also in rather numerous and prolonged storms. In the early part of the week interval there was a sharp movement of the pen-levers in the sense of tilt to eastward, followed soon by a rapid partial recovery, after which no noteworthy changes occurred.

———

June 16, 1917.

During the week ending June 15, 1917, the lava lake of Halemaumau has remained stationary except for daily fluctuations of from 10 to 15 feet, the maximum depression of the lake reaching about 90 feet below the rim of the pit. The crags have continued to subside slowly and the smoke has increased. An upward spurt of 20 feet in the level of the lake at the end of the week is probably a movement of pulsation characteristic of approach to the turning point at the solstice.

On June 9, at 4 p. m., the lava column was lower though the shore-line of the southeast pool appeared unchanged. The benches were lower by at least ten feet. The smoking area under the southeast bench had collapsed to a chasm full of debris suggestive of development of a new cove of the lake. There were new smoking cracks on the upper southeast bench. Near the former cavern locality northwest the bench crack had now developed a low cliff through subsidence of the floor on the lake side. There were new falls of wall rock on the floor west and south. The northwest arm had developed by collapse, a chasm extending westward from the lake. The floor west of the crag-mass now sloped toward the latter just as in February, the crag-mass having subsided extensively. The northwest table was lower, showing only about 20 feet of cliff above the northwest floor. The main lake was in a deep inner pit, the peninsula of the southwest islet showing walls 15 feet high above the liquid, while the eastern walls of the main lake under the several crags appeared at least 60 feet high. Fountaining was about as usual, the surface current being very slow to the southeast. The west and northwest cones were whitened with solfataric deposits and there was a glowing gash on the south side of the west cone. Smoke had generally increased.

On June 10 at 5 p. m. conditions were much the same, with evidences of continued subsidence. The southeast chasm had collapsed farther and glowing lava could be seen within it. The northeast crevasses had widened. There were some marginal falls of rock into the lake, but the shoreline level relative to the benches appeared unchanged.

At this time a very instructive growth of pressure ridges smoking strongly, was shown, one of them extending from the northwest pond locality to the northwest arm, another from the west pond locality to the west cove, and a third from the south pond locality to the south cone and chasm. Each of these ridges gave evidences of a tunnel beneath which the subsidence and compression of the bench magma had crushed in so as to arch up its roof. It was worthy of note that each of the smoke places about the benches and crags corresponded to a formerly mapped pit, chasm or tunnel in location, and dense smoke is always an evidence of an open gas chamber beneath. Such places were the southeast chasm and cone, the pressure ridges, the north and northeast depressions and the central cavern tunnel. The large crevasses do not smoke.

On Monday, June 11, at 2:30 p. m., it was evident that there had been heavy tumbles of shore into the lake north of the east island so as to widen the lake towards the north, and the northeast grotto was fountaining with great vigor.

At 3:30 p. m. on June 12 it was evident that sinking continued, as the floors which had subsided under the cliff of the southeast bench appeared lower and that cliff was scaling off from time to time. Toward the north the cliff merged into a crevasse bounded on the lower side by huge slabs tilted at a high angle, and here rocks were falling frequently.

At 11 a. m. on June 13 the southeast pool was 20 feet below the marginal bench, there was heavy fountaining in a grotto under the southeast bench, and there were falls of rock into the lake from the central peninsula and from the south margin farther east which occasioned much fountaining.

At 2 p. m. on June 14 the lake as seen from the northeast was somewhat higher, the inner cliff of the southeast pool rising only ten feet above the lake. The eastward streaming was rapid, with traveling fountains which formed from time to time in the central region and migrated through the southeast channel. The lake appeared rising, but the smoke was very dense toward the north. At 2:15 p. m. the north pool showed much fountaining. At 2:30 p. m. the lava subsided a few feet and strong fountaining developed in the central cavern. Thereafter the lake continued to sink to a depth from 15 to 20 feet below the inner bench southeast and there was a very heavy fall from the east island bank into the lake. There was glow in the southeast chasm and the south cone had developed an open pot. The crag-mass appeared distinctly lower as though slowly subsiding bodily, so that the whole lake could be seen from the northwest margin of Halemaumau over the top of the crag-mass. The northwest floor had gone down with it. The smoke at the southeast chasm had greatly diminished with the appearance there of the live lava. At the north pressure ridge, however, next west of the former north chasm, yellowish-white smoke rose rapidly in dense masses.

Measurement on June 15, 1917, at 10 a. m., determined the depression of the lake to be 71 feet below the southeast rim of the pit, a gain of two feet of elevation in seven days. In the same period, however, the crag-mass had subsided six feet and the east island four feet.

On this morning the lake was high and rising to levels above the highest spatter marks of previous days. There was strong constructional activity, building a very large crescent-shaped spatter cone under the crag-mass, and others on the northwest, west, southwest and southeast. The southwest island and peninsula were submerged. The streaming was rapid from the west toward the north and east. In the southeast chasm there was a fountaining pot between the southeast pool and the south cone. A piece of the bank fell from the south side of the southeast pool. There was strong bombardment on the north shore of the northwest arm. In the southwest cove there was one shore grotto in action, but otherwise the pool south of the submerged peninsula was crusted over. The lake overflooded the floor between the two knobs of the east island. The west and northwest cones were smoking quietly, but smoke in general had lessened. This rise reached its maximum about noon, and the lake fell away in the afternoon, revealing again the peninsula of the southwest islet.

The following report from the Whitney Laboratory of Seismology is submitted by Mr. H. O. Wood:

During the week-interval ending with June 15 three definite local earthquakes of very small seismographic amplitude have been registered; also three doubtful wave-groups of local origin, and the feebly registered chief phases of two teleseisms. Microseismic motion has been registered as usual. Volcanic vibration has continued stronger than normal, both steadily and in storms. There has not been any noteworthy shifting of the pens in the sense of tilt other than its usual diurnal changes.

June 23, 1917.

During the week ending June 22, 1917, the lava lake has subsided 44 feet, with more or less continuous clatter of falling rocks and a sinking of the inner circle of floor all around, leaving a marginal shelf on the northwest and southeast. The inner floor has carried down with it all the crags, the lake tending to keep its shore line relatively unaltered.

Measurements on Saturday, June 16, at 10 a. m., made the depression of the lake 87 feet. The crag-mass rose 60 feet above the lake and the east island 51 feet. There was strong subsidence since the previous day, and the streaming was swift to a cavern under the southeast bench, where a caldron boiled violently at the lake level. Here and elsewhere the grottoes showed stalactites. After 10 a. m. the lake appeared rising. In the main lake the streaming was outward from both the northwest and southwest coves. The spatter dome under the crag-mass had partially collapsed and the new inner bench was 10 feet above the lake. A grotto near Old Faithful was puffing. The subsidence of the crag-mass at its north end had carried down the floor west of it, leaving a south-facing escarpment in place of the pressure ridge which formerly extended westward from the northwest arm. A pressure ridge had formed across the south floor from under the south station to the south cone, marking apparently the course of a tunnel from the old south pond. There were other pressure ridges and cracks on the south floor. Fire could be seen in the west cone. Rocks were falling at the east crevasse and above the east end of the 1894 bench. Rocks were in motion, also, southwest where the floor had gaped away from the wall, forming a wall crack four feet wide. The peninsula in the southwest cove was now restored. Blue-white smoke rose in dense masses on the north and northeast, and other smoking places were the northwest and west cones, the northwest escarpment, the southwest floor, the central peninsula and the southeast cove.

During the next two days the floor on all sides subsided heavily and the smoke increased. The northwest shelf became a high cliff extending from the west station to the northwest table. The latter had lowered until its upper surface was level with the shelf. The northwest floor and crag-mass, and the northeast, east and south floors had all sunk until the floors were level, or even sloping toward the lake. The southeast chasm was now a cove of the lake on the site of the former south cone. A smoking cone or pile of slabs had developed on the floor farther west along the course of the pressure ridge. The southeast bench near its west end surmounted great yawning crevasses separated by upright slices of bench ready to fall, and the shelf was extended westward under the southwest and south stations above an inner cliff along which the floor had subsided. There was a tumbled smoky pit in the region of the north peak. The northeast peak, the east island and the south island mass remained much as before, but all had gone down en masse.

On June 19 at 3:30 p. m. the inner cliff over the lake was still only 10 to 15 feet high, and the west and northwest cones were still smoking quietly. Streaming was swift to the southwest cove and to the southeast pool from the northwest. The peninsula in the southwest cove showed a flat upper surface about six feet above the lake. There was a new narrow inner bench two feet above the lake. The principal fountaining was on the southwest, southeast and northeast.

On June 20 at 11 a. m. the benches were still lower and rocks could be heard falling almost continuously from the northeast shelf and the 1894 bench. The highest part of the northwest table at its western crag was now below the floor shelf. The lake was relatively high and appeared to be rising above the inner bench of the previous day, and some spatter benches were in process of building. The southeast cove had built a glowing blow-hole in spatter on its western bank and this was flaming and hissing strongly. Otherwise the cove was crusted over. Streaming was now outward from the southwest cove to the north and east. There was violent bubble fountaining and down-sucking at Old Faithful and heavy bombardment against the north bank of the lake. A new sulphurous spot was developing east of the east island. The general condition represented by this week's subsidence appears to be a conflict between sinking bench magma and relatively rising lake magma.

On June 21, after a slight earthquake felt at the Observatory at about 7 a. m., a visit to the lake at 9:30 a. m. revealed a lava column still low and falling. This was the day of the solstice. Rocks were falling in the northeast crevasses. There was an open pool in the crust of the southeast cove. Streaming was eastward from both the northwest and southwest. Six fountains were in action and there was evidence of spatter building on the shores. At

May 16, 1917. Elevated northwest table crag, from north station.—Photo. Jaggar.

May 16, 1917. Depressed northeast floor of overflow, from north station.—Photo. Jaggar.

the moment the lake was bordered by a rim about two feet high hanging with stalactites. There was a great splash mark across the point north of the southeast cove occasioned, evidently, by a recent tumble into the lake from the high southeast bench, the edge of which was broken and crumbling.

On Friday, June 22, 1917, at 10:30 a. m., the depression of the lake was 115 feet, showing an average fall for seven days of over six feet per day. The crag-mass stood 54 feet above the lake and the east island 39 feet. There was evidence that the low level had been reached, for the fumes were thinner and no rocks were heard falling. Between 10:30 a. m. and noon there was strong rising of about five feet, so that the lake was brimming flush with the inner bench and was easily accessible at the southeast cove.

An exploration of the northeast floor on this date showed that the subsidence of the floor had left a 15-foot cliff along the 1894 bench, making the trail down much more difficult. The northeast crevasses were six feet wide in places and the old east crag was partially buried by debris from the high southeast bench. The north ridge, formerly the east end of the northwest table, had sunk so far as to become a depression under the old north rest-house with a tumbled slope on the northwest table side. The northwest table was far below the shelf left by the May floor. A tumbled pit emitted smoke at the side of the north chasm. The northwest cone was on a slope beneath a strong straight wall made by the northwest shelf. Great crevasses had developed at the west cone and extended from these southward.

The southeast cove was open, with surface streaming to its south end. There was rapid streaming eastward in the southeast pool, a large spatter dome was building on its south side, another appeared on the west shore of the lake, and others were being constructed southwest and northeast. There was still heavy smoke from the northeast cliff over the lake.

In the evening at 9 p. m. the lake was about five feet below the inner bench, showing stalactite margins, six or seven fountains, and vigorous streaming. The fumes were somewhat thinner. There was a glowing filigree at the spatter bank of the southeast cove and a blue flame could be seen near the summit of the central peninsula. Low-roofed caverns appeared to extend under the bank at the east cove and at the central cavern, with a bright orange glow and quiet blistered skins on the still pools that could be seen inside the cavernous spaces.

On this afternoon the summit of Mauna Loa showed unusually conspicuous fume which condensed in large puffs about sundown, and drifted northward. The cloud, however, was soon dissipated and appeared to be moisture condensed above the snow drifts owing to a chance atmospheric condition. Mr. Alfred Castle and Mr. Knollenberg visited Mokuaweoweo on June 19 and found heavy snow fields in the crater on its eastern side and the usual fuming toward the west.

The following report from the Whitney Laboratory of Seismology is submitted by Mr. H. O. Wood:

During the week-interval ending with June 22 four definite local earthquakes have been registered—one of intensity barly perceptible to the senses—and three wave-groups of doubtful character. Microseismic movements have been registered as usual. The seismographic amplitudes of volcanic vibration have continued larger than usual. There has been little shifting of the pens in the sense of tilt; even the diurnal variations have been less than usual.

June 30, 1917.

During the week ending June 29, 1917, the lava lake has remained about 100 feet below the rim of Halemaumau, with small oscillations and sufficient rising to produce small overflows and a pronounced inner bench platform. The change from subsidence to slight rising on June 22 was definite, and occurred simultaneously with the solstice, but the maximum rise for the first week after the solstice has been not more than 15 feet. The broad areas of inner bench began to show pronounced tilting towards the end of the week.

On Saturday, June 23, at 9 a. m., the

fumes were thinner and the lake surface hot, with three or four fountains and with streaming motion from the north into both the southwest and southeast pools. The spatter bench was generally higher and a new spatter heap had been built at the entrance to the central cavern. The crags and floors appeared unchanged. A smoking pressure ridge had gradually developed, extending from the east cove north to the sulphur hole. A similar line of fumy broken crust, partly ridge and partly valley, extended from the southeast cove across the south floor to the southwest pool.

On June 24 at 11 a. m. the lake was rising, and at 1:30 p. m. there was slight overflow at the southeast cove. At 2 p. m. the lake subsided about four feet and there was great increase in fountaining activity.

On June 25 there was strong rising with slight overflow in the early afternoon, the high level lasting about three hours. The southeast grotto was very active and tended to undermine the wall under the southeast bench. Later there was subsidence by about five feet and increased general fountaining.

On June 26 at 7 a. m. there was strong overflow on all sides so as to flood the floors northwest, west, east and southeast. The floods left broad, flat, festooned crusts. At 2:45 p. m. the inner cliff was 10 feet high on all sides, with but little fountaining activity. The fumes appeared thicker.

At noon on June 27 the banks were only three feet high and the lake appeared quiet and rising, with some thick crusts and few fountains. The smoke was moderate. The pit under the north station had become a pronounced hole about 100 feet in diameter, containing a funnel-shaped tumble of broken rocks smoking vigorously. At 2:15 p. m. the lake lava appeared about five feet below the inner bench, with much activity on the side of the crag-mass. Across the main lake near its northeast shore Old Faithful fountain broke periodically. Fire could be seen in the sulphur hole northeast of the east island. At 2:30 p. m. the southeast pool was depressed eight feet below its banks and there was much fountaining against its south wall. There were many fountains in the main lake and continuous bombardment at the inner end of the southwest pool. At 9 p. m. the lake appeared about 11 feet below the inner bench, with strong streaming to the west and to the southeast, and fountaining southeast, southwest, near Old Faithful, and in a new cove which is developing at the north end. Blue flames played from cracks in the south floor west of the southeast cove. Some slabs were heard falling toward the northeast. Smoke was increasing along the crack east of the east island, and a ridge was developing farther east along the line of the old northeast crag of January last.

On Thursday, June 28, 1917, at 10:15 a. m., the lake was subsiding until noon. Occasional falling slabs were heard, there was rapid streaming to the southwest and southeast, with thin crusts, and five or six fountains were in action. Spatter banks fell in on the south side of the southeast pool and at the east end of the southwest pool. Inspection revealed a pronounced new inner platform all around the lake about five feet high. Pits of collapse are becoming pronounced at the north chasm and west pond.

On June 29 at 9 a. m. the lake was about 15 feet below the floors, but within an hour it had risen five feet. The main lake was crusted heavily, the streaming was slow southward, with fountaining against the crag-mass and against the south shore of the southeast pool. At 11 a. m. there was slight subsidence with reversal of streaming from slow outward to rapid inward at the southwest cove. Crusts broke up vigorously and swift streaming was resumd into the southwest and southeast coves. During the morning the very pronounced smoking of a tumble of rocks at the base of the southeast bench ceased and the stones collapsed into a pot 10 feet in diameter, where lava spurted and a great banner of blue and yellowish flame played continuously so as to stain the walls with sulphur coating.

It was now becoming evident that very marked tilting changes were going on in the bench magma. The north pit had almost entirely ceased to fume, and there were slabs falling in the northeast crevasses and under the southeast bench near the southeast cove and the east cove. The whole northeast floor appeared to be rising toward the north and sinking toward the south, while the south island mass was similarly tilting southeastward. The development of the new southeast pot was a part of this process, and the smoke cracks were increasing from these westward across the south floor. In this direction the lava of the southeast cove streamed swiftly under a tunnel roof and there was similar streaming under the south floor from the southwest pool, with very heavy smoke developing. The southern bench block apparently was breaking along this south floor line with uplift of the central crags. There was yellow sulphur stain on the south floor near the southeast cove. The spatter-margins of the southeast pool on both sides showed elevation 15 to 18 feet above the lake in the central region, whereas they showed depression at the southeast cove, the bank there being only five feet high. Angular measurement showed that the eastern and southern crags were rising. The western crag-mass, on the other hand, was slightly subsiding. This all checked with the recent weighting by overflow, which was all around the crag-mass, giving it no opportunity to tilt, whereas the southern and northeastern floor blocks were weighted only at one corner.

The following report from the Whitney Laboratory of Seismology is submitted by Mr. H. O. Wood:

During the week-interval ending with June 29 two local earthquakes have been registered, both of moderately small seismographic amplitude; and two teleseisms, one a chief phase only of a shock of low power as world-shaking earthquakes go, and one a well and completely registered shock from an origin distant approximately 1600 miles, with large seismographic amplitude. This latter probably delivered a greater quantum of energy at this station than any teleseismic disturbance hitherto recorded here. It probably emanated from a submarine origin.

Microseismic motion has been registered as usual. The seismographic amplitudes of volcanic vibration have been larger than normal—a prevailing condition for several months of late—and "storms" have been fairly frequent. Early in the interval under report there was a marked shift of the pens in the sense of tilt to west and north, followed by conspicuous fluctuations which did not produce any notable net change—that is, the shifts have remained to the time of writing.

Very respectfully,

T. A. JAGGAR JR.,
Director.

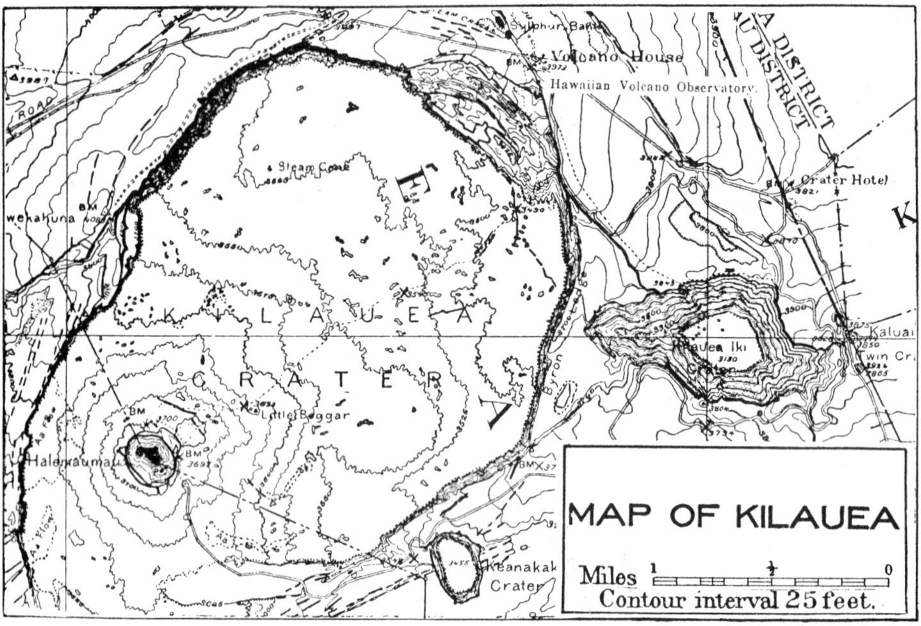

HAWAIIAN VOLCANO RESEARCH ASSOCIATION.

This society is a voluntary one, made up of subscribers to scientific work which is being executed by the Massachusetts Institute of Technology.

In 1917 there are about 150 subscribers in Hawaii and elsewhere, firms and individuals. A group of firms and persons in Hilo built the main observatory building in the spring of 1912. Publications to date have been weekly reports since the summer of 1911, now reprinted in Honolulu in monthly form. The Massachusetts Institute of Technology will publish annual reports, of which the introductory number was printed in 1912.

The weekly bulletin as it appears in the Advertiser is reprinted as a leaflet and sent to regular annual subscribers to the work of the Association. L. A. Thurston is president of the Board of Directors of the Association, and R. W. Shingle is treasurer. New subscribers who are interested in volcanoes will be welcomed in the Association. The Association aims: (1) To record volcanic activity and earthquakes in Hawaii; (2) to attract scientific men hither for special studies; (3) to promote the establishment of volcano observatories all over the world. The annual dues of regular members are $5; patrons of the Association subscribe larger amounts.

WHITNEY LABORATORY OF SEISMOLOGY.

The Whitney Laboratory of Seismology is equipped with two Bosch-Omori 100 kg tromometers registering N-S and E-W motion, a heavy Omori tromometer registering E-W motion, and an Omori "ordinary Seismograph" designed for registering strong earthquakes in all three components of motion. These are seated on concrete piers in a closed basement room having practically constant temperature, beneath the chief Observatory building near the hotel. Time is referred to a rated chronometer, checked at intervals by solar observations with a transit. Both instruments are loaned by the College of Hawaii. Hawaiian standard time (H. S. T.) is 10 hrs. 30 min. slower than Greenwich time.

CANCANI SCALE OF SEISMIC INTENSITY.

Expressed by accelerations measured in millimeters per second per second.

I.	Instrumental	0.0	2.5
II.	Very slight	2.5	5.0
III.	Slight	5.0	10.0
IV.	Sensible, mediocre	10.0	25.0
V.	Rather strong	25.0	50.0
VI.	Strong	50.0	100.0
VII.	Very strong	100.0	250.0
VIII.	Ruinous	250.0	500.0
IX.	Disastrous	500.0	1000.0
X.	Very disastrous	1000.0	2500.0
XI.	Catastrophic	2500.0	5000.0
XII.	Great catastrophe	5000.0	10000.0

Grade IV. is ordinarily the minimum perceived by the senses; and in grade XII. the acceleration, or rate of change of motion (jerk) reaches that of terrestrial gravitation.

In the standard form of report the maximum intensity or acceleration, designated by the symbol a, or max. a, is given in the conventional unit, the milligal. The milligal is a measure of acceleration, such that 1 milligal = 1/100 mm. per sec. per sec. = 10 μ per sec. per sec. The Cancani scale, here defined in terms of millimeters per sec. per sec., can therefore be expressed in **milligals by multiplying each of the numbers by 100.**

WEEKLY BULLETIN
OF THE
Hawaiian Volcano Observatory

VoI. V. HONOLULU, HAWAII, JULY, 1917. No. 7

July 7, 1917

During the week ending July 6, 1917, the lava column of Halemaumau continued to rise until Tuesday, July 3, but thereafter the lake was stationary or falling, so that the net result for the week appears to indicate stationary conditions.

On Saturday, June 30, at noon, the inner bench stood ten feet above the lake and there was great activity in the grotto on the south side of the south-east pool. There was also central fountaining in that pool and much fountaining activity in the main lake. Streaming was from the west toward the north and southeast. After 12 o'clock noon the southeast cove showed boiling and inrush under the south floor as though towards a sinkhole. At 1:30 p. m. the southwest cove, seen from the south station, showed strong bombardment in the end grotto, with a few large central fountains.

On July 1, at 1:45 p. m., it was evident that the lava lake had risen and overflowed the bank at the east cove, but, at the moment, the lake was about four feet below its shores. It was now rising rapidly with some fountaining in the middle of the southeast pool. At 3:30 p. m. the lake had risen nearly level with its banks, and at 4:30 p. m. overflow took place at the east cove and extended only about three feet beyond the previous flow. Overflow continued for about thirty minutes, followed by subsidence three feet below the bank. There was then much fountaining in all the arms of the lake and in the grotto.

On July 2, at 11:45 a. m., the lake overflowed the bank at the east cove, but this was short-lived and at 1:00 p. m. there was rapid subsidence, so that the inner cliff was ten feet high on the south side of the southeast pool. At 2:00 p. m. there was recovery which continued until the level of the lake was only two feet below its banks. Then subsidence recurred with much fountaining activity.

On Tuesday, July 3, at 2:00 p. m. the inner cliff was about seven feet high at the east cove and there was much activity in the southeast cove. There was the usual central fountaining. In the northeast arm the lava level was within three feet of overflow and slow rising appeared to be in progress. To the southwest quiet crusted conditions prevailed. On the northeast floor it was evident that there had been a flow from the east cove within a few hours, as glowing cracks were visible all over the fresh lava there.

In the later afternoon, at 4:30, it was evident that sinking had started in and the heavy fall from the south point into the channel produced strong effervescence there. Fumes appeared to be increasing toward the north.

On July 4, at 1:15 p. m., the inner bench was ten feet high all around the lake and conditions were extraordinarily quiet. There was only one active grotto on the south side of the southeast pool and central fountains were absent. At 2:40 p. m. there was little change, and the surface streaming was from the west toward the north and southeast. At 4:30 p. m. there was a heavy fall of rock from the East Island mass into the southeast pool, followed by much fountaining. At 7:00 p. m. the inner cliff was fifteen feet high and the fountaining activity was everywhere strong.

On Thursday, July 5, at 2:00 p. m. the lake was still low and there was very strong streaming, boiling and rumbling at the grotto of the southeast cove. The central cavern was also a scene of activity and all conditions

WEEKLY BULLETIN
of the
Hawaiian Volcano Observatory

Published Monthly at Honolulu, Hawaii, by the Hawaiian Volcano Research Association

L. W. de Vis-Norton........Secretary

Entered as second-class matter January 20, 1914, at the post-office at Honolulu, Hawaii, under the Act of August 24, 1912.

pointed to subsidence, following the higher levels of the early part of the week.

The following report from the Whitney Laboratory of Seismology is submitted by Mr. H. O. Wood:

During the week-interval ending with July 6, only one weak local earthquake was registered, and that had doubtful phase characteristics. Microseismic motion has been registered as usual. For many weeks the seismographic amplitudes of volcanic vibration waves have been greater than the previously normal value. This has remained true during the week under report here. Otherwise these movements have been as usual of late. Shifting of the pens in the sense of tilt to the west and north has gone on slowly and steadily in the past week, accompanied by the usual diurnal changes.

July 14, 1917.

During the week ending July 13, 1917, the Halemaumau lava pool has continued to fluctuate with some overflow of the tilted bench block of the south floor and crag. Toward the end of the week there was pronounced subsidence with undermining of the old northeast bench of 1894.

On July 8 at 2:30 p. m. the height of the inner bench was only about five feet and after 4:30 p. m. there was pronounced rising for an hour and a half. The lake at 6 p. m. was level with its margin at the east cove and at 6:10 p. m. it overflowed there slightly. Then subsidence set in with much fountaining.

On Monday, July 9, at 1:15 p. m., the lake was depressed ten feet below its margin and rising. The streaming was rapid toward the southeast, there was no fountaining in the central region, fumes were very thin and there was bombardment at the southeast grotto. At 1:40 p. m. there was a fall of rock from the east island point into the lake followed by turbulence. On the south margin of the southeast cove a blowing cone had developed and was noisy, while at the west margin of this cove there was rumbling effervescence in the cavern which appeared to lead to a sinkhole under the south floor. At 3:35 p. m. there was collapse at the southeast grotto followed by a second tumble of rock from the central peninsula into the channel.

On July 10, at 11:30 a. m., the inner wall was twenty feet high and there was active fountaining at the southeast grotto, slow streaming eastward through the channel and the fumes were thicker. There was much activity in two grottoes on the west shore of the main lake under the crag-mass. At noon it was evident that bombardment was in progress northeast and some central fountains were playing in the Old Faithful position.

On this day an examination of the south floor showed that a new long flow of considerable width had poured from the southeast cove westward and the south floor had been thereby depressed, while the central peninsula had risen. At 12:30 p. m. there was much fountaining in the north central part of the main lake and great activity at the base of the crag-mass. At 1:30 p. m. streaming was rapid through the chanbei southeastward and a pronounced rise came within a few feet of overflow at the southeast cove.

On Wednesday, July 11, 1917, at 2 p. m., it was evident that the southeast cove was nearly obliterated by overflow and half of the blowing-cone was destroyed. In the southeast pool the shore bench appeared ten feet high above the lake on the south and half that height on the north side of the pool and there was no fountaining. Fumes were thick but the lake appeared rising and there was sharp puffing occasionally, like a locomotive, from the remnants of the blowing-cone. At 2:55 p. m. a heavy avalanche fell from the northeast side of the east island. The northern cracks were fuming densely and it appeared that the northeast cliff made by the elevated May floor was becoming a rising crag.

At 1:30 p. m. on July 12 it was evident that a large block of rock had fallen away from the central peninsula. The inner cliff was 20 feet high on the south and 10 feet high on the northeast, so that the south bench was rising and the northeast bench at the east cove apparently sinking. There had been much falling away of the sides of the east island. Fountains were few. At 3 p. m. there was great activity in the south grotto but no fountains elsewhere, and the streaming to the southeast sinkhole was rapid. The 1894 bench northeast was crumbling slowly, as the talus blocks there could be seen or heard in motion every few minutes. The northeast floor beneath was slowly sinking and the large crevases under the 1894 bench were widening.

On Friday, July 13, at 1:30 p. m., the northwest margin of the main lake as seen from the north station was 10 feet high, there were a few fountains in the west arm and the fumes appeared moderately thick. The bench on the south side of the southeast pool, on the other hand, was fully 25 feet high and that pool was extremely quiet. At 3:10 p. m. there was a heavy avalanche northwest and a few minutes later another farther north, the rocks falling into the northwest arm and starting effervescence there.

The following report from the Whitney Laboratory of Seismology is submitted by Mr. H. O. Wood:

During the week ending with July 13 four small local earthquakes have been registered. The strongest of these was felt in Hilo, but not, so far as is known, in the vicinity of the Observatory. The seismographic amplitudes of microseismic motion have at times been greater than normal, but in general of usual values. The seismographic amplitudes of volcanic vibrations have continued as usual in recent weeks, stronger and stouter than the general normal. There was pronounced shifting of the pens in the sense of tilt to the west and north, necessitating readjustments, in the early part of the wek-interval followed by slight returns and then comparatively slow and small oscillations.

July 21, 1917.

During the week ending July 20, 1917, the Halemaumau lava column has risen slowly to a level not lower than 90 feet below the rim and the end of the week shows slight overflow of the inner bench southeast, renewed hissing at the northwest cone and construction of spatter domes at the lake margin. These are all signs of rising.

On Saturday, July 14, at 2 p. m., the southeast pool was fountaining in five places and its border was 20 feet high on the south and 10 feet high on the north. At 3:20 p. m. there was a strong rock slide from under the southeast bench. On this day there was much movement of loose rocks under the 1894 bench northeast. Inspection from the north at 3:40 p. m. showed that there was much fountaining in the north arm of the lake and high spurting from the Old Faithful grotto on the northwest side of the east island mass.

On July 16 the lava was higher and at 2 p. m. the west bank of the main lake appeared only five feet high and the northwest inner bench appeared submerged. There were active grottoes southeast and south and much spurting in the southeast cove. At the east cove the lake was only two to three feet below the bank. Fumes, however, were thick. At 3 p. m. there was subsidence by about two feet, streaming increased in speed and there was strong bombardment at the S. E. grotto, while five or six fountains broke into activity around the southeast pool. At 5 p. m. the writer examined the lake after an absence of two weeks and found little marked change. The south bench block showed increased tilt and there were recent flows from the southeast and east coves. The south floor exhibited a distinct valley extending from the southeast cove to the southwest cove, and the floor of this valley was much broken and smoking. The last remnant of the summit of the old east crag of January was now nearly completely buried under talus and recent flows. There was a small flaming cone west of the southeast cove. The east island had crumbled down somewhat, especially on its east and south sides, and the northeast peak was now lower than formerly and more ridge-like in form, the ridge trending north and south. The crag-mass and northwest crag both appeared lower and the north pit appeared deeper.

Measurement on Tuesday morning, July 17, 1917, indicated depression of the lake surface slightly over 100 feet. From 10 a. m. to 12 noon the lake was streaming rapidly to the southeast and showed much bubbling activity, with thin crusts. There was inrush under the bank at the west side of the southeast cove and fountains were numerous bombarding the west side of the main lake. A view of the west and northwest floor region showed the effects of continued subsidence, leaving a high shelf from the west niche southward with the bare cliff wall interrupting the shelf in two places, west and southwest. The south crags were highest on the side of the main lake. The smoke appeared thinner on this day and at the shore of the lake, under the northwest crag-mass, two inner spatter levels were visible, the upper being the floor of June 22-25 now some 20 feet above the lake. The newer inner bench was only half as high and was well marked in several places. There was smoke under the west niche, at the north margin of the lake, along the south valley and at the west cone.

In the early evening of July 18 the lake was brimming level with its banks and slightly overflowing the inner bench at the southeast cove. The streaming was from the west. There were fountains at the Old Faithful locality and at different times on the northwest, southwest, at the east cove, and under the southeast bench. In the southeast cove there was high gas pressure which caused the marginal fountain to spurt its spray from 70 to 80 feet vertically, and once a similar spurting fountain was seen to break out at the south side of the narrow leading to the southeast pool. The crusts moved along the shores with a crunching noise. There was flame and glow at the northwest cone. After descent to the shore of the lake at the east cove, the lake was seen pushing crusts eastward in overriding layers and occasionally floods of lava would overflow the stagnant crusts with a piling-up effect from west to east. The gas pressure in the lake induced continuous ballooning of the crust all over the surface, and there were many spurts of blue and some yellow flames from gases which broke through the balloons and through cracks in crust. The lake appeared not more than 90 feet below the rim. About 6:45 p. m. subsidence set in so as to lower the surface one to two feet, the crusts broke up, streaming became rapid and violent fountains developed along the shore of the east cove and migrated eastward. There was also increased fountaining elsewhere. Heavy bombardment under the southeast cliff threw spurts 60 feet into the air. After about twenty minutes the lake recovered, the surface became quiet and rising ensued.

On July 19 the lake remained high and the fumes thin. On Friday, July 20, similar conditions prevailed and slow rising of both lake and benches appeared to be in progress. The south block was more tilted down at the southeast and up toward the west. The peninsula extending west from the south crags into the southwest cove was also upraised, with its highest point at its western end some 15 feet above the lake. The west bank of the lake across the narrows leading to the southwest cove was only five feet high.

Fumes on this day were moderately thin and the streaming was from the north and northwest to the southeast, and towards a large continuous fountain at the west cove. The southwest cove was quiet. In the southeast cove the streaming had reversed and was now eastward where the current united with that from the southeast pool to expend itself in bombardment under a long spatter dome which had been built under the southeast bench. There were only five or six fountains in the lake and some large stagnant crusts. The inner bench was wholly submerged. There were no fresh overflows, however, except possibly on the east bank of the southeast cove. The northwest cone was hissing strongly and steadily, and as this cone is over a main conduit, this high gas pressure may presage a rise.

At 10:30 a. m. subsidence set in and strong fountaining appeared at three points along the northeast shore, at the north shore, and toward the southwest and southeast. The central fountain continued its activity in the western region. It appeared to indicate meeting currents from south and north.

The following report from the Whitney Laboratory of Seismology is submitted by Mr. H. O. Wood:

During the week-interval ending with July 20 four local earthquakes have been registered. One of these was felt distinctly at Kilauea as a sharp, sudden jolt. Another, a few minutes later in occurrence, was felt in Hilo, but no report of its having been felt near the station has come to hand. The remaining two shocks were of the usual unfelt sort. The motion of volcanic vibration, and microseisms, and pen-shifts in the sense of tilt have all been as usual, with no changes or events of noteworthy character.

July 28, 1917.

During the week ending July 27, 1917, the Halemaumau lava at first overflowed the benches, but since has remained stationary and the only change of importance has been a widening by collapse of the southeast cove. The depression of the lake, measured twice during the week, was 103 feet.

At 2 p. m. on Friday, July 20, the lake was level with its banks at the east cove. At 2:30 p. m. it overflowed the east side of the southeast cove and a wide flow poured over the west bank of the main lake. Thereafter the lava subsided three feet and remained so until 5:30 p. m. Rapid rising then recurred and overflow at the same places was resumed at 6:20 p. m., but in less volume.

On July 21, at 2 p. m., it was evident that there had been strong overflowing at the east cove during the morning, but now the lake was four feet below its banks. There was little fountaining and the fumes were thin. Streaming was swift southeastward.

From 10 a. m. to 2 p. m. on July 22 the lava lake was rising from a level relatively low with reference to the rim of the inner pit. The central cavern was at first open but became submerged during the morning. During the low stage the lake rushed rapidly under an arch into the tunnel at the southeast cove toward a smoking place in the south floor valley coinciding in position with the February sinkhole. In the center of the main lake continuous fountains played where currents met from north and south. There were other fountains southeast, northeast and north. Heavy shells of rock fell into the lake from under the southeast shelf and from the east island mass. The fumes were moderate. At 12:30 p. m. the lake had become coated with quiet crusts and there was hardly any streaming motion. From 1 to 2 p. m. the lava was brimming level with the bank at the east cove, and during the afternoon there was slow subsidence to a level about 10 feet below the margin.

At 9 p. m. the lake was again low relative to the inner pit and the central cavern was open. Streaming through the southeast pool was vigorous and there were fountains north, northeast, in the middle of the main lake, along the shore of the east cove and under the southeast shelf. Hanging stalactite curtains were abundant and there were glowing and flaming cracks in the floor above the southeast cavern and a high chimney on the floor of the elevated channel in the southern crag mass over the interior of the central cavern.

In the slow moving, thinly skinned, glowing lava which streamed out from the central cavern, blisters one to two feet in diameter would suddenly appear, swollen up from below through the action of rising gas. Some of these burst, leaving rings, others within the cavern were small bubble fountains. The most remarkable kind were travelling blisters, which moved rapidly sidewise with a wriggling motion and vanished, leaving a wake like a fish darting along beneath the surface of water. The cause of this travelling appeared to be a pressure impelling the gas bubble from the region of thicker and heavier crust outside the cavern toward the heated thin-skinned region within.

Measurements on Monday, July 23, 1917, at 2:15 p. m., made the depression of the lake 103 feet below the southeast station and the following were the heights of the several crags:

Central peninsula of southern block 60 feet above the lake.

Northwest table 59 feet above the lake.

East island 48 feet above the lake.

North summit northwest crag mass 48 feet above the lake.

Old summit northwest crag mass 47 feet above the lake.

Floor features were elevated as follows:

Northwest cone 22 feet above the lake.

Northeast floor 18 feet above the lake.

Margin southeast cove 7 feet above the lake.

South floor valley 7 feet above the lake.

It had now become evident that the southern crag block was rising strongly in response to the weight of recent overflows at the southeast cove. The central peninsula of this block was now the highest feature above the lake. The peninsula extension from this into the southwest cove was also much uplifted and 30 feet high at its western end, with southeastward tilt. There was also elevation in the east island mass so as to create a new straight tumbled slope southward from the northeast peak, indicating that the surface west of this line was rising higher than the remainder of the northeast floor. This was a response to the weighting effect of the fresh overflows at the east cove. That rapid motion was in progress was shown by very heavy falls of rocks from the southern mass into the channel and into the southeast pool, also from the point of the east island and from the shore of the east cove. The depression of the lake within the southeast inner pit appeared 20 feet, but this was due to rise of crags rather than sinking of lake. Toward the south-southwest there was a pronounced marginal fall-off of the southern crag block due to its rising above the western end of the valley extending from the southwest cove to the southeast cove. The old northwest crag mass appeared raised on the lake side and the northwest table appeared higher. The smoke had increased in density. Streaming was from north and south in the main lake toward the southeast pool and the central and southeast caverns were open. The northeast pit appeared to be reforming. A heavy fountain was seen to form in the southeast cove and migrate into the tunnel under the south floor changing to a swarm of bubble fountains as it did so. There were many shifting bombardments of the shores of the lake and spells of rising in the intervals. It was evident that a spasm of rising of the bench magna was in progress, the adjustments of the lake to this process causing much migratory fountaining and thin crusts. The northwest cone was no longer hissing but there was a large area near it stained with sulphur corresponding apparently to the roofed-over northwest pond beneath. The walls of the southeast pool were 40 feet high on the east, with strong bombardment at their base where the tunnel leads to the south floor.

The strong rising movements of the crags revealed clearly the fact that the east, central and southern crags and the northwest crag mass all have adjacent tunnels which would separate them off as islands if the roofs of the tunnels could be removed. In each case these roofs originated as solidified surfaces of arms of the lake just as ice persists longest in narrow channels among islands in a river. There was hot fume rising from the cracked tunnel roofs southeast, southwest, in the center, northeast and northwest, and the various pressure ridges recently reported all give evidence of tunnel locations.

On July 24, at 10:30 a. m., there was little change, the lake was slightly higher, fumes were moderate and fountains were few. At 11:30 a. m. there was subsidence with swifter streaming, eight or ten fountains developed and there was streaming into the northeast cove east of Old Faithful fountain. This cove had been enlarging at the expense of the northeast peak. There was white stain at the glowing heap over the southeast tunnel.

On July 25 from 6 to 8 p. m. there was very active streaming and high incandescence of grottoes and fountains. The inner beach at the southeast cove was 8 feet high. Streaming almost torrential at times poured southeastward

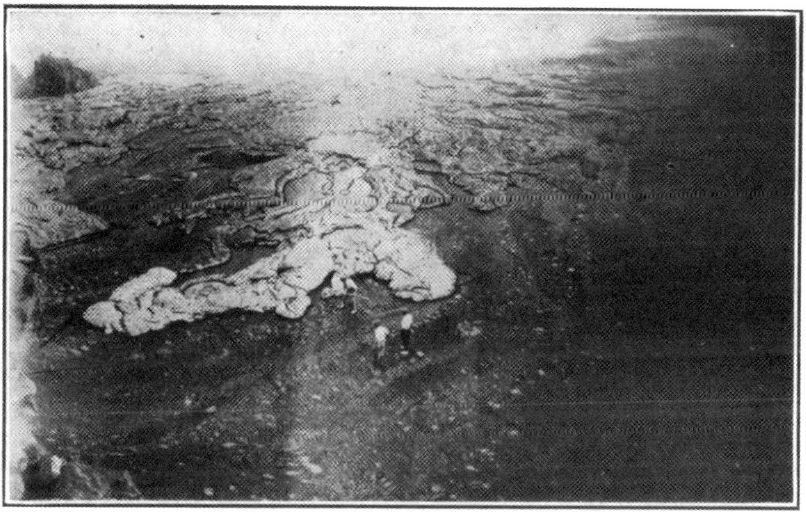

May 30, 1917. Moving lava overflow on southwest floor, men making fresh lava specimens. West cone on left, source of flows.—Photo. Jaggar.

June 14, 1917. Migrating central fountain in southeast pool, looking west from bank of lake toward central cavern.—Photo. Jaggar.

June 14, 1917. Bright lines of channel torrent of lava 50 feet away. From north bank of channel, center of pit, looking S. W.—Photo. Jaggar.

through the central channel from the north and southwest arms of the lake. The southwest cove was dark and crusted. Many large fountains travelled from the channel to the east cove and others formed under the southeast shelf. The crust at the northwest arm would occasionally break up and fountaining develop at the northwest bank. There were alternations every 20 to 30 minutes from swift streaming with fountaining to slow current and less fountaining. The general result was a rising during the evening which led to drowning of the central cavern where there was slow outward streaming, at first eastward with blistering skin, later northeastward and more rapid. There was glow and flame at the northwest cone, the central chimney and the southeast heap. There was puffing to the north. In the late evening the incandescence decreased and there was some crusting across the central channel.

On July 26 at 2 p. m. the lake was relatively high and hot, there was a new narrow inner bench, crusts were thin with rapid southeastward streaming, much bubbling and little fountaining. A crack appeared to be developing across the central peninsula above the tunnel. The shore bench of the eastern coves was from 6 to 8 feet high.

On Friday, July 27, 1917, at 11 a. m., measurement showed the depression 103 feet as on July 23 and the crags very slightly lower or unchanged. The lake was rising and crusted until 10 a. m. and thereafter it remained high, with moderate streaming from north and southwest, fumes thinner and fountains few. Fuming had increased under the west shelf. The most important change was the collapse of the southeast cove on its east side which had enlarged it to double its former size. There was bombardment at two places along its shore bench which stood five feet above the liquid.

The following report from the Whitney Laboratory of Seismology is submitted by Mr. H. O. Wood:

During the week ending with July 27 no earthquakes have been registered. Microseismic motion has been as usual. Volcanic vibration has been registered as in recent weeks, stronger than the earlier normal, but not different from recent values. There has been no noteworthy change in the position of the writing levers (tilt) except for the usual diurnal change.

August 4, 1917.

During the week ending August 3, 1917, the Kilauea lava column has maintained its level as before, only a slight net subsidence appearing by measurement at the end of the week. On Aug. 2 in the afternoon there was a magnificent breaking up of some of the benches accompanied by a sharp rise of the peak in the center of the pit and collapse of the roof of the central cavern so as to leave a chasm in the cavern's place. This cataclysm was accompanied by no special rise or fall.

On Saturday, July 28, at 2:30 p. m., it was evident that the southeast cove had widened further on its east side; this cove was very active. At 3 p. m. the inner bench was generally about ten feet high and Old Faithful could be distinguished in the northeastern part of the main lake. Fumes were thick and the lava was stagnant except for two fountaining grottoes on the southeast aspect of the northwest crag mass. At 2:50 p. m. there was renewed activity to the southeast.

On July 29 at 2:45 p. m. the inner cliff south of the southeast pool was about 20 feet high while that at the east cove was only half as high. Shore fountains were active on the south side of the southeast pool and in the southeast cove. At 3:30 p. m. the north arm was fountaining in many places, the Old Faithful interval was about 40 seconds, and the northwest grotto was noisy.

At 3 p. m. on July 30 slow rising was in progress. First there was fountaining southeast but later the lakes became very quiet and fumy. The south mass was evidently rising more, its wall over the southeast pool being now 25 feet high, whereas across the pool to the northeast there was no change and only about 10 feet of inner cliff. At 4 p. m. the grotto south of the southeast pool was spurting high, but the north pool remained quiet except for Old Faithful, which broke the surface at intervals.

On July 31 at 2:30 p. m. the north

pool was again quiet and the south grotto active. By 3 p. m. rising was in progress and the east cove bank was only six feet above the southeast pool, where rapid streaming poured southeastward to churning grottoes in the southeast cove.

On Wednesday, Aug. 1, 1917, at 1:40 p. m., there were numerous fountains. An hour later the activity had decreased except for a vigorous grotto building a spatter heap under the southeast shelf.

On Aug. 2 at 2:10 p. m., the main lake was very stagnant except for one grotto under the northwest crag mass. The bench at the west appeared 15 feet high. The southeast pool was also very quiet, its south inner cliff appearing 25 feet high. There was no change in the fumes, which were rather thick.

At 2:45 p. m. the east island began to collapse, fully half of its table falling away into the southeast pool. A few seconds later the roof of the central cavern began to fall in and portions of the adjacent south bench. Then the eastern half of the bank around the southeast cove went in with a crash and a heavy block fell from the northwest crag mass. The lake seethed with many hundreds of fountains. The central peaks adjacent to the collapsed cavern, on its north side, rose bodily about 10 feet and split asunder, so that a sharp pinnacle shaped like a steeple separated off and remained pointing upward on the eastern side of the mass. The remainder of the roof of the central cavern had now tumbled, clear through to the southwest cove, leaving a canyon floored with broken rocks, afterwards partially flooded by the lake on the east side. The raised bench clinging to the central peaks was now fully 40 feet above the lake and the south bench 30 feet high. The mass of the east island crags subsided somewhat, a channel of collapse forming over the submerged tunnel east of them.

This whole movement may be considered a readjustment of the craggy crusts of the bench magma, undermined by the central, northeastern and southeastern tunnels. Cracks developing above these tunnels have recently been mentioned, especially over the central tunnel, where there was a flaming chimney. The hot gases blowpiping through these cracks finally ate through, instantly the weights of the newly separated crust blocks were differently disposed on the pasty under-lava, this paste flowed toward the center away from the broad and heavy floors, and the central peaks, of much smaller area, were thereby lifted. The general readjustment due to this movement caused the other collapses.

Measurement on Friday, Aug. 3, 1917, at 5 p. m., gave the following data:

Depression of lava lake, 109 feet.

Height above lake of central peak, 74 feet.

Height above lake of south crag, 59 feet.

Height above lake of east crag, 49 feet.

Height above lake of southwest crag mass, 46 feet.

Height above lake of northeast floor, 23 feet.

Height above lake of south valley, 12 feet.

On this day at 2:30 p. m., looking from the north, the north side of the east island mass was seen to be fractured and tumbled, some 20 feet below the northeast inner cliff. There was much fume and few fountains. The grotto under the south bench was active and a great splash dome had been built 10 feet high and 20 feet wide under the southeast bench on the east side of the widened southeast cove. There was rapid streaming under the south floor. The east face of the central steeple showed upright laminations or beds, red and white in color, each layer four or five inches thick, similar to those formerly seen on the west side of the east island. At 5 p. m. the great southeast spatter dome completely collapsed into the lake. The northwest crag mass was now covered with rugged lumps. The floor level at the east cove appeared upraised somewhat and an inner bench only five feet high had formed under the east island remnant. Much of the south end of the east cove platform had fallen away.

The following report from the Whitney Laboratory of Seismology is submitted by Mr. H. O. Wood:

During the week-interval ending with

Aug. 3 six local earthquakes were registered. Two of these were felt plainly, one in the evening by many people and one in the early morning, which awakened some sleepers. Possibly a third was felt in structures qualified to increase the effect of the vibration. Also one teleseism of moderate to small world-shaking energy was registered. Microseismic motion has been as usual. Volcanic vibration has remained as usual recently.

Accompanying the earthquakes there were pen shifts as in the sense of tilt first one way and then the other. It is always uncertain whether such shifting is due to instrumental yieldings or to changes in position of rock blocks here. There were no net changes of noteworthy magnitude.

Very respectfully,

T. A. JAGGAR, JR.,
Director.

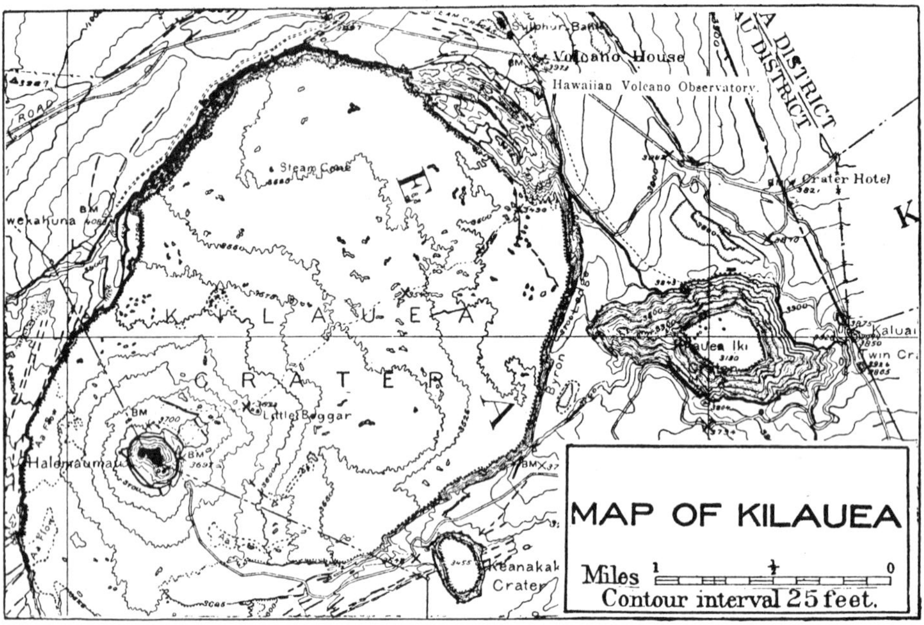

HAWAIIAN VOLCANO RESEARCH ASSOCIATION.

This society is a voluntary one, made up of subscribers to scientific work which is being executed by the Massachusetts Institute of Technology.

In 1917 there are about 150 subscribers in Hawaii and elsewhere, firms and individuals. A group of firms and persons in Hilo built the main observatory building in the spring of 1912. Publications to date have been weekly reports since the summer of 1911, now reprinted in Honolulu in monthly form. The Massachusetts Institute of Technology will publish annual reports, of which the introductory number was printed in 1912.

The weekly bulletin as it appears in the Advertiser is reprinted as a leaflet and sent to regular annual subscribers to the work of the Association. L. A. Thurston is president of the Board of Directors of the Association, and R. W. Shingle is treasurer. New subscribers who are interested in volcanoes will be welcomed in the Association. The Association aims: (1) To record volcanic activity and earthquakes in Hawaii; (2) to attract scientific men hither for special studies; (3) to promote the establishment of volcano observatories all over the world. The annual dues of regular members are $5; patrons of the Association subscribe larger amounts.

WHITNEY LABORATORY OF SEISMOLOGY.

The Whitney Laboratory of Seismology is equipped with two Bosch-Omori 100 kg tromometers registering N-S and E-W motion, a heavy Omori tromometer registering E-W motion, and an Omori "ordinary Seismograph" designed for registering strong earthquakes in all three components of motion. These are seated on concrete piers in a closed basement room having practically constant temperature, beneath the chief Observatory building near the hotel. Time is referred to a rated chronometer, checked at intervals by solar observations with a transit. Both instruments are loaned by the College of Hawaii. Hawaiian standard time (H. S. T.) is 10 hrs. 30 min. slower than Greenwich time.

CANCANI SCALE OF SEISMIC INTENSITY.

Expressed by accelerations measured in millimeters per second per second.

I.	Instrumental	0.0	2.5
II.	Very slight	2.5	5.0
III.	Slight	5.0	10.0
IV.	Sensible, mediocre	10.0	25.0
V.	Rather strong	25.0	50.0
VI.	Strong	50.0	100.0
VII.	Very strong	100.0	250.0
VIII.	Ruinous	250.0	500.0
IX.	Disastrous	500.0	1000.0
X.	Very disastrous	1000.0	2500.0
XI.	Catastrophic	2500.0	5000.0
XII.	Great catastrophe	5000.0	10000.0

Grade IV. is ordinarily the minimum perceived by the senses; and in grade XII. the acceleration, or rate of change of motion (jerk) reaches that of terrestrial gravitation.

In the standard form of report the maximum intensity or acceleration, designated by the symbol α, or max. α, is given in the conventional unit, the milligal. The milligal is a measure of acceleration, such that 1 milligal = 1/100 mm. per sec. per sec. = 10 μ per sec. per sec. The Cancani scale, here defined in terms of millimeters per sec. per sec., can therefore be expressed in **milligals by multiplying each of the numbers by 100.**

WEEKLY BULLETIN
OF THE
Hawaiian Volcano Observatory

Vol. V. HONOLULU, HAWAII, AUGUST, 1917. No. 8

Annual Address of the Director. August 23 1917

The Results of Six Years of Work

By T. A. Jaggar

Scientific Discoveries

The annual address of 1916 proposed a Kilauea volcano museum. Earlier addresses reviewed our beginnings and stimulated progress in making Mauna Loa accessible. The Observatory on July 1 completed six years of work if we include the preliminary observations in 1911 made by the Technology expedition of that year. It becomes my pleasant duty here to review very briefly the really wonderful advance in volcano knowledge that has resulted from measurements and experiments at Kilauea, an advance much assisted by the outbreaks of Mauna Loa in 1914-16 and the accessibility of Halemaumau during the past seven months.

In 1911 the volcanic heat and liquidity were supposed to increase downward indefinitely in the center of the pit. In 1917 by actual soundings, we know the lava lake to be less than 50 feet deep, occupying a saucer or channel in the cooler and stiffer lava of the lake bottom, of the islands, and of the benches.

In 1911 most geologists still thought that steam actuated volcanoes. In 1917 it is known that only 4% or less of the Kilauea lava-gas is steam and even this in part may be burnt hydrogen. Burning sulphur, hydrogen and carbon gases we now know are powerful heating and oxidizing agents in and about the liquid lava, making great natural blow-pipe flames and effervescing through the hot liquid as in a Bessemer converter.

In 1911 the lava islands were spoken of as "floating." In 1917 we know them after years of careful measurement and record to be uplifted hummocks from the bottom of the shallow pools. The consolidation of this bottom lava raised into an island, proved in February, 1917, to be clinkery lava or aa, hitherto almost unknown in Halemaumau but common on Mauna Loa.

In 1911 the main well or shaft in the crater was believed to be under "Old Faithful" fountain near the center. In 1917 at least eight such shafts are known, kept open by the rising rush of gas bubbles escaping continuously from solution in the main stiff lava column below. (Plate I). This lava foam rises to the surface, explodes in contact with air and circulates rapidly in a labyrinth of passages of its own making. Thus are produced the spectacular fountainings and streamings of the slaggy lava, so awe-inspiring to the traveller on the brink.

The maps, profiles and photographs, made at short intervals with transit and camera, give the history of measused changes of outline and relief.

In 1911, at great expense, one temperature of the liquid at the surface of the lava was obtained with an elaborate cable trolley system, after secrifice of much costly apparatus. In 1917 thirty-four measurements of temperature were made from the flaming cones on the floor and all through the lake to its bottom. This work was all done by direct

WEEKLY BULLETIN
of the
Hawaiian Volcano Observatory

Published Monthly at Honolulu, Hawaii, by the Hawaiian Volcano Research Association

L. W. de Vis-Norton........Secretary

Entered as second-class matter January 20, 1914, at the post-office at Honolulu, Hawaii, under the Act of August 24, 1912.

contact of special thermometers encased in steel pipes, and at an expense which was trivial in proportion to the results attained. These results showed that the puffing flames are hottest, the fountains and the bright lines of the lava lake less hot, the lava just below the surface still less hot, and the interior of the stiff bench lava filling the pit from side to side probably least hot of all. (Plate 2).

In 1911 no proof existed of any law or order in the risings and fallings of Kilauea and Mauna Loa lavas. In 1917, after six years of careful measurement and record, definite proof exists of half-hourly, daily, monthly, semi-annual, and longer term tides and periods in the movements of the fluid. Furthermore, response of Kilauea to the heavings of Mauna Loa was indicated in 1914-16. A diagram (Plate 3) showing the earthquake spasms and eruptions in Mauna Loa reveals five marked coincident movements of the two volcanoes in two years, and an immediate return of the lava column in great volume to the Kilauea pit after the Mauna Loa floods had ceased. This diagram records one hundred and twenty separate weekly surveys made with transit. Such charts and measurements were never made before, and these are barely a beginning. Already they have been successfully used for prediction.

Scientific Theories.

In 1911 the causes of volcanic activity were conceived in as great variety as the individuals who imagined them. A volcano was a steam engine: a volcano was not a steam engine. The earth was hotter downward: the earth was not hotter all the way down. The earth was heated from without inward: the earth was cooling from without inward. The argument in each case was based, not on accumulated measurements and records, but on the validity of this or that observer. One said, "Flames and smoke are abundant at volcanoes": his opponent replied, "Flames and smoke are unknown at volcanoes." Such arguments as "craters have steam, therefor craters are steam engines," or "lava runs like water, therefor lava on Mauna Loa cannot be connected with Kilauea," are based on false assumptions due to insufficient record of the nature, consistency, temperature and chemistry of a lava column.

In 1917 the steam engine argument falls when the lava is proved to contain little steam and the so-called visible steam proves to be warm air moistened with rain water. The argument against connection between the two volcanoes falls when we know a lava column to be a duplex substance nearly solid, full of gas, and heating itself and foaming when locally uncorked. An eruption of Mauna Loa so conceived is an opening of the vent of a pent-up furnace whose gases were previously but slightly escaping with quiet effervescence through a small orifice at Halemaumau. The effect of the unplugging immediately reacts at the smaller vent, as shown by our charts, but not at all after the fashion of a watery liquid. In 1917 I do not believe a volcano to be a steam engine, but think of it as Nature's glass factory, actuated by burning gases.

No more need be said about causes and theories. The cause of volcanic activity is subject for a volume, not for a paragraph, but every theory of value in science is essentially a grouping of hard earned facts. The cause of volcanic activity will only first be stated when at ten such stations at ours, in ten different regions of the globe, experimental records have been kept for years of the rise, heat, consistency, release, flow and cooling of lava. I have myself

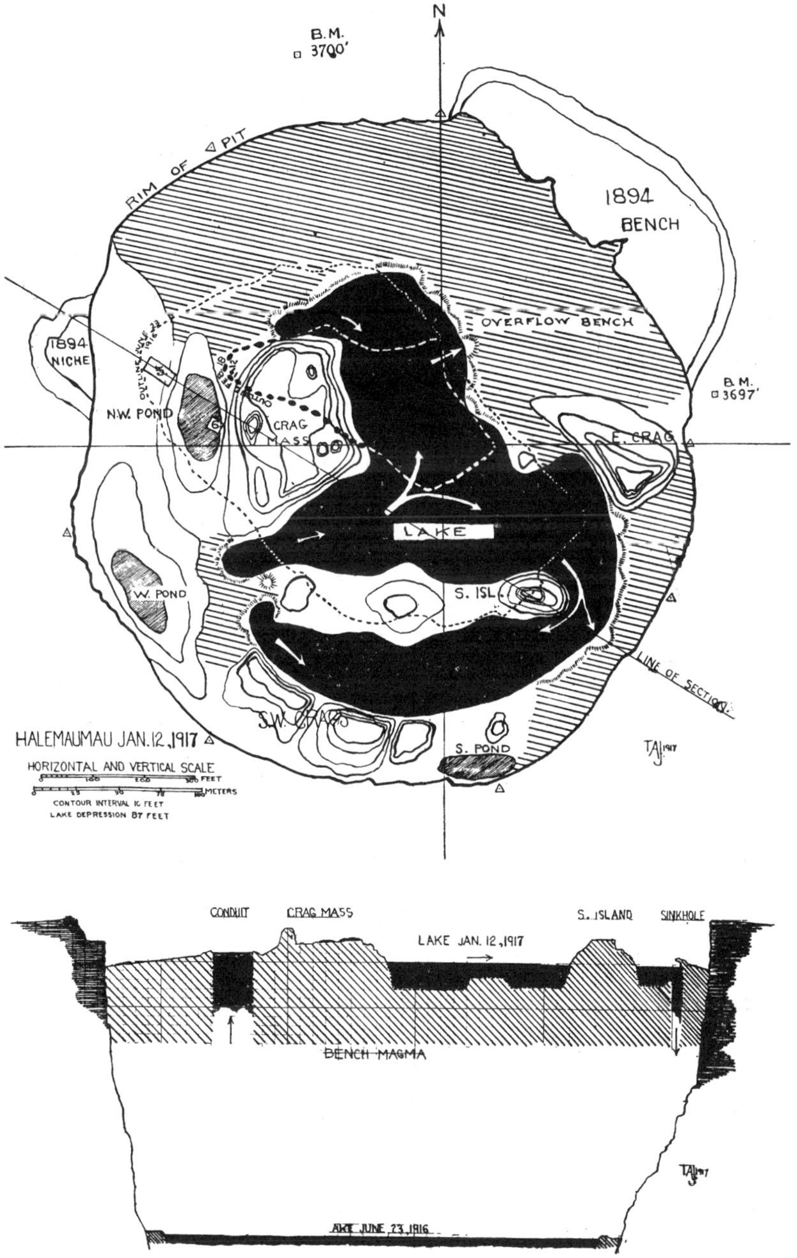

PLATE 1.—Map and diagramatic section of Halemaumau, Jan. 12, 1917. Lava lake in black, crusted conduit ponds shaded, overflow benches diagonal lines, raised crags contoured. Course dotted outline lava lake of Feb. 18, 1912. Fine dotted outline June 23, 1916. Rectangle (5) site of lava spring of June 5, 1916. Rectangle (6) west corner of pool June 6, 1916. Note that N. W. corner has been conduit source on all these dates. Slight slope lake surface from conduits W. to overflow bench E. Bench magma elevated on conduit side W. S. W., subsided on sinkhole side E. N. E. Section without vertical exaggeration, lower profile shows simple rising pool of June 23, 1916. Shoal shown in lake bottom was revealed by subsidence February, 1917. Depths from soundings and subsidence records. Note progressive shoalings from W. to E. Diagramatic sinkhole E. shows ridge of accretion on lake bottom margin which produces cascade ledge when subsidence takes place. Surveys with transit by T. A. Jaggar. Bench marks (B. M.) U. S. Geological Survey, trig stations Hawaiian Volcano Observatory. Meridian approximately 155° 17′ 8″ W., lat. 17° 24′ 33″ N. This is a typical survey of kind made frequently at Halemaumau.—*From Am. Jour. Sci., Sept., 1917.*

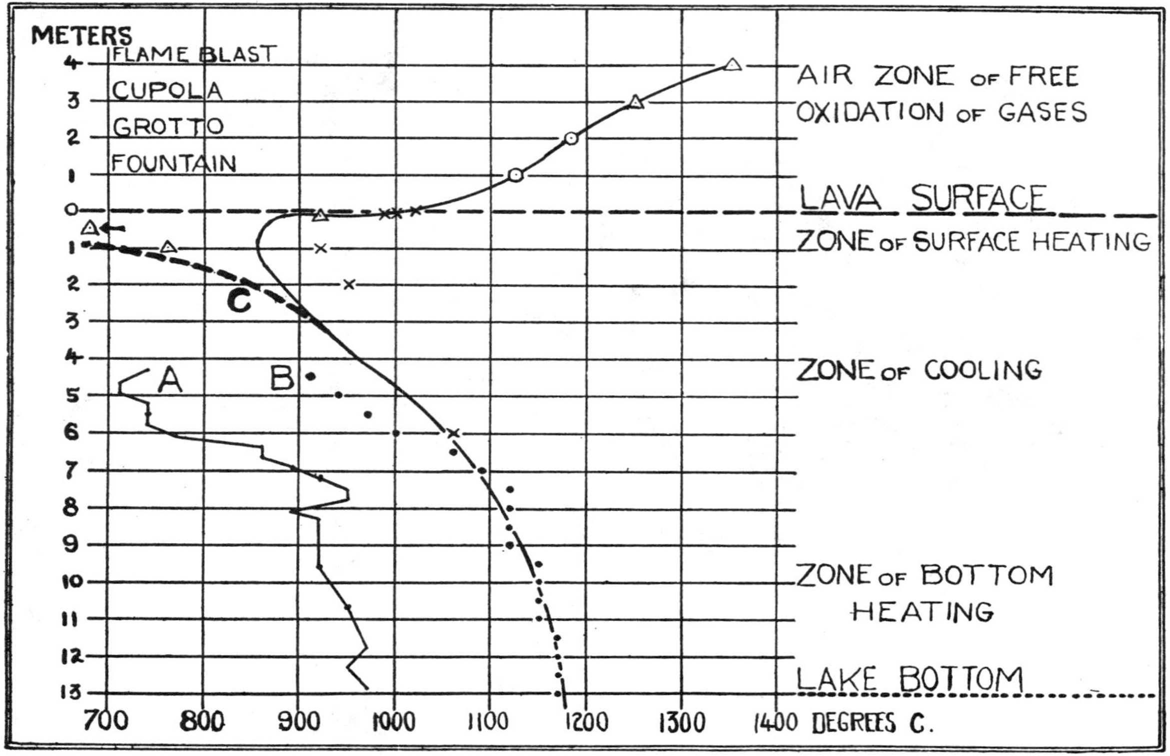

PLATE 2

Thermal gradient of Kilauea lava lake, temperatures measured with Seger cones, 1917, by T. A. Jaggar.

From Jour. Washn. Acad. Sci., July 19, 1917.

seen and studied eight different volcanic systems in eight different lands, but only as result of the six laboratory years at Kilauea have I begun to learn a little about fundamental causes.

Equipment and Output

The foregoing statement of actual discovery embodying the results of six years of progress is more formally set forth in published scientific papers. Such papers hitherto published are only a skimming of the richest surface cream which rises from the full record books now stored on the Observatory shelves. It has been my task to expend the very limited funds available for this work, so as to secure, during the first official five years of the Observatory which ended June 30, 1917, the largest possible accumulation of records, leaving the work of digesting them to the future. In view of this policy the showing made in actual experimental discovery, revealed by the contrast, not of theories, but of known facts between 1911 and 1917 gives high promise for the future.

The record books, maps, photographs, seismograms and geological collections at the Observatory, accumulated during the years, form to my thinking a vastly more valuable asset than any mere apparatus or buildings. Equipment in apparatus or buildings can always be improved or repaired with money. The equipment in records is wholly unique in preserving the sequence and dimensions of changing volcanic processes of two great volcanoes during a highly significant period. Were these records lost, they could not be duplicated even if a nation's ransom were offered as the price.

As to output, listed figures showing weekly and special reports, scientific papers, bulletins, photographs, and lantern slides were exhibited in last year's annual report. There are thousands of negatives and notes and instrumental tracings. The real output, however, of the establishment for which the subscribers of the Hawaiian Volcano Research Association are responsible, is the net effect on scientific progress of all these activities, on the community, and on the scientific and traveling world, and the example set urging others who live in volcanic lands to establish volcano observatories and so develop the science for its humane and technical ends.

Motives

The establishment has made records for six years. The Research Association has interested one hundred and fifty local people. The exchange list has reached two hundred other institutions and individuals. The work and the archives are growing in service and value, other institutions have increased their coöperation and interest and have expressed great concern at the mere mention of possible discontinuance. Discontinuance is not possible without forfeit, therefore is unthinkable. I have outlined above the scientific results of our work, but in now taking up the method of its continuance, it is necessary to analyze clearly our motives.

These motives are record, research, exhibition, publication; prevention of disaster; scientific hospitality, publicity, and propagandism. Truly a motley array of impulses, including commerce and education, foreign missions and the three-ring circus, with movie men to photograph the performers. And all to be carried by a modest wooden building on the edge of an active volcano, equipped with apparatus much of which is borrowed.

It is highly desirable to sift these aims down to their fine essentials, or to scrape off the parasitic growths and learn what is at the core of our problem. Research, publication and exhibition are matters of aftermath. Hospitality to visiting men of science and publicity are luxuries, not essentials. Prevention of disaster cannot be routine work, it is rather a goal to be striven for. There remain but two dominant, compelling and all inclusive motives for the work of the Hawaiian Volcano Observatory, these I insisted on in my first address of 1913, and these I reiterate even more strongly after showing results. The fundamental motive for an observatory is recording, and then improved recording and then more recording of a different kind. And following upon this is the propaganda of recording, extended to distant lands.

The future observatory in its scientific work will build a summit camp on Mauna Loa and make it accessible for prolonged visits. It will increase the precision and the frequency of the mappings of Halemaumau. It will collect the gases and take soundings and temperatures in many parts of the lava column. It will perfect telephotographic methods, apply the spectroscope to volcanic flames, improve scientific methods of taking moving pictures of the lava, establish voluntary earthquake stations around Mauna Loa and determine for a protracted period the daily tides in the lava lakes.

These things are all matters of recording, and improved recording means new facts. The grouping of new facts, as I have shown above, is the whole of science. These records thus improving, will always be our supreme achievements won through privilege of our possession, in Halemaumau, of the most marvelous natural geonomical laboratory on the globe. It is for you who dwell in Hawaii to say whether, with your wealth and your brains, you will build and extend this work as your own creation or whether you will yield it up to others.

Scope

Just a word in this place about expansion of the work to include studies of other geological processes. There is much to be said for Hawaii as an ideal center for geophysical measurement in the field of erosion processes on the land and deep sea processes off shore. Nearly twenty years ago I presented to the Carnegie Institution a plan for a geophysical institute in Hawaii. Still earlier there was printed in the annual report of the Director of the United States Geological Survey an estimate which I drew up for a topographic and geologic survey of this territory.

But all of this, interesting as it may be, is not the work of the Hawaiian Volcano Research Association as expressed in its constitution. Our proper work, namely **permanency** of volcanic recording and **extension** of volcano recording, is nowhere near accomplished. The first means an endowment here. The second means propagandist work in California, South America, New Zealand and Java, the Philippines, Japan and Alaska. Both of these, permanency and propagation, are absolutely essential to the determination of a volcano science, a science which by itself is of vastly too large a scope for any one man or group of men, to say nothing of the money required.

I can best illustrate this point by referring to such a laboratory as the Mt. Wilson Solar Observatory of the Carnegie Institute at Pasadena. That establishment has perhaps twenty times the income and twenty times the staff of our observatory, but it is devoted wholly to the study of the physics of the sun. I asked the Director, Dr. Hale, if he could send me a spectroscopist to study Kilauea flames, a subject certainly of interest to astronomy. His reply was that he could not afford to go outside of their proper field, namely the sun. The only distinguishing feature about Mt. Wilson for solar study is that the air is clear. In our case the distinguishing feature of the Island of Hawaii is that the two greatest and most active volcanoes on the globe are there and only there. Shall we then dissipate our energies and our money in that unique field after a start which has been concentrated and encouraging?

The Volcano Observatory Propaganda

With substantial scientific discoveries started, and invaluable record books accumulating; with bulletins, reports and articles accredited to Hawaii going into the libraries of the world; with travellers and scientists asking for photographs and asking to visit our plant; with Japan extending its volcano work; in view of all this progress, how can the Research Association join "hands around the Pacific" to get new work started in such colonies as British New Zealand or in Java?

Remembering the terrific disasters by scalding, drowning, suffocation and earthquake which these lands have suffered, conjured up in the mere names Krakatoa and Tarawera; disasters which are bound to decrease in terror with increase in knowledge, as we learn methods of prediction, of safeguard and of rescue; there should be strong appeal to the imagination of all members of this Association in the vision of new observatories in new places.

Besides the humane motive there is the scientific query, what are these distant volcanoes doing at the same time, while Kilauea lava is rising and falling? If there are summer and winter risings at Kilauea, are there summer and winter risings in New Zealand? The answer, yes or no, is a new discovery in science, yet to be made.

What use is there in knowing, do you ask? Answer, in order to discover how to predict, to determine the thickness of the earth crust, to connect volcanoes and earthquakes, to find out why the New Zealand eruptions are different from ours, and ours in turn different. In short, to solve the volcano mystery which underlies all the dwelling places of men.

But more than all these things there is the certainty of the supreme satisfaction of realizing that right here in Hawaii, on these little islands favored by possessing sugar as commercial asset and volcanoes as scientific asset, we will have built the famous center of a new science, and will hold the reins of a new chariot of enlightenment wherewith to do our bit in carrying wisdom to the remote and stricken peoples of earthquake lands.

At the moment the disaster cry is drowned by the sobbing of a war-saddened world. But the war shock has awakened our new world consciousness, and we remote from war may well give our utmost to make the rest of the world less terrible. Nature's ruthlessness has only lately stricken Salvador. The frightful disasters of Messina and San Francisco are recent memories, lives lost by scores of thousands, and property by the thousand million in money. The Whitney endowment which first sent me to Hawaii required investigations "conducted with a view to the protection of human life and property."

If the dignity of missions, to link the world in loving kindness, was worth the devotion of Ellis, Bishop, Bingham and Coan, then is the protection of life, through science, a worthy service for their successors. It is peculiarly appropriate that they should force the pagan fire goddess to give up her secrets in alleviation of distress.

The Opportunity for Hawaii

It has been asked why little Hawaii should do this? Why not some eastern endowment of millionaire origin? Answer, the eastern institutions will be only too anxious and ready to take this opportunity away from Hawaii and to build up their fame on what Hawaii rejects. The implication would be that Hawaii is not interested in her volcanoes, takes no pride in their possession, or in having started a unique scientific institution designed for the welfare of mankind, and is glad to be relieved of the financial burden of its maintenance.

Of some hot, stagnant and slipshod tropical colonies which I have visited this imputation might be true, but not of Hawaii. The volcanoes of Hawaii, which have deposited her sugar soils, are as much the property of this energetic people as the older hills which store the waters of irrigation, or the indentations of the shoreline that harbor our ships. For an educated folk possessing these things, as well say, "Why doesn't some eastern institution build our wharves and our ditches?" The issue is not ownership or responsibility. The question at stake is simply, "Will you face the responsibility of that ownership as the privilege of a wealthy and highly cultivated community, knowing that these volcanoes are famous and unique, and knowing that they may give Hawaii a world fame as a scientific center controlling subordinate stations all around the Pacific Ocean? Or will you shift the responsibility because there is little financial return?"

Is the Future Observatory to be Hawaiian?

The volcano laboratories at Kilauea have been made use of thanklessly as a convenience in the past by travellers from distant institutions. The **Hawaiian** Volcano Observatory has reached the parting of the ways. The question is squarely before Honolulu and the Territory whether you wish the present establishment to be Hawaiian and to continue to grow and deal solely with volcano research. There is no other question before this Association.

The three stated purposes of our society are to record volcanic activity, to attract scientific men and to promote volcano observatories. We have no other aims and the Observatory has no other aims. Therefore this Association is and necessarily must be opposed to giving precedence at the Observatory to any studies not volcanological. We should heartily welcome in this field an expert student of the moon with his telescope, for the lunar volcanoes teach us much concerning our own volcanoes. But we would surely not attempt to finance him. In the same spirit of hearty hospitality we would welcome a student of the deep sea bottom. But we could not afford to charter his ship. It must not be imagined that volcano research is geology. The idea of perpetual record at observatories is hardly mentioned in the geological text books. The work of our Observatory is variously physics, chemistry, surveying and meteorology unitedly concentrated on two volcanic vents. We have no aim except to study those vents and all their ramifications. The ocean may affect them, the sun and moon may affect them, but we are not specializing on ocean, sun or moon. We are specializing on volcanoes and volcanoes only, and all work must be directed to that end.

The executive Board of our Association has earnestly supported the Director of the Observatory in determining that the work shall be continued and shall deal with volcano research. It remains for this honorable society and this community, through loyalty to the Islands and pride in their fame, to decide on what scale the work shall endure, and whether the Kilauea laboratory shall be permanently **Hawaiian.**

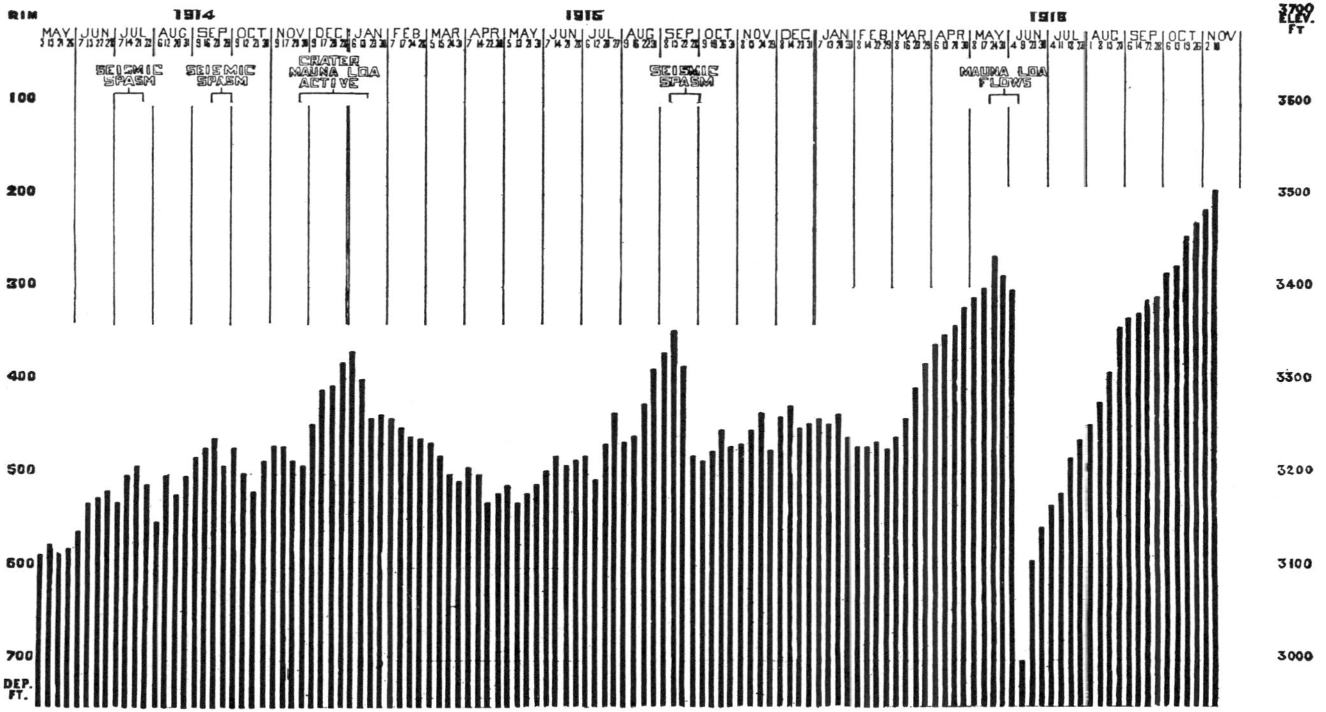

PLATE 3

Diagram showing fluctuation of level of lava in Halemaumau, in relation to seismic and volcanic activities of Mauna Loa, 1914-1916. Measurements from 120 weekly surveys by T. A. Jaggar shown.

Reprinted from Am. Jour. Sci., April, 1917.

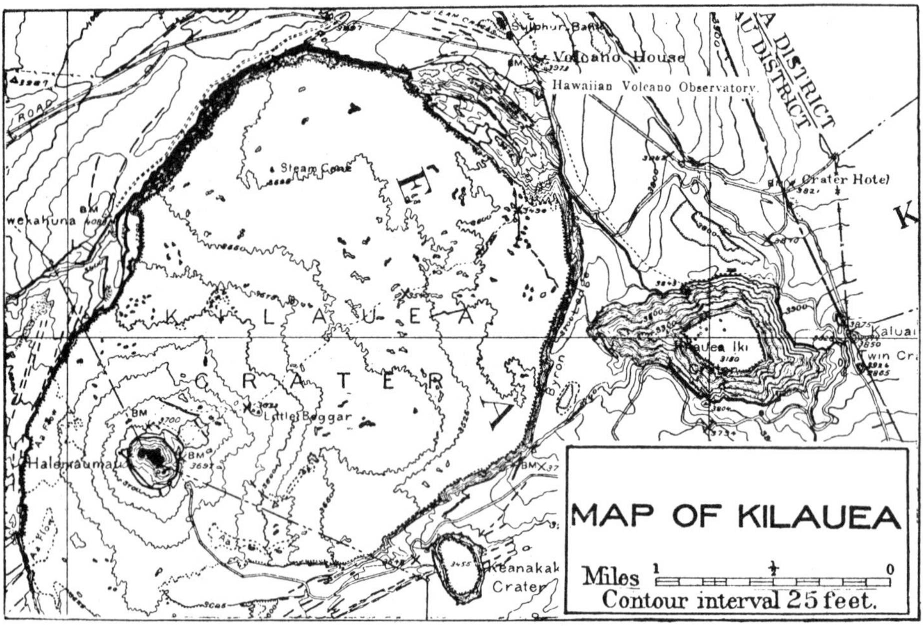

HAWAIIAN VOLCANO RESEARCH ASSOCIATION.

This society is a voluntary one, made up of subscribers to scientific work which is being executed by the Massachusetts Institute of Technology.

In 1917 there are about 150 subscribers in Hawaii and elsewhere, firms and individuals. A group of firms and persons in Hilo built the main observatory building in the spring of 1912. Publications to date have been weekly reports since the summer of 1911, now reprinted in Honolulu in monthly form. The Massachusetts Institute of Technology will publish annual reports, of which the introductory number was printed in 1912.

The weekly bulletin as it appears in the Advertiser is reprinted as a leaflet and sent to regular annual subscribers to the work of the Association. L. A. Thurston is president of the Board of Directors of the Association, and R. W. Shingle is treasurer. New subscribers who are interested in volcanoes will be welcomed in the Association. The Association aims: (1) To record volcanic activity and earthquakes in Hawaii; (2) to attract scientific men hither for special studies; (3) to promote the establishment of volcano observatories all over the world. The annual dues of regular members are $5; patrons of the Association subscribe larger amounts.

WHITNEY LABORATORY OF SEISMOLOGY.

The Whitney Laboratory of Seismology is equipped with two Bosch-Omori 100 kg tromometers registering N-S and E-W motion, a heavy Omori tromometer registering E-W motion, and an Omori "ordinary Seismograph" designed for registering strong earthquakes in all three components of motion. These are seated on concrete piers in a closed basement room having practically constant temperature, beneath the chief Observatory building near the hotel. Time is referred to a rated chronometer, checked at intervals by solar observations with a transit. Both instruments are loaned by the College of Hawaii. Hawaiian standard time (H. S. T.) is 10 hrs. 30 min. slower than Greenwich time.

CANCANI SCALE OF SEISMIC INTENSITY.

Expressed by accelerations measured in millimeters per second per second.

I.	Instrumental	0.0	2.5
II.	Very slight	2.5	5.0
III.	Slight	5.0	10.0
IV.	Sensible, mediocre	10.0	25.0
V.	Rather strong	25.0	50.0
VI.	Strong	50.0	100.0
VII.	Very strong	100.0	250.0
VIII.	Ruinous	250.0	500.0
IX.	Disastrous	500.0	1000.0
X.	Very disastrous	1000.0	2500.0
XI.	Catastrophic	2500.0	5000.0
XII.	Great catastrophe	5000.0	10000.0

Grade IV. is ordinarily the minimum perceived by the senses; and in grade XII. the acceleration, or rate of change of motion (jerk) reaches that of terrestrial gravitation.

In the standard form of report the maximum intensity or acceleration, designated by the symbol a, or max. a, is given in the conventional unit, **the milligal**. The milligal is a measure of acceleration, such that 1 milligal = 1/100 mm. per sec. per sec. = 10 μ per sec. per sec. The Cancani scale, here defined in terms of millimeters per sec. per sec., can therefore be expressed in **milligals by multiplying each of the numbers by 100.**

WEEKLY BULLETIN
OF THE
Hawaiian Volcano Observatory

Vol. V. HONOLULU, HAWAII, AUGUST-SEPTEMBER, 1917. No. 9

Editorial Note.

The October monthly report will contain full details of the proceedings of the annual meeting of the members of the Association, together with the reports of the President and Treasurer. The necessity for printing the August and September issues together has precluded publication of the financial reports until next issue.

L. W. DE VIS-NORTON,
Editor.

Volcano House, Aug. 11, 1917.

The net movement of the lava column during the week ending Aug. 10, 1917, has been by measurement in the nature of subsidence at the rate of about one foot per day. The total of eight feet difference, however, is insignificant and well within the daily range.

At 10 a. m. Saturday, Aug. 4, measurement made the depression of the lake 114 feet, of the S. crag 50 feet and of the summit of the central crag 35 feet below the S. E. station on the rim of the pit.

The lake was five feet lower than on the previous day, streaming was from the N. arm to the S. E. pool and the S. W. pool was crusted over except for a fountain in the tunnel at its inner end. There was an overflow floor in the central chasm and no visible tunnel below, and lines of vertical scraping appeared at the N. E. base of the central spine. The S. E. dome had entirely collapsed and there was only slight evidence of the S. E. tunnel. On making the circuit of Halemaumau the writer observed no marked changes N. W. and W. The peninsula extending W. from the central crag into the S. W. cove had been elevated and there was an inner overflow floor at the E. end of the S. W. cove. The sulphur stain had increased on the tumbled rocks surrounding the N. W. cone.

On the afternoon and evening of this day, with bright sunlight over Mauna Loa, whitish fume was very conspicuous above Mokuaweoweo rising in still air, while below at Kilauea the N. E. trade was blowing. This frequently happens in August owing to the combination of clear afternoon air and the seasonal declination of the sun, which brings it over the summit region.

On Aug. 6, at 3 p. m., there had been slight overflow of the inner beach at the E. cove and the lake was now about one foot below it. In the grotto under the S. bench there was much activity and also at the S. E. where there was swift inflow. There was occasional strong activity under the S. E. shelf. The S. W. cove grotto appeared quiet and most of the lake was crusted and inactive. There was occasionally quite loud puffing from the N. W. cone.

On Aug. 7 at noon the fumes appeared thinner and grotto activity was slight. The N. end of the E. island mass appeared to have recently slumped. Occasionally there was swift inflow under the floor S. E.

On Aug. 8, at 2:30 p. m., the inner bench stood 10 feet above the lake, the central crags appeared higher than ever and the central chasm had widened by collapse of its walls. The channel leading to the S. E. pool had apparently narrowed. The S. W. and N. W. coves were crusted over and streaming was outward from them to grottoes N. E. and S. E. A very large spatter dome had built over the grotto on the S. E. opposite the crevasse leading toward the S. station from the E. side of the S. E. cove and here there was a perpetual fountain within the dome with flames playing above and hot blue fume

WEEKLY BULLETIN
of the
Hawaiian Volcano Observatory

Published Monthly at Honolulu, Hawaii, by the Hawaiian Volcano Research Association

L. W. de Vis-Norton........Secretary

Entered as second-class matter January 20, 1914, at the post-office at Honolulu, Hawaii, under the Act of August 24, 1912.

of sulphurous acid rising rapidly in puffs. These fume puffs were conspicuous even at a distance. There was another high cavern grotto at the Old Faithful locality on the W. side of the E. island mass and the Old Faithful rhythmic fountaining had ceased action in the central region. The recent collapse of the E. island mass appeared to have invaded the Old Faithful sinkhole region. Slight puffing was heard toward the N. and from the N. W. cone where bright yellow sulphur was increasingly conspicuous. There was marked growth of the new inner floor at the central chasm and the E. cove. Fume was abundant, especially toward the north. No marked changes of elevation were discernible in the northwestern crags and the profiles of the old crag mass and of the E. island mass had now become singularly ragged like irregular saw teeth.

On Aug. 9, at 6 p. m., the inner bench was about eight feet above the lake at the E. island and central chasm. The raised bench at the E. cove was 20 feet high. The S. E. grotto dome was 15 feet high. As seen from the E. cove the central crag appeared an immense group of high turrets with a towering spine rising 40 feet above the lake on the eastern side of the mass. The E. face of the upper part of this spine showed vertical laminations, due probably to a former plastering of foundered crusts against the submerged N. wall of the central cavern during the spring of 1917 before the present uplift had taken place.

There were southeastward streaming, blistered thin crusts and migratory fountains. There was a flaming grotto under the S. bench. The spectacle presented by the great S. E. dome grotto as seen from the E. cove was magnificent, the continuous fountain inside the dome plashing and rumbling and building luminous stalactites which would occasionally become overweighted and bring about the collapse of huge shells of the roof into the fiery flood beneath. Occasional fountains would spatter over the surface of the E. bench. Streaming was outward from the S. W. and N. arms of the lake. The N. W. cove was crusted over and heavy crusts cracked and foundered occasionally in the middle of the N. arm, developing much bubble fountaining, while active grottoes splashed and rumbled under the E. and N. banks. The surface of the E. island and the old N. W. crag mass appeared to consist of tumbled swarms of small crags. A high ridge of broken blocks extended southward from the N. E. peak to a sagged area of the N. E. floor whence the surface sloped upward, both eastward to the cliff overhanging the E. cove and northward to the edge of the tumbled N. pit.

Measurements on Friday, Aug. 10, 1917, after 11 a. m., made the depression of the lake 117 feet beneath the S. E. station. At 11 a. m. the lake appeared low, the inner bench 12 feet high, streaming was rapid, and the fumes appeared thinner so as to make the W. side of the pit quite visible from the E. and S. E. The S. E. dome was moderately active and there were bubble fountains at the E. cove. There was a low glowing cavern under an arch of floor at the central chasm. By noon this cavern was submerged and the rising lake was quiet and crusted, with fountains at only the N. E. and S. E. grottoes.

Volcano House, Aug. 18, 1917.

During the week ending August 17, 1917, the lava lake has maintained a downward tendency similar to that of the previous week, crags and lake both subsiding. At the end of the week the lake depression was about 125 feet.

On Saturday, August 11, at 2:15 p. m., there were travelling fountains in the southeast channel and both south and southeast grottoes were active. At

3 p. m. the inner cliff was about 15 feet high in both north and southeast arms and a fall of rock from the central crag into the channel started much effervescence of bubbling fountains. There were large fountains in the north arm and the fumes on this day appeared thinner.

On August 13, at 2:45 p. m., the lake was low and the usual grottoes active; streaming was swift with central fountaining in the southeast channel. At 3:50 p. m., a large block of the spatter margin fell from the northwest point of the central crag mass and started fountaining activity in the west central region. At 4:30 p. m. there was a rock slide under the east station.

At 12:30 p. m. Tuesday, August 14, there was little change in the general appearance of the pit. The lake was about five feet below the inner bench at the east cove. It appeared relatively high and rising, with thin fumes. There was no appearance of fresh overflowing anywhere. The southeast dome was high and stained yellow with sulphur; inside was an active grotto, and from the great crevasse in the shelf above brown dusty fume arose. Streaming in the lake was towards the southeast from both the southwest and northwest arms. The peninsula in the southwest cove was unchanged. Seen from the northeast, the east island mass now appeared relatively low compared with the central crag mass.

On August 15, at 1:15 p. m., the lake was slowly rising with grotto activity south and southeast. At 2 p. m. the east cove was being bombarded and there was much fountaining in the southeast arm. At 2:15 p. m., from the west, the north cove was fountaining, but the cove under the east island was quiet. At 2:30 p. m. looking from the southwest, two large cones were seen to have been built southwest and west of the east island mass, enclosing active grottoes. This region has lately been concealed by smoke from the north bench.

On August 16, at 1:30 p. m., the lake was lower and very quiet with almost no fountaining even at the grottoes. Fumes, however, showed no increase. At 2:20 p. m. it was evident that the lake had risen about three feet and the only activity was at the grotto under the south bench. At 2:25 p. m. and again five minutes later rock falls from the spatter margin of the lake fell from the central crag mass into the channel and into the central region.

On Friday, August 17, 1917, at 1:30 p. m., the west banks were about 15 feet high, fumes appeared thicker, especially toward the north and the lake was quiet. At 1:45 p. m. looking from the northeast the only fountaining activity discernible was in the south and southeast grottoes and the streaming as usual was in their direction and comparatively slow.

The following reports from the Whitney Laboratory of Seismology are submitted by Mr. H. O. Wood:

During the week interval ending with August 10 four small local earthquakes have been registered. None were felt. Microseismic motion has been as usual. Volcanic vibration has been stronger than usual, and more sustained in the stronger spasms, even in reference to the recent weeks. Abrupt pen-shifts were produced by two of the earthquakes, otherwise pen-shifts in the sense of tilt have shown no noteworthy characteristics.

During the week interval ending with August 17 two small local earthquakes have been registered. The seismographic amplitudes of microseismic motion have varied within ordinary ranges. Volcanic vibration has been strong and spasmodic. Pen-shift in the sense of tilt was not particularly noticeable in the early part of the interval, but toward its close there has been marked eastward shifting.

Volcano House Aug. 25, 1917.

During the week ending August 24, 1917, the lava column of Halemaumau continued to subside slowly until about August 22. After that date there was rising and on August 24 there was overflow on the northwest side of the lake. There has been much falling in of lake margins during the week and at least one avalanche from the high wall of Halemaumau under the east station. Visitors are warned to give heed to the danger signs at this time.

On Saturday, August 18, 1917, at 11

a. m., the lake and crags in general appeared lower. The east island mass had so far subsided and crumbled that the north arm of the lake was clearly visible above it as seen from the southeast. The innermost spatter rim was five feet high, the west bank eight to ten feet high and the bench at the southeast cove ten to twelve feet high. There was a heavy curtain across the entrance to the southeast dome, the grotto under the south bench was active and there was vigorous fountaining along the west shore. Streaming had reversed at the west so that it was now pouring from the north arm swiftly into the southwest pool. The flow into the southeast cove was slower. There were six to eight fountains in all. Crusts were of medium thickness and the only noise was of plashing. In general the lake appeared stagnant with very slow sinking in progress. Smoking places were the southeast cove, central crag, south crag, southwest peninsula, west cone, west talus, north talus, east base of crag mass; the heaviest smoke of all was from the north bench and next in density was the fumarole at the edge of the northwest table.

There was at the northern base of the steeple crag in the center of the pit, at the top of the spatter bench, a glowing and fuming sulphurous crack which appeared to portend a coming fall of rock. The pit under the north station had increased in size and depth, and in plan was extended into a crevasse eastward. The old crag mass appeared a little lower with a strong northward slope exhibited in the recent bench levels on the lake side. From its southern base the lake shore bench rose toward the south from a level five feet above the lake to a level fifteen feet above the lake at the southwest side of the southwest cove. On the north side of the peninsula extending into the southwest cove four terraced levels appeared.

On August 19, at 2:30 p. m., the lake appeared still lower with its west bank about 15 feet high, there was much fountaining in the north arm and an active grotto was splashing at the base of the northwest crag mass. At 2:45 p. m. there were heavy falls of rock into the lake from the south and southeast benches and later there was crumbling of the margins of the lake, in the region of the east island mass.

On August 20, at 2 p. m., crumbling of the banks was still in progress and a large block fell from the northwest crag mass into the lake. After all these falls fountains boil up where the fragments sink beneath the lake. There were fountains on this day in the west central part of the lake, and in the channel leading southeast, and the south and southeast grottoes were active. There were blowing noises from the northwest cone. The fumes were thick. At 2:20 p. m. there was a prolonged avalanche on the northwest and about this time many small slides were heard from the north inner cliff. At 2:40 p. m. rising was in progress and there was noisy spurting of lava under high gas pressure from grottoes N. E. and E.

At 2 p. m., August 21, 1917, the smoke N. W. was thick and the main lake was quiet. The southeast pool showed several fountains and the usual activity in the southeast and south grottoes. There was much smoke from the south floor. At 2:45 p. m. the view from the southeast station showed great activity in the southeast cove and the northeast grotto. In the evening at 6:30 p. m. a large fragment fell from the north side of the central crag mass into the channel so that violent effervescence ensued.

On August 22, at 2 p. m., the whole lake was quiet with only slight activity at the south and southeast grottoes. At 3:20 p. m. the roof of the southeast dome grotto collapsed. A few seconds later there was a prolonged tumble of rocks from the southeast shelf followed by intense effervescence in the lake beneath.

On August 23, at 2 p. m., conditions were much the same with no fountaining except at the southern grottoes. At 2:10 p. m. a heavy avalanche fell from the upper wall under the east station and some large boulders were carried down to the floor beneath. The east island bench appeared about 10 feet above the lake which seemed to be rising.

On Friday, August 24, at 2:20 p. m., it was evident that a strong rise had taken place. The lake was level with the west bench, the northwest floor was flooded with fresh lava and there were many fountains in the north arm. Fumes were still thick toward the north. The northeast, south and southeast grottoes were spurting actively. At 3:10 p. m. a fall of rock took place from the northwest table crag and started many fountains in the northwest arm, the lake having sunk about five feet within the hour.

Volcano House, Sept. 1, 1917.

During the week ending August 31, 1917, the lava in Halemaumau pit has slowly risen without any pronounced changes. The building of spatter domes over border grottoes has been resumed and very small overflows of border benches have taken place. Fumes have diminished.

On Saturday, August 25, 1917, at 2 p. m., there was no marked change in the level of the liquid lava, the only activity was in the southeast pool and the fumes were thinner. At 2:15 p. m. streaming was rapid through the central channel southeastward, there was strong fountaining in the southern grottoes, but conditions were quiet northeast.

On August 26 at 1:15 p. m. conditions were unchanged. At 1:40 p. m. there was a fall of rock from the east island mass into the channel, followed soon after by another tumble from the central crag mass. In the course of ten minutes the lava subsided ten feet and remained so for about half an hour. Then rapid rising took place until at 4:15 p. m., there was slight overflow of the inner bench at the east cove.

On August 27, at 2 p. m., the north arm of the lake was depressed five feet below its banks, there were few fountains, fumes were thinner and there had been rock falls from the northwest face of the east island mass and from the north side of the central crag mass. Hissing from the northwest cone could be heard. At 11:30 p. m. glow could be seen at the northwest cone. There was a big flaming chimney 25 feet above the lake in the central steeple crag, and a second smaller one 15 feet above the lake on the east side of the steeple. The fissure feeding these chimneys was a crack back of the spatter veneer. From 11:30 p. m. to 2 a. m., August 28, this chimney flared continuously while a border fountain just below bombarded the lake shore on the north side of the base of the steeple. When the fountain ceased, however, the chimney flame died out and the chimney became a dull red. Repeatedly it appeared that when the fountain began the flaming was renewed and the interior of the chimney gradually acquired a yellow glow. The flame was dependent on a local fountain 25 feet below the orifice indicating clearly that the fountain set up gas combustion with an inrushing air draft as at the base of a furnace. During the night there was occasional general cracking and foundering of the crusts on the central and northern parts of the lake. The southwest arm was mostly quiet and crusted. Streaming was to the north and to the southeast. There were fountains east, southeast, south, west and northeast. The south grotto was hung with stalactites. There was occasional bright fountaining in the north corner of the lake. Fluctuations of height were very slight during the night.

Measurements on Tuesday, August 28, 1917, at 4:15 p. m., determined the depression of the lake to be 111 feet and the height of the central crag mass above the lake 74 feet.

Conditions were little changed. There were four or five fountains making blowing and plashing noises. The southern grottoes were hung with stalactites. The crusts made cracking and crunching noises. Hot bluish fume rote from the central chimneys. Streaming was outward from the southwest and north arms and carried blistered skins rather rapidly through the channel southeastward. Hot fumes arose from the east grotto. A current streamed from the northwest arm to the north bank of the lake.

On August 29 at 11 a. m. the lake was higher and rising, the liquid brimming level with the rampart of the west bench. Streaming was radial outward from the center of the lake to the north, to the southwest and to the southeast. There was central fountaining, and other fountains played southeast, south, east, in the southwest cove, against the north bank and on the north side of the east island mass. A new splash dome was being built in the southeast cove. The inner bench at the central chasm was about two feet above the lake. The central chimneys continued active. Smoke in general had diminished.

From 5 to 7 p. m. on August 30, conditions were still those of a rising lake, with streaming outward from the northwest arm to the north, to the southeast and to the southwest. There was steady hissing at the northwest cone and a new sulphur cone had formed on the bank at the east cove. The lava puffed and pounded in a grotto on the west side of the east island mass.

Examination of the southwest arm from the west showed that this arm had been widening and extending itself eastward in the directions of the south valley and the central chasm. At its extreme south corner there was a small glowing chimney 10 feet above the lake with a grotto beneath leading to the south valley tunnel. The great central crag mass, seen from the west, was a very impressive object, composed of towering peaks 70 feet high at its eastern end, flattening out to a long deck or plateau at its western end some 30 feet above the lake. This great block had parted from the south floor body at the central chasm and was now in process of rising bodily in the center of the pit. The northwest cone was a sulphurous driblet heap with a glowing crack in its summit.

A change which has gradually been taking place lately back of the edge of Halemaumau southwest is the development of a solfataric patch some 75 feet in diameter with increased heat at the cracks and deposits of bright yellow sulphur mixed with alum. There is also the odor of sulphur vapor both at this patch and the great southwest crevasse. These places lie east and west of the southwest station.

A notable feature of the bench magma in the pit at this time is the continuous valley encircling the uplifted central area. Heavy banks of Pele's hair have accumulated on the southeast shelf and on the edge of the pit above.

After dark on this day an elongate flame crack was seen above the south grotto and other flames at the central chimneys. There was strong fountaining against the north bank of the lake. Streaming was very sluggish.

On Friday, August 31, at 10 a. m., the lake was high, spatter grottoes were building, there was hissing at the inner end of the southwest cove as well as at the northwest cone, fumes were thin, the southwest cove was stagnant, streaming was to the southeast, and there were the usual chimneys and grotface of the central crag mass indicated toes. Small falls of rock from the north that that block was in motion.

For the week ending at 10 a. m. August 31, 1917, one moderate local earthquake was registered by the seismographs of the Whitney Laboratory. This happened on the afternoon of August 24. Microseisms and volcanic vibrations have both been moderate to slight in amplitude. Seismographic registration of tilt has indicated an almost stationary condition with the pens in a middle position. What movement there was toward the end of the period indicated a very slight change of tilt westward and southward.

Volcano House, Sept. 8, 1917.

During the week ending Sept. 7, 1917, the lava lake has continued to rise slowly at a rate averaging about a foot a day.

On Saturday, Sept. 1, 1917, at 1:45 p. m., the lake appeared to be rising slowly and there was strong activity in the south grotto and on the east side of the old northwest crag mass. The north arm was quiet and much concealed by smoke. There was the usual activity in the southeast grotto.

On Sept. 2 at 2:15 p. m. there was much fountaining in the north arm and west grotto. At 2:30 p. m. the southeast grotto seen from the southeast station, and also the south grotto, showed fountains and the streaming to the southeast was fairly rapid. At 3 p. m. some fifteen fountains were in action mostly in the northern and southeastern arms. A cone was forming on the new lava of the east cove overflows and spurts of fire appeared through the cracks in the summit of this dome. The dome was covered with yellow sulphur stain. From 5 to 7 p. m. the lake was clearly rising and this eastern glow cone was puffing strongly and flaming. It evidently surmounted a fountaining cavern, the presence of which was revealed by inrush and fountaining at the adjacent lake shore. The fumes were thinner on this day. There was dull glow in the central chimney and a very bright chimney surmounted the south grotto.

On Sept. 3 from 2 to 4 p. m. conditions were much the same with the lake surface about four feet below the fresh overflow of the east cove. The grottoes were mostly curtained. The east cone exhibited no gas pressure and its cracks glowed dark red. Close examination revealed smooth stalactites within these cracks and brownish spatter driblets around the orifices. Fumes on this day were moderate.

On Sept. 5 at 2 p. m. the lake was lower with considerable activity in the north arm and the west, south and southeast grottoes. The lake was subsiding and at 2:50 p. m. there was a heavy fall from the south bench at the entrance to the southeast cove. A few minutes later another block fell from the central crag mass. In both cases the debris fell into the lake and produced bubble fountaining.

On Sept. 6 at 2 p. m. the lake was nearly brimming level with the inner benches and very quiet. It was evident that there had been fresh flooding of the bench at the east cove where there was active bombardment, as also at the southeast. At 3 p. m. the lake level was within a foot of overflowing on the northwest, west and east, and these were the three principal localities of fresh overflow. Seven to eight fountains were in action and the streaming was outward from the southwest and northwest coves toward the southeast and north. The fumes were thin. The highest central crag appeared distinctly higher than the steeple crag next it on the east. There were fresh overflows on the floor of the central chasm. The central chimney was dark but the one over the south grotto was very bright. The eastern sulphurous cone of Sept. 2 was now buried under fresh flows. Spatter heaps at the lake border had been built under the old crag mass and at the south southeast and east.

Measurements at 3:15 p. m. on Friday, Sept. 7, 1917, made the lake depression 104 feet and the central crag rose 74 feet above the lake while the old crag mass was now only 38 feet above the lake.

There were four to five fountains and the streaming was outward from the northwest and southwest towards the north and southeast. The central crag appeared higher. The overflow bench appeared about three feet above the lake. The south and southeast grottoes were heavily curtained. There were fresh half-domes of spatter at the central chasm and east cove. There was fountaining northeast, north, south, southeast and west. The chimneys were fuming, but not glowing by daylight. Streaming was rapid in the southeast channel. The crusts were thin and blistered and the radiation from the lake surface was hot at the southeast station. There was occasional fountaining at the east cove. The old crag mass, the northwest table and the east island crags appeared unchanged and no fresh overflows were discernible.

On the seismographs of the Whitney Laboratory during the week ending 10 a. m. Sept. 7 only one very slight local earthquake was registered. This occurred in the early morning of Sept. 6. The microseismic and volcanic vibrations have been of small amplitude. The seismographic registration of tilt has indicated increasing inclination of the piers towards the north and west. On Sept. 6 the north-south component of the Bosch Omori pair of pendulums was restarted after several months during which the instrument has not been in operation.

Volcano House, Sept. 14, 1917.

During the week ending Sept. 14, 1917, the lava lake of Halemaumau has been essentially stationary. At the end of the week there was a slight rise and overflow of the east bench.

On Sept. 8 at 2:15 p. m. the lake appeared rising rapidly with the inner bench about 6 feet high. There was vigorous fountaining south and southeast and great activity under the new spatter dome at the eastern entrance to the central chasm. There was high spraying under the overhanging shelf southeast. The fumes were fairly thick.

On Sept. 9 at 1 p. m. the fume was thinner and there was much activity in the north arm. The inner bench stood five feet above the lake but from 5 to 7 p. m. the lake was lower with inner bench 8 to 10 feet high. There were the usual grottoes in action and occasional central fountains. There was glow in the south and central chimneys; the latter, however, greatly diminished. Occasionally the crust broke up and increased fountaining occurred. There was a spatter grotto at the east end of the southeast arm and also at the east cove.

On Monday, Sept. 10, a new east-west crack had developed extending from the south side of the east island crag across the floor of the east cove. The lake was 8 feet below the inner bench, six or seven fountains were in action, streaming was to the north, to the southeast and to the southwest, there were two active grottoes in the southeast cove, one under the south bench, one under the old crag mass, one at the east and one northwest. There were others in the north and southwest arms. The smoke and streaming were moderate and there was much spatter building. The orifice of the central chimney was sulphur stained. The central crag now appeared higher than the level of the May shelf. The east island mass was developing a wall which faced northeastward towards the chasm which separated the crags from the northeast floor. The wall on the west side of the southeast cove had broken in and a large yellow sulphur patch appeared on the floor above. It was evident that the central masses were still rising for the banks at the east and southeast coves were only three feet above the lake, whereas they rose much higher in th region of the central channel.

At 3:15 p. m. on Tuesday, ept. 11, 1917, there was no change. The central region was quiet, the fume moderate, streaming was to the southeast and four grottoes in action were visible from the northeast rim. A clear view of the old northwest crag mass showed that it had developed two benches on its east side inclined stepwise to the north about 30°, while between them was a fresh terrace or spatter bench about 10 feet above the lake which sloped very slightly north.

On Sept. 12, at 3 p. m., eight or ten fountains were in action, fumes were thick and the lake was low. About 5:50 p. m. there were two avalanches from the east island crags and ten minutes later there was a large fall from the south bench at the point marking the entrance to the southeast cove.

On Sept. 13, at 2:30 p. m., the inner bench was 10 feet high and there were fountalns in the usual grottoes except the one under the south bench which was quiet. At 3:10 p. m. the crust broke up in the southeast arm and there was cracking and foundering with many fountains.

On Sept. 14 at 3:30 p. m. there was evidence of a strong rise. The lake was very high, brimming level with the floor at the southeast cove and there was a fresh overflow at the east cove. At the west shore underneath the old crag mass a high cone had been built with a glowing chimney in its summit. The northeast chasm extending from the east cove to the north arm had widened and the rise of the lake now brought the north cove into view as seen from the southeast station. The old crag mass appeared lower as though there had been recent overflows northwest and west. At 3:40 p. m. there was a crust across the central channel, but cracking and foundering were going on in the central region and to the north. The southeast grotto was quiet and the southeast cove crusted. About 4:30 p. m. this crust broke up and there was heavy bombardment at the east end of the lake. Grottoes south, east, west, northwest and northeast were splashing and puffing and there was also fountaining against the south bank of the southwest arm where the streaming was eastward. A tumble of fresh broken masses under the middle part of the central crag mass on the south shore of the channel made a new shore point there. The northwest cove had changed its shape from a deep inlet to a shallow cove as though the bank had built out. A hot chimney was in action over the south grotto and streaming moved in a wide zone covered with festooned crust southeastward from the channel.

The seismographs of the Whitney

Laboratory have registered only one feeble local earthquake during the week ending 10 a. m., Friday, Sept. 14. Microseismic motion and volcanic vibrations have been slight. Tilting has been increasingly strong to the west and was moderately so to the north until Sept. 13, when this northward tilt suddenly decreased with great rapidity in the course of a day. Simultaneously there was a sudden change of weather with a shift of the wind from fresh northeast trade wind to calms and light southeast breezes.

Volcano House, Sept. 22, 1917.

During the week ending Sept. 21, 1917, the Halemaumau lava column has risen slightly, building pronounced spatter ramparts on the shores of the several coves and slightly overflowing the banks in those coves. The central crags have risen along with the lake.

The past three months have maintained extraordinarily uniform conditions in the Halemaumau pit. The lake has kept its level about 100 feet below the rim of the pit, and its form has changed but little. In plan it consists of three radial arms each about 400 feet long measured from the center, and each tending to bend so as to end in a hooked cove. The northern arm bends to the westward, ending in the northwest cove. The southeastern arm bends to the south and west and ends in the south east cove. The southwestern arm hooks to the eastward at its inner end. These two southern arms bend toward each other and there is strong evidence that they are connected through the central chasm and southern valley by subterranean tunnels in the bench lava. The most conspicuous object in the pit is the great central crag mass which has slowly risen during the summer until it stands 76 feet above the lake. The activity throughout the summer has been as uniform as the other features. There has been slow surface streaming from the west and northwest, ending at fountaining grottoes north, northeast, east, southeast and southwest. Rising and falling in pulsations of gas inflation, lasting each about 20 to 30 minutes, and with fluctuations from day to day of from five to twenty feet at different times, there has been a riverlike stream pouring through the central channel into the southeast arm, and the most conspicuous fountaining activity and general turbulence have been in the southeast cove. The conduit wells west and northwest from which all the streaming proceeds, have been masked under tumbled debris and crusted floor lava, but from time to time glowing and hissing cones have indicated that the wells still persist there.

This review is presented at this time because Sept. 23 is the date of the equinox, a time when changes in the crater are likely to occur. Previous experience would lead to expectation of subsidence at this time. It should be noted that the entire summer has been a period of extraordinary drought, of very little seismic activity on Hawaii and of no perceptible volcanic activity on Mauna Loa.

On Saturday, Sept. 15, 1917, from 8 to 9 p. m., the lava lake appeared relatively high with vigorous fountains east and southeast, others fairly persistent west and north and occasional outbreaks in grottoes southwest and northeast. The northern and western regions were crusted over while surface streaming poured southeastward. Flaming chimneys glowed above the west and south grottoes and there was dull glow in a chimney 20 feet above the lake on the east corner of the steeple crag which formed the eastern summit of the central crag mass. Occasionally a central fountain would break through the crust near the eastern end of the southeast arm and eject very high spray as it migrated into the southeast cove. Rising and falling motion was slight. During the subsidences the western and northwestern crust would occasionally break up with cracking and foundering and brilliant patches of upwelling melt.

On Sept. 16 from 5 to 7 p. m. there was little change. The newest overflow bench at the east cove stood five feet above the lake and on all sides a rim of overhang with stalactites hung about three feet over the liquid. Streaming was to the north, to the southeast and to the southwest. In the southwest arm the streaming was against the southern shore from the union of convergent currents jouring from both east and west. Spatter construction on this day was conspicuous. A flaming filagree cone had been built over the east grotto and there were cones at the southeast and east coves. The latter was evidently active within, as strong pulsatory heavings of the crust along the shore of the cove indicated a tunnel connection between the cove and the cone. There was high spatter overhang and a long flaming chimney above the grotto on the south side of the southeast arm and similar conditions obtained at the grotto on the east side of the old northwest crag mass. At the northeast cove marking the northern end of the cleft line that separated the east island mass from the northeast floor, a shore cone of horseshoe shape had been built with the opening toward the lake.

There was occasional violent longshore bombardment at the east and also at the southwest. In the north arm sliding heavy crusts moved over each other in a general southward direction making a noise of scraping.

The shore of the northwest cove had been so built out as to change what had been a deep inlet into a relatively slight embayment—that is, the inner part of the cove had become solid floor. Inspection of the north pit showed that it was increasingly deep with convergent talus in its bottom. The northwest table crag which appears to have changed not at all for many weeks was seen to be heavily covered with a mat of filamentous lava or Pele's hair like the southeastern shelf.

On Sept. 18 at 3:45 p. m. the general conditions were high lake with high gas pressure and constructional activity on the margins. There was stagnant crust in the conduit region west and northwest and more or less shore bombardment in other directions, but no central fountains. The eastern and southeastern spatter domes were shiftingly very noisy with gas pressure. Three or four long domes of this kind had been built towards the east. A wide streaming zone covered with festooned crust poured from the central channel southeastward, the channel itself and the central region being crusted over. Dense smoke rose from cracks at the north inner cliff above the lake. In the north arm there was cracking and foundering crust and the lava brimmed level with the rampart in the northwest cove where there appeared to be fresh overflows. There were shore fountains northwest, northeast and southwest and streaming poured from the lake center into the southwest arm. The grotto on the south side of the southeast arm was closed in by a spatter curtain but the fountaining inside kept a bellows-like wavy motion going in the outside crust, while 10 to 15 feet above in the south bench ragged crevices glowed and ejected bright jets of burning gas. Occasionally these chimneys would spurt and puff noisily with lava spray.

The east island mass now appeared to be rising highest at its southeastern end as in previous times. The central crag mass was highest in the middle. The old northwest crag mass appeared to be definitely suibsiding on its northern side and this movement was in some way connected with the flooding of the northwest floor and the building out of the shoreline there. The northwest table crag had its upper surface tilted strongly eastward and its summit remained slightly below the May bench level. This crag, along with the northeast floor and southeast shelf, has not shifted for a long time. The cone localities over the west and northwest conduit wells have lately changed very little. The bank at the east cove was only from two to three feet above the level of the lake.

On Sept. 19 from 5 to 6 p. m. the lake was brimming at the southeast and northwest ramparts, there was fresh marginal overflow at the southeast cove and the liquid stood three to four feet below the floor of the east cove. There was a spurting crack over the southeast dome. Heavy fountaining would break out occasionally in the center of the channel leading from the southeast arm to the southeast cove, and such fountains would migrate to the west bank of that cove. Other outbreaks showing sudden release of gas from beneath the lake crust took place at the east cove and the south grotto. There was the usual surface flow zone moving southeastward in the southeast arm. In the stagnant crust south of this zone large balloons were incessantly lifted by inflation of the surface crust from below. These balloons swelled to heights of four or five feet and formed in series of five or six large folds or blisters sometimes ten to twenty feet long. They would swell up until they extended themselves lengthwise to the bright line at the margin of the streaming zone where the gas would escape as the crust was lifted clear of the incandescent fluid so that the bubble would then collapse.

Until 5:30 p. m. the lake action was quiet with the north arm and central region heavily crusted and fountaining west, east and southeast. The central crag mass appeared very high. At 5:30 p. m. there was general cracking and foundering so that the lake subsided about two feet, with hundreds of bubble fountains and strong evolution of heat and gas.

Measurement on Friday, Sept, 21, 1917, at 2:30 p. m., made the depression of the lake in the central region 97 feet below the southeast station. The overflow level marking the maximum recent rise at the southeast cove was three feet higher. The central crag summit rose 76 feet above the lake. These measurements indicate a rise of the lake of 10 feet in two weeks and a rise of the central crag since Sept. 7 of two feet.

On this day the inner bench stood higher above the lake than of late, appearing about five feet high at the southeast cove and eight feet high at the east cove. There was strong shore bombardment south and southeast. Streaming was rapid to the southeast with thin blistered crusts, very hot radiation from the lake surface and no festooned flow zone. The streaming through the central channel carried along blocks of crust and there were central fountains here and in the southeast arm. Occasionally a large central fountain would form in the southeast cove. There was occasional heavy shore bombardment under the central crag mass. About 3 p. m. the heavy spatter curtain in front of the south grotto collapsed. The northern and western regions were crusted over, the central crag appeared higher than ever and fumes were thin. There was much rumbling noise and the fountains broke heavily without much gas spurting. In general the conditions indicated either subsidence or a lifting of the central crags.

The seismographs of the Whitney Laboratory for the week ending at 10 a. m. Sept. 21, 1917, registered two local earthquakes which occurred a few minutes apart in the very early morning of Sept. 15 and were generally felt in Kau and Hilo. The first earthquake at Volcano House was a prolonged rocking motion. The second one was slight. Microsesimic motion during the week has been moderate and volcanic vibration slight. The movement of the pendulums in the sense of tilt had changed from strong westward and slight northward to slight westward and stronger northward, indicating tilting motion in general to the northeast.

Volcano House, Sept. 29, 1917.

During the period immediately following the autumnal equinox of 1917 there has been no subsidence of the lava of Halemaumau but rather a rising. Crags and lake have both risen and one pronounced overflow has taken place.

On Saturday, September 22, at 4:30 p. m., the lake as seen from the northeast was high and brimming against a definite spatter rampart in the southeast cove. The shore there stood about one foot above the liquid while at the east cove and central chasm the bank was about three feet high. There was little change in general conditions. A broad festooned flow zone with blistered crusts streamed southeast from the central channel, the north and west regions were crusted over, the south chimney was flaming, the central crags appeared very high and there were occasional spells of rapid current pouring into the southeast cove. The noise to the southeast was of puffing and plashing. A row of half-dome grottoes had been built along the southeast rampart, there were strong fountains along the west bank and to the southwest and east. The spatter rampart in the southeast cove had been building out so as to widen the shore bench at the foot of the cliff under the southeast shelf.

On September 24, at 1:30 p. m., the same description would apply. The southeast domes were a little higher and another dome rampart had been built across the eastern entrance to the central chasm. The rampart activity to the southeast suggested that of January, 1917, to the northeast. The crust was folding up and ballooning on the east side of the south grotto. It was evident that there had lately been much scaling off of the high spatter veneer on the north side of the central steeple, but the central crag mass showed no signs of lowering.

On the evening of September 25 there was no change. The lake was dull and inactive and the fumes appeared a little denser.

On September 26 at 3 p. m. the only change notable was that the lake appeared depressed with reference to the central crags about five feet in excess of its stand of the previous day. The shore bench at the east cove and the central chasm appeared 8 feet high while at the southeast cove it was only 5 feet high. The northern and western parts of the lake were crusted over and the south and southeast and east grottoes were open and active. The fumes were as usual and the height of the crags with reference to the Halemaumau rim was increased rather than diminished. There were no marked falls of rock but some caving in of the lake shores was reported.

At 9 p. m. on September 27 there was strong rising in progress with pronounced overflow into the south valley from the southeast cove.

Measurements on Friday, September 28, 1917, at 11 a. m., made the depression of the south floor near the overflow of the previous evening 93 feet below the rim of Halemaumau and the depression of the lake at the moment 102 feet. These figures indicated that at the margin of the southeast cove there had been practically no change of level of the lake in seven days. (Ninety-seven feet depression of September 21.) The summit of the central crag mass, however, measured only 13 feet below the rim of Halemaumau and stood 89 feet above the lake. It had risen seven feet since September 21 and probably most of this movement took place about September 27 at the time of the southeast overflow. The east island summit stood 59 feet and the old northwest crag 47 feet above the lake, and both had risen as compared with previous measurements. It is evident, therefore, that a very pronounced displacement of the lava column in the form of sharp uplift of the central crags has followed the equinox.

The central crags were pronouncedly higher and the east island crag mass appeared broken and changed in shape. The fumes were clearly thinner and everything indicated a pronounced rise of both crags and lake. The overflow from the southeast cove southwestward was fully 100 feet long. The inner bench over the lake appeared six feet high in the center, east, west and northwest and four feet high at the southeast. The west and northwest regions were crusted over, there were migratory fountains in the center, streaming to the southeast was occasionally rapid and the lava was pounding in grottoes beneath hanging stalactites on the east and west sides of the southeast cove and under the south bench. From the east cove streaming was outward.

The record of seismicity on the Whitney seismographs for the week ending 10 a. m. September 28 shows one small local earthquake on the afternoon of September 22. Microseismic motion has been moderate. Volcanic vibrations have slightly increased, mostly as scattered tremor storms at infrequent and irregular intervals. The tilting motion shown by the instruments was at first stronger to the north and east with decrease in the north component towards the end of the period.

The fume rising from Mokuaweoweo which has been repeatedly visible during the summer under favoring weather conditions in the afternoons became strikingly conspicuous on the afternoon of September 27, rising as a column of smoke in still air, although at the lower level of the Kilauea summit fresh and gusty northeast wind was blowing.

Very respectfully,
T. A. JAGGAR, JR.,
Director.

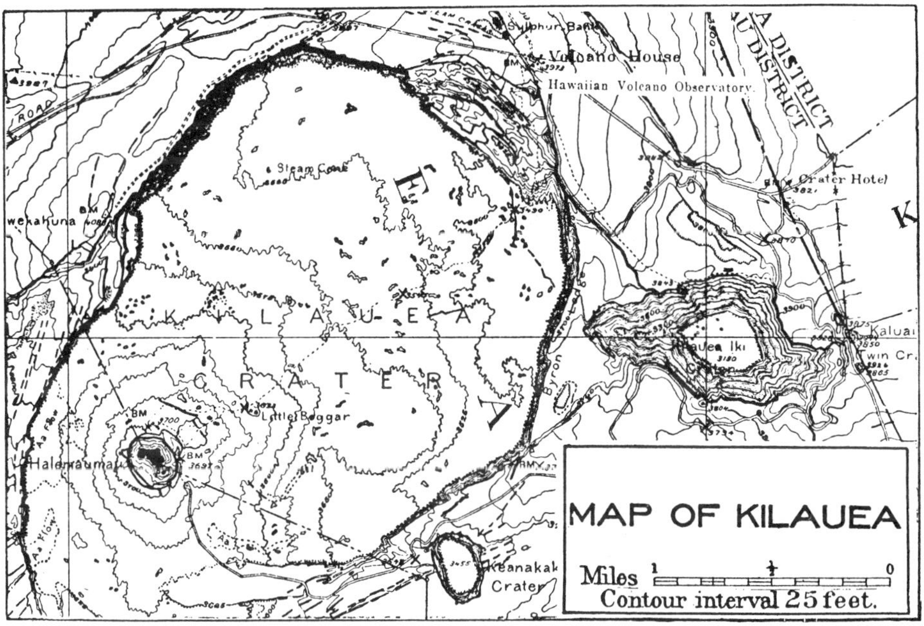

HAWAIIAN VOLCANO RESEARCH ASSOCIATION.

This society is a voluntary one, made up of subscribers to scientific work which is being executed by Dr. T. A. Jaggar, Director of the Hawaiian Volcano Observatory, Volcano House, P. O., Hawaii. **All scientific exchanges should be sent to this address.**

In 1917 there are about 150 subscribers in Hawaii **and elsewhere, firms and individuals. A group of firms and persons in Hilo built the main** observatory building in the spring of 1912. The work was founded by the Massachusetts Institute of Technology. Publications to date have been weekly reports since the summer of 1911 now reprinted in Honolulu in monthly form. There are also special reports, printed from time to time.

The weekly bulletin as it appears in the Honolulu Advertiser is reprinted as a leaflet and sent to regular annual subscribers to the work of the Association. **L. A. Thurston is president of the** Board of Directors of the Association, and L. T. Peck is treasurer. New subscribers who are **interested in volcanoes will be welcomed in the Association. The Association aims: (1) To record volcanic activity and earthquakes in Hawaii; (2) to attract scientific men hither for special studies; (3) to promote the establishment of volcano observatories all over the world. The annual dues of regular members are $5; patrons** of the Association subscribe larger amounts.

WHITNEY LABORATORY OF SEISMOLOGY.

The Whitney Laboratory of Seismology, named after an endowment fund of geophysical research held by the Massachusetts Institute of Technology, in memory of Caroline and Edward Whitney of Boston, is equipped with two Bosch-Omori 100 kg tromometers registering N-S and E-W motion, a heavy Omori tromometer registering E-W motion, and an Omori "ordinary Seismograph" designed for registering strong earthquakes in all three components of motion. These are seated on concrete piers in a closed basement room having practically constant temperature, beneath the chief Observatory building near the hotel. Time is referred to a rated chronometer, checked at intervals by solar observations with a transit. Both instruments are loaned by the College of Hawaii. Hawaiian standard time (H. S. T.) is 10 hrs. 30 min. slower than Greenwich time.

CANCANI SCALE OF SEISMIC INTENSITY.

Expressed by accelerations measured in millimeters per second per second.

I.	Instrumental	0.0	2.5
II.	Very slight	2.5	5.0
III.	Slight	5.0	10.0
IV.	Sensible, mediocre	10.0	25.0
V.	Rather strong	25.0	50.0
VI.	Strong	50.0	100.0
VII.	Very strong	100.0	250.0
VIII.	Ruinous	250.0	500.0
IX.	Disastrous	500.0	1000.0
X.	Very disastrous	1000.0	2500.0
XI.	Catastrophic	2500.0	5000.0
XII.	Great catastrophe	5000.0	10000.0

Grade IV. is ordinarily the minimum perceived by the senses; and in grade XII. the acceleration, or rate of change of motion (jerk) reaches that of terrestrial gravitation.

In the standard form of report the maximum intensity or acceleration, designated by the symbol a, or max. a, is given in the conventional unit, the **milligal**. The milligal is a measure of acceleration, such that 1 milligal = 1/100 mm. per sec. per sec. = 10 μ per sec. per sec. The Cancani scale, here **defined in terms of millimeters per sec. per sec., can therefore be expressed in milligals by multiplying each of the numbers by 100.**

WEEKLY BULLETIN
OF THE

Hawaiian Volcano Observatory

ANNUAL GENERAL MEETING AND TREASURER'S REPORT, 1917

Vol. V. HONOLULU, HAWAII, OCTOBER, 1917. No. 10

VOLCANO HOUSE, Oct. 6, 1917.— During the week ending Friday, October 5, 1917, the rising of the lava column in Halemaumau has continued, carrying up the central crags from two to five feet in different places and decreasing the measured depression of the liquid lake by 10 feet in seven days. There has been strong uplift of the east floor so as to increase the height of the cliff at the lake edge. This cliff is fast becoming a new crag or scarp with a steep backslope to the northeast.

On September 29 at 5 p. m. the general conditions in Halemaumau were much as they had been. The banks of the lake seemed a little higher and the central crags towered conspicuously. There were fountains at the base of the northwest crag mass and occasionally large central fountains would develop in the southeast arm and migrate southeastward. There was no evidence of further overflowing.

On October 1 the effect of the recent lift of the central crags was shown in the building of a new inner bench or spatter rim all around the lake, making a ledge about two feet high and some five feet below the floor level which had recently been the lake shore at the east cove and at the central chasm. The new ledge was about three feet below the rampart level at the southeast cove and from six to ten feet below the west floor on the south side of the northwest crag mass. This raised western floor level distinctly slopes downward to the southwest. At the northwest cove the inner ledge was about six feet below the floor.

That the bench magma was still in motion was evidenced on this day by rocks tumbling on a new talus slope on the northeast side of the highest eastern crag of the east island mass and also by rocks sliding on the northern talus slopes adjacent to the northwest table crag. An examination of the northwest floor showed that there were fresh overflows there and behind a spatter rampart at the north cove in the direction of the north pit. These northern overflows were probably formed simultaneously with the one southeast on September 27.

The whole lake at noon on this day was crusted except in the coves where there was streaming toward active grottoes southeast, southwest, north and northeast. The crust across the southeast arm would occasionally break up, founder and reveal southeastward streaming. Around the southeast arm and cove there were four active grottoes; at the northeast cove there were two; there was one at the north cove, and others west and southwest. Conspicuous smoking localities were northeast, north, northwest, three places west and to the southwest. The fume in the central, southern and southeastern regions was thin. The strongly smoking cliff edge at the margin of the lifted northeastern floor block stood from 30 to 40 feet above the lake on the east side of the north cove. About 12:30 p. m. the north arm crust broke up and seven fountains burst into activity, the central ones migrating to the northeast and north. These northern fountains had made much Pele's hair which formed a mat on the inclined surface of the northwest table crag.

On October 3 at 11:45 a. m. grottoes were active north, northwest and west, as well as in the more obvious southern and eastern localities. There was fresh yellow sulphur stain on the flat cone which stood as a low dome above the east cove grotto. The grotto under the southeast shelf was puffing with

WEEKLY BULLETIN
of the
Hawaiian Volcano Observatory

Published Monthly at Honolulu, Hawaii, by the Hawaiian Volcano Research Association

L. W. de Vis-Norton........Secretary

Entered as second-class matter January 20, 1914, at the post-office at Honolulu, Hawaii, under the Act of August 24, 1912.

gas pressure and a deep rumbling sound came from the south grotto. There was rapid streaming under the bank on the west side of the southeast cove, but the central channel streaming southeastward was sluggish and the northern and western regions were crusted over, with occasional cracking and foundering. The new inner spatter ledge was no longer marked. The lower floor northwest under the high shelf of May, 1917, appeared to be lowering and a large talus cone against the north-northwest wall of Halemaumau was becoming very conspicuous, its base resting on the lower eastern end of the northwest table crag.

Measurement on Friday, October 5, 1917, at 11:30 a. m., made the lake depression 92 feet below the southeast rim of Halemaumau, and the summit of the central crag was now only 10 feet below the rim of the pit and 82 feet above the lake. The east island mass had been tilting rapidly, for its western summit was now the higher for the first time, rising 53 feet above the lake, in contrast to the eastern summit, which was only 51 feet above the lake. In seven days the lake had risen 10 feet, the central crag 3 feet, the western summit of the east island crag mass 5 feet, and the eastern summit of the same only 2 feet.

On this day the bank of the lake was three to five feet high southeast and at the central chasm, and about eight feet high on the west and northwest. About noon there was sharp subsidence of the liquid, a glowing rim of overhang developed around the lake, while central and migratory fountains formed and crusts broke up. The large dome southeast had its fountains completely curtained in and rumbled with a deep note. There was fierce bombardment on the south and west sides of the southeast cove. The south grotto was open with lava pounding within. The writer descended to the east cove, which had considerably changed its shape so as to be nearly rectangular, with its eastern wall much higher than before. There was a distinct steepened ascent from the base of the northeast wall of Halemaumau to this edge of the lake. The top of the cone at the east cove was glowing and flaming in cracks, while beneath could be seen on the lake side a most spectacular grotto 8 to 10 feet high, hung with scalloped stalactites, glowing vividly and flaring with burning gas. This eastern bench over the lake had so much risen that the fountains below no longer spattered over the top of the cliff. At its southern end this cliff parted from the southeast cove rampart along a line of huge fissures, some of which went right through the middle of the eastern spatter dome.

Other signs of fresh uplift appeared along the pressure ridge on the south side of the block forming the central crag mass and also along the northeast side of the east island block. Very pronounced movement of the central region has taken place in the last ten days.

The chimney in the central steeple showed greatly increased smoking with hot brownish billows rising rapidly. There was activity in the north rampart grotto, and the northeast cove showed two active grottoes, the one a filagree flaming crack and the other a rampart dome. In the summit of the northeast inner cliff, which was shattered with huge crevasses, was found a well leading downward, now cool, but evidently formed by the melting action of hot gases. The well had irregular, smooth, lumpy, steel-gray walls with fused surfaces, and the opening descended in a somewhat spiral chimney form, two or three feet in diameter.

In the Whitney Laboratory of Seismology for the week ending 10 a. m.

Friday, October 5, 1917, five local earthquakes have been registered. Two of these were on September 30, respectively about 8 a. m. and between 3 and 4 p. m.; the other three were on October 4, respectively about 2 a. m., 12:48 p. m. and between 8 and 9 p. m. The shock of 12:48 p. m. was strong enough to start a rock slide on the face of Uwekahuna bluff Microseismic movement for the week has been moderate and the volcanic tremor continues to occur in scattered storms in the nature of minute earthquakes. The instrumental evidence of tilting showed increase of tilt to the north and west.

VOLCANO HOUSE, Oct. 13, 1917.—During the week ending October 12, 1917, lake and crags of the Halemaumau lava column have continued to rise vigorously, with increase of gas pressure and some change of habit in the way of prolonged spells of crusting, followed by general cracking up so as to make brilliant displays of fountaining and streaming. The great central crag is now plainly visible from Volcano House and the fume has become thin.

On October 7 at 10:30 a. m. it was evident that the east and northeast floor had continued to rise so that the chasm bounding the east island crag mass on its northeast side had so changed that the floor of the east cove had collapsed to a talus of tumbled blocks extending from the ruin of the east island peak to the lake shore. In this process the sulphur-stained cone of the east cove had collapsed and the cliff over the northeast shore of the southeast arm had risen higher than ever. This cliff now stood at least 30 feet above the lake. At the northeast cove, representing the other end of the chasm, there was a similar collapse and complete change of features in two days. Both the active grottoes had disappeared and in the place of the fissure grotto was a broken solfataric surface and a slope of stained debris. Where the dome grotto had been there was a small cove crusted over. A gulch full of tumbled rocks extended through from the northeast cove to the east cove. The whole east island crag mass was now a tumble of the most chaotic character, made up of stained and decomposed fragments, and this gulch marks the fissure line bounding it on the northeast. There was evidently differential movement between the crag block and the northeast floor block.

On this day there were two spatter rims at the lake shore, well marked at the east and northwest cove, showing lake levels two and four feet above the present lake. About every fifteen minutes there was a breaking up of crust across the southeast arm and a rush of streaming into the southeast cove. The north and west regions were quiet and crusted over. The north rampart grotto was closed in and rumbling. The central chimney on the north side of the steeple crag appeared inactive, but the one on the east side was open and fuming. There was no sign of cessation in the rising of the crags, and the lake appeared high in the coves, especially at the northwest, where the recent overflow rims overlapped in flat fashion as though the lake margin were gaining in height, while the northwest pond locality westward from the old crag mass appeared depressed. Other signs of building up of the rampart so as to lift the actual lake basin appeared at the north, southwest and southeast coves. If the rising continues, overflow may be expected at the coves, but elsewhere the lake is hemmed in by cliffs.

On descending to the lake shore at the east cove irrespirable sulphur fumes were encountered coming from flaming fissures in an active grotto at the tunnel leading to the northeast chasm. At the other end of the new east crag, however, a slide of rock was found between the crag and the southeast shelf which could be followed down to the edge of the lake behind and next south of the east grotto. Here there was a flaming pot and occasional heavy fountaining.

At noon on October 9 the lake was crusted over and rising. The summit of the central crag appeared much higher and nearly level with the southeast margin of Halemaumau. At 12:20 p. m. there was general breaking up of the crust, many fountains, large and small, and a rush of the surface current to the southeast. This was followed by crusting over again. A new inner ledge had been built under the central crag, and the northwest cove appeared to have a low shoreline. To show the difference in height between the main shore benches in the center of the pit and at the coves, the west rampart, central chasm and east cove floors were each from 12 to 15 feet above the lake, whereas the southeast and northwest cove margins were only from 5 to 8 feet high. The south grotto appeared deep and overhanging, and the southeast dome was closed and hissing. The chimney on the north side of the central steeple was fuming and smoke in general was moderate in volume.

On Thursday, October 11, the lake seen from the southeast and east appeared high, with strong gas pressure and much noisy puffing and spraying at the southeast, south and north grottoes. A cone with glowing fissures had been built above the southeast dome, and this emitted a sheaf of blow-pipe flame 12 inches wide and from 8 to 10 inches long, with incessant gas pressure behind it and reddish color in daylight. At night the flame appeared whitish with blue outer edge. There was streaming in a zone of wide multiple festoons from the center region to the southeast. Fountains played occasionally at the northeast cove and heavy ones spurted at the southwest cove. Fumes were thin. The southeast rampart was only one foot high. There was yellow stain on the benches at the east cove and central chasm. Both the central steeple and central crag mass beyond appeared higher than before and leaning southward. At the west cove next adjacent to the northwest crag mass the bank over the lake appeared to have subsided so that it was lower than its extension to the south. Immediately under this crag mass there was a very low place with broken rocks smoking at the lake shore. Blue fume was rising from the central chimney. At the edge of the lake beneath the east gulch the rampart had widened so as to build out in front of the east grotto of October 7.

At 5:10 p. m. the lake subsided about one foot, showing a glowing rim all around and increased fountaining. At 5:15 p. m. a large central fountain developed and migrated slowly southward with a festooned zone in its wake and a quiet crusted area east of it. This fountain migrated to the south grotto, increasing in violence, flinging high stringy masses into the air, with flame, and spray to heights of 50 feet or more. It was followed by accelerated streaming from the center of the lake in a curve to the south grotto, but when the fountain subsided the normal streaming was resumed to the southeast cove. Heat at the southeast rim of the pit was strong. The crust appeared thin, but blisters were rare. Crevasses had formed back of the edge of the east floor crag where it overhung the lake. There were glowing fissure chimneys above the west side of the southeast cove and over the south grotto.

Looking from the south station at 5:30 p. m. a heavy block of the spatter bench fell into the lake just west of the east island talus, leaving a red-hot wall as a scar. It was evident from this point of view that the southeast arm had recently increased in size by eating back both northward and eastward. The southwest arm showed low smoking flats on its southwest side sloping towards the lake, with shoreline only one to two feet high. The slope of uplift on the south side of the southern crag mass had increased in height and steepness toward the west, bending at its western end sharply into a cliff over the southwest arm. The central crag now appeared level with the brink of the pit. From the south the east island mass appeared to be bodily rising with its west end highest. At 5:50 p. m. there was general cracking, foundering and bubble fountaining all over the center of the lake, followed by the formation of a large fountain there. There was strong bombardment under the southeast shelf and about seven fountains in all in different parts of the lake. At 6 p. m. there was a prolonged quiet spell, with the whole lake heavily crusted except at the north grotto and on the west side of the southeast cove. At this place there was strong fountaining and spraying. This lasted forty minutes, until the gas pressure became so great that the crust across the southeast arm burst so that long rows of blue flames shot out along the cracks and then a great fountain explosion came suddenly through a heavy crust and was followed by a general break-up.

In the Whitney Laboratory only one small local earthquake has been registered during the week ending 10 a. m. October 12. This occurred between 8 and 9 p. m. on October 5. Microseismic motion has been ordinary and volcanic vibrations have fluctuated in intensity, with occasional stormy spells. The seismographic evidence of tilting showed increase to the north and east on October 5 and 6, followed by a reverse movement without special features on October 7, 8 and 9; on October 9, 10 and 11 the tilt became very strong to the north, with some increase to the east. On the north-south component instrument the pendulum swung to its limit in the north direction and showed tendency to remain in that position.

VOLCANO HOUSE, Oct. 20, 1917.—During the week ending Friday, October 19, 1917, the rising of the lava column has continued, taking effect in bodily uplift of the central crags, small border overflows and renewed overflow from a western blowing-cone. This last development recalls features of the great rise of a year ago.

On Saturday, October 13, it was evident that within two days there had been sufficient rising of the lake to overflow the cove margins southeast, southwest and northwest. At 5:30 p. m. on this day there was temporary subsidence of the lake of about five feet, bringing into view low-roofed tunnels at the east cove, the central chasm and on the west side of the southeast cove. A sharp rise of the central crags was manifest in the increased height of the pressure ridge or slope between the southern crag mass and the south valley. The high southeast shelf over the east gulch exhibited a large crevasse near its edge, forecasting an avalanche there.

The lake was undergoing spells of quiet crusting over, followed by times of cracking up with subsidence. During these times spatter margins along the shore would fall into the melt. There were six or seven fountains in action, stalactites hung before the north grotto, and a long curtain hung before the grotto in the southeast dome. The streaming was toward the east ledge.

On October 15 at 2 p. m. the lake was noisily puffing and rumbling at the grottoes and had been again slightly overflowing at the coves. The southeast cove overflows showed a different pattern from those seen October 13. Again the lake showed temporary depression about six feet below the southeast platform, where there was a high dome grotto. At the north cove, however, a very large dome had been built in the midst of the rampart. The southward leaning of the central steeple recorded on October 11 had now taken effect and the steeple had collapsed to two-thirds of its former height, the red oxidized debris of the ruin occupying the central chasm depression. The east ledge appeared to be lifted higher and part of the block in front of the crevasse of the southeast shelf recorded as pending on October 13 had avalanched into the east gulch below. There were eight or ten fountains in the lake, the crusts were cracking and foundering, there was fairly swift streaming to the north and to the southeast, and the smoke was troublesome, blowing from the southwest. The fountains showed heavy viscous quality in the stringy mass flung up.

On October 17 at 4 p. m. the lake was high at the southeast rampart, which stood only two feet above the liquid. The continued rising of the massive lava under the central crags, however, made the central chasm floor fully seven feet above the lake. There was much smoke from vents in the central region and towards the north and west. Two grottoes were active on the southeast, but most of the lake was crusted over. The east cove grotto was active and the southeast dome was curtained.

The west bank of the lake now appeared to be rising as a ledge like the east crag. Much of the edge of the latter had fallen away, following the line of the crevasse near the verge. At its southern highest angle this ledge was cracking profoundly at right angles to the shoreline, the pendant blocks overhanging the east gulch. There was now very heavy overhang of a turret-like mass on the south aspect of the central crag, showing every sign of an approaching crash. The west end of the northwest table had already collapsed, and the central steeple had become a rugged stump, while the lower part of the central chimney on the lake side had caved away. There was no smoke from the two chimney orifices, but much fume rose from the north and south sides of the central chasm.

During the next two days, Thursday and Friday, October 18 and 19, a change took place significant of the importance of the strong rise of the lava column which set in immediately after the autumnal equinox. This consisted in an outbreak of liquid lava through the high cracked benches at the west side of the pit where the "west pond" of 1916 has for ten months lain dormant under a tumble of smoking debris. The lava which now welled up here built a blowing-cone 15 feet high at the site of the similar cones of Janary, 1917. Piled up pahoehoe floods spread from this center in the shape of a fan, extending to and around the northwest cone. Tongues from this flood extended all over the site of the old northwest pond and in the direction of the west cove the new lava covered an oval area extending two-thirds of the distance from the west cone to the shore. The northwest cone, which has become sulphur-stained and during the summer has occasionally hissed and glowed, does not appear to have ejected any lava.

Measurement of the previous Saturday, October 13, made the depression of the lake 85 feet below the southeast station on the rim of Halemaumau. The summit of the central crag was 84 feet, and of the east island crag 60 feet above the lake. The lake had thus risen seven feet in eight days, while in the same period the central crag had risen nine feet and the east island summit 14 feet. The rate of rising of the crags was three times as fast as in the previous week, while the lake throughout the fortnight had risen and fallen irregularly within the inner pit, but by measurement maintained a rate of rising of a little over one foot per day.

The seismographs of the Whitney Laboratory for the week ending at 10 a. m. October 19, 1917, have registered three local earthquakes; two of these were trivial, respectively about 3:30 p. m. October 14 and 6:25 p. m. October 17. A more pronounced, but small, shock occurred about 7:42 p. m. October 16. Microseismic motion for the week has been moderate and volcanic vibration slightly increased in spasms towards the end of the interval. The record of tilt shown by the instruments has been remarkable, the excessive tilt to the north continuing, with, in addition, a tilting movement to the east which on one of the seismographs carried the writing stylus clear off the recording drum. The net effect of this for the two past weeks is a shifting of the plumb-line to the northeast in a series of slow pulsations which appear to be approaching a maximum. As this direction is straight away from the rising bench magma of the Halemaumau crags, the possible relation of such tilting of the ground to volcanic activity seems worthy of investigation.

VOLCANO HOUSE, Oct. 27, 1917.—During the week ending Friday, October 26, 1917, an important culmination of rising lava has taken place, followed by subsidence. The movement of rising was accompanied by extensive flooding of the western floor areas, and at the culmination, which appears to have happened during the night of October 23, the great central crag subsided and the south bench was suddenly lifted until it stood 70 feet above the lake as a peaked crag, the whole block tilting over to the west and exposing by uplift the bare rough lava wall which had been previously submerged. Before this event, a spectacular cascade from the lake into a well under the central chasm served to forecast subsidence. The highest level reached by the lake was 79 feet below the rim of the pit October 20, and the lowest to date was 98 feet on October 26. From a rate of rising of one foot or more per day, the liquid lava and the crags have subsided at an average rate of about three feet per day for the week following October 20. There was, however, pronounced spasmodic rising after that date to the night of October 23. The liquid lava showed pulsations of subsidence in advance of the bench magma.

Measurements for the week were as follows:

Oct. 20—
- Depression of lake, 79 ft. below rim.
- Depression of east island crag, 18 ft. below rim.
- Elevation of central crag, 4 ft. above rim.

Oct. 22—
- Depression of lake, 90 ft. below rim.
- Depression of east island crag, 18 ft. below rim.
- Elevation of central crag, 2 ft. above rim.

Oct. 26—
- Depression of lake, 98 ft. below rim.
- Depression of east island crag, 31 ft. below rim.
- Depression of central crag, 13 ft. below rim.
- Depression of new southeast crag, 28 ft. below rim.

On Saturday, October 20, at 9:30 a. m., the lake was crusted over and mostly quiet. There was activity in the curtained southeast grottoes, and occasional central fountains would break out. About 10 a. m. and thereafter there was general cracking of crusts, multiple fountaining and subsidence of the lake surface. Spatter margins fell into the lake at the east gulch and at the west side of the southeast cove. Rocks were heard falling at the east gulch and at the central chasm. The west cone was continuously hissing, with louder spasms at intervals. There was quick-rising hot fume at the central chimney.

The lake had overflowed extensively at the northwest cove and at the southwest cove, but not at the west. A pressure ridge and crevasses at right angles to the shoreline extended from the lake to the west cone. The southwest cove had built out its eastern shore so as to widen the platform and narrow the pool. There was no fresh overflow at the north cove. The central crag had continued to rise so that its summit was nine feet above ground level at the southeast station. The overhang of its southern turret was so strong that it seemed certain to collapse soon. The central steeple had continued to scale off on its south side, assuming again a peaked form at a lower level, with bright red smooth southern walls. The new spatter margins of the shore stood from 10 feet to 15 feet above the lake in the central region, but at the southeast cove the rampart was only 5 feet high.

On October 22 the crags still remained high, but the lake had sunk 11 feet, so that open tunnels were revealed under the central chasm, at the east cove and on the west side of the southeast cove. At 2:30 p. m. there were in addition deep wall grottoes in the south bench, at the north base of the central crag, and in the southeast and northern ramparts. The central crag grotto appeared to communicate with the chimney smoking vigorously above. Streaming was from a crust in the center of the lake toward the southeast, terminating at the several tunnels. Rocks were heard falling at the east gulch.

Within the central tunnel was a pit separated from the lake by a rampart two feet high. Active lava inside was flinging up spray from a level five or six feet below the lake. At 2:50 p. m. the lake rose, overflowed this rampart and made a cascade which poured continuously into the sinkhole under a dark arch hung with stalactites. A deep rumble came from the sinkhole, blue flame and fume shot out from the arch, and fountains became rare in the lake. At 3:10 p. m. general crusting took place after a violent bombardment at the southeast cove. The southeast tunnel became quiet and streaming poured from a bright edge of crust in the southeast arm for a distance of 50 feet straight to the cascade sinkhole. At 3:15 p. m. there was general breaking up, with streaming to the east and bombardment under the southeast shelf.

The north and west regions appeared quiet. The west cone continued its incessant hissing. The southeast rampart was about seven feet high and the central chasm floor about 14 feet high above the lake, the latter rising some two feet while it was under observation. A large block of bench on the southeast side of the east island mass had fallen into the lake since October 20 and been replaced by a new ledge three feet high, of fresh lava. Heavy smoke rose from the central, western and northern regions.

On October 23 at 2 p. m. the lake appeared higher measured by the east island but lower measured by the central cavern. Here the exposed arch was higher, the rampart prevented cascading, and the glowing pit inside the cavern showed no activity. The lake streaming was toward the rampart, but not over it. The southern crag mass appeared steeper, especially at its east point, where, at the entrance to the southeast cove, large blocks of the cliff had fallen away and the face was raw and broken clear to the southeast tunnel. The southeast rampart stood about five feet above the lake, which sank, however, some two feet. The crust was thin, blistered and moving more rapidly. Streaming was from the west and north to the east and southeast. Occasional central fountains of very large size would form in the southeast arm. At 2 p. m. there was fountaining at the southeast dome grotto, but later, during subsidence, the other grottoes became active. Very rapid hot fume rose from the central chimney and dense smoke from the south face of the steeple. Fumes as a whole were heavy and increased gas pressure was shown at the fountains. Some fountaining was seen on the east side of the southwest channel.

Inspection of the west and northwest floors showed great increase of piled up pahoehoe lava covering the northwest cone and extending all the way from the northwest cove to a point opposite the western end of the central crag mass. This lava was heaped in glistening black hummocks with short stretches of festooned flow, which indicated trickle northward and westward in the northern part of the area and rather southward and eastward in the southern part. The west cone was no longer hissing and it showed a dull stained surface. The later flows may have come from the northwest cone. The northwest table had fallen away considerably on its west side, and the debris was replaced by a wide floor of new lava built by overflow of the northwest cove.

A visit to the pit at 4:14 p. m. October 24 discovered a conspicuous change at the south point bench separating the southeast cove from the southeast arm. Within the twenty-four hours this bench, which had been scaling off and cracking the day before, had risen bodily to form a sharp peaked crag over 50 feet above the lake, the upper bench surface tipping westward at 45° and breaking away from the south crag mass, the west side of the block sliding downward along a north-south fissure extending from the middle of the central chasm southward. The great upturned section revealed a structureless gray upright wall below, recently the submerged cliff at the side of the molten lake, and this surface was irregular wavy and rough, possibly aa, in contrast to the red oxidized bedded layers above. This lower surface was more or less coated with a skin of fresh lava. It resembled the raised underpinning of the east island of February, 1917, which proved on examination to be aa, or block-lava. The new crag had scaled off on its high north side so as to make there a tumble of red talus. The south grotto was destroyed, the west side of the southeast cove was extended deeply, and a new chasm floored with fresh lava extended thence back of the new block through to the central chasm. The central cascade pot was gone.

The central crag mass and east is-

Aug. 4, 1917. Central chasm, crag and channel, east island and east cove.
Photo Jaggar

Aug. 4, 1917. Southeast shelf, cove and point. Est ledge in foreground, right.
Photo Jaggar

Aug. 18, 1917. Southeast arm, south and central crag masses, south grotto and central chasm. Photo Jaggar

Aug. 31, 1917. Central crag mass from the west. Southeast arm on left, southwest arm on right. Photo Jaggar

land mass had subsided considerably. Only a small tip of the central crag was now visible from Volcano House. The excessive central fuming had ceased, but smoke had increased at the high west peak of the east island. The northeast cove was increasing in size through the crumbling and subsidence of the east island mass. A curtained tunnel, active within, was visible at the east cove. The bench and rampart extending southward from the east gulch had fallen away and the remnant was 15 feet above the lake. The southeast rampart was high also, and overhanging. There was fountaining in the southeast tunnel, which was now farther south than before and opposite the end of the south pressure ridge. The east island spatter bench kept its level about five feet above the lake.

At 4:45 p. m. there was subsidence, accompanied by breaking up of crusts as usual, and heavy falls of spatter margin were seen at the north side of the central crag mass and at the north cove. Here the rampart fell with a heavy crash, starting excessive fountaining. The southeast dome was fuming heavily as though collapse were imminent. The lake as a whole was rather stagnant. The streaming was to the southeast, as usual.

General subsidence of the central area continued on Thursday, October 25, 1917, and the central crag disappeared from the Observatory view of the pit.

On October 26 the lake depression was 98 feet, and above it the new crag stood 70 feet, the central crag 85 feet and the east island crag 67 feet. The lake appeared subsiding, and there were rock falls from the summit of the east crag, from the south side of the new crag, and from the lake shore under it. A small avalanche fell from the outer wall of Halemaumau into the crevasses near the north pit, indicating that the subsidence was general. Activity was moderate, streaming and fountaining as usual, and the inner bench appeared 10 feet high. There were active grottoes under the central chasm and at the southeast tunnel. The old northwest crag mass had been breaking up and was much crevassed and tumbled across its middle region. There was glow and flame in the bench high above the east tunnel. The lake displayed subsidence, followed by rising. A great upright crack fissured the lower wall of the new crag on its south side. No hissing was heard from the west cone region, which was very smoky. The channel leading to the southwest cove had narrowed and the cove was quiet and crusted over.

For the Whitney Laboratory of Seismology I have to report no earthquakes registered during the week ending 10 a. m. Friday, October 26, 1917. Microseismic movement was moderate at first, strong October 23-24, slight thereafter. Volcanic vibration was spasmodic to moderate until October 23; on October 23-24 it was extraordinarily strong and stormy in the east-west component, but not in the north-south component. Thereafter it diminished greatly. Tilting to the east became excessive October 23-24, and tilt to the north continued very strong throughout the week, but decreased toward the end of the period. The correspondence of the seismic movements with the volcanic crisis of October 23-24 was remarkable.

Very respectfully,

T. A. JAGGAR, Jr.,
Director.

THE ANNUAL GENERAL MEETING AND TREASURER'S REPORT OF THE HAWAIIAN VOLCANO RESEARCH ASSOCIATION.

The annual general meeting of the Hawaiian Volcano Research Association was held at the Library of Hawaii, Honolulu, T. H., on Thursday, August 23, 1917, at 2 p. m.

Present: The Board of Directors, a large number of members, and several visitors from different parts of the world.

The President, Mr. Lorrin A. Thurston, took the chair, and opened the meeting by calling for any further nominations for directorships, and appointing a committee of scrutineers of the ballots.

ADDRESS OF THE PRESIDENT.

The President then delivered his address, which was as follows:

"Ladies and Gentlemen:

"June 30th, 1917, ends not only the fiscal year of the Hawaiian Volcano Research Association, but the five-year term during which the Association has had a working agreement with the Massachusetts Institute of Technology. It seems, therefore, a proper time to give a resumé of the work of the Association since its formation, as a basis for intelligent consideration in connection with future procedure and policy.

Origin of the Association.

"The Association is the direct outgrowth of a suggestion made by Dr. T. A. Jaggar, Professor of Geology in the Massachusetts Institute of Technology, during his visit to Honolulu in 1909 while en route to Japan to investigate volcanoes there.

"Dr. Jaggar then proposed that the Institute should establish an observatory at Kilauea, the people of Hawaii to contribute thereto the sum of five thousand dollars a year for five years, the Institute to be solely responsible for additional funds and for operating the observatory.

Failure of Institute to Act.

"The people of Honolulu met Dr. Jaggar's suggestion, but, for several reasons, the Institute did not then see its way to take action.

The Perret Expedition.

"In the spring of 1911, on the initiative of Dr. Jaggar, the Massachusetts Institute arranged with Dr. F. A. Perret, a scientist who, under the auspices of the Volcano Research Association of Springfield, Mass., has made a special study of volcanoes, to spend three months at Kilauea, making detailed observations of the volcano and collaborating with Dr. Shepherd of the Carnegie Geo-Physical Laboratory of Washington, D. C., in the measurement of the temperature of the liquid lava.

"The expedition was financed by the three above-named institutions.

Formation of the Hawaiian Volcano Research Association.

"On October 5th, 1911, upon the recommendation of Dr. Jaggar, an informal organization of this Association was formed, and later made formal by the adoption of a constitution, as an unincorporated association.

Objects of the Association.

"The objects of the Association are:

"(1) To encourage and promote investigation of and research concerning volcanoes and volcanic phenomena, and all matters connected therewith or incidental thereto.

"(2) To establish and maintain an observatory at the Volcano of Kilauea, with subordinate stations at other points, from which investigation and research may be conducted, and at which records may be made and kept for the information of all, subject to the rules of the Association.

"(3) To invite scientific institutions and observers to make use of the buildings, apparatus and facilities of the Association, subject to the rules of the Association, and, so far as possible, to assist such institutions and observers in carrying on their work.

"(4) To promote the publication and dissemination of knowledge concerning volcanology and allied subjects, and to accumulate literature, photographs, models, maps and specimens relating thereto, for the information of all, subject to the rules of the Association.

Agreement with Massachusetts Institute of Technology.

"As a result of the organization of the Association, Dr. Jaggar again visited Hawaii in January, 1912, resulting in a definite agreement with the Massachusetts Institute, in effect as follows:

"(1) That the Institute would give Dr. Jaggar a five-year leave of absence to act as Director of the Hawaiian Volcano Research Association and to conduct investigations, in the name of the Institute, of volcanic phenomena in Hawaii.

"(2) That the Association would guarantee $5000 a year towards the expenses of the Observatory.

"(3) That of this $5000, $4000 should be paid through the Institute to Dr. Jaggar as his salary, so that he might maintain his connection with the Institute as a professor therein.

"(4) That the Institute would pay towards the expenses of the investigations at the volcano, the income of the so-called Whitney Fund, such fund amounting to $35,000 and the income amounting to about $1000 per annum.

"(5) That the Institute would publish the annual report of what had been accomplished at the Observatory.

Inauguration of Work at the Volcano.

"Later in the year Dr. Jaggar returned to Honolulu for the third time, and formally began work at the volcano of Kilauea as of July 1st, 1912.

Observatory Site and Buildings.

"A lease of several acres of land near the Volcano House was secured, and, through a special contribution by the people of Hilo, an observatory building was erected thereon, containing a concrete cellar built on bed-rock for earthquake-recording instruments; a general office, working and library room; room for specimens, maps and photographs; dark and other rooms for developing and printing photographs; several storage rooms and a water-storage tank.

"The building cost approximately $2100, and additions, such as enclosing the verandas, strengthening and re-roofing the same (the roof having been blown off in a storm), and an additional tank for water, have since been made at a cost of several hundred dollars.

"Small observatory buildings have also been erected in the crater, at the edge of the central pit. These are also occupied from time to time as temporary residences by observers.

Equipment of Observatory.

"The observatory has been equipped with four seismometers and other apparatus, and somewhat meagerly with tables, chairs, shelves, filing cases and other appurtenances.

Operating Force.

"The regular operating force at the observatory consists of Dr. T. A. Jaggar, Director, in special charge of volcanic investigation; Professor H. O. Wood, in special charge of seismology, and a man of all work, Alex Lancaster.

"During the first three years of the work of the Association, Howard M. Ballou, Professor of English at the College of Hawaii, acted as the secretary of the Association and editor of its Weekly Bulletin. Mr. Ballou, having left the Territory, was succeeded by Mr. L. W. de Vis-Norton, who still efficiently fills the office.

Trail to and Rest House on Mauna Loa.

"In the Fall of 1915, by special subscription in Hilo and Honolulu, the sum of $3000 was raised with which to build a rest-house and trail direct from Kilauea to Mokuaweoweo, the summit crater on Mauna Loa, a distance of 30 miles, via the rift region at the northeast corner of Mauna Loa, the scene of the most frequent and violent activity of any on the mountain.

"With the volunteer help of a company of the 25th Infantry, a horse trail was laid out and built for 20 miles through a formerly untraversed territory to Puu Ulaula, or "Red Hill," at an elevation of 10,000 feet. Here a rest-house was built and furnished with cooking apparatus, beds and other furniture, accommodating, say, ten people, with stabling for 12 horses, and water tanks. A trail was also marked and partially constructed from Red Hill to the summit, a distance of ten miles. This trail and rest-house now make easily and quickly accessible the most vital portion of Mauna Loa both from the spectacular and research standpoint. The rest-house is available to visitors at a nominal charge of one dollar per head per day.

"The whole of the property enumerated above stands in the name of the Association.

Work Accomplished by the Association.

"The work of the Association may be analyzed as follows:

"(1) Observation of the molten lava lake and crater at Kilauea, as nearly daily as practicable, detailed records being kept of the same.

"(2) Daily photographs of the crater from a fixed point at the Observatory, showing smoke and steam formations and sources, and any changes that take place; also photos of pit from fixed points, showing action and changes, taken weekly and oftener if advisable; also frequent photographs of special features. Over 3000 such photographs have been taken.

''(3) Keeping a complete weather record, under Weather Bureau formula.

''(4) Keeping a continuous seismological record of local and distant earthquakes; also of local earth tilt and motion.

''(5) Observation and records and photographs of each new outbreak at Mokuaweoweo and lava flows therefrom.

''(6) Observation, study and record of other volcanic formations, both on Kilauea and Mauna Loa mountains.

''(7) Preparation and publication of a weekly bulletin with frequent photographs, setting forth the observations of the station, conditions and changes both at Kilauea and Mauna Loa. These are digested and printed weekly in the Hilo and Honolulu press, and 400 to 1000 copies are printed in full once a month.

''A copy of each number is mailed free to each member of the Association and to a selected list of scientists and scientific institutions all over the world, leaving quite a number of copies on hand for future use.

''(8) Daily Record. A compilation is made of the daily observations, weather record, photographs and sketches of changes and conditions which are not brought out by photographs, and other current data. This is made in duplicate, on letter paper, and each copy is bound in volumes. There are now ten such volumes, one set to be kept at the Observatory and one to be deposited at some central point available for consultation by all interested. In addition, there is a series of daily earthquake records, complete for the five years, with a few exceptions, due to accidents to the instruments.

''It will be a calamity if these observations and records are not consecutively continued.

''(9) Physical investigation of the molten lava lake is carried on whenever practicable, such as:

''(a) Measuring the heat of the same at the surface; in the fountains; in the caverns and at different depths in the lake, in different locations and under differing conditions;

''(b) Sounding the depth of the lake with iron pipe, at different times and at different points;

''(c) Securing unburned gases from the molten lava, both for quantitative and qualitative analysis, coöperating with the Carnegie Geo-physical Laboratory at Washington, D. C., for this purpose.

''(10) Collecting and arranging and labeling lava specimens and formations of all kinds in cabinets at the Observatory.

''(11) Collecting, filing and indexing, from all available sources, maps, photographs, records and publications relating to the volcano and kindred subjects.

''(12) Coöperation with and assisting scientists and scientific institutions in observations, studies and photographs of the volcano and kindred subjects.

''(13) Preparation and publication in scientific magazines as well as popular publications of articles on special subjects and phases connected with both local and distant volcanic and earthquake activity and phenomena.

''(14) Preparation of annual reports, summarizing conditions, activities and accomplishments at the station.

''The Massachusetts Institute of Technology was to have published these reports as a part of its contribution to the work of the station, and in connection with its original research work, receiving full credit for the work as though done entirely by the Institute. It published two reports, covering two years, but has published none since, having indicated its inability to do so owing to lack of available funds.

''(15) Preparation of lectures on subjects germane to the objects of the Association, and delivery of same several times a year, at different points in the Islands, with a view to educating the public to the importance of the work and creating interest in and support thereof.

"(16) Trip to Japan, in 1915. Upon the occasion of the great eruption of Sakarojima, Japan, in 1915, Dr. Jaggar went to the scene, for the purpose of examining and comparing the same with other eruptions in Japan, Hawaii and elsewhere. The expenses of this trip were borne by special contributions and not by the treasury of the Association.

"(17) Trip to Washington, in 1916. In the winter of 1915-1916, Dr. Jaggar went to Washington, representing this Association, with a view to interesting the Federal Government and Congress in volcanic, earthquake and geological investigation in Hawaii. An extremely favorable recognition was given to Dr. Jaggar and his views, a measure carrying them into effect through the medium of the Weather Bureau, almost becoming law.

"Dr. Jaggar also took an active part in securing the passage of the act creating Kilauea, Mokuaweoweo and Haleakala into a National Park; it being believed that the enactment of this measure would favorably affect the first mentioned project. The expense of this trip was partly borne by special subscription and partly by the Association.

Finances of the Association.

"The report of the Treasurer will give the details of receipts and expenditures. The following summary will, however, be appropriate for statement here:

"The receipts and expenditures of the Association from January 15th, 1912, to August 31st, 1917, both inclusive, are:

Receipts	$53,767.07
Expenditures	51,667.83
Balance on hand..	$ 2,099.24

"All obligations of the Association have been paid up.

"In order that the work of the Association might not be interrupted, pending decision as to what shall be done in the future, the directors have personally pledged the payment of all operating expenses up to September 30 next, and have raised money looking toward the continuance until December 31st next. It is calculated that, by reducing expenses to a low limit, all such expenses can be met from balance in hand and from moneys pledged.

What of the Future?

"The period of agreement between the Association and the Massachusetts Institute of Technology and with Professor Jaggar, having terminated on June 30th last, and the pledges of funds for the continuance of the work of the Association in connection with such agreement having been fulfilled, this first era in the history of the Association may be said to have closed, leaving for consideration and decision what the future course and policy of the Association shall be.

"Bearing upon this question it is probably a fact that through the medium of this Association, and the scientists who have coöperated with it, more specific knowledge concerning the make-up and workings of a volcano has been secured and made available for study, during the past five years, than has been secured during the previous nineteen hundred years of the Christian era.

"Notwithstanding this, a beginning only has been made toward securing and recording the facts which must be known if volcanology is to become anything more than mere guesswork.

"While there are many spectacular events and phenomena to be observed, studied and reported upon in connection with volcanoes, these are not as important as the unspectacular and monotonous recording of what happens day by day. Full and accurate records of such observations, made by an intelligent and experienced observer, continued over a long series of years, are what must be secured before volcanology can be reduced to an exact science or even to a basis of intelligent theorizing.

"Another factor to be considered is that Kilauea and Mauna Loa constitute a ready-at-hand laboratory for the study of volcanology which, for safety and convenience of access and continuity of action, cannot be duplicated elsewhere in the world.

"A third fact to consider is that Professor Jaggar, to whose vision this Association owes its existence, and to whose enthusiasm and patience its accomplishments are due, is not only available to continue the work, but eager to do so.

"Under these circumstances it is the earnest belief of the speaker and of the present Board of Directors of the Association, that it is the duty of this organization to use every means within its power to secure the continuance of the work which has, for the past five years, been carried on under the auspices of the Association.

"The work should be undertaken in no spirit of competition with others engaged in the same or similar work, or for the enhancement of local prestige, but upon the broadest lines as seekers for the truth, welcoming the coöperation of all organizations and individuals having the same or similar objects in view, and proffering to them every assistance and encouragement in the execution of their work which lies within the power of the Association to extend.

"For the purpose of enabling the members of this Association to definitely record their opinions and desires in this respect, and by unanimous vote of the Board of Directors, I submit resolutions intended to express the sentiments hereinbefore set forth, as follows:

" 'That it is the opinion of the Hawaiian Volcano Research Association:

" '(1) That the results already secured through the medium of this Association fully justify the efforts and expenditures made in connection therewith; call for congratulations to those who have coöperated with us, and thanks to the earnest and faithful workers who have made possible the results obtained.

" '(2) That the interests of pure science and practical humanity require that investigation, observations and records be continued on substantially the same general lines heretofore followed, the scope of the same to be expanded as opportunity and financial conditions permit.

" '(3) That this Association pledges itself to use its best endeavors to support, for not less than a further term of five years, the objects set forth in its constitution; and to endeavor to secure the assistance of others in so doing, and to endeavor to secure the coöperation of other scientific institutions and individuals to that end.

" '(4) That the officers and Directors of this Association are hereby authorized and requested to take such steps as may be necessary or proper to accomplish the objects of the Association and secure the execution of the purposes above set forth.'

"It is the earnest belief of the speaker that if the foregoing resolutions are adopted and a Board of Directors elected who are imbued with the spirit therein set forth, ways and means will be found, through some medium, to accomplish, during the next five years, results greater by far than those which have been accomplished during the past five years."

The President's address, which was received with considerable applause, was followed by an address by Professor Jaggar, the Director of the Observatory.

(Note.—Professor Jaggar's address was issued as the August number of the Bulletin of the Hawaiian Volcano Observatory.)

The Scrutineers then reported upon the ballots, with the result that the whole of the retiring Board of Directors was found to have been reëlected.

The Directors having returned thanks for their reëlection, the resolutions presented by the President came up for consideration, and after several members, and some of the distinguished visitors, among them Dr. Clay Macaulay of Japan and Mrs. Young of San Diego, California, had spoken in favor of the adoption of the resolutions in toto, the question was called for, and the resolutions unanimously adopted.

The meeting closed with hearty votes of thanks to the Directors and officers of the Association.

HAWAIIAN VOLCANO RESEARCH ASSOCIATION.

Report of the Treasurer from January 15th, 1912, to August 31st, 1917.

RECEIPTS.

Balance turned over by Professor Jaggar	$ 1,606.50
Membership dues	1,775.00
Patrons and subscriptions	40,898.50
Repairs and Washington Fund	1,113.00
Special Fund	7,975.00
Motor Cycle Fund	100.00
Lectures	254.50
Refund	44.32

PAYMENTS.

Salaries and wages	$32,137.20	
Other expenses	19,530.63	
Balance on hand Aug. 31, '17	2,099.24	
	$53,767.07	$53,767.07

CASH ACCOUNT.

Cash at Bank of Hawaii	$ 799.84	
Cash in Treasurer's hands	1,299.40	$ 2,099.24

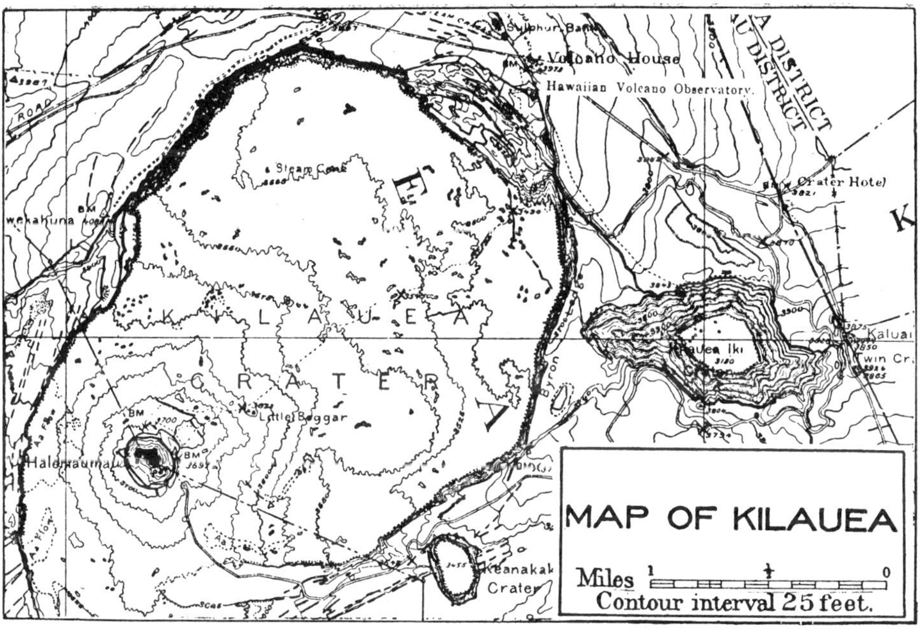

HAWAIIAN VOLCANO RESEARCH ASSOCIATION.

This society is a voluntary one, made up of subscribers to scientific work which is being executed by Dr. T. A. Jaggar, Director of the Hawaiian Volcano Observatory, Volcano House, P. O., Hawaii. **All scientific exchanges should be sent to this address.**

In 1917 there are about 150 subscribers in Hawaii and elsewhere, firms and individuals. A group of firms and persons in Hilo built the main observatory building in the spring of 1912. The work was founded by the Massachusetts Institute of Technology. Publications to date have been weekly reports since the summer of 1911 now reprinted in Honolulu in monthly form. There are also special reports, printed from time to time.

The weekly bulletin as it appears in the Honolulu Advertiser is reprinted as a leaflet and sent to regular annual subscribers to the work of the Association. L. A. Thurston is president of the Board of Directors of the Association, and L. T. Peck is treasurer. New subscribers who are interested in volcanoes will be welcomed in the Association. The Association aims: (1) To record volcanic activity and earthquakes in Hawaii; (2) to attract scientific men hither for special studies; (3) to promote the establishment of volcano observatories all over the world. The annual dues of regular members are $5; patrons of the Association subscribe larger amounts.

WHITNEY LABORATORY OF SEISMOLOGY.

The Whitney Laboratory of Seismology, named after an endowment fund of geophysical research held by the Massachusetts Institute of Technology, in memory of Caroline and Edward Whitney of Boston, is equipped with two Bosch-Omori 100 kg tromometers registering N-S and E-W motion, a heavy Omori tromometer registering E-W motion, and an Omori "ordinary Seismograph" designed for registering strong earthquakes in all three components of motion. These are seated on concrete piers in a closed basement room having practically constant temperature, beneath the chief Observatory building near the hotel. Time is referred to a rated chronometer, checked at intervals by solar observations with a transit. Both instruments are loaned by the College of Hawaii. Hawaiian standard time (H. S. T.) is 10 hrs. 30 min. slower than Greenwich time.

CANCANI SCALE OF SEISMIC INTENSITY.

Expressed by accelerations measured in millimeters per second per second.

I.	Instrumental	0.0	2.5
II.	Very slight	2.5	5.0
III.	Slight	5.0	10.0
IV.	Sensible, mediocre	10.0	25.0
V.	Rather strong	25.0	50.0
VI.	Strong	50.0	100.0
VII.	Very strong	100.0	250.0
VIII.	Ruinous	250.0	500.0
IX.	Disastrous	500.0	1000.0
X.	Very disastrous	1000.0	2500.0
XI.	Catastrophic	2500.0	5000.0
XII.	Great catastrophe	5000.0	10000.0

Grade IV. is ordinarily the minimum perceived by the senses; and in grade XII. the acceleration, or rate of change of motion (jerk) reaches that of terrestrial gravitation.

In the standard form of report the maximum intensity or acceleration, designated by the symbol a, or max. a, is given in the conventional unit, **the milligal.** The milligal is a measure of acceleration, such that 1 milligal = 1/100 mm. per sec. per sec. = 10 μ per sec. per sec. The Cancani scale, here **defined in terms of millimeters per sec. per sec., can therefore be expressed in milligals by multiplying each of the numbers by 100.**

WEEKLY BULLETIN
OF THE
Hawaiian Volcano Observatory

Vol. V. HONOLULU, HAWAII, NOVEMBER, 1917. No. 11

Volcano House, T. H., Nov. 3, 1917.

At Halemaumau during the week ending Friday, November 2, 1917, the lava lake rose relative to the crags until October 31 and appeared to subside thereafter, but this effect may have been a rising of the crag lava rather than actual sinking of the lake. There has been pronounced disturbance of the crags with a crumbling down of the greater part of the east island mass with the exception of its high western block which stands in bold relief. The lake has built a new inner bench all around and the general condition suggests rising.

On October 27 at 1:45 p. m. the fume was thin and the lava rising. The southeast grotto was active. There was streaming into a grotto on the north face of the central crag mass. At 2:10 p. m. the lava was only one foot below the floor level at the central cove. At 2:20 p. m. three large central fountains were playing in the southeast arm. At 2:30 p. m. an avalanche fell noisily from the central crag mass into the chasm south of it. At 3:10 p. m. another fall took place from the southern side of the new southeast crag, the rocks falling into the lake and starting much ebullition. At 3:40 p. m. there was violent activity in the grotto under the east gulch and ten minutes later the lake was brimming level with the inner bench at the central cove.

On October 28 at 12:45 p. m. the north arm was quiet and crusted and the pit was uniformly suffused with thin blue fume. At 1:15 p. m. it became apparent that rapid rising was in progress, the lake level being about two feet below the inner bench at the central cove. At 1:30 p. m. a fragment of this bench fell in. At 4 p. m. the lake had again fallen, the inner bench at the base of the east island mass being five feet above the lake. A large fragment of this bench subsided into the lake during a sinking spell at about 4:30 p. m. The lake was rather sluggish with streaming to the southeast as usual and crusts thin and blistered. There was glow at the east tunnel and a new half-cone had been built at the southeast grotto under and against a bank ten feet high which formed a cliff where the rampart of the southeast cove had collapsed.

At 1:30 p. m. on October 29 the inner bench around the east island mass had completely collapsed and the eastern part of that body had crumbled lower than before. The roof of the east tunnel had fallen in and there was great activity of fountaining in the east cove. All the southeastern grottoes became active at the same time. At 3:30 p. m. a large block fell from the higher east island crag into the central channel starting prolonged fountaining.

On October 30 at 3:30 p. m. the older floors at the margins of the southeast and west coves appeared to stand from ten to fifteen feet above the lake, but the new inner bench stood not more than six inches above it. The western crag of the east island mass was very high and appeared to be rising as a distinct block, the remainder of that mass being low and tumbled. The southeast half-cone was puffing continually. There was no inner bench to be seen on the south side of the east island, the raw red rock and slide slopes extending directly to the lake level. At 4:15 p. m. the lake rose and flooded the floor of the central cove. Beyond in the central chasm there were new tumbles of rock, some of the fragments standing erect ten to fifteen feet high.

WEEKLY BULLETIN
of the
Hawaiian Volcano Observatory

Published Monthly at Honolulu, Hawaii, by the Hawaiian Volcano Research Association

L. W. de Vis-Norton........Secretary

Entered as second-class matter January 20, 1914, at the post-office at Honolulu, Hawaii, under the Act of August 24, 1912.

On Wednesday, October 31, 1917, the lake at 2:15 p. m., seen from the northeast, was level with the inner bench at the central cove, active at the south east and quiet towards the north. At 2:30 p. m. the whole pit became very stagnant for an hour with practically no fountaining. Afterwards a few fountains broke into action in the north arm.

On November 1, at 11:30 a. m., the lake appeared much lower, but it had previously built up its inner bench to within five feet of the southeastern rampart level of October 20. The lake was now five feet below the inner bench and caverns were revealed on the west side of the southeast cove and at the central cove. There was also a shallow cavern on the north side of the new southeast crag. The inner bench showed much overhang and was twenty feet wide on the south side of the east island mass. A fuming hot rampart cone had been built opposite the central chasm and a new locality for hot blue fume was seen 50 feet to the north of the rampart at the north cove. The lake was evidently pulsating strongly through a ten-foot range and the crags appeared to have been both rising and crumbling. There was the puffing of gas pressure at the southeast cove, a new grotto half-dome had been built under the east gulch, but only a narrow ledge extended thence southward. The southeast half-dome collapsed with a crash at noon setting up intense fountaining against the bank which continued for fifteen minutes. At 4 p. m. the lake was about ten feet below the inner bench and there was rapid streaming and strong fountaining.

At noon the writer made a series of tests on the east floor bench to determine how the bench magma moves. A plummet pendulum was set up on the floor 40 feet from the edge of the cliff over the lake. The position of the plumb-line, indicated by a magnifying level, was recorded every five minutes for 70 minutes and the behavior of the lake watched at the same time. The pendulum showed vibration when fountains broke into action. The plumb-line swung in general from northwest to southeast, the movement being at a maximum of swing toward the southeast sink-holes while pronounced gas discharge and sinking was going on, and in the opposite direction while the lake was quiet and rising.

On Friday, November 2, at 2:40 p. m., the lake lava was within one foot of the inner bench and rising was in progress, the whole lake showing quiet crust. There was fountaining in the southeast grotto. At 3:40 p. m. the west central region broke up and rapid streaming into the southeast arm ensued.

For the week ending Friday, November 2, 1917, at 10 a. m., the seismographs of the Whitney Laboratory registered one small local earthquake about 8:40 p. m. October 27, and a very small local disturbance between 2 a. m. and 3 a. m. October 30. The amplitude of microseisms diminished during the week. Volcanic vibrations were rather strong until October 28; thereafter they were slight. Tilting was very strong throughout the week to the north and east, the eastward tilt diminishing only slightly after October 30.

Volcano House, T. H., Nov. 10, 1917.

During the week ending November 9, 1917, the lava column of Halemaumau has continued to rise about one foot per day. The liquid lake has shown tendency to fluctuate strongly within a vertical range of ten feet reaching pronounced overflow of the inner ledge on the evening of November 6. The central crags have risen at about the same rate so that the summit of the highest peak was on November 9 only seven feet below the rim of the pit. The lake has maintained an average level of about 98 feet below the rim for two weeks past, but it rose six feet higher than on November 6.

It is becoming a matter of great interest to determine in what manner the stiff bench magma really moves and whether its ordinary movements are spasmodic or gradual. The liquid lake obviously rises and falls in marked spasms. Experiments have been inaugurated designed to throw some light on this question and to measure the rising and the falling of the crags every few minutes for hours at a time in the hope that some of the sudden movements, if such occur, may be caught and measured, and the rate of the more gradual motion be determined, in relation to the horizontal plane, the rim of the pit, and the lake level respectively.

On Saturday, November 3, at 10 a. m., the lake was about five feet below the inner bench, quiet in the northwestern and central regions and active at the southeast and north coves. There were occasional migratory central fountains. A new grotto has recently formed under the north side of the central steeple and this appears to be a fairly deep cavern. The northwest cove had recently been building out its shore eastward so as to make a shallow embayment, while the north cove had eaten back northward by collapse of the rampart and so increased its indentation. The northwest table was crevassed on the lake side. No change could be seen in the vicinity of the west lava flows. The old west crag mass had a number of peaks, but still preserved the islet of August, 1916, as its westernmost summit. At its base east was an active grotto. The valley extending through from the northeast cove to the east cove had widened. At 2:30 p. m. and thereafter there was subsidence, which made the inner bench about 10 feet high above the lake by 5:30 p. m. During the subsidence there was increased streaming and fountaining.

On November 4 at 2:30 p. m. the lake was about two feet below the inner bench with activity in the southeast and east coves. At 2:45 p. m. there was relatively rapid sinking of the lake surface about three feet and numerous fountains broke into action. At 3 p. m. there was a heavy fall of the inner bench at the southeast cove followed by much fountaining.

On Monday, November 6, 1917, at 11:30 a. m., the lake was only one foot below the inner bench at the central and northwest coves, and it was evident along the base of the northeast inner cliff that the lake had recently been spattering to heights of 8 feet or more. There was fountaining on the north, west, east and southeast, with streaming into the southeastern and southwestern arms. The center and northwestern region was stagnant. The southeast dome was large and glowing. Rocks were heard falling at the north cove. Central fountains occasionally developed in the southeast arm. Puffing accompanied the noise of fountaining at the north grotto. The places of densest smoke were on the north, west and southwest. The inner floor of the northwest cove was 50 feet wide, marking the outline of the October cove when the lake was at a higher level. Still higher was a half circle of overflow formed by October flooding. The southeast crag was now well above the level of the southeast shelf. A wide rock-filled gulch had been formed between the northwest table and the northwest shelf.

On November 6 at 2:15 p. m. the lava level was three feet below the inner bench and quietly rising. There was little fountaining activity of any kind. By 4:15 the rising had overflowed the floor at the central cove and this continued for 70 minutes, the gulch west of the southeastern crag being flooded. After that subsidence set in with fountaining and the lake sank five feet below the inner bench.

On November 7 at 10:15 a. m. the new inner bench was within three feet of the floor level at the southeast cove and had built over the southeast grotto dome, but flaming holes still persisted at this locality. The floor of the gulch between the southeast and south crags had been widened, but the new overflows did not extend through to the southeast cove. The central chasm was now a widened valley owing to the crumbling of the south crag in a tumbled flowing fashion making extensive talus. In the middle of this valley was a jutting rock. The spatter bench at the east gulch had been widened and a wide inner bench built on the southeast side of the east island. Fume was rising from the east tunnel. The lake was now five feet below the inner bench with a glowing and overhanging rim. Streaming was to the southeast, fountaining was as usual, fume was moderate, there was little noise and heavy festooned crusts covered the stream through the central channel. Some blue fume rose from the pressure ridge in the south valley, and the main smoke holes were at the summit of the north inner cliff and in the western lava fields. At 10:50 a. m. there was a strong fall of the spatter bank from the north side of the central steeple. At 11:15 a. m. the wall of the southeast cove on its south side for a length of 75 feet fell into the lake, leaving a raw glowing cliff eight feet high and carrying away both the upper and inner benches. This fall made great commotion and liberated much heat in the cove.

On November 8 at 3:15 p. m. the inner bench was five feet high and there was the usual fountaining east and southeast. At 4:15 p. m. the lava had sunk two feet lower and there were migratory fountains in the middle of the southeast arm.

At 10 a. m. on Friday, November 9, measurement revealed conditions as follows:

Depression of lake, 98 feet.

Depression of central crag summit, 7 feet.

This summit thus stood 91 feet above the lake and it had risen during the week at the rate of one foot per day. The lake had risen by a similar total of six feet on the occasion of its overflows on November 6.

On this day there was little change, the lake remaining about five feet below the inner bench and general conditions indicated a stationary lake and rising crags. The bench under the east island was narrower. There was streaming to both southeast and southwest, and fountaining in northeast, southwest and southeast grottoes. Fume was dense from holes on the north, west-northwest, west and southwest, but elsewhere it was thin. There was a flaming and puffing pot over the southeast grotto.

On this day experiments were started having in view the measurement of the movements of the central crags by taking observations every fifteen minutes for several hours and repeating this process from time to time on different days. With this work in view, a new trigonometric station was established on the northeast margin of Halemaumau and a preliminary series of readings made. It is proposed to attempt direct correlation between these measurements and the seismographic records at the Observatory.

In the Whitney Laboratory of Seismology for the week ending at 2 p. m. November 9, 1917, one very small local earthquake was registered between 7 and 8 a. m., November 3. Microseismic movement has been strong to moderate, volcanic vibrations moderate, and the pendulums have shown no recovery from the excessive tilt to the north and east which has now continued for over a month. The instruments are now in process of readjustment.

Volcano House, T. H., Nov. 17, 1917.

During the week ending Friday, November 16, 1917, the Kilauea lava column has continued to rise slowly and the summit of the great central crag has again come into view above the edge of the Halemaumau pit as seen from the Volcano House. The activity during the week has been moderate with alterations of quiet inflation of the lava lake accompanied by crusting over and more tumultuous times of breaking up with fountaining and rapid streaming. There is glow at the western conduit vent and much spatter rampart construction is going on at coves.

On Saturday, November 10, at 2:15 p. m., the lava lake was four feet below the floor of the central cove, fume was heavy in the north arm and there was active fountaining at the east grotto and in the center of the southeast arm. At 2:50 p. m. inspection from the northeast showed fountaining in the west and northeast coves, the fountain at the latter locality being noisy and throwing high jets. At 2:55 p. m. there was a heavy fall of rampart material at the north cove where the north grotto was active. At 4 p. m. from the east it was evident that the lake was slowly sinking, and by 4:30 p. m. the central inner bench was seven feet high and there were many migratory fountains in the southeastern channel.

On November 11 at 2 p. m. the whole lake was quiet with inner bench five feet high. At 2:20 p. m. a large block of this bench about 50 feet long and 10 feet wide at the base of the southeast crag fell into the lake. Other fragments of the spatter rim around the southeast cove had been falling.

On November 12 between 4 and 7 p. m. the lake was sluggish with heavily crusted rising spells and breakings up at intervals. Surface streaming was to the southwest and southeast. There were fountaining grottoes on the east and west sides of the southeast cove, at the east gulch, in the southwest arm and on the northern and eastern sides of the west crag mass. The east cove tunnel exhibited a high flaming chimney in the bench back from the lake which occasionally ejected lava spray. The accumulated gas pressure breathed out from under border crusts on the lake and ballooned up the skin at the southeast cove. The west cone was visible from the south station and fumes in general were thin.

On November 13, at 2:15 p. m., the whole lake was very quiet, slow rising was in progress and some puffing came from the east grotto. This continued and at 2:30 p. m. the lake was about three feet below the inner bench. At 6:30 p. m. the rise had been so pronounced that the lake was brimming level with the inner bench at the east cove.

On Wednesday, November 14, it was evident that the rise observed on the previous day had taken effect in a rapid spurt of the movement of the crags, for the summit of the central crag was now once more plainly in view from the Observatory over two miles away. The fume as seen from a distance had been only a thin veil for the two days. When the pit was visited at 6 p. m. the crags of the central, southern and eastern regions all appeared higher and it was evident that the inner bench at the base of the southeast crag, eight feet above the lake, had been lifted with the crag, as the similar bench at the east gulch across the channel was only three feet high. The southeast bank had caved in and a new bench had been built there about three feet high.

The lake showed surface streaming from the bright edge of the dark crust southeastward from the middle of the southeast arm. There were central fountains in the southeast cove and north arm, and border fountains at the east and of the southwest cove and in the southwest channel. The north grotto was also active. There was no glow at the east chimney but a distinct glow was seen in the vicinity of the west cone. There was some appearance of fresh cracks at and under the south station as though the south valley were sinking to compensate the rising crags. The high western knob of the east island mass was markedly increasing in height with dense fume rising from its summit as though a chimney were developing there. The northeast cove and the gulch extending from it both appeared larger.

On November 15 at 2 p. m. the inner bench was from 8 to 10 feet high and some fifteen fountains were in action mostly away from the shores. From the southwest it appeared that much of the central crag mass had fallen to increase the debris slopes in the central valley and a long north-south crack appeared through the summit of this mass. At 2:45 p. m. the southwest arm was very quiet, but there was much fountaining in the central region. At 3:50 p. m. most of the east cove grotto dome collapsed. At 5:15 p. m. much of the inner bench around the base of the east island crag had fallen in and portions of the southeast shelf scaled away between the south and southeast stations. At 6:30 p. m. there was a heavy avalanche from the east island crag into the central channel and the inner bench was fully 12 feet high.

Measurement on Friday, November 16, 1917, at 11 a. m., made the depression of the lake 88 feet below the south rim of the pit. The summit of the central crag was three feet below the rim. These measurements would imply a rise of the lake amounting to 10 feet in seven days and of the crag 4 feet in the same time. The actual rise of the crag may have been greater as there was much scaling off.

The lake on this day was high and active, a row of dome shaped spatter grottoes was in process of active construction along the east bench and two of these were especially large at the east gulch and the southeast cove, both showing stalactite curtains. At 10:45 a. m. there was a heavy crust over the whole southeast region and the streaming from the southwest arm and from the central region was northward. Later in the forenoon the breaking up of the crusts revealed streaming to the southeast, but the outward streaming from the southwest arm continued. A view of the northeast cove showed that that feature had now become an important indentation of the lake. Rocks were seen falling from the south side of the central crags. The easternmost pinnacle of these exhibited a flat reddish face on its south side as though the mass were moving on a fault plane of which this surface was the upward projection. A festooned flow covered the floor of the gulch west of the southeast crag. There was a large sulphur-stained patch on the site of the former northwest cones, and puffing was heard from the west cone. The inner bench was from three to five feet high, smoke was moderate, and at noon the crusts were thin and wrinkled and the lava currents were rapid, inducing much central fountaining and breaking up of crusted areas. The lake was rising in the forenoon and sinking after about 11:30 a. m.

The seismographs of the Whitney Laboratory have registered no pronounced local earthquakes during the week ending at 2 p. m., November 16, 1917. The graph of a strong distant earthquake was traced by the instruments about 5 p. m., November 15, the wave motion continuing for over an hour. The seismogram indicates an origin about 4100 miles from the Observatory and probably in a meridional direction—that is towards the north or south. Microseismic motion has been strong and volcanic vibration slight during the week. The registration of tilting has shown some recovery from the extreme inclination of the ground to the north and east which prevailed throughout October, the recovery from the east tilt being the more pronounced.

Volcano House, T. H., Nov. 24, 1917.

During the week ending Friday, November 23, 1917, there was a pronounced subsidence of the Halemaumau lava column at first, followed by recovery which has restored the lava lake to the level 90 feet below the rim so characteristic of the past few months. Slow rising has been resumed. The effects of both subsidence and recovery were shown by the crags as well as the lake, and small local earthquake shocks accompanied the disturbance.

On November 17, at 2:15 p. m., the inner bench at the southeast arm was unusually high, standing 15 feet above the lake under the east island mass, and there was much fountain activity. Thereafter subsidence became very pronounced and the inner bench began to collapse on all sides. At 2:25 p. m. a fragment of it some 50 feet long and 5 feet wide along the southern margin of the southeast cove fell into the melt beneath. At 4:45 p. m. there was a very heavy fall whereby the entire inner bench under the east island mass and under the east ledge subsided, leaving only a talus slope under the former and a sheer cliff to the live lava under the latter. At 5:40 p. m. this collapse extended southward from the east ledge so that the whole row of spatter domes from the east gulch southward went in and much turbulence was set up in the lake. Inspection of the southwest arm showed that during the hour up to 6:50 p. m. the inner bench was there falling also with much fountaining as result. By 7 p. m. the inner wall at the central and southeast coves was fully 25 feet high.

On November 18 at 3 p. m. the lava was still low and there was vigorous streaming and fountaining in the southeast arm. The southwest arm appeared wider by reason of the fall of the benches, and it was quiet and crusted over. The north arm showed two fountains, but in general the border grottoes were very quiet.

On November 19, at 11:30 a. m., the lake showed considerable change from the previous week. The inner bench, about eight feet above the liquid, still persisted at the central cove, at the east point of the southeast crag and at the inner end of the southwest cove. Around the east cove and under the southeast shelf it was entirely gone and the lake at the moment appeared to be strongly rising as the active lava lap

Sept. 21, 1917. The S.E. crag before lifting.—Photo. Jaggar.

Nov. 5, 1917. The S.E. crag after lifting.—Photo. Jaggar.

Oct. 26, 1917. The uplifted S.E. crag.

ped against the talus of the east island mass without any traces of a fresh spatter rim. The east ledge and the high western knob of the east island mass appeared to have risen, but otherwise the central group of crags had slightly subsided. The northeast part of the east island mass was certainly lower. The eastern knob of the old west crag mass was split through by a wide north-south crack. That the crags were still undergoing adjustment was shown by avalanches in motion in the east gulch and rocks sliding on the south side of the central crag. The relatively low level of the lake revealed the tunnel entrances at the central cove, the east cove and the west side of the southeast cove, where there was much activity and rapid streaming under the bank. The southwest cove was crusted over except at a puffing grotto tunnel at its eastern end. There was puffing also at the southeast. Streaming from the southwest cove was northward and there was active pounding in the north grotto.

The next day, Tuesday, November 20, at 2:45 p. m., the lake level showed no change and the surface was quiet. At 3:10 p. m. rocks were falling from the central crag mass. At 3:25 p. m. there was a fall from the south side of the southeast crag. At 5:40 p. m. a sinking spell brought about rapid northward streaming in the north arm of the lake toward spatter grottoes under the northwest table and at the rampart of the north cove.

On November 21 at 11 a. m. it was evident that the crags had generally settled and the northwest table crag was split through the middle by a wide east-west crevasse. The east side of the west crag mass showed terraces as though blocks were subsiding parallel to the lake shore. The northeast side of the east island mass was lower and more tumbled in appearance, but the western knob stood higher than ever. The floor of the central cove stood seven feet above the lake, but there was a new bench at the lake's edge some two feet high. The lake was evidently recovering as this new bench was in evidence at the east cove, at the point of the southeast crag and also under the central crag. Streaming was outward from the southwest cove, there was a puffing small area of activity on the west side of the southeast cove and much noise was heard toward the northeast. There was also occasional fountaining under the east gulch. No slides were seen in motion. At 10:30 a. m. the lake was crusted over and rising. At 11 a. m. the crusts were broken up and there was rapid streaming. At 11:30 a. m. the quiet rising was resumed.

At 2:30 p. m. on November 22 it was evident that rising continued with activity at the central cove and a spatter dome building on the west side of the southeast cove. In the evening the inner bench was being overflowed.

Measurement on Friday, November 23, 1917, at 9:30 a. m., showed the lake depression to be 91 feet below the southeast rim of the pit, three feet lower than on November 16 and seven feet higher than on October 26. The central crag stood eight feet below the rim, 83 feet above the lake, and was five feet lower than on November 16, and five feet higher than on October 26. The triangular southeast crag stood 19 feet below the rim, 72 feet above the lake and was nine feet higher than on October 26. The high knob of the east island mass, overhanging the central channel on its northern side, was now 18 feet below the rim and 73 feet above the lake. It was 13 feet higher than on October 26. In general, therefore, it will be seen that the several crags have risen during the month at different rates, and that the lake fluctuates strongly within its inner pit. In a general way both lake and crags have risen a few feet during the month.

On this day the new inner bench about three feet high had developed and become general around the lake. There were spatter domes at the east gulch and on the west side of the southeast cove. The fume was thin, streaming was to the southeast, the southwest arm was crusted over, blowing noises could be heard and there were occasional heavy central fountains in the southeast arm. A considerable point had built out southeast-ward from the southeast crag. There was no special activity at the east tunnel locality. Under the east ledge a double spatter rim appeared in steps respectively three and five feet above the lake. There was puffing and spraying at the fountains and crunching noises in the southeast arm made by crusts overriding each other. The larger fountains would grow in size as they migrated eastward and these were followed by areas of bubble fountaining. During sinking spells there were falls of fragments of inner bench into the lake east, southeast and west, these sinking spells alternating at half-hour intervals with quiet crusting. There were active spatter grottoes northwest and north. The floor of the northwest cove had been recently much overflowed and was built out eastward.

In the Whitney Laboratory of Seismology five local earthquakes have been registered during the week ending at 2 p. m. November 23, and three of these were perceptible at the Observatory. The first was felt at about 9 p. m. November 18. On the 20th two shocks in close succession were felt about 6 a. m. and two others were recorded on the instruments at about 2 a. m. and noon.

Microseismic motion while still strong has diminished during the week and volcanic vibration has slightly increased. Tilt to the eastward has been resumed and has grown strong, while tilt to the north has increased with fluctuation.

Volcano House, T. H., Dec. 1, 1917.

During the week ending Friday, November 30, 1917, the rising tendency has been predominant in the Halemaumau lava column, culminating November 28. After that date there was slight subsidence, leaving the liquid lake about as before, 90 feet below the rim of pit, but the central crags had risen markedly, so as to be conspicuous above the edge of Halemaumau as seen from Volcano House two and a half miles away. The rising had built new ramparts and overflows at the coves and has shut off the southwest cove by building a floor across its entrance channel so as to create a separate pond there.

On Saturday, November 24, at 3 p. m., the inner bench east was five feet high, there was swift streaming from the north arm through the southeast arm to the cove at its inner end, where there was tumultuous fountaining, as also under the east gulch. At 5 p. m. the lake had risen to within one foot of the inner bench level under the east island mass. The south floor was about ten feet above the southeast cove lava.

On November 25 at 3:30 p. m. the lake at the south bench was higher, only about five feet below the floor level, and there was much fountaining east and west at the southeast cove, and at the central cove, with spraying gas pressure. At 3:50 p. m., on descending to the northeast floor, it was found that there was bombardment in progress under the north grotto dome, and a few minutes later a half of the spatter dome collapsed into the flood. An avalanche of rock fell from the north side of the east island mass into the lake starting violent ebullition. At 4:10 p. m. there was a fall of rocks from the central crag mass on its south side.

On November 26 at 3:45 p. m. the lake was high, covered with hard crust, with gas escaping from beneath this crust puffing and spraying at the border grotto southeast. Occasional heavy bursts of fountaining would break through the crust in the southeast arm, the northeast cove and elsewhere. The new inner bench was two to three feet high and there were fresh overflows across the south rampart and at the central cove, the latter flooding the gulch west of the southeast crag so as to produce a new cracked floor of smooth lava. The lake was rising and nearly overflowing the inner bench. Rocks were heard sliding in the central valley showing that the central crag-mass was in motion. About 4:30 p. m. the crust over the southwest cove was seen to break up and there was rapid inrush from the main lake to the cove and much violent fountaining. Meanwhile the general gas pressure under the crust of the lake seemed relieved by this local escape of gas and the border grottoes southeast were very sluggish while this southwest activity was in progress.

On November 27 at 2 p. m. only a few fountains were in action. The new construction by overflow at the east cove was within 15 feet of the surface of the east ledge at the east tunnel locality. At 3:30 p. m. there was subsidence by about four feet and increased fountaining. Fumes were thin and the central crags was now plainly seen from Volcano House.

On Wednesday, November 28, 1917, at 10:45 a. m., the lake was high and the inner rampart only about two feet above it all around. The central crag was so high that both horns of its summit ridge could be plainly seen from Volcano House. There were growing spatter domes at the north, southwest and southeast coves and smaller ones at the east base of the old west crag mass and at the east cove. A new festooned overflow had poured (since November 26) from the central cove through the gulch west of the southeast crag. The central crag appeared nearly level with the pit rim. The southwest cove was now shut off by a new floor across the southwest channel as though a western submerged extension of the central crag mass had risen to make a dam athwart the narrows. The southwest pond so formed was crusted over at the moment. There were fresh overflows on the northwest floor from the northwest cove. There was no hissing at the west cone, but the southeast grotto was puffing. Central fountains were rare, streaming was outward from the southwest, and inward to the southeast arm, and there were blistered crusts. At noon a very large central fountain formed at the entrance to the north arm. The inner bench was wide opposite the east gulch, at the east cove and on the south side of the southeast crag. There were occasional longshore migrating fountains from the central region to the east cove. Fume was moderate. The lake appeared to have been rising and to be now at a high limit.

This was verified the next day, November 29, when at 2:30 p. m. the inner bench was 10 feet high all around indicating that the lake had relatively subsided. The lake was quiet except for a border fountain at the southeast grotto. Smoke was thicker.

November 30 was rainy, the fume was moderate but not thin, the crag was still moderately high, but not rising as seen at a distance. The lake was stationary and low.

In the Whitney Laboratory of Seismology for the week ending at 2 p. m. November 30, 1917, one small local earthquake was registered about 12:30 a. m. November 27. Microseismic motion has been moderate, diminishing during the week. Volcanic vibration has been normal and inconspicuous. Tilting has increased to the east and fluctuated in the north-south azimuth with a tendency southward.

Very respectfully,

T. A. JAGGAR, JR.,
Director.

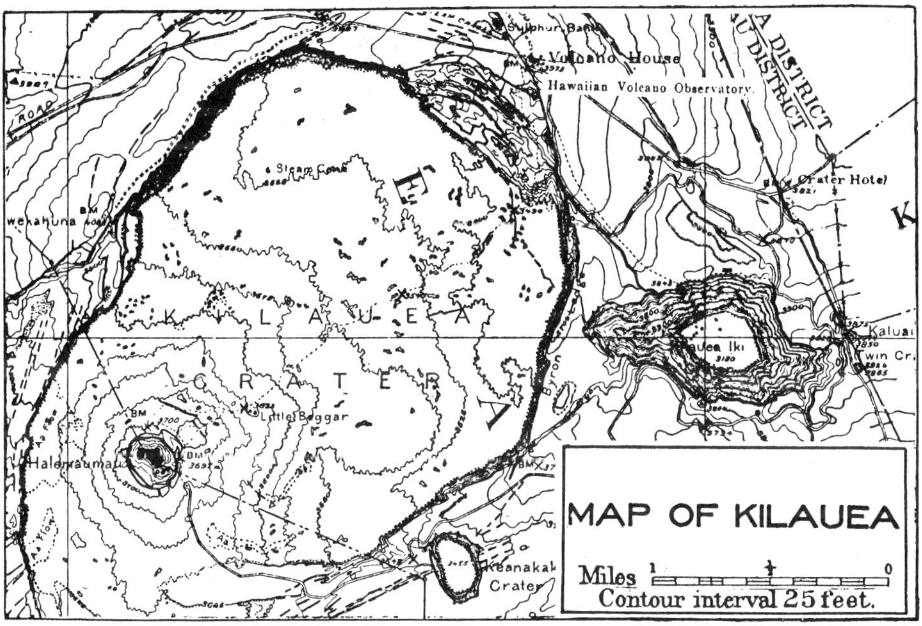

HAWAIIAN VOLCANO RESEARCH ASSOCIATION.

This society is a voluntary one, made up of subscribers to scientific work which is being executed by Dr. T. A. Jaggar, Director of the Hawaiian Volcano Observatory, Volcano House, P. O., Hawaii. **All scientific exchanges should be sent to this address.**

In 1917 there are about 150 subscribers in Hawaii and elsewhere, firms and individuals. A group of firms and persons in Hilo built the main observatory building in the spring of 1912. The work was founded by the Massachusetts Institute of Technology. Publications to date have been weekly reports since the summer of 1911 now reprinted in Honolulu in monthly form. There are also special reports, printed from time to time.

The weekly bulletin as it appears in the Honolulu Advertiser is reprinted as a leaflet and sent to regular annual subscribers to the work of the Association. L. A. Thurston is president of the Board of Directors of the Association, and L. T. Peck is treasurer. New subscribers who are interested in volcanoes will be welcomed in the Association. The Association aims: (1) To record volcanic activity and earthquakes in Hawaii; (2) to attract scientific men hither for special studies; (3) to promote the establishment of volcano observatories all over the world. The annual dues of regular members are $5; patrons of the Association subscribe larger amounts.

WHITNEY LABORATORY OF SEISMOLOGY.

The Whitney Laboratory of Seismology, named after an endowment fund of geophysical research held by the Massachusetts Institute of Technology, in memory of Caroline and Edward Whitney of Boston, is equipped with two Bosch-Omori 100 kg tromometers registering N-S and E-W motion, a heavy Omori tromometer registering E-W motion, and an Omori "ordinary Seismograph" designed for registering strong earthquakes in all three components of motion. These are seated on concrete piers in a closed basement room having practically constant temperature, beneath the chief Observatory building near the hotel. Time is referred to a rated chronometer, checked at intervals by solar observations with a transit. Both instruments are loaned by the College of Hawaii. Hawaiian standard time (H. S. T.) is 10 hrs. 30 min. slower than Greenwich time.

CANCANI SCALE OF SEISMIC INTENSITY.

Expressed by accelerations measured in millimeters per second per second.

I.	Instrumental	0.0	2.5
II.	Very slight	2.5	5.0
III.	Slight	5.0	10.0
IV.	Sensible, mediocre	10.0	25.0
V.	Rather strong	25.0	50.0
VI.	Strong	50.0	100.0
VII.	Very strong	100.0	250.0
VIII.	Ruinous	250.0	500.0
IX.	Disastrous	500.0	1000.0
X.	Very disastrous	1000.0	2500.0
XI.	Catastrophic	2500.0	5000.0
XII.	Great catastrophe	5000.0	10000.0

Grade IV. is ordinarily the minimum perceived by the senses; and in grade XII. the acceleration, or rate of change of motion (jerk) reaches that of terrestrial gravitation.

In the standard form of report the maximum intensity or acceleration, designated by the symbol a, or max. a, is given in the conventional unit, **the milligal**. The milligal is a measure of acceleration, such that 1 milligal = 1/100 mm. per sec. per sec. = 10 μ per sec. per sec. The Cancani scale, here defined in terms of millimeters per sec. per sec., can therefore be expressed in milligals by multiplying each of the numbers by 100.

WEEKLY BULLETIN
OF THE
Hawaiian Volcano Observatory

Vol. V. HONOLULU, HAWAII, DECEMBER, 1917. No. 12

Note.—The photographs presented with this issue, if taken in order from left to right, comprise a complete panorama of the present aspect of the Halemaumau pit, the active portion of the great crater of Kilauea. The indicator lines point to the sections always alluded to in our monthly reports, and will be found of advantage in locating the sites of future developments.

L. W. DE VIS-NORTON,
Editor.

VOLCANO OBSERVATORY, Dec. 8, 1917.—During the week ending December 7, 1917, the subsidence recently reported reached its lowest limit, and this crisis was accompanied by perceptible earthquakes and a readjustment of the inner lava crags. Immediately there followed a rising of both lake magma and bench magna, which has restored the crags to their high level, above the rim of the pit, and this rising is now in rapid progress in accordance with what should be expected near the December solstice. The crags are again visible from Volcano House.

On Saturday, December 1, at 10:30 a. m., the inner bench stood 10 feet above the lake and had fallen away in part at the east cove. Until 11:30 a. m. the lake rose, then followed a breaking up of crusts with subsidence. There were occasional noisy bursts of fountaining northeast. Open tunnels at the lake edge appeared at the west side of the southeast cove and at the central and east coves. There were built up ramparts at the central and southeast coves with much smoke and a glowing wall at the last locality. Rocks freshly fallen appeared at the base of the whitened south face of the steeple on the floor adjacent to the central cove. Streaming was to the southeast and into the tunnels, there was much crunching and clinking of crusts, and the fume in general was moderate. At 2:30 p. m. the lake was much lower, crusted over and very quiet. At 4:30 p. m. there was some activity in the southeast arm, which gradually increased until at 5:30 the whole lake rent its crusts asunder and streamed swiftly to the southeast.

On December 2 at 2:15 p. m. the central floor level was 25 feet above the lake and there had been much caving in of the inner bench. Fume was thick and the lake was crusted. At 2:40 p. m. there was activity in the north arm, especially at the grotto of the northeast cove. At 2:50 p. m. six or seven fountains were in action in the southeast arm.

On December 3 at 3:30 p. m. the inner bench was about 12 feet high and showed effects of caving in at the central, southeast and east coves, and fume had greatly increased. The central crags were lower, but still visible from Volcano House. Dense smoke rose from the floors above the central, southeastern and eastern tunnels and at the curtained grottoes under the east gulch and the southeast dome. There were evidently voids acting as gas condensers under these places. The condensation of unburned sulphur vapor accumulated in chambers opened by subsidence was very striking, and the marked increase of fume during temporary subsidence is due to this process. The seismographs indicated jarring at this time and visitors reported falls of inner benches.

On December 4 at 2 p. m. it was evident that a further readjustment of the southeast crag had caused its west side to sink at the central cove and its inner bench on the other side to rise—that is, the point at the entrance to the southeast cove. Fresh overflow from the lake was flooding the depressed area at the

WEEKLY BULLETIN
of the
Hawaiian Volcano Observatory

Published Monthly at Honolulu, Hawaii, by the Hawaiian Volcano Research Association

L. W. de Vis-Norton........Secretary

Entered as second-class matter January 20, 1914, at the post-office at Honolulu, Hawaii, under the Act of August 24, 1912.

central cove. There was fountaining at the southeast tunnel, the lake was elsewhere crusted over and the inner bench at the east cove was 10 feet high. At 8:30 p. m. all signs pointed to rising, the southwest arm was quiet and the north arm active, and there was much scaling away of rock from the south side of the central crag mass owing to its uplift and increased overhang there.

On Wednesday, December 5, 1917, at 11:30 a. m., the lake was rising. The eastern bench of the southeast crag showed a new lower shelf making an angle with the uplifted floor, and the east ledge also appeared as though it had been lifted. The inner bench was generally 10 feet to 12 feet above the lake level. The strong fuming of the coves had stopped as though the tunnels were filling, but there was a large sulphurous smoking patch southwest of the southwest cove. The southwest channel was again open and streaming was northward from it in a broad zone, the southeast arm being crusted over. Tunnels still showed at the central and east coves, with streaming from the lake into them. During a break-up the visible streaming southeastward was resumed. There was feeble puffing and fountaining southeast and high spatter marks were in evidence at the central cove and each gulch. At the latter locality there was glow above the lake level and a whitish flaming chimney still higher. The southeast grotto was quiet, but the southwest tunnel was noisy. There was much viscous central fountaining, bombardment was in progress along the north cove rampart, the northwest table appeared more broken, and the east island crag was cracked and stood in higher relief.

On December 6 at 11:30 a. m. the lake was higher, with new spatter margins hung with stalactites, inner bench about eight feet high, rapid streaming southeastward, smoke diminished, and crags in high relief. At 2:30 p. m. there was border fountaining at the central cove and on the north side of the central crag, but the north arm was quiet. At 3 p. m. rising was in progress and there was fountaining in the southeast arm. By 3:20 this had increased so that there was unusual gas pressure in evidence, making eight puffing border fountains and nine central fountains at the same time in this arm, the most vigorous effervescence seen here for some time. With temporary deflation of the lake and probably rising of the crags, the fresh inner bench collapsed under the east island and southeast crag masses, generating great numbers of fountains.

At this time, from the Observatory, two and a quarter miles away in a straight line, the central crag, examined with telescope, showed great increase in height above the profile of the rim of the pit, both horns and the west shoulder of the mass being plainly visible.

Measurement on Friday, December 7, 1917, at 11:30 a. m., made the depth of the lake surface 82 feet below the rim of the pit. The central crag stood 85 feet above the lake and three feet above the rim of Halemaumau. The east island stood 77 feet above the lake and five feet below the rim. As compared with November 23, two weeks previous, the lake was nine feet higher, the central crag 11 feet higher and the east island crag 13 feet higher.

At about 11:20 a. m., after a rising spell, there was general break up of crusts, swift streaming to the southeast and southwest and border fountaining. The lake stood only three feet below the inner bench. The east island, central and southeast crags all appeared higher. Heavy smoke rose from the southeast domes, the south pressure ridge, the southwest sulphurous patch, the southwest tunnel, the west floor, the old west crag mass and the north cliff. Rocks were falling from the leaning face of the central crag and a rock slide fell from the high margin of Halemaumau under the southwest crevasse. The west crag mass was split in four great crevasses at the end nearest the lake, and rocks were sliding there. The east island crag was now in view from the Observatory.

Between 8 and 9 p. m. there was increased gas pressure, the lake was at the inner level, and many fountains were pounding on the bank at the east cove, east gulch, southeast bench and west side of southeast cove. Heavy fountains burst along the eastern base of the west crag mass and others under the north rampart, and there were occasional heavy outbursts in the center, in the southeast arm and at the southwest tunnel. Streaming was from southwest to north and from the center to southeast. The southwest cove occasionally broke up with much tumult. Blue flames were playing at the central cove and from cracks above the lake at the east gulch and at the southwest tunnel. There was a glowing and flickering vent on the floor of the central cove back from the edge of the lake. No glow was seen in the west cone region. Everything indicated pronounced rising.

The seismographs of the Whitney Laboratory, for the week ending December 7 at 2 p. m., have registered three local earthquakes, two of them felt at the volcano, respectively about 12:50 a. m. and 10 p. m., December 4, and the third very small about 8:10 p. m., December 2. There have been other small jarrings. Microseismic motion has been moderate and volcanic vibration normal except for a few spasms December 4-6. Tilting has further recovered, with swinging of the pendulums to the south and west during the week.

VOLCANO OBSERVATORY, Dec. 15, 1917.—During the week ending Friday, December 14, 1917, the central group of crags in Halemaumau has maintained its great height and has risen strongly, especially at the southeast, while the liquid lake has relatively subsided so as to appear from 15 to 20 feet below the marginal bench at the southeast cove. The most rapid uplift of the crags took place between December 8 and December 10.

On Saturday morning, December 8, the east crag and the whole summit body of the central crag were plainly in view from the Observatory, and in the afternoon the lake was very quiet and crusted.

On December 9 at 6 p. m. there was much movement in the crags, falls of rock took place, and there was strong fountaining and streaming activity. The lake appeared low and the crags high.

The next morning, December 10, it was clear that strong rising of the crags had taken place, as they protruded still farther above the edge of the pit.

On December 11 between 8 and 9:30 p. m. the fume was dense, the crusts over the lake were thin and bluish flames were abundant, especially at the southeast grotto. The inner bench appeared from 12 to 15 feet high and the spatter grottoes of the southeast cove had collapsed. The inner bench had fallen away also at the central and east coves. A very wide bench had formed at the east base of the southeast crag so as to build out a point which narrowed the channel there. Streaming in the main lake was from southwest to north, and in the southeast cove was toward the usual marginal fountains there. There was also occasional streaming in evidence towards the grotto of the central cove, and bombardment at the north rampart was frequent. Occasionally the east cove crust broke up and a fountain became active at the north base of the southeast crag. A fall of inner bench material on the east side of the southeast cove made a conspicuous wave against the point opposite. Heat from the lake was strong.

On Wednesday, December 12, 1917, at 11 a. m., the lake was heavily crusted, with inner bank almost 20 feet high. There was rapid streaming into the central cove and activity on the west side of the southeast cove. The summit regions of the southeast crag and the central steeple had been scaling off and the central cove seemed more deeply indented. The older bench under the east island crag was mostly gone and a new inner bench six or eight feet lower was forming. During a break-up several small central fountains formed.

On December 13 at 11 a. m. crusts were very thick and fume had diminished, but the margin of the southeast cove seemed higher. It was evident that rising had taken place, as a crescent-shaped spatter dome had formed on the south bank and the southeast grotto was curtained with wide and long stalactites, while the opposite grotto was curtained with slender stalactites. Streaming was toward these grottoes around the long point of the southeast crag, which had greatly narrowed the channel leading to this cove. Another large horseshoe-shaped spatter cone had been built on the north side of the southeast crag without present activity, and the crag above showed scars of recent falling away. From the northeast a large tunnel could be seen on the north side of the central crag about 20 feet wide and 10 feet high. There was occasional activity here, but generally there was little noise and most of the activity was at the southeast. The central crag appeared to be crumbling and lifting so as to tilt up the slabs of recent overflow crust in the valley east of it, the botom of which in turn seemed to be subsiding. This would check with the supposition that the rise of the eastern point of the southeast crag indicated continued tilting over to the west of that crag block.

On December 14 at 5 p. m. the lake was again heavily crusted and low. A block of the west bank of the southeast cove had fallen in. There were occasional breakings-up at the southeastern grottoes. The bench point of the southeast crag had broken into slabs and a still lower inner bench was forming at the lake's edge. There was occasional fountaining with inrush to the bank on the north side of the southeast crag and also under the east island crag. The central channel was crusted over, but the crusts at the eastern coves occasionally broke up. Streaming from the southwest into the north arm continued incessantly, ending in bombardment at the north rampart, and occasional central fountains migrated along with this stream. At 6 p. m. there was spectacular cracking and foundering in the southeast cove, inaugurated by the bursting of blue flames through cracks in the thick crust, and there was left for a time a thin brilliant skin over the liquid. Flames were very conspicuous at the grottoes, and an almost steady flame played from a hole a few feet above the southeast grotto. The tunnel under the north side of the central crag was dark. An avalanche was heard from the northeast cove region. The southern and northeastern pressure ridges seemed higher, but the margin of the central cove was very low, only about four feet above the lake.

In the Whitney Laboratory during the week ending Friday, December 14, 1917, at 2 p. m. one local earthquake was registered about 1 a. m. December 11, which was felt at the Observatory as a short feeble shock. Microseismic motion has been moderate and volcanic vibration normal, with a few stronger spasms on the 7th, 9th and 12th. Tilting, which has been fairly strong of late to the south and moderate to the west, changed gradually to an eastward and northward tendency on December 13-14.

VOLCANO OBSERVATORY, Dec. 22, 1917.—During the week ending Friday, December 21, 1917, the Halemaumau column has reached a culmination closely according with the solstice and thereafter has subsided. Both the liquid lava of the lake and the group of central crags have taken part in the movements of rising and falling. The great crags in the pit have been plainly in view from the Observatory and very conspicuous in their relief above the rim of Halemaumau. High gas pressure with hissing, overflow and construction of many border cones reached a maximum on Monday, December 17.

On December 16 at 2:45 p. m. the inner bench at the central cove was only two feet high and the lake was crusted and very quiet, with much fume. It was evident that the central crag mass had risen and was well above the level of the edge of the pit, but the southeast crag had been tilting farther to the north and falling away on that side so as to destroy its summit peaks and lower it. It was evident that the floors bordering the lake were rising, especially on the northeast and south.

On December 17 at 4 p. m. the lake was in the midst of a spasm of violent rising, and during that day overflows of the lake margin had taken place at the eastern, central and northwestern coves. The latter had overflowed a large area. There were twelve border cones of crescent form in different parts of the lake, all in process of construction by border fountaining and overspatter. At the southeast cove the lake was within two feet of overbrimming the rampart. In the north central region there was a large fountain continuously active, and the streaming was there northward, while in the southeast arm it was southward. The northwest and west cone localities on the stained and smoky floor west of the old crag mass, were both glowing under blow-pipe action from beneath, the west cone evidencing this by puffing, the other by continuous hissing. The northwest table crag showed collapse of its southern half and farther uptilting of its northern half. The east ledge at the lake margin was distinctly higher. A curtain of stalactites hung across the central grotto.

On Tuesday, December 18, at 2 p. m., the maximum activity appeared to have been passed, fumes were thicker, there was little fountaining and the southeast arm was stagnant. At 2:15 there were three active border grottoes east and southeast, but otherwise the lake was heavily crusted. The southeast dome grotto was curtained and quiet, with much smoke rising from its summit. From 8:30 to 10:30 p. m. there were open grottoes at the central and southeastern coves and on the west side of the main lake. Subsidence had produced long stalactites hanging from glowing margins where the lake lapped against the crags. The stalactites were dragged with the flow of the currents which streamed into the several coves. Fourteen fountains were in action with the usual fluctuations of grotto fountaining. The east ledge was rising strongly, and the channel leading to the southeast cove had widened.

On December 19 at 4 p. m. the lake appeared relatively low and smoky. The northwest cone area still showed glow, but not the west cone, and puffing at these places had ceased. At the west cone there was noise of collapse heard as though rocks were falling into crevasses. The southeast bench appeared nine feet high and the central cove bench six feet high above the lake, while the lowest inner bench of the point of the southeast crag was three feet high. The lake was mostly crusted over. There were occasional fountains in the north arm and middle region, and there was grotto activity east and southeast and against the south side of the east island crag. Streaming was as usual to the southeast and north, and there was bombardment at the north rampart. Dense smoke rose from the south edge of the southwest cove. The northwest cove was narrow, and the fresh overflow floor stood six feet above the lake. All the spatter crescents of December 17 stood high above the lake as rampart humps at the edge of the inner bench deserted by the subsided live lava. There was some hissing from the southeast grotto curtained with stalactites across its face.

On Thursday, December 20, the high central crag mass, by measurement from the Observatory at 9 a. m., showed fully 25 feet of its turreted upper portion above the near edge of the pit as seen from a distance. This was the maximum lift of these crags for this period of rising, and the maximum had been held for the preceding twelve hours. In the afternoon of December 20 the crags were subsiding, and for the next two days they sank over four feet a day. The following were the measured vertical amounts of crag showing on successive days:

Dec. 19, 12:30 p. m.—24½ ft. showing.
Dec. 20, 9:00 a. m.—25 ft. showing.
Dec. 20, 4:30 p. m.—23 ft. showing.
Dec. 21, 9:00 a. m.—18 ft. showing.
Dec. 22, 9:00 a. m.—14 ft. showing.

On December 20 at Halemaumau the lake was still sluggish and falls of rock were seen at the southeast crag and the east island mass.

On Friday, December 21, 1917, at 4:20 p. m., measurement made the depression of the lake 92 feet below the southeast rim of Halemaumau. The position of the crags' summits was as follows: Central crag, 7 feet above edge and 8 feet lower than on the previous day; east island crag level with edge; southeast crag 27 feet below edge; east ledge 38 feet below edge. The overflow floor of the central cove was 15 feet above the lake, making the maximum level attained by the lake on December 17 approximately 77 feet down. On that date the lake had risen five feet above the level of December 7. On the morning of December 20, when the crags attained their maximum, the central and east island crags had both risen about 12 feet since December 7—averaging a little less than one foot per day. The movement, however, was by no means uniform. The accordance of the maximum with the solstice was striking.

On December 21 the lake appeared low, but much gas had accumulated beneath the thick crust and occasionally broke through it with a rush. The crust cracked with clanging noises. There were caverns revealed at the central cove and at the west side of the southeast cove. At the southeast grotto the crust was heaving and the confined gas occasionally broke out with flames. Border fountains played against the north base of the southeast crag and the south base of the east island crag. Streaming was north in the north arm. Five fountains were in action at 5:20 p. m., three in the southeast region and one each at the north and southwest. About 9 p. m. a heavy fall of the whole south margin of the southeast cove took place, and during the evening the lake was subsiding and other falls of rock were heard. Strong uplift was evident at the east ledge, the south crag and pressure ridge, the northern smoke cliff and at the remnant of the northwest table. The inner bench had fallen away at the east cove and at the east gulch, the latter now indented as a considerable cove. Rocks were falling there and from the north side of the southeast crag, and one small slide was seen in motion at the east end of the higher 1894 ledge. The long point making out southeastward from the southeast crag now exhibited four distinct benches produced by the gradual overturning of the crag to the north. The lowest of these was only four feet above the lake. The northward rotation of the mass had caused a falling off of the whole summit region on the north side so as to make that side a flat broken surface. The east ledge was now nearly as high as the southeast shelf.

For the week ending at 2 p. m. December 21, 1917, no local earthquakes have been registered on the seismograms from the Whitney Laboratory, but one powerful distant earthquake of the ''world-shaking'' class was registered about 7:40 a. m. December 21, Hawaiian time. The preliminary phase of this record developed gradually and its duration was somewhat doubtful, but an approximate estimate would make the center of the disturbance only 1300 miles away—about the distance of Fanning Island or Laysan Island. Microseismic motion and volcanic vibration have both increased moderately during the week. The tilting has progressed westward and northward, but not strongly.

VOLCANO OBSERVATORY, Dec. 29, 1917.—During the week ending Friday, December 28, 1917, the lava column of Halemaumau continued its subsidence for a time, but on December 24 it resumed rising very much as before the solstice, so that at the end of the week the depression of the liquid lake was only 75 or 80 feet and the central and east island crags were again well above the level of the edge of the pit. The solstice period has been marked by several heavy earthquakes registered on the seismographs from origins a long distance away.

On Saturday, December 22, in the morning, the lava lake was lower, rocks were falling from the north side of the southeast crag, and there were cavernous openings on the west side of the southeast cove and at the central cove. There was a new inner bench two to three feet above the lake. Smoke was increased and the rampart was cracked on the west side of the southeast cove. The crag summits as seen from the Observatory were much lower. A very heavy localized rainfall about noon over Uwekahuna bluff on the west side of Kilauea sink produced a remarkable double waterfall down the face of the cliffs under Uwekahuna, draining out from the wash valley back of the southern bench of the cliff. The waterfall continued some thirty minutes, more or less.

On December 23 the crags were stationary and the fume somewhat thinner, as though the subsidence were arrested or the lake were rising.

On December 24 at 5 p. m. the crags were much lower. The western summit of the central crag had fallen away and the east peak was now the higher and its tendency to overhang towards the south appeared increased. From the southeast station the lake appeared tumultuous, some 20 feet below the floor above the southeast cove, and general cracking and foundering and easterly streaming were in progress, with twenty or more fountains, open tunnels in the

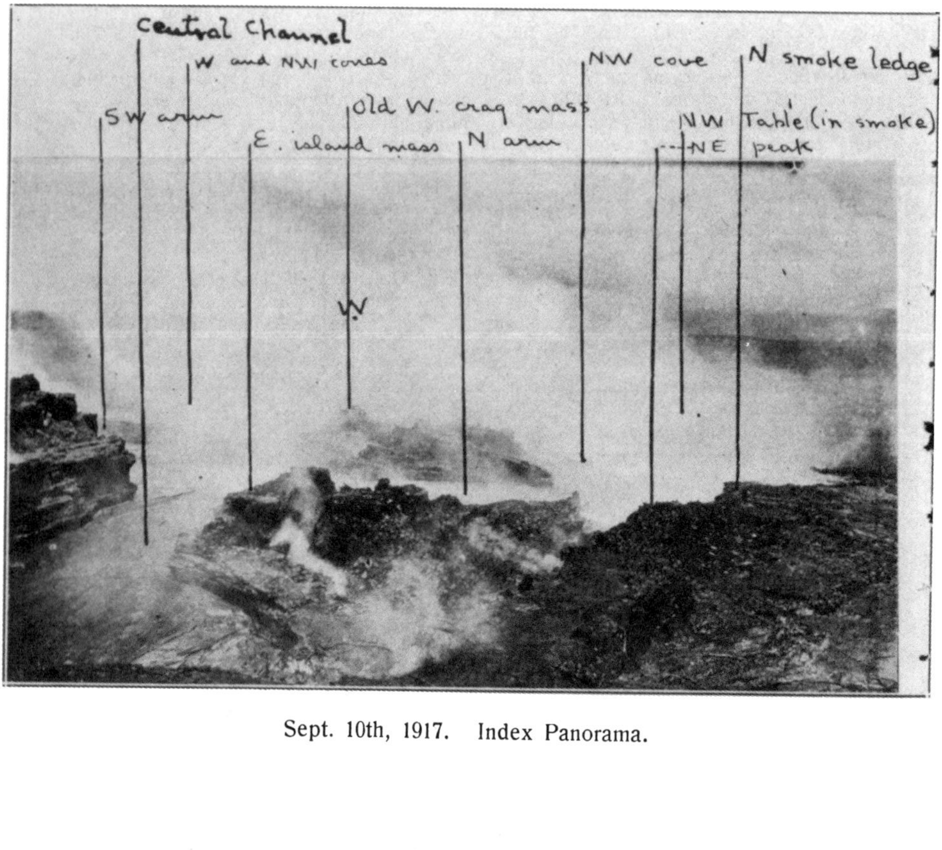

Sept. 10th, 1917. Index Panorama.

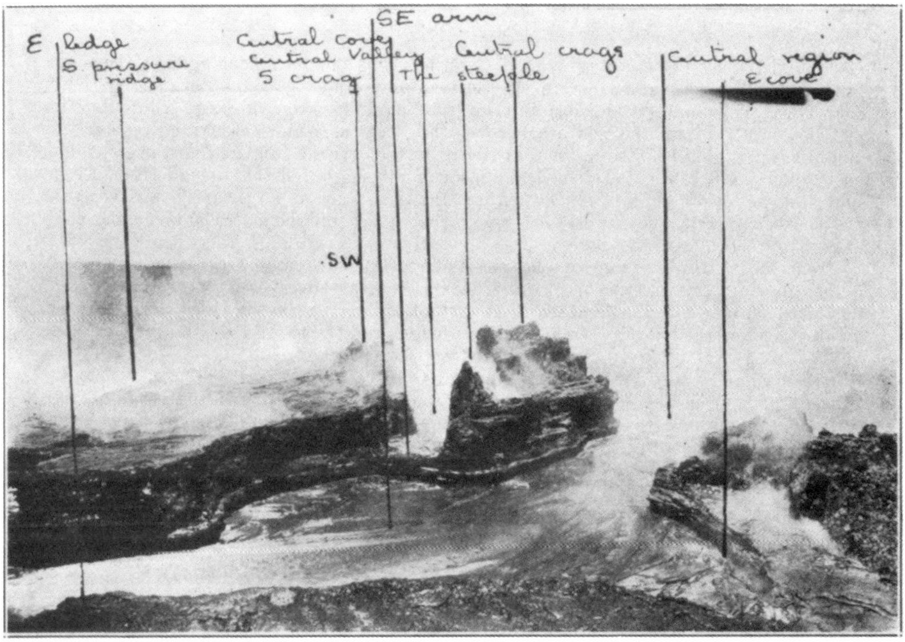

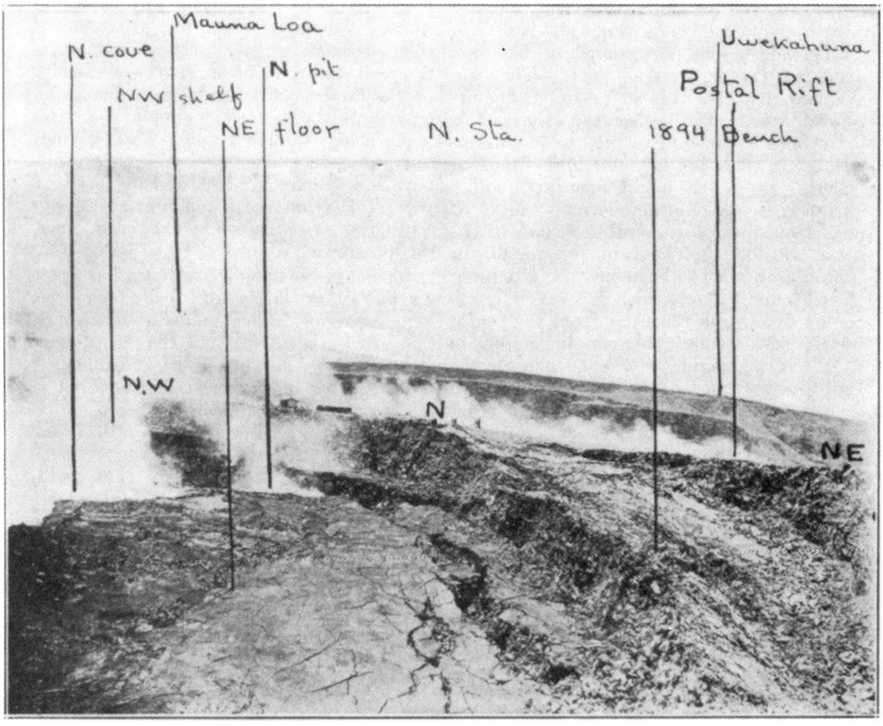

Halemaumau from East.—Photo Jaggar.

coves and stalactites hanging around the lake shores. The tunnels were at the east cove, with quietly glowing interior, on the west side of the southeast cove, rumbling and active within, and at the east gulch. Five uptilted benches were now discernible from top to bottom on the southeast crag, the lowest one being only five feet above the lake.

From the southwest edge of the pit a quiet glowing cavern was seen at the northeast corner of the southwest cove leading under the central valley. Part of the roof was seen to fall into the lava below, and there were several small falls of rock from the south face of the central crag mass. Streaming was northward out of the southwest cove through a very narrow channel some 25 feet deep, with an active grotto in its outer bend. There were places densely smoking in the southwest floor and the south pressure ridge. Hissing was heard occasionally from the direction of the southwest tunnel. There was a stained area emitting blue fames at the eastern end of the pressure ridge, suggesting the presence of a cavity below. Out in the northern, western and central parts of the lake nine fountains were counted, some of them continuous in groups on the west side of the east island mass. This was a new feature distinctive of a definite subsidence. The noise was that of a continuous plashing, and the fountains threw up much spray and high flings of melt. Both the north arm and southwest cove regions were crusted most of the time. No glow could be seen near the western cones. The benches around the middle region of the lake were irregular, 15, 20 and 30 feet high.

At 5:30 p. m., looking from the southeast, four fountains were in action in the central region and one each in the grottoes of the central and southeastern coves and on the south side of the east island. In the central cavern there was continuous fountaining, inward streaming, high incandescence and much bubbling. There was outward streaming from under the high east island crag and along the shore to the east cove tunnel. Occasionally prolonged hissing was heard in the southeast cove where the gas forced its way from under the edge of the crust which covered the greater part of the southeast arm. At 5:30 p.m. there was bombardment against the north rampart and the lake was noisy with puffing, plashing, hissing, rumbling in the caverns, and cracking crusts. A glimpse of the distant northwest table summit suggested that it had risen. From the east station no activity was seen in the cavern on the north side of the central crag. Puffing was heard at the northeast cove and from the cavern of the central cove. Several falls of rock took place from the face of the east ledge and from the north face of the southeast crag.

On December 25 at 11:30 a. m. conditions were changed and the signs of rising were unmistakable. The fume was thinner and the crags were higher. The southeast arm was crusted over and a new inner bench had been formed entirely submerging the lower bench of the previous day at the point beneath the southeast crag. The new bench stood three feet above the lake. The caverns were quite submerged and were replaced by spatter grottoes at the east gulch, the central cove, the east cove, and the northeastern and western sides of the southwest cove. Both the latter and the southeast cove were crusted over. There was an active grotto with short stalactites on the west side of the southeast cove. Four or five continuous fountains played in the central region and in the north arm. Puffing could be heard from the grottoes. The western cones were hot and fuming. There had been a fresh fall from the second bench on the south side of the southeast crag since the previous day.

It should be noted that there has been much falling lately of rock from the high edge of Halemaumau about where the great crevasses on the southwest emerge into the pit. The tumble of broken rocks is scattered on the broken and cracked floor beneath.

On Thursday, December 27, 1917, at 3 p. m., it was rainy and foggy, but, nevertheless, it was evident that both lake and crags were higher. The lake was heavily crusted, the only open place being a small area on the west side of the southeast cove where the fiery lava streamed into the southeast tunnel. There was also cracking and foundering at the margin of the east cove and occasionally some activity broke out at the east gulch.

A new inner bench had formed about one foot high above the lake, and this was a wide platform at the east cove and at the point of the southeast crag. The lake was gaining on this crag, which showed now only three inches in its profile instead of five. Again the northwest table crag appeared very high as though rising.

On December 28 the crags were distinctly higher. At 2:30 p. m. the inner bench stood two feet above the lake, which was rising, with activity at the central cove. At 2:45 there was fountaining in the north arm, and at 3 p. m. the southwest arm was seen to be broken up, with a few fountains in action there.

During the week ending at 2 p. m. December 28, 1917, the instruments of the Whitney Laboratory have registered one small local earthquake about 3 p. m., December 21, and a pronounced distant earthquake at 11 a. m., Hawaiian time, on December 28. The forephase of this seismogram is indefinite owing to heavy microseisms, so that the distance of origin is not clearly determined. Microseisms became very strong after the 24th. Volcanic vibration and movement of tilting have been moderate. The distant earthquake of December 28 may have been one of the Guatemala shocks recently reported.

Very respectfully,

T. A. JAGGAR, Jr.,

Director.

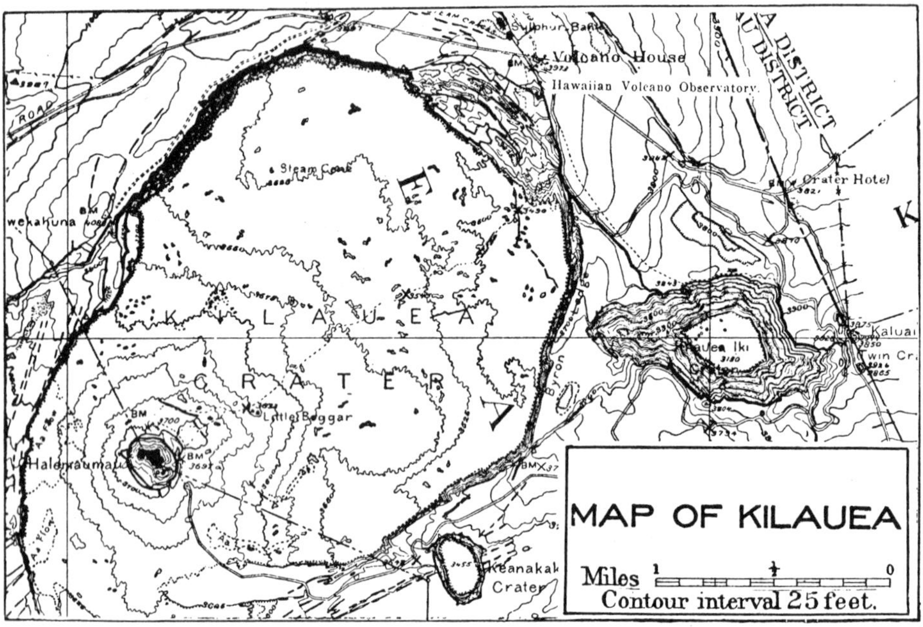

HAWAIIAN VOLCANO RESEARCH ASSOCIATION.

This society is a voluntary one, made up of subscribers to scientific work which is being executed by Dr. T. A. Jaggar, Director of the Hawaiian Volcano Observatory, Volcano House, P. O., Hawaii. **All scientific exchanges should be sent to this address.**

In 1917 there are about 150 subscribers in Hawaii and elsewhere, firms and individuals. A group of firms and persons in Hilo built the main observatory building in the spring of 1912. The work was founded by the Massachusetts Institute of Technology. Publications to date have been weekly reports since the summer of 1911 now reprinted in Honolulu in monthly form. There are also special reports, printed from time to time.

The weekly bulletin as it appears in the Honolulu Advertiser is reprinted as a leaflet and sent to regular annual subscribers to the work of the Association. L. A. Thurston is president of the Board of Directors of the Association, and L. T. Peck is treasurer. New subscribers who are interested in volcanoes will be welcomed in the Association. The Association aims: (1) To record volcanic activity and earthquakes in Hawaii; (2) to attract scientific men hither for special studies; (3) to promote the establishment of volcano observatories all over the world. The annual dues of regular members are $5; patrons of the Association subscribe larger amounts.

WHITNEY LABORATORY OF SEISMOLOGY.

The Whitney Laboratory of Seismology, named after an endowment fund of geophysical research held by the Massachusetts Institute of Technology, in memory of Caroline and Edward Whitney of Boston, is equipped with two Bosch-Omori 100 kg tromometers registering N-S and E-W motion, a heavy Omori tromometer registering E-W motion, and an Omori "ordinary Seismograph" designed for registering strong earthquakes in all three components of motion. These are seated on concrete piers in a closed basement room having practically constant temperature, beneath the chief Observatory building near the hotel. Time is referred to a rated chronometer, checked at intervals by solar observations with a transit. Both instruments are loaned by the College of Hawaii. Hawaiian standard time (H. S. T.) is 10 hrs. 30 min. slower than Greenwich time.

CANCANI SCALE OF SEISMIC INTENSITY.

Expressed by accelerations measured in millimeters per second per second.

I.	Instrumental	0.0	2.5
II.	Very slight	2.5	5.0
III.	Slight	5.0	10.0
IV.	Sensible, mediocre	10.0	25.0
V.	Rather strong	25.0	50.0
VI.	Strong	50.0	100.0
VII.	Very strong	100.0	250.0
VIII.	Ruinous	250.0	500.0
IX.	Disastrous	500.0	1000.0
X.	Very disastrous	1000.0	2500.0
XI.	Catastrophic	2500.0	5000.0
XII.	Great catastrophe	5000.0	10000.0

Grade IV. is ordinarily the minimum perceived by the senses; and in grade XII. the acceleration, or rate of change of motion (jerk) reaches that of terrestrial gravitation.

In the standard form of report the maximum intensity or acceleration, designated by the symbol a, or max. a, is given in the conventional unit, **the milligal.** The milligal is a measure of acceleration, such that 1 milligal = 1/100 mm. per sec. per sec. = 10 μ per sec. per sec. The Cancani scale, here **defined in terms of millimeters per sec. per sec., can therefore be expressed in milligals by multiplying each of the numbers by 100.**

WEEKLY BULLETIN
OF THE
Hawaiian Volcano Observatory

VOL. VI. HONOLULU, HAWAII, JANUARY, 1918. No. 1

EDITORIAL NOTES.

Supplementing our usual monthly report, we give, this month, a reprint of a recent lecture given by Dr. Jaggar, Director of the Hawaiian Volcano Observatory at Kilauea. This lecture has attracted a great deal of attention, and it is our hope, in following issues, to issue reprints of other interesting addresses recently delivered by him.

EDITOR.

January 5, 1918.

During the week ending January 4, 1918, the Halemaumau lava column rose seventeen feet and the great central crags in the pit almost as much, so that at the end of the week more than 30 feet of the crags was exposed to view across the edge of the pit as seen from Volcano House. The rapid rising is closely comparable to what happened in the first weeks of 1917 and may be expected to come to an end soon and be followed by subsidence before the March equinox. The great black crags jutting up above Halemaumau produce very much the same effect as in January, 1917. The history of the year just ended is quite accordant with what would be expected if one imagines the Mauna Loa column, after its discharge of 1916, to have risen in the Kilauea pit close to its brim and there maintained an equilibrium except for the effects of earth warpings attributable to tidal stresses. Thus we had rising in the 1916-17 winter, sinking in the early spring, rising in the early summer, a lower level thereafter and pronounced rising again for the 1917-18 winter. In October, 1917, there was some sort of a subterranean crisis following the equinox whereby the ground exhibited astonishing tiltings and there were local earthquakes. Thereafter with the rising lava these exceptional movements wholly ceased and local earthquakes have recently been at a minimum. The great earthquakes which wrecked the city of Guatemala on Saturday, December 29, were clearly recorded on the seismographs of the Whitney Laboratory.

On the morning of Saturday, December 29, the lava lake rose to the level of the inner bench and built spatter domes on both sides of the southeast cove, at the east gulch, the east cove and the central cove. The inner bench was widened to a maximum of 20 feet at the point protruding from the southeast crag and against the east island at the east cove. Elsewhere this bench was from five to ten feet wide. At the east gulch two inner benches were built, respectively six and fifteen feet above the lake, the upper one fuming and sulphur-stained. At 2 p. m. the lake had subsided five feet and was actively fountaining in the southeast cove. At 3 p. m. there was vigorous fountaining in the southwest arm and southwest cove. Looking from the south station it was evident that the south face of the central crag mass was scaling away rapidly as it rose with overhang to the south. From the southwest station it became evident that this rising of the western extension of the central crag mass was again shutting off the southwest arm by developing two bridges of crust, leaving the southwest cove an isolated pond. At 4 p. m. the streaming was to the southeast and north, cracking and foundering of the crusts were going on and there was much splashing in the grottoes with rumbling noises, especially on the west side of the southeast cove. There was much marginal overhang due to tem-

WEEKLY BULLETIN
of the
Hawaiian Volcano Observatory

Published Monthly at Honolulu, Hawaii, by the Hawaiian Volcano Research Association

L. W. de Vis-Norton........Secretary

Entered as second-class matter January 20, 1914, at the post-office at Honolulu, Hawaii, under the Act of August 24, 1912.

porary subsidence. The inner bench was about six feet below the rampart bounding the south valley at the southeast cove. Occasional migratory central fountains would form and most of the lake was covered with crusts of medium thickness separated by bright lines. Glowing orifices were seen above the shore cones at the east gulch and west of the southeast cove. Fumes in general were rather dense. At 5 p. m. a line of traveling fountains formed from the center of the southeast arm to the shore of the southeast crag and migrated eastward. This patch was followed in its progress by more rapid surface streaming from the channel eastward. The central fountains in general exhibited high gas pressure and spraying. A group of them in the middle region were in continuous effervescence. At 5:15 p. m. rising was resumed with much hissing from under border crusts.

Measurement on December 29 made the depression of the lake 78 feet below the southeast rim and the elevation of the east summit of the central crag 7 feet above the level of the rim of the pit, while the summit of the east island stood 2 feet above the rim level. These results showed that in eight days the lake had risen 14 feet, while the central crag was unchanged and the east island crag had risen only 2 feet. From this time on, however, the crags rose rapidly.

On December 30 at 5 p. m. the lake was about 10 feet below the inner bench at the southeast point. There were quiet spells followed by occasional breakings up of the crust. At first there was a rim of overhang two to three feet above the lake with glow and hanging stalactites, but after 6 p. m. this was filled by the rising fluid. Above the lake at the east gulch a glowing crack emitted flames. Central fountains broke out in the middle region and in the southeast arm, and overwhelmed the crust slowly eastward. At the northeastern corner of the southwest cove a glowing cavern led under the central valley. Fragments of the southeastern bench occasionally collapsed. Only three benches now showed in the profile of the southeast crag. There was glow from the north rampart and the fumes in general were heavy.

At 11 a. m. on Monday, December 31, 1917, the lake was higher, the fumes were much thinner, there were central fountains and the crusts were thinner with more rapid streaming. At 4:30 p. m. pronounced rising was in evidence with spatter building and much Pele's hair floating up with the puffing gases at the border grottoes. There were five or six of these, the streaming to the southeast was slow, a large dome had been built at the east cove and there was a large glowing opening at the east gulch. Central fountains were continuous. The southwest pond was now completely shut off and itself crusted over. Twenty feet to the southeast of it on the floor, above the line of the south tunnel, there was a blowing and spurting aperture, noisily building a cone. During a break-up of the pond crust with violent escape of gas and border fountains, it was evident that the gas pressure beneath was relieved and the tunnel vent ceased puffing. During the break-up the streaming was rapid from the bridge of crust on the southwest channel side eastward across the pond, and at the same time there was inrush under this bridge on the lake side, showing that there was still an open arch beneath. As soon as the crust reformed the tunnel vent resumed puffing, the crust on the pond heaving in sympathy. The west cone appeared hot but was not obviously glowing or hissing. A sulphur patch back from the high rim of Halemaumau south-southwest, which a few months ago had been fresh, was now dead and white again.

A spatter dome was building on the west side of the southeast cove. The dome at the east gulch was spurting.

At 5:30 p. m. the southeast arm and central region were crusted over, but there was open streaming from a point opposite the east gulch toward the east and to the inner end of the southeast cove. There was also a surface stream into the central cove. The lake was now two feet below the inner bench.

On January 1, 1918, at 7:30 p. m., the lake appeared about 10 feet below the inner bench, mostly crusted over, with some activity in the north arm and border fountains at the east gulch and southeast cove. No rock falls were heard.

The crags, by measurement from the Observatory, began their pronounced rising December 31 and increased their rate of rising from January 2 to January 4, the east island gaining on the central crag.

On January 3 at 10:30 a. m. the effect of the rising movement of the bench magma was inspected on the inner northeast floor where a most astonishing change of slope was revealed. The upward push of the middle portion of the stiff lava column which forms the lake bottom had lifted the east, northeast and northwest ledges bodily so as to incline them towards the peripheral wall of Halemaumau at angles near 40 degrees. The east ledge was now higher than the southeast shelf. This restores conditions similar to May of 1917. The crevasses northeast have largely closed and indeed pressure ridges have in part replaced them. The recently formed floor margin of the north cove has risen and been crushed between the rising crags east and west of it. On this day the inner bench was four feet high east and southeast, two feet high at the southwest pond and northwest cove and one foot high towards the northeast. The northeast cove valley was floored with fresh lava and the northwest cove was a narrow indentation in a wide floor area. The crusted southwest pond was heaving and the tunnel vent to the southeast of it was hissing continuously and harshly from a network of openings which glowed, flamed and showed sulphur stain.

That the crags were in motion was shown by the fall of rocks from time to time, especially towards the northeast and east. The central crag had lost its high east turret and become a jagged straight-topped ridge.

The lake was rising and crusted over with noisy central fountains near the west base of the east island crag mass. There were occasional heavy bombardments at the coves, especially at the north cove. Occasionally general breaking-up of the crust took place, there were blowing grotto fountains on the west side of the southeast cove and sometimes at the east cove and east gulch. There were spatter domes at the east, northwest, central and north cove. Streaming appeared to be outward from the northwest and southwest coves.

On Friday, January 4, the rising reached a culmination of overflow whereby the southwest pond, now partially shut off from the main lake, flooded the entire south valley from the west cone to the rampart of the southeast cove. The lake at this time was only 60 feet below the rim. So voluminous was the overflow filling of the south depression that it pooled, crusted and then the crust cracked up and foundered, leaving wide smooth surfaces with little trace of the original festooned skins. All of this suggested that the January rise of 1917 was repeating itself.

During the week ending at 2 p. m. January 4, 1918, the seismographs of the Whitney Laboratory have registered no local earthquakes, but two teleseisms, or distant great shocks, were recorded on Saturday, December 29. At least one of these originated in Guatemala, and probably both of them. The first shock began at 7:45 a. m. Hawaiian time, or about 12:15 p. m. Guatemala time. Its first preliminary phase occupied 7 min. 40 sec., corresponding to a great circle distance from Hawaii of 6070 kilometers—a close approximation to the distance of Guatemala. The second and greater shock reached the Observatory at 12:50 p. m. H. S. T. or approximately 5:20 p. m. Guatemala time and wrote its record for about 30 minutes. The preliminary phase indicated an original approximately distant about 6400 kilometers, which is near enough for the Guatemala center. The great circle distance from Honolulu to Guatemala city is approximately 3945 miles or 6365 kilometers. The first preliminary wave front sent through the earth from Guatemala should travel at a rate to reach Hawaii in about nine minutes. This would make the actual earthquakes in Guatemala 12:04 p. m. and 5:11 p. m. Guatemala time. The writer has not yet seen reported the hours of the shocks which finally wrecked the city.

Microseismic movement during the week has dwindled to nearly normal, and there has been nothing unusual in the motion of volcanic vibration. Tilting to the north and east, of no great amount, took place during the recent sharp rise of the lava in Halemaumau.

January 12, 1918.

During the week ending January 11, 1918, the rapid rising of the Halemaumau lava column has continued, and renewed activity at the old west and northwest cones above floor-cracks is interesting confirmation of the view that those places are permanent conduit wells of much importance in the mechanism of the rising lava, although they remain crusted over and obscure for months at a time. There has been a change in the habit of the lava lake since the solstice, with increased speed of streaming to the south sinkholes, thinner crusts, more fountaining, relatively sudden overflows alternating with sharp risings of the crag masses and increased gas pressure at the western conduits, building driblet cones and driblet flows from floor cracks. These effects suggest that the sun's turning point, affecting fissures underground filled with rising magma which had been under uniform stress during the sun's southing for three months, brought about a relatively sudden release of stress and reduction of pressure on gas-charged lava. Increased volumes of gas would escape from solution generating heat and inflation in the upper part of the lava column, but the net effect eventually on the magma below would be subsidence. Such explanation accounts for the paradox of subsidence symptoms such as sinkhole cascades coupled with sharp rising. This paradox was the fact at the beginning of January both last year and now. An important result of this analysis, if true, is that the observed immediate effect of an astronomical crisis on the liquid lava may not necessarily be the actual mechanical effect due to stress on the fissure system. In other words, measured rise and fall of lake magma and bench magma at the surface is not the rise and fall of the main lava column deep down, and even the lake levels and crag levels reach their culminations on different dates. To determine the critical times when the deep lava column reaches its highest and lowest, an equation must be worked out which is by no means simple.

Measurements on Saturday, January 5, 1918, at noon, made the depression of the lake 61 feet below the east rim of the pit while both the east island crag and the central crag stood 17 feet above the level of the rim. In seven days the lake had risen 17 feet and the two crags 15 feet.

Strong rising and overflowing was in progress and fumes were thin. The southeast inner bench under the southeast shelf of May, 1917, was overflowed continuously from 11 a. m. to 12:30 p. m. There was great heat on the rim, and strong gas pressure and puffing were evident at the spatter domes of the southeast cove. At the east gulch a high driblet cone with stalactites had been built. The inner bench was two to three feet high. Streaming was northward in the main lake, southeastward in the southeast arm and very rapid to the tunnel grotto at the west side of the southeast cove. The increased movement upward of the crags produced occasional falling rocks from slopes and cliffs facing away from the center of the pit. There were hot blistered thin crusts at the southeast cove and heavy polygonal crusts separated by bright lines over the central region and southeast arm. Occasional large migratory fountains would form with swarms of bubblings. At the southwest pond there was rapid streaming from west to east and the hissing vent above the tunnel extending from it southeastward was maintained through the new overflows there. So was the large smoke patch southwest of it.

At 1:30 p. m. the lake was generally crusted and high, border fountains at the southeast margin of the southwest pond splashed over into a small overflow and there was heat crackling at the hissing vent there. Tremendous fountaining was in progress at the southeast cove tunnel grotto with very rapid rush into it as though it led to a sinkhole. The margin of the summit pond was only about two feet high. The west bank of the main lake south of the old west crag mass had been warped up into a cliff 20 feet high. At 11:55 a. m. the eastern summit turret of the central crag mass, or what was left of it, fell with a crash into the central valley and a cloud of red dust shot up. At 1:45 p. m. in the southwest pond there was general breaking up and temporary subsidence with strong streaming from the west. At 2 p. m. the north arm was quiet and heavily crusted and the lake at the northwest cove was brimming level with the bank. At 2:15 p. m. there was general cracking and foundering over the whole lake with violent fountaining and temporary subsidence by about two feet. The break-up was noisy and an overhanging bright rim showed on all sides. The disturbance began with a violent fountain in the southwest arm. Between the large foundering crust area lines of bubble fountains broke out. After the breaking-up immediate recrusting set in.

The south valley was now covered with a fresh flow extending all the way from the west cone to the southeast rampart and there was a similar flow covering the whole northwest shelf to the old west crag mass. The east cove had a new overflow floor and spatter dome. The southeast cove on its south and west shores had not overflowed, owing probably to the rise of those banks along with the crags. A distinct ridge extended from the west crag mass southwestward to the west cone. The northwest crag had now become a steep hog-back with upper surface inclined eastward. The uplift of the whole central and northwestern group of crags appears to offset the flooding of the western and southern depressions. Seen from the northwest station the east ledge was now well above the southeast shelf, the southeast crag was only slightly below the edge of the pit, the east island crag towered above everything and it was evident that all the central peaks stood high above the top of the wooden A-frame at the south station.

At 3:20 p. m. there were heavy falls of rock from the central and southern crags. At 3:50 p. m. overflowing was resumed along the inner bench from the east gulch southward, building up that bench and diminishing the height of the southeast shelf above. At the southern end of this growing bench the southeast grotto was surmounted by a spatter dome and back of it ten feet from the edge of the lake a lava pot eight feet in diameter had formed whence spurts would be thrown twenty feet into the air. At 4:30 p. m., a heavy fall of rock into the lake from the north inner cliff started prolonged fountaining there.

On January 6 at 2:15 p. m. the inner bench was eight feet above the lake, there was activity at the central cove and the southeast arm was crusted. At 3:30 p. m. nearly half of the new southeastern inner bench collapsed, followed by a similar collapse of the bench protruding from the southeast crag and finally there was collapse at the southeast tunnel entrance. All of these falls made violent fountains in the southeast arm and cove. At 4:30 p. m. there was much tumbling of fragments from the sides of the east island crag. By 6 p. m. the temporary subsidence made the inner bench ten feet high and there was active fountaining everywhere and very swift rush of surface currents to the southeast tunnel.

On Jan. 7 at 11:30 a. m. the lake was high, crusted over, and the streaming with great emission of heat from the southeast point to the tunnel was estimated to flow at two feet per second. The southeast grotto continued active and the pot back of it was smaller. The dome and the bench at the east cove had collapsed, but there was a new spatter grotto forming at the east tunnel. The bench at the southeast point was six feet high but across the stream to the east the bank was only two feet high showing that the southeast crag was still rising. The floor of the east gulch appeared very low as though overflow into it were imminent. The southwest pond was crusted over, there was bubble fountaining under the isthmus bounding it on the west and a fountain noise came from the tunnel at its southeast corner. There was no hissing from the blow hole above. A large spatter dome stood on the bank of the pond northeast and in general its border was from six to eight feet above the lava within. At 11:30 a. m. rising lava overflowed the crust on the pond from west to east. The west cone ridge and west inner cliff of the lake appeared higher as though rising from the crags. Under the face of this cliff was a cavernous grotto probably where the west tunnel emerges at the lake. The northwest cone area was whitened, smoky and very hot. At noon there were fountains in the center region of the main lake and against the north and east sides of the southwest pond. There was only sluggish inflow to the tunnel at the southeast corner of this pond. The northwest crag now appeared level with the edge of the pit.

On Tuesday, January 8, at 1:30 p. m. there were twelve fountains active in the southeast arm and the lake was some ten feet below the inner bench. The north arm was crusted and the pit smoky. The southwest pond at 2:50 p. m. showed a margin 10 feet high and several active fountains. About this time there was a fall of rock from the central crag. At 6 p. m. the lake had risen about five feet and there was great activity at the southeast grottoes and swift rushing to the tunnel there.

On January 9 at 4:30 p. m. the lake was high and the southeast inner bench only one foot above it. The southeast point was five feet above it. Thin crusts covered the lake and there was swift streaming to the southeast tunnel, now very active. In the morning this tunnel had been quiet. The east ledge was now much higher than the southeast shelf and this lift was seen to extend along the inner cliff bounding the northeast floor on the lake side, clear around to the northwest crag. The fume was rather dense. Occasionally large fountains broke out in the channel leading to the southeast cove.

On January 10 at 2:30 p. m. the floor of the east gulch was found to be flooded for a long distance in the direction of the east station and the southeast inner bench showed fresh overflows. There was the same swift streaming to the southeast tunnel. At 2:40 p. m. a portion of the bench at the southeast cove collapsed, started many fountains and immediately thereafter there was subsidence of about three feet in the southeast arm. The southeast tunnel sprayed and fountained violently but the north arm remained covered with crust.

On January 11 at noon the inner bench was seen to be built up so as to make the southeast shelf much lower than the cliff above it as seen from the south station. A new twelve-foot driblet cone with a sharp pointed summit had been built at the northwest cone locality and occasional puffs were heard from it. There were glowing and puffing cracks at the base of the west driblet cone and steady hissing was heard in that vicinity. There were new festooned overflows from the northwest cove to the base of the west shelf and a long driblet flow had poured from the northwest cone to this shelf and then northward along its base for 300 feet. There were other fresh overflows from the southwest pond to the south valley and the southwest pond had contracted in size. The tunnel locality southeast of it showed glowing cracks which hissed, and sulphur stain. The west cone ridge and all the crags continued to rise. New crevasses had formed between the west and northwest cones and a great open crack extended northward from the latter along the western base of the old west crag mass.

The inner bench of the lake in general was about four feet high and around the southwest pond six feet high including a considerable rampart. Cracking and foundering was in progress at the north cove, polygonal skins moved with a rapid current in the southeast arm, there was swift rush to the southeast tunnel, dome grottoes rose above the coves and individual rocks were falling on the sides away from the lake of the several crags and ledges. This all showed that rapid upward movement was in progress. The noise of central fountains was continuous. There were solfataric smoking areas southwest of the southwest pond and south of the northwest cone. Smoke also rose from the floor opposite the northwest cove indicating the presence of the old tunnel below connecting that cove with the northwest cone conduit. There was also dense smoke from the central steeple and the north smoking crag. The east island crag now appeared unquestionably the highest object in the pit, and the east ledge appeared nearly level with the east station. The current was now out of the north arm into the southeast arm and occasional fountains in the latter would migrate around the southeast point and expend themselves against the south side of the southeast crag with swirling and very swift currents.

Measurements on this day, Friday, January 11, 1918, at 1 p. m., made the depression of the lake 57 feet below the southeast edge of Halemaumau and the bench of last overflow two feet higher. The east island crag was now above the rim of the pit 30 feet, the central crag 28 feet and the southeast crag 2 feet. The east ledge was below the rim 7 feet. These figures indicated that the lake had risen in six days 6 feet, the east island crag 13 feet and the central crag 11 feet. The crags had thus maintained their rapid rate of rising but the lake had slowed down. Since December 21, that is in three weeks, the southeast crag had risen 25 feet and the east ledge 31 feet.

In the Whitney Laboratory of Seismology for the week ending at 2 p. m. January 11, 1918, two small local earthquake shocks from origins not very near Kilauea were registered about 4:50 p. m. January 5, and about 3:02 a. m. January 7. Microseismic motion increased during the week and volcanic vibration remained slight, increasing a little. Tilt strong to the north and stronger to the east reached a maximum January 8-10 and declined on the 11th.

January 19, 1918.

During the week ending Friday, January 18, 1918, the lava column of Halemaumau has continued to rise, the lake averaging one and a half feet per day and the crags two feet per day. The east floor, where so many people descended during the summer, is now a mighty crag upheaved above the edge of the pit quite like the east crag of a year ago, and blocking the view of the lake. The rising of the week has proceeded by alternations of inflation of the lakes and rapid liftings of the crags, the latter, as before, rising more than the lake. The overflowings of the latter are small and insignificant in comparison to the bulk of new space occupied by the whole mass. Vast swellings-up of the bench magma under the floors, causing intumescence and gaping crevasses, indicate how large a part of the rise is due to this heavy mass. The bench magma fills the pit from side to side, makes the bottom of the shallow lake, and occupies a much greater area within the pit walls than the lake. In the middle of the great central crag there is one peak which has repeatedly risen, toppled southward and fallen. This appears to be the top of a rising pencil of the bench magma, like the Pelee spine in Martinique, less viscous than the shells around it, and so rising faster. Probably these shells are concentric, rising least near the outer walls, or even there subsiding in part. The bottom of the northeast valley is again far below the level of the lake, just as it was in May, 1917.

At 12:15 p. m. on Saturday, January 12, the inner bench southeast was three feet above the lake, the streaming was rapid around the bend to the southeast tunnel but the central region was quiet. At 2:30 there were eight traveling fountains migrating toward the tunnel where there was violent effervescence with rumbling. At 4:15 p. m. a block from the southeast crag fell into the lake and started great activity in the southeast arm. At 6:30 the lake had risen level with the east gulch bench.

On January 13 at 1:45 p. m. looking from the northwest the lake magma of the north arm was seen to be ten feet below the northwest floor, the north arm was quiet and crusted over and smoke in that region was thick. Looking from the north the east island crag out in the center of the pit appeared fully 30 feet higher than the north inner cliff and the northwest crag was also somewhat higher than this cliff. At 2:30 p. m. the maximum activity as usual was in the southeast cove with swift streaming toward the tunnel there. At 3 p. m. a heavy slide of rocks fell from the east summit of the central crag with much noise. At this time the southwest pond was crusted over and quiet.

On January 14 at 12:30 p. m. the lake was about ten feet below the inner bench and the latter along the east island shore showed horizontal spatter lines below and a lumpy rampart above. A large dome had been built on the south side of the central cove. There was strong rush to the southeast tunnel but elsewhere the lake was quiet. The northwest cove recently obliterated through extension of the northwest floor which probably arched over it, was found on this day to have collapsed open again to a wide and deep cove which greatly widened the north arm of the lake. In the middle of the cove a pile of crusts made an island. At its west shore the floor was swollen up and cracked. Such swelling was very conspicuous in the region which may now be called the west cone ridge, an area of intumescence extending from the west cone to the west crag mass. Here the rising had been so rapid that the west cone was now level with the west shelf and the area around it was cracked and whitened. The west and northwest cones were glowing and hissing and two smaller cones had been built in line next south of the latter. The north cove spatter dome had an open glowing gash on its summit. The west bench of the east island mass was deeply crevassed. The high crag of this mass is an upright slab, thin in the southwest-northeast direction and very wide at right angles to this. The northeast floor had now become a table crag fully 1100 feet long including the east ledge, the northeast peak and the north smoke crag, all of these now level with the edge of Halemaumau. The southwest pond had diminished in size and the tunnel southeast of it was now surmounted with an open ragged pot glowing within a half-dome of spatter and stalactites built above it. There were no fresh overflows, the strong rising being confined to the crags.

On January 15 the crags were so high that practically all of them were visible when seen through a telescope from the Observatory. This included long stretches of the east ledge, the north smoke cliff and pinnacles of the northeast peak. The fume was very thin. At 2:30 p. m. the southeast overflow bench was one foot above the lake which was quiet with very disagreeable sulphurous fumes arising from the southeast grotto. At 3:45 p. m. the lake was flush with the bench and there was much fountaining at the base of the southeast crag. There were also central fountains in the southeast arm.

On January 16 at 2:30 p. m. the southeast inner bench was three feet high, the southeast cove was active and there were fountains in the southeast arm. The continued lifting of the east crag mass had undermined the new shore bench at the east cove so that it had completely collapsed along with the spatter dome at the east tunnel. There had also been falls of bench matter at the southeast tunnel. From the south it was seen that similar collapsing had taken place at the pot over the tunnel adjacent to the southwest pond on its southeast side and there was now a glowing cavity there some ten feet in diameter. At 5:10 p. m. a portion of the southeast cove bench fell in and the lake was brimming. At 5:20 it overflowed the bench from the east gulch southward.

On January 17 at 2:15 p. m. the great activity at the southeast tunnel had ceased and the lake was high at the new bench level. There was much activity in the central cove and in a new grotto south of the central channel. Some very large boulders fell from the central crag which was continually scaling off, this indicating motion there. A grotto under the southeast crag was boiling vigorously and spurting. From the southwest station at 2:45 p. m. the southwest pond was seen to be crusted but the tunnel grotto was puffing with great activity. At 3 p. m. the pond subsided a few feet and fountains broke out there. Looking northward the lake was seen to be very quiet except in the north cove grotto. Dense smoke rose from the bench southwest of the southwest pond.

Measurements on Friday, January 18, 1918, at 11 a. m., determined the depression of the lake to be 47 feet below the rim of Halemaumau. The east ledge was now 8 feet above the rim, the east island 43 feet and the central crag 40 feet above the rim. In seven days the lake had risen 10 feet, the central crag 12 feet, the east island crag 13 feet and the east ledge 15 feet. The ledges had thus moved much faster than the lake and the maximum rising was under the great northeast floor area.

On this day the conspicuous feature was the east ledge which had so risen that the whole depression under the 1894 bench was cut off from the view of the southeast station while from the east station this ledge cut off the view of the lake except through the east gulch. This gulch had become a deep canyon leading to the V-shaped valley which now extends along nearly a half of the circumference of the pit at the base of the walls on the northeast. What had been the floor there was now tilted up at 35°, the great northeast crevasses were closed by the back pressure and this northeast ledge duplicates the 1894 ledge on a much greater scale.

In like manner the southern area had been lifted bodily and even the new south valley flows were tilted southward and swollen up along great north-south crevasses which gape open from a point under the south station across the back of the south crag and up to the central crag. This area is thus swollen up along a north-south axis. Similar swelling had continued at the west cone ridge, the general surface of which was now level with the floor of the west shelf and both the west and northwest cones were now above that level. A line of pressure ridge extended eastward from the west cone. Two new driblet peaks had formed on the north side of the northwest cone. The shores of the southwest pond and southeast cove had both been lifted. This lifting of the southwest pond basin along with the adjacent central crag is a relation precisely like what the northwest pond was to the west crag mass of November and later, 1916. The phenomenon shows that the conduit and sinkhole wells are themselves warped, lifted or depressed with the movement of the bench magma. The bench at the southeast point was upraised and there were now three benches in the profile of the southeast crag above the actual lake rim which at the time was about two feet high. Another evidence of new swelling appeared across the east island mass along a southeast-northwest axis, the broken bench on the east cove side being upraised in the middle with the two pieces tilted respectively northeast and southwest. The shores of the central region of the lake were now a complex of benches lifted to various heights. The east summit of the central crag mass showed a new proturberance toppling southward and avalanches fell from its summit. It appeared ready to fall at any moment. This was at precisely the same point where similar peaks fell twice a few weeks ago. It has been replaced in the meantime, although the west summit immediately adjacent has remained unchanged.

On this day the southwest pond was crusted over, but there was a break-up and temporary subsidence of a few feet at noon. There was a similar breaking-up in the main lake. The tunnel heap southeast of the southwest pond no longer showed an open pot and the place was quiet except for some hissing. The southeast cove was rather quiet, the southeast dome grotto high, glowing and hissing, and there was vigorous streaming and fountaining in the southeast arm. Rocks were sliding at the east gulch. There was an active grotto at the end of the west arm, probably at the tunnel under the pressure ridge which heads toward the west cone. Streaming was northeastward from the west arm and northward in the main lake.

In the Whitney Laboratory for the week ending at 2 p. m. Friday, January 18, 1918, three small local earthquakes have been registered all apparently of origin near the volcano. Two were on January 13 at 1:17 p. m. and 1:36 p. m., and the other, felt in Volcano House district, happened on the 17th at 3:18 a. m. There was a vague teleseism indicated at 7:07 a. m. on the 14th, the phases masked by microseisms. Microseisms have increased during the week, volcanic vibration has been normal. East tilt, which was very strong last week, has decreased but tilt to the south has become very strong.

January 26, 1918.

During the week ending January 25, 1918, the recent excessive rise of the lava culminated January 24, the lake reaching its limit with overflows the day before. On the 25th subsidence set in, the lake sank over twenty feet, there were profound changes in the crags, the great east island tower crumbled into the center of the lake, new islets and coves arose in the northern region and the crags generally settled to lower levels. The change was heralded in advance by whirlpool action and increased streaming and fountaining towards the southeast. All of this checks perfectly with what was to be expected when the solstice effect of sharp rising had expended itself and the reverse movement begins on approach to the equinox. It will be remembered that just such a change came at the end of January last year and it is remarkable how closely accordant in level the average maximum height has been, as reached by the liquid lava in the pit January, 1910; January, 1912; January, 1917; May, 1917, and January, 1918. All of these were just before or just after the solstice. The maximum height and volume of the visible bench magma, however, has increased greatly and progressively with the last three of these culminations, so that the mighty crags now lifted high above the rim of Halemaumau surpass anything of the kind seen here for over thirty years.

On Saturday, January 19, 1918, at 3 p. m., the inner bench was about 10 feet above the liquid lava and this may have been largely by rise of the bench magma, for the rampart material at the southeast cove had fallen leaving vertical walls and a similar effect was observed in the southwest pond. This was no longer a separate pond for the collapse had again opened the channel connecting with the main lake. Streaming was slow and the north arm was quiet and crusted over.

On January 20, at 1 p. m., the lake was heavily crusted and unchanged in apparent depression. The south bench was smoking heavily. At 1:30 p. m. a pronounced collapse was seen to have taken place in the southeast cove developing a new grotto and another fountaining cavern was noisily active under the southeast crag. Inspection of the high east island tower from the southeast showed that much of the summit region on the side toward the center of the lake had fallen away, greatly changing its profile. During the afternoon the lake was quiet but in the evening strong rising and increased gas pressure appeared and at 6:30 p. m. the surface of the lake was flush with the southeast bench. At 7 p. m. the lake overflowed at the east gulch.

On the morning of Monday, January 21, from 9:30 o'clock on the lake began a succession of powerful overflows which were destined to recur at intervals during three days. The overflows on this morning were dominantly through the east gulch into the great northeast valley, but there were others from the southwest pond into the south valley. It was evident also that there had been fresh flows recently from the northwest cove, making a new area of pooled lava which had cracked and foundered extending from the northwest crag along the base of the west shelf to near the northwest cone. Since that overflow the whole northwest floor had risen and tilted westward so as to make a new cliff over the lake. The west floor clear across the pit from the west cone ridge northward was thus another unit tilted away from the center by being swollen up from below. The west shelf above this floor was now low, the west cone was hissing and the great crevasse on the east side of the row of northwest driblet cones was filled with active lava making an elongate pond which exhibited a splashing grotto five or six feet below the base of the northwest cones. The latter stood on the western lip of the chasm. This new appearance of a western pond reaffirms the persistence there of a conduit well.

The great spectacle of this day was the torrent pouring like a mountain brook of liquid fire through the east gulch from 9:30 a. m. to 1:30 p. m. continuously. The flood moved as a rill some 300 feet and then pooled for a length of 600 feet or more under the 1894 bench. The torrent was from five to ten feet wide, hemmed in by a congealed strip on each side and moved at a rate estimated at ten miles per hour from the progress of crusts floating down the current. The under-rush beneath the surface may have been somewhat faster. The torrent seemed to erode its bed of bowlders, for the slope of rocks on the east ledge side was continually slipping so that on one occasion a tumble dammed the stream and made a temporary cascade.

There were six or more great fountaining areas in the lake, notably on the north, west, northeast, southeast and at the northwest and southwest ponds. The southeast shelf stood only about four feet above the lake with a great fountain splashing over it as on May 31 last. The resemblance to the May culmination was remarkable in other respects, such as the revival of the western cones, the formation and filling of the great northeastern valley and the uplift of the east ledge. On this morning the inner bench overflowed at the east cove and there were other flows at the northeast and central coves, the flood at the latter filling the depression west of the southeast crag. The floods filled crevasses about the southern margin of the southeast cove and new chasms filled with lava appeared in the direction of the south tunnel. The southeast crag had been tilting northward and showed a fresh broken wall and talus on that side. The core of the central crag again stood out as a turret ready to fall southward and the steeple east of it exhibited once more a sharp needle-like summit while its south face was red, smooth and perhaps striated. Rocks were tumbling into the north pit and other falls indicated instability and motion in the crags always away from the central region.

The flood into the northeast valley produced only carbon odors above. This flood did not continue long into the afternoon and the pool there was not deep like the one of May 31, 1917, but was rather a very long pahoehoe flow with festooned upper surface and toes percolating the bowlders.

Measurements on January 21 at noon determined the lake depression to be 40 feet, and the elevation of the several peaks above the rim of Halemaumau to be as follows: East island crag 40 feet, central crag 38 feet, north smoke cliff 11 feet and east ledge 8 feet. In three days the lake had risen 7 feet, the east island crag had lost 3 feet, the central crag had lost 2 feet and the east ledge was unchanged.

On January 22 at 3 p. m. the lake was flush with the bench southeast. At 3:45 p. m. slow overflow of the bench began and by 4 o'clock the flow was vigorous, pouring into the east gulch. At 4:30 the flood was level with the southeast shelf and in places overflowed it. At 11 p. m. there were extensive overflows. Throughout all of this, however, the filling of the northeast valley was only moderate, the upper surface of the flow there remaining ropy and festooned and at no time did the pool become deep enough to crack and founder as in May last. The 1894 bench remained high above the new filling and cracks in the latter indicated that the bottom of the valley subsided somewhat after the flows cooled.

On Wednesday, January 23, at noon, the lake stood two feet below its new southeastern rim. The southeast shelf was nearly completely buried under fresh flows and the new bench from lake to cliff was twice as wide as the southeast shelf had been. The flow had poured along the base of the wall southward to a point under the south station. Glow persisted in the cracks of the fresh flows. The depth of the northeast valley appeared unchanged. The southeast cove was wider and longer and south of it was a great uplifted tumble which restrained the cove from overflowing in that direction.

The lake was 22 feet below the southeast station. At 1:30 p. m. overflows began at the east gulch, southeast ledge, around the base of the old west crag mass and probably from the southwest pond also. The flow through the east gulch was not prolonged but the flooding southward was considerable. Back of the rampart at the central cove was a depression much below lake level which eventually received flows.

The southwest channel was open and when the circuit of the pit was made fresh flows were found on the floor extending southward from the southwest pond. A flat-topped islet stood in the northwest cove. The west cone had given vent to a considerable flow southward but the lava in the northwest chasm pond was quiet. The activity in the main lake showed high gas pressure, ballooning skins and flames, occasional great central fountains and five or six grotto fountains.

The crags were higher than ever and all of them above the edge of the pit except the old western crag mass. A great turret hung out ready to fall from the southern side of the summit of the central crag. As seen from the north the northwest crag and north smoke crag appeared much alike with a notch between them.

At 9 p. m. a sudden subsidence in the southeast cove developed a standing rapid at its narrowing entrance channel and a whirlpool was produced on the north side of this rapid which created a marvelous display for ten minutes.

Seen from Uwekahuna bluff at 8 p. m. the pit was an extraordinary spectacle, the crags outlined by the illumined fumes and the main lake in full view with streaming from the southwest arm to the southeast arm and a fountain against the western base of the east island crag. Glow could be seen at two places near the western cones. On this day the fountaining noises could be heard, and the splash of the fountains seen, even from Volcano House.

On January 24 at 3 p. m. there were fountains in the north arm, the southwest arm was crusted, fumes were thin and the inner bench northeast was about 5 feet high. There was fountaining at the west and southwest tunnels. At 3:30 p. m. the southeast arm was crusted and rising slowly, the southeast grotto showed a flaming pot above and there was active fountaining under the southeast crag.

From 4 to 5 p. m. the lake was 5 feet below the new southeast bench, there was streaming to the southeast tunnel, occasional migratory central fountains formed and streaming in the main lake was from the south and the north, the two currents meeting at lines of fountaining west of the east island mass. The southeastward streaming in the southeast arm occasionally became masked by crusting. During temporary subsidences wide overhanging margins two to three feet high revealed stalactites and glowing walls. Rocks were moving in the east gulch and on the northwest side of the northwest crag. The pond back of the central cove occasionally broke up with cracking and foundering and there was revealed a narrow channel leading to this pond on the west side of the southeast cove.

This time was the climax of swelling upward of the crags. On this day the north and northwest crags rose more than the others and the southeast crag had tilted over northward, its tip had fallen off, the southeast point was tilted up 8 or 10 feet above the lake. There was a fresh flow along the southeast bench and through a gap in the uplifted area under the south station, pouring thence westward the whole length of the south valley to join other festooned flows fresh from the southwest pond. The break or gap through to the central cove pond from the southeast cove appeared to be the crevasse formed by the overturning northward of the southeast crag mass. The west cone ridge had lifted higher. The floor bordering the northwest and west sides of the north arm was 8 feet high and the islet, of similar height, stood in the northwest cove as a mushroom. The north cove bank was lifted into a cliff with the spatter dome of recent formation on top.

On January 25 there was a heavy rainstorm, but the lake was reported sinking, and the east island crag crumbled to a ruin.

The seismographs of the Whitney Laboratory for the week ending at 2 p. m. January 25, 1918, have recorded seven local earthquake shocks as follows: Small shock, 7:55 a. m. Jan. 19; on Jan. 21 at 11:23 a. m., 12:59 p. m., 2:29 p. m. (the strongest), and 2:40 p. m., all small; on Jan. 23 at 4:35 p. m. and on Jan. 24 at 8:46 a. m., these also small. Microseismic motion was strong early in the week and decreased later. Volcanic vibration has been moderate, with slight increase in spasms after the 24th. Tilting increased northward and eastward, the south tilt becoming extreme Jan. 24-25. There have been thunder, lightning, hail and southwest gales during the week, extremely heavy rainfall amounting to nearly eight inches, and heavy snow has fallen on Mauna Loa and Mauna Kea.

February 2, 1918.

During the week ending Friday, February 1, 1918, the subsidence which began on January 25 continued for three days and then the lava turned and rose again after reaching a depression of approximately 50 feet below the rim of the pit. The rising has been interrupted by unusually strong pulsations of sinking and at the end of the week the depression of the liquid lake was 44 feet below the rim and the crags were stationary. The sinking spell destroyed the great East Island tower, produced strong overturning northward of the southeast crag, developed a new pond west of that crag, opened the channel to the southwest pond and developed a remarkable chasm extending from the northwest pond to the northwest cove. The topography of the north arm has completely changed.

On Saturday, January 26, from 3 to 6 p. m., a visit to the pit after and during the prolonged rainstorm which had been in progress for three days, revealed the fact that a change to subsidence had taken place, foreshadowed by the southeastern whirlpools of January 23 and the culminating rupture and overturning of the southeast crag January 24. The lake was now 30 feet below the new southeast bench, only a small low horn remained of the east island tower, and the other crags had lost height. There was vigorous southeastward streaming, border fountains surrounded the southeast cove, a cavern grotto had formed under the gateway leading to the central pond, the latter occupying the depression west of the southeast crag and showing a crusted surface 15 feet above the liquid lava of the cove. The southwest pond lay 30 feet beneath its bordering walls, showed a tunnel grotto at its northeast corner, and hot blue fumes southeast. The west cone ridge appeared lower and showed a glowing heap south of the northwest cone. At 3:20 p. m. the north arm as seen from the northwest exhibited a sudden subsidence, breaking up of crusts, violent recession of the lava to a central depression across shoals which emerged at the northeast cove and there was intense and noisy fountaining. High glowing margins were revealed. This episode was followed by a crusting-over of the lava with grotto fountaining at the north and slow rising.

At 4:30 p. m. the writer climbed to the summit of the north smoke crag and found great changes in the north arm region. This region was now the largest pond area by far, and was separated from the central region by a narrow channel. The northwest cove was greatly extended along the line of the chasm leading to the northwest cone and a high cliff had been lifted west of it. There was a new cove in the midst of the west crag mass, two peninsulas had been built out westward from the east island mass and three islands had formed in the northern lake thus isolated. The narrow channel forming its outlet southward occasionally became the scene of a steep torrent when the lava of the southeast arm subsided faster than that to the north.

At 4:30 p. m. the streaming was from the northwest cove to the active north grotto, and otherwise out of the north lake and out of the southwest arm, the two currents uniting to pour into the southeast arm. During sinking spells the crusted lava of the north lake showed cracking and foundering and the southward streaming through the narrows became almost a cascade.

The new peninsulas adjacent to the east island mass were probably built from the debris when the east island crag crumbled down. Probably the north lake bottom rose to form the islands owing to a reaction and settling back of the crags after their recent elevation.

The southeast crag had subsided bodily, lost more of its summit and a new inner bench against it had been built five feet above the lake surface. A similar lower platform bordered the east cove and the north lake. There was one heavy fall of rock into the lake from the northeast corner of the southeast crag. The great northeast crag ridge remained elevated and at the same high angle of tilt. Glow was still visible in the southeast overflows.

On January 27 at 2:30 p. m. the lake was still low and crusted except for two fountains in the southeast cove. Much of the inner bench under the east island mass had fallen away. The southwest arm was also quiet. At 3 p. m. the central pond showed two small cones, one of which was puffing, and a pot with lava three feet below the bench around it. At 6:30 p. m. the pond had grown larger and was fountaining in two places.

On January 28 the lake was low and quiet, there were some rock falls, little fountain activity and in the evening flames were abundant.

On Tuesday, January 29, 1918, the lake at the southeast cove was 20 feet below the southeast shelf, subsidence was in progress, there were many fountains in the southeast arm and a few in the north lake. At 3 p. m. the central pond, now a circular pit 20 feet deep and 20 feet across with lava at the lake level, was crusted over and hissing slightly, showing glow through cracks of the crust. The southwest pond was in process of breaking up with vigorous fountaining and streaming and the grotto at the south tunnel corner was surmounted by a puffing cone honeycombed with flaming apertures. At 4 p. m. both the southeast cove and southwest pond were 15 feet below the floors. There was the usual activity southeast with slow streaming, occasional central fountains and border fountains at the southeast grotto and the southeast tunnel. The middle of the lake was quiet, streaming was northward from the west arm and the southwest channel was open. The southwest pond was crusted over, sluggishly cracking and foundering, there was a fountain against its east bank and the skin heaved outside of the south tunnel grotto. Both the southwest and southeast coves showed a new spatter margin three feet above the lake indicating a rise and the crags were higher.

The lake was pulsating strongly. At 4:30 p. m. there was sudden subsidence leaving glowing margins three feet high and violent fountaining ensued, one of the fountains in the southeast cove migrating northward and reversing the direction of streaming for a few minutes. There were violent turbulence and cracking of crusts. Then the lake recovered. Under the heavy rain the vaporing of the recent hot flow surfaces was conspicuous and millions of steam tassels formed on the crusted portions of the lake. At 6 p. m. the lake was within one foot of its new spatter margin.

On January 30 the lava was reported very quiet and apparently sinking. On Thursday, January 31, at noon, the lake was 20 feet below the southeast bench and rising, with a new construction rim about it. A new floor and spatter dome appeared at the east cove and fresh overflow surfaces covered wide areas around the north lake and the islands and peninsulas there. The southeast chasm leading from the southeast cove to the central pond had widened. As seen from the south-southeast the profile of the gap between the steeple and the central crag had remarkable U-shape and the laminae west of this gap showed tendency to flare upward in their bedding. The south face of the steeple appeared smoothly striated vertically as though scraped by pushing upward against a fault surface. The southwest pond was low and surrounded by inner cliffs. The southeast crag showed a fresh fall of rock from the tip of its upraised southeast escarpment. This crag has recently changed position horizontally and moved northward owing to the gradual shift of its upper part west and north and the continual rebuilding of its lower part at the southeast point. Its upper escarpments show west tilt but its lower portions have been tilted northward.

The swelling up of the west ridge had now increased to such extent that a wide chasm had been developed extending all the way from the northwest cone to the west cone, the group of driblet spiracles of the northwest cone standing on its west margin. The chasm was probably increased in size by collapse of its margins when the recent subsidence withdrew the lava of the northwest pond. The west ridge on both sides of this chasm was now a swollen dome with the old west crag mass on its east flank.

The north arm had now become a large roundish lake full of islands and flats and the channel with southward streaming lava leading out of it was now a greatly constricted curving ditch almost separating it off from the southern arms. The remains of the east island turret appeared from the northwest like a narrow upright tower of great slenderness. The central crags towered up as high peaks but the northeastern crag ridge appeared lower and the lake appeared to be encroaching on the east island and western crag masses. There was a tumbled cove opening at the lake end of the west tunnel and the west cone appeared broken.

Streaming was rapid to the southeast, there were central fountains, border fountains played at the southeast cove, crusts showed tendency to balloon upward over rising gas from beneath, fumes were rather thin and there was occasional subsidence of a few feet with accelerated streaming. The islands in the north arm stood only five feet above the lake where a few fountains burst irregularly. At 2:30 p. m. the east cove bench was three feet above the lake and rising was in progress. Two fountains were in action at the central pond and the southwest pond was lively, especially at the south tunnel grotto. At 5 p. m. the lake was brimming level with the new bench at the east cove.

On Friday, February 1, 1918, at 4:30 p. m., the lake was high and rising, so that by 5:30 p. m. it was brimming level with the new marginal bench everywhere and overflowing it in places. The noise indicated high gas pressure which ballooned the crust and made many flames. Central fountains formed and migrated with the current. At 4:30 p. m. a heavy fall of rock from the north side of the southeast crag into the lake produced intense fountaining so that the rising hot gas started a whirlwind which carried up flakes of the broken lava and made a noisy display for the greater part of a minute. The fume was very thin, the crags in general remained stationary and there was much luminous fountaining in the evening, especially in the northern, central and southeastern regions.

At the time of subsidence, Saturday, January 26, at 4 p. m., rough measurements made in a rainstorm determined the depression of the lake to be 48 feet. Measurements on Friday, February 1, 1918, at 5 p. m., determined the lake depression at the southeast cove to be 44 feet below the south station. The elevation of the central crag above the south station was 46 feet and of the east ledge 17 feet. The lake thus from its high level of 22 feet below the rim, January 23, subsided in three days 26 feet and thereafter in six days recovered 4 feet. For the crags during the interval January 21-February 1 inclusive, eleven days, there was moderate rising, 8 feet for the central crag and 9 feet for the east ledge. The net movement of the lake for the same interval is slight subsidence (4 feet), for it must be remembered that the lake rose suddenly 18 feet January 21-23.

The Whitney Laboratory instruments have registered for the week ending at 2 p. m. February 1, 1918, four slight local earthquake shocks and one distant strong shock. The local earthquakes were at 11:50 p. m. January 25, 12:25 p. m. January 26, 8:37 p. m. January 28, and 5:52 a. m. February 1, the latter stronger than the others and from an origin farther from the Observatory. The teleseism was at 11:09 a. m. (H. S. T.), Wednesday, January 30, 1918, from an origin at least 4300 miles from the Observatory. Microseisms increased slightly January 27 and have decreased to rather feeble vibrations since. Volcanic vibration increased in spasms January 31-February 1. Motion of tilt increased strongly south and moderately west the early part of the week, with vigorous recovery north and east January 29-31, followed by southwest tilt again on February 1.

Very respectfully,
T. A. JAGGAR, JR.,
Director.

THE INDEX OF DANGER FROM VOLCANOES.

Lecture to Associate Engineers of Hawaii, Hilo, Jan. 16, 1918, by T. A. Jaggar.

When I was asked to speak on this subject I was given a large order. To know the index of danger means to know the subject more thoroughly than anyone has yet accomplished. The topic is an interesting one, however, and within the range of a brief discussion if my hearers will understand by it the indications which volcanoes in certain moods yield as premonitory symptoms of an outbreak dangerous to human beings. I do not understand the subject to include index of danger from earthquakes, nor can I include here a discussion of means of preventing disasters. This I must leave for the present to you engineers.

The index of danger is not quite identical with the index of eruption. For there may be great eruptions without any danger, like those on the summit of Mauna Loa, and there may be great danger from a volcano without any eruption, as in the case of the terrific earthquake on Epomeo volcano in Ischia in 1883. This was believed to be strictly volcanic, an abortive effort on the part of an internal lava column, wedging upward in a fissure which suddenly yielded without, however, releasing the volcanic fluids. The responsibility placed on an observer, therefore, to predict danger demands first foreknowledge of explosive, effusive or abortive eruption, and secondly the effect of the phenomenon on humanity.

With this preamble, and having in mind our Hawaiian volcanoes in particular, let us examine the meaning of danger, and then the expectancy of danger for Hawaii.

Danger means

(1) Explosion and suffocation, des-

truction by burial of houses under sand and stones, destruction by tornado blasts from a crater, or loss of life by direct bombardment from flying or falling stones. Falling in of roofs may be occasioned by gradual accumulation of dust or sand at some distance from the volcano.

(2) Outrush of lava from old or new crater vents, destruction of lands, houses, roads, tanks, fences, cattle, pigs, horses or men by trapping between two converging lava flows, by direct overwhelming of lava flows rapidly or by slow overwhelming through months of pushing lava. Lava flow is rarely a source of loss of life. Secondary disaster may be caused by forest fire, by damming or drying up of water-supply or by blocking of indispensable highways such as railroads.

(3) Earthquake accompanying eruption, great shocks sometimes occurring just before or during a volcanic outbreak. Falling masonry, land or mud slides, falling rocks from cliffs, wreckage from gradually increasing small shocks which have weakened buildings —all the usual earthquake effects may take place in such volcanic earthquakes just as in any other shocks, destroying life and property.

(4) Tidal waves, that is, great shock waves forced up in the sea, either through an earthquake under the sea bottom, through a volcanic convulsion in the sea bottom like a sudden explosion, or through a volcanic blast downward to the shore from a crater on the land which pushes the water away from the strand and so causes a back-wave which washes the shore disastrously. Tidal waves are worst on a shelving flat shore like Hilo bay, but they may happen on a steep off-shore bottom like Puna or Kona if earthquake faults on the land coöperate by actually depressing the land a few feet, and so drown permanently a stretch of shore. This happened on the Puna shore in 1868.

Hawaii has had **Class 1, explosion and volcanic blast,** in 1790, from Kilauea crater, when the soldiers of Keoua and their families and cattle were suffocated and burned. A repetition of that event would probably wreck the Volcano and Crater Hotels, the settlement at 29-miles, the military camp and Ainahou, the government road from west of Uwekahuna to about 26-miles, the crater road, and destroy timber and water tanks for a radius approximately six miles from Halemaumau in all directions. According to the wind direction at the time the damage would extend farther to leeward than to windward. Fine sand would fall at Glenwood, and dust would fall at Hilo during winter weather of calms and southerly winds. During trade winds the heavy ash falls would be in the Kau direction. The damage at 29-miles would probably be much less if the trade wind from east-northeast were blowing strongly. If it were really a great eruption the ash might fall on Maui and Oahu.

This Territory has had **Class 2, lava flow,** as the common and invariable accompaniment of the greater outbursts of Mauna Loa, Kilauea, Hualalai and Haleakala for hundreds of years past. The flows have run from five to sixty miles, have burst out far inland or near the sea or under the sea, have built out shorelines, and have destroyed lands, houses, roads, forests and filled river beds. The last land flow from Kilauea was in 1894 in the crater; the last from Mauna Loa was in 1916 in Kahuku and Honomalino. The last flow to break out on Kilauea mountain away from the crater was in 1868, rising through cracks in the Kau desert.

The same line of cracks extends past the crater towards the east point of the island crossing the Hilo road at about 8-miles, in the jungle to the north of the Olaa mill. There is at this moment a tremendous gas-and-lava pressure in Halemaumau, a pit at the summit of a flat inner cone or slag heap within Kilauea crater. Considered as an expansive fluid filling cracks, the apex of this lava column (the central crag) is now 30 feet above the rim of Halemaumau, 260 feet above the foot of the trail where it strikes the lava below the Volcano House, 600 feet above the bottom of Kilauea Iki and some 3400 feet above the rift line at 8-miles. A sudden release along the rift northeastward instead of southwestward as in 1868, would produce a series of Hilo earthquakes and a lava flood in the Olaa direction. 1840 produced just this effect on another rift line, namely Kapoho, and as lava floods at various places from Makaopuhi to the east-northeast, some of which reached the sea. Flows from Mauna Loa have twice threatened Hilo in the last seventy years and the 1881 flow reached and diverted the Waialama River in Waiakea, and gulches formerly filled with water were filled with a fiery flood described by Coan as moving half a mile a day. The 1855 flow poured into the upper Wailuku River and stopped five and a half miles from Hilo.

Hawaii has had **Class 3, earthquakes,** as the accompaniment of its eruptions. They have usually been numerous and small. In 1868 they were numerous and large, both on Kilauea and on Mauna Loa, with lava flows from both volcanoes. They were terrific in Kau, accompanied at Kapapala by a destructive landslide and along the coast by a tidal wave. A repetition now of that disaster would do serious damage at Kapapala, Pahala, Hilea, Honuapo, Naalehu and Waiohinu, on the new stretch of road west of Waiohinu and possibly to the hotel buildings at Kilauea. As before, the shore villages from Punaluu eastward would suffer from both earthquake and wave. Moreover the next terrific earthquake on Hawaii is not likely to be at the same place as the last one.

Hawaii has had **Class 4, tidal waves,** principally in the 1868 crisis just mentioned, but also at other times damaging Hilo and Kahului.

In considering the menace of volcanic disaster, then, there is no reason whatever to consider this Territory immune. The little ninety years since Dibble wrote the first Hawaiian history is much too short a time for volcano statistics, for the common intervals between great crisis are in multiples of sixty-five years, as has recently been shown by Omori for Asama volcano in Japan. One hundred and thirty years is a common interval between great cataclysms at the same place. This was the period since the last catastrophe by earthquake at Messina, and by eruption and earthquake at Kagoshima, Japan. 1920 will be sixty-five years since the tremendous activity of 1855 for both Kilauea and Mauna Loa. 1920 will be one hundred and thirty years since Kilauea exploded and threw out all the great rocks which one sees near Keanakakoi, and destroyed Keoua's warriors. And we know nothing of the duration of that series of explosions, nor of the lava flows and earthquakes of the period, nor of the activity of Mauna Loa. If 1868 was frightful, and involved both volcanoes, it is probable that 1790 was much worse. It is quite possible that Hualalai and Haleakala partook of that period of activity, for Hualalai was active ten years later and Haleakala hal lava flows at the south point of Maui at some time during the experience of natives who were still living when the first missionaries came here.

I do not pretend to predict anything portentous for the year 1920, but merely call attention to the sequence, the 65-year cycle having interested us at Kilauea because of agreement with theoretical considerations based on astronomic control, as discussed in Mr. Wood's paper on cyclical variations of Kilauea activity, the Second Report of the Observatory.

The commonly cited indications of coming eruption, as summarized by Mercalli, the famous director of the Vesuvian Observatory, are as follows:

(1) Earthquakes and tremors.

(2) Elevation of the land and retirement of the sea.

(3) Subterranean noises.

(4) Rise of crater floor (the top of the lava column).

(5) Rise of temperature at vents.

(6) Increased or changed gases at fumaroles.

(7) Drying up of water.

There are not mentioned in this list three other extremely important indications, which here in Hawaii are of prime significance; namely:

(8) Interval since last eruption.

(9) Nature of action at contiguous craters.

(10) Preliminary crater eruptions antecedent by some years to final lava flow eruptions.

On examining this list in the light of experience here, we may leave aside for the present noises and temperature change, gas changes and dessication. Rearranging, we have left a list of subjects of great interest because they are all related and go to the heart of the matter, namely the lava column.

(1) Interval since last eruption.

(2) Sequence of action at nearby craters.

(3) Elevation or tilting of the land.

(4) Sequence of tremors or numbers and intensities of local earthquakes.

(6) Preliminary crater eruptions.

I cannot do more today than illustrate these briefly as applied to Mauna Loa. I believe that the principles involved are fundamental and apply to any volcanic system. By volcanic system I mean an underground group of fissures charged with lava, an individual volcano being a more or less haphazard pile of slag.

The interval since last eruption is a useful index the more we know of cycles for any particular volcanic rift. This is intimately tied up with the second subject, the action at nearby craters, for the cycle in Hawaii, for instance, includes not Mauna Loa alone, but the Mauna Loa-Kilauea system. Inspection of the chart showing the movements of Kilauea lava while Mauna Loa was erupting in 1914-16 shows that Kilauea at each Mauna Loa spasm spurted and fell, the spurt being higher and the fall lower each time, until when Mauna Loa ceased activity the lava came over to the Kilauea pit and rose to a high level and stayed there.

Such a sequence in three years typifies what may be expected of the longer-term successions The Hawaiian lava column escapes to make a lava flow nowadays about once in nine years. This 1914-16 happening was an incident of that larger succession. In like manner about once in say sixty-five years a great crisis occurs, perhaps at the end of a group of incidents which occupy fifteen years or more. Thus the 1868 crisis here culminated sixteen years of unparalleled activity in both Kilauea and Mauna Loa, with immense lava floods 1852, 1855, 1859, 1868. The 1790 crisis may have accompanied a similar prolonged activity but we have no records. And on a still longer term scale there may be still bigger events which afflict the Hawaiian Islands at intervals of centuries. The shorter intervals appear closely connected with solar control and have already been used successfully here for prediction.

The sequences in dimension and distance are frequently progressive like those in time. The 1843 flow stopped twenty-five miles from Hilo, the 1852 flow stopped 12 miles from Hilo, the 1855 flow five and a half miles from Hilo, and the 1881 flow one mile from Hilo. All emerged from the same general rift line. From 1868 to 1907 there was alternation of flows first north, then south, for each eruption, and the 1916 flow broke the sequence. The 1916 flow should have had a north vent. In 1907 and 1916, two flows in succession poured out on the south side. The north flows since 1852 have been increasingly voluminous, excepting 1899; the 1916 flow was not voluminous and the high pressure at Kilauea in 1917 and at present, unequalled since 1894, attests an incompletely relieved lava column. If a new flow on the north rift should break out near the 1852 vent, which was low, Hilo would be seriously menaced, particularly as the older flows would act as confining ridges on each side.

The question of tilting of the land is tied up with the rise of the crater floor. I have recently shown that we must consider the lava column to be a hard elastic body under great tension from gases in solution. Release pressure and the gases escape, generating heat thereby and liquefying the lava. The underground column is a slow-moving affair which, however, once in so often must expand the containing fissure to the limit of gas release. This is an eruption. The upward swelling in the fissure system may be expected to actually arch the island. Hence it has been with the keenest interest that I have watched the seismographs at Kilauea crater recording an enormous variation in the vertical, an actual plumbline shift of ten seconds of arc in the course of a few days, and still more in a permanent set of the ground in the course of months. A tidal movement of **eight-tenths of a second** is considered exceptionally large elsewhere. In general the tilt has been to the west and south during sinking lava in Halemaumau, and to the east and north during rising. The pit is southwest of the Observatory, but the dominant tilts have east and west—towards or away from Mauna Loa. With and before the Mauna Loa eruptions there were strong east tilts and after them there were west tilts. The strong east tilt in 1914 began a week before Mokuaweoweo broke out. The quantitative relation of these tilts to the measured rise and fall of the lava promises important results which may enable us anywhere to locate and time the movements of lava underground. The fact that great movements of elevation before eruption and of depression after eruption in Italian and Japanese volcanoes have been verified geodetically beyond question, lends support to the seismometric data.

I have little time to take up volcanic tremors and local earthquakes. Suffice it to say that extraordinary short-period tremors are going on all the time at Kilauea and vary in intensity. Local earthquakes increased to an enormous maximum during the lava flow period of 1916 and the 1914 outbreak of November-December was heralded by seismic spasms of thirty-four shocks in July, more in September and seventy-four in November, falling off to normal (thirteen) for December after the gas pressure was released.

With regard to rise of the crater floors and premonitory crater eruptions, these are familiar happenings in Hawaii. A monumental rise of the Halemaumau floor is now in progress with the lava towering above the edge of the pit. The Kilauea sequence since Mauna Loa became sealed suggests strongly that the lava column is expanding on this side of the system and if it follows its habit it will rise and fall in Kilauea for two or three years more, then sink away and rise to a summit eruption in Mauna Loa. This will be followed by a flank eruption two or three years later. Such was the sequence in 1896-99, 1903-07, 1914-16. The next Mokuaweoweo outbreak ought to come about 1923, followed by lava flow before 1926. It will be seen that the word "eruption" means a complicated formula when two or more vents are involved.

In conclusion I might touch upon the use to which a knowledge of the "index of danger" may be put. You will see from what I have said that the subject is dependent, like insurance, on the cyclical or statistical treatment. We need observatories in Guatemala to discover the Guatemala cycles, as distinct from the Hawaiian cycles. A volcano is a vent for something accumulating, and is regular according to rate of accumulation. Great luni-solar stresses act as trigger, but the particular district has the secret of its index equation awaiting the measurements of the investigator. Widespread use of the "index of danger" can only be made when charts and tabulations have been collected for many districts and these districts arranged in orderly series showing a common origin. That has now been done for the winds and tides and movements of the stars so that we easily predict hurricanes and neap tides and comets. The inner earth would seem to be as worthy a subject, when you consider that there are at least two great volcanic disasters a year, and once in two years a city is utterly destroyed as has just been demonstrated at Guatemala. Two years before 30,000 people were killed at Avezzano in central taly. The year before 22,000 were made homeless at Sakurajima. And in 1908 130,000 were killed in Messina in five minutes, at the base of Etna volcano.

Summary.

To summarize the index of danger for Hawaii, the following puts the matter categorically, but does not pretend to be accurate or complete. It suggests the lines of reasoning based on an all too limited experience. There is here treated, in order, **Time** or expectancy, **Intensity** as marked by symptoms, **Place** as concerning danger.

TIME.

I. A great eruptive period may occur every 130 years, may affect several volcanoes together, may last 10 years or more; — Kilauea - Hualalai 1790 - 1801 (probably Mauna Loa and Haleakala also).

II. Secondary eruptive period at the half-interval 65 years, of long duration with great lava floods. Kilauea-Mauna Loa 1840-1868.

II. Accumulation and discharge once in nine years; alternation Kilauea and Mauna Loa; alternation Mauna Loa lava-flows north and south; periods of culmination in each crater about three years.

Intervals since 1868 slowly increased, volume of discharge decreased, both craters have built up their floors and confined the lava column, present condition shows high gas pressure as though a crisis were approaching.

INTENSITY, Localized Symptoms.

For the great eruptive periods,

I. A high closed dome is likely to be constructed over Halemaumau (1850).

II. Prolonged elevation or swelling of the island measurable instrumentally probably takes place. A tilting of the ground away from the center sets in for years.

III. The crater floors progressively rise.

IV. Local earthquakes increase in temporary swarms.

V. Lava gas escapes with decreased freedom at the inner craters, possibly causing decrease of volcanic tremor recorded instrumentally.

For Individual Eruptions.

I. Kilauea lava sinking slowly, portends coming eruption of Mauna Loa.

II. Earthquake spasms on Mauna Loa follow this and increase, especially at equinox. Kilauea lava spurts up with these spasms.

III. Sharp sudden tilt away from Mokuaweoweo near solstice suggests that the summit crater will erupt in a few days.

IV. At beginning of Mokuaweoweo outbreak, seismographs show unusual motions of fling. Gas-lava fountains for some months at Mokuaweoweo, lava floods there, Kilauea spurts up and subsides in sympathy. As eruption dies away, tilt is temporarily toward the center (the tilt away recovers somewhat). This is the preliminary eruption.

V. Kilauea lava rises, equinoxial earthquake spasms continue, Mauna Loa quiet one to three years. Persistent set of tilt away from Mauna Loa, and in detail possibly **away from the flank where the lava is to flow.**

VI. Explosion near summit Mauna Loa on rift which is to yield lava flow. Excessive tilt suddenly, swarms of earthquakes where lava is to come out, lava wells up and flows out flank rift.

VII. When a crisis is indicated for other reasons, the earth strain as **equinox** approaches favors earthquakes, and as **solstice** approaches favors eruption.

VIII. After Mauna Loa flow, Kilauea rises for about four or five years.

PLACE as to Danger.

I. Expectancy of alternation makes Kilauea or Mauna Loa, respectively, more dangerous.

II. It takes the north or south rifts of Mauna Ioa, respectively, more dangerous. Danger to Hilo-Hamakua north to Kona-Kau, south.

III. Coming flow promises a localized center for earthquakes, either in spasms for a long period, or in sudden increase for an immediate crisis. The locality would be Puna, Olaa or the Kau desert for a Kilauea lava-flow; the upper Wailuku, Puu Oo or Humuula for a Hilo lava-flow; Hilea for a Kau lava-flow.

IV. To localize the place of maximum danger, the most hopeful line of investigation is to determine exactly the centers of radical tilt and local earthquakes.

This could be done by having volunteer observers operate small ink-recording plumb-bob pendulums, equipped with magnifying levers. Such instruments could be made of about the size and cost of a thermograph, say for $35. The observatory would be glad to design and have made such instruments, the principles of which have already been experimented with at Kilauea. If placed at Puu Oo, Puu Lehua and Ainahou for the north flank and at Kapapala, Hilea, Kahuku Ranch and Honomalino Ranch for the south flank, it ought to be possible to determine in advance whether the next lava-flow from Mauna Loa were coming from the north or from the south, and to locate the center.

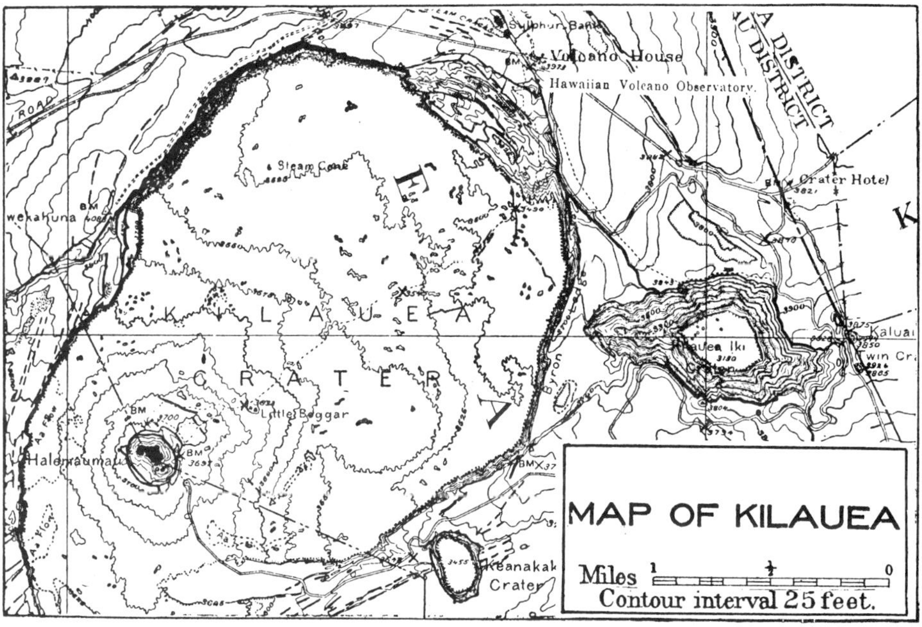

HAWAIIAN VOLCANO RESEARCH ASSOCIATION.

This society is a voluntary one, made up of subscribers to scientific work which is being executed by Dr. T. A. Jaggar, Director of the Hawaiian Volcano Observatory, Volcano House, P. O., Hawaii. **All scientific exchanges should be sent to this address.**

In 1917 there are about 150 subscribers in Hawaii and elsewhere, firms and individuals. A group of firms and persons in Hilo built the main observatory building in the spring of 1912. The work was founded by the Massachusetts Institute of Technology. Publications to date have been weekly reports since the summer of 1911 now reprinted in Honolulu in monthly form. There are also special reports, printed from time to time.

The weekly bulletin as it appears in the Honolulu Advertiser is reprinted as a leaflet and sent to regular annual subscribers to the work of the Association. L. A. Thurston is president of the Board of Directors of the Association, and L. T. Peck is treasurer. New subscribers who are interested in volcanoes will be welcomed in the Association. The Association aims: (1) To record volcanic activity and earthquakes in Hawaii; (2) to attract scientific men hither for special studies; (3) to promote the establishment of volcano observatories all over the world. The annual dues of regular members are $5; patrons of the Association subscribe larger amounts.

WHITNEY LABORATORY OF SEISMOLOGY.

The Whitney Laboratory of Seismology, named after an endowment fund of geophysical research held by the Massachusetts Institute of Technology, in memory of Caroline and Edward Whitney of Boston, is equipped with two Bosch-Omori 100 kg tromometers registering N-S and E-W motion, a heavy Omori tromometer registering E-W motion, and an Omori "ordinary Seismograph" designed for registering strong earthquakes in all three components of motion. These are seated on concrete piers in a closed basement room having practically constant temperature, beneath the chief Observatory building near the hotel. Time is referred to a rated chronometer, checked at intervals by solar observations with a transit. Both instruments are loaned by the College of Hawaii. Hawaiian standard time (H. S. T.) is 10 hrs. 30 min. slower than Greenwich time.

CANCANI SCALE OF SEISMIC INTENSITY.

Expressed by accelerations measured in millimeters per second per second.

I.	Instrumental	0.0	2.5
II.	Very slight	2.5	5.0
III.	Slight	5.0	10.0
IV.	Sensible, mediocre	10.0	25.0
V.	Rather strong	25.0	50.0
VI.	Strong	50.0	100.0
VII.	Very strong	100.0	250.0
VIII.	Ruinous	250.0	500.0
IX.	Disastrous	500.0	1000.0
X.	Very disastrous	1000.0	2500.0
XI.	Catastrophic	2500.0	5000.0
XII.	Great catastrophe	5000.0	10000.0

Grade IV. is ordinarily the minimum perceived by the senses; and in grade XII. the acceleration, or rate of change of motion (jerk) reaches that of terrestrial gravitation.

In the standard form of report the maximum intensity or acceleration, designated by the symbol a, or max. a, is given in the conventional unit, **the milligal**. The milligal is a measure of acceleration, such that 1 milligal = 1/100 mm. per sec. per sec. = 10 μ per sec. per sec. The Cancani scale, here defined in terms of millimeters per sec. per sec., can therefore be expressed in milligals by multiplying each of the numbers by 100.

WEEKLY BULLETIN
OF THE
Hawaiian Volcano Observatory

Vol. VI. HONOLULU, HAWAII, FEBRUARY, 1918. No. 2

Volcano House, Feb. 9, 1918.

During the week ending Friday, February 8, 1918, the lava lakes of the Kilauea inner pit first subsided a few feet and then recovered and at the end of the week the crags appeared slightly higher. As a whole, the tendency of the week has been a stationary condition, with the liquid lava about 40 feet below the rim of the pit.

On Saturday, February 2, at 2:30 p. m., the lake was slightly below the inner floor at the east cove, grotto fountaining was vigorous in the southeast cove, and the streaming thither through the southeast arm was rapid. The small central pond was crusted over with a glowing crack in the crusts. At 3:20 p. m. the southwest pond was level with its bordering bench and showed the usual fountaining at the south tunnel corner, where the blowing cone puffed and occasionally ejected spurts of glowing lava. There had been fresh slides on the southwest sides of the central crags, and at 6 p. m. these could be heard in motion. The movement of the southeast crag overturning northward was still in progress, for at this time there was another fall of rock from its north side into the lake.

On February 3 at 2 p. m. the inner bench was two feet high and there was an active grotto on the east side of the southeast crag. The small central pond no longer showed glow. At 2:15 p. m. the southwest pond had risen so as to overflow the crust at the entrance to the south tunnel, and the blowing cone was noisy.

On February 4 at 2:15 p. m. the lake was depressed about 4 feet below the marginal bench, the southeast arm was crusted over, but there was the usual activity in the southeast cove. The small central pond resumed activity and exhibited one fountain. At 3 p. m. the southwest pond showed central and border fountains four feet below the margin, and there was the usual activity and puffing at the south tunnel grotto and blowing cone.

On February 5, 1918, at 2:30 p. m., the lake was relatively still lower as compared with the east cove bench, which was 6 feet high. The inner shelf of recent overflow southeast was about 20 feet above the southeast channel. Slow rising appeared to be in progress. At the southwest pond the inner bench appeared 9 feet high, the pond was crusted and showed only two places of boiling, and the fumes were thick. At 5 p. m. there had evidently been subsidence, for the inner bench at the southeast cove was 10 feet high, the streaming was swift and the bombardment strong.

On February 6 at 2 p. m. the lake was so low that the southeast shelf stood fully 30 feet above it, and there was swift streaming and vigorous fountaining. There was a slight rise from 2 to 3 p. m., followed by a sinking spell, when the surface subsided about two feet, and this was followed by a very quiet interval of crusting over.

Inspection of the north lake from the inner cliff above it at 4 p. m. showed that there were two islands standing three feet above the molten lava and a peninsula attached to the east island mass so as to develop a wide floor surface there. The open channel was about 60 feet wide. There were a number of fountains and much smoke.

On February 7 at 2 p. m. the inner bench at the southeast cove was 6 feet above the lake, which was everywhere quiet and crusted. The southwest pond was in the same condition, with only the

WEEKLY BULLETIN
of the
Hawaiian Volcano Observatory

Published Monthly at Honolulu, Hawaii, by the Hawaiian Volcano Research Association

L. W. de Vis-Norton........Secretary

Entered as second-class matter January 20, 1914, at the post-office at Honolulu, Hawaii, under the Act of August 24, 1912.

south tunnel grotto rumbling. Much of the west cone had collapsed, and much smoke rose from the west cone ridge.

On Friday, February 8, 1918, at 2:30 p. m., conditions were little changed and the inner bench appeared 10 feet high. There were border fountains in the southeast cove and others in the channel leading to it, and numerous fountains migrated from the north lake southeastward. At 3 p. m., however, a sharp rise set in, so that in half an hour the height of the inner bench was reduced to less than six feet, and at 5:10 p. m. the inner bench at the east cove was overflowed in the region of the tunnel grotto there.

During the week ending at 2 p. m., Friday, February 8, 1918, the seismographs of the Whitney Laboratory registered a local earthquake at 1:34 a. m. on February 4, and spasms of volcanic vibration were strong on February 5-6. During the same interval, February 4-6, there was marked tilt to the north and east; otherwise the position of the recording pens during the week indicated tilt dominantly south and moderately or only slightly east. Microseisms were moderate, showing some increase during the vibration period above mentioned.

Volcano House, Feb. 16, 1918.

During the week ending Friday, February 15, 1918, rising of the lava of Halemaumau has increased so as to overflow the flood level bench of January 24 southeast and finally to flood the great northeast valley so voluminously that half of the 1894 bench and the valley back of it have become submerged and a new flat floor extends thence all the way to the north pit and beyond. A remarkable feature of this filling was that the lava welled up through the bottom of the 1894 depression instead of overflowing the lake margin. Other overflows have poured from the northwest pond chasm to make new fillings under the west shelf. Following these flows there have been the usual uplifts of the crags, which are now at their highest. The northeast fill, however, is still far below the level of the lake, and the latter remains as in January, about 25 feet below the rim of the pit.

On Saturday, February 9, at 2 p. m., the lake was six feet below the inner bench, streaming southeastward was swift, and there was strong fountaining in a large grotto on the south side of the southeast crag. From 2:30 to 5 p. m. rising was pronounced, so that the liquid lava nearly reached the upper surface of the inner bench. There was much tumbling of spatter margins into the lake along its eastern shores.

On February 10 at 2 p. m. the inner bench was 10 feet high and streaming and fountaining were vigorous. At 4 p. m. there had been a rise strong enough to flood the bench at the southeast tunnel. The only fountain was in the grotto under the southeast crag on its south side. At 5:30 p. m. there was collapse of the southeast crag bench and of the southeast point, into the lake, during subsidence.

Measurement on Tuesday, February 12, at 11 a. m., made the depression of the lake below the east rim of Halemaumau 33 feet. The central crag was 45 feet above the rim, and the east ledge 16 feet above it. These data showed that the lake had risen 11 feet in 11 days, or about one foot per day as an average, but the two crags were each a foot lower than on February 1.

On this day at 11 a. m. the lake was very high and rising, reaching nearly the general level of the southeast shelf of January, and at noon overflowing somewhat into the crevasses south and through the gateway leading to the central pond. The rising was marked by advancing waves of over-riding layers of the incandescent melt moving forward from the west through the southeast arm. The lake was largely crusted over, but there was bombardment at the east cove and southeast tunnel, at the east end of the southwest pond, at a high dome grotto under the north smoke cliff and occasionally at the east gulch and various points northwest and west. A high spatter rampart had been built above the southeast tunnel, and a rampart at the east end of the southwest pond had extended the floor there so much westward as to greatly shorten the pond. Streaming in the southwest pond was eastward to this rampart.

The noon rise was pronounced and threatened to flood the pit of the ceneral pond, which was at a much lower level than the southeast cove lava. At the central cove and the east cove there was strong overflowing, and all the islands and marginal plains about the north lake were drowned except the larger northwest island. The two eastern pinnacles of the west crag mass were left standing as islands. The northwest chasm under the driblet cone was filled with a pond of liquid lava at least 150 feet long, and this had been recently overflowing, along the chasm as a river bed, to the lake and it had also spilled over the lip of the chasm northwestward. At 12:15 p. m. the main flow of the day, to satisfy the noon rise, poured from this northwest pond westward to the depression at the base of the west shelf, where the flood forked right and left and then pooled in this shallow valley, the pool extending all the way to the pinnacles at the base of the northwest crag. The flow was still pouring like a river into this hollow at 1 p. m.

In this rise the lake was gaining on the crags, the southeast crag and the western and east island masses showing tendency to partial submergence. The crags showed no marked rising, and the only sliding rocks were at the east gulch. The remarkable poised block which stood erect against the summit mass of the central crag, but separated from it on its south side by a great crevasse, was seen from the west to be the top of a slab parting from the central crag mass along the east-west fissure, which sloped downward to the north at an angle of about 80°. Under the west station there were fresh falls of rock from the wall. The fumes were not especially thin.

On February 14 at 3:30 p. m. the lake was brimming level with the southeast shelf, and a fresh broad overflow from it of rough aspect had poured across the southern part of that shelf. There was high gas pressure, border fountains were numerous, streaming was rapid through the southeast arm, and new ramparts had been built southeast, east, and at the central cove. The east island and the southeast crag had been rising. At the time of its overflow the lake had been about 25 feet below the southeast station; at 4 p. m. it was a foot lower. A fresh flow had poured from the northwest pond again to the base of the west shelf, and was still glowing. At 5 p. m. there was more overflowing southeast. There had been fresh overflows also from the margin of the southwest pond, which was now again level with its bank, and crusted over. A new west cone had been built, tapering to a slender pipe above, fully 15 feet high, and on the east side of the former cone.

On Friday, February 15, 1918, in the morning, the period of high pressure reached a culmination by breaking a subterranean way for the lava through the cracks which separated the sunken crescent-shaped northeast bench of 1894 from the outer northeast wall of Halemaumau. Here the liquid melt welled up along a line following the bottom of the depression which for twenty-four years has been almost unchanged. By noon a great oblong pond filled this depression, and from it, over the eastern end of the 1894 ledge, a glowing cascade 10 to 15 feet wide poured continuously down the slope 20 feet to the northeast valley below. Here the lava pooled, and both pools kept spreading and rising all day long, the lower one gradually gaining on the upper until they came to a common level. The total filling of the northeast valley was fully 20 feet of depth, and the length of the ponded area a thousand feet. The action was extraordinarily quiet. Over the feeding fissure in the upper pond were four small driblet cones on the crust of the pond and an open pot bubbling in artesian fashion as a perpetual fountain, the westernmost of the row. This line of cones was near the wall and directly under the northeast station. The ponds remained crusted except for occasional cracking up and foundering of the crusts. Around the margins dribbling flows pushed out, making curtains, ropes and festoons of their surface skins, and new trickle flows perpetually pushed among the rocks. The cascade poured from under a ragged edge of crust of the upper pond into a swirling cauldron margined by the crust of the lower pond. At noon the surface of the lower pond showed the pattern of a festooned jumble of flows, but later in the day this crust sank into the melt beneath, leaving a smooth surface. The final result was a smooth floor of large angular units bounded by cracks like the floor of Keanakakoi crater. The only noises were the hissing and fountaining at the inlet vents and the steady rush of the cascade. The former emitted an odor of sulphurous acid, but the dominant smell was like a foundry. At 5:30 p. m. the great flood was still rising, but the two ponds had almost joined and the cascade was reduced to a torrent of slight fall. A pasty blowing cone had formed under the east station. The fill had extended to the north pit well beyond the north station, and the marginal flows were there still progressing northwestward. Only two puffing and flaming cones remained of the five feeding vents. A sudden cracking and foundering throughout the upper pond about 7 p. m. was accompanied by very bright incandescence, violent bubble fountaining, rapid spread of the action over the whole surface so as to engulf huge slabs of crust, and the cones disappeared, leaving sluggish fountains in their place. Intense heat and sulphur fume was emitted, and there was left a smooth cherry-red lake which hardened again quickly. Similar but more sluggish breaking-up happened in the lower pond. At 7:30 p. m. the northeast fill was still rising, and at least 30 feet below the lake level.

Throughout this performance the main lake remained 4 to 6 feet below the shelf-level southeast. An additional rise the previous night had extended the fresh lava on the shelf eastward to the east gulch, and had poured through the southeast gateway and filled the depression of the central pond. In the evening the lake was slightly higher than at noon, depressed three to four feet below the bench, streaming southeastward as usual, and fountaining with high spurts from the southeast crag grotto. There was a very hot tunnel grotto surmounted by a glow-cone under the central pond gate, and fountaining could be seen in that pond. The north lake and southwest pond also exhibited border fountains. During subsidence at 7:15 p. m. a red-hot margin three feet deep was revealed all around the lake, with stringy drip curtains. Large central fountains migrated southeastward, with very high fling of spray.

A small glowing pudding of lava had emerged on the south floor from a crevasse leading to the central pond. An active flow from the new west cone had filled the west pit and sent another fork eastward 50 feet. The top of the west cone was 20 feet above its base and was only about nine inches in diameter, recurved at a right angle like a bent pipe, with a fringe of stalactites hanging from the end. There was a glowing fissure at the base of the northwest cone. The recent filling of the northwest depression had been followed by more uplift of the northwest inner cliff over the lake and of the broken peaks under the northwest crag. These were now elevated and separated by a smoking chasm from the northwest crag, and beyond would be heard a rumbling lake grotto.

During the week ending at 2 p. m., Friday, February 15, the seismographs of the Whitney Laboratory have registered no earthquakes. Microseisms became strong on February 9 and decreased thereafter. Volcanic vibration increased spasmodically February 10-12 and decreased thereafter. At the same time there was an increase of tilt very strongly to the east and somewhat northward, followed by a steady decline of the east tilt for three days and a rapid increase of tilt to the south. The week has been stormy, with much rain.

Volcano House, Feb. 23, 1918.

During the week ending Friday, February 22, 1918, the lava column of Halemaumau has made a remarkable spurt in its rising, so that the lake surface at the end of the period had reached the level of the rim of the pit southeast and the overflows there were only a few inches below that rim. The imminence of overflow on that side became almost a certainty as the floods across the southeast bench dammed themselves back by congealing in the east and west gulches and so were unable to escape freely to the wall valleys northeast and southwest. At the same time much rising in the western and northeastern wall valleys took place, chiefly by welling up at the northwest chasm and around the wall fissures. The crags also rose higher than ever before. All of this culminated early Saturday morning, February 23, in an overflow of Halemaumau southeastward, destroying the road terminus.

On Saturday, February 16, 1918, at noon, the previously described upwelling in the northeast valleys continued. The lake was about four feet below the southeast bench, with the usual streaming and border fountains and much overhang showing stalactites. The southwest pond was broken up and at 1 p. m. showed border fountains, overhang and temporary subsidence. There was no flowing from the west cone. The northeast valleys showed red-hot cracks in smooth level floors about 30 feet below the lake level and flush with the eastern and middle parts of the 1894 ledge, which was submerged at those places. The two valleys were now at a common level, and the five vents were marked only by stained and smoking spots, one of which at the east was hissing, while the larger western one was a small low cone. The margins of this new floor showed trickle flows, and the north pit was now entirely filled with lumpy pahoehoe lava.

The long northeastern crag escarpment was higher and more tilted, showed a swollen bench of uplift at the southeast base of the east ledge, and here rocks were falling as though the middle part of the great scarp was swelling up. The east island mass showed increased uplift toward the center of the pit where the inner spatter margin at the lake shore was 10 feet high and sloped down toward the east cove. The southeast crag profile again showed five benches, the two upper earlier ones being tilted west, while the three lower ones of later date were tilted north.

On this day began a severe southerly rain and wind storm which threatened on February 17 to wreck the Observatory as in 1916 and destroyed roofing at the Volcano House. The week ending February 20 produced 35.72 inches of rain, the maximum being reached on February 19, with nearly 14 inches in one day.

On February 18 the lake was rising about three feet between 3 and 5:30 p. m., reaching a level one foot below the southeast bench. Activity was moderate, streaming fairly rapid, with glow lines between crusts; occasional high spraying central fountains would develop, there were large spatter domes southeast and northwest, and a new shore point protruded toward the center of the lake from the east island mass. The lake was still, however, some 25 feet below the rim.

Remarkable on this day was the pronounced uplift everywhere by intumescence. The lower bench of the southeast crag was lifted ten feet. Lifting was apparent at the edge of the southwest pond, the west cone ridge and the northwest inner cliff, all approaching the level of the Halemaumau verge. At two places the inner shelves of 1917, namely northwest and south, were uplifted bodily. The lava of the southwest pond was eight feet below the marginal rampart, the latter having been lifted along with the central crags, both of which were changed. The northeast scarp was higher, the northwest cone had fallen, and the north pit had slumped. The central pond was larger. Everything suggested that the entire lake basin along with its bottom had been lifted bodily.

The swelling effect extended even to the new northeast floors, which were much arched and higher. Little of the 1894 ledge protruded. The cone vent loudly hissed, a driblet heap over a crack in swollen up slabs. Along the crack were small driblet blowing pipes. This floor was now 20 feet below the lake level.

On February 20 at 11 a. m. the relative level of lake to bench appeared the same. Crusts were heavy, the southeast cove appeared larger and there was fresh overflow through the east gulch. Lava was welling up through the wall crack under the south station, and this crack was extending itself westward and producing fresh falls of rock. The crags were all higher and steeper, the east ledge tumbling to pinnacles. The northeast fill was still higher, and the hissing at the vents was less, giving off the odor of pure sulphur vapor. There were slight flows in the afternoon, but up to midnight there was no marked change of level in the lake, which remained 20 feet below the rim of Halemaumau.

On February 21 at 2:30 p. m. it was evident that a rising of the morning or at noon had been extraordinary. Floods from the southeast arm had so built up the bench under the southeast station that the hot crusted lava was only from 3 to 5 feet below the actual rim. It was possible that this was partly a mass uplift of the bench magma, including the bottom of the lake. At 3 p. m. the northwest chasm overflowed the west floor strongly for two hours, then the lake subsided seven feet. During this northwest flood its easternmost extension met a west-flowing stream from the northeast valley filling, on the north side of the northwest crag. At 5 p. m. and thereafter everything was flooding except the southwest valley. The southwest bench was 4 feet below the rim, covered with new flows which had poured both northward and westward. There was a flaming and blowing cone northeast and another in the west niche. The west shelf was nearly buried, and crusts were cracking and foundering. The north arm was mostly quiet, occasionally bright flaring was seen in the central region and southwest. The lake had that peculiar high pressure silent quality so distinctive of a great rise. About level with the rim of the pit the southeast lake rampart showed brimming lava carrying along tumultuous crusts, blisters and balloons of skin; noiseless fountains played in a shimmer of heat and the rampart was heaped with crusts. Voluminous overflows took place at 8 and 11 p. m., pouring west beyond the south station and north beyond the east station. The surface of these flows was finally, by measurement, only 15 inches below the rim of the pit near the southeast station, and the general level of the lake was above the rim level. Golden floods poured down the east gulch. There was a hot iron-carbon foundry smell. A bright curtained grotto gleamed under the south side of the southeast crag. Flames were numerous, bursting through crusts and balloons, a greenish flame played from a large cone at the central cove, there was a filagree cone at the east cove, there were flaming domes north, northwest, northeast, and in the northwest pond chasm, and sluggish lava was welling up below the south station, building a cone in the wall crack about 15 feet below the rim. The central pond was fountaining. The crags towered high, smoke was rather thin, and rocks fell from the east ledge and from the southeast crag. The lake was continually high until 11:45 p. m., when it subsided about a foot.

On Friday, February 22, 1918, conditions were much the same, but the flows of the southeast bench had sagged. The south wall crack produced flows spreading by driblets westward, and flows were spreading from the northwest fill eastward to the north pit. The lake fluctuated between short overflows and subsidences at about the rim level. A large double spatter cone had been built at the south corner of the southeast cove, and a bulging spatter margin surrounded the lake. Falls of rampart made waves in the lake, and streaming was swift southeastward. There were overflows at 1 and at 3 p. m. The lava pudding which rose from the wall crack south was capped with an arch of thick slabs which pulsated on either side of a crack extending 100 feet to the west, where hissing spiracles formed. The pit wall was still 30 to 40 feet high southwest, northwest and northeast. The northwest pond was fountaining, there was an active spatter dome in the west niche, there were large spatter domes in the north arm, the old west crag was a prominent tower, a cascade had poured from the north cove to the north pit, and the northeast floor was now only 15 feet below the northeast station, with a hissing spatter dome 10 feet in diameter, the counterpart of the one in the west niche. The crags were rising, as shown by rock falls under the north station, at the east ledge and at the northwest crag.

During the week ending at 2 p. m., February 22, the Whitney seismographs have recorded no definite earthquakes. During the storm, vibration was excessive and heavy microseisms followed it. East-west tilt has been slight, but tilt to the south has become excessive.

Volcano House, Mar. 2, 1918.

In order to understand the remarkable developments at Kilauea volcano during the week ending March 1, 1918, whereby

(1) The lava lake and bench of overflow, Jan. 24, 1918, from the southeast. Southeast cov
east island crag and east

(2) Halemaumau, Jan. 24, 1918, from the south showing swelling up of floors and crags above
—Februar

and central pond gate on the left, southeast crag in middle with the central peaks behind it, :dge on the right.—*February, 1918.*

ıge of pit. Depression of lakes 27 feet. Crags 40 feet above edge of pit.—Photos. Jaggar. *1918.*

for the first time in twenty-four years the lake magma has overflowed the rim of the pit Halemaumau, a brief review is necessary.

In May, 1913, the Halemaumau lava sank to smoky depths over 600 feet down. In May, 1914, the measurements revealed about 600 feet of depth; May, 1915, 500 feet; May, 1916, 300 feet; May, 1917, 20 feet. This rise during four years was interrupted temporarily in 1916 by a fall and recovery coincident with the Mauna Loa outbreak. The remarkable rapidity of that recovery to the high level of May, 1917, would lead to the belief that May of 1918 should exhibit a still higher level provided no rupture released the Hawaiian lava column somewhere in a low-level flow, causing collapse of the Kilauea crater. Throughout 1917 the lava remained high; by January, 1918, the bench magma crags were far above the rim of the pit, and on January 23 the lake was again only 20 feet down. A subsidence followed, then rising was resumed.

The January high level accords with a seasonal fluctuation which I have come to consider systematic and related to the sun's declination. There is tendency for lava to rise suddenly at solstics and to sink suddenly at equinox. This movement is complicated, however, by a secondary one, possibly due, at the two seasons respectively, to gradual restraint and gradual release of gas pressure, whereby there arises after the equinoctial fall a prolonged rising, followed by a shorter fall to solstice; while from after the solstitial rise there is apt to be a subsidence followed by a pronounced rise to the moment of the equinoctial fall. The amount of the effect of each crisis will be dependent on the equilibrium of the lava column itself with reference to its general trend upward, downward or stationary through a term of years, and it is complicated also by the relation of stiff magma underground to liquid lava. The latter is a foaming product of release of gas pressure in the stiffer substance, and consequently there arises special chemical heating. The solar effect can hardly be other than a squeezing of the rock crust of the globe causing rise or fall of the stiffer magma in the cracks, this being the mobile substance next under the rock crust. It will hence be seen that we have to do with

(1) Magma in general escaping through the ages of volcanoes, perhaps expelled by pressure downward of the crust of the earth;

(2) This magma squeezed in or under the cracked crust of the globe by the stresses induced in the equatorial protuberance of the sun's northing and southing in summer and winter;

(3) Expansion of this magma by gases in solution, when released under such changing stresses;

(4) Transformation of this magma by gases escaping from solution to bubble form, whereby gas reactions generate heat, liquidity and a foaming circulation to make what is called liquid lava.

These four motive powers, the first two terrestrial, the last two resident in the lava itself, cannot fail to complicate a curve representing the rise and fall of a lava column through the centuries, the years, and the seasons. The net result for seven years past has been tendency to gradually rising lava in May and November, falling lava in June and December, sharp rising near June 20 and December 20; and a converse tendency to gradually falling lava in February and August, rising lava in March and September, sharp sinking near March 20 and September 20. It is this calendar which led the writer to watch with interest this year 1918 a falling off of the lava column after reaching the January 20-foot level; there was depression 40 to 50 feet below the rim from January 26 to February 8, with collapse and lowering of the crags to the middle of February and every evidence of subsidence.

Then came the pre-equinoctial rise and the evidence that it was to be extraordinary was the spurting up of liquid lava, beginning February 15, around the pit margins, in depressed areas, which have since filled quietly with large crescent-shaped outlying lakes. These are quite symmetrical, lying between the three great sector crag-masses and the outer wall, the sectors being lifted at the pit center, and the older lake occupies the three rifts ebtween the sectors. This arrangement undoubtedly means a doming of the bench magma carapace, its rupture along three radial rifts and the welling up of the liquid lava through numerous shafts. The doming or intumescence of the hard floors of overflow has been the most remarkable feature of the last year, these being lifted into crags 90 feet high and more, and this hard substance has frequently risen faster than the lake so that the entire dish or saucer holding the lake has gone up bodily without any building by overflow. Recently this movement has been communicated to the outer wall of Halemaumau southwest, mashing up that margin by from 10 to 20 feet, as the swelling up of the central crags pinched the fresh fill of lava between them and the wall, and so displaced the wall.

On February 23, 1918, the lava lake overflowed the inner rim southeast at 4:55 a. m.; the outer rim, 5.09; the path from the automobile terminus was covered at 5:12; the automobile park was reached at 5:35; the park was covered at 5:41; and by 5:47 the walls surrounding it were buried. Ten minutes later it was estimated that the flow had traveled 400 yards. The total length from the edge of the pit is approximately a half mile east-southeast. By 8:30 a. m. the flow was slowing down. I am indebted to Mr. O. E. Long for the timing.

Overflows continued on this day with strong renewals about 1 and 6 p. m., and the lake was building high spatter domes, streaming eastward in both the southeast arm and the southwest pond, its rampart standing about 5 feet above the old rim of the pit, with spatter heaps 5 to 6 feet higher. The overflows buried the lip of Halemaumau from just south of the east station to the south station. The first flow was the longest, and narrow at its lower extremity but wide near the pit. It was a heavy pahoehoe with aa developed in the cracks and under layers. At the south station, 12:30 to 3:30 p. m., the old channel on the rim was filled with trickle lava welling up the wall crack there, where a fountaining and spurting pot built in three hours a driblet cone 5 feet high and 3 feet across, with gas flames flaring rhythmically from many orifices in its summit. The driblet flows from this source poured into the southwest valley.

The rising was general, a driblet fountain in the west niche contributing to the floor of the west valey, and fountains played in the northwest chasm. Remnants of the northwest shelf still protruded through the flat crust of the western fill. Small overflows had poured from the lake through the rocks to the west of the northwest crag. The northeast fill was still higher, with a large driblet dome on its eastern surface, and fresh overflows from the lake had poured through the northern gap into the north wall valley. The western and northeastern fills were about 10 feet below the lake level. The lake appeared to be gaining on the crags.

The southwest station on the edge of the pit was raised into a half-dome about 6 feet, so that the artificial rock platform was tilted southwestward.

There had been a sharp earthquake felt in Hilo about 1 p. m., February 23. On February 24 there was reaction; the overflows ceased and the lake sank about four feet, so that at 7 p. m. streaming was swift through the southeast channel; the grotto rampart stood high on all sides. There was some caving in and much rumbling in glowing caverns. During the night there had been fresh flows through the north gap and from the northwest chasm. Now the northeast floor showed slumping, but the west fill was less so, and in both places hissing cones showed gas pressure. At 9 a. m. the lake was 7 feet down, with much fountaining but steady trickle, flowing in considerable volume, spread to the south and southwest from the south station vent. Inspection of the north arm at 3 p. m. showed that there also the lava was fountaining and depressed seven feet. There was temporary rising about noon, 6 o'clock and near midnight, and this tendency to a six-hour period was noticed throughout the week. On this day the southern A-frame was destroyed by a flow.

On Monday, February 25, new flows from the southeast were flooding the former course in the early morning, and a renewal at 6 a. m. pushed out arms at the southeast, east and through the east gulch. Some 800 yards of the roadway was now buried. Flows from the south vent had half filled the southwest wall valley and the rim of the pit was buried from the east station to a point west of the south station. The northeast fill was arched up over rising lava below and new flows through the east gulch stood two feet above the ground level at the east station. At 8 a. m. flowers were here in motion, and at 9 a. m. overflow was vigorous. The crags had risen strongly. The central pond was crusted over. Rocks were falling from the east ledge. The rising of the west and northeast fills proceeded by periodical cracking and foundering of heavy crusts, driblet flows pushed out from under the margins, and flows from the lake at intervals piled up on the crust of the ponds, but eventually merged with them. The southwest valley fill was equally voluminous, but consisted of lumpy flows from the south vent. The process in general which had led to this remarkable development of new lakes in all the wall valleys may be described as prolonged intumescence followed by outburst of liquid lava up the wall crack.

At 11 a. m. there was a cascading flow from the filled and crusted northwest chasm pouring westward into the west valley. This chasm extends in a curve from a cove of the southwest channel to a circular pool at the northwest cove, and is a great rift through the west cone ridge. I was able to reach the summit of the west cone ridge and the shore of the north arm, where it was found that the formerly open arm was now replaced by a heavily crusted area with a few round pools and meandering channels. At 11:30 a. m. streaming through the southwest arm was swift to the east, but an hour later the streaming reversed and poured southward. In both cases, however, it was apparent that the northwest chasm was the source, and the pool in it stood at a higher level than the lake. There was streaming southeastward from the north arm channel, and this also came from the northwest cove pool; that is, the northern end of the northwest chasm. It is remarkable that the vents revealed by the sudden recent rising are identical with those mapped a year ago. At 1 p. m. the west niche cone suddenly broke up, liquid melt spouted like an artesian well, then with sudden tumultuous break-up the two-foot slabs of the swollen surface of the western fill cracked and foundered and splashed over the edges of the ponded area—an area, it should be noticed, distinctly higher than its margins. The surface quickly cooled to a flat expanse. I had walked over this arched area a half hour before, feeling sharp quakes occasionally in the slabs underfoot, and the cone had been four feet high and ten feet across, with a hissing gas tube of smooth lava on top.

The new aspect of Halemaumau for the week was now determined and had the following characters. A great slag heap extending 300 yards southeast across the whole eastern and southern rim sloped off beyond to new flows which persisted in activity to the south. Around the pit elsewhere great wall valleys were filling up to the pit margin and at the end of the week overflowed that margin east-northeast, north and west. The great crags rose beyond all belief, so that the higher ones overtopped the far wall of the greater Kilauea crater as seen from Volcano House. This upward movement lifted with it the shores and ramparts of the lake until the latter was near 15 feet above the old rim. As the filling of the southwest inner valley consisted of hard driblet flows, this material made a wedge between the wall of the pit and the resistless uplift of the central crags, with the result that the entire old rim from the south station westward was heaved up. This is an abbreviated description of the week's construction, and accompanying the unusual gas pressure and rapid rise of the lava were several small earth jarrings and two pronounced earthquakes. (The second one about 9 a. m., February 26.)

On February 26 general rising continued. The crust of the northeast fill was arched and broken. The west fill was much higher, about 10 feet below the shelf of the west niche, with an open pot and cone grotto in its crust. An open pond had formed in the wall crack adjacent to the west cone ,and the latter was a remarkable object 20 feet high shaped like a griffon. The southwest valley filling was only a few feet below the rim of the pit, and contained an arched oval suggesting ponding. The southwest station was now lifted 12 feet and the rim thereabouts three to five feet. The flows from the south cone vent sent out elephantine toes at the end of flows spreading like the tentacles of an octopus. At 3:15 p. m. the lake was crusted, quiet and showed a curtained grotto on the west side of the southeast cove.

Wednesday, February 27, was a rather inactive day, with lake rising and falling, continued filling of the marginal ponds, and great lift of the crags. At 7 p. m. the northeast fill was about five feet below the level of the east station, with a long arched swelling on its northeastern side, a flaring cone at its east end and a puddle of driblet flows in motion west. There was an active fountain in the north cove pond. The slag heap pond of the west niche was five feet below the margin, and glowing toes made out from its edge along the wall valley. The cone on its summit was hissing but quiet. The view of Halemaumau from the road southeast showed only an upward slope surmounted by fire-lit mountainous crags, an occasional fountain fling in the midst, the south cone flaring stationary like a lighthouse, while below in the foreground a pattern of red glowing flows made the whole smoking mass look as though it were perforated with fiery apertures. Halemaumau was no longer a pit. It was rather a rugged hill.

A walk around what had been the pit on February 28 at 11 a. m. showed upswollen flows south, with the south cone on their crest. The southwest rim had been pushed up 9 feet, the wall remaining vertical on the pit side, but showing a half-arch profile on the outer side, the ridge being 15 to 20 feet wide. The movement had been on numerous fissures concentric to the pit, the rock moving like broken wax. Evidently the movement was very gradual. As one walked around the pit the former edge for several hundred feet was a steep obstruction which cut off the view. The nature of the structure known as the "'half-dome'' which had stood on the northeast edge of Halemaumau since 1894 is explained by this uplifted southwest rim of 1918.

The filling of the southwest valley was now 12 feet above the old rim some distance west of the south station, and this sloped downward to the west, leaving only one short stretch of the old contact between floor and wall opposite the west cone. Here the floor material was a confused uplifted tumble and the west pond was an arch of crust with some slumped fresh lava north of it. The west cone ridge was now a towering crag so much uplifted that the base of the west cone was now high above the rim of the pit.

The west niche pond had an arched surface *above* the level of the margin, and trickle flows had poured out on the shelf. There were five cones close together on its surface, some of them hissing. Trickle flows were moving to the northwest crag gulch from the margins of the west niche pool, and near the old rest house north the lava was about 5 feet below the rim of the pit. The view from the west gives most strongly the impression that the central unlifted body containing the lake is a dome, and this is confirmed when one climbs to the edge of the north cove pool and finds the lake to be hardly more than a few pools in sinuous channels.

The northwest chasm had not recently been active, the lake was not now visible from any part of the rim of the pit, as it was now wholly above the rim and hidden by its own ramparts. The northeast fill was now slightly overflowing the rim of the pit east-northeast and north-northeast. Its crust was flat and a striking evidence of the very recent strong unlifting of the long escarpment of the northeast crag mass was furnished by the way this pond lapped against that mass. It lapped against a bench consisting of the upraised surface of the pond of two days before, when the pond had been at a lower level. Thus the rising crag had carried up the former pond crust with it to make a shore for the newer pond. There were no cones on the fill at this time.

The lake at 10:30 a. m. was three feet below its bank, sluggish, covered with heavy crusts, fountaining in the southeast, southwest and north cove localities. The motionless crust flats covering the greater part of the area of the north arm three to four feet above the tortuous channels which connect small ponds northeast, northwest and north with the main lake, suggest that the bottom lava has come up leaving the conduits and sink-holes open. There are at least a dozen of these known to the writer. It seems probable that the lake magma, expended in flows and fillings, is impoverishing the lake proper, while its bottom material, continuous with the material of the upswelling crag dome, is coming into view.

From 1 to 4 p. m. the lake was brimming southeast and very quiet, with occasional subsidences, one of these in the evening as much as seven feet with increased activity. High pressure everywhere continued. The south cone puffed loudly and occasionally spurted, and flows from this vent were again close to the road.

On Friday, March 1, at noon the lake was high and overflowing, the northeast fill was overflowing the old rim of the pit, and the general high pressure continued. At 7 p. m. the surface of the northeast pond was six feet above the ground level at the east station and its edge, in terraces of overlapping slag, threw out driblet flows eastward. Its surface was cracking, foundering and making fountaining pools locally, and flames burst through the crust. The lake was brimming full, and even above its rampart, hemmed in only by piled slabs and folded crusts. There were few fountains. Dribbling overflows took place.

On this day collections of gas were made with vacuum tubes at the front of the northeast flows and at gas jets flaming at the lake margin. Reports of surveys and of the Whitney Laboratory will be deferred.

Very respectfully,

T. A. JAGGAR, JR.,
Director.

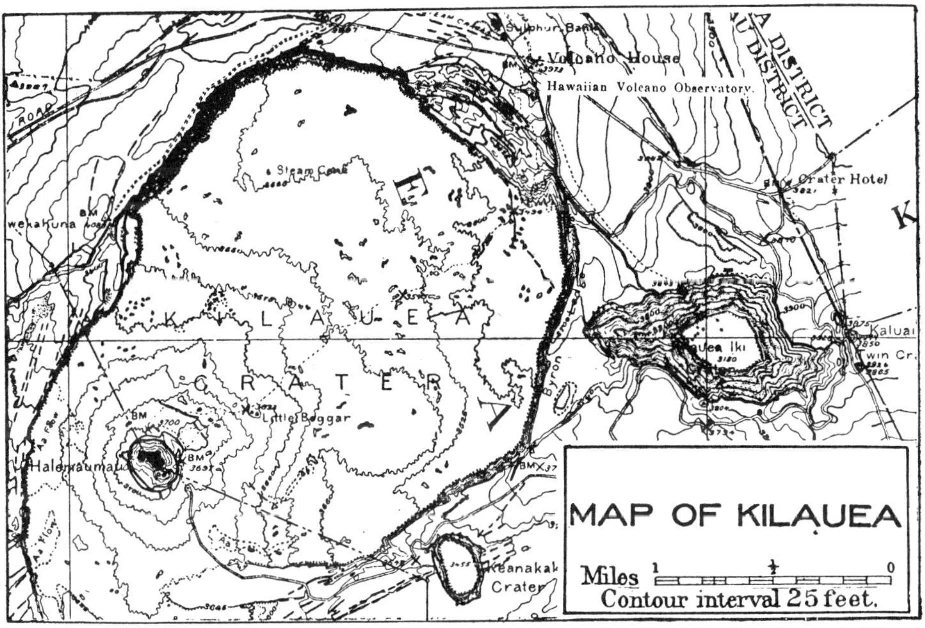

HAWAIIAN VOLCANO RESEARCH ASSOCIATION.

This society is a voluntary one, made up of subscribers to scientific work which is being executed by Dr. T. A. Jaggar, Director of the Hawaiian Volcano Observatory, Volcano House, P. O., Hawaii. **All scientific exchanges should be sent to this address.**

In 1917 there are about 150 subscribers in Hawaii and elsewhere, firms and individuals. A group of firms and persons in Hilo built the main observatory building in the spring of 1912. The work was founded by the Massachusetts Institute of Technology. Publications to date have been weekly reports since the summer of 1911 now reprinted in Honolulu in monthly form. There are also special reports, printed from time to time.

The weekly bulletin as it appears in the Honolulu Advertiser is reprinted as a leaflet and sent to regular annual subscribers to the work of the Association. L. A. Thurston is president of the Board of Directors of the Association, and L. T. Peck is treasurer. New subscribers who are interested in volcanoes will be welcomed in the Association. The Association aims: (1) To record volcanic activity and earthquakes in Hawaii; (2) to attract scientific men hither for special studies; (3) to promote the establishment of volcano observatories all over the world. The annual dues of regular members are $5; patrons of the Association subscribe larger amounts.

WHITNEY LABORATORY OF SEISMOLOGY.

The Whitney Laboratory of Seismology, named after an endowment fund of geophysical research held by the Massachusetts Institute of Technology, in memory of Caroline and Edward Whitney of Boston, is equipped with two Bosch-Omori 100 kg tromometers registering N-S and E-W motion, a heavy Omori tromometer registering E-W motion, and an Omori "ordinary Seismograph" designed for registering strong earthquakes in all three components of motion. These are seated on concrete piers in a closed basement room having practically constant temperature, beneath the chief Observatory building near the hotel. Time is referred to a rated chronometer, checked at intervals by solar observations with a transit. Both instruments are loaned by the College of Hawaii. Hawaiian standard time (H. S. T.) is 10 hrs. 30 min. slower than Greenwich time.

CANCANI SCALE OF SEISMIC INTENSITY.

Expressed by accelerations measured in millimeters per second per second.

I.	Instrumental	0.0	2.5
II.	Very slight	2.5	5.0
III.	Slight	5.0	10.0
IV.	Sensible, mediocre	10.0	25.0
V.	Rather strong	25.0	50.0
VI.	Strong	50.0	100.0
VII.	Very strong	100.0	250.0
VIII.	Ruinous	250.0	500.0
IX.	Disastrous	500.0	1000.0
X.	Very disastrous	1000.0	2500.0
XI.	Catastrophic	2500.0	5000.0
XII.	Great catastrophe	5000.0	10000.0

Grade IV. is ordinarily the minimum perceived by the senses; and in grade XII. the acceleration, or rate of change of motion (jerk) reaches that of terrestrial gravitation.

In the standard form of report the maximum intensity or acceleration, designated by the symbol a, or max. a, is given in the conventional unit, **the milligal.** The milligal is a measure of acceleration, such that 1 milligal = 1/100 mm. per sec. per sec. = 10 μ per sec. per sec. The Cancani scale, here defined in terms of millimeters per sec. per sec., can therefore be expressed in milligals by multiplying each of the numbers by 100.

WEEKLY BULLETIN
OF THE
Hawaiian Volcano Observatory

Vol. VI. HONOLULU, HAWAII, MARCH, 1918. No. 3

Volcano Observatory, Mar. 9, 1918.

During the week ending Friday, March 8, 1918, the Halemaumau lava column ceased overflowing and the liquid lava subsided 40 feet, with accompanying subsidence of the crag masses. The subsidence started suddenly in the early morning of March 3 and for the lake continued to Tuesday, March 5, when recovery set in. The crags continued to subside to March 6, and thereafter they became stationary. The recovery of the lake from March 6 to 8 amounted to a rise of 20 feet, or half of the previous subsidence. The renewal of gas pressure up to the present time has been confined to the main lake and the northeast fill, the western and southern border vents not yet taking part in it. On March 8 the depression of the lake below the southeast overflow margin of March 2 was 22 feet.

On Saturday, March 2, at noon, the pressure at Halemaumau was high and the lake about three feet below the southeast rim, with moderate marginal activity. The crags were rising to their maximum and rock slides were tumbling down the back slope of the northeast escarpment. A new point protruded from that escarpment into the lake at the east cove. The filling of the northeast valleys was domed up and flaming gases hissed through the cracks between its heavy crust blocks. There was a pool of collapse near its middle. At the west niche pond the cone locality exhibited an open pool of sluggish fountaining lava, and fresh marginal flows had pushed out to cover portions of the west niche shelf. At 5:15 p. m. the lake rose and slightly overflowed at the east gulch, sending a trickle of lava which poured some distance toward the stone shelter at the east station. At 6 p. m. the south cone source developed a strong flow which spread toward the southwest far into the night. On this evening the activity as seen from the Observatory in the distance was at its maximum, the splashing fountains being in full view at the southeast rampart, the north gap and the west niche, the crags towering high above the level of the far wall of Kilauea, and the glowing flows to the south could be seen in motion. Therefore the subsidence which set in after midnight was very marked, for at 9 a. m. on March 3 no activity was visible, the lake had sunk within its inner pit, and the crags were stationary. The effect of the sinking on the crags did not appear until the next day.

At 4 p. m. on March 3 the contrast to the previous day was remarkable, the lava appearing almost everywhere except in the lake itself as dead crusts, with hundreds of visitors swarming over places inaccessible before. The lake was 12 feet below the southeast rim, 15 feet down at the north cove pond, there was much fountaining and rumbling of the type characteristic of subsidence, and in the southeast arm the streaming was largely reversed, pouring northward and westward from the southeast channel to meet other currents along lines of turbulent fountaining which was expended in the eastern and central coves. There were the usual quiet spells accompanying risings and crustings occasioned by accumulating gas. The southeast cove showed a new indentation leading to the central pond. The lake showed an inner spatter bench three feet high around the southeast arm and making a point projecting from the east island crag into the central region.

The ponded lava fillings southwest, west and northeast all showed slumping and broken crusts. The northeast fill had an oval area near the northeast wall

WEEKLY BULLETIN
of the
Hawaiian Volcano Observatory

Published Monthly at Honolulu, Hawaii, by the Hawaiian Volcano Research Association

L. W. de Vis-Norton........Secretary

Entered as second-class matter January 20, 1914, at the post-office at Honolulu, Hawaii, under the Act of August 24, 1912.

which had broken in and subsided 10 feet. The west niche fountaining locality was now a cavern lined with stalactites at the side of a small pit about 10 feet deep, where under the overhang a sluggish fountain gurgled. The spatter cone at the north gap had broken and toppled over southward.

The south cone continued to puff and driblet flows from it continued to move at two localities near the road terminus. The heaps of lava of this driblet type near the cone had been swollen into humps with radial cracks in most remarkable fashion during the previous three days. That accumulation of expanding pasty lava within tunnels of its own crust was responsible for these swellings, was clearly shown by the heaving of the roof slabs and the welling of the paste up the cracks. The last lava in motion at the lower end of these flows glowed orange, showed few inflation bubbles, cooled less rapidly than the bubbly kinds and solidified iron gray, rough and very heavy, with aa fragments in the cracks.

On Monday, March 4, at 3 p. m., both lake and crags were subsiding rapidly, the movement of the crags being everywhere a reversal of the recent tumescence in the center of the pit. There was now a sagging toward that center. The lake at 3 p. m. was 18 feet below the southeast bench, but by 5 p. m. it was 25 feet down. Streaming was various and often westward through the southeast arm, there were many fountains, and stalactite rims were general. The summits of the southeast crag were now level with the southeast rim of overflow. The east island tower had collapsed. The north cove pond lay 15 feet below the overflow margin of the north gap, and the lava there was covered with dark thin festooned skins streaming westward to a border grotto from a glowing arch of crust two feet high which bridged the channel leading to the northeast cove. This channel meandered along the east shores of the north arm with three open ponds and three crust bridges before it emerged at the central region, and another crusted tunnel led from it to the larger pond of the northwest cove, which was 100 feet in diameter. The remainder of the north arm area consisted of solidified flats 10 feet above the ponds. There was a large fountaining grotto on the west side of the central region.

The west crag mass had sagged inward, opening wider the northwest chasm. The east island crag had sagged inward, tilting its spatter levels toward the center of the pit. The great north east escarpment had sagged inward, opening crevasses and reviving the east gulch. The southeast shelf had sagged inward, opening glowing cracks along the line of the old wall. The southwest margin was little changed, but sagging of the west cone ridge had lowered the base of the west cone below the rim of the pit, and rocks were falling in a chasm east of that cone. The south cone was flaming and lava could be heard pounding inside, but the south flows were stationary. The west niche cavern had its pasty lava pool puffing at a lower level, and there was no activity at the northeast fill.

During the night the south cone maintained its beacon light, and the glow from the active lake was very bright. The crags continued to sink.

On March 5 at noon the lava lake appeared to have reached a stationary condition. Its level was from 35 to 40 feet below the eastern overflow rim, and the spatter heapings of that upper rim had collapsed into the pit. Streaming was mostly southeastward, with occasional reversals to the central and east coves, there was a large grotto tunnel with continuous fountaining and rapid inrush at the corner, which appeared to lead toward the south cone, and the overflow rim west of this tunnel line had subsided greatly in contrast to the eastern rim, which kept its height. There was another tunnel leading to the central pond. The southeast cove was crusted, the southeast arm patterned with bright lines, and an inner bench three feet high margined the lake at the central point and the east cove. The flaming at the south cone continued. The southeast crag stood 10 feet lower than the southeast rim. The central crags had changed their shape and much had fallen away from the middle of the northeast escarpment. Falls of rock from the east ledge cliff had made a large tumble of boulders at the east gulch, and one of these had rolled out over the new lava 40 feet from the base of the cliff. The pond of the northeast fill showed fume rising from its eastern crust and a glowing cavern under the overhang of its northern margin. The crust over the west niche pond remained high. During the night the pit was less luminous.

On Wednesday, March 6, at noon, the depression was about the same, but the lake was rising. A new spatter margin had formed with crescent domes southeast, east, at the central cove, at the west, in the north arm and in the southwest arm. Streaming was swift southward from the southeast narrows, the southeast arm was crusted over, and the four grottoes of the southeast cove were spraying. The crags and floors were lower.

A new cone was developing in the northeast valley pool, and a small lava flow trickled from it over the collapsed blocks. At its source a block heaved and occasionally released a puff of gas. The pools of the north arm were slightly higher, there were five or six active fountains at the tunnels, and the crusted region stood lower. The northwest chasm contained an active lava pool 12 feet down and fully 20 feet above the lake level. The west niche cavern was nearly dead, with dull glow in the cracks. The southwest pond was bordered by a floor at its east end, which had subsided 15 feet below the level of the south margin of its pit. The liquid was 20 feet below that margin, with eastward streaming, and with fountains south and southwest. Activity at the south cone had ceased. Glow from the pit at night was moderate, and much greater southeast than northwest.

On March 7 the old edge of the crater was again defined except at the west niche and southeast rim, the crags were stationary, and the fume was somewhat denser. The fume had been thin March 4 and 5. During this day the lake rose from a depression of 30 feet at 10 a. m. to less than 25 feet at 5 p. m. Fountains were few both southeast and in the north arm. A fountain was boiling in the northwest chasm. The southwest pond was chiefly active at the south tunnel corner. In the morning the cone of the northeast pond was quiet but glowing, but at 4 p. m. it was puffing and ejecting lava spray. The west niche cavern was inactive. At 6 p. m. the lake was only three feet below the partition crust separating the southeast cove from the central pond.

On Friday, March 8, at noon, the lake was 22 feet below the southeast rim and rising, its surface level with the entrance to the central pond. It was actively building new spatter margins everywhere, the tunnels were submerged, and its inner bench was being overflowed at the central and eastern coves and across the flats of the north arm. In this northwest region it was evident that the north chasm pond was higher than the northwest cove pool, the latter higher than the north cove, and the north cove higher than the central region. There was thus a distinct grade downward from the wells of uprising west to the sinkholes southeast. There were many border grottoes and a hissing cone in the middle of the north arm showed that gas pressure had been renewed. The lake was submerging the shores of the southeast crag and the east island crag. There was as yet no renewal of rising in the crags, and hissing was not heard from the vents of the outlying ponds northeast and west, nor from the south cone. A large cone, however, had been built above the sunken slabs northeast.

A notable change, probably indicative of gas rising through the rocks, is the recent whitening by solfataric deposits of the region just north of the north station, in the vicinity of the three old driblet cones of 1894. The collection of gas samples was continued during this week.

Volcano Observatory, Mar. 16, 1918.

During the week ending March 15, 1918, the lava crags in Halemaumau have slowly risen and the liquid lake also rose, but tended to subside relative to its containing basin on Thursday and Friday, March 14 and 15. In general, the week may be said to have continued the recovery from the recent subsidence so far as the main lava column is concerned, but the liquid lake at the end of the week was 10 feet lower than at the beginning. All of this and more was recovered on March 16.

On March 9 at 10 a. m. the crags were stationary, but three hours later they were rising. The night had shown dim glow as though from a rising lake. The movements of the east ledge crag had produced a deep notch at the east gulch. At 1 p. m. the fountain of the north cove pond could be plainly seen from the Observatory. From 10 a. m. to noon there was strong rising so that the bench west of the southeast cove was flooded. Just after noon the lake subsided two feet and then recovered. At 10:30 a. m. flows were in motion from the cone in the eastern part of the northeast valley pond. At noon the north cove pond was quiet, but the northwest cove pond was brimming level with the surrounding floor and fountaining near the center with high flings. Fumes were dense in the vicinity. After 2 p. m. there were more overflows of the west shore of the southeast cove, and there were many fountains about its margins.

On March 10 at 1 p. m. the crags had risen farther. At 2:30 p. m. the lava of the southeast cove was little changed, the southeast bench standing 20 feet above it, while the bench on the south side of the cove sloped downward to the west so that in places the lake was only four feet below it. Streaming to the southwest margin was fairly rapid. At 3:30 p. m. the northwest cove pond was brimming and active, and the north cove pond quiet. At 4 p. m. the lava was high and fountaining in the northwest chasm. At 6 p. m. the lake at the southeast cove had risen flush with the floor at the gateway leading to the central pond. There was a curtained grotto farther north on the west side of the cove and a line of fountaining grottoes on the southeast side.

On Monday, March 11, the lake was a few feet lower relative to its basin, the grottoes were more active, and the streaming was swifter. There were a few fountains in the southeast arm. At 8 p. m. a small cone in the central part of the north arm was puffing loudly and occasionally ejecting spurts of molten lava. The northwest cove pond was fountaining and three feet below its marginal rim.

On March 12 at 5 p. m. inspection of the lake was difficult owing to clouds of steam from the fresh flows occasioned by heavy rain which continued for three days. Steam made an impenetrable fog so that travel in places was impossible. The lake's edge, however, was reached at the southeast bench, and the liquid showed all the signs of active rising. Fresh overflows had poured toward the hollow of the central pond, which appeared to be lower than the lake. There were fountaining grottoes southeast, a filagree curtain veiled the hissing grotto under the southeast crag, and the lake once more appeared to be gaining on the crags. There was a hissing cone in the central pond floor. The east ledge crag appeared low relative to the southeast bench as though the latter were rising. The northeast fill appeared comparatively low as though slumped, great clouds of steam rose from it, and no noise could be heard there.

On March 13 conditions were about the same. On March 14, however, there was subsidence of the lake relative to the southeast bench, which stood 30 feet above it. A circuit of the pit from 10 a. m. to 12 noon during a driving southerly rain produced the following notes. The fresh flows were followed along their southern margin to a point near the south cone, which was quiet, and no noise could be heard from the inner pits southeast or southwest. The southwest margin of the outer pit remained a high ridge as before, but near the southwest station the inner filling had been lifted higher and the base of the west cone was again above the rim of the pit. Glimpses of the crags through the rain vapor revealed them towering high. No noises of activity were heard at the western stations, but at the north a thudding rumble could be heard from the direction of the north arm. Fume mixed with the steam made the northeast rim of the pit impassable and suggested activity in the northeast fill. By making a detour the east station was reached, and during a heavy downpour strong rumbling with explosive noises and jets of blue fume started in the northeast valley. Some kind of spurting activity was going on there, which later exploration showed to be from the cone east of the north station, which ejected high spatter and a flood of very liquid lava in an unusually explosive fashion. Inspection of the hot cracks and "Pele's Kitchen" showed no changes in that region. At 4 p. m. the southeast cove was reached and the lake seen to be 12 feet below the south bench and 30 feet below the southeast bench. There was high activity and rapid streaming in the direction of the central pond, with traveling fountains and all signs of subsidence. On March 15 the low level of the lake continued, but the crags were rising.

During the past month of storms, lava overflows and exceptionally heavy rains, the seismometric records of the Whitney Laboratory have been as follows:

During the week ending at 2 p. m., February 22, 1918, no definite earthquakes were recorded either local or distant. It is doubtful whether the disastrous shocks of Amoy, China, could have been registered here owing to the excessive vibration due to high winds. The tilting of the ground became very excessive to the south, and changed from slight west to moderate east. Microseisms and volcanic (?) vibrations were excessive owing to the storm, moderating at the end of the period.

During the week ending at 2 p. m., March 1, 1918, six local earthquakes were registered, of which one was felt strongly in Hilo and another strongly felt at Volcano House. On February 23, the day of first lava overflow at Halemaumau, a small shock was registered about 4:30 a. m. and at 1:06 p. m. came the Hilo shock, of much greater amplitude on the seismogram. A small shock at 7:35 a. m. February 26 was followed at 9:42 a. m. by a smart quake which rocked the buildings and threw all the recording pens off the cylinders. On February 27 there were two small shocks at 4:27 a. m. and 6:57 a. m. and numerous vibration spasms. Tilting became so excessive to the south that the instruments were readjusted February 26—probably a fixed alteration of the vertical was indicated. Tilting increased to the east strongly, and with it there was moderate recovery to the north from February 26 to March 1. Microseismic and volcanic vibration were moderate at first; the latter became spasmodic on the 27th, and thereafter excessive wind squalls obliterated the seismic effects.

During the week ending at 2 p. m., March 8, 1918, six local earthquakes were registered and numerous spasms of volcanic vibration. Five small shocks occurred during the twenty-four hours when the Halemaumau lava changed from rising to sinking, March 3 to 4; these were at 4:07 and 5:15 p. m., March 3, and on March 4 at 2:59 and 11:20 a. m. and and at 12:08 p. m. Another shock was at 4:04 a. m., March 8. Tilting to the east and north ceased and tended rather to the west and south. North-south microseisms were strong throughout the week.

During the week ending at 2 p. m., March 15, 1918, three local earthquakes were registered. The first two of these were very small, at 6:28 p. m., March 8, and at 7:23 a. m., March 10. A stronger felt shock occurred on March 10 at 8:06 a. m. Movement of tilting increased to very strong west and south. Microseismic motion, dominantly north-south, decreased at the beginning of the period, but became strong and rhythmic later. Volcanic vibration increased to a maximum on March 14, coincident with the activity of the explosive cone in the northeast fill of Halemaumau.

Volcano Observatory, Mar. 23, 1918.

During the week ending Friday, March 22, 1918, the lava lake of Halemaumau has risen 12 feet and the crags have also risen until the high central peak is again in line with the far rim of Kilauea crater as seen from the Observatory. The fountains both east and west are again in view from Volcano House, and the level of the southeastern rampart of the lake is only about 5 feet below the level of overflow of February. The latest movement of rising has been slow, and the only outlying area to take part in it is the northeast fill, which has continued to put out sluggish flows upon the floor of its depression. The February flow area is still very hot, especially in the region of swollen domes near the south cone. The most remarkable crag uplift of the week has been the rise of the southern portion of the west cone ridge, which has created a new sharp escarpment between the west cone and the southwest channel, the whole block standing high above the old rim of the pit.

On Saturday, March 16, 1918, at noon, the lake was rising and mostly crusted over at a level in the southeast cove 18 feet below the southeast shelf and 6 feet below the south bench. Stalactites were abundant on the spatter margin above the lake, there was high gas pressure with ballooning crusts, and surfaces occasionally cracking and foundering while driblet lava pushed out from under the crust along the shores. The crags were slowly rising. An oval pot in the central pond area was pouring out driblet flows which covered the whole crust of the pond in the course of an hour. At first the pot was ballooning a flexible skin sluggishly and emitting a flame through cracks in the skin, but at 1 p. m. a noisy spurting fountain developed there, and then the lava subsided about 3 feet, leaving an oval ridge around the margin. Fumes of sulphur were rising from the south cone.

Exploration of the northeast depression revealed a remarkable change at the western cone locality. The cone was now a fuming pot 5 feet in diameter, surrounded by a splash veneer covering all the adjacent surface 50 feet or more from the center with thinly festooned and blistered glassy lava radiating in flows which must have been very liquid. This contrasted strongly with the earlier lava in its glistening gray surface and brittle smooth crusts. The ejection had been explosive, for there were solidified splashes, droplets and shreds of the melt thrown to a distance and the surface of the flow lava was pitted with the spray driblets which had fallen already solidified. This lava was in such marked contrast to all the rest that it may well have been produced on the morning of March 14 by torrents of rain water in the cracks reaching the liquid pool below. It will be remembered that an explosive rumbling was heard there through the fog at that time.

Nothing new was observed north and west except that the west cone ridge seemed higher. The southeast crag was now low and without peaks.

On March 17 at 3:30 p. m. the depression of the lake was about the same and there was lava flowing in the central pond. On visiting the north gap at 4 p. m. a new cone was found with an open pot where lava boiled and a flaming crack was active beside it. The northwest cove pond was brimming level with the edge around it and fountaining, and the pond in the northwest chasm was crusted over. At 8:30 p. m. there was some subsidence and renewed activity in the southeast cove, the southeast arm remaining crusted.

On March 19 at 9:50 a. m. the lake had risen so as to build a new rampart two feet above the level of the south floor and the lake stood three feet below this rampart. The southeast cove was crusted over and the streaming was reversed from its original course, pouring outward from the cove to the southeast arm where the current met the streaming from the west in a line of foundering and fountains, extending between the southeast crag and the east cove. A new floor platform had been built at the east cove, and a new crescent dome at the east gulch to which there was local streaming. The only dome grotto in the southeast cove was on its northwest side. All around the lake a new spatter margin had been built about three feet high. The southeast crag was greatly lifted from its former position below the level of the southeast bench, for its summit now stood fully 15 feet above that bench. The southeast bench stood 12 feet above the lake. Over the southeast tunnel grotto there was a small blowing cone on the bank, surrounded by sulphur stain. The central pond was crusted over and its cone hissing but showing no special incandescence.

The activity in the southeast cove was as follows: 9:30 a. m., temporary crusting of southeast channel, skin stagnant in southeast arm, streaming to southeast crag grotto on northwest side of southeast cove. 9:45 a. m., northward streaming resumed and southeast cove stagnant. 10 a. m., two-foot subsidence, vigorous southeast streaming restored, incaving margins and many fountains. 12:30 p. m., lake a little higher, streaming northward resumed, and heavy foun-

Feb. 23, 1918. Halemaumau overflowing, from near east station

March 8, 1918. The new overflows looking southeast, old trail on the left, from summit o

A-frame left, central crags, East Ledge Crag on right.—*Photo. Jaggar.*

East Ledge Crag. "A" on the right is where the A-frame formerly stood, at the new south cone.
—*Photo. Jaggar.*

taining at the point of conflicting currents in the southeast arm.

The south cone stood 8 feet high, with crevasses on both sides of it and a secondary cone 15 feet to the northeast of it, both of these standing on the crest of a cracked and upswollen ridge which extended for 200 feet along what had been the southern wall crack of the pit.

Exploration of the southwest pond at 9:50 a. m. revealed the fact that its southern wall margin had been lifted 20 feet and was becoming a craggy escarpment with a greatly-steepened southern slope and white smoke rising from its summit. The pond, like the rest of the lake, showed a three-foot spatter margin, an active grotto at the south tunnel, and looking across to the north it was seen that a broad new platform had been built on the northwest side of the western deck extension of the central crag mass so as to narrow the southwest channel to a long curving chasm between this platform and the west cone ridge.

The eastern depression of the northeast fill showed active driblet flows in motion and heavy glowing accumulations of lava which had welled up through cracks in the floor.

The north cove pond was now almost obliterated, built over by a heavy floor containing a spurting pot which occasionally burst into violent fountaining, and a spatter cone three feet high which sometimes hissed harshly. A little to the north where the old pond rim had been, the second active orifice was an oval glowing pot two feet across, lined with spatter stalactites, and next to it a flaming crack, over live lava which could be heard roaring below, exhibited crowded stalactites at the orifice of a glowing chamber which were unquestionably the products of remelting of the walls and suggested the cavern type. These stalactites were bearded with delicate fibrous needles.

The remainder of the north arm area showed central and northwestern ponds; the northeast cove appeared extended eastward and four or five conspicuous pinnacles margined the east island mass on its west side. An active grotto hung with an arch of stalactites was bubbling on the north side of the northwest cove pond with surface streaming towards it. The general floor of the north arm stood five feet above these ponds. Very heavy white smoke rose from cracks in the older rim of the north arm at the base of the northwest crag.

The crags had been rising slowly, especially in the center, the most marked change being the uplift of the southwest floor.

On March 20 at 4 p. m. the lake was still high and had built a very large half-dome at the south margin of the southeast cove. The pool was crusted, rising, and under high gas pressure, with spraying outbreaks at the margins, especially at the east gulch and at the south grotto. The grotto under the southeast crag was quiet and showed a high arch lined with stalactites above it. Everything indicated renewed strong gas pressure just at the equinox. At night the brilliancy of the pit as seen at a distance was increased and the actual fountains of the southeast cove could be seen from Volcano House. The crags were definitely higher, conspicuously rising above the far edge of Kilauea as seen from the Keanakakoi flats, and the uplift of the preceding twenty-four hours was specially conspicuous in the south pressure ridge and its western extension making a lifted escarpment all the way to the west cone ridge. The latter was broken through by the northwest chasm, and the southwestern half was rising higher than the northern portion, making a distinct peak above the bend of the southwest channel. This peak was much higher than the west cone itself, a prominent feature some 15 feet high and its base again above the level of the western rim of the pit. A new jutting peak of rock protruded from the summit of the south pressure ridge. The swollen new lava hills near the south cone are still hot and stand high and are much stained with gypsum, and there is similar staining elsewhere in the new flows, especially over the old wall crack and the old flaming zones. The swelling of the south cone hillocks appears to have continued after the flows ceased. A very conspicuous ridge has swollen up over the main tunnel extending southward from the south cone. Its top is the summit of the heaping and shows lengthwise cracks distended by a bulging fill of lava which rose from below and small gas spiracles are distributed along the surface of this lava.

On March 21 the high activity continued. There were occasional large central fountains, hissing and flaming glow cracks and gas spiracles were built in the bank at the southeast corner of the southeast cove. There was much ballooning of skins and southeastward streaming. The lake margin had become easily accessible at the east gulch where there was no activity. No flows were in motion at the northeast fill. The northwest cove pond was fountaining, the north cove cone was hissing strongly, and there was moderate flaming at the pot farther north. There was also an active cone in the middle region of the north arm. No activity could be seen in the northwest chasm or around the western rim. In the evening the lake flooded the bank at the east gulch and the fountains were plainly visible at Volcano House, not only southeast, but also north and northwest. Late in the evening there was temporary subsidence and a fall of the spatter bank under the southeast crag caused a strong wave.

On March 22 in the morning the lake was about 4 feet lower, fume was thin and the fountains were no longer visible from the Observatory. In the afternoon the fumes became very dense. The crags retained their height.

In the Whitney Laboratory the seismographs, for the week ending at 2 p. m., March 22, 1918, have registered faint traces of possible teleseisms or distant earthquakes March 16 and 18, on the latter date about 2 p. m., and one local earthquake about 10:54 a. m., March 22. The excessive tilt to the south and west was compensated by gradual recovery to the north and east, March 19-22. Microseismic motion diminished from strong to moderate during the week. Volcanic vibration increased and became strong on March 20, diminishing thereafter.

Volcano Observatory, Mar. 30, 1918.

During the week ending Friday, March 29, 1918, the lava lake and crags of Halemaumau continued to show the effects of the equinoctial rise until March 26, when very sharp subsidence set in which has continued so as to lower the lake 50 feet below the southeast margin, and all the crags have gone down with it. A singular coincidence of this subsidence has been a marked decrease of fume density, instead of increase such as commonly showed very promptly in the past when the lava went down. Coordinate with this has been the considerable density of fuming which marked the recent rising spells, also contrary to the rule. Assuming thin fumes due to more complete combustion of the gases, the explanation of the anomaly appears to be that increase of crusted and craggy areas over the very large surface of the upper rim of Halemaumau produced more condensation tunnels and less complete combustion, whereas the present subsidence has demolished those tunnels, opened larger liquid areas and increased both the fountaining activity and the combustion. The rapidity of the present subsidence is the greatest this year and is accompanied by southwestward tilt and numerous perceptible local earthquakes. This is in accordance with precedent for the period immediately following equinox. The nature of the subsidence appears to be a withdrawal of liquid lava through sinkholes at the east and south, and withdrawal of the bench magma vertically downward near the center of the pit. The effect of this is to flatten the hitherto steep surfaces which sloped away from the center and at the same time to produce sagging depressions and crevasses in the three great wall valleys. The crags, still in full view from the Observatory, are subsiding fast, and the fountains are no longer visible.

On Saturday, March 23, at 10 a. m., the lake was about 5 feet below the bench at the east gulch, rising about three feet towards noon. Spatter margins had been built higher and a large dome in the southeast corner showed long stalactites with glowing interstices. After a spell of breaking up the lake crusted over. The grotto on the southeast crag side had collapsed and there was a line of solfataric fume and stain extending from the lake along the boulder-filled depression of the east gulch. Heavy fountaining noises could be heard from the southwest cove. At night the fountains were very brilliant in the southeast and north arms.

On March 24 at 3:45 p. m. the southeast bench stood about 8 feet above the lake, which rose two feet in the course of two hours. The two cones of the north cove were puffing noisily, the northwest cove pond was 3 feet below its rim and crusted, and the fumes near its north bank were dense. At 6 p. m. the risen lake southeast was very quiet, with only one grotto in action. In the evening two fountains southeast and one northwest could be seen from the Observatory, but during the night the intensest illumination was in the center and the southwest cove, bringing the middle crags into silhouette.

On March 25 at 5 p. m. the southeast margin of the lake was two feet below the newest spatter rim, large domes had formed along the southern rampart, and the southeast shelf stood about 6 feet above the lake surface. At 5:30 p. m. there was subsidence of about a foot, with general break-up of crusts, very rapid streaming and enormous fountains migrating across the southeast cove with much bubbling. An open glowing cupola could be seen behind the stalactite curtain within the corner dome southeast. The central pond depression was smoking; the crags were little changed.

The east island crag had recently developed a conspicuous spire rising above its serrate top. In the northeast depression new flows were heaped up and driblet flows were in motion on the east side of the blister lava area. These came from a rough cone bearing bearded spiracles and flaming, hissing gas cracks.

At the north gap cone the pot was inactive, but a glowing crack hissed on its margin and deposited yellow sublimates. The north cove cone had small spiracle heaps on its summit and yellow stain and one of the holes was hissing and flaming. Rocks fell from the west end of the north smoke crag, which was cracking on the north station side; this crag, at the west end, seemed higher in profile than the eastern end of the northeast crag mass. The lava in the northwest cove pond was high and crusted with a sluggish fountain ballooning the crust and belching gas at the north corner. The site of the north central pond was occupied by two cones.

The west niche was dead, and in the northwest chasm the floor of crust was 12 feet down, and a bright yellow solfataric area had formed on the west margin of the rim. A hollow blowing sound could be heard below, but no glow was visible. Gas collections were made on this day southeast, northeast and north. The glow from the crater on this evening was dim.

On March 26 the crags were slightly higher, the fume was rather dense, no fountains were visible in the daytime from the Observatory, but in the evening moderate fountain action was visible.

From 4 to 5 p. m. the lake was high and little changed. The central region and southeast arm were very heavily crusted, fountains were playing in the southwest arm, on the west side of the central region, in the northwest cove pond and at the southeast cove where, as usual, the streaming was southward. At the southeast stalactite grotto there was steady inrush. At 5:30 p. m. the southeast cove fountains were throwing spray high above the south margin.

Flowing had ceased in the northeast depression. At the north gap the cones still hissed, but the rim pot was nearly dead, making much odor of free sulphur through a small glowing marginal crack, and the sulphur-colored areas were larger. The north central cones were still in place. The west end of the northeast crag mass was greatly crevassed and fallen away, and there had been much rock tumbling also at the east gulch. It was evident that motion in the crags was becoming irregular, and there was much humping and crevassing of the northeast fill, especially away from the fresh flows of the extreme northeast part. There was also bulging and sagging in the floor of the north arm area. The grotto pit of the west niche was full of broken rocks and dead. The southwest crag mass appeared higher and also the east side of the northwest chasm, but this last appearance may have been a sinking of the west side.

On March 27 at 10 a. m. the lake surface stood 12 feet below the southeast shelf, there were no marked changes, the crags were lower, but the top of the southeast crag was still higher than the southeast shelf. In the evening falls of rock were reported, and from a distance the pit appeared dull except for bright glows occasionally with sudden flaring. A small earthquake was felt.

From the Observatory at 9 a. m., March 28, it was clear that strong subsidence had started. The crags were lower and both the north and southeast lake corners were smoky. At 4 p. m. the lava southeast was 15 feet below the southeast shelf and 11 feet below the rim of recent overflow at the east gulch. The southeast cove was continuously active, with rapid southward streaming and traveling fountains. Inspection of the north arm at 5 p. m. showed that the whole east half of the floor had collapsed, making once more an open lake which joined the north central and north cove ponds. The northwest pond was still enclosed with walls about 8 feet high. At 11 p. m., seen from a distance, the crater was very bright, especially towards the north, there was much flaring during the night, and the crags subsided so that the central peak as seen from the Observatory appeared well below the southwest wall of Kilauea crater.

On March 29 at 5 a. m. another small earthquake was felt and at 8 a. m. the crags were lower and the fume was very thin. At 3:30 p. m. the lake was found to have subsided profoundly so that the southeast shelf stood 40 to 50 feet above it. The central group of crags had also sunk and the southeast crag was fully 10 feet below the surface of the southeast shelf. Crags were opening along the line from the southeast grotto to the south cone. The latter had collapsed, puffing sulphur fume rose from an open crack west of it, there was a broken area all around, and dark red glow could be seen 10 feet down the cracks. The activity was not much changed, streaming was southward in the southeast cove, while the southeast arm and middle region were crusted over except for a large fountain at the west side of the lake. There was bombardment at the base of the southern and southeastern cliffs of the southeast cove. The high cliff beneath the southeast shelf showed some overhang. The east gulch was deep at the lake shore, but choked with stones fallen from the east ledge a short distance away. The latter had subsided and flattened its back slope. The east island crag mass showed marked inclination towards the center of the pit of its spatter level of the previous day, and a glowing cavern was revealed at the east cove lake margin.

The central pond had a glowing and flaming heap on its east side. The depression northeast was lower, there were small pits of collapse and open crevasses near the northeast wall and in the middle of the northeast fill very hot air rose through big cracks from glowing depths. The north arm lakes were 30 feet down and very fumy, with sluggish activity and the cones gone. The westward slope from the northwest chasm was flatter, so that the central region was again visible from the northwest rim of Halemaumau. The southwest crag and west cone was still relatively high. At the southwest floor, however, the slope leading up to the cliff over the southwest pond was much flatter, the pond stood 30 feet below, with continuous fountaining at the south tunnel, and the southwest channel had widened. The inner bench on the east and north sides of this pond stood 10 feet above the lake, but the corresponding bench on the south side was 10 feet higher, showing that the central crag mass had subsided more than the southwest block. The pond was mostly crusted over. Huge crevasses had opened in the floor north of the south cone and everywhere around the pit. Such crevasses showed the internal incandescence of the bench magma to be only 12 to 15 feet below the surface.

In the Whitney Laboratory of Seismology nine local earthquakes have been registered during the week ending at 2 p. m., March 29, 1918, and also smaller tremors which would hardly rank as quakes. This was all accordant with the change from rising to sharply sinking lava. At least three or the shocks were felt at Volcano House. The times were 11:09 p. m., March 23; 7:23 p. m., March 25; 9:47 a. m., 8:30 a. m., 9:48 p. m. (felt), March 26; 7:38 p. m., (felt), 9:40 p. m., and many tremors March 27; 6 a. m. (felt), 9:24 a. m., March 29.

Microseisms throughout the week were moderate, volcanic vibration was at first strong continuously and later strong in shart spasms. Tilting movement, from a trend at first eastward and northward, changed on March 25 in the north-south component to strong southward, and the next day in the east-west component to westward, and thereafter the southwest tilt increased.

Very respectfully,

T. A. JAGGAR, JR., Director.

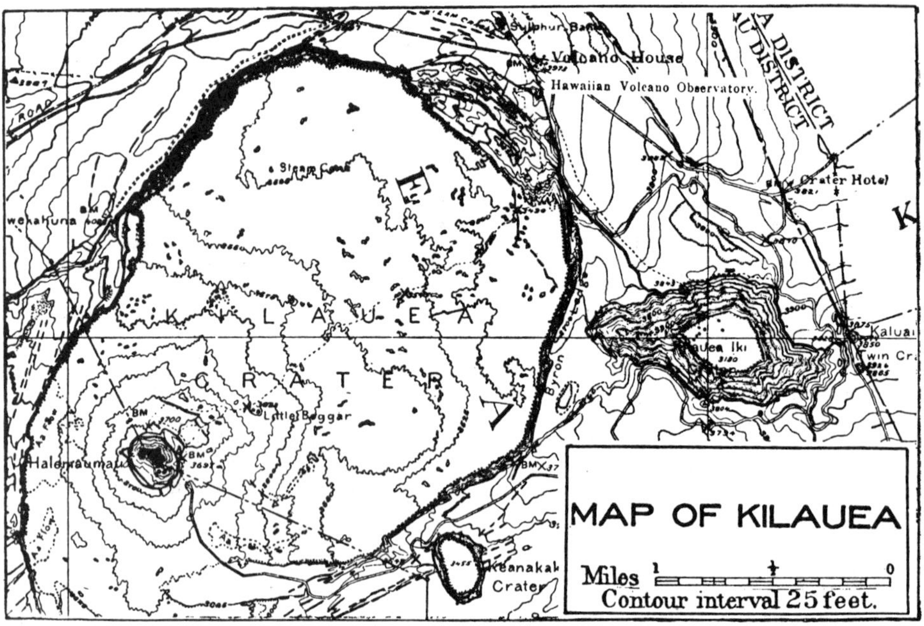

HAWAIIAN VOLCANO RESEARCH ASSOCIATION.

This society is a voluntary one, made up of subscribers to scientific work which is being executed by Dr. T. A. Jaggar, Director of the Hawaiian Volcano Observatory, Volcano House, P. O., Hawaii. **All scientific exchanges should be sent to this address.**

In 1917 there are about 150 subscribers in Hawaii and elsewhere, firms and individuals. A group of firms and persons in Hilo built the main observatory building in the spring of 1912. The work was founded by the Massachusetts Institute of Technology. Publications to date have been weekly reports since the summer of 1911 now reprinted in Honolulu in monthly form. There are also special reports, printed from time to time.

The weekly bulletin as it appears in the Honolulu Advertiser is reprinted as a leaflet and sent to regular annual subscribers to the work of the Association. L. A. Thurston is president of the Board of Directors of the Association, and L. T. Peck is treasurer. New subscribers who are interested in volcanoes will be welcomed in the Association. The Association aims: (1) To record volcanic activity and earthquakes in Hawaii; (2) to attract scientific men hither for special studies; (3) to promote the establishment of volcano observatories all over the world. The annual dues of regular members are $5; patrons of the Association subscribe larger amounts.

WHITNEY LABORATORY OF SEISMOLOGY.

The Whitney Laboratory of Seismology, named after an endowment fund of geophysical research held by the Massachusetts Institute of Technology, in memory of Caroline and Edward Whitney of Boston, is equipped with two Bosch-Omori 100 kg tromometers registering N-S and E-W motion, a heavy Omori tromometer registering E-W motion, and an Omori "ordinary Seismograph" designed for registering strong earthquakes in all three components of motion. These are seated on concrete piers in a closed basement room having practically constant temperature, beneath the chief Observatory building near the hotel. Time is referred to a rated chronometer, checked at intervals by solar observations with a transit. Both instruments are loaned by the College of Hawaii. Hawaiian standard time (H. S. T.) is 10 hrs. 30 min. slower than Greenwich time.

CANCANI SCALE OF SEISMIC INTENSITY.

Expressed by accelerations measured in millimeters per second per second.

I.	Instrumental	0.0	2.5
II.	Very slight	2.5	5.0
III.	Slight	5.0	10.0
IV.	Sensible, mediocre	10.0	25.0
V.	Rather strong	25.0	50.0
VI.	Strong	50.0	100.0
VII.	Very strong	100.0	250.0
VIII.	Ruinous	250.0	500.0
IX.	Disastrous	500.0	1000.0
X.	Very disastrous	1000.0	2500.0
XI.	Catastrophic	2500.0	5000.0
XII.	Great catastrophe	5000.0	10000.0

Grade IV. is ordinarily the minimum perceived by the senses; and in grade XII. the acceleration, or rate of change of motion (jerk) reaches that of terrestrial gravitation.

In the standard form of report the maximum intensity or acceleration, designated by the symbol a, or max. a, is given in the conventional unit, the milligal. The milligal is a measure of acceleration, such that 1 milligal = 1/100 mm. per sec. per sec. = 10 μ per sec. per sec. The Cancani scale, here defined in terms of millimeters per sec. per sec., can therefore be expressed in milligals by multiplying each of the numbers by 100.

WEEKLY BULLETIN

OF THE

Hawaiian Volcano Observatory

Vol. VI. HONOLULU, HAWAII, APRIL, 1918. No. 4

VOLCANO OBSERVATORY, April 6, 1918.—During the week ending Friday, April 6, 1918, the subsidence continued and reached its maximum movement about April 2. A comparatively stationary condition of the bench magma as represented by the central crag was indicated between April 3 and April 5 while the lava lakes during this interval rose relative to the crags. At the time of writing this rising of the lakes continues vigorously and appears to mark a distinct recovery from the subsidence. The maximum depression reached, measured roughly April 3 and April 5, was 240 feet for the lake surface below the east edge of Halemaumau near the stone shelter. The central crag stood 108 feet above the lake. Although the lake appeared to be rising and greatly flooded the floors between these dates, this action must have just compensated the subsidence for both dates gave like measurements. Hence the depression limit appears to have been reached April 4.

The sinking lava column was being withdrawn down the Halemaumau shaft from March 26 to April 4, a period of nine days, from a high level which had flooded the Kilauea inner cone for over a month, the total subsidence amounting to at least 260 feet below the overflow rim southeast. The effect of this movement was to restore the old Halemaumau pit, with its margins filled out where depressions had been and in a few places broken away where the edge had been crushed and loosened during the rise. Constructive effects have been greater than destructive so that the pit is smaller and much more symmetrical, the north-eastern and western niches being now filled with new lava. The subsidence carried down the greater crags intact, the lake maintained relation to the crags in form and action essentially unchanged. The debris slopes eventually encroached upon its outer shores. These tumbled slopes when they fell in the lake, clearly evinced the presence of a shallow lake bottom flying at flat angles by choking the channels and pools. Numerous localized small earthquakes accompanied the movement of subsidence, increasing in vehemence as it increased and ceasing completely when recovery began. During the maximum these jars were quite perceptible at the edge of the pit. The fumes have been extraordinarily thin and the presence of eighteen or more vigorous lava fountains building cones shows that combustion of the gases is very complete. A spectacular feature of the rock slides which accompanied the depression was the caving away of the still incandescent lava fillings on the northeast and west, which were sufficiently mobile to ooze outward on the broken face of the cliff as very stiff aa lava which then broke and flaked away in large blocks making by night stupendous fiery avalanches into the depths below. Halemaumau is no longer a hill, it is a pit as of old with the whole panorama of craggy hills and five bubbling fiery lakes spread out in plan beneath the visitor.

On March 30 the whole Halemaumau landscape of crags, ridges, chasms, lakes and plains very gradually subsided and so rapidly that the rocky hills which have been a feature of the view of the pit from the Observatory for over three months had disappeared by the next day, hidden by the rim of the pit. There were no avalanche clouds, small rock falls took place but no great ones and angular measurement, during the subsidence, of fixed points on the old rim, failed to detect any subsidence

WEEKLY BULLETIN
of the
Hawaiian Volcano Observatory

Published Monthly at Honolulu, Hawaii, by the Hawaiian Volcano Research Association

L. W. de Vis-Norton........Secretary

Entered as second-class matter January 20, 1914, at the post-office at Honolulu, Hawaii, under the Act of August 24, 1912.

there even when the inner crags were sinking rapidly. The fume was very thin.

At 5 p. m. the lake was over 100 feet below the rim, the new pit was defined, the southeast shelf remained erect, the lake was enlarged by marginal collapse, the central pond was active and the crags kept nearly the same relation to the lake as during the high levels. An immense overhanging cliff beneath the southeast shelf descended all the way to the liquid lava of the southeast cove, but this did not imply a sinking of the liquid within its basin by that amount, for the entire containing basin had sunk with the liquid, parting from the southeast shelf along great fault cliffs where the east gulch and south crevasses had been. In fact just at this point the subsequent fall of broken rock into the lake quickly filled it and closed the channel which had previously led to the southeast cove, showing that its basin was shallow.

The new Halemaumau rim extended the southeast shelf to follow approximately the line of the former 1894 bench on the northeast side of the pit, but at a much higher level. The old cliff line remained on the north, a new cliff crossed the west niche. The southwest margin which had been pushed up, now crumbled away somewhat, enlarging the old pit in that direction only; while from the south cone to the southeast shelf there was a new cliff considerably inside of the old pit edge.

The summit of the stiff cylinder which constituted the moving lava column inside the pit had on it as before the northeast valley floor, the northeast crag mass, the east island, the northwest, west and central crags with the outlying floors, pits, chasms and escarpments and the lake in the midst, all the activities of the whole scene, smoking vents, fountaining grottoes and streaming channels maintaining their usual habits quite regardless of the fact that the entire relief map of which they were parts was sinking into the depths at a rate which averaged more than 50 feet a day. It was an astonishingly complete demonstration that the lava lake and its feeding tubes constitute a mere surface mechanism in a substance capable of moving en masse.

On looking down on the new fill northeast occupying the old crescent-shaped 1894 wall valley somewhat outside of the true pit margin, it was seen that the drainage of remnant liquid out from under the cones which had been making flows five days before had left deep tunnels and pits all glowing within, the luminescence showing every detail of a cavernous space with a roof shell 10 feet thick, the interior, apparently 40 feet high, revealed through a ragged hole 50 feet across. When a block of the roof shell fell in, the broken rock was seen to be of bright yellow incandescence, while the cavernous space was rather orange red. Some 40 feet in front of the east shelter enormous gaping crevasses were seen at the base of the new wall. Farther west along the northeast valley and in the depression under the north station these cracks glowed inside and occasionally their walls collapsed.

Looking into the north arm of the lake the liquid of the large north pond was seen to be fountaining with high flings of melt and receiving a cascade flowing northward from the north central area. It had greatly enlarged and lowered. The lava stood some eighty feet below the north gap, but the northwest pond in its separate pit appeared to be at a much higher level and also fountaining. An isthmus separated the northern lakes from the central region.

At 6:30 p. m. the lake appeared as though rising, but the marginal cliffs appeared higher. The east ledge in subsiding was separated from the southeast shelf at what had been the east gulch by a crack which could be traced all the way to the bottom of the inner cliff and this marked the contact plane between the subsiding bench magma and that portion of it which was locked to the old rim by the new overflow—namely the southeast shelf. The summit of the east ledge was now down to the level of the southeast shelf. Only the central crags appeared still a very little above that level. The southwest pond was a deep active pit. The southeast cove had broken out an embayment in the direction of the south cone. The south floor had sunk in steps with cliffs and crevasses between it and the southeast shelf, making it now quite inaccessible, where on the day before the writer had walked across it to the central pond. Both the southeast and southwest arms had widened, there was a deep cove in the north face of the central crag mass and the whole north region of the lake looked wider. There was a glowing pit and a floor cone on the northwest side of the central cove. So much had the lake subsided that the north arm was now visible from the southeast shelf. Fountaining was moderate in the southeast cove and there was the usual broad zone of streaming to the southeast. During the night brilliant flaring could be seen above the pit.

On the morning of March 31 all but the extreme tip of the central crag had disappeared from the distant view. At 10 a. m. it was seen that the inner circle of crags had moved down more than the outer circle, the latter tending rather to hinge against the outer walls and flatten their centrifugal slopes. Between these two portions of the lava column were depressions such as the northwest chasm, the southwest and central ponds and the cove valleys. Evidently the inner lava column moved down fastest and there is probably some concentric fissuring which separated the central core from the outer ring.

The depression continued all day with small rock slides, especially west, north and east, some red dust, much opening of crevasses and thin fume. So gentle was the subsidence that the delicate sculpturing of the west cone, the east island spire and the hanging central crag pinnacle kept their positions uninjured even while being carried down bodily. Bench remnants still clung to the upper walls north, west, south and southeast. The south cone and the southeast shelf remained on the upper rim. Moderate incandescence was seen in the cracks. There was a splashing fountain in a pot in the central pond, the several lakes were surrounded by inner walls about 15 feet high, there was a live pond in the northwest chasm and ten or twelve border fountains were in action in the lakes which occasionally showed spells of breaking up and foundering crusts. Streaming was mostly to the southeast. Now and then a fall of rock into the lava would start action.

At noon Monday, April 1, the same general relations held, everything was lower, avalanches wer stronger and the highest crags were far below the rim. The southeast shelf had fallen away and was much narrower and the rock falls from it had plastered the southeast crag with sheets of lava splash. The lake had somewhat diminished in size, a fresh spatter rim five feet high was built around the main lake and streaming was westward in the northwest pond, southward in the north lake and eastward in the central lake. Encroachment of the talus had demolished the west cone. The valley floors were now sloping inward at high angles, those at the margins of the northwest chasm and the southwest pond keeping fairly horizontal. Enormous crevasses and outward leaning bench slabs between them created a very unstable condition between the outer walls and the sinking lava column and incessant crashing tumbles echoed in the cracks and formed talus below. The southeast shelf undermined by slides on both sides and with the widening old wall crack behind it became precarious as a place for spectators and many rock falls took place from its overhanging cliff into the liquid pool below. This cliff was now more than twice as high above the lake as the summit of the east ledge. In the evening the southeast shelf had crumbled all the way back to the old wall crack.

On April 2 the following record shows the progress of avalanching:

12:50 p. m., avalanche west wall, great activity north pools;

1:10 p. m., heavy avalanche north for 10 minutes, carrying down blocks 20 feet in diameter;

1:25 p. m., continuous avalanches southeast;

1:40 p. m., slides for 10 minutes under the east shelter, carrying down enormous red hot bowlders;

1:50 p. m., former southeast cove cut off as a pond by avalanche talus; some blocks 20 to 30 feet long;

2:15 p. m., inspection from southeast showed that nearly everything of the February overflow bench from the southeast side of the pit to the northeast fill had gone in, leaving the pit margin on that side essentially as of old, except for the new filling northeast, and overflow veneer southeast.

3:50 p. m., earthquake felt and slides loosened on all sides.

4:15 p. m., whole block of new bench fell just east of south cone, sending up a brown dust cloud;

4:17 p. m., block of southwest crag fell into channel, started violent fountaining which continued for an hour and more and reversed the streaming from the central region so that a continuous torrent poured westward to a place of violent bubble fountaining at the southwest bend.

From under the northeast fill just west of the east shelter and 15 feet down, aa lava was trickling out with a flaking motion very slowly.

4:20 p. m., lake rapidly sinking, showing bright rim and overhang 6 feet high. The southeast cove pond, dammed off from the main lake, did not take part in the sinking. Streaming westward from the southeast arm. While the lake sank thus the avalanches were quiet.

4:57 p. m., earthquake shock and more slides.

The depression of the lake at 3:30 p. m. was about 130 feet. There were six ponds, four north and northwest, the main lake and the southeast cove pond. The central steeple was lower than the central crag summit and the crag and bench surfaces indicated a tilt southeastward as though the subsidence were faster in that direction. The northwest crag was now buried under talus like the southeast channel.

On April 3 at 7 p. m. measurement made the lake 238 feet below the east shelter and the summit of the central crag 130 feet down. Eighteen fountains in action at fixed places were building spatter cones, while extensive floors and overflowing margins showed that the lakes were rising relative to the crags. The pools were mostly crusted, and streaming showed no fixed directions. The central region of the lake was widened northwestward, the southeast arm northeastward and the north pools both westward and eastward. Avalanching was dominantly from the faces of the northeast fill and the west niche where the incandescent lava seen on the previous day to be aa flaked off on the face of the wall, undermined everything above and so produced tremendous glowing falls of most spectacular aspect. The material appeared like banks of glowing coal. The talus would slide in incandescent streams and the cliff faces glowed red above the whole length of the former 1894 bench and the west niche bench.

Glowing spots on the face of the southeast cliff, bright red glow in cracks only a foot down on the new overflow 30 feet back from the southeast edge, and rise in the ground-temperature there, very marked during these days of subsidence, all suggested that fresh oxidation was started in the flow material beneath by exposing it to the air at the new cross section of the broken pit wall.

On April 5 at 4:30 p. m. the avalanches were few and small, fresh lava had flooded the depression east of the central crags, the northeast cove area and the northern and western pond shores and there was high gas pressure from the many blowing and fountaining cones.

On Friday, April 5, measurement at 9:15 a. m., made the depression of the lake 237 feet and of the central crag 129 feet below the east shelter, showing that subsidence had ceased. There were a few dust slides but no avalanches. Some tumbles from the east island mass and the south pressure ridge suggested rising motion in the crags. The lakes were flush with the new overflow benches, driblet flows were pushing out in the central region, all the lakes were increased by marginal building and strong blowing noises came from the center and the west chasm. Fresh overflow had poured across the west end of the southeast crag remnant from the southeast arm to the southeast pond.

The central pond had a large dome stained yellow and with a dark cavity in its summit. There was another large cone in the central floor. At the lake shore on the east side of the southwest bend there was inflow under the bank at a spatter cone and an enormous periodic fountain would explode here about once in 45 seconds like the former "Old Faithful." Relative to the central crag benches the lake appeared 15 feet higher than two days before. The talus on all sides had settled down leaving smooth walls, one large surface southwest showing vertical scorings. The former valley floors south and west now stood upright as nearly vertical slabs. Of the upturned pressure edge of the old pit wall southwest little remains, as that material caved away when the lava went down.

There was much local earthquaking during the subsidence, which ceased when the lava turned, and there was very pronounced tilt to the west and south, which changed to slow recovery east and north when the lava began to rise. The report of the Whitney Laboratory will otherwise be deferred.

VOLCANO OBSERVATORY, April 13, 1918.—During the week ending Friday, April 12, 1918, the Halemaumau lava column continued its recovery and rose some 30 feet, lifting the whole body of floor and crags by that amount until April 8. After that date subsidence was resumed until the morning of April 12 so that at the end of the week the lava was about as low as at the beginning. It now appears to be recovering. The only marked changes are further collapses of remnant benches of new lava which clung to the rim of the pit, new interior floors from overflow of the lakes, and considerable falling away of the central crag mass so as nearly to destroy its eastern steeple.

At 10:30 a. m. on Saturday, April 6, the lakes were strongly rising at a faster rate than the crags so that new overflows made new floors in all directions. There were five ponds of liquid lava as follows: (1) the main lake from southwest arm to southeast arm; (2) the north lake including both the north and northwest former coves; (3) southwest pond; (4) southeast pond; (5) the west chasm pond. In addition the crusted depression of the central pond really contained a lava pot beneath, but it was now roofed with bronzy flows and had a large hissing cone in its center stained with whitish sublimates.

The streaming was north in the north lake and east in the southwest and main lakes. There was a row of grotto cones along the northwest side of the southeast pond and one large cone on the opposite side. There were about eighteen fountaining border cones in the other lakes, occasional central fountains would break the crust and at the west end of the main lake the rhythmic fountain would occasionally explode. The channel here leading to the southwest pond was choked by falls of debris. So high was the construction by overflow that the northern peaks of the east island mass were entirely isolated, back of this mass the flows of the east and northeast coves had merged, the eastern crags of the west crag mass were nearly buried, the western deck of the central crag mass was only a few feet above the lake level, the southeastern flows were all merging and the southeast crag remnant was almost entirely submerged. The overflows of the north lake showed signs of joining through to the west chasm pond and the new floods lapped against the outer debris slopes of the pit on the west, northwest, north, southeast and southwest. There were large cones at each of the two eastern coves of the lake. The noises were of fountaining and puffing, there were occasional small adjustments of the high talus and the fume was somewhat diminished. At noon a glow edge of subsidence appeared about one foot deep around all the lakes except the southeast pond, but the latter rose and overflowed on all sides for some time before it, too, cracked up and subsided.

On April 8 at noon measurement made the depression of the summit of the central crag below the east station 103 feet and of the liquid lava in the center of the pit 198 feet. The bench magma appeared to have risen in relation to the lakes and the margins of the latter were higher towards the west and progressively lower eastward and southward. Thus the rims of the southeast pond and of the southern overflow margin of the southwest pond were only one foot high while the enclosing banks of the main lake varied from two feet high on the east to five feet high on the west. The northwest pond was again defined as a small pit of live lava with walls six feet above the liquid, and radial flows made new floor all about it. The north and west lakes were merely floors of new flows, the former being represented by a high hissing spiracle cone at the base of the cliff made by the north smoke crag. The southwest arm was again connected through to the southwest pond. The central pond cone was hissing and the southeast pond exhibited a blowing and spraying grotto.

At 6 p. m. on Thursday, April 9, after a very rainy day, the lakes appeared somewhat lower, there were more open pools, fume was increased and a small local earthquake felt during the previous night accorded with these symptoms in showing renewed subsidence. The southeast pond was crusted over within margins three feet high and two spraying vents on the north side were made by gases escaping from under the crust. The southwest pond was crusted over. Eastward streaming in the main lake carried along polygonal crusts to be engulfed at several active grottoes at the east end. There were fewer of these than a few days earlier. The southeast arm was extended eastward. There was a flaming and hissing cone on the east cove floor and another one with glowing flanks in the north central region. At the northeast cove there was a fountaining pot, and an open pool at the north pond showed three fountaining grottoes opening eastward. The lake appeared lower in the central region.

On Wednesday, April 10, at 10:30 a. m., the inner pits of the active pools were deeper, having five foot walls at the southeast pond and east arm. The entire summit block of the central steeple had fallen away on both the north and south sides leaving much talus beneath. The east arm of the lake had broken back to the east cove dome where there was inward streaming and fountaining; three fountains played on other sides of the southeast arm and two fountains north and northeast of the southeast pond. At the northeast cove there was a small open pot, much fume rose from the floors, streaming was outward from the southwest pond, all the lakes were crusted, with occasional cracking and foundering and the floor margin of the main lake appeared much increased in height westward. From 12 noon to 1 p. m. the northwest pond overflowed strongly, the flood extending itself some 300 feet along the base of the west talus. During a temporary subsidence a cavern was revealed under the southwest margin of the pond. In the north central floor there was a small open pot showing lava five feet down and farther south was a fuming vent. There was slight glow of the east side of the west chasm pond which was otherwise crusted over. The rhythmic fountain at the southwest bend still erupted every forty seconds. The bank of the main lake appeared highest in the central region. The hanging pinnacle of the central crag was still in place. White fumes still continued to raise from the south cone which makes an eminence on the southern margin of the pit.

On April 11 at 4 p. m. sharp subsidence was in progress, the inner pits were 20 feet deep and avalanches were falling around the outer walls of the main pit on all sides. At 7:30 p. m. the liquid lava appeared still lower and showed increased activity while the avalanches continued to fall. The tumbles from the new northeastern and western fills showed no incandescence.

On Friday, April 12, at 4 p. m., measurement made the depression of the central crag beneath the east station 136 feet, of the central floor bench 236 feet, and of the lake 15 feet lower. The pit was very smoky, the inner lake pits 15 feet deep towards the east and 20 feet towards the west. Both lakes and crags had greatly subsided. The activity was dull, streaming was eastward at the southwest bend, the rhythmic fountain there was smaller and showed somewhat shorter intervals, the lakes elsewhere were mostly crusted over. No avalanches were falling and the lake magma appeared to be rising. The talus summits on all sides were lower and the wall spaces above them higher. Large blocks of the March bench had fallen away from the high edge of the pit east, northeast, north and west, and there was now very little left of such new benches. The northwest triangulation station had fallen to a small remnant bench just beneath. There was a deep indentation in the north side of the central crag mass and only the eastern end of the steeple there remained. The poised pinnacle, however, was still in place.

The seismographs have recorded little earthquake activity, tilting to the west and south has been resumed, volcanic vibrations and microseisms have somewhat increased.

VOLCANO OBSERVATORY, April 20, 1918.—During the week ending April 19, 1918, the lava column has maintained a depression oscillating near the 225-foot mark for the main lava lake, the adjustments for the week being subsidences of the central crags and floors and irregular risings of the lava pools so as to overflow the floors in different places on different days. The net effect is new construction of floors at the expense of crags and talus. Thus on different days the measurement of vertical angles showed the following:

April 14, lake and floor higher, central crag lower.

April 15, lake lower, central crag and floor higher.

April 16, lake higher and overflowing, central crag and floor lower.

April 17, lake, crag and floor lower.

April 19, lake, crag and floor higher, (lake overflowing.)

On Saturday, April 13, at 2:30 p. m., the lakes were quiet and the smoke thick. The margin of the east arm pool was 10 feet high and of the southeast pond 20 feet high. Little could be seen towards the north, the ponds and floors appeared indistinguishable and puffing could be heard towards the west. For over an hour there were no slides. At 3:40 p. m., however, a strong avalanche started on the northeast wall and this was followed by others north and northwest. At the same time the southeast arm developed fountains and subsidence, indicating the close sympathy that exists between rock-sliding and lowering of the liquid lava.

On April 14 at 11 a. m. the southeast pond was somewhat higher with walls only 12 feet high, while the inner pit of the east arm remained about 10 feet deep. Rocks were sliding on the north and west, there was the occasional noise of a sharp gas blast toward the north, three border fountains played in the east arm and one or two in the southeast pond. The lake appeared to be rising but the pit was excessively smoky, especially from the north vents. The central crag pinnacle was still in place and has remained so throughout the week.

The rhythmic fountain at the west end of the main lake exploded at intervals of from 25 to 40 seconds, with sometimes a secondary explosion 10 seconds later. The fountaining took the form of an immense dome 20 feet in diameter which completely filled a caldron of the same size and at 11:40 a. m. the east wall of this cauldron caved in, producing violent turbulence and much noise. The southwest pond had become triangular and a narrow gorge containing a bridge of crust separated it from the fountaining cove. The wall around the southwest pond was 20 feet high and bench levels in general sloped strongly downward from here to the central region. There was a hissing and flaming cone in the north central floor. The northwest pond was active and there was an open pot two feet in diameter on the east side of the west pond.

The long northeast crag mass now appeared low compared with the other crags and the new flood floor north and northeast was becoming a center of accumulation which seems to go with this northeastern subsidence and the southwestern uptilting. Thus the old west crag mass had distinctly lifted the new spatter benches of the west chasm pond on its east side while the remainder of the floor of that pond sloped gently eastward. The upper surface of the west crag mass also sloped eastward.

There were small avalanches from the outer wall of the pit on all sides. Narrow remnants of the 1918 new lava still clung as benches near the upper rim of the pit under the northwest and west stations about six feet below the edge. Under the west niche a large upright block of the new bench hung out into the pit in a precarious position. At 4:30 p. m. there were slides northeast and east, some large bowlders rolling down the slope. At this time the lakes were quiet, the only active grotto being in the east cove.

On Monday, April 15, at 5:15 p. m.,

there were fewer avalanches, streaming was eastward, the central pond cone was glowing and the banks of the eastern pools were 10 feet high. Crusts broke up and foundered in the southwest pond, the west pond was crusted over and only glowing spots could be seen towards the north where the smoke was excessive. The rhythmic fountain was erupting weakly. Examination of the southwest margin of Halemaumau showed from familiar landmarks that this edge had caved back recently fully 15 feet as compared with conditions before the overflow.

On April 16 at noon, a remarkable adjustment of lake magma and bench magma was taking place, whereby the central group of crags and floors had definitely subsided since the preceding day, but the lake had just as definitely risen so that the situation was just the reverse of the intumescence or swelling of the bench magma which was so noticeable in January. The relative heights of shore lines showed how the middle had gone down. The southeast pond was 10 feet down, the east arm pool 5 feet down, while the central lake was only 2 feet down. Going farther west the southwest arm again showed a higher shore line and the southwest pond was more than 10 feet down. This all indicated subsidence of shore lines towards the center of the pit, where also there was extensive fresh overflow which radiated only from the center region. These central overflows were extensive, just as previously the northern ones had been. The lake was puffing and plashing, with new driblet cones formed and eastward streaming. The southeast pond was crusted over but an occasional rush of gas broke the crust and produced a fountain on its south side. The northwest pond was fountaining on its west margin. The main lake in its rising had become constricted and divided into pools with arches of crust between them, and the central channel was greatly narrowed.

At 12:30 p. m. the lake subsided, there was a prolonged avalanche towards the north, occasional slides were heard elsewhere and there was some tumbling of debris from the central crag. Smoke rose from several fissure lines in the northern and central floors, from the north and east crags, the central pond floor and from a wall vent at the top of the north talus.

At noon on April 17 measurements made the central pool and overflows 220 feet below the east station on the rim of Halemaumau at the stone shelter. The southeast pond was 10 feet lower than the main lake. The central crag summit was 152 feet below the rim and hence 68 feet high above its north base; its position was 25 feet farther north than in February. In like fashion the southeast pond was farther toward the center than the former southeast cove of which it was the successor. The old west crag summit was farther south than formerly and 190 feet below the rim, 30 feet above the central floor.

On this day appearances remained much the same but subsidence was dominant and avalanches were falling on all sides. Red dust slid into the smokehole half way up the north wall. The top of the lava column was subsiding as a whole, but the lake was brimming level with its margin in the central region and showed fresh overflows, while the northwest pond, the east arm and the western pools were from two to three feet beneath their margins, the southeast pond still more and the southwest pond deepest as to its marginal wall.

There were now identifiable seven pools of liquid lava; southeast, southwest, east, center, west, north and northwest. In addition there were the crusted depressions of the west and central ponds, both definite lava wells beneath. The north pool was a rather deep crack-like depression showing live lava within, and the northwest pond a shallower oval crusted oven. Blowing noise could be heard in this region. The rhythmic fountain in the west pool of the main lake was now nearly buried under crust from beneath which smothered explosions occasionally were seen. There was a glowing chimney above. The poised slab under the west niche had settled into a symmetrical upright unit parallel with the wall plane above, with crevasses on its sides, and wholly breaking the continuity of the otherwise rather continuous funnel slopes of the outer wall of the pit.

On April 18 at 4:40 p. m. there was much fountaining activity. In the southeast pond the margin was 5 feet

Feb. 22, 1918. The day before overflow, SE rim of Halemaumau; the small dome is at the lake edge.—*Photo. Jaggar.*

March 23, 1918. SW rim of Halemaumau, showing upward mashing of old edge of pit; fresh flows in foreground. The SW trig station was lifted 15 feet on the distant hump, center of picture.—*Photo. Jaggar.*

high and a few fountains broke at the edges. In the east arm streaming eastward was swift from the bridge of crust at the central channel. There were fountains at the north but the fumes were thick there. At 5:30 p. m. a noisy slide developed on the northeast talus and some smaller ones at the west. At 6 p. m. the main lake, divided into three separate ponds with bridges of crust between, showed numerous small marginal spatter grottoes building.

On Friday, April 19, at 11 a. m. and thereafter, the east arm was overflowing on all sides, there were many marginal spatter cones, much hissing noise, several filagree glowing cones and about ten fountains in all. Everything indicated strong gas pressure and rising liquid. Streaming was eastward in the main lake and southwest pond. The overflowing of the east arm was followed by similar rising and overflowing of the southeast pond, and lastly the southwest pond rose until it was only from one to two feet below its eastern and southern banks. A spouting cone had been built over the south tunnel on its southeast bank. The hole in the central pond cone appeared dark by daylight. The flood from the east arm finally poured northward through the gap on the northeast side of the east island mass. There were other fresh flows from the northern pools on the north central floor and glowing cracks could be seen beyond. About noon the lakes were rising and falling at the usual intervals of gas inflation. When the first of the temporary subsidences of the east arm took place, the southeast pond lagged behind it about 10 minutes before it, too, subsided. The subsidence amounted to about one foot.

Seventeen fume vents could be counted including wall chimneys on the north, southwest and southeast. Only two slides were seen, one in the southeast talus and another on the southwest side of the central crag.

At 8 p. m. there were many flames, puffing border grottoes, filagree cones and much spurting from under marginal crusts. The high gas pressure continued and the clear seeing gave evidence of much thinner fumes on this day. The lakes in the evening were lower than in the morning, some 5 feet below their margins and there were occasional collapses of the central channel arch. The central pond cone was glowing, flaming and spurting lava. Large banners of flame played above the grottoes of the southeast pond and the east cove and from a long crack in a cone at the north pond. Streaming was eastward, there was much rumbling, there was very little glow on the fume cloud above and the slides were trivial. The fresh floor flows showed glowing cracks. No open pools were seen at the north and no fountaining at the west arm locality, but there was a high flaming chimney there. The west chasm pond was glowing. No glow could be seen from the north wall chimney. The southeast pond had assumed hexagonal form within its new inner bench.

An interesting development at the south cone on the high margin of Halemaumau is the revelation of its interior by collapse. The roof has so fallen in as to show an open chamber some 6 feet high inside with typical cavern stalactites of the wormy type on its ceiling. As these were formed within a hot gas chamber source of active lavas less than a month ago, the proof is conclusive that such stalactites are not formed by water drip, but rather by refusion of the ceiling lava. The interior of this chamber was full of scalding vapor and too hot to explore, but from the entrance a large tube could be seen leading southward under the high pressure ridge and domes of the new overflows of March.

The following is the report of the Whitney Laboratory of Seismology for the three weeks beginning at 2 p. m. Friday, March 29, and ending at 2 p. m. Friday, April 19, 1918:

For the week of sharp subsidence of the Halemaumau lava ending April 5, forty-one local earthquakes were registered, most of these occurring March 30 to April 3.

There were fifteen shocks March 30 as follows:

3:52 a. m.	12:03 p. m.	11:16 p.m.
5:45 "	1:27 "	11:27 "
6:02 "	6:15 "	11:38 "
6:20 "	7:46 "	
7:07 " (felt)	8:23 "	
11:37 "	10:55 "	

On March 31 there were three shocks respectively 2:42 a. m., 9:43 a. m. (felt), and 5:39 p. m. On April 1 there were three shocks, 3:54 a. m., 7:06 p. m. and 7:07 p. m. (felt ?), and other slow jarrings. On April 2 there were thirteen shocks:

a. m.	p. m.	p. m.	p. m.	p. m.
12:30	3:19 (felt)	5:47 (felt)	8:15	11:28
4:53	3:49	6:46	8:31	
5:54	4:58	7:31	9:44 (felt)	

On April 3 there were five shocks, all a. m. 12:05, 1:18, 2:36, 3:19, 7:54 (felt). On April 4 there were two very slight tremors at 9:33 p. m. and 9:35 p. m.

During this week the tilting became excessive to the west and very strong to the south, microseisms were moderate and there were many spasms of volcanic vibration.

During the week ending April 12 there were only two local earthquakes, one small tremor at 6:31 a. m., April 7, and a shock at 11:10 p. m., April 8. The strong tilt to the west and south continued with fluctuations, microseisms were moderate to strong and volcanic vibration decreased.

During the present week ending April 19 there was one local tremor at 5:10 a. m., April 14, and one weakly recorded teleseism beginning 8:29 p. m., April 16, the trace of which could be detected on the seismogram for about five minutes. The record gave no indication of distance of origin. During this week the westward tilt decreased and then showed stationary tendency while the southward component fluctuated somewhat with general tendency to decrease. Microseisms somewhat increased and volcanic vibration was moderate.

VOLCANO OBSERVATORY, April 27, 1918.—During the week ending Friday, April 26, 1918, very strong rising of the lava column of Halemaumau has been in evidence with extensive flooding by lake overflow on the east side of the bottom area, and a responsive rising of the central and western crags following upon the overweighting towards the east.

Taking the lake at the central channel and the summit of the central crag as datum points, the following shows the sequence:

April 18-20, (three days), lake rose 24 feet, crag 3 feet.

April 21-23, (three days), lake rose 11 feet, crag 18 feet.

April 24-25, (two days), lake rose 5 feet, crag 7 feet.

April 26, (one day), lake rose 6 feet, crag 0 feet.

It will be seen that the movements of the crag lagged two or three days behind those of the lake and this has been usual in the past. The bench magma movements are apt to be tilting or central upswellings preceded by a gush of lake magma and high gas pressure. Furthermore the rising spell as a whole showed the following rates:

April 18-20, (lake 8 feet per day, crag 1 foot per day.

April 21-23, lake 3.6 feet per day, crag 6 feet per day.

April 24-25, lake 2.5 feet per day, crag 3.5 feet per day.

April 26, lake 6 feet per day, crag 0 feet per day.

This shows culmination for the lake April 19, and for the crag April 22. It will be seen that a renewed spasm of rising for the lake April 26 should be followed by a similar spurt for the crag and this has since happened, the end of the week exhibiting very strong rising. On April 20 the relief of the crag above the lake reached its minimum of 47 feet, but on April 26 the crag stood 50 feet above the lake, showing that its net rise during the week was greater than that of the lake.

On Saturday, April 20, at 9:45 a. m., the depression of the lake was 196 feet. The pit was more fumy with lake margins three to four feet high, fountaining, streaming and puffing, marking continued gas pressure, the appearance of lower lake magma probably due to uplift of bench magma. At noon there were strong overflows as on the previous day. One or two small rock slides were heard. The southeast pond had developed, within its inner floor by building inward, a striking hexagonal plan with rounded angles. It was in process of more and more constriction from a pond to a pot. At 3 p. m. the lake shores were five feet high. There was strong puffing to the north, a large central fountain was playing and several small ones; rock slides were occasionally seen. At 2:30 p. m. the southwest pond showed four fountains and was level with its southern bank. At

4 p. m. an unusually strong rock slide was heard toward the northwest.

On April 21 at 4:30 p. m. the southeast pond was overflowing and continued to do so for an hour, then the lava sank about four feet, leaving the pond much smaller, some 25 feet in diameter. The east arm was quiet and brimming level with its banks and when the subsidence period came it broke up and numerous fountains developed there and in the central region. The northern cones were puffing strongly and a small slide took place southwest.

Measurement on April 23 in the morning made the lake depression 185 feet. In the east arm the liquid was two feet below the margin, in the center five feet below and more farther west. At the east end were fresh overflows, a puffing filagree cone and spatter cones in process of construction, and others were forming in the central region. There were glowing heaps in the north central floor and at the north pond site, the latter hissing harshly. There was much growth of the floors and the east island remnant was nearly buried under them. The valley between the northeast crag mass and the wall of the pit was now below the floor levels and liable to invasion by flows as soon as the inner construction overtopped the lower portions of the northeast crag mass. The southeast pond region was all covered by new flows and the pond itself had become a narrow pot showing the liquid lava five feet down. A very small slide southeast was heard. The central channel was again open making one long river-like pool and streaming was eastward from under a bridge of crust over a tunnel leading from the west arm to the center. Rhythmic fountaining had ceased at the western cove. No open pools were visible north or northwest. The central and western crags appeared rising while the eastern features sank.

Measurement at 10 a. m. on Thursday, April 25, 1918, made the lake depression 180 feet. The southeast pot was still smaller. The lake was below the marginal floor three feet at the east, six feet at the center and ten feet at the west, showing that the whole floor block or crust surface of the bench magma column was being depressed at the east and lifted at the west. There were large fresh flows from the east end of the lake which had poured along the southwestern base of the northeast crag mass, showing that there was depression there. There were other fresh overflows along the base of the northern and northwestern talus, from the west pond and from the south side of the southwest pond. A wide new bench was built along the north base of the central crag mass and the fresh floor lapped high up the east base of the west crag mass. The central pond cone was half buried under new flows. On this day and the next the fume from the pit was thinner but fluctuated strongly in density within short intervals.

At 4:30 p. m. the edge of the east arm was only one foot high and the lake was quiet until 5:45, when subsidence took place for half an hour, the liquid lowering about six feet and developing the usual activity. The southeast pond site showed only small glowing apertures. Slides were few and small.

At noon April 26 the lake depression was 174 feet and the summit of the central crag was 124 feet below the rim at the east shelter. High gas pressure with rising and overflowing lakes continued. The several ponds were now mostly crusted over with surfaces continuous with the great floor area, excepting the southwest pond and the long stretch of main lake from the western to the eastern arm. The southeast pot was totally arched over during the morning by the construction of a high blowing cone over its grotto, with an open hole at the base of the cone. Streaming was eastward in the main lake, there was occasional breaking up with central fountaining, and marginal grottoes were active at the east end, on the north and south sides of the east arm and on the north and south sides of the central region. There was a glowing heap on the north central floor and at the north pond site under the north smoke crag a high stack was building. This had a circular hole some two feet in diameter across its summit and explosions inside at irregular intervals flung up an umbrella of melt. There was a bell-like ringing noise from the structure and the detonation was a muffled report like the exhaust of an explosion engine and not like the mere escape of confined gas. The noise implied a true chemical explosion of gases mixed with air and ignited. The stack at this time was over 10 feet high and quite slender.

The other cones were blowing strongly. The lake shore was two feet high east and ten feet high west. The western bridge of crust was more slender and there was violent fountaining in the west arm. The overflow pattern east and southeast was new and a wide floor of fresh overflow had built west and south of the southwest pond which was active. Rainfall produced dense steam clouds from the floors showing their high temperature. At noon rising was in progress. Much fresh flow material could be seen dimly in the northwest pond region.

In the Whitney Laboratory of Seismology during the week ending at 2 p. m. Friday, April 26, two local earthquakes have been registered respectively at 7:02 p. m., April 19, and 1:25 p. m., April 21. A teleseism identifiable as the one reported disastrous in southern California was registered at about 12:19 p. m. April 21. Microseisms have decreased from very strong to moderate and volcanic vibration has fluctuated slightly with moderate values. Movement of tilting has been steadily progressing with inclination to the east-southeast.

VOLCANO OBSERVATORY, May 4, 1918.—During the week ending May 3, 1918, the lava column has continued to rise at Kilauea, the lakes and crags continuing to alternate in their spurts upward, the ones even subsiding slightly on the days when the others rose. The sequence was as follows:

April 26-28, lake rose 5 feet (depression 174 to 169 feet); crag rose 13 feet (depression 124 to 111 feet).

April 29-30, lake rose 10 feet (depression 169 to 159 feet); crag sank 5 feet (depression 111 to 116 feet).

May 1, lake sank 4 feet (depression 159 to 163 feet); crag rose 5 feet (depression 116 to 111 feet).

The changes of the week have been similar to those of the week before, the lava floods so extending the floor area as to surround all the crags and lap the base of the talus, making an octagonal flat surface above which the crag remnants stand in relief. Three of the crags which were conspicuous objects at the time of the March subsidence have completely disappeared, buried up under talus and lava floods. These are the southeast, northwest and east island crags. The new flows have poured across and buried the east ledge and made a new ponded filling of the northeast valley. This process has now happened four times within the last fifteen months.

On Saturday, April 27, at 3:30 p. m., the inner bank of the east pool was four feet high and at the west arm much higher. The activity was sluggish and the pools crusted over with a rising tendency while spurting fountains broke from under marginal crusts. The southeast cone occasionally hissed and there was much puffing to the north and west.

When the circuit of the pit by way of the east and north rims was made flows were seen pushing across the northwestern and western floors from vents which exhibited high gas pressure at the northwest and west ponds. The north stack, formed on the previous day, was 20 feet high and now inactive. There was a flaming cone in the north central floor. Streaming was at first eastward in the central channel and the southwest pond, and westward in the west arm.

At 5 p. m. the east arm started overflowing, at 8 p. m. the southeast cone broke open and threw up a high standing fountain as the source of extensive flows, and at 9:30 p. m. the southeast pond was overflowing strongly.

The east arm overflows increased in volume from 5 to 7 p. m. with very strong spurts, so that two heavy streams were developed which poured north and south from the east end of the pool, the latter becoming covered with quiet crusts.

A sudden marked increase at the end of the first half hour of steady overflow, and at the same time the lake from the central channel westward exhibiting a glowing rim of overhang as though sinking, while the same lake in the east arm filled its basin to the brim and overflowed in strong pulsations, all gave evidence which checked with the greater height of banks westward, to the effect that the whole bench magma surface was tilting downward on the east side and upward on the west about an axial line in the narrow. At the same time there was strong cracking of crusts and fountaining in the central and western regions. The central crag summit measurably rose during the afternoon, this being a part of the western uplifted half. As the overflows shifted from (1) west to (2) north, then (3) east and southeast, and (4) southwest, it is probable that the disk of bench magma constituting the circular upper crust of the lava column, including all crags and floors, executed a somewhat spiral tilting movement as the weighting of the overflows spread in the sequence indicted. These overflows were now around the margins in contrast to the central floods of a few days before.

The eastern overflows filled the whole southeastern part of the pit surrounding the southeast cone elevation; the accumulation stagnated in the east central region and deepened until it overflowed the low saddle in the middle of the northeast crag mass. Two narrow molten streams poured down the back slope of that mass into the northeast valley and reached the foot of the talus.

The southeast cone fountain shot up 20 to 30 feet like an artesian well and continued for hours, the column lowering and the pool around it rising so that the former central pond was obliterated and the whole area east of the central crag mass ponded level with the lake surface. The southwest pond poured over its western and southern margins profusely.

Flames were abundant at the southeast cone and two glowing cones on the north central and northeastern floors. Late in the night the southeast fountain built a flaming cone about seven feet high with a spouting pot in its summit.

Near the northwest pond locality a blowing cone developed and made explosive detonations similar to the stack of the previous day and flung up umbrella-shaped blobs of melt. The growth of a driblet edifice here finally deflected the spurtings from vertical to 45° northeastward, and still later the jets were being ejected almost horizontally through the building up of a pipe which confined the blast and expelled it laterally.

Occasional fountaining was seen in the west pond and fresh floods of lava were pouring over the northwestern floor. The fume became very thin and the spectacle on this evening was magnificent. The noises were those of strong gas pressure. The only talus adjustments were small ones due to the shiftings of the bench magma.

On the morning of April 28 overflowing was still in progress southeast, and new flows had increased the bulk of the two streams on the back slope of the northeast crag mass. At 5 p. m. it was evident that overflowing continued without abatement, the floods being everywhere pooled so that toes pushed out around their margins, especially northwest and southeast. The same hissing and spurting were everywhere in progress. The following were source vents: (1) the southeast pond, (2) the northern cones, (3) the west pond and (4) the circular pot at the west bend which until recently was the site of the rhythmic fountain. From this last place the streaming was northward in the west arm and eastward in the southwest pond. The main lake was flush with its banks in the east arm and probably overflowing beneath the crusts which marked its margin. The southeast cone was a center for V-shaped glowing areas which marked flows radiating from it. The flow levels were slowly rising around the north stack.

On Monday, April 29, 1918, at 11 a. m., the gas pressure was somewhat less but the lakes were still high. There were fresh overflows on the northeast floor from the north, on the southeast floor from an oven at the southeast cone and still others from the east arm which had built a hissing filagree cone at its east end. There were other such cones southeast and north, glowing lava could be seen at the northwest pond, the northwest pond, the north stack was still standing and the strongest puffing was somewhere in that direction. The banks at the southwest pond were one foot high, at the east arm three feet. At 1 p. m. vigorous overflow began at the southwest corner of the east arm and the southwest pond appeared ready to overflow at its south margin. Both of these pools showed a lift of shorelines in the direction of the west arm. A few rock slides occurred during the morning.

The new floor surfaces were now three crescent-shaped plains which with continued growth promised to join at their horns so as to completely encircle the crags. The three crescents were northwest, east and southwest and the interruptions to the continuous circle were the junctions with the talus of the north, south and southwest crags. Everywhere the liquid lava was gaining on the crags so that these gaps must soon fill.

On Tuesday, April 30, at 4:30 p. m., it was evident that there had been excessive overflowing at noon. New glowing surfaces which were smooth as from deep pooling extended from around the east arm to the southwest pond and beyond making a new floor through the notch south of the south crag mass. There were other fresh flows west, north and northeast, the latter extending across the former east ledge and making a new floor the whole length of the northeast valley. The new flows lapped the talus under the walls of the pit everywhere except on the north and southwest.

Hissing was strong from glowing heaps southeast, east and north. There was glow at the northwest pond site and the north stack was still in place. Some rock slipping was heard. The lake margins were three feet high except for the central pool, which was somewhat higher. The former central pond was now obliterated under a flat floor and only a glowing heap of crust marked the site of the southeast pond. The southwest pond was more constricted and rounder. The west bridge was again wide.

On Wednesday, May 1, at 11:30 a. m., the floor was built still higher and the two ridges on the north and southwest which interrupted the continuous circle of new flows at the base of the talus were now flooded. A cascade had poured through from under the north station into the northeast valley and another from the west pond to the southwest floor. On this morning a standing fountain at the west pond sent a flood westward to the talus which pooled right and left, extending to the southwest pond floor and to the extreme north. The north stack now protruded only about five feet. There were new overflows from the main lake and a dome grotto at the northeast end of the east pool was half submerged under new flows. The cone at the east end was new.

While the west pond was flooding strongly, the lake at 11:30 a. m. showed five-foot margins and the southwest pond was a foot higher. An hour later both the southwest pond and the main lake rose to brimming and the lake overflowed the south margin of the central channel. Both the east and west pools showed banks a foot high at this time indicating that the floor sagged downward in the middle of the pit.

On May 2 at 5 p. m. the inner margin was four feet high at the east arm, there was much fountaining and strong blowing was heard from a cone at the west. At 6 p. m. the main lake was nearly brimming. There was some rock sliding from the southwest wall. On May 3 there were driblet flows which added to the material heaped above the sunken east ledge, but in general the heavy overflowing had ceased.

The instruments of the Whitney Laboratory of Seismology for the week ending at 2 p. m. May 3, 1918, have registered five local earthquakes, the last three being very small ones, and these were simultaneous with the excessive overflows of the Halemaumau floor. The times were 5:17 p. m. April 26, 7:40 p. m. April 28, 7:07 and 9:40 p. m. April 29, and 8:30 a. m. April 30. Microseisms have been moderate, and volcanic vibration showed occasional intense spasms until April 30, thereafter it was normal. Movement of tilting was stationary or fluctuating until April 28; thereafter it became pronounced to the east with fluctuation in the north-south component.

Very respectfully,

T. A. JAGGAR, JR.,

Director.

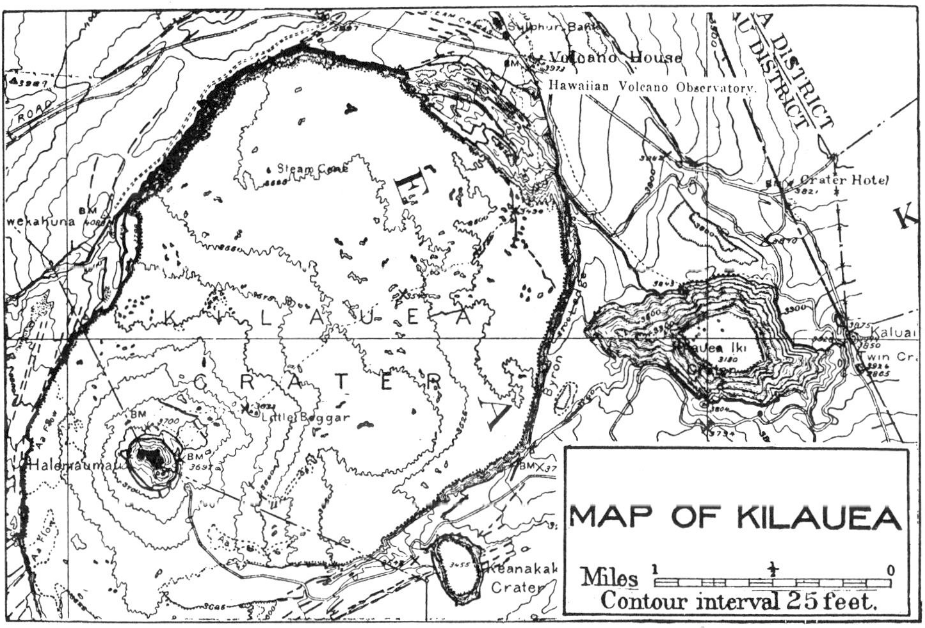

HAWAIIAN VOLCANO RESEARCH ASSOCIATION.

This society is a voluntary one, made up of subscribers to scientific work which is being executed by Dr. T. A. Jaggar, Director of the Hawaiian Volcano Observatory, Volcano House, P. O., Hawaii. **All scientific exchanges should be sent to this address.**

In 1917 there are about 150 subscribers in Hawaii and elsewhere, **firms and individuals. A group of firms and persons in Hilo built the main** observatory building in the spring of 1912. The work was founded by the Massachusetts Institute of Technology. Publications to date have been weekly reports since the summer of 1911 now reprinted in Honolulu in monthly form. There are also special reports, printed from time to time.

The weekly bulletin as it appears in the Honolulu Advertiser is reprinted as a leaflet and sent to regular annual subscribers to the work of the Association. L. A. Thurston is president of the Board of Directors of the Association, and L. T. Peck is treasurer. New subscribers who are interested in volcanoes will be welcomed in the Association. The Association aims: (1) To record volcanic activity and earthquakes in Hawaii; (2) to attract scientific men hither for special studies; (3) to promote the establishment of volcano observatories all over the world. The annual dues of regular members are $5; patrons of the Association subscribe larger amounts.

WHITNEY LABORATORY OF SEISMOLOGY.

The Whitney Laboratory of Seismology, named after an endowment fund of geophysical research held by the Massachusetts Institute of Technology, in memory of Caroline and Edward Whitney of Boston, is equipped with two Bosch-Omori 100 kg tromometers registering N-S and E-W motion, a heavy Omori tromometer registering E-W motion, and an Omori "ordinary Seismograph" designed for registering strong earthquakes in all three components of motion. These are seated on concrete piers in a closed basement room having practically constant temperature, beneath the chief Observatory building near the hotel. Time is referred to a rated chronometer, checked at intervals by solar observations with a transit. Both instruments are loaned by the College of Hawaii. Hawaiian standard time (H. S. T.) is 10 hrs. 30 min. slower than Greenwich time.

CANCANI SCALE OF SEISMIC INTENSITY.

Expressed by accelerations measured in millimeters per second per second.

I.	Instrumental	0.0	2.5
II.	Very slight	2.5	5.0
III.	Slight	5.0	10.0
IV.	Sensible, mediocre	10.0	25.0
V.	Rather strong	25.0	50.0
VI.	Strong	50.0	100.0
VII.	Very strong	100.0	250.0
VIII.	Ruinous	250.0	500.0
IX.	Disastrous	500.0	1000.0
X.	Very disastrous	1000.0	2500.0
XI.	Catastrophic	2500.0	5000.0
XII.	Great catastrophe	5000.0	10000.0

Grade IV. is ordinarily the minimum perceived by the senses; and in grade XII. the acceleration, or rate of change of motion (jerk) reaches that of terrestrial gravitation.

In the standard form of report the maximum intensity or acceleration, designated by the symbol a, or max. a, is given in the conventional unit, **the milligal.** The milligal is a measure of acceleration, such that 1 milligal = 1/100 mm. per sec. per sec. = 10 μ per sec. per sec. The Cancani scale, here **defined in terms of millimeters per sec. per sec., can therefore be expressed in milligals by multiplying each of the numbers by 100.**

WEEKLY BULLETIN
OF THE
Hawaiian Volcano Observatory

Vol. VI. HONOLULU, HAWAII, MAY, 1918 No. 5

HAWAIIAN VOLCANO OBSERVATORY, May 11, 1918.—During the week ending May 10, 1918, the lava has risen rather continuously in Halemaumau, so far as measurement of the position of the central crag is concerned, though the lake in its inner depression has had the appearance of being low and the bench magma has distinctly risen at times while the lake magma has subsided.

The following shows the progress of events whereby the central crag and the lake, as before, have alternated in their pulsations of rising:

Depression below east rim of pit:

May 5, crag summit 93 feet, lake center 166 feet;

May 6, crag summit 91 feet, lake center 159 feet;

May 7, crag summit 90 feet, lake center 166 feet;

May 8, crag summit 86 feet, lake center 167 feet;

May 10, crag summit 85 feet, lake center 157 feet.

From May 5 to 10, therefore, five days, the crag rose eight feet, an average of 1.6 feet per day, while the lake rose 9 feet, an average 1.8 feet per day; but from May 6 to 8 the lake was sinking while the crag was rising, the liquid tending to surge up and down in strong pulsations while the stiffer bench magma rose and made slower spurts. The sequence was

May 5 to 6, crag up 2 feet, lake up 7 feet;

May 6 to 7, crag up 1 foot, lake down 7 feet;

May 7 to 8, crag up 4 feet, lake down 1 foot;

May 8 to 10, crag up 1 foot, lake up 10 feet.

Saturday, May 4, 1918, was rainy but the only changes were in the nature of upward warping of the bench magma following the overflows of the previous days. A small flow poured from the southeast cone southeastward and this flow was very liquid and exhibited a glistening, glassy surface. There had been driblet puddles spreading on the northeast floor, probably of the previous day, and fresh short flows across the east ledge.

On May 5 at noon the southeast cone was glowing and puffing and there were other cones at the west pond, on the central and northeastern portions of the northern floor, two small heaps and smoking cracks at the northwest pond site and the remnant of the north stack still stood about five feet high. The banks of the east pool stood 4 feet, the central pool 6 feet, the west arm 10 feet and the southwest pond 2 feet above the liquid. Of the latter the bank of the north side was somewhat higher. The lakes were rising, the east pool was crusted over and cracking around the edges and there was cracking of crusts and bubble fountaining in the central pool. The west bridge separating the central pool from the west arm was narrow and thick with an arch three feet high beneath it. Gas pressure was moderate and there were few fountains. After 1 p. m. streaming eastward developed slowly, seven marginal grottoes showing stalactites were active in the central and eastern pools, and the west arm showed blistered skins and much bubbling. No hissing was heard from the north cones and there was now no trace of lake outlines north or northwest, only a continuous floor.

The central crag was more fallen away on its southeast side and fresh fallen rocks from it lay on the new floor. The pinnacle, part of a slab

WEEKLY BULLETIN
of the
Hawaiian Volcano Observatory

Published Monthly at Honolulu, Hawaii, by the Hawaiian Volcano Research Association

L. W. de Vis-Norton........Secretary

Entered as second-class matter January 20, 1914, at the post-office at Honolulu, Hawaii, under the Act of August 24, 1912.

south of it and separated from it by a chasm, tended to lean farther southward. A continuous train of festoons from the west pond northward indicated a last long flow in that direction. A long straight crack, gaping upward, extended from the spatter dome on the southeast edge of the east pool to the southeast talus. This and the rock slides from the central crag showed new motion in the bench magma.

Looking down from the southwest rim of the pit, the radiation of flows and streaming from that corner of the floor was striking. Considering the west pond as a center of upwelling liquid lava the streaming was southeastward in the southwest pond, eastward in the main lake, northward into tunnels of the crusted north arm and northwestward as overflows from the west pond. In the southwest pond there was a fountaining grotto tunnel in the east corner and another at the south corner.

Another striking feature of recent developments southwest was the uplift of the bench magma near this same center of outflows. The south end of the west crag mass and the deck of the central mass were both distinctly lifted.

At 4 p. m. on this day (May 5) the lake was lower relative to its banks, the east pool showed marginal cliffs 10 feet high, there was swift eastward streaming and active fountaining at the grotto under the southeast crack and another farther north. The current forked in the east pool and divided itself to rush under these two places swiftly. At 4:40 p. m. the west bridge collapsed and a few minutes later a large block of the western extension of the central crag mass fell in. At 6:20 p. m. a prolonged slide in the west talus took place and later the roof of the southeastern grotto collapsed and started much fountaining in that corner of the east pool. At this time the lakes were crusted elsewhere. The central pinnacle was still in place.

On Monday, May 6, at 5:30 p. m., both lake and central crag had risen, and the central pinnacle had fallen during the night to a jumble of immense bowlders in the notch south of it. Only its stump remained. The disturbance of the previous evening had evidently been a strong upward adjustment of the bench magma.

There was increased gas pressure, four border fountains were spurting in the main lake and the southeast floor cone was puffing. The southeast crack was more pronounced, smoking and showing glowing walls where the spatter dome had collapsed. The southern adjacent block appeared lifted. Fountains were very active in the tunnel beneath the crack. A large bowlder had fallen from the east talus to the floor on the northern or depressed side of the crack. There was a glowing heap at the lake margin under the north side of the central steeple remnant. Where the bridge had been the west arm was greatly widened. Lava was splashing inside of the northern floor cone. There was increased blue fume at the west pond, along the north central floor and west of the northwest pond site, the fume rising from many small cracks as though the lifting bench magma opened gas chambers beneath.

The southwest pond was overflooding vigorously on its southwest side, extensive moving lava streams extending all the way from the southwest crag (on the west side of the southwest pond) to a point beneath the south station. These overflows were still in motion after 6 p. m., although the main lake was depressed three feet below its margin at the east pool and more than eight feet in the west arm. Evidently the southwest pond well was independently supplied and its lava at a higher level. There were glowing cones at its eastern and southern corners.

At 6 p. m. there was glow in all the

cones, hissing toward the northwest and the lake occasionally broke up, but generally it was crusted. The south bank of the east pool was cracked and fuming.

After this spasm of overflow, inspection of the pit at 4 p. m. on May 7 showed a reaction with depression of both lake and crag and the inner walls were 8 feet high east, 10 feet at the west, while the southwest pond was only 3 feet down and its surface appeared topographically higher than the main lake. Cavernous grottoes were pounding and rumbling under the south and southeast sides of the east pool, while the streaming thither from the west was vigorous and the melt was covered with thin crust which parted along bright lines. The southeast floor cone was large, glowing and puffing. The north pot occasionally entered upon spells of prolonged blowing after accumulation of gas beneath. There was much fume west and southeast, one avalanche was heard toward the south and the floor cracks showed whitish stains.

On the morning of Wednesday, May 8, the lake was somewhat higher, the southeast cone was hissing, the marginal grottoes blowing and rumbling, streaming was eastward with some bubble fountaining and the north pot still glowed. In general the gas pressure was higher, but there were many fuming cracks and one or two rock slips were heard. Large smoking cracks with stained margins had developed in the floor about the places where lakes or pools have recently been, suggesting open chambers below. These places are in a line along the north central region, near the north stack and at the northwest and west pond sites.

On May 9 at 4 p. m. the pit was rather smoky and the lake margins 10 or 12 feet high. The lakes were very quiet. About 5 p. m. breaking up commenced toward the west and spread eastward so that streaming became visible pouring eastward with many fountains and the usual border grottoes.

On Friday, May 10, at 5:30 p. m., the pit presented the same smoky appearance and seemingly low lake, but in reality rising was in progress with the floors and crags lifting more than the liquid. Blowing cones were hissing southeast, east, north and elsewhere. The point of bench on the north side of the lake between the east and central pools was rising more than the opposite shore so that it stood 15 feet above the liquid at the same time that the cliff margin of the east pool was only 5 feet high. Measurement showed that the northeast crag had risen more than the other crags and its motion was indicated by a fall of rocks from the north wall and by the development of a second crack parallel to the long southeast floor crack on the north side of the latter. The streaming was westward in the west arm, southwestward under the bank of the southwest side of the east pool and southward in the southwest pond. Generally the main lake and east pool were crusted over. Gas pressure was moderately strong.

No earthquakes have been registered by the seismographs of the Whitney Laboratory during the week ending at 2 p. m. Friday, May 10, 1918. Microseismic and volcanic vibrations have been normal and moderate. The tilting of the ground was stationary in the east-west component the first half of the week and eastward thereafter, while at right angles to this the tilt was first southward and then northword. The amount of tilting has been moderate, with tendency to strong eastward tilt latterly.

May 18, 1918.—During the week ending Friday, May 17, 1918, the lava lakes, crags and floors of Halemaumau have risen about 20 feet, but as usual this has proceeded by alternation between the rising of the liquid lava and the bench magma respectively. The swelling up of the latter is again occasioning deep crevassing of the overflow floors and this movement during the week has lifted the shores of the east pool so that the inner cliff around the main lake is once more of uniform height.

The surveys yielded the following measurements:

May 10 to 11, central crag rose 4 feet in 1 day to depression 81 feet;

May 11 to 14, central crag rose 6 feet in 3 days to depression 75 feet;

May 14 to 17, central crag rose 11 feet in 3 days to depresion 64 feet.

May 10 to 11, lake sank 2 feet in 1 day to depression 159 feet;

May 11 to 14, lake rose 15 feet in 3 days to depression 144 feet;

May 14 to 17, lake rose 7 feet in 3 days to depression 137 feet.

May 10 to 14, crag rose 2.5 feet per day, lake 4.25 feet per day;

May 14 to 17, crag rose 3.6 feet per day, lake 2.30 feet per day.

On Saturday, May 11, 1918, at 11:30 a. m., the wall of the east pool was 8 feet high, of the central pool 12 feet, of the west arm 15 feet and of the southwest pond 4 feet. Hissing was occasionally heard toward the north and west. The crusted lakes were very quiet. At intervals, however, the grottoes rumbled and the crusts broke up and foundered. The only visible streaming was local into the grottoes or tunnels which lay on the southeast, south, northeast and northwest corners of the east pool, on the north side of the west arm and on the south side of the southwest pond.

At the southeast crack the floor on its north side had slumped and a second parallel crack a few yards farther north showed increased development. A crack of northeast trend cut the new flows where they crossed the middle of the northeast crag mass. The lifted point of bench north of the central channel had sunk back but the crags were higher. The bench magma was lifting faster than the lake magma. This produced considerable changes in the fuming; at 8 a. m. the fume rising from the pit was very thin; at noon the fume came from patches of the floor and was diffused throughout the pit in a blue haze; at 4 p. m. the general fume cloud was quite dense. The lift of bench magma had caused collapse at the flaming cones. A glowing pot had opened beside the southeast cone and the north blow hole appeared more broken.

On May 12 at 4 p. m. the lake was relatively higher, there were a few rock slides towards the northwest and there was the usual activity in the grottoes. On May 13 it was apparent that the lake magma was gaining on the solidified portion.

On Tuesday, May 14, this rising spell culminated in extensive flooded overflows which pooled in a semi-circle all the way around the base of the northern and western talus from the west pond to the northeast valley, where a heavy flow had poured through the gap between the north crag and the wall of the pit. At 6 p. m. all these flows were glowing vividly and appeared to be fed from the northern cones as well as from the west and northwest ponds. All the orifices of the floor of the pit were blowing, spurting and flaming, and the bench surrounding the eastern end of the lake appeared to be rising, for in the east pool strong cracking, foundering and collapse of banks were going on with marginal glow and streaming into the pool from under crust across the central narrows: whereas from this point westward the lake appeared quiet and crusted as though rising. This implied a new tendency whereby the bench magma was lifting towards the east and so reversing its previous habit.

Very large banners of flame played from under the bank at the northeast margin of the east pool. One strong avalanche fell from the north-northeast wall showing movements in the bench magma; a reddish cloud of dust was produced. There were other small slides east and south. The southwest pond stood one foot below its margin, and the edge was a rampart of fresh overflow. The inner cliffs of the main lake were lower than of late, but much higher than the southwest pond; they were four feet high at the east end and from eight to ten feet high in the central region and towards the west. The block subsiding between the two southeast crevasses appeared to have the pattern of a revival of the former southeast channel. Other cracks extended southward on the east side of the southeast cone. This cone was glowing, flaming and hissing and there were other flaming cones on the bench southwest of the east pool, east of the north stack remnant, at the sites of the former northwest, north and north-central ponds and on the south bank of the southwest pond. Smoke rose densely from the north central floor as though collapse might be expected there, but elsewhere the fume was rather thin.

On May 16 at 4:30 p. m. there was swift eastward streaming with several fountains in action in the main lake and four at the southwest pond. The lake rose somewhat during the next three hours and became quieter. At 6:30 p. m. the lake was crusted over, but occasionally gas would escape violently around the margin, flinging spray to great heights, breaking up the crust and occasionally downward sucking of the fragments into marginal fountains. This was seen at the east end of the main lake and on the south side of the southwest pond. The three principal places of border fountaining in the main lake were at the east end, on the north side of the central crag mass and at the north corner of the central pool. Hissing was heard from the north glow pot and from a border cone south of the southwest pond, and during a spraying outbreak at the east end of the lake there was strong hissing from a glowing crack on the bank.

A new feature, now becoming conspicuous, was the extension of floor cracking, and glow only a foot or two inside of these cracks. The largest of the cracks followed a semi-circular course about half way between the center of the pit and the east talus. This crack began west of the southeast cone which was now a flaming chasm; it passed through this chasm and extended thence to the south side of the east pool. From the north side of this pool it could be followed across the northeast floor through and beyond the north glow pot which was now a high glowing cone. The two southeast cracks extending from the east pool to the southeast talus had enlarged and gaped upward.

The walls around the east pool were 10 feet high and around the central region they were twice that much so that perhaps the concentric cracking may be accounted for by the lift of the central block. The four larger cracks radiating from the east pool suggested tumescence centering under that pool. The southwest pond banks were only 5 feet high. After nightfall there was glow in all the cones and glowing edges of crust could be seen all along the western and northwestern margins of the floor where the fresh flows abutted against the talus. Small V-shaped patches at the north appeared to indicate flows in motion. There was much fume from the north-central and northwestern regions.

At 5 p. m. on Friday, May 17, the southwest pond showed 4-foot margins and the lake 15 to 20-foot margins all around, indicating that the east pool basin had risen to a common level with the central and western basins. The radial cracking around the east pool was very pronounced and the large north crack was extended to beyond the north stack. Blowing could be heard, the lake was crusted over and explosive outbreaks from under marginal crusts had continued. Lava could be seen splashing in the southeast pot.

Evidence that the pit floor was in motion was furnished at 5 p. m. by a prolonged series of avalanches lasting three minutes or more which undermined the wall of the pit just east of the north station and finally carried away a portion of the recent lava of the northeast fill. A pink dust cloud shot up and the northeast valley floor was covered with bowlders and dust.

The instruments of the Whitney Laboratory for the week ending at 2 p. m. May 17, 1918, have registered two strong distant earthquakes. One of these began about 11:12 a. m., May 11, and the preliminary phase, which was very imperfectly registered, suggested a distance of 7600 kilometers, the distance of southern New Zealand or Costa Rica. The second began about 9:13 a. m., May 16, and appeared to be very remote, some 11,500 kilometers, equal to the distance of northern India or the Caspian Sea.

Two very small local tremors were registered at 8:51 p. m., May 12, and 5:26 a. m., May 13. Microseismic motion has been moderate and decreasing. Volcanic vibration has been ordinary with some spasms of increase between May 11 and May 13. Tilt of the ground has shown eastward tendency with stationary spells, the north-south component showing only slight fluctuations.

May 25, 1918.—During the week ending Friday, May 24, 1918, the Halemaumau lava column has continued to rise at the same rate, the central wide floors of recent overflow have swollen up and developed deep crevasses and floods of liquid lava have poured along the wall valleys. A new source of such flooding is a cone at the base of the west-southwest wall of the pit at the side of the old western well which has repeatedly developed pits and cones in the past. In contrast to the previous week, when the measured rise of the lake was somewhat greater than that of the bench magma, the latter has this week risen more than the lake so as to increase the height of the walls of the inner lake basin.

The surveys yielded the following measurements:

May 17 to 18, central crag rose 8 feet in 1 day to depression 56 feet;

May 18 to 20, central crag sank 1 foot in 2 days to depression 55 feet;

May 20 to 21, central crag rose 1 feet in 1 day to depresion 56 feet;

May 21 to 24, central crag rose 14 feet in 3 days to depression 42 feet.

May 17 to 18, lake rose 7 feet in 1 day to depression 130 feet;

May 18 to 20, lake sank 1 feet in 2 days to depression 129 feet;

May 20 to 21, lake rose 1 foot in 1 day to depression 130 feet;

May 21 to 24, lake rose 12 feet in 3 days to depression 118 feet.

May 17 to 21, crag rose 2 feet per day, lake 1.75 feet per day;

May 21 to 24, crag rose 4.6 feet per day, lake 4 feet per day.

On Saturday, May 18, 1918, about 11 a. m., there was strong overflow from the southwest pond region and from orifices at the edge of the floor west of there, and this flow poured through the south wall valley to the southeast floor along the base of the talus. Rockfalls from the north wall of the pit continued. At 2 p. m. the inner wall around the lake was 15 feet high, there was much fountaining activity in the east arm, smoke rose from many cracks in the northern floors, and the great crevasse extending from the east arm to the north pot had increased in width. This and the swollen surfaces indicated pronounced tumescence. At 1:45 p. m. there was rapid eastward streaming and some appearance of rising lake magma. Lava was splashing inside of glowing pots north and southeast and at 2:30 p. m. the southwest pond was one foot below its rampart and its south grotto was splashing; the rampart had increased in height. At 6:40 p. m. the main lake was depressed about 11 feet within its walls, the southwest pond 3 feet and the southeast pot 5 feet. All the pots and cones were glowing and flaming, including a cone beside the remnant of the north stack and the crevasse extending therefrom to the north pot, where the lava made booming noises. Under the crusted lake gas pressure was high so that there was high spraying from under the crust edges. There were high glowing streaks at the west-southwest edge of the floor as seen from the southeast. Streaming from the central pool was westward to the west grotto where the current bent northward under the bank. The east pool was mostly crusted over, with spells of temporary subsidence and breaking up preceded by violent border spraying. The floor block between the two southeast crevasses was lower. At 10:30 p. m. lava welled up from the edge of the southwest floor and poured in a narrow stream around to the southeast; at 11:10 a second flow much more voluminous followed the same course. At this time fume was thin and there was some rock sliding northwest. The north central wall over the lake was 30 feet high by uplift, while the southern wall of the east pool was only 20 feet high.

On May 20 at 6 p. m. the east pool margin was 10 feet high, that of the southwest pond 2 feet. A flow was pouring across the floor eastward on the southwest side of the southwest pond. The fresh flows of the southern floor were glowing and driblet toes were pushing out from their edges; from the edge of the southwest floor east from the lake jets of lava were flung up with an explosion noise like the exhaust of an engine. Smoke rose densely from the north central and northwestern floors. The floor north of the main lake from the narrows to the base of the west crag was evidently rising to form a scarp twice as high as the southern lake margin. The northeast crag mass also showed a crack parallel to the edge of its escarpment. There was the usual cracking, foundering and recovery of the east pool and the lava pots were flaming.

On Tuesday, May 21, at 5:30 p. m., the lake was lower with walls over 20 feet high, there were six or eight fountaining tunnels and an abandoned shore

Lava lake & NE wall valley, Halemaumau, May, 1918.—*Photo. Jaggar*

Central crag mass and S wall valley, Halemaumau, May, 1918.—*Photo. Jaggar*

rim stood 5 feet above the liquid. The southwest pond still stood at a much higher level and glowing flows lapped the talus west, southwest, south and southeast from a slag heap source against the base of the west-southwest wall of the pit. This was the site of the "griffon" cone of March. The southeast pot had collapsed to an open pit 20 feet across, containing lava 15 feet down streaming westward. The north pot had also enlarged, general crevassing had increased, the northeast talus appeared lower and smoke from many cracks was denser, the southeast floors now smoking like the northwest, but the north crag summit no longer smoked. There was strong hissing towards the west. The ring of new floor had greatly increased in width around and outside of the central, southwestern and western crag masses on the west, southwest and south sides of the bottom of the pit. The remnant of the north stack still stood. A new bridge of crust had formed across the entrance to the west arm and there were fountaining tunnels on the north and northwest sides of the central pool. The southeast region was much crevassed as though it were about to collapse to a pool and was very distinctly swollen up, so that the talus was lifted and tended to form a slumping crack between it and the wall. One small rockfall was seen to the north. Fume from the pit as a whole was greater on this day. A sharp earthquake was felt at 3:30 p. m. At 10 p. m. it was evident that flow from the southwest cone had been renewed and there was vigorous fountaining in the lake. At 11:15 p. m. flowing started again from the west cone, the top of the cone forming a boiling, standing fountain which played in artesian fashion for hours.

On the morning of May 22 there was little change. The inner pit containing the lake was deep, the fume was thinner and the fresh flows still glowed.

On May 23 at 11:30 a. m. a thunder shower with very heavy rain caused cascades to pour over Uwekahuna bluff. At the road terminus near Halemaumau, during a lull when rain was pouring down to the north, the northern part of the Kilauea crater floor showed an even vaporing all over and the heavy beat of rainfall and the rush of water into the cavernous lava made a distinct roar somewhat like wind in a forest.

On making circuit of the pit by south and west the southern inner valley showed greatly increased width of floor, the fresh flows cracking with heat and the upturned slab of old March floor which had formed the lower part of the southwest wall of the pit was now nearly buried. The new floor made a wide platform eastward as well as southward from the southwest pond. The new west cone, between the southwest and west stations was a flat slagheap some 10 feet high with a sluggish fountain boiling in a pot on its summit, feeding a dribbling cascade with festooned skins ending in a short flow which was extending itself eastward. Farther north the west pond cone was glowing and hissing. The north pot was now a pit containing a lava pond 15 feet below the edge. There was a glowing cone at the northwest pond site. The most conspicuous change observable from the northwest was the pronounced lift of the whole central and southwest region of swollen and cracked floors and tilted crags, and the subordination of the northeast crag mass, now sunken and insignificant. The northeast valley back of it was the lowest depression in the pit. The site of the former north arm emitted bluish fume from hundreds of cracks, and one greater crevasse extended from the north stack through the north pit and across the swollen surface to the east arm of the lake.

The lake margins were 15 to 20 feet high, the crust was cracking and foundering, and the lava in the southeast pit appeared to be connected with the lake through a tunnel at the southeast crevasse. Against the west base of the central crag mass, in the west arm of the lake, the rhythmic fountain was again in action sluggishly breaking at intervals of 30 seconds more or less.

At 4 p. m. the lake was very quiet. At 4:45 a large central fountain burst through the crust of the east arm and a breaking up ensued. At 5:30 p. m. flows broke out from the new west cone and the lake overflowed from its west end. The two flows joined and flooded the southwest pond depression and the flood also poured northward through the west pond depression. The eastern flow reached the base of the southeast wall of the pit. At 6:30 p. m. a prolonged avalanche fell from the north wall of the pit and smaller ones followed, showing that the upward pressure on the southwest side was depressing the bench magma under the north talus.

On Friday, May 24, 1918, at 11 a. m., the walls of the inner pit were 20 to 30 feet high and the only active spots in the lake were the southeast and west grottoes. A steel-colored, fresh, heavy, crackling flow extended all the way from the southwest cone to the base of the northwest wall of the pot where glowing toes were pushing forward. A heavy stalactite curtain hung before the southeast grotto tunnel. There was a roaring blowing noise from one of the western vents. The lava of the north pit appeared over 20 feet down. The notch made by recent avalanches east of the north station was pronounced and had carried away much of the northwestern end of the northeast fill of 1918 lava. The intumescence of the middle region is so pronounced with its somewhat radial cracking and its lens-like surface, as to afford an almost perfect demonstration of the relationship between weighting by overflow of lake magma and resultant uplift of bench magma. The overflows for weeks have been annular, following the base of the talus and the uplift is consequently central.

The registration of the seismographs of the Whitney Laboratory of Seismology for the week ending at 2 p. m. Friday, May 24, 1918, has been very remarkable in tracing the autographs of at least six strong distant earthquakes as well as one smartly felt local shock and two moderate ones.

The teleseisms were as follows, Honolulu Standard Time: 9:49 a. m., May 19, trace only; 4:26 a. m., May 20, probable distance 3880 kilometers, equal to that of Samoa, Southern California or the Alaskan peninsula; 7:42 a. m., May 20, probable distance 7110 kilometers, equal to that of Chili, where an earthquake is reported; 8:09 p. m., May 21, probable distance 4070 kilometers, equal to that of Samoa or Alaska; 1:50 a. m., May 23, a very powerful shock of doubtful distance, possibly 5900 kilometers, equal to that of the Gulf of Mexico or the Kurile Islands; lastly a doubtful trace 9:22 a. m., May 24.

The local shocks were (1) 3:30 p. m. May 21, felt at the Observatory as a prolonged north-south rocking and generally felt on this island; (2) 7:27 p. m. May 21, (3) 2:30 p. m. May 22. Microseismic motion during the week has been slight, volcanic vibration showed some spasms May 17-18 and thereafter was very slight. The tilting movements were to the east and south, May 17-19, to the west and south May 19-20, to the east and south May 20-22, and to the east and north May 22-24.

June 1, 1918.—During the week ending Friday, May 31, 1918, the lava lake and crags of Halemaumau continued to rise with some gain in the rate of rising of the liquid portion. The observed results are of the same general type as have been recorded recently, but the movements of upward swelling of the hard lava flows have culminated in the creation of new crags and the lakes have increased in size. A very marked movement May 29 to 31 lifted the marginal talus and accentuated the slopes of the crags away from the center of the pit, and at the same time a storm of volcanic tremors was recorded on the seismographs.

The following were the measured changes:

May 24 to 31, 7 days, central crag rose from depression 42 feet to 20 feet;

May 24 to 31, 7 days, lake rose from depression 118 feet to 97 feet.

The rate of rising for six weeks, taking the mean of crag and lake as representing net movement of lava column, was

April 19-26, lake 4.11′, crag 3.71′, mean 3.92′ daily;

April 26-May 3, lake 1.29′, crag 3.71′, mean 2.21′ daily;

May 3-10, lake 1.14′, crag 2.43′, mean 1.78′ daily;

April 10-17, lake 2.86′, crag 3.00′, mean 2.93′ daily;

May 17-24, lake 2.71′, crag 3.14′, mean 2.92′ daily;

May 24-31, lake 3.00′, crag 3.14′, mean 3.07′ daily.

This table is of much interest. It shows that since the strong revival of rising started there was a maximum at first with lake overflowing the bench magma; then there was a decline in the rate of rising for a fortnight, with rise of bench magma strongly dominant over rise of lake magma; next there was a fortnight of steady rising with the net rate increased 61% and the bench magma still dominant; during the last week the lake has nearly reached the bench magma rate and the net rate has increased 5%. The weekly fluctuation of the lake magma rate was much greater than that of the bench magma and during one fortnight was in the opposite direction (May 10 to 24). The crag movement was more nearly equable than that shown in either of the other columns, suggesting that the bench magma movement perhaps best represents that of the main underground lava column. A single crag does not, however, accurately represent the mean movement of the whole crater floor, which would, if measured at evenly spaced points, gives a still more equable rate.

The average of the weekly means for the composite lava column was 2.8 feet per day for the six weeks. For the lake the average was 2.5, and for the crag 3.1. The crag thus rose 24% faster than the lake and 14% faster than the imagined composite lava column (mean of crag and lake), while the lake rose 14% slower than the latter.

The upshot of this computation is that the swelling up of the pit floor three feet per day since the April rise began has proceeded nearly 25% faster than the rising of the liquid lava, and is now lifting the slide-rock slopes bodily as the circular plug of semi-solid lava pushes upward. The summit of the great central crag is now less than 20 feet below the edge of the pit; its lowest for the period was 152 feet on April 17. Just as the mass sank bodily after the 26th of March, so it is now rising en masse. The accordance with predicted fall after equinox (March 21) and rise before solstice (June 22) has been nearly perfect. A feature of the measurements which throws light on the older records of travellers is that for some weeks past an observer without instruments would have noted **a sinking lake,** for the inner basin walls were growing higher, whereas in reality both lake and margin were lifting, but the latter a quarter faster.

On Saturday, May 25, at 2:30 p. m., the north pit was seen to have increased in size, there was bubble fountaining in the pot farther north and many small lava tricklings were pushing out from the margins of flows under the west station. At 3 p. m. looking from the southwest the west arm and southwest pond were seen to have banks 5 feet high and to show some fountaining activity. A long flow was pouring eastward across the south floor at the base of the wall talus and this was spreading right and left. The east arm exhibited walls 20 feet high and was quiet and crusted over. At 3:20 p. m. the source of the southern flow revived and a fresh overflow from it welled up; this source was the west cone at the edge of the floor under the southwest wall of the pit. The new flow spread to the south a short distance.

On May 26 at 4 p. m. the lake was crusted over and the only fountaining was in the southwest pond. The southeast pit was enlarged, the north pit was more open, the walls over the lake were higher and the north pit crevasse formed an arch as seen from the north with bubbling lava beneath. There was glow also in two openings between the north pits and the central pool, one of them flaming, and another glowing pot was open in the northwest floor. Incandescent flows were sluggishly making toes here and there all over the west and southwest regions. Occasionally the rhythmic fountain would explode in the west arm. The southwest pond was continually fountaining against its northern bank and streaming in it was westward from a tunnel arch at its east end. At 5 p. m. temporary subsidence broke up the crust on the main lake, rock slides were numerous towards the northwest and at 6:10 p. m. a heavy fall into the lake from the southeast crevasse took place and started violent fountaining. Smaller falls into the southeast pool indicated that the broken bench matter between the two pools was crumbling down. This was the result of a warping upward of the bench magma which tended to make a tumble of the blocks between the crevasses. A strong slide of rocks from the northeast crag mass into the northeast valley showed that that mass was tilting farther northeastward. A similar fall from the wall of the central crag mass into the southwest pond showed that that block was also being pushed up in the center and increasing its southward slope. Glistening splash marks on the shores of the lake indicated that recent rock tumbles had been numerous. On the northeast wall of the southeast pit there was a glowing and flaming spot high above the liquid level. Small rock slides from the walls of Halemaumau occasionally took place. On the evening of May 27 large falls of rock into the southeast pool were reported.

On Tuesday, May 28, at 3 p. m., there was a fresh flood of lava in motion on the south floor, the southwest pond was overflowing and splashing against its south bank and the west cone was an additional source of flows. The whole central region appeared more uplifted, the crevasses were wider, the east and southeast pools had greatly increased in size by a falling away of the banks and the cracked isthmus separating them was much narrower. The whole southeast floor was tilted southward making the south rim of the southeast pit comparatively low. Similarly the whole northeast floor was tilted northeastward so that the east bank of the main lake was much lower than the cliff over the central region. A new escarpment rose above the north pit depression on its north side extending thence to the north side of the northwest pond depression. A new north lake was forming from a union of these two pits, the southern shore of the new lake rose by gradual slope to a second escarpment on the north side of the central pool. The recent floods west and south were apparently being compensated by upward push east and north. The enlargement of the east pool depression was in the directions of he north and southeast crevasses. The south wall valley appeared much sunken.

On Wednesday, May 29, at 5 p. m., the upward swelling continued so that the inner cliff was fully 40 feet high above the central pool, the south side of the east pool and the north side of the southeast pool. At the south side of this pool and at the east end of the lake the bluff was only 20 feet high. The pools were sluggish, showing four or five spraying fountains which would break explosively from under the crust near the margins. There were traces of a new inner spatter bench. Rocks were sliding at the southeast crevasse. Glowing flows south, southwest, west and northwest moved slowly and made crackling noises.

Looking from the north and northwest the most striking change was the irregular breaking up of the whole floor into new crags which were slowly rising and tilting. The north chasm arch had collapsed, separating the northern pond from a smaller pot north of it, the latter adjacent to the north stack remnant. A squarish block of the floor was tending to lift and tilt northward on the west side of this pot so as to create a new northwest crag. In similar fashion the floor block containing the southeast pit had risen on the side of the east pool and sunk southward, tending to form a new southeast crag. The southwest pond was high, level with its rampart and bombarding its south bank. Much smoke rose from the northern cracks. At the base of the talus north and northwest the wall valley appeared low as though that should be the next place to fill.

On May 30 at 2:30 p. m. the west side was smoky, one fountain boiled in the north pot and the main lake was quiet and crusted over. The southeast pond was enlarged and showed surface streaming westward to a grotto under the bank with steady fountaining at the entrance. At 3:10 p. m. the east pool broke up and subsided three feet but immediately crusted over and became quiet. The southwest pond at 3:20 p. m. was flush with its margins and stagnant.

On Friday, May 31, 1918, at 1 p. m., it was evident that the rising bench magma was in extraordinarily rapid motion, for small slider took place almost incessantly at the southeast crevasse, and along the top of the eastern and northeastern talus. A deep gully was forming between the top of the talus and the wall on this side in contrast to that on other sides. The floor ring south and west was greatly widened. The lake walls were 30 feet high with fresh spatter rims 10 feet above the liquid. The southwest pond, however, was only 3 feet below its rampart. The lakes were crusted over, the crusts cracking and foundering from time to time, each break-up being inaugurated by explosive blowing. The tumescence of the central region was producing marked centrifugal tilt. Thus the central crag and the entire southeast, south and southwest floor area were tilting southward so that the northern scarp of the central crag had replaced the southwestern one as its summit. Similarly the west crag was tilting westward, the new northwest crag northward and the northeast floor and crag mass eastward. The pit was quite clear on the east side but smoky towards the west. The northern pond was increasing in size.

The seismographs of the Whitney Laboratory for the week ending at 2 p. m. on Friday, May 31, 1918, registered a distant strong earthquake at 9:27 a. m. May 25. The distance indicated was approximately 3600 kilometers, probably a rift movement under the ocean. Four small local shocks were registered respectively 9:49 p. m. May 25, 4:16 a. m. May 26, 7:19 p. m. May 26 and 4:42 a. m. May 28. Microseismic movement has been moderate with slight increase. Volcanic vibration increased from moderate values beginning May 28 to stormy spells which May 30-31 became excessive. Fifteen or twenty spasms occurred each hour of the day and the number of spasms was notably greater during the hours of stronger north and east tilt. This vibration period was coincident with intense tumescence of bench magma and the lift of wall talus in the pit, but not with strong fountaining or overflowing. The daily tilting movement has tended eastward and northward, this tilting increasing strongly May 30.

Very respectfully,

T. A. JAGGAR, JR.,
Director.

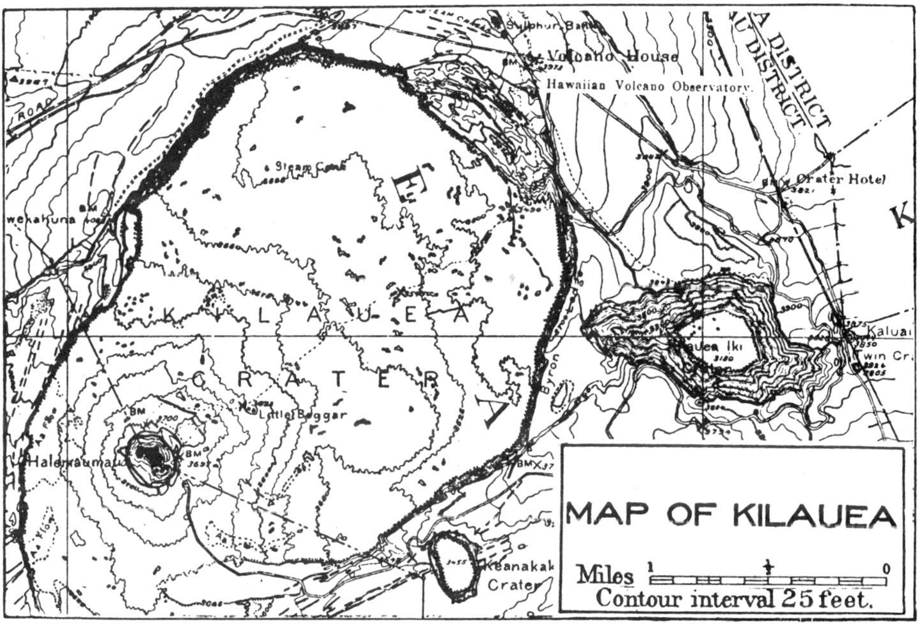

HAWAIIAN VOLCANO RESEARCH ASSOCIATION.

This society is a voluntary one, made up of subscribers to scientific work which is being executed by Dr. T. A. Jaggar, Director of the Hawaiian Volcano Observatory, Volcano House, P. O., Hawaii. **All scientific exchanges should be sent to this address.**

In 1917 there are about 150 subscribers in Hawaii and elsewhere, firms and individuals. A group of firms and persons in Hilo built the main observatory building in the spring of 1912. The work was founded by the Massachusetts Institute of Technology. Publications to date have been weekly reports since the summer of 1911 now reprinted in Honolulu in monthly form. There are also special reports, printed from time to time.

The weekly bulletin as it appears in the Honolulu Advertiser is reprinted as a leaflet and sent to regular annual subscribers to the work of the Association. L. A. Thurston is president of the Board of Directors of the Association, and L. T. Peck is treasurer. New subscribers who are interested in volcanoes will be welcomed in the Association. The Association aims: (1) To record volcanic activity and earthquakes in Hawaii; (2) to attract scientific men hither for special studies; (3) to promote the establishment of volcano observatories all over the world. The annual dues of regular members are $5; patrons of the Association subscribe larger amounts.

WHITNEY LABORATORY OF SEISMOLOGY.

The Whitney Laboratory of Seismology, named after an endowment fund of geophysical research held by the Massachusetts Institute of Technology, in memory of Caroline and Edward Whitney of Boston, is equipped with two Bosch-Omori 100 kg tromometers registering N-S and E-W motion, a heavy Omori tromometer registering E-W motion, and an Omori "ordinary Seismograph" designed for registering strong earthquakes in all three components of motion. These are seated on concrete piers in a closed basement room having practically constant temperature, beneath the chief Observatory building near the hotel. Time is referred to a rated chronometer, checked at intervals by solar observations with a transit. Both instruments are loaned by the College of Hawaii. Hawaiian standard time (H. S. T.) is 10 hrs. 30 min. slower than Greenwich time.

CANCANI SCALE OF SEISMIC INTENSITY.

Expressed by accelerations measured in millimeters per second per second.

I.	Instrumental	0.0	2.5
II.	Very slight	2.5	5.0
III.	Slight	5.0	10.0
IV.	Sensible, mediocre	10.0	25.0
V.	Rather strong	25.0	50.0
VI.	Strong	50.0	100.0
VII.	Very strong	100.0	250.0
VIII.	Ruinous	250.0	500.0
IX.	Disastrous	500.0	1000.0
X.	Very disastrous	1000.0	2500.0
XI.	Catastrophic	2500.0	5000.0
XII.	Great catastrophe	5000.0	10000.0

Grade IV. is ordinarily the minimum perceived by the senses; and in grade XII. the acceleration, or rate of change of motion (jerk) reaches that of terrestrial gravitation.

In the standard form of report the maximum intensity or acceleration, designated by the symbol a, or max. a, is given in the conventional unit, the milligal. The milligal is a measure of acceleration, such that 1 milligal = 1/100 mm. per sec. per sec. = 10 μ per sec. per sec. The Cancani scale, here defined in terms of millimeters per sec. per sec., can therefore be expressed in milligals by multiplying each of the numbers by 100.

WEEKLY BULLETIN
OF THE
Hawaiian Volcano Observatory

Vol. VI. HONOLULU, HAWAII, JUNE, 1918 No. 6

VOLCANO OBSERVATORY, June 15, 1918.—During the fortnight beginning June 1, 1918, mild subsidence has followed the previous long rising spell which culminated on June 4. On that date the summit of the central crag was depressed only 6 feet below the east rim of Halemaumau and the lake at the central cove stood 87 feet below the rim. The crag was plainly visible from Volcano House. The next day, however, it sank out of sight again and on June 15 its summit was 18 feet below the rim, while the lake had gone down still farther to a depth of 107 feet. This subsidence before the solstice is quite in accordance with the expected curve of rise and fall.

The central crag had thus sunk 12 feet in eleven days, a rate of 1.1 feet per day. The lake sank 20 feet in eleven days, a rate of 1.8 feet per day.

On Saturday, June 1, 1918, at 2 p. m., a new position of flow from the wall crack had been inaugurated under the northwest station where a powerful stream of liquid lava was welling out of the top of the talus and pouring over the rock slope to make a new fill in the depressed northern wall valley. A cone at the source was puffing loudly. The northern pond was now greatly enlarged with dimensions approximately 100 by 75 feet and two large fountains in it threw lava spray to considerable heights. At 2:30 p. m. inspection from the northeast showed that there had been much caving of the central crag and a large grotto had formed under its northern cliff. The southeast bench stood 25 feet above the east arm of the lake and there were frequent falls of rock from it. The east channel and the southeast pond were very quiet and crusted over. The southwest pond was flush with its rim on the south side.

On June 2 at 4:30 p. m. there was increased activity and swift streaming southeastward with traveling fountains. From the north at 5 p. m. the northwest wall cone was seen to be still pouring forth a flow and there was much activity in the north pond while the northern region in general was smoky. At 6 p. m. a succession of falls of rock from the raised bench on the northeast side of the east arm took place and the whole block there settled about five feet. From the east and southeast rim of the pit numerous small flows could be seen in motion in the south and west wall-valleys, those of the latter flowing northward. At 6:40 p. m. a somewhat prolonged slide was heard toward the northwest and there were some rolling rocks which plunged down the back of the northeast crag slope.

In general the scene at 7 p. m. indicated a marked change culminating the recent movement. The crags were higher though the lakes appeared relatively low and showed cavern arches at the central cove, at the cove on the north side of the east pool, and strong overhang of the inner spatter bench in the southeast pool. This bench was pronounced in both these pools some 8 feet above the liquid. A bright trickling stream of lava poured from the northwest wall cone. There were brilliantly glowing and flaming cracks in the upraised ledge next to the northwest pond on its north side and fresh glowing driblet flows covered the northwest floor. The new northwest pond was an isolated pool separated by crust from the large north lake which lay deeply sunken amid surrounding crags. A circular pit had formed between the north and the main central lakes and a deep crevasse lay between this pit and the old west crag. From a long slit in the summit of the west pond cone a blue flame was playing with hissing noise,

WEEKLY BULLETIN
of the
Hawaiian Volcano Observatory

Published Monthly at Honolulu, Hawaii, by the Hawaiian Volcano Research Association

L. W. de Vis-Norton........Secretary

Entered as second-class matter January 20, 1914, at the post-office at Honolulu, Hawaii. under the Act of August 24, 1912.

and another blowing cone had formed at the southeast base of the central crag mass. The southwest pond showed an eight-foot margin. The lake activity of streaming, fountaining and wide glow rims gave the impression of subsidence, but this may have been mostly uplift of the bench magma, for the glowing trickle flows and blowing cones indicated pronounced gas pressure.

On Monday, June 3, at 11:30 a, m.. measurement showed continued rising, the lakes appeared somewhat higher, the southern driblet flows were still in motion and the southeast cone was seen to be a small stack four feet high continuously hissing. This cone stood at the end of a vertical crack extending from the east pool along the west side of the southeast pond. There were occasional cracking and foundering of crusts in the lake and very large fountains would form in the southwest pond and in the north and east corners of the east pool. The eastern talus was still uplifting and in motion. The new northwest spatter heap was hissing and fresh lumps ejected from it had fallen on the high rim of the pit northwest while the cliff face below was plastered for half its height with the spatter from explosions of the cone. Moving trickle flows poured from the wall crack west-northwest and there were similar places all along the base of the western and southwestern walls of the pit. The west pond cone was blowing and glowing. The east side of the platform of the west crag mass was tilted up into an escarpment. The former southwest crag and also the southwest wall slab were by now entirely buried under fresh flows. The west pool of the main lake had become cut off as a small oval pond. The former south pressure ridge was nearly buried under new flows.

Tuesday, June 4, 1918, marked the culmination of rising. The back slope of the northeast crag mass was inclined fully 45° in places, while the recently uptilted floor on the northeast side of the north lake was inclined 22° to the northeast and the southern platform of the west crag mass 25° to the west. These figures give some notion of the high centrifugal tilt due to tumescence. The slope of the lava heap against the northwest wall was also about 25°.

At noon on this day the bench magma was rising strongly as shown by small rock slips south, east and northeast, many of these into the wall crack between talus and cliff. The floor crevasses southeast and north had become enormously wide. The lakes appeared low but the cavern arch on the north side of the east pool was submerged. The southwest pond, some three feet beneath its rim, sank three feet more at 12:30 p. m. and this subsidence extended to the main lake also where there was turbulent fountaining east, northeast and at the central cove accompanied by eastward streaming and formation of thin skins. A cavern under the northwest side of the southeast pond appeared as though extended in the direction of the central cove. At 12:15 p. m. there had been a strong flow from the west pond cone which welled out and spread beween the edge of the newer western flows and the slope of the west crag mass. While this flow bubbled up the lakes subsided. The northwest wall heap hissed continuously and appeared higher.

There was now a heavy filling of driblet flows in a belt 50 to 100 feet wide which extended westward and southward from under the north station. This fill had been fed from the wall crack in many places and it appeared to have weighted down the western half of the pit floor, while the eastern half was lifted. The upward swelling and cracking of bench magma appeared to center at the pools, so that there was a distinct sag between the bench slopes which radiated respectively from the northern and central pools.

Large cracks cut through the north crag. The northeast valley was now much below lake level. A glowing cavern led southward from the north lake.

In the evening the main lake was heavily crusted and higher, moving flows were seen on the southwest floor, there was glow at the base of the southeast cone and two falls from the west bridge into the lake appeared to rest on a shoal without sinking.

On June 5 at 3 p. m. the main lake was quiet and crusted over, with sinking spells about every ten minutes which revealed a glow edge around the lake a foot deep. Smoke was thick to the north, the pools there were inactive, and the northwest cone was puffing. The crag summit had subsided so as to disappear from the view of the distant observatory. The inner walls over the lake were 40 feet high, and had fallen away at the promontory north of the central channel. The southwestern and northern coves of the east pool had increased by collapse of walls. The southwest pond showed 5-foot ramparts. Flows were in sluggish motion on the south floor and at the southeastern vents. No rocks slid on the east talus but one tumble fell into the southeast crevasses about 5 p. m. The turning point from rising to sinking had been reached.

On Thursday, June 6, about 6 p. m., an important change to subsidence of the main lake was shown by a cascade into the lake from the west. An arch 10 feet high had broken away from under the west bridge, and through this from the west arm pool a cascade poured over a bench three feet higher than the level of the lake. This cascade diminished in height at 6:30 p. m. as though the lake had risen, and such fluctuations recurred, but the inrush was contiñuous, and there was inflow also from the north side of the bridge.

Other evidence of relative subsidence of the lake was furnished by a large noisy fountaining cavern opened on the north side of the east pool. Later this became quiet and a large central fountain developed in the east pool and played continuously for over an hour, engulfing crusts from east and west. Streaming in the southeast pond was slow into the large southwest grotto which glowed brilliantly. High fountain fling was seen at the southwest pond. A steady green flame burned at the southeast floor-cone without noise. A glowing cone stood high above the lake at the southwest cove of the east pool. The spatter ramparts fell into the lake from time to time and at 6:45 p. m. a large cone north of the west bridge fell into the lake in two pieces, leaving a glowing wall still incandescent a half-hour later.

On June 7, 1918, at 2:30 p. m., there was rumbling and smoke at the northern ponds but no visible fire. At 3 p. m. seen from the southeast the only activity in the main lake was at the southeast grotto, and smoke was abundant. At 3:20 p. m. the east pool broke up and this spread over the main lake, six fountains played on the margins and a central fountain broke into activity every ten or fifteen minutes.

At 3 p. m. on Saturday, June 8, the east pool again showed one central fountain tending to continuous action for a half-hour or more, and strong boiling at the southeast grotto. At 3:35 p. m. a collapse of the bench on the northeast side broke up the crust, started general effervescence, and revealed rapid streaming towards the southeast. At 4:25 p. m. a large fall of the bench on the northwest margin of the southeast pond made commotion there, followed shortly afterward by collapse at the southeast grotto of the east pool. The ''perpetual'' fountain and the many collapses gave evidence that a period of moderate subsidence was in progress.

June 9 at 4:30 p. m. conditions were unchanged, there was much activity in the pit of the southeast pond and the crumbling of the partition betweeen this pit and the east pool was marked by frequent falls of rock. Every fifteen or twenty minutes the large fountain in the east pool would break into furious activity. Border overflowing from the wall crack was renewed on this day. At 6 p. m. a flow eastward was pouring from the northwest cone under the wall, and flows were trickling on the southwest floor.

Monday, June 10, there was evidence of rising, or at least of arrested subsidence. A new inner shelf around the main lake stood five feet above it, and the lake was crusted over. At 3 p. m. there was no fountaining, there was hissing northwest, and smoke was thick. The southeast pit was dark and smoky, but rumbling.

June 11, at 3 p. m., there was little change, the inner shelf was 5 feet high, everything was crusted over and smoky. The dome over the southeast grotto collapsed, leaving a sheer wall and a few minutes later there was a rock fall into the southeast pit.

June 12 at 3 p. m. inspection from the north showed the north pools to be crusted and the northwest wall cone emitted blue fumes quietly. From the southeast the southeast pit was seen to contain a new inner bench marking a recent strong rise, and a fall of rock from the walls was seen.

On Thursday, June 13, 1918, at 7 p. m., the lakes were crusted over and very sluggish, with one or two border fountains. Breaking up took place, first in the main lake with eastward streaming, then in the southeast pit with westward streaming and a fountain on the south side; finally the southwest pond became active with a fountain on its east margin. The southwest pond stood slightly higher than the main lake. There were glowing spots in the southwest and west floors and a banner of flame played above the west side of the west bridge. Smoke was moderate, no rocks fell, and everything appeared stagnant and stationary.

The pit during these days was extraordinarily dark at night as seen from a distance. This seems to be the expected interval of subsidence and stagnation prior to the solstice, in accordance with the past habit of the lava column.

On June 14 at 6 p. m. there was little change. Both lake and southeast pond showed inner shelves five feet high, the cone on the southeast floor was smoking, a flaring pale greenish-yellow flame played above a 2-foot chimney some six feet above the lake level at the central cove (southwest side east pool). The northwest wall-cone and the west pond cone on the floor were both glowing. There were occasional blowing and spraying border fountains on the north side of the central channel and at the southeast grotto. Whitish stain appeared on the west side of the northeast crag mass.

There were now nine crusted ponds in the pit as a whole, occupying five pit depressions, one, however, being an open flat surrounded by a cone (the west pond). The north and northwest pools occupied the north pit; the north central pit lay between these and the main lake; the latter occupied an elongate large depression, with the central and east pools constituting the largest lake, while the west-arm pond and west pot were openings in the crust filling of the western part of the depression. The southeast and southwest ponds occupied small pits of their own.

Only three of the older crag masses persisted, namely the central, west and northeast. New crags in process of formation, uplifted floors, lay north and south of the north pit, and south of the east pool. A horse-shoe of flow heapings made a floor around the outside of the craggy uplifts, widest on the southwest, and extending eastward and northward for a third of the circumference in each direction.

A very pronounced earthquake, making long slow swayings, was generally felt on Hawaii at 11:13 a. m. June 14, 1918. Its record on the seismographs continued for three-quarters of an hour. The pens, which had been flung off, were immediately replaced on the drums. The long duration would suggest a near shock of great intensity. The amplitude of the first movement of the ground was sharply marked to the east and south, and eight times greater east than south, implying a horizontal thrust S. 80 E., or directly away from Mokuaweoweo, the summit crater of Mauna Loa. At Naalehu in the southern part of the island the shock was sufficiently powerful to throw things off shelves in a westerly direction (the ground beneath being displaced to the east).

VOLCANO OBSERVATORY, June 22, 1918.—During the week ending Friday, June 21, 1918, steady but almost imperceptible subsidence of the Halemaumau lava column has continued, both lake and central crag sinking 13 feet in the six days from June 15 to June 21, an average movement of 2.17

feet per day. On June 15 the central crag was 18 feet below the rim of the pit and the lake at the central cove 107 feet. On June 21 the depression of the crag was 31 feet and of the lake 120 feet.

The conspicuous features on Saturday, June 15, 1918, were the high heap of lava above the wall crack along the base of the south and west walls of the pit, making a floor sloping inward: the great height of the uplifted central floors which now cut off the views of the lake from the north and nearly obscured the view of the southwest pond from the east: and lastly the lifted marginal talus, so that it was now a ridge in many places separated from the wall by a gully. Activity was slight and smoke moderate. There was some hissing from the northern ponds and streaming in the southeast pond was towards the northwest.

On June 16 at 4 p. m. the lake was still quiet but a half hour later there was a breaking up of crust with some fountaining and eastward streaming. At 5 p. m. there was fountaining in the north lake and loud hissing from the northwest cone.

On June 18 at 4 p. m. both measurement and observation showed slow continuous subsidence. The inner cliffs appeared somewhat higher, gas puffing had ceased, the volume of smoke was moderate and the lakes were mostly crusted over. The floors of recent overflow were heavily crusted and cracked. In the main lake there was evidence of very slow streaming to the southeast shown by a zone of festooned skin extending from the central region in a curve which ended at a place of fountaining bombardment against the south bank of the east pool. At the place formerly called the west bridge, which separated the central pool from the west arm, there was now a wide beach of hard lava sloping eastward and this greatly diminished the size of that pool. There was a similar wide inner floor on the north side of the east pool. Possibly these were in part emerged flats of lake bottom. The southwest pond stood low within its pit so that a glowing cavern was revealed at its west end. No activity was discernable in the northern pools.

A visit on this day to the lava tube leading westward from the collapsed northeast fill discovered typical worm-shaped stalactites of the cavern variety up to twelve inches long, and wholly in 1918 lava which was red hot in April. It is even now so hot that the deeper portions of the tube are intolerable and specimens could not be collected with unprotected hands. There was no trace of water drip. This occurrence proves finally that such stalactites are formed by remelting in chambers freshly vacated by liquid lava and heated by hot gas. Where the cone of glassy lava had been, which it will be remembered was formed during a heavy rainstorm on March 13 last, the site now being a tumble of broken rocks, there was revealed a light porous lava lining the cavities below, greatly oxidized to a yellow ochre color, suggesting that the iron of the rock had been transformed to the hydrous oxide.

At 7 a. m. on Wednesday, June 19, the lake appeared still lower and some fresh tumbled rocks from the walls on the edge of the south floor showed that there had been mass subsidence of the lava column. Streaming was eastward in the east pool with a large central perpetual fountain in action there, and there was some fountaining in the southeast pit. Smoke was moderate and no activity was visible in the northern pools. The eastern talus ridge had somewhat subsided and there was a deep gully next to it on the wall side.

On June 20 at 7 a. m. fountaining was again seen in the center of the east pool with streaming surface currents pouring towards it from both east and west, and the effervescence occasionally took the form of lines of traveling fountains which migrated to bombard the south bank. A flaming chimney had formed above the bank of the lake on the south side of the central channel. Occasional strong hissing broke out at the southeast margin of the southeast pond, where fountaining also was seen. A smoke hole was developing high up the east talus. At 4 p. m. the lake was quiet for fountaining at the southeast bank. About 6 p. m. there was a breaking up with rapid eastward streaming. There was some fountaining in the northern ponds but the smoke rising from that region was dense.

On Friday, June 21, 1918, at noon it was evident that in general the lava column continued to subside very slowly, there was much smoke and changes were few. The southeast bench now appeared higher than the north region, as the latter was subsiding around the north lake. There were marked tunnels at the west end of the southwest pond and on the north side of the east pool. Small slides of debris took place from the northeast wall of the pit. The cliffs around the main lake showed much spatter. In the central channel there was turbulent bubble fountaining with streaming from both east and west. The inner bench around the southeast pond showed overhang with stalactites. In addition to the chimney south of the channel there was another glowing orifice some ten feet above the lake on the south side of the east pool. The north pools showed a smooth crusted surface, the main open pond being there at the east end. The northwest floor was seen to be made up of recent flows piled high against the base of the wall and sloping inward just as in the case of the fresh flows to the southwest.

A visit to the south cone on the edge of the pit showed that its summit had completely collapsed, and the interior cavernous shell was intolerably hot and coated with deposits of alum stained with sulphur. There were extensive stalactite accumulations on the northern interior of the broken dome with glossy reddish surfaces.

The following is the report of seismographic registration in the Whitney Laboratory for the three weeks, May 31 to 2 p. m. Friday, June 21, 1918.

For the week ending June 7 two strong distant earthquakes were registered, respectively June 2, 2:51 a. m., and June 4, 6:50 a. m. The phases of the first appeared to indicate a distance approximately 5000 kilometers, equal to that of Behring Straits or Fiji; the second 3650 kilometers, an origin probably under the ocean. Four local shocks occurred as follows: 2:13 p. m. May 31, 3:30 p. m. June 1, 12:49 a. m. June 6, and 12:48 p. m. June 6. Volcanic vibration was strong in the early part of the week, decreasing thereafter. Microseisms increased towards the end of the week. Tilting somewhat increased to the east and south until June 3, with recovery in the opposite direction thereafter.

During the week ending June 14 one strong distant earthquake was registered at 6:09 p. m. June 11; the distance of origin was not determinable. Local shocks occurred as follows: 2:37 a. m. June 8 (very small); 4:03 a. m. June 12 (small); 11:13 a. m. June 14, a very prolonged felt shock, which first threw the pens off the drums. After about a minute these were replaced and the movement of the ground continued for three-quarters of an hour in long slow pulsations which resembled the long waves of a distant earthquake. Volcanic vibration was slight until June 10 when very strong spasms occurred which diminished during the next three days. Microseismic motion was moderate. Tilting increased very strongly to the north until June 11 and thereafter the records indicated a stationary condition.

During the past week ending June 21 one teleseism, the long waves only, was registered at 6:04 p. m. June 20. Local earthquakes were registered at 2:54 a. m. and 3:29 p. m. June 15; 6:28 a. m. June 19 (felt). Volcanic tremor has been moderate, with some spasms June 16 to 18. Microseismic motion was moderate and decreasing. Movement of tilting has shown little change except for slight tendency west and south towards the end of the week.

Dr. Arnold Romberg, professor of physics, College of Hawaii, has accepted the position of assistant in physics at the Observatory for the summer months.

The north crater hut at Halemaumau, which has been a landmark near the pit since 1912, and was part of the original hut erected by Mr. Perret for crater experiments in 1911, was removed on June 21 and will be set up in the Observatory grounds.

VOLCANO OBSERVATORY, June 29, 1918.—During the week ending Friday, June 28, 1918, the lava column of Halemaumau responded to the solstice by ceasing subsidence and rising slightly until June 26. This was followed by depression the next day and slow rising thereafter, the central crag at the end

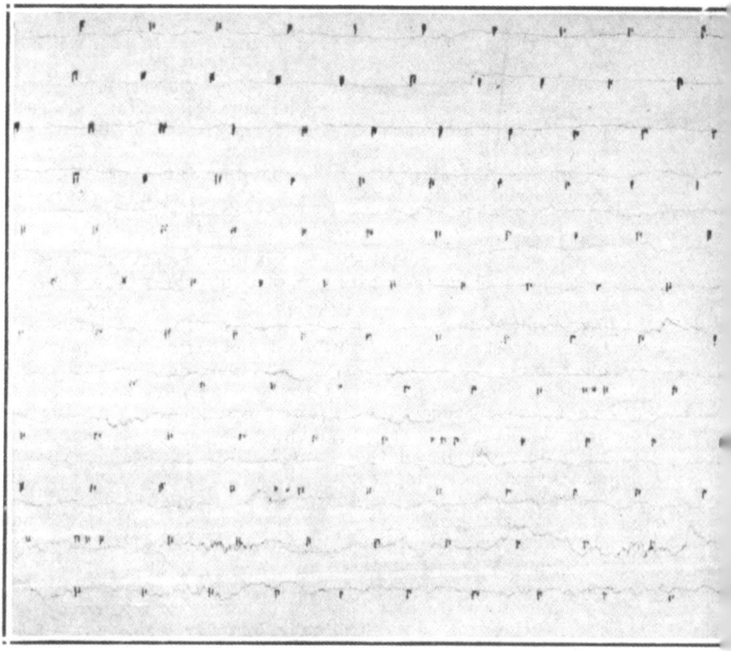

1. Seismogram, old method, showing

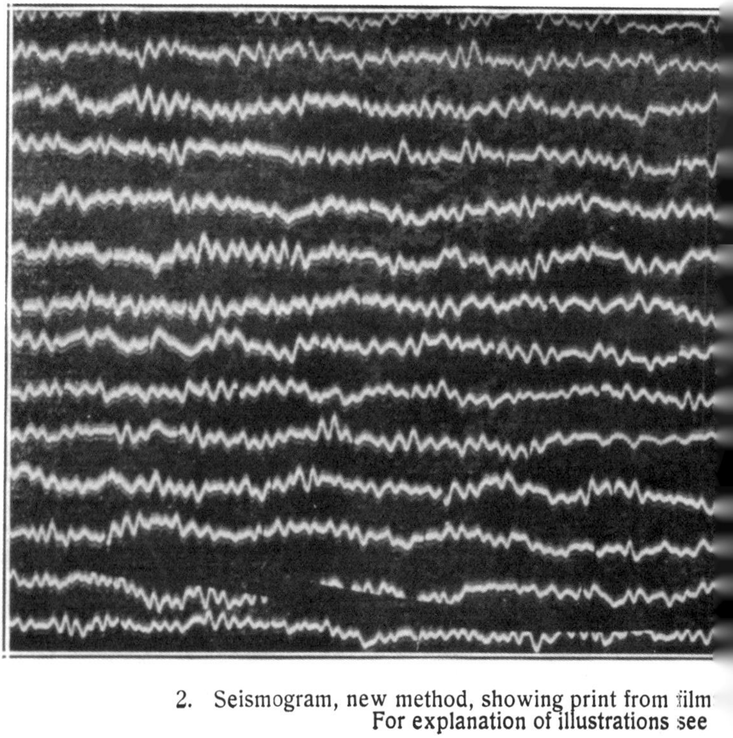

2. Seismogram, new method, showing print from film

For explanation of illustrations see

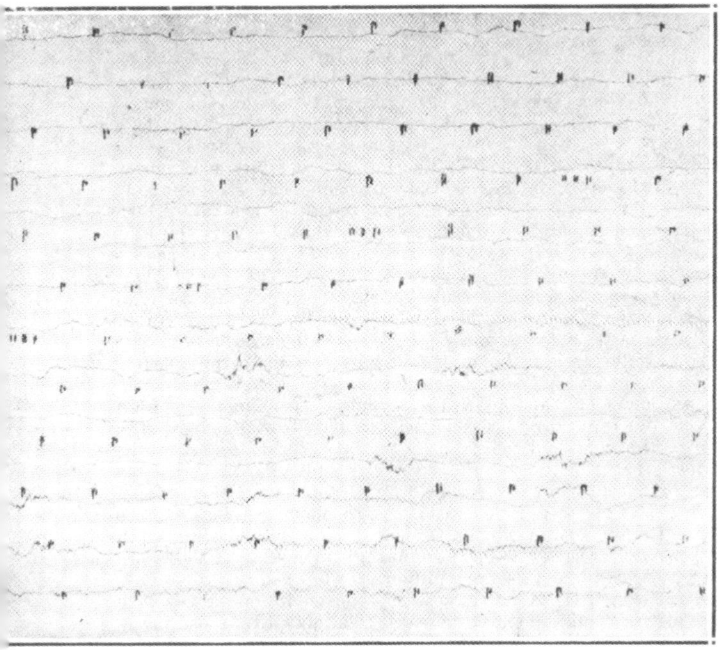

rint directly from smoked paper.

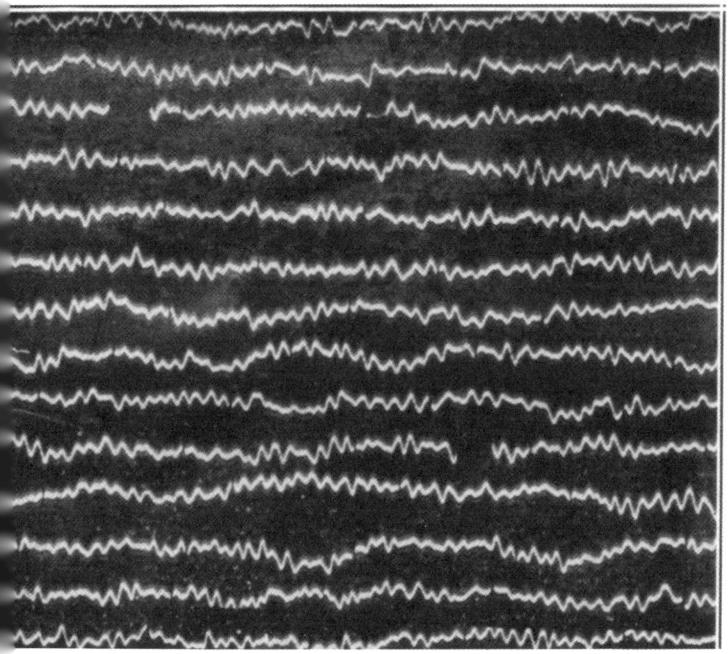

ptical registration, same pendulum as above.
te at end of report. Ed.

of the week being about 31 feet, and the lake about 125 feet below the rim of the pit. In general, the week following solstice (June 22) appears to mark arrested subsidence and a stationary condition with rising symptoms.

On Saturday, June 22, 1918, at 6 p. m., the main lake was quiet, with a fan-shaped area of glowing and streaming melt which converged to a fountain on the south bank of the east pool. Both the main and southeast pools appeared higher with reference to the inner spatter ledge. There was some hissing and spurting from under crusts. Glowing apertures had reappeared at the base of the southeast cone on the lifted floor. There was active fountaining from time to time at the east end of the north lake. Glow over the pit as a whole at night was brighter.

On June 23 at 4 p. m. the lakes were quiet and crusted, one fountain was playing on the south side of the east pool. Measurement revealed stationary condition of both lake and crags since June 21. At 5:15 p. m. a fall from the southeast ledge into the lake, followed ten minutes later by collapse of the bank north of the central narrows, indicated movement in the column, and the lake subsidized a foot or so with break-up of crusts and eastward streaming. Strong fountaining bombarded the south bank. Prior to this the crusted lake had stood one foot below the inner shelf and there were bubbling currents rushing to the bank at the southeast corner. There was continuous hissing at the cavern under the south edge of the southeast pond. The glowing edge of the north pool extended farther west than on the previous day. The flaming hole at the base of the southeast cone was conspicuous seen from the south.

The northwest cone against the wall and the west pond cone were fuming, and the latter showed a deep glowing and flaming rift on its west side. On the side of the northwest pond headed towards the west pond cone, where the former chasm and tunnel lay, there was a glowing cavern with lava pounding within. Occasionally outbursts of fountaining activity broke out at the east end of the north lake. The platform southeast of the old west crag was now a steep escarpment, itself a marked craggy eminence. In the northwest floor made of recent flows there was a collapsed oval area. Fresh fallen rocks from the wall lay on the southwest floor, and formed fresh avalanche talus. High above the southwest pond on the ledge above it south a chimney glowed and flamed. The streaming of this pond was eastward into the cavern under the chasm which bounds the cliff wall of the central crag mass on its south side. The pot of the former rhythmic fountain had become an oval pond glowing quietly. General conditions on this day showed renewed gas burning and higher temperatures, without much pressure.

On the evening of June 24 high pressure was renewed with every sign of rising lava. Ten or more fountains of the spraying and constructing type were building up the banks of the lake, glow and flames showed at the cones and gases could be heard hissing forth from confining orifices. The fumes were thinner.

This was confirmed by survey the next morning Tuesday, June 25, 1918, at 9 a. m., when the central crag was found to have risen two feet and the lake bench was built up a similar amount. The gas pressure had slackened and was now that of moderate rising, with five fountains on the edge of the main lake, a hissing fountain in the southeast pond, and hissing noise from the northwest pond and possibly from the west pond cone. Smoke had greatly diminished and small movements in the talus evidenced motion. The cavern at the west end of the southwest pond had collapsed to a channel leading toward the west arm pond. At 8:50 a. m. there was a temporary sinking spell accompanied by violent bombardment of the south bank of the east pool. Everywhere the streaming was toward the border fountains which built up the spatter banks. In the depression north of the northern lake there appeared to lie a crusted round pond.

On June 26 at 9 a. m. the levels were unchanged and at 10 a. m. the lake appeared rising. Occasional small rock slips occurred. Five or six fountains pounded on the banks of the main lake, one of these building a crescent of spatter on the south side of the east pool. Clear seeing revealed the fact that the plateau between the north and central pools had been breaking down so as to extend the north lake depression southward as though restoring the old north arm. Ocasional breakings up of crust revealed eastward streaming. The bench magma appeared to be rising most toward the east(or sinking toward the center) for it was only one foot high around the central pool, but three feet high at the east end.

The angular measurements of Thursday, June 27, made at 4 p. m., showed that both lake and central crag were slightly lower, and the crag had settled more than the lake so as to give the latter the appearance of being higher. A new spatter bench had been constructed, there was fresh festooned overflow on the inner shelf north of the central channel, a glowing chimney showed a round hole about 8 feet above the lake at the south side of the east pool and a crescent cone was in process of building on the north side. There were occasional continuous central fountains and four or five fountains played against the bank. Fuming had increased. A new crack extended from under the south station towards the southwest pond across the recent flows of the southern floor. At 6 p. m. there was fountaining in the north lake and the west pond cone was blowing noisily and occasionally ejecting spray. The next day, June 28, conditions appeared about the same with less fume and subsidence arrested.

OUR ILLUSTRATIONS.

SPECIAL NOTE—

During the recent period of moderate activity and stationary lava little work has been done at the crater, but the staff of the Observatory has been very busily engaged in instrumental problems. The Director has recently compiled the statistics of the tiltings, tremblings and quakes registered for the past five years, with the object of opening to view the seismometric problem as it directly concerns the lava column and the volcano centers of activity. Dr. Romberg comes to the Observatory in order to subject this problem to the test of experiment and is now at work with a heavy horizontal pendulum, making modifications designed especially to meet the local needs. There is, of course, no interruption to the regular routine registration with a pair of the older type instruments. The local quick-period earthquakes, the volcanic microtremor, and the extraordinary tiltings or changes of the plumb-line, are the three distinctively Hawaiian phenomena.

Pendulums recording on smoked paper lose many of the details of ground motion because of excess of friction in the apparatus; they are further inaccurate because of lack of damping designed to keep them from oscillating mechanically; and the registering clockwork mechanisms are defective in that the smoked paper moves too slowly to show plainly the important initial motion of earthquakes and the very quick motion of local ones. All the mechanical imperfections combine to yield only mediocre results, and the standard instruments, designed for cheapness and convenience of operation, are ill adapted to such special problems.

The accompanying figures show prints directly from two seismograms made before and after improvement, with the heavy pendulum and its chronographic revolving drum. They are exhibited to show the first results of improved photographic registration contrasted with the old method.

This older procedure involved an undamped pendulum, numerous pivots, a magnifying lever and needle scratching the record on smoked paper which moved only about 13 mm. per minute; the minute marks were stamped on the same paper by a separate mechanism, and this made it necessary to know and allow for the distance of minute-marker from pen in order to assign its exact time to any earthquake disturbance of the written line. This machine lost many of the distant earthquakes entirely, registered the tremors very irregularly and because of instrumental friction the needle failed to return to the safe straight line where deflected out of it. Both tilting and local earthquakes produced such deflection.

The instrument was rebuilt by Dr. Romberg with materials at hand, in consultation with the writer, so as to make its record with a ray of light from a small electric bulb. All pivots but one were eliminated and friction reduced at least 80 per cent. The light beam is projected with an ordinary camera lens through a small mirror, which is hung by silk fibre and attached to the pendulum. The image of the light is focussed on a Kodak film clamped on the revolving drum, and the film moves at more than double the former speed, namely 33 mm. per minute. To the pendulum arm is attached an openwork box of metal immersed in oil which strongly damps out mechanical vibrations, but leaves the mirror very sensitive to earth movement. The time is marked, as shown in the print, by a short extinction of the light once a minute and by a long extinction once an hour, these occultations making gaps in the record itself, instead of separate marks. The time marker is operated by an electrically connected clock. No correction is necessary other than the known error of the time-piece. The optical work is as yet imperfect owing to imperfections in available mirrors, but it will be seen in the figure how marvellously continuous are the fine microtremors and how rhythmic the grouping of the slower microseisms, the whole series showing longer slow wave movements which deserve investigation. The strong zigzags at the beginning of the record were produced artificially to show the natural decay curve of the pendulum when disturbed. The magnification and openness of the record are greatly increased over the smoked-paper registration shown in the first figure, and it will be seen that there the wave movements are illegible and irregular.

By means of small improvements over experiments made by Milne, Galitzin and others, and largely through the indefatigable spirit of Dr. Romberg in working with inadequate materials, we have succeeded in making photographic registration even of the rapid movement of local earthquakes. On July 2, 1918, a beautiful seismogram of a distant strong earthquake was obtained with the new apparatus. This will be reproduced in the next Bulletin. Suffice it to say, in reporting progress, that already the difficulties of friction, magnification, damping, opening the record and time-marking are partially overcome, and in addition the resulting seismogram is a strong transparent negative, capable of reproduction by printing on any photographic paper.

Very respectfully,

T. A. JAGGAR, JR.,

Director.

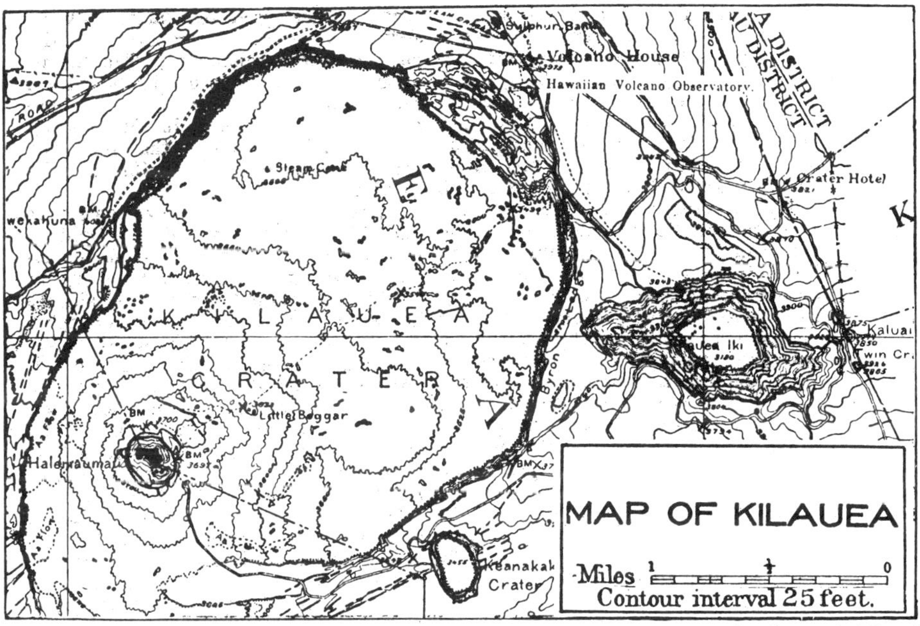

HAWAIIAN VOLCANO RESEARCH ASSOCIATION.

This society is a voluntary one, made up of subscribers to scientific work which is being executed by Dr. T. A. Jaggar, Director of the Hawaiian Volcano Observatory, Volcano House, P. O., Hawaii. **All scientific exchanges should be sent to this address.**

In 1917 there are about 150 subscribers in Hawaii and elsewhere, firms and individuals. A group of firms and persons in Hilo built the main observatory building in the spring of 1912. The work was founded by the Massachusetts Institute of Technology. Publications to date have been weekly reports since the summer of 1911 now reprinted in Honolulu in monthly form. There are also special reports, printed from time to time.

The weekly bulletin as it appears in the Honolulu Advertiser is reprinted as a leaflet and sent to regular annual subscribers to the work of the Association. L. A. Thurston is president of the Board of Directors of the Association, and L. T. Peck is treasurer. New subscribers who are interested in volcanoes will be welcomed in the Association. The Association aims: (1) To record volcanic activity and earthquakes in Hawaii; (2) to attract scientific men hither for special studies; (3) to promote the establishment of volcano observatories all over the world. The annual dues of regular members are $5; patrons of the Association subscribe larger amounts.

WHITNEY LABORATORY OF SEISMOLOGY.

The Whitney Laboratory of Seismology, named after an endowment fund of geophysical research held by the Massachusetts Institute of Technology, in memory of Caroline and Edward Whitney of Boston, is equipped with two Bosch-Omori 100 kg tromometers registering N-S and E-W motion, a heavy Omori tromometer registering E-W motion, and an Omori "ordinary Seismograph" designed for registering strong earthquakes in all three components of motion. These are seated on concrete piers in a closed basement room having practically constant temperature, beneath the chief Observatory building near the hotel. Time is referred to a rated chronometer, checked at intervals by solar observations with a transit. Both instruments are loaned by the College of Hawaii. Hawaiian standard time (H. S. T.) is 10 hrs. 30 min. slower than Greenwich time.

CANCANI SCALE OF SEISMIC INTENSITY.

Expressed by accelerations measured in millimeters per second per second.

I.	Instrumental	0.0	2.5
II.	Very slight	2.5	5.0
III.	Slight	5.0	10.0
IV.	Sensible, mediocre	10.0	25.0
V.	Rather strong	25.0	50.0
VI.	Strong	50.0	100.0
VII.	Very strong	100.0	250.0
VIII.	Ruinous	250.0	500.0
IX.	Disastrous	500.0	1000.0
X.	Very disastrous	1000.0	2500.0
XI.	Catastrophic	2500.0	5000.0
XII.	Great catastrophe	5000.0	10000.0

Grade IV. is ordinarily the minimum perceived by the senses; and in grade XII. the acceleration, or rate of change of motion (jerk) reaches that of terrestrial gravitation.

In the standard form of report the maximum intensity or acceleration, designated by the symbol a, or max. a, is given in the conventional unit, the **milligal.** The milligal is a measure of acceleration, such that 1 milligal = 1/100 mm. per sec. per sec. = 10 μ per sec. per sec. The Cancani scale, here defined in terms of millimeters per sec. per sec., can therefore be expressed in milligals by multiplying each of the numbers by 100.

WEEKLY BULLETIN
OF THE

Hawaiian Volcano Observatory

Vol. VI. HONOLULU, HAWAII, JULY, 1918 No. 7

HAWAIIAN VOLCANO OBSERVATORY, July 6, 1918.—During the week ending Friday, July 5, 1918, the lava column has fluctuated but slightly with a tendency to uplift of the northern part of the floor of the pit, including the north crag. The following measurements during the last fortnight show how stationary the lava has been:

June 21, depression of lake 129 feet, depression of central crag 31 feet.

June 23, depression of lake 130 feet, depression of central crag 30 feet.

June 25, depression of lake 130 feet, depression of central crag 31 feet.

June 26, depression of lake 129 feet, depression of central crag 29 feet.

June 27, depression of lake 131 feet, depression of central crag 34 feet.

June 29, depression of lake 131 feet, depression of central crag 31 feet.

July 2, depression of lake 129 feet, depression of central crag 33 feet.

July 4, depression of lake 132 feet, depression of central crag 36 feet.

It will be seen that the net effect is a subsidence of the lake 3 feet in 13 days and of the crag 5 feet.

On Saturday, June 29, at 1 p. m., there was strong eastward streaming in the main lake, two spatter heaps were building on the south side of the east pool and two more on the north side, one of them a large dome. The central pool was constricted by the inward construction of its marginal shelf. A flaming chimney, following contact of spatter material and inner wall, glowed about 5 feet above the lake level at the central cove. The southeast pond was flush with its inner shelf and fountaining on its south side. There was bombardment at the west end of the southeast pond. During a sinking spell when the surface of the main lake sank about a foot, a migratory central fountain was seen. A freshly formed overflow of heavy festooned lava surrounded the eastern depression of the north lake. The southeast ledge was now covered with Pele's hair. Fumes were moderate. The noises on this day were from hissing border grottoes and pounding in the caverns, while occasionally a deep toned cracking noise was audible from the region of the east ledge. In general the condition suggested rising activity.

On June 30 at 3:30 p. m. the pit was more smoky, the crags appeared lower, the lake was active and spattering over its banks, showing eastward streaming and occasional large travelling or bubble fountains which migrated to the north corner of the east pool. The southeast and main pools stood 2 feet below their inner shelves. At 5 p. m. conditions were about the same and fumes were thick in the northwest part of the pit.

On the morning of July 1 the lake was reported low with deep overhang under the inner bench on all sides, with smoke abundant.

On Tuesday, July 2, at 3:45 p. m., measurements showed the lake to be higher and the crag lower. The inner shelf had widened and was covered with fresh overflow material and exhibited spatter domes. The height of the lake had gained on the chimney at the central cove. There was much smoke, fountaining was strongest against the northern banks of the southeast pond and the east pool, streaming was eastward in a broad zone and a fountain played against the south bank of the east pool. Toward the west-northwest there was hissing, but at the northwest cone, which had broken open, there was no activity other than a little smoke.

WEEKLY BULLETIN
of the
Hawaiian Volcano Observatory

Published Monthly at Honolulu, Hawaii, by the Hawaiian Volcano Research Association

L. W. de Vis-Norton........Secretary

Entered as second-class matter January 20, 1914, at the post-office at Honolulu, Hawaii, under the Act of August 24, 1912.

Smoke rose abundantly from the west pond cone. In the west arm pond an active breaking up was seen which developed much bubble fountaining. The southwest pond was streaming eastward and fountaining against its north bank, while a new glowing chimney hole, probably flaming and showing yellow margins, was seen to have formed in the rock tumble east of the pond over the site of the central valley tunnel and under the south side of the central crag mass. There was a triangular collapsed area in the southwest flows next to the wall of the pit. A black cavern of collapse had formed in the swollen flows to the south of the south crag. Glow could no longer be seen at the southeast cone. On Wednesday, July 3, the fume from the pit was much thinner.

Measurement on July 4 at noon showed that the north crag was rising and the central region was sinking. There were fresh overflows at the margins of the north and northwest pools, and at the north pool there was puffing. Fume had greatly diminished toward the northwest, but it was thicker west of the central region and about the southeast crevasses. In the main lake the streaming was from both east and west and the currents meeting at the central channel sometimes developed there a large fountain which expressed itself in bombardment of the north bank. At the central cove also there was bombardment and the chimney there stood only 4 feet above the lake. The inner shelf showed overhang and stood two feet above the lake. The southwest and southeast ponds were about as usual with some overhang of the inner benches. Sliding was heard in the south talus. There was no action at the northwest cone. The noises were of plashing, puffing and rumbling.

On Friday, July 5, 1918, at 10 a. m., there was little change in the activity. Several fountains at the margins of the main lake continued to build up the shoreline and there were new spatter domes on the northwest shore of the north lake and on the inner shelf at the north corner of the east pool back from the edge of the lake and over the site of the northeast tunnel. There was bombardment and hissing at the southeast corner of the southwest pond. Fume was moderate. A marked change first noticed on this day was the absence of the overhanging half of the south cone on the high edge of Halemaumau, which had now fallen into the pit, leaving this cone largely demolished.

July 13, 1918.—During the week ending Friday, July 12, 1918, the Halemaumau lava column has continued slow subsidence at a faster rate than before, the central crag sinking from July 4 to July 12 nine feet or 1.1 feet per day, and the lake 12 feet or 1.5 feet per day. The measurements were as follows:

July 4, depression of lake 132 feet, depression central crag 36 feet.

July 9, depression of lake 141 feet, depression central crag 42 feet.

July 12, depression lake 144 feet, depression central crag 45 feet.

The visible changes of the week have been few and inconspicuous so that there is little of interest to report with reference to day-to-day changes.

On Monday, July 8, 1918, at 3:30 p. m., the smoke was moderately dense especially from the northern part of the pit. A cone on the border of the north lake was hissing. Streaming in the main lake was westward continuously and this phenomenon, which is unusual, has continued throughout the week. There were numerous fountains, especially on the south side of the southeast pool. This pond had completely overflowed its inner ledge and so appeared higher, while the main lake was 3 feet below its inner ledge. The northwest pond was at a pit with walls 5 or 6 feet high. The southwest pond appeared 4 or 5 feet below its inner ledge and the lava was pounding on its southeast bank. The west arm pond was low and glowed quietly. There were hot and smoky sulphurous spots at the east crevasse and in the northeast and east talus. Fuming sulphurous cones were now distributed as follows: On the southeast floor, on the ledge west of the west arm pond, at the west pond site, on the north central floor and in several places near the northern ponds.

On July 9 at 11 a. m. the streaming in the main lake exhibited a broad zone of festooning skin moving westward from the central channel to places where the lava rushed under the north bank of the central pool. Sometimes there was bombardment of the northwest bank of the east pool. Almost all the time there was fountaining bombardment at the central cove, that is the southwest side of the east pool. A slight hissing was heard at the north lake, the main lake stood two feet below its inner bench, there were occasional very slight movements of the talus on the north and east, and the fume was thin. The general appearance was as of a stationary condition.

On Friday, July 12, however, the measurement at 11:30 a. m. indicated distinct subsidence. There was dense fume rising from areas southwest, west and north, and moderate fume from the floor and talus east and southeast. Westward streaming continued. There were four or five border fountains and the lake level stood 3 to 4 feet below the main inner bench. A second newer spatter bench stood about half way between the inner bench level and the lake. There were freshly broken down places at the eastern low crags of the central crag mass, at the northeast crag mass, on the west side of the northwest pond, and on the east side of the western crag mass. The subsidence had so tilted back the central crag mass that its northern and southern peaks were now again on the same level—recently the northern one had been the higher. Wrinkled black satiny skins were streaming westward from the central channel and the current ended against the bank on the north side of the central pool. The east pool was crusted over. Two fountains played at the base of the central crag and one at the central cove. A smoking cone stood on the inner bench on the north side of the east pool. At the southeast pond the inner bench was 4 feet high with fountaining caverns under it on the north and southwest sides. The southwest pond had a high inner bench and the lava could not be seen from the southeast rim of the pit. The southeast cone had become much stained and there was a sulphur stained area above the east end of the main lake.

At 4:30 p. m. the lake was relatively much higher, the inner bench had been completely overflowed on the north sides of the central and eastern pools and was wholly submerged in the southeast pond. This meant a rise of more than four feet since morning. There were numerous puffing marginal fountains and everything suggested renewed gas pressure.

The readers of the Bulletin will be interested to know that the staff of the Observatory has recently been somewhat enlarged and on July 1 was constituted as follows:

T. A. Jaggar, Director;
Arnold Romberg, Physicist;
Isabel P. Jaggar, Recorder;
John Pekelo, General Assistant;
Alex. Lancaster, Janitor.

During the past few months the Observatory buildings have been repaired and repainted and some added accommodation secured by moving one of the crater cabins to the Observatory grounds and partitioning off the southwest verandah. During the past week work has been started on construction of new masonry surveying stations at Halemaumau to replace those destroyed by the overflow of February-March last.

Experimental work in the seismological laboratory by Dr. Romberg continues and a new upright pendulum has been built along lines designed by the writer during the past winter. This pendulum is built with the project in view of producing an accurate instrument especially adapted to determining the direction from which local earthwaves proceed. The direct determination of direction, without the intervention of rectangular coordinates, appears to have been given little attention in seismology. Several records have already been obtained optically with this instrument which show volcanic tremor, microseisms and tilt. The experiments in progress indicate definite directions for these several types of movement. It seems probable that the registration of these directions of movement for prolonged periods of time will yield new discoveries of great interest in connection with Kilauea and Mauna Loa.

The following report for the routine registration of the Bosch-Omori seismographs of the Whitney Laboratory of Seismology covers the period for the three weeks ending at 2 p. m. Friday, July 12, 1918:

During the week ending June 28 four local earthquakes have been registered as follows: June 22, 8:13 a. m.; June 24, 6:19 a. m.; June 25, 1:49 a. m.; and June 26, (felt in Hilo), 6:16 p. m. One teleseism was registered June 27, 4:25 a. m. Volcanic vibration increased from slight to strongish values during the week, and microseismic motion was strong June 26-27. Tilting increased to the north and fluctuated in the E-W component.

During the week ending July 5 three local earthquakes were registered as follows: June 29, 12:31 p. m.; June 30 (pronounced shock), 8:22 a. m.; July 4, 12:38 a. m. One teleseism was registered 8:34 p. m. July 2, which wrote a fine optical record on the rebuilt instrument and originated at about the distance of Chile. Volcanic vibration was moderate with some prolonged spasms and microseisms were of ordinary values. Tilting became excessive to the north and tended to the east, both components becoming stationary toward the end of the week.

During the week ending July 12 one local earthquake, felt here and in Hilo, occurred at 8:44 p. m. July 10, preceded by a smaller shock four minutes earlier. A teleseism was registered at 12:10 a. m. July 8. Volcanic vibration was slight during the week but showed some pronounced spasms on the afternoon of July 12. Microseismic motion was moderate. Movements of tilting fluctuated with tendency to increase towards the north and east near the end of the week.

July 20, 1918.—During the week ending Friday, July 19, 1918, the same generally stationary condition of the lava column has continued in Halemaumau with the liquid lake about 140 feet below the rim of the pit. The measurements were:

July 12, depression of lake 144 feet, depression central crag 45 feet.

July 15, depression of lake 137 feet, depression central crag 47 feet.

July 16, depression of lake 144 feet, depression central crag 45 feet.

Thus the lake rose 7 feet in three days while the crag sank 2 feet; then in one day the lake sank 7 feet while the crag rose 2 feet. Thus the alternation of movement of liquid magma and bench magma continues. Except for a marked appearance of rising of the lake on July 15, no significant changes have taken place.

On July 14 at 3:30 p. m. the streaming in the main lake was again eastward, fountaining was as usual, the inner bench was three to four feet high and there was some rock sliding in the south talus. From the southeast verge of the pit no fountains were visible in the north lake.

At 7:45 a. m. the next day, Monday, July 15, 1918, there was marked change in that fountains were visible in the north lake and the lakes generally were high and overflowing their inner benches, with puffing and splashing border fountains which were forming crescent-shaped spatter cones. There were six fountains in the main lake, two and sometimes three in the southeast pond, at least one in the south corner of the southwest pond, two in the north lake and one in the northwest pond. Streaming was eastward from the central pool and the main lake surface was greatly extended westward by overflow. Hot bluish smoke was rising from the west pond cone. There were two glowing holes through the inner shelf in the north cove of the east pool. The lakes were clearly rising but not the crags. About 1:30 p. m. the rising ceased and the lakes subsided some 5 feet; streaming changed to the west and at 4:30 p. m. the inner benches were 3 feet high. Fountaining was violent on the north side of the central pool and occasionally in the other pools. The east pool was crusted over with occasional cracking and foundering in the southeast corner. Smoke had increased.

On July 16 at 10:30 a. m. the streaming in the lake was west and north, the inner benches were higher, fountaining was ordinary and light puffing could be heard from the direction of the north lake. One glowing hole remained in the northeast inner bench. Streaming was northeastward in the southeast pond. The west arm and southwest pond were low and the streaming in the latter was southward. A heavy mass of spatter bench collapsed into the lake on the north side of the east pool. Examination of the northwest cone from the north station showed that the cone had broken asunder and the pieces lay on the talus below.

On July 17 at 7:15 a. m. the inner shelf was 5 feet high and the fume rather thin. Between 9 and 10 a. m. the lake rose until level with the shelf. At 12:30 p. m. it had again subsided about three feet and there were numerous border fountains spurting and giving evidence of considerable gas pressure. Streaming was westward.

On Thursday, July 18, at 5:30 p. m., no significant changes were discernible. The streaming was westward, four or five border fountains were playing in the main lake but no fountains were visible in the northern pools. The inner shelf stood three feet above the liquid, the northeast glow hole persisted, there were hissing noises from some of the grottoes, the southeast pond was crusted over and the southwest pond appeared relatively higher than of late. The pit was smoky.

On the morning of July 19 the lake rose from about 7 feet below the inner shelf to 3 feet below it. There was no evident visible streaming, the lake was mostly crusted over, the only fountaining being at the central cove. There was puffing towards the north. After 11 a. m. the lava was again subsiding. The southwest pond was crusted over and the southeast pond appeared 10 feet below the inner shelf. Smoke was still abundant.

The experiments in the seismological laboratory have continued during the week with improvements in sharpness of definition of optical registration, and tests with chronograph drums running at high speed. Work has been started in testing the constants of the standard instruments used for routine recording and in improving their registration appliances.

July 27, 1918.—During the week ending Friday, July 26, 1918, the Halemaumau lava column has continued stationary at a level depressed about 144 feet north, southwest and southeast. The usual slight alterations between risings and fallings of lakes and crags continue, the net result producing no essential change of level. The activity is moderate so far as fountaining, streaming and puffing are concerned, and four open lava lakes are in action, respectively in the center and at the north, southwes and southeast. The weather has been rainy and the pit consequently full of mist and fume. Seismically the present period is a quiet one.

The measurements were:

July 16, depression of lake 144 feet, depression central crag 45 feet.

July 26, depression of lake 143 feet, depression central crag 48 feet.

The general aspect of Halemaumau at present is much as it was a year ago, except that the open three-arm lake of that time is more constricted, the ends of the three arms being now separate ponds and the middle region is a longish lake of east-west trend. All four are sunk in inner pits twenty to thirty feet deep, and the margins of these pits are tumbled floors and uptilted crags. Several of the crags retain their identity year after year, and the oldest of them, the west crag, dates from August of 1916. The edge of the pit is much changed by the overflows of February-March, 1918, so that now it is a continuous unbroken circle of precipice rising 50 to 100 feet above the talus below. The talus is irregular, and has been replaced by fresh overflows on the west. The inner crags, which are in three principal bodies northeast, west and south of the center respectively, rise from 50 to 100 feet above the lake levels, and are tilted up scarps of floor matter or uplifted "islands." The highest of them now and for a year past is the south-central one, referred to as the "central crag," which at the moment of last measurement stood 95 feet above the central or main lake. The cones occasionally referred to in these pages are blowing cones built above cracks in the floors or on the margins of the lakes by the sputtering of lava charged with gas, and some of these are over the sites of lava wells known by the experience of the past and recorded in the Observatory books. The inner benches are flood margins of the several lava pools, developed by inward building of the edges of the pools and overflowing of the banks during times when rising of the liquid relative to its banks prevails.

On July 21, 1918, at 4:30 p. m., the east arm of the main lake as seen from the east was quiet and crusted and the surface stood 5 feet below the inner bench of overflow; at 4:45 p. m. the crust broke up, bubble fountaining developed and the liquid streamed westward. At 5:30 p. m. a prolonged avalanche fell from under the new northeast fill and continued off and on for ten minutes. Small readjustments of the talus followed for some time afterwards.

On Monday, July 22, 1918, at 10 a. m., the southwest pond showed fountaining and the east arm of the main lake stood five feet below the inner bench and crusted over. One fountain played for a time in the southeast pond.

July 23 at 8 a. m. the inner bench stood eight feet above the lake, five marginal fountains were in action and the surface current poured westward to the grotto on the north side of the central pool. A central fountain and some bubble fountains played in the southeast pond.

On the morning of July 24 from 9 a. m. until noon the lava column appeared quite stationary. There was sluggish bubble fountaining and some central fountains, and occasionally cracking and foundering of crusts took place in the main lake. The streaming was against the north bank. Bubble fountains were seen on the east side of the north lake and along the southeast side of the west arm pond. There was occasional violent fountaining on the south side of the southwest pond. The inner bench at the southeast pond and the east pool of the main lake was four feet high, but only two feet high at the central pool, as though the bench magma of the central part of the floor were sinking. There was some puffing noise in the fountains of the west and southwest pools. The greater part of the central pool area had now become a floor or plain, only the eastern half was an open cove. The marginal fountaining was against the north side of the channel (between east and central pools.)

July 25 at 4:30 p. m. the lake was relatively higher, two feet below the inner bench, and the reversed current now flowing southeastward gave evidence, along with all other signs, of a change to rising. There were active spatter grottoes along the margins of the main lake and in the southeast pond. At 5:30 p. m. great activity was noticed in the north lake, where five or six fountains played both along the margins and in the center. There was much smoke, however, which made it difficult to distinguish details.

Measurements Friday, July 26, 1918, at 9:30 a. m., showed that the lake had recovered to the same level as ten days before, but the crags were all very slightly lower. Relative to their margins the lakes all appeared high, the main lake standing only one foot below the inner shelf, with puffing border fountains incessantly changing position and in process of building spatter ramparts; there were four or five of them in the main lake and two in the southeast pond. The southwest pond was stagnant and crusted, but on the evening before a conspicuous flame was seen on its margin, a steady flare of burning gas. In the afternoon there was a heavy collapse of the bank of this pond on its southwest side. On this day it was very smoky and rainy. It was evident that another spasm of rising lake magma was compensating the slow subsidence of bench magma in accordance with the rhythmic action which has been the habit of the lava for many weeks.

Work on the new surveying stations at Halemaumau has proceeded rapidly so that five monuments are nearly finished. Each station consists of a level platform of concrete six feet in diameter with a concrete post in the center 2½ feet high. When finished they will be eight in number and oriented with reference to the meridian passing through nearly the center of the pit. The experimental work in seismometry continues with optical records as well

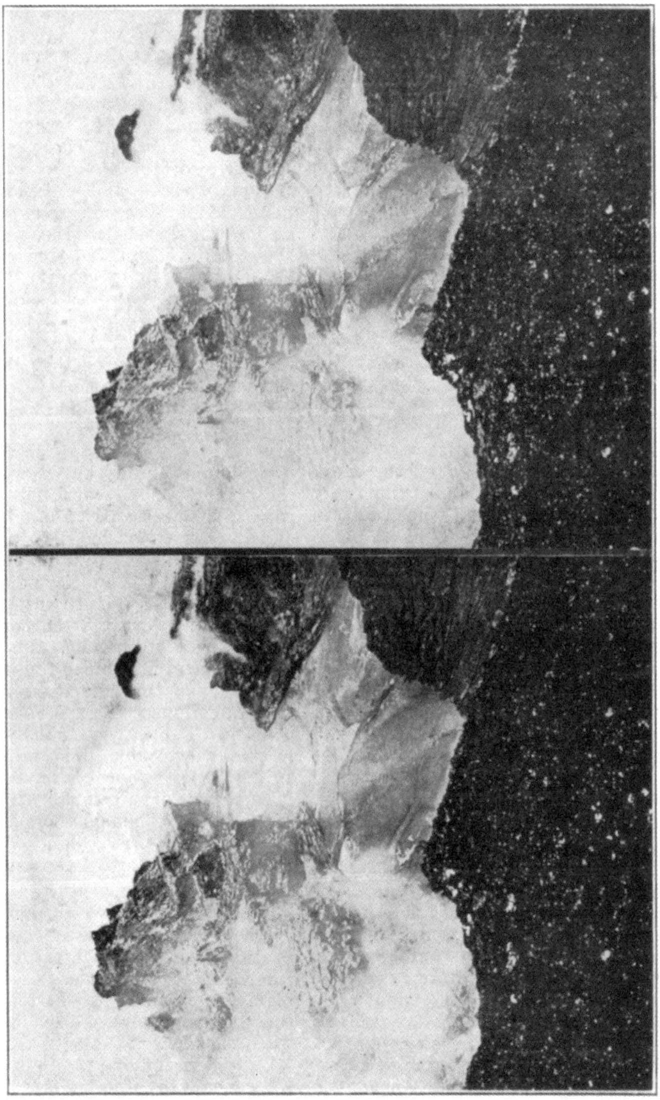

June 21, 1918. Lake and Central Crag, Halemaumau, from east verge of pit.

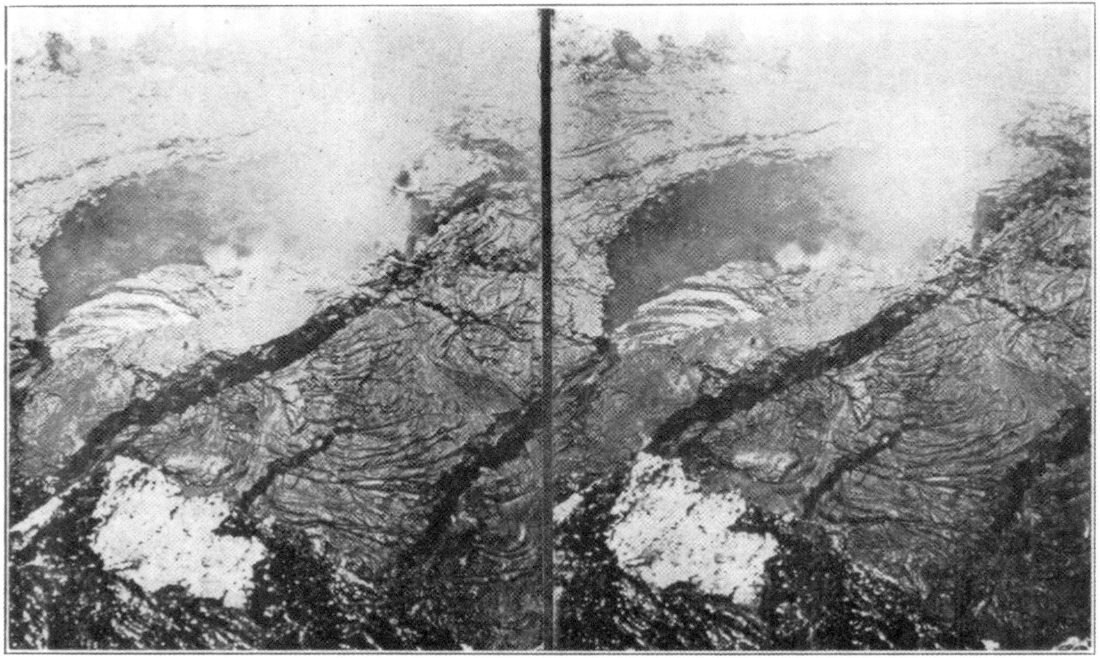

June 21, 1918. Southeast pond from southeast edge of pit.—*Photos Jaggar.*
[May be inspected with ordinary stereoscope.]

as the routine smoked paper records produced every night.

The following is the report of earthquake and other seismic registration in the Whitney Laboratory for the two weeks ending at 2 p. m. Friday, July 26, 1918:

For the week ending July 19 one teleseism was registered at 1:56 p. m. July 14, 1918, the preliminary phase indicating origin 2260 km. away, equivalent to the distance of Midway Island or the equatorial belt south of Christmas Island. Two very small local shocks happened 11:19 a. m. July 15 and 6:15 p. m. July 18. Tilting movements and volcanic vibration were slight, microseismic motion was moderate.

During the week ending July 26, a teleseism at 7:49 p. m. July 20 appeared to come from an origin about 6000 km. distant. There were small local earthquakes, 6:23 p. m. July 21, 1:58 a. m. July 24, and 2:29 p. m. July 25. Tilting showed slight tendency northward, microseisms were moderate and volcanic vibrations slight.

August 3, 1918.—During the week ending Friday, August 2, 1918, the Halemaumau lava has very slowly subsided with some increase of activity of fountaining and a deceptive appearance at times as though the lake were rising. The average rate of subsidence has been one-half a foot per day in contrast to a rate for the ten days preceding (July 16-26) of one-fifth foot per day.

The measurements were:

July 26, depression of lake 143 feet, depression of central crag 48 feet.

August 2, depression of lake 147 feet, depression of central crag 51 feet.

The week has been rainy and the pit much obscured with steam and smoke. On July 28 at 5 p. m. the inner bench around the east pool stood only one foot above the liquid and there was much fountaining under the north bank of that pool. The central pool was quiet on its north side but there were two fountaining areas at the base of the central crag mass. The north lake showed considerable activity but fumes in that region were dense. At 5:15 p. m. there was subsidence of the main lake about three feet with increased fountaining and a swift westward current. A half hour later rapid rising set in so that in twenty minutes the lake was flush with the inner bench and shortly after 6 o'clock it overflowed that bench on the northwest side of the central pool.

On Monday, July 29, at 10 a. m., the inner bench was one foot high and there were five marginal fountains along the south side of the main lake. Thin black skins covered the remainder of the lake. In the southeast pond the inner bench was four feet high and one fountain was in action. The north lake was level with its banks and marginal fountains were boiling there. At 10:30 a. m. a rock slide took place under the remains of the south cone.

On July 31 at 6 p. m. the general appearance of higher liquid lava, at least so far as relation to the surrounding bench magma was concerned, was very striking. There must have been during this time an actual rise of the lake, for some ponds and coves not previously visible came into view. Both the north lake and northwest pond were active and their surfaces in full view from the southeast station. A large cone had formed on the south bank of the north lake and a blue flame was playing through an orifice of this cone. The activity of the main lake showed high gas pressure with five spurting fountains at the inner bench level. There came a spell of breaking up when collapses of the bank on the north and west sides stimulated very rapid westward streaming; prior to that the streaming had been against the north bank. There was glow in the southeast cone and in the cone at the north corner of the east pool. The southeast pond appeared as usual with some blowing fountains and there was bright glow in the southwest pond. The northwest pond showed fountaining. The fumes were rather dense. In general the increased activity, appearing distinctly constructive in building spatter margins around the lakes, was puzzling, for other symptoms such as the fume and the crag positions indicated sinking rather than rising.

On August 1, 1918, at 5:30 p. m., the lake level, one foot below the inner bench, was unchanged and the main lake was quiet and crusted until 6:30 p. m. At that time the crust began to break up and streaming westward became rapid and tumultuous with great development of fountains. The north lake and the southwest pond also showed fountaining but the southeast pond remained quiet.

At noon on Friday, August 2, the measurements indicated slow subsidence of both lake and crag, although the lake was active and brimming level with its inner bench about the central pool. The pit as a whole was rather smoky. The southwest pond surface was now visible from the southeast rim of the pit, the northwest and north lakes were both visible and there were four or five fountains in the main lake at the bench level. A block of the upraised northeast floor appeared to have fallen from the crag overhanging the east end of the north lake and this now stood out as a pinnacle there. A considerable spatter grotto had been built up at the centrol cove (southwest side east pool). The southeast pond had become nearly circular and it appeared somewhat higher relative to the walls of its pit; a narrow inner bench of even width one foot above the pond surrounded it. There had been marked development of cracked and stained areas at the west pond cone and at the top of the inner cliff overhanging the south bank of the southwest pond, and both of these places showed increase of fuming.

During the week the first moulded concrete post, marking the new east station platform has been cast. The seismologic experiments conducted by Dr. Romberg have this week made definite progress along three lines of inquiry. A short period, highly damped, horizontal pendulum with heavy mass, recording optically on bromide paper running at high speed, has written a clear open record of a local earthquake. By relating the closeness of the lines written on the drum it has become possible to run such a high-speed record for the entire twenty-four hours each day without objectionable expense. The second accomplishment has been the discovery of a quick period vibration due to the arrangement of the heavy mass in the pendulum in question which must be a source of some instrumental error in all seismograms written by such pendulums. This arrangement was at once changed and the difficulty obviated. The third experiment has resulted in the construction of a new kind of stylus for the smoked-paper method, which promises to reduce friction. This consists in a lever made of an extremely light and fine glass tube with a minute sharp edge watchwork wheel rotating at the end in a glass bearing. The wheel itself is the writing pen and trials of its efficiency are in progress. In the course of tests of the two 100-kilogram Bosch-Omori pendulums, in order to determine experimentally the exact equivalence of their adjustments, the two instruments have been set up side by side so as to record the same earth motions in the same directions. They will be run for some time in this relation and careful tests will be made of their instrumental uniformity.

Very respectfully,

T. A. JAGGAR, JR.,
Director.

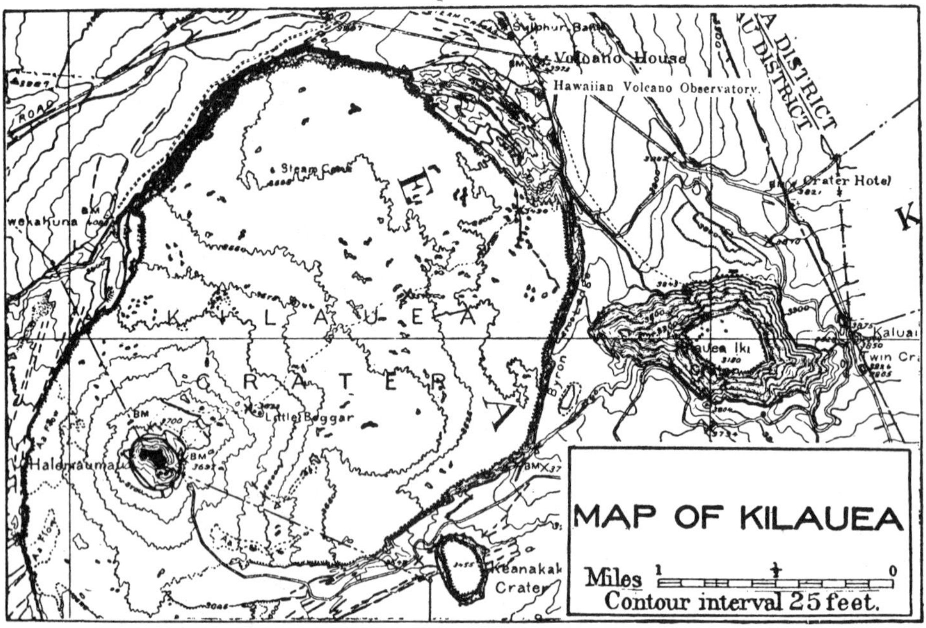

HAWAIIAN VOLCANO RESEARCH ASSOCIATION.

This society is a voluntary one, made up of subscribers to scientific work which is being executed by Dr. T. A. Jaggar, Director of the Hawaiian Volcano Observatory, Volcano House, P. O., Hawaii. **All scientific exchanges should be sent to this address.**

In 1917 there are about 150 subscribers in Hawaii and elsewhere, firms and individuals. A group of firms and persons in Hilo built the main observatory building in the spring of 1912. The work was founded by the Massachusetts Institute of Technology. Publications to date have been weekly reports since the summer of 1911 now reprinted in Honolulu in monthly form. There are also special reports, printed from time to time.

The weekly bulletin as it appears in the Honolulu Advertiser is reprinted as a leaflet and sent to regular annual subscribers to the work of the Association. L. A. Thurston is president of the Board of Directors of the Association, and L. T. Peck is treasurer. New subscribers who are interested in volcanoes will be welcomed in the Association. The Association aims: (1) To record volcanic activity and earthquakes in Hawaii; (2) to attract scientific men hither for special studies; (3) to promote the establishment of volcano observatories all over the world. The annual dues of regular members are $5; patrons of the Association subscribe larger amounts.

WHITNEY LABORATORY OF SEISMOLOGY.

The Whitney Laboratory of Seismology, named after an endowment fund of geophysical research held by the Massachusetts Institute of Technology, in memory of Caroline and Edward Whitney of Boston, is equipped with two Bosch-Omori 100 kg tromometers registering N-S and E-W motion, a heavy Omori tromometer registering E-W motion, and an Omori "ordinary Seismograph" designed for registering strong earthquakes in all three components of motion. These are seated on concrete piers in a closed basement room having practically constant temperature, beneath the chief Observatory building near the hotel. Time is referred to a rated chronometer, checked at intervals by solar observations with a transit. Both instruments are loaned by the College of Hawaii. Hawaiian standard time (H. S. T.) is 10 hrs. 30 min. slower than Greenwich time.

CANCANI SCALE OF SEISMIC INTENSITY.

Expressed by accelerations measured in millimeters per second per second.

I.	Instrumental	0.0	2.5
II.	Very slight	2.5	5.0
III.	Slight	5.0	10.0
IV.	Sensible, mediocre	10.0	25.0
V.	Rather strong	25.0	50.0
VI.	Strong	50.0	100.0
VII.	Very strong	100.0	250.0
VIII.	Ruinous	250.0	500.0
IX.	Disastrous	500.0	1000.0
X.	Very disastrous	1000.0	2500.0
XI.	Catastrophic	2500.0	5000.0
XII.	Great catastrophe	5000.0	10000.0

Grade IV. is ordinarily the minimum perceived by the senses; and in grade XII. the acceleration, or rate of change of motion (jerk) reaches that of terrestrial gravitation.

In the standard form of report the maximum intensity or acceleration, designated by the symbol a, or max. a, is given in the conventional unit, the milligal. The milligal is a measure of acceleration, such that 1 milligal = 1/100 mm. per sec. per sec. = 10 μ per sec. per sec. The Cancani scale, here defined in terms of millimeters per sec. per sec., can therefore be expressed in milligals by multiplying each of the numbers by 100.

WEEKLY BULLETIN
OF THE
Hawaiian Volcano Observatory

Vol. VI. HONOLULU, HAWAII, AUGUST, 1918 No. 8

HAWAIIAN VOLCANO OBSERVATORY.

August 10, 1918.

During the week ending Friday, August 9, 1918, the lava lake and crags of Halemaumau have risen in the pit with an extraordinary spurt which indicates that the long stagnant spell is finished. The rising of the lava column has been at the rate of at least 13 feet per day, the lake rising 85 feet in six days and the central crag 80 feet in the same time.

The measurements were:

August 2—Depression of lake, 147 feet; depression of central crag, 51 feet.

August 8—Depression of lake, 62 feet; elevation central crag above rim, 29 feet.

The manner of rising has been like that of last February and the entire episode closely resembles the remarkable rise of that time. Now as then the rapid spurt begins in the month preceding the equinoctial season. and if the present rapid rising were to continue the lake lava would be flowing over the edge of the pit before the end of August just as it did on February 23. The central bench magma has swollen up, the crags have tilted back, and the liquid has welled up the wall cracks as at that time, and even the forms and locations of the several features are similar.

On August 4, 1918, at 5 p. m., the lava of the east pool was level with the inner bench, two grottoes were boiling on the south side, and the southeast pond was quiet. From 5:30 to 6 p. m. the north and northwest pools broke into considerable activity with much fountaining.

On Monday, August 5, it became evident that lakes and crags were both rising and this sudden rise appears to have started on the preceding night. At 3:30 p. m. the central crag appeared much higher than at any time in recent days, and the northeast crag ridge showed increased backward tilt, the mass parting from the central floor crag along a crack extending from the northeast cove to the north lake. The inner benches around the main lake were uplifted and the rising talus under the east station was seen to be underlain by a block of lifting rock which slopes northward and tends to open the east wall crack and drop debris into it. The west crag mass had lifted so as to cut off the view of the west pond cone from the east station. All this jostling of crags was breaking down the partition between the southeast pond and the east pool, leaving a saddle of debris between them where rocks fell frequently. Everything indicated recurrence of central tumescence and radial tilt of the three sectors of bench magma away from the center.

That the lake magma was also rising showed at the southwest pond which was overflowing its southeast bank across what three days before had been a considerable inner cliff just to the east of the fuming cracks. Slight subsidence of about a foot succeeded the overflooding.

Because of smoke little could be seen of the northern lakes, but they appeared larger. The southwest pond ejected high spurts of lava at its south margin, and there were southern and northeastern fountains in the main lake and others on the south side of the southeast pond. The lakes were mostly covered with blistering and ballooning skins, and the fumes were thin as compared with the previous week. At 6:20 p. m. there was a heavy fall of bench matter into the lake from the point north of the narrows, leaving a notch 20 feet wide up to some 30 feet above the liquid. This produced violent fountaining. About 7:10

WEEKLY BULLETIN
of the
Hawaiian Volcano Observatory

Published Monthly at Honolulu, Hawaii, by the Hawaiian Volcano Research Association

L. W. de Vis-Norton........Secretary

Entered as second-class matter January 20, 1914, at the post-office at Honolulu, Hawaii, under the Act of August 24, 1912.

p. m. there was another collapse into the southeast pond.

On the morning of August 6 the central crag had risen above the edge of the pit and was plainly visible from a distance. At 11 a. m. it was clear that the tumescence was going on rapidly. A fresh flow had poured from the cracks north of the north lake the length of the northeast valley. The tilting away from the center was augmented by subsidence of the wall valleys, especially east and northeast, where the depression was far below lake level. The inner benches had been lifted faster than the lake. There was much sliding and tumbling in the notch between the southeast pond and the east pool. Fountaining was rather tumultuous, and in the southwest pond it took the form of cracking and foundering spells between intervals of crusting.

On Wednesday, August 7, at 1 p. m., very rapid rising of the crags had continued so that everywhere they appeared uptilted in a chaos of scarps and slopes. This, with the sinking of the wall valleys, was so continuous that the talus was slipping all along the base of the east and northeast cliffs. The upraised crags now almost wholly cut off the view of the lake from the east rim of the pit, and the northern lakes were wholly cut off. The crag overhanging the east end of the north lake was now nearly on a level with the north crag by upward tilting, and in like manner the crag overhanging the northeast side of the east arm was becoming a conspicuous scarp, and a similar scarp had developed east of the southeast pond, tipping away from the new notch between the two pools. This notch continued to widen and crumble, with an unstable pinnacle poised in its midst. A fault chasm could be seen emerging on the central cove end of the crack which separates the central crag block from that south of it, the former tending to move up on the fault plane.

The activity of the lakes was of the usual blowing, spurting and blistering type such as commonly accompanies rising lava. There was strong streaming against the bank at the south and northeast grottoes of the east pool. The fumes were not especially thin.

On August 8, with the central crag 30 feet above the rim of the pit and the lake 60 feet below it, a great change had been wrought and everything suggested the conditions of last February. Inspection at 3 p. m. showed that the deep wall valley recently depressed opposite the east-southeast end of the lake had filled through the action of lava springs welling up from beneath until it was not far below the lake and a gas vent was hissing on the surface of the crusted fill. The inner northern crag was higher than the outer, and these, along with the west crag, had come into view above the edge of the pit as seen from the distant observatory. The central steeple, a pinnacle east of the central crag, was again becoming conspicuous and the pinnacle in the southeast pond notch remained high. The new fill in the south valley had been fed from the southwest wall cracks and extended to a point beneath the south station. A puddle of fresh lava under the north station was apparently fed from the wall crack near the northwest cone; the latter was hissing. The south end of the west crag mass was upraised into a westward dipping scarp, and the mass of elevated floor on the north side of the central channel was now a crag tilted northward. A new east ledge had been built by the rapid lifting of the south end of the northeast crag mass. All the wall cracks were yawning open and everywhere talus was in motion. The crag under the east station with edge trending east-west extending from the wall to the east ledge was an extraordinary creation of this uplift, its summit being now only 30 feet below the east station and the upward thrust causing it to form a barrier across the end of the northeast valley at right angles to the other concentric features. This ledge on its south side sloped into a rock-filled gulch which had begun as the large southeast crevasse of the May rising period. This gulch is an extension of the east cove of the lake corresponding to the old east gulch, and a small fresh overflow from the lake had poured into it.

The north lake was cracking and foundering, and dense white smoke rose from a crack west of it. A pool of fresh lava which had welled up the wall crack under the west station showed cracking and foundering crusts and was spreading. There was a smoky pit probably full of lava where the west pond cone had been. The southwest pond stood about three feet below its margin. The main lake was covered with heavy folded crusts. Blisters frequently formed, there was inrush to the bank on the south side of the east arm, and occasionally tumultuous bombardment took place. There were many lines of upraised spatter rim veneering the inner pit of the main lake, and this pit showed no sign of becoming shallower. The west arm pond was extended into a gulch leading to the foot of the west wall of the pit at the site of the former west pond and west cone. Everywhere were shown the effects of a swelling up in the center, while lava welled up the wall cracks and the lakes rose in the yawning chasms between the uplifted blocks but were prevented from overflowing by the equivalent rising of those blocks.

On Friday, August 9, at 9 a. m., the rising continued, there were trickling toes at the margins of the valley fills, and slides were numerous from the rapidly tilting crag slopes. About 11 a. m. a lava spring broke its way through the talus boulders of the wall crack under the north station and made a very liquid rivulet which poured east along the base of the wall, making a new fill at the margin of the northeast valley. The dense fume at the north lake chasm was conspicuous at 9 a. m., but disappeared two hours later. The lakes tended to crack up their crusts through gas pressure from beneath from time to time, this being followed by temporary subsidence of two or three feet. At such times there was violent hissing and spurting of fountains; this was observed in all the lakes. The principal streaming in the main lake moved in a curve from the central pool eastward and then against the south bank of the east pool immediately under the saddle and pinnacle separating that pool from the southeast pond. By the evening of this day all of the larger crags were in view above the edge of the pit as seen from the Observatory.

During the week the experiments in the seismological laboratory have resulted in registration of another teleseism optically and in highly magnified registration of local earthquakes by the smoked-paper method. New concrete supports have been set up in the instrument cellar for the slow period pendulum which is destined for permanent optical registration of distant earthquakes. At the pit, work on the masonry trig stations has continued.

August 17, 1918.

During the week ending Friday, August 16, 1918, the lava column has continued to rise, but at a much slower rate, averaging 4.3 feet per day. This means that the movement throughout the week has been slowing up, for the daily measures from the Observatory of the changing height of the crags showed almost a cessation of motion on August 15. In general, lakes and crags have risen together, the net movement of the week amounting to about 30 feet.

The measurements were:

August 8—Depression of lake, 62 feet; elevation central crag above rim, 29 feet.

August 15—Depression of lake, 30 feet; elevation central crag above rim, 60 feet.

On August 15 the wall valley fill under the north station was only 24 feet down.

On Saturday, August 10, 1918, at 9:30 a. m., a circuit of the pit beginning at the south and west revealed increase of wall-valley fillings with their edges pushing out in many places. A new west cone had developed in the depression southwest of the west arm pond. An overflow had poured from the south margin of the southwest pond. A cascade was running from the rapidly growing northwest wall cone into the northwest valley. There was much fountaining on the west side of the west arm pond, and cavernous grottoes were visible at the margins of the north and northwest pools. The fresh glowing fill of the northeast valley showed crusts in process of cracking and foundering. Lava was splashing in a crack some distance to the north of the north lake. Streaming in the main lake moved from the west to terminate in bombardment at the south grotto and the northeast cove, but occasional westward streaming opposed the main current and developed traveling fountains at the central channel. There were hissing wall crack cones north, northwest, west and southeast. All the crags showed continued uptilting away from the center and much sliding of talus indicated continuing motion. The most rapidly moving crag was the one uplifted athwart the southeast end of the northeast valley with its trend at right angles to the main east ledge. It seems probable that this must be the uplifted remnant of the east gulch flows of last winter.

At 7 p. m. there was occasional cracking and foundering in the lakes, with violent fountaining and subsidence of a few feet. This in the main lake was followed by a rise with overflow of its east end so that a cascade poured down into the east valley fill. Meanwhile a ribbon cascade had been pouring along the base of the wall into this fill from a higher wall crack vent nearly under the new southeast station. The strong gas pressure developed beneath the glowing crust of this southeast fill caused bright blue flames to play over the surface of the crust, not at fixed cracks but on dark surfaces away from the glowing crevices. Apparently the gas was rising through crust pores. Sometimes the flames became bright yellow. In the main lake there were four or five large spatter cone grottoes, trickle flows continued to push out from under the wall-valley fillings, wall-crack cones northwest, north and southeast occasionally broke into spurting eruption and everything indicated continued rising without cessation.

On the morning of August 11 at 10 a. m. the crags were still rising with talus sliding, especially at the east cross ledge, and the wall valleys continued to fill. The main lake was building large grottoes south and northeast, and the southeast pond was higher, with widening inner bench. A new circular pond depression had developed around the southeast cone at the location of the former central pond, and as before a crevasse extended southward from it. A long crack extended from it in a nearly straight line to the southwest pond, marking probably the south tunnel. The streaming in the southeast pond was southward and in the main lake eastward and southward. The northeast crag mass was again becoming an upright wall in full view from Volcano House, and the north inner crag was now much higher than the outer one. The cone at the north wall crack was spurting continuously and ejecting a cascade of lava which poured eastward. The vent at the southeast wall crack was flowing sluggishly. The activity showed few changes, there was high gas pressure, cliffs 50 feet high stood over the main lake, and the fumes were thinner.

On Monday, August 12, at 10 p. m., all signs of rising continued as before. There was a flaming filagree cone built high against the wall on the south side of the southeast pond and six-foot banners of flame shot out from the grotto on the south side of the east arm. There were now seven ponds in the pit, respectively the main and north lakes, the southwest lake (consisting of southwest and west arm ponds united), and the west, northwest, southeast and central ponds. In addition, there were four marginal wall valley fillings of crusted lava fed by wells beneath, namely, the east, northeast, west, and south fills.

On August 13 at 6 p. m. it appeared that the southeast pond had overflowed into the east fill, there were grottoes with stalactites on its west side and in the northeast cove of the main lake, and a large spatter grotto had been built on the south side of the east arm. The tunnel connection from the southeast pond to the east arm appeared to lie under the northeast bank of the pond. From the west rim of the pit the central uplift was very impressive and the slope away from the center of the uplifted crag masses had developed with extraordinary rapidity, so as to produce the same effect of inner dome with lake concealed in its chasms and crevasses as was so striking last March. The main lake is nowhere visible except from the southeast. The hot fillings of the wall valleys were interrupted at only two places—one west and the other east. The south fill had recently been supplied by overflows from the southwest pond, which was fountaining violently against its south bank. The west cone was a low flat arched dome glowing inside. The ponded fill of the west valley had a flat surface and the great ledges which had slipped down in April under the west niche were almost completely submerged. The west pond was a deep chasm in the middle of the west crag mass showing the glow of activity within. The sliding slopes adjacent to the many crags gave evidence of rapid motion. The northwest cone, flaming and hissing, was built high against the wall of the pit. The northern ponds were very active. Under the old north station a horseshoe cone vomited lava beneath the crust of the northeast fill, which stood only 30 feet below the similar fill of last March. The main lake appeared high with its surface crusts drifting southward from both east and west ends and occasionally great balloons of skin were inflated from below.

On August 14 there were further overflows from the southeast and southwest ponds, and in the evening intense activity at the northwest cone produced a flood of lava which poured eastward the whole length of the northeast fill, raising the level of that ponded depression to within 15 feet of the March level.

Ou Thursday, August 15, 1918, at noon, the northeast crag mass was in motion with slides tumbling down its backslope. The north cone was low and hissing. The northwest cone had been built up to the level of the brink of the pit a few paces west of the old north resthouse and exhibited at that level several glowing, hissing and flaming orifices. Spatter from it lay on the rocks adjacent. The fill beneath was now higher than the northwest fill by some 15 feet of slope. The crags were all higher and the east ledge now wholly cut off the view of the central crag from the east shelter. The southwest pond stood two feet below its margin, the main lake and southeast pond three or four feet down, the activity was moderate, and the crust of the east fill had collapsed some six feet below its maximum level. This was the first sign of diminished gas pressure in the border fills and this checked with cessation of rising of the crags which took place on this day. Beneath the new south station the fill was only 20 feet down. This and the northwest cone locality appear likeliest places for overflows of the pit. The northwest cone was now in condition to overflow the rim at any moment.

In the Whitney Laboratory of Seismology the last stage of the summer's overhauling under Dr. Romberg has now been entered upon. This consists in setting up and adjusting the rebuilt instruments for the routine of the coming autumn and winter. The two Bosch-Omori seismographs will be operated with higher magnification, quicker moving drums and improved styluses. The registration of these instruments will be continued with smoked paper, and the new damping device consists of vanes moving in oil. This pair of instruments will record east-west and north-south components of local earthquakes, microtremors and microseisms or distant earthquakes. In this on a single drum. The time-marking device for minute marks and hour marks accomplishes with electro magnets positive lift of the scribing steel points so as to make gaps in the written line. Thus the clock time may be read directly from the seismogram and the correction for parallax is eliminated.

The second rebuilt apparatus is the Omori heavy pendulum now to be set up in the northeast-southwest azimuth as a one-component, slow-period, optically-registering instrument exclusively for teleseisms or distant earthquakes. In this instrument the iron pier has been eliminated, pivot friction is entirely removed, and the heavy mass hangs as a rigid unit on very short steel wires. By swinging the pendulum in this plane and from the rigid concrete of the corner of the cellar, it is hoped to make the free period of the pendulum slower and to reduce tilt and local tremors to a minimum.

A vertical component instrument and a special device for recording tilt are planned, as well as certain simple instruments designed to be placed in the hands of volunteer observers elsewhere on Hawaii.

August 24, 1918.

During the week ending Friday, August 23, 1918, the rising of the bench magma or lava crags has ceased and they have slightly subsided. The liquid lava has continued filling the wall valleys slowly on the southwest, northwest and northeast, but the southeast wall crack and east fill have slumped. The building up of the fillings on the north and southwest has come within a few feet of overflowing the pit rim as in February, and this upbuilding has not yet stopped. A sudden spasm of flowing might at any moment produce overflow at the southwest margin of the pit, for the driblet heap there, close to the edge for the length of a hundred feet, stands six or eight feet above the level of the edge and the flows from it are within a foot of going over. The lakes have maintained their depression 25 to 30 feet below the rim of the pit throughout the week.

On Saturday, August 17, 1918, at 6:30 p. m., the wall cracks south and east were found to have slumped while the valley fillings adjacent to them had swollen in dome fashion so as to make surfaces curving downward into the wall crack. Strong swelling was going on in the northeast fill, and lava flows were there pushing from under the crust at the east end and around the sides. Hissing gases burned from under a hinging lid at the northwest cone and the north cone was also hissing. Slides still fell from the back of the northeast ledge. There was fountaining in the northern ponds; the main lake was low, showing a tunnel at the northeast cove. There was eastward streaming and but slight activity. At 8:30 p. m. there were five or six fountains in the southeast pond, and the liquid was nearly level with the inner bench; the main lake was also high and active, and the southwest pond during the evening rose nearly to overflowing. At 9 p. m. there were more than fifteen driblet flows in motion about the northeast fill. At 10 p. m. the northwest cone had burst open and was ejecting spray thirty feet or more. There were small flows in the west wall valley.

On August 18 at 3:30 p. m. the swelling of the wall valley floors continued, so that the general level of the northeast fill was flush with the lower portions of the northeast shelf. The west fill was not quite so high. The northwest cone continued puffing and flaming. The south fill had swollen up somewhat, but the wall crack vent southeast was now a depression of collapse and the east fill a marked depression 40 feet below the southeast edge of the pit, with irregular slumped and blistered crusts for its floor.

The main lake appeared relatively low, and the southern and eastern grotto heaps now stood more than 10 feet above the liquid. There were tunnel grottoes at the northeast cove and on the west side of the southeast pond. Streaming was eastward and southward. The writer crossed the north fill without difficulty, and penetrating among the crags of the north lake found in the enclosure only tumbled rocks with both the north and northwest ponds small and inactive and six or eight feet below their margins. The floors of the wall valley fills were now easily accessible in many places and from 10 to 30 feet down. Balloons of crust and sudden heavings were notable on the north side of the main lake. Trickle flows continued to move about the northeast fill. At 5:30 p. m. the southeast pond was depressed five feet below its inner bench and very inactive. A large piece of its northwest wall fell in and started fountaining.

On the evening of August 19 the lakes were still low and sluggish with occasional explosive and ballooning bursts on the north side of the main lake. The lava fills were quiet, showing glow in the cracks. A heavy fall of rocks was reported from the north side of the central crag mass. The northwest cone was puffing occasionally. The crags were nearly stationary or slightly lower.

At 9 a. m. Tuesday, August 20, the lakes were sluggish, showed occasional fountains, and stood from 8 to 10 feet below their inner benches. The northeast fill had slightly overflowed the sunken portions of the February shelf northeast. The northwest cone was higher and stood four feet above the edge of the pit. The northwest fill was now level with the north fill, showing fresh flows and glowing crust caverns. The crags were stationary. The south valley filling showed increased arching downward toward the wall crack. The west cone depression in the southwest part of the pit had been built up by driblet flow construction to within one foot of the rim of Halemaumau opposite the great southwest crevasse. Two high puffing cones were constructing and flows were moving over a glistening pile of snaky pahoehoe which extended toward the west arm pond. This region suggested the conditions at the south cone in March, when great quantities of lava from such a driblet heap poured southward from Halemaumau for weeks.

On August 21 at 6 p. m. the main and

Aug. 23, 1918. Flame of burning gas photographed through spectroscope prism. Northwest cone, 10 p. m., flames 5 inches long. The bright bands are spectra of the melt. Wratten Panchromatic Plate. —Photo Jaggar.

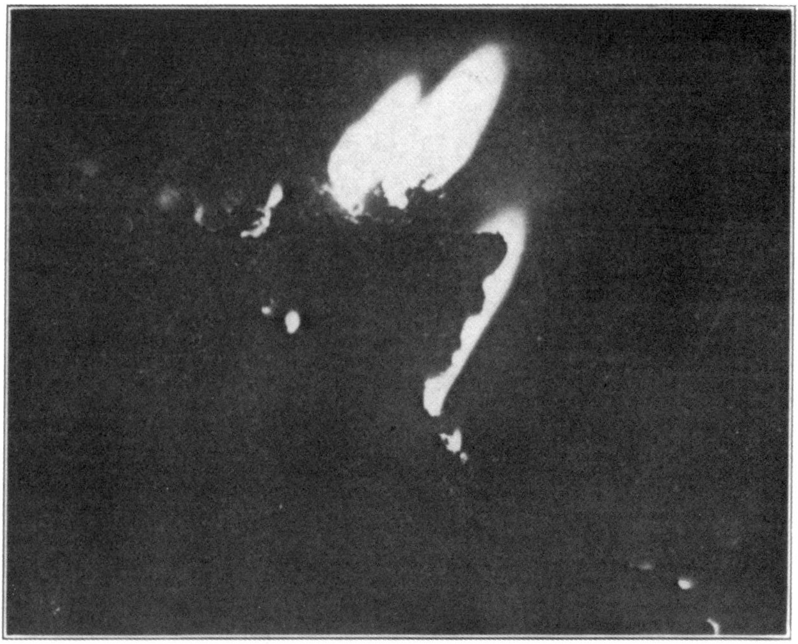

Aug. 23, 1918. Direct photograph with Wratten Panchromatic Plate of pale yellow green flames 5 inches long, 5 feet away. Northwest cone, 11 p. m. High gas pressure. The camera was set up on the side of the cone.

Aug. 23, 1918. Northwest cone where flame photographs were taken southeast lakes showed stalactitic overhang, bright fountaining and westward streaming. Some thirty feet below the southeast edge of the pit, these lakes were now barely visible owing to the uplift of the ramparts in front of them. The northern fills were glowing, and the north, northwest and west cones flaming and hissing. The southwest driblet pile was spurting and lifting a lid and emitting trickle flows fully six feet above the level of the edge of the pit. These poured into the southwest crevasse, making organ pipe cascades. Only a few feet more filling here would send an overflow down the long slope of the greater crater towards the desert. The southwest pond was spurting violently, but its surface could not be seen. There was activity in the northern lakes. The northwest cone had a filagree of glow cracks facing north on its summit, through which pale yellow flames of burning gas played with noisy blow-pipe effect. The crags were stationary.

On Thursday, August 22, at 11 a. m., activity had diminished, the pit was quiet and the crags stationary. The lakes appeared relatively higher, the southeast pond with an inner bench two feet high and the main lake six feet high. Toward a large fountain near the east end of the lake the surface currents streamed from both west and northeast. The wall cracks east and south had greatly slumped, but west and north upwelling was the rule. For a hundred feet of the southwest edge of Halemaumau the driblet flows were flush with the rim and the three cones stood high above it. There was great heat in the whitened March bench adjacent to these cones. No changes were apparent west and northeast, and the northwest cone puffed harshly. About 5 p. m. the lakes showed the usual fluctuations of activity and a tumble of rocks fell into the north lake. At 6:30 p. m. a prolonged flow started from the region of the northwest cone and extended itself the whole length of the northeast fill.

On Friday, August 23, at 6 p. m., the principal changes were increased steady gas pressure at the northwest cone with three spears of flame motionless and continuous. The nose of the blast was deafening. This increased gas pressure was accompanied by more flowing in the north and northeast fills. The writer climbed to the summit of the east crossledge for a view of the main lake. The lake showed eastward streaming and a large fountain at the east end. There were now more pronounced coves northeast, southeast, south (central cove), and at the central pool. Beside the high spatter dome at the southeast cove there was a pot flaming sluggishly and another chimney with fluttering banners of flame occupied the southeast wall of the southeast pond.

From 9 to 12 p. m., assisted by Dr. Romberg, and with the aid of a direct vision spectroscope loaned by the College of Hawaii, the writer took photographs and experimental photo-spectrographs of the continuous flames at the northwest cone. It was possible to approach within five feet of these flames and photograph them in profile against a dark background. The flames were about five inches long. The flame spectrum visually showed chiefly the sodium lines in a dark field when the flame was examined from a position which entirely cut off a view of the glowing melt. When the melt showed, the bright lines of the gas appeared against a continuous spectrum from the incandescent lava. An interesting method of identifying flames in the glowing cracks, where the incandescence was so bright as to visually conceal them, consisted in inspection of the flaming cracks through the prisms with both telescope and slit removed. The flaming gas now appeared pale yellow in natural form, while all the glow material appeared as formless parallel bright spectrum bands. The flames occupied the yellow zone of their own spectrum in each case, and an exceedingly faint band containing the green and violet could be traced extending from the flame image. This test for locating flames was applied to the fountains and grottoes of the lake and no trace of flame could be detected. When applied to the southeast pond chimney the flame again appeared in sharp outline. The illumined fume of the pit gave a continuous spectrum like the melt but less bright.

In the Whitney Laboratory the Bosch-Omori instruments have now been set up so as to write on a single drum, and the optical seismograph has also been placed in position and first tests made.

August 31, 1918.

During the week ending August 30, 1918, the first phase of the recent rise of the Halemaumau lava column had come to an end and the lava slightly subsided to a stationary condition, which continues at the present time. The lakes lie 30 to 40 feet below the rim of the pit, and the central crag stands about 60 feet above the rim. The activity of the week has been dull, blowing and flowing at wall valley cones has ceased, and while there are bright displays of fountaining in the main lake at night, such activity can be watched only by climbing down and crossing the wall valley. This stagnant spell appears to correspond to the temporary depression which took place in the first week of March last, prior to the strong rising of the equinoctial period.

On August 23 a fresh glowing flow was observed in the crevasse south of the southeast cone. On Saturday, August 24, about 8 p. m., there was an active pond in the extension of this crevasse near the southeast cone. The lakes showed increased fountaining and were relatively higher, while the crags were lower. The north wall valley showed a large turtle-back flow of fresh lava which had swollen up on the floor under the old north station and stood only 6 feet below the rim of the pit at the old north shelter. The northern ponds were active, with very high spraying fountains in three distinct depressions among the inner crags there. These local crags appeared to have risen. The west and southwest ponds were also active. The northwest cone continued to show shrieking jets of burning gas, but the upper flames had encased themselves in glassy spiracles and stood out as bluish petals around a rosette of minute orifices. When the spiracles were broken off with a stick the larger flames were restored along with the harsh hissing as before. On this night the spectroscope experiments were continued.

On August 25 at 4 p. m. the inner bench at the southeast pond stood five feet above the crusted lava surface and the east arm of the main lake was similarly inactive and low. About 6 p. m. there was breaking up and considerable activity, especially at the northeast grotto, while central fountains occasionally sprang up.

On Monday, August 26, at 11:25 a. m., the valley fills had slumped somewhat. The pit was quiet with subsiding tendency. The lakes stood 8 to 10 feet below the inner benches; their surfaces were crusted, but moderate border fountains broke through the crust now and then, with hissing at the start. There was bubbling in the southeast cone pond and much blue fume from live lava in the crevasse south of it. On crossing the south wall valley to the edge of the southwest pond the writer found the latter occupying a pit bordered on its north side by an inner bench 8 feet high, and on its southwest side by a lifted scarp 15 feet high. The channel extending eastward from it was floored with a tumble of rocks, had a width of 6 to 8 feet, and was overhung on its south side all the way to the southeast pond by an eastward extension of this southwest pond escarpment. The southwest pond was crusted over, but a fountain broke into action in the channel leading into the west arm pond.

The southwest border heap showed no activity and was now about 4 feet above the rim of the pit and from 15 to 20 feet higher than the west and south valley fills. In similar fashion the north "turtle-back" heap stood 8 to 10 feet higher than the northwest and northeast valley fills. The northwest cone could be heard bubbling inside as though its interior were a hollow chamber. There were occasional flame puffs from it, but the orifices were becoming sulphur stained; glowing cracks were numerous. Occasional fountaining noise was heard from the north lake.

The writer clambered from the east shelter through the tumbled eastern wall valley gulch and then crossed the east fill to the edge of the main lake. The latter was crusted over but periodically heavy bursts of gas broke the crust on the north side of the central channel and produced a rhythmic border fountain. There were other such fountains northeast and south with streaming to the grottoes. A raised spatter dome at the east end four feet above the lake level, and separated from the lake by a lower bench, contained an open flaming oven on the lake side filled with glowing stalactites. The lake was heavily sluggishly two feet below the innermost bench, but around most of its margins there were vertical cliffs with spatter lines 8 to 10 feet high. The southeast pond was also visited and found streaming southward to grottoes which splashed on its southeast side; the crusts were cracking and foundering. The shelf east of it stood 6 feet above the liquid. A visit to the southeast cone depression revealed only a maze of tumbled cracks, with live lava rumbling and blue fume rising only in the south crevasse. The southeast driblet cone still stood in place unaltered by its depression and the chaotic chasms about it.

On August 27 at 9 a. m. the pond margins appeared 10 feet above the pools and these were very quiet except for the outbursts on the north side of the main lake. The crags were subsiding slightly and the smoke growing thicker.

On Wednesday, August 28, at 6:30 p. m., there was little change. A large fountain was playing near the east end of the main lake, and all the pools were moderately active, including the west pond chasm and the south crevasse. The cracks of the valley fills still glowed, and the northwest cone now had open window orifices, through which flames flared up and rumbling, gurgling lava could be heard within. The southwest heap was glowing and one orifice was flaring there. The fumes were rather dense. A slab was heard to fall near the southwest pond.

On Friday, August 30, at 11 a. m., everything appeared low and stagnant. There was bright flaring at night. The crags were somewhat lowered. The lakes were nearly concealed within their ramparts, but there was bombardment at the northeast cove and occasional bright central fountains broke into action. The northwest cone was broken, showed little glow, and the interior stalactites were revealed. Thick fume rose from the southeast wall crack, the east side of the central crag mass, and many other places.

Development of the photographic plates made August 23 and 24, with and without spectroscope, at the flaming orifices of the northwest cone, produced some highly interesting pictures. The flames were positvely photographed with clear images for the first time. Furthermore, a photograph of the bright sodium line was obtained. Lastly, a photograph of the flaming and glowing orifices through the prisms alone showed not only the marked distinction between image of flame and spectrum band of melt, but also revealed flame images in the region of the green and blue of the flame spectrum proper, not detected by eye. This implied the presence of faint bright lines from the burning gases in parts of the spectrum other than the yellow. Such a result promises possibilities of spectrum analysis in determining change of gas composition at different or consecutive times at volcanic vents.

In the Whitney Laboratory of Seismology the instruments have been settling down to renewed continuous recording, and the optical apparatus promises to do good work. Dr. Romberg has made some important improvements during the week.

Very respectfully,

T. A. JAGGAR, JR.,
Director.

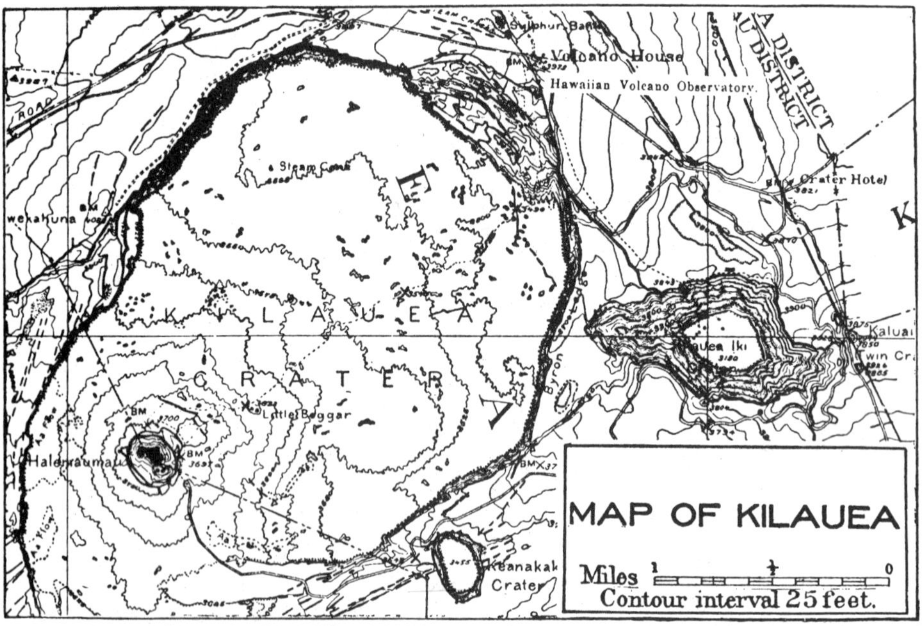

HAWAIIAN VOLCANO RESEARCH ASSOCIATION.

This society is a voluntary one, made up of subscribers to scientific work which is being executed by Dr. T. A. Jaggar, Director of the Hawaiian Volcano Observatory, Volcano House, P. O., Hawaii. **All scientific exchanges should be sent to this address.**

In 1917 there are about 150 subscribers in Hawaii and elsewhere, firms and individuals. A group of firms and persons in Hilo built the main observatory building in the spring of 1912. The work was founded by the Massachusetts Institute of Technology. Publications to date have been weekly reports since the summer of 1911 now reprinted in Honolulu in monthly form. There are also special reports, printed from time to time.

The weekly bulletin as it appears in the Honolulu Advertiser is reprinted as a leaflet and sent to regular annual subscribers to the work of the Association. L. A. Thurston is president of the Board of Directors of the Association, and L. T. Peck is treasurer. New subscribers who are interested in volcanoes will be welcomed in the Association. The Association aims: (1) To record volcanic activity and earthquakes in Hawaii; (2) to attract scientific men hither for special studies; (3) to promote the establishment of volcano observatories all over the world. The annual dues of regular members are $5; patrons of the Association subscribe larger amounts.

WHITNEY LABORATORY OF SEISMOLOGY.

The Whitney Laboratory of Seismology, named after an endowment fund of geophysical research held by the Massachusetts Institute of Technology, in memory of Caroline and Edward Whitney of Boston, is equipped with two Bosch-Omori 100 kg tromometers registering N-S and E-W motion, a heavy Omori tromometer registering E-W motion, and an Omori ''ordinary Seismograph'' designed for registering strong earthquakes in all three components of motion. These are seated on concrete piers in a closed basement room having practically constant temperature, beneath the chief Observatory building near the hotel. Time is referred to a rated chronometer, checked at intervals by solar observations with a transit. Both instruments are loaned by the College of Hawaii. Hawaiian standard time (H. S. T.) is 10 hrs. 30 min. slower than Greenwich time.

CANCANI SCALE OF SEISMIC INTENSITY.

Expressed by accelerations measured in millimeters per second per second.

I.	Instrumental	0.0	2.5
II.	Very slight	2.5	5.0
III.	Slight	5.0	10.0
IV.	Sensible, mediocre	10.0	25.0
V.	Rather strong	25.0	50.0
VI.	Strong	50.0	100.0
VII.	Very strong	100.0	250.0
VIII.	Ruinous	250.0	500.0
IX.	Disastrous	500.0	1000.0
X.	Very disastrous	1000.0	2500.0
XI.	Catastrophic	2500.0	5000.0
XII.	Great catastrophe	5000.0	10000.0

Grade IV. is ordinarily the minimum perceived by the senses; and in grade XII. the acceleration, or rate of change of motion (jerk) reaches that of terrestrial gravitation.

In the standard form of report the maximum intensity or acceleration, designated by the symbol α, or max. α, is given in the conventional unit, the milligal. The milligal is a measure of acceleration, such that 1 milligal = 1/100 mm. per sec. per sec. = 10 μ per sec. per sec. The Cancani scale, here defined in terms of millimeters per sec. per sec., can therefore be expressed in milligals by multiplying each of the numbers by 100.

WEEKLY BULLETIN
OF THE
Hawaiian Volcano Observatory

Vol. VI. HONOLULU, HAWAII, SEPTEMBER, 1918 No. 9

HAWAIIAN VOLCANO OBSERVATORY, Sept. 7, 1918.—During the week ending Friday, September 6, 1918, the Halemaumau lava column has behaved just as during the preceding week, with slight settling of the crags and moderately active lakes, the latter showing some tendency to increased gas pressure and construction of spatter margins. The crags remain in full view from Volcano House, and the smoke from their midst is rather dense. No noteworthy change of level has been recorded. This kind of activity checks with what happened last March before the equinox, when the rising of the lake from March 5 to March 8 was accompanied by stationary crags and thereafter the crags rose rapidly and continued to rise until the 26th, when strong sinking set in. The past week has been seismically quiet.

On Saturday, August 31, 1918, at 10 a. m., both lakes and crags appeared relatively low, general conditions were unchanged, and there was nothing new on the west and southwest. The main and southeast lakes were barely visible 40 feet below the rim of the pit, and the central crag towered 100 feet above them. Inspection of the north lake hollow showed that the pond there was low amid tumbled boulders and smaller inner crags. There was slight rumbling under the northwest cone.

On September 2 from 5 to 6 p. m. the stagnant condition continued, the crags were stationary, some glow could still be seen in the cracks of the valley fills, much smoke indicated the presence of open cavities below, and all the ponds occasionally showed sufficient glow to indicate general activity in the lake magma. At the northeast cove some bombardment with spraying suggested renewed gas pressure in the liquid. There was no pressure, however, at the northwest cone. The main lake was streaming from its western end toward the south and northeast grottoes, and curtained grottoes heavy with stalactites occupied the northwest side of the southeast pond, and occasionally high fountain flings were thrown up from the north lake. Sinking spells occurred as usual, with cracking and foundering of crust, followed by bubble fountaining.

On Wednesday, September 4, at 7 p. m., there was distinct increase of activity in the lakes, with puffing and spraying from border fountains. The streaming in the main lake was in a broad curved river-like zone which emerged from the tunnel on the north side of the central pool and proceeded the length of the lake in an "S" shape to the east and south. Stalactite grottoes were common to both the southeast pond and the main lake, and there was bright flaring from the southwest pond. The bright zigzag lines between skin areas over the main lake had reappeared instead of the dark crusts with angular cracks which have been much more common of late. One rock slide was seen falling from the east cross-ledge, indicating motion in the crags. A gaping crevasse in the new northeast fill parallel to the wall under the east shelter showed glow 15 feet down. This and measured slight depression of the crags indicated that the renewal of gas pressure, heating and melting processes in the lake magma was being compensated by settlement of the bench magma blocks.

On September 5 from 6 to 9 p. m. there was the same sort of activity and an increased number of border fountains, with spraying and building of spatter ramparts. A large active dome grotto with immense stalactites had been built above the northeast cove, and about 7 p. m. a long block of the spatter bench

WEEKLY BULLETIN
of the
Hawaiian Volcano Observatory

Published Monthly at Honolulu, Hawaii, by the Hawaiian Volcano Research Association

L. W. de Vis-Norton........Secretary

Entered as second-class matter January 20, 1914, at the post-office at Honolulu, Hawaii, under the Act of August 24, 1912.

on the north side of the main lake collapsed and produced much commotion in the lake during a sinking spell. The skin was ballooned and blistered by gas near the entrance to the northeast grotto, but elsewhere large crust areas were sliding over each other eastward. Streaming was from the central region to the northeast grotto, but when the south grotto suddenly broke into action with much blowing and spraying there was insuck to the bank in that direction. Streaming in the southeast pond was southward. There was great increase in slipping of rocks from the southern slope of the east cross-ledge. Many smoking areas had developed among the cracks in the crags. On the next day, Friday, September 6, conditions were unchanged.

In the Whitney Laboratory of Seismology, Dr. Arnold Romberg this week concludes his summer season of experiment and reconstruction of instruments, and the director of the Observatory takes this opportunity to express his high appreciation and that of the Research Association for the excellent work which Dr. Romberg has done. We are now equipped with four instruments especially suited to the conditions here, and designed distinctively for local earthquakes and micro-tremors, for tilting of the ground and for teleseisms. During the week the clinograph or tilt-recording instrument has been set up, a horizontal pendulum with boom 10 feet long and a natural period of 72 seconds when undamped, and without lever complications. This instrument is writing on smoked paper with clock-work which moves the paper only about two inches in twenty-four hours, so that the east-west component of tilt will be recorded strongly and measured with ease. The pendulum is hung wholly from hinges of fine taut steel wire and fitted with a micrometer adjustment for direct test of magnification under tilt. An instrument for determining the vertical component of the motion of local earthquakes is being constructed, and experiments in special study of volcanic micro-tremors will be continued.

HAWAIIAN VOLCANO OBSERVATORY, Sept. 14, 1918.—During the week ending Friday, September 13, 1918, the lava column has slowly subsided one foot per day and the activity of the liquid lava has exhibited little change from what went before. The lakes have risen and fallen through a short range, with some building of openwork grotto roofs, but the general situation has been continuation of stagnant conditions without pronounced movements of any sort.

The measurements of elevation of the central crag above the rim of the pit for the past month were as follows:

August 20, 1918—Elevation central crag above rim, 58 feet.

August 30, 1918—Elevation central crag above rim, 61 feet.

September 10, 1918—Elevation central crag above rim, 51 feet.

September 13, 1918—Elevation central crag above rim, 47 feet.

There was thus in the bench magma a rising August 21-30, for ten days, averaging .3 foot per day; August 31-September 10, eleven days, depression averaging .9 foot per day; September 11-13, three days, depression averaging 1.3 feet per day. The main lake has stood about 95 feet below the crag summit, and at present is therefore approximately 50 feet below the rim of the pit.

On Saturday, September 7, 1918, at 7 p. m., there was little change and the crags were stationary or slightly settling down. Streaming in the main lake was towards the northeast grotto and in the southeast pond towards its northwest side. Large crust areas covered the lake, the blocks sliding over each other as they moved eastward with the current. There was violent continuous blowing with flame and spatter at an orifice above the east end of the lake. No sliding was noticed at the east ledge, smoke holes were many, and there was glow in all the ponds.

On September 10 at noon the lakes appeared somewhat higher with built-up margins and great quantities of Pele's hair on the east ledge attested constructional spraying activity. The spatter margin around the southeast pond was high, with a grotto dome formed on the west side. The large dome of the northeast cove had broken down, but there was a smaller one west of it. Near the southeast edge of the main lake a central fountain threw up high viscous flings of melt.

The northeast fill showed a sagging surface, but its border against the wall of the pit was a pressure ridge surmounted by deep crevasses. These wall cracks extended through the northwest cone which was thus broken in two; the interior cupola was lined with heavy stalactites and appeared to have a flat floor without any deep well beneath. The feeding conduit may have been a relatively small gas crack. A pressure ridge apparently surmounting a tunnel extended along the wall crack eastward from the cone. Another crevassed pressure ridge had formed across the wall valley opposite the gateway between the outfacing slopes of the northwestern crags. The north lake depression seen through this gateway showed crusted lakes without evident activity.

On the southwest side of the pit the filling of the gate depression west of the west arm pond had subsided greatly, but the cones near the wall of the pit and the southwest heap still stood at a high level though they showed slumping. There had been slumping also along the line of the chasm between the southwest pond and the southeast cone depression. The bright yellow sulphur stain had developed at a very hot fuming crack on top of the cliff bounding the south side of the southeast pond; there was similar stain also on the east side of the northwest cone. Smoke holes had developed in the southeast cone crevasse and at the southeast wall crack, adding to the general fume, which was dense. The gas pressure on this day was moderate.

A circuit of the pit by the east and north sides at 5 p. m. Thursday, September 12, showed the eastern lakes to be relatively high with active border grottoes and without overhanging margins. Streaming was eastward and fume had somewhat decreased. The pinnacle between the southeast pond and the main lake had collapsed. There was a large gaping crevasse parallel to the wall of the pit in the bottom of the east fill; the wall crevasse under the east shelter had widened and hot air was rising from it, but no glow was visible. Fumes rose from the site of the former north cone and from the wall crack east of the northwest cone. The latter had broken open still farther by the gaping of the wall crack so as to show a complete cross-section of the interior of the cupola. The north lake was now a glowing molten pond. The northern escarpment bounding the depression which contains the northern lakes was lower so as to exhibit more of the interior crags and pits. The north valley fill, however, was still swollen up close to the level of the rim of the pit. The west crag escarpment was now a long wall standing high above the main lake as seen from the east, with the old west crag knob surmounting it. A smoking patch had developed in the middle of the west fill. The southwest depression was now about 25 feet below the rim of the pit. The west arm pond was fountaining continuously and noisily, with much spraying. From the tube extending from the south cone on the rim of the pit, where many of the overflows of March, 1918, had their origin, white water vapor clouds rose in abundance through the broken cone orifice.

On Friday, September 13, 1918, at 5 p. m., there was no material change in appearances, but the fumes were notably thinner and the lakes continued high and active. There were seven fountains in the main lake, two or three in the southeast pond, and spatter ramparts were building in places. Glowing filagrees of flame holes surmounted the south grotto of the main lake and the west grotto of the southeast pond. Hot solfataras with sulphur stain and puffing fumes had formed on the south side of the east cross ledge, at the southeast wall crack, and at the southeast cone crevasse. The southeast cone was still in place. While there had been recently pronounced subsidence of the small southeast crags, the east fill, the middle part of the northeast fill, and of the southwest depression, yet the broad fields of humpy lava occupying the south valley appeared swollen and the crags appeared as though the central units had subsided more than the outer ring. Streaming in the main lake was irregular but generally eastward, and occasional central fountains showed much spurting and spraying, while the marginal ones made rumbling and puffing noises. The main lake had contracted through the crusting of the western part of the central pool, where a tunnel arch leading northward had formed, and out of this poured the surface stream of the main lake in a broad zone eastward.

In the Whitney Laboratory of Seismology the week has been a notable one in that three pronounced seismic movements have tested the new instruments satisfactorily. At about 7 a. m. Saturday, September 7, the tremors of a powerful ''world-shaking'' earthquake agitated the seismographs and the optical instrument wrote a very complete and clear record of the phases. The evidence pointed to an irigin to the southeast at a distance of about 6000 kilometers. About eight hours later a pronounced earthquake-wave raised the waters of Hilo bay some four feet and was observed in the Wailoa river as a heaping of the waters which tore sampans from their moorings. This would check consistently in time of transmission of the water wave with the distance and time of the recorded teleseism originating somewhere under the Pacific to the southeast.

The next morning, September 8, about 7:40 o'clock, a local earthquake felt generally in the southern part of the island was admirably registered on the quick-moving drums of the rebuilt Bosch-Omori instruments, showing for the first time in routine registration at this station every detail of the timing and amplitude of the first preliminary tremor of a felt local earthquake.

The clinograph was adjusted on September 11 so that the smoked paper under the writing point moved at the slow rate of only 3.5 centimeters in twenty-four hours. On September 12 a pronounced tilt to the east was beautifully registered by this instrument and checked by the Bosch instruments, which indicated that the movement was to the south also. Thereafter the clinograph showed for two days tendency to accumulated westward tilt, with the diurnal curve clearly expressed as a pronounced sinusoidal line with a range or double amplitude of from 5 to 7 millimeters, the maxima of the eastward movement being reached about 8 a. m., and of the westward movement about 6 p. m., with considerable fluctuation. The westward movement was for this short period much more rapid than the eastward.

HAWAIIAN VOLCANO OBSERVATORY, Sept. 21, 1918.—During the week ending Friday, September 20, 1918, subsidence continued as measured by the summit of the bench magma at the central crag, but from about September 18 on there was pronounced revival of gas pressure in the lake magma, some compensation of subsidence of the benches by construction upward of ramparts and a rebuilding of the northwest cone over the wall crack, along with renewed hissing and flaming in other cones.

The measurements were:

September 13—Elevation central crag above southeast rim, 47 feet.

September 19—Elevation central crag above southeast rim, 38 feet.

The crag had thus subsided 9 feet in six days, making an average of downward movement of 1.5 feet per day. The lakes maintained depression of about 50 feet below the rim, and so approximately rose about 10 feet with reference to their shores.

On Saturday, September 14, it was evident that the crags were sinking somewhat faster, the lakes were lower than on the preceding day, and the pit was smoky. The main lake was moderately active, level with its spatter margin, and appeared rising. Streaming was eastward and then the currents forked toward the north and south grottoes, the stream taking its rise at the arch in crust which covered the central pool. There were occasional central fountains in the east arm. The crevasse in the bottom of the east fill appeared somewhat less open. There were slight falls of rock from the eastern outer wall of the pit near the east shelter and from the north crag.

On September 16 the crags tended to

1. August 8, 1918. South valley wall crack laking and filling.

2. August 8, 1918. North crags tipping back and northeast wall valley filling.

3. August 15, 1918. Northeast wall valley nearly full.

4. August 22, 1918. Southwest cone over wall-crack (old edge lower right corner), southwest heap overwhelming edge of pit in background.
—Photos Jaggar.

become more stationary and the glow at night was slight. From 5 to 6 p. m. the lakes showed occasional breaking-up spells with foundering of crusts, the southeast pond was crusted over, and the main lake was bombarding the bank under the northeast grotto, showed border activity at one or two other grottoes, and streamed eastward slowly. The east wall crack and the crevasse in the bottom of the east fill appeared wider. The chasm extending from the southwest pond to the southeast cone depression had now widened into a distinct inner valley which was part of the annular depression surrounding the central group of crags and bounded on the outside by the elongate escarpments which formed the inner revetments of the three great wall-valley fills, respectively northeast, west and south. This southern inner valley had been formed by down-tilting of the back slope of the central crag mass.

During the next two days, September 17 and 18, the crags showed little movement, the fume was moderate with tendency to grow thinner, and the nights showed glowing activity in the center and toward the east and but slight glow from the northern lakes. There were very slight changes in level, but the east fill rose somewhat and the smoke from the southeast cone crevasse was greatly diminished. A striking feature of this time is that it is seismically very quiet.

On Thursday, September 19, however, inspection at 2 p. m. revealed a very marked increase of gas pressure, a widening overflow rim all around the southeast pond, with a spatter grotto building on its west side, and large dome grottoes in process of building south, northeast and north of the main lake. Streaming was eastward, there were continuous noises from the fountains, and the southeast pond experienced sudden sinking spells with rapid recovery which were independent and not in sympathy with those of the main lake.

The gateway west of the northwest crag leading into the north lake enclosure presented an even floor of flows which had poured inward from the wall crack fill of the northwest cone. The writer entered the north lake enclosure through this gate and found the northwest pond to be a heavily crusted circular area with a group of hissing vents, among the tumbled rocks north of the pond, which were overhung by stalactites and building spiracles. The north lake was a small oval active pond with a large fresh spatter dome at its north end and two glowing flaming vents northwest of it which were hissing noisily. On the east bank of the lake there was a vent six inches in diameter which was continuously hissing and spurting liquid lava, forming papery sheets of the melt by a glass-blowing process around its orifice and noisily producing much Pele's hair.

The northwest cone had revived with much loud puffing and coughing. There were glowing spiracle orifices and an entirely new spatter cone some seven feet high had built on the west side of the broken cone; the new heap had an elongate orifice in its summit and its outer surface was covered with solidified trickle flows and splashes.

The west arm pond contained a vent which was blowing very noisily in spasms but could not be seen. Everything indicated strongly renewed gas pressure, and the fumes to leeward from the numerous revived vents were sharply irrespirable with sulphurous acid vapor.

On September 20, 1918, at 6 p. m., the renewed construction on the lake shores had built four high half-dome grottoes on the north side of the main lake toward which all currents streamed. There was little sign of lengthwise streaming. Six fountains were commonly in action at one time, sometimes fountaining could be seen at a grotto under the central crag mass, and occasionally central fountains would form towards the east, flinging stringy melt to great heights. Heavy curtains of stalactites had formed in front of the grottoes. The southeast pond showed glowing overhang on all sides. At night there was bright activity in the center and towards the east, the fume diminished somewhat, but the crags were lower.

In the Whitney Laboratory of Seismology progress has been made in preparing the vertical component seismograph, and the optical teleseism instrument has been completely housed in canvas screens to eliminate the effects of air currents. The instruments are recording continuously and the new routine is being improved and consolidated.

HAWAIIAN VOLCANO OBSERVATORY, Sept. 28, 1918.—During the week ending Friday, September 27, 1918, the lava crags in Halemaumau have continued to subside slowly, but no sudden or pronounced movement of any kind has as yet taken place. Except for increased smoke there is no change in the general appearance of the pit. On one day there was a revival of gas pressure in the northwest cone.

On September 22, 1918, at 11 a. m., the general fume from the pit was thinner, the crags were a little lower, and the lakes were slightly down. The southeast pond stood five feet below its recent level of inner bench and the main lake less. Here there were five puffing and plashing border grottoes with the high half-domes of recent formation somewhat broken down. There was much Pele's hair on the benches and crags, and the central pool of the main lake was all covered over with heavy crust on its north and west sides, only a small cove remaining open on its east side. The lakes appeared about 50 feet down as of late, and mostly crusted over without evidence of current, except that active pools in the crust opposite the spatter grottoes showed the usual streaming into the grottoes. Smoke was thick at the east end, obscuring the view.

The north lake stood two to three feet below its border rampart, the liquid actively fountaining, while a vent west of the pool puffed. There were conspicuous grottoes on its east and south shores, but the north dome had mostly disappeared. The northwest pond remained merely a depression floored with heavy down-slumped crust. The northwest cone was hot and fuming, and the lava inside could be heard bubbling and making a hollow sound. A crack in the fresh driblet lava which had poured from the cone extended westward from it. The surfaces all about were covered with fresh lava splashes. There was nothing new in evidence toward the west or southwest.

On Tuesday, September 24, at 2:10 p. m., a sudden sinking of the southeast pond of about three feet was observed with much bubbling and breaking up of crust. Afterwards the pond slowly recovered and crusted over. Streaming in the main lake was eastward and numerous active grottoes along its banks had built large overhanging shells hung with stalactites, some of these amounting to large half-domes. There were occasional violent spells when noisy traveling fountains developed at a plaee of conflicting currents from east and from west. The lake was covered with thin wrinkled skins. Much smoke rose from the east cross ledge. Other smoking places were the southeast wall crack, the southeast cone crevasse, the north side of the southeast crag and all along the face of the northeast escarpment. The north lakes appeared unchanged, and a striking evidence of renewed gas pressure was the revival of continuous hissing and flaming vents at the northwest cone, consisting of small spiracles on the summit of the cone. The smoke hole in the middle of the west fill was more pronounced and discolored with bright yellow patches of sulphur and alum.

On September 26 at 12:30 p. m. the lakes stood about five feet below their inner benches, a grotto on the west side of the southeast pond kept up much belching and splashing, and six or more border grottoes in the main lake were steadily active, while the dominant streaming was against the north bank. The crags were slightly lower, but no rocks were heard falling, nor was there as yet any other evidence of motion in the bench magma. The north lake was fountaining and very smoky, and the northwest cone no longer hissed. The west valley smoke heap was seen to stand opposite a crevasse gateway leading through the western dip slope to the inner lake depression. The southwest gateway depression had lowered, and through it violent fountaining could be seen at the tunnel in the north end of that extnsion arm of the southwest pond, which now occupied the site of the west arm. From the south the central and western crag masses appeared distinctly depressed inside of the outer encircling scarp. The general condition of the pit indicated continued stagnation and very slow depression.

On Friday, September 27, 1918, at 9:30 a. m., there was increased evidence of subsidence. The southeast pond was sluggish, standing some 12 feet below its inner bench, and a slide of rocks was heard from the central crag. The main lake stood similarly low within its inner pit and displayed very turbulent fountaining at its southeast cove. There were now five or six long fissures across the south valley from two to three feet wide, and a snapping was heard as though such fissuring was extending itself.

Along the wall margin of the northeast valley fill there was now a wide crevasse extending from the east shelter clear around the northeast quarter of the circumference of the pit all the way to the northwest cone. The north lake was fountaining, but obscured by smoke, and the northwest cone was quiet. The west arm grotto was about four feet high, with noisy and spectacular fountaining. Much smoke rose from the southwest region, and a fall of rocks was heard there. In general, the crags were lower and the smoke more dense.

In the Whitney Laboratory of Seismology the registration of ground movement has indicated a period seismically very quiet. Microseisms have been fairly strong, especially in the north-south directions and that at times of completely calm weather. Microtremor has been ordinary except for some prolonged very quick trembling in spasms September 27. The clinograph exhibited strong diurnal fluctuations, first east, then west, of like amount in each direction until September 24, but thereafter, until September 27, the movement has been a continuous tilt to the west with the daily eastward phase barely perceptible. The tilt change, coming just after the equinox (September 23) was very striking, and the new instrument exhibited it remarkably well.

Very respectfully,

T. A. JAGGAR, JR.,
Director.

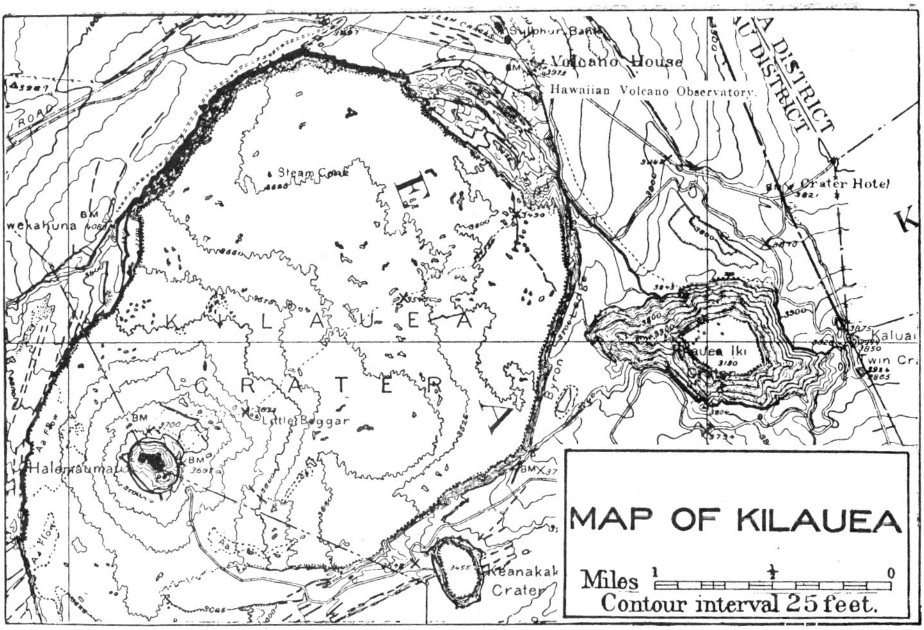

HAWAIIAN VOLCANO RESEARCH ASSOCIATION.

This society is a voluntary one, made up of subscribers to scientific work which is being executed by Dr. T. A. Jaggar, Director of the Hawaiian Volcano Observatory, Volcano House, P. O., Hawaii. **All scientific exchanges should be sent to this address.**

In 1917 there are about 150 subscribers in Hawaii and elsewhere, firms and individuals. A group of firms and persons in Hilo built the main observatory building in the spring of 1912. The work was founded by the Massachusetts Institute of Technology. Publications to date have been weekly reports since the summer of 1911 now reprinted in Honolulu in monthly form. There are also special reports, printed from time to time.

The weekly bulletin as it appears in the Honolulu Advertiser is reprinted as a leaflet and sent to regular annual subscribers to the work of the Association. L. A. Thurston is president of the Board of Directors of the Association, and L. T. Peck is treasurer. New subscribers who are interested in volcanoes will be welcomed in the Association. The Association aims: (1) To record volcanic activity and earthquakes in Hawaii; (2) to attract scientific men hither for special studies; (3) to promote the establishment of volcano observatories all over the world. The annual dues of regular members are $5; patrons of the Association subscribe larger amounts.

WHITNEY LABORATORY OF SEISMOLOGY.

The Whitney Laboratory of Seismology, named after an endowment fund of geophysical research held by the Massachusetts Institute of Technology, in memory of Caroline and Edward Whitney of Boston, is equipped with two Bosch-Omori 100 kg tromometers registering N-S and E-W motion, a heavy Omori tromometer registering E-W motion, and an Omori "ordinary Seismograph" designed for registering strong earthquakes in all three components of motion. These are seated on concrete piers in a closed basement room having practically constant temperature, beneath the chief Observatory building near the hotel. Time is referred to a rated chronometer, checked at intervals by solar observations with a transit. Both instruments are loaned by the College of Hawaii. Hawaiian standard time (H. S. T.) is 10 hrs. 30 min. slower than Greenwich time.

CANCANI SCALE OF SEISMIC INTENSITY.

Expressed by accelerations measured in millimeters per second per second.

I.	Instrumental	0.0	2.5
II.	Very slight	2.5	5.0
III.	Slight	5.0	10.0
IV.	Sensible, mediocre	10.0	25.0
V.	Rather strong	25.0	50.0
VI.	Strong	50.0	100.0
VII.	Very strong	100.0	250.0
VIII.	Ruinous	250.0	500.0
IX.	Disastrous	500.0	1000.0
X.	Very disastrous	1000.0	2500.0
XI.	Catastrophic	2500.0	5000.0
XII.	Great catastrophe	5000.0	10000.0

Grade IV. is ordinarily the minimum perceived by the senses; and in grade XII. the acceleration, or rate of change of motion (jerk) reaches that of terrestrial gravitation.

In the standard form of report the maximum intensity or acceleration, designated by the symbol α, or max. α, is given in the conventional unit, **the milligal**. The milligal is a measure of acceleration, such that 1 milligal = 1/100 mm. per sec. per sec. = 10 μ per sec. per sec. **The Cancani scale, here defined in terms of millimeters per sec. per sec., can therefore be expressed in milligals by multiplying each of the numbers by 100.**

WEEKLY BULLETIN

OF THE

Hawaiian Volcano Observatory

Vol. VI. HONOLULU, HAWAII, OCTOBER, 1918 No. 10

HAWAIIAN VOLCANO OBSERVATORY, Oct. 5, 1918.—During the week ending Friday, Oct. 4, 1918, the movement of the Kilauea lava column assumed some appearance of definite trend in relation to the recent equinox. It will be remembered that throughout September the general movement was a sluggish subsidence following the very strong rising of August. No second pronounced rising spell preceded Sept. 23, the date when the sun crossed the equator, but immediately after that date there was a very positive moderate increase of subsidence. The curve of lava movement, therefore, was a pre-equinoctial rise of 115 feet from Aug. 4 to Aug. 20, a stagnant month thereafter with slight settling of crags and fluctuations of liquid lava, and beginning Sept. 23, an increase of subsidence, averaging 2.4 feet per day, carried down the large central crag for five days. After Oct. 1 there was recovery, which may or may not continue. If it goes on, the general situation will be much like that of the autumn of 1917, when the equinoctial effect was also very slight. The principal difference lies in the fact that the lava as a whole is this year higher, so that if strong rising follows the coming December solstice, there is a prospect of still stronger overflows at Halemaumau than those of February-March, 1918.

The measures of the past fortnight were:

Sept. 19, elevation central crag above rim, 38 ft.

Sept. 24, elevation central crag above rim, 34 ft.; depression lake, 61 ft.

Sept. 29, elevation central crag above rim, 22 ft.; depression lake, 69 ft.

Oct. 1, elevation central crag above rim, 26 ft.; depression lake, 65 ft.

These figures indicate that Sept. 19-24, five days, the central crag subsided 4 feet, or 0.8 feet per day; Sept. 24-29, five days, central crag subsided 12 feet, or 2.4 feet per day; Sept. 29-Oct. 1, two days, rose 4 feet, 2 feet per day. Similarly the lake Sept. 24-29, five days, sank 8 feet, or 1.6 feet per day; Sept. 29-Oct. 1, two days, rose 4 feet, or 2 feet per day. There was thus a sinking of about 2 feet per day after the equinox, and a rising of like amount after Oct. 1, and this rising still continue (Oct. 5).

On Saturday, Sept. 28, 1918, at 9:30 a. m., a southwest wind and abundant fumes made seeing difficult. The southeast pond was heavily crusted with five-foot inner bench on its margin, and the bench around the main lake was somewhat higher. Activity was sluggish, two border fountains and one central fountain. A small slide took place at the east cross-ledge. A fountain in the southeast pond could be heard pounding and from it low marginal spray was seen rising above the edge of the inner pit for a few minutes. Much fume rose from the southwest heap. No hissing was heard. At 10:30 a. m. the lakes were heavily crusted and somewhat higher. At 9:20 p. m. the southeast pond was quiet but flaming at one side and the main lake was active with a large central fountain in addition to the marginal grottoes. Some rock slides were heard towards the south.

On Sept. 29 at 5 p. m. the inner benches were of about the same height but sharp withdrawal of the lava for several feet was observed in the southeast pond, followed by the usual recovery. Around the main lake and somewhat above the liquid level there were

WEEKLY BULLETIN
of the
Hawaiian Volcano Observatory

Published Monthly at Honolulu, Hawaii, by the Hawaiian Volcano Research Association

L. W. de Vis-Norton........Secretary

Entered as second-class matter January 20, 1914, at the post-office at Honolulu, Hawaii. under the Act of August 24, 1912.

large spatter domes covered with Pele's hair, streaming was eastward and there were active grottoes southeast and east as well as along the north bank. A glowing filagree cone stood on the bank of the lake at its northwest corner. A crack parallel to the lake shore followed the high rampart at the east-fill gap. The fountains showed spurting and blowing activity. One of the large cracks in the east fill floor appeared less open. One small rock tumble was heard from under the southeast outer cliff. The north lake was comparatively low, but active, and the active area was enlarged. There was a glowing filagree cone on the north side of the northwest pond depression. There was now pronounced inward slope of the north valley floor towards the semicircle of northern crags, which as a whole had subsided, so that the interior depression was now again in full view.

On Monday, Sept. 30, at 10:30 a. m., the edge of the southeast pond was still about 4 feet high but the main lake stood only 2 feet below the bench. There was the usual activity, and twice cavings in of the bank were observed. Snapping noise was heard from the floor of the northeast valley and rocks slipped a little on the slope of the east ledge. The bank around the north lake was 4 feet high and the northwest cone was quiet. One grotto showed fountaining in the west arm of the southwest pond under a spatter bench only a foot high.

On Oct. 1 at 11 a. m. there was the beginning of marked recovery. At first the margin of the main lake was 4 to 5 feet high, but towards noon the lake rose 2 feet. Streaming was eastward, there were numerous active grottoes and one central fountain, the latter in the east pool, and fumes were so much thinner that at times there was clear seeing to the opposite side of the pit. The north lake was moderately active and sharp hissing was continuous from one of the northern vents. The northwest cone was increasingly broken open and inactive. On descending to the edge of the southwest pond the inner cliff around it was found to be 15 to 20 feet high and the pond itself was mostly sluggish and crusted, with marginal fountains in its west arm and on its southern and eastern banks. At night the glow above Halemaumau was brighter and more extensive than at any time in recent weeks.

On Wednesday, Oct. 2, at 3:45 p. m., the lakes were high and close to the spatter bench level and the marginal fountains puffed from under the crust with the distinctive habit of rising lava. The east fill now showed marked depression as compared with the higher parts of the wall valley on the north and southwest. There was a distinct pressure ridge separating the lower level of the east fill from the higher level of the south valley and extending to the southeast smoke hole from the southeast pond as though a tunnel lay beneath. The lakes were building spatter grottoes. Thick fume rose from the several smoke holes. At 4:15 p. m. the north lake brimmed over and flooded portions of the depression around it; then there came violent fountaining on its northwest margin and rapid sinking of the liquid pool. Hissing was heard from the north central region and near the northwest pond. There was no fresh activity at the northwest cone.

On Oct. 4, at 5 p. m., the main lake stood 4 feet below the new bench of overflow. These overflow floors had greatly widened and built up, the southeast pond was constricted through marginal building out and the new overflow there had nearly passed through the gap leading to the main lake. At the east and northeast coves of the main lake the building up had obliterated the point between the coves. Streaming in the southeast pond was towards its northwest bank where a grotto rumbled somewhat; in the main lake it was westward. There was much crusted area but the open current was exposed along the north bank and the liquid moved to an active grotto at the west end. The north lake had greatly overflowed the surfaces around it which were still glowing as a wide new floor. An immense dome grotto hung with stalactites stood on the southeast side of the north lake with a flame fluttering above its entrance. A glow heap hissed at the northwest pond site. Between the west crag and the west inner escarpment there was a glowing, flaming and spurting chimney at approximately the site of the west chasm pond. There was no activity at the northwest cone. The southwest pond was fountaining.

The crags appeared lifted and the valleys relatively sunken as though strong new movement in the bench magma had commenced with upward tilting of blocks. The north fill was distinctly lower opposite the northwest gap, and the northwest valley was lower still with a break between it and the surfaces around the northwest cone. The large crevasse east of the northwest cone gaped wider on the pit side and other wall crevasses appeared bigger.

The movements registered in the Whitney Laboratory on the seismographic instruments checked with the volcanic events. Three marked spasms of tremor occurred on Oct. 4. Felt earthquakes have not occurred as yet, but on Sept 30 three small moderately distant earthquakes were registered on the photographic seismograph. Microseisms have been increasingly strong. The clinograph exhibited perfect correspondence by west tilt with the subsidence of the lava Sept. 24 to 29, and by east tilt with the rising lava Sept. 30 to Oct. 3.

Oct. 12, 1918.—During the week ending Friday, Oct. 11, 1918, the rising of the lava column at Halemaumau has continued but with diminished rapidity after Oct. 8. Up to that time the rate of something over 2 feet per day was maintained quite continuously in both crags and lakes. Beginning Oct. 8 the lakes relatively subsided but the crags continued slow rising.

The measurements were as follows:

Oct. 1, elevation central crag above southeast station, 26 feet; depression lake, 65 feet.

Oct. 7, elevation central crag above southeast station, 39 feet; depression lake, 50 feet.

In six days, thus, the central crag rose 13 feet and the lake 15 feet, the former at the rate of 2.1 feet per day and the latter 2.5 feet per day. On Oct 1 the summit of the crag stood 91 feet, and on Oct. 7, 89 feet above the lake surface.

On Oct. 6 at 12:30 p. m. the overflow margin of the southeast pond stood fully 6 feet higher than the corresponding bench around the adjacent main lake, and the pond stood 5 feet below the bench. The lake stood only about 2 feet below the greatly widened floor surrounding the east pool, but in the central region under the high crag and along the north shore of the lake the marginal benches were from 5 to 6 feet high. Apparently the central group of crags had been lifting and carrying with them the central lake margins. There were freshly constructed spatter domes and the fountaining activity was turbulent. At the southeast cone chasm the smoke had greatly diminished.

Streaming in the lake was indefinite in direction, the liquid surface being covered with quiet crusts, which extended to a large cavern at the west end of the lake, brightly luminous within above stagnant glowing liquid. The southeast pond was greatly constricted in area. The north lake was also much constricted to a small round pond at the northern base of the large spatter dome. Its overflow floor, on the other hand, was greatly extended in area. Some hissing could be heard in the northwest pond region, there was no activity at the northwest cone, and some small rock movements indicated motion in the bench magma. The main crags were all higher.

On Monday, Oct. 7, at 5 p. m., the southeast pond was flush with the bench around it and a fountain puffed from under the skin at its north margin. The southwest pond was noisily flinging lava high at the south tunnel corner. Nine fountains were in action around the main lake building a rampart which was especially high along the northern and northwestern shore. Streaming was outward from the west end, the current moving diagonally across the lake to the north bank, and there were other currents in bright marginal patches southward to fountains on the south bank. The intermediate area was mostly covered with quiet crusts. The noises were of plashing and puffing, and some rumbling in the grottoes. The widening of the platform at the east end of the lake had diminished the area of the east arm. The southeast pond, however, had enlarged since the previous day. There was much smoke. It should be noticed that the central steeple which is the eastern pinnacle of the central crag mass is again becoming a conspicuous peak standing as an isolated tower.

There was no activity at the northwest cone. Hissing continued in the northern depression. A heavy stalactite curtain had formed across the face of the north lake dome and flame banners blazed above a crack on the top of the dome. About 6 p. m. the curtain collapsed, the pond became active and the flames ceased. On the south side of the western crag mass, above the bridge separating the central pool from the west arm pool, a flaming chimney was spurting lava; another flaming hole could be seen on the west side of the west crag. Under the north station numerous crevasses in the fill along the wall crack were more widely open.

At 6 p. m. Tuesday, Oct. 8, the lakes were low relative to their banks, but the crags were higher. The banks stood 6 to 10 feet high and exhibited stalactite overhang. On the north bank of the main lake one of the spatter domes showed a large glowing chimney 15 feet above the liquid lava. Streaming was eastward, carrying broken up crusts; there were six or eight border fountains and occasionally central fountains migrated to the south grotto, where a fall from the bank was seen. There were deep glowing cavernous recesses at the lake margin on the west, south and northeast, with currents pouring inward at the last two. In the new floor at the east end of the lake a pond of collapse had formed, separated from the lake by the rampart and occupying the former east cove site. Glow could be seen above the southeast pond.

On Oct. 10 at 8 p. m. the lakes were slightly active and there was little change. A glowing chimney had formed above the west side of the southeast pond. Only one conspicuous grotto was seen in activity and that on the north side of the main lake in the middle. The lake had extended itself westward and the streaming was out from the north side of the central pool in a semicircular curve to return against the north bank farther east. There was a glowing and flaming fissure on top of the rampart southeast of the lake. Smoke was rather dense, the southwest and north lakes were glowing, one small rock tinkle was heard and the measured rising of the crag was only slight. There was new glow in some cracks which had extended themselves southward along the bottom of the east fill.

In the Whitney Laboratory of Seismology the only local earthquake registered during the week ending Friday, Oct. 11, was a moderate shock, not noticed here, about 2:25 p. m., Oct. 10. At 4 a. m. on Oct. 11 a teleseism occurred, the preliminary tremor indicating a distance of origin of some 9000 kilometers. This checks satisfactorily with a disastrous earthquake in Porto Rico just reported by the press. Microseisms have greatly increased and volcanic micro-tremors have been as usual. The clinograph showed tilt movement gradually eastward with the strong diurnal variation greatly lessened beginning Oct. 10.

Oct. 19, 1918.—During the week ending Friday, Oct. 18, 1918, the rising of the Halemaumau lava has ceased and the bench magma is practically stationary though the liquid lava has slightly subsided. There have been no marked movements during the week and the general appearance of the pit remains unchanged.

The measurements are:

Oct. 7, elevation central crag above southeast station, 39 feet; depression of lake, 50 feet.

Oct. 15, elevation central crag above southeast station, 37 feet; depression of lake, 58 feet.

Oct. 15, depression below southeast station of inner bench, 46 feet.

In eight days the crag subsided 2 feet and the lake 8 feet; the former at a rate averaging 0.25 feet per day, the latter 1 foot per day. The bench standing 12 feet above the lake represented the maximum stand of the latter about Oct. 8.

There were no essential changes in the pit Oct. 11 and Oct. 12. On Oct. 13, at 4:15 p. m., the main lake was very smoky owing to the development of the smoke holes near the east end. Both it and the southeast pond stood some 10 feet below the inner benches, some border fountains were in action and the crags were stationary. There were no marked changes of any sort. The glow at night was dimmer except for occasional spells of activity in the southwest pond, which brought out the profile of the central crag. The north lake was low within its inner pit. The floor of the east fill appeared a little higher.

On Tuesday, Oct. 15, 1918, at 10 a. m., the lakes continued dull and smoky and from the southeast station the southeast pond appeared 8 feet below its encircling floor and a spurting fountain puffed from under the crust against its north inner wall. In the main lake four or five border fountains were in action, but the direction of streaming was not evident as most of the surface was covered with crust. From the north there was no glow perceptible in the northern lakes. A fresh fall of rocks from the old wall lying on the surface of the north fill east of the north station had evidently broken away very recently. There was no gas pressure in the northwest cone. From the west, turbulent fountaining could be heard in the region of the west arm and the southwest heap appeared more broken down on the pit side. From the south no activity could be seen within the southwest pond. A sulphur-stained patch had developed at the edge of the south valley fill. The crags were stationary and the glow at night dull.

On Oct. 16 from 5 to 6 p. m. there was distinct revival of rising and gas pressure in the liquid lava, six or seven puffing and spraying fountains were in action and the lakes were bordered by marginal floors only 5 feet above the liquid. Flames played through bench cracks both north and south of the southeast pond. The southwest pond was flinging up spray. The main lake was mostly crusted except at the marginal grottoes, the crusts sometimes cracking and foundering, while the border fountains threw up lava spray, constructing spatter ramparts. The north lake was again high and visible, and active on its north and northwest sides. New glow cracks had developed on the south side of the northwest pond depression. A spraying vent was active south of the west crag mass. The crags remained stationary but the lakes were brighter at night.

From 3 to 4 p. m. on Thursday, Oct. 17, the rising activity continued and the fume as seen from a distance was much thinner. There was not much fountaining in the southeast pond but the crack in the bench northeast of it occasionally spurted lava. The banks around the lakes were about 4 feet high and there was much fountaining in the northeast and south coves of the main lake. Noisy fountaining could be heard but not seen in the north lake and the west arm.

On Friday, Oct. 18, at 6 p. m., very active rising of the lake magma was in progress and the crags also started to rise. The southeast pond showed alternations of rapid rising and sudden sinking spells, the rising overflowing the inner floor and the sinking revealing three feet of glow edge and curtains of stalactitic matter. These spells were not shared simultaneously by the main lake, which had its own breaking up spasms followed by loss of gas and subsidence. During one recovery of the southeast pond it overflowed the bench, putting out trickling toes from under a heavy skin, the latter ballooning somewhat and making flame spears through cracks in the skin. On the bench north of the pond spears of flame two feet long shot up from cracks. The streaming in the main lake was eastward in a broad zone and seven or eight fountaining grottoes played almost continuously, some of the fountains against the south bank being very explosive so as to make jets of spray 30 feet high. Flames played through cracks in the north bank and the lake appeared very large, flush with the bench and building up ramparts. There was also activity in the north and southwest ponds and the glow at night was brighter.

In the Whitney Laboratory of Seismology for the week ending Oct. 18, there were registered moderate local earthquakes at 1:23 p. m. Oct. 13; 3:43 a. m., 7:53 a. m. and 11:16 a. m., Oct. 15; and at 2:57 a. m., Oct. 17. Slight records of teleseisms appeared in the night of Oct. 13-14 and the early afternoon of Oct. 15. Microseismic movement was strong in the early part of the week, diminishing thereafter, and micro-tremors accompanied it, both reaching their maximum Oct. 14-15. The regular sinusoidal tremor has been moderately strong since, but the short-period spasmodic type of micro-tremor, much quicker than the continuous type, and frequently superposed on the latter, reached its maximum Oct. 14, with some paroxysms resembling small earthquakes. These two varieties of micro-tremor, or "volcanic vibrations," are quite distinct from the microseisms.

The clinograph, registering tilt of the ground in the east-west azimuth, (the direction of the line between Mauna Loa and Kilauea), showed eastward tilt with little diurnal fluctuation Oct. 10-13, then began and continued Oct. 14-18 more pronounced diurnal changes with gradual trend west.

Oct. 26, 1918.—During the week ending Friday, Oct. 25, 1918, the lakes and crags of Halemaumau have very slowly risen, the lakes twice as much as the crags. From the point of view of the spectator the condition of the pit has appeared wholly unchanged and the activity has been mostly sluggish.

The measurements were:

Oct. 15, elevation of central crags, 37 feet; depression of main lake, 58 feet.

Oct. 24, elevation of central crag, 40 feet; depression of main lake, 52 feet.

In nine days the central crag thus rose three feet or 0.3 feet per day and the lake six feet or 0.7 feet per day.

On Oct. 20, 1918, at 4:30 p. m., a circuit of the pit by the south and west sides showed the southeast pond to be a circular pit standing 4 feet below its surrounding floor of overflow, with a low rampart above the floor level around its margin and general appearance much like a lunar ring crater. Its annular floor stood slightly above the depression surrounding the southeast cone next adjacent to it through a gap on its southwest side. Moreover the floor stood fully 15 feet above the floor surrounding the main lake. There was a puffing and flaming cone on the floor northeast of the pond, but the pond itself was crusted and quiet.

The main lake was also 4 feet below its rampart, crusted over, and showed little border activity. The only open glowing and streaming melt was in the central pool where the current was so slow as to be indefinite but appeared to move northwestward.

The south valley floor under the south station appeared to be lifting along the wall crack, producing fresh tumbles of rock from the outer wall under the south cone. The same uplift appeared to be going on at the east cross ledge which is now a flattish pile of stones ridged along lines which trend northeast and southwest, the solfatara on the south side following one of the gullies between the ridges.

The southwest pond was active and noisy. There was much sulphur stain on top of the escarpment lying next southwest of the western crag mass. The north lake was dull and about 4 feet below its margin. The glow hole of the northwest pond depression was seen to be in the top of a small crag south of the pond. The pit as a whole was smoky and the crags stationary.

On Oct. 21 in the evening the lakes were high and active and the cone northeast of the southeast pond was puffing.

On Tuesday, Oct. 22, 1918, at 8 p. m., this rising activity continued and the lake shores were much built up. The banks around the southeast pond and main lake were about 3 feet high, the fountains were sending up high flings of melt, there was a boiling grotto on the southeast side of the southeast pond and at the cone locality northeast of it the crust had fallen in, leaving an open very bright pot with lava pounding and splashing within. A small

Aug. 22, 1918. New and old north crags formed by tilting back.

Sept. 10, 1918, northwest cone uplifted and broken over wall-crack.
—*Photos. Jaggar.*

Sept. 14, 1918, interior stalactites of northwest cone.

Sept. 1918. Lifted crags, from the west, looking across fresh flows of March, 1918: observer at level of pit rim.

flame chimney flared on the northwest side of the pond.

The main lake was streaming steadily east from the cove in the crust of the central pool. There were numerous fountains on the north and south banks and much breaking up with development of central fountains. Glowing filagree flame cracks had developed on the north and south banks of the lake. Flames played above a grotto on the southeast side. As before the lake stood 10 to 15 feet lower than the southeast pond.

The southwest pond was flinging high spray, the crags continued nearly stationary, the noises were chiefly the plash of fountains, the fume was thinner, and all the lakes showed bright glow at night.

On Oct. 24, at 11 a. m., conditions were more sluggish, the lake margins were 4 to 6 feet high and the pot east of the southeast pond had sealed up except for flaming cracks and there was left a lumpy area and a sulphur stained flattish small cone with central crater. The main lake was streaming eastward and was moderately active along the north bank and both lakes showed the usual alterations between rising and falling. No activity was visible in the north or southwest ponds. The crags were stationary and the fumes moderately dense.

On Friday, Oct. 25, 1918, at 6 p. m., the lakes were sluggish, dark and crusted. About 6:30 p. m. there were breakings up of crust in both the eastern lakes, fountains developed in the southeast pond on the northwest and south sides and in the main lake along the north, south and southeast shores. Streaming in the southeast pond poured under its northwest bank where stringy stalactites dragged in the liquid six feet below the floor above. The zone of streaming in the lake with motion eastward extended from the west end in a curve to the south grotto and a second shorter belt moved from a quiet crust in the east pool to the south grotto. From the opposite sides of the same crust there was inward streaming to the bank at the northeast grotto.

There were flaming filagree chimneys over the south grotto of the main lake and on the south and northwest banks of the southeast pond. The cone on the east side of this pond was flaming through many cracks with steady pulsations of gas pressure. There were fallings in of the banks on the northeast sides of both the central pool and the southeast pond. Some small rock falls were heard. The solfataric patch on the south side of the east cross ledge was seen to be decomposing the rocks and extending itself. The southwest and north ponds exhibited only slight activity. The night glow and general fume were both moderate.

There was registered in the Whitney Laboratory one small local earthquake about 2:30 p. m., Oct. 20; a teleseism in the night of Oct. 18-19; and an indistinct trace of one on the afternoon of Oct. 22. This latter coincides in date with a dispatch from Guatemala reporting a disaster there. Microseisms and micro-tremors of the week have been ordinary. The clinograph registered slow eastward tilt Oct. 18-20, stronger diurnal pulsations about a stationary position Oct. 21-23 and renewed eastward trend Oct. 24-25.

Nov. 2, 1918.—During the week ending Friday, Nov. 1, 1918, the recent rising of the Kilauea lava column increased strongly and somewhat suddenly beginning Oct. 29. Both crags and lakes rose and the rising became very rapid on Friday, Nov. 1. The liquid lava, which has lately lagged somewhat behind the crags in rate of uplift, began after Oct. 30 to rise faster than the crags, and this spurt reached a culmination in the early morning hours of Nov. 2. At that time, after a powerful earthquake shock just before midnight had jolted the whole island of Hawaii, molten lava welled up cracks in the rim rock of Halemaumau pit on the north side, and as much as 170 feet back from the edge, forming craterlets above two vents and sending a flood cascading into the north wall valley of the pit, as well as away from it to the north. Exactly simultaneous with the rise of the lava for four days, the ground at the Observatory tilted sharply to the north and east, and coincidently with the earthquake and lava flood, the ground recovered from this tilt instantaneously, as shown by the clinograph.

The transit measurements of the rising lava in the pit were as follows:

Oct. 24, elevation central crag above southeast rim, 40 feet; depression main lake, 52 feet.

Oct. 30, elevation central crag above southeast rim, 58 feet; depression main lake, 38 feet.

Nov. 2, elevation central crag above southeast rim, 70 feet; depression main lake, 23 feet.

These measurements imply that for the six days Oct. 24 to 30 the crag rose 18 feet or 3 feet per day, while the lake rose 14 feet or 2.3 feet per day. For the three days Oct. 30-Nov. 2 the crag rose 12 feet or 4 feet per day, while the lake rose 15 feet or 5 feet per day.

This rapid rate of rising recalls the great rise from June to December of 1916, and the spurts of rising later which finally led to the overflow of February, 1918. The present upwelling back of the north rim recalls the similar "artesian" spurt of Feb. 15 last, which was farther east on the same line of crevasses, which extend through the north driblet cones of 1894. The present situation seems to justify further the comparison made with the autumn of 1917 in the Weekly Bulletin of Oct. 5, 1918, when the prospect was pointed out of still stronger overflows.

On Saturday, Oct 26, 1918, from 3 to 4 p. m., a circuit of the pit by east and north revealed only continued sluggishness of the lakes and much crusting of their surfaces. The southeast pond lay 5 feet below its margin and appeared to be rising, covered with heavy skin. There was glow in the cone on its northeast side. At one time the crust broke up with the usual deflation and subsidence of the melt, and then the crust reformed. The main lake when first seen was similarly crusted, but one grotto later became active at the northeast corner of the lake and exhibited blowing and spraying. No activity was visible in the north lake and the smoke was there heaviest. The southwest pond was noisily fountaining. The crags continued to rise slowly and the glow at night was dim. Except for continued rising of the crags no important changes took place Oct. 27.

On Oct. 28 at 3 p. m. a circuit of the pit by way of the south and west sides was instructive because of light southwest wind which made visible places usually obscured by fume. The southeast pond and main lake were fountaining vigorously and a flaming pot northeast of the southeast pond was hung with stalactites. During a spell when the pond sank a foot or more, remarkably deep overhang extending inward at least four feet was revealed around the pond under fully three feet of thickness of platform shown in the bedded vertical wall of the pond's inner pit. Similar overhang appeared around the main lake. The lake was crusted in the center but open glowing melt streamed from a V-shaped edge of crust northeastward in the region of the northeast cove.

From the south station it was evident that the escarpment overhanging the southeast cone depression on its south side had been lifting so as to accentuate the inner annular valley and so as to cut off the view of the southeast pond. The swelling up of the south floor had produced a V-shaped gulch between it and the wall at the base of the south-southwest outer cliff of the pit. The inner valley encircling the central group of crags was very striking as one looked along the west chasm valley, now quite a wide depression extending northward from the southwest pond along the west base of the western crag mass. On its west side this valley was bounded by the infacing escarpment of the uptilted wall valley floor. The same is true on the south and northeast so that the arrangement is quite symmetrical, three elongate craggy ridges in a triangle separated at their ends by three chasms leading to the lakes within the inner depression. Each chasm corresponds to a group of lakes, respectively at the north, at the southwest and at the east.

A heavy fall of bank material was seen to tumble into the western part of the southwest pond, creating great fiery commotion and indicating movement in the bench magma. A grotto was pounding in the west arm extension of the southwest pond.

The northwest cone was sending up hot steamy fume noiselessly. The north lake was noisily fountaining, hidden by its ramparts, and there was hissing from the northwest pond vent. The east fill had now become the lowest place in the wall valley. At 3:30 p. m. the main lake and southeast pond were low with grottoes rumbling.

The sudden spurt in uplift of the bench magma on Tuesday, Oct. 29, brought the glowing chimney of the northwest pond depression into plain view from the Observatory over two miles away.

On Wednesday, Oct. 30, 1918, at 11 a. m. the writer climbed to the summit of the northeast crag mass, then along the crest descending by way of the saddle between the two north crags and explored the north lake depression. The crags had been rising strongly and the slopes were unstable. The lakes had kept pace with the crags, appearing as before about 4 feet below their inner benches. The southeast pond showed the usual alternations between crusted rising spells and tumultuous sinking ones and the main lake occasionally showed fountaining still more violent, with eastward streaming. The pot on the east side of the southeast pond was quiet and covered with Pele's hair. The southeast crags were in motion with rocks sliding. The difference in height between the depressed east fill and the lifted south valley fill was still more marked.

Looking down from the summit of the north crag mass the north lake was seen to be enlarged westward and there overhung by one of the small crags in a cavernous recess. On the western side of this crag, about 20 feet high, there was a glowing, hissing and bubbling lava chimney formed in cracks which possibly communicated with the cavernous recess mentioned. This was the glow spot visible from the Observatory. Another large filagree flaming area had formed among the crusts north of the north lake. The chasm leading northeastward from the north lake depression contained a broken driblet cone not especially fresh. Fume was still abundant and the glow at night mostly dull.

On Oct. 31 in the evening, with increased lift of the crags the lakes were also higher and were fountaining strongly. The rising continued on Nov. 1 with nothing especially novel until the great crisis of earthquake and lava outburst, mentioned in the introductory paragraph and to be more fully described in the next week's report.

In the Whitney Laboratory of Seismology a teleseism was registered about 7 a. m. Oct. 27. The first and second phases were not perfectly exhibited but the evidence pointed to an origin about 5700 kilometers away, the distance of Kamchatka, Mexico, or the New Hebrides. On Oct. 31 a local tremor occurred at 9:14 a. m. and a small quake about 3:07 p. m. Microseisms and micro-tremors have been ordinary with some increase in the former. The clinograph showed moderate daily tilt fluctuations Oct. 26-28, but this changed Oct. 28-Nov. 1 to great increase of the eastward tilt over the westward so as to net a strong eastward movement. The other instruments showed at the same time very strong north tilt indicating that the actual direction of tilting was northeasterly.

Very respectfully,

T. A. JAGGAR, JR.
Director.

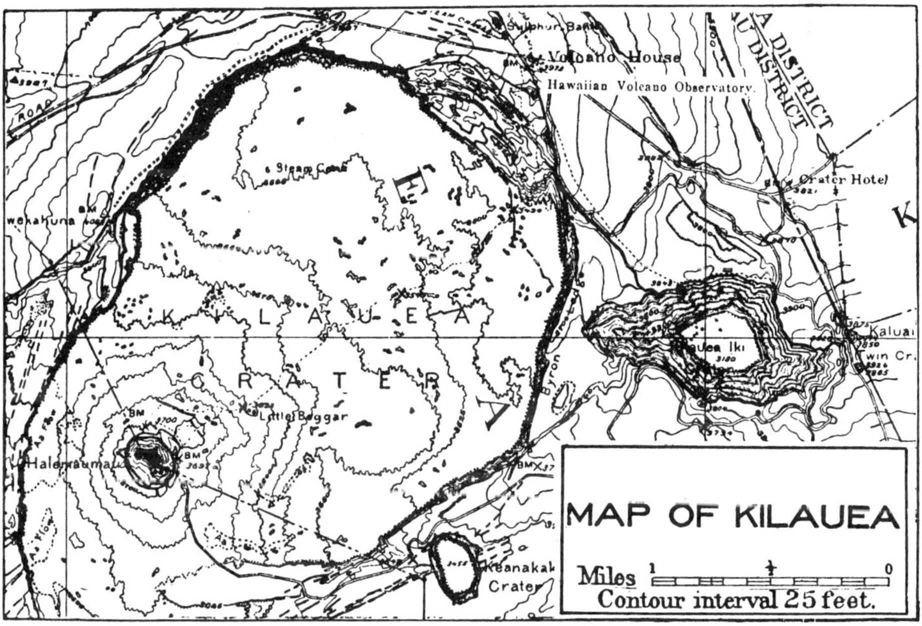

HAWAIIAN VOLCANO RESEARCH ASSOCIATION.

This society is a voluntary one, made up of subscribers to scientific work which is being executed by Dr. T. A. Jaggar, Director of the Hawaiian Volcano Observatory, Volcano House, P. O., Hawaii. **All scientific exchanges should be sent to this address.**

In 1917 there are about 150 subscribers in Hawaii and elsewhere, firms and individuals. A group of firms and persons in Hilo built the main observatory building in the spring of 1912. The work was founded by the Massachusetts Institute of Technology. Publications to date have been weekly reports since the summer of 1911 now reprinted in Honolulu in monthly form. There are also special reports, printed from time to time.

The weekly bulletin as it appears in the Honolulu Advertiser is reprinted as a leaflet and sent to regular annual subscribers to the work of the Association. L. A. Thurston is president of the Board of Directors of the Association, and L. T. Peck is treasurer. New subscribers who are interested in volcanoes will be welcomed in the Association. The Association aims: (1) To record volcanic activity and earthquakes in Hawaii; (2) to attract scientific men hither for special studies; (3) to promote the establishment of volcano observatories all over the world. The annual dues of regular members are $5; patrons of the Association subscribe larger amounts.

WHITNEY LABORATORY OF SEISMOLOGY.

The Whitney Laboratory of Seismology, named after an endowment fund of geophysical research held by the Massachusetts Institute of Technology, in memory of Caroline and Edward Whitney of Boston, is equipped with two Bosch-Omori 100 kg tromometers registering N-S and E-W motion, a heavy Omori tromometer registering E-W motion, and an Omori "ordinary Seismograph" designed for registering strong earthquakes in all three components of motion. These are seated on concrete piers in a closed basement room having practically constant temperature, beneath the chief Observatory building near the hotel. Time is referred to a rated chronometer, checked at intervals by solar observations with a transit. Both instruments are loaned by the College of Hawaii. Hawaiian standard time (H. S. T.) is 10 hrs. 30 min. slower than Greenwich time.

CANCANI SCALE OF SEISMIC INTENSITY.

Expressed by accelerations measured in millimeters per second per second.

I.	Instrumental	0.0	2.5
II.	Very slight	2.5	5.0
III.	Slight	5.0	10.0
IV.	Sensible, mediocre	10.0	25.0
V.	Rather strong	25.0	50.0
VI.	Strong	50.0	100.0
VII.	Very strong	100.0	250.0
VIII.	Ruinous	250.0	500.0
IX.	Disastrous	500.0	1000.0
X.	Very disastrous	1000.0	2500.0
XI.	Catastrophic	2500.0	5000.0
XII.	Great catastrophe	5000.0	10000.0

Grade IV. is ordinarily the minimum perceived by the senses; and in grade XII. the acceleration, or rate of change of motion (jerk) reaches that of terrestrial gravitation.

In the standard form of report the maximum intensity or acceleration, designated by the symbol a, or max. a, is given in the conventional unit, **the milligal.** The milligal is a measure of acceleration, such that 1 milligal = 1/100 mm. per sec. per sec. = 10 μ per sec. per sec. The Cancani scale, here **defined in terms of millimeters per sec. per sec., can therefore be expressed in milligals by multiplying each of the numbers by 100.**

WEEKLY BULLETIN
OF THE
Hawaiian Volcano Observatory

Vol. VI. HONOLULU, HAWAII, NOVEMBER, 1918 No. 11

WEEKLY BULLETIN OF HAWAIIAN VOLCANO OBSERVATORY.

HAWAIIAN VOLCANO OBSERVATORY, Nov. 9, 1918.—The week ending Nov. 8, 1918, has been eventful as one of the times of much volcanic activity, rising lava and seismical trembling, following upon the pronounced earthquake of Nov. 1. The lava crags have continued to rise and tilt back, more slowly than at the time of the crisis, and the liquid lava, which spurted up from new vents on Nov. 2, has flowed and built heapings on three sides of the pit and considerably filled portions of the wall valleys. The end of the week finds the lakes only a few feet below the rim of the pit, the highest crag some 80 feet above the rim and at the moment the rising has ceased. In addition to the pronounced earthquake of Nov. 1 there was a sharp shock, felt strongly in Hilo as well as here, on Nov. 7 and a powerful distant earthquake was registered in the evening of the same day.

The measurements at the pit were as follows:

Nov. 2, elevation central crag above southeast rim, 70 feet; depression of main lake, 23 feet.

Nov. 5, elevation central crag above southeast rim, 76 feet; depression of main lake, about 17 feet; depression of southeast pond rim, 13 feet.

The lakes and crags thus rose for three days after Nov. 2 about two feet per day, slowing up thereafter until Nov. 8, when they became stationary.

Press reports indicate that the earthquake of 11:33 p. m. Nov. 1 was most strongly felt at Kapapala Ranch on the southeast flank of Mauna Loa 15 miles southwest of this station. There some damage was done to such objects as water tanks and stone walls. The first two shocks at Hilea are reported as lasting three minutes and throwing down some objects such as small bottles. Mrs. de la Nux there reports the first shock at 11:36 p. m. and three others at 11:38, 11:46 and 12 midnight. Another pronounced shock was felt at 5:01 a. m. Kona and Hilo both reported strong shocks without damage and apparently somewhat stronger effects were noted on the north flank of Mauna Kea in the line of the Mauna Loa-Mauna Kea axis. At Kilauea the earthquake was prolonged with strong east-west rocking, and numerous avalanches were started from the cliffs. The very intense initial motion lasted for about a minute. All phases of the movement were registered on different instruments in the Whitney Laboratory. Like the earthquake of June 14, 1918, this shock kept the ground in vibration as recorded seismometrically for over 40 minutes. There were recurrent intense spasms during this period and three small earthquakes during the after midnight hours. The weather was still and foggy at the time of the earthquake, strong northeast wind springing up after it. The whole occurrence strongly resembled the night shock of Oct. 25, 1913.

During some time in the early morning hours of Saturday, Nov. 2, 1918, the east-west cracks on the north sides respectively of the old stone rest house ruin and of the government bench mark set in a concrete table, on the north brink of Halemaumau, opened and emitted liquid lava. At 11 a. m. cone vents in the midst of fresh flows were here spouting like artesian wells. The flood invaded the horse corral on its west side and poured from the northern-

WEEKLY BULLETIN
of the
Hawaiian Volcano Observatory

Published Monthly at Honolulu, Hawaii, by the Hawaiian Volcano Research Association

L. W. de Vis-Norton........Secretary

Entered as second-class matter January 20, 1914, at the post-office at Honolulu, Hawaii, under the Act of August 24, 1912.

most vent over 100 yards in a northwesterly direction. From the rest house vent the lava cascaded over the edge of the crater into the north wall valley of the pit on both sides of the new concrete post at the north station. The old rest house was nearly completely buried. The bench mark at the site of the former Technology Station was spattered but not injured. Heavy doming fountains of melt were bubbling at the two pots, and the solidified material was the usual glistening black pahoehoe. A little farther west the 1918 lava at the edge of the pit adjacent to the northwest cone had been uplifted 5 or 6 feet. All the sudden changes of this night were confined to the north rim.

The main lake was surrounded by uplifted banks 5 feet high and showed the usual eastward streaming, foundering crusts and active border fountains. The southeast pond was flush with its margin and the vent east of it was hissing and glowing. The north lake was fountaining at its northeast end and fresh lava occupied the floor of the northwest pond depression The southwest pond was fountaining and the escarpment south of it appeared strongly lifted at its eastern end. There was also uplift at the southwest lava heap and the crags were all rising

At 10 p. m. the night view showed plainly in the lakes the characteristics of rising activity—in the brimming lava of the southeast pond, the flaming chimneys and splashing pots, and the noiseless steady bright fountaining activity of the main lake with slow eastward streaming in straight brilliant lines. The north lake was the same and the cliff chimneys west of it and the filagree cone north of it were very brilliant. The north fill was luminous with fresh lava in motion. The vents had become flaming and hissing cones, the northern one 5 feet high. Glow could be seen in the west crag chasm.

Inspection of the Kilauea walls showed fresh earthquakes debris at two places along the Uwekahuna bluff on the west side, at the north cliff, and on the east side of Keanakakoi crater.

On Nov. 3 at 5:30 p. m. the lakes continued very brilliant and rising. The southeast pond was spraying, with blowing at the cone and flaring at the chimney west of the pond. The main lake was streaming eastward and the grottoes were heavily curtained and splashing. The southwest pond was brimming full and spraying high. The north lake was flinging up strings of melt and the other vents flaming.

The new flows had spread and greatly thickened about the rest house vent nearest the edge of the pit, this becoming the main source. The station post was now enveloped in lava. At the top of the heap a filagree flame cone stood fully 15 feet above the site of the old rest house. The fresh lava was hard enough to cross along the cascade line at the edge of the pit. Lava toes were making out sluggishly and the bottom of the north fill was much built up. At some time after 7 p. m. the southeast pond overflowed for over an hour, flooding the east wall valley all the way from the south station to the northeast valley and making a magnificent display with cracking and foundering of the new pool. The fountains could be seen from the Observatory.

On Nov. 5 at 11 a. m. the new east fill had contracted and slumped, but its surface was only about 30 feet below the rim of the pit. The solidified cascade from the southeast pond was about 15 feet wide. The main lake had not overflowed, the banks lifting with the crags and showing many cracks and a mat of Pele's hair. A high rounded driblet cone was level with the bank at the south grotto, but the lake stood 7 feet below the bank level. The cone east of the southeast pond continued flaming and hissing and burning gases continued to rise from the chimney west of the pond. The pond platform of overflow continued to stand at a level well above the floor level of the main lake and considerably above the valley depression of the old southeast driblet cone leading off to the southwest. All of the lakes were now so high that their ramparts cut off the view of the active portion most of the time.

The southeast pond and the main lake rapidly rose during the morning so that the former at 1:30 p. m. was visible from the southeast edge of the pit 3 feet below its platform and later it overflowed slightly.

Large lava heaps had now been built above the wall crack on the north and southwest sides of the pit and opposite the gateways which there, as at the east, lead inward through the crag walls to the interior lake depressions. These heapings stood above the level of the rim of the pit, both through overflow and uplift section, and from both of them flows had poured right and left along the wall valley. The source of these flows at the southwest heap was a group of hissing cones; and the strong uplift had overturned the bronzy driblet cone of August.

At the north heap flows were pushing across the surface and the rim of the pit for 200 feet was now buried to a depth of from 5 to 15 feet beneath the pile of lava poured from the old rest house vent. The flows from the northern vent had been swelling into domes. The symmetry of the three sources of overflow north, southeast, and southwest, opposite the gaps in the triangle of crags, is very striking.

The bodily uplift of the bench magma was now becoming pronounced in its effect on the flat marginal portions of the valley fills. The south valley crust was rising to become a crag, the southwest heap of August, and the northwest cone were now uplifted 10 feet over the rim of the pit, and all the crag slopes gave evidence of motion in occasional slght tumbling and rolling of rocks.

On Nov. 6 at 3 p. m. the fresh short overflows of the southeast pond were seen to terminate in elongate toes following the course of the previous cascade. The inner pit of the pond had 12-foot walls over the glowing melt with considerable overhang. The adjacent cone was hissing and flaming. Examination of the edge of the main lake showed the liquid there also to be 11 feet down, the banks east and south consisting of fissured oldish shells covered with Pele's hair. A glow hole emitted sulphurous fumes on the south side of the eastern gateway and similar fume rose from the east cross ledge. There were several high and heavily curtained grottoes, the lake streamed slowly eastward, covered with heavy folding skins and an island in the west central region about five feet high showed a row of jagged points with surfaces tipping northward.

There was now a tumbled northeast valley or chasm, a crag west of this and a slope of talus leading down to the northeast cove. The east ledge overhung a low bench at the lake shore. The central pool was bounded by cliffs on the north and south sides and a flatter floor west. Beyond, on the east and south sides of the west crag mass, were masses of choked and uplifted material.

The north lake depression showed flaming and hissing vents north, west and at the middle crag chimney, and fountaining could be heard in the lake amid much smoke

The active north rim cone was emitting a sluggish flow a few feet toward the west but otherwise the heap was stagnant As a result of uplift beneath, the northwest cone was breaking to pieces.

The crags continued to rise and the lift of the southern floor was making a strong escarpment on the west side of the southern crevasse. Glow in the evening was not bright but fountains of the southeast pond could be seen from the Observatory.

On Thursday, Nov. 7, 1918, at 5 p. m., a circuit of the pit by south and west revealed a most striking change, greatly increased upward swelling opposite the three gateways north, southwest and southeast. There was a sharp earthquake at noon followed in the afternoon by driblet flowing on the north with numerous lobes pushing out in the northeast valley. At the southeast the lakes were from 3 to 5 feet below their banks, the streaming was east, the lake surface glowed with bright lines, there were numerous fountains and grottoes and large flames played above the cracks in the cone at the southeast pond. The island seen yesterday in the main lake was now joined to the north bank. The south floor changing into a crag was now so much uplifted as to cut off from the southeast station the view of the southwest rim of the pit.

The uplift effects were repeating the

tumescence of February-March last. The southwest heap had lifted so much as to push up the old edge of the pit. The great general uplift of the west crag mass was tilting back the west floor. The uplift at the northwest cone had jammed the old rim of the pit backward so as to swell it into a half-dome. As result of this the wall crevasse showed increased gaping.

In the southwest pond there was activity at the moment only in the northwest end, but a large new spatter dome showed above the inner cliff at the southwest side of the pond. The north lake was spraying high against its north bank and the adjacent crag chimney was flaming. The north rim vent was hot and flaming and the fresh flows were swollen everywhere into domes glowing through the cracks, while moving flows sluggishly trickled in the northeast valley.

On Nov. 8 in the morning the activity was dull, the inner cliffs 6 feet or more high and the rising of the crags diminished so that the next day they were practically stationary.

During the week from 8 p. m. Friday, Nov. 1, to 8 p. m. Friday, Nov. 8, the seismographs of the Whitney Laboratory have registered one strong local shock and a succession of weak and slight ones. This followed a period of two months of seismic quiet. The strong shock occurred at 11:33 p. m. Nov. 1 with a first movement west-northwest, the direction of Mokuaweoweo. The seismic swaying of the ground in waves of long period continued until 12:26 a. m. Nov. 2, fifty-three minutes. There were recurrent quick-period shocks at 11:44, 11:52 and 12:07 superposed upon the long waves. Other shocks Nov. 2 were at 2:18 a. m., 3:01 a. m., 5 a. m. and 6:30 p. m., and two feeble shocks. Nov. 3 there were two weak shocks; Nov. 4 two feeble spasms of trembling; Nov. 5 one very feeble spasm; Nov. 6 one spasm; Nov. 7 a sharp felt shock at 12:05 p. m., two weak shocks in the afternoon, and two feeble spasms near midnight; Nov. 8 no earthquake.

A powerful teleseism Nov. 7, at 6:19 p. m., Hawaiian time, gave evidence of origin 5600 kilometers away in a direction probably either north-northwest or south-southeast. This earthquake greatly resembled the shock which gave rise to the tidal wave of Sept. 7. The origin may have been either in Kamchatka or under the South Pacific Ocean.

The microseisms and micro-tremors of the week have been ordinary. The clinograph pendulum was jolted west by the strong earthquake of Nov. 1 and remained in the offset position as though the ground had suddenly been restored from its position of eastward tilt accumulated during the previous week. From Nov. 2 to Nov. 8 the daily fluctuations of tilting have been rhythmic with slow eastward tendency.

HAWAIIAN VOLCANO OBSERVATORY, Nov. 16, 1918.—History has repeated itself at Kilauea volcano during the week ending Friday, Nov. 15, 1918, in that, after considerable flows on the floor of the greater crater, another gigantic subsidence of the lava column has taken place in a fashion which up to the present almost duplicates the events of March 26 to April 1 last. The great cylinder of stiff lava surmounted by rocky hills, yawning chasms and lava pools has sunk bodily 200 feet while the liquid lava in its midst has relatively risen and overflowed its banks. The only topographic features of the interior of Halemaumau pit disturbed by the subsidence are the marginal portions of the inner surface, broken and piled with debris from the disrupted cliffs. There is left the familiar fire pit over 200 feet deep, with bubbling lava pools amid inner craggy ridges, one of which still stands over 90 feet above the liquid. During the maximum downward movement there have been many avalanches and small earthquakes, but the fume from the pit has thinned so as to be inconspicuous and the comparatively frictionless fluent character of the movement has been its most remarkable trait. The conviction, to the writer's thinking, that the main lava column is a stiff fluid surmounted by the great crags and floors as a rifted crust, is inescapable after inspection of one of these subsidences. The liquid fills the rifts for very limited depths and wells up when the blocks are squeezed in the narrowing funnel of the true crater.

An event of no small importance on Nov. 10 and 11, dwarfed by what followed, was the voluminous outpouring of more lava flows from new vents of the north rim locality so as to send two elongate serpents of pahoehoe far across the western fields towards Uwekahuna, making an aggregate length of new flows comparable with the overflows of last February, but on the opposite side of the pit.

The measurements of the week exhibit the following remarkable changes:

Nov. 5, elevation central crag above rim, 76 feet; depression of lava lake, 17 feet.

Nov. 13, elevation central crag above rim, 69 feet; depression of lava lake, 33 feet.

Nov. 14, elevation central crag above rim, 17 feet; depression of lava lake, 72 feet.

Nov. 15, depression central crag below rim, 32 feet; depression of lava lake, 112 feet.

Nov. 16, depression central crag below rim, 142 feet; depression lava lake, 239 feet.

These figures indicate that:

Nov. 5-13, central crag sank 7 feet in 8 days, or 0.9 feet per day; lake sank 16 feet, or 2 feet per day.

Nov. 13-16, central crag sank 211 feet in 3 days, or 70 feet per day; lake sank 206 feet or 68 feet per day.

During the first of these three days the central crag sank 52 feet, the second day 49 feet and the third 110 feet.

On Saturday, Nov. 9, conditions were sluggish in the pit, crags nearly stationary, lakes low and the new cone on the north rim of the pit was hissing and building driblet spiracles which showed yellow sulphurous deposits. The concrete post of the north station was now completely surrounded by heavy flows. Glowing toes of fluid pahoehoe were in motion in the northeast valley at one place only. The tumescence had been extended to the wall valley floors, for the wall crack along the northeast margin of the northeast valley was closing together all along the rim of the pit; within two days three to five feet of gaping had closed to less than a foot. Other evidence of upward swelling was shown by the backward tilt away from the center of the pit of the fresh flows of Nov. 3 at the east end of the northeast valley floor. Furthermore the east cross ledge had been upset eastward so that bowlders had rolled down on the fresh east valley fill leaving tracks. One three-ton bowlder lay ten feet out opposite the east gateway.

A heavy rain storm for the next three days made inspection difficult. On Nov. 10 at 6: 30 p. m. the north rim vents were spurting in spasms and at this time strong revival of westward flowing started.

On Monday, Nov. 11, at 5:30 p. m., a circuit of the pit by the south and west rim revealed from the view-point of the 1894 rampart at the west niche a long glowing lava flow between there and the west wall of Kilauea crater, pushing its front southwestward. The writer crossed to its front and followed its whole length, finding its source at two new flaming and hissing cones 80 feet west of the cone at the north horse corral. From that point the course keeps parallel to the edge of Halemaumau and 200 feet back of the edge and then strikes off across the 1894 flows which are partly aa. This flow was 1500 feet long, of width varying from 30 to 80 feet. The lava is the usual black lumpy pahoehoe. The cones at the source were ten or more feet in diameter with filagree crests and small flames. The cone at the corral glowed, but slightly. The north station cones were very bright with recent swelling and fresh flows from them had piled up level with the south wall of the corral and had penetrated the corral entrance at its east end. The bench mark monument is uninjured.

The crags and floors were still more swollen, glow was conspicuous under the floor of the east fill, flames were abundant at the southeast pond cone, in cracks at the east gate and above the south grotto. The lakes stood four feet below their margins with fountains flinging visibly and there were sounds of strong activity in all the lakes. Glow could be seen in the west chasm and the inner crag vent of the north depression flared brightly. The rim of the pit at the northwest cone and southwest heap localities was now pushed up in ridges 20 feet high. The western scarp crag was lifted and the loom of all the crags suggested high pressure, agreeing with the evidence of the abundant burning gas and strong lava flow.

On the evening of Nov. 12 at 8 p. m. new fronts of the western lava flows were plainly visible in motion farther to the northwest than the first flow seen.

On Nov. 13 at 10:30 a. m. an examination of the flow locality showed the north rim cones to be inactive and the fresh flows hot but not in motion. The longer western flow was unchanged, but a second arm starting from the cone source had poured 400 yards northwest. This was the flow visible from the Observatory.

On this day the crags had begun subsidence and there was slight sliding of talus. The eastern lakes stood 5 to 8 feet below their banks, the main lake crusted and stagnant except for eastward streaming pools against the east and north banks, into the south grotto and at the west end. At the north and west there was spatter constructing and the liquid appeared rising. The east covebank had caved in, enlarging the cove. The southeast pond also appeared rising, its crusts being quiet except for fountains against the northeast bank and a collapse seen at the northwest shore. The cone east of the pond was sulphur stained and flaming. The north lake had been overflowing and extending itself voluminously so that with its overflows it had now a horseshoe shape extending around the north side of the crag west of it into the northwest pond depression. There was a fresh spatter heap at the western flame vent locality. In the evening at 11 p. m. the crags stood very high, and all the lakes were moderately bright.

In the early morning of Thursday, Nov. 14, 1918, there was an earthquake felt generally and rapid subsidence of the lava column began. At 10 a. m. everything in Halemaumau had gone down about 50 feet, the sinking was continuing very gradually, and the lakes were rising relatively to the bench magma and flooding their margins. On all sides, at the base of the outer wall of the pit, an annular zone of the wall-valley floor about 30 feet wide sloped inward at angle of 30° to 40°. The steepest of these slopes east and northeast had wide gaping crevasses at the top. Avalanches were very small but incessant. The fume had thinned. A wide platform of fresh overflows from the main lake covered the central region, and the lake was still building fresh black glistening spatter margins. The U-shaped pool of the north lake had overflowed the northwest pond depression. There were fresh flows from cracks on the wall valley floor northwest. In the northern arm of the southwest pond continuous fountains played against the base of the central crag mass. The southeast pond was brimming.

Shelves clung to the edge of the pit on all sides and the recently upheaved edges north-northwest and southwest had settled back with much cracking. There were wide wall cracks all around but the interior topography of the lava column kept its integrity. The gentlest inward slope was at the south floor. Flat areas of floor remained in the west and northeast wall valleys.

On Friday, Nov. 15, at 11:30 a. m., the column had sunk 50 feet more, but a much more rapid fall took place during the next twenty-four hours, with some spectacular red-hot avalanches at night. The subsidence continued very evenly, with continuous small avalanches, extraordinarily thin fumes, thin-shelf veneers at the recent high level mark, a cliff below 40 to 50 feet high, then the inward sloping steep ring of floor matter tending to lose its flat surfaces and break up into a talus. This outer ring slope was uniform east, north and west, but the southern floor sloped inward more gradually with some breaking down in steps. The northeast valley appeared to be the lowest depression. The southeast and southwest ponds occupied depressions 20 feet deep but were building black overflow margins as were the other lakes. Fountaining in the lakes was in progress at numerous crescent niches. The main lake at 11 a. m. had a short, violent and noisy sinking spell of four or five feet of lowering, with breaking up of crusts and a seething of multiple fountains, and similar milder spells of the same sort happened from time to time in the other ponds. Quiet crusting followed very quickly with complete recovery to the brimming level in a few minutes. The platform and cone adjacent to the southeast pond had collapsed and the pond was enlarged to a squarish shape. Streaming in the southwest pond was northward to the perpetual fountain but elsewhere streaming was indefinite. Fountains in the main lake were against the northeast and south banks and in the north lake high spatter banks were building on both the north and south sides. A small pot, with rim much higher than the north lake, fountained continuously at the northwest pond locality. The cascade locality of the new flows at the north station retained a wide overhanging shelf of fresh lava. The northwest cone had fallen and new cracks yawned in the old rim at that locality and near the old north station. Small quakes were felt on the edge of the pit, and several at the Observatory were felt during the night of Nov. 15-16 while the subsidence movement was at its maximum.

During the week ending at 8 p. m. Friday, Nov. 15, 1918, the seismographs of the Whitney Laboratory registered eighteen local shocks as follows: One small shock morning Nov. 9, and two in the night Nov. 11-12; two felt shocks in early morning Nov. 13; one felt shock in the early morning Nov. 14; two small tremors night Nov. 14-15, and ten shocks increasing in perceptibility during the day and early evening Nov. 15. Microseisms have been moderate during the week and volcanic microtremors increased Nov. 15. The tilt of the ground, shown by the east-west clinograph, was slowly eastward Nov. 9 to 13, with but slight daily fluctuation, changing Nov. 14-15 to the west, with strong diurnal movement steeply west and more gently east. The seismographs have indicated strong north tilt since the sudden spurt and earthquake of Nov. 1, and this north tilt became excessive at the time of the subsidence Nov. 14.

HAWAIIAN VOLCANO OBSERVATORY, Nov. 23, 1918.—The week ending Friday, Nov. 22, 1918, was distinguished at Halemaumau by the maximum stage of the marked subsidence reported last week, followed by recovery of the lava column. Great numbers of local earthquakes and tremblings accompanied the sinking of the lava, the earthquake frequency varying directly with the speed of the downward movement, and the seismic activity ceasing when the sinking stopped. A great quantity of liquid lava was evolv ed simultaneously with the downgoing of the bench magma along with almost complete disappearance of fumes. When the crags began to rise the smoke reappeared.

The measurements were as follows:

Nov. 16, depression central crag summit, 142 feet; main lake, 239 feet.

Nov. 18, depression central crag summit, 156 feet; main lake, 220 feet.

Nov. 20, depression central crag summit, 152 feet; main lake, 226 feet.

Other measurements Nov. 20 gave the following: Depression summit north crag, 157 feet; of summit west crag, 183 feet; of north lake flows 209 feet and southeast pond flows 219 feet.

There was thus a rise of the liquid lava Nov. 17-18, two days, of 19 feet, and depression of the central crag of 14 feet; equivalent to an actual displacement of the liquid of 33 feet. During the next two days Nov. 19-20 the lake sank 6 feet and the crag rose 4 feet, making the relative movement downward of lake magma to bench magma 10 feet. The net effects relative to a fixed station on the rim of Halemaumau were:

Nov. 17-20, 4 days, central crag subsided 10 feet, or 2.5 feet per day.

Nov. 17-20, 4 days, lake rose 13 feet, or 3.25 feet per day.

The central crag on Nov. 20 stood above the lake 74 feet, the north crag 69 feet, and the west crag 43 feet. The slope of the newly flooded floor area was downward 10 feet from the north lake depression to the southeast pond area, the former being a conduit area and the latter a sinkhole. The main lake or east pool lay in an inner pit depressed 10 feet below this floor. Just as in April, 1918, the transition from sinking to rising starts by liquid lava flooding and partial drowning of the crags. Then the crags and floors begin to swell up and smoke holes increase in number.

On Saturday, Nov. 16, 1918, at noon, there were incessant rock slides in the pit and occasional fairly heavy avalanches, making much dust. The flooded floors were increasing in size, especially in the central part of the pit. The active lakes were building spatter domes, the fountains being vigorous at the north lake, main lake, southeast pond, southwest pond and west arm pond. Occasional spells of breaking up would occur along with the development of central fountains and subsidence of the liquid surfaces, but most of the time the lakes remained crusted and showed little definite streaming. In the central region north of the central crag there was a small round pond in a crust of fresh flows. The northern shelf of fresh lava had fallen from the edge of the pit, there was still a large overhanging block clinging at the east and heavy falls were in progress at the southwest. The general condition suggested a lava column becoming stationary with free gas reactions, much heat generating liquid lava and the marginal talus approaching adjustment.

This was confirmed next day, and on Nov. 18 at 3 p. m., the crags were stationary and the lakes rising and flooding the whole central area. A steady continuous fountain bubbled up at the northwest pond locality. The general effect was like a manufacturing plant with furnaces in full blast, ten fountains could be counted and at the spatter domes and crescent niches there was much blowing and splashing and the fume was very thin. A rhythmic fountain burst about every 40 seconds at the west arm and a festooned flow poured thence northward along the gulch between the west crag mass and the western valley escarpment. The whole central area was a vast pooled flow occasionally showing cracking and foundering crusts. Large quantities of Pele's hair were rising from the pit, there were puffing cones on the north side of the north lake and the southwest side of the southeast pond, two active spatter heaps occupied the south side of the southwest pond and others indicated approximate shorelines of the main lake north, south, east and west. Excepting the southeast and southwest ponds, the lake boundaries were indistinguishably merged in overflow. The west and northeast valley floors were now mostly covered with talus. The south floor remained a bench sloping gently inward in a semicircle and east of it there was a slope composed of very large blocks. Remnant shelves of fresh lava clung to the high edge northeast and south.

The spread of the new flows on the floor tended to submerge the smaller interior crags and the western crag mass as well as the west valley escarpment. The central and northeastern crag masses remained high. The former east fill, east cross ledge and southeast pinnacles were now completely buried under talus and this region had probably sunken most. The border ring of uptilted floor material had crumbled to talus except at the base of the south-southeast and northwest cliffs. The southwestern cliff showed a burnt-looking blackish wall with vertical scrapings. The central steeple had split into two pinnacles. The profile of the edge of the pit showed new humps southwest and north made by the recent flow heapings at those places.

On Wednesday, Nov. 20, at 11 a. m., the detail of the new pit could be seen very clearly, though the smoke vents were increasing in number, especially north of the central region. The main lake had become a small kidney shaped pond at the locality of its east pool, the liquid standing 10 feet below its margin, streaming eastward, splashing in overhanging grottoes, hung with stalactites, north, south and east. The southeast pond had become converted into a flat cone with the tracery of radial flows on its surface and at its summit was a five-foot open pot leading into a brightly glowing interior. A smaller driblet cone stood at the southwest base of the larger heap. There was no trace of the pond outline and fresh flows from these cones covered the flat on their west side out as far as the base of the steeper portions of the central crag mass. The old southeast cone was still in place on the south side of this area. Other fresh overflows extended southeast from the main lake and through them only a small remnant of the southeast pinnacle projected. The north lake had become a small pot about 5 feet deep, showing liquid lava, surmounted on its north edge by a large half-dome. The northwest pond cone was now a small spatter heap and from it an elongate pool of flow lava extended southward to the base of the west crag, its crust occasionally cracking up and revealing the glowing melt beneath. The west arm pond was another small oval pit and the rhythmic fountain beneath a large spatter heap on its east side occasionally exploded. The southwest pond had become a small circular pit with margins 8 feet high.

There were frequent sinking spells in the lakes accompanied by a good deal of turbulence and at such times there was avalanching from the high walls. The west valley floor had been flooded

NEW NORTH FLOWS

Nov. 2, 1918. The fountain pot at the north corral, source of the northwest flows, 11 a. m.

Nov. 5, 1918, 11 a. m. The north station nearly overwhelmed

Nov. 2, 1918, 11 a. m. Remains of old north wall (left) and new north trig. station. Lava cascades pouring into pit.

Nov. 13, 1918, 11 a. m. North corral and government bench mark across new flows. North crag on right. Cones shown were the flow sources.

across the middle saddle of its escarpment by fresh flows which cracked up and showed liquid beneath. The general condition indicated that the stiffer lava column was beginning to rise and produce condensation chambers in the tunnels and wells beneath the floor.

On Friday, Nov 22, at 11:30 a. m., the floor was found uniformly raised by veneers of fresh lava flow all over the bottom of the pit excepting the northeast valley. The western escarpment was more submerged in its middle portions so that only small remnants stood up under the west station and at the northwest crag. The flows from the southeast and southwest ponds had increased so that the old southeast cone was now surrounded by new lava. The open pot at the southeast pond was closed, but there was slight glow in cracks southwest of it. The main lake and southwest pond were pits still smaller than before with walls 10 feet high. In the former there was fountaining in grottoes hung with stalactites north and northeast. A slightly broken down pond depression had again appeared at the base of the central crag on its north side, and a new cone had formed on the central floor near the eastern base of the west crag mass. The latter was now completely surrounded by fresh flows and appeared like a narrow elongate island with the old knob rising from its middle. The promontory of small crags which had formed an extension of the northeast crag mass toward the center of the pit was nearly obliterated under flows and only a small remnant of the small crag in the northern depression protruded above the fresh floor. The west arm pond was smaller. The ponds were mostly crusted over but occasionally a somewhat explosive fountain would break through the crust of the southwest pond. Some small rock falls took place. The areas smoking lay on the north side of the southwest pond, the west end of the main lake, at the north lake cone and at the north depression crag remnant. The margin of the pit showed no changes.

In the Whitney Laboratory for the week ending at 8 p. m., Nov. 22, 1918, there have been registered seventy-four local earthquakes and spasms of trembling, sixty-nine of which occurred during the twenty-four hours ending at 8 p. m., Saturday, Nov. 16, the day of maximum lava subsidence. The others were two shocks in the early morning, Nov. 17, and three slight spasms of trembling on the 17th, near midnight of the 18th, and in the morning of the 19th. A pronounced teleseism was registered at 7:25 a. m., Hawaiian time, Nov. 18, which gave evidence of origin about 8550 kilometers away. The microseismic vibrations increased strongly during the week, especially in the north-south azimuth as usual, and coincidently with a spell of calm weather with some very light southerly breeze. Increase of microseisms with such weather has been noticed before. Apart from the spasms of trembling above noted, the harmonic microtremor showed slight increase Nov. 20-22. The clinograph showed increase of tilt to the west until Nov. 21, then the pendulum moved slowly east with gradual decrease of the diurnal fluctuations. In the meridional azimuth there has been further slow northward tilt.

HAWAIIAN VOLCANO OBSERVATORY, Nov. 30, 1918.—The tendency reported last week for the net movement of the lava column to be downward for the bench magma and upward for the lake magma continued until Nov. 25. Then came a marked change to sharp rising of the entire lava column, the crags and floors lifting faster than the lakes. All of this has confirmed the expectation that the November subsidence, in accordance with precedent, would be a temporary one. An interesting feature of the recovery recalling again the events of last spring, has been the lagging of the stiff crag- and floor-lava behind the rise of the liquid lava by about ten days. The liquid has risen in flooding spurts with diminishing volume, while the stiffer floor matter has shown rising tendency between these spurts with very marked increase in its speed of rising as the liquid spurting spells dwindle.

The clinograph has again demonstrated perfect accordance between the west-east tilt and the measured fall and rise of the bench magma. Its movement appears to be independent of the spurting of the liquid lava. This accords with the supposition that the liquid lava is relatively local, that the bench magma is more representative of the deep lava column under Mauna Loa, and that the tilting measured is due to a swelling up or shrinking back of the heavy stiff body in the fissures under the center of the Island of Hawaii. This stiff central fluid from which the filling of the Kilauea shaft is but an offshoot, may be expected to move much more gradually than the lava in Halemaumau, this latter being subject to sudden fluctuation due to surface release of pressure. The clinograph maxima were precisely accordant with the great subsidence and the following recovery, but the progress of tilting between the turning points was much more gradual. This leads to the supposition that the excessively rapid drop of Nov. 8 and 9 was merely a culmination of the gas effervescence which had begun with the sudden lava flows of Nov. 2 and that all of this production of liquid lava was a local culminative gas-heating effect due to release of pressure when the main lava body in the deep fissures reached the limit of its upward squeezing.

A summary of November measurements with reference to the southeast rim of the pit is as follows:

Nov. 5, elevation central crag, 76 feet; depression lake, 17 feet; depression of central floor, 12 feet.

Nov. 16, depression central crag, 142 feet; depression lake, 239 feet; depression of central floor, 230 feet.

Nov. 20, depression central crag, 152 feet; depression lake, 226 feet; depression of central floor, 216 feet.

Nov. 22, depression central crag, 158 feet; depression lake, 235 feet; depression of central floor, 225 feet.

Nov. 24, depression central crag, 153 feet; depression lake, 198 feet; depression of central floor, 198 feet.

Nov. 26, depression central crag, 155 feet; depression lake, 185 feet; depression of central floor, 175 feet.

Nov. 28, depression central crag, 104 feet; depression lake, 173 feet; depression of central floor, 165 feet.

Nov. 30, depression central crag, 80 feet; depression lake, 140 feet; depression of central floor, 125 feet.

Examining first the measurements of the past ten days we find Nov. 21-22 crag subsided 6 feet, or 3 feet per day; lake 9 feet, or 4.5 feet per day. Nov. 23-24 crag rose 5 feet, or 2.5 feet per day; lake rose 37 feet, or 18.5 feet per day. Nov. 25-28 crag rose 49 feet, or 12.25 feet per day; lake rose 25 feet, or 6.25 feet per day. Nov. 29-30 crag rose 24 feet, or 12 feet per day; lake rose 33 feet, or 16.5 feet per day. This exhibits the familiar alternation between bench and lake magmas. The actual turning point of the bench magma as a whole, checked by measurements on other crags, was Nov. 25-26 and its real movement Nov. 21-25 was a slight depression with much drowning by lava floods. The lift of the bench magma from Nov. 26 to 30 was really approximately 15 feet per day.

It appears then that the lakes and floors reached their lowest Nov. 16, but the bench magma remained low to Nov. 26. The floor until the 25th was built up largely by flooding, thereafter it was lifted bodily. From Nov. 16 to 25 there was a gain of 55 feet of actual elevation of the floor by flooding while the bench magma slowly subsided 11 feet, making a net construction by lava flow veneers of 66 feet.

After that, Nov. 26 to 30, the lake rose 9 feet per day, the floor 10 feet per day and the central crag 15 feet per day. The relief of the central crag has been as follows:

Nov. 5, crag stood 93 feet above lake, 88 feet above floor.

Nov. 16, crag stood 97 feet above lake, 88 feet above floor.

Nov. 25, crag stood 30 feet above lake, 25 feet above floor.

Nov. 30, crag stood 60 feet above lake, 45 feet above floor.

On Nov. 24, 1918, at 11:30 a. m., there was almost no fume and from ten fountaining areas the floor of the pit rumbled and clanged like a factory city. The lake outlines were drowned under the spreading floods, intense heat rose from the glowing surfaces and the encroachment of the liquid lava on the crags was much the greatest since 1916. In the main lake and southeast pond areas the streaming was eastward toward fixed fountains. A flow was pouring northeastward from the central region and another westward from the north lake. The southwest region was stagnant. From time to time there was much cracking and foundering.

The northeast valley was clearly the lowest place in the pit but the flows had not yet invaded it. All the rest of the floor was one vast pool of live lava patterned with festoons or with the smooth product of the cracking and foundering process. From the southeast region flows had begun to trickle into the south chasm, the central steeple had become isolated from the central crag mass by the floods about it and only very small scarps remained of the north and south ends of the west valley ridge and of the elongate portion of the western crag mass. The middle promontory of the northeast crag mass entirely submerged as were the north central rocks, the old southeast cone and the west central floor cone of recent development.

The main lake was outlined by four fountains and an eastward streaming place at the site of the former narrows. The southeast pond was marked by bubble fountains beside a small spatter heap and the southwest pond by fountains and spatter on its south side and one fountain at the northwest corner. The west arm pond was a small circular basin with a spatter rampart on its eastern side, east of which a small orifice was blowing like a locomotive. The northwest pond was marked by a hissing black cone and the north lake by a small fountaining pool with a large dome east of it. The noises were of hissing, plashing and pounding. Whitish vapor rose at the north crag, the central steeple, at the south end of the west crag mass and at the south and southwest talus.

The new flood abutted directly against the talus north, northwest and west, covering the whole of the west valley and the sloping southern floor was covered at its two ends. Southeast the new flows lapped against the large blocks of rock at the foot of the cliff.

On Monday, Nov. 25, at 6 p. m., the flows had spread to the north-east valley through the gap at its northern end and the western crag mass was drowned with the exception of its summit knob. The entire western escarpment was now submerged. At intervals the west arm pond sent up rocket sprays of glowing lava 50 feet into the air and smaller explosions occurred at irregular intervals. On the north and east sides of the southwest pond its margin was elevated as though the central crag mass were rising, but west and south the pond merged into a flow which extended around to the west arm depression. The main lake was a small oval pool with banks 2 feet high and four spatter domes where fountains and flames played. The north lake half dome was hung with stalactites and the southeast pond cone was flaming and hissing. There were flames also at the west arm pond and at the north cone and everywhere were glowing live flows and signs of high gas pressure and much gas combustion. The fumes were very thin and the noise of slides had mostly ceased, but the remnant inner ledges of the recent high level lava on the south-southeast and north had fallen since the previous day.

On Nov. 26 at 6 p. m., the glowing fresh flows were fewer, the lakes east and southeast showed deeper inner pits and the central region north of the central crag mass appeared dark as though the floor there were lifted. Farther north, west and northeast the glow of fresh flows was bright. The central crag mass appeared higher. Flames and fountains were much before but the southwest pond again showed a definite margin 5 feet high on the south and west and the main lake banks were of similar height. The southeast cone had become a flaming filagree and there was a very marked patch of glowing filagree crust on the north bank of the main lake. The spraying from the west arm pond had decreased and there was some high spraying at the southeast corner of the main lake. The grotto on the north side of the lake was hung with stalactites. The north lake cone was bright but not active.

On Thursday, Nov. 28, 1918, at 11 a. m., the flowing had ceased and pronounced lifting and cracking of the floor and crags had set in. The whole central floor as far north as the north lake cone and east and west to the talus margins of the pit was sulphur stained along small cracks and very pronounced upward swelling was exhibited as a pressure ridge along the line of the chasm between the southwest and southeast ponds

The final flooding, presumably of the night of Nov 26, had left new festooned flows extending to the talus southeastward from a large cone at the southeast pond site and southwestward from the southwest pond, driblet flows at the northwest margin of the floor and a broad flow extending from the north lake cone southward and eastward so as to flood across the saddle of the northeast crag mass down the backslope into the northeast valley. Glistening spatter domes had been built at the southeast corners respectively of the main lake and the southwest pond. This pond was triangular as before with a low southwest shore three feet high and a 15-foot cliff on its north and east sides lifted by the swelling up of the central crag mass.

The immediate effect of the uplift, as usual in such cases, was to start collapse and enlargement of lakes, and a new small pond connected with the east pool by a tunnel beneath and forming a panhandle to that pool had opened on the northwest side of the central steeple. The walls of this pot and of the main lake were 8 feet high. Some banks were seen to collapse at the margin of the main lake.

The only wall valleys now defined were southwest and northeast, the former extending along the old south floor and thence westward, newly defined by the lift of the south chasm ridge and of a new escarpment on the east side of the tunnel connecting the southwest pond and the west arm pool.

The north cone was yellow with solfataric deposits and no pond was there visible. The main lake had widened, streaming was eastward and marginal fountains played north, south and east. The small central pond was fountaining. The southeast pond cone was hissing from one small glowing crack. The southwest pond showed a glowing cavern at the northwest tunnel, it was crusted over most of the time but the crusts occasionally broke up. Smoke had increased, especially at the southeast corner of the main lake, north and west of the central crag mass, and at the base of the north crag. Some rain steam rose from the talus, due to the excessive downpour of the previous day when nearly nine inches of rain had fallen in twenty-four hours. The central crag showed increased height, the northeast crag mass was more moderately raised and the west crag, almost submerged, showed no signs as yet of differential lifting.

In the Whitney Laboratory of Seismology for the week ending at 8 p. m., Nov. 29, 1918, there were registered local earthquake shocks Nov. 23 at 10:01 a. m. and Nov. 26 at 9:51 a. m., and two tremor spasms Nov. 24 at 5:37 a. m., and at 4:53 p. m. Microtremor has otherwise been ordinary. Microseisms increased in amplitude to very strong Nov. 25-28 during a southwesterly wind and rain storm and abated thereafter, the north-south component always the stronger, but the east-west also becoming very pronounced Nov. 27-28. The clinograph showed continued westward tilt to Nov. 25, stationary condition Nov. 26, and on Nov. 27 strong eastward tilt began which continued and increased to Nov. 29 inclusive, and thereafter. The diurnal fluctuation was very slight Nov. 25-28 and increased somewhat after that time. The meridional tilt continued northward.

Very respectfully,

T. A. JAGGAR, JR.

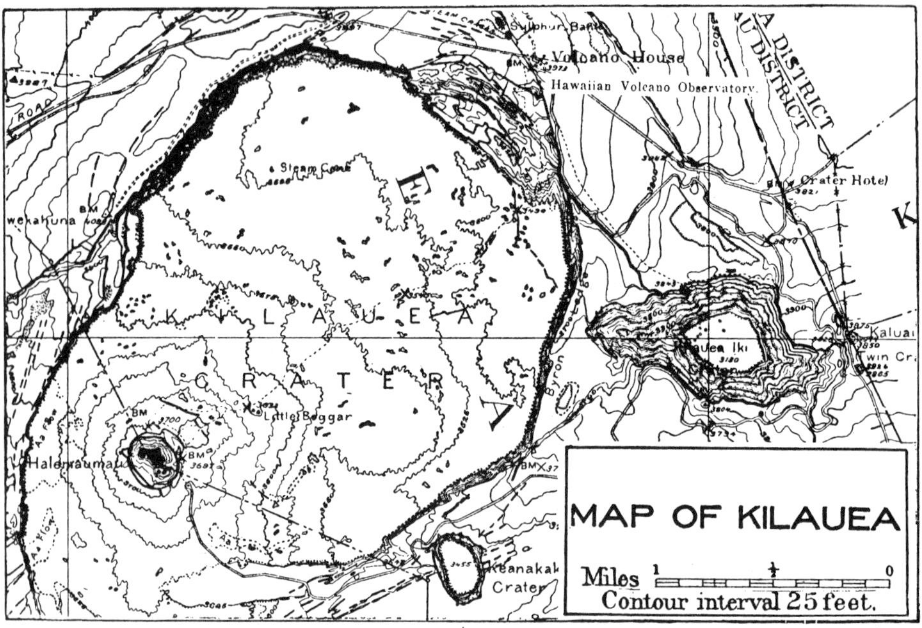

HAWAIIAN VOLCANO RESEARCH ASSOCIATION.

This society is a voluntary one, made up of subscribers to scientific work which is being executed by Dr. T. A. Jaggar, Director of the Hawaiian Volcano Observatory, Volcano House, P. O., Hawaii. **All scientific exchanges should be sent to this address.**

In 1918 there were about 150 subscribers in Hawaii and elsewhere, firms and individuals. A group of firms and persons in Hilo built the main observatory building in the spring of 1912. The work was founded by the Massachusetts Institute of Technology. Publications to date have been weekly bulletins since the summer of 1911 now reprinted in Honolulu in monthly form. There are also special reports, printed from time to time.

The monthly bulletin is sent to regular annual subscribers to the work of the Association. L. A. Thurston is president of the Board of Directors of the Association, and L. T. Peck is treasurer. New subscribers who are interested in volcanoes will be welcomed in the Association. The Association aims: (1) To record volcanic activity and earthquakes in Hawaii; (2) to attract scientific men hither for special studies; (3) to promote the establishment of volcano observatories all over the world. The annual dues of regular members are $5; patrons of the Association subscribe larger amounts.

WHITNEY LABORATORY OF SEISMOLOGY.

The Whitney Laboratory of Seismology, named after an endowment fund for geophysical research held by the Massachusetts Institute of Technology, in memory of Caroline and Edward Whitney of Boston, is equipped with the following seismometric instruments rebuilt at the station in 1918 for the special needs of volcano research: two Bosch-Omori pendulums, high speed registration of local earthquakes; one optically recording seismograph for distant earthquakes; one clinograph registering E-W tilting of the ground. A vertical component seismograph was in December, 1918, set up in experimental operation. These are seated on concrete piers in a closed basement room having practically constant temperature, beneath the chief Observatory building near the hotel. Time is referred to a rated chronometer, checked at intervals by solar observations with a transit. Both instruments are loaned by the College of Hawaii. Hawaiian standard time (H. S. T.) is 10 hrs. 30 min. slower than Greenwich time.

CANCANI SCALE OF SEISMIC INTENSITY.

Expressed by accelerations measured in millimeters per second per second.

I.	Instrumental	0.0	2.5
II.	Very slight	2.5	5.0
III.	Slight	5.0	10.0
IV.	Sensible, mediocre	10.0	25.0
V.	Rather strong	25.0	50.0
VI.	Strong	50.0	100.0
VII.	Very strong	100.0	250.0
VIII.	Ruinous	250.0	500.0
IX.	Disastrous	500.0	1000.0
X.	Very disastrous	1000.0	2500.0
XI.	Catastrophic	2500.0	5000.0
XII.	Great catastrophe	5000.0	10000.0

Grade IV. is ordinarily the minimum perceived by the senses; and in grade XII. the acceleration, or rate of change of motion (jerk) reaches that of terrestrial gravitation.

In the standard form of report the maximum intensity or acceleration, designated by the symbol a, or max. a, is given in the conventional unit, **the milligal.** The milligal is a measure of acceleration, such that 1 milligal = 1/100 mm. per sec. per sec. = 10 μ per sec. per sec. **The Cancani scale, here defined in terms of millimeters per sec. per sec., can therefore be expressed in milligals by multiplying each of the numbers by 100.**

WEEKLY BULLETIN OF THE Hawaiian Volcano Observatory

Vol. VI. HONOLULU, HAWAII, DECEMBER, 1918 No. 12

HAWAIIAN VOLCANO OBSERVATORY, Dec. 7, 1918.—During the week ending Friday, Dec. 6, 1918, the Halemaumau lava column has continued to rise over 3 feet per day with liquid flooding of the wall valley margin of the floor area dominant over bodily uplift of the bench magma. Both bench and lake magmas have risen, however, the lift of what was formerly the floor surrounding the inner pit of the main lake reaching such proportions as to convert the bottom of the crater into a pyramid or cone with the lake pit at its summit. This condition reached its maximum Dec. 2 when the lake occupied a cup in the apex of the uplifted floor some distance to the east of the center of the pit, while north, west and south the margin of the floor area subsided, reviving the wall valley in a great horseshoe. Later the liquid lava welling out from numerous vents tended to fill this horseshoe-shaped hollow. When the upheaved pyramid was at its greatest relief the pit wall on the east side was much lower than elsewhere, but the filling of the horseshoe reduced this difference. It was evident that the bench magma uplift took effect most strongly under the lake bottom, and this was not at the center of the pit but towards the east and southeast. Such an effect, if continued, would of course produce overflow first on that side of the pit and this is just what happened last February. The crag wall northeast, the so-called central crag mass lying south of the center of the pit, and the west crag were all borne on the slope of the upheaved pyramid and as parts of the flaw executed a tilting movement rather than steady elevation. Consequently the east ledge and the central crag, nearest to the lake, the peak of the pyramid, were chiefly lifted, but the old northwest crags on the side of the wall valley were depressed and partially drowned beneath the new fill. The fume from the pit remains thin but smoking vents have increased in number.

The measurements for the week were as follows:

Nov. 30, depression central crag, 80 feet; depression lake, 140 feet.

Dec. 1, depression central crag, 66 feet; depression lake, 126 feet.

Dec. 2, depression central crag, 68 feet; depression lake, 125 feet.

Nov. 6, depression central crag, 59 feet; depression lake, 116 feet.

The inner cup occupied by the lake had walls 15 feet high Nov. 30 and Dec. 6, and 20 feet high Dec. 1 and 2. These measurements indicate that the central crag rose 21 feet in six days, or 3.5 feet per day, while the lake and its inner cup rose 24 feet in six days, or 4 feet per day.

On Saturday, Nov. 30, 1918, at 11:30 a. m., the conspicuous feature in Halemaumau was strong uplift of the crater floor in an arch with its apex at the margins of the main lake and a complex of opening crevasses near the summit of this pyramid lay between the main east talus, opening of the wall crack behind it and welling out of liquid lava there. Large crevasses in the central region of the floor yawned open in lines from the north lake southward and from the main lake westward, and there were other crevasses east and north of the central crag mass, which was itself greatly raised. The northeast crag mass was somewhat lifted so as to deform the fresh flows across its saddle. One pronounced avalanche fell from the west wall of the pit and numerous rock adjustments indicated motion in the bench magma.

WEEKLY BULLETIN
of the
Hawaiian Volcano Observatory

Published Monthly at Honolulu, Hawaii, by the Hawaiian Volcano Research Association

L. W. de Vis-Norton........Secretary

Entered as second-class matter January 20, 1914, at the post-office at Honolulu, Hawaii, under the Act of August 24, 1912.

The main, central and southeast ponds were each depressed about 15 feet within their cups and the basins of the north and southwest lakes were somewhat shallower. There were occasional falls of rock from the west bank of the main lake and in that direction the lake was enlarged by union with the small pot which had opened on the north side of the central steeple. Still farther west the central pool was again open as a small pond, as were also the southeast and north lakes. Streaming was southwestward in the southeast pond and in the main lake it was indefinite, pouring inward toward the fountaining grottoes from a central crust except when the crust broke up to develop central fountains.

Wall valley flows had begun to make extensive fills from vents at the sites of the three former gateways north, east and southwest. The southwest and west arm ponds were flooding right and left along the base of the pit wall, the flows extending to the base of the northwest cliff and the whole length of the south valley; the west crag knob was now nearly submerged. The northern lake vents were flooding the north and northeast wall valleys, greatly raising and widening the northern part of the latter. The eastern vents made three talus cascades with outwelling at the top of the talus east-northeast, east and east-southeast. The two northernmost of these orifices were surmounted by hissing spiracle cones and the eastern one showed aa at the margins of the pahoehoe festoons that trickled down the sliderock slope. These flows tended to fill the southern end of the northeast valley. It was evident that the talus was lifting away from the wall where the east cross ledge had lifted in August and the gaping wall crack could be seen in places where it was not filled with the fresh lava. The filling of the wall valley had now almost completely submerged the upturned floor slabs of the November subsidence.

On Dec. 1 at 1:30 p. m. the tumescence under the main and southeast lakes had become so marked as to make the inner main lake cup the distinct summit of an unsymmetrical cone, just as Halemaumau is at the summit of a cone in Kilauea crater. This effect was most striking when the pit was viewed from its high northwest rim. From this viewpoint the floor pyramid was seen to be crowded over against the eastern wall of the pit and there lifted most strongly while the long slopes of the uplift swept down into the foreground, and right and left the crags were seen to be borne upon the flanks. Still farther right and left the northeast and south valleys made the horns of a crescent of fresh flows, the widest part of which was filling the entire northwestern .half of the bottom of the pit Around the lake as the center of the uplift there were radial cracks and these joined a long transverse crevasse extending from the north lake to the southwestern ponds. In the background, symmetrically grouped behind the pyramid, were the festooned talus cascades, the highest vents for liquid lava above the side where the uplift was highest. Here also the cliffs were less than a hundred feet high, whereas in the foreground under the observer the northwest cliff was much higher.

There was steady hissing from the east-northeast talus vent. The southern most of these vents had extended itself southward so as to make a new cascade flooding the wall valley under the southeast station. Such a valley now encircled the floor except for the interruption of the east talus. The southwest pond was fountaining on its south side and overflowing there continuously. The west pond showed fountains occasionally and adjacent vents hissed. There had been some collapse of the scarp east of it. There was fresh lava in the northeast and south valleys, the northeast fill being flatter and higher. The main lake walls were greatly increased in height, rising some 20 or 25 feet in places. There were the usual grotto fountains and a glowing vent had developed high up the wall above the northeast grotto. The north lake was now an elongate oval chasm filling, fountaining at its northeast corner. The central crag was tilting southward and smoke rose from cracks at its southern base. The fresh floor lavas were snapping, there were occasional avalanches and rocks were in motion on the crags. Large tumbled crevasses had developed along the lines connecting the main lake with the north and west ponds respectively. The valley fills southeast and south had nearly met.

On Monday, Dec. 2, at 3 p. m., it was evident that a new spell of development of liquid lava at the expense of the bench magma was in progress, for the lift had ceased and the filling greatly increased. Doubtless the wall valley bottoms were sinking and the wall cracks pulling open. Lava was pouring down the southeast talus, there were fresh cascades from the hissing cone northeast, the northeast valley was filled higher with its center smooth by cracking and foundering. The fresh flows were trickling southward on the northwest floor and the southwest wall valley was covered with new lava from the southwest pond.

The lakes were all more depressed within their basins, the main lake 25 feet, the southeast pond 15 feet, the southwest and north lakes 10 feet, and the west pond 4 feet. There was a fountain on the south side of the latter, in the main lake there was little activity except at the south grotto, the southwest and north ponds were quiet, and the liquid in the southeast pit poured rapidly southwestward as though into a cavern. Occasionally the northeast grotto of the main lake became active, but the streaming was inconstant and at one time it was westward. Great volumes of smoke rose along the immediate southwest base of the central crag, there was some slight rocksliding from the southwest wall of the pit and the floor crevasses had widened and become displaced with opposite walls at different levels.

On the evening of Dec. 4 at 7 o'clock, after the violent storm of the preceding two days, it was evident that there had been great increase of liquid lava effervescence. The fume had been notably thinner in this interval. There was now a pot in the high talus east containing a continuously fountaining puddle and snaky flows trickled down the slope to join a glowing pile of lava beneath. The high vent northeast was puffing like a locomotive and beneath it the northeast valley fill was glowing and increased in size. At the base of the northwest wall of the pit two streams were pouring from a wall crack vent feeding another broad glowing fill. The south valley fill glowed dimly and was now merged with the southeast fill. The southeast pond had sealed up and become a glowing and flaming cone. The main lake had high walls and exhibited the usual activity. The north lake was quiet with blue flames at its margin, the southwest pond was moderately active and a glowing cone stood above the west pond. The northeast valley floor was now level and continuous with the floors north and northwest.

On Friday, Dec. 6, 1918, at 1 p. m., the lava had entered upon a noisy stage owing to the confining of gas by the solidifying liquid lava, and the several vents east, north and southwest were roaring like a freight yard full of locomotives. The wall valley horseshoe was floored continuously with a broad fill so that the western pit wall was now only slightly higher than the eastern wall. The base of the old crag was submerged, but the west crag knob was still intact. The inner pyramid of uplift now stood as an island in the ring of new lava.

The sources of the flow filling have been as follows: (1), the eastern wall crack cascades; (2), the flaming cones of the north lake area; (3), the west arm pond, now surmounted by a very large blowing cone; (4), the southwest pond, small, circular and showing fresh flow festoons pouring east and west from its southern lip; and (5), the southeast pond, a black heap with a flaming orifice.

The puffing was continuous from a cone where the open puddle had been at the top of the southeastern talus. There was occasional harsh puffing from the southeast cone, the west pond cone, and loudest of all from a cone at the south end of the north lake which emitted a roar about once a minute which could be heard two miles away. At each explosion lava and flame could be seen spurting from the vent which stood at least 10 feet above the north lake.

The main lake showed a new inner floor bench 3 feet above the liquid and a 12-foot wall above that. The liquid was mostly covered with dark skin showing streaming patches where the current poured toward the several grottoes north, south and southeast, and on one occasion a marked westward streaming was observed when the crust broke up. The cracked region extending westward from the lake was smoking strongly and the smoke southwest of the central crag had diminished. The southwest pond had 3-foot banks and was somewhat active. Fountains could be seen at the north end of the north lake where a high spatter rampart had been built and the older north lake cone stood farther east on the floor. There were continuous small avalanches from the south-southeast wall of the pit which led to a heavy fall of a remnant shelf of November lava there at 2 p. m. This avalanching recurrent during the week indicated subsidence under the wall valleys.

In the Whitney Laboratory of Seismology a distant strong earthquake was registered at 10:28 p. m. Dec. 5, with greater amplitude of the long waves in the north-south component than in the east-west. The evidence of distance of origin was not shown. Local earthquakes were registered at 12:38 a. m. and at 3:29 and 5:57 p. m., Nov. 30; and a small shock at 4:28 a. m., Dec. 5. Microseisms increased to excessively strong Dec. 3-4 at the time of the northeast gale and decreased thereafter. The rhythmic microtremor tended to increase at the same time with the microseisms, but reached its maximum while the latter were decreasing and continues fairly strong at the time of writing (Dec. 7). Even the north-south component showed this tremor, which is unusual. Ordinarily the microtremor is pronounced in the east-west azimuth and the microseismic motion in the north-south.

The tilting movements were as follows: Nov. 30-Dec. 2, very strong east and north, with increasing diurnal fluctuation; Dec. 2-3, slight west and south, with strong diurnal fluctuation; Dec. 3-5, steady east and north tilt, with slight diurnal variation; Dec. 5 to the evening of Dec. 6, strong west and south, with slight diurnal movement, followed by recovery to the east and north. The net change of tilt for the week was a positive east and north movement and the deviations from this above recorded appeared to check consistently with the alternation between rising bench magma and rising lake magma, the latter agreeing with the west and south stages. In other words, the production of lava flows corresponded with sinking or stationary times in the main lava column.

HAWAIIAN VOLCANO OBSERVATORY, Dec. 14, 1918.—The second week in December has produced another of the violent reactions from uplift to temporary subsidence with liquid flooding, repeating the process described last week but with the effervescence, through blowing cones, of the gas-and-liquid floods still more intense so as to greatly increase the conquest of the crags by pooling lava. As a result the old western, southern and northern crag remnants are entirely submerged under a new flattish floor, huge blowing cones are all that mark the flood plain sites of some of the ponds, the talus is mostly submerged and the only crags that remain, besides the great central mass, are the peaks of the east ledge and the north scarp. The fume has again decreased to a very thin veil and twenty or more fountaining and puffing places are visible at one time.

The measurements for the week were as follows:

Dec. 6, depression central crag, 59 feet; depression lake, 116 feet.

Dec. 9, depression central crag, 51 feet; depression lake, 116 feet.

Dec. 12, depression central crag, 55 feet; depression lake, 115 feet.

Dec. 13, depression central crag, 47 feet; depression lake, 99 feet.

From Dec. 6 to 9, three days, the central crag rose 8 feet, or 2.7 feet per day, while the lake had actually risen 4 feet and sunk 4 feet, as indicated by a measurement Dec. 8. Dec. 9 to 12, three days, the crag sank 4 feet, or 1.3 feet per day, while the lake rose one foot. This moderate subsidence of the bench magma inaugurated a tremendous spurt of liquefaction, for the next day, Dec. 13, the lake had risen 16 feet and the entire circle of wall valley had been filled to produce the appearance of horizontality, while the crag had risen 8 feet, probably in response to the inward squeeze produced by the peripheral weighting. This bench magma uplift under the lake bottom as a center still kept the lake margin at the summit of an inner flat pyramid, for on Dec. 13 the southeast pond level was 3 feet lower than the edge of the main lake at a distance of 90 feet, and the base of the north lake cone 13 feet lower at a distance of 400 feet. These measurements imply that the seemingly flat flood plain really maintains a three per cent radial grade away from the lake basin as a center. It will be observed that for the seven days ending Dec. 13 the lake rose 17 feet, averaging 2.4 feet per day and the central crag 12 feet, averaging 1.7 feet per day; but practically all of this in the case of the lake happened during the last day of the period and two-thirds of it in the case of the crag.

On December 8, 1918, at 3:30 p. m., after a rainy day there was great increase of smoke at the pit, the bench magma was rising and the liquid lava appeared rather stagnant. The filling had continued during the preceding forty-eight hours so that the old north crag was surrounded by new floor, the northeast fill was flush with the saddle of the northeastern crag mass, the east talus vent and hardened flows from it were glowing and a fiery pot was open at the southeast pond locality. At the northeast wall vent a large double cone with a high spire appeared. The lake inner wall was 20 feet high at the west and 15 feet high at the east. The activity was mostly along the south bank with streaming in that direction and a glowing cavern overhung the western end, showing a curtain of stalactites. At long intervals the north central cone emitted a sharp hissing noise. In the evening the east talus vent was reported flowing.

At noon on Monday, Dec. 9, the increase in smoke from the pit was remarkable, coinciding with the climax of lifting bench magma. In general the pit was quiet and smoky. Puffing from the north central cone had ceased. Greatest volumes of fume rose from the central pool region where there was an open pot and tumbled crevasses over the western extension of the lake beneath. The lifting effect was shown even in the fresh smooth flows of the northeast fill which were arched up and cracked. A crescent of floor north of the lake with scarp facing southwest appeared to be rising, bounded by the western and central crevasses, and if continued this would renew the northeastern crag mass.

Flows had ceased but the adjustments of the great pool of liquid lava beneath the crust of the northeast fill produced an outflow from the edge of the pool which poured into one of the large cracks in the backslope of the north crag.

The main lake showed much bubble fountaining along its south shore and occasional large central fountains flung up stringy melt. The southwest pond region had developed lumpy cones and much smoke, the southeast region was full of smoke, the north lake was inactive and the east side of its chasm appeared rising. This was the last day to show the remnant of the west crag knob unsubmerged.

There was a heavy rain storm Dec. 10 and 11 but glimpses indicated that the fume from the pit was somewhat thinner as though liquid lava was making again.

On Thursday, Dec. 12, 1918, at 4 p. m., the crags were lower but flows had recommenced. The northeast wall vent had piled up the northeast valley fill so as to send a flow through the saddle of the northeast crag mass which then poured northward, exactly the reverse of what had happened Nov. 26 when the north lake had sent a flow across this saddle eastward.

Small rock slides especially towards the north and west occurred all afternoon showing that the wall valleys were subsiding. The liquid lava, however, was rising rapidly so that the inner walls of the main lake between 6 and 7 p. m. decreased in height from 15 to 5 feet and less. The rise was accompanied by great increase of gas pressure with violent spraying from a circle of six blowing cones all around the pit and finally tremendous river-like flows which broke out in three places.

In the early afternoon the north central cone gave out prolonged blasts of gas from a vent in its side which could be seen spraying lava. Farther north a very high spatter heap ejected spray horizontally northward. The southeast cone exhibited two open puffing vents, the northern one a spiracle three feet high. The southwest pond was small and circular with many bubble fountains and a large puffing dome lay southeast of it. The west pond cone was a broad cylinder 12 feet high, at first quiet. The central pond was open with a broken sagging crust between it and the main lake. The latter showed turbulent travelling fountains in the middle and towards the west end where east and west streaming met. Later in the evening the streaming was continuously eastward. Frequently there was violent bombardment of the southwest wall of the lake, the liquid streaming from under thin black crusts incessantly blistered and ballooned through the action of rising gas beneath. The entire pit became increasingly noisy with rumbling and puffing from the fountains and blowing cones. The smoke rising from the cracked areas was less dense than before.

After 5 p. m. the increase of gas pressure took effect in the rising of the main and central lakes, a large flaming crack was revealed between them and the group of spiracles which constituted the northeast wall cone opened low down on the pit side and ejected a rapid cascade which spread into a leaf-shaped flow on the northeast floor. The west arm cone now began throwing up liquid lava through its wide circular summit orifice and suddenly a dome of liquid spurted up through the ground beside it on the south and started a broad flow northwestward into the wall valley. This boiling source continued active for many hours. The southwest pond in a series of impulses of overflow finally poured over its ramparts in all directions, while the flaming cone southeast of it increased its violent spurting. The overflow settled down into a continuous broad flood of lava which united with the western flood and poured eastward through the south valley. The southeast wall vent revived and the southern of the southeast pond vents started to build a cone. This, the southwest and the north vents all threw spray over 50 feet. The main lake overflowed into the gaping crevasses of the southeast floor making a most spectacular display. The north central cone vent became quiet when the others burst into activity.

The north lake chasm was now a group of lumpy ramparts with the two cones as its active vents. The old north crag summit still stood above the flood but the west crag was gone.

On Friday, Dec. 13, it became evident that this spurt of the preceding day had initiated a very pronounced crisis of rising. At 3:30 p. m. the flooding was still in progress through the blowing noises were less strong. The remaining crags had risen, the floors had broadened in all directions and the only remnant of the uplifted November surface was in the region northwest of the main lake. The old south and old north crag remnants were submerged. The southeast pond district was a flat of glowing lava with a fountain in the midst. The flood had risen high around the base of the central crag, and the east ledge and north crag were only small islands in the flood.

The main lake and central pond were joined by a common flooding but the central steeple and its platform remained above them. The base of the northwest wall of the pit appeared to be the lowest place and the floods were spreading in that direction.

The west arm cone was a 7-foot dome with a glowing summit. A large double cone splashed through a gash on top where the northeastern shore of the southwest pond had been and another cone continued spurting south of it. At the north end of the north lake chasm an enormous cone 18 feet high had been built with an open triangular pot fountaining in its crest. Two other cones spurted farther north. The northeast wall cone showed a complex of spatter lumps containing a splashing pot which overflowed for a short time. The southeast wall cone had increased in size and stood on an elongate terrace of wall crack heapings at the top of some 20 feet of remaining talus. Most of the talus elsewhere was drowned. The outline of the main lake was defined by four spatter ramparts, one of which at the north collapsed and gave vent to a short festooned flow. The streaming in the lake was eastward. Fume was very thin, the smokiest place being at the north base of the central crag, and rock sliding had ceased. The night blow was very bright.

In the Whitney Laboratory for the week ending at 8 p. m., Dec. 13, 1918, the seismic events have been limited to a small local earthquake Dec. 10 at 2:56 p. m., and two teleseisms close together, the first a slight record at about 7:52 a. m., and the second a long one, beginning about 8:24 a. m. on Dec. 9. The origin would appear to be some 7300 kilometers away. Microtremor of the continuous sort increased after Dec. 11 and continued strong. Microseisms increased to Dec. 10-11 and decreased thereafter, always stronger in the north-south azimuth.

The clinograph registered an end of the westward tilting Dec. 7, slight eastward tilt to Dec. 9, very slight westward tendency to Dec. 11, and a resumption of east tilt Dec. 12-13. The daily range was strong until Dec. 7, slight Dec. 8-11, strong again after Dec. 12. As usual the more prolonged movements coincided with the rise and fall of the bench magma in Halemaumau.

HAWAIIAN VOLCANO OBSERVATORY, Dec. 21, 1918.—The week preceding the solstice at Halemaumau continued the rising spurt described last week until Dec. 14, followed by 3 days subsidence of the bench magma, the lake magma participating in this only on the first day and thereafter rising. On Dec. 20 both lake and crag were rising. Only one crag remains, the central one, as the peripheral lava floods have drowned the others. The bottom of the pit is now a continuous circular floor about 90 feet down, with the crag peak standing on it like an island 30 feet high, the three lakes east, southwest and north small pools occupying slight elevations, the eastern or main lake the largest and the other two acting as sources of many flows on the floor. The floor margin at the base of the walls has been filling extensively, with the filling compensated by subsidence below and probably by underflow toward the center, where the crag and east pool basin are lifted. The northeast fill is especially high while the western floor remains low.

The measurements for the week were as follows:

Dec. 13, depression central crag, 47 feet; depression lake, 99 feet.

Dec. 20, depression central crag, 55 feet; depression lake, 86 feet.

The net movement in seven days, therefore, was crag down 8 feet and lake up 13 feet. Other measurement showed that the north crag sank 6 feet and became submerged on the fourth day. The north lake floor and cones built up 33 feet during the week, and the southeast pond area 12 feet.

The rising and falling proceeded as follows: Dec. 13-14, 1 day, central crag went up 3 feet, north crag down 1 foot, lake up 2 feet; Dec. 15-19, 5 days, central crag down 13 feet, north crag down over 5 feet, lake up 11 feet, north lake floor up 21 feet; Dec. 19-20, 1 day, central crag up 2 feet, north crag submerged, lake stationary, north lake floor up 4 feet.

On Saturday, Dec. 14, 1918, at 5 p. m., rising and flooding continued with hissing, puffing and splashing noises and thin fume. The west cones were splashing, the southwest pond was sending a broad festoon flow northwestward. The freshest flows were west and south, but the building up elsewhere had nearly drowned the east ledge and left the north crag small. A large cone-shaped heap replaced the central pool, with a fountaining summit cap. The main lake was nearly circular and streaming from a narrow western cove to spatter ramparts north, northeast, east and south. The northeast wall-cone was half submerged and changed in shape, the eastern one built higher, and a new active one had given vent to flows under the south-southeast wall of the pit. The southeast pond was replaced by an inconspicuous spatter spot. A small remnant of the old south crag could still be detected. The main cone of the north lake was smaller and converted into an irregular group of cones.

At 3 p. m. Dec. 15 the filling and widening of the outer ring around the remnant of the lake margin uplift continued, so that the only trace of the weathered November surface was a small tumbled area northwest of the main lake. The southeast pond cone was slightly larger, the rampart grottoes of the main lake were building cavernous half-domes, the large central cone was still in place, there was fountaining at the southeast pond and north lake sites, and the east wall-cone was hissing and flaming slightly. A broad festooned flood continued to pour westward from the southwest pond, the main lake was brimming full to its banks and streaming eastward, new toes of live lava pushed out as flows from under crust in the south, west central and northwestern regions, and the northeast floor was a smoothly crusted extensive area showing the tracery of recent cracking and foundering of its crusts. The east ledge was now entirely submerged. The southwest pond in a spasm of rising overflowed its rampart eastward. Smoke rose from the central region and the north crag remnant and cracks had formed in the northeast floor parallel with the wall. The glow was bright at night and the general fume remained thin.

On Monday, Dec. 16, at noon, the flows lapped still higher up the walls of the pit and were bubbling up voluminously. A large dome fountain was spouting steadily on the south side of the north lake ones and sending a flood westward. The main lake overflowed its southern edge, the southeast pond was a bubbling spot, the southwest pond continued overflowing and large spatter heaps had built east of it. The central cone was now a roundish heap spouting on top, a hole spurted northwest of the north lake cones, little could be identified of the west arm cones, the streaming in the lake was eastward and an enclosed pot had formed on its southwest margin. The eastern wall cones appeared to be drowning themselves, the north crag was a very small remnant, the old south crag was wholly gone, and the last of the central floor crevasses of the November uplift was submerged. No talus blocks east were now visible. East and northeast the floor was smooth with cracks and founder pattern, the western fields were mostly pahoehoe trickle.

On Wednesday, Dec. 18, at 11 a. m., the marginal region appeared to be subsiding leaving the middle again in relief, fresher flows appearing all around the floor border, while the north central region showed a little cracking and gypsum stain. The east and northeast wall-cones were nearly submerged and the southeast wall-cone a fountaining puddle. The north crag was now wholly submerged. The southeast pond showed a glowing cone, the flows stood higher around the central crag, the central cone was gone, the north cones were inconspicuous and replaced by a flat crusted pool glowing on one side. The rim around the main lake stood 3 feet high, the streaming was eastward, and the southwest pond was an oval depressed three feet. A group of spatter heaps stood near the southwest pond. There were some moving flows northwest and northeast and some hissing, but the pit was much less active than before. Northeast and southeast there had been deep pooling, cracking, and foundering as before, the western region showing little of this. In the evening the pit was very dull.

On Dec. 19, 1918, at 1 p. m., the crisis of subsidence of the bench magma had been passed, it had perhaps begun to rise, there was some increase of smoke near the central crag and a notable increase of gas pressure and blowing noises. Flows had continued and a noon rise was in progress, flows pouring out southwest and west. The main lake was flush with its margin and had recently overflowed its lip northwest, and its streaming was towards big grotto domes on the north, southeast, and southwest. There were small ponds at the north and southwest lake sites, and the central cone had reformed. Flows were trickling in various places and the hissing from the east, southeast and southwest cones was loud enough to be

HALEMAUMAU FROM THE SOUTH, BEFORE AND AFTER NOVEMBER SINKING.
—Photos Jaggar.

(1) September 26, 1918: Lava column high, partly above rim of pit.

(2) December 6, 1918: Lava column low, recovering by liquid floods.
Note integrity of central crag mass, in spite of great subsidence.

heard a quarter mile away at the road terminus. The central steeple was now nearly gone. The eastern wall-crack cones had more or less reformed some distance out from the wall as the rising floods had widened the floor. The central cone was throwing up splashes and there was hissing from one of the main lake grotto domes.

On Friday, Dec. 20, at 3 p. m., the central region was lifting leaving the lakes depressed. The hissing was less and there was strong rumbling from the lake grottoes. The main lake margin was 2 to 3 feet high in shape an even oval, and there were high broad grotto domes on the east end where violent bombardment was going on. Streaming was radial from a central patch of skin, with strong inrush to southwest, to northeast and to southeast. There were occasional violent central fountains.

The southwest pond was an oval pit with the liquid lava five to ten feet below the rim, and the higher part of the verge on the east side showed deep overhang beneath and a grotto hung with stalactites where the liquid streamed eastward. Here a cone surmounted the edge, while from the opposite lower southwest edge a recent festooned overflow had poured. The west arm pond site was now a glow cone and another such flow had poured from it westward, these flows showing that the grade of this part of the floor was still to the west.

The north lake site showed a small fountaining area, a slumped crust and to the south of this a large breathing cone with glowing summit orifice. The active area showed a grotto with stalactites on the north side, the liquid within lying low. Recent flows from here had poured northwestward, and in some few places the front was pushing out live toes. The freshest flow was a large smooth area northeast and the northeast cone had revived and was spattering. The southeast pond cone and the east and southeast wall-cones were hissing a little. The central steeple was about gone and the floor about the central crag seemed to have lifted more than the crag making a ring depression about the latter. There were some fresh small rock falls along the south wall of the pit. Smoke holes had increased in number. There was some Pele's hair on the central floor and the central cone was inactive.

The week has been quiet seismically and the clinograph tilts first east, then west, then east again accorded with the rising, falling and resumed rising spells of the crags. Further experimental work in the Whitney laboratory has produced a first optical record of the vertical component seismograph, and a method of even, smooth smoking of the smoked paper sheets has been perfected.

HAWAIIAN VOLCANO OBSERVATORY, Dec. 28, 1918.—The week of the December solstice of 1918 was marked by a turning point from subsidence of the stiffer lava column or bench magma as represented by the central crag, for the crag summit reached its lowest of 57 feet below the southeast rim of the pit on Dec. 19. The lake of liquid lava, then 86 feet below the rim of the pit, rose 14 feet until Dec. 24 and thereafter became stationary. The crag rose 10 feet between Dec. 19 and 21, and for a week thereafter maintained an average level of 50 feet below the rim with day to day fluctuations of about 3 feet. The general condition of the floor of the pit, now about 65 feet down, has remained as last described a broad expanse with live flows filling the hollows, but two areas near the margins northeast and southwest have built up flat-topped slag heaps considerably above the general level of the pit floor. Latterly the vigor of flooding has decreased and smoke from solfataric areas has increased. The general tendency of the filling adjustments was to bring the levels of the floor margins to fair uniformity on Dec. 24 about 66 feet below the southeast station, but thereafter for three days, with average upbuilding of about 3 feet, the northeast slag heap pool built up 17 feet and the southwestern one 9 feet. This left the northeastern cone vent only 25 feet below the northeast rim of the pit, for the rim in that place is unusually low.

The measurements for the week were as follows:

Dec. 20, depression crag, 55 feet; lake, 86 feet; N. lake area, 79 feet.

Dec. 21, depression crag, 47 feet; lake,

80 feet; N. lake area, 79 feet; SW. pond, 76 feet.

Dec. 23, depression crag, 53 feet; lake, 74 feet.

Dec. 24, depression crag, 46 feet; lake, 72 feet; N. lake area, 70 feet; SW. pond, 69 feet.

Dec. 25, depression crag, 50 feet; lake, 72 feet.

Dec. 27, depression crag, 47 feet; lake, 74 feet; N. lake area, 64 feet; SW. pond, 67 feet.

The measurement for the seven days Dec. 21-27 indicates that the crag rose 8 feet, the lake 12 feet, the north lake area 5 feet, the southwest pond 9 feet, the northeast heap 20 feet and the southwest heap 19 feet. The net rise of the lava surface was thus about 12.15 feet or nearly like that of the lake, averaging 1.74 feet per day.

On Saturday, Dec. 21, 1918, at 4:30 p. m., activity of the spurting and flowing type with high gas pressure had been resumed, there was much puffing and hissing, while the fountains sprayed high at the east end of the lake and large dome grottoes had been built. At the north lake locality a big hissing dome stood, the east wall cones were flaming, the west floor cone ejected lava in spurts and at the base of the southwest wall of the pit a new pair of driblet cones was discovered. The central pond had reappeared, there was a fountaining vent south of the north cone and flows were moving everywhere on the floor surface with fronts alive and advancing.

About 5:30 p. m. a strong flow started to pour southward and westward from the northern fountaining vent and this was followed by heavy overflows northward and westward in pulsations from the central pond. The main lake surface showed eastward streaming.

On Dec. 22 flows continued to pour out, the northeast fill was developing a high flat plateau pool and the evening activity was dull.

On Monday, Dec. 23, at 4 p. m., the liquid flooding continued over the entire floor of Halemaumau, with the highest place apparently in the neighborhood of the southeast pond. It was becoming evident that the four lake centers of upwelling liquid east, north, southwest and in the middle of the pit were developing definite elevations with slopes away from the margins of the pools. The central crag was much more submerged, with a ring-shaped depression about its base. The surface streaming of the main lake was turbulent and mostly westward, but with some inrush to the southeast grotto. East and southwest of the lake there were somewhat raised lava pools with glowing edges and a recent flow had poured over the north lip of the lake. The northeast wall cone and a southwest pond vent were hissing strongly. The north lake heapings were steeper on their westward slope, the central pond had become a flat slag heap, the southwest pond occupied the top of a rampart ring with cones northeast of it, the west cone group was bulky and the southeastern cones were mere spatter spots. Lumpy irregularities in the floor extended from the north lake region northwestward.

From 10:30 a. m. until noon on Dec. 24 broad sheet flows were pouring out from the southwest pond and the west cone, while the high flat topped northeast pool, occupying the whole length of the former northeast valley, was putting out trickle flows around its margin. An area south of the main lake was tarnished with a mat of Pele's hair and appeared to be the surface most uplifted. The southwestern fill at the base of the wall was becoming high like the northeastern one so that there appeared to be a horseshoe of relatively high ground southwest, southeast and northeast.

The grotto domes of the main lake were less high, streaming was to the south and east and by noon the lake had sunk two feet within its basin. The eastern cones were hissing, the northeast vent had become a fountaining puddle source for the northeast pool, the solidified surface of which was now an elongate plateau falling off on all sides where trickle flows broke out along the edge, some of these being festooned streams. The surface of the pool was distinctly higher than the foot of the northeast wall of the pit and also stood above the level of the central floor.

The southern heaping of the north lake group had become a wide-angle cone and the northern one was a steeper driblet construction showing on its west side a hinged lid which opened in spasms along a glowing gash.

The west cone was half buried, acting as source for flows pouring east and west, while the southwest pond bubbled at the base of a high eastern rampart and poured out torrents which swept to the foot of the wall of the pit and flooded the whole length of the former south valley as well as the central region surrounding the base of the central crag. The annular depression around the latter was filled up and the floods were gaining on the crag though it had risen somewhat. The southeast pond region was a smooth flat with one inactive crack showing spatter markings.

On Wednesday, Dec. 25, 1918, at 2:30 p. m., the flat plateau of fill southwest and northeast had become very marked, while the center was stationary. The liquid had been building around the southeastern horseshoe of the floor margin and a perpetual fountain was pumping up through the wall cone southwest, building a large spatter heap and oven and spouting inward toward the center of the pit. Quite symmetrically opposed to this the northeast cone was spouting and building up the northeast flat. The west cone appeared to be flowing beneath a crust and at 4 p. m. the southwest pond began to renew overflow. The southeastern vents fed live flows which were cascading into the main lake over the south bank of the lake and at 4 p. m. the lake itself overflowed its northwest margin. Seen from the northwest rim of Halemaumau this arrangement exhibited right and left symmetry in the development of broad flat topped tabular crusted pools over the sites of the former southwestern and northeastern wall valleys, while an intermediate plateau formed the highest part of the floor towards the southeast. Between these slaggy up buildings, with the main lake near the top, the central floor sloped downward to the northwest along the axis of symmetry. The cones southwest, east and north were hissing, the last named very noisily. The lake streamed irregularly but mostly southward with such striking increase of bubble fountaining that twenty or more small centers of ebullition could be counted at one time in addition to the grotto splashing.

The leaf shaped crusted pool forming the flat top of the northeast plateau was now becoming a truly remarkable feature of the pit. It had the aspect of an elongate delta developed from the northeast cone vent as a source extending fully 600 feet towards the northwest with steeply sloping margins somewhat like the slag heap built from the dump of a smelter. The method of building was illustrated about 3:45 p. m. by a sudden cracking up of the heavy crusts of the pool near the spouting vent. The crust suspended and sank, the spatter cone collapsed, the melt welled up flooding adjacent crust and breaking it down, and thus the cracking and foundering spread across the entire tabular area. When this process reached the margin there was voluminous overflow sending festooned streams down the slope but lasting only a few minutes. The process evidently manifested the mechanism whereby the tabular crust was repeatedly reformed as the liquid swelled beneath it. A distinct valley was developing between this plateau and the northeastern wall of the pit. In the course of the next twenty-four hours the process led to diminution in size of the upper flat surface, indicating inward building of the margins and probably decreasing supply at the source.

Live toes and glow cracks were seen all over the floor of the pit. Smoke had very greatly increased around the crag and the central pond depression, and a new smoke hole had opened at the northwest margin of the floor. Glowing cavernous crusts lay east of the main lake. After 4 p. m. the continuous flow at the southwest wall cone became spasmodic but the southwest pond next overflowed and sent sheet floods southward.

On Dec. 26 the flooding gradually diminished and on Friday, Dec. 27, at noon, both bench and lake magma were comparatively stationary, smoke had increased and there was sharp hissing from the cones. A driblet cone 6 feet high had formed at the central depression and at 11:45 a. m., this began suddenly to roar and spit out lava and the noise become continuous. The lake was streaming to the west and north with some bubbling, the most violent bombardment being at an immense curtained grotto at its southwest end. The lake was now oval in form with thin blistering skins incessantly in motion, and its overhanging bank was about 3 feet high except during a slight noon rise. The southwest pond was crusted, quiet and 5 feet below its rim. The steeper north cone was split across its middle and glowed slightly. The smoke rose from the south and west sides of the crag, from the southeast pond site, from the west side of the lake, from the north heap and from the southwest pond.

The northeast pool vent was now two pots sluggishly heaving not more than 25 feet below the northeast edge of the pit. The flat upper surface of the pool was greatly raised and smaller, only about 200 feet long northwest-southeast, with driblet slopes away in all directions. Its plateau summit was oval.

A few flows trickled in the west central region but the intensive flooding had stopped. The floor was greatly heaped up along the base of the southwest wall of the pit all the way from the south station to the west station, and between this plateau and the northeastern one the triangular central region appeared low. In general there appeared to be a lull in the rising activity but the gas pressure continued strong.

For the fortnight ending at 8 p. m. Friday, Dec. 27, 1918, no local or distant earthquakes have been registered by the instruments of the Whitney Laboratory of Seismology. Spasms of tremor occurred as follows: Two spasms near 5 a. m., Dec. 15; others at 11:04 p. m. Dec. 16, after 1 p. m. Dec. 18, after 10 a. m. Dec. 20, and in the early morning of Dec. 23. Microseisms were moderate with temporary fluctuations until Dec. 23, when they became strong, as usual most so in the north-south azimuth, the waves decreasing to moderate after Dec. 25. Rhythmic microtremor was moderate Dec. 13-18, less Dec. 18-20, moderate with spasmodic fluctuation Dec. 20-25,, slight Dec. 25-26, strong Dec. 26-27 followed by decrease.

The movements of tilting were east and north Dec. 14-18, west and south Dec. 19-20, strong east and excessive north Dec. 21-24, and stationary with tendency southward Dec. 2527.

HAWAIIAN VOLCANO OBSERVATORY, Jan. 4, 1919.—During the New Year week ending Jan. 3, 1919, the central crag and lava lakes have subsided, the strongest downward movement beginning on Jan. 1. For the main lake the subsidence amounted to 6 feet per day after Jan. 1, though the average for the week was much less. The floor margin vents northeast and southwest have continued upward building by overflow so that the heaping of flow lava has greatly raised the floor level on these two sides, leaving the middle floor from the main lake to the northwest wall of the pit 20 to 30 feet lower. The flows from these marginal cracks dwindled during the week but there was revival of them at the southwest vent on Jan. 3. The general sequence of events since the solstice suggests that the main lava column reached its highest during the solstice week and that the release of pressure occasioned by the beginning of its subsidence generated liquid lava through the agency of gas effervescence. This liquid lava has bubbled up the wall crack and constructed slag heaps at the margins of the floor even while the central part of the lava column was sinking. The end of the week finds the pit showing all the signs of downward progress, spouting cones replaced by open inner pits containing pools of lava, great increase of smoke and sulphate stains at cracked areas, slumping of crusts recently swollen with foaming lava and slight falls of rock debris from the walls of the pit. The general floor level is about 60 feet below the rim and the liquid lakes are 20 feet lower.

Measurements for the week were as follows:

Dec. 27, depression crag, 47 feet; lake, 74 feet; NE. edge of floor, 50 feet; NW. edge of floor, 66 feet.

Jan. 3, depression crag, 52 feet; lake, 87 feet; NE. edge of floor, 36 feet; NW. edge of floor, 56 feet.

The central crag has thus subsided 5 feet in seven days, averaging .7 feet per day; the lake 13 feet, averaging 1.9 feet per day. The central floor near the lake has been slightly built up by overflow, elsewhere it is slightly lower. The floor margin northeast has been built up 14 feet, averaging 2 feet per day, and on the northwest it has been built up 10 feet, averaging 1.4 feet per day. It thus appears that the main lake sank during the week by about the same vertical amount that the marginal vents have increased their heapings.

These measurements make a striking demonstration of the thermal complexity of the upper part of a lava column and show conclusively that we have to deal with no such simple relationships as those of a floating crust on a liquid substratum. In the short period of a week a projecting peak of bench magma sinks 5 feet. The liquid in a well beside it sinks 13 feet. The liquid spurting up wall cracks at the periphery of the lava column, with maximum temperature and pressure, builds up extensive flooded heapings 14 feet. The summit of these heapings was continuously flooding at a level over 50 feet above the liquid in the well, not 600 feet distant, and both enclosed in the same pit. There is no slightest question in this limited cylinder of all being parts of the same paste and it is perfectly evident that the marginal spurtings are not in hydrostatic equilibrium with the well lava. The whole system becomes explicable, only by recognizing that the reaction heat of escaping gases from solution in a stiff glassy magma below melts out vertical channels threading the paste wherever pressure is least. In the present case the pressure is least along the wall crack because the central pencil of lava is drawing downward and the marginal portions are sucking inward. The seeming paradox of subsidence inducing lava flows thus becomes quite intelligible and it is probable that the most violent manifestations of so-called ''volcanic eruptions'' are really produced by the beginnings of subsidence.

On Saturday, Dec. 28, 1918, at 7 p. m., there was strong increase of smoke and the lakes were depressed within their cups and flaring open pots had developed at the north lake heap, the central pond cone and the southeast pond crack. Northeast and southwest high glowing slag heaps were conspicuous while the wall cones east and southwest hissed continuously. The flaring of open ponds could be seen southwest and west. Small driblet flows pushed ahead steadily at the east end of the northeast slag heap and the north end of the southwestern heap. Flames were abundant, especially at the north and central pots. The northeast cone was sputtering and the eastern one flamed through a filagree orifice. The southern and central floors were dark. Streaming in the main lake was northward across its eastern half, southward in its western half, the currents dragging thin skins to the grottoes which emitted the deep rumble of interior fountains. There was a heavy stalactite curtain across the southwest grotto. The development of open pots by collapse was a new feature indicating a turning-point towards subsidence.

On Dec. 29 the pit was smoky and the glow moderate at night, showing some flaring from the north lake. In the evening the flaming had greatly diminished and the activity was dull.

On Dec. 30, at 3:30 p. m., the southeast pond showed an opening 15 feet across leading down to a much larger chamber with overhang all around and liquid lava 10 feet below the orifice, streaming westward to a fountaining cavern. The main lake was nearly brimming, surface streaming was first west, then east and afterwards there was slight sinking. A conical heap had developed between the northeast grotto of the main lake and the north lake locality. The north cone exhibited a continnous small jet of lava, the east and southwest cones were hissing mildly, smoke was abundant, concealing the south and southwest regions, there was some slight further encroachment of lava around the base of the central crag and fountains were splashing on the east side of the southwest pond. The northeast cone stood high at the summit of a slag heap close to the northeast wall and was flinging up a little lava spatter. The high western slag heap built against the wall now extended well around from the southwest to the northwest margin of the floor. Glow at night was dim and the smoke showed considerable fluctuation in amount.

On the evening of Tuesday, Dec. 31, flows continued to pour from the northeast vent and there was slight overflows from the main lake.

On Jan. 1, 1919, during the hour following noon the lava column appeared stationary, the lakes low, solfataric stains had developed at the vents and there was much Pele's hair to leeward of the lakes. The southeast pond pit was enlarged, the surface of the liquid 15 feet down and the streaming continued westward. The main lake margins were 10 feet high and the surface was stagnant. Open pits had developed at the north and west ponds and the southwest pond continued open. The central cone was still in place with a pot beside it and the crag peak appeared unchanged. A conical heap of crust with a depression beside it occupied the middle of the south floor. There was much smoke in the central and southwestern regions. A slightly sunken glowing pool had developed in the summit of the northeast slag heap and there was glow visible at the east end of the heap. The western heap was higher with smooth upper surface and the region extending northeastward from the main lake was now a valley between these two heaps.

On Jan. 2 at 6 p. m. the inner pit of the main lake was so deep above the liquid that the latter was barely visible from the southeast rim of the pit. The liquid was fully 20 feet below the floor level and the southeast pond appeared 30 feet below the rim of its pit. Heavy stalactites hung about both pools. The north lake now occupied a large pit covering the area of the former group of cones and made a bright flare at night. The central cone had a glowing pot beside it and the southwest pond was in an enlarged pit. There was some glow at the northeast cone and east of it. Fume had increased, general appearance indicated sinking and a small earthquake was felt at noon.

On Friday, Jan. 3, 1919, at 11 a. m., the south and southeast floors showed slumped crusts as though the inflating lava had poured out from beneath. These flows when last active had almost completely buried the southwest pinnacle of the central crag, though the summit peak of the crag still stood about 18 feet above the floor level at its base. There were fresh rock falls on the edge of the floor south, southsoutheast and north, and at 12:15 p. m. a pronounced avalanche fell from under the north station. There was much smoke from the ponds, from the north side of the crag and at the east cone locality. The southeast wall vent now a glowing crack with solfataric stain was hissing slightly. The lakes rose somewhat towards noon, the main lake standing 15 feet below the edge of its pit and the southeast pond 20 feet. The central cone was now replaced by a large glowing pot sending up a dense column of smoke. The floor sagged inward toward the southwest pond pit. Noises of surging, rumbling and splashing came from beneath the heavy stalactite curtains which hung around the orifice of the southeast pond pit and across the grotto entrances of the main lake. The streaming was eastward in the southeast pond and the main lake was covered with stagnant skin. The northeastern heap was now piled conically without flat top against the wall of the pit and was surrounded by two cones. Its summit stood only 15 feet below the low northeastern edge of the pit.

The southeast cone vent close to the wall of the pit had revived and two live flows poured north and south from it. The north lake had become an oval fountaining pool over 100 feet long in the north-south direction and the liquid streamed northward beneath walls only 5 feet high. There was continuous bubbling on the north side of this lake.

For the week ending at 8 p. m. Friday, June 3, 1919, there has been registered on the seismographs of the Whitney Laboratory a teleseism of considerable intensity at 4:40 p. m. Dec. 31, 1918, with center believed to be 4350 kilometers distant, possibly Fiji or Alaska. A weakly felt local quake occurred at 12:14 p. m. Jan. 2, the first for some weeks past. Microseisms were stronger about Dec. 30-31. Microtremor has been ordinary. The tilting was west and south Dec. 28-27, east and north Dec. 29-Jan. 1, west and south Jan. 2-3 and thereafter.

Very respectfully,

T. A. JAGGAR, JR.,
Director.

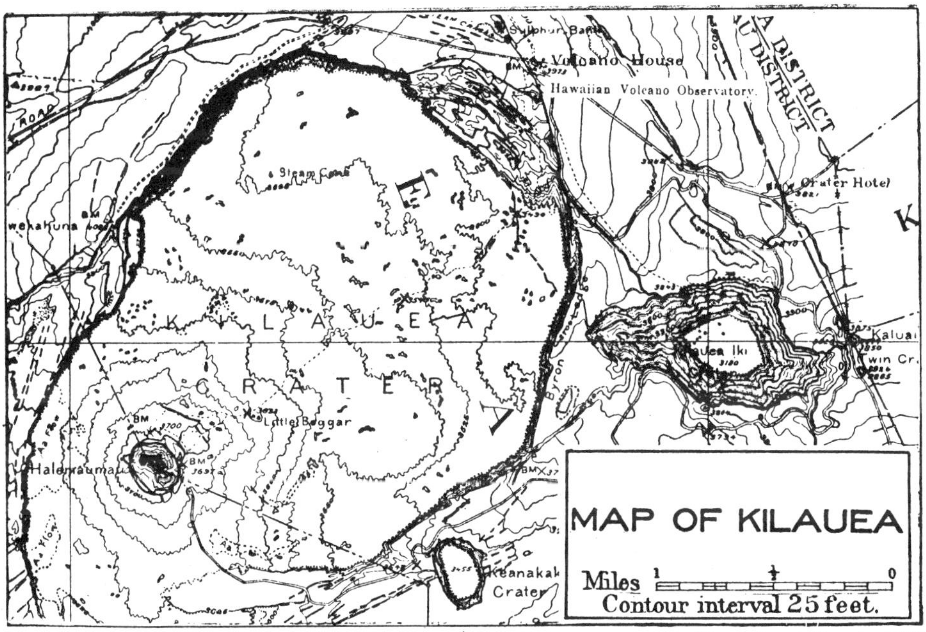

MAP OF KILAUEA

HAWAIIAN VOLCANO RESEARCH ASSOCIATION.

This society is a voluntary one, made up of subscribers to scientific work which is being executed by Dr. T. A. Jaggar, Director of the Hawaiian Volcano Observatory, Volcano House, P. O., Hawaii. **All scientific exchanges should be sent to this address.**

In 1918 there were about 150 subscribers in Hawaii and elsewhere, firms and individuals. A group of firms and persons in Hilo built the main observatory building in the spring of 1912. The work was founded by the Massachusetts Institute of Technology. Publications to date have been weekly bulletins since the summer of 1911 now reprinted in Honolulu in monthly form. There are also special reports, printed from time to time.

The monthly bulletin is sent to regular annual subscribers to the work of the Association. L. A. Thurston is president of the Board of Directors of the Association, and L. T. Peck is treasurer. New subscribers who are interested in volcanoes will be welcomed in the Association. The Association aims: (1) To record volcanic activity and earthquakes in Hawaii; (2) to attract scientific men hither for special studies; (3) to promote the establishment of volcano observatories all over the world. The annual dues of regular members are $5; patrons of the Association subscribe larger amounts.

WHITNEY LABORATORY OF SEISMOLOGY.

The Whitney Laboratory of Seismology, named after an endowment fund for geophysical research held by the Massachusetts Institute of Technology, in memory of Caroline and Edward Whitney of Boston, is equipped with the following seismometric instruments rebuilt at the station in 1918 for the special needs of volcano research: two Bosch-Omori pendulums, high speed registration of local earthquakes; one optically recording seismograph for distant earthquakes; one clinograph registering E-W tilting of the ground. A vertical component seismograph was in December, 1918, set up in experimental operation. These are seated on concrete piers in a closed basement room having practically constant temperature, beneath the chief Observatory building near the hotel. Time is referred to a rated chronometer, checked at intervals by solar observations with a transit. Both instruments are loaned by the College of Hawaii. Hawaiian standard time (H. S. T.) is 10 hrs. 30 min. slower than Greenwich time.

CANCANI SCALE OF SEISMIC INTENSITY.

Expressed by accelerations measured in millimeters per second per second.

I.	Instrumental	0.0	2.5
II.	Very slight	2.5	5.0
III.	Slight	5.0	10.0
IV.	Sensible, mediocre	10.0	25.0
V.	Rather strong	25.0	50.0
VI.	Strong	50.0	100.0
VII.	Very strong	100.0	250.0
VIII.	Ruinous	250.0	500.0
IX.	Disastrous	500.0	1000.0
X.	Very disastrous	1000.0	2500.0
XI.	Catastrophic	2500.0	5000.0
XII.	Great catastrophe	5000.0	10000.0

Grade IV. is ordinarily the minimum perceived by the senses; and in grade XII. the acceleration, or rate of change of motion (jerk) reaches that of terrestrial gravitation.

In the standard form of report the maximum intensity or acceleration, designated by the symbol a, or max. a, is given in the conventional unit, the milligal. The milligal is a measure of acceleration, such that 1 milligal = 1/100 mm. per sec. per sec. = 10 μ per sec. per sec. The Cancani scale, here defined in terms of millimeters per sec. per sec., can therefore be expressed in milligals by multiplying each of the numbers by 100.

WEEKLY BULLETIN
OF THE
Hawaiian Volcano Observatory

Vol. VII. HONOLULU, HAWAII, JANUARY, 1919 No. 1

January 11, 1919.

The subsidence of the Halemaumau lava column reported last week, compensated by extensive flooding from cones at the base of the northeast and southwest walls, has in general continued during the week ending Jan. 10, but the liquid flooding has increased in volume so that the local upbuilding, confined last week to the two margins mentioned, has extended to the regions adjacent to the eastern and northern pools. The measurements indicate that positive subsidence continued to January 6 inclusive, during the next two days there was definite rising and thereafter the average surface level of the column remained stationary, though the building by liquid flows was voluminous. This condition appears to be that of slowly subsiding bench magma compensated by layers or veneers of lava flow.

The measurements of the week were as follows:

Jan. 3, depression of lake 87 feet, of crag summit 52 feet.

Jan. 5, depression of lake 90 feet, of crag summit 53 feet.

Jan. 11, depression of lake 61 feet, of crag summit 47 feet.

For the two days Jan. 3-5 the lake thus subsided 3 feet, or 1.5 feet per day, and the crag 1 foot, or .5 foot per day. For the six days Jan. 5-11 the lake rose 29 feet, or 4.9 feet per day, and the crag 6 feet, or 1 foot per day. Other measurements showed that the summit of the northeast slag heap and the edge of the southwest pond pit were both lower on Jan. 11 than on Jan. 4.

On Saturday, Jan. 4, 1919, at 11:15 a. m. the pit was smoky, there had been general subsidence since the previous day and the main and southeast lakes were both surging cauldrons with the liquid depressed 15 feet within their respective wells. The southwest heap against the wall of Halemaumau was built up high by overflow, and cascades from it had poured into the southwest pond pit. The central pot was glowing. The north lake was throwing up flings of heavy melt. Great volumes of smoke rose from the west cone, the central pot, the central crag, the west ends of the main and north lakes, the southeast pond, cracks east of the main lake, and from the east cone. More rocks had fallen from the cliff to the south and north edges of the floor.

On Jan. 5 at 3:30 p. m. the pit continued smoky and the lakes low. The floor under the southeast wall appeared lower but the slag heaps northeast and southwest remained high. There was considerable increase of collapse about the lakes. Streaming in the north lake was northward and in the main lake southward. A large cavern extended from the latter westward toward the central pond pot and that pot was glowing and fuming. An inactive pit, oval in outline, had developed by collapse in the summit of the northeast heap. The main and southeast ponds stood 20 feet below their rims and the north lake 12 feet.

On Jan. 6 this low and smoky condition continued and at 5 p. m. the fume rising from the pit was excessively dense. About 5 a. m. the nert morning, Jan. 7, however, there was very strong flaring seen above the main lake and the roar of the fountains could be heard at the Observatory two miles away in calm air. At 11 a. m. the fume had thinned remarkably and both inspection and measurement showed that a sudden rise was in progress, taking effect most vehemently in the liquid

of the
Hawaiian Volcano Observatory

Published Monthly at Honolulu, Hawaii, by the Hawaiian Volcano Research Association

L. W. de Vis-Norton........Secretary

Entered as second-class matter January 20, 1914, at the post-office at Honolulu, Hawaii, under the Act of August 24, 1912.

lava of the lakes and cones. The lakes had risen close to brimming, the main lake had recently overflowed, there were seven or eight large fountaining spots and the southeast pond was enlarged, the liquid standing within three feet of a newly built up rampart rim. The main and north lakes also showed new spatter ramparts three to five feet high. In curious contrast to these the southwest and west ponds remained in deeper pits, their liquid surfaces fountaining beneath cliffs 10 or 15 feet high. The heap at the base of the southwest wall had completely revived its activity, showed a hot flat top of recent cracking and foundering, the crust surfaces crackling and snapping, while fresh glowing lobes with collapsed crusts extended from the heap northward. Down its eastern slope a powerful flow poured rapidly and cascaded into the west pond pit. The north lake was fountaining continuously against the south side of its center and elsewhere was covered with skin. The tendency of its streaming was northward. In the main lake the streaming was eastward in a curve toward heavy bombardment at the northeast grotto and occasional central fountains broke into action. In the southeast pond the bombardment was against the west shore and in the southwest pond against the north shore. The northeast heap remained inactive. Dense smoke clouds still rose from the north side of the central crag and there was much smoke about the southwest pond.

On Wednesday, Jan. 8, 1919, at 6 p. m. the revival of liquid lava flooding continued and the northeast heap was again in action, with its summit pit obliterated, and the northeast cone spouting and flowing. Toes were pushing out at the eastern end of the heap. The main and north lakes were brimming full and fountaining, with occasional slight sinking spells. The southeast pond, squarish in outline and about 40 feet in diameter, was full close to the edge. On the north side of the main lake a rifted grotto dome was being violently bombarded, the streaming surface skins of the lake moving toward the grotto from the west end. The north lake occasionally flung up very high strings of melt at eastern and southern grottoes. The pot in the center of the pit was glowing and splashing, the east cone was hissing and there were large fields of fresh crusted glowing lava in the eastern, southern, western and central areas, the product of spectacular flows of the previous night. No special activity was noticed in the southwest or west ponds. The western slope of the northeast heap had not been flooded by the revival. The fume from the pit as seen from a distance diminished so greatly as to be at times almost imperceptible.

During the next two days, Jan. 9 and 10, the northeast heap produced more narrow trickle flows without any increase of height. There was overflow from the eastern and northern pools and the western heap continued to put out flows. All of this tended to even up the level of the central depression so as to lessen the relief of the two slag heaps. The end of the week finds the general surface still surrounded by cliffs over 60 feet high except northeast and southwest.

The seismographs of the Whitney Laboratory for the week ending at 8 p. m., Jan. 10, 1919, have registered no teleseisms. Local earthquakes were registered as follows: 9:15 p. m. Jan. 5, perceptible; feeble shocks 9:03 p. m. Jan. 8, and about 9:45 a. m. and 6:07 p. m. Jan. 9. Microseismic motion dwindled from moderate to small amplitude during the week. Microtremor of the rhythmic type was ordinary Jan. 3-6, strongly increased in the night of Jan. 6-7, remained strong with some decrease night of Jan. 7-8, showed very rapid vibrations superposed on the rhythmic ones in the morning of Jan. 8 and occasionally thereafter, and decreased slightly Jan. 9-10. Tilting was to the west and south until the evening of Jan. 6, suddenly strong east and north on that night, this northeast tilt was continued Jan. 7-8, and after Jan. 8 the median line of the clinograph remained stationary, with diurnal fluctuations as usual. These diurnal movements of tilting appear to be southeast-northwest, and very definitely with the daily temperature range out-of-doors, but the longer term tiltings northeast-southwest accord with the lava rise and fall and depart from the longer term thermograph showings.

January 18, 1919.

The end of the week Jan. 10-17, 1919, shows a very pronounced rise of lava in progress with every prospect of overflow of the rim of the pit within a short time if the present flooding continues. (Note: Since this was written, at 8:30 a. m. Jan. 19, the lava overflowed the southwestern lip of Halemaumau.) This movement differs from the January risings of 1917 and 1918 in that the hard lava crags have disappeared, buried under layer on layer of liquid inner flows and the volume of upwelling liquid lava continually increases so that the floor of Halemaumau has become a gleaming slag heap with fountains on its crest which change position from day to day. At present the summit of the heap is toward the southwest and the recent floodings have come from three principal western vents, in locations almost identical with the feeding conduits of 1916 and 1917. The floor in general is now only 30 feet down and locally only 15 feet and easily accessible.

The confirmation of expectations based on a working theory of relationship between Mauna Loa and Kilauea which the writer has from time to time expressed and published, is very striking. The lava column is believed to be a stiff subterranean body, squeezed upward by terrestrial stresses through the ages, and charged with heating gases which effervesce and react most violently when the upward squeeze is relieved. Such effervescence generates liquid lava. The vents of Mauna Loa and Kilauea are believed to alternate in their action, 1903-07 producing Mauna Loa flow, 1908-12 intense Kilauea activity, 1914-16 Mauna Loa flow and now 1917-19 Kilauea overflow. Each eruption begins with the rise of the stiffer internal lava column and culminates with release of pressure and effervescence of liquid lava. Halemaumau in 1911 had craggy islands, in 1912 many hundreds of boiling fountains, so now in 1917-18 it had an upper surface of rocky crags, in 1919 it is developing great floods of liquid, and this year stands midway in the nine year interval between the 1914 outbreak of Mauna Loa and the next expectable Mauna Loa eruption.

The measurements of the week have been as follows:

Depression Below Southeast Section

	Main Lake...	N. Lake...	S.W. Pond...	Central Crag....	S.W. Edge Floor....	N.W. Edge Floor...
Jan. 11 ..	61	57	49	47	44	59 ft.
Jan. 16 ..	34	38	30	29	20	47 ft.

These figures show that the main lake has risen 27 feet in five days, or 5.4 feet per day, and the central crag 18 feet, or 3.6 feet per day. The spurt of most rapid rising was after Jan. 15.

On Saturday, Jan. 11, at 4:30 p. m. the flooding of the entire floor continued, the northwest portion remaining relatively low. The northeast cone showed a flaming and hissing vent in the top of a steep sided pyramid five feet high which surmounted a heap of radial flows of snaky and lumpy character. The pit formerly at the top of the heap had disappeared. The western heap showed increased height and was covered everywhere with glowing flows not conspicuously in motion. The flows had encroached upon the base of the central crag so that the latter was becoming a small inconspicuous object.

The main lake streamed continuously westward within a rim three feet high, above which huge spatter heaps made a lumpy rampart. A heavy sheet flow with slightly festooned surface had recently poured southward from the lake. The grotto and fountaining activity were moderate. The southeast pond had become a raised cone, with a large irregular cauldron full of liquid lava boiling visibly and all around were fresh glowing flows. The east cone was a small hissing filagree heap. The southwest and west ponds had now become pits and showed no special activity. The central pot glowed through cracks on its western rim and west of it live flows were in motion. The north lake threw up continuous fountains rather noiselessly against its southern and eastern banks and its ramparts were low, showing signs of extensive overflow northward. Smooth glowing flow surfaces extended along the base of the wall under the north station. The general situation revealed recurrence of strong lava flooding, but measurement made the northeast heap and the edge of the southwest pond lower than a week before.

On Monday, Jan. 13, in the evening, the spouting of the western wall cone and the line of its glowing flows could be plainly seen from the Observatory. In the daytime the southwest edge of the floor was discernible with field glasses. After midnight, with a western moon, the trail of thin Mokuaweoweo fume could be seen extending northeastward from the summit of Mauna Loa.

On Jan. 14 at noon the western wall vent was ejecting a steady spouting fountain and the building up of the heap on either side of it had become the most conspicuous feature of the pit. The northeast accumulation no longer appeared heaped up, the flows there were now irregular and lumpy and two large cones had formed. Fresh falls of wall rock near them indicated distinct subsidence of the northeast floor. The east cone, as before, was a hissing filagree heap, the southeast pond was surrounded by dull glowing cones and much Pele's hair, the main lake rim was five feet high, exhibited five grotto domes with large and vigorous fountains and northward streaming. The north lake was splashing and the southwest pond had built a high spire above its eastern rim. The west pond was indistinct in the midst of flows of the southwest heap. The central pot had become an indistinct cone, the crag was still more submerged and the smoke had increased, but remained thin above the pit as a whole.

At 8 p. m. on Jan. 15 a cone west of the north lake was spurting in high jets plainly visible from the Observatory, flows in motion could be seen at the north end of the west heap, and the splashing of the lake grottoes was also visible from a distance. The west wall cone had crusted over but the flows continued.

On Jan. 16 at 4:30 p. m. it was evident that a new fill had built a horseshoe shaped heap west, south and east, following the floor margin, with distinct fall-off to lower ground at the ends of the horseshoe northeast and northwest. At 4:45 p. m. very voluminous overflow poured from the east end of the main lake, followed by a hot welling-up and overflowing of the southeast pond, both torrents pouring to the foot of the east wall and pooling as far as the east shelter northward. Here the pool formed a flat platform and its edge sloped downward to a much lower surface at least 10 or 15 feet below, the former northeast cone being obliterated at about the place of falling off. Before the southeast pond overflowed, the ground southeast of it was seen to be greatly fissured and gaping cracks had opened along the wall. All of these were filled by the overflow.

The north lake showed a fresh glowing overflow across its northern lip. The west wall cone started a fresh flow which poured northward down the steepest face of the western heap. The cone itself was quiet, the flood pouring from a bright zigzag edge of crust. It was interesting to observe that this cone stood just where the former western wall ponds and cones had developed repeatedly, a short distance to the south of the west station.

New cones had formed, one just under the south cone heap on the Halemaumau edge and two on the floor southwest of the north lake, one of these a steep spire built by the spurting of the previous night. The west pond cone was a glowing heap, hissing and occasionally spurting. The central cone contained a large pot flaming. The east cone was flaming and spouting through the liquid lava around it. The southwest pond was crusted and mostly level with its banks, the large cone south of it glowing. The northern cones puffed somewhat.

The north and main lakes showed high grotto domes with quiet fountains puffing and spraying within them, showing high gas pressure without rumbling. At night the fountains were plainly visible from the Observatory.

The central crag summit peaks now protruded only about four or five feet above the general level of the flows. The slope of the floor was strongly northeastward from the high southwest heapings to the center of the pit and from there the grade was toward the northwest, the lowest portion of the floor lying at the base of the northwest wall. The smoke on this day was strongly variable, being thin in the morning, thicker at noon and thin again at 5 p. m.

On Friday, Jan. 17, 1919, there was revival of strong flooding from a perpetual fountain at the west pond vent about noon, plainly visible from the Observatory. This source became a standing fountain 20 feet wide backed by a crust on the south, the flood spreading from it fan-wise and then settling into a rapid river of melt pouring northward to make a fill in the northwestern part of the floor. Another flow from 2 to 4 p. m. was observed pouring steadily from the west wall cone, part flowing to the north and part to the south, the cone region itself being crusted over. The flow lava appeared under the west station as a north flowing stream and under the south station as a pool. Floor east and southwest and possibly in the center of the pit had slumped considerably. The northeast cone had resumed activity, filling the north-northeast depression and making again a northeastern heap.

The southwest pond was obscured by crust but it was marked by a high puffing and glowing cone. The main lake about five feet down its pit was surrounded by a raised rampart with high domes northeast, southwest and east, the southwestern one being closed on the lake side but open and glowing with a slit-like aperture on top. The north lake had a similar five-foot rim and raised rampart, a glowing cavernous grotto dome stood on its north bank, a group of large domes had been built east of it, while off to the southwest of the north lake and away from it on the floor stood two or three domes, one of them a spire.

At the central pond locality stood an irregular cone. The central crag remnant remained as before. At the eastern edge of the great flow there was much upending of glowing crusts. North of the west cone occasional increases in the flow pressure would burst the crust and make outflows through the cracks.

The seismographs have shown much microtremor during the intense flowing, the tilt has been first east, then west, then east again, and there have been a few small local earthquake movements, to be reported more fully later.

January 25, 1919.

During the week ending Friday, Jan. 24, 1919, it has become evident that the midwinter rise of lava in Halemaumau is to be powerful and to produce overflowing, this being the third time within a twelve-month that the liquid floods have crossed the rim of the pit. This time it is to the southwest, whereas before it was to the southeast and north. The three overflow localities have been opposite the three persistent lakes and at the places where there were open gateways for so many months between the three great crag masses.

During the past week there has been resumption of tumescence of the bench magma or central floor of the pit followed by excessive building up of the western lava heap until the latter surmounts the old rim for a quarter of the circumference and is sending sluggish flows out to the Kilauea floor as well as eastward and northward into the pit proper. The building up of the northeast and southwest heaps by overflow veneers has amounted to about as much vertically as the swelling of the bench magma beneath, so that the northeast and southwest heaps have gained elevation twice as much as the rest of the floor.

The measurements of the week expressed as depression in feet below the southeast station, except where otherwise indicated, have been as follows:

	Main Lake	Crag	N.E. Heap	S.W. Heap	
Jan. 16 ...	34	29	25	20	above rim
Jan. 18 ...	31	30	32	15	" "
Jan. 25 ...	22	13	6	14	" "

The main lake of liquid lava thus thus rose 12 feet in nine days, averaging 1.3 feet per day; the crag rose 16 feet, or 1.8 feet per day; the northeast heap rose 19 feet, or 2.1 feet per day; the southwest heap rose 34 feet, or 3.8 feet per day. As the crag and northeast heap both showed subsidence until Jan. 18, it is evident that the strongest tumescence and outflow took place after that date.

On Saturday, Jan. 18, after a night of recurrent strong fountaining at the west pond locality (now a cone high on the flank of the west heap), the entire floor of the pit appeared higher and in full view from Volcano House. At 4:30 p. m. it was evident that upward swelling was in progress under the center of the pit, and a drawing down of the crust around the edges. The flows under north station and under the east-southwest wall of the pit appeared slumped and sunken and fresh fallen stones lay on the floor at the last named locality. There was slumping also along the base of the northwest wall. In the middle region, however, and towards the south swelling and cracking could be detected. In the wall crack south lava had welled up to build a spire.

The main lake had four-foot walls, very large marginal heaps, especially at the southwest grotto, and was streaming eastward. The southeast pond cone was large with an open splashing pot. The north lake was overflowing northward and had built a high western grotto dome. The southwest pond cone was invaded by flows from the western heap which at 2 p. m. had been piling against it great slabs of crust. This was seen through the Observatory telescope. The cone maintained, however, an open splashing pot like the west pond cone farther west. The northeastern heap was higher and making flows about its edges and the cone on its summit had reformed.

The growth of the western heap was the feature most remarkable. The west wall cone was now buried under its own flows which had heaped up to make a flat plateau 400 feet long formed by the banking in of the steep marginal floods as they solidified east, northeast and north. The flat top consisted of live glowing lava streaming steadily and smoothly from a V-shaped bright line eastward. This pool stood only a foot below the southwestern rim of Halemaumau, and the indications of tumescence added to liquid rising all showed that overflow was imminent.

During the night following, the marginal driblet cone south made many brilliant flows and its heap had risen to within 15 feet of the rim of the pit the next day. This brought to a close the period of large standing fountains as feeders for the flows and on the western heap the flows moved more sluggishly.

On Jan. 19 a visit to the pit at 8:45 a. m. showed the southwest rim in process of overflowing, one tongue of lava from the western heap now extending 55 feet across the rim, headed in the direction of the 1868 cracks. Another live stream was pouring northward from the heap, flows were moving on the northeast heap, the lakes were fountaining within large dome grottoes as before and flows from the south wall cone were in motion. The lakes were brimming full and the west and southwest pond cones were splashing. The other cones were hissing and flaming. About 1 p. m. the cones had become more quiet and the flows had ceased moving. There was some slight hissing and the lakes had subsided about five feet. The longest lobe of the southwest overflow had progressed about 75 feet from the rim of the pit.

About 3:30 p. m. the northeast heap cracked up suddenly and the crusts foundered in rapid succession, making a spectacular flood for a few minutes. Just before this the north lake overflowed and the cone west of it sent out a steady flow for two hours. The main lake rose and the southeast pond overflowed slightly through an oven-like aperture, pouring into a cup in the crust east of it. The western heap renewed its northward flows and some driblet flows pushed southward.

December 13, 1918. The last of the triang

Dec. 25, 1918. The flat-topped northeast lava heap within the pit, replacing the former "wall-valley fill."

of crag masses before complete submergence.

Dec. 25, 1918. From east brink of Halemaumau; lake and submerged crag.

The evidence of central tumescence and wall crack subsidence was now strong, dense smoke rising from the cracked floor southeast, and greenish yellow sublimates lining large cracks in the center of the pit and around the main lake. The crusts of fresh flows at the base of the southeast wall had drawn away and downward, leaving on the wall the black scar of their higher position.

During the night Jan. 19-20 the pit was much less luminous and flows were inconspicuous. At 6 p. m. on Jan. 20 a new spiracle was hissing at the southeast wall cone locality and slow flows pushed out at the southwest overflow, the front being now horizontally 300 feet from the rim of the pit. The surface of the western heap stood five feet above the rim and the pool on top showed collapsed crusts and glowing edges. Lifting was in progress and high pressure was shown everywhere. The lakes were full; ten fountains splashed around the margins of the north lake and three large ones in the main lake. The northeast heap was again building up, its surface swelling and putting out marginal flows. There was great heat and pressure in the eastern cones and the cracks were opening wider.

On Tuesday, Jan. 21, at 6 p. m. the same processes continued, cherry red glow showed in the floor cracks and all the cones were flaming chimneys. There was much whitish stain beside the cracks. Immense dome grottoes had been built beside the lakes which stood four feet below their margins. The southwest overflow had become more extensive and leaf-shaped in plan, the lava being of the elephant toe variety, with lobes two to three feet thick, consisting of hollow shells which collapse on top. This characteristic made the flows on the slopes of the heap slump and leave glowing caverns. The summit of the heap cracked up and revealed a pool for a few minutes.

The northeast heap had risen so rapidly that the fill of 1918 was largely overflowed and after 6 p. m. this flood was cascading into the hot caverns under the northeast outer wall, making a most spectacular display as the melt poured from under its crust and found its way in tumbling rivulets among the debris of the 1918 pits and caves. During the night these depressions were entirely filled.

The east cone had become a splashing pot over an enlarged well beneath. The southeast pond cup depression had become a remarkable circular basin 30 feet across and 12 feet deep with the cone on its western edge. It appeared to be a sagging crust over something withdrawing below.

The general uplift had now brought the lakes and their fountains into plain view from the Observatory, the glow at night was strong and the fumes thin and even the banners of flame above the cones could be seen in the distance with field glasses and in calm weather the blowing of the cones was quite audible.

On Jan. 22 at 11 a. m. there was new welling up of lava in the southeast wall crack, increased swelling and cracking, a new spire cone at the edge of the floor south-southeast, the eastern cones were large and flaming, and even the central crag remnant appeared relatively higher, as though lifted above the floor around it. The northeast heap was higher and extended northward and the live pool on its summit streamed westward. The southwest pond was open and fountaining on the west side of its cone. The lakes were high and a cone west of the north lake had become large. The main lake was streaming eastward.

In the late afternoon the east cone burst open so as to split along a vertical east-west rift and a standing fountain gushed out on each side of the rift continuously and during the evening the flow spread into a wide pool. The lakes were brimming and streaming east and northeast. A flow poured west from under a crust in the northern part of the pit. The north cone was spouting, all the cones were flaming, there was high pressure at the southeast pond cone and the eastern flood finally spread southward and sent torrents into the eastern wall cracks which were filled from both sides. Driblet flows were making out from the northeast heap and occasional fountains were seen on the west heap but no flows.

On the following night the west heap started flowing and building again, and at 9 a. m. a flow was pouring from it toward the center of the pit. At 11 a. m., Jan. 23, the west side of the heap was visited and live streams were there travelling in several lobes, some of them reaching a speed of ten feet per minute. A meandering rivulet six feet wide poured down the upper part of the heap to feed them. Within the pit a stream ten feet wide was pouring down the north slope of the heap. All of those flows have been pouring for weeks toward the northwest wall valley, which in spite of this continues to remain the lowest part of the pit.

In contrast to the west heap activity the pit elsewhere appeared as though sinking, the lakes six to eight feet down their cups, the crusts of recent flows slumping. The northeast heap, however, was high and making driblet flows and the cones were flaming and hissing. The southwest pond appeared to have developed a small pit in the flank of the western heap.

At 5 p. m. the overflow had stopped, trickle flows moved on the northeast heap, the lakes were low but rose somewhat an hour later, and the streaming in the main lake was east and west from the center. The crusts of the previous day's flows had collapsed and the east cone was quiet, but the southeast pond cone was puffing and flaming. On walking out to the edge of the lake across the new flows, the writer found these crusts much more substantial than the hollow shells of the western overflows. This seems to indicate that the fresh rising lava of the western conduit is much more frothy and charged with gas than the lava of the eastern lakes and sinkholes. At 11 p. m. the west heap was flowing and the lakes high.

On Friday, Jan. 24, 1919, in the morning the middle region had settled, the west heap was higher and making flows north of the summit. Fresh additions had increased the thickness but not the length of the southwest overflow. The northeast heap was making driblet flows. The lakes were rather low. This condition continued into the afternoon but during the night there was revival of rising, flows from the western heap, and immense fountains splashed above the lakes and some spatter ramparts collapsed.

Tilt to the east and strong microtremor have continued and earthquake movements have been slight as instrumentally recorded, though one pronounced felt earthquake is reported from Kohala.

February 1, 1919.

The last week in January of 1919, and indeed the whole of January, have produced movements of the Halemaumau lava column much like January of 1918, except for the absence of crags this year. The past week has been notable as bringing to a close the January rise, and inaugurating a moderate subsidence which still continues. The main effects so far have consisted in withdrawal of the liquid lava more than 20 feet and a sympathetic slumping of the lake margins so as to enlarge the pools, revealing as usual larger chambers just below the surface than the actual lake areas indicated. Furthermore the southwest lava heap, source of the recent overflows has sunk more than other portions of the pit floor. This checks with other evidence to the effect that the present sinking spell is a reaction from the recent high gas pressure and generation of liquid lava, the region of the liquid lava source exhibiting the reaction most strongly. The central floor of Halemaumau has gone down but slightly, and the glowing northeast heap has even at times risen a little. The excessive hissing gas pressure so pronounced last week has ceased, and coordinate with the diminution of pressure has been the great increase of visible sulphur smoke, condensing over the subterranean voids left by the retiring liquid.

Measurements of the week expressed as depression in feet below the rim of the pit at the southeast station have been as follows:

	Main Lake....	Central Floor....	N.E. Heap	S.W. Heap	
Jan. 25....	22	16	6	14	above rim
Jan. 29....	38	23	7	1	" "

The lake thus sank 16 feet in four

days, averaging four feet per day; the southwest heap 13 feet, averaging 3.25 feet per day; the central floor seven feet, averaging 1.7 feet per day; the northeast heap one foot, averaging 0.25 foot per day. The movement of subsidence began on January 25, actual overflow continuing until the previous night.

At 5 a. m. Saturday, Jan. 25, 1919, brilliant lava flows visible from Volcano House were pouring down the east and north slopes of the southwestern heap and the lakes were brimming within their spatter ramparts and fountaining tumultously. After 8 a. m. the northern stream continued to pour from a standing fountain at the top of the heap but the lakes were lower. At 9:20 a. m. the puffing of the gas cones was plainly audible at the road terminus near the pit. The south and east wall cones and the southeast pond cone were blowing noisily. The southwest pond cone had become a high spur of the western lava heap. The central and north corner were stained with solfataric deposits. The large crusted sag basin on the east side of the southeast pond cone suggested approaching collapse, and large crevasses had opened on all sides of this depression. A strongly hissing vent had formed in the floor just east of the main lake, on the line between the lake and the east cone and burning gases played through the glowing cracks. Fume had considerably increased in the south central part of the floor.

The lake margins were about four feet high, fountaining was sluggish and streaming in the main lake was eastward. An overhanging half dome seven feet high had been built above the southwest grotto of the lake and all the ramparts were mossy with Pele's hair.

Under the east station a broad flow was pushing toward the southeast from the slope of the northeast heap. This flow piled itself up close against the front of the east shelter at the floor level of the shelter. The overflows from the southwest heap now crossed the edge of Halemaumau along a greatly widened stretch and close to the old west station. This heap was greatly increased in bulk and live overflows were pushing southwestward from it outside of Halemaumau in three places, the middle flow 15 feet wide, moving slowly and covered with heavily festooned skin. Near the top of the heap trickle flows were pushing down the north slope.

The floor of Halemaumau was lifted at the small heap at the south wall cone and thence all the way to the north lake, the uplifted region being cracked and stained and covered with Pele's hair. The lift by both tumescense and overflow had now so raised everything inside the pit that to the observer standing on the southeast margin large portions of the south, southwest and northeast cliffs were cut off from view and the lakes were hidden by their ramparts, now nearly level with the eye. The two horns of the central crag remnant still stood five or six feet above the floor level.

At 6 p. m. two flows were pouring down the northeast slope of the western heap and during the evening the lakes rose for a last display of heavy fountaining and the southwestern overflows extended themselves.

On Jan. 26 at 3 p. m. the hissing had mostly ceased, smoke had increased and the lake margins were six feet high. The southeast pond had opened to become a small well and its cone had collapsed. No flows were in motion. The last spurt of flowing had caused the northeast heap flows to overtop the uppermost northeastern shelf of March, 1918, and had extended the southwestern overflows to a distance 600 feet outside of the former southwest rim of the pit. The broad leaf-shaped areas there of fresh lobes measured 500 feet from side to side and the summit of the west heap now stood well above the post at the west station and was therefore higher than the highest part of the Halemaumau rim. The cones were all smoky and the east cone was nearly submerged under the fresh flows.

On Monday, Jan. 27, the fume showed great increase in density, rising in heavy volutes from the eastern, southern and northern floors. The live fountains could no longer be seen from the Observatory, the lakes being down. There was no special change in the general floor level.

On Jan. 28 in the morning the last trace of built up ramparts around the southeast pond had collapsed and the pond was greatly enlarged to a pool 50 feet long in the east-west direction, occupying the site of the former cone but extended so that the cup depression had become the east end of the new inner pit. The liquid stood some 20 feet below the general floor level and was mostly crusted over except for a splashing opening at the west end where a tunnel appeared to lead toward the southwest grotto of the main lake.

The main lake was surrounded by 20-foot cliffs, sluggish fountaining grottoes were hung with stalactites northeast and southwest of it, and bedded walls were mostly vertical or slightly overhanging, much Pele's hair clung to them and the surface of the pool was stagnant. The north lake was similar, its surface about 15 feet down. The large beehive cone on the floor west of the north lake had developed an open window one foot in diameter on its east side which led into a large glowing cupola with lava splashing below. The west arm cone and south wall cone were smoking but showed glow at night. The west heap remained high with a glowing cavern on top. The east cone was now a lok glowing lump. The central crag was enveloped in smoke and could not be seen. The central and southwest pond cones remained as before and there was no change in the overflow southwest. The northeast heap had slumped in places, showing glowing caverns with stalactite drip, and across its surface lines of arched crust were left in relief over tubes below whence the liquid had apparently drained downward. It was easy to walk across the floor in all directions and examine all details.

On Jan. 29 at 11 a. m. the lakes were depressed 25 feet within their inner pits and everything was stagnant and smoky. Especially dense volumes of smoke rose from the floor between the southeast pond and the south wall cone. Measurements indicated that the northeast heap had slightly risen but the western heap had settled. The large southwest grotto half dome on the edge of the main lake had fallen in and the rampart elsewhere was fast collapsing. Fountaining activity was mod- the streaming was towards the northeast grotto. There was no marked gas pressure at the cones. The floor showed increased staining along lines of cracks. The north cone was still bright and glowing. At night the glow above the lakes and cones was conspicuous, including a cone on the summit of the western heap.

At 6 p. m. on Thursday, Jan. 30, the main lake was found greatly enlarged by collapse of all its ramparts except the northeastern one and by further collapse eastward undermined by a tunnel extending toward the east cone. This lake was now 250 feet long by 100 feet wide. Its fountaining activity had increased, streaming was various, there were sharp alternations between rising and sinking spells and the glow at night was brighter. The walls of the inner pit were 30 feet high and well marked tunnels were revealed at the east and west ends of the lake, some 25 feet below the floor level. There was also suggestion of tunnels northeast and southwest. The tunnel leading eastward was circular and 10 feet in diameter.

The north cone was becoming eaten through by the gases within so that a bright filagree patch had developed on its west side. The northeast heap glowed through many cracks, there was a large flaming and glowing area around the east cone, the southeast wall cone glowed brightly and there was some fire at the south wall cone. Chimneys sent up flames at the central and western cones. The revelation of tunnels leading into the lakes about 25 feet below the floor level, at the end of the recent period of building up by overflow, is of great interest compared with the observations of 1917 which showed persistent tunnels and wells in the bottom and walls of the lake basins at depths from 25 to 45 feet.

On Friday, Jan. 31, conditions continued to be sluggish, slow sinking continued, the flaring of the chimneys decreased slightly and smoke was dense.

In the Whitney Laboratory the seismographs have registered a few local earthquakes and a near shock on the afternoon of Jan. 28 which was felt in erate, there was much crusting over and Honolulu. Microseismic motion has been ordinary, microtremor has been strong and the ground tilt has been so slight as to keep the clinograph pen nearly stationary, aside from diurnal fluctuation.

Very respectfully,

T. A. JAGGAR, JR.,
Director.

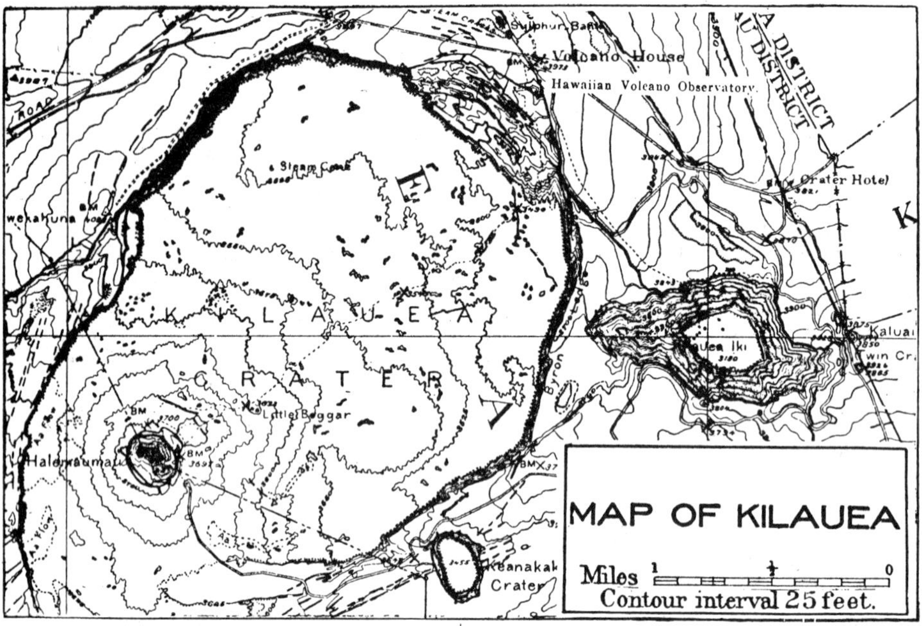

HAWAIIAN VOLCANO RESEARCH ASSOCIATION.

This society is a voluntary one, made up of subscribers to scientific work which is being executed by Dr. T. A. Jaggar, Director of the Hawaiian Volcano Observatory, Volcano House, P. O., Hawaii. **All scientific exchanges should be sent to this address.**

In 1918 there were about 150 subscribers in Hawaii and elsewhere, firms and individuals. A group of firms and persons in Hilo built the main observatory building in the spring of 1912. The work was founded by the Massachusetts Institute of Technology. Publications to date have been weekly bulletins since the summer of 1911 now reprinted in Honolulu in monthly form. There are also special reports, printed from time to time.

The monthly bulletin is sent to regular annual subscribers to the work of the Association. L. A. Thurston is president of the Board of Directors of the Association, and L. T. Peck is treasurer. New subscribers who are interested in volcanoes will be welcomed in the Association. The Association aims: (1) To record volcanic activity and earthquakes in Hawaii; (2) to attract scientific men hither for special studies; (3) to promote the establishment of volcano observatories all over the world. The annual dues of regular members are $5; patrons of the Association subscribe larger amounts.

WHITNEY LABORATORY OF SEISMOLOGY.

The Whitney Laboratory of Seismology, named after an endowment fund for geophysical research held by the Massachusetts Institute of Technology, in memory of Caroline and Edward Whitney of Boston, is equipped with the following seismometric instruments rebuilt at the station in 1918 for the special needs of volcano research: two Bosch-Omori pendulums, high speed registration of local earthquakes; one optically recording seismograph for distant earthquakes; one clinograph registering E-W tilting of the ground. A vertical component seismograph was in December, 1918, set up in experimental operation. These are seated on concrete piers in a closed basement room having practically constant temperature, beneath the chief Observatory building near the hotel. Time is referred to a rated chronometer, checked at intervals by solar observations with a transit. Both instruments are loaned by the College of Hawaii. Hawaiian standard time (H. S. T.) is 10 hrs. 30 min. slower than Greenwich time.

CANCANI SCALE OF SEISMIC INTENSITY.

Expressed by accelerations measured in millimeters per second per second.

I.	Instrumental	0.0	2.5
II.	Very slight	2.5	5.0
III.	Slight	5.0	10.0
IV.	Sensible, mediocre	10.0	25.0
V.	Rather strong	25.0	50.0
VI.	Strong	50.0	100.0
VII.	Very strong	100.0	250.0
VIII.	Ruinous	250.0	500.0
IX.	Disastrous	500.0	1000.0
X.	Very disastrous	1000.0	2500.0
XI.	Catastrophic	2500.0	5000.0
XII.	Great catastrophe	5000.0	10000.0

Grade IV. is ordinarily the minimum perceived by the senses; and in grade XII. the acceleration, or rate of change of motion (jerk) reaches that of terrestrial gravitation.

In the standard form of report the maximum intensity or acceleration, designated by the symbol α, or max. α, is given in the conventional unit, **the milligal.** The milligal is a measure of acceleration, such that 1 milligal = 1/100 mm. per sec. per sec. = 10 μ per sec. per sec. The Cancani scale, here defined in terms of millimeters per sec. per sec., can therefore be expressed in milligals by multiplying each of the numbers by 100.

U. S. DEPARTMENT OF AGRICULTURE
WEATHER BUREAU
CHARLES F. MARVIN, CHIEF

MONTHLY BULLETIN

OF THE

Hawaiian Volcano Observatory

Vol. VII. HONOLULU, HAWAII, FEBRUARY, 1919 No. 2

February 8, 1819.

Again the history of 1919 is repeating that of 1918 in seasonal mechanism of the Halemaumau lava pit, and the first week of February shows complete recovery from the preceding subsidence and the liquid lava building up rapidly above the former wall crack vents northeast and south. The lakes have recovered their brimming and overflowing condition but the southwestern border heap, which in January produced overflows outside of Halemaumau, has not yet revived at its summit. The south heap, however, overflowed the rim of the pit on Friday, February 7, and in the course of three successive impulses of overflow during the day poured 400 feet down the outer southeast slope of the Halemaumau eminence so as unfortunately to damage a small portion of the newly built trail leading from the road terminus to the pit. This trail has been graded and marked with stones and whitewash by special appropriation of the Board of Supervisors of the County, the work being barely completed when this new overflow came. This flow is in the midst of the area similarly flooded in February-March, 1918, and the cone at its source is close beside the similar "South Cone" of last year.

Measurements of the week expressed in feet below or above the southeast station have been as follows:

Main lake, Jan. 29, 38 below; central floor, 23 below; N. E. heap, 7 below; S. W. heap, 1 above. Main lake, Feb. 7, 14 below; central floor, 15 below; N. E. heap, 3 above; S. W. heap, 4 above.

The figures indicate that in nine days the lake rose 24 feet, or 2.7 feet per day; the northeast heap built itself up 10 feet, or 1.1 feet per day. Both of these were recovery by rise of liquid, the lake at a rate three-quarters as fast as the previous subsidence, and the northeast heap four times as fast. The evidence for movement of the floor in places not overflowed is furnished by the central floor at the central cone locality which rose 8 feet in nine days, or .9 feet per day, and the southwest heap which at its summit rose 3 feet, or .3 feet per day. The evidence from these two points alone is inadequate, but it would appear that the bench magma rose but little during the week and it is probable that the main lava column subsided somewhat, especially across the northwest half of the pit, compensating the effervescence of its substance in the numerous flowing vents on the other side of the circle. It should be noted that the southwest heap after recovery was still 10 feet below its maximum of Jan. 25 and the central floor had just recovered its level of that date. The repeated heavy floods which poured into the northwestern region during the week still failed to fill it or reduce the grade from the north lake in that direction, evidence favoring the view that the underpinning was subsiding. This may have been compensated by some mass uplift under the main lake and eastern vents, but there were no fixed objects there, like the former crags, to serve as bench marks for measurement.

With a view to interpretation of the probable movement of the deep lava column at such a time as this it is interesting to make comparison with the week of November 22, 1918, which ended the subsidence of November 14. On November 17-18 the liquid lava rose 19 feet and the bench magma, represented by the central crag, sank 14 feet. This was a culmination of subsidence when gas was released from confinement and induced effervescence. The present period appears to be in general a culmination of rising, with similarly a stagnation crisis in the internal pressures of the lava column and consequent release of gas inducing effervescence. It may well be true that an overflow like the one in January, abstracting many hundreds of tons weight from the top of the lava column, brings about effervescence of gas somewhat as in the case of the overflow of a geyser pool. In the geyser release of pressure lowers boiling points and explosive ebullition follows; in the lava column release of pressure lowers saturation points of gas dissolved in glass and effervescence follows. In both cases a foam forms at the expense of the fluid beneath. The excessive liquid lava of the past two months is such a foam and its rising and overflowing is not necessarily a measure of what the stiffer substance below is doing.

With this in mind it is curious to note that the clinograph, which has consistently shown eastward tilt with rising bench magma as measured by the crags, and westward tilt with sinking magma, has during the past fortnight, shown stationary or slightly eastward tilt during the spell of sinking liquid last week, and pronounced westward tilt during the time of strongly rising liquid this week. The last glimpse of the central crag was on February 1, and thereafter it disappeared, although no flows were definitely seen to drown it. In February, 1918, at the time when liquid lava welled up the 1894 depression northeast in excessive volumes, and the crater floor otherwise showed little change, there was a similar aberrant westward tilt, as though effervescence were in fact a mark of deep subsidence, not indicated at once in movements of the crater floor. Whatever the cause, it is a striking fact that the February high level of both years brings the only marked discordances between the apparent rising of lava and eastward tilt. The explanation of the discordance by lag is not tenable in the writer's judgment. Remembering the November case, when the real movement of the lava column was still downward as measured by the crags, though crags and liquid moved in opposite directions, and the tilt was to the west, agreeing rather with the crags than with the liquid, the suggestion is strong that the rise and fall of the liquid lava is not necessarily an index of the rise and fall of the lava column.

On Saturday, February 1, 1919, at 4 p. m., the lakes stood higher relative to the floor and the fumes were thinner. There was no puffing, the northeast heap and east cone glowed through cracks encrusted with salts, and the north floor cone was flaming. The main lake had 15-foot walls and was crusted over, with border fountains east and west. The southeast pond had overflowed its east end and the wall west of it was 12 feet high. A fountain bubbled up steadily on its west side and there was fountaining bombardment against its north wall. The north lake was also crusted over with 10-foot walls and border fountains northwest.

At 8 p. m. the night view showed at a distance marked increase in number of fiery areas. There were glow spots at the lakes, the central, western and northern cones and the west heap, and the spray of the main and north lakes was flung above the edge of their pits.

On February 2 at 6 p. m. the lakes were brimming and building ramparts. The north lake had overflowed extensively across the northwestern part of the floor, making a wide pool against the wall in process of cracking and foundering. The main lake was streaming eastward and bombarding its east rampart. The southeast pond overflowed eastward sluggishly with interruptions due to the bursting of its crust by gas generation of a fountain and temporary subsidence of one or two feet, followed by recovery. The southwest pond was fountaining. The south wall cone was building up by fountain splash and the east cone had become a patch of flaming and spraying cracks over a large chamber below filled with fountaining lava. Gas pressure was renewed, the north cone was flaming from glowing orifices on its west side, there was some hissing and the central and west pond cones were flaming chimneys. One of the flings of spray on the east bank of the main lake burned with a yellow flame for a few seconds as though it were a splash of kerosene.

On February 3 at 10 a. m. the lakes were overflowing so that by noon the floor was covered with fresh lava east and north from the main lake, northwest from the north lake and south a short distance from the southwest pond. The south wall cone had become a much higher ring shaped pot belching bubbles through a heavy melt, the individual bursts lifting the whole cone surrounding the pot. Next to it was a second cone hissing through a live spiracle and this relation continued throughout the week, the hissing gas vent being maintained apparently as an essential valve mechanism of the overflowing pot. The cones were about two feet below the rim of the pit and 20 feet away from and inside of the rim. A flow was pouring at noon eastward and northward from this pot along the base of the wall a few feet under the southeast station and other fresh flows had been ejected from this vent along the wall crack toward the south station. Here there was tumescence of the floor away from the wall dragging open and depressing the marginal lava.

The lakes were again contracting in area by the building inward of grotto ramparts with spatter domes over six feet high. There were four or five fountains in each of the large lakes and at least one in the southwest pond. The crag remnant had disappeared. The northeastern and southwestern heaps remained quiet.

On Tuesday, February 4, there was pronounced rising of the lakes in the morning and at 6 p. m. At 9 p. m. the lakes were depressed three feet within their cups and rose somewhat during the next two hours. The southeast pond, at first almost indistinguishable under a crust flush with the floor, finally burst its crust and revealed a circular basin 30 feet in diameter, first flames and then fountains appearing, this being followed by subsidence of the pond leaving red hot banks five feet high with stalactite drip and tumbled glowing marginal crusts overhanging in places. Thereafter the pond recovered slowly. The main lake, although only a short distance away and apparently connected with the pond, for there is a flaming vent between the two, did not partake of these movements at all. Similarly the north lake had a sinking spell quite independent of the main lake. All the lakes and lava vents are at different levels held up by differential gas pressure. The west pond is higher than the southwest pond, the latter higher than the southeast pond, the southeast pond higher than the main lake and the north lake lowest of all. The northeast heap and the south cone produce flows at still different levels.

The northeast heap had completely revived and a puddle of lava on top 10 feet in diameter was fountaining continuously and feeding flows which pushed down the western slope of the heap. The whole structure was higher. The south wall cone was flaming, the southwest and west ponds showed occasional fountains, the east cone was piled up, hissing noisily and showing sharp spears of burning gas, and flames played above the central cone. There was a period of very strong fountaining at a high level after midnight but the next morning the lakes were lower and the pit somewhat smokier. It should be said that with the revival the fume had greatly diminished.

On February 5 towards noon the lakes rose and the main lake overflowed. The northeast heap had developed a large cone on its summit. At 8 p. m. the pit was dull, but the summit crusts of the northeast heap were cracking up and sinking, showing a pool within.

On Thursday, February 6, from 1 to 4 p. m., the lakes were about the same. Streaming in the main lake was eastward and its west and northeast grottoes were curtained with stalactites. The southeast pond was somewhat lower, showing a glowing edge, and the south wall cone had recently produced heavy flows which had poured all the way to the east station. The cone at the east summit of the northeast heap had broken down on its northwestern side so as to leave an open oven over a pot eight feet in diameter covered with a heavy skin which inflated periodically like a balloon, and this was followed by a burst of gas and sputter lava from the oven opening. The whole heap elsewhere was heavily crusted with an elongate flat top extending 300 feet northwest from the oven and sloping away in all directions. The summit was now well above the level of the east shelter. At 6 p. m. there was strong fountaining and a high level with much flaming from the chimneys.

On Friday, February 7, 1919, there was another high level at 8:30 a. m. and a broad flow from the south wall cone spread across the rim of the pit and 20 feet back from the rim on the east side of the south cone of 1918 and sent its main volume northeastward just inside the rim as before. At 11 a. m. this flow had crusted over and the lakes were lower but a live flow was pouring from the west pond toward the center of the pit. At 3 p. m. the south overflow revived and pushed forward 20 feet farther back from the rim and then developed two flows just inside the rim, moving east and west, the western one cascading steeply into the wall crack under the old south cone and flowing thence to a point under the south station. The source was now 5 feet above the level of the rim of Halemaumau, an open oven towards the southeast with a hissing and flaming spiracle cone beside it. At 8 p. m. the overflows were renewed, poured in a narrow tongue 400 feet down the slope across the new trail and otherwise sent voluminous floods across the floor inside the pit, temporarily drowning the southeast pond. The end of this flow penetrated the interior of the stone shelter on the east side of the pit. Probably at the same time the north lake and main lake overflowed. The pit was a very brilliant spectacle while these night flows were in progress. The blowing cone beside the south pot burst open and fountained violently, making an exceptional display of fireworks.

During the day the northeast heap was quiet and its summit cone closed but in the evening it broke open, piled higher and drowned the former northeast station under lava and extended the heap towards the north and west.

On this day the north lake was surrounded by six symmetrical half-domes and curtained grottoes. The west pond cone on the high slope of the west heap was a fountaining pot but the summit of the heap had greatly collapsed and showed no activity. The southeast pond was crusted over and the southwest pond had built three or four spatter domes. The central and north cones had diminished in brightness of incandescence. The east cone continued to puff as a large area of glowing cracks over a concealed chamber where lava could be heard pounding.

For the week ending at 8 p. m., Feb. 7, 1919, the instruments of the Whitney Laboratory of Seismology have registered local earthquakes as follows: Feb. 1, 3:14 a. m. and 6:29 a. m.; Feb. 2, 12:47 a. m., felt; Feb. 4, 4:23 a. m., slight; Feb. 5, 3:07 a. m. and 8:24 p. m., both slight. A teleseism was registered at 1:29 p. m. Jan. 31, 1919, not reported last week. This shock showed almost no effect on the east-west instrument, and pronounced long waves only on the north-south and optical instruments, suggesting an origin either north or south of the station. The distance was not indicated.

Microseismic motion has been moderately strong north-south and slight east-west, with some temporary increase on Feb. 3 and Feb. 6. The harmonic microtremor was strong Feb. 1, Feb. 3 and Feb. 7 and strongish at other times; the spasmodic tremor of quicker period was strongest Feb. 1 and 2 and decreased thereafter with some revival Feb. 5, the maxima notably occurring on the days of local earthquakes.

The clinograph showed a turning point from slight east tilt Feb. 1 to west tilt; the seismographs showed change from north tilt to south. The westerly tilt was strong, decreasing from Feb. 2 to Feb. 6, the meridional component of the seismographs showing increasing south tilt to Feb. 4, with decrease Feb. 5 and stationary condition Feb. 6-7. On Feb. 7 the clinograph also showed stationary tendency.

Feb. 15, 1919.

During the week ending Feb. 14, 1919, the lakes have somewhat subsided within their cups, the floor has been stationary as a whole, and the northeast heap has built itself up until it stands 27 feet above the east station and has poured forth bulky overflows completely surrounding the eastern stone shelter and burying the bench mark of the United States Geological Survey which was set in a small masonry table near the back corner of the shelter.

These flows from the northeast heap pushed eastward across the rim of Halemaumau and 150 feet beyond so as to endanger the wooden hut belonging to the Observatory. The hut was accordingly removed and rebuilt on safer ground 200 yards farther north. This is the fourth time that the little wooden building has been moved. The first building was erected by Mr. Perret in 1911 on the east rim of the pit adjacent to and north of the stone shelter and its site was identical with that of the bench mark just buried up. Owing to molestation by vandals the hut was moved in 1912 to a point back of the north rim. This place proved fumy from the hot cracks and half of the building was transferred in 1916 to the position back from the east rim. In 1918 the part left at the north was torn down and rebuilt in the Observatory grounds and its former site was invaded by lava spatter with much burning of debris when the eruptive cones formed Nov. 1, 1918. February, 1919, compels another moving because of lava flow. It would be impossible to place a station anywhere near the pit margin which would be immune, unless it were built as a steel tower.

It is perhaps not generally realized that during the last year the lava column has through liquid flooding overtopped the rim of Halemaumau on eleven separate occasions and at nine different places. Six of these are considerable overflows extending more than 100 feet away from the pit and the others were driblet overflows which did not travel far. The southeast flows of Feb.-Mar., 1918, were the most extensive, those of Nov., 1918, to the north cone next in actual length and the flows of Jan.-Feb., 1919, now in progress, tend to fill some of the gaps east, south and southwest between the two earlier localities. August of 1918 produced driblet overflowing of the rim north and southwest, but no extensive flows. If the present overflowing continues as last year until the equinox and beyond, there is ample time for extensive flows yet to come.

The measurements from the rim at the southeast station have been as follows:

Main lake, Feb. 7, 14 feet below rim; Northeast heap, three feet above rim.
Main lake, Feb. 14, 25 feet below rim; Northeast heap, 16 feet above rim.

In seven days the lake sank 11 feet, or 1.6 feet per day, while the northeast heap built itself up 13 feet, or 1.9 feet per day. Other points were in general stationary.

On Saturday, Feb. 8, 1919, at noon there was no further flowing from the south cone, the floor showed increased smoke in the south central region and the lakes stood about six feet below their banks and appeared rising. The east cone was hissing. The cone on the summit of the northeast heap had become a sharp horn in profile as seen from the northeast, this structure forming the protruding cover of an oven facing north within which a circular crusted pool heaved sluggishly. From this vent extensive new flows had piled up northward and westward.

The floods from the south cone on the previous night had poured voluminously northward and southward within the pit as well as outside of it to the southeast where it had crossed the trail. The flow northward had crossed the southeast pond and evidently had cascaded into it. This had been joined by other flows from the main lake and the lava penetrated a few feet into the interior of the east shelter. The flow southward had surrounded the south station and just west of the station a stream 30 feet wide crossed the edge of the pit and flowed 200 feet beyond to the south.

Extensive fresh floods had resulted from the overbrimming of the north lake so that its rampart was all changed and the whole northwestern region covered with fresh lava. This lake was even now brimming and appeared ready to overflow again. Later about 9 p. m. more extensive flows here took place.

On February 9 there was no special activity in the morning but in the late afternoon the summit pot of the northeast heap erupted violently and changed the direction of its flows from northward to southeastward. This at once threatened the east shelter and the government bench mark. All through the evening this pot ejected a standing fountain which made a brilliant display and showed at a distance as irregular flashing. The lakes also were luminous.

At noon Monday, Feb. 10, the lakes showed inner cliffs about six feet high, the south cone was quiet and the east cone had enlarged and opened a fountaining pot in its center. At 9 a. m. the northeast heap had still maintained its standing fountain, but this had now dwindled to a sluggish fountaining pot, while trickle flows pushed ahead and piled up here and there on the slopes of the heap. The new flows had made much progress southward across the floor of the pit and a heavy block of them had pushed 100 feet eastward on the north side of the stone shelter so as to cross the old trail and head straight towards the Observatory hut 200 feet away. This flow had hardened in light brittle shells with shredded edges and some tendency to aa structure and was quite different from the masssive lumpy lava of the earlier flows from the same source.

The southwest pond had built up its spatter domes. The south oven and blowing cone were quiet. The southeast pond had 6-foot walls and a somewhat inflated crust, and a whitened spatter dome stood on the north margin of its circular pit. No such rampart elsewhere surrounded this pit as encompassed the other two lakes. The rampart around the main lake was very heavy and covered with Pele's hair and the main fountaining activity was at a double grotto northeast of the lake under a large spatter dome. Here there were great accumulations of stalactites and the gas-blistered skin on the lake surface was incessantly drawn into the grotto fountains. The grotto at the west end of the lake was a symmetrical arch with a curtain of drip across the opening which was later seen to fall. A hissing spiracle had formed above a vent midway between the southeast pond and the main lake. The north cone had become inconspicuous. The north lake had enlarged and become circular.

At 4 p. m. the action at the northeast heap had increased and flows were pouring from the summit southward. This summit now stood fully 20 feet above the floor of the east shelter, and at the east station the whole north rim of the pit was now cut off from view.

At night the view from Volcano House showed nine fiery areas at Halemaumau, making the distant view of the pit appear like the lights of a town.

On Tuesday, Feb. 11, at 9 a. m. the northeast cone was found sharp-pointed on top of the heap with secondary frozen pools or platforms adjoining it on the east which had been sources for the eastern overflows. The northern flows had stopped. The eastern flows had pushed 50 feet farther and driblet lava was in motion. A fresh lobe of the flow had piled up five feet high, almost completely filling the interior of the east shelter, and another lobe during the day surrounded the government bench mark. The lakes remained low except the north lake, which had occasional brimming spells with high fountaining. The southeast pond was generally crusted over but occasionally rose somewhat. In the afternoon the northeast cone hissed and the flows increased in vigor. Lava could be heard fountaining in the east cone pot. In the night all the fire holes were bright.

On the morning of Feb. 13 the pit was dull, there was much solfataric staining and Pele's hair and no flows were seen in motion in the forenoon. There was glow at the south, northeast, west and north cones. The main lake and southeast pond were depressed 15 feet within their shafts, the north lake ten. The grottoes were curtained and sluggish.

At the east cone one could stand on the rim and look into the open pot four feet in diameter where the lava was splashing some 15 feet below, and under the southern lip of the orifice a bright orange interior chamber was revealed, hung with delicately sculptured fiery stalactites shaped like long bunches of grapes. The entire interior including the liquid below was maintained at an even glow and at night a banner of blue-green flame fluttered above the orifice showing the presence of combustible gas. The fume to leeward was pale blue and transparent and acridly irrespirable with the acids of sulphur.

The northeast and south cones maintained hissing spiracles alongside the crusted lava pots which had been the flow sources. The flows following the sudden revival of the northeast heap of Feb. 8-9 had been brittle and papery, the later ones of Feb. 12 were heavy and bulbous.

In the afternoon there was increased hissing and at 4:04 p. m. the northeast cone, after spasmodic liftings of a lid of broken crust with some spurting of lava from within the gas cone, suddenly burst and collapsed. Instantly a large volume of very liquid lava domed up in artesian fashion, flooded the top of the heap, and then cascaded south in a rapid river of melt which progressed 100 feet in four minutes; the stream was 40 feet wide. The standing fountain was 10 feet high and 20 feet wide and explosive bursts shot up 20 feet. There was no noise worth mention, and the hissing stopped. The source quickly settled down into a rhythmically gushing spring with small bursts every five seconds emerging from a gash perhaps eighteen inches wide. The source torrent had an orange red pudding-like surface but the flow below quickly stagnated and spread sidewise, the crusts becoming rather brittle and papery, with heavier toes of the ball type emerging later. This flow continued all night, and the fountain bursts at the source dwindled after midnight. The flows were at first south, later east, mostly piling up on the previous flows. The phenomena of this outbreak were like the uncorking of champagne, and the sudden fountain was clearly a geyser effect due to release of gas pressure. This fountain, flowing for many hours, stood 40 feet above the level of the main lake of lava only 360 feet away southwest of it.

The next day, Friday, Feb. 14, 1919, the new flows were found completely surrounding the east shelter and the U. S. bench mark was buried. Slow moving toes were pushing ahead at the fronts. The east front was no farther advanced, but more spread out and piled up, but the south front had curved around the shelter, buried more of the old trail, advanced toward the east cone, and nearly reached the east station monument. The flows were now high bulbous masses of very solid pahoehoe. The cone on top of the heap was hissing slightly but not open.

There was little change in the lakes, spray could be seen in the west grotto of the main lake through an orifice above the curtain across the grotto entrance. The west cone appeared increasing in height and in the evening a revived pot on top of the west heap was fuming and flaring.

In the Whitney Laboratory of Seismology there were registered small local earthquakes at 3:44 p. m. Feb. 10, and at 12:35 a. m. and 8:08 a. m. Feb. 14. Microseismic motion and microtremor both increased to strong Feb. 10, otherwise their vibrations were moderate. The movements of tilting indicated were mostly slight or stationary, but there was strong continuous east tilt from about 2 p. m. Feb. 9 to 8 a. m. Feb. 10, and short spasms of unusually sharp east tilt on the evening of Feb. 10 and about 4 p. m. Feb. 13. The tilting was slightly west Feb. 13-14, with tendency to turn eastward on Feb. 14. The meridional component was strong north Feb. 9-10, slightly north Feb. 14, and on other days slightly southward.

Feb. 22, 1919.

During the week ending Friday, Feb. 21, 1919, the northeast cone continued its spasms of occasional overflow for a few days and then became quiet. The top of the lava column as represented by the floor and lakes has been essentially stationary, the lakes sinking and rising through a few feet. New openings filled with live lava have appeared at a pot adjacent to the central cone and in a collapsed depression at the summit of the west heap. There has been marked increase of solfataric staining extending even to the older rim south and southeast outside of the pit proper. No measurements are here recorded, as the changes of level are very small.

It may be well in this place to describe briefly the present appearance of Halemaumau, so unlike the familiar "pit" of aforetime, and also totally different from the craggy hill of last year's high levels. As one looks down upon Halemaumau from the high west bluff of Kilauea the pit rim is practically obliterated and there appears in its place a flat smoking area with three lava heaps of slight relief and three inconspicuous small circular cups containing the liquid lakes. Close inspection with a field glass shows a semicircle of low rim remaining on the northwest side, but southwest, southeast and northeast the rim is replaced by an irregular surface of humpy pahoehoe. As a whole this smoking surface is the summit of the broad flat inner cone making the bottom of the greater crater. If the "floor" of Halemaumau were now to sink bodily, preserving its integrity, the circular margin would slice in two vertically each of the three heaps southwest, southeast and northeast, carrying down the inner halves and leaving the outer halves as eminences in the new rim of the pit. Above the low cliff of the north rim there is such an eminence today, consisting of the group of cones built by the spouting lava of the extensive overflows of November, 1918. The general arrangement of the present Halemaumau floor was determined in December, 1918, that mechanism persisting ever since, viz: A semicircle of lava heaping southeast and a semicircle of never completed filling northwest. The three places of high heaping and overflow of the pit are just where there were low benches between the high crags in 1916-17; and where the crags were there are now sags between the heaps, the greatest sag of all being at the northwest where stood the great crag masses of 1917.

On Saturday, Feb. 15, at 4 p. m., the pit was dull with much smoke and no marked gas pressure and no flows in motion. The southeast and main lakes were depressed 10 feet within their cups and the north lake 20 feet. This made the latter about 17 feet lower than the main lake. The main lake was hence higher than on the previous day and the north lake lower. In the interior of the east cone the lava was surging about 12 feet down and the only departure from uniform incandescence inside was the splash on the walls which at the moment of fling was a little brighter yellow. There was glow in the west and south cones which after dark appeared as incandescent spots. At night the glow above the north and main lakes was bright, above the southeast and southwest ponds dim, and pale flame fluttered over the east cone.

On Feb. 16 about 5:30 p. m. the northeast cone, which had developed two lumpy summits, erupted again with moderate fountaining and put out more flows which piled up inside the east shelter and spread to the east, south and southwest, extending the front to the base of the east cone. After dark the northeast cone became quiet, the lakes were low and the glow dull.

Daily measurements during this period directed to numerous floor points gave evidence of a condition extraordinarily stationary, as though the top of the lava column were rigidly locked to the old rim by the new overlaps. There was none of the sensitive rising and falling of a few feet which was so characteristic of the movements of the former craggy floor.

On Monday, Feb. 17, about 5 p. m., the lakes were a little higher, the eastern ones about eight feet below their rims and the north lake 15 feet. The activity was unchanged and much smoke rose from the floor south and southwest and some smoke around the north lake. A flow trickled sluggishly on the southwest flank of the northeast heap and the northernmost of several irregular lumpy cones on the summit of the heap was hissing mildly. The north rampart of the main lake and much of the northeast grotto dome had broken down. Flames were abundant and large and appeared at the following places: A rampart pot on the west side of the north lake, the west, east and south cones, a spiracle vent between the main and southeast ponds, and filagree heaps southeast of the north lake and east of the main lake.

January 19, 1919. Margin of Halemaumau southwest overflowed, looking towards west station. (Photo Jaggar.)

February 13, 1919, 11 a. m. Incandescent interior of cavern hung with stalactites, east cone, Halemaumau floor. (Photo Jaggar.)

On Feb. 18 about 6:30 a. m. the lakes were high so that their fountains were visible at a distance. Shortly after 8 a. m. the northeast heap again burst its northernmost summit cone and started a spouting flood which deluged the slope northeastward, many bright yellow flashes of flame bursting through the red melt some distance below the summit. At 9 a. m. the flows were pushing northward and northeastward on the heap and sluggish flowing continued all day.

About 3 p. m. the summit cone of the heap had reformed and was hissing and lifting a lid of crust. Instead of bursting out through the summit, however, the pressure was relieved by an outbreak on the northeast flank of the heap and the flow overran the higher edge of Halemaumau close to the north side of the rounded pressure mound, which since 1894 has been a conspicuous eminence on the northeastern outer rim of Halemaumau. This flow poured in a tongue about 30 feet long around the mound eastward, and another tongue 50 feet long pushed northward.

This overflow filled and permanently obliterated a depressed and sheltered niche in the rim which had been used by the writer as the northeast trig station and which in December, 1916, was the station occupied by Mr. Lionel Walden when the sketches were made for the famous diorama of Halemaumau.

At 7 p. m. there were twelve flaming cones and four lakes. The northeast heap was quiet, the north lake dull and relatively low, the main lake about nine feet down, streaming eastward and bombarding its northeast grotto. Around it there were flaming vents in the rampart, on the east, north and west, the western one a high chimney pot through the top of the west grotto dome.

A pot had opened at the central cone locality and was splashing and flaming. The west cone was flaming and the southwest pond glowed dimly. Flames rose at the spiracle locality between the southeast pond and the main lake, there were high gas pressure and flames in the filagree cone on the north brink of the southeast pond and the liquid in the east cone pot was somewhat higher. The south cone flared brightly and everything indicated much flaming of gases under pressure.

On Feb. 19 the pit was smoky, there was no special change and in the evening six main glowing areas in the view as seen from a distance represented the four lakes, the west heap and the south cone.

On Thursday, Feb. 20, in the morning, the north lake was low, the main lake relatively high and the lava in the east cone appeared lower, considerably extending the grotto cavern under the cone. The main lake was thickly crusted and apparently rising. There was no gas pressure at the northeast cone, no flows were in motion and there was much smoke.

On Friday, Feb. 21, 1919, at 11 a. m., the lava of the east cone and main lake was 15 feet below the rims and the north lake was low, fountaining noisily. The interior of the east cone had diminished in brightness. Smoke rose densely from the southeastern half of the floor surface, this being notably the region occupied by the three heaps which have given vent to the recent overflows. There was great increase of solfataric staining about the smoking areas and this extended over the rim southeast and south, where disagreeable fumes of sulphurous acid rose through cracks adjacent to the southeast station and there was much deposit of yellow and white sublimates, sulphur, alum and gypsum, at this place and also near the old south cone east of the south station. The edge of the inner floor of Halemaumau just south of the southeast station appeared slightly swollen but the measurements indicated no marked changes of floor level elsewhere.

Exploration of the summit of the west heap revealed the fact that it had caved in on top and the revived pot observed glowing on the night of Feb. 14 was found in the midst of a pool area in the depression, the pool being an oval 50 feet long southeast-northwest, and the pot a cauldron seven feet long near the southern end of the pool, containing liquid lava one foot down sluggishly bubbling. The west cone was a high sulphur-stained glowing pyramid on the northeastern slope of the west heap and the southwest pond, also on the slope, was marked by rounded rampart heaps a little farther to the south.

In the evening the main lake was higher, a very large banner of flame played through the opening on top of the west grotto dome and in all seven cones were flaming and five ponds made luminous the fume above. The new west heap pond is included among these. The northeast cone was dark.

During the week ending at 8 p. m. Friday, Feb. 21, 1919, the seismographs of the Whitney Laboratory registered pronounced local earthquakes at 2:59 p. m. Feb. 15 and 6:40 a. m. Feb. 20. Microseisms and microtremors have both been moderate, the latter decreasing somewhat. Movements of tilting have been slight and variable—Feb. 15-16 to the northeast, Feb. 17 to the southwest, Feb. 18 stationary, Feb. 19-20 to the southwest, and Feb. 21 to the northeast.

March 1, 1919.

The last week in February of 1919 was strikingly repeated at the lava pit the performance of 1918, exhibiting revival of strong tumescence of the semi-solid lava around the lakes and eastern cones, and along with this mass swelling, eruptions of liquid lava making spectacular standing fountains, have, as expected for this season before the equinox, greatly extended the overflows from Halemaumau to the east, southeast and south. The lakes as well as the three lava heaps have taken part in overflowing and the swelling of the bench magma under and around the lake cups is pronounced, so that all the lakes now stand as ring-shaped basins elevated above the old rim level of the pit. There are now six lakes, the west cone having collapsed to an open pond. A conspicuous result of the renewed swelling is the mashing upward and outward of the Halemaumau pit rim southwest, south and east, so as to make a pressure ridge from 8 to 15 feet high with an elephant's-back curve on the side away from the pit. The width of the uplifted portion of the rim varies from 10 to 20 feet and for nearly a third of the circumference of Halemaumau this movement has destroyed and made unrecognizable the old rim. Similar rim crushing took place in February and October of 1918 on the southwest and north rims.

As the eruptions of the week have destroyed the three most used surveying stations, measurement for the time being is at a standstill. As the lakes have been high, at times overflowing and practically level with the adjacent floors, the net rise at the eastern surfaces has been from 10 to 15 feet and there has been overflow construction of a few feet at the northeast, south and southwest heaps. The placing of new flag stations and fresh triangulation of the altered topography is now in progress.

On Saturday, Feb. 22, 1919, at 4 p. m., it was evident that a strong rise of the liquid lava of the lakes had started. Where on the previous day the main lake and east pot lava had been 15 feet down, these places now showed the liquid only two feet below the marginal ramparts and in the southeast pond the crust was only one foot below the rim. Everything indicated increased gas pressure, marked by the steady, quiet, spraying type of fountaining. At the southeast pond the only fountain was inside of the curtained glowing cone on its north brink, elsewhere the liquid was coated with crust; the spray spurted out through the apertures of the cone. In the main lake there was steady streaming to the north and northeast grottoes, where the fountains noiselessly flung up strings of melt, the flaming gases blew incandescent spray of glass droplets across the surface skins, and these in turn were ceaselessly ballooning with gas rising from below. The ramparts were again being built up with spatter. The north lake was depressed three feet below its rim, quite circular, covered with a carpet of crust swollen in the center which was surrounded by a zone of quiet, high-flung fountaining under all the ramparts. Occasionally the gas accumulation burst the crust and started cracking and foundering of blocks and central fountaining.

The pot recently opened in the center of the floor of the pit had built a five-foot cone, which was noisily puffing through glowing apertures. The west and south cones were glowing, the east cone pot was filled with a crusted pudding which left two flaming openings on the south side, at the south cone smoke was very dense and much free sulphur vapor deposited yellow crystals back from the rim of the pit around the southeast station.

At 9 p. m. Feb. 23 the lake margins were four feet high, the cones were flaming, the activity as before, and in general the only marked change was a slight lowering of the liquid relative to its banks. At the northeast grotto of the main lake the spurts were quite rhythmic at one-second intervals, the spray was flung up from 30 to 40 feet, and outward horizontally over the crust of the lake it was hurled from 75 to 100 feet. There were occasional flings of heavy melt which slopped back on the lake surface. The streaming was towards the active corner. Occasionally the crust, about three inches thick, would break up and founder, this being as usual followed by slight subsidence due to loss of gas, whereby a red hot margin was revealed all around the lake which gained a width of about a foot before recovery set in.

On Monday, Feb. 24, no unusual activity was observed, the fume was rather dense and swelling of the bench magma southeast began to be apparent. At 10 p. m. the north lake was brimming in its basin and fountaining high, and after midnight all the lakes were high, the west heap was spurting and the central cone flaring at intervals.

Tuesday, Feb. 25, proved to be a day of sudden crisis. Measurements at 9:30 a. m. showed mass uplift of the southeast floor, northeast heap, southwest floor and at the lake ramparts and there was doubtless marked uplift in the smoky region around the south cone. The central cone had changed its shape and a new straight flow had poured from it across the floor of the pit northwestward. The lakes, observed at 10 a. m., 1 p. m. and 4 p. m., were high and brimming all day.

At 10 a. m. the southeast concrete platform used as a trig station was practically horizontal, but surrounded by cracks hot with sulphurous fumes recently developed there. During the day very rapid acceleration in tumescence of the bench magma pushed the rim of the pit up 10 feet, swelling the southeastern half of the pit floor, tilting back the concrete station at an angle of 20 degrees away from the center of the pit and keeping the relation of the inner floor to the relief of the rim about as it had been before. Just north of the southeast station the floor had stood eight feet below the rim, whereas at the station it was only two feet down; after the upheaval these relations were the same, but the pressure ridge upheaved opposite the higher rim escarpment was 12 feet high and 15 feet wide with reference to the region back of it, whereas at the station it was only about eight feet high and ten feet wide. In other words, the biggest part of the ridge of rim rock squeezed up came opposite the place where the rim had been highest above the floor. All of the rim rock involved in this pressure ridge at this place for a length of 200 feet was the overflow lava of 1918. The ridge, however, extended around the rim to the southwest, there involving the older rim made of 1894 flows.

At 4:45 p. m. the two south cones, which for some time past have been quiet and smoky, suddenly erupted a flood of liquid lava which poured westward and southward, crossing the rim of the pit as before at the south station and in the direction of the southeast trail. This outbreak was followed almost immediately by a similar flood through the orifice of the east cone, which poured straight eastward across the rim of the pit on the south side of the east station, partially submerging that station. At 5:30 p. m. there were two dome-shaped standing fountains side by side at the south cone locality, each six feet high and ten feet wide, fed from below under strong pressure like an artesian well and the pooled lava around the cones was feeding rapid hot liquid flows which cascaded southeastward and westward. The flows followed the new trail towards the road terminus for two-thirds of the way down the slope, destroying at least half of the trail and pushing twice as far as the former flow from this vent. By 5:50 p. m. the standing fountains changed to spurting vents and the flows rapidly came to rest.

The east cone also maintained a standing fountain and at 5:30 p. m. the flow had reached the former site of the Observatory hut and was advancing six feet per minute. Where the flow crossed the rim it was about 30 feet wide. This source also quieted down shortly after the other, or about 6 p. m.

During this spasm of flow the lakes were high and fountaining violently and continuously around their margins. During the night the north lake overflowed northwestward and in the evening 17 glowing points could be counted in the distant view of Halemaumau.

It is worthy of note that the sudden overflow with strong tumescence of 1918 occurred Feb. 23, whereas this year it was Feb. 25. Such intense swelling, accompanied by humping of the rim of the pit and immediately preceding in each case a spasm of strong flowing, occurred in February and November of 1918.

On Wednesday, Feb. 26, at 6:30 p. m., the fume was considerably reduced, all the vents were alive and the glow at night had increased, the pressure ridge had increased in height and the south cone was built up and spurting. The old south cone of 1918 was now entirely buried and also much of the ridge extending south from it. The east cone was flaming and the fountains of the main lake bombarded with unusual violence a long stretch of the north bank of the lake. The north lake was similarly active and the northeast heap showed summit incandescence.

On Feb. 27 the north lake was especially high, the fume was rather dense, the west heap pond had built up an inner cone and other activity continued as before.

At 2 p. m., Friday, Feb. 28, 1919, it was evident that the swelling of the bench magma included the region around the north lake and the entire southeastern half of the pit. The humped rim extended from the southwest side of the pit all around the southern margin as far as a point opposite the east cone. The continued swelling had warped the new flows of Feb. 25, broken the south cone in two and lifted its inner half so as to reveal glowing layers and in several places the inner floor layers by uplift had parted from the humped rim and so were revealed as the upheaved edge in cross section of the inner lava cylinder. The fresh flood south had extended some 600 feet beyond the south station and the southeast flows had moved a like distance but were wider and more forked. The east cone flow was about 300 feet long and had passed a short distance beyond the old hut site.

The 1918 rim was now buried under overflow from the southeast station to a point beyond the south station and from a place 30 feet south of the east station to a point 50 feet north of the northeast station. The fresh flow material south-southeast was itself mashed up to form part of the pressure rim eight to ten feet high. The south station was entirely buried, the southeast station platform borne high on the flank of the pressure rim at an angle of 40 degrees and fractured, and the east station had frozen cascades enveloping it. The highest part of the pressure rim, 100 feet north of the southeast station, stood 15 feet above the general level outside of the pit and from here it sloped down to the floor level opposite the east cone.

Looking at the Halemaumau surface from the high ground northeast of the pit, the pressure rim was seen to be a puffed up lip hemming in the uplifted floor which extended westward from it as a high flat surface with the cones, lava heaps and lake ramparts standing upon it at still higher levels. The uplift around the lakes had diminished the relative relief of the lava heaps.

The lakes were depressed about five feet within their cups, the north lake rather less than the others, moderate fountaining was in progress and dense smoke rose from the southern half of the floor. The west cone had collapsed to an open pit 50 feet in diameter, with lava splashing a short distance below the rim. The west heap pond had built up a broad cone 10 feet high, which was hissing in spasms from glowing orifices. A harsh puffing of gas was heard occasionally from one of the domes of the north lake. Short flows had recently poured out on the eastern side of the summit of the northeast heap. The northwestern floor had continued to subside and draw away from the wall of the pit; it showed marginal slumped crusts and cliff rocks which had tumbled on its surface. That tumescence was still in progress southeast was shown by incessant tumbling of fragments in the fissures of the pressure rim.

In the Whitney Laboratory of Seismology steady tilt to the east has accompanied the period of tumescence, microtremor has been strong and there have been notable local earthquakes which will be reported later. The strongest of these, at 9:24 p. m. Feb. 25, happened in the evening of the day of paroxysmal swelling and overflow, was very strongly felt and resulted in a fixed tilt of the ground to the north and east, as shown by all the instruments.

Very respectfully,
T. A. JAGGAR, JR.,
Volcanologist.

ERRATA.—January Bulletin, Vol. VII, No. 1. Page 3, for "Section," line 18, read "Station."

Page 6, line 1: The words "above rim" apply only to "S. W. Heap, January 25."

Page 8, table bottom of page: The words "above rim" apply only to "S. W. Heap."

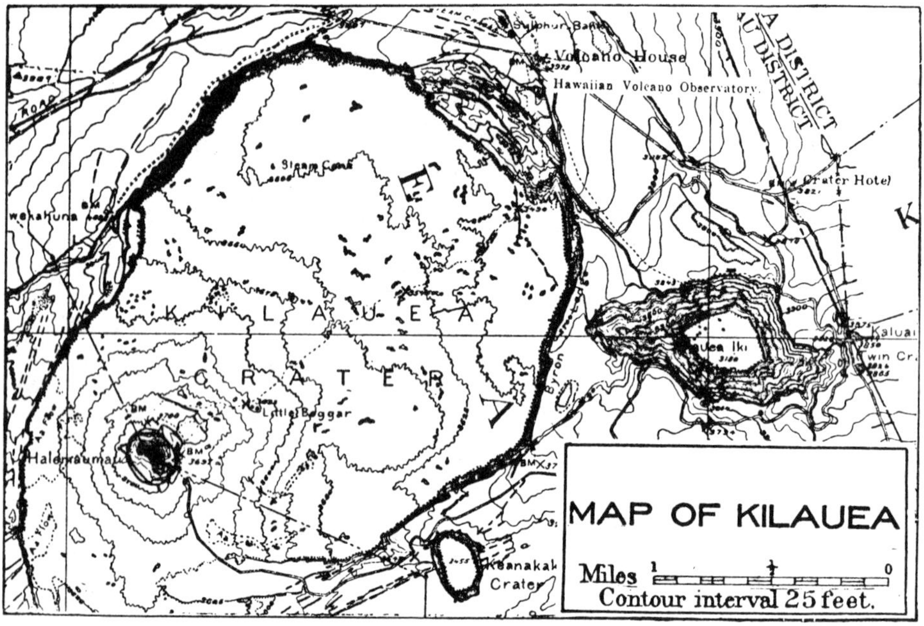

HAWAIIAN VOLCANO OBSERVATORY.

This issue of the Monthly Bulletin of the Hawaiian Volcano Observatory is the first under the authority and supervision of the U. S. Weather Bureau. In this connection, the valuable co-operation of the Hawaiian Volcano Research Association is acknowledged with gratitude.

The Observatory is equipped with the following seismometric instruments rebuilt at the station in 1918 for the special needs of volcano research: two Bosch-Omori pendulums, high speed registration of local earthquakes; one optically recording seismograph for distant earthquakes; one clinograph registering E-W tilting of the ground. A vertical component seismograph was in December, 1918, set up in experimental operation. These are seated on concrete piers in a closed basement room having practically constant temperature, beneath the chief Observatory building near the hotel. Time is referred to a rated chronometer, checked at intervals by solar observations with a transit. Both instruments are loaned by the College of Hawaii. Hawaiian standard time (H. S. T.) is 10 hrs. 30 min. slower than Greenwich time.

CANCANI SCALE OF SEISMIC INTENSITY.

Expressed by accelerations measured in millimeters per second per second.

I.	Instrumental	0.0	2.5
II.	Very slight	2.5	5.0
III.	Slight	5.0	10.0
IV.	Sensible, mediocre	10.0	25.0
V.	Rather strong	25.0	50.0
VI.	Strong	50.0	100.0
VII.	Very strong	100.0	250.0
VIII.	Ruinous	250.0	500.0
IX.	Disastrous	500.0	1000.0
X.	Very disastrous	1000.0	2500.0
XI.	Catastrophic	2500.0	5000.0
XII.	Great catastrophe	5000.0	10000.0

Grade IV. is ordinarily the minimum perceived by the senses; and in grade XII. the acceleration, or rate of change of motion (jerk) reaches that of terrestrial gravitation.

In the standard form of report the maximum intensity or acceleration, designated by the symbol a, or max. a, is given in the conventional unit, the milligal. The milligal is a measure of acceleration, such that 1 milligal = 1/100 mm. per sec. per sec. = 10 μ per sec. per sec. The Cancani scale, here defined in terms of millimeters per sec. per sec., can therefore be expressed in milligals by multiplying each of the numbers by 100.

U. S. DEPARTMENT OF AGRICULTURE
WEATHER BUREAU
CHARLES F. MARVIN, CHIEF

MONTHLY BULLETIN
OF THE
Hawaiian Volcano Observatory

VOL. VII. HONOLULU, HAWAII, MARCH, 1919 No. 3

March 8, 1919.

The changes in Halemaumau during the week ending March 7, 1919, have been occasioned by liquid overflows of the lakes and driblet flows eastward from the northeast heap. The tumescence of the floor has ceased. The cone on top of the northeast heap has developed into a steeple twelve feet high, which is a very conspicuous landmark crowning the summit of the new heapings. The longest overflow of 1919 poured south for a quarter of a mile on the afternoon of March 4.

Measurements week by week beginning Feb. 14 yield the following data showing the marked increase of rising as the equinox approaches. As the former southeast station has been destroyed measurements are now referred to the government bench mark on a concrete table back of the north rim of the pit. This mark stands 3700 feet above sea level and 11 feet below the southeast station used in recent surveys.

Feb. 14, main lake 14 feet below mark, summit cone N. E. heap 27 feet above mark.

Feb. 22, main lake 5 feet above mark, summit N. E. cone 30 feet above mark.

Feb. 28, main lake 18 feet above mark, summit N. E. cone 30 feet above mark.

March 7, main lake 37 feet above mark, summit N. E. tower 55 feet above mark.

These figures show that in eight days—February 14-22—the lake rose 19 feet, or 2.4 feet per day, and the northeast cone rose 3 feet, or .4 feet per day. In six days—February 22-28—the lake rose 13 feet, or 2.2 feet per day and the northeast cone was stationary. In seven days—February 28-March 7—the lake rose 19 feet, or 2.7 feet per day and the northeast cone rose 25 feet, or 3.6 feet per day.

On Saturday, March 1, 1919, about 6 p. m., the main lake overflowed, the flood streaming eastward past the east cone and extending to the steam cracks southeast of the former site of the wooden hut. At 9 p. m. the northeast heap erupted, producing flows which poured eastward and northwestward. A branch of the latter flow extended north in the direction of the postal crack and surrounded the arched half-dome which was formerly a conspicuous eminence bounding Halemaumau on the northeast. On this day the west heap sent a flow down its northwest slope inside the pit and the south cone area developed five spiracles of different shapes. These were scattered along the wall crack between the uplifted southeast station and the south cone of recent eruptions.

On March 2 the fume was thinner, and at 5 p m. the southeast pond was depressed five feet within its cup and covered with a blistered crust, the only fountaining being inside the curtained cone at the north margin of the pond. The main lake stood three feet below its rampart, there was the usual activity in its northeast grotto, and the surface of the lake was covered with heavy folding crusts which tended to balloon upward over rising gas, and occasional fountains would pulse under the crust, agitating it without breaking through. The north lake was nearly full to the brim with activity in several marginal grottoes. The cones elsewhere showed the usual glow and flames, the northeast cone was alive and large reddish yellow flames played through the openings of the east cone.

At 7:15 p. m. the northeast cone burst open and ejected a standing fountain for half an hour, sending out two swift flows, the longer one westward and the shorter to the east. After 7:45 the eruption dwindled.

On Monday, March 3, trickle flows were moving on the northeast heap and the summit cone had developed a high, broad tower-like structure with an open shaft where the lava was splashing and throwing up jets. Fresh flow could be seen on the northwest slope of the western heap, there were flames at the south and east cones, the swelling movement was decreasing and the pit at night was brilliant with fifteen glowing points.

Extensive forest fires had developed along a line several miles in length on the east flank of Mauna Loa, spreading rapidly in three days, owing to the lack of rain. The flames at night appeared much yellower and less red than the glow at Halemaumau, and the smoke in daylight was similar to the volcanic fume but slightly browner.

On Tuesday, March 4, 1919, the northeast cone had built up a sharp spire standing 12 feet above its base, and as this surmounted the lava heap it was the highest and most conspicuous object in Halemaumau. The view of the entire pit filling from the top of the only remaining cliff, which bounds the pit on the northwest side, showed the lakes approximately on a level with the eye, the northeast tower some 20 feet higher, and the several domes and cones rising above the flat summit of the filling within the southeastern half of the circle, while from the main lake down into the foreground at the base of the northwest cliff sweeping flows sloped downward past and around the north lake which stood as a ring-wall eminence a little to one side. The whole arrangement preserved the tendency to southeastward heaping, which began in December, when the fill was over a hundred feet down, the main difference being that this inner heap had now risen until it was above the edge of the pit.

From 6 to 7 p. m. the south cone surmounting the lifted floor at the pressure rim was spasmodically hissing and had developed a peculiar shape, hooded on top and turning an open glowing face of fiery orifices which looked southwestward. The west pond had again closed over and was surmounted by a filagree cone. The southwest pond had built two domes, and east of it a banner of flame shot upward through a crevice. The central cone was a filagree heap and the south and northeast cones were both glowing. The main lake had recently enlarged by the collapse of the west dome grotto, and in both the main and north lakes the liquid lava was splashing at about the level of the ramparts.

The pressure rim around the south and southwest edges of the pit had continued to rise so that it was now 15 feet high in places and its extension on the east-southeast side was nearly 20 feet high. On climbing to the top of the south pressure rim the uplifted inner floor of pahoehoe flows was found level with the top, an expanse of rolling and warped pahoehoe sloping away towards the center of the pit.

The east cone was flaming and the southeast pond very quiet. The northeast heap was putting out trickling toes of live lava so that the old northeast half-dome was nearly buried under them. This trickle construction was extending the heap northeastward.

At 4:30 p. m. the cone at the west heap pond erupted vigorously, making a standing fountain of very liquid lava which gave vent to the longest flow of the year to date. By 6 p. m. this flow had reached its limit, 1300 feet, to the south, a very straight stream from 50 to 100 feet wide. A second flow from the same source poured down the northwest slope of the heap. The source cone after 6 p. m. was a large open well with raised sides spurting irregularly.

On this day the fume was thinner, and in the evening there were ten incandescent points and four fuming lakes visible, the two western ponds being again converted into glowing cones.

On March 5, at 11:30 a. m., the lake margins were about five feet high, there was eastward streaming in the main lake and a spatter dome was building at its east end. Flows which appeared fresh had poured across the north rampart of the north lake and thence into the northwest wall valley, but the floor under the cliff remained low and the cliff high. The northeast cone was hissing and driblet flows from it were still in motion on the northeast side of the heap. In the evening these flows increased their vigor and during the night greatly extended the pile of driblet flows on the east side of the northeast heap, reaching out to the steam crack east of Halemaumau and covering the entire area which surrounded the former site of the Observatory hut.

On March 6, at 12:30 p. m., all tumescence appeared to have ceased, driblet flows were in motion in the vicinity of the remnant of the northeast half-dome, only the extreme summit of which remained visible. The lakes were three to four feet below their margins and the west heap pond was fountaining on the south side of the cone there. The top of the eastern stone shelter was found to be still intact at about the level of the lava heaps around it.

On Friday, March 7, 1919, there was a strong revival of rising and overflowing of liquid lava which was general throughout all the vents, excepting the south cone. Strong flows began about 8 a. m., all the lakes were high and a cascade poured across the eastern rampart of the main lake, sending a flow a few hundred feet to the east. The northeast cone tower ejected umbrella-shaped gushes through an orifice in its extreme summit. This tower was now an extraordinary steeple rising some 15 feet above its base. Driblet flows pushed out from the southeastern flank of the northeast heap. A flow poured northward from the central cone around the west side of the north lake, the cone developing into an open pot brimming with lava surging and splashing. The southwest pond overflowed southward for a short distance and built a high marginal dome. At noon the cones were hissing, the main lake brimming full and fountaining violently along its north bank and the west heap cone was an open oven ejecting lava with much fountaining, which produced a short flow southwestward. The west arm pond locality of former days was occupied by a cone hissing noisily, and the largest dome of the southwest pond was south of this and only a short distance away. The north lake was only one foot below its overflow level and its fountaining was vigorous. After this spasm of overflow there was a period of reaction, and in the evening the lakes and cones were unusually dull.

For the fortnight ending at 9 p. m. Friday, March 7, 1919, the seismographs of the Whitney Laboratory have registered the following local earthquakes: Feb. 22, 7:19 p. m., slight; Feb. 25, 9:25 p. m., strongly felt, registered for seven minutes; Feb. 26, 6:08 a. m. and 11:03 p. m., both slight; Feb. 27, 3:25 a. m., slight; March 1, 5:44 a. m., moderate; March 4, 4:54 a. m., slight; March 5, 1:33 a. m., slight; March 7, 7:08 p. m. and 7:26 p. m., both pronounced; 8:42 p. m., small.

Teleseisms, or distant earthquakes, were registered beginning 5:44 p. m. March 3 and 2:02 a. m. March 4, both of these yielding no evidence of distance and appearing much alike in energy and quality.

Microseismic movement has as usual been dominant in the north-south azimuth, moderate in amplitude Feb. 22-24, slight Feb. 25-27, stronger Feb. 28-March 5, slight March 6-7. The rhythmic microtremor has continued strong most of the time with some decrease Feb. 25 and Mar. 2-3. The spasmodic microtremor or supposed volcanic vibration has fluctuated, with strongish spasms Feb. 25-27 and March 4-5.

The tilting of the ground has also fluctuated through a small range as follows: Slightly west and south Feb. 22-24, stronger east and north Feb. 25-26, stationary Feb. 27-March 1, slight west and south March 2-3, pronounced north and east March 4-6, moderate south and west March 7.

March 15, 1919.

Continued overflow south and east from the lava heaps of Halemaumau has been the distinguishing feature of the week ending Friday, March 14, 1919. A renewal of fountaining at the wall crack south-southeast on March 11 was preceded, just as on February 25, by a swelling upward of the floor, and this was followed by a reaction during the three days following, whereby some of the ponds increased in size owing to subsidence below and collapse of the banks. These first breakdowns probably herald a large subsidence which will follow the equinox. A conspicuous feature of the northeast flow heapings which has developed during the week is the swelling up of a dozen domes or tumuli in the midst of the thickening piles of lava. It will be remembered that this happened also in March of last year in the southeastern flows toward the close of the flow period. The cause of the phenomenon appears to be increased resistance to flow as the crust thickens and the front becomes more remote, so that the advancing and expanding fluid in the ducts can find outlet most easily by swelling the roof above it.

The measurements have indicated that the southeast margin of the lava column as represented by its hardened surface rose by tumescence from two to three feet betwen March 9 and March 11 and the north lake region subsided somewhat after March 12. The lakes have fluctuated from ten to fifteen feet within their cups but the rising of the liquid lava has been expended in flows from both the lakes and the cones. The flow eastward from the northeast heap on the evening of March 12 is believed to be the longest yet poured out in 1919, measured from its tip to the former rim of Halemaumau.

On Saturday, March 8, 1919, at 9 a.m., the fume from the pit was somewhat dense and the lakes were not visible from the Observatory. During the previous night the glow had been rather dull except at 1 a. m., when the main and north lakes were fountaining at a high level. At noon the lava in the north lake was about two feet below the rampart. At 7:30 p. m. there was another high level with brilliant fountaining, followed later by subsidence. No glow was observed in the northeast cone. During the night the southwest pond exhibited brilliant activity and the large spatter dome on its margin collapsed.

On March 9 at 10 a. m. the southwest pond was high and building a new spatter dome. The north lake appeared to be overflowing, the central cone was glowing on its north side and the fume from the pit was moderately thin. About noon no flows were found in motion on the northeast heap. This heap, its summit region 40 feet above the old rim of Halemaumau, now overlapped the edge of the pit with pilings of irregular lumpy character extending several hundred feet to the east of the old east shelter.

From 4 to 6 p. m. trickle flows were pushing eastward from the flanks of the heap in several places and a remarkable development of large swollen domes had appeared in the eastern part of the heap between the east shelter and the east outlying steam crack. One of these just east of the buried stone shelter was an oval tumulus 50 feet long and 10 feet high.

The main lake at this time was four feet below its rampart with an open tunnel grotto at the west end showing glowing and dripping interior walls, while at the northeast and southeast corners there were grottoes where perpetual surges threw out a fiery surf which curved back, flinging its spray over the crust of the lake.

There were hissing and flaming vents at the south, northeast, west, east and central cones and the cone on top of the west heap was seven feet high with glowing holes in its summit that were flaming. The west pond was found to be an open circular pit 50 feet in diameter with crusted lava depressed four feet below the rim, the surface ballooning with the gas rising from below and occasionally breaking to fling up a fountain of melt. The flaming west cone stood on the east side of the pond. The central cone was now an irregular heap three feet high. East of it an open crack 12 inches wide and six feet deep showed the interior glow of the bench magma to be a dark cherry red. The north lake was only one foot below the overflow level and its surface streaming was in the direction of the northern active grottoes. Occasionally both the north and main lakes would break up and subside, showing bright edges one to two feet deep.

West of the site of the former south station the pressure rim was now fully 18 feet high in places and frozen lava cascades from the region of the southwest pond marked the places across it where that pond had recently overflowed in considerable volume.

On March 10 the only rising activity observed was shown by continued trickle flows from the northeast heap.

At 3 p. m. the gas pressure at the south wall crack spiracles was less noisy than before, the lakes stood six to seven feet below their banks, the grotto activity was unchanged and on the east side of the northeast tower there were orifices half way up where flaming gases rushed out through very small holes and built vitreous spiracles of the melted drip bubbling out with the gas. The large tumulus east of the stone shelter was giving vent to stiff lava through several cracks and this had produced a new oval patch of thick bulbous outline about the same size as the dome and south of it. The dome was clearly full of this pressing pasty lava, and its escape was both upward and sidewise through cracks. Through such a heap as this one the lava is connected by a system of tubes with the pool inside the heap, the summit cone acting as a gas vent, while the melt, partially relieved of gas, seeks outlet under pressure at the extremities of the several ducts. The swollen tumuli in the eastern extension of the heap were now some of them 15 to 20 feet high; there were about ten of them in all and live lava was trickling in several places. In the evening there was a spurt of flowing from this heap.

It was evident on this day that the southeast floor had begun to swell again and the region around the southeast pond was greatly stained with sulphur.

On Tuesday, March 11, 1919, there was repeated a day of crisis similar to February 25, just two weeks before, but with effects less strong. During the previous night a new cone four feet high was formed at the south-southeast wall crack which had poured snaky driblet cascades down the outer face of the pressure rim. The increased tumescence and yellow stain in this vicinity was pronounced. At noon the new cone was spouting from a glowing cavern on its west side, the east cone was hissing harshly and the northeast cone mildly, and flows were pushing out from the higher slopes of the northeast heap. Fresh flows of this type had again invaded the remnant of the east shelter so that all of the old stone wall was covered except the south end.

At 3 p. m. the main lake margin was six feet high, its surface was crusted and its activity was sluggish. The north lake margin was three feet high and the activity consisted of ballooning skins and bombardment along the northwest shore of the pond.

The gas pressure during the early afternoon was mild but later it was increased, and at 5:15 p. m. this took effect as effervescence and outflow of liquid lava. The north lake overflowed its north bank, the flow pouring to the wall of the pit. The northeast heap broke out in many places, building extensions to the east and north. The cones hissed noisily and the main and western lakes were fountaining in lively fashion.

The new south-southeast cone burst open and produced a standing fountain while the south cone near it spurted southward through its orifices and sent out sheets of flame. The fountaining cone developed a cascade which tumbled as a rivulet down the steep face of the cone and the pressure ridge below, making a very liquid pool which forked and spread as a thin syrup in two main streams some 300 feet to the southeast. The cascade was about five feet wide and 18 feet high. This flow solidified in smooth glassy toes, cooling through mottled purple shades and showing none of the vesicular lace work which covers the pasty bulbous toes of the northeast heap. This suggested that the long tumultuous cascade had caused unusually complete discharge of gas from the melt.

On March 12 the region adjacent to the north lake appeared slightly lower as though there had been compensatory subsidence under the north lake overflows coordinate with the tumescence southeast. In the evening at 9 p. m. a long flow had pushed out from the extreme tip of the eastward extension of the northeast heap and travelled to a point a third of a mile or more from the pit. At 9:30 p. m. a sudden flare from the southwest pond suggested collapse. The main and north lakes were fountaining high above their ramparts, the cones were puffing noisily, the pit as a whole was very brilliant and it was during this period that the southeast pond, hitherto an inconspicuous circular pit about 50 feet across, became by collapse of its banks a much larger lake.

On Thursday, March 13, it was evident that the southeast pond cone had fallen in and the central cone had collapsed to an open pot. A circuit of the pit between 4 and 7 p. m. revealed great change at the southeast pond which had become practically a large arm of the main lake, separated from the latter by only a small partition five feet thick. This southeast arm was nearly as large as the main lake, fully 150 feet long in a northwest-southeast direction and adjoined the main lake at the latter's southeast corner. The region which had collapsed followed the line of a former crack where flames were playing and spiracles were building. The streaming in the southeast pond was swift in the direction of the partition or northwestward, while in the main lake the grotto fountaining was very bright and the streaming was to the east. Both lakes stood about six feet below their banks.

The cones were hissing and flaming as usual, the west pond showed ballooning skins about five feet down and a large filagree cone above its east bank. Large yellowish and reddish flames played above this cone and another vent at the southwest pond. The north lake was bright, there were live flows on the northeast heap, one glow hole appeared low down on the south side of the northeast tower and the east cone was hissing and flaming.

On Friday, March 14, 1919, the pit had been rather dull during the night, trickle flows continued at the northeast heap and fountains were occasionally visible above the lake ramparts. In the afternoon there was pronounced subsidence, the lakes being reported over 15 feet below their banks, but after midnight they again rose to brimming levels.

In the Whitney Laboratory of Seismology the week has been seismically quiet so far as earthquakes are concerned. Microtremor has continued strong, microseisms became very strong during a period of calms and light southwesterly winds, and the tilting of the ground was eastward March 7-11, strongly westward March 12 and moderately westward March 13-14.

Gas collections with vacuum tubes have been made at several of the live vents of the crater during the week.

March 22, 1919.

The week preceding the vernal equinox of 1919 has shown the lava column of Halemaumau to stand at a constant high level so far as its crusted surface was concerned, while overflows continued from lakes and cones. The gas pressure, marked by hissing cones and spraying grottoes, has continued high, the northeast heap has remained the principal source of voluminous flowing, and the eastern lakes have exhibited a tendency to lowering within their cups. The fume has thinned.

Measurements referred to the north Government Bench Mark (3700 feet above sea level) were as follows:

March 7, main lake 37 feet above mark, N. E. tower 55 feet above mark.

March 18, main lake 35 feet above mark, N. E. tower 65 feet above mark.

The lake thus subsided two feet in eleven days, averaging 0.18 feet per day, while the northeast tower rose 10 feet, averaging 0.9 feet per day.

On Saturday, March 15, 1919, the fume was dense towards the west and southwest, new flows were pushing southward from the northeast heap and a new short fork had branched out from the easternmost flow of the heap on its north side at about the locality of the steam cracks east of Halemaumau.

At 6 p. m. the south-southeast cone was throwing up bright banners of flame with high gas pressure, the main lake and southeast pond stood six feet below their banks, the partition between them was still in place and all around the edge of the southeast pond a ballooned up crust marking a higher level had been left, now broken-in, leaving hollow shells. The pond was quiet except for a spraying fountain under its north bank.

On March 16 at noon a circuit of the pit east and north revealed a new flow from the northeast heap pushing southward along the east side of the high eastern pressure rim. The northeast tower had developed an open cavern at its base on the east side and this was hung with stalactites, while for 50 feet from it all over the top of the heap there were accumulations of recent glassy lava which appeared to have been splashed and spattered explosively from this cavern as a source. This glassy material was spread in a thin sheet with a smooth surface and appeared to have been excessively liquid when it was thrown out. There had been heavy rains during the days immediately preceding this discovery and the occurrence closely resembled a similar explosive outburst of very liquid melt which happened in this vicinity a year ago, also during heavy downpours of rain. It is possible that localized heating of rain water causes superficial steam pressure in lava chambers and so brings about an explosive eruption of the melt which is confined within the heap.

The north lake was found brimming nearly level with the lower gaps in its rim, its crust pulsing with gas inflation and fountains playing around its margins.

At noon the west and southwest ponds were brimming level with their ridges and the west pond finally welled over, both its northern and southern lips, the southern flow pushing south-southwest as an overflow outside of the pit boundaries, while the northern one spread as a sheet over 200 feet wide, pouring down the slope into the northwestern depressed part of Halemaumau. There was fountaining in the pond and high flings of melt were thrown up by the southwest pond. The west heap cone stood high and was hissing. The south cones were hissing and flaming and the other activities of the pit remained as before. As compared with the north lake the main lake stood low relative to its bank, though at all times the absolute level of the north lake basin was much lower than that of the main lake basin.

At some time later in the day the north lake overflowed and produced another flow of glassy appearance which poured toward the northwest and joined with the west pond flow. Neither of these flows reached the wall of the pit.

On Monday, March 17, in the afternoon the south and south-southeast cones were hissing noisily and the eastern lakes were low with walls ten feet high. At the north base of the east cone a driblet flow was pushing out from cracks in the ground, the gas pressure at its source lifting a lid of crust three feet square and at least six inches thick, the gas rushing out with a hissing noise at each lift of the lid which rose an inch or two at every spasm.

Live flows were in motion on the northeast heap. The summit of the heap showed two mouths, each three feet in diameter, emitting pasty flows and lifting lids of crust in the midst of circular puddings three to five feet high and 20 feet across a short distance southeast of the high tower. At the southern base of the tower spiracles were being built by gas which rushed out with strong hissing noises. The cavern under the tower contained very large stalactites covered with fresh spatter. Near the southeastern foot of the northeast heap deep caverns had been revealed by collapse, glowing inside and as much as 10 feet deep vertically. On the south slope of the northeast heap some typical aa lava appeared among the pahoehoe flows and there were very rough aa surfaces on the under side of the thin glassy shells covering the explosion area on top.

Across the central part of the floor deep cracks extended from the west end of the main lake to the north cone which is situated just south of the north lake. These cracks were two to three feet wide in places and locally showed no glow even for depths of 15 feet. The west pond surface stood two feet below its border, the skin ballooning with gas and the current streaming to a western grotto. The cone east of this pond was smaller than before and rather inactive and the pond itself had contracted so that it was not more than 20 feet across. The west heap cone was hissing and building spiracles and the central cone was hissing from large glowing orifices on its east flank. The north lake showed a margin two feet high and its activity in fountaining grottoes was around the northern semi-circle of its pit, the southern semicircle being apparently the source of rising lava. The streaming was thus northward and northeastward and the border fountains flung up stringy melt, making much new construction at large domes along the north bank.

On Tuesday, March 18, at 2 p. m., it was apparent that the pressure rim was becoming pushed back farther with a horizontal thrust and the inner floor of the pit is distinctly arched as a flat dome from the former site of the east station to that of the south station. The uplifted concrete platform of the southeast station was more broken and fallen apart owing to the tilting back. At the top of this slope the south-southeast cone had become an open dome with a glowing window two feet in diameter facing southeast and leading to the interior cupola, where the lava stood so high as to splash out through the window. A group of driblet spires and heaps stood near this cone and the older cone further south was blowing but with decreased violence. The east cone also was flaming under pressure but the area of the lifting lid of the previous day was quiet.

The southeast pond stood four feet below its rim and had risen to the brimming level within forty-eight hours as shown by an edge of crust still clinging to the margins and on the main lake side bridging the extension of the pond in that direction. The live part of the pond was circular, with overhang and active grottoes north and east, and a crust was cracking and foundering at 2:30 p. m.

The main lake appeared higher than before, standing five feet below its rampart with deep fiery grottoes northeast, southeast and west. There was much staining, smoking and cracking of the floor for 20 feet east of it. The north lake stood close to its margin and rose to brimming at 3:30 p. m. The west heap cone had built new gas spiracles on its western profile.

The northeast heap continued to show pasty bubbling lava at two craters three feet in diameter south of the high tower. Adjacent to the northeast tower on its south side was a blowing gas mouth flaming through a flap of incandescent skin and emitting a snake-like trickle of glassy lava. The mouth was three inches in diameter and the skin 18 inches long. A row of spiracles had been built near by and 50 feet away to the northeast there was a hot cavern made by a collapsed crust. At 4 p. m. the northeast heap gained pressure and broke into flows, the largest one pouring down its west flank.

At 6 p. m. strong rising occurred so that in the course of an hour the north lake overflowed northward, there were brilliant fountains at the southeast pond, the south-southeast cone increased its spitting of lava spray and flowing increased along the course of the northeast heap and at the eastern front of its flows.

On March 19 between 10 a. m. and noon the splashing window of the south-southeast cone closed to a puffing mouth. The other cones were flaming as before; the main lake, four feet down, showed the usual grotto fountains and eastward streaming with some bubble fountaining. The southeast pond had renewed its northern spatter dome and was splashing there. The west pond was overflowing in a steady stream northwestward as before. The north lake was still high, with northward streaming and grotto fountains. The fresh flow from it did not reach the north wall of the pit. The cone south of it had overflowed the surrounding floor. A new driblet cone six feet high had built beside the northeast tower on its south side and this cone was alive but the two craters farther south had solidified. Flows were in motion on the south and east flanks of the heap.

On Thursday, March 20, from 4 to 6 p. m., the high gas pressure with hissing and flaming from the cones continued, and the southeast floor showed cracks more numerous and increased in width.

The northeast heap flows were making out extensively southward so as to reach the base of the east cone and the shore of the main lake and to push past the pressure ridge outside of the Halemaumau margin 100 feet or more toward the roadway. This heap now extended over a third of a mile to the east-northeast over the Kilauea floor and many tongues projected southward from the extension.

Relative to its banks the main lake was low, with walls about 12 feet high. The rampart dome on its north side had cracked open and showed cherry red glow within. A sheet of flame shot up from cracks extending west of the lake. The north lake stood only three feet below its banks, its surface was covered with heavy crusts which occasionally broke up and its streaming continued northward to active grottoes on that side. The west pond was quiet and the southwest pond fountaining.

On the upper flanks of the northeast heap there were fresh flows and the spiracle cone south of the tower had built up a chair-like structure. An

Feb. 6, 1919. Northeast grotto of main lake, fountaining.

Feb. 6, 1919. Northeast grotto; near view.

Feb. 6, 1919. The great west grotto dome, main lake.

Feb. 7, 1919. Grotto over receding flow lava, south cone; the flow source.
—Photos Jaggar.

orifice a few feet farther east was hissing and building driblet mouths, and very smooth lava, with excessively fine grained vesiculation, flowed out sluggishly in snaky toes.

On Friday, March 21, 1919, at 6 p. m., the high gas pressure continued and small vents north of the south-southeast cone were making driblet flows. The east pressure ridge was in motion with rocks falling from both its east and west sides. A small flow on the lower southeastern flank of the northeast heap exhibited a texture entirely different from the other flows, its surface solidifying into rough steely gray ropes and the crusts at the front breaking and upending so that the paste beneath was seen to solidify in typical aa lumps which fell forward as rough clinkers. The flowing lava appeared smooth but black granular chunks could be seen developing within it.

The lakes were somewhat higher than on the previous day, the eastern ones with six-foot walls, and the east cone was ejecting lava driblets as well as flaming. There were heavy crusts on the main lake, tumultuous cracking and foundering occurred with bubble fountains, and the melt appeared somewhat more granular and pasty than at other times. The northeast heap flows had poured over the east bank of the main lake into the lake for a length of 20 feet of shore. The lake appeared to have increased in size, probably by collapse of the northern and western ramparts. The west lake was fountaining above its margins. Fume from the pit was thin, the glow was very bright in the evening and in the calm air the noise from the blowing vents could be heard over two miles away.

In the Whitney Laboratory of Seismology for the fortnight ending at 8 p. m. March 21, 1919, one teleseism was registered, beginning 5:38 p. m. March 8., without phases giving indication of distance. Local earthquakes were registered at 6:34 p. m. March 8, 4:45 p. m. March 9, and a very slight shock 12:29 a. m. March 14. Microseismic motion was relatively slight March 8-13, increasing to strong March 14-17, and thereafter was moderate March 18-21. The rhythmic microtremor has continued moderately strong with some increase on each of the dates March 8, 14 and 19. The spasmodic short-period tremor has been slight except for spasms on March 9 and 12. Tilting of the ground was slightly but continuously east and north March 8-11, strongly west and south, with rapid decrease, March 12-14, slightly east and north March 15-18, stationary March 19-20, and pronounced to the west and south March 21.

March 29, 1919.

The week following the equinox at Halemaumau has produced the expected subsidence with enlargement of all lakes and lowering of liquid lava levels to depths from 15 to 20 feet within the inner pits. The main lake which on March 20 had sunk to a depression of 12 feet within its cup, was 18 feet down on March 23, and 20 feet down on March 24 and thereafter. The first sign of enlargement of the ponds by collapse had occurred at the southeast pond during the reaction from sudden rising on March 12. On March 22 the central cone collapsed to a pond, and by March 26 all the lakes had enlarged and the west heap cone became transformed into a pond. The southeast driblet cones became an open pot March 27. By the end of the week the main lake and central pond had merged into one lake by breakdown of the subterranean channel between them and similarly the southwest and west ponds occupied a single cup. The high gas pressure and lava flows have come to an end and the fume has greatly increased.

Measurements referred to the north bench mark (3700 feet above sea level) were as follows:

March 18, main lake 35 feet above mark, N. E. tower 65 feet above mark.

March 27, main lake 23 feet above mark, N. E. tower 60 feet above mark.

In nine days the lake thus subsided 12 feet, averaging 1.3 feet per day, and the summit of the tower subsided five feet, averaging 0.6 feet per day. The floor level at the margin of the main lake was essentially unchanged, showing that the bench magma has not yet moved down bodily, and this is further evidenced by the seismicity which has continued normal without marked earthquakes.

On Saturday, March 22, 1919, the north lake could be seen fountaining above its margin in the morning. From 3 to 5 p.m. the southern cones were found still puffing but with diminished glow. The northeast heap continued to put out flows and to build driblet mouths at the summit. The flows later in the evening pushed eastward in considerable volume. No change was observed in the eastern lakes which continued to have margins about six feet high. The north lake as before was only three feet below its rim and from the north cone just south of it the chasm line leading to the main lake gaped wider open and was very hot in places. Another large crack was yawning open across the center of the floor from the main lake northwestward. The central cone had broken down, leaving an open pond 30 feet in diameter with a fountain pounding against its west shore. The west and southwest ponds had built up large spatter domes, but no new flows had poured out from them to the south or southwest. The west heap cone had become a large square topped structure like a hut about 10 feet high and 12 feet broad, with a glowing orifice near the top facing northwest. A new driblet spire three feet high and several smaller spiracles had been built near it. The northwest floor remained low and unchanged. Fume from the pit in general continued thin.

March 23 showed marked increase of smoke and lakes generally lower, with sharp fluctuations of the liquid lava up and down during the day.

At 8 p. m. the main and southeast lakes were surrounded by 18-foot cliffs and the north lake by a 12-foot margin. The lakes were crusted over, with fountaining only in the grottoes. During a rising spell from 8 to 9 p. m. extraordinary high gas pressure developed in the main lake which threw out from the northeast grotto a glassy spray at an angle of 30 degrees for a distance of fully 150 feet. The lifted crust impeded fountaining by blocking the top of the arch of the grotto and so the gas escaping from beneath the crust produced prolonged blowing against the top of the grotto chamber. The central pond was dull, the west pond bright and the southwest pond showed a glow heap. The west cone was puffing loudly but the southern cones had changed their action to quiet blowing and much flaming. The spiracles at the margin of the pit southeast had become large flaming cracks and the gas pressure was strong at the east cone and at driblet mouths which were blowing glass noisily at the south base of the northeast tower. The hissing noise had there increased and there was spurting of lava from a craterlet at the south end of the line of summit vents on the northeast heap. Flows were in motion at several places on the south side of the heap. About 9 p. m. this south flank near the summit broke open and developed two flows which originated at broken crusts about a foot square. Standing springs of lava developed at these holes, giving off sulphurous gas and sending streams of liquid pahoehoe with wrinkled skin down the slopes for a half hour or more. Bulbous flow lava from the heap had pushed out and swollen up over all the region north and east of the main lake.

Cracking had increased in the central part of the floor and continuous cracks of apparently deep origin cut through the flows of the northeast heap in the region east of the north lake. East of the main lake also there were glowing cracks behind the rampart, and the rampart elsewhere had fallen in in several places so as to enlarge the lake.

On Monday, March 24, the lakes were low, with considerable rising and falling, fumes were dense, some flows continued to push out from the northeast heap, and occasionally the fountains spurted above the level of the lake margins.

On Tuesday, March 25, there were flames at the east and southeast cones, but less incandescence, the west heap cone continued bright, the southwest pond occasionally flared brightly and visible fountaining in the larger lakes as seen from a distance had lessened, but occasionally the lava flings could be seen at the north lake. There was increase of breaking down of lake margins; fumes remained dense.

A marked change at this period was the gradual swelling up of more dome tumuli on the southern flank of the northeast heap along with occasional sluggish outflow. This became so marked that the new hillocks cut off from view of the Observatory the main lake and the east cone.

On Wednesday, March 26, at 2 p. m., the swelling of domes on the northeast heap had increased and there were fresh glowing flows on the summit and along three streams extending down the slope towards the west and north, the northern one 600 feet long. The inner cliff around the main lake was 20 feet high in places and the lake basin had a new V-shaped extension eastward, produced by caving. The lake was covered with heavy crust, three border grottoes were fountaining, the northeastern one some times throwing its spray above the rim. The cracks extending northwest and north from the main lake were 2 feet across in places, and locally these chasms were 25 feet deep without much heat evident. The central pool was perhaps 20 feet down and rumbling. The north lake was enlarged fifty per cent by breaking away of its banks southward to the north cone, and its former circular curvature was preserved only on the north side. Its northeast corner also had broken in. The lake surface was 10 feet down and a live tube was revealed about the lava level on the north side leading to a curtained grotto under a dome a few feet farther west. The tube was hung with stalactites. A half of the north cone still remained on the south brink of the pit occupied by this lake. A few feet farther south a large low sulphurous cone, bright yellow, marked the line of the crevasses. Sulphur stain had also developed in the south cone region. The blowing noise at the cones had greatly diminished, though there was some puffing from the east cone and an open pot north of the south-southeast cone emitted a large flame and the rumble of a fountaining pool could be heard below. The glow in the south-southeast cone had diminished. In the cracked ground east and south smoke had greatly increased. In the evening the brightest lights were from flames at the south-east pot and at the north grotto of the north lake, but all the ponds flared brightly on the fume cloud above.

On March 27 at 1 p. m. it was evident that the gas pressure had greatly diminished. The orifice of the southeast pot was about three by six feet in diameter, with an unstable bridge of crust across the middle, dividing a sheet of flame which rose from the wider chamber inside. This chamber, 15 feet in diameter and 20 feet deep, was incandescent, a bright orange color, and dripping with lava that splashed up from below from a narrow well at the bottom. The pot made a hollow rumble due to fountaining below and combustion above. There was much cracking and staining around the orifice.

The main lake had extended itself through to the central pond so that the combination created an inner pit over 600 feet long. The southeast pond remained separate, and was again a circular pit separated from the main lake by an isthmus 50 feet wide, where stood the abandoned shallow channel along which the southeast pond had enlarged on March 12. Both the main lake and southeast pond were depressed 20 feet within their cups.

The pressure rim around the south side of Halemaumau appeared to have slumped somewhat. The region between it and the southwest pond was covered with pahoehoe having this friable shells of crust. The southwest pond had joined its pit to that of the west pond during the general breakdown; both ponds were enlarged, but a low partition separated them only a foot or two above the lava level, which stood 15 feet below the margin of this inner pit. In the wall on the east side of each pond there was revealed the smooth cylindrical shaft opening beneath the marginal domes which had recently been the flaming and glowing indexes of the sites fo these ponds.

The west heap cone had wholly subsided into the pond beneath it, and the marginal cliff around this pond was 18 feet high. About noon a lava stream had been pouring across a terrace from a tunnel in the wall of this pond pit so as to pour downward at a flat angle into the pond. A spatter heap lay beside this half-solidified rivulet in the southern part of the bottom area, no doubt marking the site of the former cone.

The lava of the north lake was 12 feet down and fountaining only around the north margin, the rest being covered with crust. The northeast heap had ceased flowing, Halemaumau was moderately fumy, and the glow at night had become very spectacular with occasional brilliant flaring from individual ponds.

On Friday, March 28, at noon, the interior of the southeast pot had become dark, the bridge across the orifice had fallen in, and the rumble of fountaining could still be heard below. The eastern lakes were about the same, but the east floor appeared to be sagging. A shoreline mark above the lava of the main lake confirmed this, being 2 feet above the lake at the west end and sloping down to the lake level at the east. The northeast dome grotto, surmounting, above a 20 foot wall, a long and deep fountaining grotto below, appeared much shattered and ready to cave in. The streaming in the lake was northward and eastward from the edges of quiet crust, which wholly covered the western half. The north lake appeared little changed, but the yellow sulphur heap south of it was partly broken down and the chasms beyond appeared larger and more smoky all the way to the main lake.

At the northern base of the east cone there was an open hole 2 feet in diameter lined with stalactites, and other flaming orifices occupied the flanks of the cone which appeared ready to collapse. It was shattered and stained and covered with much Pele's hair, the individual strands being thickened with solfataric incrustations. Through the window the liquid lava could be seen splashing 15 feet below.

The northeast heap had developed an extraordinary explosive roar from an orifice near its summit. At irregular intervals of from five to twenty minutes a loud deep puffing noise was heard, made by gas rushing through orifices in the tower and also through a small broken-down flow-channel which led by a horizontal duct into the west side of the closed crater heaps. During the greater puffs at long intervals this tube would eject a roaring blast of gas and flame which on one occasion was prolonged for several minutes so as to bring the smooth dark interior walls of the tube to a state of incandescence. This tube was two feet high and eight inches across, and the explosive rush of gas was so strong that small rock fragments were blown out in showers.

This episode was really a miniature explosive eruption in the history of the building activity and the decline of the northeast heap, and as such is of great interest in that the explosive phenomenon did not appear until a large gas chamber had formed within the heap owing to the recession of the liquid lava.

The seismographs of the Whitney Laboratory for the week ending at 8 p. m., March 28, have registered seven small local earthquakes as follows: March 22, 12:30 a. m. and 3:52 a. m.; March 24, 1:49 a. m. and 3:45 a. m.; March 25, 3:24 p. m., very slight; March 26, 9:52 p. m., very slight; March 28, 1:40 p. m. The microseismic motion has decreased from moderately strong to slight. The harmonic microtremor, which was also moderately strong until March 25, decreased markedly thereafter. The spasmodic tremor was slight until March 25, but showed a number of spasms March 26-28. The tilting of the ground was strong to the east and north March 22-24, decreasing March 25-26, and March 27-28 became very strong to the south and slightly westward.

Very respectfully,

T. A. JAGGAR, JR.,
Volcanologist.

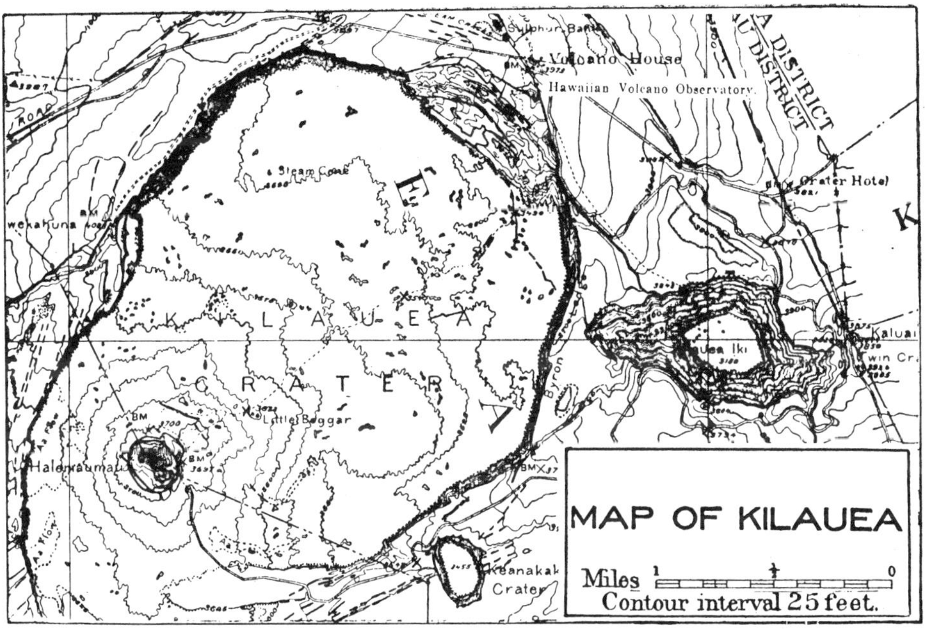

HAWAIIAN VOLCANO OBSERVATORY.

The Observatory is equipped with the following seismometric instruments rebuilt at the station in 1918 for the special needs of volcano research: two Bosch-Omori pendulums, high speed registration of local earthquakes; one optically recording seismograph for distant earthquakes; one clinograph registering E-W tilting of the ground. A vertical component seismograph was in December, 1918, set up in experimental operation. These are seated on concrete piers in a closed basement room having practically constant temperature, beneath the chief Observatory building near the hotel. Time is referred to a rated chronometer, checked at intervals by solar observations with a transit. Both instruments are loaned by the College of Hawaii. Hawaiian standard time (H. S. T.) is 10 hrs. 30 min. slower than Greenwich time.

CANCANI SCALE OF SEISMIC INTENSITY.

Expressed by accelerations measured in millimeters per second per second.

I.	Instrumental	0.0	2.5
II.	Very slight	2.5	5.0
III.	Slight	5.0	10.0
IV.	Sensible, mediocre	10.0	25.0
V.	Rather strong	25.0	50.0
VI.	Strong	50.0	100.0
VII.	Very strong	100.0	250.0
VIII.	Ruinous	250.0	500.0
IX.	Disastrous	500.0	1000.0
X.	Very disastrous	1000.0	2500.0
XI.	Catastrophic	2500.0	5000.0
XII.	Great catastrophe	5000.0	10000.0

Grade IV. is ordinarily the minimum perceived by the senses; and in grade XII. the acceleration, or rate of change of motion (jerk) reaches that of terrestrial gravitation.

In the standard form of report the maximum intensity or acceleration, designated by the symbol a, or max. a, is given in the conventional unit, the milligal. The milligal is a measure of acceleration, such that 1 milligal $= 1/100$ mm. per sec. per sec. $= 10\ \mu$ per sec. per sec. The Cancani scale, here defined in terms of millimeters per sec. per sec., can therefore be expressed in milligals by multiplying each of the numbers by 100.

U. S. DEPARTMENT OF AGRICULTURE
WEATHER BUREAU
CHARLES F. MARVIN, CHIEF

MONTHLY BULLETIN
OF THE
Hawaiian Volcano Observatory

VOL. VII. HONOLULU, HAWAII, APRIL, 1919 No. 4

HAWAIIAN VOLCANO OBSERVATORY, April 5, 1919.—The subsidence of the lava at the end of March did not prove so profound a movement as in 1918. The lowest level was reached April 1 with the eastern lakes over 30 feet below their rims, the north lake 25 feet and the west heap pond only 10 feet beneath the surrounding lava surface. The tower and general floor level of the live lava column sagged somewhat in the course of the subsidence, averaging perhaps 10 feet, but as a whole the floor was much more rigid than in the days when it was covered with crags. The liquid lava started rising rapidly on April 2 at a rate three to four times faster than its previous subsidence, taking effect first in the western ponds and the north lake, and thereafter extending to the northeast heap and the eastern lakes. General heating of the bench magma with white staining of the cracks and some upward swelling took place, and then strong lava flows.

The net effect for the week of the subsidence followed by rising is to leave the upper surfaces of both lake magma and bench magma nearly where they were before or slightly higher. The measurements, referred to the north bnch mark (3700 feet above sea level), were as follows:

March 27—Lake 23 feet above mark, NE. tower 60 feet above mark.

April 3—Lake 24 feet above mark, NE. tower 63 feet above mark.

The north lake during the same week rose about 10 feet relative to its rim.

For the entire interval of seven days the figures indicate that the main lake rose 1 foot, or .14 foot per day; the north lake rose 10 feet, or 1.4 feet per day; and the northeast tower rose 3 feet, or 0.4 foot per day. What actually happened was that the main lake sank 15 feet March 27 to April 1, or 3 feet per day, and rose 16 feet April 1 to April 3 (8 feet per day). The north lake sank 13 feet March 27 to April 1, or 2.6 feet per day, and rose 23 feet April 1 to April 3 (11.5 feet per day). At its lowest, April 1, the main lake was 8 feet above the bench mark.

On Saturday, March 29, from 2:30 to 4:30 p. m. the eastern pool of the main lake was crusted, the northeast grotto was active, and streaming was west and south in the central pool, hence reversed since the previous day. The marginal cliff around the lake was 18 feet high, heavily hung with Pele's hair and lava drip. The southeast pond cliff was 20 feet high, and here also the streaming was reversed, with bombardment against a spatter heap on the south bank. The west heap pit was shallower, with puffed-up crusts over a stagnant pond which showed a grotto overhanging quiet liquid lava at the northwest end and gas hissing from glowing cracks at the southeast margin. The pit containing the southwest and west ponds appeared enlarged, the partition between the ponds remained, and the southwest pond was quiet and heavily crusted. Not so with the west pond, however, which streamed rapidly eastward to violent marginal grottoes. The source of the current was a sluice-like channel 5 feet wide and 20 feet long at the west side, which lay on the partition floor between the two ponds, with lava rushing out from a wellspring under the cliff. This was just opposite the cavern corner of the west heap pond, which stood at a higher level, 8 feet below the floor, while the sluice was 16 feet down. The stream may have come through the tube. A spell of 4 feet of sinking reversed the torrent and reduced it to bubblings, and the lava of the pond poured into the channel, but in five or six minutes there was recovery, rising at the spring and the rush of the sluiceway was resumed. The southwest pond took no part in this rise and fall of the west pond. Its only activity was a little bubbling at the southern margin of its crust. The north lake was noisy and the smoke on this day was denser.

The blowing vent of the northeast heap glowed and faintly puffed. The cracks in the heap still glowed. The southeast pot was more broken in, showed a coffee brown drip glaze inside, and a small window below led to a fountaining chamber 25 feet down. The south-southeast cone glowed, flamed and rumbled. The breaking away of the south cone revealed an inner shell chamber and wonderfully colored stalactite lumps.

On March 30 the lakes were lower and very bright, flames were bright at the southern and central cones, and the floor remained stationary.

On Monday, March 31, at 2:30 p. m., the west heap pond had begun construction of a low hissing glow cone, the west and southwest ponds were 25 feet down, the former streaming east and the latter south. The well source was no longer a distinct channel, but merely a point of current departure, under the southwest bank of the west pond. The central floor of the pit was much shattered and the central pool of the main lake had become a gorge 40 feet deep with lava streaming west, but the east pool cliff was only 25 feet high. Glow and flame appeared at a crack in the floor north of the central pool, where a remnant of the central cone, broken in two, clung to the verge. The southeast pond had become a pit 35 feet deep to the lava level, with a spatter bank receiving bombardment at the southwest side and a tunnel leading northeast towards the east cone. The north lake had walls 25 feet high, the liquid streamed northward, and there was some fountaining south.

The northeast heap had ceased blowing. The southern cones emitted very heavy smoke. The window in the bottom of the southeast pot cavity opened into a large bright-orange colored chamber beneath, where lava surged. Dense smoke rose also from the east cone region, which showed a sulphur-stained cracked zone of 20-foot radius. The glow over the lakes was bright at night, a brilliant flame rose from the central vent, but the southeast cone glow was dim. On April 1 the lava was lower, both floor and lakes, smoke was dense, and there was a break formed in the middle of the east pressure rim.

On April 2, at 4:30 p. m., the main lake was higher, 20 feet down at the east end, and there had been more breaking back of the bank into the smoking cracked ground east. The north lake was much higher and its margin deformed, so that the liquid was 4 feet down on the north and 15 feet down on the southeast. There was a bulge in the ground between the two parts and the lake had enlarged by breaking back into the high ground of the footslopes of the northeast heap. There was much appearance of swelling in several parts of the floor of Halemaumau, accompanied by hot whitened cracks. The south end of the north lake had caved away as far as the yellow sulphur cone.

There were now five distinct inner pits: north, main, southeast, southwest, and west; the southwest one holding two ponds. The southeast old rim of Halemaumau was a pressure ridge with the lava floor overhanging it, and the northwest old rim was still a cliff 40 feet high. Northeast and southwest were great lava heapings, overlapping and burying the old rim completely, crowned by the northeast driblet tower in the one case and by the southwestern pits in the other.

On April 3 at 3:30 p. m. high gas pressure was again in evidence. The west heap pond had built a dome flush with the rim of its pit, the west and southwest ponds were only 12 feet down, and the north lake was brimming level with its north and west banks and had built two immense spatter domes on the west. The east and south cliffs of this lake were 8 feet high. The main lake was 15 feet down and enlarged both northward and eastward.

The south cones were hissing and the northeast heap puffed from the vent south of the main tower. The southeast cone, which had collapsed to an open funnel on April 1, was now closed in the funnel but showed open mouths on each side leading to high lava pounding inside. At night the north lake was brimming and the northeast tower started an eruption of umbrella splashes of melt with a loud metallic clang and a gobbling explosion noise heard two miles away. This built up a second tower the duplicate of the first on its south side, so that the striking profile, for many weeks past a landmark, was changed to a wide double-peaked turret. In the early morning hours the spouting was from a cone on the high northwest slope of the heap

On Friday, April 4, inspection at 2:30 p. m. showed that this eruption had produced two glassy smooth flows, the double tower standing above their sources, 15 feet high. A short flow had pushed north-northeast from the summit, and a long ribbon flow had poured all the way from the cone northwest of the tower to the northwest wall valley on the north side of the north lake. There was a new vent open near the south cone, and the east cone vents were flinging out black glass and dense smoke rose from the ground west of this cone.

The southeast pond was surrounded by an inner annular bench 10 feet down and the pond surface was three feet lower, streaming north with a fountain under the northeast bank. The main lake was also about 13 feet down, streaming against its north bank and showing an inner bench of recent higher level. The north lake was splashing over at its north end, the west domes were covered with Pele's hair, and deep glowing cracks had opened northeast of the lake. There was no change in the northwest wall valley. The west heap cone was becoming a large ring, and the west pond, 10 feet down, was streaming east to a closed grotto with an open pot on top. A stream mark across the isthmus from the southwest pond to the west pond indicated that a flood had passed across during the high level of the previous night. The southwest pond, as usual, was quiet and crusted over.

In the Whitney Laboratory of Seismology there were a few local earthquake shocks recorded, microseismic motion was moderate, and microtremor somewhat increasing from low values, but the striking seismic feature was the tilt, which changed about April 1 from southwest to northeast.

HAWAIIAN VOLCANO OBSERVATORY, Apr. 12, 1919.—During the week ending Friday, April 11, 1919, the Halemaumau lava column has risen slightly, but the elevation of the surface has proceeded rather by local building and filling than by lifting. There has been bench magma uplift of a few feet also, and moderate rising of the liquid lakes within their cups. The conspicuous change of the week is occasioned by the extensive flows from the northeast heap on its northwest slope inside the old pit limits, these flows spreading and swelling gradually as heavy bulbous pahoehoe in the region between the north wall of Halemaumau and the north lake. This slope has repeated the constructional activity formerly so conspicuous on the east side of the northeast heap, the high tower marking as before the center of the highest upbuilding and the greatest output of flows.

On Saturday, April 5, the crater was quiet and unchanged in the early morning, but during the forenoon the liquid lava rose to the level of the inner terraces 10 feet down in the eastern lakes. The north lake fountains were splashing over the ramparts in the afternoon, and at 9 p. m. a flow was pouring northward from a standing spring of lava on the north flank of the northeast heap. The north lake overflowed its north margin, its flows merging with those of the northeast heap. The west pond lava splashed high above its east rampart. The east cone was sputtering, the south cone flaming, the northeast tower dark, and the glow bright above the lakes.

On April 6 at 10:30 a. m. there was fresh flow lava visible across the north-northeast rim of the north lake and the west pond had built up a dome above its eastern margin. Smoke was dense at the east and south cones. The lava in the north lake was close to the rim level. A new spur of the northeast heap was building around the vent on the north flank. At 6 p. m. the north lake was brimming level with its rampart and the west pond fountaining above its margin. At 8:15 p. m. the newer southern spire of the northeast tower broke into spurting action, opening a window through its east wall and throwing out jets accompanied by muffled explosions, audible at the Observatory 2.2 miles away in a straight line. Two flows were in motion on the flank of the northeast heap in the region northeast of the north lake.

On April 7 at 4 p. m. the lakes were slightly lower, the southeast pond, a circular pool, stood 4 feet below the terrace, which was 10 feet below the cup rim. On the northeast side of the pond a spatter dome was built. The main lake stood 15 feet below the rim of its pit, crusted and with border fountains in its eastern pool, while the liquid in the channel leading to the central pool streamed westward. The north lake showed tendency to become circular again and was building up its northern and western embankment, now 3 feet above the pool, while the south and east margins, cut into the northeast heap, stood 8 feet high. The lake was covered with stagnant crust and there was marginal fountaining. The west ponds were little changed, their surfaces about 12 feet below the surrounding floor; the southwest pond was crusted, the west pond flung up heavy melt, the west heap pond was a crust with a ring-cone south of the center, and no fresh flows had poured out on the southwestern slopes of the west heap. About 6 p. m. the north lake was brimming full.

The south-southeast cone was now an open, but not fiery, pot. A hissing spiracle stood out on the inner wall of the southeast pot. Cracks in the southeast high floor had widened. The northeast tower had an added shoulder, giving it irregular form on the south face, and a new puddle of glassy lava had solidified on top of the northeast heap. On the northwestern flank of the heap a live vent was spouting and flowing and lifting a lid in spasms. From it a stream two feet wide and several hundred feet long meandered sluggishly northward. This northwestern extension of the northeast heap was now a big feature, reaching along the wall valley nearly to a point under the northwest station, the flows piling up and swelling into domes, and occupying the whole space between the north lake and the north cliff margin of Halemaumau. This width was maintained away up the flank of the heap in the direction of the northeast tower, and fresh toes of live lava even now were making out to the west of the tower.

On Tuesday, April 8, from 4 to 5 p. m., it was evident by measurement that this period represents stationary condition in the main as regards the floor. The liquid lava showed some rising and falling. A circuit of Halemaumau by way of the southern and western rims showed the west heap ring-cone to be hissing and glowing; the west pond had filagree glow heaps under its eastern cliff, rising above an inner terrace 10 feet down which encircled the pond some three feet lower. The crust over the southwest pond, which was quite inactive, stood higher than the west pond liquid level. On crossing the floor by way of the north side of the western pond group, a bright flame hole lined with stalactites, about two feet across, was found in the floor north of the central pool of the main lake. A smoking area farther west seemed to mark a tunnel line leading to the western ponds. The main lake was now some 450 feet long, a canyon-like trench 20 feet deep, 60 feet wide and 200 feet long on the west constituting the channel and central pool depressed in the higher part of the arched floor of Halemaumau, while at the east end the pool was more open, of dimensions 250 by 120 feet, and the bank only 12 feet high. This east pool showed inflated crust, border fountains, and heavy bombardment under its northwest bank, but no surface streaming. There had been more breaking back of the east end of the lake to make a terraced cove in the direction of the dense smoke which rose from the cracked region between the lake and the east cone. The east cone was noisy. There was much smoke also around the southern cones.

The northeast tower gave vent to occasional puffs of gas but the flow vents were quiet. A crack extending across the floor from the central channel of the main lake to the north lake was an open crevasse but not especially hot or fuming.

On April 9 the pit was quiet and smoky in the morning. In the afternoon the fume was thinner. At 6 p. m. the north lake was brimming high and the northeast cove of the main lake threw spray above its ramparts. At 8 p. m. fountains above the pond rim were visible also at the west pond. The northwestern footslopes of the northeast heap had now developed, by swelling from below, many dome tumuli with cracked summits.

On Thursday, April 10, at 5:30 p. m., the lakes were high, but the northeast tower and all the vents of the northeast heap had ceased to show gas pressure by hissing. The east cone was puffing and flaming from numerous orifices in its north horns. The main lake was only 10 feet down, with active border grottoes. The north lake was bombarding its banks south and west, while on the north side it was building up the rampart rapidly by high flings of lava. In the evening all the open lakes showed fountain splash above their rims, the north lake being especially vigorous in its rampart building.

On April 11 at noon there was some hissing at the southern cones and much cracking and white staining, with heat rising, east of the north lake and north of the main lake. There was snapping of the ground heard in the same regions. A large hot crevasse was discovered parallel to and a few feet farther east than the known crack leading from the main lake to the north lake. The main lake was streaming westward, 10 feet down, with grottoes northwest, north and southeast, occasional large explosive central fountains, and some bubble fountaining during sinking spells. The high level of the north lake continued and big spatter domes five feet high encased the grottoes on the north and northwest sides. A fountain was splashing against the west bank and there was some bubble fountaining out from under a terrace at the south end. There was much ballooning of skins into great blisters 10 or 15 feet across, like inflated blankets, which migrated with the current from the central part of the lake to the north. The same phenomenon was observed in the main lake. Fume from the pit was this day thinner.

A curious patch of incandescent broken lava, about two feet square, had kept its heat right on the surface of the summit floor of the northeast heap for several days, without any blowing, solfataric stain or visible flame. There was no odor. The place had exactly the appearance of a bed of hot charcoal, of cherry red heat, abruptly bounded by shells of non-incandescent lava of the same sort. The only explanation which occurred to the writer was that a slow seepage of burning gas was oxidizing the rock above some gas cavity below, not revealed on the surface.

In the Whitney Laboratory of Seismology for the fortnight ending at 8 p. m. April 11, 1919, there were registered local earthquake shocks, mostly very slight, as follows: March 29, 3:31 a. m.; March 30, 2:48 a. m.; March 31, 4:39 p. m.; April 5, 12:32 p. m. (moderate); April 7, 6:19 a. m. (felt); April 8, 4:53 a. m. and April 10, 2:11 a. m. The harmonic microtremor increased from slight values to strong about April 3 and has remained moderately strong since. The spasmodic type of tremor became strong April 7 and excessively strong April 9, vibrating the ground from 1 to 4 p. m. on that day with extraordinary continuity. On April 10 and 11 spasms of vibration continued. Microseismic movement has been ordinary with slight increase April 4 to 6 and April 9 to 10. Movement of tilting was to the south and west March 29-30, north and east March 31-April 4, south and west April 5-7, stationary April 8-9, north and east April 10-11.

HAWAIIAN VOLCANO OBSERVATORY, April 19, 1919.—During the week ending Friday, April 18, 1919, a new spasm of mass swelling of the entire hard upper surface of the lava column set in, which culminated as in February and March in a strong overflow which broke through the south pressure rim and produced the longest and most liquid flow of 1919 to date. This flow followed the same course as the flow of February 23, 1918, again covering the trail and reaching the road terminus. The three long flows of this year, extending each about one-half mile from the center of Halemaumau, lie south, southeast, and east, and were produced respectively on March 4, April 17, and March 12. Owing to the eccentric position southeastward of the axis of uplift, the extensive flows which have poured in the other direction, i. e., toward the northwest, have been confined within the old pit wall.

Approximate measurements, referred to the north bench mark (3700 feet above sea level) were as follows:

April 3, central floor 39 feet above mark, lake 24 feet above mark, northeast tower 63 feet above mark.

April 17, central floor 64 feet above mark, lake 34 feet above mark, northeast tower 60 feet above mark.

In the course of fourteen days the central floor rose 25 feet, averaging 1.8 feet per day; the main lake 10 feet, or 0.7 feet per day; and the northeast tower has subsided three feet or 0.2 feet per day.

On Saturday, April 12, the lakes in the morning were moderately high and a puddle flow covering a small area poured out from the east cone on its north side. Large spatter domes had formed in a ring around the north lake and a similar dome on the edge of the west pond had enlarged. Fume from the east and south wall crack areas was much thinner. At 8 p. m. all the lakes were high and spurting, including the southwest pond; the east cone glowed brightly and a strong swelling in the bench magma lifted the central region and caused the north lake to overflow on its northwest side. The lifting movement caused rocks to tumble from the southeast pressure ridge.

At 5 p. m. on April 13 the lifted concrete platform of the southeast station on the pressure ridge was found tilting at a higher angle, and the ridge thereabouts was 25 feet high. The wall crack between the south and south-southwest cones was flaming and the southeast pot had become a yawning chasm. A new spatter heap on the east side of the east cone showed boiling lava through the cracks and glowing cracks extended up the west face of the northeast tower. The wall enclosing the main lake was six feet high at the east end and higher farther west. The streaming was westward and from 5 to 7 p. m. the liquid subsided about three feet, with vigorous fountaining and heavy skins inflating and discharging flames. That the enclosing cliffs about the lake were lifting relative to the melt was shown by a terrace level at the east end, a high tilted scarp on the south and a broad flaming crack back from the northern verge. The region between the main and north lakes showed yawning cracks, some of them incandescent. The recent surface glow and whitening in many places were symptoms precursory of the uplift.

The north lake lava stood within a foot of its north and northwest margins but the central uplift had raised the southern margins of the lake 10 feet above the liquid. Fresh heavy flows had crossed the northwestern lip. The streaming was northward, there were flaming closed grotto domes and occasionally heavy crusts would crack and founder. The west and southwest ponds glowed brightly and later in the evening the fountains were very bright in the east cove of the main lake and around the north lake.

On Monday, April 14, the strong tumescence continued, the fume was thinner and the lakes remained high. From 6 to 7 p. m. rocks were falling from the pressure ridge, the outer face of which was nearly vertical in places, and the masonry of the southeast station had fallen in ruins. The east cone and south wall-crack were flaming as before. The east cone had been uplifted with the rising bench magma and the surface from here to the southeast pond curved up in a steep dome slope. The partition between the southeast pond and the main lake was gone, leaving an open canyon and a continuous single T-shaped lake. Streaming was mostly northward to where fountains bombarded the north bank. The bench magma was rising faster than the liquid, making the cliffs around the lake from 15 to 25 feet high.

Gas pressure continued in the northwest tower. The noise of the rising bench magma under foot was a continuous series of snapping, creaking and crunching sounds to which was added from time to time the crash of blocks falling in crevasses. The sounds were incessant and awesome in their suggestion of resistless power. The lakes during the night made bright red glare on the fume cloud.

On April 15 the mass rising continued, extending to the southwestern region and the lakes remained about as before.

At 10:15 a. m. on April 16 the floor had become a distinctly arched dome as a whole, with the center about the region of the central pool. Even the new flows of the north side of the northeast heap were arched up. The pressure rim now extended from the southeast so as to bend inward in plan through the east cone and from here northward the edge of the uplift passed under the center of the northeast heap, fracturing the summit cones and lifting the western flows of the heap to horizontality. The new fill north was so pinched by the uplift as again to tip back the old north rim of Halemaumau. The buried southwest margin of the old pit was again revealing itself as a pressure ridge so that practically the entire circle of floor was outlined by either pressure ridge or remnant cliff.

An interesting development due to fracture and collapse at the northern rim cones of November, 1918, was the revelation in the cavernous interior of these cones, only five months old, of abundant grapevine stalactites with stalagmites beneath, some of the former over 20 inches long. The shell of this cavern was only a foot thick in places and it was an incandescent gas chamber at the time of the November flows. There was no traces of water drip, and gas melting was the only possible process whereby these stalactites could have originated.

The central axis of uplift of the domed floor of Halemaumau formed craggy cliffs on both sides of the central pool of the main lake and these were now on a level with the summit of the northeast tower some 60 feet above the north bench mark of the old rim. Instead of individual craggy scarps as in former years, the whole arched floor was now one mighty tumor, as high as the former crags, with the lakes as gashes in its crest.

The south wall crack was flaming and hissing and yawning open at the cones. A chasm extended straight toward this crack, and at right angles to it, from the southeast pond. The latter was quiet, about 10 feet below its southeastern rim, but where it extended as a gorge to join the main lake the bounding cliffs were 30 feet high. The main lake streamed eastward to a spatter dome at its east end. The east cone had a splashing pot on top, the north lake was six feet down on its north side, 15 feet on the south and was quiet with curtained grottoes. The whole cup of this lake had been upheaved and tilted northward and smoking chasms extended from it towards the main lake. The west heap pond had filled up and overflowed and a trickle flow was pouring from a small splashing cone. The other two western ponds were fountaining vigorously with 5-foot margins and somewhat constricted cups. Gas vents built driblet spiracles in the southwestern wall crack region.

On Thursday, April 17, at 11 a. m., the whole region southeast of Halemaumau was found flooded with a broad lava flow of multiple forks, consisting of gleaming silvery liquid lava which hardened as very smooth dense pahoehoe. This flow had started about midnight, breaking out along a vertical chasm in the pressure rim just east of the south cone. The lips of the chasm were now plastered with spatter lava and Pele's hair, and 15 feet above the flow beneath an open window three feet in diameter revealed an incandescent vertical lava chute or sluiceway where the liquid fell rapidly and continuously through a pipe of its own making. The window was dripping with the liquid melt. The pooled lava beneath, covered with a thick shell, could be crossed in a distance of 100 yards, but the flow in the vicinity of the road terminus was 300 yards wide. The liquid was pouring through tubes to the many fronts which were building smooth, snaky toes, distributing itself widely and spreading in the course of the day over the entire trail region and as far as the front of the flow of February 23, 1918.

The pressure rim east was now 30 feet high and swelling still continued. The margin of the new uplift was increased in height at the west and south pressure rim, rocks were falling occasionally, and seen from the northwest remnant of border cliff, the central floor had become a dome above the level of one's head. The whole eastern semicircle of what had been the former rim of Halemaumau was cut off from view even as far north as the old north station, by the rising of the great swollen fill. The top of the northeast tower remained visible, and in the flank of the dome could be seen against the skyline only a little of the rim of the west pond pit and the chasm and spatter heaps occupied by the north lake. The west and north stations were both tilted away from the center of Halemaumau, the north bench mark platform 8.5 degrees from the horizontal. As this involved uplift as well as horizontal disturbance, the value of the bench mark as a levelling station is destroyed. There was no evident differential lift of the floor at the base of the northwest wall. The pressure rim effect at the north station is extended in a crushed and fractured zone up the flank of the northeast heap.

The north lake was extending its cup in a crooked crevasse headed in the direction of the main lake. Its surface streaming was north and northwest, there was some central turbulence, and the marginal cliff was eight feet high northwest and 25 feet high southeast. An inner 3-foot spatter level marked the fluctuations of the previous 24 hours. The northern border heaps were still in place and the fountains splashed below them.

The northeast heap had a hissing, glowing east-west crack through the middle of the tower and many other deep hot cracks, especially on the side of the main lake. On this side one walked uphill towards the center of Halemaumau. The latter had a 12-foot cliff at its east end, but the central floor level was 25 to 30 feet above the lake. The streaming was westward and from the southeast pond channel northward, and numerous central and travelling fountains developed from time to time. There was no evidence from the currents that the lake melt was feeding the south chasm outflow. The tunnel extending from the main lake to the east cone had now by crushing produced a pressure ridge, in contrast to the gaping effects seen along the northwest-southeast crevasses (north lake and southeast pond extensions). This was prolonged into the main outer pressure rim by way of the east cone. The cone had built a driblet slope on its northeast side 15 feet high, an open pot was splashing out lava on top, and the whole structure, with its outer base below the lake level, looked as though it might easily produce a new outflow by breaking open.

In general the fume was thinner, the glow at night brighter, the lakes hotter and more turbulent on the surface. The new outflow differed from previous ones of like rapid extension, in its smooth, hard silvery surfaces and thinly liquid habit. Like the flow of March 11 in texture, it also was fed, like that flow, by a rapid cascade capable of freeing it from gas.

On Friday, April 18, there were important changes in the extension of the swelling northwestward so as to tip and break up still further the basin of the north lake and extend it by collapse along the fissure line southwestward. The fountains splashed high at this lake and in the east cove of the main lake. The crumbling broke down some of the spatter heaps standing on top of the north lake border cliffs.

The appearance of Halemaumau as seen from the Observatory is now that of a smooth curved floor 1200 feet across, rising from the northwest rim of the former pit to a height about 50 feet above the general level of the former rim. This body falls off abruptly as an escarpment 40 feet high on the southeast at the pressure rim. The movement here has been bodily eastward, as known landmarks on the pressure rim, like the southern cones, have moved east in profile during the last few weeks. Along with this has gone the mashing up of the pressure rim, made of slabs of the rim flows, with an angular rotation from horizon-

Feb. 8, 1919. Same view five days later; the overflow which destroyed the trail. [Photos Jaggar.]

Feb. 3, 1919. South rim of Halemaumau and live flow pouring from south cone in wall-crack. From south-east station. This margin was thrust up as the great pressure rim Feb. 25 and later.

tal to vertical and beyond, so that the top of the rim is no longer defined, consisting of the old edge of the pit facing west and raised en masse, but is the rounded swollen lava floor, and is not a ridge but a scarp facing east. The upper part of the cliff so formed is the cross-section of the inner lava layers lifted clear, and the pressure rim is a tumble of talus.

In the Whitney Seismological Laboratory for the week ending at 8 p. m. Friday, April 18, 1919, there were registered six trivial local earth shocks and three distant earthquakes. The local quakes were at 7:20 p. m. April 13; 5:29 and 10:31 a. m. April 14; 5:57 and 7:19 a. m. April 17; and 7:10 a. m. April 18. The first teleseism at 12:50 a. m., H. S. T., April 17, gave evidence that the distance of its origin was about 2640 kilometers from this station, which would correspond probably to a source on the bottom of the Pacific ocean. This distance is not quite as far as the Phoenix Islands. The second teleseism was also on the 17th at 10:35 a. m. and indicated a source at 5585 kilometers, the distance of Mexico, Kamtchatka or the New Hebrides. The third teleseism at 10:51 a. m. April 18, registered pronounced long waves, but the preliminary tremor which would give evidence of distance was absent in the record.

Microseismic motion increased from slight to moderate about April 15. Both the harmonic and spasmodic types of microtremor decreased during the week from strong to slight. Movements of tilting have been remarkably slight in view of the strong swelling and overflowing at the crater, but this agrees with the February-March record as discussed in this Bulletin February 8. The general tendency of the tilt has been slight to the east and south.

HAWAIIAN VOLCANO OBSERVATORY, April 26, 1919.—The week ending April 25, 1919, at Kilauea volcano, after the long southeastward flow of the previous week, has been distinguished by intense renewed swelling of the lava floor towards the north, followed by an extraordinarily long and enduring flow, given vent, not from the pit, but from a fuming crack north-northeast of the pit approximately 790 feet from the north station. This crack has long been known as the "Postal Rift," because of its high temperature (over 300 deg. C.), making it a favorite place where travellers scorch postal cards. It marks the site of the old rim of Halemaumau prior to overflow in 1894. The long flow began Sunday morning, April 20, and at the end of the week is still progressing with front over 1.5 miles from the center of Halemaumau. The course of the flow lies north-northeast, passing on the west side of the well known steam cone which stands out on the floor of Kilauea crater towards the north. This breaking out of a flow back from the north rim recalls the similar flows of November, 1918, from sources nearer the pit.

The extension of tumescence to the old rim of Halemaumau west and north has tilted the west station 4.5 degrees to the southwest and the north bench mark platform 8.5 degrees to the north. The latter has been lifted bodily approximately eight feet, making its new elevation 3708 feet approximately above sea level. Measurements for the week with this mark as datum were as follows:

April 17, central floor 64 feet, main lake 34 feet, northeast tower 60 feet—above mark.

April 26, central floor 73 feet, main lake 38 feet, northeast tower 54 feet—above mark.

Allowing for the lift of datum mark and of the northwest station from which the angular measurements were made, the central floor rose 17 feet in nine days, averaging 1.9 feet per day; the main lake rose 12 feet, averaging 1.3 feet per day; and the northeast tower rose two feet, averaging 0.2 feet per day. Practically for the last three weeks the northeast tower has been stationary.

Approximate measurements of the progress of the front of the Postal Rift flow were as follows, the source of the flow being 1400 feet from the center of Halemaumau:

April 20, 3 p. m., front 0.4 miles from center of Halemaumau.

April 21, 10 a. m., front 0.5 miles from center of Halemaumau.

April 22, 11 a. m., front 0.6 miles from center of Halemaumau.

April 23, 10 a. m., front 0.9 miles from center of Halemaumau.

April 24, 11 a. m., front 1.2 miles from center of Halemaumau.

April 25, 12 m., front 1.4 miles from center of Halemaumau.

On Saturday, April 19, 1919, at 6 p. m., there was still glow in the southeast flow, the south wall crack was flaming and hissing and the east cone was flaming on top and splashing within. The northeast tower had cooled considerably and was quiet.

The main lake was greatly enlarged in a north-south direction along its east bank, its enclosing walls were from 15 to 25 feet high and the streaming was outward from the south arm (formerly the southeast pond). There was the usual grotto fountaining. The north lake was found surrounded by unmistakable signs of rapid extension northward of the floor swelling so conspicuous on the southeast during the previous week. As one stood on the brink of the lifted north lake cup the view all the way to the Postal Rift revealed a downward slope past and involving the north rim of Halemaumau and the driblet cones of 1894. The north lake was itself so affected by this lift that it was enlarging itself rapidly by collapse of its southeast and northwest sides. The high southeast wall crumbled into the lake in spectacular avalanches and a tumbled crevasse made a yawning chasm in the wall in the direction of the main lake. A cavern under the west bank of the lake ejected a rapid torrent of glowing melt from the direction of the western ponds and the avalanches made much tumult of boiling. The northwestern bank was a subsided flat of fractured rock submerged beneath the lava like a beach. At the northeast end of this lake two of the large spatter domes remained intact 15 feet above the lake level. There were cracks in the swollen floor with hot air rising. A crisis of northward swelling was in progress, lifting and tilting the zone of the Halemaumau rim all the way back to the old rim line of 1891.

At some time near noon on April 20 the liquid lava welled up in a standing fountain through the cracks of the Postal Rift north of Halemaumau and west of the small solfataric crater known as Pele's Kitchen. The place was within a few feet of those hottest cracks visited by tourists. There was not the slightest seismic disturbance and even the volcanic tremors were remarkably slight at this time. The lava was in great volume, of slight viscosity and flowed rapidly in rippling cascades towards the north so that by 2:30 p. m. the front was 900 feet from its source. There was at 3:41 p. m. a small local earthquake shock (instrumental, not felt). The source of this flow was visited at 7 p. m. and two small cones were found built above a crack on the north side of the densest fume of the Postal Rift. From these the stream poured steadily in the direction of Perret's Cone, widening out in shape like a laurel leaf and consisting of ordinary pahoehoe. The fountaining and spurting at the vent were moderate and commonplace.

No immediate effect at the Halemaumau lakes suggested drainage by this flow. On the contrary, the lakes were distinctly higher with pronounced gas pressure, but the tumescence of the bench magma was less. The activity of the main lake was unchanged. The north lake walls were 10 to 20 feet high, more defined on the northwest side, the caving in had ceased and the liquid had risen to drown and check the torrent from the southwest cavern. The cavern was filled up. The wall around the southeast side of the north lake had become straight and smooth.

About 10:30 p. m. the lakes rose to their levels and an overflow poured from the east end of the main lake past the east cone on its north side to the region of the old automobile terminus, some 500 feet east of Halemaumau.

About 6 p. m. on April 21 the east cone overflowed and sent a torrent eastward 600 feet overriding the lake flow of the previous night. At 9 p. m. the front of this flow was stagnant. The main lake was streaming mostly westward, with 10 to 20-foot cliffs bombarded at the lake level by violent fountains east and northeast. About every half hour the lake level suffered sudden subsidence of three to four feet with break-up of crusts and very large turbulent central fountains.

The north lake was also pulsating with rising and sinking spells and was building new curtained grottoes at its northeast end. Many cracks in the floor of Halemaumau showed incandescent bench magma beneath.

The Postal Rift flow continued its progress and had sent two narrow branches to the west in the direction of Uwekahuna. Already this flow was much the longest of the 1918-19 series.

On Tuesday, April 22, the Postal Rift source developed strong fountaining at noon so that the progress of the fronts of the flow was more rapid, the main front showing at night a shape like a glowing hand creeping in the direction of Perret''s Cone.

At 5:30 p. m. there was hissing at the south cone and the main lake showed a large continuous fountain in the southeastern part while the streaming was mostly westward and northward. The sinking spells happened suddenly at intervals of from 20 to 40 minutes, followed by quick recovery in the course of 10 minutes or less. At the beginning of the sinking spells there were very intense explosive outbursts against the wall and from under the crust margin. These outbursts began on the north and extended themselves eastward. The north lake was brimming level with its rim and rather quiet. The bench magma continued to rise but the rapid swelling had ceased. The lake fountains at night were visible from the Observatory and some high jets were seen at the west pond.

On April 23 the crater was quiet, the floor lava stationary and the lake shores caved in in places. The Postal Rift flow continued its progress with front now a mile from the center of Halemaumau and glow at the front of the upper western fork as well as at the main front near Perret's Cone. The north lake was fountaining above its rim at 7:30 p. m. and there was a very high level after midnight.

Exploration of the Postal Rift flow in the early afternoon of Thursday, April 24, showed that it consisted of moderately smooth pahoehoe lava extending beyond and west of Perret's Cone. As a whole the flow is a ribbon from 100 to 300 feet wide, spreading continuously by slowly oozing toes which are fed through tubes in the crusted upper portions of the flow. The source was still merely a small cone three feet high with hissing and flaming cracks in its summit. All the upper part of the flow was frozen solid on the surface. Active moving toes were found at 3 p. m. on the western side of the frontal lobe.

From 5 to 6 p. m. the north lake was found brimming full and dribbling over with two large high flung fountains playing continuously next to the spatter domes at the north end. The remainder of the pond was crusted over and the ravine in the direction of the main lake had widened.

The main lake was still undergoing sinking spells with northward streaming, bombardment of the north shore, and cliffs 10 feet high on the east and 30 feet high in the center. Large balloons of skin formed during the rising spells when inflation was dominant. At the west end of the central pool a chasm three to five feet wide had opened clear down to the pool level so as to connect the main lake through to the west pond. Two similar chasms less wide and not open to the liquid lava level extended from the north lake towards the main lake.

The floor was crossed on the north side of the main lake and these chasms were found to be still narrow enough to step across. The west pond was found to be circular with wall 10 to 12 feet high on the side of the chasm leading to the main lake, but on the opposite or western side the liquid stood level with the rim owing to the fact that the cup of the pond was tipped away from the center of the pit just as in the case of the north lake. A short distance farther west the west pond cone was hot and fuming and the southwest pond was in the midst of fume farther south. There were as yet no fresh flows from the western ponds.

The dome swelling of the Halemaumau floor had now lifted the floor slightly on the northwest side so as to reduce the height of the cliff there and the ends of this cliff north-northeast and west-southwest had become pressure rims so that the remnant of the old border cliff now included not more than two-fifths of the former circumference of the pit. The west station platform showed increased deformation. All tumbling of rocks at the south pressure rim, however, had now ceased and the lava column was stationary.

The sluiceway which had been the source of the flow of April 17 was now covered with a few snaky driblet trickles of solidified lava from above where there was a hissing vent. In the wall crack chasm left by the southeast pot, large masses of bright colored stalactites were revealed. The east cone continued to show flaming vents over lava surging within.

On April 25 from 2 to 3 p. m. the cliffs over the main lake were found to be somewhat higher, a 3-foot spatter margin appeared above the level of the liquid lava and the streaming was at first north and west, but this was reversed to north and east when an immense central fountain developed and migrated eastward to expend itself at the lake shore. The pulsations of rising and falling continued. The cliffs were from 15 to 30 feet high.

The north lake showed walls four feet high on the northwest side and a block of that wall was seen to collapse. There was much cracking and foundering, the usual northern border fountaining and in both the north and main lakes the ballooning of crusts was conspicuous.

Some trace of the eastern pressure rim could now be followed all the way from the southeast wall crack to the northeast tower along a line of crunched up flows, ridges and cracks marking the course of the Halemaumau pit margin beneath. Hissing continued at the south, east and northeast cones.

The Postal Rift flow was still pushing ahead and the line of active toes was bright at night as were also the glow spots at the source of the flow and at the east cone. The flow was spreading its frontal lobes eastward so as greatly to widen in a sort of a puddle the whole frontal strip. At noon the front was 1.4 miles from the center of Halemaumau and this proved to be nearly the limit of its progress.

The seismographs of the Whitney Laboratory have registered traces of two teleseisms during the week ending at 8 p. m. Friday, April 25, 1919. These were at 4:44 p. m. April 21 and 8:57 p. m. April 22, H. S. T. The evidence of distance is not clearly shown. Local earthquakes were registered at 3:41 p. m. April 20; 3:02 p. m. and 11:44 p. m. April 21, both very slight; and 10:54 a. m. April 25. Microseismic motion decreased to very slight, harmonic microtremor remained slight and the spasmodic tremor has continued abundantly in evidence with prolonged spells of several hours when it was strong.

The tilting of the ground became strong to the east and north April 19-20, reacting moderately west and south April 21-22. April 23-24 exhibited stationary tendency and April 25 there was slight tilt east and north.

HAWAIIAN VOLCANO OBSERVATORY, May 3, 1919.—During the week ending Friday, May 2, 1919, there was a short-lived sinking spell from April 25 to April 28, both the crater floor and liquid lakes taking part in the depression, and the long Postal Rift flow coming to rest. Beginning April 29, however, strong rising and overflowing were resumed, the net effect for the week being a slight rise of crater levels and voluminous new flows. The Postal Rift flow has continued to lengthen and also to spread sidewise in many places along its whole length. Its front is in the extreme north corner of Kilauea floor, against the northern end of the Uwekahuna wall, and approximately 1.6 miles from the center of Halemaumau.

The measurements of the week, above the north Halemaumau bench mark (approximately 3708 feet above sea-level) are as follows:

April 26, central floor 73 feet, main lake, 38 feet, N.E. tower 60 feet.

April 28, central floor 67 feet, main lake 27 feet, N.E. tower 60 feet.

May 2, central floor 74 feet, main lake 44 feet, N.E. tower 60 feet.

The floor thus subsided six feet in two days, or three feet per day, and the main lake 12 feet, or six feet per day. Thereafter the floor rose seven feet in four days, or 1.8 feet per day, and the lake rose 17 feet, or 4.2 feet per day. The northeast tower remained stationary. Measurements across Halemaumau from southeast to northwest show that the maximum of floor movement was adjacent to the central pool of the main lake.

On Saturday, April 26, 1919, at noon the main lake appeared lower relative to its bounding cliffs which were 15 feet high at the east end, 35 feet high on the north and 25 feet high on the south. Streaming was westward from the east end and northward from the south arm. Much of the lower spatter rim around the lake had fallen away.

The north lake was also lower and showed a wall seven feet high on the northwest side and a spatter rim of similar height under the higher bluff of the southern side of the lake. The wall at the northeast end supporting remnants of the rampart was 12 feet high and showed fresh breaks. At the southwest end this lake showed an open cavern extending under the wall.

The west and southwest ponds had both overflowed since the high level of April 24, making flows which extended 200 to 300 feet westward and southwestward across the pressure rim. These flows probably poured out in the night of April 24. The ponds were now depressed within their cups.

There was continued the gas blowing at the south and east cones and at the cone source of the "Postal Rift" flow. This flow kept pushing forward until it was nearly half way from Perret's Cone to the north wall of Kilauea, and in the evening an arm was pushing eastward on the south side of Perret's Cone.

On April 27 the front of the Postal Rift flow ceased motion and became dark, but the source continued its flaming. A pot in the south wall crack contained fountaining lava which flared on the fume cloud above. The northeast side of the north lake caved in, demolishing the rampart remnant there. The east cone continued to be a bright beacon light and the flare over the lakes was brilliant. The dome swelling of the floor of Halemaumau appeared to have lifted more towards the south and west than towards the northeast, so that the northeast sector appeared relatively depressed, bounded by the east cone pressure ridge and south cliffs of the main lake on the one side, and by the west wall of the north lake crevasse on the other.

On Monday, April 28, fume had increased slightly, the bench magma was stationary and there was some increased caving in of the banks of the lakes. The front of the Postal Rift flow remained inactive. At noon the lakes were very low, the main lake depressed 25 to 40 feet and the north lake 15 to 30 feet, with the old rampart all fallen in and the surface covered with very heavy crust. In the north lake the only fountaining was at the north corner. In the central pool of the main lake there was also a heavy crust and the streaming in the east pool was eastward with moderate border fountaining and a central fountain opposite the east cone tunnel. The high bench magma surface adjacent to the south arm was found broken up with chasms, an especially large one extending southward and narrowing from the south arm pool towards the south wall crack. This pool was crusted over and oval in form, connected with the main lake by a narrow channel. A small fountaining pond 10 feet across and 15 feet below the upper ground occupied the wall chasm near the south cone. The east cone was flaming and rumbling through vents on its west side. There was some swelling and cracking in the long southeast flow. The bench magma was snapping, indicating renewed movement, and some rocks were sliding at the pressure ridges.

During this day there was pronounced rising of the lakes and at night fountains splashed above the bank levels and the east cone flamed brightly. The Postal Rift cone made an incandescent spot which became very bright after midnight, but no glowing lava appeared at the front of the flow.

On Tuesday, April 29, there was no lift observed in the floor and no unusual activity of the lakes. At 7 p. m. an outburst of liquid lava in the middle of the frontal puddle of the Postal Rift flow in the north corner of Kileaua crater developed a standing spring with lava spreading in lobes. At 8:30 p. m. there were two such springs feeding the revived front of the flow.

On April 30 at 4:30 p. m. Halemaumau was found with generally revived flows to the southwest, north and southwest. A fresh flow of silvery lava with dense texture had pooled under a new sluiceway vent which had opened in the face of the south pressure rim a few feet farther east than the vent of April 17. This lava had sent trickling snaky toes around the upper trail monument. The wall crack pond above was boiling and fuming. The cone at the Postal Rift had increased in size and was puffing like a freight engine. The frontal pool of the flow from this cone was now midway between the north wall of Kilauea and Perret's Cone and vents in the middle of this pool opened from time to time and kept the lava working out so as to enlarge the front in different directions. The renewed trickling was now again continuous. The third region of renewed flowing was from the west ponds. The west and southwest ponds were now united in a horseshoe shaped depression at the end of the chasm leading from the main lake. This depression was indented in the southwestern flank of the dome of uplifted floor lava and in the opening of the horseshoe was the third vent (formerly the west heap pond), now a pool 20 feet across with two border spatter heaps and fountains flinging up lava which was level with the brink of the pond. Off to the southwest a broad flow had swept from these ponds as a source down the outside slope away from Halemaumau in a sheet forking into separate arms which had poured southwest out on the Kilauea floor fully a half mile from the center of Halemaumau. The end of the flow had pooled and widened on flatter ground in the direction of the 1868 cracks. Flowing had been in progress here for two days, some of the flows being freshly incandescent, others a little cooler.

The east cone was flaming and rumbling. The main lake cliffs were 12 feet high on the east and 30 feet high on the north, and the streaming was westward and northward, with fountaining under the north bank. The north lake showed a six-foot cliff on the north and 20-foot cliff on the south; streaming was northward to a line of bombarding fountains under the straight northwestern bank of the lake. These fountains occupied seven niche grottoes in a row. There were two other fountaining grottoes at the southeast bank of this lake. The north lake was now diamond shaped, its long axis trending north-northeast and south-southwest, and the northeast wall had slumped down to the lake level making an inclined surface. The south ravine leading to the main lake had enlarged and a pulpit pinnacle stood out at its entrance.

The floor continued to rise moderately. The northeast tower was smoking at its western base with mildly sulphurous fume and whitened cracks in the rock as though a slow roasting process were going on.

The tilt of the northern and western rim rock of Halemaumau was measured at 4:20 p. m. on this day with Brunton clinometer at the north bench mark and the west station platforms. The north platform surface dipped 9 deg. 5 ft. in the direction N. 10 deg. E. The west platform dipped 4 deg. 35 ft. in the direction W. S. W. There thus appears to be an arching of the north rim over the conduit leading to the Postal Rift flow as well as a pushing up of the ground away from the center of Halemaumau.

On May 1 the southwestern overflow continued and the Postal Rift flow surrounded islands of old lava, spreading so as to approach the base of the northern part of the Uwekahuna wall. In the evening there were very strong pulsations of rising and falling in the lakes and some rock fell from the walls of the main lake during sinking spells. At night the lakes were brimming level with their banks and fountaining high.

On Friday, May 2, at 3:30 p. m. there were flaming and spitting holes in the southeast chasm at the top of the pressure ridge; the main lake, five feet below its east bank, streamed westward and northward, and the north lake was covered with heavy inflated crust and building spatter domes southeast and east. The north lake was within two feet of its north brink. It had built an inner margin which was overflowed during tumultuous breaking up spells. The western ponds had made fresh flows 200 feet long in numerous lobes during the day by way of the cone pot at their gateway. The cone was built higher and splashing inside and the larger pond brimming level with its banks and fountaining. The chasm leading to the main lake here was somewhat choked below.

At 4:30 p. m. the east cone burst open and sent a double cascade down its north slope, one torrent six feet wide and the other two feet wide, uniting below into a flow which poured eastward 200 feet and spread out. The flowing ceased quite suddenly about 5:30 p. m. and the last gushes at the head of the flow were very stiff and pasty. The head of the flow solidified completely within 10 minutes so that the writer was able to cross it. This shows the enormously rapid heat radiation and solidification of such lava, and its dependence on gas supply to keep it mobile.

The main lake showed high level throughout this flowing spell and its streaming was straight away from the tunnel leading to the E cone.

In the Whitney Laboratory the seismometric instruments have registered one slight local earthquake and three teleseismic during the week ending at 8 p. m. May 2, 1919. There have also been strong spasms of tremor amounting to very small local shocks. The local quake was at 3:06 p. m. April 27. The initial movements of the teleseisms were at 8:50 p. m. April 29, 3:54 p. m. May 1, and 2:34 p. m. May 2.

The distant earthquake of April 29 was a powerful one under the Pacific several thousand kilometers away, and tidal waves were noticed the next morning at Punaluu and Hilo. I am indebted to Mr. Jas. B. Mann, an engineer in the employ of the Bishop Estate, for the following: "The morning of April 30 the water receded in Punaluu Bay first at 7:30 a. m., until almost the whole bay was dry. It came back gradually but went out rapidly again about 9 a. m. and 10:30 a. m."

The teleseism of May 1 showed obscure phases, giving no clear data for distance. The earthquake of May 2 was very plainly registered and indicated a distance of approximately 6100 kilometers.

The spasmodic microtremor was strong, especially in daytime, April 26 and May 1 and 2, developing spells of great agitation of the ground. The slower harmonic microtremor has become slight and inconspicuous. Microseismic movement has been slight to moderate. The tilting was west and south April 26, stationary April 27-28, strong east and north April 29, and steady west and south April 30 to May 2.

Very respectfully,

T. A. JAGGAR, JR.,

Volcanologist.

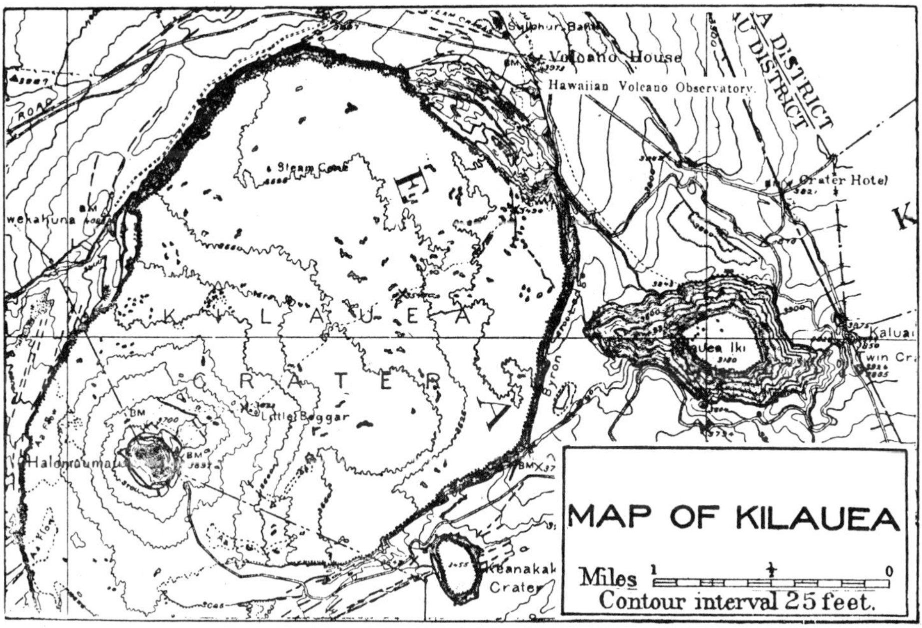

HAWAIIAN VOLCANO OBSERVATORY.

The Observatory is equipped with the following seismometric instruments rebuilt at the station in 1918 for the special needs of volcano research: two Bosch-Omori pendulums, high speed registration of local earthquakes; one optically recording seismograph for distant earthquakes; one clinograph registering E-W tilting of the ground. A vertical component seismograph was in December, 1918, set up in experimental operation. These are seated on concrete piers in a closed basement room having practically constant temperature, beneath the chief Observatory building near the hotel. Time is referred to a rated chronometer, checked at intervals by solar observations with a transit. Both instruments are loaned by the College of Hawaii. Hawaiian standard time (H. S. T.) is 10 hrs. 30 min. slower than Greenwich time.

CANCANI SCALE OF SEISMIC INTENSITY.

Expressed by accelerations measured in millimeters per second per second.

I.	Instrumental	0.0	2.5
II.	Very slight	2.5	5.0
III.	Slight	5.0	10.0
IV.	Sensible, mediocre	10.0	25.0
V.	Rather strong	25.0	50.0
VI.	Strong	50.0	100.0
VII.	Very strong	100.0	250.0
VIII.	Ruinous	250.0	500.0
IX.	Disastrous	500.0	1000.0
X.	Very disastrous	1000.0	2500.0
XI.	Catastrophic	2500.0	5000.0
XII.	Great catastrophe	5000.0	10000.0

Grade IV. is ordinarily the minimum perceived by the senses; and in grade XII. the accelerations or rate of change of motion (jerk) reaches that of terrestrial gravitation.

In the standard form of report the maximum intensity or acceleration, designated by the symbol a, or max. a, is given in the conventional unit of milligal. The milligal is a measure of acceleration, such that 1 milligal $= 1/100$ mm. per sec. per sec. $= 10\ \mu$ per sec. per sec. The Cancani scale, here defined in terms of milimeters per sec. per sec., can therefore be expresed in milligals by multiplying each of the numbers by 100.

U. S. DEPARTMENT OF AGRICULTURE
WEATHER BUREAU
CHARLES F. MARVIN, CHIEF

MONTHLY BULLETIN
OF THE
Hawaiian Volcano Observatory

VOL. VII. HONOLULU, HAWAII, MAY, 1919 No. 5

HAWAIIAN VOLCANO OBSERVATORY, May 10, 1919.—During the week ending Friday, May 9, 1919, the lift of the central floor of Halemaumau has continued at a slightly decreasing rate and the lakes have maintained high levels, building up their banks, and overflowing in the case of the western pond. The flow at the Postal Rift has widened out east and west from the source region so that the extremities of its two lateral arms are 0.7 mile apart, the one lying close to the base of the Uwekahuna wall south of the summit tripod, the other in the depression west of the Little Beggar with its front pushing parallel to the Volcano House trail. The whole flow, in shape like a bird with outstretched wings, now covers a considerable percentage of the northern half of Kilauea floor, the tail spreading on both sides of Perret's Cone and the head lying at the Postal Rift. The flow still continues to push forward energetically at its new lateral fronts, with occasional movements in its medial zone, and the source cone continues as a flaming beacon with occasional spouting spells. The backflow from these gushings has so plugged up the solfataric area of hot cracks that the voluminous fume from these cracks has greatly diminished.

As the north bench mark has continued to rise and tilt until it is now more than 10 feet above its original position, the measurements will hereafter be referred to the 3700-foot contour (original level of bench mark and of former rim of Halemaumau) and not to local marks near the crater. The following are approximate elevations above this contour:

May 2, central floor 82 ft., main lake 52 ft., N. E. tower 68 ft.

May 9, central floor 88 ft., main lake 53 ft., N. E. tower 68 ft.

The point of central floor here measured was on the south side of main lake; the northwest sector rose still more, about 10 feet during the week, making the maximum lift average 1.4 feet in the seven days. The movement, however, was not continuous, but in spurts. The rise of central floor at point measured was 6 feet, or 0.9 feet per day; of the main lake 1 foot, or 0.14 feet per day; and the northeast tower was stationary.

On Saturday, May 3, the lakes were high and brimming in their basins and the roaring of the Postal Rift source could be heard at the Observatory, the air being calm. The flow from this source was increasingly active, widening in many places, and seven moving streams were counted at one time, one of these the highest western fork, south of Uwekahuna. There were cascades over the wall of the depression containing the Pulpit Rock north of Pele's Kitchen, and an eastern arm of the flow started filling that depression. The extreme front of the main flow was moving toward the north end of the Uwekahuna wall.

On May 4 the lakes remained high, the fountains of the north lake being almost continuously visible at the Observatory. The floor of Halemaumau was rising. The reflected light from the lakes on the fume cloud at night made a brilliant display. There was dense smoke from cracks on the north side of the main lake, but elsewhere fume was thin. The Postal Rift flow made strong progress, showing a line of lights, like a city at night, across Kilauea floor from source to front, and the roar of its gas continued.

On May 5 the lakes continued high and measurement revealed a strong lift of the bench magma taking effect most around the southwest lake. Angular measurement showed also that the west and north concrete platforms had lifted farther since April 27. The Postal Rift flow was cascading into the broken ground of the Pulpit Rock depression northeast from the source and the front of the flow was against the northern base of the Uwekahuna wall. Perret's Cone was now surrounded by the flow as an island, along with some other old surface west of the cone.

At 3 p. m. the southeast wall chasm was hissing and glowing in one small hole. The uplifted crest of the arched Halemaumau floor was now 70 feet above the upper trail monument where the former southeast station had been and fully 40 feet of wall surmounted by yawning crevasses confronted the visitor approaching the so-called fire-pit—no longer a pit, but a domical hill, pitted in its crest with the fiery lakes, now occupying three chasms radiating from the center of the dome in clover-leaf pattern. The main lake, the eastern and largest of these, is forked to the south by its union with the southeast pond, so as to give to the clover a four-leaf aspect. The visitor follows the wall around to the east and climbs upward to the brink of the main lake by a pass between the east end of the wall and the heap of lava flows around the northeast tower. Here the east cone is passed, on the left, hissing and glowing, standing on the dome-slope, with the elephant-back surface arching up beyond it southward. The east bank of the lake is 6 feet above the liquid lava, which extends away into the heart of the dome for 800 feet as a canyon 40 feet deep, with the south arm another gorge forking off to the left. The traveller now walks over piles of lava between the northeast tower and the lake following around the dome slope and comes to the north lake. This is again high on the flank of the dome, with its north brink low and its south margin a high cliff on the side of the ravine leading into the heart of the dome—where a crack joins through to the central canyon of the main lake. This crack is the stem of the north clover leaf. Looking out from this north lake towards the familiar 1894 driblet cones on what was once the north edge of Halemaumau pit, we look downhill, see these cones all tipped backward to the north, and beyond them, with the steaming hot cracks no longer steaming, we find the postal Rift area a field of fresh black glistening live flows, extending away off to the north end of Kilauea crater under the Military Camp, and flooding out right and left towards the Volcano House trail and towards the high western bluff. Continuing the tramp around Halemaumau to the west side, a bit of the old wall is here preserved about 30 feet high until we pass the west niche of 1894. Inside the wall there is an upslope of flows 100 feet high to the smooth skyline profile of the great dome, and from here practically no lakes are visible. We are on the northwest slope of the dome, between the north and southwest lakes, and this is the widest unbroken sector. The southwest lake, usually shrouded in fume, is much like the north lake, but differs in that a wide chasm leads through to the central pool, and a slope of overflows, outside of Halemaumau, extends away on the southwest floor of Kilauea for half a mile. Going on around back to his starting place, the explorer picks up the wall once more, and realizes that he has to do with a great lava plug, lifted unsymmetrically above the former pit, making a wall on this southern side and a wall-valley on the northwest.

Examination on this day of the region on top of the south wall showed the pond in the wall-crack to be 50 feet long, 8 feet below the upper ground, crusted over, and with hissing gas spiracles in the crust. The ground on top thereabouts was smoking and dangerously crevassed. One looked down, forty feet below to the base of the wall here bounding abruptly the dome of uplift, and saw extending away to the southeast for a half-mile the expanse of flows which had poured over this lip and through this wall repeatedly since February of 1918. And across it all is the trail from the automobile terminus.

The main lake was streaming westward and northward. Its north bank glowed and flamed to the top and dense smoke rose from cracks above. The north lake was crusted over, two border fountains were in action, and the spatter dome on the southeast side was enlarged. The old north station was lifted more and a pressure slope of uplift extended from it towards the northeast tower, with the fresh flows from the tower lifted and broken. Similar pressure effects were seen at the west niche, where the old semi-circular ledge of 1894 was found crushed and broken.

The Postal Rift cone was covered with eight or ten gnarled spiracles hissing loudly. The cascades of this flow were pouring over the western wall of the horseshoe cliff enclosing the Pulpit Rock depression, the cascades crusted but the pool below a glistening pahoehoe flowing forward in many live toes.

The southwest lake cone (former west heap cone) was found still giving vent unremittingly to flows pushing along the southern side of the southwest heap of overflows.

May 6 proved a day of revival of gas-and-liquid flooding following the strong preceding tumescence. Shortly after midnight the Postal Rift cone burst open just as in its first spurt, and all day it sent out a surface torrent over its former flows, as well as through tubes to the fronts. The new surface floods were mostly east and west. The Pulpit Rock became surrounded with new lava and the old horseshoe tended to fill up. At 8 p. m. the cone source was still spouting. The backflow drowned out most of the Postal area smoke. The renewed cone was 5 feet high sending a 5-foot stream northward; this lava, very liquid, welled up about three feet at the orifice and swept away in its channel maintaining several standing waves. The surface flows moved west, northwest, north and northeast with fronts from 100 to 800 feet from the source, and the lower end of the original long flow pushed eastward. In the evening the freshly glowing melt made three marked arms east, north and west near the source and two, east and west, at the front near Perret's Cone .

All the while the lakes remained high. At 11 a. m. they were slightly down, the north lake, crusted but fountaining in five border grottoes, had built an inner spatter margin standing 4 feet above the melt, and some high heaps east and southeast of this lake gave evidence of a high level of the previous night when the Postal flow revived. The main lake at 11 a. m. was streaming swiftly northward and a central fountain in the east cove was the goal of local streaming from both east and west. The northeast tower smoke had become slight.

On Wednesday, May 7, at 6 p. m., the southeast wall chasm was cracked and glowing and the south chasm pond was puffing through a flaming gas cone, whence driblet streams had trickled down the outer wall of uplift. The southwest lake was noisy and bright with occasional fountaining. Short fresh flows from the southwest cone had extended the lava heap to the old west station and moved along the inside of the old wall of Halemaumau so as to override the south side of the west niche. The wall bounding the east side of the southwest lake was more lifted, the cone source was building a new lava heap, and the west station appeared still more tilted. The north lake was tending to become round again through building in of its margin which stood 7 feet above it on the north. A central fountain played at the west end of the pond, with crust ballooning near it, and two northwestern grottoes were active. From the ravine south of the north lake to within 25 feet of the central pool of the main lake a chasm 10 feet wide and 40 feet deep extended; the bottom of the chasm was covered with broken rock some 15 feet above the level of the north lake. The cliffs around the central pool were 40 feet high. The main lake stood 15 to 20 feet above the north lake. The central pool was fountaining violently against the base of its southern wall. Heavy smoke rose from the knob of cliff over the north side of the narrows between the east and central pools, as though undermining were there in progress which would eventually join through to the north lake chasm. Under this smoke a very brilliant cracked and flaming cliff surface high up the wall above the main lake suggested a closed in or curtained shaft. The main lake was comparatively high, its bank about 10 feet high at the east end, and the streaming, out from both the east cove and south arm, was swiftly westward.

The Postal Rift cone was quiet but flaming; all of the upper part of the flow was glowing and a main torrent poured from a low vent in the west lobe supplying an elongate pool parallel to and near the Uwekahuna wall south of the trig station. The glow at the Perret Cone front had ceased for a time. The east arm during the next twenty-four hours forked around the broken ground east of Pulpit Rock depression and bent north in the sag west of Little Beggar cone.

On May 8 the bench magma rising became slower, the lakes remained high. The long front flow of the Postal Rift outpouring had apparently become stiff and forced outlets east and west above, where there were two fountaining cones in a medial line besides the source cone. These seemed to be over the medial tube below, suggesting the gas cupolas along the upper course of the Thurston tube. At 11 p. m. the source cone burst and spouted lava and made a short surface flow.

On Friday, May 9, the central smoke was denser, the lakes continued high, with central and western fountains in the north lake. The Postal Rift flow continued spreading, showing a live torrent in the upper west arm in the afternoon, and in the evening two live areas revived in the Perret Cone front. From 6 to 7 p. m. all the upper part of the flow was alive as well, especially in the medial zone and cascading eastward to the east front. Beacon flames continued to burn steadily at the Postal cone and the east cone, and there was bright luminosity over the lakes and the south wall crack.

In the Whitney Laboratory of Seismology for the week ending at 8 p. m. May 9, 1919, the seismographs have registered the following local earthquakes: May 3, 8:35 a. m. (felt); May 5, 12:39 p. m.; May 6, 3:19 a. m.; May 7, 4:21 p. m. The following teleseisms have been registered, the times being initial motion: May 6, 9:34 a. m. and 7:11 p. m. The first of these was from a source about 5600 kilometers distant. Faint teleseisms were registered at 11:58 a. m. May 7 and 8:58 a. m. May 8. Microseismic movement and harmonic tremor have both been feeble during the week but spasmodic tremors have been moderate to strong. The tilting of the ground became strong to the east and north May 4-6, reacted to west and south May 7-8 and became stationary May 9.

HAWAIIAN VOLCANO OBSERVATORY, May 17, 1919.—The week preceding and incuding Friday, May 16, 1919, produced towards its close another spell of subsidence of liquid lava accompanied by inbreak of the bench magma and enlargement of the lakes. Until May 13, however, the high levels had continued and throughout even the subsidence days the Postal Rift flow has pushed ahead without cessation. The most marked topographic charges of the week have consisted in enlargement northward of the main lake, collapse and lowering of the broken ground between the main and north lakes and extension in all directions of the Postal Rift flow along with development of swollen domes in the several frontal regions of that flow.

This swelling up of tumuli, mostly 15 to 20 feet across and 5 to 10 feet high, always begins after a pahoehoe flow has progressed some distance from its source, and the swelling first is noticed in the frontal part of the flow. An individual dome forms in the course of a day or two. Usually such a dome gives vent to the lava within through the cracks. The lava welling out is generally the same as all the rest, but sometimes is very pasty and solidifies as heavy lumps with rough "shark skin" surface and even with formation of aa. This last is a rare phenomenon, observed, however, in three different flows since February of 1918. The apparent explanation of the dome swelling is that the crust and margins of the flow lobe have solidified, the lava inside has become pasty, and a revival of pressure after temporary stagnation finds swelling the path of least resistance. The forces inducing the pressure are threfold, namely gas effervescence at the source, weight of heavy fields of crust, and hydrostatic pressure in the fluid melt.

The measurements of the week expressed as approximate height of the several surfaces above the 3700-foot contour, are as follows:

May 9, central floor S. W. 88 feet, central floor N. E. 83 feet, main lake 53 feet.

May 16, central floor S. W. 87 feet, central floor N. E. 67 feet, main lake 37 feet.

These figures show the remarkable slump in the northeast summit sector of the floor along with subsidence of the main lake. The rest of the floor west and south remains a high dome as before. In seven days the central floor southwest subsided one foot but this happened May 14-16, averaging 0.5 feet per day on those two days; the central floor northeast sank 16 feet, also showing more rapid subsidence May 14-16, and averaging for the seven days 2.3 feet per day; the lake sank the same amount, namely 16 feet. The rate of sinking was really much faster, for the turning point was reached May 13, after which date the rate of subsidence for lake and northeast sector of bench for four days averaged 4 feet per day. The northeast tower continues stationary.

On Saturday, May 10, at 9 a. m., the south wall crack was hissing and flaming, the west cone was hissing and the southwest lake showed border fountains against its north and south shores. The southwestern overflowing had ceased, there was a large grotto dome in the south corner of the southwest lake. This lake had formed from the union of the former southwest and west ponds, was brimming level with its banks on the western side, but lay in the shadow of a 20-foot cliff where the great Halemaumau dome rose toward the east.

The writer climbed to the summit of this dome and stood on top of the cliff overlooking the junction of the main lake and the south arm. This cliff appeared fully 45 feet high where it overhung the central pool and from this high vantage point, looking down into the gashes occupied by the lakes, one gained the impression of being on uplifted crags, quite similar to those of 1917 and 1918. They also had surfaces sloping away from the center, and cliffs overhanging the lakes, differing only from the present situation in the lack of continuity in their outlooking slopes. The breaking up of this continuous dome surface which is going on this week so as to leave the tips of the sectors at different levels, promises to convert them into crags wholly analogous to those of former years.

The streaming in the main lake was northward and eastward. The bank at the east cove was 5 feet high. Two chasms prolonged the south arm southward, the eastern one 4 feet wide. A marginal terrace in the south arm stood 5 feet above the lake level.

The north lake was covered with crust, and spatter grottoes were building up at the southwest corner of this lake as well as on other sides. The east cone had become quieter and yellow sulphur stain had formed on the surfaces south of it. The Postal Rift cone was puffing and the flow from it progressed steadily with live toes at its three fronts northwest, north and northeast. All night long a spectacular cascade at the northeast front poured from the ponded region of the Pulpit Rock depression over the broken ground farther northeast so as to make an extensive pool in the region east of Little Beggar cone. Late at night the source cone renewed its spouting.

On May 11 the fume from the high ground north of the main lake was very dense and the central peak overhanging the east pool there collapsed. Measurements showed stationary bench magma, the lakes continued high and the Postal Rift flow continued to send out live tongues in many places so that at night the flow resembled a bed of hot coals. At midnight a new cone broke into action 20 feet northeast of the original source cone.

On May 12 at 4:30 p. m. the east

cone was noisy with gas rushing through a new summit hole. The lakes were about as before. The hot smoking ground north of the main lake was whitened by the solfataric vapors and greatly crevassed. The Postal Rift cone was covered with hissing gas spiracles and the new cone beside it was a steep spatter heap four feet high built over the heavily crusted streamway which led in the direction of the eastern lobe of the flow. For several hundred feet around these source cones the surface was smooth and the crusts several feet thick, the upper pattern giving indication of long sweeping lines of flow in the three directions of the three main arms of the flow. It is a singular characteristic of these lava flats at the source of flows that they become thicker and stronger and more heavily roofed above the lava continuously pouring through the tunnels below than any other part of the area covered by the outflow. The capacity which this Postal Rift flow shows for throwing out wings laterally is interesting evidence of the way in which the Hawaiian dome mountains like Mauna Loa and Kilauea have been built; the building is not only radial but also concentric in zones.

The Postal Rift flow had now obliterated the western wall of the Pulpit Rock depression, the Pulpit Rock itself rose only a few feet above the fill surrounding it and the lava had made an extensive flow away beyond and below this ground in the direction of Volcano House. There were also several new elongate arms of the flow trending northward from the western wing.

It was now evident that this high level of May, 1919, must be considered the equivalent of the similar high May level of 1917 and the high levels of February-March, August, and November of 1918. But the present culmination has produced much the greatest effusion of liquid lava, inducing what appears to be an equilibrium or stationary condition in the main lava column satisfied by the steady outpouring.

On May 13 the lakes continued high, dense fume rose from the region north of the main lake, the great flow continued and in the night the source cone resumed its spouting.

On May 14 at noon the south wall cones were quiet, the east cone was still less active and the main lake, about 8 feet down at the east end, was streaming to the north and east. The other lakes remained as before and the fuming had increased north of the east pool.

The Postal Rift flow was active at the west and north fronts. The source cones were partially drowned by the new lava of the previous night and this lava had very thick crusts. The cones were hissing and flaming as usual. Live lava was in motion against the base of the Uwekahuna wall northwest of Halemaumau, domes were swelling up near the front, the middle region was hot over tubes below and the east arm was stagnant.

On May 15 the dense smoke north of the main lake had disappeared and the broken ground had collapsed into the lake making a new deep northeast cove. Smoke had disappeared also from the west corner of the north lake and from the Postal crack region. In the evening the lakes were low and dull and the lights from the east and Postal Rift cones dim. The upper parts of the flow were dark but there were many live places in the west and north arms.

About 4 a. m. May 16 the Postal Rift source had started spouting again and this continued into the forenoon. It was evident that the sector of raised Halemaumau floor north of the main lake was sinking and the general surface was slightly lower.

At 6 p. m. the east cone was found with one small flaming orifice, part of the pressure ridge east of it had collapsed to a cup and the main lake was 20 feet down at the east end while the walls to the south and west remained 50 feet high, but the north walls were only 30 feet high, owing to the localized subsidence of the bench. There was great enlargement northward of the northeast cove and big rifts had formed extending westward from the end of the cove to the north lake chasm and beyond. The streaming in the main lake continued northward and eastward, there was a cavernous quiet grotto hung with stalactites at the east cove and some border bombardment in the northeast cove. The north lake had lowered but its north rim was still 10 feet high. This lake had enlarged by collapse of its spatter margins. There were very thick crusts and the lava was pasty and spattering over the crust through blowholes; the grottoes were dull.

The Postal Rift cone was puffing and flaming and the lava about it was cracked and glowing. Flows were moving at the base of Uwekahuna and the main spreading of the flow was east and west from the intermediate region south of Perret's Cone. There was much increase of white vapor in the tilted ground near the north bench mark.

The seismographs of the Whitney Laboratory for the week ending at 8 p. m., May 16, 1919, have registered the following local earthquakes, mostly feeble: 6:24 a. m. May 10; 5:26 a. m. and 12:26 p. m. May 11; 6:43 a. m., 10:45 a. m. and 3:09 p. m. May 13; 10:05 a. m. May 16. Microseismic movement has decreased from slight to very slight. Harmonic microtremor has continued slight. The spasmodic microtremor developed many strong spasms May 12-14 and continues moderate to strong; the motion is stronger east-west than north-south and stronger day-time than night. Tilting of the ground remained stationary May 10, was strong to the east and north May 11-13, and stationary with westward tendency May 14-16.

HAWAIIAN VOLCANO OBSERVATORY, May 24, 1919.—During the week ending Friday, May 23, 1919, a sluggish subsidence of the surface of the lava column amounting to about a half foot per day has been in progress, if one measures subsidence by the altitude of the hard surfaces and liquid lakes over the area which was formerly Halemaumau pit. Through all this, however, the Postal Rift flow has sent a ceaseless torrent through tubes to its northern fronts extending itself generally over the entire northern quarter of Kilauea crater, piling up along the base of Uwekahuna wall and finally obliterating the vapor vent known as Perret's Cone. A notable local subsidence of a block of the Halemaumau dome, similar to the northeastern one of last week, took place May 20-21 on the south side of the central pool, an immense cube of bench magma sinking 20 feet and causing tumult in the adjacent lake by the slumping into the lake of debris, which as usual lay as normal talus slopes, at flat angles of rest, the foundations lying on the lake bottom.

The meaurements indicate the following approximate elevations above the 3700-foot contour:

May 16, central floor S. 80 feet, central floor S. W. 87 feet, central floor N. E. 67 feet, main lake 37 feet.

May 23, central floor S. 68 feet, central floor S. W. 84 feet, central floor N. E. 62 feet, main lake 33 feet.

Thus the floor block south of the main lake sank in seven days 20 feet, or 2.9 feet per day; the crest of the Halemaumau dome southwest of the center sank 3 feet, or 0.4 feet per day; the northeast floor block sank 5 feet, or 0.7 feet per day; and the lake sank 4 feet, or 0.6 feet per day.

On Saturday, May 17, the middle part of the Postal Rift flow was spreading out in hooked and forked lobes and the front east of Perret's Cone had increased in size and changed in pattern. The upper wings of the flow had become stagnant.

The broken region north of the main lake continued to subside and increased smoke there suggested further undermining. The fountains of the north lake were high enough to show above the rim, there was some light from the south wall crack and the east cone beacon had become dim.

From 3 to 4 p. m. on May 18 no hissing could be heard at the south wall crack but lava was pounding and puffing within the east cone cupola. The walls of the main lake stood 20, 30 and 50 feet above it and the streaming was swift eastward and northeastward out of the southern and western arms. No further subsidence was noticeable in the ground north of the central pool and the fume there was not dense. On the south wall of the north lake there was a high splash mark 20 feet above the liquid believed attributable to an avalanche which had been seen at 10 a. m. to produce a puff of brown dust. The encompassing wall of the north lave was 12 feet high on the north side and 40 feet high on the south.

The southwest lake was lower, the west cone had become a pond and there was a channel depression between the two. This depression was 50 feet wide and the pond southwest of it was oval and 50 feet long in a northwest-southeast direction with lava streaming from southeast to northwest. This pond was depressed 8 feet below its margins. The southwest lake showed 15-foot walls on the southwest side and 30-foot walls on the east. Fountains were rumbling and plashing in the smoky northern part of the pond where a spatter margin 15 feet high stood across the entrance to the chasm leading to the main lake.

The Postal Rift cone was again changed in form and an open pot 18 inches in diameter on its summit led to a glowing well inside where the lava was pounding and puffing. The flow continued its steady advance at the northern fronts. The luminosity of the lakes was dull in the evening but occasional fountains could be seen at the north lake.

On Monday, May 19, the fume was somewhat denser especially at the south wall crack. The activity of the lakes remained as before and the flow was specially mobile in the north middle section and against the Uwekahuna wall. All the lakes glowed brightly at times including the south arm and the south wall crack.

The measurements of the morning of May 20 showed a distinct lowering of the block of ground west of the south arm of the main lake so that the southeast block stood as a crag making a jog in the profile of the Halemaumau dome. Fume increased in the region south of the north lake and in the evening increased water vapor was discernible about Pele's Kitchen and near the north corral. At 6:30 p. m. the fume at the south wall crack was thin, and bright banners of pinkish flame rose from the summit opening of the east cone. The marginal cliffs of the main lake were 25 feet high at the east, 50 feet high at the southeast, 40 feet high southwest and 30 feet high north. The surface streaming in a broad river northward from a dark crust which lay across the south arm expended itself in a number of border grottoes fountaining in the northeast cove, the east cove and the central pool. The southwest lake flared brightly. The north lake, with shores 10 to 15 feet high on the north and 30 to 40 feet high on the south, showed streaming currents from its south corner to its north corner and spatter domes building along its northeast shore. The crevassed summit area between the north lake and the main lake showed increase of high incandescence in chasms and much sulphurous acid fume. One deep chasm was 10 feet across and 30 feet deep. The lower part extended as a cave under an arch of debris above to the lake level at the northeast cove. The dominant rifts crossed each other, the one extending from the northeast cove towards the southwest lake and the other extending due southward from the north lake. The Postal Rift cone had glowing holes at each end and a large banner of flame in the middle.

The quiet spraying border fountains and the abundant flames indicated a renewal of rising of liquid lava perhaps induced by the rapid submergence of the south floor block which was at this time in progress.

This submergence was revealed the next morning, May 21, when this block on the west side of the south arm was found to have gone down 20 feet. At 2 p. m. this block made a cliff only 20 feet above the lake, its upper surface sloping a little eastward and its western boundary being a crevasse or fault plane extending southward from the central pool. A tumble of cliff matter lay in the lake on the north side of the sunken block. The lake appeared rather lower than before with swift streaming out of the south arm, and much heavy and tumultuous central fountaining. The southeast point stood as a crag more than 50 feet high. At the base of the crevasse leading westward from the northeast cove there was a cavern with inflow. Sometimes the streaming would bend rapidly around the corner of the southeast crag.

The north lake was lower, its northeast corner smoky and its north wall 15 feet high. Marginal construction had

Feb. 21, 1919. Southeast rim station, Halemaumau, before uplift.

Feb. 25, 1919. Standing fountain spring of lava at East Cone, the day of sudden uplift.

March 6, 1919. Southeast station after mashing up rim, which began suddenly Feb. 25.

April 17, 1919. Northeast tower and its snaky lava flows. —*Photo. Jaggar.*

ceased. The southwest lake was also lower with walls 30 to 40 feet high and the west pond, also lower, showed fallen banks at its southern corners. Both ponds were crusted over. The Postal Rift source showed two fiery places, fume was moderate and at night the lakes were dull.

The next day there was little change. On Friday, May 23, the bench magma was slightly lower and fume had become dense again in the region of central crevasses. The northern part of the Postal Rift flow was pushing forward rapidly. At 10 a. m. it was observed that the south pressure wall had been gradually breaking up of late into numerous pinnacles. The east cone was no longer noisy but had a flaming hole on top. The main lake had been about 4 feet higher as shown by a border terrace, and this terrace in the middle of the lake had formed an isthmus clear across from north to south so as once more to separate off the central pool as a distinct pond. The streaming had notably changed, the east and northeast region being stagnant while the current out of the south arm bent westward to the isthmus. The north lake also had a low marginal terrace. In the evening a window was found to have opened in the roof of the tube leading from the Postal Rift cone so that one could look into the glowing chamber where the lava, 12 feet below, was pouring steadily northward to feed the moving fronts of the flow.

During the week ending at 8 p. m. May 23 two small local earthquakes have been registered on the instruments of the Whitney Laboratory. These occurred at 12:45 a. m. May 18 and 4:53 p. m. May 23. Distant earthquakes showing no phases sufficient to identify distance were registered at 7:07 p. m. May 19 and 1:41 a. m. May 22. Spasmodic microtremor increased during the week so that it was very strong, amounting to swarms of very small earthquake shocks May 23. Harmonic microtremor has been slight with some spasmodic increase May 21-23. Microseismic motion was very slight until May 20 when it increased somewhat and then became slight again May 22-23. The tilting of the ground continued to the west and south May 17-19, was stationary May 20, slightly east and north May 21-22, and was stationary May 23.

HAWAIIAN VOLCANO OBSERVATORY, May 31, 1919.—During the week ending Friday, May 30, 1919, the continued slight subsidence of the lava column accords with what is to be expected just before solstice. This subsidence is taking the form of collapses of bench magma in numerous places, and cones have been replaced by pits owing to such breaking down over voids below. Smoke also has greatly increased over such voids beneath the crevasses in the center of the Halemaumau dome. The Postal Rift flow on the floor of Kilauea crater has continued to spread and push forward but with somewhat diminished volume.

Measurements for the week show that the liquid lava of the lakes has been stationary and the sinking of the dome sectors has been various, amounting only to a few feet. The approximate levels above the 3700 foot contour were as follows:

May 23, central floor S. 60 feet, central floor S. W. 84 feet, central floor N. E. 62 feet, main lake 33 feet.

May 30. central floor S. 54 feet, central floor S. W. 80 feet, central floor N. E. 60 feet, main lake 35 feet.

The southern block has thus subsided 6 feet in seven days, averaging 0.9 feet per day; the northeastern block 4 feet, or 0.6 feet per day; the southwestern block 2 feet, or 0.3 feet per day. The lake has risen 2 feet, or 0.3 feet per day.

On Saturday, May 24, at 8 a. m., no trace could be seen of Perret's Cone and the Postal Rift flow continued strong pushing out of toes at its northern fronts. The Halemaumau dome still stood high, its summit only slightly below the profile of the far rim of Kilauea crater as seen from the Observatory, but smoke had increased at the hot cracks north of the main lake.

From 6 to 7 p. m. the east cone was flaming and the main lake stood higher relative to its shores so that its level was nearly flush with the isthmus dividing the east pool from the central pool. There was strong northward current out of the south arm. The north lake, on the other hand, was low, showing 20-foot walls on its north and east sides. It was covered with crust which cracked and sank now and then, and a somewhat rhythmic explosive fountain burst out every two minutes from under the edge of the lake crust under the southern chasm ravine. Some northward streaming was evident in the northern part of the lake. At night this lake showed tendency to dark spells.

On the north side of the Postal Rift cone, a few feet away from the cone proper, two windows in the floor about 2 feet across each led to the tunnel beneath which was discharging continuously the flow lava northward. The northern window was clogged with glowing matter, but the other revealed brilliantly incandescent cavernous space where about 12 feet down the orange colored melt flowed northward in a majestic torrent. By looking obliquely toward the region under the cone one could see a streaming fountain feeding this flow. In the other direction the river poured northwestward in a tube and blue fume rose through cracks in the floor of hardened flow lava above. This was the wellspring which ceaselessly fed the ever pushing fronts a mile and a half away and the opening of the upper half of the tube was evidence of some decline in the volume of lava furnished.

On May 23 about 3 p. m. the isthmus shutting off the central pond was seen to be growing wider and there were live grottoes on the southeast side of the isthmus and at the northeast cove. The east pool showed central fountaining but the central pond was quiet. The north lake had a cracking crust and was increasingly dark at night, the main lake was mostly bright and the southwest lake had brightly active spells. The Postal Rift showed the same flowing in the source tube and at the fronts.

On May 26 slight continued subsidence was indicated. Smoke was increasing. The flow continued vigorous and there were bright flames at the east cone and at the Postal Rift cone.

On Tuesday, May 27, at noon the cliffs about the main lake were 20 feet high on the east, 30 feet high on the north, 25 feet on the south and 50 feet southeast and west. There were the same western and northeastern grottoes, the central pond was stagnant and more shut off, and dense fume rose from the central chasms. There appeared to be a line of breaking extending eastward from the northeast cove to the northeast tower and at the west base of the tower smoking was renewed. At 1 p. m. this place caved in and sent up a brown avalanche cloud.

The north lake showed a 15-foot wall on the north and a 40-foot wall on the south. Amid the stagnant cracking crusts there were lines of bubbling lava and a grotto cave was open on the southwest side.

The isthmus between the southwest lake and the west pond showed increased subsidence and fracture. The floor of the isthmus stood 3 feet above the lakes, whereas the wall on the southwest side of the pond stood 15 feet high and the walls bounding the lake stood 25 to 40 feet above the liquid, except at the isthmus. The lake was turbulent and smoky in its northern part and crusted toward the south. The pond had a broken tumble of rocks on its northwest side and at the opposite end a pulpit rock stood out between it and the lake.

The south wall crack was still alive, emitting pungent fume and glowing at night.

At the Postal Rift source a close inspection of the interior chamber showed it to be a large cupola under the cone where lava spouted up in gushes in two places, the one 10 feet farther east than the other. These fountains were about 15 feet below the orifices in the top of the cone. The western fountain may have fed a western tube. The eastern one fed the northern torrent which flowed north-northeast about four miles an hour, the surface of the current 12 feet below the general floor bounded on the east by a vertical wall under the window and on the west by another wall which could be seen with difficulty 15 feet to the west—making the tube 15 feet wide. Flame and sulphurous acid fume rose through the orifices and 20 feet from the cone to leeward (southwest) there was bright yellow sulphur being deposited in an oval patch 20 feet long. Similar patches of sulphur stain have recently developed to the leeward of the southwest pond and of the east cone and all of these patches smell of free sulphur. Apparently the pressure of the wind on the gas chambers underground carries the unconsumed sulphur through cracks and pores to crystallize at these places, whereas at the live vents it burns and the combustion product is sulphurous acid gas.

Exploration of the flow to the west showed that the lava was piled against the Uwekahuna cliff face for several hundred feet of length from the ash locality northward. Near the front there were high driblet heaps and swollen domes.

On May 28 at 3 p. m. the lakes were unchanged and the east cone flaming through filagree orifices in its summit. The collapse of the smoking ground under the northeast tower had produced a pit 30 feet in diameter containing a stagnant crusted lava pool in the cavity 15 feet beneath the base of the tower. There was some glow at the edge of the pool and a little gas hissing. The inner rock of the northeast heap revealed in the wall of the pit was red with abundant iron oxides. The smoking had ceased at this locality.

At the Postal Rift source the speed of current was estimated at six miles per hour in the tube. The northern part of the flow was exploded and driblet lava was found pushing through cracks in the top of a swollen ridge. The position of the first front of the flow west of the Perret Cone locality was found occupied by an elongate flat-topped swollen area. Much of the lava recently squeezed out is blue gray, heavy and smooth, rarely showing aa patches and frequently having bulbous blisters of brown glass on the surface, two or three inches in diameter. The flow has spread over all the northern part of Kilauea crater clear to the talus west of Volcano House.

On May 29 the east cone was found to have collapsed to a pit full of broken reddish rocks and the gas flames there were extinguished. The north lake was now mostly dark and crusted. The Postal Rift source region broke open in a new collapse of the main tube 200 yards northwest of the source cone.

On Friday, May 30, at 11:30 a. m., both the source cone and the new pit were emitting flame and blue fume. Exploration of the nw pit discovered the fact that the roof of the tunnel had broken in for a length of 30 feet and a width of 15 feet, revealing a lava torrent tumbling over a slope into a broad portion of the tube beyond where it flowed away into cavernous brilliant glowing depths. The part exposed to the air showed wrinkled skins. The source tunnel showed increased rapidity of flowing. It seems likely that the loss of gas from the lava as it flows through these open smoking ducts may account for the dense blue glassy lava solidifying at the frontal outlets.

The main lake was very slightly higher and the partition separating it from the central pond stood 4 feet above the liquid. Streaming was outward from the south arm and inward to the northeast cove. Fume rose densely in two columns at the northeast cove crevasse and at the north lake chasm. A new cavern of collapse with very hot air inside was revealed in the southwest summit knob of the northeast heap. The entire southern half of the northeast tower had fallen into the pit beneath choking the lava pool there so that no further activity was in evidence.

The north lake was higher, only 8 feet down on its north side, and a new spatter border had been built. A glowing vent at the lake edge south broke out more or less periodically about once in two or three minutes with a roar of rushing gas and a little lava sputter. This was a closedin grotto,for the lake crust outside would heave and break during the spasms.

The Postal Rift flow continued to glow brilliantly at night and to spread continuously and build up by many outbreaks in the middle portions. Sometimes these could be seen in daylight. The general subsidence evidenced by collapse of voids at the cones appears at the end of the week to be followed by some recovery of the liquid lava.

In the Whitney Laboratory of Seismology for the week ending Friday,

May 30, 1919, the following local earthquakes have been registered, mostly very trivial: 11:58 p. m. May 24; 9:18 a. m. May 26; 6:44 a. m. and 4.03 p. m. May 27; and 5:15 p. m. May 30. The faint trace of a teleseism was registered at 10:04 a. m. May 26 H. S. T. Spasmodic microtremor has been very strong to strong all through the week. Harmonic tremor of slower period has been moderate to slight, with a tendency to spasmodic occurrence. A remarkable spasm of slow tremor was registered about 10 to 10:20 a. m. May 28. Microseismic motion has been slight, always more in evidence north-south than east-west, which is the invariable rule here, and on May 28 there was very slight short-lived increase in amplitude. The tilting of the ground was slight to the east and north May 24, to the west and south May 25, to the west and north May 26, nearly stationary May 27-29, and strong to the west and south May 30.

Very respectfully,

T. A. JAGGAR, JR.,

Volcanologist.

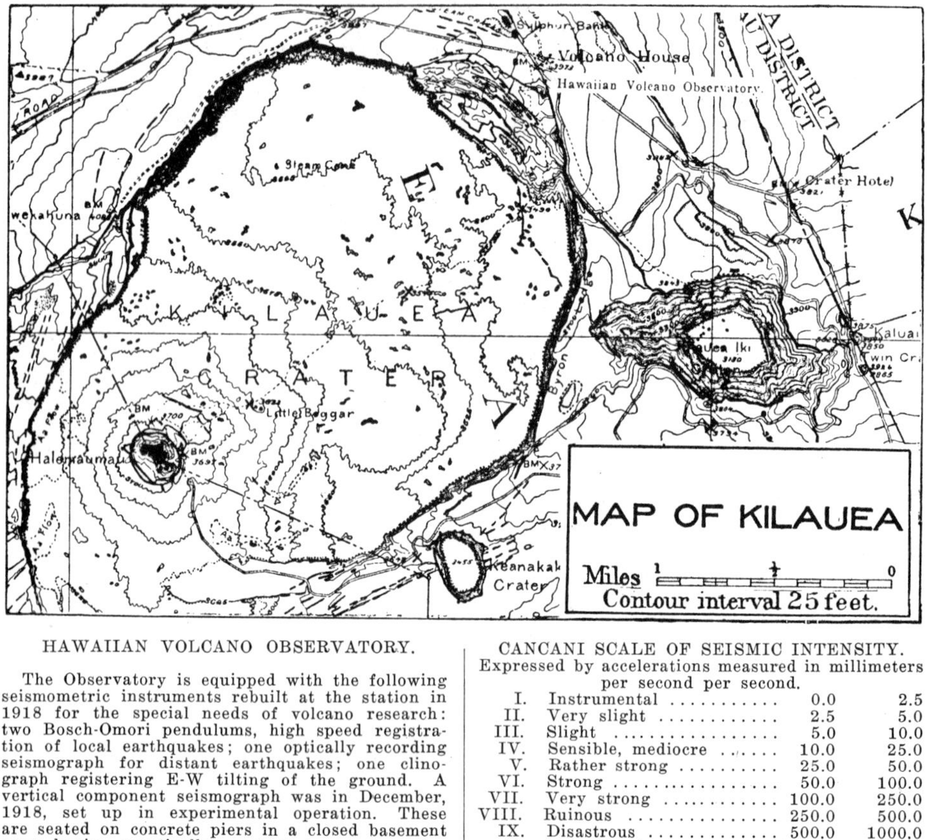

HAWAIIAN VOLCANO OBSERVATORY.

The Observatory is equipped with the following seismometric instruments rebuilt at the station in 1918 for the special needs of volcano research: two Bosch-Omori pendulums, high speed registration of local earthquakes; one optically recording seismograph for distant earthquakes; one clinograph registering E-W tilting of the ground. A vertical component seismograph was in December, 1918, set up in experimental operation. These are seated on concrete piers in a closed basement room having practically constant temperature, beneath the chief Observatory building near the hotel. Time is referred to a rated chronometer, checked at intervals by solar observations with a transit. Both instruments are loaned by the College of Hawaii. Hawaiian standard time (H. S. T.) is 10 hrs. 30 min. slower than Greenwich time.

CANCANI SCALE OF SEISMIC INTENSITY.

Expressed by accelerations measured in millimeters per second per second.

I.	Instrumental	0.0	2.5
II.	Very slight	2.5	5.0
III.	Slight	5.0	10.0
IV.	Sensible, mediocre	10.0	25.0
V.	Rather strong	25.0	50.0
VI.	Strong	50.0	100.0
VII.	Very strong	100.0	250.0
VIII.	Ruinous	250.0	500.0
IX.	Disastrous	500.0	1000.0
X.	Very disastrous	10000.0	2500.0
XI.	Catastrophic	2500.0	5000.0
XII.	Great catastrophe	5000.0	10000.0

Grade IV. is ordinarily the minimum perceived by the senses; and in grade XII. the accelerations or rate of change of motion (jerk) reaches that of terrestrial gravitation.

In the standard form of report the maximum intensity or acceleration, designated by the symbol α, or max. α, is given in the conventional unit of milligal. The milligal is a measure of acceleration, such that 1 milligal = 1/100 mm. per sec. per sec. = 10 μ. per sec. per sec. The Cancani scale, here defined in terms of millimeters per sec. per sec., can therefore be expressed in milligals by multiplying each of the numbers by 100.

U. S. DEPARTMENT OF AGRICULTURE
WEATHER BUREAU
CHARLES F. MARVIN, CHIEF

MONTHLY BULLETIN
OF THE
Hawaiian Volcano Observatory

VOL. VII. HONOLULU, HAWAII, JUNE, 1919 No. 6

June 7, 1919.

The subsidence has continued at a moderate but increasing rate during the week ending June 6, 1919. The Postal Rift flow has continued its progress, spreading voluminously under the north wall of Kilauea crater and beginning to progress from that region eastward towards the trail under Volcano House. There have been no conspicuous developments at Halemaumau, the central smoke has increased, the bench magma has slumped in places, and the lakes have been notably quiet, crusted over, and dark at night.

The measurements of approximate levels above the 3700-foot contour were as follows:

May 30—Central floor S., 54 feet; central floor SW., 80 feet; central floor NE., 60 feet; main lake, 35 feet.

June 6—Central floor S., 50 feet; central floor SW., 76 feet; central floor NE., 55 feet; main lake, 32 feet.

These figures indicate a general subsidence of about 4 feet in seven days, or 0.6 foot per day. The rate of subsidence of the bench magma has been like that of the preceding week. The liquid lava has tended to hold itself stationary, the difference shown being within the diurnal range.

On Saturday, May 31, there was much smoke and the Halemaumau dome was essentially stationary.

On June 1 at 11 a. m. exploration of the south wall-crack revealed numerous and extensive crevasses in that vicinity and the site of the former pond in the wall-crack was a jumble of crusts with live lava somewhere below which could be heard pounding beneath a pile of fuming sulphur-stained rocks. Under the spiracles at the top of the pressure wall which here bounds the Halemaumau lava column, was a partly collapsed cupola chamber. These spiracles stand at the top of the slope down which the last southeastern trickle flows poured.

The southwest wind permitted exploration of the summit of the Halemaumau dome from that side. Looking down at the main lake and central pool from the south central cliff, there was seen a depression containing the lakes, with three arms respectively northeast, west and south. The western gorge containing the central pool was floored with the isthmus separating that pond from the remainder of the main lake, and the central pond was a small circular puddle tending at the moment to overflow the isthmus. Rising of the liquid lava was in progress. The walls of this central gorge were 40 to 45 feet high on the south and 30 feet high on the north. Looking down on the south arm another gorge was seen with a narrow entrance and wider interior cup containing what was formerly the southeast pond. This arm is bounded on the west by an immense block of cliff rock which in slipping down has separated off from the dome surface beyond along a chasm trending northwest-southeast, 10 feet wide and 30 feet deep. This block stands 20 feet above the lake, while across the way the southeast crag makes a bluff 40 feet high. Turning now and looking at the larger lake consisting of the east pool and the northeast cove, we see a smoking bluff on the left 35 feet high, a low margin only 10 feet high toward the east, and the aforementioned southeast crag on the right. The liquid lava of this pool was high and crusted over, but later it broke up and showed northeastward streaming. The south arm was covered with crust. There was some spatter fountaining on the north side of the central pool. A striking feature of the summit plateau, whence these observations were made, was the accumulation of iron oxide at the edges of the hot cracks in the rock, bright orange red in color, while all around the ground was covered with a mat of Pele's hair.

The southwest lake and west pond were unusually high, the latter tending to overflow the isthmus separating it from the lake. The lake was quiet, but later developed a fountain in its southeast corner. Attached to the cliff margin of the lake southwest were several spatter-drip columns 6 feet high, made each by persistent flings at one point from fixed spraying fountains which had played against the wall like water from a hose. The effect was quite like frozen cascades.

The north lake was high and quiet, with wall 6 feet high on its north side and some general cracking and foundering which spread across the lake and left a quiet crust. The rhythmic vent under the south chasm continued to blow occasionally.

The lava in the source tunnel of the Postal Rift flow was running about 10 miles per hour and the open channel farther west still showed the cascading torrent pouring from the cavern above to the deeper tube beneath with shell-like crusts of peculiar pattern arched across the torrent in places.

On June 2 in the afternoon the lakes were somewhat lower. The main lake stood four feet below the platform separating it from the central pond; it was mostly crusted over, but there were occasional border outbursts of gas east and a sluggish grotto persisted under the sunken southwest cliff. The southwest lake was lower, with some central fountaining breaking the crusts, and there was no special change in the north lake. Very heavy smoke rose from the central chasms, which glowed brightly at night.

The Postal Rift flow was now bright enough at night to illumine the north walls of Kilauea crater and to make luminous the vapor and clouds towering above. The luminosity of the flow itself came from scattered brilliant points where the liquid lava was welling up.

The whole northern area of the flow appeared like a glowing pool, and in daytime this had a bluish tarnish different in luster from the early days of the flow. Both the tunnel openings of the source region made glow and flames visible at night. The crusted north lake at night was now notably dark, and there was no longer any fire at the east and south cones.

On June 3 there was continued slight localized sinking of the bench magma, and the lakes were still lower, the main lake wall at the east end standing 15 feet high. The central smoke was growing denser, and both Halemaumau and the Postal Rift flow were dull at night.

On Thursday, June 5, the subsidence had continued and both smoke and glow were increasing at the high crevasses in the center of Halemaumau. The east cone had slumped bodily about 10 feet, while preserving its form, the ground all around showing slope inward to a cup-like hollow. For hours during the afternoon the main lake had remained heavily crusted with curtained grottoes and its streaming concealed by the crust.

Examination of the glow locality where the dense smoke was emitted from the high ground north of the main lake revealed a tumble of crevassed rock like a bed of glowing coals, with flames playing through the interstices. This area was 20 feet in diameter, and its temperature had gradually been raised by gas seepage and oxidation over some void forming below. Dense sulphur fume and water vapor rose from the hot area, and the place appeared ready to cave in and produce a lava pot.

The north lake was crusted over except for a small liquid area under the south chasm ravine, where the rhythmic fountain broke out occasionally, and the liquid appeared to be flowing in from the south and over the crust of the lake. The occasional fountain bursts here made sudden flares at night visible from a distance as reflected from the fume cloud above.

At the Postal Rift source tube the flowing stream appeared a little higher and slower than before, and the cascade locality farther northwest was crusted across the open part, but below and beyond the broad cavern showed a steady stream pouring northward from under the crusted cascade. The front of the flow continued its spreading out and filling against the north wall of Kilauea crater so that the contact with the wall was now nearly a mile long from the northern part of the Uwekahuna bluff following around the north margin of Kilauea crater to a point under the wooded fault blocks southwest of Volcano House.

On the morning of June 6 the measurements showed marked subsidence of the central and southeastern parts of the Halemaumau dome, and the central fume column was denser. At 3 p. m. more slumping of the cup around the east cone was apparent, and the high ground south of the south arm appeared lower. There was a new tumble of rock from the cliff north of the central gorge to the isthmus floor below. The main lake had resumed its streaming from the south arm to the northeast grotto, and its level relative to the cliffs was unchanged. The north lake showed little change, there was periodic blowing from the south grotto, the north bank was 8 feet high, and a patch of crust adjacent to the west bank was in process of breaking up. At night Halemaumau showed bright activity at the east pool, south arm and southwest lake, there were flames at the central smoke patch and at the two tube vents of the Postal Rift source, and the flow showed much activity at its front which was spreading eastward in the direction of the cliff trail leading down from Volcano House.

The seismographs of the Whitney Laboratory for the week ending June 6, 1919, have registered local earthquakes as follows: Slight shocks May 31 at 1:49 a. m. and 5:16 p. m.; a very pronounced shock of large amplitude at 4:14 p. m. June 2, not felt here, but felt strongly in the district of Kau to the south; slight shocks 1:38 a. m. June 3, 10:15 p. m. June 5, and 4:50 p. m. June 6. The spasmodic microtremor was moderate May 31 to June 1, but became very strong on June 2 and remained so throughout the week, with some decrease on June 5. There were about 50 spasms of trembling June 2 to 4 inclusive. The harmonic type of tremor slightly increased June 2 to 3, and has remained somewhat stronger than before. Microseismic movement, which has been slight of late, increased a very little June 1 and 2, but became very slight after June 4, having hardly any more development in the north-south component than in the east-west, a condition very unusual here. The tilting of the ground continued strong to the south and west until June 2, when it changed and became strong to the north and moderately so to the east until June 6. It then turned again to the west and south.

June 14, 1919.

The continuation of subsidence of the Halemaumau lava column reported last week led on June 7 to the formation of a lava cascade whereby the liquid of the main lake poured over a submerged ledge into a fiery pot at the base of the northeastern marginal cliff of the lake. This phenomenon accompanying subsidence has happened frequently before, and appears to be occasioned by the faster sinking of the vesicular melt at the sinkholes of the convectional circulation. That it is a part of the normal circulation phenomena, and not an outflow, is demonstrated by the unaltered level of the lake, which remains relatively constant even when such a draining cascade continues for many days. The cascade in question has persistently poured into the gulf as a violent torrent now for a week, yet the lake feeding it has at times risen in relation to its own banks.

The other phenomena of Halemaumau have remained as before, the subsidence of the bench magma has proceeded with slight increase of rate, and the Postal Rift flow still pushes forward with somewhat diminished vigor.

The measurements indicate the following approximate levels above the 3700-foot contour:

June 6—Central floor S., 50 feet; central floor SW., 76 feet; central floor NE., 55 feet; main lake, 32 feet.

June 14—Central floor S., 40 feet; central floor SW., 70 feet; central floor NE., 50 feet; main lake, 25 feet.

These figures indicate that in eight days the south cliff block sank the most, 10 feet in all, averaging 1.2 feet per day; the central floors of the Halemaumau dome sank 6 feet, or .8 foot per day; while the main lake subsided 7 feet, or .9 foot per day.

On Saturday, June 7, 1919, in the morning the fume from the lava column appeared thinner, and it was evident that there had been some breaking back along the crevasse extending west from the northeast cove of the main lake. Measurements indicated local irregularity of movement. The Postal Rift flow was making long arms eastward from the northern part of the flow.

At noon the explanation of the change at the northeast cove was revealed when the lava pit was visited, and the main lake was found streaming rapidly from south to north as a torrent which ended in a violent cascade into a hole. This pot, 20 feet wide, lay at the north end of the northeast cove, where the grotto had been, leading into the smoking crevasse traceable on the surface above. The downpour made a roar which could be heard some distance back from the verge of the lake. Inside the cavity the liquid could be seen churning and piling up about 10 feet below the lake level. The surface streaming of the lake took its rise at the east cove, the south arm and at the isthmus in the central pool direction. For a spell the streaming changed so as to divide in the middle of the east pool and pour in part southward into the south arm.

No changes were observed at the summit smoke holes, and the north lake appeared rising, with an occasional explosion at the rhythmic fountain locality on the south side of the lake. Most of the time, night and day, this lake lay quiet under a heavy crust. The Postal Rift source tube was found unchanged at both openings, the lava current in the tube moving more slowly than before.

At 8:30 p. m. the lake cascade was found still pouring without cessation. At times the churning pool at the foot of the fall sank lower so as to make the cascade more rapid. There was no lowering of the level of the lake, the bank at the east end remained 15 feet high, and the grotto on the southwest side of the lake had built up a half dome of spatter indicating rising rather than lowering with reference to the confining cliffs of the lake cup. The embayment in the western isthmus appeared somewhat deeper than before. Blue flames played from under the marginal crusts of the lake at the east end. There was some fountaining activity in the central pond and southwest lake. Occasional movements of loose rock in the east pressure ridge gave evidence of the slow subsidence of the bench magma. A row of flames played above the source cone of the Postal Rift flow.

On June 8 the cascade continued and conditions remained as before. June 9 at 12:30 p. m. the edge of the fall was 15 feet long and curved in plan, with its concavity down stream, or toward the wall pot, and the curve ended in an angle at its west end. The fall was steeper than before and fully 20 feet high, and the boiling torrent inside the receiving pot bent westward in the cavern, where it disappeared. This direction corresponds with the large crevasse above. There were stalactites in the wall pot.

The harder substance of the lava column continued to subside slightly over the whole Halemaumau dome. The channel across the entrance to the south arm was now very narrow, and the streaming outward across the lake was from under the crust which covered this channel and the southern pool. There was a fresh tumble of rocks on the isthmus west of the east pool, which had fallen from the cliff to the south. Spatter dome grottoes stood at the shore of the pool both southwest and southeast.

At noon on June 10 the crusts of the main lake were found generally breaking up and the level of the lake somewhat higher than before. The form of the ledge over which the cascade poured had changed so that its curvature in plan was now convex down stream as though the bottom had built or swelled in that direction. This curve was the opposite of what it was the previous day. The liquid of the cascade was higher relative to the roof of the cavern into which it poured, and splashes were building an accumulation of solidified lava on the roof as well as out from the right bank of the cascade. The interior churning level was 15 feet down.

The smoke from the summit crevasses had lessened and the glow heap at the base of the smoke was much less luminous. The north lake at night resumed some of its former activity. There was slight hissing of sulphur gas in the broken east cone, and the interior cupola was hung with scores of dark reddish brown rough stalactites in close ranges, showing some feathery accumulations of iron oxides. The stalactites were from one to three inches in diameter with small globular surface accretions, from six inches to three feet long, and separated by only two to three inches, the closely packed stalks hanging side by side and filling the greater part of the cupola. This was the later development of the same interior shown glowing, in illustration of February Bulletin.

The southwest lake was found much lowered, with walls 20 to 40 feet high, a curtained grotto on the north side, and quiet crust. The small western pond was also low and crusted.

On June 11 the bench magma continued to subside so that a pronounced depression with steep slopes and open crevasses had formed around the east cone and for some distance to the north. A similar depression had by now formed west of the northeast tower. The Postal Rift flow was diminishing in volume of output and brightness of the fronts. Smoke was dense from the central chasms and the cascade continued in action.

On Thursday, June 12, the Halemaumau dome appeared lower, the fume was dense, and there was considerable heat and fume from the pit at the base of the northeast tower.

At 9 p. m. the east cone hollow, which it is necessary to cross in approaching the main lake, was found decidedly lower. The main lake was streaming brightly and rapidly toward the northeast cascade and the latter was found to have clogged its own passage with the accumulations built out from the roof and the east bank. The fall was thus largely concealed inside the curtained cavern. Marked increase of rapidity of inrush was noted at times, indicating a fluctuating level in the lower chamber whither the fall plunged. It is evident that a slight rise of this lower level to the point of complete filling of the cavern, would restore normal conditions of lake streaming and fountaining, without any change in the form of the subterranean chambers.

The north lake had curtained and upbuilding spatter grottoes on the north and northeast sides, and was mostly crusted over, with some border fountaining. The Postal Rift source vents were flaming and the lava seen pouring through the tube as revealed in the roof window was lower and more sluggish than of late. The second opening in the tube farther northwest, where the visitor could look downward obliquely and see the stream of melt pouring onward in the bright depths of the cavern, revealed distinct lowering of the surface of the melted river leaving the visible cavern roof higher. This place was now a singular structure, a true "subway entrance"; begun as a caved-in roof, with the lava revealed cascading over the debris, this was now frozen solid as a new roof; looking down the frozen cascade there remained a steeply inclined wide cavern where the molten flood could be seen emerging from beneath the crusted part. The hot gas rushing out of this cavern rose as blue fume, and on this night the writer deliberately entered this fume and breathed it. He was surprised to find it quite tolerable and largely air, with much less sulphurous acid than in the gas from the source cone.

In the Whitney Laboratory of Seismology the following local earthquakes have been registered: 4:49 a. m. June 8, slight; 10:53 a. m. June 9, pronounced; 2:06 a. m. June 11 and 7:23 p. m. June 12, both slight. A weakly recorded teleseism was registered, beginning 3:03 a. m., H. S. T., June 11. The spasmodic microtremor has continued very strong, occurring as sudden spasms, as spells several minutes long, and as prolonged vibrations lasting an hour or more. The harmonic type of slower microtremor has continued moderate to slight. Microseismic motion has been very slight. The tilting of the ground in the east-west azimuth has been various and slight; in the north-south azimuth it has been strong to the south, with rapid recovery to the north on two days, June 9 and June 12.

June 21, 1919.

During the week ending Friday, June 21, 1919, the Halemaumau lava floor has continued to subside at about the same rate as before, but the liquid lakes have shown tendency to stationary condition and some slight rising. Along with this change there has been diminution in volume of the heavy fume volutes from the central chasms, and the lava cascade of the northeast cove has from time to time ceased pouring as the liquid in the receiving funnel rose to the level of the discharging lake. The first cessation of the cascade was observed June 18, eleven days after it had commenced. The Postal Rift flow has continued spreading along the base of the extreme northern cliffs bounding Kilauea crater and the stream pouring through the source tube has been always visible, but its volume and speed have dwindled.

The measurements indicate the following approximate levels above the 3700-foot contour:

June 14—Central floor S., 40 feet; central floor SW., 70 feet; central floor NE., 50 feet; main lake, 25 feet.

June 20—Central floor S., 30 feet; central floor SW., 64 feet; central floor NE., 47 feet; main lake, 28 feet.

It thus appears that in six days the south cliff block again subsided 10 feet, averaging 1.7 feet per day; the central floors of the Halemaumau dome sank about 5 feet, or 0.9 foot per day; while the main lake rose slightly—3 feet, or 0.5 foot per day.

On Saturday, June 14, at noon the south wall crack region was found more craggy and tumbled and the slumped cup deeper around the east cone. There was much heat and some fume at the northeast tower. Fume was very dense at the summit cracks and abundant at the south wall crack and Postal Rift. A large sulphur patch had recently developed between the Postal Rift and Halemaumau, apparently above the passage connecting Halemaumau with the great flow. The latter continued flowing sluggishly. The subsidence of bench magma was evidenced by occasional rock falls observed at the main lake, the east ridge and the northeast tower.

The main lake was streaming rapidly from the closed south arm channel and had built a spatter margin recently to within 5 feet of the east verge, but at the moment the lake was there 15 feet down. The bench southwest was also only 15 feet above the lake, showing further subsidence. The southwest grotto was inactive. The cascade at the northeast cove had built a middle accumulation dividing the fall into two torrents northeast and northwest which poured into holes in the wall. The north lake was heavily crusted, occasional outbursts occurred at the southern grotto. There was northward streaming along the north border of the lake, the grottoes there were sluggish, and the liquid level appeared lower by about 5 feet.

On June 16 at 5 p. m. the general subsidence continued and there was increased fume and revived glow at the east cone. The main lake was lower, the double cascade poured into the bank as before, and its interior cavern was now obscured by crusts and curtains. The lake level stood 18 feet below the lowest part of the eastern bank and 4 feet below the central isthmus. Fume was dense from the bank bordering the cascade on the east and also from the summit crevasses.

The north and southwest lakes were both lower relative to the walls bounding them on the sides away from the center of Halemaumau, and less so with regard to their bounding walls towards the center. This arrangement appeared to indicate that a central block of the Halemaumau dome was subsiding with the lakes. Further evidence of this was shown at the south wall crack, where the line of pinnacles of the pressure ridge was beginning to form an infacing escarpment. All around Halemaumau the line of breakage bounding the sinking central block could be discerned extending from the south wall crack to the west pond, thence past the central crevasses to the north lake, and from there, by way of hot crevasses and much slumping, past the northeast tower to the east cone.

The northern wall of the north lake now stood 20 feet above the liquid, which was covered with heavy crusts that occasionally broke up. The west pond was now a deeply sunken well with 30-foot walls; the isthmus between it and the southwest lake made a 10-foot wall above the pond. A glowing cavern under the bank on the north side showed a current streaming into the pond. The pond stood much higher than the southwest lake. The southwest lake was both enlarged and very low, the walls of its pit standing 50 feet high on the west side and 60 feet high on the east. A glowing cavern hung with stalactites was revealed by the subsidence, at the southeast end of this lake, and in the northern part of the lake there was streaming towards the cavern leading in the direction of the main lake. A cavernous cove had some fountaining activity towards the northwest. Wide and deep crevasses extended from the southwest side of the lake towards the south wall crack.

The Postal Rift tube showed flow more sluggish than before, and the stream in the tube was lower. At night the flow from this source was bright in isolated spots at the base of the north wall of Kilauea.

On Tuesday, June 17, at 3 p. m. the east cone area was more sunken, and through the remnants of the cone a flaming and rumbling pot had developed.

The east bank of the main lake had caved in and the hot streaming to the cascade, with heavy smoke above, continued as before. The north lake was crusted over, the northern border fountains were making much Pele's hair, and one fountaining blow-hole was kept open through the heavy crust east of the center of the lake.

The source tube of the Postal Rift flow as revealed through its two openings contained a lava stream much lower and moving more slowly than before. Inside the northwestern opening the flowing lava far inside the cavern to the north could be seen with difficulty and at a lower level than before.

During the night June 17-18 the bright illumination above the northeast cascade ceased. Fume was denser on the morning of June 18 from the cascade locality, but during the day the fume diminished both there and at the summit smoke chasms.

A visit to the lakes at 5 p. m. revealed general rising activity in all the pools and a revival of the south wall crack pond. This pond was now a high boiling puddle 10 feet in diameter. The east cone pot had enlarged, lava was splashing within and occasional spray was thrown out.

The main lake was about 5 feet higher, and the cascade had stopped. It was replaced by a sluggishly bubbling border pot at the northeast cove. The middle part of the lake was crusted over, but border fountains were constructing spatter banks on the north and south sides of the west cove, at the east cove, and against the east-northeast bank. The characteristic northeastward streaming towards the cascade locality may have been in action under the crust, but it was not shown.

The north lake had rhythmic explosions at the south border pot, the lake had risen about 5 feet, and numerous spraying fountains around the north and east shores gave evidence of increased gas pressure.

The southwest lake and west pond were both 5 or 6 feet higher. A heavy mass of rock was seen to fall into the west pond from its south bank, leaving glowing walls. Large dome fountains burst at short intervals against the northeastern bank of the southwest lake.

The stream in the Postal Rift source tube was slightly higher and more rapid, and in the evening there were some luminous outbreaks of the flow far to the north. Fume on this day had increased at the northeast tower but was less at the central chasms. A small tunnel in the debris of these chasms led downward at a high angle to the north, showing glow in its bottom.

On June 19 the fume had greatly diminished, but mass subsidence continued. The northeast cove cascade was again in action, and the main lake showed spells of subsidence and recovery. The south arm had become an enlarged circular pond, the channel leading to the east pool being crusted. Recent risings had extended the lava floor at the lake level through the broad chasm where the southern cliff block had broken away. The upper edge of this block was now only about 6 feet above the main lake.

In the evening the cascade again ceased action, showing that the liquid lava was rising in pulsations in the subterranean voids to which the cascade poured, and the diminished fume confirms this.

On Friday, June 20, about 10 a. m. the cascade again began to develop during a spell of subsidence in the receiving pot. The lake prior to this time was crusted, with spraying border fountains building spatter banks, and there was similar activity in the north lake. Fume on this day was notably thin. During the later morning hours and again in the afternoon there were some avalanches sending up puffs of dust near the cascade locality of the northeast cove.

In the Whitney Laboratory of Seismology for the week ending Friday, June 20, 1919, registration of two slight local earthquakes is reported as follows: June 16, 3:10 a. m.; June 18, 12:53 p. m. The spasmodic type of microtremor has continued very strong with fluctuations in intensity, always stronger east-west than north-south, and strongest during the morning hours. Harmonic microtremor increased from slight to strong beginning June 18, decreasing June 20. Microseismic motion has continued very slight. Tilting of the ground has fluctuated as before, the tilt being north and east June 14-15, south and west June 16-17, north and east June 18-19, and strongly south and west on June 20.

June 28, 1919.

The June solstice of 1919 proved to be a time of pronounced change in the Halemaumau lava column. During the week ending Friday, June 27, the topography of the edge of the former pit northeast, east, south and southwest has again asserted itself as an infacing escarpment circular in plan. The mechanism bringing this about was a sharp subsidence between June 20 and June 23 of the prism of hard lava surrounding the lakes, accelerating the more gradual gentle subsidence of the last few weeks.What was before a general sagging of the surface of the Halemaumau dome, now takes definite outline as a sinking cylinder. As frequently happens in such cases, the crisis of release of pressure which lowered the bench magma also set free increased volume of gas so as to make the liquid lakes froth up to relatively higher levels within their cups. The crisis therefore has been accompanied by new gas pressure and spatter building at the border fountains, and by the renewed development of wall-crack ponds. The cascade of the northeast cove has gone out of action, but the Postal Rift flow continues to spread. The total subsidence for the week has been nearly compensated by the relative rising of the liquid, so that it is not yet evident which process is to dominate.

The measurements show that the net downward movement of bench magma for the week was not greater than during the previous weeks. On June 26, as compared with the measurements of June 20, the cliff block south of the main lake had subsided 6 feet, averaging 1 foot per day; the southwestern floor, 4 feet, or 0.7 foot per day; the north central floor block, 10 feet, or 1.7 feet per day; while the main lake remained comparatively stationary or subsided only slightly relative to fixed bench marks. Relative to its encompassing bank, the lake distinctly rose. A new triangulation and determination of levels is in progress, and the actual heights of the several lakes, in relation to sea-level, will shortly be determined.

On Saturday, June 21, at 10 a. m. the main and north lakes were high with marginal fountains building up the banks, and the southwest lake was quiet with eastward streaming. In the main lake the major constructional activity was along the south and west banks, and the streaming was northeast. The west pond stood at a level slightly higher than the southwest lake. The flow lava in the Postal Rift tube moved slowly. At 10 p. m. there was intense central fountaining in the main lake, the fountains tending to migrate towards the north.

On June 22 there was increased smoke from the south wall-crack, the northeast cove, the central chasms and at the Postal Rift. The inner circle of benches around the main lake was sinking strongly. The Postal Rift flow continued to progress sluggishly.

On June 23 conspicuous changes were evident. The sinking of the central block bounded by the northeast tower, the north and southwest lakes, and the south wall crack, had proceeded with such increased rapidity as to develop an escarpment over 15 feet high facing inward toward the center of the pit. This escarpment had now become a definite cliff under the northeast tower, also at a point a few feet east of the east cone, and along the south pressure ridge. This movement had defined anew the edge of the Halemaumau pit, leav-

1. May 6, 1919. Halemaumau a dome; southeast pressure ridge; main lake hollow to the right; former east shelter under flows in foreground.

2. May 6, 1919. Postal Rift overflowing through cracks. Halemaumau on the left. Arrow shows cone source of the great flow.

—Photos Jaggar.

ing the long pressure rim crescent and the northeast tower outside of the pit. The northeast tower wall-crack had begun again to fume and glow, a puddle of lava had formed in the hollow beside the east cone, and glow and dense fume had again developed at the south wall-crack

The westward facing cliff at the east cone now made it necessary to make a detour to the north in order to reach the main lake. Inspection 5:30 to 7 p. m. showed that the relief of cliffs around the main lake cup was not greatly changed; the lowest part of the east bank stood 15 feet above the lake, the southeast crag was 30 feet high, the northern cliff was about 25 feet high, and the western cliffs stood 40 feet over the central pool. The sunken south cliff block stood only about 8 feet above the lake.

The dominant streaming of the lake was westward, and active spatter grottoes were building on all sides. The cascade locality of the northeast cove was represented by flaming orifices puffing noisily in a spatter bench. This cove was extended 20 feet farther north by collapse, the extension being floored by tumbled debris and hardened lava. During a temporary sinking spell there was swift streaming northward under the bank and much bubble fountaining at the cascade locality.

The smoke holes of the summit of the north central region were found to have greatly diminished fume, and glow could be seen in two of them. The northernmost of these was a shaft 10 feet in diameter inclined northward at a high angle and narrowing below; 30 feet down this became a tube curved both in plan and elevation and ending at the bottom in an opening 6 feet in diameter, where lava boiled under overhanging stalactites. This liquid appeared to be about the level of the north lake, and the surging currents moved first to the south and then to the north. This deep tube was a revelation of the subterranean honeycomb of passages which connect the different lakes.

At the north lake a large flaming curtained grotto dome had been built on the north side, the usual rhythmic outbreaks took place every two or three minutes at the south corner, and there were abundant spraying border fountains building spatter benches.

In the glowing interior of the Postal Rift source cone many slender stalactites had formed of both the worm and straight types, and these hung motionless and brilliantly incandescent, added to by slow accretion of fused material from the walls, and not by splash from below. The standing fountain or cascade feeding the flow could be seen through the window of the cone about 15 feet below the surface of the ground pouring from the south toward the north. Through the window in the roof of the tube 20 feet farther north the slow steady flow continued with drawn-out bubbles bursting the surface. At night the flow under the northern Kilauea cliffs was brighter than before, and the Halemaumau lakes also made a more brilliant illumination.

On Thursday, June 24, at 6 p. m. the lakes were distinctly higher relative to their margins and exhibited high gas pressure and numerous rapidly constructing spatter half-domes and crescent niches. The south arm appeared a few feet higher than the main lake, its surface streaming was southward, and a spraying fountain was building a crescent of spatter at its south end. The central pond was sluggish and the main lake rose during an hour so that the height of all its border cliffs was lower than before by about 5 feet. The streaming was to the northeast. During the high level the western grottoes became quiet and choked with crusted lava.

The inclined shaft of the central smoke hole showed a diminished window at the bottom only 3 feet across, revealing the live lava beneath. The north lake was streaming northward and had a violent spraying fountain on its west side and several others along its north shore. Relative to its border cliffs, this lake also was 5 feet higher than on the previous day.

The sinking of the central bench magma had now brought all of the cliffs around the depression containing the two western lakes to about a common level some 25 feet above the liquid lava. The western pond was only slightly above the southwest lake level. It showed sluggish fountaining, and a small extension of its pit had opened southward by collapse. The block of ground west of this pond remained high, indicating that it would hold up as the rim of the new Halemaumau pit, continuous with the semicircular escarpment to the south.

This escarpment was now a cliff 10 feet high surmounted by broken pinnacles, the down-faulted block which created it moving on the south wall-crack as a fault plane and carrying down all the broken ground next to the north so as to close the gaping cracks there. Very large chasms concentric with the Halemaumau circle were found just back of the northeast tower and back of the station on the northwest rim of Halemaumau. This last crack was an interesting feature extending in a curve from the northwest station to the cone vents of the November flow of 1918 next to the north stone corral. This crack was the only sign of motion in the northwestern region, though measurement showed gentle subsidence of the floor west of the north lake. From this crack to the Postal Rift source a series of solfataric stained areas marked the course of the subterranean passage leading to the Postal Rift flow. These places emitted much pure sulphur vapor and were brightly colored with yellow and white coatings of sulphur, alum and sulphates.

On Wednesday, June 25, the sinking of the Halemaumau dome had reached the point where the cliff bounding the west side of the southwest lake depression had again come into view as one looked across Halemaumau from the Observatory. There was increasing smoke, but not in such concentrated masses as were present during the previous week.

On June 26 at 11:30 a. m. the south escarpment was more jagged in profile from irregular caving in, and the extension of this new rim of the pit to the east stood in such relief that the visitor could see the live lava of the main lake from the new eastern verge while yet 100 feet back from the actual edge of the lake. The lake was streaming eastward and a large elongate spatter half-dome was in violent action at the southwest shore. Here the sunken south cliff block now had the edge of its upper surface submerged under new lava. The cliffs around the lake looked lower.

The northeast tower, so long a prominent landmark, had fallen into the pit beneath it and this pit contained a new circular pool of lava at the base of the northeast heap escarpment, now a vertical cliff 15 feet high. The tower had been at the top of this cliff, another development of the wall-crack like the south escarpment. The new pool here was 50 feet in diameter and overflowing in fan-shaped outpourings of heavy bulbous pahoehoe which had spread 150 feet toward the northwest. At noon this pond was highly inflated, but the crust suddenly gave way, releasing gas with a prolonged hiss which made an overpowering odor of sulphurous acid to leeward. Much bubbling ensued, and the pond sank 15 feet during the next twenty minutes, leaving a bright glowing margin. Then the liquid recovered and crusted over and small trickle flows pushed through the new crust. A cavernous tube had been revealed by the deflation of this pond in the direction of its recent overflow.

The north lake remained as before. The lava in the Postal Rift source tube was low and flowing very slowly, estimated at half a mile per hour. The flow at night still made occasional breaks in the crust of its northern fields, where the melt would well up and spread out to fill hollows.

On June 27 from 3 to 5 p. m. the general situation indicated continued subsidence of bench magma and rising of liquid lava, and the fume was thinner. The east cone sag appeared still lower with a 20-foot cliff east of it. The lava pool of the south wall crack had revived, making at the foot of the south escarpment an elliptical pond 60 feet long fountaining at its west end. The main lake continued high, with activity as before, the cliffs about the east pool standing 20 feet high and about the central pond 30 to 40 feet high. The lowest sag of the east bank stood 12 feet above the lake. The northeast wall-crack pond was again high and fluctuating in level. The north lake had built large spatter domes on its west, north and east sides, the older banks standing 15 feet above the lake on the north and 30 feet on the south. The summit smoke hole had again opened its wide pot of fountaining lava 30 feet down, and the liquid showed northward drift of currents and occasional sudden increase of speed.

The southwest lake and west pond appeared somewhat lower with walls over 30 feet high in places, and western walls higher than eastern. The west pond was crusted over with extensions to the north and to the south, the southern one making a puffing roar of gas through the tumbled debris. The southwest lake was fountaining violently against its east bank and streaming eastward.

The registration of the seismographs in the Whitney Laboratory recorded slight local earthquakes at 8:26 p. m. June 21; 6:56 p. m. June 23, and a pronounced shock felt in Hilo at 7:37 p. m. June 26. Spasmodic microtremor continued strong during the week, and the harmonic type of tremor was moderately strong. Microseismic motion has continued very slight. The tilting of the ground became excessively strong to the north, June 22, and moderate to the east. Thereafter it recovered to the west and south, becoming strong to the west June 25; stationary tendency ensued.

July 5, 1919.

During the week ending July 4, 1919, it has become apparent that the subsidence of the Halemaumau lava column is to continue and the lakes have gone down rapidly. The central prism of bench magma and the main lake which it encloses have sunk at about the same rate as before, but the outlying lakes west and north have subsided twice as fast. The rate of lowering of the central block has decreased to stationary July 5. The Postal Rift flow has at length come to rest and the supply of liquid lava at the source tube has given out. Smoke has again increased at Halemaumau. The newly developed escarpment bounding the pit has increased in length and height, but the inner dome of bench magma and the marginal cliffs of the lakes are still in view from the Observatory.

The measurements from the Observatory on July 4 have shown depression of the various parts of the Halemaumau surface since June 26 as follows: South ridge, 2 feet; southwest cliff, 3 feet; northeast heap cliff, 1.5 feet; ground east of north lake, 2 feet; ground north of north lake, 4 feet; crags southeast of main lake, 12 feet; block north of main lake, 9 feet; block west of main lake, 13 feet; ground northwest of west lake depression, stationary. The main lake in the same interval has sunk 12 feet, the north and southwest lakes each 24 feet.

These figures indicate that the marginal ground has broken down slowly, about 2.5 feet in eight days, averaging 0.3 foot per day; the central prism around the main lake has averaged 11.3 feet in eight days, or 1.4 feet per day; while the main lake has gone down 1.5 feet per day and the north and southwest lakes 3 feet per day.

On Saturday, June 28, at 4 p. m. the main lake was slightly lower, with marginal fountains and no predominating current. The south arm pond was nearly on a level with the main lake and exhibited a single fountain at its south end. The east cone was glowing and puffing at the bottom of the funnel-shaped depression around it. The lava pool in the south wall crack was quiet, and heavy fumes were arising there and increasing in volume.

The northeast pond had increased the size of its overflow and was covered with heavy crust. The lava appeared to be rising and falling periodically, and a blast of gas through the crust was followed by a slackening of the overflow.

On June 29 from 4 to 5 p. m. the subsidence of bench magma continued and the main lake stood high relative to its banks, with strong border fountains on the west, bright lines and moving skins in the middle, and streaming first east and then west. The northeast pond was at first high, but later it broke up and developed much fume strong with sulphurous acid. The north lake showed slumping of the northern bank of its pit, the usual border grottoes were active, and at 5:30 p. m. two of these on the north and west sides caved in. The Postal Rift flow cone showed a low and sluggish stream, with more than a foot of the west wall of the tube visible above the liquid as seen through the roof window. There was glow at the base of the east cone.

On Monday, June 30, the main lake remained relatively high and covered with crust at 10 a. m., and the north lake showed increased breaking down of its northern and eastern banks. New wall-cracks had developed between the northeast pond and the north station, and there were new cracks near the northwest station. The northeast pond rose between 10 a. m. and 12:40 p. m. The well of lava at the central summit crevasse showed liquid unusually high and boiling.

The western lakes were crusted except for a violent fountain at the east corner of the southwest lake. The block of ground east of this lake had subsided and the margins of the lake showed evidence of slumping. The pit extending the west pond southward was larger, and much water vapor rose through cracks near the western end of the south pressure ridge.

The inner bank of this ridge had caved in, leaving a vertical wall over the south pool, the surface of which lay 10 feet below the general floor level. There was increased breaking down of the southwest wall of the south arm pond.

On July 1 at 10 a. m. the south pressure ridge appeared about as high above the inner flat as above the outer flows, and much smoke rose from the cracks there and from the east cone pit. There was some fresh driblet lava in this pit. The main lake stood very high relative to its banks, there was much border construction around it, and its surface stood only about 10 feet beneath the east bank. During the morning this lake rose slightly. In the west cove of this lake there was increased indentation into the isthmus leading toward the central pond, and a vigorous fountain was in action there. Like the central pond, the south arm pond was now separated by an isthmus from the main lake.

The central well was full of smoke and the bottom was not visible. The northeast pond had a circular opening in its crust about 7 feet in diameter, where sluggish glowing melt could be seen 5 feet below under the overhang. The north lake appeared as much lower (about 5 feet) than before, as the main lake appeared higher. The crevasses along the east side of the north lake had widened and let down the block on the lake side about 7 feet so as to create a new cliff margin. There was similar slumping, of more gradual slope, around the entire north margin, the crest of which stood 20 feet above the liquid lava. This lake was streaming northward to the usual border fountains. The Postal Rift flow continued in motion, and outbreaks of small streams were pushing through the surface of the flow in the north corner of Kilauea crater. Clouds of white vapor arose from the surface of the flow during rain.

On July 2 at 4 p. m. the main lake showed steady streaming from its southeast corner westward, and its border grottoes were inactive. There was some enlargement at the northeast cove. During the next hour the lake subsided 2 feet. The spatter shelf of the recent high level stood 4 feet below the east bank. The north lake appeared lower, and some breaking away of the west wall and lowering was seen during the afternoon. The western lakes also showed collapsing walls, especially northwest of the southwest lake and at the north pit of the west pond. The southwest lake was mostly crusted, but a swift current rushed toward the active grotto at the corner chasm leading to the main lake. The marginal shelf stood 5 feet above the liquid. The west pond occasionally broke up and bubbled and its level was higher than that of the southwest lake; there was a small bubbling pot in its southern corner. The northeast pond on this day appeared wholly inactive, but the cracks extending northward from the northeast heap were widened and extended to the 1894 spatter cones near the north station. The south wall crack pond was still alive, and an isolated pinnacle which had been a conspicuous landmark on the pressure ridge above it had collapsed.

On Friday, July 4, from 3 to 4 p. m. it was evident that the northern and western lakes were sinking, though the main lake showed little change relative to its banks. The southern cliff facing inward from the pressure ridge was now 30 feet high in places, with a jagged irregular crest, and the inner block next adjacent formed a sloping surface, merging with talus. So gradual had been the downward movement of the central part of the Halemaumau dome, that several flags supported by piles of stones still remained erect amid the sunken cliff blocks.

The main lake was streaming westward, and there was strong fountaining in its west cove. An open pot in the east cone was flaming above lava that could be heard rumbling within. There was a glowing pot in the middle of the crust of the northeast pond as before, but the lava inside was fully 15 feet down and smoke there had greatly increased.

The old rim of the pit was now defined by subsidence and crevassing, or by remnant rim, around its entire periphery. The north lake appeared very low, its southern cliff stood 50 feet above it, the east cliff was 30 feet high and the northern broken slope varied from 20 to 30 feet in height. There were four cavernous border grottoes and occasionally prolonged central fountains which tended to migrate slowly eastward and draw surface currents in their direction. There was no longer any rhythmic fountain at the south corner of the lake.

The roof window in the Postal Rift tube was nearly dark, but dull red glow, wholly without motion, could be seen in the hardened flow which made the bottom of the tube. The chamber under the source cone was somewhat brighter than this, but without flowing lava. A last small festooned flow glowed red-hot at the site of the former fountain, and there were many cooled stalactites in wormy and other forms. A new collapsed roof area of the tube left an open pit a few feet farther north, and here again the floor showed a narrow longitudinal ridge made by a hardened flow. The ceiling of the cavern was hung with abundant worm stalactites. The other opening farther northwest showed faint cherry red glow far within. The flow at its northern fronts no longer showed any glow at night.

The southwest lake depression was now much deeper, with walls 40 to 50 feet high, and the inner spatter rim stood 8 feet above the lake. There were violent central fountains near the north side of the lake. The west pond, at a level slightly higher, was covered with skin and cascading continuously over a fall about 3 feet high eastward into a bubbling pot which appeared to be connected by a tunnel with the southwest lake. The pot was at about the level of the latter lake. The wall bounding the west pond on the west was 50 feet high, and this promised to be continuous, with the escarpment of the pressure ridge farther south bounding the Halemaumau pit. The extensions of the west pond along the wall crack north and south were enlarged as tumbled pits full of broken rock.

The general situation appeared to indicate pronounced subsidence, with the bench magma and liquid lava alternating in spells of sinking. The liquid lava was at the moment draining downward through the north and west lakes in a spasm of retirement following upon the cessation of the Postal Rift flow. As usual in such cases, the central cylindrical body of bench magma had moved down faster than the border ring of benches, which tended to cling to the walls of the old outlying funnel.

In the Whitney Laboratory of Seismology for the week ending at 8 p. m., July 4, 1919, three local earthquakes and one distant earthquake have been registered. The local shocks were at 2:31 p. m., June 30; 8:29 p. m., July 2; and 2:35 p. m., July 3. The teleseism occurred at 1 p. m., H. S. T., June 30, and the preliminary phase of the record was well marked, giving evidence of distance of origin 7300 kilometers, equivalent to the distance from this station of Nicaragua, South Japan or New Guinea. Spasmodic microtremors have been less strong than of late, the harmonic tremor has been moderately strong, and microseismic motion has dwindled almost to the zero point—a condition very unusual here. The tilting of the ground has continued to fluctuate through a narrow range, north and east June 28-29, south and west June 30-July 1, north and slightly east July 2-3, and nearly stationary July 4.

Very respectfully,
T. A. JAGGAR, JR.,
Volcanologist.

ERRATUM.—On page 54, April Bulletin, lines 16 and 18 from the top right column, for "ft." read "min."

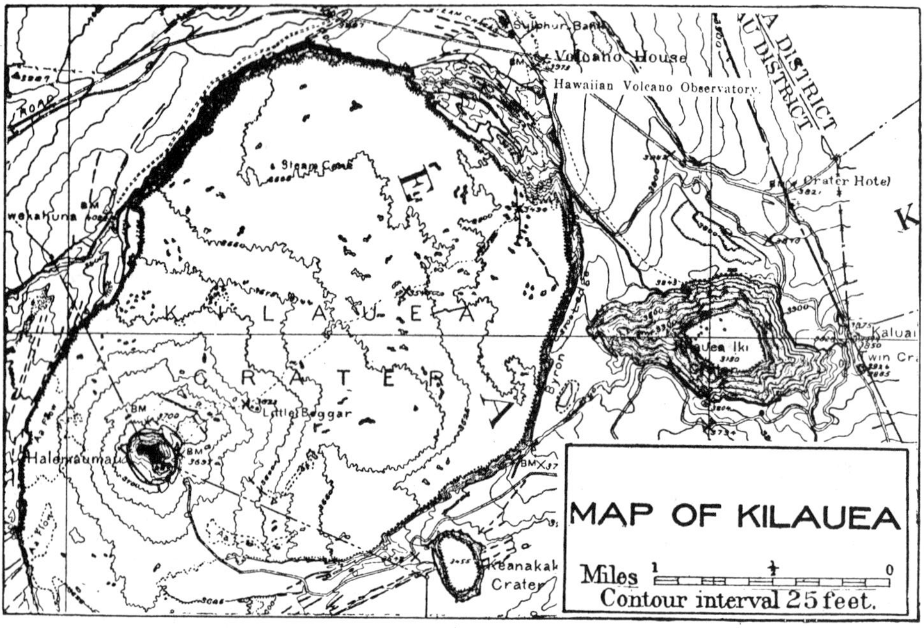

HAWAIIAN VOLCANO OBSERVATORY.

The Observatory is equipped with the following seismometric instruments rebuilt at the station in 1918 for the special needs of volcano research: two Bosch-Omori pendulums, high speed registration of local earthquakes; one optically recording seismograph for distant earthquakes; one clinograph registering E-W tilting of the ground. A vertical component seismograph was in December, 1918, set up in experimental operation. These are seated on concrete piers in a closed basement room having practically constant temperature, beneath the chief Observatory building near the hotel. Time is referred to a rated chronometer, checked at intervals by solar observations with a transit. Both instruments are loaned by the College of Hawaii. Hawaiian standard time (H. S. T.) is 10 hrs. 30 min. slower than Greenwich time.

CANCANI SCALE OF SEISMIC INTENSITY.

Expressed by accelerations measured in millimeters per second per second.

I.	Instrumental	0.0	2.5
II.	Very slight	2.5	5.0
III.	Slight	5.0	10.0
IV.	Sensible, mediocre	10.0	25.0
V.	Rather strong	25.0	50.0
VI.	Strong	50.0	100.0
VII.	Very strong	100.0	250.0
VIII.	Ruinous	250.0	500.0
IX.	Disastrous	500.0	1000.0
X.	Very disastrous	10000.0	2500.0
XI.	Catastrophic	2500.0	5000.0
XII.	Great catastrophe	5000.0	10000.0

Grade IV. is ordinarily the minimum perceived by the senses; and in grade XII. the accelerations or rate of change of motion (jerk) reaches that of terrestrial gravitation.

In the standard form of report the maximum intensity or acceleration, designated by the symbol a, or max. a, is given in the conventional unit of milligal. The milligal is a measure of acceleration, such that 1 milligal $=$ 1/100 mm. per sec. per sec. $= 10\ \mu$. per sec. per sec. The Cancani scale, here defined in terms of millimeters per sec. per sec., can therefore be expressed in milligals by multiplying each of the numbers by 100.

U. S. DEPARTMENT OF AGRICULTURE
WEATHER BUREAU
CHARLES F. MARVIN, CHIEF

MONTHLY BULLETIN
OF THE
Hawaiian Volcano Observatory

VOL. VII. HONOLULU, HAWAII, JULY, 1919 No. 7

NOTE:—Appended to this number of the Bulletin is an article by Dr. E. S. Shepherd, of the Geophysical Laboratory of the Carnegie Institution of Washington, on "The Composition of the Gases of Kilauea." The Geophysical Laboratory has honored us by permitting first publication of these important analyses in these pages, and it is believed that these are the first complete quantitative analyses ever made of gas collected directly from the flaming vesicles of live lava.

T. A. JAGGAR, Jr.

July 12, 1919.

The movement of the Halemaumau lava column for the week ending July 11, 1919, has been a continuance of subsidence at greatly diminished speed and some recovery so far as the liquid lakes are concerned. There has been nothing new in the nature of the activity. At the source opening of the recent Postal Rift flow all is now dark, and there has been much collapsing there, revealing hot caverns.

The measurements of the week directed to the visible ridges of bench magma and marginal portions of Halemaumau pit as seen from the Observatory were as follows: South ridge down 2 feet; northeast heap and west cliff stationary; ground east of north lake down 1 foot; ground north and west of main lake down 4 feet; ground north of west pond down 4 feet; and ground southwest of southwest lake down 4 feet.

These measurements show that the marginal ground has been nearly stationary, with a maximum movement in the south ridge of 2 feet in eight days, averaging 0.25 foot per day. On the other hand, the central prism of hardened lava around the central and southern group of lakes has moved down 4 feet, or 0.50 foot per day: a rate about one-third as fast as that of the previous week. The depression of the lakes within their cups indicates that they have lowered less rapidly than their surroundings, for the end of the week shows them distinctly higher relative to their adjacent banks.

The writer is indebted to Messrs. Sumner Roberts and Charles Thorndike, co-operative observers, for the following new data concerning the levels of Halemaumau features. It will be remembered that the old government bench mark on the north rim of the pit, before it was lifted and tilted in April, 1919, stood 3700 feet above sea level.

The new elevations are:

Southern wall of Halemaumau—New elevation, 3733 feet.

South-southeast wall of Halemaumau—New elevation, 3746 feet; old elevation of November, 1918, 3711 feet.

East wall of Halemaumau—New elevation, 3727 feet; old elevation of November, 1918, 3700 feet.

Northeast wall of Halemaumau—New elevation, 3733 feet.

West wall of Halemaumau—New elevation, 3728 feet; old elevation of November, 1918, 3727 feet.

Northwest wall of Halemaumau—New elevation, 3729 feet; old elevation of November, 1918, 3732 feet.

North wall of Halemaumau—New elevation, 3718 feet; old elevation of November, 1918, 3700 feet.

The lakes on July 12 stood as follows:

Main lake—22 feet below 3700-foot contour, 49 feet below east rim flag.

North lake—32 feet below 3700-foot contour, 50 feet below north rim flag.

SW.. lake—20 feet below 3700-foot contour, 53 feet below SW. rim.

W. pond—About 18 feet below 3700-foot contour, 46 feet below west station (concrete platform).

The inner cliffs relative to the several lakes stood as follows on July 12: Cliff south of north lake, 48 feet high; cliff southeast of main lake, 31 feet high; cliff north of central pond, 26 feet high; cliff east of southwest lake, 25 feet high.

These figures reveal remarkable changes which check with recent events whereby general rising of the lava column in 1918 and 1919 made its upward thrust and overflooding dominantly toward the southeast. In 1917 the highest walls of the pit were northwest and west. Now the highest walls are south and southeast and the lowest walls are north and west, and the west station is the only one of the older bench marks which is preserved at nearly its former altitude. The north flag at present, on top of the cone which was the source of the November flows of 1918, and almost directly over the site of the old stone shelter hut, stands 18 feet above the ground level of 1917 at that point, although it is now the lowest of the rim stations.

The carefully-measured lake elevations check with recent observations which have indicated all through the spring of 1919 a tendency for the southern lakes to be highest, the main lake at an intermediate level and the north lake much lower. Coordinate with this has been the tendency for actual overflow heaping in the pit to go southeast of the center and marginal subsidence to be at a maximum northwest. It will be observed that this sinking along the northwest wall-crack has now taken effect even outside of Halemaumau with downward faulting along newly-opened rifts back of the northwest station. Accordingly, the elevation of the northwest station by the new measurements is revealed to be 3 feet lower than it was in 1918.

The intense doming of the south central part of Halemaumau in February, 1919, followed by the great Postal Rift flow 800 feet north of the pit, and this latter in the direction of marginal subsidence during the doming period, accords perfectly with the supposition that the region to the north was flexed downward to the breaking point as a reaction from the flexing upward of the Halemaumau dome. The break so opened must have gaped downward in the region under the Postal Rift and so admitted the live lava from a lenticular extension of the tumescent magma underground. The Postal Rift was a natural place for such breaking, for this was the old wall of the pit of 1893, where the subterranean contacts were vertical.

On July 6 at 11 a. m. the eastern Halemaumau cliff margin stood so high above the depressed surfaces of the pit floor that the southern and western crag blocks bounding the main and southwest lakes appeared well below the eye of the visitor. The east cone at the foot of this cliff was now buried under a slope of talus, and its vent was a new glowing chimney in the slide-rock a few feet farther south. The main lake was streaming westward. The north lake showed occasional strong central fountains, a glowing and flaming high filagree of curtained lava had formed against the west wall of the lake basin, there were the usual four or five border fountains, and the depression of the lake appeared unchanged.

The source orifices of the Postal Rift were now nearly dark, but some hissing was heard in the vent under the source cone. The western tube leading from the source cone, and a few hundred feet away, had caved in, showing abundant worm stalactites. Some solfataric fume producing much white staining in the new lava rose east of the source cone where the older solfataras of the Postal Rift lay buried.

On July 7 at 6 p. m. the fume at Halemaumau was rather dense, and occasional slight adjustments whereby rocks fell in the wall-crack indicated subsidence. In addition to the flaming chimney there was a glowing puddle of lava at the east cone locality. The main lake streamed westward to spatter grottoes, the roofs of which collapsed into the lake. In the north lake large central fountains developed at intervals as the crust became inflated, and this was always followed by collapse and marginal subsidence. Flames were always abundant in border grottoes and through the crust. Streaming was southward at the south corner of the lake, but usually northward elsewhere.

On Tuesday, July 8, about 9 p. m. the apparent lake levels remained as before, there were strong central fountains, and in the north lake much gradual cracking of crusts was noticed with slow development, along extended zigzag lines of incandescence. The outbreak of central fountains in the north lake was observed first toward the northwest, migrating northward, and later towards the east, migrating eastward, the fountains expending themselves under the bank. Flaming curtained grottoes were observed in both the north and main lakes. The northeast cove of the main lake and much of the lake south of there remained continuously crusted. Streaming was from the southeast cove of the lake westward to large grottoes southwest and west, which had built heavy overhanging spatter shelves which were twice seen to cave in. The isthmus of crust leading to the south arm stood high and was covered with Pele's hair. There was some tendency to rapid flow under the bank northwest of the main lake, and there was similar rapid shoreward flow on the west side of the north lake.

The northeast and south wall-crack pools still showed the reflection of incandescence below on the fume cloud above. As seen from a distance the Postal Rift flow was no longer glowing, but glow could be found on close approach. While the liquid lakes showed no changes in relative levels, sinking continued in the north central part of the pit and some movement was noticed in the east wall-crack.

On July 9 there was continued slight subsidence in the center of Halemaumau, the smoke was rather dense and the glow moderate, and the measurements indicated an approach toward stationary condition.

At 11 a. m., July 10, the main lake appeared rather higher, with marginal fountains under shelves along the side cliffs and a slight current westward. The northeast wall-crack pond was smoky and the north lake quiet, with fresh rock slides above its north bank. The western lakes were very quiet and heavy fume rose from the west pond. The southwestern wall-crack was enlarged and very hot. The central pond was small and nearly hidden by an overhanging shelf of lava crust.

At 3 p. m. the new east wall of Halemaumau at the east cone locality was estimated to be 35 feet high, and the live chimney beneath was rumbling. One now looked from the east brink of the pit across the entire upper surface of the Halemaumau dome to the basin of the southwest lake. The north lake appeared lowered in its basin and its streaming was away from the east bank towards a new curtained grotto on the northwest side.

An examination of the northwest station on the outer rim of Halemaumau revealed the fact that the large crevasse there had developed, trending in a curve through the two sulphur patches to the Postal Rift cone. The crack departed from the edge of the pit in a tangent merging with the inner wall-crack about the west niche. The fault-block on the side toward Halemaumau had sunk from two to three feet, leaving a new wall of that height. Just behind the northwest station the crack formed a tumbled crevasse 10 feet wide, which extended narrowing toward the southwest, joining with the cracks just west of the west station.

The west pond was found to be a crusted oval about 50 feet below the western cliff, with two small pots showing the liquid lava about 4 feet below the crust. The southwest lake was fountaining in its western cove and showed westward streaming. Exploration of the flat south of it revealed nothing but a continuous plateau occupying the southwestern quadrant of Halemaumau, and the southern wall-crack pond was found to be merely a deep smoky chasm where invisible lava could be heard rumbling far below. The south arm of the main lake visited from this side showed a circular pool of glowing lava in heavy crust, the latter covered with a mat of Pele's hair. There was no notable change in conditions on July 11.

In the Whitney Laboratory the seismographic instruments have registered local earthquakes for the week ending at 8 p. m. Friday, July 11, 1919, as follows: Slight shocks at 9:51 p. m., July 5, and 2:20 a. m., July 7; a pronounced shock at 5:24 p. m., July 11. Teleseisms were registered (H. S. T.) at 8:49 p. m., July 5, probable distance of origin 6520 kilometers; 11:01 a. m., July 8, probable distance of origin 7215 kilometers; and two others, without evidence of distance, at 9:14 a. m. and 4:13 p. m. on July 9. Spasmodic microtremors increased from slight to very strong between July 5 and July 8-9, and thereafter decreased to slight on July 11. Harmonic microtremor was moderately strong throughout the week, decreasing at the end. Microseisms were very feeble. Motion of tilting was nearly stationary until July 8, when it was pronounced to the east and north, reacting to the west and south July 9-10; on July 11 the inclination was again east and north.

July 19, 1919.

The rising tendency in the lakes exhibited last week has now communicated itself to parts of the bench magma, and while the general situation in Halemaumau appears stagnant, the measurements indicate slight rising, especially at the west pond vent, which has long been a conduit source of feeding lava for the pit. Along with this rising the lakes have been notably quiet, dull, and crusted, the central and southern part of the pit has continued smoky, and changes have been slight.

Mr. Roberts made measurements during the forenoon of July 19; the several lakes, below the 3700-foot contour, were as follows, as compared with previous week:

July 13—Main lake, 22 feet; N. lake, 32; SW. lake, 20; W. pond, 18.

July 19—Main lake, 20 feet; N. lake, 33; SW. lake, 18; W. pond, 10 approximately.

The cliff south of north lake had gone down 2 feet (elevation 3713).

The cliff southeast of main lake had risen 1 foot (elevation 3711).

The cliff north of central pond had gone down 4 feet (elevation 3701).

The cliff east of southwest lake had risen 2 feet (elevation 3707).

These figures indicate slight rising south and slight sinking north. The main and southwest lakes in seven days have risen 2 feet, averaging 0.3 foot per day; the west pond has risen about 8 feet, or 1.1 feet per day; the north lake has sunk 1 foot, or 0.14 foot per day. The block south of the north lake has sunk 0.4 foot per day, but the southeast and west central blocks of bench magma have risen respectively 0.14 and 0.3 foot per day, like the adjacent lakes.

On Saturday, July 12, the fume from the northeast wall-crack, recently a pond, nearly obscured the view of the main lake from the east rim of Halemaumau. There was slight hissing from the east talus pot. The main lake seemed high with slight westward current and small grotto fountains. The north lake was low, with fountains in the west corner. The west lakes were high and very quiet, without evident current. The lava shelf around the west pond had increased so that the liquid was hardly visible, but it could be seen streaming from west to east. The cracking of the ground near the west station, especially in the newer lava of the interior of Halemaumau, had increased so as to extend from the west pond depression to the northwest station obliquely across the west niche of 1894.

On July 13 at 11 p. m. the north lake was very quiet and the main lake exhibited strong southwest streaming with bright lines and thin skins. The fountaining activity was at the southwest grottoes. There were heavy fumes from the eastern wall vents, and the odor of sulphuretted hydrogen was perceptible. The southwest lake made a faint glow.

On July 14 at 3 p. m. the north lake was higher, with curtained grottoes and glow-holes in wall northwest and west. The north grotto had collapsed and was buried under talus. There were occasional central fountains. The southwest lake was high and quiet, and the west pond was inactive. The main lake was so high as to slightly overflow the isthmus leading to the central pond. The Postal Rift source cone had caved in on top and some fresh splash material had spattered out around the orifice, but the interior was now all dark.

There was hardly any change on July 16 at 4 p. m. The cove extending west from the main lake had broken away on the south side, and the lake was quiet and crusted. The north lake had some very large central fountains, and its crust was cracking and foundering. The levels of the lakes showed nothing new, fume as a whole was rather dense, the southwest lake was bright at night, but the other lakes were dull. The Postal Rift flow was reported still glowing in places along the front.

On July 17 in the afternoon and evening the north lake was bright and active with much bubble fountaining. On July 18 at 10 a. m. a new cone was building on the west bank of the north lake, but the lake was rather quiet, with three small border fountains west, northwest and north. The southwest lake was completely crusted over, with gas hissing from under the crust at the northeast corner. On the north side of the gorge between the southwest lake and west pond, a large pulpit rock had separated off from the higher ground and tended to fall southward. The west pond had a small open circular pool, fountaining on its north side. Near the north side of the west pond depression a glow heap of tumbled rocks was flaming. The central pond was now a crusted circular pudding of hardened lava without visible pool.

In the Whitney Laboratory of Seismology for the week ending at 8 p. m. Friday, July 18, 1919, only one local earthquake was registered, July 13, 12:48 a. m. Teleseisms without clear indication of distance were registered beginning 3:38 a. m., July 14; 8 a. m., July 16, and 3:28 a. m., July 18, Hawaiian Standard Time. Spasmodic microtremor, always stronger daytime than night, was moderate to strong, and the harmonic type of microtremor slight to moderate. Microseismic motion increased slightly July 12 to 16, and then became very slight again. Tilting of the ground was strong to the north July 12, 15 and 17, with stationary condition in the intervals, and the east-west component of tilt has been gradual inclination to the west.

July 26, 1919.

During the week ending July 25, 1919, the lava column has risen sharply, carrying up both the foaming lakes and the semi-solid bench magma. This movement has had the same characters as previous risings have shown, and the principal thrust against the marginal wall of Halemaumau has been to the south and east. There has been no revival of the Postal Rift flow.

On July 19 and 20 preparations were made for beginning lava tide measurements from a tent at the north lake on July 21, with Messrs. Jaggar, Roberts, Thorndike and O. Emerson as workers. This investigation was launched July 21 to 25, and the men worked in shifts, taking observations with transit every twenty minutes night and day. It is hoped to continue these observations for a month, and the results will be compiled later. Suffice it to say at this time that the occurrence of the strong and continued rising from the first days of the work has given unexpectedly pronounced changes of angle in the measurements made, the whole surface of the lava column doming up quietly and continuously. Throughout it all, to the instrument men camped directly on the bench magma, there have come no shocks of earthquake and the entire movement has proceeded as a pasty flow. There have been creakings and snappings in the outer old wall rock of the south ridge against which the swelling lava is exerting pressure.

Measurements during the week show that from July 19 to July 25, six days, the southeast rim ridge was stationary and the northeast heap rose 2 feet. The south block of inner crags rose 4 feet, the southeast crag 11 feet, the block north of the main lake 17 feet, and the block west of the main lake 12 feet. The ground east of the north lake rose about 6 feet. The sharp rising first appeared July 21, but became very strong only after July 22. By July 23 it became apparent that a great movement was in progress.

During July 19 and 20 no marked changes were noted in Halemaumau, which continued smoky and by measurement stationary. The sinking had ceased.

On Monday, July 21, fume from the northeast wall-crack was thinner, and a strong rise of both bench magma and liquid lava of the lakes was beginning. Some sliding rocks were heard. With the coming up of the liquid, spatter ramparts were forming, with much blowing and spraying of fountains and some flaming. The main lake was streaming eastward with fountains east, northeast and southeast. The south arm of this lake and the central pond were fountaining. There was a puffing vent in the bottom of the east cone depression showing bright glow. An inner bench was building at the cove in the northwest corner of the north lake, and surface streaming was east and northwest. The southwest lake was bright, and pounding against its south shore, but the only activity in the west pond depression was the forming of a driblet cone.

At 2:45 p. m., after a series of very heavy rain showers followed by crustings of the north lake and spells of cracking and foundering, there came a violent spell of this kind, when the whole lake sank suddenly 4 feet, with hundreds of turbulent fountains developing, which expended themselves against the north bank of the lake. Otherwise on this afternoon there was the usual alternation of crusting and breaking up. At about 7 p. m. this lake overflowed the inner bench on its southwest side.

Throughout July 21 and 22 the lakes were building ramparts and contracting in area. At 10:45 a. m. on July 22 the north lake overflowed its rampart, these overflows continuing until past noon. Large gas balloons were blown in the skin of this lake, and frequent falls of rock from its southeast wall took place. Strong rising of both the bench magma and the lakes continued, the latter evidenced in the evening by a cascade of lava pouring across the crust from the south arm to the main lake.

On July 23 the fume at Halemaumau was distinctly thinner. The rising of the bench magma had now become very pronounced, amounting locally to 3 or 4 feet per day. All the lakes were building spatter cones and forming pronounced inner benches. Occasionally very large central fountains would break out and migrate to the banks, and flames were abundant at the border cones. The north lake continued to have spells of overflowing and building up its rim, alternating with marked cracking and foundering and sinking of the liquid one to two feet. There were about seven border fountains. In the southwest lake streaming was to the south corner activity, and the cone in the west pond depression was blowing.

On July 24 the fume was still thinner. The southeast crag was now in full view again from the Observatory. On the margin of the main lake large spatter domes had been built east, southeast and northeast, the east one being opposite the east cone depression. The north lake in occasional spells, as at 4 a. m., overflowed its benches so as to fill its cup all the way to the walls on all sides. Overflows of rim with large gas balloons forming, were common at other times. At times of breaking up, prior to the development of central fountains and strong cracking and foundering, the crisis would begin with hissing gas flames in serrate lines through straight cracks of crust followed by fountainings at the same spot which developed into immense areas of doming and flinging turbulence. Then would come general brilliant cracking and foundering all over the lake, with multitudes of bubble fountains, and there would be a sinking spell followed by a quick crusting and recovery. A heavy fall of cliff rock at southeast corner of north lake at 8:56 p. m. produced one of these break-ups.

All during the hours between midnight and daylight on Friday, July 25, there were high spraying fountains from border grottoes in all the lakes, but by early morning the north lake was quiet and crusted, with occasional spells of general cracking and foundering. The east cone had become a driblet spire, sputtering and blowing glass through a small orifice. The streaming in the main lake was toward the east. There was creaking in the southeast ridge and rocks were rolling down its outer slopes. From the Observatory the telescope shows that this ridge is being pushed back to the east.

August 2, 1919.

During the week ending Friday, August 1, 1919, the strong rising of both lake and bench magma in Halemaumau has continued at a rate reaching a maximum of about 4 feet per day in the uplift of the southeast crag. The lakes have mostly kept pace with the rising dome of stiff lava, though individually the lakes have risen at different rates.

The uplift has culminated as before in flows both north and south, repeating the events of the rising movements of the spring. The northern flow broke out through a vent in the Postal Rift area slightly south of the former cone source and continues to flow sluggishly a few hundred feet to the north on the east and west sides of the old crater known as Pele's Kitchen. The south flow on July 31 broke through the wall of the southern pressure ridge and made headway about 100 yards in two arms.

Measurements of the week have shown that in six days, from July 25 to 31, the southeast and east pressure rims rose 5 feet, this being the maximum movement due to mashing up of the outer rim wall of Halemaumau. The inner column of bench magma on that side of Halemaumau exhibited maximum rising of 23 feet at the southeast crag. The central cliff blocks bounding the main lake on the north and west rose 17 feet, and the ground on the northern slope of the dome east and west of the north lake rose 10 feet. The lakes have in general risen about 15 feet, the north lake thereby gaining on the adjacent ground, whereas the main lake has lagged behind its confining walls so as to seem more sunken within them. The southwest lake, the source well, has about kept pace with the rising of the bench magma.

The continuous measurement of the lava tide from a tent on the east brink of the north lake pit has been maintained unremittingly and exhibits striking fluctuations in level of both bench magma and lake magma without any perceptible quaking of the ground and few angular changes which are other than gradual.

On the morning of Saturday, July 26, the main lake had overflowed its east bank and the driblet spire at the east cone formed a pipe 6 feet high with a rectangular hook at its summit. About 7 p. m. the main lake again overflowed strongly into the east cone depression. The fountains of both the main and north lakes were in plain view from Volcano House. The north lake fluctuated in level with a tendency to overflow its banks from time to time. Its spatter margin had built out an inner floor on the east, north and west sides where the lake overflowed owing to the northward tilt of its cup. The cliff on the south side kept scaling off and the lake margin against this cliff tended to recede or remain stationary owing to the general northward tipping. The inner bench stood about 8 feet below the east rim of the cup occupied by the lake and about 5 feet below the northwest sag leading to the northern wall valley.

The southwest lake was found in the evening to be L-shaped, with arms extending southeast and northeast, and, like the other lakes, it had built up a flood bench on all sides, the flooding filling the west pond depression with a sheet of new lava. There was no open vent at the west pond. The chasm leading from the southwest lake to the main lake had opened into a canyon. The wall-crack pond on the inner side of the south ridge was flinging lava spatter over the ridge. This ridge was creaking and rising so as to loosen rocks on its southern slopes, and similar avalanches rolled down the south wall of the north lake.

On July 27 the general rising continued, but the crunching noises in the south ridge had lessened. The east cone depression was all filled up, and a small circular pond there was fountaining in a grotto on its west side. At the main lake the lift of bench magma was so much faster than that of the liquid that in the afternoon there was an inner wall 4 feet high around the lake surmounted by the inner flood bench. The south arm remained shut off from the lake, marginal fountaining was on the east side, and streaming was eastward. Streaming was eastward also in the central pond with grotto fountains at the east end of the pond.

The north lake was now nearly level with the northwestern gap, and from time to time it overflowed its widening flood bench, its actual rim tending to contract and form a circle.

The whole upper surface of the Halemaumau floor had now risen as an arch or dome, and on this day the measurements registered a curious local depression of the central blocks of the dome. From the central crevasses the fume was quite dense, but it had now almost disappeared from the northeast wall-crack. New cracks revealing glow beneath were opening northward from the north lake, but the great crack in the ground outside of Halemaumau, extending northeastward from the northwest station, was closing up, indicating a movement of uplift extending beyond the north rim flag.

In this region Professor A. Romberg had for four days been experimenting with a seismograph in a cavern, and he reported crunching noises and falling rocks in the cave July 26-27. The seismometer at the same time revealed excessive tilts, sometimes sudden, to the north; that is, away from the Halemaumau center.

At 10:28 p. m. a geyser-like rush of lava erupted through cracks about 200 feet south of the Postal Rift source cone of the April flow, and the standing fountain kept playing for some hours and developed a new flow which poured down the east side of Pele's Kitchen. This flow was a somewhat broken pahoehoe and pooled over a large area between Pele's Kitchen and the 1894 driblet cones. By the next morning the vent was a mere spatter area showing a hissing crack, heaving slabs and a gas spiracle. All that was noticed at the north lake observation camp when the lava geyser broke out was a short-lived sinking of the lake not apparently different from many other such sinkings.

On July 28 the wall around the main lake was 5 feet high and the signal flags of the south pressure ridge had fallen over owing to the continued upheaval. Inspection of the several lakes in the evening showed that the southwest lake was streaming towards a southern grotto and occasionally flung up spray above its northern wall. The cliffs surrounding the main and southwest lake-basins were about 25 feet high in general, the highest crags being those southeast and west of the main lake depression. The new north flow showed active streams pouring through the saddle east of Pele's Kitchen but no visible activity at its source. At 7:34 p. m. the crust of the main lake broke up and the whole lake streamed rapidly, with two feet or more of sinking, towards the east. There was a large dome grotto on the southeast side of this lake and other active marginal places were southwest, northwest and northeast, with occasional brilliant spraying display east. A similar cracking of the crust and streaming occurred again at 8 p. m., but no simultaneous break-ups were observed in the north lake.

From the summit of the southeast crag the south arm was seen to be a large pool streaming vigorously southward and with a stalactite grotto at southwest corner. In the high partition between the south-arm pond and the main lake was a bubbling spring of lava which appeared to well up there and pour southward towards the pond. The rampart around the pond was a 4-foot wall of the same character as that around the main lake. During the night there was much quiet crusting of the north lake and no such frequent breaking up as before.

On July 29 the north lake was mostly below its rampart until 5 a. m. Later in the day it built two very large spatter domes on its west side, and at 3 p. m., after two hours of heavy crusting, it broke up and sent driblet flows over the north rampart for a distance of about 15 feet. This lake has no spatter bench on the south cliff side owing to being tilted in its cup northward and so doing its overflowing and bench-building on the north.

The central region of Halemaumau had shown a rise in the previous twenty-four hours of 12 or 15 feet, and the northeast ridge of bench magma between the main lake and the northeast heap has risen so as to cut off the view of the tents at east side of north lake from the automobile approach above the east pond. The south ridge had also risen greatly, forming a new outer talus.

In the east cone depression there was a small circular crusted pond from which some hissing could be heard. From the Observatory at night glowing toes could be seen in the north flow on the floor of Kilauea, and bright fountains were seen in the north lake.

The process of swelling in the dome of bench magma in Halemaumau continued on July 30, with the south ridge, the southeast cliff and the west central walls the highest points of the dome. By evening the rising of the west wall profile of the north lake had nearly shut off the west station from view of the tent. Continued creaking and tum-

May 10, 1919. From summit of Halemaumau Dome,

May 6, 1919. The rush of lava from Postal Rift cone.

Dome, looking NE. across main lava lake.

May 9, 1919. Telephoto of Halemaumau dome from Uwekahuna.
Postal Rift flows in foreground.

bling of rocks were heard in the south ridge.

The north lake had a nearly circular rampart, with about twelve evenly-spaced grotto domes. These grottoes and some central fountaining could be plainly seen in the daytime from the Observatory. At noon this lake overflowed slightly and again at night strongly.

In the evening the main lake rampart wall was 8 to 10 feet high, with dome grottoes 12 to 15 feet above the lake. The west cove was deeper than before, but the crust partition between this lake and the central pond persisted. A castellate group of crags had parted from the west wall of the northeast cove, and a chasm had opened, extending northwest from this cove. There were wide gorges between the main lake and the other two lakes, all these central crevasses yawning open from uplift. At night there was a strong overflow over the east rampart of the main lake.

The flow on the north floor of Kilauea was moving at its front down the slope east of Pele's Kitchen, with nothing but strong hissing at its source.

At 6:30 a. m., July 31, the main lake was higher, with rampart from 5 to 8 feet high and a stream of liquid lava pouring across the isthmus into the south arm. The north lake had filled high the depression behind its rampart, so that the new surface was only 10 feet below the ground on which stands the tent.

At 11 a. m. lava was flowing through the south ridge at the wall-pond locality, forming a tube down the outside of the wall and pooling at its base. The flow then spread out in two lobes, each 100 yards long, one headed due south on the east side of the tunnel ridge of 1918, and the other west along the base of pressure ridge. It consisted of smooth pahoehoe like other flows characterized by a cascade at their sources.

On the floor of the west pond there was a barrel-shaped driblet cone spouting and lifting a lid on its north side while sending out a sluggish flow of lava. The southwest pond was now elongate, low and rather quiet. The north lake at this time was also very sluggish in action, changing from its previous heavy crusting with sudden bursting and sinking spells to balloon skins and more or less open soft surface, with bubbling and sinking at intervals. This means that the accumulation and release depends, not on surface crust, but on the upper viscous layer at all times subject to thickening by radiation cooling and gas expansion.

The south pressure ridge was in motion all day. At 6 p. m. large boulders were seen to roll down its outer slope in two places. It is conspicuous that the east-northeast rim of Halemau mau, just north of the east pond, is pushing up into a new pressure ridge, with rounded profile on its outer side. The lava surface inside was rising strongly and evidently lifting the east wall-opnd bodily, though the latter was raised also by numerous overflows of the main lake. The general effect of the uplift in Halemaumau is to close the crevasses outside of its rim limits and open them in the central region.

At 6 a. m. on Friday, August 1, 1919, no motion was observed at the south ridge. The east-northeast pressure ridge and the lava surface about the east pond were markedly higher. The south floor was now so greatly domed up that the inside of the south wall could not be seen from the northeast edge of Halemaumau. The view of the main lake from this same position was now cut off by its high rampart wall. The castle crags on the west side of the northeast cove o. this lake had collapsed.

There had been no revival of the flow through the south wall, but the north flow continued to push out toes at its front.

The north lake overflowed on the older ground near the tent 30 feet from its bank and extensive flows on its northwest inner bench threatened to go through the gap and out into northwest wall-valley. The inner floor or ring platform of this lake is wide east, north and northwest, while along the base of the uplifting south cliff there is only a broken shelled-off spatter scar 3 feet high; and the rampart is increasing so much in height that the view of the liquid from the tent is likely to be entirely cut off.

All the lakes have been making a brilliant display at night. There is now fume rising from the central region and some west and south.

Very respectfully,
T. A. JAGGAR, JR.,
Volcanologist.

THE COMPOSITION OF THE GASES OF KILAUEA

BY E. S. SHEPHERD

The search for the sources of energy back of volcanic phenomena requires not only a continuous observation of the physical activities of the volcano, but also an examination of the matter thrown out from the crater. This matter consists essentially of the mineral portion (lava) and the gases.

Of the various lavas and their forms we have already fairly complete information. This is not the case with the gaseous matter.

The gaseous emanations have necessarily attracted much attontion, but, from the extreme difficulty encountered in the attempt to collect them, no really satisfactory data have been obtained thus far. Of the three attempts at such collection made by the Geophysical Laboratory expeditions, only that of 1917 resulted in satisfactory samples for quantitative study. The 1912 collection was most valuable from a qualitative standpoint especially as regards the minor constituents of the gases evolved. But it did not allow a quantitative determination of the most important constituent, namely, water vapor. On the other hand, the 1917 collection, while made under less favorable conditions, develops several important facts. In this place it will suffice to state that, in 1917, vacuum tubes with soft glass plugs at one end were wired to bamboo rods and the fusible end inserted into promising flame holes as the lava crusts swept along the edge of the lake.

There are several objections to this sort of gas but it was the only one available at the time.

THE ANALYTICAL RESULTS.

The methods of analysis of such complex mixtures as one obtains from volcanoes are not altogether satisfactory. Certain constituents such as SO_2, SO_3, Cl_2 and F_2 are not easily separated where, as is too often the case, the vacuum tube does not seal perfectly, or by subsequent cracking of a tip allows the tube to fill with air before it can be properly sealed. This unfortunate condition too often results in a tube which will for analytical purposes contain ninety or more per cent of air. The volcano gas has then to be determined with this large amount of foreign gas hindering the analysis. Nevertheless, an apparatus has been developed which allows reasonably accurate determinations under such unfavorable conditions.

The analyses which follow were made with the above-mentioned apparatus, whose complete description must wait for a future publication. We would merely note that H_2O and S_2 are determined gravimetrically. SO_2 can, under our conditions, be regarded as not sharply separated, but of the correct order of magnitude. CH_4 is not tabulated; working with the best samples yet available it is not present in the fixed gases in quantities greater than 0.2% if present at all. This means that when the water is also included in the computation the amount of hydrocarbons is negligible.

In Table I are given the analyses of 10 tubes collected from the passing flames on the lake surface. In Table II is given the analysis of one of the samples obtained by Prof. Jaggar in 1918-1919. The remaining tubes of this series will be analyzed at an early date and should be the most important collection of gas yet made from any volcano. Previous collectors have necessarily been satisfied with *any* gas. This series of Prof. Jaggar's is made as opportunity offered and along certain definite lines of study. I include the analysis of No. 17 merely for comparison with the 1917 collection which was made from the lake surface.

TABLE I.

GASES COLLECTED FROM KILAUEA, 1917.

VOLUME PERCENTS AT 1200° C.

Tube	CO_2	CO	H_2	N_2	A	SO_2	S_2	Cl_2	H_2O
1*	2.65	1.04	4.22	23.22	udt	0.16	0.70	udt	67.99
2*	17.95	0.36	1.35	37.84	udt	3.51	0.49	udt	38.48
3	33.48	1.42	1.56	12.88	0.45	29.83	1.79	0.17	17.97
4	11.12	3.92	1.42	....	0.51	....	8.61	0.02	77.50
5	9.54	1.12	1.53	10.47	....	9.90	2.72	....	64.71
6	1.97	0.82	0.21	3.50	0.07	0.95	2.70	....	89.77
7	17.25	0.62	0.76	5.88	0.18	9.75	1.07	0.25	64.18
8	15.27	0.45	0.70	0.87	0.14	6.98	0.49	....	75.08
9	8.32	0.82	1.82	8.92	0.29	16.80	2.48	1.01	59.97
10	1.54	0.43	0.37	2.44	0.39	....	3.56	1.34	89.93

* Tubes 1 and 2 were analyzed before the calcium tube was added to the apparatus, so that the rare gases were not determined. Chlorine was not determined in these tubes (udt). Other blanks in the table mean that the gas was not present in determinable amounts.

TABLE II.

Tube No. 17 collected by Dr. T. A. Jaggar, Jr., March 17, 1919.

(Note:—Tip inserted in soft bursting bubble through crust of west pond.)

VOLUME PERCENTS AT 1200° C.

B is computed, neglecting water and sulfur, for comparison with the 1912 collection.

C is the analysis of Tube 16 of the 1912 collection.

Comparison of B and C shows that the source of gas in 1912 was as reliable as can be hoped for. The relative deficiency in SO_2 in C is probably due to conditions of collection and storage.

	A	Comparison of Fixed Gases	
		B	C
CO_2	11.61%	57.0%	75.77%
CO	0.37	1.8	2.31
H_2	0.58	2.8	4.44
N_2	1.29	6.4	8.22
A	0.04	0.2	0.15
SO_2	6.48	31.8	8.09
Cl_2	0.05	...	...
S_2	0.24	...	...
H_2O	79.31	...	...
F_2	trace	...	...

Examination of these tables raises more questions than it answers. The composition of the gas collected in 1917 varies greatly. Certain relations are apparent. Thus: Co is usually present in less quantity than H_2. Next to H_2O, CO_2 is the chief constituent. N_2 is usually a minor constituent and often the rare gases (computed as argon) are no more than would be required on the assumption that the nitrogen came in as air. The chlorine content is surprisingly low. On the other hand, tube 4 shows over seven per cent of sulfur, which agrees with the observation that at times fountains break which set free violet brown fumes which look like sulfur vapor.

It is clear that in most cases the gas as it reaches the surface of the lake is almost completely burned. Similarly the gas in Table II retains but very little combustible gas, although Prof. Jaggar says in his notes he regarded the sample to be as nearly perfect as one could hope to obtain.

The amount of water in all samples is surprisingly high and it is always present. Either we must allow some validity to the thesis that sea-water diffuses through the earth's crust and reappears in the volcanoes—a thesis which we have rejected for reasons stated in an earlier publication[1]—or we must agree with Jaggar's thesis that the combustible gases are burned at and below the lake's surface by air carried down by sinking crusts, air sucked down by fountaining, and oxygen diffusing into the lava as it rises in the conduits. These analyses indicate that perhaps all three of the processes postulated by Jaggar are active. Trapped air would call for a great deal more nitrogen than is present in the gases thus far collected. But this objection does not apply to oxidation along the conduits nor at the lake surface. I am at present inclined to accept the surface combustion as an important factor in the maintenance of the lake's heat supply. On the other hand, the great variations in composition of all samples collected lend support to Day's thesis that a part of the energy may be derived from the shifting gaseous equilibria due to lack of equilibrium among the gases rising in the magma, and undoubtedly the analysis of Prof. Jaggar's 1918-1919 collection as well as future systematically - taken samples will give us for the first time the data needed to establish definitely the relative importance of these various suspected sources of volcano energy. It seems to me that the further collection of gases along the lines which Prof. Jaggar is now pursuing is one of the most promising investigations now before students of volcanology.

Geophysical Laboratory,
Carnegie Institution of Washington,
Washington, D. C.,
July, 1919.

1 Day and Shepherd, Water and Volcanic Activity. Bull. Geol. Soc. Am. 24, 605. 1913.

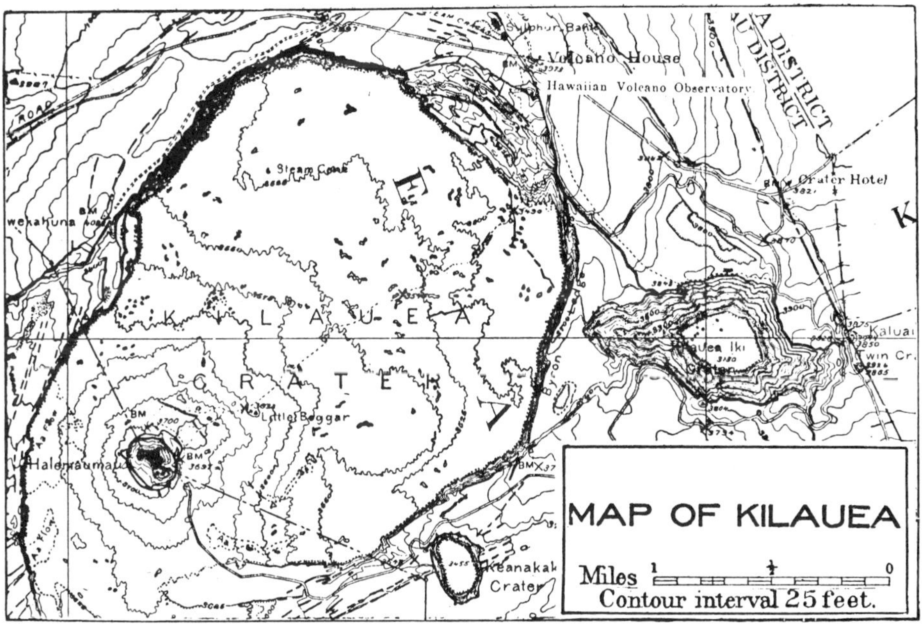

HAWAIIAN VOLCANO OBSERVATORY.

The Observatory is equipped with the following seismometric instruments rebuilt at the station in 1918 for the special needs of volcano research: two Bosch-Omori pendulums, high speed registration of local earthquakes; one optically recording seismograph for distant earthquakes; one clinograph registering E-W tilting of the ground. A vertical component seismograph was in December, 1918, set up in experimental operation. These are seated on concrete piers in a closed basement room having practically constant temperature, beneath the chief Observatory building near the hotel. Time is referred to a rated chronometer, checked at intervals by solar observations with a transit. Both instruments are loaned by the College of Hawaii. Hawaiian standard time (H. S. T.) is 10 hrs. 30 min. slower than Greenwich time.

CANCANI SCALE OF SEISMIC INTENSITY.

Expressed by accelerations measured in millimeters per second per second.

I.	Instrumental	0.0	2.5
II.	Very slight	2.5	5.0
III.	Slight	5.0	10.0
IV.	Sensible, mediocre	10.0	25.0
V.	Rather strong	25.0	50.0
VI.	Strong	50.0	100.0
VII.	Very strong	100.0	250.0
VIII.	Ruinous	250.0	500.0
IX.	Disastrous	500.0	1000.0
X.	Very disastrous	1000.0	2500.0
XI.	Catastrophic	2500.0	5000.0
XII.	Great catastrophe	5000.0	10000.0

Grade IV. is ordinarily the minimum perceived by the senses; and in grade XII. the accelerations or rate of change of motion (jerk) reaches that of terrestrial gravitation.

In the standard form of report the maximum intensity or acceleration, designated by the symbol a, or max. a, is given in the conventional unit of milligal. The milligal is a measure of acceleration, such that 1 milligal = 1/100 mm. per sec. per sec. = 10 μ. per sec. per sec. The Cancani scale, here defined in terms of millimeters per sec. per sec., can therefore be expressed in milligals by multiplying each of the numbers by 100.

U. S. DEPARTMENT OF AGRICULTURE
WEATHER BUREAU
CHARLES F. MARVIN, CHIEF

MONTHLY BULLETIN
OF THE
Hawaiian Volcano Observatory

VOL. VII. HONOLULU, HAWAII, AUGUST, 1919 No. 8

August 9, 1919.

During the week ending Friday, August 8, 1919, the strong rising of the Halemaumau lava column has continued so that the lifted dome of bench magma presents much the same appearance as it had in the spring. Again the old rim at the north station has been lifted strongly week ending Friday, August 8, 1919, the strong rising of the Halemaumau lava column has continued so that the lifted dome of bench magma presents much the same appearance as it had in the spring. Again the old rim at the north station has been lifted strongly so as to tilt back the north concrete platform and the west station has also been tilted. The new north flow from the Postal Rift area has continued to progress slowly on both sides of Pele's Kitchen so that its western front is about one half-mile from the source. Other flows have continued to pour over the south pressure ridge from a cone at the south wall-crack so that a new field of glistening glassy lava has spread in many lobes over the upper part of the trail leading from the road terminus. The southwest lake has also flowed across the outer borders of Halemaumau and also into the northwest wall-valley. A conspicuous change of the week has been the merging together of the four central pools, namely the southwest lake, central pond, main lake and south arm, so as to make one elongate trench containing liquid lava streaming rapidly from west to east.

Rising and overflow have necessitated removal and replacing of the tents where the transit observations are in progress, but this has been done without serious interruption of the work of incessant measurement of the lava tide night and day. Readings every twenty minutes have now been continued nearly three weeks. On August 3 Mr. R. H. Finch arrived from Washington to become first assistant at this station, and with his aid five men are now available for the shifting watches at the pit.

The measurements of the week have shown a lift of the south and east pressure rims of 5 feet in eight days, July 31 to August 8. In the same period the north station has been lifted 6 feet, the west station 1 foot and the northeast marginal ground appears to have been stationary. The interior central blocks of the Halemaumau dome consisting of live lava rose 13 feet at the southeast crag, 12 feet in the central region and 9 feet at the ground west of the north lake. The north lake liquid rose approximately 10 feet with much building up of its marginal bench. The main lake rose only about 6 feet and the end of the week found it lower relative to its inner bench by about the same amount. The bench had thus lifted twice as much as the lake.

On Saturday, August 2, 1919, after a stagnant spell in the early morning the north lake rose and overflowed its ramparts in the forenoon. In the afternoon it lowered again. In the evening two fountaining grottoes of this lake were in full view of the Observatory. At the east pond locality on this day a glowing cone was hissing and the surrounding surface had been lifted nearly level with the east rim of Halemaumau. From here the east margin of the main lake was now a serrate craggy mass above the observer, shutting off the lake from view. Inside its cup the lake preserved a level 6 to 8 feet below the inner wall, the south arm was continuous with the east pool, and the streaming poured from the direction of the central pond across to the east bank and in a curve through the narrows into the south arm. By measurement the central cliffs showed pronounced rising. The fume was in moderate volume. The new Postal Rift flow was hissing at the source vent and its flowing increased at the front making several glowing lobes.

At 9 a. m. on August 3 the central pool was continuous with the main lake and the streaming was swift around the bend into the south arm to a large grotto 20 feet high at the southern end of this arm. Between the central pool and the southwest lake there was still a partially closed crevasse with lava streaming eastward through openings below. In the central cracked ground between the main and north lakes the deep shaft or pot, seen glowing there previously, was now puffing with live lava below and new spray covered the orifice. A new small flow of lava had poured from the east cone and the western lakes had overflowed towards the southwest and into the northwest wall-valley.

The Postal Rift flow was swelling rapidly in a wide slag heap for several hundred feet around its source vent, the latter was glowing and hissing and toes were pushing northward at the fronts of the flow both east and west of Pele's Kitchen. In the evening on the west side of the Pele's Kitchen cone a spraying gas spiracle formed at the margin of the swollen area and gave vent to a live lobe of the flow. At about this time the old north rim of Halemaumau was lifting rapidly, as though the filling of a subterranean passage leading to the flow were also swelling. Under this stress the fissure extending northeast from the northwest station closed and its walls were compressed locally into pressure ridges. Another such pressure ridge made an arched and broken dome at the northeast base of the high ground south of the north lake.

On Monday, August 4, the east cone had been re-established well above the east rim of Halemaumau and the uplifting movement had created a new pressure ridge along the eastnortheast rim. The north lake had built up a high rampart so that in the afternoon it was necessary to move the transit station to higher ground on the north side of the north lake.

The joining through of southwest and main lakes was now so nearly complete that the surface of the lake at the east pool had changed its habit completely, and there was now a majestic river-like torrent pouring out from the central narrows with radiating bright lines on its surface, dividing into two currents which swept respectively into the northeast cove and the south arm. This arrangement shaped the lake into an elongate pool such as was repeatedly formed in 1914, 1915, 1916 and 1917 with a source-pond at the west end and a fan-shaped group of sink-holes at the east, these being fountaining grottoes east, northeast and south. The cliffs around the main lake, which had built up its spatter-margin, were now rather low, from 10 to 20 feet high, the southeast and west crags being somewhat higher.

There was strong upward lift in the night of August 4-5 followed by overflows from the north lake. The rapid flow eastward of the main lake continued, the east bench standing 5 feet above the lake and the grotto heaping still higher. The south pressure ridge was in motion, its outer face very steep, its summit over 40 feet high, and the pressure had thrust known peaks of its summit outward as well as upward with reference to the center of Halemaumau. The ridge showed two concentric walls, one within the other as seen from the south. In four days the lift of these walls had completely destroyed the frozen lava cascade which poured over the wall July 31.

About 9 a. m. August 4 the north lake overflowed voluminously on all sides and sent streams into the northwest wall-valley. In the evening at 5:30 p. m. it was evident that another lava cascade had poured down the outer side of the south pressure ridge from the south wall-crack pond which stood at a high level just inside the pressure ridge, surmounted by a spouting cone which could be seen at the top of the saddle where the flow poured over. Exploration around Halemaumau to the south and west discovered a new flow which had hardened with folded fragile crusts and had poured from the west pond flat about August 3 simultaneously with the flow which on the other side of the west pond vent had poured into the north west wall-valley. Into the northwest wall-valley other flows had coursed down the inner slope of Halemaumau from the northwest corner of the north lake.

Inspection of the southwest lake from its northern margin showed that this pool had now merged completely with the central and east pools to make one long lake through the middle of the Halemaumau dome from west to east. In the southwest pool the rampart on the west side showed distinct downward inclination from south to north. The south side of the pool was crusted over and formed the source of the rapid streaming which rushed through the narrows eastward. The narrows in question had been the crevasse separating the southwest and central pools. Here there were standing rapids and the crevasse had become a gorge leading to the central pond and beyond could be seen a current less swift sweeping from the central pond to the east pool. Another rapid current streamed from the main lake through the narrows into the south arm where a very large grotto dome received the final downrush of the circulation. The recent sudden change of habit in the activity of the main lake (east pool) from spells of crusting to continuous bright-line streaming was coincident with the yawning open and breaking down of the chasm which admitted the flood from the southwest lake.

During the night, August 5-6, the north flow cone was puffing and at the fronts the lava progressed mainly over the upper part of the former Postal Rift flow on the west side of Pele's Kitchen. During this night also the north lake had increasing high spasms of rising which culminated in strong overflows early the next morning.

About 4 a. m. on August 6 these overflows of the north lake flooded the rampart shelf and thence drained into the northwest wall valley. The spasm of rising was general and about 5 a. m. the cone in the saddle of the south pressure ridge sent a double cascade down the outer face of the ridge and this lava spread out in glistening masses of glassy lava which solidified as dense rock and covered the upper part of the new heap of such flows which radiated from this cascade locality out in the direction of the road terminus. Cascading here was repeated at 6:30 p. m.

At 3:30 p. m. August 6 the north lake again overflowed voluminously after building up its ramparts with large dome grottoes; during the afternoon it remained high with brilliant fountaining. The swelling of the bench magma had now arched the northern part of the Halemaumau dome so as greatly to lift the ground west and north of the north lake. Once more also the ground outside of the limits of the Halemaumaumau pit area was in process of strong upheaval on the west and north so that the masonry stations and signal flags were again being lifted and tilted away from the Halemaumau center. This was creating a new narrow pressure ridge at the west station and a wide zone of upheaval in the region beyond the north bench-mark.

On the morning of August 7 the tumescence culminated in extensive overflows of the north lake to the northwest and to the east, so that it was necessary to remove the small sleeping tent at the transit station to a safer place farther north. The eastern overflow extended 200 feet from the lake in a northeasterly direction to the point where the Halemaumau dome falls off in a very steep marginal slope. The uplifted bench magma here rose as an arcuate bend in the crust of the lava column, but did not exert crushing pressure outside. Farther to the south at the northeast wall pond locality a distinct pressure rim in the outside rock was developed and this became a high wall all around the southeast, south and southwest sides of Halemaumau. The materials of this wall now consisted of the semi-solid lava column as the highest tumbled wall inside marking the edges in many places of a plateau extending inward as the surface of the Halemaumau dome.

The main lake was now depressed within its cup, its east bank rising steeply into ragged crags, and a continuous crasm was developing from its northeast cove in the direction of the north lake.

On Friday, August 8, this tendency of the main lake had increased and the inner bench was 15 feet high on the south side of the lake. All around the liquid lava this rampart bench showed horizontal bedding and stood as a wall above the lake as much as 20 feet high in places on the southeastern and eastern sides and 10 feet high on the north side. The north lake at 1 p. m. was brimming level with its banks, during the afternoon it fluctuated in height and from 5 to 6 p. m. strong avalanches southeast of the lake rapidly developed the new gulch leading towards the northeast cove of the main lake.

The glassy lava of the south ridge flow had spread in many lobes covering the upper part of the trail from the road terminus and these flows on this day were hot and making progress. In the evening there was a strong spurt of flowing at this locality. The new northern flow of the Postal Rift locality was extending itself eastward.

August 16, 1919.

The high pressure under the Halemaumau lava column causing it to rise bodily and produce voluminous floods of liquid lava has continued during the second week in August. The rate of rising of the crater floors or bench magma has been slower than during the previous week, but the flooding of liquid lava has increased. One short spell of sinking, involving the craggy matter and causing the collapse of the southeast crag, took place on August 13, the Halemaumau dome sinking about a foot, and the uptilted southeast crag block breaking down into an island so as to lower its summit 14 feet. The flow from the Postal Rift has continued its progress and the north and southwest lakes have repeatedly overflowed. The south wall-crack has also continued its cascades.

Measurement has shown lift of the southern pressure ridge 1 to 2 feet and the old west and north rim stations of Halemaumau have risen 4 feet. The transit tent on the north brink of the north lake was lifted 8 feet in seven days August 8 to 15. The central blocks of the Halemaumau dome rose 6 to 9 feet in different places. The outer lakes gained somewhat on the rising bench magma so as to overflow and build up ramparts, and the main lake gained about 6 feet on its rising shores, though it was still some 9 feet beneath its rampart wall on August 15.

On Saturday, August 9, in the hours before daylight the lakes were very bright and the grotto domes of the north lake could be seen from Volcano House brilliantly fountaining. The Postal Rift flow was bright with greatest advance in its western lobe and there was glow in the southern flows. Collapse, making rock slides, developed a pronounced gulch in the middle of the wall bounding the north lake on the southeast, this being the crevasse over a subterranean tunnel connecting the main and north lakes.

At 6 a. m. the north lake was quiet and high. There had been a general breaking down of the rampart domes around the lake, only the northwestern and western ones remaining. The main lake streamed from bright lines under banks 10 to 15 feet high to an active eastern grotto. The east cone, glowing and fuming, stood over a wide crevasse in the upswollen slope leading from the east rim of Halemaumau as a steep upgrade to the verge of the lifted lake. The east pond was gone, there was left only the cone. Halemaumau was again a high hill where one looked down steep slopes towards the hut on the east and the field of Postal Rift flows towards the north. This latter field was now greatly swollen and its edge had extended itself several hundred feet to the east. In the evening the north lake was low, the rising movement lessened, and just before midnight the entire rampart block bounding the liquid lava on the southwest slowly collapsed and sank beneath the lake. At the same time the level bubble of the transit on the north side of the lake showed a sudden tilt of the ground southward. The lake remained very low for the remainder of the night, the north flow was quiet and slight earthquakes were felt at the sleeping tent.

On August 10 at 6 a. m. the southeast chasm had again increased through rock sliding and the north lake was rising slightly. At 6:30 a. m. a very exceptional condition was found in the main lake in that the current was streaming westward through the narrows leading to the southwest pool, showing that the grade of the surface was reversed, accompanied by withdrawal of lava through the western source tubes. Hitherto the eastward flow had made rapids. The fume was slightly increased. During the day, however, there was recovery and at 6 p. m. the main lake was again streaming eastward.

On August 11 there was strong revival of the new Postal Rift vent about 3 p. m. and a fountaining gush of flowing took place there. In the evening the cone was spurting high jets which fell on the surface of a new flow heap that covered the former flow for several hundred feet from the cone center. In Halemaumau occasional slips of rock were heard, the north lake was low, and there was some rising toward midnight.

On August 12 the main lake continued to stream eastward. There were fresh driblet trickles of lava through the saddle in the south pressure ridge. It was now becoming evident that the lift of the bench magma had widened the central gulches and hot cracks on the north side of the north lake, these latter marking a new mound distinct from the central Halemaumau dome and extended into farther uplift of the northern Halemaumau rim. The government bench mark there tilted northward a little over ten degrees. The northeastern pressure ridge had increased in height and steepness and the slope from the east cone up to the edge of the main lake was growing steeper. The walls east and south of the main lake cup were about 20 feet high. The block of ground between the two gulches extending south from the north lake appeared to be stationary and flat topped. About noon there was overflow from the southwest lake.

At 4:30 p. m. there was a sudden pronounced general rise of lake magma which resulted in a remarkably voluminous torrent falling as a triple cascade from the south ridge and in overflow of the north lake which sent streams over the edge of the north lake basin eastward and into the northwest wall-valley. The southern flow differed from its predecessors in the appearance and consolidation of the lava, as it tended to form broken pahoehoe slabs rather than round glistening glassy toes. As the cascades fell over the wall, the glowing melt was mottled with black blotches and fell in crumbly and stringy curtains showing a cavernous background through their interstices. The flood started with a standing fountain at the wall-crack cone and flowed for nearly an hour.

The Postal Rift cone was now about 8 feet high with gas spiracles on its crest which were hissing, and the lava inside was pushing out as toes at the fronts of the flow. This flow had now extended to the southwest as well as to the northeast, and in the new direction had broken down the roof of the cavern formerly called Pele's Reception Room and had invaded the subterranean chamber. This was the cave recently in use as a chamber for seismograph experiments.

In the forenoon of August 13 the Postal Rift cone was puffing and the new swollen flow surrounded it. The south flows were quiet. The main lake was streaming eastward. The north lake rose to a high level at about 8:30 a. m. and thereafter subsided.

Some very striking results of mass uplift were now in evidence. What had been a crack extending from the northeast cove of the main lake to the southeast wall of the north lake was now a continuous gulch from 30 to 50 feet wide, floored with tumbled rock, and the central crevasse farther west had also widened. This opening of cracks did not stop at the north lake but crossed the bottom of the lake and reappeared as huge chasms extending lake to the north wall of Halemaumau. One of these chasms was 20 feet wide, narrowing northward. Other such chasm gulches had yawned open east and south of the main lake as result of the swelling up of the Halemaumau dome, each chasm beginning as a glowing crack penetrating deeply into the crust of the bench magma. The fact that these cracks cross the lakes, and in places develop into lakes, such as the main lake channel, seems additional proof that the lake basins are shallow openings. The change in elevation of the transit shelter produced marked changes in angle of view; the old crater to the north known as Pele's Kitchen, a few days before entirely cut off from view by the slag heap of the new flow, was now again in full view so much had the shelter been lifted. On the other hand, the view of the shelter itself from the northwest station as a triangulation point had become cut off by the swelling of the ground west of the shelter.

At 5:30 p. m. the north lake rose to slightly overflowing and then sank deeply during the night, leaving the inner wall of its rampart 15 feet high. Dense puffing fume rose from the chasm gulch southeast of the north lake and rock slides there told of the undermining beneath. At midnight the Postal Rift cone was spurting with a live flow all around it. There were small earthquake shocks during the night.

About 1 o'clock in the early morning of August 14 a rift broke open in a north-south direction on the east side of the southeast crag block, this being a continuation southward of the chasm last mentioned. As a result the whole tilted summit area of the crag was carried down to a horizontal position and the block became an island mass 25 feet high, squarish in profile, standing midway between the south arm pond and the main lake, with a channel on each side of it. The movement was fairly rapid and created much disturbance in the adjacent lakes and some small earthquake shocks felt in the immediate vicinity. One of these shocks was felt at the Observatory. The sinking of the southeast crag quite changed the profile of Halemaumau as seen from Volcano House. The channels on both sides of the new island quickly crusted over so as to shut off the south arm pond from the main lake. After daylight the main lake was found with current pouring rapidly eastward through the central channel like a river, the bounding cliffs 15 to 30 feet high, and in the east pool the current spread out like a fan, carrying surface skins to the northeast cove and the southeast shore, while a large dome grotto was developing on the southwest shore. Standing on the east brink of the lake the observer could look southward through the new gap and see on the south side of the south arm pond the immense dome grotto there, 20 feet high and 40 feet broad. The north lake was now recovering and near its rampart level, and the Postal Rift cone was puffing through a high spire of its own construction.

At 6 p. m. the north lake was dribbing over its rim and a fresh flow from the Postal Rift source was pushing out to the east and also to the southwest. About noon a sharp earthquake had been recorded at Hilo. On this day the measurement had shown the first pronounced reaction from rising of the bench magma, marked by subsidence of the summit region of the Halemaumau dome by something more than a foot. Toward midnight the north lake again sank low and the southern ramparts fell in. The rising and falling spells were more frequent than at the end of July and the lake surface was more continuously broken up.

On Friday, August 15, the main lake ramparts stood from 6 to 12 feet above the liquid, a long grotto dome had formed on the southwest side and the floodings of the channel on the west side of the southeast island had almost completely drowned the sunken crag there of the June subsidence. The north lake had risen to a high level at 4 a. m.; at noon, however, it was rather low and the puffing of the Postal Rift cone was slight. This cone now occupied a hollow in the midst of an extensive swollen area, the whole flow around it being intensely inflated both locally and in general.

During the afternoon the humped ground north of the north lake and also the central Halemaumau dome were both swelling measurably, and this tumescence culminated at 6 p. m. in a rapid rise whereby the north lake overflowed quickly and voluminously in long streams eastward and northeastward. The eastern torrent went down the slope to the 1894 bench region and beyond, and lasted about a half hour. The main lake at the same time was very full and gigantic spraying fountains played beneath its eastern rampart at a level only about 6 feet below the bank. The east cone, which had recently built a new heap of gas spiracles alongside of the former cone, had now become entirely quiet. The cone in the south wall saddle was hissing and flaming and in the evening this vent erupted and sent a long flow southward and westward keeping for some distance parallel with the pressure ridge. The swollen Postal Rift area at this time was nearly dark.

The accumulating evidence from many occasions such as were illustrated on this day, indicates that each pronounced spell of localized overflowing is preceded by rapid localized swelling of the bench magma near the point where the overflow is to take place.

August 23, 1919.

During the week ending August 23, 1919, there was a pronounced lowering of the upper surface of the Halemaumau dome and of the lava lakes, simultaneous with the most voluminous flow which has yet poured out on the floor of the greater crater during the present Kilauea activity. This flow spouted from the Postal Rift vents, making new cones slightly to the west of the earlier outlets, and the flood swept in a few hours to the southwest wall of Kilauea and made an extensive pool at the foot of the southern part of Uwekahuna bluff. The new outbreak started on the afternoon of August 16 and has spread its outpourings ever since, with marked fresh gushings every evening. The sinking effects at Halemaumau were mostly between August 16 and August 20. Thereafter in the bench magma a stationary condition of adjustment to the flowing was reached, followed by recovery of the lava in the lakes.

The measurements have shown the following changes of level in seven days from August 15 to August 22: south pressure ridge down about 1.5 feet; central cliff blocks around main lake down 6 to 10 feet; east margin of main lake down about 2 feet; ground around north lake down 1 foot. The lakes lowered 30 to 40 feet August 16-17, remained low two days more, and began strong recovery August 20 so that on August 22 the north lake was again fountaining visibly above its rampart as seen from Volcano House.

At noon on August 18, the twenty-eight days of continuous measurement of tidal movement in the lava column, from a transit station at the north lake, was concluded. The writer takes this opportunity to express his appreciation, on behalf of the Observatory, of the devoted attention to duty of the volunteer and staff workers who took turns night and day in completing this task.

On Saturday, August 16, 1919, after a night of high lakes and strong flowing from the south wall-cone, the Postal Rift cone area was found intensely inflated and swollen into dome tumuli, and there was much heat from all the flow areas. The bench magma was in rapid upward movement, rocks were tumbling from the south pressure ridge almost continuously, the central crevasses and those in the northern mound were yawning open and causing rocks to fall in, and it was becoming evident at the tents near the north lake that the ground was tilting perceptibly to the east and northeast. The inclination showed in the tent poles, and the sleeping cots were so inclined that they had to be blocked up to make them level. As illustrating the nature of bench magma, red hot only a few feet down, it should be said that the tent poles of the transit shelter repeatedly caught fire during this camping venture, and had to be extinguished with water from the canteens. The cracks at the front entrance to the shelter were at all times hot enough to boil water in a few minutes.

The main lake at 6 a. m. was streaming to the east and south. The huge dome grotto in the south arm pond was again active. The wall rampart of the north lake was 6 feet high. The eastern flow from the north lake of the previous evening was about 600 feet long and now solid. The Postal cone was hissing and the bench magma rising.

About 3 p. m. a sudden outburst of spouting lava took place within the southwestern extension of the recent Postal Rift flow area, forming two new cone vents, probably over newly opened deep cracks of the underlying Postal Rift fissure system. This place was about 100 yards west of the cone source hitherto active, which in turn had broken out only a short distance southeast of the cone source of the April-May flows. The whole group of Postal Rift source cones thus lay within the strongly fuming solfataric area of whitened crevasses which for many years past have been called the "Postal Cracks." This entire area is now buried, excepting the hill with summit crater known as Pele's Kitchen. A big flood of lava rushed westward from the new vents, and immediately drained the inflated slag-heap surrounding the cone of earlier formation, causing the dome tumuli to collapse and reveal cavernous glowing interiors and broken shells. The new flow made rapid streams and delta lobes all the way to the southwest wall of Kilauea immediately west of Halemaumau and all night the lava was pooling there. The spectacular surface stream continued all night and appeared in its first rush to be much the most rapid and voluminous Kilauea flow yet produced in the 1918-19 series.

Immediately after this outbreak the north lake sank rapidly until its walls beneath the overflow bench were 30 feet high. There were many tumbles from the ramparts and at the two gulches on the south side of the lake. The main lake also lowered, its streaming still going east and northeast, and an open arch leading to the south arm pond appeared under the isthmus on the east side of the southeast island.

On August 17 at 2 p. m. the lakes remained low but showed some tendency to recovery and some spectacular fountaining. In the very early morning hours an immense block of the southeast rampart fell into the north lake making a high and brilliant puff of dust and gas. Eastward streaming continued in the main lake, and in the north lake a tube was revealed under the south chasm with liquid lava streaming out from it, like a brook, into the lake. There was continuous bubbling in front of the gulch southeast of the north lake, and the surface of the lake showed bright-line pattern and no hard crusting.

The bench magma dome had lowered along with the lakes so that the greater sinking of the central part of Halemaumau was revealed in both the main and north lakes by the greater lowering of those portions of the rampart bench which lay nearest to the central region. Thus in the main lake the east bench was high and the north benches much lower, while in the north lake the north bench was high and the rampart scar along the south wall of the lake was low with a distinct tilt between these two points.

All day the new flow was flooding northwestward from Halemaumau and about 5 p. m. there was intense revival of the flow sending streams westward on top of the solidified portion. These streams as seen in plan, looking down on them from Uwekahuna bluff, showed tendency to form a pattern like a pair of lobster claws, the main stream spreading out like a delta in arms which tended to recurve and meet. Each minor fork showed the same tendency as though forking around an obstacle and meeting on the other side.

At 6 a. m. on August 18 the main lake appeared very low with eastern rampart wall over 30 feet high and the cliff blocks north and south of the lake appeared to have slumped. The streaming was still eastward with fountaining activity east and southwest. The angles of view showed clearly that the central part of the Halemaumau dome had lowered. The rampart walls of the north lake were 15 to 30 feet high and at 5:45 a. m. strong avalanches were tumbling on the west side, removing the rampart and leaving a raw cliff of bedded flows. The stream pouring out of the cavern just west of the south gulch appeared to come from the direction of the southwest lake. At the summit crevasses the fume was still thin. During the forenoon there was some rising in the north lake but the main lake, at 3 p. m., was still very low. The north flow vent had become a hissing cone and the flow from it was crusted over during the day but at 8 p. m. a new and brilliant incandescent flow was streaming over the surface westward.

On this day at 11:40 a. m. the last watch in the series of transit measurements at the north lake was concluded, and the twenty-eight days of continuous observation, with readings every twenty

June 7, 1919. The lava cascade at the northeast cave, 9 p. m.

June 9, 1919. Cascade at the northeast cove, 12 noon; daylight view—Photos Jaggar.

minutes, was brought to a close and the camp dismantled.

On Tuesday, August 19, at 3 p. m., the measurements showed continued lowering of the bench magma. A circuit of Halemaumau starting by the east and north sides showed few changes. The main lake was streaming eastward with a rampart wall 40 feet high at the east end. The north lake stood twenty feet below its rampart edge and its activity was sluggish. The southwest lake was draining in a rushing cascade through the narrows to the central pool and the block of ground formerly high which lay south of the narrows had been tilted westward so that its western edge stood only a few feet above the southwest lake level. The rampart bench of the lake was mostly 15 to 20 feet above the liquid and the lake had enlarged considerably in the southern bay. The west pond flat was smoking. The northern flow cone was hissing and its flow crusted over in the afternoon, but at 6 p. m. voluminous spouting was resumed and a bright surface stream ensued.

Examination of the old edge of Halemaumau at the west station showed that a new narrow pressure rim had been mashed up there during the last upheaval, very similar to the northeastern pressure rim. This extended the horseshoe ridge, the middle of which lay to the south so as to encompass three-quarters of Halemaumau, while the northern quarter had been more gradually upheaved back to the place where the Postal Rift flows had welled up.

On August 20 the sinking of the bench magma continued but slightly and in the afternoon the lakes were rising strongly and the flow from the Postal Rift was gushing westward. The large grotto of the south arm pond was again active. The fume continued thin. In the evening the lakes were bright and the northern flow glowed extensively without any special bright streams.

At 6 p. m. on August 21 the source cone of the north flow contained a fountaining pot making a new pool by overflowing around it and adding to the large flow which extended west. The lakes were all higher and in the southwest and main lakes the current flowing eastward was slower. The large dome grotto of the south arm pond continued its fountaining and there were new overflows of the crust in the two channels connecting the main lake and the south pond. In the north lake the crust broke up and sank at intervals At its northwest corner there was a flaming crevasse and the remnant of spatter bench from the former high level now showed a tilt northward from the south corner of the lake indicating renewed rising of the bench magma in the center of Halemaumau. The bubbling and outward streaming, opposite the submerged southeast and south tunnels under the north lake could no longer be seen and occasionally a large fountain broke out and migrated to the bank in the northeastern part of the lake.

On August 22 the bench magma was slightly higher and from 6 to 8 p m. the northern flow was again gushing and streaming from the source cones, the lakes were all very bright and the north lake fountains were high and showed brilliantly above the rampart. The general situation indicated a recovery of the lake magma adjusted to the outflow at the new northern cones.

August 30, 1919.

During the week ending August 29, 1919, the only striking change at the Halemaumau center of activity of Kilauea volcano has been the cessation of intense fountaining at the source vents of the flow pouring from the Postal Rift region, and the transfer of such gushing to points farther west, the main stream feeding the front of the flow now travelling in an underground tube. This has been the usual history of such flows, the source region encrusting itself and forming a plateau covered with a heavy carapace from under the edge of which the moving fluid emerges.

The measurements for the six days August 22 to 28 have indicated that the lava column was essentially stationary. The main and north lakes were lower relative to their banks by about 3 feet on August 28 than on August 22 and the northern half of the bench magma showed elevation of something over one foot at the end of the interval as though the clogging effect of the restraint of the north flow by its incrustations were felt in the subterranean passages leading from Halemaumau. Otherwise there was no pronounced movement within the Halemaumau pit limits and the fluctuations of the lakes were small, the lake magma being in adjustment to the gas release of the Postal Rift overflows.

On Saturday, August 23, at 9:45 a. m. there were new spatter margins around the main lake, the liquid was level with them and spatter construction was in progress east and south. Streaming was eastward with bright lines between patches of skin. Occasionally strong fountaining would break out at the southeast bank releasing gas and lowering the lake. Considerable peninsulas of crust were built out into the meandering channel leading from the southwest lake so as to partly bridge the central pond region. The east bank of the main lake was 15 feet high and the cliffs about the lake were mostly 15 to 20 feet high. The highest cliff was towards the southwest, possibly 30 feet high. The lake was brimming hotly against the isthmus plains separating it from the south arm pond and in the latter the large dome grotto had somewhat changed its form, become partially submerged, and exhibited fountaining behind a curtained front. The activity of the lake indicated high gas pressure. A small crusted lava pond had formed in the tumbled debris of the northeast cove where a gulch floored with a jumble of rocks extended through to the north lake.

The adjustments of mass uplift of the lava column and upheaval of the northeast pressure ridge had now flattened the slope from the lake edge to the east cone, and at the same time the east bank of the lake now lay in full view of the hut and flow slope outside of Halemaumau to the northeast. This meant a restoration of the high dome of May 30, when a similar view of the whole northern floor of Kilauea crater was to be had from this point.

The north lake lay 8 to 10 feet below its rampart and was building spatter rims on the south, east and northwest. The Postal Rift cone was spurting from a small orifice and the flow heap near it was putting out live lava toes. The southwest lake was streaming slowly eastward through the narrows and had spells of breaking up and violent spraying fountains, when slight sinking occurred. This lake was very high, with a new flood plain around it which had buried the western scarp of the tilted plateau lying between this lake and the main lake. The rim cliff of Halemaumau bounding the southwest lake depression on its west side stood only 7 feet above the lake. The west pond flat showed no cone or other vent.

Examination of the south half of the Halemaumau dome surface discovered a large flat featureless area between the southwest lake and the serrate southern pressure ridge. From the south arm embayment of the main lake two large gulches had developed in place of the former crevasses, extending to the south ridge on either side of the wall-crack cone which now occupied the site of the former wall pond. This cone stood at the top of a low part of the ridge, the saddle where the cascades had poured down to build the southern flow heap. The cone consisted of four lumpy knobs each about 4 feet high with a pot in the middle where there was internal hissing and fuming and no visible live lava.

All along the inner side of the south pressure ridge the dome surface was a plateau, in places level with the top of the ridge, which could everywhere be easily reached by a climb of 10 or 15 feet, whereas the outer slope was over 40 feet high. The south arm pond was found to be circular and mostly crusted over, with occasional spells of breaking up and sinking.

The indications on this day showed strong gas pressure, high liquid lava, and some rising of bench magma. In the evening from 6 to 9 p. m. another very long and bright surface flow poured to the west from the Postal Rift. This August flow as a whole covered the floor of Kilauea crater northwest of Halemaumau out to the base of the Uwekahuna wall with deep filling for over a half mile along that wall; every evening for a week past there had been surface spurts adding layers to this flow, each spurt showing in plan the river and delta pattern. The whole area around the source cones had become an extensive plateau falling off to irregular ground with dome tumuli on the southwest, west and northwest. This evening was the last which showed violent surface flooding. The Postal Rift flow of April had shown the same characteristics, surface flooding at first, and flowing in tunnels thereafter.

On August 24 at 6 p. m. the bench magma was found stationary, the main lake high with eastward streaming and there was fountaining under the east bank and at the southwest grotto. The east bank stood about 12 feet above the liquid. The north lake stood about 8 feet below its bank and there were occasional breakings up of the surface accompanied with bubble fountaining. The most active border fountains were at the east end and there were flaming curtained grottoes at the northwest end. The Postal Rift flow area was flaming, puffing and making toes, but there was no strong surface flooding. In general the lava column appeared to be adjusting itself to the flowing conditions at the new vent so as to hold itself stationary.

On August 25 the bench magma continued stationary and the Postal Rift flow continued to push westward with out any specially bright streams. The fountains of both the main and north lakes could be seen splashing above the ramparts.

On Tuesday, August 26, at about 2:04 a. m. a local earthquake occurred, strongly felt in Hilo and in Kona and seismometrically registered at the Observatory. There was no special change at Halemaumau in the evening. Here and there brilliantly gushing vents broke out in the flow at points half way between the source cones and the west wall of Kilauea and the most conspicuous new arm of the flow lay on its northern side.

On August 27 the fume at Halemaumau was somewhat denser, the lava dome remained stationary and the flow had a spasm of renewal at 10 p. m. with gushing in its western and northern lobes.

On August 28, at 10 a. m., measurement indicated slight rising of the central and northern parts of Halemaumau but there was very little change in the main features of the pit. The main lake had constructed an inner bench which stood about 5 feet above the liquid, the older margin standing 12 feet above the lake at the east end. The streaming was sluggish eastward. The south arm pond was brightly active at times. The north lake showed a rampart edge about 9 feet high, the fountaining was moderate and ballooning skins formed on the surface. The southwest lake lay under an overhanging bench 10 feet high on the west pond side and here there was a tunnel beneath, out of which the lava flowed slowly from the direction of the west pond. The streaming in this lake was sluggish, partly southward and partly towards the main lake channel. The southern current ended at a fountaining grotto in the south arm of the lake.

The cones at the northern flow source were hissing and making gas spiracles and the top of the lava plateau west of the cones showed sweeping flat stream lines evidently over tunnels beneath which headed toward the west and northwest. There was some hissing through the heavy crusts over these tunnels, and here and there were hot semi-solidified puddles where new lava had welled up through cracks. In the evening a new northern lobe of the flow was glowing.

On Friday, August 29, there was no change in general situation, the lakes remained bright and the flow streams were far to the west, lighting up the Kilauea cliffs.

In the Whitney Laboratory of Seismology for the six weeks ending at 8 p. m., Friday, August 29, the registration of seismic events has been as follows:

For the week ending July 25 there were three local earthquakes respectively at 7:03 p. m. July 19 (slight); 6:30 p. m. July 20 (double shock); and 5:43 p. m. July 22. A slight teleseism was registered at 8:50 a. m. July 25. Spasmodic microtremor was slight, increasing somewhat July 21 to 23. The harmonic microtremor was also much less marked than before but became strongish July 22. Microseismic motion was very slight. Tilting of the ground was moderate to the west and south except on July 22 when it was to the east and north.

For the week ending August 1 there were five small local shocks as follows:

7:39 p. m. July 28; 11:05 p. m. July 29; 5:57 a. m. July 30; 8:06 p. m. July 31; 7:42 a. m. August 1. Spasmodic and harmonic microtremor were both moderate to slight, microseismic motion very slight. Tilting was to the north until July 29 with fluctuation in the east-west azimuth; July 30 to August 1 the tilting was slight and fluctuating.

For the week ending August 8 there were four local shocks as follows: 10:36 and 10:43 a. m. August 3; 7:53 a. m. and 3:43 p. m. (pronounced) August 4. Microtremor of both kinds was slight except August 6 and 8 when there were a few quick-period spasms. Microseismic motion continued very slight. Tilting continued to fluctuate through small angles, the tendency being mostly west and south with slight recoveries in the opposite directions August 3 and 5.

For the week ending August 15 there were six local shocks as follows: 9:33 p. m. (slight) August 12; 12:56 a. m. and 1:02 a. m. (both moderate) and 11:36 p. m. (double shock, slight) August 13; 11:37 a. m. (moderate) August 14; 2:12 a. m. (slight) August 15. Spasmodic microtremor tended to be very slight but there were strong spasms August 11, 14, and 15. Harmonic microtremor was slight to moderate. Microseismic motion increased from very slight to moderate in the course of the week. Tilting was strong to the south and west August 9, strongly east and north August 10-11 and nearly stationary thereafter.

For the week ending August 22 there was one slight local shock August 18 at 10:55 a. m. and a moderate distant earthquake was registered at 6:30 a. m. Spasmodic microtremor showed occasional strong spasms and the harmonic tremor was slight to moderate. Microseismic motion changed from moderate to very slight. Tilting was strongly east and north August 16-18 and strongly west and south after August 19.

For the week ending August 29 there was one moderate local shock at 2:04 a. m. August 26. Weak teleseisms occurred at 6:57 and 7:22 p. m. August 23, 2:23 a. m. August 24 and 7:50 p. m. August 28. Spasmodic microtremor became strong August 24 to 26 and showed strong spasms throughout the week. Harmonic microtremor also became strong after August 25. Microseismic motion was slight. Tilting showed mostly northward and eastward tendency, especially August 24.

Very respectfully,

T. A. JAGGAR, JR.,
Volcanologist.

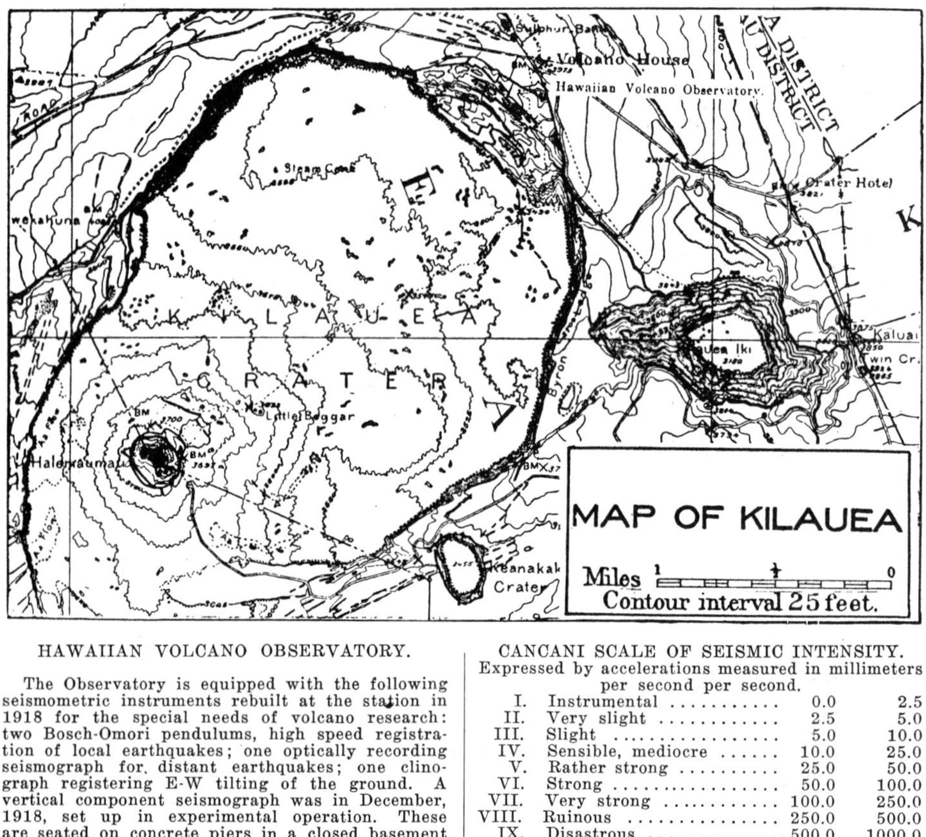

HAWAIIAN VOLCANO OBSERVATORY.

The Observatory is equipped with the following seismometric instruments rebuilt at the station in 1918 for the special needs of volcano research: two Bosch-Omori pendulums, high speed registration of local earthquakes; one optically recording seismograph for, distant earthquakes; one clinograph registering E-W tilting of the ground. A vertical component seismograph was in December, 1918, set up in experimental operation. These are seated on concrete piers in a closed basement room having practically constant temperature, beneath the chief Observatory building near the hotel. Time is referred to a rated chronometer, checked at intervals by solar observations with a transit. Both instruments are loaned by the College of Hawaii. Hawaiian standard time (H. S. T.) is 10 hrs. 30 min. slower than Greenwich time.

CANCANI SCALE OF SEISMIC INTENSITY.

Expressed by accelerations measured in millimeters per second per second.

I.	Instrumental	0.0	2.5
II.	Very slight	2.5	5.0
III.	Slight	5.0	10.0
IV.	Sensible, mediocre	10.0	25.0
V.	Rather strong	25.0	50.0
VI.	Strong	50.0	100.0
VII.	Very strong	100.0	250.0
VIII.	Ruinous	250.0	500.0
IX.	Disastrous	500.0	1000.0
X.	Very disastrous	10000.0	2500.0
XI.	Catastrophic	2500.0	5000.0
XII.	Great catastrophe	5000.0	10000.0

Grade IV. is ordinarily the minimum perceived by the senses; and in grade XII. the accelerations or rate of change of motion (jerk) reaches that of terrestrial gravitation.

In the standard form of report the maximum intensity or acceleration, designated by the symbol α, or max. α, is given in the conventional unit of milligal. The milligal is a measure of acceleration, such that 1 milligal = 1/100 mm. per sec. per sec. = 10 μ. per sec. per sec. The Cancani scale, here defined in terms of millimeters per sec. per sec., can therefore be expressed in milligals by multiplying each of the numbers by 100.

U. S. DEPARTMENT OF AGRICULTURE
WEATHER BUREAU
CHARLES F. MARVIN, CHIEF

MONTHLY BULLETIN
OF THE
Hawaiian Volcano Observatory

VOL. VII. HONOLULU, HAWAII, SEPTEMBER, 1919 No. 9

September 6, 1919.

Observations of the week ending Friday, September 5, 1919, at the inner center of lava activity of Kilauea volcano show a lowering of the lava dome over Halemaumau by a small amount, a nearly stationary condition of the liquid lava of the lakes, and continued flowing of the stream pouring out on the floor of Kilauea crater from the Postal Rift. The appearance of the lakes and crags has changed but little, smoke has slightly increased, and the glowing portions of the flow in visible motion have been altogether along the base of the western wall of Kilauea, where elongate streams have pushed northward under the Uwekahuna summit.

Measurements for the eight days August 28 to September 5 have shown that the lake margins and crag blocks of bench magma of the central region have subsided about 3 feet, the high ground north of the north lake about 4 feet, and the island remnant of the southeast crag about 8 feet. The region of Halemaumau margin west and north which was recently uplifted has sunk about 1 foot, but the east and south sides have been stationary. The lakes at the end of the week appeared, with reference to their containing basins, about 3 feet higher than at the beginning of the interval, which would mean that they are stationary as referred to fixed bench marks.

On Saturday, August 30, the bench magma was slightly lower. At 2 p. m. no changes were noticeable at the south wall cone. There was some increased sulphur fume at the east cone. The main lake continued its eastward streaming and its surface appeared low, with 30-foot rampart on the east and 12-foot inner rampart south. The north lake also appeared low with rampart wall 15 feet high and some strong fountaining near the northeast bank. Both the main and north lakes were covered with soft skins in patches, separated by bright lines. The southwest lake was high relative to its ramparts at 3 p. m., the confining walls being 6 feet high, and there was sluggish streaming eastward through the narrows leading to main lake.

The Postal Rift flow cone was hissing, and a slow flow had welled up through the top of the lava heap near the cones and south of them. A heavy shower made dense masses of vapor rise from the flow area, much denser in the western part where the surface heat was greater. The cross-section of the whole flow consists of a flat plateau near the cones, a much swollen irregular slope next to the west, and a flat pooled area under the Kilauea cliffs farther west, with flows making out at the edges. The ancient ash section at the base of the Uwekahuna wall was now nearly covered up by the new fill. In the evening, there was increase of flowing both at the source cones and farther west. In the north lake there was notably more yellow and less red in the fountain glow than in the main lake.

On August 31 at 3 p. m. fountains were vigorous in the main and north lakes, some of those in the north lake being 12 to 15 feet high and very large. Currents were slight except in the south arm pond, where there was streaming through a tunnel from the main lake, the current carrying crust fragments on its surface and exhibiting bubble fountains playing continuously, each about a foot high. The north lake stood 20 feet below its north bank. Fumes were abundant. The general situation was stationary, and the Postal Rift flow made bright streams in the evening both near the source cone and in a long lobe moving northward at the base of Uwekahuna bluff.

On September 1 stationary conditions continued and at 11 a. m. the main lake was 25 feet below its eastern bank and about 8 feet below its inner rampart, this being the level of the flats separating the lake from the south pond. Streaming was eastward through the channel leading from southwest lake, there were bright lines and ballooning skins, and large fountains broke out occasionally near the east bank. There was no specially marked border fountaining. Subsidence by gas release occurred after a spell of fountaining.

The upper rampart bank of the north lake was the level of recent overflow. The plane of this bank was now tilted relative to the lake level from southeast to northwest, the eastern bank being 15 feet high and the northwestern bank 8 feet high at the most. The cliff on the southeast side appeared as though it were arched higher than the rest. The activity was marked by alternate spells of central fountaining and quiet crusting. All the time four or five border fountains along the northern shore suggested considerable gas pressure. During a central outbreak four or five large fountains were seen in action at once, producing marginal subsidence of about 2 feet and revealing a tunnel under the bank at the south gulch. There was some tendency to ballooning skins and traces of streaming toward the north and northeast.

The Postal Rift flow cones were hissing and stained with solfataric deposits, and sulphur patches had developed southeast of them. The flow was making slender arms northward along the base of Uwekahuna.

Examination of the April flow cone and tunnel showed that the lower stretches of collapsed tunnel northwest and west were now obliterated by the new flow. There remained one upper opening, no longer very hot, into which the wind was blowing toward the source cone, and dense white water vapor arose from the cone. At the cone vent of July 27, farther east, there was a large collapsed dome area with much hot air rising, but no glow or gas pressure. The new flow surfaces between these two earlier cone sources were becoming stained with fume action from the Postal Rift cracks beneath.

On September 2 there were no changes and the pushing fronts of the flow made bright reflections on the extreme southwestern wall of Kilauea as well as under Uwekahuna.

On September 3 at 4 p. m., after heavy rains, there was increase of water vapor and summit fume from the Halemaumau dome. At the south wall cone lava could be heard bubbling beneath. The grotto dome at the south arm pond was found still large, and the pond lay 10 feet below the bank, with fluid surface and not much fountaining. A new smoke-hole had developed at the east-northeast pressure ridge. At the main lake the east wall was 40 feet high and the inner bench 10 feet high on the norh side and 20 feet high on the south side. The lake was crusted over, but streaming under the bank could be seen at the southeast and northeast corners. The north lake appeared higher, with numerous fountains along its north bank and a large central fountain near the northeast shore. The banks were from 10 to 20 feet high. The southwest lake had marginal benches 10 to 30 feet high and appeared rather low. Like the main lake, it was crusted over. There was a bridge of crust across the channel leading to the central pond, and under this appeared a cavern 10 feet high hung with stalactites. The Postal Rift flow cone hissed loudly from one orifice only, and in the evening the flow was vigorous towards the northwest and north. The general situation indicated some sinking, and slackening in the flow.

This was confirmed by the measurements of September 4, which indicated slow lowering of the bench magma, and smoke had increased at the central gulches. There was no notable change on Friday, September 5, but the flow remained bright when it was seen in evening light, and continued to spread northward in two or more narrow streams moving parallel to each other until they had passed the base of the cliff immediately under the Uwekahuna summit signal post.

In the Whitney Laboratory of Seismology during the week ending at 8 p. m., September 5, there was one local earthquake shock slightly felt here at 11:44 p. m., August 31. A slight teleseism occurred at 2:17 p. m., August 30, and another with more pronounced phases at 6:58 a. m., August 31, indicating a strong earthquake at a distance about 4085 kilometers from the station. Spasmodic microtremor alternated from moderate to strong during the week, and the harmonic tremor from slight to moderate. Microseismic motion slightly increased, but remained weak. The tilting of the ground was south and west until August 31, when it changed to north and east and remained so, the north-south component showing throughout the week more tilting than the east-west.

September 13, 1919.

During the week ending Friday, September 12, 1919, the motion of the lava column in Halemaumau crater has continued to be a slow subsidence of the bench magma compensated at the end of the week by slight rising of the lakes relative to their banks. The only notable change of activity was an increase of subsidence of the liquid lava relative to the containing basins, September 10 and 11, whereby there was established an inrush from both the north and main lakes to a sinkhole under the smoking central gulches. At the main lake this phenomenon resembled the initial stages of the cascade, which during a period of subsidence was so conspicuous a feature in June last. Smoke during the week has been on the increase at Halemaumau. The Postal Rift flow has continued its progress under Uwekahuna, the source cone hissing continuously, and bright yellow sulphur patches developing at the source region.

Measurements for the seven days September 5 to 12 have indicated a stationary condition of the south pressure ridge, a lowering of the west rim about two feet, of the north rim flag one foot, and of the new flow plateau surrounding the live flow cones two to three feet. All of these subsided points are places upheaved or upbuilded by the movement which inaugurated the flow, so that their lowering implies a waning of that force. Within the interior of Halemaumau the crag blocks around the lakes have sunk from three to five feet in the center and about two feet in the outlying floors south, east and north. Until September 11 the lakes also sank even more than the crags, but on September 12 they had recovered about five feet.

On Saturday, September 6, at 11 a. m., the main lake showed a quiet surface, eastward streaming and apparently rising activity. There was much smoke from the marginal benches and the central gulches. At the wall crack east-northeast there was new development of smoke acrid with sulphur. The north lake was high relative to its marginal cliffs and its newer inner rampart was being overflowed at the northwest corner of the lake. The lake surface was inflated, and there were several border fountains. The Postal Rift cone was hissing, there was much sulphur in the vicinity, and under Uwekahuna bluff the flow continued its progress.

From 3 to 5 p. m., September 7, there was slight lowering by measurement and little apparent change. The smoke was dense at the central gulches. The main lake was streaming eastward without much fountaining and some activity at its southwest grotto. The north lake had been comparatively high, building grotto domes at its northwest corner; it was now mostly quiet, with some founaining towards the east. The Postal Rift flow cone showed one small hissing spiracle, and the flow in the tunnel beneath continued to pour westward. The southwest lake appeared rather low, its surface streaming sweeping toward the tunnel that leads to the central channel. Against the south side of this tunnel a rhythmic fountain burst occasionally. At the west pond locality a few yards west of the southwest lake there was a tumbled depression yielding much smoke. There was also smoke at the south cone wall-crack of the pressure ridge.

On September 8 at 2:30 p. m. the main lake showed much disturbance of its surface currents. Streaming was now westward from the south pond tunnel at the southeast corner of the lake in a curved zone leading to the southwest grotto. Another current took its rise at the central canyon and swept in a curve toward the northeast and against the middle of the north bank of the lake. The northeast cove was stagnant. There had been some recent undermining by fall of banks in the central channel so that an unstable crag was protruding and overhanging the channel on its south side. The lake appeared rather low, with inner benches 15 feet high, and the confining wall of older rampart 30 feet high at the east end. The north lake was crusted over except for the usual fountain near the northeast bank. The eastern wall overhung the lake and was 15 feet high. Spatter domes had been built at the northwest corner. Portions of the heavy crust were heaving under gas pressure, lines of flame were hissing through cracks, and a break-up was imminent.

On Tuesday and Wednesday, September 9 and 10, there was at first little change, fume increased, and the flow continued its progress along the base of both the southwest and west walls of Kilauea. On September 10 the subsidence of the lakes increased, the overhanging crag south of the central channel fell, and numerous falls were reported in the evening.

On September 11 at 10:30 a. m. this sinking spell had re-established a marked inrush to two tunnels at the northeast corner of the main lake. This resembled the June cascade, but if a cassade existed, it was hidden. All that could be seen was a steady current which affected the whole lake, increasing at the northeast cove to a torrent moving about 10 miles per hour into holes in the bank without fountaining. The lake was covered with skins and bright lines. Blowing noises could be heard from the south arm pond. The rampart walls confining the main lake were 30 to 40 feet high on the east, 15 feet high on the south and 10 feet high under the north cliff. The south island cliff stood 40 feet above the lake; the south, southeast and northeast cliffs 50 feet, and the cliff west of the central pool 60 feet.

The north lake also was streaming steadily toward a central sinkhole in the region of the same gulch that received the main lake inrush. Where this gulch abutted on the north lake there was a steady streaming southward under the bank without fountaining. Otherwise the north lake exhibited three active border grottoes along its northwest shore, the surface currents migrating towards them. There was a quiet tunnel under the south gulch. East and northeast the lake was crusted. The east bank was about 18 feet high, the north bank 15 feet and the northwest rampart only 4 feet high. The south cliffs, through which the two gulches were trenched, stood 50 feet above the lake.

The Postal Rift flow cone continued its hissing, the flow moving at the fronts a mile or so from Halemaumau both to the northwest and southwest, and three sulphur patches had developed near the source cones.

On Friday, September 12, at 6:30 p. m., after considerable rain, the new smoke hole at the east-northeast wall crack was bubbling noisily with a deep, thudding sound and emitting much smoke with sulphur odor but no glow. In the afternoon during a lull in the rains, great quantities of water vapor were seen rising over the whole area covered by the 1919 flows, with greatest volume above the live western lobes of the present time. In the morning there had been a calm spell, when the vapor rose from the Halemaumau dome, dense below, thinning to a narrow stem, and bulging out above in a flower-like form, both the lower and upper parts appearing to be water vapor.

At both main and north lakes the inrushing torrents had stopped. Both appeared about five feet higher. The main lake was mostly covered with quiet ballooning skin, but there was a bright area streaming eastward, in a curve from the central channel to the southwest grotto. The central pool was crusted over. There was fountaining in the south arm pond.

In the debris of the northeast cove gulch two open pots were flaming and rumbling. The north lake had six border fountains northwest and north, large northeast occasional fountains, and the crusts were cracking and foundering. The southwest lake was occasionally very bright.

For the week ending at 8 p. m., Friday, September 12, 1919, no earthquakes have been registered in the Whitney Laboratory of Seismology. Spasmodic microtremor has diminished during the week from moderately strong to slight. The harmonic microtremor has been mostly slight. Microseismic motion has been very slight. Tilting of the ground was to the west and north September 6, nearly stationary September 7 to 9, south and west September 10 to 11, and southeast September 12.

September 20, 1919.

The principal seismo-volcanic event of importance at Kilauea volcano during the week ending September 19, 1919, was a strong earthquake which occurred at 5:20 p. m. on September 14. This was a prolonged twisting movement felt generally throughout the Island of Hawaii and slightly felt on Maui and Oahu. The maximum damage yet reported appears to have been in the Kau section, where chimneys fell and walls cracked, making the intensity approximately No. 8 of the Rossi-Forel scale. At Hilo also, objects were thrown down and much glass broken. At Kilauea crater there was strong swaying of hanging objects and a slow cumulative twisting movement which stopped a clock having torsional pendulum escapement. Rock slides were started, notably strong at the north wall of Kilauea Iki. A fairly complete record was written by the seismographs, and as in the case of some former local earthquakes registered here, the movement of the ground continued for over an hour in slow-period swayings strongly suggesting a teleseism. A similar effect was registered by Dr. Romberg in Honolulu. That the earthquake was of deep origin was indicated by the swarm of felt after-shocks which continued, gradually decreasing, for twenty-two hours at Hilea. A second strong local shock was registered at the Observatory in the very early morning of September 18 (3:37 a. m.).

The occurrence of these earthquakes with maximum effect between Kilauea and Mauna Loa and just before the equinox points toward the probability of an equinoxial volcanic crisis. Nothing, however, has occurred at Halemaumau which as yet gives evidence of what the change is to be. There was some increased gushing of the Postal Rift flow and simultaneous temporary sinking of the lava lakes during the evening of September 14.

The measurements of vertical movement of the upper surface of the Halemaumau lava column during the seven days ending September 19 indicated a slight subsidence September 12 to 15 and slight rising thereafter, the net result being a lowering of the central bench magma blocks adjacent to the lakes by one or two feet and a stationary condition elsewhere. The lake lava remained essentially stationary except for the usual daily fluctuations. The volume of flowing at the Postal Rift increased.

On Saturday, September 13, there was nothing new at Halemaumau. The bench magma was slightly falling, fume was pronounced from vents in the center, east, west, and south, and there was much vapor at the flow sources. A very smooth pool in the flow area between Halemaumau and Uwekahuna appeared to be a place of stagnant liquid lava with cracking and foundering crusts.

After the earthquake of September 14, observations of Halemaumau from 9:30 to 10 p. m. showed all the lava lakes falling rapidly, leaving a bright red margin over 10 feet deep. This was followed by landslips and caving in of lake ramparts. There was much rush of gas in the gulch north of the northeast cove of the main lake. The Postal Rift flow showed new gas pressure and new live lobes.

On September 15 from 4 to 5 p. m. the lakes appeared higher than on the previous day and the fumes rose densely from numerous vents. New cracks had developed at the south wall crack cone, and a new live vent was hissing and flaming there several feet west of the former center of activity. Two other live wall-crack vents had developed at the east cone and in the east-northeast pressure ridge, with rumbling and splashing lava beneath the surface and much flame and smoke. Smoke was issuing from several vents along the base of the northeast ridge.

The main lake was streaming sluggishly eastward with quiet wrinkled crust. The south pond grotto was more active, and a current flowed southward from the tunnel leading from the main lake. Dense fume rose at the northeast cove, and the east marginal cliff was 24 feet high. There were signs of slumping around the north lake margins, and along the north and northwest side the bank in several places was only 4 feet high. There were two persistent fountains in this lake.

The source cones of the Postal Rift flow were noisy and smoky, and at night the flow showed several bright patches under Uwekahuna.

On September 16 at 3 p. m. there was less fume from Halemaumau, but the lakes appeared four or five feet lower relative to their banks. The east wall of the main lake was 28 feet high, and the north lake stood 9 feet below its northwest bank. There was smoke from several vents along the south wall-crack. The east cone and the east-northeast wall-crack vent were both alive with much rumbling, hissing, flaming and fuming, and the lava could be heard splashing below. The main lake was streaming rapidly eastward, and there was molten lava in the bottom of the northeast cove extension. Central fountains formed in the lake and migrated to the east bank. The south pond was crusted over and quiet. In the north lake there were two continuous fountains. One of the source cones of the Postal Rift flow continued actively hissing and flaming, and this was extended along a red-hot crack south of the cone.

At 4 p. m. on September 17 the lakes appeared higher and the fumes moderate. The lava boiling beneath the east cone occasionally threw out spatter driblets, and the east-northeast vent was rumbling and fuming. The south pond was quiet except for some hissing of gas along the base of its north bank. The eastward streaming in the main lake was sluggish and one fountain was seen in the channel leading from the central pool. The east bank of the lake was about 20 feet high. There were four fountains in the north lake, which stood 4 feet below its northwest bank. The southwest lake was crusted over and quiet. The activity of the Postal Rift cone was accompanied by considerable noise and smoke, and the flow continued spreading to the west.

On September 18 at 4 p. m. the main lake was about 25 feet below its east rampart, grottoes were active south of the central channel and in the south arm pond, and the eastward streaming was barely perceptible. The east cone continued its flaming and rumbling, but the east-northeast vent was less active. The ground between the east cone and the south arm pond was in motion. The north lake crust appeared higher on the south side than on the north, and four grottoes were active along the northern banks. The crack extending southeast from the Postal Rift cone was hissing loudly.

On September 19 at 2 p. m. the lakes were higher, the fume moderate, and the eastern cones as before. Only one fountain was seen in the main lake, which stood 20 feet below the east rampart. Large fountains were playing in the south pond. The north lake was so high that its lava had overflowed the northwestern bank and drowned two spatter grottoes seen there the day before. Two fountains were in action in the center of the lake and three along the banks. The gas pressure at the Postal Rift cones was increasing, as were also the flows under Uwekahuna.

In the Whitney Laboratory of Seismology a very strong local earthquake was registered at 5:19 p. m., September 14, followed by two after-shocks within an hour. The optical instrument indicated swayings of the ground for over an hour. After-shocks felt in Hilea, and recorded by Miss Zalida de la Nux, were as follows:

September 14, 5:35 p. m., light, lasting 2 seconds.

September 14, 5:45 p. m., medium, lasting 3 seconds.

September 14, 5:55 p. m., medium, lasting two seconds.

September 14, 6:28 p. m., heavy, lasting 3 seconds.

September 14, 6:43 p. m., light.

September 14, 6:45 p. m., light.

September 14, 6:58 p. m., light.

September 14, 7:05 p. m., light.

September 14, 7:07 p. m., medium, lasting 1 second.

August 17, 1919. Lava gushing from new Postal Rift vents (liquid lava on the right). —Photos Jaggar.

August 17, 1919. New flood of lava, looking west; tilted bench-mark in foreground.

August 17, 1919. Transit shelter and sleeping tent used in lava-tide measurements for one month.

August 18, 1919. The North Lake in front of transit shelter.

September 14, 8:08 p. m., light.
September 14, 8:23 p. m., light.
September 14, 9:31 p. m., light.
September 14, 9:39 p. m., light.
September 14, 10:03 p. m., light.
Other light shocks during the night.
September 15, 4:27 a. m., light.
September 15, 6:49 a. m., medium, lasting 2 seconds.
September 15, 11:06 a. m., light.
September 15, 3:13 p. m., light.

At 3:37 a. m., September 18, there was another strong local shock and two others in the course of thirty seconds. A distant earthquake was registered at 2:35 a. m., September 13, of apparently very remote origin. The spasmodic microtremor showed tendency to few and strongish spasms at the beginning and towards the end of the week, and was only slightly in evidence September 16 and 17. The harmonic tremor, at all times slight, increased a little after September 15. Microseismic motion increased somewhat until September 17 and decreased thereafter. The tilting of the ground had southwesterly tendency until September 14; at the time of the earthquake there was an apparent shift of the pendulums, indicating strong north and east tilt, which continued September 15 and 16, and thereafter the ground remained stationary.

September 27, 1919.

An outbreak of Mauna Loa about three miles south-southwest of the southernmost pit of Mokuaweoweo at 6 p. m., September 26, revealed the meaning of the equinoxial volcanic crisis mentioned in the Bulletin a week ago. The strong earthquakes of September 14 and 18, the sudden short-lived subsidence of the Halemaumau lakes on September 14, the increase of flowing at the Postal Rift, and the strong northeast tilt of September 14-16 were now accounted for. Probably a deep rending open of the Mauna Loa rift system occurred during the earthquakes and the rising wedge of gas-charged melt attained a first explosive release of its gases September 26.

The main characteristic of the activity of the Kilauea lava column during the week has been a greatly augmented volume of flowing in the flow pouring from the Postal Rift source cones northward along the base of the Uwekahuna bluff. At one time this increase was sufficient to revive the incandescence of the flow all the way from the source cones to the front, and also to produce surface spouting from a new oven opened on top of the flow a few hundred feet west of the source vents. It must be remembered that such increase of flowing is the only measure of rising available at a time when the pit is full to the brim as at present. The activity of the week, therefore, would have been recorded as intense rising if the liquid lava had been confined within a deep pit as in former years. On the day of actual Mauna Loa outbreak there was irregular disturbance in Halemaumau, reversed streaming in the main lake, with strong fountaining and sinking bench magma, all of this having begun about September 23.

The measurements of the week indicated that the blocks of bench magma between the lakes rose about 2 feet between September 19 and September 22, and thereafter subsided from 3 to 6 feet September 23-26. The subsidence was greater in the central region and less toward the old Halemaumau border. Along with this subsidence increased smokiness occurred, westward streaming and some tumbling of talus blocks.

At 11 a. m., Saturday, September 20, all the lakes appeared higher and the fumes were thinner. Lava was bubbling noisily beneath the east cone, the splashes rising nearly to the orifice. The second rumbling vent farther north was quieter and emitted very little smoke. The liquid of the main lake stood 15 feet below the lower part of the eastern ledge and some 5 feet higher than on the previous day. The streaming was eastward, and two large fountains were in action. In the south pond there were no fountains, and the currents there were various.

The north lake was high, overflowing the gentle slope back of its northwest rampart. Six border fountains were in action along the northwest, west and southwest margins. At the Postal Rift source a new cone had formed, and the flow was spreading both eastward and southward.

On September 21 at 6 p. m. inspection of the south pressure ridge showed no marked change during the last week. The flaming and bubbling orifice of the east cone was a crack south of the cone proper. The wall-crack vent east-northeast was much stained and fuming. The main lake was quiet and crusted. There was glow in the southern grotto of the south arm pond, and a flaming chimney occupied the edge of the cliff west of the pond. The north lake showed cracking and foundering crusts, some small border fountains and occasional migratory central fountains in the northeastern region which moved toward the northeast bank. There was no change in the general height of the lake, its marginal cliff standing 10 to 15 feet above the liquid at the east and about 5 feet at the west.

Comparison of the Postal Rift cones with their appearance a week previous indicated greatly increased blowing and flaming, as new flaring cracks had opened on both the north and south sides of the northernmost of the two active cones. The flow from these cones was now very extensive and was alive along the base of the Uwekahuna bluff from a point nearly west of Halemaumau to a point midway between Uwekahuna and the north corner of Kilauea crater. An eastern arm of the flow was making out in the direction of the Volcano House trail.

The southwest lake and west pond pot were both brightly incandescent, the lake showing tendency to crust over and to rise at the time of visit. The west pot was flaming brightly. The southwest lake appeared higher than it was the week before.

On September 22, at 11 a. m., a circuit of the pit by the south and west sides revealed an active grotto in the southeast corner of the southwest lake, southward streaming in the south cove of the lake, and a level somewhat lower than on the previous day. The north lake was dull, crusted over and unchanged. The main lake was streaming slowly eastward from the central channel without much fountaining. Dense smoke rose from the summit crevasses between the main and north lakes, and the lava in the east cone vent was still pounding vigorously.

Northwest of Halemaumau, and midway between the north station and the west wall of Kilauea, live tongues of lava were found breaking out from the crust of the great flow by way of a cone formed there. A short distance south of this cone one of the tubes in the flow was found broken down, revealing in the interior cavity live gas spiracles and glow in the cracks.

At 8 p. m. the main lake was dull and there was some streaming through the central channel eastward from the southwest lake. The south wall-crack chasm at the top of the pressure ridge was glowing and fuming. Streaming in the south arm pond was southward, and the surface of the pond rose and fell at intervals, while from time to time strong fountaining and flaming would increase under and adjacent to the large south grotto dome. The lakes were sufficiently high to make the north lake fountains visible from the Observatory.

On September 24 at 12:15 p. m. a southeasterly wind made the usual approaches to the lakes very fumy. The south arm pond was lower streaming against its northwest bank, where there was violent fountaining and rumbling. There was also some fountaining in its south grotto dome. The main lake was streaming outward from its southeast corner and thence westward to a line of continuous border fountains under the southwest bank. Here there was noisy rumbling. This westward streaming in these two pools accompanied a lowering of the lake whereby the wall at the east end was 28 feet high, and the southern overflow bench 10 feet high. In the northeast cove there was some streaming under the bank. On account of the changed wind, the north lake could not be seen from its east brink because of excessive fume, but noisy rumbling fountains could be heard. The east cone vent was lower and less bright.

The Postal Rift flows were pushing far to the north along the base of the Uwekahuna wall with marked increase in the rate of lengthening northward, and the whole stretch of the flow from head to foot glowed brilliantly.

On September 25 at 3:30 p. m. there was much smoke from the border cracks and central crevasses of Halemaumau. The surface of the cliff blocks in the central region had lowered from 1 to 3 feet. The lakes appeared relatively high, especially the north lake and south arm pond. Streaming in the main lake was from the central channel to the southeast corner, and the strong fountaining along the southwest bank continued. The east bank was about 22 feet high. The south arm pond was crusted over, but a fountain was puffing from under the crust of the south grotto dome. The north lake was crusted over except for some fountaining at the northeast border, the east bank 8 feet high, and the northwest bank 2 feet high.

The main Postal Rift source cone appeared enlarged with a glowing slot in its summit. The flow seen in plan, looking down upon it from the northern end of Uwekahuna bluff, was extremely brilliant for its entire length. The flow lay against the base of the bluff on its west side, but on its east side it was sending out some ten tongues, beginning at the Postal Rift region and repeating these tongues all the way to the north end of Kilauea crater. The southern part of this great lava pudding, near the source cones, appeared just as bright as the extreme northern front. The whole mass glowed through hundreds of cracks, and live toes were pushing out all the way from the source region to the frontal lobes. In this respect the present activity of this flow differed from that of the later stages of the April flow and appeared to have a marked renewal of gas pressure to feed it.

From 7:30 to 10 p. m. on Friday, September 26, very dense fume was rising at the summit crevasses of Halemaumau. The main lake was streaming west from its east bank, the latter about 20 feet high, there were six vigorous border fountains, and the south bank of the lake was only 6 feet high. The northeast cove exhibited a flaming and fountaining pot at the entrance to the northeast gulch. Fountaining was strong in the south pond. The east cone was rumbling and hissing, and there was evidence of subsidence in the adjacent blocks. Some rocks were heard falling on the northeast ridge. The east-northeast vent at the south end of this ridge was making dense acrid fume.

The north lake appeared higher relative to its banks as though the benches had slumped, and a large east-west crevasse north of the lake had opened until it was 10 feet wide. The east rampart bench was broken and showed motion. This bank stood 8 feet above the lake; the cliff south of the north lake was 45 feet high. The fountains could be plainly seen from Volcano House, and the lake stood only 3 feet below its northwest bank.

At the Postal Rift source region, the southern cone had broken in on its south side so as to make a window revealing the bright yellow glowing interior of the cupola beneath where the lava boiled up to feed the flow. The liquid lay about 15 feet below and was streaming into tubes toward the southwest and northwest. Out of the window rose a banner of flame. There were other flaming cracks and hissing mouths at the northern cone. At 10 p. m. a cone midway between Halemaumau and the west wall of Kilauea burst open and made a very brilliant display of surface flowing, this flood pouring out toward Uwekahuna. All night long the flowing was strong and extended along the base of the bluff all the way to the north wall of Kilauea.

In the early evening of this day, September 26, a thin mantle of clouds, with clear sunset sky above, lay over Mauna Loa as seen from the Observatory. On the left the new moon was sinking in the western sky. Enough of the outline of the mountain could be seen to locate the summit. At 5:50 p. m. an explosion cloud from the upper part of the southern Mauna Loa rift punctured this veil and sent up the familiar "cauliflower" puffs or volutes of a volcanic eruption. This vapor against the light of the setting sun had chocolate-colored edges of smoky aspect, in marked contrast to the normal clouds, while the lower rising billows had a terracotta color, due either to transmitted sunlight or the luminosity of the eruption beneath. The point of explosion was practically due west of the Observatory, corresponding to the group of large cones which lies about three and a half miles southwest of the center of Mokuaweoweo. By 6:15 p. m. it was evident that there were two distinct columns side by side and perhaps a mile or so apart, just as there had been in the similar high outbreak of the morning of May 19, 1916. The culminating height of the explosion was reached at 6:30 p. m., when the top of the jet was estimated to stand 7000 feet above its base. Up to this time the northern column had seemed the stronger of the two, rising higher than the southern. Their color was now a bright orange red.

At 6:40 p. m. the sky was nearly dark except for the sinking moon on the left, and the fume stood in two pink columns, the southern one now the stronger. The explosion was now waning, and a thin ring halo of extraneous vapor encircled the two volcanic jets extending farther to the south than to the north. The jets were still boiling up in "cauliflowers," while the evening clouds on the mountain beneath had increased and obscured the mountain profile. There was evidently little wind at the scene of the eruption, the columns rising nearly vertical, and only a light air drawing out the halo toward the south, giving the whole outline something of a mushroom effect. At 7 p. m. the pile of vapor had ordinary cumulus form, lighted a pale rose color by the gushing lava foam which was flowing at the vent under the explosion clouds.

The presence of the lava was unquestionable, as the glow of the eruption was bright until midnight, and an investigation five days later by the writer revealed the presence of fresh small flows around these orifices.

At 10 p. m. the mountain was clear and only one fume jet could be seen, this apparently the upper or northern one of the two previously in action. Below this and south of it there was considerable diffuse glow, probably from the short frothy flows then spreading about the vent, the fume rising from a fountaining orifice. The glow diminished after midnight, and at 3 a. m. was no longer visible. This first eruption was very short-lived, for no fume was visible next day and in later investigations no glow was again seen at this vent.

The only local earthquakes registered in the Whitney Laboratory for the week ending at 8 p. m., September 26, 1919, occurred on September 26, the day of the Mauna Loa outbreak. These were slight, occurring at 2:20 and 2:34 p. m., and five very slight shocks at other times. The spasmodic type of microtremor was feeble except for a few strong spasms September 22 to 23 and several strong spasms September 26. The harmonic slower microtremor was slight to moderate. Microseismic motion continued very weak. The tilting of the ground was to the east September 20, west September 21, increasingly strong to the south September 22 to 24, changing to north and east September 25-26.

Very respectfully,

T. A. JAGGAR, JR.,
Volcanologist.

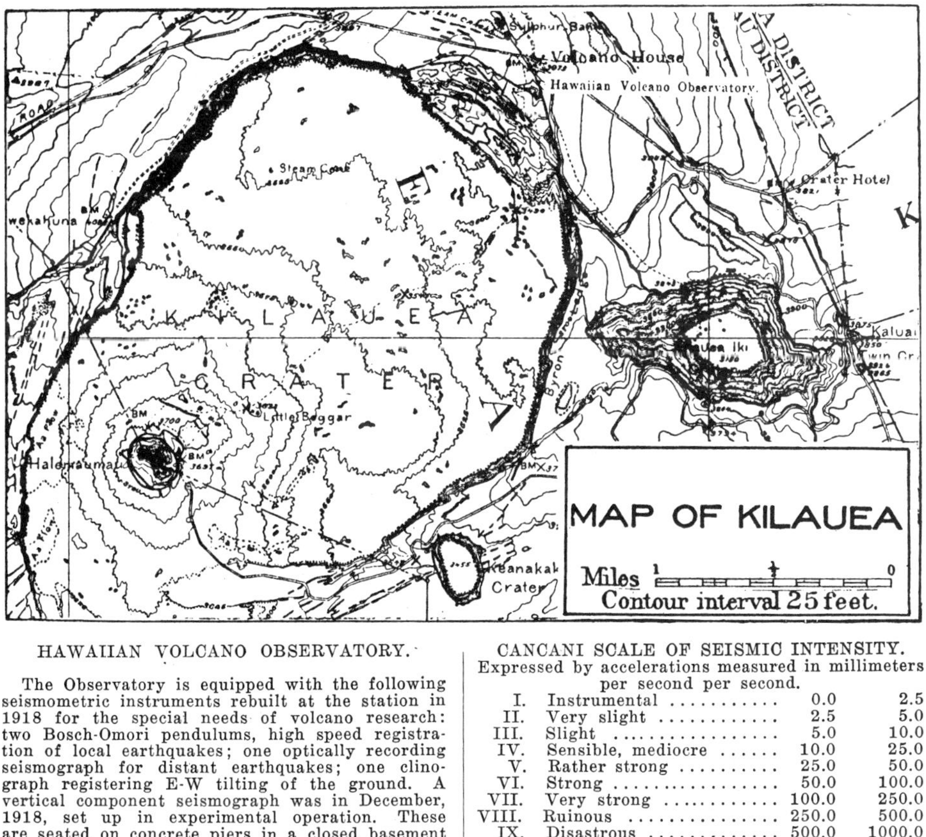

HAWAIIAN VOLCANO OBSERVATORY.

The Observatory is equipped with the following seismometric instruments rebuilt at the station in 1918 for the special needs of volcano research: two Bosch-Omori pendulums, high speed registration of local earthquakes; one optically recording seismograph for distant earthquakes; one clinograph registering E-W tilting of the ground. A vertical component seismograph was in December, 1918, set up in experimental operation. These are seated on concrete piers in a closed basement room having practically constant temperature, beneath the chief Observatory building near the hotel. Time is referred to a rated chronometer, checked at intervals by solar observations with a transit. Both instruments are loaned by the College of Hawaii. Hawaiian standard time (H. S. T.) is 10 hrs. 30 min. slower than Greenwich time.

CANCANI SCALE OF SEISMIC INTENSITY.

Expressed by accelerations measured in millimeters per second per second.

I.	Instrumental	0.0	2.5
II.	Very slight	2.5	5.0
III.	Slight	5.0	10.0
IV.	Sensible, mediocre	10.0	25.0
V.	Rather strong	25.0	50.0
VI.	Strong	50.0	100.0
VII.	Very strong	100.0	250.0
VIII.	Ruinous	250.0	500.0
IX.	Disastrous	500.0	1000.0
X.	Very disastrous	10000.0	2500.0
XI.	Catastrophic	2500.0	5000.0
XII.	Great catastrophe	5000.0	10000.0

Grade IV. is ordinarily the minimum perceived by the senses; and in grade XII. the accelerations or rate of change of motion (jerk) reaches that of terrestrial gravitation.

In the standard form of report the maximum intensity or acceleration, designated by the symbol a, or max. a, is given in the conventional unit of milligal. The milligal is a measure of acceleration, such that 1 milligal = 1/100 mm. per sec. per sec. = 10 μ. per sec. per sec. The Cancani scale, here defined in terms of millimeters per sec. per sec., can therefore be expressed in milligals by multiplying each of the numbers by 100.

U. S. DEPARTMENT OF AGRICULTURE
WEATHER BUREAU
CHARLES F. MARVIN, CHIEF

MONTHLY BULLETIN
OF THE
Hawaiian Volcano Observatory

VOL. VII. HONOLULU, HAWAII, OCTOBER, 1919 No. 10

October 4, 1919.

The week ending October 3, 1919, was characterized on Hawaii by a further outbreak of Mauna Loa with extensive lava flow from a source on the west side of the high Kahuku lands of the District of Kau and about 11 miles south-southwest of the point of outbreak of September 26. The new eruption was first seen from the Observatory location about 1:45 a. m. September 29. The source is a rift line trending S. 35° W., about half a mile to the west of the line of the 1916 rift, five miles above or north of the main 1916 source cone, and at an elevation approximately 7700 feet above sea level. As this was on the Kona flank of the mountain, a steep forested slope, the lava flood quickly descended and in twenty-four hours reached the sea along a curved path, first southwest, then west-southwest, 14 miles long. It crossed the Kona highway, twelve miles from the source, at 9:30 p. m. on the day of the outbreak, September 29, and reached the sea in the early morning hours September 30. The lands traversed are Kahuku, Kipahoehoe and Alika and the point of entry into the ocean lies two miles north of the landing at Hoopuloa village. The rate of travel of the flow from source to road measured as a smooth curve on the map was 0.6 mile per hour; the measured rate in the steep forest lands above the road about 6 p. m. September 29, according to R. McWayne, was one mile per hour. This eruption and its flowing torrent has continued throughout the week. The source fountains were reached and photographed by the writer October 1.

The changes observed at Halemaumau during this week amounted chiefly to continued subsidence of bench magma and lava lakes and some slackening of the Postal Rift flow in Kilauea crater. There was increase of fume and slight sliding of rocks, but otherwise the changes were small, gas pressure continued strong and the fountaining and streaming activities as usual. There was nothing unusual yet registered in local seismic movement.

I. Activity of Kilauea Volcano.

The measured change for the eight days ending October 4 was a subsidence of the Halemaumau rim ridges amounting to 2 feet east and south and 5 feet at the north and west stations. The inner bench magma blocks subsided over 7 feet, the greatest movement amounting to 9 feet in the region east and northeast of the main lake. The lava lakes sank about 10 feet in the seven days September 27 to October 3 inclusive.

On September 27 and 28 the lava lakes continued high, with the north lake fountains visible from the Observatory and the Postal Rift flow remained brightly glowing with high pressure behind it. The bench magma was sinkng about 2 feet per day, the rate decreasing after September 28.

At 3:30 p. m. September 29 there was increased cracking and slumping at the east cone locality, so that the small driblet heaps had sunk on the inner side of the wall crack out of sight of the trail which at the east follows the outer margin of Halemaumau. There was one glowing crack where gushing sounds could be heard from below. Rock movement was audible in the northeast pressure ridge. Dense fume rose from the solfataric area over the wall crack near the southern end of this ridge and there was much fuming also from the central crevasses.

The main lake stood high relative to its banks, the inner bench standing about 4 feet above the liquid. The cliff blocks back of this bench seemed much lower. There were five fountaining grottoes and the streaming was toward the southeast from under a crust at the central channel and from the northeast cove.

The banks of the north lake stood 5 feet above the liquid, which was streaming toward the east. There were four grottoes built up along the lake margin and much fresh spatter on the north bank. The eastern bank had lowered so as to slope toward the lake. At the eastern corner where the cliff descends to the lake level there was a blowing and flaming chimney built among old floor slabs. At 6 p. m. glow and flame could be seen in the source cone of the Postal Rift flow.

At 2:45 p. m. September 30 the main lake was streaming eastward and the north lake mostly crusted over, with two border fountains. The large grotto dome of the south arm pond showed fountaining and the east cone vent continued its flaming with bubbling noises below. The Postal Rift flow showed live toes at its front, but its vigor of flowing had decreased.

At 4 p. m. October 1 the main lake was higher with its confining rampart in places only two feet high. There was one large foutain on the east bank, the rest of the surface being quiet and crusted. The south pond was very smoky.

The north lake was also high with its northwestern bank only three feet above the liquid. A large grotto had been built on the northeast side and two others were active along the west bank. The surface currents of the lake trended northeast. Fresh cracking was in evidence about three feet from the lake margin for a length of 40 feet. There was much down-sucking along the eastern edge of the lake. The east cone locality showed increased slumping inside of the Halemaumau rim and the internal bubbling and flaming continued. The Postal Rift flow continued its progress.

At 1:30 a. m. October 2 the north lake fountains were visible from Volcano House and the Postal Rift flow glowed moderately. In the afternoon at 3:30 the east cone cracks were found flaming and rumbling as before and the inner ground north and south of this point was depressed much more than before, so that a deep wall valley was developing under the northeast ridge escarpment. Rocks were heard moving here. In general increased cracking was noticed in bench magma surfaces.

The main lake was lower with banks 7 feet high and rapid streaming from the northeast cove to the southeast bank where there was vigorous and noisy fountaining. Streaming was eastward from the central channel.

Smoke was dense from the east-northeast wall crack and the south wall crack. The north lake showed banks 11 feet high and there were six splashing grottoes around the margin, one of them under the south gulch. Rampart walls 10 feet high were revealed above the liquid lava at the mouths of the two gulches. The eastern chimney was dead. The north bank showed increased depression. Heavy crusts formed over the central parts of the lake, broken up occasionally by central fountains which migrated to whatever grotto was nearest. The Postal Rift flow showed glowing extensions in three localities.

II. Activity of Mauna Loa.

At 1:45 a. m. Monday, September 29, a moderate red glow appeared over the southern rift line of Mauna Loa at a point approximately S. 73° W. from the Observatory. Fume rose above the locality in moderate volume. There was no seismic disturbance. Both fume and glow spread to the south from the point first illumined. It was evident that the outbreak was some 5 or 6 miles north of the 1916 vent in Kahuku and near the 8000-foot level as drawn on the Government Survey map of Hawaii.

The writer by telephone at once notified Kapapala, Naalehu, Kaalualu, Kahuku and Honomalino of the coming lava flow. Mr. E. Edwards at Kaalualu near the south point of Hawaii on the shoreline could see the glow and located it as well to the north of Puu o Keokeo, the flow progressing southward.

An Observatory pack train of eight animals with supplies for a week had been previously prepared and was set in motion at 7 a. m. on the way to the source by the Kapapala-Kahuku trail. The party consisted of Messrs. Jaggar and Finch from the Observatory, John and Wale Kama, packers, from Keauhou Ranch, and across the Kapapala lands Mr. Julian Monsarrat kindly furnished the services of Kalua, as guide.

The itinerary was as follows: Left Kapapala bull pen near Halfway House 9:45 a. m.; arrived Ainapo 11 a. m.; Kahuku-Kapapala gate 3 p. m.; camped in Kahuku meadows back of Pahala 4:30 p. m. at 7000 feet above sea level. Continued with pack train September 30, 8 a. m.; camped 12 noon at forest edge inland from Hilea at a point seven or eight miles eastward from the rift line. October 1 left camp at 7 a. m.; tethered riding animals 10:30 a. m.; walked across lava flows to summit of high red hill a half mile east of source fountains, arriving at this hill at 1 p. m. In afternoon explored fountaining pit and flows and spent night in bivouac 700 feet east of fountaining pit. October 2 at 4:30 a. m. started back, arriving in camp 11:15 a. m. Broke camp 8:30 a. m. October 3, arrived Observatory 5 p. m.

From the second camp ground at 6 p. m. September 30, after heavy rain, gigantic cauliflower clouds of fume were seen over the rift osurce to the west. The highest puff was at the north end of the line of jets, direction N. 80° W., vertical angle to top of cloud 11 degrees 30 minutes. The southernmost jet lay S. 85° W. This line of clouds probably followed the course of the flow down the Kona slope. At 7 p. m. the high puff was over, but there was a bright arc of lighted fume billows with a dark zone beneath, the two vapor columns at the ends of the arc being the source of fountains on the right and the jet of steam from the foot of the flow at the shoreline on the left. The maximum distance of the high puff could not have been more than eight miles away, making the height of the column 1.6 miles.

At 8 a. m. on the morning of October 1 from the upland could be seen the two explosion vents of September 26 about 10 miles away to the north. These were gashes in the bright red oxidized rock cutting through two large cones south side. There were lines of white vapor and fresh short black lava flows, and the two cones lay perhaps a mile apart. When examined later, after nightfall, on this day these upper vents showed no glow.

The horses were left at a high flow of brown block lava and the walk to the source fountains was across some ten alternations of aa and pahoehoe. Here could be seen the line of rift cones from Puu o Keokeo northward, some forty cones visible at one time. Right ahead was a large red cone with the smoke of the eruption beyond. When this cone was climbed the source of the outbreak was revealed in panorama, consisting of a line of cones, a true fissure eruption, along a crack parallel to all the others of this rift belt, about half a mile to the west across a plain of fractured lava. Here great fountains were spouting continuously along the fissure for a thousand feet like a wall of red flames, and in detail they were seen to be made of incandescent, light, crumbly material, yellow when it shot up, and red when it came down. The noise was a roar like surf on the rocks, and was occasioned by gas rushing through a lava pool filling the rift, churning it to a foam, and flinging up the foamy matter to solidify as it fell. The bearing of the fountaining pool from the red cone was S. 80° W., and of Puu o Keokeo from the red cone S 14° W. The estimated distance of Puu o Keokeo was between four and five miles.

Northward from the large fountaining pool the fuming vents followed a rift line about one mile long, the smoking patches and driblet heaps becoming progressively smaller northward. Leveling from the summit of the red cone, which was estimated to be 175 feet high, the continuous fountains appeared to throw their denser spray jets 150 feet above the general level of the ground outside of the heapings. Individual rocket jets went higher. A very noisy cone a few feet to the north of the fountaining pool was sending up such rocket jets with angry rumbling and blowing noises amounting at times to explosive detonations.

At 3 p. m. we left the red cone and proceeded across much faulted ground to the immediate base of the rampart built by the fountains. From the east side this appeared to be a linear structure hemming in the eastern margin of the great lava lake at the southern end of the active part of the rift. At 4 p. m. we climbed over fresh flows to the southern ridge of rift construction,, now accessible, though there were small flaming cones along the crack occasionally emitting sluggish pahoehoe lava. This crack extended about two miles to the south, to judge by four vapor vents seen in that direction. The new lava floods did not there extend so far, but to the west the whole country was covered with glowing and flowing lava fields. The ridge where we stood was 50 feet above the old ground level, and 50 yards north of us stood the highest peak of the rampart wall, a singular structure when seen end on. It stood up as a narrow slab or shell confining the mighty fountains, and its height above the outside ground was about 100 feet. Next to it the fountain jets sprayed up continuously half again as high, the glowing soft fragments eternally poundng down upon the rampart, plastering it with the new matter or rolling noisily down the outer slope, gilded with a mottled fiery pattern. This eastern wall pinnacle fell off to a much lower rampart on the south, where the spatter construction was less continuous. Through the southwestern wall the lake had found an outlet, and here in a gorge 40 feet wide rushed the main lava flow like the sluiceway of a dam. This flow, only 100 feet west of us, made a fiery river with current estimated eighteen miles per hour and sweeping along a nearly straight course for 300 yards to the south, where it bent to a course about S 75° W. and appeared to plunge over a fall into a brightly glowing abyss beyond. The stream appeared shallow with many standing waves and bright grottoes along its banks. It brimmed level with these banks and occasionally overflowed them. Another stream flowing slowly lay parallel to the first one and west of it. The fume from the rift vents was oppressive and had the usual foundry smell with some sulphur in addition.

The western side of this lake of live lava was obscured by fume, but from what could be seen of the fountaining belt was not less than 100 feet wide, and this belt stood over the rift zone on the eastern side of the lake. This lake of foam could not have been less than from 200 to 300 feet wide toward the west, and some 600 feet long in a north-northeast direction. The writer obtained one glimpse of the lake surface by climbing the rampart at the northeast end where the summit was only 40 feet high and the fountaining less violent than at the south. The heat was intolerable, but by choosing a moment when the falling of fragments was at a minimum, it was possible to scramble to the edge, look in, and then beat a quick retreat. A definite lake surface of heaving, foamy lava lay about 20 feet below the edge, and the rampart curved off to the west, indicating the presence of a lower confining bench or shore in that direction of the same general quality as the spatter wall on the east. Probably the pit was somewhat of horseshoe shape with openings to the west.

Next north from the fountaining lake, following the rift line, there was a group of flaming and spraying cones containing eleven live vents and the distinctive type of activity here was violent explosion and much spilling over and rocketing. A large orifice in a cone near the south end of this group was named the "growler" because of its spasmodic awakenings when it became very noisy, some of its explosions involving distinct combustion of gas like the exhaust of a petrol engine. The noise of the main lake was compounded of rumbling due to the rush of gas through melt and a steady surf sound due to fragments falling back in a shower. The "growler" and its neighboring vents added irregular detonations and crashes to the continuous roar, so that the total was much like the noise heard when an observer looks down upon a factory city from surrounding heights. There was a distinct suggestion of traffic and metallic clangor in the hubbub, but it was not overpoweringly loud. The "growler" threw small glowing fragments to great heights, and these went up in a spray, sometimes inclined from the vertical and falling outside of the cone whence they came. The noise at rare intervals became a deep heavy booming. The group of cones here under consideration will be referred to as the middle zone lying between the main lake south, and a line of small but active vents next to the north terminated at their north end by a small cone destined to grow enormously in the course of the next three weeks. In order to simplify description, this will be referred to as the north crater, and the main lake south of the middle zone as the Alika crater, for it was at this lake that the Alika flow took its rise.

In order to show the rapid changes which were taking place at the source rift, the following notes indicate the times during this eventful night when new features developed:

7:30 p. m. During a second visit to south ridge, the flow near its cascade source seen to overflow its east bank and made a fork spreading eastward, which was short-lived.

8:00 p. m. In main lake, from a point 600 feet east, vertical angle to top of highest flung visible fragments 18°, making maximum height at this time 200 feet. Change in color of fragments from yellow (1100° C) where flung up to cherry red (800° C) in falling. Size of fragments up to maximum diameter of 4 feet, some of which dropped in showers on outside of rampart. Material basaltic pumice.

8:15 p. m. South end of main lake rampart caved in. This rampart was 100 feet high at the south, 75 feet high in the middle and 40 feet high at its north end. The "growler" vent of middle zone became more noisy and started fountaining in addition to spraying.

Flames from the end vents were seen at night to be colored bluish green to violet. Over the great fountains were banners of nearly colorless transparent flame, 200 to 300 feet higher than the fountains, surmounted by salmon colored condensing fume. A flutter of yellow-red marked these flames, and there was much bright green where the yellow reflections on fume streamers blended with the blue flame of burning gas.

The heat was sufficient to make for comfort 600 to 700 feet away, temperature of the outside night air 45° to 50° F. The light illumined the whole landscape a half-mile away.

8:30 p. m. Heavy boomings, apparently from northern part of main lake.

9:00 p. m. All three zones along the rift were in violent activity, about one hundred fountain jets in the south lake, eleven vents spraying and spilling over their flanks in the middle cones, and the north zone flaming and fuming as far as the north cone, which now began to flood its flanks in a continuous golden sheet; from its middle a lava geyser spouted up.

The middle zone now began an increase of fountaining, making overflow floods in a bright-line pattern of black and gold, and a brilliant pahoehoe flow started down the east slope from the overwash and moved southward along a depression at the immediate base of the main lake rampart.

9:30 p. m. This flow was now a strong current of lava following the general south slope of the old ground east of the rift line. A veering wind to the northwest brought pungent gas which made the eyes smart, and the great column of fume-cloud, many hundred feet high, topped by immense cumulus billows, came overhead so that a fall of light pumice lapilli showered about our bivouac.

10 to 11 p. m. The new flow moving south progressed a quarter mile or more, bushes were burning at its front, and the middle cones feeding it, including the "growler," were golden with continuous overflow. The bed of pumice lapilli between us and the main lake rampart was now buried under the new flow and it was no longer possible to reach the southern ridge for views of the Alika flow on the western side.

11:00 p. m. The "growler" was now no longer noisy. More of the gas distressing to eyes settled about us, apparently from the new flow. This gas had the foundry smell,, and seemed very heavy. A gas haze hovered low over the eastern landscape, and the upper fume column was bent over in an arch to the southwest, above the first uprush, suggesting a gas like carbon dioxide. The gas was quite irrespirable, when encountered near a vent. A white butterfly killed by the gas was found in a bed of pumice. No sulphur odor was detectable in this particular gas.

12 Midnight. About this time it became evident that the increased activity of the middle cones making the new flow had depleted the southern fountains, for their height was less and the deep rumble from them was slighter. From time to time the southern lake had revivals of great intensity, but as a whole it was less active.

The new south-moving flow on the east side kept going all night and its foot disappeared in the distance, bending apparently to the southwest, the direction of the land called Papa. It later appeared that this flow spread slightly east and moved no great distance. All of the flows near the source rift were a rough pumiceous pahoehoe on the surface, with aa efflorescence in places; the development of nearly continuous aa or clinkery surfaces took place within a mile from the source.

The great gas effervescence was what distinguished this eruption from the ordinary phenomena of Kilauea, with gases different in odor and probably rich in. carbon. The fountaining in its continuity and extent suggested Halemaumau in the summer of 1912 when there were hundreds of violent and very hot fountains playing at once. But the fluid there was stringy glass, making much Pele's hair, whereas the Mauna Loa fluid is a granular glass, making crumbly fragments of pumice from the instant the fountains form, suggesting a disintegration in the air and an even more rapid cooling effect than is present at Halemaumau. The luminosity and heat effects are much the same, but the Halemaumau grottoes and cupolas of confined viscous lava appear to the eye hotter than the Mauna Loa vents. The rapid cooling of the Mauna Loa pumiceous lava makes the fountains scarlet in daytime, whereas a bright orange is the rule at Kilauea for the grottoes and central fountains. There was no great quantity or mat of filamentous glass or Pele's hair found near the Mauna Loa vents, though pumice lapilli had short needles of such material attached.

The color effects at sundown at the rift source on Mauna Loa were gorgeous beyond description. Over the scarlet fountains rose the sheets of red and green flame topped with lilac fume, against a murky green or blue-gray background. Above rose the great buff-colored volutes of cloud, with individual billows coffee-colored or brown. All of this was backed by an outer sky of deepest cobalt blue, with normal distant horizon clouds of pearly gray.

At 4 a. m. on Thursday, October 2, 1919, the invisible gas became intolerable to both eyes and throat and we left our bivouac and moved to the east about one-third mile where the air was normal. There had been some collapse of the eastern rampart of the lake, making its profile serrate, but this was quickly repaired by backfall and splashings. When we left at daybreak the fountains were unchanged, the east flow was sluggishly pouring southward and its source cone appeared eroded down somewhat by the incessant spilling over on all sides which was still in progress. The north cone had also contributed to this flow, so that both the middle and northern zones of the rift zone were overflowing down their east flank, the floods united in a stream which moved south parallel to and beside the rift ridge; the stream had two or three marginal lobes which forked off from the main flow and trickled a few yards to the southeast.

We arrived at the place where the riding animals were tethered at 8 a. m. after three and a half hours walk, rode southeast over pahoehoe lava to the timber, and covered the way back to camp northward by the trail, arriving

11:15 a. m. Out of five days spent at this forest edge two were rainy, suggesting that this is a climatal line, with desert beyond to the west at the flow source.

The Lava Flow to the Sea. The source vents opened about midnight, September 28-29, and the flows spread to the southwest, the first rush quickly reaching the steep slope of Mauna Loa in a direction S. 60° W. and curving thence eastward to S. 78° W. through the lands of Kahuku, Kipahoehoe and Alika. At 6 p. m., September 28, the flow was reported three miles east of the main highway in Alika, at 9:30 p. m. it crossed and destroyed the road as a stream of aa some hundred yards wide in Alika, and at 4:30 a. m., September 30, the stream plunged into the sea at the Alika shore over an older flow of the same sort. This shore consists of a narrow platform of lava flows about a half mile wide, fronted with a twenty- to forty-foot cliff over the ocean, and backed by a steep bluff rounding upward into the forest lands of the mountain. The road crossing was twelve miles and the sea contact fourteen miles from the source rift following approximately the course of the flow. The stream continued to flow as a lava river for ten days.

Many persons visited the flow by sea and on land. There was a succession of short-period shallow tidal waves ranging from 3 to 14 feet in height during the flow into the sea, with maximum nearest to the flow delta, and on the third day of the period. The water was hottest north and south of the delta. Noises were heard underwater of seething and of tapping concussions. The uprush of steam where the lava made contact with the sea carried up rock fragments and sand and built a black sand cone. The lava "rafts" or blocks of bench magma which rolled down the live channel, were seen to bob up, make surface steam, and float out some distance from the shore without sinking at first, as though buoyed by the hot gas inflating them. Lightnings were seen in the steam column. There was much muddying of the water and fish were killed in considerable number.

The writer is indebted to Mrs. Jaggar for data as follows, from her observations at the points where the lava was flowing across the road and into the sea September 30 and October 1, while he was at the source. Where the flow had first crossed was 200 feet north of a lumber camp in the forest. This lava was on September 30 at 10 a. m. black aa on the surface, but glow and flames were seen all over the flow. One lobe was moving slowly down the slope 200 feet back of the houses with a rolling motion. The roadway followed the contour of the mountain toward the north, with the sea 1600 feet below on the west down a steep slope, and the hillside above whence the flow was pouring was all forested with high ohia growth. The lobe in question pushed very slowly to a pile of cordwood and set it afire.

On looking north across about 500 feet of black clinkery surface, the party could see a foaming torrent of liquid lava making a noise like running water, with speed varying at different times and in different places, estimated five to ten miles per hour. Great raft blocks of lava, red hot or black, or red below and black above, rode along with the current either smoothly or rolling over as though striking on the bottom. Sometimes these blocks broke up, either quietly or with some spraying. There were dull distant explosions heard and small nearby ones. Later at 5 p. m. these explosions were small and infrequent. An island of unconsumed trees comprising five or six acres of ground was standing on the uphill slope 100 yards from the south bank of the lava field and there some cattle were imprisoned, quietly browsing. On the ocean side a great column of vapor thousands of feet high rose from the shore, spreading above into a broad cloud. As the day advanced this made a great arch of cloud to the east, joining with the cloud from the source vents, and at intervals great drops of water fell. Two houses and a considerable quantity of the drug awa-root were said to have been burned.

Inspection of the foot of the flow at the seashore three miles north of Hoopuloa village was accomplished by riding and walking through heavy rain showers across the old lava shelf until a wall 15 feet high of glowing aa lava blocked progress. Going around a corner of this on the ocean side, with only a shelf 12 feet wide to stand on and a cliff below abutting on deep water boiling hot, all that could be seen was the fall of blocks of incandescent lava tumbling into the sea, where the water boiled and the steam vapor was so dense as to fog the view. The water was bubbling and dead fish of many colors floated in it. For 50 or more feet out to sea from the base of the great column of vapor which was rising opposite the lava channel somewhere beyond, the water was dotted with small jets and sometimes a swirling ''steam spout'' or tornado effect, a foot of two in diameter, would rise from the water a few feet away from the main steam column and join the cloud above.

Sometimes a shower of small rock fragments each two or three inches in diameter would be jetted up from a place in the water close to shore, each projectile followed by a tail of vapor, to heights 15 or 20 feet above the sea.

On returning to the flow at the road at 5 p. m., it was noticed at nightfall that the flowing lava channel had a dark zone down the middle shading off to bright red at the banks. The trees at the upper edge of the forested island broke into flames, causing the imprisoned cattle to bellow in distress.

Next day, October 1, at 12:30 p. m., the channel stream was lower and only half as wide as before. It had been about 250 feet wide and its width now was 125 feet. The island was smaller, as many trees had been overwhelmed and the marginal trees were singed. The lava field was generally less hot and its total width across the road about 1000 feet. The odors were mostly the foundry smell, but coal gas was perceptible at the edges of the flow; probably from charred vegetation. There was noticeable dizziness and shortness of breath in those who stood on the edge of the lava field for any length of time. The rafts were frequently much larger than those of the day before. The whole countryside in the evening was bright with the reflected light from the arch of cloud above. The lobe back of the houses had advanced a few feet but appeared stationary.

October 10, 1919.

The high gas pressure of the Hawaiian lava column during the week ending October 10, 1919, kept Mauna Loa in intense activity of fountaining and flowing at the Kahuku rift source, while the response at Kilauea was a continued slight subsidence of the crags in Halemaumau, the lakes tending also to sink somewhat with recovery toward the end of the week. The Alika flow from Mauna Loa ceased moving on October 10, the source vents shifting the discharge northward so as to flood new ground. The Postal Rift flow in Kilauea crater increased in volume and speed.

Observatory expeditions were made to the Alika flow October 6, and to the source rift October 8 to 11, both in charge of the writer, the last having in view the collection of gas from Mauna Loa, samples of which were obtained with vacuum tubes.

Local seismic movements in unusual number began to be registered by the instruments of the Whitney Laboratory at the Kilauea Observatory on October 5 and thereafter. Fourteen shocks were recorded in six days, as well as numerour strong spasms of micro-termor. All but two of the shocks were feeble.

I. Activity of Kilauea Volcano.

The measurements for the six days October 4 to 10 indicated continued lowering of the general level of the Halemaumau lava column but at a decreased rate. The central blocks of bench magma subsided 2 to 3 feet, and the marginal stations 1 foot or less. Until October 9 the lakes sank 4 to 5 feet, showing recovery October 10.

An examination of Halemaumau on Saturday, October 4, after the writer returned from his first Kahuku expedition, showed that there had been border slumping of the bench magma along the old wall-crack line south, southeast, east and north, there was some collapse of the central region apparent, and the eastern and northern lakes appeared rather high relative to their banks, but the southwest lake and west pond were low. The Postal Rift flow continued its outpouring with some slackening of vigor, filling the ground under the north end of Uwekahuna bluff, the gas making a great increase of yellow sulphur deposit around the source cones 100 yards north of Halemaumau.

In the region of Halemaumau proper there had been slipping of stones on the south pressure ridge and on the inner face of the northeast ridge. From the east cone locality, both to the north and to the south, the wall valley had developed extensively so that the steep infacing escarpment of the northeast ridge stood 30 feet above the smoky depression.

The south pond now was crusted over, its southern dome gotto being large with a flaming chimney on the face towards the pond. There was some breaking up along its northern margin. The main lake showed sluggish eastward streaming, and there were continuous fountains in the southeastern and northeastern parts and a steady current poured under the bank northward at the end of the northeast cove at a rate of about 4 miles per hour, suggesting the former cascade at this place. New spatter ramparts had been built around the lake. The crag block on the north side of the lake was becoming isolated like the south island, and this and the other cliffs of bench magma surrounding the lake stood from 20 to 30 feet high.

Bubbling noises were still audible under the east cone and disagreeable sulphurous fume arose there and from the wall crack farther north.

The north lake showed two or three border fountains, and while the southern wall still remained 30 to 40 feet high, the block between the two central gulches had slumped considerably. The old rampart remnant above the lake on its west side was tilted southward toward the center of Halemaumau. There was some flaming chimney action above the live grottoes. The lake stood only from 3 to 8 feet below the northern banks as the ground north and east had lowered.

The west pond was again an open pit of liquid lava, 30 feet in diameter, exhibiting surface streaming toward its southwest bank. A platform separated it from the southwest lake and the latter stood lower than the pond and 12 feet below the platform. The surface of the lake showed bright lines with streaming action towards its southeast and northeast coves. The rhythmic fountain of the latter cove had revived, exploding in large liquid domes at intervals of a minute or more against the bank on the south side of the tunnel leading to the central pond.

The two live source cones of the Postal Rift flow both had open flaming windows and a third group of cones all covered with sulphur had been formed a few paces to the south. Through the window in the middle cone the lava could still be seen boiling up and rushing westward about 15 feet below the orifice. The odor of sulphur vapor was strong. At night the lakes were very bright and the Postal Rift flow broke out and produced surface streams at several places in the northern part of Kilauea crater.

On October 5 and 6 the bench magma was stationary and the north lake fountains were high enough to be plainly visible from the Observatory. The Postal Rift flow continued its progress.

On October 7 at 5 p. m. two gas vents were spurting in the south pond and there was cracking and foundering in the main lake with slight eastward streaming. The lake stood 25 feet below the bench at the northeast cove. There was increased sinking of the bench magma adjacent to the main and north lakes on the east, and much fume rose from the inface of the northeast ridge. The north lake was quiet. The lava in the interior of the Postal Rift source cones was somewhat lower than before.

On Wednesday, October 8, at 3 p. m. the lakes appeared lower and the fumes denser. In the southwest lake a central fountain was playing and the streaming was towards the east and southeast. In the main and north lakes there were active and numerous border fountains, and again the eastward current of the main lake ended in a pronounced inrush under the bank at the northeast cove. The Postal Rift cones and the cracks adjacent covered upwelling lava as active as usual.

On October 9 at 1:30 p. m. the lakes were lower still, the fume was moderate and the lava under the source cone window of the Postal Rift flow was slightly higher. Two gas vents were flaming in the bank of the south pond, and a crevasse south of the pond was open to depths lower than the pond surface. In the main lake the east streaming continued, with numerous border fountains, and the bench at the northeast cove stood 30 feet above the lake. Two gas vents in the gulch extending back from the northeast cove and 20 feet from the lake edge were hissing loudly and spurting lava slightly. About 1:40 p. m. the north lake was seen to have a sinking spell to a level about 8 feet below the northern bank. It had been up to the level of the bank during the day and had slightly overflowed on the northwest.

On October 10 at 1 p. m. the lakes were higher, the northeast cove bench standing 25 feet above the main lake. The south pond and main lake were much as before. A current poured into a tunnel at the northeast cove and there was much noise from the gas vents in the adjacent gulch. Portions of the main lake were crusted over. The north lake was brimming level with its banks and had again overflowed its northwestern rampart, this being partly due apparently to subsidence of the bench magma. The east cone and the northeast wall crack were rumbling. Again the flow lava under the Postal Rift source cones appeared higher.

II. Activity of Mauna Loa Volcano.

On the afternoon of October 4 light southerly breezes produced general haziness, occasioned by the Kahuku eruption, the fume column of which could be seen dimly, and at 4 p. m. the sun appeared bright red. On succeeding days calm weather with some thunder and diffuse lightning was accompanied by much smokiness obscuring the view of Mauna Loa. The smoky atmosphere extended all the way to Honolulu, where it was said to fog the view of well known nearby landmarks. On October 9 the light from Mauna Loa was very bright at 8 p. m. and thereafter.

Progress of the Alika Flow. The writer visited the Alika flow at the road crossing on October 6 at 1 p. m. The flow on October 2 had made two additional short arms through the forest on the Kona or northern side, both of these crossing the road there and extending the damage already done. This made the actual length of roadway destroyed over 2000 feet. There had been tendency for the lava channel to narrow itself within definite banks, which were now about 40 feet apart, and this channel lay on the north side of the forested island, about which the flow had forked. From time to time overflows of the channel were still occurring, which added layers to the fields of rough aa on both sides of the channel and ocasionally these overflows came very suddenly and stampeded the bystanders. There were still occasional puffs from the ocean, but the continuous column of steam there had ceased.

The three features of the molten torrent which was rushing through the gorge at the time of the writer's visit, which were most impressive, were the noiselessness of the movement, the standing waves, and the rising and falling mechanism. It was now possible to walk out on the aa and stand on the river's brink. The stream was bright red, with darker blotches of rafted material, large and small, in the middle zone, and brighter incandescence along the banks. The uphill slope of the steepest part of the channel was here about 8 degrees and good-sized blocks of bowlders occasionally rode over the crest above and came down the middle of the torrent, riding easily, but sometimes surging from side to side and rolling over as though striking on the bottom. The largest blocks seen on this day were 10 to 12 feet in diameter. All along the course of the stream were standing waves such as one sees above a rapid or waterfall in a river where the irregularities of the bottom take effect in throwing the torrent into undulations. The effect in the lava stream was as though the bottom were everywhere at shallow depth, and perhaps itself shifting down hill at a slower rate than the liquid film on top. The distance from crest to crest of these standing rapids varied from 50 to 150 feet, and the crests themselves shifted somewhat and new undulations formed as the rafts came along and introduced irregularities interrupting continuity of flow.

The noise could hardly be heard at all until one stood on the hot brink of the channel. There it was a slight swishing sound, which occasionally took on a deeper note at times when the lava was rising. It should be explained that the stream came over the brow of a hill above, down a steep glen to the flat shoulder of the mountain occupied by the road, then bent off in two straight stretches of slight grade, and disappeared below toward the sea over the brow of another slight rise. The channel was a canyon with the rushing lava generally 10 or 15 feet below the bank and in places much deeper.

The mechanism of rising, at the times when the deep rumble was heard, appears to be extended the whole length of the visible stream. The lava started to rise in the channel and in a few minutes it was brimming level with the banks, as though the whole mass inflated at once. There was no wall of added liquid advancing from above, nor was there any obvious damming and pooling to make the fluid back up from below. It simply rose with a rumble and it was an even chance as to whether it would overflow somewhere or not. As a matter of fact, on this occasion it did overflow at a point on the skyline down stream where there was a short tunnel in the streamway bridged over by previous accumulations. One of the party crossed this bridge to the northern side of the flow and returned without mishap across the still glowing aa lumps of the short-lived overflow. There was much disagreeable gas with the carbon iron smell.

The melt showed a granular texture. Rows of trees, fallen but not burned, lay on the edge of the lava fields adjacent to the forest. Much of the verdure was bleached but not completely burned. Here and there the aa lava showed smooth continuous surfaces, and the stranded raft blocks were frequently rolled into ball form and exhibited layers of material which they had accumulated from the bottom of the river by rolling over and over.

After seeing the marked differentiation between the liquid lava in the channel and the evident semi-solid matter of the channel bottom and sides, this being the material of the rafts and of the still glowing lava fields covering hundreds of acres on both sides of the channel proper, the writer surmised that there were here present two kinds of magma, just as in Halemaumau. There we have the sharply differentiated lake magma and bench magma. The one flows rapidly and keeps molten through the heat of its contained gases; the other becomes half congealed, but remains mobile, owing to the porous crust which acts as a heat insulator. The islands which have appeared in the Halemaumau lakes as upraised pieces of the bottom differ from the rafts in the Mauna Loa flows only in that the one is very slow and the other is rapid; the one is produced by slowly shifting weights of crust in a pit, the other by rapidly shifting torrents rolling up and rending the substance of bottom and banks. The explanation of the dominant aa in the Mauna Loa flow is a different matter, difficult of elucidation, dependent on complex gas expansions and perhaps also peculiar oxidations of the iron in the melt.

Second Expedition to Source Rift. The itinerary of the second Observatory expedition to the Mauna Loa source rift was as follows; the route following the trail through the Kahuku Ranch from the south. Left Observatory at Volcano House P. O. October 8, 1919, 5:10 a. m., in automobile; arrive Kahuku Ranch gate 7:30 a. m.; left gate with pack train 9 a. m.; camped at forest edge approximately 7 miles southeast of flow source 3 p. m.; October 9, left camp 9 a. m., tied horses 11:30 a. m. at aa flow; started on foot 12:45 p. m., crossed lava flows westward, arriving rift source 5:45 p. m., making bivouac for the night; returning October 10, left bivouac 7:20 a. m., arrive horses 12:20 p. m.; leave the aa flow locality 1:15 p. m., arrive camp 4 p. m.; October 11, break camp 9:30 a. m., arrive Kahuku gate 2:45 p. m.; arrive Observatory by automobile 6 p. m.

The party on this occasion consisted of Mr. and Mrs. T. A. Jaggar, Dr. and Mrs. J. R. Judd, and the guides, Charles Meinecke and George Campbell. There were four pack animals and six riding horses in the train. The motive for the trip was to collect gas with vacuum tubes, to make reconnaissance of the Kahuku route, and to obtain new data on the progress of the eruption. It was hoped that by camping farther south than in the first expedition a way over smooth lava might be found for riding animals leading closer to the source rift; this effort failed, and the walking was even longer than on the first occasion, October 1. Otherwise the method of approach was much the same, crossing the upland on foot from the east. The camp ground, at elevation approximately 6000 feet, was near a good spring in a meadow to the southwest of the old aa flow called Pohaku Pohina, and near the forest reservation boundary. This was reached by the Kahuku-Kapapala trail, skirting the eastern lobes of the 1916 flow through koa forest, much of which was burned, and crossing three stretches of old aa flows beyond by a wellmarked trail.

On the afternoon of October 8 occasional distant rumbles of the fountain vents could be heard. In evening the lighted fume column was magnificent and later in the night the glow illumined a rippled cirrus. The wind was easterly and light and the weather good.

Riding northward October 9 we quickly left the timber, passing one fine speciment of silver-sword, standing about four feet high, and noting a pair of Hawaiian wild geese which seemed very tame. We followed the eastern margin of a rough brown aa flow which stood as a wall from 10 to 20 feet high, and finally penetrated a bay of this flow, tying the animals there. After making a flag station on top, we pushed on foot across this and other flows toward the source fume which lay on the left of the distant Red Cone of the first expedition; the course was west-northwest. A wide stretch of smooth lava was found which should have been reached in the first place with the horses, an old Hawaiian trail with many ancient rock shelters crossing this pahoehoe. This smooth ground appeared to extend to the timber southeast. The walking beyond was difficult as a fog of rain came on at 2:15 p. m. and we steered by compass N. 75° W. across aa and shell pahoehoe which broke in under foot. The light wind was southeast and the fountains were not noisy enough to be heard at this time. Fortunately the clouds rose and the Red Cone appeared ahead with the scarlet gashes of the old rift zone cones east of it. The fountaining was quite inaudible even to the eastern foot of this cone ridge, as this happened to be a quiet spell. The fresh red cindery aa of the last stretch was the most difficult walking of all, then came the crossing of the lava channels, one of them 20 feet deep and 50 feet wide, with steep sides. We passed around the north side of the Red Cone and sighted fountains at 5 p. m. A crevasse was crossed, 3 to 5 feet wide, deeply riven in solid rock; this and other irregular cracks in broken ground making the rift zone which extended up Mauna Loa and was here a mile wide on the east side of the 1919 vents.

We moved in close to the fountains, which were spouting along the whole line of cones much as on October 1, and at 5:45 p. m. made a first bivouac at the wall of broken rocks 700 feet from the active vents of the middle group which in the vicinity of the "growler" of October 1-2 were now strongly fountaining, but not at first overflowing on the eastern side. The activity of the week had built up and changed the outline of the several cones and ramparts. The eastern side of the Alika crater was now 150 feet high and the fountains inside shot up irregularly 50 to 100 feet above the rampart, less continuously than on October 1, and more on the north side, where the outer wall was now 40 feet high with a large flaming hole at its base outside and another in the small cone a few feet farther north, these pots being 3 to 5 feet in diameter.

The cauldrons of the middle zone showed increasing energy during the evening, throwing up geyser jets of pumiceous fountaining 200 to 300 feet high, and sometimes subsiding to growling and exploding activities which made deep thudding detonations. A northern high pot of this group was full of lava overflowing its lip sluggishly to the northwest, and also to the east, with bursts of flame through the crust on top. The largest pool here also started overflowing in spurts to the east and southeast, much as on October 1. These overflows at first were overfloodings of the rampart, which became sufficiently incessant to keep a puddle idly pushing its edge southward on the east side of the rift ridge, while the whole fountaining heap became a radiant golden overflowing bowl or chalice.

Going north from the middle zone of greatest activity, the northern zone of less active cones showed first a chimney about 15 feet high with a blue flame rising in puffs through its summit orifice. Next north was a small cone sending up rocket sprays. Much farther north was the beehive described before as the "gold cone," now about 30 feet high with a fiery filagree at its orifice, which flamed and sprayed feebly. Still farther north there was one idly flaming and fuming cone and much vapor, both along the rift and from fresh flows which fringed the eastern base of the built-up rift ridge for a width of from 100 to 200 feet.

North of the three active zones there was no glow, but a line of fuming cracks and some cones for half a mile. At the south end of the live line the extension of the rift next adjacent to the highest rampart wall of the Alika crater had been built up somewhat and was now dead. From this ridge, 75 feet above the general level, the writer climbed the south rampart of the Alika crater, a feat impossible the previous week, owing to falling fountain blobs. This bombardment was now confined to the east and north ramparts of the Alika crater and reached its maximum in the violent overflooding of the middle group of cones next to the north. The material climbed over was a talus of large light blebby blocks plastered into friable walls in the higher and steeper places, with slopes 35° below and 45° above. From the top of the south rampart the lake could be seen across three inner spatter ramparts, the intervening space exhibiting glowing beds of pumiceous fragments which resembled hot charcoal in a brazier. A curved ridge of the rim extended in closer to the lake on the left, and the dense whitish-brown fume from the "bed of coals" blew irregularly across this ridge.

About 7 p. m. I attempted to climb along this ridge, very narrow on top, so as to see the lake close at hand, but the smoke became intolerable; I could see nothing and was almost suffocated, and threw myself back down the south slope to get fresh air. I next succeeded in working along the narrow southeastern rim, a sharp arête vertical inside and steep outside, made of light basaltic pumice. I could kick away enough of this edge to get a footing, and the wind blew the dense smoke from the ember bed away and downward so that I could stand enough above it to see into the fountaining pool beyond. These rare moments revealed the lake with a granular surface dotted with black, heaving in very liquid fashion about 50 feet away across the inner ramparts and 15 feet below me. On the east side of this lake the fountains were playing up continuously to heights of from 100 to 150 feet. Beyond, in the middle of the lake, a spatter hillock could be seen standing like an island perhaps 50 feet high. Somewhere beyond through the fume and hot smother a flow could be seen pouring west. The Alika cascade from the nearer southwestern corner was cut off from view. There were no flames here from which gases could be collected, but the usual gigantic banner of flame played above the whole line of fountains. The fountaining appeared to be linear along the eastern side of the lake, its rampart was there very straight, and this appeared to be the rift line proper, the western borders of the lake being irregularly disposed.

Turning about and looking across the whole western country from this high vantage point 90 feet above the general level, the Alika flow could be seen as before, rushing off to the southwest across the upland in a meandering incandescent river, the meanders increasing their curvature in the distant downstream region, and the piling-up effect at the bends, with standing rapids, was, as before, the distinctive feature of the stream where it flowed in a straighter course near its source crater. The width of the stream was about 40 feet, the surface was granulated with a pattern of black blotches, darkest along the middle part of the current, and here and there the banks slightly overflowed.

Beyond the Alika flow to the west, just as before, there was a field of sluggish flowing lava, fed apparently from some more northern outlet of the line of pools and lakes. This appeared to be a vast puddled area, extending far away with irregular currents through it. A whirlpool formed in one place with double swirling and spurting as though the heat had started a small tornado which caught up the surface fluid. One branch current near the south edge of the fiery swamp escaped in a more definite channel and joined the Alika stream, the effect being like the distributaries and "cut-offs"' of a flooded river delta. The granulated surface of the Alika river appeared aa, but all the visible hardened lava near the source crater, so far as could be determined by the bright light of the volcanic fires, appeared to be pahoehoe. At this time, from 7 to 8 p. m. October 9, there was not the slightest sign of any diminution of the Alika flow. In fact, on this afternoon at the road crossing twelve miles below, there were overflows of the borders of the Alika channel which caused visitors to run for their lives.

The flow to the south, toward Honomalino, which we had watched forming the previous week, by overflow of the east flank of the middle zone or "growler" group of cones, was now solidified and cool over most of its course and buried under deep beds of cinder along the base of the main lake rampart. Here a glowing crack was found where the cinder which filled it was red hot—a useful camp fire for making tea and drying clothing. The outer edge on the east of this flow belt was higher than the depression at the base of the rampart, as though the former flow had somewhat drained out the middle part of its channel.

This fact determined the course of a new flow of the same character, which developed rapid progress by 11:30 p. m. The fountaining and overflow at the middle group of cones by this time had vastly increased, and the noise had changed from a mild roar like the surf on a rocky coast, to a loud thunderous pounding, with much deep rumbling along with splashing sounds. The fountains of the middle cone were now beating down and wearing away their own ramparts and extensive golden floods poured over in a steady torrent, making surges in the crater pool which piled forward to the east and south and pushed the new flow in an ever-increasing river southward along the sag at the base of Alika cone rampart. Here the flow bent eastward and sent a front 100 yards wide out into an old aa channel which was there, and thence the flow pushed towards the south-southwest and disappeared into the distance, burning bushes and making side lobes, and in general moving on the east side of and parallel to the night flow of October 1-2. The new flow continued all night.

The middle fountains increased in violence and height until the whole series of vents there became one gigantic line of geysers with maximum jets estimated 500 feet high at about 4 a. m. October 10. At the same time the former main lake, or Alika Crater, went entirely out of action so far as could be seen, though the Alika channel continued its stream.

With reference to the location of the summit of the Alika crater-cone, considered as about the middle of the 1919 rift, I am indebted to Mr. J. W. Waldron for aneroid readings made this same night on a cone one-half mile south of our location. This cone at summit his aneroid made 7700 feet, the same instrument giving 6750 at summit Puu o Keokeo on same date; true elevation Puu o Keokeo is 6870.2 by the government survey, making aneroid correction +320 feet. This would make summit of Waldron's hill 8020 feet, corrected reading. This hill could not have been over 100 feet higher than the summit of the Alika cone of 1919, which in turn was 150 feet above the general old ground level. Deducting 250 feet from 8020 gives 7770 feet as ground level at Alika Cone. The constructed summit of the Alika Cone would thus be at elevation 7920 above sea-level. The distance of the Alika Cone from Puu o Keokeo can only be approximated by angles read with transit from the Kilauea observatory on the smoke of the eruption, and by estimates made by eye. Estimates based on time of walking, in such ground, are wholly unreliable. Until Government surveys are made, the position may be provisionally stated to be five miles N. 10° E. from Puu o Keokeo.

Before midnight the flow on the east side began to burst through its western edge and send tongues in the direction of our bivouac. The line of fountains extended for a length of 400 feet through all the cones and pots of the middle zone, the southernmost of these making a torrential downpour which accumulated below in high rhythmic surges of the pond that overran the crater edge and so fed the flow; no single channel was formed. The surges filled the saddle and certainly overflowed westward also. The long rampart of the Alika Cone now stood dark and quiet against a background of fume, but there was glow beyond from the western flows. The flow on the east side moved steadily but not rapidly, and its surface bubbled, flames shot through the bubbles, it showed foundering crusts, its borders made toes of pahoehoe, and its motion was most rapid where the flow bent eastward in a kind of cascade. The new side lobes were spreading from south to north on the east side and our bivouac was hemmed in between a very rough aa channel of old blocks and the widening flow. We retreated across the aa to higher ground 200 yards farther east, and finished the night there.

On the north side of the active cones one of the vents was overflowing both west and east, and the eastern trickle here moved northward, making the accumulated pool of lava on the east side of the spilling vents a source of flowing both northward and southward. This north flow dwindled later, but the main fountaining continued strongly all night. The quality of the fountaining was frothy, just as before, the falling materials light, the shredding of the upjets very marked, and the concentrated force in a smaller area made the intensity much greater than on October 1, and the fountain jets were higher. Four-hundred-foot jets were common. In the early evening explosive rocket jets from one of the vents threw out some blocks which were like heavy aa and as much as nine inches across, but this was exceptional. No earthquakes were felt but the deep explosions of the "growler" in the early evening made concussions. The fume glow was red, the fountains in daylight were bright scarlet; at night they appeared yellow at the base and red in the trajectories and the fume above was salmon-colored. The flames were variously red, copper green and bluish.

About 9 p. m., in order to collect gas, I took vacuum tubes of 300 cubic centimeters capacity, and on attempting to reach the live flames of the northern cones found it necessary to cross to leeward of fresh flows making gas and heat which were both insupportable. The gas was quite different from the smoke of the south rampart, which had been suffocating in volume but still somewhat tolerable with the aid of a wet cloth over the nostrils. The northern gases were not visible; they had no odor except the foundry smell, but they corroded the eye tissues and gripped the lungs so as instantaneously to stop all breathing. A wet cloth produced no improvement whatever, and there was no possibility of crossing this gas belt and surviving, unless with an oxygen helmet. Accordingly I went to windward of the vents making this gas, thinly steaming hot cracks in live flows about 100 feet east of the north rift zone. The cracks had a temperature estimated 300° C. Two tubes of gas were successfully collected, breaking the tips at a depth of one foot within the crack, getting the sharp hiss reaction of the vacuum, and sealing with paraffined rubber caps, and later by fusing the glass. The insuck drew in rock powder as well as gas, and water immediately condensed on the interior of the tubes when they cooled. The samples should serve to indicate the general quality of the Mauna Loa gas, characterized by the carbonaceous foundry smell and producing the peculiar asphyxiating and enervating effects which have been described.

It was evident that we had chanced to witness an important crisis when the Alika Cone stopped functioning, for the Alika flow stopped the next morning, October 10, as reported by the guards at the road-crossing.

In the very early morning hours of this date there was some low fume drifting from the northwest which was disagreeable. At daylight the middle zone fountains and their flows continued and the Alika Cone remained dead. The great fume column above the fountains rose high in still air, drifting in a cirrus band showing flat wavy ridges far to the east overhead. There was a continuous shower of pumice during much of the night, before and after daybreak, some of the fragments one inch in diameter, light greenish gray in color. These lapilli fell two miles east of the source, frequently with drawn-out threads of Pele's hair attached, and this material must have fallen for scores of miles to the west during ordinary daytime tradewinds. We had good weather on the return and during most of the trip. The concentrated fountains of the middle zone were both noisier and higher than the distributed fountains of the previous day, for we could see them five miles across country high above the Red Cone, and could hear them far down in the Kahuku ranch lands, when we returned to the ranch gate on October 11.

Seismometric Records.

The instruments of the Whitney Laboratory, at the Observatory near Kilauea crater, registered seismic movements as follows for the fortnight September 27 to October 10, 1919.

For the week ending at 8 p. m., Friday, October 3, there were local earthquakes at 10:04 a. m. (feeble), September 27 and 4:35 a. m., September 30 (slight but well defined). A slight distant earthquake was registered 11:23 p. m. October 2. Spasmodic microtremor was mostly slight except for a few strong spasms September 27 and October 1. Harmonic microtremor was moderate to strong. Microseismic motion was slight. Tilting was notably stationary, with some north tendency September 29 and 30.

For the week ending at 8 p. m., Friday, October 10, local earthquakes were registered 7:48 a. m. October 5 (moderately strong); 4:13 a. m. October 6 (slight); October 7, 3:40 a. m., 5:36 a. m. (feeble), 1:46 p. m. (slight), 5.40 p. m. and 5:44 p. m. (both feeble); October 9, 4:25 a. m. (slight), 6:40 a. m., 10:26 a. m. (moderate), 12:30 p. m. (slight), and two other slight disturbances; October 10, 2:20 p. m. (feeble). A teleseism was registered at 2:45 p. m., October 9. Spasmodic microtremor increased from slight, to slight with occasional strong spasms after October 6. Harmonic microtremor was moderate and microseismic motion slight. Tilting was irregular and stronger than before.

October 18, 1919.

The combined activity of Mauna Loa and Kilauea together in pouring forth lava appears to have reached a culmination during the week ending October 17, though the fluid rush of lava to the ocean on Mauna Loa by the Alika channel stopped on October 10. Thereafter the fountaining of the source vents shifted northward in the Mauna Loa rift and the north crater of the series became the dominant one, with five or six other vents of the middle and northern zones rivalling it, the outpourings spreading across the upland to the west and invading the forests of Papa, Kaapuna and Opihihale, threatening more damage to cattle lands. Ultimately the flow of this later group which went farthest was in Kaapuna, and this stopped four miles east of the Kona highroad. The fountaining continued strong, with some jets rising over 400 feet occasionally. Several parties have visited the source region.

The situation in South Kona created by this uncertain condition of the lava menace above, was critically dangerous for the inhabitants, and made sharply evident the need for good topographic maps. The government contour maps on large scale are finished in some of the islands, but not in Hawaii, and should be completed at the earliest possible date. The sequence of eruptions on Mauna Loa 1914, 1916, and 1919 points to a period of unusually strong activity, especially as Kilauea keeps up high pressure and increasing overflow. Such sequences on former occasions have led to great crises of lava flow and earthquake, and the warning in the present instance should not be disregarded. In view of the menace to plantations, harbors, ranch lands, and settlements, and the presence of a National Park in the midst, it would seem that the least which can be done is to provide adequate and accurate maps of the land. There were no such maps for *any* of the land invaded by the eruptions of 1914, 1916, and 1919, and this Bulletin has set forth that fact on each occasion.

In Kilauea crater during the week ending October 17, there was continued increase of overflowing of the northern floor, compensated somewhat by continued slight sinking of the Halemaumau bench lava, the floods originating, as for months past, from vents of the Postal Rift area a few hundred feet north of the area of Halemaumau proper, and travelling through tunnels of their own incrustations to emerge as upwellings and outskirt tricklings two or three miles away, following the western and northern wall valley of the greater crater. The lava lakes of Halemaumau have changed but little, showing an adjustment to the flowing mechanism. Halemaumau has been making much smoke, and much fume rises from the Postal Rift region.

The seismic activity which began last week to be pronounced and in accord with the development of the Mauna Loa eruption, culminated on October 14 in a total of eighteen shocks in one day, registered seismographically at Kilauea Volcano. Thereafter the frequency of local shocks declined, but there were still from seven to fourteen quakes per day, mostly slight, though occasional earthquakes of wide amplitude demonstrated an increase of seismic intensity, the seismograms giving evidence of distance of earthquake centers accordant with the general distance of the Kahuku rift. No strong earthquakes have been reported from the base of Mauna Loa since the September shocks; four shocks were recorded as felt at Hilea between October 11 and 17, lasting each from one to three seconds, of intensity from No. 2 to No. 4 of Rossi-Forel scale, and of gradual development.

I. Activity of Kilauea Volcano.

Measurements of the week at the Observatory have shown at Halemaumau subsidence of the south and northeast pressure ridges by about one foot and a stationary condition at the west and north rim stations. The interior bench magma blocks adjacent to the lava lakes have subsided 4 feet on the west and south, 3 feet in the middle region, and 1 foot on the north. The ridge of fresh lava over the Postal Rift source region outside of Halemaumau and at the origin of the flow showed a lift of about one foot.

Saturday, October 11, at 11 a. m., the fume from Halemaumau was moderate and the lakes lower than on the previous day. Rocks were falling along the wall crack of the northeast ridge. The south pond was quiet, the main lake 30 feet below its bounding northeast wall, streaming was to the east, and three grottoes were in fountaining activity toward the south and southeast. In the north lake two grottoes were fountaining along the southwest border, the liquid 4 feet below the bank in general. The Postal Rift source cones continued their usual activity of subterranean fountaining and flowing, under flaming and fuming openings.

After nightfall the fountains of the north lake were visible from the Observatory, the flow on the Kilauea crater floor continued bright, and its filling under the north part of the Uwekahuna bluff had nearly submerged the locality of gypsum crystals, a white-stained patch at the base of the cliff which had long been a familiar landmark. Tongues of the newer flowing had made out eastward across the April flow area.

October 12 at 4 p. m. there was little change at Halemaumau. The main lake was high with eastward streaming, the east cone wall-cracks were noisy, the northeast wall valley appeared lower, and the north lake was one foot below its bank, showing border fountains, one central fountain during a sinking spell, and with it the usual bright edge revealed. A flaming dome had been built at the northeast corner of the north lake. The windows in the Postal Rift source cones were on the north side of the northern cone and the south side of the southern cone, the northern one revealing the fountains boiling up in the chamber below, the southern one the lava river flowing off in its tunnel to the west. There was much sulphur stain all about these cone vents. The fume from Halemaumau was not dense.

October 13 showed little change in Halemaumau, but in the evening the great flood under Uwekahuna was much increased in general brilliancy, as though swollen and incandescent all over, and especially bright under the north corner of Kilauea crater. Fountains in the north lake were still visible in the distance.

On October 14 in the evening Halemaumau was less luminous and the

Postal Rift flow was much less vigorous in its movement and brightness than on the previous evening.

On October 15 at 11 a. m. there was evidence of slight increase of subsidence of bench magma blocks, this movement by very gradual stages having been in progress since September 25. The gas pressure, however, remained high and the flowing strong.

The east cone crevasses were now wide and impassable, and the rumbling and flaming along them had shifted a few feet northward. In the south pressure ridge there was no notable change. The south arm pond was bright at night.

The main lake had four vigorous fountains around its east pool; the surface was hot and covered with thin skins moving rapidly eastward. A new cove had been built by collapse in the cliff of the east bank, the floor, however, covered with rampart and overflow material. The south island appeared lower relative to the lake. The inner bench around the lake stood 4 feet above the liquid, and back of that the cliff blocks stood 15 to 25 feet high.

The north lake was within two feet of overflow along its northwest bank and its crusted surface was slowly cracking and foundering. The dome on the northeast bank was sulphur-stained and had lost its flaming gas pressure. The marginal bench around the north lake had slumped considerably towards the east and north, showing a distinct downward bend between the southeast portion still standing high, and the bank on the east side. Back of the northern marginal bench the floor block occupied by the transit shelter in August now stood about 12 feet high.

The southwest lake had narrowed somewhat, the liquid standing 8 feet below the western margin and the cliff blocks standing from 15 to 30 feet above that. Streaming was toward the south and east and there was a grotto at the north border. The general outline of the pond was unchanged, an L-shape with the two arms pointing northeast and southeast. The west pond, depressed in the bench on the angle side of this L, was crusted over and smoking, showing two small inactive pots.

Under the Postal Rift source vents the fountaining and flowing liquid was 15 feet below the orifices, and the cone at the northern window appeared smaller, while a new spatter heap had formed by lava splashing out towards the north. The bright yellow and white accumulations of salts were increasing. Both the lava lakes and flow were brighter in the evening, and the latter more in motion than on the previous night.

On October 16 at 6 p. m. there were heavy fumes at Halemaumau. The south pond was covered with crust slowly heaving, and a glowing gas vent hissed at the south bank. The main lake was mostly crusted, with some eastward current showing, border fountains, and inpouring to a tunnel at the northeast cove The north lake appeared sinking, stood 7 feet below its bank and showed border fountains. A banner of flame 8 feet high played over one of the Postal Rift orifices. The rumbling and hissing at the east cone cracks were loud. The flow after dark showed glowing puddles over its surface and moderately rapid progress.

On Friday, October 17, at 10 a. m., the fume was rather dense, no motion could be detected in the slopes of the pressure ridges, and the liquid lava showed high gas pressure and rising. The south pond was now a circular pool with heaving crust, and a strong hissing and flaming gas vent open in the face of the large south grotto dome. At the south wall-crack cone locality there was an open break which was steaming with the inner half of the cone broken down and lowered. In the main lake the liquid stood 4 feet below the inner rampart, streaming was to the east and a spatter dome was building on the southeast. The east cone crevasses continued glowing, flaming and rumbling. Here and farther around to the south the ring of bench magma inside of the wall crack had sunk from 10 to 15 feet during the last three weeks.

The north lake was again high, standing 3 feet below its east rampart, and the northeast dome was again flaming and blowing through cracks above a large active grotto inside. There were other border fountains, the center of the lake was covered with skin, and the gas pressure was strong.

The southwest lake had recently overflowed its western bench and was streaming toward a grotto at the tun-

Mauna Loa Rift-Source from the East. Oct. 1, 1919.

Alika Lava Flow, looking upstream—road crossing. Oct. 6, 1919.

Lava Fountain 50 feet away. North Crater. Oct. 25, 1919.—Photos, Jaggar.

nel leading to the central pond. The west pond was a small round pot, with a violently hissing gas jet under the wall west of it. Both lakes and flow were high and bright in the evening.

II. Activity of Mauna Loa Volcano.

On the night of October 11 the light from the Kahuku fountains was bright. On October 12 Mauna Loa was smoky. On the night October 13-14 the smokiness cleared up and in the very early morning the fume column and source glow over Kahuku were as bright and sharply defined as at any time during the eruption.

At 7 p. m. on the evening of October 15 a clearing after rain with easterly wind revealed the Mauna Loa fume column extraordinarily bright, with a band of diffuse light on the left of it as seen from the Observatory, equivalent to a length of at least 3 or 4 miles southward from the fountain source. There was an occasional puff of vapor in this bright zone, quite removed from the fume column over the fountains. Waiohinu and Kaalualu also reported seeing this bright glow and new fume seemingly south of the fountain locality. Hilo, owing to the atmospheric conditions, reflection from high clouds and very clear air, saw very brilliant glow, and much excitement resulted.

Telephone advices stated that cattlemen from Honomalino reported continued upland pooling of a wide flow to the north of the Alika flow. There was extreme nervousness in South Kona at this time, owing to uncertainty concerning the exact direction of slopes and guiding ridges, as no accurate topographic map of the details of this country was available.

It is probable that the extreme brilliancy on this night was occasioned not only by atmospheric clearness, but by an actual culmination of intensity in fountaining and flowing, October 14-15 being the time of very pronounced seismic maximum for the whole eruptive period, as registered by the instruments of the Observatory.

October 16 produced excessive noisiness at the source region and a flow spreading in the direction of Papa and invading the timber. This occasioned great uneasiness at Honomalino ranch, causing the manager's family to move from the ranch house to a dwelling on the roadway. This flow, however, shortly came to a stop. A party which visited the source reported five fountaining vents.

On October 17 Honomalino ranch reported two branch flows, with fronts just below the timber line, to be moving very slowly, in the region between Papa and the Alika flow. The noise had greatly diminished but the flow was bright.

Some earthquakes of wide amplitude registered at the time by the seismographs, were not felt at Honomalino, and none of four strong ones registered October 16 to 18 was reported at Hilea. The distance of earthquake centers indicated by the seismograms was from 27 to 32 miles; the horizontal distance from the Observatory to the Kahuku rift fountains is approximately 32 miles, and to the upper explosion vents of September 26, twenty-four miles.

On October 17 T. C. White of Kona went to the source rift by the Kaapuna trail, making the journey in six hours of horseback and forty minutes of walking. Six fountaining vents were in action and maximum height of fountains was estimated at 300 feet. The dominant crater was the north cone, the bowl estimated 200 feet in diameter. Four live flows were found, two towards Opihihale, one towards Kaapuna, and one towards Papa. Streams of lava poured rapidly from the source vents, but the velocity was described as soon dying out when these streams mingled with the slowly-moving lava fields farther west, which were described as spreading out over the country. The Kaapuna flow at this time was 8.5 miles from the road, the Opihihale flows 13 miles from the road, and the Papa flow had its front only 3 or 4 miles southwest of the source rift. The fronts of the Opihihale flows were by aneroid 350 feet, and the Kaapuna front 1300 feet below the elevation at the source cones. The progress of the live Kaapuna flow was estimated at less than a quarter mile per hour.

III. Seismometric Record.

During the week ending at 8 p. m. Friday, October 17, 1919, the instruments of the Whitney Observatory have registered local earthquakes as follows:

Oct. 11, 1:00 a. m.—very feeble.
1:50 a. m.—very feeble.
2:15 a. m.—very feeble.
5:35 p. m.—very feeble.
6:06 p. m.—slight.
Hilea reported an additional slight shock at 7:45 p. m.
Oct. 12, 10:25 a. m.—feeble.
10:40 a. m.—very feeble.
10:50 a. m.—slight.
11:48 p. m.—very feeble.
Oct. 13, 11:25 a. m.—feeble.
3:30 p. m.—very feeble.
4:00 p. m.—slight.
6:15 p. m.—slight.
6:30 p. m.—slight.
6:48 p. m.—feeble.
9:30 p. m.—feeble.
Hilea reportod an additional moderate shock 7:15 a. m.
Oct. 14, 12:15 a. m.—slight.
4:20 a. m.—feeble.
4:25 a. m.—feeble.
6:48 a. m.—very feeble.
6:52 a. m.—moderately strong
9:20 a. m.—feeble.
11:24 a. m.—very feeble.
1:40 p. m.—feeble.
1:50 p. m.—feeble.
1:52 p. m.—slight.
2:10 p. m.—feeble.
4:47 p. m.—feeble.
11:03 p. m.—very feeble.
11:06 p. m.—slight.
And three other small disturbances.
Hilea reported an additional moderate shock at midnight.
Oct. 15, 8:28 a. m.—moderately strong (felt).
10:20 a. m.—slight.
11:10 a. m.—feeble.
1:35 p. m.—very feeble.
3:40 p. m.—slight.
7:01 p. m.—very feeble.
8:40 p. m.—very feeble.
Oct. 16, 4:15 a. m.—very feeble.
5:25 a. m.—very feeble.
7:20 a. m.—feeble.
7:30 a. m.—feeble.
7:40 a. m.—feeble.
9:00 a. m.—strong.
9:05 a. m.—slight.
11:17 a. m.—very feeble.
2:50 p. m.—very feeble.
3:35 p. m.—slight.
5:30 p. m.—very feeble.
6:40 p. m.—very feeble.
8:20 p.m.—moderately strong.
8:25 p. m.—very feeble.
Oct. 17, 8:18 a. m.—very feeble.
5:40 a. m.—slight.
8:05 a. m.—feeble.
8:35 a. m.—slight.
8:30 p. m.—feeble.
8:35 p. m.—feeble.
11:25 p.m.—moderately strong.
And three other small disturbances.
Hilea reported an additional weak shock at 9:03 p. m.

A very weak teleseism was registered at 1:35 a. m., October 11. Spasmodic microtremor throughout the week was moderate to strong. Harmonic tremor decreased during the week from strong to slight. Microseismic motion was slight. The ground tilted strongly to the east and north October 11 to 14, recovering slightly thereafter.

October 25, 1919.

During the week ending Friday, October 24, 1919, the measureable changes of the Halemaumau lava column were various, with a rising on October 18 and a sinking after October 22, both of the movements being small. In general the nature of the activity at Kilauea was quite unchanged and the flow pouring across the greater crater to the north and filling there against the wall continued unabated. On Mauna Loa the activity of the middle and northern craters of the rift continued to produce floods of lava pouring over the high land of western Kahuku and upper Kaapuna, the flow in the latter district reaching to within 4 miles of the Kona highway. The seismic record showed a decline in numbers of shocks registered daily, though individual local earthquakes had greater intensity than before.

I. Activity of Kilauea Volcano.

Measurements for the seven days ending October 24 showed a rise of the southern and eastern pressure ridges by about two feet on October 18 and a settlement of like amount thereafter. There was slight rising also of the

Halemaumau rim rock northeast and west, but the north station appeared stationary.

The inner crags of bench magma rose from 2 to 3 feet in the center of Halemaumau October 18, and sank 4 feet after October 22. This movement of subsidence was stronger than the preceding rise and affected the marginal bench magma as well as the central blocks. A similar movement of rise and fall was detected in the Postal Rift flow ridge north of Halemaumau.

On Saturday, October 18, there was pronounced rising of the lava column as indicated above, and this was responded to by the lakes and by the Postal Rift flow. The lakes in the evening were fountaining vigorously and the north lake could be plainly seen from the Observatory. So strongly was the gas pressure increased at the flow sources that a bright surface flow broke out in the slope of the new lava heap northeast of Halemaumau and streamed toward the Uwekahuna wall. Everywhere in the northern stretches of the flow there was increase of bright surface oozing, indicating a marked spurt in the flowing of liquid lava following upon the spasm of uplift of bench magma.

On October 19 there was reaction from the rising spell of the day before, shown by increased smoke, stationary bench magma, and a more sluggish condition in the flow. The lakes were fountaining very brilliantly in the evening.

On October 20 at 3 p. m. the main lake was streaming eastward from the central channel in a riverlike band covered with festooning skins, and at the northeast cove heavy crusts lay like elephant hide over the melt beneath. The inner bench around the lake stood 3 feet high and showed fresh construction all around. The cliff at the northeast corner stood 15 feet above the lake.

The south pond had built a grotto dome on its northwest side where the fountaining activity was strong, as also at the large south grotto dome. In both places stalactite curtains had formed across the ovens where the domes face the pond. The pond stood one foot below the marginal bench most of the time, but during a sinking spell it went two feet lower and developed central fountains.

The gulch extending out to the lake shore from the east cone region appeared more sunken, and the live cracks at the east cone and farther north were flaming, rumbling and smoking excessively. In the north lake a large continuous central fountain was in action, and four large border fountains; there was a flaming cone on the north side; fresh spatter ramparts gave evidence of the recent high level of October 18, as did also fresh overflows across the north and northwest ramparts. The central crevasses in the high ground south of the lake were fuming densely.

The openings at the Postal Rift source cones continued their bright flaming, the northern one over noisy fountains in the chamber beneath, which appeared higher and nearer the surface than before. The southern orifice showed steady streaming towards the southwest. Outside of the northern window, on the ground there were clusters of bright yellow sulphur needles on strands of Pele's hair and small spatter fragments, and sulphur patches had greatly increased all around the source region, emitting much sulphur odor. One strongly fuming sulphur patch lay a few yards south of the original source cones. In the evening the Postal Rift flow was moderately bright and the north lake was high.

On October 22 at 3:30 p. m., the lakes continued high, the fume moderate, the two grottoes of the south pond were in action and all of the eastward currrent of the main lake appeared to bend northward into the northeast cove. The north lake was crusted over and quiet, 3 feet below its banks, and the source cones of the flow continued their activity.

On October 23 at 1 p. m. the fume was denser and the lakes were lower, the sinking being marked just after noon. In the southwest lake there were four border fountains. Rocks were falling on the inface of the south ridge, giving evidence of subsidence of the floor beneath. Three vents were rumbling in the eastern ridge cracks. Three fountaining grottoes were active in the main lakes and the north lake stood about 7 feet below its banks. The south wall-crack cone was visited and found quietly fuming.

On October 24 at 1 p. m. it was evident that the lakes had risen and subsided again within the twenty-four hours, for there had been overflow from the main lake around both sides of the south island. That some subsidence was now in progress was shown by falling rocks at the northeast ridge. There were three border fountains in the main lake and four in the north lake. The postal Rift flow continued its progress vigorously.

II. Activity of Mauna Loa Volcano.

On the evening of October 17 Honomalino reported that three tongues at the margin of the upland flow area had penetrated the upper timber between Papa and Alika, some 8 miles from the road. The roaring noise from the fountains had diminished but the light continued very bright. The flows observed were reported moving very slowly.

On October 19 about 1 p. m. the glow over Mauna Looa was seen very dimly from the Observatory and at daylight the fume column stood as usual over the brow of the mountain. From the steamer off the south point of Hawaii the rift region was seen to be marked by a bright glare over the fountains in the early morning hours.

On October 20 South Kona reported an extensive advance of the Kaapuna flow in the valuable cattle land of the On Tai ranch, invading the trail by which the White party had made the ascent. Two other lobes of the upland flow area were said to be in the higher forests of Opihihale. There appeared to be no marked diminution of fountaining activity at the rift source, according to the reports of several parties which climbed the mountain both from the Kona and Kahuku sides. It was evident from the reports, however, that the activity was confined to the northern parts of the rift.

Visitors to the rift from the northwest side during the evening of October 23 noticed a marked increase of activity with revival of the fountains of the middle zone, beginning about 11 p. m. Extensive creeping flows were moving westward and northward across the upland, with a front in the upper Opihihale land close to the Kahuku boundary. The writer visited the rift source from the Kona side, beginning October 24, his account appearing in the Bulletin of October 25-November 1.

III. Seismometric Record.

During the week ending at 8 p. m., Friday, October 24, 1919, the seismographs of the Whitney Laboratory registered local earthquake shocks as follows:

Oct. 18, 9:10 a. m.—very feeble.
1:14 p.m.—moderately strong.
3:20 p. m.—very feeble.
3:25 p. m.—very feeble.
4:15 p. m.—very feeble.
11:30 p. m.—very feeble.
And two other small disturbances.

Oct. 19, 3:50 a. m.—slight.
6:45 a. m.—feeble.
7:05 a. m.—feeble.
7:10 a. m.—slight.
12:10 p.m.—moderately strong.
2:35 p. m.—very feeble.
4:00 p. m.—very feeble.
8:00 p. m.—very feeble.
8:35 p. m.—very feeble.
And two other small disturbances.

Oct. 20, 3:55 a. m.—very feeble.
9:55 a. m.—very feeble.
11:30 a. m.—very feeble.
11:45 a. m.—feeble.
2:45 p. m.—feeble.
3:05 p. m.—feeble.
4:20 p. m.—very feeble.

Oct. 21 12:30 a. m.—very feeble.
1:02 a. m.—feeble.
1:25 a. m.—very feeble.
3:15 a. m.—very feeble.
9:20 a. m.—feeble.
9:50 a. m.—very feeble.
11:00 a. m.—slight.
12:23 p.m.—moderately strong.
2:45 p. m.—very feeble.
9:30 p. m.—very feeble.
Hilea reported an additional weak shock at 6:45 p. m.

Oct. 22 1:10 a. m.—feeble.
3:02 a. m.—very feeble.
3:15 a. m.—very feeble.
3:25 a. m.—feeble.
6:50 a. m.—very feeble.
11:07 a. m.—feeble.
12:40 p. m.—strong.

2:08 p. m.—very strong (felt).
7:00 p. m.—very feeble.
11:24 p. m.—feeble.
Oct. 23, 12:20 a. m.—moderately strong.
4:35 p. m.—moderately strong.
And one other small disturbance.
Oct. 24. 6:05 a. m.—feeble.
6:15 a. m.—feeble.
12:30 p. m.—slight.
1:12 p. m.—very slight.
3:35 p. m.—very feeble.
3:40 p. m.—very feeble.

Spasmodic microtremor was characterized by strong spasms throughout the week. Harmonic tremor was moderate. Microseismic motion was slight. Tilting of the ground in the east-west azimuth was to the east, becoming excessively strong October 22; the north-south component fluctuated, but was northerly during the excessive eastward movement.

November 1, 1919.

During the week ending Friday, October 31, 1919, Halemaumau continued to exhibit fluctuating lava lakes and stationary bench magma with strong flowing from the Postal Rift vent, unremittingly filling the northern part of Kilauea crater with wide sheets of glowing lava. The only new feature of the fortnight at Kilauea was the tendency to pulsation up and down of the lake lava from levels of overflow of benches to depression 10 or 12 feet below benches, all within the course of single days.

The eruption on Mauna Loa continued its progress, in general diminishing, but with some increase October 25 and 26, marked by revival of the rift vents of the middle zone and by increased frequency of earthquakes registered at the Kilauea station. The only effect of this was to add some volume to the plateau, floods on the west side of the source rift, these fields of lava tending to stagnate at the western brow of the upland, where the steep forested slope above South Kona begins, and to keep widening northward on the ground nearer to the source. This mechanism accorded with the tendency at the rift to clog at the south end and develop activity northward; and it accorded also with the tendency of the flows from the beginning of the eruption to be most voluminous and elongate at first through Alika westward to the sea, and then to make progressively shorter westward arms from sources progressively northward from the Alika source-cone, so that the map of the flow-covered area presents a step-like shortening of flows from Alika through Kipahoehoe, Kaapuna and Opihihale.

Thanks to the generosity of Dr. J. R. Judd and Mr. John Guild, who equipped the expedition, the writer was able to make a third trip to the source rift from the Kona side, camping there October 24 to 27, and this time remaining continuously at the actual base of the northern fountaining cone, and securing surveys, photographs and specimens.

I. Activity of Kilauea Volcano.

Measurements at the Observatory for the seven days ending October 31, 1919, showed small and variable movements by less than a foot of both the bench magma blocks and rim stations of Halemaumau. The liquid lakes fluctuated strongly from day to day, the net effect at the end of the week being a rise of about 5 feet. The Postal Rift flow showed increase of volume, as measured by numbers of glowing puddles and toes, rate of outward spreading in area and height of the lava in the source tunnels.

On Saturday, October 25, at 1 p. m., the Halemaumau fume was moderate and the lakes higher and fluctuating rapidly. Streaming in the main lake was toward the northeast cove and there were three small border fountains. Small landslides were in motion at the northeast ridge. The north lake was only two feet below its northern and northwestern banks, and on the northwest side there had been subsidence of the bench blocks. The southwest lake was quiet and crusted over.

On October 27 at 1 p. m., there was much rumbling and flaming in the eastern wall cracks and the strong fluctuation of the lakes was marked and movements sometimes of 4 to 5 feet vertically, both up and down, occurred within an hour. The north lake was now 4 feet below its banks. There was strong activity at the Postal Rift source cones.

At 1 p. m. October 28, the fume was thicker and there had been rock tumbles on the inface of the southeast pressure ridge. The central channel region between the southwest and main lakes showed evidence of subsidence. Smoke had increased from the wall-crack along the northeast ridge at several places other than the rumbling vents east and east-northeast. The lakes did not yet show subsidence, the eastward streaming and border fountains of the main lake remaned as before, and the banks of the north lake were only 2 feet high and contained four fountaining grottoes.

At 1 p. m. on October 29, however, the lakes also exhibited unusually low levels and were mostly quiet, the north lake standing 13 feet below its bank. The south arm pond appeared smaller and was crusted. The current in the main lake was into the northeast cove and there was only one border fountain. The three eastern and northeastern wall-crack vents were rumbling loudly, and the flow source maintained its ceaseless tunnel drainage.

On October 30 there was recovery from the low stage of the preceding day, and on October 31 at 5 p. m., the lakes were all up again and the adjustment of Halemaumau pit levels to the unending flow from the postal rift was resumed as for weeks past. The flow on the Kilauea floor was voluminous, with bright surface streams and spreading edges. There was glow in the south wall-crack of Halemaumau. The south pond was very brilliant with live fountains and a flaming chimney west of it. The main lake was high, with grottoes in its southwest and eastern banks, eastward streaming, and no change in the height of the benches and cliffs around it. The eastern wall-cracks noisily bubbled and flamed as before and hot sulphurous fume was rising athwart the trail across the northeast ridge, making the trail impassable; some bubbling noise was audible here. Fume in general was dense and abundant and had recently increased in the sulphurous region around the Postal Rift source vents and the covered tunnels extending northwest from there. The north lake stood 3 feet below its northern and eastern ramparts and these were newly veneered with spatter. There were live grottoes east, northeast and north, the latter with flaming holes in its roof, and the streaming was toward the northeast bank. No special change was noticeable in the gulch crevasses extending through the sunken and broken high ground south of the north lake. The boiling and streaming lava seen through the open windows of the Postal Rift cones stood somewhat higher than before, the greater depth of the stream producing much slower flow, estimated about 5 miles per hour. Possibly also other tunnels were carrying off the drainage.

II. Activity of Mauna Loa Volcano.

The third Observatory expedition, the equipment and transportation being furnished through the kind interest of Dr. Judd and Mr. Guild on behalf of the Hawaiian Volcano Research Association, was organized with a view to making record of the progress of events at the source rift by approaching from the Kona side, a route which experience had shown must be much more direct and easy from the inhabited shore belt than the Kapapala and Kahuku routes, which the writer had followed in the first two trips. Furthermore, the great anxiety of the South Kona ranchers continued, unrelieved by any complete information as to what was going on above. A visit to Kona, moreover, was desirable in order to secure records of the happenings there and for study of the Alika flow and its delta.

The itinerary was as follows: Sailed from Honuapo 11:30 a. m. October 22, inspected Alika flow from the sea 4 p. m., arrived Napoopoo 7 p. m. October 23 visited Alika flow from Kona side and made photographs. October 24 left Kona road at Kaohe at 7 a. m. horseback, with two pack animals, guided by James On Tai, Frank Coelho and McKinley Kaupu. Arrived 10:30 a. m. On Tai mountain house in Kaohe, elevation 5000 feet; left mountain house 12:30 p. m.; arrived ridge west of active crater 3:50 p. m. Here sent back animals and on foot reached camp northwest side of north fountaining cone 4:30 p. m., Jaggar and On Tai remaining in camp here until October 27. October 27 broke camp 9:45 a. m., arrived horses 10:30 a. m., arrived mountain house 1 p. m., arrived Kona road 4 p. m. October 28 chartered sampan from Robert Leslie, towing canoe, and in company with Captain R. V. Woods made landing at delta of Alika flow for collections, notes and photographs from explosion cone there; Napoopoo to Alika delta two and a half hours by sampan. Returned by steamer from Napoopoo October 29, arriving Honuapo and Observatory October 30.

The delta or ocean end of the Alika flow, as seen from the sea, fans out on a platform of older flows of the same sort with cliff faces above the water 15 or 20 feet high on the south side of the place where the Alika lava enters the sea, and 40 feet high farther north. The channel of the new flow extends up the bluff back of this platform at a high angle, and the aa on each side of the channel is there a narrow ribbon. Other flow channels of ancient date followed nearly the same course and are seen scarring the face of the mountain as black vertical bands extending upward into the forest zone and widening at the base of the steep elephant's-back slope into leaf deltas at the shore. The new flow is merely one more veneer 10 to 15 feet thick on top of the platform beneath and spreading out in plan into a lobate front about one mile wide. Most of this front is heavy aa which crept forward and in many places crumbled, rather than flowed, over the precipice into the water, making a visible talus beneath when the water was shallow enough. Only in the middle where the channel was, did the flow actually run liquid into the ocean, and this channel is marked by a gorge 25 feet deep and 20 feet wide just above the cone at the ocean contact. This cone, at the lower terminus of the channel was built by the steam explosions resulting from the incandescent torrent rushing into water, a crater being there formed, surrounded by a heap of black sand. This horseshoe heap was 75 feet high above sea-level, and the front of it had broken down on the ocean side, revealing a section of bedded sands over a rock wall beneath. The crater was not preserved, as the last hot flows of the channel had crept down into it after the sand eruption was finished, making a fill of aa with no definite channel extending to sea-level. On either side of the sand cone similar thin last flows had crept out over the sand, these being only 3 or 4 feet thick. These differed from the earlier flows in having no sand coating on top of them. It was evident by this arrangement that the last push of the flow at the sea end was a slow-moving aa which crept across the explosion products of the former swift stream, buried up their crater and reached the water at too low a temperature to make any explosions.

The sand cone protruded as a horseshoe-shaped ridge opening towards the sea, with steeper slope of 37 degrees on the crater side and a curved outer slope of 21 to 25 degrees away from the explosion center. The ring of upper rim had a diameter of 150 feet, highest on the south and half buried under flows at the north. The material was a black and rather fine lava sand, with hard crusted surface and smooth sweeping grooved lines following the slopes, which appeared to be the result of continuous even sliding of the coarser materials of the sand shower. This pattern was quite different from the rill markings due to water wash. There were a few scattered small lava fragments on the surface of the sand. Everywhere the sand was coated with a thin film of crystalline white salt, common sea salt, to judge by the taste, and this made the cone white as seen at a distance.

On the south side of the cone where large bowlders were mantled over with sand, there were open holes with hot vapor rising from below smelling of muriatic acid. On the borders of such orifices there were zones of solfataric incrustation, dove-colored, brown, cream, orange and yellow from within outward, ending in the pure white of the general surface. Probably these coatings were iron and lime chlorides. There was much more sandfall to the south than to the north, and the cone was higher on the south side, facts which showed that the prevailing wind had been from the north during the eruption.

The channel just above the cone was a gorge in very rough and heavy aa lava, through the cracks of which bright red heat could be seen below and adjacent to these hot cracks were deposits of salts colored bright green and aquamarine. The bright green salts tasted like old brass and suggested copper. Much of the lava showed continuous rough surfaces like shark skin, with a flowering up through the cracks of rosettes or lumps of frothy hard aa. The specimens were much heavier than the rock of the flow 2000 feet higher up the mountain, just as that in turn was much heavier than the lava near the source rifts.

On the side of Hoopuloa south of the flow the vegetation was all scorched and brown for more than a mile, in contrast to the green tropical verdure beyond. A continuous sea cliff of old rock 20 feet high was here surmounted by new sand-coated lava 10 feet high.

On the northern side the higher cliffs of old rock were also surmounted by thin flows which had tumbled over into the sea and built up talus slopes beneath. The southern cliffs showed no such talus, as though the water there were deeper. At the north end of the northern cliffs one of the flow lobes had poured down a gradual slope into the sea.

Inspection of the Alika flow at the highway as approached from the Kona side, showed two tongues of the flow across the road on that side, with short stretches of roadway between. Many fallen trees lined the side of the main flow. All was now stationary and there was little fume or odor, but here and there trunks of trees were still burning. What had been the channel gorge was now 20 to 30 feet wide, full of rough aa blocks, bearing no resemblance to the smooth stream lines and standing rapids of the lava when it was in motion. In this respect aa differs utterly from pahoehoe, the latter preserving when cold every detail of its appearance while hot. The aa shrivels and tumbles into lumps of every conceivable shape and size and leaves nothing but a scoriaceous chaotic field as record of its streaming. There were tree moulds in the aa, tubular spaces which had encased burning logs. Remains of the "rafts," the large blocks of bottom lava rolled forward by the streams, could be seen here and there on the surface of the lava field as immense half-buried bowlders showing signs of being built in concentric layers.

The recent history of the rift crater on October 23, so far as it could be interpreted from rumors in Kona, was to the effect that all flows approaching the road had stopped. A party which visited the source rifts October 21 had seen one high narrow fountain in the north cone and a flow in the upland running toward the southwest. A party which spent the night October 23 at the source reported only the north cone active in the evening of that day, but just before midnight the middle craters broke out noisily and were still in action when they left. They also saw strong flowing and spreading aa on the upland west of the source craters. Honomalino on October 23 reported loud noises like rumbling or cannonading, and while no live flows were any longer in motion in the upper Papa lands, smoke and glow could be seen in the upper forest farther north towards Kona and the wind carried burnt koa leaves from that direction which fell at Honomalino. The glows over the source region as seen from Kona were moderate reflection on high cirrus in the evening October 22, very bright flaring in the early morning hours October 23, and a very dull dark red glow on low clouds in the early morning of October 24.

The route up the mountain on the Kaohe land proved to be a well marked steep jungle trail over ancient aa lava, through ohia, fern, ieie, wild taro and finally koa in the high lands. The trail is straight and very direct. This slope has heavy rainfall and the trail is muddy. In the koa here the making of dugout canoes is still an industry and we saw several logs in process of canoe-making. The rough-hewn canoe is dragged with horses all the way down to sea-level.

After leaving the upper ranch house the trail follows fence lines until it emerges from the forest into bushy country. Twenty minutes after leaving this house (12:50 p. m.) we could hear the rumble of the source fountains. We left the timber at 1:05 p. m. and saw the fume cloud ahead. At 1:40 p. m. we reached a high wall of aa known as the Kukuiopae flow, and crossed this by a beaten trail. On the opposite side of this flow we turned more to the east from a previous course southeast and followed old pahoehoe for two hours. Here we soon found ourselves travelling parallel to the front of a broad field of fresh fuming aa lava south of us, with glimpses of sluggish incandescent streams back from the front, one of these showing a cascade in a crook of the stream with black islets protruding through the falling melt. At 2:45 p. m. the fiery jets above the crater could be seen ahead and at 3:15 we reached a big crack with old but fresh-looking black glassy pahoehoe lava lining it and splashed out on both sides. This was the beginning of the rift belt on its western side, and from here on these cracks, often with cones and pits along their course, were common, the lines always trending in a general northeasterly direction toward the summit of Mauna Loa.

At 3:50 we dismounted at a ridge consisting of a long line of such cone accumulations with deep pits and impassable gulfs, and proceeded on foot, working our way across this rift and across aa fields beyond. A walk of forty minutes brought us to another line of cones which extended miles northward as a curious serrate profile. We camped near these cones and northwest of the active crater. Here we were at the edge of the live lava field of 1919, and 300 yards in front of us was the great northern cone with its fountains spurting 400 feet into the air and making the usual surf-like rumble. The northerly winds kept the fume entirely away from this side of the rift, and our camp was on moderately high ground a few hundred feet east of this last line of old rift cones and north of the hot lava fields around the base of the active cone. As we faced this cone we could see the middle crater beyond throwing up lazy flings of heavy lava, and still farther away and slightly to the right, the summits of the Alika cone could be barely discerned above the heaped-up flows which filled the whole area on the west side of the source rift. The camp ground was due north from this Alika cone, and northwest of the north cone. On our left (east) the rift line northward from the north cone exhibited no activity and little fume and consisted of only a few small conelets and sulphurous holes a foot or two in diameter. Farther east in the distance stood the familiar red hill, whence we had approached the scene in our expeditions of October 1 and 9.

In the evening there were spells of great increase in the intensity of the north crater explosions, the roar increasing and the jets spurting up 450 feet or more. The crater was an open horseshoe with a lava cascade 15 feet wide pouring from the opening northward, the lava immediately turning west and making a second fall before settling down into rather straight westward flow through a well defined channel. The highest part of the cone was its south side at the toe of the horseshoe where the summit was estimated to be 200 feet high above the general level of the old plateau land. The lava channel extended miles away to the west, a gorge within other lava spread out as hot fields on each side, these fields being themselves in motion and incandescent beneath the surface. The thickness of the lava fields may have been 40 or 50 feet above the old ground level close to the cones, thinning out to 4 or 5 feet at the edges of the field. So far as could be judged from inspection at a distance, the whole country to the west is covered with fresh lava for a width of several miles in a north-south direction. The lava field at the immediate base of the cones was rough pahoehoe with aa patches, and live aa toes occasionally pushed out from the edges of the field. Within a half-mile of the cones going west the lava became mostly aa, and beyond that it was all aa except for certain stretches where the stream channel had overflowed and made small patches of pahoehoe. The lava in the channel rose and fell from time to time, and was seen overflowing and building out a new lobe of the lava field about one mile west of the cone source at 5 p. m. At this time a great spurt of high fountaining was going on and the lava pond at the base of the fountains could be seen surging forward in its bowl and temporarily increasing the width of the outlet cascade. Later there was a reaction when the stream level lowered and a definite canyon was revealed all along the channel with walls 10 to 15 feet high. Far to the west the lava channel made other cascades which at night made a very brilliant glare on the fume above. In that direction a loud detonation was heard during the evening, like a distant blast of dynamite. This was probably an explosion of gas in old caverns adjacent to the hot flow.

On this first night (October 24) the fume column rose into a great cumulus above, the wind was at first light from the northwest and later very light from the east. The only odors of volcanic gas which were noticed happened during this last spell of east drift, when the fume from the northern extension of the 1919 rift was wafted to the camp ground. This smelled of free sulphur and was not disagreeable. There were occasional light falls of small pumice pebbles at this time. The atmospheric conditions were evidently moist and favored the development of high rain clouds above the hot lava fields, for on subsequent nights with cold northeast wind and brilliant starlight in dry air, there was no high cloud whatever over the craters, and the fume rose as thin brown smoke, which blew off to leeward without any moisture development above.

On the morning of October 25 an excursion was made around to the east side of the rift line in order to compare conditions with what had been observed in the earlier stages of the eruption. The rift line is a distinct single crack trending south-southwest and the big cone craters are developments due to lava and gas rising through this crack since September 29. This development began with the southern or Alika cone and in the course of a month has deserted that end and built up the northern cone a half-mile away. This half-mile along the crack is the line which delimits the area of big fountains; north and south from this area the crack goes on for more than a mile in each direction and is marked by small cones which were formed at the beginning of the eruption before the big vents had opened to their full size. When these latter had quarried out holes apportionate to the explosive energy of the great gas fountains, the small vents sealed themselves, leaving lines of small conelets and driblet lava solidified on each side of the crack. In going around the north side of the north crater it was necessary to cross this crack, which one might have expected to be incandescent and full of noxious gases. Strange to say it was nothing of the kind, but merely a line of small holes one or two feet in diameter, with smooth black glassy pahoehoe on the sides, red stalactites inside, and some warm air rising and smelling faintly of sulphur.

Following the edge of the lava field to the east side of the north cone, some oozing toes of red hot aa were making out in places and then came deep beds of pumice fragments from an inch to a foot in diameter. The whole east side of the line of cones was covered deeply with this material over flows below. These east flows, which had been running when seen on previous visits, trending off to the south towards Honomalino, were now entirely dead. The line of cones was now a high ridge rising in places 200 feet above the surrounding country, banked up by flows and pumice for nearly half this height, the three main eminences of the ridge being big horseshoe cones north, south and in the middle, the southern one dead, the other two alive, and the northern one roaring, fountaining and flowing continuously. There were other smaller cones as features of the ridge. The lake of lava in the middle crater would fling up a fountain above its rampart now and then, and the horseshoe of this crater, which had opened southward so as to spill both east and west, was now sealed on the east side and its opening was to the west, not visible from the eastern slopes. The great north cone seen from the east side showed slopes 45 degrees above on the south profile, and about 27 degrees on the north profile, with a spur making out on this gentler slope to confine the torrent which was pouring northward. Over the high summit lip the fountains would fling their red crumbly fragments which poured down in an endless avalanche of fire on the steep outer slope. The wind on this hot surface set up small tornadoes lasting several minutes, moving along the slope, and picking up the light pumice in violent noisy whirls. The fountains of the inner bowl, made by gas rushing continuously up through the lava lake, consisted of an endless succession of big jets, ever changing their direction and angle, and not necessarily vertical. The wind also affected them, making the heaviest avalanching of falling fragments on the side away from the wind, which was blowing from the north. There were two main noises, the deep rumble of the gas and the surf-like noise of falling, most of this last coming from the enormous showers inside the crater itself. The avalanches outside made distinct individual crashes. South of this cone in the saddle between it and the middle crater, there was a smaller cone emitting dense smoke.

Taking advantage of the long low spur on the north side, I climbed that slope in order to get an instantaneous photograph of the fountain by as close an approach as possible. It was necessary to clamber up through pumice knee deep and excessively hot. On the other side of the spur, which was the east end of the enclosing horseshoe ridge, lay the fountaining basin with its gigantic waves surging forward to the cascade outlet, and from under the back wall of this cup rose the geyser of fiery fragments 200 feet above the level of the top of the spur, the pieces bright red hot and very porous, from six inches to four feet in diameter. It was evident from occasional fragments on the ground still glowing, and from the incessant change of direction of the jets, that the nozzle might at any moment be turned in my direction, so that it required quick work to get to the summit of the spur, point and snap the camera, and get away without being bombarded. The sensation of incessantly looking up at that towering curve of rising and falling bombs, and calculating its angle, with the heat almost insupportable and the noise deafening, was an experience not soon to be forgotten. I succeeded, however, in getting to the edge of the inner declivity and taking a look down into the basin as I pointed the lens and discharged the shutter. It all had to be done in much less time than it takes to tell it, for a very few seconds of that heat would have ruined the camera. The far wall of the basin made a reflector for the heat, so that but for the wind at my back, it is doubtful whether I could have reached the edge at all. The interior of the basin was like a titanic open chalice of fiery liquor foaming in scarlet surges, these being impelled continuously forward by the geyser jets behind, the flood lifted by the jets losing its liquid aspect almost instantly, the expanding gas within the jet giving it the apearance of very loosely knitted worsted. The frothing surges were quite as liquid in appearance as any beaten foam and the mass bubbled and seethed, quickly quieting down to form black skins where the pond cascaded through the sluiceway leading to the flow channel. The nearest falling fragments at the moment of taking the picture were apparently 50 feet away.

Continuing southward past the middle crater, it became of interest to get a glimpse once more of the interior of the southern crater, whence had poured out the Alika flow prior to October 10. On October 9 I had looked into this crater and seen the liquid 15 feet below the rim. Crossing to the eastern flow channel without difficulty—it contained blocks of rough pahoehoe—I found the northern summit of the cone only 20 feet above the lava level outside, so much had that level been raised by piling flows. On climbing up, this summit was found to be the eastern lip of a large inactive crater 1000 feet in diameter and 300 feet deep. The opposite or western wall was much lower and the country beyond was all covered with fresh lava. A break in the southwest wall showed the channel of the Alika flow, the course of which could be traced in the distance. No flowing lava was to be seen. The bottom of the crater was smooth pahoehoe plastered over large balls which resembled the "raft" balls of the Alika flow. The southeastern and southern inner walls were high and nearly vertical. The edge on which I stood was traversed with cracks emitting scalding hot vapor. As this cone had been built up 150 feet at its southeastern rampart, the outer slope now being partially buried under outer accumulations, the inner depression now over 100 feet deeper must represent collapse, on the rift line, due to the eruption.

It was evident from the deep accumulations of pumice, the avalanches from the north fountains, and from disagreeable gas which in the late morning was troublesome on the east side of the rift line, just as it had been on that side during former visits, that the wind at this season is here frequently a Kona sea breeze, or else a draught from the north rather than from the east. This is due no doubt to the fact that the 1919 crack is well over on the western side of the rift zone of this district, placing it really on the Kona side of the mountain so far as climate is concerned.

At 12:30 p. m. the "growler," one of the vents of the middle crater, started noisy detonations, followed by high spraying jets of lava and a gushing fountain which drained off to the west from the southwestern spur of the middle cone. This noisy display continued until 4:30 p. m., and there were recurrences later, the flow and new geysers from the middle crater continuing in action all night and longer. The fountain of the north crater gradually became less high as the other waxed in strength. The outflow from the north crater continued to fluctuate, the cascade widening occasionally as the pool above brimmed over its lip, but the black crusts carried over the cascade increased in number. The view at 6 p. m. from the high cone west of camp, which commanded a view over the top of the live lava fields, revealed a cascade sweeping down from the new fountains of the middle zone and making a new fiery river which extended a short distance westward parallel to and south of the main flow from the north crater. Another spurting and gushing vent had developed between the north and middle cones, low down on the west side, also feeding the lava fields to the west.

In the morning, October 26, the "growler" vent was quiet and both the craters were less vigorous than before. At 12 noon the middle vent became noisy again and made sounds like the rattle of musketry or at other times like a heavy locomotive. In the evening both the craters were flowing as on the previous night, but the north crater was obviously dwindling, the cascade outlet now only 10 feet wide, and once the inner wall of the crater was seen to cave in, leaving a bright red scar. Many of the north crater jets now barely overtopped the high south rim.

On this day exploration was directed to the west, and the north edge of the extensive lava fields was followed about four miles. The channel of running lava lay parallel to this edge, often less than 100 feet back, and carrying a stream which here and there spilled over to feed the north lobes of the field. The channel stream lost speed rapidly from east to west, moving 15 miles per hour near the source, 10 miles per hour at a conspicuous bend two miles west of the source, and 3 miles per hour at a point four miles west. The channel where first visited was about 25 feet wide and had walls standing 10 or 15 feet above the liquid. The stream made a mild rippling sound like running water. Farther west at the great bend it was only 15 feet wide, and had here dwindled since first seen in the distance on October 24. This place was a crook in the gorge where large rafts frequently jammed and were seen to block the current completely for a few seconds. Then the liquid portion would percolate through the cracks and disintegrate the rafts and the masses gave way suddenly, making a flood, which poured on through two forking channels below. The raft bowlders were red hot and cheesy, and were carried along and rolled over and over at varying speeds. The ground through which the main channel was grooved was very irregular, falling off in step-like terraces of craggy tumbled aa towards the north edge of the lava field, so that many details of flow could be seen from this front of the field, by standing on knolls of the older pahoehoe. The distributive forks of the channel were frequently brimming full of slow-moving liquid, dotted with granular black lumps marking the beginnings of solidification. At the front of the lava field lobes these forks either directly fed the movement of the front, or that front was creeping by a push from below, the rates being estimated at 200 feet per hour for the first case, or 2 feet per hour for the second.

There was a second parallel lava channel about a half mile back of the first one, more to the south, and its stream also moved west and fed the lava field. Behind it farther south could be seen a fantastic wall of very rough aa pinnacles, estimated 75 feet high above the general level of the country. This southern channel was believed to be the one fed by the middle crater, and on this night that channel could be traced as a line of light from the source cone some distance westward, passing on the south side of two conspicuous ancient cones which stood as landmarks in the midst of the lava field a mile or so southwest of our camp ground. The main channel from the north crater, in its westward extension, passed to the north of these old cones.

At noon we stood on the edge of the steeper forested ground falling off to the western sea-shore, and four miles from the source cones. On our right was bushy upland merging downhill into koa forest. On our left was the lava field, its front trending east and west, a rugged tumble of aa 8 feet high, hot and occasionally crumbling forward and setting fire to bushes. Steam rose from old cavernous spaces along its front. Just 30 feet back from its front, there could be seen, by climbing a hillock or a tree, the sullen noiseless red river covered with rafts and black chunks, moving three miles per hour and spilling over its banks in places, and always spilling northward, sideways and in one direction. It was as though the river bed slid downhill sideways on the lava field of its own making. What was really happening, if one could have mapped the whole area, was a migration northward of the lava deposits of the distributing lava river system, just as a water river migrates sideways on its own delta. Somewhere downstream there was possibly forest burning, for at 10:15 a. m. we had seen soft clouds rising rapidly over hot air toward the west-southwest, and at night there was brighter glow in that direction.

Small explosions were heard in caverns; bushes burst into flame; a branch flow was found coming right out of the cracks in the ground, where a lobe had found access to an old tunnel; another poured into an old pit; numerous ancient cairns and stone shelters built by the natives here showed earthquike tumble, though similar artificial structures near our camp close to the source rift exhibited no such effects; much coal gas was perceptible due to the burning vegetation, but the flow gas was merely sulphurous and even the source fume not different from Kilauea. This was remarkable, for on October 9 the gases had been different, and often quite irrespirable. There was still much of the foundry smell. At many places the channels were visibly spilling over into new ground, always aa lava, and sometimes toes made out from under the older fields. A hot air whirlwind was seen in a patch of ohelo bushes, with rotation counter-clockwise, lasting several minutes. On returning to the great bend at 1:15 p. m. the channel flow was supplemented by new cascades pouring over the terrace, as though the liquid channel were pooled beyond.

In the evening, after return to camp, we found that the gushing of the middle crater had built out its western spur so as to cut off our view of its cascade, but its flow channel beneath on the flat was plainly seen, extending farther than the night before, and about a half-mile south of the north crater channel and parallel to it, corresponding to the second stream we had seen from farther west. These streams appeared to feed the same flow area, reaching down into the upper Opihihale forests. The lava field near camp was making many new toes, always creeping westward and northward. The whole western flow area was doing this, spilling and shifting its channels across a wide bushy upland of slight grade, and as long as this upland was available there was little danger for the lands below. No glow whatever could be seen in the extreme south where the Alika and Papa flows had been, and everything indicated that the south end of the rift was dead.

On this evening (October 26) the cones were more smoky and the fountains of both craters less high. The next morning (October 27) the activity was notably weakened. The cascade from the north crater was 10 feet wide and covered with black skins. Small flows were still glowing and moving. After leaving camp and starting back for Kona we noticed the flow spreading as on the previous day in the Kahuku upland and the Opihihale forest, but no smoke was visible to the southwest.

From Kona on October 28 and 29 the source glow was not conspicuous. At 4:30 a. m. October 30, when rounding the south point of Hawaii, from the S. S. Kilauea the writer saw a single fume jet lighted from the fountain at the rift, and a dull glow west of it from the lava fields.

III. Seismometric Record.

During the week ending at 8 p. m. Friday, October 31, 1919, the seismographs of the Whitney Laboratory registered local earthquake shocks as follows:

Oct. 25	7:03 a. m.—very feeble.
	9:48 a. m.—very feeble.
	9:57 a. m.—very feeble.
	1:20 p. m.—feeble.
	4:30 p. m.—light.
	8:00 p. m.—light.
Oct. 26	3:40 a. m.—very feeble.
	4:05 a. m.—feeble.
	4:18 a. m.—light (felt at Hilea)
	7:15 a. m.—light.
	9:58 a. m.—light.
	10:47 a. m.—very feeble.
	10:49 a. m.—light.
	12.48 a. m.—light.
	1:30 p. m.—very feeble.
	3:17 p. m.—feeble.
	6:00 p. m.—feeble.
	7:02 p. m.—light.
	8:10 p. m.—light.
	8:43 p. m.—light.
Oct. 27	1:30 a. m.—slight.
	5:17 a. m.—moderately strong.
	9:08 a. m.—very feeble.
Oct. 28	4:25 a. m.—feeble.
	2:07 p. m.—very feeble.
	3:25 p. m.—very light.
	6:35 p. m.—feeble.
	11:10 p. m.—light.
Oct. 29	5:00 a. m.—moderately strong (felt in Kona).
	6:45 a. m.—light.
	1:17 p. m.—light.
	1:19 p. m.—light.
	2:20 p. m.—very feeble.
	7:39 p. m.—light.
	7:43 p. m—light.
Oct. 30	3:45 p. m.—light.
	4:10 p. m.—feeble.
Oct. 31	4:10 a. m.—feeble.
	5:12 a. m.—moderately strong.

In view of the strong revival of earthquake frequency October 26, when the writer was in camp at the foot of the active north cone on Mauna Loa, it is remarkable that he felt no earthquakes during his stay of three nights at that camp.

Spasmodic and harmonic microtremor were mostly moderate during the week in question. Microseismic motion was slight. Tilting was north and somewhat east October 25-27, east October 28-29, west and south October 30-31.

Very respectfully,

T. A. JAGGAR, JR.,
Volcanologist.

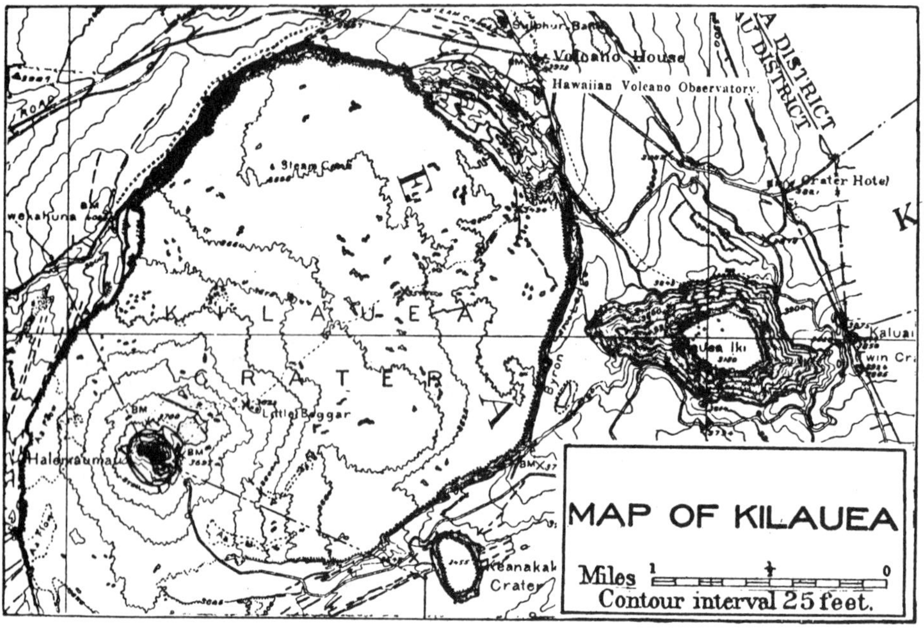

HAWAIIAN VOLCANO OBSERVATORY.

The Observatory is equipped with the following seismometric instruments rebuilt at the station in 1918 for the special needs of volcano research: two Bosch-Omori pendulums, high speed registration of local earthquakes; one optically recording seismograph for distant earthquakes; one clinograph registering E-W tilting of the ground. A vertical component seismograph was in December, 1918, set up in experimental operation. These are seated on concrete piers in a closed basement room having practically constant temperature, beneath the chief Observatory building near the hotel. Time is referred to a rated chronometer, checked at intervals by solar observations with a transit. Both instruments are loaned by the College of Hawaii. Hawaiian standard time (H. S. T.) is 10 hrs. 30 min. slower than Greenwich time.

CANCANI SCALE OF SEISMIC INTENSITY.

Expressed by accelerations measured in millimeters per second per second.

I.	Instrumental	0.0	2.5
II.	Very slight	2.5	5.0
III.	Slight	5.0	10.0
IV.	Sensible, mediocre	10.0	25.0
V.	Rather strong	25.0	50.0
VI.	Strong	50.0	100.0
VII.	Very strong	100.0	250.0
VIII.	Ruinous	250.0	500.0
IX.	Disastrous	500.0	1000.0
X.	Very disastrous	10000.0	2500.0
XI.	Catastrophic	2500.0	5000.0
XII.	Great catastrophe	5000.0	10000.0

Grade IV. is ordinarily the minimum perceived by the senses; and in grade XII. the accelerations or rate of change of motion (jerk) reaches that of terrestrial gravitation.

In the standard form of report the maximum intensity or acceleration, designated by the symbol a, or max. a, is given in the conventional unit of milligal. The milligal is a measure of acceleration, such that 1 milligal = 1/100 mm. per sec. per sec. = 10 μ. per sec. per sec. The Cancani scale, here defined in terms of millimeters per sec. per sec., can therefore be expressed in milligals by multiplying each of the numbers by 100.

U. S. DEPARTMENT OF AGRICULTURE
WEATHER BUREAU
CHARLES F. MARVIN, CHIEF

MONTHLY BULLETIN OF THE Hawaiian Volcano Observatory

VOL. VII. HONOLULU, HAWAII, NOVEMBER, 1919 No. 11

November 8, 1919.

During the week ending Friday, November 7, 1919, the effusive activity of Kilauea increased. So far as can be told by the evidence of distant glow and declining seismic motion, the Mauna Loa eruption appears to be drawing to a close. No glow has been seen there since November 5, but the cumulus billows over the Kahuku heated area continue to show. No more flows have penetrated the forests of South Kona.

Activity of Kilauea Volcano.

Measurements of the rise and fall of the crags and rim stations at Halemaumau indicate that the south and east old rims are stationary, but that the north and west stations have each risen about 1 foot. This rise was coincident with an upward swelling of the ridge formed at the source region of the Postal Rift flow of about 2 feet between November 3 and November 7. In the same interval the flow made a spurt of progress forward with rapid filling about the base of the northern cliffs of Kilauea crater, which represents a large volume of new lava poured out. The inner blocks of bench magma at Halemaumau generally rose about one foot and this movement was pronounced between November 5 and November 6, and was accompanied by strong rising of the lakes, amounting to at least 5 feet.

Recently the conditions at Halemaumau have indicated a continuance of the adjustment between the height of bench magma and lake magma which has been the characteristic of the place for many weeks past. This adjustment is dependent upon the continuous flowing of the Postal Rift stream, which since August has fluctuated but little. Consequently measurements directed to the summits of the crags around the lakes—really tabular blocks of floor—have shown an almost stationary condition, in marked contrast to the incessant fluctuation in height which was recorded before the overflows began. The rise and fall of the lava column at present, therefore, should be measured by the changing volume of outflow, a very difficult measurement to make as the flow is through tunnels and the front is a group of pools and fingering lobes. Moreover, as has been pointed out before, it is not known to what extent a real rise of the deep lava column is measured by the frothing mechanism of outflowing liquid lava charged with gas. Incidentally the Mauna Loa eruption has given further evidence of a very high gas pressure in the whole system, so that all that can be said quantitatively about the present height of the Hawaiian lava column is that it is rising and overflowing strongly.

On Saturday, November 1, 1919, at 11 a. m. the principal activity in the north lake was border fountaining against the northeast bank. Around the Postal Rift source cones there was much sulphur deposited and at the north end of Kilauea crater the flow was sending out arms rapidly in the direction of the Volcano House trail.

The topography of this flow was now divided into three parts: the source region was a closed-in heap of lava making a new ridge extending from the western part of the old Postal Rift district northeast toward Uwekahuna bluff; the pooling region was a great field of semicrusted glowing lava filling the whole north end of Kilauea crater, north of the line joining the base of the Volcano House trail with Uwekahuna trig station; the flowing region was the eastern edge of this pool, which from time to time made new lobes tending to move eastward and encircle the Halemaumau dome, the longest lobes being near the base of the Kilauea bluffs.

The source region heap is traversed by several main tubes or tunnels all leading from a single lava chamber which can be seen through the windows, open flaming orifices, of the group of source cones. Here the lava wells up below with violent fountaining all the time, and from this chamber the tubes radiate. The chamber is under the summit of the heap; it began as a spouting crack which covered itself with lava crust, and is probably by now in the nature of a small pit housed in by its own accumulations. Each tube is created through the evolution of a surface lava channel, which begins as a flood, narrows to a river, then builds in its banks with overhang until the surface crusts across, and finally the stream under this crust becomes adjusted to its enclosing shell with a cross-section much like a railroad tunnel. The marks of the original streamways on the surface are obliterated by subsequent surface flows and this thickens the roofs over the tubes. It should be understood that all of this refers only to the characteristic smooth, or pahoehoe, lava of Kilauea, the rough aa of the Mauna Loa flows behaving differently.

The pooling region of this Postal Rift flow appears at night from Uwekahuna bluff like a lighted town. The surface is dotted with incandescent points wherever active flowing is in progress, and when these are examined by nearer approach they are found to be toes of slowly-moving pahoehoe, small surface streams with festooned middle zone and lobate front, or cracks swelling open from the pressure of lava beneath so that domes are formed whence lava oozes out or gas driblet cones are built up. The latter sometimes spurt and make small explosions, building spires several feet high. Along the base of the Uwekahuna bluff the flow has now filled to depths of from 10 to 20 feet, so that the ancient ash section south of Uwekahuna summit at the base of the bluff is entirely covered up, and also the locality farther north, formerly white with gypsum crystals. The flowing region differs from the trickling lava of the pooling region only in that it spreads out over new ground, whereas the other wells up through its own crust.

On November 2 there was in the evening very strong rising of the lakes so that the main lake overflowed into the south arm pond on both sides of the south island, and the latter was seen slowly to subside. The pit was extremely brilliant. A portion of the roof of one of the main tubes of the Postal Rift flow caved in 300 yards west of the source cones, making a brilliant source of light for illumining the fumes above. The surface flows showed long stems and fingering delta fronts and the flow was particularly brilliant along the base of the cliffs in front of Volcano House.

On November 3 Halemaumau continued to have high lakes and bright fountains. Much fume had developed both from Halemaumau proper and over the source tubes of the Postal Rift flow. The latter continued its vigorous spreading and brilliant surface outpourings, one long tongue with fingering front making out in the direction of the Volcano House trail so that its extremity was east of the line joining the Observatory with the center of Halemaumau. This tongue moved parallel with the northeast cliffs of Kilauea and a few hundred feet away from them.

On November 4 at 11 a. m. the south island, which had been a tabular crag separating the south arm from the main lake, was found to have sunk out of sight, buried under new crust made by overflow of the lake. There was left a flat peninsula jutting out from the southwest shore of the main lake and standing two feet above the lake. Around the southeast end of this peninsula was an open channel which restored the south pond as an arm of the main lake. There were active grottoes in the south arm and northwest and west of the main lake, one of these being curtained. The central pond was still shut off by an isthmus of crust from the main lake. The streaming was northeast and southeast.

The east cone cracks were flaming and rumbling. The north lake stood 10 feet below its rampart and a group of perpetual fountains was in action under the gulch southeast of it. Ballooning skins tended to form here. There was fountaining on the northeast side of the lake and a curtained grotto with long stalactites had formed on the north bank.

The fume on this day was somewhat thinner. The sulphur patch south of the source cones of the Postal flow had developed incandescence and driblet lava, in the form of a ball about a foot in diameter, covered with small hissing gas mouths. Seen through the window of the south cone at the Postal Rift source the flow appeared rapid, perhaps 11 miles per hour. The new pit 300 yards farther northwest was visited and an orifice 10 feet in diameter was revealed in the side wall of the subterranean tube showing the flow inside of bright orange color, 15 feet wide, streaming north about 7 miles per hour.. The pool region of the flow continued brilliant and the eastern arm made progress.

On November 5 everything at Halemaumau continued brilliant with the flows showing marked increase of volume. There were two bright openings now in the tunnel roof northwest of the Postal Rift source. The fountains of the north lake were now continuously visible from the Observatory.

On November 6 the fume over Halemaumau appeared slightly less dense. At 5 p. m. there was an active gas vent at the edge of the south arm, the east cone cracks rumbled noisily, the main lake had eight border fountains and the north lake was nearly brimming and showed five border fountains. The gulch extending from the northeast cove to the north lake had been increasing in size by collapse and slight subsidence was indicated near the northeast edge of the north lake. Hot cracks were extending themselves east of this lake. The new driblet ball of the sulphur patch was increasing in size and hissing loudly, this noise being heard at times at the Observatory.

On Friday, November 7, at 10 a. m. the lakes were found extraordinarily high. The southwest lake had encroached upon the crag east of it and had freshly overflowed its ramparts and into the west pond depression. The streaming in the southwest lake was westward to grottoes southwest and west, an unusual condition. A partition continued to divide this lake from the central pond. The cliffs around the lake were 5 to 15 feet high. Occasional sinking spells lowered the lake surface from one to three feet.

The west pond was covered with piled circular upwellings of lava crusted over, and gas spiracles on top of this heap were flaming and hissing loudly at intervals.

The north lake was high and recently had overflowed its ramparts. The lava was pounding in the northeast grotto. A column of dense fume rose from the central crevasses. The main lake was very high, streaming to the east, its inner bench freshly built up, encroaching on the cliff blocks. Of these the northern one appeared to be tipped down on the lake side. The central pond appeared unusually high and through the gorge one could see to the southwest lake. The south arm had been overflowing into the depression southeast of it and the large grotto dome which has been a landmark on its bank for many weeks was found half-buried under fresh bench accumulations. On the south side this bench was built across a chasm 3 feet wide, this crack extending well below lake level.

The east cone cracks continued their bubbling noises and everything indicated a strong rising movement. At the south sulphur patch of the Postal Rift source the new driblet cone had grown until it was 4 feet high and its hissing and flaming continued. In the source cone cupola the lava boiled high and flowed rapidly. The northeastern tunnel from this center could be traced on the surface by hot stained cracks and thin blue fume. The pit already described west of the source was found supplemented by another break south of it with an opening facing west, showing the whole lava torrent 15 feet wide flowing rapidly northward under an overhanging shell of cavern roof standing 10 feet above the liquid. Still farther to the northwest nearer Uwekahuna another break had formed in the roof of the tube 6 feet in diameter, revealing a perilously thin shell only 8 inches thick. This led to a part of the tunnel which was 25 feet high and 20 feet wide with the lava river pouring through it in a meandering curve at a rate estimated about 5 miles per hour. These breaks in the roof of the tube probably mean a lowering of the stream level inside, but this may be occasioned quite as much by a fresh outlet from the pooled area to the north as by any diminution in supply from Halemaumau. Surface indications of fume and stain appear to indicate that there is another tunnel leading directly north from the source cones.

Activity of Mauna Loa Volcano.

The fume column and glow over the Kahuku rift of Mauna Loa continued as strong as ever apparently, up to Monday, November 3, inclusive. On the night of November 4-5 the fume column could be seen, but the glow was slight. Thereafter for two days the weather was rainy. On the morning of November 8 a large cumulus cloud could be seen. Smokiness is reported from Kona, but not any glowing radiance.

Seismometric Record.

In the Whitney Laboratory of Seismology for the week ending at 8 p. m. Friday, November 7, 1919, four local earthquakes have been registered as follows: 5:35 a. m. November 1 (very feeble); 7:50 p. m. November 1 (light); 7:56 a. m. November 3 (feeble); 5:03 p. m. November 6 (very feeble). This is a marked decrease from the earthquake frequency of mid-October when the Mauna Loa eruption was at its height. Spasmodic and harmonic microtremor have both been moderate to slight and microseismic motion slight to very slight. Movements were pronounced to the north and slightly east November 3, with recovery to the south and west during the remainder of the week.

November 15, 1919.

The week ending November 14, 1919, has apparently brought an end to all visible evidence of the Mauna Loa eruption, and the Kilauea center of volcanic activity has so increased its floods across the floor of the greater crater as to overflow the main trail leading from Volcano House to Halemaumau. This arm moved eastward from the pool in the north part of the crater, the flow thus executing an encircling movement following the Kilauea walls. The bench magma of Halemaumau has been nearly stationary, and the lake magma sank somewhat, this movement being accompanied by a swarm of ten feeble earthquakes November 11 to 13.

I. Activity of Kilauea Volcano.

Measurements have shown the Halemaumau rim to be stationary on the east and north and lowered about one foot on the south and west during the seven days ending November 14. The inner floor blocks have been stationary west and south, and lowered one to two feet in the central region. The lakes sank five or six feet beginning November 11. The ridge at the Postal Rift source has continued to rise about one foot.

On Saturday, November 8, the high levels continued and the flow remained voluminous. In the afternoon the pooled area in the northern part of Kilauea crater was putting out very rapidly a long glowing tongue of glassy bluish pahoehoe towards the Volcano House trail, and this arm advanced all the evening in the direction of the bridge where the trail crosses the 1889 crevasse. At 10 p. m. a fall of rocks was heard, perhaps at some crack invaded by the flow. After midnight in the early morning hours of November 9, a noisy blowing cone formed on a swollen tumulus of the flow under Uwekahuna Bluff, and for hours this was belching and making gobbling noises and explosions, so as to build two spires of driblet lava.

November 9 at daylight the flow was seen to have crossed the trail about 100 feet south of the crevasse bridge, and at 9 a. m. the flow was over 100 feet east of the trail. In general this tongue was a long narrow arm some 50 feet wide from the pooled area eastward. The arm was inspected and photographed at 3 p. m. It was flowing all around the edges, a sheet two to three feet thick of glassy heavy pahoehoe with bluish iridescent surface, rather rough, and making large transparent glass blisters in places. There was strong foundry smell and no such sulphurous odor as characterizes the flow nearer the source. In places the liquid was cascading into deep cracks, the walls of which would shift and tumble and snap, and some remote sounds were heard which resembled underground explosions in old caverns.

At Halemaumau at 5 p. m. the fume was moderate, the lakes high, and a brisk flow of lava poured under the tunnel windows of the Postal Source. The crack extending from the north tunnel window was covered with spatter lava.

The north lake was three feet below its bank, streaming towards the northeast grotto, and active gas vents were numerous through the ramparts. The main lake had numerous border grottoes, the current being to the east, with one sluggish branch toward the northeast cove and a very swift branch through the strait leading into the south pond. There was some falling of rocks on the inface of the northeast ridge with loud rumbling in the wall-cracks at the middle of the ridge and at the east cone.

At 11:30 a. m., November 11, all the lakes were notably low but the fume appeared slightly thinner than usual. Rumble in the east cone and the northeast ridge cracks was less loud, both groups of openings giving heat, fume and stain. The main lake stood eight feet below its inner bench, the latter overhanging at the end of the peninsula which protrudes between the main lake and the south pond. The surface of the lake was hot with thin skins, the current streaming out from a glowing tunnel under the floor which separates the central pond from the lake. In the larger pool of the lake the current divided to north and south. The northeast cove had increased in length northward by breaking back into the depression there. The bench at the east cove had slumped greatly, leaving wide crevasses north of it.

The north lake stood five feet below its bench, with general fountaining and not much streaming. A pit had formed in the bench east of the north lake rampart and fuming whitened cracks extended back from the lake in this direction. Looking south at the profile of the cliffs on the south side of the north lake they show a dome curve bending up sharply from east to west, but falling off suddenly to a lower level at the region of the central gulches. The southwest lake stood five feet below its inner bench and both this lake and the west pond heap were very smoky.

The long crack extending northward from the northwest station was again opening, as in June, to a chasm three feet wide in places. The driblet spire south of the Postal Rift source cones continued its hissing and there was extensive fuming all about and much deposition of white salts. The various openings of the flow tunnel showed the rapid lava stream as before, with slight increase of enclosing crusts.

The pool area of the flow in the north part of Kilauea crater on November 10 and 11 was slightly diminished in brightness but its extension past the Volcano House trail continued to make progress in numerous lobes towards Byron's and Waldron's Ledges. This flow had crossed and filled up portions of the 1889 chasm. A second arm of the flow was making out eastward from the pooled area at a point farther south than the arm which crosses the trail.

On November 12 at 8 p. m. the north lake was very high, with all its fountains in full view of the Observatory, and the flow was brilliant, with its arms pushing eastward rapidly. In the night times of both early morning and late evening the cone on the floor tumulus under Uwekahuna Bluff was streaming brightly and occasionally spouting, and showed growth in size.

On the morning of November 13 the lakes continued low, there was much smoke and the flow continued to progress. There were no marked changes on Friday, November 14.

II. Activity of Mauna Loa Volcano.

On the morning of November 8 a large cumulus rain cloud of ordinary form stood over the hot Kahuku source region above the south slope of Mauna Loa. No glow had been seen for two nights previously from Kona, Kaalualu or from the Observatory. South Kona reported no more flows advancing in the forests. On the afternoon of this day the sun shining through a western cloud veil was whitish and not red, in marked contrast to the blood-red effects observed when the Mauna Loa fume was rising.

At 6 p. m., November 9, there was cumulus over Kahuku and a smoking place was observed farther up the mountain slope, but not so high as the vent of September 26. There was no glow after nightfall, though the cloud could still be seen. In the very early morning of November 10 the mountain slope was perfectly clear and no glow whatever was discernible.

On the morning of November 11 there was a well developed cumulus cloud over Kahuku which showed some tendency to mushroom form, but there was little evidence of any smokiness. On November 12 and 13 even the rain cloud over the hot area ceased to form, the mountain profile was perfectly clear and not a trace of glow or localized cloud development was thereafter seen.

III. Seismometric Record.

Local earthquakes of intensities respectively 4, 5 and 1 Rossi-Forel, and lasting 10, 15 and 3 seconds, were reported at Hilea in the southern part of the Island of Hawaii at 9 a. m. November 11, 12 noon November 13, and 3:30 a. m. November 14.

In the Whitney Laboratory of Seismology local earthquakes were registered as follows for the week ending at 8 p. m. November 14, 1919: November 11, 8:42 a. m., slight; November 12, 9:17 a. m., 9:27 a. m., 9:32 a. m., 9:53 a. m., 10:40 a. m., 12 m., and 6:44 p. m., all feeble; November 13, 11:52 a. m., slight, 3:49 p. m., feeble. Spasmodic microtremor was moderate with increase in numbers of spasms during the earthquake swarm of November 11-13. Harmonic microtremor was slight throughout the week and microseismic motion also slight except for some increase November 8. Tilting was strongly to the east and north until November 14, when it recovered slightly to the south and west.

November 21, 1919.

During the week ending November 21, 1919, the gas pressure at Kilauea crater, taking effect in increased volume of outflow, has augmented so that on November 20 the flood not only surcharged the cones and tunnels of the Postal Rift area, but caused the lakes of Halemaumau to rise and overflow suddenly. This increase of outflow at Kilauea immediately follows the cessation of outflow on Mauna Loa, and in contrast to the collapse of 1916, the present situation seems rather to augur a growing pressure. This pressure reached a high value at Kilauea in August-September, a culmination disrupting Mauna Loa in September-October, and now a Kilauea revival following upon the clogging of the Mauna Loa vent. If Kilauea keeps up its voluminous discharge without any collapse as in 1916, the implication would appear to be that the eruptive period of the whole Mauna Loa-Kilauea system which began in 1914, has not yet reached its climax. It is too soon, at present, however, to assert that a strong collapse may not still be in preparation, the condition of Mauna Loa being somewhat doubtful, and the effervescence of Kilauea ambiguous with reference to the movements of the deeper lava column.

Just as in the case of previous weeks, the measurements of the Halemaumau floor crags have indicated slight subsidence, in spite of the voluminous rising and overflowing of the lake magma. The marginal ridges, east and south, were slightly up by less than a foot during the seven days ending November 21, and down by about one foot at the west and north stations and at the ridge above the tunnel feeding the Postal Rift flow. The bench magma subsided about one foot in the region between the main and north lakes. The lakes showed spurts of rising during the early part of the week and on November 20 rose and overflowed so as to make a net rise of not less than 15 feet at the time of maximum flooding.

On Saturday, November 15, at 4 p. m., there was much dense vapor from recent rainfall, but the Halemaumau fume was moderate. In the main lake the streaming was eastward, with branches into the northeast cove and south pond; there were two border fountains and an active gas vent in the south pond grotto. The north lake stood eight feet below its bank and had two border fountains and one central fountain. The wall-crack fissure of the northeast ridge continued to open and cause rocks to fall and there was slumping still in the region between the main and north lakes.

Eighty feet west of the Postal Rift source cones a new collapse over the flow tunnel showed the torrent in motion only four feet below the surface rock. At the front of the main flow near Byron's Ledge the lobes had spread backward to the west so as to cross the Volcano House trail for a second time, and small trees were burning at the foot of the cliff trail. Small underground explosions could be heard from time to time where the flow gases mixed with air in caverns.

At 11 p. m. on November 16 the cracks at the east cone were rumbling, there was slumping about the central crevasses, the central cliff block between the main and north lakes was lower, but the lakes were relatively high. The main lake had recently overflowed its banks northeast, east and south and the central pond floor west of the main lake showed fresh layers of overflow. The streaming continued eastward with very symmetrical currents diverging north and south in smooth curves at the northeast cove and at the south pond.

The southwest lake stood four feet below its west bank; its surface was crusted and the west pond was smoky. The north lake had overflowed its northwest cove extensively. There were new spatter heaps at the east border of the main lake and at the north and east borders of the north lake. The general situation indicated lower central bench magma and higher lakes.

In the Postal Rift source cones the flow lava had risen, partially sealing the orifice of the northern window and leaving a hissing flame vent. In the southern window the surface of the flow was only 10 feet down and rushing rapidly. In the new pit next to the east the torrent poured from under a crust and through the cavern beyond in a westerly direction at a rate estimated 12 miles an hour. The next two openings farther to the northwest were unchanged, but a short distance beyond disclosed a new pit leading down into the lava tunnel. This pit was 12 feet in diameter and revealed the subterranean river 20 feet wide, with a shore cavity on its north bank full of tumbled stones, all heated cherry red. The fifth opening, where the underground channel bends under Uwekahuna, remained unchanged, a thin shell above an incandescent tunnel 20 feet deep, with a broad stream moving slowly and majestically around an abrupt U-curve to flow off to the north on its underground way.

A visit to the cones on the northwest side of Kilauea crater, reached by walking over the surface of the live flow, discovered them to be a number of high swollen domes with driblet spires built by the lava oozing through summit cracks. There were no more tunnel openings in this direction, and apart from puddled moving lava in various places, the flow had crusts three or four feet thick and was extremely substantial in spite of the riverways below. The highest of the domes stood some 10 feet above the general level and was covered with spatter droplets of wormy basaltic glass, indicating the viscous character of the lava ejected on the night of November 8 and later. The normal pahoehoe of all this part of the flow, down the middle fields of the northern pooled area, showed no unusual texture and the live liquid puddles were common glistening flow lava without the bluish iridescent or sharkskin texture. The gas rising from the tubes below had dominantly the odor of sulphur. All of this was in marked contrast to the blue lava of the foot of the flow at the Volcano House trail with its foundry smell.

On November 17 and 18 the lakes were very high, so that the north lake fountains were almost continuously in view from the Observatory. Kilauea crater was never so brilliant at night within the memories of the last twenty-five years. The five bright pits leading down to the big source tunnel were rather evenly spaced to the right of Halemaumau as seen from the Observatory, each with a flaming orifice lighting fumes above, a miniature of the pits occupied by the lakes, which crowned the eminence to the left. All the foreground was a brilliant filagree of fire with ever-changing lines and streams of orange light, covering hundreds of acres across the whole northern third of the crater floor between Uwekahuna and Byron's Ledge. The flow had by now flooded the bridge on the trail and partially filled the 1889 crevasse.

On November 19 at 11 a. m. the fumes were moderate and the lakes rising. The inner benches of the eastern lakes were four to six feet high, and the rapid eastward streaming poured in swift currents into the south pond and northeast cove, where there were fountains. A break in the crust at the northeast cove showed a rapid current under the bank. The north lake stood seven feet below its rampart and was quiet except for two border grottoes. Rocks fell occasionally at the northeast ridge.

The new southern Postal Rift cone had built itself up during a spouting period at 5:30 p. m. November 18 so that it was now a large black structure seven feet high, with small flows which had poured from it into the depression east of it. A truncated cone had been built up at the first break in the flow tube, and in this cone a sluggish current could be seen joining with rapid currents which poured on each side so that all cascaded into a single tube at a lower level. The other orifices of the tunnel showed the usual volume of flowing lava.

On November 20 at 11 a. m. Halemaumau was found flooded with fresh overflows from the lakes. These flows had reached their maximum during the early morning, and were now swollen, hot and crusted over. The south pond had overflowed the entire depression of the southeast wall-valley between the south pressure ridge and the southeast crag. The main lake had overflowed the eastern wall-valley. The north lake had overflowed both to the east and to the northwest. The former overflow filled the whole northeast wall-valley, destroying much of the new trail and filling to a height above the top of trail monuments four feet high. This fill lies at a slightly lower level than the wall-valley fill made by the main lake, which had spilled over and cascaded into the northeast valley fill. On the northwest side the overflow of the north lake had filled the wall-valley under the northwest station so as to reach in places the top of the Halemaumau wall and the floor level of the west niche. The southwest lake and west pond did not overflow but the central pond had risen and overflooded the central channels, widening them and drowning the base of the cliffs.

The main lake stood very high with new spatter domes, eastward streaming and extensive new floors built far into the gulch at the northeast cove and across the peninsula separating the lake from the south pond. The cliffs around the lake were now only from 10 to 15 feet high The lava of the new wall-valley fills was pahoehoe with heavy shells which tend to collapse on cooling.

The north lake was now fountaining against a circle of new spatter domes, the new overflows standing level with the lake margins, but not visibly moving. The southwest lake had built up large spatter domes and the west pond cone was hissing. There were bubbling noises in the south wall crack cone and similar noises continued in the east and northeast wall-crack vents.

Inspection of the cliff over Kilauea crater at the northern part of Byron's Ledge showed that the bushes had burned up to the top of the cliff and the lava was still spreading over all that part of Kilauea floor. New embayments between spurs were forming where the cliff trail descends to the floor. Surface floods broke out during the evening all over the flow, and again the north lake fountains were seen at night splashing high over their ramparts. The new Postal Rift cone was also spurting.

At 10 a. m. Friday, November 21, the lakes stood two or three feet below their banks and were rather quiet, and the wall-valley fills had slumped on cooling. The west pond had a hissing vent on its southwest side and a round sulphur-stained cone in the middle. The southwest lake from time to time developed noisy bubble fountain activity. The main lake and south pond were little changed. The wall-crack of the northeast ridge was rumbling and smoking strongly, the east cone cracks

Sept. 30, 1919. Kahuku Flow source looking west at night, 8 miles away.
—Photo, Jaggar.

Oct. 1, 1919. Source fountains of Alika Flow, at night. Photo, Jaggar.

Oct. 1, 1919. Alika Flow pouring into ocean. Photo by courtesy of Rev. A. S. Baker.

Oct. 28, 1919. Foot of Alika Flow, sand cone in foreground. Photo, Jaggar.

making somewhat less noise. The north lake was surrounded with four or five immense spatter domes and remained very quiet at the time of visit. About 2 p. m., however, the north lake again overflowed with much development of marginal fountaining.

The tunnel break immediately west of the Postal Rift source cones showed a very rapid and voluminous torrent 17 feet wide and moving over 15 miles an hour. The wall-crack on the northeast side of Halemaumau showed large open chasms from recent movement, breaking across the August overflows of the north lake.

In the Whitney Laboratory for the week ending at 8 p. m. November 21, 1919, there were registered local earthquakes as follows: November 14, 11:32 p. m. (well defined); November 15, 9:30 p. m. (felt); November 16, 12:45 a. m. (very feeble), 4:05 a. m. (feeble), 5:42 p. m. (very feeble); November 18, 5:42 p. m. (very feeble). A teleseism was registered November 20 at 3:46 a. m. Spasmodic microtremors were variable throughout the week and harmonic tremors slight, increasing somewhat after November 20. Microseismic motion was slight. Tilting was strong to the south November 15, to the north and east November 16-19, and moderate to the west and south November 20-21.

November 29, 1919.

During the week ending Friday, November 28, 1919, the expected reaction at Kilauea volcano has come, from the gas and lava release of the combined Mauna Loa and Kilauea eruptions. Just as on June 5, 1916, after the Mauna Loa flow of that year, so on November 28, 1919, an even more sudden quiet drop of the Kilauea lava column took place, amounting to at least 600 feet in a single morning. As before, the subsidence was accompanied by almost continuous light local quaking of the ground, limited to the immediate vicinity of the crater. Within an hour after the disturbance started, the whole ancient pit of Halemaumau was revealed to a depth of over 400 feet, the topography of lakes and crags was largely buried under encircling talus, and a single new lake of liquid lava had started to reform in the middle of the cup. The Postal Rift flow had continued its outpouring through the source wells up to the moment of the crisis, when it on the instant ceased to flow and the tunnels were left glowing but void. There resulted in the great pooled flow of the northern part of Kilauea crater reactions of collapse and fountaining due to the withdrawal of gas pressure. The liquid lava in the bottom of Halemaumau recovered very rapidly and by November 29 was forming a large lake.

This event, culminating a sequence of explosive outbreak and flowing on Mauna Loa, with all the details analogous to the events of the combined Mauna Loa-Kilauea activities of 1914 and of 1916, appears conclusively to demonstrate a sympathy of action between the two volcanoes and proves that they are connected by underground conduits. The sequence from 1914 on has shown increase of interval, increased volume of outflow, increased height of vents, increased rapidity of the subsidence reaction, increased rapidity of the recovery, and decreased intensity of seismic crises.

All available information indicates that the Mauna Loa eruption is over. Reports from cattlemen who visited the source cones in Kahuku show that smoke was still rising there on November 19, but no moving lava was seen.

Measurements for the week indicate that for the six days, November 21-27, the marginal stations of Halemaumau were stationary on the south and west and sank about one foot on the north and northeast. The bench magma or floor lava adjacent to the three lakes subsided about one foot. The ridge adjoining the Postal Rift source cones stood stationary. The lakes remained 6 to 10 feet below their banks. At 2 a. m. November 28 the lava column, including both lake magma and bench magma, sank very suddenly, so that measurements at noon from the edge of the restored pit made the depression of the liquid surface 591 feet below the northeast rim of the pit, this having been the northeast ridge before the subsidence. The rim station was 3727 feet, and the liquid lava surface 3136 feet above sea level. The dimensions of the lava lake at the bottom of the pit were 120 x 120 x 160 feet, and the shape roughly triangular.

On Saturday, November 22, at 4 p. m., the lakes were low and appeared sinking, and the fume was rather dense. Streaming was eastward in the main lake and much fume rose at the northeast cove. The northeast ridge wall-crack was rumbling. The north lake stood 10 feet below its rampart and had two active grottoes under its north bank. The collapsed tunnel near the Postal Rift source cones contained two torrents, pouring one on each side of the black driblet cone that had formed over the edge of the hole, these coming together in the cavern beyond. In the second orifice, farther northwest, the level of the tunnel stream had lowered.

At the west pond site a gas vent was hissing, and in the southwest lake the streaming was slow towards two very large grottoes in its southeast cove. The south wall-crack cone was again glowing, fuming and rumbling.

About 4 p. m., November 23, a cloud was seen over the Kahuku rift source on Mauna Loa, which showed very hard edges and resembled the fume clouds of the eruptive period.

On this same afternoon at 5 p. m. there was a new development of marked subsidence in the south pond of Halemaumau, which suggested the beginning of a crisis. The pond had sunk 10 feet lower than the main lake, and through the channel from the main lake to the pond a cascade was falling continuously with a roar, converting the pond into a whirlpool. The channel was 20 feet wide and dark skins from the main lake were continuously carried down over the fall. The lake was slightly lower than before, exhibiting grotto caverns at the central channel and at the northeast cove. The streaming was outward from the former and inward at the latter.

The north lake stood about eight feet below its bank and was making much noisy fountaining. There was high gas pressure at the Postal Rift flow source, with much hissing and flames rising through cracks in the ground near the cones. The surface of the torrent in the tunnel opening appeared somewhat granular, like aa. The new black cone south of the Postal Rift source cones was flaming through many holes and had increased the size of its outflow area.

In the evening Halemaumau was unusually bright, owing to the brilliancy of the cascade locality, and the Postal Rift flow was also very brilliant. After midnight the south pond rose and put a stop to the cascading, and fountains could then be seen at the rampart levels at both the south pond and the north lake.

On November 24 the Postal Rift flow was unabated, the north lake fountains remained high, and while the cascade and whirlpool were not resumed in the daytime, the bright illumination of the south pond about 10 p. m. suggested a temporary renewal, which stopped later in the night. The hissing at the new north cone could be heard at the Observatory. The third tunnel opening of the Postal Rift stream had broken wider open and showed a stretch of surface flow with standing waves. The main flow surface was brightest toward the northeast, under Byron's Ledge, the pooled area of the north corner of Kilauea tending to grow darker. Extensive arms of the flow had by now developed over the middle area between Halemaumau and the Observatory.

At 11 a. m., November 26, the south pond was found with its bank five feet above the liquid and so built in that the large south grotto dome stood back from the edge of the pond, with an open glowing pot in its summit. The main lake sent a rapid stream through the channel into the south pond, and was otherwise streaming eastward without much fountaining. Evidence of motion in the bench magma was shown by a fallen block of rock on the fresh flow lava of the southeast wall-valley. The north lake stood six feet below its bank, where a very large wide spatter dome had been built on the east side. The lake was quiet, with tendency to ballooning of its crust, and a flaming grotto dome stood on its bank. The interior of the Postal Rift source cone showed high lava, streaming rapidly. The first tunnel orifice exhibited bubbles in the surface of the flowing lava, but no granulation, and a speed of about six miles per hour. The second and third openings contained a sluggish stream of dark-red color, with its banks considerably built in from the sides. The two pits of the fourth opening contained rapid streams similar to opening No. 1; a curtain of accumulation hung from the roof down to the flow surface, the latter adding to it by splashing. The new black cone south of the source vents was now 15 feet high, hissing and flaming and with new flows around it.

The Postal Rift flow, in the northern part of Kilauea crater, together with all the outflows of Halemaumau on other sides, make a covering occupying nearly a quarter of the greater crater. This flow continues to grow in area, and on this evening new fingering flows were piling on top of those already accumulated at the base of Byron's Ledge, so that a new pool was making there and widening in the direction of Halemaumau.

Up to midnight, November 27, there was nothing notably new about the condition of Halemaumau. The main lake was streaming rapidly into the south pond and northeast cove, the north lake was six to eight feet below its banks, the Postal Rift source was pouring out its torrent as before, and the northern flow area was very bright, puddling and spreading as usual.

At 1:42 a. m., November 28, earthquakes began to be registered seismometrically, and about 2 a. m. five or six pronounced quakes were felt in the course of five minutes. In all some seventy-five felt shocks occurred between 1:58 and 4 a. m. Over two hundred shocks were instrumentally registered, the half-hour following the onset being practically a continuous jarring of the ground.

With the first observed trembling, Halemaumau as seen from the Observatory became very bright in the south pond region. At 2:05 a. m. the writer was watching the cliff profile, about 40 feet high, which as seen in the distance was sharply outlined as a crag on the south side of the north lake. Hundreds of visitors have climbed the rounded slope leading to this cliff in order to view the lake from above. In less than a minute this cliff flattened out and disappeared beneath the edge of a new pit created by general subsidence, the entire Halemaumau inner dome diasppeared, and there was left a straight edge with only the south pressure ridge and the Postal Rift cones remaining as breaks in the smooth profile. It was now certain that the whole lava column was sinking quietly and very rapidly, and the five openings of the Postal Rift tunnel on the right lost brilliancy and became dull as the flow ceased within them. A few minutes after the crags sank, dense avalanche clouds of dust went up from the pit and a continuous roaring noise could be heard, partly from Uwekahuna Bluff, where sliding was started by the earthquakes.

The pooled flow in the north part of Kilauea crater grew brighter, and within an hour small ponds had been formed by collapse in western and central parts of the surface, the liquid in these ponds fountaining and spraying to considerable heights, when the steady pressure, which had been applied by the source tunnels, was withdrawn. This process continued into the forenoon, when a standing fountain was seen welling up in a small oval pond between the Observatory and Halemaumau.

Arriving at Halemaumau 3:15 a. m., the writer could hear continuous sliding of avalanches in the pit. There was no visible change in the south pressure ridge, and the trail monuments built of loose stones had not been shaken down by earthquake. The light from the lava was greatly diminished. From the platform at the east end of the pressure ridge, it appeared that the whole filling of the old circular pit of Halemaumau had gone down over 400 feet in an hour and fifteen minutes; probably the greater part of this happened in the first half-hour, for the pit was already more or less adjusted and heavy avalanches were rare. The walls were nearly vertical, the pit 1200 feet in diameter, big talus cones with glowing edges could be seen far below, and a small partly crusted lava lake was bubbling at its edge and spurting through a crust crack in the middle. The upper edge of the pit was cracked and overhanging in places, but falls from the edge were very rare and none were seen. On the rock wall inside, a layer of cracked glowing matter formed a veneer which frequently scaled off on the surface so that from the opening so formed powdery avalanches of glowing matter poured out. There was some gas puffing from vents in the floor.

The pit was extended northward through the collapsing of all the region between the northwest station and the 1894 cones, including the new large black cone. The Postal Rift source cones remained a short distance north of the new edge. This edge did not here descend to any great depth, but there was left a niche or shelf extending in irregular terraces down for perhaps 100 feet, to where the old pit margin was defined beneath as an upright cylinder. These terraces could be seen, one below the other, with ragged edges standing out in profile against the fume below.

The tunnel opening near the Postal Rift source cones was glowing brilliantly, but entirely empty. There was no hissing or flaming in the cones and the cupola beneath was glowing and empty. The stream bed of the tunnel showed a shoreline bench only 4 feet above it, indicating that the torrent had been only five or six feet deep.

Occasional heavy avalanches in the pit sent up brown dust clouds, but the continuous roar was due to the trickling slides from the glowing veneer, and to slips on the slide rock slopes below. There were some glowing cracks in the north wall, low down.

When seen by daylight at 10:30 a. m., the lava column was already in nearly complete adjustment; the pit was dusty but not very smoky, and a small triangular lake stood 591 feet below the northeast rim and lay in the northeastern corner of the floor against the talus. The floor elsewhere consisted of large surfaces of cracked bench magma, which had been lowered bodily from the Halemaumau dome above. Some traces could be made out of the original topography, and the remnant pool appeared to be the north lake. The talus slopes extended as much as a quarter of the way up the pit wall in places.

A most remarkable and interesting feature revealed by the sudden subsidence was the veneer of glowing matter moulded against the walls of the pit, and more or less striated vertically. This in daylight was a dusty brown, and had shelled off completely in places, revealing its thickness of from two to five feet. This was the wall-crack fill or dyke which had surrounded the inner hard lava column, standing between the bench magma and the old wall, and probably liquid up to the time of the subsidence. It will be remembered that the wall-crack, or contact surface between the bench magma and the confining pit, has been the source of overflows, the site of cones and flaming vents, and the place of development of ''wall valleys'' during subsidences, all of these actions being prominent since 1917. How deep the wall-crack extended has been problematical, dependent on the thickness vertically of the semi-solid lava which we call the bench magma. The revelation of this veneer to depths of over 500 feet, its inner surface the mould of an inner hard substance which confined it, demonstrates that the bench magma extended to that depth at least. It may well be that the lubricating action of the wall-crack filled with lake magma, accounts for the extraordinary quietness and quickness of the rapid descent of the column on this occasion.

The lake was crusted, with occasional cracking and foundering, two or three sluggish fountains broke through the crust, and some driblet cascades were pouring into the lake from a fissure heap on its west side. Farther west there was a puffing cone, with glowing orifices whence trickle flows had spread across an old bench magma surface coated with Pele's hair. These flows gave evidence of renewed or continued gas pressure, making lake magma.

A remarkable feature of both the east and west walls of the pit, at points exactly opposite each other, was a pair of open cracks extending straight up and down and trending northeast and southwest. These appeared to be the continuation of the same crack across the pit, a deep vertical break through the Kilauea inner cone, wherein Halemaumau is the crater. The crack opened downward and petered out upward, showing for some 400 feet above the bottom of the pit as a fissure one to two feet open. A new development of fume southwest of Halemaumau came from a fissure in line with this one, and apparently its continuation a few hundred feet outside of the pit rim.

Vapor rose densely from the ring of 1893 cracks around Halemaumau. There was much reddish grit from the avalanche clouds, which fell about the edges of the pit both in the early morning hours and in the daytime. There was some fume from the west side of the new northern shelf. The Postal Rift flow continued to make blue fume and remained bright in the evening of this day, especially near the extreme front under Bryon's Ledge. The earthquake swarming quite ceased after daylight, thereby affording additional evidence that the subsidence was completed in a few hours.

During the week ending at 8 p. m., Friday, November 28, 1919, the seismographs of the Whitney Laboratory registered local earthquakes as follows: November 22, 2:37 a. m., very feeble; November 23, 10:35 a. m., very feeble; November 25, 9:58 p. m., a near shock with origin about 110 miles away, reported strongly felt in Maui; November 26, 3:20 a. m., slight, and 3:16 p. m., feeble; November 27, 3:42 a. m., feeble (felt in Hilea). On November 28 earthquakes were registered almost continuously from 1:42 a. m. to 4:11 a. m., some seventy-five of these being perceptible between 1:58 and 4 a. m., the total number of shocks amounting to over two hundred. The heaviest and most continuous trembling was between 1:58 and 2:30 a. m., the time of the major subsidence in Halemaumau. Other earthquakes November 28, all feeble, were as follows: 8:58 a. m., 9:02 a. m., 12:45 p. m., 6:57 p. m., and 8:39 p. m.

Spasmodic microtremor during the week was slight to moderate, and harmonic tremor moderate to slight. Microseismic motion continued slight. Tilting of the ground was slight to the northwest November 22, to the southeast November 23-26, and excessive eastward and northward November 28.

Very respectfully,

T. A. JAGGAR, JR.,
Volcanologist.

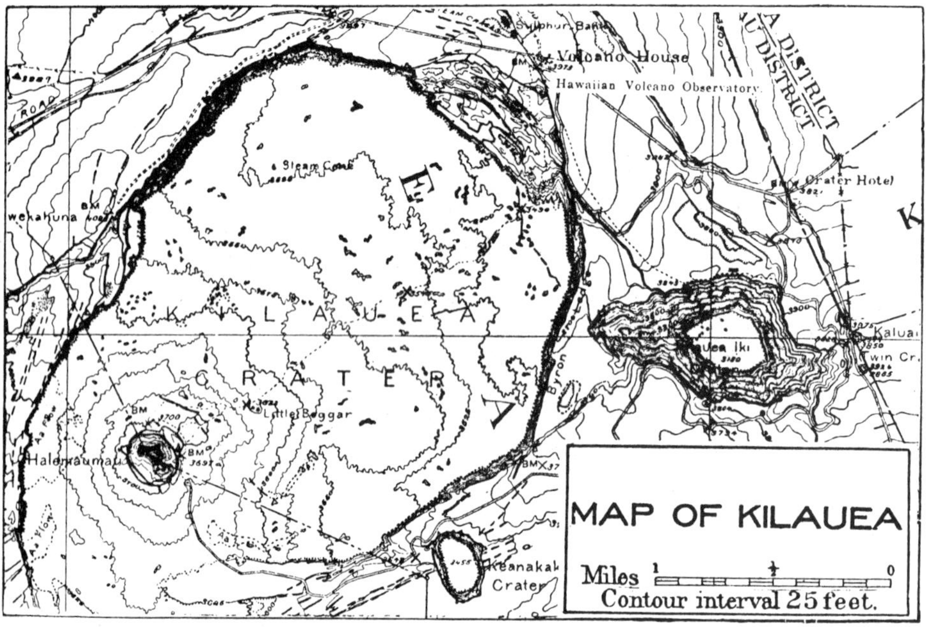

HAWAIIAN VOLCANO OBSERVATORY.

The Observatory is equipped with the following seismometric instruments rebuilt at the station in 1918 for the special needs of volcano research: two Bosch-Omori pendulums, high speed registration of local earthquakes; one optically recording seismograph for distant earthquakes; one clinograph registering E-W tilting of the ground. A vertical component seismograph was in December, 1918, set up in experimental operation. These are seated on concrete piers in a closed basement room having practically constant temperature, beneath the chief Observatory building near the hotel. Time is referred to a rated chronometer, checked at intervals by solar observations with a transit. Both instruments are loaned by the College of Hawaii. Hawaiian standard time (H. S. T.) is 10 hrs. 30 min. slower than Greenwich time.

CANCANI SCALE OF SEISMIC INTENSITY.

Expressed by accelerations measured in millimeters per second per second.

I.	Instrumental	0.0	2.5
II.	Very slight	2.5	5.0
III.	Slight	5.0	10.0
IV.	Sensible, mediocre	10.0	25.0
V.	Rather strong	25.0	50.0
VI.	Strong	50.0	100.0
VII.	Very strong	100.0	250.0
VIII.	Ruinous	250.0	500.0
IX.	Disastrous	500.0	1000.0
X.	Very disastrous	10000.0	2500.0
XI.	Catastrophic	2500.0	5000.0
XII.	Great catastrophe	5000.0	10000.0

Grade IV. is ordinarily the minimum perceived by the senses; and in grade XII. the accelerations or rate of change of motion (jerk) reaches that of terrestrial gravitation.

In the standard form of report the maximum intensity or acceleration, designated by the symbol a, or max. a, is given in the conventional unit of milligal. The milligal is a measure of acceleration, such that 1 milligal = 1/100 mm. per sec. per sec. = 10 μ. per sec. per sec. The Cancani scale, here defined in terms of millimeters per sec. per sec., can therefore be expressed in milligals by multiplying each of the numbers by 100.

U. S. DEPARTMENT OF AGRICULTURE
WEATHER BUREAU
CHARLES F. MARVIN, CHIEF

MONTHLY BULLETIN
OF THE
Hawaiian Volcano Observatory

VOL. VII. HONOLULU, HAWAII, DECEMBER, 1919 No. 12

December 6, 1919.

During the week ending Friday, December 5, 1919, the recovery of the lava column in Halemaumau pit has continued with great rapidity, developing in a few days features the equivalent of which it took weeks to produce in 1916. The liquid lava on the first day after the subsidence increased to a large lake, on the second day cascades were pouring into the lake from springs of lava which welled up behind the talus, then the ring of bench magma under the border talus rose bodily and tipped toward the lake, the gaping wall-crack so formed engulfed the talus, and finally by the end of the week long curved ponds of boiling lava developed in the encircling crack, rose to levels 100 feet or more above the central lake and cascaded inward over the ring crags so as to increase the volume of the lake.

The revelation of this encircling solid rock under what had at first appeared to be high talus cones shows that the topography of bench magma was more completely preserved during the great subsidence than appeared at the time. What had been the arched surface of flat dome shape encircling the three lakes, became after the subsidence a surface of basin shape, its edges masked by debris and a single lake in the middle. The angle of slope of the sides of this basin appears to have been increased by the weighting effect of the inflow that enlarged the lake. The semi-solid matter beneath appears to have been squeezed outward and upward, reaching the wall-crack region of less pressure and so by release of gas generating liquid magma. This is a reversal of the process so often seen in 1918 and 1919, whereby the wall-valley fill weighted the margins and pushed up the center.

Measurements on Tuesday, December 2, at 10:15 a.m., were made just after a spell of pronounced uplift of the bottom area whereby the ring of older bench had been raised as well as the lake, the bench more than the lake. There was also an inner bench or lake shore line which marked by its height above the liquid the extent to which the older basin had been lifted in excess of the rise of the lake. The depression of the lake below the northeast rim of the pit was now 446 feet, the inner bench 413 feet and the outer bench or talus 378 feet, all of these measurements being directed at the northwestern corner of the lake basin, where two days before there had been a trickling spring of lava pouring into the lake from the top of the talus. The solidified materials of this cascade were broken by the uplift. The height of the inner bench, which gave the lake the appearance of having fallen, really indicated that the annular margin of old floor had risen 33 feet in excess of the rise of the lake. The lake itself as compared with the measurements of November 28 had risen 145 feet in four days, making the average rise 36¼ feet per day. The liquid lava in the wall-crack ponds stood at levels 50 or 60 feet higher than the central lake, so that if this were compared with the liquid level of November 28 the rate of rising would be 50 feet per day. As the ring of bench magma had risen more than the lake, and confined the liquid of the wall crack, and this last had been flowing voluminously into the lake at nearly lake level on November 30, it is a fair statement of the whole rising movement to say that the lava column rose 200 feet in four days, this including the lake, its confining basin and the liquid welling up the wall-crack. The rim bench mark to which the above depression figures are referred stands 3727 feet above sea level.

A plat of the upper rim of the pit determined it to be oval in form with diameters 1200 feet east-west and 1485 feet north-south. The extra 285 feet of the north south axis is mostly made up of the northern inner shelf, the lowest terrace of which stands 85 feet below the northeastern rim of Halemaumau. The rest of the pit and the deeper portion containing the live lava column, is nearly cylindrical with walls that slope inward but slightly, so that the ring of talus, floor crags and lake has diameters of something over 1100 feet.

On Saturday, November 29, at about 4 p.m., the interior of Halemaumau was almost entirely free from fume, but the vapor from the outlying cracks was dense, especially to the southwest. The inner walls still showed the wonderful veneer of solidified wall-crack material, which gave the pit a very clean-cut upright circular appearance like the inside of a bucket. This was identical with the old shaft of 1916, but the upper rim of the pit, added to by 1918-19 overflows, showed marked changes. Among these changes are the dark colored beds of southwest overflow about 20 feet thick; the fill of the west niche formed in February, 1918; the new north shelf and a section of flows back of it; the northeast heap of 1919 built above the fill of 1918 to a depth of 40 or 50 feet with the old red scar of the 1894 bench showing in section below; and lastly the jagged profile of the south pressure ridge still standing high above the general level of the rim of the pit. Breaks in the west wall at lower levels showed at least two clean-cut unconformable bedding lines marking ancient Halemaumau rims. The only source of fume inside the pit was a stained patch at the top of the western talus.

The lake had risen to become a large pentagonal pool some 600 feet in diameter and estimated over 50 feet higher than the little pond of the previous day. The pool was quietly rising, its shores directly against the loose stones and hard rock of the talus ring without any spatter rampart or border grottoes, and its surface was covered with black skins through which four or five central fountains were breaking almost continuously. There was some bright-line pattern and occasionally the crust would crack and the blocks founder. A cracked surface of the old floor still bounded the lake on its south side.

A fragment of the east rim of the pit, which had been poised and tottering the previous day, had now fallen. A few trivial avalanches were seen. Apart from these the only noise in the pit was from the fountains. At night the pit was brighter than before. In the tumble of the northern benches no trace could be seen of the old features such as the 1894 cones and the masonry bench mark.

The Postal Rift source cone was more broken in and a large dark chamber was revealed below; a well still retaining red heat could be seen through the adjacent tunnel opening, but the tunnel itself was dark in the first three openings to the northwest. The fourth group of openings showed brilliant red heat inside and the fallen bowlders were still cherry red just as when the lava was flowing. The fifth opening was brilliantly yellow with incandescence, and the empty stream channel was six feet deep, making the height of tunnel 26 feet. The hot gas which emerged from the opening was breatheable and seemed to be merely air. The retention of heat in such large chambers having access to air suggests continued oxidation of the iron in the rock.

At night the glow spots of the Postal Rift flow were fewer and confined largely to the area under Byron's Ledge, where the lava was still spurting through openings. This revival of fountaining in a lava field cut off from a source of supply suggests gas reaction with atmospheric oxygen.

At the base of Uwekahuna Bluff in several places large and small bowlders were seen resting on the fresh lava of the Postal Rift flow, this debris having been dislodged from the bluff during the earthquakes of the early morning of November 28.

At noon on November 30 a visit to the fuming crack southwest of Halemaumau determined it to be a vertical fissure extending out radially from the pit about 300 feet from the edge and trending in the direction of the 1868 cracks. The rising smoke was dense, blue and sulphurous along some 200 feet of the fissure line, the rock of the 1919 flows was stained and the crack had a very high temperature. It was about six inches wide cutting across all the flows indiscriminately. This was much the most densely smoking vent anywhere about Halemaumau. It corresponds in position and trend with the crack in the opposite walls of the interior of Halemaumau, but the latter emits no smoke.

Halemaumau on this day was more smoky, the lake was about 40 feet higher and the wall-crack vents back of the talus were bubbling with liquid lava which cascaded into the lake across the talus on the eastern, western and southern sides of the pit. One of the western vents was spurting noisily. The old bench and slopes of slide rock were much encroached upon by the lake so that none was left on the east; on the west they were low, and the higher embankments north and south were mostly solid rock remnants with some talus on top.

The upright fracture seen cutting across the lower pit walls is of great interest on the eastern wall, in that it cracks across the wall-crack veneer, an open chasm one to three feet wide; if this veneer solidified after the early morning of November 28, then this crack across it opened still later. Its mate appearing on the southwest wall cuts across ancient bedded rocks.

The lake now showed a narrow beginning of rampart shoreline, implying the formation of a thin shell of bench magma under its bottom and sides. There were two main fountaining areas in the lake, each with two or three dome fountains of the sluggish type, the fountain sending up a blue smoke ring as it burst, and recalling the "Old Faithful" of 1911. The fountaining areas were in the north central and southwest central parts of the lake, and the crusts tended to crack in rings around the fountains. These crusts were heavier than before. The wall-crack lava of the east side accumulated in a considerable pool which drained into the lake by way of a wide cascade. The avalanches on this day were mostly under the south pressure ridge, the bowlders sometimes reaching the lake and breaking up its border crusts.

The sunken shelf at the north edge of Halemaumau lies between the cracks which formerly extended northward from the 1894 cones and from the northwest station. Before the collapse the north edge of Halemaumau was much broken up, undermined and inflated by sulphurous gases during the development of the Postal Rift flow. It seems probable that this undermining was developed by lava seepage through these two cracks, and when the drop came the whole region collapsed. Much smell of sulphur vapor still rose from the Postal Rift source region, but no glow could now be seen in the tunnel well. Luminous spots in the Postal Rift flow were now few, but the fluid was still oozing out in one place under Byron's Ledge. Blue fume rose from the flow in many places, and in some rare vents there was a puffing red fume.

On December 1 at 3:30 p.m. the fume had increased at Halemaumau and the ring of bench magma around the lake had risen about 8 feet, giving the lake the appearance of subsidence within its basin. Four fountains were playing continuously. Some light fume was issuing from a new crack northeast of Halemaumau and dense smoke rose from the southwest fissure and from several places in the old Postal Rift circle. The fourth and fifth openings of the Postal Rift flow tunnel appeared as hot as ever, the rock was red hot within two inches of the surface at the edge of a large opening and the bottom of the deep tunnel was plastic and of bright yellow incandescence. There were still numerous glow cracks in the flow covering the northern part of Kilauea crater, but no moving toes were seen.

A prolonged light earthquake in the early morning hours of December 2 was perhaps occasioned by the stress of sudden rising of the lava column. On visiting Halemaumau at 10 a.m. it was found that the encircling ring of old floor under the talus and around the lake had risen bodily and tilted inward toward the center, breaking up the solidified wall-crack cascades, opening the wall-crack until it had become a gulch and causing the talus to slump into this gulch on all sides. There was thus created an annular knife-edge ridge standing out from the wall, and on the northeast side a pool of hot liquid lava occupied the gulch and showed continuous bubble fountaining. The lake margin inside of the ring had retired from its uptilted shores leaving a sloping terrace scarred with black shore lines; this scar was 15 feet high on the northeast side and 4 feet high southwest, indicating that the uplift of the cup involved tilting from northeast to southwest. There was further evidence of this in a triangular shoal on the northeast side of the lake sloping southwestward at a flat angle, making a beach of uplifted lake bottom, with one of the fountains at its margin puffing as though building a cone. This fountain, and the persistence of the other fountaining localities, gave evidence thus of spring holes in a shallow bottom under the fountaining localities. There were still two principal fountaining areas, quiet crusts over the lake and occasionally cracking and foundering of the crusts which revealed the hot melt beneath.

There was increased smoke in the pit from talus openings north and south. Nightfall revealed glow in the northwest wall crack from lava still bubbling beneath the cascade debris. Small avalanches continued, especially southwest, the side of downward tilt of the floor.

The line of openings in the Postal Rift tunnel northwest of Halemaumau was wholly dark at the first three localities, red hot at No. 4, and at the deep pit No. 5 there was orange heat but darker than before, the rocks near the orifice being purple to cherry red. Small stones thrown in encountered a hard bottom at the stream channel and took from ten to fifteen minutes to heat up to incandescence. There was a roaring noise as of rushing air through the tunnel or its orifice, but no appearance of windy outrush was seen. It seemed possible that this noise was due to some reaction in the rock. Where the linings of the tunnel had cooled off and could be seen in daylight, the glaze was dark red with oxidation of the contained iron.

At 6 p.m. the lake was rising and had encroached upon the shoal at its border. The fountains were small, flinging a viscous melt, and the northeast wall-crack had two ponds with hundreds of small fountains making a pattern recalling the activity of 1912. Disagreeable sulphurous fume rose from these fountains at the eastern edge of the pit.

After a southwesterly storm the floor of Kilauea at 9:30 p.m. on December 4 presented dense masses of vapor and there were still scattered glowing openings in the Postal Rift flow. Halemaumau was much brighter and from its eastern edge the ring ridge could be seen to be much higher and moved inward so as to increase the width of the gulch between it and the wall. Elongate wall-crack ponds had again formed on the northeast and west, the former greatly enlarged and still boiling violently and continuously. The mottled pattern of the bubble fountaining here was what produced the bright glow from the pit, the breaking skins continuously streaming north and south from a middle dark zone. At the two ends the pond was crusted, with some spitting of small vents towards the south. At the base of the south wall of the pit the debris was sliding into a smoke hole, making small avalanches and sending up gritty dust. Some Pele's hair from the fountains fell outside of the pit.

The western wall-crack pond had two or three small fountains and was otherwise quiet. The main lake had five fountaining centers, was generally crusted and the eastern fountain was building a low cone. The spray shot up 20 or 30 feet. There was again a flat of lifted floor east of the lake.

Occasional small avalanches fell from various parts of the pit wall.

At 11 a.m. December 5 the pit was smoky, but the eastern wall-crack pond could be seen some 600 feet long and over 50 feet wide, continuously boiling and streaming northward. There were fountaining vents in the crust of the pond at its south end and farther south in the wall-crack there was noisy puffing with inward slipping talus undermined by lava below.

The main lake crust was heavier than before with three sluggish fountaining vents breaking it, the eastern one throwing up umbrella flings of melt.

The northern part of the western wall-crack pond was wide and quietly fountaining, but at its southern end this pool overflowed inward across the knife-edge ridge and sent a cascade down to the lake. The cascade was 25 feet wide and other vents in the slope below made a line of fountaining springs which flooded the western crust of the lake and made there a fresh field of pahoehoe. The large cascade fell 50 feet to the spring line, and there was about 50 feet more of drop from here to the lake surface, making the difference of level between the wall-crack pond and the lake about 100 feet.

The wall gulch on the north side was now 200 feet wide at the level of the ring ridge bordering it and the top of this ridge now stood up as a jagged crag all around the central lake. It was evident that the present rise was taking effect by lifting the margins of the old sunken floor instead of the middle, as though the weight of the lake had caused displacement outward of the plastic matter below. The intense effervescence in the wall-crack to heights greater than the lake appeared to show that marginal pressure release had converted the under paste into liquid, by release of gas from solution, and consequent heating.

The southwest fume crack showed no change. Some of the northwest edge of Halemaumau appeared to have fallen away. The debris of the inner slope of the south pressure ridge had mostly fallen, making that ridge a nearly vertical wall on the inside with an outer slope of debris.

In the Whitney Laboratory of Seismology for the week ending at midnight Friday, December 5, 1919, local earthquakes were registered as follows: November 29, 3:49 a.m.; November 30, 10:30 p.m., moderate; December 1, 3:28 a.m., slight; 9:26 a.m., very feeble; December 2, 5:36 a.m., felt; December 3, 10:23 p.m., very feeble; December 4, 2:02 a.m., light. Spasmodic tremor was weak to moderate during the week with pronounced wind effects December 4 and 5. The harmonic microtremor became excessively slight during the week. Microseismic motion was very slight, increasing a little December 4 and 5. Motion of tilting was strong to the south and moderate to the west in the early part of the week, changing on December 2 to strong east and moderate south.

On December 1, after some weeks of experimentation, a seismograph was started in operation in Hilo for the measurement of local earthquakes coordinate with the work of the Whitney Laboratory. This installation is the work of the Hawaiian Volcano Research Association, the first of a series of instruments to be placed in the hands of volunteer observers on the Island of Hawaii. The seismograph was designed by Dr. Romberg in cooperation with the writer, who has set up and modified the Hilo instrument as experiment required. Major W. V. Allen, United States Customs Collector of Hilo, has kindly consented to operate the instrument and mail the seismograms to the Observatory.

The vault used is of heavy concrete with double walls reinforced with steel, each nine inches thick and with a four-inch air space between. The roof is an arch of solid concrete fifteen inches thick. The inside space measures 14 feet 6 inches by 10 feet 8 inches, floored with concrete resting on the beach sand on land very slightly above tide water in what is known as the Ponohawai district on the north side of Kamehameha Avenue between Waiakea and Hilo town.

The use of this vault was contributed by the Hilo Mercantile Company. To this firm we are indebted for cooperation in the establishment of the seismograph, and also to the following Hilo firms and organizations who have done work on the building gratuitously through their interest in the Hawaiian Volcano Research Association: Hilo Electric Light Company, Hawaii Publicity Commission, Charles H. Will. Volcano Garage, Hawaii Consolidated Railway Company, American Factors, Ltd., and the county engineer representing the Department of Public Works.

To the last named officer we are indebted for the exact determination of the meridian, and the horizontal pendulum is set up in the meridian for registration of east-west vibration. On this site there is some artificial disturbance due to railway trains and heavy trucks, but the registration of such movement is quite distinct in character from that of earthquakes. The preliminary tests of the instrument have satisfactorily registered earthquake, tilt and microseisms, and have demonstrated that no trace of the harmonic and spasmodic microtremor, so common at Kilauea, is observed at Hilo. This seems to indicate that these tremors are distinctive of the crater region. The microseisms are stronger than at the volcano. The Maui earthquake of November 25 was registered, showing that the ground is satisfactory.

December 13, 1919.

The week ending Friday, December 12, 1919, at Kilauea Volcano has demonstrated that the rising movement of the lava of Halemaumau now in progress is the most rapid which has occurred since the Observatory was founded in 1911. The central lake area for the fourteen days following the great collapse of November 28 has risen 444 feet, averaging 31.7 feet per day. The uplift moreover up to the middle of the past week has involved the heavy prism of seemingly solid lava which we call bench magma, that filled the pit from wall to wall and had on its surface the former topography.

The movement has proceeded by alternations of spurts between the lake magma and the bench magma. For the first two days after the collapse of November 28 the lake basin filled up rapidly. For the next three days the heavy ring crag became defined and the lake was distributed into the wall-cracks and replaced by uplifted shoals. This was followed for two days more by vigorous rising of the liquid in the wall-cracks and cascading inward to fill up the basin. Beginning on December 6 for three days there was again an uplifting movement developing a great circular craggy ridge with its summit over a hundred feet above the liquid level. Then came, from December 9 to 12, a most extraordinary upwelling of violently boiling liquid, flooding the pit from wall to wall and half drowning the crag ridge so as to convert it into an island.

This last upheaval with liquid rising 40 feet per day in the upper and larger part of Halemaumau pit is a flood incomparably greater than anything heretofore seen by the writer at Kilauea. The boiling mechanism is like that of the spurts of December, 1911, and July, 1912, with thousands of fountains and intense radiation of heat. Nineteen hundred and twelve was as a whole a year of declining lava level, so that this analogy suggests that the present spasm will be short-lived and that it marks the beginning of a period of subsidence for the next two years.

The pit as a spectacle at the present time, wholly free from fume, with an enormous lake containing a great craggy island crescent, the summit of the latter only 75 feet down and the fiery turbulence made infinitely various by the rushing currents and the bombarding of ramparts, is quite comparable in magnificence to any of the phenomena of the Mauna Loa eruption.

Measurements on Tuesday, December 9, at 10 a.m., from the northeast rim station, the elevation of which is 3727 feet above sea level, determined the depression of the several features below this station to be as follows: Shore of ring pool north 267 feet; north crag peak 154 feet; central lake 270 feet; west wall-crack cones 253 feet; south wall-crack fountain 200 feet. The outside diameter of the ring pool north and south was 1000 feet and east and west 1050 feet. The width of the ring pool ribbon on the north was 100 feet and on the east 70 feet. The diameter of the central floor east-west was 760 feet.

Measurement from the same station December 12 at 10 a.m. made the depression of the north pool 147 feet and of the north crag peak 75 feet.

These measurements show that in seven days, from December 2 to December 9, the ring pool rose 129 feet, averaging 18.4 feet per day; the central lake 176 feet, averaging 25.1 feet per day; and the north crag 216 feet, averaging 31.0 feet per day. In three days, from December 9 to December 12, the lakes, now at a common level, rose 120 feet, averaging 40 feet per day, and the north crag 79 feet, averaging 29.7 feet per day.

On Saturday, December 6, at 4:30 p.m., Halemaumau contained much fume rising from the debris in the wall-cracks. A comprehensive view obtained from the south pressure-ridge showed the large lake basin of the center with a live pool on its west side, a ring ridge around it with highest summits north and south and a gulch between this ridge and the wall of the pit filled with an elongate boiling pond on the east, with rock debris north and south and with live lava cones on the west.

The changes which had occurred since the previous day were chiefly those occasioned by strong uplift of the floor on the east side. This had opened wider the eastern wall-crack pond, which had risen and was still covered with multiple fountains in its middle and northern parts, crusted over on the south and streaming northward with occasional bombardment of the walls east and west, such occasions causing a lessening of the general bubbling. The gorge occupied by this pond was extended into really profound gulches on the north and south sides of the pit.

The movement of uplift had pivoted about the contact of the floor block with the west wall so that the wall-crack on the west was narrow with spurting lava through the two cone vents. The cascade of the previous day had ceased and its frozen remnants were crushed. It had flooded the western side of the crusted central lake basin, and the new movement of eastern uplift had again followed the lead of the heavy weighting of the western floor. What was left of the central lake had moved to the west side of its basin and the whole eastern half was a cracked beach slope. At the cascade locality, the cone on top was hissing and at its base in the lake there was a sputtering fountain. The area of the lake had dwindled, probably along with the increase of the east wall pond. Three sluggish spasmodic and explosive fountains occasionally broke through the heavy crust, the northern one making a noisy report followed by a splash of falling melt. Some avalanches fell at the north end of the east pond where the liquid lava was undermining the wall-crack. The whole floor had risen even at its lowest western part.

December 7 produced much lengthening of the wall-crack pond. At 11 a.m. December 8 fume was still dense in the crater, especially at its south end. The wall-crack pond was now a crescent extended from the east to the north and south sides of the pit and the central lake had become a dark floor with two cones on its north side, one bubbling almost continuously and the other exploding at intervals with reports like a pistol shot. The streaming in the wall crack pond was from centers north, south and east, with conflicting currents and violent bubbling at the meeting points northeast and southeast. In the south wall crack there were three isolated pools. The pit at night steadily increased in brightness and the fume column rising in calm air was very brilliantly illumined by the areas of bubble fountaining beneath.

On December 9 in the forenoon, the wall-crack pool was extended in a broad ribbon around the north side of the pit and was fed from a fountain spring in the talus on the south side which stood at a much higher level than the rest of the pool. The annular ridge on the north was now lifted into a high peaked crag. The bubble fountaining was violent in the north pool as well as at the east, and rampart benches were building with crescent niches at places of continuous bombardment. Two pronounced capes or points had thus been built on the inner margin of the eastern part of the pool. The western wall-crack now contained sputtering cones all along the base of the wall, including some in a depressed ravine northwest. The central lake was now a raised floor forming the bottom of the dish surrounded by the ring or crescent of crags, and this floor was now higher than the level of the wall-crack lake. The live part of the floor was a field of overlapping pahoehoe flows fed by a sluggish fountain south of the center, which broke the crust occasionally, while at the north fountain locality a cone had formed, which belched noisily at intervals, making a patter of falling fragments after each explosion. There was another cone at the southwest corner of the floor at the cascade site.

Much smoke still rose along the west wall-crack and from parts of the southern ring crag. The currents of the annular lake moved east and west from a bridge of skin at the north, and met from north and south in the eastern pool making hundreds of bubble fountains and some travelling fountains, recalling the turbulence of 1912. The general situation indicated steady rising, with transfer of the liquid from center to periphery, and encroachment by this marginal lake upon the wall crack talus. Meanwhile the central cylinder of bench magma was lifting so as to bow its edges inward and convert them into high crags. The maximum of this lift at the north produced a peak.

On December 10 at 11 a.m. a visit to the outside fume crack southwest found it excessively hot and the fume now was thin and blue instead of the dense masses of vapor seen a week ago. No glow could be detected there. In Halemaumau the ring pool had extended itself to the southwest, where there was now a large pool of lava cascading to a lower quiet crusted puddle. At the base of the west wall the spurting cones were surrounded by crusted pools, the northern openings making fountains in grotto ovens. The north arm of the crescent lake was larger, with fountains bombarding its south bank, and this was continuous around to the east and south as a long ribbon lake from 10 to 50 feet wide, with violent bubble fountaining in several places. The continued uplift of the ring cragmass, with its culminating summit at the north, had produced a low pass at the east as though the rise north and south were breaking the dish in two. The pool within the dish was now flooding through a continuous fountain in the center which made a spread of radial flows. The blowing cone also was larger, throwing up gushes of melt. The heat from the pit had increased, the fume from the fountains was strong with sulphur, much Pele's hair was strewn about at the north, and small avalanches continued, jostled loose by the lava movements. The southern ridge of the crag mass was now straight-topped, mostly bowlders and less than half as high as the northern summit, the eastern ridge being still lower.

On Thursday, December 11, at 10 a.m., after a night of exceedingly brilliant glow at the pit, the lake was found to have welled up at an unprecedented rate north, south and west, so as to bring central and marginal pools all into one and convert the crag-mass into a crescent island with its horns pointed west. Along the foot of the west wall was a line of twelve standing fountains with some cone remnants confining them, the ring pools were boiling and the central region was a quiet flooded field covered with large areas of fresh skin which showed surface patterns like watered silk. The marginal currents diverged from the three source wells north, south and west, and converged to intermediate shifting places, where thousands of fountains, large and small, boiled up, or bombarded the walls, or built ramparts against the island. The speed of streaming was variable, but mostly swift. The avalanches were mostly at the southeast corner of the pit. The only dark skins which formed in the ring lake were at the source wells. The most violent fountains were at the east.

In the evening everything was higher and a large dome fountain bursting about eight times to a minute broke the skin of the central pool where the explosive cone had been. There was violent multiple fountaining in the ring channel southwest and in the north pool the rising lava made a pattern of golden rosettes which united in currents rushing toward the island bank. Against this bank on the north-northeast side lay a semicircle of dark skin from which streaming radiated. A torrent poured from the western cones along the wall to the north pool. Intense multiple fountaining continued at the east, and on the western side of the north pool. The heat and illumination were stronger than ever and the pit remained clear of visible fume all day.

At 10 a.m. on December 12 the concentrated intensity of the fountaining activity reached a maximum. The convection currents of the liquid lava now tended to rise along the wall of the pit, rush across the marginal lake from the wall to the island and against the island to go down in swirls and explosions of fountaining. This mechanism was strongest on the northern and southeastern sides. The heat was terrific and the uprush of gas from the pit generated troublesome whirlwinds on the edge, with showers of grit and gravel. The lake had gained on the crag mass, making the latter narrower and the former wider. The central pool, fed from the west, showed quiet cracking and foundering with one dome-fountain, almost exactly in the center, which exploded every two or three seconds. The western quarter of the ring was a line of upwelling fountains in a row, but everywhere else in the outer ring lake the fountaining was furiously tumultuous with thousands of great dome bursts of the same order of magnitude as at Halemaumau in July, 1912. The fume had slightly increased, from sources at the places of bombardment along the ring ridge. At the eastern gap in this ridge the splashing had broken through and built a spatter platform across the island There were some narrow zones of crust, especially north and southeast, at the outer border of the ring lake where the centripetal currents departed from the wall. These crusts were evenly striated in the direction of the currents. The avalanches were mostly from the south wall, strong ones being recorded, one at 9:30 a.m. and two about 12:10 p.m. The weather was calm and the roar of the fountains in the forenoon could be heard at the Observatory nearly three miles away.

A striking feature of this period of intense localized heat at the pit was the development of high cumulus clouds above the hot convection column, which showed a brown fringe beneath and a zone of transparent bluish gas between the bottom of the cloud and the edge of the pit. At sundown there was no cumulus and the fume extended far away to leeward as a thin veil hanging in flat strata. In the cool of the evening shreds of water vapor condensed irregularly in the fume cloud and a bank of fog poured over Uwekahuna Bluff like a waterfall, marking the indraught of cooler air around the margins of the hot uprush at the pit. In the evening the pit was more brilliant than at any time since 1912.

During this week the Postal Rift flow area has continued to show four or five glowing cracks as seen from the Observatory. At the source tunnel all glow has disappeared, and much hot air still rises from the openings, which have collapsed to some extent.

White localized cumulus clouds were noticed over the Kahuku source region of the recent Mauna Loa eruption in the night of December 5--6 and in the forenoons of December 10 and 11.

In the Whitney Laboratory for the week ending at midnight Friday, December 12, 1919, there have been a few very feeble local earthquakes as follows: December 9, 6:29 p.m. and 11:28 p.m.; December 10, 12:45 p.m.; December 12, 12:02 p.m. and 10:07 p.m. Spasmodic microtremors have increased from a few weak spasms per day on December 6 to several strong spasms on December 12. The harmonic microtremor has increased from almost none to slight. Microseismic motion has been moderate, and distinctly stronger than anything recorded for many weeks past. Tilting of the ground was westward and southward about December 7 and 8 and northward and eastward about December 12.

December 20, 1919.

During the week ending Friday, December 19, 1919, Kilauea has continued its remarkable performance of swift rising in Halemaumau followed by sudden outbreak of foamy thin-shelled flows through a long radial crack on the floor of Kilauea crater southwest. This action has happened twice during the week, the first outflow occasioning sudden subsidence in the pit, followed by a swarm of earthquakes, the origins of which appear from the seismograms to be nine or more miles away. The newly opened rift is continued outside of Kilauea crater for a mile and a half in the Kau desert along the line of the so-called 1868 cracks, where new hot vapor is rising and the chasms have yawned open profoundly. The activity of the liquid lava in Halemaumau continues to be marked by stormy fountaining in a lake which fills the pit from side to side, and the ring-shaped island enclosing the central lake has slowly become more and more submerged. The fountaining is still confined to an outer annular channel which has increased in width as the liquid rose in the funnel-shaped pit and gained volume at the expense of the island. The highest level was reached December 15, when the lake was in places only 20 feet below the Halemaumau rim and very near the 3700-foot contour. At present the lava appears to be rising and falling in pulsations, overflowing when it passes the level of the open southwest rift, and giving off immense quantities of gas, heat and light.

The approximate fluctuations of level of the lake at the north pool, and of the island at its northern summit for the week ending December 19 are shown in the following table, from estimates checked by transit on north-northeast rim December 16:

Dec. 12, 10:00 a. m., lake 147 feet below rim; crag 75 feet below rim. Dec. 13, 11:30 a. m., lake 90 feet below rim; crag 25 feet below rim. Dec. 14, 3:00 p. m., lake 50 feet below rim; crag 5 feet above rim. Dec. 15, 11:00 a. m., lake 35 feet below rim; crag 50 feet above rim. Dec. 15, 6:30 p. m., lake 135 feet below rim; crag 50 feet below rim. Dec. 16, 11:00 a. m., lake 148 feet below rim; crag 71 feet below rim. Dec. 17, 11:00 a. m., lake 80 feet below rim; crag 40 feet below rim. Dec. 18, 12 noon, lake 70 feet below rim; crag 40 feet below rim. Dec. 19. 6:00 p. m., lake 50 feet below rim; crag 25 feet below rim.

The figures show that during the three days December 12--15 the lake rose 112 feet or 37.5 feet per day, and the crag rose 125 feet or 41.3 feet per day; then came outflow and subsidence, from 11:25 a.m. December 15 to the same hour the next day, the lake sinking 113 feet and the crag 121 feet in one day; the recovery for three days December 16--19 lifted the lake level 98 feet, or 33 feet per day, and the crag only about half as much, 46 feet, average 15.3 feet per day; another outflow resulted.

On Saturday, December 13, at 11:30 a.m., the rise continued and at noon the crag peak was in view above the edge of Halemaumau as seen from the Observatory. The crag was coming up more than a foot per hour very steadily, but this movement was accelerated at times so as to lift the shores of the island more than the lake; in general both island and lake were keeping pace, but not uniformly. The fountains were larger, building ramparts on the outer shores of the ring-island, but the lake contact with the wall of the pit showed quiet and continuous overlap of liquid on rock with no sinking spells. The island rose most on the east and north sides so as to keep the outer ring-channel from joining across the east gap with the central basin, but on the west side the two were blended. The currents there rushed together from north and south and poured out into the basin lake. Elsewhere the marginal streaming was mostly inward from the wall against the island, except for some remnant of the north and south currents coming together on the east. The multiple fountaining had lessened. The central lake was quiet, skinned over, with some cracking and foundering of crusts. The level of the liquid lava now reached the lower edge of the north shelf of November 28. There were still occasional slides southwest. The pit at night was extremely brilliant.

At 3 p.m. December 14, the crag was well above the rim of the pit and the multiple fountaining of the ring-pool was again furious and incessant, making a loud roar like a cataract, audible three miles away (Crater Hotel). The streaming was mostly centripetal and the lake less than 50 feet down. Sulphurous acid gas was the dominant odor. The lake was gaining on the island and had reached the upper north shelf of November 28. The ring pool boiled up in hundreds of large dome fountains. Very swift currents on the west side of the pit poured from north and south around the island crags and swept inward to the central basin, sometimes making whirlpools there on the north side. In the evening the whole body of the north crag, and the fountains north, east and west were in view from the Observatory. These fountains hurled spatter lumps of dense black glass over the top of the west cliff of Halemaumau, then 60 feet high, and small spray went much higher. The ramparts were 10 or 15 feet high, built at the lake edge on the west end of the north crag, and the southwest side of the island was buried under rampart lava. The noise at the road terminus was like the roar of the surf. An occasional dome fountain burst in the central pool region. Some smoke rose from stony patches of the island where bombardment was strong. The southwest crack outside of Halemaumau was yawning open and making thin blue fume which was very hot. Avalanches were slight. The light and heat radiation at the edge of Halemaumau were now excessive.

Monday, December 15, proved to be a day of crisis. The whole crag could be seen from the Observatory, and the fountains boiled tumultuously only 20 feet below parts of the pit rim, the rising and the roaring implying a frothing up of gas and lava analogous to a Mauna Loa eruption.

At 10:30 a.m. the streaming was southward on the west side of the ring-lake, inward to the island on the south, eas tand north sides and somewhat southward on the northeast side. The ribbon of this channel was now much wider, and the island lay like an atoll in the pit, enclosing a quiet lagoon open to the west, where occasionally enormous dome fountains broke the surface crusts in the north central region. The rampart lumps of spatter were built high against the island, and the heat at the actual rim cliffs of Halemaumau was insupportable.

Examination of the southwest crack at 10:50 a.m. discovered there a bulged puddle of incandescent crusted lava 50 feet in diameter, which had welled up the crack near the smoke hole some 600 feet from the Halemaumau edge. The ground was swelling and groaning, fragments were falling in the crevasses, and small quakes could be felt underfoot and shook down loose rocks from the south pressure ridge of Halemaumau. At 11:15 I crossed the cracked zone, sulphurous hot fume was rising, and the 1919 lava of this region was freshly fissured with breaks from three to eighteen inches in diameter. Noisy intumescence was so clearly in progress that I prepared to watch for and photograph the outbreak of liquid lava which was sure to follow.

At 11:25 a.m. a puff of dust and fume shot up near the southwest edge of Kilauea crater, in the line of this rift, and under the outcrop, in the Kilauea wall, of the 1868 fissures. Instantly and quietly the ground opened, for a length of four-tenths mile, and some two hundred small fountains of very liquid lava burst out along the crack and the melt bubbled and spread right and left. This outburst was below the shoulder of ground where the first flow puddle had been observed, and down the outer slope of the Halemaumau heap some quarter mile from southwest edge of the pit. The flow-source was a single crack, curved somewhat in plan, and this crack extended to and united with the 1868 cracks, for the latter now began to show motion and avalanching on the Kilauea outer cliff. The flow spread out until it was a mile wide in the southwest Kilauea wall-valley. Molten lava could be seen flowing in the upper part of the fissure system some 15 feet below the surface, showing that the flow was fed from the lake, and that the vertical crack in the inner Halemaumau wall was really continuous with this one. Within an hour the lake had drained down to the flow-level and the flow stopped, showing in this case every appearance of hydrostatic connection. Moreover the lake went much lower and the flow became a sheet of collapsed shells, as though it had drained back through the rift when the "head" was reversed. In the afternoon, after 2 p.m., a swarm of earthquakes recorded seismometrically, indicated a sharp readjustment in the volcanic fissure system.

At the moment of the flow outbreak, both the lake and crag-mass in Halemaumau went down steadily and slowly, the center lagoon nearly keeping its level against the island, but going down a little the faster. A marginal black ledge was left against the wall of the pit all around, two or three feet wide, making a shell of that thickness with horizontal corrugations on its face marking shore levels, the upper ones one to two feet apart. These ones three to four feet apart. These shore marks gave evidence of the rhythmic jerks, with slowly increasing interval, wherewith the downward movement proceeded.

After the first ten minutes (11:35 a.m.) the column had sunk 5 feet; after 45 minutes 25 feet; after 245 minutes (3:30 p.m.) 90 feet; after 425 minutes (6:30 p.m.) 105 feet; and thereafter very little more, possibly 10 feet in 15 hours, to judge by measurements next day.

From 4 to 6 p.m. an examination of the 1868 fissures southwest of Kilauea revealed the fact that they were steaming, something unheard of for many years past, and the ground there, coated with gravel beds crusted with calcareous cement, was well suited to show the new cracking. The freshly opened zone was about a quarter mile wide and a mile and a half long, extending from the edge of Kilauea to a point 1000 feet southeast of the Cone Peak trig. station. The larger chasms had yawned open and engulfed their dirt fills; some creaking and tumbling could be heard within them. One of them was now 80 feet deep and 5 feet wide, leading down to a narrower space going to black depths. The vapor was steamy, of acid sulphurous smell, with temperature over 100 degrees F. Five conspicuous steam vents were aligned across the desert, one at the south end of the opened zone, four nearer to Kilauea in a group. The smaller fractures were of all sizes down to small fresh break lines in the dirt, and the zone petered out in a group of these minute breaks at the south end of the region indicated. Probably these chasms had opened slowly for several days, along with the opening of the smoke-hole crack near Halemaumau, but the steam was not seen before this day.

The activity of Halemaumau did not change its character. At 3:30 p.m. the lake stood 90 feet below the rim, there was the same stormy fountaining and streaming, and the even narrow black ledge all around was an impressive reminder of the recent higher level. There was no avalanching, the walls being in nice adjustment from the earlier subsidence and recovery. The island maintained its height relative to the liquid. At 6:30 p.m., however, the bench magma was sinking faster than the liquid, so that floods from the ring-pool, seeming to arise at a dark crust on the southeast border, swept around the island and across its lower parts east and south into the central lagoon. Two currents met in lines of bubbling at the west. Besides the southeast locality, there were points of departure of currents right and left at the wall margin of the north and southwest corners of the ring-pool, and these streamings were accompanied by the usual intense multiple fountaining and island bombardment which had been the distinctive feature of the last three weeks. Only once a fountain was seen in the lagoon.

At Lee's pit in the southwest part of Kilauea crater, the edge was found newly broken in from the quaking of the afternoon. Small quakes were felt about 4:10 p.m. and at 4:18 p.m. an avalanche fell from the southern part of Uwekahuna Bluff — doubtless an earthquake slide. Blue fume and flame arose from the crack where the fountains had been, white vapor rose from the next higher part of the rift towards Halemaumau, and dense whitish-brown vapor from the smoke-hole still higher a few yards from the lava pit. The flow was glowing but collapsed, friable shelly lava, and had not extended beyond what was seen at noon.

At 11 a.m. December 16 the lake was

148 feet down and the crag summit was 77 feet high above the lake. Dense fume rose from the southwest smoke-hole, twelve jets of blue fume from the source crack, and five jets of white vapor from the desert beyond.

The liquid of the lake had encroached on the southern half of the island. Streaming in the ring-pool was away from the wall on the north, southeast and southwest, intense multiple fountaining there continued, and an occasional dome-fountain broke in the north central part of the lagoon. The trace of the southwest rift-crack, up the inner wall of Halemaumau, was seen to stand open, a vertical chasm, cutting the fresh black ledge veneer, and about one foot wide. This implied its maintenance as an open crack under the lake and presumably full of liquid in the outer country up to the lake level.

The north shelf or niche of the Halemaumau rim, where vacated by the recent fill of the high level, was covered with rough black aa lava with only a few patches or crusts of pahoehoe. A little of the black ledge around the pit had scaled off. The lake appeared as though rising, it could be seen from Uwekahuna at 4:30 p.m., and at night the pit was brilliant as before.

The rising of the liquid was verified next day, for at 11:30 a.m. the lake had risen over 60 feet in twenty-four hours. The fountains were bigger and even more tumultuous, like the July demonstration of 1912 and more of them, and the foci of radial outward streaming from the wall margins of the lake were north-northeast, southeast and southwest. There was more overflowing of the south half of the island, still in progress, all except a small remnant of crag and bowlders. The north crag was surrounded by new wide fresh platforms, and appeared to be rising more than the south end of the atoll-shaped island of which it is a part. A swift torrent was again pouring south around the west end of the northern crag, making violent conflict of currents at the west with high fountains. Other such conflicts happened south and east. Large periodic dome fountains broke the skin of the central lagoon every one to two minutes, and there was a fountaining grotto built at the southwest side of this lagoon. The black ledge had scaled off more and one avalanche was seen.

From Uwekahuna at 8 p.m. both the fountains and the summit of crag were in view above the edge of the pit, which was gorgeous in its brilliancy, lighting up all the cliffs of Kilauea. No glow was seen in the southwest flow or the fuming desert cracks. The rumble of the pit was loudly audible. The Postal Rift flow, remnant from November, still shows four glowing cones, two in the north central part of Kilauea and two under Uwekahuna.

At 7:40 p.m. a detonating meteorite or bolide passed over the island, probably from northeast to southwest, making a streak of light, an explosion, and a concussion, perceived over all the eastern parts of Hawaii and from the sea to the north.

At noon December 18 the island in Halemaumau was more submerged, the lake about 70 feet down, and thousands of points of ebullition north-northeast, south and southwest made tumultuous coarse fountaining, the streaming moving out from dark skins at the wall border, north, southeast and southwest. The ring channel was wide south and north, and narrow on the west, where there were some spatter lumps marking the border of the lagoon dish. Southwest the border was marked by two large spatter lumps, one of them a grotto. The central lake had been increasing in size at the expense of the southern half of the island; the latter, however, still showed a patch of crag bowlders southeast, the island rising on the east side. The ring lake was flowing into the lagoon across its rampart west-northwest, west, southwest, south-southwest and south. The north central dome fountain in the lagoon exploded at long intervals.

The southwest crack was smoking moderately near Halemaumau and a little visible fume rose from the crack in the lower flat where the fountains had been. The crack elsewhere was yielding very hot air. It had opened one to two feet across the upper fresh lava puddle, where the rift zone was about 60 feet wide with numerous cracks and some sulphur staining. The lower crack in the flow area was lined with brownish stalactitic lava, and isolated outliers of the fissure had bubbles of lava over small vents below.

On December 19 there was enough rising in the lake to reach again the level of this outflow crack, an earthquake was felt at 6:50 a.m., and about 4:45 p.m. liquid lava again fountained up in the midst of the southwest flat and revived the flow there. This again appeared to be hydrostatic with reference to the pit. At 5:30 p.m. the flow extended right and left along the base of the Kilauea wall for three-quarters of a mile and was spreading. One large geyser of lava stood about seven feet high in the middle of the source crack, and three or four spurting cones lay along the crack on the Halemaumau side of this fountain and about 325 yards from the pit. The upper smoke hole was making thin fume and the crack above the flow was crossed without difficulty. The flowing continued steadily and the lake in Halemaumau did not go down.

The lake was about 50 feet below the rim, and the southwest crack in the inner wall was from 12 to 18 inches open. The island was more submerged southwest, south and west, the north crag standing about 35 feet above the liquid and 15 feet below the rim of the pit. The central lagoon showed a bright pattern of lines between blocks of skin, and was bordered by a broad platform on the north, part of the rampart accumulation which was burying the craggy portions of the island. The peripheral streaming was from the southwest and north, with centripetal bombardment against the island at the north and east. The noise of the endless fountaining was like a waterfall, and was audible far away. The fume continued thin and the glare brilliant.

The new situation appeared to be an adjustment of the outflow crack to the rising lake, with the rising slightly in excess of the outflow, and the mechanism tending to consume the bench magma beneath so as to lower the island relative to the liquid or frothy lava. The first outbreak of this rift December 15, with the level of liquid in the pit much above the level of outflow, and a long fissure system breaking open, produced a sudden pressure release accompanied by a reaction of subsidence. The second outbreak made no rupture and found the fissures ready and open, filled with lava which rose quietly to the level of outflow. This sequence is quite parallel in a small way to what happens in a Mauna Loa eruption.

In the Whitney Laboratory of Seismology for the week ending at midnight Friday, December 19, 1919, the following local earthquakes have been registered:

Dec. 13,	7:50	a.m.	very feeble
15,	10:56	a.m.	feeble, and four tremors
	1:30	p.m.	feeble
	1:33	"	very slight
	1:35	"	feeble
	1:36	"	slight
	1:37	"	very feeble
	1:38	"	very feeble
	1:39	"	slight
	1:41	"	very feeble
	1:42	"	moder'ly strong
	1:45	"	very slight
	1:48	"	very slight
	1:49	"	feeble
	1:51	"	very feeble
	1:52	"	feeble
	1:53	"	slight
	1:57	"	feeble
	2:00	"	slight
	2:01	"	very feeble
	2:04	"	feeble
	2:07	"	feeble
	2:17	"	very slight
	2:37	"	feeble
	3:05	"	feeble
	3:13	"	slight
	3:17	"	very feeble
	3:32	"	slight
	3:40	"	slight
	3:41	"	slight
	3:49	"	very slight
	3:50	"	very slight
	3:52	"	feeble
	3:55	"	very slight
	3:58	"	very slight
	3:59	"	very slight
	4:01	"	feeble
	4:02	"	very feeble
	4:03	"	slight
	4:04	"	moder'ly strong
	4:06	"	very feeble
	4:07	"	very feeble
	4:09	"	slight

November 28, 1919. Halemaumau pit reopened, looking southwest.

November 30. Lake in Halemaumau and ring crag under talus, looking SE.

November 30, 1919. Southwest rift in Kilauea floor, looking from Halemaumau toward 1868 cracks.

November 30, 1919. Frontal portion Postal Rift flow from Observatory, looking S.
—Photos, Jaggar.

4:11	"	very feeble
4:13	"	very feeble
4:16	"	slight
4:20	"	moder'ly strong
4:22	"	feeble
4:26	"	feeble
4:28	"	feeble
4:29	"	slight
4:30	"	2 feeble quakes
4:31	"	very slight
4:32	"	slight
4:36	"	feeble
4:38	"	slight
4:40	"	feeble
4:43	"	feeble
4:48	"	feeble
4:50	"	very slight
4:52	"	feeble
4:55	"	very feeble
5:05	"	very feeble
5:08	"	very feeble
5:09	"	feeble
5:14	"	very slight
5:15	"	slight
5:17	"	very feeble
5:33	"	very slight
5:45	"	feeble
5:50	"	slight
5:51	"	very feeble
6:07	"	feeble
6:23	"	very feeble
6:30	"	very slight
6:39	"	feeble
7:17	"	very feeble
10:02	"	slight

In all eighty-one earthquakes, eighteen of which were perceptible.

Dec. 16, 7:40 a.m. very feeble
19, 6:50 " felt

Spasmodic microtremor increased to strong December 15 and was moderate thereafter. Harmonic tremor and microseismic motion increased from slight to moderate during the week. Tilting was slightly north December 13, nearly stationary December 14-16 and then moderately west and south.

December 27, 1919.

During the week ending Friday, December 26, 1919, the Hawaiian lava column has passed through another crisis which was reached in Halemaumau exactly on the solstice, December 22. At that time the lava in the pit again gained a high level following the two spurts of rising at rates exceeding 30 feet per day described in last week's Bulletin. At the same time the rifts which had been opening in the Kau desert five miles southwest of Kilauea crater gave vent to flowing pahoehoe lava. These flows have increased throughout the week and their reaction on the pit has steadily lowered the lava lake and crag at a rate exceeding 25 feet per day, leaving the lake depressed 150 feet at the end of the week.

The rending open of the rift system southwest from Kilauea, following upon the similar outbreak of the southwest flank of Mauna Loa, recalls the events of 1823 and 1868. In those years also lava flowed from the Kau desert, and the line of the present rifting lies between the two former eruptions. In both 1868 and 1823 the Kilauea lakes were very large, and appear to have lowered greatly during the outflow. The 1823 flow originated six miles to the southwest. In 1868 both Mauna Loa and Kilauea erupted from fissures far down the southern flanks, the Kilauea outflow thirteen miles southwest of Kilauea crater. That eruption produced lava which welled out of a crack quietly without building up a source cone, and something similar appears to be the character of the 1919 outflow.

Measurements of the week have recorded in Halemaumau pit the following depressions of the lake and north crag, respectively, beneath the northeast stone monument on the edge of the pit, which stands at elevation 3727 feet above sea level:

Dec. 19, 6 p. m. lake 50 feet below rim; crag 25 feet below rim. Dec. 20, 11:00 a. m., lake 40 feet below rim; crag 20 feet below rim. Dec. 21, 11:00 a. m., lake 35 feet below rim; crag 10 feet below rim. Dec. 22, 11:00 a. m., lake 30 feet below rim; crag 0 feet below rim. Dec. 23, 11:00 a. m., lake 40 feet below rim; crag 5 feet below rim. Dec. 24, 10:00 a. m., lake 75 feet below rim; crag 45 feet below rim. Dec. 25, 11:00 a. m.. lake 110 feet below rim; crag 70 feet below rim. Dec. 26, 12:00 noon, 150 feet below rim: crag 100 feet below rim.

The movement of the lava column indicated by these figures was as follows: From December 19 to 22, three days, the bench magma rose 25 feet, or 8.3 feet per day, and the lake magma 20 feet, or 6.7 feet per day; from December 22 to 26, four days, the bench magma subsided 100 feet, or 25 feet per day, and the lake magma 120 feet, or 30 feet per day. The north crag summit is the highest point of the island in the lake and on December 21 the lake had so gained on the island that this summit stood only 20 feet above the liquid; after the subsidence, the liquid had gone down so much faster than the island that the summit stood 50 feet above the lake.

On Saturday, December 20, conditions in Halemaumau were little changed, but rising continued so that in the afternoon the crag summit came into view above the edge of the pit as seen from the Observatory. The violent boiling and streaming continued stormily in the outer ring lake surrounding a horseshoe-shaped island and the inner lagoon encircled by the island was covered with polygonal areas of skin separated from each other by bright lines. The large fountain which had burst out through the rift in the southwest part of the Kilauea floor on the previous day was now building up a broad flat-topped slag heap surmounted by an active pool. This heap lay against the southwest wall of Kilauea crater and extended from Lee's pit to the south end of Uwekahuna wall. The spreading lava at the western edges of the heap could be seen from the Observatory above the right hand profile of Halemaumau.

At 11 a.m. December 21 rising activity continued, the lake standing only 35 feet below the rim of the pit and the outer slag heap to the southwest exhibiting several standing fountains on its summit which spurted 5 or 6 feet above the surrounding pool. The southwest crevasse nearer to Halemaumau at the smoke hole stood open from 3 to 4 feet and contained live hissing lava spiracles. The multiple fountaining in the pit made a great roar, sent up much gas and radiated intense heat, and the liquid had so gained on the island that the southern side of the latter was now completely covered with rampart splashings.

The writer could see smoke in the Kau desert to the southwest beyond the first line of vapor jets. Accordingly the whole line of the rift was explored and lava was discovered overwelling the lip of the crack five miles from Kilauea and three-quarters mile west of Puu Koae.

Starting at the southwest edge of Kilauea crater, an open network of gaping fissures was found, the largest of these being a chasm 15 feet wide broken through rock below and volcanic ash above, the sand continuously slipping on the inner slopes, giving evidence of motion in progress. Vapor rose from a few of the smaller cracks, in some places smelling strongly of sulphurous acid. A second group of conspicuous cracks was found midway between the edge of Kilauea and Cone Peak. Here dense white vapor was puffing up, and down a crack 4 feet wide fluid lava could be seen 50 feet below. This was sluggish pahoehoe welling up in heavy snake-like folds, throwing out incandescent toes and making a crackling noise by reason of the heating and snapping of the adjacent rock. No visible vapor whatever arose where the lava was seen. The dense vapor always came from small cracks adjacent to the lava fillings.

A second zone of steaming cracks was found on the western side of Cone Peak and continuing thence down the mountain to the southwest. This made the active zone about a quarter mile wide and the breaking of the ground was irregular; small fractures across sand and gravel flats being frequently oblique and transverse to the general trend of the rift system. The main steaming cracks on the east and west sides of Cone Peak were usually from one to two feet wide and very continuous. In the southern hill of the Cone Peak ridge a new crack under the slope had broken down and engulfed the pumice of the cone, making a small pit about 10 feet in diameter.

The western of the two main cracks, about four and a half miles down the mountain, showed live lava inside at considerable depths, and on following the crack a half mile farther this lava rose to the surface level. It made a fill in the crack of heavy black pahoehoe, with hissing gas vents breaking through it which yielded flames and built up small spires or roundish heaving puddles. An occasional deep detonation suggested that the expanding lava was heaving open the crack. About four miles from Kilauea the lava overflowed the crack in two small puddles 30 to 50 feet in diameter which were spread out on surfaces of sand and old pahoehoe. These pools were oozing out in incandescent toes at their margins and along the fissure a line of about fifteen spitting and spurting driblet cones crossed the puddles and extended for some distance on either side. One of these was a narrow erect spire about 4 feet high. Below these flows this crack narrowed and became inconspicuous. There were vapor jets at intervals along the live line but not where the lava was most lively.

From this region for another half mile down the mountain the lava activity was offset to the eastern crack beginning a half mile west of Puu Koae and extending for a half mile farther southwest. Bluish brown fume rose densely from this area, smelling of steam and sulphurous acid, as at the old Postal Rift of Halemaumau. This crack was full of lava all along the line with spires, spiracles and heaving pudding vents, the activity appearing to have slowed down from something greater a day or two previous. The place appeared stagnating while the western crack took up the action. The eastern crack was a chasm from 2 to 4 feet wide, showing much spatter from the cones within it and some sulphurous stain. The cones were hissing and flaming but not at the moment spurting, and some of them were spires 3 to 4 feet high inside the chasm with their tops altogether below the surface of the ground. Other vents were small curled driblet spiracles where the gas escaped through a hole in a fold of heavy pahoehoe which filled the rift Many of these were level with the surface but none of the lava actually welled over the lip of the crack. At the lower end of the half-mile stretch the crack petered out.

The line of this rift system trends throughout the upper part of its course from Halemaumau through Cone Peak in the direction of Hilea and accords perfectly with the so-called 1868 cracks shown on the maps. These cracks constitute a rift belt which in places is more than four miles wide, extending from Kilauea crater to the ocean, with curvature to the east in the southern part of the belt. A dozen cones and numerous pits and deep chasms mark the course of the rift area, and in Kilauea crater itself the chasms outcrop in the face of the southern wall. Uwekahuna cliff is itself a fault face of the system and numerous cracks and fault blocks on the gravel flats near Keanakakoi lie in the rift belt. Northeast of Kilauea there is no definite evidence of any such belt. The great fractures to the southwest are ancient features and the incidents of 1868 form but a trivial part of their history.

The lava in Halemaumau on December 22 reached a maximum of fury in its boiling, the top of the crag was level with the rim and the lake about 30 feet down. The heat was so great that numerous whirlwinds were started carrying up fragments of lava and making much commotion. The fountaining pool of the southwest slag-heap continued active and the flows down the flanks of the heap reached Lee's pit so as to make a single ropy cascade across the overhanging rim of the pit which solidified, leaving a vertical column from the rim to the floor 15 feet high and one to two feet in diameter.

On this day a visit was made to the desert flow area by way of the road leading from Volcano House to Pahala. We left the road at the water tank nine miles from Volcano House and walked east across the rough aa flow for half an hour and then for one hour on smooth pahoehoe ground. This brought us to the flow at the rift west of Puu Koae. The gas pressure had ceased and the lava was not flowing. The puddles had increased in size, the largest now being 400 feet in diameter. Expansion had continued in the crack, breaking open cones and flows already solidified. In several places the surface breaking of the ground along the crack was guided by tree roots which had penetrated older fissures.

No change was observed at the smoking crack nearer to Puu Koae, but along this line two miles farther down the mountain there were new steaming fissures. The cracks were here in motion, with sand falling at the edges, occasionally deep thudding noises could be heard and several vents gave off thick white sulphurous vapor. The lava was here rising deep underground but had not yet reached the surface. The crack was extending itself in a direction which would carry it to the west of the Kamakaia hills (1823 flow) and somewhat to the east of the 1868 source vents.

At 11 a.m. December 23 Halemaumau showed the beginnings of subsidence. The ring pool was boiling evenly with inward streaming. The island stood in higher relief above the lake, its complete outline being restored at the south about 10 feet above lake level, while the north crag stood 35 feet high. Three fountains had resumed action in the central lagoon. The maximum level which had been reached the day previous was marked by a spatter margin all around the pit standing 8 feet above the lake, this being inside of the black ledge of December 15 the top of which stood 10 or 12 feet higher. It was evident that the liquid was sinking faster than the island. A broken wall 8 feet high encircled the inner lagoon. A single fountain was still in action on top of the southwest slag heap, with a cone built around it. This slag-heap was now three-fourths of a mile long and 25 feet high, built against the southwest wall of Kilauea and sloping thence rather steeply to lower ground.

Before daylight on Wednesday, December 24, travellers on the Pahala road could see flowing lava in the Kau desert. A distant view from the Uwekahuna summit at 9 a.m. revealed the gleaming surface of a flow about eight miles from Kilauea where the yawning cracks and sulphurous vapor had been seen at the lowest point reached two days before.

The lake in Halemaumau was now 75 feet down and the island stood in high relief with a large dome grotto developed on the southwest side of the inner lagoon. The crag summit was far below the rim of the pit and no longer visible from the Observatory. All fountaining had ceased at the southwest heap, and the summit pool had collapsed to a smoking pit.

At 10:30 a.m. an expedition to the desert was made by way of the Pahala road to the Kapapala bull-pen, whence the trip on foot eastward crossed smooth country so that the lower end of the new lava flow was reached in thirty minutes. This flow was found to consist of three sheets of pahoehoe lava moving steadily and slowly along the top of the rift, with rift fountains playing in a line down the middle. The total flowing area was about one and a half miles long and one-eighth mile wide at the broadest part near the lower end. This wide area was essentially a flat-topped slag-heap with slow streaming down the middle in the direction of the rift, its borders spilling over more to the west than to the east. In places the lava invaded trees and bushes which flared up, and there were some detonations of exploding gas in old caverns. The three separate sheets referred to were separated along the course of the rift by short uncovered stretches where the crack might be crossed, with live flows above and below. In the separate pools the rift line was marked by either a row of fountains or by spitting cones standing in the midst of the flow area. The lava as in the upper locality seen December 21 was chiefly porous pahoehoe with rough surface. In detail aa lava appeared locally between the pahoehoe shells.

Following the fissure below the flow, we found a place where the ground was groaning and heaving, making small earthquakes and yielding sulphurous vapor from many cracks. Sitting quietly on this ground one could feel slight shocks and hear the rock underground snapping and creaking, while pebbles and sand fell in the crevices. A mile farther down the rift there was timbered country with large sand dunes. Here the live crack was found cutting through deep banks of sand and through rock below, where incandescent lava 40 feet down was slowly welling up and making crackling noises.

It was now evident that the flow was progressing by a splitting forward of the rift and a subterranean draining of Halemaumau, each upwelling being more voluminous than the next preceding, and the individual outflows decreasing in viscosity as they gained volume.

On December 25 at 11 a.m. the lava lake in Halemaumau was about 110 feet below the rim and the crag peak could be barely seen from Uwekahuna Bluff. The fume from the pit had increased and dense vapor rose from the southwest heap.

Renewed exploration of the Kau desert flow on this day was made from the old Halfway House site fourteen miles from Volcano House on the Pahala road. Going east from here we crossed wide pahoehoe flats, one aa flow, and chasm depressions made by sunken blocks between crevasses on either side. The first of these, five miles above the beginning of the 1868 flow, has heaps of black pahoehoe lava surmounting the crack as an upper and outlying outflow of 1868. There are several wide open cracks which are very deep. Some of these appear within a mile of the road going eastward. A walk of 1 hour 50 minutes brought us to the summit trig. station of the southern Kamakaia cone. This cone is of pumice with a high lava heap beneath, and around it are the extensive flows of 1823. The view showed four localities symmetrically spaced from Kilauea for nine miles down the rift line, where fume rose. The upper of these was a quarter mile from the Kilauea edge, the second four miles, the third six miles and the lower one in the forested sand dunes nine miles from the crater. At this last locality could be seen a new flow burning the forest and making rapid progress from the source crack where on the previous day live lava had been seen in the depths.

On visiting this flow we found the rift above the upper end breaking across deep sand deposits, which occasionally slipped in, and some rumbling could be heard below. Above this crack several driblet cones had formed and these led to a wide flat flow surface 4 or 5 feet high from which streams made out laterally and on top of which there was slow streaming in a south-southwest direction and some fountaining directly over the rift line. The fronts of the live lobes were mobile pahoehoe sheets one to two feet thick, much thinner than the heaped up flows of the next higher zone of activity seen on the previous day.

There was marked increase of sharp explosions in old cavernous spaces near the live fronts, and as all of this flow was in open woodland with much burning of vegetation, it seemed probable that carbon monoxide and air were responsible for the detonations. The odor of coal gas and of burnt organic matter was more noticeable than the odor of sulphur. This flow was a half mile long and from a few yards to one-eighth mile wide. Many trees were standing in the midst of the flow and here and there they were burning and falling. The only aa noticed was on the crests of some of the driblet cones and efflorescences in cracks of pahoehoe. The live crack below this flow could be traced for only a hundred yards with some white vapor rising and no perceptible motion. A second steaming crack was found at the eastern base of the old aa flow a half mile west of this locality.

At noon Friday, December 26, the lake was lower in Halemaumau and the island stood high above it. A large dome grotto had formed against the island on the southwest side of the inner lagoon and in the middle of the latter three fountains were in action. The outer ring lake showed very intense multiple fountaining on all sides in large domes and the streaming was away from stagnant skins at localities southwest, southeast and north. The southeastern part of the island was now an uplifted flat sloping inward. The spatter rampart built against the north side of the north crag was more than half as high as the crag, and no such uplifted rampart appeared on the outer face of the island east and south. The shore of the inner lagoon showed a broken-down slope about 4 feet high. On the outer wall of the pit all around the horizontal spatter lines marking shores progressively deserted by the sinking liquid were one to two feet apart and rather closer together below than above. This black ledge makes a shell one to three feet thick. The heat and light from the stormy fountaining were intense and the visible smoke mostly from the island. The transparent fume which rises from the fountains condenses in the upper atmosphere to a reddish stratus somewhat opalescent, and this volcanic smoke is transported great distances and has been reported recently from Kona, Kohala and Honolulu.

The crack in the southwest wall of the pit was no longer open, but covered with spatter drip and showing glow spots in places. The lower northern shelf of Halemaumau, which at the end of November was covered with tumbled debris, had by overflow become a flat platform of smooth lava about 50 feet below the rim of the pit and below it the inner slope was sculptured by drip-marked horizontal terraces.

Inspection of the desert outflows on December 26 showed little progress in the lower flow area and the crack below the flow was very small and not steaming. In this lava field the fountains were vigorous and the heap piling up with tendency to outflow spreading west. The upper flow in the open country was piling up and flowing strongly. The rift under this flow as extended down hill lay a quarter mile west of the rift under the flow in the sand dunes, and from this western rift west of the sand dunes a new small flow had welled up and the ground was in motion there. Along this line some fume could be seen farther down the mountain. Cavern explosions had diminished.

During the week ending Friday, December 26, 1919, local earthquakes registered in the Whitney Laboratory have been few and very feeble, as follows: December 22, 10:30 p.m. and 11 p.m.; December 23, 4:18 a.m.; December 25, 1:25 a.m. No earthquakes whatever were felt at Hilea in southern Hawaii. This is a matter of some interest, as in 1868 some persons believed that the Kau desert rift system extended beyond Kilauea mountain in the Hilea direction. The swarm of earthquakes December 15 and others accompanying the opening of the Kau desert rift have been wholly limited to Kilauea mountain.

Spasmodic microtremor has been slight with some increase December 22--23. Harmonic tremor has been moderate. Microseismic motion was moderate to slight. Tilting became strong to the east and north December 23 and was otherwise not pronounced.

January 3, 1920.

During the week ending Friday, January 2, 1920, the lava column of Kilauea volcano again passed a critical point, the rift in the desert giving vent to a long and vigorous aa flow. This outbreak came from the midst of the upper of the two pahoehoe slag-heaps which breached itself on its eastern side and sent out a voluminous flood that travelled two miles per day. This flood was pahoehoe above but quickly changed to aa in its lower reaches and formed a straight river of lava which bent off to the south-southwest and poured down the depression immediately to the west of the Kamakaia cones. This flow in volume and steadfast progress has become comparable to the recent Alika flow on Mauna Loa and at the present time has progressed more than five miles from its source. Halemaumau has continued to show subsidence at a decreasing rate, the drainage of the lake magma becoming strikingly less when the outflows in the desert changed from pahoehoe to aa.

Measurements of depression of the lake and north crag of the island, below the northeast monument on the rim of the pit as datum (3727 feet above sea level) have been as follows. Where not otherwise indicated the lake measurements have been directed to the ring pool at north base of the north crag:

Dec. 26, 12 noon, lake 150 feet below rim; crag 100 feet below rim. Dec. 27, 2:40 p. m., lake 171 feet below rim; crag 120 feet below rim. Dec. 29, 3:00 p. m., lake 212 feet below rim; crag 154 feet below rim. Jan. 1, 11:30 a. m., lake 244 feet below rim (at north pool); crag 204 feet below rim. Jan. 1, 11.30 a. m., lake 255 feet below rim (at S. W. side lagoon).

The diameter of the lake January 1 was 1115 feet from east to west.

These figures show that for the three

days, December 26--29, prior to the outbreak of the aa flow in the desert, the lake went down 62 feet, or 20.7 feet per day, while the crag subsided 54 feet or 18 feet per day. For the next three days, however, December 29 to January 1, the lake subsided only 32 feet, or 10.7 feet per day, while the crag sank 50 feet, or 16.7 feet per day. The relief of the crag above the lake was therefore as follows:

December 26, 50 feet
27, 51 ''
29, 58 ''
January 1, 40 ''

On Saturday, December 27 at 3 p.m. the lava column of Halemaumau continued its equable subsidence, the lake receding faster than the island. The outer ramparts of the island had slumped, giving it steep walls, and cracks parallel to the walls showed tendency to further slumping. The fountaining was somewhat less intense. The evenly terraced spatter lines, marking the successive stands of the liquid against the outer wall of the pit, constituted an impressive and unbroken index of the subsidence. The fume was thin in the pit, a little rising from the island, but much vapor rose from the southwest heap in the outer crater.

In the Kau desert the flows of the middle zone six miles from Kilauea had now become specially active and were piling up an elongate terraced slag-heap along the rift for a length of two miles. This heap could be seen at night looking southward from Uwekahuna Bluff and appeared like a broad bed of coals in the midst of the open country. The glow and rumble from Halemaumau pit were now notably less, though both were still strong.

December 28 at 10 a.m. another visit was made to the lava heaps in the desert. There were now three localities where live flows had been seen and photographed, but only the two lower ones had developed imposing piles of lava. These are respectively six and nine miles from Kilauea. Both are flat-topped elongate slag-heaps with profiles not unlike the profile of Mauna Loa in miniature. Building up to heights of from 30 to 50 feet these structures, thousands of feet long, have become prominent landmarks, even rising above the tree tops as seen across the desert from the west. The upper of the two was first visited and this stands in open desert country with old pahoehoe flats on either side. At the lower end there had been no flowing forward beyond the point reached December 24, but what had then been three sheets of lava along the rift was now a series of six terraces, the one overlapping the other, following the general slope, standing over the rift line, and each surmounted by a fountaining pool which was perfectly flat, more or less crusted and occasionally spilled over its edge. By this process the terraces were increasing in height, each of them at this time from 25 to 30 feet above the general level of the country on either hand. Sluggish pahoehoe streams trickled down the outer slopes. It was possible to climb one of these slopes at an inactive area, but there was nothing on top of the heap except heavy flat crusts and a line of small fountains marking the trend of the crack beneath. Each terrace was about a third of a mile long and from one-eighth to one-quarter mile wide, the whole series making a tabular ridge extending two miles down the mountain beginning at six miles from Kilauea. There was a small patch of aa lava on the west side of the second terrace, counting from above. This entire ridge lay over the western of the two marked cracks which have been conspicuous in the present eruption. A half mile below the lower end of this ridge some small flows have welled up from the same crack.

The lower flow heap in the midst of the forested sand dunes is on the next crack to the east and so out of line with the upper ridge by about one-eighth mile. The flat summit of this heap shows numerous fountains about 40 feet above the general level of the country and on this day the flows were pushing into the forest sluggishly from the lower end of the heap. The trend of the rift cracks under both heaps is the same, S. 50° W. There was some trickling outflow on the east side of the lower heap which was burning the forest, but very little smoke or fume rose from the live lava. Neither the upper nor the lower heaps were making any definite flow down the mountain, and the splitting open of the rift system had ceased.

At 3 p.m. December 29 inspection of Halemaumau showed that the rate of lowering was less. The island stood high above the lake and the north rampart under the craggy summit of the island was seen to be breaking down with avalanches. An islet in the north pool under this rampart showed that other blocks had slipped down. There were two fountaining areas in the central lagoon near its middle and others near the western border of the lagoon where the streaming was outward toward the fountaining ring pool. The maximum boiling in this pool was along the base of the eastern wall of the pit. Other conditions remained as before.

This day was a time of crisis in the Kau desert rift, but in the forenoon the only marked change was some increase in the number of aa patches on the east flank of the upper part of the six-mile ridge. The summit of the heap was fountaining strongly, as was also the lower nine-mile heap. At some time in the afternoon of this day the upper heap broke open on its eastern side and gave vent to the great flow.

On the morning of December 30 I entered the desert from the roadway one mile below the old Halfway House site, exploring the country below the lava heaps and finding no new outbreaks. I then went up the west side of the lower heap and found that the flows in front of that heap had lengthened it until it was a mile and a half long and had completely buried the new rift at the lower end. The tabular summit at the upper end was now 60 feet high with three or four fountains playing on top in a stagnant pool that overflowed the flanks with sluggish pahoehoe streams that pushed into the sand dunes and occasionally ignited trees.

From a high dune at the north end of this heap I discovered the new aa flow a quarter mile to the east. It was a glowing river of melt extending up the country about two miles, where it bent to the west, and it evidently took its rise in the upper part of the long terraced ridge of new lava. On close examination this flow was found to be a lava band 100 yards wide, its margin a wall of rough incandescent aa 5 feet high and its middle portions creeping along about four feet to the minute. Large bowlders of accumulation lay on its surface, the edges were glowing and crumbling like cheese and the fragments which fell from the crumbling made a tinkle of hard rock. The newest of these fragments while still hot was yet intensely oxidized. Slabs of pahoehoe were scattered over the surface of the flow and the reason for this appeared when on following the flow towards its source, I found that the middle portion became increasingly pahoehoe, until at the upper half mile of the flow the material all congealed in the smooth and festooned fashion without a trace of aa.

The front of the flow lay in a fault chasm made by a sunken block 100 feet wide between two lateral rifts. The channel was about 30 feet deep with trees growing in it. The flow had increased its speed as it entered this constricted area so that it was moving approximately one-fifth mile per hour. The mass moved like a stiff glowing mud full of bowlders which would flow around the trees while they still remained upright and set them on fire. The tree trunks thus weakened finally gave way and were slowly pushed over, the tops set ablazing and finally completely engulfed by the resistless tide of molten rock. An ohia tree 35 feet high and one foot in diameter was thus swallowed up in about two minutes. The flow appeared to be making headway of about two miles per day.

Following the flow up to its source, the middle stream of pahoehoe was found travelling two to three miles per hour, and at the source itself the river, now wholly pahoehoe, moved at least eight miles per hour. Where the stream emerged from the lava heap, the eastern side of the second terrace had slumped and broken down into a ravine about 75 yards wide with walls 25 feet high. The liquid lava came from a vent in the wall as a cascade at the head of this ravine and formed rapids below over tumbled debris where a large angular fragment of the breached ridge stood as an island about 20 feet in diameter. The river was extremely liquid and from 60 to 70 feet wide within margins of its own overflow somewhat raised above the surrounding country. The whole belt of flow was 100 yards wide. Fountains could no longer be seen on top of the lava terraces of the source ridge. The breached portion of the ridge was just where the slow small aa flows in the midst of pahoehoe had been seen December 28 and December 29.

A word of explanation is necessary in speaking of live lava as **flowing pahoehoe** or **flowing aa.** The words pahoehoe and aa are commonly used of already solidified products. The difference between the two types when in motion is this: pahoehoe lava forms glistening skins which stretch and wrinkle, the lava beneath shows vesicles being drawn out, and the process of solidification leaves a highly glassy lustrous surface with rounded or ropy or serpent-like forms. As flowing lava is always congealing on the surface and at the sides, the nature of the congelation seen defines the nature of the flowing. Aa lava while in motion forms no skins on its surface and is characterized by a granular look which resembles a bed of hot anthracite coal flowing. This granular paste keeps rolling up lumpy balls of its bottom material, and these make slow moving rafts and islands. Around the edges or fronts of such a flow the glowing paste moves with an incessant cheesy crumbling and breaking. The part which is actually glowing is usually a thin layer. which rides over tumbled fragments of very rough shapes, and carries on its back other fragments of all shapes and sizes, highly scoriaceous, rusty and without any glassy surface at all. There is no bubbling or visible vesicularity to an aa front, though the rock contains irregular gas blebs when it is cold. When, as in the case of this flow, we get a transition from pahoehoe to aa in the process of flowing, the wrinkling skins and crusts of the pahoehoe phase pass down the middle of the flow and the edges start efflorescing in the cheesy aa fashion.

On December 31 Halemaumau continued its slow subsidence with the same strong boiling and intense emission of gas. Fume continued thin from the pit but dense vapor was increasing from the southwest heap and much vapor rose from the cracks near Cone Peak.

The Kau desert flow was visited by a new approach leaving the Pahala road four miles from Volcano House and heading toward Puu Koae. The upper lava crack localities of the rift were fuming slightly and flowing not at all. The head of the flow source heap was found to be a series of inactive lava pilings. The top of this heap was found to be a hard plateau pression a fine view was obtained of the flow as it poured out from its basin. This proved to be a rugged amphitheatre across the bottom of which, from west to east, flowed the lava river swiftly and silently with ripples and rapids. The river was 100 feet wide in places, flush with a bank of its own overflooding, and this sloped away on either side so as to leave the stream raised about 12 feet above the general level of the country. The whole accumulation, banks and river, thus created a lower ridge 100 yards wide with the river advancing along its middle. The source of the stream was a round opening 10 feet in diameter with a driblet rim up which the lava welled continuously in a low standing fountain rising only about three feet. This torrent bent at once into a cascade feeding the river below. The surface of the lava so emerging was full of coarse drawn-out vesicles. It made no noise and showed no gas spurting. There were a few small bubble fountains in the upper part of the river.

Keeping on the eastern side, the flow was followed about five miles to its foot. On climbing to the edge of the river in the upper part of its course, the molten stream was found brimming level with its confining margin, the surface currents progressing at different rates in separate bands lengthwise with here and there an island emerging through the surface as though the stream were very shallow.

The front of the flow lay opposite to and west of the lower Kamakaia hill. Here it was wholly aa, with a sluggish granular river showing in places, and forking about ledges which made islands in the flow. The extreme front was at the moment pouring into a chasm and setting fire to trees. The rafted blocks which made islands in the aa could be seen to move with an excessively slow creeping motion. They were evidently a part of the stiff bottom material of the stream, itself moving much more slowly than the surface river.

Fountains were still playing on top of the lower lava heap, the summit plateau of which now stood about 80 feet above the general level. A small spatter cone about three feet high stood on top of the crusted pool. At the southern end of the upper slag-heap terrace a small aa flow was oozing out and glowing.

At 9 p.m. from Uwekahuna the flow and its source heap in the distance across the desert were spectacular, the light of the source-well being reflected from the fume above while the trickle flows, the summit fountains of the southern heap and the long bright line of the flow itself made a luminous and unusual picture.

At 11:30 a.m. January 1, 1920, the lava lake in Halemaumau showed by the large spatter accumulations on the wall that its subsidence had become slow. Two flat upright slabs on the north side of the north crag had broken down into the ring pool, making islets with channels about four feet wide between them and the crag. A similar islet half filled the southeast channel and the northwest channel had greatly narrowed. The effervescence was strongest on the east, west and south. Streaming was northward on both sides of the pit, the currents meeting towards the northeast. The south and southwest channels appeared to be dividing up into fountaining pockets. Much smoke rose from the north crag. The lake had subsided sufficiently to leave a vertical wall under the north shelf and there was marked transition from the terraced spatter lines above, to the heavy border accumulations of the lake below which recorded the change from rapid to slow sinking.

On January 2 it was evident that fume from the pit was increasing and very dense vapor arose from three places along the crack in the southwest slag-heap.

On this day exploration was directed to the region below the flow in the desert by way of the old trail from the Kapapala Ranch gate across the 1868 flow. The topography slopes off more steeply towards the sea in this region, some 1300 feet above sea level. The foot of the live flow was estimated to be about 2200 feet above sea level in the vicinity of Puu Kouele and now advancing less than a half mile a day. A long smooth pahoehoe surface leads downward along a depression between the 1823 aa flow on the east and the 1868 rift escarpment on the west, and it seems probable that this will be the natural route for the new flow if it continues.

Investigation of the lower lava heap in the sand dunes revealed the fact that fountaining there had ceased. I climbed on top of the heap and found it smoking and very hot, with a summit crust about two feet thick. Some sluggish pahoehoe flows were still making out into the forest on the east side. The view from the summit showed the long aa flow as bright and vigorous as ever and following the same course as before. A second small flow was said to be making out towards the west from the upper lava heap. Glowing lava in motion could be seen near the front of the main flow near Puu Kouele and occasionally the smoke of burning forest broke out in that vicinity.

In the Whitney Laboratory of Seismology for the week ending at midnight January 2, 1920, only one very feeble local earthquake has been registered, at 1:25 a.m. on December 30, 1919. Spasmodic microtremor has been slight with a little increase December 31-January 1. Harmonic tremor was moderate and microseismic motion slight. Movement of tilting was pronounced to the east and north until December 30, when it became stationary, and on January 2 a strong reverse movement to south and west set in.

Very respectfully,

T. A. JAGGAR, JR.,

Volcanologist.

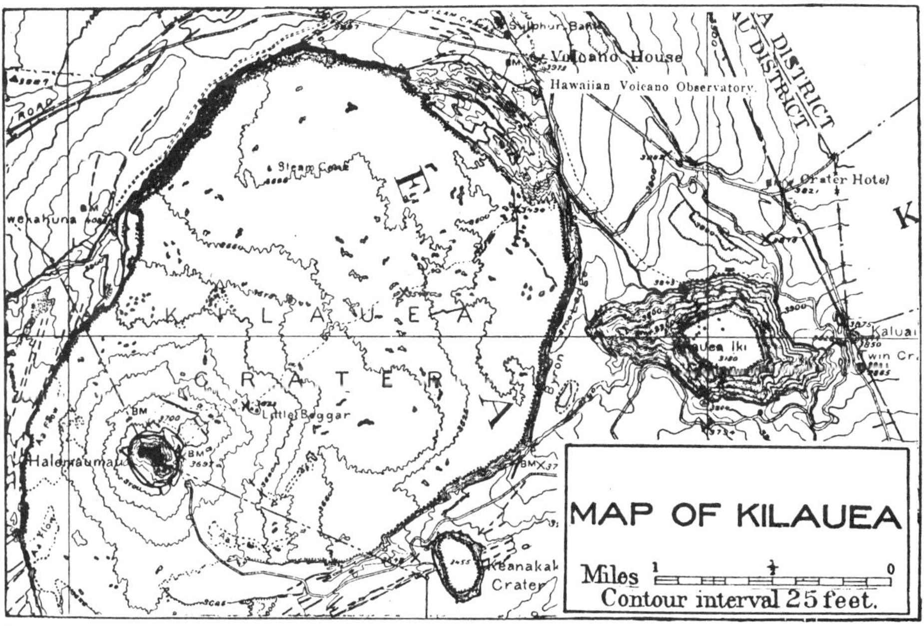

HAWAIIAN VOLCANO OBSERVATORY.

The Observatory is equipped with the following seismometric instruments rebuilt at the station in 1918 for the special needs of volcano research: two Bosch-Omori pendulums, high speed registration of local earthquakes; one optically recording seismograph for distant earthquakes; one clinograph registering E-W tilting of the ground. A vertical component seismograph was in December, 1918, set up in experimental operation. These are seated on concrete piers in a closed basement room having practically constant temperature, beneath the chief Observatory building near the hotel. Time is referred to a rated chronometer, checked at intervals by solar observations with a transit. Both instruments are loaned by the College of Hawaii. Hawaiian standard time (H. S. T.) is 10 hrs. 30 min. slower than Greenwich time.

CANCANI SCALE OF SEISMIC INTENSITY.

Expressed by accelerations measured in millimeters per second per second.

I.	Instrumental	0.0	2.5
II.	Very slight	2.5	5.0
III.	Slight	5.0	10.0
IV.	Sensible, mediocre	10.0	25.0
V.	Rather strong	25.0	50.0
VI.	Strong	50.0	100.0
VII.	Very strong	100.0	250.0
VIII.	Ruinous	250.0	500.0
IX.	Disastrous	500.0	1000.0
X.	Very disastrous	10000.0	2500.0
XI.	Catastrophic	2500.0	5000.0
XII.	Great catastrophe	5000.0	10000.0

Grade IV. is ordinarily the minimum perceived by the senses; and in grade XII. the accelerations or rate of change of motion (jerk) reaches that of terrestrial gravitation.

In the standard form of report the maximum intensity or acceleration, designated by the symbol a, or max. a, is given in the conventional unit of milligal. The milligal is a measure of acceleration, such that 1 milligal = 1/100 mm. per sec. per sec. = 10 μ. per sec. per sec. The Cancani scale, here defined in terms of millimeters per sec. per sec., can therefore be expressed in milligals by multiplying each of the numbers by 100.

U. S. DEPARTMENT OF AGRICULTURE
WEATHER BUREAU
CHARLES F. MARVIN, CHIEF

MONTHLY BULLETIN
OF THE
Hawaiian Volcano Observatory

VOL. VIII. HONOLULU, HAWAII, JANUARY, 1920 No. 1

Week Ending January 9, 1920.

Summary of Conditions.

Halemaumau is very spectacular, a circular pit 1,200 feet across, containing pools of liquid lava lapping the base of the vertical walls and fountaining intensely. A group of violently boiling marginal ponds are separated off from a central lagoon by a ridge of horseshoe shape, suggesting a coral atoll. This ridge rises from 20 to 50 feet above the liquid. The lagoon is quiet liquid with soft skins and a few fountains playing in patches. This lagoon connects at the west with the outer ring of pools. The excessive multiple fountaining has had no parallel here since 1912, and creates much brilliancy at night and an uprush of hot gas. The bottom area is 1,100 feet across, 300 feet down, and the ridge summit stands 55 feet above the lagoon.

In the Kau Desert, six miles south-southwest of Kilauea, a lava flow is quietly pouring out of the flank of a lava heap 50 feet high through a channel 40 feet wide, and is flowing towards the south. The flow is now over eight miles long, and changes from smooth lava above to clinkery lava below. The front is advancing about a half-mile per day. No such outflow on Kilauea mountain has occurred since 1868. The present outbreak began December 21, 1919. The Halemaumau lava has subsided step by step with the outflow, the present rate of subsidence being six feet per day.

Journal.

The changes of the week ending Friday, January 9, 1920, have involved further lowering of both lake and crag mass in Halemaumau by about 50 feet, the lake 4 feet in excess of the crag at the time of measurement. The slight funnelling in of the outer walls of the pit has brought about a choking of the ring pool on the north, southeast and southwest, leaving three remnants of the pool west, east and south, effervescing with multiple fountains as before. The choked portions contain slabs or shells of the island mass which have cracked off and slipped down, and isolated boiling pots of glowing lava. The crag mass is making much increased smoke through cracks, and the central lagoon has increased the turbulence of its fountaining patches. A notable change towards the end of the week was a streaming inward of the liquid from the western wall pool to the lagoon, indicating that the most rapid subsidence was at the central fountains. The rate of subsidence of the lava column as a whole continued the same.

The flow in the desert progressed but slowly, expending much of its volume in widening a large pool of aa east of Kamakaia. The flow here appears to be three-quarters of a mile wide. The extreme front at the end of the week lay on top of and was moving parallel to a pahoehoe portion of the 1823 flow two miles south-southeast of Puu Kouele. Owing to an increase of grade and concentration of the flow again into a single channel, the rate of forward movement increased from one-fifth mile per day January 4 to one-half mile per day January 9. The upper or pahoehoe portion of the lava river flowing within defined banks changed but little during the week. The two pahoehoe slag-heaps of the flow source and farther south, respectively, have both tended to break down with outflow of sluggish aa from within the heaps.

Activity of Halemaumau.

Measurements of the week at Halemaumau have been as follows:

	Lake at S.W. Grotto. Below Rim.	N. Crag Summit. Below Rim.
Jan. 1, 11:30 a.m.	255 feet	204 feet
Jan. 3, 10:25 a.m.	273 "	231 "
Jan. 5, 8:00 a.m.	287 "	238 "
Jan. 8, 10:15 a.m.	309 "	254 "

In seven days the lake sank 54 feet, or 7.7 feet per day, and the crag 50 feet, or 7.1 feet per day. The relief of the crag summit above the lagoon was:

Jan. 1	51 feet
Jan. 3	42 "
Jan. 5	49 "
Jan. 8	55 "

The above measurements of depression are referred to the northeast monument, which stands 3,727 feet above sea level.

On Saturday, January 3, at 10:25 a.m., the crag mass was 231 and the lake 273 feet below the northeast monument. It began to be apparent that the outer ring lake was receding from the higher portions of its own bottom on the north, southeast and southwest. The island horseshoe appeared very high above both the outside pools and the inner lagoon. The eastern pool was still fountaining strongly. The fountaining on the north side of the center of the lagoon was becoming continuous and developing a number of centers of effervescence, as though the shutting off of portions of the ring pool had augmented the inner gas pressure. The remains of the northern portion of the ring pool between the north crag of the island and the outer wall of the pit had become all crusted, with three islets protruding above the crust. The north crag mass had slumped into the north pool area, thus choking the pool, and diminishing the measured relief of the crag summit. Great quantities of Pele's hair rose from the pit, and the hot gases started whirlwinds outside of the pit on the northeast and south. Dense fume rose from the smoke holes of the southwest heaps on the Kilauea floor.

On January 5, at 8 a.m., the crag summit was 238 feet and the lake 287 feet below the northeast monument. The general fume from the pit had increased, and that of the southwest heap appeared less. At the rift crack in the southwest inner wall of Halemaumau the black ledge had broken away into a talus below, and the glowing cavity, making an open window along the crack, stood about 80 feet above the lake level. The ring pool here was completely choked, the east and south pools were boiling hard, the floor remnants of the north pool had slumped farther and there was a fountaining chasm at the northern base of the north crag, between it and shell crags which had slipped down. The greatest fountaining and rumbling noise originated at the west side of the pool, still loud enough to be heard at a distance. The fountaining amounted to a bombardment of the wall on the west and northeast, with streaming northward in both places, the northeast corner of the pit exhibiting a rush of travelling fountains against the wall, and the northwest corner a cascade downward into a crack between the western end of the north crag mass and the wall.

In the lagoon a fountain was still in action on the southwest, but the grotto dome there was gone. Three other fountaining areas broke the surface in the central region, and two near the western border of the lagoon. The north central fountain was continuous and noisy, the streaming from the lagoon was westward, the island stood in high relief and the narrow black ledge of plastered matter against the outer wall of the pit had shelled off extensively on the west and northwest.

At 5 p.m. on January 7 the ring pools had so dwindled that the heat at the edge of the pit was no longer excessive. A striking change was seen in the streaming on the west side of the lagoon, which was now inward, towards the center of the lagoon from the western boiling area under the wall. The impression conveyed was that the outer liquid was rising and flowing into the lagoon, and this effect was enhanced by the presence of a large standing fountain close to the southwest bank of the lagoon which played up continuously like an artesian well. Two central fountaining areas exhibited large dome fountains, whence the streaming was towards the southwest. The skins east of these fountains covering the surface of the lagoon were piled up and folded as in the case of a rising lake. The streaming along the west wall was northward as well as inward. The inner wall of the island around the lagoon was at least 18 feet high, and the outer wall at the east pool appeared still higher.

The window marking the vertical crack in the southwest wall of the pit now stood 100 feet above the lake and was larger than before. The fillings which interrupted the continuity of the ring lake on the southwest and southeast were smoky and showed some splashing pots. High slab crags in the southwest fill stood higher than the island ridge. These were shells broken away from the periphery of the ridge, beneath which the island had sunk, reversing the process seen at the north crag, where rocks were falling into chasms and shell fragments of the crag had slipped lower than the main mass. The northern fountaining chasm contained liquid which had subsided lower than on the previous day, and the northwest sink hole was now small and separated off from the western line of fountains. The east and south pools continued their boiling, but they were smaller. The smoke from the crags had lessened.

Examination of the smoking pits on top of the southwest heap, under the 1868 cracks, near the outer wall of Kilauea crater, discovered them to be large tumbled depressions with glow and probably flames in the crevices between the blocks. There were two principal pits, a northern one with dense yellow-white fume and a smaller southern one with bluish fume, both along the rift line of the present Kau desert eruption.

On January 8, at 10:15 a.m., with the lake 309 and the crag summit 254 feet below northeast rim, the slow depression continued, the crag mass more than the lake. The multiple fountains of the east pool boiled hotly in low domes. Smoke from the fractures of the north crag was less voluminous. The north central part of the lagoon showed five or six fountains in a group, and there was turbulent fountaining in the south pool.

Activity of the Kau Desert Flow.

On January 4 the upper long lava heap, source of the great flow, was found to have fresh short inactive aa flows on its southern slope, and also out from the west side of its uppermost terrace above the main flow source, which forms an amphitheatre in the east side of the second terrace. From this uppermost end of the heap there were also live pahoehoe flows dribbling down the west slope.

At the source amphitheatre the floor under the flow appeared to have built up, diminishing the cascades there, and the channel conveying the river of melt was 40 feet wide and the stream moved about six miles per hour.

The southern of the two original lava heaps had now breached its western side, causing a sink to form in its summit plateau, and through the breach had poured a sluggish mass of aa, with huge tumbled blocks of the original pahoehoe surface matter of the heap carried forward in a chaotic jumble. This aa flow was more like a landslide than a river, and proceeded only a few hundred feet, riding over the previous pahoehoe tongues of the slag heap on the western side and developing no channel. This breakdown closely resembled that of the northern heap which had given rise to the flow, only in this case there was no pressure of a well-spring behind to take advantage of the release. No pahoehoe flowed out, and the breakdown had occurred after the pahoehoe fountains of the summit pool of the heap ceased activity. The breakdown had begun by the formation of cracks extending radially down the western flank. Apparently the freezing of the summit pool, and confinement of a little of the still rising melt, burst the flank of the heap along the path of least resistance. Inspection of the front, still flowing as stiff aa in the sand dunes and timber at the foot of the heap on the west side, revealed motion and incandescence by occasional tumbling fragments, burning logs encased in the lava, deep-toned snapping noises, and the hot air vibrations and glowing crevices of live lava. There was no visible advance, though doubtless individual tongues of the melt were pushing slowly at rates measured by inches in hours. The aa was the roughest kind of red-black oxidized clinkers, matrix for huge craggy upended pahoehoe fragments, sometimes 20 feet in diameter.

The phenomenon of breakdown in its entirety conveyed the impression that the incandescent interior of the pahoehoe slag-heap is of the substance that produces aa lava when it flows and cools in the open air. This substance is in all respects similar to the bench magma of Halemaumau, which has also frequently been induced by sudden breakdowns and uplifts to produce aa. Everything in the mechanism of aa seen in this eruption indicates that its internal incandescence is lower than pahoehoe, its oxidation vastly greater, its obvious gas content less and its surface radiation of heat more rapid, perhaps because of oxidations and failure to incase itself in an insulating crust. That its motion is more viscous than pahoehoe appears to be generally true, for it forms the slower-moving underbed of a pahoehoe-making river of vitreous melt. Viscosity, however, is not a distinctive feature, for the Mauna Loa flows are highly fluent where no pahoehoe tendency is discernible, and very sluggish pahoehoe may solidify without any aa tendency.

The front of the main flow lay at the eastern base of Puu Kouele, a cone about a mile southwest of Kamakaia. The flow here and for miles upstream consisted of wide fields of aa lying between the heights of Kamakaia hills and the forested dunes of the lower lava-heap region. The extreme front lay on the smooth pahoehoe of 1823 and formed a straight wall of aa tumbling forward, advancing at a rate estimated at ten feet per hour. The total advance for the past two days was not more than a fifth of a mile per day. A much more lively arm of the flow could be seen from the summit of Puu Kouele, extended eastward from the main line to the base of Kamakaia and there flooding southward at a rate of about thirty feet per hour and tending to merge with the frontal lobes. Two other live arms were pushing, the one into the forest east of the lower lava heap, with much blazing of timber, and the other straight down the fault chasm near the front of December 31. South of Puu Kouele the ground was steaming 300 yards away from the front of the flow, a phenomenon explainable possibly by underground driving forward of water vapor through cavernous passages owing to the hot flow covering all the country to the north.

On the morning of January 6 the front of the flow east of Puu Kouele had advanced about a quarter-mile beyond its position of January 4 and was now making more rapid progress. The entire front showed definite viscous flowing at a rate estimated 80 feet per hour. The energy of the flow was still being dissipated in lateral lobes, and one such lobe was burning timber on the east side of the flow opposite the middle cone of the Kamakaia group.

Examination of the west side of the flow, on following it up the mountain, showed that it had heaped itself up into a deep pool west of the Kamakaia hills, and a new lobe, which had been seen burning the forest January 4, had penetrated the sand dune country for several hundred feet on the west side, a short distance below the southern lava heap of the first eruption. From high ground the upper stream near the source was seen to be actively flowing pahoehoe as before.

On Friday, January 9, the flow source was found quite unchanged, a steady stream poured through a channel 30 to 40 feet wide; the rate of flow was estimated to be five miles per hour, and a small cone had formed at the source vent. Opposite this cone, on top of a slag-heap terrace which had been the first structure of the eruption, the amphitheatre of discharge was found to be backed by an oval subsided area or sink, having flat floor and surrounding cliffs 10 or 12 feet high. This was similar to the sink on top of the southern lava heap.

The foot of the flow had advanced two miles south-southeast from Puu Kouele and had stopped at its extreme toe, but a lobe was moving more to the southwest, with steaming ground in front of it. All of this is on top of the pahoehoe lava of 1823.

Seismometric Record.

In the Whitney Laboratory of Seismology the following local earthquakes have been registered during the week ending at midnight January 9, 1920: January 3, 6:30 a.m., very feeble; January 5, 2:45 p.m., light; January 8, 8:53 p.m., very feeble. Spasmodic microtremor increased from slight to moderate until January 8, when there were several spasms; on January 9 the movement was slight. Harmonic tremor increased from slight to moderate, and microseismic motion from very slight to moderate, January 6-7, thereafter becoming slight again. Tilting of the ground was slight, mostly west and south.

Week Ending January 16, 1920.

Summary of Conditions.

Halemaumau remains a pit of boiling lava 337 feet deep, with a ring of marginal crags at the bottom, a large lava lake inside, and three outside pools at the base of the pit walls. Much fume rises from the fractured crags, obscuring the view in rainy weather, but in good weather the spectacle is impressive and the fountaining is strong. A new feature is the inward pouring of lava cascades from the western pool to the lake. This has been occasioned by the sinking of the latter, at a rate of five feet per day; the crags have been sinking one and a half feet per day. The subsidence ceased on January 16. The lake is 650 feet in diameter. There are glowing cracks in the wall of the pit 100 feet above the lake. The pit is a cylinder veneered with horizontal bands of clinging lava all around, left by recent subsidence. There are two shelves, twenty and eighty feet down on the north side, and a pressure ridge borders the pit on the south.

In the Kau desert six miles south-southwest of Kilauea the lava flow continues to pour out quietly, with a spectacular cascade as a new feature. The stream has shifted its course during the week, covering new ground near the source, and also on the west side of its former course. The advance of the older front has accordingly ceased. The direction of the flow is first southwest, then south-southeast. The front is four miles from the sea-coast.

Journal.

The changes of the week ending January 16 at Halemaumau have been a lessening of the rates of subsidence of both lake and crag mass, the latter slowing its downward motion much more than the lake, until finally, on January 15, the subsidence ceased and there was a reaction of rising lava January 16, the central lake rising three times as much as the north crag peak. The lowering of the liquid in excess of the lake bottom material caused the western submerged edges of the bench magma basin to emerge, and the wall-crack pond outside of this rim, remaining higher than the large lagoon inside, became the source of a cascade pouring inward to the lagoon. A similar mechanism of cascading inward to the center from the wall-crack had been in evidence during the rapid December rise, and the stages of subsidence thus repeated in inverse order the stages of the preceding inflow. The pit became increasingly smoky during the subsidence.

The lava flow in the Kau desert was found on January 12 to have stopped advancing along its extreme front below Puu Kouele, this place being on top of the 1823 flow, and about four miles from the seashore below Puu Ahi, where the 1823 flow had entered the water. At the source heap, however, the lava river continued its outpouring, dividing into several new branches near the source and making a new stream that moved for two miles southward along the western margin of the former stream. Some spectacular cascades in the upper part of this flow were occasioned by pahoehoe lava pouring over irregular ledges in the aa which had broken and rifted beneath. The fresh flows showed the same tendency as before to change into aa lava a short distance from the source. There was no marked change of volume.

Activity of Halemaumau.

Measurements of the week, expressed as depression below the northeast monument on the rim of Halemaumau (3,727 feet above sea level) have been as follows:

	Lake at SW. Grotto.	N. Crag Summit.
Jan. 8, 10:14 a.m.	309 feet	254 feet
Jan. 15, 10:30 a.m.	343 "	262 "
Jan. 16, 2:15 p.m.	337 "	260 "

In seven days the lake sank 34 feet, or 4.9 feet per day, and the crag 12 feet, or 1.7 feet per day. In one day, January 15-16, the lake rose 6 feet and the crag 2 feet. This crag summit was no longer an island, but by subsidence had become a ledge or bench against the outer wall of the pit.

On January 11, at 9:30 p.m., three fountains were playing continuously in the central lagoon, and the marginal ring pool, which had formerly been continuous around the base of the Halemaumau walls and outside of the atoll-shaped island, was now divided up into three wall-crack ponds, respectively east, south and west, the eastern one the largest and the western one still connected through the opening of the horseshoe-shaped crag mass with the large lagoon inside. This lagoon was about 650 feet in diameter and nearly circular. The intervening spaces that had formerly been occupied by the ring lake, were now clogged with debris and with the direct contact of the subsided island where it came against the inward flare of the outer walls of the pit. The eastern pool was bubbling continuously as before, with multiple fountains, some of them large. The other two wall-crack ponds were also fountaining strongly, and much fume was rising from the broken ledges of the annular crag mass.

On Monday, January 12, at 4 p.m., the pit was very smoky, the east pool was boiling hard, the streaming in the lagoon was a slow inward current from the western side and there was bubble fountaining in the center. The rift crack which rises from bottom to top of the southwest inner wall of Halemaumau as a vertical chasm giving vent subterraneously to the flows in the desert, continued at this time to show a glowing opening splashed with hanging stalactitic material, in the face of the southwest wall of the pit, about 150 feet above the lake. A visit at this time to the southwest rim of the pit, whence a view could be obtained of the northeast inner wall, revealed the fact that on the northeast wall also there is a window showing glowing lava, perhaps 50 feet above the lake and presumably on the rift crack which by previous observation is known to exist there.

At 5 p.m. January 14 the rain vapor was very dense and much fume rose from the crag mass. The speed of the current pouring from the line of western wall-crack fountains out into the lagoon had greatly increased, making a golden flocculent pattern. At the southwest grotto lava was boiling up and streaming out into the lagoon. In the center there was continuous boiling of large fountains, suggesting sinkhole action. The wall of the island remnant around the lagoon was now greatly increasing in height, as the central pool subsided faster than the ring crags. The east and south pools were boiling hard.

There had been of late some movement observable in the south pressure ridge which forms the rim of Halemaumau on that side, the bowlders slipping down the slopes and the ridge scaling off somewhat on the inner side.

At 10:30 a.m. January 15 the ledge which bounds the lagoon basin on the west, submerged during all the high levels, reappeared between the lagoon and the west wall-crack pond. A cascade was pouring into the lagoon on both sides of this ledge, the boiling wall-crack pond remaining high, while the lagoon continued to sink, draining downward through wells under the fountains of the central region. The wider cascade was on the north side of the new ledge. North of the center of the lagoon there was now a turbulent mass of bubble fountains with radial inward streaming towards the middle of the mass and concentric circles of breaking skins were continuously drawn into the vortex. It was evident that downward suction was going on there with increased fountaining. At the southwest grotto the liquid was boiling up and streaming outward as though fed by a tunnel leading from the wall-crack on the other side of the island remnant. The east pool was effervescing violently, the south pool was smaller and the west pool streamed northward into the northwest wall-crack pot as well as through the cascade above mentioned. The north crag was now a series of high steps from the wall towards the lagoon, and great quantities of smoke rose from its shattered ledges. The lagoon was now surrounded by a wall 40 feet high, consisting of the remnants of the island, the crag mass ring being restrained from subsidence by the funnelling walls of the pit. At the southwest heap outside of Halemaumau dense yellow-white fume was rising; there was also fume in a line of jets along the rift outside of Kilauea, and at night distant glow could be seen above the flows in the desert.

At 2:15 p.m., January 16, the smoke and vapor were denser than ever, and especially heavy volutes rose from the northern pit of the southwest heap. The southern pit along this rift, under the southwest wall of Kilauea crater, emitted only thin blue fume. In both these pits glow could still be seen in cracks amongst tumbled debris.

In Halemaumau the patch of central fountains of the lagoon was larger than before, and the inward streaming from all sides to the center continued. The western lip of the bench magma basin was still more lifted so that the cascade pouring from the western wall-crack pond to the lake was narrower and only a small rill remained on the south side of the ledge. The other features remained as before.

Activity of the Kau Desert Flows.

In the forenoon of January 12 there were driblet flows at several places on the summit plateau of the upper terrace of the long lava heap at the source of the main flow. The flow channel hitherto active had congealed below the bend east of the source amphitheatre, and just above the bend new streams had overflowed the river banks. One of these was making a lobe eastward from the left bank of the channel and another flooded the right bank just below the source amphitheatre and was spreading southwestward parallel with the lava heap and between it and the dome hill of older pahoehoe which had been a favorite view-point up to this time. This last arm was faced with a slow-moving wall of aa 15 feet high, over which pahoehoe lava was cascading in several places, one of the falls being 20 feet wide. With all the changes near the source, the front below Puu Kouele had necessarily ceased to flow.

On January 14 the northern part of the source heap was found to be greatly widened by recent streams down the slope toward the west and southwest. The source cone of the main river was found to be a small lava dome in a slightly tumbled depression of the main ridge. For 200 yards below this point the liquid stream was spanned by a heavy arch of crust, whence it emerged as a quietly flowing pahoehoe ribbon moving two miles per hour. A few hundred feet farther downstream, on the northeast side of the remnant of Dome Hill, the lava river greatly increased its velocity by falling over a cliff in the former river bed for a width of a hundred feet, cascading into an amphitheatre beneath, constricted to form a second cascade and a rapid pool about 60 feet wide. Apparently this fall was produced by a breakdown of the old river margin on its right bank, letting the new river form a second channel parallel to and west of the first. This river flowed away to the south to the region of the forested dunes two miles below and smoke from burning forest was there seen. There was no evident diminution in the volume of the flow. Dome Hill was largely covered by new flows, which, however, had piled up and travelled only a short distance. The terrace of the long source ridge, next below the source amphitheatre, was crossed on foot, and no activity was observed there.

On January 15 new changes took place in the source heap, probably by breaking it open along the main rift, and fresh pahoehoe streams were pouring westward, while the large eastern flow was again impoverished of supply.

Seismometric Record.

In the Whitney Laboratory of Seismology the instruments have registered the following local earthquakes, all very feeble, during the week ending at midnight January 16, 1920: January 10, 12:56 p.m.; January 11, 11:35 a.m. and 5:55 p.m.; January 14, 3:18 a.m. and 5:15 p.m.; January 15, 3:10 a.m. and 6:15 p.m. (two feeble quakes together); January 16, 8:33 a.m. Spasmodic microtremor during the week was moderate, with some wind effects. Harmonic tremor was slight, increasing January 14-15. Microseismic motion was slight. The tilting of the ground was slightly south January 10 and 11, northwest January 12, south January 13, northwest January 14, and slightly south and east January 15-16. These movements were within the limits, probably, of the diurnal temperature range.

Week Ending January 23, 1920.

Summary of Conditions.

Halemaumau and the flows pouring out in the Kau Desert continue in vigorous activity.

Halemaumau is a large pit, 1,485 feet long by 1,200 feet wide at its upper lip, with a lake of boiling lava 305 feet down. The lake is encircled by an inner craggy ridge rising 30 to 50 feet above the liquid. Three outer ponds, incessantly turbulent, with scores of fountains, lie between this ridge and the base of the outer walls of the pit.

Within the week the lake has risen 32 feet and the encircling ridge 5 feet, and this rising continues, the smoke from the cracked ridge growing less and the spectacular quality increasing. The glow at night above the pit is very uniform and bright, and the heat from the lava surface has augmented. There is dense vapor rising from a heap of new lava outside of Halemaumau in the southwest part of Kilauea crater.

This southwest heap is on the line of the gaping and steaming chasms which lead to the new flows in the desert six miles southwest of Kilauea. The flows take their rise in a mound of slaggy lava two miles long which follows the rift and is 100 feet high with three crusted pools on top. The first pool is surmounted by a low standing fountain in an oven cone; the others are fountaining spasmodically, and flows of slaggy (pahoehoe) lava have recently been spreading westward irregularly and building up the heap. The long flow of clinkery (aa) lava which was headed towards the seashore had stopped.

JOURNAL.

Activity of Halemaumau.

Measurements of the week, expressed as depression below the northeast rim of Halemaumau (3,727 feet above sea level) have been as follows:

	Lake at SW. Grotto.	N. Crag Summit.
Jan. 16, 2:15 p.m.	.337 feet	260 feet
Jan. 18, 11:25 p.m.	.333 "	260 "
Jan. 23, 9:30 a.m.	.305 "	255 "

In seven days the lake rose 32 feet, or 4.6 feet per day, and the crag 5 feet, or 0.7 foot per day. The movement of the lake magma recently in excess of the crag mass is shown by the following figures, which indicate the relief of the crag above the central lake:

Jan. 8	..........55 feet
Jan. 15	..........81 "
Jan. 16	..........77 "
Jan. 18	..........73 "
Jan. 23	..........50 "

Thus the lake until January 15 subsided more than the crag and thereafter rose, gaining on the crag.

At 11:30 a.m. January 18, there was clear seeing in Halemaumau after several days of south wind and smoky conditions. The central lake had risen and the annular crag mass surrounding it had risen most on the west side. Here a low rampart ridge, athwart the place where the cascade had been, completely shut off the west wall-crack pond from the lake. This pond was fountaining, but not so violently as the pond in the eastern trench, which remained in perpetual effervescence with some streaming out from its north-northeast corner. The south wall-crack pond was also effervescing. Streaming in the central lake was from opposite sides, west-northwest and east-southeast, the two currents meeting in a line of continuous fountaining across the center and at right angles to the directions of streaming. Here there

1. December 16, 1919. Ring island in Halemaumau
Outer ring-pool fountaining strongly,

Looking SSW. (Photo Jaggar.)
ıner lagoon quiet.

3. December 24, 1919. Rift floods in timber. (Photo Finch.)

were hundreds of small bubble fountains over a greatly increased area of activity, and the bright lines made by surface skins parting under the pull of the currents created a new pattern for this lagoon, which has hitherto been quiet. The inner wall of the crag mass stood 20 feet above the lagoon on the southwest side and only about 10 feet above it on the northeast, as though the bench magma were lifting most on the west and tilting the crag mass eastward. The northern summit crag now showed profound fractures, both radial and concentric to the pit. The fume rising from the cracks was dense and heavy; yellowish-white vapor continued to rise from the southwest heap.

On January 20, at 6 p.m., Halemaumau was inspected from its western lip. The bubble fountaining in the lagoon and the bright-line pattern of skins had increased in area over the central and southwestern parts, the blocks of skin drawing apart rapidly and the currents from east and west meeting in lines of travelling fountains across the middle. A high rampart now separated the western pool from the lake and the three marginal pools were fountaining as before. There was glow in high cracks over grottoes on the northern and southeastern sides of the lagoon, and the crag mass appeared to stand high above the lake. The pit made a bright even glare on the fume cloud at night. The lava pattern of the lake recalled the conditions of 1912 and 1913. There was strongly acid sulphurous fume rising from the southwest rift crack outside of and near Halemaumau.

On Friday, January 23, at 9:30 a.m., it was evident that the lake and crag mass were rising. New open pots of boiling lava had developed so as to extend the east trench pool northward. With clear seeing, the meaning of the flaming cracks above the lake grottoes was revealed: the annular crag mass had developed breaks traversely to its ridge in the three places where grotto fountains were playing, namely, southeast, southwest and north-northeast. The increased bubble fountaining in the lake lay in radial lines extending from the center to these three grottoes, and the streaming took its departure from triangular belts of crust which lay against the lake shores east, south and northwest. It looked as though the uplift had fractured the crag ring symmetrically in these three places, making chasms which led through from the central lake to the wallcrack of the outer ponds. These outer pools showed multiple fountaining as before, and there was much fume from the crag mass, from the smoke crack southwest near the Halemaumau rim, and from the northern pit of the southwest heap. The southern pit of that heap was no longer fuming. All of this smoke, however, did not prevent very bright glow from Halemaumau at night.

Activity of the Kau Desert Flows.

The long aa flow was explored on Saturday, January 17, during the torrential rains of a southwesterly storm. The old pahoehoe land was traversed by hundreds of brooks of running water coursing across the desert. A remarkable difference was noticed between the fresh aa areas and those of pahoehoe when drenched by rain. The aa steamed very little, whereas the pahoehoe, retaining much incondescent matter within, emitted a dense fog of steam, heaviest where the flows were new but not actually glowing on the surface. The glowing flows tended to dissipate the moisture and were more or less free from surface vapor.

The long flow was crossed above Kamakaia, and the aa was found in the channels as well as on the flats adjacent. Four distinct lava river channels were found in travelling northeast, and we passed from the aa region to the fresh pahoehoe, coming out on the east side of the whole flow belt. No live lava was found in this region, though the flows were progressively warmer towards the north. On following up the east side of the flow belt, near the old 1823 source heaps north of Kamakaia, fresher pahoehoe fronts of small flows were found making dense clouds of vapor, but none of them glowing or in motion. The only glowing lava seen was in the distance at the flow-source amphitheatre. We made the circuit of the north side of the upper end of the flow-source heap or hill, which was buried in a fog of its own steam which rose in heavy volutes. Coming down the west side of the heap a view was obtained of a part free from vapor, with lava fountains on top and overflows pouring down the western slope in two broad streams. These cascaded down the slopes, and there were fountains on the third and fourth terraces of the long lava ridge. As nearly as could be distinguished amid the heavy steam clouds, the new activity was a revival of the terraced pool next south of the source amphitheatre of the main previous flow. The longer and southernmost of the two flows pouring west had an aa front trending southwest a few hundred feet below the pahoehoe cascades and resting on the flat ground in that direction. A large fountain could be seen on the summit of the next terrace to the south. It was evident that a change of outlet was taking place in the heap, but there appeared to be ample volume of lava still flowing. This abundant flow to the westward accounted for the lack of activity east and south along the older flow course.

A visit to this locality again on the forenoon of January 21 under better seeing conditions revealed what was happening. The upper three terraces of the 1920 ridge were all fountaining on top, with pahoehoe flows pouring down the west side. The northernmost showed two cones on its summit plateau, and the larger cone was an open oven vomiting continuously a standing dome fountain six feet high of incandescent melt. This lava poured down into a pool below, which was banked against the wall of aa at the foot of the old Keamoku flow on the west. The pool was creeping forward, burning trees and bushes and making many cavern explosions where the vegetation was present. The explosions were absent where the fresh lava poured over cavernous pahoehoe of the present eruption, and this seemed good evidence that coal gas from vegetable matter makes the explosions.

On top of the second terrace a heavily crusted glowing pool was found, and in its midst a small pot was fountaining. Down the western slope a stream coursed through a sunken channel where a cavern roof had collapsed Cascades could be seen below the standing fountain of the northern summit on the western slope. Here a flow poured across the old pahoehoe below the foot of the Keamoku flow, and this had already crossed the Kapapala stone wall and spread into sparse timber which was burning. This flow was hard on top, and a place was found where the wall, a structure two feet thick and five feet high, was not yet completely covered. This stretch of wall inside the flow was perfectly aligned and showed no sign of being pushed over. Apparently the flow had overtopped the wall at its upper end and poured around it, but there was no evidence that it had knocked it down.

The third summit of the ridge showed an escarpment on top, fountains on its west slope just below the summit and short flows. There were also fountains in the profile of the ridge on top. The ridge in its entirety appeared greatly built up to a height 80 feet or more above the surrounding country.

On January 23 exploration of the rift between the southwest wall of Kilauea and Cone Peak revealed no new developments and no fresh motion in the rift cracks. There was much washing by the recent rains. Transverse cracks are common, one of them being found right across the Cone Peak ridge. Others were found extending northwest from the southwest corner of Kilauea crater, indicating that fresh movement had jostled the southern Uwekahuna block along planes at right angles to the main rift line. The westernmost of the main pair of cracks passes directly through the Cone Peak ridge, the eastern one 100 yards to the east, and these diverge farther down the mountain to a wide separation. The maximum yawning of crevasses, with much development of vapor, is about 300 yards south of the edge of Kilauea. All of these cracks could be easily crossed at the actual Kilauea edge, where the yawning open is small. The rift line across the southwest heap inside of Kilauea crater shows no sign of sufficient renewed movement to crack the smooth pahoehoe of the heap.

Seismometric Record.

In the Whitney Laboratory of Seismology during the week ending at midnight January 23, 1920, the following local earthquakes have been registered: January 17, 7:30 a.m., very feeble; January 22, 11:35 p.m., feeble; January 23, 1:30 a.m., slight, 10:40 p.m., slight. On January 18, at 8:10 a.m., an earthquake was felt at Hilea.

Spasmodic microtremor increased to several moderate spasms January 18; this motion was slighter thereafter, but slightly increased January 23. Harmonic microtremor was slight throughout the week, but increased January 23. Microseismic motion remained slight to very slight. Tilting of the ground was dominantly southward and the amount was small.

Week Ending January 30, 1920.

Summary of Conditions.

The liquid lava in Halemaumau has lowered 40 feet and then recovered 16 feet, leaving the lake 329 feet below the rim. The crag mass encircling the lake has remained nearly stationary. The pit has increased in smokiness, and dense smoke rises also from the new pits in the southwest part of Kilauea crater. In addition to the large central lake of Halemaumau there are three trench-like ponds, boiling violently with gas fountains, on the outside of the ring crag encircling the lake, between that crag and the wall of the pit. • The height of the crag summit above the lake is about 75 feet. The general movement of the week has thus been a sinking of the liquid lava in contrast to the rising of the previous week, and the pulsations up and down have increased to a rate of daily rising or sinking of 8 or 10 feet. The ring-crag has breaks across it in three places, where there are outrushing torrents of lava from the lake into grotto pots, and lines of fountains extend from the center of the lake to these places. The outer trench ponds appear lower than the lake.

The flow heap in the Kau Desert is very sluggishly active, with small flows building up the structure at its extreme upper end, six miles southwest from Kilauea crater. The flows are both slaggy and clinkery, and trickle both east and west from the rift line. The lava in the fracture appears to be solidifying from south to north, and the activity at present is dwindling.

JOURNAL.

Activity of Halemaumau.

Measurements of the week expressed as depression below the northeast rim of Halemaumau (3,727 feet above sea level) have been as follows:

	Lake at SW. Grotto.	N. Crag Summit.
Jan. 23, 9:30 a.m.	...305 feet	255 feet
Jan. 27, 5:30 p.m.	...345 "	254 "
Jan. 29, 5:40 p.m.	...329 "	...

In four days the lake sank 40 feet, or 10 feet per day, and the crag 1 foot, or 0.25 foot per day. Thereafter for two days the lake rose 16 feet, or 8 feet per day. The relief of the crag summit above the lake was:

Jan. 23 ....50 feet
Jan. 27 ....91 "

During the three days, January 24 to January 26, inclusive, the apparent changes in Halemaumau were very slight, but the lake appears to have been pulsating up and down independently of the crag mass, and the latter appears to have subsided most on its south side.

On Tuesday, January 27, at 5:30 p.m., the north crag summit was found to be nearly stationary, but the lake had subsided 40 feet as compared with January 23. The streaming in the lake from the east and west sides made a pattern of bright lines separating patches of skin which migrated to a line of fountains across the middle of the pit. The current poured out from a quiet crust at the west and incessantly created a second crust in the form of an island in the west central region. This island of crust migrated out to the fountaining belt, leaving a new patch of skin to form behind it.

The crags on opposite sides of the southwest grotto stood higher than before, and small coves or arms of the lake were being extended out through the transverse crevasses which crossed the crag mass at the three fountaining grottoes north, southwest and southeast. At all of these places there was streaming towards the grotto and away from the center. The three wall-crack pools outside of the crag ring appeared lower than the lake, as though the lava pouring towards the grottoes were draining out through tunnels to the lower level, and the wall-crack lava were sinking. The southwest rift window in the inner wall of the pit continued to glow brightly. Fume rose in large volumes from the crag mass. A dense fume column still rose from the southwest heap at the margin of the Kilauea floor.

On January 29, at 5:40 p.m., the general appearance of Halemaumau was unchanged. The streaming in the central lake poured out from dark patches of crust which lay against the shores on the west-northwest, south-southwest and east-northeast sides. The currents now met in three distinct radial lines of fountaining. These lines ended at border grottoes southwest, southeast and north-northeast. The liquid streamed into these grottoes. Two coves had now developed at the southwest grotto, the larger one sending a broad stream into a cavern and the smaller one, adjacent to it on the south, making a cascade which poured over a ledge from the lake into a border pot. The swiftest streaming was from the west, forming as before nodal centers of crusting with radial currents pouring from these centers, while the general drift carried the crusts into the fountaining zone, to be there broken up. The general arrangement of the three lines of fountaining corresponds in position to the three arms of the lake which formed in 1916 and became three distinct lakes in 1919. The noise of fountaining in the pit was no longer audible at long distances as before, and the glow at night had diminished.

Activity of the Kau Desert Flows.

In the forenoon of Saturday, January 24, the main source heap of the Kau Desert flows, six miles from Kilauea, was making trickling streams from a pool on top of its northern end, but there was no more flowing on the west side. The ridge was crossed at the second terrace, and several collapsed flat areas were found on top, with smoking vents and glowing cracks. There was no motion at the southern end of the ridge. Examination o[illegible] southern lava heap in the san[illegible] belt revealed red heat in a [illegible] a depth of about 10 feet. So[illegible]t smoking was seen in the vicin[illegible] of the long aa flow south of here. There was discovered a series of new cracks in old ground west of the middle portion of the upper main source ridge.

On January 25 the upper end of the source ridge was found to be crowned with a broken cone, whence issued a small stream of lava that flowed westward over small aa which covers the ground on the east side of the Keamoku flow. Much Pele's hair of various colors was found near this cone. The lava stream emerging from the cone was only a narrow rill, moving about twelve miles per hour. On the side of the hill a short distance below the summit a large puddle of lava had formed, from the sides of which sluggish flows pushed down to lower levels.

It was now becoming evident that the rift underneath the long tabular source ridge of the Kau Desert activity was steadily feeding a certain quantity of lava to the pools on top of and inside of this ridge, but that the escape of the lava to form flows was dependent on the paths of least resistance, and these were incessantly changing. This source ridge now stands in its highest portions from 80 to 100 feet above the surrounding country. Its length coincides in direction with the rift beneath, its upper end is about six miles and its lower end about eight miles from Kilauea. About a mile northeast of it up the rift there is the area of first outflowing, which has been inactive since the first days of the eruption (December 22). A half-mile southwest down the rift from the lower end of the source ridge, is the area of sand dunes and forest where the lower lava heap developed and built up a high flat-topped dome, then went out of action, with an aa breach in its western slope. The long source ridge, where the activity still persists, is thus the middle of the three active vents of the past six weeks. The ridge began as separate places of upwelling in a line along the crack. These formed six distinct slag-heap terraces overlapping each other down the slope of the mountain. The terrace aspect has now been largely destroyed through irregular outward building by flows, both pahoehoe and aa, which have widened the flanks and flattened the slopes so as to convert the six terraces into summit crests of a long, wide and irregular ridge, with the maximum of remnant activity at its northern or uppermost end. The great aa flow, which extends six miles down the mountain, emerged from the east side of the ridge, somewhat north of its middle. Other small aa flows burst through the flanks at the southern end of the ridge. Otherwise most of the ridge is made up of pahoehoe flows and of flat-topped summit areas of smooth lava crusts, which are simply the solidified surfaces of pools, formed in the heart of the ridge and over the rift line. The ridge with its outlying flows is nearly a half-mile wide in places, and seen from a distance it appears as a flat, silvery, low hill of wide extent, with blue fume rising in many places.

This description has seemed necessary in order to indicate the marked difference between this source vent as a flow center and the very explosive fountaining craters of the Mauna Loa type. The long Kilauea ridge has had only small fountains on top, of the type frequently described at Halemaumau as perpetual or ''artesian'' springs of lava.

The making of aa from the lava of these Kilauea slag-heaps has resulted from two distinct mechanisms. The aa of the long flow was produced where the pahoehoe gradually gave out and the under-substance of the pahoehoe bed continued to flow down the mountain. The aa which makes out directly from a breakdown of the slag-heap appears to be produced when the pahoehoe of the summit pools gives out, and the substance of its incandescent bottom bursts the bounding rampart and flows through the flank of the heap. In both cases the substance which flows as aa is the lava after it has freed itself from volcanic gas pressure and still retains sufficient mobility to flow. It is the substance which corresponds to the lake bottom material of Halemaumau.

On the afternoon of January 30 it was evident that the two northern summits of the source ridge were merging into one. Five distinct summit plateaus could be counted in the profile of the ridge as seen across the desert from the west, but the steep, even, slag-heap aspect of the outer slopes was now replaced by irregular spurs due to many small flows; some of these spread out as far as the 1823 ridge on the east and the Keamoku flow on the west. The new pahoehoe against the Keamoku aa was piled up to more than half the height of the latter, and the aa wall had been fully 15 feet high.

The western flows of the ridge were comparatively cool, so that the north summit plateau was easily reached from the west side. The only activity observed in the four southern terraces consisted in fumy orifices in the upper two. The top of the highest northern part of the fifth terrace, standing perhaps 90 feet above the surrounding country, was a flat pool of crusted live lava, showing one small oven cone and pahoehoe welling up cracks very sluggishly. There was much odor of burnt organic matter, perhaps from vegetable charcoal buried in the heap. This odor suggests the vat smells of a pork slaughter-house. A sluggish flow of brittle pahoehoe was seen moving down the eastern slope, and one recent short flow on that side had bent southward and developed into aa at its extremity. One heavy elongate mass of aa had broken out of the flank of the hill and extended about 200 feet to the southeast, this being a small breakdown, revealing the inside substance of the heap and showing at its head an amphitheatre of collapse. The top of the hill on the south side of the active pool was the usual flat plateau of heavy crusted pahoehoe, with one or two driblet heaps showing snaky trickles of frozen lava on their slopes. These probably lay over the rift line. Close by was a small flat stained yellow with sulphur and fuming.

A distant view of the southern lava heap in the sand dunes revealed no heat vibration or smoke in that direction.

Seismometric Record.

In the Whitney Laboratory of Seismology, during the week ending at midnight January 30, 1920, the following local earthquakes have been registered: January 24, 3:15 p.m., moderately strong and recorded in Hilo; the indicated distance was about 30 miles from the Observatory, and as this shock was strongly felt at Hilea as a double jolt accompanied by loud rumbling, it may be considered one of the movements of readjustment of the Kahuku rift on Mauna Loa. Another small shock was felt in Hilea January 25, 3:20 a.m. The Observatory instruments on January 28 recorded shocks at 7:55 p.m. (feeble) and 10:20 p.m. (light), both indicating distance of origin 30 miles, corresponding to the Kahuku rift, and the first of these was strongly felt in Hilea.

Spasmodic microtremor has been moderate to weak and harmonic tremor moderate throughout the week. Microseismic motion increased to moderate January 25 to 27 and thereafter decreased. Movement of tilting was slightly south and west the early part of the week and north and east thereafter.

Very respectfully,

T. A. JAGGAR, JR.,
Volcanologist.

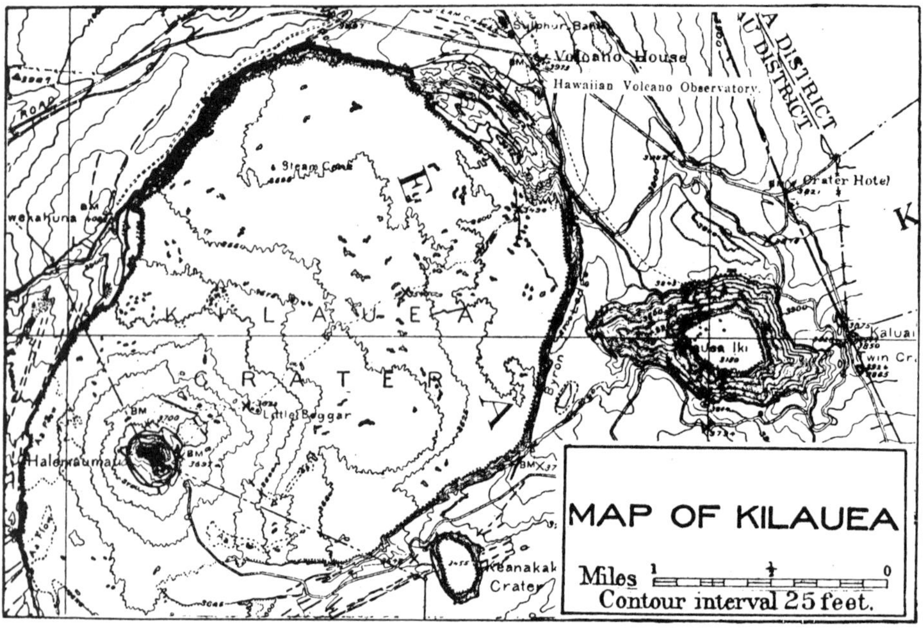

HAWAIIAN VOLCANO OBSERVATORY.

The Observatory is equipped with the following seismometric instruments rebuilt at the station in 1918 for the special needs of volcano research: two Bosch-Omori pendulums, high speed registration of local earthquakes; one optically recording seismograph for distant earthquakes; one clinograph registering E-W tilting of the ground. A vertical component seismograph was in December, 1918, set up in experimental operation. These are seated on concrete piers in a closed basement room having practically constant temperature, beneath the chief Observatory building near the hotel. Time is referred to a rated chronometer, checked at intervals by solar observations with a transit. The chronometer is loaned by the College of Hawaii. Hawaiian standard time (H. S. T.) is 10 hrs. 30 min. slower than Greenwich time.

CANCANI SCALE OF SEISMIC INTENSITY.

Expressed by accelerations measured in millimeters per second per second.

I.	Instrumental	0.0	2.5
II.	Very slight	2.5	5.0
III.	Slight	5.0	10.0
IV.	Sensible, mediocre	10.0	25.0
V.	Rather strong	25.0	50.0
VI.	Strong	50.0	100.0
VII.	Very strong	100.0	250.0
VIII.	Ruinous	250.0	500.0
IX.	Disastrous	500.0	1000.0
X.	Very disastrous	1000.0	2500.0
XI.	Catastrophic	2500.0	5000.0
XII.	Great catastrophe	5000.0	10000.0

Grade IV. is ordinarily the minimum perceived by the senses; and in grade XII. the accelerations or rate of change of motion (jerk) reaches that of terrestrial gravitation.

In the standard form of report the maximum intensity or acceleration, designated by the symbol a, or max. a, is given in the conventional unit of milligal. The milligal is a measure of acceleration, such that 1 milligal = 1/100 mm. per sec. per sec. = 10 μ. per sec. per sec. The Cancani scale, here defined in terms of millimeters per sec. per sec., can therefore be expressed in milligals by multiplying each of the numbers by 100.

U. S. DEPARTMENT OF AGRICULTURE
WEATHER BUREAU
CHARLES F. MARVIN, CHIEF

MONTHLY BULLETIN
OF THE
Hawaiian Volcano Observatory

VOL. VIII. HONOLULU, HAWAII, FEBRUARY, 1920 No. 2

Week Ending February 6, 1920.

SUMMARY OF CONDITIONS.

The lava in Halemaumau has risen during the week, the ring of crags rising more than the liquid lava. It appears that alternation of rising between lake magma and bench magma has begun again. Important changes in the topography of the bottom of the pit have begun to appear, involving development of arms of the central lake through cross fissures in the ring of crags. Opposite these arms lines of radial fountaining from the center of the pit outward have developed, the fountains tending to migrate towards the arms. These three arms are just where the three lakes were in 1919, respectively north, southeast and southwest, and they seem to mark some kind of deep fracturing in the bench magma occasioned by uplift in these three places. In all three locations the rock adjoining the chasms has lifted into crags, the ring ridge rising more there than elsewhere and hence causing the chasms to yawn open upward.

Along with this development there has been higher rising of the main lake than of the marginal ponds so that the former has been cascading into the latter and the cascades have been numerous into a wall-crack pot on the southwest. At the south side of the pit the wall veneer of hardened lava has fallen away to form a large talus slope over the site of the former south pond. All of these happenings appear to indicate a rising of the crater floor material towards the north and a sinking towards the south, amounting to a southward tipping of the ring ridge. Toward the end of the week the fume from the pit became less dense and the gas pressure greater along with the general rising.

Simultaneous with the rising in Halemaumau, there developed in the flow heap in the Kau Desert increased activity of small flows overrunning the edge of the heap at its northern end from the hot pool on top. These flows were chiefly pahoehoe until February 1, when a new breach in the east side of the heap produced a craggy and rugged short aa flow, draining the stagnant fill of pasty lava which had been formed in the core of the heap under the second terrace pool, which had recently become quiet. Other small aa flows broke out from the north flank of the heap, but those overflowing the edges of the plateau on top of the heap are always pahoehoe.

The general situation is now a condition of adjustment of the rising lava from the depths, the fountaining summit pool at Halemaumau, and the outflow source at the Kau Desert lava heap. The recovery in Halemaumau appears to indicate that the lake supply is sufficient to keep the desert outflow in operation for some time to come.

JOURNAL.

Activity of Halemaumau. Measurements of the week locating points below the northeast rim of Halemaumau (3727 feet above sea level) has been as follows:

	Lake at S. W. grotto	N. crag summit
Jan. 29, 5:40 p. m....	329 feet	(Jan. 27, 254 feet)
Feb. 1, 11:15 a. m....	324 "	239 "
5, 10:45 a. m....	315 "	231 "

In three days, January 29 to February 1, the lake rose 5 feet, or 1.7 feet per day; in four days, February 1 to 5, the lake rose 9 feet, or 2.25 feet per day. In five days, January 27 to February 1, the crag rose 15 feet, or 3 feet per day; in four days, February 1 to 5, the crag rose 8 feet, or 2 feet per day. The relief of the crag summit above the lake was

Jan. 27	91 feet
Feb. 1	85 "
5	84 "

On February 1 at 11:15 a. m. the three cross fissures in the ring crag mass had gaped open to make arms of the lake. The southeast arm was a fountaining cove without marked streaming. The southwest arm was bigger, a distinct canyon between two crags, and the lake extended through to the wall of Halemaumau with streaming that ended in a wall-crack pot that appeared to be the focus of cascading from all sides. The west wall-crack pond was cascading into this pot. The lake cascaded through a tunnel in the rampart into the west pond. The pot at the edge of the lake on the south-southwest side received a cascade from the lake which poured under a crust, and probably this pot connected underground with the wall-crack back of the crag mass. The wall-crack void which appeared to be the main cauldron receiving all these cascades lay slightly north of the Kau rift crack in the wall of the pit. Glow and puffs of blue fume from hot lava below were visible there. The rift crack could be plainly seen in the wall above where the surface veneer had fallen away. It appeared as two fractures open only a few inches. The north arm of the lake was also an elongate crevasse breaking through the north crag ridge and this also received an inrushing stream from the lake which expended itself at the end of the arm where there was a puffing gas cone glowing on the bank above.

The crags adjacent to these new arms of the lake have been lifted on each side of the cove formed by the crevasse in each case. The north crags are highest with smoking tumbled blocks, dense fume rising along the cracks and the whole mass growing to be a confused and chaotic heap. The crags on each side of the southwest arm are terraced. The uplift is less marked at the southeast arm.

The site of the former south wall-crack pond was now largely crusted over and a gas cone could be heard hissing amid much smoke. The east wall-crack pool continued to show many dome fountains but its surface appeared lower relative to the crag mass. The three wall-crack pools were distinctly lower than the lake and the ring crag summits appeared to be lifting, but this lift was in part a breaking and tilting up of surface units of the bench magma.

The alignment of fountains was now definitely three radial zones in the lake leading to the three arms along lines of turbulent travelling fountains. As the three arms were disposed at the angles of an equilateral triangle, this arrangement gave the lake a very symmetrical geometric form. There was perpetual fountaining at a central patch where the three radial lines met. In the triangular quiet spaces there was a pattern of bright lines and crusts with streaming towards the fountaining zones. An irregularity was introduced at the west where the outward streaming from the northwestern crusted region lay side by side with a conflicting current in the opposite direction that led to the cascade through the west rampart.

On Tuesday, February 3, at 10:30 a. m., the north crag appeared more lifted and all the valley matter between it and the north wall of the pit which had been the crust of the north ring pool was now part of the cracked and elevated crag mass. The lake was still streaming into the three arms and the crust on the east side of the lake appeared quiet and heavy. The cascade south-southwest was still in action. Examination of the west wall-crack pot from the west rim of Halemaumau revealed the cascade from the lake rushing out from the tunnel in the west rampart and pouring into the west pond, and this in turn was cascading under a crust into a round deep pot where brilliant lava could be seen churning and boiling at a lower level.

The fume from Halemaumau had been notably dense in the upper atmosphere of late, great volumes hanging over the flanks of Mauna Loa and obscuring the distant view of the Kau district as seen from the Observatory.

At 10:45 a. m. February 5 it was apparent that the fume rising from the southwest heap on the floor of Kilauea had greatly lessened and during this day the fume from Halemaumau diminished. There was a distinct new note in the sounds of the pit involving a heavy roar of fountaining and a sharp puffing from a cone at the northwest corner where the northern end of the west ring pool had been. Another new sound was the sliding of avalanches from the wall of the pit on the south side as though withdrawal of lava from the south ring-pool site were undermining the cliff there. The puffing and fountaining noises suggested a rising lake. There was glow in the cone at the inner end of the north arm of the lake. The east and west pools were fountaining as usual, and the south-eastern radial fountain line in the lake was interrupted by a turbulent whirlpool of fountaining east of the center. A large talus could be seen lying across the low part of the crag mass on the south side of the pit and this is where the sliding was heard.

Exploration of the upper part of the hot tunnel which had formed during the Postal Rift flow at its source showed several openings whereby the upper 200 feet of the tunnel could now be explored. At the source cone a chamber 25 feet high is revealed with an inner well leading to another oblique tunnel at a lower level. In the main tube there are shoreline marks of the lava river and much incrustation along the roof and sides with accumulations of alum and other salts and delicately colored orange, buff, yellow and white stalactites of an alabaster-like substance which appears to be gypsum.

Activity of the Kau Desert Flows. On February 1 a considerable aa outbreak took place on the west side of the second terrace of the flow heap. An exploration was made February 3 from Kilauea along the rift with a side excursion to the cone crater pits and Puu Koae. The wide open chasms of the rift near Kilauea, broken across beds of volcanic ash and gravel 20 feet thick, and basaltic rock below, present rounded buttresses and pinnacle forms which simulate in miniature some of the features of the Grand Canyon of Arizona. These crevasses stand open with walls 15 to 20 feet apart and in places there is a choking of tumbled debris below, with large wedged blocks making arches across the abyss. One of the fresh breaks of the rift system was followed for a half-mile trending southeast, showing a case of radial breaking in the mountain which extends out from the center of uplift in a direction different from the main southwest rift zone.

Nothing newly broken was found in the region of the cone crater and Puu Koae. From the summit of the latter the northern live part of the source heap could be seen off to the southwest across intervening sand flats, the heap appearing as a wide flat elevation crowned with light blue fume and glistening with fresh lava. On closer approach pahoehoe was found trickling from the summit pool all over the northern part of the heap with short flows to the east, north and west in motion.

On passing around to the west side the second hill of the long source ridge was found wholly changed down its western slope. Instead of the smooth inconspicuous field of pahoehoe which had been there before, there was now an extraordinary serrate wall or spur making a jagged profile against the sky and extending west from the summit of the heap to its base. This was a recent sluggish aa flow which had emerged from within the heap by breaking up the pahoehoe shell, turning up blocks 15 to 20 feet in diameter which still showed the smooth surfaces of the original ground. This was the jumble that had flowed on February 1 and its general character was similar to the breakdown of the southern lava heap in the sand dunes. Apparently the semi-solid bottom material of the pool in the summit of the hill had become heavy and oozed out as an aa paste carrying forward the outer shell of the hill. This flow was about 100 yards wide and a half mile long, extending westward across the stone wall and burying up the earlier pahoehoe flows which had lain against the old Keamoku aa. The new aa was piled directly against this ancient flow, overriding it slightly.

On February 6 the rift line from Kilauea to the flow was again followed, starting from Uwekahuna. On the west-southwest edge of Kilauea crater no new movement could be positively identified in cracks parallel to the edge. Following down the live rift a place was found just north of Cone Peak where the main rift from the Kilauea rim becomes divided up into the two cracks which extend on down the mountain to the two belts of flow sources which have given vent to the recent activity. This division of the rift takes place by way of a cross crack nearly at right angles to the main southwest trend, bringing the upper chasms to an end, and starting two new ones from the ends of the cross fissure. The cross fissure is thus a break concentric to the Halemaumau center.

The place of first lava outbreak, described in the Bulletin December 21-22, was found west of Puu Koae in the same condition as when last seen except that it was now wholly inactive with very little vapor rising.

The live source heap was making flows down its northern slope and both pahoehoe and aa were found side by side. The aa was flowing out of a low fracture near the base of the heap, while the pahoehoe was pouring in cascades down the flanks from the summit pool. It was of great interest to find both flows at the same locality, both alive, and from quite distinct origins. The aa was coming from the bottom material of the summit pool, the pahoehoe from the surface material. The aa was free from gas, the pahoehoe was bubbling with gas. The aa was the gas-free sediment of the pool. The pahoehoe was the gas-charged glass still making gas bubbles from gas in solution. The aa was flowing bench magma, the pahoehoe flowing lake magma. While these flows were being inspected from 12 to 2 p. m. the aa was pushing over a flowing pahoehoe tongue and was itself overridden by a flood of pahoehoe. The pahoehoe was in much greater volume than the aa and was burning bushes at the edges of the flow area and making border explosions in old caverns invaded by the carbon gas. Another small fresh aa flow was found farther south on the west side of the heap.

Seismometric Record. In the Whitney Laboratory of Seismology during the week ending at midnight February 6, 1920, the following earthquakes have been registered: February 2, 4:15 a. m., feeble; February 4, 5:35 a. m. and 10:30 p. m., both feeble; February 5, 1:25 a. m., apparent distance of origin 15 miles. A teleseism was registered at 1:00 a. m. on February 2, the preliminary phase indicating an origin about 2600 miles distant. Spasmodic microtremor increased from moderate to moderately strong towards the end of the period. Harmonic tremor was moderate January 31, slight February 1 to 5, and moderate February 6. Microseismic motion was very slight to slight. Movements of tilting changed from slightly east and north about February 1 to increasing tilt south and west, the southward movement accumulating towards the end of the week.

Week Ending February 13, 1920.

During the week ending February 13 the rising of the lava column in Halemaumau has continued, the lake more than the crags until February 9, but the crags more than the lake February 9-13. The alternation between lake and crags is thus as usual. The rate of rising continues to be 2 to 3 feet per day. The topography of the bottom of the pit is slowly changing by construction along the lake shores and by uptilting movement of crag blocks, the whole process recalling the events of the summer and autumn of 1916. Cascades from the lake outward to the wall-crack pots continued until February 12, with rising spells of the liquid which obliterated the falls, and on February 13 the cascades on the west were reversed, the liquid standing higher in the marginal pool. The fountaining is strong, the fume has diminished, and at the southwest heap on the Kilauea margin the dense fuming has been replaced by only a thin blue veil. Columns of hot vapor crowned by cumulus have risen to an immense height over the hot pit, so that the scene has been brilliant even at Hilo.

The flow heap in the Kau Desert again reached a climax of heaping whereby it broke down on the east side, developing a large depression several acres in extent and making a short aa flow eastward out of the interior matter of the broken ridge. Pahoehoe flows continued to pour from the rift orifices in the ridge, tending to fill up the depression made by the breakdown.

JOURNAL.

Activity of Halemaumau. Measurements of the week ending February 13, 1920, made the depression of points in the lava column lying below the north east rim of Halemaumau (datum 3727 feet above sea level) as follows:

	Lake at S. W. grotto	N. crag summit
Feb. 5, 10:45 a. m.	315 feet	231 feet
7, 4:15 p. m.	298 "	221 "
9, 10:00 a. m.	297 "	220 "
13, 3:30 p. m.	294 "	203 "

The lake in eight days rose 21 feet, or 2.6 feet per day and the crag 28 feet, or 3.5 feet per day. The relief of the crag was:

Feb. 5	84 feet above lake
7	77 " " "
9	77 " " "
13	91 " " "

The lake gained 14 feet on the crag between January 27 and February 9, and the crag gained 14 feet on the lake between February 9 and 13. The crag thus recovered in four days what the lake had taken thirteen days to drown.

At 4:15 p. m. Saturday, February 7, the lava lake was very hot with three radial lines of bubble fountains north, southeast and southwest, and a vortical swirl in the middle of the southeast line rotating clockwise. There were quiet patches, from which streaming radiated out to the fountaining lines, lying against the east, south and northwest shores of the lake. At the west and south-southwest, cascades were pouring outward from the lake. The western pool against the wall of the pit which received the first of these cascades itself made a large fall into the pot south of it. The northern end of this west pool had so crusted over that its roof was becoming an arch with open pots showing the lava below. The radial gulches leading out from the lake into fractures in the crag mass at the ends of the lines of fountains had penetrated through the marginal crags all the way to the wall in the cases of the southwest and southeast arms, and the north and southwest arms showed strong streaming away from the lake. A flaming cone had been built on the bank at the end of the north arm. The southeast gulch contained fountaining lava but with less rapid streaming. The south-southwest pot at the lake margin had a large flaming chimney over it. The talus at the south margin of the lake gave off much smoke from its eastern flank. All of the black ledge veneer which had covered the lower half of the south wall of the pit had scaled off to make this talus and some rock had fallen from the western part of the south pressure ridge on the upper edge of Halemaumau. There was falling off of the black ledge material from the lower part of the southwest rift crack where the southwest arm led towards and probably cascaded into the wall crack.

The crags had become high on both sides of the southwest arm and very high on both sides of the north arm. The western of these latter is the north crag which has been subject to measurement, and the summit rock of this had recently fallen, changing the profile. The upper smooth surfaces of this block showed tilt towards the center of the pit.

On February 9 at 10:00 a. m. the lake was found pulsating between very high levels, when it was continuous across the western rampart to the wall pool, and lower levels on the wall-crack side when a cascade would develop from the lake across the rampart, making a brilliant display. The west pool was churning and evidently cascading beneath a crust into the southwest wall pot. The north end of the west pool had now become a row of glowing pots and cones. Apparently rising was the dominant movement in progress for the liquid lava, for the fountaining in the lake had diminished and the fume was thinning. The streaming in the lake was mostly into the three arms as before. In the east pool along the base of the Halemaumau wall there was tendency to crust over on the wall side and to stream inward towards the crag mass, with fountaining less than before. In the evening the alternations between cascading and filling at the west continued, and the lake was covered with a brilliant pattern of bright lines between slowly drifting polyhedral crusts.

On February 11, at 6:30 p. m., there was increased fountaining and a change in the crust pattern, the main line of fountains toward which the streaming converged trending north and south. The arms of the lake southwest and southeast had enlarged and a new grotto with inrush had developed on the northeast side of the lake as though an opening had formed through the crag mass into the east pool. The whole lake was covered with the bright-line pattern, the fountains were more scattered and the lake appeared to be enlarging at the expense of the crag mass. A heavy cascade was again openly pouring into the south-southwest pot at the lake margin, and about 5 feet below the liquid lava in the pot was boiling up in a continuous dome fountain. Flings of lava shot up from wall crack activity back of the crag mass south-southwest. The east pool had become narrow and partly crusted. There was moderate streaming into the southwest, southeast and north arms and into the west pool from the lake. A high stack had been built at one of the northwest cones, and this was flinging up umbrella-shaped gushes of melt at intervals of about a half minute, with a noise like the exhaust of a gas engine. An avalanche was seen sliding at the north-northeast wall of the pit and the black ledge veneer had been scaling off in many places showing that the base of the walls was being disturbed and undermined. The fume was much thinner and in the afternoon in calm weather a very high cumulus developed over the crater showing vapor billows which boiled up rapidly.

At 3:30 p. m. February 13 the crags were evidently higher and the southwest crag adjacent to the southwest arm on its north side had developed wedge-shaped terraces on the lake side where successsive shorelines had been lifted and tilted northward. The same effect was seen on the north side of the southeast arm. New coves were developed on the northeast and northwest sides of the lake. The liquid lava of the west pool and the southwest wall pot were now up level with the lake and even higher, so that the streaming was outward into the lake through the narrows recently occupied by a cascade in the opposite direction. There was slow centrifugal flow from the lake into the north and southwest arms, but the southeast arm was stagnant. The fountaining was intense and hot, lines of travelling fountains formed irregularly, and one large fountain north of the center of the lake tended to break the surface in spasms at more or less regular intervals. The north arm had widened. The streaming was northward and southward from the current pouring into the lake at the western narrows, and on the northeast side of the lake there was streaming towards the south. At the northwest stack locality there was now a cove of the lake. The top of the north crag had developed several new pinnacles.

Examination of the rift crack near Halemaumau on the southwest showed that some gas was rising and much sulphur stain had formed. The southwest heap beyond was emitting thin blue fume.

Activity of the Kau Desert Flows. The flow heap in the desert continued its outpouring and upward building during the early part of the week and at twilight February 11 a mushroom cloud stood over the flow as seen from Kilauea, but no glow could be distinguished after dark. There was much rain vapor on the Kilauea floor at the time and thunder showers had been prevalent, developing much snow on the mountains.

Exploration of the flow February 11 showed that there was no overflow of the upper edge of the slag-heap, but a large breakdown covering several acres had opened an amphitheatre on the east side of the north end of the ridge and from this aa had spread eastward. A crag stood in the middle of the amphitheatre and the latter was bounded by a wall 20 feet in places. The newer flows of the heap on its north slope were broken by a fresh crack in line with the easternmost of the cracks of the rift system, and upon the summit in line with this fissure two fountains were splashing to a height of four feet and feeding a pahoehoe flow which poured into the eastern amphitheatre. The flow near its source was 15 feet across and moving 10 miles an hour, but below it broadened out to a width of 40 feet and slowed to 2 miles an hour. It was tending to fill up the amphitheatre.

The mechanism of the flow heap was thus repeating what had happened several times before, namely, the building up of a pahoehoe rampart around a lake on top of the heap, to the point where the substance of the lake bottom broke down the rampart on one side. This made an aa flow with more or less pahoehoe on top of it according to the topographic relations of the source wells and the breakdown. The first of the series of such breakdowns was the one which produced the long flow, and at that time the pahoehoe floods were in such volume that they carried with them as a mixture much of the aa material, themselves developing into aa as they lost gas.

Seismometric Record. In the Whitney Laboratory of Seismology during the week ending at midnight February 13, 1920, the following local earthquake has been registered: February 8, 6:05 p. m., light, distance of origin about 18 miles. A distant earthquake was feebly registered February 9, 11:00 p. m. Spasmodic microtremor was mostly weak throughout the week and harmonic tremor slight to moderate. Microseismic motion was slight to very slight. Tilting of the ground was southerly February 7, north and east February 8-9, south again February 10-11, and stationary thereafter.

Week Ending February 20, 1920.

The lava of Halemaumau pit has continued to rise with increased speed for both lake and crags, the lake gaining on the crags between February 13 and February 19. The rate of rising has been 4 to 5 feet per day. Three islands have developed in the central part of the lake adjacent to the three radial lines of fountains. It will be remembered that these three lines of fountains end at arms of the lake which began their development as crevasses through the encircling crag mass. Apparently these fissures extended under the bottom of the lake, the lines of fountains are over them and the combined lifting of the bottom sectors and piling up of foundered crusts has developed the three adjacent shoals that have become islands. The fountaining continues in the channels between the islands.

The crags adjacent to the three arms of the lake have developed three prominent uptilted blocks southwest, southeast and north, the latter the largest. These exhibit inclined terraces on the lake side which mark the stages of tilting which has progressed step by step with the rising. Each crag thus shows lines of lifted shorelines convergent as seen in elevation, the separate benches coming together at the axial point about which the block has been rotated or bent up, at the same time that it was lifted. Exactly the same phenomenon was common during the formation of the crags of 1916-17. In general the upheaval of the present ring of crag blocks appears to be away from the center so as to close the remnants of the wall-crack pond, though much activity of blowing cones continues along the wall crack, (the fissure between the lava column and the pit wall). The crowding out of the wall ponds and the development of islands and crags is diminishing the size of the liquid lake.

The flow heap in the desert southwest of Kilauea has continued at its northern end to build up as pahoehoe and break down as aa in alternations, as though there were a critical height for the heap of about 125 feet beyond which the pressure breaches the flanks and the accumulated paste inside flows out as sluggish aa. This alternation suggests interesting comparisons with the Halemaumau alternation of rising lake and lifting shores. In the Halemaumau case the rise of the lake and accumulation of bench magma beneath occasions an outward pressure of the paste which lifts the crusted marginal material. This appears to be analogous to the outward pressure that breaches the lava heap. Another suggestive comparison is the similarity of the oval amphitheatres at the head of each breach, to the oval sink craters common in Hawaii on a much grander scale. Such craters are Kilauea, Mohokea, Wood Valley at Kapapala, and Mokuaweoweo. These differ from lava pits in that they are occasioned by general sidewise withdrawal of matter below with lateral slumping, whereas lava pits like Halemaumau or Keanakakoi are the funnels over orifices whence liquid lava has been withdrawn straight down, probably through a fissure below.

The combined glow from Halemaumau and the lava flows, along with favorable atmospheric conditions was so bright at 10 p. m. February 16 that Mr. H. H. White, a yachtsman, master of the yawl Ajax, reported glow seen in the direction of Hawaii from a distance of 190 miles east-southeast.

JOURNAL.

Activity of Halemaumau. Measurements of the week ending February 20, 1920, determined the following depressions below the northeast datum at the edge of Halemaumau (3727 feet above sea level):

	Lake at S. W. grotto	N. crag summit
Feb. 13, 3:30 p. m..........	294 feet	203 feet
19, 1:30 p. m.........	265 "	180 "

The lake in six days rose 29 feet, or 4.8 feet per day, and the crag 23 feet, or 3.8 feet per day. This for the lake was nearly double the rate of rising of the previous week and for the crag only a slight increase. The relief of the crag was:

Feb. 13....................................	91 feet above lake
17....................................	84 " " "
19....................................	85 " " "

The crag had gained 14 feet on the lake between February 9 and 13, and the lake gained 6 feet on the crag between February 13 and 19. The alternation thus continued and as before, the gain made by the lake was slower than that made by the crag.

At 3 p. m. February 15 a prominent new feature discovered on the northeast side of the center of the lake was a low island shaped like a walrus, with

Dec. 15, 1919, 11:30 a.m. Lava gushing up through cracks, S.W. Kilauea floor. (Compare photo. 3, December Bulletin.)
—Photo Jaggar.

Dec. 31, 1919. Aa Lava River, lower part of flow, Kau Desert.
—Photo Finch.

Jan. 4, 1920. Explosion Hole from Coal Gas, desert flows in sand.
—Photo Jaggar.

Jan. 9, 1920. Pahoehoe Lava River, upper flow, Kau Desert.
—Photo Finch.

its head pointed southwest and its sloping back extending across the northeastern third of the lake. The mouth was a spatter grotto with hanging stalactites where inrushing currents made tumultuous fountaining. The back was washed with the lava that had splashed over it and so was a glistening surface of smooth pahoehoe. The bottom of the lake had evidently been shoaling with accumulated pyroclastic sediment and the tip of the northeastern sector of the bottom had been lifted along with the lift of the crag adjacent to the east side of the north arm of the lake. This northeastern part of the lake had recently shown dark crusts and had appeared as though an island might form just as in the case of the northern islands of August, 1916. The fountaining grotto was just where the central fountain had been, at the point where the centripetal currents had converged for many weeks.

The crags were higher, the southwest cascade continued to pour from the lake into a boiling pot, the west pool was flooded by a stream from the lake, and the east pool was still boiling in patches. The streaming was rather irregular, from the shore outward at the west side of the lake, but the lines of fountains continued to be pronounced, with some shiftings, from the center to the three arms. The currents poured into the southwest and north arms and the latter was enlarged. There was much live lava in the northern wall valley and blowing cones extended thence all along the northwest base of the wall of the pit with noisy puffing and much spouting, spraying, flaming and lifting of lids. There were other blowing cones north of the east pool. The fume from the pit was thinner.

On February 17 at noon the island had risen so that it stood 10 feet above the liquid at its southwest end. It formed an elongate body extending 200 feet towards the northeast from the center of the pit, separated from the northeastern bank of the lake by only a narrow channel between it and a new peninsula that divided the lake there into two coves.

The west pool region was flooded by the lake. A rampart had been built around a basin at the extremity of the southwest arm remote from the lake. The cascade from the lake into the south-southwest pot had widened and was falling over a curved ledge concave toward the pot. There were new crusted pools north of the north crag and the block east of the north arm was now developing into another high crag. The southwest crag showed numerous raised shorelines tilted toward the north. The blowing cones northwest continued their activity and there was much fume on the southeast side of the pit.

Thursday, February 19, at 1 p. m., the island was seen to be separated by only a narrow channel from the northeast peninsula which was larger. The island was higher and the crag on the north side of the southeast arm had been tilting eastward as well as northward, tending to close the east wall-crack pool which was now only a narrow crusted remnant at its northern end. There were large quiet crusts on the lake west and northeast with streaming from them to lines of fountains. A large pool occupied the northern wall valley with blistered crusts on its surface. A fountaining pot built against the base of the wall northwest about 10 feet above lake level, was vomiting out a cascade of molten lava that flowed down to fresh fields beneath. Other cones were spurting along the foot of the west wall. The west pool was only a small triangular remnant at the south end of the former long pool, and a stream poured from the lake into it through a tunnel. The southwest arm of the lake was greatly enlarged and the wall rift above it appeared more broken and open. The lake was streaming into the southwest pot but not conspicuously cascading.

At 6 p. m., February 20, the wind was northerly so that the seeing was from the northwest side of the pit. Two new island shoals had emerged from beneath the lake respectively west and south of the center, with the radial lines of fountains between them and separating them from the large island. They thus occupied the points of the other two sectors of the bottom that were outlined by the three lines of fountains. Here again there appeared to be emergence of these sectors as though the bench magma blocks were lifting in three triangular units and tilting away from the center, thus bringing up the lake bottom and tending to subdivide the lake into separate ponds as in 1918.

From the west side of the lake there was southeastward streaming on each side of a dark patch of crust that ended at the new island shoal. The smaller islet was on the opposite side of a channel filled with the line of fountains that leads to the southwest arm. The southwest arm was wider and becoming more irregular. There were flaming and fountaining cones northwest and north. The west pool and south-southwest pot were as before. Streaming was now outward into the lake from the three arms and a current poured from the southeast around the end of the large island meeting another current on the northwest side of the island and producing travelling fountains. The wall pot back of the southwest crag had again opened. A cone was puffing at the base of the northeast wall of the pit.

Activity of the Kau Desert Flows. On Saturday, February 14, in the forenoon moving pahoehoe lava was found over most of the northern end of the new ridge excepting the west slope. One fountain was playing above the summit pool in line with rift fissures west of the middle zone of the present live belt. Traces were found of the old Kau-Puna trail at the base of the ridge on its east side, with old native stone shelters mostly buried up by the fresh lava. Extensive aa flows that had broken out from the heap east of the northern end had spread southward nearly to the middle breakdown which had been the source of the great flow six miles long. The amphitheatre which had been observed February 11 at the head of this northeastern aa was becoming filled up with fresh pahoehoe and this region at the extreme northern end of the ridge was now an "L" of built-up ground 30 feet higher than the rest of the ridge and extending eastward.

On the afternoon of February 18 the high eastern spur of the ridge had again broken down and given vent to more aa spreading over the eastern country. The head of this breakdown was an elongate trench 150 feet wide extending northwest-southeast, with a large crag on the south side of its gateway which appeared to be a broken fragment of the ridge which had moved eastward and tilted up. Through the middle of the depression poured a river of pahoehoe which was cascading eastward past the north side of this crag. Under and around the river lay a topography of broken aa, and a few feet to the east the river changed to aa. The stream was flowing from 4 to 10 miles per hour in different places and its bed was about 20 feet wide. Upstream there was cascading and about 300 yards from the crag the torrent was found emerging from under a crust. Beyond, there was a flat mound of heavy pahoehoe that lay over the source fountain so that the mound was incessantly jarred with miniature earthquakes. This mound was 4 feet high and 20 feet in diameter, of very smooth solid lava showing glow in the cracks. Over one of these cracks there was a driblet cone with flames hissing through a glowing sponge on its summit.

The sink at the head of the western aa flow was found to be an oval bounded by vertical cliffs broken by collapse in the side of the summit plateau of the ridge. This sink was 500 feet across and the border cliffs were 10 to 15 feet high. The interior was a mass of broken and crevassed pahoehoe with a frozen aa pudding between the blocks. Where the sink opened to the large flow down the slope, there were crevasses like the seracs of a glacier. At this point the tumble of debris was thrown into high crags. In the cliff section the transition could be seen from bedded pahoehoe to a massive aa paste below. The slumped blocks at the head of the depression showed the frozen paste which had welled up the cracks. There was no pahoehoe flow on top of this breakdown, which had progressed exclusively as an oozing out of pasty aa. Not far from the head of the amphitheatre in the summit plateau and over the rift zone, an oven cone was found with a well inside 8 feet in diameter and now dead.

The average height of the northern part of the new ridge above the surrounding country was about 100 feet.

Seismometric Record. In the Whitney Laboratory of Seismology for the week ending at midnight February 20, 1920, there were registered two feeble earthquakes as follows: February 16, 6:30 p. m., and February 18, 10:05 p. m. (accompanied by slight east tilt). Spasmodic microtremor developed from weak to strongish February 17, weakening thereafter. Harmonic tremor also increased in strength February 18 and was otherwise moderate. Microseismic motion was slight. Movement of tilting was dominantly to the north during the week and strongly eastward February 14-15, the east-west component thereafter fluctuating. The accumulated tilt of the past fortnight has been strongly northward and eastward.

Week Ending February 27, 1920.

The end of February at Kilauea Volcano finds the lava of Halemaumau rising and flows pouring out of the Kau Desert rifts with increased vigor. There is no sign whatever of diminution in gas pressure and the adjustment of flows to pit source may continue for a long time. The outflows have now been running since mid-December, two and a half months, and if these are treated as a continuation of the eruption that began on Mauna Loa, the Hawaiian volcanic system has been overflowing continuously for five months. It must not be forgotten, moreover, that a large volume of lava has poured out during the past year on the floor of Kilauea which is now solidifying as a permanent addition to the land. These flows began in February, 1918, and became practically continuous after February of 1919, so that the duration of outpouring and its continuity and diversity are comparable to such periods as 1854-55 or 1879-81.

During the past week the rising of lake and crags in Halemaumau has slowed somewhat, the total gain being about 20 feet. The main changes in the pit have consisted in uplift of the islands so that the larger one became a peninsula, decrease of the fountaining and gradual replacement of the last remnants of the outer ring ponds by blowing cones. The general resemblance of conditions in the pit to the strongly rising period of 1916, with all the craggy matter developing at the expense of the lake, would seem to contradict the expectation of a year of subsidence. Subsidence seemed to be forecast by the intense fountaining of December and its resemblance to the subsidence year of 1912. It remains to be seen whether the present rise is only temporary. The lake may again foam up with hot fountaining as it did in July, 1912, and thereafter retire to lower levels, the risings being rapid and the sinkings slow. These are the distinctive features of a year of general subsidence.

The only new features in the Kau Desert flow heap are more short flows filling depressions made by breakdown, and then increasing in volume so as to flood the country north of the heap and greatly widen the skirts of the ridge of accumulation. Singularly enough, the voluminous pahoehoe has been pouring in torrents down the slopes of its selfmade eminence in a direction squarely contrary to the general slope of the country, and building extensions up the rift in the direction of the Halemaumau source.

JOURNAL.

Activity of Halemaumau. Measurements of the week ending February 28, 1920, determined the following depressions below the northeast datum at the edge of Halemaumau (3727 feet above sea-level):

	Lake at S. W. grotto	N. crag summit
Feb. 19, 1:00 p. m.........	265 feet	180 feet
28, 10:30 p. m.........	245 "	158 "

The lake in nine days rose 20 feet, or 2.2 feet per day and the crag 22 feet, or 2.4 feet per day. This for the lake was less than half the rate of rising of the previous week and for the crag somewhat more than half. The relief of the crag was

Feb. 19 .... 85 feet above the lake
28 .... 87 " " " "

The crag thus gained 2 feet on the lake between February 19 and 28, continuing the alternations between lake and crag as noted before.

On February 22 at 4 p. m. moderate rising of islands and crags was evident but in general there were few changes. The three radial lines of fountains occupied channels between the islands. In the high hollow considerably above lake level lying against the wall of the pit on the northeast side of the northeast crag, the blowing cones were replaced by a fountaining pool held as a cup at this elevation. On the west side of the lake there was a large crusted area that was seen to break up with cracking and foundering of the slabs.

At 11 a. m. February 24 the three quiet areas of the lake back of the islands were seen to be developing into pronounced sectors with the fountaining limited to the channels between them. The islands had all risen, the streaming was outward from the north arm and the former large central island had become a peninsula through uplift of the bottom of the channel that had separated the island from the northeast shore. The lake was flooding the west wall-crack area, the fountaining pots there keeping up strong activity through the crust. The east wall-pond was now entirely crusted, two fountaining pots making gas vents at the base of the northeast wall of the pit. The east bay of the lake exhibited northeastward streaming to a grotto at the bank. There were glowing cones against the wall northwest and west and a fountaining pot in the top of a cone at the northern base of the north crag. The crusted north wall-valley pool had increased in size.

Some readjustment of the lava column on this day occasioned avalanche falls which were heard toward the southeast side of the pit. Also a jumble of fresh avalanche debris was seen on the northeast wall-pond crust, the scar whence the material had fallen being visible in the wall of the pit above. It is probable that a short spell of sinking took place the next day. By the 28th, however, rising was again in evidence and flows were running over the banks of the lake and pouring from the border cones.

Activity of the Kau Desert flows. In connection with the outbreak of the Kau Desert flows in December last, a series of cracks yawned open side by side for 10 miles from Kilauea southwest, starting in the actual wall of Halemaumau first, and extending thence through the Kilauea floor and wall and out into the open country beyond. These cracks are part of a rifted belt several miles wide which ends uphill in the fissured floor and side walls of Kilauea crater itself. The floor fractures under Kilauea crater are masked by the new lavas of the last century, but at the sides the bluffs show step-faults which are planes continuous with the rift system of the desert. At the time of sudden subsidence November 28, 1919, the rift in the Halemaumau cup first appeared as a vertical crack on opposite walls southwest and northeast, an open crevasse 2 to 3 feet apart below, and closing together above. The southwest extension in plan of this crack made a new line of fuming fissures out into the desert which developed on the surface of the ground December 15 along with outflow inside the southwest wall of the larger Kilauea crater. There were great swarms of earthquakes November 28 and December 15. About December 20 the underground lava following the new fracture trickled out of the cracks on lower ground in the desert four miles southwest of Halemaumau, and thereafter split its way downhill, stopping at an orifice about nine miles down, and then settling down to determined flowing and building at a point six miles down—i. e., in the middle of the particular rift line expanded by the lava of this particular eruption. The Halemaumau lava sank from elevation

3700 and held its own at about 3400 feet above sea-level, while the main flow vent in the desert occupied approximately elevation 3000, and then built up a slagheap 100 feet high. The final flow orifice is thus 300 feet below the Halemaumau lava lake, and both are building up, or rising.

An examination on February 22 of Byron's Ledge, the downthrown fault-block separating Kilauea Iki from Kilauea crater, showed no conspicuous fresh cracking there in the vicinity of the 1832 and 1868 vents near Kilauea Iki. This is on the side of Halemaumau remote from the Kau Desert, where an extension of the flow cracks might be expected to take effect. The southeast wall of Kilauea, however, north of Keanakakoi was found to exhibit a freshly broken crack trending southwest parallel to the wall, and in the rock, along the top of the talus. This place is near an old sulphurous steam crack. On the south side of Byron's Ledge a small landslide in the talus had been started by the motion on the fissure, and this had occurred prior to December 8 as this landslide scar was first observed on that date. Therefore the movement may have taken place November 28 at the time of the great subsidence in Halemaumau. The trace of the crack rises progressively higher in the Kilauea wall going northeastward; if extended southwestward this group of fault planes would lead directly into the Kau Desert-rift system.

A study of the lava flow source ridge at its northeastern end February 23 showed that an extensive breakdown on the east side of the summit had produced a large field of aa lava extending southward a half-mile. The active summit pool now occupied an elongate wing or spur of the ridge extending eastward in an L from the north end of the main ridge, about 100 feet above the general level of the surrounding country. It should be understood that the "ridge" referred to is a lava slag-heap over the rift crack, two miles long, trending southwest, and wholly built since December 24, 1919. A similar shorter ridge said to have been formed in 1823 lies parallel to this one and a quarter-mile to the east, and the interior structure is there revealed in a series of pits which collapsed after the activity was ended. These pits are connected by arched caverns in a line the length of the heap and over the fissure-source wells below. The caverns show shore-lines of the receding inside liquid levels, and wormy stalactites and stalagmites of lava coated with gypsum crystals. On top and in the vicinity are driblet cones and heaps and the ridge is wholly of pahoehoe. The mechanism of the older ridge differed from the 1920 ridge in that the lava then drained away and flowed out lower down the mountain, whereas in 1920 that tendency has stopped, and the higher piling up followed by aa breakdowns is the method by which the lava supplied is spread out over the country; 1920 is heaping up; 1823 gained headway and drained into the sea.

On this day, February 23, the summit pool was cascading down both its slopes north and south filling up the last depression made by breakdown, and burying the former crags which the breakdown had occasioned. At the end of the spur aa was formed and the front on the east side was aa flowing forward in a jumbled paste about 20 feet per hour. An egg-shaped boulder at the front, broken open, was a lava "snow-ball" 3 feet in diameter made of a pahoehoe fragment rolled in an aa batter making a shell 3 inches thick. The ball had formed by being rolled in the paste as the flow progressed. Two large fragments were seen to pull apart as the boulders rode forward, making a cavern full of the lifeless paste, at orange heat, with coarse drawn-out vesicles. The pudding dripped from the roof after the fashion of a porous porridge, slowly freezing through shades of cherry red to purple, without any distension or inflation such as always shows in pahoehoe.

A thorough exploration of the source amphitheatre or sink at the head of the western coarse aa flow, broken out of the flank of the new ridge, revealed a mechanism much like a glacier in the arrangement of cirque, seracs and frozen river below. The aa had flowed from a fracture in the lower flank; an elliptical area 300 feet across had collapsed on top with 20-foot walls of bedded pahoehoe grading into aa paste below; step-faults formed in this area right and left; a tumble of broken slabs like floes in slush ice formed in the middle; a flat raft of plateau lava floated forward to the neck or narrows where the sink debouched, and stopped there; this was surrounded by exposed surfaces, rather smooth, of the aa paste; the margins of the narrows were overridden by the sludge and high crags there piled up; in the middle of the flow slope transverse crevasses resembled seracs; below there were stream stretches with lengthwise stream lines; everything beyond was a vast field of tumbled aa.

A night view of the flows at 10 p. m. February 26 at the north end of the ridge was extremely spectacular. Two floods of pahoehoe were sweeping as majestic rapid glowing rivers down the north and northeast flanks of the heap, fanning out below in extensive fiery fields of lava that were eating the vegetation at their edges and creeping out in all directions, sometimes cascading into the rift chasms. The light of some source fountains on top of the ridge could be seen reflected on the fume cloud above. The source ridge had now become a conspicuous feature seen across the flat desert country from the Pahala road, and the whole panorama of flowing streams and their puddled fronts, flowing directly towards Kilauea, could be seen across the old Keamoku aa as we approached from Volcano House.

Seismometric Record. In the Whitney Laboratory of Seismology for the week ending at midnight February 27, 1920, one feeble local earthquake was registered 4:20 p. m., February 25, and a feeble teleseism 1:55 p. m., February 24. Spasmodic microtremor changed from moderate to slight after February 21. Harmonic tremor fluctuated from moderate to slight. Microseismic motion was slight. Tilting of the ground was slight north and east until February 24, becoming strong west and south February 24-26, changing February 27 to strong north and east.

Very respectfully,

T. A. JAGGAR, JR.,
Volcanologist.

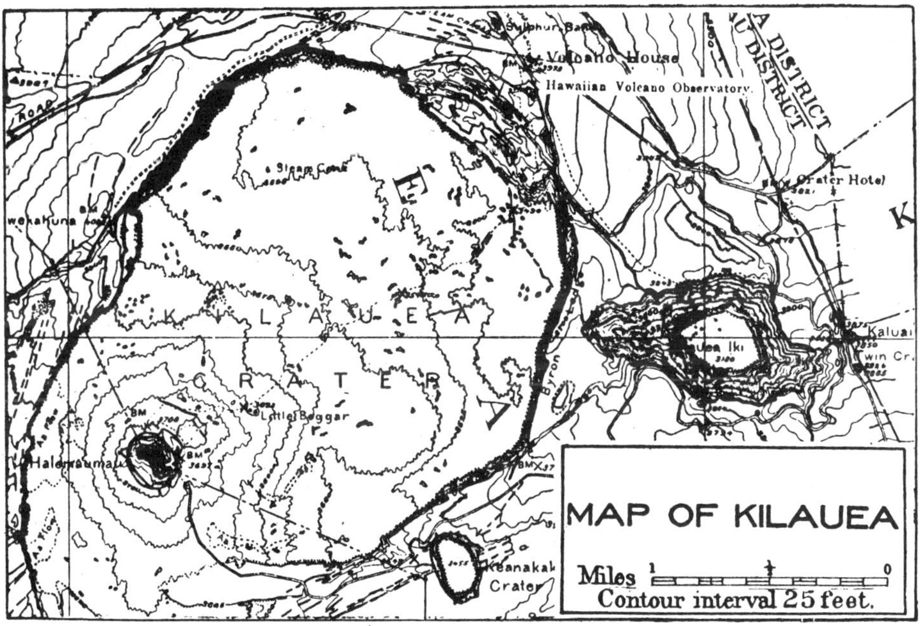

HAWAIIAN VOLCANO OBSERVATORY.

The Observatory is equipped with the following seismometric instruments rebuilt at the station in 1918 for the special needs of volcano research: two Bosch-Omori pendulums, high speed registration of local earthquakes; one optically recording seismograph for distant earthquakes; one clinograph registering E-W tilting of the ground. A vertical component seismograph was in December, 1918, set up in experimental operation. These are seated on concrete piers in a closed basement room having practically constant temperature, beneath the chief Observatory building near the hotel. Time is referred to a rated chronometer, checked at intervals by solar observations with a transit. The chronometer is loaned by the College of Hawaii. Hawaiian standard time (H. S. T.) is 10 hrs. 30 min. slower than Greenwich time.

CANCANI SCALE OF SEISMIC INTENSITY.

Expressed by accelerations measured in millimeters per second per second.

I.	Instrumental	0.0	2.5
II.	Very slight	2.5	5.0
III.	Slight	5.0	10.0
IV.	Sensible, mediocre	10.0	25.0
V.	Rather strong	25.0	50.0
VI.	Strong	50.0	100.0
VII.	Very strong	100.0	250.0
VIII.	Ruinous	250.0	500.0
IX.	Disastrous	500.0	1000.0
X.	Very disastrous	1000.0	2500.0
XI.	Catastrophic	2500.0	5000.0
XII.	Great catastrophe	5000.0	10000.0

Grade IV. is ordinarily the minimum perceived by the senses; and in grade XII. the accelerations or rate of change of motion (jerk) reaches that of terrestrial gravitation.

In the standard form of report the maximum intensity or acceleration, designated by the symbol a, or max. a, is given in the conventional unit of milligal. The milligal is a measure of acceleration, such that 1 milligal $=$ 1/100 mm. per sec. per sec. $= 10\ \mu$. per sec. per sec. The Cancani scale, here defined in terms of millimeters per sec. per sec., can therefore be expressed in milligals by multiplying each of the numbers by 100.

U. S. DEPARTMENT OF AGRICULTURE
WEATHER BUREAU
CHARLES F. MARVIN, CHIEF

MONTHLY BULLETIN
OF THE
Hawaiian Volcano Observatory

VOL. VIII. HONOLULU, HAWAII, MARCH, 1920 No. 3

Week Ending March 5, 1920.

SUMMARY OF CONDITIONS.

The lava column of Halemaumau has this week risen as of late but with the lift of the crags gaining on the lake. The evidence indicates that the nature of the uplifting movement for the bench magma which constitutes the crags is now a tumescence involving three distinct sectors of crater floor. By crater floor is meant the bottom substance of the liquid lake quite as much as the border bench material. The adjoining tips of the three sectors were a few weeks ago wholly concealed under the lake, but the divisions between the sectors, as three radial breaks in the lake bottom, were definitely marked by three lines of fountains and three crevasses athwart the shore bench. The first effects of rising produced flooding of the basin, weighting of the bottom, and lateral flow of the bottom paste under the sectors at places near the pit wall so as to elevate the three crags north, southwest and southeast, with tilting exhibited by the raised shorelines. The next phase, now in progress, was the lift of the central submerged tips of the sector blocks revealing shoals under the lake which rose as three angular islands adjoining the meeting point of the three fountaining channels The fountaining merely evidenced the rising of gas along the three radial fractures under the lake. This is an interesting revelation of the capacity of the stiff magmatic paste which forms the lake bottom to fracture in straight lines like a brittle substance. The maximum fountaining and focus of foundering crusts had been at the center, this material had piled up at the corners where the three under-lake crevasses met, and so the tumescence revealed the material first as islands. These islands in their development as rising went on clearly showed the central angles of the broken sectors. The whole arrangement is precisely as though the lake occupied a saucer which had been fractured from the center outward in three clean cut breaks, so as to let the gas come up the cracks; then the three triangular shards were lifted first by the outer corners so as to make the tilted border crags, then pushed up in the middle so as to make the three islands. Incidentally the general swelling apart of the triangular fragments along with their doming up, let the liquid into the cracks nearly to the saucer's rim and so developed three arms of the pool beyond its circular central area, like three spokes of a wheel. The islands are now increasing in size and becoming peninsulas as might be expected with continued irregular uplift of the sector blocks.

This mechanism has completely reversed the condition revealed after the great subsidence of November last. The floor matter of the crater then, by rapidly sinking most in the middle became a saucer. The rapid rising in December lifted the saucer and increased its basin curvature, the outer ring pool being the main fissure with thousands of gas fountains. The later subsidence with drainage of this ring pool in January, reversed the stresses on the saucer and fractured it, so that the rim of bench magma which had been an atoll-shaped island was let down to the point where it crowded out the ring pool and wedged against the funnelling walls of the pit. Revival of rising gas pressure now found it easiest to effervesce up the three middle cracks in the bottom of what had been the quiet central lagoon, and the doming followed the lines of maximum effervescence. This it is which has transferred all the fountaining to the central lake and now extinguished the ring pool completely, leaving only blowing cones in the wall cracks back of the marginal crags. The whole process, happening rapidly within two months, with rise and fall of the complete lava column through a range of 600 feet, has been a marvellous demonstration of the shallowness of the liquid and the rigidity of the under substance on top of which the liquid is a foam fed through the border crack and through small wells generated along fissures.

The volume of flowing lava in the Kau Desert has slightly diminished during the week but the heap of pahoehoe continues to build with a lava cascade pouring down the upper slope into a tunnel and both aa and pahoehoe spreading out on the northern and eastern sides of the north end of the flow heap.

JOURNAL.

Activity of Halemaumau. Measurements were not secured after February 28 during this week, but subsequent surveys have shown that the liquid continued to rise about 2 feet per day and the north crag about 4 feet per day. The lake on March 5 was about 229 feet below the northeast monument (which stands 3727 feet above sea-level) and the crag 135 feet, making the relief of the crag (94 feet) considerably increased since the previous week.

On February 28, 11 a. m., the lake had been overflowing its banks on the west and other signs of rising were flows from wall crack cones and greatly diminished fountaining. The west pond against the wall of the pit was now replaced by a straight line of four or five blowing and spurting cones leading from the lake towards the open southwest wall pot. There were two active wall-crack cones against the base of the northwest wall. Flows had poured down to the north pond from high wall-crack cones northwest of the north crag and at the base of the northeast wall of the pit; the north pond was a pool of crusted lava, wholly without fountains and very different from the lake which had occupied the same area in December. The streaming was into grottoes at the lake edge east and south-southwest, outward from the southeast and southwest arms of the lake towards and past the center and into the north arm. There was also streaming westward from the crust covering the east bay and eastward from that covering the west bay, this last crust being broken occasionally by a fountain in the middle. The northeast island was now a peninsula attached to the northeast crag and the island northwest of the center was growing larger and higher. This island was now 15 feet high, the small south island 5 feet high and the northeast peninsula 20 feet high. Much of the north face of the north crag had been breaking away indicating tilt northward of the sector to which it belonged. The south part of the lake was covered with bright lines and kept in motion by streaming and fountaining activities and the general trend of all the activity was towards grottoes south-southwest and at the extreme north.

An examination of the southwest heap under the Kilauea wall showed that it had ceased visible fuming and the cracks of the rift line near the Halemaumau edge were greatly stained with sulphur and giving up sulphur vapor and sulphurous acid.

At 2 p. m. February 29 a new hole had broken open in the rift crack on the inner wall of Halemaumau southwest about 50 feet above the lake. It showed no glow. The liquid lava of the lake was again cascading into the south-southwest border pot. There were hissing and flaming cones along the base of the northern and western walls of the pit and lava was slowly welling up around the edge of the crust of the north pool. Fresh floods from the lake had poured across the west border floor. On the east side of the main lake the remnant of the ring crag was very low, standing only a few feet above lake level. The tip of the northeast peninsula which had formerly been an island was now 35 feet high and dark crusts back of the several islands on the sides remote from the center suggested developing shoals.

A visit to the summit crater of the southwest heap revealed the fact that no noise nor fume was making there. Two slumped cones occupied the depression, which was an oval, about 150 feet long by 75 feet wide, filled with a tumble of broken matter quite like the amphitheatres at the heads of the breakdown aa flows which characterize the lava heap in the desert. Here as there the aa paste shows in places among the fragments and the low walls show transitions from bedded pahoehoe above to a pudding below.

On Monday, March 1, the fume from the pit was thinner and rising proceeded more rapidly. An interesting development of this period is the vapor rising as a clinging fringe along the edge of Halemaumau north and northwest. There are cracks parallel to the edge but that is not a distinctive character. This fringe of steam simulates the vapor cracks which follow the high north rim of Kilauea near Volcano House. Possibly the parallelism of the cracks in both places to the trade-wind direction accounts for the phenomenon observed.

On March 2 at 6 p. m. the islands were all higher with reference to the lake and channels and pools among them were beginning to appear like deep gorges. The west island stood 30 feet high, the northeast peninsula 45 feet and the south island 20 feet. About twenty-five fountains were playing in different places and twelve or fifteen blowing cones followed the wall crack west, northwest, north, northeast and east. The north pond showed glow lines and the streaming in the lake was complex as follows: West from southeast arm, on both sides of south island and into cascade pot south-southwest; southwest from the crust covering the east bay of the lake; southeast from the crust between the west island and the southwest crag; east from the west pool through the gap north of the west island; south from the north cove bending into the cove east of the north channel; and north through the narrows northwest and northeast of the south island. In the main channel between the northeast peninsula and the west island there were conflicting currents and travelling fountains, and currents streamed against the bank on the northeast shore of the lake. There was a large spouting open pot in the east wall crack, a noisy blowing cone northeast, occasional gushes from two cones northwest, flames from all the cones and an openwork filagree cone lay between the southwest crag and the west wall of the pit. The south side of the lake was brilliant with bright lines, moderate fountaining continued in the three channel zones, there was much turbulence in the center and at the northeast corner of the lake and bubble fountains were abundant in the southwest arm.

At 6 p. m. on March 4 the islands were found still rising and the crusted western bay appeared to have a southern outlet where rapid streaming from under the crust poured southward between the southwest crag and the western island. There was general southward streaming in the southern part of the lake with a torrent pouring into the south-southwest pot. In the middle of the west bay there was some fountaining and the wall crack cones were spreading and spurting.

At 5 p. m. March 5 the changes were slight. The whole lake showed bright-line motion with the most sluggish crusts in the west pool. There were numerour flaming and puffing cones, the greatest noise coming from the northeast wall crack. The north pool was large and crusted. Streaming poured out from the west bay on both sides of the western island and there was a current in a curved river-like zone which moved from the east bay of the lake around the south side of the north peninsula so as to bombard the bank at the end of the peninsula. Streaming otherwise was mostly centripetal, except northeast where it was against the bank. Fume was abundant, especially from the crags, fountaining moderate and the islands stood in high relief.

Activity of the Kau Desert Flow. The great rifts north of Cone Peak were visited February 29 and found unchanged. A noticeable feature of this rift system is the subsidence of certain blocks of ground between the east and west cracks of the rift belt leaving walls on each side standing up a few feet above the ground which has subsided. A distant view of the flow ridge on this day showed it to be a very wide expanse of glistening lava with fume rising from its western flank and a break in its summit open northward showing the glow of red lava inside. On March 1 some aa lava was again flowing at the north end of the ridge. On March 2 fresh pahoehoe lava flows were concentrated so as to make a bright glow on the clouds as seen in the distance in the evening.

A visit to the flow between 7 and 9 p. m. March 2 showed that there was a live sheet of sluggish but glowing pahoehoe all around the north and northwest base of the ridge with toes pushing out in places. In the northeast slope of the dome proper there was a lava cascade 15 feet wide and 10 feet high which poured into a tube below. The position of this cascade was slightly to the east of tho western rift of the live pair. A smaller lava stream of about one-third the volume of the cascade emerged from flat pahoehoe and flowed southward some distance east of the heap. A small aa flow in motion developed during the evening creeping out from a rift in the hill on the east side at the edge of the former aa breakdown. It was the cascade which made the brilliant glow on the clouds and Pele's hair forming over it was being wafted up into the air for heights of several hundred feet.

Seismometric Record. In the Whitney Laboratory of Seismology during the week ending at midnight March 5, 1920, four local earthquakes were registered as follows: February 28, 4:15 p. m., very feeble, and 10:25 p. m., moderate; March 2, 1:35 and 2:50 a. m., both very feeble. Spasmodic microtremor was mostly weak but there was development of several strong spasms March 4. Harmonic tremor was moderate to strong throughout the week. Microseismic motion remained slight. Tilting was slight or stationary until March 5 when it became extremely strong to the north and east.

Week Ending March 12, 1920.

SUMMARY OF CONDITIONS.

Until March 8 the lake and crags were rising as before, the crags more than the lake; thereafter the lake ceased to rise and the crags rose more slowly. The islands and crags have become impressive features, eight separate peaks now standing at heights from 30 to 110 feet above the lava lake, the north crag being the highest. This summit, which represents the uppermost limit of the lava column, was on March 11 only 94 feet below the lower portions of the rim of Halemaumau and only 20 to 30 feet below the north shelf, which is quite accessible from the rim. The three main fiery arms of the lava pool, with lines of fountains, are shaped like a "Y" with the currents streaming from the two arms to the stem, and the latter ending at the vertical crack which leads through the outer dome of the mountain to the flows in the desert. In between the arms stand three of the craggy peaks which started as islands and are becoming peninsulas, and back of these are three bays of the lake east, west and south, the surfaces of which are quieter than the radial arms. The western pool, however, has recently developed a tendency to a spectacular whirling of its surface impelled by a current that pours in from the northern channel, and by another that pours out through a tunnel leading towards the western wall-crack.

The crags have been cracking as though important changes were about to take place, and towards the end of the week there has been some appearance as though the crags might subside and the lake flood the benches. The fountaining has been increasing and the fume growing thinner. A crisis of subsidence is always likely to happen after the March equinox.

The desert flows were never more brilliant and have been at times as spectacular as was the Alika flow in October. A torrent 20 feet wide has been pouring first into a pit on top of the lava ridge and later down the outer slope of the ridge, from a round well at the source, and this could be approached within a few feet from the windward side, so as to observe the leaping jets of red melt as the stream escaped from under the crust and swept in cascades over terraces below. This was smooth lava, but in other places the clinkery type (aa) has been accessible, oozing out sluggishly from cracks at the ends of spurs in the source ridge.

JOURNAL.

Activity of Halemaumau. Measurements of the two weeks ending March 12, 1920, expressed as depression below the northeast monument which stands on the rim of Halemaumau at elevation 3727 feet above sea-level, have been as follows:

	Mean lake level.	North crag summit.
Feb. 28, 10:30 a. m........	242 feet	158 feet
Mar. 8, 11:00 a. m.......	217 "	111 "
" 11, 1:00 p. m.......	217 "	107 "

The lake in twelve days ending March 8 rose 25 feet, or 2.1 feet per day and in the three days thereafter ending March 11 was stationary. The crag in the twelve days rose 47 feet, or 3.9 feet per day and in the three days following rose 4 feet, or 1.3 foot per day. The relief of crag above the lake was increasing as follows:

Feb. 28, 87 feet
Mar. 8, 106 "
" 11, 110 "

On Saturday, March 6, at 6 p. m., the crags and islands were growing increasingly high and steep and the northeast and south crags, each adjacent on the east side to the north and southwest arms respectively, had now become peaks as pronounced as the others. The main streaming was inward from east and west towards the center of the lake, and dark heavy crusts covered the east and west bays. The south crag in its rising was close to the wall of the pit with narrow slab-like form. The fountaining had somewhat diminished but blowing cones were numerous around the western and northern margins of the floor area with much spurting and flaming. The current out from the east bay swept in a curve to a grotto at the end of the northeast peninsula where the liquid was sucked downward. Fume was abundant. The tip of the northeast peninsula was estimated to stand above the lake 50 feet, the west island 35 feet and the south island 25 feet.

On March 7 at 5 p. m., the lake had been overflowing the western floor against the base of the pit wall so as to drown the blowing cones there and leave them fountaining through lava crusts. A new high lava stack had been built by a gas vent in the wall-crack at the base of the south-southwest wall of the pit back of the south crag and this was throwing up umbrella flings of melt. The streaming and fountaining activities were unchanged and glowing cones continued their flaming and spurting along the north base of the north crag and in the northeast wall valley.

The crags appeared high and showed signs of breaking. Avalanches were falling from the northeast crag into the north arm of the lake. The following vertical cracks, yawning open upward, were observed in different places: (1)

across the northwest end of southwest crag with trend southwest; (2) across the high part of northeast peninsula near the center of the pit with trend east-west; (3) across the floor of the north pond trending east-west, the pond appearing uplifted and solid. Much smoke was rising from the crags, which appear generally to be smoke makers. This is probably because the dead sponge of vesicles in the bench magma acts as a condenser for such gases as sulphur and water vapor, the bench magma crust being 15 to 20 feet thick and fissured. Probably this crust absorbs much rain water.

At 11 a. m. March 8 the streaming from the west bay was eastward through the channel south of the north crag and about 11:05 a. m. a current northward through the north arm united with overflow to flood the north pond depression from the lake. This series of overflows west, north and east, while the crags are rising faster than the lake, appears to mean that the wall valley floors are not rising with the crags, but are tipping down while the crags tips up. This is in the main a tilting of the three sectors with lift in the center and sag at the walls.

In the center of the west bay there was continuous fountaining, and a current streamed southward between the northeast peninsula and the west island, bending off to the southeast. There was continuous fountaining in the narrows and also in the southwest arm. Three border cones were in action along the base of the northwest wall. The east and south sides of the floor area were very smoky.

On March 10 at 7:30 p. m. there was much rain vapor about the pit but the fume was thin. The lakes appeared to have flooded the benches excessively and the streaming was from the north arm southward and westward into the west bay. Other currents poured from the southeast arm towards the southwest and into the west bay. There had been much rising of the west island and fountains were numerous in the three arms. Gas pressure was high as evidenced by continuous loud hissing from a cone in the northeast wall crack.

At 1 p. m. March 11 it was possible to explore the southwest rim of the pit owing to southerly winds. During a thunderstorm at noon many steam spouts formed, joining the clouds above with the steam jets below, and one of the most remarkable of these formed a long horn-shaped extension downward of the thunder cloud to the flow heap in the Kau Desert.

Inspection of the south-southwest wall-crack inside the pit, which has long been concealed by smoke showed that it contained merely a tumble of broken rock covered with a mass of Pele's hair. The spalling off of the southern wall of the pit had left the pressure ridge of the upper rim standing up as a narrow shell only three feet thick in places and 10 to 12 feet high above the outer ground. It is a remarkable structure with its ragged knife-edge summit and appears very unstable.

The view of the pit seen from the southwest rim gives the impression of great symmetry in the arrangement of the three arms of the lake and the three craggy sectors of bench magma separating them. The streaming was inward to the center from the north and southeast arms and outward towards the wall in the southwest arm. The east bay was crusted, with slight streaming into the northeast corner. The west and south bays appeared symmetrical on each side of the "Y," and the three islands lay in the angles of the "Y" separating off the bays. The islands appeared as high masses with rather level spatter marks in contrast to the tilted markings of the border crags. The islands appeared to stand from 50 to 75 feet above the lake. The west island was now connected by an isthmus with the southwest crag and had become an immense uplifted mass shutting off the west bay except for the channel on the north. The south island had now joined completely with the islet southeast of it and appeared to be in process of joining with a point protruding from the south side of the lake where an oven grotto exhibited vigorous fountaining. In the southern bay and southwest arm the streaming was irregular and fountains abundant. A current rushed through the channel leading to the west bay, setting that entire pool in motion as a whirlpool slowly revolving from right to left (counter-clockwise). In the center of the whirl was a continuous fountain. On the west side of this bay a defined bench had again developed and into a tunnel under the bench a broad torrent was pouring down from the lake at about the same place as the former western cascades. The liquid appeared to be rushing under an arch into a concealed void in the wall crack and this was perhaps being drained through the fissures on that side of the pit leading to the flows in the desert.

One small avalanche was seen on the north face of the north crag showing a continuance of the tilting back of the sectors. A further evidence of such tilting was noticed along the south margin of the lake where a slightly raised shoreline bench was tilted southward away from the lake, as though the doming tendency which had lifted the central bench magma into islands, had also tilted the outer segments away from the center.

Blowing cones were numerous at the base of the walls west and northwest and in the north and northeast wall valleys. The lake had been overflowing the end of the north arm so that the north pond crust stood again nearly at lake level. There was much noisy hissing and some spouting from the blowing cones.

Activity of the Kau Desert Flows. At the flow heap or ridge at the source rift of the Kau Desert flows, six miles from Halemaumau southwest, on Saturday, March 6, 1920, in the morning, there was sluggish outflow of pahoehoe toes all about the flat of fresh lava extending west of the northern end of the ridge. There was some of the bluish "sharkskin" glassy lava. Two areas of fresh as lava had broken out of cracks in the steep part of the west side of the ridge on top of the pahoehoe flats, and the higher of these was flowing. The live pahoehoe took its origin at the north end of the ridge and flowed all the way thence about the northwest base. This came from a tube connection with the pit on the summit as described March 2, where the cascade was still pouring downward. An elliptical depression had extended the former collapsed area of the eastern lobe of the lava ridge, and this sink had vertical walls 15 feet high. Southeast from here a large block stood up with summit as high as, or higher than, the main ridge, so that it showed as a butte above the general ridge level as seen from the west.

A visit to the flow heap March 9 in the morning revealed new developments that were extremely spectacular. The west side of the northern end of the ridge was covered with heavy torrents of pahoehoe lava pouring down from the summit and forking about the small aa patches which had been inspected March 6. When the ridge was climbed to the summit area, the source pool of these new flows was found to be a circular well 40 feet in diameter, covered with crust in the middle, but from the western border of the well at the margin of the summit plateau the liquid lava escaped from under the crust and was cascading down the hill in a turbulent river of melt. Near the top of the torrent numerous fountains from released gas broke through the surface as it flowed and flung up glowing jets which resembled leaping fishes The stream below passed over a terrace and formed another cascade and pool at a lower level before it forked around the spur above the aa.

The top of the ridge showed collapse and no active streams were seen on the east side. North of the live pool a tumbled cavern showed lava below pouring downward irregularly through fissures at a depth 10 to 15 feet beneath the surface. The flows of the northern slope were hot but were not observed moving.

Seismometric Record. In the Whitney Laboratory of Seismology during the week ending at midnight Friday, March 12, 1920, three local earthquake shocks were registered, all on March 11, as follows: 12:30 p. m. feeble, 4:18 p. m. very feeble, 8:07 p. m. feeble. Spasmodic tremor increased from weak to strong March 6-10, and decreased to weak March 12. Harmonic tremor remained moderate throughout the week. Microseismic motion was mostly slight, increasing somewhat March 12. Tilting was pronounced north and west March 6, easterly March 7, then began increasing westward tilt to a maximum rate

March 10, with at that time very strong tilt to the south. This south and west tilt went on increasing moderately March 11 and 12.

Week Ending March 19, 1920.

SUMMARY OF CONDITIONS.

The lava column of Halemaumau has continued to rise slowly. During the preceding two weeks the crags rose faster than the lakes, whereas during the week ended March 19th, the lift of the lakes gained on the crags. The summit of the north crag, which continues the highest, on March 18th, was a little over 100 feet above the mean lake level. The promontory of the southwest peninsula with its horizontal terraces of old lake levels, "beach marks," resembles a truncated pyramid with a stairway on each side. The unsteadiness of the rising motion of most of the crags is evidenced both by the inclined "beach marks" and by the irregular occurrence of avalanches. The fume continues moderately thin and the fountaining is about the same as the preceding week.

The Kau Desert flow has been extending the lava ridge farther north and flooding the country for several hundred yards to the north, east, and west of the northern end of the ridge by slow moving and easily accessible pahoehoe flows. There was some renewed activity in the break down place on the western side of the ridge decribed, Feb. 1 and 3, and the junction of the aa flow from this place with the old Keomoku aa is now covered with new pahoehoe.

JOURNAL.

Activity of Halemaumau. Measurements for the two weeks ended March 19, 1920, expressed as depressions below the northeast monument on the rim of Halemaumau at an elevation of 3727 feet above sea-level are as follows:

	Mean lake level.	Summit of north crag.
Mar. 11, 1 p. m...........	217 feet	107 feet
" 18, 10 a. m...........	205 "	103 "

During the seven days ending with March 18th the lakes rose 12 feet or at an average of 1.7 feet per day. The crags during the same period rose but 4 feet or at an average of 0.6 foot per day. The relief of the crags above the lakes decreased from 110 feet on March 11th to 102 feet on March 18th.

On Saturday, March 14th, at 4 p. m., the fume was thinner than usual and the pit brighter. The west bench and the north pool were covered by glowing crusts by being flooded from the lakes. Many flaming cones were in evidence along the north and west walls of the pit, five being located near the north base of the north crag. Blowing cones and one lifting lid were observed at the base of the northeast peninsula. A whirlpool was set up in the west bay by a current in from the central channel very similar to the whirlpool observed there last week. A lava stack near the south-southwest wall was sending a flow along the wall northwestward to the head of the southwest arm. Avalanches were falling from the northeast crag and from the north side of the north crag. From beneath a dark skin patch across the east bay there was streaming both to the northeast and the southwest. The large western island is now part of a peninsula from having joined the southwest crag, while the southern island is not yet connected at the bank.

At 5:30 p. m. on March 16th the crags appeared no higher and their relief relative to the lakes seemed lower. A new islet has appeared in the central channel. The general pattern of islands, crags, and lakes strongly recalls the slight rise of March, 1913. The lakes were flooding the west bench and along both the east and west benches many of the old blowing cones were now splashing the liquid melt. Blowing cones were still puffing and coughing along the north wall. Practically all streaming was southerly. The northeast peninsula has broken down at its tip and the northeast crag appears to have cracked and broken. The fountaining was strong, everything showing high blowing pressure in the liquid lava and the fume moderate.

On March 17th at 5:30 p. m. the fume was thick over the eastern and southern portions of Halemaumau while the rest of the pit was quite clear. In the west bay one large center and one border fountain were playing. In the rest of the arms and channels there were numerous fountains with bubble fountains in the southwest arm. The lakes had risen faster than the crags so that from general appearances one would have said that the crags had sunk. Except for a sluggish streaming out of the north arm no currents were in evidence.

Measurements at 10 a. m. on March 18th showed that the lakes and crags were both rising. Avalanches had occurred from the crags of the northeast peninsula and from the north crag onto the north pool. The lakes were thinly crusted and quiet except for one fountain in the center of the west bay and a slight current out of the north arm which divided, one part going into the west bay and the other toward the southwest arm. When the fountain in the west bay ceased at 10:40 a. m. a sluggish current commenced to flow out of the bay.

Activity of the Kau Desert Flow. The flow in the Kau Desert continues with periods of slight activity and of strong rejuvenation. When the flow heap was viewed on March 15th a small aa patch, trickling sluggishly, was found on the west side of the northern end of the lava ridge. The flow center had moved from the top of the ridge and was now located at a hissing cone in the middle of the flat fill to the north of the ridge. From this center several pahoehoe flows were spreading over an area several yards wide burning trees and bushes in places. Several of the arms of the flow were making remarkably elongated toes with smaller, snaky toes making out from the larger ones. Some of the live pahoehoe was of the heavy sharkskin type. A large schollendome with fresh snaky driblets down its south side had been built up. Over 100 feet above the new lava field the new main rift was occupied by recently solidified lava that had risen from below as was shown by its flat topped filling. Another rift farther west was likewise occupied by solidified lava which showed by its festoons that it had cascaded into the rift from the adjacent lava field. This latter rift was wholly dead with no signs of recent activity but with vegetation growing in it. There were numerous freshly broken cracks in the old ground in a zone eastward from the new main rift above mentioned. On March 19th activity was confined to toeing pahoehoe flows to the north, east, and west of the north end of the lava ridge. It was found that there had been a further collapse in the sink on the western side of the ridge that produced the aa flow described on Feb. 1 and 3. Lava had cascaded into the new collapsed portion from flows that came from the high northern end of the ridge. The junction of the new aa with the old Keomoku aa and for a considerable distance on each side is now covered with new heavy pahoehoe that came around the western base of the northern end of the ridge.

Seismometric Record. During the week ended midnight March 19th 4 local earthquakes and one teleseism were registered in the Whitney Laboratory of Seismology. The dates and times of these quakes are as follows: March 13th, 10:59 p. m., strongly felt in Hilo but not recorded there because of instrumental trouble; March 15th, 1:45 a. m., slight teleseism; March 18th, 10:00 a. m. and 9:45 p. m., both feeble; and March 19th, 8 p. m., very feeble. Spasmodic microtremor increased from slight to moderate at the end of the period. Harmonic tremor was moderate. Microseismic movement was moderate to slight. The tilting of the ground was moderate west on the 14th, moderate south and east on the 15th and slight north and east thereafter.

Week Ending March 26, 1920.

SUMMARY OF CONDITIONS.

The rise of the lava column of Halemaumau continued during the week ending with March 26th, though at the end of that period the lakes and crags which had been rising as a unit appeared to be nearly stationary. The total rise during the week, 14 feet, was a little greater than the rise of the preceding week. The crags in the center of the pit have been rising with but little or no tilting, while pronounced tilting in most of the border crags has caused them to crack and break up and not increase in height as much as they otherwise would. Most of the different arms of the lava lake are getting well-defined spatter ramparts. Many of the channels are becoming more and more narrow so that the different arms are becoming more like individual lakes. Streaming has, apparently, been fortuitous, being directed towards places where large fountains were located. The fume continues moderately thin and the fountains show a tendency to become more local and larger.

The Kau Desert flow has been sending many branches around the northern end of the lava ridge and has built up a terrace there about half as high as the top of the ridge. The larger streams soon break up into numerous toeing branches. Many of these branches are of the heavy shark skin type of lava.

JOURNAL.

Activity of Halemaumau. Measurements during the week ended March 26, 1920, expressed as depressions below the northeast monument on the rim of Halemaumau at an elevation of 3727 feet above sea-level are as follows:

	Mean lake level.	Summit of north crag.
Mar. 18, 10 a. m.	205 feet	103 feet
" 20, 11:30 a. m.	...	91 "
" 22, 10:15 a. m.	193 "	...
" 25, 1 p.m.	191 "	89 "

During the seven days ending with March 25th the crags and lakes both rose 14 feet or at an average of 2 feet per day. This rate of rise is a little greater than that for the week ended March 18th. The rise of the southwest crag was a little less than that of the north crag. The relief of the north crag above the lakes is the same as last week, 102 feet.

On March 20th at 11 a. m. the streaming was slight and confined to feeding border fountains and grottos in the east arm, central channel, south arm, and west bay.

From 10 to 11 a. m. on March 22nd small avalanches were almost continuous from the north crag. The crag at the base of the northeast peninsula has almost completely broken down, leaving nothing but a narrow jagged spire with scars on all sides. Ramparts that have been built up around most of the lake arms stand from 5 to 8 feet above the liquid. Streaming was to the north in the east arm and out of the north and southwest arms to the southeast. A sluggish current was flowing into the west bay.

On March 23rd from 9:15 to 10:30 a. m. streaming was to the north in the east arm and to the south in the north arm. The lakes with their confining ramparts, 5 to 8 feet high appeared to be of the same height as on March 22nd. The vertical crack in the southwest crag, apparently, has opened slightly. A whirlpool was in action in the south-southwest pot. The grottos are becoming larger and the fountains more local and larger.

From 8 to 8:30 a. m. on March 24th there was rapid streaming out of the north arm past the center islet with a sluggish branch going into the west bay. Another current was moving west along the north side of the south island. The east arm was crusted over and rather quiet with but one fountain in the center. There was one vigorous fountain in the entrance to the west bay and three large fountains in the central channel. Fountaining was vigorous near the wall in the narrow southeast arm. The liquid lava in the west bay was from 3-5 feet below the ramparts.

The fume was moderately thick when the pit was observed at 1 p. m. on March 25th. The rapid streaming to the south past the center islet was still in evidence. A current was moving to the east out of the southwest arm. Fountains that splashed liquid over 15 feet high appeared from time to time in the central channel. The central islet has increased in width but is no higher. When the lava in the west bay fell 2 or 3 feet at 2 p. m. a current started in

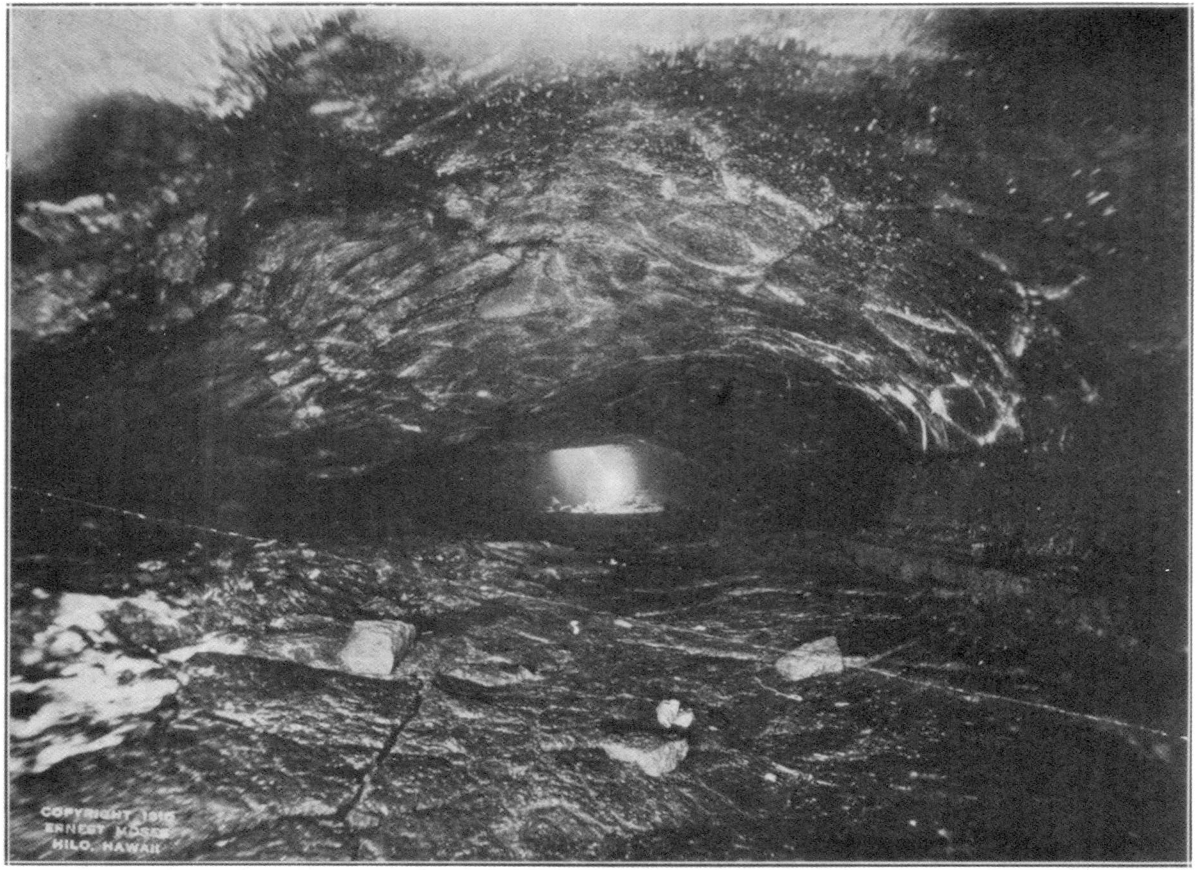

Fig. 1. "Pele's Drawing Room." Lava tube near the north brink of Halemaumau, looking north to a second opening. Destroyed by lava flows in 1918-19. —Photo by Moses.

Fig. 2. Cavern northeast of Halemaumau in Kilauea floor. This is one of the tubes of the 1894 flows whose roof has collapsed. —Photo by Moses.

Fig. 3. A lava tube supposed to be one of the Kaumana tubes of the Mauna Loa 1881 flow near Hilo. —Photo by Moses.

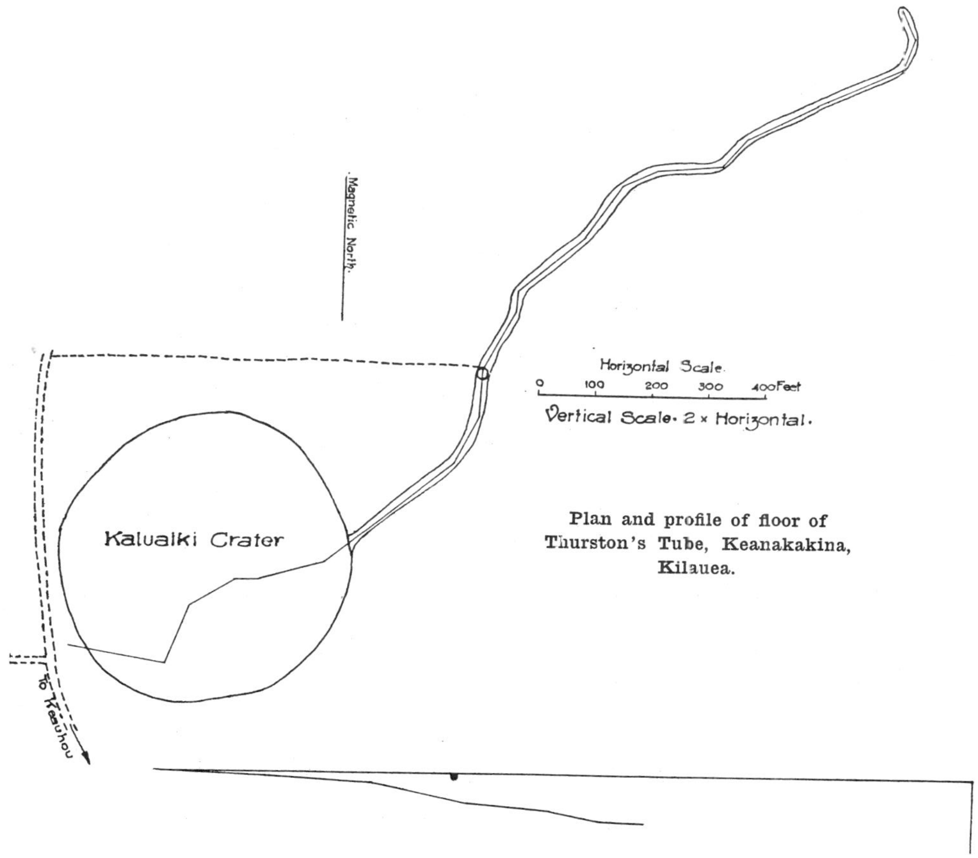

Fig. 4. Plan view of Kaluaiki crater and Thurston's tube (Keanakakina) with a profile of the tube.

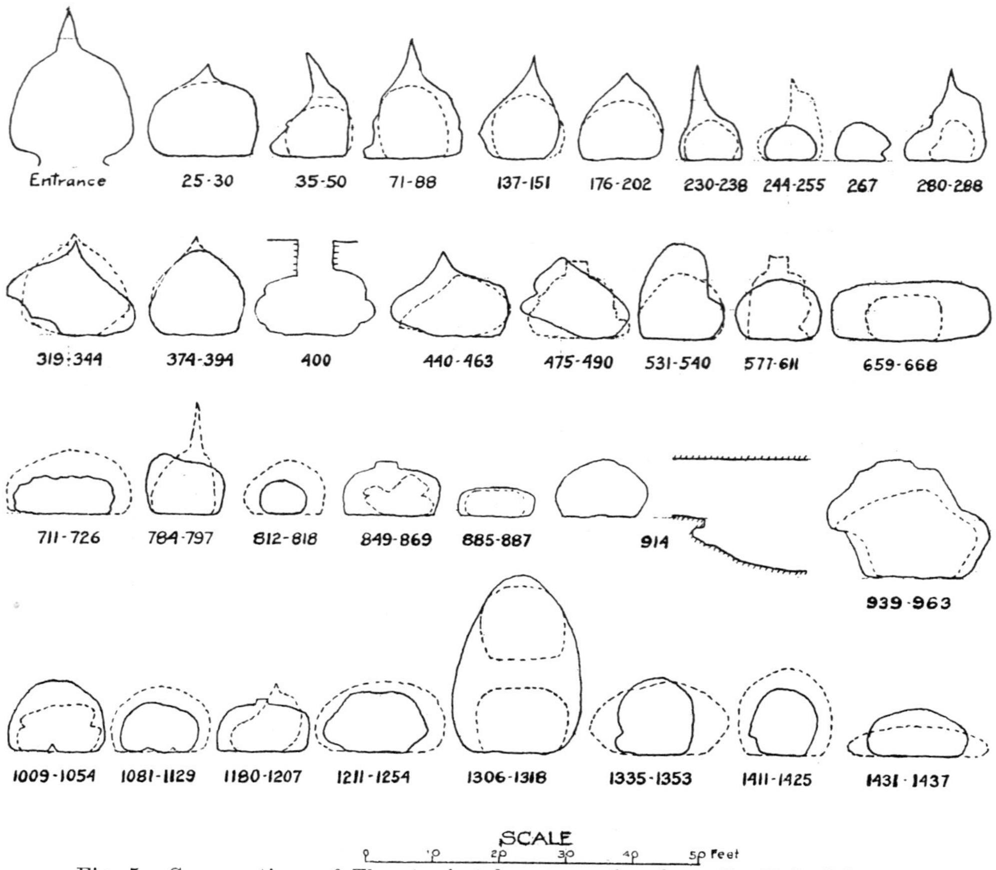

Fig. 5. Cross-sections of Thurston's tube progressing from the Kaluaiki crater to the end of the tube. The figures indicate distances in feet from the crater, where two cross-sections are superimposed; the second figure indicates the location of the dashed cross-section.

from the central channel. The bench along the wall near the base of the northeast crag has cracked considerably.

Activity of the Kau Desert Flow. When viewed on March 22nd the Kau Desert flow was found to be doing much the same as it had been during the last several weeks. The heap at the north end of the lava ridge was much higher than when last observed. The northern end of the lava ridge is now surrounded by a broad terrace that is about half as high as the highest part of the ridge. The center of the main activity was a very hot but deeply crusted pool to the northeast of the northern end of the ridge. The toes that were seen making out were of the heavy shark skin type of lava.

Seismometric Record. During the week ended midnight March 26th, 4 local earthquakes and one teleseism were registered in the Whitney Laboratory of Seismology. The dates and times are as follows: Local quakes—12:20 a. m., March 20, very feeble; March 22, 3:55 p. m., very feeble; March 24, 5:48 p. m., feeble; and March 26, 5:35 a. m., slight; distance about 30 miles. Teleseisms—March 20, 8:20 a. m., moderately strong, and March 23, 9:40 a.m., slight. Spasmodic tremor was slight on the 22, 23 and 24, and moderate on the other days during the week. Harmonic tremors were moderate and microseisms were slight.

Week Ending April 2, 1920.

SUMMARY OF CONDITIONS.

The rise of the lava during the week ending with April 1 was only 3 feet, most of this rise occurring on April 1. The nearly stationary conditions of the lakes and crags mentioned in the summary for the preceding week continued until March 31st. During this stationary period the fume from the pit was thicker than common. A cascade into a hole on the south side of the south island continued for several days and coincidental with this cascade a swift current poured into a grotto in the south crag about 70 feet away. By the end of the week a rapid rise had set in and on April 2 the north pool was flooded by overflows from the west bay and the north arm. When this rise commenced many of the cones along the wall to the north and northeast that heretofore had only been hissing spouted lava and caused small flows.

The Kau Desert flow has built up a terrace to the north and northeast of the northern end of the old fill to a height nearly as high as that of the main lava ridge. Through a narrow valley which separates this terrace from the main ridge lava rivers sometimes flow. Lava toeing out was found in all directions from the highest point at the northern end of the lava ridge.

JOURNAL.

Activity of Halemaumau. The heights of the lava and crags, expressed as depressions below the northeast monument on the rim of Halemaumau at an elevation of 3727 feet above sea-level, obtained from measurements during the week ended April 2, 1920, are as follows:

	Mean lake level.	Summit of north crag.
Mar. 25, 1 p. m.	191 feet	89 feet
" 31, 10 a. m.	191 "	88 "
Apr. 1, 1 p. m.	188 "	85 "

During the seven days ending with April 1 the lakes rose 3 feet and the crags 4 feet. About all of this rise occurred during the last day of the period. The relief of the north crag above the lakes, 103 feet, has remained about the same during the last three weeks.

From 1-2 p. m. on March 27 the fume from the crack in the floor of Kilauea to the southwest of Halemaumau was emitting much more smoke than common and the fume from the pit was moderately thick. The only streaming observed was a rapid current into the west bay. The north crag from which many avalanches have fallen is considerably cracked up at the peak.

During the afternoon of March 28 the fume was moderate. A slight vertical crack was observed in the south-southwest wall a little to the south of the crack through which the Kau Desert flow is pouring. A vigorous, broad current was rushing into a grotto on the west side of the south crag. Another current from the west bay poured into a tube near the base of the southwest crag. The southeast arm was full of fountains. Many blowing cones along the north and northeast wall could plainly be heard. The cracking and breaking up of the north crag continues. A very slender spatter spire fully 12 feet high had been built up near the base of the northeast peninsula. The south island is now a part of a peninsula from having joined the south crag. A new island, but 5 or 6 feet high and wide, has made its appearance near the south-southwest wall.

The fume interfered but slightly with good seeing from 7 to 8 p. m. on March 29 though a thunderstorm was in progress and the vapor around the pit very dense. A current was still pouring into the grotto on the west side of the south crag. From beneath a thick crust over the southern part of the east arm a current was moving to the north. A cone in the talus along the south wall was blowing very loudly.

On March 30 from 4 to 5 p. m. there was streaming in two directions in the west bay, one branch going to a grotto in the narrows leading to the central channel and another to the tube near the base of the southwest crag. The ramparts around the different lakes stood from 3-5 feet above the liquid. Small avalanches were falling from time to time from the north crag. The plaster on the inclined wall under the north ledge has slipped down in places. The current into the grotto on the west side of the south crag was flowing more vigorously than on the 29th. A narrow current was cascading into a hole in the south side of the south island with a visible drop of at least 3 feet.

At 10 a. m. on March 31 about the only activity observed was intermittent currents feeding fountains and grottoes. A few small avalanches were seen to fall from the north crag.

A small pond in the east wall crack that had recently made its appearance was observed at 1 p. m. on April 1. Many grottoes and fountains were active in all the lake arms and forming much Pele's hair. In the east arm which was covered with a thin broken crust there was a marked current to the north.

During the afternoon of April 2 there was a rapid current from the central channel into the east arm where the lava was 2 or 3 feet lower than in the rest of the lake. There was a line of fountains across the east arm starting with a border fountain at a crack through the bench magma below the northeast monument. The lava rose rapidly at 4:30 p. m. and flooded the old north pool with liquid melt. The cascade into a hole in the south side of the south island first observed on March 30th was still going on.

Activity of the Kau Desert Flow. When viewed on March 27 the Kau Desert flow was sending out slow moving pahoehoe toes over the new terrace on the west side of the northern end of the lava ridge The center of main activity was to the northeast of the lava ridge on a terrace built up there to a height nearly as great as that of the ridge itself. Numerous branches from three rivers that were flowing out from a crusted pool on top of this terrace moved in all directions except to the southwest. Between this outer terrace and the main lava ridge there is a well defined valley. On April 2 it was found that the center of activity was again at the top of the northern end of the main lava ridge. Small, slow moving flows were all that could be found by making a circuit of the place of activity.

Seismometric Record. During the week ended midnight April 2, 1920, 3 local earthquakes and one teleseism were registered in the Whitney Laboratory of Seismology The dates and times are as follows: Local quakes, 5 p. m., March 28, slight; March 30, 9:23 a. m., felt locally, dismantled instruments; March 30, 6:15 a. m., feeble. Teleseism—March 28. 6:50 p. m., moderate. Spasmodic tremor was moderately strong on March 27th and 30th and April 2, and slight on other days. Harmonic tremor was slight on March 30th and 31st and moderately strong during the rest of the period. Microseismic movement was slight.

Very respectfully,

R. H. FINCH,
Meteorologist, Temporarily in Charge.

ADDENDA.

A LAVA TUBE AT KILAUEA.

By Sidney Powers.

241 Kennedy Building, Tulsa, Okla.

INTRODUCTION.

Thurston's tube Keanakakina is one of the longest and most accessible tubes thus far found near Kilauea. This tube is named in honor of its discoverer, Mr. L. A. Thurston of Honolulu, through whose interest in Kilauea vulcanological research has been made possible on Hawaii for the past ten years. It is situated about three miles east of Halemaumau, the active pit of Kilauea, and 1,000 feet east of the rim of the pit crater Kilauea Iki. It opens into the Kaluaiki pit crater at the junction of the old Keauhou road with the road from the Volcano House to Halemaumau, and runs in a northeasterly direction. It is one of the channels by which Kaluaiki was drained not long before the lava lake finally disappeared and the crater became filled with a tumble of blocks from the walls. The lavas surrounding this crater and the original tube represent flows from the volcano Kilauea.

Kaluaiki is one of the pit craters along the long row of pit craters, cone and pit craters, cones, and finally lava flows which extends along a line of weakness from the former summit of Kilauea to the sea of Kapoho, south of Hilo. Along the same line the volcano split again in 1840 with renewed activity in the lower pit craters and below them.

Thurston's tube is described in order to give details of the size and shape of a long Hawaiian lava tube for the first time, to emphasize the comparative rarity of large tubes, and to call attention to concrete examples of "blow-piping" according to the gas fluxing hypothesis of Professor R. A. Daly. The writer is indebted to Dr. T. A. Jaggar for correcting the manuscript. With the 1918-20 activity of Kilauea and with the lava flow in Kau on December 22nd, 1919, many similar tubes have been formed which unfortunately cannot here be described.

OTHER LAVA TUBES.

Lava tubes on the floor of the Kilauea sink have been well advertised since the first visit of Ellis in 1823. One of these tubes, Fig. (1), is known as Pele's drawing room, Pele being the Hawaiian goddess of fire. It was shown many tourists and was frequently photographed before its destruction in 1918-19. These tubes are of small size and are usually single rooms. Their origin and the origin of all lava tubes is the flowing away of lava from beneath a frozen crust.

Tubes of small size and of limited length are abundant in areas covered by younger flows, but those of either large size or great length are unusual. The majority of the tubes are so low that one must crawl between rooms and the width of rooms seldom exceeds 25 feet. In the numerous palis (cliffs) which occur on nearly every island of the group lava tubes are rarely seen. On the western shore of Hawaii two caves, evidently tubes, may be seen near the triangulation station Hanakeaumoe, south of Hanamalo Bay. The diameter of these caves is about 30 feet. A mile south of Honaunau, the City of Refuge, several tubes about 6 feet wide and 4 feet high occur. On the south shore of Hawaii, at Kalapana, there is a tube 200 feet in length and large enough to crawl through. Two caves, originally tubes, are also known on the north side of the island Kauai and have already been described by the writer.

Another occurrence of tubes is in connection with craters. Lava from the Halemaumau lake poured into a tube for two days, December 28-29, 1914. This illustrates the process by which deeper tubes are almost invariably filled up; hence none are observed in the cliffs. On the Kau desert, west of Halemaumau, the pit craters are connected by a tube about 30 feet in diameter. Similarly, near the summit of Hualalai some remarkably large pit craters are connected by a tube.

Lava flows on the Island of Hawaii sometimes have tubes the roofs of which have in places collapsed (Fig. 2). Several tubes have been found near Kilauea, including one unique tube in aa lava found by H. O. Wood in the Bird Forest in 1916. Tubes in pahoehoe lava are known on the plantations between Hilo and the Volcano House and also north of Hilo. The latter are the Kaumana tubes (Fig. 3), two in number, neglecting the many branches, 4 and 5 miles from Hilo. The upper (mauka) tube is at an elevation of about 1200 feet, while the lower end of the lower (makai) tube as far as was examined had an elevation of about 925 feet. Both tubes are in the same flow, probably the flow of 1881. The upper tube was traversed for a length of about half a mile between holes in the roof, but neither end of the tube was seen. Approximate dimensions of some of the rooms are 60 feet wide, 7 feet high, 100 feet long, 20 feet wide, 3 feet high, 150 feet long. The height varies from 2½ to 15 feet, the width from 10 to 60 feet. Two tubes from the sides and one from above join the one followed. Stalactites were noted at one place, stopping of roof blocks at another, and roots such as are common in Thurston's tube have a maximum length of 7 feet. In the half mile the drop is about 30 feet. The lower tube has a reported length of over 1 mile, but it was followed only 1125 feet. Variations in height are from 2½ to 35 feet, in width from 10 to 45 feet. One conspicuous bench on either side is prolonged into a table of pahoehoe with a smooth surface 4 feet above the main tube level. Lava has run on under this table. Cupolas due to gas fluxing 3 and 5 feet high and the union of two tubes of equal size were observed.

Professor Hobbs has figured a hypothetical cross-section of a Hawaiian volcano filled with tubes of enormous size, and he explains the disappearance of the lava in Halemaumau and Mokuaweoweo (Mauna Loa) and in Matavanu (Samoa) with concomitant lava flows lower down the mountain slopes by the escape of lava through the tubular structure of the mountain flanks.* No structure of this kind on so large a scale is known in the Hawaiian Islands, and on the contrary the rifts which are developed or reopened on the flanks of the volcanoes with each eruption clearly show that the volcanoes are split from beneath, as was Sakurajima in 1914, and that the lavas escape through dikes which are formed in the rifts and which can be observed even in the walls of the Kilauean sink.

DESCRIPTION.

Measurements of Thurston's tube were made with a tape and small transit using azimuth angles, checking direction with a compass and elevation with barometers, (Figs. 4, 5). Magnetic variations of 10 degrees were noted. The length of the tube is 1494 feet, or in a straight line from entrance to end 1360 feet. The maximum height, excluding the cupola at the entrance and a collapse of the roof, is 20 feet, the maximum width 22 feet. The difference in level of

* W. H. Hobbs, buried lava tunnels as a factor in the drainage of craters of the Hawaiian type, Zeit. Vulkanologie, Bd. 1, 1914, pp. 86-88.

the entrance and end of the tube is 73 feet, representing an average drop of 4.9 feet per hundred, or 2½ degrees.

Liquid lava completely filled the tube at the initial stages of the filling, just as was the case in the Halemaumau tube above referred to. Gradually the level of the lava fell as shown by numerous benches at different parts of the tube. Finally the viscosity became so great that the surface froze. A final spurt of lava from beneath the crust is recorded near the end of the tube. The present end represents either a low place in the roof or the level to which the preexisting tube was filled. Hot lava ran down on the walls in the form of poorly developed stalactites and welled up from the floor at the farther end of the tube in many small volcanoes a foot or less in height.

During the time the lava almost completely filled the tube there was a great release of gas, especially near the entrance—the same phenomenon which may be watched in the splashing ''caves'' at the sides of the Halemaumau lake or lakes, and just as must take place as proved by the recent soundings of the Halemaumau lake by Dr. T. A. Jaggar, which showed that only the surface of the lava lake is a liquid and that this liquidity is developed by surface chemical reactions. Ths gas collected against the roof of the tube and ''blow-piped'' more than a dozen small, conical cupolas in the original, overlying lava, searing the surface of the cupolas as formed. The peaks of these cupolas are one to eight feet above the general roof level and the basal diameter is about the same as the height. Farther down the tube the narrow cupolas are replaced by large, rounded cupolas or holes as well as high rooms which have evidently been formed by stopping of lava blocks together with fluxing of the surface. Still farther along missing roof blocks must have fallen into the lava. Blow-piping was intense at the mouth of the tube where the gas release was greatest and decreased in proportion to distance from the mouth.

Since the cessation of activity at Keanakakina earthquakes have jarred loose portions of the roof making an opening to the surface at one place and causing a collapse farther along the tube which exposes a directly superimposed tube of the same dimensions, but of shorter length. The resulting cavity is 30 feet high.

One of the interesting recent developments in the tube is the penetration of long, pale yellow, filamentous roots through from 4 to at least 8 feet of roof. These roots are very abundant. Many of them are over 9 feet long below the roof and the longest measured was 12 feet. One root 9½ feet long has penetrated the floor.

Details of the tube are given in the figures and in the following table.

Details of Thurston's tube, commencing at the pit crater, which is 500 feet in diameter (Fig. 5):

Feet	
0—25	Floor of entrance collapsed contemporaneously with the subsidence of the lava in the crater leaving a U-shaped opening 25 feet long and 20 feet wide at the mouth. The pit may be entered by a ladder at the inner end of this opening. At the mouth there is the highest cupola of the tube, 24 feet above the floor. The second cupola is at 25 feet and is 16 feet high.
35	Third cupola, 18 feet high or 5½ feet above intervening roof level.
65	Six roots 10-12 feet long.
71	Fourth cupola, 20 feet high, 7½ feet above roof level.
105	Roots 9-9½ feet long; lava stalactites.
137	Fifth cupola, 17½ feet high, 6 feet above roof level.
176	Sixth cupola, 14½ feet high; root 9½ feet long growing into floor.
230	Seventh cupola, 16 feet high, 6 feet above roof level, 11 feet long, 3 feet wide.
255	Eighth cupola, 14 feet high, 8 feet above roof level, 8 feet long, 4 feet wide.
280	Ninth cupola, 16 feet high, 5 feet above roof level, 6 feet wide.
280	Ninth cupola, 16 feet high, 5 feet above roof level, 6 feet wide.
319	Tenth cupola, 15½ feet high, 3½ feet above roof level, 4 feet in diameter; roots 6½-7 feet long.
344	Dome 16½ feet high.
394	Eleventh cupola.
400	Roof collapse; roof 4 feet thick. The tube may be entered here by a ladder and a path through the forest leads from the road to this ladder. There is one small volcano near the pile of talus.
440	Long cupola, 4 feet above roof level.

475 Cupola; roots 8½-9 feet long.
490 Broad cupola, 3 feet high.
503 Hole in roof 1½ feet high, 3 feet long.
525 High room.
551 High room.
570 Hole in roof 4 feet long.
611 Hole in roof 3 feet long; 3 feet high.
625-668 Wide room, 26 feet wide in center.
700 Hole in roof 6 feet long.
717 Two blocks fallen from roof.
797 Cupola 5 feet above roof level, 6 feet long, 2 feet wide in a room.
818, 832, 841, 849 High points in roof.
893 Blocks missing from roof.
914 Lava cascade; a large room beyond.
963-990 Rock fallen from roof; 4-6 feet of roof collapsed.
1009-1038 Small volcanoes.
1054-1075 Seven large volcanoes; also small ones. Height of largest volcano 1 foot. Five of the volcanoes are on a line. An unsuccessful attempt has been made to remove the one at 1054.
1081 Small flat volcanoes.
1091 Large flat volcanoes and some small ones parallel to north wall.
1111 Four volcanoes ½ foot to 1 foot high, 3 on a line.
1129 Large volcanoes; hole in top of one 1 inch in a diameter.
1139 Line 6 feet long and parallel to wall of volcanoes 4 inches high.
1142 Block dropped off rock when lava was flowing.
1158 Hole 2 feet high in flat ceiling.
1180 Two holes in roof apparently caused by stoping.
1207 Hole 1½ feet above roof level.
1216 Lava cascade; a cave 3 feet high where lava ran from under frozen crust; also several small volcanoes on floor. From here to end of tube the lava is more ropy and has a fresher appearance indicating greater viscosity.
1234 Three small flat volcanoes.
1274 Volcano ½ foot high.
1280-1318 Collapse exposing upper tube of same size as main tube, but open for a distance of only 15 feet. Thickness of intervening rock 2-5 feet. Lava has run down lower part of sides of main tube.
1326 Volcano 10 inches high.
1335 Volcano 5 inches high with hole in top 1½ inches in diameter.
1353 Roof slightly fractured, but no blocks have fallen.
1383 Volcano 1 foot high, 1½ feet in diameter, with a 1-inch hole 1 foot deep in top.
1400 Lava cascade 1 foot high.
1437-1494 (End) Floor convex and rising to end.

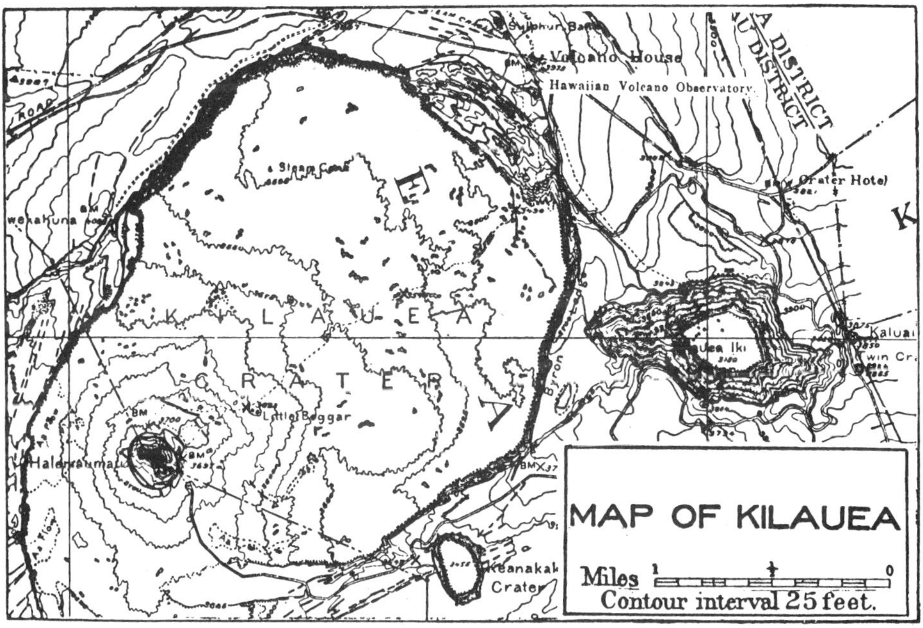

HAWAIIAN VOLCANO OBSERVATORY.

The Observatory is equipped with the following seismometric instruments rebuilt at the station in 1918 for the special needs of volcano research: two Bosch-Omori pendulums, high speed registration of local earthquakes; one optically recording seismograph for distant earthquakes; one clinograph registering E-W tilting of the ground. A vertical component seismograph was in December, 1918, set up in experimental operation. These are seated on concrete piers in a closed basement room having practically constant temperature, beneath the chief Observatory building near the hotel. Time is referred to a rated chronometer, checked at intervals by solar observations with a transit. The chronometer is loaned by the College of Hawaii. Hawaiian standard time (H. S. T.) is 10 hrs. 30 min. slower than Greenwich time.

CANCANI SCALE OF SEISMIC INTENSITY.

Expressed by accelerations measured in millimeters per second per second.

I.	Instrumental	0.0	2.5
II.	Very slight	2.5	5.0
III.	Slight	5.0	10.0
IV.	Sensible, mediocre	10.0	25.0
V.	Rather strong	25.0	50.0
VI.	Strong	50.0	100.0
VII.	Very strong	100.0	250.0
VIII.	Ruinous	250.0	500.0
IX.	Disastrous	500.0	1000.0
X.	Very disastrous	1000.0	2500.0
XI.	Catastrophic	2500.0	5000.0
XII.	Great catastrophe	5000.0	10000.0

Grade IV. is ordinarily the minimum perceived by the senses; and in grade XII. the accelerations or rate of change of motion (jerk) reaches that of terrestrial gravitation.

In the standard form of report the maximum intensity or acceleration, designated by the symbol a, or max. a, is given in the conventional unit of milligal. The milligal is a measure of acceleration, such that 1 milligal = 1/100 mm. per sec. per sec. = 10 μ. per sec. per sec. The Cancani scale, here defined in terms of millimeters per sec. per sec., can therefore be expressed in milligals by multiplying each of the numbers by 100.

U. S. DEPARTMENT OF AGRICULTURE
WEATHER BUREAU
CHARLES F. MARVIN, CHIEF

MONTHLY BULLETIN
OF THE
Hawaiian Volcano Observatory

VOL. VIII. HONOLULU, HAWAII, APRIL, 1920 No. 4

Week Ending April 9, 1920.

SUMMARY OF CONDITIONS.

The increase in the rate of rise of the lava that began last week continued during the current period and the total rise, 22 feet, was the greatest since the first week in March. The center island has been rising faster than the rest and, like the north crag, its peak is now over 100 feet above the liquid lava. The place of maximum upwelling of the liquid lava seems to be the cone areas along the north-northwest and south-southwest walls of the pit. Flows from these areas flooded the floor along the north and south walls and occasionally poured into the west bay and the southwest arm of the lake. The area of the lake has been increased both by this flooding and by the liquid encroaching upon the crags. During most of the week cascades were pouring into the east lake which is 3 or 4 feet lower than the rest and surrounded by a rampart 5 or 6 feet high.

The Kau Desert flow repeated the break-down process which seems to occur whenever a steep slag heap reaches its limiting height of about 100 feet. A break-down occurred on the east side of the terrace which had been built up to a height of about 100 feet to the northeast of the north end of the main lava ridge. Shortly after the breach in the side of the terrace was made it became the source of a good-sized lava river. Small, slow-moving pahoehoe flows were numerous over the north end of the new lava fill.

JOURNAL.

Activity of Halemaumau.—Measurements during the week ended April 9, 1920, expressed as depressions below the northeast monument on the rim of Halemaumau (3727 feet above sea level) have been as follows:

	Mean lake level.	Summit of north crag.
April 1, 1 p. m........	188 feet	85 feet
" 4, 11 a. m........	185 "	78 "
" 8, 1 p. m........	166 "	65 "

During the seven days ending with April 8th the crag rose 20 feet or at an average of 2.8 feet per day and the lake rose 22 feet or at an average of 3.1 feet. The greater part of the rise took place during the latter part of the period. The summit of the north crag and the highest part of the old central island are about 100 feet above the liquid.

The cascade into the east arm from the central channel first noticed on April 2nd was still going on at 1 p. m. April 3rd. There was also a narrow cascade into the same arm at its northern end. This latter cascade went out of action about 3 p. m. The floor along the north and east walls was being flooded with lava by overflow from cones and adjoining lake arms. About the only streaming observed was a slight current into the west bay.

On April 4 at 11 a. m. numerous border fountains were active in all arms of the lake. Flooding continued along the north and northeast walls where many coughing and hissing cones are located. The east arm of the lake has extended itself northward. At 7 p. m. there was a cascade into the east arm at its northern end. Avalanches were falling from most of the crags. A spouting cone in the talus along the south wall was fully 15 feet higher than the lake level.

At 2 p. m. on April 5th it was apparent that the lakes and crags were rising briskly. The center island was cracked and broken down on the south side. Avalanches were falling from the north crag. The streaming was to grottos and not very pronounced. A cone in the base of the north crag was hissing loudly and 3 cones along the north wall were spouting lava.

The lakes were still rising on April 6 and encroaching upon the crags. The south side of the center island was further broken up and a flat ledge but a few feet above the liquid was left on that side. The south-southwest crag was much smaller. The cascade into the tunnel in the west bay near the base of the southwest crag continues though its action is fast being obscured by the rising lava. A pronounced current that flowed into a large grotto near the south talus was very similar to one that flowed into the same place on March 27th. The small island to the south-southwest has increased in height.

On April 7 at 2 p. m. the east arm was an individual lake being 3 or 4 feet lower than the central channel and separated from the latter by a bench 5 or 6 feet high. From general appearances the lakes and crags seemed higher than on April 6th. Avalanches that fell from time to time from the north crag and central island gave evidence that some movement was in progress. The center islet has entirely disappeared. Several cracks that run lengthwise of the center island have recently developed. The southeast arm has widened both by the rising of the lava and by breaking down of the confining crags. An overflow from a cone along the north wall was flooding the north pool.

At 1 p. m. on April 8 a flow from a cone near the north wall was pouring into the west bay. The east lake which was 4 or 5 feet lower than the other arms of the lake had decreased materially in size. All of the crags appeared higher except one small crag near the north-northeast wall, which was almost drowned. A current from the southwest arm divided, one branch going to the southeast and the other toward the north arm.

On April 3 at 1 p. m. a flow from a cone near the north wall was pouring into the west bay much the same as on April 8th. Most of the bench and the talus along the south wall has been covered by flows from three high cones near the south-southwest wall. The cracks in the southwest crag have opened more. The short, east wall-crack is filled with new lava.

Activity of the Kau Desert Flow.—When the Kau Desert flow was viewed on April 5th numerous slow-moving pahoehoe toes were found on all sides of the new lava fill. A narrow black aa flow about 10 feet long had issued from the base of a large schollendom on the west side of the lava ridge. One narrow lava river rushed down the northern end of the new lava field and in places invaded new country. An April 6th numerous small flows were found much the same as on April 5th. An aa flow was moving west from the same break that produced the small aa flow on the west side of the lava heap mentioned on Feb. 6th. On April 7th the break-down process of a lava heap was again repeated. A pahoehoe river was flowing from a breach in the east side of the high terrace to the northeast of the main lava ridge.

Seismometric Record.—Two local earthquakes and one teleseism were recorded in the Whitney Laboratory of Seismology during the week ended midnight April 9, 1920. The dates and times are as follows: Local quakes, April 3, 3:20 a. m. and 9:30 p. m., both feble. Teleseism, April 6, 7.45 a. m., slight Spasmodic tremor was slight until April 5 and moderate thereafter. Harmonic tremor was moderately strong. Microseismic movement was very slight.

Week Ending April 16, 1920.

SUMMARY OF CONDITIONS.

The rise of the lava column that began on January 27, 1920, continued during the week ended April 16, 1920. The total rise of the lava during the 8 days ending with April 16 was 48 feet. The center island, which during the same period rose about 38 feet, is now the tallest, standing about 105 feet above the liquid lava. This island came into view from the Observatory about 4 p. m. on April 10. Data is not complete, but that at hand points to the conclusion that during the actual rise there was a current out of the west bay and during the short intermediary sinking spells a current flowed into the west bay. The area of the liquid lava increased considerably during the rapid rise and all of the crags but two are islands again.

Coincidental with the increase of the rate of rise of the liquid lava in Halemaumau the Kau Desert flow increased in vigor. The activity, however, was still confined to short flows that tended to increase the height of the terraces that surround the north end of the newly built lava ridge. A few small breakdowns occurred in the higher parts of the terraces.

JOURNAL.

Activity of Halemaumau.—Surveys during the week ended April 16, 1920, show the height of the lava and crags, expressed as depressions below the northeast monument on the rim of Halemaumau (3727 fet above sea level), as follows:

	Summit of north crag.	Summit of center island.	Mean lake level.
April 8, 1 p. m.......	65 feet	..	166 feet
" 10, 10 a. m.......	60 "	47 feet	150 "
" 12, 1 p. m.......	46 "	24 "	135 "
" 16, 10 a. m.......	44 "	14 "	118 "

During the 8 days ending with April 16th the north crag rose 21 feet, or at an average of 2.6 feet per day. The lake in the same period rose 48 feet, or at an average of 6 feet per day. The center island, which recently became the tallest of the crags, rose 33 feet in the 6 days ending with April 16th, or at an average of 5.5 feet per day. These rates of rise are the greatest since January 27, 1920, when the present continuous rise began. The total rise of the lava between January 27 and April 16, 1920, amounts to 227 feet.

The relief of the tallest crag above the lake was:

April 8..................................	101 feet
10..................................	103 "
12..................................	111 "
16..................................	104 "

It was noticed at 10 a. m. on April 10, 1920, that the east lake was higher than on the preceding day though still lower than the rest of the lakes. A very large section of the northeast crag was seen to fall into the lake and small avalanches fell from the other crags from time to time. All of the crags except two—one near the east-southeast wall and the other near the south-southwest wall—are islands now. The center island, which has been tilting to the north, is now very tall and came into view from the Observatory about 4 p. m.

On April 11 at 5:30 p, m. a very rapid current was pouring out of the west bay. The crags and lakes were visibly higher. At the base of the north crag, which is tilting to the north, a lava spire 5 feet high was hissing loudly. Three boiling pots were located near the wall in the north pool and three others along the northeast wall.

At 1 p. m. on April 12 the rapid current out of the west bay still continued. A small island had been formed by the breaking up of the northeast crag near the center of the pit. Another small island nearby was similarly formed from the center island. The talus along the south wall is entirely covered up with new flow.

During the forenoon of April 13 the lakes appeared to be falling rapidly and there was a current into the west bay. At about 1:30 p. m. the current into the west bay stopped and a rapid current commenced flowing out, very much as observed on the two preceding days. The center island was nearly a foot lower at 2 p. m. than it had been at 9 a. m. Many wide-mouthed cones near the south-southwest and north walls were spouting lava. The south side of the center island has been entirely covered up by the rising lava.

On April 14 at 1 p. m. currents were flowing out of the west bay, the north arm, and from under a ledge near the wall through the southeast arm. Many fountains were playing in the north end of the east lake, which now extends to the north-northeast wall. There was a cascade into a grotto in the small south-southwest crag. Avalanches were frequent from nearly all the crags.

At 10 a. m. on April 15 conditions were much the same as on the 14th. A current was flowing out of the west bay and another slower one from the southwest arm. Three fountains were playing in the west bay, 6 in the southeast arm and 6 in the southwest arm.

On April 16 at 10 a. m. a current was flowing out of the west bay. The lakes were lower than on the 15th, the east lake being 4 or 5 feet below its ramparts and the others 2 or 3 feet. Fountaining was brisk in all the arms.

Activity of the Kau Desert Flow.—Small flows were found pouring over new flows on the terrace to the north and east of the main lava ridge during the afternoon of April 11. Several hissing cones that were emitting much fume were found on top of the high terrace to the northeast. The flow was observed nearly every day during the week ending with April 16 after the 11th and each time several small lava rivers were found at different places around the north end of the new lava fill. The increase in the activity of the flow coincided with the rapid rise of the lava in Halemaumau.

Seismometric Record.—The dates and times of the 3 local earthquakes and the one teleseism that were recorded in the Whitney Laboratory of Seismology during the week ending with midnight April 16, 1920, are as follows: Local quakes, April 10, 9:40 a. m., slight; April 14, 2.05 a. m., very feeble; April 15, 8:50 a. m., very feeble. Teleseism, April 16, 12:15 p. m., slight. Spasmodic tremor was moderately strong on April 10, 12, and 14, and slight on other days. Harmonic tremor was slight until the 13th and moderately strong thereafter. Microseismic movement was notably slight. Tilting was slight in north and south directions. There was a pronounced west tilt on April 15, while on other days it was slight and mostly eastward.

Week Ending April 23, 1920.

SUMMARY OF CONDITIONS.

The rise of the lava column of Halemaumau stopped on April 16 and during the week ending with April 23 there was a fall. The crags changed but

1. Feb. 3, 1920. Along the new rift in Kau Desert near Kilauea. (Photo Finch)

2. March 2, 1920, 8 p. m. Cascade into a tube, Kau Desert flow. (Photo Finch)

3. Feb. 19, 1920. New center island in Halemaumau.
(Photo Jaggar)

4. April 8, 1920. Crags being drowned by rising lava.
(Photo Finch)

slightly while the total fall of the liquid lava was 14 feet. Several of the crags appeared to have lost in height, but most of the change in elevation of the crags was due to breaking down. A cone near the north wall ejected a considerable quantity of aa lava on April 18, after the liquid lava that had been surrounding it had drained away. The vigorous streaming that had been so pronounced for the past two weeks ceased when the lava started to fall.

The Kau Desert flow further increased in vigor and at the end of the week the output of lava was the most voluminous it had been since the first week in March. The terraces that surround the upper end of the lava ridge have increased both in height and in area, the principal increase being to the east. A lava tube on the high terrace to the northeast that has been in action for some time was revealed on April 23 by the roof breaking in. A swift lava river that has been feeding the flows on the east side was found cascading into the tube.

JOURNAL.

Activity of Halemaumau.—Surveys during the week ended April 23, 1920, gave the height of the lava and crags, expresed as depressions below the northeast monument on the rim of Halemaumau (3727 feet above sea level), as follows:

	Summit of north crag.	Summit of center island.	Mean lake level
April 16, 10 a. m.......	44 feet	14 feet	118 feet
" 20, 9 a. m.......	45 "	15 "	124 "
" 23, 3 p. m.......	40 "	20 "	132 "

The long continued rise of the lakes and crags in Halemaumau stopped about April 16 and during the week ending with April 23 the lava fell 14 feet, or at an average of 2 feet per day. The actual movement of the crags during the same period was slight. The relief of the crags above the liquid is greater than it was last week.

On April the 17th, 1920, at 1 p. m., the lakes appeared to be a trifle lower than on the 16th. There was no positive streaming to be seen. Two large lava stacks near the south-southwest wall were spouting lava. A newly built cone 10 feet high and 8 feet across near the base of the north crag, had a flaming vent on top. The 3 cones near the base of the southwest crag were rumbling loudly and spouting lava. The west bay has increased in size by taking in a part of the old north pool.

At 1 p. m. on April 18 the lakes were lower than on the preceding day. A current was flowing out of the southeast arm. A cone that has just made its appearance along the east wall was hissing loudly. A sunken place around an old cone site in the north pool became active again and was spouting aa lava—some particles being thrown over 100 feet. Both the reddish aa, ordinary, and jet black aa was being ejected. The action of this cone in ejecting aa lava immediately after the withdrawal of the shallow layer of liquid lava by the sinking of the lake is another demonstration of the sediment theory of aa formation mentioned, among other places, on page 20 of the February, 1920, Bulletin.

On April 19 at 10 a. m. it was apparent that the fall of the lava continued, all of the lake arms having well defined ramparts 4 or 5 feet high. Fountaining was vigorous in the central channel. No streaming was observed.

During the forenoon of April 20 the east lake was lower than the rest. Sluggish currents were flowing out of the north arm, the southwest arm, and the west bay. The north arm and the west bay have each increased in size and show a tendency to unite along the north wall. A cascade from a cone between the east lake and the north arm was pouring into the former. There was a pronounced whirlpool in the central channel near the point of the northeast crag.

At 1 p. m. on April 21 the lakes were lower while the crags appeared to be about the same as on the 20th. A strong current out of the west bay that joined with another from the southwest arm stopped near the point of the northeast crag and apparently went down with but little or no whirlpool motion. A slight current that started near the wall of Halemaumau moved out of the southeast arm. A small new island has appeared between the south crag and the central island.

During the forenoon of April 22 the lakes appeared to be lower. A large section of the center island broke off and fell into the central channel, followed by vigorous fountaining at the place of fall. At times a current flowed out of the west bay. The north arm and the west bay have joined completely.

At 3 p. m. currents were flowing out of the southeast arm and west bay into the southwest arm. All of the lakes were surrounded by ramparts 8-10 feet high. Vigorous fountains were playing in all lakes.

Activity of the Kau Desert Flow.—Until April 23 about all that could be seen at the Kau Desert flow were small, slow-moving pahoehoe toes around the northern end of the lava fill. These flows were especially numerous along the east side. On April 23 a vigorous lava river was found pouring into a tube on the high terrace to the northeast. The course of the flow in the tube was to the south. This river is located where the line of hissing cones were observed on April 11th. The flow in this tube is the most voluminous that has been observed since the first week in March.

Seismometric Record.—No earthquakes were recorded in the Whitney Laboratory of Seismology during the week ending with midnight April 23, 1920. Spasmodic tremor was slight until April 23 and moderately strong on that day. Harmonic tremor was slight on April 17 and moderately strong thereafter. Microseismic movement was slight. Tilting was to the south and west on the 17th; pronounced to the north and east on the 18th; and very slight on other days.

Week Ending April 30, 1920.

SUMMARY OF CONDITIONS.

The fall of the lava column of Halemaumau that began on April 16 continued during the week ended April 30, 1920. The liquid lava fell 19 feet, while the crags, as last week, changed but slightly. The relief of the tallest crags above the liquid, 105 feet, is about the same as it has been during the last several weeks. The fume has been increasing and was quite thick during the week. With this fume condition and southerly or very light winds prevailing smoke was reported from Honolulu. The most spectacular feature during the week was a lava cascade 40 feet wide that began in the southwest arm on April 29. It poured into a tunnel below as was revealed by several holes and reversing direction moved toward the crack through which the Kau Desert flow is pouring.

Coincidental with the continued fall in Halemaumau the Kau Desert flow increased its output. The river in the lava tube reported last week continued its activity. Another breakdown in the roof of this tube revealed a cascade 10 feet high.

JOURNAL.

Activity of Halemaumau.—Measurements during the week ended April 30 1920, give the height of the lakes and crags, expressed as depressions below the northeast movement on the rim of Halemaumau, as follows:

	Summit of north crag.	Summit of center island.	Mean lake level.
April 23, 3 p. m.......	40 feet	20 feet	132 feet
" 26, 1 p. m,......	40 "	40 "	140 "
" 30, 9 a. m.......	46 "	45 "	151 "

The lake level in 7 days fell 19 feet or at an average of 2.7 feet per day. The north crag sank 6 feet while the summit of the center island fell 25 feet during the week. A large part of the central island broke off which undoubtedly accounts for a large part of the apparent sinking. The increase in the height of the ramparts around the lakes from 0 on April 16 to about 30 feet on April 30th is nearly equal to the fall of the liquid lava during that time and is a further indication that the crags have been nearly stationary while the liquid lava was falling. The relief of the tallest crags above the lakes continue a little over 100 feet.

At 1 p. m. on April 24 a slight current was flowing into the west bay. Fountaining was vigorous, some fountains flinging liquid melt in umbrella-shaped patterns fully 15 feet high. The lava appeared to be lower while the crags have changed but slightly, if at all. The fume was thick, having been increasing daily since the fall started on April 16, 1920.

On April 25 at 1 p. m. the lakes were lower than on April 23. With the exception of the northeast islet which is much lower than it has been during the past several days the crags remain unchanged. A rapid current from the southwest arm poured into the central channel and a slow current moved out of the southeast arm.

It was noticed on April 26 that the central island had undergone a further breakdown, otherwise the lakes and crags appeared much the same as on the 25th. There was no streaming except for a few intermittent currents to grottos. Fountaining was vigorous in all arms.

At 3 p. m. on April 28 the cone along the east-southeast wall was an open boiling pot. A rapid current poured out of the west bay into the central channel. The floor between the east lake and the north arm has broken down. The north crag appeared to have tilted a little more to the north, which would indicate an uplift in the center of the pit.

During the afternoon of April 29 the crags and lakes appeared unchanged. A current was moving out of the west bay. A few strong fountains were playing in each arm of the lake. A cascade was observed on the east side of the southwest arm at about the same place where the rapid streaming and cascade were observed on March 28 and April 6, 1920.

On April 30 the lakes appeared to be about the same as on the 29th. Vigorous fountains were playing in all the arms except the southwest. The cascade in the southwest arm is over 40 feet wide. The lava on the southern side of the cascade poured into a pool 4 or 5 feet lower. Below the north side of the cascade the lava turned to the left, and, apparently, flowed under the central part of the south crag. Another cascade was pouring into a hole on the center side of the south crag just opposite the wide one above mentioned.

Activity of the Kau Desert Flow.—On April 28 small sluggish flows were toeing out around the north end of the lava ridge. On top of the high terrace to the northeast of the main lava ridge a lava river 12 feet wide cascaded into a tunnel with a 10-foot fall. The volume of lava in the river was considerably greater than that observed in a river at the same place on April 23. A cone some 10 or 12 feet high and about 15 feet across has been built up on the highest part of the main lava ridge. The lava inside the cone fluctuates in height—sometimes fountaining vigorously and overflowing the top, other times being 7 or 8 feet down and deeply crusted over. It is a miniature volcano.

Seismometric Reecrd.—No earthquakes were recorded in the Whitney Laboratory of Seismology during the week ending with midnight April 30, 1920. This makes two consecutive weeks during which no earthquakes were recorded—an unusually quiet period seismically. Spasmodic tremor was slight until April 28 and moderately strong thereafter. Harmonic tremor was moderately strong. Microseismic movement was moderately strong on April 24 and very slight on other days. Tilting was to the north and east on April 24 and 25 and to the south and west thereafter.

Very respectfully,
R. H. FINCH,
Meteorologist, Temporarily in Charge.

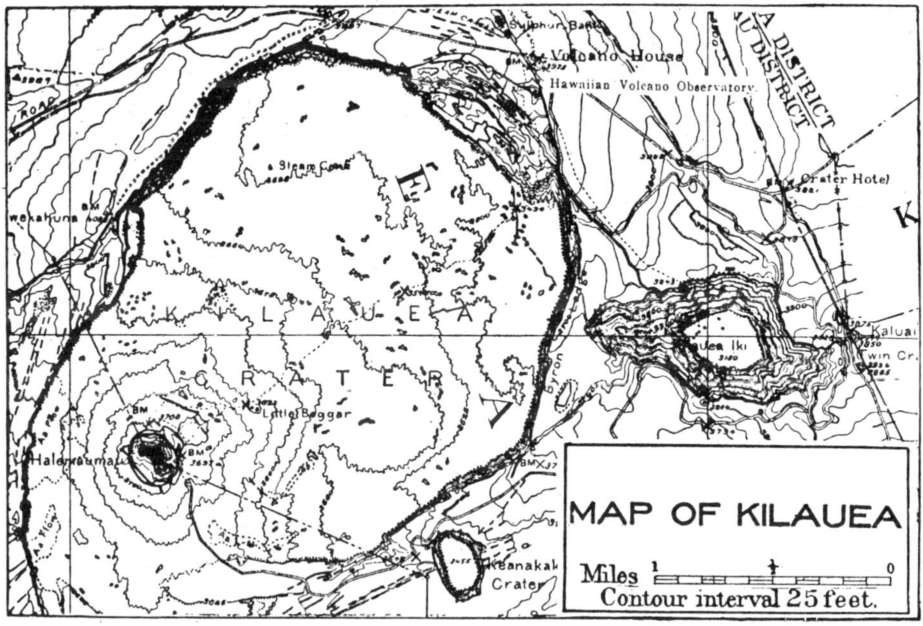

HAWAIIAN VOLCANO OBSERVATORY.

The Observatory is equipped with the following seismometric instruments rebuilt at the station in 1918 for the special needs of volcano research: two Bosch-Omori pendulums, high speed registration of local earthquakes; one optically recording seismograph for distant earthquakes; one clinograph registering E-W tilting of the ground. A vertical component seismograph was in December, 1918, set up in experimental operation. These are seated on concrete piers in a closed basement room having practically constant temperature, beneath the chief Observatory building near the hotel. Time is referred to a rated chronometer, checked at intervals by solar observations with a transit. The chronometer is loaned by the College of Hawaii. Hawaiian standard time (H. S. T.) is 10 hrs. 30 min. slower than Greenwich time.

CANCANI SCALE OF SEISMIC INTENSITY.

Expressed by accelerations measured in millimeters per second per second.

I.	Instrumental	0.0	2.5
II.	Very slight	2.5	5.0
III.	Slight	5.0	10.0
IV.	Sensible, mediocre	10.0	25.0
V.	Rather strong	25.0	50.0
VI.	Strong	50.0	100.0
VII.	Very strong	100.0	250.0
VIII.	Ruinous	250.0	500.0
IX.	Disastrous	500.0	1000.0
X.	Very disastrous	1000.0	2500.0
XI.	Catastrophic	2500.0	5000.0
XII.	Great catastrophe	5000.0	10000.0

Grade IV. is ordinarily the minimum perceived by the senses; and in grade XII. the accelerations or rate of change of motion (jerk) reaches that of terrestrial gravitation.

In the standard form of report the maximum intensity or acceleration, designated by the symbol α, or max. α, is given in the conventional unit of milligal. The milligal is a measure of acceleration, such that 1 milligal $=$ 1/100 mm. per sec. per sec. $= 10\ \mu$. per sec. per sec. The Cancani scale, here defined in terms of millimeters per sec. per sec., can therefore be expressed in milligals by multiplying each of the numbers by 100.

U. S. DEPARTMENT OF AGRICULTURE
WEATHER BUREAU
CHARLES F. MARVIN, CHIEF

MONTHLY BULLETIN
OF THE
Hawaiian Volcano Observatory

VOL. VIII. HONOLULU, HAWAII, MAY, 1920 No. 5

Week Ending May 7, 1920.

SUMMARY OF CONDITIONS.

The lava column of Halemaumau started to rise again on May 6 after falling steadily since April 16. The liquid lava on May 4 was 156 feet below the rim. The relief of the tallest crag above the lake level on that date was 110 feet. The rise of the liquid lava began when the cascade in the southwest arm stopped and is further evidence of a superficial draining away of the liquid. The height of the cascade decreased as the lake fell and, apparently, when the lake level was the same as that of the tube below the cascade, the latter ceased and the lakes started to rise. Shoals in several of the lakes were revealed when the lava was withdrawn. Several of the smaller islands rose and fell with the liquid while the larger crags moved but slightly.

The flow in the Kau Desert continues much the same: Small flows around the edge of the fill and the river in the northeast terrace active. This river is the most persistent of any phase of activity that has been observed in the Kau Desert flow. Its location was first determined on April 5th. The cone on top of the main lava ridge is rather imposing—standing 40 feet above the lava at its base.

JOURNAL.

Activity of Halemaumau. Measurements during the week ended May 7, 1920, give the height of the lakes and crags, expressed as depressions below the northeast monument on the rim of Halemaumau (3727 feet above sea level), as follows:

	Summit of north crag	Summit of center island	Mean lake level
April 30, 9 a. m......	46 feet	45 feet	151 feet
May 4, 1 p. m........	46 "	..	156 "

The lake level in 4 days fell 5 feet or at a rate of 1.2 feet per day. The actual movement of the crags, as last week, was very small.

On May 1 at 11 a. m. the cascade in the eastern part of the southwest arm was still very vigorous. The lakes appeared to be a little lower and the fume was very thick.

The cascade in the southwest arm was still the main feature of activity during the afternoon of May 2. The fall of the lava level in the lakes had decreased the drop in the cascade from over 8 feet on April 29 to about 1 foot on May 2nd. The pool below the south side of the cascade was now almost level with the lava in the southwest arm. The floor for a considerable area around the cone site near the south-southwest wall has sunk and formed a hole some 30 feet deep.

It was found during the forenoon of May 5 that the cascade in the southwest arm was much smaller, being confined to the swift northern side—next to the tube through which the flow drained. Windows in the tube below the cascade showed that the current completely reversed in direction and flowed westerly under the south crag. Slow streaming to grottos was in evidence in other arms of the lake.

During the afternoon of May 6 the cones around south and east walls were hissing loudly and splashing lava. The cascade in the southwest arm that started on April 29 had stopped. A rapid current poured out of the west bay. Sluggish streams were moving out of the southwest and the southeast arms. Everything pointed to an increase of pressure, and it was apparent that the lakes were rising. The narrow peninsula that nearly separated the southwest arm into two parts had disappeared.

At 5:30 p. m. on May 7 the lakes were much higher. The old north pool is covered with new lava. A current from the west bay was flowing under a narrow bridge that connects the north crag with the center island. A flow from a cone near the south-southwest wall was flooding the south floor.

Activity of the Kau Desert Flow. Small flows were still active, at times, around all sides of the northern end of the lava ridge. When the flow region was visited on May 3 it was found that the high cone on top of the north end of the main lava ridge had further increased in height. A small stream was pouring down the southern side of this cone. The river that flows into a tube on the high terrace to the northeast continues very vigorously. Cracking and rumbling in the lava surrounding the place where the river issued from under a crust indicated that a breakdown was beginning. The fill from this river which has been continuously active for over a month reaches to a considerable distance to the south and east. On the morning of May 7th the whole of the top of the northeast terrace was covered with slow moving pahoehoe lava. The place of issue of this flow, over the river site, was marked by large fountains.

Seismometric Record. The dates and times of the 2 local quakes and 1 teleseism that were recorded in the Whitney Laboratory of Seismology during the week ended midnight May 7, 1920, are as follows: Local quakes—May 1, 3:15 p. m., very feeble; May 4, 1:20 a. m., very feeble. Teleseism, May 7, 11:15 a. m., moderate, indicated distance to epicenter, 3600 miles. A fairly good record of this quake was obtained by the Hilo seismograph. Spasmodic tremor was slight on May 1 and 2 and moderately strong thereafter. Harmonic tremor was slight. Microseismic movement was noticeably slight. Tilting was slight throughout the week, being to the south and west until the 5th and to the north and east thereafter.

Week Ending May 14, 1920.

SUMMARY OF CONDITIONS.

The rise of the lava column of Halemaumau that started last week was of short duration, for another fall started on May 11. The liquid lava was 121 feet below the rim on May 8 and 143 feet on May 14. The relief of the tallest crag on May 14 was 113 feet. The cascade in the southwest arm that stopped on May 5 started again on May 11th. The periods of fall of the lava column during the past few weeks have coincided with the periods of activity of the above mentioned cascade and periods of rise coincided with its inactivity. The lakes started to rise on May 6 and in two days came up 35 feet. Blowing cones were much in evidence when the lakes were rising and almost absent during sinking spells. A pronounced sinking area was located at the point of the north crag during the afternoon of May 13.

The Kau Desert flow has continued to spread to the south and east, the active part being fed from the lava river flowing in the tube in the northeastern fill. The cone on top of the main lava ridge has further simulated a miniature volcano by producing small explosions after a period of quiet.

JOURNAL.

Activity of Halemaumau. Measurements during the week ended May 14, 1920, give the height of the lava and crags, expressed as depressions below the northeast monument on the rim of Halemaumau, as follows:

	Summit of north crag	Summit of central island	Mean lake level
May 4, 1 p. m.......	46 feet	..	156 feet
" 8, 1 p. m.......	27 "	23 feet	121 "
" 11, 10 a. m......	24 "	22 "	131 "
" 14, 10 a. m......	32 "	30 "	143 "

During the two days ending with May 8th the lake level rose 35 feet and the north crag rose 19 feet. By May 11th the lakes were falling again though the crags continued to rise for a short time after the lakes started to fall. During the three days ending with May 14th the lakes dropped 12 feet and the crags about 8 feet.

At 1 p. m. on May 8th there was rapid streaming out of the west bay and a small stream fed from a cone near the south-southwest wall cascaded into the eastern part of the southwest arm. A large vertical crack has developed in the northeast crag. The lakes were higher and the fume thinner. Two of the crags came into view from the observatory during the afternoon.

While the lakes were observed to be higher during the afternoon of May 9th than on May 8th it was apparent that the rate of rise was decreasing. The cascade into the southwest arm from the south floor was still active. The rapid streaming out of the west bay was much the same as on the 8th.

During the forenoon of May 11 it was apparent that the lakes were falling, though sluggish currents were pouring out of the southwest arm and out of the west bay. A cone along the south wall was hissing loudly. A rapid current cascaded into a grotto in the eastern part of the southwest arm at the same place of the vigorous cascade of April 29-May 5. The entrance to the southwest arm from the central channel had become very narrow.

At 3 p. m. of May 12 it was noticed that the fume was thicker and the lakes lower, while the crags appeared unchanged. The walls around the lakes were from 10-15 feet high. The cascade in the eastern part of the southwest arm had increased in vigor, the entire lake streaming rapidly into the cascade.

The cascade in the southwest arm continued vigorous during the afternoon of May 13th. A current from the western part of the southwest arm joined with another current from the west bay and both went down near the center point of the north crag. The lakes were lower and the fume thicker. The northeast islet was connected to the northeast crag by a narrow isthmus. The old small islands in the central channel were much higher and several new ones had appeared.

During the forenoon of May 14th there was an extremely rapid rush of lava from the west bay into the central channel through the very narrow strait that separates the north crag from the central island. There was also rapid streaming in the southwest arm, one branch feeding the cascade in the eastern part and the other going into the central channel. A few intermittent fountains were playing in each arm of the lake.

Activity of the Kau Desert Flow. When viewed on May 11th the lava river in the tube on the high northeast fill was very active. The flow from this tube reaches a long way to the south and for several hundred feet to the east. Two small aa flows pushed out of the southern side of this northeastern fill. The cone on the highest portion of the main lava ridge was quiet but emitting much smoke. Spatter from this cone was thrown over 200 feet to the east. Broken blocks of reddish lava, some of which weigh from 10-15 pounds, of the type found inside cones and lava tubes, that were strewn over the ground for several feet around the cone furnish evidence of small explosions.

Seismometric Record. The dates and times of the two local shocks and the three teleseisms that were recorded in the Whitney Laboratory of Seismology during the week ending with midnight May 14, 1920, are as follows: Local quakes—May 8, 10:25 a. m., feeble; May 9, 3:50 a. m., feeble. Teleseisms —May 8, 11 a. m. and 1 p. m., both slight; May 12, 3:30 p. m., feeble. Spasmodic tremor was moderately strong on May 8th and very slight thereafter. Harmonic tremor was moderately strong on May 8, 9, 10, and slight on other days. Microseismic movement during the week was very slight. Tilting was very slight.

Week Ending May 21, 1920.

SUMMARY OF CONDITIONS.

The lava column of Halemaumau has been slowly falling since May 11, the fall of the crags keeping pace with that of the liquid. The mean lake level on May 21 was 160 feet below the rim. The liquid lava apparently reached the level of the tunnel that had been draining the cascade in the southwest arm on May 18th, for on that day the cascade ceased, though a current into a grotto at the cascade site persisted for several days. After the cessation of the cascade, rapid streaming out of the southwest arm and west bay indicated a rising tendency but, apparently, the liquid drained away through a sink near the center of the pit. By the end of the week the crags were breaking down and the pit was quite fumy.

This week marks the end of the 5th month since the Kau Desert flow began. A considerable volume of lava is still pouring out. The active part of the flow is over 3 miles long, extending from the northern end of the new lava ridge, nearly as far north as Puu Koae to below Kamakaia. Practically all of the lava output during the week was of a moderately heavy pahoehoe type. The upper end of the 1823 flow is largely buried under the new flow.

JOURNAL.

Activity of Halemaumau. The heights of the lava and crags, expressed as depressions below the northeast monument on the rim of Halemaumau, obtained by measurements during the week ended May 21, 1920, are as follows:

	Summit of north crag	Summit of center island	Mean lake level
May 14, 10 a. m......	32 feet	30 feet	143 feet
" 21, 10 a. m......	49 "	51 "	160 "

The lake fell 17 feet during the 7 days ending with May 21, or at an average of 2.4 feet per day. The fall of the crags was practically the same as the lakes. The relief of the tallest crag above the liquid was 111 feet on May 21, which was about the same as it had been during the past several weeks.

During the afternoon of May 16 the lakes were lower and the fume moderately thick. A sluggish current was pouring out of the west bay and a rapid current was feeding the vigorous cascade in the eastern part of the southwest arm.

The cascade in the southwest arm had stopped at 1 p. m. of May 18th, though there was streaming to a grotto where the cascade had been. A rapid current was flowing out of the southwest arm and sluggish ones out of the west bay and north arm. The lakes indicated some tendency to rise.

The fume was thick during the afternoon of May 19, though the action of a few hissing cones and eastward streaming out of the west bay and southwest arm suggested a rising tendency. Avalanches were falling from many of the crags. A current was flowing to the large grotto in the eastern part of the southwest arm.

During the afternoon of May 20 the lakes were lower and the fume thicker. The entire south floor had sunk a little. The north crag was broken down by avalanches having fallen to the northeast. The peak of the center island had avalanched to the south. A sluggish current moved out of the north arm.

At 9 a. m., May 21, there was rapid streaming into the central channel out of the southwest arm and a sluggish current moving into the grotto in the eastern part of the same arm. There was an apparent down rush of lava near the center point of the center island. A few glowing places showed in many of the crags several feet above the liquid. Vigorous fountains were playing in all the arms. Small avalanches fell from the northeast crag from time to time. The west bay was separated from the central channel by a narrow isthmus.

Activity of the Kau Desert Flow. When viewed on May 15 all of the activity was confined to the eastern side of the new lava ridge. The fill to the northeast was higher than the northern part of the main ridge. Several of the breakdown sites of the tube on the northeastern fill had enlarged to holes 20-30 feet across and 15-20 feet deep with hot crusted bottoms, but no river visible except at one window part way down the southern slope of the fill. The flow to the south extends on the eastern side of the ridge that is the upper end of the 1823 flow nearly to the Kamakaia cone region. Other branches of the flow that went down the mountain to Kamakaia cone alongside the Dec. 30, 1919-Jan. 10, 1920 river course crossed over the 1823 ridge at several places. One or two small flows cascaded into a tube in the 1823 ridge.

Seismometric Record. The dates and times of the 3 local quakes that were recorded in the Whitney Laboratory of Seismology during the week ending with midnight May 21, 1920, are as follows: May 15, 2:20 a. m., moderate, felt in Honolulu, as a very perceptible shock, and in Hilea, intensity III Rossi-Forel; 1 p. m., feeble. May 20, 3:25 a. m., very feeble. Spasmodic tremor was moderately strong on May 16, 18, and 19, and slight on other days. Harmonic tremor was slight on May 15 and moderately strong thereafter. Microseismic movement was very slight. Tilting was moderate to the east on 15th, to the north of the 16th and 19th, and to the south on the 17th and 21st, with nearly stationary conditions on other days.

Week Ending May 28, 1920.

SUMMARY OF CONDITIONS.

The lava column of Halemaumau continued to fall during this week. The lake level on May 28 was 185 feet below the rim or 25 feet lower than last week. The tallest crag stood 115 feet above the liquid lava on May 28. The fall was marked by a very fumy condition of the pit. That tilting accompanies a fall as well as a rise was shown by the daily occurrence of avalanches from most of the crags. When the floor sank a ring was left around the wall of the pit as a plaster several feet thick. Coincidental with the fall narrow separations developed between the different arms of the lake so that there are now 4 separate lakes. Hissing cones and vents were notably absent.

The lava river in the tube in the northeastern fill of the Kau Desert flow has been in action nearly two months. The lava from this river has covered a considerable area to the south with a heavy and fairly level pahoehoe flow. A few large spatter cones have been built up over small lava tubes in the upper end of the lava fill. No noticeable change in the volume output of lava has accompanied the fall of Halemaumau.

JOURNAL.

Activity of Halemaumau. The heights of the lava and crags, expressed as depressions below the northeast monument on the rim of Halemaumau, obtained from measurements during the week ended May 28, 1920, are as follows:

	Summit of north crag	Summit of center island	Mean lake level
May 21, 10 a. m......	49 feet	51 feet	160 feet
" 28, 8 a. m......	70 "	85 "	185 "

During the 7 days ending with May 28 the lakes fell 25 feet or at an average of 3.6 feet per day. A part of the apparent large drop in the center island was due to the peak breaking off—the actual fall of nearly all the crags being about 21 feet or at an average of 3 feet per day.

It was apparent at 1 p. m. on May 22 that the south and east floors had sunk considerably. The center island was further broken down on the south side. The north crag was still breaking down and sinking. A current from the southwest arm appeared to sink between the center island and the south crag. There was no current in the eastern part of the southwest arm. Very large fountains were playing in the central channel.

During the afternoon of May 23, the pit was very fumy. There was rapid streaming out of the southwest arm to the strait between the center island and the south crag. A sluggish current was moving out of the southeast arm. The north crag had sunk more than the adjacent old north floor.

At 2 p. m. on May 25 the lakes were lower than on May 23 and the pit was very fumy. One current was pouring out of the southwest arm and another in the central channel moved toward the west bay. Avalanches were falling from most of the crags. Three large fountains were playing in the central channel.

During the afternoon of May 26 all of the currents that were visible through the fume were directed to grottos. A narrow ring of the old floor around the pit wall stood 10-15 feet above the new inner floor. Movements in the crag masses were evidenced by avalanches falling from time to time.

The fall of the lava column of Halemaumau still continued on May 27 and the pit was very fumy. A slow current moved out of the southwest arm. In other parts of the lakes the currents appeared fortuitous, often reversing direction within 5 minutes.

At 7:30 a. m. on May 28 there was eastward streaming in the southwest arm which was separated from the central channel by a low isthmus. The floor around the north crag sank several feet more and a large hole had developed between part of the old north floor and the north crag from which much smoke issued. Several avalanches fell from the north crag.

Activity of the Kau Desert Flow. On May 24 the Kau Desert flow was explored by going in from the Kapapala bull-pen. Flowing lava of a heavy pahoehoe type was found over a considerable area extending from below the southernmost Kamakaia cone to over a mile above, and from the aa of the Dec. 30, 1919-Jan. 10, 1920, river to within a few hundred feet of the middle Kamakaia cone. The river in the tube near the northern end of the new lava fill was very much the same as when last observed—very rapid streaming revealed through a small window surrounded by shelly lava. On May 27 a flow was

No. 1—May 8, 1920. Looking across Halemaumau from the southeast.
—Photo Finch.

No. 2—May 31, 1920. Cone in the Kau Desert flow showing explosion blocks and spatter. —Photo Finch.

No. 3—May 12, 1920. Cascade in the southwest arm.
—Photo Finch.

No. 4—Looking across Halemaumau from the northeast.
—Photo Finch.

pouring from a cone near the high cone on the northern end of the main lava ridge down the western side. The main arm of this flow went alongside the small upper aa outbreak on the western side of the lava fill and reached nearly to its edge.

Seismometric Record. The dates and times of the 3 local quakes that were recorded in the Whitney Laboratory of Seismology during the week ending with midnight May 28, 1920, are as follows: May 24, 2:20 a. m., feeble, and 6 a. m., moderate, indicated distance to origin 30 miles; felt in Hilea, intensity IV, Rossi-Forel. May 26, 1:55 a. m., moderate, indicated distance, 30 miles; felt in Hilea, intensity IV, Rossi-Forel. Spasmodic tremor was moderately strong on May 24 and slight on other days. Harmonic tremor and microseismic movement were both slight. Tilting movement was very slight and mostly to the south and west.

Respectfully,

R. H. FINCH,
Temporarily in Charge.

Two Gas Collections From Mauna Loa

By E. S. SHEPHERD

Recently we were able to report on the composition of a number of gas samples from Kilauea.* In October, 1919, Dr. T. A. Jaggar, Jr., secured two tubes from the Mauna Loa flow. Dr. Jaggar's notes are as follows:

"I have sent you two tubes from the new eruption of Mauna Loa which are the best I could do so far. They are not from live flames but from vents in a flow edge which nearly asphyxiated me. This was one hundred feet east of the live rift. I tried for the flames at the lava pots of the rift but the gas was insupportable without an oxygen helmet; a wet cloth was wholly useless. Smelt like foundry and chlorine mixed with a little CO_2 thrown in, was wet and made steam where it came out, invisible elsewhere, and knocked you flat if you got in it. Was **heavy.** Wholly unlike Kilauea. In a later expedition I found the Kilauea sulphurous smell and no trouble, but also no small flames. Shows an evolution in the course of an eruptive period. The aa flows of Mauna Loa have much heavy gas which has the foundry smell and is fearfully discouraging to breathe; one suspects iron and carbon all the time and almost no sulphur.

"**Field Notes on Tubes Sent.** Went to windward of a thinly steaming crack giving off irrespirable gas in great quantity near the eastern edge of a flow about a hundred feet east of the northern rift zone (Oct. 9, 1919, 9 p. m., Kahuku outbreak, Mauna Loa, south slope, 7700 feet above sea-level). The flow was incandescent, rough pahoehoe, glowing 3 feet below surface. Estimated temperature of crack 300° C. The tubes were broken at a depth one foot inside a crack 2 inches across, by tapping the fusible tip against the rock wall inside. Sharp hiss reaction of the vacuum obtained, drawing in rock dust as well as vapor. Tubes immediately sealed with paraffined rubber caps. Two tubes filled showing immediate condensation of water on inner walls. A third which gave no vacuum reaction was found to be cracked and was discarded. Well above the vegetation level.

"The two samples collected should serve to indicate the general quality

---

* Bull. Hawaiian Volcano Obs. VII, 94-97. July, 1919.

of the flow gas on Mauna Loa which both in 1916 and 1919 gave the foundry smell, and the analysis may account for the enervating and asphyxiating effects, an odor like pistachio, burning of the eye tissues, irrespirable and insoluble when breathed through wet cloth by way of nostrils; grips the lungs like a vise.''

These gases gave on analysis the results shown in Table I.

TABLE I. COMPOSITION OF TWO GAS SAMPLES FROM MAUNA LOA.

(Volume per cent at 1200° C. and 760 mm.*)

	* No. 1	No. 2
CO_2	3.84	6.42
CO	0.03	0.19
H_2	....	0.01
SO_2	1.22	1.95
SO_3	2.08	8.12
S_2	....	....
Cl_2	....	....
N_2	16.80	15.39
A	0.58	0.42
H_2O	75.44	67.43

The outstanding fact about these samples is the high degree of oxidation. Hydrogen is practically absent and CO is nearly as minute in quantity. Certain unexplained eccentricities in the analytical data might indicate very small amounts of hydrocarbons, but with such minute quantities a definite decision is impossible. In any case everything that could oxidize has done so, yet the amount of nitrogen is not excessive. Here, as in the Kilauea gases, the amount of nitrogen is insufficient to account for the water present.

Perhaps the next important fact is that SO_3 is present in relatively large amount and this accounts for the collector's difficulties, both in breathing and smelling. For it is truly difficult to distinguish odors in an atmosphere of sulfuric acid. It is common experience that SO_3 particles or even H_2SO_4 (as in storage battery rooms) are not easily removed from air.

The rare gases computed as argon are relatively high. Computed on the basis of the fixt gases as analyzed there is an excess of 1.2% for No. 1 and 0.05% for No. 2, over the amount which should be present if **all** N_2 came in as air. These residues have been saved and will be subjected to further study.

The absence of chlorine is interesting, since one might expect relatively large amounts in the gases which break forth after being long confined. Here, as at Kilauea, chlorine is notably lacking as compared with the Italian volcanoes.

The ''foundry smell'' noted by the collector is still unexplained. The writer has encountered it at times at Kilauea but has no explanation to offer nor can he explain its presence in a foundry. It is associated primarily with oxidizing iron or iron silicates; beyond that, information is wanting.

The water content—about seventy per cent—is similar to the Kilauea gases and in both cases is greatly in excess of any possible amount of air as shown by the nitrogen content.

The difficulties of collection are obvious from Dr. Jaggar's field notes. It

* It should be remembered that the calculation of these results to hundredths of a per cent is made necessary by the large amount of water, determined gravimetrically, which enters into the final computation, and it is not pretended that the analysis of the fixt gases is performed with any such phenomenal accuracy.

has happened to the writer as well that a red-hot crack from which flames occasionally break out and from which gas issues with vigor will show complete oxidation of gas so collected.

On the whole, these gases seem to be very like the Kilauea gases, more so than one might have expected.

Carnegie Institution of Washington,
Geophysical Laboratory,
March 22, 1920.

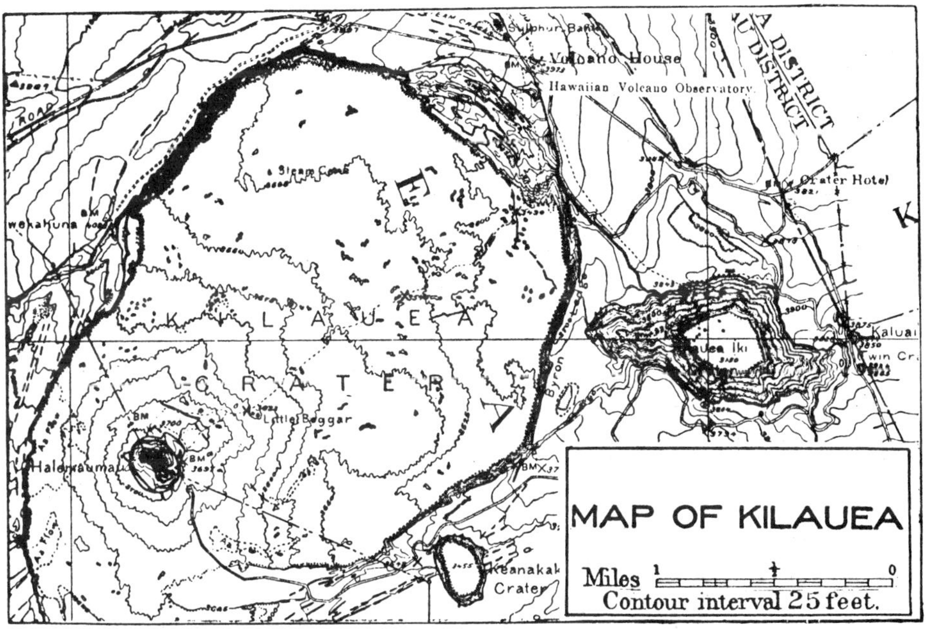

HAWAIIAN VOLCANO OBSERVATORY.

The Observatory is equipped with the following seismometric instruments rebuilt at the station in 1918 for the special needs of volcano research: two Bosch-Omori pendulums, high speed registration of local earthquakes; one optically recording seismograph for distant earthquakes; one clinograph registering E-W tilting of the ground. A vertical component seismograph was in December, 1918, set up in experimental operation. These are seated on concrete piers in a closed basement room having practically constant temperature, beneath the chief Observatory building near the hotel. Time is referred to a rated chronometer, checked at intervals by solar observations with a transit. The chronometer is loaned by the College of Hawaii. Hawaiian standard time (H. S. T.) is 10 hrs. 30 min. slower than Greenwich time.

CANCANI SCALE OF SEISMIC INTENSITY.

Expressed by accelerations measured in millimeters per second per second.

I.	Instrumental	0.0	2.5
II.	Very slight	2.5	5.0
III.	Slight	5.0	10.0
IV.	Sensible, mediocre	10.0	25.0
V.	Rather strong	25.0	50.0
VI.	Strong	50.0	100.0
VII.	Very strong	100.0	250.0
VIII.	Ruinous	250.0	500.0
IX.	Disastrous	500.0	1000.0
X.	Very disastrous	1000.0	2500.0
XI.	Catastrophic	2500.0	5000.0
XII.	Great catastrophe	5000.0	10000.0

Grade IV. is ordinarily the minimum perceived by the senses; and in grade XII, the acceleration or rate of change of motion (jerk) reaches that of terrestrial gravitation.

In the standard form of report the maximum intensity or acceleration, designated by the symbol a, or max. a, is given in the conventional unit of milligal. The milligal is a measure of acceleration, such that 1 milligal $=$ 1/100 mm. per sec. per sec. $= 10\ \mu$. per sec. per sec. The Cancani scale, here defined in terms of millimeters per sec. per sec., can therefore be expressed in milligals by multiplying each of the numbers by 100.

U. S. DEPARTMENT OF AGRICULTURE
WEATHER BUREAU
CHARLES F. MARVIN, CHIEF

MONTHLY BULLETIN
OF THE
Hawaiian Volcano Observatory

VOL. VIII. HONOLULU, HAWAII, JUNE, 1920 No. 6

Week Ending June 4, 1920.

SUMMARY OF CONDITIONS.

The fall of the lava column of Halemaumau that started on May 11, came to an end on May 30 and a rise set in. The total fall between those two dates was about 55 feet. By June 4 the lake level had regained 19 feet and stood at 166 feet below the rim. The rise of the crags during the week was slightly in excess of that of the lakes. As soon as the rise started the fume changed from very heavy to light. The place of maximum upwelling of the liquid lava seems to be in the western side of the pit, for with rising conditions there is rapid streaming out of the western arms, or the western arms stand at a higher level than the others. During the last sinking spell the area of the liquid lava was greatly diminished by new floors forming around most of the lakes.

The activity of the Kau Desert flow is again confined to a flow in a tube in the northeastern fill and spreading out to the south on the east side of the lava ridge. Rumbling and cracking noises in the north end of the lava fill have been going on for some time, but no movement has been detected save for further breakdowns around the window sites.

JOURNAL.

Activity of Halemaumau. The height of the lava and crags, expressed as depressions below the northeast monument on the rim of Halemaumau 3727 feet above sea level, obtained from measurements during the week ending June 4, 1920, are as follows:

	Summit of north crag.	Summit of center island.	Mean lake level
May 28, 8 a. m.	70 feet	85 feet	185 feet
June 4, 11 a. m.	57 feet	63 feet	166 feet

The lava column showed no signs of rising until May 30, so that most of the 19 feet rise indicated above must have taken place in five days. The rise of the center island during the same period was 22 feet.

The pit was very fumy on May 29, and about the same height as on May 28.

At 10 a. m. on May 30 the pit was less fumy than it had been during the past several days. The southeast arm is becoming narrower. The crack in the Kilauea crater floor over the Kau Desert flow has widened in several places near the Halemaumau edge, and is emitting much fume and heat. The crack line is well marked by sulphur deposits.

During the afternoon of May 31 the pit was less fumy and three or four feet higher than on May 30. Streaming was to the east in the southwest arm and to the north in the central channel. A few fountains were playing in each arm.

The lakes were higher on June 1, and the fume was very light. The level of the lava in the southwest arm appeared to be three or four feet higher than the central channel. Avalanches were falling from the central island. A current flowed northward in the central channel into the north arm.

At 9 a. m. on June 2 a rapid current was pouring out of the southwest under a bridge into the central channel. One branch from this current went into the north arm and the other into the southeast arm. The lakes were three or four feet lower than on June 1. At 11 a. m. a rapid rise set in, the liquid coming up four or five feet within an hour. Several avalanches were observed to fall from the central island during the day.

The current from the southwest arm into the central channel was still vigorous on June 3. A rapid current in the central channel was directed toward the narrow isthmus connecting the north crag and the central island. There was sluggish streaming into the southeast arm. A hissing cone was located near the northeast islet. The lakes were quiet with only a few small fountains playing and appeared to be lower than on June 2.

At 10 a. m. on June 4 the pit was more fumy than on June 3, though the lakes appeared to be about the same height. Streaming from the southwest into the central channel still continued.

Activity of the Kau Desert Flow. When the Kau Desert flow was viewed on May 31 great volumes of smoke were issuing from three breakdown sites in the lava tube on the northeast fill. Lava could be heard flowing at one of these places, about 15 feet below the crust, but could not be seen. Some movement was going on in the northeast fill as was evidenced by occasional tremblings that shook the entire mass. Occasionally heavy booming was heard that resembled the gas explosions that take place when lava invades an old pahoehoe flow covered with vegetation though no flowing lava in such a territory could be found.

Seismometric Record. The dates and times of the five local quakes and two teleseisms that were recorded in the Whitney Laboratory of Seismology during the week ending with midnight June 4, are as follows: Local quakes—May 30, 3:45 p. m. and 6:25 p. m., both feeble; June 1, 2:15 a. m. feeble, 10 a. m. light, and 5:40 p. m. feeble. Teleseisms—June 2, 12:50 p. m. feeble; June 4, 6 p. m. moderate, indicated distance 4700 miles. Spasmodic tremor was moderately strong throughout the week. Harmonic tremor was moderately strong on May 31 and June 3, and slight on other days. Microseismic movement was slight. Tilting movement was very slight—to the south and west on May 29, 30 and 31, and to the north and east on other days.

Week Ending June 11, 1920.

SUMMARY OF CONDITIONS.

The rise of the lava column of Halemaumau that started last week was of very short duration, for by the beginning of this week a fall was again in progress. The amount of the fall of the liquid during the week, 26 feet, exceeded the lift of last week by seven feet. The relief of the tallest crag continues about the same, 109 feet. The north crag which was the tallest last week is now about two-thirds of its former height. The southwest arm became visibly connected with the central channel on June 8. The pit has been quite uniformly fumy during the week and the seeing has been poor.

Except for occasional small overflows of lava around the northern end of the lava fill the activity of the Kau Desert flow is confined to a flow in a tube in the high northeastern part of the fill and the spreading out of the lava from this flow in the vicinity of Kamakaia cones. At several places where the river in the above mentioned tube was near the surface a month ago it is now 20 or more feet down. The lowering of the level of the lava in this tube is further evidence that tubes sometime increase in size by wearing away the bottom.

JOURNAL.

Activity of Halemaumau.. The height of the lava and crags, obtained by measurements during the week ended June 11, 1920, when expressed as depressions below the northeast monument on the rim of Halemaumau are as follows:

	Summit of center island	Mean lake level
June 4, 11 a. m.	63 feet	166 feet
June 11, 9 a. m.	83 feet	192 feet

The lava column started to fall about June 4 and in the week ending with June 11, the liquid fell 26 feet or at an average of 3.7 feet per day. The fall of the crag during the same period was 20 feet.

At 7 a. m. on June 5 the pit was moderately fumy and the lakes rather quiet. Three fountains were playing in the central channel and only border fountains and grottos active in the other arms. A current in the central channel was streaming toward the west bay.

The amount of the fume, the lake level, fountaining, and streaming was very much the same on June 6 as on June 5.

At 1 p. m. on June 7 a current was moving southward out of the north arm through the central channel. The pit was moderately fumy. Vigorous fountains were playing in the central channel.

On June 8 at 1 p. m. the fume was moderately thick. The peak of the north crag avalanched to the southeast, leaving the crag only about two-thirds as high as formerly. The fall of the peak was almost opposite in direction to the maximum rise of the crag during uplift. There was northward streaming in the central channel, one branch going toward the west bay and the other into the north arm, which was partially filled up by the avalanches from the north crag. The southwest arm is again connected with the central channel by a narrow gorge, out of which there was rapid streaming.

The pit was very fumy at 1 p. m. on June 9. A large part of the southwest crag has broken off. There was brisk northward streaming in the central channel.

At 10 a. m., on June 11 the pit was very fumy and the lakes quiet. A few small fountains were playing in the central channel and border fountains were active in the west bay and the southeast arm.

Activity of the Kau Desert Flow. When the Kau Desert flow was observed during the forenoon of June 10, the high cone on the north end of the main lava ridge was emitting much more smoke than when last observed. Immense quantities of smoke were also being emitted from an old window in the lava tube in the northeast fill. A lava river 20 feet below the crust was observed through a window on the south side of the northeast fill at the same place which has been open for over a month. Practically all of the activity is on the east side of the lava fill and to the south towards the Kamakaia cones.

Seismometric Record. The one feeble, local earthquake that was recorded in the Whitney Laboratory of Seismology during the week ending with midnight, June 11, 1920, occurred at 12:25 p. m., June 9. Spasmodic tremor was moderately strong throughout the week. Harmonic tremor was slight. Microseismic movement was moderately strong on the 6th and 7th and slight on other days. Tilting movement was moderate to the east on the 5th, moderate to the north on the 11th, and slight or nearly stationary on other days.

Week Ending June 18, 1920.

SUMMARY OF CONDITIONS.

The fall of the lava column of Halemaumau that started last week continued slowly during the current week. The fall of the liquid lava during the week, 6 feet, is the smallest weekly change in level that has occurred since the first week of May, 1920. The relief of the tallest crag above the liquid has commenced to decrease and was 102 feet on June 18. There were four separate lakes again, though a tunnel connecting the southwest arm with the central channel was visible. That all the different lakes have tunnel connections was shown by all the lakes falling quite uniformly when a cascade was in action in the east lake on June 17. Northward streaming in the central channel and into the north arm has been nearly continuous during the week.

At the Kau Desert flow there has been some flowing to the south from the high northern end of the main lava ridge, though the main activity is much the same as during the past several weeks—a river in a tube leading south from the northeastern fill and spreading out of the lava from tubes in the vicinity of the Kamakaia cones. A fountaining lava lake was revealed by a breakdown near the tall cone on the northern end of the main lava ridge during the morning of June 17.

JOURNAL.

Activity of Halemaumau. The height of the lava and crags, expressed as depressions below the northeast monument on the rim of Halemaumau, obtained from measurements during the week ending June 18, 1920, are as follows:

	Peak center island	Mean lake level
June 11, 9 a. m.	83 feet	192 feet
June 18 8:30 p. m.	96 feet	198 feet

The fall of the liquid lava during the seven days ending with June 18, was but six feet. During the same period the peak of the center island fell 13 feet. The relief of the tallest crag above the liquid was seven feet less on June 18 than on June 11.

At 5 p. m. on June 12 the pit was fumy with the odor of hydrogen sulphide very pronounced. A current was flowing out of the southwest arm through a tunnel into the central channel. Large border fountains and grottos were playing in all arms of the lake.

The pit was very fumy at 10 a. m., on June 13. The current through the tunnel from the southwest arm into the central pool was still vigorous. The lake level appeared to be much the same as on June 12.

At 3 p. m., on June 14 the pit was very fumy and the liquid at about the same level as during the past several days. There was pronounced streaming to a large grotto in the southeast arm and out of the southwest arm through the tunnel leading into the central channel. Three large fountains were almost continuous in the central channel and border fountains and grottos were playing in the other arms of the lake.

At 4 p. m. on June 15 all arms of the lake were rather quiet and the pit fumy. No currents except sluggish streaming to a few grottos were observed.

The lakes were about 10 feet below the lower inner ramparts at 8:30 a. m. on June 16, or about 4 feet lower than on the 15th. At 2 p. m. the lakes had risen so that the liquid was only about five feet below their ramparts. A northward moving current in the central channel went into the north arm, where it was directed to a border fountain on the east side. The pit was less fumy than on the 15th.

At 1 p. m. on June 17 the pit was so fumy that but little could be seen. Judging from the noise, however, fountaining was very vigorous in all of the lakes. At about 9 p. m. the lakes fell rapidly when a cascade in the northern end of the east lake commenced.

A rapid current out of the southwest arm was observed at 8 p. m. on June 18. Very vigorous currents were, at times, directed to grottos in the southeast arm. There was slow streaming to the north in the central channel. Numerous border fountains were active in all the lakes. Two large fountains were continuously playing in the central channel.

Activity of the Kau Desert Flow. When the Kau Desert flow was observed during the forenoon of June 16, much smoke was issuing from the large cone on the northern end of the main lava ridge and from windows in the tube in the northeastern fill. The lava river below the large window on the south slope of the northeastern fill has sealed over. Another small window was found a few feet to the south with its walls incandescent to within a few inches of the top. A flow from the north end of the main lava ridge, the height of which has recently increased about 25 feet, cascaded into the breakdown amphitheater mentioned on Feb. 1 and 3 and March 19, 1920. During the morning of June 17 a collapse occurred on the southeast side of the tall cone on the northern end of the main lava ridge and revealed a fountaining lake about 25 feet across.

Seismometric Record. The dates and times of the three local quakes that were recorded in the Whitney Laboratory of Seismology during the week ending with midnight June 18, 1920, are as follows: June 13, 12:20 p. m. slight, felt in Hilo; June 13, 1:45 p. m., very feeble; June 14, 8 a. m., very feeble. Spasmodic tremor was moderately strong until the 15th and slight thereafter. Harmonic tremor and microseisms were slight. Tilting movement was moderately strong to the north and west on the 16th, to the south and east on the 17th and to the west on the 18th. On other days the movement was slight or stationary.

Week Ending June 25, 1920.

SUMMARY OF CONDITIONS.

The subsidence of the lava column was more rapid during the current week than during the past. The level of the liquid lava on June 26 was 234 feet below the rim, having fallen 36 feet during the eight days ending on that date. The relief of the tallest crag above the liquid continues to decrease and was 92 feet on June 26. The pit was quite uniformly smoky during the week. Avalanches from the crags and walls were more or less daily occurrences. Northward streaming in the central channel was again almost continuous during the week.

At the Kau Desert flow, the small lava lake on the summit of the main lava fill at its northern end continues to simulate a small volcano by alternate crusting over and breaking out with explosive fountains. A flow in a tube from this region comes to the surface below the Kamakaia cones and toes out as the heavy sharkskin type of pahoehoe lava. Several of these toes invaded wooded regions and made tree molds.

JOURNAL.

Activity of Halemaumau. The height of the lava and crags, expressed as depressions below the northeast monuments (3727 ft.) on the rim of Halemaumau, obtained from measurements during the week ending June 26, 1920 are as follows:

	Mean lake level	Peak center island
June 18, 8:30 p. m.	198 feet	96 feet
June 26, 3 p. m.	234 feet	142 feet

During the eight days ending with June 26, the liquid fell 36 feet, or at an average of 4.5 feet per day. During the same period the peak of the center island was lowered 46 feet; a part of this lowering, however, was due to the island breaking down. The relief of the tallest crag has been decreasing during the last two weeks and on June 26, it was 92 feet above the liquid.

At 4 p. m. on June 19, 1920, the pit was less fumy than during the past several days. A vigorous current was flowing out of the southeast arm, one branch from which went to a grotto at the entrance to the arm and the other into the central channel. A rapid current was moving northward in the central channel. Avalanches fell from the south crag. Four or five fountains were playing continuously in the central channel.

The pit was moderately fumy at 4 p. m. on June 20. A northward moving current in the central channel went into the north arm.

The smoke from the Kau Desert flow was plainly visible from the volcano road during the afternoon on June 21. A hissing vent near the entrance to the southeast arm of the lake was making much noise. This is the first hissing vent or cone that has been heard in over 2 weeks. The east lake was fountaining more vigorously than usual. A sluggish current flowed through a tunnel from the southwest arm into the central channel. There was but very little streaming in any of the lake arms. The fume was moderately thick.

At 1 p. m. on June 22, there was rapid streaming into the north arm and slow streaming out of the southwest arm. Avalanches fell from the north crag. The pit was less fumy than on the 21st, and the lakes about the same height. More fume than common was issuing from the southwest floor crack near the rim of Halemaumau.

The pit was moderately fumy during the forenoon of June 23 and the lake level lower than on June 22. The north arm was heavily crusted over and all the lakes were rather quiet, only a few border fountains playing in each arm. A large sector of the "plaster" on the south-southwest wall fell off.

At 8 p. m. on June 25, a slow current was pouring through the tunnel leading from the southwest arm to the central channel. There was slight northward streaming in the central channel. A current moved from under a crust in the recess between the north crag and the central island. Most of the northward streaming went into the narrow arm. Avalanches fell from the south crag.

Activity of the Kau Desert Flow. The Kau Desert flow was observed over its entire length on June 25 by going in at its northern end, and then walking down the east side of the new flow along the 1823 ridge. The only visible activity at the northern end, aside from several densely smoking vents at breakdown sites in the lava tube in the northeastern fill, was the crusted summit pond on the main lava ridge. This pond broke out with explosive fountains several times during the day. On going south along the new flow belt the lava got hotter in the vicinity of the middle Kamakaia cone and in the frontal region, about one mile above Puu Kouele, there were numerous surface streams of the sharkskin type. Along the edges of the flow there was burning timber and many explosions in old caverns were heard. The eastern branch of the January, 1920, aa flow in this region has been buried in many places by heavy pahoehoe. A wooded kipuka between the January aa courses had just been invaded by the new flow and many glowing tree molds with the wood still burning inside were observed. The lava feeding this front is all coming through tubes from away up at the head of Mauna Iki and this mechanism is closely analagous to the Postal Rift flow of October-November, 1919. Returning by the lower lava heap in the sand dunes it was found that the rift crack along the east side of the foot of the heap showed renewed steaming and was quite hot. There were no signs of any activity in the heap.

Seismometric Record. The dates and times of the six local quakes that were recorded in the Whitney Laboratory of Seismology during the week ending with midnight June 25, are as follows: June 19, 5:50 a. m., 12:15 p. m., and 7:00 p. m., all very feeble. June 22, 7:15 a. m feeble, and 2:25 p. m., very feeble. June 23, 12:40 p. m., feeble. Spasmodic tremor was slight on June 22nd and moderately strong on other days. Harmonic tremor was slight.

1. Pit and cave in 1823 ridge, 1920 ridge in background: Kau Desert. (Photo Finch)

2. 1823 cave, gypsum sheets and stalactites. (Photo Jaggar)

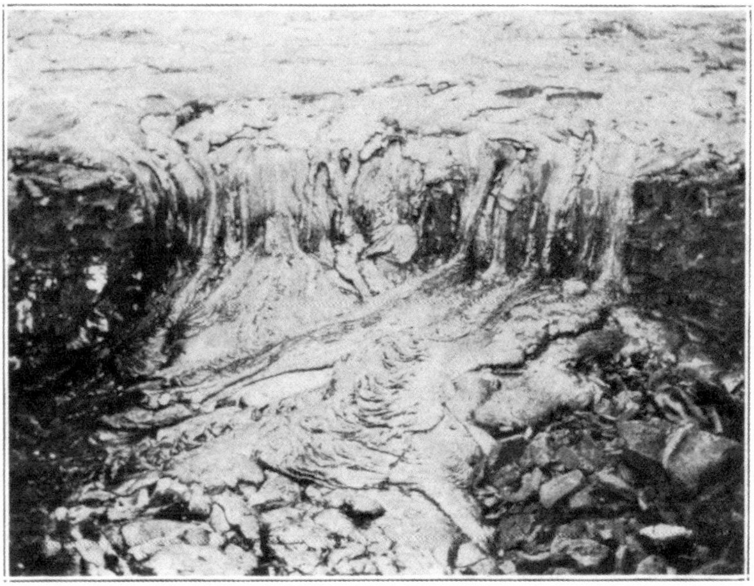

3. Cascade of 1920 lava in 1823 pit; May, 1920. (Photo Finch)

4. June 25, 1920: pahoehoe front of 1920 flow below Kamakaia Hills. (Photo Jaggar)

Microseismic movement was moderately strong on June 25, and slight on other days. Tilting movement was slight and irregular during the week.

Week Ending July 2, 1920.

SUMMARY OF CONDITIONS.

The beginning of July finds the lava pit of Halemaumau a large circular cauldron occupied by lava lakes and crags and much smoke. There are two inner shelves on the north side of the pit. During the week there has been increased subsidence with falling of debris from the crags and walls, a more or less regular central fountain and streaming outward from the southwest lake towards the center of the pit. Great masses of Pele's hair have accumulated in mossy banks on the northeast wall of the pit. The volume of fume is sufficient to obscure the view in daytime from all but the northern and western sides. There has been some blowing noise from lake margins, where crusting confines the gas.

The flow in the Kau Desert continues a slow but steady progress, pahoehoe lava creeping through tunnels of its own crust for a distance of about five miles from a source at the northern end of the January ridge, now spoken of as the "little mountain" or Mauna Iki. At the source there is only a small pond which is spasmodically active, and a fuming east-west fissure across the northern brow of the ridge. The pahoehoe flood has moved parallel with the January aa flow, and on the eastern side of that flow, being banked up against it, and even overflowing it in places. The whole tract of country a quarter to a half mile wide between the January flow and the Kamakaia hills is flooded with the new pahoehoe and the advancing front is a mile or so south of these hills.

On June 29 an expedition was made to the summit crater Mokuaweoweo on Mauna Loa, by way of Puu Ulaula. No new activity was apparent in Mokuaweoweo and there was no sign of any ejects later than 1914. Riding and pack mules were taken all the way to the summit by the northern route, which has hitherto been considered impassable for animals.

JOURNAL.

Activity of Halemaumau. Measurements during the week ending July 3, 1920, expressed as depression below the northeast monument on the rim of Halemaumau (3727 feet above sea-level) have been as follows:

	Mean lake level	Peak central island
June 26, 3 p. m.	234 feet	142 feet
July 3, 1 p. m.	259 feet	———

During the seven days ending July 3 the lake subsided 25 feet, averaging 3.6 feet per day. The peak of the central island was too smoky for measurement on July 3, but it appeared to stand about 95 feet above the lake level.

There was little noticeable change in the general condition of the pit at 3 p. m. Saturday, June 26. Some falls of rock were heard along the northwest wall and from the north crag and center island. There was a large intermittent rhythmic central fountain in the central channel and another fountain broke the surface of the center of the west pond. All the arms of the lake showed border fountaining. The southwest peak of the central crag mass appeared higher than the northeast peak and emitted much smoke from chasms and cracks. A slight current poured through a tunnel from the southwest lake into the central channel and there was some streaming northward into the north arm.

On June 27 at 4 p. m. the large central fountain broke noisily at about 30-second intervals. The west lake inspected from the west side of the pit was seen to have become a remarkable cauldron hemmed in by a semicircle of uplifted crag matter, showing horizontal spatter marks except for a serrate row of upturned benches on its crest. The horizontal marks reached to the May high level, which had left an inner shelf depressed about 100 feet below the rim of the pit around the northern and western sides. The fountaining in the west pool was variable and the streaming was toward a persistent grotto on its western side.

The southwest lake had become an arm of the main lake, with a torrent pouring from it northeastward through a narrow canyon into the central pool. The southwest pool was stagnant and showed some border fountains. Streaming in the southeast arm was mostly southeastward. A broad upheaved flat separated this arm from the east lake, which is entirely shut off as a separate pond. There is another lifted flat area separating the southeast arm from the southwest lake. A high northeastern crag separated the east lake from the north arm and there were high peaks north and south of the west pool, but the south crag lying on the east side of the south pool outlet was relatively low. The remnants of the former marginal crags west and southwest had largely tumbled into confused talus heaps.

Dense fume was rising from the southwest rift where it crossed the Kilauea floor at the base of the southwestern slag-heap that had been piled against the Kilauea wall in December, 1919. Near the instrument hut northeast of Halemaumau a new hot solfataric patch is giving off blue fume.

On June 28 at 6 p. m., the pit was fumy, the central pool appeared wider, the narrow torrent continued to lead northward from the southwest pool and some small avalanches fell from the south wall of the pit. The central fountain continued to explode periodically and the lakes elsewhere appeared more crusted.

On June 29 at 2 p. m. the west pond was covered with smooth crust except at its west end, where there were bright lines and occasional fountains. Fountaining and blowing noises came from the center of the pit and the southeast arm was crusted. In the central channel the lake appeared wider and higher. A southern avalanche was heard at 2:40 p. m. The liquid had risen around the small islet in the central channel.

On June 30 at 2 p. m., the west pond bank stood about one foot above the lake and travelling fountains were moving northward along the southwest pool outlet. The southeast arm appeared slightly lower and several rock falls were heard from the south wall of the pit, one of these quite heavy at 2:20 p. m.

At 10 a. m. Friday, July 2, the fresh border bench of the southeast arm stood five or six feet above the liquid and the streaming was from the central region into this arm and from the end of the arm northwestward, the two currents bending northward to bombard the shore with the constant fountaining. Some fountaining could be seen in the east lake. The west pond was stagnant and five feet below its banks. The current out of the southwest pool swept northward as a narrow brook between two flat promontories and, emerging into the central pool, the lava poured southeastward on both sides of an islet and westward to three fountaining border grottoes. The regular central fountain lay west of the islet and erupted about every half minute. Small rock movements were frequently heard in the talus east and south.

Seismometric Record. During the week ending midnight July 2, 1920, two local earthquakes and one teleseism were registered, as follows. Local shocks, June 30, 5:40 a. m., very feeble, and July 1, 3:15 a. m., feeble. Teleseism, very slight, June 28, 12:30 p. m. Spasmodic tremor increased somewhat during the week, the maximum being several strong spasms July 1. Harmonic tremor was slight, with increase to moderate June 30. Microseismic motion was slight, increasing slightly June 29. Tilting was dominantly northerly and slight, at a maximum July 1, and but little movement in the east-west azimuth.

Expedition to Mauna Loa. The writer, R. H. Finch, John Kama (guide) and Joseph Kaipalaoa (packer) left Keauhou Ranch June 29 at 8 a. m. for the annual inspection of Mokuaweoweo, the summit crater of Mauna Loa. The equipage consisted of four riding and three pack mules. The rest house at Puu Ulaula was reached at 2:15 p. m. On June 30 with one pack and four saddle animals, the party entered on the upper trail at 8 a. m., and reached Mokuaweoweo at 1 p. m. This was the first time that this trail had been traversed with a complete pack-train.

The animals and guides were sent back to the rest house, and Messrs. Jaggar and Finch camped in a cavern near a waterhole and explored the floor of Mokuaweoweo. Photographs were obtained of the northern pit crater, the walls of the north, middle and south craters, the central cones, the great south cone and pit of 1914, and some details of lava texture. There was no evidence of recent activity, though the cones and western lava fields of 1914 were stained and fuming with solfataric emanations. A line of old rifts trending northwest from the extreme northern brink of the north bay of Mokuaweoweo was found, and believed to lead to the 1859 source cones. The minimum temperature registered was 28° F. and the maximum 73°. The weather was fine and calm, and the air excessively dry.

We left the summit at 3:20 p. m. July 1 and camped near one of the northeast rift cones at elevation 11,900 feet. July 2 we met the pack-train a few miles farther down the trail and returned the same day to the Observatory, arriving about 5 p. m.

Very respectfully,

T. A. JAGGAR, Jr.
Volcanologist.

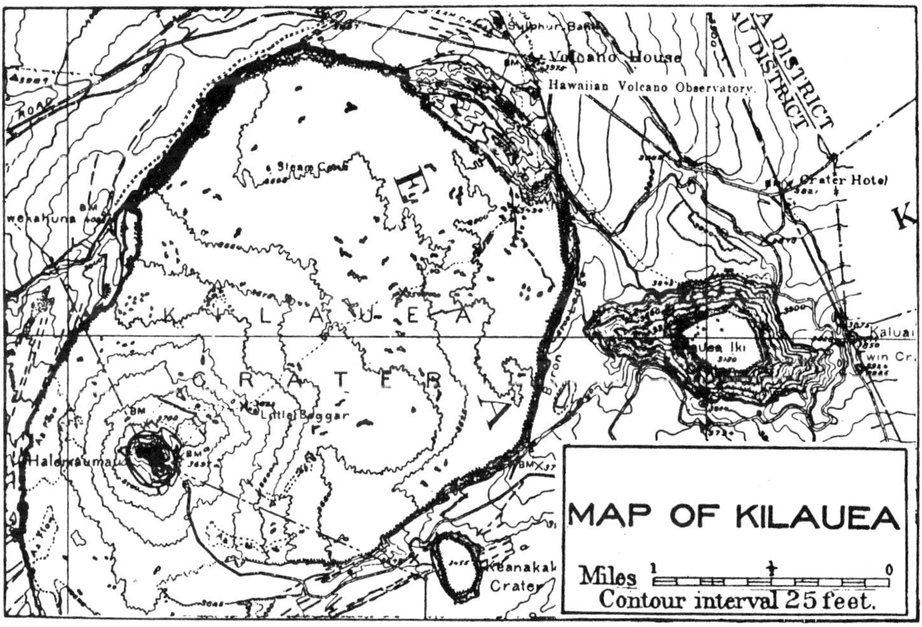

HAWAIIAN VOLCANO OBSERVATORY.

The Observatory is equipped with the following seismometric instruments rebuilt at the station in 1918 for the special needs of volcano research: two Bosch-Omori pendulums, high speed registration of local earthquakes; one optically recording seismograph for distant earthquakes; one clinograph registering E-W tilting of the ground. A vertical component seismograph was in December, 1918, set up in experimental operation. These are seated on concrete piers in a closed basement room having practically constant temperature, beneath the chief Observatory building near the hotel. Time is referred to a rated chronometer, checked at intervals by solar observations with a transit. The chronometer is loaned by the College of Hawaii. Hawaiian standard time (H. S. T.) is 10 hrs. 30 min. slower than Greenwich time.

CANCANI SCALE OF SEISMIC INTENSITY.

Expressed by accelerations measured in millimeters per second per second.

I.	Instrumental	0.0	2.5
II.	Very slight	2.5	5.0
III.	Slight	5.0	10.0
IV.	Sensible, mediocre	10.0	25.0
V.	Rather strong	25.0	50.0
VI.	Strong	50.0	100.0
VII.	Very strong	100.0	250.0
VIII.	Ruinous	250.0	500.0
IX.	Disastrous	500.0	1000.0
X.	Very disastrous	1000.0	2500.0
XI.	Catastrophic	2500.0	5000.0
XII.	Great catastrophe	5000.0	10000.0

Grade IV. is ordinarily the minimum perceived by the senses; and in grade XII, the acceleration or rate of change of motion (jerk) reaches that of terrestrial gravitation.

In the standard form of report the maximum intensity or acceleration, designated by the symbol a, or max. a, is given in the conventional unit of milligal. The milligal is a measure of acceleration, such that 1 milligal = 1/100 mm. per sec. per sec. = 10 μ. per sec. per sec. The Cancani scale, here defined in terms of millimeters per sec. per sec., can therefore be expressed in milligals by multiplying each of the numbers by 100.

U. S. DEPARTMENT OF AGRICULTURE
WEATHER BUREAU
CHARLES F. MARVIN, CHIEF

MONTHLY BULLETIN
OF THE
Hawaiian Volcano Observatory

VOL. VIII. HONOLULU, HAWAII, JULY, 1920 No. 7

Week Ending July 9, 1920.

SUMMARY OF CONDITIONS.

The sinking of the Halemaumau lava column has passed the 300-foot depression line and the general situation at the end of the week finds the crags sinking rapidly and the lava lakes tending to crust over and to become smoky and sluggish. The period has been notable for several spells of pronounced displacement of the liquid by the subsiding bench magma, whereby the lakes have risen strongly relative to their shorelines and so new marginal benches have been built. The total downward movement appears to have passed its maximum and the lakes show some symptoms of the beginning, of recovery though the crags continue to go down. Avalanches have been frequent from the walls of the pit.

The level of the lava in the source pond of the Kau Desert flow fluctuates in height and the stream flowing in tunnels can be seen through a roof-window. The whole arrangement is much the same as in the case of the Postal Rift flow on the Kilauea floor in November, 1919. The front of the flow has filled in the country between the lower Kamakaia hill and Puu Kouele and is progressing very sluggishly by welling up and spreading out as a vast hot pudding of smooth lava with a crust only a few inches thick, and liquid pahoehoe welling up here and there.

JOURNAL.

Activity of Halemaumau.—Measurements during the week ending July 9, 1920, expressed as depression below the northeast monument (3727 feet above sea level) have been as follows:

	Mean lake level	Peak Central Island
July 3, 1 p. m.	259 feet	
July 9, 4 p. m.	301 feet	207 feet

During the six days ending July 9 the lake subsided 42 feet, averaging seven feet per day. The crag summit of the central island had gone down since June 26 sixty-five feet, averaging five feet per day. On June 26 its relief above the lake was 92 feet, and on July 9, 94 feet.

At 1 p. m. July 3 the fume was dense in the pit and there was rumbling noise from the border fountains. A current poured through a narrow channel from the southwest arm into the central pool of the main lake. In this pool two central fountains played occasionally. The north arm was heavily crusted. The lakes appeared to be lower relative to their banks and numerous border fountains were in action. At 9:30 p. m. the marginal benches stood about five feet above the lakes and the maximum fountaining activity was in the center. Two avalanches occurred at the southeast wall of the pit. At 11 p. m. the liquid lava had risen about three feet, and continued to rise.

On July 4, at 3 to 5 p. m. the fume was thick on the east and south sides of the pit, but the seeing was moderately good from the northwest. A remarkable rise took place during the afternoon. At 3 p. m. the lakes stood about three feet below their marginal shelves and a narrow rivulet poured through the channel from the southwest pond to the center. In the central pool a rhythmic fountain burst from time to time. Some sliding was heard toward the south and east. About 4 p. m. the lakes had begun to rise rapidly and at 5 p. m. the liquid was at least 20 feet higher than when first seen. The border shelves were all drowned under new floods, and pronounced blowing noises gave evidence of strong gas pressure. The southwest pond was now connected with the center by a broad channel, and a second channel connected it with the southeastern arm of the lake through an eastern chasm in the southern crag mass, the crag being thus converted into an island. Overflows were pouring southward from the eastern end of the southeast arm so as to flood the floor leading thence toward the southwest pond. A cone in the middle of this latter pond was puffing and being rapidly drowned by the rising lava. The banks of the central rivulet were completely flooded across so as to drown the peninsula which had separated that rivulet from the southeast arm. All avalanching noises entirely ceased during the rising spell.

An exploration of the Postal Rift tunnel on this day revealed a large chamber inclined downward under the source cone. This cavern trended southward in the direction of Halemaumau and on climbing down into it, the wrter found three feeding wells narrowing to irregular inclined fissures a few feet across. These fissures dipped in the direction of the pit and showed trends, the one toward the southeast, the other toward the southwest. The general arrangement showed an increase in size of the vent upward as though the melt under pressure below, opened a larger orifice for itself above when relieved of pressure. The same arrangement was found in a second tunnel leading southward from the forks of the cavern. This also ended in a rift trending towards the southwest and showed strong inclination downward in the direction of Halemaumau. On looking down the narrow fissure in which the cavern ended two orifices could be seen over 20 feet below admitting daylight, possibly from windows in the northern well of Halemaumau above the north shelf.

On following the tube away from Halemaumau to the openings where large stalactites of magnesium sulphate were collected in January 1920, these coatings of soluble salts were found to have become dry and powdery and great quantities of the white powder lay on the floor of the cavern. A quarter mile farther from the source along the cavern the interior became intolerably hot and here fresh sulphate stalactites hung from the roof.

On Monday, July 5, at 5 p. m., the smoke in Halemaumau had increased and the lakes had again subsided relative to the crags. There was sluggish fountaining in ten or twelve border grottoes and the rhythmic central fountain broke the surface in large dome bursts. The stream from the southwest lake was again a rivulet between banks, which marked a winding chasm in a flat overflow platform between the central and southern crags. This stream flowed rapidly and was covered with an arch of crust in two places. The banks of fresh lava formed by the rise of the previous day stood in different places from 8 to 15 feet above the lake levels. One strong avalanche was heard. A pulpit rock about 15 feet high was observed on the east side of the east lake. Dense fume puffed from a hole under the lower north shelf and also from the summit of the central crag. In the Kilauea floor a quarter mile from Halemaumau two fuming holes sent up dense masses of vapor from the southwest rift leading to the Kau flow.

On July 6, at 5 p. m., the fume had diminished and the lakes were higher.

There was a blowing cone on the bench east of the central pool and two more under the south crag, these at times being very noisy. The central fountain continued its activity and avalanches fell from both the walls and crags. The streaming had diminished and for a time a current was seen pouring from the central pool towards the southwest arm, reversing the former direction of flow. The north arm remained crusted.

At 8 p. m. July 7 the former rivulet had become a separate pool with tunnels on each side of it through which the current poured from the southwest arm towards the center of the pit. There had been a recent overflow of the benches as shown by glowing crusts on the south floor between the southeast arm and the southwest pond. The flats around the south crag contained numerous glowing holes, some of which were flaming, and these holes reached some distance up the flank of the crag. The rhythmic fountain in the center had become continuous and there were times when the current poured out of the central pool into the southwest arm.

At 4 p. m. July 8, there was smoke all around the walls and from the central crag. The principal noises were of fountaining and a rumbling accompanied with puffing from the south grotto. Clinging crag remnants could be seen at the base of the southwest wall of the pit 100 feet above the bottom. Avalanches were common and a strong one fell from the south wall at 4:55 p. m. There were numerous grottoes hung with stalactites about the lakes. The southeast arm was fountaining in six places, its banks were 10 feet high and along with the strong southeastward streaming there were occasional travelling fountains. The north arm showed four fountains with steaming to the grottoes and some sliding at the north talus. The west arm of the central pool was stagnant, except for two border grottoes and had banks 10 feet high. The west pond was oval in shape and appeared higher than the central pool. Its inner bench stood 10 feet high at the north end and five feet high at the south. There were slides in motion on the southwest talus. The upper inner bench around the west pond stood five feet above the lower bench at the north end, and two feet above it at the south end. Above the southwest talus there was an open crack which made the talus stand out from the wall of the pit. The general situation around the west pond suggested that the bench magma was lowering most at the south end. The pond was crusted except at the west grotto. The bedding or terracing on the central crag was horizontal and there were strong cracks athwart the crag. In the south crag there were fuming and glowing patches and the terracing on the sides of the crag dipped towards the south. On the north crag these terrace marks were horizontal below and upturned above. The northeast crag exhibited a large scar of broken wall overhanging the central pool. On this pool there were polyhedral patches of skin and the streaming poured through the central rivulet from the southwest lake under arches through a gorge 10 feet deep in the new bench. The southwest lake had an occasional central fountain and showed heavy stalactites in its south grotto.

On July 9 at 4 p. m., the lakes again appeared lower and there were avalanches from the walls of the pit. Part of the floor between the south and center crags had collapsed, but the current still poured through the gorge from the southwest pond to the central pool. There was much crust on the lakes and fountaining continued in the central region. There were the usual border grottoes.

Activity of Kau Desert Flow.—At 1 p. m. July 4, the lava pond on the summit of Mauna Iki was visited. The level of the lava was found to fluctuate through a range of six or seven feet and occasionally the crust broke up with very explosive fountaining. The flow eastward through the tube that feeds the front by Kamakaia could barely be seen through a small window in the roof.

On July 7 the foot of the flow was visited and the whole region between the January aa and the lower Kamakaia hill was found covered with a very not lava field that was flowing sluggishly. This was all pahoehoe and was riding over the January aa from east to west. Pushing toes were seen here and there on the surface of the flow, partly of the shark-skin texture, but mostly of glistening smooth lava with a crust only a few inches thick. Some bushes were burning at the margin of the flow.

At the edge of a river-way in the midst of the hardened aa lava there was found a zone of remarkable arborescent red oxide of iron where apparently burning gas had played out from the shearing crack between the bank lava and the moving stream.

Seismometric Record.—During the week ending at midnight, July 9, 1920, two local earthquakes and one teleseism were registered as follows. Local shocks: July 6, 3:20 a. m., perceptible, awakening some sleepers; July 7, 6:50 a. m., feeble. Teleseism July 5, 4:30 p. m. Spasmodic and harmonic tremor were both slight during the week. Microseismic motion was slight. Tilting was moderate to the southwest until July 6 inclusive, then moderate to the northeast July 7 and 8, and stationary July 9.

Week Ending July 16, 1920.

SUMMARY OF CONDITIONS.

There has been very little change in Halemaumau during the week, and the rate of subsidence has decreased to less than two feet per day. The crags have distinctly lowered faster than the lakes, the latter tending to crust over and form blowing cones.

The source pond of the Mauna Iki lava flow continues to fluctuate through a small range and has slightly enlarged, and there are occasional spells of breaking up of the crust with fountaining.

During this week the first party of tourists has gone through to Mokuaweoweo on muleback from the house at Puu Ulaula and back, making the journey from camp to summit in 4.5 hours and the return in four hours. This route is now therefore practicable for riding animals, as determined by the Observatory party June 30.

JOURNAL.

Activity of Halemaumau.—Measurements during the week ending July 17, 1920, expressed as depression below the northeast monument (3727 feet above sea level) have been as follows:

	Mean Lake Level.	Peak Central Island.
July 9, 4 p. m.	301 feet	207 feet
July 17, 8 p. m.	314 feet	

In eight days the lake subsided 13 feet, averaging 1.6 feet per day. The relief of the island peak had diminished at the end of the week, but on account of smoke it was not measurable.

At noon Saturday, July 10, the fume was somewhat thinner but the seeing was poor. Avalanches continued and the lakes stood high relative to the crags. The south crag appeared to be sinking relative to the lake level so that the overflow floors were increasing around it. The west pond had also flooded its banks. About twelve fountains could be counted, including an occasional central fountain. The rivulet from the southwest lake to the central pool was covered with an arch of crust in its middle portions. Along the rift on the Kilauea floor southwest there was much sulphur deposited and two marked smoke holes were in action.

At 11 a. m. July 11, some rock slides were heard and the streaming in the main lake was somewhat towards the center from the north, west and southwest. Elsewhere the lakes were stagnant. The channel arch was broken so that the southwest rivulet occupied a continuous gorge. It is worthy of note that the three outlying lakes east, west and southwest lie directly against the vertical wall of the pit on their outer sides as though each of these were fed by the wall-crack.

July 31 at 11 a. m. the lakes showed idle marginal fountaining and the east pond was boiling on its north side. A deep cavern could be seen under the central platform on the west side of the central pool. Rock slides were observed on the north and south sides of the pit. There was some noisy puffing from the central grottoes. Dense fume rose from the southwest rift in the Kilauea floor. The remnants of the May shelf 100 feet below the Kilauea rim could be seen still clinging to the wall of the pit on its east and southeast sides.

At 6 p. m. July 14 the crags appeared lower and the north, west, central and southwest pools were crusted and showed a tendency to form pot-hole fountains in the midst of heavy shells. Eight fountains were counted. On the platform west of the central channel a glowing filagree heap had formed where there was violent discharge of gas which lifted a lid on the side of the heap. The rivulet channel showed no flowing and had become a series of crusted pools. The streaming in the central pool was from the west arm to the southeast arm and the latter showed bright lines and thin skin. Only a few stones were heard falling. Fountaining in the east pond was against the northeast bank.

At 3 p. m. July 16 the lakes were somewhat lower with benches six to eight feet above them. The central rivulet had become a small pond, no streaming was detected and some avalanches fell from the walls of the pit.

Activity of the Kau Desert Flow.—On July 10 the source pond on Mauna Iki was reported enlarging by collapse of the margins with some fountaining. On July 13 the lake was still larger, five feet below the edge, and occasionally fountaining. This kind of activity continued without change.

Seismometric Record.—During the week ending midnight, July 16, two local earthquakes and one teleseism were registered as follows: Local shocks July 10, 4:30 a. m., feeble; 11:10 p. m., very feeble. Teleseism July 10, 2:20 p. m., light. A moderate local shock was felt in Hilea at 12:40 a. m., July 15. Spasmodic tremor increased from a few weak spasms per day to several moderate spasms per day. Harmonic microtremor increased from slight to moderate. Microseismic motion was mostly slight. Movement of tilting was at first stationary, then slightly to the south and west July 12-13, changing thereafter to east and north with strong eastward tendency July 15.

Week Ending July 23, 1920.

SUMMARY OF CONDITIONS.

The third week in July shows a further diminution in rate of sinking of the lakes of Halemaumau, now less than a foot per day, the crags subsiding much faster than the lakes and so lessening their relief. The pit continues smoky and the only changes are increased building out of the marginal benches around the lakes.

The lake at the source of the Kau Desert flow has subsided in its pit 15 to 20 feet and a second live pit with lava in its bottom has collapsed at the smoke vents on the northern brow of the Mauna Iki ridge. The flowing lava can no longer be seen in the roof-window of the flow tube. A considerable deposit of blue copper sulphate was found on the edges of cracks in incandescent rock near the north pit where the tube leading from the pit had slumped.

JOURNAL.

Activity of Halemaumau.—Measurements during the week ending July 24, 1920, expressed as depression below the northeast monument (3727 feet below sea level) have been as follows:

	Mean Lake Level	Peak Central Island.
July 17, 8 p. m.	314 feet	
July 24, 2 p. m.	320 feet	252 feet

In the seven days ending July 24 the lake has subsided six feet, averaging 0.9 feet per day and in 15 days from July 9 to July 24 the crag summit has gone down 45 feet, averaging three feet per day. The relief of the crag above the mean lake level has thus changed from 94 feet to 68 feet.

On Saturday, July 17, at 7 p. m. there was a sluggish current out of the central pool through the tunnels leading to the southwest arm. The west bay of the central pool was deeply crusted. The south grotto was persistently active.

On July 18 the pit was emitting dense smoke. At 11 a. m. July 20, there was some seeing from the northwest rim at intervals. A new bench of overflow around the lakes stood about eight feet above the liquid lava making an extensive platform around the south crag on the southwest pond side as well as in the center of the pit. The south crag accordingly appeared much submerged. The rivulet from the southwest arm was covered over by the platform, but it was visibly streaming through its tunnel at the outlet into the central pool. In the corner of the west arm of the central pool, at the northern base of the central crag, a flaming cone had formed with a glowing orifice one foot in diameter in its summit. The west pond had built a new flood bench which lapped up against the southwest talus. The southeast arm was alive and fountaining and several active grottoes were visible at the margin of the southwest pond. Avalanches were numerous.

On July 21 at 7 a. m., seeing was difficult, but no streaming was detected. The large south grotto was active and there was noisy fountaining at the region of the north arm. No avalanches were heard.

At 11 a. m. July 22 the pit continued smoky and quiet. A bench on the west side of the central pool was seen to fall in, the liquid standing 10 feet below the platform. The fountaining noises were moderate and most of the smoke appeared to be coming from the central crag and the marginal talus heaps as usual. Beginning on the evening of July 23, there was marked thinning of the fumes as though the lakes were rising, and the combustion of the gases becoming more complete.

Activity of the Kau Desert Flow.—A visit to the flow source 10 to 12 a. m. on July 18 determined the source pond to be 75 feet long east-west by 50 feet wide north-south. The crusted pond lay 10 feet below the edge. There was glow at the edges and the heavy crust was swollen upward, occasionally releasing gas with a hissing noise. Visitors reported that the crust broke up and foundered with violent fountaining at long intervals, not oftener than once or twice a day.

A second pit was found farther north where the smoky cracks had been and live lava was seen at the bottom of this pit. The depression was 30 feet deep and 50 feet across, with a tumble of rocks on one side. The ground east from here was broken down apparently along a collapsed tube and glow could be seen in the cracks.

At one of the larger cracks for a distance of about 20 feet gaping open from six to twelve inches, with incandescence below indicating a temperature not less than 800° C., there was found on the walls of the fissure a mass of salts subliming from a vaporized condition. These salts appeared bright yellow below, green in an intermediate zone and blue on the cooler edges. When collected with a stick the salts instantly changed completely to an azure blue color. They were somewhat waxy while hot. The stick instantly caught fire one foot above the crack. A solution of the salts afterwards tested with ammonia turned deep blue, showing the presence of copper. The salt is probably copper sulphate. A large incandescent stalactite could be seen down the crack and this appeared to consist of the same salt.

1. Pit at base of cone in Mokuaweoweo.

2. July 18, 1920. Deposit of copper salts in a hot crack, Kau Desert flow. (Photo Finch)

A 1914 cone at the left.
(Photo Finch)

3. July 18, 1920. Crusted source pond, Kau Desert Flow.
(Photo Jaggar)

A visit to the pits along the main tube eastward from the Mauna Iki pond showed an interior through one of the windows excessively hot and emitting irrespirable gas, with the floor of the tube about 15 feet below, but no incandescence visible in daylight. Fume and stain could be seen along the line of the tube in the direction toward Kamakaia.

At 3 p. m. on July 21 the Mauna Iki pond had subsided so that its surface stood 25 feet below the rim and the crust was cracking and foundering slightly along the edge under deeply overhanging banks. There had been some fountaining earlier in the day. The northern pit had increasingly slumped, and but little live lava was visible. The copper locality was still in action.

Seismometric Record.—During the week ending midnight, July 23, two very feeble local earthquakes were registered as follows: July 18, 9:10 p. m; July 20, 3:10 p. m. Spasmodic microtremor was moderate and harmonic tremor slight. Microseismic motion was also slight. There was very little tilting motion except for a westward tendency July 18.

Week Ending July 30, 1920.

SUMMARY OF CONDITIONS.

The rate of sinking of the Halemaumau lava column, which has been decreasing during the month of July reached its limit on July 24, and during the current week the level of the lava remained unchanged. The crags continued to subside for a short time after the lakes had become stationary. The fume has materially decreased in density. A large section of the "plaster" on the west wall fell during the stationary condition of the liquid. There was a tendency for eastward streaming throughout the week.

The lakes in the pits at the upper end of the Kau Desert low fluctuated in height and the crusts that formed over them broke up with vigorous fountaining from time to time. At the lower end of the flow, in the vicinity of the Kamakaia cones, the activity was confined to a few trickling toes.

JOURNAL.

Activity of Halemaumau.—Measurements during the week ended July 30, expressed as depressions below the northeast monument on the rim of Halemaumau, show that the lava was stationary at 320 feet. The crags continued to fall slightly, averaging less than one foot per day.

During the afternoon of July 24 the pit was less smoky than common. A sluggish current was pouring out of the southwest arm into the central channel. A blowing cone in the flat by the central crag was making considerable noise. The liquid lava stood about five feet below the central platform. The indications pointed to a rising tendency of the lava column. The northeast islet had broken down and was but a few feet above the liquid. One brisk fountain was playing in the central pool and border fountains only were active in other arms of the lake. The crust over the west pool was foundering. Small avalanches were heard.

Fairly good seeing was obtained during clearing spells, while making a circuit of the pit during the forenoon of July 26th. The southwest lake appeared to be considerably lower than the west lake. The central peninsula had become an island 10-15 feet high and tipped westward. The central platform appeared to be breaking up as though the side of the south crag were subsiding and the side of the central crag staying up. Occasional blasts were heard from some of the numerous grottos and the roofs of a few of these grottos were seen to fall in. Nine or ten fountains were playing at all times. The west pool was observed cracking and foundering from east to west. This lake was about 6 feet below its surrounding bench that was covered by a fresh overflow. The western part of the southwest lake was crusted over, while the eastern part of the same lake was cracking and foundering with fountains at its eastern end. Three open glowing pots were located near this eastern end—two on the confining bench and one on the west side of the south crag. There was a general tendency for eastward streaming.

While the fume was quite dense during the afternoon of July 28 the lakes appeared to be at the same height as on July 24th. Two large grottoes in the southwest arm were active. Very little persistent streaming was observed. Large sections of the "plaster" had fallen off the western wall.

During the evening of July 30 the fume was moderately thick. Sluggish currents were pouring out of the southwest arm into the central channel through two separate tunnels. One fountain, surrounded by a thick crust, was playing in the central pool. All arms of the lake were heavily crusted. These crusts would founder after quiet intervals, often several hours long.

Activity of the Kau Desert Flow. But few signs of actually flowing lava were found at the lower end of the Kau Desert flow on July 28. The front of the flow showed three or more tongues of cold pahoehoe lava just east of Puu Kouele. Live lava was found opposite lower Kamakaia, but not visibly flowing. A white salt deposit that tasted like acetic acid was found over spots where ohia trees had been buried by live lava. Many small tree moulds were observed. The crusted ponds at the source region of the flow were observed to break up and fountain on several different days.

Seismometric Record.—Two very feeble earthquakes were registered during the week ending midnight, July 30, 1920, as follows: July 25, 1:41 a. m.; July 30, 7:13 a. m. Spasmodic tremor was moderate on July 26 and 27 and slight on other days. Harmonic tremor and microseismic movement were both slight. There was very little tilting during the week.

Very respectfully,

T. A. JAGGAR, Jr.
Volcanologist.

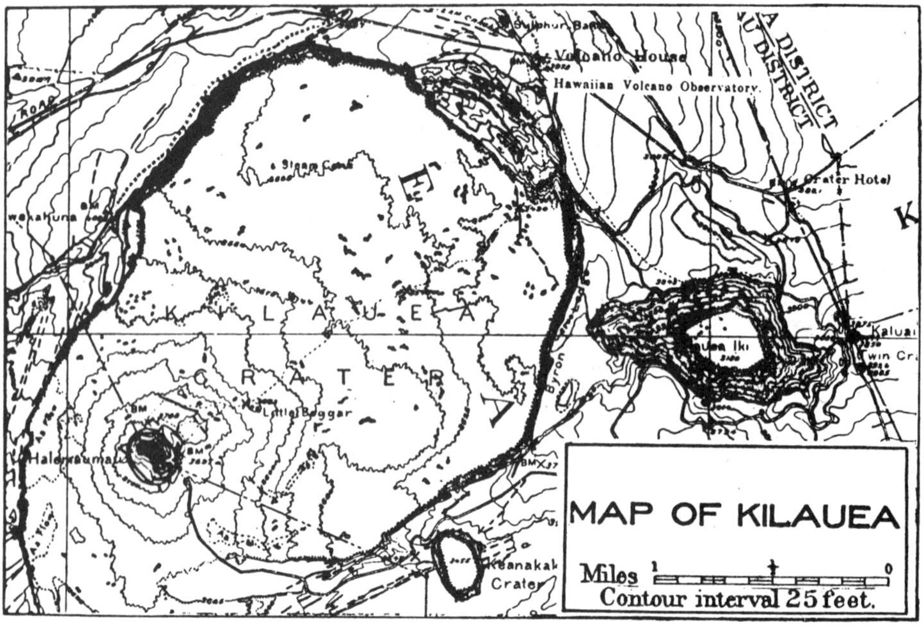

HAWAIIAN VOLCANO OBSERVATORY.

The Observatory is equipped with the following seismometric instruments rebuilt at the station in 1918 for the special needs of volcano research: two Bosch-Omori pendulums, high speed registration of local earthquakes; one optically recording seismograph for distant earthquakes; one clinograph registering E-W tilting of the ground. A vertical component seismograph was in December, 1918, set up in experimental operation. These are seated on concrete piers in a closed basement room having practically constant temperature, beneath the chief Observatory building near the hotel. Time is referred to a rated chronometer, checked at intervals by solar observations with a transit. The chronometer is loaned by the College of Hawaii. Hawaiian standard time (H. S. T.) is 10 hrs. 30 min. slower than Greenwich time.

CANCANI SCALE OF SEISMIC INTENSITY.

Expressed by accelerations measured in millimeters per second per second.

I.	Instrumental	0.0	2.5
II.	Very slight	2.5	5.0
III.	Slight	5.0	10.0
IV.	Sensible, mediocre	10.0	25.0
V.	Rather strong	25.0	50.0
VI.	Strong	50.0	100.0
VII.	Very strong	100.0	250.0
VIII.	Ruinous	250.0	500.0
IX.	Disastrous	500.0	1000.0
X.	Very disastrous	1000.0	2500.0
XI.	Catastrophic	2500.0	5000.0
XII.	Great catastrophe	5000.0	10000.0

Grade IV. is ordinarily the minimum perceived by the senses; and in grade XII, the acceleration or rate of change of motion (jerk) reaches that of terrestrial gravitation.

In the standard form of report the maximum intensity or acceleration, designated by the symbol a, or max. a, is given in the conventional unit of milligal. The milligal is a measure of acceleration, such that 1 milligal = 1/100 mm. per sec. per sec. = 10 μ. per sec. per sec. The Cancani scale, here defined in terms of millimeters per sec. per sec., can therefore be expressed in milligals by multiplying each of the numbers by 100.

U. S. DEPARTMENT OF AGRICULTURE
WEATHER BUREAU
CHARLES F. MARVIN, CHIEF

MONTHLY BULLETIN
OF THE
Hawaiian Volcano Observatory

VOL. VIII. HONOLULU, HAWAII, AUGUST, 1920 No. 8

Week Ending August 6, 1920.

SUMMARY OF CONDITIONS.

The sinking of the Halemaumau lava column came to a stop August 1 after having been nearly stationary for a week at 320 or 325 feet below the rim. The crags appeared to recover from the sinking spell more rapidly than the liquid and rose 38 feet while the lakes rose 27 feet. The fume gradually decreased in density and when the rise was well under way became very thin. A new lake appeared in the east floor during this rise but disappeared after having been active for a day.

The Kau Desert flow showed no signs of activity during the week beyond emitting considerable quantities of smoke.

JOURNAL.

Activity of Halemaumau.—The height of the lava and crags, obtained by measurements during the two weeks ended Aug. 6, 1920, when expressed as depressions below the northeast monument on the rim of Halemaumau (3727 feet above sea-level) are as follows:

	Mean lake level.	Peak center island.
July 24, 2 p. m.	320 feet	252 feet
August 1, 10 a. m.	321 "	258 "
August 6, 9 a. m.	294 "	220 "

The lava and crags after having been nearly stationary for a week started to rise August 1st and during the 5 days ended August 6th the lakes rose 27 feet or at an average of 5.4 feet per day. During the same period the crag rose 38 feet.

At 10 a. m. of August 1 the pit was moderately fumy. All lakes were crusted over except the southwest arm, which was fountaining vigorously. One fountain in the central pool was nearly continuous while surrounded by a heavy crust. The lava was apparently rising and was about 2 feet below the inner confining banks. Avalanches fell from the west wall.

During the afternoon of August 2nd the pit was less fumy than common. The southeast arm was nearly separated from the central pool. Fountains were playing in all arms and the crusts which had formed were breaking up. A part of the May shelf along the north wall had scaled off.

The fume was very thin at 1 p. m. on August 4th and the entire pit could be clearly seen from any position on the rim. The lakes were visibly higher than on the 2nd. Most of the floor surrounding the lakes had recently been flooded. A new small lake had appeared between the southeast arm and the east lake near the point of the east crag. The east lake was 3 or 4 feet lower than the others. A cone near the south edge of the southwest arm was hissing loudly. All of the lakes were crusted over.

At 10 a. m. on August 5th the pit was very clear. There was streaming out of the southwest arm into the central pool. The new lake observed on the 4th had gone out of action, leaving a hole several feet deep. The lakes were down 3 or 4 feet from what they had been a few hours previous, as shown by the still glowing overflows. Border fountains were active in all the lakes.

During the forenoon of August 6th the fume was very thin and the lakes were higher than on the 5th. A flow was pouring over the surface from the southeast arm into the east lake. All crags, except the one to the west, were islands by flooding around their bases. A current was flowing out of the southwest arm into the central pool. One fountain was playing in the middle of the central pool. A flow had poured from the north arm around the east crag into the northern end of the east lake.

Activity of the Kau Desert Flow.—When observed during the forenoon of August 3rd both pits at the upper end of the Kau Desert flow contained no live lava though much smoke was being emitted. The western and larger of the two pits had further increased in size by the wall having fallen in. There were numerous very hot cracks close to the eastern of the two pits but no glowing places were found.

Seismometric Record.—The dates and times of the two teleseisms and one local earthquake that were recorded during the week ended midnight August 6th are as follows: Teleseisms—August 2, 5:55 p. m., very feeble; August 3, 10:10 a. m., light. Local shock, August 6, 5:50 p. m., very feeble. Spasmodic and harmonic tremors were both slight to moderate during the week. Microseismic motion was again slight. Tilting movement was variable, being moderate to the west on the 1st and 3rd and moderate to the east on the 2nd and 4th.

Week Ending August 13, 1920.

SUMMARY OF CONDITIONS.

The rise of the lava column of Halemaumau that started on August 1 continued during the current week and on August 11 the liquid was 261 feet below the rim. The pit was very free from smoke during the week and the seeing was good. During a visitation of the Pan-Pacific Scientific Conference at the pit during the evening of August 8th a cascade poured from the west pond into the central pool. When the platform at the base of the central crag collapsed on August 7th and enlarged the central pool 3 small islands were formed from the remnants of this platform. Rapid eastward streaming out of the southwest arm was almost continuous during the week.

There was renewed activity at the western source pond of the Kau Desert flow during the week and a small hissing cone was formed in the center of the new crusted fill in this pond.

JOURNAL.

Activity of Halemaumau:—Measurements during the week ended August 13, 1920, expressed as depressions below the northeast monument on the rim of Halemaumau, gave results as follows:

	Mean lake level.	Peak center island.
August 6, 9 a. m.	294 feet	220 feet
August 11, 10 a. m.	261 "	198 "

The lake level rose 33 feet during the 5 days ending with August 11, or at an average of 6.6 feet per day. The crag during the same 5 days rose 22 feet. The rise of the crag during the preceding week exceeded that of the liquid by 11 feet, while during the current week the liquid rose 11 feet more than the crag, the total rise of each between August 1 and August 11 being 60 feet. The relief of the central crag was changed but slightly during the past several weeks.

At 3 p. m. on August 7 the connection between the southwest arm and the central pool was an open channel. A rapid current was flowing through this channel into the central pool. There were three small islands in the central pool which appeared to be remnants of the sunken platform that had surrounded the base of the central crag. The central pool was considerably enlarged by the collapse of this platform. The liquid was 4 or 5 feet below the inner confining benches and was rising.

The lakes were very high at 9 p. m. on August 8. Fresh, glowing flows were in evidence on all benches. There was rapid eastward streaming out of the southwest arm to the center. The arrangement of the streaming and the slope of the bottom was definitely from the west pond to the southeast. This arrangement produced two fountaining grottoes at the east end of the southwest arm, some near the wall in the southeast arm, several around the east pond, and some in the north arm. The west pond tended to remain crusted except for occasional breaking up. A cascade some 30 feet wide and 8 feet high poured from beneath a crust that covered the west pond into the central pool. Flames were issuing from a filagree patch just north of the north arm. A grotto in the southeast arm was puffing strongly. The east lake appeared to be a few feet lower than the central pool. A part of the south bank of this lake collapsed.

At 10 a. m. on August 9 the fume was thin and the lakes high. The liquid was about 4 feet below the bench at the southwest and the north, thence to the east lake and the southeast arm the bench became progressively lower. The west pond was crusted over with only a few grottos in action. A marked rise occurred about noon and flooded the lowest benches around the east lake and the southeast arm.

Some greenish and stained salt that appeared to be ferrous sulphate was found in the Postal Rift flow cavern.

At 10 a. m. on August 11 the fume was very thin. The lakes were crusted over and rising. One branch from the very rapid current out of the southwest arm went into the southeast arm and the other to the north. Two border fountains and one central fountain were active in the central pool, while only grottos were active in the other arms. A glowing hole some 10 feet above the lake level was observed in the southwest wall near the beginning of the Kau Desert rift crack.

The fume was still very light at 10 a. m., August 12. The current out of the southwest arm was much the same as on the 11th. The 3 central islets were higher above the liquid than during the past several days. The glowing window in the southwest wall showed very plainly. The west pond was crusted over and 4 or 5 feet higher than the central pool until 11 a. m. when the crust foundered and the level decreased 3 or 4 feet.

At 10 a. m. on August 13 the lakes appeared to be nearly stationary. The current from the southwest arm to the central pool varied from very sluggish to rapid. The west pond was higher than the central pool. The east lake had further decreased in area. A deep crust had formed over the small, narrow north arm.

Activity of the Kau Desert Flow.—When the Kau Desert flow was observed during the forenoon of August 10 it was found that the western, or larger, of the two source ponds had renewed its activity since the preceding week. A new crusted lava pool had partly covered the rock talus around the walls of the pit. No other activity was noted though there were many hot cracks on the top of the new lava ridge.

Seismometric Record.—The dates and times of the 5 local earthquakes that were recorded during the week ending with midnight, August 13, are as follows: August 7, 11 p. m., feeble; August 11, 3:30 p. m., very feeble; August 12, 4:50

a. m., feeble; August 13, 1:10 a. m. and 4:35 p. m., both very feeble. Spasmodic tremor was slight on August 8 and 13, and moderately strong on other days during the week. Harmonic tremor was moderately strong, having increased when the lava started to rise about August 1. Microseismic movement continued slight during the week. Tilting was slight and irregular.

Week Ending August 20, 1920.

SUMMARY OF CONDITIONS.

The lava lakes and crags of Halemaumau have risen continuously with a strong spurt upward of the crags and benches preceding a spell of voluminous overflowing of the benches by the lakes. At the rift opening in the southwest wall of the pit leading to the Kau Desert flows, a cascade of liquid lava poured out of a hole in the wall down to the lake beneath at about the time (August 16th) when the Kau flow ceased action. At the same time there was voluminous flooding of the benches and a small felt earthquake, as though the flow fissure to the southwest had sealed and the liquid had backed up to Halemaumau. The opening in the wall continued glowing and fuming. The overflows from the lakes built up the platforms around the crags. One of the islets in the central pool disappeared during the week.

The Kau Desert flow heap shows increased collapse of the source pit and no sign of flowing activity in tunnels or otherwise has been discernible since August 15. The first outflow on this rift line in Kilauea Crater was on December 15, 1919, so that the flow continued for eight months.

JOURNAL.

Activity of Halemaumau.—The movement of the liquid lava and crags is indicated for the first three days of the week by the following measurements, expressed as depressions below the northeast monument on the rim of Halemaumau (3727 feet above sea level):

	Mean lake level.	Peak western crag (hitherto called central island)
August 11, 10 a. m......	261 feet	198 feet
August 14, 10 a. m......	258 "	189 "

It is thus evident that in three days the lake rose only three feet and the crag nine feet, but this swelling upward of the bench magma was followed, as is usually the case, by flooding overflows from the lakes during the remainder of the week. The relief of the crag above the lake on August 14 was 69 feet as against 63 feet, August 11.

On Saturday, August 14, from 10 to 11 a. m., fume had increased and the benches around the lakes were 4 feet higher than on the previous day. The margin around the west pond was 5 feet high. The east pond had decreased in size. The streaming was rapid from the southwest to the central pool.

At 4 p. m., August 15, the visible fume had been decreasing in volume and the lakes were higher.

August 16, at 5 p. m., strong overflow of the benches was in progress from all the pools and a cascade was pouring into the pit from a hole in the southwest wall a few feet above the lake bench. Here glow had been visible in the rift crack leading to the Kau Desert flow for several days. About 7:20 p. m. an earthquake was felt (at both Halemaumau and at the Observatory), and there were falls of rock from Halemaumau on the north side. Other slight falls were noticed during the evening, some of the boulders breaking through the crusts of the new flows on the floor.

August 17, at 11 a. m., the fume from the pit was thin and the central lake had lowered 10 feet within the banks, the east pond 12 to 14 feet. Fresh lava covered most of the benches, and the small round island and middle island of

August 11, 1920. High lake overflowing its banks.
Photo Finch.

August 14, 1920. Showing lower lake and increase of fume.
Photo Finch.

Kau Desert flow first rising through rift near Puu Koae, December 22, 1919.
Photo Jaggar.

Flowing lava of Kau Desert, near Kamakaia, July 25, 1920. Photo Jaggar.

the central pool were veneered over with new lava. The cascade from the southwest hole had solidified with a pile of pahoehoe on the bench at its foot, and no glow could be detected at its source cavity in daylight. An east-west crack had opened across the southern end of the northeast crag. Streaming in the lake was from the southwest. An inspection of the Kau Desert rift line on the Kilauea floor southwest found the ground hot and fuming with much red and yellow deposit in patches. There was a noon rise of the liquid lava until the lakes brimmed almost level with their banks, and the two smaller islands were nearly submerged by 12:30 p. m. After this there was slight subsidence.

August 18, at 11 a. m., the pit was very clear and the liquid lava was below its margins 5 feet in the west pond, and 10 feet in the central and east lakes. The southern arms and west pond were crusted over. There were border fountains and a central fountain in the central pool. At the north end of the middle island a large spatter grotto with stalactites had been built since the previous day, and here there was incessant fountaining. The last high level had enlarged this island, and the small round island west of it had disappeared. There had been fresh flows, one from the west pond flooding on both sides of the north crag remnant and across the north floor nearly to the east pond, one from the southeast arm towards the east pond, and overflow from the southwest arm all around. More avalanches were indicated by fresh talus and pink dust from the east wall of the pit on the floor south of the east pond. In the southwest arm one large grotto was fountaining and the current from this arm poured through the channel to the center where it diverged about the islands. The uplift of the promontories adjacent to the entrance channel of the southeast arm suggested a tilting up due to the weight of the new bench flows farther east. No glow could be discovered in the southwest rift crack but a filagree cone was glowing on the south bank of the southeast arm. At 11:40 a. m. a sinking spell occurred in the central pool and the east pond, not affecting the west pond.

On the morning of August 19 the relief of the crags and benches above the lakes was about three feet higher than on the previous day. The lakes were more stagnant. Examination of the Postal Rift tunnel showed that the temperature in its inner recesses is decreasing.

Activity of the Kau Desert Flow.—Inspection of Mauna Iki at 8 a. m. August 15 showed that much smoke was rising from the western source pit. The floor of this pit had again collapsed after emitting a small amount of lava around the hissing central vent observed on August 10. No activity was discernible anywhere here or at the second pit.

Seismometric Record.—One teleseism and three local earthquakes were registered during the week ending at midnight August 20, as follows: August 14, teleseism, 7:55 p. m.; local earthquakes, August 16, 1:15 p. m., feeble, and 7:20 p. m., moderately strong, felt at Observatory and in Hilea, estimated distance of source 25 miles; also August 17, 1:10 p. m., very feeble. Spasmodic and harmonic microtremors were moderate to strong. Microseismic motion was slight. Tilting was to the north and east August 14-15; then westward and somewhat southward for most of the remainder of the week.

Week Ending August 27, 1920.

SUMMARY OF CONDITIONS.

The reaction of marked rising which was noted earlier in the month tended to approach a culmination during the past week and the overflowing from the lakes ceased. The fume has been thin and the arrangement of features seen in the bottom of the pit gives evidence of a bilateral symmetry about a northwest-southeast axis such as has been noticed before in Halemaumau, the northwest pond being the source well and the southeast arm the sinkhole, with a down grade between them. This west pond comes first with crags on both sides; next comes the long central and southeastern pools with crags on both sides; and right and left lie the two outlying lakes more or less connected with arms of the central pool. These are respectively the southwest arm and the east pond. The tunnel connection of the east pond with the north cove of the central pool is shown by a northern flaming pit with a glowing cone beside it and a fuming area marking an underground condensation chamber.

There is no more glowing at the front of the Kau Desert flows near Kamakaia, and only smoke rises at the sourrce wells on Mauna Iki.

JOURNAL.

Activity of Halemaumau.—Measurements during the week ending August 27, 1920, expressed as depressions below the northeast monument on the Halemaumau rim (3727 feet above sea level) have been as follows:

	Mean lake level.	Peak of northeast crag.	Peak of west crag.
August 14, 10 a. m.......	258 feet	...	189 feet
August 25, 10 a. m.......	244 "	180 feet	184 "

In eleven days the lake rose 14 feet, averaging 1.3 feet per day, and the west crag rose 5 feet, averaging 0.45 foot per day. The relief of this crag thus decreased from 69 feet to 60 feet, and the relief of the northeast crag August 25 was 64 feet above the lake.

On Saturday, August 21, at 9:30 a. m., the liquid lava almost filled the cups of the east and west ponds, and the main lake and its arms were nearly level with the bordering benches. There were strong surface currents from the southwest arm forking around the west island and meeting in a line of two or three very large fountains in the central pool. These were accompanied by many bubble fountains. The arms of the lake were heavily crusted and the west pond especially so, the latter with some border spraying about 11 a. m. from under its crust along its northeast margin. The east pond showed border fountains and at 10:45 a .m. it overflowed its east bank in two places. There were a few short leaf-shaped flows of recent date around the edges of the west pond, but no extensive overflows had taken place for two days. Smoke had increased from cracks in the benches and rock had freshly fallen below the north shelf. The middle island was now as high as the east island.

At 2 p. m., August 22, the growth of the platform at the expense of the crags during the last fortnight was conspicuous to an observer returning after an absence, and the northeast crag had grown to be a peak equal to the west crag, formerly called the "central" crag. The glowing wall chimney at the base of the southwest wall was a solfataric heap built over the crack leading to the Kau Desert rift. The cone on the bench near the north cove was emitting a spear of greenish flame a foot long. There was circular streaming counter clockwise around the western island. Gas pressure was strong, as shown by the spraying and travelling fountains which formed where the currents met north of the island, and by a spraying fountain which developed in the east pond after a spell of crusting. There was occasional cracking and foundering of crusts in the west pond.

August 25 at 10 a. m. the fume was still moderately thin but the lakes were 9 feet below their surrounding platforms, excepting the east pond, which was only 5 feet down. The rotary current around the island continued, the latter standing one foot above the liquid, and a second stream poured into the southeast arm. There were two glowing vents at the north flame pot. Grottoes were active in the west cove and on the south side of the west pond.

August 26 the gas pressure had diminished and the fume increased. A pot and filagree flame cone were still full of burning gases on the north platform.

Streaming out of the southwest channel was slow. Fountains were few and the lakes stood about 6 feet below their banks.

August 27 at 4 p. m. the lakes were 6 or 7 feet below their banks. The southeastern islet stood only 3 feet above the liquid, while the northern one stood 6 feet high. There was rapid streaming out of the southwest arm but all the pools tended to sluggishness and a crusted condition. The southwest bench solfatara at the crack in the wall of the pit showed a glowing vent at the top of a talus heap.

Condition of the Kau Desert Flow.—A visit to the widely open part of the 1920 rift a quarter mile southwest of Kilauea Crater on the morning of August 23 revealed no changes there, some hot vapor was still rising, and the rift chasm showed no tendency to close. It remains a canyon-like cleft 20 feet wide in places and from 50 to 100 feet deep in those places where the bottom debris can be seen. It was a crack which yawned open last December, breaking across beds of ash above solid rock below. This crack extends on down the mountain and five miles to the southwest passes under Mauna Iki as a vent only one or two feet wide, the source of the whole great slag heap and its flows.

There are no new developments at Mauna Iki. The source pond locality was smoking strongly on August 22. During an excursion with the visiting geologists on August 25 the lower end of the 1920 flows was visited in the region near Kamakaia. The pahoehoe flows were still hot but not flowing and exhibited no new extrusions. They stopped in the ground between Kamakaia and Puu Kouele. There was slight fuming from Mauna Iki along the line of the tunnels in pahoehoe which fed the frontal region, until recently in motion.

Seismometric Record.—During the week ending at midnight August 27, 1920, five local earthquakes and one distant shock were registered at the Observatory, as follows: Local earthquakes—August 22, 10 p. m., feeble, and 11:58 p. m., very feeble; August 23, 6:45 a. m., slight, origin distance 12 miles; August 26, 4:21 p. m., very feeble; August 27, 3:20 a. m., very feeble Spasmodic microtremor was moderate. Harmonic microtremor was strongish August 21, moderate to slight thereafter. Microseismic motion remained slight. Tilting was slight or absent until August 26-27 when it increased to the east and north.

T. A. JAGGAR, JR.,
Volcanologist.

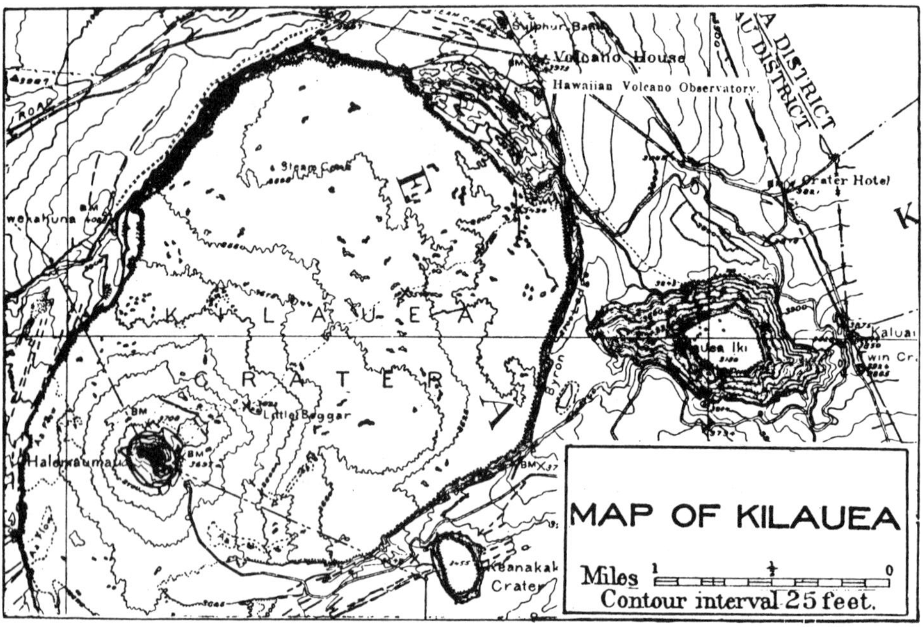

HAWAIIAN VOLCANO OBSERVATORY.

All exchanges should be addressed to
HAWAIIAN VOLCANO OBSERVATORY,
Volcano House, P. O. Hawaii.

The Observatory is equipped with the following seismometric instruments rebuilt at the station in 1918 for the special needs of volcano research: two Bosch-Omori pendulums, high speed registration of local earthquakes; one optically recording seismograph for distant earthquakes; one clinograph registering E-W tilting of the ground. A vertical component seismograph was in December, 1918, set up in experimental operation. These are seated on concrete piers in a closed basement room having practically constant temperature, beneath the chief Observatory building near the hotel. Time is referred to a rated chronometer, checked at intervals by wireless signal from the Pearl Harbor Naval Station. The chronometer is loaned by the College of Hawaii. Hawaiian standard time (H. S. T.) is 10 hrs. 30 min. slower than Greenwich time.

CANCANI SCALE OF SEISMIC INTENSITY.

Expressed by accelerations measured in millimeters per second per second.

I.	Instrumental	0.0	2.5
II.	Very slight	2.5	5.0
III.	Slight	5.0	10.0
IV.	Sensible, mediocre	10.0	25.0
V.	Rather strong	25.0	50.0
VI.	Strong	50.0	100.0
VII.	Very strong	100.0	250.0
VIII.	Ruinous	250.0	500.0
IX.	Disastrous	500.0	1000.0
X.	Very disastrous	1000.0	2500.0
XI.	Catastrophic	2500.0	5000.0
XII.	Great catastrophe	5000.0	10000.0

Grade IV. is ordinarily the minimum perceived by the senses; and in grade XII, the acceleration or rate of change of motion (jerk) reaches that of terrestrial gravitation.

In the standard form of report the maximum intensity or acceleration, designated by the symbol α, or max. α, is given in the conventional unit of milligal. The milligal is a measure of acceleration, such that 1 milligal = 1/100 mm. per sec. per sec. = 10 μ. per sec. per sec. The Cancani scale, here defined in terms of millimeters per sec. per sec., can therefore be expressed in milligals by multiplying each of the numbers by 100.

U. S. DEPARTMENT OF AGRICULTURE
WEATHER BUREAU
CHARLES F. MARVIN, CHIEF

MONTHLY BULLETIN
OF THE
Hawaiian Volcano Observatory

VOL. VIII. HONOLULU, HAWAII, SEPTEMBER, 1920 No. 9

Week Ending September 3, 1920.

SUMMARY OF CONDITIONS.

The lava lakes of Kilauea in Halemaumau pit at the beginning of September show subsidence of about 10 feet during the week so that the liquid pool in the center stands 257 feet below the rim. Four crags stand as peaks above the floor which forms the banks of the several lakes. The highest of these on the northeast stands 76 feet above the central pool. One of the two islands in this pool broke in two during the week leaving three islets with flat tops which stand only a few feet above the liquid lava, and the latter rises and falls sometimes submerging one of them. There is a large central lake with three arms, and two outlying ponds under the walls of the pit, the western one standing some 12 feet higher than the main lake. This west pond appears to be the source of rising liquid lava, which flows thence through tunnels to the other lakes, rising highest in the source pond by reason of the foaming action of its gases. There is a variable streaming from the source to the several arms of the main lake, and fountains develop variably, mostly against the banks, sometimes a dozen in action at once. With the sinking of the lava there has been some falling of rocks from the walls to the marginal talus slopes.

No further action has been reported from the lava flow in the Kau Desert 6 miles southwest of Kilauea crater. The source ponds of the flow have collapsed and show no gas pressure, and the tunnels which led to the front are increasingly caving in. At the head of the rift inside of Kilauea crater and close to Halemaumau dense masses of acid fume are rising and decomposing the surface lava with development of brilliantly colored solfataric patches.

JOURNAL.

Activity of Halemaumau.—Measurements during the week ending Sept. 4, 1920, expressed as depressions below the northeast monument on the rim of Halemaumau (3727 feet above sea-level), have been as follows:

	Mean lake level.	Peak of northeast crag.	Peak of west crag.
Aug. 25, 10 a. m.....	244 feet	180 feet	184 feet
Aug. 29, 3 p. m.....	248 "	180 "	183 "
Sept. 4, 2 p. m.....	257 "	181 "	...

During the 10 days from Aug. 25th to Sept. 4th the lakes subsided 13 feet, averaging 1.3 feet per day. The crags tended to be stationary or sank but slightly. The relief of both the west and northeast crags above the lakes was on Sept. 4th about 76 feet, an increase for the northeast crag of 12 feet in 10 days. In the previous 11 days the relief of the crags had decreased by a similar amount, showing that the culmination of rising liquid and the beginning of subsidence were marked by nearly stationary bench magma while the liquid lava foamed up and sank back.

At 3 p. m. Aug. 29 the fume in the pit was thin, 11 fountains were in action and the streaming of the main lake was towards the ends of the three arms and northeastward from the southwestern channel into the central pool where the currents tended to encircle the two islands. There was occasional strong bombardment with fountaining at the west cove and on the north side of the west island. Sometimes rapid streaming developed into the north cove where a tunnel led under the bench to chambers over which the surface was smoking and sulphur stained. A similar tunnel could be seen on the north side of the east pond, and this may lead through to the north cove. The west pond showed thin skins and bright lines and this was the general habit of the other pools also. There were loud hissing and growling noises which developed from time to time toward the north and east probably from the vicinity of the northeast tunnel, and much rumbling was made by the grotto on the north side of the west island.

The chimney fuming at the talus level at the base of the southwestern wall of the pit was seen to be directly at the place where the Kau Desert rift emerges inside of Halemaumau. An examination of the upper veneers of plastered shore lines on the walls of the pit, remnant from the subsidence of December, 1919, showed that this material had fallen away much on the lower northeast and east sides, the lowest part of it had scaled off on all sides and the upper bench lines were preserved except at the west and south.

At 4:50 p. m. Aug. 30th the east pond was found overflowing its banks and a small adjacent pot was spurting. The other pools exhibited much rapid streaming and were lower relative to their banks so that the spatter accumulations tended to break off and fall in. After 5 p. m. the outline of the east pond became defined within its banks but the other pools rose, the west pond and southwest arm becoming heavily crusted over. On the west pond surface a small spurting cone remained open at the southwest end and from under the crust of the southwest arm a live current poured through the channel to the central pool. There were soft thin skins and bright glow lines over the central pool and the southeast arm.

A grotto was continuously active at the north end of the west island and occasionally a prolonged fountaining with much spurting would develop in the north central region and migrate to the west cove of the lake. There were four or five other variable fountains against the banks. Numerous flaming vents became visible in the evening towards the north, southeast, and south, at the rift vent in the talus southwest, and next to the east pond on the southeast side. There was much blowing noise indicating strong gas pressure. The streaming tended to encircle the west island counterclockwise and poured past the southeast island into the southeast arm. The east pond remained high during the 2 hours of observation.

On August 31st from 10 p. m. to 12 mid. the lakes appeared stationary with banks 7 to 8 feet high around the central pool and west pond, but the southeast arm appeared relatively higher. The streaming out of the southwest arm continued. There were many flaming vents at different points on the floor and 3 or 4 of them were clustered at the southwest rift vent about 15 feet above the liquid lava of the southwest arm.

On the morning of Friday, Sept. 3rd, the western island in the central pool was found broken in two, leaving a pulpit rock standing above the liquid at its southern half and a flat shoal on the north against which there was fountaining. During a spell of deflation with breaking up of crusts the lakes exhibited

12 fountains of which 9 were in the main lake. The liquid appeared to be rising after 10 a. m. in the main and eastern pools, but not in the west pond, so that these pools appeared to be lifted to the west pond level. Around the latter there was a margin 8 feet high whereas the bank was only 3 feet high around the central pool. During the rise the island shoal became entirely submerged and the pulpit rock was barely above the liquid level. In the southwest arm the streaming was from its west end and diverging so that one current poured to its eastern end and the other through the channel to the central pool. In the center there was slow circular movement around the 2 islets, through the channels to the southeastern and northern arms and northward through the channel between the islets and the western crag mass. Around the west pond there were four vigorous border grottos showing overhang and stalactites. There were occasional central fountains sometimes prolonged. Flaming holes appeared at the north, east and southeast, and at the talus against the southwest rift. The latter is a vent at the top of the talus, sulphur stained and appears to be a cone cementing the broken rocks. Fume was moderate from the floors and crags, and above the fountains rose volutes of pale blue transparent gas.

Condition of the Kau Desert Rift.—The Mauna Iki source region of the recent Kau Desert flow was visited during the forenoon of Aug. 31. The source pond appeared to be more caved in than when seen Aug. 10th. The walls of the pit are about 30 feet high and the floor has slumped showing a cone in the shape of a flat pudding which had welled up at the center. Caving in of the sides was still in progress at this time as two falls of rock from the walls were seen in the course of 20 minutes. There was no hissing of gas but very hot smoke rose above the tunnel outlet on the east side of the pit. Bright red iron oxide stained the broken rocks.

Three hundred yards to the east of this pit a new opening in the roof of the tunnel was found with hot air rising through it at a temperature of over 200° C. Worm stalactites could be seen inside the tunnel, an interesting feature of which was their occurrence in part on broken surfaces on the roof wall in isolated groups.

At the northern pit on the summit of Mauna Iki no activity was observed but there was much heat along the tunnel lines and some copper salts were still in process of deposition at the locality where they were found before.

The morning was cloudy and cool and vapor could be seen rising along both of the 1919-20 rift cracks in the region west of Puu Koae. In the other direction towards Kamakaia bluish fume rose along the tunnel line leading to the front of the recent pahoehoe flows.

On Sept. 3rd the cracks trending southwest 100 yards from Halemaumau in the floor of Kilauea crater were explored. These cracks are definitely aligned with the Kau Desert rift and it was here that the first outflow occurred Dec. 15, 1919. The ground in spots was wet with steam and bluish or brownish steaming vapor rose from the cracks, very dense in places and wholly irrespirable, containing large quantities of sulphuric acid. Measurements of the temperature at one locality showed 170° C. Here the surface lava which dates from 1918-1919 is completely altered and where the fume is hottest and densest the coloring of the solfataric salts is a bright scarlet varying to terra cotta, orange, and sulphur yellow in bands towards the outer margins of the patches. The brightest red occurs where the fume is densest, hottest, and most acid. The main rift crack is ordinarily bright yellow with sulphur and there is also much waxy yellow salt that tastes of alum. The decomposition of the rock along the vapouring crack is very complete. Examination of the southwest heap under the wall of Kilauea crater showed the summit craters tumbled in but not fuming.

Seismometric Record.—During the week ending midnight Sept. 3, 1920, three local earthquakes and two teleseisms were registered as follows: Local shocks—Aug. 28, 3:45 a. m. and 4:55 a. m., both feeble; Sept. 2, 6:50 p. m., very slight. Teleseisms—Aug. 29th, 2:40 a. m., slight, and Sept. 1, 4:36 p. m., slight. Spasmodic tremor increased after Aug. 29, then decreased and on Sept. 3 increased to numerous weak spasms. Harmonic tremor varied from slight to moderate. Microseismic motion was slight. Tilt was moderate to west and south until Aug. 31, became strong to the east on Sept. 1 and strong to the north on Sept. 3.

Week Ending September 10, 1920.

SUMMARY OF CONDITIONS.

The liquid lava of Halemaumau sank 16 feet during the week while the higher crags remained stationary. The liquid was thus drained away through the wells which penetrate the bench magma and this undermined the heavy platforms and crags causing them to fracture along huge crevasses which formed in 3 places. In 2 of these the liquid from the lakes poured into the breaches and new glowing pools were formed, one of them showing a fiery cascade from the lake to the outlying pot. Shoals have built up around the islands as the central lake subsided and there have been rapid fluctuations of level whereby one of the islands disappeared and then developed again by accretion. The southwestern arm, through the draining away of the liquid has revealed a shoal which tends to become an island. All of this lowering of the liquid and opening of new pots has increased the number of separate pools to 8 which are more or less connected and there are 5 distinct crag peaks large and small.

JOURNAL.

Activity of Halemaumau.—Measurements for the week ending Sept. 10, 1920, expressed as depressions below the northeast monument on the rim of Halemaumau (3727 feet above sea-level), have been as follows:

	Mean lake level.	Peak of northeast crag.	Peak of west crag.
Sept. 4, 2 p. m....	257 feet	181 feet	...
Sept. 10, 11 a. m....	273 "	181 "	182 feet

In 6 days the lake thus sank 16 feet averaging 2.5 feet per day and the crags were essentially stationary, the relief of the northeast crag increasing from 76 feet to 92 feet.

On Saturday, Sept. 4th, at 2 p. m., the fume had become thicker though there was still good seeing at the pit. The streaming was moderately rapid toward the center from the southwest arm, the current dividing in the central pool into 2 branches moving respectively northwest and southeast. A large fountaining grotto had developed against the southern bank of the central pool. There were 3 islands in the central pool, the northern one the smallest and east of this islet a continuous fountain was in action. The lakes stood from 8-10 feet below their banks.

On Sept. 5th at 4 p. m. there were only 2 islands in the lake, respectively the southeastern and northwestern ones, and the absence of the island at the entrance to the southwest channel produced a greatly widened space of liquid lava in the central pool. The fume in the pit was rather thin though smoke rose from cracks in the islands, crags and floors. From time to time spells of rapid streaming towards the southeast developed through the narrows leading to the southeast arm. On the south side of the southwest channel a pulpit rock had developed from fracture of the south crag mass. There was much turbulent fountaining along the base of the bank on the south side of the southeast channel. Strong central fountaining was seen on one occasion to develop in the southwest arm and this fountain migrated to the eastern bank. On the east pond there was a heavy crust which finally broke up with southward migration of the cracking and foundering blocks. The southwest rift solfatara at the base of the wall appeared very hot, fumy and sulphurous and there was stain on the rift crack above for 1-3 of the height of the wall. The southwest arm lava appeared high, the banks of the west pond were 4 feet high, at the central pool, east pond and southeast arm the banks were 6 feet high and the 2 points confining the southeast channel were 10 feet high.

At 11 a. m. Sept. 7th, the 3 islands of the central pool were again restored, the southwestern islet occupying that corner of the pool which is opposite the current pouring inward from the southwest channel. Its development appeared to be an accretionary growth, upward from a shoal on the bottom under the dividing place of the current.

The west pond remained quiet and crusted over most of the time. There were large continuous fountains in the north part of the central pool. The speed of the streaming fluctuated. Abundant smoke arose from the fractures in the northeast crag.

On Sept. 9th at 3:30 p. m. conspicuous new developments were noticeable in the form of fractures through the bench magma indicating a tendency to break down under the drainage which had been lowering the liquid lava. It will be remembered that a small outlying pond was reported between the east pond and southeast arm during the first week in August. At this locality there had now developed an east-west crevasse extending eastward from the east cove of the central lake and through this chasm which was about 4 feet wide a cascade torrent from the central pool was rushing eastward and downward into a void under the platform. The visible drop of the liquid was 15 feet.

Another east-west crack extended through a rocky western extension of the northeast crag from the north cove of the central pool and had created a new open pot of liquid lava about 8x15 feet in size to the east of that cove. In general line with this crack a large fracture across the northern arm of the northeast crag was seen.

Another fracture line which had developed extending northward from the eastern end of the southwest arm tended to extend that arm L-shape in the direction of the north-south chasm which cuts athwart the south crag mass.

The general appearance of all these breaks seems to indicate a very pronounced jostling and breaking up of the large sector blocks of bench magma such as on past occasions has preceded strong sinking movements. The pouring of cascades into voids is particularly distinctive of such subsidences and gives subsidence character to the whole crisis as distinct from similar fractures which sometimes occur during a general uplift of bench magma.

On this day the banks of the lakes were from 4 to 12 feet high, the highest ones being at the east pond and southeast arm. The rim of the west pond was 5 feet high and the shore at the narrows at the southwest channel stood only 2 feet above the liquid.

On Sept. 10 at 11 a. m. the streaming in the main lake was from the southwest as before and much of the current was directed to the east cove where the cascade continued to pour eastward through the chasm into the new east pot. The east pond appeared increased in size. The west pond was heavily crusted over and stood from 12-15 feet below its banks. In the new north pot there was some fountaining. The south side of the pit was smoky and the seeing there was poor.

Experiments with Fume Humidity, and Special Collections.—Accompanied by geologists of the Pan-Pacific Scientific Conference [H. S. Washington and J. A. Thomson] the writer made the following experiment on the afternoon of Sept. 9th at the margin of Halemaumau on the leeward side. Dr. Washington had suggested that as a smouldering torch makes apparent by nucleation the water vapor in many of the small cracks emitting hot gases, a similar effect should appear at the edge of Halemaumau where the most concentrated gas from the fountains is pouring over the leeward edge of the pit. The gas analyses published by Shepherd [This Bulletin, Vol. 7, No. 7, July, 1919], show water content of the flaming gases from the fountaining lava of Halemaumau of from 60-90 volume per cent at 1200° C. In discussion with the visiting men of science, the writer had called attention to the singular fact, seemingly paradoxical, that the gas from the hot lava rises in great quantities from the pit, and when it is in greatest volume from thousands of fountains as in July, 1912, and December, 1919, there is not the least visible steam.

An iron pipe was fitted with a wad of cotton waste at one end, dipped in kerosene, and ignited. This was carried as a torch to the southwestern rim where the blue fume of the fountains was pouring up from below in its most disagreeable form. The experiment was tried in 2 places, the torch was thrust over the edge of the pit so that it would be fully immersed in the gas and the waste was thrust into the gas in both the flaming and smouldering conditions. No nucleation could be perceived in the crater fume, and there was not the slightest trace of increase in visible vapor.

It should be noted that on Dec. 15, 1919, and thereafter, there were strong lava fountains in the southwest heap a few hundred feet directly to the leeward from Halemaumau making clouds of sulphurous gas full of particles perfectly devised for the nucleation of the vast volumes of gas from the crater itself. At this time also the crater was doing its maximum fountaining. No development of water vapor cloud occurred where the crater fume swept across the fume from the southwest heap, nor was any (water) cumulus developed farther to leeward.

That the fume particles of the crater cloud itself are adapted for nucleating water vapor is abundantly shown on the Kilauea floor. Here when the wind is in the southwest the fume cloud from Halemaumau sweeps across the field of cracked lava where moist hot air is rising through the cracks and these so-called steam jets are made visible abundantly along the track of fume. The analyses of the most continuously visible of these yields only 8 or 10% of water and 70 or 80% of air, while the others, strongly nucleated by the sulphur fume contain only minute quantities of water vapor. It is therefore difficult to understand why the cloud of blue fume from Halemaumau rapidly cooled and in very humid atmosphere fails to nucleate its own water vapor to the leeward of the pit although analysis shows as much as 90% of water.

Another interesting event in the visit of these geologists was the collection of petrological specimens from the large boulders southeast of Halemaumau thrown out in 1790. The rock is a fine grained dense igneous mass with vugs containing crystals of hematite and other minerals, some of them spherical and white like analcite and others resembling nepheline. This hematite-bearing rock is a distinct product of deep ejection and it is a matter of great interest what conditions produced this special oxidization of the iron and what the mineral association really is.

Seismometric Record.—During the week ending midnight Sept. 10, 1920, two local earthquakes and one teleseism were registered as follows: Local shocks—Sept. 5, 12:50 p. m., feeble; Sept. 9, 11:59 p. m., slight, approximate distance to origin, 27 miles. Teleseism—Sept. 7, 3:24 p. m., approximate distance to origin, 3100 miles. Spasmodic microtremor diminished during the week from moderately strong to slight and harmonic tremor showed similar diminution. Microseisms continued slight. Movements of tilting were westward with strong fluctuations in the north-south direction until Sept. 8 and thereafter the movement was moderate to the north and east.

Week Ending September 17, 1920.

SUMMARY OF CONDITIONS.

The lava lakes of Halemaumau pit continued to subside throughout the week but at a rate only one-half as fast as that of the preceding week. The scene at the end of the week was unusually spectacular owing to the development of a strong lava cascade where the southeast pool had gone down more than the central lake and the whole flood of molten stuff rushed over a ledge of the concealed lake bottom into the swirling cauldron of glowing lava below. The usual streaming across the lake and between the islands and crags became faster, giving the tortuous basin the appearance of a lava river sweeping from west to east. An irregular block of crags and floors near the center of the pit broke away from the marginal portions and subsided with the lakes, while the outer ring of higher crags clung to the walls of the funnel with only a slight sagging inward of the summits.

This tendency of the bench magma to break down in annular steps with the inner rings going down farthest during a subsidence period has been observed before and appears to indicate that the withdrawal of the main pasty mass of the lava column beneath is at a maximum in the center of the pit, the funnel walls of the pit tending to retard the down-sinking of the outer annulus of semi-hardened substance.

JOURNAL.

Activity of Halemaumau.—Measurements for the week ending Sept. 17, 1920, expressed as depressions beneath the northeast monument on the rim of Halemaumau (3727 feet above sea-level), have been as follows:

	Mean lake level.	Peak of west crag.
Sept. 10, 11 a. m................	273 feet	182 feet
Sept. 16, 10 a. m................	280 "	184 "

In six days the lake sank 7 feet, averaging 1.2 feet per day and the crag 2 feet averaging 0.3 foot per day. The relief of the crag thus increased from 91 to 96 feet.

On Saturday, Sept. 11, at 2:30 p. m., the walls of the individual lake basins were mostly about 20 feet high and the islands had increased in size showing nearly vertical sides from 10-20 feet high. The lakes were sluggish with slow streaming toward the center from the southwest arm and there were crusted pools in the new eastern and northern pots, the last showing crusts at two levels, the inner one occupying a cavern.

A distinct new island had formed southwest of the center of the southwest arm, the mass standing high and showing a flat shoal east of it. At 3:10 p. m. the crusts south of this island broke away and a bubbling torrent poured eastward from the channel between the island and the south shore.

There was some bubbling fountaining in the east pond and the noises in the pit were chiefly those of plashing fountains of which not more than 5 or 6 were in action at one time. The bank at the south side of the entrance to the southeast arm had collapsed leaving an islet in the entrance channel and a talus slope against the bank. Probably some similar mechanism had produced the island in the southwest arm from collapse of the southwestern point of the south crag mass. The crevasse which had produced the eastern pot was now extended as an open chasm through to the northeastern margin of the southeast arm. There was a new tumble of rocks on the north-northeast floor of the pit made by a recent avalanche. Much smoke rose from the western and southern crag masses.

On Sept. 12 at 3 p. m. the pit was moderately fumy and inner platforms along the lake shores had been built since the previous day. The streaming from the southwest arm forked in the central pool so that one branch of the current led into the southeast arm through a narrow entrance only 5 feet wide and the other led to the north cove ending in a long patch of border fountains. The 3 islands of the central pool each showed a marginal platform standing about 2 feet above the liquid. A similar platform at the southern side of the channel leading to the southeast arm had been developed from the islet of the previous day. There was live lava in the east and north pots. The west pond appeared unusually low with a glowing margin as though subsidence were in progress. There were no central fountains in any of the pools.

At 3 p. m., Sept. 13, the inner marginal platform had increased and was building out the north shore of the central lake and tending to choke the region surrounding the island in the southwest arm. The lakes showed rapid fluctuations of level, 9 fountains were in action in different parts of the pit and the new pots were crusted over but exhibited glowing lava. The cliffs above the inner lake platforms still appeared to be from 15-20 feet high.

On the afternoon of Sept. 14 strong fluctuations of level of the lakes were still in evidence, for the lake was level with the new inner platforms at 3 p. m. but had sunk 5 feet below them at 4 p. m. so that the north islet stood like a mushroom with overhang on all sides. Rocks were heard falling from the northeast wall of the pit. Streaming in the channel was vigorous to the east and north. About 3 p. m. there was much puffing at the east pond. Seven or eight fountains were in action.

On Sept. 15 the lakes were much the same, some avalanches were seen and there were spells of very rapid streaming through the narrows from the central pool into the southeast arm.

On Sept. 16 at 10 a. m. it was evident that certain portions of the crag masses adjacent to the central lake were slipping downward along fracture planes more or less concentric with the pit. Outside of this a ring of floor surfaces representing the bottom of the pit remained at a higher level approximately 15 feet above the liquid of the lake. The inner group of benches had subsided along with the sinking of the liquid so that they stood only about 8 feet above it and at still lower levels were the new platforms of overflow at the edge of the lake only 2-3 feet high. The area included by the line of fracture involved the north and west points or capes which protrude into the central pool, and the west point including the southeastern half of the west crag mass. There is also included the western part of the south crag mass bounded by the southwest arm and the new chasm which extends that arm northward from its eastern end. The two western islands are comparatively low and belong to the sunken blork, the southwestern one showing a 2-foot platform around it. The southeast island, on the other hand, stands from 12-15 feet above the lake and seems to be a part of the outer floor like the walls of the southeast arm. The northeast crag mass is still high though the cracks through it on the north and south sides mark breaks extending from the central downsunken prism somewhat tangential to the plan of that prism. With the subsidence the bench magma has thus tended to fault concentrically with the central prism downthrown.

From 10-11 a. m. there were quiet skins over the east and west ponds and the walls inclosing these ponds were 15 feet high. A soft skin over lava pulsating beneath covered the eastern pot. The streaming of the central pool took its origin as usual from the southwest and radiated to the northwest and northeast, and through the southeast channel into the southeast arm. There was some fountaining against the eastern banks of both the east and west ponds. Much vapor rose from the southwest wall vent and the fume from the pit as a whole was at this time abundant, though at 6 a. m. it had been very thin.

Sept. 7, 1920. Halemaumau from lower north shelf,

Sept. 7, 1920. Lower North Shelf in Halemaumau, looking east.

ooking south and southwest. Photos, Jaggar.

Sept 7, 1920. Cavern of Postal Rift flow, third opening.

At 11 a. m. a remarkably rapid subsidence of the liquid lava developed in the southeast arm so that the difference in level between the liquid in that arm and in the central pool was about 12 feet, and an immense cascade was produced pouring from the lake into the southeast arm cauldron. All the currents of the southeast arm were reversed, the surface lava rushing northwestward from the end of the arm to the vortex at the base of the fall. The walls around the cauldron were now fully 25 feet high. On the right bank of the fall there was revealed by the lowering a rounded bench of red hot structureless paste below the level spatter markings of the evacuated shore higher up. During all of this crisis the eastern pot remained low with an inner shelf 15 feet down and the liquid lava visible 5 feet lower. The cascade made a dull roaring noise and vast quantities of fume rose from the churning liquid.

During the 30 minutes that the torrent was under observation there was no other evident change in the lakes, none of the other pools lowered, the cascade maintained its volume and height and the only effect was an acceleration of the surface streaming from west to east. The eastern pot was clearly connected with the southeast arm for the level of its lava was unusually low.

This cascade development was accordant with the unusually swift flow at the southeast narrows which had been repeatedly noticed as occurring in spasms since Sept. 5. On Sept. 15 a spasm of rapid inflow into the southeast arm was estimated to move 2 meters per second by Dr. F. Omori, a visitor here at this time. There was a similar cascade in the south arm of the lake system Nov. 23, 1919, just before the great subsidence of that month.

At 3 p. m. Sept. 17th the lake appeared lower and the cascade was still in action. Strong surface flowing crossed the southern side of the central pool from the region of the southwest pool; the eastern part of the southwest arm was crusted and motionless. The walls of the southeast arm cauldron were now 30 feet high, of the southwest arm 20 feet high, of the central depression 25 feet high, and of the west pond 15 feet high. The cascade was flowing at a flatter angle as though it had eroded its bottom, but the action at its foot was very violent. The newer islands and shore platforms were now 6 feet above the liquid. The southeastern part of the west crag mass and other portions of the inner subsided ring appeared lower than before and the isolation given to the southeastern floor block by the strong lowering of the two southern arms made it stand up in relief like a new tilted crag mass.

Seismometric Record.—During the week ending midnight Sept. 17, 1920, the only earthquake registered was a very feeble local one on Sept. 17th, 8:05 a. m. Spasms of microtremor during the week were few and weak to moderate. Harmonic tremor and microseismic motion were both slight. Tilting was nearly stationary with slight north and east tendency Sept. 16th.

Week Ending September 24, 1920.

SUMMARY OF CONDITIONS.

The subsidence of the lava lakes of Halemaumau which had amounted to 36 feet between Aug. 25th and Sept. 16 and probably to as much as 40 feet by Sept. 18th came to an end on the last named date and very rapid recovery set in whereby there was rising of the liquid lava of over 30 feet in two days. The day of flood tide in this spasm of sudden rising was Sept. 20th so that the whole movement may be considered to be closely related to the autumnal equinox.

The fume has become very thin, the cascade which was pouring to the southeast ceased, hot fountaining ensued in the lakes and the liquid lava tended to drown the low islets and points of platform jutting into the lakes. During the equinoctial week the rising tendency has continued with constriction of area of the lakes owing to growth of overflow platforms and the formation of arched crusts across the channels leading to the southeastern and southwestern arms. The inner basins of these arms have thus tended to become separate ponds. Along with the rising movement flaming cracks have developed marginal to the lakes and glowing cones which resemble beds of hot embers.

There has been no revival of the Kau Desert flows. An area about 200 feet back from the rim of Halemaumau on the northeast side, in old rock, that has been fuming since March, 1920, has developed solfataric action with hot sulphurous fumes and deposits of yellow and white salts. The area lies nearly in the line with an extension across the pit of the Kau Desert rift.

JOURNAL.

Activity of Halemaumau.—Measurements during the week ending Sept. 24, 1920, expressed as depressions below the northeast monument on the rim of Halemaumau (3727 feet above sea-level), have been as follows:

	Mean lake level.	Peak of northeast crag.	Peak of west crag.
Sept. 16, 10 a. m....	280 feet	...	184 feet
Sept. 22, 11 a. m....	255 "	182 feet	180 "

In 6 days the lake had risen 25 feet averaging 4.2 feet per day and the west crag rose 4 feet averaging 0.7 foot per day. The relief of the crag has thus diminished from 96 feet, Sept. 16th, to 75 feet, Sept. 22nd. The rising, in fact, had been much more rapid than these figures indicate, for on Sept. 18th the lake was lower than on Sept 16th and the bench of overflow during the maximum flooding of Sept. 20th stood 251 feet below the rim. The measured change between Sept. 16 and Sept. 20, therefore, was a rise of 29 feet in 4 days, but actually all of this and somewhat more took place between Sept. 18th and Sept. 20th. During these 2 days, therefore, there was certainly a rising of the liquid of more than 15 feet per day. On Sept. 22, the depression of the west pond which is the high source well of the system was 240 feet making it 15 feet higher than that main lake. The main lake at this time, measured on the west side of the central pool, stood 4 feet below the bench of overflow of Sept. 20th.

On Saturday, Sept. 18, observations of the lake from 11 a. m. to 4 p. m. showed that considerable fluctuations were in progress, the net result of which was pronounced rising with increase of fountains and thinning of the fume which permitted of clear seeing. The southeast cascade had ceased and there were spells of rising, with an appearance of sinking of the liquid at noon which may have been in part a rising of the bench magma.

In the forenoon the walls around the lake cups appeared about 15 feet high and the central lake had so risen that the liquid connected through to the east and north pots, by way of the chasms which had formed those depressions. The fracture block south of the eastern pot had thus become a nearly isolated table sloping toward the southeast arm. The cascade narrows leading to that arm was only about 4 feet wide. From the fracture block a new point of shore protruded southward into the southeast arm, built up of overflow material. This arm was quiet until the afternoon.

The streaming was moderate and in the usual direction from west to east with much tearing of black satiny skins making bright line patterns on the lakes. There were occasional large central fountains. Some talus slipping was heard. Above the inner recesses of the north pot a glowing flame hole had developed with puffing dense yellow and blue vapor above it, while underneath 2 tunnelways appeared to extend eastward and northeastward from this arm of the lake, best revealed during the noon sinking spell.

The southwest arm, west pond and east pond were at first quiet. After 1 p. m. there developed more intense fountaining and streaming with apparently lower lakes and in the west pond the crusts cracked and foundered and there was much caving in of spatter margins with strong central and marginal fountaining, sending up puffs of blue gas.

Caving in of spatter margins was seen in the main and southwest lakes also. From the west part of the southwest arm the streaming forked to the southeast and northeast. Some fountaining developed in the east pond. The small north island appeared like a low cake with stalactites hanging around it, the southwest island was slightly higher, and the southeast island was a pulpit rock 10 feet high.

By 4 p. m. there was a return of strong rising with development of a swift current into the southeast arm, the 2 pots were again flooded from the lake, the platform shore points were submerged and the north island was nearly submerged.

All day on Sept. 19th the fume was thin and the rising continued and on Sept. 20 at 10:30 a. m. the fume was very thin and the lakes were greatly enlarged by the flooding of their banks. At this time the symmetry of the lake basins about an axis, northwest-southeast, was very marked, the ground plan appearing like a bird on its back, the west pond the head, the east and southwest pools the wings, and the southeast pool the tail. The islets and central banks were only 1 foot high, the surfaces were generally quiet and from 9-11 border fountains were puffing and splashing. Streaming was slight and the surfaces were covered with black soft skins. The lake cups of August outside the inner platforms showed the following heights of inclosing cliffs: west pond, 12 feet; central lake, 15 feet; southeast arm, 10 feet; southwest arm, 8 feet; and east pond, 5 feet.

An appearance of subsidence began at 10:30 a. m. New flood platforms were revealed and an arch of crust was left between the southwest arm island and the south crag mass. Under this arch there was eastward streaming to the inner part of the southwest arm. The southwest wall fumarole continued its activity.

At 4:30 p. m. Sept. 21 the lake was down 3-4 feet relative to its new benches and these had been built to a level even higher than that recorded on the previous day. The flood level had reached the edge of the east pot fracture block on the southeast arm side and the base of the several crag masses had been flooded with new platform material so as to diminish their relief. The cliffs of the lake cups recorded on the previous day as 8-15 feet high were now only 5-10 feet high. The banks of the actual lake in the central region were in general 4 feet high and the marginal ponds showed 3-foot rims. The development of the platform made the lake narrower than when seen Sept. 20th.

Such platform construction of the pools was especially in evidence through the building of bridges on the north and south sides of the island in the southwest arm and across the entrance to the southeast arm, for the time shutting off these arms as separate ponds. From the tunnel under these bridges there was eastward streaming, making 3 marked bands of festooned surface skins and there were two other such bands appearing like separate rivers flowing eastward across the central pool on each side of the southwest island. In general there were from 5-7 fountains and an occasional central fountain was developed in the north part of the central pool. The fume was very thin.

Sept. 22 at 11 a. m. the fume continued thin, there was the same eastward streaming, the bridges persisted, and an additional bridge had been formed between the southeast island and the southeast shore. A considerable platform had been built out into the central lake on its northeast side. The north pot was quiet. On the east side of the southeast island a large grotto was in action and there were intermittent central fountains, sometimes two at once. The shore line banks were 3-4 feet high.

On Sept. 23 at 2:30 p. m. a circuit of the pit by the way of the east and north sides showed that the lakes were high with their inner platforms only 1 foot above the liquid. The outer cliffs inclosing the lake cups were about 7 feet high at the west pond, in the center and at the southwest arm, and only 2-3 feet high at the southwest side of the southwest arm and at the east pond. There were 10-12 fountains in action and the streaming eastward was as usual. The eastern portion of the southwest arm and the whole of the southeast arm were still more isolated as separate lakes by the heavy bridges formed at their connection channels, but the bridge connecting the southeast island with the shore had broken down. The strongest and most continuous grotto fountaining was on the southeast side of this island. The cracks in the north floor of the pit near the north pot were again fuming and stained with solfataric deposits. There had been more overflows of the north cove and the east chasm. Such overflowing of the lake shores made the southern crag mass appear to be dwindling in size owing to the overflow platform growing around it. The fume from the southwest wall vent was slight. There was fluctuations from rising to sinking between 2 and 3 p. m.

The fume from the pit itself was thin but from the southwest crack in the Kilauea floor outside of Halemaumau the acid fume appears to be increasingly thick and the solfataras there are increasingly hot and brightly colored, with very poisonous vapor rising.

Seismometric Record.—During the week ending midnight, Sept. 24, 1920, one local quake and 3 teleseisms were registered as follows: Local quake—Sept. 21, 10:40 a. m., very feeble. Teleseisms—Sept. 20, 4:14 a. m., strong, apparent distance of origin, 3200 miles; Sept. 21, 7:24 a. m., slight; Sept. 24, 11:59 a. m., slight. Spasmodic microtremor was moderate during the week and harmonic tremor slight to moderate. Microseismic movement increased from slight to moderate. Tilting was northward during the early part of the week with fluctuations in the east-west direction and became strongish to the east about Sept. 23

Week Ending October 1, 1920.

SUMMARY OF CONDITIONS.

The rising of liquid lava in Halemaumau which was so conspicuous at the time of the equinox has continued during the past week so that the entire inner circular landscape of lakes, hills, and plains 1100 feet in diameter is seen to be rising bodily. The crag peaks have risen more than the rest, 13-15 feet in a week, the lakes in the same time rising only 4 or 5 feet. The tunnels which formed where the narrows leading to arms of the lake had crusted over and made lava bridges, have been so wrenched by the rising movement that one of them on the southeast arm has broken down before the crushing forces of the uplifting crag blocks and there is left a narrow chasm with a rifted promontory beside it.

As usual in the case of a rising movement the second stage after strong rising of the lakes is an uplift of the crags with maximum upward thrust in the center tending to tilt the crag blocks and adjacent floors away from the center. This centrifugal tilt is very marked in the present rising spell so that the shores of the three-armed lake tend to become lower from the center toward the walls of the pit, new escarpments in the central region recently shore lines are lifted to become crag ridges, and the marginal ponds have their entire cups titlted centrifugally so that their liquid lava in rising overflows only on the side away from the center. In the course of the disturbances of the week the northern of the 3 islands in the central lake has collapsed and disappeared.

JOURNAL.

Activity of Halemaumau.—Measurements during the week ending Oct. 1, 1920, expressed as depressions below the northeast monument on the rim of Halemaumau (3727 feet above sea-level), have been as follows:

	Mean lake level.	Peak of northeast crag.	Peak of west crag.
Sept. 22, 11 a. m...	255 feet	182 feet	180 feet
Sept. 29, 2 p. m...	253 "	167 "	167 "

In 7 days the lake rose 2 feet averaging 0.3 foot per day and each crag rose about 14 feet averaging 2 feet per day. Both crags on Sept. 29 had thus increased their relief from about 75 feet to 86 feet. The base of the crags on their outer or wall sides had not taken part in this rising movement, for the east, west, and southwest pools overflowed these surface without any coniderable rising of the liquid. Therefore it would seem that a central tumescence or doming of the lake bottom material was the prime cause of the movement and the 3 triangular sectors of which the crag masses are the peaks, executed pivotal movements about axes along the base of the walls of the pit, respectively, northeast, northwest and south.

On Saturday, Sept. 25, 1920, at 9 p. m., there were streaming bands of liquid lava pouring from under arches of crust at the southeast and southwest arms. The west pond stood lower relative to its banks than the eastern pool. There was a flaming crack at the north pot and at a glowing filagree cone built over a grotto at the east end of the southwest arm. There was another glowing crack, probably flaming, at the base of the southwest wall of the pit over the rift opening. Twelve fountains were in action, from 1 to 5 of these being in the north central region of the main lake where sometimes these would merge into one large continuous fountain. Streaming was as usual from the southwest bay to the central pool. The fume was moderately thin.

On Sept. 26 at 10 a. m., it was evident that the liquid lava stood at a very high level in most of the pools and had been overflowing at the east pond. The north island had disappeared, the west pond was singularly low with banks at least 12 feet high, and a torrent poured from the central pool under an arch of crust into the southeast arm. The marginal bench around the main lake was only 2-3 feet high, but the southwest island appeared somewhat increasing in height and dense vapor rose as though from a chimney in the summit of the west crag, though no smoke whatever rises from the similar summit peak of the northeast crag.

On Sept. 27 at 4 p. m. the lakes were high and the fume had been notably thin all day. Both the east and west ponds were now only 1 to 2 feet below their banks and there was much gas puffing at the east pond where a filagree cone showed a flaming vent on the southern margin of the pond. The southern arms were sluggish, there was the usual streaming from the southwest arm and the 2 islands stood from 6-8 feet above the liquid. Differential uplift of the floor surfaces was beginning to be manifest, the south bank of the southeast arm standing high and showing that the southern floor was tilting southward, whereas the platform built around the island in the southwest arm was tilting to the northwest. There were 12 fountains in action and the fume was mostly from the top of the west crag.

At 4:30 p. m. the heavy crusts which had accumulated around the tunnel entrance in the southeast arm suddenly broke away and for 15 minutes a rapid torrent poured from the central pool under the arch into the southeast arm, recalling the mechanism of the recent cascade. Then there was a slowing down and the surfaces crusted over.

On Sept. 28 at 3 p. m. the east and west ponds were still high and the central region showed banks standing 4-6 feet above the liquid lava. The tilting of the crag sectors was now becoming pronounced, the southeastern floor and peaks were lifting toward the center and dipping towards the southeast so that the inner shelf south of the southeastern narrows showed a distinct tilting up. It was evident moreover that the escarpment south of the west crag mass, recently a shore line, was being tilted up northward. The eastern and northern benches were beginning to show signs of a tilt northeastward. The sectors are not tilted straight away from the center but somewhat obliquely and irregularly.

On this day there were from 12 to 15 fountains in action and at about 3:30 p. m. another breaking up of crusts was seen in the southeast arm followed by a southeast torrent under the bridge. During all of this the east pond remained high and puffing. There were signs at the north cove of fresh overflows.

At 1:30 p. m. Sept. 29 the east and west ponds stood 3 feet below their banks and streaming was in progress under the bridge leading into the southeast arm. Later the east pond rose to overflowing and the liquid lava of the southeast arm appeared to back up and cause the torrent to slow its movement. At the north pot there was a bubbling pond of molten lava oval in form and 10 feet in diameter. The liquid in the pot appeared higher than that in the central lake.

On Oct. 1 at 10:30 a. m. the fume in the pit was thin but at the rift solfatara southwest it was increasingly dense. The most conspicuous change in Halemaumau was the disappearance of the bridge across the channel leading from the central lake to the southeast arm. There was now an open channel which showed fluctuating spells of rapid streaming into the arm. No such breakdown had yet occurred at the bridges north and south of the island in the southwest arm. There were 6-8 fountains in the lakes and the height of the banks was 3-4 feet at the outer pools and 8-10 feet at the shores and islands in the center. Fresh overflows were visible on the northeast side of the east pond and on the south side of the southwest arm. The fume chimney on top of the west crag has now become a conspicuous feature of the pit.

Seismometric Record.—During the week ending midnight Oct. 1, 3 local earthquakes were registered as follows: Sept. 28, 6:40 a. m., apparent distance to origin 13 miles, felt in this vicinity; Sept. 29, 2:20 p. m., slight; and Sept. 29, 7:49 p. m., very feeble. Spasmodic microtremor increased during the week to moderately strong. Harmonic tremor remained slight to moderate. Microseismic motion was slight the early part of the week and increased to moderate after Sept. 29th. Tilting was westward, Sept. 25, stationary, Sept. 26-27, and pronounced to the north and east Sept. 29-30, with some recovery to the southwest Oct. 1.

T. A. JAGGAR,
Volcanologist.

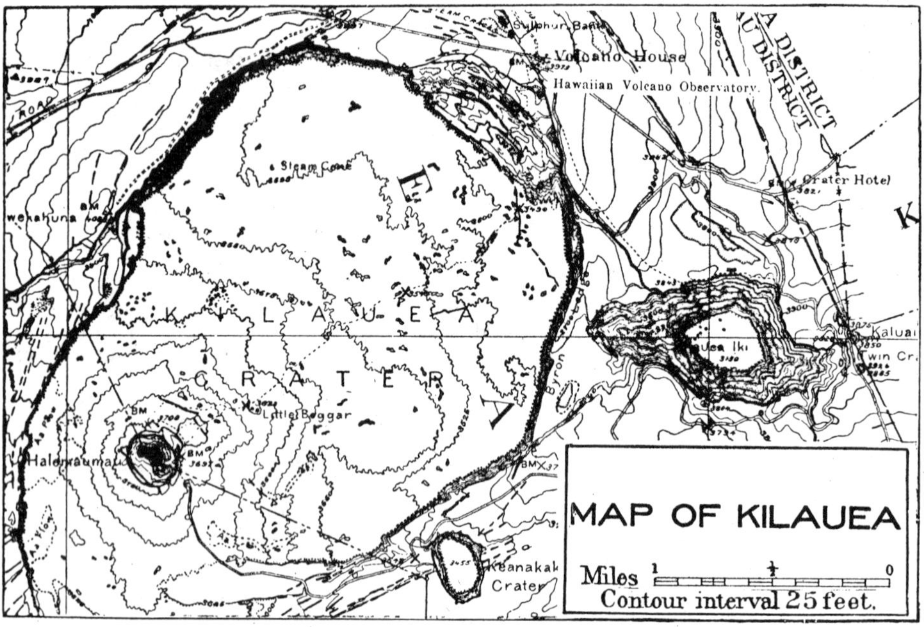

HAWAIIAN VOLCANO OBSERVATORY.

All exchanges should be addressed to
HAWAIIAN VOLCANO OBSERVATORY,
Volcano House, P. O. Hawaii.

The Observatory is equipped with the following seismometric instruments rebuilt at the station in 1918 for the special needs of volcano research: two Bosch-Omori pendulums, high speed registration of local earthquakes; one optically recording seismograph for distant earthquakes; one clinograph registering E-W tilting of the ground. A vertical component seismograph was in December, 1918, set up in experimental operation. These are seated on concrete piers in a closed basement room having practically constant temperature, beneath the chief Observatory building near the hotel. Time is referred to a rated chronometer, checked at intervals by wireless signal from the Pearl Harbor Naval Station. The chronometer is loaned by the College of Hawaii. Hawaiian standard time (H. S. T.) is 10 hrs. 30 min. slower than Greenwich time.

CANCANI SCALE OF SEISMIC INTENSITY.

Expressed by accelerations measured in millimeters per second per second.

I.	Instrumental	0.0	2.5
II.	Very slight	2.5	5.0
III.	Slight	5.0	10.0
IV.	Sensible, mediocre	10.0	25.0
V.	Rather strong	25.0	50.0
VI.	Strong	50.0	100.0
VII.	Very strong	100.0	250.0
VIII.	Ruinous	250.0	500.0
IX.	Disastrous	500.0	1000.0
X.	Very disastrous	1000.0	2500.0
XI.	Catastrophic	2500.0	5000.0
XII.	Great catastrophe	5000.0	10000.0

Grade IV. is ordinarily the minimum perceived by the senses; and in grade XII, the acceleration or rate of change of motion (jerk) reaches that of terrestrial gravitation.

In the standard form of report the maximum intensity or acceleration, designated by the symbol a, or max. a, is given in the conventional unit of milligal. The milligal is a measure of acceleration, such that 1 milligal = 1/100 mm. per sec. per sec. = 10 μ. per sec. per sec. The Cancani scale, here defined in terms of millimeters per sec. per sec., can therefore be expressed in milligals by multiplying each of the numbers by 100.

U. S. DEPARTMENT OF AGRICULTURE
WEATHER BUREAU
CHARLES F. MARVIN, CHIEF

MONTHLY BULLETIN
OF THE
Hawaiian Volcano Observatory

VOL. VIII. HONOLULU, HAWAII, OCTOBER, 1920 No. 10

Week Ending October 8, 1920.

SUMMARY OF CONDITIONS.

The activity of the week at Halemaumau has recalled the conditions of the autumn of 1916, when there was similar steady rising of the lava column with alternations between liquid flooding and lift of the crag sectors, and such phenomena occurred as are now conspicuous, radiating bright lines of streaming from the west, migratory and large fountains, tipping crags, tilting cups of the ponds, islands making and disappearing, and overflows filling the downtilted margin along the wall cracks.

The fountains have been increasing in number so that from 12 to 14 are often in action at one time, and central continuous fountaining jets which migrate with the currents are common. The benches have been overflowed from the southwest bay and from the east and west ponds. There has been more glowing and hissing at the inner wall-vent of the southwest rift, and the Red Solfatara (southwest of Halemaumau) makes increasingly dense fume, though the fume in the pit is thin. More lift of the south crag mass has broken down the bridge south of it, connecting the southwest arm again with the southwest bay. The west crag mass in scraping against the wall of the pit on its west side has made a chasm there. The southwestern island toppled over southward, then became joined by a bridge to the south shoreline of the lake, and now is lifting and extending itself eastward. The east pot has been lifted on the back of the northeastern crag mass and has become apparently extinct. For a second time the uplifted shoreline flat, south of the southeastern narrows has broken down along a crevasse and created a fracture block sagging towards the lake. Both the east and west ponds have developed the habit of breaking up from time to time with much spraying of fountains and foundering of crusts, this being followed by slight subsidence, a period of crusting over and a subsequent rise. Spatter ramparts have begun to appear in several places.

JOURNAL.

Activity of Halemaumau.—Measurements during the week ending October 8, 1920, expressed as depressions below the northeast monument on the rim of Halemaumau (3727 feet above sea level), have been as follows:

	Mean lake level.	Northeast peak.	Southeast peak.	West peak.
Sept. 29, 2 p. m.....	253 feet	167 feet	....	167 feet
Oct. 7, 2 p. m.....	245 feet	173 feet	205 feet	162 feet

In 8 days the lake rose 8 feet, averaging 1 foot per day, the northeast crag sank 6 feet averaging 0.7 foot per day, and the west crag rose 5 feet averaging 0.6 foot per day. The relief of the northeast crag thus decreased from 86 feet to 72 feet and that of the west crag from 86 feet to 83 feet.

On October 3 at 9:30 a. m. there was slow streaming, 5 fountains were in action, quiet skins covered the lakes, and there was a noisy blowing grotto on the southeast side of the southeast island. This island remained about 10 feet high but the southwestern island appeared to have overturned toward the south and to be eroded away on its northwest side leaving a large channel in that direction and a small channel south of it. This island was smaller than before, stood only 3 feet above the liquid and its surface sloped southeast. Crusts tended to accumulate on its southeast side.

The lift of the crag sectors was now conspicuous in the southeast peak, the cliffs on both sides of that peak appearing higher than before. Along with this uplift the bench south of the narrows leading to the southeast arm had broken down in a square block leaving a wide crevasse between it and the southeast peak. The whole bench of the southern crag mass along the south side of the central pool was uplifted and the southern flat areas showed tilt to the southeast and south.

A similar tilt of the west crag mass appeared to be toward the north creating a new scarp 20 feet high with cliff face to the south, on the west side of the southwest bay. The lift of the northeast crag mass had left the east pot crusted and dead and stained with sulphur.

The evidence of these tiltings was shown in the relatively low banks at the west pond, east pond, southwest bay, and north side of the southeast arm, only 3-4 feet high. The margins of the central lake and the north shore of the southwest arm pond stood 6-8 feet high and the cliff on the south side of the southeast arm showed an upward slope from east to west of its crest level above the liquid lava of from 10 to 15 feet.

Dense fume rose from the summit of the west crag and moderate fume from the south crag mass and from the southeast island above the large grotto. As a whole the fume in the pit was thin.

The talus accumulations tend to be grouped along the base of the northern, eastern, and southern walls of the pit and to be less conspicuous on the side of the western walls. This is largely inherited material from an earlier stage so that this arrangement probably means that the center of upbuilding has been against the west wall of the pit.

At 10:30 a. m. the southwest bay and the east pond were rising and the lakes were generally higher. The southwest rift wall-vent was hissing. The south arm pond now appeared to be quite shut off except for some streaming through the tunnel on the north side of the island partition which had grown between this pond and the southwest bay.

On October 4 at 5 p. m. the lakes were lower, the southwest wall-vent was hissing and glowing, 11-14 fountains were in action and the bright lines of streaming radiated eastward in the southwest arm pond, in the central pool and in the southeast arm. Central fountains tended to develop in lines and these would migrate with the currents, the fountains growing in size as they progressed. Three large central fountains were seen simultaneously in different places, one in the west pond migrating to the north bank, one in the central pool migrating to the northeast cove, and one in the southeast arm migrating to the southeast end of the arm.

The southwest island was now 5 feet high and had increased in size. The southeast island stood 8 feet high. The shore margin of the previous day was everywhere upraised relative to the liquid. The west pond gave pronounced evidence that its cup was tilted northwestward by the uplift of the west crag sector, for its confining rim on the southeast side was 8 feet high, while on the northwest side it was only 3 feet high. The east pond showed similar evidence, its southwestern margin standing 5 feet high and its northeastern bank 3 feet high. Similarly the southwest bay showed a 3-foot bank on its west side and a 6-foot bank on the east. The margins of the main lake were generally 8-10 feet high.

There was much noise of plashing and puffing fountains. There were the usual fluctuations of sinking and rising, and during a sinking spell the south chasm showed a tunnel on the central pool side. The north pot was small and glowing. A crevasse could be seen on the southwestern face of the northeast crag mass trending southeast-northwest. This appeared to check with the downfaulting of the central prism noted on September 17th.

At 2:30 p. m. on October 5th the lake had again risen and the southwest island showed an eastward extension and a bridge connecting it with the south crag mass. The east pond was in process of overflowing on the northeast side for 50 feet to the north, its surface flush with the bank on the southwest side. The west pond was 1 foot below its bank on the northwest side and 5 feet down on the southeast side. The point south of the entrance to the southeast arm, the fracture block, had sunk about 5 feet in 2 days and was now a low platform only about 4 feet above the liquid. The main lake had been overflowing its north cove extension, and the north pot had enlarged with development of a glowing fracture area west of it. The southwest wall-vent continued its hissing.

The west pond was crusted at first, but a spurting fountain broke out against the bank in the west corner of the pond and finally developed a fountaining area 20 feet in diameter with spraying jets that shot 80 feet into the air. Sheets of yellow-green flame and puffs of semi-transparent fume rising from this violent fountain suggested, on a small scale, the Alika source fountains on Mauna Loa seen in October, 1919. The fountaining activity gradually spread across the south side of the pond so that the crust broke up, then there was general bubble fountaining, the entire pond became deflated and sank about 3 feet.

Since the north island disappeared there has been no trace of any shoal in that vicinity. The island growth appears to depend on current transportation of foundered material and deposition where the bottom is least eroded and the current velocity dwindles.

On October 7 at 2 p. m. the southwest arm was found to be again connected by a wide channel with the southwest bay, the bridge being entirely destroyed. There was strong streaming into it from the southwest bay and many shore fountains along its southern margin. There were large spraying central fountains seen in several places. The channel leading to the southeast arm was narrow. A rampart with flaming holes and spatter cones was being built on the east side of the east pond and 5 fountains were in action in that pond. There had been recent overflow southward from this pond as well as northward. It was now about 1 foot below its bank.

The north pot was brimming level with its banks and crusted over. The west pond was brimming on its northwest side, showed a wall 8 feet high on its southeast side and at 2:15 p. m. there was breaking up of its surface and a subsidence of 2 feet with much bubble fountaining. Fresh driblet overflow had recently flooded the north bank of the pond. In the central pool the north bay was crusted over, 4 central fountains were in action at one time, and other features remained unchanged. Blue smoke appeared to be increasing from cracks in the isthmus separating the west pond from the central pool. An east-west crack had developed across the fracture block south of the southeast narrows.

It was evident that the southwest scarp of the west crag mass was still lifting and against the wall of the pit west of it there was a sag and a pressure ridge where the floor had met friction in crushing along the wall. An avalanche was heard in that vicinity.

At 10 a. m. October 8, general rising continued with thin fume from the pit, but dense white vapor rose from the summit of the west crag and increasing volumes of fume were puffing up from the Red Solfatara.

Inspection of the southwest arm from the south side of the pit showed that there was still a bridge and tunnel south of the island in that arm but a broad open channel lay north of the island where the streaming was eastward from the southwest bay. The only change noted in the central pool was the more massive development of the east extension of the southwest island. A large fall of spatter bank was seen at the south side of the central pool. About 16 fountains were in action in different parts of the pit. The west pond exhibited again a breaking up of crust followed by subsidence and recovery. Both the east and west ponds stood high, the east pond puffing loudly along its northeast border. The north pot was at first quiet, then the crust broke up with much fountaining and the liquid lava sank about 3 feet and continued boiling.

A considerable chasm was now developed along the wall crack west of the west crag. Just south of this place the southwest bay had been overflowing its banks.

Seismometric Record.—During the week ending midnight October 8, 1920, 6 local earthquakes were registered as follows: October 3, 11:56 a. m. very feeble; 11:30 p. m. slight, apparent distance to origin 14 miles; October 5, 4:28 a. m., two feeble shocks a few seconds apart; 9:44 p. m. very feeble; and October 8, 2:11 a. m. feeble. Spasmodic microtremor was moderate in the early part of the week developing strong spasms October 5 and October 7. Harmonic tremor increased from moderate to strongish. Microseismic motion also increased during the week from moderate to moderately strong. Tilting was slight southward and westward October 2, eastward October 3-5, pronounced to the west and south October 6-8.

Week Ending October 15, 1920.

SUMMARY OF CONDITIONS.

The rising of the lava in Halemaumau continued during this week, the crags lifting three times as fast as the lake and so greatly increasing their relief. The lakes have overflowed the margins of the floor of the pit, the north pot has enlarged, a new pot has formed against the base of the southwest wall, and at the place where the Kau Desert crack emerges inside the pit there has developed a cone 10 feet high which gives vent to liquid lava. This lava floods the black ledge southward for a long distance a few feet above the lake level, and at times has cascaded from the bank into the lake. There are now four outlying ponds respectively southwest, east, north, and west, four crag masses south, northeast, west, and north (the latter a small remnant), and a large central lake with long arms southeast and southwest and two islands in the central pool. The perceptible heat at the edge of Halemaumau has increased with the more rapid streaming and the increase in numbers of fountains, of which twenty are sometimes in action at once. New cracks have formed where flat surfaces of floor swelled upward, and the disturbances of the floors have set loose some avalanches from the walls.

JOURNAL.

Activity of Halemaumau.—Measurements for the week ending October 15, 1920, expressed as depressions below the northeast monument on the rim of Halemaumau (3727 feet above sea level), have been as follows:

	Mean lake level.	Northeast peak.	Southeast peak.	West peak.
Oct. 7, 2 p. m.....	245 feet	173 feet	205 feet	162 feet
Oct. 14, 10 a. m.	237 feet	154 feet	198 feet	140 feet

In seven days the lake rose 8 feet, averaging 1.1 feet per day; the northeast crag 19 feet, averaging 2.7 feet; the southeast crag 7 feet, averaging 1 foot; and the west crag 22 feet, averaging daily 3.1 feet. The relief of the southeast peak decreased from 40 feet to 39 feet, but the others increased, the northeast from 72 feet to 83 feet and the west peak from 83 feet to 97 feet.

On Saturday, October 9, the activity was as before, with spells of breaking up in the west pond and some overflowing there. The fume from the pit was thin, and that from the Red Solfatara was dense.

October 10 at 11:15 a. m. there was increased overflowing of marginal areas in evidence. The west pond had overflowed along the base of the wall from a point beneath the west station to the northern floor, cascading through the gap between the north crag remnant and the lower north shelf. The southwest arm and the bay leading to it had both overflowed the black ledge southwest and south. The east pond had overflowed east and north and the north pot or north pond had sent a stream to the base of the north wall of the pit and another westward. This niche adjacent to the north cove of the central lake had also been overflowed from the lake itself, which had flooded also the western point of its shore.

The lift of the crags north and south of the southeast arm had so raised the cup of the latter that the pool was stagnant and so incapable of overflowing, but spatter ramparts were being built at its eastern end.

During a depression spell from 18 to 20 fountains were seen in action at once, whereas during rising only 7 or 8 were playing. The streaming during this lowering was from the southwest channel to the northeast cove, with migrating large fountains in the center. Several caverns were revealed as the liquid sank, at the east, south, and west coves, the south side of the southwestern channel and the south corner of the southwest bay. The noises of the pit were chiefly plashing from the fountains, with puffing in addition at the east pond. The islands stood high as large masses, the western one 10 feet, the eastern 15 feet above the liquid. The bench on the south side of the southeast narrows had again lifted until it stood 10 feet above the lake.

This lifting action was shown in many ways elsewhere, as though the border fills had weighted down the crag blocks marginally and tilted them up centrally. Cracks showed swelling effect on the northern floor slopes of the west crag mass, on the floor northeast of the north pot, and on the floor south of the southeast arm. All the east pot region was tilted up, sloping northward. The north pot had caved back and become enlarged so that it was 50 feet long, with lava inside streaming northeastward to a fountaining cavern. The north point protruding into the central lake had been lifted until it was now 18 feet high, and raised inner benches could be seen all around the lake. A small pressure ridge trending east-west, apparently thrust from the south, was discernible on the north floor of the pit between new flows from both sides. Another cracked and swollen area was in the black ledge adjacent to the southwest bay of the lake, just against the Kau rift crack. A conspicuous crack trending southwest crossed the ledge, while on either side there were overflows from the lake. There was much fume from the crags and floors.

Much activity of fountaining and overflowing was reported for the afternoon of October 11, and on October 12 at 5 p. m. the lakes were found rather quiet, 9 or 10 fountains were in action, the southwest and southeast arms crusted over, except when the former had a breaking-up spell. There had been a new overflow of its bank by the west pond, the stream extending eastward along the base of the north talus to join with a stream from the north pot. The southwest wall vent was spurting and glowing and live lava on the bench southeast from it showed that flows from this vent were moving. The west island was connected by a bridge of crust with the south crag mass. The east pond was but slightly depressed below its banks, the west pond somewhat more, and the other pools 6 to 8 feet.

October 14 at 10 a. m. there were 10 fountains in action and toward 11 a. m. the liquid lava was rising. The central pool was surrounded by uplifted walls 20 feet high above the inner marginal platforms of fresh accretion which stood 2 feet above the liquid lava on the west and north. In contrast to the raised central area the outlying pools lay only 1 or 2 feet below their banks. The west island had built out at lake level towards the northeast and stood 15 feet high. The east island had lifted until it was 20 feet high and there was violent fountaining in the channel south of it. In the northwest bay of the lake a big fall of spatter bank accumulations was seen.

The bench magma of the middle region was evidently rising, for the surface which had been the crust over the northeast cove was now, along with the pulpit rock north of it, lifted into a crag. The north pot adjacent to this crag was now an oval east-west pond and east of it the ground had swollen up still more opening wider the crevasses. Along the south side of the west pond there were other new crevasses parallel to the edge of the pond, which was becoming larger by infall on that side. This was all part of the northwestern backslope of the west crag mass, and on the opposite, or southeast, side of the crag, at the base of the steep part, the portions which had slipped downward recently were fast becoming engulfed by the overflows and bench building of the rising lake.

On the southwest black ledge against the wall of the pit there was a new pot of live lava 15 feet in diameter just north of the Kau rift crack. At the rift crack a driblet cone, 10 feet high, was flaming. The whole southern black ledge was covered with live flows from this cone, which drained in a small cascade 2 feet wide from the bench into the southwest arm of the lake, falling about 2 feet. There were snaky piles of pahoehoe lava near the cone, and along the south talus the flows were pushing eastward and filling hollows.

The overflows on the north floor from the west pond and north pot were united, but those from the east pond did not yet extend so far. There was fresh avalanche debris northwest on the new flow surfaces. Streaming in the lake was from the southwest and to the southeast, and in the west pond the current was northward. Dense white fume rose from the cracks in the summit of the west crag, and bluer fume from the north base of the crag. Steamy fume rose from many fissures in the south crag mass. In general fume from the benches is blue, that from the summits appears more like steam. The noises of the pit were of quiet plashing.

At 10:50 a. m. there was sudden violent fountaining in the tunnel under the overhang at the east end of the north pot. Then at the west end of this cauldron there began a rapid upwelling of foaming lava like an artesian fountain, dome shaped, there was intense bubble fountaining, and the basin filled to brimming but stopped and failed to overflow. Then the froth subsided a foot or two and became quiet. The current was from west to east and it appeared that the breaking up of crust had released gas pressure and so started a small local eruption.

At 6 p. m. October 15th, the relative heights of pools and shorelines were about the same, eleven fountains were in action, there were no fresh flows, a considerable bay was forming on the north side of the southeast arm, and the west island was connected by a bridge of crust with the south crag mass. The cone at the southwest rift crack was flaming, and there were flames through perforations in the roofs of grottos at the eastern ends of the southern arms of the lake and at other places. Streaming was swift through the southwest channel to the center of the lake, and thence to the southeast arm.

Seismometric Record.—During the week ending midnight, October 15, 1920, seven local earthquakes and one teleseism were registered as follows: Local shocks—October 9, 1:21 a. m. feeble, 4:43 a. m. very feeble; October 10, 10:14 a. m. very feeble; October 11, 7:16 a. m. very feeble; October 12, 9:10 a. m. and 10:02 p. m., both very feeble; October 13, 8:50 p. m. very feeble. The distant earthquake was slight, at 4:05 a. m. October 15. Spasmodic microtremor was moderate to strong, harmonic tremor moderate, with some increase on October 11, and microseismic motion was slight to moderate. Tilting was moderate to the north and east October 9 to 11, stationary October 12-14, and strong to the southeast October 15.

Week Ending October 22, 1920.

SUMMARY OF CONDITIONS.

The lava of Halemaumau has risen 20 to 30 feet during the week and the excessive rising of the crags in the previous week was conpensated by excessive rising of the lakes this week. This flooding of the liquid has steadily increased the overflows on the benches and all through the week these overflows have been in progress until they nearly completely encircle the crag masses. The main lake is now only 207 feet below the rim of the pit. During all of this rising the wall-cone at the southwest rift crack has remained a center of lava emission, making a broad flat heap and feeding flows in the south wall-valley.

Observations on October 16 and 20, and reports from cattlemen and others, suggest that some increased fuming has occurred on Mauna Loa at the summit crater and also on the southern slope. There have been pronounced swarms of small local earthquakes registered instrumentally.

JOURNAL.

Activity of Halemaumau.—Measurements for the week ending October 22, 1920, expressed as depressions below the northeast monument on the rim of Halemaumau (3727 feet above sea level) have been as follows:

	Mean lake level.	Northeast peak.	West peak.
Oct. 14, 10 a. m.............	237 feet	154 feet	140 feet
Oct. 21, 4 p. m.............	207 feet	130 feet	116 feet

In seven days the lake rose 30 feet, averaging 4.3 feet per day, and the northeast and west crags each 24 feet, averaging 3.4 feet. The relief of the northeast peak above the lake, owing to flooding by the latter, decreased from 83 to 77 feet, and of the west peak from 97 to 91 feet.

On Saturday, October 16, at 3:30 p. m., the lakes were quiet at first, but this was followed by a breaking up and sinking of crusts with 7 or 8 fountains. The outer pools showed low shorelines, but the central pool showed shoreline bluffs 10 to 15 feet high. New cracks were forming on the north backslope of the west crag due to caving in of the west pond banks on that side under the perpetual tilting uplift of the crag mass. A glowing cone had formed at the south corner of the southwest arm. A fall of marginal spatter was seen from the south side of the southwest channel. From the north and south edges of the west pond there was fresh driblet overflow. The former island in the southwest arm was now a peninsula, as a fill of fresh flows had choked the channel southwest of it. The north pot and the cove near it were crusted over, but at 3:45 p. m. the crust on the pot broke up. The east island in the central lake was now high and narrow and leaning southeastward as though it might fall over.

At 11:30 a. m., October 17, the lake was hotly fountaining and streaming from west to east and the floor lava was rising obviously. Nine fountains were counted. There was much caving in of spatter banks, and the southwest wall cone and its flows were glowing. The portions of the west crag which had slipped down on the lake side were becoming submerged, only a few jagged red remnants of rock protruding above the overflow bench. On the western side of this crag mass a heavy avalanche had been seen at 8 a. m. sending up a cloud of red dust. This was where the end of the crag being tilted northward came against the west wall of the pit and so created dragging friction. Fresh driblet overflows indicated recent spasms of brimming at the southwest arm, west pond, and east pond. The streaming from the innermost end of the southwest arm was westward, and thence northeastward through the channel leading to the central pool.

A visit to the Red Solfatara or smoke hole southwest of Halemaumau on the Kau rift at 4:30 p. m., October 18, found this place puffing up soft, white steamy volutes of volcanic fume after the recent heavy rains, making the vent very conspicuous. The bright red alteration of the surface lava was now more rusty in color, the yellow sulphurous patches being still very abundant. The fume from Halemaumau was thin. The wind being southerly the view of the pit from the south and southwest rim was very clear. A large wall-crack chasm had opened next to the west crag, and on the lake side the pinnacles of the west crag fault-block were now mostly an overflow bench.

The lakes were overflowing strongly. The southeast arm had overbrimmed its end, the flow pouring northward to merge with flows from the east pond. Streaming on the surface of this arm swept in a curve from the narrows to the south shore. On the southeast bank there was a flaming cone. The east pond overflows were moving both north and south and had pooled under the northern shelves of the pit, merging with flows from the west pond and the north pot. The west pond was overflowing both north and south lips. The north cove was now a continuous arm through to the north pot. The northeast cove of the central lake was surmounted by a lifted platform 20 feet high with deep cavernous overhang beneath where a tunnel appeared to lead under the northeast crag towards the east pond. A new islet had appeared near the northeast point of the lake shore. The streaming across the lake was towards this point and into the north arm. The east island had toppled over as expected in a southerly direction leaving a scarp with inclined backslope.

From 7 to 20 fountains were seen in action at different times. The southwest wall-cone now was built up to a height of at least 20 feet above the southwest arm, and had become a wide flat cone-heap flaming on top, showing collapsed glowing pits and tumescence cracks. The southwest arm was crusted at first, with blowing fountains at the borders and puffing filagree cones flaming at the east end. Later there was a rapid breaking up with brilliant display of upwelling melt and sinking blocks along with much bubble fountaining. Fresh avalanche material (of the previous day as reported) lay on the black ledge west of the southwest bay. Everything indicated that a pronounced flooding by liquid lava was following the strong lift of the crags reported last week.

October 19 at 6 p. m. the flooding continued from east and west ponds, there were new glowing flows trickling on the southwest bench, and the lake was so high that it flooded through the east crevasse to the east pot. The streaming was west and then northeast from the extreme east end of the bent southwest arm of the lake. There was still a flame hole in the southwest wall-cone. The north pot remained an arm of the lake. There were many flames and border grottos, the largest of the latter an immense half dome on the south face of the uplifted north point of the lake-shore. Nine fountains were counted in action.

October 20 Halemaumau lava was still high and active with some overflowing and occasional avalanches from the walls. October 21 at 4 p. m. the flowing was confined to the southwest wallcone vent where fresh floods on the black ledge extended from the base of the west crag mass to the wall valley east of the southwest arm. There were now only two interruptions to a ring of newly flooded floor all around the pit, one the chasm between the west crag and the wall, and the other a short stretch along the talus for 100 feet south of the southeast arm. Here some driblet flowing had trickled only a little way south from the southeast arm.

The east and west ponds stood about 1 foot below their banks. Streaming was still out from the innermost end of the southwest arm. More blocks of rock appeared to have slid down the southeastern fault-face of the west crag mass. The northeast crag was now very steep and its extension northwest lying between the northeast cove and the north arm stood from 30 to 40 feet above the lake. The east island had accumulated a new platform at its base, both islands being connected by bridges of crust with the south crag mass. There was again a separate east pot. At 4:15 p. m. a small slide occurred under the northwest wall of the pit. The lakes were quiet with only five or six fountains. Fume had increased and was very dense from the west crag and the Red Solfatara.

On Friday, October 22, at 8:30 p. m., the air was calm and a heavy vapor cumulus occasioned by atmospheric convection stood over Halemaumau. Dense fume rose from the Red Solfatara. The walls around the main lake appeared high with continued lift of the bench magma. The east and west ponds were brimming full and the southwest and southeast arm nearly so. The bay at the north side of the southeast arm appeared to be enlarging. There were bridges of crust most of the time between the islands and the south crag mass. A heavy pudding

May 23, 1920. Halemaumau from

September 14, 1920. Halemaumau

the north shelf.—Photo Morihiro.

from the north shelf.—Photo Jaggar.

of fresh glowing flow lava filled the south wall valley far to the east of the southwest arm, fed from the southwest rift vent, the front trickling and the source cone showing a glow hole. There was a bridge between the east pot and the central pool, and the crag block south of this pot stood 30 feet high.

From 9 to 15 fountains in action at once were seen at different times, 6 being counted in the central pool. Streaming was out of the southwest arm, and there were heavy fountaining bombardments at the northwest cove and at the south side of the southeast arm. Blowing fountains sent spray far over the banks from under the crust at the south side of the east pond; on the north side there was a flaming cone. The west pond showed similar activity. The lakes were crusted, with bubbling breakings up at intervals. A torrent swept through the narrows to the southeast arm from under a heavy crust that covered part of the central pool; then a fountain ploughed its way from the center to the narrows, cracking up the crust as it progressed until there was a general foundering for a distance of 100 feet. This relieved the congestion at the narrows, the southeast arm lava rose to the common level, and the torrent slowed down. The drainage of the arm through wells beneath had been faster than the supply through the narrows which were perhaps dammed by the accretion of bottom debris and the jam of surface crust.

Mauna Loa Fume.—October 16 the cattlemen of Keauhou Ranch reported a fume column over the Kahuku source locality above Puu o Keokeo, about where the 1919 flow from Mauna Loa had its vent. At 6 p. m. the writer saw a wisp of fume at the same place and some smoky appearance in the sky. The fume disappeared and there was no glow at night.

At 6:30 a. m., October 20, there was distinct brown fume over Mokuaweoweo, the summit crater of Mauna Loa, in a small jet making a trail of smoke northward.

Seismometric Record.—During the week ending midnight, October 22, 14 local earthquakes and 3 teleseisms were registered as follows: Local shocks—October 16, 11:26 a. m. and 12:55 p. m., very feeble, and 5:58 p. m., feeble; October 17, 12:45 a. m., very feeble, and 11:27 p. m., feeble; October 19, 9:12 a. m., very feeble, estimated origin distance 18 miles, 11:28 a. m., 6:37 p. m., and 11:43 p. m., very feeble; October 20, 9:32 p. m., very feeble; October 21, 5:22 a. m., very feeble, estimated distance 19 miles; October 22, 4:41 a. m., 4:36 p. m., and 7:57 p. m., all very feeble. Distant shocks—October 17, 9:50 p. m., moderate intensity, estimated distance 3600 miles; October 18, 2:00 a. m. and 2:35 a. m., both slight. Spasmodic microtremor has been moderate, harmonic tremor mostly strong, microseismic motion moderate, and tilting strong north and east October 15, then south and west until October 20, when a reaction to north and east set in.

Week Ending October 29, 1920.

SUMMARY OF CONDITIONS.

The welling up of torrents of liquid lava reached a climax, in Halemaumau, on October 23 when the whole bottom area of the pit was flooded and the crag hills were isolated for a time. Thereafter the lakes and crags tended to maintain a stationary level, the former settling back within their cups and leaving the new fill to solidify, thus widening the floor area peripheral to the crag masses. The total rising of the week was only 4 or 5 feet and the lakes at the end of the period were several feet lower than they had been about October 23, when their depression was slightly less than 200 feet below the rim datum mark. The summit of the highest of the crags, a smoking peak on the west side of the central lake, is 111 feet below the rim.

The islands have changed their shapes and tend to become peninsulas. There have been small falls of debris from the wall of the pit. After a smart earthquake which was generally felt in the Hilo district in the early morning of October 27 there were signs of renewed rising at Halemaumau, blowing and flaming grottos became conspicuous, and a new driblet flow appeared at the margin of the floor where the Kau Desert rift crack intersects the pit wall.

JOURNAL.

Activity of Halemaumau.—Measurements for the week ending October 29, 1920, expressed as depressions below the northeast monument on the rim of Halemaumau (3727 feet above sea level) have been as follows:

	Mean lake level.	Northeast peak.	West peak.
Oct. 21, 4 p. m.............	207 feet	130 feet	116 feet
Oct. 24, noon	200 feet	126 feet	111 feet
Oct. 29, 10 a. m.............	203 feet	125 feet	111 feet

In eight days the lake rose 4 feet, averaging 0.5 foot per day, and the northeast and west crags each 5 feet, averaging 0.6 foot per day, but the actual maximum was reached October 24 for both crags and liquid lava, and the rate of rising per day October 21-24 was 2.3 feet for the liquid and about 1.7 feet for the crags. The liquid lava thereafter subsided 3 feet and the crags remained essentially stationary. The relief of the northeast peak increased in the 8 days, October 21-29, from 77 to 78 feet above the lake, and that of the west peak from 91 to 92 feet.

Saturday, October 23, was an eventful day at the lava pit. At 10:15 a. m. the fume was thin, there was much plashing of fountains, the radiant heat was strong, and the lakes were high, the western pools overflowing their banks voluminously. Eight fountains were in action. A festooned torrent from the southwest bay of the main lake had drowned the wall-cone at the rift. Two torrents pouring southward from the southwest arm were flooding the talus at the base of the south wall of the pit. The island, which had been close to shore in this arm of the lake was backed on the southwest side by floods of lava covering the adjacent ''black ledge'' or bench so as to be left surrounded by liquid and the banks of the lake were obliterated. This flood had penetrated the space between the west crag mass and the wall of the pit. The west pond was overflowing northeastward.

At 10:20 a. m. the southeast arm of the lake began overflowing from its south corner, the stream lapping the wall talus. There were smooth-topped pools of glowing lava following the floor margin all around the east and north sides of the pit, fed from overflow of the southeast arm and east pond. The live flow from the west pond joined this flood at the north, and the smooth crust showed that the annular lagoon so formed was deep and had been breaking and swallowing its crust and deflating its vesicles, leaving a slightly raised edge and lowered medial portion. The bridge between the central lake and the east pot was nearly flooded across. The greater part of the downsunken half of the west crag mass, on the side of the central lake, was covered over and becoming drowned. There were still isthmus connections between the south crag mass and the east and west islands.

At 10:30 a. m. the cracking and foundering process broke out through the crusts of the fill occupying the north floor and spread across the filled area with much bubbling loss of gas. The shell left clinging all around the east and north sides of the pit at the base of the wall after the lowering occasioned by this compacting process stood 1 to 2 feet higher than the resulting surface of new crust. Migratory lines of fountains in the central pool at this time moved from west to east.

At 10:35 a. m. the southeast arm overflowed its northeast corner in slow pahoehoe toes and this started a flow in the direction of the east pond.

At 10:45 a. m. a great flood of overflow like a river started over the northern lip of the west pond, and majestically marched eastward along the base of the north wall of the pit.

By 11 a. m. this torrent had reached the east pond and was cascading into it with a fall of about 2 feet, the volumes of lava on the bench surrounding the cup of the pond and continuing southward. All of these flows, it will be observed, assumed annular courses along the wall-valley, that is, they followed the depression between the uplifted crag masses of the central region and the wall of the pit, thus encircling the crags, the grades at first being mostly downward to a lowest level in the southeast region. The first effect of the cascade into the east pond was not to fill it up, but by breaking up its crust to start fountaining in the pond with release of gas and so to lower the pond level about 2 feet more by deflation. The largest cascades were on the east and north sides of the cup, now falling 4 feet.

The rapid rise at the west pond had by 11:15 a. m. flooded the gap south of the west pond between the wall of the pit and the west crag, so that the festooned front of this flow could now be seen headed toward the southwest bay of the lake on the southern side of the west crag mass. Meantime the flow past the east pond had progressed southward a short distance toward the southeast arm.

At 11:30 a. m. the scene at the bottom of the pit presented the appearance of three powerful torrents radiating from the west crag region, the southwest arm prolonging itself into a river flooding the south talus, the west pond being continuous with the flow circling the north and east side of the pit, and the main lake resolving itself into a meandering stream ending in overflow at the southeast arm. The last two had reached convectional adjustment with the sinkholes of the east pond and the southeast arm, but the southwest arm overflow was deepening the pool that it fed. A wide flow from the west pond southward between the crag mass and the wall had become stagnant. The north arm of the lake was brimming full and level with the flow from the west pond. It only remained for the southern flow to join through to the southeast arm in order to completely isolate the three crag masses. The arrangement of quiet crusts at the origins and fountains at the destinations of the several streams indicated that the west pond and southwest bay are source wells, and the east pond, east pot, north arm, and southeast arm are sink holes for the convectional circulation. Probably the east end of the southwest arm leads to a sink hole also, but at this time it was overflowed.

At 11:50 a. m. there was a breaking up of crusts with violent fountaining on the west side of the southwest bay.

At 12:05 p. m. the west pond subsided sufficiently to show its edges. The first great rise of the day thus ended at noon. The south flow had nearly joined the overflow at the southeast arm.

At 3:30 p. m. the lakes were 2 to 3 feet down, and the east pond 5 feet down. A continuous fountain played in the east part of the central pool, and migratory fountains moved from here to the bank at the northeast crag. The current from the southwest diverged to the east and to a long fountaining grotto northwest. A noisy grotto developed fountaining on the south side of the southeast arm. The east island showed a bridge connection to the south shore. The lakes sank lower about 1 foot at 4 p. m.

From 9 to 11 p. m. a new period of flooding started but the torrents over the benches arose at the east ends of the southeast and southwest arms. The sinking spell of the afternoon appears to have reversed the grade of the floor, for the southeast corner became the origin of immense volumes of peripheral flowing. The end of the southeast arm overflowed both north and south along the base of the wall. The south branch joined with the new flood from the southwest arm, pooling and filling still more the south wall valley. The north branch joined with a southward flow from the east pond, overmastered it, and then swept on northward encountering an overflow westward from the north arm and merging with it. All this time the west pond, which had been the main source in the morning, remained 1 or 2 feet below its bank with marginal fountains blowing and spurting, and a high-pressure flaming cone on its west bank. The north floor depression was pooled and filled. Enormous volumes poured for more than two hours from the southeast finding a downgrade to the north, exactly the opposite of the grade found by the morning flood. An axis of uplift must lie across the pit from northwest to southeast, and somehow the marginal fills and the reactions due to settling by loss of gas determine the slight grades which govern the peripheral flowing.

The quiet center of dispersion of most of the flowing this evening was as usual the southwest bay, covered by a dark crust, from the edges of which the flows moved southwestward against the wall of the pit, northeastward and across the main lake to feed the overflows from the southeast arm, and eastward through the southwest arm to the south fill.

At noon, October 24, there were 11 fountains in the lava lakes and the flows on the floors were glowing, with occasional spells of cracking up of crusts which sank in the melt beneath. The lakes showed defined borders a foot or two high. At the southwest rift corner there was trace of a gas vent. Nearly all the talus slopes were buried under the new flows. The streaming was as usual from the southwest bay eastward and northeastward. The east and west islands showed bridge connections southward. Large grottos had developed at the east end of the southwest arm. The backslope east of the northeast crag had caved in and tumbled to a talus below. There was a continuous ring of new floor all around in which the crag masses stood like islands, and the edge of this floor against the pit wall stood higher than the middle portions, like a beach, as the middle portions had slumped through loss of gas. Around the central lake the promontories of fresh bench lava northeast, west, and south showed uplift and centrifugal tilt. The new floor was now continuous from the southwest arm to southeast arm, and the crags showed partial submergence under the new floods, especially the south crag mass.

In the evening the lakes were very quiet and covered with crust except in the central pool and southwest channel. The ponds were one or two feet below their rims. Six fountains were counted. The new flows showed glowing cracks in heavy shells of crust.

At 9 p. m. the west pond rose and overflowed its lip all around, making short streams northeast and south which quickly stopped. After this time there was a breaking up of crusts and a slight lowering of lakes, 11 fountains appeared, the streaming into the southeast arm became rapid, and large spurting and spraying fountains broke out around the edges of the west pond. A small avalanche fell from the northeast wall.

At 10 p. m. the west pond was full again and dribbling over slightly. All the evening the east pond remained crusted with slight border fountaining.

On October 25, at 5:30 p. m., the lakes were depressed about four feet and there was little sign of tilting in the shorelines. At different times from 11 to 18 fountains were in action. There was little glow left in the new flows. There was no conspicuous blowing, a filagree cone occupied the west side of the east pond, the fountains were both central and marginal, there was steady eastward streaming with bright lines on the lake surface, and overhang of banks showing stalactites was common. Tunnels were visible under thick bridges of crust between the islands and the south shore, and also under the bench matter of the south chasm which divided the two halves of the southern crag mass. The east pot was wholly crusted over. The west pond was slightly higher than the other pools, perhaps 3 feet below its rim.

At 6 p. m., October 26, there was variable streaming out of the southwest channel, sometimes sending a branch northward, and at all times curving to pour into the southeast arm. The lakes remained about 4 feet below their banks. There was much crusting over with subsequent foundering. A blow hole at the east pot locality hissed loudly from time to time, and a rock slide fell from the east side of the northeast crag.

At 3 p. m., October 27, the border lakes were 4 to 5 feet down and the central pool 6 to 7 feet down. The lakes were sluggish, the north cove and southeast arm crusted over, and streaming from the southwest channel was slow. Nine fountains were in action, and the tunnels remained open. No marked evidence of tilting shorelines appeared, nor of cracks in the floors due to uplift. Most of the fume in the pit rose from the west and south crags.

October 28 at noon the lakes were found rising, standing 3 to 6 feet below their banks, the southwest arm, southeast arm and east pond building filagree cones with burning gas puffing through the orifices. At first only 3 fountains were in action, but later the number increased to 8. Fresh avalanche material had fallen from the southeast wall of the pit. Streaming was eastward in all arms.

Examination of the smoking chimney crag on the west side of the pit revealed the fact that two large vertical east-west chasms or cracks extend down the west side of the crag mass from the glowing smoke holes on top to and under the floor of new flows below. Evidently these rifts are part of the mechanism which has created the glowing summit chimney.

New driblet flows had poured out on the black ledge from the southwest rift crack, making a small flat area of pahoehoe toes radial from the origin, one tongue of which had overrun the bank and cascaded into the southwest bay of the lake. At the east pot a small broken hole had opened. On the southeast side of the west crag a sharp pinnacle had become isolated. Much smoke rose from the south crag mass. At the Red Solfatara very dense rapidly rising billows of whitish fume rose.

At 10 a. m., October 29, the main lake was streaming slowly eastward with quiet wrinkled skins on its surface, and the ponds were quiet. Five or six fountains were in action, mostly at fixed grottos on the southern sides of the southeast arm, the east side of the east pond, the southeast side of the north arm, the north side of the west pond, the east end of the southwest arm where there is a filagree flame-cone, on the south side of the central lake between the two peninsulas, and in the east cove. These places were not all fountaining at once. A new narrow inner platform about 1 foot high had formed around the central lake. There was no such platform around the outlying ponds, which were 2 to 4 feet below their marginal banks. An occasional prolonged central fountain would migrate east in the main lake. The point south of the southeast channel had newly broken down, involving the east island peninsula, leaving an east-west chasm between the broken blocks and the southeast crag. The remnant ledge of the east island was now small within the surrounding shell of new flow matter. The west island rock on the other hand had become a large raised peninsula. A small new cove had formed west of the southwest channel, eroded out of the overflow platform which there covered the debris of a portion of the west crag mass that has been slipping down for months past. This platform now stood about 4 feet above the lake.

At 6 p. m. there was tendency for the current from the central lake into the southeast arm to become a torrent occasionally, leading to a border fountain at the end of the arm. Four or five migratory central fountains would form in the main lake, and a large grotto was continuously active at the north promontory. Flames at the border cone of the southwest arm shot 5 or 6 feet into the air. The smoke from the south and west crags was at this time always conspicuous, in contrast to its absence north and northeast.

Seismometric Record.—During the week ending midnight, October 29, 8 local earthquakes were registered as follows: October 23, 1:54 p. m., felt locally, estimated distance of origin, 5 miles; 10:20 p. m., very feeble; 11:23 p. m., feeble, distance, 14 miles; October 24, 6:28 a. m., very feeble; October 25, 3:06 a. m. and 4:50 a. m., both very feeble; October 27, 5:33 a. m, felt, distance about 5 miles, direction, N. W. or S. E. from station; 11:34 p. m., very feeble. Spasmodic and harmonic microtremor were moderate to strong. Microseismic motion was moderate, with some increase October 24-26. Tilting was southward October 23-24, northward and somewhat east, October 25-26, and slight thereafter.

T. A. JAGGAR, Jr.
Volcanologist.

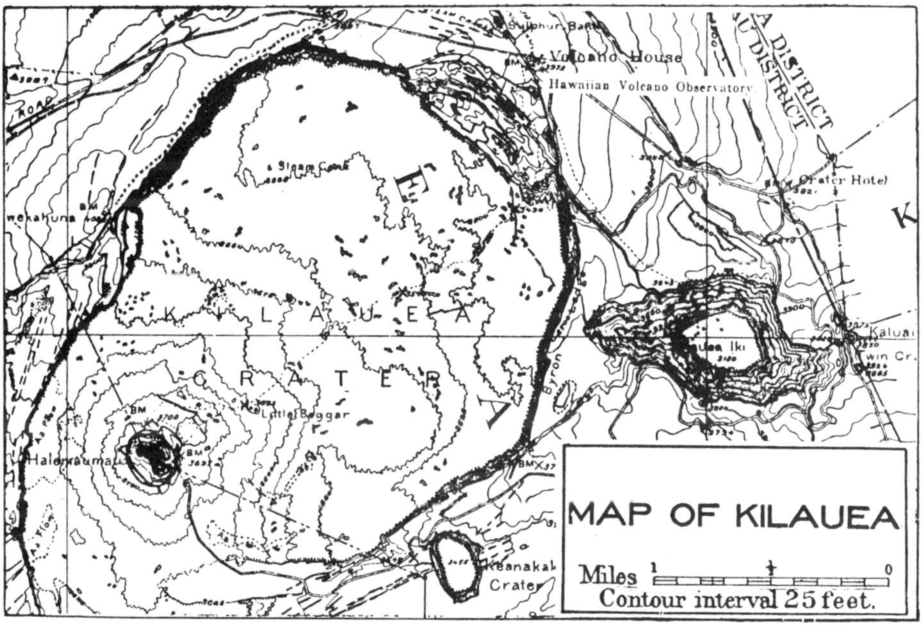

HAWAIIAN VOLCANO OBSERVATORY.

All exchanges should be addressed to
HAWAIIAN VOLCANO OBSERVATORY,
Volcano House, P. O. Hawaii.

The Observatory is equipped with the following seismometric instruments rebuilt at the station in 1918 for the special needs of volcano research: two Bosch-Omori pendulums, high speed registration of local earthquakes; one optically recording seismograph for distant earthquakes; one clinograph registering E-W tilting of the ground. A vertical component seismograph was in December, 1918, set up in experimental operation. These are seated on concrete piers in a closed basement room having practically constant temperature, beneath the chief Observatory building near the hotel. Time is referred to a rated chronometer, checked at intervals by wireless signal from the Pearl Harbor Naval Station. The chronometer is loaned by the College of Hawaii. Hawaiian standard time (H. S. T.) is 10 hrs. 30 min. slower than Greenwich time.

CANCANI SCALE OF SEISMIC INTENSITY.

Expressed by accelerations measured in millimeters per second per second.

I.	Instrumental	0.0	2.5
II.	Very slight	2.5	5.0
III.	Slight	5.0	10.0
IV.	Sensible, mediocre	10.0	25.0
V.	Rather strong	25.0	50.0
VI.	Strong	50.0	100.0
VII.	Very strong	100.0	250.0
VIII.	Ruinous	250.0	500.0
IX.	Disastrous	500.0	1000.0
X.	Very disastrous	1000.0	2500.0
XI.	Catastrophic	2500.0	5000.0
XII.	Great catastrophe	5000.0	10000.0

Grade IV. is ordinarily the minimum perceived by the senses; and in grade XII, the acceleration or rate of change of motion (jerk) reaches that of terrestrial gravitation.

In the standard form of report the maximum intensity or acceleration, designated by the symbol α, or max. α, is given in the conventional unit of milligal. The milligal is a measure of acceleration, such that 1 milligal = 1/100 mm. per sec. per sec. = 10 μ. per sec. per sec. The Cancani scale, here defined in terms of millimeters per sec. per sec., can therefore be expressed in milligals by multiplying each of the numbers by 100.

U. S. DEPARTMENT OF AGRICULTURE
WEATHER BUREAU
CHARLES F. MARVIN, CHIEF

MONTHLY BULLETIN
OF THE
Hawaiian Volcano Observatory

VOL. VIII. HONOLULU, HAWAII, NOVEMBER, 1920 No. 11

Week Ending November 5, 1920.

SUMMARY OF CONDITIONS.

The week has been characterized by the beginnings of subsidence, with strong tilting up of the crags at first and some flooding by the lakes making an appearance of rising. The net effect, however, was a readjustment of the crag and floor blocks and a sinking away of the lakes within their cups, the bench magma actually going down very little. The movement produced numerous small avalanches from crags and pit walls. In general the sink-hole pools on the east side of Halemaumau lowered more than the rest, and on one occasion a cascade poured from the central lake into the north pot.

After the rising spell reported for the previous week the liquid flooding appears to have culminated October 31st, and the rising of the bench magma about November 2nd.

JOURNAL.

Activity of Halemaumau. Measurements for the week ending November 5, 1920, expressed as depression below the northeast monument on the rim of Halemaumau (3727 feet above sea level) have been as follows:

	Mean lake level	Northeast peak	West peak
October 29, 10 a. m.	203 feet	125 feet	111 feet
November 5, 11 a. m.	219 "	126 "	115 "

In seven days the lake lowered 16 feet, averaging 2.3 feet per day, the northeast crag one foot, averaging per day 0.14 foot, and the west crag 4 feet, averaging 0.6 foot. In the same period the relief of the northeast crag peak above the lake increased from 78 to 93 feet, and that of the west peak from 92 to 104 feet.

At 10:15 a. m., October 31, a flooding by the lake magma was in progress from the southwest bay as a source; the western and southern banks of the central lake were drowned, and the isthmuses which had connected the east and west islands to the lakeshore were more or less obliterated. The point of "land" on the west side of the lake was covered to the base of the west pinnacle. The newly broken down block of the peninsula on the south side of the southeast narrows was entirely submerged. The east island stood as a little peaked rock only 4 feet high. The peninsular remnant of the island in the southwest arm was nearly submerged. That arm of the lake was stagnant, with a glowing cone at its eastern end; the central pool also was quiet, and only four or five fountains were in action in the other pools.

The liquid lava of the southwest bay stood 1 foot below the bank, of the southeast arm 2 feet below, of the north arm the same, of the east pond 4 feet, and of the west pond 5 feet below its banks. At the east pot there was a small opening. The surface streamings were northward in the east pond, southward in the west pond, outward into the central lake from the southwest bay, and the southeast arm was full of clogged festoons of skin. Fresh stone falls lay on the floor of the pit north, northeast and east.

On the afternoon of November 1 the east pond showed lower level 9 feet below its bank, the surface being quiet. The streaming from the southwest in the central lake diverged to northeast and southeast. Slow foundering of crust was going on in the east pot, and a sluggish current poured in from the central lake. The west island peninsula had so built out from the south crag mass as to create a narrows less than 100 feet wide between it and the northeast peninsula. Rocks had fallen from the north side of the southeast crag. The only active grottoes were in the southwest arm and the northeast cove; at 3 p. m. a short-lived fountain broke out in the middle of the central pool. A cascade with a visible drop of at least five feet and a width of about six feet was pouring from the central lake into the north pot. Occasional fountaining activity broke out in the south chasm, which divides the south crag mass in two, and on the central lake side. The east island remained isolated. The center of the pit was comparatively free from fume, but the southwest and northeast sides were smoky.

At 4:45 p. m., November 2, the lakes were covered with thin skins showing the bright-line pattern in the center and southeast. The streaming was eastward, with occasional migratory small central fountains. There were only three or four border fountains. The inner shore platforms of the central lake were 2 feet high at the west and 3 feet high around the island masses; the west pond bank was 4 feet high, the southwest bay 5 feet, the east pond and southeast arm 7 feet, and the north pot 8 feet. The north pot cascade had ceased, a narrow bridge separated the pot from the north cove, and the lava in the pot was crusted. So were the east and west ponds, with some puffing of gas from under border skins. There was new smoke from the bank of the east pond, and from a rising crag block south of the east pot, which had become crevassed. The east pot was again a cove of the central pool. The south side of the southeast narrows again had broken down, making a pulpit rock. The east island, on the other hand, was again connected by a bridge of crust with the southeast crag. The crag sectors appeared newly uplifted, the southeast peak being higher, also the west island peninsula, and there were new cracks in the eastern floor and a pressure ridge along the edge of the floor south-southeast. The northeast promontory was now lifted to become a large crag.

At 9:15 a. m., November 4, the central lake was becoming constricted by the uplift of shoals east and north and the widening of its marginal platforms. Strong disturbance of the bench magma was indicated by new heavy tumbles of rock lying on the floor southeast, east, north-northeast and southwest. The uplift of the northeast point now showed in elevation on its south face two convergent bench levels dipping northeast, the upper at a high angle, the lower flat. The shoals making islets lay north of the east island, at the tip of the north point crag—here connected to shore by a narrow isthmus of crust—and in the north cove opposite the bridge leading to the north pot. The northwest bank of the central lake appeared to be lifting to become a crag tilted north-northwest, involving the old north crag remnant. The east island was again isolated, but like the rest of the lake shore possessed a wide base platform. The cove of the south chasm had become enlarged and the cleft widened into a smoky gorge extending through to the southwest arm. The north side of the west crag had now become a knife-edge by complete collapse of the floor surface uplifted between it and the west pond. The greater recent motion, however, had been in the east and north crags.

There was the usual streaming from the southwest, the border pools were crusted over, there was deep rumbling from a fountain in the north pot, and only three or four small grottoes were in action. The southeast arm was enlarged by collapse on its north side. At 9:45 a. m. a violent fountain burst through the crust on the southeast side of the west pond sending jets of lava spray 30 feet into the air, breaking up the crust, and lowering the pond 2 feet. Some stones were heard falling, but generally the pit was quiet except for the north pot rumble and slight hissing noise. The banks of the lakes were 5 feet high at the west and southwest pools and 8 feet east and southeast.

At 11 a. m. Friday, November 5, it was evident that the crag masses were in strong motion and the liquid lava showed marked differences of level in separate lakes, and rapid circulation. There were almost no fountains. The differences of depression within their cups of the several pools were as follows: West pond 2 feet, rising and crusted; central pool 5 feet below the new platforms; east pond 10 feet; southwest arm and bay 12 feet, rising to 10 feet; southeast arm most depressed of all, 15 feet. The outlying pools were crusted over, but the streaming was rapid from the southwest bay to the central lake, and still swifter thence through the southeast narrows. The island blocks stood high, there was crust over the north cove, the chasms of the east pot and the south gorge were enlarged, and that motion was in progress was evident from the noise of falling talus fragments at the northeast crag and from the walls of the pit. From the cliff on the south side of the southeast arm there was frequent caving in, a noisy avalanche tumbling there at 10:19 a. m. New taluses against the southeast and north-northeast walls of Halemaumau had increased in size. At 11:45 a. m. a fountain developed in the south chasm cove and there was a rush of streaming thither with migratory fountains in the current.

Seismometric Record. During the week ending midnight November 5 seven local earthquakes were registered, as follows: Nov. 2, 3:23 a. m., very feeble; Nov. 3, 9:33 a. m., weak, apparent origin 10 miles distant S. W. or N. E.; Nov. 4, 7:05 p. m., feeble; Nov. 5, 1:01 a. m., 9:14 a. m., 11:40 a. m., 2:47 p. m., all very feeble. Spasmodic microtremor was moderate to strong, harmonic tremor slight to moderate, and microseismic motion strong, decreasing towards the end of the interval. Tilt was east and north until Nov. 2, south and west Nov. 3-5, being pronounced in the directions specified Oct. 30-31 and Nov. 3-4.

Week Ending November 12, 1920.

SUMMARY OF CONDITIONS.

The scene at Halemaumau presented to the visitor during this week as he looked down from the high rim was a vast circular pit 1200 to 1400 feet in diameter, with nearly vertical walls, and at the bottom lay an inner landscape of smoking crags, marginal floors reaching out to the walls, and pools of incandescent lava large and small, the largest an octopus affair with its tentacles forming a fiery stream which swept in a torrent from one side of the bottom to the other. The stream ended in a cascade forking about a ledge and falling in brilliant rapids to a lower pool, where the glowing melt surged and swirled with scintillating golden pattern. The pool where the stream arose on the southwest side was at least 15 feet higher than the southeast sinkhole pool where it ended in a fall. All of this flowing is part of the convectional circulation whereby the hotter and more foamy lava rises at the west, and the cooled and heavier substance sinks away at the east. The underground tubes which convey this effervescing fluid ramify through the paste that forms the crags and floors, which paste extends indefinitely downward. That these crags are red hot is shown by the west peak, which, until November 12th, had a summit chimney consisting of a mass of cracks glowing and flaming, and in daylight ejecting puffs of dense white fume.

The mechanism whereby such crag peaks become undermined by gas fluxing was illustrated on the morning of that date, when this summit collapsed and left a pit where bubbling lava was welling up amid the fallen debris. The lakes had been slowly subsiding relative to their cups, so that the banks became from 15 to 20 feet high, and it is this lowering of the liquid level, different in the separate pools and in the concealed walls and tunnels, which produces collapse after undermining. The dense smoke disappeared when the condensing chamber was destroyed. The open cracks of the Red Solfatara southwest of Halemaumau, also emitting dense clouds of poisonous acid vapor, have recently become red hot close to the surface, where by measurement early in September the temperature was less than 200 degrees Centigrade.

JOURNAL.

Activity of Halemaumau. Measurements for the week ending November 12, 1920, expressed as depression below the northeast monument on the rim of Halemaumau (3727 feet above sea level) have been as follows:

	Mean lake level	Northeast peak	West peak
November 5, 11 a. m.	219 feet	126 feet	115 feet
November 12, 10 a. m.	233 "	133 "	118 "

In seven days the lake subsided 14 feet, averaging 2 feet per day; the northeast peak 7 feet, averaging 1 foot; and the west peak 3 feet, averaging 0.4 foot. The relief of the northeast crag increased from 93 to 100 feet above the lake, and of the west crag from 104 to 115 feet.

The rate of subsidence, therefore, was similar to that of the preceding week, but the sinking of the bench magma represented by the crags was faster than before.

At 8 a. m. Saturday, November 6, an increased sinking of the level of the southeast arm produced a cascade through the narrows leading to this pool from the central lake. At 8:50 a. m. a heavy slide of rocks fell from the south side of the narrows. This cascade is a repetition of what happened September 16, 1920, in the same place. There was now a double fall around a ledge in the middle of the narrows, the ledge a new one possibly broken down from one of the shelves at the side. The drop was about six feet in an irregular jumble of rapids, the filling and falling of the lower pool changing the height from time to time. Toward the vortex at the base of the fall rushed the surface current from the east end of the pool, reversing the usual streaming here. The currents of the main lake were speeded up by this terminal torrent, presenting the appearance of a river of melt meandering from the southwest bay across the central lake, everything being lowered by the drainage so that the channels between the islands and promontories were more constricted. Into the northern cove of the southeast arm from the notch in the bank a current occasionally bubbled up from below, coming through the tunnel of the east pot chasm which there connects through from the central lake.

General subsidence had produced marked change in the west pond since the previous day, the crusted pool now standing 18 feet below its banks. The spatter margin was seen breaking off and falling into the pond below, and most of this veneer had already fallen from the west side, and was in process of falling from the north and south sides. The platforms around the main lake were 4 or 5 feet high, the east pond 15 feet, and the southwest arm 20 feet, as though the liquid lava were relatively highest in the central region. There were 8 or 9 fountains in action, including some migratory central ones, the north cove was crusted over, and during the writer's visit from 4 to 6 p. m. the crusts on the north pot and the east pond broke up a little.

As darkness approached a bright flame chimney could be seen amid cracks in the high peak of the west crag, 110 feet above the central lake, where for many weeks very dense acid fume has been rising from the summit. These fumes, whatever may be their actual content of water vapor, are capable of raising the temperature of the rock through which they percolate to bright scarlet glow, and finally of exhibiting definite flames of burning gas. As has been stated in the preamble, the same kind of glowing this week appeared at the Red Solfatara outside of Halemaumau. In both cases gas-charged lava lies below, and the rock brought to incandescence by the burning gas is solidified pahoehoe lava. It is incredible that this gas prior to its exothermic reactions in the cracks can contain any very large percentage of water vapor. A gas so lean in combustibles as to contain 95 per cent of water, nitrogen and carbonic acid (see analyses, E. S. Shepherd, this Bulletin, July, 1919) cannot burn with visible flames and heat rocks to redness. The conclusion is inescapable that the gases collected by Dr. Shepherd and the writer were burned gases.

That the crags were cracking and in motion on this day was attested by falls of rock from the north side of the northeast crag, from the southeast crag, from the sides of the chasm through the south crag and from the west crag mass. The island in the southwest arm had broken away from the southwest bank, to which it had been attached by a bridge and its top was now a few feet below the bank level. A big crack 3 feet wide had opened through the northeast crag, extending southeastward from the north pot.

At 2 p. m. on November 7 the cascade in the southeast arm was lower and partially arched with crust. The depression of this pool was 18 feet within its cup, of the east and west ponds 15 feet, and of the southwest arm 12 feet. The central lake appeared still more like a river with one of its distributaries bending southward through a narrow pass between the east and west islands to the south chasm. The southwest arm was crusted over, and the main current took its rise at the bright edge of a dark crust in the southwest bay, making a bright-line pattern as it progressed. Two falls of rock were seen from the old veneer on the high southeast wall of Halemaumau, and a large new talus had accumulated below, lying against the base of the wall at the edge of the southeast arm. This undermining was due to the subsidence of the bench magma on that side. The streaming in the east pond was southward.

From 10 a. m. to noon, November 9, the lakes were found higher and the southeast cascade had disappeared. A general shoaling about the southeastern part of the central lake had produced new shoreline flats between the east and west islands, and also protruding out from the point south of the narrows where the cascade had been. There was fountaining at the south side of the east island making a spatter dome with stalactites; otherwise only three or four small fountains were seen, except during a breaking-up spell on the northeast side of the west pond.

The north pot had welled up and filled its cup to within four feet of the upper bank, joining through again to the north cove, but remaining crusted except for two pots; the one on the north cove side was seen to break up, produce a fountain, and lower its level. The ponds and pools were mostly 10 or 12 feet below their banks. There was much smoke.

The writer was able to climb down to the inner north floor without difficulty by way of a chasm in the east end of the lower north shelf. The edge of the lake at the north cove was found quite accessible, and also the divide between the central pool and the west pond. The detail of lava texture, streaming, fountaining and height of shores and crags recalled conditions in the summer of 1917.

At 11:30 a. m., November 10, the cascade conditions were restored, the walls of the southeast pool were 20 feet high, and the east and west ponds were 15 feet below their banks. There were now two cascades, one as before into the southeast arm, but directed differently, and another southward through the narrows between the east and west island platforms to the pool at the south chasm. The new direction to the torrent leading into the southeast arm was occasioned by the new flat built out on the south side of the narrows, which forced the channel over against the east pot entrance, and made the fall tumble southward instead of southeastward as before. The whole fall had migrated slightly northward. Large high platforms now surrounded the islands. Amid these shoalings the winding torrent swept from the southwest bay across the lake eastward, with but few fountains, the gas release for the whole lake system being satisfied by the raging cauldrons at the bottoms of the two cascades. As before, the streaming in the southeast arm was northwestward to the vortex at the foot of the fall. There was some streaming from the central lake into the east pot cove. A few falls of rock were heard.

On November 11 a singular change had occurred. At 2 p. m. the two cascades of the day before were found replaced by one steeper fall in a different place, namely, from the central pool into the east pot, the level of which had fallen 12 feet. The new fall was a straight chute of that height into this small cauldron which became a covered tunnel below. This had now become the dominant sink hole of the system, and the southeast arm had risen and was crusted over, its current draining out into the central pool through the narrows, and thence around the bend into the east pot. In the bottom of the east pot cauldron a westward set of the currents could be seen, rushing to the vortex at the foot of the cascade. An irregular splash at the verge of the cascade showed where a rock protruded through the falling melt, part of the ledge over which the fall tumbled. Another such evidence of a shallow bottom was seen in a standing rapid 50 feet west of the cascade in the narrows between the northeast point and the east island. This northeast point had risen and lifted the shallow lake bottom with it, extending itself into a cape and constricting the lake still more. The standing rapid in question remained fixed at one place in what had been the middle of the lake, but was now a swift river-like current. There was no question but that an obstruction or accretion lay below, and that the east side of the lake bottom was rapidly shoaling.

Between the two islands in the lake there was southward streaming and this current circled around the east island. The fountains observed were on the southwest side of the island in the southwest arm, at the east end of that arm, and in the east pond. The depressions of the pools within their cups were: Central lake below island platforms 6 feet; east, west and southwest pools 15 feet; southeast arm 18 feet; east pot, beneath the raised floor encircling it on the east, 25 feet. There was hot rapid streaming across the lake from the southwest bay to the cascade. The subsidence had revealed tunnels adjacent to the lake bottom at the northeast cove and at the west margin of the southwest bay. Rocks were occasionally sliding from the southeast crag.

A visit to the Red Solfatara on this date showed that the surface deposits around the hottest smoke hole, where heavy billows of dense whitish fume were puffing up, were pale yellow, and the open chasms of the rift were glowing cherry red three feet down, at a temperature at least 800 degrees Cent. The hot rocks were hissing as the rain fell on them. No lava was visible in the cracks, and the heat must be attributed to the work of the rising gases. The temperature has risen 600 degrees Cent. in two months.

At 10 a. m. November 12 the cascade into the east pot continued and a current southeastward into the southeast arm had been restored. The standing rapid in the central pool was as before, but later, at 9 p. m., a new islet had been formed by accretion up from the lake bottom at the site of this rapid. The island in the southwest arm on this day appeared as though it had moved eastward. A ledge west of the southwest channel had slumped down and made a new cove. Seven or eight fountains were in action, the banks of the east and west ponds were about 12 feet high, there were spells of breaking up in the southeast arm, north cove and west pond, an avalanche fell on the southwest black ledge, and a heavy block of the southwest bank of the west pond collapsed, making a splash and a wave across the heavy fluid. There was a flaming glow hole in the bank of the east pond on its south side.

At 10:40 a. m. the whole smoking top of the west crag collapsed inward and sent up a cloud of dust and sand. There remained a pit in the top of the crag mass, and the dense vapor, which had been pouring forth for months, wholly ceased. Thin blue fume rose from the new pit, the dimensions of which were 50 by 100 feet in plan and about 50 feet deep. There were some readjustments of talus, and on looking down into the hole from the west rim of Halemaumau one could see a pool of black crusted slowly upwelling pahoehoe lava, gradually burying a pile of debris that lay against the north side of the bottom area.

Only a narrow partition stood between the new pit and the west pond, and the bottom of the pit appeared about 20 feet deeper than the level of the west pond lava. There had certainly been a large void inside the crag stoped out by gas fluxing or some such process, and this had been the condensing chamber for the thick fume which had so long risen from the summit. The cavity may in part have owed its origin to the tilting up of a pre-existing lava tunnel.

Seismometric Record. During the week ending midnight November 12, fourteen local earthquakes were registered, as follows:

November 6, 2:52 p. m.—Very feeble.
November 7, 4:11 a. m.—Very feeble.
November 7, 4:23 a. m.—Feeble, apparent distance 11 miles.
November 7, 5:53 a. m.—Very feeble.
November 7, 8:30 a. m.—Very feeble, apparent distance 11 miles.
November 7, 5:14 p. m.—Feeble.
November 7, 5:39 p. m.—Feeble.
November 7, 6:37 p. m.—Feeble.
November 9, 12:53 a. m.—Very feeble.
November 9, 6:13 a. m.—Very feeble.
November 9, 10:36 p. m.—Very feeble.
November 11, 10:20 a. m.—Very slight.
November 11, 1:15 p. m.—Feeble.
November 12, 4:46 a. m.—Very feeble.

Both spasmodic and harmonic forms of microtremor decreased from moderate to slight. Microseismic motion also decreased to slight. Tilting was northward and eastward November 7-8, westward and southward November 11-12.

Week Ending November 19, 1920.

SUMMARY OF CONDITIONS.

The Halemaumau pit exhibits a spectacular changing jumble of lava pools, overflow platforms, islands and crags. The lakes have come up a little and the crags have slightly subsided. The cups containing the four outer pools have confining walls 10 or 12 feet high, but the central lake has built new flood platforms about its margins. These have constricted the lake to narrow meandering channels and have formed bridges shutting off two pools which were parts of the lake before. The general effect of this is to give the appearance of pronounced rising, especially for the central lake, to be followed later perhaps by a lift of the crag masses.

The activity has been mostly confined to five or six large fountaining grottoes, and swift surface streaming of the main lake in golden torrents, these in places acquiring standing rapids over obstructing hummocks of the lake bottom. Such hummocks have grown to islets, showing how shallow are the pools. The torrents have changed to cascades from time to time, tumbling into two eastern pools through narrow gorges, when these pools lowered faster than the central lake. Part of the time these cascades have flowed under arches of crust. About November 15th and thereafter the rising of the liquid lava became pronounced, and this showed itself by building up the bottom of the new pit where last week a crag chimney collapsed, and also in the upbuilding of large flats of overflow lava around the remnants of former islands in the lake.

Red heat continues in the Red Solfatara; the rift in the Kau Desert four miles from Kilauea retains only a slight vaporing from the recent outflow activity, and the summit fume on Mauna Loa is pronounced, but not exceptionally so.

JOURNAL.

Activity of Halemaumau. Measurements for the week ending November 19, 1920, expressed as depression below the northeast monument on the rim of Halemaumau (3727 feet above sea level) have been as follows:

	Mean lake level	Northeast peak	West peak
November 12, 10 a. m.	233 feet	133 feet	118 feet
November 18, 11 a. m.	230 "	136 "	145 "

In six days the lake rose 3 feet, averaging 0.5 foot per day, and the northeast peak subsided 3 feet, averaging 0.5 foot. The west peak became much lower by collapse on November 12 after the measurements were made, the measurements of November 18 being directed to the north horn of the remnant mass.

The relief above the lake of the northeast crag decreased from 100 to 94 feet, that of the west crag from 115 to 85 feet.

On Saturday, November 13, from 10 to 11 a. m. the cascade from the central lake was still rushing into the east pot, and the islet which had been a standing rapid had increased in size. The main lake as before had the appearance of a torrent sweeping from west to east. There were five or six fountains in action. In marked contrast to the times when the chimney of the west crag had been smoking, Halemaumau now sent up only pale blue fume, but dense white fume was rising from the Red Solfatara to the southwest. The several outlying pools next to the walls of Halemaumau lay depressed within their cups from 15 to 25 feet. About 7 p. m. the cascade ceased.

At 3 p. m., November 14, the cascade was found transferred to the narrows leading to the southeast arm. The east pot entrance was crusted, and the pond there had risen level with the lake. The new cascade was rather a series of rapids, one of them a small fall. The central lake was high, flooding its west point. The outlying pools had also risen a little, their banks standing from 12 to 15 feet above the liquid. There were occasional border fountains in the east and west ponds, and a few fountains in the main lake, notably under the new high crag point northeast. The pool in process of becoming enclosed south of the two island platforms was seen to have its crusts break up and founder. A fountain played in the channel between the island and the bank in the southwest arm. In the west crag pit black pahoehoe lava had welled up. The fume from Halemaumau was thin and diffused.

At 10 a. m., November 15, rising continued, and new platforms 1 foot high were built about the central lake. This lake had become greatly constricted in area during the past week; new shore had been built out southward from the crag mass of the northeast point, which had now become a big addition to the northeast crag; more shore had been built northward about the two islands and from the southwest side of the southeast narrows; the west point had become a large low promontory, and the north arm and much of the north cove were lifted surfaces. The pool enclosed by the islands and extending to the south chasm was nearly shut off, resolving the main lake into a meandering stream with quiet adjacent lagoons.

Rapid currents were now rushing into both the east pot and southeast arm from the lake, the east pot stream the swifter. Four or five puffing fountains were in action. The pools were higher, with walls of cups 6 feet high at the east pond, 8 feet at the southwest bay, and 12 feet at the west pond and southeast arm. The north arm was now floored with a pudding of frozen pahoehoe 3 feet above the lake level. There was a standing rapid south of the north point peninsula. At 10:15 a. m. the west point was being flooded and at 10:30 all the platforms were overflowed. Patches of fume were rising from the crags, the net output being thin and diffuse.

At 11 a. m., November 16, inspection of Halemaumau from Uwekahuna bluff revealed dense fume puffing up from the Red Solfatara and moderate fume in the pit. The fountaining rumble at that distance was occasionally noisy.

Halemaumau at 7 p. m. had the cascade again pouring into the southeast arm and the current from the end of the arm rushing to the vortex. From the east central narrows of the lake the swift torrent showed a golden "epaulette" pattern. There was some glow in the west crag pit. The ponds were quiet and occasional fountains broke the surface of the north cove.

Sept. 16, 1920. West side of Halemaumau.

Sept. 26, 1920. Halemaumau from the northwest. – *Photos. By T. A. Jaggar.*

On November 17, in the morning at eight o'clock the benches had been flooded, followed by 5 feet of subsidence at 10:30 a. m. The cascade was reported to have begun at noon. It had stopped at 2 p. m., five to seven fountains were in action with noisy puffing, and the building of wide marginal platforms 1 to 2 feet high had now shut off the south central pond and bridged the narrows leading to the southeast arm. The island in the southwest arm was surrounded by a wide egg-shaped platform, and both this arm and the southeast pool were covered with crust. Streaming was north-northeast from the southwest channel and east through the east central channel. The banks were 5 feet high in the east pond, 8 feet in the southwest arm, 10 feet in the west pond, and 12 feet in the southeast pool.

Two terrace levels of uplifted bench magma were in evidence at the northeast cove, and a crust over the east pot was uplifted to the level of the lake platforms. These platforms, it should be noted, were not formed around the east and west ponds. The remnants of the central islands, submerged under this platform accretion, were now very small. A pulpit rock had formed by the breaking away of a block of raised bench south of the entrance to the east pot. There were two patches on the southwest bench opposite the southwest rift line, and one on the north floor, where small cracks were stained white and glow could be seen. All of these facts gave evidence that the bench magma was swelling and cracking, and that it was lifting the lake bottom material in the central region, for the shoals which developed into platform shores became permanent additions to floors and crags.

In the west crag pit the black lava had piled higher, fresh debris lay upon it and rocks were falling. In the main lake three half-dome spatter-grottoes had formed on the east, north and northwest sides, and at 2:30 p. m. there was a breaking up of crust in the southwest arm with eastward streaming and the development of a fountain at the east end of the island there.

November 18 at 11 a. m. the liquid lava appeared to be quietly rising, and on the previous night the diminished general glow above Halemaumau suggested the crusted lakes of a rising spell. A rapid stream was pouring through the southeast arm narrows and there was the usual current from the southwest channel. Occasionally big fountains would break out in the north cove and in the center, the latter migrating to the east banks of the lake, and these expenditures of gas would lower the lake about one foot. Sometimes there were breakings-up and lowerings in the east and west ponds, the border cliffs of the ponds standing about 12 feet above the liquid. The marginal platforms of the central pool were now 4 feet high. There were many white-stained glowing and fuming patches on the floors, especially on the increase on the southwest black ledge. An inspection of the lake margin from the north floor showed that there were heavy folded "elephant hide" skins over the north cove and an open hole at the north pot; at the base of the north wall the edge of the floor was raised and drawn out from the cliff, with a very hot wall-crack behind it, which it was necessary to step across in order to reach the floor. A spell of breaking up and subsiding was noticed in the south central pond. Smoke was rising in the west crag pit.

Seismometric Record. During the week ending midnight, November 19, nine local earthquakes were registered, as follows:

November 13, 3:01 a. m.—Very feeble.
November 13, 1:37 p. m.—Very feeble.
November 13, 5:03 p. m.—Feeble, apparent distance 4 miles.
November 14, 11:31 p. m.—Feeble, apparent distance 9 miles.
November 15, 12:42 a. m.—Very feeble.
November 16, 2:00 a. m.—Feeble.
November 16, 6:11 a. m.—Very feeble.
November 16, 9:03 a. m.—Very feeble.
November 18, 4:45 a. m.—Very feeble.

Spasmodic tremor was mostly weak and harmonic tremor slight during the week. Microseismic motion was slight to moderate. Tilting was dominantly to the north and east.

Week Ending November 26, 1920.

SUMMARY OF CONDITIONS.

The lakes and crags of Halemaumau have risen a foot a day or more during this week, the rising taking effect as overflow only from the central lake as yet, flooding the benches around its margin and also the north floor of the pit. The outer pools of the area have risen 10 or 15 feet with reference to their cups. The early part of the week showed the crags and floors rising, the bench margin of the western pond completely caving in on one side and enlarging the pool. About November 23 the great rise began for the central lake, in pulsations about once a day, and the fresh inner platform around this lake increased in area, gradually encroaching upon five small ponds in the platform, which were all that was left of the eastern part of the lake.

The fluctuations of rising and falling were marked respectively by thinning and thickening of fume in the course of the hour that led to the change. During the high flooding there was a notable absence of fountains. The former islands in the lake are buried under the new platform shorelines. One of the small central ponds must have been a feeding well under the central lake before its enclosure, for it became a cone on the platform with lava streaming from its central orifice. The surface current in the main lake, which for months has swept from west to east, became temporarily reversed towards the southwest on November 26th.

JOURNAL.

Activity of Halemaumau. Measurements for the week ending November 26, 1920, expressed as depression below the northeast monument on the rim of Halemaumau (3727 feet above sea level) have been as follows:

	Mean lake level	Northeast peak	West peak
November 18, 11 a. m.	230 feet	136 feet	145 feet
November 25, 10 a. m.	223 "	137 "	139 "

In seven days the lake rose 7 feet, averaging 1 foot per day, the northeast peak subsided 1 foot, averaging 0.14 foot, and the west peak rose 6 feet, averaging 0.9 foot. The relief of the northeast crag above the lake thus decreased from 94 to 86 feet, and that of the west crag from 85 to 84 feet.

On Saturday, November 20, the fume had increased in Halemaumau, and the outlying pools lay depressed 15 to 20 feet below the edges of their cups. Six fountains were in action in noisy rumbling grottoes. At the southeast arm about 5 p. m. a fall of rock took place on the south side of the narrows leading from the central lake, this channel being now bridged over by an arch of crust. There were cracks in the marginal rock of this arm on the north side. A second bridge of crust lay across the east central narrows, and the lava was bubbling up from under the east side of the bridge. Near here a narrow cascade was seen pouring toward the east pot from under a crust. So far as could be seen, the liquid lava reached the southeast arm from the main lake by way of the south central pond and thence in a loop under the southeast arm bridge. The southwest bay was crusted, and a flaming chimney had formed on the bank northeast of it.

At 10:30 a. m., November 21, flaming vents and blowing fountains appeared to indicate the gas pressure which goes with rising, but the rising of the bench magma seemed dominant, for all the crags stood high and crowded and the lake channels were narrow. Smoke rose from the southwest black ledge and from all the crags. A large talus had developed under the southwest rift. The west pond stood 20 feet below its brink, and its south wall appeared to be lifting. The east pond was also low in its cup, and the southwest channel where the current flowed northeast to the central lake was a narrow gorge between platforms six feet high.

The floor of the west crag pit held a glowing orifice over a cupola where a fountain was noisily pounding below. There was eastward streaming between the black ledge and the island in the southwest arm. No visible cascade could be detected at the east pot, though such falls may flow under crust. The arch across the east central narrows was 4 feet thick. The west pond was covered with bright lines and exhibited two fountains. Five or six fountains were all that could be seen at one time in the pit, including grottoes at the north shore of the main lake, and at the east ends of the southern arms, these being hung with stalactites.

The Red Solfatara was emitting dense fume from glowing cracks, and the patches of bright red and orange alteration products could still be seen on the rock surfaces north of the smoke hole.

November 22 at 11:45 a. m. the floor surrounding the west pond had entirely caved in on the northwest side, between the pond and the wall of Halemaumau, greatly enlarging the pool and giving it in plan two square corners on that side. The central lake had risen to within 3 feet of the platform level. The southeast arm pool was now entirely shut off by the growth of the platform in the east central region, and the small pots in the platform were becoming obliterated. The west pond lay 20 feet below the edge of its cup and the east pond 10 feet.

Rapid fluctuations in thickness of fume from Halemaumau on November 23, dense at 8 a. m., thin at 9:30, thicker again at 10:30, gave warning of spells of rising liquid lava accompanying the thinning. Fresh dribbling overflows on the platform around the central pool confirmed this, and also a fresh spatter level around the west pond 3 feet above the liquid. There had been more collapse of the east bank of the west pond, the surface of which stood 15 feet below the surrounding floor. The east pond stood 10 feet down and was covered with heavy crust. The central lake in the forenoon was 2½ feet beneath the platform, and in this platform on the east and southeast five ponds could be counted, one each south, southeast and east of the central lake and two in the east pot region. During rises, these ponds, usually crusted over, effaced themselves, but during sinkings they came into view. The southeast pools appeared lower than the central lake, and the latter lower than the west pond. Four or five fountains were in action, two continuous ones bombarding the base of the northeast crag mass. An occasional fountain appeared in the south central pond. The southwest channel had recently narrowed, and the north arm had become a crusted niche, fuming. After 10:40 a. m. the number of fountains increased. The partitions of crumbling crag matter north and southwest of the west crag pit were becoming lower.

At 11:30 a. m., November 24, a strong rise of the liquid lava was going on and the fumes were very thin. The central lake was flooding all its margins, the last peak of the former west island was drowned and the small eastern ponds obliterated, and the flooding surface was continuous from the lake into the east pot, southeast arm and southwest arm. There were new flows into the north arm niche and the base of the south crag was flooded on both sides. The tip of the east island still protruded and the island in the southwest arm was nearly covered. The lake was covered with black satiny skins, the current pouring from the southwest and dividing in the central region to north, east and south. The outer pools were not so high relative to their banks, which stood 4 feet above the east pond, 5 feet above the west pond, 7 feet above the southwest arm at the peripheral black ledge, and 8 feet above the southeast arm.

The west crag pit had no glow in the cone on its floor, and chasms had opened through the crag remnant from the pit towards the west pond northward and towards the southwest black ledge. The west pond was heavily crusted until noon, when it broke up with fountaining and subsidence. The northern arête of the west crag had now become a narrow knife-edge wall, disjoined from the northern escarpment of the crag mass, which latter retained a flat surface dipping northward on the west side of the west pond. Ordinarily there were only 2 or 3 fountains in the central lake during this morning, and 2 in the east pond. The downgrade from the western pools to the eastern was pronounced.

November 25 at 9 a. m. the central pools were 3 feet below the new flood platform, including the four ponds, and the southeast arm was again detached. The north niche pot was filled to the brim, at a higher level than the north cove of the lake. There were fountains on the west side of the east pond, in the southeast pool and at one or two other places.

At 9:20 a. m. the liquid rose rapidly as on the day before, flooded the platforms, joined through from the central lake to the southeast arm, and by 9:45 a. m. brimmed over the north arm and started a flow on the north floor of the pit. The east island remnant and the island in the southwest arm were entirely submerged. The south chasm was flooded through, isolating the south crag. The fume grew thin. There were quiet satiny skins on the lake and no fountaining except in the east pond, which remained depressed 6 feet. The west pond remained 8 feet down its cup.

At 10 a. m. the banks of the southwest arm on the wall side were 4 feet high, of the southeast arm 8 feet along the south margin, the north floor was flooded half way across, and the platforms were all submerged.

At 10:15 a. m. the only noises in the pit were the crunching and crackling of invaded talus, the snapping of cooling crust, and a little gas blowing. There was some bubbling in the southeast arm, but no other fountaining. By way of the east pot chasm the liquid had nearly opened a new strait through to the eastern end of the southeast arm.

At 10:25 a. m. the benches north of the east pot and southeast arm were only 2 feet high and the east crag block was an island. A black pudding of pahoehoe lava was spreading over the floor of the west crag pit. The hot lake surface was still without fountains, the southwest bay acting as the main apparent source of the upwelling. The east and west ponds had each risen 2 feet. It was worthy of note at this time, in the absence of fountains, that there was no "blue gas" rising, only pale whitish steamy fume from the crags.

At 11 a. m. the streaming was slower, the rise appeared to be near its limit, the banks southwest and southeast were in places only one or two feet high, and the southwest pool maintained a heavy crust, from the bright line at the edge of which the streaming proceeded eastward. The lava was creeping up the south slope of the east crag block.

All the exposed broken walls of the interior and exterior of the collapsed west crag were red, purple and sulphur yellow with excessive oxidation. A small black hole in the wall lay on the south side of the west crag pit.

At the Red Solfatara a crack on the north side of the big smoke hole, at a lower temperature, was still making brilliantly colored deposits. The main smoking crack was two feet wide, the only noise a purring sound, the deposits on the margins of the red heat a pale buff brown, dense fume condensing above, and no sound of lava splashing below could yet be detected.

November 26, from 3 to 5 p. m., there was reaction from the previous high level and the main lake was 7 to 8 feet below its banks. The streaming was from the southwest arm to two border fountains on the east side of the central lake, otherwise there was one border fountain in the southeast pool, one in the west pond and one in the southwest arm. At times a central fountain would develop. Sometimes the current would bend to a grotto on the west side. The west pond was crusted over.

9 to 10 p. m. the lake was higher, with 7 or 8 puffing fountains, and the streaming reversed to southwest from the central pool. The new flows on the north floor were glowing. There were quiet crusted spells, followed by times of breaking up with sinking crusts. There was a spectacular breaking up of the

west pond surface with fountaining, 10 feet or more below its banks, and the other outlying pools were 7 or 8 feet depressed within their cups. At the site of the southeast central pot, near the former east island locality, the orifice was built up with narrow cascades pouring down a slope into the depression of the east pot, the liquid passing under a shell. Some of the border fountains on this evening were building chair-shaped niches.

Notes on Mauna Loa and the Kau Desert. On November 18 the summit fume on Mauna Loa had been very plainly visible.

At 3 p. m., November 25, blue smoke was seen in the direction of the Kau Desert, though as the event proved, this was probably beyond in the Pahala cane fields.

In the forenoon of November 26 an expedition was made from the Kapapala Bullpen eastward across the desert to the rifts of 1919-20, but no activity was found. The western side of the aa flow of January, 1920, was followed up to the sand-dune slag heap of that period. From the summit a good view of the lower country was obtained. Some hot steaming cracks were found on the western rift just north of the dune area, where a small lava outbreak took place last year, but there was nothing new about this vaporing.

Seismometric Record. During the week ending midnight, November 26, five local earthquakes were registered, as follows:

November 20, 10:18 a. m.—Very slight instrumentally, apparent distance of origin about 16 miles, felt north of Hilo.
November 21, 2:26 a. m.—Feeble.
November 22, 4:56 a. m.—Feeble.
November 26, 12:29 a. m.—Feeble.
November 26, 11:10 p. m.—Very feeble.

Spasmodic microtremor increased from weak to moderate. Harmonic tremor was slight, increasing a little. Microseismic motion was moderate, decreasing. Tilting motion was rather stationary, with a movement eastward Nov. 22, compensated by a westward tilt Nov. 24, and a flurry of north-south fluctuations Nov. 25-26.

Week Ending December 3, 1920.

SUMMARY OF CONDITIONS.

The rising in Halemaumau which began on November 14 gradually increased at the beginning of December, becoming a tremendous flood from all the lakes on the 2nd, the rise netting over 5 feet per day for the week. The rise of the lakes was twice as great as that of the crags and floors, so that the crags were flooded about their bases with new floor-making material and became smaller. The whole floor area was flooded from wall to wall, the rising being at the west and the lowest point the east pond, the latter sometimes sinking while flows were progressing so as to receive the glowing floods as spectacular cascades. While the strong flooding is in progress the lakes lose their identity, the heat from the immense glowing surfaces is intense, and the crags appear like islands.

From 10 to 20 ordinary fountains have been in action and on the 2nd a standing fountain of the artesian type acted as central source for a flow sweeping eastward from the site of the recent pot which lay southeast of the central lake.

A notable development of symmetry has appeared in the arrangement of the lakes since the southeast pool became separated off from the central lake. The four outer pools lie at the corners of a square, with the central lake in the middle, and on the intermediate diagonals between the outer pools lie the four pots, east, north, in the west crag, and in the south chasm. All of these pots have formed in crag fissures.

JOURNAL.

Activity of Halemaumau. Measurements for the week ending December 3,

1920, expressed as depression below the northeast monument on the rim of Halemaumau (3727 feet above sea level) have been as follows:

	Mean lake level	Northeast peak	West peak
November 25, 10 a. m.	223 feet	137 feet	139 feet
December 4, 10 a. m.	173 "	114 "	112 "

In nine days the lake rose 50 feet, averaging 5.5 feet per day, the northeast peak 23 feet, averaging 2.5 feet, and the west peak 27 feet, averaging 3.0 feet. The relief of the northeast peak decreased from 86 to 59 feet, and of the west peak from 84 to 61 feet.

At noon Saturday, November 27, the central and western lakes were up to within 1 foot of their banks, and the east pond and north cove were overflowing. The flow from the north cove swept across the north floor and bent eastward until it reached the east pond, and the latter was dribbling over its south margin. In all the lakes there were from 15 to 20 fountains of the puffing niche-building variety, and the streaming was northward to the central lake from the southwest pool. At 12 noon all the platforms and central ponds were obliterated by the rise, and the southern sides of the east crag block and the south crag mass were covered with new lava. At 12:15 the lakes lowered, and there was left a broad western point, and platforms over the east central region and against the south base of the south crag. Depressed in the platform there was a pond adjacent to the south crag on its north side, with a fountaining grotto against the base of the crag, and another pond occupying what had been the south chasm, between the south and southeast crags. There were doubtful openings in the platform at the east pot and at the site of the former northeast cove. The island in the southwest arm was revealed intact as a flat-topped table when the liquid went down. The fume from Halemaumau was very thin on this day, but that from the Red Solfatara continued dense.

November 28 the lava continued high and the fume thin. November 29 at 10:30 a. m. there had been recent flows from the central lake over the east pot area, and no pot was now defined. There were broad festoons over a new flow extending northeastward from the north cove, the north niche of the lake shore was entirely gone and the north pot not defined. The south and southeast crags were becoming small by submergence. The island in the southwest arm appeared to be slowly pushing eastward, perhaps by accretion at its east end and caving away at the west.

The lake was rising from 10 to 10:30, but at 10:35 there was breaking up with subsidence in the center and at the west pond with development of large fountains migrating to the banks. Streaming was to the northeast and east in the southwest arm, the northeast current bending in the central lake southeastward through tunnels to the end of the southeast arm. Ten to seventeen fountains were in action. Fume from the crag masses was moderately abundant.

The southeast pool was now effectively shut off and the symmetry of the five lakes was apparent. The platforms stood one to three feet above the lakes. The main lake and the southwest arm were two similar pools with a channel between them 15 feet wide, and there were two remnant ponds south of the center. The west pond was flush with its rim on the southwest side, 1 foot below the rim northeast, the east pond stood 2 feet below its rim, and the southeast pool 3 to 4 feet below. The west crag pit had developed much talus, the notches northeast and southwest of it caving away, and the bottom showed no fresh lava and a dead-looking spiracle on its southwest side. The talus on the black ledge at the southwest rift was large, and suggested some movement in the rift. Fume was dense and rose rapidly at the Red Solfatara.

In the forenoon of December 1 the lakes were high and had been generally overflowing the floors. There were new overflows from the southwest bay on the black ledge, from the southwest arm to the south floor, and across the platforms eastward from the main lake. Here there were only slight signs of the east and south central ponds in the shape of slightly slumped areas in the platform, and at the east pot also there was only a small sag. Other overflows were from the east pond southward for 100 feet, and northward from the west pond and the north cove. The platforms about the main lake had been tilting up centrifugally so that they stood 4 feet above the liquid, while the benches of the outlying pools were only about 2 feet high. There was a big newly fallen talus under the southwest station. Some falling rocks were seen at the notches adjacent to the west crag pit. Migratory central fountains were moving northeast, spatter heaps had formed, the lakes radiated much heat, and at noon the west pond was brimming full. There was some appearance of a source of dribbling lava on the bench opposite the southwest rift, where smoking cracks have recently opened parallel to the wall.

The pit was making very little fume, but the Red Solfatara, after recent rains, was making a very large and dense cloud from the same crack that showed bright glow only a few feet down.

High lava and increasing overflows continued on December 2, and from 6 to 10 p. m. this developed into a crisis of intense effervescence of liquid lava like that of October 23 this year.

At 6 p. m. the southeast arm overflowed in the direction of the east pond, the flow reaching the pond and stopping there.

About 7 p. m. the west pond overflowed and sent a big torrent across the north floor nearly to the east pond.

Both of these preliminary upwellings ended with breakings-up of crust at the ponds and temporary lowerings accompanied by fountaining.

After 7:45 came the grand climax of flooding. All the pools rose and overflowed; the southwest bay appeared to be the main center of dispersal, with current south through this arm, northeastward through the channel to the main lake, and northward on the west side of the west crag mass by a backing up and filling process until a flowing front was seen headed toward the west pond from the south. The north cove was overflowing to join with the floods which covered the north floor. A standing fountain started southeast of the center of the pit, and sent a torrent east, both the dome-shaped artesian upwelling and the stream continuing after 10 p. m., when the writer left Halemaumau. From 10 to 20 fountains were in action at different times. The lowest point to which all floods converged was the east pond.

The fill finally assumed a nearly level aspect, with a smooth glowing edge against the wall of the pit all around, and the crags stood as islands in the flat flood, which became evenly crusted, the shells cracking and foundering in different places. The end of the southeast arm maintained large spurting fountains, but all of the pools lost their identity of outline and the raised liquid level reduced the relief of the crags. There were occasional falls of rock from the walls around the edges of the bottom area, especially on the east side.

At 10 p. m. the flood was at its height and the fountains few, but no signs of cessation of the rise had yet appeared. Definite flow zones marked the surface with festoons of skin and bordering bright-line curtains, moving east from the standing fountain, north, northeast, and south from the dark southwestern area, and northeast from the site of the west pond.

December 3 in the forenoon the lakes were high. A flow from the west pond that started about 11 a. m. followed around the base of the north wall and cascaded into the east pond, which had remained depressed several feet. A branch from this flow cascaded into the north end of the main lake for a short time at noon. At 5 p. m. the lakes were down a few feet below their banks, with central and border fountains in action.

Seismometric Record. During the week ending midnight, December 3, eight local earthquakes were registered, as follows:

November 27, 5:39 p. m.—Very feeble.
November 29, 9:36 a. m.—Very feeble.
December 1, 5:24 a. m.—Feeble.
December 1, 10:01 a. m.—Feeble.
December 2, 3:31 p. m.—Feeble.
December 2, 11:50 p. m.—Very feeble.
December 3, 12:41 a. m.—Very feeble.
December 3, 7:30 p. m.—Very feeble.

Spasmodic microtremor varied from moderate to strong; harmonic tremor from slight to moderate. Microseismic motion decreased from moderate to slight. Motion of tilting became strong to the east and north November 28-29, with strong reaction to the south December 1, and some westward tendency.

T. A. JAGGAR,
Volcanologist.

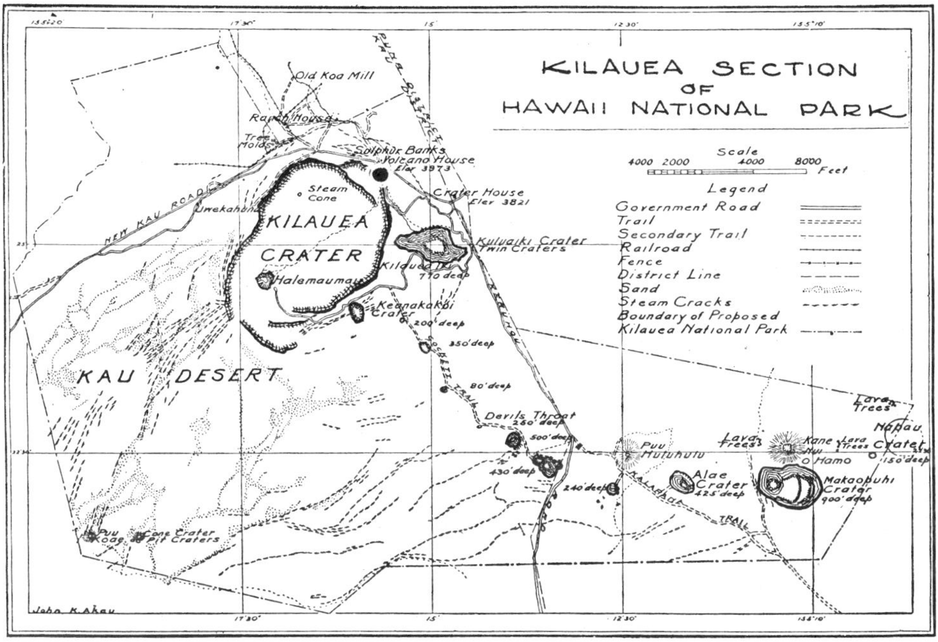

All exchanges should be addressed to

HAWAIIAN VOLCANO OBSERVATORY,

Volcano House P. O., Hawaii.

The Observatory is equipped with the following seismometric instruments rebuilt at the station in 1918 for the special needs of volcano research: two Bosch-Omori pendulums, high-speed registration of local earthquakes; one optically recording seismograph for distant earthquakes; one clinograph registering E-W tilting of the ground. A vertical component seismograph was in December, 1918, set up in experimental operation. These are seated on concrete piers in a closed basement room having practically constant temperature, beneath the chief Observatory building near the hotel. Time is referred to a rated chronometer, checked at intervals by wireless signal from the Pearl Harbor Naval Station. The chronometer is loaned by the College of Hawaii. Hawaiian standard time (H. S. T.) is 10 hrs. 30 min. slower than Greenwich time.

HAWAII NATIONAL PARK.

This park was created by act of Congress August 1, 1916, and includes three famous volcanoes—Kilauea and Mauna Loa on Hawaii and Haleakala on Maui. Frequent passenger steamers ply between these islands and Honolulu.

Haleakala Section—Haleakala, "house built by the sun," a peak more than 10,000 feet high, carries an immense fissure-like crater 8 miles long and 3 miles wide, with walls 2000 feet high. Here, as well as on Mauna Loa and Mauna Kea, grows the Silver-Sword (Argyroxiphium). Thirteen volcanic cones lie wholly within the crater, some rising nearly to the height of the summit. The scene at sunrise is marvelously beautiful.

Wailuku is the point of departure, automobiles taking the traveler to Olinda, a summer residence settlement 4043 feet high. After 2 hours drive to this point, saddle horses are taken to the summit, a ride of 3½ hours. Here is a fine concrete rest house, built by the citizens of Maui, and fully equipped with iron beds, blankets, stoves and cooking utensils.

Mauna Loa Section—Mauna Loa, a vast dome 13,675 feet high, reached through forests of Hawaiian mahogany (koa) and tree fern, then up brilliantly colored lava slopes, has a summit crater 3 miles long by 1½ miles wide, with walls 700 feet high, and when in action fountains of fire froth are here jetted 500 feet into the air. Every five or ten years splendid spectacles of lava eruption are staged on the mountain, sometimes from the lower flanks.

There are trails on the Kona side, and also from the southwest, but the usual and best route is with saddle mules from the Kilauea section to Puu Ulaula (9800 feet), a ride of six hours. Here there is a fully equipped cottage with stables and water supply. From this point on the second day a four-hour ride takes the visitor to the summit crater, where there is water. A right of way within the park connects Kilauea with Mauna Loa, where eventually a road will be constructed. The views are glorious and the chasms, cones and contorted lavas indescribably chaotic.

Kilauea Section—The lakes of foaming fiery lava within the crater of Kilauea form the most spectacular exhibit in the Hawaii National Park, if not in the world. The pit of fire, Halemaumau, is inside of the main crater, at the apex of a broad, flat, inner cone. Kilauea is a dome volcano 4000 feet high, overridden by the lava slopes of Mauna Loa on the west, so that it seems but a spur of the greater, and perhaps younger, slag-heap mountain.

The Kilauea Park and the inner pit itself are both reached directly by automobile from Hilo, the second city of the Territory of Hawaii, and there are excellent hotel accommodations. The distance from Hilo is 30 miles. Within the park there are 15 miles of roads and about 20 miles of trails. As shown on the map, there are a dozen ancient pits within the area of the park, as well as cones, caverns and hot solfataras and a strange desert where lava flows have poured out of cracks as recently as 1920.

The live pit of Halemaumau is easily accessible and not dangerous. Frequently one can walk to the actual edge of the splashing, fountaining lava lakes, the lava column rising and falling from year to year so that its most distinctive character is ceaseless change. At night the spectacle is full of marvelous color, and the region is a paradise for artists, photographers and naturalists.

The several sections are under the control of the National Park Service of the Department of the Interior. The United States Weather Bureau maintains the Hawaiian Volcano Observatory, which stands on the brink of the greater crater within the Kilauea Park.

U. S. DEPARTMENT OF AGRICULTURE
WEATHER BUREAU
CHARLES F. MARVIN, CHIEF

MONTHLY BULLETIN
OF THE
Hawaiian Volcano Observatory

VOL. VIII. HONOLULU, HAWAII, DECEMBER, 1920 No. 12

Week Ending December 10, 1920.

SUMMARY OF CONDITIONS.

The lava column in Halemaumau pit has gone on rising five feet a day, sometimes the floors and sometimes the lakes rising the more, with some suggestion of a daily alternation between the two, the lake overflows being conspicuous about noon. There was an interruption of the strong overflowing for two days, December 6 and 7, but after the 8th the lakes again overran their edges with increasing floods for three days.

The interruption was a time of uplift of the central crags, with break-down of western crag blocks to form a new island and a peninsula, and a rising of other shore points added to the northeast crag mass.

Incidentally the whole floor area rose more on the western side and subsided on the eastern, relative to the wall of the pit, for avalanches at the southeast wall indicated undermining by withdrawal of the floor.

The liquid also rose most in the western wells, so that the flows sweeping across the floor of the pit cascaded into the eastern wells, which had remained depressed within their cups.

JOURNAL.

Activity of Halemaumau. Measurements for the week ending December 10, 1920, expressed as depression below the northeast monument on the rim of Halemaumau (3727 feet above sea level) have been as follows:

	Mean lake level	Northeast peak	West peak
December 4, 10 a. m.	173 feet	114 feet	112 feet
December 9, 11 a. m.	148 "	97 "	80 "

In 5 days the lake rose 25 feet, averaging 5 feet per day, the northeast peak 17 feet, averaging 3.4 feet, and the west peak 32 feet, averaging per day 6.4 feet. The relief of the northeast peak above the lake decreased from 59 to 51 feet, that of the west peak increased from 61 to 68 feet.

At 10 a. m. Saturday, December 4, 1920, the entire floor of the pit apart from the crag peaks was covered with flowing lava. The currents flowed from the west side along the base of the walls around the periphery and across the center to the east pond, where the flood terminated in a circular cascade pouring into the cup of that pond. The cup was very small and the drop to the liquid surface within was 9 feet. Two small cascades or rapids with a drop of one or two feet marked overflow of the eastern edge of the main lake, except for this none of the lakes except the east pond had any outline. The cup of the west pond was revealed for a few minutes at 10:30 a. m., when a fountain broke out and relieved gas pressure sufficiently to lower the liquid two feet, but within 10 minutes the pond was again brimming. Overflow northward out of the main lake ceased for a while at 11 a. m. Throughout the morning there was constant flow from the southeast arm to the east pond. There was northward flowing on the west side of the west crag into the west pond. Much blue fume arose from the cascade at the east pond.

The two halves of the south crag mass had now become very small, about 14 to 16 feet above the flood at their bases. At 11:30 a. m. a fountain broke out in the central lake at the eastern base of the west crag, and rapid streaming from the southwest arm at once set in towards the fountain. Again the effect of gas relief showed in cessation of overflow from that lake.

At 10 a. m. December 5 the lakes had lowered relative to their banks five to six feet, the east pond remaining very low, a small pit with crusted pool inside 10 feet down. In the central lake border fountains broke out occasionally at two or three places, always drawing towards them a surface streaming out of the southwest channel, but at other times the lake was quiet. There were border fountains in the eastern part of the west pond.

From 10:15 to 10:30 a. m. the main lake and southwest arm rose about five feet, the other lakes lagging behind these in rising. By 10:40 these two were overflowing. All the lakes, including the east pond, were now rising, and at 11 a. m. they had lost their outlines. The east pond rose 10 feet in less than an hour. The central lake overflowed to the north and southeast, the southwest arm to the southwest, and the southeast arm to the southeast.

December 6 from 1 to 2 p. m. the lakes had lowered again. They were mostly 5 to 6 feet down, but the west pond was only 3 to 4 feet. A small east central pond started fountaining at 2 p. m. and suddenly sank 10 feet. There was streaming from the southwest arm across the main lake to a border fountain at the north end. Two grottoes were active on the south side of the southeast pool; there was some fountaining in the east pond. There was a small glowing cone near the east pond on the side of the northeast crag.

The indications on December 7 at 1 p. m. were that the central benches and crags had risen while the liquid remained relatively stationary. This was shown as follows: the bank of the southwest arm on the wall side stood 1 foot above the liquid; the banks on the northeast side of this arm, and around most of the central lake, were from 7 to 9 feet high.

The west crag mass was lifting, and the south bank of the west pond was about 8 feet high. The pond in the west crag pit appeared dead, with its floor dipping north. An island block on the east side of the west crag mass had broken away, its upper surface dipping north, so that its south end stood 9 feet above the lake and its north end 2 feet. The east pond had enlarged a little and had 5-foot walls. The southeast pond had 4-foot walls. The east central little pond was crusted over and depressed within its cup about 2 feet.

December 8 at 10 a. m. the pit was more fumy, as is usual when the crags rise, and this rising had been carried farther. The eastern banks of the main lake, 8 to 10 feet high, in contrast to the other shores 6 to 8 feet high, are part of the crag mass tilting eastward, and the lifting floor at the lake edge on the northeast side was making a new addition to the western extension of the northeast crag. Another evidence of movement in the bench magma was a fresh crack in the floor extending southeast from the center lake past the small pond there, zigzagging across to the southeast pool. Further development of the island which had slipped down into the main lake from a break in the west crag mass was submergence under the lake of the low north end of the island. Another block nearer the west peak had also sunk down with northward tilt, its north end 7 feet below the old floor level and its south end 5 feet below. On the southeast floor of the pit fresh avalanche material from the wall had fallen, this again suggesting downtilt there, compensating uptilt in the center. The western crag mass in tilting northward had lifted a portion of the clinging floor on the south side 8 feet above its adjacent part.

The level of the outer pools was 2 to 7 feet below the banks as before, and at 11 a. m. the southwest bay and arm were overflowing southward in two streams and northward on the west side of the west crag. The west pond on the wall side rose to brimming. The east pond remained depressed 6 feet. Streaming was southwestward and northward from the southwest channel. There were two border fountains in the southwest arm, one or two in the southeast arm and one in the west pond. The southeast arm overflowed and one of its two fountains went out of action.

From 10:30 a. m. to 12 noon December 9 the fume was very thin, overflows were in action and the lakes were high. Four vigorous grotto fountains were pounding the shores of the southeast lake, and there was one active grotto each in the main lake and the west pond. The southeast arm was one foot below overflow level, the east pond was brimming, the southwest arm was overflowing, and the west pond was source of a flow still in motion that reached around to the east pond and beyond by way of the north floor. At 11 a. m. there was overflowing lava on the platform southeast of the main lake which for a few minutes cascaded into the small pond there. A crack had been enlarging extending northeast from the north pot region.

December 10 at 1 p. m. tremendous floods of liquid lava were pouring over the floor of the pit as on December 2. Two streams from the southwest pool covered the south floor, the one going directly across from the end of the arm to the southeast lake, the other following around the wall from the southwest bay. Both cascaded down 4 feet as they drained into the southeast lake. A long stream across the north floor from the west pond was joined by one from the north side of the main lake and the joint flood cascaded with a drop of 10 feet into the east pond pit. A new small pot in the southeast central floor was fountaining. The island and adjacent fracture block on the west side of the main lake were drowned. The east part of the south crag mass was almost drowned. The liquid lava stood at least 7 feet higher relative to the floors than on the 9th.

Seismometric Record. During the week ending midnight December 10, seventeen local earthquakes and one distant earthquake were registered, as follows:

Local shocks:
December 4, 2:08 a. m.—Feeble.
December 4, 4:20 a. m.—Feeble.
December 4, 12:10 p. m.—Very feeble.
December 5, 5:03 a. m.—Very feeble.
December 6, 5:27 a. m.—Feeble.
December 6, 6:05 a. m.—Feeble.
December 6, 8:02 p. m.—Very feeble.
December 7, 3:40 p. m.—Very feeble.
December 8, 6:11 a. m.—Very feeble.
December 8, 10:26 a. m.—Feeble.
December 9, 12:58 a. m.—Slight.
December 9, 2:42 a. m.—Very feeble.
December 9, 7:03 a. m.—Very feeble.
December 9, 5:36 p. m.—Very feeble.
December 9, 7:08 p. m.—Very feeble.
December 9, 10:43 p. m.—Very feeble.
December 10, 4:48 p. m.—Very feeble.
Teleseism:
December 9, 6:40 p. m.—Moderate.

Spasmodic microtremor and harmonic tremor were moderate to strong.

Microseismic motion was moderate. Tilting was to the east and north until December 8, thereafter it was stationary with southerly tendency.

Week Ending December 17, 1920.

SUMMARY OF CONDITIONS.

This week fulfilled the expectation that the December solstice would produce a strong rise of the Kilauea lava. Never was the fire pit more brilliant and spectacular, with lakes of molten lava only 100 feet below the rim. The slaggy streams of glowing stuff have been overflowing the lips of the several pools, flooding the floors and cascading into the lowest of the wells, the net rise amounting to seven feet per day. The craggy peaks between the lakes have lifted and tipped over bodily, averaging four to five feet per day, gaining on the lakes for two days at a time, and then in turn being flooded about their bases for a similar period, the rise of the lake levels as a whole surpassing the rise of the peaks by from 16 to 20 feet.

The floor of the pit has become easily accessible when the flows cool and harden. There are now four pools with marginal spatter domes, many bubblings and fifteen to twenty large spraying fountains which send up clouds of tangled Pele's hair. The fountains have increased in size, numbers and brilliancy, and from the west bluff of Kilauea crater the splashing lakes and jagged peaks inside the pit have become plainly visible. From the observatory the fume column is brilliantly lighted up at night, and the sky reflections have been seen far out to sea and at Hilo. Between the lakes are the three crag masses, the larger ones forty to fifty feet high, smoking profusely through chasms which yawn open and show glow within as the dense lava underlying them swells upward. The high northeast crag came into view above the rim of the pit as seen from the observatory on December 16. The numbers of overflows from the lakes have increased until sometimes they occur several times a day. Two of the lakes have increased in size during spells of crag uplift, the east pond from a small cup 20 feet in diameter to a long lake 200 feet in length following the margin of the floor area.

On the afternoon of December 15, from 3:30 to 5 p. m. the high region southwest of the summit of Mauna Loa, at an elevation from 11,000 to 12,000 feet, exhibited several thin but definite fume jets, the smoke drifting off to the southwest. No glow could be seen there after dark, and there were no later developments of activity at Mauna Loa.

JOURNAL.

Activity of Halemaumau. Measurements for the week ending December 18, 1920, expressed as depression below the northeast monument on the rim of Halemaumau (3727 feet above sea level) have been as follows:

	Mean lake level	Northeast crags		West crag
		Old peak	West summit	
December 9, 11 a. m.	148 feet	97 feet	......	80 feet
December 11, 10 a. m.	147 "	92 "	......	72 "
December 18, 10 a. m.	99 "	60 "	47 feet	44 "

In 7 days the lake rose 48 feet, averaging 6.9 feet per day, the northeast peak 32 feet, averaging 4.6 feet, and the west crag 28 feet, averaging per day 4 feet. The northeast crag had now started to rise faster than the west crag, which had before been in the lead, and the new northwestern summit of the northeast crag stood 13 feet higher than the older summit. The relief of this older summit of the northeast crag above the lakes had decreased from 55 to 39 feet (the new summit stood 52 feet above them) and the relief of the west crag had decreased from 75 to 55 feet. The lakes had appeared seven or eight feet higher on the 10th than on the 11th, indicating that strong pulsations of rising and falling were in progress from day to day.

On Saturday, December 11, 10 to 11 a. m., the fume was thin but more dense than on the previous day and the lakes were lower. The southwest arm stood 3 feet below its southern banks, the southeast arm 6 feet depressed, the east pond 10 feet, and the main lake and west pond 8 feet. The island in the southwest arm was uplifted, standing 6 feet higher than the adjacent black ledge. The west crag mass was rising and tilting northwestward, and avalanches fell from the eastern flank of the northeast crag. A small slide fell from the lower part of the crater wall between the east and southeast pools. A glowing cone had built up over the east central pot that had been the scene of the recent ''artesian'' source well.

At 5 p. m., December 12, the floors built by recent overflowing were swollen up, sloping away from the center of pit, and were cracked radially and showed glow down cracks. Great floods of overflow from the pools had just started and from 15 to 17 fountains were in action.

The southeast pool was sending a rapid flow northward which cascaded into the east pond pit. The southwest arm was overflowing its margins to southwest and to southeast, the west pond was overflowing both north and south, the southern flow passing by the west crag pit and flooding its floor. The stream pouring to the north floor followed the wall-valley around to the east pond, which was gradually obliterated when this flow met the torrent coming in the opposite direction.

The north bank of the main lake was too much uplifted to permit overflow there, and the tumescence cracks in the floor extended north and northeast from that region. All the crag masses had been lifting up in the central region and tilting away, the west crag the most so, so that its southern peak was now much higher than its northern one, and the adjacent lake bench was becoming another raised scarp. This, the island and the northeast bench of the central lake stood 15 to 20 feet above the liquid.

The streaming was from the southwest bay to the central lake fan-wise on each side of the island, and with bright-line pattern these currents ended at fountaining border grottoes at the northwest, north and northeast. The depression east of the center of the pit showed an upwelling pool of live lava, and the cone south of this had grown to be a large flaming dome. The north and south shores of the main lake stood 10 feet above the liquid.

The fume from the pit was thin but from the fissure of the Red Solfatara dense white fume arose in volutes. Glow could be seen in one place along this fissure, of bright scarlet incandescence 10 feet down. Apparently gas was burning in the crack and the dense fume was the combustion product.

At 5 p. m., December 13, there were fresh glowing flows from the lakes on all sides and a live flow from the southeast pool was cascading in a heavy porridge-like mass into the east pond pit with a drop of 15 feet, to which depth the surface of that pond had retreated. The flaming dome southeast of the center was blowing loudly. The lower north shelf in the Halemaumau wall was now slightly over-ridden by the last flow from the west pond. The northward streaming in the central lake reached a row of grotto niches bombarded by high spraying fountains on the west side of the north end of the lake. There were 13 fountains in the several lakes, some of them spraying 50 feet vertically, the marginal grottoes of the southeast pool being on its north side, and of the east pond on its southwest side.

At 6 p. m. the southeast pool had increased its fountaining and was subsiding so as to stop the overflow, and the cascade into the east pond became sluggish and small. The east pond had risen until its surface was only eight feet down.

December 14 at 11 a. m. the lakes were 8 to 10 feet down, the northeast crag was rising strongly, the central dome had stopped roaring, smoke had increased, and only about 10 fountains were in action. No flows were in motion. The gain of the floors on the crags by flow construction had buried the old north crag completely about December 5, and now the southeast crag also was completely submerged, leaving of the south crag mass only a small western remnant.

The writer crossed the north floor and inspected the main and west lakes from their shores. The flow on the north floor was very hot and fresh with its medial belt of festooned crust slumped to form a depression. There were large dome grottoes, especially on the northwest side of the main lake, and large migratory central fountains were in action. High flings of melt were thrown up by the fountains of the west pond. The southwest arm appeared to be the highest of the pools, and the west pond, central lake, and southeast pool progressively lower; the east pond was only 5 feet below its margins. There was rapid streaming to the northwest grottoes of the main lake. A large grotto had formed on the southwest side of the east pond and several on the banks of the southeast pool.

An escarpment five feet high had formed, facing southwest, breaking across the narrow ledge between the wall of the pit and the east corner of the southeast pool. The north wall of the pool had lifted with the rising northeast crag mass.

In the evening the lakes were still depressed and the crags smoky.

December 15, at 10 a. m., the east pond was found enlarged by northward collapse of its banks, so that its area was increased about nine times, and it had become an elongate lake following the curvature of the northeast wall of the pit with development of bubble fountaining as a conspicuous feature. The abundant small fountains were on the southwest side of the pond, migratory to grottoes there.

Two persistent islands maintained themselves on the west side of the central pool and at the southwest side of the southwest pool. There was smoke from the uplifted portions of all the crags, especially on the central pool side of the northeast crag mass. The south crag remnant was now very low. The southern peak of the west crag mass and the northwestern peak of the northeast mass had grown higher than the old peaks by uptilt, and the eastern outlook surface of the old northeast peak was now nearly vertical. It was originally a flat floor.

There were 10 to 15 fountaining areas in the pit and at 10 a. m. strong overflows were just commencing. The noises were of plashing and puffing, and the crisp tinkling of cooling surfaces. Large quiet migratory fountains developed in different places from time to time.

The flows were from the west pond to the east pond by the north floor, there were short overflows north and south from the southeast pool, long flows crossed the south floor from the southwest bay, and other floods poured south from the west pond. Filling was evidently in excess of the rising of the crags. The north flow from the west pond made a low cascade falling into the east pond, and the surface of the east pond held its level remarkably, for small frozen cascade shells at its border adjacent to the main fall were not deranged by any fluctuation of level. The porridge-like pahoehoe pouring into the pond from under the breaking crusts of the flow showed hundreds of bursting bubbles from 1 to 3 inches in diameter, and so did the whirlpool of lava a foot beyond where the torrent went into the pond. This minute bubbling and blistering is a distinctive character of pahoehoe melt, in marked contrast to aa.

Traveling fountains were seen in a line on the north side of the island in the central pool. The banks of that pool were 3 to 10 feet high, of the east and west ponds 1 to 3 feet high, and of the southeast and southwest arms 0 to 6 feet high. At 11:15 a. m. the flows appeared stagnant and the central lake was lowering. At 11:25 the east pond had sunk two feet and developed border fountaining, while the west pond simultaneously started renewed overflows. From 4 to 6 p. m. the pit was moderately fumy, and central fountains were playing in all the cups. There were two large grottoes in the southeast pool, two others in the west pond, the locality of fountaining in the east pond corresponding to the site of the former small pool, and the crusts were foundering in the new north extension of that pond. There was occasional rapid streaming out of the southwest arm to the main lake. The southeast pool was enlarging itself along a crack leading to the central lake. The overflows had stopped and all the lakes were depressed about 5 feet except the central one, which had still higher banks. After nightfall a flaming vent was seen in the southeast corner of the west pond, and the central cone was flaming brightly.

At noon, December 17, much fume was rising from the middle of the northeast crag mass, where what was formerly the shoreline of the northeast cove of the central lake had been tilted up until it was now a smoking chimney on the crest of the ridge. That the bench magma was lifting was indicated by new open tumescence cracks radial from the center of the pit. Near one of these extending northeast from the central lake, at the site of the former north pot, there was a fuming and flaming hole. A glowing craterlet had formed in the central cone. There was fresh avalanche tumble from the older part of the northeast crag at its southern end. The north floor appeared about 100 feet below the rim of the pit.

The glow from the pit had been very bright the previous night. The central lake stood 8 or 10 feet below its uplifted banks, the southeast pool had 4-foot banks, the banks at the southwest arm and west pond were 3 feet high, and the east pond was brimming level with its rim. There had been some rising, there was much turbulent continuous fountaining and also bubble fountaining, and from 15 to 20 large fountains could be counted. There were some travelling fountains in lines. A zone of bubble fountains formed across the middle of the east pond, ending in bombardment grottoes northeast and southwest. The central pools had large fountains and changeable currents, mostly towards the north and southeast.

The continued enlargement of the east pond had lengthened it, mostly towards the north, until it was 200 feet long. The northwest end of the southeast pool had enlarged in a curve or hook.

Very hot fume was rising in puffs from the Red Solfatara.

Seismometric Record. During the week ending midnight, December 17, five local earthquakes and two teleseisms were registered, as follows:

Local earthquakes—
December 11, 6:20 a. m.—Feeble.
December 11, 7:15 a. m.—Feeble.
December 11, 6:45 p. m.—Very feeble.
December 12, 3:10 p. m.—Feeble.
December 13, 4:20 a. m.—Very feeble.
Teleseisms—
December 13, 5:35 p. m.—Slight.
December 16, 1:49 a. m.—Moderate, estimated distance 5,930 miles.

Spasmodic and harmonic microtremor were both moderate during the week, increasing December 16 and 17. Microseismic motion was slight to moderate. Tilting was pronounced to the west December 11-12, to the east and north December 13-14 and thereafter slightly northward and westward.

Week Ending December 24, 1920.

SUMMARY OF CONDITIONS.

The Christmas season of 1920 has been marked at Halemaumau by a great crisis of high rising lava with the scene enhanced in beauty and awesomeness by a southerly storm, the torrents of rain adding clouds of steam to the brilliant floods of lava. The rising has continued without abatement, with increase of bubble fountaining, recalling the December crisis of 1919. There are hundreds of fountains great and small, high grottoes are hung with curtains of stalactites, flames burst from the inflated skins on the streaming lava everywhere, and the floods of overflow within the limits of the pit make an almost continuous expanse of molten lava for a diameter of 1400 feet.

These overflows have been almost continuous, leaving the lakes unrecognizable at times and outlined by only their rows of spatter grottoes, these tending to space out in rhythmic scalloped rows like beach cusps. Cones have formed at the west, north, and in the center, and the two islands have maintained themselves. Cascading from the border fills into the east pond has happened repeatedly. The northeast crag has risen above the rim of the pit about ten feet.

In addition to the activity of Halemaumau itself, the 1919 rift crack leading southwest has produced close to the surface a blowing vent of glowing lava and burning gas, inside of Kilauea crater, and about 500 feet outside of Halemaumau. This crack roars and sends up jets of flame over a veritable furnace of boiling lava below, and at any moment the place may give vent to a lava flow that will relieve the pressure in the pit.

JOURNAL.

Activity of Halemaumau. Observations of level during the week made the lakes 99 feet below the Northeast Monument December 18, about 70 feet December 23 and about 60 feet December 24. The rate of rising continued about 7 feet per day for the lakes and the northeast crag.

From 10 a. m. to noon Saturday, December 18, the marginal lakes were repeatedly overflowing. At 10:15 the east lake overflowed, mostly northward. There were violent spraying fountains at this pool, with puffing flame bursts and great quantities of Pele's hair. The southeast pool had been brimming over its lip, but it lowered slightly when the east lake overflowed. During the morning the southwest arm overflowed the whole south floor. About 11:15 the west pond flooded the north floor and continued overflowing after noon. The flows were not very voluminous and there was considerable smoke from the crags. Apart from the bubble fountaining there were from 15 to 20 major fountains to be seen at one time in the pit. All the pools were bubbling and ballooning the surface skins. The wall of the pit in several places stood only about 80 feet above the floor. Yawning radial cracks at the north edge of the central lake showed that the ground was swelling upward.

Inspection close at hand of the moving front of the flow from the west pond, revealed minute bubblings along the bright lines at the edge of the belt of festooned crust, and such bubbling was at a maximum where the flow emerged from under crust at the edge of the lake, was less where fresh breaks let the melt well out to form branch flows, and was least where the baggy toes swelled out along the front from under the crustal skirts. This relation suggested that the diminution of bubbling was coordinate with increase of viscosity and restraint of gas escaping from solution. The grand maximum in this case was in the lake itself, where a coalescence of bubbles just beneath the thick viscous surface melt, ruptures that layer and so maintains the perpetual fountains and high flings.

At 1:30 p. m., December 19, there was a lull in the overflowing and the marginal lakes were 2 feet down and the central lake 5 feet down, all with abundant fountains. By 2:30, however, the southwest arm was overflowing southward and a trickling overflow was beginning at the east bank of the west pond. The southeast and east pools were now brimming full. A cone in the midst of the west crag remnants was hissing loudly and throwing out lava spurts. Rumbling was heard at the Red Solfatara.

At 4 p. m., December 19, rising of crags was dominant, though there were flows on the floor fresh from the marginal lakes. There were 20 to 25 major fountains and much bubbling, grotto domes were being built up, there were noises of puffing and splashing, fume rose from the crags, and dense fume arose at the Red Solfatara. Streaming was southwestward in the southwest bay. The tilt of the northeast crag mass had by now so pushed back the lower and older

Dec. 31, 1920. Halemaumau

Nov. 15, 1920. Dense Fume at Red Solfatara.

from the North. (Photos. Jaggar).

Dec. 28, 1920. Rift Cone and Flows at Red Solfatara.

peaks that their surfaces, originally flat floors, were practically vertical. The east shore bench of the central pool had been lifting up and tilting southeast, and back of this point at the site of the former east pot the south end of the crag mass was caving away, so that the southeast pool had extended itself in that direction, forming a hooked cove.

At 3 p. m., December 20, it was evident—and this was confirmed by visitors—that on the previous night new floods from the lakes had drowned the floors and cascaded into the east pond. The northeast crag had been rising strongly. The marginal lakes were now flush with the new fill, and the latter had a crust 2 inches thick which was cracking and foundering in the southern region and by release of gas lowering the surface below the wall margin. Enormous fountains occasionally broke out in the center and at the southwest, and there was steady bombarding of large ramparts by fountains on the western sides of the east and southeast pools. The number of larger fountains in the pit was from 20 to 30. At the northwest corner of the north cove an enormous spatter dome had been built. The central cone (southeast of the central lake) had become a large flaming dome.

At 11 a. m., December 21, the border lakes were overflowing, the molten intervening fills cracking and foundering, and at the north floor this fill, fed from the west pond, stood 6 feet or more above the east pond. An elongate cascade or chute of liquid lava descended from this north fill to the east pond. The overflows in motion poured from the southwest arm eastward along the wall valley, and from the southeast pool northward; the streaming was to the northwest and southeast from the middle of the southwest bay, to the southeast and to the northwest in the southeast pool, and to the north and east in the east pond. A long row of high scalloped ramparts had developed on the northwest shore of the central lake, and other ramparts were building on the north and east shores of the east pond. At noon the whole rampart at the southeast end of the southeast pool collapsed.

The south crag remnant was becoming mostly submerged. The southwest and central islands still held their own above the rising lakes. Rocks fell from the overturned east face of the old northeast peak, now a small affair at the base of the new crag. The north shelf of the Halemaumau rim now stood only about 15 feet above the inner floor. Abundant smoke rose from the crags and from the Red Solfatara.

About fifteen major fountains were in action. The central cone had changed its shape and was hissing through a new spiracle on its summit. A large cone had formed at the north pond site, northeast of the central lake.

At 10 a. m., December 23, a rainy day with light southwest wind, the pit was floored with a new glowing flood from wall to wall, the north shelf was submerged, and the streaming was reversed from its usual course, pouring out of the central region to the southwest. The northeast crag summit was now well above the far rim of the pit as seen from the south. There were hot bubblings and ten or twelve fountaining grottoes, the outlines of the pools being marked only by some of the ramparts. A large flood was pouring from the southeast pool to the east pond and the central cone had become an open ring with a splashing orifice two feet wide.

At 11 a. m. the streaming in the southwest bay, which had been pouring northwestward behind the west crag, changed to an eastward course. Only small ramparts preserved the outline of the north cove, but two uptilted bench crags had risen at the west shore of the central lake. As a whole the main west crag mass was greatly drowned and the south crag remnant was now only 7 feet high. The island in the southwest arm had become a low partially drowned peninsula. The wall of Halemaumau under the northeast station appeared 75 feet high. At this time the central pool lowered about 1 foot. The maximum of bubble fountaining was at the east pond and in the north cove. Liquid lava was welling up at the west pond, southwest bay, and the central cone.

Light southwest wind made it possible to approach the Red Solfatara from the south, and the red hot crack there was found to be 2 feet wide with live lava inside 11 feet down, making black pahoehoe about its edges. This was rumbling, puffing and flaming, indicating a chamber over live lava directly connected with Halemaumau and liable to flow out at any minute. The depressed ground immediately southwest in the line of the crack stood 15 feet lower than the liquid in the chamber. There was no perceptible movement of the 1919 rift farther to the southwest.

At 11:30 a. m. the central lake had lowered 3 feet and the other pools were slightly down, the southeast arm still overflowing. Fountaining had increased. The crusts over the fresh fill south were cracking and foundering.

At 5 p. m. the southwest bay was freshly overflowing the floor adjacent, and the southeast arm had stopped doing so, as though the entire underlying bench magma block had toppled over westward. There was abundant fountaining, thin blistered skins covered the lakes, flaming gases broke through the skins, and a cone was flaming in the hollow west of the west crag. A row of grotto caverns, evenly spaced, had formed on the northern side of the southwest arm.

At this time a rod was placed in the desert at the steaming rift chasm lying across the crack where it was four feet wide, in order to serve as a marker in case of movement on the crack subsequently. The location was the 1919 rift a few hundred feet southwest of Kilauea crater. It may be said here that no movement on the rift was detected by this device during the next two months.

On December 24 at 4 p. m. during a southwesterly storm the lava in the pit was found about 50 feet down, with fresh floods on the floors not so voluminous as before. The banks of the central pool were 4 to 5 feet high. The lava in the glowing orifice of the Red Solfatara was lower and less noisy. A spurting cone was in action about the middle of the west crag mass.

Seismometric Record. During the week ending midnight, December 24, eleven local earthquakes were registered, as follows:

December 18, 11:02 a. m.—Feeble.
December 18, 6:42 p. m.—Very feeble.
December 19, 1:49 a. m.—Very feeble.
December 19, 11:56 a. m.—Feeble.
December 20, 5:47 a. m.—Very feeble.
December 20, 2:49 p. m.—Feeble.
December 21, 5:27 p. m.—Feeble.
December 21, 6:03 p. m.—Very feeble.
December 21, 7:37 p. m.—Very feeble.
December 22, 6:53 p. m.—Very feeble.
December 24, 4:17 a. m.—Very feeble.

Spasmodic microtremor was moderate to strong. Harmonic tremor was moderate. Microseismic motion became strongish December 24th. Tilting was southerly throughout the week, strongest December 19-20, and at that time combined with westward tilt.

Week Ending December 31, 1920.

SUMMARY OF CONDITIONS.

The high rise of the Halemaumau lava continued to the New Year, producing a flow from the cones of the 1919 rift outside of the pit on the southwest side and slightly overflowing the rim of the pit directly from the eastern lake. The lava thus rose to the level of the Halemaumau margin and stopped there, for as soon as the overflows occurred the rapid rising ceased. The first positive outflow was on December 27.

Before this date the liquid lava had been rising over 6 feet per day and the northeast crag in the midst of the floods had lifted itself bodily over 8 feet per day. The whole lava column including lakes and crags had risen 158 feet since

December 4. From the bluffs around Kilauea crater the scene at the fire pit became marvelous at night, the lakes gleaming with lines of splashing fountains of glowing melt, the southwestern flow making a fiery trail out on the Kilauea floor, the blowing cones shooting sprays of lava like rockets 40 or 50 feet into the air, and over all the great crag silhouetted against a luminous mist of volcanic fume. The noises of puffing and pounding were heard far away, and the bright light on the cloud was visible for many miles. The lava lakes necessarily became larger. Owing to the irregularities, some portions of the Halemaumau rim still remained elevated 15 or 20 feet above the lake level. When the flows began the dense smoke which had been pouring out of the rift crack ceased entirely and new cones were built up at the source of the flow, about 100 yards outside of the pit on the Kau side. At the end of the year the flow had progressed about a quarter mile.

JOURNAL.

Activity of Halemaumau. Measurements of the fortnight ending December 31, 1920, expressed as elevations relative to the northeast monument on the rim of Halemaumau (3727 feet above sea level), have been as follows:

	Mean Lake Level	Northeast Crag Old Peak	Northeast Crag West Summit	West Crag
December 18...	99 feet below	60 feet below	47 feet below	44 feet below
December 29...	32 feet below	10 feet below	44 feet above	11 feet below

In 11 days the lake rose 67 feet, averaging 6.1 feet per day, the old northeast crag rose 50 feet, averaging 4.5 feet per day, the new summit of the northeast crag rose 91 feet averaging 8.3 feet per day, and the west crag 33 feet averaging 3 feet per day. The relief of the northeast summit above the lake level thus increased from 52 feet to 76 feet and that of the west crag had decreased from 55 to 21 feet. The rate of rising decreased sharply on December 27, the date of the first outflow to the southwest.

On Saturday, December 25, the southwestern storm continued and so far as known the activity remained the same with lakes 40-45 feet below the rim and flooding of the floors still in progress.

December 26 the storm continued with thunder and lightning but the strong wind ceased. From 5-6 p. m. the pit was found flooded from wall to wall as before, the lake areas showing hundreds of bubble fountains, ballooning skins, flames through the crevices of the balloons, large border grottoes hung with stalactites, and some spurting cones. The lava appeared about 30 feet below the north rim, 35 feet at the southwest, 40 feet at the southeast, and 50 feet beneath the high northeastern and western rims. The west crag now appeared low with a large spurting cone east of it. The island and northern ramparts of the central lake had risen. So had the southern crag mass and the island in the southwest arm, but the liquid had gained around their bases making them relatively less high than before; only the northeast crag had held its own and indeed gained on the lakes.

The floods of liquid lava were now nearly level with the upper bench on the north side of the pit and from north to south there was an expanse of 1300 feet of nearly continuous liquid across the pit. Streaming was generally northward. Large grottoes outlined the several lake cups within the more extensive flooded areas of quietly crusted lava which covered the floor platforms. The fountains of the west pond were now in view from the Observatory. In the east pond the bubbling made hundreds of golden rosettes within a brilliantly incandescent pudding.

At the Red Solfatara a blowing cone had formed 3 feet above the ground level, surmounted by a glowing filagree with spears of flame 3 feet long. Below was a chamber where lava was effervescing noisily and appeared ready to flow at any moment.

At midnight, December 26, flaming and spurting vents were conspicuous. The streaming to the northeast out of the southwest arm was rapid and border fountains along the east bank of that arm threw the melt 40 feet into the air. The cone at the west crag mass sent spurts 80 feet at times, and large flame banners shot up from the central pot. The cone at the Red Solfatara hissed loudly and ejected flames and occasionally lava jets.

December 27, at 5 p. m., the lakes were obviously several feet higher and the last flow on the north platform was only 9 feet below the low north rim of the pit. All the lake cups were brimming full except for the rampart spatter elevations. Flames and spurts of lava were seen at a summit orifice in a closed grotto at the northwest end of the east lake, lava spurted 5 feet high at the west cone, and at the southwest rift outside of Halemaumau a new cone had started rocket spurts 25 feet high from a vent about 200 feet nearer the pit than the first cone, and also sent a driblet flow along the rift crack. The older vent had built a spiracle 2 feet in diameter and 6 feet high, and here the sprays shot up 40 feet. Both cones were spinning much Pele's hair. About 6 p. m. the spattering accumulated into a weak driblet flow southward. At 7 p. m. this increased and a second stream started from the side of the cone, each making a ribbon about 4 feet wide, and the two joining below into a single flow. The upper cone ceased its rocketing when the lower flows began. These flows progressed some 300 feet in a southwest direction during evening.

The southwest arm during the evening overflowed southward a little way. The crack leading northward from the central lake showed a small boiling pot. A glowing filagree had developed at the north base of the northeast crag. From the Observatory on this evening the fountains of the east pool had become visible.

December 28, at 10 a. m., inspection of the Kau Desert cracks and of the marker there showed no movement on the rift and no activity in the desert.

At Halemaumau southeast the highest level reached by the liquid floods had been about 20 feet below the rim. The lower parts of the rim southwest and north appeared 10 to 15 feet high above the inner levels. The higher parts northeast and west were still about 30 feet above the lakes. It was evident that the central floors and the northeast crag had been lifting rapidly, the latter becoming very conspicuous at a distance; indeed nearly the whole interior of Halemaumau was now in view from the Observatory. The pools were from 2 to 8 feet below their edges, except where the east and west ponds were overflowing slightly. A row of five big spatter domes had formed on the northern side of the southwest arm, and others were at the ends of the east pond. In the southwest bay, the north cove, and the east pond there was much bubbling, and the noise of the pit was chiefly plashing. Large cones had formed at the north pot. On the north and south sides of the pit there were wide flat floors with thick crusts. The old south crag was but a small remnant buried in flows and the west crag had greatly dwindled. Towards noon the lakes settled within their cups and appeared to be in adjustment with outflow at the rift. The northeast crag also, by measurement from the observatory, ceased rising during this day.

The new developments along the southwest rift were as follows: The upper cone, 300 feet from Halemaumau, lay in the rift crack, showed driblet spiracles, and stood 4 feet high; the main cone was 500 feet from the pit, a double dome 10 feet high standing on a glistening heap of glassy pahoehoe made by its own outpourings. The flow covered the rift crack down to the valley in the Kilauea floor between this point and the southwest heap of December, 1919, building a pooled area in the valley with front turned to the northwest. The total length of flow so far was over 500 feet with slow-pushing toes at the front. The cones were making little noise, and the splashing at the vents had stopped. There was no longer any dense fume rising at the vents. No sign of fault movement on the rift was apparent, nor of action at the southwest heap or the hot "Postal Card" crack on the opposite side of Halemaumau.

Between morning and night of December 29 the fountains of the southern pools came into view from the Observatory. Spray from the northern fountains sometimes shot up as high as the large crag, over 70 feet. Collapse of banks of the border pools east, southeast and southwest was repeatedly noticed, greatly enlarging the lakes, and this while the cups were brimming full and even overflowing the margins. At 11 a. m. the liquid lava was only five feet below the lowest notch of the northeast Halemaumau rim. Some fume was rising from the crags, the central lake shores had risen, a new flow lay on the north floor, and the island in the southwest arm had disappeared. A large dome grotto had formed on the northwest bank of the east lake. The rift cones were hissing and the flow appeared sluggish. At 5 p. m. the lakes were flooding the pit to within 3 feet of overflow at the northeast gap, and at 6 p. m. voluminous new flows burst from the lower rift cone.

The puffing of the vents at Halemaumau could now be heard at the Observatory two miles away and there were hundreds of bubble fountains and many large ones in all the lakes. Most of the grotto domes in the border lakes were formed on the side toward the center of the pit. The puffing gas produced great quantities of Pele's hair. December 30, at 4 p. m., the lakes were nearly flush with their banks which had been built up to within 1 foot of the low gap northeast, the northern floods filling the uppermost niche remnant of the north shelves. An island had formed in the southeast channel apparently by subsidence of a portion of the east crag mass standing about 4 feet above the liquid. The central island and the west shorelines of the main lake were tilting up and increasing in relative height. The rift flow had been reported inactive in the forenoon, but was now moving as a rivulet of lava and both the cones were hissing.

At 10 a. m., December 31, the quantity of gas rising through the lakes was evidently vastly greater than the week before, as shown by the ballooning skins and scores of large dome-shaped fountain bursts indicating that the lakes were intensely inflated as a lava froth. The southeast pool had large spatter domes at the east end and currents meeting in the middle. The southwest pool was greatly enlarged eastward and southward with built up spatter domes along the shore. The east pond had become a long lake against the northeast margin of the pit with large spatter domes and a rapid rush of currents to grottoes on its southwest side. The north pot had become a cove of the central lake containing high funtains surrounded by a large rampart. It was prolonged into a fissure eastward over which a hissing filagree cone was flaming. Northwest of the east lake another trench-like cove had formed containing fountains enclosed by a rampart. The west pond was in constant effervescence with balloon crusts migrating to its east margin and the liquid filling it to the brim. A large cone 11 feet high was spurting on the east side of the west crag. The streaming was from the central pool to the southwest arm accompanied by strong fountaining in both pools. The fume from the pit was very irrespirable though transparent, indicating the presence of large quantities of sulphurous gas.

At the southwest rift the lower cone had increased in size and was hissing, and the flow in the southwest valley was growing in volume. The upper cone had become an arch, from which lava was being vomited on both sides, making a fresh flow with front progressing to the southwest.

From 12:30 to 3 p. m. there were fresh overflows from the east and west ponds and the east pond was level with the northeast gap in the Halemaumau rim. Both of these lakes appeared to be acting as source wells for the rising lava, and building themselves up as slag heaps above the level of the north floor. All the outlying pools tended to show surface streaming toward the center and away from the Halemaumau wall, as though the liquid were rising up the wall-crack. The crags had been lifting centrally and tipping away from the center of Halemaumau and the island in the central lake had become a high tabular mass tilted to the northwest. At 3 p. m. the south pools were overflowing their banks. From the Observatory at 5 p. m. the northeast peak was seen to be level with the far cliff of Kilauea crater.

From 9 p. m. until midnight, December 31, the high pressure with outflow from the rift cones continued, and the flow was moving both northwest and southeast from the valley fill in the southwest part of Kilauea crater. Both source cones were spouting lava. At 9 p. m. there was slow overflow from the west lake to the north floor. At 11 p. m. the east lake and the southeast arm overflowed so that the floods joined and this rise produced a small overflow of the Halemaumau rim at the northeast gap. By midnight the east lake had so built up its margin that the lava in the lake stood 5 feet above the level of the rim of the pit. In the northeast crag mass on its southern face a glowing vent could be seen about 50 feet above the lake level. At the east end of the southeast arm the grotto fountaining hurled spray 50 feet into the air.

A remarkable phenomenon observed at the west pond at 10 p. m., and repeated several times, was the production of distinct white flames issuing from cracks near the wall back of the lake. Small explosions could be heard from time to time where the flames occurred, the detonations sometimes preceding the appearance of the flames.

Seismometric Record. During the week ending at midnight, December 31, one feeble local earthquake was registered, December 30, at 12:36 p. m. Spasmodic microtremor was moderate to strong. Harmonic tremor was moderate. Microseismic motion decreased from strong to feeble during the week. Tilting of the ground was pronounced to the south December 25-26, stationary December 27, and became very strong to the east and north for the remainder of the week.

T. A. JAGGAR,
Volcanologist.

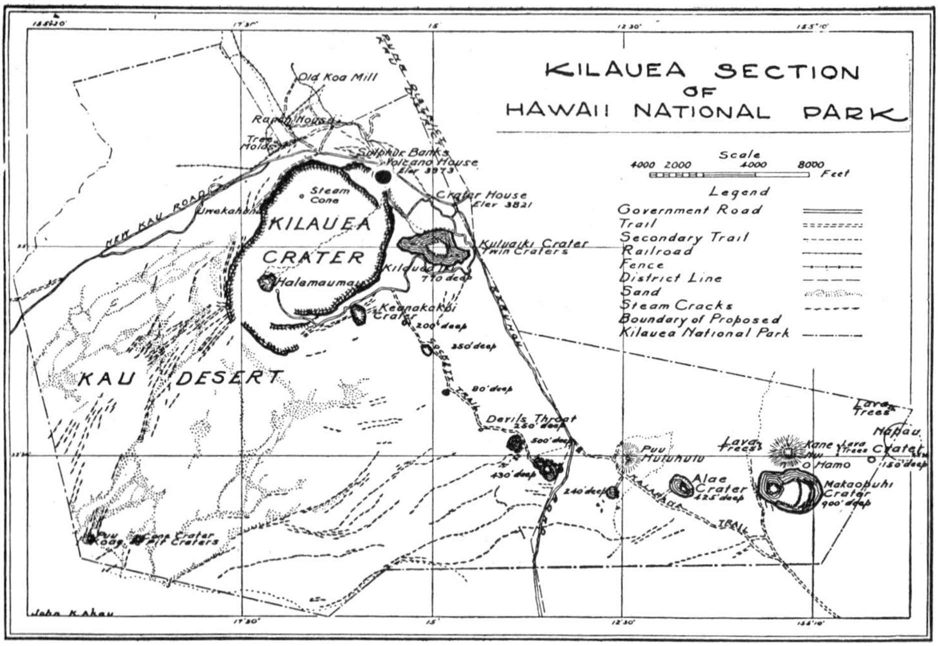

Black spot shows location of Observatory.

All exchanges should be addressed to

HAWAIIAN VOLCANO OBSERVATORY,

Volcano House P. O., Hawaii.

The Observatory is equipped with the following seismometric instruments rebuilt at the station in 1918 for the special needs of volcano research: two Bosch-Omori pendulums, high-speed registration of local earthquakes; one optically recording seismograph for distant earthquakes; one clinograph registering E-W tilting of the ground. A vertical component seismograph was in December, 1918, set up in experimental operation. These are seated on concrete piers in a closed basement room having practically constant temperature, beneath the chief Observatory building near the hotel. Time is referred to a rated chronometer, checked at intervals by wireless signal from the Pearl Harbor Naval Station. The chronometer is loaned by the University of Hawaii. Hawaiian standard time (H. S. T.) is 10 hrs. 30 min. slower than Greenwich time.

HAWAII NATIONAL PARK.

This park was created by act of Congress August 1, 1916, and includes three famous volcanoes—Kilauea and Mauna Loa on Hawaii and Haleakala on Maui. Frequent passenger steamers ply between these islands and Honolulu.

Haleakala Section—Haleakala, "house built by the sun," a peak more than 10,000 feet high, carries an immense fissure-like crater 8 miles long and 3 miles wide, with walls 2000 feet high. Here, as well as on Mauna Loa and Mauna Kea, grows the Silver Sword (Argyroxiphium). Thirteen volcanic cones lie wholly within the crater, some rising nearly to the height of the summit. The scene at sunrise is marvelously beautiful.

Wailuku is the point of departure, automobiles taking the traveler to Olinda, a summer residence settlement 4043 feet high. After 2 hours drive to this point, saddle horses are taken to the summit, a ride of 3½ hours. Here is a fine concrete rest house, built by the citizens of Maui, and fully equipped with iron beds, blankets, stoves and cooking utensils.

Mauna Loa Section—Mauna Loa, a vast dome 13,675 feet high, reached through forests of Hawaiian mahogany (koa) and tree fern, then up brilliantly colored lava slopes, has a summit crater 3 miles long by 1½ miles wide, with walls 700 feet high, and when in action fountains of fire froth are here jetted 500 feet into the air. Every five or ten years splendid spectacles of lava eruption are staged on the mountain, sometimes from the lower flanks.

There are trails on the Kona side, and also from the southwest, but the usual and best route is with saddle mules from the Kilauea section to Puu Ulaula (9800 feet), a ride of six hours. Here there is a fully equipped cottage with stables and water supply. From this point on the second day a four-hour ride takes the visitor to the summit crater, where there is water. A right of way within the park connects Kilauea with Mauna Loa, where eventually a road will be constructed. The views are glorious and the chasms, cones and contorted lavas indescribably chaotic.

Kilauea Section—The lakes of foaming fiery lava within the crater of Kilauea form the most spectacular exhibit in the Hawaii National Park, if not in the world. The pit of fire, Halemaumau, is inside of the main crater, at the apex of a broad, flat, inner cone. Kilauea is a dome volcano 4000 feet high, overridden by the lava slopes of Mauna Loa on the west, so that it seems but a spur of the greater, and perhaps younger, slag-heap mountain.

The Kilauea Park and the inner pit itself are both reached directly by automobile from Hilo, the second city of the Territory of Hawaii, and there are excellent hotel accommodations. The distance from Hilo is 30 miles. Within the park there are 15 miles of roads and about 20 miles of trails. As shown on the map, there are a dozen ancient pits within the area of the park, as well as cones, caverns and hot solfataras and a strange desert where lava flows have poured out of cracks as recently as 1920.

The live pit of Halemaumau is easily accessible and not dangerous. Frequently one can walk to the actual edge of the splashing, fountaining lava lakes, the lava column rising and falling from year to year so that its most distinctive character is ceaseless change. At night the spectacle is full of marvelous color, and the region is a paradise for artists, photographers and naturalists.

The several sections are under the control of the National Park Service of the Department of the Interior. The United States Weather Bureau maintains the Hawaiian Volcano Observatory, which stands on the brink of the greater crater within the Kilauea Park.

Index

aa. *See* lava flow
accretionary lava balls. *See* lava flow: ball lava
Alaska, Katmai, 48*p*, 49*p*
Alika flow. *See* Mauna Loa: eruptions: 1919
Aso. *See* Japan
Bandai. *See* Japan
bench magma. *See* Kilauea: Halemaumau: lava lake
caldera. *See* crater, origin; Kilauea: crater
Central America, seismicity, 383
collapse, volcanic. *See* Kilauea: Halemaumau: collapse
crater, origin, 1112. *See also* Kilauea: crater
cycles, volcanic. *See* eruption periodicity
Day, A.L., and Shepherd, E.S. (1913), "Water and Volcanic Activity," 229-235
driblet cone, 309*p*
earthquakes. *See* Hawaii, island of: seismicity; seismicity
Epomeo. *See* Ischia
eruption mechanism, 298–300, 906–907
eruption periodicity, 719–721
  Kilauea, 296, 297
  Mauna Loa, 296, 297, 455
eruption precursors
  Mauna Loa, 235, 237, 243, 302, 1005
  Sakurajima, 129
  seismicity, 719–722, 1005
  tilt, 49, 720–722
eruption prediction, 719–722
  Kilauea, 294
  Mauna Loa, 242, 248, 291, 294, 296, 301, 455
Finch, R.H., joins HVO, 982
Franklin, E.C., Halemaumau visit, 201
fumarole, 93, 533. *See also* Kilauea: Halemaumau: solfatara
gas, volcanic
  explosions related to vegetation, 1081, 1099
  magmatic. *See* Kilauea: Halemaumau: lava lake: gas; Mauna Loa: gas
geodesy. *See* ground deformation surveys, Hawaii
geophysics. *See also* ground deformation surveys, Hawaii; seismicity
geophysics
  magnetism, studies by J.W. Green, 35, 41, 43, 51, 59, 62
Green, W. L., (1887), review, 133
ground deformation surveys, Hawaii
  tilt. *See also* eruption precursors; Kilauea: Halemaumau: lava lake
    clinograph, 818, 820
    effect of rainfall, 30, 381
Guatemala, 1918 earthquake, 705–706
Haleakala, 145*p*
Halemaumau. *See* Kilauea
Hawaii, island of, 163*m*, 319*m*
  Hilo, seismograph station, 1065, 1066
  seismicity, 315–327. *See also* Kilauea: seismicity; Mauna Loa: seismicity
    earthquake swarms
      1914, 243, 302. *See also* Mauna Loa: eruption: 1914
      1915, Sept., 359–360
      1916, May, 450, 453. *See also* Mauna Loa: eruption: 1916
      1919, Kilauea, 1057, 1072. *See also* Kilauea: Halemaumau: collapse, 1919
    earthquakes, individually noted
      1913, 62–65
      1918, Hilo, 840
      1919, 1001
    weekly/monthly summaries
      1913, 1–84
      1914, 85-262
      1915, 263-382
      1916, 383-547
      1917, 548-702
      1918, 703-871
      1919, 872-1087
      1920, 1088-1268
  tsunami
    1918, Hilo, 820
    1919, Punaluu, 932
    danger to Hilo, 718, 719
Hawaii National Park, 87*m*
  description, 427–430
  legislation establishing, 396, 406-407, 424–431
Hawaiian Volcano Observatory
  aims, 10, 292, 408, 415, 417–418
  annual address (1916), 405–413
  annual address (1917), 639–646

Key: *d* = line drawing; *m* = map; *p* = photograph; *t* = table

Hawaiian Volcano Observatory
buildings, 1*p*, 11*p*, 121*p*, 889
east shelter, 502
instrument house, 4*p*, 12*p*
Technology Station, 4*p*, 196*p*
history, 414–415
monitoring methods, 292–293, 413-414
publications (1911–1915), 431–434
report, weekly, 10
storm damage (1915), 385–387, 392
summary of work (1911–1915), 413
United States government sponsorship, proposed, 406–407, 414, 416, 422–424
Hawaiian Volcano Research Association
aims, 10, 405–413, 643–646, 673
annual meeting (1917), 672–678
board of directors, 97
buildings, 674
finances, 676, 678
funding, 170–171, 209
meetings, 94, 97, 98, 156–158, 210-212
membership, 158
museum, proposed, 407–413
publications, 210–211, 292
records, 643
summary of work (1911–1915), 405-406
summary of work (1911–1917), 639-643, 673–676
weekly bulletins, 488
hazard
earthquake, 718–719
volcanic, Jaggar lecture, 717–722
intrusion, processes described, 261
Ischia, Epomeo volcano, 1883 earthquake, 717
Jaggar, T.A., 95*p*
trip to Japan (1913). *See* Japan
Japan
Aso, 150–151
Bandai, 151
Jaggar, T.A., 1913 trip, 94, 128–132, 150–152, 156–157
Kirishima, 150
Sakurajima, 94, 128–132, 421, 132*m*, 153*p*
compared to Martinique, 130, 132
Yakeyama, 335
Katmai. *See* Alaska
Kilauea, 327*m*
crater, 3*p*, 91*m*
faults related to eruptive fissure, 320
eruption. *See also* eruption mechanism; eruption periodicity; eruption precursors; eruption prediction
1790, summit
boulders, 1204
1919, summit, 926–1007, 1010, 1017–1019, 1026–1035, 1045-1059, 1003*p*. *See also* Kilauea: Halemaumau: collapse 1919; Kilauea: Postal Rift
end of eruption, 1055
new outbreaks, 972, 988
1919–1920, southwest rift zone, 1070–1201, 1113–1114*p*, 1148*p*, 1097*p*, 1160*p*, 1172-1173*p*, 1184–1185*p*, 1194*p*. *See also* Mauna Iki
beginning of rifting, 1096*p*
chronology of vent openings, 1118–1119
collapse, 1190
comparison with 1823 and 1868, 1077, 1119
end of activity, 1192
example of miniature volcano, 1152, 1155, 1156
graben formation, 1125
lava pond, summit of Mauna Iki, 1128, 1182, 1183
shield–building mechanism, 1108, 1111, 1112
gas. *See* gas, volcanic; Kilauea: Halemaumau: lava lake
Halemaumau
activity in (weekly and monthly summaries)
1913, 1–84
1914, 85–262
1915, 263–382
1916, 383–547
1917, 548–702
1918, 703–871
1919, 872–1087
1920, 1088–1268
collapse, 1916, 463–466
collapse, 1919, associated with end of 1919 eruption, 1055, 1057–1059

Key: *d* = line drawing; *m* = map; *p* = photograph; *t* = table

Kilauea
Halemaumau
connection with southwest rift zone, 1192
crack measurements, 305–308
crater bird rescued, 559
depth
1914, 162, 200, 219
1915, 269, 279, 285
1916, 463–465
dimensions
1913, 74
1914, 219
1915, 283, 285
1916, 442, 465, 493, 507, 520
1917, 636
1919, 1062
1920, 1095
dome, changed appearance in 1919, 892, 935, 944, 966, 971
lava lake
bench magma, 681, 682, 709, 711, 777, 778, 850–851, 855, 859, 1058, 1061
circulation, 1236
crags, 242, 342–343
crust, formation, 225, 484
crustal foundering, 589, 592
drainback, 272, 273, 485
fountains, 489, 681
gas
collection methods, 551-553, 617, 997
composition, 977–980, 978*t*, 980*t*
flames, 1237–1238
spectroscopic measurement, 813-815
mechanism of release, 298, 732, 886
oxidation experiments, 552, 589, 600, 605
release, periodic, 185, 224, 294, 881, 886, 956, 976, 1259
"Water and volcanic activity," 229–235
islands, 440, 461, 503, 569, 632, 636, 639
levee formation, 1111
level, 6, 295*d (1912-1914),* 463–466, 647*d* (1914–1916), 965–966

Kilauea
Halemaumau
lava lake
level
related to earthquakes, 733, 751, 755, 780, 836
pressure ridges, 617, 618
sample, 550
sounding, 557, 583
subsidence, 752, 843, 951, 956, 1058. *See also* Kilauea: Halemaumau: collapse, 1916, 1919
talus, effect on, 59, 63, 161, 174, 322, 589
temperatures, 551–553, 556-557, 559, 587, 589, 599-600, 642*d* (thermal gradient)
tidal fluctuations, 73, 293-298, 732
measurements (1919), 969, 971, 982, 988, 1004*p*
tilt, relation to activity, 720, 836, 850, 886
uplift, 711, 1065, 1122, 1213
maps and photos
1909, 181*p*
1910, 167*p*
1913 lava lake, 15–17*p*
1914 lava lake, 99*p*, 125*p*
1915, 303*p*, 313*p*
1916, 467–468*p*, 494–495*p*, 505–506*p*, 517–518*p*, 531-532*p*, 542–543*p*
1917, 554–555*p*, 567–568*p*, 580–581*p*, 593–594*p*, 607-608*p*, 621–622*p*, 633-634*p*, 641*m*, 670–671*p*, 686–687*p*, 698–699*p* (features labelled)
1918, 730–731*p*, 744–745*p*, 759–760*p*, 774–775*p*, 800-801*p*, 811–812*p*, 822-823*p*, 834–835*p*, 848-849*p*, 863*p*, 878–879*p*
1919, 893–894*p*, 909–910*p*, 924–925*p*, 942–943*p*, 957-958*p*, 990–991*p*, 1004*p*, 1075–1076*p*, 1096– 1097*p*
1920, 1149*p*, 1160–1161*p*, 1193*p*, 1208–1209*p*, 1226-1227*p*, 1242–1243*p*, 1260–1261*p*

Key: *d* = line drawing; *m* = map; *p* = photograph; *t* = table

Kilauea
Halemaumau
northwest station, 108*p*
solfatara, development, 654
sounding, 557, 583
spectroscope experiments, 811*p*, 813–815
surveying stations, 799
wall veneer, 1058, 1062
magnetism. *See* geophysics
Mauna Iki. *See also* Kilauea: eruption: 1919–1920
growth of, 1101–1102, 1118, 1119, 1171
named, 1174
Mauna Loa, relation to, 243, 293, 296, 297, 306, 455, 459, 460, 578, 720, 874, 1045, 1050, 1055
model, 408, 410, 411
Pele's Drawing Room, 52, 447, 1139, 1132*p*
Postal Rift, 174, 439, 447
source of 1919 eruption, 926
temperatures, 43, 36*p*
rainfall, effects, 255
steam cracks, 202, 384
Red Solfatara, 1217
rift zones, summary, 318–324
seismicity, 323*d*. *See also* Hawaii, island of: seismicity; seismicity
Sulphur Bank, 20*p*, 112*p*
tephra, 39*p*
Uwekahuna Bluff, 109*p*
Kirishima. *See* Japan
lava flow
aa
formation, 457, 1102, 1108, 1150
relation to paheoehoe, 1037-1038, 1084–1085, 1091, 1098, 1108, 1124
ball–lava, 1119
into sea, 1016, 1017, 1036, 1037
mechanism, 939
molds and casts, 141*p* (tree mold)
pahoehoe
characteristics, 192, 1051, 20*p*, 33*p*, 117*p*, 124*p*, 137*p*, 299*p*
formation, 457, 549
relation to aa. *See* lava flow: aa: relation to pahoehoe
tumuli, 937, 938, 988
lava lake. *See* Kilauea: Halemaumau
lava tube, 959, 960, 992, 1107, 1119, 1171, 1179, 1133p (Kilauea, 1894),
lava tube, cont., 1134*p* (1881 Mauna Loa), 1172 (Kilauea, 1823), 1209*p* (Kilauea, 1920)
formation, 192, 1046–1048
Thurston's, 22, 1139–1141, 27*p*, 28*p*, 1132–1134*p*, 1135–1136, 1141–1142*t*
Maui. *See* Haleakala
Mauna Iki. *See* Kilauea
Mauna Kea, 113*p*, 215*p*, 245*p*
Mauna Loa, 327*m*
eruptions. *See also* eruption periodicity; eruption precursors; eruption prediction
1914, summit, 235, 237–238, 263, 266, 291–292, 300–304, 228*p*, 257–258*p*, 259*m*, 307*p*
1916, southwest rift zone, 450-459, 469–475, 481, 444-446*p*
Kahuku flow, 469–475, 481
1919, southwest rift zone, 1005, 1007–1008, 1010, 1011–1017, 1019–1026, 1030, 1033–1034, 1035–1043, 1050, 1055, 1028-1029*p*, 1053–1054*p*
Alika flow, 1016, 1036–1037
facilities needed, 253, 301–304
fissure of 1868 eruption, 475
gas
collection, 1162–1164
Alika flow, 1024
composition, 1162–1164, 1163*t*
Kilauea, relation to. *See* Kilauea
Mokuaweoweo, 52–53*p*, 56–57*p*, 247*m*
1913 expedition, 49, 51, 60*p*, 175*p*
1915 expedition, 348, 350, 354
1920 expedition, 1175–1176
faults, related to eruptive fissure, 320
northeast rift zone, 51
Puu o Keokeo, 475
Red Hill, resthouse and stable, 481
rift zones, summary, 318–324
seismicity, 323*d*. *See also* Hawaii, island of: seismicity; seismicity
earthquake swarms
1914, 235, 237, 243, 302
1920, 1223
trail and resthouse, 361, 365–367, 372–374, 391, 674
Pacific Panama Fair Exhibit, 211–212, 311, 339

Key: *d* = line drawing; *m* = map; *p* = photograph; *t* = table

pahoehoe. *See* lava flow
Perret, F.A., collecting Kilauea gas, 1914, 179–180
Peru, Caraveli, 1913 earthquake, 26
photography, aerial, Powers, S., 275
rainfall, effect on ground tilt. *See* ground deformation surveys, Hawaii: tilt
Romberg, A., seismograph work, 787, 791, 792, 796, 803, 809, 813, 818, 972
Sakurajima. *See* Japan
seismicity. *See also* Hawaii, island of: seismicity; Kilauea: seismicity; Mauna Loa: seismicity
  earthquake
    epicentral distance, 316*t*, 321*t*, 323*d*
    mechanism, 318–326
    tectonic *vs*. volcanic, 318–326
  harmonic tremor, 19, 225, 322, 359, 1057, 1070, 1072
  intensity, scales, Cancani, 2
  relation to eruption, 719–722, 836
  teleseism, 820, 932
  volcanic, description, 315–326
seismogram, 788–789*p*
seismograph, 796–798, 803, 807, 809, 818, 824, 972
  Hilo, newly installed 1919, 1065
  microseismic noise, 127, 381
  optical, 791–792
  portable, Omori, 151–152
seismology and volcanology contrasted, 417
Shepherd, E.S., gas collection at Kilauea, 1911-12, 617
stalactites, lava, 590, 746, 761, 786, 922, 959
stalagmites, lava, 22
sublimates, 217, 1179, 1183, 1191
Sulphur Bank. *See* Kilauea
temperature. *See* Kilauea: Halemaumau: lava lake; Kilauea: Postal Rift
tide, earth. *See* Kilauea: Halemaumau: lava lake: tidal fluctuations
tilt. *See also* eruption precursors; ground deformation surveys, Hawaii; Kilauea: Halemaumau: lava lake
volcanic plumbing, speculations on, 322–326
volcano observatories, proposed, 419-423
volcano studies, Pacific, to 1915, 421-422
Whitney Laboratory of Seismology, 315
  building improvements, 807, 824
Yakeyama. *See* Japan

Key: *d* = line drawing; *m* = map; *p* = photograph; *t* = table

This book was reprinted and bound
by Edwards Brothers, Incorporated,
Ann Arbor, Michigan,
on 40 lb. Cougar, Dynawhite,
acid-free paper.

The title pages, preface,
acknowledgment, introduction,
bibliography, and indices were
prepared on a Macintosh
using Microsoft Word.